ROYAL HISTORICAL SOCIETY

GUIDES AND HANDBOOKS

No. 10

GUIDE TO THE

LOCAL ADMINISTRATIVE UNITS OF ENGLAND

ROYAL HISTORICAL SOCIETY

GUIDES AND HANDBOOKS

1. *Guide to English commercial statistics, 1696-1782*. By G. N. Clark and Barbara M. Franks. 1938.
2. *Handbook of British chronology*. Edited by F. M. Powicke, Charles Johnson and W. J. Harte. 1939. 2nd edition, edited by F. M. Powicke and E. B. Fryde, 1961.
3. *Medieval libraries of Great Britain: a list of surviving books*. By N. R. Ker. 1941. 2nd edition, 1964.
4. *Handbook of dates for students of English history*. By C. R. Cheney. 1945. Reprinted, 1955.
5. *Guide to the national and provincial directories of England and Wales, excluding London, published before 1856*. By Jane E. Norton. 1950.
6. *Handbook of oriental history*. Edited by C. H. Phillips. 1951.
7. *Texts and Calendars. An analytical guide to serial publications*. By E. L. C. Mullins. 1958.
8. *Anglo-Saxon Charters. An annotated list and bibliography*. By P. H. Sawyer. 1968.
9. *A Centenary Guide to the publications of the Royal Historical Society 1868-1968 and of the former Camden Society 1838-1897*. By Alexander Taylor Milne. 1968.

Guide to the Local Administrative Units of England

VOLUME I: Southern England

BY
FREDERIC A. YOUNGS, JR.

LONDON
OFFICES OF THE ROYAL HISTORICAL SOCIETY
UNIVERSITY COLLEGE LONDON, GOWER STREET
LONDON WC1E 6BT
1979

FOR CHRISTINE

ISBN 0 901050 67 9

Printed in Great Britain by Butler & Tanner Ltd., Frome and London

CONTENTS

PREFACE

It is a pleasure to thank those whose assistance has been so important in this project. Mrs. Dorothy M. Owen was instrumental in supporting it in the early stages and I have benefited greatly from her knowledge and assistance. Several members of the Royal Historical Society have assisted in their official capacities, especially Dr. Ian Roy, Mr. Keith Thomas and Dr. Valerie Pearl as literary directors and Professor G. R. Elton as President. Mr. Christopher Elrington, Editor of the Victoria History of the Counties of England, has been most generous and gracious with his time and experience.

My debt to archivists and librarians is extensive. Mr. David Armstrong, Records Officer for the Church Commissioners, afforded me every facility and assistance over a long period of time at his office. The staff of the State Paper Room at the British Library has been very cooperative. I have learned much not only of their respective counties but of cooperative scholarship from the county archivists acknowledged below.

Support from my own university has been particularly appreciated, especially the efforts of Professor John L. Loos and Dean Henry L. Snyder. Judge M. D. Miller. Jr., and Mrs. Ruth Loyd Miller have been a great encouragement and in particular assisted the project by making available their electronic composer. Assistance in answering a string of queries has been provided by Messrs. Ronald Fritze and Graham Haslam.

My greatest debt is to my wife, Christine M. Youngs, who has assisted me at every stage of the work, with help in tedious research and with support through all stages of a complex undertaking. It is only fitting that this volume be dedicated to her.

Frederic A. Youngs, Jr.
Louisiana State University
Baton Rouge

ACKNOWLEDGEMENTS

Bedfordshire Record Office, Miss Patricia L. Bell. Berkshire Record Office, Miss A. Green, Mr. Gillies. Bristol Record Office, Miss Mary E. Williams. British Library (State Papers Room), Mr. Patrick Veysey. Buckinghamshire Record Office, Mr. H. A. Hanley. Cambridgeshire County Record Office, Mr. J. M. Farrar. Church Commissioners, Mr. David Armstrong. Cornwall County Record Office, Mr. P. L. Hull. Corporation of London Record Office, Miss Betty R. Masters. Devon Record Office, Mr. M. G. Dickinson, Mrs. M. M. Rowe, Mr. P. A. Kennedy, Mr. Chell (Plymouth). Dorset County Record Office, Miss Margaret E. Holmes. Ely Diocesan Records (University Library, Cambridge), Mrs. Dorothy M. Owen. Essex Record Office, the late K. C. Newton, Miss Nancy Briggs. Gloucestershire Record Office, Mr. Brian S. Smith. Greater London Record Office (County Hall and Middlesex Records), Mr. W. J. Smith, Mr. A. R. Neate, Miss J. Coburn. Guildhall Library (London), Mr. Christopher Cooper, Mr. G. E. Yeo. Hampshire Record Office, Miss Margaret E. Cash, Mr. C. R. Davey. Hertfordshire Record Office, Mr. Peter Walne. Huntingdon and Peterborough (now Cambs) Record Office, Mr. A. D. Hill, Mr. P. J. Locke. Kent Archives Office, Dr. Felix Hull. Norfolk Record Office, Miss Jean M. Kennedy. Oxford Diocesan Records (Bodleian Library), Dr. D. M. Barratt. Oxfordshire Record Office, Miss S. J. Barnes. Somerset Record Office, Mr. Derek M. Shorrocks, Mr. Ivor P. Collis. Suffolk Record Office (Ipswich Branch), Mr. William Serjeant. Surrey Record Office, Dr. D. B. Robinson. East Sussex Record Office, Mr. A. A. Dibben. West Sussex Record Office, Mrs. Patricia Gill. Wiltshire Record Office, Mr. K. H. Rogers, Mr. Maurice G. Rathbone.

HOW TO USE THE GUIDE

THE SCOPE AND USE OF THE GUIDE

The basis of the *Guide* is the parish, a unit of medieval origins which at first had solely ecclesiastical rights and obligations. From the late sixteenth century civil responsibilities were imposed upon it, and when parliamentary constituencies were restructured in the nineteenth and twentieth centuries, they were defined in terms of governmental units comprised of parishes. Thus in time the parish became a fundamental unit in the civil, parliamentary and ecclesiastical organisation of England, important both for royal and local government.

This is the first of a two volume project. The twenty-one ancient counties and the City of London include southern England and are south of a line drawn roughly from the Severn to the Wash. The division was made in part because the entries would be of roughly equal length with the northern counties and in part because the choice did the least violence to the arrangement of dioceses within the church, which in only a few cases include parishes in counties which are included in the two separate volumes.

These introductory pages provide the information and procedures necessary to use the *Guide.* First there is a section on ORGANISATION AND FORMAT which explains the plan of the entire *Guide* and of the many types of entries within it. It will be noted here and also in the third section, ABBREVIATIONS, that numerous devices have been employed to express information as succinctly as possible—a necessity considering that over 10,000 parishes are included, each with a multiplicity of detail. The second section, DEFINITIONS OF TERMS, supplies a basic understanding not only of the nature of the units but also of the sources used in gathering information about each of them. The final section, DATES, is necessary because unlike a gazeteer which deals with areas at one fixed moment in time, the *Guide* presents information which on the ecclesiastical and parliamentary side dates from the middle ages, and on the civil side from the late sixteenth century—all in a continuous presentation up to 1 April 1974.

It is important to note what the *Guide* is not intended to do. On the ecclesiastical side, it is not concerned with the medieval origin of the parish. There has been no original research to date the inception of a parish, but of course where the research of others has made this clear, the information is provided. For the period after the Reformation, the *Guide* deals only with the established Church of England, so that there is no information about the organisation of dissenters, catholics or non-Christian groups.

On the civil side, the *Guide* is concerned with administrative and not judicial organisation. It makes no attempt to date the medieval origins of boroughs but does indicate the first date at which a borough was represented in the House of Commons. The *Guide* deals only with local governmental units which either had an exceptional importance over a long period of time (the hundred, for example) or which are important links in the historical evolution of major administrative units (the poor law unions became the basis for the structure of the sanitary districts, which in turn became the basis of administrative county districts from 1894). Thus many important units such as highway districts or town improvement commissions are not included. It will be appreciated that it was necessary to exclude a number of areas in order to keep the size of the *Guide* manageable.

Several comments about completeness of detail and accuracy are needed. Any historian's work reductively depends on the completeness of sources; in a work which intends to deal with the totality of the parishes the problem becomes particularly acute. It will be clear from the description of sources used that an effort was made to use as wide a range of sources as possible, and to use them as checks on each other. It must be realised that in spite of this there are many instances in which information cannot be found, and that there is a limit on reconstruction. For example, there has not been an attempt to date to deal with the question of how many hundreds there were in Kent or with their parochial composition. After a discussion with the county archivist, the compiler prepared a *variorum* summary based on the major authorities. Yet in cases like these, exact answers are beyond the possibility of historical certainty. It should also be noted that a goal of the *Guide* is to furnish not only the dates of changes but also the exact authority for the change. In many cases dates are generally understood but formal orders lacking, so that the date is noted but the footnote will indicate 'authority not found'.

Finally, every attempt has been made to be accurate. Citations and information have been compared and checked. The compiler has visited each county record office at least twice and sent a copy of the results to the county for the archivist's review. Naturally any errors which remain are the sole responsibility of the compiler. Readers detecting errors or omissions are invited to send them to the compiler so that corrigenda can be included in the second volume.

ORGANISATION AND FORMAT

PART I: THE PARISHES OF ENGLAND

This part is arranged alphabetically by ancient counties, and within each by its constituent parishes in alphabetical order. To the extent allowed by the nature of each parish, a variety of information is presented.

Information:

Creation, Abolition.

For each civil parish (CP) and ecclesiastical parish (EP), the date of creation, the names of other parishes from which it was formed and a footnote reference to the authority for the creation. For each ancient parish (AP), CP and EP, the date of the abolition (if any), the names of the parishes into which its territory was dispersed and a footnote reference to the authority for the abolition. It is possible for a parish to be abolished for one purpose and continue to exist for the other, e.g., an AP which loses its civil identity to an expanding nearby town while remaining ecclesiastically separate.

Alterations of Boundaries.

For all parishes, the dates when boundaries were altered, for any purpose, with a footnote reference to the authority for the change. The names of other parishes affected are not generally cited for economy of space, except when the change resulted in the creation of a new parish, when another parish was gained in its entirety, when the boundary of a county was altered (changes in APs, CPs) or when the boundary of a diocese was affected (APs, EPs).

Civil Organisation.

For APs and CPs, to the extent that the parish was in existence at any time, inclusion in hundreds (late 16th cent–1889), boroughs (at any time), poor law unions (1830s–1930), sanitary districts (1875–94) and administrative county units (1894–1974).

Parliamentary Organisation.

For APs and CPs, to the extent that the parish was in existence at any time, inclusion in parliamentary boroughs (at any time) and divisions or county constituencies (after 1832).

Ecclesiastical Organisation.

For APs and EPs, the rural deaneries in which the parish was organised. A reference to the entries at the beginning of the county's section will indicate how the rural deaneries were organised in dioceses and archdeaconries.

Sample Entries:

For the instances below and for all entries, reference must be made both to the General Abbreviations (below in this section), applicable throughout the *Guide*, and to the abbreviations particular to each county, found at the beginning of its entries in Part I.

EXAMPLE A: HILDERSHAM
Cambs AP *LG* Seq 5. *Parl* Seq 1. *Eccl* Seq 1.

EXAMPLE B: TORTWORTH
Glos AP *LG* Seq 18. Transf 1974 to Avon.[4] *Parl* W'rn Dv (1832–85), Mid Dv (1885–1918), Thornb. Dv (1918–48), Stroud & Thornb. CC (1948–55), S Glos CC (1955–*). *Eccl* Seq 21.

EXAMPLE C: PENZANCE
Cornw Bor and chap in Madron AP, sep EP 1741 as 'Penzance St Mary',[79] qv, sep CP 1866.[8] *LG* Penw. Hd, Penz. PLU, pt Penz. USD, pt Madron USD, Penz. MB. Civ bdry: 1894 (the pt in Madron USD cr Penzance in Madron CP),[17] 1934.[6] *Parl* West Dv (1867–1918), St Ives CC (1918–*).

EXAMPLE D: RYE PARK
Herts
EP Cr 1937 from Hoddesdon EP, Great Amwell AP.[20] Ware RDn (1937–70), Cheshunt RDn (1970–*).

EXAMPLE E: CANN HALL
Essex
CP Cr 1894 from the pt of Wanstead AP in Leyton USD.[115] *LG* W Ham PLU, Leyton UD (1894–1926), MB (1926–65). Transf 1965 to Gtr London (Waltham Forest LB). *Parl* Leyton East Parl Bor (1918–48), Leyton BC (1948–70), Gtr London thereafter.

Creation, Abolition.

Cann Hall (E) is a civil parish only and its formation from Wanstead, while reducing the latter for civil purposes, in no way affected it for ecclesiastical purposes. Rye Park (D) is an ecclesiastical parish only, and its formation did not affect Great Amwell for civil purposes. Penzance (C) was a subordinate part of Madron, gaining separate ecclesiastical status as a parish in 1741 (although the common ecclesiastical name included the saint to whom the parish church was dedicated, so that a separate entry follows below for its ecclesiastical organisation) and the title of civil parish only in 1866. Hildersham (A) and Tortworth (B) are ancient parishes and the *Guide* does not attempt to date their medieval origins.

Alteration of Boundaries.

Hildersham (A) underwent no boundary changes whatsoever. Cann Hall (F) as a CP was capable only of civil boundary alterations, Rye Park (E) only of ecclesiastical. The changes in Penzance (C) in 1894 and 1934 are labelled 'civ bdry' because, even though the names differed for civil and ecclesiastical purposes, the parish was one in origin. The change for 1934 is cited by year only because no new parishes were created or existing ones gained, but there is an elaboration for 1894 because the change resulted in the creation of a new parish. The boundary of Essex was affected in 1965 when Cann Hall was transferred to help create Greater London, so that details are provided.

Civil Organisation.

The arrangement of the parish within the civil structure of its county is marked off in examples A, B, C and E by *LG* for *Local Government*; Rye Park (D) has no civil status. For Hildersham (A) and Tortworth (B) an abbreviated entry prefixed by 'Seq' is used to shorten the entry. By reference to the initial page of the entry for Cambs under 'Local Government Sequences' it will be found that Hildersham and other parishes with Sequence 5 were in Chilford Hd, Linton PLU and RSD, in Linton RD from 1894–1934 and in South Cambridgeshire RD 1934–74. The organisation is presented in full for Penzance (C) because it was partly in one unit and partly in another at some stage of its organisation and because it like Cann Hall (E) was organised in urban units, nearly always a unique arrangement.

Parliamentary Organisation.

The abbreviation *Parl* sets off the arrangement of A, B, C and E for parliamentary constituencies. The inclusive years within particular constituencies were shown because the arrangement would apply not only to general but also to bye elections. The abbreviated sequence is used again for Hildersham (A) because it shared that arrangement with other Cambs parishes. Tortworth (B) had a unique arrangement within constituencies so that they are presented in full detail. Penzance (C) and Cann Hall (E) are in full because they existed only part of the period covered by the sequence and thus the sequence would not be applicable to them.

Ecclesiastical Organisation.

The appropriate entries for examples A, B and D are set off with *Eccl*; Cann Hall (F) had no separate ecclesiastical status and the ecclesiastical entries for Penzance (C) are found under the parish's usual ecclesiastical name of 'Penzance St Mary'. Sequences can be used for Hildersham (A) and Tortworth (B) but not for Rye Park (D) because it did not exist for the entire time period expressed by the arrangement of sequences.

Sample Entry for Major Urban Area:

Part of the entry for Dover (Kent) is presented in order to illustrate a special form of abbreviated entry.

DOVER

The following have 'Dover' in their names. Insofar as any existed at a given time: *LG* Dover Bor/MB, Cq Pt of Dover, River PLU (renamed Dover in 1840s), Dover USD. *Parl* Dover Parl Bor (1558–1918), Dover Dv/CC (1918–70), Dover & Deal CC (1970–*). *Eccl* Dover RDn.

CP1–DOVER–Cr 1896 by union AP5, AP1, Hougham AP.[182] Bdry: 1903,[249] 1931,[250] 1934,[19] 1951.[251]

CP2–DOVER CASTLE–Ex-par, sep CP 1858.[163] *LG* In Dover Bor from 1814, PLU (1858[120]–1930). Abol 1934 ent to Dover CP.[19]

EP1–DOVER, CHARLTON–Cr 1972 by union Charlton by Dover St Bartholomew EP, Charlton-by-Dover St Peter and St Paul EP.[184]

AP1–DOVER ST JAMES THE APOSTLE–Civ bdry: 1883.[8] Abol 1896 to help cr CP1.[182] Exempt from Archdeacon (until 1845). Eccl bdry: 1857,[252] 1873 (incl gains ex-par East Cliffe).[239]

Many of the details of the entries follow the norms expressed above: civil and ecclesiastical boundary alterations are clearly separated (Dover St James the Apostle), some units have only civil status (Dover) so that the boundary alterations are of necessity only civil and so forth. The principal change is the indication of a parish's name by a special entry (CP1, EP1, AP1) so that the name need not be repeated each time in which it was involved in changes with other parishes in Dover (to which alone the arrangement is restricted). The saving in space is substantial, particularly when applied to all the parishes in the City of London. The other change is that the organisation for civil, parliamentary and ecclesiastical purposes is expressed once only, in the headnote. Unless stated otherwise in the entry for particular parishes (as it is, for example, in CP2 which was not in the borough until 1814), it is assumed that each parish was for civil purposes in the borough, cinque port and so on, to the extent possible given the nature of each unit (only the arrangement in Dover RDn will apply to EP1, for example, because it had no civil status).

PART II: LOCAL GOVERNMENT UNITS

The entries in this Part summarise from a different aspect information provided in Part I. Here the perspective is the composition in their totality of local government units rather than the place of the individual parish.

Arrangement by Counties.

The basic arrangement is alphabetical by ancient county, but because these were followed by administrative and then metropolitan and non-metropolitan counties, a partial rearrangement has been necessary. As regards *administrative counties*, East Suffolk and West Suffolk are presented with Suffolk, East Sussex and West Sussex with Sussex, the Isle of Ely and also Cambridgeshire and the Isle of Ely with Cambridgeshire, the Isle of Wight with Hampshire and Huntingdon and Peterborough with Huntingdonshire. As regards *non-metropolitan counties*, Avon is presented separately before Bedfordshire, East Sussex and West Sussex are with Sussex and the Isle of Wight is with Hampshire.

Alterations in County Boundaries.

For each of the ancient, administrative and non-metropolitan counties there is a summary of the changes in county boundaries, arranged by the years in which the alterations took place. It will be necessary to note the parishes affected and then to refer to Part I to determine the nature of the change each underwent.

Organisation within Local Government Units.

The major portion of Part II consists of summary lists of constituent parishes for the hundreds, boroughs, poor law unions, sanitary districts and administrative county districts within the county.

EXAMPLE – HUNDREDS

CHARLTON HD

Barkham, Broad Hinton (from 1866), Earley[2] (from 1866), Finchampstead, pt Hurst (1844–66), pt Shinfield[2] (ent from 1844), pt Sonning[2] (until 1866), pt Swallowfield, Whistley (from 1866)

In this example from Berkshire, it will be noted that parishes may be assumed to be within the hundred throughout their entire history unless their place in it is limited by dates of inclusion. Parishes in the hundred which were partly or entirely within a borough at some time before 1889 are marked in each case, here with the superscript '2'. The principles stated here apply to the other entries in Part II. It will be noted that Poor Law Unions were entirely within the county unless noted otherwise; in the latter instance, it will be necessary to look under each county indicated to ascertain the complete parochial composition of the union.

PART III: PARLIAMENTARY CONSTITUENCIES

The entries in this Part are similar to those in Part II in that there are summary lists of the composition of each parliamentary constituency. It is possible to shorten the entries substantially because the practice from 1832–85 was to express divisions in terms of hundreds and liberties and from 1918 onward in terms of administrative county units. As will be noted below the dates at which boroughs first sent representatives to parliament are based on the lists of MPs in *Parliamentary Papers* and not on original research, and that it has been necessary to provide a complete survey of the parochial composition of county divisions for 1885–1918 because the latter were expressed in terms of petty sessional divisions.

PART IV: THE DIOCESES OF ENGLAND

Part IV is similar to Parts II and III in that it is a summary of infomation presented in Part I, but differs in that there are no summary lists of the parochial composition because of limitations of space. Instead the summary lists are of rural deaneries within the respective dioceses and archdeaconries. The dates and authorities for changes in these units are also summarised.

DEFINITIONS OF TERMS

PRELIMINARY NOTE:

The *definitions* below are for the purposes of the *Guide* only. A full definition would include the powers assigned to each unit and thus would introduce matters outside the *Guide's* scope which is limited to the areas in which those powers were used.

Sources used for particular districts are specified. In addition there was an extensive use of *The Victoria History of the Counties of England*, directories, topographical and historical works particular to each county, gazeteers such as Samuel Lewis, *A Topographical Dictionay of England* and Oliver Mason, *The Gazeteer of England*, internal memoranda and manuscript sources in county record offices, and maps such as the Ordnance Survey and Speed's. Many of these are cited in the footnotes.

ADMINISTRATIVE COUNTY–See COUNTY
ANCIENT COUNTY–See COUNTY
ANCIENT PARISH–See PARISH
ANCIENT TOWN–See CINQUE PORT
ARCHDEACONRY–See DIOCESE
BOROUGH

Borough ('Bor').

There is agreement neither on what constitutes a borough in the early period, nor on how many there were. Some towns had ancient charters, others claimed the right by prescription, some were incorporated and some had several claims to the title. Among distinguishing marks were the borough's own offices and institutions which included some degree of exemption from the county's jurisdiction, special schemes of taxation, the right to hold fairs and markets and the right to representation in parliament. Since the *Guide* is not concerned with the medieval origins of units, the inclusion of a unit as a borough is based on the research of others (see *Sources* below). Because many boroughs disappeared early or because the extent of the borough gradually increased or was even in dispute, the inclusion of a parish as a constituent part of a particular borough must be provisional, and it cannot be assumed that the parish's area was entirely subject to the borough's jurisdiction. Some boroughs were of such importance that they gained the status of 'counties of themselves' (see COUNTY).

Municipal Borough ('MB').

These were established by authority of the Municipal Corporations Act, 1835 (5 & 6 Wm. IV., *c* 76), either by inclusion in the schedule to the act of 1835 or by later charter. A number of earlier boroughs were not made municipal boroughs, and those which did not gain the status by the mid-1880s were disfranchised. The scheme of municipal boroughs was ended in 1974, so that if inclusive dates are not expressed in Part II of the *Guide* after a borough's name, it is to be understood that it was in existence from 1835 to 1974.

County Borough ('CB').

Towns of exceptional importance were made county boroughs, either by inclusion in the original schedule in the Local Government Act, 1888 (51 & 52 Vict., *c* 41, effective 1889) or by later charter. This status carried complete exemption from the jurisdiction of the surrounding or adjacent administrative county (see COUNTY), but it was common to include returns of the area in census and other reports along with the county with which they were 'associated', usually the area from which they first won independence. This procedure is followed in the *Guide*; a table later in this section lists county boroughs alphabetically and the names of the 'associated' counties. This scheme was also terminated in 1974, so that a lack of dates by a name in Part II of the *Guide* indicates the county borough's existence from 1889 to 1974.

Wards.

Boroughs, municipal boroughs and county boroughs of any size were divided into wards, the composition of which varied over the years. Because the wards only rarely coincided with parishes, the basic unit of the *Guide*, schemes of wards are generally ignored. The two exceptions are the wards of the City of London because of their special importance (see LONDON) and the constitution of parliamentary constituencies when stated in terms of wards. The former are included in Part II of the *Guide* under London, the latter in Part III under the respective counties when needed.

Sources and Boundaries.

The inclusion of a borough of medieval origin rests primarily upon M. W. Beresford and H. P. R. Finberg, *English Medieval Boroughs: A Hand-List* (1973), on other secondary sources and on consultation with the archivists of the various counties, but not on original research. Schedules of municipal and county boroughs appear in the original acts and later incorporations are summarised in the census returns. At the time the act of 1835 was contemplated, a survey was made of the then existing boroughs, with results published in *Parliamentary Papers.* The returns were voluntary and thus incomplete, but valuable particulars of changes in boundaries in the early periods are often included. For the period 1875–94 when municipal boroughs were also urban sanitary districts (see SANITARY DISTRICTS), changes in the boundaries of one did not automatically alter the other, and differences are noted in Part II of the *Guide* under each county. Thereafter alterations in the boundaries of constituent parishes also altered the boundaries of the municipal or county borough.

See also: Metropolitan Boroughs and *London Boroughs* under LONDON.

BOROUGH CONSTITUENCY–See PARLIAMENTARY CONSTITUENCIES

BOUNDARY ALTERATIONS–See each major unit where boundary alterations particular to it are noted

CHAPELRY–See PARISH

CINQUE PORT

From early times the *Cinque Ports ('Cq Pt')* have had a special and privileged place in the shipping and naval activities of England, and an identity distinct from the counties in which they were located. The original five ports were Hastings in Sussex and Romney, Hythe, Dover and Sandwich in Kent, to which were added early the two *Ancient Towns ('Anc Towns')* of Winchelsea and Rye, both in Sussex. Many of the seven ports had dependent members, some at a good distance (Sandwich, for example, included Brightlingsea in Essex). Details of the organisation are noted for each parish in Part I of the *Guide*, and organisation by port in Part II under Kent and Sussex.

CIVIL PARISH–See PARISH

COUNTY

Ancient County ('Anc Co').

Counties are geographic entities whose origins reach back into the pre-Conquest period. They were derived either from Anglo-Saxon kingdoms whose size made them suitable administrative units when England was unified in the tenth century, or as artificial creations formed from larger kingdoms. The number of 'shires' (the Anglo-Saxon term) or 'counties' (Norman term) varied in the medieval period, particularly in the north of England.

Ancient counties were divided into *Hundreds ('Hd')*, the origins and roles of which are debated by historians. Hundreds were comprised of vills in the medieval period, and of parishes only by the late sixteenth century, thus providing the starting point for the *Guide*. The vast restructuring of hundreds in the middle ages thus falls outside the scope of the *Guide*. By the later nineteenth century hundreds had lost administrative importance. They are thus ignored in the *Guide* after 1889, at which time ancient counties were supplanted by administrative counties.

Administrative County ('Adm Co').

A new scheme of administrative counties was created in 1889 by the Local Government Act, 1888 (51 & 52 Vict., *c* 41, effective 1889). The new counties consisted of Municipal Boroughs (see BOROUGHS) and, from 1894, Urban and Rural Districts (as established by the Local Government Act, 1894, 57 & 58 Vict., *c* 58). *Urban Districts ('UD')* and *Rural Districts ('RD')* were either successors to previously existing urban or rural sanitary districts (see SANITARY DISTRICTS) or were created by later order. The scheme of administrative counties and constituent units was abolished in 1974.

County Boroughs ('CB').

The Local Government Act, 1888, also conferred on a number of important boroughs the status of county borough which entailed complete independence from the surrounding or adjacent county from which it had once been dependent. For details, see BOROUGHS.

Metropolitan and Non-Metropolitan Counties.

The Local Government Act, 1972 (20 & 21 Eliz. II, *c* 70, effective 1974) supplanted administrative counties and county boroughs with a new scheme of six metropolitan and thirty-nine non-metropolitan counties (excluding Greater London as constituted in 1965; see LONDON). The new counties were divided respectively into metropolitan districts and districts; all of the metropolitan counties are in the north of England and fall within the scope of Volume II of the *Guide*. This new arrangement provided a logical terminus for the *Guide*, which does, however, state in Part II the constitution of each non-metropolitan county in southern England as of its erection on 1 April 1974.

County of Itself.

Certain important towns enjoyed the right to name their own sheriffs and were known as 'counties of themselves', 'counties of cities' or 'counties of towns'. In addition to London these included the following in southern England (list and dates from which sheriffs appointed kindly supplied by *VCH*): Bristol (1373), Southampton (1447), Canterbury (1471), Gloucester (1483), Exeter (1537), Poole (1571).

Poor Law Counties (or Registration Counties).

When the Poor Law Commissioners organised poor law unions after 1834 (see POOR LAW), the unions of parishes often included parishes in two or more ancient counties. The census returns from 1851 created an artificial 'poor law' or 'registration' county, grouping under one county those unions predominantly comprised of parishes within that ancient county. The arrangement is ignored in Part I of the *Guide* but is reflected in Part II where poor law unions are identified as belonging to one or the other poor law county. Where a union included parishes from several counties, it will be necessary to refer to each county involved to ascertain the complete composition of the union.

Sources and Boundaries.

The schedules to the acts of 1888 and 1972 are the initial source, modified by later governmental orders (see PARISHES, *Sources and Boundaries* where the agencies are stated). In Part I of the *Guide* any changes which affected the boundary of a county are indicated under the name of the border parishes affected, with the names of parishes affected in the adjacent county or county borough as well. In Part II all changes which affected county boundaries are summarised by year in the initial entry 'Alterations in County Boundaries'.

See also: City of London, London Administrative County, Greater London under LONDON.

COUNTY BOROUGH–See BOROUGH and COUNTY
COUNTY CONSTITUENCY–See PARLIAMENTARY CONSTITUENCIES
COUNTY OF ITSELF–See COUNTY

DIOCESE

Diocese ('Dioc').

The diocese was the basic geographical division of the church from the earliest times. There was a continual rearrangement of dioceses before the Normans, but the system established by them in the eleventh century remained until the nineteenth century, altered only slightly in the sixteenth century. The *Guide* includes all dioceses of the established church from the Norman period until 1974, the terminal date for all entries, even though the ecclesiastical structure remains after that date with no loss in continuity. Dioceses are directed by a *bishop ('bp')* with ordinary jurisdiction, and the town in which his cathedral is located is properly called a *city*. On occasion the term 'city' has been granted to other towns by royal letters patent (Cambridge and Southampton in this century, for example).

Archdeaconries ('AD') and Rural Deaneries ('RDn').

From the twelfth and thirteenth centuries dioceses were divided into archdeaconries, geographic areas with special administrative and judicial roles under the direction of an archdeacon. These in turn were divided into rural deaneries, 'rural' used to distinguish them from the dean and chapter of the cathedral of the diocese. The system of rural deaneries was in abeyance from the sixteenth to the early nineteenth century when it was revived.

Rearrangements of dioceses, archdeaconries and rural deaneries were frequent from the early nineteenth century. To note all three jurisdictions in each of the parochial entries would expand the *Guide* to unmanageable size, so only the rural deaneries in which a parish was organised are noted. At the beginning of the entries for each county in Part I, the arrangement of rural deaneries in which that county's parises were organised is specified, with details of the organisation of the rural deaneries within dioceses and archdeaconries. Part IV of the *Guide* lists the complete composition of the dioceses, regardless of the counties in which constituent parishes were located.

Peculiars.

A number of parishes were geographically within the area of a diocese yet exempt in part or entirely from the jurisdiction of the bishop, archdeacon, other official or ecclesiastical courts. These *peculiar jurisdictions ('pec jurisd')* are specified in Part I of the *Guide* only. Most peculiar jurisdictions were abolished in the late 1840s but some persist; the terminal date of inclusion with the peculiar is noted.

Sources and Boundaries.

Changes in dioceses in Henry VIII's reign were made by letters patent, printed in Rymer's *Foedera.* Since the nineteenth century the new dioceses have been created by statutory authority, brought into effect by orders in council published in the *London Gazette.* The effective date of the change was usually the date gazetted, but sometimes at a later specified date or upon the vacancy of an incumbent.

Arrangements of parishes within the diocesan framework are noted for the mid-twelfth century in detail in William E. Lunt (ed.) *The Valuation of Norwich* (1926), for 1291 in *Taxatio Ecclesiastica Angliae et Walliae Auctoritate P. Nicholai IV* (1802), for the 1530s in *Valor Ecclesiasticus Temp. Henr. VIII. Auctoritate Regia Institutus* (1817), and for later times in John Bacon, *Liber Regis vel Thesaurus Rerum Ecclesiasticarum* (1786 edition used). Rearrangements since the later nineteenth century were made by gazetted orders in council; changes before 1875 were often on the bishop's authority and not published. In these cases the date cited in the *Guide* is the date in which the changes first appeared in the *Clergy List.*

There were other ways for the composition of a rural deanery to be changed in addition to an explicit order: constituent parishes could be abolished or new ones created; alterations of boundaries involving parishes in different dioceses, archdeaconries or rural deaneries could occur; or parishes could become organised in unions of benefices with parishes in adjacent jurisdictions, and thereby be drawn into the ecclesiastical organisation of the neighboring parish.

DISTRICT–See *Metropolitan District* and *District* under COUNTY, *Urban District* and *Rural District* under COUNTY, *Urban Sanitary District* and *Rural Sanitary District* under SANITARY DISTRICTS

DIVISION–See PARLIAMENTARY CONSTITUENCIES

ECCLESIASTICAL PARISH–See PARISH

EXTRA-PAROCHIAL

Certain geographic areas were not organised as parishes and hence were called *extra-parochial ('ex-par').* There were a variety of reasons, including association with the crown (Windsor Castle), with a religious house before the Dissolution or with a cathedral chapter, or with other corporate bodies such as inns of court. An attempt was made to extinguish these for civil purposes in the 1850s, notably in the statute 20 Vict., *c* 19, effective 1 Jan 1858, which stipulated that these places should either become separate civil parishes or be incorporated into an adjacent civil parish. Although this established the principle, a series of supplementary orders was often required to make the plan uniform (see PARISHES, *Sources and Boundaries*). These civil changes had no effect whatsoever on the ecclesiastical status of the extra-parochial places and a good many remain in that status. Over the years many have been altered, made parishes or amalgamated with other units, and these are indicated in the *Guide*.

GILBERT UNION–See POOR LAW
HAMLET–See PARISH
HUNDRED–See COUNTY
INCORPORATION–See BOROUGH, POOR LAW
LIBERTY–See PARISH
LONDON

The City of London.

The City enjoyed independence as a county of itself (see COUNTY) from early times. It was subdivided into *wards* which only rarely coincided with the parishes; the wards are listed in Part II of the *Guide* only.

The Metropolis.

As the population spilled out beyond the City's original limits of about a square mile, there then existed no single governmental unit to exercise authority over the enlarged area. The Metropolitan Management Act, 1855 (18 & 19 Vict., *c* 120) created a *Metropolitan Board of Works* to undertake sanitary responsibilities for the area which by then included parts of Middlesex, Surrey and Kent, without however altering jurisdictions in any other matters. The Board was comprised of *Vestries* in the case of important parishes and of *Boards of Works* for unions of two or more parishes.

London Administrative County.

The area of the Metropolis (with minor boundary alterations) became a separate county in 1889 when the general system of administrative counties was established (see COUNTY). As a result of the London Government Act, 1899 (62 & 63 Vict., *c* 14, effective 1900) London Administrative County was subdivided into *Metropolitan Boroughs ('Metrop Bor')*, in great part following the earlier divisions into Vestries and Boards of Works, in some instances earlier parliamentary arrangements.

Greater London.

The London Government Act, 1963 (11 & 12 Eliz. II, *c* 33, effective 1965) replaced the older scheme with Greater London, an area comprised of London Administrative County, the entire county of Middlesex, parts of Surrey, Kent, Essex and Hertfordshire, and several county boroughs. A provision of the act stipulated that no area was to be in a parish, but rather in newly constituted *London Boroughs.*

London and the Arrangement of the Guide.

Because 'London' now includes all or part of many ancient counties, the normal arrangement of entries in the *Guide* must be altered. All *ecclesiastical* changes are therefore noted in the entries for the ancient counties and the City of London in which they were originally located, regardless of the then-existing civil arrangement. For *civil* purposes there is a fourfold listing : the City of London (with civil and ecclesiastical entries); the ancient counties partly or wholly included in London at some date (with civil arrangements only until subsumed, ecclesiastical at any time); London Administrative County (civil details only); and Greater London (civil details only, by London Borough).

Sources and Boundaries.

These are the same as for alterations in parishes and counties (see PARISH, COUNTY)

LONDON BOROUGH–See LONDON
LORDSHIP–See PARISH
METROPOLIS–See LONDON
METROPOLITAN BOARD OF WORKS–See LONDON
METROPOLITAN BOROUGH–See LONDON
METROPOLITAN COUNTY–See COUNTY
MUNICIPAL BOROUGH–See BOROUGH
NON-METROPOLITAN COUNTY–See COUNTY
PARISH

There can be no single definition of 'parish'–ineed, the parish in origin was more a conglomeration of rights than a specific geographic area. Because the *Guide* deals with the areas in which these rights were exercised, the definition must be subdivided into ancient, civil and ecclesiastical parishes.

Ancient Parish ('AP').

As used for the purposes of the *Guide*, an ancient parish is one which existed at first for ecclesiastical purposes, as an area under the jurisdiction of a clergyman with cure of souls, but which gained secular functions in later periods. The first secular function was the relief of the poor, under successive statutory authorities beginning with the Elizabethan poor law of 1597. Therefore 'ancient parish' is used for a parish which existed before 1597 and which thereafter served both secular and ecclesiastical roles.

Civil Parish ('CP').

These units served only civil roles. It was common to define parishes in this sense as areas 'for which a separate poor rate is or can be assessed', a definition of no use after 1930. The existence, alteration or abolition of these units made no effect on the ecclesiastical arrangement of the identical geographic area.

Many civil parishes were in effect areas at first subordinate to a mother parish which came in time to enjoy independence. These units were variously called *hamlets ('hmlt'*, small settlements), *tithings ('tg')* or *townships ('tp')* (generallly subdivisions for poor law purposes), *chapelries ('chap'*, areas with a clergyman dependent upon the incumbent of the mother parish), *liberties ('lbty')* or *lordships* (areas with an early dependence upon a secular or ecclesiastical lord), or were called by a variety of other names with local importance. If a separate poor law rate was levied in the subordinate unit, it was then called by its own 'rank' such as hamlet and/or as 'parish'. To avoid this confusion the Poor Law Amendment Act, 1866 (29 & 30 Vict., *c* 113) stipulated that these areas should thereafter be called 'parishes'. It has been noted elsewhere (see EXTRA-PAROCHIAL) that many areas not within the parochial framework also became civil parishes, particularly in 1858.

Ecclesiastical Parishes ('EP').

These units came into existence after 1597 to serve only ecclestical roles. The number of these was much greater than for civil parishes, particularly as efforts were made to build new churches in increasingly populated urban areas. Many ecclesiastically subordinate areas within parishes such as chapelries were raised to parochial rank, and many formed with no earlier status. The Commissioners of Queen Anne's Bounty provided financial assistance to clergymen with inadequate financial resources, after which the benefice was styled a 'perpetual curacy'. This had no effect on the independence of previously separate parishes, but 'augmentation' of revenues for hitherto subordinate units gave them new independent status (1 Geo. I, *c* 10), and many ecclesiastical parishes therefore date from that augmentation. In the nineteenth and twentieth centuries a number of statutory provisions allowed the creation of many different types of ecclesiastical parishes, alike only in the newly independent status. It was thus not unusual for a parish to be 'refounded' to gain privileges and rights according to newer statutes which it had not earlier enjoyed as a perpetual curacy. The various types of ecclesiastical parishes are ignored because the reference to the original order will make the status clear; an exception is made for *particular districts ('part dist')* which are mentioned in the footnotes because their creation often rested on the authority of the particular bishop or other agency and because these orders were not generally published in the *London Gazette.*

Sources and Boundaries.

Civil parishes have been created and abolished, and their boundaries altered, by parliamentary statutes and by orders of a succession of governmental agencies (the Local Government Board, the Ministry of Health, the Ministry of Housing and Local Government and the Department of the Environment). The census has been the main source for these changes because the orders published in the intercensal periods are recapitulated in every new census.

The archives of the Church Commissioners (originally Ecclesiastical Commissioners) have been used to trace the ecclesiastical changes. For the period to 1939 the orders in council making the changes were published as an appendix to the Commissioners' report to parliament, so that one need not work through the bulky *London Gazette*, nor sort through the files of copies of the records in the diocesan record offices. Since 1939 the *London Gazette* is the principal source, although lately the orders have been published by name only, so that one must consult the originals.

Full details of all parishes affected by creations and abolitions of civil and ecclesiastical parishes are provided, with a footnote reference to the authority. Boundary alterations are cited by date with footnote reference to the authority, without further details, except when the alteration affected the boundaries of the county (civil parishes) or diocese (ecclesiastical parish), in which cases full particulars are included.

A particularly complicating element arises because many parishes consisted of two or more geographically separate portions. The elements of a parish existing apart were called 'detached parts', and conversely elements of other parishes included within a parish were called 'foreign parts'. A determined effort was made in the 1880s to eliminate these for civil purposes, notably in the statute 45 & 46 Vict., *c* 58 (effective 1883) which ordered that detached parts be incorporated into the parish which surrounded them or with which they enjoyed the longest common boundary. A series of orders was needed, however, to implement the principle fully; orders in the 1880s changing civil boundaries are nearly all of this type. These changes had no effect whatsoever on the ecclesiastical constitution of the parish, unless separate orders in council to that purpose were issued later.

PARLIAMENTARY BOROUGH–See PARLIAMENTARY CONSTITUENCIES

PARLIAMENTARY CONSTITUENCIES

Rearrangements of Constituencies.

Representatives of the counties of England in the House of Commons were called knights of the shire, with two representing each county. From 1832 onwards a number of statutes divided counties for parliamentary purposes: from 1832 to 1948 these were called *divisions ('Dv')* of the county, and since 1948 *county constituencies ('CC')*. A large number of boroughs were also represented in the House of Commons, called *parliamentary boroughs ('Parl Bor')* until 1948, *borough constituencies ('BC')* thereafter. Other interests such as the universities were also represented at different times.

In 1832 and 1867, with a few exceptions, county divisions were expressed in terms of hundreds and liberties. In 1885 the definition was in terms of *Petty Sessional Divions ('PSD')*, judicial units with which the *Guide* is not otherwise concerned. It has been necessary, therefore, to provide the parochial composition of the constituencies in the period 1885–1918 in Part III of the *Guide*. From 1918 onward the elements were stated in administrative county units.

Sources and Boundaries.

Dates of medieval representation of boroughs in parliament have been taken from the list of MPs in *Parliamentary Papers*, with no additional research other than secondary sources. Dates are shown as inclusive between alterations rather than by date of general elections (e.g., 1832–67) since bye elections would be based on the earlier arrangement. Changes from 1832–1918 and for 1948 are based on schedules in the following acts: 1832 (2 & 3 Wm. IV, *c* 45); 1867 (30 & 31 Vict., *c* 102); 1885 (48 & 49 Vict., *c* 3, 23); 1918 (7 & 8 Geo. V, *c* 64); 1948 (11 & 12 Geo. VI, *c* 65). Changes in 1945 and 1970 rest on schedules published as statutory instruments (1945/701, 1970/1674). From 1951 onward a number of changes are made on specific individual cases without awaiting a general rearrangement; these are published as statutory instruments. Many of the latter also change boundaries for parliamentary purposes, usually to bring the boundaries of borough constituencies into line with altered boundaries of municipal and county boroughs.

PARTICULAR DISTRICT–See PARISH

PECULIARS–See DIOCESE

PETTY SESSIONAL DIVISION–See PARLIAMENTARY CONSTITUENCIES

POOR LAW

The Elizabethan Poor Law.

The poor law acts of 1597 and 1601 assigned to the parishes the responsibility for administering the relief of the poor. These and numerous acts thereafter also allowed units within the parishes but without parochial status (chapelries, hamlets and the like) to be distinct and separate poor law units. It is impossible to date when most of these units assumed those responsibilities, but at the time they did so they became civil parishes (see PARISHES). This assumption of status is indicated in the *Guide* by the entry 'separate civil identity early'.

Incorporations and Gilbert Unions.

From the eighteenth century there was a growing awareness that a regional and/or particular rather than a parochial approach was needed in poor law matters. A number of parishes and groups of parishes sought special provisions through acts in parliament and are thus called *incorporations ('incorp')* for poor law purposes. The necessity for seeking special privileges through legislation was obviated by the permissive 'Gilbert's Act' of 1783 (22 Geo. III, *c* 83) which allowed voluntary associations of parishes for poor law purposes.

Poor Law Unions ('PLU').

The next step in forming unions of parishes was compulsory: the Poor Law Amendment Act,

1834 (4 & 5 Wm. IV, *c* 76) authorised Poor Law Commissioners to create poor law unions throughout the realm. Many of the parishes and groups of parishes already under incorporations or Gilbert unions were subsumed into the new poor law unions, but others remained separate for varying periods of time. For the purposes of the *Guide*, incorporations and Gilbert unions are not included unless they maintained their independence after the scheme of poor law unions. The Local Government Act, 1929 (19 & 20 Geo. V, *c* 17, effective 1930) abolished poor law unions and transferred those functions to the county councils of the administrative counties.

Sources and Boundaries.

The Poor Law Commissioners made annual reports to parliament in which the establishment of and changes in poor law unions can be found, particularly in 1835 and 1836 (published in *Parliamentary Papers*). Many changes of parishes from one union to another are recorded only in the minute books of the unions, usually held now in county record offices; since many of these are lost, it is sometimes possible to date changes only by reference to county directories, looking for the first appearance of a parish in a new union.

See also: Poor Law County under COUNTY

POOR LAW COUNTY–See COUNTY
POOR LAW UNION–See POOR LAW
RURAL DEANERY–See DIOCESE
RURAL DISTRICT–See COUNTY
RURAL SANITARY DISTRICT–See SANITARY DISTRICTS
SANITARY DISTRICTS

Urban Sanitary Districts ('USD') and Rural Sanitary Districts ('RSD').

The Public Health Acts of 1873 and 1875 (35 & 36 Vict., *c* 79, effective 1875, and 38 & 39 Vict., *c* 55) created new authorities with responsibilities in public health. Urban areas, already included in municipal boroughs or other bodies such as towns with improvement commissioners, were to form uban sanitary districts, the number of which was gradually enlarged in succeeding years. The remainder of the realm was to be divided into rural sanitary districts to be co-terminous with poor law unions less the areas in urban sanitary districts. The system was abolished by the Local Government Act, 1894 (57 & 58 Vict., *c* 58) which transformed existing urban and rural sanitary districts into general-purpose *urban districts ('UD')* and *rural districts ('RD')* respectively, in the new scheme of administrative counties (see COUNTY).

Sources and Boundaries.

Creations, abolitions and changes in these units are summarised in the census reports. The incorporation of a town as a municipal borough (see BOROUGHS) also made it an urban sanitary district. Changes in the boundaries of one did not always affect the other; changes are specified in Part II of the *Guide* under sanitary districts.

TITHING–See PARISH
TOWNSHIP–See PARISH
URBAN DISTRICT–See COUNTY
URBAN SANITARY DISTRICT–See SANITARY DISTRICTS
VESTRY–See LONDON
WARDS–See *City of London* under LONDON and PARLIAMENTARY CONSTITUENCIES

GENERAL ABBREVIATIONS

MONARCHS, MONTHS

The usual abbreviations are used for names of monarchs and of months of the year.

ABBREVIATIONS PARTICULAR TO COUNTIES

These are the initial entries for each county in Part I of the *Guide.*

COUNTIES

Beds	Bedfordshire	Bucks	Buckinghamshire
Berks	Berkshire	Cambs	Cambridgeshire

Cornw	Cornwall	IoW	Isle of Wight
Glos	Gloucestershire	Middx	Middlesex
Hants	Hampshire	Northants	Northamptonshire
Herts	Hertfordshire	Oxon	Oxfordshire
Hunts	Huntingdonshire	Warws	Warwickshire
IoE	Isle of Ely	Wilts	Wiltshire

DIOCESES

Canterb	Canterbury	Roch	Rochester
Chelm	Chelmsford	St Edm & Ipsw	St Edmundsbury and Ipswich
Glouc	Gloucester	Swk	Southwark
Guildf	Guildford	Winch	Winchester
Norw	Norwich	Worc	Worcester
Portsm	Portsmouth		

TERMS

abol	abolished	Hd	Hundred
AD	Archdeaconry	hmlt	hamlet
addtl	additional	incl	included
Adm	Administrative	incorp	incorporated
alt	alteration	Instr	Instrument
Anc	Ancient	jurisd	jurisdiction
AP	Ancient Parish	LB	London Borough
apptd	appointed	lbty	liberty
Archbp	Archbishop	LG	Local Government
BC	Borough Constituency	LGB	Local Government Board
Bd	Board	LGBO	Local Government Board Order
bdry	boundary	lic min	effective when a minister licensed to the cure
Bor	Borough		
Bp	Bishop	*Lond Gaz*	*London Gazette*
c	chapter (statute)	MB	Municipal Borough
ca	*circa*	mediev	medieval
Cath	Cathedral	Metrop	Metropolitan
CB	County Borough	mbr(s)	Member(s)
CBC	Church Building Commissioners	MHealthO	Ministry of Health Order
CC	County Constituency	MHousLGO	Ministry of Housing and Local Government Order
chap	chapel(ry)		
civ	civil	N (N'rn)	North (Northern)
Co	County	No	Number
conf	confirmed	O	Order
consecr	consecration	OC	Order in Council
Const	Constituency	orig	original
CP	Civil Parish	o'wise	otherwise
Cq Pt	Cinque Port	par(s)	parish(es)
cr	created	Parl	Parliamentary
d	*dorse*	Part Dist	Particular District
Decl	Declaration	PC	Perpetual Curacy
Dept	Department	pec	peculiar
dioc	diocese	PLU	Poor Law Union
Dist	District	prev	previous
Dv	Division	prob	probably
E (E'rn)	East (Eastern)	ProvO	Provisional Order
eccl	ecclesiastical	PSD	Petty Sessional Division
ent	entire(ly)	pt	part(ly)
Envirn	Environment	QAB	augmented by Commissioners of Queen Anne's Bounty
EP	Ecclesiastical Parish		
ex-par	extra-parochial	qv	for which see the separate entry
Gt	Great	RD	Rural District
Gtr	Greater	RDn	Rural Deanery

RO	Record Office	*temp*	*tempore*
RSD	Rural Sanitary District	tg	tithing
S (S'rn)	South (Southern)	transf	transferred
sep	separate	twnshp	township
Seq	Sequence	UD	Urban District
SI	Statutory Instrument	USD	Urban Sanitary District
St	Saint	vac	effective upon vacancy
supp	supplemental	W (W'rn)	West (Western)

FREQUENTLY CITED SOURCES

Beresford & Finberg	M. W. Beresford and H. P. R. Finberg *English Medieval Boroughs: A Hand-List*
Liber Regis	John Bacon, *Liber Regis*
Lond Gaz	*London Gazette*
VCH	*Victoria History of the Counties of England*
Valor Eccl	*Valor Ecclesiasticus*

DATES

The terminal date of the *Guide* is 1 April 1974 at which time the Local Government Act, 1972, became effective. Since that act did not affect the ecclesiastical or parliamentary units, the character * is used to indicate that the ecclesiastical or parliamentary units continued to exist after 1 April 1974.

'ASSOCIATED' COUNTY BOROUGHS AND COUNTIES OF THEMSELVES

The entry in italics was a county of itself only. Those marked with † were counties of themselves and later county boroughs. For London's unique situation see LONDON above in DEFINITIONS OF TERMS. The entry is paired with the name of the 'associated' county with which its entries are found in the *Guide.*

Bath	Somerset	London	City of London
Bournemouth	Hants	Ipswich	Suffolk
Brighton	Sussex	Luton	Beds
Bristol†	Glos	Norwich	Norfolk
Canterbury†	Kent	Oxford	Oxon
Croydon	Surrey	Plymouth	Devon
Devonport	Devon	*Poole*	Dorset
Eastbourne	Sussex	Portsmouth	Hants
Exeter†	Devon	Reading	Berks
Gloucester†	Glos	Southampton†	Hants
East Ham	Essex	Southend on Sea	Essex
West Ham	Essex	Torbay	Devon
Hastings	Sussex	Great Yarmouth	Norfolk

Part I: The Parishes of England

BEDFORDSHIRE

ABBREVIATIONS

Abbreviations particular to Beds follow. Those general abbreviations in use throughout the *Guide* are found on page xix.

Ampt.	Ampthill
Bedf.	Bedford
Biggl.	Biggleswade
Clap.	Clapham
Dunst.	Dunstable
Felm.	Felmersham
Leigh. Buz.	Leighton Buzzard
Mansh.	Manshead
Redb.	Redbourne
Sharnb.	Sharnbrook
Sheff.	Shefford
Stod.	Stodden
Wixamt.	Wixamtree
Wob.	Woburn

SEQUENCES

An abbreviated entry prefixed by 'Seq' is used in the parochial entries to avoid repeating often the names of superior units of administration. The content of each sequence is shown below.

Local Government Sequences ('LG')

SEQ 1 Barford Hd, Bedf. PLU, RSD, RD
SEQ 2 Biggl. Hd, PLU, RSD, RD
SEQ 3 Clifton Hd, Biggl. PLU, RSD, RD
SEQ 4 Flitt Hd, Ampt. PLU, RSD, RD
SEQ 5 Flitt Hd, Luton PLU, RSD, RD
SEQ 6 Mansh. Hd, Leigh. Buz. PLU, RSD, Eaton Bray RD (1894–1933), Luton RD (1933–74)
SEQ 7 Mansh. Hd, Wob. PLU (1835–99), RSD, Ampt. PLU (1899–1930), RD
SEQ 8 Mansh. Hd, Wob. PLU (1835–99), RSD, Leigh. Buz. PLU (1899–1930), Eaton Bray RD (1894–1933), Luton RD (1933–74)
SEQ 9 Redb. Hd, Ampt. PLU, RSD, RD
SEQ 10 Redb. Hd, Bedf. PLU, RSD, RD
SEQ 11 Stod. Hd, Bedf. PLU, RSD, RD
SEQ 12 Stod. Hd, St Neot's PLU, Eaton Socon RD (1894–1934), Bedf. RD (1934–74)
SEQ 13 Willey Hd, Bedf. PLU, RSD, RD
SEQ 14 Wiley Hd, Wellingborough PLU, RSD, Bedf. RD
SEQ 15 Wixamt. Hd, Bedf. PLU, RSD, RD
SEQ 16 Wixamt. Hd, Biggl. PLU, RSD, RD

Parliamentary Sequences ('Parl')

SEQ 1 N'rn Dv (1885–1918), Bedf. Dv/CC (1918–*)
SEQ 2 N'rn Dv (1885–1918), Bedf. Dv (1918–48), Mid CC (1948–*)
SEQ 3 N'rn Dv (1885–1918), Mid Dv/CC (1918–*)
SEQ 4 S'rn Dv (1885–1918), Luton Dv (1918–48), South CC (1948–*)
SEQ 5 S'rn Dv (1885–1918), Mid Dv/CC (1918–*)
SEQ 6 S'rn Dv (1885–1918), Mid Dv (1918–48), South CC (1948–*)

Ecclesiastical Sequences ('Eccl')

SEQ 1 Bedf. RDn (until 1866), Bedf. RDn First Dv (1866–80), Bedf. RDn (1880–*)
SEQ 2 Bedf. RDn (until 1866), Bedf. RDn Second Dv (1866–80), Haynes RDn (1880–1918), Bedf. RDn (1918–*)
SEQ 3 Clap. RDn (until 1866), Clap. RDn E'rn Dv (1866–80), Felm. RDn (1880–1970), Sharnb. RDn (1970–*)
SEQ 4 Clap. RDn (until 1866), Clap. RDn W'rn Dv (1866–80), Felm. RDn (1880–1970), Sharnb. RDn (1970–*)
SEQ 5 Dunst. RDn (until 1866), Dunst. RDn First Dv (1866–80), Ampt. RDn (1880–*)
SEQ 6 Dunst. RDn (until 1866), Dunst. RDn First Dv (1866–80), Dunst. RDn(1880–*)
SEQ 7 Dunst. RDn (until 1866), Dunst. RDn Second Dv (1866–80), Dunst. RDn (1880–*)
SEQ 8 Dunst. RDn (until 1866), Dunst. RDn

Second Dv (1866–80), Luton RDn (1880–*)

SEQ 9 Eaton RDn (until 1866), Eaton RDn S'rn Dv (1866–80), Eaton RDn (1880–1917), Bedf. RDn (1917–22), Riseley RDn (1922–70), Sharnb. RDn (1970–*)

SEQ 10 Eaton RDn (until 1866), Eaton RDn S'rn Dv (1866–80), Eaton RDn (1880–1917), Biggl. RDn (1917–*)

SEQ 11 Eaton RDn (until 1866), Eaton RDn S'rn Dv (1866–80), Eaton RDn (1880–1917), Riseley RDn (1917–70), Sharnb. RDn (1970–*)

SEQ 12 Eaton RDn (until 1866), Eaton RDn N'rn Dv (1866–80), Riseley RDn (1880–1970), Sharnb. RDn (1970–*)

SEQ 13 Fleete RDn (until 1866), Fleete RDn E'rn Dv (1866–80), Ampt. RDn (1880–*)

SEQ 14 Fleete RDn (until 1866), Fleete RDn W'rn Dv (1866–80), Fleete RDn (1880–1970), Ampt. RDn (1970–*)

SEQ 15 Sheff. RDn (until 1866), Sheff. RDn E'rn Dv (1866–80), Biggl. RDn (1880–*)

SEQ 16 Sheff. RDn (until 1866), Sheff. RDn E'rn Dv (1866–80), Sheff. RDn (1880–*)

SEQ 17 Sheff. RDn (until 1866), Sheff. RDn W'rn Dv (1866–80), Biggl. RDn (1880–*)

SEQ 18 Sheff. RDn (until 1866), Sheff. RDn W'rn Dv (1866–80), Sheff. RDn (1880–*)

DIOCESES AND ARCHDEACONRY

With a few exceptions noted below in the parochial entries, Beds pars were in Bedford AD which was in Lincoln dioc until 1837, in Ely dioc 1837–1914, and in St Albans dioc from 1914.

THE PARISHES OF BEDFORDSHIRE

AMPTHILL

AP *LG* Redb. Hd, Ampt. PLU, RSD (1875–93), USD (1893–94), UD. *Parl* Seq 3. *Eccl* Seq 13.

ARLESEY

AP *LG* Seq 3. Civ bdry: 1947 (incl gains pt Ickleford CP, Herts),[1] 1956 (incl gains pt Ickleford CP, Herts).[2] *Parl* Seq 3. *Eccl* Seq 16.

ASPLEY GUISE

AP *LG* Seq 7. Civ bdry: 1883 (cr Aspley Heath CP),[3] 1934,[4] 1956,[5] 1965 (exchanges pts with Woburn Sands CP, Bucks).[6] *Parl* Seq 5. *Eccl* Seq 14.

ASPLEY HEATH

CP Cr 1883 from Aspley Guise AP.[3] *LG* Mansh. Hd, Wob. PLU (1883–99), RSD, Ampt. PLU (1899–1930), RD. Bdry: 1885 (gains pt Wavendon AP, Bucks),[7] 1965 (exchanges pts with Wavendon AP, loses pt to Woburn Sands CP, both Bucks).[6] *Parl* Seq 5.

ASTWICK

Chap in Studham AP, sep par between 1242–91.[8] *LG* Seq 2. *Parl* Seq 3. *Eccl* Seq 16.

GREAT BARFORD

AP *LG* Seq 1. *Parl* Seq 2. *Eccl* Seq 10.

LITTLE BARFORD

AP *LG* Biggl. Hd, St Neot's PLU, RSD, Eaton Socon RD (1894–1934), Bedf. RD (1934–74). *Parl* Seq 2. *Eccl* Sheff. RDn (until 1866), Sheff. RDn W'rn Dv (1866–80), Biggl. RDn (1880–1972). Abol eccl 1972 to help cr Tempsford with Little Barford EP.[9]

BARTON IN THE CLAY

AP Usual civ spelling until renamed 1956 'Barton-le-Cley'[10]; for eccl see following entry. *LG* Flitt Hd, Luton PLU, RSD, RD. *Parl* S'rn Dv (1885–1918), Luton Dv (1918–48), South CC 70).

BARTON-LE-CLEY

AP Usual eccl spelling, civ spelling after 1956 when 'Barton in the Clay' renamed.[10] *LG* Luton RD. *Parl* S CC (1970–*). *Eccl* Seq 5.

BATTLESDEN

AP *LG* Seq 7. Civ bdry: 1956.[11] *Parl* Seq 5. *Eccl* Dunst. RDn (until 1866), Dunst. RDn First Dv (1866–80), Fleete RDn (1880–1928). Abol eccl 1928 to help cr Battlesden with Pottesgrove EP.[12]

BATTLESDEN WITH POTTESGROVE

EP Cr 1928 by union Battlesden AP, Pottesgrove AP.[12] Fleete RDn (1928–70), Ampt. RDn (1970–*).

BEDFORD

The following have 'Bedford' in their name. Insofar as any existed at a given time: *LG* Willey Hd, Bedf. Bor/MB, PLU, USD. *Parl* Bedf. Parl Bor (1295–1918), Bedf. Dv/CC (1918–*). *Eccl* Bedf. RDn (until 1866), Bedf. RDn First Dv (1866–80), Bedf. RDn (1880–*).

CP1–BEDFORD–Cr 1934 by union AP2, AP3, AP4, AP5, AP6.[13] Bdry: 1968.[14]

AP1–BEDFORD ALL SAINTS–disappeared by early 17th cent, possibly absorbed in AP5.[15]

EP1–BEDFORD ALL SAINTS–Cr 1916 from AP5.[16] Bdry: 1944.[17]

EP2–BEDFORD CHRIST CHURCH–Cr 1958 from AP2.[18]

EP3–BEDFORD HOLY TRINITY–Cr 1840 from AP5.[19] Bdry: 1894,[20] 1896 (cr EP6).[21]

EP4–BEDFORD ST ANDREW–Cr 1915 from AP6.[22]

AP2–BEDFORD ST CUTHBERT–Abol civ 1934 to help cr CP1.[13] Eccl bdry: 1958 (cr EP2).[18]

AP3–BEDFORD ST JOHN–Abol civ 1934 to help cr CP1.[13] Eccl bdry: 1995,[24] 1956 (help cr

EP7).[25]

EP5–BEDFORD ST LEONARD–Cr 1889 from AP4.[23] Bdry: 1955.[24]

EP6–BEDFORD ST MARTIN–Cr 1896 from EP3.[21]

AP4–BEDFORD ST MARY–Abol civ 1934 to help cr CP1.[13] Eccl bdry: 1889 (cr EP5),[23] 1955,[24] 1956 (help cr EP7).[25]

EP7–BEDFORD ST MICHAEL AND ALL ANGELS–Cr 1956 from AP3, AP4, Caddington AP.[25]

AP5–BEDFORD ST PAUL–Abol civ 1934 to help cr CP1.[13] Civ and eccl bdry: possibly absorbed AP7 in 1545, AP1 in 17th cent.[15] Addtl eccl bdry alt: 1840 (cr EP3),[19] 1894,[20] 1916 (cr EP1).[16]

AP6–BEDFORD ST PETER [de MERTON]–Abol civ 1934 to help cr CP1.[13] Eccl bdry: 1915 (cr EP4).[22]

AP7–BEDFORD ST PETER DUNSTABLE–Pulled down 1545, possibly absorbed in AP4.[15]

BIDDENHAM

AP *LG* Seq 13. Civ bdry: 1934.[13] *Parl* Seq 1. *Eccl* Seq 1. Eccl bdry: 1944.[17]

BIGGLESWADE

AP *LG* Bigg. Hd, Bor (13th to 17th cent),[50] PLU, RSD (1875–92), USD (1892–94), UD. Civ bdry: 1920 (bdry with Langford AP confirmed),[26] 1933.[4] *Parl* Seq 3. *Eccl* Pec jurisd of Biggl. (until 1852), Seq 15 thereafter.

BILLINGTON

Chap and hmlt in Leighton Buzzard AP, sep EP 1810,[19] sep CP 1866.[27] *LG* Seq 6. *Parl* Seq 6. *Eccl* Pec jurisd of Leigh. Buz. (1810–52), Seq 7 thereafter.

BISCOT

Hmlt in Luton AP, sep EP 1866.[28] Dunst. RDn First Dv (1866–80), Luton RDn (1880–*). Bdry: 1903,[29] 1940,[30] 1942,[31] 1954 (help cr Leagrave EP),[32] 1971 (cr Limbury EP).[33]

BLETSOE

AP *LG* Seq 13. Civ bdry: 1933.[34] *Parl* Seq 1. *Eccl* Seq 3.

BLUNHAM

AP Incl hmlt Moggerhanger (sep EP 1860,[35] sep CP 1866[27]). *LG* Seq 16. *Parl* Seq 3. *Eccl* Seq 17.

BOLNHURST

AP *LG* Stod. Hd, Bedf. PLU, RSD, RD. Civ bdry: 1879.[36] Abol civ 1934 to help cr Bolnhurst and Keysoe CP.[13] *Parl* N'rn Dv (1885–1918), Bedf. Dv (1918–48). *Eccl* Seq 11.

BOLNHURST AND KEYSOE

CP Cr 1934 by union Bolnhurst AP, Keysoe AP.[13] *LG* Bedf. RD. Bdry: 1948,[37] 1956.[38] *Parl* Bedf. CC (1948–*). Parl bdry: 1955.[42]

BROMHAM

AP *LG* Seq 13. Civ bdry: 1934 (help cr Bedford CP),[13] 1948.[37] *Parl* Seq 1. Parl bdry: 1955.[42] *Eccl* Clap. RDn (until 1866), Clap. RDn E'rn Dv (1866–80), Bedf. RDn (1880–1922), Felm. RDn (1922–30), Bedf. RDn (1930–*).

CADDINGTON

AP Pt Beds (Flitt Hd), pt Herts (Dacorum Hd), made 1894 2 sep CPs, one in each co.[39] *LG* Luton PLU, RSD. *Parl* Beds pt, N'rn Dv (1885–1918). *Eccl* Seq 8. Eccl bdry: 1940,[30] 1954 (help cr Leagrave EP),[32] 1961.[43]

CP Cr 1894 from the Beds pt of Caddington AP.[39] *LG* Luton PLU, RD. Civ bdry: 1897 (gains ent Caddington CP, Herts, and help cr Markyate CP, Herts),[40] 1907 (loses pt to Flamstead AP, gains pt Markyate CP, both Herts),[26] 1933,[4] 1964 (loses pt to Luton CB and CP),[41] 1965 (gains pt Flamstead AP, pt Markyate CP, both Herts).[6] *Parl* Luton Dv (1918–48), South CC (1948–*).

CALDECOTE

EP Cr 1928 from Northill AP.[44] Biggl. RDn.

CAMPTON

AP Incl twnshp Shefford (sep CP 1866[27]). *LG* Seq 3. Civ bdry: 1933.[4] *Parl* Seq 3. *Eccl* Seq 18.

CARDINGTON

AP Incl hmlts Cotton End, Harrowden, Fenlake (made one CP 1866 as 'Eastcotts'[27]). *LG* Seq 15. Addtl civ bdry alt: 1934,[13] 1968.[14] *Parl* Seq 2. *Eccl* Seq 2. Eccl bdry: 1956 (help cr Bedford St Michael and All Angels EP).[25]

CARLTON

AP *LG* Willey Hd, Bedf. PLU, RSD, RD. Abol civ 1934 to help cr Carlton and Chellington CP.[13] *Parl* N'rn Dv (1885–1918), Bedf. Dv (1918–48). *Eccl* Clap. RDn (until 1866), Clap. RDn W'rn Dv (1866–80), Felm. RDn (1880–1970), Sharnb. RDn (1970–72). Abol eccl 1972 to help cr Carlton with Chellington EP.[45]

CARLTON AND CHELLINGTON

CP Cr 1934 by union Carlton AP, Chellington AP.[13] *LG* Bedf. RD. Civ bdry: 1948.[37] *Parl* Bedf. CC (1948–*). Parl bdry: 1955.[42]

CARLTON WITH CHELLINGTON

EP Cr 1972 by union Carlton AP, Chellington AP.[45] Sharnb. RDn.

CHALGRAVE

AP *LG* Seq 8. Civ bdry: 1929.[46] *Parl* Seq 6. *Eccl* Seq 7. Eccl bdry: 1931.[47]

CHELLINGTON

AP Organisation as for Charlton AP.

CHICKSANDS

Ex-par place, sep CP 1858,[48] eccl ex-par status retained as 'Chicksands Priory'. *LG* Seq 3. *Parl* Seq 3.

CLAPHAM

Chap in Oakley AP, sep par 1545.[49] *LG* Seq 11. Civ bdry: 1934 (help cr Bedford CP),[13] 1948,[37] 1968.[14] *Parl* Seq 1. Parl bdry: 1955.[42] *Eccl* Clap. RDn (1545–1866), Clap. RDn E'rn Dv (1866–80), Bedf. RDn (1880–*).

CLIFTON

AP *LG* Seq 3. Civ bdry: 1933.[4] *Parl* Seq 3. *Eccl* Seq 18.

CLOPHILL

AP *LG* Seq 4. *Parl* Seq 3. *Eccl* Fleete RDn (until 1866), Fleete RDn E'rn Dv (1866–80), Ampt. RDn (1880–1970), Sheff. RDn (1970–*).

COLMWORTH

AP *LG* Seq 1. Civ bdry: 1948,[37] 1956.[38] *Parl* Seq

2. Parl bdry: 1955.[42] *Eccl* Seq 11.

COLWORTH FARM
Ex-par place, sep CP 1858.[48] *LG* Willey Hd, Bedf. PLU, RSD, RD. Abol 1895 ent to Sharnbrook AP.[51]

COPLE
AP *LG* Seq 15. *Parl* Seq 2. *Eccl* Bedf. RDn (until 1866), Bedf. RDn Second Dv (1866–80), Haynes RDn (1880–1918), Bedf. RDn (1918–74), Biggl. RDn (1974–*).

CRANFIELD
AP *LG* Seq 9. *Parl* Seq 3. *Eccl* Seq 14.

DEAN
AP *LG* Stod. Hd, St Neot's PLU, RSD, Eaton Socon RD. Abol civ 1934 to help cr Dean and Shelton CP.[13] *Parl* N'rn Dv (1885–1918), Bedf. Dv (1918–48). *Eccl* Seq 12.

DEAN AND SHELTON
CP Cr 1934 by union Dean AP, Shelton AP.[13] *LG* Bedf. RD. *Parl* Bedf. CC (1948–*).

DUNSTABLE
AP *LG* Mansh. Hd, Dunst. Bor (12th to 16th cent), MB (1864–1974),[52] Luton PLU, Dunst. USD. Civ bdry: 1907,[53] 1933,[4] 1954,[54] 1964.[41] *Parl* Dunst. Parl Bor (1312 only), Seq 4. *Eccl* Seq 6. Eccl bdry: 1961.[43]

DUNTON
AP *LG* Seq 2. *Parl* Seq 3. *Eccl* Seq 15.

EASTCOTTS
Twnshp in Cardington AP (consisting of the three hmlts of Cotton End, Harrowden, Fenlake), sep CP 1866.[27] *LG* Seq 15. Bdry: 1934 (help cr Bedford CP),[13] 1968.[14] *Parl* Seq 2.

EATON BRAY
AP *LG* Mansh. Hd, Luton PLU (1835–40s), Leigh. Buz. PLU (1840s–1930), RSD, Eaton Bray RD
Bray (1835–40s), Eggington, Heath and Reach, Hockliffe (1899–1930), Leighton Buzzard, Stanbridge. Tilsworth (1899–1930)

EATON SOCON
AP *LG* Barford Hd, St Neot's PLU, RSD, Eaton Socon RD (1894–1934), Bedf. RD (1934–65). Civ bdry: 1956.[38] Abol civ 1965 pt to Roxton AP, pt to help cr Staploe CP, pt to St Neot's UD and CP, Hunts.[6] *Parl* N'rn Dv (1885–1918), Bedf. Dv (1918–48), Mid CC (1948–70). *Eccl* Seq 10.

EDWORTH
AP *LG* Seq 2. *Parl* Seq 3. *Eccl* Sheff. RDn (until 1866), Sheff. RDn E'rn Dv (1866–80), Biggl. RDn (1880–*).

EGGINGTON
Hmlt and chap in Leighton Buzzard AP, sep EP 1810,[19] sep CP 1866.[27] *LG* Seq 6. *Parl* Seq 6. *Eccl* Pec jurisd of Leigh. Buz. (1810–52), Dunst. RDn (1852–66), Dunst. RDn Second Dv (1866–80), Dunst. RDn (1880–*).

ELSTOW
AP *LG* Seq 10. Civ bdry: 1934 (help cr Bedford CP),[13] 1934.[13] *Parl* Seq 2. *Eccl* Seq 2. Eccl bdry: 1955.[24]

EVERSHOLT
AP *LG* Seq 7. *Parl* Seq 5. *Eccl* Seq 14.

EVERTON
AP Incl hmlt Tetworth (pt Beds [Biggl. Hd], pt Hunts [Toseland Hd], considered a CP since 1810,[55] the pt in Beds transf to Hunts 1832 for parl purposes, 1844 for civ purposes[56]). *LG* Biggl. Hd, PLU, RSD, RD. Addtl civ bdry alt: 1933,[4] 1965 (gains pt Gamlingay AP, Cambs, and pt Tetworth CP, Hunts).[56] *Parl* Seq 3. *Eccl* St Neots RDn, Hunts AD.

EYEWORTH
AP *LG* Seq 2. Civ bdry: 1883.[57] *Parl* Seq 3. *Eccl* Seq 15.

FARLEY HILL
EP Renaming 1967 of Luton St Michael and St George, Farley Hill EP.[58] Luton RDn.

FARNDISH
AP Pt Beds (Willey Hd), pt Northants (Higham Ferrers Hd). *LG* Wellingborough PLU, RSD. Abol civ 1884 ent to Podington AP.[59] *Eccl* Clap. RDn (until 1866), Clap. RDn W'rn Dv (1866–80), Felm. RDn (1880–1970), Sharnb. RDn (1970). Abol eccl 1970 to help cr Podington with Farndish EP.[60]

FELMERSHAM
AP Incl chap Pavenham (sep civ identity early, sep EP 1859[61]). *LG* Seq 13. *Parl* Seq 1. *Eccl* Seq 3.

FLITTON
AP Incl hmlt Silsoe (sep EP 1846,[62] sep CP 1866[27]). *LG* Seq 4. *Parl* Seq 5. *Eccl* Seq 13.

FLITWICK
AP *LG* Seq 9. *Parl* Seq 5. *Eccl* Seq 13.

GOLDINGTON
AP *LG* Barford Hd, Bedf. PLU, RSD, RD. Abol civ 1934 pt to Ravensden AP, pt to Renhold AP, pt to help cr Bedford CP.[13] *Parl* N'rn Dv (1885–1918), Bedf. Dv (1918–48). *Eccl* Seq 1.

GRAVENHURST
CP Cr 1888 by union Lower Gravenhurst AP, Upper Gravenhurst AP.[63] *LG* Ampt. PLU, RSD, RD. *Parl* Mid Dv/CC (1918–*).

LOWER GRAVENHURST
AP *LG* Flitt Hd, Ampt. PLU, RSD. Abol civ 1888 to help cr Gravenhurst CP.[63] *Parl* S'rn Dv (1885–1918). *Eccl* Fleete RDn (until 1866), Fleete RDn E'rn Dv (1866–80), Sheff. RDn (1880–1972). Abol eccl 1972 to help cr Upper with Lower Gravenhurst EP.[64]

UPPER GRAVENHURST
Chap in Shillington AP from 14th cent, sep par *temp* Elizabeth I.[65] *LG* Flitt Hd, Ampt. PLU, RSD. Abol civ 1888 to help cr Gravenhurst CP.[63] *Parl* S'rn Dv (1885–1918). *Eccl* Sheff. RDn (*temp* Elizabeth I–1866), Sheff. RDn W'rn Dv (1866–80), Sheff. RDn (1880–1972). Abol eccl 1972 to help cr Upper with Lower Gravenhurst EP.[64]

UPPER WITH LOWER GRAVENHURST
EP Cr 1972 by union Upper Gravenhurst AP, Lower Gravenhurst AP.[64] Sheff. RDn.

HARLINGTON
AP *LG* Seq 7. Civ bdry: 1933.[4] *Parl* Seq 5. *Eccl* Fleete RDn (until 1866), Fleete RDn E'rn Dv

(1866–80), Luton RDn (1880–*). Eccl bdry: 1957.[66]

HARROLD

AP *LG* Seq 13. *Parl* Seq 1. *Eccl* Seq 4.

COCKAYNE HATLEY

AP Earlier, 'Hatley Port'. *LG* Seq 2. Civ bdry: 1883.[57] *Parl* Seq 3. *Eccl* Seq 15.

HAYNES

AP Earlier often 'Hawnes'. *LG* Seq 4. *Parl* Seq 3. *Eccl* Fleete RDn (until 1866), Fleete RDn E'rn Dv (1866–80), Haynes RDn (1880–1918), Ampt. RDn (1918–70), Sheff. RDn (1970–*).

HEATH AND REACH

Hmlt in Leighton Buzzard AP, sep EP 1826,[19] sep CP 1866.[27] *LG* Seq 6. Civ bdry: 1933,[4] 1956.[11] *Parl* Seq 6. *Eccl* Pec jurisd of Leigh. Buz. (1826–52), Seq 7 thereafter.

HENLOW

AP *LG* Seq 3. Civ bdry: 1947.[1] *Parl* Seq 3. *Eccl* Seq 16.

HIGHAM GOBION

AP *LG* Seq 4. Civ bdry: 1933.[4] *Parl* Seq 5. *Eccl* Seq 5.

HOCKLIFFE

AP *LG* Seq 8. Civ bdry: 1929,[46] 1956.[11] *Parl* Seq 6. *Eccl* Seq 7. Eccl bdry: 1931.[27]

HOLCOT

AP Sometimes 'Hulcote', the form used when new CP, EP formed from this par. *LG* Mansh. Hd, Wob. PLU (1835–99), RSD, Ampt. PLU (1899–1930), RD. Abol civ 1933 to help cr Hulcote and Salford CP.[4] *Parl* S'rn Dv (1885–1918), Mid Dv (1918–48). *Eccl* Fleete RDn. Abol eccl 1750 to help cr Hulcote with Salford EP.[67]

HOLWELL

AP *LG* Clifton Hd, Hitchin PLU, RSD, sep RD (1894–97). Civ bdry: 1897.[69] Transf 1897 to Herts.[68] *Parl* N'rn Dv (1885–1918), Herts thereafter. *Eccl* Sheff. RDn (until 1866), Sheff. RDn W'rn Dv (1866–80), Sheff. RDn (1880–1914), Hitchin RDn (St Albans AD, 1914–*).

HOUGHTON CONQUEST

AP *LG* Seq 9. *Parl* Seq 3. *Eccl* Bedf. RDn (until 1866), Bedf. RDn Second Dv (1866–80), Haynes RDn (1880–1918), Ampt. RDn (1918–*).

HOUGHTON REGIS

AP *LG* Mansh. Hd, Luton PLU, RSD, RD. Civ bdry: 1897 (loses pt to help cr Markyate CP, Herts),[40] 1907,[53] 1928,[70] 1933,[4] 1954.[54] *Parl* Seq 4. *Eccl* Seq 7. Eccl bdry: 1961,[43] 1967 (help cr Luton St Hugh, Lewsey EP).[71]

HULCOTE AND SALFORD

CP Cr 1933 by union Holcot AP, Salford AP.[4] *LG* Ampt. RD. Bdry: 1956 (incl exchanges pts with Wavendon AP, Bucks).[5] *Parl* Mid CC (1948–*).

HULCOTE WITH SALFORD

EP Cr 1750 by union Holcot AP, Salford AP.[67] Fleete RDn (1750–1866), Fleete RDn W'rn Dv (1866–80), Fleete RDn (1880–1970), Ampt. RDn (1970–*).

HUMBERSHOE

Hmlt in Studham AP, sep CP 1866.[27] *LG* Mansh. Hd, Luton PLU, RSD, RD. Abol 1897 to help cr Markyate CP, Herts.[40] *Parl* S'rn Dv (1885–1918).

HUSBORNE CRAWLEY

AP *LG* Seq 7. *Parl* Seq 5. *Eccl* Seq 14.

HYDE

Hmlts East Hyde, West Hyde in Luton AP, sep EP 1859 as 'East Hyde',[72] sep CP 1896 as 'Hyde' (from Luton Rural CP).[70] *LG* Luton PLU, RD. Civ bdry: 1907 (exchanges pts with Flamstead AP, Harpendon Rural CP, both Herts),[26] 1928,[70] 1933,[4] 1939,[73] 1964 (loses pt to Luton CB and CP),[41] 1965 (exchanges pts with Flamstead AP, Herts).[6] *Parl* Luton Dv (1918–48), South CC (1948–*). *Eccl* Dunst. RDn (1859–66), Dunst. RDn First Dv (1866–80), Luton RDn (1880–*).

EAST HYDE—See prev entry

ICKLEFORD

Chap (pt Herts [Hitchin Hd], pt Beds [Clifton Hd]) in Pirton AP (o'wise Herts), sep civ identity early early, the pt in Beds transf to Herts 1832 for parl purposes, 1844 for civ purposes,[56] sep EP 1847.[42] See main entry in Herts.

KEMPSTON

AP *LG* Redb. Hd, Bedf. PLU, RSD, RD (1894–96), Kempston UD (1896–1974). Civ bdry: 1896 (the pt not made UD to cr Kempston Rural CP),[74] 1934.[13] *Parl* N'rn Dv (1885–1918), Bedf. Dv/CC (1918–*). *Eccl* Seq 2. Eccl bdry: 1955.[24]

KEMPSTON RURAL

CP Cr 1896 from the pt of Kempston AP not made UD.[74] *LG* Bedf. PLU, RD. Bdry: 1934,[13] 1937,[77] 1948.[37] *Parl* Bedf. Dv (1918–48), Mid CC (1948–*). Parl bdry: 1955.[42]

KENSWORTH

AP In Herts (Dacorum Hd), transf 1897 to Beds.[68] *LG* Luton PLU, RSD, sep RD in Herts (1894–97), Luton RD (1897–1974). *Parl* In Herts until 1918), Luton Dv (1918–48), South CC (1948–*). *Eccl* Berkhampstead RDn (until 1907), St Albans RDn (1907–30)(both in St Albans AD), Dunst. RDn (1930–*). Eccl bdry: 1961.[75]

KEYSOE

AP *LG* Stod. Hd, Bedf. PLU, RSD, RD. Abol civ 1934 to help cr Bolnhurst and Keysoe CP.[13] *Parl* N'rn Dv (1885–1918), Bedf. Dv (1918–48). *Eccl* Eaton RDn (until 1866), Eaton RDn S'rn Dv (1866–80), Riseley RDn (1880–1970), Sharnb. RDn (1970–*).

KNOTTING

Chap in Melchbourne AP, sep par 1176.[76] *LG* Stod. Hd, Bedf. PLU, RSD, RD. Abol civ 1934 to help cr Knotting and Souldrop CP.[13] *Parl* N'rn Dv (1885–1918), Bedf. Dv (1918–48). *Eccl* Seq 3.

KNOTTING AND SOULDROP

CP Cr 1934 by union Knotting AP, Souldrop AP.[13] *LG* Bedf. RD. *Parl* Bedf. CC (1948–*).

LANGFORD

AP *LG* Seq 2. Civ bdry: 1920.[78] *Parl* Seq 3. *Eccl* Sheff. RDn (until 1866), Sheff. RDn E'rn Dv (1866–80), Sheff. RDn (1880–99), Biggl. RDn (1899–1918), Sheff. RDn (1918–*).

LEAGRAVE

Hmlt in Luton AP, sep CP 1896 (from Luton Rural CP),[79] sep EP 1954 (from Biscot EP, Caddington AP, Toddington AP).[32] *LG* Luton PLU, RD. Abol civ 1928 pt to Houghton Regis AP, pt to Luton CP, pt to Sundon AP.[70] *Parl* Luton Dv (1918–48). *Eccl* Luton RDn. Eccl bdry: 1965,[80] 1967 (help cr Luton St Hugh, Lewsey EP).[71]

LEIGHTON BUZZARD

AP Incl chap and hmlt Billington (sep EP 1826,[19] sep CP 1866[27]), hmlt Heath and Reach (sep EP 1826,[19] sep CP 1866[27]), hmlt and chap Ellington (sep EP 1810,[19] sep CP 1866[27]), chap Stanbridge (sep EP 1735,[19] sep CP 1866[27]). *LG* Mansh. Hd, Leigh. Buz soke (13th to 17th cent), PLU, RSD (1875–91), USD (1891–94), UD. Civ bdry: 1933.[4] Abol civ 1965 to help cr Leighton-Linslade UD and CP.[81] *Parl* S'rn Dv (1885–1918), Mid Dv (1918–48), South CC (1948–70). *Eccl* Pec jurisd Leigh. Buz. (until 1852), Seq 7 thereafter.

LEIGHTON-LINSLADE

CP Cr 1965 by union Leighton Buzzard AP, pt Linslade AP, Bucks.[81] *LG* Leigh.-Linslade UD. *Parl* South CC (1970–*).

LIDLINGTON

AP *LG* Seq 9. *Parl* Seq 3. *Eccl* Seq 14.

LIMBURY

Hmlt in Luton AP, sep CP 1896 (from Luton Rural CP),[79] sep EP 1971 (from Biscot EP).[33] *LG* Luton PLU, RD. Abol civ 1928 pt to Luton AP, pt to Streatley AP, pt to Stopsley CP, pt to Sundon AP.[70] *Parl* Luton Dv (1918–48). *Eccl* Luton RDn.

LUTON

The following have 'Luton' in their names. Insofar as any existed at a given time: *LG* Flitt Hd, Luton Bor, PLU, MB (pt 1876–94, ent 1894–1964), pt Luton USD (1876–94), Luton RSD (ent 1875–76, pt 1876–94), CB (1964–74). *Parl* S'rn Dv (1885–1918), Luton Dv (1918–48), sep noted thereafter. *Eccl* Dunst. RDn (until 1866), Dunst. RDn First Dv (1866–80), Luton RDn (1880–*).

AP1–LUTON [ST MARY]–Incl hmlt Leagrave (sep CP 1896 [from area CP2],[79] sep EP 1954 [from Biscot EP, Caddington AP, Toddington AP][32]), hmlt Limbury (sep CP 1896 [from area CP2],[79] sep EP 1971 [from Biscot EP][33]), hmlt Stopsley (sep CP 1896 [from area CP2],[79] sep EP 1861[82]), hmlts East Hyde, West Hyde (sep EP 1869 as 'East Hyde',[72] sep CP 1896 as 'Hyde' [from area CP2][79]), hmlt Biscot (sep EP 1866[28]). Abol civ 1894 the pt in the MB to cr CP3, the remainder to cr CP2.[83] Addl eccl bdry alt: 1861 (cr EP2),[84] 1877 (cr EP6),[85] 1895 (cr EP8),[86] 1930,[87] 1958,[89] 1959 (help cr EP4),[88] 1960.[90]

CP1–LUTON–Renaming 1896 of CP3 when CP2 abol.[79] Bdry: 1928,[70] 1933,[4] 1939,[73] 1964.[41] *Parl* Pt South CC, pt Luton BC (1948–70), pt Luton East BC, pt Luton West BC (1970–*) [see Part III of the *Guide* for composition of the CC and BCs since 1948 by wards of the MB/CB].

EP1–LUTON ALL SAINTS–Cr 1922 from EP2.[91] Bdry: 1930,[30] 1965.[80]

EP2–LUTON CHRIST CHURCH–Cr 1861 from AP1.[84] Bdry: 1893 (cr EP9),[92] 1903,[29] 1922 (cr EP1),[91] 1930,[87] 1933 (help cr EP3),[93] 1940,[30] 1954.[44]

CP2–LUTON RURAL–Cr 1894 from the pt of AP1 not in the MB.[83] Bdry: 1895.[94] Abol 1896 to cr the 4 sep CPs of Hyde, Leagrave, Limbury, Stopsley.[79]

EP3–LUTON ST ANDREW–Cr 1933 from EP2, Biscot EP.[93] Bdry: 1940.[30]

EP4–LUTON ST CHRISTOPHER, ROUND GREEN–Cr 1959 from AP1, EP6, Stopsley EP.[88]

EP5–LUTON ST HUGH, LEWSEY–Cr 1967 from Houghton Regis AP, Leagrave EP.[71]

EP6–LUTON ST MATTHEW, HIGH TOWN–Cr 1877 from AP1, EP2.[85] Bdry: 1930,[87] 1959 (help cr EP4).[88]

EP7–LUTON ST MICHAEL AND ST GEORGE, FARLEY HILL–Cr 1969 from EP9.[95] Renamed 1967 'Farley Hill' EP.[58]

EP8–LUTON ST PAUL–Cr 1895 from AP1.[86] Bdry: 1930.[87]

EP9–LUTON ST SAVIOUR–Cr 1893 from EP2.[92] Bdry: 1930,[87] 1954,[97] 1969 (cr EP7).[95]

CP3–LUTON URBAN–Cr 1894 from the pt of AP1 in the MB.[83] Renamed 1896 as CP1 when CP2 abol.[83]

MARKYATE

CP Cr 1897 from Humbershoe AP, Houghton Regis AP and the Herts pt of Caddington AP,[99] to be in Herts, qv.

MARKYATE STREET

EP Cr 1877 as 'Markyate Street' or 'Market Street' from Houghton Regis AP, Studham AP, Caddington AP (Beds, Herts), Flamstead AP (Herts).[98] Berkhampstead RDn (1877–1907), St Albans RDn (1907–30)(both St Albans AD), Luton RDn (1930–70), Wheathampstead RDn (St Albans AD, 1970–*).

MARSTON MORETAINE

AP Usual civ spelling; for eccl see following entry. *LG* Seq 9. *Parl* Seq 3.

MARSTON MORETEYNE

AP Usual eccl spelling; for civ see prev entry. *Eccl* Seq 14.

MAULDEN

AP *LG* Seq 9. *Parl* Seq 3. *Eccl* Seq 13.

MELCHBOURNE

AP Incl chap Knotting (se par 1176[76]). *LG* Stod. Hd, Bedf. PLU, RSD, RD. Abol civ 1934 to help cr Melchbourne and Yelden CP.[13] *Parl*

N'rn Dv (1885–1918), Bedf. Dv (1918–48). *Eccl* Seq 12.

MELCHBOURNE AND YELDEN

CP Sometimes 'Melchbourne and Yielden'. Cr 1934 by union Melchbourne AP, Yelden AP.[13] *LG* Bedf. RD. Bdry: 1965 (exchanges pts with Chelveston cum Caldecott AP, Northants).[6] *Parl* Bedf. CC (1948–*).

MEPPERSHALL

AP Pt Beds (Clifton Hd), pt Herts (Dacorum Hd), the latter transf to Beds 1832 for parl purposes, 1844 for civ purposes.[56] *LG* Biggl. PLU, RSD, RD. Civ bdry: 1933.[4] *Parl* Seq 3. *Eccl* Seq 18. Eccl bdry: 1938.[100]

MILLBROOK

AP *LG* Redb. Hd, Ampt. PLU, RSD, RD. *Parl* Seq 3. *Eccl* Fleete RDn (until 1866), Fleete RDn W'rn Dv (1866–80), Ampt. RDn (1880–*).

MILTON BRYAN

AP *LG* Seq 7. Civ bdry: 1956.[11] *Parl* Seq 5. *Eccl* Dunst. RDn (until 1866), Dunst. RDn First Dv (1866–80), Fleete RDn (1880–1970), Ampt. RDn (1970–*).

MILTON ERNEST

AP *LG* Seq 11. *Parl* Seq 1. *Eccl* Seq 3.

MOGGERHANGER

Hmlt in Blunham AP, sep EP 1860,[35] sep CP 1866.[27] *LG* Seq 16. Civ bdry: 1883.[57] *Parl* Seq 3. *Eccl* Sheff. RDn (1860–66), Sheff. RDn W'rn Dv (1866–80), Biggl. RDn (1880–*).

NORTHILL

AP Collegiate church 1404–1547.[101] *LG* Seq 16. Civ bdry: 1883,[57] 1933.[4] Bdry with Sandy AP conf 1914.[102] *Parl* Seq 3. *Eccl* Seq 17. Eccl bdry: 1928 (cr Caldecote EP).[44]

OAKLEY

AP Incl chap Clapham (sep par 1545[49]). *LG* Seq 11. Civ bdry: 1948.[37] *Parl* Seq 1. Parl bdry: 1955.[42] *Eccl* Clap. RDn (until 1866), Clap. RDn E'rn Dv (1866–80), Bedf. RDn (1880–1922), Felm. RDn (1922–30), Bedf. RDn (1930–*).

ODELL

AP *LG* Seq 13. Civ bdry: 1883.[57] *Parl* Seq 1. *Eccl* Seq 4.

PAVENHAM

Chap in Felmersham AP, sep civ identity early, sep EP 1859.[61] *LG* Seq 13. *Parl* Seq 1. *Eccl* Clap. RDn (1859–66), Clap. RDn E'rn Dv (1866–80), Felm. RDn (1880–1970), Sharnb. RDn (1970–*).

PERTENHALL

AP *LG* Stod. Hd, St Neot's PLU, RSD, Eaton Socon RD (1894–1934), Bedf. RD (1934–74). Civ bdry: 1879.[103] *Parl* Seq 1. *Eccl* Seq 12.

PODINGTON

AP *LG* Willey Hd,. Wellingborough PLU, RSD, Bedf. RD. Civ bdry: 1883,[57] 1884.[59] *Parl* Seq 1. *Eccl* Clap. RDn (until 1866), Clap. RDn W'rn Dv (1866–80), Felm. RDn (1880–1970), Sharnb. RDn (1970). Abol eccl 1970 to help cr Podington with Farndish EP.[60]

PODINGTON WITH FARNDISH

EP Cr 1970 by union Podington AP, Farndish AP.[60] Sharnb. RDn.

POTSGROVE

AP Usual civ spelling; for civ see following entry. *LG* Seq 7. *Parl* Seq 5.

POTTESGROVE

AP Usual eccl spelling; for civ see prev entry. *Eccl* Dunst. RDn (until 1866), Dunst. RDn First Dv (1866–80), Fleete RDn (1880–1928). Abol eccl 1928 to help cr Battlesden with Pottesgrove EP.[12]

POTTON

AP *LG* Seq 2. Civ bdry: 1933.[4] *Parl* Seq 3. *Eccl* Seq 15.

PULLOXHILL

AP *LG* Seq 4. Civ bdry: 1933,[4] 1933.[104] *Parl* Seq 5. *Eccl* Seq 13.

RAVENSDEN

AP *LG* Seq 1. Civ bdry: 1934,[13] 1948,[37] 1968.[14] *Parl* Seq 1. Parl bdry: 1955.[42] *Eccl* Seq 9.

RENHOLD

AP *LG* Seq 1. Civ bdry: 1934,[13] 1948,[37] 1968.[14] *Parl* Seq 2. Parl bdry: 1955.[42] *Eccl* Eaton RDn (until 1866), Eaton RDn S'rn Dv (1866–80), Eaton RDn (1880–1917), Bedf. RDn (1917–*).

RIDGMONT

AP Orig dependent on Segenhoe, the latter soon accounted as a hmlt in Ridgmont.[105] *LG* Redb. Hd, Wob. PLU (1835–99), RSD, Ampt. PLU (1899–1930), RD. *Parl* Seq 5. *Eccl* Seq 14.

RISELEY

AP *LG* Seq 11. *Parl* Seq 1. *Eccl* Seq 12.

ROXTON

AP *LG* Seq 1. Civ bdry: 1965.[6] *Parl* Seq 2. *Eccl* Seq 10.

SALFORD

AP Abol eccl 1750[67] and civ 1933[4] to help cr Hulcote and Salford EP, CP respectively. *LG* Mansh. Hd, Wob. PLU (1835–99), RSD, Ampt. PLU (1899–1930), RD. *Parl* S'rn Dv (1885–1918), Mid Dv (1918–48). *Eccl* Fleete RDn.

SANDY

AP *LG* Pt Biggl. Hd, pt Wixamt. Hd, Biggl. PLU, RSD, RD (1894–1927), Sandy UD (1927–74). Civ bdry: 1883,[57] 1933.[4] Bdry with Northill AP conf 1914.[102] *Parl* N'rn Dv (1885–1918), Mid Dv/CC (1918–*). *Eccl* Seq 15.

SEGENHOE–See Ridgmont

SHARNBROOK

AP *LG* Seq 13. Civ bdry: 1895,[51] 1933.[34] *Parl* Seq 1. *Eccl* Seq 3.

SHEFFORD

Twnshp in Campton AP, sep CP 1866,[27] sep EP 1903 (from Campton AP, Clifton AP, Southill AP, ex-par place of Shefford Hardwick).[106] *LG* Seq 3. Civ bdry: 1933.[4] *Parl* Seq 3. *Eccl* Sheff. RDn. Eccl bdry: 1938.[100]

SHEFFORD HARDWICK

Ex-par place, sep CP 1858.[48] *LG* Clifton Hd, Biggl. PLU (1858[96]–1930), RSD, RD. Abol 1933 ent to Shefford CP.[4] *Parl* N'rn Dv (1885–1918), Mid Dv (1918–48). *Eccl* Ex-par. Bdry:

1903 (help cr Shefford EP).[106]

SHELTON

AP *LG* Stod. Hd, St Neot's PLU, RSD, Eaton Socon RD. Abol civ 1934 to help cr Dean and Shelton CP.[13] *Parl* N'rn Dv (1885–1918), Bedf. Dv (1918–48). *Eccl* Seq 12.

SHILLINGTON

AP Incl chap Upper Gravenhurst (from 14th cent, sep par *temp* Elizabeth I[65]). *LG* Pt Herts (Odsey Hd), pt Beds (Clifton Hd, Flitt Hd), Ampt. PLU, RSD, pt sep RD in Herts (1894–97), Ampt. RD (pt 1894–97, ent 1897–1974). Civ bdry: 1897 (incl loses pt in Herts to Pirton AP, Ickleford CP, both Herts),[69] 1907 (exchanges pts with Offley AP, Herts).[26] *Parl* Pt Herts until 1918, Beds pt Seq 5. *Eccl* Seq 18.

SILSOE

Hmlt in Flitton AP, sep EP 1846,[62] sep CP 1866.[27] *LG* Seq 4. *Parl* Seq 5. *Eccl* Fleete RDn (1846–66), Fleete RDn E'rn Dv (1866–80), Ampt. RDn (1880–*).

SOULDROP

AP *LG* Willey Hd, Bedf. PLU, RSD, RD. Abol civ 1934 to help cr Knotting and Souldrop CP.[13] *Parl* N'rn Dv (1885–1918), Bedf. Dv (1918–48). *Eccl* Seq 3.

SOUTHILL

AP *LG* Seq 16. Civ bdry: 1933.[4] *Parl* Seq 3. *Eccl* Seq 18. Eccl bdry: 1903 (help cr Shefford EP).[106]

STAGSDEN

AP *LG* Seq 13. Civ bdry: 1948.[37] *Parl* Seq 2. Parl bdry: 1955.[42] *Eccl* Clap. RDn (until 1866), Clap. RDn W'rn Dv (1866–80), Bedf. RDn (1880–1922), Felm. RDn (1922–70), Bedf. RDn (1970–*).

STANBRIDGE

Chap in Leighton Buzzard AP before 1344,[107] sep EP 1735,[19] sep CP 1866.[27] *LG* Seq 6. *Parl* Seq 6. *Eccl* Pec jurisd of Leigh. Buz. (1750–1852), Seq 7 thereafter.

STAPLOE

CP Cr 1965 from Eaton Socon AP.[6] *LG* Bedf. RD. *Parl* Mid CC (1970–*).

LITTLE STAUGHTON

AP *LG* Stod. Hd, St Neot's PLU, RSD, Eaton Socon RD (1894–1934), Bedf. RD (1934–74). Civ bdry: 1879.[108] *Parl* Seq 1. *Eccl* Eaton RDn (until 1866), Eaton RDn S'rn Dv (1866–80), Riseley RDn (1880–1970), Sharnb. RDn (1970–*).

STEPPINGLEY

AP *LG* Seq 9. *Parl* Seq 5. *Eccl* Fleete RDn (until 1866), Fleete RDn W'rn Dv (1866–80), Fleete RDn (1880–1930), Ampt. RDn (1930–*).

STEVINGTON

AP *LG* Seq 13. Civ bdry: 1948.[37] *Parl* Seq 1. Parl bdry: 1955.[42] *Eccl* Seq 4.

STEWARTBY

CP Cr 1937 from Kempston Rural CP, Wootton AP.[27] *LG* Bedf. RD. *Parl* Mid CC (1948–*).

UPPER STONDON

AP *LG* Seq 3. *Parl* Seq 3. *Eccl* Seq 18.

STOPSLEY

Hmlt in Luton AP, sep EP 1861,[82] sep CP 1896 (from Luton Rural CP).[79] *LG* Luton PLU, RD. Civ bdry: 1928.[70] Abol civ 1933 pt to Luton CP, pt to Hyde CP, pt to Streatley AP.[4] *Parl* Luton Dv (1918–48). *Eccl* Dunst. RDn (1861–66), Dunst. RDn First Dv (1866–80), Luton RDn (1880–*). Eccl bdry: 1930,[87] 1951 (help cr Luton St Christopher, Round Green EP),[88] 1960.[90]

STOTFOLD

AP *LG* Seq 3. Civ bdry: 1965 (loses pt to Letchworth AP, Herts).[6] *Parl* Seq 3. *Eccl* Seq 16.

STREATLEY

AP Sometimes 'Streatley with Sharpenhoe'. *LG* Flitt Hd, Luton PLU, RSD, RD. Civ bdry: 1928,[70] 1933,[4] 1964 (loses pt to Luton CB and CP).[41] *Parl* Seq 4. *Eccl* Dunst. RDn (until 1866), Dunst. RDn First Dv (1866–80), Luton RDn (1880–*). Eccl bdry: 1942.[31]

STUDHAM

AP Incl chap Astwick (sep par between 1242–91[8]), hmlt Humbershoe (sep CP 1866[27]). Pt Beds (Mansh. Hd), pt Herts (Hitchin and Pirton Hd), pt of the latter transf to Beds 1832 for parl purposes, 1844 for civ purposes.[56] *LG* Luton PLU, RSD. Made 2 sep CPs 1894, each 'Studham', one in each co,[39] qv. *Parl* Pt Herts until 1918, Beds pt S'rn Dv (1885–1918). *Eccl* Seq 7.

CP Cr 1894 from the Beds pt of Studham AP.[39] *LG* Luton PLU, RD. Civ bdry: 1897 (gains Studham CP, Herts),[40] 1907 (exchanges pts with Little Gaddesden AP, Herts).[26] *Parl* Luton Dv (1918–48), S CC (1948–*).

SUNDON

AP *LG* Flitt Hd, Luton PLU, RSD, RD. Civ bdry: 1928,[70] 1964 (loses pt to Luton CB and CP).[41] *Parl* Seq 4. *Eccl* Dunst. RDn (until 1866), Dunst. RDn First Dv (1866–80), Luton RDn (1880–*). Eccl bdry: 1942.[31]

SUTTON

AP *LG* Seq 2. *Parl* Seq 3. *Eccl* Seq 15.

SWINESHEAD

AP In Hunts (Leightonstone Hd), transf 1888 to Beds.[109] *LG* St Neots PLU, RSD, Eaton Socon RD (1894–1934), Bedf. RD (1934–74). *Parl* In Hunts until 1918, Bedf. Dv/CC (1918–*). *Eccl* Leightonstone RDn (until 1863), St Neots RDn (1863–78), Kimbolton RDn (1878–1914)(all Ely dioc, Huntingdon AD), Riseley RDn (1914–70), Sharnb. RDn (1970–*).

TEMPSFORD

AP *LG* Seq 2. Civ bdry: 1933,[4] 1965 (gains pt Gamlingay AP, Cambs, pt Tetworth AP, Hunts).[110] *Parl* Seq 3. *Eccl* Sheff. RDn (until 1866), Sheff. RDn W'rn Dv (1866–80), Biggl. RDn (1880–1972). Abol eccl 1972 to help cr Tempsford with Little Barford EP.[9]

TEMPSFORD WITH LITTLE BARFORD

EP Cr 1972 by union Tempsford AP, Little Barford AP.[9] Biggl. RDn.

TETWORTH

Hmlt (pt Beds [Biggl. Hd], pt Hunts [Toseland Hd]) in Everton AP (o'wise Beds), considered a CP since 1810,[55] no sep eccl identity, the pt in Beds transf to Hunts 1832 for parl purposes, 1844 for civ purposes.[56] See main entry in Hunts.

THURLEIGH

AP *LG* Seq 13. *Parl* Seq 1. *Eccl* Eaton RDn (until 1866), Eaton RDn N'rn Dv (1866–80), Eaton RDn (1880–1917), Felm. RDn (1917–70), Sharnb. RDn (1970–*).

TILBROOK

AP *LG* Stod. Hd, St Neots PLU, RSD. Transf 1896 from Beds to Hunts.[109] *Parl* N'rn Dv (1885–1918), Hunts thereafter. *Eccl* Eaton RDn (until 1866), Eaton RDn N'rn Dv (1866–80), Riseley RDn (1880–1914), Kimbolton RDn (1914–64), Leightonstone RDn (1964–*)(latter two in Huntingdon AD).

TILSWORTH

AP *LG* Seq 8. *Parl* Seq 6. *Eccl* Seq 7.

TINGRITH

AP *LG* Seq 7. Civ bdry: 1888.[111] *Parl* Seq 5. *Eccl* Fleete RDn (until 1866), Fleete RDn W'rn Dv (1866–80), Fleete RDn (1880–1957), Ampt. RDn (1957–*).

TODDINGTON

AP *LG* Mansh. Hd, Wob. PLU (1835–99), RSD, Ampt. PLU (1899–1930), RD (1894–1933), Luton RD (1933–74). Civ bdry: 1933,[4] 1956,[11] 1964 (loses pt to Luton CB and CP).[41] *Parl* S'rn Dv (1885–1918), Mid Dv (1918–48), S CC (1948–*). *Eccl* Seq 6. Eccl bdry: 1954 (help cr Leagrave EP).[32]

TOTTERNHOE

AP *LG* Mansh. Hd, Luton PLU, RSD, RD. Civ bdry: 1933.[4] *Parl* Seq 4. *Eccl* Seq 7.

TURVEY

AP *LG* Seq 13. Civ bdry: 1948.[37] *Parl* Seq 1. Parl bdry: 1955.[42] *Eccl* Clap. RDn (until 1866), Clap. RDn W'rn Dv (1866–80), Felm. RDn (1880–1970), Bedf. RDn (1970–74), Sharnb. RDn (1974–*).

OLD WARDEN

AP *LG* Seq 16. Civ bdry: 1933.[4] *Parl* Seq 3. *Eccl* Seq 17.

WESTONING

AP *LG* Mansh. Hd, Ampt. PLU, RSD, RD. Civ bdry: 1888,[111] 1933.[4] *Parl* Seq 5. *Eccl* Seq 13. Eccl bdry: 1957.[66]

WHIPSNADE

AP Possibly orig a free chapel, sep par before 1291.[112] *LG* Pt Beds (Mansh. Hd), pt Herts (Dacorum Hd), Luton PLU, RSD, pt sep RD in Herts (1894–97), Luton RD (pt 1894–97, ent 1897–1974). Civ bdry: 1897 (loses the Herts pt to help cr Markyate CP, Herts).[113] *Parl* Pt Herts until 1918, Beds pt Seq 4. *Eccl* Seq 7.

WILDEN

AP *LG* Seq 1. Civ bdry: 1956.[38] *Parl* Seq 2. *Eccl* Seq 9.

WILLINGTON

AP *LG* Seq 15. *Parl* Seq 2. *Eccl* Bedf. RDn (until 1866), Bedf. RDn Second Dv (1866–80), Haynes RDn (1880–1922), Biggl. RDn (1922–*).

WILSHAMSTEAD

AP *LG* Seq 10. *Parl* Seq 2. *Eccl* Seq 2.

WOBURN

AP *LG* Seq 7. *Parl* Seq 5. *Eccl* Seq 14.

WOBURN SANDS

EP Cr 1867 from Aspley Guise AP, Wavendon AP (Bucks).[114] Fleete RDn W'rn Dv (1867–80), Fleete RDn (1880–1970), Ampt. RDn (1970–*).

WOODSIDE

EP Cr 1892 from Caddington AP.[115] Luton RDn. Bdry: 1930,[87] 1961.[43]

WOOTTON

AP *LG* Seq 10. Civ bdry: 1937.[27] *Parl* Seq 2. *Eccl* Seq 2.

WRESTLINGWORTH

AP *LG* Seq 2. Civ bdry: 1883.[57] *Parl* Seq 3. *Eccl* Seq 15.

WYMINGTON

AP *LG* Willey Hd, Wellingborough PLU, RSD, Bedf. RD. Civ bdry: 1965 (loses pt to Rushden AP, Northants).[6] *Parl* Seq 1. *Eccl* Seq 4.

YELDEN

AP Sometimes 'Yielden'. *LG* Stod. Hd, Bedf. PLU, RSD, RD. Abol civ 1934 to help cr Melchbourne and Yelden CP.[13] *Parl* N'rn Dv (1885–1918), Bedf. Dv (1918–48). *Eccl* Seq 12.

BERKSHIRE

ABBREVIATIONS

Abbreviations particular to Berkshire follow. Those general abbreviations in use throughout the *Guide* are found on page xix.

Abing.	Abingdon
Beyn.	Beynhurst
Bradf.	Bradfield
Charl.	Charlton
Cook.	Cookham
Easth.	Easthampstead
Fairc.	Faircross
Ganf.	Ganfield
Hungf.	Hungerford
Kintb.	Kintbury
Maid.	Maidstone
Newb.	Newbury
Read.	Reading
Rippl.	Ripplesmere
Shriv.	Shrivenham
Sonn.	Sonning
Vale WH	Vale of the White Horse
Wall.	Wallingford
Want.	Wantage
Warg.	Wargrave
Wind.	Windsor
Wok.	Wokingham

SEQUENCES

An abbreviated entry prefixed by 'Seq' is used in the parochial entries to avoid repeating often the names of superior units of administration. The content of each sequence is shown below.

Local Government Sequences ('LG')

SEQ 1 Beyn. Hd, Cook. PLU (1835–99), RSD, Maid. PLU (1899–1930), Cook. RD
SEQ 2 Charl. Hd, Wok. PLU, RSD, RD
SEQ 3 Compton Hd, Want. PLU, RSD, RD
SEQ 4 Fairc. Hd, Bradf. PLU, RSD, RD
SEQ 5 Fairc. Hd, Newb. PLU, RSD, RD
SEQ 6 Fairc. Hd, Want. PLU, RSD, RD
SEQ 7 Ganf. Hd, Faringdon PLU, RSD, RD
SEQ 8 Hormer Hd, Abing. PLU, RSD, RD
SEQ 9 Kintb. Eagle Hd, Hungf. PLU (1835–96), RSD, Hungf. & Ramsb. PLU (1896–1930), Hungf. RD
SEQ 10 Kintb. Eagle Hd, Newb. PLU, RSD, RD
SEQ 11 Kintb. Eagle Hd, Want. PLU, RSD, RD
SEQ 12 Moreton Hd, Bradf. PLU, RSD, RD
SEQ 13 Moreton Hd, Wall. PLU, RSD, RD
SEQ 14 Ock Hd, Abing. PLU, RSD, RD
SEQ 15 Ock Hd, Wall. PLU, RSD, RD
SEQ 16 Read. Hd, Bradf. PLU, RSD, RD
SEQ 17 Rippl. Hd, Easth. PLU, RSD, RD
SEQ 18 Shriv. Hd, Faringdon PLU, RSD, RD
SEQ 19 Theale Hd, Bradf. PLU, RSD, RD
SEQ 20 Want. Hd, PLU, RSD, RD

Parliamentary Sequences ('Parl')

SEQ 1 E'rn Dv (1885-1918), Newb. Dv (1918-48), Wok. CC (1948–70), Read S CC (1970–*)
SEQ 2 E'rn Dv (1885-1918), Wind. Dv/CC (1918–70), Wind. & Maid. CC (1970–*)
SEQ 3 E'rn Dv (1885–1918), Wind. Dv (1918–48), Wok. CC (1948–*)
SEQ 4 N'rn Dv (1885–1918), Abing. Dv/CC (1918–*)
SEQ 5 S'rn Dv (1885–1918), Abing. Dv/CC (1918–*)
SEQ 6 S'rn Dv (1885–1918), Abing. Dv (1918–48), Newb. CC (1948–*)

SEQ 7 S'rn Dv (1885-1918), Newb. Dv/CC (1918–*)

Ecclesiastical Sequences ('Eccl')

SEQ 1 Abing. RDn
SEQ 2 Abing. RDn (until 1865), Vale WH RDn (1865–*)
SEQ 3 Abing. RDn (until 1865), Wall. RDn (1865–*)
SEQ 4 Abing. RDn (until 1865), Want. RDn (1865–*)
SEQ 5 Newb. RDn (until 1865), Bradf. RDn (1865–*)
SEQ 6 Newb. RDn
SEQ 7 Read. RDn (until 1865), Bradf. RDn (1865–*)
SEQ 8 Read. RDn (until 1865), Maid. RDn (1865–*)
SEQ 9 Read. RDn (until 1915), Maid. RDn (1915–21), Sonn. RDn (1921–*)
SEQ 10 Read. RDn
SEQ 11 Read. RDn (until 1874), Sonn. RDn (1874–*)
SEQ 12 Wall. RDn

DIOCESES AND ARCHDEACONRY

With a few exceptions noted below in the parochial entries, the Berks pars were in Berkshire AD which was in Sarum dioc until 1836 and in Oxford dioc thereafter.

THE PARISHES OF BERKSHIRE

ABINGDON
CP Cr 1894 by the union of the pars in Abing. MB, viz., pt Abingdon St Helen AP, pt Abingdon St Nicholas AP (to which the pt of Culham AP, Oxon, in the MB was added[1]), pt Sutton Wick CP.[2] *LG* Abing. PLU, MB. Civ bdry: 1934,[3] 1952.[4] Transf 1974 to Oxon.[5] *Parl* Abing. Dv/CC (1918–*).

ABINGDON ST HELEN
AP Incl chap Drayton (sep civ identity early); for cr Drayton EP and other EPs from united EP of Abingdon St Helen and St Nicholas, see following entry. *LG* Hormer Hd, Abing. PLU, pt Abing. Bor/MB, pt Abing. USD (enlarged pt 1890[9]–94), pt Abing. RSD. Civ bdry: 1883,[10] 1885.[11] Abol civ 1894 the pt in the MB to help cr Abingdon CP, the remainder to help cr Abingdon St Helen Without CP.[2] *Parl* Pt Abing. Parl Bor (1556–1885), N'rn Dv (1885–1918). *Eccl* Abing. RDn. Abol eccl 1508 to help cr Abingdon St Helen with St Nicholas EP.[12]

ABINGDON ST HELEN WITH ST NICHOLAS
EP Cr 1508 by union Abingdon St Helen AP, Abingdon St Nicholas AP.[12] Incl chap Drayton (sep civ identity early from Abingdon St Helen alone, sep EP 1876 from this united par[6]), chap Shippon (sep EP 1865[7]), chap Dry Sandford (sep EP 1867[8]). Abing. RDn.

ABINGDON ST HELEN WITHOUT
CP Cr 1894 from the pt of Abingdon St Helen AP and Abingdon St Nicholas AP not in Abing. MB.[2] *LG* Abing. PLU, RD. Bdry: 1934,[3] 1952.[4] Transf 1974 to Oxon.[5] *Parl* Abing. Dv/CC (1918–*).

ABINGDON ST NICHOLAS
AP *LG* Hormer Hd, Abing. PLU, Bor, MB/USD (ent until bdry alt 1883,[10] pt 1883–94). Abol civ 1894 (the pt in the MB having gained the pt of Culham AP, Oxon in the MB[1]), the pt in the MB to help cr Abingdon CP, the remainder to help cr Abingdon St Helen Without CP.[2] *Parl* Abing. Parl Bor (1556–1885), N'rn Dv (1885–1918). *Eccl* Abing. RDn. Abol eccl 1508 to help cr Abingdon St Helen with St Nicholas EP.[12]

ALDERMASTON
AP *LG* Aldermaston Bor, disappeared by 16th cent,[13] Seq 19. Civ bdry: 1934.[3] *Parl* Seq 7. *Eccl* Seq 7. Eccl bdry: 1973 (help cr North Tadley EP, to be in Winch dioc).[210]

ALDWORTH
AP *LG* Seq 3. Civ bdry: 1934.[3] *Parl* Seq 5. *Eccl* Newb. RDn (until 1866), Wall. RDn (1866–1915), Bradf. RDn (1915–*).

APPLEFORD
Chap in Sutton Courtenay AP, sep CP 1866.[14] *LG* Seq 14. Transf 1974 to Oxon.[5] *Parl* Seq 4.

APPLETON
AP Incl Besselsleigh for a brief time late 16th or early 17th cent.[15] Usual eccl spelling; for civ see following entry. *Eccl* Seq 1. Eccl bdry: 1954.[16]

APPLETON WITH EATON
AP Usual civ spelling; for eccl and temporary incl of Besselsleigh, see prev entry. *LG* Seq 14. Transf 1974 to Oxon.[5] *Parl* Seq 4.

ARBORFIELD
Chap in Sonning AP, sep par *ca* 16th cent.[17] *LG* Sonn. Hd, Wok. PLU, RSD, RD. Abol civ 1948 to help cr Arborfield and Newland CP.[18] *Parl* E'rn Dv (1885–1918), Newb. Dv (1918–48). *Eccl* Pec jurisd Dean of Sarum (until 1846), Seq 11 thereafter.

ARBORFIELD AND NEWLAND
CP Cr 1948 by union Arborfield AP, Newland CP.[18] *LG* Wok. RD. *Parl* Read. S CC (1970–*).

ARDINGTON
AP *LG* Seq 20. Civ bdry: 1883,[10] 1887.[19] Transf

1974 to Oxon.[5] *Parl* Seq 4. *Eccl* Seq 4.

SOUTH ASCOT

EP Cr 1898 from Ascot Heath EP, Sunningdale EP.[20] Maid. RDn (1898–1921), Sonn. RDn (1921–*).

ASCOT HEATH

EP Cr 1865 from Cranbourne EP, Sunninghill AP, Bracknell EP.[21] Maid. RDn (1865–1921), Sonn. RDn (1921–*). Bdry: 1898 (help cr South Ascot EP).[20]

ASHAMPSTEAD

Chap in Basildon AP, frequently called sep par,[22] sep civ identity early, sep EP 1847.[23] *LG* Seq 12. *Parl* Seq 6. *Eccl* Wall. RDn (1847–75), Bradf. RDn (1875–*).

ASHBURY

AP *LG* Seq 18. Transf 1974 to Oxon.[5] *Parl* Seq 4. *Eccl* Seq 2.

ASTON TIRROLD

AP *LG* Seq 13. Civ bdry: 1883,[10] 1934.[3] Transf 1974 to Oxon.[5] *Parl* Seq 4. *Eccl* Seq 3.

ASTON UPTHORPE

Chap in Blewbury AP, sep EP1862 (combined with chap Upton in same par as 'Upton with Aston Upthorpe EP'[24] qv), sep CP 1866.[14] *LG* Seq 13. Civ bdry: 1883,[10] 1934.[3] Transf 1974 to Oxon.[5] *Parl* Seq 4.

AVINGTON

AP *LG* Kintb. Eagle Hd, Hungf. PLU (1835–96), RSD, Hungf. & Ramsbury PLU (1896–1930), Hungf. RD. Abol civ 1894 ent to Kintbury AP.[3] *Parl* S'rn Dv (1885–1918), Newb. Dv (1918–48). *Eccl* Seq 6.

BAGLEY WOOD

Ex-par place, sep CP 1858.[25] *LG* Hormer Hd, Abing. PLU, RSD, RD. Abol 1900 ent to Radley AP.[26] *Parl* N'rn Dv (1885–1918).

GREAT BARINGDON

AP Pt Glos (Slaughter Hd), pt Berks (Faringdon Hd), the latter transf to Glos 1832 for parl purposes, 1844 for civ purposes.[27] See main entry in Glos.

BARKHAM

AP *LG* Seq 2. *Parl* Seq 1. *Eccl* Read. RDn (until 1915), Sonn. RDn (1915–*).

BASILDON

AP Incl chap Ashampstead (sometimes called sep par,[22] sep civ identity early, sep EP 1847[23]). *LG* Seq 12. *Parl* Seq 6. *Eccl* Wall. RDn (1847–1956), Bradf. RDn (1956–*).

BAULKING

Chap in Uffington AP, sep CP 1866,[14] sep EP 1848 when combined with Woolstone chap in same par as 'Baulking with Woolstone' EP[29] (divided 1917, Baulking made sep EP, Woolstone reunited with Uffington AP to cr Uffington with Woolstone EP[31]). *LG* Seq 18. Civ bdry: 1883,[10] 1888.[30] Transf 1974 to Oxon.[5] *Parl* Seq 4. *Eccl* Vale WH RDn.

BAULKING WITH WOOLSTONE

EP Cr 1848 by union chap Baulking, chap Woolstone, both in Uffington AP.[29] Abing RDn (1848–65), Vale WH RDn (1865–1917). Abol 1917, Baulking made sep EP, Woolstone reunited with Uffington AP to cr Uffington with Woolstone EP.[31]

BEAR WOOD

EP Cr 1846 from Hurst EP, Wokingham AP.[28] Read. RDn (1846–74), Sonn. RDn (1874–*).

BEECH HILL

Tg and chap in Berks pt of Stratfield Saye AP (Hants, Berks), sep CP 1866,[14] sep EP 1868.[32] *LG* Seq 16. Civ bdry: 1934.[3] *Parl* Seq 7. *Eccl* Basingstoke RDn N-E'rn Dv (Winch dioc, 1868–69), Read. RDn (1869–*).

BEEDON

Chap in Chieveley AP, sep par *ca* 1526–38.[33] *LG* Seq 6. Civ bdry: 1934.[3] *Parl* Seq 5. *Eccl* Seq 6.

BEENHAM

AP Usual civ spelling; for eccl see following entry. *LG* Seq 16. Civ bdry: 1883,[10] 1934.[3] *Parl* Seq 7.

BEENHAM VALENCE

AP Usual eccl spelling; for civ see prev entry. *Eccl* Seq 7.

BESSELSLEIGH

AP Prob incl within Appelton AP for brief time in late 16th or early 17th cent.[15] *LG* Seq 8. Transf 1974 to Oxon.[5] *Parl* Seq 4. *Eccl* Seq 1. Eccl bdry: 1954.[16]

BINFIELD

AP *LG* Cook. Hd, Easth. PLU, RSD, RD. Civ bdry: 1955 (help cr Bracknell CP).[34] *Parl* Seq 3. *Eccl* Read. RDn (until 1865), Maid. RDn (1865–1921), Sonn. RDn (1921–*).

BISHAM

AP *LG* Seq 1. *Parl* Great Marlow Parl Bor (mostly in Bucks, 1832–85), Seq 2 thereafter. *Eccl* Seq 8. Eccl bdry: 1856 (help cr Stubbings EP).[35]

BLEWBURY

AP *LG* Pt Read. Hd, pt Moreton Hd (the chaps of Aston Upthorpe, Upton, sep EP 1862 as 'Upton with Aston Upthorpe',[24] 2 sep CPs 1866 of Upton, Aston Upthorpe[14]), thus ent Read. Hd from 1866, Want. PLU, RSD, RD. Transf 1974 to Oxon.[5] *Parl* Seq 4. *Eccl* Pec jurisd Dean of Sarum (until 1846), Seq 3 thereafter.

BOURTON

Tg in Shrivenham AP, sep CP 1866,[14] sep EP 1867.[36] *LG* Seq 18. Transf 1974 to Oxon.[5] *Parl* Seq 4. *Eccl* Vale WH RDn.

BOXFORD

AP *LG* Pt Fairc. Hd, pt Kintb. Eagle Hd, Newb. PLU, RSD, RD. *Parl* Seq 7. *Eccl* Seq 6.

BOYNE HILL

EP Cr 1857 from Bray AP.[37] Read. RDn (1857–65), Maid. RDn (1865–*). Bdry: 1904.[38] Now called 'Maidenhead All Saints'.

BRACKNELL

EP Chap in Warfield AP, Winkfield AP, sep EP 1851.[39] Read. RDn (1851–65), Maid. RDn (1865–1921), Sonn. RDn (1921–*). Bdry: 1865 (help cr Ascot Heath EP),[21] 1953.[40]

CP Cr 1955 from Binfield AP, Easthampstead AP,

Warfield AP, Winkfield AP.[34] *LG* Easth. RD. Civ bdry: 1965.[41] *Parl* Wok. CC (1970–*).

BRADFIELD

AP *LG* Seq 19. Civ bdry: 1968.[42] *Parl* Seq 7. *Eccl* Seq 7.

BRAY

AP Incl pt Maidenhead (sep CP 1894 [from the pts of Bray AP, Cookham AP within Maid. MB],[43] sep EP 1720 [as 'Maidenhead St Luke' from area within Cookham AP only][44]). *LG* Bray Hd, perhaps Bray mediev Bor,[45] Cook. PLU (1835–99), Maid. PLU (1899–1930), pt Maid. Bor/MB (until 1894), pt Maid. USD, pt Cook. RSD, Cook. RD. Addtl civ bdry alt: 1894 (loses pt in Maid. MB to help cr Maidenhead CP),[43] 1934.[3] *Parl* Seq 2. *Eccl* Seq 8. Eccl bdry: 1858 (cr Boyne Hill EP, now called 'Maidenhead All Saints'),[37] 1871 (help cr Bray Wood EP),[46] 1875 (help cr Maidenhead St Andrew and St Mary Magdalen EP).[47]

BRAY WOOD

EP Cr 1871 from Bray AP, Winkfield AP, Cranbourne EP.[46] Maid. RDn. Bdry: 1960.[48]

BRIGHTWALTON

AP *LG* Seq 6. *Parl* Seq 5. *Eccl* Seq 6.

BRIGHTWELL

AP Prob in Sotwell AP in 10th cent, sep thereafter.[49] *LG* Moreton Hd, Wall. PLU, RSD, RD. Civ bdry: 1934.[3] Abol civ 1948 to help cr Brightwell-cum-Sotwell CP.[50] *Parl* Wall. Parl Bor (1832–85), N'rn Dv (1885–1918), Abing. Dv (1918–48). *Eccl* Wall. RDn. Reconstituted 1868, gaining Sotwell chap from Wallingford St Leonard AP and loses pt to latter, hence thereafter 'Brightwell with Sotwell' EP.[51]

BRIGHTWELL-CUM-SOTWELL

CP Cr 1948 by union Brightwell AP, Sotwell CP.[50] *LG* Wall. RD. Transf 1974 to Oxon.[5] *Parl* Abing. CC (1970–*).

BRIGHTWELL WITH SOTWELL

EP Cr 1868 by union pt Brightwell AP, chap Sotwell of Wallingford St Leonard AP.[51] Wall. RDn.

BRIMPTON

AP *LG* Seq 5. *Parl* Seq 7. *Eccl* Newb. RDn (until 1865), Bradf. RDn (1865–1958), Newb. RDn (1958–73), Bradf. RDn (1973–*). Eccl bdry: 1953,[52] 1958.[53]

BRITWELL

CP Cr 1974 from the pt of Burnham AP, Bucks, to be in Berks.[5]

BUCKLAND

AP *LG* Seq 7. Transf 1974 to Oxon.[5] *Parl* Seq 4. *Eccl* Seq 2.

BUCKLEBURY

AP *LG* Seq 16. Civ bdry: 1883,[10] 1934,[3] 1968,[42] 1969.[54] *Parl* Seq 7. Parl bdry: 1972.[55] *Eccl* Seq 6.

BURGHFIELD

AP *LG* Theale Hd, Bradf. PLU, RSD (ent 1875–87 and 1889–94, pt 1887–89), pt Read. CB/USD (1887[80]–89), Theale RD. Civ bdry: 1889 (loses pt in Read. CB to Reading St Giles AP).[56] *Parl* Seq 7. *Eccl* Seq 7.

BUSCOT

AP *LG* Seq 18. Transf 1974 to Oxon.[5] *Parl* Seq 4. *Eccl* Seq 2.

CATMORE

AP *LG* Seq 3. *Parl* Seq 5. *Eccl* Seq 6.

CHADDLEWORTH

AP *LG* Seq 11. *Parl* Seq 4. *Eccl* Seq 6.

EAST CHALLOW

Chap and pt of twnshp of Challow in Letcombe Regis AP, sep CP 1866[14] (for eccl see following entry). *LG* Seq 11. Civ bdry: 1887.[57] Transf 1974 to Oxon.[5] *Parl* Seq 4.

EAST CHALLOW WITH WEST CHALLOW

EP Cr 1852 from the 2 chaps (and 1 twnshp of Challow) of East Challow, West Challow in Letcombe Regis AP,[58] sometimes now called 'Challow'. Abing. RDn (1852–65), Want. RDn (1865–*). Bdry: 1930.[59]

WEST CHALLOW

CP Chap and pt of twnshp of Challow in Letcombe Regis AP, sep CP 1866[14] (for eccl see prev entry). *LG* Seq 11. Civ bdry: 1887.[57] Transf 1974 to Oxon.[5] *Parl* Seq 4.

CHANDLINGS FARM

Ex-par place, sep CP 1858.[25] *LG* Hormer Hd, Abing. PLU, RSD, RD. Abol 1900 ent to Radley CP.[26] *Parl* N'rn Dv (1885–1918).

CHARLTON

Hmlt in Wantage AP, sep CP 1866.[14] *LG* Want. Hd, PLU, RSD, RD. Abol 1934 pt to help cr Lockinge CP, pt to Wantage AP, pt to Grove CP.[3] *Parl* N'rn Dv (1885–1918), Abing. Dv (1918–48).

CHARNEY BASSETT

Chap in Longworth AP, sep CP 1866,[14] eccl severed 1947 to help cr Lyford with Charney Bassett EP.[60] *LG* Seq 7. Transf 1974 to Oxon.[5] *Parl* Seq 4.

CHARVIL

Cr 1970 from Woodley and Sandford CP.[61] *LG* Wok. RD.

CHIEVELEY

AP Incl Peasmore (sep par *ca* 1104–05[62]), chap Beedon (sep par *ca* 1526–38[33]), chap Leckhampstead (sep CP 1866,[14] sep EP 1882[63]), chap Winterbourne (sep CP 1866[14]). *LG* Seq 5. Addtl civ bdry alt: 1959.[54] *Parl* Seq 7. Parl bdry: 1972.[55] *Eccl* As 'Chieveley with Winterbourne and Oare', Seq 6. Addtl eccl bdry alt: 1966.[64]

CHILDREY

AP *LG* Seq 20. Civ bdry: 1883,[10] 1887.[57] Transf 1974 to Oxon.[5] *Parl* Seq 4. *Eccl* Seq 4. Eccl bdry: 1930.[59]

CHILTON

AP *LG* Seq 3. Transf 1974 to Oxon.[5] *Parl* Seq 5. *Eccl* Abing. RDn (until 1865), Want. RDn (1865–1970), Wall. RDn (1970–*).

CHILTON FOLIAT

AP Pt Wilts (Kinwardstone Hd), pt Berks (Kintb. Eagle Hd). *LG* Hungf. PLU, RSD, pt sep RD in Wilts (1894–95), pt Hungf. RD (1894–95), the Berks pt transf 1895 to Hungerford AP and the par ent Wilts (Ramsbury RD) thereafter. See main entry in Wilts.

CHOLSEY

AP Incl chap Moulsford (sep civ identity early, sep EP 1845[66]). *LG* Read. Hd, Wall. PLU, RSD, RD. Addtl civ bdry alt: 1948.[67] Transf 1974 to Oxon.[5] *Parl* Seq 4. *Eccl* Seq 12. Addtl eccl bdry alt: 1951.[68]

CLAPCOT

Lbty in Wallingford All Hallows AP, sep CP 1894 (from the pt of Wallingford All Hallows AP and the pt of Wallingford Castle Precincts CP in Wall. MB).[69] *LG* Wall. PLU, RD. Abol civ 1934 pt to Wallingford AP, pt to Stowell AP.[3] *Parl* Abing. Dv (1918–48).

CLEWER

AP *LG* Rippl. Hd, Wind. PLU, pt New Wind. MB 1835–67, enlarged pt 1867–94), pt New Wind. USD, pt Wind. RSD. Civ bdry: 1878.[70] Abol civ 1894 the pt in the MB to cr Clewer Within CP, the remainder to cr Clewer Without CP.[71] *Parl* Pt New Wind. Parl Bor (1832–1918), pt E'rn Dv (1885–1918). *Eccl* Seq 8. Eccl bdry: 1843 (cr New Windsor Holy Trinity EP),[72] 1872 (cr Clewer St Stephen EP).[73]

CLEWER ST STEPHEN

EP Cr 1872 from Clewer AP.[73] Maid. RDn.

CLEWER WITHIN

CP Cr 1894 from the pt of Clewer AP in New Wind. MB.[71] *LG* Wind. PLU, New Wind. MB. *Parl* Wind. Dv/CC (1918–70), Wind. & Maid. CC (1970–*).

CLEWER WITHOUT

CP Cr 1894 from the pt of Clewer AP not in New Wind. MB.[71] *LG* Wind. PLU, RD (1894–1920), New Wind. MB (1920–74). Bdry: 1920.[74] *Parl* Wind. Dv/CC (1918–70), Wind. & Maid. CC (1970–*).

COLD ASH

Pt of Thatcham AP, sep EP 1865,[75] sep CP 1894.[76] *LG* Newb. PLU, RD. Civ bdry: 1934.[3] *Parl* Newb. Dv/CC (1918–*). *Eccl* Newb. RDn. Eccl bdry: 1956.[77]

COLESHILL

AP Pt Wilts (Highworth, Cricklade and Staple Hd), pt Berks (Shriv. Hd), the former transf 1881 to Inglesham AP (Wilts) and par ent Berks thereafter.[78] *LG* Faringdon PLU, RSD, RD. Addtl civ bdry alt: 1940.[79] Transf 1974 to Oxon.[5] *Parl* Berks pt, Seq 4. *Eccl* Seq 2. Eccl bdry: 1840 (help cr Highworth with Sevenhampton and Inglesham EP, to be in Bristol dioc).[211]

COMBE

AP In Hants (Padstow Hd), transf 1895 to Berks.[65] *LG* Hungf. PLU (1835–96), Hungf. & Ramsbury PLU (1896–1930), Hungf. RD. *Parl* Hants until 1918, Newb. Dv/CC (1918–*). *Eccl* Andover RDn (until 1858), Andover RDn N-W'rn Dv (1858–71), N Andover RDn (1871–92), Kingsclere RDn (1892–1913), Andover RDn (1913–*) (all Winch dioc).

COMPTON

AP *LG* Seq 3. *Parl* Seq 5. *Eccl* Newb. RDn (until 1866), Wall. RDn (1866–1915), Newb. RDn (1915–*).

COMPTON BEAUCHAMP

AP *LG* Seq 18. Civ bdry: 1888.[30] Transf 1974 to Oxon.[5] *Parl* Seq 4. *Eccl* Seq 2.

COOKHAM

AP Incl pt Maidenhead (sep CP 1894 [from the pt of Cookham AP, Bray AP in Maid. MB],[43] sep EP 1720 [from this par only] as 'Maidenhead St Luke'[44]). *LG* Cook. Hd, PLU (1835–99), Maid. PLU (1899–1930), pt Maid. Bor/MB (until 1894), pt Maid. USD, pt Cook. RSD, Cook. RD. Addtl civ bdry alt: 1934.[3] *Parl* Seq 2. *Eccl* Seq 8. Addtl eccl bdry alt: 1846 (cr Cookham Dean EP),[81] 1928 (help cr Furze Platt EP, now commonly called 'Maidenhead St Peter').[82]

COOKHAM DEAN

EP Cr 1846 from Cookham AP.[81] Read. RDn (1846–65), Maid. RDn (1865–*). Bdry: 1856 (help cr Stubbings EP),[35] 1904,[83] 1928 (help cr Furze Platt EP, now commonly called 'Maidenhead St Peter').[82]

GREAT COXWELL

AP *LG* Faringdon Hd, PLU, RSD, RD. Transf 1974 to Oxon.[5] *Parl* Seq 4. *Eccl* Seq 2.

LITTLE COXWELL

Chap in Great Faringdon AP, sep CP 1866.[14] *LG* Faringdon Hd, PLU, RSD, RD. Transf 1974 to Oxon.[5] *Parl* Seq 4.

CRANBOURNE

EP Cr 1851 from Winkfield AP, Sunninghill AP, Old Windsor AP.[84] Read. RDn (1851–65), Maid. RDn (1865–*). Bdry: 1865 (help cr Ascot Heath EP),[21] 1871 (help cr Bray Wood EP),[46] 1960.[48]

CROWTHORNE

Chap in Sandhurst CP, EP, sep EP 1874,[86] sep CP 1894.[85] *LG* Easth. PLU, RD. *Parl* Wind. Dv (1918–48), Wok. CC (1948–*). *Eccl* Sonn. RDn.

CULHAM

AP Pt Oxon (Dorchester Hd), pt Berks (Ock Hd), the latter transf 1894 to Abingdon St Helen AP and par ent Oxon thereafter.[1] *LG* Abing. PLU, pt Abing. MB/USD (1890–94), Abing. RSD (ent 1875–90, pt 1890–94). *Parl* Berks pt, N'rn Dv (1885–1918). *Eccl* Cuddesdon RDn (Oxford AD).

CUMNOR

AP Incl chap South Hinksey (sep civ identity early, sep EP 1723,[116] eccl refounded 1885[87]), chap Wootton (sep civ identity early, sep EP 1885[87]). *LG* Seq 8. Addtl civ bdry alt: 1934.[3] Transf 1974 to Oxon.[5] *Parl* Seq 4. *Eccl* Seq 1.

DATCHET

AP In Bucks, qv, transf 1974 to Berks.[5]

DENCHWORTH

AP *LG* Want. Hd (ent until 1831, pt thereafter), pt Ock Hd (from 1831),[88] Want. PLU, RSD, RD. Transf 1974 to Oxon.[5] *Parl* Seq 4. *Eccl* Seq 4.

DENFORD

EP Cr 1833 from Kintbury AP.[89] Newb. RDn.

Abol 1952 to help cr Hungerford and Denford EP.[90]

DIDCOT

AP *LG* Seq 13. Civ bdry: 1935.[91] Transf 1974 to Oxon.[5] *Parl* Seq 4. *Eccl* Seq 3. Eccl bdry: 1915 (help cr Northbourne EP).[92]

DIDCOT ST PETER

EP Renaming 1965 of Northbourne EP.[209] Wall. RDn.

DRAYCOT MOOR

Hmlt in Longworth AP, sep CP 1866.[14] *LG* Ock Hd, Abing. PLU, RSD, RD. Abol 1971 to help cr Kingston Bagpuize with Southmoor CP.[93] *Parl* N'rn Dv (1885–1918), Abing. Dv/CC (1918–*).

DRAYTON

Chap in Abingdon St Helen AP, sep civ identity early, sep EP 1867 (from Abingdon St Helen with St Nicholas EP).[6] *LG* Seq 14. Civ bdry: 1883,[10] 1934.[3] Transf 1974 to Oxon.[5] *Parl* Seq 4. *Eccl* Abing. RDn.

EARLEY

Lbty in Sonning AP, sep EP 1843,[94] sep CP 1866.[14] *LG* Charl. Hd, Wok. PLU, RSD (ent 1875–87 and 1889–94, pt 1887–89), pt Read. CB/USD (1887[80]–89), Wok. RD. Civ bdry: 1889 (loses the pt in Read. CB to Reading St Giles AP).[56] *Parl* S'rn Dv (1885–1918), Newb. Dv (1918–48), Wok. CC (1948– 70), Read. S CC (1970–*). *Eccl* Read. RDn (1843–74), Sonn. RDn (1874–1915), Read. RDn (1915–*). Eccl bdry: 1877 (cr Earley St Bartholomew EP),[95] 1957,[96] 1959,[97] 1973 (help cr Reading St Barnabas EP).[98]

EARLEY ST BARTHOLOMEW

EP Cr 1877 from Earley AP.[95] Sonn. RDn (1877–1915), Read. RDn (1915–*). Bdry: 1957.[96]

EASTBURY

EP Cr 1867 from Lambourn AP.[99] Newb. RDn.

EASTGARSTON

AP Usual eccl spelling; for civ see 'East Garston'. *Eccl* Seq 6.

EASTHAMPSTEAD

AP *LG* Seq 17. Civ bdry: 1955 (help cr Bracknell AP),[34] 1965.[41] *Parl* Seq 3. *Eccl* Read. RDn (until 1865), Maid. RDn (1865–74), Read. RDn (1874–1915), Maid. RDn (1915–21), Sonn. RDn (1921–*).

EATON HASTINGS

AP *LG* Seq 18. Transf 1974 to Oxon.[5] *Parl* E'rn Dv (1885–1918), Abing. Dv/CC (1918–*). *Eccl* Seq 2.

ENBORNE

AP *LG* Seq 10. Civ bdry: 1934.[3] *Parl* Seq 7. *Eccl* Seq 6. Eccl bdry: 1963 (help cr Newbury St George the Martyr, Wash Common EP).[100]

ENGLEFIELD

AP *LG* Seq 19. *Parl* Seq 7. *Eccl* Seq 7.

ETON

CP In Bucks, transf 1974 to Berks.[5]

FARINGDON WITH LITTLE COXWELL

AP Usual eccl spelling; for civ and for chaps see following entry. *Eccl* Pec jurisd of Faringdon (until 1846), Seq 2 thereafter.

GREAT FARINGDON

AP Usual civ spelling; for eccl see prev entry. Incl chap Little Coxwell (sep CP 1866[14]), Tg Littleworth (sep EP 1843,[94] sep CP 1952[138]). *LG* Pt Faringdon Hd, pt Shriv. Hd, Faringdon Bor (status not sustained), PLU, RSD, RD. Transf 1974 to Oxon.[5] *Parl* Seq 4.

LITTLE FARINGDON

Tg in Langford AP (Oxon, Berks), sep EP 1864.[136] Witney RDn, Oxford AD.

FARNBOROUGH

AP *LG* Seq 3. *Parl* Seq 5. *Eccl* Newb. RDn (until 1865), Want. RDn (1865–*).

FAWLEY

AP Incl Whatcombe (sep par until 12th or 13th cent[101]). *LG* Seq 11. *Parl* Seq 4. *Eccl* Seq 4.

FERNHAM

Hmlt in Shrivenham AP, sep CP 1866,[14] eccl made pt of Longcot EP 1846.[102] *LG* Seq 18. Transf 1974 to Oxon.[5] *Parl* Seq 4.

FINCHAMPSTEAD

AP *LG* Seq 2. *Parl* Seq 1. *Eccl* Read. RDn (until 1915), Sonn. RDn (1915–*).

FRILFORD

Twnshp in Marcham AP, sep CP 1866.[14] *LG* Seq 14. Civ bdry: 1883,[10] 1934.[3] Transf 1974 to Oxon.[5] *Parl* Seq 4.

FRILSHAM

AP *LG* Seq 4. Civ bdry: 1934.[3] *Parl* Seq 6. *Eccl* Newb. RDn (until 1866), Wall. RDn (1866–75), Bradf. RDn (1875–*).

FURZE PLATT

EP Cr 1928 from Maidenhead St Luke EP, Cookham AP, Cookham Dean EP, Stubbings EP.[82] Maid. RDn. Now usually called 'Maidenhead St Peter'.

FYFIELD

AP *LG* Ock Hd, Abing. PLU, RSD, RD. Abol civ 1952 to help cr Fyfield and Tubney CP.[103] *Parl* N'rn Dv (1885–1918), Abing. Dv/CC (1918–70). *Eccl* Abing. RDn. Abol eccl 1952 to help cr Fyfield with Tubney EP.[104]

FYFIELD AND TUBNEY

CP Cr 1952 by union Fyfield AP, Tubney AP.[103] *LG* Abing. RD. Transf 1974 to Oxon.[5] *Parl* Abing. CC (1970–*).

FYFIELD WITH TUBNEY

EP Cr 1952 by union Fyfield AP, Tubney AP.[104] Abing. RDn. Bdry: 1954.[16]

GARFORD

Chap in Marcham AP, sep CP 1866.[14] *LG* Seq 14. Civ bdry: 1883,[10] 1934.[3] Transf 1974 to Oxon.[5] *Parl* Seq 4.

EAST GARSTON

AP Usual civ spelling; for eccl see 'Eastgarston'. *LG* Pt Lambourn Hd, pt Moreton Hd, pt Want. Hd, Hungf. PLU (1835–96), RSD, Hungf. & Ramsbury PLU (1896–1930), Hungf. RD. *Parl* Seq 7.

GOOSEY

Chap in Stanford in the Vale AP, sep CP 1866.[14] *LG* Ock Hd, Want. PLU, RSD, RD. Transf 1974 to Oxon.[5] *Parl* Seq 4.

GRAZELEY

Tg in Sulhamstead Abbots AP, sep EP 1860 (from Sulhamstead Abbots AP, Sulhamstead Banninster AP, and ent Lambwood Hill EP),[105] sep CP 1866 (from Sulhamstead Abbots AP alone).[14] *LG* Seq 16. *Parl* Seq 7. *Eccl* Donative, Read. RDn. Eccl bdry: 1913.[106]

GREENHAM

Chap and Tg in Thatcham AP, pt made sep EP 1857[107] (the remainder 1859 help cr Newbury St John the Evangelist EP[108]), sep CP 1866.[14] *LG* Fairc. Hd, Newb. PLU, pt Newb. MB/USD (1878[108]–94), Newb. RSD (ent 1875–78, pt (1878–94), Newb. RD. Civ bdry: 1894 (loses the pt in the MB to Newbury AP),[109] 1934.[3] *Parl* Seq 7. *Eccl* Newb. RDn. Eccl bdry: 1859 (help cr Newbury St John the Evangelist EP).[108]

GROVE

Chap in Wantage AP, sep EP 1835,[126] sep CP 1866.[14] *LG* Seq 20. Civ bdry: 1934.[3] Transf 1974 to Oxon.[5] *Parl* Seq 4. *Eccl* Abing. RDn (1835–65), Want. RDn (1865–*).

HAGBOURNE

AP Incl Liberties East Hagbourne, West Hagbourne (each a sep CP 1866[14]) so that after 1866 Hagbourne has no civ identity. *LG* Moreton Hd. *Eccl* Chap in West Hagbourne prob destroyed at Reformation and church in East Hagbourne continues as 'Hagbourne', Seq 3. Eccl bdry: 1915 (help cr Northbourne EP),[92] 1942.[110]

EAST HAGBOURNE

Lbty in Hagbourne AP, sep CP 1866.[14] *LG* Seq 13. Bdry: 1935.[91] Transf 1974 to Oxon.[5] *Parl* Seq 4.

WEST HAGBOURNE

Status, organisation, and bdry alt as for East Hagbourne.

HAMPSTEAD MARSHALL

AP *LG* Seq 10. *Parl* Seq 7. *Eccl* Seq 6.

HAMPSTEAD NORRIS

AP Usual civ spelling; for eccl spelling and civ name after 1969, see following entry. *LG* Fairc. Hd, Want. PLU, RSD, RD. Civ bdry: 1934,[3] 1948 (cr Hermitage CP).[111] Abol civ 1969 pt to Bucklebury AP, remainder renamed 'Hampstead Norreys' CP.[54] *Parl* S'rn Dv (1885–1918), Abing. Dv/CC (1918–70).

HAMSTEAD NORREYS

AP Usual eccl spelling and civ spelling after 1969 when main pt of Hampstead Norris AP renamed (remainder transf to Bucklebury AP).[54] *LG* Want. RD. *Parl* Abing. CC (1972[55]–*). *Eccl* Newb. RDn (until 1866), Wall. RDn (1866–1915), Newb. RDn (1915–*).

EAST HANNEY

Twnshp in West Hanney AP, sep CP 1866.[14] *LG* Ock Hd, Want. PLU, RSD, RD. Civ bdry: 1887.[57] Transf 1974 to Oxon.[5] *Parl* Seq 4.

WEST HANNEY

AP Incl Twnshp East Hanney (sep CP 1866[14]), twnshp and chap Lyford (sep EP 1845,[112] sep CP 1866[14]). *LG* Pt Want. Hd, pt Ock Hd (Lyford) hence ent Want. Hd from 1866, Want. PLU, RSD, RD. Addtl civ bdry alt: 1887.[57] Transf 1974 to Oxon.[5] *Parl* Seq 4. *Eccl* Seq 4.

HARWELL

AP *LG* Moreton Hd, Want. PLU, RSD, RD. Civ bdry: 1935.[91] Transf 1974 to Oxon.[5] *Parl* Seq 4. *Eccl* Abing. RDn (until 1865), Want. RDn (1865–1970), Wall. RDn (1970–*).

HATFORD

AP *LG* Seq 7. Transf 1974 to Oxon.[5] *Parl* Seq 4. *Eccl* Abing. RDn (until 1865), Vale WH RDn (1865–1973). Abol eccl 1973 to help cr Stanford in the Vale with Goosey and Hatford EP.[113]

EAST HENDRED

AP *LG* Seq 20. Civ bdry: 1883,[10] 1887.[19] Transf 1974 to Oxon.[5] *Parl* Seq 4. *Eccl* Seq 4.

WEST HENDRED

AP *LG* Seq 20. Civ bdry: 1887.[57] Transf 1974 to Oxon.[5] *Parl* Seq 4. *Eccl* Seq 4.

HERMITAGE

Area in Hampstead Norris (eccl, 'Hampstead Norreys') AP, sep EP 1840,[114] sep CP 1948.[111] *LG* Want. RD. Civ bdry: 1969 (incl help cr Hampstead Norreys CP).[54] *Parl* Abing. CC (1970–*). *Eccl* Newb. RDn. Eccl bdry: 1966.[64]

NORTH HINKSEY

Chap in Cumnor AP, sep civ identity early, sep EP 1726.[94] *LG* Hormer Hd, Abing. PLU, pt Oxford USD (1875–94), pt Oxford MB (1889–90), CB (1900–94), pt Abing. RSD, Abing. RD. Civ bdry: 1885 (loses pt to Oxford St Aldate AP and Oxford MB),[115] 1894 (loses the pt in the CB to Oxford St Thomas AP so that the par ent Berks thereafter),[1] 1934.[3] Transf 1974 to Oxon.[5] *Parl* Seq 4. *Eccl* Oxford RDn (Berks AD 1726–1915, Oxford AD 1915–*).

SOUTH HINKSEY

Chap in Cumnor AP, sep civ identity early, sep EP 1723.[116] *LG* Hormer Hd, Abing. PLU, pt Oxford MB (1889–90), CB (1900–94), pt Oxford USD (1889–94), Abing. RSD (ent 1875–89, pt 1889–94), Abing. RD. Civ bdry: 1885,[117] 1894 (loses the pt in the CB to Oxford St Aldate AP so that the par ent Berks thereafter),[103] 1936 (help cr Kennington CP).[117] Transf 1974 to Oxon.[5] *Parl* Pt Oxford Parl Bor (1867–1918), remainder and later, Seq 4. *Eccl* As for North Hinksey.

BROAD HINTON

Lbty in Hurst parochial chap, sep CP 1866.[14] Ent in Wilts (Amesbury Hd), transf to Berks 1832 for par purposes, 1844 for civ purposes.[27] *LG* Charl. Hd (from 1866), Wok. PLU, RSD. Civ bdry: 1883,[10] 1894 (help cr Twyford CP).[119] Abol 1894 to help cr Hurst St Nicholas CP.[120] *Parl* E'rn Dv (1885–1918).

HINTON WALDRIST

AP *LG* Seq 7. Transf 1974 to Oxon.[5] *Parl* Seq 4. *Eccl* Seq 2.

HORTON

AP Ent in Bucks, qv, transf 1974 to Berks.[5]

HUNGERFORD

AP Prob pt of Kintbury AP, sep par early.[121] *LG* Pt Berks (Kintb. Eagle Hd, Hungf. Bor, status not sustained[160]), pt Wilts (Kinwardstone Hd), the latter transf 1895 to Berks,[65] Hungf. PLU (1835–96), RSD, Hungf. & Ramsbury PLU (1896–1930), pt sep RD in Wilts (1894–95), Hungf. RD (pt 1894–95, ent 1895–1974). Addtl civ bdry alt: 1883.[10] *Parl* Berks pt, S'rn Dv (1885–1918), Newb. Dv/CC (1918–*). *Eccl* Pec jurisd Dean & Canons of Windsor (until 1846), Newb. RDn (1846– 1952). Abol eccl 1952 to help cr Hungerford and Denford EP.[90]

HUNGERFORD AND DENFORD

EP Cr 1952 by union Hungerford AP, Denford EP.[90] Newb. RDn.

HURLEY

AP *LG* Seq 1. *Parl* Seq 2. *Eccl* Seq 8. Eccl bdry: 1842 (help cr Knowl End EP).[122]

HURST

Parochial chap in Sonning AP, sep civ identity early, sep EP 1831.[94] *LG* Pt Berks (Newland Lbty, Winnersh Lbty, both in Sonn. Hd; Whistley Lbty in Charl. Hd), pt Wilts (Broad Hinton Lbty in Amesbury Hd), latter transf to Berks (Charl. Hd) 1832 for parl purposes, 1844 for civ purposes.[27] Broad Hinton, Newland, Whistley, Winnersh were each sep rated for poor law purposes and each became sep CP 1866[14] (none ever had sep eccl identity) so 'Hurst' had no sep civ identity after 1866. *Eccl* Pec jurisd Dean of Sarum (1831–46), Read. RDn (1846–74), Sonn. RDn (1874–*). Eccl bdry: 1846 (help cr Bear Wood EP),[28] 1876 (cr Twyford EP).[123]

HURST ST NICHOLAS

CP Cr 1894 from Broad Hinton CP, Whistley CP.[120] *LG* Wok. PLU, RD. Bdry: 1952.[124] *Parl* Newb. Dv (1918–48), Wok. CC (1948–*).

EAST ILSLEY

AP *LG* Seq 3. *Parl* Seq 5. *Eccl* Seq 6.

WEST ILSEY

AP *LG* Seq 3. *Parl* Seq 5. *Eccl* Pec jurisd Dean & Canons of Windsor (until 1846), Newb. RDn (1846–1930), Want. RDn (1930–*).

INGLESHAM

AP Pt Wilts (Highworth Hd), pt Berks (Faringdon Hd), latter transf to Wilts 1832 for par purposes, 1844 for civ purposes.[27] See main entry in Wilts.

INKPEN

AP *LG* Seq 9. Civ bdry: 1934.[3] *Parl* Seq 7. *Eccl* Seq 6.

KENNINGTON

Twnshp in Radley AP, Sunningwell AP, sep EP 1866,[125] sep CP 1936 (from Radley AP, South Hinksey CP).[118] *LG* Abing. RD. Transf 1974 to Oxon.[5] *Parl* Abing. CC (1948–*). *Eccl* Abing. RDn. Spelling of dedication changed from 'St Swithin' to 'St Swithun' in 1958.[127]

KIDMORE END

EP Cr 1854 from Sonning AP and from the Oxon pars of Caversham AP, Shiplake AP.[128] Henley RDn (Oxford AD).

KINGSTON BAGPUIZE

AP Orig pt of Lolworth AP, sep by 16th cent.[129] *LG* Ock Hd, Abing. PLU, RSD, RD. Abol civ 1971 to help cr Kingston Bagpuize with Southmoor CP.[93] *Parl* N'rn Dv (1885–1918), Abing. Dv/CC (1918–*). *Eccl* Seq 1. Eccl bdry: 1958.[130]

KINGSTON BAGPUIZE WITH SOUTHMOOR

CP Cr 1971 by union Kingston Bagpuize AP, Draycott Moor CP.[93] *LG* Abing. RD. Transf 1974 to Oxon.[5]

KINGSTON LISLE

Chap in Sparsholt AP (with attached Hmlt of Fawler, hence sometimes 'Kingston Lisle with Fawler') , sep CP 1866.[14] *LG* Seq 18. Civ bdry: 1883,[10] 1888.[30] Transf 1974 to Oxon.[5] *Parl* Seq 4.

KINTBURY

AP Prob incl Hungerford (sep par early[121]). *LG* Seq 9. Civ bdry: 1934.[3] *Parl* Seq 7. *Eccl* Seq 6. Eccl bdry: 1833 (cr Denford EP).[89]

KNOWL HILL

EP Cr 1842 from Hurley AP, Wargrave AP.[122] Read. RDn (1842–65), Maid. RDn (1865–*). Bdry: 1954.[131]

LAMBOURN

AP Incl twnshp Hadley with Blagrave (sep EP 1838 as 'Lambourn Woodlands'[133]), chap Eastbury (sep EP 1867[99]). *LG* Lambourn Hd, Bor (status not sustained beyond 15th cent[132]), Hungf. PLU (1835–96), RSD, Hungf. & Ramsbury PLU (1896–1930), Hungf. RD. *Parl* Seq 7. *Eccl* Seq 6. Addtl eccl bdry alt: 1891.[134]

LAMBOURN WOODLANDS

EP Cr 1838 from Lambourn AP.[133] Newb. RDn. Bdry: 1891.[134]

LAMBWOOD HILL

EP Cr 1854 from Shinfield AP.[135] Read. RDn. Abol 1860 to help cr Grazeley EP.[105]

LANGFORD

AP Incl Tg Little Faringdon (sep EP 1864[136]). *LG* Pt Oxon (Bampton Hd), pt Berks (Faringdon Hd, incl Little Faringdon), latter transf to Oxon 1832 for parl purposes, 1844 for civ purposes.[27] *Eccl* Pec jurisd of Langford (until 1846), Witney RDn (Oxford AD, 1846–*) See main entry in Oxon.

LECKHAMPSTEAD

Chap in Chieveley AP, sep CP 1866,[14] sep EP 1882.[63] *LG* Seq 5. *Parl* Seq 7. *Eccl* Newb. RDn.

LETCOMBE BASSETT

AP *LG* Seq 11. Civ bdry: 1883,[10] 1887.[57] Transf 1974 to Oxon.[5] *Parl* Seq 4. *Eccl* Seq 4. Eccl bdry: 1930.[59]

LETCOMBE REGIS

AP Incl twnshp Challow, sep CP 1866,[14] comprised of 2 chaps of East Challow, West Challow, sep EP 1852 as 'East Challow with West Challow'.[58] *LG* Seq 11. Civ bdry: 1887.[19] Transf 1974 to Oxon.[5] *Parl* Seq 4. *Eccl* Seq 4. Eccl bdry: 1930.[59]

LITTLEWICK

EP Cr 1894 from White Waltham AP.[137] Maid. RDn. Bdry: 1954.[131]

LITTLEWORTH

Tg in Great Faringdon AP, sep EP 1842 (incl Tg Thrup and Wadley),[94] sep CP 1952.[138] *LG* Faringdon RD. Transf 1974 to Oxon.[5] *Parl* Abing. CC (1970–*). *Eccl* Abing. RDn (1842–65), Vale WH RDn (1865–*).

LOCKINGE

CP Cr 1934 by union East Lockinge AP, West Lockinge CP.[3] *LG* Want. RD. Transf 1974 to Oxon.[5] *Parl* Abing. CC (1948–*).

EAST LOCKINGE

AP *LG* Want. Hd, PLU, RSD, RD. Civ bdry: 1883,[10] 1887.[19] Abol civ 1934 to help cr Lockinge CP.[3] *Parl* N'rn Dv (1885–1918), Abing. Dv (1918–48). *Eccl* Seq 4.

WEST LOCKINGE

Hmlt in Wantage AP, sep CP 1866.[14] *LG* Want. Hd, PLU, RSD, RD. Civ bdry: 1887.[139] Abol 1934 to help cr Lockinge CP.[3] *Parl* N'rn Dv (1885–1918), Abing. Dv (1918–48).

LONGCOTT

Chap in Shrivenham AP, sep EP 1846 (incl Fernham Hmlt),[102] sep CP 1866.[14] *LG* Seq 18. Transf 1974 to Oxon.[5] *Parl* Seq 4. *Eccl* Abing. RDn (1846–65), Vale WH RDn (1865–*).

LONGWORTH

AP Incl chap Kingston Bagpuize (sep par by 16th cent[129]), chap Charney Bassett (sep CP 1866,[14] eccl severed 1947 to help cr Lyford with Charney Bassett EP[60]), hmlt Draycot Moor (sep CP 1866[14]). *LG* Pt Ganf. Hd, pt Ock Hd (Draycot Moor) hence ent Ganf. Hd from 1866, Faringdon PLU, RSD, RD. Transf 1974 to Oxon.[5] *Parl* Seq 4. *Eccl* Seq 2.

LYFORD

Chap and twnshp in West Hanney AP, sep EP 1845,[112] sep CP 1866.[14] *LG* Seq 14. Transf 1974 to Oxon.[5] *Parl* Seq 4. *Eccl* Abing. RDn (1845–65), Want. RDn (1865–1947). Reconstituted 1947 gaining Charney Bassett chap from Longworth AP to cr Lyford with Charney Bassett EP.[60]

LYFORD WITH CHARNEY BASSETT

EP Cr 1947 by union Lyford AP, Charney Bassett chap of Longworth AP.[60] Vale WH RDn.

MAIDENHEAD

CP Cr 1894 from the pts of Bray AP, Cookham AP in Maid. MB.[43] *LG* Cook. PLU (1894–99), Maid. PLU (1899–1930), MB. Civ bdry: 1934.[3] *Parl* Wind. Dv/CC (1918–70), Wind. & Maid. CC (1970–*).

MAIDENHEAD ST ANDREW AND ST MARY MAGDALEN

EP Cr 1875 from Maidenhead St Luke EP, Bray AP.[47] Maid. RDn.

MAIDENHEAD ST LUKE

EP Cr 1720 from Cookham AP.[44] Read. RDn (1720–1865), Maid. RDn (1865–*). Bdry: 1875 (help cr Maidenhead St Andrew and St Mary Magdalen EP),[47] 1904,[38] 1928 (help cr Furze Platt EP, now called 'Maidenhead St Peter').[82]

MAIDENHEAD ST PETER

EP Name used now for EP cr 1928 as 'Furze Platt', qv.

MARCHAM

AP Incl twnshp Frilford (sep CP 1866[14]), chap Garford (sep CP 1866[14]). *LG* Seq 14. Civ bdry: 1883,[10] 1934.[3] Transf 1974 to Oxon.[5] *Parl* Seq 4. *Eccl* Seq 1. Eccl bdry: 1937.[140]

MIDGHAM

Chap in Thatcham AP, sep EP 1857,[107] sep CP 1866.[14] *LG* Seq 5. *Parl* Seq 7. *Eccl* Newb. RDn (1857–1973), Bradf. RDn (1973–*).

MILTON

AP *LG* Seq 14. Transf 1974 to Oxon.[5] *Parl* Seq 4. *Eccl* Seq 1.

NORTH MORETON

AP *LG* Seq 13. Transf 1974 to Oxon.[5] *Parl* Wall. Parl Bor (1832–85), Seq 4 thereafter. *Eccl* Seq 3.

SOUTH MORETON

AP Organisation as for North Moreton.

MORTIMER WEST END

Tg in Stratfield Mortimer AP (Hants, Berks), sep CP 1866 in Hants (Holdshott Hd), sep EP 1870.[141] For civ see main entry in Hants. *Eccl* Read. RDn (1870–1952), Bradf. RDn (1952–*).

MOULSFORD

Chap in Cholsey AP, sep civ identity early, sep EP 1845.[66] *LG* Seq 13. Civ bdry: 1948.[67] Transf 1974 to Oxon.[5] *Parl* Seq 4. *Eccl* Wall. RDn. Eccl bdry: 1951.[68]

NEWBURY

AP Sometimes considered chap to Thatcham AP, pt prob in Speen AP, sep par by 14th cent.[100] *LG* Fairc. Hd, Newb. PLU, Bor/MB, USD. Civ bdry: 1934.[3] *Parl* Seq 7. *Eccl* Newb. RDn. Eccl bdry: 1859 (help cr Newbury St John the Evangelist EP).[108] Abol eccl 1973 to help cr Newbury with Speenhamland EP.[143]

NEWBURY ST GEORGE THE MARTYR, WASH COMMON

EP Cr 1963 from Newbury St John the Evangelist EP, Enborne AP.[100] Newb. RDn.

NEWBURY ST JOHN THE EVANGELIST

EP Cr 1859 from Newbury AP, Greenham EP.[108] Newb. RDn. Bdry: 1963 (help cr Newbury St George the Martyr, Wash Common EP).[100]

NEWBURY WITH SPEENHAMLAND

EP Cr 1973 by union Newbury AP, Speenhamland EP.[143] Newb. RDn.

NEWLAND

Lbty in Hurst parochial chap, sep CP 1866.[14] *LG* Sonn. Hd, Wok. PLU, RSD, RD. Civ bdry: 1883.[10] Abol 1948 to help cr Arborfield and Newland CP.[18] *Parl* E'rn Dv (1885–1918), Newb. Dv (1918–48).

NORTHBOURNE

EP Cr 1915 from Hagbourne AP, Didcot AP.[92] Wall. RDn. Bdry: 1942.[110] Renamed 1965 'Didcot St Peter'.[209]

OXFORD ST ALDATE

AP Principal pt in Oxford Bor/MB/CB, but tg Grandpont in Berks (Hormer Hd), pt Oxf. USD (1875–89), the par ent Oxon from 1889,[144] the area in Oxford Parl Bor from 1867. See main entry in Oxon.

PADWORTH

AP *LG* Seq 19. Civ bdry: 1883,[10] 1934.[3] *Parl* Seq 7. *Eccl* Seq 7.

PANGBOURNE

AP *LG* Seq 16. *Parl* Seq 7. *Eccl* Seq 7.

PEASEMORE

AP Orig pt of Chieveley AP, sep par *ca* 1104–05.[62] *LG* Seq 6. *Parl* Seq 5. *Eccl* Seq 6.

PURLEY

AP *LG* Seq 19. Civ bdry: 1883,[10] 1894,[145] 1934.[3] *Parl* Seq 7. *Eccl* Seq 7.

PUSEY

AP *LG* Seq 7. Transf 1974 to Oxon.[5] *Parl* Seq 4. *Eccl* Seq 2.

RADLEY

Chap in Abingdon St Helen AP, sep civ identity early, claimed to be eccl sep and treated as Donative. Incl pt twnshp Kennington (sep EP 1866,[125] sep CP 1936[118] [see Kennington for complete composition of CP, EP]). *LG* Seq 8. Addtl civ bdry alt: 1885,[111] 1894,[26] 1934,[3] 1952.[118] Transf 1974 to Oxon.[5] *Parl* Seq 4. *Eccl* Abing. RDn.

READING

The following have 'Reading' in their names. Insofar as any existed at a given time: *LG* Read. Hd, PLU [Bor/MB/CB, RSD, USD sep noted]. *Parl* sep noted. *Eccl* Read. RDn.

CP1–READING–Cr 1905 by union AP1, AP2, AP3.[147] *LG* Read. CB. Bdry: 1911 (gains Caversham UD, Oxon),[148] 1919.[149] *Parl* Read. Parl Bor (1918–48); pt Read. N BC pt Read. S BC (1948–55); pt Read. BC (1955–70), pt Newb. CC (1955–70); pt Read. N BC, pt Read. S BC (1970–*). [See Part III of the *Guide* for the composition of the constituencies by wards of the CB].

EP1–READING CHRIST CHURCH–Name commonly used now for EP cr 1863 as 'Whitley', qv.

EP2–READING GREY FRIARS–Cr 1864 from AP2, AP3.[150] Bdry: 1892,[151] 1957,[96] 1973.[152]

EP3–READING HOLY TRINITY–Cr 1875 from AP3.[153] Bdry: 1892,[154] 1957.[96]

EP4–READING ST BARNABAS–Cr 1973 from Shinfield AP, Whitley EP, Earley EP.[98]

AP1–READING ST GILES–*LG* Pt Read. Hd (until 1835), Read. Bor/MB (pt until 1835, ent 1835–89), pt Read. RSD (1875–87), Read. USD (pt 1875–87, ent 1887–94), Read. CB. Civ bdry: 1889 (gains the pts of Shinfield AP, Burghfield AP, Earley AP in the CB).[56] Abol civ 1905 to help cr CP1.[147] *Parl* Pt Read. Parl Bor (1295–1918), pt S'rn Dv (1885–1918). Eccl bdry: 1863 (cr Whitley EP, now called as EP1),[155] 1874 (cr EP5),[156] 1912 (help cr EP6),[157] 1957,[96] 1973.[152]

EP5–READING ST JOHN THE EVANGELIST–Cr 1874 from AP1.[156]

AP2–READING ST LAWRENCE–*LG* Read. Bor/MB/CB, USD. Abol civ 1905 to help cr CP1.[147] *Parl* Read. Parl Bor (1295–1918). Eccl bdry: 1864 (help cr EP2).[150]

EP6–READING ST LUKE–Cr 1912 from AP1, Whitley EP.[157] Bdry: 1957.[96]

AP3–READING ST MARY–*LG* Pt Read. Hd (until 1835), Read. Bor/MB (pt until 1835, ent 1835–89), pt Read. RSD (1875–87), Read. USD (pt 1875–87, ent 1887–94), Read. CB. Civ bdry: 1889 (gains the pt of Tilehurst AP in the CB).[56] Abol civ 1905 to help cr CP1.[147] *Parl* Pt Read. Parl Bor (1295–1918), pt S'rn Dv (1885–1918). Eccl bdry: 1864 (help cr EP2),[150] 1875 (cr EP3),[153] 1892,[154] 1957,[96] 1973.[152]

REMENHAM

AP *LG* Beynh. Hd, Henley PLU (1835–94), RSD, Wok. PLU (1894–1930), RD. *Parl* Seq 3. *Eccl* Seq 11.

RUSCOMBE

Chap in Sonning AP, sep civ identity early, sep EP before 1835.[158] *LG* Sonn. Hd, Wok. PLU, RSD, RD. *Parl* Seq 3. *Eccl* Pec jurisd Dean of Sarum (until 1847), Read. RDn (1847–74), Sonn. RDn (1874–1973). Abol eccl 1973 to help cr Ruscombe and Twyford EP.[161]

RUSCOMBE AND TWYFORD

EP Cr 1973 by union Ruscombe EP, Twyford EP.[161] Sonn. RDn.

DRY SANDFORD

EP Cr 1867 (as 'Sandford St Helen') from Abingdon St Helen with St Nicholas EP.[8] Abing. RDn. Bdry: 1937.[140]

SANDHURST

Chap by 1220 to Sonning AP,[162] sep civ identity early, sep EP 1756.[94] Incl chap Crowthorne (sep EP 1874,[86] sep CP 1894[85]). *LG* Sonn. Hd, Easth. PLU, RD. *Parl* Seq 3. *Eccl* Pec jurisd Dean of Sarum (1756–1846), Read. RDn (1846–65), Maid. RDn (1865–74), Sonn. RDn (1874–*).

SANDLEFORD

Ex-par place, orig priory, sep CP 1858.[25] *LG* Fairc. Hd, Newb. PLU, RSD, RD. Abol 1934 pt to Newbury AP, pt to Greenham CP.[3] *Parl* S'rn Dv (1885–1918), Newb. Dv (1918–48).

SEACOURT

Church in ruins by 15th cent, treated later as free chapel then as ex-par place, sep CP 1858.[25] *LG* Pt Berks (Hormer Hd), pt Oxford CB, Abing. PLU, pt Abing. RSD, pt Oxford USD. Made 2 sep CPs 1894, one in each county,[163] qv. *Parl* N'rn Dv (1885–1918).

CP Cr 1894 from the Berks pt of Seacourt CP.[163] *LG* Abing. PLU, RD. Abol 1900 ent to Wytham AP.[164]

SHALBOURNE

AP Pt Wilts (Kinwardstone Hd), pt Berks (Oxenwood Tg, Bagshot Tg, both in Kintb. Eagle Hd),

Oxenwood Tg transf to Wilts 1832 for parl purposes, 1844 for civ purposes,[27] the remainder transf 1895 to Wilts.[165] *LG* Hungf. PLU, RSD, pt sep RD in Wilts (1894–95), pt Hungf. RD (1894–95) before transf. Civ bdry: 1883.[10] *Parl* Berks pt, S'rn Dv (1885–1918), Wilts thereafter. *Eccl* Pec jurisd Dean & Canons of Windsor (until 1846), Newb. RDn (1846–1956), Pewsey RDn (dioc Sarum, Wilts AD, 1956–*).

SHAW CUM DONNINGTON

AP *LG* Seq 5. *Parl* Seq 7. *Eccl* Seq 6. Eccl bdry: 1956.[77]

EAST SHEFFORD

AP Sometimes 'Little Shefford'. *LG* Seq 9. *Parl* Seq 7. *Eccl* Newb. RDn. Abol eccl 1926 to help cr West with East Shefford EP.[166]

GREAT SHEFFORD

EP Renaming 1973 of West with East Shefford EP.[167] Newb. RDn.

WEST SHEFFORD

AP Sometimes 'Great Shefford'. Organisation as for East Shefford.

WEST WITH EAST SHEFFORD

EP Cr 1926 by union East Shefford AP, West Shefford AP.[166] Newb. RDn. Renamed 1973 'Great Shefford'.[67]

SHELLINGFORD

AP *LG* Seq 7. Transf 1974 to Oxon.[5] *Parl* Seq 4. *Eccl* Seq 2.

SHILTON

AP Pt Oxon (Bampton Hd), pt Berks (Faringdon Hd), the latter transf to Oxon 1832 for parl purposes, 1844 for civ purposes.[27] See main entry in Oxon.

SHINFIELD

AP Incl chap Swallowfield (Wilts, Berks, sep civ identity early [qv for later division into 2 CPs], sep EP 1854[168]). Pt Berks (Charl. Hd, Theale Hd), pt Wilts (Amesbury Hd), latter transf to Berks 1832 for parl purposes, 1844 for civ purposes.[27] *LG* Wok. PLU, pt Reading MB/CB/USD (1887[80]–89), Wok. RSD (ent 1875–87 and 1889–94, pt 1887–89), Wok. RD. Addtl civ bdry alt: 1889 (loses the pt in the CB to Reading St Giles AP),[56] 1934.[3] *Parl* Pt Wilts until 1832, S'rn Dv (1885–1918), Newb. Dv (1918–48), Wok. CC (1948–70), Read S CC (1970–*). *Eccl* Seq 10. Addtl eccl bdry alt: 1854 (help cr Lambwood Hill EP),[135] 1913 (help cr Spencer's Wood EP),[106] 1974 (help cr Reading St Barnabas EP).[98]

SHIPPON

EP Cr 1865 from Abingdon St Helen with St Nicholas EP.[7] Abing. RDn.

SHOTTESBROOKE

AP *LG* Seq 1. Civ bdry: 1887.[169] *Parl* Seq 2. *Eccl* Orig priory church, Read. RDn. Abol eccl 1744 to help cr White Waltham with Shottesbrooke EP.[170]

SHRIVENHAM

AP Incl chap Bourton (sep CP 1866,[14] sep EP 1867[36]), chap Watchfield (sep CP 1866[14]), hmlt Fernham, hmlt Longcot (each a sep CP 1866,[14] united eccl 1846 to cr 'Longcott' EP[102]). *LG* Seq 18. Transf 1974 to Oxon.[5] *Parl* Seq 4. *Eccl* Seq 2.

SLOUGH

CP Ent in Bucks, transf 1974 to Berks.[5]

SONNING

AP Incl chap Arborfield (sep par *ca* 16th cent[17]), chap Wokingham (sep par early[171]), parochial chap Hurst (sep civ identity early, sep EP 1831[94]), chap Sandhurst (sep civ identity early, sep EP 1756[94]), chap Ruscombe (sep civ identity early, sep EP before 1835[158]), chap Woodley (sep CP 1866 as 'Woodley and Sandford',[14] sep EP 1881 as 'Woodley'[172]), lbty Earley (sep EP 1843,[94] sep CP 1866[14]), lbty Eye and Dunsden (in Oxon, Binfield Hd, sep CP 1866 in Oxon,[14] sep EP 1876 as 'Dunsden'[173]). *LG* Pt Berks (main pt and Woodley in Sonn. Hd, Earley in Charl. Hd), pt Oxon (Eye and Dunsden), Wok. PLU, pt Read. CB/USD (1887[80]–89), Wok. RSD (ent 1875–87 and 1889–94, pt 1887–89), Wok. RD. Addtl civ bdry alt: 1889 (loses the pt in the CB to Reading St Giles AP),[174] 1970.[61] *Parl* Pt Oxon until 1867, E'rn Dv (1885–1918), Newb. Dv (1918–48), Wok. CC (1970–*). *Eccl* Pec jurisd Dean of Sarum (until 1847), Seq 11 thereafter. Addtl eccl bdry alt: 1854 (help cr Kidmore End EP).[128]

SOTWELL

Chap in Wallingford St Lucian (until disappeared 14th cent), then to Wallingford St Leonard AP, sep civ identity early, eccl severed 1868 to help cr Brightwell with Stowell EP.[60] *LG* Moreton Hd, Wall. PLU, RSD, RD. Civ bdry: 1934.[3] Abol civ 1948 to help cr Brightwell-cum-Sotwell CP.[3] *Parl* Wall. Parl Bor (1832–85), N'rn Dv (1885–1918), Abing. Dv/CC (1918–70).

SPARSHOLT

AP Incl chap Kingston Lisle (sep CP 1866,[14] no sep eccl identity). *LG* Pt Want. Hd, pt Shriv. Hd (Kingston Lisle) thus ent Want. Hd from 1866, Want. PLU, RSD, RD. Civ bdry: 1887.[57] Transf 1974 to Oxon.[5] *Parl* Seq 4. *Eccl* Often as 'Sparsholt with Kingston Lisle', Seq 4.

SPEEN

AP Prob incl pt of Newbury at an early date, sep by 14th cent.[142] *LG* Pt Fairc. Hd, pt Kintb. Eagle Hd, Newb. PLU, pt Newb. MB (1878–94), pt Newb. USD (1878–94), Newb. RSD (ent 1875–78, pt 1878–94), Newb. RD. Civ bdry: 1894 (loses the pt in the MB to Newbury AP),[109] 1934.[3] *Parl* Seq 7. *Eccl* Seq 6. Eccl bdry: 1844 (cr Speenhamland EP, sometimes later called 'Newbury St Mary the Virgin'),[175] 1848 (cr Stockcross EP).[176]

SPEENHAMLAND

EP Cr 1844 from Speen AP.[175] Sometimes later called 'Newbury St Mary the Virgin'. Newb. RDn. Abol 1973 to help cr Newbury with Speenhamland EP.[143]

SPENCER'S WOOD
EP Cr 1913 from Shinfield AP, Swallowfield EP, Grazeley EP.[106] Read. RDn.

STANFORD DINGLEY
AP *LG* Seq 4. Civ bdry: 1883.[10] *Parl* Seq 7. *Eccl* Seq 5.

STANFORD IN THE VALE
AP Incl chap Goosey (sep CP 1866,[14] no sep eccl identity). *LG* Pt Ganf. Hd, pt Ock Hd (Goosey), thus ent Ganf. Hd from 1866, Faringdon PLU, RSD, RD. Transf 1974 to Oxon.[5] *Parl* Seq 4. *Eccl* As 'Stanford in the Vale with Goosey', Abing. RDn (until 1865), Vale WH RDn (1865–1973). Abol eccl 1973 to help cr Stanford in the Vale with Goosey and Hatford EP.[113]

STANFORD IN THE VALE WITH GOOSEY–see prev entry

STANFORD IN THE VALE WITH GOOSEY AND HATFORD
EP Cr 1973 by union Stanford in the Vale with Goosey AP, Hatford AP.[113] Vale WH RDn.

STEVENTON
AP *LG* Seq 14. Transf 1974 to Oxon.[5] *Parl* Seq 4. *Eccl* Seq 1.

STOCKCROSS
EP Cr 1848 from Speen AP.[176] Newb. RDn.

STRATFORD MORTIMER
AP Incl Tg Wokefield (sep CP 1866[14]),Tg Mortimer West End (Holdshott Hd, Hants, sep CP 1866 in Hants,[14] sep EP 1870[141]). *LG* Read. Hd (until mid-17th cent), Theale Hd (from mid-17th cent),[177] Bradf. PLU, RSD, RD. *Parl* Seq 7. *Eccl* Read. RDn (until 1952), Bradf. RDn (1952–*).

STRATFIELD SAYE
AP In Hants (Holdshot Hd) but incl hmlt Beech Hill in Berks (Read. Hd, sep CP 1866 in Berks,[14] sep EP 1868[32]), thus this par ent Hants from 1866, qv for main entry.

STREATLEY
AP *LG* Seq 12. *Parl* Seq 6. *Eccl* Seq 12.

STUBBINGS
EP Cr 1856 from Bisham AP, Cookham Dean EP.[35] Read. RDn (1856–65), Maid. RDn (1865–*). Bdry: 1904,[83] 1928 (help cr Furze Platt EP, now called 'Maidenhead St Peter').[82]

SULHAM
AP *LG* Seq 19. Civ bdry: 1883,[10] 1934.[3] *Parl* Seq 7. *Eccl* Seq 7.

SULHAMSTEAD
CP Cr 1934 by union Sulhamstead Abbots AP, Sulhamstead Bannister Upper End CP.[3] *LG* Bradf. RD. *Parl* Newb. CC (1948–*).

SULHAMSTEAD ABBOTS
AP Incl Tg Grazeley (sep CP 1866,[14] sep EP 1860 from Sulhamstead Abbots AP, Sulhamstead Bannister AP, ent Lambwood Hill EP[105]). *LG* Read. Hd, Bradf. PLU, RSD, RD. *Parl* S'rn Dv (1885–1918), Newb. Dv (1918–48). *Eccl* Read. RDn (until 1865), Bradf. RDn (1865–1966). Abol eccl 1966 to help cr Sulhamstead Abbots and Bannister EP.[178]

SULHAMSTEAD ABBOTS AND BANNISTER
EP Cr 1966 by union Sulhamstead Abbots AP, Sulhamstead Bannister AP.[178] Bradf. RDn.

SULHAMSTEAD BANNISTER
AP *LG* Theale Hd. Sulhamstead Bannister Lower End, Sulhamstead Bannister Upper End were each sep rated for poor law purposes and became sep CPs 1866,[14] thus this par had no civ identity after 1866. *Eccl* Read. RDn (until 1865), Bradf. RDn (1865–1966). Eccl bdry: 1860 (help cr Grazeley EP).[105] Abol eccl 1966 to help cr Sulhamstead Abbots and Bannister EP.[178]
CP Cr 1934 by union Sulhamstead Bannister Lower End CP, pt Wokefield AP.[3] *LG* Bradf. RD. *Parl* Newb. CC (1948–*).

SULHAMSTEAD BANNISTER LOWER END
Pt of Sulhamstead Bannister AP, sep CP 1866.[14] *LG* Theale Hd, Bradf. PLU, RSD, RD. Abol 1934 to help cr Sulhamstead Bannister CP.[3] *Parl* S'rn Dv (1885–1918), Newb. Dv (1918–48).

SULHAMSTEAD BANNISTER UPPER END
Pt of Sulhamstead Bannister AP, sep CP 1866.[14] *LG* Theale Hd, Bradf. PLU, RSD, RD. Abol 1934 to help cr Sulhamstead CP.[3] *Parl* S'rn Dv (1885–1918), Newb. Dv (1918–48).

SUNNINGDALE
Pt of Old Windsor AP, sep EP 1841 (from Berks APs of Old Windsor, Sunninghill, and Surrey APs of Windlesham, Egham, Chobham),[179] sep CP 1894 (from Old Windsor AP alone).[180] *LG* Wind. PLU, RD. *Parl* Wind. Dv/CC (1918–70), Wind. & Maid. CC (1970–*). *Eccl* Read. RDn (1841–65), Maid. RDn (1865–1921), Sonn. RDn (1921–*). Eccl bdry: 1890 (help cr South Ascot EP),[20] 1904.[181]

SUNNINGHILL
AP *LG* Cook. Hd, Wind. PLU, RSD, RD. Civ bdry: 1878.[182] *Parl* Seq 2. *Eccl* Read. RDn (until 1865), Maid. RDn (1865–1921), Sonn. RDn (1921–*). Eccl bdry: 1841 (help cr Sunningdale EP),[179] 1851 (help cr Cranbourne EP),[84] 1865 (help cr Ascot Heath EP).[20]

SUNNINGWELL
AP Incl pt twnshp Kennington (sep EP 1866 [from Radley AP, Sunningwell AP],[14] sep CP 1936 [from Radley AP, South Hinksey CP][118]). *LG* Seq 8. Civ bdry: 1883,[10] 1885.[11] Transf 1974 to Oxon.[5] *Parl* Seq 4. *Eccl* Seq 1.

SUTTON COURTENAY
AP Incl twnshp Sutton Wick, chap Appleford (each a sep CP 1866,[14] neither with sep eccl identity). *LG* Seq 14. Civ bdry: 1883,[10] 1887,[183] 1934.[3] Transf 1974 to Oxon.[5] *Parl* Seq 4. *Eccl* As 'Sutton Courtenay with Appleford', Seq 1.

SUTTON WICK
Twnshp in Sutton Courtenay AP, sep CP 1866,[14] no sep eccl identity. *LG* Ock Hd, Abing. PLU, pt Abing. MB (1868–94), pt Abing. USD, (enlarged pt 1890–94), pt Abing. RSD, Abing. RD. Civ bdry: 1883,[10] 1894 (the pt in the MB to help cr Abingdon CP).[2] Abol 1934 pt to

Abingdon CP, pt to Drayton CP, pt to Sutton Courtenay AP.[3] *Parl* Pt Abing. Parl Bor (1868–85), N'rn Dv (1885–1918), Abing. Dv (1918–48).

SWALLOWFIELD
Chap in Shinfield AP, sep civ identity early, sep EP 1854.[168] Pt Berks (Charl. Hd, Read. Hd), pt Wilts (Amesbury Hd), the latter transf to Berks 1832 for parl purposes, 1844 for civ purposes.[27] The two pts of this par, East Swallowfield, West Swallowfield, sep rated and each a sep CP 1866,[14] thus this par has no civ identity after 1866. *Parl* Pt Wilts until 1832; see following entries for period after 1832. *Eccl* Read. RDn. Eccl bdry: 1913 (help cr Spencer's Wood EP).[106]

CP Cr 1894 by union East Swallowfield CP, West Swallowfield CP.[184] *LG* Wok. PLU, RD. *Parl* Newb. Dv (1918–48), Wok. CC (1948–70), Read. S CC (1970–*).

EAST SWALLOWFIELD
CP Pt of Swallowfield CP, sep CP 1866.[14] *LG* Wok. PLU, RSD. Abol 1894 to help cr Swallowfield CP.[184] *Parl* E'rn Dv (1885–1918).

WEST SWALLOWFIELD
CP Organisation as for East Swallowfield.

THATCHAM
AP Incl Tg and chap Greenham, Midgham (each a sep EP 1857,[107] each a sep CP 1866[14]), area of Cold Ash (sep EP 1865,[75] sep CP 1894[76]), claimed to incl chap Newbury (sep par 14th cent[142]). *LG* Pt Read. Hd, Thatcham Bor (status not sustained),[185] pt Fairc. Hd (Greenham, Midham), thus ent Read. Hd from 1866, Newb. PLU, RSD, RD. Addtl civ bdry alt: 1934.[3] *Parl* Seq 7. *Eccl* Seq 6. Addtl eccl bdry alt: 1953.[52]

THEALE
Tg in Tilehurst AP, sep EP 1820,[186] sep CP 1894.[187] *LG* Bradf. PLU, RD. Civ bdry: 1911.[148] *Parl* Newb. Dv/CC (1918–*). *Eccl* Read. RDn (1820–65), Bradf. RDn (1865–*).

TIDMARSH
AP *LG* Seq 19. *Parl* Seq 7. *Eccl* Seq 7.

TILEHURST
AP *LG* Read. Hd, Bradf. PLU, RSD (ent 1875–87 and 1889–94, pt 1887–89), pt Read MB/CB/USD (1887[80]–89), Bradf. RD. Civ bdry: 1889 (loses the pt in the CB to Reading St Giles AP),[56] 1894 (cr Theale CP),[187] 1911.[148] *Parl* Seq 7. *Eccl* Read. RDn (until 1865), Bradf. RDn (1865–1915), Read. RDn (1915–*). Eccl bdry: 1882 (cr Tilehurst St George EP),[188] 1957.[96]

TILEHURST ST GEORGE
EP Cr 1882 from Tilehurst AP.[188] Bradf. RDn (1882–1915), Read. RDn (1915–*). Bdry: 1957.[96]

TUBNEY
AP *LG* Ock Hd, Abing. PLU, RSD, RD. Civ bdry: 1883,[10] 1934.[3] Abol civ 1952 to help cr Fyfield and Tubney CP.[103] *Parl* N'rn Dv (1885–1918), Abing. Dv/CC (1918–70). *Eccl* Abing. RDn. Abol eccl 1952 to help cr Fyfield with Tubney EP.[104]

TWYFORD
EP Area in Hurst EP, sep EP 1848,[123] sep CP 1894 (from Broad Hinton CP).[119] *LG* Wok. PLU, RD. *Parl* Wind. Dv (1918–48), Wok. CC (1948–*). *Eccl* Read. RDn (1848–74), Sonn. RDn (1874–*). Bdry: 1967.[189] Abol eccl 1973 to help cr Ruscombe and Twyford EP.[82]

UFFINGTON
AP Incl chap Baulking, chap Woolstone (each sep CP 1866,[14] combined 1848 into one EP 'Baulking with Woolstone[29]). *LG* Seq 18. Transf 1974 to Oxon.[5] *Parl* Seq 4. *Eccl* Abing. RDn (until 1865), Vale WH RDn (1865–68). Abol eccl 1868 when united with Woolstone EP to cr Uffington with Woolstone EP.[190]

UFFINGTON WITH WOOLSTONE
EP Cr 1868 by union Uffington AP, Woolstone EP.[190] Vale WH RDn.

UFTON NERVET
Orig two churches, Ufton Robert (St Peter), Ufton Richard (St John the Baptist), united 1434–35 with the former to be the parish church, the latter pulled down 1886.[191] *LG* Seq 19. *Parl* Seq 7. *Eccl* Seq 7.

UPTON
Chap in Blewbury AP, sep CP 1866,[14] eccl combined 1862 with chap Aston Upthorpe in same par to cr 'Upton with Aston Upthorpe' EP,[24] qv. *LG* Moreton Hd, Want. PLU, RSD, RD. Transf 1974 to Oxon.[5] *Parl* Seq 4.

UPTON WITH ASTON UPTHORPE
EP Cr 1862 by union chap Upton, chap Aston Upthorpe, both in Blewbury AP.[24] Abing. RDn (1862–65), Wall. RDn (1865–*).

WALLINGFORD
The following have 'Wallingford' in their name. Insofar as any existed at a given time: *LG* Moreton Hd, Wall. PLU, Bor/MB, USD. *Parl* Wall. Parl Bor (1295–1885), N'rn Dv (1885–1918), Abing. Dv/CC (1948–*). *Eccl* Wall. RDn.

CP1–WALLINGFORD–Cr 1919 by union AP1, AP4, AP7, AP10.[192] Civ bdry: 1934.[3] Transf 1974 to Oxon.[5]

AP1–WALLINGFORD ALL HALLOWS–*LG* Pt Wall. Bor/MB, pt Wall. USD, pt Wall. RSD. Civ bdry: 1894 (the pt not in the MB to help cr Clapcot CP, and gains the pt of CP2 not in the MB).[69] Abol civ 1919 to help cr CP1.[192] *Parl* Pt Wall. Parl Bor (1295–1885), N'rn Dv (1885–1918), Abing. Dv (1918–48). *Eccl* Abol eccl 1648 after destruction in Civil War to help cr EP1.[193]

CP2–WALLINGFORD CASTLE PRECINCTS–Ex-par place, sep CP 1858.[25] *LG* Pt Wall. Bor/MB, pt Wall. USD, pt Wall. RSD. Abol 1894 the pt in the MB to AP1, the remainder to help cr Clapcot CP.[69] *Parl* Pt Wall. Parl Bor (1866–85), N'rn Dv (1885–1918).

AP2–WALLINGFORD HOLY TRINITY–Pt conventual church, pt parochial, dissolved 16th cent and merged into AP7.[194]

AP3–WALLINGFORD ST JOHN UNDER THE WATER–united 1419 with AP7.[195]

AP4–WALLINGFORD ST LEONARD–Gains AP5, AP11 in 14th cent[196]; incl chap Sotwell after 14th cent (prev in AP5; sep civ identity early, eccl severed 1868 to help cr Brightwell with Sotwell EP[51]). Abol civ 1919 to help cr CP1.[192] Abol eccl 1971 to help cr EP2.[197]

AP5–WALLINGFORD ST LUCIAN–Incl chap Sotwell; the par and the chap merged into AP4 in 14th cent.[196]

AP6–WALLINGFORD ST MARTIN–In disuse by end of 14th cent, merged into AP7.[195]

AP7–WALLINGFORD ST MARY LE MORE–Gains AP6 in 14th cent,[195] AP3 in 1419,[195] AP2 in 16th cent.[194] Abol civ 1919 to help cr CP1.[192] Abol eccl 1648 to help cr EP1.[193]

EP1–WALLINGFORD ST MARY LE MORE WITH ALL HALLOWS–Cr 1648 by union AP1, AP7.[193] Abol 1971 to help cr EP2.[197]

EP2–WALLINGFORD ST MARY LE MORE WITH ALL HALLOWS WITH ST LEONARD AND ST PETER–Cr 1971 by union EP1, AP4, AP10.[197]

AP8–WALLINGFORD ST MARY THE LESS–Absorbed 1374 into AP10.[198]

AP9–WALLINGFORD ST MICHAEL–Absorbed 1374 into AP10.[198]

AP10–WALLINGFORD ST PETER–Gains 1374 AP8, AP9.[198] Abol civ 1919 to help cr CP1.[192] Abol eccl 1971 to help cr EP2.[197]

AP11–WALLINGFORD ST RUMBOLD–Absorbed into AP4 in 14th cent.[196]

WHITE WALTHAM

AP *LG* Seq 1. Civ bdry: 1877.[199] *Parl* Seq 2. *Eccl* Read. RDn. Abol eccl 1744 to help cr White Waltham with Shottesbrooke EP.[170]

WHITE WALTHAM WITH SHOTTESBROOKE

EP Cr 1744 by union White Waltham AP, Shottesbrooke AP.[170] Read. RDn (1744–1865), Maid. RDn (1865–*). Bdry: 1894 (cr Littlewick EP).[137]

WALTHAM ST LAWRENCE

AP *LG* Warg. Hd, Cook. PLU (1835–99), RSD, Maid. PLU (1899–1930), Cook. RD. *Parl* Seq 2. *Eccl* Seq 8.

WANTAGE

AP Incl hmlt Charlton, hmlt West Locking (each sep CP 1866,[14] neither with sep eccl identity), chap Grove (sep EP 1835,[126] sep CP 1866[14]). *LG* Want. Hd, PLU, USD, UD. Civ bdry: 1887,[57] 1934.*3* Transf 1974 to Oxon.[5] *Parl* Seq 4. *Eccl* Pec jurisd Dean & Canons of Windsor (until 1846), Seq 4 thereafter.

WARFIELD

AP Incl pt chap Bracknell (sep EP 1851,[39] sep CP 1955,[34] in each case also pt cr from Winkfield AP). *LG* Warg. Hd, Easth. PLU, RSD, RD. *Parl* Seq 3. *Eccl* Read. RDn (until 1865), Maid. RDn (1865–1921), Sonn. RDn (1921–*). Addtl eccl bdry alt: 1953.[40]

WARGRAVE

AP *LG* Warg. Hd, perhaps Warg. Bor (status not sustained),[200] Wok. PLU, RSD, RD. *Parl* Seq 3. *Eccl* Seq 11. Eccl bdry: 1842 (help cr Knowl Hill EP).[122]

WASING

AP *LG* Seq 5. *Parl* Seq 7. *Eccl* Seq 5. Eccl bdry: 1958.[53]

WATCHFIELD

Chap in Shrivenham AP, sep CP 1866.[14] *LG* Seq 18. Transf 1974 to Oxon.[5] *Parl* Seq 4.

WELFORD

AP *LG* Seq 5. *Parl* Seq 7. *Eccl* Seq 6.

WEXHAM COURT

CP Cr 1974 from the pt of Wexham AP, Bucks, to be in Berks.[5]

WHATCOMBE

AP Sep identity lost early, now Tp in Fawley AP.[201]

WHISTLEY

Lbty in Hurst CP, sep CP 1866.[14] *LG* Charl. Hd, Wok. PLU, RSD. Civ bdry: 1883,[10] 1894 (help cr Twyford CP).[119] Abol 1894 to help cr Hurst St Nicholas CP.[120] *Parl* E'rn Dv (1885–1918).

WHITCHURCH

AP *LG* Pt Oxon (Langtree Hd), pt Berks (Read. Hd), Bradf. PLU, RSD. Civ bdry: 1883.[10] The pt in Berks transf 1894 to Purley AP[145] and the par ent Oxon thereafter, qv for main entry.

WHITLEY

EP Cr 1863 from Reading St Giles AP.[155] Sometimes called 'Reading Christ Church'. Read. RDn. Bdry: 1912 (help cr Reading St Luke EP),[157] 1957,[96] 1973 (help cr Reading St Barnabas EP),[161] 1973.[152]

NEW WINDSOR

AP *LG* Pt Rippl. Hd, Wind. PLU, New Wind. Bor MB (pt until 1880s, ent 1880s–1974), New Wind. USD. Civ bdry: 1878.[70] *Parl* New Wind. Parl Bor (pt 1302–1868, ent 1868–1918), Wind. Dv/CC (1918–70), Wind. & Maid. CC (1970–*). *Eccl* Seq 8.

NEW WINDSOR HOLY TRINITY

EP Cr 1843 from the pt of Clewer AP in New Wind. MB.[72] Read. RDn (1843–65), Maid. RDn (1865–*).

OLD WINDSOR

AP Incl Sunningdale (sep EP 1841,[179] sep CP 1894[180]). *LG* Rippl. Hd, perhaps Old Wind. Bor,[202] Wind. PLU, RSD, RD. Addtl civ bdry alt: 1878.[182] *Parl* Seq 2. *Eccl* Seq 8. Addtl eccl bdry alt: 1851 (help cr Cranbourne EP).[84]

WINDSOR CASTLE

Ex-par place divided into Upper and Lower wards, latter incl 1886 in New Wind. PLU, MB for rating purposes.[203] *Parl* Pt in MB, Wind. Dv/CC (1918–70), Wind. & Maid. CC (1970–*).

WINKFIELD

AP Incl pt Bracknell (sep EP 1851,[39] sep CP 1955,[34] in each case also pt cr from Warfield AP). *LG* Seq 17. Addtl civ bdry alt: 1965.[41] *Parl* Seq 3. *Eccl* Seq 8. Addtl eccl bdry alt: 1851 (help cr Cranbourne EP),[84] 1871 (help cr Bray Wood EP),[46] 1953,[40] 1960.[48]

WINNERSH
Lbty in Hurst CP, sep CP 1866.[14] *LG* Sonn. Hd, Wok. PLU, RSD, RD. Bdry: 1952.[124] *Parl* Seq 1.

WINTERBOURNE
Chap in Chieveley AP, sep CP 1866.[14] *LG* Seq 5. *Parl* Seq 7.

LITTLE WITTENHAM
AP Sometimes 'Abbots Wittenham' or 'East Wittenham'. *LG* Seq 15. Early bdry with Long Wittenham differs from present.[204] Transf 1974 to Oxon.[5] *Parl* Seq 4. *Eccl* Seq 1.

LONG WITTENHAM
AP Sometimes 'Earls Wittenham' or 'West Wittenham'. *LG* Seq 15. Early bdry with Little Wittenham differs from present.[204] Transf 1974 to Oxon.[5] *Parl* Seq 4. *Eccl* Seq 1.

WOKEFIELD
Tg in Stratfield Mortimer AP, sep CP 1866.[14] *LG* Seq 19. Bdry: 1934 (help cr Sulhamstead Bannister CP).[3] *Parl* Seq 7.

WOKINGHAM
Chap in Sonning AP, sep civ identity early, sep EP 1812.[94] Pt Berks (Sonn. Hd), pt Wilts (Amesbury Hd), the latter transf to Berks 1832 for parl purposes, 1844 for civ purposes.[27] *LG* Wok. PLU, pt Wok. Bor/MB, pt Wok. USD, pt Wok. RSD. Addtl civ bdry alt: 1883.[10] Abol civ 1894 the pt in the MB to cr Wokingham Within CP, the remainder to cr Wokingham Without CP.[205] *Parl* E'rn Dv (1885–1918). *Eccl* Pec jurisd Dean of Sarum (1812–46), Read. RDn (1846–65), Maid. RDn (1865–74), Sonn. RDn (1874–*). Addtl eccl bdry alt: 1863 (cr Wokingham St Paul EP),[206] 1864 (help cr Bear Wood EP),[28] 1871 (help cr Wokingham St Sebastian EP).[207]

WOKINGHAM ST PAUL
EP Cr 1863 from Wokingham EP.[206] Read. RDn (1863–65), Maid. RDn (1865–74), Sonn. RDn (1874–*). Bdry: 1871 (help cr Wokingham St Sebastian EP).[207]

WOKINGHAM ST SEBASTIAN
EP Cr 1871 from Wokingham EP, Wokingham St Paul EP.[207] Maid. RDn (1871–74), Sonn. RDn (1874–*).

WOKINGHAM WITHIN
CP Cr 1894 from the pt of Wokingham CP in Wok. MB.[205] *LG* Wok. PLU, MB. Bdry: 1927.[208] *Parl* Newb. Dv (1918–48), Wok. CC (1948–*).

WOKINGHAM WITHOUT
CP Cr 1894 from the pt of Wokingham CP not in Wok. MB.[205] *LG* Wok. PLU, RD. *Parl* Newb. Dv (1918–48), Wok. CC (1948–*).

WEST WOODHAY
AP *LG* Seq 9. *Parl* Seq 7. *Eccl* Seq 6.

WOODLEY
Lbty in Sonning AP, sep CP 1866 as 'Woodley and Sandford',[14] sep EP 1881 as 'Woodley'.[172] *LG* Sonn. Hd, Wok. PLU, RSD, RD. Civ bdry: 1970 (incl cr Charvil EP).[61] *Parl* Seq 1. *Eccl* Sonn. RDn (1881–1959), Read. RDn (1959–*). Eccl bdry: 1959.[97]

WOODLEY AND SANDFORD–see prev entry

WOOLHAMPTON
AP *LG* Theale Hd, Newb. PLU, RSD, RD. Civ bdry: 1934.[3] *Parl* Seq 7. *Eccl* Seq 7.

WOOLSTONE
Chap in Uffington AP, sep CP 1866,[14] combined eccl 1848 with chap Baulking in same par to cr Baulking with Woolstone EP,[29] qv; latter dissolved 1868, Baulking becomming sep EP, Woolstone reunited with Uffington to cr Uffington with Woolstone EP.[190] *LG* Seq 18. Civ bdry: 1888.[30] Transf 1974 to Oxon.[5] *Parl* Seq 4.

WOOTTON
Chap in Cumnor AP, sep civ identity early, sep EP 1723.[94] *LG* Seq 8. Civ bdry: 1885.[11] Transf 1974 to Oxon.[5] *Parl* Seq 4. *Eccl* Oxford RDn (Oxford AD, 1723–1915), Abing. RDn (1915–*).

WRAYSBURY
AP In Bucks, usually 'Wyrardisbury' before 1974, transf 1974 to Berks.[5]

WYTHAM
AP *LG* Seq 8. Civ bdry: 1900.[164] Transf 1974 to Oxon.[5] *Parl* Seq 4. *Eccl* Abing. RDn (until 1915), Oxford RDn (Oxford AD, 1915–*).

YATTENDON
AP *LG* Seq 4. *Parl* Seq 6. *Eccl* Newb. RDn (until 1866), Wall. RDn (1866–75), Bradf. RDn (1875–*).

BUCKINGHAMSHIRE

ABBREVIATIONS

Abbreviations particular to Buckinghamshire follow. Those general abbreviations in use throughout the *Guide* are found on page xix.

Amer.	Amersham
Ash.	Ashendon
Aylb.	Aylesbury
Beac.	Beaconsfield
Blet.	Bletsoe
Buck.	Buckingham
Burn.	Burnham
Ches.	Chesham
Clay.	Claydon
Cott.	Cottesloe
Cren.	Crendon
Desb.	Desborough
Hamb.	Hambledon
Iving.	Ivinghoe
Milt. Keyn.	Milton Keynes
Murs.	Mursley
Newp.	Newport
Pagn.	Pagnall
Stratf.	Stratford
Wend.	Wendover
Wins.	Winslow
Wolv.	Wolverton
Wyc.	Wycombe

SEQUENCES

An abbreviated entry prefixed by 'Seq' is used in the parochial entries to avoid repeating often the names of superior units of administration. The content of each sequence is show below.

Local Government Sequences ('LG')

SEQ 1 Ash. Hd, Aylb. PLU, RSD, RD
SEQ 2 Ash. Hd, Thame PLU, RSD, Long Cren. RD (1894–1934), Aylb. RD (1934–74)
SEQ 3 Ash. Hd, Wins. PLU, RSD, RD
SEQ 4 Aylb. Hd, PLU, RSD, RD
SEQ 5 Aylb. Hd, Wyc. PLU, RSD, Aylb. RD
SEQ 6 Buck. Hd, Brackley PLU, RSD, Buck. RD
SEQ 7 Buck. Hd, PLU, RSD, RD
SEQ 8 Burn. Hd, Amer. PLU, RSD, RD
SEQ 9 Burn. Hd, Eton PLU, RSD, RD
SEQ 10 Cott. Hd, Aylb. PLU, RSD, RD
SEQ 11 Cot. Hd, Aylb. PLU, RSD, RD (1894–1934), Wing RD (1934–74)
SEQ 12 Cott. Hd, Leighton Buzzard PLU, RSD, Wing RD
SEQ 13 Cott. Hd, Wins. PLU, RSD, RD
SEQ 14 Desb. Hd, Wyc. PLU (1835–45), Henley PLU (1845–1930), RSD, Hamb. RD (1894–1934), Wyc. RD (1934–74)
SEQ 15 Desb. Hd, Wyc. PLU, RSD, RD
SEQ 16 Newp. Hd, Newp. Pagn. PLU, RSD, RD
SEQ 17 Stoke Hd, Eton PLU, RSD, RD

Parliamentary Sequences ('Parl')

SEQ 1 Mid Dv (1885–1918), Aylb. Dv/CC (1918–*)
SEQ 2 Mid Dv (1885–1918), Aylb. Dv/CC (1918–70), Ches. & Amer. CC (1970–*)
SEQ 3 Mid Dv (1885–1918), Aylb. Dv/CC (1918–48), S Bucks CC (1948–70), Ches. & Amer. CC (1970–*)
SEQ 4 Mid Dv (1885–1918), Aylb. Dv (1918–45), Wyc. Dv/CC (1945–70), Aylb. CC (1970–*)
SEQ 5 Mid Dv (1885–1918), Buck. Dv/CC (1918–*)
SEQ 6 N'rn Dv (1885–1918), Buck. Dv/CC (1918–*)
SEQ 7 N'rn Dv (1885–1918), Buck. Dv (1918–48), Aylb. CC (1948–*)
SEQ 8 S'rn Dv (1885–1918), Aylb. Dv (1918–

48), S Bucks CC (1948–70), Ches. & Amer. CC (1970–*)

SEQ 9 S'rn Dv (1885–1918), Wyc. Dv (1918–45), Eton & Slough Dv (1945–48), S Bucks CC (1948–70), Beac. CC (1970–*)

SEQ 10 S'rn Dv (1885–1918), Wyc. Dv/CC (1918–*)

SEQ 11 S'rn Dv (1885–1918), Wyc. Dv/CC (1918–70), Beac. CC (1970–*)

Ecclesiastical Sequences ('Eccl')

SEQ 1 Buck. RDn (until 1865), Buck. RDn First Dv (1865–74), Buck. RDn (1874–*)

SEQ 2 Buck. RDn (until 1855), Stony Stratf. RDn (1855–65), Buck. RDn Second Dv (1865–74), Buck. RDn (1874–*)

SEQ 3 Buck. RDn (until 1855), Clay. RDn (1855–*)

SEQ 4 Buck. RDn (until 1855), Stony Stratf. RDn (1855–65), Buck. RDn Second Dv (1865–74), Buck. RDn (1874–1915), Wolv. RDn (1915–70), Buck. RDn (1970–*)

SEQ 5 Burn. RDn

SEQ 6 Burn. RDn (until 1855), Amer. RDn (1855–*)

SEQ 7 Murs. RDn (until 1855), S Murs. RDn (1855–74), Iving. RDn (1874–1964), Murs. RDn (1964–*)

SEQ 8 Murs. RDn (until 1855), N Murs. RDn (1855–74), Murs. RDn (1874–*)

SEQ 9 Murs. RDn (until 1855), N Murs. RDn (1855–74), Murs. RDn (1874–1964), Clay. RDn (1964–*)

SEQ 10 Murs. RDn (until 1855), Wend. RDn First Dv (1855–74), Wend. RDn (1874–*)

SEQ 11 Newp. RDn (until 1855), Newp. RDn First Dv (1855–74), Newp. RDn (1874–*)

SEQ 12 Newp. RDn (until 1855), Newp. RDn Second Dv (1855–74), Blet. RDn (1874–1970), Milt. Keyn. RDn (1970–*)

SEQ 13 Newp. RDn (until 1855), Newp. RDn Second Dv (1855–74), Blet. RDn (1874–1970), Murs. RDn (1970–*)

SEQ 14 Newp. RDn (until 1855), Stony Stratf. RDn (1855–65), Buck. RDn Second Dv (1865–74), Buck. RDn (1874–1915), Wolv. RDn (1915–70), Milt. Keyn. RDn (1970–*)

SEQ 15 Pec jurisd St Albans (until 1846), Buck. RDn (1846–55), Clay. RDn (1855–*)

SEQ 16 Wadd. RDn

SEQ 17 Wadd. RDn (until 1855), Clay. RDn (1855–*)

SEQ 18 Wadd. RDn (until 1855), Clay. RDn (1855–74), Wadd. RDn (1874–*)

SEQ 19 Wend. RDn (until 1855), Wend. RDn First Dv (1855–74), Wend. RDn (1874–*)

SEQ 20 Wend. RDn (until 1855), Wend. RDn Second Dv (1855–74), Aylb. RDn (1874–*)

SEQ 21 Wyc. RDn (until 1865), Aylb. RDn (1865–74), Wyc. RDn (1874–*)

SEQ 22 Wyc. RDn (until 1865), Burn. RDn (1865–74), Wyc. RDn (1874–*)

SEQ 23 Wyc. RDn (until 1865), Marlow RDn (1865–74), Wyc. RDn (1874–*)

DIOCESES AND ARCHDEACONRY

With a few exceptions noted below in the parochial entries,
Bucks pars were in Lincoln dioc until 1837 and in Oxford dioc thereafter.
The RDns were always in Buckingham AD.

THE PARISHES OF BUCKINGHAMSHIRE

ADDINGTON
AP *LG* Seq 7. *Parl* Seq 1. *Eccl* Seq 3.

ADSTOCK
AP *LG* Seq 7. *Parl* Seq 6. *Eccl* Buck. RDn (until 1855), Clay. RDn (1855–70), Buck. RDn (1970–*).

AKELEY
AP *LG* Seq 7. *Parl* Seq 6. *Eccl* Seq 2.

AMERSHAM
AP Incl hmlt Coleshill (pt Bucks [Burn. Hd], pt Herts [Dacorum Hd], the latter transf to Bucks 1832 for parl purposes, 1844 for civ purposes,[1] sep CP 1866[2]). Usual civ spelling; for eccl see 'Amersham with Coleshill'. *LG* Burn. Hd (pt until 1844, ent from 1844), Amer. Bor, PLU, RSD, RD. Addtl civ bdry alt: 1934,[3] 1956.[4] *Parl* Amer. Parl Bor (1300–09, 1624–1832), N'rn Dv (1918–48), S Bucks CC (1948–70), Ches. & Amer. CC (1970–*)

AMERSHAM ON THE HILL
EP Cr 1973 from Amersham with Coleshill AP.[5] Amer. RDn.

AMERSHAM WITH COLESHILL
AP Usual eccl spelling; for civ see 'Amersham'. *Eccl* Seq 6. Eccl bdry: 1952,[6] 1966 (help cr Chenies and Little Chalfont EP),[7] 1973 (cr Amersham on the Hill EP).[5]

ASHENDON
AP *LG* Seq 1. *Parl* Seq 7. *Eccl* Wadd. RDn. Abol eccl 1921 to help cr Wotton Underwood with Ashendon EP.[8]

ASHLEY GREEN

Pt of Chesham AP, sep EP 1875,[9] sep CP 1897.[10] *LG* Amer. PLU, RD. Civ bdry: 1900,[11] 1907 (exchanges pts with Bovingdon CP, Northchurch AP, both Herts),[12] 1934.[3] *Parl* Aylb. Dv/CC (1918–70), Ches. & Amer. CC (1970–*). *Eccl* Amer. RDn.

ASTON ABBOTS

AP *LG* Seq 11. *Parl* Seq 1. *Eccl* Pec jurisd St Albans (dioc London, until 1846), Seq 8 thereafter.

ASTON CLINTON

AP *LG* Seq 4. Civ bdry: 1934 (help cr Cholesbury cum St Leonards CP).[3] *Parl* Aylb. Parl Bor (1804–85), Seq 1 thereafter. *Eccl* Seq 19. Eccl bdry: 1860 (cr Aston Clinton St Leonard EP).[13]

ASTON CLINTON ST LEONARD

Chap in Aston Clinton AP, ruins by 17th cent, rebuilt and EP 1860.[13] Wend. RDn First Dv (1860–74), Wend. RDn (1874–*).

ASTON SANDFORD

AP *LG* Seq 1. *Parl* Seq 1. *Eccl* Wadd. RDn (until 1855), Wend. RDn Second Dv (1855–65), Aylb. RDn (1865–*).

ASTWOOD

AP *LG* Seq 16. Civ bdry: 1886,[14] 1957.[15] *Parl* Seq 6. *Eccl* Seq 11.

AYLESBURY

AP Incl chap Bierton, chap Broughton (sep par 1294[16] as 'Bierton with Broughton',[17] qv for later eccl spearation), chap Stoke Mandeville, chap Buckland (each with sep civ identity early from Bierton with Broughton, sep EP 1858 as 'Stoke Mandeville with Buckland',[18] qv for later eccl separation), chap Walton (sep EP 1846[19]). *LG* Aylb. Hd, Aylb. Bor (pt until 1835, ent thereafter), PLU, USD, UD (1894–1917), MB (1917–74). Addtl civ bdry alt: 1883,[20] 1886,[21] 1896,[22] 1958.[23] *Parl* Aylb. Parl Bor (pt 1554–1804, ent 1804–85), Seq 1 thereafter. *Eccl* Pec jurisd as Lincoln prebend (until 1846), Seq 20 thereafter. Addtl eccl bdry alt: 1852 (help cr Prestwood EP from Stoke Mandeville chap),[24] 1955.[25]

BARTON HARTSHORN

AP *LG* Seq 7. *Parl* Seq 6. *Eccl* Buck. RDn. Abol eccl 16th cent to help cr Chetwode with Barton Hartshorn EP.[26]

BEACHAMPTON

AP *LG* Seq 7. *Parl* Seq 6. *Eccl* Seq 4.

BEACONSFIELD

AP *LG* Burn. Hd, Amer. PLU, Beac. USD, UD. Civ bdry: 1934.[3] *Parl* Seq 8. *Eccl* Burn. RDn (until 1865), Aylb. RDn (1865–74), Burn. RDn (1874–1973), Buck. RDn (1973–*).

BECKLEY

AP Pt Oxon (Bullingdon Hd), pt Bucks (hmlt of Studeley, Ash. Hd), the latter transf to Oxon 1832 for parl purposes. 1844 for civ purposes.[1] See main entry in Oxon.

BIDDLESDEN

AP *LG* Seq 6.[27] Civ bdry: 1884 (incl loses pt to Syresham AP, Northants).[28] *Parl* Seq 6. *Eccl* Seq 3.

BIERTON WITH BROUGHTON

AP The chaps of Bierton, Broughton in Aylesbury AP made sep par 1294 as 'Bierton with Broughton'.[16] Incl chaps Stoke Mandeville, Buckland (each with sep civ identity early, sep EP 1858 as 'Stoke Mandeville with Buckland',[18] the latter divided 1887 into sep EPs of Stoke Mandeville, Buckland[29]), chap Quarrendon (sep civ identity early, no sep eccl identity). *LG* Seq 4. Addtl civ bdry alt: 1883,[20] 1885,[30] 1886,[21] 1896.[22] *Parl* Aylb. Parl Bor (1804–85), Seq 1 thereafter. *Eccl* Often as 'Bierton with Quarrendon', pec jurisd Dean & Chapter of Lincoln (until 1846), Wend. RDn (1846–55), Wend. RDn Second Dv (1855–65), Wend. RDn First Dv (1865–74), Wend. RDn (1874–1915), Aylb. RDn (1915–*). Addtl eccl bdry alt: 1850 (help cr Prestwood EP from Stoke Mandeville chap).[24]

BLEDLOW

AP *LG* Aylb. Hd, Wyc. PLU, RSD, RD. Abol civ 1934 pt to help cr Bledlow cum Saunderton CP, pt to Princes Risborough CP.[3] *Parl* Aylb. Parl Bor (1804–85), Mid Dv (1885–1918), Aylb. Dv (1918–45). *Eccl* Wend. RDn (until 1855), Wyc. RDn (1855–65), Aylb. RDn (1865–1973). Eccl bdry: 1968 (cr Bledlow Ridge EP).[31] Abol eccl 1973 to help cr Bledlow with Saunderton and Horsenden EP.[32]

BLEDLOW CUM SAUNDERTON

CP Cr 1934 by union Horsendon AP, Saunderton AP, Bledlow AP.[3] *LG* Wyc. RD. *Parl* Wyc. CC (1948–70), Aylb. CC (1970–*).

BLEDLOW RIDGE

EP Cr 1868 from Bledlow AP.[31] Aylb. RDn (1868–74), Wyc. RDn (1874–*).

BLEDLOW WITH SAUNDERTON AND HORSENDEN

EP Cr 1973 by union Bledlow AP, Saunderton AP, Horsenden AP.[32] Aylb. RDn.

BLETCHLEY

AP Incl pt chap and twnshp Fenny Stratford (sep EP 1730,[33] sep CP 1866[2]), twnshp Water Eaton (sep CP 1866,[2] sep EP 1974[34]). *LG* Newp. Hd, incl pt Fenny Stratf. Bor, Newp. Pagn. PLU, RSD, RD (1894–98), Fenny Stratf. UD (1898–1911), Blet. UD (1911–74). Addtl civ bdry alt: 1934,[3] 1953.[35] *Parl* Seq 6. *Eccl* Seq 12. Addtl eccl bdry alt: 1951,[36] 1973.[37]

BOARSTALL

Chap in Oakley AP, sep civ identity early, eccl united 1740 with Brill chap in same par to cr 'Brill with Boarstall' EP.[38] *LG* Ash. Hd, Bicester PLU, RSD, Long Cren. RD (1894–1934), Aylb. RD (1934–74). *Parl* Seq 7.

BOURNE END

EP Cr 1974 from Wooburn AP.[39] Wyc. RDn.

BOVENEY

Chap or lbty in Burnham AP, sep CP 1866,[2] eccl severed 1911 to help cr Eton with Boveney EP.[40] *LG* Burn. Hd, Eton PLU, RSD, RD. Abol civ 1934 pt to Eton AP, pt to Dorney AP.[3] *Parl* S'rn Dv (1885–1918), Wyc. Dv (1918–45).

BRADENHAM
AP *LG* Seq 15. Civ bdry: 1885.[41] *Parl* Seq 4. *Eccl* Seq 23.

BRADWELL
AP *LG* Seq 16. Civ bdry: 1919 (the pt of the par constituted Stratf. & Wolv. UD cr 'New Bradwell' CP),[42] 1923.[43] *Parl* Seq 6. *Eccl* Newp. RDn (until 1855), Stony Stratf. RDn (1855–65), Buck. RDn Second Dv (1865–74), Buck. RDn (1874–1915), Wolv. RDn (1915–70), Milt. Keyn. RDn (1970–74). Eccl bdry: 1857 (help cr New Bradwell with Stantonbury EP),[44] 1961.[45] Abol eccl 1974 to help cr Stantonbury EP.[34]

BRADWELL ABBEY
Ex-par place, sep CP 1858.[46] *LG* Seq 16.[47] *Parl* Seq 6.

NEW BRADWELL
CP Cr 1919 from the pt of Bradwell AP cr Stratf. & Wolv. UD.[42] *LG* Newp. Pagn. PLU, Stratf. & Wolv. UD (1919–20), Wolv. UD (1920–34). Bdry: 1923.[48] Abol 1934 ent to Wolverton AP.[3]

NEW BRADWELL AND STANTONBURY
EP Cr 1857 from Stantonbury AP, pt Bradwell AP.[44] Stony Stratf. RDn (1857–65), Buck. RDn (1874–1915), Wolv. RDn (1915–70), Milt. Keyn. RDn (1970–74). Bdry: 1961.[45] Abol 1974 to help cr Stantonbury EP.[34]

COLD BRAYFIELD
Vicarage ordained 13th cent, civ identity maintained, sep eccl identity not maintained and considered later as chap in Lavendon AP.[49] *LG* Seq 16. *Parl* Seq 6.

BOW BRICKHILL
AP *LG* Seq 16. *Parl* Seq 6. *Eccl* Seq 13. Eccl bdry: 1974 (help cr Woughton EP).[34]

GREAT BRICKHILL
AP *LG* Newp. Hd, Newp. Pagn. PLU, RSD, RD (1894–1934), Wing RD (1934–74). Civ bdry: 1934.[3] *Parl* Seq 6. *Eccl* Seq 13. Eccl bdry: 1955.[50]

LITTLE BRICKHILL
AP *LG* Seq 16. *Parl* Seq 6. *Eccl* Pec jurisd Archbp Canterb (until 1846), Seq 13 thereafter.

BRILL
Chap in Oakley AP, sep civ identity early, eccl united 1740 with Boarstall chap in same par as 'Brill with Boarstall'.[38] *LG* Brill Bor (until 14th cent), Seq 2. Civ bdry: 1886,[51] 1934.[3] *Parl* Seq 7.

BRILL WITH BOARSTALL
Union 16th cent for eccl purposes as two curacies of Brill, Boarstall chaps of Oakley AP, sep EP 1740,[38] civ identities maintained separately. Wadd. RD.

BROUGHTON
AP *LG* Seq 16 (for the Broughton in Aylb. Hd, see 'Bierton with Broughton'). Civ bdry: 1956.[52] *Parl* Seq 6. *Eccl* Seq 12.

BUCKINGHAM
AP Incl Gawcot (sep EP 1818[53]). *LG* Buck. Hd, Bor/MB, PLU, USD. Civ bdry: 1934,[3] 1956.[54] *Parl* Buck. Parl Bor (1529–1885), Seq 6 thereafter. *Eccl* Pec jurisd as Lincoln prebend (until 1846), Seq 1 thereafter.

BUCKLAND
Chap in Aylesbury AP, then in Bierton with Broughton when latter made sep par 1294,[16] sep civ identity early, sep EP 1858 when combined with Stoke Mandeville chap in same par as 'Stoke Mandeville and Buckland',[18] the latter divided 1887 into two EPs of Stoke Mandeville, Buckland.[29] *LG* Seq 4. *Parl* Aylb. Parl Bor (1804–85), Seq 1 thereafter. *Eccl* Wend. RDn (1887–*).

BURNHAM
AP Incl chap Boveney (sep CP 1866,[2] eccl severed 1911 to help cr Eton with Boveney EP[40]). *LG* Seq 9. Addtl civ bdry alt: 1883,[20] 1930,[56] 1934,[3] 1974 (the pt transf to Berks cr Britwell CP).[55] *Parl* Seq 9. Parl bdry: 1945.[196] *Eccl* Seq 5. Addtl eccl bdry alt: 1867 (help cr Dropmore EP),[57] 1959.[58]

CADMORE END
EP Cr 1852 from Fingest AP, Lewknor AP (Bucks, Oxon), Stokenchurch AP (Oxon, in Bucks from 1895).[59] Aston RDn (Oxford AD, 1852–65), Marlow RDn (1865–74), Wyc. RDn (but in Oxford AD, 1874–1915), Aston RDn (Oxford AD, 1915–73), Wyc. RDn (1973–*).

CALVERTON
AP *LG* Newp. Hd, Potterspury PLU,[60] RSD, Stratf. & Wolv. RD (1894–1919), UD (1919–20), Wolv. UD (1920–27). Civ bdry: 1883.[20] Abol civ 1927 ent to Wolverton AP.[61] *Parl* N'rn Dv (1885–1918), Buck. Dv (1918–48). *Eccl* Newp. RDn (until 1855), Stony Stratf. RDn (1855–65), Buck. RDn Second Dv (1865–74), Buck. RDn (1874–1915), Wolv. RDn (1915–70), Buck. RDn (1970–*). Eccl bdry: 1870 (help cr Wolverton St Mary EP),[62] 1954,[63] 1968.[64]

CASTLETHORPE
Chap in Hanslope AP, sep civ identity early, no sep eccl identity. *LG* Seq 16. Civ bdry: 1965.[65] *Parl* Seq 6.

CAVERSFIELD
AP *LG* Buck. Hd, transf to Oxon 1832 for parl purposes, 1844 for civ purposes.[1] See main entry in Oxon. *Parl* Bucks until 1832, Oxon thereafter. *Eccl* Buck. RDn (until 1855), Bicester RDn (1855–1956), Bicester & Islip RDn (1965–*)(latter two RDns in Oxford AD).

CHALFONT ST GILES
AP *LG* Seq 8. Civ bdry: 1934.[3] *Parl* Seq 8. *Eccl* Seq 6. Eccl bdry: 1952,[6] 1966.[7]

CHALFONT ST PETER
AP *LG* Seq 8. Civ bdry: 1895 (help cr Gerrard's Cross CP),[23] 1907 (exchanges pts with Rickmansworth Rural CP, loses pt to Chorleywood CP, both Herts),[12] 1934.[3] *Parl* Seq 8. *Eccl* Seq 6. Eccl bdry: 1963 (help cr Chorleywood St Andrew EP, to be in St Alb dioc).[66]

CHARNDON
Hmlt in Twyford AP, sep CP 1866.[2] *LG* Seq 7. *Parl* Seq 6.

CHARTRIDGE
CP Cr 1899 from Chesham AP.[67] *LG* Amer. PLU, RD. *Parl* Aylb. Dv/CC (1918–70), Ches. & Amer. CC (1970–*).

CHEARSLEY
Chap in Long Crendon AP, sep par 1458.[68] *LG* Seq 1. *Parl* Seq 7. *Eccl* Seq 16.

CHEDDINGTON
AP *LG* Seq 12. Civ bdry: 1884.[69] *Parl* Seq 5. *Eccl* Seq 7.

CHENIES
AP *LG* Seq 8. Civ bdry: 1907 (loses pt to Chorleywood CP, Herts),[12] 1934.[3] *Parl* Seq 3. *Eccl* Burn. RDn (until 1855), Amer. RDn (1855–1966). Eccl bdry: 1963 (help cr Chorleywood St Andrew EP, to be in St Alb dioc).[66] Reconstituted 1966, gains pt Amersham with Coleshill AP and renamed 'Chenies and Little Chalfont' EP.[7]

CHENIES AND LITTLE CHALFONT
EP Cr 1966 when Chenies AP gains pt Amersham with Coleshill AP.[7] Amer. RDn.

CHESHAM
AP Incl Chesham Bois (some independent rights 14th–15th cent, sep thereafter[70]), chap Latimer (sep EP 1868 [from Chesham AP, Flaunden EP (Herts)],[71] sep CP 1899 [from Chesham AP alone][67]). *LG* Burn. Hd, Amer. PLU, RSD (1875–92), Ches. USD (1892–94), UD. Addtl civ bdry alt: 1899 (cr Chartridge CP),[67] 1900,[11] 1934.[3] *Parl* Seq 3. *Eccl* Seq 6. Addtl eccl bdry alt: 1867 (help cr Chesham Christ Church EP),[72] 1973.[73]

CHESHAM BOIS
Chap in Chesham AP, some independent rights 14th–15th cent, sep thereafter.[70] *LG* Seq 8. Civ bdry: 1934.[3] *Parl* Seq 3. *Eccl* Seq 6.

CHESHAM CHRIST CHURCH
EP Cr 1867 from Chesham AP.[72] Amer. RDn.

CHETWODE
Priory church, parochial since 1480.[74] *LG* Seq 7. Civ bdry: 1956 (incl exchange pts with Godington AP, Oxon).[75] *Parl* Seq 6. *Eccl* Buck. RDn. United 16th cent with Barton Hartshorn AP to cr Chetwode with Barton Hartshorn EP.[26]

CHETWODE WITH BARTON HARTSHORN
EP Cr 16th cent by union Chetwode AP, Barton Hartshorne AP.[26] Buck. RDn (16th cent–1865), Buck. RDn First Dv (1865–74), Buck. RDn (1874–1970), Clay. RDn (1970–*).

CHICHELEY
AP *LG* Seq 16. Civ bdry: 1956.[76] *Parl* Seq 6. *Eccl* Seq 11.

CHILTON
AP Incl chap Dorton (sep civ identity early, sep EP 1788[33]). *LG* Seq 2. *Parl* Seq 7. *Eccl* Often as 'Chilton cum Easington', Seq 16.

CHOLESBURY
AP No presentations from 1416 for long period, sep civ identity maintained, sometimes deemed chap to Drayton Beauchamp AP, sep eccl status regained 1756.[33] *LG* Cott. Hd, Aylb. PLU, RSD, RD. Abol civ 1934 to help cr Cholesbury cum St Leonards CP.[3] *Parl* Mid Dv (1885–1918), Aylb. Dv (1918–48). *Eccl* Seq 10.

CHOLESBURY CUM ST LEONARDS
CP Cr 1934 by union Cholesbury AP, Hawridge AP, and pts of Aston Clinton AP, Buckland AP, Drayton Beauchamp AP.[3] *LG* Amer. RD. *Parl* Aylb. CC (1948–70), Ches. & Amer. CC (1970–*).

CHORLEYWOOD ST ANDREW
EP Cr 1963 from Chorley Wood Christ Church EP (Herts, St Alb dioc), Chalfont St Peter AP, Chenies AP, to be ent St Alb dioc, Watford RDn.[66]

EAST CLAYDON
AP *LG* Seq 3. Civ bdry: 1956.[77] *Parl* Seq 6. *Eccl* Wadd. RDn. Gains eccl in 17th cent Hogshaw AP.[78] Abol eccl 1821 to help cr Middle Claydon with East Claydon EP.[79]

MIDDLE CLAYDON
AP *LG* Ash. Hd, Buck. PLU, RSD, RD. *Parl* Seq 6. *Eccl* Wadd. RDn. Abol eccl 1821 to help cr Middle Claydon with East Claydon EP.[79]

MIDDLE CLAYDON WITH EAST CLAYDON
EP Cr 1821 by union Middle Claydon AP, East Claydon AP.[79] Wadd. RDn (1821–55), Clay. RDn (1855–*).

STEEPLE CLAYDON
AP *LG* Seq 7. Civ bdry: 1956.[75] *Parl* Seq 6. *Eccl* Seq 3. Eccl bdry: 1967.[80]

CLIFTON REYNES
AP *LG* Seq 16. *Parl* Seq 6. *Eccl* Seq 11.

COLESHILL
Hmlt in Amersham AP, pt Bucks (Burn. Hd), pt Herts (Dacorum Hd), the latter transf to Bucks 1832 for parl purposes, 1844 for civ purposes,[1] sep CP 1866,[2] no sep eccl identity. *LG* Amer. PLU, RSD, RD. Bdry: 1956.[4] *Parl* Seq 8.

COLNBROOK
EP Cr 1853 from Langley Marish chap in Wyrardisbury AP, Horton AP, Stanwell AP (Middx, London dioc).[81] Burn. RDn. Bdry: 1873.[82]

NORTH CRAWLEY
AP *LG* Seq 16. Civ bdry: 1886,[14] 1956,[76] 1957.[15] *Parl* Seq 6. *Eccl* Seq 11.

LONG CRENDON
AP Incl chap Chearsley (sep par 1458[68]), chap Lower Winchendon (sep civ identity early, sep EP 1744 as 'Nether Winchendon'[33]). *LG* Seq 2. Addtl civ bdry alt: 1886.[51] *Parl* Seq 7. *Eccl* Seq 16.

CRESLOW
AP *LG* Seq 10. *Parl* Seq 1. *Eccl* Murs. RDn. Rectory suppressed *temp* Elizabeth I, later deemed pt Whitchurch AP.[83]

CUBLINGTON
AP *LG* Seq 11. *Parl* Seq 1. *Eccl* Seq 8.

CUDDINGTON
Chap in Haddenham AP, sep civ identity early, sep EP 1855.[84] *LG* Seq 4. *Parl* Aylb. Parl Bor (1804–85), Seq 1 thereafter. *Eccl* Seq 20.

DATCHET
AP Incl chap Fulmer (sep par 1553[85]). *LG* Seq 17.

Civ bdry: 1934.[3] Transf 1974 to Berks.[194] *Parl* Seq 9. *Eccl* Seq 5.

DENHAM

AP *LG* Seq 17. Civ bdry: 1907 (exchanges pts with Rickmansworth Rural CP, Herts),[12] 1934.[3] *Parl* Seq 9. *Eccl* Seq 6.

DINTON

AP Usual eccl spelling; for civ see following entry. *Eccl* Murs. RDn (until 1855), Wend. RDn First Dv (1855–65), Aylb. RDn (1865–*).

DINTON-WITH-FORD AND UPTON

AP Usual civ spelling; for eccl see prev entry. *LG* Pt Ash. Hd, pt Aylb. Hd, pt Desb. Hd, Aylb. PLU, RSD, RD. *Parl* Aylb. Parl Bor (pt 1804–67, ent 1867–85), Seq 1 thereafter.

DORNEY

AP *LG* Seq 9. Civ bdry: 1883,[20] 1930,[56] 1934.[3] *Parl* Seq 9. *Eccl* Seq 5.

DORTON

Chap in Chilton AP, sep civ identity early, sep EP 1788.[33] *LG* Seq 2. *Parl* Seq 7. *Eccl* Wadd. RDn. Eccl bdry: 1867 (help cr Dropmore EP).[57]

DRAYTON BEAUCHAMP

AP *LG* Seq 10. Civ bdry: 1883 (loses pt to Tring AP, Herts),[20] 1886,[21] 1934 (help cr Cholesbury cum St Leonards CP).[3] *Parl* Seq 1. *Eccl* Murs. RDn (until 1855), S Murs. RDn (1855–74), Iving. RDn (1874–1915), Wend. RDn (1915–*). Eccl bdry: 1867 (help cr Long Marston EP, to be in Roch dioc).[86]

DRAYTON PARSLOW

AP *LG* Seq 13. Civ bdry: 1956,[65] 1965.[87] *Parl* Seq 6. *Eccl* Seq 8.

DROPMORE

EP Cr 1867 from Burnham AP, Dorney EP, Hitcham AP, Taplow AP.[57] Burn. RDn.

DUNTON

AP *LG* Seq 13. *Parl* Seq 6. *Eccl* Murs. RDn (until 1855), N Murs. RDn (1855–1964), Clay. RDn (1964–*).

EDGCOTT

AP *LG* Seq 7. *Parl* Seq 6. *Eccl* Seq 3.

EDLESBOROUGH

AP *LG* Seq 12. Civ bdry: 1883,[20] 1885 (loses pt to Little Gaddesden AP, Herts),[88] 1907 (gains pt from Little Gaddesden AP, Herts).[12] *Parl* Aylb. Parl Bor (1804–85),Seq 5 thereafter. *Eccl* Seq 7.

ELLESBOROUGH

AP *LG* Aylb. Hd, Wyc. PLU, RSD, RD. Civ bdry: 1934.[3] *Parl* Seq 4. *Eccl* Seq 19.

EMBERTON

AP *LG* Seq 16. Civ bdry: 1886.[14] *Parl* Seq 6. *Eccl* Seq 11.

ETON

AP *LG* Stoke Hd, Eton PLU, pt Eton USD, pt Eton RSD, Eton UD. Civ bdry: 1894 (the pt not in the USD cr Eton Wick CP),[89] 1900,[57] 1921,[90] 1934.[3] Transf 1974 to Berks.[194] *Parl* Pt New Wind. Parl Bor (primarily Berks, 1867–1918), pt S'rn Dv (1885–1918), Wyc. Dv (1918–45), Eton & Slough Dv (1945–48), BC (1948–*). *Eccl* Burn. RDn. Reconstituted 1911 as 'Eton with Boveney', gaining chap Boveney from Burnham AP.[40]

ETON WICK

CP Cr 1894 from the pt of Eton AP not in Eton USD.[89] *LG* Eton PLU, RD. Civ bdry: 1900,[91] 1921.[90] Abol 1934 ent to Eton AP.[3] *Parl* Wyc. Dv (1918–45).

ETON WITH BOVENEY

EP Cr 1911 by union Eton AP, chap Boveney of Burnham AP.[40] Burn. RDn.

FARNHAM ROYAL

AP Incl hmlt Seer Green (sep EP 1847,[92] sep CP 1866[2]), hmlt Hedgerley Dean (sep CP 1866[2]). *LG* Seq 9. Civ bdry: 1930,[56] 1934.[3] *Parl* Seq 9. *Eccl* Seq 5. Eccl bdry: 1959.[58]

FAWLEY

AP *LG* Seq 14. *Parl* Seq 10. *Eccl* Wyc. RDn (until 1865), Marlow RDn (1865–74), Wyc. RDn (1874–*).

FILGRAVE

AP *LG* Newp. Hd. *Eccl* Newp. RDn. Abol 1639 to help cr Tyringham with Filgrave.[93]

FINGEST

AP Incl pt chap Cadmore End (sep EP 1852 [from Fingest AP, Lewknor AP, Stokenchurch AP][59]). *LG* Desb. Hd, Wyc. PLU, RSD, RD. Civ bdry: 1934.[3] Renamed 1937 'Fingest and Lane End' CP.[94] *Parl* S'rn Dv (1885–1918), Wyc. Dv (1918–48). *Eccl* Seq 23. Addtl eccl bdry alt: 1867 (help cr Lane End EP).[95]

FINGEST AND LANE END

CP Renaming 1937 of Fingest AP.[94] *LG* Wyc. RD. *Parl* Wyc. CC (1948–*).

FOSCOTT

AP Sometimes 'Foxcote'. *LG* Seq 7. *Parl* Seq 6. *Eccl* Buck. RDn (until 1855), Stony Stratf. RDn (1855–65), Buck. RDn Second Dv (1865–74), Buck. RDn (1874–1972). Abol eccl 1972 to help cr Maids Moreton with Foscott EP.[96]

FULMER

Chap in Datchett AP, sep par 1553.[85] *LG* Seq 17. Civ bdry: 1895 (help cr Gerrard's Cross CP),[23] 1934.[3] *Parl* Seq 9. *Eccl* Seq 6. Eccl bdry: 1959.[97]

GAWCOTT

EP Cr 1818 from Buckingham AP.[53] Buck. RDn (1818–65), Buck. RDn First Dv (1865–74), Buck. RDn (1874–*).

GAYHURST

AP *LG* Seq 16. Civ bdry: 1883,[20] 1886.[14] *Parl* Seq 6. *Eccl* Newp. RDn. Abol eccl 1736 to help cr Stoke Goldington with Gayhurst EP.[98]

GERRARD'S CROSS

Chap in Chalfont St Peter AP, Fulmer AP, Iver AP, Langley Marish CP/EP, Upton cum Chalvey AP, sep EP 1861,[99] sep CP 1895.[23] *LG* Eton PLU, RD. Civ bdry: 1907 (gains pt Rickmansworth Rural CP, Herts),[12] 1934,[100] 1934.[3] *Parl* Wyc. Dv (1918–45), Eton & Slough Dv (1945–48), S Bucks CC (1948–70), Beac. CC (1970–*). *Eccl* Amer. RDn. Eccl bdry: 1959.[97]

GRANBOROUGH

Chap in Winslow AP, sep par 16th cent.[101] *LG* Seq 2. Civ bdry: 1956.[77] *Parl* Seq 6. *Eccl* Seq

15 (London dioc until 1845, Oxford thereafter).

GRENDON UNDERWOOD
AP *LG* Seq 1. Civ bdry: 1886.[21] *Parl* Seq 7. *Eccl* Seq 17.

GROVE
AP *LG* Seq 12. Civ bdry: 1956.[102] *Parl* Seq 5. *Eccl* Murs. RDn (until 1855), S Murs. RDn (1855–74), Iving. RDn (1874–1964), Murs. RDn (1964–73). Abol eccl 1973 to help cr Wing with Grove EP.[103]

HADDENHAM
AP Incl chap Cuddington (sep civ identity early, sep EP 1855[84]). *LG* Seq 4. *Parl* Aylb. Parl Bor (1804–85), Seq 1 thereafter. *Eccl* Seq 20.

HALTON
AP *LG* Seq 4. *Parl* Aylb. Parl Bor (1804–85), Seq 1 thereafter. *Eccl* Pec jurisd Archbp Canterb (until 1846), Seq 19 thereafter.

HAMBLEDEN
AP *LG* Seq 14. Civ bdry: 1934.[3] *Parl* Seq 10. *Eccl* Seq 23. Eccl bdry: 1867 (help cr Lane End EP).[95]

GREAT HAMPDEN
AP *LG* Aylb. Hd, Wyc. PLU, RSD. Abol civ 1885 to help cr Great and Little Hampden CP.[104] *Parl* Aylb. Parl Bor (1804–85), Mid Dv (1885–1918). *Eccl* Wend. RDn (until 1855), Wyc. RDn (1855–65), Aylb. RDn (1865–92). Abol eccl 1892 to help cr Great Hampden with Little Hampden EP.[105]

GREAT AND LITTLE HAMPDEN
CP Cr 1885 by union Great Hampden AP, pt Little Hampden CP, pt Stoke Mandeville AP.[104] *LG* Aylb. Hd, Wyc. PLU, RSD, RD. Bdry: 1934.[3] *Parl* Aylb. Dv (1918–45), Wyc. Dv/CC (1945–70), Aylb. CC (1970–*).

GREAT HAMPDEN WITH LITTLE HAMPDEN
EP Cr 1892 by union Great Hampden AP, Little Hampden chap of Hartwell AP.[105] Aylb. RDn.

LITTLE HAMPDEN
Chap in Hartwell AP, sep civ identity early, eccl severed 1892 to help cr Great Hampden with Little Hampden EP.[105] *LG* Aylb. Hd, Wyc. PLU, RSD. Abol civ 1885 to help cr Great and Little Hampden CP.[104] *Parl* Aylb. Parl Bor (1804–85), Mid Dv (1885–1918).

HANSLOPE
AP Incl chap Castlethorpe (sep civ identity early, no sep eccl identity). Pt Bucks (Newp. Hd), pt Northants (Cleley Hd), Newp. Pagn. PLU, RSD, RD. Addtl civ bdry alt: 1894 (loses the pt in Northants to Hartwell AP, Northants),[106] 1956.[65] *Parl* Bucks pt, N'rn Dv (1885–1918), Buck. Dv/CC (1918–*). *Eccl* As 'Hanslope with Castlethorpe', Newp. RDn (until 1855), Newp. RDn First Dv (1855–74), Newp. RDn (1874–1915), Wolv. RDn (1915–70), Newp. RDn (1970–*).

HANSLOPE WITH CASTLETHORPE—See prev entry

HARDMEAD
AP *LG* Seq 16. Civ bdry: 1886.[14] *Parl* Seq 6. *Eccl* Seq 11.

HARDWICK
AP Incl hmlt Weedon (sep CP 1866[2]). *LG* Seq 10. *Parl* Seq 1. *Eccl* Murs. RDn (until 1855), N Murs. RDn (1855–74), Murs. RDn (1874–1964), Aylb. RDn (1964–*).

HARTWELL
AP Incl chap Little Hampden (sep civ identity early, eccl severed 1892 to help cr Great Hampden with Little Hampden EP[105]). *LG* Seq 4. Civ bdry: 1883,[20] 1887.[107] *Parl* Aylb. Parl Bor (1804–85), Seq 1 thereafter. *Eccl* Wend. RDn (until 1855), Wend. RDn Second Dv (1855–65), Aylb. RDn (1865–1953). Abol eccl 1953 to help cr Stone with Bishopstone and Hartwell EP.[108]

HAVERSHAM
AP *LG* Newp. Hd, Newp. Pagn. PLU, RSD, RD. Abol civ 1934 to help cr Haversham cum Little Linford CP.[3] *Parl* N'rn Dv (1885–1918), Buck. Dv (1918–48). *Eccl* Newp. RDn (until 1855), Newp. RDn First Dv (1855–1915), Wolv. RDn (1915–70), Newp. RDn (1970–73). Abol eccl 1973 to help cr Haversham with Little Linford EP.[109]

HAVERSHAM CUM LITTLE LINFORD
CP Cr 1934 by union Haversham AP, Little Linford CP.[3] *LG* Newp. Pagn. RD. *Parl* Buck. CC (1948–*).

HAVERSHAM WITH LITTLE LINFORD
EP Cr 1973 by union Haversham AP, Little Linford EP.[109] Newp. RDn.

HAWRIDGE
AP *LG* Cott. Hd, Aylb. PLU, RSD, RD. Civ bdry: 1907 (loses pt to Northchurch AP, Wiggington CP, both Herts).[12] Abol civ 1934 to help cr Cholesbury cum St Leonards CP.[3] *Parl* Mid Dv (1885–1918), Aylb. Dv (1918–48). *Eccl* Seq 10.

HAZLEMERE
EP Cr 1847 from Hughenden AP, Penn AP, High Wycombe AP.[110] Wyc. RDn (1847–65), Amer. RDn (1865–74), Wyc. RDn (1874–*). Bdry: 1863 (help cr Tyler's Green EP).[111]

HEDGERLEY
AP *LG* Seq 17. Civ bdry: 1934,[100] 1934.[3] *Parl* Seq 9. *Eccl* Seq 5.

HEDGERLEY DEAN
Hmlt in Farnham Royal AP, sep CP 1866.[2] *LG* Burn. Hd, Eton PLU, RSD, RD. Civ bdry: 1934.[100] Abol civ 1934 pt to Farnham Royal AP, pt to Gerrard's Cross CP.[3] *Parl* S'rn Dv (1885–1918), Wyc. Dv (1918–45).

HEDSOR
AP *LG* Seq 15. Civ bdry: 1883.[20] *Parl* Seq 11. *Eccl* Seq 22.

HILLESDEN
AP *LG* Seq 7. Civ bdry: 1956.[75] *Parl* Buck. Parl Bor (1832–85), Seq 6 thereafter. *Eccl* Buck. RDn (until 1865), Buck. RDn First Dv (1865–74), Buck. RDn (1874–97), Clay. RDn (1897–1961), Buck. RDn (1961–*).

HITCHAM
AP *LG* Burn. Hd, Eton PLU, RSD, RD. Abol civ 1934 pt to Burnham AP, pt to Dorney AP, pt

to Taplow AP.[3] *Parl* S'rn Dv (1885–1918), Wyc. Dv (1918–45). *Eccl* Seq 5. Eccl bdry: 1867 (help cr Dropmore EP).[57]

HOGGESTON
AP *LG* Seq 13. *Parl* Seq 6. *Eccl* Seq 8.

HOGSHAW
AP *LG* Seq 3. Civ bdry: 1934.[3] *Parl* Seq 6. *Eccl* Wadd. RDn. Church in ruins by 17th cent, consolidated with East Claydon AP.[78]

HORSENDEN
AP *LG* Aylb. Hd, Wyc. PLU, RSD, RD. Abol civ 1934 pt to help cr Bledlow cum Saunderton CP, pt to Princes Risborough CP.[3] *Parl* Aylb. Parl Bor (1804–85), Mid Dv (1885–1918), Aylb. Dv (1918–45). *Eccl* Wend. RDn (until 1865), Wend. RDn Second Dv (1865–74), Aylb. RDn (1874–1973). Abol eccl 1973 to help cr Bledlow with Saunderton and Horsenden EP.[32]

HORTON
AP *LG* Seq 17. Civ bdry: 1930,[56] 1934.[3] Transf 1974 to Berks.[194] *Parl* Seq 9. *Eccl* Seq 5. Eccl bdry: 1853 (help cr Colnbrook EP).[81]

GREAT HORWOOD
AP *LG* Seq 13. *Parl* Seq 6. *Eccl* Seq 9.

LITTLE HORWOOD
Chap in Winslow AP, sep par by 1535.[112] *LG* Seq 13. *Parl* Seq 6. *Eccl* St Albans AD (London dioc, until 1846), Murs. RDn (1846–55), N Murs. RDn (1855–74), Murs. RDn (1874–1964), Clay. RDn (1964–68), Murs. RDn (1968–*).

HUGHENDEN
AP *LG* Seq 15. Civ bdry: 1928,[113] 1934 (incl loses pt to help cr West Wycombe Rural CP.[3] *Parl* Aylb. Parl Bor (1804–85), Mid Dv (1885–1918), Aylb. Dv (1918–45), Wyc. Dv/CC (1945–*). *Eccl* Seq 21. Eccl bdry: 1847 (help cr Hazlemere EP),[110] 1850 (help cr Prestwood EP),[24] 1968.[114]

HULCOTT
AP *LG* Seq 4. Civ bdry: 1885.[115] *Parl* Aylb. Parl Bor (1804–85), Seq 1 thereafter. *Eccl* Seq 20.

IBSTONE
AP Usual civ spelling, sometimes 'Ipstone'; for eccl see 'Ipsden'. In Oxon (Pirton Hd), transf 1896 to Bucks.[116] *LG* Wyc. PLU, RSD, RD. *Parl* Oxon (until 1918), Wyc. Dv/CC (1918–70), Aylb. CC (1970–*).

ICKFORD
AP Pt Bucks (Ash. Hd), pt Oxon (Ewelme Hd), the latter transf 1886 to Waterstock AP, Oxon, and par ent Bucks thereafter.[117] *LG* Thame PLU, RSD, Long. Cren. RD (1894–1934), Aylb. RD (1934–74). *Parl* Pt Oxon, pt Bucks (N'rn Dv, 1885–1918), Buck. Dv (1918–48), Aylb. CC (1948–*). *Eccl* Seq 16.

ILMER
AP *LG* Ash. Hd, Wyc. PLU, RSD, RD. Civ bdry: 1886.[118] Abol civ 1934 to help cr Longwick cum Ilmer CP.[3] *Parl* Mid Dv (1885–1918), Aylb. Dv (1918–45). *Eccl* Wadd. RDn (until 1865), Aylb. RDn (1865–1973). Abol eccl 1973 to help cr Princes Risborough with Ilmer EP).[32]

IVER
AP *LG* Seq 17. Civ bdry: 1895 (help cr Gerrard's Cross CP),[23] 1934.[3] *Parl* Seq 9. *Eccl* Burn. RDn (until 1874), Amer. RDn (1874–1970), Burn. RDn (1970–*). Eccl bdry: 1862 (cr Iver Heath EP),[119] 1873.[82]

IVER HEATH
EP Cr 1862 from Iver AP.[119] Burn. RDn (1862–74), Amer. RDn (1874–1970), Burn. RDn (1970–*).

IVINGHOE
AP *LG* Seq 12. Civ bdry: 1883,[20] 1884,[120] 1885,[121] 1895 (loses pts to Little Gaddesden AP, Nettleden CP, former in Herts, latter transf at that time to Herts).[122] *Parl* Seq 5. *Eccl* Murs. RDn (until 1855), S Murs. RDn (1855–74), Iving. RDn (1874–1964), Murs. RDn (1964–73). Eccl bdry: 1939.[123] Abol eccl 1973 to help cr Ivinghoe with Pitstone EP.[124]

IVINGHOE WITH PITSTONE
EP Cr 1973 by union Ivinghoe AP, Pitstone AP.[124] Murs. RDn.

GREAT KIMBLE
AP *LG* Aylb. Hd, Wyc. PLU, RSD. Civ bdry: 1883.[20] Abol civ 1885 to help cr Great and Little Kimble CP.[104] *Parl* Aylb. Parl Bor (1804–85), Mid Dv (1885–1918). *Eccl* Wend. RDn (until 1865), Aylb. RDn (1865–95). Abol eccl 1895 to help cr Great Kimble with Little Kimble EP.[125]

GREAT AND LITTLE KIMBLE
CP Cr 1885 by union Great Kimble AP, Little Kimble AP.[104] *LG* Aylb. Hd, Wyc. PLU, RSD, RD. *Parl* Aylb. Dv (1918–45), Wyc. Dv/CC (1945–70), Aylb. CC (1970–*).

GREAT KIMBLE WITH LITTLE KIMBLE
EP Cr 1895 by union Great Kimble AP, Little Kimble AP.[125] Aylb. RDn (1895–1966), Wend. RDn (1966–*).

LITTLE KIMBLE
AP *LG* Aylb. Hd, Wyc. PLU, RSD, RD. Abol civ 1885 to help cr Great and Little Kimble CP.[104] *Parl* Aylb. Parl Bor (1804–85), Mid Dv (1885–1918). *Eccl* Wend. RDn (until 1855), Wend. RDn First Dv (1855–74), Aylb. RDn (1874–95). Abol eccl 1895 to help cr Great Kimble with Little Kimble EP.[125]

KINGSEY
AP Pt Oxon (Lewknor Hd), pt Bucks (Ash. Hd). *LG* Thame PLU, RSD, pt Thame RD in Oxon (1894–95), pt sep RD in Bucks (1894–95). Civ bdry: 1886.[118] The Bucks pt transf 1895 to Oxon[116] and par ent Oxon until transf 1933 back to Bucks.[126] *LG* Aylb. RD (1933–74). *Parl* Pt Oxon, pt Bucks (Mid Dv, 1885– 1918), in Oxon, qv, (1918–48), Aylb. CC (1948–*). *Eccl* Wadd. RDn (until 1874), Aylb. RDn (1874–1925), Aston RDn (Oxford AD, 1925–*).

KINGSWOOD
Hmlt in Ludgershall AP, sep CP 1866.[2] *LG* Seq 1. *Parl* Seq 7.

LACEY GREEN
Area in Princes Risborough AP, sep EP 1821,[127]

sep CP 1934.[3] *LG* Wyc. RD. *Parl* Wyc. CC (1948–70), Aylb. CC (1970–*). *Eccl* Wend. RDn (1826–55), Wyc. RDn (1855–65), Aylb. RDn (1865–*).

LANE END
EP Cr 1867 from Fingest AP, Great Marlow AP, West Wycombe AP, Hambleden AP.[95] Marlow RDn (1867–74), Wyc. RDn (1874–*). Bdry: 1968.[114]

LANGLEY MARISH
Chap in Wyrardisbury AP,[128] sep civ identity early, sep EP 1856.[129] *LG* Stoke Hd, Eton PLU, RSD, RD. Civ bdry: 1895 (help cr Gerrard's Cross CP),[23] 1900,[130] 1930.[56] Abol civ 1934 pt to Fulmer AP, pt to Iver AP, pt to Wexham AP.[3] *Parl* S'rn Dv (1885–1918), Wyc. Dv (1918–45). *Eccl* Burn. RDn. Eccl bdry: 1853 (while still chap, help cr Colnbrook EP),[81] 1959.[97]

LATHBURY
AP *LG* Seq 16. Civ bdry: 1883,[20] 1886.[14] *Parl* Seq 6. *Eccl* Seq 11.

LATIMER
Hmlt and chap in Chesham AP, sep EP 1868,[71] sep CP 1899.[67] *LG* Amer. PLU, RD. Civ bdry: 1907 (gains pt Bovingdon CP, exchanges pts with Flaunden CP, both Herts),[12] 1934.[3] *Parl* Aylb. Dv/CC (1918–70), Ches. & Amer. CC (1970–*). *Eccl* Amer. RDn. Abol eccl 1876 to help cr Latimer with Flaunden EP.[131]

LATIMER WITH FLAUNDEN
EP Cr 1876 by union Latimer EP, Flaunden EP (Herts, Roch dioc) to be ent in Oxford dioc.[131] Amer. RDn.

LAVENDON
AP Incl Cold Brayfield (vicarage ordained 13th cent, sep civ identity maintained, sep eccl status not sustained and later considered as a chap in this par[49]). *LG* Seq 16. Civ bdry: 1886.[14] *Parl* Seq 6. *Eccl* Seq 11.

LECKHAMPSTEAD
AP *LG* Seq 7. *Parl* Seq 6. *Eccl* Seq 2.

LEE
Chap in Weston Turville AP, sep par by 1535.[183] Usual civ spelling until renamed 1954 'The Lee', the usual eccl spelling.[132] *LG* Aylb. Hd, Amer. PLU,[133] RSD, RD. Civ bdry: 1911.[134] *Parl* Aylb. Parl Bor (1804–85), Mid Dv (1885–1918), Aylb. Dv/CC (1918–70).

THE LEE
Usual eccl spelling, and civ spelling from 1954 of par prev 'Lee', qv for sep identity from Weston Turville AP.[132] *LG* Amer. RD. *Parl* Ches. & Amer. CC (1970–*). *Eccl* Seq 19.

LEWKNOR
AP In Oxon, incl Lewknor Uphill (pt Bucks, pt Oxon; see following entry), which when becomes sep CP 1866 with pt in ea co[2] renders Lewknor ent Oxon thereafter. See main entry in Oxon. Eccl bdry: 1852 (help cr Cadmore End EP).[59]

LEWKNOR UPHILL
Comprised of 3 detached pts in Lewknor AP, pt Oxon (Lewknor Hd), pt Bucks (Desb. Hd), the area of the former increased and the latter decreased when chap Ackhampstead transf from Bucks to Oxon 1832 for parl pruposes, 1844 for civ purposes,[1] sep CP 1866 with area in ea co.[2] *LG* Wyc. PLU, RSD. Abol 1885 the pt in Oxon to Stokenchurch CP, the pt in Bucks to Great Marlow AP.[135] *Parl* Bucks pt, Mid Dv (1885–1918).

LILLINGSTONE DAYRELL
AP *LG* Seq 7. Civ bdry: 1878,[136] 1956.[137] *Parl* Seq 6. *Eccl* Seq 3.

LILLINGSTONE LOVELL
AP In Oxon (Ploughley Hd), transf to Bucks 1832 for parl purposes, 1844 for civ purposes.[1] *LG* Buck. Hd (from 1844), PLU, RSD, RD. Civ bdry: 1878,[136] 1956.[137] *Parl* Oxon (until 1832), Seq 6 thereafter. *Eccl* Bicester RDn (Oxford AD, until 1920), Buck. RDn (1920–*).

GREAT LINFORD
AP *LG* Seq 16. *Parl* Seq 6. *Eccl* Newp. RDn (until 1855), Newp. RDn First Dv (1855–74), Newp. RDn (1874–1970), Milt. Keyn. RDn (1970–74). Abol eccl 1974 to help cr Stantonbury EP.[34]

LITTLE LINFORD
Chap in Newport Pagnell AP, sep civ identity early, sep EP 1735.[33] *LG* Newp. Hd, Newp. Pagn. PLU, RSD, RD. Abol civ 1934 to help cr Haversham cum Little Linford CP.[3] *Parl* N'rn Dv (1885–1918), Buck. Dv (1918–48). *Eccl* Newp. RDn (1735–1855), Newp. RDn First Dv (1855–74), Newp. RDn (1874–1973). Abol eccl 1973 to help cr Haversham with Little Linford EP.[109]

LINSLADE
AP *LG* Cott. Hd, Leighton Buzzard PLU, RSD, Wing RD (1874–97), Linslade UD (1897–1965). Abol civ 1965 pt to Soulbury AP, pt to help cr Leighton-Linslade UD and CP, to be ent Beds.[138] *Parl* Mid Dv (1885–1918), Buck. Dv/CC (1918–70). *Eccl* Seq 7.

LONGWICK CUM ILMER
CP Cr 1934 by union Ilmer AP, Monks Risborough AP, pt Princes Risborough AP, pt Towersey CP.[3] *LG* Wyc. RD. *Parl* Wyc. CC (1948–70), Aylb. CC (1970–*).

LOUDWATER
EP Cr 1792 from High Wycombe AP.[139] Marlow RDn (1792–1874), Wyc. RDn (1874–*).

LOUGHTON
AP Cr 1409 by union Great Loughton AP, Little Loughton AP.[140] *LG* Seq 16. *Parl* Seq 6. *Eccl* Seq 5.

GREAT LOUGHTON
AP Newp. RDn, abol 1409 to help cr Loughton AP.[140]

LITTLE LOUGHTON
AP Organisation as for Great Loughton AP.

LUDGERSHALL
AP Incl hmlt Kingswood (sep CP 1866[2]). *LG* Seq 1. Addtl civ bdry alt: 1886.[51] *Parl* Seq 7. *Eccl*

Seq 18.

LUFFIELD ABBEY

Ex-par place, pt Bucks (Buck. Hd), pt Northants (Greens Norton Hd), the latter transf to Silverstone AP, Northants, 1832 for parl purposes, 1844 for civ purposes,[1] sep CP 1858.[46] *LG* Buck. PLU, RSD, RD. *Parl* Pt Northants (until 1832), Seq 6 thereafter.

GREAT MARLOW

AP *LG* Seq 15. Civ bdry: 1885,[135] 1896 (cr Marlow Urban CP and Great Marlow UD),[141] 1934 (incl help cr High Wycombe CP).[3] *Parl* Great Marlow Parl Bor (1300–09, 1624–1885), Seq 10 thereafter. *Eccl* Seq 23. Eccl bdry: 1867 (help cr Lane End EP),[95] 1968.[114]

LITTLE MARLOW

AP *LG* Seq 15. Civ bdry: 1883,[20] 1934.[3] *Parl* Great Marlow Parl Bor (1832–85), Seq 10 thereafter. *Eccl* Seq 23. Eccl bdry: 1954.[142]

MARLOW URBAN

CP Cr 1896 from the pt of Great Marlow AP constituted Great Marlow UD.[141] *LG* Wyc. PLU, Great Marlow UD (1896–97), Marlow UD (1897–1974). *Parl* Wyc. Dv/CC (1918–*).

MARSH GIBBON

AP *LG* Seq 7. Civ bdry: 1956 (loses pt to Piddington AP, Oxon).[197] *Parl* Seq 6. *Eccl* Seq 3.

FLEET MARSTON

AP *LG* Seq 1. *Parl* Seq 1. *Eccl* Wadd. RDn (until 1855), Clay. RDn (1855–74), Wadd. RDn (1874–1973). Abol eccl 1973 to help cr Waddesdon with Over Winchendon and Fleet Marston EP).[143]

LONG MARSTON

EP Cr 1867 from Drayton Beauchamp AP, Marsworth AP, Tring AP (Herts), to be in Roch dioc.[86] Berkhampstead RDn. Bdry: 1910.[144]

NORTH MARSTON

AP *LG* Seq 3. *Parl* Seq 6. *Eccl* Seq 17.

MARSWORTH

AP *LG* Cott. Hd, Berkhampstead PLU, RSD, Wing RD. Civ bdry: 1883 (incl lose pt to Tring AP, Herts),[3] 1888 (loses pt to Puttenham AP, Herts).[145] *Parl* Seq 5. *Eccl* Seq 7. Eccl bdry: 1867 (help cr Long Marston EP, to be in Roch dioc).[86]

MEDMENHAM

AP *LG* Seq 14. *Parl* Great Marlow Parl Bor (1832–85), Seq 10 thereafter. *Eccl* Seq 23.

MENTMORE

AP *LG* Seq 12. Civ bdry: 1956.[102] *Parl* Seq 5. *Eccl* Seq 7.

MILTON KEYNES

AP *LG* Seq 16. Civ bdry: 1956.[52] *Parl* Seq 6. *Eccl* Seq 12.

GREAT MISSENDEN

AP *LG* Aylb. Hd, Amer. PLU, RSD, RD. Civ bdry: 1911,[134] 1934.[3] *Parl* Aylb. Parl Bor (1804–85), Seq 2 thereafter. *Eccl* Seq 19. Eccl bdry: 1850 (help cr Prestwood EP),[24] 1973.[73]

LITTLE MISSENDEN

AP *LG* Aylb. Hd, Wyc. PLU (1835–1901), RSD, Amer. PLU (1901–30), Wyc. RD (1894–1901), Amer. RD (1901–74). *Parl* Aylb. Parl Bor (1804–85), Seq 2 thereafter. *Eccl* Wend. RDn (until 1855), Amer. RDn (1855–*). Eccl bdry: 1850 (help cr Penn Street EP),[146] 1973.[73]

MAIDS' MORETON

AP *LG* Seq 7. Civ bdry: 1934,[3] 1956.[54] *Parl* Buck. Parl Bor (1832–85), Seq 6 thereafter. *Eccl* As 'Maids Moreton', Buck. RDn. Abol eccl 1972 to help cr Maids Moreton with Foscott EP.[96]

MAIDS MORETON WITH FOSCOTT

EP Cr 1972 by union Maids Moreton AP, Foscott AP.[96] Buck. RDn.

MOULSOE

AP *LG* Seq 16. Civ bdry: 1956.[52] *Parl* Seq 6. *Eccl* Newp. RDn (until 1855), Newp. RDn First Dv (1855–74), Blet. RDn (1874–1970), Milt. Keyn. RDn (1970–*).

MURSLEY

AP *LG* Seq 13. *Parl* Seq 6. *Eccl* Seq 8.

NASH

Hmlt in Whaddon AP, sep CP 1866,[2] eccl severed 1854 to help cr Thornton and Nash EP, now usually called 'Nash and Thornton'.[147] *LG* Seq 13. *Parl* Seq 6.

NASH AND THORNTON

EP Usual name now for EP cr 1854 as 'Thornton and Nash', qv.

NETTLEDEN

Chap in Pitstone AP, sep EP 1737,[33] sep CP 1866.[2] *LG* Cott. Hd, Berkhampstead PLU, RSD, sep RD (1894–95). Transf 1895 to Herts.[122] *Parl* Mid Dv (1885–1918), Herts thereafter. *Eccl* Murs. RDn (1737–1874), N Murs. RDn (1874–77), Berkhampstead RDn (St Alb dioc, 1877–*). Addtl eccl bdry alt: 1939.[123]

NEWPORT PAGNELL

AP Incl chap Little Linford (sep civ identity early, sep EP 1735[33]). *LG* Newp. Hd, Newp. Pagn. Bor (until 17th cent), PLU, RSD, RD (1894–97), UD (1897–1974). Addtl civ bdry alt: 1956.[76] *Parl* Seq 6. *Eccl* Seq 11. Addtl eccl bdry alt: 1973,[148] 1974 (help cr Stantonbury EP).[34]

NEWTON BLOSSOMVILLE

AP *LG* Seq 16. *Parl* Seq 6. *Eccl* Seq 11.

NEWTON LONGVILLE

AP *LG* Newp. Hd, Newp. Pagn. PLU, RSD, RD (1894–1934), Wins. RD (1934–74). Civ bdry: 1934,[3] 1953,[35] 1956,[149] 1974.[55] *Parl* Seq 6. *Eccl* Seq 13.

OAKLEY

AP Incl chap Boarstall, chap Brill (the latter a Bor until 14th cent; each with sep civ identity early, sep EP 1740 as 'Brill with Boarstall'[38]). *LG* Seq 2. Addtl civ bdry alt: 1886,[117] 1934.[3] *Parl* Seq 7. *Eccl* Seq 16.

OLNEY

AP Incl hmlt Warrington (sep CP 1866[2]), chap Weston Underwood (sep civ identity early, sep EP 1778[150]). *LG* Olney Bor (status not sustained), Seq 16. *Parl* Seq 6. *Eccl* Incl Olney Park Farm,[151] Seq 11.

OLNEY PARK FARM
Ex-par place, sep CP 1858,[46] eccl incl in Olney AP.[151] *LG* Seq 16. *Parl* Seq 6.

OVING
AP *LG* Seq 1. *Parl* Seq 1. *Eccl* Wadd. RDn (until 1855), Clay. RDn (1855–1902). Abol eccl 1902 to help cr Oving with Pitchcott EP.[152]

OVING WITH PITCHCOTT
EP Cr 1902 by union Oving AP, Pitchcott AP.[152] Clay. RDn.

PADBURY
AP *LG* Seq 7. *Parl* Buck. Parl Bor (1832–85), Seq 6 thereafter. *Eccl* Buck. RDn (until 1874), Clay. RDn (1874–1970), Buck. RDn (1970–*).

PENN
AP *LG* Seq 8. Civ bdry: 1956.[4] *Parl* Seq 8. *Eccl* Seq 6. Eccl bdry: 1847 (help cr Hazlemere EP),[110] 1850 (help cr Penn Street EP),[146] 1863 (help cr Tyler's Green EP).[111]

PENN STREET
EP Cr 1850 from Little Missénden AP, Penn AP.[146] Burn. RDn (1850–55), Amer. RDn (1855–*).

PETSOE MANOR
Ex-par place, sep CP 1858.[46] *LG* Seq 16. *Parl* Seq 6.

PITCHCOTT
AP *LG* Seq 1. *Parl* Seq 1. *Eccl* Wadd. RDn (until 1855), Clay. RDn (1855–1902). Abol eccl 1902 to help cr Oving with Pitchcott EP.[152]

PITSTONE
AP Incl chap Nettleden (sep EP 1737,[33] sep CP 1866,[2] transf 1895 to Herts[122]). Sometimes 'Pightlesthorne' but civ name declared 1923 to be 'Pitstone'.[153] *LG* Cott. Hd, Berkhampstead PLU (1835–1923), RSD, Leigh. Buz. PLU (1923–30), Wing RD. Addtl civ bdry alt: 1884.[154] *Parl* Seq 5. *Eccl* Murs. RDn (1855–74), Iving. RDn (1874–1964), Murs. RDn (1964–73). Abol eccl 1973 to help cr Ivinghoe with Pitstone EP.[124]

POUNDON
Hmlt in Twyford AP, sep CP 1866.[2] *LG* Seq 7. *Parl* Seq 6.

PRESTON BISSETT
AP *LG* Seq 7. Civ bdry: 1956.[75] *Parl* Buck. Parl Bor (1832–85), Seq 6 thereafter. *Eccl* Buck. RDn (until 1970), Clay. RDn (1970–*).

PRESTWOOD
EP Cr 1850 from Hughenden AP, Great Missenden AP, Stoke Mandeville chap in Bierton with Broughton AP.[24] Wyc. RDn (1852–55), Amer. RDn (1855–65), Aylb. RDn (1865–1966), Wend. RDn (1966–*).

QUAINTON
AP Incl hmlt Shipton Lee (sep CP 1866[2]). *LG* Seq 1. Civ bdry: 1885,[155] 1934.[3] *Parl* Seq 1. *Eccl* Seq 17.

QUARRENDON
Chap in Aylesbury AP, then in Bierton with Broughton when latter made sep par 1294; sep civ identity early, no sep eccl identity. *LG* Seq 1. *Parl* Seq 1.

RADCLIVE
AP Usual eccl spelling; for civ see following entry. *Eccl* Seq 1.

RADCLIVE-CUM-CHACKMORE
AP Usual civ spelling; for eccl see prev entry. *LG* Seq 7. Civ bdry: 1934.[3] *Parl* Buck. Parl Bor (1832–85), Seq 6 thereafter.

RADNAGE
AP *LG* Seq 15. *Parl* Seq 4. *Eccl* Seq 21.

RAVENSTONE
AP *LG* Seq 16. Civ bdry: 1886.[14] *Parl* Seq 6. *Eccl* Seq 11.

MONK'S RISBOROUGH
AP *LG* Aylb. Hd, Wyc. PLU, RSD, RD. Abol civ 1934 pt to help cr Longwick cum Ilmer CP, pt to Princes Risborough AP, pt to Great and Little Hampden CP.[3] *Parl* Aylb. Parl Bor (1804–85), Mid Dv (1885–1918), Aylb. Dv (1918–45). *Eccl* Pec jurisd Archbp Canterb (until 1846), Wend. RDn (1846–55), Wyc. RDn (1855–65), Aylb. RDn (1865–*).

PRINCES RISBOROUGH
AP Incl Lacey Green (sep EP 1821,[77] sep CP 1934[3]). *LG* Aylb. Hd, Wyc. PLU, RSD, RD. Addtl civ bdry alt: 1934 (incl help cr Longwick cum Ilmer CP).[3] *Parl* Aylb. Parl Bor (1804–85), Seq 4 thereafter. *Eccl* Wend. RDn (until 1855), Wyc. RDn (1855–65), Aylb. RDn (1865–1973). Abol eccl 1973 to help cr Princes Risborough with Ilmer EP.[32]

PRINCES RISBOROUGH WITH ILMER
EP Cr 1973 by union Princes Risborough AP, Ilmer AP.[32] Aylb. RDn.

SAUNDERTON
AP Cr before 1535 by union Saunderton St Nicholas AP, Saunderton St Mary AP.[156] *LG* Desb. Hd, Wyc. PLU, RSD, RD. Civ bdry: 1885.[157] Abol civ 1934 to help cr Bledlow cum Saunderton CP.[3] *Parl* Mid Dv (1885–1918), Aylb. Dv (1918–45). *Eccl* Wyc. RDn (before 1535–1865), Aylb. RDn (1865–1973). Abol eccl 1973 to help cr Bledlow with Saunderton and Horsenden EP.[32]

SAUNDERTON ST MARY
AP Wyc. RDn, abol before 1535 to help cr Saunderton AP.[156]

SAUNDERTON ST NICHOLAS
AP Organisation as for Saunderton St Mary AP.

SEER GREEN
Hmlt in Farnham Royal AP, sep EP 1847,[92] sep CP 1866.[2] *LG* Seq 8. *Parl* Seq 8. *Eccl* Burn. RDn (1847–55), Amer. RDn (1855–*).

SHABBINGTON
AP *LG* Seq 2. Civ bdry: 1886.[117] *Parl* Seq 7. *Eccl* Seq 16.

SHALSTONE
AP *LG* Seq 7. *Parl* Seq 6. *Eccl* Seq 1.

SHENLEY
AP *LG* Pt Cott. Hd (Brook End), pt Newp. Hd (Church End), seach sep rated for poor law purposes and each CP 1866,[2] thus civ identity of Shenley ends at 1866. *Eccl* Seq 14.

SHENLEY BROOK END
Pt of Shenley AP, sep CP 1866.[2] *LG* Seq 13. Civ bdry: 1974 (loses pt in Milt. Keyn. Dist to Whaddon AP).[55] *Parl* Seq 6.

SHENLEY CHURCH END
Pt of Shenley AP, sep CP 1866.[2] *LG* Seq 16. *Parl* Seq 6.

SHERINGTON
AP *LG* Seq 16. *Parl* Seq 6. *Eccl* Seq 11.

SHIPTON LEE
Hmlt in Quainton AP, sep CP 1866.[2] *LG* Ash. Hd, Aylb. PLU, RSD. Abol civ 1886 ent to Quainton AP.[155] *Parl* Mid Dv (1885–1918).

SIMPSON
AP Incl pt chap and twnshp Fenny Stratford (sep EP 1730,[33] sep CP 1866,[2] in both cases with pt also from Bletchley AP). *LG* Newp. Hd, pt Fenny Stratf. Bor, Newp. Pagn. PLU, RSD, RD (1894–95), Fenny Stratf. UD (1895–1911), Blet. UD (1911–34). Abol civ 1934 ent to Bletchley AP.[3] *Parl* N'rn Dv (1885–1918), Buck. Dv (1918–48). *Eccl* Newp. RDn (until 1855), Newp. RDn Second Dv (1855–74), Blet. RDn (1874–1970), Milt. Keyn. RDn (1970–74). Addtl eccl bdry alt: 1951,[36] 1973.[37] Abol eccl 1974 to help cr Woughton EP.[34]

SLAPTON
AP *LG* Seq 12. Civ bdry: 1883,[20] 1884,[154] 1885.[158] *Parl* Seq 5. *Eccl* Seq 7.

SLOUGH
Pt of Upton cum Chalvey AP, sep CP 1894 (the pt in Slough UD),[89] sep EP 1904 (from Upton cum Chalvey AP, Stoke Poges AP).[159] *LG* Eton PLU, Slough UD (1894–1938), MB (1938–74). Civ bdry: 1896,[160] 1900,[130] 1934.[3] Transf 1974 to Berks.[194] *Parl* Wyc. Dv (1918–45), Eton & Slough Dv (1945–48), BC (1948–*). *Eccl* Burn. RDn.

SOULBURY
AP *LG* Seq 12. Civ bdry: 1934,[3] 1956,[65] 1956,[87] 1965.[161] *Parl* Seq 5. *Eccl* Murs. RDn (until 1855), S Murs. RDn (1855–74), Iving. RDn (1874–1957), Blet. RDn (1957–70), Murs. RDn (1970–*). Eccl bdry: 1955.[50]

STANTONBURY
AP *LG* Seq 16. *Parl* Seq 6. *Eccl* Newp. RDn (until 1855), Stony Stratf. RDn (1855–57). Abol eccl 1857 to help cr New Bradwell with Stantonbury EP.[44]
EP Cr 1974 by union Bradwell AP, New Bradwell with Stantonbury EP, Great Linford AP, pt Newport Pagnell AP.[34] Milt. Keyn. RDn.

STEWKLEY
AP *LG* Seq 13. Civ bdry: 1956.[87] *Parl* Seq 5. *Eccl* Seq 8.

STOKE GOLDINGTON
AP *LG* Seq 16. *Parl* Seq 6. *Eccl* Newp. RDn. Abol eccl 1736 to help cr Stoke Goldington with Gayhurst EP.[98]

STOKE GOLDINGTON WITH GAYHURST
EP Cr 1736 by union Stoke Goldington AP, Gayhurst AP.[98] Newp. RDn (1736–1855), Newp. RDn First Dv (1855–74), Newp. RDn (1874–*).

STOKE HAMMOND
AP *LG* Newp. Hd, Leighton Buzzard PLU, RSD, Wing RD. Civ bdry: 1934,[3] 1956.[87] *Parl* Seq 6. *Eccl* Seq 13.

STOKE IN SLOUGH
CP Cr 1894 from the pt of Stoke Poges AP in Slough USD.[89] *LG* Eton PLU, Slough UD. Abol 1896 ent to Slough CP.[160]

STOKE MANDEVILLE
Chap in Aylesbury AP, then in Bierton with Broughton when latter made sep par 1294; sep civ identity early, combined 1858 with Buckland chap in same par as 'Stoke Mandeville and Buckland EP',[18] divided 1887 into 2 EPs of Stoke Mandeville, Buckland.[29] *LG* Seq 5. Civ bdry: 1883,[20] 1885 (incl help cr Great and Little Hampden CP),[104] 1887,[107] 1934,[3] 1958.[162] *Parl* Aylb. Parl Bor (1804–85), Seq 1 thereafter. *Eccl* Wend. RDn. Eccl bdry: 1850 (while chap, help cr Prestwood EP).[24]

STOKE MANDEVILLE AND BUCKLAND
EP Cr 1858 by union of chap Stoke Mandeville, chap Buckland, both in Bierton with Broughton AP.[18] Wend. RDn First Dv (1858–74), Wend. RDn (1874–87). Abol 1887 to cr 2 EPs of Stoke Mandeville, Buckland.[29]

STOKE POGES
AP *LG* Stoke Hd, Eton PLU, pt Eton RSD, pt Slough USD, Eton RD. Civ bdry: 1894 (the pt in the USD to cr Stoke in Slough CP),[89] 1900,[130] 1930,[56] 1934.[3] *Parl* Seq 9. *Eccl* Seq 5. Eccl bdry: 1959.[97]

STOKENCHURCH
Chap in Aston Rowant AP in Oxon (Lewknor Hd), sep civ identity early in Oxon, sep EP 1844,[163] transf civ 1895 to Bucks.[164] *LG* Wyc. PLU, RSD, Thame RD in Oxon (1894–95), Wyc. RD (1895–1974). *Parl* Oxon until 1918, Wyc. Dv/CC (1918–70), Aylb. CC (1970–*). *Eccl* Aston RDn (Oxford AD, 1844–1973), Wyc. RDn (1973–*).

STONE
AP Usual civ spelling; for eccl see following entry. *LG* Seq 4. Civ bdry: 1883.[20] *Parl* Aylb. Parl Bor (1804–85), Seq 1 thereafter.

STONE WITH BISHOPSTONE
AP Usual eccl spelling; for civ see prev entry. *Eccl* Wend. RDn (until 1855), Wend. RDn Second Dv (1855–65), Aylb. RDn (1865–1953). Abol eccl 1953 to help cr Stone with Bishopstone and Hartwell EP.[108]

STONE WITH BISHOPSTONE AND HARTWELL
EP Cr 1953 by union Stone with Bishopstone AP, Hartwell AP.[108] Aylb. RDn.

FENNY STRATFORD
Chap and twnshp in Bletchley AP, Simpson AP, sep EP 1730,[33] sep CP 1866.[2] *LG* Newp. Hd, Newp. Pagn. PLU, RSD, RD (1894–95), Fenny Stratf. UD (1895–1911), Blet. UD (1911–34). Abol civ 1934 ent to Bletchley AP.[3] *Parl* N'rn Dv (1885–1918), Buck. Dv (1918–48). *Eccl* Seq 12. Eccl bdry: 1951,[36] 1974.[34]

STONY STRATFORD
The 2 chaps of St Giles (in Calverton AP), St Mary Magdalen (in Wolverton AP), sep civ identity together early as 'Stony Stratford', sep EP 1767[33]; divided late 18th cent into Stony Stratford East CP, Stony Stratford West CP.[165] *LG* Newp. Hd. *Eccl* Newp. RDn (1767–1855), Stony Stratf. RDn (1855–65), Buck. RDn Second Dv (1865–74), Buck. RDn (1874–1915), Wolv. RDn (1915–68). Abol eccl 1968 to help cr Stony Stratford St Mary and St Giles EP.[166]

STONY STRATFORD EAST
CP Cr late 18th cent from Stony Stratford CP.[165] *LG* Newp. Hd, Potterspury PLU,[60] Stratf. & Wolv. RD (1894–1919), UD (1919–20), Wolv. UD (1920–27). Abol 1927 ent to Wolverton AP.[61] *Parl* N'rn Dv (1885–1918), Buck. Dv (1918–48).

STONY STRATFORD WEST
CP Organisation as for Stony Stratford East CP, but with bdry alt 1883[167] in addition.

STONY STRATFORD ST MARY AND ST GILES
EP Cr 1968 by union Stony Stratford EP, Stony Stratford St Mary the Virgin EP.[166] Wolv. RDn (1968–70), Milt. Keyn. RDn (1970–*). Bdry: 1968,[64] 1973.[168]

STONY STRATFORD ST MARY THE VIRGIN
EP Renaming 1953 of Wolverton St Mary EP.[169] Wolv. RDn. Bdry: 1954.[63] Abol 1968 to help cr Stony Stratford St Mary and St Giles EP.[166]

STOWE
AP Incl hmlt or twnshp Boycott (situated in Oxon, transf to Bucks 1832 for parl purposes, 1844 for civ purposes[1]). *LG* Seq 7. *Parl* Seq 6. *Eccl* Seq 2.

WATER STRATFORD
AP *LG* Seq 7. *Parl* Seq 6. *Eccl* Seq 1.

STRATTON AUDLEY
Chap in Bicester AP, Oxon, prob sep par 1455.[170] Pt Oxon (Ploughley Hd), pt Bucks (Buck. Hd), the latter transf to Oxon 1832 for parl purposes when Caversfield AP transf, 1844 for civ purposes.[1] See main entry in Oxon.

SWANBOURNE
AP *LG* Seq 13. Civ bdry: 1956.[77] *Parl* Seq 6. *Eccl* Murs. RDn (until 1855), N Murs. RDn (1855–74), Murs. RDn (1874–1964), Clay. RDn (1964–68), Murs. RDn (1968–*).

TAPLOW
AP *LG* Seq 9. Civ bdry: 1934.[3] *Parl* Seq 9. Parl bdry: 1945.[196] *Eccl* Seq 5. Eccl bdry: 1867 (help cr Dropmore EP).[57]

TATTENHOE
Chap in Lavendon AP, sep civ identity early, sep eccl since 1636 as Donative.[171] *LG* Seq 13. Civ bdry: 1974 (loses pt in Milt. Keyn. Dist to Shenley Brook End CP, loses pt in Aylb. Vale Dist to Whaddon AP).[55] *Parl* Seq 6. *Eccl* Murs. RDn (1636–1855), N Murs. RDn (1855–74), Murs. RDn (1874–1964), Wolv. RDn (1964–70), Buck. RDn (1970–*).

TERRIERS
EP Cr 1937 from High Wycombe AP.[172] Wyc. RDn. Bdry: 1973.[173]

THORNBOROUGH
AP *LG* Seq 7. Civ bdry: 1934.[3] *Parl* Buck. Parl Bor (1832–85), Seq 6 thereafter. *Eccl* Seq 2.

THORNTON
AP *LG* Seq 7. *Parl* Seq 6. *Eccl* Buck. RDn. Abol eccl 1854 when united with Nash chap of Whaddon AP to cr Thornton and Nash EP, often now called 'Nash and Thornton'.[147]

THORNTON AND NASH
EP Cr 1854 by union Thornton AP, Nash chap of Whaddon AP.[147] Buck. RDn (1854–55), Stony Stratf. RDn (1855–65), Buck. RDn Second Dv (1865–74), Buck. RDn (1874–1915), Wolv. RDn (1915–70), Buck. RDn (1970–*). Now often called 'Nash and Thornton'.

TINGEWICK
AP *LG* Seq 7. *Parl* Buck. Parl Bor (1832–85), Seq 6 thereafter. *Eccl* Seq 1.

TOWERSEY
Chap in Thame AP, Oxon, sep civ identity early in Bucks (Ash. Hd), sep EP 1841.[174] *LG* Thame PLU, RSD, Long Cren. RD. Transf 1934 to Oxon except for pt left in Bucks to help cr Longwick cum Ilmer CP.[175] *Parl* Mid Dv (1885–1918), Aylb. Dv (1918–48), Oxon thereafter. *Eccl* Pec jurisd Dean & Chapter of Lincoln (1841–46), Wend. RDn (1846–55), Wadd. RDn (1855–74), Aylb. RDn (1874–1973), Aston RDn (Oxford AD, 1973–*).

TURVILLE
AP *LG* Seq 15. *Parl* Seq 10. *Eccl* Seq 23.

TURWESTON
AP *LG* Seq 6.[27] *Parl* Seq 6. *Eccl* Seq 1.

TWYFORD
AP Incl hmlt Poundon (sep CP 1866[2]). *LG* Seq 7. *Parl* Seq 6. *Eccl* Buck. RDn (until 1961), Sonning RDn (Berkshire AD, 1961–*).

TYLER'S GREEN
EP Cr 1863 from Hazlemere EP, High Wycombe AP, Penn AP.[111] Amer. RDn (1863–1915), Wyc. RDn (1915–*). Bdry: 1955.[176]

TYRINGHAM
AP *LG* Newp. Hd. *Eccl* Newp. RDn. Abol 1639 to help cr Tyringham with Filgrave.[93]

TYRINGHAM WITH FILGRAVE
Cr 1639 by union Tyringham AP, Filgrave AP.[93] *LG* Seq 16. *Parl* Seq 6. *Eccl* Seq 11.

UPTON CUM CHALVEY
AP Incl Slough (sep CP 1894 [the pt in Slough USD],[89] sep EP 1904 [from Upton cum Chalvey AP, Stoke Poges AP][159]). *LG* Stoke Hd, Eton PLU, pt Slough USD, pt Eton RSD, Eton RD. Addtl civ bdry alt: 1895 (help cr Gerrard's Cross CP),[23] 1900.[177] Abol civ 1901 ent to Wexham AP.[178] *Parl* S'rn Dv (1885–1918). *Eccl* Seq 5. Addtl eccl bdry alt: 1959.[58]

WADDESDON
AP Incl hmlt Westcott (sep CP 1866[2]), hmlt Woodham (sep CP 1866[2]). *LG* Seq 1. Addtl civ bdry

alt: 1886.[21] *Parl* Seq 1. *Eccl* Wadd. RDn (until 1855), Clay. RDn (1855–74), Wadd. RDn (1874–1973). Abol eccl 1973 to help cr Waddesdon with Over Winchendon and Fleet Marston EP.[143]

WADDESDON WITH OVER WINCHENDON AND FLEET MARSTON
EP Cr 1973 by union Waddesdon AP, Over Winchendon AP, Fleet Marston AP.[143] Wadd. RDn.

WALTON
AP *LG* Seq 16. *Parl* Aylb. Parl Bor (1804–85), Seq 6 thereafter. *Eccl* Newp. RDn (until 1855), Newp. RDn Second Dv (1855–74), Blet. RDn (1874–1970), Milt. Keyn. RDn (1970–74). Abol eccl 1974 pt to help cr Woughton EP, pt to help cr Wavendon with Walton EP.[34]

WALTON HOLY TRINITY
EP Cr 1846 from Aylesbury AP.[19] Wend. RDn (1846–55), Wend. RDn Second Dv (1855–65), Aylb. RDn (1865–*). Bdry: 1955.[25]

WARRINGTON
Hmlt in Olney AP, sep CP 1866.[2] *LG* Seq 16. Civ bdry: 1886.[14] *Parl* Seq 6.

WATER EATON
Twnshp in Bletchley AP, sep CP 1866,[2] sep EP 1974.[34] *LG* Newp. Hd, Newp. Pagn. PLU, RSD, RD. Abol civ 1934 ent to Bletchley AP.[3] *Parl* N'rn Dv (1885–1918), Buck. Dv (1918–48). *Eccl* Milt. Keyn. RDn.

WAVENDON
AP *LG* Seq 16. Civ bdry: 1885,[179] 1907 (help cr Woburn Sands CP),[180] 1956 (incl exchanges pts with Hulcote and Salford CP, Beds),[52] 1965 (gains pt Aspley Heath CP, Beds).[181] *Parl* Seq 6. *Eccl* Newp. RDn (until 1855), Newp. RDn Second Dv (1855–74), Blet. RDn (1874–1970), Milt. Keyn. RDn (1970–74). Abol eccl 1974 to help cr Wavendon with Walton EP.[34]

WAVENDON WITH WALTON
EP Cr 1974 by union Wavendon AP, pt Walton AP, pt Bow Brickhill AP.[34] Milt. Keyn. RDn.

WEEDON
Hmlt in Hardwick AP, sep CP 1866.[2] *LG* Seq 10. Bdry: 1883,[20] 1886.[21] *Parl* Seq 1.

WENDOVER
AP *LG* Aylb. Hd, Wend. Bor, Wyc. PLU, RSD, Aylb. RD. Civ bdry: 1885,[30] 1911,[134] 1934.[3] *Parl* Wend. Parl Bor (1300–09, 1625–1832), Aylb. Parl Bor (1804–85), Seq 1 thereafter. *Eccl* Seq 19.

WESTBURY
AP *LG* Seq 6.[27] Civ bdry: 1884.[182] *Parl* Seq 6. *Eccl* Seq 1.

WESTCOTT
Hmlt in Waddesdon AP, sep CP 1866.[2] *LG* Seq 1. *Parl* Seq 1.

WESTON TURVILLE
AP Incl chap Lee (sep par by 1535 [eccl, 'The Lee'][183]). *LG* Seq 4. Addtl civ bdry alt: 1958.[162] *Parl* Aylb. Parl Bor (1804–85), Seq 1 thereafter. *Eccl* Wend. RDn (until 1855), Wend. RDn Second Dv (1855–65), Aylb. RDn (1865–1974). Wend. RDn (1974–*).

WESTON UNDERWOOD
Chap in Olney AP, sep civ identity early, sep EP 1778.[150] *LG* Seq 16. *Parl* Seq 6. *Eccl* Seq 11.

WEXHAM
AP *LG* Seq 16. Civ bdry: 1901,[178] 1934,[3] 1974 (the pt transf to Berks cr Wexham Court CP).[55] *Parl* Seq 9. *Eccl* Seq 5.

WHADDON
AP Incl hmlt Nash (sep CP 1866,[2] eccl severed 1854 to help cr Thornton and Nash EP[147]). *LG* Seq 13. Addtl civ bdry alt: 1974 (loses pt in Milt. Keyn. Dist to Shenley Brook End CP).[55] *Parl* Seq 6. *Eccl* Murs. RDn (until 1855), N Murs. RDn (1855–74), Murs. RDn (1874–1964), Wolv. RDn (1964–70), Buck. RDn (1970–*).

WHITCHURCH
AP *LG* Seq 10. *Parl* Seq 1. *Eccl* Seq 9. Incl eccl Creslow (which maintained sep civ identity) after latter's eccl suppression *temp* Eliz. I.[83]

WILLEN
AP *LG* Newp. Hd, Newp. Pagn. PLU, RSD, RD. Abol civ 1934 to help cr Woolstone cum Willen CP.[3] *Parl* N'rn Dv (1885–1918), Buck. Dv (1918–48). *Eccl* Newp. RDn (until 1855), Newp. RDn Second Dv (1855–74), Blet. RDn (1874–1958), Newp. RDn (1958–70), Milt. Keyn. RDn (1970–*). Eccl bdry: 1973.[184]

LOWER WINCHENDON
Chap in Long Crendon AP, sep civ identity early. Usual civ spelling; for eccl spelling and sep eccl status see following entry. *LG* Seq 1. *Parl* Seq 1.

NETHER WINCHENDON
Chap in Long Crendon AP, sep EP 1744.[33] Usual eccl spelling; for civ see prev entry. *Eccl* Seq 16.

OVER WINCHENDON
AP Usual eccl spelling; for civ see following entry. *Eccl* Wadd. RDn. Abol eccl 1973 to help cr Waddesdon with Over Winchendon and Fleet Marston EP.[143]

UPPER WINCHENDON
AP Usual civ spelling; for eccl see prev entry. *LG* Seq 1. *Parl* Seq 1.

WING
AP *LG* Seq 12. Civ bdry: 1956.[102] *Parl* Seq 5. *Eccl* Murs. RDn (until 1855), S Murs. RDn (1855–74), Iving. RDn (1874–1964), Murs. RDn (1964–73). Abol eccl 1973 to help cr Wing with Grove EP.[103]

WING WITH GROVE
EP Cr 1973 by union Wing AP, Grove AP.[103] Murs. RDn.

WINGRAVE
AP Usual eccl spelling; for civ see following entry. *Eccl* Seq 7.

WINGRAVE WITH ROWSHAM
AP Usual civ spelling; for eccl see prev entry. *LG* Seq 11. Civ bdry: 1886.[21] *Parl* Seq 1.

WINSLOW
AP Incl chap Granborough (sep par 16th cent[101]), chap Little Horwood (sep par before 1535[112]).

LG Seq 13. Addtl civ bdry alt: 1956.[77] *Parl* Seq 6. *Eccl* Seq 15 (London dioc until 1845, Oxford thereafter).

WOBURN SANDS

CP Cr 1907 from Wavendon AP.[180] *LG* Newp. Pagn. PLU, RD. Civ bdry: 1965 (exchanges pts with Aspley Guise AP, gains pt Aspley Heath CP, both Beds).[181] *Parl* Buck. Dv/CC (1918–*).

WOLVERTON

AP *LG* Newp. Hd, Potterspury PLU,[60] RSD, Stratf. & Wolv. RD (1894–1919), UD (1919–20), Wolv. UD (1920–*). Civ bdry: 1927 (gains the other pars in the UD),[61] 1934.[3] *Parl* Seq 6. *Eccl* Seq 14. Eccl bdry: 1843 (cr Wolverton St George EP),[185] 1870 (help cr Wolverton St Mary EP),[62] 1973.[168]

WOLVERTON ST GEORGE

EP Cr 1843 from Wolverton EP.[185] Newp. RDn (1843–55), Stony Stratf. RDn (1855–65), Buck. RDn Second Dv (1865–74), Buck. RDn (1874–1915), Wolv. RDn (1915–70), Milt. Keyn. RDn (1970–*). Bdry: 1868.[186]

WOLVERTON ST MARY

EP Cr 1870 from Calverton AP, Wolverton AP.[62] Buck. RDn Second Dv (1870–74), Buck. RDn (1874–1915), Wolv. RDn (1915–53). Renamed 1953 'Stony Stratford St Mary the Virgin' EP.[169]

WOOBURN

AP *LG* Seq 15. Civ bdry: 1883,[20] 1934.[3] *Parl* Seq 11. Parl bdry: 1945.[196] *Eccl* Seq 22. Eccl bdry: 1954,[142] 1964,[187] 1974 (cr Bourne End EP).[39]

WOODHAM

Hmlt in Waddesdon AP, sep CP 1866.[2] *LG* Seq 10. Civ bdry: 1886.[21] *Parl* Seq 7.

GREAT WOOLSTONE

AP *LG* Newp. Hd, Newp. Pagn. PLU, RSD, RD. Abol civ 1934 to help cr Woolstone cum Willen CP.[3] *Parl* N'rn Dv (1885–1918), Buck. Dv (1918–48). *Eccl* Newp. RDn (until 1855), Newp. RDn Second Dv (1855–74), Blet. RDn (1874–1958), Newp. RDn (1958–70), Milt. Keyn. RDn (1970–74). Abol eccl 1974 to help cr Woughton EP.[34]

LITTLE WOOLSTONE

AP Organisation as for Great Woolstone AP.

WOOLSTONE CUM WILLEN

CP Cr 1934 by union Great Woolstone AP, Little Woolstone AP, Willen AP.[3] *LG* Newp. Pagn. RD. *Parl* Buck. CC (1948–*).

WORMINGHALL

AP *LG* Seq 2. *Parl* Seq 7. *Eccl* Seq 16.

WOTTON UNDERWOOD

AP *LG* Seq 1. Civ bdry: 1886.[51] *Parl* Seq 7. *Eccl* Wadd. RDn (until 1855), Clay. RDn (1855–74), Wadd. RDn (1874–192). Abol eccl 1921 to help cr Wotton Underwood with Ashendon EP.[8]

WOTTON UNDERWOOD WITH ASHENDON

EP Cr 1921 by union Wotton Underwood AP, Ashendon AP.[8] Wadd. RDn.

WOUGHTON

EP Cr 1974 by union Great Woolstone AP, Little Woolstone AP, Woughton on the Green AP, Simpson AP, pt Walton AP, pt Bow Brickhill AP.[34] Milt. Keyn. RDn.

WOUGHTON ON THE GREEN

AP *LG* Seq 16. *Parl* Seq 6. *Eccl* Newp. RDn (until 1855), Newp. RDn Second Dv (1855–74), Blet. RDn (1874–1970), Milt. Keyn. RDn (1970–74). Eccl bdry: 1973.[37] Abol eccl 1974 to help cr Woughton EP.[34]

WRAYSBURY–See WYRARDISBURY

WYCOMBE

Area of the Bor/MB of Chepping Wycombe, in Chepping Wycombe AP, sep CP 1866.[2] *LG* Wyc. PLU, Chepping Wyc. MB, USD. Abol 1896 to help cr High Wycombe CP.[188] *Parl* Chepping Wyc. Parl Bor (1866–85), S'rn Dv (1885–1918).

CHEPPING WYCOMBE

AP Usual civ spelling; for eccl see 'High Wycombe'. Incl Wycombe (area of Bor/MB, sep CP 1866[2]). *LG* Desb. Hd, Wyc. PLU, pt Chepping Wyc. Bor/MB, pt Wyc. RSD, pt Chepping Wyc. USD. Abol civ 1894 the pt in the MB to cr Chepping Wycombe Urban CP, the remainder to cr Chepping Wycombe Rural CP.[89] *Parl* Chepping Wyc. Parl Bor (pt 1300–1832, ent 1832–85), S'rn Dv (1885–1918).

CP Renaming 1949 of Chepping Wycombe Rural CP.[189] *LG* Wyc. RD. *Parl* Wyc. CC (1970–*).

CHEPPING WYCOMBE RURAL

CP Cr 1894 from the pt of Chepping Wycombe AP not in Chepping Wyc. MB.[89] *LG* Wyc. PLU, RD. Civ bdry: 1901,[190] 1928.[113] 1934.[3] Renamed 1949 'Chepping Wycombe'.[189] *Parl* Wyc. Dv/CC (1918–70). Parl bdry: 1945.[196]

CHEPPING WYCOMBE URBAN

CP Cr 1894 from the pt of Chepping Wycombe AP in Chepping Wyc. MB.[89] *LG* Wyc. PLU, Chepping Wyc. MB. Abol 1896 to help cr High Wycombe CP.[188]

HIGH WYCOMBE

AP Usual eccl spelling; for civ see 'Chepping Wycombe'. *Eccl* Wyc. RDn (until 1855), Amer. RDn (1855–74), Wyc. RDn (1874–*). Eccl bdry: 1792 (cr Loudwater EP),[139] 1847 (help cr Hazlemere EP),[110] 1863 (help cr Tyler's Green EP),[111] 1897 (cr High Wycombe Christ Church EP),[191] 1937 (cr Terriers EP),[172] 1919,[192] 1955,[176] 1967 (gains High Wycombe Christ Church EP),[193] 1968.[114]

CP Cr 1896 by union Chepping Wycombe Urban CP, Wycombe CP.[188] *LG* Wyc. PLU, Chepping Wyc. MB (1896–1946), High Wyc. MB (1946–74). Bdry: 1901,[190] 1928,[113] 1934.[3] *Parl* Wyc. Dv/CC (1918–*). Parl bdry: 1945.[196]

HIGH WYCOMBE CHRIST CHURCH

EP Cr 1897 from High Wycombe AP.[191] Wyc. RDn. Bdry: 1919.[192] Abol 1967 ent to High Wycombe AP.[193]

WEST WYCOMBE

AP *LG* Desb. Hd, Wyc. PLU, RSD, RD. Civ bdry: 1901,[190] 1928.[113] Abol civ 1934 pt to help cr West Wycombe Rural CP, pt to High Wycombe CP, pt to Fingest AP, pt to Hughenden AP.[3] *Parl* S'rn Dv (1885–1918), Wyc. Dv (1918–45). *Eccl* Seq 23. Eccl bdry: 1867 (help cr Lane End EP),[95] 1968.[114]

WEST WYCOMBE RURAL

CP Cr 1934 from Hugenden AP, West Wycombe AP.[3] *LG* Wyc. RD. *Parl* Wyc. CC (1948–*).

WYRARDISBURY

AP Incl chap Langley Marish (sep civ identity early, sep EP 1856[129]; Colnbrook EP cr from Langley Marish chap 1853 before latter a sep EP[81]). Sometimes 'Wraysbury', a name more commonly used now. *LG* Seq 17. Addtl civ bdry alt: 1934.[3] Transf 1974 to Berks.[194] *Parl* Seq 9. *Eccl* Seq 5.

CAMBRIDGESHIRE

ABBREVIATIONS

Abbreviations particular to Cambridgeshire follow. Those general abbreviations in use throughout the *Guide* are found on page xix.

Abing.	Abingdon
Armingf.	Armingford
Arr.	Arrington
Camb.	Cambridge
Cax.	Caxton
Chatt.	Chatteris
Chest.	Chesterton
Chev.	Cheveley
Chilf.	Chilford
Flend.	Flendish
Ford.	Fordham
Knap.	Knapwell
Melb.	Melbourn
Nwmkt.	Newmarket
Papw.	Papworth
Radf.	Radfield
Stap.	Staploe
Thrip.	Thriplow
Weth.	Wetherley
Whittl.	Whittlesey
Wilb.	Wilbraham
Wisb.	Wisbech
Wittl.	Wittlesford

SEQUENCES

An abbreviated entry prefixed by 'Seq' is used in the parochial entries to avoid repeating often the names of superior units of administration. The content of each sequence is shown below.

Local Government Sequences ('LG')

(Seqs 1–22 were in Cambs Anc Co then in Cambs Adm Co [1889–1965]; Seqs 23–26 were in Cambs Anc Co then in IoE Adm Co [1889–1965]; all were in Cambs & IoE Adm Co [1965–74])

SEQ 1	Armingf. Hd, Cax. PLU, RSD, Cax. & Arr. RD (1894–1934), S Cambs RD (1934–74)
SEQ 2	Armingf. Hd, Royston PLU, RSD, Melb. RD (1894–1934), S Cambs RD (1934–74)
SEQ 3	Chest. Hd, PLU, RSD, RD
SEQ 4	Chev. Hd, Nwmkt. PLU, RSD, RD
SEQ 5	Chilf. Hd, Linton PLU, RSD, RD (1894–1934), S Cambs RD (1934–74)
SEQ 6	Flend. Hd, Chest. PLU, RSD, RD
SEQ 7	Longstow Hd, Cax. PLU, RSD, Cax. & Arr. RD (1894–1934), Chest. RD (1934–74)
SEQ 8	Longstow Hd, Cax. PLU, RSD, Cax. & Arr. RD (1894–1934), S Cambs RD (1934–74)
SEQ 9	Northstow Hd, Chest. PLU, RSD, RD
SEQ 10	Papw. Hd, Cax. PLU, RSD, Cax. & Arr. RD (1894–1934), Chest. RD (1934–74)
SEQ 11	Papw. Hd, St Ives PLU, RSD, Swavesey RD (1894–1934), Chest. RD (1934–74)
SEQ 12	Radf. Hd, Linton PLU, RSD, RD (1894–1934), S Cambs RD (1934–74)
SEQ 13	Radf. Hd, Nwmkt. PLU, RSD, RD
SEQ 14	Staine Hd, Chest. PLU, RSD, RD
SEQ 15	Staine Hd, Nwmkt. PLU, RSD, RD
SEQ 16	Stap. Hd, Nwmkt. PLU, RSD, RD
SEQ 17	Thrip. Hd, Chest. PLU, RSD, RD
SEQ 18	Thrip. Hd, Royston PLU, RSD, Melb. RD (1894–1934), S Cambs RD (1934–74)
SEQ 19	Weth. Hd, Cax. PLU, RSD, Cax. & Arr. RD (1894–1934), S Cambs RD (1934–74)
SEQ 20	Weth. Hd, Chest. PLU, RSD, RD
SEQ 21	Weth. Hd, Royston PLU, RSD, Melb. RD (1894–1934), S Cambs RD (1934–74)
SEQ 22	Wittl. Hd, Linton PLU, RSD, RD (1894–1934), S Cambs RD (1934–74)
SEQ 23	Ely Hd, PLU, RSD, RD

SEQ 24 Wisb. Hd, PLU, RSD, RD
SEQ 25 N Witchf. Hd, PLU, RSD, RD
SEQ 26 S Witchf. Hd, Ely PLU, RSD, RD

Parliamentary Sequences ('Parl')

SEQ 1 E'rn Dv (1885–1918), Cambs Parl Co (1918–70), Cambs & IoE Parl Co (Cambs CC, 1970–*)
SEQ 2 E'rn Dv (1885–1918), IoE Parl Co (1918–70), Cambs & IoE Parl Co (IoE CC, 1970–*)
SEQ 3 N'rn Dv (1885–1918), IoE Parl Co (1918–70), Cambs & IoE Parl Co (IoE CC, 1970–*)
SEQ 4 W'rn Dv (1885–1918), Cambs Parl Co (1918–70), Cambs & IoE Parl Co (Cambs CC, 1970–*)
SEQ 5 W'rn Dv (1885–1918), IoE Parl Co (1918–70), Cambs & IoE Parl Co (IoE CC, 1970–*)

Ecclesiastical Sequences ('Eccl')

(Barton RDn orig called 'Harston' and Knapwell RDn orig called 'Papworth')

In Ely dioc orig:
SEQ 1 Abing. RDn (until 13th cent), Camps RDn (13th cent–1862), Camps RDn Second Dv (1862–99), Camps RDn (1899–*)
SEQ 2 Barton RDn
SEQ 3 Bourn RDn
SEQ 4 Camb. RDn
SEQ 5 Camb. RDn (until 1899), Quy RDn (1899–*)
SEQ 6 Chest. RDn (until 1899), Quy RDn (1899–*)
SEQ 7 Chest. RDn (until 1899), N Stowe RDn (1899–*)
SEQ 8 Ely RDn
SEQ 9 Ely RDn (until 1884), March RDn (1884–*)
SEQ 10 Knap. RDn (until 13th cent), Bourn RDn (13th cent–*)
SEQ 11 Knap. RDn (until 13th cent), Bourn RDn (13th cent–1899), N Stowe RDn (1899–*)
SEQ 12 Shingay RDn
SEQ 13 Wilb. RDn (until 13th cent), Camps RDn (13th cent–1862), Camps RDn First Dv (1862–99), Camps RDn (1899–*)
SEQ 14 Wilb. RDn (until 13th cent), Camps RDn (13th cent–1862), Camps RDn First Dv (1862–99), Quy RDn (1899–*)
SEQ 15 Wilb. RDn (until 13th cent), Camps RDn (13th cent–1862), Ford. RDn Camb. Dv (1862–84), Ford. RDn (1884–1917), Chev. RDn (1917–*)
SEQ 16 Wisb. RDn

In Norwich dioc orig:
SEQ 17 Ford. RDn (until 1862), Ford. RDn Camb. Dv (1862–84), Ford. RDn (1884–*)
SEQ 18 Ford. RDn (until 1862), Ford. RDn Camb. Dv (1862–84), Thurlow RDn (1884–1917), Chev. RDn (1917–*)
SEQ 19 Ford. RDn (until 1862), Ford. RDn Suffolk Dv (1862–84), Mildenhall RDn (1884–1917), Ford. RDn (1917–*)

DIOCESE AND ARCHDEACONRIES

All Cambs pars are in Ely dioc except a few noted below in the parochial entries and those in Fordham RDn (in Norw dioc until 1837, in Ely thereafter). The RDns were arranged in ADs as follows.

ELY AD
Abing. RDn (until 13th cent), Barton RDn,[1] Bourn RDn, Camb. RDn, Camps RDn (13th cent–1837), Camps RDn (1899–*), Camps RDn First Dv (1877–99), Camps RDn Second Dv (1877–99), Chest. RDn (until 1899), Chev. RDn (1917–*), Ford. RDn (1914–*), Harston RDn,[1] Knap. RDn[2] (until 13th cent), Papw. RDn,[2] Quy RDn (1899–*), Shingay RDn, N Stowe RDn (1899–*), Wilb. RDn (until 13th cent)

ISLE OF ELY AD (1884–1915[3])
Ely RDn, March RDn,[4] Wisb. RDn

SUDBURY AD[5]
Camps RDn (1837–62), Camps RDn First Dv (1862–77), Camps RDn Second Dv (1862-77), Ford. RDn (until 1862), Ford. RDn (1884–1914), Ford. RDn Camb. Dv (1862–84), Ford. RDn Suffolk Dv (1862–84), Mildenhall RDn (1884–1914), Thurlow RDn (1884–1914)

WISBECH AD (1915–*[3])
Ely RDn, March RDn, Wisb. RDn

THE PARISHES OF CAMBRIDGESHIRE

GREAT ABINGTON
AP *LG* Seq 5. *Parl* Seq 1. *Eccl* Seq 1.

LITTLE ABINGTON
AP *LG* Seq 5. *Parl* Seq 1. *Eccl* Seq 1.

ABINGTON PIGOTTS
AP *LG* Seq 2. *Parl* Seq 4. *Eccl* Seq 12.

ARRINGTON
AP *LG* Seq 19. *Parl* Seq 4. *Eccl* Seq 2.

ASHLEY
AP *LG* Chev. Hd. *Eccl* Ford. RDn. United before 1535 with Silverley AP, union civ called 'Ashley' but eccl 'Ashley with Silverley',[6] qv. After 1535: *LG* Seq 4. *Parl* Seq 1.

ASHLEY WITH SILVERLEY
AP Usual eccl name for union before 1535 of Ashley AP, Silverley AP (for civ see prev entry).[6] *Eccl* Ford. RDn (before 1535–1862), Ford. RDn Camb. Dv (1862–84), Ford. RDn (1884–1917), Chev. RDn (1917–*).

BABRAHAM
AP *LG* Seq 5. *Parl* Seq 1. *Eccl* Seq 1.

BALSHAM
AP *LG* Seq 12. *Parl* Seq 1. *Eccl* Seq 13.

BAR HILL
CP Cr 1966 from Dry Drayton AP.[7] *LG* Chest. RD. *Parl* Cambs CC (1970–*).

BARRINGTON
AP *LG* Seq 21. *Parl* Seq 4. *Eccl* Seq 2.

BARTLOW
AP *LG* Seq 5. Civ bdry: 1965 (exchanges pts with Ashdon AP, Essex).[8] *Parl* Seq 4. *Eccl* Seq 1.

BARTON
AP *LG* Seq 20. *Parl* Seq 4. *Eccl* Seq 2.

BASSINGBOURN
AP Incl Hmlt Kneesworth (sep CP 1866[9]; this hmlt incl pt Royston, sep par 1540[10] *LG* Armingf. Hd, Royston PLU, RSD, Melb. RD (1894–1934), S Cambs RD (1934–66). Civ bdry: 1896 (loses pt to cr South Bassingbourn CP, to be in Herts).[11] Abol civ 1966 to help cr Bassingbourn cum Kneesworth CP.[12] *Parl* W'rn Dv (1885–1918). *Eccl* Seq 12. Eccl bdry: 1890.[13]

BASSINGBOURN CUM KNEESWORTH
CP Cr 1966 by union Bassingbourn AP, Kneesworth CP.[12] *LG* S Cambs RD. *Parl* Cambs CC (1970–*).

BENWICK
Chap in Doddington AP, sep EP 1847,[14] sep CP 1866.[9] *LG* Seq 25. Civ bdry: 1965 (gains pt Ramsey UD & AP, Hunts & Peterborough).[8] *Parl* Seq 3. *Eccl* Ely RDn (1847–84), March RDn (1884–*).

BOTTISHAM
AP Incl Lode (sep EP 1852 from this par and from Swaffham Bulbeck AP as 'Bottisham Lode and Long Meadow',[15] now usually called 'Lode', sep CP from this par alone 1894[16]). *LG* Seq 15. *Parl* Seq 1. *Eccl* Seq 14.

BOTTISHAM LODE AND LONG MEADOW
EP Cr 1852 from Bottisham AP, Swaffham Bulbeck AP.[15] Camps RDn (1852–62), Camps RDn First Dv (1862–99), Quy RDn (1899–*). Now usually called 'Lode'.

BOURN
AP *LG* Seq 7. Civ bdry: 1949.[17] *Parl* Seq 4. *Eccl* Seq 3.

BOXWORTH
AP *LG* Seq 11. *Parl* Seq 4. *Eccl* Seq 10.

BRINKLEY
AP *LG* Seq 13. Civ bdry: 1885.[18] *Parl* Seq 1. *Eccl* Seq 15.

HELION BUMPSTEAD
AP Pt Essex (Freshwell Hd), pt Cambs (Chilf. Hd), the latter transf 1885 to Castle Camps AP and the par ent in Essex thereafter.[19] See main entry in Essex.

BURROUGH GREEN
AP *LG* Seq 13. *Parl* Seq 1. *Eccl* Seq 15.

BURWELL
Cr in 17th or 18th cent by union Burwell St Andrew AP, Burwell St Mary AP.[20] *LG* Seq 16. Civ bdry: 1954 (help cr Reach CP).[21] *Parl* Seq 1. *Eccl* Ford. RDn (until 1862), Ford. RDn Camb. Dv (1862–84), Ford. RDn (1884–*). Eccl bdry: 1961.[22]

BURWELL ST ANDREW
AP *LG* Stap. Hd. *Eccl* Ford. RDn. Abol in 17th or 18th cent to help cr Burwell CP, EP.[20]

BURWELL ST MARY
AP Organisation as for Burwell St Andrew.

CALDECOTE
AP *LG* Seq 7. Civ bdry: 1949.[17] *Parl* Seq 4. *Eccl* Bourn RDn. Abol eccl 1972 to help cr Caldecote with Childerley EP.[23]

CALDECOTE WITH CHILDERLEY
EP Cr 1972 by union Caldecote AP, Childerley AP.[23] Bourn RDn.

CAMBRIDGE
The following have 'Cambridge' in their names. Insofar as any existed at a given time: *LG* Flend. Hd, PLU, Bor/MB (made a city 1951[58]), USD. *Parl* Camb. Parl Bor/BC (1295–*). *Eccl* Camb. RDn.

CP1–CAMBRIDGE–Cr 1900 by union AP2, AP3, AP4, AP5, AP6, AP7, AP8, AP9, AP10, AP11, AP13, AP14, AP15.[24] Bdry: 1923,[25] 1934.[26]

AP1–CAMBRIDGE ALL SAINTS [BY THE CASTLE]–Abol 1365 ent to AP11.[27]

AP2–CAMBRIDGE ALL SAINTS [IN THE JEWRY or BY THE HOSPITAL]– Abol civ 1900 to help cr CP1.[24] Eccl bdry: between 1248–58 (cr AP17), gained back 1857.[28] Abol eccl 1973 to help cr EP1.[29]

AP3–CAMBRIDGE HOLY SEPULCHRE–Usual civ spelling. Abol civ 1900 to help cr CP1.[24] Eccl, 'St Sepulchre', abol eccl 1973 to help cr EP1.[29]

EP1–CAMBRIDGE HOLY SEPULCHRE WITH ALL SAINTS–Cr 1973 by union AP2, AP3.[29]

AP4–CAMBRIDGE HOLY TRINITY–Civ bdry: 1883.[30] Abol civ 1900 to help cr CP1.[24] Eccl bdry: 1940.[31]

AP5–CAMBRIDGE ST ANDREW THE GREAT–Civ bdry: 1883,[30] 1885.[32] Abol civ 1900 to help cr CP1.[24] Eccl bdry: 1845 (help cr EP10).[33]

AP6–CAMBRIDGE ST ANDREW THE LESS–Sometimes 'Barnwell', parochial in early 13th cent.[34] Civ bdry: 1883,[30] 1885.[32] Abol civ 1900 to help cr CP1.[24] Eccl bdry: 1845 (help cr EP10),[33] 1870 (cr EP9),[36] 1888 (help cr EP2),[35] 1940,[31] 1952.[37]

EP2–CAMBRIDGE ST BARNABAS–Cr 1888 from EP9, EP10, AP6.[35] Eccl bdry: 1903 (cr EP11),[38] 1961 (help cr EP6).[39]

AP7–CAMBRIDGE ST BENEDICT [ST BENE'T] – Civ bdry: 1883.[30] Abol civ 1900 to help cr CP1.[24] Eccl bdry: 1940.[31]

AP8–CAMBRIDGE ST BOTOLPH–Civ bdry: 1885.[32] Abol civ 1900 to help cr CP1.[24] Eccl bdry: 1940.[31]

AP9–CAMBRIDGE ST CLEMENT–Abol civ 1900 to help cr CP1.[24]

AP10–CAMBRIDGE ST EDWARD [eccl, ST EDWARD KING AND MARTYR]–Gains 1446 AP12.[40] Abol civ 1900 to help cr CP1.[24]

AP11–CAMBRIDGE ST GILES–Civ bdry: 1886 (gains AP16).[41] Abol civ 1900 to help cr CP1.[24] Eccl bdry: 1918 (help cr EP6),[42] 1940.[31] Abol eccl 1971 to help cr EP3.[43]

EP3–CAMBRIDGE ST GILES WITH ST PETER–Cr 1971 by union AP11, AP16.[43]

EP4–CAMBRIDGE ST JAMES–Cr 1972 from Cherry Hinton AP, Cherry Hinton St John the Evangelist EP (the latter now commonly called 'Cambridge St John').[44]

EP5–CAMBRIDGE ST JOHN–Common name now for EP cr 1897 as 'Cherry Hinton St John the Evangelist', qv.

AP12–CAMBRIDGE ST JOHN ZACHARY [or ST JOHN BAPTIST]– Abol 1446, united to AP10.[40]

EP6–CAMBRIDGE ST MARK–Cr 1918 from Grantchester AP, AP11.[42] Bdry: 1940.[31]

EP7–CAMBRIDGE ST MARTIN–Cr 1961 from EP2, EP10, EP11, Cherry Hinton AP, Cherry Hinton St John the Evangelist EP (the latter now commonly called 'Cambridge St John').[39]

AP13–CAMBRIDGE ST MARY THE GREAT–Orig 'St Mary the Virgin'. Abol civ 1900 to help cr CP1.[24] Abol eccl 1954 to help cr EP8.[45]

EP8–CAMBRIDGE ST MARY THE GREAT WITH ST MICHAEL–Cr 1954 by union AP13, AP15.[45]

AP14–CAMBRIDGE ST MARY THE LESS–Orig 'St Peter outside Trumpington Gates'. Civ bdry: 1885.[32] Abol civ 1900 to help cr CP1.[24] Eccl bdry: 1940.[31]

EP9–CAMBRIDGE ST MATTHEW–Cr 1870 from AP6.[36] Bdry: 1888 (help cr EP2).[35]

AP15–CAMBRIDGE ST MICHAEL–Abol civ 1900 to help cr CP1.[24] Abol eccl 1954 to help cr EP8.[45]

EP10–CAMBRIDGE ST PAUL– Cr 1845 from AP5, AP6.[33] Eccl bdry: 1888 (help cr EP2),[35] 1940,[31] 1961,[46] 1961 (help cr EP7).[43]

AP16–CAMBRIDGE BY PETER [BY THE CASTLE OR BEYOND THE BRIDGE]– Abol civ 1886 ent to AP11.[41] Abol eccl 1971 to help cr EP3.[43]

–CAMBRIDGE ST PETER OUTSIDE TRUMPINGTON GATES–See AP14

EP11–CAMBRIDGE ST PHILIP–Cr 1903 from EP2.[38] Bdry: 1961 (help cr EP7).[39]

AP17–CAMBRIDGE ST RADEGUND–Cr between 1246–58 from AP2 into which reabsorbed 1857.[28]

–CAMBRIDGE ST SEPULCHRE–See AP3

CP2–CAMBRIDGE WITHOUT–Cr 1912 from Cherry Hinton AP, Grantchester AP, Trumpington AP.[47] *LG* Chest. PLU, RD. Abol 1923 ent to CP1.[25] *Parl* Cambs Parl Co (1918–48).

UNIVERSITY OF CAMBRIDGE
The various colleges were ex-par until 1856, absorbed within the respective pars in which they were situated thereafter. *Parl* Sep Parl Bor (1604–1948).

CASTLE CAMPS
AP *LG* Seq 5. Civ bdry: 1885 (gains the Cambs pt of Helion Bumpstead AP),[19] 1965 (exchanges pts with each of Ashdon AP, Helion Bumpstead AP, Hempstead AP, all in Essex).[8] *Parl* Seq 1. *Eccl* Seq 1.

SHUDY CAMPS
AP *LG* Seq 5. *Parl* Seq 1. *Eccl* Seq 1.

CARLTON
AP Wilb. RDn (until 13th cent), Camps RDn (13th cent–abol), united before 1535 with Willingham AP the union civ called 'Carlton' but eccl 'Carlton cum Willingham'.[48] *LG* Seq 12. *Parl* Seq 1.

CARLTON CUM WILLINGHAM
AP Usual eccl name (for civ see prev entry) of union before 1535 of Carlton AP, Willingham AP.[48] *Eccl* Camps RDn (cr–1862), Camps RDn First Dv (1862–77), Ford. RDn (1877–1917), Chev. RDn (1917–*).

CAXTON
AP *LG* Seq 7. *Parl* Seq 4. *Eccl* Seq 3.

CHATTERIS
AP *LG* N Witchf. Hd, PLU, Chatt. USD, UD. Civ bdry: 1960,[49] 1965 (gains pt Somersham AP, Hunts).[8] *Parl* Seq 3. *Eccl* Seq 9.

CHERRY HINTON
AP *LG* Flend. Hd, Chest. PLU, RSD, RD. Civ bdry: 1912 (help cr Cambridge Without CP).[47] Abol civ 1934 ent to Cambridge CP.[26] *Parl* Seq 1. *Eccl* Seq 4. Eccl bdry: 1897 (help cr Cherry Hinton St John the Evangelist EP [now commonly called 'Cambridge St John']),[50] 1961 (help cr Cambridge St Martin EP),[39] 1972 (help cr Cambridge St James EP).[44]

CHERRY HINTON ST JOHN THE EVANGELIST
EP Cr 1897 from Cherry Hinton AP, Trumpington AP.[50] Camb. RDn. Bdry: 1961,[46] 1961 (help cr Cambridge St Martin EP),[39] 1972 (help cr Cambridge St James EP).[44] Now commonly called 'Cambridge St John'.

CHESTERTON
AP *LG* Chest. Hd, PLU, USD, UD (1894–1912), Camb. MB (1912–23). Civ bdry: 1912 (loses pt to Milton AP and remainder transf to the MB).[47]

Abol civ 1923 ent to Cambridge CP.[25] *Parl* Camb. Parl Bor (pt 1867–1918, ent 1918–48), pt W'rn Dv (1885–1918). *Eccl* Chest. RDn (until 1899), Camb. RDn (1899–*). Eccl bdry: 1881 (cr Chesterton St Luke EP),[51] 1938 (cr Chesterton St George EP),[52] 1966.[53]

CHESTERTON THE GOOD SHEPHERD

EP Cr 1969 from Chesterton St Luke EP.[54] Camb. RDn.

CHESTERTON ST GEORGE

EP Cr 1938 from Chesterton AP.[52] Camb. RDn. Bdry: 1966.[53]

CHESTERTON ST LUKE

EP Cr 1881 from Chesterton AP.[51] Chest. RDn (1881–99), Camb. RDn (1899–*). Bdry: 1940,[31] 1966,[53] 1969 (cr Chesterton The Good Shepherd EP).[54]

CHETTISHAM

EP Chap in Ely St Mary AP, sep EP 1726.[55] Ely RDn. Bdry: 1876.[56]

CHEVELEY

AP *LG* Seq 4. *Parl* Seq 1. *Eccl* Seq 18. Eccl bdry: 1949.[57]

CHILDERLEY

AP *LG* Seq 3. *Parl* Seq 4. *Eccl* Knap. RDn (until 13th cent), Bourn RDn (13th cent–1972). Abol eccl 1972 to help cr Caldecote with Childerley EP.[23]

CHIPPENHAM

AP *LG* Seq 16. *Parl* Seq 1. *Eccl* Seq 19.

GREAT CHISHILL

AP Sometimes spelled 'Great Chishall', name declared as above 1929.[58] In Essex (Uttlesford Hd), transf 1895 to Cambs.[59] *LG* Royston PLU, sep RD (1894–95), Melb. RD (1895–1934), S Cambs RD (1934–68). Civ bdry: 1965 (exchanges pts with Chrishall AP, Essex).[11] Abol civ 1968 to help cr Great and Little Chishill CP.[60] *Parl* In Essex until 1918, Cambs Parl Co (1918–70). *Eccl* Newport RDn (until 1847), Saffron Walden RDn (1847–*) and thus in London dioc (until 1845), Roch. dioc (1845–1914), Chelm. dioc (1914–*).

GREAT AND LITTLE CHISHILL

CP Cr 1968 by union Great Chishill AP, Little Chishill AP.[60] *LG* S Cambs RD. *Parl* Cambs CC (1970–*).

LITTLE CHISHILL

AP Sometimes spelled 'Little Chishall', name declared as above 1929.[58] Organisation as for Great Chishill.

CLAPTON

AP Singay RDn, united prob in 17th cent with Croydon AP the union civ called 'Croydon' but eccl 'Croydon cum Clapton'.[61] See the respective entries.

COATES

EP Cr 1843 from Whittlesey St Mary AP.[62] ElyRDn (1843–84), March RDn (1884–*).

COLDHAM

EP Cr 1874 from Friday Bridge EP.[63] Wisb. RDn.

COMBERTON

AP *LG* Seq 20. *Parl* Seq 4. *Eccl* Seq 2.

CONINGTON

AP *LG* Seq 11. *Parl* Seq 4. *Eccl* Seq 11.

COTON

AP Orig in Grantchester AP, sep par before 13th cent.[64] *LG* Seq 20. *Parl* Seq 4. *Eccl* Seq 2.

COTTENHAM

AP *LG* Seq 3. *Parl* Seq 4. *Eccl* Seq 7.

COVENEY

AP Incl chap Manea (sep CP 1866,[9] sep EP 1883[65]). *LG* Seq 26. Civ bdry: 1884.[66] *Parl* Seq 3. *Eccl* Seq 8.

CROXTON

AP *LG* Seq 7. *Parl* Seq 4. *Eccl* Seq 3.

CROYDON

AP Shingay RDn, united prob in 17th cent with Clapton AP the union civ called 'Croydon' but eccl 'Croydon cum Clapton'.[61] *LG* Seq 1. Civ bdry: 1956.[67] *Parl* Seq 4.

CROYDON CUM CLAPTON

EP Usual eccl name (for civ see prev entry) for union prob in 17th cent of Croydon AP, Clapton AP.[61] *Eccl* Shingay RDn.

FEN DITTON

AP *LG* Seq 6. Civ bdry: 1934.[26] *Parl* Seq 1. *Eccl* Seq 5. Eccl bdry: 1952.[37]

WOOD DITTON

AP Incl pt chap Newmarket All Saints (sep civ identity early, sep EP 1747[55]). *LG* Chev. Hd, Nwmkt. PLU, pt Nwmkt. USD, pt Nwmkt. RSD. Becomes 1894 2 sep CPs,[69] one in Cambs (Nwmkt. RD), one in W Suffolk (Nwmkt. UD, abol 1895 ent to Newmarket All Saints CP[68]). *Parl* Seq 1. *Eccl* Seq 17.

DODDINGTON

AP Incl chap Wimblington (sep CP 1866,[9] sep EP 1874[70]), chap March [St Wendreda] (sep CP 1866,[9] sep EP 1868[71]), chap Benwick (sep CP 1866,[9] sep EP 1868[14]). *LG* Seq 25. *Parl* Seq 3. *Eccl* Seq 9. Addtl eccl bdry alt: 1872 (cr March St John EP),[70] 1873 (cr March St Mary EP),[70] 1881 (cr March St Peter EP).[70]

DOWNHAM

AP *LG* Seq 23. Civ bdry: 1933.[72] *Parl* Seq 3. *Eccl* As 'Little Downham', Seq 8. Eccl bdry: 1878 (help cr Littleport St Matthew EP).[73]

LITTLE DOWNHAM–See prev entry

DRY DRAYTON

AP *LG* Seq 3. Civ bdry: 1966 (cr Bar Hill CP).[7] *Parl* Seq 4. *Eccl* Seq 7.

FEN DRAYTON

AP *LG* Seq 11. *Parl* Seq 4. *Eccl* Seq 11.

DULLINGHAM

AP *LG* Seq 13. *Parl* Seq 1. *Eccl* Seq 15.

DUXFORD

The 2 APs of Duxford St John, Duxford St Peter united early for civ purposes as 'Duxford', united eccl 1874.[74] *LG* Seq 22. *Parl* Seq 1. *Eccl* Camps RDn Second Dv (1874–99), Camps RDn (1899–*).

DUXFORD ST JOHN

AP *LG* Wittl. Hd. *Eccl* Abing. RDn (until 13th cent), Camps RDn (13th cent–1862), Camps RDn Second Dv (1862–74). Abol eccl 1874 to help cr Duxford EP.[74]

DUXFORD ST PETER

AP Organisation as for Duxford St John.

ELM

AP Incl chap and hmlt Emneth (pec jurisd Bp of Ely, in Norfolk [Freebridge Marshland Hd], sep civ identity early in Norfolk, sep EP 1841[75]). *LG* Seq 24. Addtl civ bdry alt: 1933,[72] 1934 (gains pt Emneth CP, Norfolk).[76] *Parl* Seq 3. *Eccl* Seq 16. Addtl eccl bdry alt: 1860 (cr Friday Bridge EP).[77]

ELSWORTH

AP *LG* Seq 10. *Parl* Seq 4. *Eccl* Seq 10.

ELTISLEY

AP *LG* Seq 7. *Parl* Seq 4. *Eccl* Seq 3.

ELY COLLEGE

Ex-par place, sep CP 1858.[78] *LG* Ely Hd, PLU (1858[79]–1930), USD, UD. *Parl* Seq 2.

ELY HOLY TRINITY

AP Usual eccl spelling; for civ see 'Ely Trinity'. *Eccl* Ely RDn. Eccl bdry: 1726 (cr Stuntney EP),[55] 1878 (help cr Prickwillow EP).[80] Abol eccl 1938 to help cr Ely Holy Trinity with St Mary EP.[81]

ELY HOLY TRINITY WITH ST MARY

CP Cr 1933 by union Ely Trinity AP, Ely St Mary AP.[82] *LG* Ely UD. Bdry: 1934.[72]

EP Cr 1938 by union Ely Holy Trinity AP, Ely St Mary AP.[81] Ely RDn.

ELY ST MARY

AP *LG* Ely Hd, Bor/MB, USD, UD. Civ bdry: 1884,[83] 1886.[84] Abol civ 1933 to help cr Ely Holy Trinity with St Mary CP.[82] *Parl* E'rn Dv (1885–1918), IoE Parl Co (1918–48). *Eccl* Ely RDn. Abol eccl 1938 to help cr Ely Holy Trinity with St Mary EP.[81] Eccl bdry: 1876,[56] 1878 (help cr Littleport St Matthew EP).[73]

ELY TRINITY

AP Usual civ spelling; for eccl see 'Ely Holy Trinity'. *LG* Ely Hd, Bor/MB, USD, UD. Civ bdry: 1884.[83] Abol civ 1933 to help cr Ely Holy Trinity with St Mary CP.[82] *Parl* E'rn Dv (1885–1918), IoE Parl Co (1918–48). *Eccl* As for Ely St Mary, incl bdry alt.

GREAT EVERSDEN

AP *LG* Seq 8. *Parl* Seq 4. *Eccl* Seq 3.

LITTLE EVERSDEN

AP *LG* Seq 8. *Parl* Seq 4. *Eccl* Seq 3.

EXNING WITH LANDWADE

Exning AP (Suffolk, Lackford Hd) incl chap Landwade (Cambs), sep civ identity early, qv, no sep eccl identity.

FORDHAM

AP *LG* Seq 16. Civ bdry: 1953.[85] *Parl* Seq 1. *Eccl* Seq 17.

FOWLMERE

AP *LG* Seq 18. Civ bdry: 1965 (gains pt Chrishall AP, Essex).[8] *Parl* Seq 4. *Eccl* Seq 2.

FOXTON

AP *LG* Seq 18. *Parl* Seq 4. *Eccl* Seq 2.

FRIDAY BRIDGE

EP Cr 1860 from Elm AP.[77] Wisb. RDn. Bdry: 1874 (cr Coldham EP).[63]

FULBOURN

The 2 APs of Fulbourn All Saints, Fulbourn St Vigoris united 1765 for civ purposes,[86] 1876 for eccl purposes.[87] *LG* Seq 6. *Parl* Seq 1. *Eccl* Camb. RDn.

FULBOURN ALL SAINTS

AP *LG* Flend. Hd. *Eccl* Camb. RDn. Abol civ 1765,[86] eccl 1876,[87] to help cr Fulbourn CP, EP respectively.

FULBOURN ST VIGORIS

AP Organisation as for Fulbourn All Saints.

GAMLINGAY

AP *LG* Seq 8. Civ bdry: 1958,[88] 1965 (loses pts to Everton AP, Tempsford AP, both Beds, pt to Tetworth AP, Hunts, gains pt Waresley AP, Hunts).[89] *Parl* Seq 4. *Eccl* Seq 3.

GIRTON

AP *LG* Seq 9. Civ bdry: 1934,[90] 1953,[91] 1954.[92] *Parl* Seq 4. *Eccl* Seq 7. Eccl bdry: 1961.[93]

GOREFIELD

EP Cr 1870 from Leverington AP.[94] Wisb. RDn.

LITTLE GRANSDEN

AP *LG* Seq 8. *Parl* Seq 4. *Eccl* Exempt jurisd of Bp until end 19th cent,[95] thereafter Bourn RDn (until 1928), St Neots RDn (Huntingdon AD, 1928–*).

GRANTCHESTER

AP Incl Coton (sep par by 13th cent[64]). *LG* Seq 20. Civ bdry: 1912 (help cr Cambridge Without CP),[47] 1934.[26] *Parl* Seq 4. *Eccl* Seq 2.

GRAVELEY

AP *LG* Papw. Hd, St Neots PLU, RSD, RD, Cax. & Arr. RD (1894–1934), Chest. RD (1934–74). *Parl* Seq 4. *Eccl* Seq 10.

GRUNTY FEN

Ex-par place, sep CP 1858.[78] *LG* S Witchf. Hd, Ely PLU (1858[79]–1930), RSD, RD. Bdry: 1886.[84] Abol 1933 ent to Wilburton AP.[72] *Parl* W'rn Dv (1885–1918), IoE Parl Co (1918–48).

GUYHIRNE WITH RINGSEND

EP Cr 1749 from Wisbech St Peter AP.[96] Wisb. RDn.

HADDENHAM

AP *LG* Seq 26. *Parl* Seq 5. *Eccl* Seq 8.

HARDWICK

AP *LG* Seq 7. *Parl* Seq 4. *Eccl* Seq 3.

HARLTON

AP *LG* Seq 20. *Parl* Seq 4. *Eccl* Seq 2.

HARSTON

AP *LG* Seq 17. Civ bdry: 1934.[90] *Parl* Seq 4. *Eccl* Seq 2.

HASLINGFIELD

AP *LG* Seq 20. Civ bdry: 1934.[26] *Parl* Seq 4. *Eccl* Seq 2.

HATLEY

CP Cr 1957 by union East Hatley AP, Hatley St George AP, pt Taplow AP.[97] *LG* S Cambs RD. Bdry: 1958.[88] *Parl* Cambs CC (1970–*).

EAST HATELY

AP *LG* Armingf. Hd, Cax. PLU, RSD, Cax. & Arr. RD (1894–1934), S Cambs RD (1934–57). Abol civ 1957 to help cr Hatley CP.[97] *Parl* W'rn Dv (1885–1918), Cambs Parl Co (1918–70). *Eccl* Seq 12.

HATLEY ST GEORGE
AP *LG* Longstow Hd, Cax. PLU, RSD, Cax. & Arr. RD (1894–1934), S Cambs RD (1934–57). Abol civ 1957 to help cr Hatley CP.[97] *Parl* W'rn Dv (1885–1918), Cambs Parl Co (1918–70). *Eccl* Seq 3.

HAUXTON
AP *LG* Seq 17. Civ bdry: 1934.[90] *Parl* Seq 4. *Eccl* Seq 2.

HEYDON
AP In Essex (Uttlesford Hd), transf 1895 to Cambs.[59] *LG* Royston PLU, RSD, sep RD (1894–95), Melb. RD (1895–1934), S Cambs RD (1934–74). Civ bdry: 1965 (gains pt Chrishall AP, Essex).[8] *Parl* In Essex until 1918, Cambs Parl Co (1918–70), Cambs CC (1970–*). *Eccl* As for Great Chishill.

HILDERSHAM
AP *LG* Seq 5. *Parl* Seq 1. *Eccl* Seq 1.

HINXTON
AP *LG* Seq 22. Civ bdry: 1886.[98] *Parl* Seq 1. *Eccl* Seq 1.

HISTON
The 2 APs of Histon St Andrew, Histon St Etheldreda united late 18th or early 19th cent as 'Histon'.[99] *LG* Seq 3. Civ bdry: 1883,[30] 1886,[100] 1934 (incl gains pt West Walton CP, Norfolk),[90] 1954.[92] *Parl* Seq 4. *Eccl* Chest. RDn (cr–1899), N Stowe RDn (1899–*). Eccl bdry: 1961.[93]

HISTON ST ANDREW
AP *LG* Chest. Hd. *Eccl* Chest. RDn. Abol late 18th or early 19th cent to help cr Histon CP, EP.[99]

HISTON ST ETHELDREDA
AP Organisation as for Histon St Andrew.

HORNINGSEA
AP *LG* Seq 6. *Parl* Seq 1. *Eccl* Seq 5.

HORSEHEATH
AP *LG* Seq 5. *Parl* Seq 1. *Eccl* Seq 1.

ICKLETON
AP *LG* Seq 22. Civ bdry: 1886,[19] 1965 (gains pt Chrishall AP, exchanges pts with Great Chesterford AP, both Essex).[8] *Parl* Seq 1. *Eccl* Seq 1.

IMPINGTON
AP *LG* Seq 9. Civ bdry: 1883,[30] 1886,[100] 1912,[101] 1934,[26] 1953.[91] *Parl* Seq 4. *Eccl* Seq 7. Eccl bdry: 1961.[93]

ISLEHAM
AP *LG* Seq 16. *Parl* Seq 1. *Eccl* Pec jurisd of King's College, Cambridge (until 1852), Ford. RDn (1852–62), Ford. RDn Camb. Dv (1862–84), Ford. RDn (1884–*).

KENNETT
AP *LG* Seq 16. *Parl* Seq 1. *Eccl* Seq 19.

KINGSTON
AP *LG* Seq 8. *Parl* Seq 4. *Eccl* Seq 3.

KIRTLING
AP *LG* Seq 4. *Parl* Seq 1. *Eccl* Seq 18.

KNAPWELL
AP *LG* Seq 10. *Parl* Seq 4. *Eccl* Seq 10.

KNEESWORTH
Hmlt in Bassingbourn AP, sep CP 1866.[9] Incl pt Royston, sep par 1540.[10] *LG* Armingf. Hd, Royston PLU, RSD, Melb. RD (1894–1934), S Cambs RD (1934–66). Bdry: 1896 (loses pt to cr South Kneesworth CP, to be in Herts).[11] Abol 1966 to help cr Bassingbourn cum Kneesworth CP.[12] *Parl* W'rn Dv (1885–1918), Cambs Parl Co (1918–70).

LAND COMMON TO ELY TRINITY AND ELY ST MARY–See respective pars for organisation; abol 1933 pt to help cr Ely Holy Trinity with St Mary CP, pt to Downham CP, pt to Littleport AP, pt to Witchford AP.[72]

LANDBEACH
AP *LG* Seq 9. *Parl* Seq 4. *Eccl* Seq 6.

LANDWADE
Chap (Cambs, Stap. Hd) in Exning AP (Suffolk, Lackford Hd), sep civ identity early, no sep eccl identity. *LG* Nwmkt. PLU, RSD, RD. Abol 1953 ent to Fordham AP.[85] *Parl* E'rn Dv (1885–1918), Cambs Parl Co (1918–70).

LEVERINGTON
AP Incl chap Parson Drove (sep CP 1866,[9] sep EP 1870[94]). *LG* Seq 24. Addtl civ bdry alt: 1933,[72] 1934 (gains pt Walsoken AP, Norfolk).[76] *Parl* Seq 3. *Eccl* Seq 16. Addtl eccl bdry alt: 1869 (help cr Wisbech St Augustine EP),[55] 1870 (cr Gorefield EP, help cr Southea cum Murrow EP).[94]

LINTON
AP *LG* Mediev Bor, status not sustained,[102] Seq 5. Civ bdry: 1965 (exchanges pts with Hadstock AP, gains pt Great Chesterford AP, both Essex).[8] *Parl* Seq 1. *Eccl* Seq 1.

LITLINGTON
AP *LG* Seq 2. *Parl* Seq 4. *Eccl* Seq 12.

LITTLEPORT
AP *LG* Seq 23. Civ bdry: 1885 (gains pt Hilgay AP, Norfolk),[103] 1933.[72] *Parl* Seq 3. *Eccl* Seq 8. Eccl bdry: 1866 (help cr Little Ouse EP),[104] 1878 (help cr Prickwillow EP),[80] 1878 (help cr Littleport St Matthew EP).[73]

LITTLEPORT ST MATTHEW
EP Cr 1878 from Littleport AP, Ely St Mary AP, Ely Holy Trinity EP, Downham AP.[73] Ely RDn.

LODE
Area cr sep EP 1852 as 'Bottisham Lode and Long Meadow' qv (from Bottisham AP, Swaffham Bulbeck AP),[15] usually eccl called 'Lode' now, sep CP 1894 as 'Lode' (from Bottisham AP).[16] *LG* Nwmkt. PLU, RD. *Parl* Cambs Parl Co (1918–70), Cambs CC (1970–*).

LOLWORTH
AP *LG* Northstow Hd, St Ives PLU, RSD, Swavesey RD (1894–1934), Chest. RD (1934–74). *Parl* Seq 4. *Eccl* Seq 11.

LONGSTANTON
CP Cr 1953 by union Long Stanton All Saints AP, Long Stanton St Michael AP.[105] *LG* Chest. RD. *Parl* Cambs CC (1970–*).

LONGSTOWE
AP *LG* Seq 8. *Parl* Seq 4. *Eccl* Seq 3.

MADINGLEY
AP *LG* Seq 9. *Parl* Seq 4. *Eccl* Seq 7.

MANEA
Chap in Coveney AP, sep CP 1866,[9] sep EP 1883.[65] *LG* S Witchf. Hd, N Witchf. PLU, RSD, RD. Civ bdry: 1884,[106] 1960.[49] *Parl* Seq 3. *Eccl* Ely RDn (1883–84), March RDn (1884–*).

MARCH
Chap in Doddington AP, sep CP 1866,[9] sep EP [St Wendreda] 1868.[71] *LG* N Witchf. Hd, PLU, March USD, UD. Civ bdry: 1933,[72] 1935.[76] *Parl* Seq 3. *Eccl* Ely RDn (1868–84), March RDn (1884–*).

MARCH ST JOHN
EP Cr 1872 from Doddington AP.[70] Ely RDn (1872–84), March RDn (1884–*).

MARCH ST MARY
EP Cr 1873 from Doddington AP.[70] Ely RDn (1873–84), March RDn (1884–*).

MARCH ST PETER
EP Cr 1881 from Doddington AP.[70] Ely RDn (1881–84), March RDn (1884–*).

MELBOURN
AP Incl pt Royston, sep par 1540.[10] *LG* Seq 2. Civ bdry: 1883,[30] 1896 (cr South Melbourn CP, to be in Herts).[11] *Parl* Seq 4. *Eccl* Seq 12. Eccl bdry: 1890.[13]

MELDRETH
AP *LG* Seq 2. Civ bdry: 1883,[30] 1955.[107] *Parl* Seq 4. *Eccl* Seq 12.

MEPAL
AP *LG* Seq 26. Civ bdry: 1884.[83] *Parl* Seq 5. *Eccl* Seq 8.

MILTON
AP *LG* Seq 9. Civ bdry: 1912,[47] 1912,[101] 1934.[26] *Parl* Seq 4. *Eccl* Seq 6.

GUILDEN MORDEN
AP *LG* Seq 2. *Parl* Seq 4. *Eccl* Seq 12.

STEEPLE MORDEN
AP *LG* Seq 2. *Parl* Seq 4. *Eccl* Seq 12.

NEWMARKET ALL SAINTS
Chap in Newmarket St Mary AP (Suffolk, Lackford Hd), Wood Ditton AP, sep civ identity early in Cambs, sep EP 1747.[55] *LG* Chev. Hd, Nwmkt. PLU, USD. Civ bdry: 1885.[108] Transf 1889 to W Suffolk.[109] *Parl* E'rn Dv (1885–1918), W Suffolk thereafter. *Eccl* Ford. RDn (1747–1862), Ford. RDn Camb. Dv (1862–84), Ford. RDn (1884–1914), Thurlow RDn (1914–16), Nwmkt. RDn (1916–*), and thus in St Edm & Ipsw dioc from 1914. Eccl bdry: 1870,[139] 1948,[140] 1949.[57]

NEWTON
AP *LG* Seq 17. *Parl* Seq 4. *Eccl* Seq 2.

NEWTON
AP Usual civ spelling; for eccl see following entry. *LG* Seq 24. Civ bdry: 1934 (gains pt West Walton AP, Norfolk).[76] *Parl* Seq 3.

NEWTON IN THE ISLE
AP Usual eccl spelling; for civ see previous entry. *Eccl* Seq 16.

OAKINGTON
AP Incl Hmlt Westwick (sep CP 1866[9]). *LG* Pt Chest. Hd (Westwick), pt Northstow Hd (ent from 1866), Chest. PLU, RSD, RD. Addtl civ bdry alt: 1954.[92] *Parl* Seq 4. *Eccl* Seq 7.

ORWELL
AP *LG* Seq 19. *Parl* Seq 4. *Eccl* Seq 2.

LITTLE OUSE
EP Cr 1866 from Littleport AP and from Norfolk pars of Hilgay AP, Feltwell St Mary and St Nicholas EP, pt Feltwell Anchor ex-par place, to be in Ely dioc.[104] Ely RDn. Bdry: 1878 (help cr Prickwillow EP).[80]

OUTWELL
AP Incl chap Welney (prob of 17th cent origin, sep EP 1862,[110] sep CP 1866[9]). *LG* Pt Cambs (IoE, Wisb. Hd), pt Norfolk (Clackclose Hd), Wisb. PLU, RSD. Divided 1889 into 2 CPs, one in ea co,[111] qv. *Parl* Cambs pt N'rn Dv (1885–1918). *Eccl* Fincham RDn (until 1917), Wisb. RDn (1917–*) and thus in Norw. dioc until 1914 (Norfolk AD until 1894, Lynn AD 1894–1914) and Ely dioc from 1914 (IoE AD 1914–15, Wisb. AD thereafter). Eccl bdry: 1909 (from Norfolk area, help cr Nordleph EP).[129]
CP Cr 1888 from Cambs pt of Outwell AP.[111] *LG* Wisb. PLU, RSD, RD. Civ bdry: 1934 (exchanges pts with Emneth CP, Norfolk).[76] *Parl* IoE Parl Co (1918–70), IoE CC (1970–*).

OVER
AP *LG* Seq 11. *Parl* Seq 4. *Eccl* Seq 7.

PAMPISFORD
AP *LG* Seq 5. *Parl* Seq 1. *Eccl* Seq 1.

PAPWORTH EVERARD
AP *LG* Seq 10. Civ bdry: 1904.[112] *Parl* Seq 4. *Eccl* Seq 10.

PAPWORTH ST AGNES
AP Pt Cambs (Papw. Hd), pt Hunts (Toseland Hd), the latter transf 1895 to Cambs.[113] *LG* Cax. PLU, RSD, pt sep RD in Hunts (1894–95), Cax. & Arr. RD (pt 1894–95, ent 1895–1934), Chest. RD (1934–74). Addtl civ bdry alt: 1904.[112] *Parl* Cambs pt, W'rn Dv (1885–1918), Cambs Parl Co (1918–70), Cambs CC (1970–*). *Eccl* Seq 10.

PARSON DROVE
Chap in Leverington AP, sep CP 1866,[9] sep EP 1870.[94] *LG* Seq 24. Civ bdry: 1934 (exchanges pts with Sutton St Edmunds CP, gains pt Tydd St Mary AP, both Lincs [Pts of Holland]).[76] *Parl* Seq 3. *Eccl* Wisb. RDn.

POND'S BRIDGE
EP Cr 1866 from Whittlesey St Andrew with St Guthlac AP , Stanground AP (Cambs, Hunts), and from Hunts pars of Ramsey AP, Ramsey St Mary EP.[114] St Ives RDn (Huntingdon AD).

PRICKWILLOW
EP Cr 1878 from Ely Holy Trinity AP, Littleport AP, Little Ouse EP (Cambs, Norfolk), and from Suffolk pars of Mildenhall AP, Lakenheath AP, to be in Ely dioc.[80] Ely RDn.

QUY
AP Wilb. RDn, united before 13th cent with Stow AP to cr Stow cum Quy AP,[116] eccl usually called 'Quy'.

RAMPTON
AP *LG* Seq 9. Civ bdry: 1884.[117] *Parl* Seq 4. *Eccl*

Seq 12.

RAMSEY

AP Pt Hunts (Hurstingstone Hd), pt Cambs (IoE, N Witchford Hd), considered ent Hunts by 1871.[137] See main entry in Hunts.

REACH

CP Cr 1954 from Burwell CP, Swaffham Prior CP.[21] *LG* Nwmkt. RD. *Parl* Cambs CC (1970–*).

REDMERE

Ex-par place in Norfolk (Clackclose Hd), sep CP 1858,[78] transf. 1895 to IoE.[59] *LG* Ely PLU, RSD, sep RD (1894–95), Ely RD (1895–1933). Abol 1933 ent to Littleport AP.[72] *Parl* Norfolk until 1918, IoE Parl Co (1918–48).

ROYSTON

AP Dist in Cambs APs (Armingf. Hd) of Melbourn, Kneesworth (in Bassingbourn Hmlt) and in Herts APs (Odsey Hd) of Barkway, Reed, Therfield, sep par 1540.[10] *LG* Royston PLU, RSD, pt Royston RD in Herts (1894–96), pt sep RD in Cambs (1894–96). Civ bdry: 1896 (Cambs pt cr North Royston CP to be in Herts),[11] and main pt of par ent Herts thereafter, qv for main entry. *Parl* Cambs pt, W'rn Dv (1885–1918), Herts thereafter. *Eccl* See main entry in Herts.

SAWSTON

AP *LG* Seq 22. *Parl* Seq 1. *Eccl* Seq 1.

GREAT SHELFORD

AP *LG* Seq 17. Civ bdry: 1934.[26] *Parl* Seq 4. *Eccl* Seq 2.

LITTLE SHELFORD

AP *LG* Seq 17. *Parl* Seq 4. *Eccl* Seq 2.

SHEPRETH

AP *LG* Seq 21. *Parl* Seq 4. *Eccl* Seq 2.

SHINGAY

AP *LG* Armingf. Hd, Royston PLU, RSD, Melb. RD (1894–1934), S Cambs RD (1934–57). Civ bdry: 1956.[67] Abol civ 1957 to help cr Shingay cum Wendy CP.[118] *Parl* W'rn Dv (1885–1918), Cambs Parl Co (1918–70). *Eccl* Seq 12.

SHINGAY CUM WENDY

CP Cr 1957 by union Shingay AP, Wendy AP.[118] *LG* S Cambs RD. *Parl* Cambs CC (1970–*).

SILVERLEY

AP *LG* Chev. Hd. *Eccl* Ford. RDn. United before 1535 with Ashley AP, union civ called 'Ashley' but eccl 'Ashley with Silverley'.[6]

SNAILWELL

AP *LG* Seq 16. *Parl* Seq 1. *Eccl* Ford. RDn (until 1862), Ford. RDn Suffolk Dv (1862–84), Ford. RDn (1884–*).

SOHAM

AP Usual civ spelling; for eccl see following entry. *LG* Seq 16. *Parl* Seq 1.

SOHAM WITH BARWAY

AP Usual eccl spelling; for civ see prev entry. *Eccl* Seq 17.

SOUTHEA CUM MURROW

EP Cr 1870 from Leverington AP, Wisbech St Mary EP.[119] Wisb. RDn.

STANGROUND

AP Pt Hunts (Norman Cross Hd), pt Cambs (IoE, N Witchford Hd), the Hunts pt cr 1905 'Stanground South' CP, the IoE pt 'Stanground North' CP.[121] Incl chap Farcet (sep EP 1851,[138] sep CP in Hunts 1866[9]). *LG* Peterborough PLU, RSD, pt Thorney RD in IoE (1894–1905), pt Norman Cross RD in Hunts (1894–1905). *Parl* Cambs pt, N'rn Dv (1885–1918). *Eccl* Yaxley RDn (Huntingdon AD).

STANGROUND NORTH

CP Cr 1905 from the IoE pt of Stanground AP.[121] *LG* Peterborough PLU, Thorney RD. *Parl* IoE Parl Co (1918–70), IoE CC (1970–*).

LONG STANTON ALL SAINTS

AP *LG* Northstow Hd, Chest. PLU, RSD, RD. Abol civ 1953 to help cr Longstanton CP.[105] *Parl* W'rn Dv (1885–1918), Cambs Parl Co (1918–70). *Eccl* Chest. RDn (until 1899), N Stowe RDn (1899–1959). Abol eccl 1959 to help cr Long Stanton St Michael and All Saints EP.[122]

LONG STANTON ST MICHAEL

AP Organisation as for Long Stanton All Saints.

LONG STANTON ST MICHAEL AND ALL SAINTS

EP Cr 1959 by union Long Stanton St Michael AP, Long Stanton All Saints AP.[122] N Stowe RDn.

STAPLEFORD

AP *LG* Seq 17. *Parl* Seq 4. *Eccl* Seq 2.

STETCHWORTH

AP *LG* Seq 13. *Parl* Seq 1. *Eccl* Seq 15.

STOW

AP Wilb. RDn, united before 13th cent with Quy AP to cr Stow cum Quy AP,[116] eccl usually called 'Quy'.

STOW CUM QUY

AP Cr before 13th cent by union Stow AP, Quy AP.[116] *LG* Seq 14. *Parl* Seq 1. *Eccl* Usually called 'Quy', Seq 14.

STRETHAM

AP Incl chap Thetford (sep CP 1866,[9] no sep eccl identity). *LG* Seq 26. *Parl* Seq 5. *Eccl* As 'Stretham with Little Thetford', Seq 8.

STRETHAM WITH LITTLE THETFORD–see prev entry

STUNTNEY

Chap in Ely Holy Trinity AP, sep EP 1726.[55] Ely RDn.

SUTTON

AP *LG* Seq 26. *Parl* Seq 5. *Eccl* Seq 8.

SWAFFHAM BULBECK

AP *LG* Seq 15. *Parl* Seq 1. *Eccl* Wilb. RDn (until 13th cent), Camps RDn (13th cent–1862), Camps RDn First Dv (1862–84), Ford. RDn Camb. Dv (1884–1917), Ford. RDn.

SWAFFHAM PRIOR

Cr 1667 by union Swaffham Prior St Mary AP, Swaffham Prior St Cyriac and St Jolitta AP.[123] *LG* Seq 15. Civ bdry: 1954 (help cr Reach CP).[21] *Parl* Seq 1. *Eccl* Camps RDn (1667–1862), Camps RDn First Dv (1862–99), Quy RDn (1899–1917), Ford. RDn (1917–*). Eccl bdry: 1961.[22]

SWAFFHAM PRIOR ST CYRIAC

AP *LG* Staine Hd. *Eccl* Wilb. RDn (until 13th cent), Camps RDn (13th cent–abol). Abol before

1535 to help cr Swaffham Prior St Cyriac and St Jolitta.[124]

SWAFFHAM PRIOR ST CYRIAC AND ST JOLITTA
AP Cr before 1535 by union Swaffham Prior St Cyriac AP, Swaffham Prior St Jolitta AP.[124] *LG* Staine Hd. *Eccl* Camps RDn. Abol 1667 to help cr Swaffham Prior.[123]

SWAFFHAM PRIOR ST JOLITTA
AP Organisation as for Swaffham Prior St Cyriac.

SWAFFHAM PRIOR ST MARY
AP *LG* Staine Hd. *Eccl* Wilb. RDn (until 13th cent), Camps RDn (13th cent–1667). Abol 1667 to help cr Swaffham Prior.[123]

SWAVESEY
AP *LG* Mediev bor, status not sustained,[125] Seq 11. *Parl* Seq 4. *Eccl* Seq 11.

TADLOW
AP *LG* Seq 1. Civ bdry: 1958 (help cr Hatley CP).[97] *Parl* Seq 4. *Eccl* Seq 12.

TEVERSHAM
AP *LG* Seq 6. *Parl* Seq 1. *Eccl* Seq 5.

THETFORD
Chap in Stretham AP, sep CP 1866,[9] no sep eccl identity. *LG* Seq 26. Civ bdry: 1933.[72] *Parl* Seq 5.

THORNEY
AP Usual civ spelling; for eccl see following entry. *LG* Wisb. Hd, Peterborough PLU, RSD, Thorney RD. Civ bdry: 1933.[72] *Parl* Seq 3.

THORNEY ABBEY
AP Usual eccl spelling; for civ see prev entry. *Eccl* Pec jurisd (until 1852), Seq 16 thereafter.

THRIPLOW
AP *LG* Seq 18. *Parl* Seq 4. *Eccl* Seq 2.

TOFT
AP *LG* Seq 7. *Parl* Seq 4. *Eccl* Seq 3.

TRUMPINGTON
AP *LG* Thrip. Hd, Chest. PLU, RSD, RD. Civ bdry: 1912 (help cr Cambridge Without CP).[47] Abol civ 1934 pt to Cambridge CP, pt to Grantchester AP, pt to Haslingfield AP.[26] *Parl* W'rn Dv (1885–1918), Cambs Parl Co (1918–48). *Eccl* Barton RDn (until 1961), Camb. RDn (1961–*). Eccl bdry: 1897 (help cr Cherry Hinton St John the Evangelist EP, now commonly called 'Cambridge St John').[50]

TYDD ST GILES
AP *LG* Seq 24. Civ bdry: 1934 (exchanges pts with Tydd St Mary AP, Lincs [Pts of Holland], gains pt from West Walton AP, loses pt to Walpole St Peter AP, the last 2 in Norfolk).[76] *Parl* Seq 3. *Eccl* Seq 16.

UPWELL
AP *LG* Pt Cambs (IoE, Wisb. Hd), pt Norfolk (Clackclose Hd), Wisb. PLU, RSD. Civ bdry: 1884.[126] Divided 1889 into 2 CPs, one in each co,[111] qv. *Parl* Cambs pt, N'rn Dv (1885–1918). *Eccl* Fincham RDn (until 1917), Wisb. RDn (1917–*)(ADs as for Outwell). Eccl bdry: 1866 (cr Upwell Christ Church EP),[127] 1909 (help cr Nordelph EP from the Norfolk pt of the par).[128]
CP Cr 1888 from the IoE pt of Upwell AP.[111] *LG* Wisb. PLU, RSD, RD. Bdry: 1934 (loses pt to Upwell CP, Norfolk).[76] *Parl* IoE Parl Co (1918–70), IoE CC (1970–*).

UPWELL CHRIST CHURCH
EP Cr 1869 from Upwell AP.[127] Fincham RDn (1869–1917), March RDn (1917–*)(ADs as for Outwell).

WATERBEACH
AP *LG* Seq 9. *Parl* Seq 4. *Eccl* Seq 6.

WELCHES DAM
Ex-par place, sep CP 1858.[78] *LG* S Witchf. Hd, N Witchf. PLU, RSD, RD. Abol 1960 pt to Chatteris AP, pt to Manea CP.[49] *Parl* N'rn Dv (1885–1918), IoE Parl Co (1918–70).

WELNEY
Chap in Outwell AP prob of 17th cent origin,[115] sep EP 1862,[110] sep CP 1866.[9] *LG* Pt in Cambs (IoE, Wisb. Hd), pt in Norfolk (Clackclose Hd), Downham PLU, RSD. Divided 1889 into 2 sep CPs, one for each co,[111] qv. *Parl* Cambs pt, N'rn Dv (1885–1918). *Eccl* Fincham RDn (1862–1917), March RDn (1917–*)(ADs as for Outwell).
CP Cr 1888 from the IoE pt of Welney CP.[111] *LG* Downham PLU, RSD, sep RD (1894–95), transf 1895 to Norfolk as 'West Welney'.[59]

WENDY
AP *LG* Armingf. Hd, Royston PLU, RSD, Melb. RD (1894–1934), S Cambs RD (1934–57). Civ bdry: 1956.[67] Abol civ 1957 to help cr Shingay cum Wendy CP.[118] *Parl* Seq 4. *Eccl* Shingay RDn. Abol eccl before 1535 to help cr Wendy with Shingay EP.[129]

WENDY WITH SHINGAY
EP Cr before 1535 by union Wendy AP, Shingay AP.[129] Shingay RDn.

WENTWORTH
AP *LG* Seq 26. Civ bdry: 1884,[130] 1896.[84] *Parl* Seq 5. *Eccl* Seq 8.

WESTLEY WATERLESS
AP *LG* Seq 13. *Parl* Seq 1. *Eccl* Seq 15.

WESTON COLVILLE
AP *LG* Seq 12. *Parl* Seq 1. *Eccl* Seq 15.

WESTWICK
Hmlt in Oakington AP, sep CP 1866.[9] *LG* Chest. Hd, PLU (1866[79]–1930), RSD, RD. *Parl* Seq 4.

WHADDON
AP *LG* Seq 2. Civ bdry: 1955.[107] *Parl* Seq 4. *Eccl* Seq 12.

WHITTLESEY
CP Cr 1926 by union Whittlesey Rural CP, Whittlesey Urban CP.[131] *LG* Whittl. PLU, UD. Bdry: 1933.[72] *Parl* IoE Parl Co (1948–70), IoE CC (1970–*).

WHITTLESEY RURAL
CP Cr 1894 from the pt of Whittlesey St Mary and St Andrew CP not in Whittl. USD.[132] *LG* Whittl. PLU, RD. Abol 1926 to help cr Whittlesey CP.[131] *Parl* IoE Parl Co (1918–48).

WHITTLESEY ST ANDREW
AP *LG* N Witchf. Hd, Whittl. PLU. Abol civ 1850 to help cr Whittlesey St Mary and St Andrew

CP.[133] *Eccl* Seq 9. Eccl bdry: 1866 (help cr Pond's Bridge EP).[114]

WHITTLESEY ST MARY

AP *LG* N Witchf. Hd, Whittl. PLU. Abol civ 1850 to help cr Whittlesey St Mary and St Andrew CP.[133] *Eccl* Seq 9. Eccl bdry: 1843 (cr Coates EP).[62]

WHITTLESEY ST MARY AND ST ANDREW

CP Cr 1850 by union Whittlesey St Mary AP, Whittlesey St Andrew AP.[133] *LG* N Witchf. Hd, Whittl. PLU, pt Whittl. USD, pt Whittl. RSD. Bdry: 1883.[30] Abol 1894 the pt in the USD to cr Whittlesey Urban CP, the remainder to cr Whittlesey Rural CP.[132] *Parl* N'rn Dv (1885–1918).

WHITTLESEY URBAN

CP Cr 1894 from the pt of Whittlesey St Mary and St Andrew CP in Whittl. USD.[132] *LG* Whittl. PLU, UD. Abol 1926 to help cr Whittlesey CP.[131] *Parl* IoE Parl Co (1918–48).

WHITTLESFORD

AP *LG* Seq 22. *Parl* Seq 1. *Eccl* Seq 1.

WICKEN

AP *LG* Seq 16. *Parl* Seq 1. *Eccl* Seq 17.

WEST WICKHAM

AP *LG* Seq 5. *Parl* Seq 1. *Eccl* Seq 1.

GREAT WILBRAHAM

AP *LG* Seq 14. *Parl* Seq 1. *Eccl* Seq 14.

LITTLE WILBRAHAM

AP *LG* Seq 14. *Parl* Seq 1. *Eccl* Seq 14.

WILBURTON

AP *LG* Seq 26. Civ bdry: 1933.[72] *Parl* Seq 5. *Eccl* Seq 8.

WILLINGHAM

AP *LG* Papw. Hd, Chest. PLU, RSD, RD. Civ bdry: 1884.[117] *Parl* Seq 4. *Eccl* Seq 7.

WILLINGHAM

AP Wilb. RDn (until 13th cent), Camps RDn (13th cent–abol). United before 1535 with Carlton AP the union civ called 'Carlton' but eccl 'Carlton cum Willingham'.[44]

WIMBLINGTON

Chap in Doddington AP, sep CP 1866,[9] sep EP 1874.[70] *LG* Seq 25. *Parl* Seq 3. *Eccl* Ely RDn (1874), March RDn (1874–84).

WIMPOLE

AP *LG* Seq 19. *Parl* Seq 4. *Eccl* Seq 2.

WISBECH ST AUGUSTINE

EP Chap in Wisbech St Peter and St Paul AP, sep EP 1869 (from that par and from Leverington AP).[55] Wisb. RDn. Bdry: 1971.[134]

WISBECH ST MARY

Chap in Wisbech St Peter AP (eccl, Wisbech St Peter and St Paul), sep civ identity early, sep EP 1854.[135] *LG* Seq 24. Civ bdry: 1933.[72] *Parl* Seq 3. *Eccl* Wisb. RDn.

WISBECH ST PETER

AP Usual civ spelling for eccl see following entry. Incl chap Wisbech St Mary (sep civ identity early, sep EP 1854[135]). *LG* Wisb. Hd, PLU, USD, UD. Addtl civ bdry alt: 1933,[72] 1934 (gains pt Walsoken AP, pt Emneth CP, both Norfolk).[76] *Parl* Seq 3.

WISBECH ST PETER AND ST PAUL

AP Usual eccl spelling for civ see prev entry. Incl chap Wisbech St Mary (sep civ identity early, sep EP 1854[135]). *Eccl* Seq 16. Addtl eccl bdry alt: 1749 (cr Guyhirne with Ringsend EP),[96] 1869 (help cr Wisbech St Augustine EP),[55] 1971.[134]

WITCHAM

AP *LG* S Witchf. Hd, Ely PLU, RSD, RD (ent until 1884, pt 1884–94), USD (pt 1884–94), RD. Civ bdry: 1884 (incl gains pt Ely Trinity AP, pt Ely St Mary AP, and thus this par pt in Ely USD),[136] 1894 (loses the pt in the USD to cr Witcham Gravel CP),[132] 1933.[72] *Parl* Seq 5. *Eccl* Seq 8.

WITCHAM GRAVEL

CP Cr 1894 from the pt of Witcham AP in Ely USD.[132] *LG* Ely PLU, UD. Abol 1933 ent to Witcham AP.[72] *Parl* IoE Parl Co (1918–48).

WITCHFORD

AP *LG* Seq 26. Civ bdry: 1884,[106] 1886,[84] 1933.[72] *Parl* Seq 5. *Eccl* Seq 8.

WEST WRATTING

AP *LG* Seq 12. *Parl* Seq 1. *Eccl* Seq 13.

CORNWALL

ABBREVIATIONS

Abbreviations particular to Cornwall follow; those general abbreviations in use throughout the *Guide* are found on page xix.

Bodm.	Bodmin
Call.	Callington
Camb.	Camborne
Camelf.	Camelford
Carnm.	Carnmarth
Falm.	Falmouth
Helst.	Helston
Kerr.	Kerrier
Launc.	Launceston
Lesnw.	Lesnwith
Lisk.	Liskeard
Lostw.	Lostwithiel
Newq.	Newquay
Pad.	Padstow
Penr.	Penryn
Penw.	Penwith
Penz.	Penzance
Powd.	Powder
Redr.	Redruth
St Aust.	St Austell
St Col. Maj.	St Columb Major
St Germ.	St Germans
Salt.	Saltash
Strat.	Stratton
Trigg Maj.	Trigg Major
Trigg Min.	Trigg Minor
Wadebr.	Wadebridge

SEQUENCES

An abbreviated entry prefixed by 'Seq' is used in the parochial entries to avoid repeating often the names of superior units of administration. The content of each sequence is shown below.

Local Government Sequences ('LG')

SEQ 1 East Hd, Launc. PLU, RSD, RD
SEQ 2 East Hd, Lisk. PLU, RSD, RD
SEQ 3 East Hd, St Germ. PLU, RSD, RD
SEQ 4 Kerr. Hd, Falm. PLU, RSD, E Kerr. RD (1894–1934), Kerr. RD (1934–74)
SEQ 5 Kerr. Hd, Falm. PLU, RSD, E Kerr. RD (1894–1934), Truro RD (1934–74)
SEQ 6 Kerr. Hd, Helst. PLU, RSD, RD (1894–1934), Kerr. RD (1934–74)
SEQ 7 Lesnw. Hd, Camelf. PLU, RSD, RD
SEQ 8 Lesnw. Hd, Launc. PLU, RSD, RD
SEQ 9 Lesnw. Hd, Strat. PLU, RSD, RD
SEQ 10 Penw. Hd, Penz. PLU, RSD, W Penw. RD
SEQ 11 Powd. Hd, St Aust. PLU, RSD, RD
SEQ 12 Powd. Hd, Truro PLU, RSD, RD
SEQ 13 Pyder Hd, Bodm. PLU, RSD, RD (1894–1934), Wadebr. RD (1934–68), Wadebr. & Pad. RD (1968–74)
SEQ 14 Pyder Hd, St Col. Maj. PLU, RSD, RD (1894–1934), St Aust. RD (1934–74)
SEQ 15 Pyder Hd, St Col. Maj. PLU, RSD, RD (1894–1934), Truro RD (1934–74)
SEQ 16 Pyder Hd, St Col. Maj. PLU, RSD, RD (1894–1934), Wadebr. RD (1934–68), Wadebr. & Pad. RD (1968–74)
SEQ 17 Pyder Hd, Truro PLU, RSD, RD
SEQ 18 Strat. Hd,. Bodm. PLU, RSD, RD
SEQ 19 Trigg Hd, Bodm. PLU, RSD, RD (1894–1934), Wadebr. RD (1934–68), Wadebr. & Pad. RD (1968–74)
SEQ 20 Trigg Hd, Camelf. PLU, RSD, RD
SEQ 21 West Hd, Bodm. PLU, RSD, RD (1894–1934), Lisk. RD (1934–74)
SEQ 22 West Hd, Lisk. PLU, RSD, RD

Parliamentary Sequences ('Parl')

SEQ 1 East Dv (1832–85), Mid Dv (1885–1918), N'rn Dv (1918–48), N Cornw CC (1948–*)
SEQ 2 East Dv (1832–85), Mid Dv (1885–1918), Penr. & Falm. Dv (1918–48), Truro CC (1948–*)
SEQ 3 East Dv (1832–85), N-E'rn Dv (1885–1918), Bodm. Dv/CC (1918–*)
SEQ 4 East Dv (1832–85), N-E'rn Dv (1885–1918), N'rn Dv (1918–48), N Cornw CC (1948–*)
SEQ 5 East Dv (1832–85), S-E'rn Dv (1885–1918), Bodm. Dv/CC (1918–*)
SEQ 6 West Dv (1832–85), Mid Dv (1885–1918), N'rn Dv (1918–48), Truro CC (1948–*)
SEQ 7 West Dv (1832–85), Mid Dv (1885–1918), Penr. & Falm. Dv (1918–48), Truro CC (1948–*)
SEQ 8 West Dv (1832–85), Truro Dv (1885–1918), Camb. Dv (1918–48), Falm. & Camb. CC (1948–*)
SEQ 9 West Dv (1832–85), Truro Dv (1885–1918), Penr. & Falm. Dv (1918–48), Truro CC (1948–*)
SEQ 10 West Dv (1832–85), Truro Dv (1885–1918), St Ives Dv/CC (1918–*)
SEQ 11 West Dv (1832–85), W'rn Dv (1885–1918), St Ives Dv/CC (1918–*)

Ecclesiastical Sequences ('Eccl')

SEQ 1 East RDn
SEQ 2 East RDn (until 1875), Trigg Maj. RDn (1875–*)
SEQ 3 East RDn (until 1924), West RDn (1924–*)
SEQ 4 Kerr. RDn
SEQ 5 Kerr. RDn (until 1875), Carnm. RDn (1875–1915), Carnm. N RDn (1915–*)
SEQ 6 Kerr. RDn (until 1875), Carnm. RDn (1875–1915), Carnm. S RDn (1915–*)
SEQ 7 Penw. RDn
SEQ 8 Penw. RDn (until 1875), Carnm. RDn (1875–1915), Carnm. N RDn (1915–*)
SEQ 9 Powd. RDn
SEQ 10 Powd. RDn (until 1875), Bodm. RDn (1915–*)
SEQ 11 Powd. RDn (until 1875), St Aust. RDn (1875–*)
SEQ 12 Pydar RDn
SEQ 13 Pydar RDn (until 1875), Bodm. RDn (1875–*)
SEQ 14 Pydar RDn (until 1875), Powd. RDn (1875–*)
SEQ 15 Trigg Maj. RDn
SEQ 16 Trigg Maj. RDn (until 1875), Strat. RDn (1875–*)
SEQ 17 Trigg Maj. RDn (until 1875), Trigg. Min. RDn (1875–*)
SEQ 18 Trigg. Min. RDn
SEQ 19 Trigg Min. RDn (until 1875), Bodm. RDn (1875–*)
SEQ 20 Trigg Min. RDn (until 1875), Bodm. RDn (1875–1972), Trigg Min. RDn (1972–*)
SEQ 21 West RDn
SEQ 22 West RDn (until 1875), Bodm. RDn (1875–*)

DIOCESES AND ARCHDEACONRIES

With a few exceptions noted below in the parochial entries, Cornwall pars were in Exeter dioc until 1876 and in Truro dioc thereafter. The RDns were organised in ADs as follows:

BODMIN AD (1878–*)
Bodm., East, Strat., Trigg Maj., Trigg Min., West

TRURO AD
Bodm. (until 1878), Carnm. (1876–1915), Carnm. N (1915–*), Carnm. S (1915–*), East (until 1878), Kerr., Penw., Powd., Pydar, St Aust., Strat. (until 1878), Trigg Maj. (until 1878), Trigg. Min. (until 1878), West (until 1878)

THE PARISHES OF CORNWALL

ADVENT
Chap in Lanteglos (eccl, 'Lanteglos by Camelford'), sep civ identity early, no sep eccl identity. *LG* Seq 7. *Parl* Seq 4.

ALTARNON
AP Usual eccl spelling; for civ see following entry. *Eccl* Seq 15. Eccl bdry: 1849 (help cr Bolventor EP).[1]

ALTARNUN
AP Usual civ spelling; for civ see prev entry. *LG* Seq 8. *Parl* Seq 4.

ANTONY
AP Incl chap Torpoint (sep EP 1821,[2] sep CP 1904[3]). *LG* Seq 3. *Parl* Seq 5. *Eccl* Seq 1. Eccl bdry: 1973.[4]

BALDHU
EP Cr 1847 from Kenwyn AP, Kea chap in Kenwyn AP, Chacewater EP.[5] Powd. RDn

BLISLAND
AP *LG* Seq 19. Civ bdry: 1934.[6] *Parl* East Dv

(1832–85), N-E'rn Dv (1885–1918), Bodm. Dv/CC (1918–*). *Eccl* Trigg Min. RDn (until 1875), Bodm. RDn (1875–1972). Abol eccl 1972 to help cr Blisland with Temple EP.[7]

BLISLAND WITH TEMPLE

EP Cr 1972 by union Blisland AP, Temple AP.[7] Bodm. RDn.

BOCONNOC

AP *LG* Seq 22. *Parl* Seq 5. *Eccl* Pec jurisd Dean & Chapter of Exeter (until 1848), Seq 21 thereafter.

BODMIN

AP *LG* Trigg Hd, pt Bodm. Bor/MB (this pt cr 1866 Bodmin Borough CP[8]), Bodm. PLU, RSD, RD. Abol civ 1934 pt to Bodmin Borough CP, pt to help cr Bodmin Rural CP.[6] *Parl* Bodm. Parl Bor (pt 1295–1832, ent 1832–85), S-E'rn Dv (1885–1918), Bodm. Dv (1918–48). *Eccl* Seq 19.

BODMIN BOROUGH

CP Cr 1866 from the pt of Bodmin AP in Bodm. MB.[8] *LG* Bodm. PLU, USD, MB. *Parl* Bodm. Parl Bor (1867–85), S-E'rn Dv (1885–1918), Bodm. Dv/CC (1918–*).

BODMIN RURAL

CP Cr 1934 from Bodmin AP.[6] *LG* Wadebr. RD. Abol 1939 pt to Helland CP, pt to Lanivet AP.[9]

BOLVENTOR

EP Cr 1849 from Altarnon AP, Cardynham AP, St Neot AP.[1] Trigg Maj. RDn.

BOTUS FLEMING

AP *LG* Seq 3. *Parl* Seq 5. *Eccl* Seq 1. Eccl bdry: 1963.[10]

BOYTON

Called both 'par' and 'chap' at early date, sep civ identity clear, certainly EP 1768.[11] Pt Cornw (Strat. Hd), pt Devon (Northcott hmlt in Black Torrington Hd), the latter transf to Devon 1832 for parl purposes, 1844 for civ purposes[12] (became sep CP 1866 in Devon, qv). *LG* Launc. PLU, RSD, RD. Addtl civ bdry alt: 1966 (incl gains pt Northcott CP, pt Luffincott AP, pt St Giles in the Heath AP, all in Devon).[24] *Parl* Cornw pt, Seq 4. *Eccl* Seq 15.

BRADOC

AP Usual eccl spelling; for civ see 'Broadoak'. *Eccl* Pec jurisd Dean & Chapter of Exeter (until 1848), Seq 21 thereafter.

BREAGE

AP Sometimes 'St Breock in Kerrier'. Incl chaps Cury, Gunwalloe, Germoe (each with sep civ identity early, the first two combined 1836 into one EP 'Cury with Gunwalloe',[13] Germoe had no sep eccl identity, hence usual eccl spelling for this par 'Breage with Germoe'; see following entry). *LG* Seq 6. Civ bdry: 1934.[6] *Parl* Seq 10.

BREAGE WITH GERMOE

AP Usual eccl spelling; for civ and other chaps orig in Breage see prev entry. *Eccl* Seq 4. Eccl bdry: 1846 (cr Godolphin EP).[14]

BRIDGERULE

AP Pt Devon (Holsworthy Hd), pt Cornw (Strat. Hd), the latter transf to Devon 1832 for parl purposes, 1844 for civ purposes.[12] See main entry in Devon.

BROADOAK

AP Usual civ spelling; for eccl see 'Bradoc'. *LG* Seq 22. *Parl* Seq 5.

BRYHER

Island in the Isles of Scilly, sep CP 1866.[8] *LG* Isles of Scilly PLU, RSD, RD (technically not pt of Cornw Anc, Adm, or Non-Metrop Co). *Parl* Seq 11.

BUDE HAVEN

EP Cr 1836 from Stratton AP.[15] Trigg. Maj. RDn (1836–75), Strat. RDn (1875–*).

BUDOCK

AP Orig sep par, absorbed eccl into St Gluvias AP by 16th cent and considered its chap until sep EP 1890,[16] sep civ identity maintained. Incl Falmouth (sep par 1664[45]). *LG* Kerr. Hd, Falm. PLU, pt Falm. MB, USD (1892–94), Falm. RSD (ent 1875–92, pt 1892–94). Abol civ 1894 the pt in the MB to cr Budock Urban CP, the remainder to cr Budock Rural CP.[17] *Parl* Penr. Parl Bor (until 1832), pt Penr. & Falm. Parl Bor (1832–1918), pt West Dv (1832–85), pt Truro Dv (1885–1918). *Eccl* Carnm. RDn (1890–1915), Carnm. S RDn (1915–*). Addtl eccl bdry alt: 1848 (when still chap, cr Penwerris EP),[18] 1924 (help cr Falmouth All Saints EP),[19] 1957,[20] 1966.[21]

CP Cr 1934 from Budock Rural CP.[6] *LG* Kerr. RD. *Parl* Falm. & Camb. CC (1948–*).

BUDOCK RURAL

CP Cr 1894 from the pt of Budock CP not in Falm. MB.[17] *LG* Falm. PLU, E Kerr. RD. Abol 1934 pt to Falmouth CP, pt to Penryn CP, pt to cr Budock CP.[6] *Parl* Penr. & Falm. Dv (1918–48).

BUDOCK URBAN

CP Cr 1894 from the pt of Budock CP in Falm. MB.[17] *LG* Falm. PLU, MB. Abol 1920 ent to Falmouth CP.[22] *Parl* Penr. & Falm. Dv (1918–48).

CALLINGTON

Bor in South Hill AP, perhaps sep par early and maintains sep civ identity, no sep eccl identity. *LG* East Hd, Call. Bor,[23] Lisk. PLU, RSD, RD (1894–1901), Call. UD (1901–34), St Germ. RD (1934–74). Civ bdry: 1934.[6] *Parl* Call. Parl Bor (1584–1832), Seq 3 thereafter.

CALSTOCK

AP *LG* East Hd, Tavistock PLU, RSD, RD (1894–1934), St Germ. RD (1934–74). Civ bdry: 1966 (loses pts to Lamerton AP, Tavistock Hamlet CP, both Devon).[24] *Parl* East Dv (1832–85), N-E'rn Dv (1885–1918), N'rn Dv (1918–48), Bodm. CC (1948–*). *Eccl* Seq 1.

CAMBORNE

AP *LG* Penw. Hd, Redr. PLU, Camb. USD, UD. Abol civ 1934 to help cr Camborne-Redruth CP.[6] *Parl* West Dv (1832–85), N-W'rn Dv (1885–1918), Camb. Dv (1918–48). *Eccl* Seq 8. Eccl bdry: 1844 (help cr Tuckingmill EP),[25]

1845 (cr Treslothan EP),[26] 1847 (cr Penponds EP).[27]

CAMBORNE-REDRUTH
CP Cr 1934 by union Camborne AP, pt Gwennap AP, pt Illogan AP.[6] *LG* Camb.-Redr. UD. *Parl* Falm. & Camb. CC (1948–*).

CAMELFORD
CP Cr 1934 from Lanteglos AP (eccl, 'Lanteglos by Camelford').[6] *LG* Camelf. RD. *Parl* N Cornw CC (1948–*).

CARBIS BAY
EP Cr 1948 from Lelant AP.[28] Penw. RDn. Bdry: 1969.[29]

CARDINHAM
AP Usual civ spelling; for eccl see following entry. *LG* West Hd, Bodm. PLU, RSD, RD (1894–1934), Wadebr. RD (1934–68), Wadebr. & Pad. RD (1968–74). Civ bdry: 1934.[6] *Parl* Seq 5.

CARDYNHAM
AP Usual eccl spelling; for civ see prev entry. *Eccl* Seq 22. Eccl bdry: 1849 (help cr Bolventor EP).[1]

CARNMENELLIS
EP Cr 1846 from Wendron AP.[30] Kerr. RDn (1846–1924), Carnm. N RDn (1924–69). Bdry: 1881 (help cr Pencoys EP),[31] 1964.[32] Abol 1969 to help cr Pencoys with Carnmenellis EP.[33]

CHACEWATER
Chap in Kenwyn AP, sep EP 1829,[34] sep CP 1934 (from Kenwyn Rural CP, Kea CP).[6] *LG* Truro RD. *Parl* Truro CC (1948–*). *Eccl* Powd. RDn. Eccl bdry: 1846 (help cr Mithian EP),[35] 1847 (help cr Baldhu EP).[5]

CHARLESTOWN
EP Cr 1846 from St Austell AP.[36] Powd. RDn (1846–75), St Aust. RDn (1875–*).

COLAN
AP Sometimes 'Little Colan'. *LG* Seq 14. Civ bdry: 1934.[6] *Parl* Seq 1. *Eccl* Seq 12.

CONSTANTINE
AP *LG* Seq 4. *Parl* Seq 8. *Eccl* Seq 4.

CORNELLY
AP Anciently 'Grogoth'. Chap in Probus AP, sep par 1532.[37] *LG* Powd. Hd, Truro PLU, RSD, RD. Abol civ 1934 ent to Tregoney CP.[6] *Parl* West Dv (1832–85), Mid Dv (1885–1918), Penr. & Falm. Dv (1918–48). *Eccl* Powd. RDn.

CRANTOCK
AP *LG* Pyder Hd, St Col. Maj. PLU, pt Newq. USD (1892–94), St Col. Maj. RSD (ent 1875–92, pt 1892–94). Abol civ 1894 the pt in the USD to cr Crantock Urban CP, the remainder to cr Crantock Rural CP.[17] *Parl* West Dv (1832–85), Mid Dv (1885–1918). *Eccl* Pydar RDn.

CRANTOCK RURAL
CP Cr 1894 from the pt of Crantock AP not in Newq. USD.[17] *LG* St Col. Maj. PLU, RD. Civ bdry: 1902.[38] Abol 1934 pt to Newquay CP, pt to Cubert AP.[6] *Parl* N'rn Dv (1918–48).

CRANTOCK URBAN
CP Cr 1894 from the pt of Crantock AP in Newq. USD.[17] *LG* St Col. Maj. PLU, Newq. UD. Abol 1902 ent to Newquay CP.[38]

CREED
AP Incl pt Bor and twnshp Grampound (sep CP 1866[8]). *LG* Seq 11. *Parl* Pt Grampound Parl Bor (1553–1824), Seq 7 thereafter. *Eccl* Powd. RD. Renamed 1974 Grampound with Creed EP.[39]

CROWAN
AP *LG* Penw. Hd, Helst. PLU, RSD, RD (1894–1934), Kerr. RD (1934–74). *Parl* West Dv (1832–85), N-W'rn Dv (1885–1918), Camb. Dv (1918–48), Falm. & Camb. CC (1948–*). *Eccl* Penw. RDn (until 1875), Kerr. RDn (1875–*).

CUBERT
AP Sometimes anc 'St Cuthbert'. *LG* Seq 15. Civ bdry: 1934.[6] *Parl* Seq 6. *Eccl* Seq 12.

CUBY
Chap (eccl, 'St Cuby') in Tregoney AP, sep civ identity early, no sep eccl identity. *LG* Pt Tregoney Bor,[23] Powd. Hd, Truro PLU, RSD, RD. *Parl* Pt Tregoney Parl Bor (1295–1307, 1563–1832), Seq 7 thereafter.

CURY
Chap in Breage AP, sep civ identity early; for eccl see following entry. *LG* Seq 6. *Parl* Seq 10.

CURY WITH GUNWALLOE
EP Cr 1836 by union chaps Cury, Gunwalloe, both in Breage AP (eccl, usually 'Breage with Germoe' after cr of this par).[13] Kerr. RDn.

DAVIDSTOW
AP *LG* Seq 7. *Parl* Seq 4. *Eccl* Seq 17.

DEVORAN
EP Cr 1873 from Feock AP.[41] Powd. RDn.

DULOE
AP *LG* Seq 22. *Parl* Seq 5. *Eccl* Seq 21. Eccl bdry: 1851 (help cr Herodsfoot EP).[42]

DUNHEVED–See LAUNCESTON (OTHERWISE DUNHEVED)

EGLOSHAYLE
AP *LG* Seq 19. Civ bdry: 1898 (help cr Wadebridge CP).[43] *Parl* Seq 4. *Eccl* Pec jurisd Bp Exeter (until 1848), Seq 19 thereafter.

EGLOSKERRY
AP Incl chap Tremaine (sep civ identity early, sep EP 1723[44]). *LG* Seq 1. *Parl* Seq 4. *Eccl* Trigg Maj. RDn.

ENDELLION–See ST ENDELLION

FALMOUTH
Cr 1664 from Budock chap of St Gluvias AP.[45] *LG* Kerr. Hd, Falm. PLU, pt Falm. Bor/MB (this pt cr 1866 Falmouth Borough CP),[8] Falm. MB (1892–1974), Falm. Parish USD (1875–92), Falm. USD (1892–94). *Parl* Penr. & Falm. Parl Bor (1832–1918), Penr. & Falm. Dv (1918–48), Falm. & Camb. CC (1948–*). *Eccl* Pec jurisd Bp Exeter (1664–1848), Kerr. RDn (1848–75), Carnm. RDn (1875–1915), Carnm. S RDn (1915–*). Eccl bdry: 1924 (help cr Falmouth All Saints EP).[19]

FALMOUTH ALL SAINTS
EP Cr 1924 from Falmouth EP, Budock EP.[19] Carnm. S RDn (1924–*). Bdry: 1966.[21]

FALMOUTH BOROUGH
CP The pt of Falmouth CP in Falm. Bor/MB, sep CP 1866.[8] Sometimes 'Falmouth Town'. *LG* Falm. PLU, USD, MB. Abol 1920 ent to Falmouth CP.[15] *Parl* Penr. & Falm. Parl Bor (1867–1918), Penr. & Falm. Dv (1918–48).

FEOCK
AP Sometimes 'St Feock'. *LG* Seq 12. *Parl* Seq 9. *Eccl* Seq 9. Eccl bdry: 1873 (help cr Devoran EP).[41]

FLUSHING
EP Cr 1844 from Mylor AP.[46] Kerr. RDn (1844–75), Carnm. RDn (1875–1915), Carnm. S RDn (1915–*).

FORRABURY
AP Abol civ 1919, eccl 1958, in each instance united with Minster AP to cr Forrabury and Minster CP,[47] EP[48] respectively. *LG* Lesnw. Hd, Camelf. PLU, RSD, RD. *Parl* East Dv (1832–85), N-E'rn Dv (1885–1918), N'rn Dv (1918–48). *Eccl* Trigg Min. RDn.

FORRABURY AND MINSTER
Cr civ 1918[47] and eccl 1958[48] by union Forrabury AP, Minster AP. *LG* Camelf. PLU, RD. *Parl* N Cornw CC (1948–*). *Eccl* Trigg Min. RDn.

GERMOE
Chap in Breage AP, sep civ identity early, no sep eccl identity. *LG* Seq 6. *Parl* Seq 10.

GERRANS
AP Usual civ spelling; for eccl see 'St Gerrans'. Incl St Anthony in Roseland (sep civ identiy early, priory church treated after Dissolution in 16th cent as curacy, sometimes as chap in Gerrans AP, but retained sep identity). *LG* Seq 12. Civ bdry: 1934.[6] *Parl* Seq 7.

GODOLPHIN
EP Cr 1846 from Breage with Germoe AP.[14] Kerr. RDn.

GOLANT–See ST SAMPSON

GORRAN
AP Common name formerly 'St Goran'. *LG* Seq 11. Civ bdry: 1934 (help cr St Austell CP).[6] *Parl* Seq 2. *Eccl* Seq 11.

GRADE
AP *LG* Kerr. Hd, Helst. PLU, RSD, RD. Civ bdry: 1882.[49] Abol civ 1934 to help cr Grade Ruan CP.[6] *Parl* West Dv (1832–85), Truro Dv (1885–1918), St Ives Dv (1918–48). *Eccl* Kerr. RDn. Abol eccl 1958 to help cr St Ruan with St Grade EP.[50]

GRADE RUAN
CP Cr 1934 by union Grade AP, Ruan Major AP, Ruan Minor AP.[6] *LG* Kerr. RD. *Parl* St Ives CC (1948–*).

GRAMPOUND
CP Bor and twnshp in Creed AP, Probus AP, sep CP 1866.[8] *LG* Powd. Hd, Grampound Bor,[23] St Aust. PLU, RSD, RD. *Parl* Grampound Parl Bor (1553–1824), East Dv (1867–85), Mid Dv (1885–1918), Penr. & Falm. Dv (1918–48), Truro CC (1948–*).

GRAMPOUND WITH CREED
EP Renaming 1974 of Creed AP.[39] Powd. RDn.

GULVAL
AP Anciently sometimes 'Lanesly'. *LG* Penw. Hd, Penz. PLU, RSD, W Penw. RD. Abol civ 1934 pt to Penzance CP, pt to Madron CP, pt to Ludgvan AP.[6] *Parl* West Dv (1832–1918), St Ives Dv (1918–48). *Eccl* Seq 7.

GUNWALLOE
Chap in Breage AP, sep civ identity early, eccl united 1836 with chap Cury in same par to cr one EP 'Cury with Gunwalloe'.[13] *LG* Seq 6. *Parl* Seq 10.

GWENNAP
AP *LG* Kerr. Hd, Redr. PLU, RSD, RD (1894–1934), Truro RD (1934–74). Civ bdry: 1934 (help cr Camborne-Redruth CP).[6] *Parl* West Dv (1832–85), N-W'rn Dv (1885–1918), Camb. Dv (1918–48), Falm. & Camb. CC (1948–*). *Eccl* Seq 5. Eccl bdry: 1829 (cr St Day EP),[51] 1844 (cr Lannarth EP, now commonly called 'Lanner').[52]

GWINEAR
AP *LG* Penw. Hd, Redr. PLU, RSD, RD. Abol civ 1934 to help cr Gwinear-Gwithian CP.[6] *Parl* West Dv (1832–85), N-W'rn Dv (1885–1918), Camb. Dv (1918–48). *Eccl* Seq 7.

GWINEAR-GWITHIAN
CP Cr 1934 by union Gwinear AP, Gwithian CP.[6] *LG* W Penw. RD. Civ bdry: 1938.[53] *Parl* Falm. & Camb. CC (1948–*).

GWITHIAN
Chap in Phillack AP, sep civ identity early, no sep eccl identity. *LG* Penw. Hd, Redr. PLU, RSD, RD. Abol 1934 to help cr Gwinear-Gwithian CP.[6] *Parl* West Dv (1832–85), N-W'rn Dv (1885–1918), Camb. Dv (1918–48).

HALSETOWN
EP Cr 1846 from St Ives AP.[54] Penw. RDn. Bdry: 1969.[29]

HAYLE
Town and dist in Phillack AP, sep EP 1870,[55] sep CP 1934 as renaming of St Erth Urban CP.[6] *LG* W Penw. RD. Civ bdry: 1935,[56] 1938.[53] *Parl* Falm. & Camb. CC (1948–*). *Eccl* Pewn. RDn.

HELLAND
AP *LG* Seq 19. Civ bdry: 1939.[57] *Parl* Bodm. Parl Bor (1832–85), S-E'rn Dv (1885–1918), Bodm. Dv/CC (1918–*). *Eccl* Seq 19.

HELSTON
Chap and bor in Wendron AP, sep EP 1845,[58] sep CP 1866.[8] *LG* Kerr. Hd, Helst. PLU, MB, USD. Civ bdry: 1934.[6] *Parl* Helst. Parl Bor (1867–85), Truro Dv (1885–1918), Camb. Dv (1918–48), St Ives CC (1948–*). *Eccl* Kerr. RDn.

HERODSFOOT
EP Cr 1851 from Duloe AP, Lannreath AP, St Pinnock AP.[42] West RDn.

HESSENFORD
EP Cr 1834 from St Germans EP.[59] East RDn. Bdry: 1973.[60]

NORTH HILL
AP *LG* Seq 1. *Parl* Seq 4. *Eccl* Seq 2.

SOUTH HILL
AP Incl bor Callington (sep civ identity as CP early, no sep eccl identity, hence usual eccl spelling 'South Hill with Callington', qv). *LG* Seq 2. *Parl* Pt Call. Parl Bor (1584–1832), Seq 3 thereafter.

SOUTH HILL WITH CALLINGTON
AP Usual eccl spelling; for civ see South Hill, Callington. *Eccl* Seq 1.

ILLOGAN
AP *LG* Penw. Hd, Redr. PLU, RSD, RD. Abol civ 1934 pt to help cr Camborne-Redruth CP, pt to St Agnes CP.[6] *Parl* West Dv (1832–85), N-W'rn Dv (1885–1918), Camb. Dv (1918–48). *Eccl* Seq 8. Eccl bdry: 1844 (help cr Tuckingmill EP),[25] 1846 (help cr Mount Hawke EP),[61] 1973.[62]

JACOBSTOW
AP *LG* Seq 18. Civ bdry: 1884.[63] *Parl* Seq 4. *Eccl* Seq 16.

KEA
AP Orig sep par, united with Kenwyn AP by 16th cent and deemed its chap, sep civ identity early, sep EP 1883 as 'St Kea',[64] qv. *LG* Seq 12. Civ bdry: 1934 (help cr Chacewater CP).[6] *Parl* Seq 9.

KENWYN
AP Gains before 16th cent Kea AP (regains sep civ identity early, eccl deemed chap to Kenwyn AP until sep EP 1883 as 'St Kea'[64]); incl chap Chacewater (sep EP 1829,[34] sep CP 1934 [from Kenwyn Rural CP, Kea CP][6]). *LG* Powd. Hd, Truro PLU, pt Truro Bor/MB (enlarged pt 1832–85), pt Truro USD, pt Truro RSD. Abol civ 1894 the pt in the MB to cr Kenwyn Urban CP, the remainder to cr Kenwyn Rural CP.[17] *Parl* Pt Truro Parl Bor (1295–1885), pt West Dv (1832–85), Truro Dv (1885–1918). *Eccl* Sometimes 'Kenwyn with Kea' before latter cr sep EP 1883, Powd. RDn. Addtl eccl bdry alt: 1846 (help cr Mithian EP),[35] 1846 (cr Kenwyn St George EP, now called 'Truro St George'),[65] 1847 (help cr Baldhu EP),[5] 1865 (cr Kenwyn St John EP, now called 'Truro St John'),[66] 1963.[10]
CP Cr 1934 from Tregavethan CP, pt Kenwyn Rural CP.[6] *LG* Truro RD. *Parl* Truro CC (1948–*).

KENWYN RURAL
CP Cr 1894 from the pt of Kenwyn AP not in Truro MB.[17] *LG* Truro PLU, RD. Abol 1934 to help cr 3 CPs of Chacewater, Truro, Kenwyn.[6] *Parl* Camb. Dv (1918–48).

KENWYN ST GEORGE
EP Cr 1846 from Kenwyn AP.[65] Powd. RDn. Bdry: 1963.[10] Now called 'Truro St George'.

KENWYN ST JOHN
EP Cr 1865 from Kenwyn AP.[66] Powd. RDn. Bdry: 1963.[10] Now called 'Truro St John'.

KENWYN URBAN
CP Cr 1894 from the pt of Kenwyn AP in Truro MB.[17] *LG* Truro PLU, MB. Abol 1934 to help cr Truro CP.[6] *Parl* Penr. & Falm. Dv (1918–48).

KENWYN WITH KEA–See KENWYN

KILKHAMPTON
AP *LG* Kilkhampton Bor (status not sustained), Seq 18. Civ bdry: 1934,[6] 1966 (loses pt to Bradworthy AP, exchanges pts with Pancrasweek CP, both Devon).[24] *Parl* Seq 4. *Eccl* Seq 16.

LADOCK
AP *LG* Seq 12. Civ bdry: 1934.[6] *Parl* Seq 2. *Eccl* Seq 9.

LAMORRAN
AP *LG* Powd. Hd, Truro PLU, RSD, RD. Abol civ 1934 ent to St Michael Penkevil AP.[6] *Parl* West Dv (1832–85), Mid Dv (1885–1918), Penr. & Falm. Dv (1918–48). *Eccl* Seq 9. Eccl bdry: 1957.[67]

LAND COMMON TO PHILLEIGH AND RUAN LANIHORNE
See the sep pars for Hd, PLU, RSD. *LG* Truro RD. Abol 1934 pt to each of the pars.[6] *Parl* Penr. & Falm. Dv (1918–48).

LANDEWEDNACK
AP *LG* Seq 6. *Parl* Seq 10. *Eccl* Seq 4.

LANDRAKE WITH ST ERNEY
AP St Erney was the orig mother church of Landrake, united and subordinated to it by 16th cent.[68] *LG* Seq 3. *Parl* Seq 5. *Eccl* Pec jurisd Bp Exeter (until 1848), Seq 1 thereafter.

LANDULPH
AP *LG* Seq 3. *Parl* Seq 5. *Eccl* Seq 1.

LANEAST
AP *LG* Pt East Hd, pt Lesnw. Hd, Launc. PLU, RSD, RD. *Parl* Seq 4. *Eccl* Seq 15.

LANHYDROCK
AP *LG* Seq 13. Civ bdry: 1934.[6] *Parl* Bodm. Parl Bor (1832–85), S-E'rn Dv (1885–1918), Bodm. Dv/CC (1918–*). *Eccl* Seq 13.

LANIVET
AP *LG* Seq 13. Civ bdry: 1939.[57] *Parl* Bodm. Parl Bor (1832–85), S-E'rn Dv (1885–1918), Bodm. Dv/CC (1948–*). *Eccl* Seq 13.

LANLIVERY
AP Incl Penkneth Bor, early absorbed into Lostw. Bor and no sep civ or eccl identity as par. *LG* Powd. Hd, pt Lostw. Bor/MB, Bodm. PLU, pt Lostw. USD, pt Bodm. RSD. Abol civ 1894 the pt in the MB to cr Lanlivery Urban CP, the remainder to cr Lanlivery Rural CP.[17] *Parl* Pt Lostw. Parl Bor (1304–1832), East Dv (1832–85), S-E'rn Dv (1885–1918). *Eccl* Seq 10. Eccl bdry: 1956.[69]
CP Renaming 1934 of Lanlivery Rural CP.[6] *LG* St Aust. RD. *Parl* Bodm. CC (1948–*).

LANLIVERY RURAL
CP Cr 1894 from the pt of Lanlivery AP not in Lostw. MB.[17] *LG* Bodm. PLU, RD. Renamed 1934 'Lanlivery'.[6] *Parl* Bodm. Dv (1918–48).

LANLIVERY URBAN
CP Cr 1894 from the pt of Lanlivery AP in Lostw. MB.[17] *LG* Bodm. PLU, Lostw. MB. Abol 1896 ent to Lostwithiel AP.[70]

LANNARTH
EP Cr 1844 from Gwennap AP.[52] Kerr. RDn (1844–75), Carnm. RDn (1875–1915), Carnm.

N RDn (1915–*). Now commonly called 'Lanner'.

LANNER–See LANNARTH

LANREATH

AP *LG* Seq 22. *Parl* Seq 5. *Eccl* Seq 21. Eccl bdry: 1851 (help cr Herodsfoot EP).[42]

LANSALLOS

AP *LG* Seq 22. Civ bdry: 1934.[6] *Parl* Seq 5. *Eccl* Seq 21.

LANTEGLOS

AP Usual civ spelling; for eccl see 'Lanteglos by Camelford'. Incl chap Advent (sep civ identity early, no sep eccl identity hence eccl often 'Lanteglos by Camelford with St Adwena'). *LG* Lesnw. Hd, pt Camelf. Bor,[23] Camelf. PLU, RSD, RD. Abol civ 1934 pt to cr Camelford CP, pt to Tintagel AP.[6] *Parl* Pt Camelf. Parl Bor (1553–1832), East Dv (1832–85), N-E'rn Dv (1885–1918), N'rn Dv (1918–48).

LANTEGLOS

AP Usual civ spelling; for eccl see 'Lanteglos by Fowey'. *LG* West Hd, pt Fowey Bor,[23] Lisk. PLU, RSD, RD. *Parl* Seq 5.

LANTEGLOS BY CAMELFORD

AP Usual eccl spelling; for civ and sep chap Advent see the first 'Lanteglos' above. *Eccl* Often as 'Lanteglos by Camelford with St Adwena', Seq 18.

LANTEGLOS BY CAMELFORD WITH ST ADWENA–See prev entry

LANTEGLOS BY FOWEY

AP Usual eccl spelling; for civ see second 'Lanteglos' above. *Eccl* Seq 21.

LAUNCELLS

AP *LG* Seq 18. Civ bdry: 1966 (exchanges pts with Pancrasweek CP, gains pt Bridgerule CP, both Devon).[24] *Parl* Seq 4. *Eccl* Seq 16.

LAUNCESTON (OTHERWISE DUNHEVED)

CP Cr 1922 by union St Mary Magdalene AP, Lawhitton Urban CP, St Thomas the Apostle Urban CP, St Thomas Street CP, St Stephens by Launceston Urban CP.[71] *LG* Launc. PLU, MB. *Parl* N Cornw CC (1948–*).

LAUNCESTON ST MARY MAGDALENE

AP Usual eccl spelling; for civ see 'St Mary Magdalene'. Incl chap Launceston St Thomas (sep civ identity early as 'St Thomas the Apostle', sep EP 1726[44]). *Eccl* Seq 15.

LAUNCESTON ST THOMAS

Chap in Launceston St Mary Magdalene AP (civ, 'St Mary Magdalene'), sep civ identity early as 'St Thomas the Apostle' (qv), sep EP 1726.[44] *Eccl* Trigg Maj. RDn.

LAWHITTON

AP *LG* East Hd, Launc. PLU, Launc. Bor/MB (pt until 1835, ent 1835–89, pt 1889–94), Launc. USD (ent 1875–89, pt 1889–94), pt Launc. RSD (1889–94). Abol civ 1894 the pt in the MB to cr Lawhitton Urban CP, the remainder to cr Lawhitton Rural CP.[17] *Parl* Launc. Parl Bor (pt 1295–1832, ent 1832–85), N-E'rn Dv (1885–1918). *Eccl* Pec jurisd Bp Exeter (until 1848), Seq 2 thereafter.

LAWHITTON RURAL

CP Cr 1894 from the pt of Lawhitton AP not in Launc. MB.[17] *LG* Launc. PLU, RD. *Parl* N'rn Dv (1918–48), N Cornw CC (1948–*).

LAWHITTON URBAN

CP Cr 1894 from the pt of Lawhitton AP in Launc. MB.[17] *LG* Launc. PLU, MB. Abol 1922 to help cr Launceston (otherwise Dunheved) CP.7

LAWHITTON URBAN

CP Cr 1894 from the pt of Lawhitton AP in Launc. MB.[17] *LG* Launc. PLU, MB. Abol 1922 to help cr Launceston (otherwise Dunheved) CP.[71] *Parl* N'rn Dv (1918–48).

LELANT

AP Usual eccl spelling; for civ see 'Uny Lelant'. Incl chap St Ives (sep civ identity early, sep EP 1826[44]), chap Towednack (sep civ identity early, sep EP 1902[72]). *Eccl* Seq 7. Addtl eccl bdry alt: 1948 (cr Carbis Bay EP).[28]

LESNEWTH

AP *LG* Seq 7. *Parl* Seq 4. *Eccl* Seq 18.

LEWANNICK

AP *LG* Seq 1. *Parl* Seq 4. *Eccl* Seq 2.

LEZANT

AP *LG* Seq 1. *Parl* Seq 4. *Eccl* Pec jurisd Bp Exeter (until 1848), Seq 2 thereafter.

LINKINHORNE

AP *LG* Seq 2. *Parl* Seq 3. *Eccl* Seq 3.

LISKEARD

AP *LG* West Hd, Lisk. PLU, pt Lisk. Bor (enlarged pt from 1587), pt Lisk. MB (most of which cr 1866 Liskeard Borough CP[8] [the remainder in MB and Lisk. USD added 1884 to Liskeard Borough CP[73]]), Lisk. RSD (pt 1875–84, ent 1884–94), RD. *Parl* Lisk. Parl Bor (pt 1295–1587, enlarged pt 1587–1832, ent 1832–85), S-E'rn Dv (1885–1918), Bodm. Dv/CC (1918–*). *Eccl* Seq 21.

LISKEARD BOROUGH

CP Cr 1866 from most of the pt of Liskeard AP in Lisk. MB.[8] *LG* Lisk. PLU, MB, USD. Civ bdry: 1884 (gains the pts of Liskeard AP and of St Cleer AP in Lisk. MB).[73] *Parl* Lisk. Parl Bor (1867– 85), S-E'rn Dv (1885–1918), Bodm. Dv/CC (1918–*).

LOOE

CP Cr 1934 by union East Looe CP, West Looe CP, pt Talland AP.[6] *LG* Looe UD. *Parl* Bodm. CC (1948–*).

EP Usual name now for EP cr 1845 as 'East and West Looe', qv.

EAST LOOE

CP Chap in St Martin AP (often merely 'Looe'), sep CP 1866[8] (for eccl see following entry). *LG* West Hd, E Looe Bor,[23] Lisk. PLU, RSD, RD (1894–98), Looe UD (1898–1934). Abol 1934 to help cr Looe CP.[6] *Parl* East Dv (1867–85), S-E'rn Dv (1885–1918), Bodm. Dv (1918–48).

EAST AND WEST LOOE

EP Cr 1845 from the areas of East Looe (in St Martin AP) and West Looe (in Talland AP).[74] West RDn. Bdry: 1961.[75] Now usually called

'Looe'.

WEST LOOE

CP Sometimes 'Portbyan' or 'Portbighan'. Town in Talland AP, sep CP 1866[8] (for eccl see prev entry). *LG* West Hd, W Looe Bor,[23] Lisk. PLU, RSD, RD (1894–98), Looe UD (1898–1934). Bdry: 1898.[76] Abol 1934 to help cr Looe CP.[6] *Parl* As for East Looe.

LOSTWITHIEL

AP *LG* Powd. Hd, Bodm. PLU, Lostw. Bor,[77] Bodm. RSD (1875–85), Lostw. MB (1885–1968), USD (1885–94), St Aust. RD (1968–74). Civ bdry: 1896,[70] 1934.[6] *Parl* Lostw. Parl Bor (1304–1832), East Dv (1832–85), S-E'rn Dv (1885–1918), Bodm. Dv/CC (1918–*). *Eccl* Seq 10. Eccl bdry: 1956.[69]

LUDGVAN

AP *LG* Penw. Hd, Penz. PLU, Ludgvan USD, UD (1894–1934), W Penw. RD (1934–74). Civ bdry: 1934.[6] *Parl* Seq 11. *Eccl* Seq 7.

LUXULYAN

AP Sometimes 'Luxulian' but correct spelling as above specified 1934.[6] *LG* Powd. Hd, Bodm. PLU, RSD, RD (1894–1934), St Aust. RD (1934–74). *Parl* Seq 5. *Eccl* Seq 10.

MABE

Chap in Mylor AP, sep civ identity early, sep EP 1868.[78] *LG* Seq 4. Civ bdry: 1934.[6] *Parl* Seq 8. *Eccl* Kerr. RDn (1868–75), Carnm. RDn (1875–1915), Carnm. S RDn (1915–*). Eccl bdry: 1966.[21]

MADRON

AP Incl chap Morvah (sep civ identity early, no sep eccl identity, thus eccl 'Madron with Morvah', qv), chap Penzane (sep EP 1741 as 'Penzance St Mary',[79] most of Madron in Penz. MB cr 1866 Penzance CP[8]). *LG* Penw. Hd, Penz. PLU, pt Penz. Bor/MB (until 1894, reduced pt 1866–94), pt Penz. USD, pt Penz. RSD, Madron UD (1894–1934), W Penw. RD (1934–74). Addtl civ bdry alt: 1894 (the pt in Penz. MB cr Madron in Penzance CP),[17] 1934.[6] *Parl* Seq 11.

MADRON IN PENZANCE

CP Cr 1894 from the pt of Madron AP in Penz. MB.[17] *LG* Penz. PLU, MB. Abol 1934 ent to Penzance CP.[6] *Parl* St Ives Dv (1918–48).

MADRON WITH MORVAN

AP Usual eccl name; for civ and sep of chap Morvah, see Madron, Morvah. *Eccl* Seq 7. Eccl bdry: 1741 (cr Penzance St Mary EP),[79] 1848 (help cr Newlyn St Peter EP).[80]

MAKER

AP Pt Cornw (East Hd), pt Devon (Roborough Hd), the latter transf to Cornw 1832 for parl purposes, 1844 for civ purposes.[12] Incl chap Millbrook (sep EP 1869,[81] sep CP 1896[82]). *LG* St Germ. PLU, RSD, RD. Abol civ 1950 to help cr Maker with Rame CP.[83] *Parl* East Dv (1832–85), S-E'rn Dn (1885–1918), Bodm. Dv/CC (1918–70). *Eccl* East RDn. Eccl bdry: 1878.[84] Abol eccl 1943 to help cr Maker with Rame EP.[85]

MAKER WITH RAME

Cr civ 1950[83] and eccl 1943[85] by union Maker AP, Rame AP. *LG* St Germ. RD. *Parl* Bodm. CC (1970–*). *Eccl* East RDn.

MANACCAN

AP *LG* Seq 6. *Parl* Seq 10. *Eccl* Seq 4.

MARAZION

Chap in St Hilary AP, sep civ identity early, sep EP 1823.[86] *LG* Seq 10. *Parl* West Dv (1867–1918), St Ives Dv/CC (1918–*). *Eccl* Penw. RDn.

MARHAMCHURCH

AP *LG* Seq 18. *Parl* Seq 4. *Eccl* Seq 16.

MAWGAN IN MENEAGE

AP Usual civ spelling; for eccl see 'St Mawgan'. *LG* Seq 6. *Parl* Seq 10.

MAWGAN IN PYDER

AP *LG* Seq 14. Civ bdry: 1934.[6] *Parl* Seq 1. *Eccl* Seq 12.

MAWNAN

AP *LG* Seq 4. Civ bdry: 1934.[6] *Parl* West Dv (1832–85), Truro Dv (1885–1918), Penr. & Falm. Dv (1918–48), Falm. & Camb. CC (1948–*). *Eccl* Kerr. RDn (until 1915), Carnm. S RDn (1915–*).

MENHENIOT

AP *LG* Seq 2. *Parl* Seq 5. *Eccl* Seq 3.

MERTHER

Chap in Probus AP, sep civ identity early, sep EP 1787.[87] *LG* Powd. Hd, Truro PLU, RSD, RD. Abol civ 1934 ent to St Michael Penkevil AP.[6] *Parl* West Dv (1832–85), Mid Dv (1885–1918), Penr. & Falm. Dv (1918–48). *Eccl* Powd. RDn.

MEVAGISSEY

AP *LG* Powd. Hd, St Aust. PLU, RSD, RD. Abol civ 1934 to help cr St Austell CP.[6] *Parl* East Dv (1832–85), Mid Dv (1885–1918), Penr. & Falm. Dv (1918–48). *Eccl* Seq 11.

MICHAELSTOW

AP *LG* Seq 7. *Parl* Seq 4. *Eccl* Seq 18.

MILLBROOK

Chap in Maker AP, sep EP 1869,[81] sep CP 1896.[82] *LG* St Germ. PLU, RD. *Parl* Bodm. Dv/CC (1918–*). *Eccl* East RDn. Eccl bdry: 1878.[84]

MINSTER

AP Abol civ 1919, eccl 1958, in each instance united with Forrabury AP to cr Forrabury and Minster CP,[47] EP[48] respectively. Incl Boscastle Bor (status not sustained), no sep civ or eccl identity as par. *LG* Lesnw. Hd, Camelf. PLU, RSD, RD. *Parl* East Dv (1832–85), N-E'rn Dv (1885–1918). *Eccl* Trigg Min. RDn.

MITHIAN

EP Cr 1846 from Kenwyn AP, Kea chap in Kenwyn AP, Perranzabuloe AP, St Agnes EP, Chacewater EP.[35] Pydar RDn (1846–75), Powd. RDn (1875–*).

MORVAH

Chap in Madron AP, sep civ identity early, no sep eccl identity. *LG* Seq 10. *Parl* Seq 11.

MORVAL

AP *LG* Seq 22. *Parl* Seq 5. *Eccl* Seq 21.

MORWENSTOW
AP *LG* Seq 18. Civ bdry: 1966 (loses pt to Bradworthy AP, Devon).[24] *Parl* Seq 4. *Eccl* Seq 16.
MOUNT HAWKE
EP Cr 1846 from St Agnes EP, Illogan AP.[61] Pydar RDn (1846–75), Carnm. RDn (1875–1915), Carnm. N RDn (1915–58), Powd. RDn (1958–*).
MULLION
AP *LG* Seq 6. *Parl* Seq 10. *Eccl* Seq 4.
MYLOR
AP Incl chap Mabe (sep civ identity early, sep EP 1868[78]). *LG* Seq 5. *Parl* West Dv (ent 1832–67, pt 1867–85), pt Penr. & Falm. Parl Bor (1867–1918), pt Truro Dv (1885–1918), Penr. & Falm. Dv (1918–48), Truro CC (1948–*).
NEWLYN
AP Usual civ spelling; for eccl see following entry. *LG* Incl pt Michell Bor, Seq 15. Civ bdry: 1934.[6] *Parl* Pt Michell Bor (1553–1832), Seq 6 thereafter.
NEWLYN EAST
AP Usual eccl spelling, sometimes 'St Newlyn'; for civ see prev entry. *Eccl* Seq 12.
NEWLYN ST PETER
EP Cr 1848 from Madron AP, Paul AP.[80] Penw. RDn.
NEWQUAY
Chap in St Columb Minor AP, sep CP 1894 (from the pt in Newq. USD),[17] sep EP 1918.[88] *LG* St Col. Maj. PLU, Newq. UD. Civ bdry: 1902,[38] 1934.[6] *Parl* N'rn Dv (1918–48), N Cornw CC (1948–*). *Eccl* Pydar RDn.
OTTERHAM
AP *LG* Seq 7. *Parl* Seq 4. *Eccl* Seq 17.
PADSTOW
AP *LG* Pyder Hd, Pad. Bor (14th cent, status not sustained), St Col. Maj. PLU, pt Pad. USD, pt St Col. Maj. RSD. Abol civ 1894 the pt in the USD to cr Padstow Urban CP, the remainder to cr Padstow Rural CP.[17] *Parl* East Dv (1832–85), Mid Dv (1885–1918). *Eccl* Pec jurisd Bp Exeter (until 1848), Seq 12 thereafter.
CP Renaming 1968 of Padstow Urban CP.[108] *LG* Wadebr. & Pad. RD. *Parl* N Cornw CC (1970–*).
PADSTOW RURAL
CP Cr 1894 from the pt of Padstow AP not in Pad. USD.[17] *LG* St Col. Maj. PLU, RD. Abol 1934 ent to Padstow Urban CP.[6] *Parl* N'rn Dv (1918–48).
PADSTOW URBAN
CP Cr 1894 from the pt of Padstow AP in Pad. USD.[17] *LG* St Col. Maj. PLU, Pad. UD. Renamed 1968 'Padstow' CP.[108] *Parl* N'rn Dv (1918–48), N Cornw CC (1948–70).
PAR
EP Cr 1846 from St Blazey EP, Tywardreath AP, St Austell AP, ex-par Par Harbour and sands.[89] Powd. RDn (1846–75), St Aust. RDn (1875–*).
PAUL
AP Incl Mousehole Bor (status not sustained, no sep civ or eccl identity as par). *LG* Penw. Hd, Penz. PLU, RSD (1875–91), Paul USD (1891–94), UD (1894–1934), W Penw. RD (1934–74). Civ bdry: 1934.[6] *Parl* Seq 11. *Eccl* Seq 7.
PELYNT
AP *LG* Seq 22. *Parl* Seq 5. *Eccl* Seq 21.
PENCOYS
EP Cr 1881 from Carnmenellis EP.[31] Kerr. RDn (1881–1924), Carnm. N RDn (1924–69). Abol 1969 to help cr Pencoys with Carnmenellis EP.[33]
PENCOYS WITH CARNMENELLIS
EP Cr 1969 by union Pencoys EP, Carnmenellis EP.[33] Carnm. N RDn. Abol 1972 ent to Redruth AP.[90]
PENDEEN
EP Cr 1846 from St Just in Penwith AP.[91] Penw. RDn.
PENPONDS
EP Cr 1847 from Camborne AP.[27] Penw. RDn (1847–75), Carnm. RDn (1875–1915), Carnm. N RDn (1915–*).
PENRYN
CP Bor in St Gluvias AP, sep CP 1866.[8] *LG* Kerr. Hd, Falm. PLU, Penr. Bor/MB, USD. Civ bdry: 1934.[6] *Parl* Penr. Parl Bor (1553–1832), Penr. & Falm. Parl Bor (1832–1918), Penr. & Falm. Dv (1918–48), Falm. & Camb. CC (1948–*).
PENWERRIS
EP Cr 1848 from Budock chap in St Gluvias AP.[18] Kerr. RDn (1848–75), Carnm. RDn (1875–1915), Carnm. S RDn (1915–*). Eccl bdry: 1957.[20]
PENZANCE
Bor and chap in Madron AP, sep EP 1741 as 'Penzance St Mary',[79] qv, sep CP 1866.[8] *LG* Penw. Hd, Penz. PLU, pt Penz. USD, pt Madron USD, Penz. MB. Civ bdry: 1894 (the pt in Madron USD cr Penzance in Madron CP),[17] 1934.[6] *Parl* West Dv (1867–1918), St Ives CC (1918–*).
PENZANCE IN MADRON
CP Cr 1894 from the pt of Penzance CP in Madron USD.[17] *LG* Penz. PLU, Madron UD. Abol 1934 ent to Penzance CP.[6] *Parl* St Ives Dv (1918–48).
PENZANCE ST JOHN THE BAPTIST
EP Cr 1882 from Penzance St Mary EP.[93] Penw. RD. Bdry: 1898.[94]
PENZANCE ST MARY
Chap in Madron AP, sep EP 1741,[79] sep CP 1866 as 'Penzance',[8] qv. Penw. RDn. Bdry: 1867 (cr Penzance St Paul EP),[92] 1882 (cr Penzance St John the Baptist EP),[93] 1898.[94] Abol 1973 to help cr Penzance St Mary with St Paul EP.[95]
PENZANCE ST MARY WITH ST PAUL
EP Cr 1973 by union Penzance St Mary EP, Penzance St Paul EP.[95] Penw. RDn.
PENZANZE ST PAUL
EP Cr 1867 from Penzance St Mary EP.[92] Penw. RDn. Bdry: 1958.[94] Abol 1973 to help cr Penzance St Mary with St Paul EP.[95]
PERRAN-AR-WORTHAL–See following entry
PERRANARWORTHAL
Chap in Stithians AP, sep civ identity early as

above, sep curacy and eccl identity early as 'Perran-ar-worthal'. *LG* Seq 5. *Parl* West Dv (1832–85), Truro Dv (1885–1918), Camb. Dv (1918–48), Truro CC (1948–*). *Eccl* Carnm. N RDn.

PERRANUTHNOE

AP *LG* Seq 10. *Parl* Seq 11. *Eccl* Seq 7.

PERRANZABULOE

AP Incl chap St Agnes (sep civ identity early, sep EP 1846[97]). *LG* Seq 17. *Parl* West Dv (1832–85), Mid Dv (1885–1918), Camb. Dv (1918–48), Truro CC (1948–*). *Eccl* Pec jurisd Dean & Chapter of Exeter (until 1848), Seq 14 thereafter. Eccl bdry: 1846 (help cr Mithian EP).[35]

LITTLE PETHERICK

AP Usual civ spelling; for eccl see 'St Petroc Minor'. *LG* Pyder Hd, St Col. Maj. PLU, RSD, RD. Abol civ 1934 ent to St Issey AP.[6] *Parl* East Dv (1832–85), Mid Dv (1885–1918), N'rn Dv (1918–48).

NORTH PETHERWIN

AP *LG* East Hd, Launc. PLU. Transf to Devon 1832 for parl purposes, 1844 for civ purposes[12] and in Devon (qv for this period) until transf 1966 to Cornw (Launc. RD).[126] *Parl* Cornw (until 1832), Devon (1832–1970, qv), N Cornw CC (1970–*).*Eccl* Seq 15.

SOUTH PETHERWIN

AP Incl chap Trewen (sep civ identity early, no sep eccl identity, hence eccl 'South Petherwin with Trewen', qv). *LG* East Hd, Launc. PLU, Launc. Bor/MB (pt until 1835, ent 1835–89), Launc. USD (1875–89), RSD (1889–94), RD. *Parl* Launc. Parl Bor (pt 1295–1832, ent 1832–85), N-E'rnDv(1885–1918),Bodm.Dv/CC(1918–*).

SOUTH PETHERWIN WITH TREWEN

AP Usual eccl spelling; for civ and sep chap Trewen see prev entry. *Eccl* Pec jurisd Bp Exeter (until 1848), Seq 15 thereafter.

PHILLACK

AP Incl chap Gwithian (sep civ identity early, no sep eccl identity hence eccl 'Phillack with Gwithian', qv), dist Hayle (sep EP 1870,[55] sep CP 1934 as renaming of St Erth Urban CP[6]). *LG* Penw. Hd, Redr. PLU, pt Hayle USD, pt Redr. RSD. Abol civ 1894 the pt in the USD to cr West Phillack CP, the remainder to cr East Phillack CP.[17] *Parl* West Dv (1832–85), N-W'rn Dv (1885–1918).

PHILLACK WITH GWITHIAN

AP Usual eccl spelling; for civ and sep chap Gwithian, Hayle see prev entry. *Eccl* Seq 7.

EAST PHILLACK

CP Cr 1894 from the pt of Phillack AP not in Hayle USD.[17] *LG* Redr. PLU, Phillack UD. Abol 1935 ent to Hayle CP.[56] *Parl* Camb. Dv (1918–48).

WEST PHILLACK

CP Cr 1894 from the pt of Phillack AP in Hayle USD.[17] *LG* Redr. PLU, UD (1894–1934), W Penw. RD (1934–38). Abol 1938 ent to Hayle CP.[53] *Parl* Camb. Dv (1918–48).

PHILLEIGH

AP See also Land Common to Philleigh and Ruan Lanihorne, abol 1934 with pt to this par.[6] *LG* Seq 12. *Parl* Seq 7. *Eccl* Seq 9.

PILLATON

AP *LG* Seq 3. Civ bdry: 1894.[98] *Parl* Seq 3. *Eccl* Seq 1. Eccl bdry: 1963.[10]

PORTHLEVEN

EP Cr 1840 from Sithney AP.[99] Kerr. RDn.

PORT ISAAC

EP Cr 1913 from St Endellion AP.[100] Bodm. RDn (1913–72), Trigg Min. RDn (1972–*).

POUGHILL

AP *LG* Strat. Hd, PLU, RSD, RD. Civ bdry: 1900 (help cr Stratton and Bude CP).[101] Abol civ 1934 pt to Kilkhampton AP, pt to Stratton and Bude CP.[6] *Parl* East Dv (1832–85), N-E'rn Dv (1885–1918), N'rn Dv (1918–48). *Eccl* Trigg Maj. RDn (until 1875), Strat. RDn (1875–*).

POUNDSTOCK

AP *LG* Seq 9. *Parl* Seq 4. *Eccl* Seq 16.

PROBUS

AP Incl pt bor and twnshp Grampound (sep CP 1866[8]), chap Cornelly (sep par 1532[37]), chap Merther (sep civ identity early, sep EP 1787[87]). *LG* Seq 12. *Parl* Pt Grampound Par Bor (1553–1824), Seq 9 thereafter. *Eccl* Seq 9. Eccl bdry: 1957.[67]

QUETHIOCK

AP *LG* Seq 3. *Parl* Seq 3. *Eccl* Seq 1.

RAME

AP Abol civ 1950 and eccl 1943 , in each case united with Maker AP to cr Maker with Rame CP,[83] EP[85] respectively. *LG* East Hd, St Germ. PLU, RSD, RD. *Parl* East Dv (1832–85), S-E'rn Dv (1885–1918), Bodm. Dv/CC (1918–70). *Eccl* East RDn.

REDRUTH

AP *LG* Penw. Hd, Redr. PLU, USD, UD. Abol civ 1934 to help cr Camborne-Redruth CP.[6] *Parl* West Dv (1832–85), N-W'rn Dv (1885–1918), Camb. Dv (1918–48). *Eccl* Seq 8. Eccl bdry: 1846 (cr Treleigh EP),[102] 1852,[103] 1972,[90] 1973.[62]

ROCHE

AP *LG* Seq 11. Civ bdry: 1934 (help cr St Austell CP).[6] *Parl* Seq 2. *Eccl* Seq 11.

RUAN LANIHORNE

AP See also Land Common to Philleigh and Ruan Lanihorne, abol 1934 with pt to this par.[6] *LG* Seq 12. *Parl* Seq 7. *Eccl* Seq 9.

RUAN MAJOR

AP *LG* Kerr. Hd, Helst. PLU, RSD, RD. Civ bdry: 1882.[104] Abol civ 1934 to help cr Grade Ruan CP.[6] *Parl* West Dv (1832–85), Truro Dv (1885–1918), St Ives Dv (1918–48). *Eccl* Kerr. RDn. Abol eccl 1958 to help cr St Ruan with St Grade EP.[50]

RUAN MINOR

AP *LG* Kerr. Hd, Helst. PLU, RSD, RD. Abol civ 1934 to help cr Grade Ruan CP.[6] *Parl* West Dv (1832–85), Truro Dv (1885–1918), St Ives Dv (1918–48). *Eccl* Kerr. RDn. Abol eccl

1958 to help cr St Ruan with St Grade EP.[50]

ST AGNES

Chap in Perranzabuloe AP, sep civ identity early, sep EP 1846.[97] *LG* Seq 17. *Parl* West Dv (1832–1918), Camb. Dv (1918–48), Truro CC (1948–*). *Eccl* Pec jurisd Dean & Chapter of Exeter (1846–48), Pydar RDn (1848–75), Powd. RDn (1875–*). Eccl bdry: 1846 (help cr Mount Hawke EP),[61] 1846 (help cr Mithian EP).[35]

ST AGNES

CP Island in the Isles of Scilly, sep CP 1866.[8] *LG* Isles of Scilly PLU, RSD, RD (technically not pt of Cornw Anc, Adm, or Non-Metrop Co). *Parl* Seq 11.

ST ALLEN

AP *LG* Seq 12. *Parl* Seq 9. *Eccl* Seq 9.

ST ANTHONY IN MENEAGE

AP *LG* Seq 6. *Parl* Seq 10. *Eccl* Seq 4.

ST ANTHONY IN ROSELAND

Priory church treated after Dissolution in 16th cent as curacy, sometimes as chap in Gerrans AP, sep civ and eccl identity maintained. *LG* Powd. Hd, Truro PLU, RSD, RD. Abol civ 1934 ent to Gerrans AP.[6] *Parl* West Dv (1832–85), Mid Dv (1885–1918), Penr. & Falm. Dv (1918–48). *Eccl* Pec jurisd Bp Exeter (until 1848), Powd. RDn (1848–1915), Carnm. S RDn (1915–48). Abol eccl 1948 to help cr St Gerrans with St Anthony in Roseland EP.[106]

ST AUSTELL

AP Incl chap St Blazey (sep civ identity early, sep EP 1844[107]). *LG* Powd. Hd, St Aust. PLU, pt St Aust. USD, pt St Aust. RSD. Abol civ 1894 the pt in the USD to cr St Austell Urban CP, the remainder to cr St Austell Rural CP.[17] *Parl* East Dv (1832–85), Mid Dv (1885–1918). *Eccl* Seq 11. Addtl eccl bdry alt: 1846 (help cr Par EP),[89] 1846 (cr Charlestown EP, Treverbyn EP).[36]

CP Cr 1934 by union St Austell Rural CP, St Austell Urban CP, St Blazey CP, Mevagissey AP, pts of Roche AP, St Ewe AP.[6] *LG* St Aust. UD (1934–68), St Aust. with Fowey MB (1968–74). *Parl* Truro CC (1948–*).

ST AUSTELL RURAL

CP Cr 1894 from the pt of St Austell AP not in St Aust. USD.[17] *LG* St Aust. PLU, RSD, RD. Civ bdry: 1925.[105] Abol 1934 to help cr St Austell CP.[6] *Parl* Penr. & Falm. Dv (1918–48).

ST AUSTELL URBAN

CP Cr 1894 from the pt of St Austell AP in St Aust. USD.[17] *LG* St Aust. PLU, UD. Civ bdry: 1925.[105] Abol 1934 to help cr St Austell CP.[6] *Parl* Penr. & Falm. Dv (1918–48).

ST BALZEY

AP Orig sep par at least through 13th cent, deemed chap in St Austell AP by 16th cent, sep civ identity maintained, sep EP 1844.[107] *LG* Powd. Hd, St Aust. PLU, RSD, RD. Abol civ 1934 to help cr St Austell CP.[6] *Parl* East Dv (1832–85), Mid Dv (1885–1918), Penr. & Falm. Dv (1918–48). *Eccl* Powd. RDn (1844–75), St Aust. RDn (1875–*). Eccl bdry: 1846 (help cr Par EP).[89]

ST BREOCK

AP Usual civ spelling; for eccl see following entry. *LG* Seq 16. Civ bdry: 1898 (help cr Wadebridge CP).[43] *Parl* Seq 1.

ST BREOKE

AP Usual eccl spelling; for civ see prev entry. *Eccl* Pec jurisd Bp Exeter (until 1848), Seq 12 thereafter.

ST BREWARD

AP Sometimes 'Simonward'. *LG* Seq 20. *Parl* Seq 4. *Eccl* Seq 18.

ST BUDEAUX

Chap in Plymouth St Andrew AP, Devon (Roborough Hd), small pt in Cornw (East Hd), the latter transf 1894 to Devon.[109] *LG* Plympton St Mary PLU, RSD; see main entry in Devon for period after 1894. *Parl* Cornw pt, E'rn Dv (1832–85), S-E'rn Dv (1885–1918); see Devon for remainder. *Eccl* See main entry in Devon.

ST BURYAN

AP Incl Sennen, St Levan (each sep civ identity early, each sep EP 1850[119]). *LG* Seq 10. *Parl* Seq 11. *Eccl* Pec RDn of St Buryan[110] (until 1430), royal pec (1430–1848), Seq 7 thereafter.

ST CLEER

AP *LG* West Hd, Lisk. PLU, pt Lisk. Bor (enlarged pt from 1587), pt Lisk. MB (1835–84), pt Lisk. USD (1875–84), Lisk. RSD (pt 1875–84, ent 1884–94), Lisk. RD. Civ bdry: 1884 (loses the pt in the MB to Liskeard Borough CP).[73] *Parl* Pt Lisk. Parl Bor (1295–1885), pt East Dv (1832–85), S-E'rn Dv (1885–1918), Bodm. Dv/CC (1918–*). *Eccl* Seq 21.

ST CLEMENT

AP *LG* Powd. Hd, Truro PLU, pt Truro MB, pt Truro USD, pt Truro RSD. Abol civ 1894 the pt in the MB to cr St Clement Urban CP, the remainder to cr St Clement Rural CP.[17] *Parl* Pt Truro Parl Bor (1832–85), pt West Dv (1832–85), Truro Dv (1885–1918). *Eccl* Seq 9. Eccl bdry: 1865 (cr Truro St Paul EP),[111] 1963.[10]

CP Cr 1934 from St Clement Rural CP, St Erme AP.[6] *LG* Truro RD. *Parl* Truro CC (1948–*).

ST CLEMENT RURAL

CP Cr 1894 from the pt of St Clement AP not in Truro MB.[17] *LG* Truro PLU, RD. Abol 1934 pt to help cr Truro CP, pt to help cr St Clement CP.[6] *Parl* Penr. & Falm. Dv (1918–48).

ST CLEMENT URBAN

CP Cr 1894 from the pt of St Clement AP in Truro MB.[17] *LG* Truro PLU, MB. Abol 1934 to help cr Truro CP.[6] *Parl* Penr. & Falm. Dv (1918–48).

ST CLETHER

AP *LG* Seq 7. *Parl* East Dv (1832–85), N-E'rn Dv (1885–1918), N'rn Dv (1918–48), N Cornw CC (1948–*). *Eccl* Trigg Maj. RDn (until 1875), Trigg Min. RDn (1875–1946), Trigg Maj. RDn (1946–*).

ST COLUMB MAJOR

AP *LG* Seq 14. *Parl* Seq 1. *Eccl* Seq 12.

ST COLUMB MINOR
AP Incl chap Newquay (sep CP 1894 [the pt in Newq. USD],[17] sep EP 1918[88]). *LG* Pyder Hd, St Col. Maj. PLU, pt Newq. USD, pt St Col. Maj. RSD. Abol civ 1894 the pt not cr Newquay CP to cr St Columb Minor Rural CP.[17] *Parl* East Dv (1832–85), Mid Dv (1885–1918). *Eccl* Seq 12.

ST COLUMB MINOR RURAL
CP Cr 1894 from the pt of St Columb Minor AP not in Newq. USD.[17] *LG* St Col. Maj. PLU, RD. Civ bdry: 1902.[38] Abol 1934 pt to Newquay CP, pt to Colan AP.[6] *Parl* N'rn Dv (1918–48).

ST CUBY–See CUBY for civ, TREGONEY WITH ST CUBY for eccl

ST DAY
EP Perhaps once sep par,[112] prob only chap in Gwennap AP, sep EP 1829.[51] Kerr. RDn (1829–75), Carnm. RDn (1875–1915), Carnm. N RDn (1915–*). Bdry: 1886.[113]

ST DENNIS
Chap in St Michael Carhays AP, sep civ identity early, sep EP 1850.[114] *LG* Seq 11. Civ bdry: 1971.[115] *Parl* Seq 2. *Eccl* Powd. RDn (1850–75), St Aust. RDn (1875–*).

ST DOMINIC
AP Usual eccl spelling; for civ see following entry. *Eccl* Seq 1.

ST DOMINICK
AP Usual civ spelling; for eccl see prev entry. *LG* East Hd, Lisk. PLU, RSD, RD (1894–1934), St Germ. RD (1934–74). *Parl* Seq 3.

ST ENDELLION
AP Often 'Endellion' now. *LG* Seq 19. *Parl* Seq 4. *Eccl* Trigg Min. RDn (until 1875), Bodm. RDn (1875–1972), Trigg Min. RDn (1972–*). Eccl bdry: 1913 (cr Port Isaac EP).[100]

ST ENODER
AP *LG* Pt Powd. Hd, pt Pyder Hd (ent Pyder by 19th cent[116]), Seq 14 thereafter. Civ bdry: 1934.[6] *Parl* West Dv (1832–85), Mid Dv (1885–1918), N'rn Dv (1918–48), N Cornw CC (1948–*). *Eccl* Seq 12.

ST ERME
AP *LG* Seq 12. Civ bdry: 1934 (help cr St Clement CP).[6] *Parl* West Dv (1832–1918), Penr. & Falm. Dv (1918–48), Truro CC (1948–*). *Eccl* Seq 9. Eccl bdry: 1957,[67] 1963.[10]

ST ERNEY–See LANDRAKE WITH ST ERNEY

ST ERTH
AP *LG* Penw. Hd, Penz. PLU, pt Hayle USD, pt Penz. RSD. Abol civ 1894 the pt in the USD to cr St Erth Urban CP, the remainder to cr St Erth Rural CP.[17] *Parl* W'rn Dv (1832–1918). *Eccl* Seq 7.
CP Renaming 1934 of St Erth Rural CP.[6] *LG* W Penw. RD. Civ bdry: 1938.[53] *Parl* St Ives CC (1948–*).

ST ERTH RURAL
CP Cr 1894 from the pt of St Erth AP not in Hayle USD.[17] *LG* Penz. PLU, W Penw. RD. Renamed 1934 'St Erth'.[6] *Parl* St Ives Dv (1918–48).

ST ERTH URBAN
CP Cr 1894 from the pt of St Erth AP in Hayle USD.[17] *LG* Penz. PLU, Hayle UD. Renamed 1934 'Hayle'.[6] *Parl* Camb. Dv (1918–48).

ST ERVAN
AP *LG* Seq 16. *Parl* Seq 1. *Eccl* Pec jurisd Bp Exeter (until 1848), Seq 12 thereafter.

ST EVAL
AP *LG* Seq 16. *Parl* Seq 1. *Eccl* Pec jurisd Bp Exeter (until 1848), Seq 12 thereafter.

ST GERMANS
Priory church, sep civ and eccl identity early.[117] *LG* Incl Cuddenbeak Bor which became St Germ. Parl Bor; Seq 3. *Parl* St Germ. Parl Bor (1563–1832), Seq 5 thereafter. *Eccl* Pec jurisd Bp Exeter (until 1848), Seq 1 thereafter. Eccl bdry: 1834 (cr Hessenford EP),[59] 1847 (cr Tideford EP),[118] 1973.[60]

ST GERRANS
AP Usual eccl spelling; for civ see 'Gerrans'. Incl St Anthony in Roseland (sep civ identity early, priory church treated after Dissolution in 16th cent as curacy, sometimes as chap in this par but retained sep status). *Eccl* Pec jurisd Bp Exeter (until 1848), Powd. RDn (1848–1915), Carnm. S RDn (1915–48). Abol eccl 1948 to help cr St Gerrans with St Anthony in Roseland EP.[106]

ST GERRANS WITH ST ANTHONY IN ROSELAND
EP Cr 1948 by union St Gerrans AP, St Anthony in Roseland EP.[106] Carnm. S RDn (1948–63), Powd. RDn (1963–*).

ST GLUVIAS
AP Incl Budock (orig sep par but deemed chap to this par by 16th cent, retained sep civ identity, sep EP 1890[16]), Falmouth (sep par 1664[45]). *LG* Kerr. Hd, pt Penr. Bor/MB (until 1866), Falm. PLU, RSD, E Kerr. RD (1894–1934), Kerr. RD (1934–74). Addtl civ bdry alt: 1866 (the pt in Penr. MB cr Penryn CP).[8] *Parl* Pt Penr. Parl Bor (1553–1832), pt Penr. & Falm. Parl Bor (1832–1918), pt West Dv (1832–85), pt Truro Dv (1885–1918), Penr. & Falm. Dv (1918–48), Falm. & Camb. CC (1948–*). *Eccl* Usually 'St Gluvias with Budock' before latter's sep 1890, 'St Gluvias' thereafter; pec jurisd Bp Exeter (until 1848), Kerr. RDn (1848–75), Carnm. RDn (1875–1915), Carnm. S RDn (1915–*). Addtl eccl bdry alt: 1966.[16]

ST GORAN–See GORRAN

ST HILARY
AP Incl chap and bor Marazion (sep civ identity early, sep EP 1823[86]). *LG* Seq 10. *Parl* Seq 11. *Eccl* Seq 7.

ST ISSEY
AP *LG* Seq 16. Civ bdry: 1934.[6] *Parl* Seq 1. *Eccl* Pec jurisd Bp Exeter (until 1848), Seq 12 thereafter.

ST IVE
AP *LG* Seq 2. *Parl* Seq 3. *Eccl* East RDn (until 1924), West RDn (1924–*).

ST IVES
Chap in Uny Lelant (eccl, 'Lelant'), sep civ identity early, sep EP 1826.[44] *LG* Penw. Hd, St Ives Bor/MB, USD. Civ bdry: 1934.[6] *Parl* St

Ives Parl Bor (1558–1885), W'rn Dv (1885–1918), St Ives Dv/CC (1918–*). *Eccl* Penw. RDn. Eccl bdry: 1969.[29]

ST JOHN

AP Pt Devon (Roborough Hd), pt Cornw (East Hd), the former transf to Cornw 1832 for parl purposes, 1844 for civ purposes.[12] *LG* St Germ. PLU, RSD, RD. *Parl* Pt Devon before 1832, Seq 5 thereafter. *Eccl* Seq 1. Eccl bdry: 1846 (cr Halsetown EP).[54]

ST JULIOT

AP *LG* Seq 7. *Parl* Seq 4. *Eccl* Seq 17.

ST JUST IN PENWITH

AP *LG* Penw. Hd, Penz. PLU, RSD, W Penw. RD (1894–97), St Just UD (1897–1974). *Parl* Seq 11. *Eccl* Seq 7. Eccl bdry: 1846 (cr Pendeen EP).[91]

ST JUST IN ROSELAND

AP *LG* Incl bor St Mawes,[23] Seq 12. *Parl* Pt St Mawes Parl Bor (1563–1832), Seq 7 thereafter. *Eccl* Powd. RDn (until 1915), Carnm. S RDn (1915–63), Powd. RDn (1963–*).

ST KEA

Orig sep par, deemed chap in Kenwyn AP by 16th cent, sep civ identity maintained as 'Kea', qv, sep EP 1883.[64] *Eccl* Powd. RDn. Eccl bdry: 1846 (when still chap, help cr Mithian EP),[35] 1847 (when still chap, help cr Baldhu EP),[5] 1963.[10]

ST KEVERNE

AP *LG* Seq 6. *Parl* Seq 10. *Eccl* Seq 4.

ST KEW

AP *LG* Seq 19. *Parl* Seq 4. *Eccl* Seq 20.

ST KEYNE

AP *LG* Seq 22. *Parl* Seq 5. *Eccl* Seq 21.

ST LEVAN

Pt of St Buryan AP, sep civ identity early, sep EP 1850.[119] *LG* Seq 10. *Parl* Seq 11. *Eccl* Seq 7.

ST MABYN

AP *LG* Seq 19. *Parl* East Dv (1832–85), N-E'rn Dv (1885–1918), Bodm. Dv (1918–48), N Cornw CC (1948–*). *Eccl* Seq 19.

ST MARTIN

AP Usual civ spelling; for eccl see 'St Martin by Looe'. Incl bor East Looe (sep CP 1866[8]). *LG* West Hd, pt E Looe Bor,[23] Lisk. PLU, RSD, RD. Civ bdry: 1934 (help cr Looe CP).[6] *Parl* E Looe Parl Bor (1563–1832), Seq 5 thereafter.

ST MARTIN'S

Island in the Isles of Scilly, sep CP 1866.[8] *LG* Isles of Scilly PLU, RSD, RD (technically not pt of Cornw Anc, Adm, or Non-Metrop Co). *Parl* Seq 11.

ST MARTIN BY LOOE

AP Usual eccl spelling; for civ see 'St Martin'. *Eccl* Seq 21. Eccl bdry: 1845 (help cr East and West Looe EP.[74]

ST MARTIN IN MENEAGE

AP *LG* Seq 6. *Parl* Seq 10. *Eccl* Kerr. RDn. Abol eccl before 1521 to help cr St Mawgan with St Martin in Meneage EP.[120]

ST MARY'S

Island in the Isles of Scilly, sep CP 1866.[8] *LG* Isles of Scilly PLU, RSD, RD (technically not in Cornw Anc, Adm, or Non-Metrop Co). *Parl* Seq 11.

ST MARY MAGDALENE

AP Usual civ spelling; for eccl see 'Launceston St Mary Magdalene'. Incl chap St Thomas the Apostle (sep civ identity early, sep EP 1726 as 'Launceston St Thomas'[44]), bor Dunheved (early united with Launc. Bor). *LG* East Hd, Launc. Bor/MB, USD. Abol civ 1922 to help cr Launceston (otherwise Dunheved) CP.[71] *Parl* Launc. Parl Bor (1295–1885), N-E'rn Dv (1885–1918), N'rn Dv (1918–48).

ST MAWGAN

AP Usual eccl spelling; for civ see 'Mawgan'. *Eccl* Kerr. RDn. Abol before 1521 to help cr St Mawgan with St Martin in Meneage EP.[120]

ST MAWGAN WITH ST MARTIN IN MENEAGE

EP Cr before 1521 by union St Mawgan AP, St Martin in Meneage AP.[120] Kerr. RDn.

ST MELLION

AP *LG* Seq 3. *Parl* Seq 3. *Eccl* Seq 1.

ST MERRYN

AP *LG* Seq 16. *Parl* Seq 1. *Eccl* Pec jurisd Bp Exeter (until 1848), Seq 12 thereafter.

ST MEWAN

AP *LG* Seq 11. Civ bdry: 1925,[105] 1934.[6] *Parl* Seq 2. *Eccl* Seq 11.

ST MICHAEL CARHAYS

AP Sometimes 'St Michael Caerhays'. Incl chap St Dennis (sep civ identity early, sep EP 1850[114]). *LG* Seq 11. *Parl* Seq 2. *Eccl* Seq 11.

ST MICHAEL PENKEVIL

AP *LG* Seq 12. Civ bdry: 1934.[6] *Parl* Seq 9. *Eccl* Seq 9.

ST MICHAEL'S MOUNT

Ex-par place, sep CP 1858.[121] *LG* West Hd, Penz. PLU (1858[122]–1930), RSD, W Penw. RD. *Parl* West Dv (1867–1918), St Ives Dv/CC (1918–*).

ST MINVER

AP *LG* Trigg Hd. Incl St Minver Highlands, St Minver Lowlands, each sep rated for poor and CP 1866[8] so that St Minver has no sep civ identity thereafter. *Parl* East Dv (1832–67). *Eccl* Trigg Min. RDn (until 1875), Bodm. RDn (1875–1972), Trigg Min. RDn (1972–*).

ST MINVER HIGHLANDS

CP Pt of St Minver AP, sep CP 1866.[8] *LG* Trigg Hd, Bodm. PLU, RSD, RD (1894–1934), Wadebr. RD (1934–68), Wadebr. & Pad. RD (1968–74). *Parl* East Dv (1867–85), N-E'rn Dv (1885–1918), N'rn Dv (1918–48), N Cornw CC (1948–*).

ST MINVER LOWLANDS

CP Organisation as for St Minver Highlands.

ST NEOT

AP *LG* Seq 22. *Parl* Seq 5. *Eccl* Seq 21. Eccl bdry: 1849 (help cr Bolventor EP).[1]

ST PETROC MINOR

AP Usual eccl spelling; for civ see 'Little Petherick'. *Eccl* Pec jurisd Bp Exeter (until 1848), Seq 12 thereafter.

ST PINNOCK
AP *LG* Seq 22. *Parl* Seq 5. *Eccl* Seq 21. Eccl bdry: 1851 (help cr Herodsfoot EP).[42]

ST RUAN WITH ST GRADE
EP Cr 1958 by union Grade AP, Ruan Major AP, Ruan Minor AP.[50] Kerr. RDn.

ST SAMPSON
Sometimes 'Golant' or 'St Sampson (or Golant).' Chap in Tywardreath AP, sep civ identity early, sep EP 1737[44] (perhaps in 1507[123]). *LG* Seq 11. *Parl* Seq 5. *Eccl* Powd. RDn (1737–1875), St Aust. RDn (1875–*).

ST STEPHEN IN BRANNEL
AP *LG* Seq 11. Civ bdry: 1971.[115] *Parl* Seq 2. *Eccl* Seq 11.

ST STEPHENS
AP Usual civ spelling; for eccl see 'St Stephens by Launceston'. Priory church, parochial since Dissolution in 16th cent. *LG* East Hd, pt Newport Bor,[23] Launc. PLU, MB (ent 1835–89, pt 1889–94), USD (ent 1875–89, pt 1889–94), pt Launc. RSD (1889–94). Abol civ 1894 the pt in the MB to cr St Stephens by Launceston Urban CP, the remainder to cr St Stephens by Launceston Rural CP.[17] *Parl* Pt Newport Parl Bor (1553–1832), Launc. Parl Bor (1832–85), N-E'rn Dv (1885–1918).

ST STEPHENS
AP Usual civ spelling; for eccl see 'St Stephens by Saltash'. Incl chap Saltash (sep EP 1815,[127] sep CP 1866[8]). Pt Cornw (East Hd), pt Devon (Roborough Hd), the latter transf 1895 to St Budeaux CP, Devon, and St Stephens ent Cornw thereafter.[124] *LG* Pt Saltash Bor,[125] pt Trematon Bor, St Germ. PLU, RSD, RD. Abol civ 1934 ent to Saltash CP.[6] *Parl* Pt Saltash Parl Bor (1553–1832), East Dv (1832–85), S-E'rn Dv (1885–1918).

ST STEPHENS BY LAUNCESTON
AP Usual eccl spelling; for civ see first 'St Stephens' above. *Eccl* Trigg Maj. RDn.

ST STEPHENS BY LAUNCESTON RURAL
CP Cr 1894 from the pt of St Stephens AP not in Launc. MB.[17] *LG* Launc. PLU, RD. Civ bdry: 1966 (gains pt Werrington AP as it is transf from Devon to Cornw).[126] *Parl* N'rn Dv (1918–48), N Cornw CC (1948–*).

ST STEPHENS BY LAUNCESTON URBAN
CP Cr 1894 from the pt of St Stephens AP in Launc. MB.[17] *LG* Launc. PLU, MB. Abol 1922 to help cr Launceston (otherwise Dunheved) CP.[71] *Parl* N'rn Dv (1918–48).

ST STEPHENS BY SALTASH
AP Usual eccl spelling; for civ see second 'St Stephens' above. Incl chap Saltash (sep EP 1815,[127] sep CP 1866[8]). *Eccl* Seq 1. Eccl bdry: 1881 (cr Saltash St Nicholas and St Faith EP),[128] 1963.[10]

ST STITHIANS
AP Usual eccl spelling; for civ and sep chap Perranarworthal see 'Stithians'. *Eccl* Seq 5.

ST TEATH
Collegiate, parochial since Dissolution. *LG* Seq 20. *Parl* Seq 4. *Eccl* Trigg Min. RDn.

ST THOMAS THE APOSTLE
Chap in St Mary Magdalene AP (eccl, 'Launceston St Mary Magdalene'), sep civ identity early, sep EP 1726 as 'Launceston St Thomas'.[44] Incl hmlt St Thomas Street (sep CP 1866[8]). *LG* East Hd, Launc. PLU, pt Launc. Bor, Launc. MB (ent 1835–89, pt 1889–94), Launc. USD (ent 1875–89, pt 1889–94), pt Launc. RSD (1889–94). Abol civ 1894 the pt in the MB to cr St Thomas the Apostle Urban CP, the remainder to cr St Thomas the Apostle Rural CP.[17] *Parl* Launc. Parl Bor (pt 1295–1832, ent 1832–85), N-E'rn Dv (1885–1918).

ST THOMAS THE APOSTLE RURAL
CP Cr 1894 from the pt of St Thomas the Apostle CP not in Launc. MB.[17] *LG* Launc. PLU, RD. *Parl* N'rn Dv (1918–48), N Cornw CC (1948–*).

ST THOMAS THE APOSTLE URBAN
CP Cr 1894 from the pt of St Thomas the Apostle CP in Launc. MB.[17] *LG* Launc. PLU, MB. Abol 1922 to help cr Launceston (otherwise Dunheved) CP.[71] *Parl* N'rn Dv (1918–48).

ST THOMAS STREET
CP Hmlt in St Thomas the Apostle CP, sep CP 1866.[8] *LG* East Hd, Launc. PLU, MB, USD. Abol 1922 to help cr Launceston (otherwise Dunheved) CP.[71] *Parl* Launc. Parl Bor (1867–85), N-E'rn Dv (1885–1918), N'rn Dv (1918–48).

ST TUDY
AP *LG* Seq 19. *Parl* East Dv (1832–85), N-E'rn Dv (1885–1918), Bodm. Dv (1918–48), N Cornw CC (1948–*). *Eccl* Seq 20.

ST VEEP
AP *LG* Seq 22. *Parl* Seq 5. *Eccl* West RDn (until 1964), Bodm. RDn (1964–*).

ST WENN
AP *LG* Seq 14. *Parl* Seq 1. *Eccl* Seq 12.

ST WINNOW
AP *LG* Seq 21. Civ bdry: 1934.[6] *Parl* Seq 5. *Eccl* Pec jurisd Dean & Chapter of Exeter (until 1848), Seq 22 thereafter.

SALTASH
Bor and chap in St Stephens AP, sep EP 1815,[127] sep CP 1866.[8] *LG* East Hd, St Germ. PLU, RSD (1875–85), Saltash MB (1885–1974), USD (1885–94). Civ bdry: 1934.[6] *Parl* East Dv (1867–85), S-E'rn Dv (1885–1918), Bodm. Dv/CC (1918–*). *Eccl* East RDn.

SANCREED
AP *LG* Seq 10. *Parl* Seq 11. *Eccl* Seq 7.

ISLES OF SCILLY
AP Technically not in Cornw Anc, Adm, or Non-Metrop Co. *LG* Divided 1866 into sep CPs of Bryher, St Agnes, St Martin's, St Mary's, Tresco.[8] The RD for the Isles was constituted 1890.[129] *Parl* West Dv (1832–67); see the sep CPs thereafter. *Eccl* Declared 1838 to be in Penw. RDn.[130]

SENNEN
Daughter church to St Buryan AP, sep civ identity early, sep EP 1850.[119] *LG* Seq 10. *Parl* Seq

11. *Eccl* Seq 7.

SHEVIOCK

AP Incl mediev bor Crafthole (status not sustained beyond 16th cent). *LG* Seq 3. *Parl* Seq 5. *Eccl* Seq 1. Eccl bdry: 1973.[60]

SITHNEY

AP *LG* Kerr. Hd, Helst. PLU, RSD, RSD, RD (1894–1934), Kerr. RD (1934–74). *Parl* Helst. Parl Bor (1832–85), W'rn Dv (1885–1918), St Ives CC (1918–*). *Eccl* Seq 4. Eccl bdry: 1840 (cr Porthleven EP).[99]

STITHIANS

AP Usual civ spelling; for eccl see 'St Stithians'. Incl chap Perranarworthal (sep civ identity early, curacy and sep eccl identity early as 'Perran-ar-worthal'). *LG* Kerr. Hd, Redr. PLU, RSD, RD (1894–1934), Kerr. RD (1934–74). *Parl* West Dv (1832–85), Truro Dv (1885–1918), Camb. Dv (1918–48), Falm. & Camb. CC (1948–*).

STOKE CLIMSLAND

AP *LG* Seq 1. Civ bdry: 1934,[6] 1966 (loses pts to Dunterton AP, Lamerton AP, Milton Abbot AP, Sydenham Damerel AP, all Devon).[24] *Parl* Seq 4. *Eccl* Seq 2.

STRATTON

AP *LG* Strat. Hd, PLU, RSD, RD. Civ bdry: 1900 (help cr Stratton and Bude CP).[98] Abol civ 1935 pt to Stratton and Bude CP, pt to Kilkhampton AP.[6] *Parl* East Dv (1832–85), N-E'rn Dv (1885–1918), N'rn Dv (1918–48). *Eccl* Seq 16. Eccl bdry: 1836 (cr Bude Haven EP).[15]

STRATTON AND BUDE

CP Cr 1900 from Stratton AP, Poughill AP.[98] *LG* Strat. PLU, Strat. & Bude UD. Renamed 1934 'Bude-Stratton' and enlarged when Strat. UD constituted.[6] *Parl* N'rn Dv (1918–48).

TALLAND

AP Incl West Looe Bor (sep CP 1866[8]). *LG* West Hd, pt W Looe Bor,[23] Lisk. PLU, RSD, RD. Civ bdry: 1898.[76] Abol civ 1934 pt to cr Looe CP, pt to Lansallos AP.[6] *Parl* Pt W Looe Parl Bor (1553–1832), East Dv (1832–85), S-E'rn Dv (1885–1918), Bodm. Dv (1918–48). *Eccl* Seq 21. Eccl bdry: 1845 (cr East and West Looe EP, now commonly called 'Looe'),[74] 1961.[75]

NORTH TAMERTON

AP Pt Cornw (Strat. Hd), pt Devon (Roborough Hd), the latter transf to Cornw 1832 for parl purposes, 1844 for civ purposes.[12] *LG* Holsworthy PLU, RSD, RD (1894–1934, the only Cornish par in this RD otherwise ent Devon), Strat. RD (1934–74). Addtl civ bdry alt: 1966 (exchanges pts with Luffincott AP, loses pt to Tetcott AP, both Devon).[24] *Parl* Pt Devon until 1832, Seq 4 thereafter. *Eccl* Seq 18.

TEMPLE

AP *LG* Trigg Hd, Bodm. PLU, RSD, RD. Abol civ 1934 ent to Blisland AP.[6] *Parl* East Dv (1832–85), N-E'rn Dv (1885–1918), Bodm. Dv (1918–48). *Eccl* Trigg Min. RDn (until 1875), Bodm. RDn (1875–1972). Abol eccl 1972 to help cr Blisland with Temple EP.[8]

TIDEFORD

EP Cr 1847 from St Germans AP.[118] East RDn.

TINTAGEL

AP Incl Bossiney Bor,[23] no sep identity as par. *LG* Seq 7. Civ bdry: 1934.[6] *Parl* Pt Bossiney Parl Bor (1553–1832), Seq 4 thereafter. *Eccl* Seq 18.

TORPOINT

Chap in Antony AP, sep EP 1821,[2] sep CP 1904.[3] *LG* St Germ. PLU, Torpoint UD. *Parl* Bodm. Dv/CC (1918-*). *Eccl* East RDn. Eccl bdry: 1973.[4]

TOWEDNACK

Chap in Uny Lelant (eccl, 'Lelant'), sep civ identity early, sep EP 1902.[131] *LG* Seq 10. Civ bdry: 1934.[6] *Parl* St Ives Parl Bor (1832–85), W'rn Dv (1885–1918), St Ives Dv/CC (1918–*). *Eccl* Penw. RDn.

TREGAVETHAN

CP Detached pt of Kea CP, sep CP 1866.[6] *LG* Powd. Hd, Truro PLU, RSD, RD. Abol 1934 to help cr Kenwyn CP.[6] *Parl* East Dv (1867–85), Truro Dv (1885–1948).

TREGONY

AP Incl chap and bor Cuby (sep CP 1866,[8] no sep eccl identity, hence eccl 'Tregony with St Cuby', qv). *LG* Powd. Hd, Truro PLU, RSD, RD. Civ bdry: 1934.[6] *Parl* West Dv (1867–85), Mid Dv (1885–1918), Penr. & Falm. Dv (1918–48). Truro CC (1948–*).

TREGONY WITH ST CUBY

AP Usual eccl spelling; for civ and sep chap Cuby see prev entry. *Eccl* Powd. RDn.

TRELEIGH

EP Cr 1846 from Redruth AP.[102] Penw. RDn (1846–75), Carnm. RDn (1875–1915), Carnm. N RDn (1915–*). Bdry: 1852,[103] 1886,[113] 1973.[62]

TREMAINE

Chap in Egloskerry AP, sep civ identity early, sep EP 1719.[44] *LG* Seq 1. *Parl* Seq 4. *Eccl* Trigg Maj. RDn. Abol eccl 1940 to help cr Tresmere with Tremaine EP,[132] but the two constituent pars in 1940 were disunited in 1962,[133] hence once again Trigg Maj. RDn.

TRENEGLOS

AP Incl chap Warbstow (sep civ identity early, sep EP 1926[134]). *LG* Seq 8. *Parl* Seq 4. *Eccl* Trigg Maj. RDn (until 1964), Strat. RDn (1964–*).

TRESCO

Island in the Isles of Scilly, sep CP 1866.[8] *LG* Isles of Scilly PLU, RSD, RD (technically not pt of Cornw Anc, Adm, or Non-Metrop Co). *Parl* Seq 11.

TRESLOTHAN

EP Cr 1845 from Camborne AP.[26] Penw. RDn (1845–75), Carnm. RDn (1875–1915), Carnm. N RDn (1915–*).

TRESMEER

AP Usual civ spelling; for eccl see following entry. *LG* Seq 1. *Parl* Seq 4.

TRESMERE

AP Usual eccl spelling; for civ see prev entry. *Eccl*

Trigg Maj. RDn. Abol eccl 1940 to help cr Tresmere with Tremaine EP,[132] but the two constituent pars in 1940 were disunited in 1962,[133] hence once again Trigg Maj. RDn.

TRESMERE WITH TREMAINE

EP Cr 1940 by union Tresmere AP, Tremaine EP.[132] Trigg Maj. RDn. Abol 1962, the constituent pars of 1940 separated into orig pars.[133]

TREVALGA

AP *LG* Seq 7. *Parl* Seq 4. *Eccl* Seq 18.

TREVERBYN

EP Cr 1846 from St Austell AP.[36] Powd. RDn (1846–75), St Aust. RDn (1875–*).

TREWEN

Chap in South Petherwin AP, sep civ identity early, no sep eccl identity. *LG* Seq 1. *Parl* Seq 4.

TRURO

CP Cr 1934 by union Truro St Mary AP, St Clement Urban CP, Kenwyn Urban CP, and pts of Kenwyn Rural CP, St Clement Rural CP.[6] *LG* Truro MB. *Parl* Truro CC (1948–*).

TRURO ST GEORGE

EP Name commonly used now for par cr as 'Kenwyn St George', qv.

TRURO ST JOHN

EP Name commonly used now for par cr as 'Kenwyn St John', qv.

TRURO ST MARY

AP *LG* Powd. Hd, Truro Bor/MB, PLU, USD. Abol civ 1934 to help cr Truro CP.[6] *Parl* Truro Parl Bor (1295–1885), Truro Dv (1885–1918), Penr. & Falm. Dv (1918–48). *Eccl* Seq 9. Eccl bdry: 1963.[10]

TRURO ST PAUL

EP Cr 1865 from St Clement AP.[135] Powd. RDn. Eccl bdry: 1963.[10]

TUCKINGMILL

EP Cr 1844 from Camborne AP, Illogan AP.[25] Penw. RDn (1844–75), Carnm. RDn (1875–1915), Carnm. N RDn (1915–*).

TYWARDREATH

AP Incl chap St Sampson (sep civ identity early, sep EP 1737[44] [perhaps 1507[130]]). *LG* Powd. Hd, St Aust. PLU, RSD, RD (1894–1934), St Aust. UD (1934–68), St Aust. with Fowey MB (1968–74). *Parl* East Dv (1832–85), S-E'rn Dv (1885–1918), Bodm. Dv (1918–48), Truro CC (1948–*). *Eccl* Seq 11.

UNY LELANT

AP Usual civ spelling; for eccl see 'Lelant'. Incl chap St Ives (sep civ identity early, sep EP 1826[44]). *LG* Penw. Hd, Penz. PLU, RSD, W Penw. RD. Abol civ 1934 pt to St Ives CP, pt to Ludgvan AP.[6] *Parl* St Ives Parl Bor (1832–85), West Dv (1885–1918), St Ives Dv (1918–48).

VERYAN

AP *LG* Seq 12. *Parl* Seq 7. *Eccl* Seq 9.

WADEBRIDGE

CP Cr 1898 from Egloshayle AP, St Breock AP.[43] *LG* Bodm. PLU, Wadebr. UD (1894–1934), Wadebr. RD (1934–68), Wadebr. & Pad. RD (1968–74). *Parl* N'rn Dv (1918–48), N Cornw CC (1948–*).

WARBSTOW

Chap in Treneglos AP, sep civ identity early, sep EP 1926.[134] *LG* Seq 8. *Parl* Seq 4. *Eccl* Strat. RDn.

WARLEGGAN

AP *LG* Seq 21. *Parl* Seq 5. *Eccl* Seq 22.

WEEK ST MARY

AP *LG* Week St Mary Bor (status not sustained), Seq 18. Civ bdry: 1884.[63] *Parl* Seq 4. *Eccl* Seq 16.

WENDRON

AP Incl chap and bor Helston (sep EP 1845,[58] sep CP 1866[8]). *LG* Kerr. Hd, pt Helst. Bor/MB (until 1866), Helst. PLU, RSD, RD (1894–1934), Kerr. RD (1934–74). Civ bdry: 1934 (incl help cr Camborne-Redruth CP).[6] *Parl* Pt Helst. Parl Bor (1298–1885, enlarged pt 1832–85), Truro Dv (1885–1918), Camb. Dv (1918– 48), St Ives CC (1948–*). *Eccl* Seq 4. Eccl bdry: 1964.[32]

WERRINGTON

AP Pt Devon (Black Torrington Hd), pt Cornw (East Hd), the latter transf to Devon 1832 for civ purposes, 1844 for civ purposes[12] and in Devon qv) until transf 1966 to Cornw (gains at same time pt St Giles on the Heath CP, Devon).[126] *Parl* Cornw (until 1832), Devon (1832–1970), N Cornw CC (1970–*). *Eccl* Trigg Maj. RDn. Abol eccl 1973 to help cr Werrington with St Giles on the Heath and Virginstow EP.[136]

WERRINGTON WITH ST GILES ON THE HEATH AND VIRGINSTOW

EP Cr 1973 by union Werrington AP, St Giles on the Heath AP (Devon), Virginstow EP (Devon).[136] Trigg Maj. RDn.

WITHIEL

AP *LG* Seq 13. *Parl* East Dv (1932–85), Mid Dv (1885–1918), Bodm. Dv/CC (1918–*). *Eccl* Pydar RDn (until 1875), Bodm. RDn (1875–1963), St Aust. RDn (1963–*).

WHITSTONE

AP *LG* Seq 18. Civ bdry: 1966 (loses pts to Bridgerule CP, Pyworthy AP, both Devon).[24] *Parl* Seq 4. *Eccl* Seq 16.

WOLFE ROCK LIGHTHOUSE

Ex-par place. *LG* Penz. PLU, W Penw. RD.

ZENNOR

AP *LG* Seq 10. *Parl* Seq 11. *Eccl* Seq 7.

DEVON

ABBREVIATIONS

Abbreviations particular to Devon follow. Those general abbreviations in use throughout the *Guide* are found on page xix.

Axmin.	Axminster
Aylb.	Aylesbeare
Bamp.	Bampton
Barnst.	Barnstaple
Bidef.	Bideford
Braun.	Braunton
Broadwoodw.	Broadwoodwidger
Budl.	Budleigh
Cadb.	Cadbury
Chum.	Chumleigh
Coler.	Coleridge
Cred.	Crediton
Cull.	Cullompton
Dartm.	Dartmouth
Dunk.	Dunkeswell
Erming.	Ermington
Exmin.	Exminster
Frem.	Fremington
Halb.	Halberton
Hayr.	Hayridge
Holsw.	Holsworthy
Hon.	Honiton
Ipp.	Ipplepen
Ivybr.	Ivybridge
Kingsbr.	Kingsbridge
Molt.	Molton
Moret.	Moreton
Newt. Abb.	Newton Abbot
Okeh.	Okehampton
Ott.	Ottery
Plymp.	Plympton
Plymt.	Plymtree
Rob.	Roborough
Sheb.	Shebbear
Shirw.	Shirwell
Stanb.	Stanborough
Tam.	Tamerton
Tav.	Tavistock
Tawt.	Tawton
Teigm.	Teignmouth
Teignbr.	Teignbridge
Tiv.	Tiverton
Torq.	Torquay
Torr.	Torrington
Tot.	Totnes
Wink.	Winkleigh
With.	Witheridge
Wonf.	Wonford
Woodl.	Woodleigh

SEQUENCES

An abbreviated entry prefixed by 'Seq' is used in the parochial entries to avoid repeating often the names of superior units of administration. The content of each sequence is show below.

Local Government Sequences ('LG')

SEQ 1 Axmin. Hd, PLU, RSD, RD
SEQ 2 Axmin. Hd, Hon. PLU, RSD, RD
SEQ 3 Bamp. Hd, Tiv. PLU, RSD, RD
SEQ 4 Braun. Hd, Barnst. PLU, RSD, RD
SEQ 5 Braun. Hd, S Molt. PLU, RSD, RD
SEQ 6 E Budl. Hd, St Thomas PLU, RSD, RD
SEQ 7 W Budl. Hd, Cred. PLU, RSD, RD
SEQ 8 Cliston Hd, St Thomas PLU, RSD, RD
SEQ 9 Coler. Hd, Kingsbr. PLU, RSD, RD
SEQ 10 Coler. Hd, Tot. PLU, RSD, RD
SEQ 11 Colyton Hd, Axmin. PLU, RSD, RD
SEQ 12 Colyton Hd, Hon. PLU, RSD, RD
SEQ 13 Cred. Hd, PLU, RSD, RD
SEQ 14 Eming. Hd, Kingsbr. PLU, RSD, RD
SEQ 15 Erming. Hd, Plymp. St Mary PLU, RSD, RD
SEQ 16 Exmin. Hd, Newt. Abb. PLU, RSD, RD
SEQ 17 Exmin. Hd, St Thomas PLU, RSD, RD
SEQ 18 Frem. Hd, Barnst. PLU, RSD, RD
SEQ 19 Frem. Hd, Torr. PLU, RSD, RD
SEQ 20 Halb. Hd, Tiv. PLU, RSD, RD
SEQ 21 Hartland Hd, Bidef. PLU, RSD, RD
SEQ 22 Hayr. Hd, Hon. PLU, RSD, RD
SEQ 23 Hayr. Hd, Tiv. PLU, RSD, RD
SEQ 24 Haytor Hd, Tot. PLU, RSD, RD
SEQ 25 Haytor Hd, Newt. Abb. PLU, RSD, RD
SEQ 26 Hemyock Hd, Hon. PLU, RSD, RD
SEQ 27 Hemyock Hd, Wellington PLU, RSD, Culmstock RD (1894–1935), Tiv. RD (1935–74)
SEQ 28 Lifton Hd, Okeh. PLU, RSD, RD
SEQ 29 Lifton Hd, Tav. PLU, RSD, RD
SEQ 30 S Molt. Hd, Barnst. PLU, RSD, RD
SEQ 31 S Molt. Hd, PLU, RSD, RD
SEQ 32 Plymp. Hd, Plymp. St Mary PLU, RSD, RD
SEQ 33 Rob. Hd, Tav. PLU, RSD, RD
SEQ 34 Sheb. Hd, Bidef. PLU, RSD, RD
SEQ 35 Sheb. Hd, Okeh. PLU, RSD, RD
SEQ 36 Sheb. Hd, Torr. PLU, RSD, RD
SEQ 37 Shirw. Hd, Barnst. PLU, RSD, RD
SEQ 38 Stanb. Hd, Kingsbr. PLU, RSD, RD
SEQ 39 Stanb. Hd, Tot. PLU, RSD, RD
SEQ 40 Tav. Hd, PLU, RSD, RD
SEQ 41 N Tawt. with Wink. Hd, Cred. PLU, RSD, RD
SEQ 42 N Tawt. with Wink. Hd, Okeh. PLU, RSD, RD
SEQ 43 N Tawt. with Wink. Hd, Torr. PLU, RSD, RD
SEQ 44 Teignb. Hd, Newt. Abb. PLU, RSD, RD
SEQ 45 Tiv. Hd, PLU, RSD, RD
SEQ 46 Black Torr. Hd, Holsw. PLU, RSD, RD
SEQ 47 Black Torr. Hd, Okeh. PLU, RSD, RD
SEQ 48 With. Hd, Cred. PLU, RSD, RD
SEQ 49 With. Hd, S Molt. PLU, RSD, RD
SEQ 50 With. Hd, Tiv. PLU, RSD, RD
SEQ 51 Wonf. Hd, Cred. PLU, RSD, RD
SEQ 52 Wonf. Hd, Newt. Abb. PLU, RSD, RD
SEQ 53 Wonf. Hd, Okeh. PLU, RSD, RD
SEQ 54 Wonf. Hd, St Thomas PLU, RSD, RD

Parliamentary Sequences ('Parl')

SEQ 1 N'rn Dv (1832–67), North Dv (1867–85), E'rn Dv (1885–1918), Hon. Dv/CC (1918–*)
SEQ 2 N'rn Dv (1832–67), North Dv (1867–1918), S Molt. Dv (1918–48), N Devon CC (1948–*)
SEQ 3 N'rn Dv (1832–67), North Dv (1867–1918), S Molt. Dv (1918–48), W Devon CC (1948–*)
SEQ 4 N'rn Dv (1832–67), North Dv (1867–1918), S Molt. Dv (1918–48), Torr. CC (1948–70), W Devon CC (1970–*)
SEQ 5 N'rn Dv (1832–67), North Dv (1867–1918), S Molt. Dv (1918–48), Torr. CC (1948–70), Tiv. CC (1970–*)
SEQ 6 N'rn Dv (1832–67), N Dv (1867–85), N-E'rn Dv (1885–1918), Hon. Dv/CC (1918–*)
SEQ 7 N'rn Dv (1832–67), North Dv (1867–85), N-E'rn Dv (1885–1918), Tiv. Dv/CC (1918–*)
SEQ 8 N'rn Dv (1832–67), North Dv (1867–85), N-W'rn Dv (1885–1918), Barnst. Dv (1918–48), N Devon CC (1948–*)
SEQ 9 N'rn Dv (1832–67), North Dv (1867–85), N-W'rn Dv (1885–1918), Barnst. Dv (1918–48), Torr. CC (1948–70), N Devon CC (1970–*)
SEQ 10 N'rn Dv (1832–67), South Dv (1867–85), W'rn Dv (1885–1918), S Molt. Dv (1918–48), Torr. CC (1948–70), W Devon CC (1970–*)
SEQ 11 N'rn Dv (1832–67), South Dv (1867–85), W'rn Dv (1885–1918), Tav. Dv/CC (1918–70), W Devon CC (1970–*)
SEQ 12 S'rn Dv (1832–67), East Dv (1867–85), E'rn Dv (1885–1918), Hon. Dv/CC (1918–*)
SEQ 13 S'rn Dv (1832–67), East Dv (1867–85),

Mid Dv (1885–1918), S Molt. Dv (1918–48), Torr. CC (1948–70), W Devon CC (1970–*)
SEQ 14 S'rn Dv (1832–67), East Dv (1867–85), Mid Dv (1885–1918), S Molt. Dv (1918–48), Torr. CC (1948–70), Tiv. CC (1970–*)
SEQ 15 S'rn Dv (1832–67), East Dv (1867–85), Mid Dv (1885–1918), Tiv. Dv/CC (1918–*)
SEQ 16 S'rn Dv (1832–67), East Dv (1867–85), Mid Dv (1885–1918), Tot. Dv/CC (1918–*)
SEQ 17 S'rn Dv (1832–67), East Dv (1867–85), N-E'rn Dv (1885–1918), Tiv. Dv/CC (1918–*)
SEQ 18 S'rn Dv (1832–67), South Dv (1867–85), S'rn Dv (1885–1918), Tav. Dv/CC (1918–70), W Devon CC (1970–*)
SEQ 19 S'rn Dv (1832–67), South Dv (1867–85), W'rn Dv (1885–1918), Tot. Dv/CC (1918–*)
SEQ 20 S'rn Dv (1832–67), South Dv (1867–85), W'rn Dv (1885–1918), S Molt. Dv (1918–48), Torr. CC (1948–70), W Devon CC (1970–*)
SEQ 21 S'rn Dv (1832–67), South Dv (1867–85), W'rn Dv (1885–1918), Tav. Dv/CC (1918–70), W Devon CC (1970–*)

Ecclesiastical Sequences ('Eccl')

In Exeter AD orig:
SEQ 1 Aylb. RDn
SEQ 2 Aylb. RDn (until 1875), Ott. RDn (1875–*)
SEQ 3 Cadb. RDn
SEQ 4 Christianity RDn
SEQ 5 Dunk. RDn (until 1875), Dunk. & Hon. RDn (1875–1902), Hon. RDn (1902–*)
SEQ 6 Dunsford RDn (until 1875), Kenn RDn (1875–*)
SEQ 7 Dunsford RDn (until 1875), Okeh. RDn (1875–*)
SEQ 8 Hon. RDn (until 1875), Dunk. & Hon. RDn (1875–1902), Hon. RDn (1902–*)
SEQ 9 Hon. RDn (until 1875), Ott. RDn (1875–1902), Hon. RDn (1902–*)
SEQ 10 Kenn RDn
SEQ 11 Plymt. RDn (until 1875), Aylb. RDn (1875–*)
SEQ 12 Plymt. RDn (until 1875), Ott. RDn (1875–*)
SEQ 13 Plymt. RDn (until 1875), Tiv. E RDn (1875–1902), Cull. RDn (1902–*)
SEQ 14 Tiv. RDn (until 1875), Tiv. E RDn (1875–1902), Cull. RDn (1902–*)
SEQ 15 Tiv. RDn (until 1875), Tiv. W RDn (1875–1902), Tiv. RDn (1902–*)

In Barnstable AD orig:
SEQ 16 Barnst. RDn
SEQ 17 Barnst. RDn (until 1875), S Molt. RDn (1875–*)
SEQ 18 Barnst. RDn (until 1875), Shirw. RDn (1875–*)
SEQ 19 Barnst. RDn (until 1875), Torr. RDn (1875–*)
SEQ 20 Chum. RDn
SEQ 21 Hartland RDn
SEQ 22 Hartland RDn (until 1875), Torr. RDn (1875–*)
SEQ 23 S Molt. RDn
SEQ 24 S Molt. RDn (until 1875), Chum. RDn (1875–*)
SEQ 25 S Molt. RDn (until 1875), Tiv. W RDn (1875–1902), Tiv. RDn (1902–*)
SEQ 26 Shirw. RDn
SEQ 27 Shirw. RDn (until 1875), Barnst. RDn (1875–*)
SEQ 28 Torr. RDn
SEQ 29 Torr. RDn (until 1875), Chum. RDn (1875–*)

In Totnes AD orig:
SEQ 30 Holsw. RDn
SEQ 31 Ipp. RDn
SEQ 32 Ipp. RDn (until 1875), Moret. RDn (1875–*)
SEQ 33 Ipp. RDn (until 1875), Tot. RDn (1875–*)
SEQ 34 Moret. RDn
SEQ 35 Okeh. RDn
SEQ 36 Plymp. RDn
SEQ 37 Tam. RDn (until 1875), Tav. RDn (1875–*)
SEQ 38 Tav. RDn
SEQ 39 Tot. RDn
SEQ 40 Woodl. RDn

DIOCESE AND ARCHDEACONRIES

With a few exceptions noted below in the parochial entries, Devon pars were in Exeter dioc. The RDns were organised in ADs as follows:

BARNSTAPLE AD
Barnst. RDn, Chum. RDn, Hartland RDn, Holsw. RDn (1848–1918), S Molt. RDn, Plymt. RDn (until 1875), Shirw. RDn, Torr. RDn

EXETER AD
Aylb. RDn, Cadb. RDn, Christianity RDn, Cull. RDn (1902–*), Dunk. RDn (until 1875), Dunk. & Hon. RDn (1875–1902), Dunsford RDn (until

1875), Hon. RDn (until 1875 and 1902–*), Kenn RDn, Ott. RDn (1875–*), Tiv. RDn (until 1875 and 1902–*), Tiv. E RDn (1875–1902), Tiv. W RDn (1875–1902)

PLYMOUTH AD (1918–*)
Plymouth RDn (1954–*), Plymp. RDn, Tav. RDn, Three Towns RDn (1918–54)

TOTNES AD
Holsw. RDn (until 1848 and 1918–*), Ipp. RDn, Moret. RDn, Okeh. RDn, Plymp. RDn (until 1918), Tam. RDn (until 1875), Tav. RDn (until 1918), Three Towns RDn (1875–1918), Tot. RDn, Woodl. RDn

THE PARISHES OF DEVON

ABBOTSHAM
AP *LG* Seq 34. Civ bdry: 1935.[1] *Parl* Seq 9. *Eccl* Seq 21.

ABBOTSKERSWELL
AP *LG* Haytor Hd, Newt. Abb. PLU, RSD, RD. Abol civ 1935 to help cr Kerswells CP.[1] *Parl* S'rn Dv (1832–67), East Dv (1867–85), Mid Dv (1885–1918), Tot. Dv (1918–48). *Eccl* Seq 32.

ALFINGTON
EP Cr 1882 from Ottery St Mary AP.[2] Ott. RDn.

EAST ALLINGTON
AP *LG* Seq 38. *Parl* Seq 19. *Eccl* Seq 40.

ALPHINGTON
AP *LG* Alphington Bor (status not sustained), Seq 54. Civ bdry: 1884,[3] 1913,[4] and loses pts to Exeter CB and St Thomas the Apostle AP in each of 1937,[5] 1940,[6] 1966.[7] *Parl* Seq 17. *Eccl* Seq 10.

ALVERDISCOTT
AP *LG* Seq 19. *Parl* Seq 3. *Eccl* Seq 22.

WEST ALVINGTON
AP Incl chap South Huish (sep civ identity early, sep EP 1877[8]), chap Malborough (sep civ identity early, perhaps 17th cent bor,[9] sep EP 1877[10] [this chap incl Salcombe, sep EP 1803[11]]), chap South Milton (sep civ identity early, sep EP 1886[12]). *LG* West Alvington Bor (status not sustained), Seq 38. Civ bdry: 1884,[13] 1894,[14] 1896.[15] *Parl* Seq 19. *Eccl* Seq 40.

ALWINGTON
AP *LG* Seq 34. *Parl* Seq 9. *Eccl* Seq 21.

EAST ANSTEY
AP *LG* Seq 31. Civ bdry: 1966 (exchanges pts with Brushford AP, loses pt to Dulverton AP, both Somerset).[16] *Parl* Seq 2. *Eccl* Seq 23.

WEST ANSTEY
AP *LG* Seq 31. *Parl* Seq 2. *Eccl* Seq 23.

APPLEDORE
EP Cr 1841 from Northam AP.[17] Hartland RDn.

ARLINGTON
AP *LG* Seq 37. *Parl* Seq 8. *Eccl* Detached from but subject to Exeter AD (until 1848), Shirw. RDn (1848–1944). Abol eccl 1944 to help cr East Down with Arlington EP.[18]

ASHBURTON
AP Incl chap Bickington (sep civ identity early, sep EP 1861[19]), chap Buckland in the Moor (sep civ identity early, sep EP between 1878–1910[20]). *LG* Ashburton Bor, Teignbr. Hd, Newt. Abb. PLU, RSD, RD (1894–98), Ashburton UD (1898–1974). Civ bdry: 1935.[1] *Parl* Ashburton Parl Bor (1298, 1407–1918), Tot. Dv/CC (1918–*). *Eccl* Pec jurisd Dean & Chapter of Exeter (until 1848), Seq 34 thereafter.

ASHBURY
AP *LG* Seq 47. *Parl* Seq 10. *Eccl* Seq 35.

ASHCOMBE
AP *LG* Seq 17. *Parl* Seq 17. *Eccl* Seq 10.

ASHFORD
AP *LG* Seq 4. *Parl* Seq 8. *Eccl* Barnst. RDn. Abol eccl 1945 to help cr Pilton with Ashford EP.[21]

ASHPRINGTON
AP *LG* Seq 10. Civ bdry: 1884.[22] *Parl* Seq 19. *Eccl* Seq 39.

ASHREIGNEY
AP Sometimes 'Ring Ash'. *LG* Seq 43. *Parl* Seq 3. *Eccl* Seq 29.

ASHTON
AP *LG* Seq 17. Civ bdry: 1884.[23] *Parl* Seq 17. *Eccl* Seq 6.

ASHWATER
AP *LG* Seq 46. *Parl* Seq 11. *Eccl* Seq 30.

ATHERINGTON
AP *LG* N Tawt. with Wink. Hd, Barnst. PLU, RSD, RD. *Parl* Seq 8. *Eccl* Seq 16.

AVETON GIFFORD
AP *LG* Aveton Gifford Bor (status not sustained), Seq 14. Civ bdry: 1885.[24] *Parl* Seq 19. *Eccl* Seq 40.

AWLISCOMBE
AP *LG* Seq 26. Civ bdry: 1884.[25] *Parl* Seq 1. *Eccl* Seq 5.

AXMINSTER
AP Incl chaps Kilmington, Membury (each with sep civ identity early, each sep EP 1911[26]). Pt Devon (Axmin. Hd), pt Dorset (Whitchurch Canonicorum Hd), the latter transf to Devon 1832 for parl purposes, 1844 for civ purposes.[27] *LG* Axmin. Bor (status not sustained), PLU, RSD, RD. Civ bdry: 1884,[28] 1889.[29] Abol civ 1915 pt to cr Axminster Hamlets CP, pt to cr Amnin. UD and Axminster Town CP.[30] *Parl* S'rn Dv (1832–67), East Dv (1867–85), E'rn Dv (1885–1918). *Eccl* Seq 8.
CP Renaming 1953 of Axminster Town CP when Axmin. UD abol.[31] *LG* Axmin. RD. Bdry: 1962.[32] *Parl* Hon. CC (1970–*).

AXMINSTER HAMLETS
CP Cr 1915 from the pt of Axminster AP not cr Axmin. UD.[30] *LG* Axmin. PLU, RD. Abol 1962 pt to Axminster AP, pt to Chardstock AP.[32] *Parl* Hon. Dv/CC (1918–70).

AXMINSTER TOWN
CP Cr 1915 from the pt of Axminster AP cr Axmin. UD.[30] *LG* Axmin. PLU, UD. Renamed 1953 'Axminster' when UD abol.[31] *Parl* Hon. Dv/CC (1918–70).

AXMOUTH
AP *LG* Seq 1. Civ bdry: 1939 (help cr Combpyne Rousdon CP).[33] *Parl* Seq 12. *Eccl* Seq 8.

AYLESBEARE
AP Incl chap and bor Newton Poppleford (bor status not sustained, sep EP 1862,[34] sep CP 1898[35]). *LG* Seq 6. Addtl civ bdry alt: 1884.[3] *Parl* Seq 12. *Eccl* Seq 1.

BABBACOMBE
EP Cr 1868 from St Marychurch AP.[36] Ipp. RDn.

BAMPTON
AP Incl chap Petton (sep EP between 1879–82[37]). *LG* Bamp. Bor (status not sustained), Bamp. Hd, Tiv. PLU, pt Bamp. USD, pt Tiv. RSD, Bamp. UD (1894–1935), Tiv. RD (1935–74). Civ bdry: 1894 (the pt not in the USD added to UD).[38] *Parl* Seq 7. *Eccl* Seq 15.

BARNSTAPLE
AP *LG* Braun. Hd, Barnst. Bor/MB, PLU, USD. Civ bdry: 1885 (gains the pt of Bishop's Tawton AP in Barnst. MB),[39] 1899.[40] *Parl* Barnst. Parl Bor (1295–1885), N-W'rn Dv (1885–1918), Barnst. Dv (1918–48), N Devon CC (1948–*). *Eccl* Seq 16. Eccl bdry: 1844 (cr Barnstaple St Mary Magdalene EP),[41] 1846 (cr Barnstaple Holy Trinity EP),[42] 1886,[43] 1905,[44] 1923,[45] 1956 (help cr Sticklepath EP).[46]

BARNSTAPLE HOLY TRINITY
EP Cr 1846 from Barnstaple AP.[42] Barnst. RDn. Bdry: 1905,[44] 1923.[45]

BARNSTAPLE ST MARY MADGALENE
EP Cr 1844 from Barnstaple AP.[41] Barnst. RDn. Bdry: 1886.[43]

BEAFORD
AP *LG* Seq 36. *Parl* Seq 3. *Eccl* Seq 28.

BEAWORTHY
AP *LG* Seq 47. *Parl* Seq 10. *Eccl* Okeh. RDn (until 1920), Holsw. RDn (1920–*).

BEER
Chap in Seaton and Beer AP, sep CP 1894,[47] sep EP 1905.[48] *LG* Axmin. PLU, RD. *Parl* Hon. Dv/CC (1918–*). *Eccl* Hon. RDn.

BELSTONE
AP *LG* Seq 47. *Parl* Seq 10. *Eccl* Sometimes as 'Belstone with Sticklepath', Seq 35. Eccl bdry: 1929.[49]

BERE FERRERS
AP Incl Bere Alston Bor (no sep status as par). *LG* Seq 33. *Parl* Pt Bere Alston Parl Bor (1584–1832), Seq 21. *Eccl* As 'Bere Ferrers with Bere Alston', Seq 37.

BERE FERRERS WITH BERE ALSTON–see prev entry

BERRY POMEROY
AP *LG* Haytor Hd, Tot. PLU, pt Tot. MB (1835–94), pt Tot. USD, pt Tot. RSD, Tot. RD. Civ bdry: 1894 (loses the pt in the MB to Totnes AP),[50] 1897.[51] *Parl* Pt Totnes Parl Bor (1832–1918), pt S'rn Dv (1832–67), pt East Dv (1867–85), pt S'rn Dv (1885–1918), Tot. Dv/CC (1918–*). *Eccl* Ipp. RDn (until 1848), Tot. RDn (1848–*). Eccl bdry: 1968.[52]

BERRYNARBOR
AP *LG* Seq 4. *Parl* Seq 8. *Eccl* Seq 26.

BICKINGTON
Chap in Ashburton AP, sep civ identity early, sep EP 1861.[19] *LG* Seq 44. Civ bdry: 1935.[1] *Parl* Seq 16. *Eccl* Moret. RDn. Eccl bdry: 1928.[53]

ABBOTS BICKINGTON
AP Incl chap Bulkworthy (sep civ identity early, no sep eccl identity, hence eccl 'Abbots Bickington with Bulkworthy, qv). *LG* Seq 46. *Parl* Seq 11.

ABBOTS BICKINGTON WITH BULKWORTHY
AP Usual eccl spelling; for civ and sep chap Bulkworthy see prev entry. *Eccl* Seq 30.

HIGH BICKINGTON
AP *LG* Seq 43. Civ bdry: 1884.[54] *Parl* Seq 3. *Eccl* Barnst. RDn (until 1875), Torr. RDn (1875–1956), Barnst. RDn (1956–*).

BICKLEIGH
AP Sometimes 'Bickleigh near Tiverton'. *LG* Seq 23. *Parl* Seq 7. *Eccl* Tiv. RDn (until 1875), Tiv. E RDn (1875–1902), Tiv. RDn (1902–*).

BICKLEIGH
AP Sometimes 'Bickleigh near Plymouth'. Incl chap Sheepstor (sep civ identity early, sep EP 1875[44]). *LG* Rob. Hd, Plymp. St Mary PLU, RSD, RD. Civ bdry: 1939,[55] 1951 (incl loss pt to Plymouth CB and CP).[57] *Parl* S'rn Dv (1832–67), South Dv (1867–85), W'rn Dv (1885–1918), Tav. Dv (1918–48), Plymouth Sutton BC (1948–70), W Devon CC (1970–*). Parl bdry: 1951.[56] *Eccl* As 'Bickleigh with Sheepstor' before 1875 and 'Bickleigh' thereafter, Tam. RDn (until 1875), Plymp. RDn (1875–*).

BICKLEIGH WITH SHEEPTSTOR–See prev entry

BICTON
AP *LG* Seq 6. *Parl* Seq 12. *Eccl* Aylb. RDn. Abol eccl 1926 to help cr East Budleigh with Bicton EP.[59]

BIDEFORD
AP *LG* Sheb. Hd, Bidef. Bor/MB, PLU, USD. Civ bdry: 1935.[1] *Parl* Seq 9. *Eccl* Seq 21. Eccl bdry: 1973.[60]

BIGBURY
AP *LG* Seq 14. Civ bdry: 1884.[13] *Parl* Seq 19. *Eccl* Seq 40. Eccl bdry: 1923.[61]

BISHOPSNYMPTON
AP Usual eccl spelling; for civ see 'Bishop's Nympton'. *Eccl* Pec jurisd Bp Exeter (until 1848), Seq 23 thereafter.

BISHOPSTEIGNTON
AP Incl chap and bor West Teignmouth (sep civ identity early, bor status not sustained, sep EP 1842[62]). *LG* Exmin. Hd, Newt. Abb. PLU, pt Teignm. USD (1883–94), Newt. Abb. RSD (ent 1875–83, pt 1883–94), Newt. Abb. RD. Civ bdry: 1883,[48] 1894 (loses the pt in the USD to West Teignmouth AP),[64] 1935.[1] *Parl* Seq 16. *Eccl* Pec jurisd Bp Exeter (until 1848), Seq

10 thereafter. Eccl bdry: 1886 (cr Luton EP).[65]

BITTADON

AP *LG* Seq 4. *Parl* Seq 8. *Eccl* Seq 27. Eccl bdry: 1926.[66]

BLACKAWTON

AP Incl chap Strete (sep EP 1881 [orig called 'Street' but Strete later][67] sep CP 1935 as 'Strete'[1]). *LG* Seq 9. Addtl civ bdry alt: 1884.[68] *Parl* Seq 19. *Eccl* Tot. RDn (until 1875), Woodl. RDn (1875–*).

BLACKBOROUGH

AP *LG* Hayr. Hd, Tiv. PLU; although sep rated orig in PLU, soon deemed pt of Kentisbeare AP for civ purposes (eccl independence maintained) as had been customary before. *Parl* N'rn Dv (1832–67). *Eccl* Seq 13.

BONDLEIGH

AP *LG* Seq 42. Civ bdry: 1884.[69] *Parl* Seq 4. *Eccl* Seq 20. Eccl bdry: 1928.[70]

NORTH BOVEY

AP *LG* Seq 44. Civ bdry: 1885.[71] *Parl* Seq 16. *Eccl* Seq 34.

BOVEY TRACEY

AP *LG* Bovey Tracey Bor (status not sustained), Seq 44. Civ bdry: 1882,[72] 1885,[73] 1957.[74] *Parl* Seq 16. *Eccl* Seq 34. Eccl bdry: 1880 (help cr Chudleigh Knighton EP),[75] 1895 (help cr Bovey Tracey St John the Evangelist EP),[76] 1956.[77]

BOVEY TRACEY ST JOHN THE EVANGELIST

EP Cr 1895 from Bovey Tracey AP.[76] Moret. RDn.

BOW

AP Sometimes 'Nymet Tracey'. *LG* Bow Bor (status not sustained), Seq 41. Civ bdry: 1884.[78] *Parl* Seq 5. *Eccl* Chum. RDn (until 1875), Cadb. RDn (1875–*). Eccl bdry: third quarter 17th cent (gains Broad Nymet AP).[79]

BOYTON

Called both 'par' and 'chap' at early date, sep civ identity clear, certainly EP 1768.[80] Pt Cornw (Stratton Hd), pt Devon (Northcott hmlt in Black Torr. Hd), the latter retained in Devon 1832 for parl purposes, 1844 for civ purposes,[27] sep CP 1866,[81] qv. See main entry in Cornw.

BRADFORD

AP *LG* Seq 46. Civ bdry: 1884.[78] *Parl* Seq 11. *Eccl* Seq 30.

BRADNINCH

AP *LG* Hayr. Hd, Bradninch Bor, Tiv. PLU, RSD, RD. *Parl* Bradninch Parl Bor (1303 only, excused from sending MPs *temp* Henry VII[79]), Seq 7. *Eccl* Plymt. RDn (until 1875), Tiv. E RDn (1875–1902), Cull. RDn (1902–*).

BRADNINCH–See EXETER BRADNINCH PRECINCT

BRADSTONE

AP *LG* Seq 29. *Parl* Seq 21. *Eccl* Tav. RDn. Abol eccl 1923 to help cr Kelly with Bradstone EP.[82]

BRADWORTHY

AP Incl chap Pancrasweek (sep civ identity early, eccl [as 'Pancraswyke'] severed 1959 to help cr Pyworthy with Pancraswyke EP[83]). *LG* Black Torr. Hd, Bidef. PLU (1835–before 1850), Holsw. PLU (before 1850–1930),[84] Holsw. RSD, RD. Addtl civ bdry alt: 1966 (gains pt Kilkhampton AP, pt Morwenstow AP, both Devon).[16] *Parl* Seq 11. *Eccl* As 'Bradworthy with Pancraswyke' before 1959 and 'Bradworthy' thereafter, Holsw. RDn.

BRADWORTHY WITH PANCRASWYKE–See prev entry

BRAMPFORD SPEKE

AP *LG* Seq 54. Civ bdry: 1884,[3] 1940.[6] *Parl* Seq 17. *Eccl* Seq 3. Incl Cowley, sep EP 1867[11] but independent status not sustained and now deemed chap in this par.

BRANSCOMBE

AP *LG* Seq 12. *Parl* Seq 12. *Eccl* Pec jurisd Dean & Chapter of Exeter (until 1848), Seq 2 thereafter.

BRATTON CLOVELLY

AP *LG* Seq 28. Civ bdry: 1885.[85] *Parl* Seq 20. *Eccl* Okeh. RDn (until 1952), Tav. RDn (1952–*). Eccl bdry: 1958.[86]

BRATTON FLEMING

AP *LG* Seq 4. *Parl* Seq 8. *Eccl* Seq 26.

BRAUNTON

AP Usual civ name; for eccl see following entry. *LG* Seq 4. *Parl* Seq 8.

BRAUNTON WITH SAUNTON AND KNOWLE

AP Usual eccl spelling; for civ see prev entry. *Eccl* Pec jursid Dean of Exeter (until 1848), Seq 27 thereafter.

HIGH BRAY

AP *LG* Seq 37. Civ bdry: 1883.[63] *Parl* Seq 8. *Eccl* Seq 26. Eccl bdry: 1945.[87]

BRENDON

AP *LG* Seq 37. *Parl* Seq 8. *Eccl* Seq 26.

SOUTH BRENT

AP *LG* Seq 39. Civ bdry: 1950.[88] *Parl* Seq 19. *Eccl* Seq 39. Eccl bdry: 1960.[89]

BRENTOR

AP Usual civ spelling; for eccl see 'Brent Tor'. *LG* Seq 40. Civ bdry: 1880,[90] 1885.[91] *Parl* Seq 21.

BRIDESTOWE

AP Incl chap Stourton (sep civ identity early, sep EP 1889[92]). *LG* Seq 28. Civ bdry: 1884.[93] *Parl* Seq 20. *Eccl* As 'Bridestowe with Sourton' before 1889 and 'Bridestowe' thereafter, Tav. RDn (until 1875), Okeh. RDn (1875–1964), Tav. RDn (1964–*).

BRIDESTOWE WITH SOURTON–See prev entry

BRIDFORD

AP *LG* Seq 54. *Parl* Seq 15. *Eccl* Seq 6.

BRIDGERULE

AP Pt Cornw (Stratton Hd), pt Devon (Black Torr. Hd), the former transf to Devon 1832 for parl purposes, 1844 for civ purposes.[27] The two pts of Bridgerule East, Bridgerule West sep rated for poor and each a sep CP 1866,[81] (qv) so that this par has no civ identity after 1866. *Parl* Devon pt, N'rn Dv (1832–67). *Eccl* Seq 30.

CP Cr 1950 by union Bridgerule East CP, Bridgrule West CP.[94] *LG* Holsw. RD. Civ bdry: 1966 (gains pt Whitstone AP, loses pt to Launcells AP, both Cornw).[16] *Parl* W Devon CC (1970–*).

BRIDGERULE EAST
CP Cr 1866 from Bridgerule AP.[81] *LG* Black Torr. Hd, Holsw. PLU, RSD, RD. Civ bdry: 1884.[95] Abol 1950 to help cr Bridgerule CP.[94] *Parl* W'rn Dv (1885–1918), Tav. Dv/CC (1948–70).

BRIDGERULE WEST
CP Organisation as for Bridgerule East, but no bdry alt in 1884.

BRIXHAM
AP Incl chap Churston Ferrers (sep civ identity early, sep EP by 1850[96]). *LG* Haytor Hd, Tot. PLU, pt Lower Brixham USD, pt Tot. RSD, Lower Brixham UD (1894–95), Brixham UD (1895–1967). Addtl civ bdry alt: 1894 (pt outside the UD brought within it).[97] Abol civ 1967 pt to help cr Torbay CB and CP, pt to Kingswear AP.[98] *Parl* S'rn Dv (1832–67), East Dv (1867–85), Torq. Dv (1885–1948), Torq. BC (1948–70). *Eccl* Seq 31. Addtl eccl bdry alt: 1825 (help cr Lower Brixham EP),[99] 1830,[100] 1954 (help cr Churston Ferrers with Goodrington EP).[101]

LOWER BRIXHAM
EP Cr 1852 from Brixham AP.[99] Ipp. RDn. Bdry: 1830.[100]

BRIXTON
Chap in Plympton St Maurice AP, sep civ identity early, sep EP 1814.[11] *LG* Plymp. Earle Bor, Seq 32. Civ bdry: 1884,[102] 1966 (loses pt to Plymouth CB and CP).[103] *Parl* Pt Plymp. Earle Parl Bor (1295–1832), Seq 18 thereafter. *Eccl* Plymp. RDn. Eccl bdry: 1962.[104]

BROADHEMBURY
AP *LG* Seq 22. *Parl* Seq 6. *Eccl* Seq 12.

BROADHEMPSTON
AP *LG* Seq 25. Civ bdry: 1884.[105] *Parl* Seq 16. *Eccl* Ipp. RDn (until 1875), Tot. RDn (1875–1938). Abol eccl 1938 to help cr Broadhempston and Woodland EP.[106] Eccl bdry: 1928.[53]

BROADHEMPSTON AND WOODLAND
EP Cr 1938 by union Broadhempston AP, Woodland EP.[106] Tot. RDn.

BROADWOOD KELLY
AP Usual civ spelling; for eccl see following entry. *LG* Seq 47. Civ bdry: 1885.[107] *Parl* Seq 10.

BROADWOODKELLY
AP Usual eccl spelling; for civ see prev entry. *Eccl* Okeh. RDn (until 1967), Chum. RDn (1967–*).

BROADWOODWIDGER
AP *LG* Lifton Hd, Holsw. PLU(1837–52), Launceston PLU (1852–1930), RSD, Broadwoodw. RD (1894–1966), Holsw. RD (1966–74). Civ bdry: 1884,[108] 1885.[85] *Parl* Seq 21. *Eccl* Tav. RDn (until 1875), Trigg Major RDn (Truro dioc, 1875–1922), Tav. RDn (1922–*). Eccl bdry: 1958.[86]

BRUSHFORD
AP *LG* Seq 41. *Parl* Seq 5. *Eccl* Seq 20.

BUCKERELL
AP *LG* Seq 26. Civ bdry: 1884.[25] *Parl* Seq 1. *Eccl* Seq 12.

BUCKFASTLEIGH
AP *LG* Stanb. Hd, Tot. PLU, RSD (ent 1875–94, pt Jan–apptd day 1894), pt Buckfastleigh UD (Jan–apptd day 1894). Abol civ 1894 the pt in the USD to cr East Buckfastleigh CP, the remainder to cr West Buckfastleigh CP.[47] *Parl* S'rn Dv (1832–67), South Dv (1867–85), S'rn Dv (1885–1918). *Eccl* Seq 39.

EAST BUCKFASTLEIGH
CP Cr 1894 from the pt of Buckfaslteigh AP in Buckfastleigh USD.[47] *LG* Tot. PLU, Buckfastleigh UD. *Parl* Tot. Dv/CC (1918–*).

WEST BUCKFASTLEIGH
CP Cr 1894 from the pt of Buckfastleigh AP not in Buckfastleigh USD.[47] *LG* Tot. PLU, RD. *Parl* Tot. Dv/CC (1918–*).

EAST BUCKLAND
AP *LG* Seq 5. *Parl* Seq 2. *Eccl* Seq 17.

EGG BUCKLAND
AP *LG* Rob. Hd, Plymp. St Mary PLU, RSD, RD. Civ bdry: 1896 (loses pt to Plymouth CB and Plymouth Charles AP).[109] Abol civ 1939 pt to Plymouth CB and CP, pt to Bickleigh AP.[55] *Parl* S'rn Dv (1832–67), South Dv (1867–85), W'rn Dv (1885–1918), Tav. Dv (1918–48). *Eccl* Tam. RDn (until 1848), Plymp. RDn (1848–1954), Plymouth RDn (1954–*). Eccl bdry: 1931 (help cr Laira EP),[110] 1958 (help cr Plymouth Crownhill (Church of the Ascenseion) EP).[111]

WEST BUCKLAND
AP *LG* Seq 5. Civ bdry: 1884.[112] *Parl* Seq 2. *Eccl* Shirw. RDn (until 1875), S Molt. RDn (1875–*).

BUCKLAND BREWER
AP Incl chap East Putford (sep civ identity early, no sep eccl identity, later associated with West Putford, qv). *LG* Seq 34. Civ bdry: 1883,[63] 1885.[113] *Parl* Seq 9. *Eccl* Seq 21.

BUCKLAND FILLEIGH
AP *LG* Seq 36. *Parl* Seq 3. *Eccl* Seq 28.

BUCKLAND IN THE MOOR
Chap in Ashburton AP, sep civ identity early, sep EP between 1878–1910.[20] *LG* Seq 25. *Parl* Seq 16. *Eccl* Moret. RDn.

BUCKLAND MONACHORUM
AP Incl chap Horrabridge (sep EP 1867,[114] sep CP 1950[115]). *LG* Seq 33. *Parl* Seq 21. *Eccl* Seq 37. Addtl eccl bdry alt: 1935 (cr Yelverton EP).[116]

BUCKLAND TOUT SAINTS
Chap in Charleton AP, sep CP 1866,[115] no sep eccl identity. *LG* Seq 9. Civ bdry: 1884.[13] *Parl* South Dv (1867–85), S'rn Dv (1885–1918), Tot. Dv/CC (1918–*).

BUCKS MILLS
EP Cr 1862 from Woolfardisworthy West AP, Parkham AP.[118] Hartland RDn.

EAST BUDLEIGH
AP Incl chap Withycombe Raleigh (sep civ identity early, sep EP 1850[119]), chap Budleigh Salterton (sep CP 1894 [the pt of East Budleigh in Budl. Salterton USD],[47] sep EP 1900[120]). *LG* E Budl. Hd, St Thomas PLU, pt Budl. Salterton USD, pt St Thomas RSD, St Thomas RD. *Parl* Seq 12. *Eccl* Aylb. RDn. Abol eccl 1926 to

help cr East Budleigh with Bicton EP.[59]

EAST BUDLEIGH WITH BICTON
EP Cr 1926 by union East Budleigh AP, Bicton AP.[59] Aylb. RDn.

BUDLEIGH SALTERTON
Chap in East Budleigh AP, sep CP 1894 (the pt in Budl. Salterton USD),[47] sep EP 1900.[120] *LG* St Thomas PLU, Budl. Salterton UD. Civ bdry: 1896.[121] *Parl* Hon. Dv/CC (1918–*). *Eccl* Aylb. RDn.

BULKWORTHY
Chap in Abbots Bickington AP, sep civ identity early, no sep eccl identity. *LG* Seq 34. Civ bdry: 1883,[63] 1885.[122] *Parl* Seq 9.

BURLESCOMBE
AP *LG* Pt Bamp. Hd, pt Halb. Hd, Wellington PLU, RSD, Culmstock RD (1894–1935), Tiv. RD (1935–74). Civ bdry: 1884.[123] *Parl* Seq 7. *Eccl* Seq 14.

BURRINGTON
AP *LG* N Tawt. with Wink. Hd, S Molt. PLU, RSD, RD. *Parl* Seq 2. *Eccl* Seq 20.

BUTTERLEIGH
AP *LG* Cliston Hd, Tiv. PLU, RSD, RD. *Parl* Seq 17. *Eccl* Seq 13.

CADBURY
AP *LG* Seq 23. *Parl* Seq 7. *Eccl* Seq 3.

CADELEIGH
AP *LG* Seq 23. *Parl* Seq 7. *Eccl* Cadb. RDn (until 1875), Tiv. W RDn (1875–1902), Tiv. RDn (1902–*).

CALVERLEIGH
AP *LG* Tiv. Hd, PLU, RSD. Abol civ 1885 ent to Loxbeare AP.[124] *Parl* N'rn Dv (1832–67), North Dv (1867–85), N-E'rn Dv (1885–1918). *Eccl* Seq 15.

CATTEDOWN
EP Cr 1911 from Sutton on Plym EP.[125] Three Towns RDn. Abol 1954 ent to Sutton on Plym EP.[126]

CHAGFORD
AP *LG* Seq 53. *Parl* Seq 13. *Eccl* Dunsford RDn (until 1875), Moret. RDn (1875–*).

CHALLCOMBE
AP *LG* Seq 37. *Parl* Seq 8. *Eccl* Seq 26.

CHARDSTOCK
AP In Dorset (Beaminster Hd). *LG* Axmin. PLU, RSD, sep RD in Dorset (1894–96). Civ bdry: 1884 (loses pt to Membury CP, Devon).[127] Transf 1896 to Devon,[126] after which civ: *LG* Axmin. RD. Civ bdry: 1966 (loses pt to Chard AP, Wambrook AP, both Somerset).[16] *Parl* In Dorset until 1918, Hon. Dv/CC (1918–*). *Eccl* Bridport RDn (until 1872), Beaminster RDn (1872–*) and thus in Sarum dioc until 1542 and from 1836–*, Bristol dioc 1542–1836.

CHARDSTOCK ALL SAINTS
EP Cr 1841 from Chardstock AP (Dorset), Axminster AP (Devon)[132] and thus primarily Dorset, qv for main entry.

CHARLES
AP *LG* Shirw. Hd, S Molt. PLU, RSD, RD. *Parl* Seq 2. *Eccl* Shirw. RDn (until 1875), S Molt. RDn (1875–1945), Shirw. RDn (1945–*).

CHARLETON
AP Incl chap Buckland Tout Saints (sep civ identity early, no sep eccl identity, hence eccl 'Charleton with Buckland Tout Saints', qv). *LG* Seq 9. Civ bdry: 1884.[13] *Parl* Seq 19.

CHARLETON WITH BUCKLAND TOUT SAINTS
AP Usual eccl spelling; for civ and sep chap Buckland Tout Saints see prev entry. *Eccl* Seq 40. Eccl bdry: 1938.[128]

CHAWLEIGH
AP *LG* Chawleigh Bor (status not sustained), Seq 41. *Parl* Seq 5. *Eccl* Seq 20.

CHELDON
AP *LG* Seq 49. *Parl* Seq 2. *Eccl* Seq 24.

CHELSON MEADOW
Ex-par place, sep CP 1858.[129] *LG* Plymp. Hd, situated in Plymp. Earle Bor, Plymp. St Mary PLU, RSD. Abol 1894 ent to Plympton St Mary CP.[130] *Parl* Situated in Plympton Earle Parl Bor (1295–1832), South Dv (1867–85), S'rn Dv (1885–1918).

CHERITON BISHOP
AP *LG* Seq 51. *Parl* Seq 14. *Eccl* Seq 6.

CHERITON FITZPAINE
AP *LG* Seq 7. Civ bdry: 1884.[131] *Parl* Seq 5. *Eccl* Seq 3.

CHEVITHORNE
EP Cr 1889 from Tiverton AP.[133] Tiv. W RDn (1889–1902), Tiv. RDn (1902–*). Bdry: 1958.[134]

CHITTLEHAMHOLT
Chap in Chittlehampton AP, sep EP 1839,[136] sep CP 1866.[81] *LG* S Molt. Hd, PLU,[135] RSD, RD. Civ bdry: 1885.[137] *Parl* North Dv (1867–85), N'rn Dv (1885–1918), S Molt. Dv (1918–48), N Devon CC (1948–*). *Eccl* Barnst. RDn (1839–75), S Molt. RDn (1875–*).

CHITTLEHAMPTON
AP Incl chap Chittlehamholt (sep EP 1839,[136] sep CP 1866[81]). *LG* Seq 31. Addtl civ bdry alt: 1884,[112] 1885.[137] *Parl* Seq 2. *Eccl* Seq 17.

CHIVELSTONE
Chap in Stokenham AP, sep civ identity early, eccl severed 1932 to help cr South Pool with Chivelstone EP.[138] *LG* Seq 9. *Parl* Seq 19.

CHRISTOW
AP *LG* Seq 54. *Parl* Seq 17. *Eccl* Seq 6.

CHUDLEIGH
AP *LG* Chudleigh Bor (status not sustained), Seq 16. *Parl* Seq 16. *Eccl* Pec jurisd Bp Exeter (until 1848), Kenn RDn (1848–75), Moret. RDn (1875–*).

CHUDLEIGH KNIGHTON
EP Chap pt in Hennock AP, pt in Bovey Tracey AP, sep EP 1852.[75] Moret. RDn. Bdry: 1956.[77]

CHUMLEIGH
AP *LG* Chum. Bor (status not sustained), Seq 49. *Parl* Seq 2. *Eccl* Seq 20.

CHURCHSTANTON
AP *LG* Hemyock Hd, Taunton PLU, RSD, sep RD in Devon (1894–96). Transf 1896 to Somer-

set.[126] *Parl* N'rn Dv (1832–67), North Dv (1867–85), E'rn Dv (1885–1918), Somerset thereafter. *Eccl* Dunk. RDn (until 1875), Dunk. & Hon. RDn (1875–1902), Hon. RDn (1902–early 1960s), Taunton RDn (early 1960s–63), Taunton S RDn (1963–*) (last 2 in Bath & Wells dioc).

CHURCHSTOW
AP *LG* Seq 38. Civ bdry: 1884,[13] 1896,[15] 1935.[1] *Parl* Seq 19. *Eccl* Seq 40.

CHURSTON FERRERS
Chap in Brixham AP, sep civ identity early, sep EP by 1850.[96] *LG* Haytor Hd, Tot. PLU, RSD, RD. Abol civ 1967 pt to help cr Torbay CB and CP, pt to Kingswear CP.[98] *Parl* S'rn Dv (1832–67), East Dv (1867–85), Torq. Dv (1885–1948), Torbay BC (1948–70). *Eccl* Ipp. RDn. Abol eccl 1954 to help cr Churston Ferrers with Goodrington EP.[101]

CHURSTON FERRERS WITH GOODRINGTON
EP Cr 1954 by union Churston Ferrers EP, pt Brixham AP, pt Paignton AP.[101] Ipp. RDn.

CLANNABOROUGH
AP *LG* Seq 41. Civ bdry: 1884.[139] *Parl* Seq 5. *Eccl* Chum. RDn (until 1875), Cadb. RDn (1875–*).

CLAWTON
Curacy to Cornworth Priory, independent status as par maintained. *LG* Seq 46. *Parl* Seq 11. *Eccl* Holsw. RDn.

CLAYHANGER
AP *LG* Seq 3. *Parl* Seq 7. *Eccl* Tiv. RDn (until 1875), Tiv. E RDn (1875–1902), Cull. RDn (1902–68), Tiv. RDn (1968–*).

CLAYHIDON
AP *LG* Seq 27. Civ bdry: 1966 (loses pt to West Buckland CP, Somerset).[124] *Parl* Seq 7. *Eccl* Dunk. RDn (until 1875), Dunk. & Hon. RDn (1875–1902), Cull. RDn (1902–*). Eccl bdry: 1844 (help cr Dunkeswell Abbey EP),[140] 1958.[141]

CLOVELLY
AP *LG* Seq 21. *Parl* Seq 9. *Eccl* Seq 21.

BROAD CLYST
AP *LG* Seq 8. Civ bdry: 1966.[7] *Parl* Seq 17. *Eccl* Seq 1.

CLYST HONITON
AP *LG* Seq 6. *Parl* Seq 12. *Eccl* Pec jurisd Dean & Chapter of Exeter (until 1848), Seq 1 thereafter.

CLYST HYDON
AP *LG* Seq 8. Civ bdry: 1884.[3] *Parl* Seq 17. *Eccl* Plymt. RDn (until 1875), Aylb. RDn (1875–1902), Ott. RDn (1902–*).

CLYST ST GEORGE
AP *LG* Seq 6. Civ bdry: 1966.[7] *Parl* Seq 12. *Eccl* Seq 1.

CLYST ST LAWRENCE
AP *LG* Seq 8. Civ bdry: 1884.[3] *Parl* Seq 17. *Eccl* Seq 11.

CLYST ST MARY
AP *LG* Seq 6. *Parl* Seq 12. *Eccl* Seq 1. Eccl bdry: 1931.[142]

COCKINGTON
Curacy in Tormoham AP, civ and eccl identity as par maintained. *LG* Haytor Hd, Newt. Abb. PLU, RSD (1875–Jan 1894), Cockington USD (Jan–apptd day 1894), Cockington UD (1894–1900), Newt. Abb. RD (1900–28). Civ bdry: 1900.[143] Abol civ 1928 ent to Torquay CP.[144] *Parl* S'rn Dv (1832–67), East Dv (1867–85), Torq. Dv (1885–1948), Tot. CC (1948–*). *Eccl* Pec jurisd Manor of Cockington (until 1848), Ipp. RDn thereafter. Eccl bdry: 1881.[145]

COFFINSWELL
Chap in St Marychurch AP, sep civ identity early, sep EP 1913.[79] *LG* Seq 25. Civ bdry: 1967 (help cr Torbay CB and CP).[98] *Parl* Seq 16. *Eccl* Ipp. RDn.

COFTON
EP Cr 1864 from Starcross EP.[146] Kenn RDn.

COLATON RALEIGH
AP *LG* Seq 6. Civ bdry: 1883,[63] 1894.[147] *Parl* Seq 12. *Eccl* Seq 1. Eccl bdry: 1845 (help cr Salterton EP, now called 'Woodbury Salterton').[148]

COLDRIDGE
AP *LG* Seq 41. *Parl* Seq 5. *Eccl* Seq 20.

COLEBROOKE
AP *LG* Seq 13. Civ bdry: 1884.[149] *Parl* Seq 5. *Eccl* Pec jurisd Dean & Chapter of Exeter (until 1848), Seq 3 thereafter.

COLLATON
EP Cr 1864 from Paignton AP.[150] Ipp. RDn.

COLYTON
AP Incl bor Colyford (status not sustained, no sep identity as par), chap Monkton (sep civ identity early, sep EP 1867[151]), chap and bor Shute (sep identity as bor not sustained, civ identity as par early, sep EP 1860[152]). *LG* Seq 11. Civ bdry: 1885,[153] 1935.[1] *Parl* Seq 12. *Eccl* Pec jurisd Dean & Chapter of Exeter (until 1848), Seq 8 thereafter.

COMBE IN TEIGNHEAD
AP *LG* Wonf. Hd, Newt. Abb. PLU, RSD. Abol civ 1885 pt to help cr Haccombe with Combe CP, pt to Stokeinteignhead AP.[154] *Parl* S'rn Dv (1832–67), East Dv (1867–85). *Eccl* Kenn RDn (until 1848), Ipp. RDn (1848–75), Moret. RDn (1875–*).

COMBE MARTIN
AP *LG* Combe Martin Bor (status not sustained), Seq 4. *Parl* Seq 8. *Eccl* Seq 26.

COMBE RALEIGH
AP *LG* Seq 2. Civ bdry: 1884.[25] *Parl* Seq 12. *Eccl* Seq 5.

COMBE PYNE
AP Usual eccl spelling; for civ see 'Combpyne'. *Eccl* Hon. RDn (until 1875), Dunk. & Hon. RDn (1875–1902), Hon. RDn (1902–72). Abol eccl 1972 to help cr Combe Pyne with Rousdon EP.[155]

COMBE PYNE WITH ROUSDON
EP Cr 1972 by union Combe Pyne AP, Rousdon AP.[155] Hon. RDn.

COMBE RALEIGH
AP *LG* Seq 2. Civ bdry: 1884.[25] *Parl* Seq 12. *Eccl* Seq 5.

COMBPYNE
AP Usual civ spelling; for eccl see 'Combe Pyne'. *LG* Axmin. Hd, PLU, RSD, RD. Abol civ 1939 to help cr Combpyne Rousdon CP.[33] *Parl* S'rn Dv (1832–67), East Dv (1867–85), E'rn Dv (1885–1918), Hon. Dv (1918–48).

COMBPYNE ROUSDON
CP Cr 1939 by union Combpyne AP, Rousdon AP, pt Axmouth AP.[33] *LG* Axmin. RD. *Parl* Hon. CC (1948–*).

COMPTON GIFFORD
Chap in Plymouth Charles CP/EP, sep CP 1866,[156] sep EP 1871.[155] *LG* Rob. Hd, Plymp. St Mary PLU, Compton Gifford USD, UD (1894–96), Plymp. St Mary RD (1896–1939). Civ bdry: 1896 (loses pt to Plymouth CB and Plymouth Charles CP),[109] 1935.[1] Abol civ 1939 ent to Plymouth CB and CP.[55] *Parl* South Dv (1867–85), W'rn Dv (1885–1918), Tav. Dv (1918–48). *Eccl* Plymp. RDn (1871–75), Three Towns RDn (1875–1954), Plymouth RDn (1954–*). Eccl bdry: 1880,[157] 1889 (help cr Plymouth St Matthias EP),[158] 1905 (help cr Plymouth St Augustine EP),[159] 1905,[160] 1910 (help cr Plymouth St Gabriel, Peverell Park EP),[161] 1972.[162]

COOKBURY
Chap in Milton Damerel AP, sep civ identity early, eccl severed 1954 to help cr Holsworthy with Cookbury EP.[163] *LG* Seq 46. *Parl* Seq 11.

CORNWOOD
AP Incl chap Ivybridge (sep EP 1835,[164] sep CP 1894 [the pt in Ivybr. USD][165]). *LG* Erming. Hd, Plymp. St Mary PLU, pt Ivybr. USD, pt Plymp. St Mary RSD, Plymp. St Mary RD. *Parl* Seq 18. *Eccl* Seq 36.

CORNWORTHY
AP *LG* Seq 10. *Parl* Seq 19. *Eccl* Seq 39.

CORYTON
AP *LG* Seq 29. Civ bdry: 1884.[93] *Parl* Seq 21. *Eccl* Seq 38.

COTLEIGH
AP *LG* Seq 12. *Parl* Seq 12. *Eccl* Seq 8.

COUNTISBURY
Chap in Lynton AP, sep civ identity early, sep EP 1747.[166] *LG* Seq 37. Civ bdry: 1866,[167] 1935.[1] *Parl* Seq 8. *Eccl* Shirw. RDn.

COVE
EP Cr 1886 from Tiverton AP.[133] Tiv. W RDn (1886–1902), Tiv. RDn (1902–*).

COWLEY–See BRAMPFORD SPEKE

CREACOMBE
AP *LG* Seq 49. Civ bdry: 1884.[112] *Parl* Seq 2. *Eccl* Seq 23.

CREDITON
AP Incl chap Kennerleigh (sep civ identity early, sep EP 1752[11]), chap Sandford (sep civ identity early, eccl severed 1928 to help cr Sandford with Upton Hellions EP[168]). *LG* Cred. Hd, Bor (status not sustained), PLU, pt Cred. USD, pt Cred. RSD. Addtl civ bdry alt: 1884.[169] Abol civ 1894 the pt in the USD to cr Crediton Town CP, the remainder to cr Crediton Hamlets CP.[170] *Parl* Cred. Parl Bor (1303 only), N'rn Dv (1832–67), North Dv (1867–85), N'rn Dv (1885–1918), S Molt. Dv (1918–48). *Eccl* Pec jurisd Bp Exeter (until 1848), Kenn RDn (1848–75), Cadb. RDn (1875–*).

CREDITON HAMLETS
CP Cr 1894 from the pt of Crediton AP not in Cred. USD.[170] *LG* Cred. PLU, RD. *Parl* S Molt. Dv (1918–48), Torr. CC (1948–70), Tiv. CC (1970–*).

CREDITON TOWN
CP Cr 1894 from the pt of Crediton AP in Cred. USD.[170] *LG* Cred. PLU, UD. *Parl* S Molt. Dv (1918–48), Torr. CC (1948–70), Tiv. CC (1970–*).

CRUWYS MORCHARD
AP *LG* Seq 50. Civ bdry: 1884.[171] *Parl* Seq 7. *Eccl* Seq 25.

CULLOMPTON
AP *LG* Perhaps Cull. Bor (17th cent, status not sustained),[172] Seq 23. Civ bdry: 1883.[63] *Parl* Seq 7. *Eccl* Seq 13.

CULMSTOCK
AP *LG* Seq 27. *Parl* Seq 7. *Eccl* Pec jurisd Dean & Chapter of Exeter (until 1848), Seq 14 thereafter.

DALWOOD
Hmlt (Dorset, Fordington Lbty) in Stockland AP (Dorset, Whitchurch Canonicorum Hd), the par and hmlt both transf to Devon 1832 for parl purposes, 1844 for civ purposes,[27] Dalwood sep CP 1866[81] but no sep civ identity.
LG Axmin. Hd (from 1844), PLU, RSD, RD. *Parl* In Dorset until 1832, East Dv (1867–85), E'rn Dv (1885–1918), Hon. Dv/CC (1918–*).

DARTINGTON
AP Incl bor North Ford (status not sustained, no sep identity as par), Seq 39. Civ bdry: 1884,[22] 1897.[51] *Parl* Seq 19. *Eccl* Often as 'Dartington with St Barnabas', Seq 39. Eccl bdry: 1968.[52]

DARTMOUTH
CP Cr 1891 by union St Petrox AP, St Saviour CP, Townstall AP (qv also for Dartm. Bor).[173] *LG* Tot. PLU, Dartm. USD, MB. *Parl* Torq. Dv (1918–48), Tot. CC (1948–*).

DARTMOUTH ST PETROX
Usual eccl spelling; for civ see 'St Petrox'. Prob chap in Townstall AP, sep civ identity early, sep EP 1748.[11] *Eccl* Tot. RDn (1748–1875), Ipp. RDn (1875–*).

DAWLISH
AP Incl chap East Teignmouth (sep civ identity early, sep EP 1777[11]). *LG* Exmin. Hd, Newt. Abb. PLU, pt Dawlish USD, pt Teignm. USD (1883–94), pt Newt. Abb. RSD. Civ bdry: 1883,[63] 1885.[174] Abol civ 1894 the pt in Dawlish USD to cr East Dawlish CP, the remainder to cr West Dawlish CP.[47] *Parl* S'rn Dv (1832–67), East Dv (1867–85), Mid Dv (1885–1918). *Eccl* Sometimes as 'Dawlish with St Marks's and Holcombe', pec jurisd Dean & Chapter of Exeter (until 1848), Seq 10 thereafter. St Mark was cr sep EP 1850[11] but did not sustain

independent status.

DAWLISH WITH ST MARK'S AND HOLCOMBE–
See prev entry

EAST DAWLISH
CP Cr 1894 from the pt of Dawlish AP in Dawlish USD.[47] *LG* Newt. Abb. PLU, Dawlish UD. Civ bdry: 1928,[175] 1935.[1] *Parl* Tiv. Dv/CC (1918–*).

WEST DAWLISH
CP Cr 1894 from the pt of Dawlish AP not in Dawlish USD.[47] Civ bdry: 1928,[175] 1935.[1] *Parl* Tiv. Dv/CC (1918–*).

DEAN PRIOR
AP *LG* Seq 39. *Parl* Seq 19. *Eccl* Seq 39.

DENBURY
AP *LG* Denbury Bor (status not sustained), Haytor Hd, Newt. Abb. PLU, RSD. Abol civ 1885 ent to Torbryan AP.[176] *Parl* S'rn Dv (1832–67), East Dv (1867–85). *Eccl* Seq 32. Eccl bdry: 1928.[53]

DEVON COUNTY BUILDINGS AREA
Reanming 1963 of Devon Prison and Constabulary Barracks as latter transf from Exeter CB to Devon Adm Co, not to be in any co div.[209]

DEVON PRISON AND CONSTABULARY BARRACKS
Situated in Exeter St David CP but not pt of it, within Exeter Bor/MB/CB until transf 1963 to Devon Adm Co as 'Devon County Buildings Area', not to be in any co div.[209]

DEVONPORT
The following have 'Devonport' in their names. Insofar as any existed at a given time: *LG* Rob. Hd, Stoke Damerel incorp for poor (from 1888, Devonport Parish incorp), Devonport USD, MB (1837–89), CB (1889–1914), Plymouth CB (1914–74). *Parl* Devonport Parl Bor (1832–1918). *Eccl* Plymp. RDn (until 1875), Three Towns RDn (1875–1954), Plymouth RDn (1954–*).

CP1–DEVONPORT–Renaming 1824 of Plymouth Docks area. Civ bdry: 1888 (gains Stoke Damerel AP, pt Pennycross CP, pt St Budeaux CP when constituted CB),[165] 1900.[177]

EP1–DEVONPORT ST AUBYN–Cr 1882 from Stoke Damerel AP, EP11.[178] Bdry: 1887 (help cr EP6).[190] Reconstituted 1958 gaining EP6, EP8, EP11, EP12.[179]

EP2–DEVONPORT ST BARNABAS–Cr 1904 from Stoke Damerel AP.[180] Bdry: 1954,[181] 1965.[182]

EP3–DEVONPORT ST BARTHOLOMEW–Cr 1965 from Stoke Damerel AP, Pennycross EP, EP2.[182]

EP4–DEVONPORT ST BONIFACE–Cr 1916 from St Budeaux EP.[183] Bdry: 1933 (help cr Weston Mill EP),[184] 1933,[185] 1954.[186]

EP5–DEVONPORT ST JAMES–Cr 1846 from Stoke Damerel AP.[187] Bdry: 1874,[188] 1885 (help cr EP7).[161] Sometimes 'Devonport St James the Great'. Abol 1958 pt to help cr EP10, pt to North Keynham EP.[179]

EP6–DEVONPORT ST JOHN THE BAPTIST–Cr 1887 from Stoke Damerel AP, EP1.[190] Abol 1958 ent to EP1.[179]

EP7–DEVONPORT ST MARK, FORD–Cr 1885 from Stoke Damerel AP, EP9, EP5, Plymouth St Andrew EP.[189] Bdry: 1895,[191] 1954,[186] 1957 (help cr Plymouth St James the Less, Ham EP),[192] 1929 (help cr North Keynham EP, now commonly called 'Devonport St Thomas').[193]

EP8–DEVONPORT ST MARY–Cr 1846 from Stoke Damerel AP.[194] Abol 1958 ent to EP1.[179]

EP9–DEVONPORT ST MICHAEL–Cr 1873 from Stoke Damerel AP.[194] Bdry: 1885 (help cr EP7),[189] 1895,[191] 1954.[186] Abol 1958 ent to EP10.[179]

EP10–DEVONPORT ST MICHAEL, STOKE–Cr 1958 from ent EP9, pt EP5.[179]

EP11–DEVONPORT ST PAUL–Cr 1846 from Stoke Damerel AP.[195] Bdry: 1882 (help cr EP1).[178] Abol 1958 ent to EP1.[179]

EP12–DEVONPORT ST STEPHEN–Cr 1846 from Stoke Damerel AP.[195] Abol 1958 ent to EP1.[179]

– –DEVONPORT ST THOMAS–Common name now for EP cr 1929 as 'North Keynham' qv.

DIPTFORD
AP *LG* Seq 39. *Parl* Seq 19. *Eccl* Seq 39.

DITTISHAM
AP *LG* Seq 10. *Parl* Seq 19. *Eccl* Seq 39.

DODBROOKE
AP *LG* Dodbrooke Bor (status not sustained), Coler. Hd, Kingsbr. PLU, RSD (until 4 Mar 1893), Kingsbr. & Dodbrooke USD (4 Mar–26 Mar 1893). Civ bdry: 1884.[13] Abol civ 26 Mar 1893 to help cr Kingsbridge and Dodbrooke CP.[196] *Parl* S'rn Dv (1832–67), South Dv (1867–85), S'rn Dv (1885–1918). *Eccl* Seq 40.

DODDISCOMBSLEIGH
AP *LG* Seq 17. *Parl* Seq 17. *Eccl* Seq 6.

DOLTON
AP *LG* Seq 43. *Parl* Seq 3. *Eccl* Seq 28.

DOTTON
Ex-par place, sep EP 1858.[197] *LG* E Budl. Hd, St Thomas PLU, RSD. Abol 1894 ent to Colaton Raleigh AP.[147] *Parl* South Dv (1867–85), E'rn Dv (1885–1918).

DOWLAND
AP *LG* Seq 43. *Parl* Seq 3. *Eccl* Seq 28.

EAST DOWN
AP *LG* Seq 4. *Parl* Seq 8. *Eccl* Shirw. RDn. Abol eccl 1944 to help cr East Down with Arlington EP.[18]

EAST DOWN WITH ARLINGTON
EP Cr 1944 by union East Down AP, Arlington AP.[18] Shirw. RDn.

WEST DOWN
AP *LG* Seq 4. *Parl* Seq 8. *Eccl* Seq 27.

DOWN ST MARY
AP *LG* Seq 41. Civ bdry: 1884.[139] *Parl* Seq 5. *Eccl*

Seq 3.

DREWSTEIGNTON

AP *LG* Seq 53. Civ bdry: 1885.[198] *Parl* Seq 13. *Eccl* Seq 7.

DUNCHIDEOCK

AP *LG* Seq 17. *Parl* Seq 17. *Eccl* Seq 10.

DUNKESWELL

AP *LG* Seq 26. *Parl* Seq 1. *Eccl* Dunk. RDn (until 1875), Dunk. & Hon. RDn (1875–1902), Hon. RDn (1902–29). Eccl bdry: 1844 (help cr Dunkeswell Abbey EP).[140] Abol eccl 1929 to help cr Dunkeswell with Dunkeswell Abbey EP.[199]

DUNKESWELL ABBEY

EP Cr 1844 from Dunkeswell AP, Clayhidon AP, Hemyock AP.[140] Dunk. RDn (1844–75), Dunk. & Hon. RDn (1875–1902), Hon. RDn (1902–29). Abol 1929 to help cr Dunkeswell with Dunkeswell Abbey EP.[199]

DUNKESWELL WITH DUNKESWELL ABBEY

EP Cr 1929 by union Dunkeswell AP, Dunkeswell Abbey EP.[199] Hon. RDn.

DUNSFORD

AP *LG* Seq 54. *Parl* Seq 15. *Eccl* Seq 6.

DUNTERTON

AP *LG* Seq 29. Civ bdry: 1966 (gains pt Stoke Climsland AP, Cornw).[16] *Parl* Seq 21. *Eccl* Tav. RDn. Abol eccl 1921 to help cr Milton Abbot with Dunterton EP.[200]

EGGESFORD

AP *LG* Seq 41. *Parl* Seq 5. *Eccl* Seq 20.

ELBURTON

EP Cr 1973 from Plymstock AP.[201] Plymouth RDn.

ELLACOMBE

EP Cr 1868 from Upton EP.[202] Ipp. RDn. Bdry: 1966.[203] Abol 1974 to help cr Central Torquay EP.[204]

ERMINGTON

AP Incl chap Kingston (sep civ identity early, eccl severed 1934 to help cr Ringmore with Kingston EP[61]), dist Ivybridge (sep EP 1835,[164] sep CP 1894 [the pt in Ivybr. USD][165]). *LG* Erming. Hd, Plymp. St Mary PLU, RD. *Parl* Seq 18. *Eccl* As 'Ermington with Kingston' before 1835 and 'Ermington' thereafter, Plymp. RDn. Eccl bdry: 1934.[104]

ERMINGTON WITH KINGSTON–See prev entry

ERNSETTLE

EP Cr 1958 from St Budeaux EP.[205] Plymouth RDn.

ESCOT

EP Cr 1844 from Ottery St Mary AP, Talaton AP.[206] Aylb. RDn (1844–75), Ott. RDn (1875–*).

EXBOURNE

AP *LG* Seq 47. *Parl* Seq 10. *Eccl* Seq 35.

NETHER EXE

Chap in Thorverton AP, sep civ identity early, sep EP 1730.[11] *LG* Hayr. Hd, St Thomas PLU, RSD, RD. *Parl* Seq 7. *Eccl* Cadb. RDn. Abol eccl 1937 to help cr Rewe with Nether Exe EP.[207]

WEST EXE

EP Cr 1856 from Tiverton AP.[208] Tiv. RDn (1856–75), Tiv. W RDn (1875–1902), Tiv. RDn (1902–*).

EXETER

The following have 'Exeter' in their names. Insofar as any existed at a given time: *LG* Wonf. Hd, Exeter incorp for poor (1697–1930), Bor/MB/CB, USD. *Parl* Exeter Parl Bor/BC. *Eccl* Christianity RDn. The area of the Devon Prison and Constabulary Barracks was not in any CP until (along with pt St Leonard AP) added 1963 to Exeter CP.[209]

CP1–EXETER CP–Cr 1901 by union all APs below, CP2, CP3, CP4.[210] Civ bdry: 1913,[4] 1940,[6] 1963 (gains Devon Prison and Constabulary Barracks, pt St Leonard AP),[209] 1966.[7]

EP1–CENTRAL EXETER–Cr 1974 by union EP8, EP12, EP14.[211]

AP1–EXETER ALLHALLOWS, GOLDSMITH STREET–Abol civ 1901 to help cr CP1.[210] Abol eccl 1934 to help cr EP4.[212]

AP2–EXETER ALL HALLOWS ON THE WALLS–Abol civ 1901 to help cr CP1.[210] Abol eccl 1939 to help cr EP12.[213]

CP2–EXETER BEDFORD CIRCUS–Ex-par place, sep CP 1858.[129] Abol civ 1901 to help cr CP1.[210] Abol eccl 1954 to help cr EP8.[214]

CP3–EXETER BRADNINCH PRECINCT (civ, 'BRADNINCH')–Ex-par place, sep CP 1858.[129] Abol civ 1901 to help cr CP1.[210] Abol eccl 1956 to help cr EP8.[214]

CP4–EXETER CASTLE YARD–Ex-par place, sep CP 1858.[129] Abol civ 1963 ent to CP1.[219] Abol eccl 1956 to help cr EP8.[214]

–EXETER CATHEDRAL PRECINCTS (civ, 'CLOSE OF ST PETER'S CATHEDRAL')–Ex-par place not made CP, eccl loses pt 1956 to help cr EP8.[214]

EP2–EXETER EMMANUEL–Cr 1910 from Exeter St Thomas AP, Exwick EP.[215] Bdry: 1956,[214] 1958.[216]

AP3–EXETER HOLY TRINITY–Chap in Heavitree AP, sep civ identity early in the Bor, sep eccl identity early. Abol civ 1901 to help cr CP1.[210] Abol eccl 1969 to help cr EP6.[217] Eccl bdry: 1956.[214]

AP4–EXETER ST DAVID–Chap in Heavitree AP, sep civ identity early in the Bor, sep EP 1826.[11] Abol civ 1901 to help cr CP1.[210] Incl Exeter St Michael, sep EP 1868[11] but sep status not maintained, hence this par eccl sometimes 'Exeter St David with St Michael and All Angels'. Addtl eccl bdry alt: 1956.[214]

AP5–EXETER ST EDMUND–Abol civ 1901 to help cr CP1.[210] Abol eccl 1956 pt to AP13, pt to Exeter St Thomas AP.[214]

AP6–EXETER ST GEORGE THE MARTYR (eccl, 'EXETER ST GEORGE')– Abol civ 1901 to help cr CP1.[210] Abol eccl 1935 to help cr EP10.[218]

EP3–EXETER ST JAMES–Cr 1838 from AP18.[219] Sometimes 'Exeter St James the Great'. Bdry: 1883,[220] 1883 (help cr EP11),[225] 1956.[214]

AP7–EXETER ST JOHN–Abol civ 1901 to help cr CP1.[210] Abol eccl 1935 to help cr EP10.[218]
AP8–EXETER ST KERRIAN–Abol civ 1901 to help cr CP1.[210] Abol eccl 1934 to help cr EP9.[218]
AP9–EXETER ST LAWRENCE–Abol civ 1901 to help cr CP1.[210] Abol eccl 1930 to help cr EP5.[221]
EP4–EXETER ST LAWRENCE WITH ALLHALLOWS (GOLDSMITH STREET), ST MARTIN, ST PAUL AND ST STEPHEN–Cr 1934 by union EP5, AP1.[212] Abol 1956 to help cr EP8.[214]
EP5–EXETER ST LAWRENCE WITH ST STEPHEN AND ST MARTIN–Cr 1930 by union AP9, AP10, AP19.[221] Abol 1934 to help cr EP4.[212]
–EXETER ST LEONARD–Usual eccl spelling; for civ see 'St Leonard'. Abol eccl 1969 to help cr EP6.[217]
EP6–EXETER ST LEONARD WITH HOLY TRINITY–Cr 1969 by union Exeter St Leonard AP, AP3.[217]
EP7–EXETER ST MARK–Cr 1930 from Heavitree AP.[222] Bdry: 1956.[214]
AP10–EXETER ST MARTIN–Abol civ 1901 to help cr CP1.[210] Abol eccl 1930 to help cr EP5.[221]
EP8–EXETER ST MARTIN, ST STEPHEN, ST LAWRENCE WITH ALLHALLOWS (GOLDSMITH STREET) AND ST PAUL–Cr 1956 by union EP4, CP2, CP3, CP4, pt CP5, EP4, AP16.[214] Abol 1974 to help cr EP1.[211]
AP11–EXETER ST MARY ARCHES–Abol civ 1901 to help cr CP1.[210] Abol eccl 1934 to help cr EP9.[212]
EP9–EXETER ST MARY ARCHES WITH ST KERRIAN AND ST PANCRAS–Cr 1934 by union AP8, AP11, AP15.[212]
AP12–EXETER ST MARY MAJOR–Abol civ 1901 to help cr CP1.[210] Abol eccl 1935 to help cr EP10.[218]
EP10–EXETER ST MARY MAJOR WITH ST GEORGE, ST JOHN AND ST PETROCK–Cr 1935 by union AP6, AP7, AP12, AP17.[218] Renamed 1970 as EP14.[223]
AP13–EXETER ST MARY STEPS–Abol civ 1901 to help cr CP1.[210] Eccl bdry: 1939,[213] 1956.[224]
EP11–EXETER ST MATTHEW, NEWTOWN–Cr 1883 from AP18, EP3.[225] Bdry: 1956.[214]
–EXETER ST MICHAEL–See EXETER ST DAVID
AP14–EXETER ST OLAVE–Abol civ 1901 to help cr CP1.[210] Abol eccl 1939 to help cr EP12.[213]
EP12–EXETER ST OLAVE WITH ALLHALLOWS ON THE WALL–Cr 1939 by unon AP2, AP14.[213] Abol 1974 to help cr EP1.[211]
AP15–EXETER ST PANCRAS–Abol civ 1901 to help cr CP1.[210] Abol eccl 1934 to help cr EP9.[212]
AP16–EXETER ST PAUL–Abol civ 1901 to help cr CP1.[210] Abol eccl 1956 to help cr EP8.[214]
EP13–EXETER ST PAUL–Cr 1964 from Wear EP (now commonly called 'Countess Wear').[226]
AP17–EXETER ST PETROCK–Abol civ 1901 to help cr CP1.[210] Abol eccl 1935 to help cr EP10.[214]
EP14–EXETER ST PETROCK WITH ST MARY MAJOR–Renaming 1970 of EP10.[223] Abol 1974 to help cr EP1.[211]
AP18–EXETER ST SIDWELL–Chap in Heavitree AP, sep civ identity early in Bor, sep EP 1825.[11] Abol civ 1901 to help cr CP1.[210] Eccl bdry: 1838 (cr EP3),[219] 1883 (help cr EP11),[225] 1956.[214]
AP19–EXETER ST STEPHEN–Abol civ 1901 to help cr CP1.[210] Abol eccl 1930 to help cr EP5.[221]
–EXETER ST THOMAS–Usual eccl spelling; for civ see 'St Thomas the Apostle'. Kenn RDn (until 1875), Christianity RDn (1875–*). Eccl bdry: 1793 (cr Oldridge EP),[11] 1872 (cr Exwick EP),[227] 1910,[228] 1910 (help cr EP2).[215]

EXMINSTER
AP *LG* Seq 17. Civ bdry: 1884,[3] 1940 (loses pt to Exeter CB and CP),[6] 1966 (loses pt to Exeter CB and St Thomas the Apostle AP).[7] *Parl* Seq 17. *Eccl* Seq 10.

EXMOOR
Ex-par place, sep CP 1858,[129] sep EP 1857.[230] Pt Somerset (Carhampton Hd), pt Devon (S Molt. Hd). *LG* S Molt. PLU, RSD. The pt in Devon added 1884 to North Molton AP[229] and par ent Somerset thereafter. *Parl* Pt in Devon uninhabited; see entry in Somerset. *Eccl* See main entry in Somerset.

EXWICK
EP Cr 1872 from Exeter St Thomas AP.[227] Kenn RDn (1872–75), Christianity RDn (1875–*). Bdry: 1910,[228] 1910 (help cr Exeter Emmanuel EP),[215] 1956,[214] 1958.[216]

FARRINGDON
AP *LG* Seq 6. Civ bdry: 1884.[3] *Parl* Seq 12. *Eccl* Seq 1. Eccl bdry: 1931.[142]

FARWAY
AP *LG* Seq 12. Civ bdry: 1935.[1] *Parl* Seq 12. *Eccl* Seq 9.

FENITON
AP *LG* Seq 22. *Parl* Seq 1. *Eccl* Seq 12.

FILLEIGH
AP *LG* Seq 5. *Parl* Seq 2. *Eccl* Seq 17.

FREMINGTON
AP *LG* Fremington Bor (status not sustained), Seq 18. *Parl* Fremington Parl Bor (1332 only), Seq 8. *Eccl* Seq 16. Eccl bdry: 1923,[231] 1956 (help cr Sticklepath EP).[46]

FRITHELSTOCK
AP *LG* Seq 36. Civ bdry: 1883,[63] 1884,[232] 1885.[233] *Parl* Seq 3. *Eccl* Seq 22.

GEORGEHAM
AP *LG* Seq 4. Civ bdry: 1884.[234] *Parl* Seq 8. *Eccl* Seq 27.

GERMANSWEEK
AP Sometimes 'Week St Germans'. *LG* Seq 28. *Parl* Seq 20. *Eccl* Seq 38.
GIDLEIGH
AP *LG* Seq 53. *Parl* Seq 13. *Eccl* Seq 7.
GITTISHAM
AP *LG* E Budl. Hd, Hon. PLU, RSD, RD. Civ bdry: 1884.[25] *Parl* Seq 12. *Eccl* Hon. RDn (until 1875), Ott. RDn (1875–1902), Hon. RDn (1902–*).
GOODLEIGH
AP *LG* Seq 4. *Parl* Seq 8. *Eccl* Seq 26.
GULWORTHY
EP Name commonly used now for EP cr 1858 as 'Tavistock St Paul', qv.
HACCOMBE
AP Incl area Milber (sep CP 1901 [from area Haccombe with Combe],[235] sep EP 1963[280]). *LG* Wonf. Hd, Newt. Abb. PLU, RSD. Abol civ 1885 to help cr Haccombe with Combe CP.[154] *Parl* S'rn Dv (1832–67), East Dv (1867–85), Mid Dv (1885–1918). *Eccl* Ipp. RDn (until 1875), Moret. RDn (1875–1913), Ipp. RDn (1913–*).
HACCOMBE WITH COMBE
CP Cr 1885 by union Haccombe AP, pt Combe in Teignhead AP.[154] *LG* Wonf. Hd, Newt. Abb. PLU, RSD, RD. Bdry: 1901 (cr Milber CP).[235] *Parl* Tot. Dv/CC (1918–*).
HALBERTON
AP *LG* Seq 20. *Parl* Seq 7. *Eccl* Sometimes as 'Halberton with Ash Thomas', Seq 14.
HALWELL
AP *LG* Seq 10. Civ bdry: 1884.[236] *Parl* Seq 19. *Eccl* Seq 39.
HALWILL
AP *LG* Seq 46. *Parl* Seq 10. *Eccl* Seq 30.
HARBERTON
AP *LG* Seq 10. Civ bdry: 1884.[237] *Parl* Seq 19. *Eccl* Seq 39. Eccl bdry: 1860 (cr Harbertonford EP).[238]
HARBERTONFORD
EP Cr 1860 from Harberton AP.[238] Tot. RDn.
HARFORD
AP *LG* Erming. Hd, Plymp. St Mary PLU, pt Ivybr. USD, pt Plymp. St Mary RSD, Plymp. St Mary RD. Civ bdry: 1894 (the pt in the USD to help cr Ivybridge CP).[165] *Parl* Seq 18. *Eccl* Seq 36.
HARPFORD
AP Incl chap Venn Ottery (sep civ and eccl identity early). *LG* E Budl. Hd, Hon. PLU, RSD, RD (1894–1935), St Thomas RD (1935–68). Civ bdry: 1935.[1] Renamed 1968 'Newton Poppleford and Harpford'.[239] *Parl* S'rn Dv (1832–67), East Dv (1867–85), E'rn Dv (1885–1918), Hon. Dv (1918–48), Tiv. CC (1948–70). *Eccl* Aylb. RDn (until 1875), Ott. RDn (1875–*).
HARTLAND
AP Incl bor Harton (status not sustained, no sep identity as par). *LG* Seq 21. *Parl* Seq 9. *Eccl* Seq 21.
HATHERLEIGH
AP *LG* Hatherleigh Bor (status not sustained), Seq 47. *Parl* Seq 10. *Eccl* Seq 35.
HAWKCHURCH
AP In Dorset (pt Cerne, Totcombe and Modbury Hd, pt Uggscombe Hd), transf 1896 to Devon.[240] *LG* Axmin. PLU, RSD, sep RD in Dorset (1894–96), Axmin. RD (1896–1974). Civ bdry: 1966 (loses pts to Marshwood CP, Thorncombe AP, Whitechurch Canonicorum AP, Wootton Fitzpaine AP, all Dorset).[16] *Parl* In Dorset until 1918, Hon. Dv/CC (1918–*). *Eccl* Bridport RDn (until 1872), Beaminster RDn (1872–*)(Sarum dioc until 1542 and from 1836, Bristol dioc 1542–1836).
HEANTON PUNCHARDON
AP *LG* Seq 4. *Parl* Seq 8. *Eccl* Seq 27.
HEAVITREE
AP Incl chap Exeter St David (sep civ identity early in Exeter Bor, sep EP 1826[11]), chap Exeter St Sidwell (sep civ identity early in Exeter Bor, sep EP 1825[11]), chap Exeter Holy Trinity (sep civ identity early in Exeter Bor, sep eccl identity early). *LG* Wonf. Hd, St Thomas PLU, RSD, RD (1894–96), Heavitree UD (1896–1913). Addtl civ bdry alt: 1879.[241] Abol civ 1913 pt to Exeter CB and CP, pt to Alphington AP, pt to Pinhoe AP, pt to Topsham AP.[4] *Parl* S'rn Dv (1832–67), East Dv (1867–85), N-E'rn Dv (1885–1918). *Eccl* Pec jurisd Dean & Chapter of Exeter (until 1848), Seq 4 thereafter. Addtl eccl bdry alt: 1930 (cr Exeter St Mark EP),[222] 1931,[142] 1934,[242] 1938 (help cr Whipton EP),[243] 1964,[226] 1968.[52]
LITTLE HEMPSTON
AP Usual civ spelling; for eccl see 'Littlehempston'. *LG* Seq 24. Civ bdry: 1897.[51] *Parl* S'rn Dv (1832–67), East Dv (1867–85), S'rn Dv (1885–1918), Tot. Dv/CC (1918–*).
HEMYOCK
AP *LG* Seq 27. Civ bdry: 1966 (loses pt to Wellington Without CP, Somerset).[16] *Parl* Seq 7. *Eccl* Dunk. RDn (until 1875), Tiv. E RDn (1875–1902), Cull. RDn (1902–*).
HENNOCK
AP *LG* Seq 44. Civ bdry: 1883,[63] 1885.[73] *Parl* Seq 16. *Eccl* Seq 34. Eccl bdry: 1852 (help cr Chudleigh Knighton EP).[75]
HIGHAMPTON
AP *LG* Seq 47. Civ bdry: 1884.[244] *Parl* Seq 10. *Eccl* Okeh. RDn (until 1936), Torr. RDn (1936–*).
HIGHLEY ST MARY
Ex-par place, sep CP 1858.[129] *LG* With. Hd, Tiv. PLU,[135] RSD. Abol civ 1894 ent to Newton St Cyres AP.[245] *Parl* East Dv (1867–85), N-E'rn Dv (1885–1918).
HIGHWEEK
Chap in Kingsteignton AP, sep civ identity early, sep EP 1864 as 'Highweek with Abbotsbury',[246] qv. *LG* Teignbr. Hd, Newt. Abb. PLU, RSD, RD (1894–1901), UD (1901–74). Civ bdry: 1883,[63] 1885.[73] *Parl* Seq 16.
HIGHWEEK WITH ABBOTSBURY
Chap in Kingsteignton AP, sep civ identity

early as 'Highweek', qv, sep EP 1864.[246] Moret. RDn. Eccl bdry: 1928.[53]

WEST HILL

EP Cr 1863 from Ottery St Mary AP.[247] Aylb. RDn (1863–75), Ott. RDn (1875–*).

HITTISLEIGH

AP *LG* Seq 51. Civ bdry: 1885.[198] *Parl* Seq 14. *Eccl* Dunsford RDn (until 1875), Cadb. RDn (1875–1973), Okeh. RDn (1973–*).

HOCKWORTHY

AP *LG* Seq 3. Civ bdry: 1884.[248] *Parl* Seq 7. *Eccl* Seq 14.

HOLBETON

AP *LG* Seq 15. Civ bdry: 1884,[102] 1935 (help cr Newton and Noss CP).[1] *Parl* Seq 18. *Eccl* Seq 36. Eccl bdry: 1961.[104]

HOLCOMBE BURNELL

AP *LG* Seq 54. *Parl* Seq 17. *Eccl* Seq 6.

HOLCOMBE ROGUS

AP *LG* Bamp. Hd, Tiv. PLU (1835–before 1850), Wellington PLU (before 1850–1930), RSD, Culmstock RD (1894–1935), Tiv. RD (1935–74). Civ bdry: 1966 (loses pt to Thorne St Margaret CP, Somerset).[16] *Parl* Seq 7. *Eccl* Seq 14.

HOLLACOMBE

AP *LG* Seq 46. *Parl* Seq 11. *Eccl* Seq 30.

HOLNE

AP *LG* Seq 39. *Parl* S'rn Dv (1832–67), South Dv (1867–85), Mid Dv (1885–1918), Tot. Dv/CC (1918–*). *Eccl* Seq 39.

HOLSWORTHY

AP *LG* Holsw. Bor (status not sustained), Black Torr. Hd, Holsw. PLU, RSD, RD (1894–1900), UD (1900–64), RD(1964–74). Civ bdry: 1900 (the pt not constituted Holsw. UD cr Holsworthy Hamlets CP).[249] *Parl* Seq 11. *Eccl* Holsw. RDn. Reconstitued eccl 1954 when gains chap Cookbury of Milton Damerel with Cookbury AP, to cr 'Holsworthy with Cookbury' EP.[163]

HOLSWORTHY HAMLETS

CP Cr 1900 from the pt of Holsworthy AP not constituted Holsw. UD.[249] *LG* Holsw. PLU, RD. *Parl* Tav. Dv/CC (1918–70), W Devon CC (1970–*).

HOLSWORTHY WITH COOKBURY

EP Cr 1954 by union Holsworthy AP, chap Cookbury of Milton Damerel with Cookbury AP.[163] Holsw. RDn. Bdry: 1959.[83]

HONEYCHURCH

AP *LG* Black Torr. Hd, Okeh. PLU, RSD. Civ bdry: 1884.[69] Abol civ 1894 ent to Sampford Courtenay AP.[245] *Parl* S'rn Dv (1832–67), South Dv (1867–85), W'rn Dv (1885–1918). *Eccl* Seq 35. Eccl bdry: 1928.[70]

HONITON

AP *LG* Axmin. Hd, Hon. Bor, MB (1846–1974), PLU, USD. Civ bdry: 1935.[1] *Parl* Hon. Parl Bor (1300–11, 1640–1867), East Dv (1867–85), E'rn Dv (1885–1918), Hon. Dv/CC (1918–*). *Eccl* Seq 8.

HONICKNOWLE

EP Cr 1956 from St Budeaux EP, Pennycross EP.[250] Plymouth RDn.

HOOE

EP Cr 1855 from Plymstock AP.[251] Plymouth RDn. Bdry: 1954.[252]

HORRABRIDGE

Chap in Buckland Monachorum AP, Sampford Spiney AP, Walkhampton AP, Whitchurch AP, sep EP 1867 (also incl pt Peter Tavy AP),[114] sep CP 1950 (not incl pt Petertavy AP).[115] *LG* Tav. RD. *Parl* W Devon CC (1970–*). *Eccl* Tam. RDn (1867–75), Tav. RDn (1875–*). Eccl bdry: 1920.[253]

HORWOOD

AP *LG* Seq 18. *Parl* Seq 8. *Eccl* Seq 16.

HUISH

AP *LG* Seq 36. *Parl* Seq 3. *Eccl* Seq 28.

NORTH HUISH

AP *LG* Seq 39. Civ bdry: 1950.[88] *Parl* Seq 19. *Eccl* Sometimes as 'North Huish with Avonwick', Plymp. RDn (until 1875), Tot. RDn (1875–*). Eccl bdry: 1960.[89]

SOUTH HUISH

Chap in West Alvington AP, sep civ identity early, sep EP 1877.[8] *LG* Seq 38. *Parl* Seq 19. *Eccl* Woodl. RDn.

HUNTSHAM

AP *LG* Seq 45. Civ bdry: 1884.[248] *Parl* Seq 7. *Eccl* Tiv. RDn (until 1875), Tiv. E RDn (1875–1902), Cull. RDn (1902–68), Tiv. RDn (1968–*).

HUNTSHAW

AP *LG* Seq 19. *Parl* Seq 3. *Eccl* Seq 19.

HUXHAM

AP *LG* Seq 54. Civ bdry: 1966 (exchanges pts with Exeter CB and CP).[7] *Parl* Seq 17. *Eccl* Seq 1.

IDDESLEIGH

AP *LG* Seq 35. *Parl* N'rn Dv (1832–67), North Dv (1867–85), W'rn Dv (1885–1918), S Molt. Dv (1918–48), Torr. CC (1948–70), W Devon CC (1970–*). *Eccl* Seq 28.

IDE

AP *LG* Seq 17. Civ bdry: 1884.[3] *Parl* Seq 17. *Eccl* Pec jurisd Dean & Chapter of Exeter (until 1848), Seq 10 thereafter.

IDEFORD

AP *LG* Seq 44. *Parl* Seq 16. *Eccl* Seq 34.

ILFRACOMBE

AP *LG* Ilfracombe Bor (status not sustained), Braun. Hd, Barnst. PLU, Ilfracombe USD, UD. *Parl* Seq 8. *Eccl* Seq 27. Eccl bdry: 1857 (cr Ilfracombe St Philip and St James EP),[254] 1869 (help cr Lee EP).[255]

ILFRACOMBE ST PHILIP AND ST JAMES

EP Cr 1857 from Ilfracombe AP.[254] Shirw. RDn (1857–75), Barnst. RDn (1875–*).

ILSHAM

EP Cr 1880 from Torwood EP.[256] Ipp. RDn.

ILSINGTON

AP *LG* Seq 44. *Parl* Seq 16. *Eccl* Seq 34.

INSTOW

AP *LG* Seq 18. Civ bdry: 1883.[63] *Parl* Seq 8. *Eccl*

Seq 16.

INWARDLEIGH

AP *LG* Seq 47. *Parl* Seq 10. *Eccl* Seq 35.

IPPLEPEN

AP Incl chap Kingswear (sep civ identity early, sep EP 1720[11]), chap Woodland (sep civ identity early, sep EP 1754[11]). *LG* Seq 25. Civ bdry: 1884,[257] 1885.[73] *Parl* Seq 16. *Eccl* Seq 31. Eccl bdry: 1928.[53]

IVYBRIDGE

Dist in Cornwood AP, Ermington AP, Ugborough AP, sep EP 1835,[164] sep CP 1894 (the pt in Ivybr. USD).[165] *LG* Plymp. St Mary PLU, Ivybr. UD (1894–1935), Plymp. St Mary RD (1935–74). *Parl* Tav. Dv/CC (1918–70), W Devon CC (1970–*). *Eccl* Plymp. RDn.

JACOBSTOWE

AP *LG* Seq 47. *Parl* Seq 10. *Eccl* Seq 35.

KELLY

AP *LG* Seq 29. *Parl* Seq 21. *Eccl* Tav. RDn. Abol eccl 1923 to help cr Kelly with Bradstone EP.[82]

KELLY WITH BRADSTONE

EP Cr 1923 by union Kelly AP, Bradstone AP.[82] Tav. RDn.

KENN

AP Incl Kennford Bor (status not sustained, no sep identity as par). *LG* Seq 17. Civ bdry: 1884.[3] *Parl* Seq 17. *Eccl* Seq 10.

KENNERLEIGH

Chap in Crediton AP, sep civ identity early, sep EP 1752.[11] *LG* Seq 13. *Parl* Seq 5. *Eccl* Pec jurisd Bp Exeter (1752–1848), Cadb. RDn (1848–*).

KENTISBEARE

AP Incl Blackborough (once sep par, orig rated sep for poor law purposes but deemed later as before civ pt of this par). *LG* Seq 23. Civ bdry: 1883,[63] 1935.[1] *Parl* Seq 7. *Eccl* Seq 13.

KENTISBURY

AP *LG* Seq 4. *Parl* Seq 8. *Eccl* Seq 26.

KENTON

AP *LG* Kenton Bor (status not sustained), Seq 17. Civ bdry: 1884,[3] 1885.[174] *Parl* Seq 17. *Eccl* Seq 10. Eccl bdry: 1829 (help cr Starcross EP).[258]

KERSWELLS

CP Cr 1935 by union Abbotskerswell AP, Kingskerswell AP.[1] *LG* Newt. Abb. RD. Civ bdry: 1967 (help cr Torbay CB and CP).[98] *Parl* Tot. CC (1948–*).

NORTH KEYNHAM

EP Cr 1929 from Devonport St Mark, Ford EP.[193] Now commonly called 'Devonport St Thomas'. Three Towns RDn (1929–54), Plymouth RDn (1954–*). Eccl bdry: 1933 (help cr Weston Mill EP).[184]

KILMINGTON

Chap in Axminster AP, sep civ identity early, sep EP 1911.[26] *LG* Seq 1. *Parl* Seq 12. *Eccl* Hon. RDn.

KINGSBRIDGE

AP *LG* Stanb. Hd, Kingsbr. Bor (status not sustained), PLU, RSD (until 4 Mar 1893), Kingsbr. & Dodbrooke USD (4 Mar–26 Mar 1893). Abol civ 26 Mar 1893 to help cr Kingsbridge and Dodbrooke CP.[196] *Parl* S'rn Dv (1832–67), South Dv (1867–85), S'rn Dv (1885–1918). *Eccl* Seq 40.

KINGSBRIDGE AND DODBROOKE

CP Cr 1893 by union Kingsbridge AP, Dodbrooke AP.[196] *LG* Kingsbr. PLU, Kingsbr. & Dodbrooke USD, UD. Civ bdry: 1896,[15] 1935.[1] *Parl* Tot. Dv/CC (1918–*).

KINGSKERSWELL

Chap in St Mary Church (eccl, 'St Marychurch') AP, sep civ identity early, sep EP 1829.[11] *LG* Haytor Hd, Newt. Abb. PLU, RSD, RD. Civ bdry: 1883,[63] 1884.[259] Abol civ 1935 to help cr Kerswells CP.[1] *Parl* S'rn Dv (1832–67), East Dv (1867–85), Mid Dv (1885–1918), Tot. Dv (1918–48). *Eccl* Pec jurisd Dean & Chapter of Exeter (1829–1848), Ipp. RDn (1848–*). Eccl bdry: 1956 (help cr Shipway Collaton EP),[260] 1960 (help cr Torquay St Martin, Barton EP).[261]

KINGSNYMPTON

AP Usual eccl spelling; for civ see 'Kings Nympton'. *Eccl* Seq 23.

KINGSTEIGNTON

AP Incl chap Highweek (sep civ identity early, sep EP 1864;[246] this chap incl bors Newton Abbot, Newton Bushnell, neither sustains status, neither with sep identity as par). *LG* Seq 44. *Parl* Seq 16. *Eccl* Seq 34. Addtl eccl bdry alt: 1880 (help cr Chudleigh Knighton EP).[75]

KINGSTON

Chap in Ermington AP, sep civ identity early, eccl severed 1934 pt to help cr Ringmore with Kingston EP, pt to Bigbury AP.[61] *LG* Seq 14. Civ bdry: 1884,[13] 1885.[24] *Parl* Seq 19.

KINGSWEAR

Chap in Ipplepen AP, sep civ identity early, sep EP 1720.[11] *LG* Seq 24. Civ bdry: 1879.[98] *Parl* S'rn Dv (1832–67), East Dv (1867–85), Torq. Dv (1885–1948), Torq. BC (1948–70), Tot. CC (1970–*). *Eccl* Ipp. RDn.

KNOWSTONE

AP *LG* Seq 31. *Parl* Seq 2. *Eccl* Seq 23.

LAIRA

EP Cr 1931 from Egg Buckland AP, Plymouth St Augustine EP, ent ex-par place Laira Green.[110] Plymp. RDn (1931–54), Plymouth RDn (1954–*). Eccl bdry: 1956.[262]

LAIRA GREEN

Ex-par place, sep CP 1858,[129] abol eccl 1931 to help cr Laira EP.[110] *LG* Rob. Hd, Plymp. St Mary PLU,[135] RSD, RD. Abol civ 1896 pt to Plymstock AP, pt to Plymouth CB and Plymouth Charles CP.[109] *Parl* South Dv (1867–85), W'rn Dv (1885–1918).

LAMERTON

AP *LG* Seq 29. Civ bdry: 1885,[91] 1966 (gains pt Calstock AP, pt Stoke Climsland AP, both Cornw).[16] *Parl* Seq 21. *Eccl* Tav. RDn. Abol eccl 1938 to help cr Lamerton with Sydenham Damerel EP.[263]

LAMERTON WITH SYDENHAM DAMEREL
EP Cr 1938 by union Lamerton AP, Sydenham Damerel AP.[263] Tav. RDn.
LAND COMMON TO AXMINSTER AND KILMINGTON
See the sep pars for Hd, PLU, RSD. *LG* Axmin. RD. Renamed 1915 'Land Common to Axminster Hamlets and Kilmington' when Axminster AP abol.[30]
LAND COMMON TO AXMINSTER HAMLETS AND KILMINGTON
Renaming 1915 (when Axminster Hamlets cr) of Land Common to Axminster and Kilmington.[30] *LG* Axmin. RD.
LAND COMMON TO BRIDESTOWE AND SOURTON
See the sep pars for Hd, PLU, RSD. *LG* Okeh. RD.
LANDCROSS
AP *LG* Seq 34. *Parl* Seq 9. *Eccl* Seq 21.
LANDKEY
Chap in Bishop's Tawton AP, sep civ identity early, sep EP 1775.[11] *LG* Seq 30. *Parl* Seq 8. *Eccl* Pec jurisd Bp Exeter (1775–1848), Barnst. RDn (1848–75), Shirw. RDn (1875–*).
LANDSCOVE
EP Cr 1852 from Staverton AP.[264] Ipp. RDn (1852–75), Tot. RDn (1875–*).
LANGTREE
AP *LG* Seq 36. Civ bdry: 1884.[265] *Parl* Seq 3. *Eccl* Seq 28.
LAPFORD
AP *LG* Seq 41. Civ bdry: 1885.[266] *Parl* Seq 5. *Eccl* Seq 20.
LEE
EP Cr 1869 from Ilfracombe AP, Mortehoe AP.[255] Shirw. RDn (1869–75), Barnst. RDn (1875–*).
LEUSDEN
EP Cr 1864 from Widecombe in the Moor AP.[267] Moret. RDn.
LEW TRENCHARD
AP Usual eccl spelling; for civ see following entry. *Eccl* Tav. RDn. Abol eccl 1922 to help cr Lew Trenchard with Thrushelton EP.[268]
LEW TRENCHARD WITH THRUSHELTON
EP Cr 1922 by union Lew Trenchard AP, chap Thrushelton and other pts of Marystowe with Thrushelton AP.[268] Tav. RDn.
LEWTRENCHARD
AP Usual civ spelling; for eccl see 'Lew Trenchard'. *LG* Seq 29. Civ bdry: 1885.[269] *Parl* Seq 21.
LIFTON
AP *LG* Seq 29. Civ bdry: 1884.[108] *Parl* Seq 21. *Eccl* Seq 38.
LITTLEHAM
AP Sometimes 'Littleham by Bideford'. *LG* Seq 34. *Parl* Seq 9. *Eccl* Seq 21.
LITTLEHAM
AP Sometimes civ 'Littleham with Exmouth', usual eccl 'Littleham cum Exmouth', qv. *LG* E Budl. Hd, St Thomas PLU, pt Exmouth USD, pt St Thomas RSD, Exmouth UD (pt 1894–96, ent 1896–1974), pt St Thomas RD (1894–96). Civ bdry: 1896 (the pt not in the UD added to the UD),[270] 1896.[121] *Parl* S'rn Dv (1832–67), East Dv (1867–85), N-E'rn Dv (1885–1918), Hon. Dv/CC (1918–*).
LITTLEHAM CUM EXMOUTH
AP Usual eccl name; for civ see prev entry. *Eccl* Pec jurisd Dean & Chapter of Exeter (until 1848), Aylb. RDn (1848–*).
LITTLEHEMPSTON
AP Usual eccl spelling; for civ see 'Little Hempston'. *Eccl* Ipp. RDn (until 1848), Tot. RDn (1848–*).
LODDISWELL
AP *LG* Pt Coler. Hd, pt Stanb. Hd, Kingsbr. PLU, RSD, RD. *Parl* Seq 19. *Eccl* Seq 40. Eccl bdry: 1938.[128]
LOXBEARE
AP *LG* Seq 45. Civ bdry: 1885.[124] *Parl* Seq 7. *Eccl* Tiv. RDn (until 1875), Tiv. W RDn (1875–1902), Tiv. RDn (1902–24). Abol eccl 1924 to help cr Templeton with Loxbeare EP.[271]
LOXHORE
AP *LG* Seq 37. *Parl* Seq 8. *Eccl* Seq 26.
LUFFINCOTT
AP *LG* Seq 46. Civ bdry: 1883,[272] 1966 (exchanges pts with North Tamerton AP, loses pt to Boyton CP, both Cornw).[16] *Parl* Seq 11. *Eccl* Seq 30.
LUNDY
AP Usual eccl spelling; for civ see following entry. *Eccl* Hartland RDn.
LUNDY ISLAND
AP Usual civ spelling; for eccl see prev entry. *LG* Seq 34. *Parl* Seq 9 (mention omitted by mistake in schedule to 1948 act, supplied by supplemental order 1951[273]).
LUPPITT
AP *LG* Seq 2. *Parl* Seq 12. *Eccl* Seq 5.
LUSTLEIGH
AP *LG* Seq 44. Civ bdry: 1885,[71] 1957.[74] *Parl* Seq 16. *Eccl* Seq 34.
LUTON
EP Cr 1866 from Bishopsteignton AP.[65] Kenn RDn.
LYDFORD
AP *LG* Lydford Bor (status not sustained), Seq 29. *Parl* Lydford Parl Bor (1300 only), Seq 21. *Eccl* Seq 38. Eccl bdry: 1912 (help cr Princetown EP).[274]
LYMPSTONE
AP *LG* Seq 6. *Parl* Seq 12. *Eccl* Seq 1.
LYNTON
AP Incl chap Countisbury (sep civ identity early, sep EP 1747[166]). *LG* Shirw. Hd, Barnst. PLU, Lynton USD, UD. Civ bdry: 1935.[1] *Parl* Seq 8. *Eccl* Seq 26.
MAKER
AP Pt Cornw (East Hd), pt Devon (Rob. Hd), the latter transf to Cornw 1832 for parl purposes, 1844 for civ purposes.[27] Incl chap Millbrook (sep EP 1869,[275] sep CP 1896 in Cornw[276]). See main entry in Cornw.
MALBOROUGH
Chap in West Alvington AP, sep civ identity early, sep EP 1877[10]. Incl chap Salcombe (sep

EP 1803,[11] sep CP 1894 [the pt in Salcombe USD][47]). *LG* Malborough Bor (perhaps 17th cent bor while still in West Alvington AP,[9] status not sustained), Kingsbr. PLU, pt Salcombe USD, pt Kingsbr. RSD, Kingsbr. RD. Addtl civ bdry alt: 1896.[277] *Parl* Seq 19. *Eccl* Woodl. RDn.

MAMHEAD
AP *LG* Seq 17. *Parl* Seq 17. *Eccl* Seq 10.

MANATON
AP *LG* Seq 44. *Parl* Seq 16. *Eccl* Seq 34.

MARIANSLEIGH
AP *LG* Seq 49. *Parl* Seq 2. *Eccl* Seq 23.

MARLDON
Chap in Paignton AP, sep civ identity early, sep EP before 1878.[278] *LG* Seq 24. Civ bdry: 1884,[257] 1967 (help cr Torbay CB and CP).[98] *Parl* S'rn Dv (1832–67), East Dv (1867–85), Torq. Dv (1885–1948), Tot. CC (1948–*). *Eccl* Ipp. RDn. Eccl bdry: 1928.[53]

MARTINHOE
AP *LG* Seq 37. *Parl* Seq 8. *Eccl* Seq 26.

MARWOOD
AP *LG* Seq 4. *Parl* Seq 8. *Eccl* Seq 27. Eccl bdry: 1926.[66]

MARYSTOW
AP Usual civ spelling; for eccl see following two entries. Incl chap Thrushelton (sep civ identity early, eccl severed 1922 to help cr Lew Trenchard with Thrushelton EP[268]). *LG* Seq 29. *Parl* Seq 21.

MARYSTOWE
AP Usual eccl spelling after 1922 when chap Thrushelton eccl severed to help cr Lew Trenchard with Thrushelton EP;[268] for civ see prev entry. *Eccl* Tav. RDn.

MARYSTOWE WITH THRUSHELTON
AP Usual eccl spelling until 1922; for civ and sep chap Thrushelton see two prev entries. *Eccl* Tav. RDn.

MARYTAVY
AP Usual civ spelling; for eccl see 'Mary Tavy'. Sometimes 'Tavy St Mary'. *LG* Seq 29. Civ bdry: 1885.[91] *Parl* Seq 21.

MEAVY
AP *LG* Seq 33. *Parl* Seq 21. *Eccl* Seq 37.

MEETH
AP *LG* Seq 35. *Parl* Seq 10. *Eccl* Seq 28.

MEMBURY
Chap in Axminster AP, sep civ identity early, sep EP 1911.[26] *LG* Seq 1. Civ bdry: 1884 (gains pt Chardstock AP, Dorset).[279] *Parl* Seq 12. *Eccl* Hon. RDn.

MERTON
AP *LG* Seq 36. *Parl* Seq 3. *Eccl* Seq 28.

MESHAW
AP *LG* Seq 49. Civ bdry: 1885.[266] *Parl* Seq 2. *Eccl* Seq 23.

MILBER
Area in Haccombe AP, sep CP 1901 (from Haccombe with Combe CP),[235] sep EP 1963.[280] *LG* Newt. Abb. PLU, UD. *Parl* Tot. Dv/CC (1918–*). *Eccl* Moret. RDn.

SOUTH MILTON
Chap in West Alvington AP, sep civ identity early, sep EP 1886.[12] *LG* Seq 38. *Parl* Seq 19. *Eccl* Woodl. RDn.

MILTON ABBOT
AP *LG* Seq 40. Civ bdry: 1966 (gains pt Stoke Climsland AP, Cornw).[16] *Parl* Seq 21. *Eccl* Tav. RDn. Abol eccl 1921 to help cr Milton Abbot with Dunterton EP.[200]

MILTON ABBOT WITH DUNTERTON
EP Cr 1921 by union Milton Abbot AP, Dunterton AP.[200] Tav. RDn.

MILTON DAMEREL
AP Usual civ spelling, eccl spelling from 1954 when time loses chap Cookbury (civ identity early) to help cr Holsworthy with Cookbury EP.[163] *LG* Seq 46. *Parl* Seq 11. *Eccl* Holsw. RDn.

MILTON DAMEREL WITH COOKBURY
AP Usual eccl spelling until 1954 when loses chap Cookbury to help cr Holsworthy with Cookbury EP;[163] for civ and eccl after 1954 see prev entry. *Eccl* Holsw. RDn.

MODBURY
AP *LG* Modbury Bor (status not sustained), Seq 14. Civ bdry: 1884.[281] *Parl* Modbury Parl Bor (1360 only), Seq 19. *Eccl* Sometimes as 'Modbury with Brownston', Seq 36. Eccl bdry: 1963.[282]

MOLLAND
AP *LG* Seq 31. *Parl* Seq 2. *Eccl* Seq 23.

NORTH MOLTON
AP Incl chap Twitchen (sep civ identity early, sep EP before 1850[290]). *LG* N Molton Bor (status not sustained), Seq 31. Civ bdry: 1882,[3] 1884.[283] *Parl* Seq 2. *Eccl* Seq 23. Eccl bdry: 1945.[87]

SOUTH MOLTON
AP *LG* S Molt. Hd, Bor, PLU, S Molt. MB (1835–1967; disputed whether ent or only pt in the MB before 1894), USD, RD (1967–74). Civ bdry: 1894 (the disputed pt, deemed not in MB, cr Queensnympton CP).[47] *Parl* S Molt. Parl Bor (1302 only), Seq 2. *Eccl* S Molt. RDn. Abol eccl 1945 to help cr South Molton with Nymet St George EP.[284]

SOUTH MOLTON WITH NYMET ST GEORGE
EP Cr 1945 by union South Molton AP, Nymet St George AP.[284] S Molt. RDn.

MONKLEIGH
AP *LG* Seq 34. *Parl* Seq 9. *Eccl* Seq 21.

MONKTON
Chap in Colyton AP, sep civ identity early, sep EP 1867.[151] *LG* Seq 12. Civ bdry: 1884.[25] *Parl* Seq 12. *Eccl* Hon. RDn (1867–75), Dunk. & Hon. RDn (1875–1902), Hon. RDn (1902–*).

MONKTON WYLD
EP Cr 1850 from Whitchurch Canonicorum AP (Dorset), Uplyme AP.[285] See main entry in Dorset.

MORCHARD BISHOP
AP *LG* Seq 13. *Parl* Seq 5. *Eccl* Pec jurisd Bp Exeter (until 1848), Seq 3 thereafter.

MOREBATH
AP *LG* Bamp. Hd, Tiv. PLU (1835–56), Dulverton PLU (1856–94), RSD, Tiv. PLU (1894–1930), RD. *Parl* Seq 7. *Eccl* Seq 15.

MORELEIGH
AP *LG* Seq 39. Civ bdry: 1884.[286] *Parl* Seq 19. *Eccl* Woodl. RDn (until 1875), Tot. RDn (1875–*). Eccl bdry: 1931.[287]

MORETONHAMPSTEAD
AP *LG* Moretonhampstead Bor (status not sustained), Seq 44. Civ bdry: 1885.[71] *Parl* Seq 16. *Eccl* Seq 34.

MORTEHOE
AP *LG* Seq 4. Civ bdry: 1884.[234] *Parl* Seq 8. *Eccl* Seq 37. Eccl bdry: 1869 (help cr Lee EP),[255] 1922 (cr Woolacombe EP).[288]

MUSBURY
AP *LG* Seq 1. *Parl* Seq 12. *Eccl* Seq 8.

NEWPORT
EP Cr 1847 from Bishop's Tawton AP (qv for Newport Bor [status not sustained]).[289] Barnst. RDn. Bdry: 1905.[160]

NEWTON AND NOSS
CP Cr 1935 by union Revelstone CP, Newton Ferrers AP, pt Holbeton AP.[1] *LG* Plymp. St Mary RD. *Parl* Tav. CC (1948–70), W Devon CC (1970–*).

NEWTON FERRERS
AP *LG* Newton Ferrers Bor (status not sustained), Erming. Hd, Plymp. St Mary PLU, RSD, RD. Civ bdry: 1884.[102] Abol civ 1935 to help cr Newton and Noss CP.[1] *Parl* S'rn Dv (1832–67), South Dv (1867–85), S'rn Dv (1885–1918), Tav. Dv (1918–48). *Eccl* Seq 36. Eccl bdry: 1961.[104]

NEWTON POPPLEFORD
Chap in Aylesbeare AP, sep EP 1761,[34] sep CP 1898.[35] *LG* St Thomas PLU, RD. Abol civ 1935 ent to Harpford AP.[1] *Parl* Tiv. Dv (1918–48). *Eccl* Aylb. RDn (1761–1902), Ott. RDn (1902–*).

NEWTON POPPLEFORD AND HARPFORD
CP Renaming 1968 of Harpford AP.[239] *LG* St Thomas RD. *Parl* Hon. CC (1970–*).

NEWTON ST CYRES
AP *LG* Seq 13. Civ bdry: 1884.[245] *Parl* Seq 5. *Eccl* Seq 3.

NEWTON ST PETROCK
AP *LG* Seq 34. Civ bdry: 1885.[291] *Parl* Seq 9. *Eccl* Torr. RDn (until 1954), Holsw. RDn (1954–*).

NEWTON TRACEY
AP *LG* Seq 18. *Parl* Seq 8. *Eccl* Seq 16. Eccl bdry: 1923.[231]

NORTHAM
AP *LG* Sheb. Hd, Bidef. PLU, Northam USD, UD. Civ bdry: 1935.[1] *Parl* Seq 9. *Eccl* Sometimes as 'Northam with Westward Ho!', Seq 21. Eccl bdry: 1841 (cr Appledore EP),[17] 1973.[60]

NORTHCOTT
Hmlt (Devon, Black Torr. Hd) in Boyton AP (Cornw, Stratton Hd), the former transf to Devon 1832 for parl purposes, 1844 for civ purposes,[27] sep CP 1866.[81] *LG* Holsw. PLU (1837–52), Launceston PLU (1852–1930), RSD, Broadwoodw. RD (1894–1966). Civ bdry: 1888.[293] Transf 1966 to Cornw (Launceston RD).[292] *Parl* South Dv (1867–85), W'rn Dv (1885–1918), Tav. Dv/CC (1918–70), Cornw thereafter.

NORTHLEIGH
AP *LG* Seq 12. Civ bdry: 1884.[25] *Parl* Seq 12. *Eccl* Seq 8.

NORTHLEW
AP *LG* Seq 47. *Parl* Seq 20. *Eccl* Seq 35.

BROAD NYMET
AP *LG* N Tawt. and Wink. Hd. Abol civ between 1820–50 ent to North Tawton AP.[84] *Eccl* Chum. RDn. Abol eccl third quarter 17th cent ent to Bow AP.[79]

NYMET ROWLAND
AP *LG* Seq 41. *Parl* Seq 5. *Eccl* Seq 20.

NYMET ST GEORGE
AP Usual eccl spelling; for civ see 'George Nympton'. *Eccl* S Molt. RDn. Abol eccl 1945 to help cr South Molton with Nymet St George EP.[284]

BISHOP'S NYMPTON
AP Usual civ spelling; for eccl see 'Bishopsnympton'. *LG* Seq 49. *Parl* Seq 2.

GEORGE NYMPTON
AP Usual civ spelling; for eccl see 'Nymet St George'. *LG* Seq 31. *Parl* Seq 2.

KING'S NYMPTON
AP Usual civ spelling; for eccl see 'Kingsnympton'. *LG* Seq 49. *Parl* Seq 2.

OAKFORD
AP *LG* Seq 50. Civ bdry: 1894.[245] *Parl* Seq 7. *Eccl* Seq 25.

OFFWELL
AP *LG* Seq 12. Civ bdry: 1884,[25] 1935.[1] *Parl* Seq 12. *Eccl* Seq 8.

OGWELL
CP Cr 1895 by union East Ogwell AP, West Ogwell AP.[294] *LG* Newt. Abb. PLU, RD. *Parl* Tot. CC (1918–*).

EAST OGWELL
AP *LG* Wonf. Hd, Newt. Abb. PLU, pt Wolborough USD (1885–94), pt Newt. Abb. RSD (ent 1875–85, pt 1885–94). Civ bdry: 1885.[73] Abol civ 1894 to help cr Ogwell CP.[294] *Parl* S'rn Dv (1832–67), East Dv (1867–85), Mid Dv (1885–1918). *Eccl* Kenn RDn (until 1848), Ipp. RDn (1848–75), Moret. RDn (1875–*).

WEST OGWELL
AP *LG* Wonf. Hd, Newt. Abb. PLU, RSD. Abol civ 1894 to help cr Ogwell CP.[294] *Parl, Eccl* Organisation as for East Ogwell.

OKEHAMPTON
AP *LG* Pt Lifton Hd, pt Black Torr. Hd, Okeh. PLU, MB (pt 1885–94, ent 1894–1974), pt Okeh. USD (1885–94), Okeh. RSD (ent 1875–85, pt 1885–94). Civ bdry: 1894 (the pt not in the MB cr Okehampton Hamlets CP),[47] 1935.[1] *Parl* Okeh. Parl Bor (1300–13, 1640–1832), pt N'rn Dv & pt S'rn Dv (1832–67), South Dv (1867–85), W'rn Dv (1885–1918), S Molt. Dv (1918–48), Torr. CC (1948–70), W Devon CC

(1970–*). *Eccl* Seq 35.

MONK OKEHAMPTON
AP Usual civ spelling; for eccl see 'Monkokehampton'. *LG* Seq 47. Civ bdry: 1885.[107] *Parl* Seq 10.

OKEHAMPTON HAMLETS
CP Cr 1894 from the pt of Okehampton AP not in Okeh. MB.[47] *LG* Okeh. PLU, RD. *Parl* S Molt. Dv (1918–48), Torr. CC (1948–70), W Devon CC (1970–*).

OLDRIDGE
Chap in Exeter St Thomas AP (civ, 'St Thomas the Apostle'), sep EP 1793,[11] no sep civ identity.

OTTERTON
AP *LG* Seq 6. Civ bdry: 1935.[1] *Parl* Seq 12. *Eccl* Seq 1.

OTTERY ST MARY
AP *LG* Ott. St Mary Hd, Hon. PLU, Ott. St Mary USD, UD. *Parl* Seq 12. *Eccl* Seq 2. Eccl bdry: 1841 (cr Tipton EP),[295] 1844 (help cr Escot EP),[206] 1863 (cr West Hill EP),[247] 1882 (cr Alfington EP).[2]

VENN OTTERY
Chap in Harpford AP, sep civ and eccl identity early. *LG* E Budl. Hd, Hon. PLU, RSD, RD. Abol civ 1935 ent to Harpford AP.[1] *Parl* S'rn Dv (1832–67), East Dv (1867–85), E'rn Dv (1885–1918), Hon. Dv (1918–48). *Eccl* Ott. RDn. Abol eccl 1933 to help cr Tipton St John with Venn Ottery EP.[296]

PAIGNTON
AP Incl chap Marldon (sep civ identity early, sep EP before 1878[278]). *LG* Paignton Bor (status not sustained), Haytor Hd, Tot. PLU, Paignton USD, UD. Abol civ 1967 to help cr Torbay CB and CP.[98] *Parl* S'rn Dv (1832–67), East Dv (1867–85), Torq. Dv (1885–1948), Torq. BC (1948–70). *Eccl* Pec jurisd Bp Exeter (until 1848), Seq 31 thereafter. Eccl bdry: 1864 (help cr Collaton EP),[150] 1889 (cr Paignton Christ Church EP),[297] 1948 (cr Paignton St Paul, Preston EP),[298] 1954 (help cr Churston Ferrers with Goodrington EP).[101]

PAIGNTON CHRIST CHURCH
EP Cr 1889 from Paignton AP.[297] Ipp. RDn.

PAIGNTON ST PAUL, PRESTON
EP Cr 1948 from Paignton AP.[298] Ipp. RDn.

PANCRASWEEK
Chap in Bradworthy with Pancraswyke AP, sep civ identity early as 'Pancrasweek', eccl severed 1959 to help cr Pyworthy with Pancraswyke EP.[83] *LG* Seq 46. Civ bdry: 1884,[299] 1966 (exchanges pts with Kilkhampton AP, Launcells AP, both Cornw).[16] *Parl* Seq 11.

PARKHAM
AP *LG* Seq 34. Civ bdry: 1885.[113] *Parl* Seq 9. *Eccl* Seq 21. Eccl bdry: 1862 (help cr Bucks Mills EP).[118]

PARRACOMBE
AP *LG* Seq 37. *Parl* Seq 8. *Eccl* Seq 26.

PAYHEMBURY
AP *LG* Seq 22. *Parl* Seq 6. *Eccl* Seq 12.

PENNYCROSS
Chap in Plymouth St Andrew AP, sep CP 1866,[81] sep EP 1898.[300] *LG* Rob. Hd, Plymp. St Mary PLU, RSD, RD. Civ bdry: 1888 (loses pt to Devonport CP when latter constituted CB),[165] 1896 (loses pt to Plymouth CB and Plymouth St Andrew AP).[109] Abol civ 1898 pt to Devonport CB and CP, pt to St Budeaux CP.[301] *Parl* South Dv (1867–85), S'rn Dv (1885–1918). *Eccl* Three Towns RDn (1898–1954), Plymouth RDn (1954–*). Eccl bdry: 1910 (help cr Plymouth St Gabriel, Peverell Park EP),[161] 1956 (help cr Honicknowle EP),[250] 1956,[302] 1957 (help cr Plymouth St James the Less, Ham EP),[192] 1958 (help cr Plymouth Crownhill (Church of the Ascension) EP),[111] 1965 (help cr Devonport St Bartholomew EP).[182]

PETERS MARLAND
AP Usual civ spelling; for eccl see following entry. *LG* Seq 36. Civ bdry: 1884.[303] *Parl* Seq 3.

PETERSMARLAND
AP Usual eccl spelling; for civ see prev entry. *Eccl* Seq 28.

PETERTAVY
AP Usual civ spelling; for eccl see 'Peter Tavy'. Sometimes 'Tavy St Peter'. *LG* Pt Lifton Hd, pt Rob. Hd, Tav. PLU, RSD, RD. Civ bdry: 1885.[91] *Parl* Seq 21.

NORTH PETHERWIN
AP In Cornw (East Hd), transf to Devon 1832 for parl purposes, 1844 for civ purposes.[27] *LG* Black Torr. Hd (from 1844), Launceston PLU, RSD, Broadwoodw. RD (1894–1966). Transf 1966 to Cornw (Launceston RD).[292] *Parl* In Cornw before 1832, N'rn Dv (1832–67), South Dv (1867–85), W'rn Dv (1885–1918), Tav. Dv (1918–70), Cornw thereafter. *Eccl* Trigg Major RDn (Exeter dioc until 1876, Truro thereafter [Truro AD until 1878, Bodmin AD thereafter]).

PETROCKSTOW
AP Usual civ spelling; for eccl see following entry. *LG* Seq 36. *Parl* Seq 3.

PETROCKSTOWE
AP Usual eccl spelling; for civ see prev entry. *Eccl* Seq 28.

PETTON
EP Chap in Bampton AP, sep EP between 1879–82,[37] no sep civ identity. Tiv. RDn.

PILTON
AP *LG* Pilton Bor (status not sustained), Braun. Hd, Barnst. PLU, pt Barnst. USD, pt Barnst. RSD. Abol civ 1894 the pt in the USD to cr East Pilton CP, the remainder to cr West Pilton CP.[47] *Parl* N'rn Dv (1832–67), North Dv (1867–85), N-W'rn Dv (1885–1918). *Eccl* Barnst. RDn. Abol eccl 1945 to help cr Pilton with Ashford EP.[21]

EAST PILTON
CP Cr 1894 from the pt of Pilton AP in Barnst. USD.[47] Barnst. PLU, MB. Civ bdry: 1899.[40] *Parl* Barnst. Dv (1918–48), N Devon CC (1948–*).

WEST PILTON
CP Cr 1894 from the pt of Pilton AP not in Barnst. USD.[47] *LG* Barnst. PLU, RD. Civ bdry: 1899.[40] *Parl* As for East Pilton.

PILTON WITH ASHFORD
EP Cr 1945 by union Pilton AP, Ashford AP.[21] Barnst. RDn.

PINHOE
AP *LG* Wonf. Hd, St Thomas PLU, RSD, RD (1894–1966). Civ bdry: 1913,[4] 1940 (loses pt to Exeter CB and CP).[6] Abol civ 1966 pt to Exeter CB and CP, pt to Broad Clyst AP.[7] *Parl* S'rn Dv (1832–67), East Dv (1867–85), N-E'rn Dv (1885–1918), Tiv. Dv/CC (1918–70). *Eccl* Seq 1. Eccl bdry: 1938 (help cr Whipton EP).[243]

PLYMOUTH
Sutton Prior bor incorp 1439 as 'Plymouth'.[304] The following have 'Plymouth' in their names. Insofar as any existed at a given time: *LG* Rob. Hd, Plymouth incorp for poor (1708–1930), Bor/MB/CB, USD. *Parl* Plymouth Parl Bor (1298–1328, 1442–1918), divided thereafter into 3 Parl Bors/BCs of Plymouth Devonport, Plymouth Drake, Plymouth Sutton (see Part III of the *Guide* for constitutions by wards of the CB). *Eccl* Plymp. RDn (until 1875), Three Towns RDn (1875–1954), Plymouth RDn (1954–*). There were several ex-par places in Plymouth of which only one became sep par, 'Laira Green' CP in 1858,[129] EP 1931 as 'Laira' (also from Egg Buckland AP, EP10).[110]

CP1–PLYMOUTH–Cr 1898 by union AP1, AP2.[305] Bdry: 1899,[306] 1939,[55] 1951,[57] 1966.[103]

EP1–PLYMOUTH ALL SAINTS–Cr 1875 from EP18.[307] Abol 1958 ent to EP18.[179]

AP1–PLYMOUTH CHARLES–Cr 1641 from AP2.[308] Civ bdry: 1896,[109] 1897.[309] Abol civ 1898 to help cr CP1.[305] Eccl bdry: 1844 (help cr Sutton on Plym EP),[310] 1871 (cr Compton Gifford EP),[155] 1874 (help cr EP16),[311] 1877 (help cr EP15),[312] 1883,[313] 1889 (help cr EP17),[158] 1905 (help cr EP10).[159] Abol eccl 1954 to help cr EP2.[126]

EP2–PLYMOUTH CHARLES WITH ST LUKE–Cr 1954 by union AP1, EP16.[126] Abol 1964 pt to help cr EP3, pt to EP8.[314]

EP3–PLYMOUTH CHARLES WITH ST MATTHIAS–Cr 1964 from EP17, EP2.[314]

EP4–PLYMOUTH CHRIST CHURCH–Cr 1846 from AP2.[315] Bdry: 1866,[316] 1871,[317] 1889 (help cr EP17),[158] 1964.[248] Church closed in 1965.

EP5–PLYMOUTH CROWNHILL (CHURCH OF THE ASCENSION)–Cr 1958 from Egg Buckland AP, Pennycross EP, St Budeaux EP, Tamerton Foliot AP.[111]

–PLYMOUTH DOCKS–Ex-par, eccl 'Great Western Docks', eccl abol 1954 pt to EP8, pt to EP18.[126]

EP6–PLYMOUTH HOLY TRINITY–Cr 1842 from AP2.[318] Incl chap St Saviour (sep EP 1883 as EP19[319]). Addtl bdry alt: 1884.[320] Abol 1930 to help cr EP7.[321]

EP7–PLYMOUTH HOLY TRINITY AND ST SAVIOUR–Cr 1930 by union EP6, EP19.[321] Abol 1954 ent to EP8.[126]

–PLYMOUTH LIGHTHOUSE–Ex-par

AP2–PLYMOUTH ST ANDREW–Incl chap St Budeaux (sep civ identity early outside the Bor [pt Devon, pt Cornw, qv], sep EP between 1822–50[84]), chap East Stonehouse (sep civ identity early outside the Bor, sep EP 1746[11]). Addtl civ and eccl bdry alt early: 1641 (cr AP1).[308] Abol civ 1898 to help cr CP1.[305] Addtl eccl bdry alt: 1823 (cr EP11),[322] 1842 (cr EP6),[318] 1846 (cr EP4),[315] 1847 (help cr EP13),[311] 1866,[316] 1870,[323] 1880,[157] 1885 (help cr Devonport St Mark, Ford EP),[189] 1898 (cr Pennycross EP).[300] Abol eccl 1930 to help cr EP9.[324]

EP8–PLYMOUTH ST ANDREW–Cr 1954 by union EP9, EP7, pt EP13, pt Sutton on Plym EP, pt Great Western Docks.[126] Bdry: 1964.[314]

EP9–PLYMOUTH ST ANDREW WITH ST CATHERINE–Cr 1930 by union AP2, EP11.[324] Abol 1954 to help cr EP8.[126]

EP10–PLYMOUTH ST AUGUSTINE–Cr 1905 from EP17, AP1, EP15, Compton Gifford EP.[159] Bdry: 1931 (help cr Laira EP),[110] 1954,[126] 1956.[262]

EP11–PLYMOUTH ST CATHERINE–Cr 1823 from AP2.[322] Abol 1930 to help cr EP9.[324]

EP12–PLYMOUTH ST GABRIEL, PEVERELL PARK–Cr 1910 from Compton Gifford EP, Pennycross EP.[161] Bdry: 1954,[126] 1956.[77]

EP13–PLYMOUTH ST JAMES–Cr 1847 from AP2.[311] Bdry: 1870.[325] Abol 1954 pt to help cr EP8, pt to EP18.[126]

EP14–PLYMOUTH ST JAMES THE LESS, HAM–Cr 1957 from Devonport St Mark, Ford EP, Pennycross EP, Weston Mill EP.[192]

EP15–PLYMOUTH ST JUDE–Cr 1877 from AP1, addtl ex-par land.[312] Bdry: 1905 (help cr EP10),[159] 1908 (cr EP20).[326]

EP16–PLYMOUTH ST LUKE–Cr 1874 from AP1.[311] Bdry: 1883,[313] 1889 (help cr EP17).[158] Abol 1954 to help cr EP2.[126]

EP17–PLYMOUTH ST MATTHIAS–Cr 1889 from AP1, EP16, EP4, Compton Gifford EP.[158] Bdry: 1905 (help cr EP10),[159] 1905.[160] Abol 1964 to help cr EP3.[314]

EP18–PLYMOUTH ST PETER–Cr 1847 from AP2, East Stonehouse EP.[311] Bdry: 1875 (cr EP1),[307] 1954,[126] 1958,[179] 1964.[314]

EP19–PLYMOUTH ST SAVIOUR–Chap in EP6, sep EP 1883.[319] Abol 1930 to help cr EP7.[311]

EP20–PLYMOUTH ST SIMON–Cr 1908 from EP15.[326] Bdry: 1954.[126]

PLYMPTON ST MARY
Chap in Plympton St Maurice AP, sep civ and eccl identity early. Incl Chelson Meadow ex-par place (sep CP 1858[129]). *LG* Plymp. Hd, pt Plymp. Earle Bor, Plymp. St Mary PLU, RSD, RD. Civ bdry: 1894.[130] Renamed 1966 'Sparkwell' after alt in area.[103] *Parl* Pt Plymp. Parl

Bor (1295–1832), S'rn Dv (1832–67), South Dv (1867–85), S'rn Dv (1885–1918), Tav. Dv/CC (1918–*). *Eccl* Plymp. RDn. Eccl bdry: 1884 (help cr Sparkwell EP).[327]

PLYMPTON ST MAURICE

AP Sometimes 'Plympton Earle' or 'Plympton Morris'. Incl chap Brixton (sep civ identity early, sep EP 1814[11]), chap Sampford Spiney (sep civ identity early, sep EP 1772[11]), chap Plympton St Mary (sep civ and eccl identity early), chap Shaugh Prior (sep civ identity early, sep EP 1810[11]). *LG* Plymp. Hd, Plymp. Earle Bor, Plymp. St Mary PLU, RSD, RD. Abol civ 1966 pt to Plymouth CB and CP, pt to Brixton CP.[103] *Parl* Plymp. Parl Bor (1295–1832), thereafter as for Plympton St Mary. *Eccl* Seq 36.

PLYMSTOCK

AP *LG* Plymp. Hd, Plymp. St Mary PLU, RSD, RD. Civ bdry: 1896,[109] 1897 (loses pt to Plymouth CB and Plymouth Charles AP),[309] 1939 (loses pt to Plymouth CB and CP).[55] Abol civ 1966 pt to Plymouth CB and CP, pt to Brixton CP, pt to Wembury AP.[103] *Parl* S'rn Dv (1832–67), South Dv (1867–85), S'rn Dv (1885–1918), Tav. Dv/CC (1918–70). *Eccl* Seq 36. Eccl bdry: 1855 (cr Hooe EP),[251] 1954,[252] 1973 (cr Elburton EP).[201]

PLYMTREE

AP *LG* Seq 22. *Parl* Seq 6. *Eccl* Seq 12.

POLTIMORE

AP *LG* Seq 54. Civ bdry: 1966 (exchanges pts with Exeter CB & CP).[7] *Parl* Seq 17. *Eccl* Seq 1.

SOUTH POOL

AP *LG* Seq 9. Civ bdry: 1884.[13] *Parl* Seq 9. *Eccl* Subject to jurisd of but detached from Exeter AD (until 1848), Woodl. RDn. Reconstituted 1932, gaining chap Chivelstone of Stokenham AP to cr South Pool with Chivelstone EP.[328]

SOUTH POOL WITH CHIVELSTONE

EP Cr 1932 by union South Pool AP, chap Chivelstone of Stokenham AP.[328] Woodl. RDn.

EAST PORTLEMOUTH

AP *LG* Seq 9. *Parl* Seq 19. *Eccl* Seq 40.

POUHGILL

AP *LG* Seq 7. *Parl* Seq 5. *Eccl* Seq 3.

POWDERHAM

AP *LG* Seq 17. *Parl* Seq 17. *Eccl* Seq 10.

PRINCETOWN

EP Cr 1912 from Lydford AP.[274] Now usually called 'Princetown with Postbridge and Huccaby'. Tav. RDn. Bdry: 1919.[329]

PUDDINGTON

AP *LG* Seq 48. *Parl* Seq 5. *Eccl* Seq 25.

PUTFORD

EP Renaming 1971 of West Putford with East Putford AP.[330] Holsw. RDn.

EAST PUTFORD

Chap in Buckland Brewer AP, sep civ identity maintained, eccl later considered area in West Putford AP. *LG* Seq 34. Civ bdry: 1883.[63] *Parl* Seq 9.

WEST PUTFORD

AP Usual civ name; for eccl and eccl association of East Putford see following entry. *LG* Black Torr. Hd, Bidef. PLU (1835–97), RSD, Holsw. PLU (1897–1930), RD. *Parl* Seq 11.

WEST PUTFORD WITH EAST PUTFORD

AP Usual eccl name after West Putford AP gains chap East Putford from Buckland Brewer AP. *Eccl* Holsw. RDn. Renamed 1971 'Putford' EP.[330]

PYWORTHY

AP *LG* Seq 46. Civ bdry: 1884,[95] 1966 (gains pt Whitstone AP, Cornw).[16] *Parl* Seq 11. *Eccl* Holsw. RDn. Reconstituted 1959, gaining chap Pancraswyke of Bradworthy with Pancraswyke AP, pt Sutcombe AP, to cr Pyworthy with Pancraswyke EP.[83]

PYWORTHY WITH PANCRASWYKE

EP Cr 1959 by union Pyworthy AP, chap Pancraswyke of Bradworthy with Pancraswyke AP, pt Sutcombe AP.[83] Holsw. RDn.

QUEENSNYMPTON

CP Cr 1894 from the pt of South Molton AP not in S Molt. MB.[47] *LG* S Molt. PLU, RD. *Parl* S Molt. Dv (1918–48), N Devon CC (1948–*).

RACKENFORD

AP *LG* Rackenford Bor (status not sustained), Seq 49. *Parl* Seq 2. *Eccl* S Molt. RDn (until 1902), Tiv. RDn (1902–*).

RATTERY

AP *LG* Seq 39. Civ bdry: 1884.[22] *Parl* Seq 19. *Eccl* Seq 39.

REVELSTOKE

Chap in Yealmpton AP, sep civ identity early (incl when chap Noss Mayo Bor [status not sustained]), sep EP 1856.[331] *LG* Plymp. Hd, Plymp. St Mary PLU, RSD, RD. Abol civ 1935 to help cr Newton and Noss EP.[1] *Parl* S'rn Dv (1832–67), South Dv (1867–85), S'rn Dv (1885–1918), Tav. Dv (1918–48). *Eccl* Plymp. RDn. Eccl bdry: 1962.[104]

REWE

AP *LG* Pt Hayr. Hd, pt Wonf. Hd, St Thomas PLU, RSD, RD. *Parl* Seq 17. *Eccl* Plymt. RDn (until 1875), Aylb. RDn (1875–1937). Abol eccl 1937 to help cr Rewe with Nether Exe EP.[207]

REWE WITH NETHER EXE

EP Cr 1937 by union Rewe AP, Nether Exe EP.[207] Aylb. RDn.

RINGMORE

AP *LG* Seq 14. *Parl* Seq 19. *Eccl* Woodl. RDn. Abol eccl 1934 to help cr Ringmore with Kingston EP.[61]

RINGMORE WITH KINGSTON

EP Cr 1934 by union Ringmore AP, pt chap Kingston of Ermington with Kingston AP.[61] Woodl. RDn.

ROBOROUGH

AP *LG* Seq 19. *Parl* Seq 3. *Eccl* Seq 28.

ROCKBEARE

AP *LG* Seq 6. *Parl* Seq 12. *Eccl* Seq 1.

ROMANSLEIGH

AP *LG* Seq 49. *Parl* Seq 2. *Eccl* Seq 23.

ROSE ASH

AP *LG* Seq 49. Civ bdry: 1884.[112] *Parl* Seq 2. *Eccl*

Seq 23.

ROUSDON

AP *LG* Axmin. Hd, PLU, RSD, RD. Abol civ 1939 to help cr Combpyne Rousdon CP.[33] *Parl* S'rn Dv (1832–67), East Dv (1867–85), E'rn Dv (1885–1918), Hon. Dv (1918–48). *Eccl* Hon. RDn (until 1875), Dunk. & Hon. RDn (1875–1902), Hon. RDn (1902–72). Abol eccl 1972 to help cr Combe Pyne with Rousdon EP.[155]

ST BUDEAUX

Chap in Plymouth St Andrew AP, sep civ identity early, sep EP between 1822–50.[84] *LG* Pt Devon (Rob. Hd), pt Cornw (East Hd), Plymp. St Mary PLU, RSD, RD. Civ bdry: 1888 (loses pt to Devonport CB and CP),[165] 1894 (par made ent Devon),[332] 1895,[334] 1898 (loses pt to Devonport CB and CP),[301] 1899 (loses pt to Plymouth CB and CP),[306] 1935,[1] 1939 (loses pt to Plymouth CB and CP).[55] Abol civ 1951 ent to Plymouth CB and CP.[57] *Parl* S'rn Dv (1832–67), South Dv (1867–85), W'rn Dv (1885–1918), Tav. Dv/CC (1918–70). *Eccl* Plymp. RDn (between 1822/50–75), Three Towns RDn (1875–1954), Plymouth RDn (1954–*). Eccl bdry: 1916 (cr Devonport St Boniface EP),[183] 1933,[185] 1933 (help cr Weston Mill EP),[184] 1956 (help cr Honicknowle EP),[250] 1958 (help cr Plymouth Crownhill (Church of the Ascension) EP),[111] 1958 (cr Ernesettle EP).[153]

ST JOHN

AP Pt Cornw (East Hd), pt Devon (Rob. Hd), the latter transf to Cornw 1832 for parl purposes, 1844 for civ purposes.[27] See main entry in Cornw.

ST GILES IN THE WOOD

AP *LG* Seq 19. *Parl* Seq 3. *Eccl* Subject to but detached from Exeter AD (until 1848), Seq 28 thereafter.

ST GILES ON THE HEATH

AP *LG* Black Torr. Hd, Holsw. PLU (1837–52), Launceston PLU (1852–1930), RSD, Broadwoodw. RD (1894–1966), Holsw. RD (1966–74). Civ bdry: 1966 (loses pt to Boyton CP, Cornw, and to Werrington AP as latter transf to Cornw).[292] *Parl* Seq 11. *Eccl* Trigg Major RDn (Exeter dioc until 1876, Truro thereafter [Truro AD until 1878, Bodmin AD thereafter]). Abol eccl 1973 to help cr Werrington with St Giles on the Heath and Virginstow EP.[335]

ST LEONARD

AP Usual civ spelling; for eccl see 'Exeter St Leonard'. *LG* Wonf. Hd, Exeter Bor, St Thomas PLU, RSD, RD (1894–1900), Exeter CB (1900–74). Civ bdry: 1879.[241] *Parl* Exeter Parl Bor/BC (1832–*).

ST MARK–See DAWLISH

ST MARY CHURCH

AP Usual civ spelling; for eccl see following entry. Incl chap Coffinswell (sep civ identity early, sep EP 1913[79]), chap Kingskerswell (sep civ identity early, sep EP 1829[11]). *LG* Haytor Hd, Newt. Abb. PLU, pt St Mary Church USD, pt Newt. Abb. RSD, St Mary Church UD (1894–1900), Torq. MB (1900–24). Addtl civ bdry alt: 1883,[63] 1884,[259] 1894 (the pt not in the UD added to it),[336] 1900 (the pt not transf to the MB lost to Newton Abbot CP).[337] Abol civ 1924 to help cr Torquay CP.[338] *Parl* S'rn Dv (1832–67), East Dv (1867–85), Torq. Dv (1885–1948).

ST MARYCHURCH

AP Usual eccl spelling; for civ and chaps Coffinswell, Kingskerswell, see prev entry. Pec jurisd Dean & Chapter of Exeter (until 1848), Ipp. RDn (1848–*). Addtl eccl bdry alt: 1868 (cr Babbacombe EP),[36] 1956 (help cr Shiphay Collaton EP),[339] 1960 (help cr Torquay St Martin, Barton EP).[261]

ST NICHOLAS

AP *LG* Wonf. Hd, Newt. Abb. PLU, Teignm. USD, UD. Civ bdry: 1884 (gains pts Stokeinteignhead AP in Teignm. USD),[340] 1967.[98] *Parl* S'rn Dv (1832–67), East Dv (1867–85), Mid Dv (1885–1918), Tot. Dv (1918–48), Tiv. CC (1948–*). *Eccl* Kenn RDn (until 1848), Ipp. RDn (1848–*). Now usually eccl called 'Shaldon'.

ST PETROX

Prob chap to Townstall, sep civ identity early, sep EP 1748 as 'Dartmouth St Petrox', qv.[11] *LG* Coler. Hd, Tot. PLU, Dartm. Bor/MB, USD. Civ bdry: 1883,[63] 1885 (gains the pt of Stoke Fleming AP in Dartm. MB).[341] Abol civ 1891 to help cr Dartmouth CP.[173] *Parl* Dartm. Parl Bor (1298–1918).

ST SAVIOUR

Chap in Townstall AP, sep civ identity early, no sep eccl identity. *LG* Coler. Hd, Tot. PLU, Dartm. Bor/MB, USD. Abol civ 1891 to help cr Dartmouth CP.[173] *Parl* Dartm. Parl Bor (1298–1918).

ST STEPHENS

AP Usual civ spelling; usual eccl 'St Stephens by Saltash'. Incl Saltash (bor in Cornw, sep EP 1815,[353] sep CP 1866 in Cornw[27]), bor Trematon in Cornw (status not sustained). *LG* Pt Cornw (East Hd), pt Devon (Rob. Hd), St Germans PLU, RSD, pt sep RD in Devon (1894–95), St Germans RD (Cornw, pt 1894–95, ent 1895–1934). Civ bdry: 1895 (the pt in Devon transf to Cornw).[334] For period after 1895 see main entry in Cornw. *Parl* Saltash Parl Bor (the Cornw pt, 1553–1832), Devon pt, S'rn Dv (1832–67), South Dv (1867–85), W'rn Dv (1885–1918), ent Cornw thereafter. *Eccl* Trigg Major RDn (Exeter dioc until 1876, Truro thereafter [Truro AD until 1878, Bodmin AD thereafter]). Addtl eccl bdry alt: 1881 (cr Saltash St Nicholas and St Faith EP)[354]; for period after 1895 see entry in Cornw.

ST THOMAS THE APOSTLE

AP Usual civ spelling; for eccl see 'Exeter St Thomas'. *LG* Wonf. Hd, St Thomas PLU, St Thomas the Apostle USD, UD (1894–1900), Exeter CB (1900–74). Civ bdry: 1884,[3] 1900 (the pt not transf to Exeter CB lost to Whitestone AP),[343] 1937,[5] 1940,[6] 1966.[7] *Parl*

S'rn Dv (1832–67), East Dv (1867–85), N-E'rn Dv (1885–1918), Exeter Parl Bor/BC (1918–*).

SALCOMBE
Chap in Malborough AP, sep EP 1844,[344] sep CP 1894 (the pt in Salcome USD).[47] *LG* Kingsbr. PLU, Salcome UD. Civ bdry: 1896.[277] *Parl* Tot. Dv/CC (1918–*). *Eccl* Pec jurisd Dean & Chapter of Exeter (1844–48), Woodl. RDn (1848–*).

SALCOMBE REGIS
AP *LG* E Budl. Hd, Hon. PLU, RSD, RD. Civ bdry: 1894,[147] 1899.[345] Abol civ 1931 ent to Sidmouth AP.[346] *Parl* S'rn Dv (1832–67), East Dv (1867–85), E'rn Dv (1885–1918), Hon. Dv (1918–48). *Eccl* Seq 2.

SALTERTON
EP Cr 1845 from Colaton Raleigh AP, Woodbury AP.[347] Now usually called 'Woodbury Salterton'. Aylb. RDn.

SAMPFORD COURTENAY
AP *LG* Seq 47. Civ bdry: 1894.[245] *Parl* Seq 10. *Eccl* Seq 35. Eccl bdry: 1929.[49]

SAMPFORD PEVERELL
AP *LG* Sampford Peverell Bor (status not sustained), Seq 20. Civ bdry: 1884.[123] *Parl* Seq 7. *Eccl* Seq 14.

SAMPFORD SPINEY
Chap in Plympton St Maurice AP, sep civ identity early, sep EP 1772.[11] Incl Horrabridge (sep EP 1867,[114] sep CP 1950[115]). *LG* Seq 33. *Parl* Seq 21. *Eccl* Tam. RDn (until 1875), Tav. RDn (1875–*).

SANDFORD
Chap in Crediton AP, sep civ identity early, eccl severed 1928 to help cr Sandford with Upton Hellions EP.[168] *LG* Seq 13. Civ bdry: 1894.[170] *Parl* Seq 5.

SANDFORD WITH UPTON HELLIONS
EP Cr 1928 by union chap Sandford in Crediton AP, Upton Hellions AP.[168] Cadb. RDn.

SATTERLEIGH
AP *LG* S Molt. Hd, PLU, RSD. Abol civ 1894 to help cr Satterleigh and Warkleigh CP.[245] *Parl* N'rn Dv (1832–67), North Dv (1867–85), N'rn Dv (1885–1918). *Eccl* Seq 23.

SATTERLEIGH AND WARKLEIGH
CP Cr 1894 by union Satterleigh AP, Warkleigh AP.[245] *LG* S Molt. PLU, RD. *Parl* S Molt. Dv (1918–48), N Devon CC (1948–*).

SEATON
CP Cr 1894 from the pt of Seaton and Beer AP in Seaton USD.[47] *LG* Axmin. PLU, Seaton UD. *Parl* Hon. Dv/CC (1918–*).
EP Cr 1905 when Seaton and Beer AP divided into 2 EPs of Seaton, Beer.[48] Hon. RDn.

SEATON AND BEER
AP *LG* Colyton Hd, Axmin. PLU, pt Seaton USD, pt Axmin. RSD. Abol civ 1894 the pt in the USD cr Seaton CP, the remainder cr Beer AP.[47] *Parl* S'rn Dv (1832–67), East Dv (1867–85), E'rn Dv (1885–1918). *Eccl* Hon. RDn (until 1875), Dunk. & Hon. RDn (1875–1902), Hon. RDn (1902–05). Divided 1905 into 2 EPs of Seaton, Beer.[48]

SHALDON–See ST NICHOLAS

SHAUGH PRIOR
Chap in Plympton St Maurice AP, sep civ identity early, sep EP 1810.[11] *LG* Seq 32. *Parl* Seq 21. *Eccl* Plymp. RDn.

SHEBBEAR
AP Incl chap and bor Sheepwash (bor status not sustained, sep civ identity early as par, sep EP 1884[348]). *LG* Seq 36. *Parl* Seq 3. *Eccl* Torr. RDn.

SHEEPSTOR
Chap in Bickleigh AP, sep civ identity early, sep EP 1832[44]). *LG* Seq 33. *Parl* Seq 21. *Eccl* Plymp. RDn (1875–1929), Tav. RDn (1929–*).

SHEEPWASH
Chap and bor in Shebbear AP, bor status not sustained, sep civ identity as par early, sep EP 1884.[348] *LG* Seq 36. *Parl* Seq 10. *Eccl* Torr. RDn.

SHELDON
AP *LG* Seq 22. Civ bdry: 1935.[1] *Parl* Seq 1. *Eccl* Dunk. RDn (until 1875), Dunk. & Hon. RDn (1875–1902), Hon. RDn (1902–68), Cull. RDn (1968–72), Hon. RDn (1972–*).

SHERFORD
Chap in Stokenham AP, sep civ identity early, no sep eccl identity. *LG* Seq 9. *Parl* Seq 19.

SHERWOOD VILLA
Ex-par place, sep CP 1858.[129] *LG* Cred. Hd, PLU,[135] RSD. Abol civ 1894 ent to Newton St Cyres AP.[245] *Parl* North Dv (1867–85), N'rn Dv (1885–1918).

SHILLINGFORD ST GEORGE
AP *LG* Seq 17. *Parl* Seq 17. *Eccl* Seq 10.

SHIPHAY COLLATON
EP Cr 1956 from St Marychurch AP, Kingskerswell AP, Tormoham AP.[339] Ipp. RDn.

SHIRWELL
AP *LG* Seq 37. *Parl* Seq 8. *Eccl* Seq 26.

SHOBROOKE
AP *LG* Seq 7. Civ bdry: 1884.[349] *Parl* Seq 5. *Eccl* Seq 3.

SHUTE
Chap and bor in Colyton AP, bor status not sustained, sep civ identity as par early, sep EP 1860.[152] *LG* Seq 11. *Parl* Seq 12. *Eccl* Hon. RDn (1860–75), Dunk. & Hon. RDn (1875–1902), Hon. RDn (1902–*).

SIDBURY
AP *LG* E Budl. Hd, Hon. PLU, RSD, RD. Abol civ 1931 ent to Sidmouth AP.[346] *Parl* S'rn Dv (1832–67), East Dv (1867–85), E'rn Dv (1885–1918), Hon. Dv (1918–48). *Eccl* Often as 'Sidbury with Sidford', pec jurisd Dean & Chapter of Exeter (until 1848), Seq 2 thereafter.

SIDBURY WITH SIDFORD–See prev entry

SIDMOUTH
AP *LG* E Budl. Hd, Hon. PLU, Sidmouth USD, UD. Civ bdry: 1899,[345] 1931,[346] 1935.[1] *Parl* Seq 12. *Eccl* Aylb. RDn (until 1875), Ott. RDn (1875–1973). Renamed 1973 'Sidmouth with

Woolbrook'.[350]

SIDMOUTH WITH WOOLBROOK

EP Renaming 1973 of Sidmouth AP.[350] Ott. RDn.

SILVERTON

AP *LG* Silverton Bor (status not sustained), Seq 23. *Parl* Seq 7. *Eccl* Seq 13.

SLAPTON

AP Collegiate until Dissolution 16th cent, parochial thereafter. *LG* Seq 9. *Parl* Seq 19. *Eccl* Seq 40.

SOURTON

Chap in Bridestowe AP, sep civ identity early, sep EP 1889.[92] *LG* Seq 28. *Parl* Seq 20. *Eccl* Okeh. RDn (1889–1964), Tav. RDn (1964–*).

SOUTHLEIGH

AP Incl bor Wiscombe (status not sustained, no sep identity as par). *LG* Seq 12. Civ bdry: 1885,[153] 1935.[1] *Parl* Seq 12.

SOUTHWAY

EP Cr 1971 from Tamerton Foliot AP.[333] Plymouth RDn.

SOWTON

AP *LG* Seq 54. Civ bdry: 1884,[3] 1940 (loses pt to Exeter CB and CP),[6] 1966 (exchanges pts with Exeter CB and CP).[7] *Parl* Seq 12. *Eccl* Seq 1. Eccl bdry: 1931.[142]

SPARKWELL

EP Cr 1884 from Plympton St Mary EP.[327] Plymp. RDn. Bdry: 1963.[282]

CP Renaming 1966 of Plympton St Mary CP when area alt.[103] *LG* Plymp. St Mary RD. *Parl* W Devon CC (1970–*).

SPREYTON

AP *LG* Seq 53. *Parl* Seq 13. *Eccl* Dunsford RDn (until 1875), Okeh. RDn (1875–1902), Cadb. RDn (1902–73), Okeh. RDn (1973–*).

STARCROSS

EP Cr 1829 from Dawlish AP, Kenton AP.[258] Kenn RDn. Bdry: 1864 (cr Cofton EP).[146]

STAVERTON

AP *LG* Seq 24. Civ bdry: 1884.[105] *Parl* Seq 16. *Eccl* Pec jurisd Dean & Chapter of Exeter (until 1848), Seq 33 thereafter. Eccl bdry: 1852 (cr Landscove EP).[264]

STICKLEPATH

EP Cr 1956 from Barnstaple AP, Fremington AP, Tawstock AP.[46] Barnst. RDn.

STOCKLAND

AP In Dorset (Whitchurch Canonicorum Hd), incl hmlt Dalwood (Dorset, Fordington Lbty); both transf to Devon 1832 for parl purposes, 1844 for civ purposes[27] (Dalwood sep CP 1866[81] but no sep eccl identity, hence usual eccl spelling 'Stockland with Dalwood' qv). *LG* Axmin. Hd (from 1844), PLU, RSD, RD. *Parl* Dorset until 1832, Seq 12 in Devon thereafter.

STOCKLAND WITH DALWOOD

AP Usual eccl spelling; for civ, transf from Dorset to Devon, and civ sep of chap Dalwood see prev entry. *Eccl* Bridport RDn (until 1836 [Sarum dioc until 1542, Bristol dioc 1542–1836]), Hon. RDn (1836–75), Dunk. & Hon. RDn (1875–1902), Hon. RDn (1902–*).

STOCKLEIGH ENGLISH

AP *LG* Seq 7. *Parl* Seq 5. *Eccl* Seq 3.

STOCKLEIGH POMEROY

AP *LG* Seq 7. *Parl* Seq 5. *Eccl* Seq 3.

STOKE CANON

AP *LG* Seq 54. Civ bdry: 1940 (loses pt to Exeter CB and CP),[6] 1966.[7] *Parl* Seq 17. *Eccl* Pec jurisd Dean & Chapter of Exeter (until 1848), Seq 1 thereafter.

STOKE DAMEREL

AP *LG* Rob. Hd, Stoke Damerel incorp for poor, Devonport MB, USD. Abol civ 1888 ent to Devonport CP.[165] *Parl* Devonport Parl Bor (1832–1918). *Eccl* Tam. RDn (until 1848), Plymp. RDn (1848–75), Three Towns RDn (1875–1954), Plymouth RDn (1954–*). Eccl bdry: 1846 (cr Devonport St James EP),[187] 1846 (cr Devonport St Mary EP, Devonport St Paul EP, Devonport St Stephen EP),[195] 1873 (cr Devonport St Michael EP),[194] 1874,[188] 1882 (help cr Devonport St Aubyn EP),[175] 1885 (help cr Devonport St Mark, Ford EP),[189] 1887 (help cr Devonport St John the Baptist EP),[190] 1895,[191] 1904 (cr Devonport St Barnabas EP),[180] 1965 (help cr Devonport St Bartholomew EP).[182]

STOKE FLEMING

AP *LG* Coler. Hd, Kingsbr. PLU, pt Dartm. MB (1835–85), pt Dartm. USD (1875–85), Kingsbr. RSD (pt 1875–85, ent 1885–94), RD. Civ bdry: 1885 (loses pt in MB,USD to St Petrox AP).[341] *Parl* Seq 19. *Eccl* Ipp. RDn (until 1848), Tot. RDn (1848–75), Ipp. RDn (1875–*).

STOKE GABRIEL

AP *LG* Seq 24. *Parl* S'rn Dv (1832–67), East Dv (1867–85), Torq. Dv (1885–1918), Tot. Dv/CC (1918–*). *Eccl* Pec jurisd Bp Exeter (until 1848), Seq 33 thereafter.

STOKEINTEIGNHEAD

AP *LG* Wonf. Hd, Newt. Abb. PLU, pt Teignm. USD (1875–84), Newt. Abb. RSD (pt 1875–84, ent 1884–94), RD. Civ bdry: 1884 (loses pt in USD to St Nicholas AP),[340] 1885,[154] 1935,[1] 1967.[98] *Parl* S'rn Dv (1832–67), East Dv (1867–85), Mid Dv (1885–1918), Torq. Dv (1918–48), Tot. CC (1948–*). *Eccl* Kenn RDn (until 1848), Ipp. RDn (1848–1952), Moret. RDn (1952–*).

STOKENHAM

AP Incl chap Chivelstone (sep civ identity early, eccl severed 1932 to help cr South Pool with Chivelstone EP[138]), chap Sherford (sep civ identity early, no sep eccl identity, hence this par eccl 'Stokenham with Sherford and Beesands', qv). *LG* Seq 9. *Parl* Seq 19.

STOKENHAM WITH SHERFORD AND BEESANDS

AP Usual eccl spelling; for civ and sep chap Chivelstone, chap Sherford see prev entry. *Eccl* Seq 40.

EAST STONEHOUSE

Chap in Plymouth St Andrew AP, sep civ identity early outside the bor, sep EP 1746.[11] *LG* Rob. Hd, E Stonehouse incorp for poor, USD, UD (1894–1914), Plymouth CB (1914–74). *Parl* Devonport Parl Bor (1832–1918), thereafter in Plymouth Parl Bors/BCs (see Part III of the *Guide*). *Eccl* Plymp. RDn (1746–1875), Three Towns RDn (1875–1954). Eccl bdry: 1847 (help cr Plymouth St Peter EP),[311] 1876 (cr East Stonehouse St Matthew EP),[351] 1883 (cr East Stonehouse St Paul EP).[352] Abol eccl 1954 pt to Plymouth St Peter EP, pt to help cr East Stonehouse St George with St Paul EP.[126]

EAST STONEHOUSE ST GEORGE WITH ST PAUL
EP Cr 1954 by union East Stonehouse St Paul EP, pt East Stonehouse EP, pt Great Western Docks.[106] Plymouth RDn.

EAST STONEHOUSE ST MATTHEW
EP Cr 1876 from East Stonehouse EP.[351] Three Towns RDn. Abol 1954 ent to Plymouth St Peter EP.[126]

EAST STONEHOUSE ST PAUL
EP Cr 1883 from East Stonehouse EP.[352] Three Towns RDn. Abol 1954 to help cr East Stonehouse St George with St Paul EP.[126]

STOODLEIGH
AP *LG* Seq 50. *Parl* Seq 7. *Eccl* Seq 25.

STOWFORD
AP *LG* Seq 29. *Parl* Seq 21. *Eccl* Seq 38.

STREET–See following entry

STRETE
Chap in Blackawton AP, sep EP 1881 as 'Street'[67] but commonly now 'Strete', sep CP 1935 as 'Strete'.[1] *LG* Kingsbr. RD. *Parl* Tot. Dv/CC (1948–*). *Eccl* Woodl. RDn.

SUTCOMBE
AP *LG* Seq 46. Civ bdry: 1884.[299] *Parl* Seq 11. *Eccl* Seq 30. Eccl bdry: 1959.[83]

SUTTON ON PLYM
EP Cr 1844 from Plymouth Charles EP.[310] Plymouth RDn (1844–75), Three Towns RDn (1875–1954), Plymouth RDn (1954–*). Bdry: 1884,[320] 1911 (cr Cattedown EP),[125] 1954.[126]

SUTTON PRIOR–See PLYMOUTH

SWIMBRIDGE
AP *LG* Seq 30. *Parl* Seq 8. *Eccl* Pec jurisd Bp Exeter (until 1848), Barnst. RDn (1848–75), Shirw. RDn (1875–*).

SYDENHAM DAMEREL
AP *LG* Seq 29. Civ bdry: 1966 (gains pt Stoke Climsland AP, Cornw).[16] *Parl* Seq 21. *Eccl* Tav. RDn. Abol eccl 1938 to help cr Lamerton with Sydenham Damerel EP.[263]

TALATON
AP *LG* Seq 22. *Parl* Seq 1. *Eccl* Seq 12. Eccl bdry: 1844 (help cr Escot EP).[206]

TAMERTON FOLIOT
AP *LG* Rob. Hd, Tamerton Foliot Bor (status not sustained), Plymp. St Mary PLU, RSD, RD. Civ bdry: 1939 (loses pt to Plymouth CB and CP).[55] Abol civ 1951 pt to Plymouth CB and CP, pt to Bickleigh AP.[57] *Parl* S'rn Dv (1832–67), South Dv (1867–85), W'rn Dv (1885–1918), Tav. Dv (1918–48), Plymouth Devonport BC (1948–70). Parl bdry: 1951.[56] *Eccl* Tam. RDn (until 1875), Plymp. RDn (1875–1954), Plymouth RDn (1954–*). Eccl bdry: 1956,[250] 1958 (help cr Plymouth Crownhill (Church of the Ascension) EP),[111] 1971 (cr Southway EP).[333]

TAVISTOCK
AP *LG* Tav. Hd, Bor, PLU, RSD, RD (1894–98), UD (1898–1966), RD (1966–74). Civ bdry: 1885,[91] 1898 (the pt not constituted Tav. UD cr Tavistock Hamlets CP),[355] 1911,[356] 1935.[1] *Parl* Pt Tav. Parl Bor (1295–1885), pt S'rn Dv (1832–67), pt South Dv (1867–85), W'rn Dv (1885–1918), Tav. Dv/CC (1918–70), W Devon CC (1970–*). *Eccl* Seq 38. Eccl bdry: 1858 (cr Tavistock St Paul EP).[357]

TAVISTOCK HAMLETS
CP Cr 1898 from the pt of Tavistock AP not constituted Tav. UD.[355] *LG* Tav. PLU, RD. Civ bdry: 1966 (gains pt Calstock AP, Cornw).[16] *Parl* Tav. Dv/CC (1918–70), W Devon CC (1970–*).

TAVISTOCK ST PAUL
EP Cr 1858 from Tavistock AP.[357] Tav. RDn. Now usually called 'Gulworthy'.

MARY TAVY
AP Usual eccl spelling; for civ see 'Marytavy'. *Eccl* Seq 37.

PETER TAVY
AP Usual eccl spelling; for civ see 'Petertavy'. *Eccl* Seq 37. Eccl bdry: 1867 (help cr Horrabridge EP).[114]

TAWSTOCK
AP *LG* Seq 18. Civ bdry: 1899.[40] *Parl* Seq 8. *Eccl* Often as 'Tawstock with Harracott', Seq 16. Eccl bdry: 1956 (help cr Sticklepath EP).[46]

BISHOP'S TAWTON
AP Incl bor Newport (status not sustained, no sep identity as par). *LG* S Molt. Hd, Barnst. PLU, pt Barnst. USD (1875–85), Barnst. RSD (pt 1875–85, ent 1885–94), RD. Civ bdry: 1885 (loses pt in USD to Barnstable AP).[39] *Parl* Seq 8. *Eccl* Sometimes as 'Bishop's Tawton with Herner', Seq 16. Eccl bdry: 1847 (cr Newport EP).[289]

NORTH TAWTON
AP *LG* N Tawt. Bor, Seq 42. *Parl* Seq 4. *Eccl* Chum. RDn (until 1875), Okeh. RDn (1875–*).

SOUTH TAWTON
AP Usual civ spelling; incl bor South Zeal (status not sustained, no sep identity as par, but incl in eccl spelling, qv in following entry). *LG* Seq 53. *Parl* Seq 13.

SOUTH TAWTON WITH SOUTH ZEAL
AP Usual eccl spelling; for civ and bor South Zeal (no sep identity as par) see prev entry. *Eccl* Seq 7.

TEDBURN ST MARY
AP *LG* Seq 54. *Parl* Seq 15. *Eccl* Seq 6. Eccl bdry: 1970.[358]

TEIGNGRACE
AP *LG* Seq 44. Civ bdry: 1883,[63] 1885.[73] *Parl* Seq 16. *Eccl* Seq 34. Eccl bdry: 1956.[77]

TEIGNMOUTH
CP Cr 1909 by union East Teignmouth CP, West Teignmouth CP.[359] *LG* Newt. Abb. PLU, Teignm. UD. Civ bdry: 1935.[1] *Parl* Tot. Dv (1918–48), Tiv. CC (1948–*).

EAST TEIGNMOUTH
Chap in Dawlish AP, sep civ identity early, sep EP 1777.[11] *LG* E Teignm. Bor (when still chap, status not sustained), Exmin. Hd, Newt. Abb. PLU, Teignm. USD, UD. Civ bdry: 1883.[63] Abol civ 1909 to help cr Teignmouth CP.[359] *Parl* S'rn Dv (1832–67), East Dv (1867–85), Mid Dv (1885–1918). *Eccl* Pec jurisd Dean & Chapter of Exeter (1777–1848), Kenn RDn (1848–*).

WEST TEIGNMOUTH
Chap in Bishopsteignton AP, sep civ identity early, sep EP 1842.[62] *LG* W Teignm. Bor (when still chap, status not sustained), Exmin. Hd, Newt. Abb. PLU, Teignm. USD, UD. Civ bdry: 1883.[63] Abol civ 1909 to help cr Teignmouth CP.[359] *Parl* As for East Teignmouth. *Eccl* Pec jurisd Bp Exeter (1842–48), Kenn RDn (1848–*).

TEMPLETON
AP *LG* Seq 50. *Parl* Seq 7. *Eccl* Tiv. RDn (until 1875), Tiv. W RDn (1875–1902), Tiv. RDn (1902–24). Abol eccl 1924 to help cr Templeton with Loxbeare EP.[271]

TEMPLETON WITH LOXBEARE
EP Cr 1924 by union Templeton AP, Loxbeare AP.[271] Tiv. RDn.

TETCOTT
AP *LG* Seq 46. Civ bdry: 1883,[272] 1966 (gains pt North Tamerton AP, Cornw).[16] *Parl* Seq 11. *Eccl* Seq 30.

THELBRIDGE
AP *LG* Seq 48. Civ bdry: 1885.[266] *Parl* Seq 5. *Eccl* Seq 24.

THORNBURY
AP *LG* Seq 46. *Parl* Seq 11. *Eccl* Seq 30.

THORNCOMBE
AP In Dorset (Whitechurch Canonicorum Hd), transf to Devon 1832 for par purposes, 1844 for civ purposes,[27] transf 1896 back to Dorset.[360] *LG* Axmin. Hd (from 1844), PLU (1836–94), RSD, RD (1894–96), Beaminster PLU (1894–1930). Civ bdry: 1884.[29] *Parl* Dorset until 1832, S'rn Dv (1832–67), East Dv (1867–85), E'rn Dv (1885–1918), Dorset thereafter. *Eccl* Hon. RDn (until 1836), Bridport RDn (1836–72), Lyme RDn (1872–1970), Beaminster RDn (1970–*)(last three in Sarum dioc).

THORVERTON
AP Incl chap Nether Exe (sep civ identity early, sep EP 1730[11]). *LG* Seq 23. *Parl* Seq 7. *Eccl* Seq 3.

THROWLEIGH
AP *LG* Seq 53. *Parl* Seq 13. *Eccl* Seq 7.

THRUSHELTON
Chap in Marystowe AP, sep civ identity early, eccl severed 1922 (along with other pts of Marystowe AP) to help cr Lew Trenchard with Thrushelton EP.[268] *LG* Seq 29. Civ bdry: 1885.[269] *Parl* Seq 21.

THURLESTONE
AP *LG* Seq 38. *Parl* Seq 19. *Eccl* Seq 40.

TIPTON ST JOHN
EP Cr 1841 from Ottery St Mary AP[295] as 'Tipton', later usually called 'Tipton St John'. Aylb. RDn (1841–75), Ott. RDn (1875–1933). Abol 1933 to help cr Tipton St John with Venn Ottery EP.[296]

TIPTON ST JOHN WITH VENN OTTERY
EP Cr 1933 by union Titpton St John EP, Venn Ottery AP.[296] Ott. RDn.

TIVERTON
AP *LG* Tiv. Hd, PLU, Bor/MB, USD. *Parl* Tiv. Parl Bor (1621–1885), N-E'rn Dv (1885–1918), Tiv. Dv/CC (1918–*). *Eccl* Seq 15. Eccl bdry: 1856 (cr West Exe EP).[208] Par divided (per scheme 1886) into AP and 4 EPs, effective dates as follows: Cove, 1886; Chevithorne, 1889; Withleigh, 1890; Tiverton St George, 1896.[133] Later eccl bdry alt: 1960 (help cr Tiverton St Andrew EP).[162]

TIVERTON ST ANDREW
EP Cr 1960 from Tiverton AP, Tiverton St George EP.[162] Tiv. RDn.

TIVERTON ST GEORGE
EP Cr 1896 from Tiverton AP.[133] Tiv. RDn. Bdry: 1960 (help cr Tiverton St Andrew EP).[162]

TOPSHAM
AP *LG* Wonf. Hd, Topsham Bor (status not sustained), St Thomas PLU, RSD, RD. Civ bdry: 1913,[4] 1940.[6] Abol civ 1966 pt to Exeter CB and CP, pt to Clyst St George AP, pt to Woodbury AP.[7] *Parl* S'rn Dv (1832–67), East Dv (1867–85), N-E'rn Dv (1885–1918), Tiv. Dv/CC (1970–*). *Eccl* Pec jurisd Dean & Chapter of Exeter (until 1848), Seq 1 thereafter. Eccl bdry: 1840 (cr Wear EP, now commonly called 'Countess Wear'),[361] 1931,[142] 1961.[362]

BRENT TOR
AP Usual eccl spelling; for civ see 'Brentor'. *Eccl* Seq 38.

TORBAY
CP Cr 1967 from Brixham AP, Churston Ferrers CP, Coffinswell CP, Kerswells CP, Marldon CP, Paignton AP, Torquay CP, ent Mew Stone and Cod Rock Islands (not in any CP).[98] *LG* Torbay CB. *Parl* Torbay BC (1970–*).

TORBRYAN
AP *LG* Seq 25. Civ bdry: 1885.[363] *Parl* Seq 16. *Eccl* Ipp. RDn (until 1875), Moret. RDn (1875–1928), Ipp. RDn (1928–*).

TORMOHAM
AP Usual civ spelling; for eccl see following entry. Incl curacy Cockington (sep civ and eccl identity sustained). *LG* Haytor Hd, Newt. Abb. PLU, Torq. MB, USD. Addtl civ bdry alt: 1900.[364] Abol civ 1924 to help cr Torquay CP.[338] *Parl* S'rn Dv (1832–67), East Dv (1867–85), Torq. Dv (1885–1948).

TORMOHUN
AP Usual eccl spelling; for civ and curacy Cockington see prev entry. *Eccl* Ipp. RDn. Addtl eccl bdry alt: 1855 (help cr Torwood EP),[365] 1861 (help cr Torquay St John EP),[366] 1869 (help cr Torquay St Luke EP).[367]

TORQUAY
CP Cr 1924 by union St Mary Church AP, Tormoham AP.[338] *LG* Newt. Abb. PLU, Torq. MB. Civ bdry: 1928,[144] 1935.[1] Abol 1967 pt to help cr Torbay CB and CP, pt to Coffinswell CP, pt to St Nicholas AP, pt to Stokeinteignhead AP.[98] *Parl* Torq. BC (1948–70).

CENTRAL TORQUAY
EP Cr 1974 by union Torquay St John EP, Tormohun AP, Ellacombe EP.[204] Ipp. RDn.

TORQUAY HOLY TRINITY
EP Cr 1896 from Torwood EP.[368] Ipp. RDn.

TORQUAY ST JAMES, UPTON
EP Cr 1910 from Upton EP.[369] Ipp. RDn.

TORQUAY ST JOHN
EP Cr 1825 from Tormohun AP, Upton EP.[366] Ipp. RDn. Bdry: 1966.[203] Abol 1974 to help cr Central Torquay EP.[204]

TORQUAY ST LUKE
EP Cr 1869 from Tormohun AP, Upton EP.[267] Ipp. RDn. Bdry: 1966.[203]

TORQUAY ST MARTIN, BARTON
EP Cr 1960 from St Marychurch AP, Kingskerswell AP.[261] Ipp. RDn.

BLACK TORRINGTON
AP *LG* Seq 46. Civ bdry: 1884.[370] *Parl* Seq 11. *Eccl* Seq 30.

GREAT TORRINGTON
AP *LG* Pt Frem. Hd (until 1617), Torr. Bor (pt until 1617, ent from 1617), Torr. PLU, Great Torr. MB, USD. *Parl* Pt Torr. Parl Bor (1295–1330), Seq 4. *Eccl* Seq 28.

LITTLE TORRINGTON
AP *LG* Seq 36. *Parl* Seq 3. *Eccl* Seq 28.

TORWOOD
EP Cr 1855 from St Marychurch AP, Tormohun AP.[365] Ipp. RDn. Bdry: 1880 (cr Ilsham EP),[256] 1896 (cr Torquay Holy Trinity EP).[368]

TOTNES
AP Incl Little Totnes Bor, Bridgetown Pomeroy Bor (neither sustains status). *LG* Coler. Hd, Tot. PLU, Bor/MB, USD. Civ bdry: 1894 (gains the pt of Berry Pomeroy AP in the MB),[50] 1897.[51] *Parl* Tot. Parl Bor (pt 1295–1832, ent 1832–1918), Tot. Dv/CC (1918–*). *Eccl* Sometimes as 'Totnes with Bridgetown', Seq 39. Eccl bdry: 1968.[52]

TOWNSTALL
AP Incl chap St Petrox (sep civ identity early, sep EP 1748[11]), chap St Saviour (sep civ identity early, no sep eccl identity, hence this par eccl 'Townstall with St Saviour', qv). *LG* Coler. Hd, Tot. PLU, Dartm. USD, pt Dartm. MB. Civ bdry: 1883.[63] Abol civ 1891 to help cr Dartmouth CP.[173] *Parl* Dartm. Parl Bor (1298–1918).

TOWNSTALL WITH ST SAVIOUR
AP Usual eccl spelling; for civ and chaps St Petrox, St Saviour, see prev entry. *Eccl* Seq 31.

TRENTISHOE
AP *LG* Seq 4. *Parl* Seq 8. *Eccl* Seq 26.

TRUSHAM
AP *LG* Seq 16. Civ bdry: 1884.[371] *Parl* Seq 16. *Eccl* Kenn RDn (until 1875), Moret. RDn (1875–1922), Kenn RDn (1922–*).

TWITCHEN
Chap in North Molton AP, sep civ identity early, sep EP before 1850.[290] *LG* Seq 31. *Parl* Seq 2. *Eccl* S Molt. RDn.

UFFCULME
AP *LG* Seq 3. *Parl* Seq 7. *Eccl* Pec jurisd as Sarum prebend (until 1847), Seq 14 thereafter.

UGBOROUGH
AP *LG* Erming. Hd, Tot. PLU, pt Ivybr. USD, pt Tot. RSD, Tot. RD. Civ bdry: 1894 (the pt in the USD to help cr Ivybridge CP),[165] 1950.[70] *Parl* Seq 19. *Eccl* Seq 36. Eccl bdry: 1835 (help cr Ivybridge EP),[164] 1960,[89] 1965.[282]

UPLOWMAN
AP *LG* Pt Halb. Hd, pt Tiv. Hd, Tiv. PLU, RSD, RD. Civ bdry: 1884.[372] *Parl* Seq 7. *Eccl* Seq 14.

UPLYME
AP *LG* Seq 1. Civ bdry: 1884.[28] *Parl* Seq 12. *Eccl* Seq 8. Eccl bdry: 1850 (help cr Monkton Wyld EP [primarily in Dorset]).[285]

UPOTTERY
AP *LG* Axmin. Hd, Hon. PLU, RSD, RD. Civ bdry: 1966 (exchanges pts with Churchstanton AP, Somerset).[16] *Parl* Seq 12. *Eccl* Dunk. RDn (until 1875), Dunk. & Hon. RDn (1875–1902), Hon. RDn (1902–*).

UPTON
EP Cr 1848 from Tormohun AP.[373] Ipp. RDn. Bdry: 1825 (help cr Torquay St John EP),[366] 1868 (cr Ellacombe EP),[202] 1869 (help cr Torquay St Luke EP),[367] 1910 (cr Torquay St James, Upton EP),[369] 1966.[203]

UPTON HELLIONS
AP *LG* Seq 7. *Parl* Seq 5. *Eccl* Cadb. RDn. Abol eccl 1928 to help cr Sandford with Upton Hellions EP.[168]

UPTON PYNE
AP *LG* Seq 54. Civ bdry: 1884,[3] 1940 (loses pt to Exeter CB and CP).[6] *Parl* Seq 17. *Eccl* Seq 3.

VIRGINSTOW
AP *LG* Lifton Hd, Holsw. PLU (1837–52), Launceston PLU (1852–1930), RSD, Broadwoodw. RD (1894–1966), Holsw. RD (1966–74). *Parl* Seq 21. *Eccl* Tav. RDn (until 1875), Trigg Major RDn (Exeter dioc 1875–76, Truro dioc thereafter [Truro AD until 1878, Bodmin AD 1878–1973]). Abol eccl 1973 to help cr Werrington with St Giles on the Heath and Virginstow EP.[335]

WALKHAMPTON
AP *LG* Seq 33. Civ bdry: 1950 (help cr Horrabridge CP).[115] *Parl* Seq 21. *Eccl* Seq 37. Eccl bdry: 1867 (help cr Horrabridge EP),[114] 1919.[329]

WARKLEIGH
AP *LG* S Molt. Hd, PLU, RSD. Abol civ 1894 to help cr Satterleigh and Warkleigh CP.[245] *Parl* S'rn Dv (1832–67), North Dv (1867–85), N'rn Dv (1885–1918). *Eccl* Seq 23.

WASHFIELD
AP *LG* W Budl. Hd, Tiv. PLU, RSD, RD. *Parl* Seq 7. *Eccl* Seq 15.

WASHFORD PYNE
AP *LG* Seq 48. *Parl* Seq 5. *Eccl* Seq 25.

WEAR
EP Cr 1840 from Topsham AP.[361] Now usually called 'Countess Wear'. Aylb. RDn (1840–1902), Christianity RDn (1902–*). Bdry: 1934,[242] 1961,[362] 1964 (cr Exeter St Paul EP).[226]

COUNTESS WEAR–See prev entry

WEARE GIFFARD
AP *LG* Seq 36. *Parl* Seq 3. *Eccl* Seq 21.

WELCOMBE
AP *LG* Seq 21. *Parl* Seq 9. *Eccl* Seq 21.

WEMBURY
AP *LG* Seq 32. Civ bdry: 1966.[103] *Parl* Seq 18. *Eccl* Seq 36.

WEMBWORTHY
AP Usual civ spelling; for eccl see following entry. *LG* Seq 41. *Parl* Seq 5.

WEMBWORTHY WITH BRUSHFORD
AP Usual eccl spelling; for civ see prev entry. *Eccl* Seq 20.

WERRINGTON
AP *LG* Black Torr. Hd, Launceston PLU, RSD, Broadwoodw. RD. Civ bdry: 1888.[293] Transf 1966 to Cornw (Launceston RD).[292] *Parl* N'rn Dv (1832–67), South Dv (1867–85), W'rn Dv (1885–1918), Tav. Dv/CC (1918–70), Cornw thereafter. *Eccl* Trigg Major RDn (Exeter dioc until 1876, Truro thereafter [Truro AD until 1878, Bodmin AD 1878–1973]). Abol eccl 1973 to help cr Werrington with St Giles on the Heath and Virginstow EP.[335]

WERRINGTON WITH ST GILES ON THE HEATH AND VIRGINSTOW
EP Cr 1973 by union Werrington AP, St Giles on the Heath AP, Virginstow AP.[335] Trigg Major RDn (Truro dioc).

WESTLEIGH
AP *LG* Seq 18. Civ bdry: 1883.[63] *Parl* Seq 8. *Eccl* Seq 16.

WESTON MILL
EP Cr 1933 from St Budeaux EP, Devonport St Boniface EP, North Keynham EP.[184] Three Towns RDn (1933–54), Plymouth RDn (1954–*). Eccl bdry: 1957 (help cr Plymouth St James the Less, Ham EP).[192]

WESTON PEVERELL
CP Cr 1899 from St Budeaux CP.[306] *LG* Plymp. St Mary PLU, RD. Bdry: 1900 (loses pt to Devonport CB and CP).[177] Abol 1935 pt to Compton Gifford CP, pt to St Budeaux CP.[1] *Parl* Tav. Dv (1918–48).

WHIMPLE
AP *LG* Seq 8. *Parl* S'rn Dv (1832–67), East Dv (1867–85), E'rn Dv (1885–1918), Tiv. Dv/CC (1918–*). *Eccl* Seq 1.

WHIPTON
EP Cr 1938 from Heavitree AP, Pinhoe AP.[243] Christianity RDn.

WHITCHURCH
AP Incl pt chap Horrabridge (sep EP 1867,[114] sep CP 1950[115]). *LG* Seq 33. Addtl civ bdry alt: 1885,[191] 1935.[1] *Parl* Seq 21. *Eccl* Seq 37. Addtl eccl bdry alt: 1920.[253]

WHITESTONE
AP *LG* Seq 54. Civ bdry: 1884,[3] 1900,[343] 1940 (loses pt to Exeter CB and St Thomas the Apostle AP).[6] *Parl* Seq 17. *Eccl* Seq 6. Eccl bdry: 1970.[358]

WHITLEIGH
EP Cr 1956 from St Budeaux EP.[250] Plymouth RDn.

WIDECOMBE IN THE MOOR
AP *LG* Seq 25. *Parl* Seq 16. *Eccl* Seq 34. Eccl bdry: 1864 (cr Leudsen EP).[267]

WIDWORTHY
AP *LG* Seq 12. *Parl* Seq 12. *Eccl* Seq 8.

WILLAND
AP *LG* Seq 20. *Parl* Seq 7. *Eccl* Seq 14.

WINKLEIGH
AP *LG* Winkleigh Bor (status not sustained), Seq 43. *Parl* Seq 3. *Eccl* Seq 29.

WITHERIDGE
AP *LG* Witheridge Bor (status not sustained), Seq 49. Civ bdry: 1885.[374] *Parl* Seq 2. *Eccl* Seq 23.

WITHLEIGH
EP Cr 1890 from Tiverton AP.[133] Tiv. RDn.

WITHYCOMBE RALEIGH
Chap in East Budleigh AP, sep civ identity early, sep EP 1850 as 'Withycombe Raleigh with Exmouth All Saints',[119] qv. *LG* E Budl. Hd, St Thomas PLU, pt Exmouth USD, pt St Thomas RSD, Exmouth UD. Addtl civ bdry alt: 1883,[63] 1894 (pt outside the UD added to it).[270] *Parl* Seq 12

WITHYCOMBE RALEIGH WITH EXMOUTH ALL SAINTS
Chap in East Budleigh AP, sep civ identity early as 'Withycombe Raleigh', qv, sep EP 1850.[119] Aylb. RDn.

WOLBOOUGH
AP Incl bors Newton Abbot, Newton Bushel (neither sustains status). *LG* Haytor Hd, Newt. Abb. PLU, Wolborough USD (1875–4 Aug 1894), Newt. Abb. USD (4 Aug 1894–apptd day 1894), UD. Civ bdry: 1885.[73] *Parl* Seq 16. *Eccl* Donative. Ipp. RDn (until 1875), Moret. RDn (1875–*).

WOODBURY
AP Usual civ spelling; for eccl see following entry. *LG* Woodbury Bor (status not sustained), Seq 6. Civ bdry: 1884,[3] 1966.[7] *Parl* Seq 12.

WOODBURY WITH EXTON
AP Usual eccl spelling; for civ see prev entry. *Eccl* Pec jurisd Vicars Choral of Exeter (until 1848), Seq 1 thereafter. Eccl bdry: 1845 (help cr Salterton EP, now usually called 'Woodbury Salterton'.[347]

WOODLAND
Chap in Ipplepen AP, sep civ identity early, sep EP 1754.[11] *LG* Seq 25. *Parl* Seq 16. *Eccl* Ipp. RDn (until 1875), Moret. RDn (1875–1938). Eccl bdry: 1928.[53] Abol eccl 1938 to help cr Broadhempston and Woodland EP.[106]

WOODLEIGH
AP *LG* Seq 38. Civ bdry: 1884.[286] *Parl* Seq 19. *Eccl* Seq 40. Eccl bdry: 1931.[287]

WOOLACOMBE
EP Cr 1922 from Mortehoe AP.[288] Barnst. RDn.

WOOLFARDISWORTHY
AP Usual civ spelling; for eccl see 'Woolfardisworthy East'. *LG* Seq 48. Civ bdry: 1884,[139] 1885.[266] *Parl* Seq 5.

WOOLFARDISWORTHY
AP Usual civ spelling; for eccl see 'Woolfardisworthy West'. *LG* Seq 21. *Parl* Seq 9.

WOOLFARDISWORTHY EAST
AP Usual eccl spelling; for civ see 1st 'Woolfardisworthy' above. *Eccl* S Molt. RDn (until 1875), Cadb. RDn (1875–*).

WOOLFARDISWORTHY WEST
AP Usual eccl spelling; for civ see 2nd 'Woolfardisworthy' above. *Eccl* Seq 21. Eccl bdry: 1862 (cr Bucks Mills EP).[118]

EAST WORLINGTON
AP *LG* Seq 49. Civ bdry: 1882,[266] 1885.[375] *Parl* Seq 2. *Eccl* Seq 24.

WEST WORLINGTON
AP *LG* With. Hd, S Molt. PLU, RSD. Abol civ 1885 ent to East Worlington AP.[375] *Parl* N'rn Dv (1832–67), North Dv (1867–1918). *Eccl* Seq 24.

YARCOMBE
AP *LG* Axmin. Hd, Chard PLU (1836–94), RSD, Hon. PLU (1894–1930), RD. Civ bdry: 1884.[376] *Parl* Seq 12. *Eccl* Seq 5.

YARNSCOMBE
AP *LG* Hartland Hd, Torr. PLU, RSD, RD. Civ bdry: 1884.[54] *Parl* Seq 3. *Eccl* Seq 19.

YEALMPTON
AP Incl chap Revelstoke (sep civ identity early [incl bor Noss Mayo, status not sustained], sep EP 1856[331]). *LG* Seq 32. Addtl civ bdry alt: 1884,[102] 1935.[1] *Parl* Seq 18. *Eccl* Seq 36. Addtl eccl bdry alt: 1962.[104]

YELVERTON
EP Cr 1935 from Buckland Monachorum AP.[116] Tav. RDn.

ZEAL MONACHORUM
AP *LG* Seq 41. *Parl* Seq 5. *Eccl* Seq 20.

DORSET

ABBREVIATIONS

Abbreviations particular to Dorset follow. Those general abbreviations in use throughout the *Guide* are found on page xix.

Abbotsb.	Abbotsbury
Badb.	Badbury
Beam.	Beaminster
Blackm.	Blackmore
Blandf.	Blandford
Bridp.	Bridport
Browns.	Brownshall
Buck.	Buckland
Can.	Canonicorum
Cerne, Tot. & Modb.	Cerne, Totcombe and Modbury
Cogd.	Cogdean
Cranb.	Cranborne
Cull. Tree	Culliford Tree
Dorch.	Dorchester
Egg.	Eggerton
Framp.	Frampton
Gill.	Gillingham
Hundredsb.	Hundredsbarrow
Knowlt.	Knowlton
Melc.	Melcombe
Milt.	Milton
Newt.	Newton
Pimp.	Pimperne
Purb.	Purbeck
Redl.	Redlane
Rowb.	Rowberrow
Shaft.	Shaftesbury
Sherb.	Sherborne
Sixp.	Sixpenny
Sturm.	Sturminster
Toll.	Tollerford
Uggsc.	Uggscombe
Wareh.	Wareham
Weym.	Weymouth
Whitch.	Whitchurch
Wimb.	Wimborne
Winf.	Winfrith
Yetm.	Yetminster

SEQUENCES

An abbreviated entry prefixed by 'Seq' is used in the parochial entries to avoid repeating often the names of superior units of administration. The content of each sequence is shown below. Because Cranborne PLU and Purbeck PLU each existed only for half a year before being absorbed respectively into Wimborne PLU (to cr Wimborne and Cranborne PLU) and into Wareham PLU (to cr Wareham and Purbeck PLU), the two short lived PLUs are not noted in the parochial entries, although they are noted in Part II of the *Guide*.

Local Government Sequences ('LG')

SEQ 1 Badb. Hd, Wimb. & Cranb. PLU, RSD, RD
SEQ 2 Beam. Hd, PLU, RSD, RD
SEQ 3 Bindon Lbty, Wareh. & Purb. PLU, RSD, RD
SEQ 4 Browns. Hd, Sturm. PLU, RSD, RD
SEQ 5 Buck. Newt. Hd, Dorch. PLU, RSD, RD (1894–1933), Sturm. RD (1933–74)
SEQ 6 Cerne, Tot. & Modb. Hd, Dorch. PLU, RSD, RD
SEQ 7 Cogd. Hd, Poole PLU, RSD, RD (1894–1933), Wareh. & Purb. RD (1933–74)
SEQ 8 Cogd. Hd, Wimb. & Cranb. PLU, RSD, RD
SEQ 9 Coombs Ditch Hd, Blandf. PLU, RSD, RD
SEQ 10 Cranb. Hd, Blandf. PLU, RSD, RD
SEQ 11 Cranb. Hd, Wimb. & Cranb. PLU, RSD, RD
SEQ 12 Cull. Tree Hd, Dorch. PLU, RSD, RD
SEQ 13 Framp. Hd, Dorch. PLU, RSD, RD
SEQ 14 George Hd, Dorch. PLU, RSD, RD
SEQ 15 Gill. Hd, Shaft. PLU, RSD, RD
SEQ 16 Hasilor Hd, Wareh. & Purb. PLU, RSD, RD
SEQ 17 Hundredsb. Hd, Wareh. & Purb. PLU, RSD, RD
SEQ 18 Knowlt. Hd, Wimb. & Cranb. PLU, RSD, RD
SEQ 19 Piddletown Hd, Dorch. PLU, RSD, RD
SEQ 20 Pimp. Hd, Blandf. PLU, RSD, RD
SEQ 21 Pimp. Hd, Sturm. PLU, RSD, RD
SEQ 22 Redl. Hd, Shaft. PLU, RSD, RD
SEQ 23 Redl. Hd, Sturm. PLU, RSD, RD
SEQ 24 Rowb. Hd, Wareh. & Purb. PLU, RSD, RD
SEQ 25 Sherb. Hd, PLU, RSD, RD
SEQ 26 Sixp. Hadley Hd, Shaft. PLU, RSD, RD
SEQ 27 Sturm. Newt. Hd, Sturm. PLU, RSD, RD
SEQ 28 Toll. Hd, Beam. PLU, RSD, RD
SEQ 29 Toll. Hd, Dorch. PLU, RSD, RD
SEQ 30 Uggsc. Hd, Bridp. PLU, RSD, RD
SEQ 31 Uggsc. Hd, Dorch. PLU, RSD, RD
SEQ 32 Uggsc. Hd, Weym. PLU, RSD, RD (1894–1933), Dorch. RD (1933–74)
SEQ 33 Whitch. Can. Hd, Beam. PLU, RSD, RD
SEQ 34 Whitch. Can. Hd, Bridp. PLU, RSD, RD
SEQ 35 Whiteway Hd, Blandf. PLU, RSD, RD
SEQ 36 Whiteway Hd, Sturm. PLU, RSD, RD
SEQ 37 Winf. Hd, Wareh. & Purb. PLU, RSD, RD
SEQ 38 Yetm. Hd, Dorch. PLU, RSD, RD (1894–1933), Sherb. RD (1933–74)
SEQ 39 Yetm. Hd, Sherb. PLU, RSD, RD

Parliamentary Sequences ('Parl')

SEQ 1 E'rn Dv (1885–1948), North CC (1948–*)
SEQ 2 E'rn Dv (1885–1918), N'rn Dv (1918–48), North CC (1948–*)
SEQ 3 E'rn Dv (1885–1948), South CC (1948–*)
SEQ 4 E'rn Dv (1885–1918), S'rn Dv (1918–48), South CC (1948–*)
SEQ 5 N'rn Dv (1885–1948), North CC (1948–*)
SEQ 6 N'rn Dv (1885–1948), West CC (1948–*)
SEQ 7 S'rn Dv (1885–1948), South CC (1948–*)
SEQ 8 S'rn Dv (1885–1918), W'rn Dv (1918–48), West CC (1948–*)
SEQ 9 W'rn Dv (1885–1918), N'rn Dv (1918–48), West CC (1948–*)
SEQ 10 W'rn Dv (1885–1948), West CC (1948–*)

Ecclesiastical Sequences ('Eccl')

SEQ 1 Bridp. RDn (until 1872), Bridp. RDn First Dv/Abbotsb. (1872–1970), Dorch. RDn (1970–*)
SEQ 2 Bridp. RDn (until 1872), Bridp. RDn First Dv/Abbotsb. (1872–1970), Lyme Bay RDn (1970–*)
SEQ 3 Bridp. RDn (until 1872), Bridp. RDn First Dv/Abbotsb. (1872–1970), Weym. RDn (1970–*)
SEQ 4 Bridp. RDn (until 1872), Bridp. RDn Second Dv/Bridp. (1872–1954), Beam. RDn (1955–*)
SEQ 5 Bridp. RDn (until 1872), Bridp. RDn Second Dv/Bridp. (1872–1970), Lyme Bay RDn (1970–*)
SEQ 6 Bridp. RDn (until 1872), Bridp. RDn Third Dv/Lyme (1872–1970), Beam. RDn (1970–*)
SEQ 7 Bridp. RDn (until 1872), Bridp. RDn Third Dv/Lyme (1872–1970), Beam. RDn (1970–*)
SEQ 8 Bridp. RDn (until 1872), Bridp. RDn Fourth Dv/Beam. (1872–*)
SEQ 9 Dorch. RDn (until 1872), Dorch. RDn First Dv/Dorch. (1872–*)
SEQ 10 Dorch. RDn (until 1872), Dorch. RDn First Dv/Dorch. (1872–1916), Abbotsb. RDn (1916–70), Dorch. RDn (1970–*)
SEQ 11 Dorch. RDn (until 1872), Dorch. RDn Second Dv/Weym. RDn (1872–*)
SEQ 12 Dorch. RDn (until 1872), Dorch. RDn Third Dv/Purb. (1872–*)
SEQ 13 Pimp. RDn (until 1872), Pimp. RDn First Dv/Blandf. (1872–1970), Milt. & Blandf. RDn (1970–*)

SEQ 14 Pimp. RDn (until 1872), Pimp. RDn Second Dv/Wimb. (1872–*)
SEQ 15 Shaft. RDn (until 1872), Shaft. RDn First Dv/Shaft. (1872–1973), Blackm. Vale RDn (1973–*)
SEQ 16 Shaft. RDn (until 1872), Shaft. RDn Second Dv/Stalbridge (1872–1954), Sherb. RDn (1955–*)
SEQ 17 Shaft. RDn (until 1872), Shaft. RDn Second Dv/Stalbridge (1872–1954), Sturm. Newt. RDn (1955–73), Blackm. Vale RDn (1973–*)
SEQ 18 Shaft. RDn (until 1872), Shaft. RDn Third Dv/Sherb. (1872–*)
SEQ 19 Shaft. RDn (until 1872), Shaft. RDn Third Dv/Sherb. (1872–1916), Cerne RDn (1916–54), Beam. RDn (1955–*)
SEQ 20 Shaft. RDn (until 1872), Shaft. RDn Fourth Dv/Sturm. Newt. (1872–1972), Blackm. Vale RDn (1973–*)
SEQ 21 Shaft. RDn (until 1872), Shaft. RDn Fourth Dv/Sturm. Newt. (1872–1954), Shaft. RDn (1955–73), Shaft. & Tisbury RDn (1973–*)
SEQ 22 Whitch. RDn (until 1872), Whitch. RDn First Dv/Bere Regis (1872–1972), Dorch. RDn (1973–*)
SEQ 23 Whitch. RDn (until 1872), Whitch. RDn First Dv/Bere Regis (1872–1916), Cerne RDn (1916–54), Dorch. RDn (1955–*)
SEQ 24 Whitch. RDn (until 1872), Whitch. RDn Second Dv/Poole (1872–*)
SEQ 25 Whitch. RDn (until 1872), Whitch. RDn Second Dv/Poole (1872–1962), Milton RDn (1962–70), Purb. RDn (1970–*)
SEQ 26 Whitch. RDn (until 1872), Whitch. RDn Third Dv/Cerne (1872–1954), Beam. RDn (1955–*)
SEQ 27 Whitch. RDn (until 1872), Whitch. RDn Third Dv/Cerne (1872–1954), Dorch. RDn (1955–*)
SEQ 28 Whitch. RDn (until 1872), Whitch. RDn Third Dv/Cerne (1872–1954), Sherb. RDn (1955–*)
SEQ 29 Whitch. RDn (until 1872), Whitch. RDn Fourth Dv/Milton (1872–1970), Milt. & Blandf. RDn (1970–*)

DIOCESES AND ARCHDEACONRIES

SARUM DIOC (until 1542)
Dorset AD: Bridp. RDn, Dorch. RDn, Pimp. RDn, Shaft. RDn, Whitch. RDn

BRISTOL DIOC (1542–1836)
Dorset AD: Bridp. RDn, Dorch. RDn, Pimp. RDn, Shaft. RDn, Whitch. RDn

SARUM DIOC (1836–*)
Dorset AD: Abbotsb. RDn (1872–1916), Beam. RDn (1872–1916), Bere Regis RDn (1872–1916), Blackm. Vale RDn (1973–*), Blandf. RDn (1872–1970), Bridp. RDn (until 1872), Bridp. RDn (1872–1916), Cerne RDn (1872–1916), Dorch. RDn (until 1872), Dorch. RDn (1872–1916), Lyme RDn (1872–1916), Milt. RDn (1872–1970), Milt. & Blandf. RDn (1970–*), Pimp. RDn (until 1872), Poole RDn (1872–*), Purb. RDn (1872–*), Shaft. RDn (until 1872), Shaft. RDn (1872–1972), Shaft. & Tisbury RDn (1973–*), Sherb. RDn (1872–1916), Stalbridge RDn (1872–1954), Sturm. Newt. RDn (1872–1972), Weym. RDn (1872–1916), Whitch. RDn (until 1872), Wimb. RDn (1872–*)
Sherborne AD (1916–):* Abbotsb. RDn (1916–70), Beam. RDn, Bere Regis RDn, Bridp. RDn (1916–70), Cerne RDn (1916–54), Dorch. RDn, Lyme RDn (1916–70), Lyme Bay RDn (1970–*), Sherb. RDn, Weym. RDn

Note: From 1872–1954 RDns in Sarum were known both as divisions of the orig RDns and by the names used invariably later; the seq numbers above use the former, the organisation of RDns in ADs and the parochial entries the latter. The double names may be paired as follows:
Bridp. First–Fourth Dvs: Abbotsb., Bridp., Lyme, Beam., respectively
Dorch. First–Third Dvs: Dorch., Weym., Purb., respectively
Pimp. First–Second Dvs: Blandf., Wimb. respectively
Shaft. First–Fourth Dvs: Shaft., Stalbridge, Sherb., Sturm. Newt., respectively
Whitch. First–Fourth Dvs: Bere Regis, Poole, Cerne, Milton, respectlvely

THE PARISHES OF DORSET

ABBOTSBURY
AP *LG* Seq 32. Civ bdry: 1894,[1] 1933.[2] *Parl* Seq 10. *Eccl* Seq 3.

AFFPUDDLE
AP *LG* Seq 17. *Parl* Seq 7. *Eccl* Whitch. RDn (until 1872), Bere Regis RDn (1872–1970). Abol eccl 1970 to help cr Affpuddle with Turnerspuddle EP.[3]

AFFPUDDLE WITH TURNERSPUDDLE
EP Cr 1970 by union Affpuddle AP, Turnerspuddle AP.[3] Bere Regis RDn (1970–72), Dorch. RDn (1973–*). Bdry: 1971.[4]

ALCESTER
CP Cr 1894 from Shaftesbury St James AP.[5] *LG* Shaft. PLU, RD. Abol 1921 ent to Shaftesbury CP.[6] *Parl* N'rn Dv (1918–48).

ALDERHOLT
Chap in Cranborne AP, sep EP 1849,[7] sep CP 1894.[8] *LG* Wimb. & Cranb. PLU, RD. *Parl* N'rn Dv (1918–48), North CC (1948–*). *Eccl* Pimp. RDn (1849–72), Wimb. RDn (1872–*).

ALLINGTON
AP *LG* Godderthorne Hd, Bridp. PLU, pt Bridp. MB (1835–94), pt Bridp. USD, pt Bridp. RSD, Bridp. RD. Civ bdry: 1884,[9] 1894 (loses the pt in the MB to Bridport AP),[10] 1954.[178] *Parl* Pt Bridp. Parl Bor (1832–85), Seq 10 thereafter. *Eccl* Orig sep par, later deemed free chap, sep par again 1820.[11] Seq 5. Eccl bdry: 1927.[12]

ALMER
AP *LG* Loosebarrow Hd, Blandf. PLU (1835–94), RSD, Wimb. & Cranb. PLU (1894–1930), RD. Abol civ 1935 ent to Sturminster Marshall AP.[2] *Parl* E'rn Dv (1885–1948). *Eccl* Whitch. RDn (until 1872), Poole RDn (1872–1962), Milt. RDn (1962–70), Purb. RDn (1970–72). Abol eccl 1972 to help cr Almer and Charborough EP.[13]

ALMER AND CHARBOROUGH
EP Cr 1972 by union Almer AP, Charborough AP.[13] Purb. RDn.

ALTON PANCRAS
AP *LG* Alton Pancras Lbty, Cerne PLU, RSD, RD (1894–1933), Dorch. RD (1933–74). *Parl* Seq 10. *Eccl* Pec jurisd Cath Chapter of Sarum (until 1847), Seq 22 thereafter.

ANDERSON
AP Usual civ spelling; for eccl see 'Winterborne Anderson'. Free chap said by some to have been chap in Bere Regis AP, sep par by 14th cent.[14] *LG* Seq 9. Civ bdry: 1933.[2] *Parl* Seq 5.

ARNE
Chap in Wareham Holy Trinity AP, sep civ identity early, no sep eccl identity. *LG* Seq 16. Bdry: 1894,[15] 1931.[16] *Parl* Wareh. Parl Bor (1832–85), Seq 4 thereafter.

ASHMORE
AP *LG* Cranb. Hd, Shaft. PLU, RSD, RD. *Parl* Seq 5. *Eccl* Pimp. RDn (until 1872), Blandf. RDn (1872–1961), Shaft. RDn (1961–72), Blackm. Vale RDn (1973–*).

ASKERSWELL
AP *LG* Egg. Hd, Bridp. PLU, RSD, RD. Civ bdry: 1884.[9] *Parl* Seq 10. *Eccl* Seq 5.

ATHELHAMPTON
AP *LG* Seq 19. *Parl* Seq 10. *Eccl* Whitch. RDn (until 1872), Bere Regis RDn (1872–1967). Abol eccl 1967 to help cr Puddletown with Athelhampton and Burleston EP.[17]

AXMINSTER
AP Incl chaps Kilmington, Membury (each with sep civ identity early in Devon, each sep EP 1911[36]). Pt Devon (Axminster Hd), pt Dorset (Whitch. Can. Hd), the latter transf to Devon 1832 for parl purposes, 1844 for civ purposes.[37] See main entry in Devon.

BATCOMBE
AP *LG* Seq 38. *Parl* Seq 9. *Eccl* Dorch. RDn (until 1872), Sherb. RDn (1872–1916), Abbotsb. RDn (1916–25), Sherb. RDn (1925–*).

BEAMINSTER
Chap in Netherbury AP, sep civ identity early, sep EP 1849.[18] *LG* Seq 2. *Parl* Seq 10. *Eccl* Bridp. RDn (1849–72), Beam. RDn (1872–*).

BEER HACKETT
AP *LG* Seq 25. *Parl* Seq 6. *Eccl* Pec jurisd Cath Chapter of Sarum (until 1847), Seq 18 thereafter.

BELCHALWELL
AP *LG* Cranb. Hd, Sturm. PLU, RSD. Abol civ 1884 pt to Okeford Fitzpaine AP, pt to Fifehead Neville AP.[19] *Eccl* Sometimes deemed chap to Fifehead Neville AP but sep identity maintained, Shaft. RDn (until 1872), Milt. RDn (1872–1954), Sturm. Newt. RDn (1955–72), Blackm. Vale RDn (1973–*). Eccl bdry: 1974.[20]

BERE REGIS
AP Usual civ name, eccl name from 1972 when loses chap of Winterbourne Kingston (sep civ identity early), the latter made sep EP[21]; for eccl before 1972 see following entry. Also incl hmlt Milborne Stileham (sep CP 1866,[22] eccl severed 1890 and transf to Milborne St Andrew with Dewlish AP[23]), perhaps incl chap Anderson (eccl, 'Winterbourne Anderson', sep par by 14th cent[14]). *LG* Bere Regis Hd, Wareh. PLU & Purb. PLU, RSD. RD. *Parl* Wareh. Parl Bor (1832–85), Seq 4 thereafter.
EP Cr 1972 when Bere Regis with Winterbourne Kingston AP divided into 2 EPs of Bere Regis, Winterbourne Kingston.[21] Milt. & Blandf. RDn.

BERE REGIS WITH WINTERBOURNE KINGSTON
AP Usual eccl spelling; for civ and sep of other dependent units see prev entry. *Eccl* Pec jurisd Cath Chapter of Sarum (until 1847), Whitch. RDn (1847–72), Bere Regis RDn (1872–1972). Abol eccl 1972, divided into 2 EPs of Bere Regis, Winterbourne Kingston.[21]

BETTISCOMBE
AP *LG* Frampt. Lbty, Beam. PLU, RSD, RD. Civ bdry: 1883,[24] 1884.[25] *Parl* Seq 10. *Eccl* Seq 6.[26] Eccl bdry: 1953 (gains chaps Marshwood, Fishpond from Whitchurch Canonicorum AP).[27]

BEXINGTON
AP Bridp. RDn, united 1451 to Puncknowle AP.[26]

BINCOMBE
AP *LG* Frampt. Lbty, Weym. PLU, RSD, RD (1894–1933), Dorch. RD (1933–74). Civ bdry: 1933.[2] *Parl* Seq 7. *Eccl* Dorch. RDn (until 1872), Weym. RDn (1872–1970). Abol eccl 1970 to help cr Bincombe with Broadway EP.[28]

BINCOMBE WITH BROADWAY
EP Cr 1970 by union Bincombe AP, Broadway AP.[28] Weym. RDn.

BLANDFORD FORUM
AP *LG* Coombs Ditch Hd, Blandf. PLU, Blandf. Forum Bor/MB (pt until 1896, ent 1896–1974), pt Blandf. Forum USD, pt Blandf. RSD. Civ bdry: 1896 (gains the pts of Bryanston AP, Blandford St Mary AP in the MB),[30] 1896 (the pt not in the MB lost to Bryanston AP, pt to Pimperne AP),[31] 1930.[32] *Parl* Pt Bladf. Parl

Bor (1304–49), Seq 5 thereafter. *Eccl* Seq 13. Eccl bdry: 1972.[33]

BLANDFORD ST MARY

AP Incl Littleton AP (orig sep par, united 1430 with Blandford St Mary[34]). *LG* Coombs Ditch Hd, Blandf. PLU, USD, pt Blandf. Forum MB (1889–96), Blandf. RD (pt 1894–96, ent 1896–1974). Civ bdry: 1887,[35] 1896 (loses the pt in the MB to Blandford Forum AP),[30] 1933.[2] *Parl* Seq 5. *Eccl* Seq 29. Eccl bdry: 1972.[33]

BLOXWORTH

AP *LG* Coombs Ditch Hd, Wareh. & Purb. PLU, RSD, RD. *Parl* Seq 4. *Eccl* Pec jurisd Cathedral Chapter of Sarum (until 1847), Seq 25 thereafter. Eccl bdry: 1960.[38]

NEW BOROUGH AND LEIGH

EP Cr 1877 from Wimborne Minster AP.[39] Wimb. RDn. Bdry: 1903 (help cr Colehill EP).[40]

BOTHENHAMPTON

AP *LG* Loders & Bothenhampton Lbty, Bridp. PLU, pt Bridp. MB (1835–94), pt Bridp. USD, pt Bridp. RSD, Bridp. RD. Civ bdry: 1884,[9] 1894 (incl loses the pt in the MB to Bridport AP).[10] *Parl* Pt Bridp. Parl Bor (1832–85), Seq 10 thereafter. *Eccl* Donative, Seq 5. Eccl bdry: 1927.[12]

BOURNEMOUTH ST JOHN THE EVANGELIST

EP Cr 1891 from Kinson EP, Bournemouth St Peter EP (Hants), Bournemouth St Stephen EP (Hants).[41] See main entry in Hants. Bdry: 1892,[42] 1925.[71]

BOURTON

Chap in Gillingham AP, sep EP 1847,[43] sep CP 1866.[22] *LG* Gill. Lbty, Mere PLU (1835–94), RSD, Shaft. PLU (1894–1930), RD. Civ bdry: 1883,[24] 1885.[44] *Parl* Seq 5. *Eccl* Shaft. RDn (1847–1972), Blackm. Vale RDn (1973–*).

BRADFORD ABBAS

AP *LG* Seq 25. *Parl* Seq 6. *Eccl* Sometimes as 'Bradford Abbas with Clifton Maybank' after gains 1824 Clifton Maybank AP,[45] Seq 18. Addtl eccl bdry alt: 1954,[46] 1966.[47]

BRADFORD ABBAS WITH CLIFTON MAYBANK– See prev entry

BRADFORD PEVERELL

AP *LG* Seq 14. Civ bdry: 1894,[48] 1900,[49] 1933.[2] *Parl* Seq 8. *Eccl* Seq 9.

BRADPOLE

AP *LG* Beam. Forum & Redhone Hd, Bridp. PLU, pt Bridp. MB (1835–94), pt Bridp. USD, pt Bridp. RSD, Bridp. RD. Civ bdry: 1894 (incl loses the pt in the MB to Bridport AP),[10] 1901.[50] *Parl* Pt Bridp. Parl Bor (1832–85), Seq 10 thereafter. *Eccl* Seq 5.

BRANKSEA

EP Cr 1855 from Studland AP.[51] Dorch. RDn (1855–72), Purb. RDn (1872–74), Poole RDn (1874–1971). Abol eccl 1971 to help cr Parkstone St Peter with Branksea EP.[52]

BRANKSOME

CP Cr 1894 from the pt of Kinson CP in Kinson USD.[53] *LG* Poole PLU, Branksome UD. Abol 1905 to help cr Poole CP.[54]

BRANKSOME ST ALDHELM

EP Cr 1930 from Branksome Park EP, Parkstone St Osmund EP.[55] Poole RDn.

BRANKSOME ST CLEMENT

EP Cr 1904 from Kinson EP.[56] Poole RDn. Bdry: 1953,[57] 1964.[58]

BRANKSOME PARK

EP Cr 1878 from Parkstone St Peter EP, Kinson EP.[59] Poole RDn. Bdry: 1927,[60] 1930 (help cr Branksome St Aldhelm EP).[55]

LONG BREDY

AP Incl chap Littlebredy (sep civ identity early, no sep eccl identity), hmlt and tg Kingston Russell (sep civ identity early, eccl ex-par[62]). *LG* Egg. Hd, Dorch. PLU, RSD, RD. Addtl civ bdry alt: 1894.[1] *Parl* Seq 10. *Eccl* Seq 2.

BRIDPORT

AP *LG* Whitch. Can. Hd, Bridp. PLU, Bor/MB, USD. Civ bdry: 1894 (gains the pts of the other pars in the MB, *viz.*, Allington AP, Bothenhampton AP, Bradpole AP, Burton Bradstock AP, Symondsbury AP, Walditch AP),[10] 1901,[50] 1923,[63] 1954.[178] *Parl* Bridp. Parl Bor (1295–1885), Seq 10 thereafter. *Eccl* Seq 5. Eccl bdry: 1927.[12]

BROADMAYNE

AP *LG* Seq 14. *Parl* Seq 8. *Eccl* Seq 9.

BROADSTONE

EP Cr 1906 from Great Canford AP, Longfleet EP.[64] Poole RDn.

BROADWAY

AP *LG* Cull. Tree Hd, Weym. PLU, RSD, RD. Abol civ 1933 pt to Weymouth CP, pt to Bincombe AP.[2] *Parl* S'rn Dv (1885–1918), W'rn Dv (1918–48). *Eccl* Dorch. RDn (until 1872), Weym. RDn (1872–1970). Eccl bdry: 1952.[65] Abol eccl 1970 to help cr Bincombe with Broadway EP.[66]

BROADWINDSOR

AP *LG* Broadwindsor Lbty, Beam. PLU, RSD, RD. Civ bdry: 1966 (gains pt Wayford AP, pt Winsham AP, loses pt to West Crewkerne CP, all Somerset).[179] *Parl* Seq 10. *Eccl* Bridp. RDn (until 1872), Beam. RDn (1872–1971). Abol eccl 1971 to help cr Broadwindsor with Burstock EP.[67]

BROADWINDSOR WITH BURSTOCK

EP Cr 1971 by union Broadwindsor AP, Burstock AP.[67] Beam. RDn.

BRYANSTON

AP *LG* Pimp. Hd, Blandf. PLU, pt Blandf. Forum USD, pt Blandf. MB (1889–96), pt Blandf. RSD, Blandf. RD (pt 1894–96, ent 1896–1974). Civ bdry: 1887,[35] 1894,[31] 1896 (incl loses the pt in the MB to Blandford Forum AP),[30] 1897,[68] 1930.[32] *Parl* Seq 5. *Eccl* Seq 29.

BUCKHORN WESTON

AP *LG* Redl. Hd, Wincanton PLU (1835–94), RSD, Shaft. PLU (1894–1930), RD. Civ bdry: 1966 (exchanges pts with Wincanton CP, Somerset).[179] *Parl* Seq 5. *Eccl* Seq 15.

BUCKLAND NEWTON
AP Incl chap Plush (no sep civ identity, eccl severed 1937 to help cr 2 EPs of Piddletrenthide with Plush, Mappowder[69]). *LG* Buck. Newt. Hd, Cerne PLU, RSD, RD (1894–1933), Dorch. RD (1933–74). *Parl* Seq 10. *Eccl* Seq 28.

BUCKLAND RIPERS
AP *LG* Cull. Tree Hd, Weym. PLU, RSD. Abol civ 1894 ent to Radipole AP.[70] *Parl* S'rn Dv (1885–1918). *Eccl* Seq 11.

BURLESTON
AP *LG* Seq 19. *Parl* Seq 8. *Eccl* Whitch. RDn (until 1872), Bere Regis RDn (1872–1967). Abol eccl 1967 to help cr Puddletown with Athelhampton and Burleston EP.[17]

BURSTOCK
AP *LG* Seq 33. *Parl* Seq 10. *Eccl* Bridp. RDn (until 1872), Beam. RDn (1872–1971). Abol eccl 1971 to help cr Broadwindsor with Burstock EP.[67]

LONG BURTON
EP Cr 1929 when Long Burton with Holnest AP divided, Long Burton to be a sep EP and Holnest to help cr Wootton Glanville with Holnest EP.[72] Stalbridge RDn (1929–55), Sherb. RDn (1955–*).

LONG BURTON WITH HOLNEST
AP Usual eccl spelling; for civ and civ sep of Holnest chap see 'Longburton'. Shaft. RDn (until 1872), Stalbridge RDn (1872–1929), Abol eccl 1929, Long Burton to be a sep EP, Holnest to help cr Wootton Glanville with Holnest EP.[72]

BURTON BRADSTOCK
AP Incl chap Shipton George (sep civ identity early, no sep eccl identity, hence usual eccl name 'Burton Bradstock with Shipton George', qv). *LG* Framp. Lbty, Bridp. PLU, pt Bridp. MB (1835–94), pt Bridp. USD, pt Bridp. RSD, Bridp. RD. Addtl civ bdry alt: 1884,[9] 1894 (loses the pt in the MB to Bridport AP).[10] *Parl* Pt Bridp. Parl Bor (1832–85), Seq 10 thereafter.

BURTON BRADSTOCK WITH SHIPTON GEORGE
AP Usual eccl spelling; for civ and civ sep of Shipton George chap see prev entry. *Eccl* Bridp. RDn. Eccl bdry: 1927.[12] Abol eccl 1954 to help cr Burton Bradstock with Shipton George and Chilcombe EP.[73]

BURTON BRADSTOCK WITH SHIPTON GEORGE AND CHILCOMBE
EP Cr 1954 by union Burton Bradstock with Shipton George AP, Chilcombe AP.[73] Bridp. RDn (1954–70), Lyme Bay RDn (1970–*).

GREAT CANFORD
AP Usual eccl spelling; for civ and sep, civ and eccl, of chaps, see 'Canford Magna'. *Eccl* Royal pec jurisd (until 1847), Whitch. RDn (1847–72), Poole RDn (1872–1916), Wimb. RDn (1916–*). Addtl eccl bdry alt: 1834 (help cr Parkstone St Peter EP),[74] 1906 (help cr Broadstone EP),[64] 1964.[58]

CANFORD CLIFFS AND SANDBANKS
EP Cr 1956 from Parkstone St Peter EP.[75] Poole RDn.

CANFORD MAGNA
AP Usual civ spelling; for eccl see 'Great Canford'. Incl chap Poole St James (sep par 1538[76]), hmlt & tg Longfleet (sep EP 1837,[77] sep CP 1866[22]), tg Kinson (sep EP 1865,[78] sep CP 1866[22]). *LG* Cogd. Hd, Poole PLU, pt Poole MB (1835–66), Poole RSD, RD. Abol civ 1933 pt to Poole CP, pt to Pamphill CP.[2] *Parl* Pt Poole Parl Bor (1832–67), E'rn Dv (1885–1918).

CANN
AP Usual civ spelling; for eccl see 'Shaftesbury St Rumbold alias Cann'. *LG* Seq 26. Civ bdry: 1894,[5] 1921,[6] 1933.[2] *Parl* Shaft. Parl Bor (1832–85), Seq 5 thereafter.

CASTLETON
Chap and bor (status not sustained) in Oborne AP, sep civ identity early, sep EP 1716.[79] *LG* Sherb. Hd, PLU, pt Sherb. USD, pt Sherb. RSD, Sherb. RD. Addtl civ bdry alt: 1894 (loses the pt in the USD to Sherborne AP and gains a pt of the latter not in the USD),[80] 1929.[81] *Parl* Seq 6. *Eccl* Shaft. RDn (1716–1872), Sherb. RDn (1872–1970). Abol eccl 1970 to help cr Sherborne with Castleton EP.[66]

CATHERSTON LEWESTON
AP *LG* Seq 34. *Parl* Seq 10. *Eccl* Seq 7.

CATTISTOCK
AP *LG* Seq 6. *Parl* Seq 10. *Eccl* Seq 1.

BISHOP'S CAUNDLE
AP *LG* Seq 25. Civ bdry: 1886.[82] *Parl* Seq 6. *Eccl* Seq 16.

MARSH CAUNDLE
AP Usual eccl spelling; for civ see 'Caundle Marsh'. *Eccl* Pec jurisd Cath Chapter of Sarum (until 1847), Seq 16 thereafter.

PURSE CAUNDLE
AP *LG* Seq 25. *Parl* Seq 6. *Eccl* Sometimes as 'Caundle Purse', Seq 16.

STOURTON CAUNDLE
AP *LG* Seq 4. *Parl* Seq 5. *Eccl* Donative, sometimes 'Caundle Stourton', Seq 16.

CAUNDLE MARSH
AP Usual civ spelling; for eccl see 'Marsh Caundle'. *LG* Seq 25. Civ bdry: 1886.[82] *Parl* Seq 6.

NETHER CERNE
AP *LG* Seq 6. *Parl* Seq 10. *Eccl* Donative, Whitch. RDn (until 1872), Bere Regis RDn (1872–74), Cerne RDn (1874–1954), Dorch. RDn (1955–71). Abol eccl 1971 ent to Cerne Abbas AP.[83]

UP CERNE
AP Usual civ spelling; for eccl see 'Upcerne'. *LG* Sherb. Hd, Cerne PLU, RSD, RD (1894–1933), Dorch. RDn (1933–74). *Parl* Seq 10.

CERNE ABBAS
AP *LG* Seq 6. *Parl* Seq 10. *Eccl* Whitch. RDn (until 1872), Bere Regis RDn (1872–74), Cerne RDn (1874–1954), Dorch. RDn (1955–*). Eccl bdry: 1971 (gains Upcerne AP),[84] 1971 (gains

Nether Cerne AP).[83]

CHALBURY

AP *LG* Seq 1. Civ bdry: 1886,[85] 1953.[180] *Parl* Seq 1. *Eccl* Seq 14.

CHALDON BOYS

AP Dorch. RDn, united 1446 to Chaldon Herring AP.[86]

CHALDON HERRING

AP Sometimes anc 'East Chaldon'. Gains 1446 Chaldon Boys AP.[86] *LG* Seq 3. *Parl* Seq 7. *Eccl* Seq 12.

CHARBOROUGH

AP Orig sep AP, civ status not sustained and later deemed hmlt in Morden AP, eccl status sustained. *Eccl* Whitch. RDn (until 1872), Poole RDn (1872–1962), Purb. RDn (1962–72). Abol eccl 1972 to help cr Almer and Charborough EP.[13]

CHARDSTOCK

AP *LG* Beam. Hd, Axminster PLU, RSD, sep RD (1894–96). Civ bdry: 1884 (loses pt to Membury CP, Devon).[87] Transf 1896 to Devon.[88] *Parl* W'rn Dv (1885–1918), Devon thereafter. *Eccl* Pec jurisd Cath Chapter of Sarum (until 1847), Seq 6 thereafter. Eccl bdry: 1841 (help cr Chardstock All Saints EP).[89]

CHARDSTOCK ALL SAINTS

EP Cr 1841 from Chardstock AP, Axminster AP (Devon).[89] Bridp. RDn (1841–72), Lyme RDn (1872–1970), Beam. RDn (1970–*).

CHARLTON MARSHALL

Chap in Spetisbury AP, sep civ identity early, no sep eccl identity. *LG* Cogd. Hd, Blandf. PLU, RSD, RD. *Parl* Seq 5.

CHARMINSTER

AP Incl chap Stratton (sep civ identity early, sep EP 1742[79]). *LG* Seq 14. Civ bdry: 1883,[24] 1885,[93] 1901,[49] 1933.[2] *Parl* Seq 8. *Eccl* Whitch. RDn (until 1872), Dorch. RDn (1872–*).

CHARMOUTH

AP *LG* Charmouth Bor (status not sustained), Whitch. Can. Hd, Axminster PLU (1836–94), RSD, Bridp. PLU (1894–1930), RD. *Parl* Lyme Regis Parl Bor (1832–85), Seq 10 thereafter. *Eccl* Seq 7.

CHEDINGTON

AP *LG* Seq 2.[90] *Parl* Seq 10. *Eccl* Bridp. RDn (until 1872), Beam. RDn (1872–1971). Abol eccl 1971 to help cr South Perrot with Mosterton and Chedington EP.[91]

EAST CHELBOROUGH

AP Sometimes 'Luccombe'. *LG* Seq 28. *Parl* Seq 10. *Eccl* Seq 8.

WEST CHELBOROUGH

AP *LG* Seq 28. *Parl* Seq 10. *Eccl* Seq 8.[92]

CHESELBOURNE

AP *LG* Whiteway Hd, Cerne PLU, RSD, RD (1894–1933),[94] Dorch. RD (1933–74). Civ bdry: 1880.[94] *Parl* Seq 10. *Eccl* Whitch. RDn (until 1872), Bere Regis RDn (1872–1925), Milt. RDn (1925–70), Milt. & Blandf. RDn (1970–*).

CHETNOLE

Chap in Yetminster AP, sep CP 1866,[22] eccl severed 1955 to help cr Leigh with Chetnole EP.[95] *LG* Seq 39. Civ bdry: 1886.[82] *Parl* Seq 9.

CHETTLE

AP *LG* Monkton up Wimb. Hd, Wimb. & Cranb. PLU (1835–94), RSD, Blandf. PLU (1894–1930), Wimb. & Cranb. RD. *Parl* Seq 5. *Eccl* Seq 8.

CHICKERELL

AP *LG* Pt Cull. Tree Hd, pt Sutton Poyntz Lbty, Weym. PLU, RSD, RD (1894–1933), Dorch. RD (1933–74). Civ bdry: 1933.[2] *Parl* Seq 7. *Eccl* Seq 11. Eccl bdry: 1956 (help cr Weymouth St Edmund EP).[96]

CHIDEOCK

Chap in Whitchurch Canonicorum AP, sep civ identity early, sep EP 1886.[97] *LG* Seq 34. *Parl* Seq 10. *Eccl* Lyme RDn (1886–1970), Lyme Bay RDn (1970–*).

CHILCOMBE

AP *LG* Seq 30. *Parl* Seq 10. *Eccl* Bridp. RDn. Abol eccl 1954 to help cr Burton Bradstock with Shipton George and Chilcombe EP.[73]

CHILFROME

AP *LG* Seq 29. *Parl* Seq 10. *Eccl* Seq 1.

CHURCH KNOWLE

AP *LG* Seq 16. *Parl* Seq 4. *Eccl* Seq 12.

CLIFTON MAYBANK

AP *LG* Seq 39. *Parl* Seq 6. *Eccl* Dorch. RDn. Abol eccl 1824 ent to Bradford Abbas AP.[45]

COLEHILL

CP Cr 1896 from Holt CP.[113] *LG* Wimb. & Cranb. PLU, RD. Bdry: 1913,[98] 1921,[99] 1933,[2] 1956.[175] *Parl* E'rn Dv (1918–48), North CC (1948–*).

EP Cr 1903 from Wimborne Minster AP, Hampreston AP, New Borough and Leigh EP.[40] Wimb. RDn. Bdry: 1954.[100]

NETHER COMPTON

AP *LG* Seq 35. Civ bdry: 1894.[80] *Parl* Seq 6. *Eccl* Pec jurisd Cath Chapter of Sarum (until 1847), Seq 18 thereafter.

OVER COMPTON

AP *LG* Seq 25. *Parl* Seq 6. *Eccl* Pec jurisd Cath Chapter of Sarum (until 1847), Seq 18 thereafter. Eccl bdry: 1954.[46]

WEST COMPTON

AP Usual civ spelling; for eccl see 'Compton Abbas West'. *LG* Seq 6. *Parl* Seq 10.

COMPTON ABBAS

AP *LG* Seq 26. Civ bdry: 1886.[14] *Parl* Shaft. Parl Bor (1832–85), Seq 5 thereafter. *Eccl* Seq 21.

COMPTON ABBAS WEST

AP Usual eccl spelling; for civ see 'West Compton'. *Eccl* Seq 1.

COMPTON VALENCE

AP Sometimes anc 'East Compton'. *LG* Seq 13. *Parl* Seq 10. *Eccl* Dorch. RDn (until 1949), Abbotsb. RDn (1949–70), Lyme Bay RDn (1970–*).

COOMBE KEYNES
AP *LG* Seq 37. *Parl* Seq 7. *Eccl* Dorch. RDn (until 1872), Purb. RDn (1872–1974). Eccl bdry: 1844 (cr Wool EP).[101] Abol eccl 1974 to help cr Wool, East Burton and Coombe Keynes EP.[102]

CORFE CASTLE
AP Incl chap Kingston (sep EP 1877,[103] no sep civ identity). *LG* Corfe Castle Hd, Bor, Wareh. & Purb. PLU, RSD, RD. *Parl* Corfe Castle Parl Bor (1572–1832), Wareh. Parl Bor (1832–85), Seq 4 thereafter. *Eccl* Royal pec (until 1847), Seq 12 thereafter.

CORFE MULLEN
Chap in Sturminster Marshall AP, sep civ identity early, sep EP 1858.[104] *LG* Seq 8. Civ bdry: 1886,[85] 1930,[105] 1958.[181] *Parl* Seq 1. *Eccl* Whitch. RDn (1858–72), Poole RDn (1872–1970), Wimb. RDn (1970–*).

CORSCOMBE
AP *LG* Seq 2. Civ bdry: 1884.[106] *Parl* Seq 10. *Eccl* Seq 8. Eccl bdry: 1871 (cr Toller Whelme EP),[107] 1939 (gains Toller Whelme EP).[108]

CRANBORNE
AP Incl chap Alderholt (sep EP 1849,[7] sep CP 1894[8]), hmlts Verwood, Three Legged Cross (united with hmlt West Moors in West Parley AP 1887 to cr 'Verwood and West Moors' EP,[109] sep CP 1894 as 'Verwood'[8]), chap Boveridge (no sep civ identity, hence this par eccl 'Cranborne with Boveridge', qv). *LG* Pt Cranb. Hd, pt Monkton Up Wimb. Hd, Wimb. & Cranb. PLU, RSD, RD. Addtl civ bdry alt: 1886.[85] *Parl* Seq 2.

CRANBORNE WITH BOVERIDGE
AP Usual eccl spelling; for civ and sep, civ and eccl, of chaps, see prev entry. *Eccl* Seq 14. Addtl eccl bdry alt: 1958.[110]

LONG CRICHEL
AP *LG* Seq 18. *Parl* Seq 2. *Eccl* Pimp. RDn (until 1872), Wimb. RDn (1872–1960). Abol eccl 1960 to help cr Long Crichel with Moor Crichel EP.[111]

LONG CRICHEL WITH MOOR CRICHEL
EP Cr 1960 by union Long Crichel AP, Moor Crichel AP.[111] Wimb. RDn.

MOOR CRICHEL
AP *LG* Seq 1. Civ bdry: 1886.[85] *Parl* Seq 1. *Eccl* Pimp. RDn (until 1872), Wimb. RDn (1872–1960). Abol eccl 1960 to help cr Long Crichel with Moor Crichel EP.[111]

DEWLISH
AP Once sep AP,[112] later deemed chap in Milborne St Andrew AP, civ identity regained, no later sep eccl identity. *LG* Dewlish Lbty, Dorch. PLU, RSD, RD. *Parl* Seq 8.

DORCHESTER
CP Cr 1927 by union Dorchester All Saints AP, Dorchester St Peter AP.[115] *LG* Dorch. PLU, MB. Bdry: 1933.[2] *Parl* West CC (1948–*).
EP Cr 1973 by union Dorchester St Peter and All Saints EP, Dorchester Holy Trinity with Frome Whitfield EP, Fordington AP, West Fordington EP.[116] Dorch. RDn.

DORCHESTER ALL SAINTS
AP *LG* Uggsc. Hd, Dorch. Bor/MB, PLU, USD. Civ bdry: 1894 (incl gains pt of the pt of Fordington AP in the MB),[48] 1900.[49] Abol civ 1927 to help cr Dorchester CP.[115] *Parl* Dorch. Parl Bor (1295–1885), S'rn Dv (1885–1918), W'rn Dv (1918–48). *Eccl* Dorch. RDn. Abol eccl 1962 to help cr Dorchester St Peter and All Saints EP.[117]

DORCHESTER HOLY TRINITY
AP Gains 1610 Frome Whitfield AP, the union civ called 'Dorchester Holy Trinity', eccl 'Dorchester Holy Trinity with Frome Whitfield', qv.[118] *LG* Uggsc. Hd, Dorch. PLU, pt Dorch. Bor/MB, pt Dorch. USD, pt Dorch. RSD. Civ bdry: 1885.[93] Abol civ 1894 the pt in the MB to Dorchester St Peter AP, the remainder to Stinsford AP.[48] *Parl* Pt Dorch. Parl Bor (1295–1885), S'rn Dv (1885–1918). *Eccl* Dorch. RDn.

DORCHESTER HOLY TRINITY WITH FROME WHITFIELD
EP Cr 1610 by union Dorchester Holy Trinity AP, Frome Whitfield AP.[118] Dorch. RDn. Bdry: 1957.[119] Abol ecl 1973 to help cr Dorchester EP.[116]

DORCHESTER ST PETER
AP *LG* Uggsc. Hd, Dorch. Bor/MB, PLU, USD. Civ bdry: 1894 (incl gains the pt of Dorchester Holy Trinity AP and pt of the pt of Fordington AP in the MB),[48] 1900.[49] Abol civ 1927 to help cr Dorchester CP.[115] *Parl* Dorch. Parl Bor (1295–1885), S'rn Dv (1885–1918), W'rn Dv (1918–48). *Eccl* Dorch. RDn. Abol eccl 1962 to help cr Dorchester St Peter and All Saints EP.[117]

DORCHESTER ST PETER AND ALL SAINTS
EP Cr 1962 by union Dorchester St Peter AP, Dorchester All Saints AP.[117] Dorch. RDn. Abol 1973 to help cr Dorchester EP.[116]

DURWESTON
AP Gains 1381 Knighton AP.[152] *LG* Seq 20. *Parl* Seq 5. *Eccl* Seq 29.

EDMONDSHAM
AP *LG* Pt Bindon Lbty, pt Cranb. Hd, Wimb. & Cranb. PLU, RSD, RD. Civ bdry: 1886.[85] *Parl* Seq 2. *Eccl* Seq 14.

ENSBURY
EP Cr 1967 from Talbot Village EP, Kinson EP.[120] Poole RDn.

EVERSHOT
Chap in Frome St Quintin AP, sep civ identity early, no sep eccl identity. *LG* Seq 28. *Parl* Seq 10.

FARNHAM
AP *LG* Cranb. Hd, Wimb. & Cranb. PLU (1835–94), RSD, RD (1894–1933), Blandf. PLU (1894–1930), RD (1933–74). Civ bdry: 1885.[122] *Parl* Seq 5. *Eccl* Seq 31.

FARRINGDON
AP Dorch. RDn, united early to Iwerne Courtney AP,[123] eccl severed 1952 and united with East

Orchard with Margaret Marsh EP.[124]

FIFEHEAD MAGDALEN

AP *LG* Seq 23. Civ bdry: 1966 (incl gains pt Henstridge AP, Somerset).[179] *Parl* Seq 5. *Eccl* Seq 15.

FIFEHEAD NEVILLE

AP *LG* Seq 21. Civ bdry: 1884.[19] *Parl* Seq 5. *Eccl* Whitch. RDn (until 1872), Milt. RDn (1872–1955), Sturm. Newt. RDn (1955–*).

FLEET

AP *LG* Seq 32. *Parl* Seq 7. *Eccl* Seq 11.

FOLKE

AP *LG* Seq 25. *Parl* Seq 6. *Eccl* Pec jurisd Cath Chapter of Sarum (until 1847), Shaft. RDn (1847–72), Stalbridge RDn (1872–1954), Sherb. RDn (1955–72). Abol eccl 1972 to help cr Folke, North Wootton and Haydon EP.[125]

FOLKE, NORTH WOOTTON AND HAYDON

EP Cr 1972 by union Folke AP, North Wootton EP, Haydon AP.[125] Sherb. RDn.

FONTMELL MAGNA

AP Incl chap West Orchard (sep civ identity early, eccl severed 1952 and transf to East Orchard with Margaret Marsh EP[124]). *LG* Seq 26. *Parl* Pt Shaft. Parl Bor (1832–85), Seq 5 thereafter. *Eccl* Seq 20.

FORDINGTON

AP *LG* Fordington Lbty, Dorch. PLU, pt Dorch. MB (1835–94), pt Dorch. USD, pt Dorch. RSD, Dorch. RD. Civ bdry: 1883,[24] 1885,[93] 1894 (incl loses the pt in the MB pt to Dorchester All Saints AP, pt to Dorchester St Peter AP).[48] Abol civ 1900 pt to Dorchester All Saints AP, pt to Dorchester St Peter AP.[49] *Parl* Pt Dorch. Parl Bor (1832–85), S'rn Dv (1885–1918). *Eccl* Pec jurisd Cath Chapter of Sarum (until 1847), Dorch. RDn (1847–197). Eccl bdry: 1847 (cr West Fordington EP).[121] Abol eccl 1973 to help cr Dorchester EP.[116]

WEST FORDINGTON

EP Cr 1847 from Fordington AP.[121] Dorch. RDn. Bdry: 1957.[119] Abol 1973 to help cr Dorchester EP.[116]

FRAMPTON

AP *LG* Seq 13. Civ bdry: 1885.[93] *Parl* Seq 10. *Eccl* Seq 9.

FRIERMAYNE

AP Dorch. RDn, united 1563 to West Knighton AP.[126]

FROME BILLETT

AP Dorch. RDn, united 1470 to West Stafford AP.[126]

FROME ST QUINTIN

AP *LG* Toll. Hd, Cerne PLU, RSD, RD (1894–1933), Dorch. RD (1933–74). *Parl* Seq 10. *Eccl* Seq 26.

FROME VAUCHURCH

AP *LG* Seq 29. Civ bdry: 1885.[127] *Parl* Seq 10. *Eccl* Dorch. RDn (until 1916), Abbotsb. RDn (1916–25). Abol eccl 1925 to help cr Maiden Newton with Frome Vauchurch EP.[128]

FROME WHITFIELD

AP *LG* George Hd. *Eccl* Dorch. RDn. Abol 1610 united with Dorchester Holy Trinity AP, the union civ called 'Dorchester Holy Trinity', eccl 'Dorchester Holy Trinity with Frome Whitfield'.[118]

GILLINGHAM

AP Incl chap Motcombe (sep civ identity early, sep EP 1883 as 'Motcombe with Enmore Green'[129]), chap Bourton (sep EP 1847,[43] sep CP 1866[22]), chaps East Stour, West Stour (each with sep civ identity early, neither with sep eccl identity). *LG* Seq 15. *Parl* Seq 5. *Eccl* Royal Pec (until 1847), Seq 15 thereafter.

GOATHILL

AP In Somerset (Horethorne Hd), transf 1895 to Dorset.[130] *LG* Sherb. PLU, sep RD in Somerset (1894–95), Sherb. RD (1895–1974). *Parl* Somerset until 1918, N'rn Dv (1918–48), West CC (1948–*). *Eccl* See entry in Somerset.

GODMANSTON

AP Usual civ spelling until renamed 1966 'Godmanstone';[182] for civ after 1966 and eccl see following entry. *LG* Cerne, Tot. & Modb. Hd, Dorch. PLU, RSD, RD. *Parl* W'rn Dv (1885–1948), West CC (1948–70).

GODMANSTONE

AP Usual eccl spelling; and civ spelling after 1966 when 'Godmanston' renamed.[182] *LG* Dorch. RD. *Parl* West CC (1970–*). *Eccl* Seq 23.

GOREWOOD

Ex-par place, sep CP 1858.[131] *LG* Piddletrenthide Lbty, Cerne PLU, RSD, RD. Abol 1933 ent to Minterne Magna AP.[2] *Parl* W'rn Dv (1885–1948).

GUSSGAE ALL SAINTS

AP *LG* Seq 18. Civ bdry: 1886.[85] *Parl* Seq 2. *Eccl* Seq 14.

GUSSAGE ST MICHAEL

AP *LG* Seq 1. Civ bdry: 1886.[85] *Parl* Seq 2. *Eccl* Seq 14. Eccl bdry: 1926 (help cr Woodlands EP).[132]

HALSTOCK

AP *LG* Halstock Lbty, Beam. PLU, RSD, RD. *Parl* Seq 10. *Eccl* Pec jurisd Cath Chapter of Sarum (until 1847), Shaft. RDn (1847–72), Beam. RDn (1872–*).

HAMMOON

AP *LG* Seq 21. *Parl* Seq 5. *Eccl* Pimp. RDn (until 1872), Sturm. Newt. RDn (1872–1971). Abol eccl 1971 to help cr Childe Okeford and Manston with Hammoon EP.[133]

HAMPRESTON

AP *LG* Pt Dorset (Cranb. Hd), pt Hants (Westover Lbty), the latter transf to Dorset in the 1860s.[134] *LG* Wimb. PLU (1835–94), RSD, Wimb. & Cranb. PLU (1894–1930), RD. Addtl civ bdry alt: 1888,[135] 1913,[98] 1956.[175] *Parl* Dorset pt, Seq 1. *Eccl* Seq 14. Eccl bdry: 1903 (help cr Colehill EP).[40]

HAMWORTHY

Chap in Sturminster Marshall AP, sep civ identity

early, sep EP 1858.[104] *LG* Cogd. Hd, Poole PLU, USD, MB (1835–1905). Abol civ 1905 to help cr Poole CP.[54] *Parl* Poole Parl Bor (1832–85), E'rn Dv (1885–1918). *Eccl* Whitch. RDn (1858–72), Poole RDn (1872–*).

HANDLEY–See following entry

SIXPENNY HANDLEY

AP Sep par, united 1327 to Iwerne Minster AP[136] and soon after deemed latter's chap, sep civ identity regained early, sep EP 1844 as 'Handley', the latter incl hmlt Gussage St Andrew.[137] Sometimes 'Sixpenny Hanley'. *LG* Sixp. Handley Hd, Wimb. & Cranb. PLU, RSD. RD. *Parl* Seq 2. *Eccl* Shaft. RDn (before 1327 and 1844–72), Blandf. RDn (1970–*). Eccl bdry: 1925,[138] 1958.[110]

HANFORD

AP Orig sep par, later deemed civ ex-par but eccl status retained, sep CP 1858.[13] *LG* Redl. Hd, Sturm. PLU (1858[232]–1930), RSD, RD. *Parl* Seq 5. *Eccl* Seq 20.

HASELBURY BRYAN

EP Renaming 1972 of Hazelbury Bryan AP.[139] Sturm. Newt. RDn (1972), Blackm. Vale RDn (1973–*).

HAWKCHURCH

AP *LG* Pt Cerne, Tot. & Modb. Hd, pt Uggsc. Hd, Axminster PLU, RSD, sep RD (1894–96). Transf 1896 to Devon.[88] *Parl* W'rn Dv (1885–1918), Devon thereafter. *Eccl* Seq 6.

HAYDON

AP *LG* Seq 25. Civ bdry: 1886.[82] *Parl* Seq 6. *Eccl* Pec jurisd Cath Chapter of Sarum (until 1847), Shaft. RDn (1847–72), Stalbridge RDn (1872–1954), Sherb. RDn (1955–72). Abol eccl 1972 to help cr Folke, North Wootton and Haydon EP.[125]

HAZELBURY BRYAN

AP *LG* Seq 21. *Parl* Seq 5. *Eccl* Whitch. RDn (until 1872), Cerne RDn (1872–1954), Sturm. Newt. RDn (1955–72). Renamed 1972 'Haselbury Bryan'.[139]

HEATHERLANDS

EP Cr 1886 from Kinson EP.[140] Poole RDn. Bdry: 1953.[57]

HERMITAGE

AP *LG* Fordington Lbty, Cerne PLU, RSD, RD (1894–1933), Shaft. RD (1933–74). *Parl* Seq 10. *Eccl* Pec jurisd Cath Chapter of Sarum (until 1847), Shaft. RDn (1847–72), Sherb. RDn (1872–1916), Cerne RDn (1916–54), Sherb. RDn (1955–*).

HILFIELD

Parochial chap in Sydling St Nicholas AP, sep civ identity early, sep EP 1850.[141] *LG* Cerne, Tot. & Modb. Hd, Cerne PLU, RSD, RD (1894–1933), Sherb. RD (1933–74). Civ bdry: 1885.[142] *Parl* Seq 10. *Eccl* Shaft. RDn (1850–72), Cerne RDn (1872–1954), Sherb. RDn (1955–*).

HILTON

AP *LG* Seq 34. *Parl* Seq 5. *Eccl* Seq 29.

HINTON MARTEL

AP Usual eccl spelling; for civ see following entry. *Eccl* Seq 14.

HINTON MARTELL

AP Usual civ spelling; for eccl see prev entry. *LG* Seq 1. Civ bdry: 1886,[85] 1953.[180] *Parl* Seq 1.

HINTON PARVA

AP Sometimes 'Stanbridge'. *LG* Seq 1. Civ bdry: 1886.[85] *Parl* Seq 1. *Eccl* Seq 14.

HINTON ST MARY

Chap in Iwerne Minster AP, sep civ identity early, sep EP 1863.[143] *LG* Seq 27. *Parl* Seq 5. *Eccl* Shaft. RDn (1863–72), Sturm. Newt. RDn (1872–1972), Blackm. Vale RDn (1973–*).

EAST HOLME

AP *LG* Seq 16. *Parl* Seq 4. *Eccl* Seq 12.[144]

HOLNEST

Chap in Longburton AP (eccl 'Long Burton with Holnest'), sep civ identity early, eccl severed 192 to help cr Wootton Glanville with Holnest EP, the remainder cr Long Burton EP.[72] *LG* Seq 25. Civ bdry: 1886.[82] *Parl* Seq 6.

HOLT

Tg in Wimborne Minster AP, sep EP 1882,[145] sep CP 1894 (from the pt of the par not in Wimb. Minster USD).[146] *LG* Wimb. & Cranb. PLU, RD. Civ bdry: 1896 (cr Colehill CP),[113] 1956 (help cr West Moors CP).[175] *Parl* E'rn Dv (1918–48), North CC (1948–*). *Eccl* Wimb. RDn. Eccl bdry: 1927.[147]

HOLWELL

AP In Somerset (Horethorne Hd), transf to Dorset (Browns. Hd) 1832 for parl purposes, 1844 for civ purposes.[37] *LG* Sherb. PLU, RSD, RD. *Parl* Somerset until 1832, Seq 6 thereafter. *Eccl* Seq 16.

HOOKE

AP *LG* Egg. Hd, Beam. PLU, RSD, RD. Civ bdry: 1884.[106] *Parl* Seq 10. *Eccl* Bridp. RDn (until 1916), Beam. RDn (1916–30), Bridp. RDn (1930–70), Beam. RDn (1970–*).

HORTON

AP Incl chap Woodlands (sep civ identity early, sep EP 1926 [from Horton AP, Gussage St Michael AP, Wimborne St Giles AP][132]). *LG* Seq 1. *Parl* Seq 2. *Eccl* Seq 14.

IBBERTON

AP *LG* Seq 36. *Parl* Seq 5. *Eccl* Whitch. RDn (until 1872), Milt. RDn (1872–1954), Sturm. Newt. RDn (1955–72), Blackm. Vale RDn (1973–*).

IWERNE COURTNEY

AP Sometimes 'Shroton'. Incl Farringdon AP, gained early[123] (eccl severed 1952 and transf to East Orchard with Margaret Marsh EP[124]). *LG* Redl. Hd, Blandf. PLU, RSD, RD. Civ bdry: 1915.[148] *Parl* Seq 5. *Eccl* Shaft. RDn (until 1872), Sturm. Newt. RDn (1872–1954), Blandf. RDn (1955–70), Milt. & Blandf. RDn (1970–*).

IWERNE MINSTER

AP Gains 1327 Sixpenny Handley AP[136] (later

deemed chap to this par, civ identity regained early, sep EP 1844 as 'Handley' [incl hmlt Gussage St Andrew][136]), chaps East Orchard, Margaret Marsh (each with sep civ identity early, one EP 1863 as 'East Orchard with Margaret Marsh'[143]), chap Hinton St Mary (sep civ identity early, sep EP 1863[143]). *LG* Seq 26. Civ bdry: 1915.[148] *Parl* Seq 5. *Eccl* Seq 20.

IWERNE STEPLETON

AP *LG* Seq 20. Civ bdry: 1887.[35] *Parl* Seq 5. *Eccl* Seq 13.

KIMMERIDGE

AP *LG* Seq 16. *Parl* Seq 4. *Eccl* Donative, Seq 12.

KINGSTON

Chap in Corfe Castle AP, no sep civ identity, sep EP 1877.[103] Purb. RDn.

KINGSTON LACEY

EP Cr 1922 from Wimborne Minster AP.[149] Wimb. RDn.

KINGSTON RUSSELL

Hmlt & tg in Long Bredy AP, sep civ identity early, eccl ex-par.[62] *LG* Seq 31. *Parl* Seq 10.

KINGTON MAGNA

AP *LG* Redl. Hd, Wincanton PLU (1835–94), RSD, Shaft. PLU (1894–1930), RD. Civ bdry: 1966 (exchanges pts with Henstridge AP, Somerset).[179] *Parl* Seq 5. *Eccl* Seq 15.

KINSON

Tg in Canford Magna AP (eccl, 'Great Canford'), sep EP 1865,[78] sep CP 1866.[22] *LG* Cogd. Hd, Poole PLU, pt Kinson USD (1892–94), Poole RSD (ent 1875–92, pt 1892–94), Poole RD. Civ bdry: 1888,[135] 1894 (loses the pt in the USD to cr Branksome CP).[53] Abol civ 1931 ent to Bournemouth CB and CP (associated with Hants Adm Co).[151] *Parl* E'rn Dv (1885–1948). *Eccl* Whitch. RDn (1865–72), Poole RDn (1872–*). Eccl bdry: 1878 (help cr Branksome Park EP),[59] 1886 (cr Heatherlands EP),[140] 1891 (help cr Bournemouth St John the Evangelist EP, to be in Winch dioc),[41] 1892 (loses pt to Bournemouth St John the Evangelist EP and thus to Winch dioc),[42] 1904 (cr Branksome St Clement EP),[56] 1919 (cr Talbot Village EP),[150] 1927,[60] 1967 (help cr Ensbury EP).[120]

KNIGHTON

AP Whitch. RDn, united 1381 to Durweston AP.[152]

WEST KNIGHTON

AP Incl Friermayne AP gained 1563.[126] *LG* Seq 12. Civ bdry: 1883.[24] *Parl* Seq 8. *Eccl* Seq 9. Eccl bdry: 1969.[153]

LANGTON HERRING

AP *LG* Seq 32. *Parl* Seq 10. *Eccl* Seq 3.

LANGTON LONG

AP Usual eccl spelling; for civ see following entry. *Eccl* Seq 13. Eccl bdry: 1972.[33]

LANGTON LONG BLANDFORD

AP Usual civ spelling; for eccl see prev entry. *LG* Seq 20. Civ bdry: 1930,[32] 1933.[2] *Parl* Seq 5.

LANGTON MATRAVERS

AP *LG* Seq 24. Civ bdry: 1933.[2] *Parl* Seq 4. *Eccl* Seq 12. Eccl bdry: 1954.[154]

LAZERTON

AP Pimp. RDn, united 1431 to Stourpaine AP.[155]

LEIGH

Tg and chap in Yetminster AP, sep EP 1849,[156] sep CP 1866.[22] *LG* Seq 39. Civ bdry: 1885,[142] 1886.[82] *Parl* Seq 9. *Eccl* Shaft. RDn (1849–72), Sherb. RDn (1872–1955). Reconstituted 1955 as 'Leigh with Chetnole' when gains chap Chetnole of Yetminster with Chetnole AP.[95]

LEIGH WITH CHETNOLE

EP Cr 1955 by union Leigh EP, chap Chetnole of Yetminster with Chetnole AP.[95] Sherb. RDn.

LEWESTON

Ex-par place, sep CP 1858,[131] eccl abol 1927 ent to Lillington AP.[157] *LG* Seq 25. *Parl* Seq 6.

LILLINGTON

AP *LG* Seq 25. *Parl* Seq 6. *Eccl* Pec jurisd Cath Chapter of Sarum (until 1847), Seq 18 thereafter. Eccl bdry: 1927.[157]

LILLIPUT

EP Cr 1962 from Parkstone St Peter EP.[158] Poole RDn.

LITTLEBREDY

Chap in Long Bredy AP, sep civ identity early, no sep eccl identity. *LG* Seq 31. *Parl* Seq 10.

LITTLETON

AP Whitch. RDn, united 1430 to Blandford St Mary AP.[34]

LITTON CHENEY

AP *LG* Seq 30. Civ bdry: 1884,[9] 1894.[1] *Parl* Seq 10. *Eccl* Seq 2.

LODERS

AP *LG* Loders & Bothenhampton Lbty, Bridp. PLU, RSD, RD. Civ bdry: 1884.[9] *Parl* Seq 10. *Eccl* Seq 5.

LONGBURTON

AP Usual civ spelling; for eccl see 'Long Burton with Holnest'. Incl chap Holnest (sep civ identity early, eccl severed 1929 to help cr Wootton Glanville with Holnest EP, leaving Long Burton sep EP[72]), area of ex-par place of Leweston (sep CP 1858[131]). *LG* Seq 25. *Parl* Seq 6.

LONGFLEET

Hmlt and tg in Canford Magna (eccl, 'Great Canford'), sep EP 1837,[77] sep CP 1866.[22] *LG* Cogd. Hd, Poole PLU, MB (1835–1905), USD. Abol civ 1905 to help cr Poole CP.[54] *Parl* Poole Parl Bor (1867–85), E'rn Dv (1885–1918). *Eccl* Whitch. RDn (1837–72), Poole RDn (1872–*). Eccl bdry: 1906 (help cr Broadstone EP),[64] 1946 (cr Oakdale EP),[159] 1952.[124]

EAST LULWORTH

AP *LG* Seq 37. *Parl* Seq 7. *Eccl* Seq 12. Eccl bdry: 1959.[160]

WEST LULWORTH

Chap in Winfrith Newburgh AP, sep civ identity early, sep EP 1863.[161] *LG* Seq 3. Civ bdry: 1883,[24] 1888.[162] *Parl* Seq 7. *Eccl* Dorch. RDn (1863–72), Purb. RDn (1872–*). Eccl bdry: 1959.[160]

LYDLINCH

AP *LG* Browns. Hd, Sturm. PLU, RSD, RD. Civ bdry: 1884.[163] *Parl* Seq 5. *Eccl* Seq 17.

LYME REGIS
AP *LG* Whitch. Can. Hd, Axminster PLU, pt Lyme Regis Bor, Lyme Regis MB (pt 1835–99, ent 1899–1974), USD. *Parl* Pt Lyme Regis Parl Bor (1295–1885), Seq 10 thereafter. *Eccl* Pec jurisd Cath Chapter of Sarum (until 1847), Seq 7 thereafter.

LYTCHETT MATRAVERS
AP *LG* Seq 7. Civ bdry: 1888.[135] *Parl* Seq 3. *Eccl* Seq 24.

LYTCHETT MINSTER
Chap in Sturminster Marshall AP, sep civ identity early, sep EP 1858.[104] *LG* Seq 7. Civ bdry: 1930.[105] *Parl* Seq 3. *Eccl* Whitch. RDn (1858–72), Poole RDn (1872–*).

MAIDEN NEWTON
AP *LG* Seq 29. *Parl* Seq 10. *Eccl* Bridp. RDn (until 1872), Abbotsb. RDn (1872–1925). Abol eccl 1925 to help cr Maiden Newton with Frome Vauchurch EP.[128]

MAIDEN NEWTON WITH FROME VAUCHURCH
EP Cr 1925 by union Maiden Newton AP, Frome Vauchurch AP.[128] Abbotsb. RDn (1925–70), Dorch. RDn (1970–*).

MANSTON
AP *LG* Seq 23. *Parl* Seq 5. *Eccl* Shaft. RDn (until 1872), Sturm. Newt. RDn (1872–1971). Abol eccl 1971 to help cr Childe Okeford and Manston with Hammoon EP.[133]

MAPPERTON
AP *LG* Beam. Forum & Redhone Hd, Beam. PLU, RSD, RD. *Parl* Seq 10. *Eccl* Pec jurisd Cath Chapter of Sarum (until 1847), Bridp. RDn (1847–72), Beam. RDn (1872–1971). Abol eccl 1971 to help cr Melplaish with Mapperton EP.[164]

MAPPOWDER
AP *LG* Seq 5. *Parl* Seq 10. *Eccl* Whitch. RDn (until 1872), Cerne RDn (1872–193). Reconstituted 1937 as 'Mappowder with Plush' when gains pt Buckland Newton AP incl Plush.[69]
EP Cr 1954 when Mappowder with Plush EP loses Plush to help cr Piddletrenthide with Plush and remainder reconstituted as 'Mappowder'.[46] Cerne RDn (1954), Sturm. Newt. RDn (1955–72), Blackm. Vale RDn (1973–*).

MAPPOWDER WITH PLUSH
EP Cr 1937 by union Mappowder AP, pt Buckland Newton AP incl Plush.[69] Cerne RDn. Abol 1954 when Plush transf to help cr Piddletrenthide with Plush EP, remainder reconstituted 'Mappowder'.[46]

MARGARET MARSH
Chap in Iwerne Minster AP, sep civ identity early, eccl severed 1863 and united with chap East Orchard in the same par as 'East Orchard with Margaret Marsh' EP.[143] *LG* Sturm. Newt. Hd, Shaft. PLU, RSD, RD. *Parl* Shaft. Parl Bor (1832–85), Seq 5 thereafter.

MARNHULL
AP *LG* Seq 27. *Parl* Seq 5. *Eccl* Shaft. RDn (until 1920s), Sturm. Newton RDn (1920s–1972), Blackm. Vale RDn (1973–*).

MARSHWOOD
Chap in Whitchurch Canonicorum AP, sep civ identity early, eccl severed 1953 and transf to Bettiscombe AP.[27] *LG* Seq 33. Civ bdry: 1884,[25] 1966 (gains pt Hawkchurch AP, Devon).[179] *Parl* Seq 10.

MELBURY ABBAS
AP *LG* Seq 26. *Parl* Shaft. Parl Bor (1832–85), Seq 5 thereafter. *Eccl* Shaft. RDn (until 1872), Sturm. Newt. RDn (1872–1954), Shaft. RDn (1955–*).

MELBURY BUBB
AP *LG* Seq 38. *Parl* Seq 10. *Eccl* Shaft. RDn (until 1872), Sherb. RDn (1872–1916), Cerne RDn (1916–54), Beam. RDn (1955–*).

MELBURY OSMOND
AP *LG* Yetm. Hd, Beam. PLU, RSD, RD. *Parl* Seq 10. *Eccl* Shaft. RDn (until 1872), Sherb. RDn (1872–1972). Eccl bdry: 1959 (gains Stockwood AP).[166] Abol eccl 1972 to help cr Melbury Osmond with Melbury Sampford EP.[165]

MELBURY OSMOND WITH MELBURY SAMPFORD
EP Cr 1972 by union Melbury Osmond AP, Melbury Sampford AP.[165] Sherb. RDn.

MELBURY SAMPFORD
AP *LG* Seq 28. *Parl* Seq 10. *Eccl* Shaft. RDn (until 1872), Sherb. RDn (1872–1972). Abol eccl 1972 to help cr Melbury Osmond with Melbury Sampford EP.[165]

MELCOMBE HORSEY
AP *LG* Whiteway Hd, Cerne PLU, RSD, RD (1894–1933), Dorch. RD (1933–74). *Parl* Seq 10. *Eccl* Seq 29.

MELCOMBE REGIS
Chap in Radipole AP, sep par 1606.[73] *LG* Cull. Tree Hd, Melc. Regis Bor (when chap, until 1571), Weym. & Melc. Regis Bor (from 1571)/ MB, USD, Weym. PLU. Civ bdry: 1894 (gains the pt of Radipole AP in the MB),[70] 1895.[167] Abol civ 1920 ent to Weymouth AP.[168] *Parl* Melc. Regis Parl Bor (1304, 1328–1832), Weym. & Melc. Regis Parl Bor (1832–85), S'rn Dv (1885–1948). *Eccl* Dorch. RDn (1606–1872), Weym. RDn (1872–*).

MELPLAISH
EP Cr 1847 from Netherbury AP, Powerstock AP.[169] Bridp. RDn (1847–72), Beam. RDn (1872–1971). Abol 1971 to help cr Melplaish with Mapperton EP.[164]

MELPLAISH WITH MAPPERTON
EP Cr 1971 by union Melplaish EP, Mapperton AP.[164] Beam. RDn.

MILBORNE
CP Cr 1933 by union Milborne St Andrew AP, Milborne Stileham CP.[2] *LG* Blandf. RD. *Parl* North CC (1948–*).

MILBORNE ST ANDREW
AP Incl Dewlish (once sep AP,[112] later deemed chap in this par, civ identity regained, no later sep eccl identity hence eccl 'Milborne St Andrew with Dewlish', qv). *LG* Pt Puddletown Lbty, pt Dewlish Lbty, Blandf. PLU, RSD, RD. Abol civ

1933 to help cr Milborne CP.[2] *Parl* N'rn Dv (1885–1948).

MILBORNE ST ANDREW WITH DEWLISH

AP Usual eccl spelling; for civ and civ sep Dewlish see prev entry. *Eccl* Whitch. RDn (until 1872), Milt. RDn (1872–1970), Bere Regis RDn (1970–72), Dorch. RDn (1973–*). Eccl bdry: 1890 (gains hmlt and tg Milborne Stileham from Bere Regis with Winterborne Kingston AP).[23]

MILBORNE STILEHAM

Hmlt and tg in Bere Regis with Winterborne Kingston AP, sep CP 1866,[22] eccl severed 1890 and transf to Milborne St Andrew with Dewlish AP.[23] *LG* Bere Regis Hd, Blandf. PLU, RSD, RD. Abol 1933 to help cr Milborne CP.[2] *Parl* N'rn Dv (1885–1948).

MILTON ABBAS

AP *LG* Seq 35. Civ bdry: 1880,[170] 1883,[24] 1933.[2] *Parl* Seq 5. *Eccl* Seq 29. Eccl bdry: 1954.[171]

MINTERNE MAGNA

AP *LG* Pt Piddletrenthide Lbty, pt Fordington Lbty, Cerne PLU, RSD, RD. Civ bdry: 1933.[2] *Parl* Seq 10. *Eccl* Seq 27.

MONKTON WYLD

EP Cr 1850 from Whitchurch Canonicorum AP, Uplyme AP (Devon).[172] Bridp. RDn (1850–72), Lyme RDn (1872–1970), Beam. RDn (1970–*).

WEST MOORS

EP Cr 1922 when Verwood and West Moors EP divided into 2 EPs of Verwood, West Moors.[174] Wimb. RDn. Bdry: 1927.[147]

CP Cr 1956 from Holt CP, West Parley AP.[175] *LG* Wimb. & Cranb. RD. *Parl* North CC (1970–*).

MORDEN

AP *LG* Loosebarrow Hd, Wareh. & Purb. PLU, RSD, RD. Civ bdry: 1894 (incl cr St Martin CP).[176] *Parl* Seq 4. *Eccl* Whitch. RDn (until 1872), Poole RDn (1872–1962), Milt. RDn (1962–70), Purb. RDn (1970–*). Eccl bdry: 1958.[177]

MORETON

AP *LG* Pt Bindon Lbty, pt Winfrith Hd, Wareh. & Purb. PLU, RSD, RD. *Parl* Seq 7. *Eccl* Dorch. RDn (until 1872), Weym. RDn (1872–1916), Dorch. RDn (1916–*).

MOSTERTON

Chap in South Perrot AP, sep civ identity early, no sep eccl identity. *LG* Beam. Forum & Redhone Hd, Beam. PLU, RSD, RD. *Parl* Seq 10.

MOTCOMBE

Chap in Gillingham AP, sep civ identity early, sep EP 1883 as 'Motcombe with Enmore Green',[129] qv. *LG* Seq 15. Civ bdry: 1933.[2] *Parl* Shaft. Parl Bor (1832–85), Seq 5 thereafter.

MOTCOMBE WITH ENMORE GREEN

Chap in Gillingham AP, sep civ identity early as 'Motcombe', qv, sep EP 1883.[129] *Eccl* Shaft. RDn (1883–1973), Shaft. & Tisbury RDn (1973–*).

NETHERBURY

AP Incl chap Beaminster (sep civ identity early, sep EP 1849[18]). *LG* Seq 2. *Parl* Seq 10. *Eccl* Pec jurisd Cath Chapter of Sarum (until 1847), Seq 8 thereafter. Addtl eccl bdry alt: 1847 (help cr Melplaish EP).[169]

OAKDALE

EP Cr 1946 from Longfleet EP.[159] Poole RDn. Bdry: 1964.[58]

OBORNE

AP Incl chap and bor Castleton (bor status not sustained, sep civ identity early, sep EP 1716[79]). *LG* Seq 25. *Parl* Seq 6. *Eccl* Pec jurisd Cath Chapter of Sarum (1716–1847), Seq 18 thereafter.

CHILDE OKEFORD

AP *LG* Seq 23. Civ bdry: 1884.[183] *Parl* Seq 5. *Eccl* Shaft. RDn (until 1872), Sturm. Newt. RDn (1872–1971). Abol eccl 1971 to help cr Childe Okeford and Manston with Hammoon EP.[133]

CHILDE OKEFORD AND MANSTON WITH HAMMOON

EP Cr 1971 by union Childe Okeford AP, Manston AP, Hammoon AP.[133] Sturm. Newt. RDn (1971–72), Blackm. Vale RDn (1973–*). Bdry: 1974.[20]

SHILLING OKEFORD–See SHILLINGSTONE

OKEFORD FITZPAINE

AP *LG* Seq 27. Civ bdry: 1884.[184] *Parl* Seq 5. *Eccl* Seq 20. Eccl bdry: 1974.[20]

EAST ORCHARD

Chap in Iwerne Minster AP, sep civ identity early, eccl joined with chap Margaret Marsh in the same par to cr East Orchard with Margaret Marsh EP.[143] *LG* Seq 26. Civ bdry: 1886.[114] *Parl* Seq 5.

EAST ORCHARD WITH MARGARET MARSH

EP Cr 1863 by union chaps East Orchard, Margaret Marsh, both in Iwerne Minster AP.[143] Shaft. RDn (1863–72), Sturm. Newt. RDn (1872–1972), Blackm. Vale RDn (1973–*). Bdry: 1952 (gains West Orchard chap of Fontmell Magna AP).[124]

WEST ORCHARD

Chap in Fontmell Magna AP, sep civ identity early, eccl severed 1952 and transf to East Orchard with Margaret Marsh EP.[124] *LG* Seq 26. *Parl* Seq 5.

OSMINGTON

AP *LG* Cull. Tree Hd, Weym. PLU, RSD, RD (1894–1933), Dorch. RD (1933–74). *Parl* Seq 7. *Eccl* Dorch. RDn (until 1872), Weym. RDn (1872–1969). Abol eccl 1969 to help cr Osmington with Poxwell EP.[185]

OSMINGTON WITH POXWELL

EP Cr 1969 by union Osmington AP, Poxwell AP.[185] Weym. RDn.

OWERMOIGNE

AP *LG* Owermoigne Lbty, Weym. PLU, RSD, RD (1894–1933), Dorch. RD (1933–74). Civ bdry: 1880.[186] *Parl* Seq 7. *Eccl* Dorch. RDn (until 1872), Weym. RDn (1872–1949), Dorch. RDn (1949–*). Eccl bdry: 1954.[171]

PAMPHILL
CP Cr 1894 from the pt of Wimborne Minster AP not in Wimb. Minster USD.[146] *LG* Wimb. & Cranb. PLU, RD. Bdry: 1933,[2] 1958.[181] *Parl* E'rn Dv (1918–48), North CC (1948–*).

PARKSTONE
Dist in Kinson tg of Canford Magna AP (eccl, 'Great Canford'), sep EP 1834 as 'Parkstone St Peter',[74] qv, sep CP 1866 as 'Parkstone'.[22] *LG* Cogd. Hd, Poole PLU, MB, USD. Abol civ 1905 to help cr Poole CP.[54] *Parl* Poole Parl Bor (1867–85), E'rn Dv (1885–1918).

PARKSTONE ST LUKE
EP Cr 1903 from Parkstone St Peter EP.[187] Poole RDn.

PARKSTONE ST OSMUND
EP Cr 1911 from Parkstone St Peter EP.[188] Poole RDn. Bdry: 1930 (help cr Branksome St Aldhelm EP),[55] 1933.[189]

PARKSTONE ST PETER
Dist in Kinson tg of Canford Magna AP (eccl, 'Great Canford'), sep EP 1834,[74] sep CP 1866 as 'Parkstone',[22] qv. *Eccl* Whitch. RDn (1834–72), Poole RDn (1872–*). Eccl bdry: 1903 (cr Parkstone St Luke EP),[187] 1911 (cr Parkstone St Osmund EP),[188] 1933,[189] 1952,[124] 1956 (cr Canford Cliffs and Sandbanks EP),[75] 1962 (cr Lilliput EP).[158] Abol eccl 1971 to help cr Parkstone St Peter with Branksea EP.[52]

PARKSTONE ST PETER WITH BRANKSEA
EP Cr 1970 by union Parkstone St Peter EP, Branksea EP.[52] Poole RDn.

WEST PARLEY
AP Incl hmlt West Moors (united 1887 with hmlts Verwood, Three Legged Cross in Cranborne AP to cr Verwood and West Moors EP [qv for later division into sep EPs Verwood, West Moors][109]; West Moors CP cr 1956 fron West Parley AP, Holt CP[175]). *LG* Seq 11. Addtl civ bdry alt: 1886,[85] 1947 (exchanges pts with St Leonards and St Ives CP, Hants).[235] *Parl* Seq 1. *Eccl* Seq 14.

PENTRIDGE
AP *LG* Seq 11. Civ bdry: 1933 (gains East Woodyates CP, West Woodyates EP).[2] *Parl* Seq 2. *Eccl* Pimp. RDn (until 1872), Wimb. RDn (1872–1925), Blandf. RDn (1925–70), Milt. & Blandf. RDn (1970–*). Eccl bdry: 1925.[138]

SOUTH PERROT
AP Incl chap Mosterton (sep civ identity early, no sep eccl identity hence this par eccl 'South Perrot with Mosterton', qv). *LG* Beam. Forum & Redhone Hd, Beam. PLU, RSD, RD. Addtl civ bdry alt: 1966 (loses pt to Misterton AP, Somerset).[179] *Parl* Seq 10.

SOUTH PERROT WITH MOSTERTON
AP Usual eccl spelling; for civ and civ sep chap Mosterton see prev entry. *Eccl* Bridp. RDn (until 1872), Beam. RDn (1872–1971). Abol eccl 1971 to help cr South Perrot with Mosterton and Chedington EP.[91]

SOUTH PERROT WITH MOSTERTON AND CHEDINGTON
EP Cr 1971 by union South Perrot with Mosterton AP, Chedington AP.[91] Beam. RDn.

PIDDLEHINTON
AP *LG* Piddlehinton Lbty, Dorch. PLU, RSD, RD. Civ bdry: 1885.[93] *Parl* Seq 8. *Eccl* Seq 22. Eccl bdry: 1933,[190] 1940.[191]

PIDDLETRENTHIDE
AP *LG* Piddletrenthide Lbty, Cerne PLU, RSD, RD (1894–1933), Dorch. RD (1933–74). Civ bdry: 1933.[2] *Parl* Seq 10. *Eccl* Whitch. RDn (until 1872), Bere Regis RDn (1872–1954). Eccl bdry: 1940.[191] Reconstituted 1954 as 'Piddletrenthide with Plush' when gains pt Mappowder with Plush AP, the remainder to constitute 'Mappowder' EP.[46]

PIDDLETRENTHIDE WITH PLUSH
EP Cr 1954 by union Piddletrenthide AP, pt Mappowder with Plush EP.[46] Bere Regis RDn (1954–72), Dorch. RDn (1973–*).

PILSON
AP *LG* Seq 33. *Parl* Seq 10. *Eccl* Seq 6.

PIMPERNE
AP *LG* Seq 20. Civ bdry: 1887,[192] 1894,[31] 1897,[68] 1930,[32] 1933.[2] *Parl* Seq 5. *Eccl* Seq 13. Eccl bdry: 1937,[193] 1972.[33]

POOLE
CP Cr 1905 by union Poole St James AP, Branksome CP, Hamworthy CP, Longfleet CP, Parkstone CP.[54] *LG* Poole PLU, MB. Bdry: 1933.[2] *Parl* E'rn Dv (1918–48), Poole BC (1948–*).

POOLE ST JAMES
Chap in Canford Magna AP (eccl, 'Great Canford'), sep par 1538.[76] Incl chap Parkstone (sep EP 1834 as 'Parkstone St Peter',[74] sep CP 1866 as 'Parkstone'[22]). *LG* Hasilor Hd, Poole Bor/MB, PLU, USD. Abol civ 1905 to help cr Poole CP.[54] *Parl* Poole Parl Bor (1362–1885), E'rn Dv (1885–1918). *Eccl* Royal pec (1538–1847), Whitch. RDn (1847–72), Poole RDn (1872–*). Addtl eccl bdry alt: 1853 (cr Poole St Paul EP).[195] Abol eccl 1957 to help cr Poole St James and St Paul EP.[194]

POOLE ST JAMES AND ST PAUL
EP Cr 1957 by union Poole St James AP, Poole St Paul EP.[194] Poole RDn.

POOLE ST PAUL
EP Cr 1853 from Poole St James AP.[195] Whitch. RDn (1853–72), Poole RDn (1872–1957). Abol 1957 to help cr Poole St James and St Paul EP.[194]

NORTH POORTON
AP *LG* Beam. Forum & Redhone Hd, Beam. PLU, RSD, RD. Civ bdry: 1884.[196] *Parl* Seq 10. *Eccl* Bridp. RDn (until 1970), Lyme Bay RDn (1970–71). Abol eccl 1971 to help cr Powerstock with West Milton, Witherstone and North Poorton EP.[52]

PORTESHAM
AP *LG* Seq 32. *Parl* Seq 10. *Eccl* Seq 3.

PORTLAND
AP *LG* Isle of Portland Lbty, Weym. PLU, Portland USD, UD. *Parl* Seq 7. *Eccl* Dorch. RDn (until 1872), Weym. RDn (1872–1966). Eccl bdry: 1841 (cr Portland St John EP),[79] 1873 (cr Portland St Peter EP).[197] Abol eccl 1966 to help cr Portland All Saints with St Peter EP.[198]

PORTLAND ALL SAINTS WITH ST PETER
EP Cr 1966 by union Portland AP, Portland St Peter EP.[198] Weym. RDn.

PORTLAND ST JOHN
EP Cr 1841 from Portland AP.[79] Dorch. RDn (1841–72), Weym. RDn (1872–*).

PORTLAND ST PETER
EP Cr 1873 from Portland AP.[197] Weym. RDn. Abol 1966 to help cr Portland All Saints with St Peter EP.[198]

POWERSTOCK
AP Usual civ spelling; for eccl see following entry. *LG* Pt Egg. Hd, pt Powerstock Lbty, Beam. PLU, RSD, RD. Civ bdry: 1884.[196] *Parl* Seq 10.

POWERSTOCK WITH WEST MILTON
AP Usual eccl spelling; for civ see prev entry. *Eccl* Bridp. RDn (until 1970), Lyme Bay RDn (1970–71). Eccl bdry: 1847 (help cr Melplaish EP).[169] Abol eccl 1971 to help cr Powerstock with West Milton, Witherstone and North Poorton EP.[52]

POWERSTOCK WITH WEST MILTON, WITHERSTONE AND NORTH POORTON
EP Cr 1971 by union Powerstock with West Milton AP, Witherstone AP, North Poorton AP.[52] Lyme Bay RDn.

POXWELL
AP *LG* Winf. Hd, Weym. PLU, RSD, RD. Civ bdry: 1933.[2] *Parl* Seq 7. *Eccl* Dorch. RDn (until 1872), Weym. RDn (1872–1969). Abol eccl 1969 to help cr Osmington with Poxwell EP.[185]

POYNTINGTON
AP In Somerset (Horethorne Hd), transf 1895 to Dorset.[130] *LG* Sherb. PLU, RSD, sep RD in Somerset (1894–95), Sherb. RD (1895–1974). *Parl* Somerset until 1918, N'rn Dv (1918–48), West CC (1948–*). *Eccl* Merston RDn (Bath & Wells dioc, Wells AD, until 1929), Sherb. RDn (1929–*).

PRESTON
AP *LG* Sutton Poyntz Lbty, Weym. PLU, RSD, RD. Abol civ 1933 pt to Weymouth AP, pt to Bincombe AP, pt to Poxwell AP.[2] *Parl* S'rn Dv (1885–1918), W'rn Dv (1918–48). *Eccl* Sometimes as 'Preston with Sutton Poyntz', pec jurisd Cath Chapter of Sarum (until 1847), Seq 11 thereafter.

PUDDLETOWN
AP *LG* Seq 19. Civ bdry: 1885.[93] *Parl* Seq 8. *Eccl* Whitch. RDn (until 1872), Bere Regis RDn (1872–1967). Eccl bdry: 1930.[190] Abol eccl 1967 to help cr Puddletown with Athelhampton and Burleston EP.[17]

PUDDLETOWN WITH ATHELHAMPTON AND BURLESTON
EP Cr 1967 by union Puddletown AP, Athelhampton AP, Burleston AP.[17] Bere Regis RDn (1967–72), Dorch. RDn (1973–*).

PULHAM
AP *LG* Pt Buck. Newt. Hd, pt Bindon Lbty, Cerne PLU, RSD, RD (1894–1933), Sturm. RD (1933–74). *Parl* Seq 10. *Eccl* Seq 28.

PUNCKNOWLE
AP Gains 1451 Bexington AP.[26] *LG* Seq 30. Civ bdry: 1894.[1] *Parl* Seq 10. *Eccl* Seq 2.

RADIPOLE
AP Incl chap Melcombe Regis (sep par 1606[73]). *LG* Cull. Tree Hd, Weym. PLU, pt Melc. Regis Bor (until 1571), pt Weym. & Melc. Regis Bor (1571–1606), pt Weym. & Melc. Regis MB (1832–94), pt Weym. & Melc. Regis USD, pt Weym. RSD, Weym. RD. Addtl civ bdry alt: 1894 (loses the pt in the MB to Melcombe Regis AP, pt of the remainder to cr East Radipole CP, the residue combined with pt Buckland Ripers AP as reconstituted Radipole par),[15] 1895.[167] Abol civ 1933 pt to Weymouth AP, pt to Chickerell AP.[2] *Parl* Pt Melc. Regis Parl Bor (until 1606), pt Weym. & Melc. Regis Parl Bor (1832–85), S'rn Dv (1885–1948). *Eccl* Seq 11. Addtl eccl bdry alt: 1926 (cr Weymouth St Mary EP),[199] 1951,[200] 1952,[65] 1956 (help cr Weymouth St Edmund EP),[96] 1957.[201]

EAST RADIPOLE
CP Cr 1894 from pt of the pt of Radipole AP not in Weym. & Melc. Regis MB.[15] *LG* Weym. PLU, RD. Abol 1895 pt to Melcombe Regis AP, pt to Radipole AP.[167]

RAMPISHAM
AP *LG* Seq 28. *Parl* Seq 10. *Eccl* Seq 4.

RYME INSTRINSECA
AP *LG* Ryme Instrinseca Lbty, Sherb. PLU, RSD, RD. Civ bdry: 1886.[82] *Parl* Seq 9. *Eccl* Pec jurisd Cath Chapter of Sarum (until 1847), Seq 18 thereafter.

ST MARTIN
CP Cr 1894 from Morden AP.[176] *LG* Wareh. & Purb. PLU, RD. Bdry: 1931.[16] *Parl* S'rn Dv (1918–48), South CC (1948–*).

SANDFORD ORCAS
AP In Somerset (Horethorne Hd), transf 1895 to Dorset.[130] *LG* Sherb. PLU, RSD, sep RD in Somerset (1894–95), Sherb. RD (1895–1974). Civ bdry: 1966 (gains pt Corton Denham AP, Somerset).[179] *Parl* Somerset until 1918, N'rn Dv (1918–48), West CC (1948–*). *Eccl* Merston RDn (until 1917), Milborne Port RDn (1917–55), Merston RDn (1955–72) (all in Bath & Wells dioc, Wells AD), Sherb. RDn (1973–*).

SEABOROUGH
AP In Somerset (Crewkerne Hd), transf 1895 to Dorset.[130] *LG* Beam. PLU, RSD, RD, sep RD in Somerset (1894–95), Sherb. RD (1895–

1974). *Parl* Somerset until 1918, W'rn Dv (1918–48), West CC (1948–*). *Eccl* Crewkerne RDn (Bath & Wells dioc, Taunton AD, until 1971), Beam. RDn (1971–*).

SHAFTESBURY

The following have 'Shaftesbury' in their names. Insofar as any existed at a given time: *LG* Monkton Up Wimb. Hd, Shaft. incorp for poor (until 1880s), PLU (1880s–1930) (Bor/MB, USD, RSD sep noted). *Parl* Before 1885, sep noted; N'rn Dv (1885–1918), North CC (1918–*). *Eccl* Shaft. RDn (until 1972), Shaft. & Tisbury RDn (1973–*).

CP1–SHAFTESBURY–Cr 1894 by union of the pts of AP2, AP5, AP9 in Shaft. MB.[5] *LG* Shaft. MB. Bdry: 1921,[6] 1933.[2]

AP1–SHAFTESBURY ALL SAINTS–United 1423 to AP5.[45]

AP2–SHAFTESBURY HOLY TRINITY–Gains 1534 AP7.[45] *LG* Pt Shaft. Bor/MB, pt Shaft. USD, pt Shaft. RSD. Abol civ 1894 the pt in the MB to help cr CP1, the remainder to Cann AP.[5] *Parl* Shaft. Parl Bor (pt 1295–1832, ent 1832–85). *Eccl* Abol eccl 1967 to help cr EP2.[203]

EP1–SHAFTESBURY HOLY TRINITY–Renaming 1972 of EP2.[204]

EP2–SHAFTESBURY HOLY TRINITY WITH ST PETER AND ST RUMBOLD–Cr 1967 by union AP2, AP9, AP10.[203] Renamed 1972 EP1.[204]

AP3–SHAFTESBURY ST ANDREW–United 1534 to AP9.[45]

AP4–SHAFTESBURY ST EDWARD–United 1423 to AP5.[45]

AP5–SHAFTESBURY ST JAMES–Gains 1423 AP1, AP4, gains 1446 AP6.[45] *LG* Pt Shaft. Bor/MB, pt Shaft. USD, pt Shaft. RSD. Abol civ 1894 the pt in the MB to help cr CP1, pt to Cann AP, pt to cr Alcester CP.[5] *Parl* Shaft. Parl Bor (pt 1295–1832, ent 1832–85).

AP6–SHAFTESBURY ST JOHN–United 1446 to AP5.[45]

AP7–SHAFTESBURY ST LAWRENCE–United 1534 to AP2.[45]

AP8–SHAFTESBURY ST MARTIN–United 1534 to AP9.[45]

AP9–SHAFTESBURY ST PETER–Gains 1534 AP3, AP8.[45] *LG* Pt Shaft. Bor/MB, pt Shaft. USD, pt Shaft. RSD. Abol civ 1894 the pt in the MB to help cr CP1, the remainder to Cann AP.[5] *Parl* Shaft. Parl Bor (pt 1295–1832, ent 1832–85). *Eccl* Abol eccl 1967 to help cr EP2.[203]

AP10–SHAFTESBURY ST RUMBOLD–Usual eccl spelling; for civ see 'Cann'. *Eccl* Eccl bdry: 1952.[205] Abol eccl 1967 to help cr EP2.[203]

SHAPWICK

AP *LG* Seq 1. Civ bdry: 1886,[85] 1888.[206] *Parl* Seq 1. *Eccl* Pimp. RDn (until 1872), Blandf. RDn (1872–1949), Wimb. RDn (1949–*). Eccl bdry: 1959.[207]

SHERBORNE

AP Incl chap North Wootton (sep civ identity early, sep EP 1812[79]). *LG* Sherb. Hd, PLU, pt Sherb. Bor, pt Sherb. USD, pt Sherb. RSD, Sherb. UD. Addtl civ bdry alt: 1894 (loses the pt not in the USD to Castleton AP, Nether Compton AP, gains the pt of Castleton AP in the USD),[80] 1929.[208] *Parl* Pt Sherb. Parl Bor (1338 only), Seq 6 thereafter. *Eccl* Shaft. RDn (until 1872), Sherb. RDn (1872–1970). Addtl eccl bdry alt: 1966.[47] Abol eccl 1970 to help cr Sherborne with Castleton EP.[66]

SHERBORNE WITH CASTLETON

EP Cr 1970 by union Sherborne AP, Castleton EP.[66] Sherb. RDn.

SHILLINGSTONE

AP Sometimes 'Shilling Okeford'. *LG* Cranb. Hd, Sturm. PLU, RSD, RD. *Parl* Seq 5. *Eccl* Whitch. RDn (until 1872), Milt. RDn (1872–1970), Sturm. Newt. RDn (1970–72), Blackm. Vale RDn (1973–*).

SHIPTON GEORGE

Parochial chap in Burton Bradstock AP, sep civ identity early, no sep eccl identity. *LG* Godderthorne Hd, Bridp. PLU, RSD, RD. Civ bdry: 1884.[9] *Parl* Seq 10.

SILTON

AP *LG* Redl. Hd, Mere PLU (1835–94), RSD, Shaft. PLU (1894–1930), RD. Civ bdry: 1883,[24] 1885.[44] *Parl* Seq 5. *Eccl* Seq 15.

SPETISBURY

AP Usual eccl spelling, civ spelling from 1955 as renaming of Spletisbury[209]; for civ before 1955 see following entry. Incl chap Charlton Marshall (sep civ identity early, no sep eccl identity). *LG* Blandf. RD. *Parl* North CC (1970–*). *Eccl* Seq 28. Eccl bdry: 1972.[33]

SPLETISBURY

AP Usual civ spelling before 1955 when renamed 'Spetisbury'[209]; for civ after 1955, eccl, civ sep chap Charlton Marshall, see prev entry. *LG* Loosebarrow Hd, Blandf. PLU, RSD, RD. *Parl* N'rn Dv (1885–1948), North CC (1948–70).

WEST STAFFORD

AP Gains 1470 Frome Billett AP.[126] *LG* Seq 12. Civ bdry: 1933.[2] *Parl* Seq 8. *Eccl* Seq 9.

STALBRIDGE

AP *LG* Seq 4. *Parl* Seq 5. *Eccl* Seq 17.

STANTON ST GABRIEL

Parochial chap in Whitchurch Canonicorum AP, sep civ identity early, no sep eccl identity. *LG* Seq 34. *Parl* Seq 10.

STEEPLE

AP *LG* Seq 16. *Parl* Seq 4. *Eccl* Dorch. RDn (until 1872), Purb. RDn (1872–1952). Abol eccl 1952 pt to help cr Steeple with Tyneham EP, pt to Wareham AP.[210]

STEEPLE WITH TYNEHAM

EP Cr 1952 by union Tyneham AP, pt Steeple AP.[210] Purb. RDn.

STINSFORD

AP *LG* Seq 14. Civ bdry: 1894,[48] 1933.[2] *Parl* Seq 8. *Eccl* Whitch. RDn (until 1872), Bere Regis

RDn (1872–1970), Dorch. RDn (1970–*).

STOCK GAYLARD

AP *LG* Browns. Hd, Sturm. PLU, RSD. Abol civ 1884 ent to Lydlinch AP.[163] *Eccl* Seq 17.

STOCKLAND

AP *LG* Pt Whitch. Can. Hd, pt Fordington Lbty (Dalwood chap), main pt of par and the chap transf to Devon 1832 for parl purposes, 1844 for civ purposes[37] (Dalwood became sep CP 1866 in Devon,[22] no sep eccl identity, hence this par eccl 'Stockland with Dalwood', qv). See entry in Devon for Stockland, Dalwood in civ and parl organisation after 1832/44.

STOCKLAND WITH DALWOOD

AP Usual eccl spelling; for civ, transf to Devon, and civ sep chap Dalwood see prev entry. *Eccl* Bridp. RDn (until 1836), Honiton RDn (1836–75), Dunkeswell & Honiton RDn (1875–1902), Honiton RDn (1902–*)(all after 1836 in Exeter dioc, Exeter AD).

STOCKWOOD

AP *LG* Sutton Poyntz Lbty, Sherb. PLU, RSD, RD. *Parl* Seq 9. *Eccl* Pec jurisd Cath Chapter of Sarum (until 1847), Shaft. RDn (1847–72), Sherb. RDn (1872–1959). Abol eccl 1959 ent to Melbury Osmond AP.[166]

EAST STOKE

AP *LG* Seq 37. Civ bdry: 1883,[24] 1888.[162] *Parl* Pt Wareh. Parl Bor (1832–85), Seq 4 thereafter. *Eccl* Seq 12. Eccl bdry: 1954,[100] 1959.[160]

STOKE ABBOTT

AP *LG* Seq 2. *Parl* Seq 10. *Eccl* Seq 8.

STOKE WAKE

AP *LG* Seq 36. *Parl* Seq 5. *Eccl* Whitch. RDn (until 1872), Milt. RDn (1872–1930), Cerne RDn (1930–54), Sturm. Newt. RDn (1955–72), Blackm. Vale RDn (1973–*).

EAST STOUR

Chap in Gillingham AP, sep civ identity early, no sep eccl identity. *LG* Seq 22. *Parl* Shaft. Parl Bor (1832–85), Seq 5 thereafter.

WEST STOUR

Chap in Gillingham AP, seq civ identity early, no sep eccl identity. *LG* Seq 22. *Parl* Seq 5.

STOUR PROVOST

AP *LG* Stour Provost Lbty, Shaft. PLU, RSD, RD. *Parl* Shaft. Parl Bor (1832–85), Seq 5 thereafter. *Eccl* Seq 15.

STOURPAINE

AP Gains 1431 Lazerton AP.[155] *LG* Seq 20. *Parl* Seq 5. *Eccl* Pec jurisd Cath Chapter of Sarum (until 1847), Seq 13 thereafter.

STRATTON

Chap in Charminster AP, sep civ identity early, sep EP 1742.[79] *LG* Seq 14. *Parl* Seq 8. *Eccl* Whitch. RDn (1742–1872), Dorch. RDn (1872–*).

STUDLAND

AP *LG* Pt Newton Bor (status not sustained), Seq 24. Civ bdry: 1894.[211] *Parl* Seq 4. *Eccl* Seq 12. Eccl bdry: 1855 (cr Branksea EP),[51] 1954.[154]

STURMINSTER MARSHALL

AP Incl chaps Lytchett Minster, Corfe Mullen, Hamworthy (each with sep civ identity early, each sep EP 1858[104]). *LG* Seq 8. Addtl civ bdry alt: 1886,[85] 1888,[212] 1933 (gains Almer AP).[2] *Parl* Seq 1. *Eccl* Royal pec (until 1847), Whitch. RDn (1847–72), Poole RDn (1872–1962), Milt. RDn (1962–70), Wimb. RDn (1970–*).

STURMINSTER NEWTON

AP *LG* Seq 27. *Parl* Seq 5. *Eccl* Seq 20.

SUTTON WALDRON

AP *LG* Seq 22. *Parl* Seq 5. *Eccl* Seq 20.

SWANAGE

AP *LG* Rowb. Hd, Wareh. & Purb. PLU, Swanage USD, UD. Civ bdry: 1894,[211] 1933.[2] *Parl* Seq 4. *Eccl* Seq 12. Eccl bdry: 1954.[154]

SWYRE

AP *LG* Seq 30. *Parl* Seq 10. *Eccl* Seq 2.

SYDLING ST NICHOLAS

AP Incl chap Hillfield (sep civ identity early, sep EP 1850[141]). *LG* Sydling St Nicholas Lbty, Cerne PLU, RSD, RD (1894–1933), Dorch. RD (1933–74). *Parl* Seq 10. *Eccl* Seq 23.

SYMONDSBURY

AP Usual civ spelling; for eccl see following entry. *LG* Whitch. Can. Hd, Bridp. PLU, pt Bridp. MB (1835–94), pt. Bridp. USD, pt Bridp. RSD, Bridp. RD. Civ bdry: 1884,[9] 1894 (loses the pt in the MB to Bridport AP),[10] 1923,[63] 1954.[178] *Parl* Pt Bridp. Parl Bor (1832–85), Seq 10 thereafter.

SYMONDSBURY WITH EYPE AND BROADOAK

AP Usual eccl spelling; for civ see prev entry. *Eccl* Bridp. RDn (until 1872), Lyme RDn (1872–1916), Bridp. RDn (1916–70), Lyme Bay RDn (1970–*). Eccl bdry: 1927.[12]

TALBOT VILLAGE

EP Cr 1919 from Kinson EP.[150] Poole RDn. Bdry: 1953,[57] 1967 (help cr Ensbury EP).[120]

TARRANT CRAWFORD

AP *LG* Badb. Hd, Blandf. PLU, RSD, RD. Civ bdry: 1888.[213] *Parl* Seq 2. *Eccl* Pimp. RDn (until 1872), Blandf. RDn (1872–1937). Abol eccl 1937 to help cr Tarrant Gunville with Tarrant Rushton, Tarrant Rawston, Tarrant Keynston and Tarrant Crawford EP.[193]

TARRANT GUNVILLE

AP *LG* Seq 10. *Parl* Seq 5. *Eccl* Pimp. RDn (until 1872), Blandf. RDn (1872–1928). Abol eccl 1928 to help cr Tarrant Gunville with Tarrant Rushton and Tarrant Rawston EP.[214]

TARRANT GUNVILLE WITH TARRANT RUSHTON AND TARRANT RAWSTON

EP Cr 1928 by union Tarrant Gunville AP, Tarrant Rushton AP, Tarrant Rawston AP.[214] Blandf. RDn. Abol 1932 to help cr Tarrant Gunville with Tarrant Rushton and Tarrant Rawston with Tarrant Keynston EP.[215]

TARRANT GUNVILLE WITH TARRANT RUSHTON AND TARRANT RAWSTON AND TARRANT KEYNSTON

EP Cr 1932 by union Tarrant Gunville with Tarrant Rushton and Tarrant Rawston EP, Tarrant Keynston EP.[215] Blandf. RDn. Abol 1937 to help cr Tarrant Gunville with Tarrant Rushton,

Tarrant Rawston, Tarrant Keynston and Tarrant Crawford EP.[193]

TARRANT GUNVILLE WITH TARRANT RUSHTON, TARRANT RAWSTON, TARRANT KEYNSTON AND TARRANT CRAWFORD

EP Cr 1937 by union Tarrant Gunville with Tarrant Rushton and Tarrant Rawston and Tarrant Keynston EP, Tarrant Crawford AP.[193] Blandf. RDn (1937–70), Milt. & Blandf. RDn (1970–*).

TARRANT HINTON

AP *LG* Seq 20. Civ bdry: 1933.[2] *Parl* Seq 5. *Eccl* Pimp. RDn (until 1872), Blandf. RDn (1872–1970), Milt. & Blandf. RDn (1970–*). Eccl bdry: 1937.[193]

TARRANT KEYNSTON

AP *LG* Seq 20. Civ bdry: 1887.[35] *Parl* Seq 5. *Eccl* Pimp. RDn (until 1872), Blandf. RDn (1872–1932). Abol eccl 1932 to help cr Tarrant Gunville with Tarrant Rushton and Tarrant Rawston and Tarrant Keynston EP.[215]

TARRANT LAUNCESTON

Tg and chap in Tarrant Monkton AP, sep civ identity early, eccl taken down 1762 and no sep eccl identity.[216] *LG* Seq 20. Civ bdry: 1933.[2] *Parl* Seq 5.

TARRANT MONKTON

AP Incl tg and chap Tarrant Launceston (sep civ identity early, eccl taken down 1762 and no sep eccl identity, hence this par eccl 'Tarrant Monkton with Tarrant Launceston', qv). *LG* Monkton Up Wimb. Hd, Blandf. PLU, RSD, RD. Civ bdry: 1933.[2] *Parl* Seq 5.

TARRANT MONKTON WITH TARRANT LAUNCESTON

AP Usual eccl spelling; for civ and civ sep chap Tarrant Launceston see prev entry. *Eccl* Pimp. RDn (until 1872), Blandf. RDn (1872–1928). Abol eccl 1928 to help cr Tarrant Gunville with Tarrant Rushton and Tarrant Rawston EP.[214]

TARRANT RAWSTON

AP *LG* Seq 20. *Parl* Seq 5. *Eccl* Pimp. RDn (until 1872), Blandf. RDn (1872–1928). Abol eccl 1928 to help cr Tarrant Gunville with Tarrant Rushton and Tarrant Rawston EP.[214]

TARRANT RUSHTON

AP *LG* Seq 10. Civ bdry: 1887,[35] 1888.[217] *Parl* Seq 2. *Eccl* Pimp. RDn (until 1872), Blandf. RDn (1872–1928). Abol eccl 1928 to help cr Tarrant Gunville with Tarrant Rushton and Tarrant Rawston EP.[214]

THORNCOMBE

AP In Dorset (Whitch. Can. Hd), transf to Devon 1832 for parl purposes, 1844 for civ purposes (Axminster Hd),[37] transf back to Dorset 1896.[218] *LG* Axminster PLU (1836–94), RSD, Beam. PLU (1894–1930), sep RD in Devon (1894–96), Beam. RD (1896–1974). Civ bdry: 1884,[219] 1966 (exchanges pts with Chard AP, Somerset, gains pt Hawkchurch AP, Devon).[179] *Parl* Dorset until 1832, Devon 1832–1918 (qv), W'rn Dv (1918–48), West CC (1948–*). *Eccl* Honiton RDn (Exeter dioc, until 1836), Bridp. RDn (1836–72), Lyme RDn (1872–1970), Beam. RDn (1970–*).

THORNFORD

AP *LG* Seq 25. *Parl* Seq 6. *Eccl* Pec jurisd Cath Chapter of Sarum (until 1847), Seq 18 thereafter.

TINCLETON

AP *LG* Seq 19. *Parl* Seq 8. *Eccl* Donative, Whitch. RDn (until 1872), Bere Regis RDn (1872–1916), Dorch. RDn (1916–*). Eccl bdry: 1971.[4]

TODBER

AP Usual civ spelling; for eccl see following entry. *LG* Seq 22. *Parl* Seq 5.

TODBERE

AP Usual eccl spelling; for civ see prev entry. *Eccl* Seq 15.

TOLLARD ROYAL

AP Pt Dorset (Cranb. Hd), pt Wilts (Chalke Hd), the former transf to Wilts in 1880s.[220] For civ and parl organisation after 1880s see main entry in Wilts. *Eccl* Chalke RDn (until 1872), Chalke RDn Second Portion/Tisbury (1872–1925)(both in Salisbury AD), Blandf. RDn (1925–70), Milt. & Blandf. RDn (1970–*).

TOLLER FRATRUM

AP Incl parochial chap Wynford Eagle (sep civ identity early, sep EP 1911[221]). *LG* Seq 29. *Parl* Seq 10. *Eccl* Dorch. RDn (until 1916), Bridp. RDn (1916–30), Abbotsb. RDn (1930–70), Dorch. RDn (1970–*).

TOLLER PORCORUM

AP *LG* Pt Beam. Forum & Redhone Hd, pt Toll. Hd, Dorch. PLU, RSD, RD. *Parl* Seq 10. *Eccl* Bridp. RDn (until 1970), Beam. RDn (1970–*).

TOLLER WHELME

EP Cr 1871 from Corscombe AP.[107] Bridp. RDn (1871–72), Beam. RDn (1872–1939). Abol 1939 ent to Corscombe AP.[108]

TOLPUDDLE

AP *LG* Seq 19. *Parl* Seq 8. *Eccl* Seq 22.

TRENT

AP In Somerset (Horethorne Hd), transf 1895 to Dorset.[130] *LG* Sherb. PLU, RSD, sep RD in Somerset (1894–95), Sherb. RD (1895–1974). *Parl* Somerset until 1918, N'rn Dv (1918–48), West CC (1948–*). *Eccl* Merston RDn (Bath & Wells dioc, Wells AD, until 1973), Sherb. RDn (1973–*).

TURNERS PUDDLE

AP Usual civ spelling; for eccl see following entry. *LG* Seq 17. *Parl* Seq 7.

TURNERSPUDDLE

AP Usual eccl spelling; for civ see prev entry. *Eccl* Pec jurisd Cath Chapter of Sarum (until 1847), Whitch. RDn (1847–72), Bere Regis RDn (1872–1970). Abol eccl 1970 to help cr Affpuddle with Turnerspuddle EP.[3]

TURNWORTH

AP *LG* Seq 10. Civ bdry: 1887.[35] *Parl* Seq 5. *Eccl* Seq 29.

TYNEHAM

AP *LG* Seq 16. *Parl* Seq 4. *Eccl* Dorch. RDn (until

1872), Purb. RDn (1872–1952). Abol eccl 1952 to help cr Steeple with Tyneham EP.[210]

UPCERNE

AP Usual eccl spelling; for civ see 'Up Cerne'. *Eccl* Whitch. RDn (until 1872), Bere Regis RDn RDn (1872–74), Cerne RDn (1874–1954), Dorch. RDn (1955–71). Abol eccl 1971 ent to Cerne Abbas AP.[84]

UPWEY

AP *LG* Pt Wabyhouse Lbty, pt Cull. Tree Hd, Weym. PLU, RSD, RD. Abol civ 1933 pt to Weymouth AP, pt to Bincombe AP, pt to Chicherell AP.[2] *Parl* S'rn Dv (1885–1918), W'rn Dv (1918–48). *Eccl* Seq 11.

VERWOOD

Hmlt in Cranborne AP, sep CP 1894,[8] eccl united 1887 with hmlt Three Legged Cross in Cranborne AP and hmlt West Moors in West Parley AP to cr 'Verwood and West Moors' EP,[109] (qv), the latter divided 1922 into the 2 EPs of Verwood, West Moors.[174] *LG* Wimb. & Cranb. PLU, RD. Civ bdry: 1956.[175] *Parl* N'rn Dv (1918–48), North CC (1948–*). *Eccl* Wimb. RDn.

VERWOOD AND WEST MOORS

EP Cr 1887 by union hmlts Verwood, Three Legged Cross in Cranborne AP, hmlt West Moors in West Parley AP.[174] Wimb. RDn. Abol 1922, divided into the 2 EPs of Verwood, West Moors.[174]

WALDITCH

AP *LG* Godderthorne Hd, Bridp. PLU, pt Bridp. MB (1835–94), pt Bridp. USD, pt Bridp. RSD. Abol civ 1894 the pt in the MB to Bridport AP, the remainder to Bothenhampton AP.[10] *Parl* W'rn Dv (1885–1918). *Eccl* Seq 5. Eccl bdry: 1927.[12]

WAMBROOK

AP Chap in Netherbury AP, sep par 1405.[222] *LG* Beam. Hd, Chard PLU, RSD, sep RD (1894–95). Transf 1895 to Somerset.[130] *Parl* W'rn Dv (1885–1918), Somerset thereafter. *Eccl* Pec jurisd Cath Chapter of Sarum (until 1847), Seq 6 thereafter.

WAREHAM

EP Cr 1678 by union Wareham Holy Trinity AP, Wareham Lady St Mary AP, Wareham St Martin AP.[223] Whitch. RDn (1678–1872), Poole RDn (1872–1916), Purb. RDn (1916–*). Eccl bdry: 1952,[210] 1954,[100] 1958.[177]

WAREHAM HOLY TRINITY

AP Incl chap Arne (sep civ identity early, no sep eccl identity), bor Stoborough (no sep civ identity, status not sustained). *LG* Winf. Hd, Wareh. & Purb. PLU, pt Wareh. Bor, pt Wareh. MB & USD (1886–94), Wareh. & Purb. RSD (ent 1875–86, pt 1886–94). Abol civ 1894 the pt in the MB to Wareham Lady St Mary AP, the remainder to Arne CP.[15] *Parl* Wareh. Parl Bor (pt 1302–1832, ent 1832–85), E'rn Dv (1885–1918). *Eccl* Whitch. RDn. Abol eccl 1678 to help cr Wareham EP.[233]

WAREHAM LADY ST MARY

AP Gains early Wareham St Michael AP.[224] *LG* Winf. Hd, Wareh. & Purb. PLU, pt Wareh. Bor, Wareh. MB & USD (1886–1974). Civ bdry: 1888,[162] 1894 (gains the pts of Wareham Holy Trinity AP, Wareham St Martin AP in the MB, loses pt to Arne CP),[15] 1931.[16] *Parl* Wareh. Parl Bor (pt 1302–1832, ent 1832–85), Seq 4 thereafter. *Eccl* As for Wareham Holy Trinity.

WAREHAM ST MARTIN

AP *LG* Organisation as for Wareham Holy Trinity. Civ bdry: 1888.[162] Abol civ 1894 the pt in the MB to Wareham Lady St Mary AP, the remainder to Morden AP.[15] *Parl*, *Eccl* as for Wareham Holy Trinity.

WAREHAM ST MICHAEL

AP Whitch. RDn, united early to Wareham Lady St Mary AP.[224]

WARMWELL

AP *LG* Winf. Hd, Dorch. PLU, RSD, RD. Civ bdry: 1883.[24] *Parl* Seq 8. *Eccl* Dorch. RDn (until 1872), Weym. RDn (1872–1953), Dorch. RDn (1953–*). Eccl bdry: 1969.[153]

WATERCOMBE

Ex-par place, sep CP 1858,[131] eccl abol 1969 ent to Warmwell AP.[153] *LG* Winf. Hd, Dorch. PLU, RSD, RD. *Parl* Seq 8.

WEYMOUTH

Chap in Wyke Regis AP, sep civ identity early, sep EP 1836.[225] *LG* Uggsc. Hd, Weym. PLU, Weym. Bor (until 1571), Weym. & Melc. Regis Bor (from 1571)/MB, USD. Civ bdry: 1894 (gains the pt of Wyke Regis AP in the MB),[70] 1895,[167] 1920 (gains ent Melcombe Regis AP),[168] 1933.[2] *Parl* Weym. Parl Bor (1348–1832), Weym. & Melc. Regis Parl Bor (1832–85), Seq 7 thereafter. *Eccl* Dorch. RDn (1836–72), Weym. RDn (1872–*). Eccl bdry: 1956.[226]

WEYMOUTH ST EDMUND

EP Cr 1956 from Wyke Regis AP, Weymouth St Paul EP, Radipole AP, Chickerell AP.[96] Weym. RDn.

WEYMOUTH ST JOHN

EP Cr 1856 from Melcombe Regis AP.[227] Dorch. RDn (1856–72), Weym. RDn (1872–*). Bdry: 1951.[200]

WEYMOUTH ST MARY

EP Cr 1926 from the detached pt of Radipole AP.[199] Weym. RDn.

WEYMOUTH ST PAUL

EP Cr 1901 from Wyke Regis AP.[228] Bdry: 1956 (help cr Weymouth St Edmund EP),[96] 1956,[226] 1957.[201]

WHITCOMBE

AP *LG* Seq 12. *Parl* Seq 8. *Eccl* Donative, Dorch. RDn. Abol eccl 1971 to help cr Winterbourne Came with Whitcombe EP.[229]

WHITCHURCH CANONICORUM WITH STANTON ST GABRIEL

AP Usual eccl spelling; for civ and sep of chaps, civ and eccl, see following entry. *Eccl* Seq 7.

Addtl eccl bdry alt: 1850 (help cr Monkton Wyld EP).[172]

WHITECHURCH CANONICORUM

AP Usual civ spelling. Incl chap Chideock (sep civ identity early, sep EP 1886[97]), chap Marshwood (sep civ identity early, eccl severed 1953 and transf to Bettiscombe AP[27]), chap Fishponds (no sep civ or eccl identity, eccl severed 1953 and transf to Bettiscombe AP[27]), chap Stanton St Gabriel (sep civ identity early, no sep eccl identity hence this par eccl 'Whitchurch Canonicorum with Stanton St Gabriel', qv). *LG* Seq 34. Addtl civ bdry alt: 1884,[230] 1966 (gains pt Hawkchurch AP, Devon).[179] *Parl* Seq 10.

WIMBORNE ALL SAINTS

AP *LG* Wimb. St Giles Hd. *Eccl* Pimp. RDn. Abol civ and eccl 1732 ent to Wimborne St Giles AP.[231]

WIMBORNE MINSTER

AP Incl chap Holt (sep EP 1882,[185] sep CP 1894[146]). *LG* Badb. Hd, Wimb. Minster Bor (status not sustained), Wimb. & Cranb. PLU, pt Wimb. Minster USD (1892–94), Wimb. & Cranb. RSD (ent 1875–92, pt 1892–94), Wimb. Minster UD. Addtl civ bdry alt: 1886,[85] 1888,[135] 1894 (the pt not in the USD to cr the 2 CPs of Holt, Pamphill),[146] 1921,[99] 1933.[2] *Parl* Seq 1. *Eccl* Royal pec (until 1847), Seq 14 thereafter. Addtl eccl bdry alt: 1877 (cr New Borough and Leigh EP),[39] 1922 (cr Kingston Lacey EP),[149] 1954.[100]

WIMBORNE ST GILES

AP Gains 1732 Wimborne All Saints AP.[231] *LG* Wimb. St Giles Hd, Wimb. & Cranb. PLU, RSD, RD. Civ bdry: 1886.[85] *Parl* Seq 2. *Eccl* Seq 14. Eccl bdry: 1926 (help cr Woodlands EP),[132] 1958.[110]

WINFRITH NEWBURGH

AP Incl chap West Lulworth (sep civ identity early, sep EP 1863[161]). *LG* Seq 37. Civ bdry: 1946.[236] *Parl* Seq 7. *Eccl* Seq 12.

WINTERBORNE CAME

AP Usual civ spelling; for eccl see 'Winterbourne Came'. Gains by 1291 Winterborne Faringdon AP[123] (the latter incl hmlt Winterborne Herringston which claimed to be ex-par, sep civ identity early, eccl remains in Winterbourne Came AP). *LG* Pt Cull. Tree Hd, pt Framp. Lbty, Dorch. PLU, RSD, RD. *Parl* Seq 8.

WINTERBORNE CLENSTON

AP Usual civ spelling; for eccl see 'Winterbourne Clenstone'. Gains 1435 Winterborne Phillipston AP, Winterborne St Nicholas AP.[224] *LG* Seq 9. Civ bdry: 1887.[35] *Parl* Seq 5.

WINTERBORNE FARINGDON

AP Decayed by 1291 and incl in Winterborne Came AP (eccl, 'Winterbourne Came').[232] Incl hmlt Winterborne Herringston (claimed to be ex-par, sep civ identity early from Winterborne Came, in which latter remained eccl).

WINTERBORNE HERRINGSTON

Hmlt in Winterborne Faringdon, the latter decayed by 1291 and this hmlt thereafter in Winterborne Came AP (eccl, 'Winterbourne Came'), claimed to be ex-par and sep civ identity early, remained eccl in Winterbourne Came AP. *LG* Seq 12. Civ bdry: 1894,[48] 1900.[49] *Parl* Seq 8.

WINTERBORNE HOUGHTON

AP Usual civ spelling; for eccl see 'Winterbourne Houghton'. *LG* Seq 20. *Parl* Seq 5.

WINTERBORNE KINGSTON

Chap in Bere Regis AP, sep civ identity early, sep EP 1972 as 'Winterbourne Kingston',[21] qv. *LG* Bere Regis Hd, Blandf. PLU, RSD, RD. *Parl* Seq 2.

WINTERBORNE MONKTON

AP Usual civ spelling; for eccl see 'Winterbourne Monkton'. *LG* Seq 12. Civ bdry: 1894,[48] 1900.[49] *Parl* Seq 8.

WINTERBORNE PHILLOPSTON

AP Whitch. RDn, united 1435 to Winterborne Clenston AP (eccl, 'Winterbourne Clenstone').[224]

WINTERBORNE ST MARTIN

AP Usual civ spelling; for eccl see 'Winterbourne St Martin'. *LG* Seq 14. *Parl* Seq 8.

WINTERBORNE ST NICHOLAS

AP Whitch. RDn, united 1435 to Winterborne Clenston (eccl, 'Winterbourne Clenstone').[224]

WINTERBORNE STEEPLETON

AP Usual civ spelling; for eccl see 'Winterbourne Steepleton'. *LG* Seq 31. *Parl* Seq 10.

WINTERBORNE STICKLAND

AP Usual civ spelling; for eccl see 'Winterbourne Stickland'. *LG* Seq 20. Civ bdry: 1887,[35] 1897.[68] *Parl* Seq 5.

WINTERBORNE TOMSON

AP Usual civ spelling; for eccl see 'Winterbourne Tomson'. *LG* Coombs Ditch Hd, Blandf. PLU, RSD, RD. Abol civ 1933 ent to Anderson AP.[2] *Parl* N'rn Dv (1885–1948).

WINTERBORNE WHITECHURCH

AP Usual civ spelling; for eccl see 'Winterbourne Whitchurch'. *LG* Seq 9. *Parl* Seq 5.

WINTERBORNE ZELSTON

AP Usual civ spelling; for eccl see 'Winterbourne Zelstone'. *LG* Rushmore Hd, Blandf. PLU, RSD, RD. *Parl* Seq 5.

WINTERBOURNE ABBAS

AP *LG* Egg. Hd, Dorch. PLU, RSD, RD. *Parl* Seq 10. *Eccl* Seq 1.

WINTERBOURNE ANDERSON

AP Usual eccl spelling; for civ see 'Anderson'. Free chapel said by some to have been chap in Bere Regis AP, sep par by 14th cent.[14] Whitch. RDn (until 1872), Poole RDn (1872–1962), Milt. RDn (1962–70), Purb. RDn (1970–72). Eccl bdry: 1960.[38] Abol eccl 1972 to help cr Winterbourne Zelstone with Tomson and Anderson EP.[13]

WINTERBOURNE CAME

AP Usual eccl spelling; for civ and early bdry alt, see 'Winterborne Came'. *Eccl* Dorch. RDn. Abol eccl 1971 to help cr Winterbourne Came with Whitcombe EP.[229]

WINTERBOURNE CAME WITH WHITCOMBE
EP Cr 1971 by union Winterbourne Came AP, Whitcombe AP.[229] Dorch. RDn.

WINTERBOURNE CLENSTONE
AP Usual eccl spelling; for civ and early bdry alt, see 'Winterborne Clenston'. *Eccl* Seq 29.

WINTERBOURNE HOUGHTON
AP Usual eccl spelling; for civ see 'Winterborne Houghton'. *Eccl* Seq 29.

WINTERBOURNE KINGSTON
Chap in Bere Regis AP, sep civ identity early as 'Winterborne Kingston', qv, sep EP 1972.[21] Milt. & Blandf. RDn.

WINTERBOURNE MONKTON
AP Usual eccl spelling; for civ see 'Winterborne Monkton'. *Eccl* Seq 9.

WINTERBOURNE ST MARTIN
AP Usual eccl spelling; for civ see 'Winterborne St Martin'. *Eccl* Seq 9.

WINTERBOURNE STEEPLETON
AP Usual eccl spelling; for civ see 'Winterborne Steepleton'. *Eccl* Seq 1.

WINTERBOURNE STICKLAND
AP Usual eccl spelling; for civ see 'Winterborne Stickland'. *Eccl* Seq 29.

WINTERBOURNE TOMSON
AP Usual eccl spelling; for civ see 'Winterborne Tomson'. *Eccl* Pec jurisd Cath Chapter of Sarum (until 1847), Whitch. RDn (1847–72), Poole RDn (1872–1962), Milt. RDn (1962–70), Milt. & Blandf. RDn (1970–72). Abol eccl 1972 to help cr Winterbourne Zelstone with Tomson and Anderson EP.[13]

WINTERBOURNE WHITCHURCH
AP Usual eccl spelling; for civ see 'Winterborne Whitechurch'. *Eccl* Seq 29.

WINTERBOURNE ZELSTONE
AP Usual eccl spelling; for civ see 'Winterborne Zelston'. *Eccl* Whitch. RDn (until 1872), Poole RDn (1872–1962), Milt. RDn (1962–70), Milt. & Blandf. RDn (1970–72). Abol eccl 1972 to help cr Winterbourne Zelstone with Tomson and Anderson EP.[13]

WINTERBOURNE ZELSTONE WITH TOMSON AND ANDERSON
EP Cr 1972 by union Winterbourne Zelstone AP, Winterbourne Tomson AP, Winterbourne Anderson AP.[13] Milt. & Blandf. RDn.

WITCHAMPTON
AP *LG* Seq 11. Civ bdry: 1886.[85] *Parl* Seq 1. *Eccl* Seq 14. Eccl bdry: 1954,[100] 1959.[207]

WITHERSTONE
AP Orig sep par, no civ identity sustained (deemed pt of Powerstock AP). Sinecure rectory. Bridp. RDn (until 1970), Lyme Bay RDn (1970–71). Abol eccl 1971 to help cr Powerstock with West Milton, Witherstone and North Poorton EP.[52]

WOODSFORD
AP *LG* Winf. Hd, Dorch. PLU, RSD, RD. *Parl* Seq 8. *Eccl* Seq 9.

WOODLANDS
Chap in Horton AP, sep civ identity early, sep EP 1926 (from Horton AP, Wimborne St Giles AP, Gussage St Michael AP).[132] *LG* Seq 18. *Parl* Seq 2. *Eccl* Wimb. RDn.

EAST WOODYATES
Ex-par place, sep CP 1858,[131] abol eccl 1925 ent to Pentridge AP.[138] *LG* Cranb. Hd, Wimb. & Cranb. PLU,[232] RSD, RD. Abol 1933 ent to Pentridge AP.[2] *Parl* E'rn Dv (1885–1918), N'rn Dv (1918–48).

WEST WOODYATES
Orig sep par[233] later claimed to be ex-par, sep CP 1858,[131] abol eccl 1925 ent to Handley EP.[138] *LG* Wimb. St Giles Hd, Wimb. & Cranb. PLU, RSD, RD. Abol 1933 ent to Pentridge AP.[2] *Parl* E'rn Dv (1885–1918), N'rn Dv (1918–48).

WOOL
Chap in Coombe Keynes AP, sep civ identity early, sep EP 1844.[101] *LG* Seq 3. Civ bdry: 1946.[236] *Parl* Seq 7. *Eccl* Dorch. RDn (1844–72), Purb. RDn (1872–1974). Later called Wool with East Burton. Abol eccl 1974 to help cr Wool, East Burton and Coombe Keynes EP.[102]

WOOL, EAST BURTON AND COOMBE KEYNES
EP Cr 1974 by union Wool with East Burton EP, Coombe Keynes AP.[102] Purb. RDn.

WOOLAND
AP *LG* Seq 36. *Parl* Seq 5. *Eccl* Donative, Whitch. RDn (until 1872), Milt. RDn (1872–1954), Sturm. Newt. RDn (1955–72), Blackm. Vale RDn (1973–*).

GLANVILLES WOOTTON
AP Usual civ spelling; for eccl see 'Wootton Glanville'. *LG* Seq 5. *Parl* Seq 10.

NORTH WOOTTON
Chap in Sherborne AP, sep civ identity early, sep EP 1812.[79] *LG* Seq 25. *Parl* Seq 6. *Eccl* Shaft. RDn (1812–72), Stalbridge RDn (1872–1954), Sherb. RDn (1955–72). Abol eccl 1972 to help cr Folke, North Wootton and Haydon EP.[125]

WOOTTON FITZPAINE
AP *LG* Seq 35. Civ bdry: 1883,[24] 1884.[9] *Parl* Seq 10. *Eccl* Seq 7.

WOOTTON GLANVILLE
AP Usual eccl spelling; for civ see 'Glanvilles Wootton'. *Eccl* Whitch. RDn (until 1872), Cerne RDn (1872–1929). Abol eccl 1929 to help cr Wootton Glanville with Holnest EP.[72]

WOOTTON GLANVILLE WITH HOLNEST
EP Cr 1929 by union Wootton Glanville AP, pt Long Burton with Holnest AP, pt Haydon AP.[72] Cerne RDn (1929–54), Sherb. RDn (1955–*).

WORTH MATRAVERS
AP *LG* Seq 24. *Parl* Seq 4. *Eccl* Seq 12.

WRAXALL
AP *LG* Egg. Hd, Beam. PLU, RSD, RD. *Parl* Seq 10. *Eccl* Seq 4.

WYKE REGIS
AP Incl chap & bor Weymouth (sep civ identity early, bor merged 1571 into Weym. & Melc. Regis Bor, sep EP 1836[225]). *LG* Wimb. St Giles

Hd, Weym. PLU, pt Weym. & Melc. Regis MB (1835–94), pt Weym. & Melc. Regis USD, pt Weym. RSD, Weym. RD. Addtl civ bdry alt: 1894 (loses the pt in the MB to Weymouth CP),[70] 1895.[167] Abol civ 1933 pt to Weymouth CP, pt to Chickerell AP.[2] *Parl* Pt Weym. Parl Bor (until Weymouth gains sep identity), pt Weymouth & Melc. Regis Parl Bor (1832–85), S'rn Dv (1885–1948). *Eccl* Seq 11. Addtl eccl bdry alt: 1901 (cr Weymouth St Paul EP),[228] 1956 (help cr Weymouth St Edmund EP),[96] 1956.[226]

WYNFORD EAGLE

Parochial chap in Toller Fratrum AP, sep civ identity early, sep EP 1911.[221] *LG* Seq 29. *Parl* Seq 10. *Eccl* Dorch. RDn (1911–16), Abbotsb. RDn (1916–70), Dorch. RDn (1970–*).

YETMINSTER

AP Usual civ spelling, eccl spelling after 1955 when loses chap Chetnole to help cr Leigh with Chetnole EP.[95] Incl chap Leigh (sep EP 1849,[156] sep CP 1866[22]), chap Chetnole (sep civ identity early, no sep eccl identity, hence until 1955 this par eccl 'Yetminster with Chetnole', qv). *LG* Seq 39. Addtl civ bdry alt: 1886.[82] *Parl* Seq 9. *Eccl* Sherb. RDn (1955–*).

YETMINSTER WITH CHETNOLE

AP Usual eccl spelling; for civ and sep of chaps, see prev entry. *Eccl* Pec jurisd Cath Chapter of Sarum (until 1847), Pimp. RDn (1847–72), Blandf. RDn (1872–1955). Reconstituted as 'Yetminster' (qv) 1955 when loses chap Chetnole to help cr Leigh with Chetnole EP.[95]

ESSEX

ABBREVIATIONS

Abbreviations particular to Essex follow. Those general abbreviations in use throughout the *Guide* are found on page xix.

Ardl.	Ardleigh
Bark.	Barking
Barst.	Barstable
Belch.	Belchamp
Bill.	Billericay
Braint.	Braintree
Brentw.	Brentwood
Bump.	Bumpstead
Canew.	Canewdon
Chaf.	Chafford
Chelm.	Chelmsford
Chigw.	Chigwell
Clav.	Clavering
Cogg.	Coggeshall
Colch.	Colchester
Danb.	Danbury
Ep.	Epping
Freshw.	Freshwell
Halst.	Halstead
Harw.	Harwich
Hatf. Pev.	Hatfield Peverel
Hav.	Havering
Heding.	Hedingham
Hinckf.	Hinckford
Ingat.	Ingatestone
Lamb.	Lambourne
Lexd.	Lexden
Nwpt.	Newport
Ong.	Ongar
Ors.	Orsett
Redbr.	Redbridge
Rochf.	Rochford
Saff. Wald.	Saffron Walden
Sampf.	Sampford
S'end	Southend
Stan.	Stanstead
Tendr.	Tendring
Thurst.	Thurstable
Uttl.	Uttlesford
Walt'stow	Walthamstow
Wanst.	Wanstead
Wickf.	Wickford
Winst.	Winstree
Woodf.	Woodford
Yeld.	Yeldham

SEQUENCES

An abbreviated entrry prefixed by 'Seq' is used in the parochial entries to avoid repeating often the names of superior units of administration. The content of each sequence is shown below.

Local Government Sequences ('LG')

SEQ 1 Chelm. Hd, PLU, RSD, RD
SEQ 2 Clav. Hd, Bishop's Stortford PLU, RSD, Stan. RD (1894–1934), Saff. Wald. RD (1934–74)
SEQ 3 Clav. Hd, Saff. Wald. PLU, RSD, RD
SEQ 4 Dengie Hd, Maldon PLU, RSD, RD
SEQ 5 Dunmow Hd, Chelm. PLU, RSD, RD
SEQ 6 Dunmow Hd, PLU, RSD, RD
SEQ 7 Freshw. Hd, Dunmow PLU, RSD, RD (1894–1934), Braint. RD (1934–74)
SEQ 8 Freshw. Hd, Saff. Wald. PLU, RSD, RD
SEQ 9 Harlow Hd, Bishop's Stortford PLU, RSD, Stan. RD (1894–1934), Dunmow RD (1934–74)
SEQ 10 Harlow Hd, Ep. PLU, RSD, RD (1894–1955), Ep. & Ong. RD (1955–74)
SEQ 11 Hinckf. Hd, Braint. PLU, RSD, RD
SEQ 12 Hinckf. Hd, Dunmow PLU, RSD, RD
SEQ 13 Hinckf. Hd, Halst. PLU, RSD, RD
SEQ 14 Hinckf. Hd, Risbridge PLU, RSD, Bump. RD (1894–1934), Halst. RD (1934–74)
SEQ 15 Hinckf. Hd, Sudbury PLU, RSD, Belch. RD (1894–1934), Halst. RD (1934–74)
SEQ 16 Lexd. Hd, Halst. PLU, RSD, RD
SEQ 17 Lexd. Hd, Lexd. & Winst. PLU, RSD, RD
SEQ 18 Ong. Hd, Ep. PLU, RSD, RD (1894–1955), Ep. & Ong. RD (1955–74)
SEQ 19 Ong. Hd, PLU, RSD, RD (1894–1955), Ep. & Ong. RD (1955–74)
SEQ 20 Rochf. Hd, PLU, RSD, RD
SEQ 21 Tendr. Hd, PLU, RSD, RD
SEQ 22 Thurst. Hd, Maldon PLU, RSD, RD
SEQ 23 Uttl. Hd, Bishop's Stortford PLU, RSD, Stan. RD (1894–1934), Saff. Wald. RD (1934–74)
SEQ 24 Uttl. Hd, Saff. Wald. PLU, RSD, RD
SEQ 25 Winst. Hd, Lexd. & Winst. PLU, RSD, RD
SEQ 26 Witham Hd, Braint. PLU, RSD, RD
SEQ 27 Witham Hd, Maldon PLU, RSD, RD

Parliamentary Sequences ('Parl')

SEQ 1 N'rn Dv (1832–67), N-E Dv (1867–85), E'rn Dv (1885–1918), Colch. Dv/CC (1918–*)
SEQ 2 N'rn Dv (1832–67), N-E Dv (1867–85), E'rn Dv (1885–1918), Maldon Dv/CC (1918–*)
SEQ 3 N'rn Dv (1832–67), N-E Dv (1867–85), E'rn Dv (1885–1918), Maldon Dv/CC (1918–70), Braint. CC (1970–*)
SEQ 4 N'rn Dv (1832–67), N-E Dv (1867–85), E'rn Dv (1885–1918), Saff. Wald. Dv/CC (1918–*)
SEQ 5 N'rn Dv (1832–67), N-E Dv (1867–85), N-E'rn Dv (1885–1918), Harw. Dv/CC (1918–*)
SEQ 6 N'rn Dv (1832–67), N-E Dv (1867–85), N'rn Dv (1885–1918), Saff. Wald. Dv/CC (1918–*)
SEQ 7 N'rn Dv (1832–67), N-W Dv (1867–85), Mid Dv (1885–1918), Chelm. Dv/CC (1918–70), Braint. CC (1970–*)
SEQ 8 N'rn Dv (1832–67), N-W Dv (1867–85), N'rn Dv (1885–1918), Saff. Wald. Dv/CC (1918–*)
SEQ 9 S'rn Dv (1832–67), N-E Dv (1867–85), S-E'rn Dv (1885–1918), Maldon Dv/CC (1918–*)
SEQ 10 S'rn Dv (1832–67), N-W Dv (1867–85), Mid Dv (1885–1918), Chelm. Dv/CC (1918–*)
SEQ 11 S'rn Dv (1832–67), N-W Dv (1867–85), Mid Dv (1885–1918), Chelm. Dv/CC (1918–70), Braint. CC (1970–*)
SEQ 12 S'rn Dv (1832–67), N-W Dv (1867–85), W'rn Dv (1885–1918), Ep. Dv/CC (1918–70), Brentw. & Ong. CC (1970–*)
SEQ 13 S'rn Dv (1832–67), N-W Dv (1867–85), W'rn Dv (1885–1918), Ep. Dv/CC (1918–70), Ep. Forest CC (1970–*)
SEQ 14 S'rn Dv (1832–67), N-W Dv (1867–85), W'rn Dv (1885–1918), Ep. Dv/CC (1918–55), Chigw. CC (1955–70), Harlow CC (1970–*)
SEQ 15 S'rn Dv (1832–67), N-W Dv (1867–85), W'rn Dv (1885–1918), Saff. Wald. Dv/CC (1918–*)
SEQ 16 S'rn Dv (1832–67), South Dv (1867–85), S-E'rn Dv (1885–1948), Bill. CC (1948–55), S E Essex (1955–*)
SEQ 17 S'rn Dv (1832–67), South Dv (1867–85), S-E'rn Dv (1885–1948), Southend East BC (1948–70), Maldon CC (1970–*)

Ecclesiastical Sequences ('Eccl')

In Colchester AD orig:
SEQ 1 Colch. RDn
SEQ 2 Lexd. RDn (until 1847), Cogg. RDn (1847–1907), Cogg. & Tey RDn (1907–*)
SEQ 3 Lexd. RDn (until 1847), Cogg. RDn

(1847–1907), Witham RDn (1907–*)
SEQ 4 Lexd. RDn (until 1847), Dedham RDn (1847–*)
SEQ 5 Lexd. RDn (until 1847), Halst. RDn (1847–1907), Cogg. & Tey RDn (1907–*)
SEQ 6 Lexd. RDn (until 1847), Halst. RDn (1847–1907), Halst. & Heding. RDn (1907–*)
SEQ 7 Lexd. RDn (until 1847), Mersea RDn (1847–1907), Colch. RDn (1907–*)
SEQ 8 Nwpt. RDn (until 1907), Nwpt. & Stan. RDn (1907–*)
SEQ 9 Nwpt. RDn (until 1847), Saff. Wald. RDn (1847–*)
SEQ 10 Sampf. RDn (until 1907), Dunmow RDn (1907–*)
SEQ 11 Sampf. RDn (until 1847), Nwpt. RDn (1847–1907), Nwpt. & Stan. RDn (1907–*)
SEQ 12 Sampf. RDn (until 1907), Saff. Wald. RDn (1907–*)
SEQ 13 Tendr. RDn (until 1847), Ardl. RDn (1847–95), Ardl. & Harw. RDn (1895–1907), Harw. RDn (1907–*)
SEQ 14 Tendr. RDn (until 1847), Harw. RDn (1847–95), Ardl. & Harw. RDn (1895–1907), Harw. RDn (1907–*)
SEQ 15 Tendr. RDn (until 1847), Harw. RDn (1847–95), St Osyth RDn (1895–*)
SEQ 16 Tendr. RDn (until 1847), St Osyth RDn (1847–*)
SEQ 17 Witham RDn
SEQ 18 Witham RDn (until 1907), Braint. RDn (1907–*)
SEQ 19 Witham RDn (until 1847), Hatf. Pev. RDn (1847–1907), Maldon RDn (1907–*)
SEQ 20 Witham RDn (until 1847), Hatf. Pev. RDn (1847–1907), Witham RDn (1907–*)

In Essex AD orig:

SEQ 21 Barst. RDn (until 1895), Danb. RDn (1895–1907), Wickf. RDn (1907–*)
SEQ 22 Barst. RDn (until 1895), Ors. RDn (1895–1907), Ors. & Grays RDn (1907–*)
SEQ 23 Barst. RDn (until 1845), Bill. RDn (1845–95), Barst. RDn (1895–1907), Barst. o'wise Brentw. RDn (1907–*)
SEQ 24 Barst. RDn (until 1845), Bill. RDn (1845–95), Ingat. RDn (1895–1907), Barst. o'wise Brentw. RDn (1907–*)
SEQ 25 Barst. RDn (until 1845), Ors. RDn (1845–1907), Ors. & Grays RDn (1907–55), Basildon RDn (1955–*)
SEQ 26 Barst. RDn (until 1845), Ors. RDn (1845–1907), Ors. & Grays RDn (1907–*)
SEQ 27 Chaf. RDn (until 1966), Hav. RDn (1966–*)
SEQ 28 Chaf. RDn (until 1845), Bill. RDn (1845–95), Barst. RDn (1895–1907), Barst. o'wise Brentw. RDn (1907–*)
SEQ 29 Chaf. RDn (until 1845), Ors. RDn (1845–1907), Ors. & Grays RDn (1907–*)
SEQ 30 Chaf. RDn (until 1907), Ors. & Grays RDn (1907–52), Chaf. o'wise Romford RDn (1952–66), Hav. RDn (1966–*)
SEQ 31 Chelm. RDn
SEQ 32 Chelm. RDn (until 1956), Roding RDn (1956–*)
SEQ 33 Chelm. RDn (until 1845), Ingat. RDn (1845–1907), Barst. o'wise Brentw. RDn (1907–*)
SEQ 34 Chelm. RDn (until 1845), Danb. RDn (1845–1907), Chelm. RDn (1907–*)
SEQ 35 Chelm. RDn (until 1845), Danb. RDn (1845–1907), Wickf. RDn (1907–*)
SEQ 36 Dengie RDn
SEQ 37 Dengie RDn (until 1845), Maldon RDn (1845–*)
SEQ 38 Ong. RDn (until 1845), Lamb. RDn (1845–1907), Chigw. RDn (1907–*)
SEQ 39 Ong. RDn
SEQ 40 Rochf. RDn (until 1845), Canew. RDn (1845–1907), Canew. & S'end RDn (1907–*)
SEQ 41 Rochf. RDn (until 1907), Canew. & S'end RDn (1907–*)
SEQ 42 Rochf. RDn (until 1907), Wickf. RDn (1907–*)

In Middx AD orig:

SEQ 43 Dunmow RDn
SEQ 44 Dunmow RDn (until 1845), Roding RDn (1845–1922), Harlow RDn (1922–*)
SEQ 45 Harlow RDn
SEQ 46 Heding. RDn (until 1907), Belch. RDn (1907–*)
SEQ 47 Heding. RDn (until 1895), Braint. RDn (1895–*)
SEQ 48 Heding. RDn (until 1907), Halst. & Heding RDn (1907–*)
SEQ 49 Heding. RDn (until 1895), Halst. RDn (1895–1907), Halst. & Heding. RDn (1907–*)
SEQ 50 Heding. RDn (until 1847), Yeld. RDn (1847–1907), Belch. RDn (1907–*)
SEQ 51 Heding. RDn (until 1847), Yeld. RDn (1847–1907), Halst. & Heding RDn (1907–*)

DIOCESES AND ARCHDEACONRIES

The Essex pars were in London dioc until 1846, in Roch dioc 1846–77, in St Albans dioc 1877–1914 and in Chelm dioc from 1914. The major exception was Bark. RDn, pt of which was kept in London dioc 1846–67 then transf to Roch dioc as the other pt of the RDn had been in 1846. Details of Bark. RDn before 1867 are sep noted below. RDns were organised in ADs as follows:

COLCHESTER AD
Ardl. RDn (1847–95), Ardl. & Harw. RDn (1895–1907), Belch. RDn (1907–*), Braint. RDn (1847–*), Cogg. RDn (1847–1907), Cogg. & Tey RDn (1907–*), Colch. RDn, Dedham RDn (1847–*), Dunmow RDn (1907–*), Halst. RDn (1847–1907), Halst. & Heding. RDn (1907–*), Harw. RDn (1847–95), Harw. RDn (1907–*), Hatf. Pev. RDn (1847–1907), Heding. RDn (1845–1907), Lexd. RDn (until 1847), Mersea RDn (1847–1907), Nwpt. RDn (until 1907), Nwpt. & Stan. RDn (1907–*), Saff. Wald. RDn (1847–*), St Osyth RDn (1847–*), Sampf. RDn (until 1907), Tendr. RDn (until 1847), Jurisd Waltham (until 1847), Witham RDn, Yeldham RDn (1847–1907)

ESSEX AD (until 1922, then renamed 'West Ham')
Bark. (until 1895 [see note above on diocs]), Bark. RDn (1907–22), N Bark. RDn (1895–1907), S Bark. RDn (1895–1907), W Bark. RDn (1895–1907), Barst. RDn (until 1907), Barst. o'wise Brentw. RDn (1907–22), Bill. RDn (1845–95), Canew. RDn (1845–1907), Canew. & S'end RDn (1907–22), Chaf. RDn (until 1907), Chaf. o'wise Romford RDn (1907–22), Chelm. RDn, Chigw. RDn (1883–1922), Danb. RDn (1845–1907), Dengie RDn, Dunmow RDn (1845–1907), Ep. RDn (1845–62), W Ham RDn (1907–22), Harlow RDn (1845–1922), Ingat. RDn (1845–1907), Lamb. RDn (1845–1907), Leyton RDn (1916–22), Maldon RDn (1845–1922), Ong. RDn, Ors. RDn (1845–1907), Ors. & Grays RDn (1907–22), Rochf. RDn (until 1907), Roding RDn (1862–1922), Romford RDn (1862–8), Walt'stow & Chingford RDn (1916–22), Walt'stow & Leyton RDn (1907–16), Wanst. & Woodf. RDn (1916–22), Wickf. RDn (1907–22)

WEST HAM AD (1922–*, renaming of Essex AD)
Bark. RDn, Chaf. o'wise Romford RDn (1922–66), Chigw. RDn, West Ham RDn (1922–66), Harlow RDn (1952–*), Hav. RDn (1966–*), Leyton RDn (1922–66), Newham RDn (1966–*), Ong. RDn (1952–*), Ors. & Grays RDn (1922–52), Redbr. RDn (1966–*), Walt'stow & Chingford RDn (1922–66), Wanst. & Woodf. RDn (1922–66), Waltham Forest RDn (1966–*)

pt of MIDDLESEX AD (until 1845)
Dunmow RDn, Harlow RDn, Heding. RDn

SOUTHEND AD (1922–*)
Barst. o'wise Brentw. RDn, Basildon RDn (1955–*), Canew. & S'end RDn, Chelm. RDn, Dengie RDn, Harlow RDn (1922–52), Maldon RDn, Ong. RDn (1922–52), Ors. & Grays RDn, Roding RDn, Wickf. RDn

THE PARISHES OF ESSEX

ABBERTON
AP *LG* Seq 25. *Parl* N'rn Dv (1832–67), N-E Dv (1867–85), N-E'rn Dv (1885–1918), Colch. Dv/CC (1918–*). *Eccl* Lexd. RDn (until 1847), Mersea RDn (1847–1907), Colch. RDn (1907–61). Abol eccl 1961 to help cr Abberton with Langenhoe EP.[1]

ABBERTON WITH LANGENHOE
EP Cr 1961 by union Abberton AP, Langenhoe AP.[1] Colch. RDn.

ALDBOROUGH HATCH
EP Cr 1863 from Great Ilford EP, Barkingside Trinity EP.[2] Bark. RDn (1863–95 [London dioc 1863–67]), S Bark. RDn (1895–1907), Bark.RDn (1907–66), Redbr. RDn (1966–*). Bdry: 1934 (help cr Barkingside St Laurence EP),[3] 1934,[4] 1939,[5] 1960 (help cr Chadwell Heath St Mark, Mark's Gate EP).[6]

ALDERSBROOK
EP Cr 1914 from Wanstead AP, Little Ilford AP.[10] Walt'stow & Leyton RDn (1914–16), Wanst. & Woodf. RDn (1916–66), Redbr. RDn (1966–*).

ALDHAM
AP *LG* Seq 17. Civ bdry: 1883,[8] 1889,[7] 1949 (incl help cr Eight Ash Green CP).[9] *Parl* Seq 1. *Eccl* Lexd. RDn (until 1847), Halst. RDn (1847–68), Dedham RDn (1868–1907), Cogg. & Tey RDn (1907–*).

ALL SAINTS IN STANWAY AND LEXDEN
EP Cr 1845 from Stanway AP, Lexden AP.[11] Cogg. RDn (1845–95), Colch. RDn (1895–1962). Bdry: 1955,[12] 1956.[13] Renamed 1962 'Shrub

End'.[14]

ALPHAMSTONE

AP *LG* Seq 15. Civ bdry: 1883,[8] 1885.[15] *Parl* Seq 4. *Eccl* Seq 48.

ALRESFORD

AP *LG* Seq 21. Civ bdry: 1948.[16] *Parl* Seq 5. *Eccl* Seq 16.

ALTHORNE

AP *LG* Seq 4. Civ bdry: 1934.[17] *Parl* Seq 9. *Eccl* Seq 36.

ARDLEIGH

AP Incl former ex-par area of No Man's Land. *LG* Seq 21. Civ bdry: 1934.[17] *Parl* Seq 5. *Eccl* Tendr. RDn (until 1847), Ardl. RDn (1847–95), Ardl. & Harw. RDn (1895–1907), Dedham RDn (1907–*). Eccl bdry: 1868 (help cr Colchester St John EP).[18]

ARKESDEN

AP *LG* Seq 24. Civ bdry: 1883.[8] *Parl* Seq 8. *Eccl* Newp. RDn (until 1895), Saff. Wald. RDn (1895–1907), Newp. & Stan. RDn (1907–*).

ASHDON

AP Incl hmlt Bartlow End (sep CP 1866[19]). *LG* Seq 8. Addtl civ bdry alt: 1883,[8] 1946,[20] 1965 (exchanges pts with Bartlow AP, Castle Camps AP, both Cambs & IoE).[21] *Parl* Seq 8. *Eccl* Seq 12.

ASHELDHAM

AP *LG* Seq 4. Civ bdry: 1889.[22] *Parl* Seq 9. *Eccl* Seq 36.

ASHEN

AP *LG* Seq 14. Civ bdry: 1883,[8] 1885.[23] *Parl* Seq 6. *Eccl* Seq 50.

ASHINGDON

AP *LG* Seq 20. Civ bdry: 1946.[20] *Parl* Seq 17. *Eccl* Seq 41.

AVELEY

AP *LG* Chaf. Hd, Ors. PLU, RSD, RD (1894–1929), Purfleet UD (1929–36). Civ bdry: 1883.[8] Abol civ 1936 to help cr Thurrock CP.[24] *Parl* S'rn Dv (1832–67), South Dv (1867–85), S-E'rn Dv (1885–1948). *Eccl* Seq 29. Eccl bdry: 1958 (help cr Belhus Park EP).[25]

GREAT BADDOW

AP *LG* Seq 1. Civ bdry: 1946.[20] *Parl* Seq 10. *Eccl* Seq 31. Eccl bdry: 1874 (help cr Galleywood Common EP).[26]

LITTLE BADDOW

AP *LG* Seq 1. *Parl* Seq 10. *Eccl* Seq 31.

BALLINGDON

AP Sometimes 'Ballingdon cum Brundon'. Orig AP but church in ruins and deemed chap in Sudbury All Saints (Suffolk), sep civ identity retained (pt Suffolk [Babergh Hd], pt Essex [Hinckf. Hd]), the Essex pt lost 1896 to Sudbury MB and CP and ent W Suffolk thereafter.[27] *LG* Sudbury PLU, pt Sudbury MB (1892–96), pt Sudbury USD (1883–94), Sudbury RSD (ent 1875–83, pt (1892–94), pt Belch. RD (1894–96). Civ bdry: 1883.[8] *Parl* Essex pt, North Dv (1832–67), N-E Dv (1867–85), N'rn Dv (1885–1918). *Eccl* See main entry in Suffolk.

GREAT BARDFIELD

AP Incl hmlt and chap Bardfield Saling (eccl, 'Little Saling', sep par 1574[28]). *LG* Great Bardfield Bor (status not sustained), Seq 7. Addtl civ bdry alt: 1883,[8] 1889,[29] 1955.[30] *Parl* Seq 8. *Eccl* Seq 10.

LITTLE BARDFIELD

AP *LG* Freshw. Hd, Dunmow PLU, RSD, RD. Civ bdry: 1883,[8] 1889,[29] 1956.[30] *Parl* Seq 8. *Eccl* Seq 10.

BARDFIELD SALING

AP Usual civ spelling; for eccl see 'Little Saling'. Hmlt and chap in Great Barfield, sep par 1574.[28] *LG* Seq 7. Civ bdry: 1888.[31] *Parl* Seq 8.

BARKING

AP Incl Great Ilford (orig sep AP, later considered ward of Barking, some sep civ rights regained early, sep EP 1830,[33] sep CP 1866[32] as 'Ilford'). *LG* Becontree Hd, Romford PLU, Bark. Town USD (pt 1882–85, ent 1885–94), Romf. RSD (ent 1875–82, pt 1882–85), Bark. Town UD (1894–1931), Bark. MB (1931–65). Addtl civ bdry alt: 1893,[34] 1907,[35] 1934.[36] Transf 1965 to Gtr London (pt Bark. LB, pt Newham LB).[37] *Parl* S'rn Dv (1832–67), South Dv (1867–85), S'rn Dv (1885–1918), Romf. Dv (1918–45), Bark. BC (1945–70), Gtr London thereafter. *Eccl* Bark. RDn (until1895 [London dioc until 1867]), S Bark. RDn (1895–1907), Bark. RDn (1907–73). Addtl eccl bdry alt: 1914 (help cr Goodmayes All Saints EP),[38] 1913 (help cr Becontree St Elizabeth EP),[39] 1934 (help cr Becontree St John EP),[40] 1934 (help cr Barking St Erkenwald EP),[41] 1934 (help cr Becontree St Alban EP),[42] 1935 (help cr Becontree St Mary EP),[43] 1936 (help cr Becontree St Cedd EP),[44] 1938 (help cr Barking St Patrick EP),[45] 1971.[46] Abol eccl 1973 to help cr Barking St Mary with St Patrick EP.[47]

BARKING ST ERKENWALD

EP Cr 1934 from Barking AP, Goodmayes All Saints EP.[41] Bark. RDn.

BARKING ST MARY WITH ST PATRICK

EP Cr 1973 by union Barking AP, Barking St Patrick EP.[47] Bark. RDn.

BARKING ST PATRICK

EP Cr 1938 from Barking AP.[45] Bark. RDn. Abol 1973 to help cr Barking St Mary with St Patrick EP.[47]

BARKING ROAD

EP Cr 1868 from Plaistow St Mary EP, West Ham AP.[48] Bark. RDn (1868–95), W Bark. RDn (1895–1907), W Ham RDn (1907–61). Abol 1961 pt to Victoria Docks St Luke EP, pt to Canning Town St Cedd EP.[49]

BARKINGSIDE ST CEDD

EP Cr 1961 from Wanstead Holy Trinity, Hermon Hill EP, Barkingside Trinity EP, Barkingside St George EP.[50] Bark. RDn (1961–66), Redbr. RDn (1966–*).

BARKINGSIDE ST FRANCIS OF ASSISI

EP Cr 1956 from Barkingside Trinity EP.[51] Bark. RDn (1956–66), Redbr. RDn (1966–*).

BARKINGSIDE ST GEORGE

EP Cr 1928 from Barkingside Trinity EP, Great Ilford EP.[52] Bark. RDn (1928–66), Redbr. RDn (1966–*). Bdry: 1961 (help cr Barkingside St Cedd EP).[50]

BARKINGSIDE ST LAURENCE

EP Cr 1934 from Barkingside Trinity EP, Great Ilford EP, Aldborough Hatch EP.[3] Bark. RDn (1934–66), Redbr. RDn (1966–*).

BARKINGSIDE TRINITY

EP Cr 1841 from Great Ilford EP.[53] Bark. RDn (1841–95 [London dioc 1841–67]), S Bark. RDn (1895–1907), Bark. RDn (1907–66), Redbr. RDn (1966–*). Bdry: 1863 (help cr Aldborough Hatch EP),[2] 1928 (help cr Barkingside St George EP),[52] 1934 (help cr Barkingside St Laurence EP),[3] 1934,[4] 1956 (help cr Barkingside St Francis of Assisi EP),[51] 1961 (help cr Hainault EP),[54] 1961 (help cr Barkingside St Cedd EP).[50]

BARLING

AP Usual civ spelling; for eccl see 'Barling Magna'. *LG* Rochf. Hd, PLU, RSD, RD. Civ bdry: 1883.[8] Abol civ 1946 to help cr Barling Magna CP.[20] *Parl* S'rn Dv (1832–67), South Dv (1867–85), S-E'rn Dv (1885–1948).

BARLING MAGNA

AP Usual eccl spelling; for civ see prev entry. *Eccl* Pec jurisd Dean & Chapter of St Paul's, London (until 1845), Seq 40 thereafter.

CP Cr 1946 by union Barling AP, pt Great Wakering AP, pt Little Wakering AP.[20] *LG* Rochf. RD. *Parl* Southend East BC (1948–70), Maldon CC (1970–*).

BARNSTON

AP *LG* Seq 6. Civ bdry: 1883,[8] 1889.[29] *Parl* Seq 8. *Eccl* Seq 43.

BARTLOW END

Hmlt in Ashdon AP, sep CP 1866.[19] *LG* Freshw. Hd, Linton PLU,[66] RSD, Saff. Wald. RD. Abol 1946 ent to Ashdon AP.[20] *Parl* N-W Dv (1867–85), N'rn Dv (1885–1918), Saff. Wald. Dv (1918–48).

BASILDON

Chap in Laindon (sep CP 1866,[19] no sep eccl identity though sometimes called 'rectory'[55]). *LG* Barst. Hd, Bill. PLU, RSD, RD (1894–1935), Bill. UD (1935–37). Abol 1937 to help cr Billericay CP.[56] *Parl* S'rn Dv (1832–67), South Dv (1867–85), Mid Dv (1885–1918), S-E'rn Dv (1918–48).

BASILDON ST ANDREW

EP Cr 1957 from Laindon AP, Nevendon AP, Pitsea AP, Vange AP, Ramsden Crays AP.[57] Basildon RDn.

BEAUMONT

AP *LG* Tendr. Hd. *Eccl* Tendr. RDn. United 1678 with Moze AP, the union civ called 'Beaumont cum Moze', eccl 'Beaumont with Moze'.[58]

BEAUMONT CUM MOZE

Civ spelling of par cr 1678 by union Beaumont AP, Moze AP (for eccl see following entry).[58] *LG* Seq 21. *Parl* Seq 5.

BEAUMONT WITH MOZE

Eccl spelling of par cr 1678 by union Beaumont AP, Moze AP (for civ see prev entry).[58] *Eccl* Seq 15.

BECONTREE ST ALBAN

EP Cr 1934 from Barking AP, Dagenham St Martin EP.[42] Bark. RDn.

BECONTREE ST CEDD

EP Cr 1936 from Barking AP.[44] Bark. RDn.

BECONTREE ST ELIZABETH

EP Cr 1931 from Barking AP, Dagenham AP.[39] Bark. RDn.

BECONTREE ST GEORGE

EP Cr 1935 from Dagenham AP.[59] Chaf. RDn (1935–66), Bark. RDn (1966–*).

BECONTREE ST JOHN

EP Cr 1934 from Barking AP.[40] Bark. RDn.

BECONTREE ST MARY

EP Cr 1935 from Dagenham AP.[43] Chaf. RDn (1935–66), Bark. RDn (1966–*). Bdry: 1969 (help cr Rush Green EP).[60]

BECONTREE ST PETER

EP Cr 1931 from Dagenham AP, Becontree St Thomas EP.[61] Chaf. RDn (1931–66), Bark. RDn (1966–*).

BECONTREE ST THOMAS

EP Cr 1922 from Goodmayes All Saints EP, Dagenham AP.[62] Bark. RDn. Bdry: 1931 (help cr Becontree St Peter EP).[61]

HIGH BEECH

EP Cr 1836 from Waltham Abbey AP.[63] Romf. RDn (1836–83), Chigw. RDn (1883–*). Bdry: 1957,[64] 1972.[65]

BELCHAMP OTTEN

AP *LG* Seq 15. Civ bdry: 1885.[15] *Parl* Seq 6. *Eccl* Seq 50.

BELCHAMP ST PAUL

AP *LG* Seq 15. Civ bdry: 1888.[67] *Parl* Seq 6. *Eccl* Pec jurisd Dean & Chapter of St Paul's, London (until 1845), Seq 50 thereafter.

BELCHAMP WALTER

AP *LG* Seq 15. Civ bdry: 1885.[15] *Parl* Seq 6. *Eccl* Seq 46.

BELHUS PARK

EP Cr 1958 from Aveley AP, South Ockendon AP, Stifford AP.[25] Ors. & Grays RDn. Bdry: 1970.[68]

NORTH BENFLEET

AP Incl pt Canvey Island (sep EP 1739,[70] sep CP 1880[90]). *LG* Barst. Hd, Bill. PLU, RSD, RD (1894–1935), Bill. UD (1935–37). Addtl civ bdry alt: 1880.[69] Abol civ 1937 to help cr Billericay CP.[56] *Parl* S'rn Dv (1832–67), South Dv (1867–85), Mid Dv (1885–1918), S-E'rn Dv (1918–48). *Eccl* Barst. RDn (until 1845), Rochf. RDn (1845–1907), Wickf. RDn (1907–55), Basildon RDn (1955–*). Addtl eccl bdry alt: 1964 (help cr New Thundersley EP).[71]

SOUTH BENFLEET

AP Incl pt Canvey Island (sep EP 1739,[70] sep CP 1880[90]). *LG* Barst. Hd, Bill. PLU (1835–47), Rochf. PLU (1847–1930), RSD, RD (1894–1929), Benfleet UD (1929–74). Addtl civ bdry alt: 1880.[69] *Parl* Seq 16. *Eccl* Barst. RDn (until

1845), Rochf. RDn (1845–1907), Canew. & S'end RDn (1907–*). Addtl eccl bdry alt: 1964 (help cr New Thundersley EP).[71]

GREAT BENTLEY
AP *LG* Seq 21. *Parl* Seq 5. *Eccl* Seq 16.

LITTLE BENTLEY
AP *LG* Seq 21. *Parl* Seq 5. *Eccl* Tendr. RDn (until 1847), Ardl. RDn (1847–95), Ardl. & Harw. RDn (1895–1907), Harw. RDn (1907–69), St Osyth RDn (1969–*).

BERDEN
AP *LG* Berden Bor (status not sustained), Seq 2. *Parl* Seq 8. *Eccl* Seq 8.

BERECHURCH
AP Chap in Colchester Holy Trinity, sep par 1536.[73] *LG* Lexd. Hd, Colch. PLU, Bor/MB, USD. Abol civ 1897 to help cr Colchester CP.[74] *Parl* Colch. Parl Bor (until 1918). *Eccl* Seq 1. Eccl bdry: 1955.[12]

WEST BERGHOLT
AP *LG* Seq 17. Civ bdry: 1883,[8] 1889,[7] 1934,[17] 1938,[75] 1955.[76] *Parl* Seq 1. Parl bdry: 1956.[424] *Eccl* Seq 4.

BIRDBROOK
AP *LG* Seq 14. Civ bdry: 1885.[91] *Parl* Seq 6. *Eccl* Seq 50. Eccl bdry: 1842 (help cr Cornish Hall End EP).[92]

BILLERICAY
EP Cr 1823 from Great Burstead AP.[77] Barst. RDn (1823–45), Bill. RDn (1845–1907), Barst. o'wise Brentw. RDn (1907–*). Bdry: 1883,[78] 1956.[79]
CP Cr 1937 by union Basildon CP, Bowers Gifford AP, Great Burstead AP, Laindon AP, Nevendon AP, North Benfleet AP, Pitsea AP, Vange AP, Wickford AP, Lee Chapel CP, Little Burstead AP.[56] *LG* Bill. UD (1937–55), Basildon UD (1955–74). Bdry: 1938.[80] *Parl* Bill. CC (1948–70), Basildon BC (1970–*).

BIRCH
Cr eccl 1813,[82] civ 1816[81] by union Great Birch AP, Little Birch AP. *LG* Seq 17. Civ bdry: 1883,[8] 1889,[7] 1949.[9] *Parl* Seq 1. *Eccl* Lexd. RDn (1813–47), Cogg. RDn (1847–1907), Cogg. & Tey RDn (1907–*).

GREAT BIRCH
AP *LG* Lexd. Hd. *Eccl* Lexd. RDn. Abol eccl 1813[82] and civ 1816[81] to help cr Birch EP, CP respectively.

LITTLE BIRCH
AP Organisation as for Great Birch.

BIRCHANGER
AP *LG* Seq 23. Civ bdry: 1953.[83] *Parl* Seq 8. *Eccl* Seq 8.

BLACKMORE
AP *LG* Chelm. Hd, Ong. PLU, RSD, RD (1894–1955), Epp. & Ong. RD (1955–74). *Parl* South Dv (1832–67), N-W Dv (1867–85), W'rn Dv (1885–1918), Chelm. Dv/CC (1918–55), Chigw. CC (1955–70), Brentw. & Ong. CC (1970–*). *Eccl* Chelm. RDn (until 1845), Ingat. RDn (1845–1907), Ong. RDn (1907–*).

BOBBINGWORTH
AP *LG* Seq 19. Civ bdry: 1946.[20] *Parl* Seq 12. *Eccl* Seq 39.

BOCKING
AP *LG* Hinckf. Hd, Braint. PLU, RSD, RD. Abol civ 1934 pt to help cr Braintree and Bocking CP, pt to Stisted AP, pt to Gosfield AP.[17] *Parl* N'rn Dv (1832–67), N-E Dv (1867–85), E'rn Dv (1885–1918), Maldon Dv (1918–48). *Eccl* Pec jurisd Archbp Canterb (Bocking RDn, until 1845), Braint. RDn (1845–*). Eccl bdry: 1906 (cr Bocking St Peter EP).[85]

BOCKING ST PETER
EP Cr 1906 from Bocking AP.[85] Braint. RDn.

BOREHAM
AP *LG* Seq 1. *Parl* Seq 11. *Eccl* Seq 31.

BORLEY
AP *LG* Seq 15. *Parl* Seq 6. *Eccl* Pec jurisd Archbp Canterb (Bocking RDn, until 1845), Heding. RDn (1845–1907), Belch. RDn (1907–69). Abol eccl 1969 to help cr Liston and Borley EP.[86]

BOWERS GIFFORD
AP Incl pt Canvey Island (sep EP 1739,[88] sep CP 1880[90]). *LG* Barst. Hd, Bill. PLU, RSD, RD (1894–1935), Bill. UD (1935–37). Civ bdry: 1889,[87] 1935.[24] Abol civ 1937 to help cr Billericay CP.[56] *Parl* S'rn Dv (1832–67), South Dv (1867–85), Mid Dv (1885–1918), S-E'rn Dv (1918–48). *Eccl* Barst. RDn (until 1895), Rochf. RDn (1895–1955), Basildon RDn (1955–*).

BOXTED
AP *LG* Seq 17. *Parl* Seq 1. *Eccl* Seq 4.

BRADFIELD
AP Incl pt chap and bor Manningtree (bor status not sustained, sep civ identity as par early, sep EP 1840[89]). *LG* Seq 21. *Parl* Seq 5. *Eccl* Seq 13.

BRADWELL
AP Usual civ spelling; for eccl see following entry. *LG* Seq 26. Civ bdry: 1889,[93] 1949.[9] *Parl* Seq 3.

BRADWELL BY COGGESHALL
AP Usual eccl spelling; for civ see prev entry. *Eccl* Seq 18.

BRADWELL ON SEA
AP *LG* Seq 4. *Parl* Seq 9. *Eccl* Seq 36.

BRAINTREE
AP *LG* Hinckf. Hd, Braint. PLU, USD, UD. Civ bdry: 1883.[8] Abol civ 1934 pt to help cr Braintree and Bocking CP, pt to Black Notley AP, pt to Stisted AP.[17] *Parl* N'rn Dv (1832–67), N-E Dv (1867–85), E'rn Dv (1885–1918), Maldon Dv (1918–48). *Eccl* Seq 47.

BRAINTREE AND BOCKING
CP Cr 1934 from Black Notley AP, Bocking AP, Braintree AP, Gosfield AP, Rayne AP, Stisted AP.[17] *LG* Braint. & Bocking UD. *Parl* Maldon CC (1948–70), Braint. CC (1970–*).

GREAT BRAXTED
AP *LG* Witham Hd, PLU (1835–83), RSD (1875–83), Maldon PLU (1883–1930), RSD (1883–

94), RD. Civ bdry: 1956.[94] *Parl* Seq 2. *Eccl* Seq 17.

LITTLE BRAXTED

AP *LG* Witham Hd, PLU (1835–83), RSD (1875–83), Maldon PLU (1883–1930), RSD (1883–94), RD. *Parl* Seq 2. *Eccl* Seq 17.

BRENTWOOD

Chap and twnshp in South Weald, sep EP 1738,[95] sep CP 1866.[19] *LG* Chaf. Hd, Bill. PLU, RSD, RD (1894–99), Brentw. UD (1899–1974). Civ bdry: 1883,[8] 1908,[98] 1934.[17] *Parl* South Dv (1867–85), Mid Dv (1885–1918), Chelm. Dv (1918–48), Romf. BC (1948–55), Bill. CC (1955–70), Brentw. & Ong. CC (1970–*). *Eccl* Chaf. RDn (1738–1907), Barst. o'wise Brentw. RDn (1907–*). Eccl bdry: 1956,[96] 1961 (cr Brentwood St George the Martyr EP).[97]

BRENTWOOD ST GEORGE THE MARTYR

EP Cr 1961 from Brentwood EP.[97] Barst. o'wise Brentw. RDn.

BRIGHTLINGSEA

AP *LG* Tendr. Hd, Lexd. & Winst. PLU (1836–80), RSD (1875–80), Tendr. PLU (1880–1930), RSD (1880–94), RD (1894–96), Brightlingsea UD (1896–1974). *Parl* Seq 5. *Eccl* Seq 16.

GREAT BROMLEY

AP *LG* Seq 21. *Parl* Seq 5. *Eccl* Seq 13.

LITTLE BROMLEY

AP *LG* Seq 21. *Parl* Seq 5. *Eccl* Seq 13.

BROOMFIELD

AP *LG* Seq 1. Civ bdry: 1883,[8] 1888,[99] 1888,[100] 1889,[101] 1934,[17] 1946.[20] *Parl* Seq 11. *Eccl* Seq 31. Eccl bdry: 1893,[102] 1930 (help cr Chelmsford The Ascension EP),[103] 1958 (help cr Chelmsford St Andrew EP).[104]

BROXTED

AP Sometimes 'Chawreth'. *LG* Seq 6. Civ bdry: 1883.[8] *Parl* Seq 8. *Eccl* Dunmow RDn. Abol eccl 1972 to help cr Broxted with Chickney EP.[105]

BROXTED WITH CHICKNEY

EP Cr 1972 by union Broxted AP, Chickney AP.[105] Dunmow RDn.

BUCKHURST HILL

Chap in Chigwell AP, sep EP 1838,[106] sep CP 1894.[107] *LG* Ep. PLU, Buckhurst UD (1894–1933), Chigw. UD (1933–74). *Parl* Ep. CC (1918–48), Woodf. BC (1948–55), Chigw. CC (1955–70), Ep. Forest CC (1970–*). *Eccl* Ong. RDn (1838–45), Lamb. RDn (1845–62), Romf. RDn (1862–83), Chigw. RDn (1883–*).

BULMER

AP *LG* Seq 15. Civ bdry: 1883,[8] 1885.[15] *Parl* Seq 6. *Eccl* Seq 46.

BULPHAN

AP *LG* Barst. Hd, Ors. PLU, RSD, RD. Abol civ 1936 to help cr Thurrock CP.[24] *Parl* S'rn Dv (1832–67), South Dv (1867–85), S-E'rn Dv (1885–1948). *Eccl* Barst. RDn (until 1845), Ors. RDn (1845–1907), Ors. & Greys RDn (1907–64), Barst. o'wise Brentw. RDn (1964–*).

HELION BUMPSTEAD

AP Pt Essex (Freshw. Hd), pt Cambs (Chilford Hd), the latter lost 1885 to Castle Camps AP, Cambs, and par ent Essex thereafter.[108] *LG* Risbridge PLU, RSD, Bump. RD (1894–1934), Halst. RD (1934–74). Addtl civ bdry alt: 1965 (exchanges pts with Castle Camps AP, Cambs & IoE).[109] *Parl* Pt N'rn Dv (1885–1918), Saff. Wald. Dv/CC (1918–*). *Eccl* Sometimes as 'Helions Bumpstead', Sampf. RDn (until 1907), Saff. Wald. RDn (1907–55), Belch. RDn (1955–*).

STEEPLE BUMPSTEAD

AP *LG* Seq 14. Civ bdry: 1883,[8] 1895.[91] *Parl* Seq 6. *Eccl* Seq 50.

BURES

Hmlt (Hinckf. Hd) in Bures St Mary AP (Suffolk, Babergh Hd), sep CP 1866 in Essex.[19] *LG* Sudbury PLU, RSD, Belch. RD (1894–1934), Halst. RD (1934–74). Bdry: 1884,[110] 1885.[15] *Parl* N-E Dv (1867–85), N'rn Dv (1885–1918), Saff. Wald. Dv/CC (1918–*).

BURES ST MARY

AP In Suffolk (Babergh Hd), incl hmlt Bures (Essex, Hinckf. Hd, sep CP 1866 in Essex[19] and Bures St Mary ent Suffolk thereafter). See main entry in Suffolk.

MOUNT BURES

AP *LG* Seq 17. Civ bdry: 1884,[11] 1889.[7] *Parl* Seq 1. *Eccl* Lexd. RDn (until 1847), Halst. RDn (1847–1907), Dedham RDn (1907–*).

BURNHAM

AP Usual civ spelling; for eccl see following entry. *LG* Dengie Hd, Maldon PLU, RSD, RD (1894–98), Burnham on Crouch UD (1898–1974). Civ bdry: 1934.[17] *Parl* Seq 9.

BURNHAM ON CROUCH

AP Usual eccl spelling; for civ see prev entry. *Eccl* Seq 36.

GREAT BURSTEAD

AP Incl chap Billericay (sep EP 1823[77] [CP cr 1937 (qv) formed in pt from this ent par]). *LG* Barst. Hd, Bill. PLU, RSD, RD (1894–1935), Bill. UD (1935–37). Addtl civ bdry alt: 1934,[17] 1936.[111] Abol civ 1937 to help cr Billericay CP.[56] *Parl* S'rn Dv (1832–67), South Dv (1867–85), Mid Dv (1885–1918), S-E'rn Dv (1918–48). *Eccl* Seq 24. Addtl eccl bdry alt: 1883.[78]

LITTLE BURSTEAD

AP *LG* Barst. Hd, Bill. PLU, RSD, RD (1894–1935), Bill. UD (1935–37). Civ bdry: 1934.[17] Abol civ 1937 to help cr Billericay CP.[56] *Parl* S'rn Dv (1832–67), South Dv (1867–85), Mid Dv (1885–1918), S-E'rn Dv (1918–48). *Eccl* Seq 23. Eccl bdry: 1883,[78] 1972.[112]

BUSH END

EP Cr 1860 from Hatfield Broad Oak AP.[113] Harlow RDn.

BUTTSBURY

AP *LG* Chelm. Hd, PLU, RSD, RD. Abol civ 1935 pt to Great Burstead AP, pt to Stock AP.[24] *Parl* S'rn Dv (1832–67), N-W Dv (1867–85), Mid Dv (1885–1918), Chelm. Dv (1918–48). *Eccl*

Seq 33. Eccl bdry: 1956.[79]

CANEWDON

AP *LG* Seq 20. Civ bdry: 1934,[17] 1946.[20] *Parl* Seq 17. *Eccl* Seq 40.

GREAT CANFIELD

AP *LG* Seq 6. Civ bdry: 1949.[114] *Parl* Seq 8. *Eccl* Dunmow RDn (until 1907), Roding RDn (1907–*).

LITTLE CANFIELD

AP *LG* Seq 6. Civ bdry: 1949.[114] *Parl* Seq 8. *Eccl* Seq 43.

CANN HALL

CP Cr 1894 from the pt of Wanstead AP in Leyton USD.[115] *LG* W Ham PLU, Leyton UD (1894–1926), MB (1926–65). Transf 1965 to Gtr London (Waltham Forest LB). *Parl* Leyton East Parl Bor (1918–48), Leyton BC (1948–70), Gtr London thereafter.

CANNING TOWN ST CEDD

EP Cr 1937 from Plaistow St Andrew EP.[116] W Ham RDn (1937–66), Newham RDn (1966–*). Bdry: 1961 (incl pt to help reconstitute Victoria Docks the Ascension EP),[49] 1972.[117]

CANNING TOWN ST GABRIEL

EP Cr 1879 from West Ham AP, Plaistow St Mary EP, Plaistow St Andrew EP.[118] Bark. RDn (1879–95), W Bark. RDn (1895–1907), W Ham RDn (1907–61). Bdry: 1908 (help cr Canning Town St Matthias EP),[119] 1961.[49] Abol 1961 pt to Canning Town St Matthias, pt to help reconstitute Victoria Docks The Ascension EP).[49]

CANNING TOWN ST MATTHIAS

EP Cr 1908 from Canning Town St Gabriel EP, Plaistow St Mary EP, Plaistow St Andrew EP.[119] W Ham RDn (1908–66), Newham RDn (1966–*). Reconstituted 1961 by gaining pts of Canning Town St Gabriel EP, Barking Road EP, West Ham AP, losing pt to Plaistow St Andrew EP.[49]

CANVEY ISLAND

Island in river Thames, pt in Barst. Hd (APs of North Benfleet, South Benfleet, Bowers Gifford, Laindon, Pitsea, Vange), pt in Rochf. Hd (APs of Prittlewell, Southchurch), sep EP 1739,[88] sep CP 1880.[90] *LG* Rochf. PLU,[120] RSD, RD (1894–1926), Canvey Island UD (1926–74). Civ bdry: 1880.[69] *Parl* S-E'rn Dv (1885–1948), Bill. CC (1948–55), S-E CC (1955–*). *Eccl* Barst. RDn (1739–1845), Rochf. RDn (1845–1907), Canew. & S'end RDn (1907–*).

CHADWELL HEATH

EP Cr 1895 from Dagenham AP, Great Ilford EP.[122] Chaf. o'wise Romf. RDn (1895–1966), Bark. RDn (1966–*). Bdry: 1914 (help cr Goodmayes All Saints EP),[38] 1917 (cr Goodmayes St Paul EP),[123] 1927 (help cr Romford The Ascension, Collier Row EP),[124] 1960 (help cr Chadwell Heath St Mark, Mark's Gate EP).[6]

CHADWELL HEATH ST MARK, MARK'S GATE

EP Cr 1960 from Aldborough Hatch EP, Romford The Ascension, Collier Row EP, Chadwell Heath EP, Romford St John the Divine EP.[6] Chaf. o'wise Romf. RDn (1960–66), Bark. RDn (1966–*).

CHADWELL ST MARY

AP *LG* Barst. Hd, Ors. PLU, RSD, RD (1894–1912), Tilbury UD (1912–36). Abol civ 1936 to help cr Thurrock CP.[24] *Parl* S'rn Dv (1832–67), South Dv (1867–85), S-E'rn Dv (1885–1948). *Eccl* Seq 26. Eccl bdry: 1903 (cr Tilbury Docks EP).[121]

CHAPPEL

Chap in Great Tey AP, sep rights from 1553.[125] Sometimes 'Chapel' or 'Pontesbright'. *LG* Seq 17. Civ bdry: 1889.[7] *Parl* Seq 1. *Eccl* Lexd. RDn (until 1862), Halst. RDn (1862–1907), Cogg. & Tey RDn (1907–*).

CHELMSFORD

AP *LG* Chelm. Hd, Bor, PLU, USD, MB (1888–1974). Civ bdry: 1888,[100] 1889,[101] 1897,[127] 1907,[126] 1934.[17] *Parl* Chelm. Parl Bor (1337 only), Seq 10. *Eccl* Chelm. RDn. Eccl bdry: 1838 (help cr Chelmsford The Ascension EP).[103] Renamed 1960 'Chelmsford St Mary the Virgin, St Peter and St Cedd'.[129]

CHELMSFORD ALL SAINTS

EP Cr 1962 from Chelmsford The Ascension EP, Writtle AP.[130] Chelm. RDn.

CHELMSFORD THE ASCENSION

EP Cr 1930 from Chelmsford AP, Broomfield AP, Writtle AP.[103] Chelm. RDn. Bdry: 1958 (help cr Chelmsford St Andrew EP),[104] 1962,[131] 1962 (help cr Chelmsford All Saints EP).[130]

CHELMSFORD ST ANDREW

EP Cr 1958 from Writtle AP, Broomfield AP, Chignall St James AP, Chignall Smealy AP, Chelmsford The Ascension EP.[104] Chelm. RDn.

CHELMSFORD ST MARY THE VIRGIN, ST PETER AND ST CEDD

EP Renaming 1960 of Chelmsford AP.[129] Chelm. RDn. Bdry: 1962.[131]

GREAT CHESTERFORD

AP *LG* Seq 24. Civ bdry: 1954,[132] 1965 (exchanges pts with Ickleton AP, loses pt to Linton AP, both Cambs & IoE).[109] *Parl* Seq 8. *Eccl* Sampf. RDn (until 1847), Saff. Wald. RDn (1847–*).

LITTLE CHESTERFORD

AP *LG* Seq 24. Civ bdry: 1883.[8] *Parl* Seq 8. *Eccl* Sampf. RDn (until 1847), Saff. Wald. RDn (1847–*).

CHICKNEY

AP *LG* Seq 6. *Parl* Seq 8. *Eccl* Dunmow RDn. Abol eccl 1972 to help cr Broxted with Chickney EP.[105]

CHIGNALL

CP Cr 1888 by union Chignall Smealy AP, pt Chignall St James AP, pt Writtle AP, pt Broomfield AP.[133] *LG* Chelm. PLU, RSD, RD. Bdry: 1946.[20] *Parl* Chelm. Dv/CC (1918–70), Braint. CC (1970–*).

CHIGNALL ST JAMES

AP *LG* Chelm. Hd, PLU, RSD. Abol civ 1888 pt to help cr Chignall CP, pt to Writtle AP, pt to Broomfield AP.[133] *Parl* South Dv (1832–67), N-E Dv (1867–85), Mid Dv (1885–1918).

Eccl Seq 31. Eccl bdry: 1958 (help cr Chelmsford St Andrew EP).[104]

CHIGNALL SMEALY

AP *LG* Chelm. Hd, PLU, RSD. Abol civ 1888 to help cr Chignall CP.[133] Civ bdry: 1883.[8] *Parl*, *Eccl*, Eccl bdry alt as for Chignall St James.

CHIGWELL

AP Incl Buckhurst Hill (sep EP 1838,[106] sep UD and CP 1894[107]). *LG* Ong. Hd, Ep. PLU, RSD, RD (1894–1933), Chigw. UD (1933–74). Addtl civ bdry alt: 1965 (loses pt to Gtr London to help cr Redbr. LB).[37] *Parl* S'rn Dv (1832–67), N-W Dv (1867–85), W'rn Dv (1885–1918), Ep. Dv/CC (1918–55), Chigw. CC (1955–70), Ep. Forest CC (1970–*). *Eccl* Ong. RDn (until 1845), Lamb. RDn (1845–62), Romf. RDn (1862–83), Chigw. RDn (1883–*). Addtl eccl bdry alt: 1860 (cr Chigwell Row EP),[134] 1961 (help cr Hainault EP).[54]

CHIGWELL ROW

EP Cr 1860 from Chigwell AP.[134] Lamb. RDn (1860–62), Romf. RDn (1862–83), Chigw. RDn (1883–*). Bdry: 1957,[135] 1961 (help cr Hainault EP).[54]

CHILDERDITCH

AP *LG* Chaf. Hd, Bill. PLU, RSD, RD. Abol civ 1934 pt to Little Burstead AP, pt to Brentwood CP.[17] *Parl* S'rn Dv (1832–67), South Dv (1867–85), Mid Dv (1885–1918), S-E'rn Dv (1918–48). *Eccl* Seq 28.

CHINGFORD

AP *LG* Waltham Hd, Ep. PLU, RSD, Chingford UD (1894–1938), MB (1938–65). Civ bdry: 1883,[8] 1934.[17] Transf 1965 to Gtr London (Waltham Forest LB).[37] *Parl* S'rn Dv (1832–67), N-W Dv (1867–85), W'rn Dv (1885–1918), Ep. Dv/CC (1918–70), Gtr London thereafter. *Eccl* Bark. RDn (until 1895 [London dioc until 1867]), N Bark. RDn (1895–1907), Walt'stow & Leyton RDn (1907–16), Walt'stow & Chingford RDn (1916–66), Waltham Forest RDn (1966–*). Eccl bdry: 1922 (help cr Chingford St Edmund EP),[137] 1954,[138] 1956 (help cr Chingford St Anne EP).[136]

CHINGFORD ST ANNE

EP Cr 1956 from Chingford AP, Highams Park EP, Walthamstow St Peter EP.[136] Walt'stow & Chingford RDn (1956–66), Waltham Forest RDn (1966–*).

CHINGFORD ST EDMUND

EP Cr 1922 from Chingford AP, Walthamstow AP.[137] Walt'stow & Chingford RDn (1922–66), Waltham Forest RDn (1966–*).

GREAT CHISHILL

AP *LG* Uttl. Hd, Royston PLU, RSD, sep RD in Essex (1894–95). Transf. 1895 to Cambs.[139] *Parl* N'rn Dv (1832–67), N-W Dv (1867–85), N'rn Dv (1885–1918), Cambs thereafter. *Eccl* Seq 9.

LITTLE CHISHILL

AP Organisation as for Great Chishill.

CHRISHALL

AP *LG* Seq 24. Civ bdry: 1883,[8] 1946,[20] 1965 (exchanges pts with Great Chishill AP, gains pt Little Chishill AP, loses pts to Duxford AP, Fowlmere AP, Heydon AP, Ickleton AP, all Cambs & IoE).[109] *Parl* Seq 8. *Eccl* Pec jurisd Dean & Chapter of Westminster (until 1845), Seq 9 thereafter.

GREAT CLACTON

AP *LG* Tendr. Hd, PLU, RSD (1875–91), Great Clacton USD, UD (renamed 1895 'Clacton' UD). Civ bdry: 1934.[17] *Parl* N'rn Dv (1832–67), N-E Dv (1867–85), N-E'rn Dv (1885–1918), Harw. Dv/CC (1918–*). *Eccl* Seq 16. Eccl bdry: between 1768–1810 (gains ent Little Holland AP),[291] 1878 (cr Clacton-on-Sea St Paul EP),[142] 1907 (help cr Clacon-on-Sea St James EP).[141]

LITTLE CLACTON

AP *LG* Seq 21. Civ bdry: 1934.[17] *Parl* Seq 5. *Eccl* Seq 16.

CLACTON-ON-SEA ST JAMES

EP Cr 1907 from Clacton-on-Sea St Paul EP, Great Clacton AP.[141] St Osyth RDn.

CLACTON-ON-SEA ST PAUL

EP Cr 1878 from Great Clacton AP.[142] St Osyth RDn. Bdry: 1907 (help cr Clacton-on-Sea St James EP).[141]

CLAVERING

AP Incl chap Langley (sep civ identity early, sep EP 1875[143]). *LG* Seq 3. *Parl* Seq 8. *Eccl* Seq 8.

COGGESHALL

AP Usual eccl spelling; for civ see 'Great Coggeshall'. *Eccl* Lexd. RDn (until 1847), Cogg. RDn (1847–1907), Cogg. & Tey RDn (1907–32). Abol eccl 1932 to help cr Coggeshall with Markshall EP.[144]

CP Cr 1949 by union Great Coggeshall AP, Markshall AP, pt Feering AP, pt Little Coggeshall AP, pt Pattiswick AP.[9] *LG* Braint. RD. *Parl* Braint. CC (1970–*).

COGGESHALL WITH MARKSHALL

EP Cr 1932 by union Coggeshall AP, Markshall AP.[144] Cogg. & Tey RDn.

GREAT COGGESHALL

AP Usual civ spelling; for eccl see 'Coggeshall'. *LG* Lexd. Hd, Witham PLU (1835–83), RSD (1875–83), Braint. PLU (1883–1930), RSD (1883–94), Braint. RD. Abol civ 1949 to help cr Coggeshall CP.[144] *Parl* N'rn Dv (1832–67), N-E Dv (1867–85), E'rn Dv (1885–1918), Madon Dv/CC (1918–70).

LITTLE COGGESHALL

AP *LG* Witham Hd, PLU (1835–83), RSD (1875–83), Braint. PLU (1883–1930), RSD (1883–94), Braint. RD. Civ bdry: 1883,[8] 1889.[93] Abol civ 1949 pt to help cr Coggeshall CP, pt to Feering AP.[9] *Parl* As for Great Coggeshall. *Eccl* Pec jurisd Archbp Canterb (Bocking RDn); presumed benefice always held jointly with Great Coggeshall so no sep eccl identity.[145]

COLCHESTER

The following have 'Colchester' in their names. Insofar as any existed at a given time: *LG* Lexd. Hd, Colch. PLU, Bor/MB, USD. *Parl* Colch. Parl

Bor (1295–1918), Colch. Dv/CC (1918–*). *Eccl* Colch. RDn.

CP1–COLCHESTER–Cr 1897 by union AP1 through AP12, Berechurch AP, Greenstead AP, Lexden AP, Mile End St Michael AP.[74] Bdry: 1934.[17]

AP1–COLCHESTER ALL SAINTS–Abol civ 1897 to help cr CP1.[74] Eccl bdry: 1868 (help cr EP6).[18] Abol eccl 1953 pt to help cr EP4, pt to help cr EP5, pt to AP11.[146]

AP2–COLCHESTER HOLY TRINITY–Incl chap Berechurch (sep par 1536[73]). Civ bdry: 1883.[8] Abol civ 1897 to help cr CP1.[74] Abol eccl 1940 to help cr EP1.[147]

EP1–COLCHESTER HOLY TRINITY WITH ST MARTIN–Cr 1940 by union AP2, AP7.[147] Abol 1953 pt to help cr EP4, pt to help cr EP5, pt to AP8, pt to AP11.[146]

EP2–COLCHESTER ST ANNE–Cr 1959 from EP5, Greenstead AP.[148]

EP3–COLCHESTER ST BARNABAS, OLD HEATH–Cr 1951 from AP4, AP3, East Donyland AP.[149]

AP3–COLCHESTER ST BOTOLPH–Civ bdry: 1883.[8] Abol civ 1897 to help cr CP1.[74] Eccl bdry: 1868 (help cr EP6),[18] 1951 (help cr EP3).[149] Abol eccl 1953 pt to help cr EP4, pt to help cr EP5, pt to AP6, pt to AP9.[146]

EP4–COLCHESTER ST BOTOLPH WITH HOLY TRINITY AND ST GILES–Cr 1953 by union pt AP3, pt EP1, pt AP4, pt AP1, pt AP10, pt AP5, pt AP9.[146] Bdry: 1953 (cr EP8),[150] 1955.[12]

AP4–COLCHESTER ST GILES–Civ bdry: 1883.[8] Abol civ 1897 to help cr CP1.[74] Eccl bdry: 1950,[151] 1951 (help cr EP3).[149] Abol eccl 1953 pt to help cr EP4, pt to AP8.[146]

AP5–COLCHESTER ST JAMES–Abol civ 1897 to help cr CP1.[74] Abol eccl 1953 pt to help cr EP4, pt to help cr EP5, pt to Greenstead AP, pt to EP6.[146]

EP5–COLCHESTER ST JAMES WITH ALL SAINTS AND ST NICHOLAS AND ST RUNWALD–Cr 1953 by union pt AP5, pt AP1, pt AP10, AP12, pt AP3, pt Myland St Michael (o'wise Mile End St Michael) AP, pt EP1, pt AP9, pt Greenstead AP.[146] Bdry: 1959 (help cr EP2).[148]

EP6–COLCHESTER ST JOHN–Cr 1868 from Greenstead AP, Myland St Michael (o'wise Mile End St Michael) AP, Langham AP, Ardleigh AP, AP1, AP3.[18] Bdry: 1953,[146] 1961.[227]

AP6–COLCHESTER ST LEONARD–Abol civ 1897 to help cr CP1.[74] Eccl bdry: 1953.[146]

AP7–COLCHESTER ST MARTIN–Abol civ 1897 to help cr CP1.[74] Abol eccl 1940 to help cr EP1.[147]

AP8–COLCHESTER ST MARY AT THE WALLS–Civ bdry: 1883.[8] Abol civ 1897 to help cr CP1.[74] Eccl bdry: 1953,[146] 1956.[13]

AP9–COLCHESTER ST MARY MAGDALEN–Civ bdry: 1883.[8] Abol civ 1897 to help cr CP1.[74] Eccl bdry: 1953 (incl help cr EP5).[146]

AP10–COLCHESTER ST NICHOLAS–Abol civ 1897 to help cr CP1.[74] Abol eccl 1953 pt to help cr EP4, pt to help cr EP5, pt to AP11.[146]

EP7–COLCHESTER ST PAUL–Cr 1879 from Lexden AP.[152] Bdry: 1953.[146]

AP11–COLCHESTER ST PETER–Abol civ 1897 to help cr CP1.[74] Eccl bdry: 1953.[146]

AP12–COLCHESTER ST RUNWALD–Civ bdry: 1883.[8] Abol civ 1897 to help cr CP1.[74] Abol eccl 1953 to help cr EP5.[146]

EP8–COLCHESTER ST STEPHEN–Cr 1953 from EP4.[150] Bdry: 1955.[12]

COLLIER ROW

EP Cr 1955 from Romford EP, Romford The Ascension Collier Row EP, Havering-atte-Bower AP.[153] Chaf. o'wise Romford RDn (1955–66), Hav. RDn (1966–*). Bdry: 1971.[154]

EARLS COLNE

AP *LG* Seq 16. Civ bdry: 1883.[8] *Parl* Seq 4. *Eccl* Seq 6.

WAKES COLNE

AP *LG* Seq 17. Civ bdry: 1883,[8] 1889.[7] *Parl* Seq 1. *Eccl* Lexd. RDn (until 1847), Halst. RDn (1847–1907), Cogg. & Tey RDn (1907–*).

WHITE COLNE

AP *LG* Seq 16. Civ bdry: 1883,[8] 1885.[155] *Parl* Seq 6. *Eccl* Seq 6.

COLNE ENGAINE

AP *LG* Seq 16. Civ bdry: 1883,[8] 1885.[155] *Parl* Seq 6. *Eccl* Seq 6.

COOPERSALE

EP Cr 1852 from Theydon Garnon AP.[156] Lamb. RDn (1852–1907), Chigw. RDn (1907–*).

COPFORD

AP *LG* Seq 17. Civ bdry: 1883,[8] 1889,[7] 1949 (incl help cr Eight Ash Green CP).[9] *Parl* Seq 1. *Eccl* Seq 2.

CORNISH HALL END

EP Cr 1842 from Finchingfield AP, Birdbrook AP, Ridgewell AP.[92] Heding. RDn (1842–62), Braint. RDn (1862–*).

CORRINGHAM

AP *LG* Barst. Hd, Ors. PLU, RSD, RD. Civ bdry: 1889.[157] Abol civ 1936 to help cr Thurrock CP, pt to Bowers Gifford AP.[24] *Parl* S'rn Dv (1832–67), South Dv (1867–85), S-E'rn Dv (1885–1948). *Eccl* Seq 22. Eccl bdry: 1962.[158]

CRANHAM

AP *LG* Chaf. Hd, Romford PLU, RSD, RD (1894–1934), Hornchurch UD (1934–65). Civ bdry: 1934,[17] 1936.[24] Transf 1965 to Gtr London (Hav. LB).[37] *Parl* S'rn Dv (1832–67), South Dv (1867–85), Mid Dv (1885–1918), Romford Dv (1918–45), Hornchurch Dv (1945–48), BC (1948–70), Gtr London thereafter. *Eccl* Seq 27. Eccl bdry: 1957 (help cr Cranham Park EP).[159]

CRANHAM PARK

EP Cr 1957 from Cranham AP, Upminster AP.[159] Chaf. o'wise Romford RDn (1957–66), Hav. RDn (1966–*).

CREEKSEA

AP Usual civ spelling; for eccl see 'Cricksea'. *LG*

Dengie Hd, Maldon PLU, RSD, RD. Abol civ 1934 pt to Burnham AP, pt to Canewdon AP.[17] *Parl* S'rn Dv (1832–67), N-E Dv (1867–85), S-E'rn Dv (1885–1918), Maldon Dv (1918–48).

CRESSING

AP *LG* Seq 26. Civ bdry: 1889.[93] *Parl* Seq 3. *Eccl* Seq 18.

CRICKSEA

AP Usual eccl spelling; for civ see 'Creeksea'. *Eccl* Seq 36.

DAGENHAM

AP *LG* Becontree Hd, Romford PLU, RSD, RD (1894–1926), Dagenham UD (1926–38), MB (1938–74). Civ bdry: 1934,[36] 1946,[160] 1965 (loses pt to Gtr London [pt Redbr. LB, pt Bark. LB]).[37] *Parl* S'rn Dv (1832–67), South Dv (1867–85), S'rn Dv (1885–1918), Romford Dv (1918–48), Dagenham BC (1948–*). *Eccl* Bark. RDn (until 1862 [London dioc until 1846]), Romford RDn (1862–68), Chaf. RDn (1868–1907), Chaf. o'wise Romford RDn (1907–66), Bark. RDn (1966–*). Eccl bdry: 1895 (help cr Chadwell Heath EP),[122] 1914 (help cr Goodmayes All Saints EP),[38] 1922 (help cr Becontree St Thomas EP),[62] 1927 (cr Dagenham St Martin EP),[162] 1931 (help cr Becontree St Peter EP, help cr Becontree St Elizabeth EP),[39] 1935 (cr Becontree St George EP),[59] 1969 (help cr Rush Green EP).[161]

DAGENHAM ST MARTIN

EP Cr 1927 from Dagenham AP.[162] Chaf. o'wise Romford RDn (1927–66), Bark. RDn (1966–*). Bdry: 1934 (help cr Becontree St Alban EP).[42]

DANBURY

AP *LG* Seq 1. Civ bdry: 1888.[163] *Parl* Seq 10. *Eccl* Pt (Runsell) pec jurisd Archbp Canterb (Bocking RDn, until 1845), Seq 34 thereafter.

DEBDEN

AP *LG* Seq 24. *Parl* Seq 8. *Eccl* Sampf. RDn (until 1847), Saff. Wald. RDn (1847–*).

DEDHAM

AP *LG* Seq 17. Civ bdry: 1938.[75] *Parl* Seq 1. *Eccl* Seq 4.

DENGIE

AP *LG* Seq 4. Civ bdry: 1889.[22] *Parl* Seq 9. *Eccl* Seq 36. Eccl bdry: 1933.[164]

DODDINGHURST

AP *LG* Barst. Hd,[171] Ong. PLU, RSD, RD (1894–1955), Ep. & Ong. RD (1955–74). *Parl* S'rn Dv (1832–67), South Dv (1867–85), Mid Dv (1885–1918), Chelm. Dv/CC (1918–70), Brentw. & Ong. CC (1970–*). *Eccl* Barst. RDn (until 1845), Ingat. RDn (1845–80s), Bill. RDn (1880s–95), Ingat. RDn (1895–1907), Barst. o'wise Brentw. RDn (1907–*).

EAST DONYLAND

AP *LG* Seq 17. Civ bdry: 1889,[7] 1934,[17] 1946.[20] *Parl* Seq 1. *Eccl* Seq 7. Eccl bdry: 1950,[151] 1951 (help cr Colchester St Barnabas, Old Heath EP).[149]

DOVERCOURT

AP Incl chap Harwich St Nicholas (sep civ identity early in Harw. Bor, sep EP 1871[165]). *LG* Tendr. Hd, PLU (1838–1930), Harw. Bor/MB, USD. Abol civ 1925 to help cr Harwich CP.[166] *Parl* Harw. Parl Bor (1604–1885), N-E'rn Dv (1885–1918), Harw. Dv/CC (1918–*). *Eccl* Seq 14.

DOWNHAM

AP *LG* Barst. Hd, Bill. PLU, RSD, RD. Civ bdry: 1883,[8] 1888,[167] 1889.[87] Abol civ 1934 pt to Great Burstead AP, pt to South Hanningfield AP.[17] *Parl* S'rn Dv (1832–67), South Dv (1867–85), Mid Dv (1885–1918), S-E'rn Dv (1918–48). *Eccl* Seq 21.

GREAT DUNMOW

AP *LG* Seq 6. Civ bdry: 1883,[8] 1889.[29] *Parl* Seq 8. *Eccl* Seq 43.

LITTLE DUNMOW

AP *LG* Seq 6. *Parl* Seq 8. *Eccl* Seq 43.

DUNTON

AP Usual civ spelling; for eccl see following entry. *LG* Barst. Hd, Bill. PLU, RSD, RD. Civ bdry: 1889.[157] Abol civ 1934 pt to Little Burstead AP, pt to Brentwood CP.[17] *Parl* S'rn Dv (1832–67), South Dv (1867–85), Mid Dv (1885–1918), S-E'rn Dv (1918–48).

DUNTON WAYLETT

AP Usual eccl spelling; for civ see prev entry. *Eccl* Barst. RDn (until 1845), Bill. RDn (1845–95), Barst. RDn (1895–1907), Barst. o'wise Brentw. RDn (1907–55), Basildon RDn (1955–64), Brentw. RDn (1964–*).

GOOD EASTER

AP *LG* Seq 5. Civ bdry: 1888.[168] *Parl* Seq 7. *Eccl* Pec jurisd Good Easter (until 1845), Seq 44 thereafter.

HIGH EASTER

AP *LG* Seq 6. Civ bdry: 1888,[169] 1889.[29] *Parl* Seq 8. *Eccl* Seq 44.

EASTHORPE

AP *LG* Lexd. Hd, Lex. & Winst. PLU, RSD, RD. Civ bdry: 1883,[8] 1889.[7] Abol civ 1949 pt to Copford AP, pt to Marks Tey AP, pt to Messing cum Inworth CP.[9] *Parl* N'rn Dv (1832–67), N-E Dv (1867–85), E'rn Dv (1885–1918), Colch. Dv/CC (1918–70). *Eccl* Seq 2.

GREAT EASTON

AP *LG* Seq 6. *Parl* Seq 8. *Eccl* Seq 43. Eccl bdry: 1880.[170]

LITTLE EASTON

AP *LG* Seq 6. *Parl* Seq 8. *Eccl* Seq 43.

EASTWOOD

AP *LG* Rochf. Hd, PLU, RSD, RD. Civ bdry: 1913 (loses pt to help cr Southend on Sea CB and CP),[173] 1926,[172] 1933 (loses pt to Southend on Sea CB and CP),[111] 1934.[17] Abol civ 1946 ent to Canewdon AP.[20] *Parl* S'rn Dv (1832–67), South Dv (1867–85), S-E'rn Dv (1885–1948). *Eccl* Seq 41. Eccl bdry: 1951 (help cr Prittlewell St Peter EP),[174] 1952 (cr Leigh-on-Sea St James EP),[177] 1954 (help cr Prittlewell St Stephen EP),[175] 1956 (help cr Leigh-on-Sea St Aidan, The Fairway EP),[178] 1962 (cr Eastwood St David EP).[176]

EASTWOOD ST DAVID
EP Cr 1962 from Eastwood AP.[176] Canew. & S'end RDn.

EIGHT ASH GREEN
CP Cr 1949 from Aldham AP, Copford AP, Fordham AP, Stanway AP.[9] *LG* Lexd. & Winst. RD. *Parl* Colch. CC (1970–*).

ELMDON
AP *LG* Seq 24. Civ bdry: 1883.[8] *Parl* Seq 8. *Eccl* Nwpt. RDn (until 1847), Saff. Wald. RDn (1847–1931). Abol eccl 1931 to help cr Wendon Lofts with Elmdon EP.[179]

ELMSTEAD
AP *LG* Seq 21. Civ bdry: 1897,[180] 1948.[16] *Parl* Seq 5. *Eccl* Seq 13.

ELSENHAM
AP *LG* Seq 23. Civ bdry: 1946,[20] 1953.[83] *Parl* Seq 8. *Eccl* Seq 11.

EPPING
AP Orig subordinate to Epping Upland mother church[203] but superseded the latter early (Epping Upland regains civ identity 1896 [the pt of Epping not constituted Ep. UD],[181] sep EP 1912[182]). *LG* Waltham Hd, Ep. PLU, RSD, RD (1894–96), Ep. UD (1896–1974).Addtl civ bdry alt: 1896 (gains pt Theydon Bois AP, Theydon Garnon AP to form expanded Epping UD and AP),[181] 1934.[17] *Parl* Seq 13. *Eccl* Jurisd Waltham (until 1845), Ep. RDn (1845–62), Romford RDn (1862–83), Chigw. RDn (1883–*).

EPPING UPLAND
Orig mother church to Epping, subordinated early,[203] regains identity 1896 as CP (the pt of Epping not constituted Ep. UD),[181] sep EP 1912.[182] *LG* Ep. PLU, RD (1896–1955), Ep. & Ong. RD (1955–74). Bdry: 1934,[17] 1946,[20] 1949,[114] 1955 (incl pt to Harlow AP to help constitute Harlow UD).[183] *Parl* Ep. Dv/CC (1918–70), Ep. Forest CC (1970–*). *Eccl* Chigw. RDn.

FAIRSTEAD
AP *LG* Witham Hd, PLU (1835–83), RSD (1875–83), Braint. PLU (1883–1930), RSD (1883–94), Braint. RD. Civ bdry: 1883,[8] 1889.[93] *Parl* Seq 3. *Eccl* Seq 17.

NORTH FAMBRIDGE
AP *LG* Seq 4. *Parl* Seq 9. *Eccl* Chelm. RDn (until 1845), Maldon RDn (1845–*).

SOUTH FAMBRIDGE
AP *LG* Rochf. Hd, PLU, RSD, RD. Abol civ 1949 ent to Ashingdon AP.[9] *Parl* S'rn Dv (1832–67), South Dv (1867–85), S-E'rn Dv (1885–1948), Southend East BC (1948–70). *Eccl* Seq 41.

FARNHAM
AP *LG* Seq 2. *Parl* Seq 8. *Eccl* Seq 8.

FAULKBOURNE
AP *LG* Witham Hd, PLU (1835–83), RSD (1875–83), Braint. PLU (1883–1930), RSD (1883–94), Braint. RD. Civ bdry: 1883,[8] 1933.[184] *Parl* Seq 3. *Eccl* Seq 17.

FEERING
AP Incl Pattiswick (sep par 1313[185]). *LG* Lexd. Hd, Witham PLU (1835–83), RSD (1875–83), Braint. PLU (1883–1930), RSD (1883–94), Braint. RD. Civ bdry: 1889,[93] 1934,[17] 1949 (incl help cr Coggeshall CP).[9] *Parl* Seq 3. *Eccl* Seq 2.

FELSTED
AP *LG* Seq 12. Civ bdry: 1934.[17] *Parl* Seq 4. *Eccl* Seq 47.

FINCHINGFIELD
AP *LG* Seq 11. Civ bdry: 1883,[8] 1955.[30] *Parl* N'rn Dv (1832–67), N-E Dv (1867–85), N'rn Dv (1885–1918), Maldon Dv/CC (1918–70), Braint. CC (1970–*). *Eccl* Seq 47. Eccl bdry: 1842 (help cr Cornish Hall End EP).[92]

FINGRINGHOE
AP *LG* Seq 25. Civ bdry: 1889.[7] *Parl* Seq 1. *Eccl* Seq 7. Eccl bdry: 1955.[12]

FOBBING
AP *LG* Barst. Hd, Ors. PLU, RSD, RD. Civ bdry: 1889.[157] Abol civ 1936 pt to help cr Thurrock CP, pt to Lee Chapel CP.[24] *Parl* S'rn Dv (1832–67), South Dv (1867–85), S-E'rn Dv (1885–1948). *Eccl* Seq 22.

FORD END
EP Cr 1871 from Great Waltham EP.[186] Chelm. RDn (1871–1956), Roding RDn (1956–*).

FORDHAM
AP *LG* Seq 17. Civ bdry: 1889,[7] 1949 (help cr Eight Ash Green CP).[9] *Parl* Seq 1. *Eccl* Seq 4.

FOREST GATE [EMMANUEL]
EP Cr 1852 from East Ham AP, West Ham AP.[187] Bark. RDn (1852–95 [London dioc 1852–67]), W Bark. RDn (1895–1907), W Ham RDn (1907–62). Bdry: 1881 (help cr Forest Gate St James EP),[188] 1884 (cr Forest Gate St Saviour EP),[189] 1886 (cr Forest Gate All Saints EP),[190] 1894 (help cr Upton Cross EP),[191] 1894 (help cr Forest Gate St Mark EP).[192] Abol 1962 to help cr Forest Gate Emmanuel with Upton Cross St Peter EP.[193]

FOREST GATE ALL SAINTS
EP Cr 1886 from Forest Gate EP.[190] Bark. RDn (1886–95), S Bark. RDn (1895–1907), Bark. RDn (1907–66), Newham RDn (1966–*). Bdry: 1894 (help cr Forest Gate St Mark EP),[192] 1901 (help cr Forest Gate St Edmund EP).[194]

FOREST GATE EMMANUEL WITH UPTON CROSS ST PETER
EP Cr 1962 by union Forest Gate EP, Upton Cross EP.[193] W Ham RDn (1962–66), Newham RDn (1966–*).

FOREST GATE ST EDMUND
EP Cr 1901 from Forest Gate All Saints EP, Little Ilford AP, Upton Park St Stephen EP.[194] S Bark. RDn (1901–07), Bark. RDn (1907–66), Newham RDn (1966–*). Bdry: 1953.[195]

FOREST GATE ST JAMES
EP Cr 1881 from Forest Gate EP, Stratford EP, West Ham AP.[188] Bark. RDn (1881–95), W Bark. RDn (1895–1907), W Ham RDn (1907–66), Newham RDn (1966). Bdry: 1895 (help cr Wanstead Slip EP),[196] 1961.[49] Abol 1966 to

help cr Stratford St John and Christ Church with Forest Gate St James EP.[197]

FOREST GATE ST MARK
EP Cr 1894 from Forest Gate EP, Forest Gate All Saints EP.[192] Bark. RDn (1894–95), W Bark. RDn (1895–1907), W Ham RDn (1907–66), Newham RDn (1966–*).

FOREST GATE ST SAVIOUR
EP Cr 1884 from Forest Gate EP.[189] Bark. RDn (1884–95), W Bark. RDn (1895–1907), W Ham RDn (1907–66), Newham RDn (1966–*).

FOULNESS
Sep EP 1548, sep CP 1601.[198] *LG* Rochf. Hd, PLU,[66] RSD, RD. Civ bdry: 1946.[20] *Parl* Seq 17. *Eccl* Seq 40.

FOXEARTH
AP *LG* Seq 15. Civ bdry: 1885.[110] *Parl* Seq 6. *Eccl* Seq 46.

FRATING
AP *LG* Seq 21. Civ bdry: 1888.[199] *Parl* Seq 5. *Eccl* Seq 16.

FRINTON
AP *LG* Tendr. Hd, PLU, RSD, RD (1894–1901), Frinton on Sea UD (1901–34). Civ bdry: 1883,[8] 1888,[201] 1905.[200] Abol civ 1934 to help cr Frinton and Walton CP.[17] *Parl* N'rn Dv (1832–67), N-E Dv (1867–85), N-E'rn Dv (1885–1918), Harw. Dv (1918–48). *Eccl* Seq 16.

FRINTON AND WALTON
CP Cr 1934 by union Frinton AP, Great Holland AP, Walton le Soken AP, pt Kirby le Soken AP.[17] *LG* Frinton & Walton UD. *Parl* Harw. CC (1948–*).

FRYERNING
AP *LG* Chelm. Hd, PLU, RSD. Abol civ 1889 to help cr Ingatestone and Fryerning CP.[202] *Parl* S'rn Dv (1832–67), N-W Dv (1867–85), Mid Dv (1885–1918). *Eccl* Seq 33.

FYFIELD
AP *LG* Seq 19. *Parl* Seq 12. *Eccl* Seq 39.

GALLEYWOOD COMMON
EP Cr 1874 from Great Baddow AP, West Hanningfield AP, Moulsham EP, Orsett AP.[26] Chelm. RDn.

GESTINGTHORPE
AP *LG* Seq 15. *Parl* Seq 6. *Eccl* Seq 46.

GIDEA PARK
EP Cr 1933 from Squirrel's Heath EP.[204] Chaf. o'wise Romford RDn (1933–66), Hav. RDn (1966–*). Bdry: 1957.[135]

GOLDHANGER
AP *LG* Seq 19. Civ bdry: 1889,[22] 1934.[17] *Parl* Seq 2. *Eccl* Seq 19.

GOODMAYES ALL SAINTS
EP Cr 1914 from Barking AP, Great Ilford St Mary EP, Chadwell Heath EP, Dagenham AP.[38] Bark. RDn (1914–66), Redbr. RDn (1966–*). Bdry: 1922 (help cr Becontree St Thomas EP),[62] 1934 (help cr Barking St Erkenwald EP).[41]

GOODMAYES ST PAUL
EP Cr 1917 from Chadwell Heath EP.[123] Bark. RDn (1917–66), Redbr. RDn (1966–*). Bdry: 1939.[5]

GOSFIELD
AP *LG* Seq 13. Civ bdry: 1934 (incl help cr Braintree and Bocking CP).[17] *Parl* Seq 6. *Eccl* Seq 49.

GRAYS
EP Cr 1926 from Grays Thurrock AP, Little Thurrock AP.[205] Ors. & Grays RDn.

GREENSTEAD
AP *LG* Colch. Hd, PLU, Bor/MB, USD. Abol civ 1897 to help cr Colchester CP.[74] *Parl* Colch. Parl Bor (1295–1918). *Eccl* Seq 1. Eccl bdry: 1868 (help cr Colchester St John EP),[18] 1953 (incl help cr Colchester St James with All Saints and St Nicholas and St Runwald EP),[146] 1959 (help cr Colchester St Anne EP),[148] 1961.[227]

GREENSTEAD
AP *LG* Ong. Hd, PLU, RSD, RD (1894–1955), Ep. & Ong. RD (1955–65). Abol civ 1965 to help cr Ongar CP.[206] *Parl* South Dv (1832–67), N-W Dv (1867–85), W'rn Dv (1885–1918), Chelm. Dv/CC (1918–55), Chigw. CC (1955–70). *Eccl* Seq 39.

GREENSTEAD GREEN
EP Cr 1845 from Halstead Holy Trinity EP.[207] Heding. RDn (1845–47), Halst. RDn (1847–1907), Halst. & Heding. RDn (1907–*).

HADLEIGH
AP *LG* Rochf. Hd, PLU, RSD, RD (1894–1929), Benfleet UD (1929–74). Civ bdry: 1880,[69] 1934.[17] *Parl* Seq 16. *Eccl* Seq 41. Eccl bdry: 1739 (help cr Canvey Island EP),[88] 1958 (help cr Hadleigh St Barnabas EP).[208]

HADLEIGH ST BARNABAS
EP Cr 1958 from Hadleigh AP,[208] Leigh-on-Sea EP, Leigh-on-Sea St James EP.[208] Canew. & S'end RDn.

HADSTOCK
AP *LG* Freshw. Hd, Linton PLU, RSD, Saff. Wald. RD. Civ bdry: 1965 (exchanges pts with Linton AP, Cambs & IoE).[109] *Parl* Seq 8. *Eccl* Seq 12.

HAINAULT
EP Cr 1961 from Romford The Ascension, Collier Row EP, Barkingside Trinity EP, Chigwell AP, Chigwell Row EP.[54] Chigw. RDn (1961–66), Redbr. RDn (1966–*). Bdry: 1974.[228]

HALE END ALL SAINTS, HIGHAMS PARK–See HIGHAMS PARK

GREAT HALLINGBURY
AP *LG* Seq 9. Civ bdry: 1953.[83] *Parl* Seq 15. *Eccl* Seq 45. Eccl bdry: 1961.[209]

LITTLE HALLINGBURY
AP Organisation as for Great Hallingbury.

HALSTEAD
AP *LG* Hinckf. Hd, Halst. PLU, pt Halst. USD, pt Halst. RSD. Civ bdry: 1883.[8] Abol civ 1894 the pt in the USD to cr Halstead Urban CP, the remainder to cr Halstead Rural CP.[115] *Parl* N'rn Dv (1832–67), N-E Dv (1867–85), E'rn Dv (1885–1918). *Eccl* Seq 49. Eccl bdry: 1844 (cr Halstead Holy Trinity EP).[210]

HALSTEAD HOLY TRINITY
EP Cr 1844 from Halstead AP.[210] Heding. RDn (1844–47), Halst. RDn (1847–1907), Halst. &

Heding. RDn (1907–*). Bdry: 1845 (cr Greenstead Green EP).[211]

HALSTEAD RURAL

CP Cr 1894 from the pt of Halstead AP not in Halst. USD.[115] *LG* Halst. PLU, RD. Bdry: 1934,[17] 1954.[212] *Parl* Saff. Wald. Dv/CC (1918–*).

HALSTEAD URBAN

CP Cr 1894 from the pt of Halstead AP in Halst. USD.[115] *LG* Halst. PLU, UD. Bdry: 1934,[17] 1954.[212] *Parl* Saff. Wald. Dv/CC (1918–*).

EAST HAM

AP *LG* Becontree Hd, W Ham PLU, RSD (1875–79), E Ham USD (1879–94), UD (1894–1904), MB (1904–15), CB (1915–65). Civ bdry: 1893,[34] 1900 (gains ent Little Ilford AP in the UD),[214] 1901,[213] 1907.[35] Transf 1965 to Gtr London (Newham LB).[37] *Parl* S'rn Dv (1832–67), South Dv (1867–85), Romf. Dv (1885–1918), pt E Ham North Parl Bor/BC (1918–70), pt E Ham South Parl Bor/BC (1918–70) [see Part III of the *Guide* for composition of these constituencies by wards of the CB], Gtr London thereafter. *Eccl* Bark. RDn (until 1895 [London dioc until 1867]), S Bark. RDn (1895–1907), Bark. RDn (1907–66), Newham RDn (1966–*). Eccl bdry: 1852 (help cr Forest Gate EP),[187] 1864 (help cr Victoria Docks St Mark EP),[215] 1888 (help cr Upton Park St Stephen EP),[216] 1901 (help cr Little Ilford St Barnabas EP),[217] 1923 (cr East Ham St George EP),[218] 1924 (cr East Ham St Paul EP).[219] Abol eccl 1968 to help cr East Ham with Upton Park St Alban EP.[220]

EAST HAM ST GEORGE

EP Cr 1923 from East Ham AP.[218] Bark. RDn (1923–66), Newham RDn (1966–*).

EAST HAM ST PAUL

EP Cr 1924 from East Ham AP.[219] Bark. RDn (1924–66), Newham RDn (1966–*).

EAST HAM WITH UPTON PARK ST ALBAN

EP Cr 1968 by union East Ham AP, Upton Park St Alban EP.[220] Newham RDn.

WEST HAM

AP *LG* Becontree Hd, W Ham PLU, USD, MB (1886–88), CB (1888–1965). Civ bdry: 1887.[221] Transf 1965 to Gtr London (Newham LB).[37] *Parl* S'rn Dv (1832–67), South Dv (1867–85), pt W Ham North Parl Bor (1885–1918), pt W Ham South Parl Bor (1885–1918), pt W Ham Plaistow Parl Bor (1918–48), pt W Ham Silvertown Parl Bor (1918–48), pt W Ham Stratford Parl Bor (1918–48), pt W Ham Upton Parl Bor (1918–48), pt W Ham North BC (1948–70), pt W Ham South BC (1948–70) [see Part III of the *Guide* for composition of these constituences by wards of the CB], Gtr London thereafter. *Eccl* Bark. RDn (until 1895 [London dioc until 1867]), W Bark. RDn (1895–1907), W Ham RDn (1907–66), Newham RDn (1966–*). Eccl bdry: 1844 (cr Stratford St John EP, cr Plaistow St Mary EP),[222] 1844 (cr Stratford Marsh EP),[223] 1852 (help cr Forest Gate EP),[187] 1868 (help cr Barking Road EP),[53] 1879 (help cr Leytonstone Holy Trinity, Harrow Green EP),[226] 1879 (help cr Canning Town St Gabriel EP),[118] 1881 (help cr Forest Gate St James EP),[188] 1888 (help cr Upton Park St Stephen EP),[216] 1891 (cr West Ham St Thomas EP),[224] 1894 (help cr Upton Cross EP),[191] 1897 (cr West Ham St Matthew EP),[225] 1961.[49]

WEST HAM ST MATTHEW

EP Cr 1897 from West Ham AP.[225] W Bark. RDn (1897–1907), W Ham RDn (1907–66), Newham RDn (1966–*). Bdry: 1961.[49]

WEST HAM ST THOMAS

EP Cr 1891 from West Ham AP.[224] Bark. RDn (1891–95), W Bark. RDn (1895–1907), W Ham RDn (1907–61). Abol eccl 1961 pt to help cr Stratford St John with Christ Church EP), pt to West Ham AP.[49]

EAST HANNINGFIELD

AP *LG* Seq 1. Civ bdry: 1888,[229] 1946.[20] *Parl* Seq 10. *Eccl* Chelm. RDn (until 1845), Danb. RDn (1845–1907), Wickf. RDn (1907–72), Chelm. RDn (1972–*).

SOUTH HANNINGFIELD

AP *LG* Seq 1. Civ bdry: 1887,[167] 1934,[17] 1946,[20] 1955.[230] *Parl* Seq 10. *Eccl* Seq 35.

WEST HANNINGFIELD

AP *LG* Seq 1. Civ bdry: 1946,[20] 1955.[230] *Parl* Seq 10. *Eccl* Seq 35. Eccl bdry: 1874 (help cr Galleywood Common EP).[26]

HARLOW

AP *LG* Harlow Hd, Bor (status not sustained), Ep. PLU, RSD, RD (1894–1955), Harlow UD (1955–74). Civ bdry: 1883,[8] 1946,[20] 1949,[9] 1955 (area enlarged when constituted UD to incl pts of Netteswell AP, Epping Upland CP, Great Parndon AP, Roydon AP, losing pts to North Weald Bassett AP, Matching AP, Sheering AP).[183] *Parl* Seq 14. *Eccl* Seq 45. Eccl bdry: 1857 (cr Harlow St John the Baptist EP),[231] 1865 (cr Harlow St Mary Magdalen EP),[232] 1923 (gains ent Harlow St John the Baptist EP).[233]

HARLOW ST JOHN THE BAPTIST

EP Cr 1857 from,[231] and abol 1923 back into[233] Harlow AP. Harlow RDn.

HARLOW ST MARY MAGDALEN

EP Cr 1865 from Harlow AP.[232] Harlow RDn.

HARLOW NEW TOWN ST PAUL WITH LITTLE PARNDON ST MARY

EP Renaming 1957 of Little Parndon AP after the latter exchanges pts with Great Parndon AP and gains pt Netteswell AP, Latton AP.[234] Harlow RDn.

HAROLD HILL ST GEORGE

EP Cr 1956 from Romford EP.[235] Chaf. o'wise Romford RDn (1956–66), Hav. RDn (1966–*).

HAROLD HILL ST PAUL

EP Cr 1956 from Harold Wood EP.[236] Chaf. o'wise Romford RDn (1956–66), Hav. RDn (1966–*).

HAROLD WOOD

EP Cr 1938 from Hornchurch AP.[237] Chaf. o'wise

Romford RDn (1938–66), Hav. RDn (1966–*). Bdry: 1954,[238] 1956 (cr Harold Hill St Paul EP).[236] Now sometimes called 'Harold Hill St Peter'.

HARWICH

CP Cr 1925 by union Dovercourt AP, Harwich St Nicholas CP.[166] *LG* Harw. MB. *Parl* Harw. CC (1948–*).

HARWICH ST NICHOLAS

Chap in Dovercourt AP, sep civ rights from 16th cent,[289] sep EP 1871.[165] *LG* Tendr. Hd, PLU (1838–1925), Harw. Bor/MB, USD. Abol civ 1925 to help cr Harwich CP.[166] *Parl* Harw. Parl Bor (1604–1885), N-E'rn Dv (1885–1918), Harw. Dv (1918–48). *Eccl* Seq 14.

HATFIELD BROAD OAK

AP Sometimes 'Hatfield Regis'. *LG* Harlow Hd, Hatfield Regis Bor (status not sustained), Dunmow PLU, RSD, RD. Civ bdry: 1949.[114] *Parl* Seq 15. *Eccl* Seq 45. Eccl bdry: 1860 (cr Bush End EP, cr Hatfield Heath EP).[113]

HATFIELD HEATH

EP Cr 1860 from Hatfield Broad Oak AP.[113] Harlow RDn.

HATFIELD PEVEREL

AP *LG* Witham Hd, PLU (1835–83), RSD (1875–83), Braint. PLU (1883–1930), RSD (1883–94), Braint. RD. Civ bdry: 1883.[8] *Parl* Seq 3. *Eccl* Witham RDn (until 1847), Hatf. Pev. RDn (1847–1907), Witham RDn (1907–74). Abol eccl 1974 to help cr Hatfield Peverel with Ulting EP.[239]

HATFIELD PEVEREL WITH ULTING

EP Cr 1974 by union Hatfield Peverel AP, Ulting AP.[239] Witham RDn.

HAVENGORE

Ex-par island, pt cr sep CP 1858, remainder to Little Wakering AP.[311] *LG* Rochf. Hd, PLU,[120] RSD, RD. Abol 1946 ent to Foulness CP.[20] *Parl* South Dv (1867–85), S-E'rn Dv (1885–1948).

HAVERHILL

AP Pt Suffolk (Risbridge Hd), pt Essex (Hinckf. Hd), the latter lost 1879 to Sturmer AP in exchange of territory and par ent Suffolk thereafter.[240] *LG* Risbridge PLU, RSD. For organisation after 1879 see main entry in Suffolk. *Parl* Essex pt, N'rn Dv (1832–67), N-E Dv (1867–85). *Eccl* See main entry in Suffolk.

HAVERING-ATTE-BOWER

Ward in Hornchurch AP, first termed CP 1790, sep EP 1836.[242] *LG* Hav.-atte-Bower Lbty, Romford PLU, RSD, RD (1894–1934), Romford UD (1934–37), MB (1937–65). Transf 1965 to Gtr London (Hav. LB).[37] *Parl* S'rn Dv (1832–67), South Dv (1867–85), S'rn Dv (1885–1918), Romford Dv (1918–48), Romford BC (1948–70), Gtr London thereafter. *Eccl* Pec jurisd Hornchurch (until 1845), Bark. RDn (1845–62 [Roch dioc 1846–62]), Lamb. RDn (1862–1907), Chaf. o'wise Romford RDn (1907–66), Hav. RDn (1966–*). Eccl bdry: 1955 (help cr Collier Row EP),[153] 1956.[243]

HAWKWELL

AP *LG* Seq 20. *Parl* Seq 17. *Eccl* Seq 41.

HAZELEIGH

AP *LG* Seq 4. Civ bdry: 1883.[8] *Parl* S'rn Dv (1832–67), South Dv (1867–85), S-E'rn Dv (1885–1918), Mald. Dv/CC (1918–*). *Eccl* Dengie RDn (until 1845), Maldon RDn (1845–1932). Abol eccl 1932 to help cr Woodham Mortimer with Hazeleigh EP.[244]

CASTLE HEDINGHAM

AP *LG* Seq 13. Civ bdry: 1883.[8] *Parl* Seq 6. *Eccl* Donative, Seq 48.

SIBLE HEDINGHAM

AP *LG* Seq 13. Civ bdry: 1883,[8] 1885.[155] *Parl* Seq 6. *Eccl* Seq 48.

HEMPSTEAD

AP *LG* Seq 8. Civ bdry: 1965 (exchanges pts with Castle Camps AP, Cambs & IoE).[21] *Parl* Seq 8. *Eccl* Seq 12.

HENHAM

AP *LG* Pt Clav. Hd, pt Uttl. Hd, Bishop's Stortford PLU, RSD, Stan. RD (1894–1935), Saff. Wald. RD (1935–74). Civ bdry: 1946.[20] *Parl* Seq 8. *Eccl* Seq 11.

GREAT HENNY

AP *LG* Seq 15. Civ bdry: 1885.[15] *Parl* Seq 6. *Eccl* Heding. RDn (until 1907), Halst. & Heding. RDn (1907–67). Abol eccl 1967 to help cr Great and Little Henny EP.[245]

GREAT AND LITTLE HENNY

EP Cr 1967 by union Great Henny AP, Little Henny AP.[245] Halst. & Heding. RDn.

LITTLE HENNY

AP *LG* Seq 15. *Parl* Seq 6. *Eccl* As for Great Henny.

HEYBRIDGE

AP *LG* Thurst. Hd, Maldon PLU, RSD, RD. Civ bdry: 1883.[8] Abol civ 1934 pt to help cr Maldon CP, pt to Great Totham AP.[17] *Parl* Maldon Parl Bor (1832–85), S-E'rn Dv (1885–1918), Maldon Dv (1918–48). *Eccl* Pec jurisd Dean & Chapter of St Paul's, London (until 1845), Seq 19 thereafter.

HEYDON

AP *LG* Uttl. Hd, Royston PLU, RSD, sep RD in Essex (1894–95). Transf 1895 to Cambs.[139] *Parl* N'rn Dv (1832–67), N-W Dv (1867–85), N'rn Dv (1885–1918), Cambs thereafter. *Eccl* Seq 9.

HIGHAMS PARK

EP Cr 1912 from Walthamstow St John EP, Walthamstow St Peter EP.[246] Walt'stow & Leyton RDn (1912–16), Walt'stow & Chingford RDn (1916–66), Waltham Forest RDn (1966–*). Bdry: 1956 (help cr Chingford St Anne EP).[136] Now sometimes called 'Hale End All Saints, Highams Park'.

HIGHWOOD

Chap in Writtle AP, sep EP 1875,[247] sep CP 1954.[248] *LG* Chelm. RD. *Parl* Chelm. CC (1970–*). *Eccl* Chelm. RDn.

HOCKLEY

AP *LG* Seq 20. Civ bdry: 1926,[172] 1929 (loses pt

South Dv (1867–85), S-W'rn Dv (1885–1918), pt Leyton East Parl Bor (1918–48), pt Leyton West Parl Bor (1918–48) [see Part III of the *Guide* for the composition of these constituencies by wards of the UD], Leyton BC (1948–70), Gtr London thereafter. *Eccl* Bark. RDn (until 1895 [London dioc until 1867]), N Bark. RDn (1895–1907), Walt'stow & Leyton RDn (1907–16), Leyton RDn (1916–66), Waltham Forest RDn (1966–69). Eccl bdry: 1845 (cr Leytonstone EP),[296] 1879 (help cr Leytonstone Holy Trinity, Harrow Green EP),[297] 1881 (help cr Walthamstow St Stephen EP),[298] 1885,[301] 1886 (help cr Leyton All Saints EP),[299] 1894 (cr Leyton St Catherine EP),[300] 1904,[302] 1907 (cr Leyton St Paul EP),[303] 1932 (help cr Leyton St Luke EP),[304] 1933 (cr Leyton St Edward EP),[305] 1935 (cr Leyton Emmanuel EP).[306] Abol eccl 1969 to help cr Leyton St Mary with St Edward EP.[307]

LEYTON ALL SAINTS

EP Cr 1886 from Leyton AP, Walthamstow St James EP.[299] Bark. RDn (1886–95), N Bark. RDn (1895–1907), Walt'stow & Leyton RDn (1907–16), Leyton RDn (1916–66), Waltham Forest RDn (1966–*).

LEYTON CHRIST CHURCH

EP Cr 1904 from Leyton St Catherine EP, Leytonstone EP.[308] N Bark. RDn(1904–07),Walt'stow & Leyton RDn (1907–16), Leyton RDn (1916–66), Waltham Forest RDn (1966–*).

LEYTON EMMANUEL

EP Cr 1935 from Leyton All Saints EP.[306] Leyton RDn (1935–66), Waltham Forest RDn (1966–*).

LEYTON ST CATHERINE

EP Cr 1894 from Leyton AP.[300] Bark. RDn (1894–95), N. Bark. RDn (1895–1907), Walt'stow & Leyton RDn (1907–16), Leyton RDn (1916–66), Waltham Forest RDn (1966–*). Bdry: 1904 (help cr Leyton Christ Church EP),[308] 1904.[302]

LEYTON ST EDWARD

EP Cr 1933 from Leyton AP.[305] Leyton RDn (1933–66), Waltham Forest RDn (1966–69). Abol 1969 to help cr Leyton St Mary with St Edward EP.[307]

LEYTON ST LUKE

EP Cr 1932 from Leytonstone Holy Trinity, Harrow Green EP, Leyton AP.[304] Leyton RDn (1932–66), Waltham Forest RDn (1966–*).

LEYTON ST MARY WITH ST EDWARD

EP Cr 1969 by union Leyton AP, Leyton St Edward EP.[307] Waltham Forest RDn.

LEYTON ST PAUL

EP Cr 1907 from Leyton AP.[303] Walt'stow & Leyton RDn (1907–16), Leyton RDn (1916–66), Waltham Forest RDn (1966–*).

LEYTONSTONE

EP Cr 1845 from Leyton AP.[296] Bark. RDn (1845–95 [London dioc 1845–67]), N Bark. RDn (1895–1907), Walt'stow & Leyton RDn (1907–16), Leyton RDn (1916–66), Waltham Forest RDn (1966–*). Bdry: 1879 (help cr Leytonstone Holy Trinity, Harrow Green EP),[297] 1888 (cr Leytonstone St Andrew EP),[309] 1893 (help cr Leytonstone St Margaret EP),[310] 1904 (help cr Leyton Christ Church EP).[308]

LEYTONSTONE HOLY TRINITY, HARROW GREEN

EP Cr 1879 from Leytonstone EP, Leyton AP, Wanstead AP, West Ham AP, Stratford New Town EP.[297] Bark. RDn (1879–95), N Bark. RDn (1895–1907), Walt'stow & Leyton RDn (1907–16), Leyton RDn (1916–66), Waltham Forest RDn (1966–*). Bdry: 1893 (help cr Leytonstone St Margaret EP),[310] 1895 (help cr Wanstead Slip EP),[196] 1932 (help cr Leyton St Luke EP).[304]

LEYTONSTONE ST ANDREW

EP Cr 1888 from Leytonstone EP.[309] Bark. RDn (1888–95), N Bark. RDn (1895–1907), Walt'stow & Leyton RDn (1907–16), Leyton RDn (1916–66), Waltham Forest RDn (1966–*).

LEYTONSTONE ST MARGARET

EP Cr 1893 from Leytonstone Holy Trinity, Harrow Green EP, Leytonstone EP.[310] Bark. RDn (1893–95), N Bark. RDn (1895–1907), Walt'stow & Leyton RDn (1907–16), Leyton RDn (1916–53). Abol 1953 to help cr Leytonstone St Margaret with St Columba EP.[146]

LEYTONSTONE ST MARGARET WITH ST COLUMBA

EP Cr 1953 by union Leytonstone St Margaret EP, Wantead Slip [St Columba] EP.[146] Leyton RDn (1953–66), Waltham Forest RDn (1966–*).

LINDSELL

AP *LG* Seq 6. *Parl* Seq 8. *Eccl* Seq 43.

LISTON

AP *LG* Seq 15. Civ bdry: 1885.[15] *Parl* Seq 6. *Eccl* Heding. RDn (until 1907), Belch. RDn (1907–69). Abol eccl 1969 to help cr Liston and Borley EP.[86]

LISTON AND BORLEY

EP Cr 1969 by union Liston AP, Borley AP.[86] Belch. RDn.

LITTLEBURY

AP *LG* Seq 24. Civ bdry: 1954.[132] *Parl* Seq 8. *Eccl* Seq 9. Eccl bdry: 1889.[312]

LOUGHTON

AP *LG* Ong. Hd, Ep. PLU, RSD, RD (1894–1900), Loughton UD (1900–33), Chigw. UD (1933–74). *Parl* S'rn Dv (1832–67), N-W Dv (1867–85), W'rn Dv (1885–1918), Ep. Dv (1918–48), Woodf. BC (1948–70), Ep. Forest CC (1970–*). *Eccl* Bark. RDn (until 1845), Ep. RDn (1845–62), Romford RDn (1862–83), Chigw. RDn (1883–*). Eccl bdry: 1887 (cr Loughton St Mary the Virgin EP),[313] 1972.[314]

LOUGHTON ST MARY THE VIRGIN

EP Cr 1887 from Loughton AP.[313] Chigw. RDn. Bdry: 1972.[314]

1. *Eccl* Lexd. RDn (until 1847), Mersea RDn (1847–1907), Colch. RDn (1907–61). Abol eccl 1961 to help cr Abberton with Langenhoe EP.[1]

LANGFORD

AP *LG* Seq 22. Civ bdry: 1883,[8] 1888,[273] 1889,[22] 1934 (help cr Maldon CP).[17] *Parl* Seq 2. *Eccl* Seq 19.

LANGHAM

AP *LG* Seq 17. *Parl* Seq 1. *Eccl* Seq 4. Eccl bdry: 1868 (help cr Colchester St John EP).[18]

LANGLEY

Chap in Clavering AP, sep civ identity early, sep EP 1875.[143] *LG* Seq 3. *Parl* Seq 8. *Eccl* Nwpt. RDn (until 1907), Nwpt. & Stan. RDn (1907–*).

LATCHINGDON

AP *LG* Seq 4. United both civ and eccl mid 18th cent with Snoreham AP, the union usually civ called 'Latchingdon' but eccl and often civ 'Latchingdon with Snoreham'.[274] Addtl civ bdry alt: 1946.[275] *Parl* Seq 9. *Eccl* Pec jurisd Archbp Canterb (Bocking RDn, until 1845), Dengie RDn (1845–1954). Abol eccl 1954 to help cr Latchingdon with Mundon EP.[277]

LATCHINGDON WITH MUNDON

EP Cr 1954 by union Latchingdon with Snoreham EP, Mundon AP.[277] Dengie RDn. Bdry: 1973.[276]

LATCHINGDON WITH SNOREHAM–See LATCHINGDON

LATTON

AP *LG* Harlow Hd, Ep. PLU, RSD, RD. Civ bdry: 1883.[8] Abol civ 1949 pt to Harlow AP, pt to North Weald Bassett AP.[9] *Parl* S'rn Dv (1832–67), N-W Dv (1867–85), W'rn Dv (1885–1918), Ep. Dv/CC (1918–70). *Eccl* Harlow RDn. Renamed 1957 'Mark Hall St Mary at Latton' after exchanges pts with Harlow AP and with Netteswell AP and loses pt to help cr Harlow New Town St Paul with Little Parndon St Mary EP.[234]

HIGH LAVER

AP *LG* Seq 19. *Parl* Seq 12. *Eccl* Seq 39. Eccl bdry: 1944.[288]

LITTLE LAVER

AP *LG* Seq 19. *Parl* Seq 12. *Eccl* Seq 39.

MAGDALEN LAVER

AP *LG* Seq 18. Civ bdry: 1883,[8] 1946.[20] *Parl* Seq 14. *Eccl* Seq 39.

LAWFORD

AP *LG* Seq 21. *Parl* Seq 5. *Eccl* Seq 13.

LAYER BRETON

AP *LG* Seq 25. Civ bdry: 1889.[7] *Parl* Seq 1. *Eccl* Seq 2.

LAYER DE LA HAYE

AP *LG* Seq 25. Civ bdry: 1889,[7] 1953 (incl help cr Great and Little Wigborough CP).[83] *Parl* Seq 1. *Eccl* Seq 7.

LAYER MARNEY

AP *LG* Seq 25. Civ bdry: 1889,[7] 1934.[8] *Parl* Seq 1. *Eccl* Seq 2.

LEE CHAPEL

Ex-par place, sep CP 1858,[311] abol eccl 1957 pt to Langdon Hills AP, pt to Laindon AP.[272] *LG* Barst. Hd, Bill. PLU,[120] RSD, RD (1894–1935), Bill. UD (1935–37). Civ bdry: 1889,[157] 1935,[14] 1936.[24] Abol 1937 to help cr Billericay CP.[56] *Parl* South Dv (1867–85), Mid Dv (1885–1918), S-E'rn Dv (1918–48). Eccl bdry: 1883.[78]

LEIGH

AP Usual civ spelling; for eccl see following entry. *LG* Rochf. Hd, PLU, RSD, RD (1894–97), Leigh on Sea UD (1897–1913). Abol civ 1913 to help cr Southend on Sea CB and CP.[173] *Parl* S'rn Dv (1832–67), South Dv (1867–85), S-E'rn Dv (1885–1918).

LEIGH-ON-SEA

AP Usual eccl spelling; for civ see prev entry. *Eccl* Seq 41. Eccl bdry: 1929 (cr Leigh-on-Sea St Margaret EP),[294] 1951 (help cr Leigh-on-Sea St James EP).[295]

LEIGH-ON-SEA ST AIDAN, THE FAIRWAY

EP Cr 1956 from Eastwood AP.[178] Canew. & S'end RDn.

LEIGH-ON-SEA ST JAMES

EP Cr 1952 from Leigh-on-Sea AP, Eastwood AP.[177] Canew. & S'end RDn. Bdry: 1958 (help cr Hadleigh St Barnabas EP).[208]

LEIGH-ON-SEA ST MARGARET

EP Cr 1929 from Leigh-on-Sea AP.[294] Canew. & S'end RDn. Bdry: 1958 (help cr Hadleigh St Barnabas EP).[208]

GREAT LEIGHS

AP *LG* Pt Witham Hd, pt Chelm. Hd, Chelm. PLU,[66] RSD, RD. Abol civ 1949 pt to help cr Great and Little Leighs CP, pt to Little Waltham AP.[114] *Parl* Pt N'rn Dv, pt S'rn Dv (1832–67), pt N-E Dv, pt N-W Dv (1867–85), Mid Dv (1885–1918), Chelm. Dv (1918–70). *Eccl* Seq 32.

GREAT AND LITTLE LEIGHS

CP Cr 1949 by union Little Leighs AP, pt Great Leighs AP, pt Little Waltham AP.[114] *LG* Chelm. RD. *Parl* Braint. CC (1970–*).

LITTLE LEIGHS

AP Organisation as for Great Leighs except abol civ 1934 ent to help cr Great and Little Leighs CP.[114]

LEXDEN

AP *LG* Lexd. Hd, Colch. Bor/MB, USD. Civ bdry: 1883.[8] Abol civ 1897 to help cr Colchester CP.[74] *Parl* Colch. Parl Bor (1295–1918). *Eccl* Seq 1. Eccl bdry: 1845 (help cr All Saints in Stanway and Lexden EP),[11] 1879 (help cr Colchester St Paul EP),[152] 1956.[13]

LEYTON [ST MARY]

AP Sometimes anc 'Low Leyton'. *LG* Becontree Hd, W Ham PLU, Leyton USD (ent 1875–83 and 1887–94, pt 1883–87), pt Wanstead USD (1883–87), Leyton UD (1894–1926), MB (1926–65). Transf 1965 to Gtr London (Waltham Forest LB).[37] *Parl* S'rn Dv (1832–67), ford St Andrew EP),[265] 1928 (help cr Barkingside St George EP),[52] 1934 (help cr Barkingside St Laurence EP),[3] 1958 (cr Great Ilford St Alban EP).[266]

GREAT ILFORD ST ALBAN

EP Cr 1958 from Great Ilford EP.[266] Bark. RDn (1958–66), Redbr. RDn (1966–*).

GREAT ILFORD ST ANDREW

EP Cr 1923 from Great Ilford EP.[265] Bark. RDn (1923–66), Redbr. RDn (1966–*).

GREAT ILFORD ST JOHN THE EVANGELIST

EP Cr 1904 from Great Ilford EP.[263] S Bark. RDn (1904–07), Bark. RDn (1907–66), Redbr. RDn (1966–*).

GREAT ILFORD ST LUKE

EP Cr 1916 from Great Ilford EP.[264] Bark. RDn (1916–66), Redbr. RDn (1966–*).

GREAT ILFORD ST MARY

EP Cr 1904 from Great Ilford EP.[263] S Bark. RDn (1904–07), Bark. RDn (1907–66), Redbr. RDn (1966–*). Bdry: 1914 (help cr Goodmayes All Saints EP),[38] 1971.[46]

LITTLE ILFORD

AP *LG* Becontree Hd, W Ham PLU, RSD (1875–86), E Ham USD (1886–94), UD (1894–1900). Abol civ 1900 ent to East Ham AP.[267] *Parl* S'rn Dv (1832–67), South Dv (1867–85), S'rn Dv (1885–1918). *Eccl* Bark. RDn (until 1895 [London dioc until 1867]), S Bark. RDn (1895–1907), Bark. RDn (1907–66), Newham RDn (1966–*). Eccl bdry: 1901 (help cr Little Ilford St Barnabas EP),[217] 1901 (help cr Forest Gate St Edmund EP),[194] 1914 (help cr Aldersbrook EP).[10]

LITTLE ILFORD ST BARNABAS

EP Cr 1901 from Little Ilford AP, East Ham AP.[217] S Bark. RDn (1901–07), Bark. RDn (1907–66), Newham RDn (1966–*).

INGATESTONE

AP *LG* Chelm. Hd, PLU, RSD. Abol civ 1889 to help cr Ingatestone and Fryerning CP.[202] *Parl* S'rn Dv (1832–67), N-W Dv (1867–85), Mid Dv (1885–1918). *Eccl* Seq 33.

INGATESTONE AND FRYERNING

CP Cr 1889 by union Ingatestone AP, Fryerning AP.[202] *LG* Chelm. PLU, RSD, RD. Bdry: 1950.[268] *Parl* Chelm. Dv/CC (1918–*).

INGRAVE

AP *LG* Barst. Hd, Bill. PLU, RSD, RD. Abol civ 1934 ent to Brentwood CP.[17] *Parl* S'rn Dv (1832–67), South Dv (1867–85), Mid Dv (1885–1918), Chelm. Dv (1918–48). *Eccl* Barst. RDn. Abol eccl 1712 to help cr West Horndon with Ingrave EP.[259]

EP Cr 1961 when West Horndon with Ingrave EP abol, Ingrave made sep EP, the remainder to help cr East with West Horndon EP.[257]

INWORTH

AP *LG* Lexd. Hd, Witham PLU (1835–83), RSD (1875–83), Lexd. & Winst. PLU (1883–1930), RSD (1883–94), RD. Civ bdry: 1889.[7] Abol civ 1934 pt to help cr Messing cum Inworth CP, pt to Feering AP, pt to help cr Tiptree CP.[17] *Parl* N'rn Dv (1832–67), N-E Dv (1867–85), E'rn Dv (1885–1918), pt Colch. Dv (1918–48 [a detached pt]), pt Maldon Dv (1918–48). *Eccl* Seq 3. Eccl bdry: 1859 (help cr Tiptree Heath EP).[269]

KEDINGTON

AP Pt Suffolk (Risbridge Hd), pt Essex (Hinckf. Hd), the latter transf 1895 to W Suffolk[139] and par ent Suffolk thereafter. *LG* Risbridge PLU, RSD, pt Bump. RD in Essex (1894–95), pt Risbridge RD in Suffolk (1894–95). Civ bdry: 1883.[8] See main entry in Suffolk for later organisation. *Parl* Essex pt, N'rn Dv (1832–67), N-E Dv (1867–85), N'rn Dv (1885–1918). *Eccl* See main entry in Suffolk.

KELVEDON

AP *LG* Witham Hd, PLU (1835–83), RSD (1875–83), Braint. PLU (1883–1930), RSD (1883–94), Braint. RD. Civ bdry: 1883,[8] 1889,[93] 1933,[184] 1956.[270] *Parl* Seq 3. *Eccl* Seq 17.

KELVEDON HATCH

AP *LG* Seq 19. *Parl* Seq 12. *Eccl* Ong. RDn (until 1845), Lamb. RDn (1845–1907), Ong. RDn (1907–53), Barst. o'wise Brentw. RDn (1953–*).

KIRBY LE SOKEN

AP *LG* Tendr. Hd, PLU, RSD, RD. Civ bdry: 1883.[8] Abol civ 1934 pt to help cr Frinton and Walton CP, pt to Thorpe le Soken AP.[17] *Parl* N'rn Dv (1832–67), N-E Dv (1867–85), N-E'rn Dv (1885–1918), Harw. Dv (1918–48). *Eccl* Pec jurisd of the Sokens (until 1845), Seq 15 thereafter.

LAINDON

AP Incl chap Basildon (sep civ identity early, no sep eccl identity though sometimes called 'rectory'[55]), pt Canvey Island (sep EP 1739,[88] sep CP 1880[90]). *LG* Barst. Hd, Bill. PLU, RSD, RD (1894–1935), Bill. UD (1935–37). Addtl civ bdry alt: 1880,[69] 1889.[271] Abol civ 1937 to help cr Billericay CP.[56] *Parl* S'rn Dv (1832–67), South Dv (1867–85), Mid Dv (1885–1918), S-E'rn Dv (1918–48). *Eccl* Barst. RDn (until 1907), Barst. o'wise Brentw. RDn (1907–55), Basildon RDn (1955–*). Addtl eccl bdry alt: 1883,[78] 1957,[272] 1957 (help cr Basildon St Andrew EP).[57]

LAINDON HILLS–See LANGDON HILLS

LAMARSH

AP *LG* Seq 15. Civ bdry: 1883,[8] 1885.[15] *Parl* Seq 6. *Eccl* Seq 48.

LAMBOURNE

AP *LG* Seq 19. *Parl* Seq 12. *Eccl* Usually as 'Lambourne with Abridge', Seq 38.

LANGDON HILLS

AP Sometimes 'Laindon Hills'. *LG* Barst. Hd, Ors. PLU, RSD, RD. Civ bdry: 1889.[157] Abol civ 1936 pt to help cr Thurrock CP, pt to Lee Chapel CP.[24] *Parl* S'rn Dv (1832–67), South Dv (1867–85), S-E'rn Dv (1885–1948). *Eccl* Seq 25.

LANGENHOE

AP *LG* Seq 25. Civ bdry: 1934,[17] 1946.[20] *Parl* Seq

to Rawreth AP as latter helps constitute Rayleigh UD),[152] 1934,[17] 1946,[20] 1960,[249] 1964 (cr Hullbridge CP).[250] *Parl* Seq 17. *Eccl* Seq 42.

GREAT HOLLAND

AP *LG* Tendr. Hd, PLU, RSD, RD. Civ bdry: 1888.[251] Abol civ 1934 ent to Frinton and Walton CP.[17] *Parl* N'rn Dv (1832–67), N-E Dv (1867–1918), Harw. Dv (1918–48). *Eccl* Seq 16.

LITTLE HOLLAND

AP *LG* Tendr. Hd, PLU, RSD, RD. Abol civ 1934 ent to Great Clacton AP.[17] *Parl* N'rn Dv (1832–67), N-E Dv (1867–85), N-E'rn Dv (1885–1918), Harw. Dv (1918–48). *Eccl* Tendr. RDn. Abol between 1768–1810 ent to Great Clacton AP.[291]

GREAT HORKESLEY

AP *LG* Seq 17. Civ bdry: 1883,[8] 1955.[76] *Parl* Seq 1. *Eccl* Seq 4.

LITTLE HORKESLEY

AP *LG* Seq 17. Civ bdry: 1883,[8] 1889,[7] 1955.[76] *Parl* Seq 1. *Eccl* Seq 4.

HORNCHURCH

AP Incl lbty and ward Havering-atte-Bower (first termed CP 1790, sep EP 1836[242]), chap Romford (sep civ identity early, sep EP *ca* 1840[292]). *LG* Hav.-atte-Bower Lbty, Romford PLU, RSD, RD (1894–1926), Hornchurch UD (1926–65). Addtl civ bdry alt: 1934,[17] 1946.[160] Transf 1965 to Gtr London (Hav. LB).[37] *Parl* S'rn Dv (1832–67), South Dv (1867–85), S'rn Dv (1885–1918), Romford Dv (1918–45), Hornchurch Dv (1945–48), Hornchurch BC (1948–70), Gtr London thereafter. *Eccl* Pec jurisd Hornchurch (until 1845), Bark. RDn (1845–62 [Roch dioc 1846–62]), Romford RDn (1862–68), Chaf. RDn (1868–1966), Hav. RDn (1966–*). Addtl eccl bdry alt: 1925 (cr Hornchurch Holy Cross EP),[253] 1926 (cr Hornchurch St Nicholas, Elm Park EP),[254] 1926 (help cr Squirrel's Heath EP),[255] 1938 (cr Harold Wood EP),[237] 1954,[256] 1957.[135]

HORNCHURCH HOLY CROSS

EP Cr 1925 from Hornchurch AP.[253] Chaf. o'wise Romford RDn (1925–66), Hav. RDn (1966–*). Bdry: 1969 (help cr Rush Green EP),[161] 1971.[293]

HORNCHURCH ST NICHOLAS, ELM PARK

EP Cr 1957 from Hornchurch AP.[254] Chaf. o'wise Romford RDn (1957–66), Hav. RDn (1966–*).

EAST HORNDON

AP *LG* Barst. Hd, Bill. PLU, RSD, RD. Abol civ 1934 pt to Little Burstead AP, pt to Brentwood CP.[17] *Parl* S'rn Dv (1832–67), South Dv (1867–85), Mid Dv (1885–1918), S-E'rn Dv (1918–48). *Eccl* Barst. RDn (until 1845), Bill. RDn (1845–95), Barst. RDn (1895–1907), Barst. o'wise Brentw. RDn (1907–61). Abol eccl 1961 to help cr East with West Horndon EP.[257]

EAST AND WEST HORNDON

EP Renaming 1972 of East with West Horndon EP.[258] Barst. o'wise Brentw. RDn.

EAST WITH WEST HORNDON

EP Cr 1961 by union East Horndon AP, remaining area of West Horndon with Ingrave EP when Ingrave made sep EP.[257] Barst. o'wise Brentw. RDn. Renamed 1972 'East and West Horndon'.[258]

WEST HORNDON

AP *LG* Barst. Hd, Bill. PLU, RSD, RD. Abol civ 1934 pt to Little Burstead AP, pt to Brentwood CP.[17] *Parl* S'rn Dv (1832–67), South Dv (1867–85), Mid Dv (1885–1918), S-E'rn Dv (1918–48). *Eccl* Barst. RDn. Abol 1712 to help cr West Horndon with Ingrave EP.[259]

WEST HORNDON WITH INGRAVE

EP Cr 1712 by union West Horndon AP, Ingrave AP.[259] Barst. RDn (until 1845), Bill. RDn (1845–95), Barst. RDn (1895–1907), Barst. o'wsie Brentw. RDn (1907–61). Bdry: 1956.[96] Abol 1961, Ingrave reconstituted sep EP, West Horndon to help cr East with West Horndon EP.[257]

HORNDON ON THE HILL

AP *LG* Barst. Hd, Ors. PLU, RSD, RD. Civ bdry: 1910.[260] Abol civ 1936 to help cr Thurrock CP.[24] *Parl* S'rn Dv (1832–67), South Dv (1867–85), S-E'rn Dv (1885–1948). *Eccl* Seq 26. Eccl bdry: 1954.[261]

HULLBRIDGE

CP Cr 1964 from Hockley AP.[250] *LG* Rochf. RD. *Parl* Maldon CC (1970–*).

HUTTON

AP *LG* Barst. Hd, Bill. PLU, RSD, RD. Abol civ 1934 ent to Brentwood CP.[17] *Parl* S'rn Dv (1832–67), South Dv (1867–85), Mid Dv (1885–1918), Chelm. Dv (1918–48). *Eccl* Seq 23. Eccl bdry: 1956.[96]

ILFORD

Great Ilford (qv) orig a sep AP, later considered pt of Barking AP, sep CP 1866 as 'Ilford'[32] (for eccl see following entry). *LG* Becontree Hd, Romford PLU,[120] RSD (1875–90), Ilford USD (1890–94), UD (1894–1926), MB (1926–65). Bdry: 1907,[35] 1934,[36] 1956.[262] Transf 1965 to Gtr London (Redbr. LB).[37] *Parl* South Dv (1867–85), S'rn Dv (1885–1918), Ilford Parl Bor (1918–45), pt Ilford North BC (1945–70), pt Ilford South BC (1945–70) [see Part III of the *Guide* for composition of these constituencies by wards of the MB], Gtr London thereafter. Parl bdry: 1960.[427]

GREAT ILFORD [ST CLEMENT]

AP Orig sep AP, later considered pt of Barking AP, sep civ identity regained 1966 as 'Ilford' CP (qv), sep EP 1830.[33] Bark. RDn (1830–95 [London dioc 1830–67]), S Bark. RDn (1895–1907), Bark. RDn (1907–66), Redbr. RDn (1966–*). Bdry: 1841 (cr Barkingside Trinity EP),[53] 1863 (help cr Aldborough Hatch EP),[2] 1895 (help cr Chadwell Heath EP),[122] 1904 (cr Great Ilford St Mary EP, cr Great Ilford St John the Evangelist EP),[263] 1916 (cr Great Ilford St Luke EP),[264] 1923 (cr Great Il-

MALDON
CP Cr 1934 by union Maldon All Saints AP, Maldon St Mary AP, Maldon St Peter AP, and pts of Goldhanger AP, Heybridge AP, Great Totham AP, Langford AP, Little Totham AP, Mundon AP, Steeple AP, Tolleshunt Major AP.[17] *LG* Maldon MB. *Parl* Maldon CC (1948–*).

MALDON ALL SAINTS
AP *LG* Dengie Hd, Maldon PLU, Bor/MB, USD. Abol civ 1934 to help cr Maldon CP.[17] *Parl* Maldon Parl Bor (1334–1885), Maldon Dv (1885–1948). *Eccl* Chelm. RDn. Maldon All Saints AP and Maldon St Peter AP united 1306 although some sep rights retained until 18th cent (see following entry), incl sep civ identity from 16th cent.[315]

MALDON ALL SAINTS WITH ST PETER
EP Cr 1306 (although some sep rights kept until 18th cent) by union Maldon All Saints AP, Maldon St Peter AP.[315] *Eccl* Seq 37.

MALDON ST MARY
AP *LG* Dengie Hd, Maldon PLU, Bor/MB, USD. Civ bdry: 1883,[8] 1889.[22] Abol civ 1934 to help cr Maldon CP.[17] *Parl* Maldon Parl Bor (1334–1885), Maldon Dv (1885–1948). *Eccl* Pec jurisd Dean & Chapter of Westminster (until 1845), Seq 37 thereafter.

MALDON ST PETER
AP *LG* Dengie Hd, Maldon PLU, Bor/MB, USD. Civ bdry: 1883,[8] 1889.[22] Abol civ 1934 to help cr Maldon CP.[17] *Parl*, *Eccl* as for Maldon All Saints.

MANNINGTREE
Chap and bor in Mistley AP, Bradfield AP, bor status not sustained, sep civ identity as par early, sep EP 1840.[89] *LG* Seq 21. *Parl* Seq 5. *Eccl* Tendr. RDn (until 1847), Ardl. RDn (1847–95), Ardl. & Harw. RDn (1895–1907), Harw. RDn (1907–67). Abol eccl 1967 to help cr Mistley with Manningtree EP.[316]

MANUDEN
AP *LG* Seq 2. *Parl* Seq 8. *Eccl* Seq 8.

GREAT MAPLESTEAD
AP *LG* Seq 13. Civ bdry: 1883,[8] 1885.[155] *Parl* Seq 6. *Eccl* Seq 48.

LITTLE MAPLESTEAD
AP Organisation as for Great Maplestead.

MARGARETTING
AP *LG* Seq 1. Civ bdry: 1950,[268] 1954.[248] *Parl* Seq 10. *Eccl* Seq 33.

MARK HALL ST MARY AT LATTON
EP Renaming 1957 of Latton AP after the latter exchanged pts with Harlow AP, Netteswell AP, and lost pt to help cr Harlow New Town with Little Parndon EP.[234] Harlow RDn.

MARKSHALL
AP *LG* Lexd. Hd, Witham PLU (1835–83), RSD (1875–83), Braint. PLU (1883–1930), RSD (1883–94), Braint. RD. Abol civ 1949 to help cr Coggeshall CP.[9] *Parl* N'rn Dv (1832–67), N-E Dv (1867–85), E'rn Dv (1885–1918), Maldon Dv (1918–70). *Eccl* Lexd. RDn (until 1847), Halst. RDn (1847–1907), Cogg. & Tey RDn (1907–32). Abol eccl 1932 to help cr Coggeshall with Markshall EP.[144]

MASHBURY
AP *LG* Seq 5. Civ bdry: 1885,[229] 1888.[317] *Parl* Seq 7. *Eccl* Dunmow RDn (until 1920s), Chelm. RDn (1920s–*).

MATCHING
AP *LG* Seq 10. Civ bdry: 1883,[8] 1955.[317] *Parl* Seq 14. *Eccl* Seq 45. Eccl bdry: 1944.[288]

MAYLAND
AP *LG* Seq 4. Civ bdry: 1889.[22] *Parl* Seq 9. *Eccl* Seq 36. Eccl bdry: 1973.[276]

EAST MERSEA
AP *LG* Seq 25. *Parl* Seq 1. *Eccl* Seq 7.

WEST MERSEA
AP *LG* Winst. Hd, Lexd. & Winst. PLU, RSD, RD (1894–1926), W Mersea UD (1926–74). Civ bdry: 1953.[83] *Parl* Seq 1. *Eccl* Seq 7.

MESSING
AP *LG* Lexd. Hd, Witham PLU (1835–83), RSD (1875–83), Lexd. & Winst. PLU (1883–1930), RSD (1883–94), Lexd. & Winst. RD. Civ bdry: 1883,[8] 1889,[7] 1934 (help cr Tiptree CP, help cr Messing cum Inworth CP).[17] Abol civ 1949 ent to Birch AP.[9] *Parl* N'rn Dv (1832–67), N-E Dv (1867–85), E'rn Dv (1885–1918), Colch. Dv/CC (1918–70). *Eccl* Seq 3. Eccl bdry: 1859 (help cr Tiptree Heath EP).[269]

MESSING CUM INWORTH
CP Cr 1934 by union pt Inworth AP, pt Messing AP.[270] *LG* Lexd. & Winst. RD. *Parl* Colch. CC (1948–*).

MIDDLETON
AP *LG* Seq 15. Civ bdry: 1885.[15] *Parl* Seq 6. *Eccl* Seq 48.

MILE END ST MICHAEL
AP Usual civ spelling; for eccl see 'Myland St Michael (otherwise Mile End St Michael)'. *LG* Lexd. Hd, Colch. PLU, Bor/MB, USD. Abol civ 1897 to help cr Colchester CP.[74] *Parl* Colch. Parl Bor (1295–1918). *Eccl* Seq 1. Eccl bdry: 1868 (help cr Colchester St John EP),[18] 1953 (incl help cr Colchester St James with All Saints and St Nicholas and St Runwald EP).[146]

MISTLEY
AP Incl pt chap and bor Manningtree (sep bor status not sustained, sep civ identity as par early, sep EP 1840[89]). *LG* Seq 21. *Parl* Seq 5. *Eccl* Tendr. RDn (until 1847), Ardl. RDn (1847–95), Ardl. & Harw. RDn (1895–1907), Harw. RDn (1907–67). Abol eccl 1967 to help cr Mistley with Manningtree EP.[316]

MISTLEY WITH MANNINGTREE
EP Cr 1967 by union Mistley AP, Manningtree EP.[316] Harw. RDn.

MOZE
AP *LG* Tendr. Hd. *Eccl* Tendr. RDn. United 1678 with Beaumont AP, the union civ called 'Beaumont cum Moze', eccl 'Beaumont with Moze'.[58]

MUCKING
AP *LG* Barst. Hd, Ors. PLU, RSD, RD. Civ bdry: 1888,[320] 1910.[260] Abol civ 1936 to help cr Thurrock CP.[24] *Parl* S'rn Dv (1832–67), South

Dv (1867–85), S-E'rn Dv (1885–1948). *Eccl* Barst. RDn (until 1845), Ors. RDn (1845–1907), Ors. & Grays RDn (1907–73). Eccl bdry: 1963.[321] Abol eccl 1973 to help cr Stanford-le-Hope with Mucking EP.[322]

MUNDON

AP *LG* Seq 4. Civ bdry: 1934 (help cr Maldon CP),[17] 1946,[323] 1955.[324] *Parl* Seq 9. *Eccl* 1934), Chelm. RD (1934–74). Civ bdry: 1934,[17] 1936.[111] *Parl* Seq 10. Parl bdry: 1945.[426] *Eccl* Chelm. RDn (until 1845), Bill. RDn (1845–95), Barst. o'wise Brentw. RDn (1907–*). Eccl bdry: 1956.[79]

MORETON

AP *LG* Seq 19. Civ bdry: 1946.[20] *Parl* Seq 12. *Eccl* Seq 39. Eccl bdry: 1933.[318]

MOULSHAM

EP Cr 1838 from Chelmsford AP.[128] Chelm. RDn. Bdry: 1874 (help cr Galleywood Common EP),[26] 1956.[319]

MOUNTNESSING

AP *LG* Chelm. Hd, Bill. PLU, RSD, RD (1894–Chelm. RDn (until 1845), Maldon RDn (1845–1954). Abol eccl 1954 to help cr Latchingdon with Mundon EP.[277]

MYLAND ST MICHAEL (OTHERWISE MILE END ST MICHAEL)

AP Usual eccl spelling; for civ see 'Mile End St Michael'. *Eccl* Seq 1. Eccl bdry: 1868 (help cr Colchester St John EP),[18] 1953 (incl help cr Colchester St James with All Saints and St Nicholas and St Runwald EP).[146]

NAVESTOCK

AP *LG* Seq 19. *Parl* Seq 12. *Eccl* Pec jurisd Dean & Chapter of St Paul's, London (until 1845), Lamb. RDn (1845–1907), Barst. o'wise Brentw. RDn (1907–*).

NAZEING

AP *LG* Waltham Hd, Ep. PLU, RSD, RD (1894–1955), Ep. & Ong. RD (1955–74). Civ bdry: 1946.[20] *Parl* Seq 14. *Eccl* Bark. RDn (until 1862 [London dioc until 1846]), Harlow RDn (1862–*).

NETTESWELL

AP *LG* Harlow Hd, Ep. PLU, RSD, RD. Civ bdry: 1946,[9] 1949.[20] Abol civ 1955 ent to Harlow AP when latter constituted UD.[325] *Parl* S'rn Dv (1832–67), N-W Dv (1867–85), W'rn Dv (1885–1918), Ep. Dv/CC (1918–70). *Eccl* Harlow RDn. Renamed 1957 'Tye Green with St Andrew' after exchanged pts with Latton AP, and lost pts to Great Parndon AP, Little Parndon AP.[234]

NEVENDON

AP *LG* Barst. Hd, Bill. PLU, RSD, RD (1894–1935), Bill. UD (1935–37). Civ bdry: 1883,[8] 1889.[87] Abol civ 1937 to help cr Billericay CP.[56] *Parl* S'rn Dv (1832–67), South Dv (1867–85), Mid Dv (1885–1918), S-E'rn Dv (1918–48). *Eccl* Barst. RDn (until 1895), Danb. RDn (1895–1955), Basildon RDn (1955–*). Eccl bdry: 1957 (help cr Basildon St Andrew EP).[57]

NEWPORT

AP *LG* Nwpt. Bor (status not sustained), Seq 24. Civ bdry: 1883,[8] 1946,[20] 1960.[326] *Parl* Seq 8. *Eccl* Pec jurisd Dean & Chapter of Westminster (until 1845), Seq 8 thereafter.

NOAK HILL

CP Cr 1895 from Romford Rural CP.[327] *LG* Romford PLU, RD (1894–1934), UD (1934–37), MB (1937–65). Transf 1965 to Gtr London (Hav. LB).[37] *Parl* Romford Dv (1918–45), Romford BC (1945–70), Gtr London thereafter.

COLD NORTON

AP *LG* Seq 4. *Parl* Seq 9. *Eccl* Seq 37.

NORTON MANDEVILLE

Area in High Ongar AP, sep identity as par late 12th cent.[328] *LG* Ong. Hd, PLU, RSD, RD (1894–1955), Ep. & Ong. RD (1955–68). Civ bdry: 1946.[20] Abol civ 1968 ent to High Ongar AP.[329] *Parl* S'rn Dv (1832–67), N-W Dv (1867–85), W'rn Dv (1885–1918), Chelm. Dv/CC (1918–70). *Eccl* Seq 39.

BLACK NOTLEY

AP *LG* Seq 26. Civ bdry: 1889,[93] 1934 (incl help cr Braintree and Bocking CP).[17] *Parl* Seq 3. *Eccl* Seq 18.

WHITE NOTLEY

AP *LG* Seq 26. Civ bdry: 1888,[273] 1889.[93] *Parl* Seq 3. *Eccl* Seq 17.

GREAT OAKLEY

AP *LG* Seq 21. *Parl* Seq 5. *Eccl* Seq 14.

LITTLE OAKLEY

AP *LG* Seq 21. *Parl* Seq 5. *Eccl* Tendr. RDn (until 1847), Harw. RDn (1847–95), Ardl. & Harw. RDn (1895–1907), Harw. RDn (1907–73). Abol eccl 1973 to help cr Ramsey with Little Oakley EP.[330]

NORTH OCKENDON

AP *LG* Chaf. Hd, Ors. PLU, RSD, RD. Abol civ 1936 pt to help cr Thurrock CP, pt to Cranham AP.[24] *Parl* S'rn Dv (1832–67), South Dv (1867–85), S-E'rn Dv (1885–1948). *Eccl* Seq 27.

SOUTH OCKENDON

AP *LG* Chaf. Hd, Ors. PLU, RSD, RD (1894–1929), Purfleet UD (1929–35). Civ bdry: 1888.[320] Abol civ 1936 to help cr Thurrock CP.[24] *Parl* S'rn Dv (1832–67), South Dv (1867–85), S-E'rn Dv (1885–1948). *Eccl* Seq 29. Eccl bdry: 1958 (help cr Belhus Park EP),[25] 1970.[68]

ONGAR

CP Cr 1965 by union Chipping Ongar AP, Greenstead AP, Shelley AP, pt High Ongar AP.[331] *LG* Ep. & Ong. RD. *Parl* Brentw. & Ong. CC (1970–*).

CHIPPING ONGAR

AP *LG* Ong. Hd, PLU, RSD, RD (1894–1955), Ep. & Ong. RD (1955–68). Abol civ 1965 to help cr Ongar CP.[331] *Parl* S'rn Dv (1832–67), N-W Dv (1867–85), W'rn Dv (1885–1918), Chelm. Dv/CC (1918–70). *Eccl* Seq 39.

HIGH ONGAR

AP Incl Norton Mandeville (sep par late 12th cent[328]). *LG* Seq 19. Addtl civ bdry alt: 1946,[20] 1965 (help cr Ongar CP),[331] 1968.[329] *Parl* S'rn Dv (1832–67), N-E Dv (1867–85), W'rn Dv (1885–1918), Ep. Dv/CC (1918–70), Brentw. & Ong. CC (1970–*). *Eccl* Seq 39. Eccl bdry: 1955.[84]

ORSETT

AP *LG* Barst. Hd, Ors. PLU, RSD, RD. Civ bdry: 1881,[332] 1888.[320] Abol civ 1936 to help cr Thurrock CP.[24] *Parl* S'rn Dv (1832–67), South Dv (1867–85), S-E'rn Dv (1885–1948). *Eccl* Seq 26. Eccl bdry: 1874 (help cr Galleywood Common EP).[26]

OVINGTON

AP *LG* Seq 14. Civ bdry: 1885.[91] *Parl* Seq 6. *Eccl* Seq 50.

PAGLESHAM

AP *LG* Seq 20. Civ bdry: 1946.[20] *Parl* Seq 17. *Eccl* Seq 40.

PANFIELD

AP *LG* Seq 11. *Parl* Seq 3. *Eccl* Seq 47.

GREAT PARNDON

AP *LG* Harlow Hd, Ep. PLU, RSD, RD. Civ bdry: 1883,[8] 1934 (gains pt Eastwick AP, Herts).[333] Abol civ 1955 pt to Harlow AP and to help constitute Harlow UD, pt to Epping Upland CP, pt to North Weald Bassett AP, pt to Roydon AP.[183] *Parl* S'rn Dv (1832–67), N-W Dv (1867–85), W'rn Dv (1885–1918), Ep. Dv/CC (1918–70). *Eccl* Seq 45.

LITTLE PARNDON

AP *LG* Harlow Hd, Ep. PLU, RSD, RD. Civ bdry: 1883.[8] Abol civ 1949 ent to Netteswell AP.[9] *Parl* As for Great Parndon. *Eccl* Harlow RDn. Renamed 1957 'Harlow New Town St Paul with Little Parndon St Mary' after exchanging pts with Great Parndon AP.[234]

PATTISWICK

Chap and donative in Feering AP, sep par 1313.[185] *LG* Lexd. Hd, Braint. PLU, RSD, RD. Civ bdry: 1883,[8] 1889.[93] Abol civ 1949 pt to help cr Coggeshall CP, pt to Bradwell AP.[9] *Parl* N'rn Dv (1832–67), N-E Dv (1867–85), E'rn Dv (1885–1918), Maldon Dv/CC (1918–70). *Eccl* Lexd. RDn (until 1847), Halst. RDn (1847–1907), Braint. RDn (1907–*).

PEBMARSH

AP *LG* Seq 13. *Parl* Seq 6. *Eccl* Seq 48.

PELDON

AP *LG* Seq 25. Civ bdry: 1889,[7] 1953.[83] *Parl* Seq 1. *Eccl* Seq 7.

PENTLOW

AP *LG* Seq 15. *Parl* Seq 6. *Eccl* Seq 50.

PITSEA

AP Incl pt Canvey Island (sep EP 1739,[88] sep CP 1880[90]). *LG* Barst. Hd, Bill. PLU, RSD, RD (1894–1935), Bill. UD (1935–37). Addtl civ bdry alt: 1880,[69] 1889.[87] Abol civ 1937 to help cr Billericay CP.[56] *Parl* S'rn Dv (1832–67), South Dv (1867–85), Mid Dv (1885–1918), S-E'rn Dv (1918–48). *Eccl* Barst. RDn (until 1895), Rochf. RDn (1895–1907), Ors. & Greys RDn (1907–55), Basildon RDn (1955–*). Addtl eccl bdry alt: 1957 (help cr Basildon St Andrew EP).[57]

PLAISTOW ST ANDREW

EP Cr 1871 from Plaistow St Mary EP.[334] Bark. RDn (1871–95), W Bark. RDn (1895–1907), W Ham RDn (1907–66), Newham RDn (1966–*). Bdry: 1879 (help cr Canning Town St Gabriel EP),[118] 1908 (help cr Canning Town St Matthias EP),[119] 1937 (cr Canning Town St Cedd EP),[116] 1961.[49]

PLAISTOW ST MARY

EP Cr 1844 from West Ham AP.[222] Bark. RDn (1844–95 [London dioc 1844–67]), W Bark. RDn (1895–1907), W Ham RDn (1907–66), Newham RDn (1966–*). Bdry: 1864 (help cr Victoria Docks St Mark EP),[215] 1868 (help cr Barking Road EP),[48] 1871 (cr Plaistow St Andrew EP),[334] 1875,[335] 1879 (help cr Canning Town St Gabriel EP),[118] 1888 (help cr Upton Park St Stephen EP),[216] 1894 (help cr Upton Cross EP),[191] 1908 (help cr Canning Town St Matthias EP).[119]

PLESHY

AP *LG* Pleshy Bor (status not sustained), Seq 5. Civ bdry: 1949,[20] 1969.[336] *Parl* N'rn Dv (1832–67), N-W Dv (1867–85), W'rn Dv (1885–1918), Chelm. Dv/CC (1918–70), Braint. CC (1970–*). *Eccl* Seq 44.

PRITTLEWELL

AP Incl pt Canvey Island (sep EP 1739,[88] sep CP 1880[90]). *LG* Rochf. Hd, PLU, Southend on Sea USD, MB (1892–1913). Addtl civ bdry alt: 1880.[69] Abol civ 1913 to help cr Southend on Sea CB and CP.[173] *Parl* S'rn Dv (1832–67), South Dv (1867–85), S-E'rn Dv (1885–1918). *Eccl* Pt (Milton) pec jurisd Archbp Canterb (Bocking RDn, until 1845), Seq 40 thereafter. Addtl eccl bdry alt: 1842 (cr Southend St John EP),[337] 1877 (help cr Prittlewell All Saints EP),[338] 1901 (cr Southend-on-Sea St Alban the Martyr, West Cliff EP),[339] 1911 (cr Southend-on-Sea St Saviour, Westcliff EP),[340] 1922 (help cr Westcliff St Paul EP),[341] 1931 (help cr Prittlewell St Luke EP),[342] 1951 (help cr Prittlewell St Peter EP),[174] 1954 (help cr Prittlewell St Stephen EP).[175]

PRITTLEWELL ALL SAINTS

EP Cr 1877 from Prittlewell AP.[338] Canew. RDn (1877–95), Canew. & S'end RDn (1970–74). Bdry: 1922 (help cr Westcliff St Paul EP),[341] 1931 (help cr Prittlewell St Luke EP),[342] 1971.[344] Abol 1974 to help cr Southend St John with St Mark, All Saints with St Francis and St Erkenwald EP.[343]

PRITTLEWELL ST LUKE

EP Cr 1931 from Prittlewell AP, Prittlewell All Saints EP.[342] Canew. & S'end RDn.

PRITTLEWELL ST PETER

EP Cr 1951 from Prittlewell AP, Eastwood AP.[174] Canew. & S'end RDn. Bdry: 1963 (cr Westcliff St Cedd and the Saints of Essex EP).[345]

PRITTLEWELL ST STEPHEN
EP Cr 1954 from Prittlewell AP, Eastwood AP.[175] Canew. & S'end RDn.

PURLEIGH
AP *LG* Seq 4. Civ bdry: 1883,[8] 1888,[163] 1889,[22] 1955.[324] *Parl* Seq 9. *Eccl* Seq 37.

QUENDON
AP *LG* Uttl. Hd, Saff. Wald. PLU, RSD, RD. Abol civ 1946 to help cr Quendon and Rickling CP.[114] *Parl* N'rn Dv (1832–67), N-W Dv (1867–85), N'rn Dv (1885–1918), Saff. Wald. Dv (1918–48). *Eccl* Seq 8.

QUENDON AND RICKLING
CP Cr 1946 by union Quendon AP, Ricking AP.[14] *LG* Saff. Wald. RD. *Parl* Saff. Wald. CC (1948–*).

RADWINTER
AP *LG* Seq 8. Civ bdry: 1965 (exchanges pts with Castle Camps AP, Cambs & IoE).[109] *Parl* Seq 8. *Eccl* Seq 12.

RAINHAM
AP *LG* Chaf. Hd, Romford PLU, RSD, RD (1894–1934), Hornchurch UD (1934–65). Transf 1965 to Gtr London (Hav. LB).[37] *Parl* S'rn Dv (1832–67), South Dv (1867–85), S-E'rn Dv (1885–1918), Romford Dv (1918–48), Hornchurch CC (1945–48), Hornchurch BC (1948–70), Gtr London thereafter. *Eccl* Seq 30. Eccl bdry: 1954.[256]

RAMSDEN BELLHOUSE
AP *LG* Barst. Hd, Bill. PLU, RSD, RD. Civ bdry: 1888,[167] 1889.[87] Abol civ 1934 pt to Great Burstead AP, pt to South Hanningfield AP.[17] *Parl* S'rn Dv (1832–67), South Dv (1867–85), Mid Dv (1885–1918), S-E'rn Dv (1918–48). *Eccl* Barst. RDn (until 1880s), Ingat. RDn (1880s–1907), Wickf. RDn (1907–*).

RAMSDEN CRAYS
AP *LG* Barst. Hd, Bill. PLU, RSD, RD. Abol civ 1934 pt to Great Burstead AP, pt to South Hanningfield AP.[17] *Parl* As for Ramsden Bellhouse. *Eccl* Barst. RDn (until 1895), Ingat. RDn (1895–1907), Wickf. RDn (1907–*).

RAMSEY
AP *LG* Seq 21. *Parl* Seq 5. *Eccl* Tendr. RDn (until 1847), Harw. RDn (1847–95), Ardl. & Harw. RDn (1895–1907), Harw. RDn (1907–73). Abol eccl 1973 to help cr Ramsey with Little Oakley EP.[330]

RAMSEY WITH LITTLE OAKLEY
EP Cr 1973 by union Ramsey AP, Little Oakley AP.[330] Harw. RDn.

RAWRETH
AP *LG* Rochf. Hd, PLU, RSD, RD (1894–1929), Rayleigh UD (1929–74). Civ bdry: 1926,[172] 1929 (gains pt Hockley AP when this par helps constitute Rayleigh UD).[252] *Parl* Seq 16. *Eccl* Seq 42.

RAYLEIGH
AP *LG* Rochf. Hd, PLU, RSD, RD (1894–1929), Rayleigh UD (1929–74). Civ bdry: 1926,[172] 1929 (pt to help constitute Rayleigh UD, the remainder lost to Thundersley AP to help constitute Thundersley UD),[252] 1934,[17] 1960.[249] *Parl* S'rn Dv (1832–67), South Dv (1867–85), S-E'rn Dv (1885–1948), Bill. CC (1948–70), S E Essex CC (1970–*). *Eccl* Seq 42.

RAYNE
AP *LG* Seq 11. Civ bdry: 1934 (incl help cr Braintree and Bocking CP).[17] *Parl* Seq 3. *Eccl* Seq 47.

RETTENDON
AP *LG* Seq 1. Civ bdry: 1888,[229] 1946,[114] 1949.[20] *Parl* Seq 10. *Eccl* Seq 35.

RICKLING
AP *LG* Uttl. Hd, Saff. Wald. PLU, RSD, RD. Abol civ 1946 to help cr Quendon and Rickling CP.[114] *Parl* N'rn Dv (1832–67), N-W Dv (1867–85), N'rn Dv (1885–1918), Saff. Wald. Dv (1918–48). *Eccl* Seq 8.

RIDGEWELL
AP *LG* Seq 13. Civ bdry: 1885,[155] 1956.[346] *Parl* Seq 6. *Eccl* Seq 50. Eccl bdry: 1842 (help cr Cornish Hall End EP).[92]

RIVENHALL
AP *LG* Witham Hd, PLU (1835–83), RSD (1875–83), Braint. PLU (1883–1930), RSD (1883–94), Braint. RD. Civ bdry: 1889.[93] Abol civ 1933 ent to Witham AP.[184] *Parl* N'rn Dv (1832–67), N-E Dv (1867–85), E'rn Dv (1885–1918), Maldon Dv (1918–48). *Eccl* Seq 17.

ROCHFORD
AP *LG* Seq 20. Civ bdry: 1934.[17] *Parl* Seq 17. *Eccl* Seq 41.

ABBESS RODING
AP *LG* Pt Ong. Hd, pt Dunmow Hd,[347] Ong. PLU, RSD, RD. Abol civ 1946 to help cr Abbess Beauchamp and Berners Roding CP.[20] *Parl* Pt N'rn, pt S'rn Dv (1832–67), N-W Dv (1867–85), W'rn Dv (1885–1918), Chelm. Dv (1918–48). *Eccl* Ong. RDn (until 1907), Roding RDn (1907–*).

ABBESS BEAUCHAMP AND BERNERS RODING
CP Cr 1946 by union Abbess Roding AP, Beauchamp Roding AP, Berners Roding AP.[20] *LG* Ong. RD (1946–55), Ep. & Ong. RD (1955–74). *Parl* Brentw. & Ong. CC (1970–*).

AYTHORPE RODING
AP *LG* Seq 6. *Parl* Seq 8. *Eccl* Seq 44.

BEAUCHAMP RODING
AP *LG* Ong. Hd, PLU, RSD, RD. Abol civ 1946 to help cr Abbess Beauchamp and Berners Roding CP.[20] *Parl* S'rn Dv (1832–67), N-W Dv (1867–85), W'rn Dv (1885–1918), Chelm. Dv (1918–48). *Eccl* Ong. RDn (until 1907), Roding RDn (1907–*).

BERNERS RODING
AP *LG* Dunmow Hd, Ong. PLU, RSD, RD. Abol civ 1946 to help cr Abbess Beauchamp and Berners Roding CP.[20] *Parl* N'rn Dv (1832–67), N-W Dv (1867–85), W'rn Dv (1885–1918), Chelm. Dv (1918–48). *Eccl* Seq 44.

HIGH RODING
AP *LG* Seq 6. Civ bdry: 1883,[8] 1889.[29] *Parl* Seq 8. *Eccl* Seq 44.

LEADEN RODING
AP *LG* Seq 6. *Parl* Seq 8. *Eccl* Seq 44.

MARGARET RODING
AP *LG* Seq 6. Civ bdry: 1888.[348] *Parl* Seq 8. *Eccl* Seq 44.

MORELL RODING
AP Orig sep par, now considered hmlt to White Roding AP.[349] *LG* Ong. Hd. *Eccl* Dunmow RDn.

WHITE RODING
AP Incl Morell Roding, orig sep par and now considered this par's hmlt.[349] *LG* Seq 6. *Parl* Seq 8. *Eccl* Seq 44.

ROMFORD
Chap in Hornchurch AP, sep civ identity early, sep EP *ca* 1840.[292] *LG* Hav.-atte-Bower Lbty, Romford PLU, pt Romford USD, pt Romford RSD. Abol civ 1894 the pt in the USD to cr Romford Urban CP, the remainder to cr Romford Rural CP.[115] *Parl* S'rn Dv (1832–67), South Dv (1867–85), S'rn Dv (1885–1918). *Eccl* Pec jurisd Hornchurch (until 1845), Bark. RDn (1845–62 [Roch dioc 1846–62]), Romford RDn (1862–68), Chaf. RDn (1868–1907), Chaf. o'wise Romford RDn (1907–66), Hav. RDn (1966–*). Eccl bdry: 1853 (cr Romford St Andrew EP),[351] 1926 (help cr Squirrel's Heath EP),[255] 1927 (help cr Romford The Ascension, Collier Row EP),[124] 1928 (help cr Romford St John the Divine EP),[350] 1953,[238] 1955 (help cr Collier Row EP),[153] 1956 (cr Harold Hill St George EP),[235] 1971.[154]
CP Cr 1900 by union Romford Rural CP, Romford Urban CP.[352] *LG* Romford PLU, UD (1900–37), MB (1937–65). Bdry: 1934.[17] Transf 1965 to Gtr London (Hav. LB).[37] *Parl* Romford Dv (1918–45), Romford BC (1945–70), Gtr London thereafter.

ROMFORD THE ASCENSION, COLLIER ROW
EP Cr 1927 from Romford EP, Chadwell Heath EP.[124] Chaf. o'wise Romford RDn (1927–66), Hav. RDn (1966–*). Bdry: 1935 (help cr Romford The Good Shepherd, Collier Row EP),[353] 1955 (help cr Collier Row St James EP),[153] 1956,[243] 1957,[135] 1960 (help cr Chadwell Heath St Mark, Mark's Gate EP),[6] 1961 (help cr Hainault EP),[54] 1971.[154]

ROMFORD THE GOOD SHEPHERD, COLLIER ROW
EP Cr 1935 from Romford The Ascension, Collier Row EP, Romford St John the Divine EP.[353] Chaf. o'wise Romford RDn (1935–66), Hav. RDn (1966–*). Bdry: 1971.[154]

ROMFORD RURAL
CP Cr 1894 from the pt of Romford CP not in Romford USD.[115] *LG* Romf. PLU, RD. Bdry: 1895 (cr Noak Hill CP).[327] Abol 1900 to help cr Romford CP.[354]

ROMFORD ST ALBAN
EP Cr 1952 from Romford St Andrew EP.[355] Chaf. o'wise Romford RDn (1952–66), Hav. RDn (1966–*). Bdry: 1957,[135] 1972.[293]

ROMFORD ST ANDREW
EP Cr 1853 from Romford EP.[351] Romford RDn (1853–62), Chaf. RDn (1862–1907), Chaf. o'wise Romford RDn (1907–66), Hav. RDn (1966–*). Bdry: 1926 (help cr Squirrel's Heath EP),[255] 1928 (help cr Romford St John the Divine EP),[350] 1952 (cr Romford St Alban EP),[355] 1969 (help cr Rush Green EP).[161]

ROMFORD ST JOHN THE DIVINE
EP Cr 1928 from Romford EP, Romford St Andrew EP.[350] Chaf. o'wise Romford RDn (1928–66), Hav. RDn (1966–*). Bdry: 1935 (help cr Romford The Good Shepherd, Collier Row EP),[353] 1960 (help cr Chadwell Heath St Mark, Mark's Gate EP).[6]

ROMFORD URBAN
CP Cr 1894 from the pt of Romford CP in Romford USD.[115] *LG* Romford PLU, UD. Abol 1900 to help cr Romford CP.[354]

ROXWELL
Chap in Writtle AP, sep par 1597.[356] *LG* Seq 1. *Parl* Seq 11. *Eccl* Pec jurisd Writtle with Roxwell (until 1845), Seq 31 thereafter.

ROYDON
AP *LG* Pt Harlow Hd, pt Waltham Hd, Ep. PLU, RSD, RD (1894–1955), Ep. & Ong. RD (1955–74). Civ bdry: 1946,[20] 1955 (incl loses pt to Harlow AP to help constitute Harlow UD).[183] *Parl* Seq 14. *Eccl* Seq 45.

RUNWELL
AP *LG* Chelm. Hd, PLU,[66] RSD, RD. Civ bdry: 1888.[167] *Parl* Seq 10. *Eccl* Seq 35.

RUSH GREEN
EP Cr 1969 from Romford St Andrew EP, Dagenham AP, Hornchurch Holy Cross EP, Becontree St Mary EP.[161] Hav. RDn.

SAFFRON WALDEN
AP *LG* Uttl. Hd, Saff. Wald. PLU, MB (184 – 1974), USD. Civ bdry: 1883.[8] *Parl* N'rn Dv (1832–67), N-W Dv (1867–85), N'rn Dv (1885–1918), Saff. Wald. Dv/CC (1918–*). *Eccl* Sampf. RDn (until 1847), Saff. Wald. RDn (1847–*). Eccl bdry: 1889.[312]

ST LAWRENCE
AP Usual civ spelling; for eccl see following entry. *LG* Seq 4. Civ bdry: 1883,[8] 1889.[22] *Parl* Seq 9.

ST LAWRENCE NEWLAND
AP Usual eccl spelling; for civ see prev entry. *Eccl* Seq 36. Eccl bdry: 1933.[164]

ST OSYTH
AP *LG* Seq 21. Civ bdry: 1883,[8] 1934.[17] *Parl* Seq 5. *Eccl* Seq 16.

SALCOT
AP Salcot, Virley sep civ pars, Salcot Virley (qv) one EP.[357] *LG* Seq 25. *Parl* N'rn Dv (1832–67), N-E Dv (1867–85), N-E'rn Dv (1885–1918), Colch. Dv/CC (1918–*).

SALCOT VIRLEY
One EP, but Salcot, Virley have sep civ identities (qv).[357] *Eccl* Lexd. RDn (until 1847), Mersea RDn (1847–1907), Witham RDn (1907–70), Colch. RDn (1970–*).

GREAT SALING
AP *LG* Seq 11. Civ bdry: 1888.[31] *Parl* Seq 3. *Eccl* Seq 47.

LITTLE SALING

AP Usual eccl spelling; for civ see 'Bardfield Saling'. Hmlt & chap in Great Bardfield AP, sep par 1574.[28] *Eccl* Sampf. RDn (until 1907), Braint. RDn (1907–*).

GREAT SAMPFORD

AP *LG* Seq 8. Civ bdry: 1878.[358] *Parl* Seq 8. *Eccl* Seq 12.

LITTLE SAMPFORD

AP Organisation as for Great Sampford.

SANDON

AP *LG* Seq 1. Civ bdry: 1883,[8] 1946.[20] *Parl* Seq 10. *Eccl* Seq 34.

SHALFORD

AP *LG* Seq 11. Civ bdry: 1883.[8] *Parl* Seq 3. *Eccl* Seq 47.

SHEERING

AP *LG* Seq 10. Civ bdry: 1883,[8] 1955.[183] *Parl* Seq 14. *Eccl* Seq 45.

SHELLEY

AP *LG* Ong. Hd, PLU, RSD, RD (1894–1955), Ep. & Ong. RD (1955–65). Abol civ 1965 to help cr Ongar CP.[331] *Parl* S'rn Dv (1832–67), N-W Dv (1867–85), W'rn Dv (1885–1918), Chelm. Dv (1918–70). *Eccl* Seq 39. Eccl bdry: 1933.[318]

SHELLOW BOWELLS

AP *LG* Dunmow Hd, Ong. PLU, RSD, RD. Abol civ 1946 to help cr Willingdale CP.[20] *Parl* N'rn Dv (1832–67), N-W Dv (1867–85), W'rn Dv (1885–1918), Chelm. Dv (1918–48). *Eccl* Dunmow RDn (until 1845), Roding RDn (1845–1928). Abol eccl 1928 to help cr Willingale with Shellow EP.[359]

SHENFIELD

AP *LG* Barst. Hd, Bill. PLU, RSD, RD. Abol civ 1934 pt to Brentwood CP, pt to Mountnessing AP.[17] *Parl* S'rn Dv (1832–67), South Dv (1867–85), Mid Dv (1885–1918), Chelm. Dv (1918–48). *Eccl* Seq 23. Eccl bdry: 1855 (help cr Great Warley Christ Church EP),[360] 1956.[96]

NORTH SHOEBURY

AP *LG* Rochf. Hd, PLU, RSD, RD. Abol civ 1933 pt to Southend on Sea CB and CP, pt to Great Wakering AP.[111] *Parl* S'rn Dv (1832–67), South Dv (1867–85), S-E'rn Dv (1885–1948). *Eccl* Seq 40.

SOUTH SHOEBURY

AP *LG* Rochf. Hd, PLU, RSD, S Shoebury UD (renamed 1895 'Shoeburyness' UD). Abol civ 1933 ent to Southend on Sea CB and CP.[111] *Parl* S'rn Dv (1832–67), South Dv (1867–85), S-E'rn Dv (1885–1948). *Eccl* Seq 40.

SHOPLAND

AP *LG* Rochf. Hd, PLU, RSD, RD. Abol civ 1933 pt to Southend on Sea CB and CP, pt to Sutton AP.[111] *Parl* S'rn Dv (1832–67), South Dv (1867–85), S-E'rn Dv (1885–1948). *Eccl* Rochf. RDn (until 1845), Canew. RDn (1845–1907), Canew. & S'end RDn (1907–*).

SHRUB END

EP Renaming 1962 of 'All Saints in Stanway and Lexden' EP.[14] Colch. RDn.

WEST SILVERTOWN

EP Cr 1926 from Victoria Docks St Mark EP, Victoria Docks St Luke EP.[361] W Ham RDn (1926–66), Newham RDn (1966–*).

SNOREHAM

AP *LG* Dengie Hd. *Eccl* Dengie RDn. United both civ and eccl mid 18th cent with Latchingdon AP, the union usually civ called 'Latchingdon' but eccl and often civ 'Latchingdon with Snoreham',[274] qv.

SOUTHCHURCH

AP Incl pt Canvey Island (sep EP 1739,[88] sep CP 1880[90]). *LG* Rochf. Hd, PLU, RSD, Southend on Sea USD, MB (1892–1913). Civ bdry: 1880.[69] Abol civ 1913 to help cr Southend on Sea CB and CP.[173] *Parl* S'rn Dv (1832–67), South Dv (1867–85), S-E'rn Dv (1885–1918). *Eccl* Pec jurisd Archbp Canterb (Bocking RDn, until 1845), Seq 40 thereafter. Eccl bdry: 1921 (cr Thorpe Bay EP),[362] 1923 (cr Southend Christ Church EP).[363]

SOUTHEND CHRIST CHURCH

EP Cr 1923 from Southchurch AP.[363] Canew. & S'end RDn.

SOUTHEND ST ERKENWALD

EP Cr 1911 from Southend St John the Baptist EP.[364] Canew. & S'end RDn. Abol 1974 to help cr Southend St John with St Mark, All Saints with St Francis and St Erkenwald EP.[343]

SOUTHEND ST JOHN THE BAPTIST

EP Cr 1842 from Prittlewell AP.[337] Rochf. RDn (1842–62), Canew. RDn (1862–1907), Canew. & S'end RDn (1907–74). Bdry: 1911 (cr Southend St Erkenwald EP).[364] Abol 1974 to help cr Southend St John with St Mark, All Saints with St Francis and St Erkenwald EP.[343]

SOUTHEND ST JOHN WITH ST MARK, ALL SAINTS WITH ST FRANCIS AND ST ERKENWALD

EP Cr 1974 by union Prittlewell All Saints EP, Southend St Erkenwald EP, Southend St John the Baptist EP.[343] Canew. & S'end RDn.

SOUTHEND ON SEA

CP Cr 1913 by union Leigh AP, Prittlewell AP, Southchurch AP, pt Eastwood AP.[173] *LG* Rochf. PLU, Southend on Sea MB (1913–14), CB (1914–*). Bdry: 1933.[111] *Parl* Southend on sea Parl Bor (ent 1918–45, pt 1945–48 [excluding the pt not in the CP in 1918 but added 1933, the latter remaining in S-E'rn Dv]), pt Southend East BC, pt Southend West BC (1948–70)[see Part III of the *Guide* for the composition of these constituencies by wards of the CB and other units]. Parl bdry: 1955.[428]

SOUTHEND-ON-SEA ST ALBAN THE MARTYR, WEST CLIFF

EP Cr 1901 from Prittlewell AP.[365] Canew. RDn (1901–07), Canew. & S'end RDn (1907–*). Bdry: 1922 (help cr Westcliff St Paul EP).[341]

SOUTHEND-ON-SEA ST SAVIOUR, WESTCLIFF

EP Cr 1911 from Prittlewell AP.[340] Canew. & S'end RDn. Bdry: 1923 (cr Westcliff St Michael and All Angels EP),[366] 1930 (cr Westcliff St Andrew EP).[367]

SOUTHMINSTER

AP *LG* Seq 4. Civ bdry: 1889.[22] *Parl* Seq 9. *Eccl* Seq 36.

SPRINGFIELD

AP *LG* Seq 1. Civ bdry: 1888,[229] 1907,[126] 1934.[17] *Parl* Seq 11. *Eccl* Seq 31. Eccl bdry: 1930 (cr Springfield Holy Trinity EP).[368]

SPRINGFIELD HOLY TRINITY

EP Cr 1930 from Springfield AP.[368] Chelm. RDn.

SQUIRREL'S HEATH

EP Cr 1926 from Romford EP, Hornchurch AP, Romford St Andrew EP.[255] Chaf. o'wise Romford RDn (1926–66), Hav. RDn (1966–*). Bdry: 1933 (cr Gidea Park EP),[204] 1957.[135]

STAMBOURNE

AP *LG* Seq 13. Civ bdry: 1883,[8] 1885.[155] *Parl* Seq 6. *Eccl* Seq 51.

STAMBRIDGE

Cr civ 1934,[17] eccl 1958[369] by union Great Stambridge AP, Little Stambridge AP. *LG* Rochf. RD. *Parl* Southend East BC (1948–70), Maldon CC (1970–*). Parl bdry: 1945.[426] *Eccl* Canew. & S'end RDn.

GREAT STAMBRIDGE

AP Abol civ 1934,[17] eccl 1958[369] to help cr Stambridge CP, EP respectively. *LG* Rochf. Hd, PLU, RSD, RD. *Parl* S'rn Dv (1832–67), South Dv (1867–85), S-E'rn Dv (1885–1948). *Eccl* Rochf. RDn (until 1845), Canew. RDn (1845–1907), Canew. & S'end RDn (1907–58).

LITTLE STAMBRIDGE

AP Organisation as for Great Stambridge.

STANFORD LE HOPE

AP Usual civ spelling; for eccl see following entry. *LG* Barst. Hd, Ors. PLU, RSD, RD. Civ bdry: 1888,[320] 1910.[270] Abol civ 1936 to help cr Thurrock CP.[24] *Parl* S'rn Dv (1832–67), South Dv (1867–85), S-E'rn Dv (1885–1948).

STANFORD-LE-HOPE

AP Usual eccl spelling; for civ see prev entry. *Eccl* Barst. RDn (until 1895), Ors. RDn (1895–1907), Ors. & Grays RDn (1907–73). Eccl bdry: 1954,[261] 1962.[158] Abol eccl 1973 to help cr Stanford-le-Hope with Mucking EP.[332]

STANFORD-LE-HOPE WITH MUCKING

EP Cr 1973 by union Stanford-le-Hope AP, Mucking AP.[322] Ors. & Grays RDn.

STANFORD RIVERS

AP *LG* Seq 19. *Parl* Seq 12. *Eccl* Ong. RDn (until 1845), Lamb. RDn (1845–1907), Ong. RDn (1907–*).

STANSTEAD MOUNTFITCHET

AP *LG* Pt Clav. Hd, pt Uttl. Hd, Bishop's Stortford PLU, RSD, Stan. RD (1894–1934), Saff. Wald. RD (1934–74). Civ bdry: 1946,[20] 1953.[83] *Parl* Seq 8. *Eccl* Seq 11.

STANWAY

AP *LG* Seq 17. Civ bdry: 1883,[8] 1934,[17] 1949 (incl help cr Eight Ash Green CP).[9] *Parl* Seq 1. *Eccl* Seq 2. Eccl bdry: 1845 (help cr All Saints in Stanway and Lexden EP).[11]

STAPLEFORD ABBOTTS

AP *LG* Seq 19. *Parl* Seq 12. *Eccl* Seq 38.

STAPLEFORD TAWNEY

AP *LG* Seq 19. *Parl* Seq 12. *Eccl* Seq 38.

STEBBING

AP *LG* Seq 12. *Parl* N'rn Dv (1832–67), N-E Dv (1867–85), W'rn Dv (1885–1918), Saff. Wald. Dv/CC (1918–*). *Eccl* Heding. RDn (until 1862), Braint. RDn (1862–1907), Dunmow RDn (1907–*).

STEEPLE

AP *LG* Seq 4. Civ bdry: 1883,[8] 1889,[22] 1934 (help cr Maldon CP).[17] *Parl* Seq 9. *Eccl* Seq 36.

STIFFORD

AP *LG* Chaf. Hd, Ors. PLU, RSD, RD. Civ bdry: 1888.[320] Abol civ 1936 to help cr Thurrock CP.[24] *Parl* S'rn Dv (1832–67), South Dv (1867–85), S-E'rn Dv (1885–1948). *Eccl* Chaf. RDn (until 1862), Ors. RDn (1862–1907), Ors. & Grays RDn (1907–*). Eccl bdry: 1958 (help cr Belhus Park EP),[25] 1970.[68]

STISTED

AP *LG* Hinckf. Hd, Braint. PLU, RSD (ent 1875–83, pt 1883–89, ent 1889–94), pt Braint. USD (1883–89), Braint RD. Civ bdry: 1883,[8] 1889,[93] 1934 (incl help cr Braintree and Bocking CP),[17] 1949.[9] *Parl* Seq 3. *Eccl* Pec jurisd Archbp Canterb (Bocking RDn, until 1845), Seq 47 thereafter.

STOCK

AP Usual civ spelling; for eccl see following entry. *LG* Seq 1. Civ bdry: 1881,[332] 1935,[24] 1955.[230] *Parl* Seq 10.

STOCK HARVARD

AP Usual eccl spelling; for civ see prev entry. *Eccl* Chelm. RDn (until 1862), Ingat. RDn (1862–1907), Wickf. RDn (1907–*).

STONDON MASSEY

AP *LG* Seq 19. *Parl* Seq 12. *Eccl* Ong. RDn (until 1862), Lamb. RDn (1862–1907), Ong. RDn (1907–*).

STOW MARIES

AP *LG* Seq 4. Civ bdry: 1889.[22] *Parl* Seq 9. *Eccl* Seq 37.

STRATFORD ST JOHN

EP Cr 1844 from West Ham AP.[222] Bark. RDn (1844–95 [London dioc 1844–67]), W Bark. RDn (1895–1907), W Ham RDn (1907–61). Bdry: 1865 (cr Stratford New Town EP),[370] 1881 (help cr Forest Gate St James EP).[188] Abol 1961 to help cr Stratford St John with Christ Church EP).[49]

STRATFORD ST JOHN WITH CHRIST CHURCH

EP Cr 1961 by union Stratford St John EP, Stratford Marsh EP.[49] W Ham RDn. Abol 1966 to help cr Stratford St John and Christ Church with Forest Gate St James EP.[197]

STRATFORD ST JOHN AND CHRIST CHURCH WITH FOREST GATE ST JAMES

EP Cr 1966 by union Stratford St John with Christ Church EP, Forest Gate St James EP.[197] W Ham RDn (1966), Newham RDn (1966–*).

STRATFORD MARSH

EP Cr 1852 from West Ham AP.[223] Bark. RDn (1852–95 [London dioc 1852–67]), W Bark. RDn (1895–1907), W Ham RDn (1907–*). Abol 1961 to help cr Stratford St John with Christ Church EP.[49]

STRATFORD NEW TOWN

EP Cr 1865 from Stratford St John EP.[370] Bark. RDn (1865–95 [London dioc 1865–67]), W Bark. RDn (1895–1907), W Ham RDn (1907–66), Newham RDn (1966–*). Bdry: 1879 (help cr Leytonstone Holy Trinity, Harrow Green EP).[297]

STRETHALL

AP *LG* Seq 24. *Parl* Seq 8. *Eccl* Seq 9.

STURMER

AP *LG* Seq 14. Civ bdry: 1879 (exchanges pts with Haverhill AP, Suffolk),[240] 1883 (loses pt to Kedington AP, Suffolk),[8] 1884 (loses pt to Wixoe AP, Suffolk),[371] 1885 (exchanges pts with Haverhill AP, Suffolk).[372] *Parl* Seq 6. *Eccl* Seq 50.

SUTTON

AP *LG* Seq 20. Civ bdry: 1933.[111] *Parl* Seq 17. *Eccl* Rochf. RDn (until 1862), Canew. RDn (1862–1907), Canew. & S'end RDn (1907–*).

TAKELEY

AP *LG* Uttl. Hd, Dunmow PLU, RSD, RD. Civ bdry: 1949.[114] *Parl* Seq 8. *Eccl* Sampf. RDn (until 1847), Nwpt. RDn (1847–1907), Dunmow RDn (1907–*).

TENDRING

AP *LG* Seq 21. *Parl* Seq 5. *Eccl* Seq 15.

TERLING

AP *LG* Witham Hd, PLU (1835–83), RSD (1875–83), Braint. PLU (1883–1930), RSD (1883–94), Braint. RD. Civ bdry: 1883,[8] 1889.[93] *Parl* Seq 3. *Eccl* Seq 17.

GREAT TEY

AP Incl chap Chappel (sep rights from 1553[125]). *LG* Seq 17. Addtl civ bdry alt: 1883,[8] 1889.[7] *Parl* Seq 1. *Eccl* Seq 5.

LITTLE TEY

AP *LG* Lexd. Hd, Lexd. & Winst. PLU, RSD, RD. Civ bdry: 1883,[8] 1889.[7] Abol civ 1949 ent to Marks Tey AP.[9] *Parl* N'rn Dv (1832–67), N-E Dv (1867–85), E'rn Dv (1885–1918), Colch. Dv/CC (1918–70). *Eccl* Seq 5.

MARKS TEY

AP *LG* Seq 17. Civ bdry: 1889,[7] 1949.[9] *Parl* Seq 1. *Eccl* Seq 5.

THAXTED

AP *LG* Thaxted Bor (status not sustained), Seq 6. *Parl* Seq 8. *Eccl* Seq 43.

THEYDON BOIS

AP *LG* Seq 18. Civ bdry: 1896 (loses pt to Epping AP to help constitute Ep. UD),[181] 1934,[17] 1946,[20] 1949.[114] *Parl* Seq 13. *Eccl* Seq 38.

THEYDON GARNON

AP *LG* Seq 18. Civ bdry: 1896 (loses pt to Epping AP to help constitute Ep. UD),[181] 1934,[17] 1946,[20] 1949.[114] *Parl* Seq 13. *Eccl* Seq 38. Eccl bdry: 1852 (cr Coopersale EP).[156]

THEYDON MOUNT

AP *LG* Seq 19. *Parl* Seq 12. *Eccl* Seq 38.

THORPE LE SOKEN

AP *LG* Seq 21. Civ bdry: 1883,[8] 1934.[17] *Parl* Seq 5. *Eccl* Pec jurisd of the Sokens (until 1845), Seq 15 thereafter.

THORPE BAY

EP Cr 1921 from Southchurch AP.[362] Canew. & S'end RDn.

THORINGTON

AP Usual eccl spelling; for civ see following entry. *Eccl* Seq 16.

THORRINGTON

AP Usual civ spelling; for eccl see prev entry. *LG* Seq 21. Civ bdry: 1888.[199] *Parl* Seq 5.

THUNDERSLEY

AP *LG* Pt Barst. Hd, pt Rochf. Hd, Bill. PLU (1835–47), Rochf. PLU (1847–1930), RSD, RD (1894–1929), Benfleet UD (1929–74). Civ bdry: 1926,[172] 1929 (loses pt to Rayleigh AP to help constitute Rayleigh UD, the remainder to help constitute Benfleet UD).[252] *Parl* Seq 16. *Eccl* Barst. RDn (until 1845), Rochf. RDn (1845–1907), Wickf. RDn (1907–*). Eccl bdry: 1964 (help cr New Thundersley EP).[71]

NEW THUNDERSLEY

EP Cr 1964 from Thundersley AP, North Benfleet AP, South Benfleet AP.[71] Wickf. RDn.

THURROCK

CP Cr 1936 by union Aveley AP, Bulphan AP, Chadwell St Mary AP, East Tilbury AP, Grays Thurrock AP, Horndon on the Hill AP, Little Thurrock AP, Mucking AP, Orsett AP, South Ockendon AP, Stanford le Hope AP, Stifford AP, West Thurrock AP, West Tilbury AP, and pts of Corringham AP, Fobbing AP, Langdon Hills AP, North Ockendon AP.[24] *LG* Thurrock UD. Bdry: 1938.[373] *Parl* Thurrock CC (1948–70), BC (1970– *).

GRAYS THURROCK

AP *LG* Chaf. Hd, Ors. PLU, RSD (1875–86), Grays Thurrock USD (1886–94), UD. Civ bdry: 1893.[374] Abol civ 1936 to help cr Thurrock CP.[24] *Parl* S'rn Dv (1832–67), South Dv (1867–85), S-E'rn Dv (1885–1948). *Eccl* Seq 26. Eccl bdry: 1926 (help cr Grays EP),[205] 1934 (help cr Little Thurrock St John EP).[375]

LITTLE THURROCK

AP *LG* Barst. Hd, Ors. PLU, RSD, RD. Civ bdry: 1888,[320] 1893.[374] Abol civ 1936 to help cr Thurrock CP.[24] *Parl* As for Grays Thurrock. *Eccl* Seq 26. Eccl bdry: 1926 (help cr Grays EP),[205] 1934 (help cr Little Thurrock St John EP).[375]

LITTLE THURROCK ST JOHN

EP Cr 1934 from Little Thurrock AP, Grays Thurrock AP.[375] Ors. & Grays RDn.

WEST THURROCK

AP *LG* Chaf. Hd, Ors. PLU, RSD, RD (1894–1929), Purfleet UD (1929–35). Abol civ 1935 to help cr Thurrock CP.[24] *Parl* As for Grays Thurrock. *Eccl* Seq 29.

EAST TILBURY
AP *LG* Barst. Hd, Ors. PLU, RSD, RD. Abol civ 1936 to help cr Thurrock CP.[24] *Parl* As for Grays Thurrock. *Eccl* Seq 26. Eccl bdry: 1963.[321]
WEST TILBURY
AP *LG* Barst. Hd, Ors. PLU, RSD, RD. Abol civ 1936 to help cr Thurrock CP.[24] *Parl* As for Grays Thurrock. *Eccl* Seq 26.
TILBURY DOCKS
EP Cr 1903 from Chadwell St Mary EP.[121] Ors. RDn (1903–07), Ors. & Grays RDn (1907–*).
TILBURY JUXTA CLARE
AP *LG* Seq 13. Civ bdry: 1883,[8] 1885,[376] 1888,[67] 1946,[20] 1956.[346] *Parl* Seq 6. *Eccl* Seq 50.
TILLINGHAM
AP *LG* Seq 4. Civ bdry: 1883.[8] *Parl* Seq 9. *Eccl* Pec jurisd Dean & Chapter of St Paul's, London (until 1845), Seq 36 thereafter.
TILTY
AP *LG* Seq 6. Civ bdry: 1883.[8] *Parl* Seq 8. *Eccl* Seq 43. Eccl bdry: 1880.[170]
TIPTREE
CP Cr 1934 from Inworth AP, Messing AP, Tolleshunt d'Arcy AP, Tolleshunt Knights AP.[24] *LG* Lexd. & Winst. RD. *Parl* Colch. CC (1948–*).
EP Renaming 1957 of Tiptree Heath EP.[377] Witham RDn. Abol 1961 to help cr Tolleshunt Knights with Tiptree EP.[378]
TIPTREE HEATH
EP Cr 1859 from Inworth AP, Messing AP, Tollesbury AP, Tolleshunt d'Arcy AP, Tolleshunt Knights AP, Great Wigborough AP, and the ex-par place Long Legs.[269] Cogg. RDn (1859–1907), Witham RDn (1907–57). Renamed 1957 'Tiptree'.[377]
TOLLESBURY
AP *LG* Seq 22. Civ bdry: 1888,[379] 1889.[22] *Parl* Seq 2. *Eccl* Seq 20. Eccl bdry: 1859 (help cr Tiptree Heath EP).[269]
TOLLESHUNT D'ARCY
AP *LG* Seq 22. Civ bdry: 1889,[22] 1934 (help cr Tiptree AP).[17] *Parl* Seq 2. *Eccl* Seq 20. Eccl bdry: 1859 (help cr Tiptree Heath EP).[269]
TOLLESHUNT KNIGHTS
AP *LG* Seq 22. Civ bdry: 1888,[380] 1889,[22] 1934 (help cr Tiptree CP).[24] *Parl* Seq 2. *Eccl* Witham RDn (until 1847), Hatf. Pev. RDn (1847–1907), Witham RDn (1907–61). Eccl bdry: 1859 (help cr Tiptree Heath EP).[269] Abol eccl 1961 to help cr Tolleshunt Knights with Tiptree EP.[378]
TOLLESHUNT KNIGHTS WITH TIPTREE
EP Cr 1961 by union Tolleshunt Knights AP, Tiptree EP.[378] Witham RDn.
TOLLESHUNT MAJOR
AP *LG* Seq 22. Civ bdry: 1889,[22] 1934 (help cr Maldon CP).[17] *Parl* Seq 2. *Eccl* Seq 20.
TOPPESFIELD
AP *LG* Seq 13. Civ bdry: 1820,[389] 1883,[8] 1885,[155] 1954.[381] *Parl* Seq 6. *Eccl* Seq 51.
GREAT TOTHAM
AP *LG* Seq 22. Civ bdry: 1883,[8] 1889,[22] 1934 (incl help cr Maldon CP).[17] *Parl* Seq 2. *Eccl* Seq 20.
LITTLE TOTHAM
AP *LG* Seq 22. Civ bdry: 1883,[9] 1889,[22] 1934 (incl help cr Maldon CP).[17] *Parl* Seq 2. *Eccl* Seq 19.
TWINSTEAD
AP *LG* Seq 15. Civ bdry: 1883,[8] 1885.[15] *Parl* Seq 6. *Eccl* Seq 48.
TYE GREEN WITH ST ANDREW
EP Renaming 1957 of Netteswell AP after the latter exchanged pts with Latton AP and lost pts to Great Parndon AP, Little Parndon AP.[234] Harlow RDn.
UGLEY
AP *LG* Seq 2. *Parl* Seq 8. *Eccl* Seq 11.
ULTING
AP *LG* Witham Hd, PLU (1835–83), RSD (1875–83), Maldon PLU (1883–1930), RSD (1883–94), Maldon RD. Civ bdry: 1883,[8] 1889.[22] *Parl* Seq 2. *Eccl* Witham RDn (until 1847), Hatf. Pev. RDn (1847–1907), Witham RDn (1907–74). Abol eccl 1974 to help cr Hatfield Peverel with Ulting EP.[239]
UNNAMED
CP Cr 1894 from the pt of Witham AP not in Witham USD.[115] *LG* Braint. RD. Abol 1903 ent to Witham AP.[390]
UPMINSTER
AP *LG* Chaf. Hd, Romford PLU, RSD, RD (1894–1934), Hornchurch UD (1934–65). Civ bdry: 1934.[17] Transf 1965 to Gtr London (Hav. LB).[37] *Parl* S'rn Dv (1832–67), South Dv (1867–85), Mid Dv (1885–1918), Romford Dv (1918–45), Hornchurch Dv (1945–48), Hornchurch BC (1948–70), Gtr London thereafter. Parl bdry: 1945.[426] *Eccl* Seq 27. Eccl bdry: 1957 (help cr Cranham Park EP).[159]
UPTON CROSS
EP Cr 1894 from West Ham AP, Plaistow St Mary EP, Forest Gate EP, Upton Park St Stephen EP.[191] Bark. RDn (1894–95), W Bark. RDn (1895–1907), W Ham RDn (1907–62). Bdry: 1961.[49] Abol 1962 to help cr Forest Gate Emmanuel with Upton Cross St Peter EP.[193]
UPTON PARK ST ALBAN
EP Cr 1903 from Upton Park St Stephen EP.[391] S Bark. RDn (1903–07), Bark. RDn (1907–66), Newham RDn (1966–68). Bdry: 1953.[195] Abol 1968 to help cr East Ham with Upton Park St Alban EP.[220]
UPTON PARK ST STEPHEN
EP Cr 1887 from East Ham AP, West Ham AP, Plaistow St Mary EP.[216] Bark. RDn (1887–95), S Bark. RDn (1895–1907), Bark. RDn (1907–53). Bdry: 1894 (help cr Upton Cross EP),[191] 1901 (help cr Forest Gate St Edmund EP),[194] 1903 (cr Upton Park St Alban EP).[391] Abol 1953 pt to Forest Gate St Edmund EP, pt to Upton Park St Alban EP.[195]
VANGE
AP Incl pt Canvey Island (sep EP 1739,[88] sep CP 1880[90]). *LG* Barst. Hd, Bill. PLU, RSD, RD

(1894–1935), Bill. UD (1935–37). Addtl civ bdry alt: 1880.[69] Abol civ 1937 to help cr Billericay CP.[56] *Parl* S'rn Dv (1832–67), South Dv (1867–85), Mid Dv (1885–1918), S-E'rn Dv (1918–48). *Eccl* Seq 25. Addtl eccl bdry alt: 1957 (help cr Basildon St Andrew EP).[57]

VICTORIA DOCKS THE ASCENSION

EP Cr 1904 from Victoria Docks St Luke EP.[392] W Bark. RDn (1904–07), W Ham RDn (1907–66), Newham RDn (1966–*). Bdry: 1961,[49] 1972.[117]

VICTORIA DOCKS ST LUKE

EP Cr 1875 from Victoria Docks St Mark EP.[393] Bark. RDn (1875–95), W Bark. RDn (1895–1907), W Ham RDn (1907–66), Newham RDn (1966–*). Bdry: 1904 (cr Victoria Docks The Ascension EP),[392] 1920 (cr Victoria Docks St Matthew EP),[395] 1926 (help cr West Silvertown EP),[361] 1961.[49]

VICTORIA DOCKS ST MARK

EP Cr 1864 from Plaistow St Mary EP, East Ham AP, Woolwich AP (Kent).[215] Bark. RDn (1864–95 [London dioc 1864–67]), W Bark. RDn (1895–1907), W Ham RDn (1907–66), Newham RDn (1966–*). Bdry: 1875 (help cr Victoria Docks St Luke EP),[393] 1877 (cr North Woolwich EP),[394] 1926 (help cr West Silvertown EP).[361]

VICTORIA DOCKS ST MATTHEW

EP Cr 1920 from Victoria Docks St Luke EP.[395] W Ham RDn. Abol 1961 pt to Victoria Docks The Ascension EP, pt to Victoria Docks St Luke EP.[49]

VIRLEY

AP Salcot, Virley sep civ pars, Salcot Virley (qv) one EP.[357] *LG* Seq 25. Civ bdry: 1888,[379] 1889.[7] *Parl* N'rn Dv (1832–67), N-E Dv (1867–85), N-E'rn Dv (1885–1918), Colch. Dv/CC (1918–*).

GREAT WAKERING

AP *LG* Seq 20. Civ bdry: 1933 (loses pt to Southend on Sea CB and CP),[111] 1946 (incl help cr Barling Magna CP).[20] *Parl* Seq 17. *Eccl* Seq 40.

LITTLE WAKERING

AP Incl the pt of Havengore Island not made sep CP 1858.[311] *LG* Rochf. Hd, PLU, RSD, RD. Civ bdry: 1883.[8] Abol civ 1946 pt to help cr Barling Magna CP, pt to Great Wakering AP, pt S'rn Dv (1832–67), South Dv (1867–85), S-E'rn Dv (1885–1948). *Eccl* Seq 40.

GREAT WALTHAM

AP *LG* Seq 1. Civ bdry: 1883,[8] 1949,[114] 1969.[336] *Parl* Seq 11. *Eccl* Seq 32. Eccl bdry: 1871 (cr Ford End EP).[186]

LITTLE WALTHAM

AP *LG* Seq 1. Civ bdry: 1883,[8] 1888,[229] 1949.[114] *Parl* Seq 11. *Eccl* Seq 32.

WALTHAM ABBEY

AP Usual eccl spelling (sometimes 'Waltham Holy Cross otherwise Waltham Abbey'); for civ see following entry. *Eccl* Donative, Jurisd Waltham (until 1845), Ep. RDn (1845–62), Romford RDn (1862–83), Chigw. RDn (1883–*). Eccl bdry: 1836 (cr High Beech EP),[63] 1954,[138] 1957,[64] 1972.[65]

WALTHAM HOLY CROSS

AP Usual civ spelling; for eccl see prev entry. *LG* Waltham Hd, Bor (status not sustained), Edmonton PLU, Waltham Holy Cross USD, UD. Civ bdry: 1934.[17] *Parl* Seq 13.

WALTHAMSTOW [ST MARY]

AP *LG* Becontree Hd, W Ham PLU, Walt'stow USD, UD (1894–1926), MB (1926–65). Civ bdry: 1877,[396] 1883.[8] Transf 1965 to Gtr London (Waltham Forest LB).[37] *Parl* S'rn Dv (1832–67), South Dv (1867–85), S-W'rn Dv (1885–1918), pt Walt'stow East Parl Bor/BC, pt Walt' stow West Parl Bor/BC (1918–70) [see Part III of the *Guide* for the composition of these constituencies by wards of the UD/MB], Gtr London thereafter. *Eccl* Bark. RDn (until 1895 [London dioc until 1867]), N Bark. RDn (1895–1907), Walt'stow & Leyton RDn (1907–16), Walt'stow & Chingford RDn (1916–66), Waltham Forest RDn (1966–69). Eccl bdry: 1844 (cr Walthamstow St James EP, Walthamstow St John EP, Walthamstow St Peter EP),[397] 1881 (help cr Walthamstow St Stephen EP),[298] 1887 (help cr Walthamstow St Michael and All Angels EP),[398] 1901 (help cr Walthamstow St Barnabas EP),[399] 1903 (help cr Walthamstow St Luke EP),[400] 1904 (help cr Walthamstow St James the Greater EP),[401] 1919 (help cr Walthamstow St Gabriel EP),[402] 1922 (help cr Chingford St Edmund EP).[137] Abol eccl 1969 to help cr Walthamstow St Mary with St Stephen EP.[403]

WALTHAMSTOW ST ANDREW

EP Cr 1911 from Walthamstow St John EP.[404] Walt'stow & Leyton RDn (1911–16), Walt'stow & Chingford RDn (1916–66), Waltham Forest RDn (1966–*).

WALTHAMSTOW ST BARNABAS

EP Cr 1901 from Walthamstow St James EP, Walthamstow AP.[399] N Bark. RDn (1901–07), Walt'stow & Leyton RDn (1907–16), Walt'stow & Chingford RDn (1916–66), Waltham Forest RDn (1966–*).

WALTHAMSTOW ST GABRIEL

EP Cr 1919 from Walthamstow AP, Walthamstow St John EP.[402] Walt'stow & Chingford RDn (1919–66), Waltham Forest RDn (1966–*).

WALTHAMSTOW ST JAMES

EP Cr 1844 from Walthamstow AP.[397] Commonly called 'Walthamstow St Saviour' and so renamed 1967.[405] RDns as for Walthamstow AP for 1844–1967. Bdry: 1886 (help cr Leyton All Saints EP),[299] 1887 (help cr Walthamstow St Michael and All Angels EP),[398] 1901 (help cr Walthamstow St Barnabas EP),[399] 1904 (help cr Walthamstow St James the Greater EP).[401]

WALTHAMSTOW ST JAMES THE GREATER

EP Cr 1904 from Walthamstow St James EP, Walthamstow AP.[401] RDns as for Walthamstow St Barnabas. Bdry: 1955.[406]

WALTHAMSTOW ST JOHN
EP Cr 1844 from Walthamstow AP.[397] Bark.RDn (1844–95 [London dioc 1844–67]), N Bark. RDn (1895–1907), Walt'stow & Leyton RDn (1907–16), Walt'stow & Chingford RDn (1916–66), Waltham Forest RDn (1966–*). Bdry: 1903 (help cr Walthamstow St Luke EP),[400] 1911 (cr Walthamstow St Andrew EP),[404] 1912 (help cr Highams Park EP),[246] 1919 (help cr Walthamstow St Gabriel EP).[402]

WALTHAMSTOW ST LUKE
EP Cr 1903 from Walthamstow AP, Walthamstow St John EP.[400] RDns as for Walthamstow St Barnabas.

WALTHAMSTOW ST MARY WITH ST STEPHEN
EP Cr 1969 by union Walthamstow AP, Walthamstow St Stephen EP.[405] Waltham Forest RDn.

WALTHAMSTOW ST MICHAEL AND ALL ANGELS
EP Cr 1887 from Walthamstow AP, Walthamstow St James EP.[398] Bark. RDn (1887–95), N Bark. RDn (1895–1907), Walt'stow & Leyton RDn (1907–16), Walt'stow & Chingford RDn (1916–66), Waltham Forest RDn (1966–*). Bdry: 1924 (cr Walthamstow St Oswald EP),[407] 1955.[406]

WALTHAMSTOW ST OSWALD
EP Cr 1924 from Walthamstow St Michael and All Angels EP.[407] Walt'stow & Chingford RDn. Abol 1955 pt to Walthamstow St James the Greater EP, pt to Walthamstow St Michael and All Angels EP.[406]

WALTHAMSTOW ST PETER
EP Cr 1844 from Walthamstow AP.[397] RDns as for Walthamstow St John. Bdry: 1875 (help cr Woodford Wells EP),[408] 1912 (help cr Highams Park EP),[246] 1956 (help cr Chingford St Anne EP).[136]

WALTHAMSTOW ST SAVIOUR
EP Renaming 1967 of Walthamstow St James EP.[405] Waltham Forest RDn.

WALTHAMSTOW ST STEPHEN
EP Cr 1881 from Walthamstow AP, Leyton AP.[298] RDns as for Walthamstow St Michael and All Angels for 1881–1969. Abol 1969 to help cr Walthamstow St Mary with St Stephen EP.[403]

WALTON LE SOKEN
AP *LG* Tendr. Hd, PLU, Walton on the Naze USD, UD. Civ bdry: 1883,[8] 1905.[200] Abol civ 1934 to help cr Frinton and Walton CP.[17] *Parl* N'rn Dv (1832–67), N-E Dv (1867–85), N-E'rn Dv (1885–1918), Harw. RDn (1918–48). *Eccl* Pec jurisd of the Sokens (until 1845), Seq 15 thereafter.

WANSTEAD
AP *LG* Becontree Hd, W Ham PLU, Wanst. USD (ent 1875–83, pt 1883–94), pt Leyton USD (1883–94), Wanst. UD (1894–1934), Wanst. & Woodf. UD (1934–37), MB (1937–65). Civ bdry: 1883,[409] 1887,[221] 1887,[410] 1894 (the pt in Leyton USD to cr Cann Hall CP),[115] 1899,[411] 1901,[213] 1926,[172] 1956.[212] Transf 1965 to Gtr London (Redbr. LB).[37] *Parl* S'rn Dv (1832–67), South Dv (1867–85), S'rn Dv (1885–1918), Ep. Dv (1918–48), Woodf. BC (1948–70), Gtr London thereafter. Parl bdry: 1960.[427] *Eccl* Bark. RDn (until 1895 [London dioc until 1867]), N Bark. RDn (1895–1907), Walt'stow & Leyton RDn 1907–16), Wanst. & Woodf. RDn (1916–66), Redbr. RDn (1966–*). Eccl bdry: 1879 (help cr Leytonstone Holy Trinity, Harrow Green EP),[297] 1888 (help cr Wanstead Holy Trinity, Hermon Hill EP),[412] 1914 (help cr Aldersbrook EP),[10] 1962,[413] 1963 (help cr South Woodford EP).[414]

WANSTEAD HOLY TRINITY, HERMON HILL
EP Cr 1888 from Wanstead AP, Woodford St Mary AP.[412] Bark. RDn (1888–95), N Bark. RDn (1895–1907), Walt'stow & Leyton RDn (1907–16), Wanstead & Woodf. RDn (1916–66), Redbr. RDn (1966–*). Bdry: 1961 (help cr Barkingside St Cedd EP),[50] 1962,[413] 1963 (help cr South Woodford EP).[414]

WANSTEAD SLIP
EP Cr 1895 from Forest Gate St James EP, Leytonstone Holy Trinity, Harrow Green EP.[196] Bark. RDn (1895), N Bark. RDn (1895–1907), Walt'stow & Leyton RDn (1907–16), Leyton RDn (1916–53). Abol 1953 to help cr Leytonstone St Margaret with St Columba EP).[146]

GREAT WARLEY
AP *LG* Chaf. Hd, Romford PLU, RSD, RD (1894–1934), Hornchurch UD (1934–65). Civ bdry: 1904,[415] 1934.[17] Transf 1965 to Gtr London (Hav. LB).[37] *Parl* S'rn Dv (1832–67), South Dv (1867–85), Mid Dv (1885–1918), Romford Dv (1918–45), Hornchurch CC (1945–48), Hornchurch BC (1948–70), Gtr London thereafter. Parl bdry: 1945.[426] *Eccl* Chaf. RDn (until 1907), Barst. o'wise Brentw. RDn (1907–*). Eccl bdry: 1855 (help cr Great Warley Christ Church EP).[360]

GREAT WARLEY CHRIST CHURCH
EP Cr 1855 from Great Warley AP, Shenfield AP, South Weald AP.[360] Chaf. RDn (1855–1907), Barst. o'wsie Brentw. RDn (1907–*). Bdry: 1956.[96]

LITTLE WARLEY
AP *LG* Chaf. Hd, Bill. PLU, RSD, RD. Civ bdry: 1889.[157] Abol civ 1934 pt to Little Burstead AP, pt to Brentwood CP.[17] *Parl* S'rn Dv (1832–67), South Dv (1867–85), Mid Dv (1885–1918), S-E'rn Dv (1918–48). *Eccl* Seq 28.

NORTH WEALD
AP Usual eccl spelling; for civ see following entry. *Eccl* Seq 39.

NORTH WEALD BASSETT
AP Usual civ spelling; for eccl see prev entry. *LG* Pt Harlow Hd, pt Ong. Hd, Ep. PLU, RSD, RD (1894–1955), Ep. & Ong. RD (1955–74). Civ bdry: 1883,[8] 1946,[20] 1949,[9] 1955.[183] *Parl* Seq 14.

SOUTH WEALD
AP Incl chap and twnshp Brentwood (sep EP 1837,[95] sep CP 1866[19]). *LG* Chaf. Hd, Bill. PLU, RSD, RD. Addtl civ bdry alt: 1883,[8]

1904,[415] 1908.[98] Abol civ 1934 ent to Brentwood CP.[17] *Parl* S'rn Dv (1832–67), South Dv (1867–85), Mid Dv (1885–1918), Chelm. Dv (1918–48). *Eccl* Chaf. RDn (until 1907), Barst. o'wise Brentw. RDn (1907–*). Addtl eccl bdry alt: 1855 (help cr Great Warley Christ Church EP),[360] 1951 (cr Bentley Common EP),[72] 1956.[96]

WEELEY
AP *LG* Seq 21. Civ bdry: 1883.[8] *Parl* Seq 5. *Eccl* Seq 16.

GREAT WENDEN
AP *LG* Uttl. Hd. *Eccl* Nwpt. RDn. Abol 1662 to help cr Wendens Ambo.[416]

LITTLE WENDEN
AP Organisation as for Great Wenden.

WENDENS AMBO
Cr 1662 by union Great Wenden AP, Little Wenden AP.[416] *LG* Seq 24. *Parl* Seq 8. *Eccl* Seq 9.

WENDON LOFTS
AP *LG* Seq 24. Civ bdry: 1946.[20] *Parl* Seq 8. *Eccl* Nwpt. RDn (until 1847), Saff. Wald. RDn (1847–1931). Abol eccl 1931 to help cr Wendon Lofts with Elmdon EP.[179]

WENDON LOFTS WITH ELMDON
EP Cr 1931 by union Wendon Lofts AP, Elmdon AP.[179] Saff. Wald. RDn.

WENNINGTON
AP *LG* Chaf. Hd, Romford PLU, RSD, RD (1894–1934), Hornchurch UD (1934–65). Transf 1965 to Gtr London (Hav. LB).[37] *Parl* S'rn Dv (1832–67), South Dv (1867–85), S-E'rn Dv (1885–1918), Romford Dv (1918–45), Hornchurch CC (1945–48), Hornchurch BC (1948–70), Gtr London thereafter. *Eccl* Seq 30.

WESTCLIFF ST ANDREW
EP Cr 1930 from Southend-on-Sea St Saviour EP.[367] Canew. & S'end RDn.

WESTCLIFF ST CEDD AND THE SAINTS OF ESSEX
EP Cr 1963 from Prittlewell St Peter EP.[345] Canew. & S'end RDn.

WESTCLIFF ST MICHAEL AND ALL ANGELS
EP Cr 1923 from Southend-on-Sea St Saviour EP.[366] Canew. & S'end RDn.

WESTCLIFF ST PAUL
EP Cr 1922 from Southend-on-Sea St Alban the Martyr, West Cliff EP.[341] Canew. & S'end RDn.

WETHERSFIELD
AP *LG* Seq 11. Civ bdry: 1883.[8] *Parl* Seq 3. *Eccl* Seq 47.

WICKEN BONHUNT
AP *LG* Seq 24. *Parl* Seq 8. *Eccl* Nwpt. RDn (until 1880s), Saff. Wald. RDn (1880s–1907), Nwpt. & Stan. RDn (1907–*).

WICKFORD
AP *LG* Barst. Hd, Bill. PLU, RSD, RD. Civ bdry: 1888.[167] Abol civ 1937 to help cr Billericay CP.[56] *Parl* S'rn Dv (1832–67), South Dv (1867–85), Mid Dv (1885–1918), S-E'rn Dv (1918–48). *Eccl* Seq 21.

WICKHAM BISHOPS
AP *LG* Thurst. Hd, Witham PLU (1835–83), RSD (1875–83), Maldon PLU (1883–1930), RSD (1883–94), Maldon RD. Civ bdry: 1883,[8] 1889.[22] *Parl* Seq 2. *Eccl* Seq 20.

WICKHAM ST PAUL
AP *LG* Seq 15. *Parl* Seq 8. *Eccl* Pec jurisd Dean & Chapter of St Paul's, London (until 1845), Seq 48 thereafter.

WIDDINGTON
AP *LG* Seq 24. Civ bdry: 1883,[8] 1946,[20] 1960.[326] *Parl* Seq 8. *Eccl* Seq 11.

WIDFORD
AP *LG* Chelm. Hd, PLU, RSD, RD. Civ bdry: 1889.[101] Abol civ 1934 pt to Chelmsford MB and AP, pt to Writtle AP.[17] *Parl* S'rn Dv (1832–67), N-W Dv (1867–85), Mid Dv (1885–1918), Chelm. Dv (1918–48). *Eccl* Chelm. RDn (until 1845), Ingat. RDn (1845–95), Chelm. RDn (1895–*). Eccl bdry: 1956.[319]

GREAT WIGBOROUGH
AP *LG* Winst. Hd, Lexd. & Winst. PLU, RSD, RD. Civ bdry: 1888,[380] 1889.[7] Abol civ 1953 to help cr Great and Little Wigborough CP.[83] *Parl* N'rn Dv (1832–67), N-E Dv (1867–85), E'rn Dv (1885–1918), Colch. Dv/CC (1918–70). *Eccl* Seq 7. Eccl bdry: 1859 (help cr Tiptree Heath EP).[269]

GREAT AND LITTLE WIGBOROUGH
CP Cr 1953 by union Great Wigborough AP, Little Wigborough AP, pt Layer de la Haye AP.[83] *LG* Lexd. & Winst. RD. *Parl* Colch. CC (1970–*).

LITTLE WIGBOROUGH
AP *LG* Winst. Hd, Lexd. & Winst. PLU, RSD, RD. Civ bdry: 1889.[7] Abol civ 1953 to help cr Great and Little Wigborough CP.[83] *Parl* As for Great Wigborough. *Eccl* Seq 7.

WILLINGALE
CP Cr 1946 by union Willingale Doe AP, Willingale Spain AP, Shellow Bowells AP.[20] *LG* Ong. RD (1946–55), Ep. & Ong. RD (1955–74). *Parl* Chelm. CC (1948–70), Brentw. & Ong. CC (1970–*).

WILLINGALE DOE
AP *LG* Dunmow Hd, Ong. PLU, RSD, RD. Civ bdry: 1883.[8] Abol civ 1946 to help cr Willingale CP.[20] *Parl* N'rn Dv (1832–67), N-W Dv (1867–85), W'rn Dv (1885–1918), Chelm. Dv (1918–48). *Eccl* Dunmow RDn (until 1845), Roding RDn (1845–1928). Abol eccl 1928 to help cr Willingale with Shellow EP.[359]

WILLINGALE SPAIN
AP Organisation as for Willingale Doe.

WILLINGALE WITH SHELLOW
EP Cr 1928 by union Willingale Doe AP, Willingale Spain AP, Shellow Bowells AP.[359] Roding RDn.

WIMBISH
AP *LG* Seq 24. *Parl* Seq 8. *Eccl* Dunmow RDn (until 1895), Sampf. RDn (1895–1907), Saff. Wald. RDn (1907–*).

WITHAM
AP *LG* Witham Hd, Bor (status not sustained), PLU

(1835–83), Braint. PLU (1883–1930), Witham USD (ent 1875–83, pt 1883–94), pt Braint. RSD (1883–94), Witham UD. Civ bdry: 1883,[8] 1894 (the pt not in the USD cr Unnamed CP),[115] 1903 (gains the Unnamed CP),[390] 1933,[184] 1956.[94] *Parl* Seq 3. *Eccl* Seq 17.

WIVENHOE
AP *LG* Lexd. Hd, Lexd. & Winst. PLU, RSD, RD (1894–98), Wivenhoe UD (1898–1974). Civ bdry: 1897,[180] 1934.[17] *Parl* N'rn Dv (1832–67), N-E Dv (1867–85), E'rn Dv (1885–1918), Harw. Dv/CC (1918–*). *Eccl* Lexd. RDn (until 1847), Dedham RDn (1847–1907), Colch. RDn (1907–*).

WIX
AP *LG* Seq 21. *Parl* Seq 5. *Eccl* Seq 13.

NORTH WOOD
The 2 ex-par places of Belchamp North Wood, Belchamp North End made single CP 1858 as 'North Wood'.[425] *LG* Hinckf. Hd, Sudbury PLU, RSD, Belch. RD (1894–1934), Halst. RD (1934–46). Abol 1946 pt to Little Yeldham AP, pt to Tilbury juxta Clare AP.[20] *Parl* N-E Dv (1867–85), N'rn Dv (1885–1918), Saff. Wald. Dv (1918–48).

WOODFORD
AP Often 'Woodford St Mary', the name declared 1926 to be 'Woodford'.[423] *LG* Becontree Hd, W Ham PLU, Woodf. USD, UD (1894–1934), Wanstead & Woodf. UD (1934–37), Wanstead & Woodf. MB (1937–65). Civ bdry: 1883,[409] 1899,[411] 1901,[417] 1926.[172] Transf 1965 to Gtr London (Redbr. LB).[37] *Parl* S'rn Dv (1832–67), South Dv (1867–85), S-W'rn Dv (1885–1918), Ep. Dv (1918–48), Woodf. BC (1948–70), Gtr London thereafter. *Eccl* Bark. RDn (until 1895) [London dioc until 1867]), N Bark. RDn (1895–1907), Walt'stow & Leyton RDn (1907–16), Wanstead & Woodf. RDn (1916–66), Redbr. RDn (1966–71). Eccl bdry: 1834 (cr Woodford Bridge EP),[419] 1875 (help cr Woodford Wells EP),[408] 1888 (help cr Wanstead Holy Trinity, Hermon Hill EP),[412] 1962,[413] 1963 (help cr South Woodford EP).[417] Abol eccl 1971 to help cr Woodford St Mary with St Philip and St James EP.[418]

WOODFORD ST BARNABAS
EP Cr 1911 from Woodford Bridge EP, Woodford Wells EP, Wanstead Holy Trinity, Hermon Hill EP.[420] Walt'stow & Leyton RDn (1911–16), Wanstead & Woodf. RDn (1916–66), Redbr. RDn (1966–*).

WOODFORD ST MARY–See WOODFORD

WOODFORD ST MARY WITH ST PHILIP AND ST JAMES
EP Cr 1971 by union Woodford AP, South Woodford EP.[418] Redbr. RDn.

SOUTH WOODFORD
EP Cr 1963 from Woodford AP, Wanstead AP, Wanstead Holy Trinity, Hermon Hill EP.[414] Wanstead & Woodf. RDn (1963–66), Redbr. RDn (1966–71). Abol 1971 to help cr Woodford St Mary with St Philip and St James EP.[418]

WOODFORD BRIDGE
EP Cr 1834 from Woodford AP.[419] Bark. RDn (1844–95 [London dioc 1844–67]), N Bark. RDn (1895–1907), Walt'stow & Leyton RDn (1907–16), Wanstead & Woodf. RDn (1916–66), Redbr. RDn (1966–*). Bdry: 1911 (help cr Woodford St Barnabas EP).[420]

WOODFORD WELLS
EP Cr 1875 from Woodford AP, Walthamstow St Peter EP.[408] RDns as for Woodford Bridge for 1875–*. Bdry: 1911 (help cr Woodford St Barnabas EP).[420]

SOUTH WOODHAM
EP Cr 1971 from Woodham Ferrers AP.[421] Wickf. RDn.

WOODHAM FERRERS
AP *LG* Chelm. Hd, PLU,[66] RSD, RD. Civ bdry: 1934.[17] *Parl* Seq 10. *Eccl* Seq 35. Eccl bdry: 1971 (cr South Woodham EP).[421]

WOODHAM MORTIMER
AP *LG* Seq 4. *Parl* Seq 9. *Eccl* Dengie RDn (until 1845), Maldon RDn (1845–1932). Abol eccl 1932 to help cr Woodham Mortimer with Hazeleigh EP.[244]

WOODHAM MORTIMER WITH HAZELEIGH
EP Cr 1932 by union Woodham Mortimer AP, Hazeleigh AP.[244] Maldon RDn.

WOODHAM WALTER
AP *LG* Seq 4. *Parl* Seq 9. *Eccl* Seq 37.

NORTH WOOLWICH
EP Cr 1877 from Victoria Docks St Mary EP (Essex, Kent).[394] Bark. RDn (1877–95), S Bark. RDn (1895–1907), Bark. RDn (1907–66), Newham RDn (1966–*).

WORMINGFORD
AP *LG* Seq 17. Civ bdry: 1889,[7] 1955.[76] *Parl* Seq 1. Parl bdry: 1956.[424] *Eccl* Seq 4.

WRABNESS
AP *LG* Seq 21. *Parl* Seq 5. *Eccl* Seq 14.

WRITTLE
AP Incl chap Roxwell (sep par 1597[356]), chap Highwood (sep EP 1875,[247] sep CP 1954[248]). *LG* Writtle Bor (status not sustained), Seq 1. Addtl civ bdry alt: 1883,[8] 1888,[422] 1888,[100] 1889 (incl help cr Chignall CP),[100] 1889,[101] 1897,[127] 1907,[126] 1934,[17] 1946,[20] 1953,[268] 1956.[319] *Parl* Seq 11. *Eccl* Pec jurisd Writtle with Roxwell (until 1845), Seq 31 thereafter. Addtl eccl bdry alt: 1930 (help cr Chelmsford The Ascension EP),[103] 1958 (help cr Chelmsford St Andrew EP),[104] 1962 (help cr Chelmsford All Saints EP).[130]

GREAT YELDHAM
AP *LG* Seq 13. Civ bdry: 1820,[389] 1883,[8] 1885,[155] 1954.[381] *Parl* Seq 6. *Eccl* Seq 51.

LITTLE YELDHAM
AP *LG* Seq 13. Civ bdry: 1885,[155] 1888,[67] 1946,[20] 1954.[381] *Parl* Seq 6. *Eccl* Seq 50.

GLOUCESTERSHIRE

ABBREVIATIONS

Abbreviations particular to Glos follow. Those general abbreviations in use throughout the *Guide* are found on page xix.

Almond.	Almondsbury
Bart. Reg.	Barton Regis
Berk.	Berkeley
Bled.	Bledisloe
Brightw. Bar.	Brightwells Barrow
Camp.	Campden
Chelt.	Cheltenham
Chip. Sodb.	Chipping Sodbury
Cirenc.	Cirencester
Cotsw.	Cotswold
Crowt. & Min.	Crowthorne and Minety
Dudst. & K's Bart.	Dudstone and King's Barton
Durs.	Dursley
For.	Forest
Glouc.	Gloucester
Grumb.	Grumbalds
Hawk.	Hawkesbury
Kiftsg.	Kiftsgate
Lanc.	Lancaster
Lang. & Swin.	Langley and Swinehead
Longt.	Longtree
Marst. Sic.	Marston Sicca
N'leach	Northleach
Puck.	Pucklechurch
Rapsg.	Rapsgate
St Briav.	St Briavels
Slaugh.	Slaughter
Sodb.	Sodbury
Stap.	Stapleton
Stoneh.	Stonehouse
Tetb.	Tetbury
Tewk.	Tewkesbury
Thornb.	Thornbury
Tibald.	Tibaldstone
W'bury.	Westbury
W'minst.	Westminster
Wheath.	Wheathampstead
Whits.	Whitstone
Winch.	Winchcombe

SEQUENCES

An abbreviated entry prefixed by 'Seq' is used in the parochial entries to avoid repeating often the names of superior units of administration. The content of each sequence is shown below.

Local Government Sequences ('LG')

SEQ 1 Berk. Hd, Durs. PLU, RSD, RD
SEQ 2 Berk. Hd, Tetb. PLU, RSD, RD
SEQ 3 Berk. Hd, Thornb. PLU, RSD, RD
SEQ 4 Bisley Hd, Cirenc. PLU, RSD, RD
SEQ 5 Bisley Hd, Stroud PLU, RSD, RD
SEQ 6 Bled. Hd, Chepstow PLU, RSD, Lydney RD
SEQ 7 Botloe Hd, Newent PLU, RSD, RD
SEQ 8 Bradley Hd, N'leach PLU, RSD, RD

SEQ 9 Brightw. Bar. Hd, Cirenc. PLU, RSD, RD
SEQ 10 Brightw. Bar. Hd, N'leach PLU, RSD, RD
SEQ 11 Crowt. & Min. Hd, Cirenc. PLU, RSD, RD
SEQ 12 Deerhurst Hd, Chelt. PLU, RSD, RD
SEQ 13 Duchy of Lanc. Hd, W'bury on Severn PLU, RSD, E Dean & United Pars RD (1894–1935), E Dean RD (1935–74)
SEQ 14 Dudst. & K's Bart. Hd, Glouc. Bor & Co (1483–1672), Chelt. PLU, RSD, RD
SEQ 15 Dudst. & K's Bart. Hd, Glouc. Bor & Co (1483–1672), Glouc. PLU, RSD, RD
SEQ 16 Grumb. Ash Hd, Chip. Sodb. PLU, RSD, RD (1894–1935), Sodb. RD (1935–74)
SEQ 17 Grumb. Ash Hd, Tetb. PLU, RSD, RD
SEQ 18 Grumb. Ash Hd, Thornb. PLU, RSD, RD
SEQ 19 Kiftsg. Hd, Evesham PLU, RSD, Pebworth RD (1894–1931), Camp. RD (1931–35), N Cotsw. RD (1935–74)
SEQ 20 Kiftsg. Hd, Shipston on Stour PLU, RSD, Camp. RD (1894–1935), N Cotsw. RD (1935–74)
SEQ 21 Kiftsg. Hd, Stow on the Wold PLU, RSD, RD (1894–1935), N Cotsw. RD (1935–74)
SEQ 22 Kiftsg. Hd, Winch. PLU, RSD, RD (1894–1935), Chelt. RD (1935–74)
SEQ 23 Lang. & Swin. Hd, Chip. Sodb. PLU, RSD, RD (1894–1935), Sodb. RD (1935–74)
SEQ 24 Longt. Hd, Stroud PLU, RSD, RD
SEQ 25 Longt. Hd, Tetb. PLU, RSD, RD
SEQ 26 Puck. Hd, Chip. Sodb. PLU, RSD, RD (1894–1935), Sodb. RD (1935–74)
SEQ 27 Rapsg. Hd, Chelt. PLU, RSD, RD
SEQ 28 Rapsg. Hd, Cirenc. PLU, RSD, RD
SEQ 29 St Briav. Hd, Chepstow PLU, RSD, Lydney RD
SEQ 30 St Briav. Hd, Monmouth PLU, RSD, W Dean RD
SEQ 31 St Briav. Hd, W'bury on Severn PLU, RSD, E Dean & United Pars RD (1894–1935), E Dean RD (1935–74)
SEQ 32 Slaugh. Hd, N'leach PLU, RSD, RD
SEQ 33 Slaugh. Hd, Stow on the Wold PLU, RSD, RD (1894–1935), N Cotsw. RD (1935–74)
SEQ 34 Tewk. Hd, PLU, RSD, RD (1894–1935), Chelt. RD (1935–74)
SEQ 35 Tewk. Hd, Winch. PLU, RSD, RD (1894–1935), Chelt. RD (1935–74)
SEQ 36 W'bury Hd, Chepstow PLU, RSD, Lydney RD
SEQ 37 W'minst. Hd, Shipton on Stour PLU, RSD, Camp. RD (1894–1935), N Cotsw. RD (1935–74)
SEQ 38 Whits. Hd, Stroud PLU, RSD, RD
SEQ 39 Whits. Hd, Wheath. PLU, RSD, RD (1894–1935), Glouc. RD (1935–74)

Parliamentary Sequences ('Parl')

SEQ 1 E'rn Dv (1832–1918), Cirenc. & Tewk. Dv/CC (1918–*)
SEQ 2 E'rn Dv (1832–1918), Cirenc. & Tewk. Dv/CC (1918–55), Stroud. CC (1955–*)
SEQ 3 E'rn Dv (1832–85), Mid Dv (1885–1918), Stroud Dv (1918–48), Stroud & Thornb. CC (1948–55), Stroud CC (1955–*)
SEQ 4 E'rn Dv (1832–85), N'rn Dv (1885–1918), Cirenc. & Tewk. Dv/CC (1918–*)
SEQ 5 E'rn Dv (1832–85), N'rn Dv (1885–1918), Cirenc. & Tewk. Dv (1918–48), W Glos CC (1948–*)
SEQ 6 E'rn Dv (1832–85), N'rn Dv (1885–1918), Stroud Dv (1918–48), Cirenc. & Tewk. CC (1948–*)
SEQ 7 E'rn Dv (1832–85), N'rn Dv (1885–1918), Stroud Dv (1918–48), Stroud & Thornb. CC (1948–55), Stroud CC (1955–*)
SEQ 8 E'rn Dv (1832–85), N'rn Dv (1885–1918), Stroud Dv (1918–48), W Glos CC (1948–*)
SEQ 9 Stroud Parl Bor (1832–85), Mid Dv (1885–1918), Stroud Dv (1918–48), Stroud & Thornb. CC (1948–55), Stroud CC (1955–*)
SEQ 10 W'rn Dv (1832–85), E'rn Dv (1885–1918), Cirenc. & Tewk. Dv/CC (1918–55), Stroud CC (1955–*)
SEQ 11 W'rn Dv (1832–85), For. Dean Dv (1885–1948), W Glos CC (1948–*)
SEQ 12 W'rn Dv (1832–85), Mid Dv (1885–1918), Stroud Dv (1948–55), Stroud CC (1955–*)
SEQ 13 W'rn Dv (1832–85), Mid Dv (1885–1918), Thornb. Dv (1918–48), S Glos CC (1948–*)
SEQ 14 W'rn Dv (1832–85), S'rn Dv (1885–1918), Thornb. Dv (1918–48), S Glos CC (1948–*)
SEQ 15 W'rn Dv (1832–85), S'rn Dv (1885–1918), Thornb. Dv (1918–48), Stroud & Thornb. CC (1948–55), S Glos CC (1955–*)

Ecclesiastical Sequences ('Eccl')

Orig in Hereford dioc:
SEQ 1 For. RDn (until 1866), For. North RDn (1866–*)
SEQ 2 For. RDn (until 1866), For. South RDn (1866–*)
SEQ 3 For. RDn (until 1866), For. South RDn (1866–1907), For. North RDn (1907–*)
SEQ 4 Ross RDn (until 1836), For. RDn (1836–66), For. South RDn (1866–*)

Orig in Worcester dioc:
SEQ 5 Bibury pec jurisd (until 1847), Fairford RDn (1847–*)
SEQ 6 Blockley jurisd (until 1847), Camp. RDn (1847–1907), Stow RDn (1907–*)
SEQ 7 Bristol RDn (until 1866), Bristol (Rural Dv) RDn (1866–87), Stap. RDn (1887–1927), Almond. RDn (1927–49), Clifton RDn (1949–73), W'bury & Severnside

RDn (1973–*)

SEQ 8 Bristol RDn (until 1866), Bristol (Rural Dv) RDn (1866–87), Stap. RDn (1887–1927), Almond. RDn (1927–73), Horfield RDn (1973–*)

SEQ 9 Bristol RDn (until 1866), Bristol (Rural Dv) RDn (1866–87), Stap. RDn (1887–1927), Almond. RDn (1927–49), Stap. RDn (1949–*)

SEQ 10 Bristol RDn (until 1866), Bristol (Rural Dv) RDn (1866–87), Stap. RDn (1887–1927), Almond. RDn (1927–73), W'bury & Severnside RDn (1973–*)

SEQ 11 Camp. RDn.

SEQ 12 Camp. RDn (until 1907), Winch. RDn (1907–*)

SEQ 13 Cirenc. RDn

SEQ 14 Cirenc. RDn (until 1836), N'leach RDn (1836–66), N'leach South RDn (1866–87), N'leach RDn (1887–*)

SEQ 15 Durs. RDn (until 1901), Tetb. RDn (1901–*)

SEQ 16 Fairford RDn

SEQ 17 Glouc. RDn (until 1907), Bisley RDn (1907–*)

SEQ 18 Glouc. RDn (until 1952), Glouc. City RDn (1952–*)

SEQ 19 Glouc. RDn (until 1952), Glouc. North RDn (1952–*)

SEQ 20 Glouc. RDn (until 1952), Glouc. South RDn (1952–*)

SEQ 21 Hawk. RDn (until 1866), Hawk. North RDn (1866–87), Hawk. RDn (1887–*)

SEQ 22 Hawk. RDn (until 1866), Hawk. South RDn (1866–87), Bitton RDn (1887–*)

SEQ 23 Hawk. RDn (until 1866), Hawk. South RDn (1866–87), Bitton RDn (1887–1949), Stap. RDn (1949–*)

SEQ 24 Stoneh. RDn (until 1866), Stoneh. North RDn (1866–87), Bisley RDn (1887–*)

SEQ 25 Stoneh. RDn (until 1866), Stoneh. North RDn (1866–87), Bisley RDn (1887–1907), Cirenc. RDn (1907–*)

SEQ 26 Stoneh. RDn (until 1866), Stoneh. South RDn (1866–87), Stoneh. RDn (1887–*)

SEQ 27 Stoneh. RDn (until 1866), Stoneh. South RDn (1866–87), Tetb. RDn (1887–*)

SEQ 28 Stow RDn

SEQ 29 Stow RDn (until 1836), N'leach RDn (1836–66), N'leach North RDn (1866–87), N'leach RDn (1887–*)

SEQ 30 Winch. RDn (until 1866), Winch. North RDn (1866–87), Winch. RDn (1887–1907), Glouc. RDn (1907–52), Glouc. North RDn (1952–*)

SEQ 31 Winch. RDn (until 1866), Winch. North RDn (1866–87), Winch. RDn (1887–1901), Tewk. RDn (1901–*)

SEQ 32 Winch. RDn (until 1866), Winch. South RDn (1866–87), Chelt. RDn (1887–*)

DIOCESES AND ARCHDEACONRIES

Glos pars were organised in dioceses and archdeaconries as follows.

BRISTOL DIOC (1542–1836)
Bristol AD: Bristol RDn

BRISTOL DIOC (1897–*)
Bristol AD: Almond. RDn (1927–73), Bitton RDn, Bristol RDn (1897–1901), Bristol City RDn (1901–*), E Bristol RDn (1901–49), Clifton RDn (1901–*), Horfield RDn (1973–*), Stap. RDn (1897–1927), Stap. RDn (1949–*), W'bury. & Severnside RDn (1973–*)

GLOUCESTER DIOC (1541–1836)
Glouc. AD: Bristol RDn (1541–42), Camp. RDn, Cirenc. RDn, Durs. RD, Fairford RDn, Glouc. RDn, Hawk. RDn, Stoneh. RDn, Stow RDn, Winch. RDn
Hereford AD: For. RDn

GLOUCESTER DIOC (1897–*)
Chelt. AD (1919–):* Camp. RDn, Chelt. RDn, Cirenc. RDn, Fairford RDn, N'leach. RDn, Stow RDn, Tetb. RDn, Winch. RDn
Cirenc. AD (1897–1919): Camp. RDn, Cirenc. RDn, Fairford RDn, N'leach. RDn, Stow RDn, Winch. RDn (1907–19)
Glouc. AD: Bisley RDn, Chelt. RDn (1897–1919), Durs. RDn, For. North RDn, For. South RDn, Glouc. RDn (1897–1952), Glouc. City RDn (1952–*), Glouc. North RDn (1952–*), Glouc. South RDn (1952–*), Hawk. RDn, Stoneh. RDn, Tetb. RDn (1907–19), Tewk. RDn (1907–*), Winch. RDn (1897–1907)

GLOUCESTER AND BRISTOL DIOC (1836–97)
Bristol AD: Bitton RDn (1887–97), Bristol RDn (1836–66), Bristol RDn (1887–97), Bristol (City Dv) RDn (1866–87), Bristol (Rural Dv) RDn (1866–87), Cirenc. RDn (1836–82), Fairford RDn (1836–82), Hawk. RDn (1836–66), Hawk. RDn (1887–97), Hawk. North RDn (1866–87), Hawk. South RDn (1866–87), Stap. RDn (1887–97)
Cirenc. AD (1882–97): Camp. RDn, Cirec. RDn, Fairford RDn, Stow RDn, N'leach RDn (1887–97), N'leach North RDn (1882–87)
Glouc. AD: Bisley RDn (1887–97), Camp. RDn (1836–82), Chelt. RDn (1887–97), Durs. RDn, For. RDn (1836–66), For. North RDn (1866–97), For. South RDn (1866–97), Glouc. RDn, N'leach. RDn (1836–66), N'leach. North RDn (1866–82), N'leach. South RDn (1866–97), Stoneh. RDn (1836–66), Stoneh. RDn (1887–97), Stoneh. North RDn (1866–87), Stoneh. South RDn (1866–97), Stow RDn (1836–82), Winch. RDn (1836–66), Winch. RDn (1887–

97), Winch. North RDn (1866–87), Winch. South RDn (1866–87)

THE PARISHES OF GLOUCESTERSHIRE

ABENHALL
AP Sometimes 'Abinghall'. *LG* St Briav. Hd, W'bury on Severn PLU, RSD, E Dean & United Pars RD. Civ bdry: 1885.[1] Abol civ 1935 ent to Mitcheldean AP.[2] *Parl* W'rn Dv (1832–85), For. Dean Dv (1885–1948). *Eccl* Seq 3.

ABSON AND WICK–See WICK AND ABSON

IRON ACTON
AP *LG* Pt Thornb. Hd, pt Grumb. Ash Hd, Chip. Sodb. PLU, RSD, RD (1894–1935), Sodb. RD (1935–74). Civ bdry: 1883.[3] Transf 1974 to Avon.[4] *Parl* Seq 14. *Eccl* Seq 23.

ACTON TURVILLE
AP United 1344 to Tormarton AP[5] and considered its chapel, sep civ identity early, sep EP 1870.[6] *LG* Seq 16. Transf 1974 to Avon.[4] *Parl* Seq 14. *Eccl* Seq 21.

ADLESTROP
Chap in Broadwell (sometimes described as sep par united early to Broadwell[7]), sep civ identity early, eccl severed 1937 to help cr Oddington with Adlestrop EP.[8] *LG* Seq 33. Civ bdry: 1935.[2] *Parl* Seq 1.

ADMINGTON
Hmlt in Quinton AP, sep CP 1866.[9] *LG* Kiftsg. Hd, Shipston on Stour PLU, RSD, Camp. RD. Transf 1935 to Warws.[10] *Parl* E'rn Dv (1867–1918), Cirenc. & Tewk. Dv (1918–48), Warws therafter.

ALDERLEY
AP *LG* Seq 16. Civ bdry: 1883,[3] 1885.[11] *Parl* Seq 14. *Eccl* Seq 21.

ALDERTON
AP *LG* Seq 35. Civ bdry: 1957.[12] *Parl* Seq 4. *Eccl* Seq 12.

ALDSWORTH
AP Sep par sometimes accounted chap in Turkdean AP.[13] *LG* Seq 10. *Parl* Seq 1. *Eccl* Pec jurisd Bibury (until 1847), Fairford RDn (1847–87), N'leach RDn (1887–*). Eccl bdry: 1934.[14]

ALKINGTON
Tg in Berkeley AP, sep CP 1866.[9] *LG* Seq 3. Civ bdry: 1884.[15] *Parl* W'rn Dv (1867–85), N'rn Dv (1885–1918), Thornb. Dv (1918–48), Stroud & Thornb. CC (1948–55), S Glos CC (1955–*).

ALMONDSBURY
AP *LG* Pt Berk. Hd, pt Lang. & Swin. Hd, pt Thornb. Hd, Thornb. PLU, RSD, RD. Civ bdry: 1935,[2] 1953 (cr Patchway CP),[16] 1966 (loses pt to Bristol CB and CP),[17] 1970.[18] Transf 1974 to Avon.[4] *Parl* Seq 14. *Eccl* Seq 10. Eccl bdry: 1881 (help cr Pilning EP),[19] 1964 (help cr Patchway EP).[20]

ALSTONE
Hmlt in Overbury AP (Worcs), transf to Glos 1832 for parl purposes, 1844 for civ purposes,[21] sep CP 1866.[9] *LG* Kiftsg. Hd, Winch. PLU, RSD, RD. Abol 1935 ent to Teddington AP.[2] *Parl* E'rn Dv (1867–85), N'rn Dv (1885–1918), Cirenc. & Tewk. Dv (1918–48).

ALVESTON
AP *LG* Lang. & Swin. Hd, Thornb. PLU, RSD, RD. Civ bdry: 1883.[3] Transf 1974 to Avon.[4] *Parl* Seq 15. *Eccl* Seq 10.

ALVINGTON
Chap in Woolaston AP, sep civ identity early, no sep eccl identity. *LG* Seq 6. Civ bdry: 1935.[2] *Parl* Seq 11.

AMBERLEY
EP Cr 1840 from Minchinhampton AP.[22] Stoneh. RDn (1840–66), Stoneh. South RDn (1866–87), Stoneh. RDn (1887–*). Bdry: 1895 (help cr Nailsworth EP).[23]

DOWN AMPNEY
AP *LG* Seq 11. Civ bdry: 1894.[24] *Parl* Seq 1. *Eccl* Seq 16.

AMPNEY CRUCIS
AP *LG* Seq 11. Civ bdry: 1883,[3] 1894,[25] 1935.[2] *Parl* Seq 1. *Eccl* Seq 13.

AMPNEY ST MARY
AP *LG* Seq 11. Civ bdry: 1894.[25] *Parl* Seq 1. *Eccl* Seq 13.

AMPNEY ST PETER
AP *LG* Seq 11. Civ bdry: 1883,[3] 1894.[25] *Parl* Seq 1. *Eccl* Seq 13.

ANDOVERSFORD
CP Cr 1956 from Dowdeswell AP, Shipton CP, Whittington AP, Withington AP.[26] *LG* N'leach RD. *Parl* Cirenc. & Tewk. CC (1970–*).

APPERLEY
Chap in Deerhurst AP, sep EP 1856[13] but status not sustained and considered chap in Deerhurst.

ARLINGHAM
AP *LG* Berk. Hd, Wheath. PLU, RSD, RD (1894–1935), Glouc. RD (1935–74). *Parl* W'rn Dv (1832–85), N'rn Dv (1885–1918), Stroud Dv (1918–48), Stroud & Thornb. CC (1948–55), Stroud CC (1955–*). *Eccl* Seq 20. Eccl bdry: 1855 (help cr Framilode EP).[27]

ASHCHURCH
AP Chap to Tewk. Abbey, sep status as curacy after 16th cent Dissolution.[28] *LG* Seq 34. Civ bdry: 1935,[2] 1965 (loses pt to Beckford AP, Worcs).[29] *Parl* Seq 4. *Eccl* Seq 31.

ASHLEWORTH
AP *LG* Berk. Hd, Glouc. PLU, RSD, RD. *Parl* W'rn Dv (1832–85), N'rn Dv (1885–1918), For. Dean Dv (1918–48), W Glos CC (1948–*). *Eccl* Seq 19.

ASHLEY
AP In Wilts, one of the Wilts mbrs of Tetb. RD, transf 1931 to Glos.[401] *LG* Tetb. RD. Civ bdry: 1935.[2] *Parl* In Wilts until 1948, Cirenc. & Tewk. CC (1948–55), Stroud CC (1955–*).

COLD ASHTON
AP *LG* Seq 26. Transf 1974 to Avon.[4] *Parl* Seq 14. *Eccl* Seq 22.

ASHTON UNDER HILL
Chap in Beckford AP, sep civ identity early, no sep eccl identity. *LG* Tibald. Hd, Evesham PLU, RSD, Pebworth RD (1894–1931). Transf 1931 to Worcs.[30] *Parl* E'rn Dv (1832–85), N'rn Dv (1885–1918), Cirenc. & Tewk. Dv (1918–48), Worcs thereafter.

COLD ASTON
AP Usual eccl spelling; for civ see following entry. *Eccl* Seq 29.

ASTON BLANK
AP Usual civ spelling; for eccl see prev entry. *LG* Seq 8. *Parl* Seq 1.

ASTON MAGNA
Hmlt in Blockley AP (Worcs until 1931, Glos thereafter), sep EP 1847.[31] Worcester dioc (see entry in Worcs) until 1919, Camp. RDn (1919–*).

ASTON SOMERVILLE
AP *LG* Kiftsg. Hd, Evesham PLU, RSD, Pebworth RD (1894–1931). Transf 1931 to Worcs.[30] *Parl* E'rn Dv (1832–85), N'rn Dv (1885–1918), Cirenc. & Tewk. Dv (1918–48), Worcs. thereafter. *Eccl* Seq 12.

ASTON SUB EDGE
AP Usual eccl spelling; for civ see following entry. *Eccl* Camp. RDn. Abol eccl 1930 to help cr Weston sub Edge with Aston sub Edge EP.[32]

ASTON SUBEDGE
AP Usual civ spelling; for eccl see prev entry. *LG* Seq 19. *Parl* Seq 1.

AUST
Tg in Henbury AP, sep CP 1866.[9] *LG* Henbury Hd, Thornb. PLU, RSD, RD. Bdry: 1885,[33] 1935.[2] Transf 1974 to Avon.[4] *Parl* W'rn Dv (1867–85), S'rn Dv (1885–1918), Thornb. Dv (1918–48), Stroud & Thornb. CC (1948–55), S Glos CC (1955–*).

AVENING
AP Incl pt chap Nailsworth (sep CP 1866,[9] sep EP 1895[23]). *LG* Longt. Hd, Stroud PLU (1836–94), RSD, Tetb. PLU (1894–1930), RD. Addtl civ bdry alt: 1935.[2] *Parl* Stroud Parl Bor (1832–85), Mid Dv (1885–1918), Cirenc. & Tewk. Dv/CC (1918–55), Stroud CC (1955–*). *Eccl* Seq 27.

AVONMOUTH
EP Cr 1917 from Shirehampton AP.[34] Stap. RDn (1917–19), Clifton RDn (1919–73), W'bury & Severnside RDn (1973–*).

AWRE
AP *LG* Bled. Hd, W'bury on Severn PLU, Awre USD, UD (1894–1935), E Dean RD (1935–74). Civ bdry: 1935,[2] 1953.[35] *Parl* Seq 11. *Eccl* Seq 1. Eccl bdry: 1853 (cr Blakeney EP).[36]

AYLBURTON
Tg and chap in Lydney AP, sep CP 1866,[9] no sep eccl identity. *LG* Seq 6. *Parl* W'rn Dv (1867–85), For. Dean Dv (1885–1948), W Glos CC (1948–*).

BADGEWORTH
AP Incl chap Shurdington (sep civ identity early, sep EP 1887[37] [Shurdington incl Up Hatherley,[38] orig sep par, considered chap since 17th cent, sep civ identity early, sep EP 1887[37]]). *LG* Seq 14. Addtl civ bdry alt: 1894.[39] *Parl* Seq 6. *Eccl* Seq 32. Addtl eccl bdry alt: 1887 (gains pt Shurdington when latter made sep EP),[37] 1933,[40] 1933.[41]

BADMINTON
AP Usual eccl spelling; for civ see following entry. *Eccl* Seq 21.

GREAT BADMINTON
AP Usual civ spelling; for eccl see prev entry. *LG* Grumb. Ash Hd, Chip. Sodb. PLU, RSD, RD (1894–1935), Sodb. RD (1935–74). Civ bdry: 1883.[3] Transf 1974 to Avon.[4] *Parl* Seq 15.

BAGENDON
AP *LG* Seq 11. *Parl* Seq 1. *Eccl* Seq 13.

BARNSLEY
AP *LG* Seq 9. *Parl* Seq 1. *Eccl* Seq 5.

BARNWOOD
AP *LG* Dudst. & K's Bart. Hd, Glouc. Bor & Co (1463–1672), Glouc. PLU, RSD, RD. Civ bdry: 1883,[3] 1885,[43] 1900 (loses pt to Gloucester CB and CP),[42] 1935 (incl loses pt to Gloucester CB and CP, help cr Longlevens CP),[2] 1951 (loses pt to Gloucester CB and CP).[46] Abol civ 1966 pt to Gloucester CB and CP, pt to Upton St Leonards AP, pt to Hucclecote CP.[44] *Parl* E'rn Dv (1832–85), N'rn Dv (1885–1918), S'rn Dv (1918–48), Glouc. BC (1948–70). Parl bdry: 1951.[45] *Eccl* Seq 18. Eccl bdry: 1930 (help cr Gloucester St Aldate, Finley Road EP),[47] 1932 (help cr Wotton St Mary Without EP),[48] 1935 (help cr Coney Hill EP, now commonly called Gloucester St Oswald EP).[49]

BARRINGTON
CP Cr 1935 by union Great Barrington AP, Little Barrington AP, pt Eastleach Turville AP.[2] *LG* N'leach RD. *Parl* Cirenc. & Tewk. CC (1948–*).

GREAT BARRINGTON
AP Incl chap Little Barrington, chap Windrush (both sep pars in Glos in 14th cent[50]). Pt Berks (Faringdon Hd), pt situated in Glos (Slaugh. Hd), the former transf to Glos 1832 for parl purposes, 1844 for civ purposes.[51] *LG* Stow on the Wold PLU, RSD, RD. Addtl civ bdry alt: 1882,[52] 1883.[3] Abol civ 1935 to help cr Barrington CP.[2] *Parl* Glos pt, E'rn Dv (1832–1918), Cirenc. & Tewk. Dv (1918–48). *Eccl* Stow RDn (until 1907), N'leach RDn (1907–*).

LITTLE BARRINGTON
AP Chap in Great Barrington AP, sep par 14th cent.[50] *LG* Slaugh. Hd, N'Leach PLU, RSD, RD. Civ bdry: 1882,[52] 1883,[3] 1883.[46] Abol civ 1935 to help cr Barrington CP.[2] *Parl* E'rn Dv (1832–1918), Cirenc. & Tewk. Dv (1918–48). *Eccl* Seq 29.

BARTON HILL CHRIST CHURCH
EP Cr 1886 from Bristol St George EP, Bristol Holy Trinity EP, Barton Hill St Luke EP.[133] Bristol (City Dv) RDn (1886–87), Bristol RDn (1887–

1901), E Bristol RDn (1901–49), Bitton RDn (1949–54). Bdry: 1868 (help cr Bristol St Silas EP).[129] Abol 1954 to help cr Barton Hill St Luke with Christ Church EP.[135]

BARTON HILL ST LUKE

EP Cr 1850 from Bristol St George EP, Bristol Holy Trinity EP.[134] Bristol RDn (1850–66), Bristol (City Dv) RDn (1866–87), Bristol RDn (1887–1901), E Bristol RDn (1901–49), Bitton RDn (1949–54). Bdry: 1865 (help cr Bristol The Unity EP [now commonly called 'Bristol Emmanuel']),[97] 1866,[115] 1868 (help cr Bristol St Silas EP),[129] 1886 (help cr Barton Hill Christ Church EP).[133] Abol 1954 to help cr Barton Hill St Luke with Christ Church EP.[135]

BARTON HILL ST LUKE WITH CHRIST CHURCH

EP Cr 1954 by union Barton Hill St Luke EP, Barton Hill Christ Church EP.[135] Bitton RDn (1954–73), Bristol City RDn (1973–*). Bdry: 1970 (gains Bedminster St Luke with St Silas EP).[136]

BARTON ST MARY, BARTON ST MICHAEL–See GLOUCESTER BARTON ST MARY, GLOUCSTER BARTON ST MICHAEL

BATSFORD

AP *LG* Pt Glos (Kiftsg. Hd), pt Worcs (Oswalslow Hd), Shipston on Stour PLU, RSD, pt sep RD in Worcs (1894–96), Camp. RD (pt 1894–96, ent 1896–1935), N Cotsw. RD (1935–74). Civ bdry: 1896 (the pt in Worcs transf to Glos),[54] 1935,[2] 1936.[55] *Parl* Glos pt, Seq 1. *Eccl* Blockley jurisd (until 1847), Camp. RDn (1847–87). Gains 1887 Moreton in Marsh chap from Bourton on the Hill AP, hence thereafter 'Batsford with Moreton in Marsh',[56] qv.

BATSFORD WITH MORETON IN MARSH

EP Cr 1887 by union Batsford AP, Moreton in Marsh chap of Bourton on the Hill AP.[56] Camp. RDn (1887–1907), Stow RDn (1907–*).

BAUNTON

AP *LG* Seq 11. Civ bdry: 1935.[2] *Parl* Seq 1. *Eccl* Seq 13.

BEACHLEY

EP Cr 1850 from Tidenham AP.[57] For. RDn (1850–66), For. South RDn (1866–*).

BEARSE COMMON

Ex-par place, absorbed into St Briavels AP civ 1858,[58] eccl 1932.[59]

BECKFORD

AP Incl chap Ashton under Hill (sep civ identity early, no sep eccl identity hence this par eccl 'Beckford with Ashton under Hill', qv), chap Great Washbourne (sep 1177[60]). *LG* Tibald. Hd, Winch. PLU, RSD, RD. Transf 1931 to Worcs.[30] *Parl* E'rn Dv (1832–85), N'rn Dv (1885–1918), Cirenc. & Tewk. Dv (1918–48), Worcs thereafter.

BECKFORD WITH ASHTON UNDER HILL

AP Usual eccl spelling; for civ and sep of chaps, see prev entry. *Eccl* Camp. RDn (until 1907), Tewk. RDn (1907–*).

BERKELEY

AP Incl chap & tg Breadstone (sep CP 1866,[9] no sep eccl identity), tg Ham and chap Stone (sep CP 1866 as 'Ham and Stone',[9] no sep eccl identity), and the following tgs, each sep CP 1866[9] but no sep eccl identities: Alkington, Hamfallow, Hinton. *LG* Berk. Bor (status not sustained), Seq 3. Addtl civ bdry alt: 1883,[3] 1935.[2] *Parl* W'rn Dv (1832–85), N'rn Dv (1885–1918), Thornb. Dv (1918–48), Stroud & Thornb. CC (1948–55), S Glos CC (1955–*). *Eccl* Seq 32.

BEVERSTON

AP Usual eccl spelling; for civ and sep chap see following entry. *Eccl* Seq 15.

BEVERSTONE

AP Incl chap Kingscote (sep civ identity early, no sep eccl identity). Usual civ spelling; for eccl see prev entry. *LG* Seq 2. Addtl civ bdry alt: 1935.[2] *Parl* Seq 10.

BIBURY

AP Incl chap Winson (sep CP 1866,[9] no sep eccl identity hence this par eccl 'Bibury with Winson', qv). *LG* Pt Bradley Hd, pt Brightw. Bar. Hd, N'leach PLU, RSD, RD. *Parl* Seq 1.

BIBURY WITH WINSON

AP Usual eccl spelling; for civ and civ sep chap Winson see prev entry. *Eccl* Seq 5.

ENGLISH BICKNOR

AP *LG* Seq 30. Civ bdry: 1935 (incl help cr Lydbrook CP),[2] 1965 (loses pt to Goodrich AP, Hereford).[29] *Parl* Seq 11. *Eccl* Seq 4. Eccl bdry: 1852 (help cr Lydbrook EP),[61] 1972.[62]

BISHOP'S WOOD

EP Cr 1845 from Walford AP (Hereford), Ruardean EP.[63] See main entry in Hereford.

BISLEY

AP Incl chap Stroud (sep civ identity early, sep EP 1723[13]), chap Chalford (sep EP 1842,[13] sep CP 1894[64]). *LG* Bisley Hd, Stroud PLU, Bisley USD (ent 1875–83, pt 1883–94), pt Stroud RSD (1883–94). Addtl civ bdry alt: 1883,[3] 1885.[65] Abol civ 1894 the main pt to help cr Bisley with Lypiatt CP, the chap to cr Chalford CP.[64] *Parl* Stroud Parl Bor (1832–85), Mid Dv (1885–1918). *Eccl* Seq 24. Addtl eccl bdry alt: 1848 (cr Bussage EP),[66] 1849 (cr Oakridge EP),[67] 1894 (help cr France Lynch EP).[68]

BISLEY WITH LYPIATT

CP Cr 1894 by union Lypiatt CP, the pt of Bisley AP exclusive of chap Chalford (made sep CP).[64] *LG* Stroud PLU, RD. Bdry: 1935,[2] 1936,[69] 1958.[70] *Parl* Stroud Dv (1918–48), Stroud & Thornb. CC (1948–51), Stroud CC (1951–*).

BITTON

AP Incl chap and hmlt Hanham (sep EP 1841,[71] sep CP 1866[9]), chap and hmlt Oldland (sep EP 1861,[37] sep CP 1866[9]). *LG* Lang. & Swin. Hd, Keynsham PLU, RSD, Warmley RD. Addtl civ bdry alt: 1966 (gains pt North Stoke AP, Somerset).[72] Transf 1974 to Avon.[4] *Parl* W'rn Dv (1832–85), Mid Dv (1885–1918), Thornb. Dv (1918–48), S Glos CC (1948–70), Kingswood CC (1970–*). *Eccl* Seq 22. Addtl eccl bdry alt: 1851 (help cr Warmley EP).[73]

BLAISDON
AP *LG* W'bury Hd, W'bury on Severn PLU, RSD, pt sep RD in Hereford (1894–96), E Dean & United Pars RD (pt 1894–96, ent 1896–1935), E Dean RD (1935–74). Civ bdry: 1883,[74] 1890 (gains pt Lea Bailey CP and thus incl pt of Hereford),[75] 1896 (par to be ent Glos),[54] 1935.[2] *Parl* Seq 11. *Eccl* Seq 1.

BLAKENEY
EP Cr 1853 from Awre AP.[36] For. RDn (1853–66), For. North RDn (1866–*).

BLEDINGTON
AP *LG* Seq 33. *Parl* Seq 1. *Eccl* Seq 28.

BLOCKLEY
AP In Worcs, transf 1931 to Glos.[76] *LG* Camp. RD (1931–35), N Cotsw. RD (1935–74). Civ bdry: 1935.[2] *Parl* Worcs until 1948, Cirenc. & Tewk. CC (1948–*). *Eccl* Worc dioc until 1919, Camp. RDn (1919–*).

BODDINGTON
Chap in Staverton AP, sep civ identity early, no sep eccl identity. *LG* Pt W'minst. Hd, pt Tewk. Hd, Tewk. PLU, RSD, RD (1894–1935), Chelt. RD (1935–74). *Parl* Seq 4.

BOURTON ON THE HILL
AP Incl chap Moreton in Marsh (sep civ identity early, eccl severed 1887 to help cr Batsford with Moreton in Marsh EP[56]). *LG* Pt Tewk. Hd, pt W'minst. Hd, Shipton on Stour PLU, RSD, Camp. RD (1894–1935), N Cotsw. RD (1935–74). *Parl* Seq 1. *Eccl* Seq 6.

BOURTON ON THE WATER
AP Incl chap Clapton, chap Lower Slaughter (each with sep civ identity early, each early reputed as sep eccl par). *LG* Seq 33. *Parl* Seq 1. *Eccl* Stow RDn. Abol eccl 1953 to help cr Bourton on the Water with Clapton EP.[77]

BOURTON ON THE WATER WITH CLAPTON
EP Cr 1953 by union Bourton on the Water AP, Clapton EP.[77] Stow RDn.

BOXWELL WITH LEIGHTERTON
AP *LG* Grumb. Ash Hd, Tetb. PLU, RSD, RD. *Parl* Seq 10. *Eccl* Hawk. RDn (until 1866), Hawk. North RDn (1866–87), Hawk. RDn (1887–1907), Tetb. RDn (1907–*).

BREADSTONE
Tg and chap in Berkeley AP, sep CP 1866,[9] no sep eccl identity. *LG* Berk. Hd, Thornb. PLU, RSD, RD. Abol 1935 ent to Hamfallow CP.[2] *Parl* W'rn Dv (1867–85), N'rn Dv (1885–1918), Thornb. Dv (1918–48).

BREAM
EP Cr 1752 from Newland AP (when reconstituted 1854 gains pt Dean Forest St Paul EP).[78] For. RDn (1752–1866), For. South RDn (1866–*).

BRIMPSFIELD
AP *LG* Seq 28. Civ bdry: 1935.[2] *Parl* Seq 1. *Eccl* Stoneh. RDn (until 1866), Stoneh. North RDn (1866–87), Bisley RDn (1887–1972). Abol eccl 1972 to help cr Brimpsfield and Syde EP.[80]

BRIMPSFIELD AND SYDE
EP Cr 1972 by union Brimpsfield AP, Syde AP.[80] Cirenc. RDn.

BRIMSCOMBE
EP Cr 1840 from Minchinhampton AP.[22] Stoneh. RDn (1840–66), Stoneh. South RDn (1866–87), Stoneh. RDn (1887–*). Bdry: 1973.[81]

BRISTOL
The following have 'Bristol' in their names. Insofar as any existed at a given time: *LG* Bristol Bor & Co/MB/CB, Bristol Incorp for Poor, USD. *Parl* Bristol Parl Bor (1295–1885); for 1885–1918 divided into Bristol Parl Bor, pt East Dv, pt North Dv, pt South Dv, pt West Dv; after 1918, pts in following: Bristol Central Parl Bor/BC (1918–70), Bristol East Parl Bor (1918–70), Bristol North Parl Bor (1918–48), Bristol North East BC (1948–*), Bristol North West BC (1948–*), Bristol South Parl Bor/BC (1918–*), Bristol South East BC (1948–*), Bristol West Parl Bor/BC (1918–*). [See Part III of the *Guide* for composition of the constituencies by pars and wards]. Parl bdry: 1952.[24] *Eccl* The most general combinations used below (for the periods in which individual pars existed): Seq 'A', Bristol RDn (until 1866), Bristol (City Dv) RDn (1866–87), Bristol RDn (1887–1901), Bristol City RDn (1901–*); Seq 'B', Bristol RDn (until 1866), Bristol (City Dv) RDn (1866–87), Bristol RDn (1887–1901), E Bristol RDn (1901–49), Bristol City RDn (1949–*); other combinations sep noted.

CP1–BRISTOL–Cr 1898 by union CP2, CP3, CP4, CP6, Stapleton AP.[90] Bdry: 1898,[82] 1901,[83] 1902,[84] 1904,[85] 1918,[86] 1933,[87] 1935,[2] 1951,[88] 1966.[83] Transf 1974 to Avon.[4]

CP2–CENTRAL BRISTOL–Cr 1896 by union AP1, CP5, AP2, AP3, AP4, CP7, AP6, AP8, AP9, Bristol St Mary Redcliffe CP, AP10, AP11, CP9, AP13, CP10, AP15, Bristol St Thomas CP, Bristol Temple CP.[89] Abol 1898 to help cr CP1.[90]

–EAST BRISTOL ST GEORGE–Eccl name commonly used now for EP14, qv.

CP3–NORTH BRISTOL–Cr 1896 by union Clifton AP, Redland CP, CP8, CP11, pt Henbury AP, pt Shirehampton CP.[89] Abol 1898 to help cr CP1.[90]

CP4–SOUTH BRISTOL–Cr 1896 by union Bedminster AP (Somerset), and the pts in Bristol CB of the following Somerset pars: Abbots Leigh CP, Easton in Gordano AP, Long Ashton AP, Portbury AP, Portishead AP.[89] Bdry: 1898.[91] Abol 1898 to help cr CP1.[90]

AP1–BRISTOL ALL SAINTS–Gains civ 1876 AP16.[132] Abol civ 1896 to help cr CP2.[89] *Eccl* Seq 'A'. Abol eccl 1958 to help cr EP31.[92]

CP5–BRISTOL CASTLE PRECINCTS–Ex-par place, sep CP 1858.[58] Abol 1896 to help cr CP2.[89]

AP2–BRISTOL CHRIST CHURCH–Usual eccl spelling; for civ see 'Bristol Christchurch'. *Eccl* Bristol RDn. Abol eccl 1787 to help cr EP1.[93]

EP1–BRISTOL CHRIST CHURCH WITH ST EWEN–Cr 1787 by union AP2, AP4.[93] Eccl

Seq 'A'. Abol 1973 to help cr EP2.[94]

EP2–BRISTOL CHRIST CHURCH WITH ST EWEN AND ALL SAINTS–Renaming 1973 of EP1 when gains the pt of EP31 containing All Saints.[94] Bristol City RDn.

–BRISTOL CHRIST THE SERVANT, STOCKWOOD–Cr from territory in anc Somerset, qv.

AP2–BRISTOL CHRISTCHURCH–Usual civ spelling; for eccl see 'Bristol Christ Church'. Abol civ 1896 to help cr CP2.[90]

–BRISTOL EMMANUEL–Name commonly used for EP32, qv.

–BRISTOL HOLY CROSS INNS COURT–Cr from territory in anc Somerset, qv.

EP3–BRISTOL HOLY TRINITY–Cr 1834 from AP14.[95] Bristol RDn (1834–66), Bristol (City Dv) RDn (1866–87), Bristol RDn (1887–1901), E Bristol RDn (1901–27), Bristol RDn (1927–*). Bdry: 1844 (cr EP18), cr EP 29),[96] 1850 (help cr Barton Hill St Luke EP),[134] 1865 (help cr EP32),[97] 1870 (cr EP 13),[98] 1883 (help cr EP20),[96] 1886 (help cr Barton Hill Christ Church EP),[133] 1954.[99] Commonly called 'Bristol Holy Trinity, St Philip' or 'Bristol St Philip and St Jacob Without'.

–BRISTOL HOLY TRINITY, ST PHILIP–Name commonly used for EP3, qv.

EP4–BRISTOL ST AGNES–Cr 1883 from EP10.[100] Eccl Seq 'B'. Abol 1956 to help cr EP5.[101]

EP5–BRISTOL ST AGNES WITH ST SIMON–Cr 1956 by union EP4, EP29, pt EP 25, pt Montpelier EP.[101] Bristol City RDn.

EP6–BRISTOL ST AIDAN–Cr 1905 from Two Mile Hill EP, EP14.[102] E Bristol RDn (1905–49), Bitton RDn (1949–*).

EP7–BRISTOL ST AMBROSE, WHITEHALL–Cr 1915 from EP14, Moorfields EP.[103] E Bristol RDn (1915–49), Bitton RDn (1949–*).

EP8–BRISTOL ST ANDREW WITH ST BARTHOLOMEW–Cr 1958 by union pt Montpelier EP, pt EP11.[104] Almond. RDn (1958–73), Horfield RDn (1973–*).

AP3–BRISTOL ST AUGUSTINE–Sometimes 'Bristol St Augustine the Less'. Abol civ 1896 to help cr CP2.[89] *Eccl* Seq 'A'. Eccl bdry: 1832 (cr EP 15).[105] Abol eccl 1938 to help cr EP9.[106]

EP9–BRISTOL ST AUGUSTINE WITH ST GEORGE–Cr 1938 by union EP15, AP3.[106] Bristol City RDn.

EP10–BRISTOL ST BARNABAS–Cr 1843 from AP12.[107] *Eccl* Seq 'B'. Bdry: 1876,[132] 1883 (cr EP4).[100] Abol 1955 to help cr EP25.[108]

EP11–BRISTOL ST BARTHOLOMEW–Cr 1861 from AP5.[109] Bristol RDn (1861–66), Bristol (City Dv) RDn (1861–87), Bristol RDn (1887–1901), E Bristol RDn (1901–49), Almond. RDn (1949–58). Abol 1958 pt to help cr EP8, pt to Bishopston St Michael and All Angels EP.[104]

EP12–BRISTOL ST CLEMENT–Cr 1855 from AP12.[110] Eccl Seq 'A'. Abol 1943 to help cr EP 26.[111]

AP4–BRISTOL ST EWEN–Abol civ 1896 to help cr CP2.[89] *Eccl* Bristol RDn. Abol eccl 1787 to help cr EP1.[93]

EP13–BRISTOL ST GABRIEL–Cr 1870 from EP3.[98] Eccl Seq 'B'. Abol 1954 to help cr Easton St Gabriel with St Lawrence EP.[99]

EP14/CP6–BRISTOL ST GEORGE–Cr 1756 from the outparish pt of AP14.[112] *LG* Bart. Reg. Hd, PLU, St George USD, UD. Abol civ 1898 to help cr CP1.[90] *Parl* W'rn Dv (1832–85), Bristol Parl Bor, East Dv (1885–1918). *Eccl* Bristol RDn (1756–1866), Bristol (City Dv) RDn (1866–87), Bristol RDn (1887–1901), E Bristol RDn (1901–49), Bitton RDn (1949–*). Eccl bdry: 1845 (cr Two Mile Hill EP),[113] 1848 (help cr Easton St Mark EP),[114] 1850 (help cr Barton Hill St Luke EP),[134] 1866,[115] 1873 (help cr Moorfield EP),[116] 1886 (help cr Barton Hill Christ Church EP),[133] 1905 (help cr EP6),[102] 1915 (help cr EP7),[103] 1925 (help cr EP21).[117] Now commonly called 'East Bristol St George'.

EP15–BRISTOL ST GEORGE, BRANDON HILL–Cr 1832 from AP13.[105] Bristol RDn (1832–66), Bristol (City Dv) RDn (1866–87), Bristol RDn (1887–1901), Clifton RDn (1901–27), Bristol City RDn (1927–38). Abol 1938 to help cr EP9.[106]

AP5–BRISTOL ST JAMES–*LG* Pt Bart. Reg. Hd, pt Bristol Bor; subdivided, the former combined with outparish pt of AP12 to cr CP8, the latter to cr CP7, so that AP5 has no civ identity after 1866.[9] *Parl* Pt Bristol Parl Bor (until 1867), pt W'rn Dv (1832–67). *Eccl* Seq 'A'. Eccl bdry: 1850 (help cr Kingsdown St Matthew EP),[118] 1861 (cr EP11).[109] Abol eccl 1957 to help cr EP16.[119]

CP7–BRISTOL ST JAMES IN–The pt of AP5 in Bristol Bor. Abol 1896 to help cr CP2.[89]

CP8–BRISTOL ST JAMES AND ST PAUL OUT–Combined outparish pts of AP5, AP12, as one CP. *LG* Bart. Reg. Hd, PLU, Bristol MB (1868–89), USD, CB. Abol 1896 to help cr CP3.[89] *Parl* W'rn Dv (1832–67), Bristol Parl Bor (1867–1918).

EP16–BRISTOL ST JAMES WITH ST PETER–Cr 1957 by union AP5, AP13, AP9.[119] Bristol City RDn.

AP6–BRISTOL ST JOHN THE BAPTIST–Gains 1587 AP7.[120] Abol civ 1896 to help cr CP2.[89] *Eccl* Seq 'A'. Because of united benefice cr 1957, name as for EP 17 used.[121]

EP17–BRISTOL ST JOHN THE BAPTIST WITH ST MARY LE PORT–Name 1957 of united benefice, not affecting pars.[121]

EP18–BRISTOL ST JUDE–Cr 1844 from EP3.[96] Eccl Seq 'A'. Abol 1942 to help cr EP19.[122]

EP19–BRISTOL ST JUDE WITH ST MATTHIAS–Cr 1942 by union EP18, The Weir (St Matthias) EP.[122] Bristol City RDn.

AP7–BRISTOL ST LAWRENCE–Bristol RDn. United 1578 with AP6.[120]

EP20–BRISTOL ST LAWRENCE–Cr 1883 from EP3, Moorfields EP.[96] Eccl Seq 'B', Abol 1954 pt to help cr Easton St Gabriel with St Lawrence EP, pt to EP3.[99]

AP8–BRISTOL ST LEONARD–Abol civ 1896 to help cr CP2.[89] *Eccl* Bristol RDn. Abol eccl 1766 to help cr EP24.[123]

EP21–BRISTOL ST LEONARD, REDFIELD–Cr 1925 from EP14, Moorfields EP.[117] E Bristol RDn (1925–49), Bitton RDn (1949–*).

AP9–BRISTOL ST MARY LE PORT–Abol civ 1896 to help cr CP2.[89] *Eccl* Seq 'A'. Abol eccl 1957 to help cr EP16.[119]

EP22–BRISTOL ST MARY MAGDALENE WITH ST FRANCIS, LOCKLEAZE–Cr 1961 from Horfield AP, Horfield St Gregory EP, Stapleton AP.[124] Almond. RDn (1961–73), Horfield RDn (1973–*).

–BRISTOL ST MARY REDCLIFFE–Cr from territority in anc Somerset, qv.

–BRISTOL ST MARY REDCLIFFE WITH BRISTOL TEMPLE–Cr from territory in anc Somerset, qv.

–BRISTOL ST MARY REDCLIFFE WITH BRISTOL TEMPLE AND BEDMINSTER ST JOHN THE BAPTIST–Cr from territory in anc Somerset, qv.

AP10–BRISTOL ST MICHAEL–Usual civ spelling; for eccl see following entry. Abol civ 1896 to help cr CP2.[89]

AP10–BRISTOL ST MICHAEL AND ALL ANGELS–Usual eccl spelling; for civ see prev entry. *Eccl* Seq 'A'. Bdry: 1874 (help cr Tyndall's Park EP).[397]

EP23–BRISTOL ST NATHANAEL WITH ST KATHERINE–Cr 1954 by union Kingsdown St Nathanael EP, pt Bishopston St Katherine EP, pt Redland EP.[125] Almond. RDn (1954–73), Horfield RDn (1973–*).

AP11–BRISTOL ST NICHOLAS–Abol civ 1896 to help cr CP2.[89] *Eccl* Bristol RDn. Abol 1766 to help cr EP24.[123]

EP24–BRISTOL ST NICHOLAS WITH ST LEONARD–Cr 1766 by union AP11, AP8.[123] Eccl Seq 'A'. Abol 1958 to help cr EP31.[92]

AP12–BRISTOL ST PAUL–*LG* Pt Bart. Reg. Hd, pt Bristol Bor; subdivided, the former combined with outparish pt of AP5 to cr CP8, the remainder to cr CP9, so that AP12 has no later civ identity. *Eccl* Seq 'A'. Eccl bdry: 1843 (cr EP10),[107] 1845 (help cr Montpelier EP),[126] 1846 (help cr The Weir EP),[398] 1847,[399] 1855 (cr EP12).[110] Abol eccl 1943 to help cr EP26.[111]

CP9–BRISTOL ST PAUL IN–The pt of AP12 in Bristol Bor. Abol 1896 to help cr CP2.[89]

EP25–BRISTOL ST PAUL WITH ST BARNABAS–Cr 1955 by union EP26, EP10.[108] Bristol City RDn. Bdry: 1956 (help cr EP5),[101] 1958.[127]

EP26–BRISTOL ST PAUL WITH ST CLEMENT–Cr 1943 by union EP12, AP12.[111] Bristol City RDn. Abol 1955 to help cr EP25.[108]

AP13–BRISTOL ST PETER–Abol civ 1896 to help cr CP2.[89] *Eccl* Seq 'A'. Bdry: 1846 (help cr The Weir EP).[398] Abol eccl 1957 to help cr EP16.[119]

AP14–BRISTOL ST PHILIP AND ST JACOB–*LG* Pt Bart. Reg. Hd, pt Bristol Bor. Subdivided 1720 the pt in the Bor as CP10, the remainder as CP11,[128] hence AP14 has no civ identity after 1720. *Eccl* Seq 'A'. Eccl bdry: 1756 (the outparish pt cr EP14),[112] 1834 (cr EP3),[125] 1846 (help cr The Weir EP),[398] 1865 (help cr EP32),[97] 1868 (help cr EP28).[129] Abol eccl 1938 to help cr EP27.[130]

CP10–ST PHILIP AND ST JACOB IN–Cr 1720 from the pt of AP14 in Bristol Bor.[128] Abol 1896 to help cr CP2.[89]

CP11–BRISTOL ST PHILIP AND ST JACOB OUT–Cr 1720 from the pt of AP14 in Bart. Reg. Hd.[128] *LG* Bart. Reg. PLU (1836–1840s), Clifton PLU (1840s–96), Bristol MB (1868–89), USD, CB. Abol 1896 to help cr CP2.[89] *Parl* W'rn Dv (1832–67), Bristol Parl Bor (1867–1918).

–BRISTOL ST PHILIP AND ST JACOB WITHOUT–Name commonly used for EP3, qv.

EP27–BRISTOL ST PHILIP AND ST JACOB WITH EMMANUEL–Cr 1938 by union AP14, EP32.[130] Bristol City RDn. Bdry: 1956.[131]

EP28–BRISTOL ST SILAS–Cr 1868 from EP3, Barton Hill St Luke EP).[129] Bristol (City Dv) RDn (1868–87), Bristol RDn (1887–1901), Bristol City RDn (1901–27), Bedminster RDn (1927–56). Abol 1956 pt to help cr Bedminster St Luke with St Silas EP, pt to EP27.[131]

EP29–BRISTOL ST SIMON–Cr 1844 from EP3.[96] Eccl Seq 'B' Abol 1956 to help cr EP5.[101]

AP15–BRISTOL ST STEPHEN–Abol civ 1896 to help cr CP2.[89] *Eccl* Seq 'A'. Abol eccl 1958 to help cr EP31.[92]

EP30–BRISTOL ST STEPHEN WITH ST NICHOLAS AND ST LEONARD–Renaming 1973 of EP31 when latter loses pt (containing All Saints) to help cr EP2.[94] Bristol City RDn.

EP31–BRISTOL ST STEPHEN WITH ST NICHOLAS AND ST LEONARD AND ALL SAINTS–Cr 1958 by union AP15, EP24, AP1.[92] Bristol City RDn. Renamed 1973 EP30 when loses pt (containing All Saints) to help cr EP2.[94]

–BRISTOL ST THOMAS–Cr from territory in anc Somerset, qv.

AP16–BRISTOL ST WERBURGH–Civ abol 1876, absorbed into AP1, eccl taken down but new church rebuilt with same dedication after bdry alt.[132] *Eccl* Seq 'B'.

–BRISTOL TEMPLE–Cr from territory in anc Somerset, av.

EP32–BRISTOL THE UNITY–Cr 1856 from AP14, Barton Hill St Luke EP, EP3.[97] *Eccl* Seq 'A'. Abol 1938 to help cr EP27.[130] Commonly called 'Bristol Emmanuel'.

BROADWELL

AP Usual civ spelling. Incl chap Adlestrop (orig sep par, early united with Broadwell, sep civ identity early, eccl severed 1937 to help cr Oddington with Adlestrop EP,[8] hence this par eccl 'Broadwell with Adlestrop' until that time, 'Broadwell' thereafter). *LG* Seq 33. Addtl civ bdry alt: 1935.[2] *Parl* Seq 1. *Eccl* Stow RDn (1937–*).

BROADWELL WITH ADLESTROP

AP Usual eccl spelling until loses 1937 chap Adlestrop (orig sep par, early united with Broadwell) to help cr Oddington with Adlestrop EP[8]; for civ, civ sep chap, and eccl after 1937 see prev entry. *Eccl* Stow RDn.

BROCKWORTH

AP *LG* Seq 15. *Parl* E'rn Dv (1832–85), N'rn Dv (1885–1918), Stroud Dv (1918–48), Glouc. BC (1948–70), W Glos CC (1970–*). *Eccl* Winch. RDn (until 1866), Winch. South RDn (1866–87), Glouc. RDn (1887–1952), Glouc. North RDn (1952–*).

BROMSBERROW

AP *LG* Seq 7. *Parl* Seq 11. *Eccl* Seq 1.

BROOKTHORPE

AP *LG* Dudst. & K's Bart. Hd, Glouc. Bor & Co (1483–1672), Wheath. PLU, RSD, RD (1894–1935), Glouc. RD (1935–56). Civ bdry: 1884,[137] 1885,[138] 1951 (loses pt to Glouc. CB and CP).[46] Renamed 1956 'Brookthorpe-with-Whaddon'.[139] *Parl* E'rn Dv (1832–67), pt E'rn Dv, pt Stroud Parl Bor (1867–85), N'rn Dv (1885–1918), Stroud Dv (1918–48), Stroud & Thornb. CC (1948–55), Stroud CC (1955–70). Parl bdry: 1951.[401] *Eccl* Seq 20. Eccl bdry: 1873,[140] 1873 (help cr The Edge EP),[141] 1885,[142] 1932.[143]

BROOKTHORPE-WITH-WHADDON

CP Renaming 1956 of Brookthorpe AP.[139] *LG* Glouc. RD. *Parl* Stroud CC (1970–*).

BROUGHTON POGGS

AP In Oxon (Bampton Hd), pt (Great Lemhill Farm) situated in Glos, transf to Lechlade AP 1832 for parl purposes, 1844 for civ purposes,[21] so that the par ent Oxon thereafter, qv.

BUCKLAND

AP *LG* Seq 22. *Parl* Seq 4. *Eccl* Seq 12.

BULLEY

Chap in Churcham AP, sep civ identity early, no sep eccl identity. *LG* Duchy Lanc. Hd, W'bury on Severn PLU, RSD, E Dean & United Pars RD. Abol 1935 ent to Churcham AP.[2] *Parl* W'rn Dv (1832–85), N'rn Dv (1885–1918), For. Dean Dv (1918–48).

BUSSAGE

EP Cr 1848 from Bisley AP.[66] Stoneh. RDn (1848–66), Stoneh. North RDn (1866–87), Bisley RDn (1887–*). Bdry: 1973.[81]

CAINSCROSS

Chap in Stonehouse AP, sep EP 1838,[144] sep CP 1894 (from Stonehouse AP, Stroud CP).[145] *LG* Stroud PLU, RD. Abol civ 1936 pt to Stroud CP, pt to King's Stanley AP.[69] *Parl* Stroud Dv (1918–48). *Eccl* Stoneh. RDn (1838–66), Stoneh. South RDn (1866–87), Stoneh. RDn (1887–*).

CAM

AP *LG* Seq 1. Civ bdry: 1883,[3] 1883,[146] 1935,[2] 1951.[147] *Parl* Seq 12. *Eccl* Seq 32. Eccl bdry: 1888 (help cr Lower Cam EP).[148]

LOWER CAM

EP Cr 1888 from Cam AP, Stinchcombe AP.[148] Durs. RDn.

CHIPPING CAMPDEN

AP *LG* Chip. Camp. Bor (status not sustained), Seq 20. Civ bdry: 1965 (gains pt Broadway AP, Worcs).[29] *Parl* Seq 1. *Eccl* Seq 11.

NORTH CERNEY

AP *LG* Seq 28. Civ bdry: 1935.[2] *Parl* Seq 1. *Eccl* Seq 13.

SOUTH CERNEY

AP *LG* Seq 11. *Parl* Seq 1. *Eccl* Sometimes as 'South Cerney with Cerney Wick', Seq 13.

CHACELEY

AP In Worcs, transf 1931 to Glos.[76] *LG* Tewk. RD (1931–35), Glouc. RD (1935–74). Civ bdry: 1965 (loses pt to Eldersfield AP, Worcs).[29] *Parl* Worcs until 1948, W Glos CC (1948–*). *Eccl* Worc dioc until 1919 (see entry in Worcs), Tewk. RDn (1919–*).

CHALFORD

Chap in Bisley AP, sep EP 1842,[13] sep CP 1894.[64] *LG* Stroud PLU, RD. Civ bdry: 1959.[149] *Parl* Stroud Dv (1918–48), Stroud & Thornb. Dv (1948–51), Stroud Dv (1951–*). *Eccl* Stoneh. RDn (1842–66), Stoneh. North RDn (1866–87), Bisley RDn (1887–*).

CHARFIELD

AP *LG* Seq 18. Civ bdry: 1935.[2] Transf 1974 to Avon.[4] *Parl* W'rn Dv (1832–85), Mid Dv (1885–1918), Thornb. RDn (1918–48), Stroud & Thornb. CC (1948–55), S Glos CC (1955–*). *Eccl* Seq 21.

CHARLTON ABBOTS

AP *LG* Kiftsg. Hd, Winch. PLU, RSD, RD. Civ bdry: 1883.[150] Abol civ 1935 to help cr Sudbury CP.[2] *Parl* E'rn Dv (1832–85), N'rn Dv (1885–1918), Cirenc. & Tewk. Dv (1918–48). *Eccl* Winch. RDn (until 1866), Winch. South RDn (1866–87), Chelt. RDn (1887–*).

CHARTLON KINGS

Chap in Cheltenham AP, sep civ identity early, sep EP 1814.[13] *LG* Chelt. Hd, PLU, Charlton Kings USD (ent 1875–92, pt 1892–94), pt Chelt. MB/USD (1892–94), Charlton Kings UD. Civ bdry: 1894 (loses the pt in Chelt. MB to Cheltenham AP),[151] 1935.[2] *Parl* E'rn Dv (1832–85), Chelt. Parl Bor/BC (1885–*). *Eccl* Seq 32. Eccl bdry: 1885 (cr Charlton Kings The Holy Apostle EP).[152]

CHARLTON KINGS THE HOLY APOSTLES

EP Cr 1885 from Charlton Kings EP.[152] Winch. South RDn (1885–87), Chelt. RDn (1887–*).

CHEDWORTH

AP *LG* Rapsg. Hd, N'leach PLU, RSD, RD. *Parl* Seq 1. *Eccl* Seq 14.

CHELTENHAM
The following have 'Cheltenham' in their names. Insofar as any existed at a given time: *LG* Chelt. Hd, PLU, Bor, MB (1885–1974), USD. *Parl* Chelt. Parl Bor (1832–*). *Eccl* Seq 32.

AP1–CHELTENHAM–Incl chap Charlton Kings (sep civ identity early, sep EP 1814[13]). Civ bdry: 1894 (gains the pts of Charlton Kings CP, Leckhampton AP in the MB),[153] 1935.[2] *Eccl* bdry: 1845 (cr EP11),[154] 1846 (cr EP10),[155] 1855 (cr EP6),[156] 1862 (cr EP8),[157] 1865 (cr EP1),[158] 1866 (cr EP5),[159] 1869 (cr Pittville EP, now commonly called 'Cheltenham All Saints'),[160] 1898 (cr EP3),[161] 1916 (cr EP4).[162]

–CHELTENHAM ALL SAINTS–Name commonly used now for EP cr 1869 as 'Pittville', qv.

EP1–CHELTENHAM CHRIST CHURCH–Cr 1865 from AP1.[158] Bdry: 1884 (cr EP12),[163] 1934.[164]

EP2–CHELTENHAM EMMANUEL–cr 1922 from EP6.[165]

EP3–CHELTENHAM HOLY TRINITY–Cr 1898 from AP1.[161]

EP4–CHELTENHAM ST JAMES–Cr 1916 from AP1.[162] Abol 1972 to help cr Leckhampton St Philip and St James with Cheltenham St James EP.[166]

EP5–CHELTENHAM ST JOHN–Cr 1866 from AP1.[159] Abol 1967 to help cr EP7.[167]

EP6–CHELTENHAM ST LUKE–Cr 1855 from AP1.[156] Bdry: 1922 (cr EP2).[165] Abol 1967 to help cr EP7.[167]

EP7–CHELTENHAM ST LUKE AND ST JOHN–Cr 1967 by union EP6, EP5.[167]

EP8–CHELTENHAM ST MARK–Cr 1862 from AP1.[157] Bdry: 1934,[164] 1968.[168]

EP9–CHELTENHAM ST MICHAEL–Renaming 1966 of Lynworth EP.[169]

EP10–CHELTENHAM ST PAUL–Cr 1846 from AP1.[155]

EP11–CHELTENHAM ST PETER–Cr 1845 from AP1.[154]

EP12–CHELTENHAM ST STEPHEN–Cr 1884 from EP1.[163] Bdry: 1968.[168]

CHERINGTON
AP *LG* Seq 25. Civ bdry: 1935.[2] *Parl* Seq 2. *Eccl* Seq 27.

CHILD'S WICKHAM
AP *LG* Kiftsg. Hd, Evesham PLU, RSD, Pebworth RD. Transf 1931 to Worcs.[30] *Parl* W'rn Dv (1832–85), N'rn Dv (1885–1918), Cirenc. & Tewk. Dv (1918–48), Worcs thereafter. *Eccl* Camp. RDn (until 1907), Winch. RDn (1907–73). Renamed 1973 'Childswyckham'.[170]

CHILDSWYCKHAM
EP Eccl renaming 1973 of Child's Wickham AP.[170] Winch. RDn.

CHURCHAM
AP Incl hmlts Highnam, Over, Linton (sep CP 1866 as 'Highnam Over and Linton'[9]), chap Bulley (sep civ identity early, no sep eccl identity hence this par eccl 'Churcham with Bulley', qv). *LG* Pt Dudst. & K's Bart. Hd (this pt in Glouc. Bor and Co 1483-1672), pt W'bury Hd, W'bury on Severn PLU, RSD, E Dean & United Pars RD (1894–1935), E Dean RD (1935–74). Addtl civ bdry alt: 1935.[2] *Parl* Pt E'rn Dv, pt W'rn Dv (1832–85), N'rn Dv (1885–1918), For. Dean Dv (1918–48), W Glos CC (1948–*).

CHURCHAM WITH BULLEY
AP Usual eccl spelling; for civ and civ sep chap Bulley see prev entry. *Eccl* Seq 1.

CHURCHDOWN
AP Incl chap and hmlt Hucclecote (sep EP 1851,[171] sep CP 1866[9]). *LG* Seq 15. Addtl civ bdry alt: 1883,[3] 1935 (incl help cr Longlevens CP).[2] *Parl* Seq 8. *Eccl* Seq 19. Addtl eccl bdry alt: 1932 (help cr Wotton St Mary Without EP).[48]

CHURCHDOWN ST JOHN THE EVANGELIST
EP Cr 1963 from Wotton St Mary Without EP.[172] Glouc. North RDn.

CINDERFORD
Pt of East Dean CP/EP, sep EP 1845,[173] sep CP 1953.[174] *LG* E Dean RD. *Parl* W Glos CC (1970–*). *Eccl* For. RDn (1845–66), For. South RDn (1866–*). Eccl bdry: 1880 (help cr Woodside EP).[175]

CIRENCESTER
AP *LG* Crowt. & Min. Hd, Cirenc. Bor, PLU, USD, UD. Civ bdry: 1935.[2] *Parl* Cirenc. Parl Bor (1572–1885), E'rn Dv (1885–1918), Cirenc. & Tewk. Dv/CC (1918– *). *Eccl* Seq 13.

CLAPTON
Chap in Bourton on the Water AP, sep civ identity early, early reputed as sep eccl par. *LG* Seq 33. *Parl* Seq 1. *Eccl* Stow RDn. Abol eccl 1953 to help cr Bourton on the Water with Clapton EP.[77]

CLEARWELL
EP Cr 1856 from Newland AP, Dean Forest St Paul EP.[176] For. RDn (1856–66), For. South RDn (1866–*). Bdry: 1890.[177]

BISHOP'S CLEEVE
AP Incl hmlt and chap Southam and Brockhampton (sep CP 1866[9]), hmlt and chap Stoke Orchard (sep CP 1866,[9] eccl severed 1953 to help cr Tredington with Stoke Orchard and Hardwicke EP[178]), hmlt Woodmancote (sep CP 1866[9]), hmlt Gotherington (sep CP 1866,[9] eccl severed 1933 to help cr Woolstone with Gotherington EP[179]). *LG* Bishop's Cleeve Hd, Winch. PLU, RSD, RD (1894–1935), Chelt. RD (1935–74). Addtl civ bdry alt: 1950,[180] 1953.[181] *Parl* Seq 4. *Eccl* Limited pec jurisd (16th–18th cent[182]), Seq 31 thereafter.

CLIFFORD CHAMBERS
AP *LG* Tewk. Hd, Stratford on Avon PLU, RSD, Marston Sicca RD. Transf 1931 to Warws.[10] *Parl* E'rn Dv (1832–1918), Cirenc. & Tewk. Dv (1918–48), Warws thereafter. *Eccl* Seq 11. Eccl bdry: 1928.[183]

CLIFTON
The following have 'Clifton' in their names. Insofar as any existed at a given time: *LG* Bart. Reg. Hd, PLU (1836–1840s), Clifton PLU

(1840s–96), Bristol MB (1868–89), USD, CB. *Parl* Bristol Parl Bor (1867–1918). *Eccl* Bristol RDn (until 1866), Bristol (City) RDn (1866–87), Bristol RDn (1887–1901), Clifton RDn (1901–*).

AP1–CLIFTON [ST ANDREW]–Abol civ 1898 to help cr North Bristol CP.[89] Eccl bdry: 1841 (cr King's Parade EP, now commonly called EP9),[184] 1844 (cr EP3),[185] 1859 (cr EP10),[186] 1863 (cr EP6),[187] 1864 (cr Clifton Wood EP),[188] 1864,[199] 1877,[189] 1881 (cr EP8).[190] Abol eccl 1952 pt to EP3, pt to EP7.[191]

EP1–CLIFTON ALL SAINTS–Cr 1868 from EP9.[192] Bdry: 1877.[189] Abol 1962 to help cr EP2.[193]

EP2–CLIFTON ALL SAINTS WITH TYNDALL'S PARK–Cr 1962 by union EP1, Tyndall's Park EP.[193]

EP3–CLIFTON CHRIST CHURCH–Cr 1844 from AP1.[185] Bdry: 1869 (cr EP5),[194] 1952.[195] Abol 1963 to help cr EP4.[196]

EP4–CLIFTON CHRIST CHURCH WITH EMMANUEL–Cr 1963 by union EP3, EP5.[196]

EP5–CLIFTON EMMANUEL–Cr 1869 from EP3.[194] Abol 1963 to help cr EP4.[196]

EP6–CLIFTON HOLY TRINITY–Cr 1863 from AP1.[187] Abol 1939 to help cr EP7.[197]

EP7–CLIFTON HOLY TRINITY, ST ANDREW THE LESS AND ST PETER–Cr 1939 by union EP8, EP6, Clifton Wood EP.[197] Bdry: 1952.[191]

EP8–CLIFTON ST ANDREW THE LESS, DOWRY SQUARE–Cr 1881 from AP1.[190] Abol 1939 to help cr EP7.[197]

EP9–CLIFTON ST JOHN THE EVANGELIST–Cr 1841 as 'King's Parade' from Westbury on Trym AP, AP1.[184] Commonly called later as EP9. Bdry: 1868 (cr EP1),[192] 1877,[189] 1882 (help cr Woolcott Park EP).[198]

EP10–CLIFTON ST PAUL–Cr 1859 from AP1.[186] Bdry: 1864.[199]

CLIFTON WOOD

EP Cr 1856 from Clifton AP.[188] Bristol RDn (1856–66), Bristol (City Dv) RDn (1866–87), Bristol RDn (1887–1901), Clifton RDn (1901–39). Abol 1939 to help cr Clifton Holy Trinity, St Andrew the Less and St Peter EP.[197]

CLOPTON

Hmlt in Mickleton AP, sep CP 1866.[9] *LG* Kiftsg. Hd, Shipston on Stour PLU, RSD, Camp. RD. Transf 1935 to Warws.[10] *Parl* E'rn Dv (1867–1918), Cirenc. & Tewk. Dv (1918–48), Warws thereafter.

COALEY

AP Sometimes 'Cowley'. *LG* Seq 1. Civ bdry: 1883,[3] 1883.[200] *Parl* Seq 12. *Eccl* Seq 32.

COALPIT HEATH

EP Cr 1845 from Frampton Cotterell AP, Westerleigh AP.[201] Hawk. RDn (1845–66), Hawk. South RDn (1866–87), Bitton RDn (1887–1949), Stap. RDn (1949–*). Bdry: 1942.[202]

COATES

AP *LG* Seq 11. Civ bdry: 1883,[3] 1935.[2] *Parl* Seq 1. *Eccl* Seq 13.

COBERLEY

AP *LG* Seq 27. *Parl* Seq 6. *Eccl* Stoneh. RDn (until 1866), Stoneh. North RDn (1866–87), Chelt. RDn (1887–1951), Cirenc. RDn (1951–*).

COLEFORD

Chap in Newland AP, sep EP 1782,[13] refounded eccl 1872,[203] sep CP 1894 (the pt in Coleford USD).[242] *LG* Monmouth PLU, Coleford UD (1894–1935), W Dean RD (1935–74). *Parl* For. Dean Dv (1918–48), W Glos CC (1948–*). *Eccl* For. RDn (1772–1866), For. South RDn (1866–*). Eccl bdry: 1890.[177]

COLESBOURNE

AP *LG* Seq 28. *Parl* Seq 1. *Eccl* Winch. RDn (until 1866), Winch. South RDn (1866–87), Chelt. RDn (1887–1951), Cirenc. RDn (1951–*).

COLN ROGERS

AP *LG* Bradley Hd, N'leach PLU, RSD, RD. Abol civ 1935 ent to Coln St Dennis AP.[2] *Parl* E'rn Dv (1832–1918), Cirenc. & Tewk. Dv (1918–48). *Eccl* Seq 14.

COLN ST ALDWYN

AP *LG* Brightw. Bar. Hd, N'leach PLU, RSD, RD. Civ bdry: 1935.[2] Renamed 1959 'Coln St Aldwyns'.[204] *Parl* E'rn Dv (1832–1918), Cirenc. & Tewk. Dv/CC (1948–70). *Eccl* Seq 16. Eccl bdry: 1934.[14]

COLN ST ALDWYNS

CP Renaming 1959 of Coln St Aldwyn AP.[204] *LG* N'leach RD. *Parl* Cirenc. & Tewk. CC (1970–*).

COLN ST DENNIS

AP *LG* Deerhurst Hd, N'leach PLU, RSD, RD. Civ bdry: 1935.[2] *Parl* Seq 1. *Eccl* Sometimes as 'Coln St Denys', Seq 14.

LITTLE COMPTON

AP In Glos (Deerhurst Hd), situated in Warws to which transf 1832 for parl purposes, 1844 for civ purposes.[51] See main entry in Warws. *Eccl* Stow RDn (until 1919), Chipping Norton RDn (Oxford dioc and AD, 1919–*).

COMPTON ABDALE

AP *LG* Seq 8. Civ bdry: 1883.[53] *Parl* Seq 1. *Eccl* Seq 14.

COMPTON GREENFIELD

AP *LG* Henbury Hd, Bart. Reg. PLU (called 'Clifton' PLU 1840s–80s), RSD. Civ bdry: 1883.[3] Abol civ 1886 ent to Henbury AP.[205] *Parl* W'rn Dv (1832–85), S'rn Dv (1885–1918). *Eccl* Seq 7.

CONDICTOTE

AP Perhaps pt dependent on Oddington, sep par by 16th cent.[206] *LG* Pt Kiftsg. Hd, pt Slaugh. Hd, Stow on the Wold PLU, RSD, RD (1894–1935), N Cotsw. RD (1935–74). Civ bdry: 1883.[3] *Parl* Seq 1. *Eccl* Pec jurisd Blockley (until 16th cent),[206] Seq 28 thereafter.

CONEY HILL

EP Cr 1935 from Barnwood AP, Gloucester St Aldate, Finlay Road EP, pt ex-par place Wotton Vill.[49] Glouc. RDn (1935–52), Glouc. City RDn (1952–*). Commonly called 'Gloucester

St Oswald'.

CORSE

AP *LG* W'minst. Hd, Newent PLU, RSD, RD. *Parl* E'rn Dv (1832–85), For. Dean RDn (1885–1948), W Glos CC (1948–*). *Eccl* Seq 30.

COWLEY

AP *LG* Seq 27. Civ bdry: 1935.[2] *Parl* Seq 6. *Eccl* Stoneh. RDn (until 1866), Stoneh. North RDn (1866–87), Chelt. RDn (1887–1951), Cirenc. RDn (1951–*).

CRANHAM

AP *LG* Rapsg. Hd, Stroud PLU, pt Bisley USD (1883–94), Stroud RSD (ent 1875–83, pt 1883–94), Stroud RD. Civ bdry: 1883,[3] 1885,[65] 1894.[56] *Parl* Seq 9. *Eccl* Seq 24.

CROMHALL

AP *LG* Seq 3. Civ bdry: 1955.[207] Transf 1974 to Avon.[4] *Parl* W'rn Dv (1832–85), Mid Dv (1885–1918), Thornb. Dv (1918–48), Stroud & Thornb. CC (1948–55), S Glos CC (1955–*). *Eccl* Seq 21.

CUTSDEAN

Chap in Temple Guiting AP, sep civ identity early in Worcs, no sep eccl identity. Transf 1931 to Glos.[30] *LG* Winch. RD (1931–35), N Cotsw. RD (1935–74). Civ bdry: 1935.[2] *Parl* Worcs until 1948, Cirenc. & Tewk. CC (1948–*).

DAGLINGWORTH

AP *LG* Seq 11. Civ bdry: 1935.[2] *Parl* Seq 1. *Eccl* Seq 13.

DAYLESFORD

AP In Worcs, transf 1931 to Glos.[30] *LG* Stow on the Wold RD. Abol civ 1935 ent to Adlestrop AP.[2] *Parl* Worcs until 1948. *Eccl* See entry in Worcs.

EAST DEAN

Twnshp formed 1844 from ex-par For. of Dean.[173] *LG* St Briav. Hd, W'bury on Severn PLU, RSD, E Dean & United Pars RD (1894–1935), E Dean RD (1935–74). Bdry: 1883,[3] 1883,[208] 1884,[209] 1885,[1] 1935 (incl help cr Lydbrook CP).[2] Abol 1953 pt to Cinderford CP, pt to cr Drybrook CP, pt to cr Ruspidge CP, pt to Awre AP, pt to Littledean AP, pt to Mitcheldean AP.[35] *Parl* W'rn Dv (1867–85), For. Dean Dv (1885–1948), W Glos CC (1948–70).

WEST DEAN

Twnshp formed 1844 from ex-par For. of Dean.[173] *LG* Seq 30. Bdry: 1935.[2] *Parl* W'rn Dv (1867–85), For. Dean Dv (1885–1948), Stroud & Thornb. CC (1948–70), W Glos CC (1970–*).

DEAN FOREST CHRIST CHURCH

EP Cr 1817 and refounded 1844 from pt of ex-par For. of Dean.[210] For. RDn (1844–66), For. South RDn (1866–*). Bdry: 1890,[177] 1972.[62] Now commonly called 'Christ Church'.

DEAN FOREST HOLY TRINITY

EP Cr 1817 and refounded 1844 from pt of ex-par For. of Dean.[211] For. RDn (1817–66), For. South RDn (1866–*). Bdry: 1852 (help cr Lydbrook EP),[61] 1880 (help cr Woodside EP).[175] Now commonly called 'Drybrook'.

DEAN FOREST ST PAUL

EP Cr 1822 and refounded 1844 from pt of ex-par For. of Dean.[210] For. RDn (1822–66), For. South RDn (1866–*). Bdry: 1854 (help refound Bream EP),[78] 1856 (help cr Clearwell EP),[176] 1866 (cr Viney Hill EP),[212] 1890,[177] 1909.[213] Now commonly called 'Parkend'.

DEERHURST

AP Incl chap Elmstone Hardwicke (sep par by 1296),[214] chap Tirley (sep par by 1316),[217] chap Staverton (sep par by 1297),[216] chap Leigh (sep par 1540),[215] chap Hasfield (sep par 1317 but independence still questioned 16th cent),[219] chap Apperley (sep EP 1856,[145] sep eccl identity not sustained); Woolstone ptly dependent on this par but independence sustained.[218] *LG* Pt Deerhurst Hd, pt W'minst. Hd, Tewk. PLU, RSD, RD (1894–1935), Chelt. RD (1935–74). *Parl* Seq 4. *Eccl* Seq 31. The 'pec' of Deerhurst seemingly not exempt.[220]

DIDBROOK

AP Incl eccl since 1737 chap Hailes (sep civ identity maintained[221]), tp Pinnock and Hyde (sep CP 1866[9]). *LG* Kiftsg. Hd, Winch. PLU, RSD, RD. Addtl civ bdry alt: 1883,[150] 1883.[222] Abol civ 1935 pt to Stanway AP, pt to Toddington AP.[2] *Parl* E'rn Dv (1832–85), N'rn Dv (1885–1918), Cirenc. & Tewk. Dv (1918–48). *Eccl* Seq 12.

DIDMARTON

AP *LG* Seq 17. Civ bdry: 1935,[2] 1966 (exchanges pts with Sherston AP, loses pt to Sopworth AP, both Wilts).[72] *Parl* Seq 10. *Eccl* Hawk. RDn. Abol before 19th cent to help cr Didmarton with Oldbury on the Hill EP.[223]

DIDMARTON WITH OLDBURY ON THE HILL

EP Cr before 19th cent by union Didmarton AP, Oldbury on the Hill AP.[223] Hawk. RDn (until 1866), Hawk. North RDn (1866–87), Hawk. RDn (1887–1907), Tetb. RDn (1907–*).

DODINGTON

AP *LG* Seq 16. Civ bdry: 1935.[2] Transf 1974 to Avon.[4] *Parl* Seq 14. *Eccl* Hawk. RDn (until 1866), Hawk. South RDn (1866–87), Bitton RDn (1887–1949), Stap. RDn (1949–53). Abol eccl 1953 to help cr Wapley with Codrington and Dodington EP.[224]

DONNINGTON

Hmlt in Stow on the Wold AP, sep CP 1866.[9] *LG* Seq 33. *Parl* E'rn Dv (1867–1918), Cirenc. & Tewk. Dv/CC (1918–*).

DORSINGTON

AP *LG* Kiftsg. Hd, Stratford on Avon PLU, RSD, Marst. Sic. RD (1894–1931). Transf 1931 to Warws.[251] *Parl* E'rn Dv (1832–1918), Cirenc. & Tewk. Dv (1918–48), Warws thereafter. *Eccl* Camp. RDn. Abol eccl 1964 to help cr Pebworth with Dorsington EP.[225]

DOWDESWELL

AP *LG* Seq 8. Civ bdry: 1883,[53] 1956 (help cr Andoversford CP).[26] *Parl* Seq 1. *Eccl* Pec jurisd Withington (until 1847), Seq 32 thereafter.

DOWNEND
EP Chap in Mangotsfield AP, sep EP 1874.[226] Bristol (Rural Dv) RDn (1847–87), Stap. RDn (1887–1927), Almond. RDn (1927–49), Stap. RDn (1949–*). Bdry: 1924 (help cr Soundwell EP),[227] 1942.[202]

DOYNTON
AP *LG* Seq 23. Transf 1974 to Avon.[4] *Parl* Seq 14. *Eccl* Seq 22.

DRIFFIELD
AP *LG* Seq 11. Civ bdry: 1935.[2] *Parl* Seq 1. *Eccl* Seq 13.

DRYBROOK
EP Name commonly used now for EP cr 1817 as 'Dean Forest Holy Trinity', qv.
CP Cr 1953 from East Dean CP.[174] *LG* E Dean RD. Bdry: 1957,[228] 1965 (gains pt Hope Mansell AP, Hereford).[29] *Parl* W Glos CC (1970–*).

DUMBLETON
AP *LG* Seq 22. Civ bdry: 1935,[2] 1965 (loses pt to Beckford AP, Worcs).[29] *Parl* Seq 4. *Eccl* Seq 12.

DUNTISBOURNE ABBOTS
AP *LG* Pt Crowt. & Min. Hd, pt Rapsg. Hd, Cirenc. PLU, RSD, RD. *Parl* Seq 1. *Eccl* Cirenc. RDn. Abol eccl 1972 to help cr The Duntisbournes EP.[229]

DUNTISBOURNE ROUSE
AP *LG* Seq 11. *Parl* Seq 1. *Eccl* Cirenc. RDn. Eccl bdry: 1932.[230] Abol eccl 1972 to help cr The Duntisbournes EP.[229]

THE DUNTISBOURNES
EP Cr 1972 by union Duntisbourne Abbots AP, Duntisbourne Rouse AP.[229] Cirenc. RDn.

DURSLEY
AP *LG* Dursley Bor (status not sustained), Seq 1. Civ bdry: 1883,[3] 1883,[231] 1935,[2] 1951.[147] *Parl* Seq 12. *Eccl* Seq 32.

DYMOCK
AP *LG* Dymock Bor (status not sustained), Seq 7. Civ bdry: 1935.[2] *Parl* Seq 11. *Eccl* Seq 1. Eccl bdry: 1873.[232]

DYRHAM
AP Usual eccl spelling; for civ see following entry. *Eccl* Hawk. RDn (until 1866), Hawk. South RDn (1866–87), Bitton RDn (1887–1955), Stap. RDn (1955–*).

DYRHAM AND HINTON
AP Usual civ spelling; for eccl see prev entry. *LG* Seq 16. Transf 1974 to Avon.[4] *Parl* Seq 14.

EASTINGTON
AP *LG* Whits. Hd, Wheath. PLU, RSD, RD (1894–1935), Glouc. RD (1935–74). Civ bdry: 1883,[3] 1884,[233] 1935.[2] *Parl* E'rn Dv (1832–85), Mid Dv (1885–1918), S'rn Dv (1918–48), Stroud & Thornb. CC (1948–55), Stroud CC (1955–*). *Eccl* Seq 26. Eccl bdry: 1855 (help cr Framilode EP).[27]

EASTINGTON
Tg and chap in Northleach AP, sep CP 1866,[9] no sep eccl identity. *LG* Bradley Hd, N'leach PLU, RSD, RD. Abol 1950 to help cr Northleach with Eastington CP.[40] *Parl* E'rn Dv (1867–1918), Cirenc. & Tewk. Dv/CC (1918–51).

EASTLEACH
CP Cr 1935 by union Eastleach Martin AP, pt Eastleach Turville AP.[2] *LG* N'leach RD. *Parl* Cirenc. & Tewk. CC (1948–*).

EASTLEACH MARTIN
AP *LG* Brightw. Bar. Hd, N'leach PLU, RSD, RD. Civ bdry: 1883.[53] Abol civ 1935 to help cr Eastleach CP.[2] *Parl* E'rn Dv (1832–1918), Cirenc. & Tewk. Dv (1918–48). *Eccl* Seq 16.

EASTLEACH TURVILLE
AP *LG* Brightw. Bar. Hd, N'leach PLU, RSD, RD. Civ bdry: 1883.[53] Abol civ 1935 pt to help cr Barrington CP, pt to help cr Eastleach CP.[2] *Parl*, *Eccl* as for Eastleach Martin.

EASTON ALL HALLOWS
EP Cr 1893 from Easton St Mark EP.[293] Bristol (Rural Dv) RDn (1893–1901), E Bristol RDn (1901–49), Bristol City RDn (1949–*).

EASTON ST GABRIEL WITH ST LAWRENCE
EP Cr 1954 by union Bristol St Gabriel EP, pt Bristol St Lawrence EP.[99] Bristol City RDn.

EASTON ST MARK
EP Cr 1848 from Bristol St George EP, Stapleton AP.[114] Bristol RDn (1848–87), Bristol (City Dv) RDn (1887–1901), E Bristol RDn (1901–49), Bristol City RDn (1973–*). Bdry: 1893 (cr Easton All Hallows EP).[293]

EASTVILLE
EP Cr 1889 from Easton St Mark EP, Fishponds EP.[234] Bristol RDn (1889–1901), E Bristol RDn (1901–49), Stap. RDn (1949–*). Bdry: 1910 (help cr Fishponds All Saints EP).[235]

EBRINGTON
AP *LG* Seq 20. Civ bdry: 1935.[2] *Parl* Seq 1. *Eccl* Seq 11.

THE EDGE
EP Cr 1873 from Painswick AP, Harescombe AP, Brookthorpe AP.[141] Winch. South RDn (1873–87), Glouc. RDn (1887–1907), Bisley RDn (1907–*). Bdry: 1932.[92]

EDGEWORTH
AP *LG* Seq 4. Civ bdry: 1935.[2] *Parl* Seq 1. *Eccl* Stoneh. RDn (until 1866), Stoneh. North RDn (1866–87), Bisley RDn (1887–1901), Cirenc. RDn (1901–49), Bisley RDn (1949–*).

ELBERTON
AP *LG* Berk. Hd, Thornb. PLU, RSD, RD. Abol civ 1935 ent to Aust CP.[2] *Parl* W'rn Dv (1832–85), S'rn Dv (1885–1918), Thornb. Dv (1918–48). *Eccl* Seq 10.

ELKSTONE
AP *LG* Seq 28. *Parl* Seq 1. *Eccl* Stoneh. RDn (until 1866), Stoneh. North RDn (1866–87), Bisley RDn (1887–1901), Chelt. RDn (1901–49), Cirenc. RDn (1949–*).

ELMORE
AP *LG* Seq 15. Civ bdry: 1883,[3] 1884,[236] 1884,[237] 1885.[238] *Parl* Seq 7. *Eccl* Seq 20.

ELMSTONE HARDWICKE
AP Chap in Deerhurst AP, sep par by 1296.[214] Incl hmlt Uckington (sep CP 1866,[9] no sep eccl identity hence this par eccl 'Elmstone Hardwicke

with Uckington', qv). *LG* Pt Deerhurst Hd, pt W'minst. Hd, Tewk. PLU, RSD, RD (1894–1935), Chelt. RD (1935–74). *Parl* Seq 4.

ELMSTONE HARDWICKE WITH UCKINGTON

AP Chap in Deerhurst AP, sep par by 1296.[214] Usual eccl spelling; for civ and civ sep Uckington, see prev entry. *Eccl* Winch. RDn (until 1866), Winch. North RDn (1866–87), Winch. RDn (1887–1907), Tewk. RDn (1907–22), Chelt. RDn (1922–53). Abol eccl 1953 to help cr Tredington with Stoke Orchard and Hardwicke EP.[239]

EVENLODE

AP In Worcs, transf 1931 to Glos.[76] *LG* Stow on the Wold RD (1931–35), N Cotsw. RD (1935–74). *Parl* Worcs until 1948, Cirenc. & Tewk. CC (1948–*). *Eccl* Worc dioc until 1919, Stow RDn (1919–*).

EYFORD

AP Sep par which disappeared, civ identity regained, eccl ex-par[240] and now pt of Upper and Lower Slaughter with Eyford EP, qv. *LG* Slaugh. Hd, Stow on the Wold PLU, RSD, RD. Abol civ 1935 ent to Upper Slaughter AP.[2] *Parl* E'rn Dv (1832–1918), Cirenc. & Tewk. Dv (1918–48).

FAIRFORD

AP *LG* Fairford Bor (status not sustained), Seq 9. *Parl* Seq 1. *Eccl* Seq 16.

FALFIELD

Chap in Thornbury AP, sep EP 1863,[241] sep CP 1894.[242] *LG* Thornb. PLU, RD. Civ bdry: 1935,[2] 1955.[207] Transf 1974 to Avon.[4] *Parl* Thornb. Dv (1918–48), Stroud & Thornb. CC (1948–55), S Glos CC (1955–*). *Eccl* Durs. RDn (1863–1907), Hawk. RDn (1907–*).

FARMINGTON

AP *LG* Seq 8. *Parl* Seq 1. *Eccl* Seq 14.

FILTON

AP *LG* Berk. Hd, Bart. Reg. PLU [called Clifton 1840s–80s] (1836–94), RSD, Chip. Sodb. PLU (1894–1930), Chip. Sodb. RD (1894–1935), Sodb. RD (1935–74). Civ bdry: 1883,[3] 1885,[243] 1935 (loses pt to Bristol CB and CP),[2] 1951,[244] 1966 (loses pt to Bristol CB and CP).[17] Transf 1974 to Avon.[4] *Parl* Seq 14. *Eccl* Seq 8. Eccl bdry: 1929 (help cr Horfield St Gregory EP).[245]

FISHPONDS

EP Cr 1869 from Stapleton AP.[246] Bristol (Rural Dv) RDn (1869–87), Stap. RDn (1887–1901), E Bristol RDn (1901–49), Stap. RDn (1949–*). Bdry: 1889 (help cr Eastville EP),[234] 1910 (cr Fishponds All Saints EP),[235] 1911 (cr Fishponds St John EP).[247]

FISHPONDS ALL SAINTS

EP Cr 1910 from Fishponds EP, Eastville EP.[235] E Bristol RDn (1910–49), Stap. RDn (1949–*).

FISHPONDS ST BEDE

EP Cr 1929 from Fishponds St John EP.[248] E Bristol RDn (1929–49), Stap. RDn (1949–62). Abol 1962 ent to Fishponds St John EP.[249]

FISHPONDS ST JOHN

EP Cr 1911 from Fishponds EP.[247] E Bristol RDn (1911–49), Stap. RDn (1949–*). Bdry: 1929 (cr Fishponds St Bede EP),[248] 1962 (gains back Fishponds St Bede EP when latter abol).[249]

FLAXLEY

AP *LG* St Briav. Hd, W'bury on Severn PLU, RSD, E Dean & United Pars RD. Civ bdry: 1883,[3] 1883,[208] 1883.[250] Abol civ 1935 ent to Blaisdon AP.[2] *Parl* W'rn Dv (1832–85), For. Dean Dv (1885–1948). *Eccl* Seq 1. Eccl bdry: 1880 (help cr Woodside EP).[175]

FOREST FENCE AND THE FENCE

Eccl ex-par place, abol ent to St Briavels AP.[5]

FORTHAMPTON

AP *LG* Tewk. Hd, PLU, RSD, RD (1894–1935), Glouc. RD (1935–74). Civ bdry: 1965 (loses pt to Eldersfield AP, Worcs).[29] *Parl* Seq 5. *Eccl* Seq 31.

FRAMILODE

EP Cr 1855 from Saul AP, Arlingham AP, Fretherne EP, Eastington AP, Wheatenhurst otherwise Whitminster AP, Moreton Valence AP, Standish AP.[27] Glouc. RDn. Abol eccl 1949 to help cr Fretherne with Framilode EP.[252]

FRAMPTON COTTERELL

AP *LG* Seq 23. Civ bdry: 1885,[11] 1935.[2] Transf 1974 to Avon.[4] *Parl* Seq 14. *Eccl* Seq 23. Eccl bdry: 1845 (help cr Coalpit Heath EP),[201] 1942.[202]

FRAMPTON ON SEVERN

AP *LG* Seq 39. Civ bdry: 1883,[3] 1935.[2] *Parl* Seq 7. *Eccl* Durs. RDn (until 1922), Glouc. RDn (1922–52), Glouc. South RDn (1952–*).

FRANCE LYNCH

EP Cr 1894 from Bisley AP, Chalford EP, Oakridge EP.[68] Bisley RDn.

FRENCHAY

EP Cr 1836 from Winterbourne AP.[253] Bristol RDn (1836–66), Bristol (Rural Dv) RDn (1866–87), Stap. RDn (1887–1927), Almond. RDn (1927–49), Stap. RDn (1949–*). Bdry: 1861 (help cr Winterbourne Down EP).[254]

FRETHERNE

AP *LG* Whits. Hd, Wheath. PLU, RSD. Reconstituted 1884 as 'Fretherne with Saul' when gains pt Saul, loses pt to Eastington AP.[233] *Parl* E'rn Dv (1832–85). *Eccl* Glouc. RDn. Abol eccl 1949 to help cr Fretherne with Framilode EP.[252]

FRETHERNE WITH FRAMILODE

EP Cr 1949 by union Fretherne AP, Framilode EP.[252] Glouc. RDn. Abol eccl 1950 to help cr Saul with Fretherne, Framilode and Whitminster EP.[259]

FRETHERNE WITH SAUL

CP Cr 1884 by union Fretherne AP, pt Saul AP.[233] *LG* Wheath. PLU, RSD, RD (1894–1935), Glouc. RD (1935–74). *Parl* N'rn Dv (1885–1918), Stroud Dv (1918–48), Stroud & Thornb. CC (1948–55), Stroud CC (1955–*).

FROCESTER

AP *LG* Seq 39. *Parl* E'rn Dv (1832–85), Mid Dv (1885–1918), Stroud Dv (1918–48), Stroud & Thornb. CC (1948–55), Stroud CC (1955–*). *Eccl* Seq 26.

GLOUCESTER

The following have 'Gloucester' in their names. Insofar as any existed at a given time: *LG* Dudst. & K's Bart. Hd, Glouc. PLU, Bor/MB/CB, USD. *Parl* Glouc. Parl Bor/BC (1295–*). *Eccl* Glouc. RDn (until 1952), Glouc. City RDn (1952–*).

CP1–GLOUCESTER–Cr 1896 by union of pars in Glouc. CB: CP2, AP2, CP6, CP5, AP3, AP6, AP5, AP7, AP8, AP9, AP10, AP11, AP12, Littleworth CP, Wotton St Mary Within CP.[256] Bdry: 1900,[42] 1910,[85] 1932,[2] 1951,[46] 1957,[260] 1966.[44] Parl bdry: 1951,[401] 1960.[402]

AP1–GLOUCESTER ALL SAINTS–Early united to AP7.[257]

EP1–GLOUCESTER ALL SAINTS–Cr 1876 from EP5.[258]

CP2–GLOUCESTER BARTON ST MARY–Hmlt in AP9, sep CP 1866.[9] *LG* Pt Dust. & K's Bart. Hd (1866–1885), Glouc. MB (pt 1866–85, ent 1885–88), CB (1888–96). Bdry: 1883,[3] 1885.[43] Abol 1896 to help cr CP1.[256]

CP3–GLOUCESTER BARTON ST MICHAEL–Hmlt in AP10, sep CP 1866.[9] *LG* Pt Dudst. & K's Bart. Hd, pt Glouc. MB. Abol 1885 pt to CP2, pt to Wotton St Mary Within CP, pt to CP6, pt to Upton St Leonards CP.[238]

EP2–GLOUCESTER CHRIST CHURCH–Cr 1877 from EP9, AP9, pt of eccl ex-par South Hamlet (pt of area of CP5), ent ex-par Littleworth (area of Littleworth CP).[261] Bdry: 1937.[262]

AP2–GLOUCESTER HOLY TRINITY–Eccl identity lost before 18th cent, united eccl to AP9,[263] abol civ 1896 to help cr CP1.[256]

CP4–GLOUCESTER NORTH HAMLET–Ex-par, sep CP 1858,[58] abol eccl 1877 ent to AP5.[265] *LG* Pt Dudst. & K's Bart. Hd, pt Glouc. MB. Civ bdry: 1883.[3] Abol civ 1885 pt to Highnam Over and Linton CP, pt to Wotton St Mary Within CP, pt to AP5, pt to AP11, pt to AP6.[238] *Parl* Pt Glouc. Parl Bor (1867–1918), pt E'rn Dv (1867–85), pt N'rn Dv (1885–1918). Eccl bdry: 1868.[264]

CP5–GLOUCESTER SOUTH HAMLET–Ex-par, sep CP 1858,[58] eccl ex-par status retained. *LG* Pt Dudst. & K's Bart. Hd (until 1885), Glouc. MB (pt 1858–85, ent 1885–89), CB (1889–96). Civ bdry: 1883,[3] 1885.[238] Abol civ 1896 to help cr CP1.[256] *Parl* Glouc. Parl Bor (1867–1918). Eccl bdry: 1868 (help cr EP6),[264] 1877 (help cr EP2),[261] 1971 (help cr EP4).[266]

CP6–GLOUCESTER POOL MEADOW–Ex-par, sep CP 1858.[58] Abol 1896 to help cr CP1.[256]

AP3–GLOUCESTER ST ALDATE–Abol civ 1896 to help cr CP1,[256] abol eccl 1931 to help cr EP10.[267]

EP3–GLOUCESTER ST ALDATE, FINLAY ROAD–Cr 1930 from EP14, EP5, Matson AP, Barnwood AP, AP9, Hempsted AP.[47] Bdry: 1935 (help cr Coney Hill EP, now commonly called 'Gloucester St Oswald').[49] This par commonly called 'Gloucester St Aldate'.

AP4–GLOUCESTER ST AUDONEI–Early united to AP7.[268]

–GLOUCESTER ST BARNABAS–Name commonly used for EP cr as 'Tuffley', qv.

AP5–GLOUCESTER ST CATHERINE–Orig priory chapel, sep identity early. Incl hmlt Longford St Catherine (sep CP 1866[9]), hmlt Kingsholme St Catherine (no sep identity). *LG* Pt Dudst. & K's Bart. Hd (until 1885), Glouc. Bor/MB/CB (pt until 1885, ent 1885–96). Addtl civ bdry alt: 1883,[3] 1885.[238] Abol civ 1896 to help cr CP1.[256] *Parl* Glouc. Parl Bor (pt 1295–1867, ent 1867–1918), pt E'rn Dv (1832–67). Eccl bdry: 1842 (help cr EP5),[269] 1844 (help cr Twigworth EP),[271] 1846 (help cr EP8),[270] 1877,[265] 1932 (help cr Wotton St Mary Without EP).[48]

EP4–GLOUCESTER ST GEORGE–Cr 1971 from Hempsted AP, EP7, EP14, Tuffley EP, Whaddon AP, Quedgeley AP, pt ex-par South Hamlet (pt of area of CP5).[266]

EP5–GLOUCESTER ST JAMES–Cr 1842 from AP10, AP9, AP5, Upton St Leonards EP, pt ex-par Ville of Wotton.[269] Bdry: 1844 (help cr EP14),[272] 1876 (cr EP1),[258] 1930 (help cr EP3).[47]

AP6–GLOUCESTER ST JOHN THE BAPTIST–Civ bdry: 1885.[238] Abol civ 1896 to help cr CP1.[256] Eccl bdry: 1846 (help cr EP8).[270] Abol eccl 1931 to help cr EP10.[267]

EP6–GLOUCESTER ST LUKE–Cr 1868 from ex-par South Hamlet (pt of area of CP5), AP9, Hempsted AP, Upton St Leonards EP, AP11, ent ex-par Ville of Wotton, ent ex-par North Hamlet (area of CP4).[265] Bdry: 1884 (help cr EP14),[272] 1909 (help cr EP7).[273] Abol 1937 pt to EP14, pt to EP2, pt to EP7.[262]

EP7–GLOUCESTER ST LUKE THE LESS–Cr 1909 from EP6, EP14, Hempsted AP.[273] Bdry: 1937,[262] 1971 (help cr EP4).[266] Commonly called 'Gloucester St Stephen'.

EP8–GLOUCESTER ST MARK–Cr 1846 from AP5, AP6, AP9.[270]

AP7–GLOUCESTER ST MARY DE CRYPT–Gains early AP1,[267] gains early AP4,[268] gains 1643 AP12 (sep 1660 but later considered subordinate to this par[257]), thereafter known as EP9, qv. Abol civ 1896 to help cr CP1.[256]

EP9–GLOUCESTER ST MARY DE CRYPT WITH ALL SAINTS AND ST OWEN–Name used from 1643 when AP12 added to earlier union of AP7, AP1, AP4.[257] Bdry: 1877 (help cr EP2).[261] Abol 1931 to help cr EP10.[267]

EP10–GLOUCESTER ST MARY DE CRYPT WITH ALL SAINTS AND ST OWEN WITH ST JOHN THE BAPTIST–Cr 1931 by union EP9, AP6, AP3.[267] Abol 1952 to help cr EP11.[259]

EP11–GLOUCESTER ST MARY DE CRYPT WITH ALL SAINTS AND ST OWEN AND ST MICHAEL WITH ST MARY DE GRACE–Cr

1952 by union EP10, AP10, AP8.[259] Sometimes called 'St Mary de Crypt with St John the Baptist'.

AP8–GLOUCESTER ST MARY DE GRACE–Abol 1896 to help cr CP1.[256] Abol eccl 1952 to help cr EP11.[259]

AP9–GLOUCESTER ST MARY DE LODE–Gains AP2 before 18th cent (and thus eccl sometimes called as EP13). Incl chap Maisemore (sep civ identity early, sep EP1733[145]), chap Upton St Leonards (sep civ identity early, sep EP 1781[145]), hmlt and chap Twigworth (sep EP 1844 [from this par and AP5][271] sep CP 1866 [from this par alone][9]), hmlt Tuffley (sep CP 1866,[9] sep EP 1930[275]), hmlt Barton St Mary (sep CP [CP2] 1866[9]), hmlt Longford St Mary (sep CP 1866[9]), hmlt Wotton St Mary (sep CP 1866[9]), hmlt Kingsholme St Mary (no sep identity). *LG* Pt Dudst. & K's Bart. Hd (the area of hmlts, until 1866), Glouc. Bor/MB (pt until 1866, ent 1866–88), CB (1888–96). Addtl civ bdry alt: 1883,[3] 1885.[238] Abol civ 1896 to help cr CP1.[256] *Parl* Glouc. Parl Bor (pt 1295–1867, ent 1867–1918), pt E'rn Dv (1832–67). Addtl eccl bdry alt: 1842 (help cr EP5),[269] 1846 (help cr EP8),[270] 1868 (help cr EP6),[264] 1876,[80] 1877 (help cr EP2),[261] 1930 (help cr EP3),[47] 1932 (help cr Wotton St Mary Without EP).[48] Abol eccl 1971 to help cr EP12.[274]

EP12–GLOUCESTER ST MARY DE LODE AND ST NICHOLAS–Cr 1971 by union AP9, AP11.[274]

EP13–GLOUCESTER ST MARY DE LODE WITH HOLY TRINITY–See AP9.

AP10–GLOUCESTER ST MICHAEL–Incl hmlt Barton St Michael (sep CP [CP3] 1866[9]). *LG* Pt Dudst. & K's Bart. Hd (the area of hmlt, until 1866), Glouc. Bor/MB (pt until 1866, ent 1866–88), CB (1888–96). Abol civ 1896 to help cr CP1.[256] *Parl* Glouc. Parl Bor (pt until 1867, ent 1867–1918), pt E'rn Dv (1832–67). Eccl bdry: 1842 (help cr EP5),[269] 1868 (help cr EP6).[264] Abol eccl 1952 to help cr EP11.[259]

AP11–GLOUCESTER ST NICHOLAS–Orig chap to St Bartholomew hospital, sep identity early. Civ bdry: 1885.[238] Abol civ 1896 to help cr CP1.[256] Abol eccl 1971 to help cr EP12.[274]

–GLOUCESTER ST OSWALD–Name commonly used for EP cr as 'Coney Hill', qv.

AP12–GLOUCESTER ST OWEN–Incl chap Quedgeley (sep civ and eccl identity early). Abol civ 1896 to help cr CP1.[256] Destroyed 1643 and eccl united to AP7.[257]

EP14–GLOUCESTER ST PAUL–Cr 1884 from EP6, EP5.[272] Bdry: 1885,[93] 1909 (help cr EP7),[273] 1930 (help cr EP3),[47] 1930 (help cr Tuffley EP),[275] 1971 (help cr EP4).[266]

–GLOUCESTER ST STEPHEN–Name commonly used for EP cr as EP7, qv.

GORSLEY WITH CLIFFORD'S MESNE
EP Cr 1872 from Newent AP, Linton AP (Hereford).[276] For. North RDn.

GOTHERINGTON
Hmlt in Bishop's Cleeve AP, sep CP 1866,[9] eccl severed 1933 to help cr Woolstone with Gotherington EP.[179] *LG* Bishop's Cleeve Hd, Winch. PLU, RSD, RD (1894–1935), Chelt. RD (1935–74). *Parl* E'rn Dv (1867–85), N'rn Dv (1885–1918), Cirenc. & Tewk. Dv/CC (1918–*).

GREENBANK
EP Cr 1926 from Easton St Mark EP.[277] E Bristol RDn (1926–49), Stap. RDn (1949–*).

LOWER GUITING–See GUITING POWER

TEMPLE GUITING
AP Incl chap Cutsdean (sep civ identity early in Worcs, no sep eccl identity thus this par eccl 'Temple Guiting with Cutsdean', qv). *LG* Kiftsg. Hd, Winch. PLU, RSD, RD (1894–1935), N Cotsw. RD (1935–74). Civ bdry: 1935.[2] *Parl* Seq 4.

TEMPLE GUITING WITH CUTSDEAN
AP Usual eccl spelling; for civ and civ sep chap Cutsdean see prev entry. *Eccl* Seq 28.

GUITING POWER
AP Sometimes 'Lower Guiting'. Usual civ spelling; for eccl see following entry. *LG* Kiftsg. Hd, Winch. PLU, RSD, RD (1894–1935), N Cotsw. RD (1935–74). Civ bdry: 1883.[150] *Parl* E'rn Dv (1832–85), N'rn Dv (1885–1918), Cirenc. & Tewk. Dv/CC (1918–*).

GUITING POWER WITH FARMCOTE
AP Usual eccl spelling; for civ see prev entry. *Eccl* Seq 28.

HAILES
Chap since 1738 in Didbrook AP, sep civ identity maintained,[221] sep EP 1837[145] but status not sustained and remains chap in Didbrook. *LG* Kiftsg. Hd, Winch. PLU, RSD, RD. Abol civ 1935 pt to Stanway AP, pt to Toddington AP.[2] *Parl* E'rn Dv (1832–85), N'rn Dv (1885–1918), Cirenc. & Tewk. Dv (1918–48).

HAM AND STONE
Ham tg, Stone chap, both in Berkeley AP, united for relief of poor, sep CP 1866.[9] *LG* Seq 3. *Parl* W'rn Dv (1867–85), N'rn Dv (1885–1918), Thornb. Dv (1918–48), Stroud & Thornb. CC (1948–55), S Glos CC (1955–*).

HAMFALLOW
Tg in Berkeley AP, sep CP 1866.[9] *LG* Seq 3. Civ bdry: 1935.[2] *Parl* W'rn Dv (1867–85), N'rn Dv (1885–1918), Thornb. Dv (1918–48), Stroud & Thornb. CC (1948–55), S Glos CC (1955–*).

HAMPNETT
AP Gains eccl 1660 Stowell AP,[284] each retaining sep civ identity, thus for eccl see 'Hampnett with Stowell'. *LG* Seq 8. Civ bdry: 1950 (help cr Northleach with Eastington CP).[40] *Parl* Seq 1.

EP Cr 1964 when Hampnett with Stowell and Yanworth EP divided into 2 EPs of Hampnett, Yanworth and Stowell.[280] N'leach RDn.

HAMPNETT WITH STOWELL

EP Cr 1660 by union Hampnett AP, Stowell AP.[284] Cirenc. RDn (until 1836), N'leach RDn (1836–66), N'leach South RDn (1866–87), N'leach RDn (1887–1938). Reconstituted 1938 when gains Yanworth chap of Haselton with Yanworth AP to cr Hampnett with Stowell and Yanworth EP.[279]

HAMPNETT WITH STOWELL AND YANWORTH

EP Cr 1938 by union Hampnett with Stowell EP, chap Yanworth of Haselton with Yanworth AP.[279] Abol 1964, divided into 2 EPs of Hampnett, Yanworth and Stowell.[280]

HANHAM

Chap in Bitton AP, sep EP 1841,[71] sep CP 1866.[9] *LG* Lang. & Swin. Hd, Keynsham PLU, pt Kingswood USD, pt Keynsham RSD. Abol civ 1894 the pt in the USD to help cr Kingswood CP, the remainder to cr Hanham Abbots CP.[342] *Parl* W'rn Dv (1867–85), S'rn Dv (1885–1918). *Eccl* Hawk. RDn (1841–66), Hawk. South RDn (1866–87), Bitton RDn (1887–*).

HANHAM ABBOTS

CP Cr 1894 from the pt of Hanham CP not in Kingswood USD.[342] *LG* Keynsham PLU, Warmley RD. Civ bdry: 1898.[82] Transf 1974 to Avon.[4] *Parl* Thornb. Dv (1918–48), S Glos CC (1948–70), Kingswood CC (1970–*).

HARDWICKE

Chap in Standish AP, sep civ identity early, no sep eccl identity. *LG* Seq 39. Civ bdry: 1883,[3] 1884,[237] 1885,[238] 1935.[2] *Parl* Seq 7.

HARESCOMBE

AP *LG* Dudst. & K's Bart. Hd (Glouc. Bor & Co 1483–1672), Wheath. PLU, RSD, RD (1894–1935), Glouc. RD (1935–74). Civ bdry: 1885,[281] 1885.[283] *Parl* Seq 7. *Eccl* Glouc. RDn until 1901), Bisley RDn (1901–30s), Glouc. RDn (1930s–52), Glouc. South RDn (1952–*). Eccl bdry: 1873,[140] 1873 (help cr The Edge EP),[141] 1932.[148]

HARESFIELD

AP *LG* Seq 39. Civ bdry: 1884,[282] 1885,[238] 1885,[281] 1885.[283] *Parl* Seq 7. *Eccl* Seq 20. Eccl bdry: 1873,[140] 1873 (help cr The Edge EP),[141] 1932.[148]

HARNHILL

AP *LG* Crowt. & Min. Hd, Cirenc. PLU, RSD, RD. Abol civ 1935 ent to Driffield AP.[2] *Parl* E'rn Dv (1832–1918), Cirenc. & Tewk. Dv (1918–48). *Eccl* Seq 13.

HARTPURY

AP *LG* Dudst. & K's Bart. Hd (Glouc. Bor & Co 1483–1672), Newent PLU, RSD, RD. *Parl* E'rn Dv (1832–85), N'rn Dv (1885–1918), For. Dean Dv (1918–48), W Glos CC (1948–*). *Eccl* Seq 19.

HASFIELD

AP Chap in Deerhurst AP, sep par 1317 but independence still questioned 16th cent.[219] *LG* W'minst. Hd, Tewk. PLU, RSD, RD (1894–1935), Glouc. RD (1935–74). *Parl* Seq 5. *Eccl* Seq 31.

HASELTON

AP Incl chap Yanworth (sep civ identity early, eccl severed 1938 to help cr Hampnett with Stowell and Yanworth EP,[279] hence this par eccl before 1938 'Haselton with Yanworth', qv). *LG* Seq 8. Civ bdry: 1935.[2] *Parl* Seq 1.

EP Renaming 1938 when loses chap Yanworth to help cr Hampnett with Stowell and Yanworth EP.[279] N'leach RDn.

HASELTON WITH YANWORTH

AP Usual eccl spelling until 1938; for civ see 'Haselton'. Stow RDn (until 1836), N'leach RDn (1836–66), N'leach North RDn (1866–87), N'leach RDn (1887–1938). Abol eccl 1938 when chap Yanworth severed to help cr Hampnett with Stowell and Yanworth EP,[279] Haselton remaining sep EP.

DOWN HATHERLEY

AP *LG* Seq 15. Civ bdry: 1883.[3] *Parl* Seq 8. *Eccl* Seq 30. Eccl bdry: 1932 (help cr Wotton St Mary Without EP).[48]

UP HATHERLEY

AP Orig sep par, civ identity maintained, eccl deemed chap to Shurdington chap of Badgeworth AP from 17th cent,[38] sep EP 1887.[37] *LG* Seq 14. Civ bdry: 1935.[2] *Parl* Seq 6. *Eccl* Winch. RDn (1887), Chelt. RDn (1887–*). Eccl bdry: 1933,[40] 1968.[168]

HATHEROP

AP *LG* Seq 9. Civ bdry: 1935.[2] *Parl* Seq 1. *Eccl* Seq 16. Eccl bdry: 1934.[14]

HAWKESBURY

AP Incl chap Hillesley (sep EP 1852[300]). *LG* Seq 16. Civ bdry: 1883,[3] 1885,[11] 1935.[2] Transf 1974 to Avon.[4] *Parl* Seq 14. *Eccl* Seq 21.

HAWLING

AP *LG* Seq 22. Civ bdry: 1883,[150] 1935.[2] *Parl* Seq 4. *Eccl* Stow RDn (until 1929), N'leach RDn (1929–53), Chelt. RDn (1953–*).

HAYWARDS FIELD

Ex-par place, sep CP 1858.[58] *LG* Whitst. Hd, Stroud PLU, RSD. Abol 1884 ent to Stonehouse AP.[285] *Parl* E'rn Dv (1867–85).

HEMPSTED

AP *LG* Dudst. & K's Bart. Hd (Glouc. Bor and Co 1483–1672), Glouc. PLU, RSD, RD. Civ bdry: 1883,[3] 1885,[238] 1900 (loses pt to Glouc. CB and CP),[42] 1935 (loses pt to Glouc. CB and CP),[2] 1951 (loses pt to Glouc. CB and CP),[46] 1954.[286] Abol civ 1966 pt to Glouc. CB and CP, pt to Highnam CP, pt to Minsterworth AP.[44] *Parl* E'rn Dv (ent 1832–67, pt 1867–85), pt Glouc. Parl Bor (1867–85), N'rn Dv (1885–1918), Stoud Dv (1918–48), Glouc. BC (1948–70). Parl bdry: 1951.[45] *Eccl* Seq 18. Eccl bdry: 1868 (help cr Gloucester St Luke EP),[264] 1909 (help cr Gloucester St Luke the Less EP),[273] 1930 (help cr Gloucester St Aldate, Finlay Road EP),[47] 1930 (help cr Tuffley EP),[275] 1937,[262] 1971 (help cr Gloucester St George EP).[266]

HENBURY

AP Incl tg Aust (sep CP 1866,[9] eccl severed 1954 and transf to Olveston AP[294]), tg Redwick and Northwick (sep CP 1866,[9] eccl severed 1885 and transf to Pilning EP[288]). *LG* Pt Henbury Hd, pt Berk. Hd, Bart. Reg. PLU [called 'Clifton' 1840s–80s] (1836–1904), RSD, RD (1894–1904), Thornb. PLU (1904–30), RD (1904–35). Addtl civ bdry alt: 1883,[3] 1885,[290] 1885,[291] 1896 (help cr North Bristol CP to be in Bristol CB),[89] 1901 (loses pt to Bristol CB and CP),[83] 1902 (loses pt to Bristol CB and CP),[84] 1904 (loses pt to Bristol CB and CP).[287] Abol civ 1935 pt to Bristol CB and CP, pt to Almondsbury AP, pt to Redwick and Northwick CP.[2] *Parl* W'rn Dv (1832–85), S'rn Dv (1885–1918), Thornb. Dv (1918–48). *Eccl* Seq 7. Addtl eccl bdry alt: 1881 (help cr Pilning EP),[19] 1929 (cr Sea Mills EP),[289] 1962 (incl help cr Lawrence Weston EP).[292]

HENLEAZE

EP Cr 1926 from Westbury on Trym AP.[295] Clifton RDn.

HEWELSFIELD

Chap in Lydney AP, sep civ identity early, sep EP 1855.[296] *LG* Seq 29. Civ bdry: 1935.[2] *Parl* Seq 11. *Eccl* For. RDn (1855–66), For. South RDn (1866–*). Eccl bdry: 1932.[59]

HIDCOTE BARTRIM

Hmlt in Mickleton AP, sep CP 1866.[9] *LG* Kiftsg. Hd, Shipston on Stour PLU, RSD, Camp. RD. Abol 1935 ent to Ebrington AP.[2] *Parl* E'rn Dv (1867–1918), Cirenc. & Tewk. Dv (1918–48).

HIGHLEADON

Hmlt in Rudford AP, sep CP 1866.[9] *LG* Dudst. & K's Bart. Hd, Newent PLU, RSD, RD. Abol 1935 ent to Rudford AP.[2] *Parl* E'rn Dv (1867–85), For. Dean Dv (1885–1948).

HIGHNAM

EP Cr 1851 from Churcham AP.[297] For. RDn (1851–66), For. North RDn (1866–1922). Abol 1922 to help cr Highnam with Lassington EP.[298]

CP Cr 1935 by union Highnam Over and Linton CP, Lassington CP.[2] *LG* Glouc. RD. Bdry: 1966 (incl loses pt to Glouc. CB and CP).[44] *Parl* W Glos CC (1948–*).

HIGHNAM OVER AND LINTON

Three sep hmlts in Churcham AP, made single CP 1866.[9] *LG* Dudst. & K's Bart. Hd, Glouc. PLU, RSD, RD. Civ bdry: 1883,[3] 1883.[299] Abol 1935 to help cr Highnam CP.[2] *Parl* E'rn Dv (1867–85), N'rn Dv (1885–1918), For. Dean Dv (1918–48).

HIGHNAM WITH LASSINGTON

EP Cr 1922 by union Highnam EP, Lassington AP.[298] For. North RDn.

HILL

AP *LG* Seq 3. Transf 1974 to Avon.[4] *Parl* W'rn Dv (1832–85), S'rn Dv (1885–1918), Thornb. Dv (1918–48), Stroud & Thornb. CC (1948–55), S Glos CC (1955–*). *Eccl* Donative, Durs. RDn.

HILLESLEY

Chap in Hawkesbury AP, sep EP 1852.[300] Hawk. RDn (1852–66), Hawk. North RDn (1866– 87), Hawk. RDn (1887–*).

HINDERS LANE AND DOCKHAM

Ex-par place, sep CP 1858,[58] abol eccl 1880 to help cr Woodside EP.[175] *LG* St Briav. Hd, W'bury on Severn PLU, RSD. Abol 1884 ent to East Dean CP.[209] *Parl* W'rn Dv (1867–85).

HINTON

Tg in Berkeley AP, sep CP 1866.[9] *LG* Seq 3. *Parl* W'rn Dv (1867–85), N'rn Dv (1885–1918), Thornb. Dv (1918–48), Stroud & Thornb. CC (1948–55), S Glos CC (1955–*).

HINTON ON THE GREEN

AP *LG* Tibald. Hd, Evesham PLU, RSD, Pebworth RD (1894–1931). Transf 1931 to Worcs.[30] *Parl* E'rn Dv (1832–85), N'rn Dv (1885–1918), Cirenc. & Tewk. Dv (1918–48), Worcs thereafter. *Eccl* Camp. RDn (until 1907), Tewk. RDn (1907–19), Worc dioc thereafter; see entry in Worcs.

CHURCH HONEYBOURNE

AP In Worcs (Blackenhurst Hd), incl chap Cow Honeybourne (sep civ identity early in Glos [Kiftsg. Hd], eccl united early to Church Honeybourme, union reaffirmed 1885[301]). See main entry in Worcs.

COW HONEYBOURNE

Chap in Church Honeybourne AP (Worcs, Blackenhurst Hd), sep civ identity early in Glos (Kiftsg. Hd), eccl united early to Church Honeybourne, union reaffirmed 1885.[301] *LG* Evesham PLU, RSD, Pebworth RD (1894–1931). Transf 1931 to Worcs.[30] *Parl* E'rn Dv (1832–1918), Cirenc. & Tewk. Dv (1918–48).

HORFIELD

AP *LG* Berk. Hd, Bart. Reg. PLU [called 'Clifton' 1840s–80s], Horfield USD (pt 1875–81, ent 1881–94), pt Bart. Reg. RSD (1875–81), Horfield UD. Civ bdry: 1883,[3] 1885.[243] Abol civ 1904 ent to Bristol CB and CP.[287] *Parl* W'rn Dv (1832–85), Bristol Parl Bor, West Dv (1885–1918). *Eccl* Bristol RDn (until 1866), Bristol (Rural Dv) RDn (1866–87), Stap. RDn (1887–1901), Clifton RDn (1901–49), Almond. RDn (1949–73), Horfield RDn (1973–*). Eccl bdry: 1845 (help cr Montpelier EP),[126] 1929 (help cr Horfield St Gregory EP),[245] 1961 (help cr Bristol St Mary Magdalene with St Francis, Lockleaze EP),[124] 1961.[302]

HORFIELD ST GREGORY

EP Cr 1929 from Horfield AP, Filton AP.[245] Clifton RDn (1929–49), Almond. RDn (1949–73), Horfield RDn (1973–*). Bdry: 1961 (help cr Bristol St Mary Magdalene with St Francis, Lockleaze EP).[124]

HORSLEY

AP Incl pt chap Nailsworth (sep CP 1892,[340] sep EP 1895[23]). *LG* Seq 24. Addtl civ bdry alt: 1935.[2] *Parl* Seq 9. *Eccl* Seq 26.

HORTON

AP *LG* Seq 16. Transf 1974 to Avon.[4] *Parl* Seq 14.

Eccl Seq 21.

HUCCLECOTE

Chap and hmlt in Churchdown AP, sep EP 1851,[171] sep CP 1866.[9] *LG* Seq 15. Civ bdry: 1935 (incl help cr Longlevens CP),[2] 1966 (incl loses pt to Glouc. CB and CP).[44] *Parl* E'rn Dv (1867–85), N'rn Dv (1885–1918), Stroud Dv (1918–48), Glouc. BC (1948–70), W Glos CC (1970–*). *Eccl* Glouc. RDn (1851–1952), Glouc. City RDn (1952–*).

HUDNALLS WITH ST BRIAVEL'S COMMON

Eccl ex-par, abol 1932 pt to Hewelsfield EP, pt to St Briavels EP.[59]

HUNTLEY

AP *LG* Seq 13. *Parl* Seq 11. *Eccl* Seq 1.

ICOMB

AP Incl hmlt Church Icomb (in Worcs, Oswaldslow Hd, transf to Glos 1832 for parl purposes, 1844 for civ purposes,[21] sep CP 1866[9]). *LG* Slaugh. Hd, Stow on the Wold PLU, RSD, RD (1894–1935), N Cotsw. RD (1935–74). Addtl civ bdry alt: 1935.[2] *Parl* Seq 1. *Eccl* Seq 28.

CHURCH ICOMB

Hmlt in Icomb AP, situated in Worcs (Oswaldslow Hd), transf to Glos (Slaugh. Hd) 1832 for parl purposes, 1844 for civ purposes,[21] sep CP 1866.[9] *LG* Stow on the Wold PLU, RSD, RD. Abol 1935 ent to Icomb AP.[2] *Parl* E'rn Dv (1832–1918), Cirenc. & Tewk. Dv (1918–48).

ILMINGTON

AP *LG* Pt Glos (Kiftsg. Hd), pt Warws (Kington Hd), Shipston on Stour PLU, RSD. The Glos pt transf to Warws 1894 and the par ent Warws thereafter[341]; see main entry in Warws. *Parl* Glos pt, E'rn Dv (1832–85), N'rn Dv (1885–1918). *Eccl* See entry in Warws.

INNSWORTH

CP Renaming 1967 of Longlevens CP.[303] *LG* Glouc. RD. *Parl* W Glos CC (1970–*).

KEMBLE

AP In Wilts (Malmesbury Hd), transf 1897 to Glos.[304] *LG* Cirenc. PLU, RSD, sep RD in Wilts (1894–97), Cirenc. RD (1897–1974). Civ bdry: 1935.[2] *Parl* In Wilts until 1918, Cirenc. & Tewk. Dv/CC (1918–*). *Eccl* Sarum dioc until 1897 (see entry in Wilts), Cirenc. RDn (1897–*).

KEMERTON

AP *LG* Tewk. Hd, PLU, RSD, Winch. RD (1894–1931). Transf 1931 to Worcs.[251] *Parl* E'rn Dv (1832–85), N'rn Dv (1885–1918), Cirenc. & Tewk. Dv (1918–48), Worcs thereafter. *Eccl* Camp. RDn (until 1887), Winch. RDn (1887–1907), Tewk. RDn (1907–*).

KEMPLEY

AP *LG* Seq 7. Civ bdry: 1965 (gains pt Upton Bishop AP, Hereford).[29] *Parl* Seq 11. *Eccl* Seq 1.

KEMPSFORD

AP *LG* Seq 9. *Parl* Seq 1. *Eccl* Sometimes as 'Kempsford with Whelford', Seq 16.

KING'S PARADE

EP Cr 1841 from Clifton AP, Westbury on Trym AP.[184] Bristol RDn (1841–66), Bristol (City Dv) RDn (1866–87), Bristol RDn (1887–1901), Clifton RDn (1901–*). Now commonly called 'Clifton St John the Evangelist'.

POOLE KEYNES

AP In Wilts (Malmesbury Hd), transf 1897 to Glos.[304] *LG* Cirenc. PLU, RSD, sep RD in Wilts (1894–97), Cirenc. RD (1897–1974). *Parl* In Wilts until 1918, Cirenc. & Tewk. Dv/CC (1918–*). *Eccl* Sarum dioc until 1897 (see entry in Wilts), Cirenc. RDn (1897–*).

SOMERFORD KEYNES

AP In Wilts (Highworth, Cricklade and Staple Hd), transf 1897 to Glos.[304] *LG* Cirenc. PLU, RSD, sep RD in Wilts (1894–97), Cirenc. RD (1897–1974). Civ bdry: 1894.[306] *Parl* In Wilts until 1918, Cirenc. & Tewk. Dv/CC (1918–*). *Eccl* Sarum dioc (see entry in Wilts).

KINGSCOTE

Chap in Beverstone, sep civ and eccl identity early. *LG* Seq 2. Civ bdry: 1883,[3] 1883,[307] 1935.[2] *Parl* Seq 10. *Eccl* Durs. RDn (until 1907), Tetb. RDn (1907–*).

KINGSDOWN ST MATTHEW

EP Cr 1850 and refounded 1870 from Bristol St James AP, Montpelier EP, Westbury on Trym AP.[118] Bristol RDn (1850–66), Bristol (City Dv) RDn (1866–87), Bristol RDn (1887–1901), Clifton RDn (1901–49), Almond. RDn (1949–73), Horfield RDn (1973–*). Bdry: 1876 (help cr Kingsdown St Nathanael EP),[308] 1958.[104]

KINGSDOWN ST NATHANAEL

EP Cr 1876 from Kingsdown St Matthew EP, Westbury on Trym AP.[308] Bristol (City Dv) RDn (1876–87), Bristol RDn (1887–1901), Clifton RDn (1901–49), Almond. RDn (1949–54). Abol 1954 to help cr Bristol St Nathanael with St Katherine EP.[125]

KINGSWOOD

AP In Wilts (Chippenham Hd), situated in Glos, transf to Glos (Berk. Hd) 1832 for parl purposes, 1844 for civ purposes.[21] *LG* Durs. PLU, RSD, RD. *Parl* W'rn Dv (1832–85), Mid Dv (1885–1918), Stroud Dv (1918–48), Stroud & Thornb.CC (1948–55), Stroud CC (1955–*). *Eccl* Pec jurisd Consistory Court of Glouc. (until 1847), Seq 32 thereafter.

KINGSWOOD

Hmlt in Bitton AP, sep EP 1821,[310] sep CP 1894 (from the pts of Hanham CP, Mangotsfield AP, Oldland CP in Kingswood UD).[342] *LG* Keynsham PLU, Kingswood UD. Civ bdry: 1966 (exchanges pts with Bristol CB and CP).[17] Transf 1974 to Avon.[4] *Parl* Thornb. Dv (1918–48), S Glos CC (1948–70), Kingswood CC (1970–*). *Eccl* Hawk. RDn (1821–66), Hawk. South RDn (1866–87), Bitton RDn (1887–1934), E Bristol RDn (1934–49), Bitton RDn (1949–*). Eccl bdry: 1851 (help cr Warmley EP),[73] 1874,[309] 1924 (help cr Soundwell EP).[227]

LANCAUT

Chap eccl attached to Woolaston AP from 1711[343] until severed 1932 to help cr Tidenham with Lancaut EP,[200] civ attached to Tidenham AP until sep CP 1866.[9] *LG* W'bury Hd, Chepstow PLU, RSD, Lydney RD. Abol 1935 ent to Tidenham AP.[2] *Parl* W'rn Dv (1867–85), For. Dean Dv (1885–1948).

LASBOROUGH

AP Orig sep AP, depopulated late 14th cent and united civ with Westonbirt by mid 17th cent (the union usually called 'Westonbirt', sometimes 'Westonbirt with Lasborough'), sep eccl identity maintained.[344] *LG* Longt. Hd. *Eccl* Seq 25.

LASSINGTON

AP *LG* Dudst. & K's Bart. Hd (Glouc. Bor and Co 1483–1672), Glouc. PLU, RSD, RD. Abol civ 1935 to help cr Highnam CP.[2] *Parl* E'rn Dv (1832–85), N'rn Dv (1885–1918), For. Dean Dv (1918–48). *Eccl* Pec St Oswald (Archbp of York, until 1847), Glouc. RDn (1847–1907), For. North RDn (1907–22). Abol eccl 1922 to help cr Highnam with Lassington EP.[298]

LAWRENCE WESTON

EP Cr 1962 from Henbury AP, Westbury on Trym AP.[292] Clifton RDn (1962–73), W'bury & Severnside RDn (1973–*).

LEA

Chap in Linton AP (Hereford), sep civ identity early, sep EP early 19th cent[145]; pt Glos (St Briav. Hd), pt Herford (Greytree Hd), the former transf to Hereford 1832 for parl purposes, 1844 for civ purposes.[21] See main entry in Hereford. *Eccl* Irchingfield RDn (cr–1836), For. RDn (1836–66), For. North RDn (1866–*).

LEA BAILEY

Tg in Newland AP (Hereford), sep CP 1866 in Glos (St Briav. Hd).[9] *LG* Ross PLU, RSD. Bdry: 1884.[209] Abol 1890 pt to Blaisdon AP, pt to Lea CP.[75] *Parl* W'rn Dv (1867–85), For. Dean Dv (1885–1918).

LECHLADE

AP Gains the pt of Broughton Poggs AP, Oxon, situated in Glos, 1832 for parl purposes, 1844 for civ purposes.[21] *LG* Brightw. Bar. Hd, Faringdon PLU, RSD, RD (the only Glos par in this RD o'wise ent Berks, 1894–1935), Cirenc. RD (1935–74). Addtl civ bdry alt: 1886 (gains pt Broughton Poggs AP, Oxon).[403] *Parl* Seq 1. *Eccl* Seq 16.

LECKHAMPTON

AP *LG* Chelt. Hd, PLU, pt Chelt. MB, pt Chelt. USD, pt Chelt. RSD, Chelt. RD. Civ bdry: 1894 (loses the pt in the MB to Cheltenham AP),[311] 1935.[2] *Parl* E'rn Dv (ent 1832–67, pt 1867–85), pt Chelt. Parl Bor (1867–1918), pt N'rn Dv (1885–1918), Stroud Dv (1918–48), Cirenc. & Tewk. CC (1948–*). *Eccl* Seq 32. Eccl bdry: 1869 (cr Leckhampton St Philip and St James EP).[312]

LECKHAMPTON ST PHILIP AND ST JAMES

EP Cr 1869 from Leckhampton AP.[312] Winch. South RDn (1869–87), Chelt. RDn (1887–1972). Abol 1972 to help cr Leckhampton St Philip and St James with Cheltenham St James EP.[166]

LECKHAMPTON ST PHILIP AND ST JAMES WITH CHELTENHAM ST JAMES

EP Cr 1972 by union Leckhampton St Philip and St James EP, Cheltenham St James EP.[166] Chelt. RDn.

LEIGH

AP Chap in Deerhurst AP, sep par 1540.[313] *LG* Pt Deerhurst Hd, pt W'minst. Hd, Tewk. PLU, RSD, RD (1894–1935), Chelt. RD (1935–74). *Parl* Seq 4. *Eccl* Winch. RDn (until 1866), Winch. North RDn (1866–87), Winch. RDn (1887–1907), Tewk. RDn (1907–52), Glouc. North RDn (1952–*).

LEMINGTON

Usual eccl spelling; for status and independence as par see following entry. *Eccl* Camp. RDn (until 1907), Stow RDn (1907–34). Abol eccl 1934 to help cr Todenham with Lower Lemington EP.[314]

LOWER LEMINGTON

Chap in Stanway AP, by 16th cent chap in Tewkesbury AP, sep civ identity early, eccl independence in doubt 16th-17th cent, later maintained.[345] Usual eccl spelling 'Lemington', qv. *LG* Tewk. Hd, Shipston on Stour PLU, RSD, Camp. RD. Abol civ 1935 ent to Batsford AP.[2] *Parl* E'rn Dv (1832–1918), Cirenc. & Tewk. Dv (1918–48).

LINTON

AP In Hereford, incl chap Lea (sep civ identity early [pt Glos (St Briav. Hd), pt Hereford (Greytree Hd), the former transf to Hereford 1832 for parl purposes, 1844 for civ purposes[21]], sep EP early 19th cent[145]). See main entry in Hereford.

LITTLEDEAN

AP *LG* St Briav. Hd, W'bury on Severn PLU, pt W'bury on Severn USD (1883–94), W'bury on Severn RSD (ent 1875–83, pt 1883–94), E Dean & United Pars RD (1894–1935), E Dean RD (1935–74). Civ bdry: 1883,[315] 1884,[209] 1894 (loses the pt in the USD to Westbury on Severn AP),[402] 1935.[35] *Parl* Seq 11. *Eccl* Seq 2.

WEST LITTLETON

Chap in Tormarton AP, sep civ identity early, no sep eccl identity. *LG* Grumb. Ash Hd, Chip. Sodb. PLU, RSD, RD. Abol 1935 ent to Tormarton AP.[2] *Parl* W'rn Dv (1832–85), S'rn Dv (1885–1918), Thornb. Dv (1918–48).

LITTLETON ON SEVERN

AP Usual eccl spelling; for civ see following entry. *Eccl* Seq 10.

LITTLETON UPON SEVERN

AP Usual civ spelling; for eccl see prev entry. *LG* Lang. & Swin. Hd, Thornb. PLU, RSD, RD. Abol civ 1935 ent to Aust CP.[2] *Parl* W'rn Dv (1832–85), S'rn Dv (1885–1918), Thornb. Dv (1918–48).

LITTLEWORTH

Ex-par lbty, sep CP 1858.[58] *LG* Glouc. PLU,

MB, CB, USD. Abol 1896 to help cr Gloucester CP.[256] *Parl* Glouc. Parl Bor (1867–1918).

LONGBOROUGH

AP Usual civ spelling; for eccl see following entry. *LG* Seq 21. Civ bdry: 1883.[316] *Parl* Seq 1.

LONGBOROUGH WITH SEZINCOTE

AP Usual eccl spelling (Sezincote a destroyed church now deemed a chap); for civ see prev entry. *Eccl* Seq 21. Eccl bdry: 1927.[317]

LONGFORD

CP Cr 1885 from Longford St Catherine CP, Longford St Mary CP, Wootton St Mary AP, Sandhurst AP, Twigworth EP, Barnwood AP, Gloucester St Mary de Lode AP, Gloucester Barton St Mary CP.[238] *LG* Dudst. & K's Bart. Hd, Glouc. PLU, RSD, RD. Bdry: 1935 (loses pt to Glouc. CB and CP),[2] 1966 (exchanges pts with Glouc. CB and CP).[44] *Parl* Stroud Dv (1918–48), W Glos CC (1948–*).

LONGFORD ST CATHERINE

Hmlt in Gloucester St Catherine AP, sep CP 1866.[9] *LG* Pt Dudst. & K's Bart. Hd, Glouc. PLU, pt Glouc. MB, pt Glouc. USD, pt Glouc. RSD. Bdry: 1883.[3] Abol 1885 pt to Barnwood AP, pt to help cr Wootton St Mary Without CP, pt to help cr Longford CP, pt to Gloucester St Catherine AP.[238] *Parl* Pt E'rn Dv (1867–85), pt N'rn Dv (1885–1918), pt Glouc. Parl Bor (1867–1918).

LONGFORD ST MARY

Hmlt in Gloucester St Mary de Lode AP, sep CP 1866.[9] *LG* Pt Dudst. & K's Bart Hd, Glouc. PLU, pt Glouc. MB, pt Glouc. USD, pt Glouc. RSD. Abol 1885 pt to help cr Wootton St Mary Without CP, pt to help cr Longford CP, pt to Gloucester St Catherine AP, pt to Gloucester St John the Baptist AP, pt to Gloucester Barton St Mary CP, pt to Gloucester South Hamlet CP, pt to Matson AP, pt to Barnwood AP, pt to help cr Wootton St Mary Within CP.[238] *Parl* As for Longford St Catherine.

LONGHOPE

AP *LG* Seq 13. Civ bdry: 1935,[2] 1965 (loses pt to Lea CP, Hereford).[29] *Parl* Seq 11. *Eccl* Seq 1.

LONGLEVENS

CP Cr 1935 from Barnwood AP, Churchdown AP, Hucclecote CP, Wootton St Mary Without CP.[2] *LG* Glouc. RD. Bdry: 1951 (loses pt to Glouc. CB and CP),[46] 1966 (loses pt to Glouc. CB and CP).[44] Renamed 1967 'Innsworth'.[303] *Parl* W Glos CC (1948–70).

EP Name commonly used now for EP cr as 'Wootton St Mary Without', qv.

LONGNEY

AP *LG* Seq 39. Civ bdry: 1884.[346] *Parl* Seq 7. *Eccl* Seq 20.

LYDBROOK

EP Cr 1852 from Dean Forest Holy Trinity EP, English Bicknor AP, Ruardean AP, Newland AP.[61] For. RDn (1852–66), For. South RDn (1966–*).

CP Cr 1935 from East Dean CP, English Bicknor AP, Ruardean AP, West Dean CP.[2] *LG* W Dean RD. *Parl* W Glos CC (1948–*).

LYDNEY

AP Incl chap Aylburton (sep CP 1866,[9] no sep eccl identity, hence this par eccl sometimes 'Lydney with Aylburton'), chaps Hewelsfield, St Briavels (each sep civ identity early, each sep EP 1855[296]). *LG* Seq 6. Addtl civ bdry alt: 1935.[2] *Parl* Seq 11. *Eccl* Seq 2.

LYDNEY WITH AYLBURTON–See prev entry

LYNWORTH

EP Cr 1953 from Pittville EP, Prestbury AP.[318] Chelt. RDn. Reanmed 1966 'Cheltenham St Michael'.[169]

MAISEMORE

Chap in Gloucester St Mary de Lode AP, sep civ identity early, sep EP 1733.[145] *LG* Seq 15. Civ bdry: 1883,[3] 1935 (loses pt to Glouc. CB and CP),[2] 1966 (incl loses pt to Glouc. CB and CP).[44] *Parl* Seq 8. *Eccl* Seq 19.

MANGOTSFIELD

AP Incl chap Downend (sep EP 1874[226]). *LG* Bart. Reg. Hd, Keynsham PLU, pt Kingswood USD (1890–94), Keynsham RSD (ent 1875–90, pt 1890–94), Warmley RD. Civ bdry: 1894 (the pt in the USD help cr Kingswood CP).[342] Abol civ 1927 pt to cr Mangotsfield Urban CP and Mangotsfield UD, the remainder to cr Mangotsfield Rural CP.[319] *Parl* W'rn Dv (1832–85), S'rn Dv (1885–1918), Thornb. Dv (1918–48). *Eccl* Seq 9. Addtl eccl bdry alt: 1874,[309] 1924 (help cr Soundwell EP).[227]

MANGOTSFIELD RURAL

CP Cr 1927 from the pt of Mangotsfield AP not constituted Mangotsfield UD.[319] *LG* Keynsham PLU, Warmley RD. Bdry: 1935.[2] Transf 1974 to Avon.[4] *Parl* S Glos CC (1948–70), Kingswood CC (1970–*).

MANGOTSFIELD URBAN

CP Cr 1927 from the pt of Mangotsfield AP constituted Mangotsfield UD.[319] *LG* Keynsham PLU, Mangotsfield UD. Bdry: 1935,[2] 1966 (loses pt to Bristol CB and CP).[17] Transf 1974 to Avon.[4] *Parl* S Glos CC (1948–55), Bristol South East BC (1955–70), Kingswood CC (1970–*).

MARSHFIELD

AP *LG* Marshfield Bor (status not sustained), Thornb. Hd, Chip. Sodb. PLU, RSD, RD (1894–1935), Sodb. RD (1935–74). *Parl* Seq 14. *Eccl* Seq 22.

MARSTON SICCA

AP *LG* Kiftsg. Hd, Stratford on Avon PLU, RSD, Marst. Sic. RD. Transf 1931 to Warws.[251] *Parl* E'rn Dv (1832–1918), Cirenc. & Tewk. Dv (1918–48), Warws thereafter. *Eccl* Seq 11. Eccl bdry: 1930.[320]

MATSON

AP *LG* Dudst. & K's Bart. Hd (Glouc. Bor and Co 1483–1672), Glouc. PLU, RSD, RD. Civ bdry: 1883,[3] 1885,[238] 1900 (loses pt to Glouc. CB and CP).[42] Abol civ 1935 pt to Glouc. CB and CP, pt to Brookthorpe AP, pt to Upton St Leonards AP.[2] *Parl* E'rn Dv (1832–85), N'rn

Dv (1885–1918), Stroud Dv (1918–48). *Eccl* Seq 18. Eccl bdry: 1892,[321] 1930 (help cr Tuffley EP),[275] 1930 (help cr Gloucester St Aldate, Finlay Road EP),[47] 1967.[104]

MAUGERSBURY

Hmlt in Stow on the Wold AP, sep CP 1866.[9] *LG* Slaugh. Hd, Stow on the Wold PLU, pt Stow on the Wold USD, pt Stow on the Wold RSD, Stow on the Wold RD (1894–1935), N Cotsw. RD (1935–74). Bdry: 1894 (loses the pt in the USD to Stow on the Wold AP),[322] 1935,[2] 1939.[323] *Parl* E'rn Dv (1867–1918), Cirenc. & Tewk. Dv/CC (1918–*).

MEYSEY HAMPTON

AP Sometimes 'Maiseyhampton'. *LG* Seq 11. *Parl* Seq 1. *Eccl* Seq 16.

MICKLETON

AP Incl hmlt Clopton, hmlt Hidcote Bartrim (each sep CP 1866[9]). *LG* Seq 20. *Parl* Seq 1. *Eccl* Seq 11.

MINCHINHAMPTON

AP Incl chap Nailsworth (sep CP 1892,[340] sep EP 1895[23]), chap Rodborough (sep civ identity early, sep EP 1840[22]); in 1840 two other EPs, Amberley, Brinscombe, were cr along with Rodborough[22]. *LG* Minchinhampton Bor (status not sustained), Seq 24. Addtl civ bdry alt: 1959.[149] *Parl* Seq 9. *Eccl* Seq 26.

MINETY

AP Glos par (Crowt. & Min. Hd) situated in Wilts, transf to Wilts 1832 for parl purposes, 1844 for civ purposes.[21] See entry in Wilts.

MINSTERWORTH

AP Chap in Westbury on Severn AP, sep par by 1309.[354] *LG* Duchy Lanc. Hd, W'bury on Severn PLU, RSD, E Dean & United Pars RD (1894–1935), Glouc. RD (1935–74). Civ bdry: 1884,[236] 1966 (incl exchanges pts with Glouc. CB and CP).[44] *Parl* W'rn Dv (1832–85), N'rn Dv (1885–1918), For. Dean RDn (1918–48), W Glos CC (1948–*). *Eccl* Seq 1.

MISERDEN

AP *LG* Bisley Hd, Cirenc. PLU, pt Bisley USD (1883–94), Cirenc. RSD (ent 1875–83, pt 1883–94), Cirenc. RD. Civ bdry: 1883,[3] 1885,[65] 1894 (loses the pt in the USD to help cr Bisley with Lypiatt CP),[64] 1958.[70] *Parl* Seq 3. *Eccl* Seq 24.

MITCHELDEAN

AP *LG* Seq 31. Civ bdry: 1883,[3] 1935,[2] 1953,[35] 1965 (loses pts to Hope Mansell AP, Weston under Penyard AP, Lea CP, all Hereford).[29] *Parl* Seq 11. *Eccl* Seq 3.

MOCKING HAZELL WOOD

Eccl ex-par place, abol 1932 ent to St Briavels EP.[59]

MONTPELIER

EP Cr 1845 from Bristol St Paul AP, Horfield AP.[126] Bristol RDn (1845–66), Bristol (City Dv) RDn (1866–87), Bristol RDn (1887–1901), E Bristol RDn (1901–49), Bristol City RDn (1949–56). Bdry: 1850 (help cr Kingsdown St Matthew EP),[118] 1876,[132] 1956.[101] Abol 1958 pt to Kingsdown St Matthew EP, pt to Bristol St Paul with St Barnabas EP, pt to Bristol St Nathanael with St Katherine EP.[104]

MOORFIELDS

EP Cr 1873 from Easton St Mark EP, Bristol St George EP.[116] Bristol (City Dv) RDn (1873–87), Bristol RDn (1887–1901), E Bristol RDn (1901–49), Bitton RDn (1949–*). Bdry: 1883 (help cr Bristol St Lawrence EP),[97] 1893 (help cr Easton All Hallows EP),[324] 1915 (help cr Bristol St Ambrose, Whitehall EP),[103] 1925 (help cr Bristol St Leonard, Redfield EP).[117]

MORETON IN MARSH

Chap in Bourton on the Hill AP, sometimes with independent parochial rights,[355] sep civ identity early, transf eccl 1887 to Batsford as its chap[56] and hence this par has no sep eccl identity. *LG* Moreton in Marsh Bor (status not sustained), Seq 37. Civ bdry: 1936.[55] *Parl* Seq 1.

MORETON VALENCE

AP Incl chap Whaddon (prob not orig dependent on this par, sep civ identity early, eccl regarded as its chap until 1840 when transf to Brookthorpe AP[356]). *LG* Seq 39. Addtl civ bdry alt: 1883,[3] 1884,[233] 1884,[325] 1886.[326] *Parl* Seq 7. *Eccl* Seq 20. Addtl eccl bdry alt: 1855 (help cr Framilode EP).[27]

NAILSWORTH

Chap in Minchinhampton AP, Horsley AP, Avening AP, sep CP 1892,[340] sep EP 1895 (also from pt Amberley EP).[23] *LG* Longt. Hd, Stroud PLU, RSD, Nailsworth UD. Civ bdry: 1935.[2] *Parl* E'rn Dv (1867–85), Mid Dv (1885–1918), Stroud Dv (1918–48), Stroud & Thornb. CC (1948–55), Stroud CC (1955–*). *Eccl* Stoneh. RDn.

NAUNTON

AP *LG* Pt Bradley Hd, pt Slaugh. Hd, Stow on the Wold PLU, RSD, RD (1894–1935), N Cotsw. RD (1935–74). Civ bdry: 1935.[2] *Parl* Seq 1. *Eccl* Seq 28.

NEWENT

AP *LG* Newent Bor (status not sustained), Seq 7. Civ bdry: 1965 (gains pt Aston Ingham AP, Hereford).[29] *Parl* Seq 11. *Eccl* Seq 1. Eccl bdry: 1872 (help cr Gorsley with Clifford's Mesne EP).[276]

NEWINGTON BAGPATH

AP Incl chap Owlpen (sep civ and eccl identity early). *LG* Berk. Hd, Tetb. PLU, RSD, RD. Addtl civ bdry alt: 1883,[307] 1884.[327] Abol civ 1935 ent to Kingscote CP.[2] *Parl* W'rn Dv (1832–85), E'rn Dv (1885–1918), Cirenc. & Tewk. Dv (1918–48). *Eccl* Seq 15.

NEWLAND

AP Incl tg Lea Bailey (sep CP 1866[9]), chap Bream (sep EP 1756, refounded 1854[78]), chap Coleford (sep EP 1782,[13] refounded 1872,[203] sep CP 1894 [the pt in Coleford USD][242]). *LG* St Briav. Hd, Monmouth PLU, pt Coleford USD, pt Monmouth RSD, W Dean RD. Addtl civ bdry alt: 1883,[3] 1883,[357] 1935.[2] *Parl* Seq 11. *Eccl* Sometimes as 'Newland with Redbrook', Seq 4. Addtl eccl bdry alt: 1852 (help cr Lydbrook EP),[61] 1856 (help cr Clearwell EP),[176] 1909,[213] 1972.[62]

NEWNHAM

AP Chap in Westbury on Severn AP, sep par 14th cent.[358] *LG* Newnham Bor (status not sustained), W'bury Hd, W'bury on Severn PLU, RSD, Newnham USD, UD (1894–1935), Glouc. RD (1935–74). *Parl* Seq 11. *Eccl* Seq 1.

LONG NEWNTON

AP In Wilts, transf 1931 to Glos.[401] *LG* Tetb. RD. Civ bdry: 1966 (loses pt to Brokenborough AP, Wilts).[72] *Parl* In Wilts until 1948, Cirenc. & Tewk. CC (1948–55), Stroud CC (1955–*).

NORTH NIBLEY

Chap in Wotton under Edge AP, sep civ identity early, sep EP 1743.[145] *LG* Seq 1. Civ bdry: 1883,[3] 1883,[146] 1885,[328] 1951.[147] *Parl* Seq 12. *Eccl* Seq 32.

NORTHLEACH

AP Incl tg Eastington (sep CP 1866[9]). *LG* Bradley Hd, N'leach Bor (status not sustained), N'leach PLU, RSD, RD. Abol civ 1950 to help cr Northleach with Eastington CP.[40] *Parl* E'rn Dv (1832–1918), Cirenc. & Tewk. Dv (1918–55). *Eccl* Seq 14.

NORTHLEACH WITH EASTINGTON

CP Cr 1935 by union Northleach AP, Eastington CP, Hampnett AP.[40] *LG* N'leach RD. *Parl* Cirenc. & Tewk. CC (1951–*).

NORTON

AP *LG* Seq 15. Civ bdry: 1883.[3] *Parl* Seq 8. *Eccl* Seq 19.

NOTGROVE

AP *LG* Bradley Hd, Stow on the Wold PLU, RSD, RD (1894–1935), N'leach RD (1935–74). *Parl* Seq 1. *Eccl* Seq 29.

NYMPSFIELD

AP Perhaps once pt of Frocester AP.[359] *LG* Seq 1. Civ bdry: 1883,[146] 1935.[2] *Parl* Seq 12. *Eccl* Stoneh. RDn (until 1866), Stoneh. South RDn 1866–87), Stoneh. RDn (1887–1966), Durs. RDn (1966–*).

OAKRIDGE

EP Cr 1849 from Bisley AP.[67] Stoneh. RDn (1849–66), Stoneh. North RDn (1866–87), Bisley RDn (1887–*). Bdry: 1894 (help cr France Lynch EP).[68]

ODDINGTON

AP Perhaps incl pt Condicote (sep par by 16th cent[206]). *LG* Seq 33. *Parl* Seq 1. *Eccl* Stow RDn. Abol eccl 1937 to help cr Oddington with Adlestrop EP.[8]

ODDINGTON WITH ADLESTROP

EP Cr 1937 by union Oddington AP, chap Adlestrop of Broadwell with Adlestrop AP.[8] Stow RDn.

OLDBURY ON THE HILL

AP *LG* Grumb. Ash Hd, Tetb. PLU, RSD. Abol civ 1883 ent to Didmarton AP.[222] *Parl* W'rn Dv (1832–85). *Eccl* Hawk. RDn. Abol before 19th cent to help cr Didmarton with Oldbury on the Hill EP.[223]

OLDBURY UPON SEVERN

Chap in Thornbury AP, sep EP 1863,[329] sep CP 1894.[330] *LG* Thornb. PLU, RD. Transf 1974 to Avon.[4] *Parl* Thornb. Dv (1918–48), Stroud & Thornb. CC (1948–55), S Glos CC (1955–*). *Eccl* Durs. RDn (1863–1907), Hawk. RDn (1907–*).

OLDLAND

Hmlt and chap in Bitton AP, sep EP 1861,[331] sep CP 1866.[9] *LG* Lang. & Swin. Hd, Keynsham PLU, pt Kingswood USD, pt Keynsham RSD, Warmley RD. Bdry: 1894 (loses the pt in the USD to help cr Kingswood CP).[342] Transf 1974 to Avon.[4] *Parl* W'rn Dv (1867–85), S'rn Dv (1885–1918), Thornb. Dv (1918–48), S Glos CC (1948–70), Kingswood CC (1970–*). *Eccl* Hawk. RDn (1861–66), Hawk. South RDn (1866–87), Bitton RDn (1887–*).

OLVESTON

AP Incl chap Alveston (sep civ identity early, sep EP 1846[360]). *LG* Lang. & Swin. Hd, Thornb. PLU, RSD, RD. Addtl civ bdry alt: 1885,[332] 1935.[2] *Parl* Seq 15. *Eccl* Seq 10.

OVERBURY

AP In Worcs, incl hmlt Little Washbourne (transf to Glos 1832 for parl purposes, 1844 for civ purposes,[21] sep CP 1866[9] in Glos). See main entry in Worcs.

OWLPEN

Chap in Newington Bagpath AP, sep civ and eccl identity early. *LG* Seq 1. Civ bdry: 1883,[3] 1883,[146] 1884.[327] *Parl* Seq 12. *Eccl* Seq 32.

OXENHALL

AP *LG* Seq 7. Civ bdry: 1883.[333] *Parl* Seq 11. *Eccl* Seq 1.

OXENTON

Chap in Tewkesbury AP, sep civ identity early, sep EP from 16th cent.[361] *LG* Seq 34. Civ bdry: 1935.[2] *Parl* Seq 4. *Eccl* Seq 31.

OZLEWORTH

AP *LG* Seq 2. *Parl* Seq 10. *Eccl* Seq 15.

PAINSWICK

AP *LG* Painswick Bor (status not sustained), Seq 5. Civ bdry: 1883,[3] 1936,[69] 1958.[70] *Parl* Seq 9. *Eccl* Seq 24. Eccl bdry: 1821 (cr Sheepscombe EP),[334] 1844 (cr Slad EP),[362] 1873 (help cr The Edge EP).[141]

PARKEND

EP Name commonly used for EP cr as 'Dean Forest St Paul', qv.

PATCHWAY

CP Cr 1953 from Almondsbury AP.[16] *LG* Thornb. RD. Bdry: 1970.[18] Transf 1974 to Avon.[4] *Parl* S Glos CC (1955–*).

EP Cr 1964 from Almondsbury AP, Stoke Gifford AP.[20] Almond. RDn (1964–73), Horfield RDn (1973–*).

PAUNTLEY

AP *LG* Seq 7. Civ bdry: 1883.[333] *Parl* Seq 11. *Eccl* Seq 1.[363]

PEBWORTH

AP *LG* Kiftsg. Hd, Evesham PLU, RSD, Pebworth RD (1894–1931). Transf 1931 to Worcs.[30]

Parl E'rn Dv (1832–1918), Cirenc. & Tewk. Dv (1918–48), Worcs thereafter. *Eccl* Camp. RDn. Abol eccl 1964 to help cr Pebworth with Dorsington EP.[225]

PEBWORTH WITH DORSINGTON

EP Cr 1964 by union Pebworth AP, Dorsington AP.[225] Camp. RDn.

PILNING

EP Cr 1881 from Almondsbury AP, Henbury AP.[19] Bristol (Rural Dv) RDn (1881–87), Stap. RDn (1887–1927), Almond. RDn (1927–49), Clifton RDn (1949–73), W'bury & Severnside RDn (1973–*). Bdry: 1885.[288]

PILNING AND SEVERN BEACH

CP Renaming 1965 of Redwick and Northwick CP.[336] *LG* Thornb. RD. Bdry: 1966 (loses pt to Bristol CB and CP).[17] Transf 1974 to Avon.[4] *Parl* S Glos CC (1970–*).

PINNOCK AND HYDE

Tp in Didbrook AP, sep CP 1866.[9] *LG* Kiftsg. Hd, Winch. PLU, RSD, RD. Bdry: 1883.[150] Abol 1935 ent to Temple Guiting AP.[2] *Parl* E'rn Dv (1867–85), N'rn Dv (1885–1918), Cirenc. & Tewk. CC (1918–48).

PITCHCOMBE

AP *LG* Dudst. & K's Bart. Hd (Glouc. Bor and Co 1483–1672), Stroud PLU, RSD, RD. Civ bdry: 1884,[137] 1884.[337] *Parl* Seq 9. *Eccl* Seq 17. Eccl bdry: 1873,[140] 1932.[143]

PITTVILLE

EP Cr 1869 from Cheltenham AP.[160] Winch. South RDn (1869–87), Chelt. RDn (1887–*). Bdry: 1953 (help cr Lynworth EP).[318] Now called 'Cheltenham All Saints'.

POULTON

AP In Wilts (Highworth, Cricklade and Staple Hd) situated in Glos, transf to Glos 1832 for parl purposes, 1844 for civ purposes (Crowt. & Min. Hd).[21] *LG* Cirenc. PLU, RSD, RD. *Parl* Seq 1. *Eccl* Cricklade RDn (until 1887 [Sarum dioc until 1837]), Faiford RDn (1887–*).

PRESCOTT

Ex-par place, sep CP 1858.[58] *LG* Tewk. Hd, Winch. PLU, RSD, RD (1894–1935), Chelt. RD (1935–74). Civ bdry: 1883,[150] 1935.[2] *Parl* E'rn Dv (1867–85), N'rn Dv (1885–1918), Cirenc. & Tewk. Dv/CC (1918–*).

PRESTBURY

AP *LG* Prestbury Bor (status not sustained), Seq 12. Civ bdry: 1935.[2] *Parl* Seq 4. *Eccl* Seq 32. Eccl bdry: 1869 (help cr Pittville EP),[318] 195 (help cr Lynworth EP).[318]

PRESTON

AP *LG* Seq 11. *Parl* Seq 1. *Eccl* Sometimes as 'Preston All Saints', Seq 13.

PRESTON

AP *LG* Dudst. & K's Bart. Hd (Glouc. Bor and Co 1483–1672), Newent PLU, RSD, RD. Abol civ 1935 ent to Dymock AP.[2] *Parl* E'rn Dv (1832–1918), For. Dean Dv (1918–48). *Eccl* Sometimes as 'Preston St John the Baptist', Ross RDn (until 1836), For. RDn (1836–66), For. North RDn (1866–*).

PRESTON ON STOUR

AP *LG* Deerhurst Hd, Stratford on Avon PLU, RSD, Mar. Sic. RD (1894–1931). Transf 1931 to Warws.[251] *Parl* E'rn Dv (1832–1918), Cirenc. & Tewk. Dv (1918–48), Warws thereafter. *Eccl* Camp. RDn (until 1930s), Cov & Lichf dioc thereafter (see entry in Warws).

PRINKNASH PARK

Ex-par place, sep CP 1858.[58] *LG* Dudst. & K's Bart. Hd, Glouc. PLU, RSD, RD. Abol 1935 ent to Upton St Leonards AP.[2] *Parl* E'rn Dv (1867–85), N'rn Dv (1885–1918), Stroud Dv (1918–48).

PUCKLECHURCH

AP Incl chap Westerleigh (sep civ identity early, sep EP 1886[9]), chap Abson and area Wick (sep civ identity early as 'Wick and Abson', Wick made EP 1880[338] so this par eccl usually 'Pucklechurch and Abson', qv). *LG* Seq 26. Addtl civ bdry alt: 1885.[11] Transf 1974 to Avon.[4] *Parl* Seq 14.

PUCKLECHURCH AND ABSON

AP Usual eccl spelling; for civ and sep chaps, see prev entry. *Eccl* Hawk. RDn (until 1866), Hawk. South RDn (1866–87), Bitton RDn (1887–1949), Stap. RDn (1949–*).

QUEDGELEY

Chap in Gloucester St Owen AP, claimed independent status early, later treated as donative.[364] *LG* Pt Dudst. & K's Bart. Hd (pt Glouc. Bor and Co 1483–1672, pt Whits. Hd, Glouc. PLU, RSD, RD. Civ bdry: 1883,[3] 1885,[238] 1900,[42] 1935 (incl loses pt to Glouc. CB and CP),[2] 1951 (loses pt to Glouc. CB and CP),[46] 1954.[286] *Parl* E'rn Dv (1832–85), N'rn Dv (1885–1918), Stroud Dv (1918–48), Stroud & Thornb. CC (1948–55), Stroud CC (1955–*). Parl bdry: 1951.[401] *Eccl* Seq 20. Eccl bdry: 1967,[339] 1971 (help cr Gloucester St George EP).[266]

QUENINGTON

AP *LG* Seq 9. Civ bdry: 1935.[2] *Parl* Seq 1. *Eccl* Seq 16.

QUINTON

AP Incl hmlt Admington (sep CP 1866[9]). *LG* Kiftsg. Hd, Shipston on Stour PLU, RSD, Camp. RD (1894–1931). Transf 1931 to Warws.[251] *Parl* E'rn Dv (1832–1918), Cirenc. & Tewk. Dv (1918–48), Warws thereafter. *Eccl* Seq 11. Eccl bdry: 1930.[320]

RANDWICK

Chap in Standish AP, sep civ identity early, curates early, sep EP 1733.[365] *LG* Seq 38. Civ bdry: 1883,[3] 1885,[283] 1885,[65] 1886,[326] 1894.[347] *Parl* Seq 9. *Eccl* Glouc. RDn (until 1907), Bisley RDn (1907–*).

RANGEWORTHY

Chap in Thornbury AP, sep EP 1745,[145] sep CP 1866.[9] *LG* Thornb. Hd, PLU, RSD, RD. Transf 1974 to Avon.[4] *Parl* W'rn Dv (1867–85), S'rn Dv (1885–1918), Thornb. Dv (1918–48), Stroud & Thornb. CC (1948–55), S Glos CC (1955–*). *Eccl* Seq 21.

REDLAND
Chap in Westbury on Trym AP, sep CP 1894 (from the pt in Bristol CB),[242] sep EP 1925.[348] *LG* Bristol PLU, CB. Abol 1896 to help cr North Bristol CP.[89] *Eccl* Clifton RDn (1925–49), Almond. RDn (1959–73), Horfield RDn (1973–*). Bdrv: 1954.[125]

REDMARLEY D'ABITOT
AP In Worcs (see entry there), from 1894 in Unnamed RD administered by Newent RD Council until transf 1931 to Glos.[76] *LG* Newent RD. Civ bdry: 1965 (gains pt Eldersfield AP, exchanges pts with Pendock AP, both Worcs).[29] *Parl* Worcs until 1948, W Glos CC (1948–*). *Eccl* See entry in Worcs.

REDWICK AND NORTHWICK
Tg in Henbury AP, sep CP 1866.[9] *LG* Henbury Hd, Thornb. PLU, RSD, RD. Civ bdry: 1883,[3] 1935.[2] Renamed 1965 'Pilning and Severn Beach'.[336] *Parl* W'rn Dv (1867–85), S'rn Dv (1885–1918), Thornb. Dv (1918–48), Stroud & Thornb. CC (1948–55), S Glos CC (1955–70).

RENDCOMBE
AP *LG* Seq 28. Civ bdry: 1935.[2] *Parl* Seq 1. *Eccl* Seq 13.

GREAT RISSINGTON
AP *LG* Seq 33. *Parl* Seq 1. *Eccl* Seq 28.

LITTLE RISSINGTON
AP *LG* Seq 33. *Parl* Seq 1. *Eccl* Seq 28.

WICK RISSINGTON
AP Usual civ spelling; for eccl see following entry. *LG* Seq 33. *Parl* Seq 1.

WYCK RISSINGTON
AP Usual eccl spelling; for civ see prev entry. *Eccl* Seq 28.

ROCKHAMPTON
AP *LG* Pt Berk. Hd, pt Lang. & Swin. Hd, Thornb. PLU, RSD, RD. Civ bdry: 1885.[332] Transf 1974 to Avon.[4] *Parl* Seq 15. *Eccl* Durs. RDn (until 1907), Hawk. RDn (1907–*). Eccl bdry: 1956.[349]

RODBOROUGH
Chap in Minchinhampton AP, sep civ identity early, sep EP 1840.[22] *LG* Seq 24. Civ bdry: 1936.[69] *Parl* Seq 9. *Eccl* Stoneh. RDn (1840–66), Stoneh. South RDn (1866–87), Stoneh. RDn (1887–*).

RODMARTON
AP *LG* Longt. Hd, Cirenc. PLU, RSD, RD. Civ bdry: 1935.[2] *Parl* Seq 1. *Eccl* Seq 27.

ROEL
Ex-par place, sep CP 1858.[58] *LG* Kiftsg. Hd, Winch. PLU, RSD, RD. Abol 1935 ent to Hawling AP.[2] *Parl* E'rn Dv (1867–85), N'rn Dv (1885–1918), Cirenc. & Tewk. Dv (1918–48).

RUARDEAN
Chap in Walford AP (Hereford), sep civ identity early in Glos, sep EP 1842.[350] *LG* St Briav. Hd, Ross PLU, RSD, E Dean & United Pars RD (1894–1935), E Dean RD (1935–74). Civ bdry: 1935 (incl help cr Lydbrook CP),[2] 1957.[228] *Parl* Seq 11. *Eccl* For. RDn (1842–66), For. South RDn (1866–*). Eccl bdry: 1845 (help cr Bishop's Wood EP),[63] 1852 (help cr Lydbrook EP).[201]

RUDFORD
AP Incl hmlt Highleadon (sep CP 1866[9]). *LG* Pt Botloe Hd, pt Dudst. & K's Bart. Hd (pt Glouc. Bor and Co 1483–1672), Newent PLU, RSD, RD. Addtl civ bdry alt: 1883,[299] 1935.[2] *Parl* Pt E'rn Dv, pt W'rn Dv (1832–85), N'rn Dv (1885–1918), For. Dean Dv (1918–48), W Glos CC (1948–*). *Eccl* Seq 1.

RUSPIDGE
CP Cr 1953 from East Dean CP.[174] *LG* E Dean RD. *Parl* W Glos CC (1970–*).

ST BRIAVELS
Chap in Lydney AP, sep civ identity early, sep EP 1855.[296] *LG* St Briav. Bor (status not sustained), Seq 29. *Parl* Seq 11. *Eccl* For. RDn (1855–66), For. South RDn (1866–*). Eccl bdry: 1932 (gains ent ex-par places of St Briavels Castle, Bearse Common, Forest Fence and the Fence, Mocking Hazel Wood, pt Hudnalls with St Briavel's Common).[59]

ST BRIAVELS CASTLE
Eccl ex-par place, abol 1932 ent to St Briavels EP.[59]

ST NICHOLAS WITHOUT
CP Cr 1894 from the pt of Gloucester St Nicholas AP not in Glouc. CB.[242] *LG* Glouc. PLU, CB. Abol 1896 to help cr Gloucester CP.[256]

SAINTBURY
AP *LG* Seq 19. *Parl* Seq 1. *Eccl* Jurisd Blockley (until 1847), Camp. RDn (1847–*).

SALPERTON
AP Usual civ spelling; for eccl see following entry. *LG* Bradley Hd, N'leach PLU, RSD, RD. Abol civ 1935 ent to Hasleton AP.[2] *Parl* E'rn Dv (1832–1918), Cirenc. & Tewk. Dv (1918–48).

COLD SALPERTON
AP Usual eccl spelling; for civ see prev entry. *Eccl* Seq 29.

SANDHURST
AP *LG* Seq 15. Civ bdry: 1883,[3] 1885.[238] *Parl* Seq 8. *Eccl* Seq 19.

SAPPERTON
AP *LG* Seq 4. Civ bdry: 1883,[3] 1935.[2] *Parl* Seq 1. *Eccl* Sometimes as 'Sapperton with Frampton Mansell', Seq 25. Eccl bdry: 1932.[230]

SAUL
Prob orig sep AP, chap to Standish from 13th cent,[352] sep civ identity early, sep EP 1740.[145] *LG* Whits. Hd, Wheath. PLU, RSD. Abol civ 1884 pt to Standish AP, pt to Moreton Valence AP, pt to Fretherne AP and the last mentioned becomes 'Fretherne with Saul' CP.[233] *Parl* E'rn Dv (1832–85). *Eccl* Glouc. RDn. Abol eccl 1937 to help cr Saul with Whitminster EP.[351]

SAUL WITH FRETHERNE AND FRAMILODE
EP Cr 1961 when Whitminster severed from Saul with Fretherne, Framilode and Whitminster EP.[175] Glouc. South RDn.

SAUL WITH FRETHERNE, FRAMILODE AND WHITMINSTER
EP Cr 1950 by union Saul with Whitminster EP, Fretherne with Framilode EP.[259] Glouc. RDn (1950–52), Glouc. South RDn (1952–61). Abol 1961 when Whitminster becomes sep EP, the remainder reconstituted as Saul with Fretherne and Framilode EP.[175]

SAUL WITH WHITMINSTER
EP Cr 1937 by union Saul AP, Whitminster AP.[351] Glouc. RDn. Abol 1950 to help cr Saul with Fretherne, Framilode and Whitminster EP.[259]

SEA MILLS
EP Cr 1929 from Henbury AP.[289] Almond. RDn (1929–34), Clifton RDn (1934–73), W'bury & Severnside RDn (1973–*). Bdry: 1951.[366]

SELSEY
EP Cr 1863 from King's Stanley AP.[334] Stoneh. RDn (1863–66), Stoneh. South RDn (1866–87), Stoneh. RDn (1887–*).

SEVENHAMPTON
AP *LG* Seq 8. Civ bdry: 1935 (help cr Sudeley CP).[2] *Parl* Seq 1. *Eccl* Seq 32.

SEZINCOTE
AP Destroyed church, sep civ identity maintained, eccl deemed chap in Longborough hence the latter eccl 'Longborough with Sezincote', qv. *LG* Seq 21. *Parl* Seq 1.

SHEEPSCOMBE
EP Cr 1821 from Painswick AP.[334] Stoneh. RDn (1821–66), Stoneh. North RDn (1866–87), Bisley RDn (1887–*).

SHENINGTON
AP Glos par (Tewk. Hd) situated in Oxon, transf to Oxon 1832 for parl purposes, 1844 for civ purposes.[21] See entry in Oxon.

SHERBORNE
AP *LG* Seq 32. *Parl* Seq 1. *Eccl* Seq 14.

SHIPTON
CP Cr 1871 by union Shipton Oliffe AP, Shipton Sollars AP.[367] *LG* Bradley Hd, N'leach PLU, RSD, RD. Civ bdry: 1883,[53] 1956 (help cr Andoversford CP).[26] *Parl* E'rn Dv (1885–1918), Cirenc. & Tewk. Dv/CC (1918–*).

SHIPTON MOYNE
AP *LG* Seq 25. Civ bdry: 1935.[2] *Parl* E'rn Dv (1832–1918), Cirenc. & Tewk. Dv/CC (1918–55), Stroud CC (1955–*). *Eccl* Seq 27.

SHIPTON OLIFFE
AP *LG* Bradley Hd, N'leach PLU, RSD. Abol civ 1871 to help cr Shipton CP.[367] *Parl* E'rn Dv (1832–85). *Eccl* Winch. RDn (until 1836), N'leach RDn (1836–66), N'leach North RDn (1866–87), N'leach RDn (1887–*).

SHIPTON SOLLARS
AP *LG* Bradley Hd, N'leach PLU, RSD. Abol civ 1871 to help cr Shipton CP.[367] *Parl* E'rn Dv (1832–85). *Eccl* Seq 29.

SHIREHAMPTON
Chap and tg in Westbury on Trym AP, sep EP 1844,[368] sep CP 1866.[9] *LG* Henbury Hd, Bart. Reg. PLU (called 'Clifton' 1840s–80s), RSD, RD. Civ bdry: 1885,[290] 1896 (help cr North Bristol CP to be in Bristol CB),[89] 1901 (loses pt to Bristol CB and CP),[83] 1902 (loses pt to Bristol CB and CP).[84] Abol civ 1904 ent to Bristol CB and CP.[287] *Parl* W'rn Dv (1867–85), S'rn Dv (1885–1918). *Eccl* Bristol RDn (1844–66), Bristol (Rural Dv) RDn (1866–87), Stap. RDn (1887–1919), Clifton RDn (1919–73), W'bury & Severnside RDn (1973–*). Eccl bdry: 1917 (cr Avonmouth EP).[34]

SHURDINGTON
Chap in Badgeworth AP, sep civ identity early, all (except pt lost to Badgeworth AP) cr sep EP 1887.[37] Shurdington incl Up Hatherley (orig sep par, considered chap since 17th cent,[38] sep civ identity early, also EP 1887[37]). *LG* Seq 14. Addtl civ bdry alt: 1894.[39] *Parl* Seq 6. *Eccl* Chelt. RDn.

SIDDINGTON
AP *LG* Seq 11. *Parl* Seq 1. *Eccl* Seq 13.

SISTON
AP Usual civ spelling; for eccl see 'Syston'. *LG* Puck. Hd, Keynsham PLU, RSD, Warmley RD. Civ bdry: 1935.[2] Transf 1974 to Avon.[4] *Parl* W'rn Dv (1832–85), S'rn Dv (1885–1918), Thornb. Dv (1918–48), S Glos CC (1948–70), Kingswood CC (1970–*).

SLAD
EP Cr 1844 from Painswick AP.[362] Stoneh. RDn (1844–66), Stoneh. North RDn (1866–87), Bisley RDn (1887–*).

LOWER SLAUGHTER
Chap in Bourton on the Water AP, sep civ identity early, eccl independence much questioned, won by late 18th or early 19th cent.[382] *LG* Seq 33. *Parl* Seq 1. *Eccl* Stow RDn.

UPPER SLAUGHTER
AP *LG* Seq 33. Civ bdry: 1884,[370] 1935.[2] *Parl* Seq 1. *Eccl* Seq 28.

SLIMBRIDGE
AP *LG* Seq 1. Civ bdry: 1883,[3] 1883.[146] *Parl* Seq 12. *Eccl* Seq 32.

SNOWSHILL
Chap in Staunton AP, sep civ and eccl identity early. *LG* Seq 22. *Parl* Seq 4. *Eccl* Seq 12.

SODBURY
CP Cr 1946 by union Chipping Sodbury CP, Old Sodbury AP.[371] *LG* Sodb. RD. Transf 1974 to Avon.[4] *Parl* S Glos CC (1970–*).

CHIPPING SODBURY
Daughter church to Old Sodbury, sep civ identity early, sep EP 1831.[145] *LG* Grumb. Ash Hd, Chip. Sodb. Bor (status not sustained), Chip. Sodb. PLU, RSD, RD (1894–1935), Sodb. RD (1935–46). Abol civ 1946 to help cr Sodbury CP.[371] *Parl* W'rn Dv (1832–85), S'rn Dv (1885–1918), Thornb. Dv (1918–48). *Eccl* Hawk. RDn (1831–66), Hawk. North RDn (1866–87), Hawk. RDn (1887–*).

LITTLE SODBURY
AP *LG* Seq 16. Civ bdry: 1883.[3] Transf 1974 to Avon.[4] *Parl* Seq 14. *Eccl* Seq 21.

OLD SODBURY
AP Incl chap and bor Chipping Sodbury (bor status

not sustained, sep civ identity early, sep EP 1831[145]). *LG* Grumb. Ash Hd, Chip. Sodb. PLU, RSD, RD (1894–1935), Sodb. RD (1935–46). Abol civ 1946 to help cr Sodbury CP.[371] *Parl* W'rn Dv (1832–85), S'rn Dv (1885–1918), Thornb. Dv (1918–48). *Eccl* Seq 21.

SOUNDWELL
EP Cr 1924 from Downend EP, Mangotsfield AP, Kingswood EP.[227] Almond. RDn (1924–49), Stap. RDn (1949–73), Bitton RDn (1973–*).

SOUTHAM
CP Cr 1935 from Southam and Brockhampton CP.[2] *LG* Chelt. RD. *Parl* Cirenc. & Tewk. CC (1948–*).

SOUTHAM AND BROCKHAMPTON
Hmlt in Bishop's Cleeve AP, sep CP 1866.[9] *LG* Bishop's Cleeve Hd, Winch. PLU, RSD, RD. Abol 1935 pt to cr Southam CP, pt to Swindon AP.[2] *Parl* E'rn Dv (1867–85), N'rn Dv (1885–1918), Cirenc. & Tewk. Dv (1918–48).

SOUTHMEAD
EP Cr 1936 from Westbury on Trym AP.[372] Clifton RDn (1936–49), Stap. RDn (1949–73), W'bury & Severnside RDn (1973–*).

SOUTHROP
AP *LG* Seq 10. Civ bdry: 1883.[53] *Parl* Seq 1. *Eccl* Seq 16.

STANDISH
AP Incl chap Hardwicke (sep civ identity early, no sep eccl identity hence this par eccl 'Standish with Hardwicke', qv), chap Randwick (sep civ identity early, curates early, sep EP 1733[145]), chap Saul (prob orig sep AP, chap to Standish from 13th cent,[352] sep civ identity early, sep EP 1740[145]). *LG* Seq 39. Addtl civ bdry alt: 1883,[3] 1884,[403] 1885.[404] *Parl* Seq 7.

STANDISH WITH HARDWICKE
AP Usual eccl spelling; for civ and civ sep chaps, see prev entry. *Eccl* Seq 20. Addtl eccl bdry alt: 1855 (help cr Framilode EP),[27] 1932.[143]

KING'S STANLEY
AP *LG* King's Stanley Bor (status not sustained), Seq 38. Civ bdry: 1936,[69] 1959.[149] *Parl* Seq 9. *Eccl* Seq 26. Eccl bdry: 1863 (cr Selsey EP).[334]

LEONARD STANLEY
AP *LG* Seq 38. Civ bdry: 1884,[373] 1959.[149] *Parl* Pt Stroud Parl Bor, pt E'rn Dv (1832–85), Mid Dv (1885–1918), Stroud Dv (1918–48), Stroud & Thornb. CC (1948–55), Stroud CC (1955–*). *Eccl* Seq 26.

STANLEY PONTLARGE
Chap in Toddington AP, sep civ identity early, no sep eccl identity. *LG* Kiftsg. Hd, Winch. PLU, RSD, RD. Abol 1935 ent to Prescott CP.[2] *Parl* E'rn Dv (1832–85), N'rn Dv (1885–1918), Cirenc. & Tewk. Dv (1918–48).

STANTON
AP *LG* Seq 22. Civ bdry: 1883.[150] *Parl* Seq 4. *Eccl* Seq 12.

STANWAY
AP Incl chap Lower Lemington (until 16th cent, thereafter chap in Tewkesbury AP, sep civ identity early, eccl independence in doubt 16th-17th cent, later maintained as 'Lemington'[345]). *LG* Seq 35. Civ bdry: 1883,[150] 1935.[2] *Parl* Seq 4. *Eccl* Seq 12.

STAPLETON
AP *LG* Bart. Reg. Hd, PLU (called 'Clifton' 1840s–80s), Stap. USD, UD. Abol civ 1898 to help cr Bristol CP in Bristol CB.[90] *Parl* W'rn Dv(1832–85), Bristol Parl Bor, North Dv (1885–1918), S'rn Dv (1885–1918). *Eccl* Bristol RDn (until 1866), Bristol (Rural Dv) RDn (1866–87), Stap. RDn (1887–1927), E Bristol RDn (1927–49), Stap. RDn (1949–*). Eccl bdry: 1848 (help cr Easton St Mark EP),[114] 1869 (cr Fishponds EP),[246] 1961 (help cr Bristol St Mary Magdalene with St Francis, Lockleaze EP).[124]

STAUNTON
AP Incl chap Snowshill (sep civ and eccl identity early). *LG* Seq 30. *Parl* Seq 11. *Eccl* Irchingfield RDn (until 1836), For. RDn (1836–66), For. South RDn (1866–*).

STAUNTON
AP In Worcs, from 1894 in Unnamed RD administered by Newent RD Council, transf 1931 to Glos.[76] *LG* Newent RD. Civ bdry: 1965 (loses pt to Eldersfield AP, Worcs).[29] *Parl* Worcs until 1948, W Glos CC (1948–*). *Eccl* Worc dioc until 1952, Glouc. North RDn (1952–*).

STAVERTON
AP Chap in Deerhurst AP, sep par by 1297.[216] Incl chap Boddington (sep civ identity early, no sep eccl identity, hence this par eccl 'Staverton with Boddington', qv). *LG* Seq 12. Civ bdry: 1935.[2] *Parl* Seq 6.

STAVERTON WITH BODDINGTON
AP Usual eccl spelling; for civ and civ sep chap, see prev entry. *Eccl* Winch. RDn (until 1866), Winch. North RDn (1866–1907), Chelt. RDn (1907–*). Eccl bdry: 1933,[41] 1963.[374]

STINCHCOMBE
AP *LG* Seq 1. Civ bdry: 1883,[3] 1883,[328] 1884,[375] 1935.[2] *Parl* Seq 12. *Eccl* Seq 32. Eccl bdry: 1888 (help cr Lower Cam EP).[148]

STOKE BISHOP
EP Cr 1859 from Westbury on Trym AP.[239] Bristol RDn (1860–66), Bristol (Rural Dv) RDn (1866–87), Stap. RDn (1887–1919), Clifton RDn (1919–73), W'bury & Severnside RDn (1973–*).

STOKE GIFFORD
AP *LG* Henbury Hd, Bart. Reg. PLU (1836–1904, called 'Clifton' 1840s–80s), RSD, RD (1894–1904), Chip. Sodb. PLU (1904–30), RD (1904–35), Sodb. RD (1935–74). Civ bdry: 1885,[243] 1935 (gains pt Bristol CB and CP),[2] 1951,[244] 1966 (loses pt to Bristol CB and CP).[17] Transf 1974 to Avon.[4] *Parl* W'rn Dv (1832–85), S'rn Dv (1885–1918), Thornb. Dv (1918–48), Stroud & Thornb. CC (1948–55), S Glos CC (1955–*). *Eccl* Seq 8. Eccl bdry: 1964 (help cr Patchway EP).[20]

STOKE ORCHARD
Hmlt in Bishop's Cleeve AP, sep CP 1866,[9] eccl

severed 1953 to help cr Tredington with Stoke Orchard and Hardwicke EP.[178] *LG* Orig in Tewk. Hd, later Bishop's Cleeve Hd, Tewk. PLU, RSD, RD (1894–1935), Chelt. RD (1935–74). Addtl civ bdry alt: 1935,[2] 1951.[180] *Parl* E'rn Dv (1867–85), N'rn Dv (1885–1918), Cirenc. & Tewk. Dv/CC (1918–*).

STONEHOUSE
AP *LG* Seq 38. Civ bdry: 1883,[3] 1884,[285] 1884,[376] 1885,[65] 1894,[347] 1935.[2] *Parl* Stroud Parl Bor (1832–85), Mid Dv (1885–1918), Stroud Dv (1918–48), Stroud & Thornb. CC (1948–55), Stroud CC (1955–*). *Eccl* Seq 26. Eccl bdry: 1838 (cr Cainscross EP).[144]

STOW-ON-THE-WOLD
AP Incl hmlt Donnington, hmlt Maugersbury (each sep CP 1866,[9] neither with sep eccl identity). *LG* Stow on the Wold Bor (status not sustained), Slaugh. Hd, Stow on the Wold PLU, USD, UD (1894–1935), N Cotsw. RD (1935–74). Addtl civ bdry alt: 1894 (gains the pt of Maugersbury CP in the USD),[322] 1935,[2] 1939.[323] *Parl* Seq 1. *Eccl* Seq 28. Eccl bdry: 1927,[327] 1927,[317] 1937.[8]

STOWELL
AP *LG* Bradley Hd, N'leach PLU, RSD, RD. Abol civ 1935 ent to Yanworth CP.[2] *Parl* E'rn Dv (1832–1918), Cirenc. & Tewk. Dv (1918–48). *Eccl* Cirenc. RDn. Abol eccl 1660 to help cr Hampnett with Stowell EP.[284]

STRATTON
AP *LG* Crowt. & Min. Hd, Cirenc. PLU, RSD, RD. Abol civ 1935 pt to Cirencester AP, pt to Baunton AP, pt to Daglingworth AP.[2] *Parl* E'rn Dv (1832–67), Cirenc. Parl Bor (1867–85), E'rn Dv (1885–1918), Cirenc. & Tewk. Dv (1918–48). *Eccl* Seq 13.

STROUD
Chap in Bisley AP,[369] sep civ identity early, sep EP 1723.[145] Incl chap Whiteshill (sep EP 1844,[378] sep CP 1894[379]). *LG* Bisley Hd, Stroud PLU, pt Stroud USD, pt Stroud RSD, Stroud UD. Addtl civ bdry alt: 1883,[3] 1884,[376] 1900,[347] 1935,[2] 1936.[69] *Parl* Seq 9. *Eccl* Stoneh. RDn (1723–66), Stoneh. North RDn (1866–87), Bisley RDn (1887–*). Addtl eccl bdry alt: 1879 (cr Stroud Holy Trinity EP).[380]

STROUD HOLY TRINITY
EP Cr 1879 from Stroud EP.[380] Stoneh. North RDn (1879–87), Bisley RDn (1887–*). Bdry: 1973.[81]

SUDELEY
CP Cr 1935 by union Charlton Abbots AP, Sudeley Manor AP, pt Sevenhampton AP.[2] *LG* Chelt. RD. *Parl* Cirenc. & Tewk. CC (1948–*).

SUDELEY MANOR
AP *LG* Kiftsg. Hd, Winch. PLU, RSD, RD. Civ bdry: 1883.[3] Abol civ 1935 to help cr Sudeley CP.[2] *Parl* E'rn Dv (1832–85), N'rn Dv (1885–1918), Cirenc. & Tewk. Dv (1918–48). *Eccl* Winch. RDn (until 1866), Winch. North RDn (1866–87), Winch. RDn (1887–1931). Abol eccl 1931 to help cr Winchcombe with Gretton and Sudeley Manor EP.[381]

SUTTON-UNDER-BRAILES
AP Glos par (W'minst. Hd) situated in Warws, transf to Warws 1832 for parl purposes, 1844 for civ purposes.[21] See entry in Warws. *Eccl* Stow RDn (until 1919), Cov & Lichf dioc thereafter (see entry in Warws).

SWELL
CP Cr 1935 by union pt Upper Swell AP, pt Lower Swell AP.[2] *LG* N Cotsw. RD. *Parl* Cirenc. & Tewk. CC (1948–*).

LOWER SWELL
AP *LG* Slaugh. Hd, Stow on the Wold PLU, RSD, RD. Abol civ 1935 pt to Stow on the Wold AP, pt to help cr Swell CP.[2] *Parl* E'rn Dv (1832–1918), Cirenc. & Tewk. Dv (1918–48). *Eccl* Sometimes as 'Nether Swell', Seq 28. Eccl bdry: 1973.[8]

UPPER SWELL
AP *LG* Kiftsg. Hd, Stow on the Wold PLU, RSD, RD. Abol civ 1935 pt to Stow on the Wold AP, pt to help cr Swell CP.[2] *Parl* E'rn Dv (1832–1918), Cirenc. & Tewk. Dv (1918–48). *Eccl* Seq 28. Eccl bdry: 1927,[377] 1973.[8]

SWINDON
AP *LG* Chelt. Hd, PLU, RSD, RD. Civ bdry: 1935,[2] 1950.[180] *Parl* Seq 4. *Eccl* Seq 32.

SYDE
AP *LG* Seq 28. *Parl* Seq 1. *Eccl* Stoneh. RDn (until 1866), Stoneh. North RDn (1866–87), Bisley RDn (1887–1907), Cirenc. RDn (1907–72). Abol eccl 1972 to help cr Brimpsfield and Syde EP.[80]

SYSTON
AP Usual eccl spelling; for civ see 'Siston'. *Eccl* Seq 22. Eccl bdry: 1851 (help cr Warmley EP).[73]

TAYNTON
AP *LG* Seq 7. *Parl* Seq 11. *Eccl* Seq 1.

TEDDINGTON
AP In Worcs, since 1894 in Tewk. RD although remains in Worcs, transf 1931 to Glos.[76] *LG* Tewk. RD (1931–35), Chelt. RD (1935–74). Civ bdry: 1935,[2] 1965 (exchanges pts with Beckford AP, Worcs).[29] *Parl* Worcs until 1948, Cirenc. & Tewk. CC (1948–*). *Eccl* See entry in Worcs.

TETBURY
AP *LG* Tetb. Bor (status not sustained), Longt. Hd, Tetb. PLU, RSD, pt Tetb. USD, pt Tetb. RSD, Tetb. UD (1894–1935), Tetb. RD (1935–74). Civ bdry: 1894 (the pt not in the USD cr Tetbury Upton CP),[383] 1955.[384] *Parl* Seq 2. *Eccl* Seq 27.

TETBURY UPTON
CP Cr 1894 from the pt of Tetbury AP not in Tetb. USD.[383] *LG* Tetb. PLU, RD. Bdry: 1935,[2] 1955.[384] *Parl* Cirenc. & Tewk. Dv/CC (1918–55), Stroud CC (1955–*).

TEWKESBURY
AP Incl chap Tredington (sep par from 12th cent[385]), chap Lower Lemington (orig chap in Stanway AP, chap in Tewkesbury by 16th cent,

sep civ identity early, eccl independence in doubt 16th-17th cent, later maintained[345]), chap Walton Cardiff (sep par late 17th cent[386]), chap Oxenton (sep civ identity early, sep EP 1746[145]). *LG* Tewk. Hd, Bor/MB, PLU, USD. Addtl civ bdry alt: 1935,[2] 1965 (gains pt Bredon AP, Worcs).[29] *Parl* Tewk. Parl Bor (pt 1604–1832, ent 1832–85), N'rn Dv (1885–1918), Cirenc. & Tewk. Dv/CC (1918–*). *Eccl* Seq 31. Addtl eccl bdry alt: 1848 (cr Tewkesbury Holy Trinity EP),[387] 1964.[388]

TEWKESBURY HOLY TRINITY
EP Cr 1848 and refounded 1893 from Tewkesbury AP.[387] Winch. RDn (1893–1901), Tewk. RDn (1901–*).

THORNBURY
AP Incl chap Oldbury upon Severn (sep EP 1863,[329] sep CP 1894[330]), chap Rangeworthy (sep EP 1745,[145] sep CP 1866[9]), chap Falfield (sep EP 1863,[241] sep CP 1894[330]). *LG* Thornb. Hd, PLU, Bor (status not sustained), RSD, RD. Addtl civ bdry alt: 1885.[332] Transf 1974 to Avon.[4] *Parl* W'rn Dv (1832–85), S'rn Dv (1885–1918), Thornb. Dv (1918–48), Stroud & Thornb. CC (1948–55), S Glos CC (1955–*). *Eccl* Durs. RDn (until 1907), Hawk. RDn (1907–*).

THRUPP
CP Cr 1894 from Stroud CP.[379] *LG* Stroud PLU, RD. Bdry: 1936.[69] *Parl* Stoud Dv (1918–48), Stroud & Thornb. CC (1948–55), Stroud CC (1955–*).

TIBBERTON
AP *LG* Duchy Lanc. Hd, Newent PLU, RSD, RD. *Parl* Seq 11. *Eccl* Seq 1.

TIDENHAM
AP *LG* Seq 36. Civ bdry: 1935.[2] *Parl* Seq 11. *Eccl* For. RDn (until 1866), For. South RDn (1866–1932). Eccl bdry: 1850 (cr Beachley EP).[57] Abol eccl 1932 to help cr Tidenham with Lancaut EP.[200]

TIDENHAM WITH LANCAUT
EP Cr 1932 by union Tidenham AP, Lancaut chap of Woolaston AP.[200] For. South RDn.

TIRLEY
AP Chap in Deerhurst AP, sep par by 1316.[217] *LG* Pt Deerhurst Hd, pt W'minst. Hd, Tewk. PLU, RSD, RD. *Parl* Seq 5. *Eccl* Seq 31.

TODDINGTON
AP Incl chap Stanley Portlarge (sep civ identity early, no sep eccl identity hence this par eccl 'Toddington with Stanley Portlarge', qv). *LG* Seq 22. Civ bdry: 1883,[150] 1935,[2] 1957.[12] *Parl* Seq 4.

TODDINGTON WITH STANLEY PORTLARGE
AP Usual eccl spelling; for civ and civ sep chap, see prev entry. *Eccl* Seq 12.

TODENHAM
AP *LG* Seq 37. *Parl* Seq 1. *Eccl* Camp. RDn (until 1907), Stow RDn (1907–34). Abol eccl 1934 to help cr Todenham with Lower Lemington EP.[314]

TODENHAM WITH LOWER LEMINGTON
EP Cr 1928 by union Todenham AP, Lemington EP.[314] Stow RDn.

TORMARTON
AP Incl chap Acton Turville (orig sep AP, united 1344 to Tormarton,[5] sep civ identity early, sep EP 1870[6]), chap West Littleton (sep civ identity early, no sep eccl identity). *LG* Seq 16. Civ bdry: 1935.[2] Transf 1974 to Avon.[4] *Parl* Seq 14. *Eccl* Hawk. RDn (until 1866), Hawk. South RDn (1866–97), Bitton RDn (1897–1949), Chippenham RDn (1949–73), Bitton RDn (1973–*).

TORTWORTH
AP *LG* Seq 18. Transf 1974 to Avon.[4] *Parl* W'rn Dv (1832–85), Mid Dv (1885–1918), Thornb. Dv (1918–48), Stroud & Thornb. CC (1948–55), S Glos CC (1955–*). *Eccl* Seq 21.

TREDINGTON
AP Chap in Tewkesbury AP, sep par from 12th cent.[385] *LG* Tewk. Hd, PLU, RSD, RD. Abol civ 1935 pt to Tewkesbury AP, pt to Stoke Orchard CP.[2] *Parl* E'rn Dv (1832–85), N'rn Dv (1885–1918), Cirenc. & Tewk. Dv (1918–48). *Eccl* Winch. RDn (until 1866), Winch. North RDn (1866–87), Winch. RDn (1887–1901), Tewk. RDn (1901–53). Abol eccl 1953 to help cr Tredington with Stoke Orchard and Hardwicke EP.[239]

TREDINGTON WITH STOKE ORCHARD AND HARDWICKE
EP Cr 1953 by union Tredington AP, Stoke Orchard chap in Bishop's Cleeve AP, Elmstone Hardwicke with Uckington AP.[178] Tewk. RDn.

TUFFLEY
Hmlt in Gloucester St Mary de Lode AP, sep CP 1866,[9] sep EP 1930 from Gloucester St Paul EP, Hempsted AP, Matson AP.[275] *LG* Dudst. & K's Bart. Hd, Glouc. PLU, RSD, RD. Abol civ 1900 pt to Gloucester CB and CP, pt to Quedgeley AP, pt to Whaddon AP.[42] *Parl* E'rn Dv (1867–85), N'rn Dv (1885–1918). *Eccl* Glouc. RDn (1930–52), Glouc. City RDn (1952–*). Bdry: 1876,[389] 1885,[142] 1967,[339] 1971 (help cr Gloucester St George EP).[266] This par commonly called 'Gloucester St Barnabas'.

TURKDEAN
AP Sometimes Aldsworth accounted chap in this par but seems to have had independent status. *LG* Seq 8. *Parl* Seq 1. *Eccl* Seq 29.

TWIGWORTH
Hmlt in Gloucester St Mary de Lode AP, sep CP 1866,[9] sep EP 1844 from Gloucester St Mary de Lode AP, Gloucester St Catherine AP.[271] *LG* Dudst. & K's Bart. Hd, Glouc. PLU, RSD, RD. Civ bdry: 1883,[3] 1885.[238] *Parl* E'rn Dv (1867–85), N'rn Dv (1885–1918), Stroud Dv (1918–48), W Glos CC (1948–*). *Eccl* Glouc. RDn (1844–1952), Glouc. North RDn (1952–*). Eccl bdry: 1932 (help cr Wootton St Mary Without EP).[48]

TWO MILE HILL
EP Cr 1845 from Bristol St George EP.[113] Bristol

RDn (1845–66), Bristol (Rural Dv) RDn (1866–87), Stap. RDn (1887–1901), E Bristol RDn (1901–49), Bitton RDn (1949–*). Bdry: 1905 (help cr Bristol St Aidan EP).[102]

TWYNING

AP *LG* Kiftsg. Hd, Tewk. PLU, RSD, RD (1894–1935), Chelt. RD (1935–74). *Parl* Seq 4. *Eccl* Seq 31.

TYNDALL'S PARK

EP Cr 1874 from Westbury-on-Trym AP, Bristol St Michael and All Angels AP.[397] Bristol (Rural Dv) RDn (1874–87), Bristol RDn (1887–1901), Clifton RDn (1901–62). Bdry: 1877.[189] Abol 1962 to help cr Clifton All Saints with Tyndall's Park EP.[193]

TYTHERINGTON

AP *LG* Pt Henbury Hd, pt Thornb. Hd, Thornb. PLU, RSD, RD. Civ bdry: 1935.[2] Transf 1974 to Avon.[4] *Parl* Seq 15. *Eccl* Seq 21.

UCKINGTON

Hmlt in Elmstone Hardwicke AP, sep CP 1866.[9] *LG* Deerhurst Hd, Chelt. PLU, RSD, RD. *Parl* E'rn Dv (1867–85), N'rn Dv (1885–1918), Cirenc. & Tewk. Dv/CC (1918–*).

ULEY

AP *LG* Seq 1. Civ bdry: 1883,[3] 1883,[231] 1883.[146] *Parl* Seq 12. *Eccl* Seq 32.

UPLANDS

CP Cr 1894 from the pt of Painswick AP in Stroud USD.[379] *LG* Stroud PLU, UD. Abol 1936 ent to Stroud CP.[69] *Parl* Stroud Dv (1918–48).

UPLEADON

AP *LG* Seq 7. *Parl* Seq 11. *Eccl* Seq 1.

UPTON ST LEONARDS

Chap in Gloucester St Mary de Lode AP, sep civ identity early, sep EP 1781.[145] *LG* Seq 15. Civ bdry: 1883,[3] 1885,[238] 1900 (loses pt to Glouc. CB and CP),[42] 1935 (incl loses pt to Glouc. CB and CP),[2] 1957 (loses pt to Glouc. CB and CP),[260] 1966 (incl loses pt to Glouc. CB and CP).[44] *Parl* E'rn Dv (ent 1832–67, pt 1867–85), pt Glouc. Parl Bor (1867–85), N'rn Dv (1885–1918), Stroud Dv (1918–48), Stroud & Thornb.CC (1948–55), Stroud CC (1955–*). Parl bdry: 1960.[402] *Eccl* Glouc. RDn (1781–1952), Glouc. North RDn (1952–*). Eccl bdry: 1842 (help cr Gloucester St James EP),[269] 1868 (help cr Gloucester St Luke EP),[264] 1892.[321]

VINEY HILL

EP Cr 1866 from Dean Forest St Paul EP.[212] For. South RDn.

WALFORD

AP In Hereford, incl chap Ruardean (sep civ identity early in Glos, sep EP 1842[350]). See main entry in Hereford.

WALTON CARDIFF

Chap in Tewkesbury AP, sep par from late 17th cent.[386] *LG* Seq 34. Civ bdry: 1935.[2] *Parl* Seq 4. *Eccl* Seq 31.

WAPLEY AND CODRINGTON

AP Usual civ spelling; for eccl see following entry. *LG* Grumb. Ash Hd, Chip. Sodb. PLU, RSD, RD. Abol civ 1935 ent to Dodington AP.[2] *Parl* W'rn Dv (1832–85), S'rn Dv (1885–1918), Thornb. Dv (1918–48).

WAPLEY WITH CODRINGTON

AP Usual eccl spelling; for civ see prev entry. *Eccl* Hawk. RDn (until 1866), Hawk. South RDn (1866–87), Bitton RDn (1887–1949), Stap. RDn (1949–53). Abol eccl 1953 to help cr Wapley with Codrington and Dodington EP.[224]

WAPLEY WITH CODRINGTON AND DODINGTON

EP Cr 1953 by union Dodington AP, Wapley with Codrington AP.[224] Stap. RDn.

WARMLEY

EP Cr 1851 from Syston AP, Bitton AP, Kingswood EP.[73] Hawk. RDn (1851–66), Hawk. South RDn (1866–87), Bitton RDn (1887–*).

GREAT WASHBOURNE

AP *LG* Tewk. Hd, Winch. PLU, RSD, RD. Abol civ 1935 ent to Dumbleton AP.[2] *Parl* E'rn Dv (1832–85), N'rn Dv (1885–1918), Cirenc. & Tewk. Dv (1918–48). *Eccl* Seq 12.

LITTLE WASHBOURNE

Hmlt in Overbury AP (Worcs), the hmlt transf to Glos 1832 for parl purposes, 1844 for civ purposes,[21] sep CP 1866.[9] *LG* Kiftsg. Hd, Winch. PLU, RSD, RD. Abol 1935 ent to Dumbleton AP.[2] *Parl* E'rn Dv (1867–85), N'rn Dv (1885–1918), Cirenc. & Tewk. Dv/CC (1918–*).

THE WEIR

EP Cr 1846 from Bristol St Paul AP, Bristol St Peter AP, Bristol St Philip and St Jacob EP.[398] Bristol RDn (1846–66), Bristol (City Dv) RDn (1866–87), Bristol RDn (1887–1901), Bristol City RDn (1901–42). Abol eccl 1942 to help cr Bristol St Jude with St Matthias EP.[122]

WELFORD

AP Pt Glos (Deerhurst Hd), pt Warws (Barlichway Hd), the latter transf to Glos in the 1880s.[391] *LG* Stratford on Avon PLU, RSD, Marst. Sic. RD (1894–1931). Transf 1931 to Warws.[251] *Parl* Glos pt, E'rn Dv (1832–1918), Cirenc. & Tewk. Dv (1918–48), Warws thereafter. *Eccl* Seq 11.

WESTBURY-ON-SEVERN

AP Incl chaps Newnham, Minsterworth (each sep par by 1309[358]). *LG* Pt Duchy Lanc. Hd, pt W'bury Hd, W'bury on Severn PLU, USD (ent 1875–83, pt 1883–94), UD. Civ bdry: 1883,[3] 1883,[315] 1894 (made ent UD and gains the pt of Littledean AP in the USD).[402] *Parl* Seq 11. *Eccl* Seq 1.

WESTBURY-ON-TRYM

AP Incl chap Redland (sep CP 1894 [the pt in Bristol CB][242] sep EP 1925[348]), tg Shirehampton (sep CP 1844,[368] sep CP 1866[9]). *LG* Henbury Hd, Bart. Reg. PLU (called 'Clifton' 1840s–80s), pt Bristol MB/CB (1880s–94), pt Bristol USD, pt Bart. Reg. RSD, Bart. Reg. RD. Addtl civ bdry alt: 1883,[3] 1885,[290] 1885.[243] Abol civ 1904 ent to Bristol CB and CP.[287] *Parl* W'rn Dv (1832–85), S'rn Dv (1885–1918), *Eccl* Bristol RDn (until 1866), Bristol (Rural

Dv) RDn (1866–87), Stap. RDn (1887–1901), Clifton RDn (1901–73), W'bury & Severnside RDn (1973–*). Addtl eccl bdry alt: 1841 (help cr King's Parade EP [now called 'Clifton St John the Evangelist']),[295] 1850 (help cr Kingsdown St Matthew EP),[118] 1859 (help cr Stoke Bishop EP),[239] 1874 (help cr Tyndall's Park EP),[397] 1877,[189] 1913 (cr Westbury-on-Trym St Alban EP [now called 'Westbury Park']),[392] 1926 (cr Henleaze EP),[295] 1936 (cr Southmead EP),[372] 1951,[366] 1962 (incl help cr Lawrence Weston EP).[292]

WESTBURY-ON-TRYM ST ALBAN
EP Cr 1913 from Westbury-on-Trym AP.[392] Clifton RDn. Now commonly called 'Westbury Park'.

WESTBURY PARK–See prev entry.

WESTCOTE
AP *LG* Seq 33. *Parl* Seq 1. *Eccl* Seq 28.

WESTERLEIGH
Chap in Pucklechurch AP, sep civ identity early, sep EP 1886.[394] *LG* Seq 26. Civ bdry: 1885,[393] 1885,[11] 1935.[2] Transf 1974 to Avon.[4] *Parl* Seq 14. *Eccl* Hawk. South RDn (1886–87), Bitton RDn (1887–1949), Stap. RDn (1949–*). Eccl bdry: 1845 (when still chap, cr Coalpit Heath EP).[201]

WESTON-ON-AVON
AP Pt Glos (Kiftsg. Hd), pt Warws (Barlichway Hd), the latter transf to Glos in 1880s.[395] *LG* Stratford on Avon PLU, RSD, Marst. Sic. RD (1894–1931). Transf 1931 to Warws.[251] *Parl* Glos pt, E'rn Dv (1832–1918), Cirenc. & Tewk. Dv (1918–48), Warws thereafter. *Eccl* Sometimes as 'Weston', Seq 11. Eccl bdry: 1928.[183]

WESTON-SUB-EDGE
AP Usual eccl spelling; for civ see 'Weston Subedge'. *Eccl* Camp. RDn. Abol eccl 1930 to help cr Weston-sub-Edge with Aston-sub-Edge EP.[32]

WESTON-SUB-EDGE WITH ASTON-SUB-EDGE
EP Cr 1930 by union Weston-sub-Edge AP, Aston-sub-Edge AP.[32] Camp. RDn.

WESTON SUBEDGE
AP Usual civ spelling; for eccl see 'Weston-sub-Edge'. *LG* Seq 19. Civ bdry: 1965 (exchanges pts with Honeybourne AP, Worcs).[29] *Parl* Seq 1.

WESTONBIRT
AP Gains civ Lasborough AP (depopulated late 14th cent) by mid 17th cent, the civ union usually called 'Westonbirt' but sometimes 'Westonbirt with Lasborough', eccl remains distinct.[344] *LG* Seq 25. Civ bdry: 1935,[2] 1966 (exchanges pts with Sherston AP, Wilts).[72] *Parl* Seq 2. *Eccl* Seq 25.

WESTONBIRT WITH LASBOROUGH–See prev entry

WHADDON
AP *LG* Dudst. & K's Bart. Hd (Glouc. Bor. and Co. 1483–1672), Glouc. PLU, RSD, RD. Civ bdry: 1883,[3] 1885,[238] 1900.[42] Abol civ 1935 pt to Glouc. CB and CP, pt to Brockthorpe AP.[2] *Parl* E'rn Dv (1832–85), N'rn Dv (1885–1918), Stroud Dv (1918–48). *Eccl* Seq 20. Eccl bdry: 1873,[146] 1876,[389] 1932,[143] 1967,[339] 1971 (help cr Gloucester St George EP).[266]

WHEATENHURST
AP Usual civ name until renamed 1945 'Whitminster'[396]; for civ after 1945 and eccl see 'Whitminster'. *LG* Whits. Hd, Wheath. PLU, RSD, RD (1894–1935), Glouc. RD (1935–45). *Parl* E'rn Dv (1832–85), N'rn Dv (1885–1918), Stroud Dv (1918–48).

WHITESHILL
Chap in Stroud CP/EP, sep EP 1844,[378] sep CP 1894.[379] *LG* Stroud PLU, RD. Bdry: 1935,[2] 1936.[269] *Parl* Stroud Dv (1918–48), Stroud & Thornb. CC (1948–55), Stroud CC (1955–*). *Eccl* Stoneh. RDn (1844–66), Stoneh. North RDn (1866–87), Bisley RDn (1887–*).

WHITMINSTER
AP Usual eccl spelling, civ spelling from 1945 when 'Wheatenhurst' renamed Whitminster[396]; for civ before 1945 see the former. *LG* Glouc. RD. *Parl* Stroud & Thornb. CC (1948–55), Stroud CC (1955–*). *Eccl* Glouc. RDn. Abol 1937 to help cr Saul with Whitminster EP.[351]
EP Cr 1961 when Saul with Fretherne, Framilode and Whitminster EP divided into 2 EPs of Whitminster, Saul with Fretherne and Framilode.[175] Glouc. South RDn.

WHITTINGTON
AP *LG* Seq 8. Civ bdry: 1956 (help cr Andoversford CP).[26] *Parl* Seq 1. *Eccl* Seq 32.

WICK–See following entry

WICK AND ABSON
Chap in Pucklechurch AP, sep civ identity early as 'Wick and Abson', pt made sep EP 1880 as 'Wick' EP,[338] so that the mother par usually 'Pucklechurch and Abson', qv. *LG* Puck. Hd, Chip. Sodb. PLU, RSD, RD (1894–1935), Sodb. RD (1935–74). Civ bdry: 1885,[11] 1935.[2] Transf 1974 to Avon.[4] *Parl* Seq 14. *Eccl* As 'Wick', Hawk. South RDn (1880–87), Bitton RDn (1887–*).

WICKWAR
AP *LG* Wickwar Bor (status not sustained), Seq 16. Civ bdry: 1935.[2] Transf 1974 to Avon.[4] *Parl* Seq 14. *Eccl* Seq 21.

WIDFORD
AP In Glos (Slaugh. Hd) situated in Oxon, transf to Oxon 1832 for parl purposes, 1844 for civ purposes.[21] See entry in Oxon.

WILLERSEY
AP *LG* Kiftsg. Hd, Evesham PLU, RSD, Pebworth RD (1894–1931), Camp. RD (1931–35), N Cotsw. RD (1935–74). Civ bdry: 1965 (loses pt to Broadway AP, Worcs).[29] *Parl* Seq 1. *Eccl* Seq 11.

WINCHCOMBE
AP Usual civ spelling; for eccl see following entry. *LG* Winchcombe Bor (status not sustained), Seq 22. Civ bdry: 1883,[3] 1883,[150] 1935.[2] *Parl* Seq 4.

WINCHCOMBE WITH GRETTON
AP Usual eccl spelling; for civ see prev entry. *Eccl* Winch. RDn (until 1866), Winch. North RDn (1866–87), Winch. RDn (1887–1931). Abol eccl 1931 to help cr Winchcombe with Gretton and Sudeley Manor EP.[381]

WINCHCOMBE WITH GRETTON AND SUDELEY MANOR
EP Cr 1931 by union Winchcombe with Gretton AP, Sudeley Manor AP.[381] Winch. RDn.

WINDRUSH
AP Chap in Great Barrington AP (Glos, Berks), sep par in Glos in 14th cent.[50] *LG* Seq 32. *Parl* Seq 1. *Eccl* Stow RDn (until 1836), N'leach RDn (1836–66), N'leach South RDn (1866–87), N'leach RDn (1887–*).

WINSON
Chap in Bibury AP, sep CP 1866.[9] *LG* Bradley Hd, N'leach PLU, RSD, RD. *Parl* E'rn Dv (1867–1918), Cirenc. & Tewk. Dv/CC (1918–*).

WINSTONE
AP *LG* Bisley Hd, Cirenc. PLU, RSD, RD. *Parl* Seq 1. *Eccl* Seq 25.

WINTERBOURNE
AP *LG* Lang. & Sein. Hd, Bart. Reg. (called 'Clifton' 1840s–80s) PLU (1836–1904), RSD, RD (1894–1904), Chip. Sodb. PLU (1904–30), RD (1904–35), Sodb. RD (1935–74). Civ bdry: 1883,[3] 1885,[393] 1935,[244] 1935 (incl loses pt to Bristol CB and CP),[2] 1966 (exchanges pts with Bristol CB and CP).[17] Transf 1974 to Avon.[4] *Parl* Seq 1. *Eccl* Seq 9. Eccl bdry: 1836 (cr Frenchay EP),[253] 1861 (help cr Winterbourne Down EP),[254] 1942.[202]

WINTERBOURNE DOWN
EP Cr 1861 from Winterboune AP, Frenchay EP.[254] Bristol RDn (1861–66), Bristol (Rural Dv) RDn (1866–87), Stap. RDn (1887–1927), Almond. RDn (1927–49), Stap. RDn (1949–*). Bdry: 1942.[202]

GREAT WITCOMBE
AP *LG* Seq 14. *Parl* Seq 6. *Eccl* Pec jurisd St Oswald (1837–1952), Glouc. North RDn (1952–*). Eccl bdry: 1928.[79]

WITHINGTON
AP *LG* Seq 8. Civ bdry: 1883,[53] 1956 (help cr Andoversford CP).[26] *Parl* Seq 1. *Eccl* Winch. RDn (until 1866), Winch. South RDn (1866–87), Chelt. RDn (1887–1948), N'leach RDn (1948–*).

WOODCHESTER
AP *LG* Seq 24. *Parl* Seq 9. *Eccl* Seq 26.

WOODMANCOTE
Hmlt in Bishop's Cleeve Hd, sep CP 1866.[9] *LG* Bishop's Cleeve Hd, Winch. PLU, RSD, RD (1894–1935), Chelt. RD (1935–74). Civ bdry: 1953.[181] *Parl* E'rn Dv (1867–85), N'rn Dv (1885–1918), Cirenc. & Tewk. Dv/CC (1918–*).

WOODSIDE
EP Cr 1880 from Flaxley AP, Newland AP, Cinderford EP, Dean Forest Holy Trinity EP, ent expar Hinders Lane and Dockham.[175] For. South RDn.

WOOLASTON
AP Incl chap Alvington (sep civ identity early, no sep eccl identity hence this par eccl 'Woolaston with Alvington', qv), chap Lancaut (attached to this par 1711,[343] severed 1932 to help cr Tidenham with Lancaut EP,[202] civ attached to Tidenham until sep CP 1866[9]). *LG* Seq 36. Civ bdry: 1935.[2] *Parl* Seq 11.

WOOLASTON WITH ALVINGTON
AP Usual eccl spelling; for civ and sep chaps, see prev entry. *Eccl* Seq 2.

WOOLCOTT PARK
EP Cr 1882 from Tyndall's Park EP, King's Parade EP.[198] Bristol (Rural Dv) RDn (1882–87), Bristol RDn (1887–1901), Clifton RDn (1901–*).

WOOLSTONE
AP Ptly dependent upon Deerhurst AP, independence sustained.[218] *LG* Deerhurst Hd, Tewk. PLU, RSD, RD. Abol civ 1935 ent to Oxenton AP.[2] *Parl* E'rn Dv (1832–85), N'rn Dv (1885–1918), Cirenc. & Tewk. Dv (1918–48). *Eccl* Winch. RDn (until 1866), Winch. North RDn (1866–87), Winch. RDn (1887–1907), Tewk. RDn (1907–33). Abol eccl 1933 to help cr Woolstone with Gotherington EP.[179]

WOOLSTONE WITH GOTHERINGTON
EP Cr 1933 by union Woolstone AP, Gotherington chap of Bishop's Cleeve AP.[179] Tewk. RDn.

WORMINGTON
AP *LG* Kiftsg. Hd, Winch. PLU, RSD, RD. Abol civ 1935 ent to Dumbleton AP.[2] *Parl* E'rn Dv (1832–85), N'rn Dv (1885–1918), Cirenc. & Tewk. Dv (1918–48). *Eccl* Seq 23.

VILLE OF WOTTON
Usual civ spelling for ex-par place (eccl, 'Wotton Ville', qv), sep CP 1858.[58] *LG* Glouc. PLU, MB, USD. Bdry: 1883.[3] Abol 1885 pt to help cr Wotton St Mary Within CP, pt to Gloucester St Catherine AP, pt to Gloucester Barton St Mary CP, pt to Gloucester South Hamlet CP.[238] *Parl* Glouc. Parl Bor (1867–1918).

WOTTON ST MARY
Hmlt in Gloucester St Mary de Lode AP, sep CP 1866.[9] *LG* Pt Dudst. & K's Bart. Hd, pt Glouc. MB, Glouc. PLU, pt Glouc. USD, pt Glouc. RSD. Abol 1885 pt to help cr Wotton St Mary Within CP, pt to help cr Wotton St Mary Without CP.[238] *Parl* Pt Glouc. Parl Bor (1867–1918), pt E'rn Dv (1867–85), pt N'rn Dv (1885–1918)

WOTTON ST MARY WITHIN
CP Cr 1885 from Gloucester North Hamlet CP, Gloucester St Catherine AP, Gloucester Barton St Michael CP, Gloucester Barton St Mary CP, Gloucester South Hamlet CP, Ville of Wotton CP, Wotton St Mary CP.[238] *LG* Glouc. PLU, Glouc. MB/CB (pt 1885–94, ent 1894–98), pt Glouc. USD, pt Dudst. & K's Bart. Hd, pt Glouc. RSD. Bdry: 1894 (loses the pt not in the CB to cr Wotton Vill CP).[242] Abol 1898 to help cr Gloucester CP.[256]

WOTTON ST MARY WITHOUT

CP Cr 1885 from Wotton St Mary CP, Barnwood AP, Longford St Catherine CP.[238] *LG* Dudst. & K's Bart. Hd, Glouc. PLU, RSD, RD. Abol 1935 pt to Glouc. CB and CP, pt to Barnwood AP, pt to Churchdown AP, pt to help cr Longlevens CP.[2] *Parl* Stroud Dv (1918–48).

EP Cr 1932 from Gloucester St Mary de Lode AP, Gloucester St Catherine AP, Barnwood AP, Churchdown AP, Down Hatherley AP, Twigworth EP, ex-par Wotton Ville.[48] Glouc. RDn (1932–52), Glouc. City RDn (1952–*). Now called 'Longlevens'. Bdry: 1940,[400] 1963 (incl cr Churchdown St John the Evangelist EP).[172]

WOTTON UNDER EDGE

AP Incl chap North Nibley (sep civ identity early, sep CP 1743[145]). *LG* Wotton under Edge Bor, Seq 1. Civ bdry: 1883,[3] 1883,[146] 1883,[231] 1935.[2] *Parl* Seq 12. *Eccl* Seq 32.

WOTTON VILL

CP Cr 1894 from the pt of Wotton St Mary Within CP not in Glouc. CB.[242] *LG* Glouc. PLU, RD. Bdry: 1910 (loses pt to Glouc. CB and CP).[85] Abol 1951 ent to Gloucester CP.[46] *Parl* Stroud Dv (1918–48), Glouc. BC (1948–51).

WOTTON VILLE

Usual eccl spelling for ex-par place (civ, 'Ville of Wotton', qv). Eccl bdry: 1842 (help cr Gloucester St James EP),[269] 1868 (help cr Gloucester St Luke EP),[264] 1877,[265] 1932 (help cr Wotton St Mary Without EP),[48] 1935 (help cr Coney Hill EP, now called 'Gloucester St Oswald').[49]

YANWORTH

Chap in Haselton AP, sep CP 1866.[9] *LG* Seq 8. Bdry: 1935.[2] *Parl* E'rn Dv (1867–1918), Cirenc. & Tewk. Dv/CC (1918–*).

YANWORTH AND STOWELL

EP Cr 1964 from Hampnett with Stowell and Yanworth EP.[280] N'leach. RDn.

YATE

AP *LG* Henbury Hd, Chip. Sodb. PLU, RSD, RD (1894–1935), Sodb. RD (1935–74). Transf 1974 to Avon.[4] *Parl* Seq 14. *Eccl* Seq 21.

HAMPSHIRE

ABBREVIATIONS

Abbreviations particular to Hants follow. Those general abbreviations in use throughout the *Guide* are found on page xix.

Aldsh.	Aldershot
Alresf.	Alresford
Alv.	Alverstoke
Andv.	Andover
Basingst.	Basingstoke
Berm.	Bermondspit
Bountb.	Bountisborough
Bournem.	Bournemouth
Buddl.	Buddlesgate
Cath.	Catherington
Chilb.	Chilbolton
Christch.	Christchurch
Droxf.	Droxford
E'leigh.	Eastleigh
Farnb.	Farnborough
Finchd.	Finchdean
For.	Forest
Fordbr.	Fordingbridge
Hart. Wit.	Hartley Witney
Kingscl.	Kingsclere
Landp.	Landport
Lym.	Lymington
Lyndh.	Lyndhurst
Mainsbr.	Mainsbridge
Micheld.	Micheldever
Petf.	Peterfield
Portsd.	Portsdown
Ports. Isl.	Portsea Island
Portsm.	Portsmouth
Ringw.	Ringwood
Silch.	Silchester
(K's) Somb.	(King's) Somborne
S'htn.	Southampton
Stockb.	Stockbridge
Ston.	Stoneham
Bp's Sutton	Bishop's Sutton
Thorng.	Thorngate
Bp's Walth.	Bishop's Waltham
Whitch.	Whitchurch
Winch.	Winchester

SEQUENCES

An abbreviated entry prefixed by 'Seq' is used in the parochial entries to avoid repeating often the names of superior units of administration. The content of each sequence is shown below.

Local Government Sequences ('LG')

SEQ 1	Alton	Hd,	PLU,	RSD,	RD
SEQ 2	Andv.	Hd,	PLU,	RSD,	RD
SEQ 3	Basingst.	Hd,	PLU,	RSD,	RD
SEQ 4	Berm. Hd,	Alton	PLU,	RSD,	RD
SEQ 5	Berm. Hd,	Basingst.	PLU,	RSD,	RD
SEQ 6	Buddl. Hd,	Winch.	PLU,	RSD,	RD
SEQ 7	Crondall Hd,	Hart. Wit.	PLU,	RSD,	RD
SEQ 8	Dibden Lbty,	New For.	PLU,	RSD,	RD

SEQ 9 Evingar Hd, Kingscl. PLU, RSD, RD (1894–1932), Kingscl. & Whitch. RD (1932–74)
SEQ 10 Evingar Hd, Whitch. PLU, RSD, RD (1894–1932), Kingscl. & Whitch. RD (1932–74)
SEQ 11 Fawley Hd, Alresf. PLU, RSD, RD (1894–1932), Winch. RD (1932–74)
SEQ 12 Fawley Hd, Winch. PLU, RSD, RD
SEQ 13 Finchd. Hd, Pet. PLU, RSD, RD
SEQ 14 Fordbr. Hd, PLU, RSD, RD (1894–1932), Ringw. & Fordbr. RD (1932–74)
SEQ 15 Holdshot Hd, Basingst. PLU, RSD, RD
SEQ 16 Mainsbr. Hd, S Ston. PLU, RSD, RD (1894–1932), Winch. RD (1932–74)
SEQ 17 Meonstoke Hd, Droxf. PLU, RSD, RD
SEQ 18 Odiham Hd, Hart. Wit. PLU, RSD, RD
SEQ 19 Overton Hd, Basingst. PLU, RSD, RD
SEQ 20 Overton Hd, Whitch. PLU, RSD, RD (1894–1932), Kingscl. & Whitch. RD (1932–74)
SEQ 21 Pastrow Hd, Andv. PLU, RSD, RD
SEQ 22 Portsd. Hd, Fareham PLU, RSD, RD (1894–1932), Droxf. RD (1932–74)
SEQ 23 Selborne Hd, Alton PLU, RSD, RD
SEQ 24 Bp's Sutton Hd, Alresf. PLU, RSD, RD (1894–1932), Alton RD (1932–74)
SEQ 25 Bp's Sutton Hd, Alresf. PLU, RSD, RD (1894–1932), Winch. RD (1932–74)
SEQ 26 Bp's Sutton Hd, Alton PLU, RSD, RD
SEQ 27 Thorng. Hd, Romsey PLU, RSD, RD (1894–1932), Romsey & Stockb. RD (1932–74)
SEQ 28 Thorng. Hd, Stockb. PLU, RSD, RD (1894–1932), Romsey & Stockb. RD (1932–74)
SEQ 29 Bp's Walth. Hd, Droxf. PLU, RSD, RD
SEQ 30 Wherwell Hd, Andv. PLU, RSD, RD
SEQ 31 [IoW] E Medina Lbty, IoW PLU, RSD, [IoW Adm Co] RD
SEQ 32 [IoW] W Medina Lbty, IoW PLU, RSD, [IoW Adm Co] RD

Parliamentary Sequences ('Parl')

SEQ 1 N'rn Dv (1832–85), E'rn Dv (1885–1918), Petf. Dv/CC (1918–*)
SEQ 2 N'rn Dv (1832–85), E'rn Dv (1885–1918), Pet. Dv (1918–48), Winch. CC (1948–*)
SEQ 3 N'rn Dv (1832–1918), Aldsh. Dv/CC (1918–*)
SEQ 4 N'rn Dv (1832–1918), Aldsh. Dv/CC (1918–70), Basingst. CC (1970–*)
SEQ 5 N'rn Dv (1832–1918), Basingst. Dv/CC (1918–*)
SEQ 6 N'rn Dv (1832–85), W'rn Dv (1885–1918), Basingst. Dv/CC (1918–*)
SEQ 7 N'rn Dv (1832–85), W'rn Dv (1885–1918), Basingst. Dv/CC (1918–55), Winch. CC (1955–*)
SEQ 8 N'rn Dv (1832–85), W'rn Dv (1885–1918), Basingst. Dv/CC (1918–70), Winch. CC (1970–*)
SEQ 9 N'rn Dv (1832–85), W'rn Dv (1885–1918), Winch. Dv/CC (1918–*)
SEQ 10 S'rn Dv (1832–85), New For. Dv (1885–1918), New For. & Christch. Dv (1918–48), New For. CC (1948–*)
SEQ 11 S'rn Dv (1832–85), New For. Dv (1885–1918), New For. & Christch. Dv (1918–48), Winch. CC (1948–*)
SEQ 12 S'rn Dv (1832–85), New For. Dv (1885–1918), New For. & Christch. Dv (1918–48), Winch. CC (1948–70), E'leigh. CC (1970–*)
SEQ 13 S'rn Dv (1832–85), New For. Dv (1885–1918), Winch. Dv/CC (1918–55), E'leigh. CC (1955–*)
SEQ 14 S'rn Dv (1832–1918), Fareham Dv (1918–48), Petf. CC (1948–*)
SEQ 15 S'rn Dv (1832–1918), Winch. Dv (1918–48), Petf. CC (1948–55), E'leigh. CC (1955–*)
SEQ 16 S'rn Dv (1832–85), W'rn Dv (1885–1918), Basingst. Dv/CC (1918–55), Winch. CC (1955–*)
SEQ 17 IoW Dv (1832–1918), IoW Parl Co (1918–*)

Ecclesiastical Sequences ('Eccl')

SEQ 1 Alresf. RDn
SEQ 2 Alresf. RDn (until 1856), W Meon RDn (1856–71), Alresf. RDn (1871–*)
SEQ 3 Alresf. RDn (until 1856), Micheld. RDn (1856–71), Alresf. RDn (1871–*)
SEQ 4 Alresf. RDn (until 1892), Winch. RDn (1892–*)
SEQ 5 Alton RDn (until 1856), W Alton RDn (1856–92), Alton RDn (1892–*)
SEQ 6 Andv. RDn (until 1856), N-E Andv. RDn (1856–71), N Andv. RDn (1871–92) Kingscl. RDn (1892–1928), Whitch. RDn (1928–*)
SEQ 7 Andv. RDn (until 1856), N-W Andv. RDn (1856–71), W Andv. RDn (1871–92), Andv. RDn (1892–*)
SEQ 8 Andv. RDn (until 1856), S-W Andv. RDn (1856–71), W Andv. RDn (1871–92), Andv. RDn (1892–*)
SEQ 9 Andv. RDn (until 1856), S-W Andv. RDn (1856–71), W Andv. RDn (1871–92), Stockb. RDn (1892–1900), Andv. RDn (1900–*)
SEQ 10 Andv. RDn (until 1856), Chilb. RDn (1856–71), S Andv. RDn (1871–92), Stockb. RDn (1892–1922), Andv. RDn (1922–*)
SEQ 11 Basingst. RDn (until 1856), N-E Basingst. RDn (1856–92), Aldsh. RDn (1892–1928), Odiham RDn (1928–*)
SEQ 12 Basingst. RDn (until 1856), N-E Basingst. (1856–71), Odiham RDn (1871–92), Basingst. RDn (1892–1928), Odiham

RDn (1928–*)
SEQ 13 Basingst. RDn (until 1856), N-E Andv. RDn (1856–92), Silch. RDn (1892–1928), Basingst. RDn (1928–*)
SEQ 14 Basingst. RDn (until 1856), N-E Basingst. RDn (1856–92), Silch. RDn (1892–1928), Odiham RDn (1928–*)
SEQ 15 Basingst. RDn (until 1856), S-W Basingst. RDn (1856–92), Basingst. RDn (1892–*)
SEQ 16 Basingst. RDn (until 1856), S-W Basingst. RDn (1856–71), N-E Basingst. RDn (1871–92), Silch. RDn (1892–1928), Basingst. RDn (1928–*)
SEQ 17 Basingst. RDn (until 1856), Odiham RDn (1856–92), Aldsh. RDn (1892–1928), Odiham RDn (1928–*)
SEQ 18 Droxf. RDn (until 1856), N-E Droxf. RDn (1856–71), Havant RDn (1871–92), Landp. RDn (1892–1900), Havant RDn (1900–*)
SEQ 19 Droxf. RDn (until 1856), N-E Droxf. RDn (1856–71), Havant RDn (1871–92), Petf. RDn (1892–1900), Havant RDn (1900–*)
SEQ 20 Droxf. RDn (until 1856), N-W Droxf. RDn (1856–71), Bp's Walth. RDn (1871–*)
SEQ 21 Droxf. RDn (until 1856), S-W Droxf. RDn (1856–71), Alv. & Ports. Isl. RDn (1871–79), Alv. RDn (1879–*)
SEQ 22 Droxf. RDn (until 1856), W Meon RDn (1856–71), Petf. RDn (1871–*)
SEQ 23 Droxf. RDn (until 1856), W Meon RDn (1856–71), Bp's Walth. RDn (1871–*)
SEQ 24 Fordbr. RDn (until 1856), E Fordbr. RDn (1856–92), Lyndh. RDn (1892–*)
SEQ 25 Fordbr. RDn (until 1856), W Fordbr. RDn (1856–92), Christch. RDn (1892–1908), Ringw. RDn (1908–12), Christch. RDn (1912–*)
SEQ 26 Somb. RDn (until 1856), S-W Somb. (1856–71), Romsey RDn (1871–*)
SEQ 27 S'htn. RDn
SEQ 28 Winch. RDn
SEQ 29 [IoW] IoW RDn (until 1850), E Medine RDn (1850–71), N-E Medine RDn (1871–92), W Wight RDn (1892–*)
SEQ 30 [IoW] IoW RDn (until 1850), E Medine RDn (1850–71), S-E Medine RDn (1871–92), E Wight RDn (1891–*)
SEQ 31 [IoW] IoW RDn (until 1850), W Medine RDn (1850–92), W Wight RDn (1892–*)

DIOCESES AND ARCHDEACONRIES

Hants pars were organised in dioceses and archdeaconries as follows.

GUILDFORD DIOC (1927–*)
Surrey AD: Aldsh. RDn
PORTSMOUTH DIOC (1927–*)
Portsm. AD: Alv. RDn, Havant RDn, Odiham RDn, Portsm. RDn, Bp's Walth. RDn
IoW AD: E Wight RDn, W Wight RDn
WINCHESTER DIOC
Basingst. AD (1927–):* Aldsh. RDn (1927), Alresf. RDn (1948–*), Alton RDn, Andv. RDn, Basingst. RDn, Kingscl. RDn (1927–28), Odiham RDn (1928–*), Silch. RDn (1927–28), Whitch. RDn (1928–*)
Portsm. AD (1925–27): Alv. RDn, Havant RDn, Petf. RDn, Portsm. RDn, Bp's Walth. RDn
IoW AD (1871–1927): E Medine RDn (1871–72), N-E Medine RDn (1872–92), S-E Medine RDn (1872–92), W Medine RDn (1871–92), E Wight RDn (1892–1927), W Wight RDn (1892–1927)
Winch. AD: Aldsh. RDn (1892–1927), Alresf. RDn (until 1948), Alton RDn (until 1856), Alton RDn (1892–1927), E Alton RDn (1856–71), W Alton RDn (1856–92), Alv. RDn (1879–1925), Alv. & Ports. Isl. RDn (1871–79), Andv. RDn (until 1856), Andv. RDn (1892–1927), N Andv. RDn (1871–92), N-E Andv. RDn (1856–71), N-W Andv. RDn (1856–71), S Andv. RDn (1871–92), S-W Andv. RDn (1856–71), W Andv. RDn (1871–92), Basingst. RDn (until 1856), Basingst. RDn (1892–1927), N-E Basingst. RDn (1856–92), S-W Basingst. RDn (1856–92), Bournem. RDn (1928–*), Chilb. RDn (1856–71), Christch. RDn (1892–*), Droxf. RDn (until 1856), N-E Droxf. RDn (1856–71), N-W Droxf. RDn (1856–71), S-E Droxf. RDn (1856–71), S-W Droxf. RDn (1856–71), Fawley RDn (1856–92), Fordbr. RDn (until 1856), E Fordbr. RDn (1856–92), W Fordbr. RDn [sometimes 'Vale of Avon' after 1871] (1856–92), Havant RDn (1871–92), Havant RDn (1900–25), Kingscl. RDn (1892–1927), Landp. RDn (1892–1900), Lyndh. RDn (1892–*), E Medine RDn (1850–71), W Medine RDn (1850–71), W Meon RDn (1856–71), Micheld. RDn (1856–71), Odiham RDn (1856–92), Petf. RDn (1871–1925), Ports. Isl. RDn (1879–92), Portsm. RDn (1892–1925), Ringw. RDn (1908–12), Romsey RDn (1871–*), S'htn. RDn, Silch. RDn (1892–1927), Somb. RDn (until 1856), S-W Somb. RDn (1856–71), Stockb. RDn (1892–1922), Bp's Walth. RDn (1871–1925), IoW RDn (until 1850), Winch. RDn

THE PARISHES OF HAMPSHIRE

ABBOTS ANN
AP*LG* Pt Andv. Hd, pt Wherwell Hd (until 1834), ent Wherwell Hd (from 1834), Andv. PLU, RSD, RD. Civ bdry: 1932.[1] *Parl* Seq 8. *Eccl*

As 'Abbot's Ann', Seq 8. Eccl bdry: 1956 (help cr Andover St Michael and All Angels EP).[2]

ABBOTS BARTON

CP Cr 1894 from the pt of Winchester St Bartholomew AP not in Winch. MB.[3] *LG* Winch. PLU, RD. Bdry: 1900,[4] 1932,[1] 1969.[5] *Parl* Winch. Dv/CC (1918–*).

ABBOTSTONE

AP Orig sep AP in Alresf. RDn, early united to Itchen Stoke AP, the union civ called 'Itchen Stoke', eccl 'Itchen Stoke with Abbotstone'.[6]

ALDERSHOT

Chap in Crondall AP, sep civ identity early, sep EP 1819.[7] *LG* Crondall Hd, Farnham PLU, Aldsh. USD, UD (1894–1922), MB (1922–74). *Parl* Seq 3. *Eccl* Basingst. RDn (1819–56), Odiham RDn (1856–92), Aldsh. RDn (1892–*). Eccl bdry: 1878 (cr Aldershot Holy Trinity EP),[8] 1958 (cr Aldershot St Augustine EP).[9]

ALDERSHOT HOLY TRINITY

EP Cr 1878 from Aldershot EP.[8] Odiham RDn (1878–92), Aldsh. RDn (1892–*).

ALDERSHOT ST AUGUSTINE

EP Cr 1958 from Aldershot EP.[9] Aldsh. RDn.

ALRESFORD

Usual eccl spelling. Chap in Old Alresford AP, sep civ identity early as 'New Alresford', qv, sep EP 1850 as 'Alresford'.[10] *Eccl* Alresf. RDn.

NEW ALRESFORD

Usual civ spelling. Chap in Old Alresford AP, sep civ identity early as 'New Alresford', sep EP 1850 as 'Alresford', qv.[10] *LG* Alresf. Lbty and Bor, Fawley Hd, Alresf. PLU, RSD, RD (1894–1932), Winch. RD (1932–74). *Parl* New Alresf. Parl Bor (1295, 1300–01, 1306, 1306–07 only), Seq 2 thereafter.

OLD ALRESFORD

AP Incl chap New Alresford (sep civ identity early as 'New Alresford', sep EP 1850 as 'Alresford'[10]). *LG* Orig Alresf. Lbty, in Fawley Hd from 15th cent,[11] Seq 11 thereafter. Addtl civ bdry alt: 1932 (gains Godsfield CP).[1] *Parl* Seq 2. *Eccl* Pec jurisd (until 1845), Seq 1 thereafter.

ALTON

AP Incl chap Holybourne (sep civ identity early, sep EP 1862[12]). *LG* Alton Hd, Bor, PLU, USD, UD. Addtl civ bdry alt: 1932 (incl help cr Worldham CP).[1] *Parl* Alton Parl Bor (1295 only), Seq 1 thereafter. *Eccl* Seq 4. Addtl eccl bdry alt: 1875 (cr Alton All Saints EP).[13]

ALTON ALL SAINTS

EP Cr 1875 from Alton AP.[13] W Alton RDn (1875–92), Alton RDn (1892–*). Bdry: 1965.[14]

ALVERSTOKE

AP Incl chap Gosport (sep EP 1732,[7] refounded eccl 1860,[15] no sep civ identity). *LG* Alv. Lbty, Alv. incorp for poor (1799–1852), PLU (1852–1930), USD (ent 1875–83, pt 1883–91), pt Gosport & Alv. USD (1891–94), pt Alv. RSD (1883–94), Gosport & Alv. UD (1894–1922), Gosport MB (1922–74). Addtl civ bdry alt: 1883,[16] 1886,[17] 1894 (ent par incl in UD, gains the pt of Rowner AP in the USD),[3] 1922 (gains pt Portsm. CB and AP),[18] 1930,[19] 1932 (gains Lee on the Solent CP, gains Rowner AP),[1] 1940 (gains pt Portsm. CB and AP).[20] *Parl* S'rn Dv (1832–1918), Fareham Dv (1918–48), Gosport & Fareham BC (1948–70), Gosport BC (1970–*). *Eccl* Pec jurisd (until 1845), Seq 21 thereafter. Addtl eccl bdry alt: 1841 (cr Forton EP),[21] 1845 (cr Gosport St Matthew EP),[22] 1845 (cr Elson EP),[23] 1913 (cr Gosport Christ Church EP).[24]

AMPFIELD

Chap in Hursley AP, sep EP 1841,[7] sep CP 1894.[25] *LG* Hursley PLU, RD (1894–1932), Winch. RD (1932–74). Civ bdry: 1897 (help cr Chandlers Ford CP),[26] 1963.[27] *Parl* Winch. Dv/CC (1918–70), E'leigh. CC (1970–*). *Eccl* Winch. RDn (1841–1949), Romsey RDn (1949–*). Eccl bdry: 1855 (help cr Braishfield EP),[28] 1910 (help cr Chandler's Ford EP).[29]

AMPORT

AP Incl chap Appleshaw (sep civ identity early, sep EP 1864[30]). *LG* Seq 2. *Parl* Seq 8. *Eccl* Seq 8. Eccl bdry: 1924.[31]

ANDOVER

AP Incl chap Foxcott (sep civ identity early, no sep eccl identity hence this par eccl 'Andover with Foxcott', qv). *LG* Andv. Hd, PLU, Bor/MB (ent until 1883, pt 1883–94, ent 1894–1974), USD (ent 1875–83, pt 1883–94). Addtl civ bdry alt: 1883 (gains Knights Enham AP [area not in MB or USD]),[16] 1894 (the pt not in the MB cr Knights Enham CP),[3] 1932 (incl cr Smannell CP and gains Knights Enham CP).[1] *Parl* Andv. Parl Bor (1295, 1302–07, 1586–1885), W'rn Dv (1885–1918), Basingst. Dv/CC (1918–70), Winch. CC (1970–*).

ANDOVER ST MICHAEL AND ALL ANGELS

EP Cr 1956 from Andover with Foxcott AP, Abbot's Ann AP.[2]

ANDOVER WITH FOXCOTT

AP Usual eccl spelling, sometimes 'Andover with Foxcote'; for civ and civ sep chap Foxcott, see 'Andover'. *Eccl* Seq 8. Eccl bdry: 1858 (cr Smannell with Hatherden EP),[426] 1965 (cr Andover St Michael and All Angels EP).[2]

ANDWELL

Ex-par place, sep CP 1858.[32] *LG* Basingst. Hd, PLU, RSD, RD. Bdry: 1879.[33] Abol 1932 to help cr Mapledurwell and Up Nately CP.[1] *Parl* N'rn Dv (1867–1918), Basingst. Dv (1918–48).

APPLESHAW

Chap in Amport AP, sep civ identity early, sep EP 1864.[30] *LG* Seq 2. *Parl* Seq 8. *Eccl* S-W Andv. RDn (1864–71), W Andv. RDn (1871–92), Andv. RDn (1892–*). Eccl bdry: 1939.[34]

ARRETON

AP *LG* E Medina Hd/Lbty, IoW PLU, RSD. Abol civ 1894 pt to cr North Arreton CP, pt to cr South Arreton CP.[36] *Parl* IoW Dv (1832–1918). *Eccl* IoW RDn (until 1850), E Medine RDn (1850–72), N-E Medine RDn (1872–92), W Wight RDn (1892–1959), E Wight RDn (1959–*). Eccl bdry: 1853 (help cr Haven

Street EP).[35]

NORTH ARRETON

CP Cr 1894 from Arreton AP.[36] *LG* IoW PLU, RD. Bdry: 1895.[38] Abol 1907 ent to Whippingham AP.[37]

SOUTH ARRETON

CP Cr 1894 from Arreton AP.[36] *LG* IoW PLU, RD. Bdry: 1898.[39] *Parl* IoW Parl Co (1918–*).

ASHE

AP *LG* Overton Hd, Whitch. PLU, RSD, RD. Abol civ 1932 pt to Steventon AP, pt to Overton AP.[1] *Parl* N'rn Dv (1832–85), W'rn Dv (1885–1918), Basingst. Dv (1918–48). *Eccl* Basingst. RDn (until 1856), S-W Basingst. RDn (1856–92), Basingst. RDn (1892–*). Eccl bdry: 1952.[40]

ASHLEY

AP *LG* K's Somb. Hd (until 1834), Buddl. Hd (from 1834), Stockb. PLU, RSD, RD (1894–1932), Romsey & Stockb. RD (1932–74). Civ bdry: 1883,[41] 1895.[38] *Parl* Seq 7. *Eccl* Seq 26.

ASHLEY

CP Cr 1894 from the pt of Ryde CP not in Ryde MB.[3] *LG* IoW PLU, RD. Abol 1933 pt to Ryde CP, pt to Newchurch AP.[42] *Parl* IoW Parl Co (1918–48).

ASHLEY WALK

CP Cr 1868 from ex-par places in New For. (pt Godshill, Godshill Inclosure, Ashley Walk, Ashley Lodge, Mudmore, Ogdens, Amberwood, Eyeworth Lodge, Telegraph Toll Gate, Miller's Ford, Greenhouse Farm).[43] *LG* Fordbr. Hd, PLU, RSD, RD. Abol 1932 ent to Fordingbridge AP.[1] *Parl* New For. Dv (1885–1918), New For. & Christch. Dv (1918–48).

ASHMANSWORTH

Chap in East Woodhay AP, sep par at Reformation in 16th cent, sep civ identity maintained, eccl absorbed back into East Woodhay in 18th cent,[44] sep EP again 1884.[45] *LG* Seq 9. Civ bdry: 1932 (gains Crux Easton AP).[1] *Parl* Seq 6. *Eccl* Pec jurisd when sep par 16th–18th cent, N Andv. RDn (1884–92), Kingscl. RDn (1892–1922), Whitch. RDn (1922–*).

AVINGTON

AP *LG* Fawley Hd, Winch. PLU, RSD, RD. Civ bdry: 1889.[46] Abol civ 1932 to help cr Itchen Valley CP.[1] *Parl* N'rn Dv (1832–85), W'rn Dv (1885–1918), Winch. Dv (1918–48). *Eccl* Alresf. RDn (until 1892), Winch. RDn (1892–1928), Alresf. RDn (1928–*).

AWRIDGE

EP Cr 1877 from Michelmersh AP, Romsey AP, ent ex-par Dunwood.[47] Romsey RDn.

NORTH BADDESLEY

AP Incl pt chap Rownhams (sep EP 1856,[48] sep CP 1897[49]). *LG* Mainsbr. Hd (until 1834), K's Somb. Hd (from 1834), Hursley PLU, RSD, RD (1894–1932), Romsey & Stockb. RD (1932–74). Addtl civ bdry alt; 1897 (help cr Chandlers Ford CP),[26] 1932,[2] 1954,[50] 1964.[51] *Parl* Seq 13. *Eccl* Donative, pec jurisd (until 1845), S'htn. RDn (1845–56), S-W Somb. RDn (1856–71), Romsey RDn (1871–*). Addtl eccl bdry alt: 1910 (help cr Chandler's Ford EP),[29] 1951,[52] 1958.[53]

SOUTH BADDESLEY

EP Cr 1859 from Boldre AP.[54] E Fordbr. RDn (1859–71), Fawley RDn (1871–92), Lyndh. RDn (1892–*).

BARTON

EP Cr 1843 from Whippingham AP.[55] IoW RDn (1843–50), E Medine RDn (1850–72), N-E Medine RDn (1872–92), W Wight RDn (1892–*).

BARTON STACEY

AP *LG* Barton Stacey Hd, Andv. PLU, RSD, RD. *Parl* Seq 8. *Eccl* Somb. RDn (until 1856), Chilb. RDn (1856–71), S Andv. RDn (1871–92), Stockb. RDn (1892–1922), Whitch. RDn (1928–*).

BASING

AP Orig sep AP with chap Basingstoke, the latter sep par 1244 and Basing soon considered chap in Basingstoke,[56] sep civ identity for Basing early, eccl united 1864 with chap Up Nately in same par as Basing cum Up Nately EP,[30] qv. *LG* Basingst. Hd, Bor/MB, PLU, USD. Civ bdry: 1879,[57] 1894,[58] 1932.[1] *Parl* Seq 5.

EP Cr 1934 when chap Up Nately of Basing cum Up Nately EP severed to help cr Greywell with Up Nately EP, the remainder to be Basing EP.[59] Sometimes 'Old Basing'. Basingst. RDn. Bdry: 1958.[60]

BASING CUM UP NATELY

EP Cr 1864 by union chap Basing, chap Up Nately, each in Basingstoke AP.[30] S-W Basingst. RDn (1864–71), Odiham RDn (1871–92), Basingst. RDn (1892–1934). Bdry: 1918.[61] Abol 1934 the chap Up Nately severed to help cr Greywell with Up Nately EP, the remainder to be Basing EP (sometimes 'Old Basing').[59]

OLD BASING–See BASING

BASINGSTOKE

AP Orig chap in Basing AP, sep par 1244, Basing soon considered chap in this par; incl also chap Up Nately (each sep civ identity early, the two chaps united 1864 to cr Basing cum Up Nately EP[30]). *LG* Basingst. Hd, PLU, Bor/MB, USD. Addtl civ bdry alt: 1879,[62] 1891 (gains the pt of Eastrop AP in Basingst. MB),[63] 1932,[1] 1965,[64] 1970.[65] *Parl* Basingst. Parl Bor (1295, 1302, 1306 only), Seq 5 thereafter. *Eccl* Seq 15. Addtl eccl bdry alt: 1958,[60] 1959.[66]

BAUGHURST

AP *LG* Seq 9. Civ bdry: 1932 (incl gains Ewhurst AP),[1] 1956.[67] *Parl* Seq 6. *Eccl* Pec jurisd (until 1845), Seq 13 thereafter. Eccl bdry: 1939,[68] 1973 (help cr North Tadley EP).[69]

BEAULIEU

AP *LG* Beaulieu Lbty, New For. PLU, RSD, RD. *Parl* Seq 10. *Eccl* Donative, S'htn. RDn (until 1856), Fawley RDn (1856–92), Lyndh. RDn (1892–*). Eccl bdry: 1946.[70]

BEAUWORTH

Chap in Cheriton AP, sep civ identity early, eccl

united 1879 with chap Kilmeston in same par as Kilmeston with Beauworth EP.[71] *LG* Seq 11. Civ bdry: 1888,[72] 1932.[1] *Parl* Seq 2.

BEDHAMPTON

AP *LG* Portsd. Hd, Havant PLU, RSD, RD. Civ bdry: 1901.[73] Abol civ 1932 pt to help cr Rowlands Castle CP, pt to Havant AP.[1] *Parl* S'rn Dv (1832–1918), Fareham Dv (1918–48). *Eccl* Seq 18. Eccl bdry: 1968 (help cr Leigh Park EP).[74]

BEMBRIDGE

Chap in Brading AP, sep EP 1828,[7] eccl refounded 1884 (incl territory reclaimed from sea in Brading Harbour),[75] sep CP 1896.[76] *LG* IoW PLU, RD. Civ bdry: 1933.[42] *Parl* IoW Parl Co (1918–*). *Eccl* IoW RDn (1828–50), E Medine RDn (1850–72), S-E Medine RDn (1872–92), E Wight RDn (1892–*).

BENTLEY

Chap (situated in Hants) in Farnham AP (Surrey), at times such as 1573 considered in Surrey for some purposes,[77] sep civ identity early in Hants, sep EP 1727.[7] *LG* Bentley Lbty, Alton PLU, RSD, RD. Civ bdry: 1932 (gains Coldrey CP).[1] *Parl* Seq 1. *Eccl* Alton RDn (1727–1856), W Alton RDn (1856–92), Farnham RDn (Surrey AD, 1892–* [dioc Guildf 1927–*]).

BENTWORTH

AP *LG* Odiham Hd (until 1834), Berm. Hd (from 1834), and Seq 4 thereafter. *Parl* Seq 1. *Eccl* Seq 5.

BERNARD STREET

EP Cr 1853 from Southampton St Mary AP.[78] Sometimes 'Southampton St James, Bernard Street'. S'htn. RDn. Bdry: 1954.[79] Abol 1968 to help cr Southampton St Michael with Holy Rood, St Lawrence and St John and St James Docks EP.[80]

BIGHTON

AP *LG* Seq 25. *Parl* Seq 2. *Eccl* Seq 1.

BINSTEAD

AP *LG* W Medina Hd/Lbty, IoW PLU, RSD, RD. Abol civ 1933 pt to Ryde CP, pt to Newport CP.[42] *Parl* IoW Dv/Parl Co (1832–1948). *Eccl* Pec jurisd (until 1845), IoW RDn (1845–50), E Medine RDn (1850–72), N-E Medine RDn (1872–92), E Wight RDn (1872–*).

BINSTED

Chap in Alton AP, sep civ identity early, eccl united 1853 with chap Kingsley in same par to cr Binsted with Kingsley EP.[81] *LG* Seq 1. Civ bdry: 1932.[1] *Parl* Seq 1.

BINSTED WITH KINGSLEY

EP Cr 1853 by union chap Binsted, chap Kingsley, each in Alton AP.[81] Alton RDn (1853–56), W Alton RDn (1856–92), Alton RDn (1892–*). Bdry: 1871 (help cr Rowledge EP [mostly in Surrey]).[408]

BISHOPSTOKE

AP Incl chap Fair Oak (sep EP 1871,[82] sep CP 1894[83]). *LG* Fawley Hd, Winch. PLU (1835–1920), E'leigh. PLU (1920–30), Winch. RSD, RD (1894–99), E'leigh. UD (1899–1932). Addtl civ bdry alt: 1899 (the pt not transf to E'leigh. UD cr Stoke Park CP).[84] Abol civ 1932 ent to Eastleigh CP.[1] *Parl* N'rn Dv (1832–85), W'rn Dv (1885–1918), Winch. Dv (1918–48). *Eccl* Pec jurisd (until 1845), Winch. RDn (1845–71), Bp's Walth. RDn (1871–1925), S'htn. RDn (1925–*).

BITTERNE

Area in South Stoneham AP, sep EP 1853 (incl pt from West End EP),[85] sep CP 1894 (from South Stoneham alone).[86] *LG* S Ston. PLU (1894–1924), S'htn. PLU (1924–30), S Ston. RD (1894–1920), S'htn. CB (1920–25). Civ bdry: 1895.[87] Abol civ 1925 ent to S'htn. CB and CP.[88] *Parl* S'htn. Parl Bor (1918–48). *Eccl* S'htn. RDn. Eccl bdry: 1905 (help cr Bitterne Park EP),[89] 1916 (help refound St Mary Extra EP [sometimes 'Southampton St Mary Extra']),[90] 1918,[91] 1949,[92] 1965.[93]

BITTERNE PARK

EP Cr 1905 from Bitterne EP, South Stoneham AP.[89] S'htn. RDn. Bdry: 1916 (help refound St Mary Extra EP [sometimes 'Southampton St Mary Extra']),[90] 1949,[92] 1961,[94] 1965.[93]

BLACKMOOR

EP Cr 1867 from Selborne AP.[95] W Alton RDn (1867–92), Alton RDn (1892–1925), Petf. RDn (1925–*). Bdry: 1926,[96] 1957.[97]

BLENDWORTH

AP *LG* Finchd. Hd, Cath. PLU, RSD, RD. Abol civ 1932 pt to help cr Horndean CP, pt to help cr Rowlands Castle CP, pt to Havant AP.[1] *Parl* N'rn Dv (1832–85), E'rn Dv (1885–1918), Petf. Dv (1918–48). *Eccl* Seq 19. Eccl bdry: 1955.[98]

BOARHUNT

AP *LG* Portsd. Hd, Fareham PLU, RSD, RD (1894–1932), Droxf. RD (1932–74). Civ bdry: 1888.[99] *Parl* Seq 14. *Eccl* Droxf. RDn. Abol eccl prob in 18th cent, certainly by 1876 to help cr Southwick and Boarhunt EP.[100]

BOLDRE

AP Incl area Sway (sep EP 1841,[101] sep CP 1866[102]), chap Lymington (sep civ identity early, pt in Lym. Bor, sep EP 1869[103]), area East Boldre (sep EP 1845,[7] sep CP 1929[105]). *LG* Pt New For. Hd, pt Christch. Hd, Lym. PLU, RSD, RD (1894–1932), New For. RD (1932–74). Addtl civ bdry alt: 1878.[106] *Parl* Pt Lym. Parl Bor (until Lymington par has sep civ identity), Seq 10 thereafter. *Eccl* Seq 24. Addtl eccl bdry alt: 1859 (cr South Baddesley EP).[54]

EAST BOLDRE

Area in Boldre AP, sep EP 1845,[7] sep CP 1929.[105] *LG* Lym. PLU, RD (1929–32), New For. RD (1932–74). *Parl* New For. CC (1948–*). *Eccl* Fordbr. RDn (1845–56), Fawley RDn (1856–92), Lyndh. RDn (1892–*). Eccl bdry: 1964.[70]

BONCHURCH

AP Incl chap Shanklin (sep civ identity early, sep

EP 1853[107]). *LG* E Medine Hd/Lbty, IoW PLU, RSD, RD. Abol civ 1933 pt to help cr Sandown-Shanklin CP, pt to Ventnor CP.[42] *Parl* IoW Dv/Parl Co (1832–1948). *Eccl* Seq 30.

BOSCOMBE

EP Cr 1890 from Bournemouth St Clement EP.[82] W Fordbr. RDn (1890–92), Christch. RDn (1892–1928), Bournem. RDn (1928–*).

BOSCOMBE ST ANDREW

EP Cr 1929 from Pokesdown EP.[108] Bournem. RDn.

BOSSINGTON

Chap in Broughton AP, sep civ identity early, no sep eccl identity.[109] *LG* Thorng. Hd, Stockb. PLU, RSD, RD (1894–1932), Romsey & Stockb. RD (1932–74). Civ bdry: 1883,[16] 1883.[110] *Parl* Seq 16.

BOTLEY

AP Incl pt chap Hedge End (sep EP 1876,[111] sep CP 1894[86]). *LG* Seq 16. Addtl civ bdry alt: 1884,[112] 1897,[86] 1932.[1] *Parl* Seq 15. *Eccl* S'htn. RDn (until 1856), N-W Droxf. RDn (1856–71), Bp's Walth. RDn (1871–*). Addtl eccl bdry alt: 1874.[113]

BOURNEMOUTH

The following have 'Bournemouth' in their names. Insofar as any existed at a given time: *LG* Bournem. Par (poor law purposes), MB (1890–1900), CB (1900–74). *Parl* Bournem. Parl Bor (1918–48), pt Bournem. East and Christch. BC, pt Bournem. West BC (1948–70), pt Bournem. East BC, pt Bournem. West BC (1970–*) [see Part III of the *Guide* for the composition of these constituencies by wards of the CB]. *Eccl* Fordbr. RDn (1845–56), E Fordbr. RDn (1856–71), W Fordbr. RDn (1871–92), Christch. RDn (1892–1928), Bournem. RDn (1928–*).

CP1–BOURNEMOUTH–Cr 1894 from the pts of Christchurch AP, Holdenhurst CP in Bournem. MB.[114] Bdry: 1901,[115] 1902 (gains Winton CP, Pokesdown CP, Southbourne CP),[116] 1914,[117] 1931 (incl gains Kinson AP [Dorset]),[118] 1932.[119] Transf 1974 to Dorset.[141]

EP1–BOURNEMOUTH [ST PETER]–Cr 1845 from main pt Christchurch AP, chap Holdenhurst of Christchurch AP.[120] Bdry: 1867 (cr EP2),[95] 1871 (cr EP8),[82] 1874 (cr EP13),[121] 1874 (help cr Moordown EP),[122] 1882 (cr EP16),[123] 1891 (help cr EP10),[124] 1920,[125] 1921 (cr EP5),[126] 1922 (help cr EP12).[127] Abol 1973 to help cr EP15.[128]

EP2–BOURNEMOUTH HOLY EPIPHANY–Cr 1953 from Moordown EP, Holdenhurst EP, EP9.[129]

EP3–BOURNEMOUTH HOLY TRINITY–Cr 1867 from EP1.[95] Bdry: 1890 (cr EP14),[130] 1908 (help cr EP7),[132] 1914 (help cr EP4),[104] 1919 (help cr EP6).[133] Abol 1973 to help cr EP15.[128]

EP4–BOURNEMOUTH ST ALBAN–Cr 1914 from EP7, EP3, Moordown EP.[104] Bdry: 1929 (help cr EP9),[134] 1929.[135]

EP5–BOURNEMOUTH ST AMBROSE–Cr 1921 from EP1.[126] Bdry: 1925.[136]

EP6–BOURNEMOUTH ST ANDREW–Cr 1919 from EP3, Holdenhurst EP.[133]

EP7–BOURNEMOUTH ST AUGUSTIN–Cr 1900 from EP3, Moordown EP, EP16.[132] Bdry: 1908,[137] 1914 (help cr EP4).[104]

EP8–BOURNEMOUTH ST CLEMENT–Cr 1871 from EP1.[82] Bdry: 1890 (cr Boscombe St John the Evangelist EP).[82]

EP9–BOURNEMOUTH ST FRANCIS–Cr 1929 from Holdenhurst EP, Moordown EP, EP4.[134] Bdry: 1951,[59] 1953 (help cr EP2).[129]

EP10–BOURNEMOUTH ST JOHN THE EVANGELIST–Cr 1891 from Kinson AP (Dorset, dioc Sarum), EP1, EP16.[138] Bdry: 1892,[139] 1925.[136]

EP11–BOURNEMOUTH ST LUKE–Cr 1917 from Moordown EP, EP16.[140]

EP12–BOURNEMOUTH ST MARY–Cr 1922 from EP1, Pokesdown EP, Holdenhurst EP.[127]

EP13–BOURNEMOUTH ST MICHAEL–Cr 1874 from EP1.[121] Bdry: 1920.[125]

EP14–BOURNEMOUTH ST PAUL–Cr 1890 from EP3.[130]

EP15–BOURNEMOUTH ST PETER WITH ST SWITHUN, HOLY TRINITY AND ST STEPHEN–Cr 1973 by union EP1, EP3, EP16.[128]

EP16–BOURNEMOUTH ST STEPHEN–Cr 1882 from EP1.[123] Bdry: 1891 (help cr EP10),[138] 1900 (help cr EP7),[132] 1917 (help cr EP11),[140] 1920,[125] 1925.[136] Abol 1973 to help cr EP15.[128]

BRADING

AP Incl area Sandown (sep EP 1848,[7] sep CP 1894 [the pt in Sandown USD][3]), chap Bembridge (sep EP 1828,[7] refounded eccl 1884 [incl area in Brading Harbour reclaimed from sea],[75] sep CP 1896[76]). *LG* E Medina Hd/Lbty, Brading Bor, IoW PLU, pt Sandown USD, pt Shanklin USD, pt IoW RSD, IoW RD. Addtl civ bdry alt: 1894 (the pt in Shanklin USD cr East Shanklin CP),[42] 1895,[142] 1899,[143] 1933 (incl help cr Sandown-Shanklin CP).[42] *Parl* Seq 17. *Eccl* Seq 30.

BRADLEY

AP *LG* Overton Hd (until 1834), Berm. Hd (from 1834), Basingst. PLU, RSD, RD. *Parl* Seq 5. *Eccl* Alresf. RDn (until 1856), Micheld. RDn (1856–71), W Alton RDn (1871–92), Alton RDn (1892–1953), Alresf. RDn (1953–*).

BRAISHFIELD

Chap in Michelmersh AP, sep EP 1855 (incl pts from Romsey AP, Ampfield AP),[28] sep CP 1951 (from Michelmersh alone).[144] *LG* Romsey & Stockb. RD. *Parl* Winch. CC (1955–70), E'leigh. CC (1970–*). *Eccl* Somb. RDn (1855–56), S-W Somb. RDn (1856–71), Romsey RDn (1871–*).

BRAMDEAN

AP *LG* Seq 25. Civ bdry: 1932 (gains Hinton Ampner CP).[1] *Parl* Seq 2. *Eccl* Seq 2.

BRAMLEY

AP *LG* Seq 3. *Parl* Seq 5. *Eccl* Basingst. RDn (until 1856), N-E Basingst. RDn (1856–92), Silch. RDn (1892–1928), Basingst. RDn (1928–*).

BRAMSHAW

AP Pt Wilts (Cawden & Cadworth Hd), pt Hants (New For. Hd [until 1834], Redbr. Hd [from 1834]), made 2 sep CPs 1894, each 'Bramshaw', one in ea co.[3] *LG* New For. PLU, RSD. *Parl* Hants pt, S'rn Dv (1832–85), New For. Dv (1885–1918). *Eccl* Orig pec jurisd in Sarum dioc; for then and later, see entry in Wilts.

CP Cr 1894 from the Hants pt of Bramshaw AP (Hants, Wilts).[3] *LG* New For. PLU, RD. Bdry: 1932 (gains East Bramshaw CP).[1] *Parl* New For. & Christch. Dv (1918–48), New For. CC (1948–*).

EAST BRAMSHAW

CP Renaming 1895 of Bramshaw CP, Wilts (cr 1894 from the Wilts pt of Bramshaw AP [Hants, Wilts] [3]) when transf to Hants.[145] *LG* New For. PLU, RD. Abol 1932 ent to Bramshaw CP.[1] *Parl* New For. & Christch. Dv (1918–48).

BRAMSHILL

Tg in Eversley AP, sep CP 1866.[122] *LG* Situated in Holdshot Hd (until 1834), Odiham Hd (from 1834), Hart. Wit. PLU, RSD, RD. Bdry: 1932.[1] *Parl* N'rn Dv (1867–1918), Aldsh. Dv/CC (1918–70), Basingst. CC (1970–*).

BRAMSHOTT

AP Pt Hants (Alton Hd [until 1834], Finchd. Hd [from 1834]), pt Sussex (Dumpford Hd), par made ent Hants 1895.[146] Gains pt Rogate AP (Sussex) 1832 for parl purposes, 1844 for civ purposes.[147] *LG* Headley incorp for poor (until 1869), Petf. PLU (1869–1930), RSD, pt sep RD in Sussex (1894–95), Petf. RD (pt 1894–95, ent 1895–1974). Addtl civ bdry alt: 1932.[1] *Parl* Hants pt, Seq 1. *Eccl* Alton RDn (until 1856), E Alton RDn (1856–71), Petf. RDn (1871–*).

BRANSGORE

CP Cr 1974 from the pt of Christchurch East CP retained in Hants (the remainder transf to Dorset).[141]

EP Cr 1832,[7] refounded 1875[148] from Christchurch AP. Fordbr. RDn (1823–56), E Fordbr. RDn (1856–71), W Fordbr. RDn (1871–92), Christch. RDn (1892–*).

BREAMORE

AP Orig priory church. Gains early for eccl purposes the pts of North Charford AP, South Charford AP on west bank of river Avon,[82] the same gained civ 1932.[1] *LG* Breamore Lbty, Fordbr. PLU, RSD, RD (1894–1932), Ringw. & Fordbr. RD (1932–74). Addtl civ bdry alt: 1883,[16] 1888.[149] *Parl* Seq 10. *Eccl* Fordbr. RDn (until 1856), W Fordbr. RDn (1856–92), Christch. RDn (1892–1908), Ringw. RDn (1908–12), Christch. RDn (1912–*).

BRIGHTSTONE

AP Usual eccl spelling; for civ see following entry. *Eccl* Pec jurisd (until 1845), Seq 31 thereafter.

BRIXTON

AP Usual civ spelling; for eccl see prev entry. *LG* Seq 32. Civ bdry: 1883,[16] 1889,[150] 1933 (gains Mottistone AP).[42] *Parl* Seq 17.

BROCKENHURST

Chap in Boldre AP, sep civ identity early, sep EP 1862.[104] *LG* New For. Hd, Lym. PLU, RSD, RD (1894–1932), New For. RD (1932–74). Civ bdry: 1934.[151] *Parl* Seq 10. *Eccl* E Fordbr. RDn (1862–92), Lyndh. RDn (1892–*).

BROOK

AP Usual civ spelling; for eccl see following entry. *LG* W Medina Hd/Lbty, IoW PLU, RSD, RD. Civ bdry: 1889.[150] Abol civ 1933 ent to Brixton AP.[42] *Parl* IoW Dv/Parl Co (1832–1948).

BROOKE

AP Usual eccl spelling; for civ see prev entry. *Eccl* Seq 31.

BROOMY

CP Cr 1868 from ex-par places in New For. (Broomy Lodge, Broomy New Enclosure Cottage, Linford, Linford New Enclosure Lodge, Linwood, Roe Enclosure Cottage, Shobley Hall, Holly Hatch).[43] *LG* Fordbr. Hd, Ringw. PLU, RSD, RD. Abol 1932 ent to Ellingham AP.[1] *Parl* New For. Dv (1885–1918), New For. & Christch. Dv (1918–48).

BROUGHTON

AP Orig chap in Mottisfont AP, sep par early.[152] Gains early Pittleworth AP.[463] Incl chap Bossington (sep civ identity early, no sep eccl identity hence this par eccl 'Broughton with Bossington', qv). *LG* Seq 28. Addtl civ bdry alt: 1883,[16] 1883.[153] *Parl* Seq 16.

BROUGHTON WITH BOSSINGTON

AP Usual eccl spelling; for civ and civ sep chap Bossington, see prev entry. *Eccl* Seq 26. Eccl bdry: 1972.[154]

BUCKHOLT

Ex-par place (comprised of East Buckholt, West Buckholt), sep CP 1858,[32] eccl abol 1972 pt to West Tytherley AP, pt to East Tytherley AP, pt to Broughton with Bossington AP.[154] *LG* Seq 28. Bdry: 1883.[155] *Parl* Seq 16.

BULLINGTON

Chap in Wherwell AP, sep civ identity early, eccl gains 1852 chap Tufton so that this par from then eccl 'Bullington with Tufton',[156] as such sep EP 1857,[157] qv. *LG* Seq 30. *Parl* Seq 8.

EP Cr 1929 when chap Tufton of Bullington with Tufton EP severed to help cr Hurstbourne Priors with Tufton EP, the remainder to be Bullington EP.[158] Whitch. RDn.

BULLINGTON WITH TUFTON

EP Cr 1857 from Wherwell AP.[157] Chilb. RDn (1857–71), S Andv. RDn (1871–92), Stockbr. RDn (1892–1922), Whitch. RDn (1922–28), Whitch. RDn (1928–29). Abol 1929 the chap of Tufton severed to help cr Hurstbourne Priors with Tufton EP, the remainder to be Bullington EP.[158]

BURGHCLERE

AP Incl chap Newtown (sep civ identity early, no

sep eccl identity hence this par eccl 'Burghclere with Newtown', qv). *LG* Evingar Hd (pt until 1834, ent from 1834), pt Kingscl. Hd (tg Earlstone, transf 1834 to Evingar Hd), Kingscl. PLU, RSD, RD (1894–1932), Kingscl. & Whitch. RD (1932–74). *Parl* Seq 6.

BURGHCLERE WITH NEWTOWN
AP Usual eccl spelling; for civ and civ sep chap and bor Newtown, see prev entry. *Eccl* Seq 6.

BURITON
AP Incl chap and bor Petersfield (sep civ identity early, sep EP 1886[159]). *LG* Finchd. Hd, pt Petf. Bor (until Petersfield sep CP), Petf. PLU, pt Petf. USD (1893–94), Petf. RSD (ent 1875–93, pt 1893–94), Petf. RD. Addtl civ bdry alt: 1894 (loses the pt in the USD to Petersfield CP),[160] 1932.[1] *Parl* Petf. Parl Bor (pt until Petersfield sep CP, ent 1832–85), E'rn Dv (1885–1918), Petf. Dv/CC (1918–*). *Eccl* Droxf. RDn (until 1856), E Alton RDn (1856–71), Petf. RDn (1871–*).

BURLEY
CP Cr 1868 from ex-par places in New For. (Burley Walk, Holmsley Walk, Burley Ville Tp).[43] *LG* New For. Hd, Ringw. PLU, RSD, RD (1894–1932), Ringw. & Fordbr. RD (1932–74). Bdry: 1876,[161] 1932.[1] *Parl* New For. Dv (1885–1918), New For. & Christch. Dv (1918–48), New For. CC (1948–*).

BURSLEDON
Chap in Hamble le Rice AP (eccl, 'Hamble'), sep civ identity early, sep EP 1850.[7] *LG* Bp's Walth. Hd (until 1834), Mainsbr. Hd (from 1834), and Seq 16 thereafter. Civ bdry: 1894,[163] 1908,[164] 1932,[1] 1955.[165] *Parl* Seq 15. *Eccl* S'htn. RDn (1850–71), Bp's Walth. RDn (1871–1925), S'htn. RDn (1925–*). Eccl bdry: 1959.[166]

BURTON
EP Cr 1877 from Christhcurch AP.[167] E Fordbr. RDn (1877–80s), W Fordbr. RDn (1880s–92), Christch. RDn (1892–*).

CALBOURNE
AP Incl chap and bor Newtown (sometimes bor 'Francheville', no sep civ identity, sep EP 1871 [incl pt from Shinfleet AP][168]). *LG* Seq 32. Civ bdry: 1889,[150] 1933.[42] *Parl* Pt Newtown Parl Bor (1584–1832), Seq 17 thereafter. *Eccl* Pec jurisd (until 1845), Seq 31 thereafter.

CALSHOT
Ex-par area in Dibden Lbty, orig sep rated in New For. PLU but sep civ status not sustained and later incl in Fawley AP.

BROWN CANDOVER
AP Incl chap Woodmancott (sep civ identity early, eccl as 'Woodmancote' severed 1847 to help cr Woodmancote and Popham EP[169]). *LG* Mainsbr. Hd, Alresf. PLU, RSD, RD. Addtl civ bdry alt: 1888.[72] Abol civ 1932 to help cr Candovers CP.[1] *Parl* N'rn Dv (1832–85), E'rn Dv (1885–1918), Petf. Dv (1918–48). *Eccl* Alresf. RDn. Abol eccl 1847 to help cr Brown Candover with Chilton Candover EP.[170]

BROWN CANDOVER WITH CHILTON CANDOVER
EP Cr 1847 by union Brown Candover AP, Chilton Candover AP.[170] Alresf. RDn (1847–56), Micheld. RDn (1856–71), Alresf. RDn (1871–*).

CHILTON CANDOVER
AP *LG* Mainsbr. Hd, Alresf. PLU, RSD, RD. Abol civ 1932 to help cr Candovers CP.[1] *Parl* As for Brown Candover. *Eccl* Alresf. RDn. Abol eccl 1847 to help cr Brown Candover with Chilton Candover EP.[170]

PRESTON CANDOVER
AP *LG* Seq 5. *Parl* Seq 5. *Eccl* Alresf. RDn. Gains eccl Nutley AP (sep civ identity retained), perhaps in 1688,[171] thereafter eccl 'Preston Candover with Nutley', qv.

PRESTON CANDOVER WITH NUTLEY
EP Cr perhaps in 1688[171] by union Preston Candover AP, Nutley AP (sep civ identity retained). *Eccl* Seq 3.

CANDOVERS
CP Cr 1932 by union Brown Candover AP, Chilton Candover AP.[1] *LG* Basingst. RD. *Parl* Basingst. CC (1948–*).

CARISBROOKE
AP Incl chap and bor Newport (sep civ identity early, sep EP 1858[172]), civ incl area Parkhurst Forest (orig ex-par, eccl abol 1968, pt to this par, pt to Newport EP[175]). *LG* W Medina Hd/Lbty, pt Newport Bor/MB, IoW incorp for poor (1770–1865), PLU (1865–1930), pt Newport USD, pt IoW RSD, IoW RD. Addtl civ bdry alt: 1883,[16] 1889,[150] 1894 (incl loses the pt in the MB to Newport CP),[173] 1894.[73] Abol civ 1933 ent to Newport CP.[42] *Parl* Pt Newport Parl Bor (1295 [jointly with Yarmouth], 1584–1867, extended pt 1867–85), IoW Dv/Parl Co (pt 1832–85, ent 1885–1948). *Eccl* Seq 31. Addtl eccl bdry alt: 1806 (cr West Cowes EP),[7] 1850 (cr Carisbrooke St John EP),[7] 1934,[174] 1968.[175]

CARISBROOKE ST JOHN
EP Cr 1850 from Carisbrooke AP.[7] W Medine RDn (1850–92), W Wight RDn (1892–*). Bdry: 1968.[175]

CARISBROOKE ST NICHOLAS–See ST NICHOLAS

CATHERINGTON
AP *LG* Finchd. Hd, Cath. PLU, RSD, RD. Abol civ 1932 pt to help cr Horndean CP, pt to Havant AP.[1] *Parl* N'rn Dv (1832–85), E'rn Dv (1885–1918), Petf. Dv (1918–48). *Eccl* Seq 19. Eccl bdry: 1881 (help cr Denmead EP [orig pec jurisd]),[176] 1955.[98]

CHALE
AP *LG* Seq 32. *Parl* Seq 17. *Eccl* Seq 31.

CHALTON
AP Incl chap Idsworth (sep CP 1866,[102] no sep eccl identity hence this par eccl 'Chalton with Idsworth', qv). *LG* Finchd. Hd, Cath. PLU, RSD, RD. Abol civ 1932 pt to help cr Rowlands Castle CP, pt to Clanfield AP.[1] *Parl* N'rn Dv (1832–

85), E'rn Dv (1885–1918), Petf. Dv (1918–48).

CHALTON WITH IDSWORTH

AP Usual eccl spelling; for civ and civ sep chap Idsworth, see prev entry. *Eccl* Seq 19. Eccl bdry: 1921,[177] 1955.[98]

CHANDLER'S FORD

EP Cr 1910 from Ampfield EP, North Stoneham AP, Otterbourne EP, North Baddesley AP, Eastleigh EP.[29] S'htn. RDn.

CHANDLERS FORD

CP Cr 1897 from Ampfield AP, North Baddesley AP, North Stoneham AP, Otterbourne AP, South Stoneham AP.[26] *LG* Hursley PLU, RD. Abol 1932 pt to Eastleigh CP, pt to North Baddesley AP.[1] *Parl* Winch. Dv (1918–48).

NORTH CHARFORD

AP Decayed AP, sep civ identity maintained, eccl abol early, the pt on the east bank of the river Avon annexed to Hale AP, the pt on the west bank to Breamore AP,[178] abol civ 1932 in same way.[1] *LG* Fordbr. Hd, PLU, RSD, RD. *Parl* S'rn Dv (1832–85), New For. Dv (1885–1918), New For. & Christch. Dv (1918–48). *Eccl* Fordbr. RDn.

SOUTH CHARFORD

AP Organisation as for North Charford, incl civ and eccl abol.

CHAWTON

AP *LG* Seq 1. Civ bdry: 1932.[1] *Parl* Seq 1. *Eccl* Seq 5. Eccl bdry: 1965,[14] 1973 (help cr Four Marks EP).[179]

CHERITON

AP Incl chap Tichborne (sep civ identity early, no sep eccl identity hence this par sometimes eccl 'Cheriton with Tichborne'), chap Kilmeston, chap Beauworth (each with sep civ identity early, eccl combined 1879 to cr Kilmeston with Beauworth EP[71]). *LG* Seq 11. Addtl civ bdry alt: 1883,[16] 1888.[72] *Parl* Seq 2. *Eccl* Pec jurisd (until 1845), Seq 2 thereafter.

CHERITON WITH TICHBORNE–See prev entry

CHILBOLTON

AP *LG* Buddl. Hd (until 1834), Wherwell Hd (from 1834), and Seq 30 thereafter. *Parl* Seq 8. *Eccl* Pec jurisd (until 1845), Somb. RDn (1845–56), Chilb. RDn (1856–71), S Andv. RDn (1871–92), Stockb. RDn (1892–1922), Andv. RDn (1922–*).

CHILCOMB

AP *LG* Fawley Hd, Winch. PLU, pt Winch. MB (1835–94), pt Winch. USD, pt Winch. RSD. Abol civ 1894 the pt in the MB to cr Chilcomb Within CP, the remainder to cr Chilcomb Without CP.[3] *Parl* Pt Winch. Parl Bor (1832–1918), pt N'rn Dv (1832–85), pt W'rn Dv (1885–1918). *Eccl* Pec jurisd (until 1845), Winch. RDn (1845–1950). Abol eccl 1950 to help cr Chilcomb with Winchester St Peter Chesil EP.[182]

CP Cr 1932 from Chilcomb Without CP.[1] *LG* Winch. RD. *Parl* Winch. CC (1948–*).

CHILCOMB WITH WINCHESTER ST PETER CHESIL

EP Cr 1950 by union Chilcomb AP, Winchester St Peter Chesil AP (civ, 'Winchester St Peter Cheesehill').[182] Winch. RDn. Renamed 1972 'Winchester All Saints with Chilcomb St Andrew and Chesil St Peter'.[48]

CHILCOMB WITHIN

CP Cr 1894 from the pt of Chilcomb AP in Winch. MB.[3] *LG* Winch. PLU, MB. Bdry: 1900.[4] Abol 1902 to help cr Winchester CP.[183]

CHILCOMB WITHOUT

CP Cr 1894 from the pt of Chilcomb AP not in Winch. MB.[3] *LG* Winch. PLU, RD. Bdry: 1894 (gains the pts of the following not in Winch. MB: Milland CP, Winchester St John AP, Winchester St Peter Cheesehill AP, Winnall AP),[184] 1900.[4] Abol 1932 pt to help cr Chilcomb CP, pt to Winchester CP.[1] *Parl* Winch. Dv (1918–48).

CHILWORTH

AP *LG* Mainsbr. Hd, S Ston. PLU (1835–1920), E'leigh. PLU (1920–30), S Ston. RSD, RD (1894–1932), Romsey & Stockb. RD (1932–74). Civ bdry: 1932,[51] 1954 (incl gains pt S'htn. CB and CP),[185] 1964.[51] *Parl* Seq 13. *Eccl* S'htn. RDn (until 1871), Romsey RDn (1871–1922), S'htn. RDn (1922–*). Eccl bdry: 1958.[53]

CHINEHAM

AP Orig AP, united early to Monk Sherborne AP.[463]

CHRISTCHURCH

AP Incl area Highcliffe (sep EP 1862,[7] sep CP 1879 [from Christchurch East CP][186]), chap Holdenhurst (sep civ identity early, sep EP 1876[111]), chap Pokesdown (sep EP 1859,[196] sep CP 1894[189]). *LG* Christch. Hd (ent until 1834), pt from 1834), pt Ringw. Hd (from 1834 [tg North Ashley]), pt Christch. Bor, Bournem. & Christch. PLU (1835–1900), Christch. PLU (1900–30), Christch. MB (pt 1886–94, ent 1894–1974), pt Christch. USD (1886–94), pt Bournem. MB (1890–94), pt Bournem. USD (1890–94), pt Bournem. & Christch. RSD (1875–84, reduced pt 1884–86, further reduced 1886–94). Addtl civ bdry alt: 1887,[187] 1892,[188] 1894 (help cr Christchurch East CP, cr Hurn CP, cr Southbourne CP,[189] loses the pt in Bournem. MB to help cr Bournemouth CP[114]), 1894,[190] 1912,[191] 1932 (loses pt to Bournem. CB and CP),[119] 1932,[192] 1932,[1] 1961,[193] 1971.[194] Transf 1974 to Dorset.[141] *Parl* Pt Christch. Parl Bor (1571–1832, extended pt 1832–1918), pt S'rn Dv (1832–85), pt New For. Dv (1885–1918), New For. & Christch. Dv (1918–48), Bournem. East & Christch. BC (1948–70), Christch. & Lym. BC (1970–*). Parl bdry: 1964,[461] 1973.[462] *Eccl* Fordbr. RDn (until 1856), E Fordbr. RDn (1856–71), W Fordbr. RDn (1871–92), Christch. RDn (1892–*). Addtl eccl bdry alt: 1816 (cr Hinton

Admiral EP,[7] refounded 1867 as 'Hinton Admiral with Beckley',[195] but now commonly called 'Hinton Admiral'), 1823 (cr Bransgore EP,[7] refounded 1875[148]), 1845 (cr Bournemouth EP [from main pt of par and from pt chap Holdenhurst]),[120] 1874 (from area chap Holdenhurst, help cr Moordown EP),[122] 1877 (cr Burton EP),[167] 1882,[197] 1892,[199] 1970 (help cr St Leonards and St Ives EP).[200]

CHRISTCHURCH EAST

CP Cr 1894 from Christchurch AP, Milton AP.[189] *LG* Christch. PLU, RD (1894–1932), Ringw. & Fordbr. RD (1932–74). Bdry: 1897 (cr Highcliffe CP [chap in Christchurch AP, qv for eccl sep status]),[186] 1961.[193] Abol 1974 the pt remaining in Hants cr Bransgore CP, the pt transf to Dorset cr Burton CP in that co.[141] *Parl* New For. & Christch. Dv (1918–48), New For. CC (1948–*). Parl bdry: 1964.[461]

CLANFIELD

AP *LG* Finchd. Hd, Cath. PLU, RSD, RD (1894–1932), Petf. RD (1932–74). Civ bdry: 1932.[1] *Parl* Seq 1. *Eccl* Seq 19. Eccl bdry: 1955.[98]

GOODWORTH CLATFORD

AP *LG* Seq 30. *Parl* Seq 8. *Eccl* Seq 10.

UPPER CLATFORD

AP *LG* Andv. Hd (until 1834), Pastrow Hd (from 1834), Andv. PLU, RSD, RD. *Parl* Seq 8. *Eccl* Seq 10.

CLIDDESDEN

AP Incl Hatch (orig sep AP, incl in this par after 1380[201]). *LG* Seq 3. Civ bdry: 1932,[1] 1965.[64] *Parl* Seq 5. *Eccl* Seq 15. Eccl bdry: 1958.[60]

COLBURY

EP Cr 1872 from North Eling EP, Marchwood EP.[202] E Fordbr. RDn (1872–92), Lyndh. RDn (1892–*).

CP Cr 1894 from Eling AP.[203] *LG* New For. PLU, RD. Abol 1934 pt to Denny Lodge CP,[205] pt to Eling AP.[205] *Parl* New For. & Christch. Dv (1918–48).

COLDEN COMMON

Chap in Owlesbury AP, Twyford AP, sep EP 1844 (orig cr as 'Coldon' but 'Colden Common' long used),[206] sep CP 1932.[1] *LG* Winch. RD. *Parl* Winch. CC (1948–*). *Eccl* Droxf. RDn (1844–56), N-W Droxf. RDn (1856–71), Bp's Walth. RDn (1871–1908), Winch. RDn (1908–*).

COLDON–See prev entry

COLDREY

Ex-par place, sep CP 1858.[32] *LG* Alton Hd, PLU, RSD, RD. Abol 1932 ent to Bentley CP.[1] *Parl* N'rn Dv (1867–85), E'rn Dv (1885–1918), Petf. Dv (1918–48).

COLEMORE

AP Usual civ spelling; for eccl see 'Colmer'. Incl chap Priors Dean (sep civ identity early, eccl as 'Prior's Dean' severed 1949 to help cr Hawkley with Prior's Dean EP[80]). *LG* Barton Stacey Hd (until 1834), E Meon Hd (from 1834), Petf. PLU, RSD, RD. Abol civ 1932 to help cr Colemore and Priors Dean CP.[1] *Parl* N'rn Dv (1832–85), E'rn Dv (1885–1918), Petf. Dv (1918–48).

COLEMORE AND PRIORS DEAN

CP Cr 1932 by union Colemore AP, Priors Dean CP.[1] *LG* Petf. RD. *Parl* Petf. CC (1948–*).

COLMER

EP Cr 1949 when chap Prior's Dean eccl severed from Colmer with Prior's Dean AP to help cr Hawkley with Prior's Dean EP, the remainder to be Colmer.[80] Alton RDn. Abol 1972 to help cr East Tisted and Colemore EP.[207]

COLMER WITH PRIOR'S DEAN

AP Usual eccl spelling; for civ and civ sep chap Priors Dean, see 'Colemore'. *Eccl* Alton RDn (until 1856), E Alton RDn (1856–71), Petf. RDn (1871–1900), Alton RDn (1900–49). Abol eccl 1949 when chap Prior's Dean severed to help cr Hawkley with Prior's Dean EP, the remainder to be Colmer EP.[80]

COMBE

AP *LG* Pastrow Hd, Hungerford PLU, RSD, sep RD in Hants (1894–95). Transf 1895 to Berks.[208] *Parl* N'rn Dv (1832–85), W'rn Dv (1885–1918), Berks thereafter. *Eccl* Andv. RDn (until 1856), N-W Andv. RDn (1856–71), N Andv. RDn (1871–92), Kingscl. RDn (1892–1913), Andv. RDn (1913–*).

COMPTON

AP *LG* Seq 6. Civ bdry: 1900,[4] 1932,[1] 1956 (cr Olivers Battery CP).[209] *Parl* Seq 9. *Eccl* Seq 28.

COPYTHORNE

CP For eccl area see 'North Eling'. Cr 1894 from Eling AP.[203] *LG* New For. PLU, RD. Bdry: 1932,[1] 1934.[205] *Parl* New For. & Christch. Dv (1918–48), New For. CC (1948–*).

CORHAMPTON

AP Gains early Lomer AP.[210] *LG* Meonstoke Hd, Droxf. PLU, RSD, RD. Civ bdry: 1884.[211] Abol civ 1932 to help cr Corhampton and Meonstoke CP.[1] *Parl* N'rn Dv (1832–85), E'rn Dv (1885–1918), Petf. Dv (1918–48). *Eccl* Seq 23.

CORHAMPTON AND MEONSTOKE

CP Cr 1932 by union Corhampton AP, Meonstoke AP.[1] *LG* Droxf. RD. *Parl* Petf. CC (1948–*).

COSHAM

CP Cr 1894 by union Widley AP, Wymering AP.[212] *LG* Fareham PLU, RD. Bdry: 1904 (loses pt to Portsm. CB and AP),[213] 1920 (loses pt to Portsm. CB and AP).[214] Renamed 1921 'Widley'.[460] *Parl* Fareham Dv (1918–48).

EP Cr 1936 from Wymering AP, Widley AP.[215] Havant RDn.

COVE

Tg in Yateley AP, sep EP 1845,[7] sep CP 1866.[102] *LG* Crondall Hd, Farnb. incorp for poor (1794–1869), Hart. Wit. PLU (1869–1930), RSD, RD. Abol civ 1932 pt to help cr Hawley CP, pt to Farnborough AP.[1] *Parl* N'rn Dv (1867–1918), Aldsh. Dv (1918–48). *Eccl* Basingst. RDn (1845–56), Odiham RDn (1856–92), Aldsh. RDn (1892–*). Eccl bdry: 1862 (help cr Fleet EP,[7] refounded 1863[123]), 1874 (help cr Minley EP).[137]

COWES
Chap in Northwood AP, sep EP 1806 (as 'West Cowes [St Mary]'),[7] eccl refounded 1927 (as 'Cowes'),[216] sep CP 1894 (the pt in W Cowes USD).[3] *LG* IoW PLU, Cowes UD. Civ bdry: 1923,[217] 1933 (incl gains East Cowes CP).[42] *Parl* IoW Parl Co (1918–*). *Eccl* IoW RDn (1806–50), W Medine RDn (1850–92), W Wight RDn (1892–*).

EAST COWES
Chap in Whippingham AP, sep EP 1843,[55] sep CP 1894 (the pt in E Cowes USD).[3] *LG* IoW PLU, E Cowes UD (1894–1933). Civ bdry: 1897.[218] Abol civ 1933 ent to Cowes CP.[42] *Parl* IoW Parl Co (1918–48). *Eccl* IoW RDn (1843–50), E Medine RDn (1850–72), N-E Medine RDn (1872–92), W Wight RDn (1892–*).

WEST COWES
EP Cr 1862 (as 'West Cowes Holy Trinity') from Carisbrooke AP.[7] W Medine RDn (1862–92), W Wight RDn (1892–*).

WEST COWES [ST MARY] –See COWES

COWES ST FAITH
EP Cr 1970 from Northwood AP.[219] W Wight RDn.

CRAWLEY
AP Incl chap Hunton (sep CP 1866,[102] eccl severed 1938 to help cr Stoke Charity with Hunton EP[131]). *LG* Seq 6. *Parl* Seq 9. *Eccl* Pec jurisd (until 1845), Winch. RDn (1845–56), Chilb. RDn (1856–71), Winch. RDn (1871–*).

CROFTON
Chap in Titchfield AP, sep EP 1871,[220] sep CP 1894.[221] *LG* Fareham PLU, RD. Civ bdry: 1930 (help cr Lee on Solent CP).[19] Abol civ 1932 ent to Fareham AP.[192] *Parl* Fareham Dv (1918–48). *Eccl* Alv. & Ports. Isl. RDn (1871–79), Alv. RDn (1879–*). Eccl bdry: 1935 (cr Lee on the Solent EP).[364]

CRONDALL
AP Incl chap Yateley (sep civ identity early,[222] sep EP 1809[7]), chap Aldershot (sep civ identity early, sep EP 1819[7]), chap Long Sutton (sep civ identity early, sep EP 1816[7]). Gains early Ewshott AP[463] (eccl severed 1842 to cr Crookham-cum-Ewshott EP[225]; Ewshott EP cr 1886 from latter and from Crondall AP[226]). *LG* Seq 7. Addtl civ bdry alt: 1883,[16] 1894 (cr Crookham CP, cr Fleet CP),[223] 1952 (cr Crookham Village CP).[224] *Parl* Seq 3. *Eccl* Basingst. RDn (until 1856), Odiham RDn (1856–92), Aldsh. RDn (1892–1928), Alresf. RDn (1928–*).

CROOKHAM
CP Cr 1894 from Crondall AP.[223] *LG* Hart. Wit. PLU, RD. Abol 1932 pt to Fleet CP, pt to Crondall AP.[1] *Parl* Aldsh. Dv (1918–48).
EP Renaming 1957 of Crookham-cum-Ewshott EP, losing pt at same time to Fleet EP.[227] Alresf. RDn.

CROOKHAM-WITH-EWSHOTT
EP Cr 1842 from Crondall AP.[225] Basingst. RDn (1842–56), Odiham RDn (1856–92), Aldsh. RDn (1892–1928), Alresf. RDn (1928–57). Bdry: 1862 (help cr Fleet EP,[7] refounded 1863[123]), 1886 (help cr Ewshott EP),[226] 1891.[228] Renamed 1957 'Crookham', losing pt at same time to Fleet EP.[227]

CROOKHAM VILLAGE
CP Cr 1952 from Crondall AP.[224] *LG* Hart. Wit. RD. *Parl* Aldsh. CC (1955–*).

CROWN FARM
Ex-par place, sep CP 1858.[32] *LG* Thorng. Hd, Stockb. PLU (1858[229]–83), RSD. Abol 1883 pt to East Tytherley AP, pt to Bossington CP.[155] *Parl* S'rn Dv (1867–85).

CRUX EASTON
AP *LG* Pastrow Hd, Kingscl. PLU, RSD, RD. Abol civ 1932 ent to Ashmanworth CP.[1] *Parl* N'rn Dv (1832–85), W'rn Dv (1885–1918), Basingst. Dv (1918–48). *Eccl* Andv. RDn (until 1856), N-W Andv. RDn (1856–71), N Andv. RDn (1871–92), Kingscl. RDn (1892–1928), Whitch. RDn (1928–*).

CURBRIDGE
CP Cr 1932 from the pts of Sarisbury CP, Titchfield AP not absorbed into Fareham UD and CP.[192] *LG* Droxf. RD. Abol 1952 pt to Curdridge CP, pt to Wickham AP.[230] *Parl* Petf. CC (1948–55).

CURDRIDGE
Chap in Bishops Waltham AP (eccl, 'Bishop's Waltham'), sep EP 1838,[231] sep CP 1894.[232] *LG* Droxf. PLU, RD. Civ bdry: 1952,[230] 1967.[233] *Parl* Petf. Dv/CC (1918–*). *Eccl* Droxf. RDn (1853–56), N-W Droxf. RDn (1856–71), Bp's Walth. RDn (1871–*). Eccl bdry: 1971 (loses pt to Shidfield EP as latter renamed 'Shedfield').[234]

DAMERHAM
AP Sometimes 'South Damerham'. In Wilts (Damerham Hd), transf 1895 to Hants.[145] Incl chap Martin (sep civ identity early in Wilts, sep EP 1854,[7] also transf civ 1895 to Hants[145]). *LG* Fordbr. PLU, RSD, sep RD in Wilts (1894–95), Fordbr. RD (1895–1932), Ringw. & Fordbr. RD (1932–74). *Parl* Wilts until 1918, New For. & Christch. Dv (1918–48), New For. CC (1948–*). *Eccl* Sarum dioc; see main entry in Wilts.

EAST DEAN
Chap in Mottisfont AP, sep civ identity early, eccl combined 1884 with chap Lockerley in same par to cr Lockerley with East Dean EP.[235] *LG* Seq 27. *Parl* Seq 11.

PRIORS DEAN
Chap (eccl, 'Prior's Dean') in Colemore AP (eccl, 'Colmer'), sep civ identity early, eccl severed 1949 to help cr Hawkley with Prior's Dean EP.[80] *LG* Barton Stacey Hd (until 1834), E Meon Hd (from 1834), Petf. PLU, RSD, RD. Abol civ 1932 to help cr Colemore and Priors Dean CP.[1] *Parl* N'rn Dv (1832–85), E'rn Dv (1885–1918), Petf. Dv (1918–48).

VERNHAMS DEAN
Chap in Hurstbourne Tarrant AP, sep civ identity early, sep EP 1871.[220] *LG* Seq 21. Civ bdry: 1883,[16] 1888.[236] *Parl* Seq 8. *Eccl* W

Andv. RDn (1871–92), Andv. RDn (1892–*).

WEST DEAN

AP Pt Wilts (Alderbury Hd), pt Hants (Thorng. Hd). *LG* Stockb. PLU, RSD. Civ bdry: 1883 (loses the pt in Hants to West Tytherley AP and the par ent Wilts thereafter).[237] *Parl* Hants pt, S'rn Dv (1832–85). *Eccl* Sarum dioc; see main entry in Wilts.

DEANE

AP *LG* Seq 19. *Parl* Seq 5. *Eccl* Basingst. RDn (until 1856), S-W Basingst. RDn (1856–92), Basingst. RDn (1892–1928), Whitch. RDn (1928–*). Eccl bdry: 1930,[238] 1952.[40]

DENMEAD

Chap (pec jurisd) in Hambledon AP, sep EP 1881 (incl pt Catherington AP, ent ex-par Little Creech),[176] sep CP 1932 (from Hambledon alone).[1] *LG* Droxf. RD. Civ bdry: 1958.[239] *Parl* Petf. CC (1948–*). *Eccl* Havant RDn (1881–92), Petf. RDn (1892–1900), Havant RDn (1900–*).

DENNY LODGE

CP Cr 1868 from ex-par places in New For. (Ramnor Cottage, New Enclosure Cottage, Lady Cross Lodge, Whitley Ridge Lodge, Gardner's House in Whitley Ridge Walk, Denny Lodge and Beaulieu Road or Blackdown in Denny Lodge Walk; Kingshot, Sandy Hill, Ipersbridge, Gatesbridge, Cowlease, Otterwood, Hill Top, all mostly in Denny Hill Lodge Walk; Decoy Pond Farm, Calverley Cottage, pt Ipley Farm).[240] *LG* Beaulieu Lbty, New For, PLU (1868–1930), RSD, RD. Bdry: 1934,[204] 1934.[205] *Parl* New For. Dv (1885–1918), New For. & Christch. Dv (1918–48), New For. CC (1948–*).

DIBDEN

AP *LG* Seq 8. Civ bdry: 1913.[241] *Parl* Seq 10. *Eccl* S'htn. RDn (until 1856), Fawley RDn (1856–92), S'htn. RDn (1892–1922), Lyndh. RDn (1922–*). Eccl bdry: 1921.[242]

DOCKENFIELD

Tg in Frensham AP (Surrey), ex-par otherwise, situated in Hants and CP in Hants 1858.[32] *LG* Alton Hd, Farnham PLU, RSD, sep RD in Hants (1894–95). Transf 1895 to Surrey.[243] *Parl* N'rn Dv (1867–85), E'rn Dv (1885–1918), Surrey thereafter.

DOGMERSFIELD

AP *LG* Seq 18. Civ bdry: 1932.[1] *Parl* Seq 4. *Eccl* Seq 17.

DROXFORD

AP Incl chap Shidfield (sep EP 1837,[7] eccl refounded 1843 [qv for later renaming 'Shedfield'],[90] sep CP 1894 as 'Shedfield'[244]), pt chap Swanmore (sep EP 1846,[245] sep CP 1894[244]). *LG* Seq 29. Addtl civ bdry alt: 1884.[246] *Parl* Seq 1. *Eccl* Pec jurisd (until 1845), Seq 20 thereafter.

DUMMER

AP Sometimes 'Dummer with Kempshott'. *LG* Seq 5. Civ bdry: 1879,[247] 1932.[1] *Parl* Seq 5. *Eccl* Seq 15. Eccl bdry: 1931,[248] 1960.[249]

DUMMER WITH KEMPSHOTT–See prev entry

DUNWOOD

Ex-par place, sep CP 1858,[32] eccl abol 1877 to help cr Awridge EP.[47] *LG* Thorng. Hd, Romsey PLU (1858[229]–1930), RSD, RD. Abol 1932 ent to Sherfield English AP.[1] *Parl* S'rn Dv (1867–85), New For. Dv (1885–1918), New For. & Christch. Dv (1918–48).

DURLEY

Chap (pec jurisd) in Upham AP, sep civ identity early, sep EP 1855.[195] *LG* Seq 29. *Parl* Seq 1. *Eccl* Droxf. RDn (1855–56), N-W Droxf. RDn (1856–71), Bp's Walth. RDn (1871–*).

EASTLEIGH

Tg in South Stoneham AP, sep EP 1868,[250] sep CP 1894 (the pt in E'leigh. USD).[251] *LG* S Ston. PLU, E'leigh. UD (1894–99), E'leigh. & Bishopstoke UD (1899–1932), E'leigh. UD (1932–36), MB (1936–74). Civ bdry: 1898,[252] 1932 (incl gains Bishopstoke AP).[1] *Parl* Winch. Dv/CC (1918–55), E'leigh. CC (1955–*). *Eccl* S'htn. RDn (1868–71), Bp's Walth. RDn (1871–1925), S'htn. RDn (1925–*). Eccl bdry: 1954.[253]

EASTON

AP *LG* Fawley Hd, Winch. PLU, RSD, RD. Civ bdry: 1889.[46] Abol civ 1932 to help cr Itchen Valley CP.[1] *Parl* N'rn Dv (1832–85), W'rn Dv (1885–1918), Winch. Dv (1918–48). *Eccl* Pec jurisd (until 1845), Seq 4 thereafter.

EASTROP

AP Sometimes early called chap. *LG* Basingst. Hd, PLU, pt Basingst. MB & USD (1879–91), Basingst. RSD (ent 1875–79, pt 1879–91, ent 1891–94), Basingst. MB (1894–1932). Civ bdry: 1891 (loses the pt in the MB to Basingstoke AP),[63] 1894 (loses pts to Rotherwick AP, Basing AP before made pt MB).[58] Abol civ 1932 ent to Basingstoke AP.[1] *Parl* N'rn Dv (1832–1918), Basingst. Dv (1918–48). *Eccl* Seq 15. Eccl bdry: 1958.[60]

ECCHINSWELL

Chap in Kingsclere AP, sep civ identity early, eccl united 1853 with chap Sydmonton in same par to cr Ecchinswell and Sydmonton EP.[254] *LG* Evingar Hd, Kingscl. PLU, RSD, RD. Abol civ 1932 to help cr Ecchinswell and Sydmonton CP.[1] *Parl* N'rn Dv (1832–85), W'rn Dv (1885–1918), Basingst. Dv (1918–48).

ECCHINSWELL AND SYDMONTON

EP Cr 1852 by union chap Ecchinswell, chap Sydmonton, both in Kingsclere AP.[254] Basingst. RDn (1852–56), N-E Andv. RDn (1856–71), N Andv. RDn (1871–92), Kingscl. RDn (1892–1928), Whitch. RDn (1928–*).

CP Cr 1932 by union Ecchinswell CP, Sydmonton CP.[1] *LG* Kingscl. & Whitch. RD. *Parl* Basingst. CC (1948–*).

ELDON–See following entry

UPPER ELDON

AP Orig sep AP, later civ incl in Kings Somborne AP (eccl, 'King's Somborne'),[255] sep eccl identity retained and usually 'Eldon', sep

CP 1866 as 'Upper Eldon'.[102] *LG* K's Somb. Hd, Stockb. PLU, RSD, RD. Abol civ 1932 ent to Kings Somborne AP.[1] *Parl* S'rn Dv (1832–85), W'rn Dv (1885–1918), Basingst. Dv (1918–48). *Eccl* Somb. RDn (until 1856), S-W Somb. RDn (1856–71), Romsey RDn (1871–1972). Abol eccl 1972 to help cr Michelwersh with Eldon EP.[256]

ELING

AP Incl chap Marchwood (sep EP 1846,[7] sep CP 1894[203]). *LG* Pt Redbridge Hd, pt Thorng. Hd, New For. PLU, RSD. RD. Addtl civ bdry alt: 1894 (cr Colbury CP, cr Copythorne CP [civ area of North Eling EP], cr Netley Marsh CP),[203] 1932,[1] 1934,[205] 1954.[185] *Parl* S'rn Dv (1832–85), New For. Dv (1885–1918), New For. & Christch. Dv (1918–48), New For. CC (1948–55), E'leigh. CC (1955–70), New For. CC (1970–*). *Eccl* S'htn. RDn (until 1856), Fawley RDn (1856–71), E Fordbr. RDn (1871–92), Lyndh. RDn (1892–*). Addtl eccl bdry alt: 1837 (cr North Eling EP [eccl area of Copythorne CP]),[257] 1855 (cr Netley EP),[174] 1937 (help cr Testwood EP).[258]

NORTH ELING

EP Cr 1837 from Eling AP.[131] For civ jurisd in this area, see Copythorne CP. S'htn. RDn (1837–56), Fawley RDn (1856–71), E Fordbr. RDn (1871–92), Lyndh. RDn (1892–*). Bdry: 1872 (help cr Colbury EP).[202]

ELLINGHAM

AP *LG* Fordbr. Hd (until 1834), Ringw. Hd (from 1834), Ringw. PLU, RSD, RD (1894–1932), Ringw. & Fordbr. RD (1932–74). Civ bdry: 1932 (gains Broomy CP).[1] *Parl* Seq 10. *Eccl* Seq 25.

ELLISFIELD

AP *LG* Seq 5. *Parl* Seq 5. *Eccl* Seq 15.

ELSON

EP Cr 1845 from Alverstoke AP.[23] Droxf. RDn (1845–56), S-W Droxf. RDn (1856–71), Alv. & Ports. Isl. RDn (1871–79), Alv. RDn (1879–*). Bdry: 1949.[23]

ELVETHAM

AP *LG* Odiham Hd, Hart. Wit. PLU, RSD, RD. Civ bdry: 1883,[16] 1926.[259] Abol civ 1932 pt to Fleet AP, pt to Hartley Witney AP.[1] *Parl* N'rn Dv (1832–1918), Aldsh. Dv (1918–48). *Eccl* Basingst. RDn (until 1856), N-E Basingst. RDn (1856–92), Aldsh. RDn (1892–1928), Odiham RDn (1928–67). Eccl bdry: 1862 (help cr Fleet EP,[7] refounded 1863[123]), 1891,[228] 1957.[227] Abol eccl 1967 to help cr Hartley Witney and Elvetham EP.[260]

EMERY DOWN

EP Cr 1864 from chap Lyndhurst of Minstead AP.[216] Fawley RDn (1864–71), E Fordbr. RDn (1871–92), Lyndh. RDn (1892–*).

EMPSHOTT

AP *LG* Selborne Hd, Petf. PLU, RSD, RD. Abol civ 1932 ent to Hawkley AP.[1] *Parl* N'rn Dv (1832–85), E'rn Dv (1885–1918), Petf. Dv (1918–48). *Eccl* Alton RDn (until 1856), E Alton RDn (1856–71), Petf. RDn (1871–*).

EMSWORTH

EP Cr 1841 from Warblington AP.[261] Droxf. RDn (1841–56), N-E Droxf. RDn (1856–71), Havant RDn (1871–92), Landp. RDn (1892–1900), Havant RDn (1900–31). Abol 1931 to help cr Warblington with Emsworth EP.[262]

KNIGHTS ENHAM

AP *LG* Andv. Hd, PLU, RSD. Abol civ 1883 ent to Andover AP.[16] *Parl* Andv. Parl Bor (1832–85). *Eccl* As 'Knight's Enham', Seq 8. Eccl bdry: 1973 (exchanges pts with Smannel EP which is then renamed 'Smannel with Ernham Alamein').[263]

CP Cr 1894 from the pt of Andover AP not in Andv. MB.[3] *LG* Andv. PLU, RD. Abol 1932 ent to Andover AP.[1] *Parl* Basingst. Dv (1918–48).

EVERSLEY

AP *LG* Holdshot Hd (ent until 1834, pt 1834–66, ent from 1866), pt Odiham Hd (tg Bramshill, transf to this Hd in 1830s, sep CP in Odiham Hd 1866[102] so that Eversley again ent Holdshot Hd), Hart. Wit. PLU, RSD, RD. *Parl* Seq 4. *Eccl* Seq 11.

EWHURST

AP *LG* Kingscl. Hd, PLU, RSD, RD. Abol civ 1932 ent to Baughurst AP.[1] *Parl* N'rn Dv (1832–85), W'rn Dv (1885–1918), Basingst. Dv (1918–48). *Eccl* Basingst. RDn (until 1856), N-E Andv. RDn (1856–71), N-E Basingst. RDn (1871–92), Silch. RDn (1892–1928), Basingst. RDn (1928–71). Eccl bdry: 1939.[68] Abol eccl 1971 to help cr Wolverton cum Ewhurst EP.[264]

EWSHOTT

AP Orig AP, incl early in Crondall AP,[463] incl in area EP Crookham-cum-Ewshott cr 1886,[225] 'Ewshott' EP cr 1886 from latter and from Crondall AP.[226] Odiham RDn (1886–92), Aldsh. RDn (1892–*).

EXBURY

Chap in Fawley AP, sep civ identity early, sep EP 1863.[265] Sometimes 'Exbury and Lepe'. *LG* New For. Hd (until late 18th cent), Bp's Walth. Hd (from late 18th cent), New For. PLU, RSD, RD. *Parl* N'rn Dv (1832–85), New For. Dv (1885–1918), New For. & Christch. Dv (1918–48), New For. CC (1948–*). *Eccl* Fawley RDn (1863–92), S'htn. RDn (1892–1900), Lyndh. RDn (1900–*).

EXTON

AP *LG* Fawley Hd (until 1834), Meonstoke Hd (from 1834), and Seq 17 thereafter. Civ bdry: 1884,[211] 1932.[1] *Parl* Seq 1. *Eccl* Pec jurisd (until 1845), Seq 23 thereafter.

FACCOMBE

AP Incl chap Tangley (sep civ identity early, sep EP 1898[266]). *LG* Seq 21. *Parl* Seq 8. *Eccl* Seq 7.

FAIR OAK

Chap in Bishopstoke AP, sep EP 1871,[82] sep CP 1894.[83] *LG* Winch. PLU, RD. Bdry: 1932.[1] *Parl* Winch. Dv/CC (1918–*). *Eccl* Bp's Walth. RDn (1871–1925), S'htn. RDn (1925–*).

FAREHAM
AP Gains early Whipstrode AP.[463] *LG* Fareham Hd, Bor, PLU, USD, UD. Civ bdry: 1932 (incl gains Crofton CP, Hook with Warsash CP, pts Portchester CP, Sarisbury CP, Titchfield AP),[192] 1932.[1] *Parl* Fareham Parl Bor (1306 only), S'rn Dv (1832–1918), Fareham Dv (1918–48), Gosport & Fareham BC (1948–70), Fareham BC (1970–*). *Eccl* Pec jurisd (until 1845), Seq 21 thereafter. Eccl bdry: 1837 (cr Fareham Holy Trinity EP).[267]

FAREHAM HOLY TRINITY
EP Cr 1837 from Fareham AP.[267] Droxf. RDn (1837–56), S-W Droxf. RDn (1856–71), Alv. & Ports. Isl. RDn (1871–79), Alv. RDn (1879–*). Bdry: 1849,[268] 1957 (cr Fareham St John the Evangelist EP).[269]

FAREHAM ST JOHN THE EVANGELIST
EP Cr 1956 from Fareham Holy Trinity EP.[269] Alv. RDn.

FARINGDON
AP Usual eccl spelling; for civ see 'Farringdon'. *Eccl* Seq 5. Eccl bdry: 1937 (help cr Four Marks EP).[179]

FARLEIGH WALLOP
AP *LG* Seq 5. Civ bdry: 1932,[1] 1971.[65] *Parl* Seq 5. *Eccl* Seq 15.

FARLEY CHAMBERLAYNE
AP *LG* K's Somb. Hd (until 1834), Micheld. Hd (from 1834), Hursley PLU, RSD, RD. Abol civ 1932 ent to Hursley AP.[1] *Parl* N'rn Dv (1832–85), W'rn Dv (1885–1918), Winch. Dv (1918–48). *Eccl* Winch. RDn (until 1856), S-W Somb. RDn (1856–71), Romsey RDn (1871–*).

FARLINGTON
AP *LG* Portsd. Hd, Havant PLU, RSD, RD. Civ bdry: 1886.[270] Abol civ 1932 pt to help cr Southwick and Widley CP, pt to Havant AP,[1] pt to Portsm. CB and AP.[119] *Parl* S'rn Dv (1832–1918), Fareham Dv (1918–48). *Eccl* Seq 18. Eccl bdry: 1858 (help cr Purbrook EP),[271] 1870 (help cr Portsdown EP),[388] 1913,[447] 1968.[272]

FARNBOROUGH
AP *LG* Crondall Hd, Farnb. incorp for poor (1794–1869), Hart. Wit. PLU (1869–1930), RSD, RD (1894–96), Farnb. UD (1896–1974). Civ bdry: 1932,[1] 1953.[273] *Parl* Seq 3. *Eccl* Basingst. RDn (until 1856), Odiham RDn (1856–1928), Aldsh. RDn (1928–*). Eccl bdry: 1906 (cr South Farnborough EP).[274]

SOUTH FARNBOROUGH
EP Cr 1906 from Farnborough AP.[274] Aldsh. RDn.

FARNHAM
AP In Surrey (Farnham Hd and Bor), incl several chaps ent in Surrey and also chap Bentley (in Hants, at times such as 1573 considered in Surrey for some purposes,[77] sep civ identity early in Hants so that Farnham ent Surrey thereafter). Farnham was orig chap in Frensham AP (Surrey), and became sep par by 1553.[217] Eccl bdry: 1871 (help cr Rowledge EP [mostly in Surrey]).[408] For other chaps and all aspects of Farnham's organisation, see main entry in Surrey.

FARRINGDON
AP Usual civ spelling; for eccl see 'Faringdon'. *LG* Seq 23. Civ bdry: 1932 (help cr Four Marks CP).[1] *Parl* Seq 1.

FAWLEY
AP Incl chap Exbury (sep civ identity early, sep EP 1863[30]). *LG* Pt New For. Hd, pt Bp's Walth. Hd (1662–late 18th cent), pt Redbridge Hd (until 1834), Dibden Lbty (from late 18th cent), New For. PLU, RSD, RD. Addtl civ bdry alt: 19th cent (gains area Calshot, ex-par, orig sep rated in New For. PLU, status not sustained and thereafter incl in this par), 1913.[241] *Parl* Seq 10. *Eccl* Pec jurisd (until 1845), S'htn. RDn (1845–56), Fawley RDn (1856–92), S'htn. RDn (1892–1908), Lyndh. RDn (1908–*). Addtl eccl bdry alt: 1840 (cr Hythe EP,[7] refounded 1841[275]), 1960.[276]

FLEET
EP Cr 1862,[7] refounded 1863[123] from Crookham-cum-Ewshott EP, Cove EP, Elvetham AP. Odiham RDn (1862–92), Aldsh. RDn (1892–*). Bdry: 1891,[228] 1957.[227]
CP Cr 1894 from Crondall AP.[223] *LG* Hart. Wit. PLU, RD (1894–1904), Fleet UD (1904–74). Bdry: 1926,[259] 1932.[1] *Parl* Aldsh. Dv/CC (1918–*).

FORDINGBRIDGE
AP Incl chap Ibsley (sep civ identity early, at one time deemed sep eccl[277] but now eccl incl in this par). *LG* Fordbr. Hd, PLU, RSD, RD (1894–1932), Ringw. & Fordbr. RD (1932–74). Addtl civ bdry alt: 1883,[16] 1888,[149] 1932 (gains Ashley Walk CP),[1] 1963.[278] *Parl* Seq 10. *Eccl* Seq 25. Addtl eccl bdry alt: 1855 (cr Hyde Common EP).[279]

FORTON
EP Cr 1841 from Alverstoke AP.[21] Droxf. RDn (1841–56), S-W Droxf. RDn (1856–71), Alv. & Ports. Isl. RDn (1871–79), Alv. RDn (1879–*).

FOUR MARKS
CP Cr 1932 from East Tisted AP, Farringdon AP, Medstead AP, Newton Valence AP, Ropley AP.[1] *LG* Alton RD. *Parl* Petf. CC (1948–*).
EP Cr 1973 from Medstead AP, Chawton AP, Faringdon AP, Ropley EP.[179] Alton RDn.

FOXCOTT
Chap in Andover AP, sep civ identity early, no sep eccl identity. *LG* Andv. Hd, PLU, RSD, RD. Bdry: 1888.[280] Abol 1932 pt to Andover AP, pt to Tangley CP.[1] *Parl* Andv. Parl Bor (1832–85), W'rn Dv (1885–1918), Basingst. Dv (1918–48).

FREEFOLK
Chap (pec jurisd) in Whitchurch AP, sep civ identity early, eccl severed 1872 to help cr Laverstoke with Freefolk EP, sometimes 'Laverstoke with Freefolk Syfrewaste'.[281] *LG* Evingar Hd, Whitch. PLU, RSD, RD. Usually called 'Freefolk Manor'. Abol 1932 ent to Laverstoke AP.[2] *Parl* N'rn Dv (1832–85), W'rn Dv (1885–

1918), Basingst. Dv (1918–48).

FREEMANTLE

EP Cr 1866 from Millbrook AP.[282] S'htn. RDn. Bdry: 1954.[79]

FRENCHMOOR

Ex-par place, sep CP 1858.[32] *LG* Seq 28. *Parl* S'rn Dv (1867–85), W'rn Dv (1885–1918), Basingst. Dv/CC (1918–55), Winch. CC (1955–*).

FRENSHAM

AP Chap in Farnham AP (Surrey), sep par by 1553.[217] Pt Surrey (Farnham Hd), pt Hants (Dockenfield hmlt, Alton Hd), the latter sep CP 1866 in Hants,[102] so that Frensham ent Surrey thereafter. See main entry in Surrey.

FRESHWATER

AP *LG* Seq 32. Civ bdry: 1894 (cr Totland CP).[283] *Parl* Seq 17. *Eccl* Seq 31. Eccl bdry: 1875 (cr Totland Bay EP).[284]

FROXFIELD

Chap in East Meon AP, sep civ identity early, sep EP 1867.[285] *LG* E Meon Hd, Petf. PLU, RSD, RD. Civ bdry: 1932 (gains Privett CP),[1] 1971.[286] *Parl* Petf. Parl Bor (1832–85), E'rn Dv (1885–1918), Petf. Dv/CC (1918–*). *Eccl* W Meon RDn (1867–71), Petf. RDn (1871–*). Eccl bdry: 1871 (help cr Langrish EP),[287] 1956.[288]

FROYLE

AP *LG* Seq 1. Civ bdry: 1932.[1] *Parl* Seq 1. *Eccl* Seq 5.

FYFIELD

AP *LG* Seq 2. Civ bdry: 1888.[236] *Parl* Seq 8. *Eccl* Seq 8.

GATCOMBE

AP *LG* Seq 32. Civ bdry: 1883,[16] 1894.[289] *Parl* Seq 17. *Eccl* Seq 31. Eccl bdry: 1934,[174] 1968.[175]

GATTEN

EP Cr 1876 from Sandown EP.[290] S-E Medine RDn (1876–92), E Wight RDn (1892–*). Now called 'Shanklin St Paul'. Bdry: 1930 (help cr Lake EP).[216]

GODSFIELD

Ex-par place, sep CP 1858.[32] *LG* Bountb. Hd, Alresf. PLU (1858[229]–1930), RSD, RD. Abol 1932 ent to Old Alresford AP.[1] *Parl* N'rn Dv (1867–85), E'rn Dv (1885–1918), Petf. Dv (1918–48).

GODSHILL

AP Incl pt chap Whitwell (sep civ identity early, sep EP 1867[291]). *LG* Seq 32. Addtl civ bdry alt: 1896,[292] 1898,[293] 1933.[42] *Parl* Seq 17. *Eccl* Seq 30. Addtl eccl bdry alt: 1968.[294]

GOSPORT

EP Cr 1732,[7] refounded 1860 from Alverstoke AP.[15] Pec jurisd (1732–1845), Droxf. RDn (1845–56), S-W Droxf. RDn (1856–71), Alv. & Ports. Isl. RDn (1871–79), Alv. RDn (1879–*). Bdry: 1950 (gains Gosport St Matthew EP).[295]

GOSPORT CHRIST CHURCH

EP Cr 1913 from Alverstoke AP.[24] Alv. RDn.

GOSPORT ST MATTHEW

EP Cr 1845 from Alverstoke AP.[22] RDns as for Gosport from 1845–1950. Abol 1950 ent to Gosport EP.[295]

GRATELEY

AP *LG* Seq 2. *Parl* Seq 8. *Eccl* Seq 9.

GRAYSHOTT

CP Cr 1902 from Headley AP.[297] *LG* Alton PLU, RD. Bdry: 1921,[298] 1932.[1] *Parl* Petf. Dv/CC (1918–*).

GREATHAM

AP *LG* Alton Hd (until 1834), Finchd. Hd (from 1834), and Seq 13 thereafter. Civ bdry: 1929 (incl help cr Whitehill CP),[299] 1971.[286] *Parl* Seq 1. *Eccl* Alton RDn (until 1856), E Alton RDn (1856–71), Petf. RDn (1871–*). Eccl bdry: 1955,[97] 1967.[300]

GREYWELL

Chap in Odiham AP, sep civ identity early, sep EP 1901.[301] *LG* Seq 18. *Parl* Seq 4. *Eccl* Aldsh. RDn (1901–22), Basingst. RDn (1922–28), Odiham RDn (1928–34). Reconstituted 1934 as Greywell with Up Nately when gains chap Up Nately of Basing cum Up Nately EP.[59]

EP Reconstitution 1955 of Greywell with Up Nately EP when chap Up Nately severed to help cr Mapledurwell with Up Nately EP, the remainder to be Greywell.[176] Odiham RDn.

GREYWELL WITH UP NATELY

EP Cr 1934 by union Greywell EP, chap Up Nately of Basing cum Up Nately EP.[59] Odiham RDn. Abol 1955 when chap Up Nately severed to help cr Mapledurwell with Up Nately EP, the remainder to be Greywell.[176]

HALE

AP Gains early eccl the pts of North Charford AP, South Charford AP on east bank of river Avon,[178] gains the same pts civ 1932.[1] *LG* Seq 14. *Parl* Seq 10. *Eccl* Seq 25.

HAMBLE

AP Usual eccl spelling; for civ see following entry. Incl chap Bursledon (sep civ identity early, sep EP 1850[7]). *Eccl* Pec jurisd (until 1845), S'htn. RDn (1845–71), Bp's Walth. RDn (1871–1922), S'htn. RDn (1922–*).

HAMBLE LE RICE

AP Usual civ spelling, sometimes 'Hamble', the latter the invariable eccl spelling (qv, incl civ and eccl sep chap Bursledon). *LG* Seq 16. Addtl civ bdry alt: 1902,[302] 1925,[303] 1952.[304] *Parl* Seq 15.

HAMBLEDON

AP Incl chap Denmead (sep EP 1881 [qv for other pars from which cr as well],[176] sep CP 1932 [from Hambledon alone][1]). *LG* Hambledon Hd, Droxf. PLU, RSD, RD. *Parl* Seq 1. *Eccl* Pec jurisd (until 1845), Droxf. RDn (1845–56), N-E Droxf. RDn (1856–71), Havant RDn (1871–92), Petf. RDn (1892–1900), Havant RDn (1900–66), Bp's Walth. RDn (1966–*). Addtl eccl bdry alt: 1851 (help cr Newtown EP).[94]

HAMPRESTON
AP In Dorset (Cranborne Hd), pt in Hants (from at least 1595, Westover Lbty),[305] the latter transf to Holdenhurst CP in 1860s[296] so that Hampreston ent Dorset thereafter. *LG* Wimborne PLU. *Parl* Hants pt, S'rn Dv (1832–67). See main entry in Dorset.

HANNINGTON
AP *LG* Chuteley Hd, Kingscl. PLU, RSD, RD. Civ bdry: 1883.[16] Abol civ 1932 pt to Baughurst AP, pt to Kingsclere AP.[1] *Parl* N'rn Dv (1832–85), W'rn Dv (1885–1918), Basingst. Dv (1918–48). *Eccl* Pec jurisd (until 1845), Basingst. RDn (1845–56), N-E Basingst. RDn (1856–71), S-W Basingst. RDn (1871–92), Kingscl. RDn (1892–1908), Basingst. RDn (1908–*). Eccl bdry: 1939.[18]

HARBRIDGE
AP *LG* Ringw. Hd, PLU, RSD, RD. Abol civ 1932 to help cr Harbridge and Ibsley CP.[1] *Parl* S'rn Dv (1832–85), New For. Dv (1885–1918), New For. & Christch. Dv (1918–48). *Eccl* Pec jurisd (until 1845), Fordbr. RDn (1845–56), W Fordbr. RDn (1856–92), Christch. RDn (1892–*).

HARBRIDGE AND IBSLEY
CP Cr 1932 by union Harbridge AP, Ibsley CP.[1] *LG* Ringw. & Fordbr. RD. *Parl* New For. CC (1948–*).

HARTLEY MAUDITT
AP *LG* Alton Hd, PLU, RSD, RD. Abol civ 1932 to help cr Worldham CP.[1] *Parl* N'rn Dv (1832–85), E'rn Dv (1885–1918), Petf. Dv (1918–48). *Eccl* Alton RDn (until 1856), W Alton RDn (1856–92), Alton RDn (1892–1944). Abol eccl 1944 to help cr Hartley Mauditt with West Worldham EP.[306]

HARTLEY MAUDITT WITH WEST WORLDHAM
EP Cr 1944 by union Hartley Mauditt AP, West Worldham AP.[306] Alton RDn.

HARTLEY WESPALL
AP *LG* Seq 15. Civ bdry: 1879,[307] 1883,[16] 1932.[1] *Parl* Seq 5. *Eccl* Basingst. RDn (until 1856), N-E Basingst. RDn (1856–92), Silch. RDn (1892–1928), Odiham RDn (1928–73). Abol eccl 1973 to help cr Stratfield Saye with Hartley Wespall EP.[54]

HARTLEY WINTNEY
AP *LG* Odiham Hd, Farnb. incorp for poor (1798–1827), Hart. Wit. PLU, RSD, RD. Civ bdry: 1932.[1] *Parl* Seq 4. *Eccl* Basingst. RDn (until 1856), N-E Basingst. RDn (1856–92), Aldsh. RDn (1892–1928), Odiham RDn (1928–67). Abol eccl 1967 to help cr Hartley Wintney and Elvetham EP.[260]

HARTLEY WINTNEY AND ELVETHAM
EP Cr 1967 by union Hartley Wintney AP, Elvetham AP.[260] Odiham RDn.

HATCH
AP Orig AP, Basingst. RDn, incl in Cliddesden AP after 1380.[201]

HATHERDEN
EP Cr 1874 from Smannell with Hatherden EP,[308] the latter thereafter 'Smannell'. W Andv. RDn (1874–92), Andv. RDn (1892–*).

HAVANT
AP *LG* Havant Lbty, Havant PLU, USD, UD (1894–1932), Havant & Waterloo UD (1932–74). Civ bdry: 1901,[73] 1902 (cr North Havant CP),[309] 1902,[310] 1932,[1] 1952,[311] 1958,[239] 1964.[312] *Parl* S'rn Dv (1832–1918), Fareham Dv (1918–48); Portsm., Langstone BC (1948–70); Havant & Waterloo BC (1970–*). *Eccl* Pec jurisd (until 1845), Seq 18 thereafter. Eccl bdry: 1839 (help cr Redhill EP,[7] refounded 1840[176]), 1968 (incl help cr Leigh Park EP).[74]

NORTH HAVANT
CP Cr 1902 from Havant AP.[309] *LG* Havant PLU, RD. Abol 1932 pt to help cr Rowlands Castle CP, pt to Havant AP.[1] *Parl* Fareham Dv (1918–48).

HAVEN STREET
EP Cr 1853 from Newchurch AP, Arreton AP.[35] E Medine RDn (1853–72), N-E Medine RDn (1872–92), E Wight RDn (1892–*).

HAWKLEY
Chap in Newton Valence AP, sep civ identity early, sep EP 1860.[313] *LG* Selborne Hd, Petf. PLU, RSD, RD. Civ bdry: 1932 (gains Empshott AP),[1] 1971.[286] *Parl* Seq 1. *Eccl* E Alton RDn (1860–71), Petf. RDn (1871–1949). Abol eccl 1949 to help cr Hawkley with Prior's Dean EP.[80]

HAWKLEY WITH PRIOR'S DEAN
EP Cr 1949 by union Hawkley AP, chap Prior's Dean of Colmer with Prior's Dean AP.[80] Petf. RDn. Bdry: 1956,[288] 1957.[97]

HAWLEY
EP Cr 1842 from Yateley EP.[7] Basingst. RDn (1842–56), N-E Basingst. RDn (1856–92), Aldsh. RDn (1892–*). Bdry: 1874 (help cr Minley EP).[137]
CP Cr 1932 from Cove AP, Hawley with Minley CP, Yateley CP.[1] *LG* Hart. Wit. RD. Bdry: 1953,[273] 1958.[315] *Parl* Aldsh. CC (1955–*).

HAWLEY WITH MINLEY
CP Cr 1866 by union tg Hawley, tg Minley, both in Yateley CP.[102] *LG* Crondall Hd (pt until 1834, ent from 1834), pt Holdshot Hd (tg Minley, until 1834), Farnb. incorp for poor (1794–1869), Hart. Wit. PLU (1869–1930), RSD, RD. Abol 1932 pt to help cr Hawley CP, pt to Farnborough AP, pt to Fleet AP.[1] *Parl* N'rn Dv (1867–85), Aldsh. Dv (1918–48).

NORTH HAYLING
Chap in South Hayling AP, sep civ identity early, no sep eccl identity.[316] Sometimes 'Northwood'. *LG* Bosmere Hd, Havant PLU, RSD, RD. Abol 1932 ent to Havant AP.[1] *Parl* S'rn Dv (1832–1918), Fareham Dv (1918–48).

SOUTH HAYLING
AP Incl chap North Hayling (sometimes 'Northwood', sep civ identity early, no sep eccl identity[316]). Sometimes 'Southwood'. *LG*, civ abol, *Parl* as for North Hayling. *Eccl* Seq 18.

HEADLEY

AP *LG* Bp's Sutton Hd (until 1834), Alton Hd (from 1834), Headley incorp for poor (until 1869), Alton PLU (1869–1930), RSD, RD. Civ bdry: 1902 (cr Grayshott CP),[297] 1921,[298] 1929 (help cr Whitehill CP).[299] *Parl* Seq 1. *Eccl* Alton RDn (until 1856), E Alton RDn (1856–71), Petf. RDn (1871–78), Godalming RDn (1878–1928), Farnham RDn (1928–*) [Guildford dioc from 1927].

HECKFIELD

AP Incl tg and chap Mattingley (sep EP 1863,[318] sep CP 1866[102]). *LG* Holdshot Hd, Hart. Wit. PLU, RSD, RD. Addtl civ bdry alt: 1932.[1] *Parl* Seq 4. *Eccl* Basingst. RDn (until 1856), N-E Basingst. RDn (1856–92), Silch. RDn (1892–1928), Odiham RDn (1928–72). Abol eccl 1972 to help cr Heckfield with Mattingley EP.[319]

HECKFIELD WITH MATTINGLEY

EP Cr 1972 by union Heckfield AP, Mattingley EP.[319] Odiham RDn.

HEDGE END

EP Cr 1876 from Botley AP, West End EP, ex-par No Man's Land.[111] Bp's Walth. RDn (1876–1925), S'htn. RDn (1925–*). Bdry: 1957,[320] 1959.[166]

CP Cr 1894 from South Stoneham AP, Botley AP.[86] *LG* S Ston. PLU (1894–1920), E'leigh. PLU (1920–30), S Ston. RD (1894–1932); Winch. RD (1932–74). Bdry: 1932.[1] *Parl* Winch. Dv (1918–48), Petf. CC (1948–55), E'leigh. CC (1955–*).

HERRIARD

AP *LG* Pt Odiham Hd (until 1834), Berm. Hd (pt until 1830s, ent from 1834), and Seq 5 thereafter. *Parl* Seq 5. *Eccl* Seq 15.

HIGHCLERE

AP *LG* Seq 9. *Parl* Seq 6. *Eccl* Pec jurisd (until 1845), Seq 6 thereafter.

HIGHCLIFFE

Area in Christchurch AP, sep EP 1862,[7] sep CP (from Christchurch East CP) 1897.[186] *LG* Bournem. & Christch. PLU (1897–1900), Christch. PLU (1900–30), RD. Civ bdry: 1901,[213] 1912.[191] Abol civ 1933 ent to Christchurch AP.[119] *Parl* New For. & Christch. Dv (1918–48). *Eccl* E Fordbr. RDn (1862–71), W Fordbr. RDn (1871–92), Christch. RDn (1892–*).

HINTON ADMIRAL–See following entry

HINTON ADMIRAL WITH BECKLEY

EP Cr 1816 from Christchurch AP as 'Hinton Admiral',[7] refounded 1867 as 'Hinton Admiral with Beckley',[321] now usually called 'Hinton Admiral'. Fordbr. RDn (1816–56), E Fordbr. RDn (1856–71), W Fordbr. RDn (1871–92), Christch. RDn (1892–*).

HINTON AMPNER

AP *LG* Fawley Hd, Alresf. PLU, RSD, RD. Abol civ 1932 ent to Bramdean AP.[1] *Parl* N'rn Dv (1832–85), E'rn Dv (1885–1918), Petf. Dv (1918–48). *Eccl* Seq 2.

HOLDENHURST

Chap (pec jurisd) in Christchurch AP, sep civ identity early, sep EP 1876.[111] *LG* Westover Lbty, Bournem. & Christch. PLU (1835–1900), Christch. PLU (1900–1930), pt Bournem. USD (1875–84, extended pt 1884–94), pt Bournem. MB (1890–94), pt Christch. RSD (1875–84, reduced pt 1884–94), Christch. RD. Civ bdry: 1860s (gains the pt of Hampreston AP [Dorset, Hants] in Hants so that Hampreston ent Dorset thereafter),[296] 1877,[322] 1894,[190] 1894 (cr Winton CP),[323] 1894 (loses the pt in the MB to help cr Bournemouth CP),[114] 1895,[324] 1901 (incl loses pt to Bournem. CB and CP),[115] 1914 (loses pt to Bournem. CB and CP).[117] Abol civ 1931 pt to Bournem. CB and CP, pt to Hurn CP.[118] *Parl* Christch. Parl Bor (1832–1918), New For. & Christch. Dv (1918–48). *Eccl* W Fordbr. RDn (1876–92), Christch. RDn (1892–1948), Bournem. RDn (1948–*). Eccl bdry: while still chap, 1845 (help cr Bournemouth EP),[120] 1874 (help cr Moordown EP)[157]; when sep EP, 1882,[197] 1919 (help cr Bournemouth St Andrew EP),[133] 1922 (help cr Bournemouth St Mary EP),[127] 1929 (help cr Bournemouth St Francis EP),[134] 1929,[135] 1953 (help cr Bournemouth Holy Epiphany EP),[129] 1969,[199] 1970 (help cr St Leonards and St Ives EP).[200]

HOLYBOURNE

Chap in Alton AP, sep civ identity early, sep EP 1862.[12] Incl tg Neatham (sep CP 1866,[102] no sep eccl identity hence this par sometimes eccl 'Holybourne with Neatham'). *LG* Alton Hd, PLU, RSD, RD. Abol civ 1932 pt to Alton AP, pt to Froyle AP.[1] *Parl* N'rn Dv (1832–85), E'rn Dv (1885–1918), Petf. Dv (1918–48). *Eccl* W Alton RDn (1862–92), Alton RDn (1892–*).

HOLYBOURNE WITH NEATHAM–See prev entry

HOOK

CP Cr 1932 from Nateley Scures AP, Up Nateley CP, Newnham AP, Odiham AP.[1] *LG* Hart. Wit. RD. *Parl* Aldsh. CC (1948–70), Basingst. CC (1970–*).

EP Cr 1955 from Newnham AP, Nateley Scures AP, Odiham AP.[176] Odiham RDn.

HOOK WITH WARSASH

EP Cr 1872 from Sarisbury EP, Titchfield AP.[325] Alv. & Ports. Isl. RDn (1872–79), Alv. RDn (1879–*). Bdry: 1893 (help cr Lock's Heath EP).[464]

HORDLE

Chap in Milford AP, sep civ identity early, sep EP 1860.[326] *LG* Christch. Hd, Lym. PLU, RSD, RD. Civ bdry: 1905.[327] Abol civ 1932 pt to Lymington CP, pt to Sway CP.[1] *Parl* S'rn Dv (1832–85), New For. Dv (1885–1918), New For. & Christch. Dv (1918–48). *Eccl* E Fordbr. RDn (1860–92), Lyndh. RDn (1892–*). Eccl bdry: 1951,[288] 1956.[28]

HORNDEAN

CP Cr 1932 from Blendworth AP, Catherington AP.[1] *LG* Petf. RD. *Parl* Petf. CC (1948–*).

HOUGHTON
AP *LG* Buddl. Hd (until 1834), K's Somb. Hd (from 1834), Stockb. PLU, RSD, RD (1894–1932), Romsey & Stockb. RD (1932–74). *Parl* Seq 16. *Eccl* Seq 26.

HOUND
AP Incl chap Burlesdon (sep civ identity early, sep EP 1850[169]). *LG* Seq 16. Addtl civ bdry alt: 1894,[163] 1894 (cr Sholing CP),[124] 1902,[302] 1908,[164] 1925,[303] 1952,[304] 1954 (loses pt to S'htn. CB and CP),[185] 1955.[165] *Parl* Seq 15. *Eccl* S'htn. RDn (until 1871), Bp's Walth. RDn (1871–1908), S'htn. RDn (1908–*). Eccl bdry: 1864 (help cr Woolston EP),[328] 1867 (help cr Sholing EP [orig 'Scholing']),[332] 1916 (help refound Southampton St Mary Extra EP),[90] 1959.[166]

HUNTON
Chap in Crawley AP, sep CP 1866,[102] eccl severed 1938 to help cr Stoke Charity with Hunton EP.[131] *LG* Buddl. Hd, Winch. PLU, RSD, RD. Abol 1932 ent to Wonston AP.[1] *Parl* N'rn Dv (1867–85), W'rn Dv (1885–1918), Winch. Dv (1918–48).

HURN
CP Cr 1894 from Christchurch AP.[189] *LG* Bournem. & Christch. PLU (1894–1900), Christch. PLU (1900–30), Christch. RD (1894–1932), Ringw. & Fordbr. RD (1932–74). Bdry: 1912,[191] 1931,[118] 1932 (incl help cr St Leonards and St Ives CP),[1] 1971.[194] Transf 1974 to Dorset incl gains the pt of Sopley AP also transf to Dorset.[141] *Parl* New For. & Christch. Dv (1918–48), New For. CC (1948–*). Parl bdry: 1973.[462]

HURSLEY
AP Incl chap Ampfield (sep EP 1841,[7] sep CP 1894[25]), chap Otterbourne (sep civ identity early, sep EP 1876[329]). *LG* Buddl. Hd, Hursley PLU, RSD, RD (1894–1932), Winch. RD (1932–74). Addtl civ bdry alt: 1932 (incl gains Farley Chamberlayne AP).[1] *Parl* Seq 9. *Eccl* Pec jurisd (until 1845), Seq 28 thereafter.

HURSTBOURNE PRIORS
AP Incl chap St Mary Bourne (sep civ identity early, sep EP 1928[330]). *LG* Seq 10. Addtl civ bdry alt: 1932 (gains Tufton CP).[1] *Parl* Seq 6. *Eccl* Pec jurisd (until 1845), Andv. RDn (1845–56), N-W Andv. RDn (1856–71), W Andv. RDn (1871–92), Andv. RDn (1892–1928), Whitch. RDn (1928–29). Reconstituted eccl 1929 gaining chap Tufton of Bullington with Tufton EP to cr Hurstbourne Priors with Tufton EP.[158]
EP Cr 1954 when chap Tufton of Hurstbourne Priors with Tufton EP severed to help cr Whitchurch with Tufton EP, the remainder to be Hurstbourne Priors EP.[331] Whitch. RDn.

HURSTBOURNE PRIORS WITH TUFTON
EP Cr 1929 by union Hurstbourne Priors AP, chap Tufton of Bullington with Tufton EP.[158] Whitch. RDn. Abol 1954 when chap Tufton severed to help cr Whitchurch with Tufton EP, the remainder to be Hurstbourne Priors EP.[331]

HURSTBOURNE TARRANT
AP Incl chap Vernhams Dean (sep civ identity early, sep EP 1871[220]). *LG* Seq 21. Addtl civ bdry alt: 1883,[16] 1888.[236] *Parl* Seq 8. *Eccl* Seq 7.

HYDE COMMON
EP Cr 1855 from Fordingbridge AP.[279] Fordbr. RDn (1855–56), E Fordbr. RDn (1856–71), W Fordbr. RDn (1871–92), Christch. RDn (1892–1908), Ringw. RDn (1908–12), Christch. RDn (1912–*).

HYTHE
EP Cr 1840 from Fawley AP,[7] refounded 1841.[275] Pec jurisd (1840–45), S'htn. RDn (1845–56), Fawley RDn (1856–92), S'htn. RDn (1892–1928), Lyndh. RDn (1928–*). Bdry: 1921.[242]

IBSLEY
Chap in Fordingbridge AP, sep civ identity early, at one time deemed eccl sep[277] but now incl in Fordingbridge. *LG* Fordbr. Hd, Ringw. PLU, RSD, RD. Abol 1932 to help cr Harbridge and Ibsley CP.[1] *Parl* S'rn Dv (1832–85), New For. Dv (1885–1918), New For. & Christch. Dv (1918–48).

IDSWORTH
Chap in Charlton AP, sep CP 1866,[102] no sep eccl identity. *LG* Finchd. Hd, Cath. PLU, RSD, RD. Abol 1932 to help cr Rowlands Castle CP.[1] *Parl* N'rn Dv (1867–85), E'rn Dv (1885–1918), Petf. Dv (1918–48).

IFORD
EP Cr 1936 from Pokesdown EP.[215] Bournem. RDn.

ITCHEN
CP Cr 1903 by union St Mary Extra CP, Sholing CP.[333] *LG* S Ston. PLU, Itchen UD (1903–20), S'htn. CB (1920–25). Abol 1925 ent to Southampton CP.[88] *Parl* S'htn. Parl Bor (1918–48).

ITCHEN ABBAS
AP *LG* Bountb. Hd, Winch. PLU, RSD, RD. Civ bdry: 1889.[46] Abol civ 1932 to help cr Itchen Valley CP.[1] *Parl* N'rn Dv (1832–85), W'rn Dv (1885–1918), Winch. Dv (1918–48). *Eccl* Seq 1.

ITCHEN STOKE
AP Gains early Abbotstone AP,[6] the union civ called 'Itchen Stoke', eccl 'Itchen Stoke with Abbotstone', qv. *LG* Bountb. Hd, Alresf. PLU, RSD, RD. Addtl civ bdry alt: 1889.[46] Abol civ 1932 to help cr Itchen Stoke and Ovington CP.[1] *Parl* N'rn Dv (1832–85), E'rn Dv (1885–1918), Petf. Dv (1918–48).

ITCHEN STOKE AND ABBOTSTONE
AP Usual eccl spelling for union early of Abbotstone AP, Itchen Stoke AP[6]; for civ see prev entry. *Eccl* Alresf. RDn. Abol eccl 1973 to help cr Ovington and Itchen Stoke EP.[263]

ITCHEN STOKE AND OVINGTON
CP Cr 1932 by union Itchen Stoke AP, Ovington AP.[1] *LG* Winch. RD. *Parl* Winch. CC (1948–*).

ITCHEN VALLEY
CP Cr 1932 by union Avington AP, Easton AP, Itchen Abbas AP, Martyr Worthy AP.[1] *LG*

Winch. RD. *Parl* Winch. CC (1948–*).

JESUS CHAPEL–See ST MARY EXTRA

KEMPSHOTT

AP Orig AP, Basingst. RDn, united 1393 to Winslade AP.[334]

KILMESTON–See KILMISTON

KILMESTON WITH BEAUWORTH

EP Cr 1879 by union chap Kilmeston (civ, 'Kilmiston'), chap Beauworth, both in Cheriton AP.[71] Basingst. RDn.

KILMISTON

Chap in Cheriton AP, sep civ identity early as 'Kilmiston', eccl as 'Kilmeston' united 1879 with chap Beauworth in same par to cr Kilmeston with Beauworth EP.[71] *LG* Seq 11. Addtl civ bdry alt: 1888.[72] *Parl* Seq 2.

KIMPTON

AP *LG* Seq 2. *Parl* Seq 8. *Eccl* Seq 8.

KINGSCLERE

AP Incl chap Ecchinswell (Evingar Hd), chap Sydmonton (each sep civ identity early, eccl united 1852 to cr Ecchinswell with Sydmonton EP[254]). *LG* Kingscl. Hd (pt until Ecchinswell gains sep civ identity in Evingar Hd, ent thereafter), Kingscl. PLU, RSD, RD (1894–1932), Kingscl. & Whitch. RD (1932–74). Addtl civ bdry alt: 1883,[16] 1932,[1] 1956.[67] *Parl* Seq 6. *Eccl* Basingst. RDn (until 1856), N-E Andv. RDn (1856–71), N Andv. RDn (1871–92), Kingscl. RDn (1892–1928), Whitch. RDn (1928–*). Addtl eccl bdry alt: 1846 (cr Woodlands EP [area incl Headley, so that often 'Woodlands with Headley']),[335] 1939.[68]

KINGSCLERE-WOODLANDS WITH HEADLEY–See WOODLANDS

KINGSLEY

Chap in Alton AP, sep civ identity early, eccl united 1853 with chap Binsted in same par to cr Binsted with Kingsley EP.[81] *LG* Alton Hd, Headley incorp for poor (until 1869), Alton PLU (1869–1930), RSD, RD. Addtl civ bdry alt: 1929 (help cr Whitehill CP).[299] *Parl* Seq 1.

KINGSTON

AP *LG* W Medina Hd/Lbty, IoW incorp for poor (1770–1865), PLU (1865–1930), RSD, RD. Civ bdry: 1883,[16] 1889.[150] Abol civ 1933 ent to Shorewell CP.[42] *Parl* IoW Dv/Parl Co (1832–1948). *Eccl* Seq 31.

LAINSTON

AP Orig AP, church later ruinous and considered ex-par place, sep CP 1858.[32] *LG* Buddl. Hd, Winch. PLU, RSD, RD. Abol 1932 ent to Sparsholt AP.[1] *Parl* N'rn Dv (1867–85), W'rn Dv (1885–1918), Winch. Dv (1918–48).

LAKE

EP Cr 1930 from Sandown EP, Gatten EP.[216] E Wight RDn.

LANDPORT

EP Cr 1898 from Portsea All Saints EP, Portsmouth AP.[40] Landp. RDn (1898–1900), Portsm. RDn (1900–55). Abol 1955 ent to Portsea All Saints EP.[336]

LANGRISH

Chap in East Meon AP, sep EP 1871 (incl pt from Froxfield EP),[287] sep CP 1894 (from East Meon alone).[337] *LG* Petf. PLU, RD. Bdry: 1932.[1] *Parl* Petf. Dv/CC (1918–*). *Eccl* Petf. RDn.

LASHAM

AP *LG* Odiham Hd (until 1834), Berm. Hd (from 1834), and Seq 4 thereafter. *Parl* Seq 1. *Eccl* Alton RDn (until 1856), W Alton RDn (1856–92), Alton RDn (1892–1928), Basingst. RDn (1928–*).

LAVERSTOKE

AP *LG* Seq 20. Civ bdry: 1932 (gains Freefolk CP).[1] *Parl* Seq 6. *Eccl* Basingst. RDn (until 1856), N-W Andv. RDn (1856–71), S-W Basingst. RDn (1871–72). Reconstituted 1872 gaining chap Freefolk in Whitchurch AP to cr Laverstoke with Freefolk EP,[281] sometimes 'Laverstoke with Freefolk Syfrewaste'.

LAVERSTOKE WITH FREEFOLK

EP Cr 1872 by union Laverstoke AP, chap Freefolk of Whitchurch AP.[281] Sometimes 'Laverstoke with Freefolk Syfrewaste'. S-W Basingst. RDn (1872–92), Basingst. RDn (1892–1928), Whitch. RDn (1928–*).

LECKFORD

AP *LG* K's Somb. Hd (until 1834), Thorng. Hd (from 1834), and Seq 28 thereafter. *Parl* Seq 7. *Eccl* Somb. RDn (until 1856), Chilb. RDn (1856–71), S Andv. RDn (1871–92), Stockb. RDn (1892–1922), Romsey RDn (1922–28), Andv. RDn (1928–*).

LEE ON THE SOLENT

CP Cr 1930 from Crofton CP, Rowner AP.[19] *LG* Gosport MB. Abol 1932 ent to Alverstoke AP.[1]

EP Cr 1935 from Crofton EP.[364] Alv. RDn.

LEIGH PARK

EP Cr 1968 from Bedhampton AP, Havant AP, Rowlands Castle EP.[74] Havant RDn.

LINKENHOLT

AP *LG* Seq 21. *Parl* Seq 8. *Eccl* Andv. RDn (until 1856), N-W Andv. RDn (1856–71), N Andv. RDn (1871–92), Kingscl. RDn (1892–1919), Andv. RDn (1919–*).

LISS

AP Orig AP, sep civ identity maintained, eccl absorbed into Odiham AP,[338] sep EP again 1819.[7] *LG* Odiham Hd (until 1834), Finchd. Hd (from 1834), and Seq 13 thereafter. Civ bdry: 1932.[1] *Parl* Petf. Parl Bor (1832–85), E'rn Dv (1885–1918), Petf. Dv/CC (1918–*). *Eccl* Basingst. RDn (orig as AP, again 1819–56), E Alton RDn (1856–71), Petf. RDn (1871–*). Eccl bdry: 1967.[300]

LITCHFIELD

AP *LG* Kingscl. Hd, PLU, RSD, RD. Abol civ 1932 to help cr Litchfield and Woodcott CP.[1] *Parl* N'rn Dv (1832–85), W'rn Dv (1885–1918), Basingst. Dv (1918–48). *Eccl* Andv. RDn (until 1856), N-E Andv. RDn (1856–71), N Andv.

RDn (1871–92), Kingscl. RDn (1892–1928), Whitch. RDn (1928–68). Abol eccl 1968 to help cr Whitchurch with Tufton and Litchfield EP.[339]

LITCHFIELD AND WOODCOTT

CP Cr 1932 by union Litchfield AP, Woodcott AP, pt St Mary Bourne CP.[1] *LG* Kingscl. & Whitch. RD. *Parl* Basingst. CC (1948–*).

LITTLETON

AP *LG* Seq 6. Civ bdry: 1932.[1] *Parl* Seq 9. *Eccl* Pec jurisd (until 1845), Seq 28 thereafter. Eccl bdry: 1967.[340]

LOCKERLEY

Chap in Mottisfont AP, sep civ identity early, eccl united 1884 with chap East Dean in same par to cr Lockerley with East Dean EP.[235] *LG* Seq 27. Bdry: 1888.[341] *Parl* Seq 11.

LOCKLERLEY WITH EAST DEAN

EP Cr 1884 by union chap Lockerley, chap East Dean, both in Mottisfont AP.[235] Romsey RDn. Bdry: 1972.[342]

LOCK'S HEATH

EP Cr 1893 from Sarisbury EP, Titchfield AP, Hook with Warsash EP.[464] Alv. RDn.

LOMER

AP Orig AP, Droxf. RDn, early incl in Corhampton AP.[210]

LONGPARISH

AP Anc 'Middleton'. *LG* Seq 30. Civ bdry: 1888,[236] 1932.[1] *Parl* Seq 8. *Eccl* Andv. RDn (until 1856), Chilb. RDn (1856–71), S Andv. RDn (1871–92), Stockb. RDn (1892–1922), Andv. RDn (1922–28), Whitch. RDn (1928–*).

LONGSTOCK

AP *LG* K's Somb. Hd (until 1834), Thorng. Hd (from 1834), and Seq 28 thereafter. *Parl* Seq 7. *Eccl* Somb. RDn (until 1856), Chilb. RDn (1856–71), S Andv. RDn (1871–92), Stockb. RDn (1892–1922), Romsey RDn (1922–52), Andv. RDn (1952–*). Eccl bdry: 1962.[343]

LYMINGTON

Chap in Boldre AP, sep civ identity early, sep EP 1869.[103] *LG* New For. Hd, Lym. PLU, Bor/MB (pt until 1889, ent 1889–1974), Lym. USD (pt 1875–89, ent 1889–94), pt Lym. RSD (1875–89). Civ bdry: 1932 (incl gains Milford on Sea CP, Milton CP, Pennington CP).[1] *Parl* Lym. Parl Bor (pt 1584–1832, ent 1832–85), New For. Dv (1885–1918), New For. & Christch. Dv (1918–48), New For. CC (1948–70), Christch. & Lym. BC (1970–*). *Eccl* E Fordbr. RDn (1869–92), Lyndh. RDn (1892–*).

LYNDHURST

Chap in Minstead AP, sep civ identity early, sep EP 1928.[325] *LG* New For. Hd (until 1834), Thorng. Hd (from 1834), New For. PLU, RSD, RD. Civ bdry: 1934.[204] *Parl* Seq 10. *Eccl* Lyndh. RD. Eccl bdry: 1864 (when still chap, cr Emery Down EP).[216]

MAPLEDURWELL

Chap in Newnham AP, sep civ identity early, sep EP 1918.[61] *LG* Basingst. Hd, PLU, RSD, RD. Abol civ 1932 to help cr Mapledurwell and Up Nately CP.[1] *Parl* N'rn Dv (1832–1918), Basingst. Dv (1918–48). *Eccl* Odiham RDn. Reconstituted eccl 1955 gaining chap Up Nately of Greywell with Up Nately to help cr Mapledurwell with Up Nately EP.[176]

MAPLEDURWELL AND UP NATELY

CP Cr 1932 by union Mapledurwell CP, Andwell CP, pt Up Nately CP.[1] *LG* Basingst. RD. *Parl* Basingst. CC (1948–*).

MAPLEDURWELL WITH UP NATELY

EP Cr 1955 by union Mapledurwell AP, chap Up Nately of Greywell with Up Nately EP.[176] Odiham RDn.

MARCHWOOD

Chap in Eling AP, sep EP 1846,[7] sep CP 1894.[203] *LG* New For. PLU, RD. Civ bdry: 1932.[1] *Parl* New For. & Christch. Dv (1918–48), New For. CC (1948–*). *Eccl* S'htn. RDn (1846–56), Fawley RDn (1856–71), E Fordbr. RDn (1871–92), Lyndh. RDn (1892–*). Eccl bdry: 1872 (help cr Colbury EP).[202]

MARTIN

Chap in Damerham AP (Wilts, Damerham Hd, the par sometimes 'South Damerham'), sep civ identity early in Wilts, transf 1895 to Hants,[145] sep EP 1854.[7] *LG* Fordbr. PLU, RSD, sep RD in Wilts (1894–95), Fordbr. RD (1895–1932), Ringw. & Fordbr. RD (1932–74). Civ bdry: 1932 (gains Toyd Farm and Allenford CP).[1] *Parl* Wilts until 1918, New For. & Christch. Dv (1918–48), New For. CC (1948–*). *Eccl* Sarum dioc; see entry in Wilts.

MATTINGLEY

Tg and chap in Heckfield AP, sep EP 1863 as 'Mattingley',[318] sep CP 1866 as 'Mattingly'.[102] Sometimes civ 'Mattingly with Hazely'. *LG* Holdshot Hd, Hart. Wit. PLU, RSD, RD. Civ bdry: 1902.[344] *Parl* N'rn Dv (1867–1918), Aldsh. Dv/CC (1918–70), Basingst. CC (1970–*). *Eccl* N-E Basingst. RDn (1863–92), Silch. RDn (1892–1928), Odiham RDn (1928–72). Abol eccl 1972 to help cr Heckfield with Mattingley EP.[319]

MATTINGLY–See prev entry

MEDSTEAD

Chap (pec jurisd) in Old Alresford AP, sep civ identity early, sep EP 1850.[10] *LG* Orig Alresf. Lbty, in Fawley Hd (15th cent[11]– 1834), Bp's Sutton Hd (from 1834), and Seq 26 thereafter. Civ bdry: 1932 (incl help cr Four Marks CP).[1] *Parl* Seq 1. *Eccl* Alresf. RDn (1850–56), W Alton RDn (1856–92), Alton RDn (1892–*). Eccl bdry: 1973 (help cr Four Marks EP).[179]

MELCHET PARK

Ex-par place in Wilts (Alderbury Hd), sep CP 1858 in Wilts,[32] transf 1895 to Hants.[145] *LG* Romsey PLU, RSD, sep RD in Wilts (1894–95), Romsey RD (1895–1932). Abol 1932 to help cr Melchet Park and Plaitford CP.[1] *Parl* In Wilts until 1918, New For. & Christch. Dv (1918–48).

MELCHET PARK AND PLAITFORD

CP Cr 1932 by union Melchet Park CP, Plaitford

AP.[1] *LG* Romsey & Stockb. RD. *Parl* Winch. CC (1948–70), E'leigh. CC (1970–*).

EAST MEON

AP Incl chap Froxfield, chap Steep (each sep civ identity early, each sep EP 1867[285]), chap Langrish (sep EP 1871 [incl pt from Froxfield EP],[287] sep CP 1894 [from East Meon alone][337]). *LG* E Meon Hd, Petf. PLU, RSD, RD. *Parl* Pt Petf. Parl Bor (1832–85), remainder and later, Seq 1. *Eccl* Pec jurisd (until 1845), Seq 22 thereafter.

WEST MEON

AP Incl chap Privett (sep civ identity early, sep EP 1872[345]). *LG* Fawley Hd (until 1834), Meonstoke Hd (from 1834), and Seq 17 thereafter. *Parl* Seq 1. *Eccl* Pec jurisd (until 1845), Seq 22 thereafter.

MEONSTOKE

AP Incl chap Soberton (sep civ identity early, sep EP 1897[346]). *LG* Meonstoke Hd, Droxf. PLU, RSD, RD. Abol civ 1932 to help cr Corhampton and Meonstoke CP.[1] *Parl* N'rn Dv (1832–85), E'rn Dv (1885–1918), Petf. Dv (1918–48). *Eccl* Pec jurisd (until 1845), Seq 23 thereafter. Eccl bdry: 1851 (from area chap Soberton, help cr Newtown EP).[94]

MICHELDEVER

AP Incl chap Popham (sep civ identity early, eccl severed 1847 to help cr Woodmancote and Popham EP[169]), chap Northington (sep civ identity early, eccl severed 1847 to help cr Swarraton with Northington EP[347]), chap East Stratton (sep civ identity early, sep EP 1931[348]). *LG* Micheld. Hd, Winch. PLU, RSD, RD. Addtl civ bdry alt: 1932 (gains East Stratton CP).[1] *Parl* Seq 9. *Eccl* Somb. RDn (until 1856), Micheld. RDn (1856–71), Alresf. RDn (1871–1908), Winch. RDn (1908–*).

MICHELMERSH

AP Incl chap Braishfield (sep EP 1855 [incl pts from Romsey AP, Ampfield AP],[28] sep CP 1951 [from Michelmersh alone][144]). *LG* Buddl. Hd (until 1834), Thorng. Hd (from 1834), and Seq 27 thereafter. Addtl civ bdry alt: 1883,[16] 1888,[349] 1932 (incl gains Timsbury AP).[1] *Parl* Seq 12. *Eccl* Pec jurisd (until 1845), Somb. RDn (1845–56), S-W Somb. RDn (1856–71), Romsey RDn (1871–1972). Addtl eccl bdry alt: 1877 (help cr Awbridge EP).[47] Abol eccl 1972 to help cr Michelmersh with Eldon EP.[256]

MICHELMERSH WITH ELDON

EP Cr 1972 by union Michelmersh AP, Eldon AP (orig 'Upper Eldon').[256] Romsey RDn.

MIDDLETON–See LONGPARISH

MILFORD

AP Incl chap Milton (sep civ identity early, sep EP 1791[7]), chap Hordle (sep civ identity early, sep EP 1860[326]), chap Pennington (sep EP 1843,[351] sep CP 1911 [from pt of Milford when abol[352]]). *LG* Pt Christch. Hd, pt Ringw. Hd, Lym. PLU, RSD, RD. Addtl civ bdry alt: 1905.[327] Abol civ 1911 pt to help cr Milford on Sea CP, pt to help cr Pennington CP.[352] *Parl* S'rn Dv (1832–85), New For. Dv (1885–1918), New For. & Christch. Dv (1918–48). *Eccl* Seq 24. Addtl eccl bdry alt: 1951.[288]

MILFORD ON SEA

CP Cr 1911 from Milford AP.[352] *LG* Lym. PLU, RD. Abol 1932 ent to Lymington CP.[1] *Parl* New For. & Christch. Dv (1918–48).

MILLAND

Ex-par ville in Winchester Soke & Lbty, sep CP 1858.[32] *LG* Winch. PLU, MB (ent 1835–89, pt 1889–94, ent 1894–1902), pt Winch. USD, pt Winch. RSD. Bdry: 1889,[181] 1894 (loses the pt not in the MB to help cr Chilcomb Without CP).[184] Abol 1902 to help cr Winchester CP.[183] *Parl* Winch. Parl Bor (1832–1918).

MILLBROOK

AP Incl Shirley (orig sep AP, incl in this par 1574,[463] sep EP 1839,[7] sep CP 1894 (the pt in Shirley & Freemantle USD[3]). *LG* Buddl. Hd (until 1834), Mainsbr. Hd (from 1834), S Ston. PLU (1835–1920), E'leigh. PLU (1920–30), pt Shirley USD (1875–81), extended pt Shirley & Freemantle USD (1881–94), pt S Ston. RSD (1875–81, reduced pt 1881–94), S Ston. RD (1894–1932), Romsey & Stockb. RD (1932–54). Addtl civ bdry alt: 1895.[354] Abol civ 1954 pt to S'htn. CB and CP, pt to Eling AP.[185] *Parl* S'rn Dv (1832–1918), Winch. Dv (1918–48), S'htn. Test BC (1948–55). *Eccl* Seq 27. Addtl eccl bdry alt: 1866 (cr Freemantle EP),[282] 1939 (help cr Southampton St Peter, Maybush EP),[355] 1954.[148]

MILTON

Chap in Milford AP, sep civ identity early, sep EP 1791.[7] *LG* Christch. Hd, Lym. PLU, RSD, RD (1894–1926), Milton UD (1926–32). Civ bdry: 1894 (help cr Christchurch East CP),[189] 1926.[356] Abol civ 1932 ent to Lymington CP.[1] *Parl* S'rn Dv (1832–85), New For. Dv (1885–1918), New For. & Christch. Dv (1918–48). *Eccl* Fordbr. RDn (1791–1856), E Fordbr. RDn (1856–92), Lyndh. RDn (1892–1928), Christch. RDn (1928–*).

MILTON

EP Cr 1844 from Portsea AP.[357] Droxf. RDn (1844–56), S-E Droxf. RDn (1856–71), Alv. & Ports. Isl. RDn (1871–79), Ports. Isl. RDn (1879–92), Landp. RDn (1892–1900), Portsm. RDn (1900–*). Bdry: 1851 (help cr Southsea St Jude EP),[358] 1862 (help cr Southsea St Bartholomew EP),[359] 1886,[360] 1906 (help cr Portsea St Stephen EP),[361] 1907,[362] 1916 (cr Portsea St Cuthbert EP).[363]

MINLEY

EP Cr 1874 from Cove EP, Hawley EP.[137] N-E Basingst. RDn (1874–92), Aldsh. RDn (1892–*).

MINSTEAD

AP Incl chap Lyndhurst (sep civ identity early, sep EP 1928[325]). *LG* New For. Hd (until 1834), Thorng. Hd (from 1834), New For. PLU, RSD, RD. Addtl civ bdry alt: 1932.[1] *Parl* Seq 10. *Eccl* Fordbr. RDn (until 1856), Fawley RDn (1856–

71), E Fordbr. RDn (1871–92), Lyndh. RDn (1892–*). Addtl eccl bdry alt: 1864 (from area chap Lyndhurst, cr Emery Down EP).[216]

MONXTON

AP *LG* Seq 2. *Parl* Seq 8. *Eccl* Seq 9. Eccl bdry: 1939.[34]

MOORDOWN

EP Cr 1874 from chap Holdenhurst in Christchurch AP, Bournemouth EP.[122] W Fordbr. RDn (1874–92), Christch. RDn (1892–1928), Bournem. RDn (1928–*). Bdry: 1900 (help cr Bournemouth St Augustin EP),[132] 1908,[137] 1914 (help cr Bournemouth St Alban EP),[104] 1917 (help cr Bournemouth St Luke EP),[140] 1929 (help cr Bournemouth St Francis EP),[134] 1953 (help cr Bournemouth Holy Epiphany EP),[129] 1951.[59]

MORESTEAD

AP *LG* Fawley Hd, Winch. PLU, RSD, RD. Civ bdry: 1889.[181] Abol civ 1932 ent to Owslebury AP.[1] *Parl* N'rn Dv (1832–85), W'rn Dv (1885–1918), Winch. Dv (1918–48). *Eccl* Pec jurisd (until 1845), Seq 28 thereafter.

MORTIMER WEST END

Tg (Hants, Holdshot Hd) in Stratfield Mortimer AP (Berks, Theale Hd), sep CP 1866 in Hants[102] so that Stratfield Mortimer ent Berks thereafter, sep EP 1870.[365] *LG* Basingst. PLU (1866[229]–1930), RSD, RD. *Parl* N'rn Dv (1867–1918), Basingst. Dv/CC (1918–*). *Eccl* Oxf dioc; see entry in Berks.

MOTTISFONT

AP Incl chap Broughton (sep par early[152]), chap East Dean, chap Lockerley (each sep civ identity early, eccl united 1884 to cr Lockerley with East Dean EP[235]), chap East Tytherley (sep par early[366]). *LG* Seq 27. Addtl civ bdry alt: 1883.[16] *Parl* Seq 11. *Eccl* Seq 26. Addtl eccl bdry alt: 1927.[342]

MOTTISTONE

AP *LG* W Medina Hd/Lbty, IoW incorp for poor (1770–1865), PLU (1865–1930), RSD, RD. Abol civ 1933 ent to Brixton AP (eccl, 'Brightstone').[42] *Parl* IoW Dv/Parl Co (1832–1948). *Eccl* Seq 31.

UP NATELY

Chap in Basingstoke AP, sep civ identity early, eccl united 1864 with chap Basing (orig AP) in same par to cr Basing cum Up Nately EP.[30] *LG* Basingst. Hd, PLU, RSD, RD. Civ bdry: 1879.[367] Abol civ 1932 pt to help cr Mapledurwell and Up Nately CP, pt to help cr Hook CP.[1] *Parl* N'rn Dv (1832–1918), Basingst. Dv (1918–48).

NATELY SCURES

AP *LG* Basingst. Hd, PLU, RSD, RD. Civ bdry: 1879.[368] Abol civ 1932 pt to help cr Hook CP, pt to Newnham AP.[1] *Parl* N'rn Dv (1832–1918), Basingst. Dv (1918–48). *Eccl* Seq 12. Eccl bdry: 1918,[61] 1955 (help cr Hook EP).[279]

NEATHAM

Tg in Holybourne CP, sep CP 1866.[102] *LG* Alton Hd, PLU, RSD, RD. Abol 1932 pt to Alton AP, pt to Binsted CP, pt to Froyle AP.[1] *Parl* N'rn Dv (1867–85), E'rn Dv (1885–1918), Petf. Dv (1918–48).

NETLEY

EP Cr 1855 from Eling AP.[174] S'htn. RDn (1855–56), Fawley RDn (1856–71), E Fordbr. RDn (1871–92), Lyndh. RDn (1892–*). Bdry: 1937 (help cr Testwood EP).[258]

NETLEY MARSH

CP Cr 1894 from Eling AP.[203] *LG* New For. PLU, RD. Bdry: 1934.[205] *Parl* New For. & Christch. Dv (1918–48), New For. CC (1948–55), E'leigh. CC (1955–70), New For. CC (1970–*).

NEWCHURCH

AP Incl area Ryde (sep CP/EP 1866[369]), chap Wroxall (sep CP 1894,[370] sep EP 1908[9]). *LG* Seq 31. Addtl civ bdry alt: 1933.[42] *Parl* Seq 17. *Eccl* Seq 30. Addtl eccl bdry alt: 1846 (cr Ryde Holy Trinity EP),[182] 1846 (cr Swanmore St Michael and All Angels EP),[108] 1853 (help cr Haven Street EP).[35]

NEWNHAM

AP Incl chap Mapledurwell (sep civ identity early, sep EP 1918[61]). *LG* Seq 3. Addtl civ bdry alt: 1879,[371] 1932 (incl help cr Hook CP).[1] *Parl* Seq 5. *Eccl* Seq 12. Addtl eccl bdry alt: 1955 (help cr Hook EP).[176]

NEWPORT

Chap in Carisbrooke AP, sep civ identity early, sep EP 1918.[61] *LG* W Medina Hd/Lbty, Newport Bor/MB, USD, IoW incorp for poor (1770–1865), PLU (1865–1930). Civ bdry: 1894 (gains the pts of the following pars in Newport MB: St Nicholas AP, Carisbrooke AP, Whippingham AP),[173] 1933 (incl gains Carisbrooke AP).[42] *Parl* Newport Parl Bor (1295 jointly with Yarmouth, Newport alone 1584–1885), IoW Dv/Parl Co (1885–*). *Eccl* W Medine RDn (1858–92), W Wight RDn (1892–*). Eccl bdry: 1968.[175]

NEWTON VALENCE

AP Incl chap Hawkley (sep civ identity early, sep EP 1860[313]). *LG* Seq 23. Addtl civ bdry alt: 1932 (help cr Four Marks CP).[1] *Parl* Seq 1. *Eccl* Seq 5.

NEWTOWN

Chap and bor in Burghclere AP, sep civ identity early, no sep eccl identity. Sometimes 'Sandleford'. *LG* Evingar Hd, Newtown Bor, Newbury PLU (1835–94), RSD, Kingscl. PLU (1894–1930), RD (1894–1932), Kingscl. & Whitch. RD (1932–74). Civ bdry: 1932.[1] *Parl* Seq 6.

NEWTOWN

EP Cr 1851 from Soberton chap in Meonstoke AP.[94] Droxf. RDn (1851–56), N-W Droxf. RDn (1856–71), Bp's Walth. RDn (1871–*).

NEWTOWN

EP Cr 1871 from Calbourne AP, Shalfleet AP.[168] W Medine RDn (1871–92), W Wight RDn (1892–*).

NEWTOWN ST LUKE

EP Cr 1853 from Southampton St Mary AP, Portswood EP.[85] S'htn. RDn. Bdry: 1866 (help cr

Southampton St Matthew EP),[206] 1893 (cr Southampton St Barnabas EP),[372] 1925.[373] Abol 1973 to help cr Southampton (City Centre) EP.[374]

NITON

AP Incl chap Whitwell (sep civ identity early, sep EP 1867[291]). *LG* Seq 31. Addtl civ bdry alt: 1933.[42] *Parl* Seq 17. *Eccl* Seq 30.

NORTHAM

EP Cr 1853 from Southampton St Mary AP.[85] S'htn. RDn. Abol 1973 to help cr Southampton (City Centre) EP.[374]

NORTHINGTON

Chap in Micheldever AP, sep civ identity early, eccl united 1847 with Swarraton AP to help cr Swarraton with Northington EP.[347] *LG* Micheld. Hd, Alresf. PLU, RSD, RD (1894–1932), Winch. RD (1932–74). Civ bdry: 1888,[72] 1932 (gains Swarraton AP).[1] *Parl* Seq 2.

NORTHWOOD–See NORTH HAYLING

NORTHWOOD

AP Incl chap Cowes (sep CP 1894 [the pt in W Cowes USD],[3] sep EP 1927[216]). *LG* W Medina Hd/Lbty, IoW incorp for poor (1770–1865), PLU (1865–1930), pt Newport Bor/MB (until 1876), pt Newport USD (1875–76), pt W Cowes USD (1875–82, extended pt 1882–94), pt IoW RSD (1875–76, extended pt 1876–82, reduced pt 1882–94), IoW RD. Abol civ 1933 pt to Cowes CP, pt to Newport CP, pt to Calbourne AP.[42] *Parl* Pt Newport Parl Bor (1584–1867), IoW Dv/Parl Co (pt 1832–67, ent 1867–1948). *Eccl* Seq 31. Addtl eccl bdry alt: 1968,[175] 1970 (cr Cowes St Faith EP).[219]

NURSLING

AP Incl pt chap Rownhams (sep EP 1856,[48] sep CP 1897[49]). *LG* Buddl. Hd (until 1834), Redbridge Hd (from 1834), Romsey PLU, RSD, RD. Abol civ 1932 to help cr Nursling and Rownhams CP.[1] *Parl* S'rn Dv (1832–85), New For. Dv (1885–1918), New For. & Christch. Dv (1918–48). *Eccl* S'htn. RDn (until 1871), Romsey RDn (1871–1949), S'htn. RDn (1949–55), Romsey RDn (1955–68). Abol eccl 1968 to help cr Nursling and Rownhams EP.[256]

NURSLING AND ROWMHAMS

Cr civ 1932,[1] eccl 1968[256] by union Nursling AP, Rownhams CP/EP. *LG* Romsey & Stockb. RD. Civ bdry: 1954 (exchanges pts with S'htn. CB and CP),[185] 1967 (loses pt to S'htn. CB and CP).[375] *Parl* Winch. CC (1948–55), E'leigh. CC (1955–*). *Eccl* Romsey RDn.

NUTLEY

AP Orig sep AP, Alresf. RDn, sep civ identity maintained, later eccl incl in Preston Candover AP (perhaps in 1688[376]), no sep eccl identity thereafter. *LG* Seq 5. *Parl* Seq 5.

OAKFIELD

EP Cr 1844 from St Helens AP.[377] IoW RDn (1844–50), E Medine RDn (1850–72), S-E Medine RDn (1872–92), E Wight RDn (1892–*). Now called 'Ryde St John Baptist'.

OAKLEY

AP Usual civ spelling; for eccl see following entry. *LG* Chuteley Hd, Basingst. PLU, RSD, RD. Civ bdry: 1968.[378] *Parl* Seq 5.

CHURCH OAKLEY

AP Usual eccl spelling; for civ see prev entry. *Eccl* Seq 15.

ODIHAM

AP Incl chap Rotherwick (sep civ identity early, sep EP 1817[7]), chap Greywell (sep civ identity early, sep EP 1901[30]), tg Bramshill (sep CP 1866,[102] in Holdshot Hd until 1834, Odiham Hd from 1834), chap Weston Patrick (sep civ identity early, sep EP 1815[7]); gains eccl early Liss AP[338] (sep civ identity retained, sep EP again 1819[7]). *LG* Until 1834, pt Odiham Hd, pt Holdshot Hd, thereafter Odiham Hd, Hart. Wit. PLU, RSD, RD. Addtl civ bdry alt: 1932 (incl help cr Hook CP).[1] *Parl* Seq 4. *Eccl* Basingst. RDn (until 1856), Odiham RDn (1856–92), Aldsh. RDn (1892–1922), Basingst. RDn (1928–*). Addtl eccl bdry alt: 1955 (help cr Hook EP).[176]

OLIVERS BATTERY

CP Cr 1956 from Compton AP.[209] *LG* Winch. RD. *Parl* Winch. CC (1970–*).

OTTERBOURNE

Chap in Hursley AP, sep civ identity early, sep EP 1876.[329] *LG* Buddl. Hd, Hursley PLU, RSD, RD (1894–1932), Winch. RD (1932–74). Civ bdry: 1883,[16] 1897 (help cr Chandlers Ford CP),[26] 1932.[1] *Parl* Seq 9. *Eccl* Winch. RDn. Eccl bdry: 1910 (help cr Chandler's Ford EP).[29]

OVERTON

AP Incl chap Tadley (sep civ identity early, sep EP 1878[379]). *LG* Overton Bor (status not sustained), Seq 20. Addtl civ bdry alt: 1932.[1] *Parl* Seq 6. *Eccl* Pec jurisd (until 1846), Basingst. RDn (1846–56), N-E Basingst. RDn (1856–71), S-W Basingst. RDn (1871–92), Basingst. RDn (1892–1928), Whitch. RDn (1928–*). Eccl bdry: 1869 (from area chap Tadley, help cr Ramsdale EP).[357]

OVINGTON

AP *LG* Fawley Hd, Alresf. PLU, RSD, RD. Abol civ 1932 to help cr Itchen Stoke and Ovington CP.[1] *Parl* N'rn Dv (1832–85), E'rn Dv (1885–1918), Petf. Dv (1918–48). *Eccl* Pec jurisd (until 1845), Alresf. RDn (1845–1973). Abol eccl 1973 to help cr Ovington and Itchen Stoke EP.[263]

OVINGTON AND ITCHEN STOKE

EP Cr 1973 by union Itchen Stoke and Abbotstone AP, Ovington AP.[263] Alresf. RDn.

OWSLEBURY

AP *LG* Seq 12. Civ bdry: 1932 (incl gains Morestead AP, help cr Colden Common CP).[1] *Parl* Seq 9. *Eccl* Pec jurisd (until 1845), Droxf. RDn (1845–56), N-W Droxf. RDn (1856–71), Bp's Walth. RDn (1871–1908), Winch. RDn (1908–*). Eccl bdry: 1844 (help cr Coldon EP).[206]

PAMBER
Attached to Sherborne Priory, thereafter chap in Sherborne AP, sep civ identity early, eccl severed 1930 to help cr Monk Sherborne with Pamber EP.[380] *LG* Barton Stacey Hd (until 1834), Basingst. Hd (from 1834), and Seq 3 thereafter. Bdry: 1932,[1] 1956.[381] *Parl* Seq 5.

PARK HOUSE
Ex-par area in Andv. Hd, sep rated in Andv. PLU but sep civ status not sustained and later incl in Thruxton AP.

PARKHURST FOREST
Ex-par area, later civ incl in Carbisbrooke AP, eccl abol 1968 pt to Carisbrooke AP, pt to Newport EP.[175]

PAULSGROVE
EP Cr 1955 from Wymering AP, Portchester AP.[382] Havant RDn.

PENNINGTON
Chap in Milford AP, sep EP 1843,[351] sep CP 1911.[352] *LG* Lym. PLU, RD. Abol civ 1932 ent to Lymington CP.[1] *Parl* New For. & Christch. Dv (1918–48). *Eccl* Fordbr. RDn (1843–56), E Fordbr. RDn (1856–92), Lyndh. RDn (1892–*). Eccl bdry: 1956.[28]

PENTON GRAFTON
AP Usual civ spelling, sometimes 'Weyhill', qv for usual eccl spelling. *LG* Seq 2. Civ bdry: 1888.[236] *Parl* Seq 8.

PENTON MEWSEY
AP *LG* Seq 2. *Parl* Seq 8. *Eccl* Seq 8.

PETERSFIELD
Chap and bor in Buriton AP, sep civ identity early, sep EP 1886 as 'Petersfield with Sheet'.[159] Incl tg Sheet (sep CP 1866,[102] no sep eccl identity). *LG* Finchd. Hd, Petf. Bor, PLU, pt Petf. USD (1893–94), Petf. RSD (ent 1875–93, pt 1893–94), Petf. UD. Addtl civ bdry alt: 1894 (gains the pts of Buriton AP, Sheet CP in Petf. USD),[160] 1932.[1] *Parl* Petf. Parl Bor (pt 1306–07, 1553–1832, ent 1832–85), E'rn Dv (1885–1918), Petf. Dv/CC (1918–*). *Eccl* Petf. RDn.

PITTLEWORTH
AP Orig AP, Somb. RDn, abol early to Broughton AP.[463]

PLAITFORD
Chap in Wilts (Amesbury Hd) in West Grimstead AP, sep civ identity early in Wilts, sep EP 1856,[383] civ transf 1895 to Hants.[145] *LG* Romsey PLU, RSD, sep RD in Wilts (1894–95), Romsey RD (1895–1932). Civ bdry: 1885.[387] Abol civ 1932 to help cr Melchet Park and Plaitford CP.[1] *Parl* In Wilts until 1918, New For. & Christch. Dv (1918–48). *Eccl* Sarum dioc; see entry in Wilts.

POKESDOWN
EP Cr 1856,[7] refounded 1859[196] from Christchurch AP. E Fordbr. RDn (1856–71), W Fordbr. RDn (1871–92), Christch. RDn (1892–1928), Bournem. RDn (1892–*). Bdry: 1887 (cr Southbourne-on-Sea EP),[384] 1892,[325] 1910,[385] 1922 (help cr Bournemouth St Mary EP),[127] 1929 (cr Boscombe St Andrew EP),[108] PLU, RD (1894–95), Pokesdown UD (1895–1901), Bournem. CB (1901–02). Abol 1902 ent to Bournem. CB and CP.[116]

POKESDOWN ST JAMES
EP Cr 1931 from Pokesdown EP.[123] Bournem. RDn.

POPHAM
Chap in Micheldever AP, sep civ identity early, eccl severed 1847 to help cr Woodmancote and Popham EP.[169] *LG* Micheld. Hd (until 1834), Berm. Hd (from 1834), and Seq 5 thereafter. Civ bdry: 1932.[1] *Parl* Seq 5.

PORTCHESTER
AP *LG* Portsd. Hd, Portchester Bor (status not sustained), Fareham PLU, RSD, RD. Abol civ 1932 pt to Portsm. CB and AP, pt to Fareham AP.[1] *Parl* S'rn Dv (1832–1918), Fareham Dv (1918–48). *Eccl* Droxf. RDn (until 1856), S-E Droxf. RDn (1856–71), Alv. & Ports. Isl. RDn (1871–79), Alv. RDn (1879–92), Landp. RDn (1892–1900), Havant RDn (1900–70), Alv. RDn (1970–*). Eccl bdry: 1955 (help cr Paulsgrove EP).[382]

PORTSDOWN
EP Cr 1870 from Widley AP, Farlington AP, Purbrook EP.[388] Alv. & Ports. Isl. RDn (1870–71), Alv. RDn (1871–92), Landp. RDn (1892–1900), Havant RDn (1900–*). Bdry: 1968.[272]

PORTSEA
The following have 'Portsea' in their names. Insofar as any existed at a given time: *LG* Pt Portsd. Hd (until 1835), pt [The Guildable] in Lbty Portsm., Portsm. Bor/MB/CB (pt until 1835, ent 1835–1900), Ports. Isl. PLU, Portsm. USD. *Parl* Portsm. Parl Bor (1832–1918). *Eccl* Droxf. RDn (until 1856), S-E Droxf. RDn (1856–71), Alv. & Ports. Isl. RDn (1871–79).

AP1–PORTSEA [ST MARY]–Civ bdry: 1883.[16] Abol civ 1900 ent to Portsm. CB and AP.[389] Eccl bdry: 1819 (cr EP7,[7] refounded 1875 [incl pt from EP4][391]), 1824 (cr EP8,[7] refounded 1835[390]), 1835 (cr EP1),[393] 1835 (cr EP14),[390] 1842 (cr EP4),[393] 1844 (cr Milton EP),[357] 1865 (cr EP11),[359] 1875 (cr EP12),[13] 1882 (help cr EP13),[394] 1886,[360] 1906 (help cr EP16),[361] 1955.[336]

EP1–PORTSEA ALL SAINTS–Cr 1835 from AP1.[393] Bdry: 1898 (help cr Landport EP),[40] 1906 (help cr EP16),[361] 1907,[362] 1917 (help cr EP9),[395] 1955.[336] Abol 1971 to help cr EP2.[396]

EP2–PORTSEA ALL SAINTS WITH RUDMORE ST JOHN THE BAPTIST–Cr 1971 by union EP1, EP10.[396]

EP3–PORTSEA THE ASCENSION–Cr 1929 from EP12.[397]

EP4–PORTSEA HOLY TRINITY–Cr 1842 from AP1.[393] Bdry: 1875 (help refound EP7).[391] Abol 1906 pt to EP7, pt to EP8.[361]

EP5–PORTSEA ST ALBAN–Cr 1914 from EP16, EP12.[398]

EP6–PORTSEA ST CUTHBERT–Cr 1916 from Milton EP.[363]

EP7–PORTSEA ST GEORGE–Cr 1819 from

AP1,[7] refounded 1875 from AP1, EP4.[391] RDns as for AP1 (1819–92), Portsm. RDn (1892–1955). Bdry: 1906.[361] Abol 1955 ent to Portsmouth AP.[336]

EP8–PORTSEA ST JOHN –Cr 1824,[7] refounded 1835[390] from AP1. RDns as for AP1 (1824–92), Portsm. RDn (1892–*). Bdry: 1906.[361] Abol 1955 ent to Portsmouth AP.[336]

EP9–PORTSEA ST JOHN RUDMORE–Cr 1917 from EP12, EP1.[395] Reconstituted 1955 as EP10 when gains EP15.[336]

EP10–PORTSEA ST JOHN THE BAPTIST, RUDMORE–Cr 1955 by union EP9, EP15.[336] Abol 1971 to help cr EP2.[396]

EP11–PORTSEA ST LUKE–Cr 1865 from AP1.[359] RDns as for AP1 (1865–92), Portsm. RDn (1892–*). Bdry: 1882 (help cr EP13),[394] 1955 (incl gains EP14).[336]

EP12–PORTSEA ST MARK, NORTH END–Cr 1875 from AP1.[13] Alv. & Ports. Isl. RDn (1875–79), Ports. Isl. RDn (1879–92), Portsm. RDn (1892–*). Bdry: 1906 (help cr EP16),[361] 1907,[362] 1914 (help cr EP5),[398] 1917 (help cr EP9),[395] 1929 (cr EP3, cr EP15),[397] 1955.[336]

EP13–PORTSEA ST MICHAEL AND ALL ANGELS–Cr 1882 from AP1, EP11, EP14.[394] Ports. Isl. RDn (1882–92), Portsm. RDn (1892–1955). Abol 1955 pt to Portsmouth AP, pt to EP11.[336]

EP14–PORTSEA ST PAUL–Cr 1835 from AP1.[393] RDns as for AP1 (1835–92), Portsm. RDn (1892–1955). Bdry: 1851 (help cr Southsea St Jude EP),[358] 1882 (help cr EP13).[394] Abol 1955 pt to Portsmouth AP, pt to Southsea St Jude EP, pt to EP11.[336]

EP15–PORTSEA ST SAVIOUR–Cr 1929 from EP12.[397] Abol 1955 to help cr EP10.[336]

EP16–PORTSEA ST STEPHEN–Cr 1906 from EP12, Milton EP, AP1, EP1.[361] Bdry: 1914 (help cr EP5).[398] Abol 1955 pt to AP1, pt to EP13.[336]

PORTSMOUTH

AP *LG* Lbty Portsm. & Ports. Isl., Ports. Isl. PLU (1836–89), Portsm. Par (poor law, 1889–1930), Portsm. Bor/MB/CB, USD. Civ bdry: 1883,[16] 1900 (gains Great Salterns CP, Portsea AP),[389] 1904,[213] 1920,[214] 1922 (loses pt to Alverstoke AP),[18] 1940 (loses pt to Alverstoke AP),[20] 1967 (gains Spitbank Fort and Horse Sand Fort in Solent).[399] *Parl* Portsm. Parl Bor (1295–1918); pt Portsm. Central Parl Bor, pt Portsm. North Parl Bor, pt Portsm. South Parl Bor (1918–48); pt Portsm. Langstone BC, pt Portsm. South BC, pt Portsm. West BC (1948–70); pt Portsm. North BC, pt Portsm. South BC (1970–*) [see Part III of the *Guide* for composition of these constituencies by wards of the CB]. *Eccl* Droxf. RDn (until 1856), S-E Droxf. RDn (1856–71), Alv. & Ports. Isl. RDn (1871–79), Ports. Isl. RDn (1879–92), Portsm. RDn (1892–*). Eccl bdry: 1898 (help cr Landport EP),[40] 1955 (incl gains Portsea St John EP, Portsea St

PORTSWOOD

Chap in South Stoneham AP, sep EP 1847,[7] refounded eccl 1848,[400] sep CP 1894 (the pt in S'htn. CB).[3] *LG* S Ston. PLU (1894–1908), S'htn. incorp for poor (1908–09), PLU (1909–12), S'htn. CB. Abol civ 1912 to help cr Southampton CP.[401] *Eccl* S'htn. RDn. Bdry: 1853 (help cr Newtown St Luke EP),[85] 1867 (cr Portswood St Deny's EP).[402]

PORTSWOOD ST DENY'S

EP Cr 1867 from Portswood EP.[402] S'htn. RDn.

PRIVETT

Chap in West Meon AP, sep civ identity early, sep EP 1872.[345] *LG* Fawley Hd (until 1834), E Meon Hd (from 1834), Petf. PLU, RSD, RD. Abol civ 1932 ent to Froxfield AP.[1] *Parl* N'rn Dv (1832–85), E'rn Dv (1885–1918), Petf. Dv (1918–48). *Eccl* Petf. RDn.

PURBROOK

EP Cr 1858 from Farlington AP.[271] N-E Droxf. RDn (1858–71), Havant RDn (1871–92), Landp. RDn (1892–1900), Havant RDn (1900–*). Bdry: 1870 (help cr Portsdown EP).[388]

QUARLEY

AP *LG* Seq 2. *Parl* Seq 8. *Eccl* Seq 9. Eccl bdry: 1939,[14] 1955.[403]

RAMSDALE

EP Cr 1869 from Wootton St Lawrence AP, Monk Sherborne AP, Tadley EP.[357] S-W Basingst. RDn (1869–92), Silch. RDn (1892–1928), Basingst. RDn (1928–*).

REDHILL

EP Cr 1839,[7] refounded 1840[127] from Havant AP, Warblington AP. Droxf. RDn (1839–56), N-E Droxf. RDn (1856–71), Havant RDn (1871–92), Landp. RDn (1892–1900), Havant RDn (1900–53). Bdry: 1921.[177] Renamed 1953 'Rowlands Castle'.[390]

RHINEFIELD

CP Cr 1868 from pts of ex-par New For. (pts Rhinefield and Wilverley Walks [incl Rhinefield Lodge, Rhinefield, Sandys Cottage, Latchmore, Wilverley Lodge, Set and Horns Inclosure Cottage]).[404] *LG* Pt New For. Hd, pt Christch. Hd, Lym. PLU, RSD, RD (1894–1932), New For. RD (1932–74). Bdry: 1926.[356] *Parl* New For. Dv (1885–1918), New For. & Christch. Dv (1918–48), New For. CC (1948–*).

RINGWOOD

AP *LG* Ringw. Hd, PLU, RSD, RD (1894–1932), Ringw. & Fordbr. RD (1932–74). Civ bdry: 1876,[161] 1892,[188] 1932 (incl help cr St Leonards and St Ives CP).[1] *Parl* Seq 10. *Eccl* Sometimes as 'Ringwood with Poulner and Bisterne', pec jurisd (until 1845), Seq 25 thereafter. Eccl bdry: 1840 (help cr Burley Ville EP),[162] 1969,[199] 1970 (help cr St Leonards and St Ives EP).[200]

ROCKBOURNE

AP *LG* Seq 14. Civ bdry: 1883,[16] 1888.[149] *Parl* Seq 10. *Eccl* Donative, Seq 25.

ROMSEY

AP *LG* K's Somb. Hd, pt Romsey Bor/MB, Romsey PLU. Abol civ 1866 pt of the pt in the MB cr Romsey Infra CP, the remainder in the MB and the pt not in the MB cr Romsey Extra CP.[102] *Parl* S'rn Dv (1832–67). *Eccl* Seq 26. Eccl bdry: 1855 (help cr Braishfield EP),[28] 1856 (help cr Rownhams EP),[48] 1877 (help cr Awbridge EP),[47] 1931,[405] 1951.[260]

ROMSEY EXTRA

CP Cr 1866 from the pt of Romsey AP not in Romsey MB, and from pt of Romsey AP in the MB.[102] *LG* K's Somb. Hd, Romsey PLU, pt Romsey MB, pt Romsey USD, pt Romsey RSD, Romsey RD (1894–1932), Romsey & Stockb. RD (1932–74). Bdry: 1883,[16] 1888,[349] 1894 (loses the pt in the MB to Romsey Infra CP),[406] 1897 (help cr Rownhams CP),[49] 1932,[1] 1954,[50] 1963.[27] *Parl* S'rn Dv (1867–85), New For. Dv (1885–1918), New For. & Christch. Dv (1918–48), Winch. CC (1948–70), E'leigh. CC (1970–*).

ROMSEY INFRA

CP Cr 1866 from pt of the pt of Romsey AP in Romsey MB.[102] *LG* Romsey PLU, MB, USD. Bdry: 1894 (gains the pt of Romsey Extra CP in Romsey MB),[406] 1932.[1] *Parl* As for Romsey Extra.

ROPLEY

Chap in Bishop's Sutton AP, sep civ identity early, sep EP 1882.[407] *LG* Seq 24. Civ bdry: 1932 (incl help cr Four Marks CP).[1] *Parl* Seq 1. *Eccl* Alresf. RDn. Eccl bdry: 1973 (help cr Four Marks EP).[179]

ROTHERWICK

Chap in Odiham AP, sep civ identity early, sep EP 1817.[7] *LG* Seq 18. Civ bdry: 1894,[58] 1932.[1] *Parl* Seq 4. *Eccl* Basingst. RDn (1817–56), N-E Basingst. RDn (1856–92), Silch. RDn (1892–1928), Odiham RDn (1928–*). Eccl bdry: 1958.[60]

ROWLANDS CASTLE

CP Cr 1932 from Bedhampton AP, Blendworth AP, Charlton AP, North Havant CP, Warblington AP, ent Idsworth CP.[1] *LG* Petf. RD. Bdry: 1952.[311] *Parl* Petf. CC (1948–*).

EP Renaming 1953 of Redhill EP.[390] Havant RDn. Bdry: 1968 (incl help cr Leigh Park EP).[74]

ROWLEDGE

EP Cr 1871 from Binsted with Kingsley EP (Hants) and from Wrecclesham EP, Frensham AP (both Surrey).[408] See main entry in Surrey.

ROWNER

AP *LG* Titchfield Hd, Fareham PLU, pt Alv. USD (1883–91), pt Gosport & Alv. USD (1891–94), Fareham RSD (ent 1875–83, pt 1883–94), Fareham RD. Civ bdry: 1883,[16] 1886,[17] 1894 (loses the pt in the USD to Alverstoke AP),[3] 1930 (incl help cr Lee on Solent CP).[19] Abol civ 1932 ent to Alverstoke AP.[1] *Parl* S'rn Dv (1832–1918), Fareham Dv (1918–48). *Eccl* Seq 21. Eccl bdry: 1949.[23]

ROWNHAMS

EP Cr 1856 from North Baddesley AP, Romsey AP, Nursling AP.[48] S-W Somb. RDn (1856–71), Romsey RDn (1871–1968). Bdry: 1958.[53] Abol 1968 to help cr Nursling and Rownhams EP.[256]

CP Cr 1897 from North Baddesley AP, Nursling AP, Romsey Extra CP.[49] *LG* Romsey PLU, RD. Abol 1932 to help cr Nursling and Rownhams CP.[1] *Parl* New For. & Christch. Dv (1918–48).

RYDE

Area in Newchurch AP, sep CP/EP 1866.[369] *LG* E Medina Hd/Lbty, IoW PLU, Ryde MB (pt 1868–94, ent 1894–1974), pt Ryde USD, pt IoW RSD. Civ bdry: 1894 (loses the pt not in the MB to cr Ashey CP),[3] 1894 (gains the pt of St Helens AP in Ryde MB),[409] 1933 (incl gains St Helens AP),[42] 1967 (gains No Man's Land and St Helens Fort in Solent).[399] *Parl* IoW Parl Dv/Co (1867–*). *Eccl* E Medine RDn (1866–72), N-E Medine RDn (1872–92), E Wight RDn (1892–*). Eccl bdry: 1961.[410]

RYDE HOLY TRINITY

EP Cr 1846 from Newchurch AP.[182] IoW RDn (1846–50), E Medine RDn (1850–72), N-E Medine RDn (1872–92), E Wight RDn (1892–*).

ST FAITH

AP Usual civ spelling; for eccl see 'Winchester St Faith'. *LG* Buddl. Hd, pt Winch. Bor/MB, Winch. PLU, pt Winch. USD, pt Winch. RSD. Abol civ 1894 the pt in the MB cr St Faith Within CP, the remainder cr St Faith Without CP.[3] *Parl* Pt Winch. Parl Bor (1295–1918), pt N'rn Dv (1832–85), pt W'rn Dv (1885–1918).

ST FAITH WITHIN

CP Cr 1894 from the pt of St Faith AP in Winch. MB.[3] *LG* Winch. PLU, MB. Bdry: 1900.[4] Abol 1902 to help cr Winchester CP.[183]

ST FAITH WITHOUT

CP Cr 1894 from the pt of St Faith AP not in Winch. MB.[3] *LG* Winch. PLU, RD. Abol 1900 pt to St Faith Within CP, pt to Compton AP.[4]

ST HELENS

AP *LG* E Medina Hd/Lbty, IoW incorp for poor (1770–1865), PLU (1865–1930), pt Ryde MB (1868–94), pt St Helens USD, pt Ryde USD, pt IoW RSD, St Helens UD. Civ bdry: 1894 (loses the pt in the MB to Ryde CP and made ent St Helens UD),[409] 1899.[43] Abol civ 1933 ent to Ryde CP.[42] *Parl* IoW Dv/Parl Co (1832–1948). *Eccl* Seq 30. Eccl bdry: 1844 (cr Oakfield EP),[377] 1907 (cr Seaview EP).[411]

ST LAWRENCE

AP *LG* E Medina Hd/Lbty, IoW incorp for poor (1770–1865), PLU (1865–1930), RSD, RD. Abol civ 1933 ent to Ventnor CP.[42] *Parl* IoW Dv/Parl Co (1832–1948). *Eccl* Seq 30.

ST LEONARDS AND ST IVES

CP Cr 1932 from Hurn CP, Ringwood AP.[1] *LG* Ringw. & Fordbr. RD. Bdry: 1947.[412] Transf 1974 to Dorset.[141] *Parl* New For. CC (1948–*).

EP Cr 1970 from Ringwood AP, Christchurch AP, Holdenhurst EP.[200] Christch. RDn.

ST MARY BOURNE

Chap (pec jurisd) in Hurstbourne Priors AP, sep civ identity early, sep EP 1928.[330] *LG* Seq 10. Civ bdry: 1932 (incl help cr Litchfield and Woodcott CP).[1] *Parl* Seq 6. *Eccl* Whitch. RDn.

ST MARY EXTRA

Chap in Southampton St Mary AP (erected as chap 1617,[413] usually known as 'Jesus Chapel'), sep civ identity early, sep EP 1714,[7] eccl sep status seemingly not sustained, eccl refounded 1923 from Southampton St Mary AP, Hound AP, Sholing EP, Bitterne EP, Bitterne Park EP.[90] *LG* Mainsbr. Hd (until **1834**), Bp's Walth. (from **1834**), S Ston. PLU, RSD, RD (1894–98), Itchen UD (1898–1903). Abol civ 1903 to help cr Itchen CP.[333] *Parl* S'rn Dv (1832–1918), Winch. Dv (1918–48). *Eccl* Sometimes as 'Southampton St Mary Extra', S'htn. RDn. Eccl bdry: 1866 (cr Weston EP),[339] 1867 (help cr Sholing EP [orig 'Scholing']).[414]

ST NICHOLAS

Chap in Carisbrooke Castle, sep civ identity early, sep eccl identity early as sinecure. *LG* W Medina Hd/Lbty, IoW incorp for poor (1770–1865), PLU (1865–94), pt Newport Bor/MB, pt Newport USD, pt IoW RSD. Civ bdry: 1883,[16] 1889.[150] Abol civ 1894 the pt in the MB to Newport CP, pt of remainder to Northwood AP, remainder to Carisbrooke AP.[73] *Parl* IoW Dv/Parl Co (1832–1918). *Eccl* Seq 31. Eccl bdry: 1968.[175] Now eccl called 'Carisbrooke St Nicholas'.

GREAT SALTERNS

Ex-par place, sep CP 1858,[32] eccl bdry alt 1907.[362] *LG* Portsd. Hd, Ports. Isl. PLU (1858[229]–1900), RSD, RD (1894–95), Portsm. CB (1895–1900). Abol 1900 ent to Portsm. CB and AP.[389] *Parl* S'rn Dv (1867–1918).

SANDOWN

Area in Brading AP, sep EP 1848,[7] sep CP 1894 (the pt in Sandown USD).[3] *LG* IoW PLU, Sandown UD. Bdry: 1895.[143] Abol 1933 to help cr Sandown-Shanklin CP.[42] *Parl* IoW Parl Co (1918–48). *Eccl* IoW RDn (1848–50), E Medine RDn (1850–72), S-E Medine RDn (1872–92), E Wight RDn (1892–*). Eccl bdry: 1876 (cr Gatten EP [now called 'Shanklin St Paul']),[290] 1881 (cr Lower Sandown EP),[415] 1930 (help cr Lake EP).[216]

LOWER SANDOWN

EP Cr 1881 from Sandown EP.[415] S-E Medine RDn (1881–92), E Wight RDn (1892–*).

SANDOWN-SHANKLIN

EP Cr 1933 by union Sandown CP, Shanklin AP and pts Bonchurch AP, Brading AP, Yaverland AP.[42] *LG* Sandown-Shanklin UD. *Parl* IoW Parl Co (1948–*).

SARISBURY

Chap in Titchfield AP, sep EP 1836,[7] eccl refounded 1837,[416] sep CP 1894.[221] *LG* Fareham PLU, RD. Abol civ 1932 pt to Fareham AP, pt to help cr Curbridge AP.[192] *Parl* Fareham Dv (1918–48). *Eccl* Droxf. RDn (1837–56), S'htn. RDn (1856–71), Alv. & Ports. Isl. RDn (1871–79), Alv. RDn (1879–*). Eccl bdry: 1872 (help cr Hook with Warsash EP),[325] 1893 (help cr Lock's Heath EP).[464]

SCHOLING–See SHOLING

SEAVIEW

EP Cr 1907 from St Helens AP.[411] E Wight RDn.

SELBORNE

AP *LG* Seq 23.[417] Civ bdry: 1929 (help cr Whitehill CP).[299] *Parl* Seq 1. *Eccl* Seq 5. Eccl bdry: 1867 (cr Blackmoor EP),[95] 1870.[131]

SHALDEN

AP *LG* Odiham Hd (until **1834**), Alton Hd (from **1834**), and Seq 1 thereafter. Civ bdry: 1932.[1] *Parl* Seq 1. *Eccl* Seq 5.

SHALFLEET

AP *LG* Seq 32. Civ bdry: 1889.[150] *Parl* Seq 17. *Eccl* Seq 31. Eccl bdry: 1871 (help cr Newtown EP),[168] 1968.[175]

SHANKLIN

Chap in Bonchurch AP, sep civ identity early, sep EP 1853.[107] *LG* E Medina Hd/Lbty, IoW incorp for poor (1770–1865), PLU (1865–1930), pt Shanklin USD, pt IoW RSD, Shanklin UD. Civ bdry: 1894 (made ent Shanklin UD),[3] 1898 (gains East Shanklin CP).[418] Abol civ 1933 to help cr Sandown-Shanklin CP.[42] *Parl* IoW Dv/Parl Co (1832–1948). *Eccl* E Medine RDn (1853–72), S-E Medine RDn (1872–92), E Wight RDn (1892–*). Eccl bdry: 1869 (cr Shanklin St Saviour EP).[419]

EAST SHANKLIN

CP Cr 1894 from the pt of Brading AP in Shanklin AP.[3] *LG* IoW PLU, Shanklin UD. Bdry: 1895.[142] Abol 1898 ent to Shanklin AP.[418]

SHANKLIN ST SAVIOUR

EP Cr 1869 from Shanklin EP.[419] E Medine RDn (1869–72), S-E Medine RDn (1872–92), E Wight RDn (1892–*).

SHEDFIELD

CP Cr1894 from Droxford AP.[244] *LG* Droxf. PLU, RD. Bdry: 1932,[1] 1967.[233] *Parl* Petf. Dv/CC (1918–*).

EP Renaming 1971 of Shidfield EP, gaining at same time pts Swanmore EP, Bishop's Waltham AP, Curdridge EP.[420] Bp's Walth. RDn.

SHEET

Tg in Petersfield CP, sep CP 1866,[102] no sep eccl identity. *LG* Finchd. Hd, Petf. PLU, pt Petf. USD (1893–94), Petf. RSD (ent 1875–93, pt 1893–94), Petf. RD. Bdry: 1894 (loses the pt in the USD to Petersfield CP).[160] Abol 1932 pt to Petersfield CP, pt to Buriton AP, pt to Steep AP.[1] *Parl* N'rn Dv (1867–85), E'rn Dv (1885–1918), Petf. Dv (1918–48).

MONK SHERBORNE

AP Anc also 'West Sherborne'. Gains early Chineham AP.[463] *LG* Pt Chuteley Hd, pt Basingst. Hd (until 1834), ent Basingst. Hd (from 1834), Basingst. PLU, RSD, RD. Civ bdry: 1879,[421] 1932.[1] *Parl* Seq 5. *Eccl* Basingst. RDn (until 1856), S-W

Basingst. RDn (1856–71), N-E Basingst. RDn (1871–92), Silch. RDn (1892–1928), Basingst. RDn (1928–30). Eccl bdry: 1869 (help cr Ramsdale EP).[357] Abol eccl 1930 to help cr Monk Sherborne with Pamber EP.[380]

MONK SHERBORNE WITH PAMBER

EP Cr 1930 by union Monk Sherborne AP, ex-par places Sherborne Priory, Pamber.[380] Basingst. RDn. Bdry: 1972.[422]

SHERBORNE ST JOHN

AP *LG* Seq 3. Civ bdry: 1932,[1] 1965.[64] *Parl* Seq 5. *Eccl* Seq 16.

SHERFIELD ENGLISH

AP *LG* Seq 27. Civ bdry: 1932 (incl gains Dunwood CP).[1] *Parl* Seq 12. *Eccl* Seq 26.

SHERFIELD-ON-LODDON

AP Sometimes civ 'Sherfield upon Loddon'. *LG* Odiham Hd (until 1830s), Basingst. Hd (from 1830s) and Seq 3 thereafter. *Parl* Seq 5. *Eccl* Seq 16.

SHERFIELD UPON LODDON–See prev entry

SHIDFIELD

EP Cr 1837,[7] refounded 1843 from Droxford AP.[423] Droxf. RDn (1837–56), N-W Droxf. RDn (1856–71), Bp's Walth. RDn (1871–1971). Bdry: 1874.[113] Renamed 1971 'Shedfield' gaining at same time pts Swanmore EP, Bishop's Waltham AP, Curdridge EP.[420]

SHIPTON BELLINGER

AP *LG* Thorng. Hd (until 1834), Andv. Hd (from 1834), and Seq 2 thereafter. *Parl* Seq 8. *Eccl* Seq 8.

SHIRLEY

AP Orig sep AP, united 1574 to Millbrook AP,[463] sep EP status regained 1839,[7] sep civ status 1894 (the pt in Shirley & Freemantle USD).[3] *LG* S Ston. PLU (1894–1908), S'htn. incorp for poor (1908–09), PLU (1909–12), Shirley & Freemantle UD (1894–95), S'htn. CB (1895–1912). Civ bdry: 1895.[354] Abol 1912 to help cr Southampton CP.[401] *Eccl* S'htn. RDn. Eccl bdry: 1891 (cr Southampton St Mark EP),[271] 1939 (help cr Southampton St Peter, Maybush EP),[355] 1956 (cr Southampton St Jude Warren Avenue EP).[424]

SHOLING

EP Cr 1867 from St Mary Extra EP, Hound AP.[414] Orig 'Scholing', later usually 'Sholing'. S'htn. RDn. Bdry: 1916 (help refound St Mary Extra EP),[90] 1918,[91] 1957,[320] 1971 (help cr Southampton St Christopher, Thornhill EP).[425]

CP Cr 1894 from Hound AP.[114] *LG* S Ston. PLU, RD (1894–98), Itchen UD (1898–1903). Abol 1903 to help cr Itchen CP.[333]

SHORWELL

AP *LG* Seq 32. Civ bdry: 1883,[16] 1889,[150] 1932 (gains Kingston AP).[42] *Parl* Seq 17. *Eccl* Seq 31. Eccl bdry: 1968.[175]

SILCHESTER

AP *LG* Seq 15. *Parl* Seq 5. *Eccl* Seq 13.

SMANNELL

EP Cr 1858 from Andover with Foxcott AP as 'Smannell with Hatherden'.[426] from cr 1874 of Hatherden EP from the par[308] called 'Smannell'. Andv. RDn (1858–71), W Andv. RDn (1871–92), Andv. RDn (1892–1973). Renamed 1973 'Smannell with Enham Alamein' after exchanges pts with Knight's Enham AP.[263]

CP Cr 1932 from Andover AP.[1] *LG* Andv. RD. *Parl* Basingst. CC (1948–70), Winch. CC (1970–*).

SMANNELL WITH ENHAM ALAMEIN

EP Renaming 1973 of Smannell EP after exchanges pts with Kinght's Enham AP.[263] Andv. RDn.

SMANNELL WITH HATHERDEN–see SMANNELL

SOBERTON

Chap in Meonstoke AP, sep civ identity early, sep EP 1897.[346] *LG* Seq 17. Civ bdry: 1884.[427] *Parl* Seq 1. *Eccl* Bp's Walth. RDn. Eccl bdry: 1851 (when still chap, cr Newtown EP).[94]

KINGS SOMBORNE

AP Incl chap Little Somborne (sep civ identity early, no sep eccl identity), chap and bor Stockbridge (sep civ identity early, sep EP 1842[428]). *LG* K's Somb. Hd, Stockb. PLU, RSD, RD (1894–1932), Romsey & Stockb. RD (1932–74). Addtl civ bdry alt: 1883,[429] 1932 (gains Upper Eldon CP).[1] *Parl* Seq 16. *Eccl* As 'King's Somborne', Seq 26. Eccl bdry: 1962.[343]

LITTLE SOMBORNE

Chap in Kings Somborne AP (eccl, 'King's Somborne'), sep civ identity early, no sep eccl identity. *LG* K's Somb. Hd (until 1834), Buddl. Hd (from 1834), Stockb. PLU, RSD, RD (1894–1932), Romsey & Stockb. RD (1932–74). Bdry: 1883.[430] *Parl* Seq 16.

SOPLEY

AP *LG* Christch. Hd, Bournem. & Christch. PLU (1835–89), Christch. PLU (1889–1930), RSD, RD (1894–1932), Ringw. & Fordbr. RD (1932–74). Civ bdry: 1877,[431] 1974 (the pt transf to Dorset added to Hurn CP as latter also transf to Dorset).[141] *Parl* Seq 10. *Eccl* Fordbr. RDn (until 1856), E Fordbr. RDn (1856–71), W Fordbr. RDn (1871–92), Christch. RDn (1892–1908), Ringw. RDn (1908–12), Christch. RDn (1912–*). Eccl bdry: 1969.[199]

SOUTHAMPTON

The following have 'Southampton' in their names. Insofar as any exitsed at a given time: *LG* S'htn. Bor/MB/CB, Co, incorp for poor (1772–1909), PLU (1909–30), USD. Made 'City and Co' 1964.[432] *Parl* Southampton Parl Bor (1295–1948); pt Southampton, Itchen BC, pt Southampton, Test BC (1948–*) [see Part III of the *Guide* for composition of these BCs by wards of the CB]. *Eccl* S'htn. RDn.

CP1–SOUTHAMPTON–Cr 1912 by union Portswood CP, Shirley CP, AP1, AP2, AP3, AP4, AP5, AP6.[401] Bdry: 1925 (gains Bitterne CP, Itchen CP, CP2),[88] 1967 (gains Nursling and Rownhams CP).[375]

AP1–SOUTHAMPTON ALL SAINTS–Abol civ 1912 to help cr CP1.[401] Eccl bdry: 1861 (cr EP15),[433] 1863 (cr EP14).[339] Abol eccl 1954 pt to help cr EP10, pt to help cr EP16, pt to help cr EP12, pt to Bernard Street EP.[79]

EP1–SOUTHAMPTON (CITY CENTRE)–Cr 1973 by union Northam EP, Newtown St Luke EP, EP10, EP11, EP13, EP16.[374]

AP2–SOUTHAMPTON HOLY ROOD–Sometimes eccl 'Southampton St Cross'. Abol civ 1912 to help cr CP1.[401] Abol eccl 1923 to help cr EP2.[434]

EP2–SOUTHAMPTON HOLY ROOD WITH ST LAURENCE AND ST JOHN–Cr 1923 by union AP2, EP8.[434] Abol 1954 to help cr EP12.[79]

EP3–SOUTHAMPTON HOLY TRINITY–Cr 1848 from AP5.[131] Bdry: 1854,[89] 1866 (help cr EP11).[206] Abol 1954 pt to help cr EP10, pt to EP11.[79]

EP4–SOUTHAMPTON ST ALBAN–Cr 1932 from South Stoneham AP.[40]

EP5–SOUTHAMPTON ST BARNABAS–Cr 1893 from Newtown St Luke EP.[372] Bdry: 1925.[373]

EP6–SOUTHAMPTON ST CHRISTOPHER, THORNHILL–Cr 1971 from West End EP, Sholing EP.[425]

–SOUTHAMPTON ST CROSS–See AP2

–SOUTHAMPTON ST JAMES, BERNARD STREET–See BERNARD STREET

AP3–SOUTHAMPTON ST JOHN–Abol civ 1912 to help cr CP1.[401] Abol eccl 1708 to help cr EP8.[435]

EP7–SOUTHAMPTON ST JUDE WARREN AVENUE–Cr 1956 from Shirley EP.[424]

–SOUTHAMPTON ST LAURENCE–See AP4

EP8–SOUTHAMPTON ST LAURENCE WITH ST JOHN–Cr 1708 by union AP4, AP3.[435] Abol 1923 to help cr EP2.[434]

AP4–SOUTHAMPTON ST LAWRENCE–Usual civ spelling and usual eccl spelling in united pars from 1954 (see EP12, EP13); usual eccl spelling earlier 'Southampton St Laurence'. Abol civ 1912 to help cr CP1.[401] Abol eccl 1708 to help cr EP8.[435]

EP9–SOUTHAMPTON ST MARK–Cr 1892 from Shirley EP.[276] Bdry: 1954 (incl help cr EP12, help cr EP16).[79]

AP5–SOUTHAMPTON ST MARY–Incl chap St Mary Extra (erected as chap 1617,[413] usually known as 'Jesus Chapel', sep civ identity early, sep EP 1714,[7] eccl sep status seemingly not sustained, eccl refounded 1923 from Southampton St Mary AP, Hound AP, Sholing EP, Bitterne EP, Bitterne Park EP[90]). Abol civ 1912 to help cr CP1.[401] Addtl eccl bdry alt: 1848 (cr EP3),[131] 1853 (cr Bernard Street EP [sometimes 'Southampton St James, Bernard Street']),[78] 1853 (help cr Newtown St Luke EP, cr Northam EP),[85] 1864 (help cr Woolston EP),[328] 1866 (cr Weston EP),[339] 1866 (help cr EP11),[206] 1918.[91] Abol eccl 1954 to help cr EP10.[79]

–SOUTHAMPTON ST MARY EXTRA–See ST MARY EXTRA

EP10–SOUTHAMPTON ST MARY WITH HOLY TRINITY–Cr 1954 by union AP5, pts EP3, AP1.[79] Abol 1973 to help cr EP1.[374]

EP11–SOUTHAMPTON ST MATTHEW–Cr 1866 from AP5, EP3, Newtown St Luke EP.[206] Bdry: 1954.[79] Abol 1973 to help cr EP1.[374]

AP6–SOUTHAMPTON ST MICHAEL–Abol civ 1912 to help cr CP1.[401] Abol eccl 1954 to help cr EP12.[79]

EP12–SOUTHAMPTON ST MICHAEL WITH HOLY ROOD, ST LAWRENCE AND ST JOHN–Cr 1954 by union AP6, EP2 and pts AP1, EP9.[79] Abol 1968 to help cr EP13.[80]

EP13–SOUTHAMPTON ST MICHAEL WITH HOLY ROOD, ST LAWRENCE AND ST JOHN AND ST JAMES DOCKS–Cr 1968 by union EP12, Bernard Street EP.[80] Abol 1973 to help cr EP1.[374]

CP2–SOUTHAMPTON ST NICHOLAS–Cr 1920 from North Stoneham AP, South Stoneham AP.[436] Abol 1925 ent to CP1.[88]

EP14–SOUTHAMPTON ST PAUL–Cr 1863 from AP1.[339] Abol 1954 to help cr EP16.[79]

EP15–SOUTHAMPTON ST PETER–Cr 1861 from AP1.[433] Abol 1954 to help cr EP16.[79]

EP16–SOUTHAMPTON ST PETER AND ST PAUL WITH ALL SAINTS–Cr 1954 by union EP15, EP14 and pts AP1, EP9.[79] Abol 1973 to help cr EP1.[374]

EP17–SOUTHAMPTON ST PETER, MAYBUSH–Cr 1939 from Shirley EP, Millbrook EP.[355] Bdry: 1954.[148]

SOUTHBOURNE

CP Cr 1894 from Christchurch AP.[189] *LG* Christch. PLU, RD. Bdry: 1901.[213] Abol 1902 ent to Bournem. CB and CP.[116]

SOUTHBOURNE-ON-SEA

EP Cr 1887 from Pokesdown EP.[384] W Fordbr. RDn (1887–92), Christch. RDn (1892–1928), Bournem. RDn (1928–*). Bdry: 1910.[385]

SOUTHSEA

The following have 'Southsea' in their names. Insofar as any existed at a given time: *Eccl* Droxf. RDn (cr–1856), S-E Droxf. RDn (1856–71), Alv. & Ports. Isl. RDn (1871–79), Ports. Isl. RDn (1879–92), Portsm. RDn (1892–*).

EP1–SOUTHSEA THE HOLY SPIRIT–Cr 1948 by union EP2, EP4.[437]

EP2–SOUTHSEA ST BARTHOLOMEW–Cr 1862 from Milton EP.[359] Bdry: 1886,[360] 1904 (cr EP4).[438] Abol 1948 to help cr EP1.[437]

EP3–SOUTHSEA ST JUDE–Cr 1851 from Portsea St Paul EP, Milton EP.[358] Bdry: 1862 (cr EP6),[359] 1883 (cr EP5),[425] 1955.[336]

EP4–SOUTHSEA ST MATTHEW–Cr 1904 from EP2.[438] Abol 1948 to help cr EP1.[437]

EP5–SOUTHSEA ST PETER–Cr 1883 from EP3.[425] Bdry: 1886,[360] 1955.[366]

EP6–SOUTHSEA ST SIMON–Cr 1862 from EP3.[359]

SOUTHWICK

AP Gains early Wanstead AP.[463] *LG* Portsd. Hd, Fareham PLU, RSD, RD. Civ bdry: 1883,[16] 1886.[439] Abol civ 1932 pt to help cr Southwick and Widley CP, pt to Havant AP.[1] *Parl* S'rn Dv (1832–1918), Fareham Dv (1918–48). *Eccl* Donative, Droxf. RDn. Abol eccl prob in 18th cent, certainly by 1876, to help cr Southwick and Boarhunt EP.[100]

SOUTHWICK AND BOARHUNT

EP Cr prob in 18th cent, certainly by 1876, by union Southwick AP, Boarhunt AP.[100] Droxf. RDn (cr–1856), S-W Droxf. RDn (1856–71), Alv. & Ports. Isl. RDn (1871–79), Alv. RDn (1879–*).

SOUTHWICK AND WIDLEY

CP Cr 1932 by union pts Farlington AP, Southwick CP, Waterloo CP, and ent Widley CP.[1] *LG* Droxf. RD. Bdry: 1952,[311] 1964.[312] *Parl* Petf. CC (1948–*).

SPARSHOLT

AP *LG* Seq 6. Civ bdry: 1932 (incl gains Lainston CP).[1] *Parl* Seq 9. *Eccl* Seq 28.

STANMORE

EP Cr 1954 from Winchester St Faith AP, Winchester Christ Church EP.[440] Winch. RDn. Bdry: 1973.[342]

STEEP

Chap in East Meon AP, sep civ identity early, sep EP 1867.[285] Incl tgs North Ambersham, South Ambersham (each situated in Easebourne Hd, Sussex, each transf to Selham AP, Sussex, 1832 for parl purposes, 1844 for civ purposes,[147] [so that Steep ent Hants thereafter] each sep CP 1866 in Sussex,[102] each transf 1916 from dioc Winch to dioc Chich[444]). *LG* E Meon Hd, Petf. PLU, RSD, RD. Addtl civ bdry alt: 1883,[16] 1932.[1] *Parl* Hants pt, Petf. Parl Bor (1832–67); afterwards ent Hants, Petf. Parl Bor (1867–85), E'rn Dv (1885–1918), Petf. Dv/CC (1918–*). *Eccl* W Meon RDn (1867–71), Petf. RDn (1871–*).

STEVENTON

AP *LG* Basingst. Hd (until 1834), Overton Hd (from 1834), and Seq 19 thereafter. Civ bdry: 1932.[1] *Parl* Seq 6. *Eccl* Seq 15. Eccl bdry: 1930.[238]

STOCKBRIDGE

Chap in King's Somborne AP, sep civ identity early, sep EP 1842.[428] *LG* Stockb. Bor, K's Somb. Hd (until 1834), Thorng. Hd (from 1834), and Seq 28 thereafter. Civ bdry: 1883.[441] *Parl* Stockb. Parl Bor (1563–1832), Seq 7 thereafter. *Eccl* Somb. RDn (1842–56), Chilb. RDn (1856–71), S Andv. RDn (1871–92), Stockb. RDn (1892–1922), Romsey RDn (1922–*). Eccl bdry: 1962.[343]

STOKE CHARITY

AP *LG* Buddl. Hd, Winch. PLU, RSD, RD. Abol civ 1932 ent to Wonston AP.[1] *Parl* N'rn Dv (1832–85), W'rn Dv (1885–1918), Winch. Dv (1918–48). *Eccl* Somb. RDn (until 1856), Micheld. RDn (1856–71), Winch. RDn (1871–1938). Abol eccl 1938 to help cr Stoke Charity with Hunton EP.[131]

STOKE CHARITY WITH HUNTON

EP Cr 1938 by union Stoke Charity AP, chap Hunton of Crawley AP.[131] Winch. RDn.

STOKE PARK

CP Cr 1899 from Bishopstoke AP.[84] *LG* Winch. PLU, RD. Abol 1932 pt to Eastleigh CP, pt to Fair Oak CP.[1] *Parl* Winch. Dv (1918–48).

NORTH STONEHAM

AP *LG* Mainsbr. Hd, S Ston. PLU (ent 1835–1924, pt 1924–30), pt S'htn. PLU (1924–30), S Ston. RSD, RD. Civ bdry: 1897 (help cr Chandlers Ford CP),[26] 1898,[252] 1920 (help cr Southampton St Nicholas CP [to be in S'htn. CB]).[436] Abol civ 1932 pt to Eastleigh CP, pt to Chilworth AP.[1] *Parl* S'rn Dv (1832–85), New For. Dv (1885–1918), New For. & Christch. Dv (1918–48). *Eccl* Seq 27. Eccl bdry: 1910 (help cr Chandler's Ford EP),[29] 1954.[253]

SOUTH STONEHAM

AP Incl chap Portswood (sep EP 1847,[7] eccl refounded 1858,[400] sep CP 1894 [the pt of South Stoneham in S'htn. Bor/MB/CB][3]), tg Eastleigh (sep EP 1868,[200] sep CP 1894 [the pt in E'leigh. USD][251]), chap West End (sep EP 1840,[268] sep CP 1894[86]), area Bitterne (sep EP 1853 [incl pt from West End EP],[85] sep CP 1894 [from South Stoneham only][86]). *LG* Mainsbr. Hd, S Ston. PLU, pt E'leigh. USD (1893–94), pt S'htn. Bor/MB/CB [Portswood] (until 1894), pt S'htn. USD, pt S Ston. RSD, S Ston. RD. Addtl civ bdry alt: 1894 (incl help cr Hedge End CP),[86] 1895,[87] 1897 (help cr Chandlers Ford CP),[26] 1898.[87] Abol civ 1920 pt to help cr Southampton St Nicholas CP (to be in S'htn. CB), pt to West End CP.[436] *Parl* Pt S'htn. Parl Bor (1295–1918), pt S'rn Dv (1832–85), pt Winch. Dv (1885–1918). *Eccl* Pec jurisd (until 1845), Seq 27 thereafter. Addtl eccl bdry alt: 1905 (help cr Bitterne Park EP),[89] 1925,[373] 1932 (cr Southampton St Alban EP),[40] 1961,[94] 1965.[70]

STRATFIELD MORTIMER

AP In Berks (Theale Hd), incl tg Mortimer West End (in Hants, Holdshot Hd), the latter sep CP 1866[102] in Hants so that Stratfield Mortimer ent Berks thereafter. See main entry in Berks.

STRATFIELD SAYE

AP In Hants (Holdshot Hd), incl chap and tg Beech Hill (in Berks, Reading Hd, sep CP 1866 in Berks[102] so that Stratfield Saye ent Hants thereafter, sep EP 1868[451]). *LG* Basingst. PLU, RSD, RD. *Parl* Hants pt, Seq 5. *Eccl* Basingst. RDn (until 1856), N-E Basingst. RDn (1856–92), Silch. RDn (1892–1928), Odiham RDn (1928–73). Abol eccl 1973 to help cr Stratfiel Saye with Hartley Wespall EP.[234]

STRATFIELD SAYE WITH HARTLEY WESPALL

EP Cr 1973 by union Stratfield Saye AP, Hartley Wespall AP, Stratfield Turgis AP.[234] Odiham RDn.

STRATFIELD TURGIS

AP *LG* Seq 15. Civ bdry: 1879,[307] 1883,[16] 1932.[1] *Parl* Seq 5. *Eccl* Basingst. RDn (until 1856), N-E Basingst. RDn (1856–92), Silch. RDn (1892–1928), Odiham RDn (1928–73). Abol eccl 1973 to help cr Stratfield Saye with Hartley

Wespall EP.[234]

EAST STRATTON

Chap in Micheldever AP, sep civ identity early, sep EP 1931.[348] *LG* Micheld. Hd, Winch. PLU, RSD, RD. Abol civ 1932 ent to Micheldever AP.[1] *Parl* N'rn Dv (1832–85), W'rn Dv (1885–1918), Winch. Dv (1918–48). *Eccl* Winch. RDn.

BISHOPS SUTTON

AP Incl chap Ropley (sep civ identity early, sep EP 1883[407]). *LG* Seq 25. *Parl* Seq 2. *Eccl* As 'Bishop's Sutton', Seq 2.

LONG SUTTON

Chap in Crondall AP, sep civ identity early, sep EP 1816.[7] *LG* Crondall Hd, Ash incorp for poor (until 1869), Hart. Wit. PLU (1869–1930), RSD, RD. Civ bdry: 1932.[1] *Parl* Seq 4. *Eccl* Basingst. RDn (1816–56), Odiham RDn (1856–92), Basingst. RDn (1892–1928), Odiham RDn (1928–*).

SWANMORE

Chap pt in Bishops Waltham AP (eccl, 'Bishop's Waltham'), pt in Droxford AP, sep EP 1846,[247] sep CP 1894.[244] *LG* Droxf. PLU, RD. Civ bdry: 1967.[233] *Parl* Petf. Dv/CC (1918–*). *Eccl* Droxf. RDn (1846–56), N-W Droxf. RDn (1856–71), Bp's Walth. RDn (1871–*). Eccl bdry: 1961,[410] 1971 (loses pt to Shidfield EP as latter renamed 'Shedfield').[420]

SWANMORE ST MICHAEL AND ALL ANGELS

EP Cr 1864 from Newchurch AP.[108] E Medine RDn (1864–71), N-E Medine RDn (1871–92), E Wight RDn (1892–*).

SWARRATON

AP *LG* Bountb. Hd (until **1834**), Micheld. Hd (from **1834**), Alresf. PLU, RSD, RD. Abol civ 1932 ent to Northington CP.[1] *Parl* N'rn Dv (1832–85), E'rn Dv (1885–1918), Petf. Dv (1918–48). *Eccl* Alresf. RDn. Reconstituted 1847 gaining chap Northington in Micheldever AP to cr Swarraton with Northington EP.[347]

SWARRATON WITH NORTHINGTON

EP Cr 1847 by union Swarraton AP, chap Northington in Micheldever AP.[347] Alresf. RDn (1847–56), Micheld. RDn (1856–71), Alresf. RDn (1871–*).

SWAY

Area in Boldre AP, sep EP **1841**,[101] sep CP 1866.[102] *LG* New For. Hd, Lym. PLU (1866[229]–1930), RSD, RD (1894–1932), New For. RD (1932–74). Civ bdry: 1878,[106] 1932.[1] *Parl* S'rn Dv (1867–85), New For. Dv (1885–1918), New For. & Christch. Dv (1918–48), New For. CC (1948–*). *Eccl* Fordbr. RDn (1839–56), E Forbdr. RDn (1856–92), Lyndh. RDn (1892–*). Eccl bdry: 1956.[28]

SYDMONTON

Chap in Kingsclere AP, sep civ identity early, eccl united 1853 with chap Ecchinswell in same par to cr Ecchinswell and Sydmonton EP.[7] *LG* Kingscl. Hd, PLU, RSD, RD. Abol 1932 to help cr Ecchinswell and Sydmonton CP.[1] *Parl* N'rn Dv (1832–85), W'rn Dv (1885–1918), Basingst. Dv (1918–48).

TADLEY

Chap in Overton AP, sep civ identity early, sep EP 1878.[379] *LG* Overton Hd, Kingscl. PLU, RSD, RD (1894–1932), Kingscl. & Whitch. RD (1932–74). Civ bdry: 1932,[1] 1956.[87] *Parl* Seq 6. *Eccl* N-E Basingst. RDn (1878–92), Silch. RDn (1892–1928), Basingst. RDn (1928–*). Eccl bdry: 1869 (when chap, help cr Ramsdale EP),[357] 1972,[472] 1973 (help cr North Tadley EP).[69]

NORTH TADLEY

EP Cr 1973 from Aldermaston AP (Berks, dioc Oxford), Baughurst AP, Tadley AP, to be in dioc Winch.[69] Basingst. RDn.

TANGLEY

Chap in Faccombe AP, sep civ identity early, sep EP 1898.[266] *LG* Pastrow Hd (until **1834**), Andv. Hd (from **1834**), and Seq 2 thereafter. Civ bdry: 1888,[443] 1932.[1] *Parl* Seq 8. *Eccl* Alresf. RDn.

SOUTH TEDWORTH

AP Usual civ spelling; for eccl see 'South Tidworth'. *LG* Seq 2. *Parl* Seq 8.

TESTWOOD

EP Cr 1937 from Eling AP, Netley AP.[258] Lyndh. RDn.

THORLEY

AP *LG* E Medina Hd/Lbty, IoW incorp for poor (1770–1865), PLU (1865–1930), IoW RSD, RD. Abol civ 1933 ent to Yarmouth AP.[42] *Parl* IoW Dv/Parl Co (1832–1948). *Eccl* Seq 31.

THRUXTON

AP Incl area Park House (orig ex-par, sep rated in Andv. PLU but sep civ status not sustained). *LG* Andv. Hd (until **1834**), Pastrow Hd (from **1834**), Andv. PLU, RSD, RD. Addtl civ bdry alt: 1888.[236] *Parl* Seq 8. *Eccl* Seq 8.

TICHBORNE

Chap in Cheriton AP, sep civ identity early, no sep eccl identity. *LG* Seq 11. Civ bdry: 1883,[16] 1888.[72] *Parl* Seq 2.

SOUTH TIDWORTH

AP Usual eccl spelling; for civ see 'South Tedworth'. *Eccl* Seq 8.

TIMSBURY

AP *LG* K's Somb. Hd, Romsey PLU, RSD, RD. Civ bdry: 1888.[349] Abol civ 1932 ent to Michelmersh AP.[1] *Parl* S'rn Dv (1832–85), New For. Dv (1885–1918), New For. & Christch. Dv (1918–48). *Eccl* Seq 26. Eccl bdry: 1931.[405]

EAST TISTED

AP *LG* Pt Selborne Hd, pt Alton Hd (until **1834**), ent Selborne Hd (from **1834**), and Seq 23 thereafter. Civ bdry: 1932 (help cr Four Marks CP).[1] *Parl* Seq 1. *Eccl* Alton RDn (until 1856), W Alton RDn (1856–92), Alton RDn (1892–1972). Abol eccl 1972 to help cr East Tisted with Colemore EP.[207]

EAST TISTED WITH COLEMORE

EP Cr 1972 by union East Tisted AP, Colmer EP.[207] Alton RDn.

WEST TISTED

AP *LG* Seq 24. *Parl* Seq 1. *Eccl* Donative, Seq 2.

TITCHFIELD

AP Incl chap Crofton (sep EP 1871,[220] sep CP 1894[221]). *LG* Titchfield Hd, Fareham PLU, RSD, RD. Abol civ 1932 pt to Fareham AP, pt to help cr Curbridge CP.[192] *Parl* S'rn Dv (1832–1918), Fareham Dv (1918–48). *Eccl* Seq 21. Eccl bdry: 1836 (cr Sarisbury EP,[7] refounded 1837[416]), 1872 (help cr Hook with Warsash EP),[325] 1893 (help cr Lock's Heath EP).[464]

TOTLAND

CP Cr 1894 from Freshwater AP.[253] *LG* Iow PLU, RD. *Parl* IoW Parl Co (1918–*).

TOTLAND BAY

EP Cr 1875 from Freshwater AP.[284] W Medine RDn (1875–92), W Wight RDn (1892–*).

TOYD FARM AND ALLENFORD

Ex-par area in Wilts (Damerham Hd), sep CP 1858 in Wilts,[32] transf 1895 to Hants.[145] *LG* Fordbr. PLU, RSD, sep RD in Wilts (1894–95), Fordbr. RD (1895–1932). Abol 1932 ent to Martin CP.[1] *Parl* In Wilts until 1918, New For. & Christch. Dv (1918–48).

TUFTON

Chap in Wherwell AP, sep civ identity early, eccl severed 1852 and united to Bullington AP as Bullington with Tufton,[156] as such sep EP 1857.[157] *LG* Wherwell Hd (until 1834), Evingar Hd (from 1834), Whitch. PLU, RSD, RD. Abol 1932 ent to Hurstbourne Priors AP.[1] *Parl* N'rn Dv (1832–85), W'rn Dv (1885–1918), Basingst. Dv (1918–48).

TUNWORTH

AP *LG* Seq 3. Civ bdry: 1932.[1] *Parl* Seq 5. *Eccl* Basingst. RDn (until 1856), S-W Basingst. RDn (1856–71), Odiham RDn (1871–92), Basingst. RDn (1892–1954), Odiham RDn (1954–*).

TWYFORD

AP Incl pt chap Colden Common (sep EP 1844 [orig as 'Coldon' but 'Colden Common' commonly used later],[206] sep CP 1932[1]). *LG* Seq 12. Addtl civ bdry alt: 1883.[16] *Parl* Seq 9. *Eccl* Pec jurisd (until 1845), Seq 28 thereafter.

EAST TYTHERLEY

AP Chap in Mottisfont AP, sep par early.[366] *LG* Seq 28. Civ bdry: 1883,[16] 1883,[445] 1888.[341] *Parl* Seq 16. *Eccl* Donative, Seq 26. Eccl bdry: 1972.[154]

WEST TYTHERLEY

AP *LG* Seq 28. Civ bdry: 1883 (gains the pt of West Dean AP [Wilts, Hants] in Hants so that West Dean ent Wilts thereafter).[237] *Parl* Seq 16. *Eccl* Seq 26. Eccl bdry: 1972.[154]

UPHAM

AP Incl chap Durley (sep civ identity early, sep EP 1855[195]). *LG* Bp's Walth. Hd (until 1834), pt Fawley Hd, pt Meonstoke Hd (from 1834), Droxf. PLU, RSD, RD. Addtl civ bdry alt: 1932.[1] *Parl* Seq 1. *Eccl* Pec jurisd (until 1845), Seq 20 thereafter.

UPTON GRAY

AP *LG* Seq 5. Civ bdry: 1879,[449] 1902,[344] 1932.[1] *Parl* Seq 5. *Eccl* Basingst. RDn (until 1856), Odiham RDn (1856–92), Basingst. RDn (1892–1928), Odiham RDn (1928–*).

VENTNOR

Area in Newchurch AP, sep EP 1862,[7] sep CP 1866.[102] *LG* E Medina Hd/Lbty, IoW incorp for poor (1770–1865), PLU (1865–1930), pt Ventnor USD, pt IoW RSD, Ventnor UD. Civ bdry: 1894 (made ent within UD),[3] 1896,[292] 1933 (incl gains St Lawrence AP).[42] *Parl* IoW Dv/Parl Co (1867–*). *Eccl* E Medine RDn (1862-72), S-E Medine RDn (1872–92), E Wight RDn (1892–*). Bdry: 1862 (cr Ventnor Holy Trinity EP),[450] 1968.[294]

VENTNOR HOLY TRINITY

EP Cr 1862 from Ventnor EP.[450] RDns as for Ventnor.

WALLESWORTH

AP Orig sep AP, Droxf. RDn, united 1426 to Widley AP.[465]

NETHER WALLOP

AP *LG* Seq 28. *Parl* Seq 7. *Eccl* Andv. RDn (until 1856), Chilb. RDn (1856–71), W Andv. RDn (1871–92), Stockb. RDn (1892–1922), Romsey RDn (1922–57), Andv. RDn (1957–*). Eccl bdry: 1972.[342]

OVER WALLOP

AP *LG* Seq 28. *Parl* Seq 7. *Eccl* Andv. RDn (until 1856), Chilb. RDn (1856–71), W Andv. RDn (1871–92), Stockb. RDn (1892–1922), Romsey RDn (1922–28), Andv. RDn (1928–*).

BISHOPS WALTHAM

AP Incl pt chap Swanmore (sep EP 1846,[245] sep CP 1894[244]), chap Curdridge (sep EP 1838,[231] sep CP 1894[232]). *LG* Seq 29. Addtl civ bdry alt: 1967.[233] *Parl* Seq 1. *Eccl* As 'Bishop's Waltham', pec jurisd (until 1845), Seq 20 thereafter. Addtl eccl bdry alt: 1971 (loses pt to Shedfield EP as latter renamed 'Shidfield').[420]

NORTH WALTHAM

AP *LG* Overton Hd (until 1834), Holdshot Hd (from 1834), Basingst. PLU, RSD, RD. *Parl* Seq 5. *Eccl* Pec jurisd (until 1845), Seq 15 thereafter.

WANSTEAD

AP Orig sep AP, Droxf. RDn, early incl in Southwick AP though sometimes called par early 17th cent.[463]

WARBLINGTON

AP *LG* Bosmere Hd, Havant PLU, RSD, Warblington UD (1894–1932). Civ bdry: 1902.[310] Abol civ 1932 pt to help cr Rowlands Castle CP, pt to Havant AP.[1] *Parl* S'rn Dv (1832–1918), Fareham Dv (1918–48). *Eccl* Droxf. RDn (until 1856), N-E Droxf. RDn (1856–71), Havant RDn (1871–92), Landp. RDn (1892–1900), Havant RDn (1900–31). Eccl bdry: 1839 (help cr Redhill EP,[7] refounded 1840[127]), 1841 (cr Emsworth EP).[261] Abol eccl 1931 to help cr Warblington with Emsworth EP.[262]

WARBLINGTON WITH EMSWORTH

EP Cr 1931 by union Warblington AP, Emsworth EP.[262] Havant RDn.

SOUTH WARNBOROUGH

AP *LG* Berm. Hd (until 1834), Odiham Hd (from

1834), and Seq 18 thereafter. Civ bdry: 1883,[16] 1932.[1] *Parl* Seq 4. *Eccl* Basingst. RDn (until 1856), Odiham RDn (1856–92), Basingst. RDn (1892–1928), Odiham RDn (1928–*).

WARNFORD

AP *LG* Seq 17. *Parl* Seq 1. *Eccl* Pec jurisd (until 1845), Seq 22 thereafter.

WATERLOO

Ex-par place, sep CP 1858,[32] sep EP 1856 as 'Waterlooville',[7] eccl refounded 1910.[446] *LG* Portsd. Hd, Cath. PLU, RSD, RD. Abol civ 1932 pt to help cr Southwick and Widley CP, pt to Havant AP.[1] *Parl* S'rn Dv (1867–1918), Petf. Dv (1918–48).

WATERLOOVILLE

Ex-par place, sep CP 1858 as 'Waterloo',[32] sep EP 1856,[7] eccl refounded 1910.[446] N-E Droxf. RDn (1856–71), Havant RDn (1871–92), Landp. RDn (1892–1900), Havant RDn (1900–*). Bdry: 1913.[447]

WEEKE

AP Chap in Winchester St Mary of the Valleys AP, sep par 1493 incl gains parochial rights of Winchester St Anastasius AP.[448] *LG* Buddl. Hd, Winch. PLU, pt Winch. Bor/MB, pt Winch. USD, pt Winch. RSD. Abol civ 1894 the pt in the MB to cr Weeke Within CP, the remainder to cr Weeke Without CP.[3] *Parl* Pt Winch. Parl Bor (1295–1918), pt N'rn Dv (1832–85), pt W'rn Dv (1885–1918). *Eccl* Seq 28. Eccl bdry: 1967,[340] 1973.[342]

WEEKE WITHIN

CP Cr 1894 from the pt of Weeke AP in Winch. MB.[3] *LG* Winch. PLU, MB. Bdry: 1900.[4] Abol 1902 to help cr Winchester CP.[183]

WEEKE WITHOUT

CP Cr 1894 from the pt of Weeke AP not in Winch. MB.[3] *LG* Winch. PLU, RD. Bdry: 1900.[4] Abol 1932 pt to Winchester CP, pt to Hursley AP.[1] *Parl* Winch. Dv (1918–48).

WELLOW

CP Cr 1932 by union East Wellow AP, West Wellow CP.[1] *LG* Romsey & Stockb. RD. *Parl* Winch. CC (1948–70), E'leigh. CC (1970–*).

EAST WELLOW

AP In Hants (Thorng. Hd), incl tg West Wellow (in Wilts, Amesbury Hd, sep civ identity early in Wilts, transf civ 1895 to Hants,[145] no sep eccl identity). *LG* Romsey PLU, RSD, RD. Addtl civ bdry alt: 1883.[16] Abol civ 1932 to help cr Wellow CP.[1] *Parl* S'rn Dv (1832–85), New For. Dv (1885–1918), New For. & Christch. Dv (1918–48). *Eccl* Seq 26.

WEST WELLOW

Tg (in Wilts, Amesbury Hd) in East Wellow AP (Hants, Thorng. Hd), sep civ identity early in Wilts, transf 1895 to Hants,[145] no sep eccl identity. *LG* Romsey PLU, RSD, sep RD in Wilts (1894–95), Romsey RD (1895–1932). Abol 1932 to help cr Wellow CP.[1] *Parl* In Wilts until 1918, New For. & Christch. Dv (1918–48).

WEST END

Chap in South Stoneham AP, sep EP 1840,[268] sep CP 1894.[86] *LG* S Ston. PLU (1894–1920), E'leigh. PLU (1920–30), S Ston. RD (1894–1932), Winch. RD (1932–74). Civ bdry: 1920,[436] 1932,[1] 1954 (loses pt to S'htn. CB and CP).[185] *Parl* Winch. Dv (1918–48), Petf. CC (1948–55), E'leigh. CC (1955–*). *Eccl* S'htn. RDn. Eccl bdry: 1853 (help cr Bitterne EP),[85] 1874,[113] 1876 (help cr Hedge End EP),[111] 1957,[320] 1971 (help cr Southampton St Christopher, Thornhill EP).[425]

WESTON

EP Cr 1866 from St Mary Extra EP (sometimes 'Southampton St Mary Extra').[339] S'htn. RDn.

WESTON CORBETT

AP Orig sep AP, later deemed ex-par place, sep CP 1858.[32] *LG* Berm. Hd, Basingst. PLU, RSD, RD. *Parl* N'rn Dv (1867–1918), Basingst. Dv/CC (1918–*).

WESTON PATRICK

Chap in Odiham AP, sep civ identity early, sep EP 1815.[7] *LG* Odiham Hd (until 1834), Berm. Hd (from 1834), Basingst. PLU, RSD, RD. Civ bdry: 1879,[449] 1883,[16] 1932.[1] *Parl* Seq 5. *Eccl* Basingst. RDn (1815–56), Odiham RDn (1856–92), Basingst. RDn (1892–1928), Odiham RDn (1928–*).

WEYHILL

AP Usual eccl spelling, sometimes civ spelling; for usual civ spelling see 'Penton Grafton'. *Eccl* Seq 8. Eccl bdry: 1924,[31] 1939.[34]

WHERWELL

AP Incl chap Bullington, chap Tufton (each sep civ identity early, eccl united 1852 as Bullington with Tufton,[156] and as such sep EP 1857[157]). *LG* Seq 30. Addtl civ bdry alt: 1888.[236] *Parl* Seq 8. *Eccl* Seq 10.

WHIPPINGHAM

AP Incl chap East Cowes (sep EP 1843,[55] sep CP 1894 [the pt in E Cowes USD][3]). *LG* E Medina Hd/Lbty, IoW incorp for poor (1770–1865), PLU (1865–1930), pt E Cowes USD, pt Newport Bor/MB, pt Newport USD, pt IoW RSD, IoW RD. Addtl civ bdry alt: 1894 (loses the pt in Newport MB to Newport CP),[19] 1894,[289] 1897,[218] 1907 (gains North Arreton CP).[37] *Parl* Pt Newport Parl Bor (1295 jointly with Yarmouth, 1584–1867, extended pt 1867–85), IoW Dv/Parl Co (pt 1832–67, reduced pt 1867–85, ent 1885–*). *Eccl* Seq 29. Addtl eccl bdry alt: 1843 (cr Barton EP).[55]

WHIPSTRODE

AP Orig sep AP, Droxf. RDn, united early to Fareham AP.[463]

WHITCHURCH

AP *LG* Whitch. Bor, Seq 10. Civ bdry: 1932.[1] *Parl* Whitch. Parl Bor (1586–1832), Seq 6 thereafter. *Eccl* Pec jurisd (until 1845), Andv. RDn (1845–56), N-W Andv. RDn (1856–71), S-W Basingst. RDn (1871–92), Basingst. RDn (1892–1908), Kingscl. RDn (1908–28), Whitch. RDn (1928–54). Reconstituted eccl 1954 gaining chap Tufton of Hurstbourne Priors with Tufton AP and another pt of Hurstbourne

Priors to cr Whitchurch with Tufton EP.[331]

WHITCHURCH WITH TUFTON

EP Cr 1954 by union Whitchurch AP, chap Tufton of Hurstbourne Priors with Tufton AP, another pt Hurstbourne Priors.[331] Whitch. RDn. Abol 1968 to help cr Whitchurch with Tufton and Litchfield EP.[339]

WHITCHURCH WITH TUFTON AND LITCHFIELD

EP Cr 1968 by union Whitchurch with Tufton EP, Litchfield AP.[339] Whitch. RDn.

WHITEHILL

CP Cr 1929 from Greatham AP, Headley AP, Kingsley CP, Selborne AP.[299] *LG* Alton PLU, RD. *Parl* Petf. CC (1948–*).

WHITSBURY

AP In Wilts (Cawden & Cadworth Hd), transf 1895 to Hants.[145] *LG* Fordbr. PLU, RSD, sep RD in Wilts (1894–95), Fordbr. RD (1895–1932), Ringw. & Fordbr. RD (1932–74). *Parl* In Wilts until 1918, New For. & Christch. Dv (1918–48), New For. CC (1948–*). *Eccl* Seq 25.

WHITWELL

Chap pt in Niton AP, pt in Godshill AP, sep civ identity early, sep EP 1867.[291] *LG* E Medina Hd/Lbty, IoW incorp for poor (1770–1865), PLU (1865–1930), RSD, RD. Abol civ 1933 pt to Ventnor CP, pt to Niton AP.[42] *Parl* IoW Dv/Parl Co (1832–1948). *Eccl* E Medine RDn (1867–72), S-E Medine RDn (1872–92), E Wight RDn (1892–*).

WICKHAM

AP *LG* Titchfield Hd, Fareham PLU, RSD, RD (1894–1932), Droxf. RD (1932–74). Civ bdry: 1932,[1] 1952.[230] *Parl* Seq 14. *Eccl* Seq 20.

WIDLEY

AP Gains 1426 Wallesworth AP.[465] *LG* Portsd. Hd, Fareham PLU, RSD. Abol civ 1894 to help cr Cosham CP.[212] *Parl* S'rn Dv (1832–1918). *Eccl* Droxf. RDn (until 1856), S-E Droxf. RDn (1856–71), Alv. & Ports. Isl. RDn (1871–79), Alv. RDn (1879–92), Landp. RDn (1892–1900), Havant RDn (1900–68). Eccl bdry: 1870 (help cr Portsdown EP),[388] 1936 (help cr Cosham EP).[215]

CP Renaming 1921 of Cosham CP.[460] *LG* Fareham PLU, RD. Abol 1932 to help cr Southwick and Widley CP.[1]

WIELD

AP *LG* Orig pt Alresf. Lbty, in Fawley Hd (15th cent[11]–1834), Bp's Sutton (from 1834), and Seq 26 thereafter. *Parl* Seq 1. *Eccl* Alresf. RDn (until 1856), Micheld. RDn (1856–71), Alresf. RDn (1871–92), Alton RDn (1892–*).

WINCHFIELD

AP *LG* Seq 18. Civ bdry: 1932.[1] *Parl* Seq 4. *Eccl* Seq 17.

WINCHESTER

The following have 'Winchester' in their names. The list must be taken as provisional until further research into the mediev period is done, and represents the present state of information at the Hants RO.[452] *LG* Winch. PLU (Bor from 16th cent, MB, Soke, USD sep noted). *Parl* Winch. Parl Bor (1295–1918), Winch. Dv/CC (1918–*). *Eccl* Winch. RDn.

CP1–WINCHESTER–Cr 1902 by union Chilcomb Within CP, Milland CP, St Faith Within CP, Weeke Within CP, Winnall AP, AP6, AP12, AP15, AP22, AP26, AP27, AP30, AP31, AP40, AP41.[183] *LG* Winch. MB. Bdry: 1932,[1] 1969.[5]

AP1–WINCHESTER ALL SAINTS, GOLDSMITH STREET–Or 'All Hallows'. Abol 1529 ent to AP41.

AP2–WINCHESTER ALL SAINTS IN VINEIS–Abol before 1535.

EP1–WINCHESTER ALL SAINTS WITH CHILCOMB ST ANDREW AND CHESIL ST PETER–Renaming 1972 of Chilcomb with Winchester St Peter Chesil EP.[48]

–WINCHESTER CATHEDRAL YARD–Ex-par place, incl 1858[32] in 'Winchester The Close' CP (sep civ identity not sustained).

EP2–WINCHESTER CHRIST CHURCH–Cr 1861 from AP9.[453] Bdry: 1954 (help cr Stanmore EP),[440] 1973.[342]

–WINCHESTER THE CLOSE–Ex-par place, sep CP 1858[32] (incl area Winchester Cathedral Yard, Winchester Morley's College) (sep civ identity not sustained)

–WINCHESTER COLLEGE MILL–Ex-par place, incl 1858[32] in 'Winchester St Mary's College' CP (sep civ identity not sustained)

–WINCHESTER COLLEGE WHARF–Ex-par place, incl 1858[32] in 'Winchester St Mary's College' CP (sep civ identity not sustained)

EP3–WINCHESTER HOLY TRINITY–Cr 1855 from AP26, AP22.[361] Bdry: 1973.[342]

–WINCHESTER MORLEY'S COLLEGE–Ex-par place, incl 1858[32] in 'Winchester The Close' CP (sep civ status not sustained)

AP3–WINCHESTER ST ALPHEGE–Abol 1st half 15th cent ent to AP41.

AP4–WINCHESTER ST ANASTASIUS–Sometimes 'St Anastasia'. Gains 1st half 15th cent AP24. Abol 1493, parochial rights transf to help cr Weeke AP.[448]

AP5–WINCHESTER ST ANDREW–Abol 1st half 15th cent.

AP6–WINCHESTER ST BARTHOLOMEW HYDE–*LG* Winch. Bor/MB (pt until 1894, ent 1894–1902), pt Winch. Soke, pt Fawley Hd, pt Winch. USD, pt Winch. RSD. Civ bdry: 1889,[181] 1894 (the pt not in the MB cr Abbots Barton CP),[3] 1900.[4] Abol civ 1902 to help cr CP1.[183] *Parl* Pt Winch. Parl Bor (1295–1918), pt N'rn Dv (1832–85), pt W'rn Dv (1885–1918). Eccl bdry: 1973.[342]

AP7–WINCHESTER ST CATHERINE–Perhaps not an AP but rather chap in Chilcombe AP, in which now located.

AP8–WINCHESTER ST CLEMENT–Gains by 1537 AP33. Abol 1652 ent to AP41.

–WINCHESTER ST CROSS–Ex-par place, sep CP 1858[32] as 'Winchester St Cross Hospital' (sep civ status not sustained). Gains between

1500–28 AP9, thereafter eccl sometimes 'Winchester St Cross with St Faith'. Eccl bdry: 1861 (cr EP2),[453] 1954 (help cr Stanmore EP),[440] 1973.[342]

–WINCHESTER ST CROSS HOSPITAL–See prev entry

–WINCHESTER ST CROSS HOSPITAL PRECINCTS–Ex-par place, sep CP 1858[32] (sep civ status not sustained)

–WINCHESTER ST CROSS WITH ST FAITH–See WINCHESTER ST CROSS

AP9–WINCHESTER ST FAITH–Usual eccl spelling; for civ see 'St Faith'. Abol eccl between 1500–28 ent to Winchester St Cross, the union sometimes 'Winchester St Cross with St Faith'.

AP10–WINCHESTER ST GEORGE–Abol by 1615 ent to AP26.

AP11–WINCHESTER ST JAMES–Abol by 1535.

AP12–WINCHESTER ST JOHN [THE BAPTIST]–Sometimes 'St John on the Hill' or 'St John in the Soke'. United to AP30 in 1525 but sep identity regained 18th cent. *LG* Winch. Bor/MB (pt until 1894, ent 1894–1902), pt Winch. Soke, pt Buddl. Hd, pt Winch. USD, pt Winch. RSD. Civ bdry: 1894 (the pt not in the MB lost to Chilcomb Without CP).[184] Abol civ 1902 to help cr CP1.[183] *Parl* As for AP6. Abol eccl 1970 to help cr EP4.[454]

AP13–WINCHESTER ST JOHN DE HOSPITALI–Abol 1st half 15th cent.

AP14–WINCHESTER ST JOHN PORT LATIN, BUCKSTREET–Abol 1st half 15th cent.

AP15–WINCHESTER ST LAWRENCE–*LG* Winch. Bor/MB, USD. Abol civ 1902 to help cr CP1.[183] Abol eccl 1955 to help cr EP6.[403]

EP5–WINCHESTER ST LAWRENCE AND ST MAURICE WITH ST SWITHUN-UPON-KINGSGATE–Renaming 1974 of EP6.[227]

EP6–WINCHESTER ST LAWRENCE WITH ST MAURICE–Cr 1955 by union AP15, AP26.[403] Renamed 1974 as EP5.[227]

AP16–WINCHESTER ST MARGARET'S–Abol 1st half 15th cent.

AP17–WINCHESTER ST MARTIN, ALWARD STREET–Sometimes 'St Martin's, Parchment Street'. Abol by 1535.

AP18–WINCHESTER ST MARTIN, GAR STREET–Abol by 1535.

AP19–WINCHESTER ST MARTIN'S WITHOUT KINGSGATE–Abol by 1535.

AP20–WINCHESTER ST MARTIN, WOOD STREET–Or 'St Martin outside Westgate'. Decayed mid-14th cent.

AP21–WINCHESTER ST MARY DE LA WODE–Or 'St Mary de Linea Selda' or 'St Mary de Linea Tela' or 'St Mary Ode'. United by 1556 to AP26.

–WINCHESTER ST MARY'S COLLEGE–Ex-par place, sep CP 1858[32] incl ex-par places College Wharf, College Mill (sep civ status not sustained), eccl enlarged 1964 when gains pt EP7.[455]

AP22–WINCHESTER ST MARY KALENDAR–Gains between 1500–28 AP36. Abol eccl 1652 ent to AP26. *LG* Winch. Bor/MB, USD. Abol civ 1902 to help cr CP1.[183]

AP23–WINCHESTER ST MARY NEAR GOLD STREET–Abol by 1535.

AP24–WINCHESTER ST MARY OF THE VALLEYS–Incl chap Weeke (sep par 1493, gaining parochial rights AP4[448]). United early 15th cent with AP4, pulled down 1493.

AP25–WINCHESTER ST MARY, TANNER STREET–Abol 1528 ent to AP26.

AP26–WINCHESTER ST MAURICE–Gains 1526 AP29, gains 1528 AP25, gains by 1556 AP21, gains by 1615 AP10 and AP21, gains eccl 1652 AP22, AP31, hence sometimes eccl 'Winchester St Maurice with St George, St Mary de Wode, St Mary Kalendar and St Peter Colebrook'. *LG* Winch. Bor/MB, USD. Abol civ 1902 to help cr CP1.[183] Addtl eccl bdry alt: 1855 (help cr EP3).[361]

AP27–WINCHESTER ST MICHAEL–Or 'St Michael in Kingsgate Street' or 'St Michael in the Soke'. *LG* Winch. Bor/MB, Soke, USD. Abol civ 1902 to help cr CP1.[183] Abol eccl 1926 to help cr EP8.[457]

EP7–WINCHESTER ST MICHAEL WITH ST SWITHUN–Cr 1926 by union AP27, AP39.[456] Bdry: 1964.[455] Abol eccl 1967 to help cr EP8.[457]

AP28–WINCHESTER ST NICHOLAS, KINGSGATE–Or 'St Nicholas outside the Walls'. Abol 1st half 15th cent.

AP29–WINCHESTER ST PANCRAS–Abol 1526 ent to AP26.

AP30–WINCHESTER ST PETER CHEESEHILL–Usual civ spelling; usual eccl 'Winchester St Peter Chesil'. Gains 1525 AP12 (regains sep identity 18th cent). *LG* Winch. Bor/MB (pt until 1894, ent 1894–1902), Winch. Soke, pt Winch. USD, pt Winch. RSD. Civ bdry: 1894 (the pt not in the MB lost to Chilcomb Without CP).[184] Abol civ 1902 to help cr CP1.[183] Abol eccl 1950 to help cr Chilcomb with Winchester St Peter Chesil EP.[182]

–WINCHESTER ST PETER CHESIL–See AP30

AP31–WINCHESTER ST PETER COLEBROOK Abol eccl 1652 ent to AP26. *LG* Winch. Bor/MB, USD. Abol civ 1902 to help cr CP1.[183]

AP32–WINCHESTER ST PETER IN MACELLIS–Or 'St Peter in the Shambles'. Abol 1577 ent to AP41.

AP33–WINCHESTER ST PETER WHITEBREAD–Abol before 1527 ent to AP8.

AP34–WINCHESTER ST PETER WITHOUT SOUTHGATE–Abol by 1535.

AP35–WINCHESTER ST PETROC–Renamed mid-15th cent as AP41.

AP36–WINCHESTER ST RUMBOLD–Or 'St Ruel'. United 1528 to AP22.

AP37–WINCHESTER ST SAVIOUR, BURDON STREET–Abol 1st half 15th cent.

AP38–WINCHESTER ST SAVIOUR KINGSGATE–Abol by 1535.

AP39–WINCHESTER ST STEPHEN BY WOLVESEY–Abol by 1535.

AP40–WINCHESTER ST SWITHIN–Usual civ spelling, sometimes 'St Swithin upon Kingsgate'; eccl 'Winchester St Swithun'. *LG* Winch. Bor/MB, Soke, USD. Abol civ 1902 to help cr CP1.[183] Abol eccl 1926 to help cr EP7.[457]

–WINCHESTER ST SWITHUN–See prev entry

AP41–WINCHESTER ST THOMAS–Sometimes 'St Thomas the Martyr'. Renaming mid-15th cent of AP35. Gains 1st half 15th cent AP3, gains 1529 AP1, gains 1577 AP32, gains 1652 AP8, hence sometimes eccl 'Winchester St Thomas with St Clement'. *LG* Winch. Bor/MB, USD. Abol civ 1902 to help cr CP1.[183] Abol eccl 1967 to help cr EP8.[457]

–WINCHESTER ST THOMAS WITH ST CLEMENT–See prev entry

AP42–WINCHESTER ST THOMAS AND ST CLEMENT WITH ST MICHAEL AND ST SWITHUN–Cr 1967 by union AP41, EP7.[457] Bdry: 1973.[342]

AP43–WINCHESTER ST VALERY–Or 'St Waleric'. Abol by 1535.

–WINCHESTER THE WEIRS–Ex-par place, sep CP 1858[32] (sep civ status not sustained).

–WINCHESTER WOLVESEY–Ex-par place, sep CP 1858[32] (sep civ status not sustained).

WINNALL

AP *LG* Fawley Hd, Winch. PLU, Winch. MB (pt 1835–94, ent 1894–1902), pt Winch. USD, pt Winch. RSD. Civ bdry: 1894 (loses the pt not in the MB to Chilcomb Without CP).[184] Abol civ 1902 to help cr Winchester CP.[183] *Parl* Pt Winch. Parl Bor (1832–1918), pt N'rn Dv (1832–85), pt W'rn Dv (1885–1918). *Eccl* Pec jurisd (until 1845), Winch. RDn (1845–1970). Abol eccl 1970 to help cr Winchester St John the Baptist with Winnall St Martin EP.[454]

WINSLADE

AP Incl Kempshott (orig AP, united 1393 with Winslade[334]). *LG* Seq 3. Civ bdry: 1879,[247] 1932.[1] *Parl* Seq 5. *Eccl* Seq 15. Eccl bdry: 1931.[248]

WINTON

CP Cr 1894 from Holdenhurst CP.[323] *LG* Bournem. & Christch. PLU (1894–1900), Christch. PLU (1900–02), Winton UD (1898–1901), Bournem. CB (1901–02). Abol 1902 ent to Bournemouth CP.[116]

WOLVERTON

AP *LG* Kingscl. Hd, PLU, RSD, RD. Civ bdry: 1883.[16] Abol civ 1932 pt to Baughurst AP, pt to Kingsclere AP.[1] *Parl* N'rn Dv (1832–85), W'rn Dv (1885–1918), Basingst. Dv (1918–48). *Eccl* Basingst. RDn (until 1856), N-E Andv. RDn (1856–71), N-E Basingst. RDn (1871–92), Silch. RDn (1892–1928), Basingst. RDn (1928–71). Eccl bdry: 1939.[68] Abol eccl 1971 to help cr Wolverton cum Ewhurst EP.[264]

WOLVERTON CUM EWHURST

EP Cr 1971 by union Wolverton AP, Ewhurst AP.[264] Basingst. RDn.

WONSTON

AP *LG* Barton Stacey Hd (until 1834), Buddl. Hd (from 1834), and Seq 6 thereafter. Civ bdry: 1932 (gains Hunton CP, Stoke Charity AP).[1] *Parl* Seq 9. *Eccl* Pec jurisd (until 1845), Somb. RDn (1845–56), Chilb. RDn (1856–71), Winch. RDn (1871–*).

WOODCOTT

AP *LG* Pastrow Hd, Kingscl. PLU, RSD, RD. Abol civ 1932 to help cr Litchfield and Woodcott CP.[1] *Parl* N'rn Dv (1832–1918), W'rn Dv (1918–48), Basingst. Dv (1918–48). *Eccl* Donative, Andv. RDn (until 1856), N-W Andv. RDn (1856–71), N Andv. RDn (1871–92), Kingscl. RDn (1892–1920s), Whitch. RDn (1920s–*).

WOODGREEN

Ex-par place, sep CP 1858.[32] *LG* Fordbr. Hd, PLU, RSD, RD (1894–1932), Ringw. & Fordbr. RD (1932–74). Bdry: 1932,[1] 1963.[278] *Parl* S'rn Dv (1867–85), New For. Dv (1885–1918), New For. & Christch. Dv (1918–48), New For. CC (1948–*).

EAST WOODHAY

AP Incl chap Asmansworth (sep par at Reformation in 16th cent, sep civ identity maintained, eccl absorbed back into this par in 18th cent,[44] sep EP again 1884[45]). *LG* Seq 9. *Parl* Seq 6. *Eccl* Seq 6. Addtl eccl bdry alt: 1850 (cr Woolton Hill EP).[458]

WOODLANDS

EP Cr 1846 from Kingsclere AP.[335] Incl area Headley so that sometimes 'Woodlands with Headley', now called 'Kingsclere-Woodlands with Headley'. Basingst. RDn (1846–56), N-E Andv. RDn (1856–71), N Andv. RD (1871–92), Kingscl. RDn (1892–1928), Whitch. RDn (1928–*). Bdry: 1926.[91]

WOODLANDS WITH HEADLEY–See WOODLANDS

WOODMANCOTE–See WOODMANCOTT

WOODMANCOTE AND POPHAM

EP Cr 1847 by union chap Woodmancote (civ, 'Woodmancott') in Brown Candover AP, chap Popham in Micheldever AP.[169] Alresf. RDn (1847–56), Micheld. RDn (1856–71), Alresf. RDn (1871–1900), Winch. RDn (1900–28), Basingst. RDn (1928–31), Winch. RDn (1931–*).

WOODMANCOTT

Chap in Brown Candover AP, sep civ identity early, eccl as 'Woodmancote' severed 1847 to help cr Woodmancote and Popham EP.[169] *LG* Mainsbr. Hd (until 1830s), Holdshot Hd (from 1830s) and Seq 15 thereafter. *Parl* Seq 5.

WOOLSTON

EP Cr 1864 from St Mary Extra EP (sometimes 'Southampton St Mary Extra'), Hound AP.[328] S'htn. RDn.

WOOLTON HILL

EP Cr 1850 from East Woodhay AP.[458] Andv. RDn (1850–56), N-E Andv. RDn (1856–71), N Andv. RDn (1871–92), Kingscl. RDn (1892–1928), Whitch. RDn (1928–*).

WOOTTON

AP *LG* E Medina Hd/Lbty, IoW incorp for poor (1770–1865), PLU (1865–94), RSD. Civ bdry: 1883.[16] Abol civ 1894 pt to Gatcombe AP, pt to Whippingham AP.[289] *Parl* IoW Dv/Parl Co (1832–1918). *Eccl* Seq 29. Eccl bdry: 1934.[174]

WOOTTON ST LAWRENCE

AP *LG* Chuteley Hd (until 1834), Basingst. Hd (from 1834), and Seq 3 thereafter. Civ bdry: 1879,[421] 1932,[1] 1956,[381] 1968.[378] *Parl* Seq 5. *Eccl* Seq 15. Eccl bdry: 1869 (help cr Ramsdale EP),[357] 1960.[249]

WORLDHAM

CP Cr 1932 by union East Worldham AP, West Worldham AP, Hartley Mauditt AP, pt Alton AP.[1] *LG* Alton RD. *Parl* Petf. CC (1948–*).

EAST WORLDHAM

AP *LG* Alton Hd, PLU, RSD, RD. Civ bdry: 1883.[16] Abol civ 1932 to help cr Worldham CP.[1] *Parl* N'rn Dv (1832–85), E'rn Dv (1885–1918), Petf. Dv (1918–48). *Eccl* Seq 5.

WEST WORLDHAM

AP *LG* Alton Hd, PLU, RSD, RD. Civ bdry: 1888.[459] Abol civ 1932 to help cr Worldham CP.[1] *Parl* As for East Worldham. *Eccl* Alton RDn (until 1856), W Alton RDn (1856–92), Alton RDn (1892–1944). Abol eccl 1944 to help cr Hartley Mauditt with West Worldham EP.[306]

ABBOTTS WORTHY

AP Orig sep AP, united mid-16th cent to Kings Worthy AP.[463]

HEADBOURNE WORTHY

AP *LG* Barton Stacey Hd (until 1834), Fawley Hd (from 1834), and Seq 12 thereafter. Civ bdry: 1883.[16] *Parl* Seq 9. *Eccl* Winch. RDn (until 1856), Alresf. RDn (1856–92), Winch. RDn (1892–*).

KINGS WORTHY

AP Gains mid-16th cent Abbotts Worthy AP.[463] *LG* Barton Stacey Hd (until 1834), pt Fawley Hd, pt Micheld. Hd (from 1834), Winch. PLU, RSD, RD. Civ bdry: 1883,[16] 1889.[181] *Parl* Seq 9. *Eccl* Seq 4.

MARTYR WORTHY

AP *LG* Fawley Hd, Winch. PLU, RSD, RD. Abol civ 1932 to help cr Itchen Valley CP.[1] *Parl* N'rn Dv (1832–85), W'rn Dv (1885–1918), Winch. Dv (1918–48).

WORTING

AP *LG* Chuteley Hd (until 1834), Basingst. Hd (from 1834), Basingst. PLU, RSD, RD. Abol civ 1932 pt to Basingstoke AP, pt to Wootton St Lawrence AP.[1] *Parl* N'rn Dv (1832–1918), Basingst. Dv (1918–48). *Eccl* Seq 15. Eccl bdry: 1959.[66]

WROXALL

Chap in Newchurch AP, sep CP 1894,[390] sep EP 1908.[9] *LG* IoW PLU, RD. Abol 1933 pt to Ventnor CP, pt to Newchurch AP.[42] *Parl* IoW Parl Co (1918–48). *Eccl* E Wight RDn.

WYMERING

AP *LG* Portsd. Hd, Fareham PLU, RSD. Civ bdry: 1886.[99] Abol civ 1894 to help cr Cosham CP.[212] *Parl* S'rn Dv (1832–1918). *Eccl* Droxf. RDn (until 1856), S-E Droxf. RDn (1856–71), Alv. & Ports. Isl. RDn (1871–79), Alv. RDn (1879–92), Landp. RDn (1892–1900), Havant RDn (1900–68). Eccl bdry: 1907,[262] 1936 (help cr Cosham EP),[215] 1955 (help cr Paulsgrove EP).[382] Abol eccl 1968 pt to help cr Wymering with Widley EP, pt to Portsdown EP.[272]

WYMERING WITH WIDLEY

EP Cr 1968 by union pt Wymering AP, pt Widley AP.[272] Havant RDn.

YARMOUTH

AP *LG* Yarmouth Bor, Seq 32. Civ bdry: 1933 (gains Thorley AP).[42] *Parl* Yarmouth Parl Bor (1295 jointly with Newport, Yarmouth 1584–1832), Seq 17 thereafter. *Eccl* Seq 31.

YATELEY

Chap in Crondall AP, sep civ identity early, sep EP 1809.[7] Incl tg Minley, chap and tg Hawley (united civ 1866 to form Hawley and Minley CP,[106] Minley sep EP 1874 [from Hawley EP, Cove EP],[137] Hawley sep EP 1842 [from Yateley alone] [7]), tg Cove (sep CP 1866,[102] sep EP 1845 [7]). *LG* Cronall Hd, Farnb. incorp for poor (1794–1869), Hart. Wit. PLU (1869–1930), RSD, RD. Addtl civ bdry alt: 1932 (incl help cr Hawley CP).[1] *Parl* Seq 3. *Eccl* Basingst. RDn (1809–56), N-E Basingst. RDn (1856–92), Aldsh. RDn (1892–1928), Odiham RDn (1928–*).

YAVERLAND

AP *LG* E Medina Hd/Lbty, IoW incorp for poor (1770–1865), PLU (1865–1930), RSD, RD. Abol civ 1933 pt to help cr Sandown-Shanklin CP, pt to Bembridge CP, pt to Brading AP.[42] *Parl* IoW Dv/Parl Co (1832–1948). *Eccl* IoW RDn (until 1850), E Medine RDn (1850–72), S-E Medine RDn (1872–92), E Wight RDn (1892–*).

HERTFORDSHIRE

ABBREVIATIONS

Abbreviations particular to Herts follow. Those general abbreviations in use throughout the *Guide* are found on page xix.

Ald.	Aldenham
Benn.	Bennington
Berk.	Berkhampstead
Bp's Stortf.	Bishop's Stortford
Braugh.	Braughing
Broadw.	Broadwater
Buntf.	Buntingford
Dac.	Dacorum
Edw.	Edwinstree
Hatf.	Hatfield
Hem. Hemp.	Hemel Hempstead
Hertf.	Hertford
Rickm.	Rickmansworth
Roys.	Royston
St Alb.	St Albans
Stev.	Stevenage
Watf.	Watford
Wheath.	Wheathampstead

SEQUENCES

An abbreviated entry prefixed by 'Seq' is used in the parochial entries to avoid repeating often the names of superior units of administration. The content of each sequence is shown below.

Local Government Sequences ('LG')

SEQ 1 Braugh. Hd, Bp's Stortf. PLU, RSD, RD (1894–95), Hadham RD (1895–1935), Braugh. RD (1935–74)
SEQ 2 Braugh. Hd, Ware PLU, RSD, RD
SEQ 3 Broadw. Hd, Hertf. PLU, RSD, RD
SEQ 4 Broadw. Hd, Hitchin PLU, RSD, RD
SEQ 5 Broadw. Hd, Ware PLU, RSD, RD
SEQ 6 Cashio Hd, Barnet PLU, RSD, RD (1894–1941), Elstree RD (1941–74)
SEQ 7 Cashio Hd, Hitchin PLU, RSD, RD
SEQ 8 Cashio Hd, Watf. PLU, RSD, RD
SEQ 9 Dac. Hd, Berk. PLU, RSD, RD (1894–1937), Berkhamstead RD (1937–74)
SEQ 10 Dac. Hd, Hem. Hemp. PLU, RSD, RD
SEQ 11 Edw. Hd, Bp's Stortf. PLU, RSD, RD (1894–95), Hadham RD (1895–1935), Braugh. RD (1935–74)
SEQ 12 Edw. Hd, Buntf. PLU, RSD, RD (1894–1935), Braugh. RD (1935–74)
SEQ 13 Edw. Hd, Roys. PLU, RSD, Ashwell RD (1894–1935), Hitchin RD (1935–74)
SEQ 14 Hertf. Hd, PLU, RSD, RD
SEQ 15 Hitchin Hd, PLU, RSD, RD
SEQ 16 Odsey Hd, Buntf. PLU, RSD, RD (1894–1935), Braugh. RD (1935–74)
SEQ 17 Odsey Hd, Hitchin PLU, RSD, RD
SEQ 18 Odsey Hd, Roys. PLU, RSD, Ashwell RD (1894–1935), Hitchin RD (1935–74)

Parliamentary Sequences ('Parl')

SEQ 1 E'rn Dv (1885–1918), Hertf. Dv/CC (1918–55), E Herts CC (1955–*)
SEQ 2 E'rn Dv (1885–1918), Hertf. Dv/CC (1918–70), Hertf. & Stev. CC (1970–*)
SEQ 3 Mid Dv (1885–1918), Hem. Hemp. Dv/CC (1918–*)
SEQ 4 Mid Dv (1885–1918), St Alb. Dv (1918–45), Barnet Dv/CC (1945–70), S Herts CC (1970–*)
SEQ 5 Mid Dv (1885–1918), St Alb. Dv (1918–45), Barnet CC (1945–55), Hertf. CC (1955–70), Welwyn & Hatf. CC (1970–*)
SEQ 6 N'rn Dv (1885–1918), Hertf. Dv/CC (1918–55), E Herts CC (1955–*)
SEQ 7 N'rn Dv (1885–1918), Hitchin Dv/CC (1918–*)
SEQ 8 N'rn Dv (1885–1918), Hitchin Dv/CC (1918–55), E Herts CC (1955–*)
SEQ 9 N'rn Dv (1885–1918), Hitchin Dv/CC (1918–55), Hertf. CC (1955–70), Hertf. & Stev. CC (1970–*)

SEQ 10 N'rn Dv (1885–1918), Hitchin Dv (1918–48), St Alb. CC (1948–55), Hertf. CC (1955–70), Welwyn & Hatf. CC (1970–*)
SEQ 11 W'rn Dv (1885–1918), Hem. Hemp. Dv/CC (1918–*)
SEQ 12 W'rn Dv (1885–1918), Hem. Hemp. Dv (1918–48), S W Herts CC (1948–*)

Ecclesiastical Sequences ('Eccl')

SEQ 1 Baldock RDn (until 1970), Buntf. RDn (1970–*)
SEQ 2 Baldock RDn (until 1970), Stev. RDn (1970–*)
SEQ 3 Baldock RDn (until 1845), Benn. RDn (1845–82), Benn. & Buntf. RDn (1882–92), Benn. RDn (1892–1922), Buntf. RDn (1922–*)
SEQ 4 Baldock RDn (until 1845), Benn. RDn (1845–82), Benn. & Buntf. RDn (1882–92), Benn. RDn (1892–1922), Welwyn RDn (1922–70), Stev. RDn (1970–*)
SEQ 5 Berk. RDn (until 1970), Berkhamsted RDn (1970–*)
SEQ 6 Braugh. RDn (until 1845), Buntf. RDn (1845–82), Benn. & Buntf. RDn (1882–92), Buntf. RDn (1892–*)
SEQ 7 Braugh. RDn (until 1845), Buntf. RDn (1845–82), Benn. & Buntf. RDn (1882–92), Buntf. RDn (1892–1922), Bp's Stortf. RDn (1922–*)
SEQ 8 Braugh. RDn (until 1845), Bp's Stortf. RDn (1845–*)
SEQ 9 Braugh. RDn (until 1845), Ware RDn (1845–1970), Cheshunt RDn (1970–*)
SEQ 10 Braugh. RDn (until 1845), Ware RDn (1845–1970), Hertf. RDn (1970–*)
SEQ 11 Hertf. RDn
SEQ 12 Hertf. RDn (until 1845), Welwyn RDn (1845–1970), Hatf. RDn (1970–*)
SEQ 13 Hertf. RDn (until 1845), Welwyn RDn (1845–1970), Stev. RDn (1970–*)
SEQ 14 Hitchin RDn
SEQ 15 Hitchin RDn (until 1970), Stev. RDn (1970–*)
SEQ 16 St Alb. RDn
SEQ 17 St Alb. RDn (until 1845), Barnet RDn (1845–*)
SEQ 18 St Alb. RDn (until 1845), Watf. RDn (1845–*)
SEQ 19 St Alb. RDn (until 1845), Watf. RDn (1845–1970), Rickm. RDn (1970–*)
SEQ 20 St Alb. RDn (until 1970), Wheath. RDn (1970–*)

DIOCESES AND ARCHDEACONRIES

Most Herts pars were in Huntingdon AD in Lincoln dioc until 1845; a few were in Middlesex AD in London dioc, in a unit usually called Braughing RDn, although the exact status of these units remains uncertain. From 1845–77 the Herts pars were in Roch dioc, in the Jurisd of St Albans (1863–77) which was renamed 1863 'Rochester and St Albans AD'. Since 1877 the pars have been in St Albans dioc, in St Albans AD.

THE PARISHES OF HERTFORDSHIRE

ALBURY

AP *LG* Seq 11. *Parl* Seq 6. *Eccl* Pec jurisd Dean & Chapter of St Paul's, London (until 1845), Seq 8 thereafter.

ALDBURY

AP *LG* Seq 9. Civ bdry: 1888,[1] 1937.[2] *Parl* Seq 11. *Eccl* Seq 5. Eccl bdry: 1910.[3]

ALDENHAM

AP *LG* Pt Dac. Hd, pt Cashio Hd, Watf. PLU, RSD, RD. Civ bdry: 1935,[4] 1952,[5] 1968.[6] *Parl* Mid Dv (1885–1918), Watf. Dv (1918–48), S W Herts CC (1948–70), S Herts CC (1970–*). *Eccl* Berk. RDn (until 1845), Watf. RDn (1845–1970), Ald. RDn (1970–*). Eccl bdry: 1865 (cr Radlett EP),[7] 1885,[8] 1969.[92]

AMERSHAM

AP In Bucks (Burnham Hd), incl hmlt Coleshill (pt Bucks [Burn. Hd], pt Herts [Dac. Hd], the hmlt transf to Bucks 1832 for parl purposes, 1844 for civ purposes[9]). See main entry in Bucks.

GREAT AMWELL

AP Incl pt hmlt and chap Hoddesdon (sep EP 1844,[10] sep CP 1866[11]), prob incl Stanstead St Margarets (sep par 13th cent[12]). *LG* Hertf. Hd, Ware PLU, pt Ware RSD, pt Ware USD, pt Hertf. MB (1885–97), pt Hertf. USD (1885–94), Ware RD (pt 1894–97, ent 1897–1974). Civ bdry: 1883,[13] 1894 (pt of the pt in Hertf. MB help cr Hoddesdon Urban CP,[14] the pt in Ware USD help cr Ware Urban CP[15]), 1897 (loses the remainder of the pt in the MB to St John Urban CP),[16] 1904,[17] 1935 (help cr Hoddesdon CP).[4] *Parl* Seq 1. *Eccl* Seq 10. Eccl bdry: 1858 (help cr Ware Christ Church EP),[18] 1864 (help cr Little Amwell EP),[19] 1937 (help cr Rye Park EP),[20] 1938.[21]

LITTLE AMWELL

Lbty in Waltham Abbey, then in Hertford All Saints AP,[22] sep EP 1864 (from Great Amwell AP, Hertford All Saints and St John EP),[19] sep CP 1866 (from Hertford All Saints AP alone).[11]

LG Hertf. Hd, PLU (1866[23]–1930), pt Hertf. MB (1835–94), pt Ware USD (1875–88), pt Hertf. RSD, pt Hertf. USD, Hertf. RD. Civ bdry: 1883,[13] 1888 (the pt in Ware USD cr Unnamed CP),[24] 1894 (the pt in the MB help cr St John Urban CP),[25] 1904,[17] 1920,[26] 1935,[4] 1959.[27] *Parl* Seq 2. *Eccl* Hertf. RDn.

ANSTEY

AP *LG* Seq 12. *Parl* Seq 8. *Eccl* Seq 6.

APSLEY END

EP Cr 1872 from Abbots Langley AP, King's Langley AP, Leverstock Green EP, Boxmoor EP.[28] Watf. RDn (1872–1907), Berk. RDn (1907–70), Berkhamsted RDn (1970–*). Bdry: 1912,[29] 1960.[30]

ARDELEY

AP Often 'Yardeley'. *LG* Odsey Hd (until 1843), Edw. Hd (from 1843), Buntf. PLU, RSD, RD (1894–1935), Braugh. RD (1935–74). *Parl* Seq 8. *Eccl* Seq 3. Eccl bdry: 1933.[31]

ARKLEY

CP Cr 1894 from the pt of Chipping Barnet CP not in Barnet USD or E Barnet Valley USD.[32] *LG* Barnet PLU, RD (1894–1905), UD (1905–65). Civ bdry: 1897.[33] Transf 1965 to Gtr London (Barnet LB).[34] *Parl* St Alb. Dv (1918–45), Barnet Dv/CC (1945–70), Gtr London thereafter.

EP Cr 1905 from Chipping Barnet EP, Shenley AP, Ridge AP, Elstree AP, Mill Hill St Paul EP (Middx).[35] Barnet RDn. Bdry: 1957.[36]

ASHWELL

AP *LG* Ashwell Bor (11th–15th cent),[43] Seq 18. *Parl* Seq 7. *Eccl* Seq 1.

ASPENDEN

AP Incl Wakeley (once a free chapel and perhaps a sep par, later deemed ex-par,[37] sep CP 1858[38]). *LG* Seq 12. Civ bdry: 1883,[39] 1937 (help cr Buntingford CP),[40] 1952.[41] *Parl* Seq 8. *Eccl* Seq 3. Eccl bdry: 1938.[42]

ASTON

AP *LG* Seq 3. Civ bdry: 1883,[13] 1888,[44] 1953,[45] 1974 (the pt in Stev. Dist [in Stevenage New Town] not to be in any par).[264] *Parl* Seq 9. *Eccl* Seq 4. Eccl bdry: 1958.[46]

AYOT ST LAWRENCE

AP Sometimes 'Great Ayot'. *LG* Broadw. Hd, Welwyn PLU, RSD, RD. *Parl* Seq 10. *Eccl* Seq 12. Eccl bdry: 1923.[47]

AYOT ST PETER

AP Sometimes 'Little Ayot' or 'Ayot Montfitchet'. *LG* Broadw. Hd, Welwyn PLU, RSD, RD. Civ bdry: 1951.[48] *Parl* Seq 10. *Eccl* Seq 12.

BALDOCK

AP In Weston AP, sep par *ca* 1199.[49] *LG* Baldock Bor (from 11th cent, later only market town),[50] Broadw. Hd, Hitchin PLU, Baldock USD, UD. Civ bdry: 1881,[51] 1909,[52] 1913,[53] 1928.[54] *Parl* Seq 7. *Eccl* Seq 2. Eccl bdry: 1933.[31]

BARKWAY

AP Incl pt Royston (sep par 1540[55]). *LG* Seq 13. *Parl* Seq 7. *Eccl* Seq 6.

BARLEY

AP Incl hmlt Nuthampstead (sep CP 1866[11]). *LG* Edw. Hd (until 1841), Odsey Hd (from 1841), Roys. PLU, RSD, Ashwell RD (1894–1935), Hitchin RD (1935–74). *Parl* Seq 7. *Eccl* Seq 6.

CHIPPING BARNET

Chap in East Barnet AP, sep civ identity early, sep EP 1866.[56] *LG* Cashio Hd, Barnet PLU, pt Barnet USD, pt E Barnet Valley USD, pt Barnet RSD, Barnet UD (1894–1965). Civ bdry: 1894 (loses the pt in RSD to cr Arkley CP, the pt in E Barnet Valley USD to cr Barnet Vale CP),[32] 1897.[33] Transf 1965 to Gtr London (Barnet LB).[34] *Parl* Mid Dv (1885–1918), St Alb. Dv (1918–45), Barnet Dv/CC (1945–70), Gtr London thereafter. *Eccl* Barnet RDn. Eccl bdry: 1869 (help cr Lyonsdown EP),[57] 1899 (cr Barnet Vale EP).[58]

EAST BARNET

AP Incl chap Chipping Barnet (sep civ identity early, sep EP 1866[56]). *LG* Cashio Hd, Barnet PLU, E Barnet Valley USD, UD (1894–1935), E Barnet UD (1935–65). Transf 1965 to Gtr London (Barnet LB).[34] *Parl* Mid Dv (1885–1918), St Alb. Dv (1918–45), Barnet Dv/CC (1945–70), Gtr London thereafter. *Eccl* Seq 17. Addtl eccl bdry alt: 1869 (help cr Lyonsdown EP),[57] 1906 (cr South Barnet EP),[59] 1911 (help cr New Barnet EP),[60] 1972,[61] 1974.[62]

NEW BARNET

EP Cr 1911 from Lyonsdown EP, East Barnet AP.[60] Barnet RDn.

SOUTH BARNET

EP Cr 1906 from East Barnet AP.[59] Barnet RDn. Renamed 1951 'New Southgate St Michael and All Angels EP'.[63]

BARNET VALE

CP Cr 1894 from the pt of Chipping Barnet CP in E Barnet Valley USD.[32] *LG* Barnet PLU, E Barnet Valley UD (1894–1935), E Barnet UD (1935–65). Transf 1965 to Gtr London (Barnet LB).[34] *Parl* St Alb. Dv (1918–45), Barnet Dv/CC (1945–70), Gtr London thereafter.

EP Cr 1899 from Chipping Barnet EP.[58] Barnet RDn.

SOUTH BASSINGBOURN

CP Cr 1896 from Bassingbourn AP (Cambs), to be in Herts.[64] *LG* Roys. PLU, Ashwell RD. Abol 1897 ent to Royston AP.[65]

BAYFORD

Chap in Essendon AP, sep civ identity early, sep EP 1867.[66] *LG* Seq 14. Civ bdry: 1880,[44] 1935.[4] *Parl* Seq 2. *Eccl* Hertf. RDn. Eccl bdry: 1931.[67]

BENGEO

AP *LG* Hertf. Hd, PLU, pt Hertf. USD, pt Hertf. RSD, pt Hertf. MB (1868–94). Abol civ 1894 the pt in the MB to cr Bengeo Urban CP, the remainder to cr Bengeo Rural CP.[25] *Parl* E'rn Dv (1885–1918). *Eccl* Hertf. RDn. Eccl bdry: 1869 (help cr Benge Christ Church EP),[68] 1908 (help cr Waterford EP).[69] Abol eccl 1969 to help cr Bengeo (Holy Trinity with Christ Church) EP.[70]

BENGEO (HOLY TRINITY WITH CHRIST CHURCH

EP Cr 1969 by union Bengeo AP, Bengeo Christ Church EP.[70] Hertf. RDn.

BENGEO CHRIST CHURCH

EP Cr 1869 from Bengeo AP, Hertford St Andrew with St Nicholas and St Mary EP.[68] Hertf. RDn. Abol 1969 to help cr Bengeo (Holy Trinity with Christ Church) EP.[70]

BENGEO RURAL

CP Cr 1894 from the pt of Bengeo AP not in Hertf. MB.[25] *LG* Hertf. PLU, RD. Civ bdry: 1920,[26] 1935,[4] 1937.[71] *Parl* Hertf. Dv/CC (1918–70), Hertf. & Stev. CC (1970–*).

BENGEO URBAN

CP Cr 1894 from the pt of Bengeo AP in Hertf. MB.[25] *LG* Hertf. PLU, MB. Abol 1900 to help cr Hertford CP.[72]

BENINGTON

AP *LG* Seq 3. Civ bdry: 1888.[73] *Parl* Seq 9. *Eccl* Seq 4.

BERKHAMPSTEAD

AP Usual civ spelling; for eccl see 'Great Berkhampstead'. *LG* Berk. Bor (from 11th cent, market town later),[74] Dac. Hd, Berk. PLU, pt Gt Berk. USD, pt Berk. RSD, pt Gt Berk. UD (1894–98), pt Berk. RD (1894–98). Abol civ 1898 the pt in the UD to cr Great Berkhampstead Urban CP, the remainder to cr Great Berkhampstead Rural CP.[75] *Parl* W'rn Dv (1885–1918).

BERKHAMPSTEAD ST MARY–See NORTHCHURCH

GREAT BERKHAMPSTEAD

AP Usual eccl spelling (sometimes 'Berkhampstead St Peter'); for civ see 'Berkhampstead'. *Eccl* Seq 5. Eccl bdry: 1894 (cr Potten End EP).[76]

GREAT BERKHAMPSTEAD RURAL

CP Cr 1898 from the pt of Berkhampstead AP not in Gt Berk. UD.[75] *LG* Berk. PLU, RD. Civ bdry: 1935.[4] Abol 1937 pt to help cr Nettleden with Potten End CP, pt to Northchurch AP.[2] *Parl* Hem. Hemp. Dv (1918–48).

GREAT BERKHAMPSTEAD URBAN

CP Cr 1898 from the pt of Berkhampstead AP in Gt Berk. UD.[75] *LG* Berk. PLU, Gt Berk. UD. Bdry: 1909,[77] 1935.[4] Renamed 1937 'Berkhamsted Urban CP'.[77] *Parl* Hem. Hemp. Dv (1918–48).

LITTLE BERKHAMPSTEAD

AP *LG* Seq 14. Civ bdry: 1888.[44] *Parl* Seq 2. *Eccl* Seq 11. Eccl bdry: 1931.[67]

BERKHAMSTED URBAN

CP Renaming 1937 of Great Berkhampstead Urban CP.[78] *LG* Berkhamsted UD. Civ bdry: 1961.[79] *Parl* Hem. Hemp. CC (1948–*).

BOREHAM WOOD ALL SAINTS

EP Cr 1909 from Elstree AP, Radlett EP.[80] St Alb. RDn (1909–70), Ald. RDn (1970–*). Bdry: 1957,[36] 1958 (help cr Boreham Wood St Michael and All Angels EP).[81]

BOREHAM WOOD ST MICHAEL AND ALL ANGELS

EP Cr 1958 from Radlett EP, Boreham Wood All Saints EP, Ridge AP.[81] Barnet RDn (1958–70), Ald. RDn (1970–*).

BOURNE END

EP Cr 1915 from Sunnyside EP, Bovingdon EP, Boxmoor EP, Hemel Hempstead AP.[82] Berk. RDn (1915–70), Berkhamsted RDn (1970–*).

BOVINGDON

Chap in Hemel Hempstead AP, sep EP 1834,[83] sep CP 1866.[11] *LG* Seq 10. Civ bdry: 1907 (exchanges pts with Ashley Green CP, loses pt to Latimer CP, both Bucks),[84] 1935.[4] *Parl* Seq 11. *Eccl* Berk. RDn (1834–45), St Alb. RDn (1845–1907), Berk. RDn (1907–70), Berkhamsted RDn (1970–*). Eccl bdry: 1915 (help cr Bourne End EP),[82] 1960.[30]

BOXMOOR

EP Cr 1830 from Hemel Hempstead AP.[83] Berk. RDn (1830–45), St Alb. RDn (1845–1907), Berk. RDn (1907–70), Berkhamsted RDn (1970–*). Bdry: 1872 (help cr Apsley End EP),[28] 1912,[29] 1915 (help cr Bourne End EP),[82] 1960.[30]

BRAMFIELD

AP Sometimes 'Braintfield'. *LG* Cashio Hd, Hertf. PLU, RSD, RD. Civ bdry: 1920,[26] 1935.[4] *Parl* Seq 2. *Eccl* Welwyn RDn (until 1929), Hertf. RDn (1929–*). Eccl bdry: 1908 (help cr Waterford EP).[69]

BRAUGHING

AP *LG* Seq 1. Civ bdry: 1935,[4] 1937 (help cr Hormead CP).[40] *Parl* Seq 6. Parl bdry: 1945.[264] *Eccl* Braugh. RDn (until 1845), Bp's Stortf. RDn (1845–1922), Buntf. RDn (1922–70), Bp's Stortf. RDn (1970–*).

BRICKENDON

Lbty in Waltham Abbey, then in Hertford All Saints AP, sep CP 1866.[11] *LG* Hertf. PLU, pt Hertf. MB (1866–92, enlarged pt 1892–94), pt Hertf. USD, pt Hertf. RSD. Abol 1894 the pt in the MB to cr Brickendon Urban CP, the remainder to cr Brickendon Rural CP.[25] *Parl* E'rn Dv (1885–1918).

BRICKENDON LIBERTY

CP Cr 1928 by union Brickendon Rural CP, St John Rural CP.[85] *LG* Hertf. PLU, RD. Bdry: 1935,[4] 1959.[27] *Parl* Hertf. CC (1948–70), Hertf. & Stev. CC (1970–*).

BRICKENDON RURAL

CP Cr 1894 from the pt of Brickendon AP not in Hertf. MB.[25] *LG* Hertf. PLU, RD. Abol 1929 to help cr Brickendon Liberty CP.[85] *Parl* Hertf. Dv (1918–48).

BRICKENDON URBAN

CP Cr 1894 from the pt of Brickendon AP in Hertf. MB.[25] *LG* Hertf. PLU, MB. Abol 1900 to help cr Hertford CP.[72]

BROADFIELD

Chap in Rushden AP, eccl in disuse by 16th cent, sep civ identity early, eccl attached to Cottered AP by 18th cent.[86] *LG* Odsey Hd, Buntf. PLU, RSD, RD (1894–1935), Braugh. RD (1935–55). Abol civ 1955 ent to Cottered AP.[87] *Parl* N'rn Dv (1885–1918), Hitchin

Dv/CC (1918–70).
BROXBOURNE
AP Incl pt hmlt and chap Hoddesdon (sep EP 1844,[10] sep CP 1866[11]). *LG* Hertf. Hd, Ware PLU, RSD, RD. Abol civ 1935 pt to help cr Hoddesdon CP, pt to Brickendon Liberty CP.[4] *Parl* E'rn Dv (1885–1918), Hertf. Dv (1918–48). *Eccl* Braugh. RDn (until 1845), Ware RDn (1845–70), Cheshunt RDn (1970–*).
BUCKLAND
AP *LG* Seq 12. Civ bdry: 1935.[4] *Parl* Seq 8. *Eccl* Seq 6. Eccl bdry: 1857.[88]
BUNTINGFORD
Chap in Layston AP, sep CP 1937 (from Aspenden AP, Layston AP, Throcking AP, Wyddial AP).[40] *LG* Braugh. RD. Civ bdry: 1952.[41] *Parl* Hitchin CC (1948–55), E Herts CC (1955–*).
BUSHEY
AP In Watford AP, sep par by 1166.[89] *LG* Dac. Hd, Watf. PLU, pt Watf. USD, pt Watf. RSD. Abol civ 1894 the pt in the USD to cr Bushey Urban CP, the remainder to cr Bushey Rural CP.[32] *Parl* W'rn Dv (1885–1918). *Eccl* St Alb. RDn (until 1845), Watf. RDn (1845–1970), Ald. RDn (1970–*). Eccl bdry: 1879 (help cr Oxhey St Matthew EP),[90] 1889 (cr Bushey Heath EP),[91] 1969.[92]
CP Renaming 1906 of Bushey Rural CP when transf to Bushey UD.[93] *LG* Watf. PLU, Bushey UD. Bdry: 1935.[4] *Parl* Watf. Dv (1918–48), S W Herts CC (1948–*).
BUSHEY HEATH
EP Cr 1889 from Bushey AP.[91] Watf. RDn (1889–1970), Ald. RDn (1970–*). Bdry: 1969.[92]
BUSHEY RURAL
CP Cr 1894 from the pt of Bushey AP not in Watf. USD.[32] *LG* Watf. PLU, RD. Renamed 1906 'Bushey CP' when made pt of Bushey UD.[93]
BUSHEY URBAN
CP Cr 1894 from the pt of Bushey AP in Watf. USD.[32] *LG* Watf. PLU, UD. Renamed 1906 'Oxhey CP'.[94]
BYGRAVE
AP *LG* Seq 17. Civ bdry: 1881,[51] 1913,[53] 1928.[54] *Parl* Seq 7. *Eccl* Seq 2. Eccl bdry: 1933.[31]
CADDINGTON
AP Pt in Herts (Dac. Hd), pt in Beds (Flitt Hd), made 2 sep CPs 1894, one in each co, qv.[95] *LG* Luton PLU, RSD. *Parl* Herts pt, Mid Dv (1885–1918). *Eccl* See main entry in Beds.
CP Cr 1894 from the pt of Caddington AP in Herts.[95] *LG* Hem. Hemp. RD. Abol 1897 to help cr Markyate CP.[75]
CALDECOTE
AP *LG* Seq 17. *Parl* Seq 7. *Eccl* Seq 1.
CHESHUNT
AP *LG* Hertf. Hd, Edmonton PLU, Cheshunt USD, UD. Civ bdry: 1935.[4] *Parl* Seq 1. *Eccl* Seq 9. Eccl bdry: 1855 (cr Waltham Cross Holy Trinity EP),[97] 1871 (cr Goff's Oak EP).[98]
CHIPPERFIELD
EP Cr 1848 from Abbots Langley AP, King's Langley AP, Watford AP.[83] Watf. RDn (1848–1970), Rickm. RDn (1970–*). Bdry: 1964.[99]
CP Cr 1958 from King's Langley AP.[100] *LG* Hem. Hemp. RD. *Parl* Hem. Hemp. CC (1970–*).
CHIVESFIELD–see GRAVELEY
CHORLEY WOOD CHRIST CHURCH
EP Cr 1845 from Rickmansworth AP.[83] Watf. RDn (1845–1970), Rickm. RDn (1970–*). Bdry: 1875 (help cr Mill End EP),[101] 1963 (help cr Chorleywood St Andrew EP).[102]
CHORLEYWOOD
CP Cr 1898 from the pt of Rickmansworth AP not in Rickm. UD.[65] *LG* Watf. PLU, RD (1898–1913), Chorleywood UD (1913–74). Civ bdry: 1907 (gains pt Chalfont St Peter AP, Chenies AP, both Bucks),[84] 1938.[103] *Parl* Watf. Dv (1918–48), S W Herts CC (1948–*).
CHORLEYWOOD ST ANDREW
EP Cr 1963 from Chorley Wood Christ Church EP, Chalfont St Giles AP (Bucks), Chenies AP (Bucks).[102] Watf. RDn (1963–70), Rickm. RDn (1970–*).
CLOTHALL
AP *LG* Seq 17. Civ bdry: 1881.[51] *Parl* Seq 7. *Eccl* Seq 2. Eccl bdry: 1933.[31]
CODICOTE
AP *LG* Seq 7. *Parl* Seq 7. *Eccl* St Alb. RDn (until 1845), Welwyn RDn (1845–1970), Hatf. RDn (1970–*). Eccl bdry: 1923.[47]
COLNEY
EP Sometimes 'London Colney'. Cr 1827 from St Albans St Peter AP, St Albans St Stephen AP, Shenley AP.[83] St Alb. RDn (1827–45), Barnet RDn (1845–1907), St Alb. RDn (1907–70), Ald. RDn (1970–*). Bdry: 1962.[104]
LONDON COLNEY
CP Cr 1947 from St Peter Rural CP.[105] *LG* St Alb. RD. *Parl* St Alb. CC (1948–70), S Herts CC (1970–*).
COLNEY HEATH
EP Cr 1847 from Ridge EP.[83] St Alb. RDn (1847–1970), Hatf. RDn (1970–*). Bdry: 1959.[106]
CP Cr 1947 from St Peter Rural CP.[107] *LG* St Alb. RD. Bdry: 1962.[108] *Parl* St Alb. CC (1948–70), S Herts CC (1970–*).
COTTERED
AP *LG* Seq 16. Civ bdry: 1955.[87] *Parl* Seq 8. *Eccl* Incl Broadfield chap since 18th cent,[86] Seq 3.
CROXLEY GREEN ALL SAINTS
EP Cr 1872 from Rickmansworth AP, Watford AP.[109] Watf. RDn (1872–1970), Rickm. RDn (1970–*). Bdry: 1896,[110] 1957 (cr Croxley Green St Oswald EP),[111] 1964.[99]
CROXLEY GREEN ST OSWALD
EP Cr 1957 from Croxley Green All Saints EP).[111] Watf. RDn (1957–70), Rickm. RDn (1970–*).
DATCHWORTH
AP *LG* Seq 3. Civ bdry: 1883,[13] 1911,[112] 1953,[45] 1964,[113] 1974 (the pt in Stev. Dist [in Stev. New Town] not to be in any par).[264] *Parl* Seq 9. *Eccl* Seq 13. Eccl bdry: 1916,[114] 1958.[46]
DIGSWELL
AP *LG* Broadw. Hd, Welwyn PLU, RSD, RD. Civ bdry: 1883,[13] 1921 (help cr Welwyn Garden

City CP).[115] Abol civ 1935 ent to Welwyn AP.[4] *Parl* N'rn Dv (1885–1918), Hitchin Dv (1918–48). *Eccl* Hertf. RDn (until 1907), Welwyn RDn (1907–70), Hatf. RDn (1970–*). Eccl bdry: 1968.[116]

EASTWICK

AP *LG* Seq 2. Civ bdry: 1935 (incl gain pt Great Parndon AP, pt Roydon AP, both Essex),[4] 1937.[117] *Parl* Seq 1. *Eccl* Braugh. RDn (until 1845), Ware RDn (1845–1922), Bp's Stortf. RDn (1922–55). Abol eccl 1955 to help cr Gilston with Eastwick EP.[118]

ELSTREE

AP *LG* Seq 6. Civ bdry: 1935 (incl help cr Rowley CP),[4] 1951,[119] 1957,[120] 1968.[6] *Parl* Seq 4. *Eccl* St Alb. RDn (until 1845), Watf. RDn (1845–1907), St Alb. RDn (1907–70), Ald. RDn (1970–*). Eccl bdry: 1885,[8] 1905 (help cr Arkley EP),[35] 1909 (help cr Boreham Wood All Saints EP).[80]

ENFIELD

AP In Middx (Edmonton Hd). *LG* Edmonton PLU, pt Enfield USD, pt E Barnet Valley USD (1888–94), pt Barnet RSD (two detached pts, transf 1888 to E Barnet Valley USD). A detached pt gained 1779[122] from Monken Hadley AP then lost back to that par 1883,[13] thus became pt of Herts when Monken Hadley transf 1889 from Middx to Herts.[123] The two detached pts in E Barnet Valley USD transf 1894 to Monken Hadley and thus also became pt of Herts.[121] See main entry in Middx.

ESSENDON

AP Incl chap Bayford (sep civ identity early, sep EP 1867[66]). *LG* Hertf. Hd, PLU, RSD, RD. *Parl* Seq 5. *Eccl* Hertf. RDn. Abol eccl 1959 to help cr Essendon and Woodhill EP.[106]

ESSENDON AND WOODHILL

EP Cr 1959 by union Essendon AP, the pt of Bishop's Hatfield AP which incl chap Woodhill, pt North Mymms AP.[106] Hertf. RDn (1959–70), Hatf. RDn (1970–*).

FLAMSTEAD

AP Chap in Redbourn AP, sep par beginning 12th cent.[124] *LG* Seq 10. Civ bdry: 1897 (gains the Beds pt of Whipsnade AP and help cr Markyate CP),[125] 1907 (exchanges pts with Hyde CP, gains pt Caddington AP, both Beds),[126] 1935,[4] 1937,[71] 1965 (exchanges pts with Hyde CP, Beds).[127] *Parl* Seq 3. *Eccl* Berk. RDn (until 1907), St Alb. RDn (1907–70), Wheath. RDn (1970–*). Eccl bdry: 1877 (help cr Markyate Street EP).[195]

FLAUNDEN

Chap in Hemel Hempstead AP, sep EP 1834,[83] sep CP 1866.[11] *LG* Seq 10. Civ bdry: 1907 (exchanges pts with Latimer CP, Bucks).[84] *Parl* Seq 11. *Eccl* Berk. RDn (1834–45), St Alb. RDn (1845–76). Abol eccl 1876 to help cr Latimer with Flaunden EP, to be in Oxford dioc (Amersham RDn, 1876–*).[128]

FROGMORE

EP Cr 1859 from St Albans St Stephen AP.[129] St Alb. RDn (1859–1970), Ald. RDn (1970–*). Bdry: 1969.[92]

GREAT GADDESDEN

AP *LG* Seq 10. Civ bdry: 1935.[4] *Parl* Seq 3. *Eccl* Seq 5. Eccl bdry: 1926,[130] 1938.[131]

LITTLE GADDESDEN

AP *LG* Seq 9. Civ bdry: 1885 (gains pt Edlesborugh AP, Bucks),[132] 1895 (gains pt Ivinghoe AP, pt Nettleden AP, both Bucks),[133] 1907 (loses pt to Edlesborough AP, Bucks),[84] 1907 (exchanges pts with Studham AP, Beds),[126] 1937.[2] *Parl* Seq 3. *Eccl* Seq 5. Eccl bdry: 1939.[134]

GILSTON

AP *LG* Seq 2. Civ bdry: 1935 (gains pt Netteswell AP, Essex).[4] *Parl* Seq 1. *Eccl* Braugh. RDn (until 1845), Bp's Stortf. RDn (1845–1955). Abol eccl 1955 to help cr Gilston with Eastwick EP.[118]

GILSTON WITH EASTWICK

EP Cr 1955 by union Gilston AP, Eastwick AP, pt High Wych EP.[118] Bp's Stortf. RDn.

GOFF'S OAK

EP Cr 1871 from Cheshunt AP.[98] Ware RDn (1871–1970), Cheshunt RDn (1970–*).

GRAVELEY

AP Incl Chivesfield (sometimes distinct until united *ca* 1445 with Graveley as its chapel, dismantled 1750[135]). *LG* Seq 4. Civ bdry: 1935,[4] 1953,[45] 1955,[136] 1969.[137] *Parl* Seq 7. Parl bdry: 1971.[265] *Eccl* As 'Graveley with Chivesfield', Seq 15. Eccl bdry: 1958.[46]

GRAVELEY WITH CHIVESFIELD—see prev entry

LITTLE HADHAM

AP Sep par, united *ca* 1300 to Much Hadham AP as the latter's chapel,[138] sep civ identity maintained, sep EP 1870.[139] *LG* Seq 11. *Parl* Seq 1. *Eccl* Bp's Stortf. RDn.

MUCH HADHAM

AP Incl chap Little Hadham (from *ca* 1300, formerly sep par, sep civ identity maintained, sep EP 1870[139]). *LG* Seq 11. *Parl* Seq 1. *Eccl* Seq 8.

HADLEY

CP Cr 1894 from the pt of Monken Hadley AP in Barnet USD.[32] *LG* Barnet PLU, UD. Transf 1965 to Gtr London (Barnet LB).[34] *Parl* St Alb. Dv (1918–45), Barnet Dv/CC (1945–70), Gtr London thereafter.

MONKEN HADLEY

AP In Middx (Edmonton Hd). *LG* Barnet PLU, pt Barnet USD, pt E Barnet Valley USD. Transf 1889 to Herts,[140] E Barnet Valley UD (1894–1935), E Barnet UD (1935–65). Civ bdry: 1779 (loses detached pt to Enfield AP),[122] 1883 (regains same pt),[13] 1894 (gains the pt of Enfield AP, Middx, in E Barnet Valley USD, loses the pt in Barnet USD to cr Hadley CP).[32] Transf 1965 to Gtr London (Barnet LB).[34] *Parl* Middx until 1918, St Alb. Dv (1918–45), Barnet Dv/CC (1945–70), Gtr London thereafter. *Eccl* Donative until 1777,[141] Enfield RDn (1858–1967), Central Barnet RDn (1967–*) (both in London dioc).

HARPENDEN
Chap in Wheathampstead AP, sep civ identity early, sep EP 1859.[142] *LG* Dac. Hd, St Alb. PLU, RSD, RD (1894–98). Abol civ 1898 pt to cr Harpenden UD and Harpenden Urban CP, the remainder to cr Harpenden Rural CP.[143] *Parl* Mid Dv (1885–1918). *Eccl* St Alb. RDn (1859–1970), Wheath. RDn (1970–*). Eccl bdry: 1936 (help cr Harpenden St John the Baptist EP),[144] 1949.[145]

HARPENDEN RURAL
CP Cr 1898 from the pt of Harpenden CP not made UD.[143] *LG* St Alb. PLU, RD. Civ bdry: 1907 (exchanges pts with Hyde CP, Beds),[126] 1935,[4] 1937.[146] *Parl* Hem. Hemp. Dv/CC (1918–70), St Alb. CC (1970–*).

HARPENDEN ST JOHN THE BAPTIST
EP Cr 1936 from Harpenden EP, Wheathampstead AP, Redbourn AP.[144] St Alb. RDn (1936–70), Wheath. RDn (1970–*).

HARPENDEN URBAN
CP Cr 1898 from the pt of Harpenden CP constitututed Harpenden UD.[143] *LG* St Alb. PLU, Harpenden UD. Civ bdry: 1935.[4] *Parl* Hem. Hemp. Dv/CC (1918–70), St Alb. CC (1970–*).

HATFIELD
CP Cr 1951 from Bishop's Hatfield AP, Welwyn Garden City CP.[147] *LG* Hatf. RD. *Parl* Hertf. CC (1955–70), Welwyn & Hatf. CC (1970–*).

HATFIELD HYDE
EP Cr 1927 from Bishop's Hatfield AP.[148] Welwyn RDn (1927–70), Hatf. RDn (1970–*).

HATFIELD ST MARY
EP Cr 1849 from Bishop's Hatfield AP.[83] Hertf. RDn. Reconstituted 1912 as Ponsbourne EP.[149]

BISHOP'S HATFIELD
AP Incl chap Totteridge (sep civ identity early, sep EP 1892[150]). *LG* Broadw. Hd, Hatf. PLU, RSD, RD. Civ bdry: 1921 (help cr Welwyn Garden City CP),[115] 1935.[4] Abol civ 1951 pt to help cr Hatfield CP, pt to Welwyn Garden City CP.[151] *Parl* Mid Dv (1885–1918), St Alb. Dv (1918–45), Barnet Dv/CC (1945–55). *Eccl* Often as 'Hatfield', Hertf. RDn (until 1970), Hatf. RDn (1970–*). Addtl eccl bdry alt: 1849 (cr Hatfield St Mary EP,[83] reconstituted 1912 as Ponsbourne EP[149]), 1858 (cr Lemsford EP),[152] 1927 (help cr Welwyn Garden City EP),[153] 1927 (cr Hatfield Hyde EP),[148] 1959 (help cr Essendon and Woodhill EP).[106]

LITTLE HEATH
EP Cr 1894 from North Mymms AP.[154] Barnet RDn (1894–1970), Cheshunt RDn (1970–*).

HEMEL HEMPSTEAD
AP Incl chaps Bovingdon, Flaunden (each sep EP 1834,[83] each sep CP 1866[11]). *LG* Dac. Hd, Hem. Hemp. Bor (early status uncertain),[155] PLU, RSD, RD (1894–98), MB (1898[156]–1974). Civ bdry: 1935.[4] *Parl* Seq 11. *Eccl* Berk. RDn (until 1845), St Alb. RDn (1845–1907), Berk. RDn (1907–70), Berkhamsted RDn (1970–*). Addtl eccl bdry alt: 1830 (cr Boxmoor EP),[83] 1850 (help cr Leverstock Green EP),[47] 1878 (cr Hemel Hempstead St Paul EP),[157] 1915 (cr Bourne End EP),[82] 1926,[130] 1938,[131] 1960.[30]

HEMEL HEMPSTEAD ST PAUL
EP Cr 1878 from Hemel Hempstead AP.[157] St Alb. RDn (1878–1907), Berk. RDn (1907–60). Abol 1960 pt to Hemel Hempstead AP, pt to Leverstock Green EP.[30]

HERTFORD
The following have 'Hertford' in their names. Insofar as any existed at a given time: *LG* Hertf. Hd, PLU [Bor/MB, USD, RSD sep noted]. *Parl* Sep noted; Hertf. Parl Bor returned members irregularly 1298–1376, regularly 1624–1885. *Eccl* Hertf. RDn.

CP1–HERTFORD–Cr 1900 by union of pars in Hertf. MB: AP1, St Andrew Urban CP, St John Urban CP, Bengeo Urban CP, Brickendon Urban CP.[72] *LG* Hertf. MB. Civ bdry: 1920.[26] *Parl* Hertf. Dv/CC (1918–70), Hertf. & Stev. CC (1970–*).

AP1–HERTFORD ALL SAINTS–Incl lbty Brickendon (lbty to Waltham Abbey until 16th cent, orig outside Bor, sep CP 1866[11]), lbty Little Amwell (lbty to Waltham Abbey until 16th cent, orig outside Bor, sep EP 1864 [from EP1, Great Amwell AP],[19] sep CP 1866 [from AP1 alone][11]). *LG* Hertf. Bor/MB (pt until 1866, ent from 1866), USD. Abol civ 1900 to help cr CP1.[72] *Parl* Hertf. Parl Bor (pt until 1866, ent 1866–85), E'rn Dv (1885–1918). *Eccl* Abol eccl *ca* 1640 to help cr EP1.[158]

EP1–HERTFORD ALL SAINTS WITH ST JOHN–Cr *ca* 1640 by union AP1, AP3.[158] Bdry: 1864 (help cr Little Amwell EP),[19] 1931.[67]

AP2–HERTFORD ST ANDREW–*LG* Pt Hertf. Bor/MB (enlarged pt 1835–94), pt Hertf. USD, pt Hertf. RSD. Abol civ 1894 the pt in the MB to cr St Andrew Urban CP, the remainder to cr St Andrew Rural CP.[25] *Parl* Pt Hertf. Parl Bor (until 1885), E'rn Dv (1885–1918). *Eccl* Abol eccl before 1535 to help cr EP2.[159]

EP2–HERTFORD ST ANDREW WITH ST NICHOLAS AND ST MARY–Cr before 1535 by union AP2, AP4, AP5.[159] Bdry: 1869 (help cr Bengeo Christ Church EP),[68] 1969.[160]

AP3–HERTFORD ST JOHN–*LG* Pt Hertf. Bor/MB, pt Hertf. USD, pt Hertf. RSD. Civ bdry: 1883.[13] Abol civ 1894 the pt in the MB to cr St John Urban CP, the remainder to cr St John Rural CP.[25] *Parl* Pt Hertf. Parl Bor (until 1885), E'rn Dv (1885–1918). *Eccl* Abol eccl *ca* 1640 to help cr EP1.[158]

AP4–HERTFORD ST MARY–No sep civ functions; abol by 1535 to help cr EP2.[159]

AP5–HERTFORD ST NICHOLAS–No sep civ functions; abol by 1535 to help cr EP2.[159]

HERTINGFORDBURY
AP *LG* Seq 14. Civ bdry: 1924,[161] 1935,[4] 1951.[151] *Parl* Seq 2. *Eccl* Seq 11. Eccl bdry: 1968.[116]

HEXTON
AP *LG* Seq 7. *Parl* Seq 7. *Eccl* St Alb. RDn (until 1845), Hitchin RDn (1845–*). Eccl bdry: 1942.[162]

HIGH CROSS
EP Cr 1845 from Standon AP.[163] Bp's Stortf. RDn (1845–1907), Ware RDn (1907–70), Hertf. RDn (1970–*).

HINXWORTH
AP *LG* Seq 18. *Parl* Seq 7. *Eccl* Seq 1.

HITCHIN
AP Incl chap Great Wymondley (sep par by 13th cent[164]), chap Ippolyts (sep par 16th cent [eccl, 'St Ippolyts'][165]). *LG* Hitchin Hd, Bor (12th–14th cent, market town later),[166] PLU, pt Hitchin USD, pt Hitchin RSD. Abol civ 1894 the pt in the USD to cr Hitchin Urban CP, the remainder to cr 3 sep CPs for 3 hmlts, Langley, Preston, Walsworth.[167] *Parl* N'rn Dv (1885–1918). *Eccl* Seq 14. Addtl eccl bdry alt: 1864 (cr Hitchin St Saviour EP),[83] 1968.[168]

HITCHIN ST SAVIOUR
EP Cr 1864 from Hitchin AP.[83] Hitchin RDn.

HITCHIN URBAN
CP Cr 1894 from the pt of Hitchin AP in Hitchin USD.[167] *LG* Hitchin PLU, UD. Bdry: 1921,[169] 1935.[4] *Parl* Hitchin Dv/CC (1918–*).

HOCKERILL
EP Cr 1852 from Bishop's Stortford AP.[170] Bp's Stortf. RDn.

HODDESDON
Hmlt and chap (14th–17th cent[171]) in Broxbourne AP and in Great Amwell AP, sep EP 1844,[10] sep CP 1866.[11] *LG* Hertf. Hd, Ware PLU (1866[23]–94), pt Hoddesdon USD, pt Ware RSD. Civ bdry: 1883.[13] Abol civ 1894 the pt in the USD to help cr Hoddesdon Urban CP, the remainder to cr Hoddesdon Rural CP.[14] *Parl* E'rn Dv (1885–1918). *Eccl* Braugh. RDn (1844–45), Ware RDn (1845–1970), Cheshunt RDn (1970–*). Eccl bdry: 1937 (help cr Rye Park EP),[20] 1938.[21]
CP Cr 1935 from Broxbourne AP, Great Amwell AP, Hoddesdon Rural CP, Stanstead Abbots AP, Wormley AP, ent Hoddesdon Urban CP.[4] *LG* Hoddesdon UD. *Parl* Hertf. CC (1948–55), E Herts CC (1955–*).

HODDESDON RURAL
CP Cr 1894 from the pt of Hoddesdon CP not in Hoddesdon USD.[14] *LG* Ware PLU, RD. Abol 1935 pt to help cr Hoddesdon CP, pt to Brickendon Liberty CP.[4] *Parl* Hertf. Dv (1918–48).

HODDESDON URBAN
CP Cr 1894 from the pt of Hoddesdon CP in Hoddesdon USD, and from Great Amwell AP.[14] *LG* Ware PLU, Hoddesdon UD. Abol 1935 to help cr Hoddesdon CP.[4] *Parl* Hertf. Dv (1918–48).

HOLWELL
AP In Beds (Clifton Hd), transf 1897 to Herts (incl gains pt Shillington AP [prev in both Beds, Herts]).[172] *LG* Hitchin PLU, RD. Civ bdry: 1901,[173] 1956.[174] *Parl* Beds until 1918, Hitchin Dv/CC (1918–*). *Eccl* Shefford RDn (until 1866), Shefford RDn W'rn Dv (1866–80), Shefford RDn (1880–1914)(all in Bedford AD), Hitchin RDn (1914–*).

HORMEAD
CP Cr 1937 by union Great Hormead AP, Little Hormead AP, pt Layston AP, pt Braughing AP.[40] *LG* Braugh. RD. *Parl* Hitchin Dv/CC (1945–55), E Herts CC (1955–*).

GREAT HORMEAD
AP *LG* Edw. Hd, Buntf. PLU, RSD, RD (1894–1935), Braugh. RD (1935–37). Civ bdry: 1883.[13] Abol civ 1937 to help cr Hormead CP.[40] *Parl* N'rn Dv (1885–1918), Hitchin Dv (1918–48). *Eccl* Seq 6. Eccl bdry: 1938.[42]

LITTLE HORMEAD
AP Organisation as for Great Hormead except no eccl bdry alt.

HUNSDON
AP *LG* Seq 2. Civ bdry: 1883,[13] 1888.[175] *Parl* Seq 1. *Eccl* Seq 10.

WEST HYDE
EP Cr 1846 from Rickmansworth AP.[176] Watf. RDn (1846–1970), Rickm. RDn (1970–*).

ICKLEFORD
Chap in Pirton AP, sep civ identity early, sep EP 1847.[177] Pt Herts (Hitchin Hd), pt Beds (Clifton Hd), the latter transf to Herts 1832 for parl purposes, 1844 for civ purposes.[9] *LG* Hitchin PLU, RSD, RD. Civ bdry: 1897,[178] 1947 (gains pt Arlesley AP, Beds),[179] 1956 (incl gains pt Arlesley AP, Beds).[174] *Parl* Herts pt, Seq 7. *Eccl* Seq 14.

IPPOLLITTS
Usual civ spelling; for eccl see 'St Ippolyts'. Chap in Hitchin AP, sep par 16th cent.[165] *LG* Seq 15. Civ bdry: 1935,[4] 1937 (help cr Wymondley CP),[105] 1953,[45] 1955.[180] *Parl* Seq 7.

KELSHALL
AP *LG* Seq 18. *Parl* Seq 7. *Eccl* Seq 1.

KENSWORTH
AP *LG* Dac. Hd, Luton PLU, RSD, sep RD (1894–97). Transf 1897 to Beds.[172] *Parl* Mid Dv (1885–1918), Beds thereafter. *Eccl* Berk. RDn (until 1907), St Alb. RDn (1907–30), Dunstable RDn (Bedford AD, 1930–*). Eccl bdry: 1961.[181]

KIMPTON
AP *LG* Seq 15. Civ bdry: 1935.[4] *Parl* Seq 7. *Eccl* Hitchin RDn (until 1845), Welwyn RDn (1845–1970), Wheath. RDn (1970–*). Eccl bdry: 1923.[47]

KNEBWORTH
AP *LG* Seq 4. Civ bdry: 1883,[13] 1908,[172] 1911,[112] 1953.[45] *Parl* Seq 7. *Eccl* Hitchin RDn (until 1845), Welwyn RDn (1845–1970), Stev. RDn (1970–*). Eccl bdry: 1916,[114] 1958.[46]

SOUTH KNEESWORTH
CP Cr 1896 from Kneesworth CP (Cambs) to be in Herts.[182] *LG* Roys. PLU, Ashwell RD. Abol 1897 ent to Royston AP.[64]

LANGLEY
CP Hmlt in Hitchin AP, sep CP 1894 from pt of the pt of Hitchin AP not in Hitchin USD.[167]

LG Hitchin PLU, RD. Civ bdry: 1953.[45] *Parl* Hitchin Dv/CC (1918–*).

ABBOTS LANGLEY

AP *LG* Seq 8. Civ bdry: 1935 (incl help cr Watford CP),[4] 1952,[5] 1974 (the pt in Dac. Dist cr Nash Mills CP).[264] *Parl* W'rn Dv (1885–1918), Hem. Hemp. Dv (1918–48), S W Herts CC (1948–*). Parl bdry: 1945.[264] *Eccl* Seq 18. Eccl bdry: 1848 (help cr Chipperfield EP),[83] 1850 (help cr Leverstock Green EP),[47] 1864 (help cr Langleybury EP),[83] 1872 (help cr Apsley End EP),[28] 1883,[183] 1919.[184]

KING'S LANGLEY

AP *LG* Seq 10. Civ bdry: 1935,[4] 1958 (cr Chipperfield CP).[100] *Parl* Seq 11. *Eccl* Berk. RDn (until 1845), Watf. RDn (1845–1970), Berk. RDn (1970–*). Eccl bdry: 1848 (help cr Chipperfield EP),[83] 1872 (help cr Apsley End EP),[28] 1883,[183] 1919.[184]

LANGLEYBURY

EP Cr 1864 from Watford AP, Abbots Langley AP.[83] Watf. RDn. Bdry: 1883,[183] 1956,[185] 1964.[99]

LAYSTON

AP Incl chap Buntingford, thus for eccl spelling see following entry. *LG* Edw. Hd, Buntf. PLU, RSD, RD (1894–1935), Braugh. RD (1935–37). Civ bdry: 1883.[186] Abol civ 1937 pt to help cr Buntingford CP, pt to help cr Hormead CP, pt to Wyddial AP.[40] *Parl* N'rn Dv (1885–1918), Hitchin Dv (1918–48).

LAYSTON WITH BUNTINGFORD

AP Usual eccl spelling; for civ see prev entry. *Eccl* Seq 6. Eccl bdry: 1932,[187] 1938.[42]

LEAVSDEN

EP Cr 1853 from St Albans St Stephen AP, Watford AP.[188] Watf. RDn. Bdry: 1931,[189] 1961 (help cr Watford St Peter EP),[190] 1969.[92]

LEMSFORD

EP Cr 1858 from Bishop's Hatfield AP.[152] Hertf. RDn (1858–1970), Hatf. RDn (1970–*). Bdry: 1927 (help cr Welwyn Garden City EP).[153]

LETCHWORTH

AP *LG* Broadw. Hd, Hitchin PLU, RSD, RD (1894–1919), Letchworth UD (1919–*). Civ bdry: 1908,[191] 1935,[4] 1965.[127] *Parl* Seq 7. *Eccl* Seq 14. Eccl bdry: 1916.[114]

LETCHWORTH ST PAUL

EP Cr 1963 from Willian AP.[192] Hitchin RDn.

LEVERSTOCK GREEN

EP Cr 1850 from Abbots Langley AP, Hemel Hempstead AP, St Albans St Michael AP.[47] St Alb. RDn (1850–1960), Berk. RDn (1960–*). Bdry: 1872 (help cr Apsley End EP).[28]

LILLEY

AP *LG* Seq 15. Civ bdry: 1883,[13] 1937.[193] *Parl* Seq 7. *Eccl* Seq 14. Eccl bdry: 1958.[194]

LYONSDOWN

EP Cr 1869 from Chipping Barnet EP, East Barnet AP.[57] Barnet RDn. Bdry: 1911 (help cr New Barnet EP).[60]

MARKYATE

CP Cr 1897 from Caddington AP (Beds, Herts), Flamstead AP, Humbershoe CP, Houghton Regis AP (Beds).[125] *LG* Hem. Hemp. PLU, RD. Civ bdry: 1907 (exchanges pts with Caddington AP, Beds),[126] 1937,[71] 1965.[127] *Parl* Hem. Hemp. Dv/CC (1918–*).

MARKYATE STREET

EP Cr 1877 from Flamstead AP, Caddington AP (Beds, Herts), Studham AP (Beds), Houghton Regis AP (Beds).[195] Berk. RDn (1877–1907), St Alb. RDn (1907–30), Luton RDn (Bedford AD, 1930–70), Wheath. RDn (1970–*).

LONG MARSTON

EP Cr 1867 from Tring AP, Marsworth AP (Bucks), Drayton Beauchamp AP (Bucks).[196] Berk. RDn. Bdry: 1910.[3]

MEESDEN

AP *LG* Seq 12. *Parl* Seq 8. *Eccl* Seq 6.

SOUTH MELBOURN

CP Cr 1896 from Melbourn AP (Cambs) to be in Herts.[182] *LG* Roys. PLU, Ashwell RD. Abol 1897 ent to Royston AP.[64]

MEPPERSHALL

AP Pt Beds (Clifton Hd), pt Herts (Dac. Hd), the latter transf to Beds 1832 for parl purposes, 1844 for civ purposes.[9] *LG* Biggleswade PLU; see Beds for later organisation. *Parl* See Beds. *Eccl* Shefford RDn (until 1866), Shefford RDn W'rn Dv (1866–80), Shefford RDn (1880–*) (all in Bedford AD). Eccl bdry: 1938.[197]

MILL END

EP Cr 1875 from Rickmansworth AP, Chorley Wood Christ Church EP.[101] Watf. RDn (1875–1970), Rickm. RDn (1970–*).

NORTH MIMMS

AP Usual civ spelling; for eccl see 'North Mymms'. *LG* Dac. Hd, Hatf. PLU, RSD, RD. Civ bdry: 1935.[4] *Parl* Seq 5.

SOUTH MIMMS

AP Pt Middx (Edmonton Hd), pt Herts (Cashio Hd). *LG* Barnet PLU, pt S Mimms RSD, pt Barnet RSD (1875–88), pt E Barnet Valley USD (1888–94), pt Barnet USD (pts in USDs in Herts). Civ bdry: 1894 (loses the pt in Barnet USD to cr South Mimms Urban CP to be in Herts, loses the pt in E Barnet Valley USD to Monken Hadley AP),[198] thus South Mimms ent Middx (qv) until transf 1965 to Herts[34]; from 1965, Potter's Bar UD. *Parl* Pt Mid Dv (1885–1918), Middx 1918–70, S Herts CC (1970–*). *Eccl* Usually as 'South Mymms'; see entry in Middx.

SOUTH MIMMS URBAN

CP Cr 1894 from the pt of South Mimms AP in Barnet UD.[198] *LG* Barnet PLU, UD. Transf 1965 to Gtr London (Barnet LB).[34] *Parl* St Alb. Dv (1918–45), Barnet Dv/CC (1945–70), Gtr London thereafter.

GREAT MUNDEN

AP *LG* Seq 5. Civ bdry: 1883,[13] 1888,[175] 1937,[199] 1959.[200] *Parl* Seq 6. *Eccl* Baldock RDn (until 1845), Benn. RDn (1845–82), Benn. & Buntf. RDn (1882–92), Benn. RDn (1892–1922), Buntf. RDn (1922–70), Stev. RDn (1970–*).

LITTLE MUNDEN
AP *LG* Seq 5. Civ bdry: 1883,[13] 1888,[201] 1937,[199] 1959.[200] *Parl* Seq 6. *Eccl* Baldock RDn (until 1845), Benn. RDn (1845–82), Benn. & Buntf. RDn (1882–92), Benn. RDn (1892–1922), Ware RDn (1922–29), Buntf. RDn (1929–70), Stev. RDn (1970–*).

NORTH MYMMS
AP Usual eccl spelling; for civ see 'North Mimms'. *Eccl* Berk. RDn (until 1845), Barnet RDn (1845–1970), Hatf. RDn (1970–*). Eccl bdry: 1894 (cr Little Heath EP),[154] 1959 (help cr Essendon and Woodhill EP).[106]

NASH MILLS
CP Cr 1974 from the pt of Abbots Langley AP to be in Dac. Dist.[264]

NETTLEDEN
Chap in Pitstone AP, sep civ identity early, sep EP 1737.[83] In Bucks (Cottesloe Hd), transf 1895 to Herts (gains pt Ivinghoe AP, Bucks, at that time).[133] *LG* Berk. PLU, RD. Civ bdry: 1935.[4] Abol civ 1937 to help cr Nettleden with Potten End CP.[2] *Parl* Bucks until 1918, Hem. Hemp. Dv (1918–48). *Eccl* Mursley RDn (1737–1874), N Mursley RDn (1874–77)(both in Oxford dioc), Berk. RDn (1877–*). Eccl bdry: 1926,[202] 1938,[131] 1939.[134]

NETTLEDEN WITH POTTEN END
CP Cr 1937 by union Nettleden CP, pt Great Berkhampstead Rural CP, pt Northchurch AP.[2] *LG* Berkhamsted RD. *Parl* Hem. Hemp. CC (1948–*).

NEWNHAM
AP *LG* Seq 7. *Parl* Seq 7. *Eccl* St Alb. RDn (until 1845), Baldock RDn (1845–1970), Buntf. RDn (1970–*).

NORTHAW
Chap in St Albans St Peter AP, sep par *ca* 1540.[203] *LG* Cashio Hd, Hatf. PLU, RSD, RD. *Parl* E'rn Dv (1885–1918), St Alb. Dv (1918–45), Barnet Dv/CC (1945–55), Hertf. CC (1955–70), Welwyn & Hatf. CC (1970–*). *Eccl* St Alb. RDn (*ca* 1540–1845), Barnet RDn (1845–1970), Cheshunt RDn (1970–*).

NORTHCHURCH
AP Sometimes 'Berkhampstead St Mary' or 'North Berkhampstead'. *LG* Seq 9. Civ bdry: 1907 (gains pt Hawridge AP, pt Ashley Green AP, both Bucks),[84] 1909,[77] 1935,[4] 1937,[2] 1961.[70] *Parl* Seq 11. *Eccl* Seq 5. Eccl bdry: 1909 (cr Sunnyside EP),[204] 1926.[202]

NORTHWOOD HOLY TRINITY
EP Cr 1854 from Ruislip EP (Middx), Watford AP, Rickmansworth AP,[205] to be in London dioc. See main entry in Middx.

NORTON
AP *LG* Cashio Hd, Hitchin PLU, RSD, RD. Civ bdry: 1881.[51] Abol civ 1908 ent to Letchworth AP.[191] *Parl* N'rn Dv (1885–1918). *Eccl* St Alb. RDn (until 1845), Baldock RDn (1845–1970), Hitchin RDn (1970–*). Eccl bdry: 1933.[31]

NUTHAMPSTEAD
Hmlt in Barkway AP, sep CP 1866.[11] *LG* Seq 13. *Parl* Seq 7.

OFFLEY
AP *LG* Seq 15. Civ bdry: 1883,[13] 1907 (exchanges pts with Shillington AP, Beds),[126] 1937.[193] *Parl* Seq 7. *Eccl* Seq 14. Eccl bdry: 1958.[194]

OXHEY
CP Renaming 1906 of Bushey Urban CP.[94] *LG* Watf. PLU, UD (1906–22), MB (1922–35). Abol 1935 to help cr Watford CP.[4] *Parl* Watf. Dv (1918–48).

OXHEY ALL SAINTS
EP Cr 1961 from Oxhey St Matthew EP.[206] Watf. RDn.

OXHEY ST MATTHEW
EP Cr 1879 from Watford AP, Bushey AP.[90] Watf. RDn. Bdry: 1961 (cr Oxhey All Saints EP).[206]

BRENT PELHAM
AP *LG* Seq 11. *Parl* Seq 6. *Eccl* Pec jurisd Dean & Chapter of St Paul's, London (until 1845), Buntf. RDn (1845–82), Benn. & Buntf. RDn (1882–92), Buntf. RDn (1892–1922), Bp's Stortf. RDn (1922–28), Buntf. RDn (1928–*).

FURNEUX PELHAM
AP *LG* Seq 11. *Parl* Seq 6. *Eccl* Pec jurisd Dean & Chapter of St Paul's, London (until 1845), Buntf. RDn (1845–82), Benn. & Buntf. RDn (1882–92), Buntf. RDn (1892–1922), Bp's Stortf. RDn (1922–*).

STOCKING PELHAM
AP *LG* Seq 11. *Parl* Seq 1. *Eccl* Braugh. RDn (until 1845), thereafter as for Furneux Pelham.

PIRTON
AP Incl chap Ickleford (pt Herts [Hitchin Hd], pt Beds [Clifton Hd] until 1844, ent Herts thereafter, sep civ identity early, sep EP 1847[177]). *LG* Seq 15. Civ bdry: 1883,[13] 1897,[178] 1901.[173] *Parl* Seq 7. *Eccl* Seq 14.

PONSBOURNE
EP Reconstitution 1912 of Hatfield St Mary EP (sep EP 1849[83] from Bishop's Hatfield AP).[149] Hertf. RDn.

POTTEN END
EP Hmlt in Great Berkhampstead AP, sep EP 1894[76]; for civ see Nettleden with Potten End CP. Berk. RDn. Bdry: 1926.[130]

PRESTON
CP Hmlt in Hitchin AP, sep CP 1894 from pt of the pt of Hitchin AP not in Hitchin USD.[167] *LG* Hitchin PLU, RD. Civ bdry: 1955.[180] *Parl* Hitchin Dv/CC (1918–*).

PUTTENHAM
AP *LG* Dac. Hd, Berk. PLU, RSD, RD (1894–1937), Berkhamsted RD (1937–64). Civ bdry: 1888 (gains pt Marsworth AP, Bucks).[207] Abol civ 1964 ent to Tring Rural CP.[208] *Parl* W'rn Dv (1885–1918), Hem. Hemp. Dv/CC (1918–70). *Eccl* Seq 5.

RADLETT
EP Cr 1865 from Aldenham AP.[7] Watf. RDn (1865–1907), St Alb. RDn (1907–70), Ald. RDn (1970–*). Bdry: 1909 (help cr Boreham Wood All Saints EP),[80] 1958 (help cr Boreham Wood St Michael and All Angels EP),[81] 1969.[92]

RADWELL
AP *LG* Odsey Hd, Hitchin PLU, RSD, RD. *Parl* Seq 7. *Eccl* Seq 1.

REDBOURN
AP Incl chap Flamstead (sep par 12th cent[124]). *LG* Cashio Hd, St Alb. PLU, RSD, RD. Civ bdry: 1935,[4] 1937,[146] 1974 (the pt in Dac. Dist [in Hem. Hemp. New Town] not to be in any par).[264] *Parl* Mid Dv (1885–1918), Hem. Hemp. Dv/CC (1918–70), St Alb. CC (1970–*). *Eccl* Seq 20. Eccl bdry: 1936 (help cr Harpenden St John the Baptist EP).[144]

REED
AP Incl pt Royston (sep par 1540[55]). *LG* Seq 18. Civ bdry: 1935.[4] *Parl* Seq 7. *Eccl* Seq 6.

RICKMANSWORTH
AP *LG* Cashio Hd, Watf. PLU, RSD, RD. Abol civ 1898 pt to cr Rickm. UD and Rickmansworth Urban CP, the remainder to cr the 2 CPs of Chorleywood, Rickmansworth Rural.[65] *Parl* W'rn Dv (1885–1918). *Eccl* Seq 19. Eccl bdry: 1846 (cr West Hyde EP),[176] 1848 (cr Chorleywood Christ Church EP),[83] 1854 (help cr Northwood Holy Trinity EP),[205] 1872 (help cr Croxley Green All Saints EP),[109] 1875 (help cr Mill End EP),[101] 1896.[110]

RICKMANSWORTH RURAL
CP Cr 1898 from the pt of Rickmansworth AP not constituted Rickm. UD.[65] *LG* Watf. PLU, RD. Bdry: 1907 (exchanges pts with Denham AP, Chalfont St Peter AP, loses pt to Gerrard's Cross CP, all Bucks),[84] 1913,[209] 1924.[210] Abol 1935 pt to Rickmansworth Urban CP, pt to Sarratt AP.[4] *Parl* Watf. Dv (1918–48).

RICKMANSWORTH URBAN
CP Cr 1898 from the pt of Rickmansworth AP constituted Rickm. UD.[65] *LG* Watf. PLU, Rickm. UD. Bdry: 1913.[209] 1924,[210] 1935.[4] *Parl* Watf. Dv (1918–48), S W Herts CC (1948–*).

RIDGE
AP Chap in St Albans St Peter AP, sep par by 1349.[211] *LG* Seq 6. Civ bdry: 1926 (exchanges pts with South Mimms AP, Middx),[212] 1935 (incl help cr Rowley CP).[4] *Parl* Seq 4. *Eccl* Seq 17. Eccl bdry: 1847 (cr Colney Heath EP),[83] 1905 (help cr Arkley EP),[35] 1957,[36] 1958 (help cr Boreham Wood St Michael and All Angels EP).[81]

ROWLEY
CP Cr 1935 from Elstree AP, Ridge AP, Shenley AP.[4] *LG* Barnet UD. Transf 1965 to Gtr London (Barnet LB).[34] *Parl* Barnet CC (1945–70), Gtr London thereafter.

ROYSTON
AP District in Herts pars of Barkway, Reed, Therfield (Odsey Hd) and in Cambs pars of Melbourn, Kneesworth (Armingford Hd), sep par 1540.[55] *LG* Roys. PLU, RSD, pt sep RD in Cambs (1894–96) until area cr North Royston CP to be in Herts,[182] Roys. RD (pt 1894–96, ent 1896–97), Roys. UD (1897–1974). Addtl civ bdry alt: 1897 (gains North Royston CP, South Bassingbourn CP, South Kneesworth CP, pt Therfield AP when Roys. UD constituted),[64] 1935.[4] *Parl* Herts pt Seq 7. *Eccl* Braugh. RDn (1540–1845), Buntf. RDn (1845–82), Benn. & Buntf. RDn (1882–84), Baldock RDn (1884–1970), Buntf. RDn (1970–*). Eccl bdry: 1857,[88] 1890.[213]

NORTH ROYSTON
CP Cr 1896 from the Cambs pt of Royston AP, to be in Herts.[182] *LG* Roys. PLU, Ashwell RD. Abol 1897 ent to Royston AP.[64]

RUSHDEN
AP Incl chap Broadfield (in disuse by 16th cent, sep civ identity maintained, eccl attached to Cottered AP by 18th cent[86]). *LG* Seq 16. *Parl* Seq 7. *Eccl* Baldock RDn (until 1845), Benn. RDn (1845–82), Baldock RDn (1882–1970), Buntf. RDn (1970–*).

RYE PARK
EP Cr 1937 from Hoddesdon EP, Great Amwell AP.[20] Ware RDn (1937–70), Cheshunt RDn (1970–*).

SACOMBE
AP *LG* Seq 3. Civ bdry: 1935.[4] *Parl* Seq 9. *Eccl* Hertf. RDn (until 1845), Welwyn RDn (1845–1907), Benn. RDn (1907–22), Ware RDn (1922–29), Welwyn RDn (1929–70), Stev. RDn (1970–*).

ST ALBANS
The following have 'St Albans' in their names. Insofar as any existed at a given time: *LG* Cashio Hd, St Alb. PLU [Bor/MB, USD, RSD sep noted]. *Parl* St Alb. Parl Bor (1300–36, 1553–1852[215]), Mid Dv (1885–1918), St Alb. Dv/CC (1918–*). *Eccl* St Alb. RDn.

AP1–ST ALBANS–Former abbey church, parochial needs served first by chap St Andrew (in AP3) which was then superseded by this church after Dissolution in 16th cent,[214] cathedral since 1877. *LG* St Alb. Bor/MB, USD. Civ bdry: 1894 (gains the pt of St Stephen AP in St Alb. MB),[216] 1898 (gains the CPs in the MB: St Michael Urban, St Peter Urban, Sandridge Urban),[217] 1913,[218] 1935.[4] *Parl* St Alb. Parl Bor (until 1852). Eccl bdry: 1859 (help cr EP1).[219]

EP1–ST ALBANS CHRIST CHURCH–Cr 1859 from AP1, AP2.[219] Bdry: 1971.[220]

EP2–ST ALBANS ST MARY, MARSHALWICK–Cr 1972 from EP3, EP4, Sandridge AP.[221]

AP2–ST ALBANS ST MICHAEL–*LG* Pt St Alb. Bor/MB, pt St. Alb. USD, pt St Alb. RSD. Abol civ 1894 the pt in the MB to cr St Michael Urban CP, the remainder to cr St Michael Rural CP.[216] *Parl* Pt St Alb. Parl Bor (until 1852). Eccl bdry: 1850 (help cr Leverstock Green EP),[222] 1859 (help cr EP1),[219] 1969,[92] 1971.[220]

EP3–ST ALBANS ST PAUL–Cr 1910 from AP3.[223] Bdry: 1930,[224] 1962,[225] 1972 (help cr EP2).[221]

AP3–ST ALBANS ST PETER–Incl chap St Andrew (which served parochial needs until Dissolution in 16th cent[214] but did not attain independent identity), chap Ridge, chap Sandridge (each sep par by 1349[211]), chap Northaw (sep par *ca* 1540[203]). *LG* Pt St Alb. Bor/MB, pt St Alb. USD, pt St Alb. RSD. Addtl civ bdry alt: 1879.[226] Abol civ 1894 the pt in the MB to cr St Peter Urban CP, the remainder to cr St Peter Rural CP.[216] Addtl eccl bdry alt: 1827 (help cr Colney EP),[83] 1910 (cr EP3),[223] 1930,[224] 1962,[104] 1972 (help cr EP2).[221]

EP4–ST ALBANS ST SAVIOUR–Cr 1905 from Sandridge AP.[227] Bdry: 1972 (help cr EP2).[221]

AP4–ST ALBANS ST STEPHEN–Usual eccl spelling; for civ see 'St Stephen'. Eccl bdry: 1827 (help cr Colney EP),[83] 1853 (help cr Leavesden EP),[188] 1859 (cr Frogmore EP),[129] 1969.[92]

ST ANDREW RURAL

CP Cr 1894 from the pt of Hertford St Andrew AP not in Hertf. MB.[25] *LG* Hertf. PLU, RD. Civ bdry: 1920.[26] Abol 1924 ent to Hertingfordbury AP.[16] *Parl* Hertf. Dv (1918–48).

ST ANDREW URBAN

CP Cr 1894 from the pt of Hertford St Andrew AP in Hertf. MB.[25] *LG* Hertf. PLU, MB. Abol 1900 to help cr Hertford CP.[72]

ST IPPOLYTS

AP Usual eccl spelling; for civ see 'Ippollitts'. Chap in Hitchin AP, sep par 16th cent.[165] *Eccl* Seq 14. Eccl bdry: 1968.[168]

ST JOHN RURAL

CP Cr 1894 from the pt of Hertford St John AP not in Hertf. MB.[25] *LG* Hertf. PLU, RD. Bdry: 1920.[26] Abol 1929 to help cr Brickendon Liberty CP.[85] *Parl* Hertf. Dv (1918–48).

ST JOHN URBAN

CP Cr 1894 from the pt of Hertford St John AP in Hertf. MB.[25] *LG* Hertf. PLU, MB. Bdry: 1897 (gains the pts of Great Amwell AP, Ware AP in Hertf. MB).[16] Abol 1900 to help cr Hertford CP.[72]

ST MICHAEL RURAL

CP Cr 1894 from the pt of St Albans St Michael AP not in St Alb. MB.[216] *LG* St Alb. PLU, RD. Bdry: 1913,[218] 1935,[4] 1974 (the pt in Dac. Dist. [in Hem. Hemp. New Town] not to be in any par).[264] *Parl* St Alb. Dv/CC (1918–*).

ST MICHAEL URBAN

CP Cr 1894 from the pt of St Albans St Michael AP in St Alb. MB.[216] *LG* St Alb. PLU, MB. Abol 1898 ent to St Albans AP.[217]

ST PETER RURAL

CP Cr 1894 from the pt of St Albans St Peter AP not in St Alb. MB.[216] *LG* St Alb. PLU, RD. Civ bdry: 1913,[218] 1935.[4] Abol 1947 pt to cr Colney Heath CP, pt to cr London Colney CP.[107] *Parl* St Alb. Dv (1918–48).

ST PETER URBAN

CP Cr 1894 from the pt of St Albans St Peter AP in St Alb. MB.[216] *LG* St Alb. PLU, MB. Abol 1898 ent to St Albans AP.[217]

ST STEPHEN

AP Usual civ spelling; for eccl see 'St Albans St Stephen'. *LG* Cashio Hd, St Alb. PLU, pt St Alb. MB (1835–94), pt St Alb. USD, pt St Alb. RSD, St Alb. RD. Civ bdry: 1879,[226] 1894 (loses the pt in the MB to St Albans AP),[216] 1913,[218] 1935.[4] *Parl* Mid Dv (1885–1918), St Alb. Dv/CC (1918–70), S Herts CC (1970–*).

SANDON

AP *LG* Odsey Hd, Buntf. PLU, RSD, RD (1894–1935), Hitchin RD (1935–74). *Parl* Seq 7. *Eccl* Seq 1.

SANDRIDGE

AP Chap in St Albans St Peter AP, sep par by 1349.[211] *LG* Cashion Hd, St Alb. PLU, pt St Alb. MB (1877–94), pt St Alb. USD, pt St Alb. RSD. Abol civ 1894 the pt in the MB to cr Sandridge Urban CP, the remainder to cr Sandridge Rural CP.[216] *Parl* Mid Dv (1885–1918). *Eccl* Seq 20. Eccl bdry: 1923,[47] 1972 (help cr St Albans St Mary, Marshalwick EP).[221]

CP Renaming 1957 of Sandridge Rural CP.[228] *LG* St Alb. RD. Bdry: 1962.[108] *Parl* St Alb. CC (1970–*).

SANDRIDGE RURAL

CP Cr 1894 from the pt of Sandridge AP not in St Alb. MB.[216] *LG* St Alb. PLU, RD. Bdry: 1913,[218] 1935.[4] Renamed 1957 'Sandridge CP'.[228] *Parl* St Alb. Dv/CC (1918–*).

SANDRIDGE URBAN

CP Cr 1894 from the pt of Sandridge AP in St Alb. MB.[216] *LG* St Alb. PLU, MB. Abol 1898 ent to St Albans AP.[217]

SARRATT

AP *LG* Seq 8. Civ bdry: 1935,[4] 1938,[103] 1952.[5] *Parl* Seq 12. Parl bdry: 1945.[264] *Eccl* Seq 19.

SAWBRIDGEWORTH

AP Incl hmlt High Wych (sep EP 1862,[229] sep CP 1901[230]). *LG* Braugh. Hd, Bp's Stortf. PLU, RSD, RD (1894–95), Hadham RD (1895–1901), Sawbridgeworth UD (1901-74). *Parl* E'rn Dv (1885–1918), Hertf. Dv/CC (1918–55), E Herts CC (1955–*). *Eccl* Seq 8.

SHENLEY

AP *LG* Dac. Hd, Barnet PLU, RSD, RD (1894–1941), Elstree RD (1941–74). Civ bdry: 1926 (gains pt Hendon AP, Middx),[212] 1935 (incl help cr Rowley CP),[4] 1951,[119] 1957.[120] *Parl* Seq 4. *Eccl* Berk. RDn (until 1845), Barnet RDn (1845–1922), St Alb. RDn (1922–70), Ald. RDn (1970–*). Eccl bdry: 1827 (help cr Colney EP),[83] 1905 (help cr Arkley EP),[35] 1957.[36]

SHEPHALL

AP *LG* Cashio Hd, Hitchin PLU, RSD, RD (1894–1953), Stev. UD (1953–74). *Parl* N'rn Dv (1885–1918), Hitchin Dv/CC (1918–70), Hertf. & Stev. CC (1970–*). *Eccl* St Alb. RDn (until 1845), Welwyn RDn (1845–1958). Abol eccl 1958 ent to Steveneage AP.[46]

SHILLINGTON

AP Incl chap Upper Gravenhurst (from 14th cent, in Beds and sep par in that co *temp* Eliz. I[231]). Pt

Herts (Odsey Hd), pt Beds (Clifton Hd, Ampthill Hd). *LG* Ampthill PLU, RSD, pt sep RD in Herts (1894–97), pt Ampthill RD in Beds (1894–97). Civ bdry: 1897 (loses pt to Holwell AP as the latter transf to Herts, and pts to Ickleford CP, Pirton AP as well, so that par ent Beds thereafter).[172] *Parl* Herts pt, S'rn Dv (1885–1918), ent Beds thereafter. *Eccl* See main entry in Beds, incl eccl bdry alt 1942.[162]

NEW SOUTHGATE ST MICHAEL AND ALL ANGELS

EP Renaming 1951 of South Barnet EP.[63] Barnet RDn. Abol 1972 ent to New Southgate St Paul EP (London dioc).[61]

STANDON

AP *LG* Standon Bor (13th–17th cent, market town thereafter),[232] Seq 2. Civ bdry: 1935,[4] 1952.[232] *Parl* Seq 1. *Eccl* Seq 8. Eccl bdry: 1845 (cr High Cross EP).[163]

STANSTEAD ABBOTS

AP *LG* Perhaps mediev Stanstead Abbots Bor,[234] Seq 2. Civ bdry: 1883,[13] 1935 (help cr Hoddesdon CP).[4] *Parl* Seq 1. *Eccl* Seq 10.

STANSTEAD ST MARGARET

AP Prob pt of Great Amwell AP, sep par 13th cent.[12] Sometimes 'Thele'. *LG* Hertf. Hd, Ware PLU, RSD, RD. *Parl* Seq 1. *Eccl* Seq 9.

STAPLEFORD

AP *LG* Seq 14. Civ bdry: 1937.[71] *Parl* Seq 2. *Eccl* Hertf. RDn (until 1845), Welwyn RDn (1845–1907), Hertf. RDn (1907–*).

STEVENAGE

AP *LG* Broadw. Hd, Hitchin PLU, Stev. USD, UD. Civ bdry: 1935,[4] 1953,[45] 1969.[137] *Parl* Seq 9. Parl bdry: 1971.[265] *Eccl* Seq 15. Eccl bdry: 1958,[46] 1971 (cr the 6 EPs as in following 6 entries).[235]

STEVENAGE HOLY TRINITY
STEVENAGE ST FRANCIS, PIN GREEN
STEVENAGE ST HUGH, CHELLS
STEVENAGE ST MARY SHEPHALL
STEVENAGE ST NICHOLAS
STEVENAGE ST PETER, BROADWATER

Each of the 6 named immediately above cr EP 1971 from Stevenage AP.[235] Each Stev. RDn.

BISHOP'S STORTFORD

AP Usually 'Stortford' before 17th cent. *LG* Braugh. Hd, Bp's Stortf. PLU, USD, UD. Civ bdry: 1910,[236] 1935.[4] *Parl* Bp's Stortf. Parl Bor (1311–41), E'rn Dv (1885–1918), Hertf. Dv/CC (1918–55), E Herts CC (1955–70), Hertf. & Stev. CC (1970–*). *Eccl* Seq 8. Eccl bdry: 1852 (cr Hockerill EP),[170] 1860 (cr Bishop's Stortford New Town EP).[237]

BISHOP'S STORTFORD NEW TOWN

EP Cr 1860 from Bishop's Stortford AP.[237] Bp's Stortf. RDn. Abol 1973 to help cr Thorley with Bishop's Stortford Holy Trinity EP.[238]

STUDHAM

AP Pt Beds (Manshead Hd), pt Herts (Dac. Hd). *LG* Luton PLU, RSD. Civ bdry: 1844 (a pt in Herts transf to Beds).[9] Made 1894 2 sep CPs, one in each co, qv.[95] *Parl* Herts pt (reduced pt 1832–1918), S'rn Dv (1885–1918), ent Beds thereafter. *Eccl* See main entry in Beds.

CP Cr 1894 from the Herts pt of Studham AP.[95] *LG* Luton PLU, Sep RD (1894–97). Abol 1897 when this par and Studham CP, Beds, reunited, to be in Beds.[239]

SUNNYSIDE

EP Cr 1909 from Northchurch AP.[204] Berk. RDn (1909–70), Berkhamsted RDn (1970–*). Bdry: 1915 (help cr Bourne End EP),[82] 1926.[130]

TEWIN

AP *LG* Seq 14. Civ bdry: 1921 (help cr Welwyn Garden City CP),[115] 1951,[151] 1964.[113] *Parl* Seq 2. *Eccl* Seq 12.

THERFIELD

AP Incl pt Royston (sep par 1540[55]). *LG* Seq 18. Addtl civ bdry alt: 1897,[64] 1935.[4] *Parl* Seq 7. *Eccl* Seq 1. Eccl bdry: 1857.[88]

THORLEY

AP *LG* Seq 1. Civ bdry: 1910,[236] 1935.[4] *Parl* Seq 1. *Eccl* Braugh. RDn (until 1845), Bp's Stortf. RDn (1845–1973). Abol eccl 1973 to help cr Thorley with Bishop's Stortford Holy Trinity EP.[238]

THORLEY WITH BISHOP'S STORTFORD HOLY TRINITY

EP Cr 1973 by union Thorley AP, Bishop's Stortford New Town EP.[238] Bp's Stortf. RDn.

THROCKING

AP *LG* Edw. Hd, Buntf. PLU, RSD, RD (1894–1935), Braugh. RD (1935–55). Civ bdry: 1883,[240] 1937 (help cr Buntingford CP).[40] Abol civ 1955 ent to Cottered AP.[87] *Parl* N'rn Dv (1885–1918), Hitchin Dv/CC (1918–70). *Eccl* Seq 3. Eccl bdry: 1932.[187]

THUNDRIDGE

AP Chap in Ware AP, sep par 16th cent.[241] *LG* Seq 2. Civ bdry: 1952.[232] *Parl* Seq 1. *Eccl* Seq 10. Eccl bdry: 1844 (help cr Wareside EP).[242]

TOTTERIDGE

Chap in Bishop's Hatfield AP, sep civ identity early, sep EP 1892.[150] *LG* Broadw. Hd, Barnet PLU, RSD, RD (1894–1914), UD (1914–65). Transf 1965 to Gtr London (Barnet LB).[34] *Parl* Mid Dv (1885–1918), St Alb. Dv (1918–45), Barnet Dv/CC (1945–70), Gtr London thereafter. *Eccl* Barnet RDn.

TRING

AP Incl chap Wigginton (from 1328 but retained some parochial rights,[243] sep civ identity early, sep EP 1748[83]). *LG* Dac. Hd, Berk. PLU, pt Tring USD, pt Berk. RSD. Addtl civ bdry alt: 1883 (gains pt Marsworth AP, Bucks),[13] 1888.[1] Abol civ 1894 the pt in the USD to cr Tring Urban CP, the remainder to cr Tring Rural CP.[32] *Parl* W'rn Dv (1885–1918). *Eccl* Seq 5. Addtl eccl bdry alt: 1867 (help cr Long Marston EP),[196] 1910.[3]

TRING RURAL

CP Cr 1894 from the pt of Tring AP not in Tring USD.[32] *LG* Berk. PLU, RD (1894–1937), Berkhamsted RD (1937–74). Civ bdry: 1964.[208] *Parl* Hem. Hemp. Dv/CC (1918–*).

TRING URBAN
CP Cr 1894 from the pt of Tring AP in Tring USD.[32] *LG* Berk. PLU, Tring UD. *Parl* Hem. Hemp. Dv/CC (1918–*).

UNNAMED
CP The pt of Little Amwell CP in Ware USD made 1894 sep but unnamed CP.[95] *LG* Hertf. PLU, Ware UD. Abol 1904 ent to Ware Urban CP.[17]

WAKELEY
Free chapel, perhaps parochial, later considered ex-par lbty in Aspenden AP,[37] sep CP 1858.[38] *LG* Edw. Hd, Roys. PLU, RSD. Abol 1883 ent to Westmill AP.[244]

KING'S WALDEN
AP *LG* Seq 15. Civ bdry: 1955.[180] *Parl* Seq 7. *Eccl* Seq 14. Eccl bdry: 1968.[168]

ST PAUL'S WALDEN
AP *LG* Seq 7. *Parl* Seq 7. *Eccl* St Alb. RDn (until 1845), Welwyn RDn (1845–95), Hitchin RDn (1895–*).

WALKERN
AP *LG* Seq 3. *Parl* Seq 9. *Eccl* Baldock RDn (until 1845), Benn. RDn (1845–82), Baldock RDn (1882–92), Benn. RDn (1892–1922), Hitchin RDn (1922–70), Stev. RDn (1970–*).

WALLINGTON
AP *LG* Odsey Hd, Buntf. PLU, RSD, RD (1894–1935), Hitchin RDn (1935–74). *Parl* Seq 7. *Eccl* Seq 1.

WALSWORTH
Hmlt in Hitchin AP, sep CP 1894 from pt of the pt of Hitchin AP not constituted Hitchin UD.[167] *LG* Hitchin PLU, RD. Abol 1921 ent to Hitchin Urban CP.[169] *Parl* Hitchin Dv (1918–48).

WALTHAM CROSS
EP Cr 1855 as 'Waltham Cross Holy Trinity EP' from Cheshunt AP,[97] renamed 1974 'Waltham Cross Christ Church EP'.[245] Ware RDn (1855–1970), Cheshunt RDn (1970–*).

WARE
AP Incl chap Thundridge (sep par 16th cent[241]). *LG* Braugh. Hd, Ware Bor (1199–16th cent),[246] PLU, pt Hertf. USD, pt Ware USD, pt Ware RSD, pt Hertf. MB (1888–94). Addtl civ bdry alt: 1888,[24] 1894 (the pt in Ware USD to help cr Ware Urban CP, the pt in Hertf. MB remains in the MB, the remainder to cr Ware Rural CP).[15] Abol civ 1897 ent to St John Rural CP.[16] *Parl* E'rn Dv (1885–1918). *Eccl* Seq 10. Addtl eccl bdry alt: 1844 (help cr Wareside EP),[247] 1858 (help cr Ware Christ Church EP).[18]

WARE CHRIST CHURCH
EP Cr 1858 from Ware AP, Great Amwell AP.[18] Ware RDn (1858–1970), Hertf. RDn (1970–*).

WARE RURAL
CP Cr 1894 from the pt of Ware AP not in Ware USD or Hertf. MB.[15] *LG* Ware PLU, RD. Civ bdry: 1935,[4] 1952,[232] 1961.[248] *Parl* Hertf. Dv/CC (1918–55), E Herts CC (1955–*).

WARE URBAN
CP Cr 1894 from the pt of Ware AP and of Great Amwell AP in Ware UD.[15] *LG* Ware PLU, UD. Civ bdry: 1904 (gains Unnamed CP in Ware UD),[17] 1935,[4] 1961.[248] *Parl* Hertf. Dv/CC (1918–55), E Herts CC (1955–70), Hertf. & Stev. CC (1970–*). Parl bdry: 1945.[264]

WARESIDE
EP Cr 1844 from Thundridge AP, Ware AP.[247] Braugh. RDn (1844–45), Ware RDn (1845–1970), Hertf. RDn (1970–*).

WATERFORD
EP Cr 1908 from Bengeo AP, Bramfield AP.[69] Hertf. RDn. Bdry: 1969.[160]

WATFORD
The following have 'Watford' in their names. Insofar as any existed at a given time: *LG* Cashio Hd, Watf. Bor (13th cent, market town thereafter),[249] PLU [USD, RSD, UD, MB sep noted]. *Parl* W'rn Dv (1885–1918), Watf. Dv (1918–48), organisation after 1948 sep noted. *Eccl* St Alb. RDn (until 1845), Watf. RDn (1845–*).

AP1–WATFORD–Incl Bushey (sep par by 1176[89]). *LG* Pt Watf. USD, pt Watf. RSD. Abol civ 1894 the pt in the USD to cr CP3, the remainder to cr CP2.[32] Eccl bdry: 1848 (help cr Chipperfield EP),[83] 1853 (help cr Leavesden EP),[188] 1854 (help cr Northwood Holy Trinity EP),[205] 1857 (cr EP2),[83] 1864 (help cr Langleybury EP),[83] 1872 (help cr Croxley Green All Saints EP),[109] 1879 (help cr Oxhey St Matthew EP),[90] 1904 (help cr EP4),[250] 1905 (cr EP6),[251] 1913 (cr EP3),[252] 1956,[185] 1956 (cr EP5),[253] 1973.[254]

CP1–WATFORD–Cr 1935 by union CP3, Oxhey CP, pt Abbots Langley AP, pt CP2.[4] *LG* Watf. MB. *Parl* Watf. BC (1948–*).

EP1–WATFORD CHRIST CHURCH–Cr 1909 from EP2.[255]

CP2–WATFORD RURAL–Cr 1894 from the pt of AP1 not in Watf. USD.[32] *LG* Watf. RD. Bdry: 1901,[256] 1904,[257] 1909,[258] 1921,[259] 1924,[260] 1926,[212] 1935 (help cr CP1),[4] 1952.[5] *Parl* Watf. Dv (1918–48), S W Herts CC (1948–*).

EP2–WATFORD ST ANDREW–Cr 1857 from AP1.[83] Bdry: 1904 (help cr EP4),[250] 1909 (cr EP1),[255] 1961 (help cr EP7).[190]

EP3–WATFORD ST JAMES–Cr 1913 from AP1.[252] Abol 1973 ent to AP1.[254]

EP4–WATFORD ST JOHN–Cr 1904 from AP1, EP2.[250]

EP5–WATFORD ST LUKE–Cr 1956 from AP1.[253]

EP6–WATFORD ST MICHAEL–Cr 1905 from AP1.[251] Bdry: 1956.[185]

EP7–WATFORD ST PETER–Cr 1961 from EP2, Leavesden EP.[190]

CP3–WATFORD URBAN–Cr 1894 from the pt of AP1 in Watf. USD.[32] *LG* Watf. PLU, UD (1894–1922), MB (1922–35). Civ bdry: 1901,[256] 1904,[257] 1909,[258] 1921,[259] 1924,[260] 1926.[212] Abol 1935 to help cr CP1.[4]

WATTON AT STONE
AP *LG* Seq 3. Civ bdry: 1883,[13] 1888.[44] *Parl* Seq 9. *Eccl* Seq 13.

WELWYN

AP *LG* Broadw. Hd, Welwyn PLU, RSD, RD. Civ bdry: 1883,[13] 1911,[112] 1921 (help cr Welwyn Garden City CP),[115] 1935,[4] 1951,[48] 1953,[151] 1964.[113] *Parl* Seq 10. *Eccl* Seq 12. Eccl bdry: 1916.[114]

WELWYN GARDEN CITY

CP Cr 1921 from Digswell AP, Welwyn AP, Bishop's Hatfield AP, Tewin AP.[115] *LG* Welwyn PLU, RD (1921–27), Welwyn Garden City UD (1927–74). Civ bdry: 1935,[4] 1951.[151] *Parl* Hitchin Dv (1918–45), St Alb. CC (1945–55), Hertf. CC (1955–70), Welwyn & Hatf. CC (1970–*).

EP Cr 1927 from Bishop's Hatfield AP, Lemsford EP.[153] Welwyn RDn (1927–70), Hatf. RDn (1970–*).

WESTMILL

AP *LG* Braugh, Hd, Buntf. PLU, RSD, RD (1894–1935), Braugh. RD (1935–74). Civ bdry: 1883,[244] 1935.[4] *Parl* Seq 8. Parl bdry: 1945.[264] *Eccl* Seq 3.

WESTON

AP Incl Baldock (sep par *ca* 1199[49]). *LG* Seq 4. Civ bdry: 1881,[51] 1913,[53] 1928,[54] 1935.[4] *Parl* Seq 7. *Eccl* Baldock RDn (until 1845), Benn. RDn (1845–82), Baldock RDn (1882–1970), Stev. RDn (1970–*).

WHEATHAMPSTEAD

AP Incl chap Harpenden (sep civ identity early, sep EP 1859[142]). *LG* Dac. Hd, St Alb. PLU, RSD, RD. Civ bdry: 1935.[4] *Parl* Mid Dv (1885–1918), Hem. Hemp. Dv (1918–48), St Alb. CC (1948–*). Parl bdry: 1945.[264] *Eccl* Berk. RDn (until 1845), St Alb. RDn (1845–1970), Wheath. RDn (1970–*).

WHIPSNADE

AP Possibly free chapel, par before 1291.[261] Pt Beds (Manshead Hd), pt Herts (Dac. Hd), the latter transf 1897 to Flamstead AP so par ent Beds thereafter.[125] *LG* Luton PLU, pt Luton RD in Beds (1894–97), pt sep RD in Herts (1894–97). *Parl* Herts pt, Mid Dv (1885–1918), Beds thereafter. *Eccl* See main entry in Beds.

WIDFORD

AP *LG* Seq 2. *Parl* Seq 1. *Eccl* Braugh. RDn (until 1845), Bp's Stortf. RDn (1845–1907), Ware RDn (1907–70), Hertf. RDn (1970–*).

WIGGINTON

Chap in Tring AP (from 1328, but retained some parochial rights[243]), sep civ identity early, sep EP 1748.[83] *LG* Seq 9. Civ bdry: 1907 (gains pt Hawridge AP, Bucks).[84] *Parl* Seq 11. *Eccl* Berk. RDn (1748–1970), Berkhamsted RDn (1970–*).

WILLIAN

AP *LG* Broadw. Hd, Hitchin PLU, RSD, RD. Civ bdry: 1881,[51] 1908,[191] 1909,[52] 1928.[54] Abol civ 1935 ent to Letchworth AP.[4] *Parl* N'rn Dv (1885–1918), Hitchin Dv (1918–48). *Eccl* Baldock RDn (until 1845), Hitchin RDn (1845–*). Eccl bdry: 1933.[31]

WORMLEY

AP *LG* Hertf. Hd, Ware PLU, RSD, RD. Abol civ 1935 pt to Cheshunt AP, pt to help cr Hoddesdon CP, pt to Brickendon Liberty CP.[4] *Parl* E'rn Dv (1885–1918), Hertf. Dv (1918–48). *Eccl* Seq 9. Eccl bdry: 1963 (help cr Letchworth St Paul EP).[192]

HIGH WYCH

Hmlt in Sawbridgeworth AP, sep EP 1862,[229] sep CP 1901.[230] *LG* Bp's Stortf. PLU, Hadham RD (1901–35), Braugh. RD (1935–74). Civ bdry: 1935.[4] *Parl* Hertf. Dv (1918–48), Hitchin CC (1948–55), E Herts CC (1955–*). *Eccl* Bp's Stortf. RDn. Eccl bdry: 1955 (help cr Gilston with Eastwick EP).[118]

WYDDIAL

AP *LG* Seq 12. Civ bdry: 1883,[13] 1883,[262] 1937 (incl help cr Buntingford CP).[40] *Parl* Seq 8. *Eccl* Seq 6. Eccl bdry: 1938.[42]

WYMONDLEY

CP Cr 1937 by union Great Wymondley AP, Little Wymondley AP, pt Ippolyts AP.[105] *LG* Hitchin RD. Bdry: 1953,[45] 1955.[136] *Parl* Hitchin CC (1948–*).

GREAT WYMONDLEY

AP Chap in Hitchin AP, sep par by 13th cent.[164] *LG* Broadw. Hd, Hitchin PLU, RSD, RD. Civ bdry: 1935.[4] Abol civ 1937 to help cr Wymondley CP.[105] *Parl* N'rn Dv (1885–1918), Hitchin Dv (1918–48). *Eccl* Seq 14. Eccl bdry: 1958.[46]

LITTLE WYMONDLEY

AP Sep par before 1235.[263] *LG* Broadw. Hd, Hitchin PLU, RSD, RD. Civ bdry: 1935.[4] Abol civ 1937 to help cr Wymondley CP.[105] *Parl* N'rn Dv (1885–1918), Hitchin Dv (1918–48). *Eccl* Seq 14. Eccl bdry: 1958.[46]

YARDELEY–See ARDELEY

HUNTINGDONSHIRE

ABBREVIATIONS

Abbreviations particular to Hunts follow. Those general abbreviations in use throughout the *Guide* are found on page xix.

Hunt.	Huntingdon
Hurst.	Hurstingstone
Kimb.	Kimbolton
Leight.	Leightonstone
Norm. Cr.	Norman Cross
Peterb.	Peterborough
Thrap.	Thrapston
Tosel.	Toseland
Yax.	Yaxley

SEQUENCES

An abbreviated entry prefixed by 'Seq' is used in the parochial entries to avoid repeating often the names of superior units of administration. The content of each sequence is shown below.

Local Government Sequences ('LG')

SEQ 1 Hurst. Hd, St Ives PLU, RSD, RD
SEQ 2 Leight. Hd, Hunt. PLU, RSD, RD
SEQ 3 Leight. Hd, Oundle PLU, RSD, RD (1894–1935), Hunt. RD (1935–74)
SEQ 4 Leight. Hd, St Neots PLU, RSD, RD
SEQ 5 Leight. Hd, Thrap. PLU, RSD, RD (1894–1935), St Neots RD (1935–74)
SEQ 6 Norm. Cr. Hd, Hunt. PLU, RSD, RD
SEQ 7 Norm. Cr. Hd, Peterb. PLU, RSD, Norm. Cr. RD
SEQ 8 Tosel. Hd, Caxton PLU, RSD, St Neots RD
SEQ 9 Tosel. Hd, St Ives PLU, RSD, RD
SEQ 10 Tosel. Hd, St Neots PLU, RSD, RD

Parliamentary Sequences ('Parl')

SEQ 1 N'rn Dv (1885–1918), Hunts Parl Co (1918–70), Hunts & Peterb Parl Co (Hunts CC, 1970–*)
SEQ 2 S'rn Dv (1885–1918), Hunts Parl Co (1918–70), Hunts & Peterb Parl Co (Hunts CC, 1970–*)

Ecclesiastical Sequences ('Eccl')

SEQ 1 Leight. RDn (until 1863), Leight. RDn First Dv (1863–78), Kimb. RDn (1878–1964), Leight. RDn (1964–*)
SEQ 2 Leight. RDn (until 1863), Leight. RDn Second Dv (1863–78), Leight. RDn (1878–*)
SEQ 3 Leight. RDn (until 1863), Leight. RDn Second Dv (1863–78), Leight. RDn (1878–1964), Hunt. RDn (1964–*)
SEQ 4 St Ives RDn
SEQ 5 St Ives RDn (until 1878), Hunt. RDn (1878–*)
SEQ 6 St Ives RDn (until 1863), Leight. RDn First Dv (1863–78), Hunt. RDn (1878–*)
SEQ 7 St Neots RDn
SEQ 8 St Neots RDn (until 1863), Leight. RDn First Dv (1863–78), Hunt. RDn (1878–*)
SEQ 9 Yax. RDn

DIOCESES AND ARCHDEACONRY

With a few exceptions noted below in the parochial entries, Hunts pars were in Huntingdon AD which was in Lincoln dioc until 1837 and in Ely dioc thereafter.

THE PARISHES OF HUNTINGDONSHIRE

ABBOTSLEY
AP *LG* Seq 10. *Parl* Seq 2. *Eccl* Seq 7.

ALCONBURY
AP Incl area Alconbury Weston (sep civ identity early, no sep eccl identity, hence usual eccl spelling 'Alconbury with Alconbury Weston', qv). *LG* Seq 2. *Parl* Seq 2.

ALCONBURY WESTON
Area in Alconbury AP, sep civ identity early, no sep eccl identity. *LG* Perhaps mediev bor,[1] Seq 2. *Parl* Seq 2.

ALCONBURY WITH ALCONBURY WESTON
AP Usual eccl spelling; for civ see Alconbury, Alconbury Weston. *Eccl* Seq 3.

ALWALTON
AP *LG* Seq 7. Civ bdry: 1956 (exchanges pts with Castor AP, Soke of Peterb).[2] *Parl* Seq 1. *Eccl* Seq 9.

BARHAM
Chap to prebend of Stow Longa (civ, 'Stow'), sep civ identity early, eccl usually presented with Spaldwick AP[3] until sep EP 1802.[4] *LG* Leight. Hd, Hunt. PLU, RSD, RD. Abol civ 1935 to help cr Barham and Woolley CP.[5] *Parl* S'rn Dv (1885–1918), Hunts Parl Co (1918–48). *Eccl* Pec jurisd Stow Longa (1802–39), Leight. RDn (1839–78), Kimb. RDn (1878–1964), Leight. RDn (1964–65). Abol eccl 1965 to help cr Barham and Woolley EP.[6]

BARHAM AND WOOLLEY
Cr civ 1935,[5] eccl 1965[6] by union Barham AP, Woolley AP. *LG* Hunt. RD. *Parl* Hunts Parl Co (1948–70), Hunts CC (1970–*). *Eccl* Leight. RDn.

BLUNTISHAM
AP Usual eccl name; for civ and sep chap Earith see 'Bluntisham cum Earith'. *Eccl* Seq 4.
CP Cr 1948 from Bluntisham cum Earith AP.[7] *LG* St Ives RD. *Parl* Hunts CC (1970–*).

BLUNTISHAM CUM EARITH
AP Usual civ name; for eccl see 'Bluntisham' AP. Incl chap Earith (sep CP when Bluntisham cum Earith AP dissolved 1948[7]). *LG* Hurst. Hd, St Ives PLU, RSD, RD. Civ bdry: 1884,[8] 1885.[9] Abol civ 1948, divided into 2 CPs of Bluntisham, Earith.[7] *Parl* N'rn Dv (1885–1918), Hunts Parl Co (1918–70).

BOTOLPHBRIDGE
AP *LG* Norm. Cr. Hd. *Eccl* Yax. RDn. United 1702 with Orton Longueville AP, the union civ called simply 'Orton Longueville' eccl 'Orton Longueville with St Botolphbridge'.[10]

BRAMPTON
AP *LG* Perhaps mediev bor,[1] Seq 2. *Parl* Seq 2. *Eccl* Pec jurisd Brampton (until 1839), Leight. RDn (1839–63), Leight. RDn First Dv (1863–78), Hunt. RDn (1878–*).

BRINGTON
AP Incl chap Bythorn (sep civ identity early, eccl severed 1936 to help cr Keyston and Bythorn EP[11]), chap Old Weston (orig sep AP, subordinated to Brington after 13th cent,[12] sep civ identity regained early, no sep eccl identity). Usual civ spelling; for eccl before 1936 see 'Brington with Bythorn and Old Weston', after 1936 'Brington with Old Weston'. *LG* Leight. Hd, Thrap. PLU, RSD, RD. Abol civ 1935 to help cr Brington and Molesworth CP.[5] *Parl* S'rn Dv (1885–1918), Hunts Parl Co (1918–48).

BRINGTON AND MOLESWORTH
CP Cr 1935 by union Brington AP, Molesworth AP.[5] *LG* Hunt. RD. Civ bdry: 1965 (gains pt Clopton AP, Northants).[13] *Parl* Hunts Parl Co (1948–70), Hunts CC (1970–*).

BRINGTON WITH BYTHORN AND OLD WESTON
AP Usual eccl spelling until 1936 when chap Bythorn (sep civ identity early) eccl severed to help cr Keyston and Bythorn EP,[11] thereafter this par 'Brington with Old Weston', qv; for civ and sep civ identities of Bythorn, Old Weston, see 'Brington'. *Eccl* Leight. RDn (until 1863), Leight. RDn First Dv (1863–78), Kimb. RDn (1878–1936).

BRINGTON WITH OLD WESTON
AP Usual eccl spelling after 1936 when Brington with Bythorn and Old Weston eccl loses chap Bythorn (see prev entry).[11] *Eccl* Kimb. RDn (1936–64), Leight. RDn (1964–*).

BROUGHTON
AP *LG* Seq 1. *Parl* Seq 1. *Eccl* St Ives RDn. Eccl reconstituted 1968 when gains chaps Old Hurst, Woodhurst from St Ives with Old Hurst and Woodhurst AP, thereafter 'Broughton with Old Hurst and Woodhurst',[14] qv.

BROUGHTON WITH OLD HURST AND WOODHURST
EP Cr 1968 by union Broughton AP, chaps Old Hurst, Woodhurst of St Ives with Old Hurst and Woodhurst AP.[14] St Ives RDn.

BUCKDEN
AP *LG* Seq 10. *Parl* Seq 2. *Eccl* Pec jurisd Buckden (until 1839), Leight. RDn (1839–63), St Neots RDn (1863–*).

BUCKWORTH
AP *LG* Seq 2. *Parl* Seq 2. *Eccl* Seq 3.

BURY
AP Orig chap to Wistow AP, became the par church by 1178 with Wistow its chap (regains sep identity 1351[16]), later Bury gains chaps Upwood, Little Raveley (each with sep civ identity early, Little Raveley sep EP 1746,[17] Upwood united 1819 with Great Raveley AP [no church] to cr Upwood with Great Raveley EP[4]). *LG* Seq 1. Civ and eccl bdry alt: 16th cent at Dissolution (gains pt Ramsey AP).[15] Addtl civ bdry alt: 1883.[18] *Parl* Seq 1. *Eccl* Seq 4.

BYTHORN
Chap in Broughton AP (eccl, 'Broughton with

Bythorn and Old Weston'), sep civ identity early, eccl severed 1936 to help cr Keyston and Bythorn EP.[5] *LG* Leight. Hd, Thrap. PLU, RSD, RD. Abol civ 1935 to help cr Bythorn and Keyston CP.[5] *Parl* S'rn Dv (1885–1918), Hunts Parl Co (1918–48).

BYTHORN AND KEYSTON

CP Cr 1935 by union Bythorn CP, Keyston AP.[5] *LG* Hunt. RD. Civ bdry: 1965 (loses pt to Titchmarsh AP, Northants).[13] *Parl* Hunts Parl Co (1948–70), Hunts CC (1970–*).

CALDECOTE

AP *LG* Norm. Cr. Hd, Peterb. PLU, RSD, Norm. Cr. RD. Abol civ 1935 to help cr Denton and Caldecote CP.[5] *Parl* N'rn Dv (1885–1918), Hunts Parl Co (1918–48). *Eccl* Yax. RDn. Abol eccl 1962 to help cr Caldecote and Denton EP.[19]

CALDECOTE AND DENTON

EP Cr 1962 by union Caldecote AP, Denton EP.[19] Yax. RDn.

CATWORTH

CP Cr 1885 by union Great Catworth AP, Little Catworth CP.[20] *LG* Leight. Hd, St Neots PLU, RSD, RD. *Parl* Hunts Parl Co (1918–70), Hunts CC (1970–*).

GREAT CATWORTH

AP *LG* Leight. Hd, St Neots PLU, RSD. Civ bdry: 1780,[21] 1879.[22] Abol civ 1885 to help cr Catworth CP.[20] *Parl* S'rn Dv (1885–1918). *Eccl* Seq 1.

LITTLE CATWORTH

Chap in Stow AP (eccl, 'Stow Longa'), sep civ identity early, no sep eccl identity. *LG* Leight. Hd, St Neots PLU, RSD. Civ bdry: 1780,[21] 1879.[22] Abol 1885 to help cr Catworth CP.[20] *Parl* S'rn Dv (1885–1918).

CHESTERTON

AP *LG* Seq 7. Civ bdry: 1956 (exchanges pts with Castor AP, Soke of Peterb).[2] *Parl* Seq 1. *Eccl* Seq 9.

COLNE

Chap in Somersham AP, sep civ identity early, no sep eccl identity. *LG* Seq 1. Civ bdry: 1884.[8] *Parl* Seq 1.

CONINGTON

AP *LG* Seq 6. *Parl* Seq 1. *Eccl* Yax. RDn (until 1863), Leight. RDn Second Dv (1863–78), Leight. RDn (1878–1964), Yax. RDn (1964–*).

COPMANFORD

AP Usual eccl spelling; for civ see following entry. *Eccl* Leight. RDn. Abol eccl 1465 to help cr Upton and Copmanford EP.[23]

COPPINGFORD

AP Usual civ spelling; for eccl see prev entry. *LG* Leight. Hd, Hunt. PLU, RSD, RD. Abol civ 1935 to help cr Upton and Coppingford CP.[5] *Parl* S'rn Dv (1885–1918), Hunts Parl Co (1918–48).

COVINGTON

AP *LG* Seq 5. *Parl* Seq 2. *Eccl* Seq 1.

DENTON

AP *LG* Norm. Cr. Hd, Peterb. PLU, RSD, Norm. Cr. RD. Abol civ 1935 to help cr Denton and Caldecote CP.[5] *Parl* N'rn Dv (1885–1918), Hunts Parl Co (1918–48). *Eccl* Yax. RDn. Abol eccl 1962 to help cr Caldecote and Denton EP.[19]

DENTON AND CALDECOTE

CP Cr 1935 by union Denton AP, Caldecote AP.[5] *LG* Norm. Cr. RD. Civ bdry: 1965 (gains pt Lutton AP, Northants).[13] *Parl* Hunts Parl Co (1948–70), Hunts CC (1970–*).

DIDDINGTON

AP *LG* Seq 10. *Parl* Seq 2. *Eccl* Seq 7.

EARITH

Chap in Bluntisham cum Earith AP, sep CP when latter dissolved 1948 into the 2 CPs of Bluntisham, Earith.[7] *LG* St Ives RD. *Parl* Hunts CC (1970–*).

EASTON

AP *LG* Seq 2. *Parl* Seq 2. *Eccl* Pec jurisd Stow Longa (until 1839), Leight. RDn (1839–78), Kimb. RDn (1878–1964), Leight. RDn (1964–*).

ELLINGTON

AP *LG* Seq 2. *Parl* Seq 2. *Eccl* Seq 1.

ELTON

AP Pt Hunts (Norm. Cr. Hd), pt Northants (Polebrook Hd), considered ent Hunts by 1851,[24] Oundle PLU, RSD, RD (1894–1935), Norm. Cr. RD (1935–74). Civ bdry: 1965 (exchanges pts with Fortheringay AP, gains pt Warmington AP, loses pt to Nassington AP, all Northants).[13] *Parl* Seq 1. *Eccl* Seq 9.

EVERTON

AP Main pt of par in Beds, incl hmlt Tetworth (pt Beds [Biggleswade Hd), pt Hunts [Tosel. Hd], considered a CP since 1810,[25] no sep eccl identity hence this par eccl 'Everton with Tetworth', qv, the pt in Beds transf to Hunts 1832 for parl purposes, 1844 for civ purposes[26]). See main entry in Beds and Tetworth below.

EVERTON WITH TETWORTH

AP Usual eccl spelling; for civ and civ sep chap Tetworth see prev entry. *Eccl* Seq 7.

EYNESBURY

AP *LG* Tosel. Hd, St Neots PLU, pt St Neots USD, pt St Neots RSD, pt St Neots RD (1894–95), St Neots UD (pt 1894–95, ent 1895–1974). Civ bdry: 1895 (the pt not in the USD cr Eynesbury Hardwicke CP).[27] *Parl* Seq 2. *Eccl* Seq 7.

EYNESBURY HARDWICKE

CP Cr 1895 from the pt of Eynesbury AP not in St Neots UD.[27] *LG* St Neots PLU, RD. Civ bdry: 1968.[28] *Parl* Hunts Parl Co (1918–70), Hunts CC (1970–*).

FARCET

Chap in Stanground AP, sep EP 1851,[29] sep CP 1866.[30] *LG* Norm. Cr. Hd, Peterb. PLU,[31] RSD, Norm. Cr. RD. Civ bdry: 1886,[32] 1935.[5] *Parl* Seq 1. *Eccl* Yax. RDn.

FENSTANTON

AP Incl chap Hilton (sep civ identity early, sep EP

1873[33]). *LG* Tosel. Hd, St Ives PLU, pt St Ives MB (1874–96), pt St Ives USD, pt St Ives RSD, St Ives RD (pt 1894–96, ent 1896–1974). Civ bdry: 1896 (loses the pt in the MB to St Ives AP).[34] *Parl* Seq 1. *Eccl* Seq 8.

FLETTON

AP *LG* Norm. Cr. Hd, Peterb. PLU, pt Peterb. MB (1874–94 [thus this pt Soke of Peterb Adm Co 1889–94]), pt Peterb. USD, pt Peterb. RSD. Abol civ 1894 the pt in the MB to cr Fletton Urban CP (sometimes 'New Fletton'), the remainder to cr Fletton Rural CP (sometimes 'Old Fletton').[35] *Parl* N'rn Dv (1885–1918). *Eccl* Seq 9.

CP Renaming 1938 of Fletton Rural CP.[36] *LG* Old Fletton UD. *Parl* Hunts Parl Co (1948–70), Hunts CC (1970–*).

OLD FLETTON–See FLETTON RURAL

FLETTON RURAL

CP Cr 1894 from the pt of Fletton AP not in Peterb. MB.[35] Sometimes 'Old Fletton'. *LG* Peterb. PLU, Norm. Cr. RD (1894–1905), Old Fletton UD (1905–38). Renamed 1938 'Fletton'.[36] *Parl* Hunts Parl Co (1918–48).

FOLKSWORTH

AP *LG* Norm. Cr. Hd, Peterb. PLU, RSD, Norm. Cr. RD. Abol civ 1935 to help cr Folksworth and Washingley CP.[5] *Parl* N'rn Dv (1885–1918), Hunts Parl Co (1918–48). *Eccl* Seq 9.

FOLKSWORTH AND WASHINGLEY

CP Cr 1935 by union Folksworth AP, Washingley AP.[5] *LG* Norm. Cr. RD. *Parl* Hunts Parl Co (1948–70), Hunts CC (1970–*).

GREAT GADDESDEN

AP *LG* Seq 8. *Parl* Seq 2. *Eccl* Seq 7.

GREAT GIDDING

AP *LG* Seq 3. Civ bdry: 1965 (loses pt to Luddington AP, Northants).[13] *Parl* Seq 2. *Eccl* Leight. RDn (until 1863), Leight. RDn Second Dv (1863–78), Leight. RDn (1878–1973). Abol eccl 1973 to help cr Great with Little and Steeple Gidding EP.[37]

GREAT WITH LITTLE AND STEEPLE GIDDING

EP Cr 1973 by union Great Gidding AP, Little Gidding AP, Steeple Gidding AP.[37] Leight. RDn.

LITTLE GIDDING

AP *LG* Seq 3. *Parl* Seq 2. *Eccl* As for Great Gidding.

STEEPLE GIDDING

AP *LG* Seq 2. *Parl* Seq 2. *Eccl* As for Great Gidding.

GLATTON

AP Incl hmlt, chap and bor Holme (bor status not sustained, sep EP 1857,[38] sep CP 1866[30]). *LG* Seq 7. *Parl* Seq 1. *Eccl* Yax. RDn (1857–63), Leight. RDn Second Dv (1863–78), Leight. RDn (1878–1964), Yax. RDn (1964–*).

GODMANCHESTER

AP *LG* Tosel. Hd, Hunt. PLU, Godmanchester Bor/MB, USD. Abol civ 1961 to help cr Huntingdon and Godmanchester CP.[61] *Parl* S'rn Dv (1885–1918), Hunts Parl Co (1918–70). *Eccl* Seq 8.

GRAFHAM

AP *LG* Seq 4. *Parl* Seq 2. *Eccl* Seq 1.

HADDON

AP *LG* Seq 7. *Parl* Seq 1. *Eccl* Seq 9. Eccl bdry: 1959.[39]

HAMERTON

AP *LG* Seq 2. *Parl* Seq 2. *Eccl* Seq 2.

HARTFORD

AP Gains *ca* 1858 ex-par Sapley (orig royal forest),[40] so that often 'Hartford and Sapley'. *LG* Perhaps mediev bor,[1] Hurst. Hd, Hunt. PLU, RSD, RD. Abol civ 1935 pt to Huntingdon CP, pt to help cr Houghton and Wyton CP, pt to Kings Ripton AP.[5] *Parl* S'rn Dv (1885–1918), Hunts Parl Co (1918–48). *Eccl* Seq 6.

HARTFORD AND SAPLEY–See prev entry

HEMINGFORD ABBOTS

AP *LG* Seq 9. *Parl* Seq 1. *Eccl* Seq 8.

HEMINGFORD GREY

AP *LG* Tosel. Hd, St Ives PLU, pt St Ives MB (1889–96), pt St Ives USD (1889–94), St Ives RSD (ent 1875–89, pt 1889–94), St Ives RD (pt 1894–96, ent 1896–1974). Civ bdry: 1896 (loses the pt in the MB to St Ives AP).[34] *Parl* Seq 1. *Eccl* Seq 8.

HILTON

Chap in Fenstanton AP, sep civ identity early, sep EP 1873.[33] *LG* Seq 9. *Parl* Seq 1. *Eccl* Leight. RDn First Dv (1873–78), Hunt. RDn (1878–*).

HOLME

Hmlt, chap and bor in Glatton AP, bor status not sustained, sep EP 1857,[38] sep CP 1866.[30] *LG* Seq 7. Civ bdry: 1935.[5] *Parl* Seq 1. *Eccl* Leight. RDn (1857–63), Leight. RDn Second Dv (1863–78), Leight. RDn (1878–1964), Yax. RDn (1964–*).

HOLYWELL CUM NEEDINGWORTH

AP *LG* Seq 1. *Parl* Seq 1. *Eccl* Seq 4.

HOUGHTON

AP *LG* Hurst. Hd, St Ives PLU, RSD, RD. Abol civ 1935 to help cr Houghton and Wyton CP.[5] *Parl* N'rn Dv (1885–1918), Hunts Parl Co (1918–48). *Eccl* Seq 5.

HOUGHTON AND WYTON

CP Cr 1935 by union Houghton AP, Wyton AP, pt Hartford AP.[5] *LG* St Ives RD. *Parl* Hunts Parl Co (1948–70), Hunts CC (1970–*).

HUNTINGDON

The following have 'Huntingdon' in their names. Insofar as any existed at a given time: *LG* Hurst. Hd, Hunt. PLU, USD, Bor/MB (1835–1961), Hunt. & Godmanchester MB (1961–74). *Parl* Hunt. Parl Bor (1295–1885), S'rn Dv (1885–1918), Hunts Parl Co (1918–70), Hunts CC (1970–*). *Eccl* Hunt. RDn.

CP1–HUNTINGDON–Cr 1921 by union AP1, AP4, AP10, AP13.[41] Bdry: 1935.[5] Abol 1961 to help cr CP2.[61]

CP2–HUNTINGDON AND GODMANCHESTER–Cr 1961 by union CP1, Godmanchester AP.[61]

AP1–HUNTINGDON ALL SAINTS–Abol civ 1921 to help cr CP1.[41] Abol eccl 1667 to help cr EP1.[42]

EP1–HUNTINGDON ALL SAINTS WITH ST JOHN–Cr 1667 by union AP1, AP10.[42]

AP2–HUNTINGDON HOLY TRINITY–Derelict by 14th cent.[42]

AP3–HUNTINGDON ST ANDREW–In decay after 1529.[43]

AP4–HUNTINGDON ST BENEDICT–Abol civ 1921 to help cr CP1.[41] Abol eccl 1668 to help cr EP2.[42]

AP5–HUNTINGDON ST BOTOLPH–Site unknown.[43]

AP6–HUNTINGDON ST CLEMENT–No mention after 1372.[42]

AP7–HUNTINGDON ST EDMUND–United 1312 to AP13.[42]

AP8–HUNTINGDON ST GEORGE–Mentioned only in 17th cent.[43]

AP9–HUNTINGDON ST GERMAIN–On 17th cent map, no earlier mention.[43]

AP10–HUNTINGDON ST JOHN–Abol civ 1921 to help cr CP1.[41] Abol eccl 1667 to help cr EP1.[42]

AP11–HUNTINGDON ST LAWRENCE–No mention after 13th cent.[43]

AP12–HUNTINGDON ST MARTIN–United 1343 to AP13.[42]

AP13–HUNTINGDON ST MARY–Gains 1312 AP7,[42] gains 1343 AP12.[42] Abol civ 1921 to help cr CP1.[41] Abol eccl 1668 to help cr EP2.[42]

EP2–HUNTINGDON ST MARY AND ST BENEDICT–Cr 1668 by union AP13, AP4.[42]

AP14–HUNTINGDON ST MICHAEL–In ruins by 16th cent, incl in AP16.[42]

AP15–HUNTINGDON ST NICHOLAS–Site unknown.[43]

AP16–HUNTINGDON ST PETER–In ruins by 16th cent, incl AP14.[43]

OLD HURST

Chap in St Ives AP, sep civ identity early, eccl severed 1968 to help cr Broughton with Old Hurst and Woodhurst EP.[14] *LG* Seq 1. *Parl* Seq 1.

KEYSTON

AP *LG* Leight. Hd, Thrap. PLU, RSD, RD. Abol civ 1935 to help cr Bythorn and Keyston CP.[5] *Parl* S'rn Dv (1885–1918). *Eccl* Leight. RDn (until 1863), Leight. RDn First Dv (1863–78), Kimb. RDn (1878–1936). Reconstituted 1936 when gains Bythorn chap of Brington with Bythorn and Old Weston AP to cr Keyston and Bythorn EP.[11]

KEYSTON AND BYTHORN

EP Cr 1936 by union Keyston AP, Bythorn chap of Brington with Bythorn and Old Weston AP.[11] Kimb. RDn (1936–64), Leight. RDn (1964–*).

KIMBOLTON

AP *LG* Seq 4. *Parl* Seq 2. *Eccl* Leight. RDn (until 1863), St Neots RDn (1863–78), Kimb. RDn (1878–1964), Leight. RDn (1964–*).

LEIGHTON

AP Usual civ spelling; for eccl see following entry. *LG* Seq 2. *Parl* Seq 2.

LEIGHTON BROMSWOLD

AP Usual eccl spelling; for civ see prev entry. *Eccl* Pec jurisd Prebend of Leighton Bromswold (until 1839), Leight. RDn (1839–63), Leight. RDn First Dv (1863–78), Kimb. RDn (1878–1964), Leight. RDn (1964–*).

LUDDINGTON IN THE BROOK

AP Pt Hunts (Leight. Hd), pt Northants (Polebrook Hd), the former transf 1895 to Northants.[44] *LG* Oundle PLU, RSD, pt sep RD in Hunts (1894–95). See main entry in Northants. *Parl* Hunts pt, N'rn Dv (1885–1918). *Eccl* See main entry in Northants.

LUTTON

AP Sometimes 'Luddington in the Wold'. Pt Hunts (Norm. Cr. Hd), pt Northants (Willybrook Hd), the former transf 1895 to Northants.[44] *LG* Oundle PLU, RSD, pt sep RD in Hunts (1894–95). See main entry in Northants. *Parl* Hunts pt, N'rn Dv (1885–1918). *Eccl* Gains 1512 Washingley AP.[45] See main entry in Northants.

MIDLOE

Ex-par place, sep CP 1858.[46] *LG* Tosel. Hd, St Neots PLU, RSD, RD. Abol civ 1935 to help cr Southoe and Midloe CP.[5] *Parl* S'rn Dv (1885–1918), Hunts Parl Co (1918–48).

MOLESWORTH

AP *LG* Leight. Hd, Thrap. PLU, RSD, RD. Abol civ 1935 to help cr Brington and Molesworth CP.[5] *Parl* S'rn Dv (1885–1918), Hunts Parl Co (1918–48). *Eccl* Seq 1.

MORBORNE

AP *LG* Seq 7. Civ bdry: 1965 (gains pt Warmington AP, Northants).[13] *Parl* Seq 1. *Eccl* Seq 9.

OFFORD CLUNY

AP *LG* Perhaps Offord Cluny mediev bor,[47] Seq 10. *Parl* Seq 2. *Eccl* Seq 7.

OFFORD D'ARCY

AP *LG* Seq 10. *Parl* Seq 2. *Eccl* Seq 7.

ORTON LONGUEVILLE

AP Gains 1702 Botolphbridge AP, union civ called 'Orton Longueville', eccl 'Orton Longueville with St Botolphbridge', qv.[10] *LG* Seq 7. Addtl civ bdry alt: 1956 (exchanges pts with Peterborough MB and CP, Soke of Peterb).[2] *Parl* Seq 1. *Eccl* Yax. RDn.

ORTON LONGUEVILLE WITH ST BOTOLPHBRIDGE

EP Eccl spelling for union 1702 of Orton Longueville AP, Botolphbridge AP[10]; for civ see prev entry. Yax. RDn. Bdry: 1959.[39]

ORTON WATERVILLE

AP *LG* Seq 7. Civ bdry: 1956.[2] *Parl* Seq 1. *Eccl* Seq 9. Eccl bdry: 1959.[39]

PAPWORTH ST AGNES

AP Pt Hunts (Tosel. Hd), pt Cambs (Papworth Hd), the former transf 1895 to Cambs.[48] *LG* Caxton PLU, RSD, pt sep RD in Hunts (1894–95). See main entry in Cambs. *Parl* Hunts pt, N'rn Dv (1885–1918). *Eccl* See main entry in Cambs.

GREAT PAXTON

AP Incl chaps Little Paxton, Toseland (each with sep civ identity early, neither with sep eccl identity). *LG* Seq 10. *Parl* Seq 2. *Eccl* Seq 7.

LITTLE PAXTON

Chap in Great Paxton AP, sep civ identity early, no sep eccl identity. *LG* Seq 10. *Parl* Seq 2.

PIDLEY CUM FENTON

Chap in Somersham AP, sep civ identity early, no sep eccl identity. *LG* Seq 1. Civ bdry: 1935.[5] *Parl* Seq 1.

POND'S BRIDGE

EP Cr 1866 from Ramsey AP, Ramsey St Mary EP, Stanground AP (Hunts, Cambs), Whittlesey St Mary with St Guthlac AP (Cambs).[49] St Ives RDn. Bdry: 1951.[50]

RAMSEY

AP Pt Hunts (Hurst. Hd), pt Cambs (N Witchford Hd, IoE), considered ent Hunts by 1871.[51] Loses pt 16th cent to Bury AP at Dissolution.[15] *LG* Hunt. PLU, Ramsey USD, UD. Addtl civ bdry alt: 1935,[5] 1965 (loses pt to Benwick CP, Cambs & IoE).[52] *Parl* Seq 1. *Eccl* Seq 4. Addtl eccl bdry alt: 1860 (cr Ramsey St Mary EP),[53] 1866 (help cr Pond's Bridge EP),[49] 1951.[50]

RAMSEY ST MARY

EP Cr 1860 from Ramsey AP.[53] St Ives RDn. Bdry: 1866 (help cr Pond's Bridge EP),[49] 1951.[50]

GREAT RAVELEY

AP *LG* Hurst. Hd, Hunt. PLU, RSD, RD. Abol civ 1935 to help cr Upwood and the Raveleys CP.[5] *Parl* N'rn Dv (1885–1918), Hunts Parl Co (1918–48). *Eccl* St Ives RDn. Abol eccl 1819 to help cr Upwood with Great Raveley EP.[4]

LITTLE RAVELEY

Chap in Wistow AP until 1351, then to Bury AP, sep civ identity early, sep EP 1746.[17] *LG* Hurst. Hd, Hunt. PLU, RSD, RD. Abol civ 1935 to help cr Upwood and the Raveleys CP.[5] *Parl* N'rn Dv (1885–1918), Hunts Parl Co (1918–48). *Eccl* St Ives RDn.

ABBOTS RIPTON

AP *LG* Hurst. Hd, Hunt. PLU, RSD, RD. *Parl* Seq 1. *Eccl* St Ives RDn (until 1922), Hunt. RDn (1922–*).

KINGS RIPTON

AP *LG* Perhaps Kings Ripton mediev bor,[47] Hurst. Hd, Hunt. PLU, RSD, RD. Civ bdry: 1935.[5] *Parl* Seq 1. *Eccl* St Ives RDn (until 1971), Hunt. RDn (1971–*).

ST IVES

AP Usual civ spelling; for eccl see 'St Ives with Old Hurst and Woodhurst'. *LG* Hurst. Hd, St Ives PLU, MB (1874–1974), USD. Civ bdry: 1896 (gains the pts of Fenstanton AP, Hemingford Grey AP in St Ives MB).[34] *Parl* Seq 1.

EP Renaming 1968 when St Ives with Old Hurst and Woodhurst loses its chaps to help cr Broughton with Old Hurst and Woodhurst EP.[14] St Ives RDn.

ST IVES WITH OLD HURST AND WOODHURST

AP Usual eccl spelling; for civ see 'St Ives'. St Ives RDn. Renamed 'St Ives' 1968 when loses its chaps to help cr Broughton with Old Hurst and Woodhurst EP.[14]

ST NEOTS

AP *LG* Tosel. Hd, St Neots PLU, pt St Neots USD, pt St Neots RSD, pt St Neots RD (1894–95), St Neots UD (pt 1894–95, ent 1895–1974). Civ bdry: 1895 (the pt not in the UD cr St Neots Rural CP),[27] 1965 (gains pt Eton Socon AP, Beds),[13] 1968.[28] *Parl* Seq 2. *Eccl* Seq 7.

ST NEOTS RURAL

CP Cr 1895 from the pt of St Neots AP not in St Neots UD.[27] *LG* St Neots PLU, RD. *Parl* Hunts Parl Co (1918–70), Hunts CC (1970–*).

SAPLEY

Ex-par place, formerly royal forest, absorbed *ca* 1858 into Hartford AP so that the latter sometimes called 'Hartford and Sapley',[40] qv.

SAWTRY

CP Cr 1935 by union Sawtry All Saints and St Andrew CP, Sawtry St Judith CP.[5] *LG* Hunt. RD. *Parl* Hunts Parl Co (1948–70), Hunts CC (1970–*).

EP Common name now for EP cr 1873 as 'Sawtry All Saints and St Andrew', qv.

SAWTRY ALL SAINTS

AP Abol civ 1886,[54] eccl 1873[54] to help cr Sawtry All Saints and St Andrew CP, EP respectively. *LG* Norm. Cr. Hd, Hunt. PLU, RSD. *Parl* N'rn Dv (1885–1918). *Eccl* Yax. RDn (until 1863), Leight. RDn Second Dv (1863–73).

SAWTRY ALL SAINTS AND ST ANDREW

Cr civ 1886,[54] eccl 1873[55] by union Sawtry All Saints AP, Sawtry St Andrew AP. *LG* Norm. Cr. Hd, Hunt. PLU, RSD, RD. Abol civ 1935 to help cr Sawtry CP.[5] *Parl* Hunts Parl Co (1918–48). *Eccl* Leight. RDn Second Dv (1873–78), Leight. RDn (1878–1964), Yax. RDn (1964–*). Eccl bdry: 1959.[56]

SAWTRY ST ANDREW

AP Organisation as for Sawtry All Saints.

SAWTRY ST JUDITH

Ex-par place, sep CP 1858,[46] eccl abol 1969 ent to Sawtry [All Saints and St Andrew] EP.[56] *LG* Norm. Cr. Hd, Hunt. PLU,[31] RSD, RD. Abol 1935 to help cr Sawtry CP.[5] *Parl* N'rn Dv (1885–1918), Hunts Parl Co (1918–48).

SIBSON CUM STIBBINGTON

AP Usual civ spelling; for eccl see 'Stibbington'. *LG* Norm. Cr. Hd, Stamford PLU, RSD, sep unnamed RD (1894–1935, administered by Barnack RD Council, Soke of Peterb), Norm. Cr. RD (1935–74). *Parl* Seq 1.

SOMERSHAM

AP Incl chaps Colne, Pidley cum Fenton (each with sep civ identity early, neither with sep eccl identity). *LG* Seq 1. Addtl civ bdry alt: 1884,[8] 1965 (loses pt to Chatteris UD and AP, Cambs & IoE).[52] *Parl* Seq 1. *Eccl* Seq 4.

SOUTHOE

AP Incl chap Hail Weston (sep civ identity early, some sep eccl rights 13th cent and vicarage ordained, sep eccl status not sustained and treated as chap to this par, hence eccl 'Southoe with Hail Weston', qv). *LG* Tosel. Hd, St Neots PLU, RSD, RD. Abol civ 1935 to help cr Southoe and Midloe CP.[5] *Parl* S'rn Dv (1885–1918), Hunts Parl Co (1918–48).

SOUTHOE AND MIDLOE

CP Cr 1935 by union Southoe AP, Midloe AP.[5] *LG* St Neots RD. *Parl* Hunts Parl Co (1948–70), Hunts CC (1970–*).

SOUTHOE WITH HAIL WESTON

AP Usual eccl spelling; for civ and sep chap Hail Weston see 'Southoe'. *Eccl* Seq 7.

SPALDWICK

AP *LG* Seq 2. *Parl* Seq 2. *Eccl* Pec jurisd Stow Longa (until 1839), Leight. RDn (1839–63), Leight. RDn First Dv (1863–78), Kimb. RDn (1878–1964), Leight. RDn (1964–*). Eccl bdry: 1958.[57]

STANGROUND

AP Pt Hunts (Norm. Cr. Hd), pt Cambs (IoE, N Witchford Hd), the Hunts pt made a sep CP 1905 as 'Stanground South', the pt in IoE cr 'Stanground North' CP.[58] Incl chap Farcet (sep EP 1851,[29] sep CP in Hunts 1866[30]). *LG* Peterborough PLU, RSD, pt Thorney RD in IoE (1894–95), pt Norm. Cr. RD in Hunts (1894–95). *Parl* Hunts pt, N'rn Dv (1885–1918). *Eccl* Seq 9. Eccl bdry: 1866 (help cr Pond's Bridge EP).[49]

STANGROUND SOUTH

CP Cr 1905 from the Hunts pt of Stanground AP.[58] *LG* Peterborough PLU, Old Fletton UD. *Parl* Hunts Parl Co (1918–70), Hunts CC (1970–*).

GREAT STAUGHTON

AP *LG* Seq 10. *Parl* Seq 2. *Eccl* Seq 7.

STIBBINGTON

AP Usual eccl spelling; for civ see 'Sibson cum Stibbington'. *Eccl* Seq 9.

STILTON

AP *LG* Seq 7. *Parl* Seq 1. *Eccl* Seq 9.

STOW

AP Usual civ spelling; for eccl see following entry. Incl chap Little Catworth (sep civ identity early, no sep eccl identity). *LG* Leight. Hd, St Neots PLU, RSD, RD. Civ bdry: 1780.[21] Renamed 1955 'Stow Longa'.[59] *Parl* S'rn Dv (1885–1918), Hunts Parl Co (1918–70).

STOW LONGA

AP Usual eccl spelling; for civ before 1955 see 'Stow'. *Eccl* Pec jurisd Stow Longa (until 1839), Leight. RDn (1839–63), Leight. RDn First Dv (1863–78), Kimb. RDn (1878–1964), Leight. RDn (1964–*). Eccl bdry: 1958.[57]

CP Renaming 1955 of Stow AP.[59] *LG* St Neots RD. *Parl* Hunts CC (1970–*).

GREAT STUKELEY

AP *LG* Hurst. Hd, Hunt. PLU, RSD, RD. Abol civ 1935 pt to help cr The Stukeleys CP, pt to Huntingdon CP.[5] *Parl* S'rn Dv (1885–1918), Hunts Parl Co (1918–48). *Eccl* Seq 6.

LITTLE STUKELEY

AP *LG* Hurst. Hd, Hunt. PLU, RSD, RD. Abol civ 1935 to help cr The Stukeleys CP.[5] *Parl*, *Eccl* as for Great Stukeley.

THE STUKELEYS

CP Cr 1935 by union Little Stukeley AP, pt Great Stukeley AP.[5] *LG* Hunt. RD. *Parl* Hunts Parl Co (1948–70), Hunts CC (1970–*).

SWINESHEAD

AP *LG* Leight. Hd, St Neots PLU, RSD. Transf 1896 to Beds.[60] *Parl* S'rn Dv (1885–1918). See Beds for civ, parl thereafter. *Eccl* Leight. RDn (until 1863), St Neots RDn (1863–78), Kimb. RDn (1878–1914), Riseley RDn (1914–70), Sharnbrook RDn (1970–*)(the last two in Bedford AD).

TETWORTH

Hmlt in Everton AP, the latter in Beds except for Tetworth (pt Hunts [Tosel. Hd], pt Beds [Biggleswade Hd]), sep CP since 1810,[25] no sep eccl identity, the pt in Beds transf to Hunts 1832 for parl purposes, 1844 for civ purposes.[26] *LG* St Neots PLU, RSD, RD. Civ bdry: 1965 (gains pt Gamlingay AP, Cambs & IoE, loses pts to Everton AP, Tempsford AP, both Beds).[13] *Parl* Seq 2.

THURNING

AP Pt Hunts (Leight. Hd), pt Northants (Polebrook Hd), the former transf 1895 to Northants.[44] *LG* Oundle PLU, RSD, pt sep RD in Hunts (1894–95). See main entry in Northants. *Parl* Hunts pt, N'rn Dv (1885–1918). *Eccl* Leight. RDn (until 1863), Leight. RDn Second Dv (1863–78), Leight. RDn (1878–1929). For organisation in Peterb dioc thereafter, see main entry in Northants.

TILBROOK

AP In Beds (Stodden Hd), transf 1896 to Hunts.[60] *LG* St Neots PLU, RSD, RD. *Parl* Hunts Parl Co (1918–70), Hunts CC (1970–*). *Eccl* Eaton RDn (until 1866), Eaton RDn N'rn Dv (1866–80), Riseley RDn (1880–1914)(all in Bedford AD), Kimb. RDn (1914–64), Leight. RDn (1964–*).

TOSELAND

Chap in Great Paxton AP, sep civ identity early, no sep eccl identity. *LG* Seq 10. *Parl* Seq 2.

UPTON

AP *LG* Leight. Hd, Hunt. PLU, RSD, RD. Abol civ 1935 to help cr Upton and Coppingford CP.[5] *Parl* S'rn Dv (1885–1918), Hunts Parl Co (1918–48). *Eccl* Leight. RDn. Abol eccl 1465 to help cr Upton and Copmanford EP.[23]

UPTON AND COPMANFORD

EP Cr 1465 by union Upton AP, Copmanford AP (civ, 'Coppingford'; see following entry).[23] Leight. RDn (1465–1863), Leight. RDn Second Dv (1863–78), Leight. RDn (1878–1964), Yax. RDn (1964–71), Leight. RDn (1971–*).

UPTON AND COPPINGFORD

CP Cr 1935 by union Upton AP, Coppingford AP (eccl, 'Copmanford'; see prev entry).[5] *LG* Hunt. RD. *Parl* Hunts Parl Co (1948–70), Hunts CC (1970–*).

UPWOOD

Chap in Wistow AP until 1351, then to Bury

AP, sep civ identity early, sep EP 1819 when joined with Great Raveley AP (no church) as 'Upwood with Great Raveley',[4] qv. *LG* Hurst. Hd, Hunt. PLU, RSD, RD. Civ bdry: 1884.[18] Abol civ 1935 to help cr Upwood and the Raveleys CP.[5] *Parl* N'rn Dv (1885–1918), Hunts Parl Co (1918–48).

UPWOOD AND THE RAVELEYS

CP Cr 1935 by union Upwood CP, Great Raveley AP, Little Raveley CP.[5] *LG* Hunt. RD. *Parl* Hunts Parl Co (1948–70), Hunts CC (1970–*).

UPWOOD WITH GREAT RAVELEY

EP Cr 1819 by union Upwood chap of Bury AP, Great Raveley AP.[4] St Ives RDn.

WOOD WALTON

AP *LG* Seq 6. Civ bdry: 1935.[5] *Parl* Seq 1. *Eccl* Yax. RDn (until 1878), Leight. RDn (1878–1964), Hunt. RDn (1964–*).

WARBOYS

AP *LG* Seq 1. Civ bdry: 1935.[5] *Parl* Seq 1. *Eccl* Seq 4.

WARESLEY

AP *LG* Seq 10. Civ bdry: 1965 (loses pt to Gamlingay AP, Cambs).[52] *Parl* Seq 2. *Eccl* Seq 7.

WASHINGLEY

AP *LG* Norm. Cr. Hd, Peterb. PLU, RSD, Norm. Cr. RD. Abol civ 1935 to help cr Folksworth and Washingley CP.[5] *Parl* N'rn Dv (1885–1918), Hunts Parl Co (1918–48). *Eccl* Oundle RDn (Northampton AD). Abol 1512 ent to Lutton AP.[45]

WATER NEWTON

AP *LG* Seq 7. *Parl* Seq 1. *Eccl* Seq 9.

HAIL WESTON

Chap in Southoe AP, sep civ identity early, some sep eccl rights 13th cent and vicarage ordained, sep civ identity regained early, sep eccl status not sustained and treated as chap to Southoe thus eccl 'Southoe and Hail Weston', qv. *LG* Seq 10. *Parl* Seq 2.

OLD WESTON

AP Sep status as par lost and deemed chap to Brington AP from 13th cent, sep civ identity regained early; see Brington with Bythorn and Old Weston for later eccl organisation of this chap. *LG* Seq 5. *Parl* Seq 2.

WINWICK

AP Pt Hunts (Leight. Hd), pt Northants (Polebrook Hd), the latter transf 1895 to Hunts.[44] *LG* Oundle PLU, RSD, RD (pt 1894–94, ent 1895–1935), Hunt. RD (1935–74). Addtl civ bdry alt: 1965 (loses pts to Barnwell CP, Clopton AP, both Northants).[13] *Parl* Pt N'rn Dv (1885–1918), Hunts Parl Co (1918–70), Hunts CC (1970–*). *Eccl* Seq 2.

WISTOW

AP Orig sep par with chap Bury dependent, the latter parochial by 1178 with Wistow its chap, Wistow sep again 1351.[16] *LG* Seq 1. *Parl* Seq 1. *Eccl* Seq 4.

WOODHURST

Chap in St Ives AP, sep civ identity early, eccl severed 1968 to help cr Broughton with Old Hurst and Woodhurst EP.[14] *LG* Seq 1. Addtl civ bdry alt: 1884,[18] 1885.[9] *Parl* Seq 1. *Eccl* Seq 4.

WOODSTON

AP *LG* Norm. Cr. Hd, Peterb. PLU, pt Peterb. MB/USD (1874–94 [thus this pt Soke of Peterb Adm Co 1888–94]), pt Peterb. RSD. Abol civ 1894 the pt in the MB to cr Woodston Urban CP, the remainder to cr Woodston Rural CP.[35] *Parl* N'rn Dv (1885–1918). *Eccl* Seq 9.

CP Renaming 1938 of Woodston Rural CP.[36] *LG* Old Fletton UD. *Parl* Hunts Parl Co (1948–70), Hunts CC (1970–*).

WOODSTON RURAL

CP Cr 1894 from the pt of Woodston AP not in Peterb MB.[35] *LG* Peterb. PLU, Norm. Cr. RD (1894–1905), Old Fletton UD (1905–38). Renamed 1938 'Woodston'.[36]

WOOLLEY

AP *LG* Leight. Hd, Hunt. PLU, RSD, RD. Abol civ 1935 to help cr Barham and Woolley CP.[5] *Parl* S'rn Dv (1885–1918), Hunts Parl Co (1918–48). *Eccl* Leight. RDn (until 1863), Leight. RDn First Dv (1863–78), Kimb. RDn (1878–1964), Leight. RDn (1964–65). Abol eccl 1965 to help cr Barham and Woolley EP.[6]

WYTON

AP *LG* Hurst. Hd, St Ives PLU, RSD, RD. Abol civ 1965 to help cr Houghton and Wyton CP.[5] *Parl* N'rn Dv (1885–1918), Hunts Parl Co (1918–70). *Eccl* Seq 5.

YAXLEY

AP *LG* Seq 7. Civ bdry: 1935.[5] *Parl* Seq 1. *Eccl* Seq 9. Eccl bdry: 1959.[39]

YELLING

AP *LG* Seq 8. *Parl* Seq 2. *Eccl* St Neots RDn (until 1929), Bourn RDn (Ely dioc, 1929–*).

KENT

ABBREVIATIONS

Abbreviations particular to Kent follow. Those general abbreviations in use throughout the *Guide* are found on page xix.

Aloesb.	Aloesbridge
Ashf.	Ashford
Ayl.	Aylesford
Beck.	Beckenham
Bewsb.	Bewsborough
Birch.	Bircholt
Blackb.	Blackbourne
Blackh.	Blackheath
Bleang.	Bleangate
Bough.	Boughton
Bren. & Horsm.	Brenchley and Horsmonden
Brom.	Bromley
Canterb.	Canterbury
Char.	Charing
Chisl.	Chislehurst
Cob.	Cobham
Codsh.	Codsheath
Corn.	Cornillo
Cranb.	Cranbrook
Dartf.	Dartford
Deptf.	Deptford
Downh.	Downhamford
Fav.	Faversham
Felb.	Felborough
Folk.	Folkestone
Gill.	Gillingham
Grav.	Gravesend
Greenw.	Greenwich
Hollingb.	Hollingbourn
Ivybr.	Ivybridge
Kingh.	Kinghamford
Larkf.	Larkfield
Littlef.	Littlefield
Longbr.	Longbridge
Loningb.	Loningborough
Lym.	Lympne
Maid.	Maidstone
Mall.	Malling
Orp.	Orpington
Ospr.	Ospringe
Recul.	Reculver
Ring.	Ringslow
Roch.	Rochester
Rolv.	Rolveden
Rom.	Romney
Sandw.	Sandwich
Selbrit.	Selbrittenden
Seven.	Sevenoaks
Shamw.	Shamwell
Shep.	Sheppey
Shor.	Shoreham
Sitt.	Sittingbourne

Stow.	Stowting
Tent.	Tenterden
Tolt.	Toltingtrough
Tonbr.	Tonbridge
Tunbr. Wells	Tunbridge Wells
Washl.	Washlingstone
Westb.	Westbere
Whit.	Whitstable
Wilm.	Wilmington
Woolw.	Woolwich

SEQUENCES

An abbreviated entry prefixed by 'Seq' is used in the parochial entries to avoid repeating often the names of superior units of administration. The content of each sequence is shown below.

Local Government Sequences ('LG')

Lathe of Aylesford

SEQ 1 Eyhorne Hd, Hollingb. PLU, RSD, RD
SEQ 2 Eyhorne Hd, Maid. PLU, RSD, RD
SEQ 3 Hoo Hd, PLU, RSD, RD (1894–1935), Strood RD (1935–74)
SEQ 4 Larkf. Hd, Mall. PLU, RSD, RD
SEQ 5 Littlef. Hd, Mall. PLU, RSD, RD
SEQ 6 Maid. Hd, Hollingb. PLU, RSD, RD
SEQ 7 Maid. Hd, PLU, RSD, RD
SEQ 8 Shamw. Hd, N Ayl. PLU (1835–84), RSD (1875–84), Strood PLU (1884–1930), RSD (1884–94), Strood RD
SEQ 9 Tolt. Hd, N Ayl. PLU (1835–84), RSD (1875–84), Strood PLU (1884–1930), RSD (1884–94), Strood RD
SEQ 10 Twyford Hd, Maid. PLU, RSD, RD
SEQ 11 Twyford Hd, Mall. PLU, RSD, RD
SEQ 12 Wash. Hd, Tonbr. PLU, RSD, RD
SEQ 13 Wrotham Hd, Mall. PLU, RSD, RD

Lathe of St Augustine

SEQ 14 Bewsb. Hd, River PLU (renamed Dover in 1840s), Dover RSD, RD
SEQ 15 Bleang. Hd, Blean PLU, RSD, RD (1894–1934), Bridge-Blean RD (1934–74)
SEQ 16 Bridge & Petham Hd, Bridge PLU, RSD, RD (1894–1934), Bridge-Blean RD (1934–74)
SEQ 17 Corn. Hd, Eastry PLU, RSD, RD
SEQ 18 Downh. Hd, Bridge PLU, RSD, RD (1894–1934), Bridge-Blean RD (1934–74)
SEQ 19 Eastry Hd, PLU, RSD, RD
SEQ 20 Kingh. Hd, Bridge PLU, RSD, RD (1894–1934), Bridge-Blean RD (1934–74)
SEQ 21 Wingham Hd, Eastry PLU, RSD, RD

Lathe of Scray

SEQ 22 Bough. under Blean Hd, Fav. PLU, RSD, RD (1894–1934), Swale RD (1934–74)
SEQ 23 Calehill Hd, W Ashf. PLU, RSD, RD
SEQ 24 Chart & Longbr. Hd, E Ashf. PLU, RSD, RD
SEQ 25 Chart & Longbr. Hd, W Ashf. PLU, RSD, RD
SEQ 26 Cranb. Hd, PLU, RSD, RD
SEQ 27 Fav. Hd, PLU, RSD, RD (1894–1934), Swale RD (1934–74)
SEQ 28 Felb. Hd, E Ashf. PLU, RSD, RD
SEQ 29 Milton Hd, PLU, RSD, RD (1894–1934), Swale RD (1934–74)
SEQ 30 Teynham Hd, Fav. PLU, RSD, RD (1894–1934), Swale RD (1934–74)
SEQ 31 Wye Hd, E Ashf. PLU, RSD, RD

Lathe of Shepway

SEQ 32 Birch. Franchise/Birch. Franchise & Barony, E Ashf. PLU, RSD, RD
SEQ 33 Folk. Hd, River PLU (renamed Dover in 1840s), Dover RSD, RD
SEQ 34 Folk. Hd, Elham PLU, RSD, RD
SEQ 35 Hayne Hd, Elham PLU, RSD, RD
SEQ 36 Loningb. Hd, Elham PLU, RSD, RD
SEQ 37 Rom. Marsh Lbty, PLU, RSD, RD
SEQ 38 Stow. Hd, Elham PLU, RSD, RD

Lathe of Sutton at Hone

SEQ 39 Axton/Axton, Dartf. & Wilm. Hd, Dartf. PLU, RSD, RD
SEQ 40 Codsh. Hd, Seven. PLU, RSD, RD
SEQ 41 Somerden Hd, Seven. PLU, RSD, RD
SEQ 42 Westerham Hd, Seven. PLU, RSD, RD

Parliamentary Sequences ('Parl')

SEQ 1 E'rn Dv (1832–1918), Canterb. Dv/CC (1918–*)
SEQ 2 E'rn Dv (1832–1918), Canterb. Dv (1918–48), Folk. & Hythe CC (1948–*)
SEQ 3 E'rn Dv (1832–1918), Dover Dv/CC (1918–70), Dover & Deal CC (1970–*)
SEQ 4 E'rn Dv (1832–85), N-E'rn Dv (1885–1918), Fav. Dv/CC (1918–*)
SEQ 5 E'rn Dv (1832–85), S'rn Dv (1885–1918), Ashf. Dv/CC (1918–*)
SEQ 6 E'rn Dv (1832–85), S'rn Dv (1885–1918), Ashf. Dv (1918–48), Folk. & Hythe CC (1948–*)
SEQ 7 E'rn Dv (1832–85), Isle of Thanet Dv/CC

(1885–1970), Thanet West BC (1970–*)
SEQ 8 W'rn Dv (1832–67), Mid Dv (1867–1918), Grav. Dv/CC (1918–*)
SEQ 9 W'rn Dv (1832–67), Mid Dv (1867–1918), Maid. Dv/CC (1918–*)
SEQ 10 W'rn Dv (1832–67), Mid Dv (1867–1918), Seven. Dv/CC (1918–70), Tonbr. & Mall. CC (1970–*)
SEQ 11 W'rn Dv (1832–67), Mid Dv (1867–85), S'rn Dv (1885–1918), Ashf. Dv/CC (1918–*)
SEQ 12 W'rn Dv (1832–67), Mid Dv (1867–85), S'rn Dv (1885–1918), Ashf. Dv/CC (1918–70), Royal Tunbr. Wells CC (1970–*)
SEQ 13 W'rn Dv (1832–67), Mid Dv (1867–85), S'rn Dv (1885–1918), Maid. Dv/CC (1918–*)
SEQ 14 W'rn Dv (1832–67), Mid Dv (1867–85), S-W'rn Dv (1885–1918), Maid. Dv/CC (1918–*)
SEQ 15 W'rn Dv (1832–67), Mid Dv (1867–85), S-W'rn Dv (1885–1918), Seven. Dv/CC (1918–70), Tonbr. & Mall. CC (1970–*)
SEQ 16 W'rn Dv (1832–67), Mid Dv (1867–85), S-W'rn Dv (1885–1918), Tonbr. Dv/CC (1918–70), Royal Tunbr. Wells CC (1970–*)
SEQ 17 W'rn Dv (1832–67), West Dv (1867–85), N-W'rn Dv (1885–1918), Chisl. Dv/CC (1918–55), Dartf. CC (1955–*)
SEQ 18 W'rn Dv (1832–67), West Dv (1867–85), N-W'rn Dv (1885–1918), Chisl. Dv (1918–48), Orp. CC (1948–55), Dartf. CC (1955–70), Seven. CC (1970–*)
SEQ 19 W'rn Dv (1832–67), West Dv (1867–85), S-W'rn Dv (1885–1918), Seven. Dv/CC (1918–*)
SEQ 20 W'rn Dv (1832–67), West Dv (1867–85), W'rn Dv (1885–1918), Seven. Dv/CC (1918–*)

Ecclesiastical Sequences ('Eccl')

Orig Canterb dioc:
SEQ 1 Bridge RDn (until 1873), E Bridge RDn (1873–*)
SEQ 2 Bridge RDn (until 1873), W Bridge RDn (1873–*)
SEQ 3 Canterb. RDn
SEQ 4 Canterb. RDn (until 1864), E Charing RDn (1864–*)
SEQ 5 Canterb. RDn (until 1864), W Charing RDn (1864–*)
SEQ 6 Dover RDn
SEQ 7 Dover RDn (until 1895), Elham RDn (1895–*)
SEQ 8 Elham RDn
SEQ 9 Elham RDn (until 1895), N Lym. RDn (1895–*)
SEQ 10 Lym. RDn (until 1864), N Lym. RDn (1864–*)
SEQ 11 Lym. RDn (until 1864), N Lym. RDn (1864–1914), E Charing RDn (1914–*)
SEQ 12 Lym. RDn (until 1864), S Lym. RDn (1864–*)
SEQ 13 Ospr. RDn
SEQ 14 Sandw. RDn
SEQ 15 Sandw. RDn (until 1914), Dover RDn (1914–*)
SEQ 16 Sitt. RDn
SEQ 17 Sutton RDn
SEQ 18 Westb. RDn (until 1930), Thanet RDn (1930–*)
SEQ 19 Westb. RDn (until 1930), Canterb. RDn (1930–*)
SEQ 20 Westb. RDn (until 1914), Canterb. RDn (1914–71), Recul. RDn (1971–*)

Orig Roch dioc:
SEQ 21 Dartf. RDn (until 1864), E Dartf. RDn (1864–1909), Dartf. RDn (1909–*)
SEQ 22 Dartf. RDn (until 1864), E Dartf. RDn (1864–1909), Dartf. RDn (1909–36), Chisl. RDn (1936–65), Sidcup RDn (1965–*)
SEQ 23 Dartf. RDn (until 1845), Greenw. RDn (1861–86), Lew. RDn (1886–*)
SEQ 24 Mall. RDn (until 1864), N Mall. RDn (1864–1906), Mall. RDn (1906–*)
SEQ 25 Mall. RDn (until 1864), N Mall. RDn (1864–1906), Mall. RDn (1906–54), Tonbr. RDn (1954–*)
SEQ 26 Mall. RDn (until 1864), S Mall. RDn (1864–84), Tonbr. RDn (1884–*)
SEQ 27 Mall. RDn (until 1864), S Mall. RDn (1864–1906), Tunbr. Wells RDn (1906–*)
SEQ 28 Roch. RDn (until 1909), Cliffe at Hoo RDn (1909–54), Strood RDn (1954–*)
SEQ 29 Roch. RDn (until 1862), Cob. RDn (1862–*)
SEQ 30 Roch. RDn (until 1862), Cob. RDn (1862–1936), Grav. RDn (1936–*)
SEQ 31 Roch. RDn (until 1862), Cob. RDn (1862–1954), Roch. RDn (1954–*)
SEQ 32 Roch. RDn (until 1862), Cob. RDn (1862–1909), Shor. RDn (1909–54), Cob. RDn (1954–*)
SEQ 33 Roch. RDn (until 1862), Grav. RDn (1862–*)
SEQ 34 Roch. RDn (until 1954), Strood RDn (1954–*)

Pec jurisd Archbp Canterb, in Cby dioc from 1845 (see next section for later):
SEQ 35 Shor. RDn
SEQ 36 Shor. RDn (until 1864), N Mall. RDn (1864–1906), Mall. RDn (1906–*)
SEQ 37 Shor. RDn (until 1864), S Mall. RDn (1864–84), Tonbr. RDn (1884–*)
SEQ 38 Shor. RDn (until 1909), Seven. RDn (1909–*)

DIOCESES AND ARCHDEACONRIES

CANTERBURY DIOC

Canterb. AD: Bridge RDn (until 1873), E Bridge RDn (1873–*), W Bridge RDn (1873–*), Canterb. RDn, Char. RDn (until 1841), Dover RDn, Elham RDn, Lym. RDn (until 1864), N Lym. RDn (1864–1914), S Lym. RDn (1864–1914), Ospr. RDn, Recul. RDn (1971–*), Sandw. RDn, Sitt. RDn (until 1841), Sutton RDn (until 1841), Thanet RDn (1930–*), Westb. RDn (until 1930)

Croydon AD (1930–):* Croydon RDn

Maid. AD (1841–):* Char. RDn (1841–64), E Char. RDn (1864–*), W Char. RDn (1864–*), Croy. RDn (1873–1930), Dartf. RDn (1845–64), E Dartf. RDn (1864–1905), W Dartf. RDn (1864–1905), N Lym. RDn (1914–*), S Lym. RDn (1914–*), Mall. RDn (1845–64), N Mall. RDn (1864–1905), S Mall. RDn (1864–1905), Shor. RDn (1845–1905), Sitt. RDn, Sutton RDn, Tonbr. RDn (1884–1905)

LONDON DIOC

A small number of Kent pars, sep noted in the parochial entries, were in this dioc 1845–68; these pars were not in a RDn until 1861, after which Greenw. RDn, Woolw. RDn

ROCHESTER DIOC

Brom. AD (1955–):* Beck. RDn, Brom. RDn, Chisl. RDn (1955–65), Dartf. RDn (1955–65), Erith RDn (1960–*), Orp. RDn, Sidcup RDn (1965–*)

Roch. AD (1863–77 only, 'Roch. & St Albans'): Beck. RDn (1909–55), Brom. RDn (1909–55), Chisl. RDn (1936–55), Cliffe at Hoo RDn (1909–54), Cob. RDn (1862–*), Dartf. RDn (until 1845), Dartf. RDn (1909–55), Dartf. RDn (1965–*), E Dartf. RDn (1905–09), W Dartf. RDn (1905–09), Deptf. RDn (1879–86), Gill. RDn (1954–*), Grav. RDn (1862–*), Greenw. RDn (1868–1905), Lew. RDn (1886–1905), Mall. RDn (until 1845), N Mall. RDn (1905–06), S Mall. RDn (1905–06), Orp. RDn (1954–55), Roch. RDn, Shor. RDn (1905–06), Strood RDn (1954–*), Tonbr. RDn (1905–06), Woolw. RDn (1868–1905)

Tonbr. AD (1906–):* Mall. RDn, Seven. RDn (1909–*), Shor. RDn, Tonbr. RDn, Tunbr. Wells RDn

SOUTHWARK DIOC

No AD within this dioc (1905–06): Greenw. RDn, Lew. RDn, Woolw. RDn

Lew. AD (1906–):* Eltham RDn (1962–66), Greenw. RDn (1906–54), Greenw. RDn (1966–*), Greenw. & Deptf. RDn (1954–66), Lew. RDn, Woolw. RDn

THE PARISHES OF KENT

ABBEY WOOD

EP Renaming 1965 of Plumstead St Michael and All Angels EP.[1] Woolw. RDn (1965–66), Greenw. RDn (1966–*). Bdry: 1973 (help cr Thamesmead EP).[2]

ACOL

Ville in Minster AP, sep CP 1866,[3] eccl severed 1871 and united with Birchington chap in Monkton AP to cr Birchington with Acol EP, qv.[4] Sometimes 'Wood'. *LG* Ring. Hd, non-corp mbr of Cq Pt Dover, in lbties of Dover, Thanet PLU, RSD, Isle of Thanet RD (1894–1935), Eastry RD (1935–74). Bdry: 1894 (help cr Westgate on Sea CP),[5] 1935 (incl help cr Margate CP).[6] *Parl* E'rn Dv (1867–85), Isle of Thanet Dv/CC (1885–1970), Thanet West BC (1970–*).

ACRISE

AP *LG* Pt Loningb. Hd, pt Folk. Hd, Elham PLU, RSD, RD. Civ bdry: 1959.[7] *Parl* Seq 2. *Eccl* Seq 8.

ADDINGTON

AP *LG* Seq 4. Civ bdry: 1883,[8] 1888.[9] *Parl* Seq 10. *Eccl* Mall RDn (until 1864), N Mall. RDn (1864–1906), Mall. RDn (1906–*). Eccl bdry: 1934.[10]

ADISHAM

AP Incl chap Staple (sep civ identity early, sep EP 1863[11]). *LG* Seq 18. Addtl civ bdry alt: 1889,[12] *Parl* Seq 1. *Eccl* Exempt from Archdeacon (until 1845), Seq 1.

ALDINGTON

AP Incl chap Smeeth (sep civ identity early, sep EP 1868[13]). *LG* Pt Bircholt Franchise/Bircholt Franchise & Barony, pt Rom. Marsh Lbty, pt Hythe Bor/MB (this pt in Cq Pt of Hythe), pt Hythe USD, pt Rom. Marsh RSD, E Ashf. RD. Addtl civ bdry alt: 1883,[8] 1888 (loses the pt in the MB to St Leonard Hythe CP),[14] 1934 (incl help cr Hythe CP).[6] *Parl* Pt Hythe Parl Bor (1558–1918), pt E'rn Dv (1832–1918), Ashf. Dv/CC (1918–*). *Eccl* Exempt from Archdeacon (until 1845), Seq 10.

ALKHAM

AP Incl chap Capel-le-Ferne (sep civ identity early, no sep eccl identity hence this par eccl 'Alkham with Capel-le-Ferne', qv). *LG* Seq 33. Addtl civ bdry alt: 1883,[8] 1960 (incl help cr Temple Ewell with River CP).[16] *Parl* Seq 3.

ALKHAM WITH CAPEL-LE-FERNE

AP Usual eccl spelling; for civ and civ sep chap Capel-le-Ferne, see prev entry. *Eccl* Seq 6.

ALLHALLOWS

AP *LG* Seq 3. Civ bdry: 1963.[17] *Parl* Seq 8. *Eccl* Seq 28.

ALLINGTON

AP *LG* Larkf. Hd, Mall. PLU, RSD, RD. Civ bdry:

1932.[18] Abol civ 1934 ent to Maidstone AP.[19] *Parl* W'rn Dv (1832–67), Mid Dv (1867–1918), Seven. Dv (1918–48). *Eccl* Mall. RDn (until 1864), N Mall. RDn (1864–1901), Sutton RDn (1891–1905), N Mall. RDn (1905–06), Mall. RDn (1906–36), Sutton RDn (1936–*). Eccl bdry: 1952,[20] 1963.[21] Dedication changed 1974 to 'St Nicholas'.[22]

APPLEDORE

AP Incl chap Ebony (sep civ identity early, eccl severed 1928 to help cr Stone with Ebony EP[23]; this par before 1928 eccl 'Appledore with Ebony', thereafter 'Appledore'). *LG* Pt Blackb. Hd, pt Lbty of New Rom. & Cq Pt New Rom., pt Rom. Marsh Lbty, Tent. PLU, RSD, RD. Addtl civ bdry alt: 1934.[19] *Parl* Seq 11. *Eccl* Seq 12. Eccl bdry: 1935.[25]

APPLEDORE WITH EBONY–See prev entry

ASH

AP Chap in Wingham AP, sep par 1286.[26] Sometimes 'Ash St Nicholas' or 'Ash-next-Sandwich'. *LG* Wingham Hd, Eastry PLU, RSD, RD. Civ bdry: 1935.[6] *Parl* Seq 3. *Eccl* Pec jurisd Wingham (until 1546), exempt from Archdeacon (until 1845), Bridge RDn (until 1873), E Bridge RDn (1873–1967). Eccl bdry: 1849 (cr West Marsh EP).[27] Abol eccl 1967 to help cr Ash with Westmarsh EP.[28]

ASH

AP Sometimes 'Ash next Ridley'. *LG* Axton/Axton, Dartf. & Wilm. Hd, Dartf. PLU, RSD, RD. Civ bdry: 1934.[19] Abol civ 1955 pt to help cr Ash-cum-Ridley CP (later called 'Ash-with-Ridley'), pt to West Kingsdown CP.[29] *Parl* W'rn Dv (1832–67), West Dv (1867–85), N-W'rn Dv (1885–1918), Chisl. Dv (1918–48), Orp. CC (1948–55), Dartf. CC (1955–70). *Eccl* Seq 32.

ASH-CUM-RIDLEY

CP Cr 1955 by union Ridley AP, pt Ash AP.[29] Now called 'Ash-with-Ridley'. *LG* Dartf. RD. *Parl* Seven. CC (1970–*).

ASH-WITH-RIDLEY–See prev entry

ASH WITH WESTMARSH

EP Cr 1967 by union Ash AP, West Marsh EP.[28] E Bridge RDn.

ASHFORD

AP *LG* Chart & Longbr. Hd (pt in Ashf. Lbty), W Ashf. PLU (1836–1930), Ashf. USD, UD. Civ bdry: 1934.[19] *Parl* Seq 5. *Eccl* Seq 4. Eccl bdry: 1959 (incl help cr South Ashford EP).[30]

SOUTH ASHFORD

EP Cr 1959 from Ashford AP, Kingsnorth AP.[30] E Char. RDn.

ASHURST

AP *LG* Washl. Hd, Tonbr. PLU, RSD, RD. Abol civ 1934 ent to Speldhurst AP.[19] *Parl* W'rn Dv (1832–67), Mid Dv (1867–85), S-W'rn Dv (1885–1918), Tonbr. Dv (1918–48). *Eccl* Seq 27.

AYLESFORD

AP *LG* Seq 4. Civ bdry: 1888,[9] 1934.[19] *Parl* Seq 10. *Eccl* Roch. RDn (until 1862), Cob. RDn (1862–1954), Mall. RDn (1954–*). Eccl bdry: 1934,[10] 1963,[21] 1966,[31] 1967 (incl help cr Chatham St William EP).[37]

AYLESHAM

CP Cr 1951 from Nonington AP.[32] *LG* Eastry RD. *Parl* Dover & Deal CC (1970–*).

BADLESMERE

AP *LG* Fav. Hd, PLU, RSD, RD (1894–1935), Swale RD (1935–74). Civ bdry: 1935.[6] *Parl* Seq 4. *Eccl* Seq 13.

BAPCHILD

AP *LG* Seq 29. Civ bdry: 1883,[8] 1930 (help cr Sittingbourne and Milton CP),[33] 1935.[15] *Parl* Seq 4. *Eccl* Seq 16. Eccl bdry: 1957.[34]

BARFRESTON

AP Usual civ spelling; for eccl see following entry. *LG* Eastry Hd, PLU, RSD, RD. Abol civ 1935 ent to Eythorne AP.[15] *Parl* E'rn Dv (1832–1918), Dover Dv (1918–48).

BARFREYSTONE

AP Usual eccl spelling; for civ see prev entry. *Eccl* Seq 15.

BARHAM

Chap in Bishopsbourne AP, sep civ identity early, sep EP 1845.[35] *LG* Seq 20. Civ bdry: 1934.[19] *Parl* Seq 1. *Eccl* Bridge RDn (1845–73), E Bridge RDn (1873–*). Eccl bdry: 1891.[36]

BARMING

CP Cr 1934 by union pt East Barming AP, ent West Barming CP.[19] *LG* Maid. RD. *Parl* Maid. CC (1948–*).

EAST BARMING

AP Sometimes 'Barming'. Civ incl West Barming (orig AP, eccl included in Nettlestead AP,[38] sep CP 1866[3]). *LG* Seq 7. Abol civ 1934 pt to help cr Barming CP, pt to Maidstone AP.[19] *Parl* W'rn Dv (1832–67), Mid Dv (1867–1918), Maid. Dv (1918–48). *Eccl* Seq 24.

WEST BARMING

AP Orig AP, later deemed civ within East Barming AP, eccl within Nettlestead AP,[38] sep civ identity regained 1866.[3] *LG* Maid. Hd, PLU (1866[120]–1930), RSD, RD. Abol 1934 to help cr Barming CP.[19] *Parl* Mid Dv (1867–1918), Maid. Dv (1818–48).

BARMING HEATH

EP Cr 1930 from Maidstone St Michael and All Angels EP.[39] Sutton RDn. Now called 'Maidstone St Andrew'.

BARNEHURST

EP Cr 1937 from Bexley Heath Christ Church EP, Crayford AP, Erith St Paul, Northumerland Heath EP.[40] Dartf. RDn (1937–60), Erith RDn (1960–*). Bdry: 1972.[41]

BEARSTEAD

AP *LG* Orig pt Eyhorne Hd, pt Maid. Hd, by 19th cent ent Eyhorne Hd,[44] Seq 2 thereafter. Civ bdry: 1883,[8] 1888,[45] 1889,[46] 1934.[19] *Parl* Seq 9. *Eccl* Seq 17. Eccl bdry: 1940,[47] 1971 (help cr Maidstone All Saints with St Philip and Holy Trinity EP),[48] 1972.[49]

BEAUFIELD–See WHITFIELD

BECKENHAM

The following have 'Beckenham' in their names. Insofar as any existed at a given time: *LG* Brom. & Beck. Hd, Brom. PLU, USD, UD (1894–1935), MB (1935–65). Transf 1965 to Gtr London (Brom. LB).[51] *Parl* W'rn Dv (1832–67), West Dv (1867–85), N-W'rn Dv (1885–1918), Brom. Parl Bor (1918–48), Beck. BC (1948–70), Gtr London thereafter. *Eccl* Dartf. RDn (until 1864), W Dartf. RDn (1864–1909), Beck. RDn (1909–*).

AP1–BECKENHAM [ST GEORGE]–Civ bdry: 1902,[50] 1934.[19] Eccl bdry: 1870 (cr Shortlands EP),[52] 1872 (cr EP7),[53] 1877 (cr EP3),[54] 1878 (cr EP1),[55] 1878 (cr Penge Lane EP, now called 'Beckenham Holy Trinity'),[56] 1899,[57] 1907 (cr EP6),[58] 1924 (cr EP4),[59] 1945 (cr EP2).[62]

EP1–BECKENHAM CHRIST CHURCH–Cr 1878 from AP1.[55] Bdry: 1899,[57] 1931,[60] 1936 (help cr EP5).[61]

–BECKENHAM HOLY TRINITY–Name used now for EP cr 1878 as Penge Lane, qv.

EP2–BECKENHAM ST AUGUSTINE–Cr 1945 from AP1.[62]

EP3–BECKENHAM ST BARNABAS–Cr 1877 from AP1.[54] Bdry: 1936 (help cr EP5),[61] 1938 (help cr West Wickham St Mary of Nazareth EP).[63]

EP4–BECKENHAM ST JAMES, ELMERS END–Cr 1924 from AP1.[59] Bdry: 1931.[60]

EP5–BECKENHAM ST JOHN THE BAPTIST–Cr 1936 from EP1, EP3.[61]

EP6–BECKENHAM ST MICHAEL AND ALL ANGELS–Cr 1907 from AP1.[58]

EP7–NEW BECKENHAM–Cr 1872 from AP1.[53] Bdry: 1899.[57]

BEKESBOURNE

AP *LG* Bridge & Petham Hd, non-corporate mbr Cq Pt of Hastings (concurrent county jurisd from 1811), Bridge PLU, pt Canterb. MB/CB (1868–94), pt Canterb. USD, pt Bridge RSD, Bridge RD (1894–1934), Bridge-Blean RD (1934–74). Civ bdry: 1889,[12] 1894 (loses the pt in the CB to Canterbury St Paul AP),[42] 1958.[43] *Parl* Seq 1. *Eccl* Seq 1.

BELLINGHAM

EP Cr 1940 from Lewisham St John, Southend EP, Lower Sydenham EP.[64] Lewisham RDn.

BELVEDERE ALL SAINTS

EP Cr 1861 from Erith AP.[65] Dartf. RDn (1861–64), E Dartf. RDn (1864–1909), Dartf. RDn (1909–60), Erith RDn (1960–*). Bdry: 1917 (help cr Belvedere St Augustine EP),[66] 19 (help cr Bexleyheath St Peter EP).[67]

BELVEDERE ST AUGUSTINE

EP Cr 1917 from Belvedere All Saints EP, Erith AP.[67] Dartf. RDn (1917–60), Erith RDn (1960–*). Bdry: 1927,[68] 1973 (help cr Thamesmead EP).[2]

BENENDEN

AP *LG* Orig pt Rolv. Hd, pt Selbrit. Hd, pt Berkeley Hd, pt Carnb. Hd, ent Rolv. Hd by 19th cent,[44] Cranb. PLU, RSD, RD. *Parl* Seq 12. *Eccl* Seq 5.

BETHERSDEN

AP *LG* Orig. pt Chart & Longbr. Hd, pt Blackb. Hd, pt Calehill Hd, by 19th cent ent Chart & Longbr. Hd,[44] Seq 25 thereafter. *Parl* Seq 5. *Eccl* Char. RDn (until 1864), W Char. RDn (1864–1914), E Char. RDn (1914–*).

BETTESHANGER

AP *LG* Eastry Hd, PLU, RSD, RD. Abol civ 1935 ent to Northbourne AP.[6] *Parl* E'rn Dv (1832–1918), Dover Dv (1918–48). *Eccl* Sandw. RDn. Eccl bdry: 1894.[69] Abol eccl 1973 to help cr Betteshanger and Ham EP.[70]

BETTESHANGER AND HAM

EP Cr 1973 by union Betteshanger AP, Ham AP.[70] Sandw. RDn.

BEXLEY

AP *LG* Orig ent Ruxley Hd, by 19th cent pt Ruxley Hd, pt Codsh. Hd,[44] Dartf. PLU, Bexley USD, UD (1894–1937), MB (1937–65). Civ bdry: 1902 (gains East Wickham CP),[470] 1910,[71] 1934,[19] 1937.[72] Transf 1965 to Gtr London (Bexley LB).[51] *Parl* W'rn Dv (1832–67), West Dv (1867–85), W'rn Dv (1885–1918), Dartf. Dv (1918–45), Bexley BC (1945–70). Gtr London thereafter. *Eccl* Pec jurisd Shor. (until 1845), Seq 22 thereafter. Eccl bdry: 1866 (cr Bexley Heath Christ Church EP),[73] 1878 (cr Lamorbey Holy Trinity EP),[362] 1936 (help cr Bexley St John EP),[74] 1961,[75] 1969 (help cr Sidcup St Andrew EP),[76] 1972.[77]

BEXLEY ST JOHN

EP Cr 1936 from Bexley AP, Lamorbey Holy Trinity EP, Welling St John EP.[74] Chisl. RDn (1936–65), Sidcup RDn (1965–*). Bdry: 1936.[74]

BEXLEY HEATH CHRIST CHURCH

EP Cr 1866 from Bexley AP.[73] E Dartf. RDn (1866–1909), Dartf. RDn (1909–60), Erith RDn (1960–*). Bdry: 1926 (help cr Welling St John EP),[79] 1937 (help cr Barnehurst EP),[40] 1937,[58] 1955 (help cr Bexleyheath St Peter EP),[78] 1961,[75] 1972.[41]

BEXLEYHEATH ST PETER

EP Cr 1955 from Bexley Heath Christ Church EP, Belvedere All Saints EP.[78] Dartf. RDn (1955–60), Erith RDn (1960–*).

BICKLEY

EP Cr 1866 from Bromley AP.[80] W Dartf. RDn (1866–1909), Brom. RDn (1909–*). Bdry: 1906 (help cr Chislehurst Christ Church EP),[81] 1907,[82] 1934 (help cr Bromley Common St Augustine EP),[81] 1938,[83] 1957.[84]

BICKNOR

AP *LG* Orig pt Eyhorne Hd, perhaps pt Isle of Shep. Lbty or pt Milton Hd,[85] ent Eyhorne Hd by 19th cent, Seq 1 thereafter. *Parl* Seq 9. *Eccl* Sitt. RDn. Gains before 1905 chap Huckinge from Hollingbourn AP,[86] thereafter 'Bicknor with Huckinge' until 1972, at which time divided into 2 EPs of Bicknor, Huckinge.[87] After 1972, Sitt. RDn.

BICKNOR AND HUCKINGE
EP Cr before 1905 by union Bicknor AP, chap Huckinge in Hollingbourn AP.[86] Sitt. RDn. Divided 1972 into 2 EPs of Bicknor, Huckinge.[87]

BIDBOROUGH
AP *LG* Seq 12. Civ bdry: 1886,[88] 1934.[19] *Parl* Seq 16. *Eccl* Seq 26. Eccl bdry: 1968.[89]

BIDDENDEN
AP *LG* Orig pt Berkeley Hd, pt Cranb. Hd, ent Berkeley Hd by 19th cent,[44] Tent. PLU, RSD, RD. *Parl* Seq 11. *Eccl* Seq 5.

BIGGIN HILL
EP Cr 1928 from Cudham AP.[90] Beck. RDn (1928–36), Brom. RDn (1936–*).

BILSINGTON
AP *LG* Pt Newchurch Hd, pt Rom. Marsh Lbty, E Ashf. PLU, RSD, RD. Civ bdry: 1934.[19] *Parl* Seq 5. *Eccl* Seq 10.

BIRCHINGTON
Chap in Monkton AP, sep civ identity early, eccl severed 1871 and united with chap Acol (or 'Wood') of Minster AP to cr Birchington with Acol EP,[4] qv. *LG* Ring. Hd, non-corporate mbr Cq Pt of Dover, in Lbties of Dover, Thanet PLU, RSD, RD. Abol civ 1935 pt to Acol CP, pt to help cr Margate CP.[6] *Parl* E'rn Dv (1832–85), Isle of Thanet Dv (1885–1948).

BIRCHINGTON WITH ACOL
EP Cr 1871 by union chap Birchington of Monkton AP, chap Acol (or 'Wood') of Minster AP.[4] Westb. RDn (1871–1930), Thanet RDn (1930–*). Bdry: 1884 (help cr Westgate on Sea EP).[91]

BIRCHOLT
AP *LG* Birch. Barony/Birch. Franchise & Barony, E Ashf. PLU, RSD, RD. Abol civ 1934 ent to Brabourne AP.[19] *Parl* E'rn Dv (1832–85), S'rn Dv (1885–1918), Ashf. Dv (1918–48). *Eccl* Elham RDn (until 1895), N Lym. RDn (1895–1956). Abol eccl 1956 ent to Brabourne AP.[92]

BIRLING
AP *LG* Seq 4. Civ bdry: 1888,[9] 1898.[93] *Parl* Seq 10. *Eccl* Seq 24. Eccl bdry: 1911 (cr Lower Birling EP).[94]

LOWER BIRLING
EP Cr 1911 from Birling AP.[94] Mall. RDn (1911–36), Cob. RDn (1936–*).

BISHOPSBOURNE
AP Incl chap Barham (sep civ identity early, sep EP 1845[35]). *LG* Seq 20. *Parl* Seq 1. *Eccl* Seq 1.

BLACKHEATH ALL SAINTS
EP Cr 1859 from Lewisham AP.[95] [London dioc 1859–68], Greenw. RDn (1861–86), Lewisham RDn (1886–*). Bdry: 1884,[87] 1960.[96]

BLACKHEATH THE ASCENSION
EP Cr 1883 from Lewisham AP.[97] Greenw. RDn (1883–86), Lewisham RDn (1886–*). Bdry: 1951.[98]

BLACKHEATH ST JOHN THE EVANGELIST
EP Cr 1854, refounded 1868 from Greenwich AP.[99] Greenw. RDn (1868–1954), Greenw. & Deptf. RDn (1954–66), Greenw. RDn (1966–*).

BLACKHEATH PARK
EP Cr 1886 from Charlton next Woolwich AP.[100] Woolw. RDn (1886–1950), Greenw. RDn (1950–54), Greenw. & Deptf. RDn (1954–66), Greenw. RDn (1966–*). Bdry: 1960,[96] 1974.[101]

BLACKMANSTONE
AP *LG* Worth Hd, ent Rom. Marsh Lbty by 19th cent,[44] Rom. Marsh PLU, RSD, RD. Abol civ 1934 pt to Burmarsh AP, pt to Newchurch AP, pt to St Mary in the Marsh AP.[19] *Parl* E'rn Dv (1832–85), S'rn Dv (1885–1918), Ashf. Dv (1918–48). *Eccl* Lym. RDn (until 1873), S Lym. RDn (1873–1963). Abol eccl 1963 ent to Burmarsh AP.[102]

BLEAN
AP Usual eccl spelling; for civ see 'St Cosmus and St Damian in the Blean'. *Eccl* Seq 3.

BOBBING
AP *LG* Seq 29. Civ bdry: 1930.[103] *Parl* Seq 4. *Eccl* Seq 16.

BONNINGTON
AP *LG* Orig Street Hd, by 19th cent pt Street Hd, pt Rom. Marsh Lbty,[44] E Ashf. PLU, RSD, RD. Civ bdry: 1934.[19] *Parl* W'rn Dv (1832–67), West Dv (1867–85), S'rn Dv (1885–1918), Ashf. Dv/CC (1918–*). *Eccl* Seq 10.

BORDEN
AP *LG* Seq 29. Civ bdry: 1930 (help cr Sittingbourne and Milton CP),[33] 1935.[6] *Parl* Seq 4. *Eccl* Seq 16.

BOROUGH GREEN
Cr civ 1934,[19] eccl 1974[104] from Ightham AP, Wrotham AP. *LG* Mall. RD. *Parl* Seven. CC (1948–70), Tonbr. & Mall. CC (1970–*). *Eccl* Shor. RDn.

BORSTAL
EP Cr 1901 from Rochester St Margaret AP.[96] Roch. RDn.

BOUGHTON ALUPH
AP *LG* Seq 31. Civ bdry: 1934.[19] *Parl* Seq 5. *Eccl* Bridge RDn (until 1873), W Bridge RDn (1873–91), E Char. RDn (1891–*).

BOUGHTON MALHERBE
AP *LG* Seq 1. *Parl* Seq 9. *Eccl* Char. RDn (until 1864), E Char. RDn (1864–72), Sutton RDn (1972–*).

BOUGHTON MONCHELSEA
AP *LG* Orig Eyhorne Hd, pt Maid. Hd, pt Eyhorne Hd by 19th cent,[44] Maid. PLU, RSD, RD. Civ bdry: 1888,[105] 1934.[19] *Parl* Seq 9. *Eccl* Seq 17. Eccl bdry: 1970.[106]

BOUGHTON UNDER BLEAN
AP *LG* Seq 22. Civ bdry: 1883,[8] 1934.[19] *Parl* Seq 4. *Eccl* Exempt from Archdeacon (until 1845), Seq 13.

BOXLEY
AP *LG* Seq 6. Civ bdry: 1932.[107] *Parl* Seq 9. *Eccl* Seq 17. Eccl bdry: 1963,[21] 1971 (help cr Maidstone All Saints with St Philip and Holy Trinity EP).[48]

BRABOURNE
AP *LG* Orig pt Wye Hd, pt Birch. Barony, ent Birch. Franchise & Barony by 19th cent,[44] Seq 32 thereafter. Civ bdry: 1934.[19] *Parl* Seq 5.

Eccl Seq 9. Eccl bdry: 1956 (gains Bircholt AP).[92]

BRASTED

AP *LG* Orig pt Westerham Hd, pt Brasted Ville, by 19th cent pt Codsh. Hd, pt Westerham Hd,[44] Seven. PLU, RSD, RD. Civ bdry: 1934.[19] *Parl* Seq 20. *Eccl* Seq 38. Eccl bdry: 1880 (help cr Four Elms EP),[108] 1907.[109]

BREDGAR

AP *LG* Seq 29. *Parl* Seq 4. *Eccl* Seq 16.

BREDHURST

Chap in Hollingbourne AP, sep civ identity early, curacy & self-styled vicarage, eccl sep status sustained.[110] *LG* Seq 1. Civ bdry: 1934.[19] *Parl* Seq 9. *Eccl* Exempt from Archdeacon (until 1845), Sutton RDn (until 1938), Roch. RDn (1938–54), Gill. RDn (1954–72). Eccl bdry: 1884,[112] 1938,[121] 1943,[111] 1963.[21] Abol eccl 1972 to help cr South Gillingham EP.[113]

BRENCHLEY

AP *LG* Orig pt Bren. & Horsm. Hd, pt Twyford Hd (also pt in town Aylesford), ent Bren. & Horsm. Hd by 19th cent,[44] Tonbr. PLU, RSD, RD. Civ bdry: 1934,[19] 1955 (cr Paddock Wood CP).[114] *Parl* Seq 16. *Eccl* Seq 27. Eccl bdry: 1860 (help cr Paddock Wood EP),[115] 1875 (cr Matfield EP).[111]

THE BRENTS

EP Cr 1881 from Preston next Faversham EP, Faversham AP.[116] Ospr. RDn. Bdry: 1947.[117] Abol eccl 1966 to help cr The Brents and Davington EP.[118]

THE BRENTS AND DAVINGTON

EP Cr 1966 by union The Brents EP, Davington AP.[118] Ospr. RDn.

BRENZETT

AP *LG* Orig Aloesb. Hd, by 19th cent pt Aloesb. Hd, pt Rom. Marsh Lbty, pt Cq Pt of New Rom. and Lbties New Rom.,[44] Rom. Marsh PLU, RSD, RD. Civ bdry: 1934.[19] *Parl* Seq 6. *Eccl* Seq 12. Eccl bdry: 1962.[24]

BRIDGE

Chap in Patrixbourne AP, sep civ identity early, no sep eccl identity. *LG* Seq 16. *Parl* Seq 1.

BROADSTAIRS

EP Cr 1850 from St Peter in Thanet AP.[119] Westb. RDn (1850–1930), Thanet RDn (1930–*).

BROADSTAIRS AND ST PETER'S

CP Cr 1935 by union pts Garlinge CP, Ramsgate CP, St Peter CP.[6] *LG* Broadstairs and St Peter's UD. *Parl* Isle of Thanet CC (1948–70), Thanet East BC (1970–*).

BROADWATER

EP Cr 1867 from Frant AP (Sussex, Kent), Eridge Green EP (Sussex),[53] to be in Chich dioc. See entry in Sussex. Bdry: 1889 (help cr Tunbridge Wells King Charles the Martyr EP),[2] 1921.[96]

BROADWATER DOWN

CP Cr 1894 from the Kent pt of Frant AP (Sussex, Kent) in Tunbr. Wells MB.[122] *LG* Ticehurst PLU, Tunbr. Wells MB. Bdry: 1900 (gains pt Frant AP, E Sussex).[147] Abol 1934 ent to Tunbridge Wells MB and CP.[19] *Parl* Tonbr. Dv (1918–48).

BROCKLEY

EP Cr 1901 from Lewisham AP.[123] Lewisham RDn. Abol 1960 pt to help cr Crofton Park St Hilda with St Cyprian EP, pt to Deptford St Peter EP, pt to Lewisham AP.[124]

BROCKLEY HILL

EP Cr 1867 from Forest Hill Christ Church EP.[118] [London dioc 1867–68], Greenw. RDn (1867–86), Lewisham RDn (1886–*). Bdry: 1900 (help cr Crofton Park EP).[100]

BROMLEY

The following have 'Bromley' in their names. Insofar as any existed at a given time: *LG* Brom. & Beck. Hd, Brom. PLU, USD, UD (1894–1903), MB (1903–65). Transf 1965 to Gtr London (Brom. LB).[51] *Parl* W'rn Dv (1832–67), West Dv (1867–85), W'rn Dv (1885–1918), Brom. Parl Bor/BC (1918–70), Gtr London thereafter. *Eccl* Dartf. RDn (until 1864), W Dartf. RDn (1864–1909), Brom. RDn (1909–*).

AP1–BROMLEY [ST PETER AND ST PAUL]–Civ bdry: 1902,[50] 1934 (incl help cr Chislehurst and Sidcup CP).[19] Eccl bdry: 1842 (cr EP2, refounded 1843),[125] 1863 (cr Plaistow EP, refounded 1864),[126] 1866 (cr Bickley EP),[80] 1880 (help cr EP4),[127] 1887,[128] 1906,[129] 1907,[82] 1938 (help cr West Wickham St Mary of Nazareth EP),[63] 1938,[83] 1948 (cr EP5),[130] 1955 (help cr EP1),[131] 1966.[132]

EP1–BROMLEY CHRIST CHURCH–Cr 1955 from AP1, Plaistow EP.[131] Bdry: 1963.[53]

EP2–BROMLEY HOLY TRINITY–Cr 1842, refounded 1843 from AP1.[125] Bdry: 1889 (cr EP7),[2] 1934 (help cr EP6),[81] 1957.[84] Sometimes called 'Bromley Common Holy Trinity'.

EP3–BROMLEY ST ANDREW–Cr 1927 from Plaistow EP.[133] Bdry: 1938.[83]

EP4–BROMLEY ST JOHN THE EVANGELIST–Cr 1880 from AP1, Plaistow EP.[127] Bdry: 1907,[82] 1938.[83]

EP5–BROMLEY ST MARK–Cr 1948 from AP1.[130] Bdry: 1957.[84]

–BROMLEY COMMON HOLY TRINITY–See EP2.

EP6–BROMLEY COMMON ST AUGUSTINE–Cr 1934 from EP7, EP2, Bickley EP.[81] Bdry: 1957.[84]

EP7–BROMLEY COMMON ST LUKE–Cr 1889 from EP2.[2] Bdry: 1907,[82] 1934 (help cr EP6).[81]

BROMPTON

EP Cr 1847 from Chatham AP, Gillingham AP.[134] Roch. RDn (1847–1954), Gill. RDn (1954–56). Abol 1956 to help cr Gillingham St Mark EP.[135]

NEW BROMPTON ST LUKE

EP Cr 1909 from New Brompton St Mark EP, Gillingham AP.[136] Roch. RDn (1909–54), Gill. RDn (1954–*). Now called 'Gillingham St

Luke'.

NEW BROMPTON ST MARK

EP Cr 1863 from Gillingham AP.[137] Roch. RDn (1863–1954), Gill. RDn (1954). Bdry: 1892 (help cr Gillingham St Barnabas EP),[138] 1909 (help cr New Brompton St Luke EP),[136] 1935.[139] Abol 1954 to help cr Gillingham St Mark EP.[135]

BROOK

AP *LG* Orig Wye Hd, pt Wye Hd, pt Chart. & Longb. Hd by 19th cent,[44] E Ashf. PLU, RSD, RD. Civ bdry: 1934.[19] *Parl* Seq 5. *Eccl* Bridge RDn (until 1891),[145] N Lym. RDn (1891–1962), E Char. RDn (1962–69), W Bridge RDn (1969–*).

BROOKLAND

AP *LG* Orig Aloesb. Hd, by 19th cent pt Aloesb. Hd, pt Lbty Cq Pt of New Rom., pt Rom. Marsh Lbty,[44] Rom. Marsh PLU, RSD, RD. Civ bdry: 1883,[8] 1934.[19] *Parl* Seq 5. *Eccl* Seq 12. Eccl bdry: 1935,[25] 1962.[24]

BROOMFIELD

Chap in Leeds AP, sep civ identity early, no sep eccl identity. *LG* Seq 1. *Parl* Seq 9.

BROOMHILL

AP Pt Sussex (Goldspur Hd, Lbty Anc Town/Cq Pt of Winchelsea), pt Kent (Lbty Cq Pt of New Rom.), the latter transf 1895 to E Sussex and the par ent E Sussex thereafter.[146] *LG* Rye PLU, RSD, pt sep RD in Kent (1894–95). *Parl* Kent pt, E'rn Dv (1832–85), S'rn Dv (1885–1918). *Eccl* Church destroyed, early incl in Lydd AP, qv incl the cr of Rye Harbour EP.

BUCKLAND

AP Usual civ spelling; for eccl see 'Buckland near Dover'. *LG* Bewb. Hd, pt Dover Bor, Dover MB (pt 1835–94, ent 1894–96), pt Dover Cq Pt, pt Dover USD, pt Dover RSD. Civ bdry: 1894 (loses the pt not in the MB to River AP),[140] 1895.[141] Abol civ 1896 to help cr Dover CP.[142] *Parl* Pt Dover Parl Bor (1558–1918), pt E'rn Dv (1832–1918).

BUCKLAND

AP *LG* Seq 27. Civ bdry: 1935.[6] *Parl* Seq 4. *Eccl* Ospr. RDn. Eccl bdry: 1940.[117] Abol 1957 ent to Teynham AP.[95]

BUCKLAND NEAR DOVER

AP Usual eccl spelling; for civ see first Buckland above. *Eccl* Exempt from Archdeacon (until 1845), Seq 6. Eccl bdry: 1903 (cr Buckland St Barnabas EP),[129] 1953.[143]

BUCKLAND ST BARNABAS

EP Cr 1903 from Buckland near Dover AP.[129] Dover RDn. Abol 1953 pt to help cr Charlton-near-Dover St Peter and St Paul EP, pt to Buckland near Dover AP.[143]

BURHAM

AP *LG* Seq 4. Civ bdry: 1883,[8] 1888.[9] *Parl* Seq 10. *Eccl* Seq 31. Eccl bdry: 1963,[21] 1966.[31]

BURMARSH

AP *LG* Worth Hd, Rom. Marsh Lbty by 19th cent,[44] Seq 37 thereafter. Civ bdry: 1888 (gains the pt of West Hythe AP not in Hythe MB),[144] 1934 (incl help cr Hythe CP).[19] *Parl* Seq 6. *Eccl* Lym. RDn (until 1873), N Lym. RDn (1873–1914), S Lym. RDn (1914–*). Eccl bdry: 1963 (gains Eastbridge AP, Blackmanstone AP, Orgarswick AP).[102]

CANTERBURY

The following have 'Canterbury' in their names. Insofar as any existed at a given time: *LG* Canterb. Bor/MB/CB, USD, incorp for poor. *Parl* Canterb. Parl Bor (1295–1918), Canterb. Dv/CC (1918–*). *Eccl* Canterb. RDn.

CP1–CANTERBURY–Cr 1897 by union AP1, CP3, CP5, CP6, AP2, AP3, AP4, CP7, AP7, CP9, AP8, AP9, AP10, AP11, AP13, AP14, AP17, AP18, AP19, CP10.[148] Bdry: 1912 (gains CP2, CP4, CP8, Holy Cross Westgate Within CP, St Dunstan Within CP, Thanington Within CP, Staplegate CP),[149] 1934.[150]

AP1–CANTERBURY ALL SAINTS–Abol civ 1897 to help cr CP1.[148] Abol eccl 1938 to help cr EP1.[151]

CP2–CANTERBURY THE ARCHBISHOP'S PALACE PRECINCTS–Ex-par, sep CP 1858.[163] Not in Bor, but in MB/CB. Abol 1912 ent to CP1.[149] *Parl* Canterb. Parl Bor (1832–1918). Retains eccl ex-par status.

CP3–CANTERBURY BLACK PRINCE'S CHANTRY–Ex-par, sep CP 1858.[163] Inclusion in Bor/MB/CB, Parl Bor as for CP2. Abol civ 1897 to help cr CP1,[148] abol eccl 1959 ent to EP2.[152]

CP4–CANTERBURY CHRISTCHURCH–Ex-par, sep CP 1858.[163] Inclusion in Bor/MB/CB, Parl Bor as for CP2. Abol civ 1912 ent to CP1,[149] eccl retains ex-par status. Eccl bdry: 1959.[152]

CP5–CANTERBURY EAST BRIDGE HOSPITAL–Ex-par, sep CP 1858.[163] Inclusion in Bor/MB/CB, Parl Bor as for CP2. Abol civ 1897 to help cr CP1,[148] abol eccl 1959 ent to EP2.[152]

CP6–CANTERBURY OLD CASTLE–Ex-par, sep CP 1858.[163] Inclusion in Bor/MB/CB, Parl Bor as for CP2. Abol civ 1897 to help cr CP1.[148]

AP2–CANTERBURY HOLY CROSS WESTGATE–Pt Canterb. Bor/MB/CB (this pt in Canterb. Incorp [poor], Canterb. USD), pt Westgate Hd (this pt Bridge PLU, Bridge RSD). Abol civ 1894 the pt in the CB to cr Holy Cross Westgate Within CP, the remainder to cr Holy Cross Westgate Without CP.[122] Eccl bdry: 1959.[152] Abol eccl 1965 to help cr EP3.[92]

AP3–CANTERBURY ST ALPHEGE–Abol civ 1897 to help cr CP1.[148] Exempt from Archdeacon (until 1845). Abol eccl 1938 to help cr EP1.[151]

EP1–CANTERBURY ST ALPHEGE AND ST MARY AND ALL SAINTS–Cr 1938 by union AP3, AP14, AP1.[151] Abol 1957 to help cr EP2.[153]

EP2–CANTERBURY ST ALPHEGE WITH ST MARGARET–Cr 1957 by union EP1, EP5.[153] Bdry: 1959 (incl gains areas of CP10, CP5, CP3, Staplegate).[152] Abol 1973 to help cr EP8.[68]

AP4–CANTERBURY ST ANDREW–Abol civ 1897 to help cr CP1.[148] Abol eccl 1888 to help cr EP5.[154]

CP7–CANTERBURY ST AUGUSTINE–Ex-par, sep CP 1858.[163] Inclusion in Bor/MB/CB, Parl Bor as for CP2. Abol 1897 to help cr CP1.[148]

AP5–CANTERBURY ST DUNSTAN–Usual eccl spelling; for civ see 'St Dunstan'. Eccl bdry: 1959.[152] Abol eccl 1965 to help cr EP3.[92]

EP3–CANTERBURY ST DUNSTAN WITH HOLY CROSS–Cr 1965 by union AP5, AP2.[92]

AP6–CANTERBURY ST EDMUND–Abol 1349 ent to AP10.[155]

AP7–CANTERBURY ST GEORGE THE MARTYR–Abol civ 1897 to help cr CP1.[148] Abol eccl 1959 pt to AP10, pt to AP18, pt to EP2.[152]

CP8/EP4–CANTERBURY ST GREGORY THE GREAT–Priory, ex-par within area AP14, sep EP 1852,[156] sep CP 1858.[163] Inclusion in Bor/MB/CB, Parl Bor as for CP2. Abol civ 1912 ent to CP1.[149] Eccl bdry: 1887.[157]

AP8–CANTERBURY ST JOHN–Abol 1349 ent to AP12.[158]

CP9–CANTERBURY ST JOHN'S HOSPITAL–Ex-par, sep CP 1858.[163] Inclusion in Bor/MB/CB, Parl Bor as for CP2. Abol 1897 to help cr CP1.[148]

AP8–CANTERBURY ST MARGARET–Abol civ 1897 to help cr CP1.[148] Abol eccl 1888 to help cr EP5.[154]

EP5–CANTERBURY ST MARGARET WITH ST ANDREW AND ST MARY–Cr 1888 by union AP8, AP4, AP11.[154] Abol 1957 to help cr EP2.[153]

AP9–CANTERBURY ST MARTIN–Civ bdry: 1894 (gains the pt of Littlebourne AP in Canterb. CB).[42] Abol civ 1897 to help cr CP1.[148] Exempt from Archdeacon (until 1845). Abol eccl 1971 to help cr EP6.[159]

EP6–CANTERBURY ST MARTIN AND ST PAUL–Cr 1971 by union AP9, AP18.[159]

AP10–CANTERBURY ST MARY BREDIN–Gains 1349 AP6.[155] Civ bdry: 1894 (gains the pt of Nackington AP in Canterb. CB).[42] Abol civ 1897 to help cr CP1.[148] Eccl bdry: 1959.[152]

AP11–CANTERBURY ST MARY BREDMAN–Abol civ 1897 to help cr CP1.[148] Abol eccl 1888 to help cr EP5.[154]

AP12–CANTERBURY ST MARY DE CASTRO–Gains 1349 AP8.[158] Abol 1684 to AP17, the union civ called as AP17, eccl as EP7.[160]

AP13–CANTERBURY ST MARY MAGDALEN–Gains at unknown mediev date AP16.[162] Abol civ 1897 to help cr CP1.[148] Abol eccl 1959 pt to EP2, pt to eccl ex-par area of CP4.[152]

AP14–CANTERBURY ST MARY NORTHGATE–Civ bdry: 1894 (gains the pts of Fordwich AP, Hackington AP, Sturry AP in Canterb. CB).[42] Abol civ 1897 to help cr CP1.[148] Eccl bdry: 1752 (cr EP4), wich AP, Hackington AP, Sturry AP in Canterb. CB).[42] Abol civ 1897 to help cr CP1.[148] Eccl bdry: 1852 (cr EP4),[156] 1887.[157] Abol eccl 1938 to help cr EP1.[151]

AP15–CANTERBURY ST MARY QUEENGATE–Abol by 1381 to AP16.[161]

AP16–CANTERBURY ST MICHAEL BURGATE–Gains by 1381 AP15.[16] Abol at unknown mediev date to AP13.[162]

AP17–CANTERBURY ST MILDRED–Gains 1684 AP12, the union civ called as AP17, eccl as EP7.[160] Abol civ 1897 to help cr CP1.[148]

EP7–CANTERBURY ST MILDRED WITH ST MARY DE CASTRO–Eccl name for union 1684 of AP17, AP12 (for civ see prev entry).[160]

AP18–CANTERBURY ST PAUL–Civ bdry: 1894 (gains the pts of Beakesbourne AP, Patrixbourne AP in Canterb. CB).[42] Abol civ 1897 to help cr CP1.[148] Eccl bdry: 1959.[152] Abol eccl 1971 to help cr EP6.[159]

AP19–CANTERBURY ST PETER–Abol civ 1897 to help cr CP1.[148] Abol eccl 1973 to help cr EP9.[68]

EP8–CANTERBURY ST PETER AND ST ALPHEGE WITH ST MARGARET–Cr 1973 by union EP2, AP19.[68]

CP10–CANTERBURY WHITE FRIARS–Ex-par, sep CP 1858.[163] Inclusion in Bor/MB/CB as for CP2. Abol civ 1897 to help cr CP1,[148] abol eccl 1959 ent to EP2.[152]

CAPEL

Chap in Tudeley AP, sep civ identity early, sep EP by 1868.[472] *LG* Orig pt Tonbr. Lowey, pt Twyford Hd, pt Washl. Hd, by 19th cent pt Washl. Hd, pt Tonbr. Lowey,[44] Tonbr. PLU, RSD, RD. Bdry: 1883,[8] 1885,[164] 1935.[19] *Parl* Seq 16. *Eccl* Tonbr. RDn. Eccl bdry: 1962.[409]

CAPEL-LE-FERNE

Chap in Alkham AP, sep civ identity early, no sep eccl identity. *LG* Seq 33. Bdry: 1934.[19] *Parl* Seq 3.

CATFORD ST ANDREW

EP Cr 1905 from Catford St Laurence EP.[165] Lewisham RDn. Bdry: 1934.[166]

CATFORD ST LAURENCE

EP Cr 1888 from Lewisham AP.[167] Lewisham RDn. Bdry: 1905 (cr Catford St Andrew EP),[165] 1916 (help cr Lewisham St John, Southend EP),[61] 1934.[166]

CATFORD (SOUTHEND) AND DOWNHAM

EP Renaming 1973 of Lewisham St John, Southend EP.[168] Lewisham RDn.

CHALK

AP *LG* Shamw. Hd, N Ayl. PLU (1835–84), RSD (1875–84), Strood PLU (1884–1930), RSD (1884–94), RD. Civ bdry: 1887.[169] Abol civ

1935 ent to Gravesend AP.[6] *Parl* W'rn Dv (1832–67), Mid Dv (1867–1918), Grav. Dv (1918–48). *Eccl* Seq 33. Eccl bdry: 1934 (help cr Higham with Merston EP),[171] 1954,[170] 1959 (help cr Gravesend St Aidan EP).[172]

CHALLOCK
Chap in Godmersham AP, sep civ identity early, sep EP 1870.[173] *LG* Seq 28. Civ bdry: 1968.[174] *Parl* Seq 5. *Eccl* Exempt from Archdeacon (until 1845), Bridge RDn (until 1873), W Bridge RDn (1873–1928). Abol eccl 1928 to help cr Challock and Molash EP.[175]

CHALLOCK AND MOLASH
EP Cr 1928 by union Molash EP, Challock EP.[175] W Bridge RDn. Bdry: 1965.[176]

CHARING
AP Incl chap Egerton (sep civ identity early, sep EP 1814[177]). *LG* Seq 23. Addtl civ bdry alt: 1935,[6] 1957.[178] *Parl* Seq 5. *Eccl* Exempt from Archdeacon (until 1845), Seq 4. Addtl eccl bdry alt: 1874 (incl cr Charing Heath EP),[179] 1940,[180] 1970.[181]

CHARING HEATH
EP Cr 1874 from Charing AP, Lenham AP.[179] E Char. RDn.

CHARLTON
AP Usual civ spelling; for eccl see following entry. *LG* Bewsb. Hd, pt Dover Bor, Dover MB (pt 1835–94, ent 1894–96), pt Cq Pt of Dover, River PLU (renamed Dover in 1840s), pt Dover USD, pt Dover RSD. Civ bdry: 1894 (loses the pt not in the MB to Guston AP),[140] 1895.[141] Abol civ 1896 to help cr Dover CP.[182] *Parl* Pt Dover Parl Bor (1558–1918), pt E'rn Dv (1832–1918).

CHARLTON BY DOVER
AP Usual eccl spelling; for civ see prev entry. *Eccl* Dover RDn. Eccl bdry: 1877 (cr Charlton by Dover St Bartholomew EP).[183] Abol eccl 1953 pt to help cr Charlton-by-Dover St Peter and St Paul EP, pt to Dover St Mary the Virgin AP.[143]

CHARLTON BY DOVER ST BARTHOLOMEW
EP Cr 1877 from Charlton by Dover AP.[183] Dover RDn. Abol 1972 to help cr Dover, Charlton EP.[184]

CHARLTON-BY-DOVER ST PETER AND ST PAUL
EP Cr 1953 by union pt Charlton by Dover AP, pt Buckland St Barnabas EP.[143] Dover RDn. Abol 1972 to help cr Dover, Charlton EP.[184]

CHARLTON NEXT WOOLWICH
AP *LG* Blackh. Hd, Lewisham PLU (1836–68), Woolw. PLU (1868–89), Plumstead Dist (Metrop Bd Wks). Transf 1889 to London.[190] *Parl* Greenw. Parl Bor (pt 1832–67, ent 1867–1918), London thereafter. *Eccl* Dartf. RDn (until 1845), [London dioc 1845–68], Greenw. RDn (1861–68), Woolw. RDn (1868–1908). Eccl bdry: 1845 (help cr Woolwich St Thomas EP),[138] 1862 (cr Charlton St Paul EP),[185] 1867 (help cr Kidbrooke EP),[191] 1886 (cr Blackheath Park EP).[100] Abol eccl 1908 to help cr Old Charlton St Luke with St Paul EP.[57]

CHARLTON ST PAUL
EP Cr 1862 from Charlton next Woolwich AP.[185] [London dioc 1862–68], Greenw. RDn (1862–68), Woolw. RDn (1868–1908). Bdry: 1886 (cr New Charlton EP).[186] Abol 1908 to help cr Old Charlton St Luke with St Paul EP.[57]

NEW CHARLTON
EP Cr 1886 from Charlton St Paul EP.[186] Woolw. RDn (1886–1947), Greenw. RDn (1947–54), Greenw. & Deptf. RDn (1954–66), Greenw. RDn (1966–*).

OLD CHARLTON ST LUKE WITH ST PAUL
EP Cr 1908 by union Charlton next Woolwich AP, Charlton St Paul EP.[57] RDns as for New Charlton, from 1908. Bdry: 1935,[187] 1937,[188] 1953.[189]

GREAT CHART
AP *LG* Orig pt Calehill Hd, pt Chart & Longb. Hd, ent Chart & Longb. Hd by 19th cent,[44] Seq 25 thereafter. *Parl* Seq 5. *Eccl* Seq 4.

LITTLE CHART
AP *LG* Calehill Hd, W Ashf. PLU (1836–1930), RSD, RD. Civ bdry: 1935,[6] 1957.[178] *Parl* Seq 5. *Eccl* Seq 4. Eccl bdry: 1970.[181]

CHARTHAM
AP *LG* Orig pt Felb. Hd, pt Bridge & Petham Hd, by 19th cent pt Felb. Hd, pt Westgate Hd,[44] Bridge PLU, RSD, RD (1894–1934), Bridge-Blean RD (1934–74). *Parl* Seq 1. *Eccl* Seq 2.

CHATHAM
The following have 'Chatham' in their names. Insofar as any existed at a given time: *LG* Chatham & Gill. Hd, pt Roch. Bor, Medway PLU, Chatham MB (pt 1890–1934, ent 1934–74), Medway RSD (ent 1875–90, pt 1890–94), pt Chatham USD (1890–94), pt Roch. MB (1894–1934), pt Gill. UD (1894–1903), pt Gill. MB (1903–06). *Parl* Pt Chatham Parl Bor (1832–1918), pt W'rn Dv (1832–67), pt Mid Dv (1867–1918); for 1918–48, pt Roch., Gill. Parl Bor, pt Roch., Chatham Parl Bor; Roch. & Chatham BC (1948–*). *Eccl* Roch. RDn.

AP1–CHATHAM [ST MARY]–Civ bdry: 1894 (gains the pt of Gillingham AP in Chatham MB),[192] 1906 (loses the pt in Gill. MB to Gillingham AP),[193] 1934 (loses the pt in Roch. MB to help cr Rochester CP).[19] Eccl bdry: 1842 (cr Luton EP, refounded 1852),[195] 1847 (help cr Brompton EP),[134] 1852 (cr EP2),[196] 1855 (help cr EP4).[197] Abol eccl 1964 to help cr EP3.[194]

EP1–CHATHAM ALL SAINTS–Cr 1914 from Luton EP, EP4.[129]

EP2–CHATHAM ST JOHN–Cr 1852 from AP1.[196] Bdry: 1855 (help cr EP4),[197] 1954 (help cr EP6),[198] 1955 (help cr EP5).[199] Abol 1964 to help cr EP3.[194]

EP3–CHATHAM ST MARY AND ST JOHN–Cr 1964 by union AP1, EP2.[194]

EP4–CHATHAM ST PAUL–Cr 1855 from AP1, Gillingham AP, EP2.[197] Bdry: 1954 (help cr EP6).[198]

EP5–CHATHAM ST PHILIP AND ST JAMES–Cr 1955 from EP2, Luton EP.[199] Bdry: 1963,[21] 1966,[31] 1967 (incl help cr EP7).[37]

EP6–CHATHAM ST STEPHEN–Cr 1954 from Rochester St Peter EP, EP2, EP4.[198] Bdry: 1966.[31]

EP7–CHATHAM ST WILLIAM–Cr 1967 from EP5, Aylesford AP.[37]

CHELSFIELD

AP Incl chap Farnborough (sep civ identity early, sep EP 1876[200]). *LG* Ruxley Hd, Brom. PLU, RSD, RD. Abol civ 1934 ent to Orpington AP.[19] *Parl* W'rn Dv (1832–67), West Dv (1867–85), W'rn Dv (1885–1918), Chisl. Dv (1918–48). *Eccl* Dartf. RDn (until 1864), W Dartf. RDn (1864–1909), Brom. RDn (1909–54), Orp. RDn (1954–*). Eccl bdry: 1938,[203] 1938 (cr Greenstreet Green EP),[201] 1940 (help cr Orpington Christ Church EP).[202]

CHERITON

AP Incl chap Sandgate (sep EP 1854 [see Sandgate for all pars involved in this cr],[204] sep CP 1894 [the pt in Sandgate USD][122]). *LG* Folk. Hd, Elham PLU, pt Sandgate USD, pt Elham RSD, Elham RD (1894–98), Cheriton UD (1898–1934). Addtl civ bdry alt: 1886 (loses the pt in Hythe Parl Bor [not prev in Hythe MB] to St Leonard Hythe CP).[205] Abol civ 1934 pt to help cr Hythe CP, pt to Folkestone CP.[19] *Parl* Hythe Parl Bor (pt 1832–1918, ent 1918–48), pt E'rn Dv (1832–1918). *Eccl* Seq 7. Addtl eccl bdry alt: 1892 (help cr Cheriton Street EP),[206] 1938.[207]

CHERITON STREET

EP Cr 1892 from Cheriton AP, Folkestone AP.[206] Elham RDn. Bdry: 1953.[167]

CHEVENING

AP *LG* Orig pt Codsh. Hd, pt Somerden Hd, ent Codsh. Hd by 19th cent,[44] Seq 40 thereafter. *Parl* Seq 20. *Eccl* Seq 38. Eccl bdry: 1852 (help refound Ide Hill EP [cr 1818 from Sundridge AP]).[208]

CHIDDINGSTONE

AP *LG* Orig pt Somerden Hd, pt Ruxley Hd, by 19th cent ent Somerden Hd,[44] Penshurst PLU (1835–1840s), Seven. PLU (1840s–1930), RSD, RD. Civ bdry: 1934.[19] *Parl* Seq 19. *Eccl* Seq 37. Eccl bdry: 1852 (help refound Ide Hill EP [cr 1818 from Sundridge AP]),[208] 1880 (help cr Four Elms EP),[108] 1906 (help cr Chiddingstone Causeway EP).[209]

CHIDDINGSTONE CAUSEWAY

EP Cr 1906 from Chiddingstone AP, Leigh AP, Penshurst AP.[209] Tonbr. RDn.

CHILHAM

AP Incl chap Molash (sep civ identity early, sep EP 1871[4]). *LG* Seq 28. Addtl civ bdry alt: 1935.[6] *Parl* Seq 5. *Eccl* Seq 2.

CHILLENDEN

AP *LG* Eastry Hd, PLU, RSD, RD. Abol civ 1935 ent to Godnestone AP.[6] *Parl* E'rn Dv (1832–1918), Dover Dv (1918–48). *Eccl* Bridge RDn (until 1873), E Bridge RDn (1873–1940). Abol eccl 1940 to help cr Chillenden with Knowlton EP.[180]

CHILLENDON WITH KNOWLTON

EP Cr 1940 by union Chillendon AP, Knowlton AP.[180] E Bridge RDn.

CHISLEHURST

AP *LG* Orig pt Blackh. Hd, pt Ruxley Hd, ent Ruxley Hd by 19th cent,[44] Brom. PLU, RSD, RD (1894–1900), Chisl. UD (1900–34). Abol civ 1934 pt to help cr Chislehurst and Sidcup CP, pt to Bromley AP, pt to Orpington AP.[19] *Parl* W'rn Dv (1832–67), West Dv (1867–85), W'rn Dv (1885–1918), Chisl. Dv (1918–45). *Eccl* Dartf. RDn (until 1864), W Dartf. RDn (1864–1909), Brom. RDn (1909–36), Chisl. RDn (1936–65), Brom. RDn (1965–*). Eccl bdry: 1843 (cr Sidcup St John EP, refounded 1844),[211] 1875 (cr Chislehurst The Annunciation EP),[111] 1906,[129] 1906 (help cr Chislehurst Christ Church EP),[81] 1935 (help cr Petts Wood EP),[82] 1938,[83] 1940,[180] 1959 (help cr St Paul's Cray St Barnabas EP).[210]

CHISLEHURST THE ANNUNCIATION

EP Cr 1875 from Chislehurst AP.[111] RDns as for Chislehurst AP, from 1875. Bdry: 1938,[83] 1954.[166]

CHISLEHURST CHRIST CHURCH

EP Cr 1906 from Chislehurst AP, Bickley EP.[81] RDns as for Chislehurst AP, from 1906. Bdry: 1938.[83]

CHISLEHURST AND SIDCUP

CP Cr 1934 by union North Cray AP, Mottingham CP, Sidcup CP, and pts of St Mary Cray CP, St Paul's Cray CP, Orpington AP, Chislehurst AP, Bromley AP.[19] *LG* Chisl. & Sidcup UD (1934–65). Bdry: 1937.[72] Transf 1965 to Gtr London (pt Bexley LB, pt Brom. LB).[51] *Parl* Chisl. CC (1945–70), Gtr London thereafter.

CHISLET

AP *LG* Bleang. Hd, pt Lbty Fordwich and thus pt Fordwich corporate mbr Cq Pt of Sandw., Blean PLU, RSD, RD (1894–1934), Bridge-Blean RD (1934–74). Civ bdry: 1934.[19] *Parl* Seq 1. *Eccl* Westb. RDn (until 1930), Canterb. RDn (1930–*). Eccl bdry: 1960.[212]

CHRISTCHURCH–See CANTERBURY CHRISTCHURCH

CLIFFE

AP Usual civ spelling; for eccl see 'Cliffe at Hoo'. *LG* Seq 8. Civ bdry: 1968.[213] *Parl* Seq 8.

EAST CLIFFE

Ex-par, sep CP 1858,[163] eccl abol 1873 ent to Dover St James AP.[239] *LG* Not in Dover Bor, pt Cq Pt of Dover, Dover MB (1835–96), USD (1875–94). Bdry: 1894 (gains the pt of Guston AP in Dover MB),[140] 1895.[141] Abol 1896 to help cr Dover CP.[182] *Parl* Dover Parl Bor (1835–1918).

WEST CLIFFE

AP *LG* Bewsb. Hd, River PLU (renamed Dover in 1840s), Dover RSD, RD. Abol civ 1934 pt to East Langdon AP, pt to St Margaret's at Cliffe AP.[19] *Parl* E'rn Dv (1832–1918), Dover Dv

(1918–48). *Eccl* Seq 6.

CLIFFE AT HOO

AP Usual eccl spelling; for civ see 'Cliffe'. *Eccl* Pec jurisd Cliffe at Hoo (until 1845), Roch. RDn (1845–62), Grav. RDn (1862–1909), Cliffe at Hoo RDn (1909–54), Strood RDn (1954–58). Eccl bdry: 1949.[31] Abol eccl 1958 to help cr Cliffe at Hoo with Cooling EP.[214]

CLIFFE AT HOO WITH COOLING

EP Cr 1958 by union Cliffe at Hoo EP, Cooling AP.[218] Strood RDn.

CLIFTONVILLE

EP Cr 1874 from Margate Trinity EP.[215] Westb. RDn (1874–1930), Thanet RDn (1930–*). Now called 'Margate St Paul'.

COBHAM

AP *LG* Orig pt Hoo Hd, pt Shamw Hd, by 19th cent ent Shamw. Hd,[44] Seq 8 thereafter. Civ bdry: 1935,[6] 1962,[216] 1963.[213] *Parl* Seq 8. Parl bdry: 1964.[480] *Eccl* Seq 29. Eccl bdry: 1939.[217]

COLDRED

AP *LG* Bewsb. Hd, River PLU (renamed Dover in 1840s), Dover RSD, RD. Abol civ 1963 to help cr Shepherdswell with Coldred CP.[219] *Parl* E'rn Dv (1832–1918), Dover Dv/CC (1918–70). *Eccl* Sandw. RDn. Eccl bdry: 1970.[221] Abol eccl 1970 to help cr Sibertswold with Coldred EP.[220]

COLLIER STREET

EP Cr 1858 from Yalding AP.[221] Mall. RDn (1858–64), N Mall. RDn (1864–1906), Mall. RDn (1906–*). Bdry: 1860 (help cr Paddock Wood EP).[115]

COOLING

AP *LG* Shamw. Hd, Hoo PLU, RSD, RD (1894–1935), Strood RD (1935–74). Civ bdry: 1887,[223] 1963 (help cr Hoo St Werburgh CP).[213] *Parl* Seq 8. *Eccl* Roch. RDn (until 1862), Grav. RDn (1862–1909), Cliffe at Hoo RDn (1909–). Abol eccl 19 to help cr Cliffe at Hoo with Cooling EP.[218]

COWDEN

AP *LG* Orig pt Axton/Axton, Dartf. & Wilm. Hd, pt Somerden Hd, pt Westerham Hd, by 19th cent pt Somerden Hd, pt Westerham Hd,[44] Penshurst PLU (1835–1840s), Seven. PLU (1840s–1930), RSD, RD. *Parl* Seq 19. *Eccl* Seq 26. Eccl bdry: 1839 (help cr Mark Beech EP).[224]

COXHEATH

CP Cr 1964 from East Farleigh AP, Hunton AP, Linton AP, Loose AP.[225] *LG* Maid. RD. *Parl* Maid. CC (1970–*).

CRANBROOK

AP *LG* Orig pt Cranb. Hd, pt E Barnfield Hd, pt Berkeley Hd, by 19th cent ent Cranb. Hd,[44] Seq 26 thereafter. *Parl* Seq 12. *Eccl* Seq 5. Eccl bdry: 1842 (cr Sissinghurst [or Trinity, Cranbrook] EP).[226]

FOOTS CRAY

AP Sometimes 'Footscray'. *LG* Ruxley Hd, Brom. PLU, RSD, RD (1894–1902), Foots Cray UD (1902–21), Sidcup UD (1921–25). Civ bdry: 1883,[8] 1910.[71] Renamed civ 1925 'Sidcup'.[240] *Parl* W'rn Dv (1832–67), West Dv (1867–85), N-W'rn Dv (1885–1918), Chisl. Dv (1918–45). *Eccl* Seq 22. Eccl bdry: 1938,[83] 1968,[227] 1969 (help cr Sidcup St Andrew EP).[76]

NORTH CRAY

AP *LG* Ruxley Hd, Brom. PLU, RSD, RD. Abol civ 1934 to help cr Chislehurst and Sidcup CP.[19] *Parl* As for Foots Cray. *Eccl* Seq 22. Eccl bdry: 1968,[227] 1969 (help cr Sidcup St Andrew EP),[76] 1972.[77]

ST MARY CRAY

Chap in Orpington AP, sep civ identity early, sep EP 1867.[228] *LG* Ruxley Hd, Brom. PLU, RSD, RD. Abol civ 1934 pt to help cr Chislehurst and Sidcup CP, pt to Orpington AP.[19] *Parl* As for Foots Cray. *Eccl* Shor. RDn (until 1845), Dartf. RDn (1845–64), W Dartf. RDn (1864–1909), Brom. RDn (1909–54), Orp. RDn (1954–*). Eccl bdry: 1852 (when chap, cr Crocken Hill EP),[229] 1938,[83] 1959 (help cr St Paul's Cray St Barnabas EP).[210]

ST PAUL'S CRAY

AP *LG* Ruxley Hd, Brom. PLU, RSD, RD. Abol civ 1934 pt to help cr Chislehurst and Sidcup CP, pt to Orpington AP.[19] *Parl* As for Foots Cray. *Eccl* Dartf. RDn (until 1864), thereafter as for St Mary Cray. Eccl bdry: 1938,[83] 1959 (help cr St Paul's Cray St Barnabas EP),[210] 1968.[227]

ST PAUL'S CRAY ST BARNABAS

EP Cr 1959 from Chislehurst AP, St Paul's Cray AP, St Mary Cray EP.[210] Orp. RDn.

CRAYFORD

AP *LG* Lessness Hd, Dartf. PLU, RSD, RD (1894–1920), Crayford UD (1920–65). Civ bdry: 1934.[19] Transf 1965 to Gtr London (Bexley LB).[51] *Parl* W'rn Dv (1832–67), West Dv (1867–85), N-W'rn Dv (1885–1918), Dartf. Dv (1918–45), Dartf. BC (1945–55), Erith & Chatham BC (1955–70), Gtr London thereafter. *Eccl* Shor. RDn (until 1845), Dartf. RDn (1845–64), E Dartf. RDn (1864–1909), Dartf. RDn (1909–65), Erith RDn (1965–*). Eccl bdry: 1880,[230] 1925 (help cr Slade Green EP),[231] 1937 (help cr Barnehurst EP).[40]

CROCKEN HILL

EP Cr 1852 from Eynsford AP, chap St Mary Cray of Orpington AP.[229] Dartf. RDn (1852–64), E Dartf. RDn (1864–1909), Brom. RDn (1909–36), Chisl. RDn (1936–65), Dartf. RDn (1965–*). Bdry: 1868,[27] 1901 (help cr Swanley St Mary EP),[232] 1969.[87]

CROCKHAM HILL

EP Cr 1863 from Westerham AP.[177] Shor. RDn (1863–1909), Seven. RDn (1909–73), Tonbr. RDn (1973–*). Bdry: 1880 (help cr Four Elms EP).[108]

CROFTON ST PAUL

EP Cr 1959 from Orpington AP.[233] Brom. RDn. Bdry: 1957.[84]

CROFTON PARK

EP Cr 1900 from Lewisham AP, Brockley Hill EP, Perry Hill EP.[100] Lewisham RDn. Abol 1960 to help cr Crofton Park St Hilda with St Cyprian EP.[124]

CROFTON PARK ST HILDA WITH ST CYPRIAN
EP Cr 1960 by union Crofton Park EP, pt Brockley EP, pt Lewisham AP.[124] Lewisham RDn.

CRUNDALE
AP *LG* Seq 31. Civ bdry: 1934.[19] *Parl* Seq 5. *Eccl* Seq 2.

CUDHAM
AP *LG* Ruxley Hd, Brom. PLU, RSD, RD. Abol civ 1934 ent to Orpington AP.[19] *Parl* W'rn Dv (1832–67), West Dv (1867–85), W'rn Dv (1885–1918), Chisl. Dv (1918–48). *Eccl* Dartf. RDn (until 1864), W Dartf. RDn (1864–1909), Beck. RDn (1909–36), Seven. RDn (1936–54), Orp. RDn (1954–*). Eccl bdry: 1928 (cr Biggin Hill EP),[90] 1938,[203] 1970.[234]

CUXTON
AP *LG* Seq 8. Civ bdry: 1934,[19] 1962,[216] 1963.[213] *Parl* Seq 8. Parl bdry: 1964.[480] *Eccl* Seq 34.

DARENTH
AP *LG* Seq 39. Civ bdry: 1955.[29] *Parl* Seq 17. *Eccl* Shor. RDn (until 1845), Roch. RDn (1845–62), Grav. RDn (1862–1936), Dartf. RDn (1936–*).

DARTFORD
AP *LG* Dartf. & Wilm. Hd/Axton, Dartf. & Wilm. Hd, Dartf. PLU, USD, UD (1894–1933), MB (1933–74). Civ bdry: 1934.[19] *Parl* W'rn Dv (1832–67), West Dv (1867–85), N-W'rn Dv (1885–1918), Dartf. Dv (1918–45), BC (1945–55), CC (1955–*). *Eccl* Seq 22. Eccl bdry: 1903 (cr Dartford St Alban EP),[235] 1910 (cr Dartford Christ Church EP).[236]

DARTFORD CHRIST CHURCH
EP Cr 1910 from Dartford AP.[236] Dartf. RDn. Bdry: 1972.[77]

DARTFORD ST ALBAN
EP Cr 1903 from Dartford AP.[235] E Dartf. RDn (1903–09), Dartf. RDn (1909–*). Bdry: 1956 (help cr Dartford St Edmund, King and Martyr EP).[237]

DARTFORD ST EDMUND, KING AND MARTYR
EP Cr 1956 from Dartford St Alban EP, Stone AP.[237] Dartf. RDn.

DAVINGTON
AP *LG* Fav. Hd, PLU, RSD, RD. Abol civ 1935 pt to help cr Faversham CP, pt to Luddenham AP, pt to Oare AP.[6] *Parl* E'rn Dv (1832–85), N-E'rn Dv (1885–1918), Fav. Dv (1918–48). *Eccl* Ospr. RDn. Abol eccl 1966 to help cr The Brents and Davington EP.[118]

DEAL
AP *LG* Orig pt Bewsb. Hd, pt Corn. Hd, ent Bewsb. Hd by 19th cent,[44] Deal Bor/MB, USD and thus corporate mbr Cq Pt of Sandw. (under jurisd Sandw. until 1835), Eastry PLU (1836–1930). Civ bdry: 1935.[6] *Parl* Sandw. Parl Bor (1832–85), E'rn Dv (1885–1918), Dover Dv/CC (1918–70), Dover & Deal CC (1970–*). *Eccl* Exempt from Archdeacon (until 1845), Seq 14. Eccl bdry: 1852 (cr Deal St Andrew EP, Deal St George EP),[238] 1963.[102]

DEAL ST ANDREW
EP Cr 1852 from Deal AP.[238] Sandw. RDn. Bdry: 1963.[102]

DEAL ST GEORGE
EP Cr 1852 from Deal AP.[238] Sandw. RDn. Bdry: 1963.[102]

DENTON
AP *LG* Pt Kingh. Hd, pt Eastry Hd (perhaps ent Eastry Hd at early date[241]), River PLU (renamed Dover in 1840s), Dover RSD, RD. Civ bdry: 1934.[19] Abol civ 1963 to help cr Denton with Wootton CP.[219] *Parl* E'rn Dv (1832–1918), Dover Dv/CC (1918–70). *Eccl* Elham RDn (until 1895), Dover RDn (1895–*).

DENTON
AP *LG* Shamw. Hd, N Ayl. PLU (1835–84), RSD (1875–84), Strood PLU (1884–1930), RSD (1884–94), Strood RD. Abol civ 1935 ent to Gravesend AP.[6] *Parl* W'rn Dv (1832–67), Mid Dv (1867–1918), Grav. Dv (1918–48). *Eccl* Seq 8.

DENTON WITH WOOTTON
CP Cr 1963 by union Denton AP, Wootton AP.[219] *LG* Dover RD. *Parl* Dover & Deal CC (1970–*).

DEPTFORD
The following have 'Deptford' in their names. Insofar as any existed at a given time: *LG* Hd sep noted, Greenw. PLU, Dist (Metrop Bd Wks). Transf 1889 to London.[190] *Parl* W'rn Dv (1832–67), West Dv (1867–85), 1885–1918 sep noted, London thereafter. *Eccl* Dartf. RDn (until 1845), [London dioc 1845–68], Greenw. RDn (1861–79), Deptf. RDn (1879–86), Greenw. RDn (1886–1954), Greenw. & Deptf. RDn (1954–66), Lewisham RDn (1966–*).

EP1–DEPTFORD CHRIST CHURCH–Cr 1871 from EP6.[242] Abol 1936 to help cr EP5.[74]

EP2–DEPTFORD ST JOHN–Cr 1855 from EP6.[243] Bdry: 1871 (cr EP8),[244] 1887.[77]

EP3–DEPTFORD ST LUKE–Cr 1873 from EP6.[59] Bdry: 1951.[98]

EP4–DEPTFORD ST MARK–Cr 1884 from EP6.[245] Abol 1921 to help cr EP7.[227]

AP1–DEPTFORD ST NICHOLAS–*LG* Pt Kent (Blackh. Hd), pt Surrey (Hatcham, in Brixton Hd). In 1730, CP1/EP6 cr from this par from the Surrey pt and pt of the area in Kent, so that AP1 ent Kent thereafter.[246] *Parl* Greenw. Parl Bor (1832–1918), London thereafter. Abol eccl 1936 to help cr EP5.[74]

EP5–DEPTFORD ST NICHOLAS WITH CHRIST CHURCH–Cr 1936 by union AP1, EP1.[74] Bdry: 1951.[98]

CP1/EP6–DEPTFORD ST PAUL–Cr 1730 from the Surrey pt (Hatcham, in Brixton Hd), and pt of the area in Kent of AP1.[246] *Parl* Greenw. Parl Bor (1832–85), Deptf. Parl Bor (1885–1918), London thereafter. Eccl bdry: 1845 (cr Hatcham St James EP, in Surrey),[248] 1855 (cr EP2),[243] 1871 (cr EP1),[242] 1873 (cr EP3),[59] 1884 (cr EP4).[245] Abol eccl 1921 to help cr EP7.[227]

EP7–DEPTFORD ST PAUL WITH ST MARK–Cr 1921 by union EP6, EP4.[227] Bdry: 1951.[98]
EP8–DEPTFORD ST PETER–Cr 1871 from EP2.[244] Bdry: 1960.[124]

DETLING
Chap in Maidstone AP, sep par by 1643.[247] *LG* Seq 6. *Parl* Seq 9. *Eccl* Exempt from Archdeacon (until 1845), Seq 17. Eccl bdry: 1963.[21]

DITTON
AP *LG* Seq 4. Civ bdry: 1888.[9] *Parl* Seq 10. *Eccl* Seq 24.

DODDINGTON
AP *LG* Seq 30. Civ bdry: 1935.[6] *Parl* Seq 4. *Eccl* Seq 13.

DOVER
The following have 'Dover' in their names. Insofar as any existed at a given time: *LG* Dover Bor/MB, Cq Pt of Dover, River PLU (renamed Dover in 1840s), Dover USD. *Parl* Dover Parl Bor (1558–1918), Dover Dv/CC (1918–70), Dover & Deal CC (1970–*). *Eccl* Dover RDn.
CP1–DOVER–Cr 1896 by union AP5, AP1, Hougham AP.[182] Bdry: 1903,[249] 1931,[250] 1934,[19] 1951.[251]
CP2–DOVER CASTLE–Ex-par, sep CP 1858.[163] *LG* In Dover Bor from 1814, PLU (1858[120]–1930). Abol 1934 ent to Dover CP.[19]
EP1–DOVER, CHARLTON–Cr 1972 by union Charlton by Dover St Bartholomew EP, Charlton-by-Dover St Peter and St Paul EP.[184]
AP1–DOVER ST JAMES THE APOSTLE–Civ bdry: 1883.[8] Abol 1896 to help cr CP1.[182] Exempt from Archdeacon (until 1845). Eccl bdry: 1857,[252] 1873 (incl gains ex-par East Cliffe).[239]
AP2–DOVER ST JOHN–Early destroyed.
EP2–DOVER ST MARTIN–Cr 1903 from Hougham-in-Dover EP.[253]
AP3–DOVER ST MARTIN THE GREATER–Early destroyed.
AP4–DOVER ST MARTIN THE LESS–Early destroyed.
AP5–DOVER ST MARY THE VIRGIN–Civ bdry: 1883.[8] Abol civ 1896 to help CP1.[182] Exempt from Archdeacon (until 1845). Eccl bdry: 1841 (cr EP3),[254] 1885,[255] 1953.[244]
AP6–DOVER ST NICHOLAS–Early destroyed.
AP7–DOVER ST PETER–Early destroyed.
EP3–DOVER TRINITY–Cr 1841 from AP5.[254] Bdry: 1854,[256] 1857,[252] 1885,[255] 1901,[133] 1934.[80] Abol 1953 ent to AP5.[244]

DOWNE
Chap in Orpington AP, sep civ identity early, sep EP 1861.[177] *LG* Ruxley Hd, Brom. PLU, RSD, RD. Abol civ 1934 ent to Orpington AP.[19] *Parl* W'rn Dv (1832–67), West Dv (1867–85), W'rn Dv (1885–1918), Chisl. Dv (1918–48). *Eccl* Shor. RDn (1861–64), W Dartf. RDn (1864–1909), Beck. RDn (1909–36), Brom. RDn (1936–54), Orp. RDn (1954–*).

DUNKIRK
Ex-par ville or lbty, sep CP 1858,[163] sep EP 1916.[257] *LG* Westgate Hd, Fav. PLU, RSD, RD (1894–1934), Swale RD (1934–74). Civ bdry: 1934 (incl help cr Whitstable CP).[19] *Parl* E'rn Dv (1867–85), N-E'rn Dv (1885–1918), pt Fav. Dv, pt Canterb. Dv (1918–48), Fav. CC (1948–*). *Eccl* Exempt from Archdeacon (until 1845), Ospr. RDn.

DUNTON GREEN
Cr eccl 1890,[242] civ 1909[258] from Otford AP. *LG* Seven. PLU, RD. *Parl* Seven. Dv/CC (1918–*). *Eccl* Shor. RDn (1890–1909), Seven. RDn (1909–*).

DYMCHURCH
AP *LG* Orig Worth Hd, Rom. Marsh Lbty by 19th cent,[44] Seq 37 thereafter. Civ bdry: 1883,[8] 1886,[259] 1934,[19] 1951.[260] *Parl* Seq 6. *Eccl* Seq 12. Eccl bdry: 1927,[201] 1933.[261]

EASTBRIDGE
AP *LG* Orig Worth Hd, Rom. Marsh Lbty by 19th cent,[44] Rom. Marsh PLU, RSD, RD. Abol civ 1934 ent to Burmarsh AP.[19] *Parl* E'rn Dv (1832–85), S'rn Dv (1885–1918), Ashf. Dv (1918–48). *Eccl* Lym. RDn (until 1873), S Lym. RDn (1873–1963). Abol eccl 1963 ent to Burmarsh AP.[102]

EASTCHURCH
AP *LG* Isle of Sheppey Lbty (perhaps orig Milton Hd[262]), Sheppey PLU, RSD, RD. Abol civ 1968 to help cr Queenborough-in-Sheppey MB and CP.[263] *Parl* E'rn Dv (1832–85), N-E'rn Dv (1885–1918), Fav. Dv/CC (1918–70). *Eccl* Seq 16. Eccl bdry: 1962.[264]

EASTLING
AP *LG* Seq 27. *Parl* Seq 4. *Eccl* Seq 13.

EASTRY
AP Incl chap Worth (sep civ identity early, sep EP 1854[265]). *LG* Pt Eastry Hd, pt Wingham Hd (perhaps ent Eastry Hd at early date[266]), Eastry PLU, RSD, RD. Addtl civ bdry alt: 1935.[6] *Parl* Seq 3. *Eccl* Exempt from Archdeacon (until 1845), Seq 14. Eccl bdry: 1894.[69]

EASTWELL
AP *LG* Seq 31. Civ bdry: 1934.[19] *Parl* Seq 5. *Eccl* Seq 4.

EBONY
Chap in Appledore AP, sep civ identity early, eccl severed 1928 to help cr Stone with Ebony EP,[23] the latter divided 1972 into 2 EPs of Stone, Ebony,[267] Ebony EP less orig detached pt. *LG* Pt Tent. Hd, pt Tent. Bor/MB, pt Tent. corporate mbr Anc Town/Cq Pt of Rye, Tent. PLU, pt Tent. USD, pt Tent. RSD. Abol civ 1894 the pt in the MB to Tenterden AP, the remainder to help cr Stone cum Ebony CP.[268] *Parl* Pt E'rn Dv (1832–85), pt W'rn Dv (1832–67), pt Mid Dv (1867–85), S'rn Dv (1885–1918). *Eccl* S Lym. RDn (1972–*).

EDENBRIDGE
Chap in Westerham AP, sep civ identity early, sep EP 1814.[177] *LG* Westerham Hd (perhaps orig pt Somerden Hd, pt Westerham Hd[269]), Penshurst PLU (1835–1840s), Seven. PLU (1840s–1930), RSD, RD. Civ bdry: 1934.[19] *Parl* Seq 19. *Eccl* Seq 26. Eccl bdry: 1880 (help

cr Four Elms EP).[108]

EGERTON

Chap in Charing AP, sep civ identity early, sep EP 1814.[177] *LG* Seq 23. Civ bdry: 1935.[6] *Parl* Seq 5. *Eccl* Exempt from Archdeacon (until 1845), Canterb. RDn (1814–64), E Char. RDn (1864–*).

ELHAM

AP *LG* Seq 36. Civ bdry: 1959.[7] *Parl* Seq 2. *Eccl* Seq 8.

ELMLEY

AP Sometimes 'Isle of Elmley'. *LG* Isle of Sheppey Lbty (perhaps orig Milton Hd[271]), Sheppey PLU, RSD, RD. Abol civ 1968 to help cr Queenborough-in-Sheppey MB and CP.[263] *Parl* E'rn Dv (1832–85), N-E'rn Dv (1885–1918), Fav. Dv/CC (1918–70). *Eccl* Sitt. RDn. Abol eccl 1954 ent to Minster in Sheppey AP.[135]

ELMSTED

AP *LG* Seq 38. Civ bdry: 1886,[272] 1957.[273] *Parl* Seq 2. *Eccl* Elham RDn (until 1895), W Bridge RDn (1895–*).

ELMSTONE

AP *LG* Preston Hd, Eastry PLU, RSD, RD. Abol civ 1935 pt to Preston AP, pt to Wingham AP.[6] *Parl* E'rn Dv (1832–1918), Dover Dv (1918–48). *Eccl* Seq 1.

ELTHAM

The following have 'Eltham' in their names. Insofar as any existed at a given time: *LG* Blackh. Hd, Lewisham PLU, Plumstead Dist (Metrop Bd Wks). Transf 1889 to London.[190] *Parl* W'rn Dv (1832–67), West Dv (1867–85), Woolw. Parl Bor (1885–1918), London thereafter. *Eccl* Dartf. RDn (until 1845), [London dioc 1845–68], Greenw. RDn (1861–68), Woolw. RDn (1868–1962), Eltham RDn (1962–66), Greenw. RDn (1966–*).

AP1–ELTHAM [ST JOHN THE BAPTIST]–Incl chap Mottingham (sep EP 1866,[8] sep EP 1884[278]). Addtl eccl bdry alt: 1865 (help cr Plumstead Christ Church, Shooter's Hill EP),[275] 1869 (cr EP1),[276] 1871 (help cr EP4),[277] 1909 (cr EP3),[279] 1913,[83] 1928,[98] 1931 (help cr EP5),[280] 1931,[106] 1931,[281] 1937,[282] 1951,[283] 1960.[96]

EP1–ELHAM HOLY TRINITY–Cr 1869 from AP1.[276] Bdry: 1913,[83] 1929 (cr EP6),[121] 1931,[106] 1937,[282] 1954.[166]

EP2–ELTHAM ST BARNABAS–Cr 1928 from AP1.[98] Bdry: 1937,[188] 1948.[284]

EP3–ELTHAM ST LUKE, WELL HALL–Cr 1909 from AP1.[279] Renamed 1963 as EP7.[104]

EP4–ELTHAM ST PETER–Cr 1871 from AP1, Lee Park EP.[277] Woolw. RDn. Bdry: 1931.[281] Abol 1960 pt to help cr Lee The Good Shepherd with St Peter EP, pt to AP1.[96]

EP5–ELTHAM ST SAVIOUR–Cr 1931 from AP1, EP4.[280] Bdry: 1951,[283] 1974.[101]

EP6–NEW ELTHAM–Cr 1929 from EP1.[121] Bdry: 1931,[106] 1937,[282] 1954.[166]

EP7–ELTHAM PARK ST LUKE–Renaming 1963 of EP3.[104]

ERITH

AP *LG* Lessness Hd, Dartf. PLU, Erith USD, UD (1894–1938), MB (1938–65). Civ bdry: 1934,[19] 1937.[72] Transf 1965 to Gtr London (Bexley LB).[51] *Parl* W'rn Dv (1832–67), West Dv (1867–85), N-W'rn Dv (1885–1918), Dartf. Dv (1918–45), BC (1945–55), Erith & Chatham BC (1955–70), Gtr London thereafter. *Eccl* Dartf. RDn (until 1864), E Dartf. RDn (1864–1909), Dartf. RDn (1909–60), Erith RDn (1960–*). Eccl bdry: 1861 (cr Belvedere All Saints EP),[65] 1874 (cr Erith Christ Church EP),[285] 1905 (cr Erith St Paul, Northumberland Heath EP),[286] 1917 (help cr Belvedere St Augustine EP),[66] 1971.[287]

ERITH CHRIST CHURCH

EP Cr 1874 from Erith AP.[285] RDns as for Erith AP, from 1874. Bdry: 1880,[230] 1925 (help cr Slade Green EP),[231] 1971.[287]

ERITH ST PAUL, NORTHUMBERLAND HEATH

EP Cr 1905 from Erith AP.[286] RDns as for Erith AP, from 1905. Bdry: 1937 (help cr Barnehurst EP),[40] 1937,[58] 1971.[287]

TEMPLE EWELL

AP *LG* Bewsb. Hd, River PLU (renamed Dover in 1840s), Dover RSD, RD. Abol civ 1960 pt to help cr Temple Ewell with River CP, pt to Lydden AP, pt to Whitfield AP.[288] *Parl* E'rn Dv (1832–1918), Dover Dv/CC (1918–70). *Eccl* Seq 6. Eccl bdry: 1924.[289]

TEMPLE EWELL WITH RIVER

CP Cr 1960 by union pts Temple Ewell AP, River AP, Alkham AP.[288] *LG* Dover RD. *Parl* Dover & Deal CC (1970–*).

EYNSFORD

AP *LG* Seq 39. Civ bdry: 1955 (incl help cr Swanley CP).[29] *Parl* Seq 18. *Eccl* Shor. RDn (until 1864), E Dartf. RDn (1864–1909), Brom. RDn (1909–36), Shor. RDn (1936–*). Eccl bdry: 1852 (help cr Crocken Hill EP),[229] 1963.[290]

EYTHORNE

AP Incl chap Oxney (sep civ identity early, no sep eccl identity). *LG* Seq 19. Civ bdry: 1935.[6] *Parl* Seq 3. *Eccl* Sandw. RDn (until 1962), Dover RDn (1962–*).

FAIRFIELD

AP *LG* Aloesb. Hd, Rom. Marsh PLU, RSD, RD. Abol civ 1934 pt to Snargate AP, pt to Stone cum Ebony CP.[19] *Parl* E'rn Dv (1832–85), S'rn Dv (1885–1918), Ashf. Dv (1918–48). *Eccl* Exempt from Archdeacon (until 1845), Seq 12. Eccl bdry: 1962.[24]

EAST FARLEIGH

AP *LG* Seq 7. Civ bdry: 1887,[291] 1934,[19] 1964 (incl help cr Coxheath CP).[225] *Parl* Seq 9. *Eccl* Seq 36. Eccl bdry: 1841 (help cr Tovil EP, refounded 1843),[292] 1971.[293]

WEST FARLEIGH

AP *LG* Seq 10. *Parl* Seq 9. *Eccl* Seq 24.

FARNBOROUGH

Chap in Chelsfield AP, sep civ identity early, sep EP 1876.[200] *LG* Ruxley Hd, Brom. PLU, RSD, RD. Abol civ 1934 pt to Bromley AP, pt to Orpington AP.[19] *Parl* W'rn Dv (1832–67), West Dv (1867–85), W'rn Dv (1885–1918), Chisl. Dv (1918–48). Parl bdry: 1945.[481] *Eccl* W Dartf. RDn (1876–1909), Brom. RDn (1909–54), Orp. RDn (1909–*). Eccl bdry: 1938.[203]

FARNINGHAM

AP *LG* Seq 39. Civ bdry: 1955 (incl help cr Swanley CP).[29] *Parl* Seq 18. *Eccl* Shor. RDn (until 1864), E Dartf. RDn (1864–1909), Dartf. RDn (1909–*). Eccl bdry: 1963,[290] 1969.[87]

FAVERSHAM

AP *LG* Fav. Hd, pt Fav. Bor/MB, pt Fav. corporate mbr Cq Pt of Dover, Fav. PLU, pt Fav. USD, pt Fav. RSD. Abol civ 1894 the pt in the MB to cr Faversham Within CP, the remainder to cr Faversham Without CP.[294] *Parl* E'rn Dv (1832–85), N-E'rn Dv (1885–1918). *Eccl* Seq 13. Eccl bdry: 1881 (help cr The Brents EP),[116] 1930,[295] 194 .[117]

CP Cr 1935 by union Faversham Within CP, North Preston Without CP, Preston Within CP, and pts of Davington AP, Faversham Without CP, Luddenham AP, Ospringe AP, South Preston Without CP.[6] *LG* Fav. MB. *Parl* Fav. CC (1948–*).

FAVERSHAM WITHIN

CP Cr 1894 from the pt of Faversham AP in Fav. MB.[294] *LG* Fav. PLU, MB. Abol 1935 to help cr Faversham CP.[6] *Parl* Fav. Dv (1918–48).

FAVERSHAM WITHOUT

CP Cr 1894 from the pt of Faversham AP not in Fav. MB.[294] *LG* Fav. PLU, RD (1894–1934), Swale RD (1934–74). Bdry: 1935 (help cr Faversham CP).[6] *Parl* Fav. Dv/CC (1918–*).

FAWKHAM

AP *LG* Seq 39. Civ bdry: 1955.[29] *Parl* Seq 18. *Eccl* Seq 29.

FOLKESTONE

The following have 'Folkestone' in their names. Insofar as any existed at a given time: *LG* Folk. Hd, Elham PLU (1836–1930), (Bor, MB, USD, pt in Cq Pt sep noted). *Parl* E'rn Dv (1832–1918), Hythe Parl Bor (1918–48), Folk. & Hythe CC (1948–*). *Eccl* Dover RDn (until 1895), Elham RDn (1895–*).

AP1–FOLKESTONE [ST MARY AND ST EANSWYTHE]–*LG* Pt Folk. Bor/MB, pt Folk. corporate mbr Cq Pt of Dover, pt Folk. USD, pt Sandgate USD (this pt in Folk. MB), pt Elham RSD. Abol civ 1886 the pt in the MB to cr CP3, the remainder to Hawkinge AP.[274] Eccl bdry: 1850 (cr EP1),[296] 1854 (help cr Sandgate EP),[204] 1868 (cr EP5),[281] 1874,[298] 1881 (cr EP4),[297] 1885 (help cr EP6),[297] 1892 (help cr Cheriton Street EP),[206] 1899,[289] 1953.[167]

CP1–FOLKESTONE–Renaming before 1891 of CP3. Bdry: 1894 (loses the pt in Sandgate USD to cr CP2),[122] 1934.[19]

EP1–FOLKESTONE CHRIST CHURCH–Cr 1850, refounded 1851 from AP1.[296] Bdry: 1868 (cr EP2),[300] 1883 (cr Foord EP, now called 'Folkestone St John the Baptist'),[255] 1899.[299] Abol 1953 pt to help cr EP3, pt to AP1.[167]

EP2–FOLKESTONE HOLY TRINITY–Cr 1868 from EP1.[300] Bdry: 1899,[299] 1938.[207] Abol 1953 to help cr EP3.[167]

EP3–FOLKESTONE HOLY TRINITY WITH CHRIST CHURCH–Cr 1953 by union EP2, pt EP1.[167]

–FOLKESTONE ST JOHN THE BAPTIST–Name used now for EP cr 1883 as 'Foord', qv.

CP2–FOLKESTONE NEXT SANDGATE–Cr 1894 from the pt of AP1 in Sandgate USD.[122] *LG* Pt Sandgate UD, pt Folk. MB. Abol 1934 ent to CP1.[19]

EP4–FOLKESTONE ST MICHAEL AND ALL ANGELS–Cr 1881 from AP1.[297] Bdry: 1885 (help cr EP6),[297] 1899.[299] Abol 1953 ent to AP1.[167]

EP5–FOLKESTONE ST PETER–Cr 1868 from AP1.[281]

EP6–FOLKESTONE ST SAVIOUR–Cr 1885 from EP4, AP1.[297] Bdry: 1953.[167]

CP3–FOLKESTONE TOWN–Cr 1886 from the pt of AP1 in Folk. MB.[274] Renamed before 1891 as CP1.

FOORD

EP Cr 1883 from Folkestone Christ Church EP.[255] Dover RDn (1883–95), Elham RDn (1895–*). Bdry: 1899,[299] 1953.[167] Now called 'Folkestone St John the Baptist'.

FOOTSCRAY–See FOOTS CRAY

FORDCOMBE

EP Cr 1870 from Penshurst AP.[301] S Mall. RDn (1870–84), Tonbr. RDn (1884–1954), Tunbr. Wells RDn (1954–*).

FORDWICH

AP *LG* Downh. Hd, pt Fordwich Bor, pt corporate mbr Cq Pt of Sandw, pt Canterb. Bor/MB/CB, Bridge PLU, pt Canterb. USD, pt Bridge RSD, Bridge RD (1894–1934), Bridge-Blean RD (1834–74). Civ bdry: 1894 (loses the pt in Canterb. CB to Canterbury St Mary North Gate AP),[42] 1934.[19] *Parl* Pt Canterb. Parl Bor (1295–1918), remainder and later, Seq 1. *Eccl* Seq 3. Eccl bdry: 1930.[302]

FOREST HILL CHRIST CHURCH

EP Cr 1855 from Lewisham AP.[303] [London dioc 1855–68], Greenw. RDn (1861–86), Lewisham RDn (1886–*). Bdry: 1866 (help cr Sydenham Christ Church EP),[304] 1867 (cr Brockley Hill EP),[118] 1874 (cr Forest Hill St Augustine Honor Oak Park EP),[305] 1879 (help cr Lower Sydenham EP),[295] 1880,[130] 1880 (help cr Perry Hill EP),[134] 1887 (cr Forest Hill St Paul EP).[306]

FOREST HILL ST AUGUSTINE HONOR OAK PARK

EP Cr 1874 from Forest Hill Christ Church EP.[305] Greenw. RDn (1874–86), Lewisham RDn (1886–*). Bdry: 1921 (incl gains pt area anc Surrey),[307] 1925,[74] 1936.[61]

FOREST HILL ST PAUL

EP Cr 1887 from Forest Hill Christ Church EP.[306] Lewisham RDn. Bdry: 1921,[307] 1936 (incl gains pt area anc Surrey),[61] 1960.[124]

FOUR ELMS

EP Cr 1880 from Brasted AP, Hever AP, Chiddingstone AP, Edenbridge EP, Crockham Hill EP.[108] S Mall. RDn (1880–84), Tonbr. RDn (1884–*). Bdry: 1907.[109]

FRANT

AP Pt Sussex (Rotherfield Hd), pt Kent (Washl. Hd). *LG* Ticehurst PLU, pt Tunbr. Wells MB & USD (1888–94), Ticehurst RSD (ent 1875–88, pt 1888–94). Civ bdry: 1894 (pt of the Kent pt to help cr Tonbridge Rural CP,[308] the remainder to cr Broadwater Down CP,[122] both in Kent, so that Frant ent E Sussex thereafter. *Parl* Kent pt, W'rn Dv (1832–67), Mid Dv (1867–85), S-W'rn Dv (1885–1918). For later organisation and for eccl in Chich dioc, see main entry in Sussex.

FRINDSBURY

AP Incl chap Strood (sep par *temp* Richard I[309]). *LG* Shamw. Hd, pt Roch. MB (1835–94), N Ayl. PLU (1835–84), pt N Ayl. RSD (1875–84), Strood PLU (1884–94), pt Strood RSD (1884–94), pt Roch. USD. Civ bdry: 1887.[223] Abol civ 1894 the pt in the MB to cr Frindsbury Intra CP, the remainder to cr Frindsbury Extra CP.[310] *Parl* Pt Roch. Parl Bor (1832–1918), pt W'rn Dv (1832–67), pt Mid Dv (1867–1918). *Eccl* Roch. RDn (until 1909), Cliffe at Hoo RDn (1909–36), Roch. RDn (1936–54), Strood RDn (1954–67). Eccl bdry: 1869 (help cr Strood St Mary EP),[170] 1878 (cr Upnor EP),[56] 1935,[134] 1949.[31] Abol eccl 1967 to help cr Frindsbury with Upnor EP.[28]

FRINDSBURY EXTRA

CP Cr 1894 from the pt of Frindsbury AP not in Roch. MB.[310] *LG* Strood PLU, RD. Bdry: 1934 (help cr Rochester CP),[19] 1963 (incl help cr Hoo St Werburgh CP).[213] *Parl* Grav. Dv/CC (1918–*).

FRINDSBURY INTRA

CP Cr 1894 from the pt of Frindsbury AP in Roch. MB.[310] *LG* Strood PLU, Roch. MB. Abol civ 1934 to help cr Rochester CP.[19] *Parl* Pt Roch., Chatham Parl Bor, pt Roch., Gill. Parl Bor (1918–48).

FRINDSBURY WITH UPNOR

EP Cr 1967 by union Frindsbury AP, Upnor EP.[28] Strood RDn. Abol 1972 ent to Strood AP.[311]

FRINSTED

AP *LG* Seq 1. *Parl* Seq 9. *Eccl* Sutton RDn (until 1914), Sitt. RDn (1914–*).

FRITTENDEN

AP *LG* Orig pt Berkeley Hd, pt Cranb. Hd, ent Cranb. Hd by 19th cent,[44] Seq 26 thereafter. *Parl* E'rn Dv (1832–85), S'rn Dv (1885–1918), Ashf. Dv/CC (1918–70), Royal Tunbr. Wells CC (1970–*). *Eccl* Seq 5.

GARLINGE

CP Cr 1894 from pt of the pt of Margate St John the Baptist AP not in Margate MB.[5] *LG* Thanet PLU, RD. Bdry: 1913,[103] 1914.[312] Abol 1935 pt to help cr Broadstairs and St Peter's CP, pt to help cr Margate CP, pt to Ramsgate CP.[6] *Parl* Isle of Thanet Dv (1918– 48).

GILLINGHAM

The following have 'Gillingham' in their names. Insofar as any existed at a given time: *LG* Chatham and Gill. Hd, Medway PLU, pt Chatham MB & USD (188 –94), Gill. USD (ent 1875–90, pt 1890–94), Gill. UD (1894–1903), MB (1903–74). *Parl* Pt Chatham Parl Bor (1832–1918), pt W'rn Dv (1832–67), pt Mid Dv (1867–1918), Roch., Gill. Parl Bor (1918–48), Gill. BC (1948–*). *Eccl* Shor. RDn (until 1845), Roch. RDn (1845–1954), Gill. RDn (1954–*).

AP1–GILLINGHAM [ST MARY THE VIRGIN]– Civ bdry: 1894 (loses the pt in Chatham MB to Chatham AP),[192] 1906 (gains Grange CP),[313] 1906 (gains the pt of Chatham AP in Gill. MB),[193] 1913,[314] 1929,[315] 1934,[19] 1938.[121] Eccl bdry: 1847 (help cr Brompton EP),[134] 1855 (help cr Chatham St Paul EP),[197] 1863 (cr New Brompton St Mark EP),[137] 1892 (help cr EP3),[138] 1909 (help cr New Brompton St Luke EP),[136] 1935,[232] 1938,[121] 1956 (help cr EP1),[316] 1956 (help cr Wigmore with Hempstead EP).[317]

EP1–GILLINGHAM HOLY TRINITY–Cr 1956 from Rainham AP, AP1.[316]

EP2–GILLINGHAM ST AUGUSTINE–Cr 1917 from EP3, Luton EP.[70] Bdry: 1935,[232] 1972.[113]

EP3–GILLINGHAM ST BARNABAS–Cr 1892 from AP1, New Brompton St Mark EP.[138] Bdry: 1917 (help cr EP2),[70] 1935.[232]

–GILLINGHAM ST LUKE–Name used now for EP cr 1909 as New Bromton St Luke, qv.

EP4–GILLINGHAM ST MARK–Cr 1956 by union Brompton EP, New Brompton St Mark EP.[135]

–GILLINGHAM ST MATTHEW–Name used until 1972 (when abol) for EP cr 1956 as Wigmore with Hempstead, qv.

EP5–SOUTH GILLINGHAM–Cr 1972 by union Bredhurst EP, pt Wigmore with Hempstead EP, Rainham AP.[113]

GODMERSHAM

AP Incl chap Challock (sep civ identity early, sep EP 1870[173]). *LG* Seq 28. Addtl civ bdry alt: 1934.[19] *Parl* Seq 5. *Eccl* Exempt from Archdeacon (until 1845), Seq 2. Addtl eccl bdry alt: 1965.[176]

GOODNESTONE

AP Area in Wingham AP, sep par 1286.[318] *LG* Seq 21. Civ bdry: 1935.[6] *Parl* Seq 3. *Eccl* Pec jurisd Wingham (until 1846), exempt from Archdeacon (until 1845), Seq 1.

GOODNESTONE

AP *LG* Seq 27. Civ bdry: 1930,[295] 1935.[6] *Parl* Seq 4. *Eccl* Ospr. RDn. Eccl bdry: 194 .[117] Abol eccl 1973 to help cr Goodnestone with Graveney EP.[319]

GOODNESTONE WITH GRAVENEY

EP Cr 1973 by union Goodnestone AP, Graveney

AP.[319] Ospr. RDn.

GOUDHURST

AP *LG* Orig pt Cranb. Hd, pt Marden Hd, pt W Barnfield Hd, by 19th cent pt Cranb. Hd, pt Marden Hd,[44] Cranb. PLU, RSD, RD. *Parl* Seq 12. *Eccl* Sutton RDn (until 1891), W Char. RDn (1891–*). Eccl bdry: 1843 (cr Kilndown EP).[39]

GRAIN

AP Usual eccl spelling; for civ see following entry. *Eccl* Shor. RDn (until 1845), Roch. RDn (1845–1909), Cliffe at Hoo RDn (1909–54), Strood RDn (1954–*).

ISLE OF GRAIN

AP Usual civ spelling; for eccl see prev entry. *LG* Orig Chatham & Gill. Hd, Hoo Hd by 19th cent,[44] Seq 3 thereafter. *Parl* Seq 8.

GRANGE

Hmlt in Gillingham AP, sep CP 1866.[3] *LG* Chatham & Gill. Hd, non-corporate mbr Cq Pt of Hastings (concurrent jurisd in county Kent from 1811), Medway PLU, RSD, RD (1894–1903), Gill. MB (1903–06). Abol 1906 ent to Gillingham AP.[313] *Parl* Mid Dv (1867–1918).

GRAVENEY

AP *LG* Seq 22. Civ bdry: 1883,[8] 1934 (help cr Whitstable CP),[19] 1935.[6] *Parl* Seq 4. *Eccl* Ospr. RDn. Abol eccl 1973 to help cr Goodnestone with Graveney EP.[319]

GRAVESEND

The following have 'Gravesend' in their names. Insofar as any existed at a given time: *LG* Tolt. Hd, Grav. & Milton PLU, Grav. MB, USD. *Parl* W'rn Dv (1832–67), Grav. Parl Bor (1867–1918), Grav. Dv/CC (1918–*). *Eccl* Roch. RDn (until 1862), Grav. RDn (1862–*).

AP1–GRAVESEND [ST GEORGE]–Civ bdry: 1915 (gains Milton AP),[320] 1935.[6] Eccl bdry: 1852 (cr EP3),[321] 1951 (incl help cr EP4).[322] Abol eccl 1952 ent to EP3.[323]

EP1–GRAVESEND ST AIDAN–Cr 1959 from Chalk AP.[172]

EP2–GRAVESEND ST GEORGE–Renaming 1967 of EP3.[324]

EP3–GRAVESEND ST JAMES–Cr 1852 from AP1.[321] Bdry: 1952 (gains AP1, Milton Holy Trinity EP).[323] Renamed 1967 as EP2.[324]

EP4–GRAVESEND ST MARY–Cr 1951 from AP1, Perry Street EP.[322]

GREENHITHE

EP Cr 1857 from Swanscombe AP, Stone AP.[325] Roch. RDn (1857–62), Grav. RDn (1862–1954), Dartf. RDn (1954–*). Bdry: 1899,[326] 1971.[327]

GREENSTREET GREEN

EP Cr 1938 from Chelsfield AP.[201] Brom. RDn (1938–54), Orp. RDn (1954–*). Bdry: 1970.[234]

GREENWICH

The following have 'Greenwich' in their names. Insofar as any existed at a given time: *LG* Blackh. Hd, Greenw. PLU, Dist (Metrop Bd Wks). Transf 1889 to London.[190] *Parl* Greenw. Parl Bor (pt 1832–85, ent 1885–1918), pt W'rn Dv (1832–67), pt West Dv (1867–85), London thereafter. *Eccl* Dartf. RDn (until 1845), [London dioc 1845–68], Greenw. RDn (1861–1954), Greenw. & Deptf. RDn (1954–66), Greenw. RDn (1966–*).

AP1–GREENWICH [ST ALFEGE]–Sometimes anc 'St Alphege'. Eccl bdry: 1840 (cr EP5, refounded 1868),[329] 1849 (cr EP8, refounded 1868),[204] 1854 (cr Blackheath St John the Evangelist EP, refounded 1868),[99] 1864 (cr EP3).[56] Abol eccl 1951 pt to help cr EP1, pt to help cr EP2.[98]

EP1–GREENWICH HOLY TRINITY AND ST PAUL–Cr 1951 by union pt EP3, pt EP8, pt AP1.[98]

EP2–GREENWICH ST ALFEGE WITH ST PETER–Cr 1951 by union pt AP1, pt EP3, ent EP4.[98]

EP3–GREENWICH ST PAUL–Cr 1864 from AP1.[56] Bdry: 1867 (cr EP4).[328] Abol 1951 pt to help cr EP1, pt to help cr EP2.[98]

EP4–GREENWICH ST PETER–Cr 1867 from EP3.[328] Bdry: 1867.[206] Abol 1951 to help cr EP2.[98]

EP5–EAST GREENWICH CHRIST CHURCH–Cr 1840, refounded 1868 from AP1.[329] Bdry: 1901 (cr Westcombe Park EP),[138] 1902 (cr EP7).[329] Abol 1951 to help cr EP6.[330]

EP6–EAST GREENWICH CHRIST CHURCH WITH ST ANDREW AND ST MICHAEL–Cr 1951 by union EP5, EP7.[330]

EP7–EAST GREENWICH ST ANDREW AND ST MICHAEL–Cr 1902 from EP5.[329] Abol 1951 to help cr EP6.[330]

EP8–WEST GREENWICH–Cr 1849, refounded 1868 from AP1.[204] Bdry: 1886.[77] Abol 1951 pt to help cr EP1, pt to Blackheath The Ascension EP.[98]

GUSTON

AP Incl area ex-par East Cliffe (sep CP 1858,[163] eccl severed 1873 ent to Dover St James AP[239]). *LG* Bewsb. Hd, pt Dover Bor/MB, pt Cq Pt of Dover, River PLU (renamed Dover in 1840s), pt Dover USD, pt Dover RSD, Dover RD. Civ bdry: 1894 (loses the pt in the MB to East Cliffe CP, gains the pt of Charlton AP not in the MB),[140] 1895,[141] 1934,[19] 1951.[251] *Parl* Pt Dover Parl Bor (1558–1918), remainder and later, Seq 3. *Eccl* Exempt from Archdeacon (until 1845), Seq 6.

HACKINGTON

AP Sometimes 'St Stephen'. *LG* Orig pt Bridge & Petham Hd, pt Westgate Hd, pt Downh. Hd, by 19th cent pt Bleang. Hd, pt Westgate Hd,[44] pt Canterb. Bor/MB/CB, Blean PLU, pt Canterb. USD, pt Blean RSD, Blean RD (1894–1934), Bridge-Blean RD (1934–74). Civ bdry: 1883,[8] 1894 (loses the pt in the CB to Canterbury St Mary North Gate AP),[42] 1934 (loses pt to Canterbury CB and CP).[150] *Parl* Pt Canterb. Parl Bor (1295–1918), remainder and later, Seq 1. *Eccl* Seq 3. Eccl bdry: 1938,[331]

1959.[152]

HADLOW

AP *LG* Orig pt Littlef. Hd, pt Tonbr. Lowey, ent Tonbr. Lowey by 19th cent,[44] Tonbr. PLU, RSD, RD. Civ bdry: 1883,[8] 1928.[332] *Parl* W'rn Dv (1832–67), Mid Dv (1867–85), S-W'rn Dv (1885–1918), Tonbr. Dv/CC (1918–70), Tonbr. & Mall. CC (1970–*). *Eccl* Seq 25. Eccl bdry: 1954.[134]

HIGH HALDEN

AP *LG* Pt Berkeley Hd, pt Blackb. Hd, Tent. PLU, RSD, RD. *Parl* Seq 11. *Eccl* Seq 5.

HALLING

AP *LG* Seq 8. *Parl* Seq 8. *Eccl* Seq 29.

HALSTEAD

AP *LG* Seq 40. Civ bdry: 1956.[333] *Parl* Seq 20. *Eccl* Seq 38. Eccl bdry: 1938,[203] 1970.[234]

HIGH HALSTOW

Incl land common to this par and to St Mary Hoo AP, called 'The Mean', transf civ 1935 ent to the latter,[6] transf eccl 1949 ent to the former.[31] *LG* Seq 3. *Parl* Seq 8. *Eccl* Seq 28.

LOWER HALSTOW

AP *LG* Seq 29. Civ bdry: 1883.[8] *Parl* Seq 4. *Eccl* Seq 16. Eccl bdry: 1961.[75]

HAM

AP *LG* Eastry Hd, PLU, RSD, RD. Abol civ 1935 ent to Northbourne AP.[6] *Parl* E'rn Dv (1832–1918), Dover Dv (1918–48). *Eccl* Sandw. RDn. Abol eccl 1973 to help cr Betteshanger and Ham EP.[70]

HARBLEDOWN

AP *LG* Westgate Hd, Bridge PLU, RSD, RD (1894–1934), Bridge-Blean RD (1934–74). Civ bdry: 1883,[8] 1889 (gains Mint CP),[334] 1894,[42] 1934 (incl loses pt to Canterbury CB and CP).[150] *Parl* Seq 1. *Eccl* Pt exempt from Archdeacon (until 1845), Seq 3. Eccl bdry: 1959.[152]

LOWER HARDRES

AP *LG* Seq 16. Civ bdry: 1934.[19] *Parl* Seq 1. *Eccl* Canterb. RDn (until 1914), W Bridge RDn (1914–21). Abol eccl 1921 to help cr Lower Hardres and Nackington EP.[335]

LOWER HARDRES AND NACKINGTON

EP Cr 1921 by union Lower Hardres AP, Hackington AP.[335] E Bridge RDn. Bdry: 1970.[224]

UPPER HARDRES

AP Incl chap Stelling (sep civ identity early, no sep eccl identity). *LG* Orig pt Bridge & Petham Hd, pt Loningb. Hd, by 19th cent ent Bridge & Petham Hd,[44] Seq 16 thereafter. *Parl* Seq 1. *Eccl* Seq 2.

HARRIETSHAM

AP *LG* Seq 1. *Parl* Seq 9. *Eccl* Seq 17.

HARTLEY

AP *LG* Seq 39. Civ bdry: 1955.[29] *Parl* Seq 18. *Eccl* Seq 29.

HARTLIP

AP *LG* Seq 29. *Parl* Seq 4. *Eccl* Seq 16. Eccl bdry: 1963.[21]

HARTY

AP *LG* Fav. Hd, Shep. PLU, RSD, RD. Abol civ 1968 to help cr Queenborough-in-Sheppey MB and CP.[263] *Parl* E'rn Dv (1832–85), N-E'rn Dv (1885–1918), Fav. Dv/CC (1918–70). *Eccl* Ospr. RDn (until 1892), Sitt. RDn (1892–*).

HASTINGLEIGH

AP *LG* Birch. Barony (perhaps pt Birch. Barony, pt Birch. Franchise[336])/Birch. Franchise & Barony, Seq 32 thereafter. Civ bdry: 1883,[337] 1934.[19] *Parl* Seq 5. *Eccl* Elham RDn (until 1895), W Bridge RDn (1895–*).

HATCHAM ST CATHERINE

EP Cr 1891 from Hatcham Park EP (Surrey, Kent), Lewisham AP.[338] Greenw. RDn (1891–1954), Greenw. & Deptf. RDn (1954–66), Lewisham RDn (1966–*). Bdry: 1936,[60] 1957.[340]

HATCHAM ST JAMES

EP Cr 1845 from the Surrey pt of Deptford St Paul EP (Kent, Surrey).[242] Deptf. RDn (1845–86), Greenw. RDn (1886–1954), Greenw. & Deptf. RDn (1954–66), Lewisham RDn (1966–*). Bdry: 1851 (incl gains area in anc Kent),[341] 1872 (cr Hatcham Park EP [Kent, Surrey]),[232] 1886 (help cr Rotherhithe St Katherine EP [in Surrey]).[232]

HATCHAM PARK

EP Cr 1872 from Hatcham St James EP (Kent, Surrey).[232] RDns as for Hatcham St James, from 1872. Bdry: 1888 (help cr Camberwell St Bartholomew EP [Surrey]),[342] 1891 (help cr Hatcham St Catherine EP [Surrey, Kent]),[338] 1960.[124]

HAWKHURST

AP *LG* Orig pt Kent (pt E Barnfield Hd, pt Cranb. Hd, pt Selbrit. Hd), pt Sussex (Henhurst Hd), by 19th cent pt Kent (E Barnfield Hd), pt Sussex (Henhurst Hd),[44] the latter lost civ 1886 to Etchingham AP in Sussex[339] and this par ent Kent thereafter. *LG* Cranb. PLU, RSD, RD. Addtl civ bdry alt: 1883.[8] *Parl* Kent pt, W'rn Dv (1832–67), Mid Dv (1867–85), S'rn Dv (1885–1918), Ashf. Dv/CC (1918–70), Royal Tunbr. Wells CC (1970–*). *Eccl* Seq 5. Eccl bdry: 1930.[185]

HAWKINGE

AP *LG* Seq 34. Civ bdry: 1886 (gains the pt of Folkestone AP not in Folk. MB),[274] 1934.[19] *Parl* Seq 2. *Eccl* Seq 7. Eccl bdry: 1874 (gains hmlt Uphill from Folkestone AP).[298]

HAYES

AP *LG* Ruxley Hd, Brom. PLU, RSD, RD. Abol civ 1934 pt to Beckenham AP, pt to Bromley AP.[19] *Parl* W'rn Dv (1832–67), West Dv (1867–45), W'rn Dv (1885–1918), Chisl. Dv (1918–48). *Eccl* Shor. RDn (until 1864), W Dartf. RDn (1864–1909), Beck. RDn (1909–36), Brom. RDn (1936–*). Eccl bdry: 1938 (help cr West Wickham St Mary of Nazareth EP),[63] 1938,[83] 1957.[84]

HEADCORN

AP *LG* Orig pt Eyhorne Hd, pt Teynham Hd, pt Berkeley Hd, pt Calehill Hd, pt Cranb. Hd, by 19th cent ent Eyhorne Hd,[44] Seq 1 thereafter. Civ bdry: 1888.[343] *Parl* Seq 9. *Eccl* Char. RDn (until 1864), W Char. RDn (1864–1914), E

Char. RDn (1914–62), Sutton RDn (1962–*).

HERNE

AP *LG* Bleang. Hd, Blean PLU, pt Herne Bay USD, pt Blean RSD, Blean RD. Civ bdry: 1894 (loses the pt in the USD to cr Herne Bay CP),[122] 1900.[344] Abol civ 1934 ent to Herne Bay CP.[19] *Parl* E'rn Dv (1832–1918), Canterb. Dv (1918–48). *Eccl* Exempt from Archdeacon (until 1845), Seq 20. Eccl bdry: 1849 (cr Herne Bay Christ Church EP),[345] 1906,[152] 1936 (cr Herne Bay St Bartholomew EP),[346] 1960.[212]

HERNE BAY

CP Cr 1894 from the pt of Herne AP in Herne Bay USD.[122] *LG* Blean PLU, Herne Bay D. Bdry: 1900,[344] 1934.[19] *Parl* Canterb. Dv/CC (1918– *).

HERNE BAY CHRIST CHURCH

EP Cr 1849 from Herne AP.[345] Westb. RDn (1849–1914), Canterb. RDn (1914–71), Recul. RDn (1971–*). Bdry: 1906.[152] Often called 'Herne Bay Christ Church with St John the Evangelist'.

HERNE BAY ST BARTHOLOMEW

EP Cr 1936 from Herne AP.[346] Canterb. RDn (1936–71), Recul. RDn (1971–*).

HERNHILL

AP *LG* Seq 22. Civ bdry: 1934 (incl help cr Whitstable CP).[19] *Parl* E'rn Dv (1832–85), N-E'rn Dv (1885–1918); pt Canterb. Dv, pt Fav. Dv (1918–48); Fav. CC (1948–*). *Eccl* Exempt from Archdeacon (until 1845), Seq 13.

HEVER

AP *LG* Orig pt Ruxley Hd, pt Somerden Hd, ent Somerden Hd by 19th cent,[44] Seq 41 thereafter. Civ bdry: 1934.[19] *Parl* Seq 19. *Eccl* Seq 37. Eccl bdry: 1839 (help cr Mark Beech EP),[224] 1880 (help cr Four Elms EP),[108] 1907.[109]

HIGHAM

AP *LG* Seq 8. Civ bdry: 1887,[169] 1963.[213] *Parl* Seq 8. *Eccl* Roch. RDn (until 1862), Grav. RDn (1862–1909), Cliffe at Hoo RDn (1909–34). Abol eccl 1934 to help cr Higham with Merston EP.[171]

HIGHAM WITH MERSTON

EP Cr 1934 by union Higham AP, Mareston otherwise Merston AP, pt Chalk AP.[171] Cliffe at Hoo RDn (1934–54), Strood RDn (1954–*). Bdry: 1957.[153]

HILDENBOROUGH

EP Cr 1844 from Tonbridge AP, Leigh AP.[227] Mall. RDn (1844–64), S Mall. RDn (1864–84), Tonbr. RDn (1884–*). Bdry: 1954.[134]

CP Cr 1894 from Tonbridge Rural CP.[347] *LG* Tonbr. PLU, RD. Bdry: 1928,[332] 1934 (incl help cr Tonbridge CP).[19] *Parl* Tonbr. Dv/CC (1918–70), Tonbr. & Mall. CC (1970–*).

HINXHILL

AP *LG* Seq 24. Civ bdry: 1883,[8] 1934.[19] *Parl* Seq 5. *Eccl* Lym. RDn (until 1864), N Lym. RDn (1864–1962), E Char. RDn (1962–*).

HOATH

Chap in Reculver AP, sep civ identity early, no sep eccl identity. *LG* Seq 15. Civ bdry: 1934.[19] *Parl* Seq 1.

HOLLINGBOURNE

AP Incl chap Bredhurst (sep civ identity early, eccl curacy, self-styled vicarage, eccl sep status sustained[110]), chap Hucking (sep civ identity early, eccl [as 'Huckinge'] severed before 1905 to help cr Bicknor with Huckinge EP,[86] qv for later division into EPs Bicknor, Huckinge). *LG* Seq 1. *Parl* Seq 9. *Eccl* Exempt from Archdeacon (until 1845), Seq 17.

HOLY CROSS WESTGATE WITHIN

CP Cr 1894 from the pt of Canterbury Holy Cross Westgate AP in Canterb. CB.[122] *LG* Canterb. Incorp (poor), CB. Abol 1897 to help cr Canterbury CP.[148]

HOLY CROSS WESTGATE WITHOUT

CP Cr 1894 from pt of the pt of Canterbury Holy Cross Westgate AP not in Canterb. CB.[122] *LG* Bridge PLU, RD. Abol 1912 ent to Canterbury CB and CP.[149]

HOO

AP Usual civ spelling; for eccl see following entry. *LG* Hoo Hd, PLU, RSD, RD (1894–1935), Swale RD (1935–68). Abol civ 1968 pt to help cr Hoo St Werburgh CP, pt to Frindsbury Extra CP.[213] *Parl* W'rn Dv (1832–67), Mid Dv (1867–1918), Grav. Dv/CC (1918–70).

HOO ST WERBURGH

AP Usual eccl spelling; for civ see prev entry. *Eccl* Seq 28.

CP Cr 1968 by union pts Hoo AP, Cooling AP, Frindsbury Extra CP.[213] *LG* Strood RD. *Parl* Grav. CC (1970–*).

ST MARY HOO

AP Incl land common to this par and to High Halstow AP, called 'The Mean', transf civ 1935 ent to the former,[6] transf eccl 1949 ent to the latter.[31] *LG* Seq 3. *Parl* Seq 8. *Ecci* Seq 28.

HOPE

AP Usual eccl spelling; for civ see following entry. *Eccl* Lym. RDn. Abol eccl 1840 to help cr New Romney with Hope EP.[348]

HOPE ALL SAINTS

AP Usual civ spelling; for eccl see prev entry. *LG* Orig pt Langport Hd, pt St Martin Ivychurch Hd, ent Rom. Marsh Lbty by 19th cent,[44] Rom. Marsh PLU, RSD, RD. Civ bdry: 1883.[8] Abol civ 1934 pt to Newchurch AP, pt to Old Romney AP, pt to St Mary in the Marsh AP.[19] *Parl* E'rn Dv (1832–85), S'rn Dv (1885–1918), Ashf. Dv (1918–48).

HORSMONDEN

AP Orig pt Kent (pt Bren. & Horsm. Hd, pt Larkf. Hd [pt also in town Aylesford]), pt Sussex (Loxfield Pelham Hd), by 19th cent pt Kent (Bren. & Horsm. Hd), pt Sussex (Loxfield Pelham Hd),[44] the par made ent Kent 1895.[146] *LG* Tonbr. PLU, RSD, RD (pt 1894–95, ent 1895–1974), pt sep RD in E Sussex (1894–95). Civ bdry: 1934.[19] *Parl* Kent pt, W'rn Dv (1832–67), Mid Dv (1867–1885), S'rn Dv (1885–1918), Tonbr. Dv/CC (1918–70), Royal Tunbr. Wells CC (1970–*). *Eccl* Seq 27.

HORTON KIRBY

AP *LG* Seq 39. Civ bdry: 1955 (incl help cr Swanley CP).[29] *Parl* Seq 18. *Eccl* Seq 21. Eccl bdry: 1938,[151] 1969.[87]

HOTHFIELD

AP *LG* Orig pt Chart & Longbr. Hd, pt Calehill Hd, ent Chart & Longbr. Hd by 19th cent,[44] Seq 25 thereafter. Civ bdry: 1957.[178] *Parl* Seq 5. *Eccl* Seq 4. Eccl bdry: 1970.[181]

HOUGHAM

AP *LG* Pt Bewsb. Hd, pt Folk. Hd, pt Dover Bor, pt Cq Pt of Dover, Dover MB (pt 1835–94, ent 1894–96), River PLU (renamed Dover in 1840s), pt Dover USD, pt Dover RSD. Civ bdry: 1894 (loses the pt not in the MB to cr Hougham Without CP),[140] 1895.[141] Abol civ 1896 to help cr Dover CP.[182] *Parl* Pt Dover Parl Bor (1558–1918), pt E'rn Dv (1832–1918). *Eccl* Seq 6. Incl eccl Poulton (orig AP, long in ruins). Addtl eccl bdry alt: 1844 (the pt in the Bor to cr Hougham-in-Dover EP),[349] 1901.[33]

HOUGHAM-IN-DOVER

EP Cr 1844 from Hougham AP (the area in the Bor).[349] Dover RDn. Bdry: 1901,[133] 1903 (cr Dover St Martin EP),[253] 1934.[80]

HOUGHAM WITHOUT

CP Cr 1894 from the pt of Hougham AP not in Dover MB.[140] *LG* Dover PLU, RD. Bdry: 1895,[141] 1934.[19] *Parl* Dover Dv/CC (1918–70), Dover & Deal CC (1970–*).

HUCKING

Chap in Hollingbourne AP, sep civ identity early, eccl (as 'Huckinge') severed before 1905 to help cr Bicknor with Huckinge EP,[86] the latter divided 1972 into 2 EPs of Bicknor, Huckinge[87]; see following entry for the latter. *LG* Seq 1. *Parl* Seq 9.

HUCKINGE

EP Cr 1972 when Bicknor with Huckinge EP divided into 2 EPs of Bicknor, Huckinge.[87] Sitt. RDn. See prev entry for early organisation of this chap.

HUNTON

AP *LG* Orig pt Twyford Hd, pt Larkf. Hd, pt Maid. Hd, by 19th cent ent Twyford Hd,[44] Seq 10 thereafter. Civ bdry: 1968 (help cr Coxheath CP).[225] *Parl* Seq 14. *Eccl* Shor. RDn (until 1864), N Mall. RDn (1864–1906), Mall. RDn (1906–71). Abol eccl 1971 pt to help cr Linton with Hunton CP, pt to East Farleigh AP.[293]

HURST

AP *LG* Pt Street Hd, pt Rom. Marsh Lbty, E Ashf. PLU, RSD, RD. Civ bdry: 1886.[350] Abol civ 1934 pt to Aldington AP, pt to Burmarsh AP.[19] *Parl* E'rn Dv (1832–1918), Ashf. Dv (1918–48). *Eccl* Sometimes eccl 'Falconhurst' or 'Fawkenhurst', Seq 12. Eccl bdry: 1927,[201] 1930.[351]

HYTHE

EP Chap in Saltwood AP, sep civ identity early as 'St Leonard Hythe', qv, sep EP 1844 as 'Hythe'.[352] Exempt from Archdeacon (1844–45), Elham RDn. Bdry: 1930.[351]

CP Cr 1934 by union pts Aldington AP, Burmarsh AP, Cheriton AP, St Leonard Hythe CP, Lympne AP, Saltwood AP, Sandgate CP.[19] *LG* Hythe RD. *Parl* Folk. & Hythe CC (1948–*).

NEW HYTHE

EP Cr 1948 from East Malling AP.[40] Mall. RDn. Renamed 1964 'Larkfield'.[194]

ST LEONARD HYTHE

Chap in Saltwood AP, sep civ identity early, sep EP 1844 as 'Hythe',[352] qv. *LG* Hythe Hd, Bor/MB, Cq Pt of Hythe, Eastry PLU, Hythe USD. Civ bdry: 1883,[8] 1886 (gains the pts of Cheriton AP, Newington AP, Saltwood AP in Hythe Parl Bor [but not prev in the MB]),[353] 1888 (gains the pts of Aldington AP, West Hythe AP in Hythe MB).[14] Abol civ 1934 pt to help cr Hythe CP, pt to Lympne AP, pt to Burmarsh AP.[19] *Parl* Hythe Parl Bor (1558–1948). (until 1914), E Bridge RDn (1914–40). Abol eccl 1940 to help cr Chillendon with Knowlton EP.[180]

WEST HYTHE

AP *LG* Orig pt Worth Hd, pt Hythe Hd, pt Hythe Bor, pt Cq Pt Hythe (former non-corp mbr), by 19th cent pt Hythe Bor & Cq Pt, pt Rom. Marsh Lbty,[44] Rom. Marsh PLU, pt Hythe MB (1835–88), pt Hythe USD, pt Rom. Marsh RSD. Abol civ 1888 the pt in the MB to St Leonard Hythe CP, the remainder to Burmarsh AP.[355] *Parl* Hythe Parl Bor (1558–1918). *Eccl* Seq 10.

ICKHAM

AP Usual eccl spelling; for civ and occasional eccl see following entry. *Eccl* Exempt from Archdeacon (until 1845), Seq 1.

ICKHAM AND WELL

AP Usual civ spelling and occasional eccl; for usual eccl see prev entry. *LG* Seq 18. Civ bdry: 1889,[12] 1958.[43] *Parl* Seq 1.

IDE HILL

EP Cr 1818 from Sundridge AP, refounded 1852 from Sundridge AP, Chevening AP, Chiddingstone AP.[208] Shor. RDn (1818–1909), Seven. RDn (1909–73). Abol eccl 1973 to help cr Sundridge with Ide Hill EP.[356]

IFIELD

AP *LG* Tolt. Hd, N Ayl. PLU (1835–84), RSD (1875–84), Strood PLU (1884–1930), RSD (1884–94), Strood RD. Abol civ 1935 pt to Gravesend AP, pt to Cobham AP.[6] *Parl* W'rn Dv (1832–67), Mid Dv (1867–1918), Grav. Dv (1918–48). *Eccl* Shor. RDn (until 1845), Roch. RDn (1845–62), Grav. RDn (1862–1901), Cob. RDn (1901–36), Grav. RDn (1936–*). Eccl bdry: 1887,[357] 1939,[217] 1957.[119]

IGHTHAM

AP *LG* Seq 13. Civ bdry: 1934 (incl cr Borough Green CP).[19] *Parl* Seq 10. *Eccl* Seq 35. Eccl bdry: 1966,[331] 1974 (help cr Borough Green EP).[104]

IVYCHURCH

AP *LG* Orig pt St Martin Ivychurch Hd, pt Rom. Marsh Lbty, pt Lbty Cq Pt of New Rom., pt

Aloesb. Hd, by 19th cent as before except pt no longer in Aloesb. Hd,[44] Rom. Marsh PLU, RSD, RD. Civ bdry: 1883,[8] 1934.[19] *Parl* Seq 6. *Eccl* Exempt from Archdeacon (until 1845), Seq 12. Eccl bdry: 1935.[25]

IWADE
Chap in Teynham AP, sep civ identity early, sep EP 1730.[177] *LG* Milton Hd (perhaps orig pt Milton Hd, pt Teynham Hd[358]), Seq 29 thereafter. *Parl* Seq 4. *Eccl* Sitt. RDn.

KEMSING
AP Incl chap Seal (sep civ identity early, sep EP 1874[26]). *LG* Seq 40. Civ bdry: 1934.[19] *Parl* Seq 20. *Eccl* Seq 35. Eccl bdry: 1867 (cr Seal St Laurence EP).[359]

KENARDINGTON
AP *LG* Orig pt Blackb. Hd, pt Ham Hd, pt Lbty Cq Pt of New Rom., by 19th cent pt Blackb. Hd, pt Rom. Marsh Lbty, pt Lbty Cq Pt of New Rom.,[44] Tent. PLU, RSD, RD. Civ bdry: 1883,[8] 1934.[19] *Parl* Seq 5. *Eccl* Seq 12. Eccl bdry: 1962.[24]

KENNINGTON
AP *LG* Chart & Longbr. Hd, E Ashf. PLU, RSD, RD. Abol civ 1934 pt to Ashford AP, pt to Boughton Aluph AP, pt to Hinxhill AP, pt to Wye AP.[150] *Parl* E'rn Dv (1832–85), S'rn Dv (1885–1918), Ashf. Dv (1918–48). *Eccl* Seq 4.

KESTON
AP *LG* Ruxley Hd, Brom. PLU, RSD, RD. Abol civ 1934 pt to Bromley CP, pt to Orpington AP.[19] *Parl* W'rn Dv (1832–67), West Dv (1867–85), W'rn Dv (1885–1918), Chisl. Dv (1918–45). *Eccl* Shor. RDn (until 1864), W Dartf. RDn (1864–1909), Beck. RDn (1909–36), Brom. RDn (1936–*).

KIDBROOKE
Orig AP, church long demolished, later deemed a lbty, sep civ status regained as CP 1866,[3] sep EP 1867 (from the lbty and pt Charlton next Woolwich AP).[191] *LG* Blackh. Hd, Lewisham PLU (1836–68), Woolw. PLU (1868–89), Plumstead Dist (Metrop Bd Wks). Transf 1889 to London.[190] *Parl* W'rn Dv (1832–67), West Dv (1867–85), Greenw. Parl Bor (1885–1918), London thereafter. *Eccl* [London dioc 1867–68], Greenw. RDn (1867–68), Woolw. RDn (1868–1950), Greenw. RDn (1950–54), Greenw. & Deptf. RDn (1954–66), Greenw. RDn (1966–*). Eccl bdry: 1904,[128] 1937,[188] 1948,[248] 1960 (incl help cr Lee The Good Shepherd with St Peter EP),[96] 1974.[101]

KILNDOWN
EP Cr 1841, refounded 1843 from Goudhurst AP.[39] Sutton RDn (1843–91), W Char. RDn (1891–*).

KINGSDOWN
AP *LG* Seq 29. *Parl* Seq 4. *Eccl* Sitt. RDn (until 1955), Ospr. RDn (1955). Abol eccl 1955 to help cr Lynsted with Kingsdown EP.[360]

KINGSDOWN
AP Usual civ spelling; for eccl see 'Kingsdown with Mappiscombe'. *LG* Pt Axton/Axton, Dartf. & Wilm. Hd, pt Codsh. Hd, Dartf. PLU, RSD, RD. Civ bdry: 1934.[19] Renamed civ 1948 'West Kingsdown'.[361] *Parl* W'rn Dv (1832–67), West Dv (1867–85), N-W'rn Dv (1885–1918), Chisl. Dv (1918–48), Orp. CC (1948–70).

KINGSDOWN ST JOHN
EP Cr 1850 from Ringwould AP.[56] Sandw. RDn. Bdry: 1963.[102]

KINGSDOWN WITH MAPPISCOMBE
AP Usual eccl spelling; for civ see second Kingsdown above. *Eccl* Roch. RDn (until 1862), Cob. RDn (1862–1909), Shor. RDn (1909–*). Eccl bdry: 1963.[290]

WEST KINGSDOWN
CP Renaming 1948 of Kingsdown AP (second Kingsdown above).[361] *LG* Dartf. RD. Bdry: 1955 (incl help cr Ash-cum-Ridley CP).[29] *Parl* Seven. CC (1970–*).

KINGSNORTH
AP *LG* Seq 25. Civ bdry: 1934,[19] 1935.[6] *Parl* Seq 5. *Eccl* Seq 11. Eccl bdry: 1959 (incl help cr South Ashford EP).[30]

KINGSTON
AP *LG* Seq 20. Civ bdry: 1889.[12] *Parl* Seq 1. *Eccl* Seq 1.

KIPPINGTON
EP Cr 1877 from Sevenoaks AP, Riverhead EP.[362] Shor. RDn (1877–1909), Seven. RDn (1909–*).

KNOCKHOLT
Chap in Orpington AP, sep civ and eccl identity early. *LG* Ruxley Hd, Brom. PLU, RSD, RD. Abol civ 1934 ent to Orpington AP.[19] *Parl* W'rn Dv (1832–67), West Dv (1867–85), W'rn Dv (1885–1918), Chisl. Dv (1918–48). *Eccl* Shor. RDn (until 1909), Seven. RDn (1909–54), Orp. RDn (1954–70), Seven. RDn (1970–*). Eccl bdry: 1970.[234]
CP Cr 1969 from Bromley LB and AP (Gtr London), to be in Kent.[364] *LG* Seven. RD. *Parl* Seven. CC (1970–*).

KNOWLTON
AP *LG* Eastry Hd, PLU, RSD, RD. Abol civ 1935 ent to Goodnestone AP.[6] *Parl* E'rn Dv (1832–1918), Dover Dv (1918–48). *Eccl* Sandw. RDn (until 1914), E Bridge RDn (1914–40). Abol eccl 1940 to help cr Chillendon with Knowlton EP.[180]

LAMBERHURST
AP Pt Kent (Bren. & Horsm. Hd), pt Sussex (Loxfield Pelham Hd), the par made ent Kent 1895.[146] *LG* Ticehurst PLU, RSD, pt sep RD in Sussex (1894–95), Tonbr. RD (pt 1894–95, ent 1895–1974). *Parl* Kent pt, W'rn Dv (1832–67), Mid Dv (1867–85), S-W'rn Dv (1885–1918), Tonbr. Dv/CC (1918–70), Royal Tunbr. Wells CC (1970–*). *Eccl* Seq 27.

LAMORBEY HOLY REDEEMER
EP Cr 1934 from Lamorbey Holy Trinity EP, Welling St John EP.[108] Dartf. RDn (1934–36), Chisl. RDn (1936–65), Sidcup RDn (1965–*). Bdry: 1937,[282] 1954.[166]

LAMORBEY HOLY TRINITY
EP Cr 1878 from Bexley AP.[362] Dartf. RDn (1878–

64), E Dartf. RDn (1864–1909), Dartf. RDn (1909–36), Chisl. RDn (1936–65), Sidcup RDn (1965–*). Bdry: 1926 (help cr Welling St John EP),[79] 1934 (help cr Lamorbey Holy Redeemer EP),[108] 1936 (help cr Bexley St John EP),[74] 1937,[282] 1968,[227] 1969 (help cr Sidcup St Andrew EP).[76]

LAND COMMON TO HIGH HALSTOW AND ST MARY HOO–See THE MEAN

LANGDON

CP Cr 1963 by union East Langdon AP, West Langdon AP.[219] *LG* Dover RD. *Parl* Dover & Deal CC (1970–*).

EAST LANGDON

AP *LG* Corn. Hd, River PLU (renamed Dover in 1840s), Dover RSD, RD. Civ bdry: 1934.[19] Abol civ 1963 to help cr Langdon CP.[219] *Parl* E'rn Dv (1832–1918), Dover Dv/CC (1918–70). *Eccl* Seq 15.

WEST LANGDON

AP *LG* Bewsb. Hd, River PLU (renamed Dover in 1840s), Dover RSD, RD. Civ abol, *Parl*, *Eccl* as for East Langdon.

LANGLEY

AP *LG* Seq 1. Civ bdry: 1833,[105] 1934.[19] *Parl* Seq 9. *Eccl* Seq 17. Eccl bdry: 1970,[106] 1971.[48]

LANGTON GREEN

EP Cr 1880 from Speldhurst AP.[365] S Mall. RDn (1880–1906), Tunbr. Wells RDn (1906–*). Bdry: 1971.[366]

LARKFIELD

EP Renaming 1964 of West Hythe EP.[194] Mall. RDn.

LEAVELAND

AP *LG* Seq 27. *Parl* Seq 4. *Eccl* Seq 13.

LEE

The following have 'Lee' in their names. Insofar as any existed at a given time: *LG* Blackh. Hd, Lewisham PLU, Plumstead Dist (Metrop Bd Wks). Transf 1889 to London.[190] *Parl* W'rn Dv (1832–67), West Dv (1867–85), Lewisham Parl Bor (1885–1918), London thereafter. *Eccl* [London dioc 1845–68], Seq 23.

AP1–LEE [ST MARGARET]–Eccl bdry: 1854 (cr EP6),[253] 1863 (cr EP3),[367] 1881 (help cr EP5),[109] 1888 (help cr EP1),[280] 1904,[128] 1960,[96] 1972.[368]

EP1–LEE THE GOOD SHEPHERD–Cr 1888 from AP1, EP6.[280] Bdry: 1904.[128] Abol 1960 to help cr EP2.[96]

EP2–LEE THE GOOD SHEPHERD WITH ST PETER–Cr 1960 by union EP1, and pts of EP6, AP1, EP3, Eltham St Peter EP, Kidbrooke St James EP.[96] Bdry: 1968,[227] 1972.[368]

EP3–LEE HOLY TRINITY–Cr 1863 from AP1.[367] Bdry: 1904.[128] Abol 1960 pt to AP1, pt to help cr EP2.[96]

EP4–LEE ST AUGUSTINE, GROVE PARK–Cr 1891 from EP5.[338] Bdry: 1934,[166] 1950,[370] 1952 (help cr Mottingham St Edward the Confessor EP).[369]

EP5–LEE ST MILDRED, BURNT ASH HILL–Cr 1881 from AP1, EP6.[109] Bdry: 1891 (cr EP4),[338] 1904.[128]

EP6–LEE PARK–Cr 1854 from AP1.[253] Bdry: 1871 (help cr Eltham St Peter EP),[277] 1881 (help cr EP5),[109] 1888 (help cr EP1),[280] 1904.[128] Abol 1960 pt to AP1, pt to help cr EP2, pt to Blackheath All Saints EP.[96]

LEEDS

AP Incl chap Broomfield (sep civ identity early, no sep eccl identity, thus this par eccl 'Leeds with Broomfield', qv). *LG* Seq 1. *Parl* W'rn Dv (1832–67), Mid Dv (1867–1918), Maid. Dv/CC (1918–*).

LEEDS WITH BROOMFIELD

AP Usual eccl spelling; for civ and civ sep chap Broomfield see prev entry. *Eccl* Seq 17.

LEIGH

AP *LG* Orig pt Washl. Hd, pt Codsh. Hd, pt Somerden Hd, by 19th cent pt Codsh. Hd, pt Somerden Hd,[44] Penshurst PLU (1835–1840s), Seven. PLU (1840s–1930), RSD, RD. Civ bdry: 1894,[347] 1934.[19] *Parl* Seq 19. *Eccl* Seq 26. Eccl bdry: 1844 (help cr Hildenborough EP),[227] 1906 (help cr Chiddingstone Causeway EP).[209]

LENHAM

AP *LG* Orig pt Eyhorne Hd, pt Calehill Hd, by 19th cent ent Eyhorne Hd,[44] Seq 1 thereafter. Civ bdry: 1888.[343] *Parl* Seq 9. *Eccl* Seq 17. Eccl bdry: 1874 (help cr Charing Heath EP).[179]

LEWISHAM

The following have 'Lewisham' in their names. Insofar as any existed at a given time: *LG* Blackh. Hd, Lewisham PLU, Dist (Metrop Bd Wks). Transf 1889 to London.[190] *Parl* W'rn Dv (1832–67), West Dv (1867–85), Lewisham Parl Bor (1885–1918), London thereafter. *Eccl* [London dioc 1845–68], Seq 23.

AP1–LEWISHAM [ST MARY]–Eccl bdry: 1855 (cr Sydenham St Bartholomew EP, cr Forest Hill Christ Church EP),[303] 1859 (cr Blackheath All Saints EP),[95] 1865 (cr EP3),[372] 1871 (cr EP2),[371] 1879 (help cr Lower Sydenham EP),[295] 1880 (help cr Perry Hill EP),[134] 1883 (cr Blackheath The Ascension EP),[97] 1884,[87] 1888 (cr EP5),[342] 1900 (help cr Crofton Park EP),[100] 1901 (cr Brockley EP),[123] 1904,[87] 1905 (cr Catford St Laurence EP),[167] 1916 (help cr EP1),[61] 1960 (incl help cr Crofton Park St Hilda with St Cyprian EP),[124] 1968.[227]

EP1–LEWISHAM ST JOHN, SOUTHEND–Cr 1916 from AP1, Catford St Laurence EP.[61] Bdry: 1934,[166] 1940 (help cr Bellingham EP),[64] 1963.[53] Renamed 1973 'Catford (Southend) and Downham'.[168]

EP2–LEWISHAM ST MARK–Cr 1871 from AP1.[371] Bdry: 1904,[128] 1960.[96] Abol 1968 pt to help cr EP4, pt to AP1, pt to EP5, pt to Lee The Good Shepherd with St Peter EP.[227]

EP3–LEWISHAM ST STEPHEN–Cr 1865 from AP1.[372] Bdry: 1884,[87] 1904.[87] Abol 1968 to help cr EP4.[227]

EP4–LEWISHAM ST STEPHEN AND ST MARK–Cr 1968 by union EP3, pt EP2.[227]

EP5–LEWISHAM ST SWITHUN, HITHER GREEN–Cr 1888 from AP1.[342] Bdry: 1904,[128] 1934,[166] 1968.[227]

LEYBOURNE

AP *LG* Seq 4. Civ bdry: 1934.[19] *Parl* Seq 10. *Eccl* Seq 24. Eccl bdry: 1934.[10]

LEYSDOWN

AP *LG* Isle of Shep. Lbty, Shep. PLU, RSD, RD. Renamed civ 1949 'Leysdown-on-Sea'.[373] *Parl* E'rn Dv (1832–85), N-E'rn Dv (1885–1918), Fav. Dv/CC (1918–70). *Eccl* Seq 16. Eccl bdry: 1962.[264]

LEYSDOWN-ON-SEA

CP Renaming 1949 of Leysdown AP.[373] *LG* Shep. RD. Abol 1968 to help cr Queenborough-in-Sheppey MB and CP.[263]

LIDSING

Ville and chap in Gillingham AP, sep CP 1866.[3] *LG* Chatham & Gill. Hd, Medway PLU, RSD, RD (1894–1903), Gill. MB (1903–13). Abol 1913 ent to Gillingham AP.[314] *Parl* Mid Dv (1867–1918).

LINTON

AP *LG* Seq 7. Civ bdry: 1883,[374] 1964 (incl help cr Coxheath CP).[225] *Parl* Seq 9. *Eccl* Sutton RDn. Eccl bdry: 1970.[106] Abol eccl 1971 pt to help cr Linton with Hunton EP (to be in Roch dioc), pt to East Farleigh AP.[293]

LINTON WITH HUNTON

EP Cr 1971 by union pt Linton AP, pt Hunton AP.[293] Mall. RDn.

LITTLEBOURNE

AP *LG* Downh. Hd, Bridge PLU, pt Canterb. Bor/MB/CB, pt Canterb. USD, pt Bridge RSD, Bridge RD. Civ bdry: 1889,[12] 1894 (loses the pt in the CB to Canterbury St Martin AP),[42] 1934,[19] 1958.[43] *Parl* Pt Canterb. Parl Bor (1295–1918), remainder and later, Seq 1. *Eccl* Seq 1.

LONGFIELD

AP *LG* Seq 39. Civ bdry: 1955.[29] *Parl* Seq 18. *Eccl* Seq 29. Eccl bdry: 1938.[151]

LOOSE

Chap in Maidstone AP, sep civ identity early, sep EP 1858.[177] *LG* Seq 7. Addtl civ bdry alt: 1887,[291] 1934,[19] 1964 (incl help cr Coxheath CP).[225] *Parl* Seq 9. *Eccl* Seq 17. Eccl bdry: 1841 (help cr Tovil EP, refounded 1843),[292] 1970,[106] 1971,[48] 1971.[293]

LUDDENHAM

AP *LG* Seq 27. Civ bdry: 1930,[103] 1935 (incl help cr Faversham CP).[6] *Parl* Seq 4. *Eccl* Ospr. RDn. Abol eccl 1926 to help cr Luddenham with Stone EP.[117]

LUDDENHAM WITH STONE

EP Cr 1926 by union Luddenham AP, Stone AP, pt Murston AP, pt Buckland AP, losing area to Ospringe AP, Goodnestone AP, The Brents EP, Preston next Faversham AP.[375] Ospr. RDn. Abol 1966 to help cr Oare and Luddenham EP.[375]

LUDDESDOWN

AP *LG* Seq 9. *Parl* Seq 8. *Eccl* Roch. RDn (until 1862), Cob. RDn (1862–*). Renamed eccl 1934 'Luddesdown with Dode' when gains contiguous ex-par places.[81]

LUDDESDOWN WITH DODE–See prev entry

LULLINGSTONE

AP *LG* Axton/Axton, Dartf. & Wilm. Hd, Dartf. PLU, RSD, RD. Abol civ 1955 ent to Eynsford AP.[29] *Parl* W'rn Dv (1832–67), West Dv (1867–85), N-W'rn Dv (1885–1918), Chisl. Dv (1918–55), Dartf. CC (1955–70). *Eccl* Dartf. RDn (until 1864), E Dartf. RDn (1864–1909), Brom. RDn (1909–36), Shor. RDn (1936–*).

LUTON

EP Cr 1842, refounded 1852 from Chatham AP.[195] Roch. RDn. Bdry: 1914 (help cr Chatham All Saints EP),[129] 1917 (help cr Gillingham St Augustine EP),[70] 1938,[121] 1955 (help cr Chatham St Philip and St James EP),[199] 1956 (help cr Wigmore with Hempstead EP).[317]

LYDD

AP *LG* Orig Langport Hd, pt Lydd Bor and thus this pt corp mbr Cq Pt of New Romney, later pt Rom. Marsh Lbty,[44] Rom. Marsh PLU, Lydd MB (1885–1974), Rom. Marsh RSD

LYDDEN

AP *LG* Orig pt Bewsb. Hd, pt Folk. Hd, ent Bewsb. Hd by 19th cent,[44] Seq 14 thereafter. Civ bdry: 1883,[8] 1934,[19] 1960 (incl help cr Temple Ewell and River CP).[208] *Parl* Seq 3. *Eccl* Seq 6. Eccl bdry: 1924.[289]

LYMINGE

AP Incl chap Stanford (sep civ identity early, sep EP 1853[376]). *LG* Seq 36. *Parl* Seq 2. *Eccl* Exempt from Archdeacon (until 1845), Seq 8.

LYMPNE

AP *LG* Orig pt Hayne Hd, pt Street Hd, pt Worth Hd, by 19th cent pt Street Hd, pt Rom. Marsh Lbty,[44] Elham PLU, RSD, RD. Civ bdry: 1883,[8] 1886,[377] 1891,[354] 1934 (incl help cr Hythe CP).[19] *Parl* Seq 2. *Eccl* Seq 10. Eccl bdry: 1930.[351]

LYNSTEAD

AP Usual eccl spelling; for civ see following entry. *Eccl* Ospr. RDn. Abol eccl 1955 to help cr Lynstead with Kingsdown EP.[360]

LYNSTEAD WITH KINGSDOWN

EP Cr 1955 by union Lynstead AP, Kingsdown EP.[360] Ospr. RDn. Bdry: 1963.[378]

LYNSTED

AP Usual civ spelling; for eccl see 'Lynstead'. *LG* Seq 30. *Parl* Seq 4.

MAIDSTONE

The following have 'Maidstone' in their names. Insofar as any existed at a given time: *LG* Maid. Hd, Bor/MB, PLU, USD. *Parl* Maid. Parl Bor (1553, 1572–1918), Maid. Dv/CC (1918–*). *Eccl* Exempt from Archdeacon (until 1845), Sutton RDn.

AP1–MAIDSTONE [ALL SAINTS]–Incl chap Detling (sep par by 1643[247]), chap Loose (sep civ identity early, sep EP 1858[177]). Addtl civ bdry alt: 1883,[374] 1932,[107] 1934.[19] Addtl eccl bdry alt: 1841 (cr Tovil EP, refounded 1843),[292] 1841 (cr EP2, cr EP9),[384] 1861 (cr EP11),[385] 1861 (cr EP4).[95]

EP1–MAIDSTONE ALL SAINTS WITH ST PHILIP–Cr 1962 by union AP1, EP11.[379] Abol 1971 pt to help cr EP2, pt to EP7, pt to Tovil EP.[106]

EP2–MAIDSTONE ALL SAINTS WITH ST PHILIP AND HOLY TRINITY–Cr 1971 by union pts of EP1, EP3, EP5, Boxley AP, EP7, EP9, Bearstead AP.[48]

EP3–MAIDSTONE HOLY TRINITY–Cr 1841 from AP1.[384] Bdry: 1841,[170] 1861 (cr EP8),[1] 1871 (cr EP4),[371] 1895 (help cr EP6).[321] Abol 1971 pt to help cr EP2, pt to EP6.[48]

–MAIDSTONE ST ANDREW–Name used now for EP cr 1930 as Barming Heath, qv.

EP4–MAIDSTONE ST FAITH–Cr 1871 from AP1.[371]

EP5–MAIDSTONE ST JOHN THE EVANGELIST–Cr 1861 from AP1.[95] Bdry: 1933 (help cr EP7),[380] 1933.[381] Abol 1971 pt to help cr EP2, pt to EP7, pt to Bearstead AP, pt to Otham AP.[48]

EP6–MAIDSTONE ST LUKE–Cr 1895 from EP9, EP3.[321] Bdry: 1971.[48]

EP7–MAIDSTONE ST MARTIN–Cr 1933 from EP11, EP5.[380] Bdry: 1971 (incl help cr EP2).[48]

EP8–MAIDSTONE ST MICHAEL AND ALL ANGELS–Cr 1877 from EP10.[382] Bdry: 1913,[383] 1930 (cr Barming Heath EP, now called 'Maidstone St Andrew').[39]

EP9–MAIDSTONE ST PAUL–Cr 1861 from EP3.[1] Bdry: 1895 (help cr EP6),[321] 1971 (help cr EP2).[48]

EP10–MAIDSTONE ST PETER–Cr 1841 from AP1.[384] Bdry: 1877 (cr EP8),[382] 1913,[383] 1952.[20]

EP11–MAIDSTONE ST PHILIP–Cr 1861 from AP1.[385] Bdry: 1933 (help cr EP6),[380] 1933.[381] Abol 1962 to help cr EP1.[379]

EAST MALLING
AP *LG* Larkf. Hd, Mall. PLU, RSD, RD. Renamed civ 1962 'East Malling and Larkfield'.[386] *Parl* W'rn Dv (1832–67), Mid Dv (1867–1918), Seven. Dv/CC (1918–70). *Eccl* Seq 36. Eccl bdry: 1948 (cr New Hythe EP).[40]

EAST MALLING AND LARKFIELD
CP Renaming 1962 of East Malling AP.[386] *LG* Mall. RD. *Parl* Tonbr. & Mall. CC (1970–*).

WEST MALLING
AP *LG* Seq 4. *Parl* Seq 10. *Eccl* Seq 24.

MARDEN
AP *LG* Orig pt Marden Hd, pt Eyhorne Hd, pt Maid. Hd, pt Twyford Hd, ent Marden Hd by 19th cent,[44] Maid. PLU, RSD, RD. *Parl* Seq 13. *Eccl* Sutton RDn (until 1914), W Char. RDn (1914–*).

MARESTON OTHERWISE MERSTON
AP *LG* Shamw. Hd, sep identity lost civ early and incl in Shorne AP. *Eccl* Roch. RDn (until 1862), Cob. RDn (1862–1934). Abol eccl 1934 to help cr Higham with Merston EP.[171]

MARGATE
CP Cr 1935 by union Margate St John the Baptist AP, Westgate on Sea CP, and pts of Acol CP, Minster AP, Birchington CP, Garlinge CP, St Peter CP.[6] *LG* Margate MB. *Parl* Isle of Thanet CC (1948–70), Thanet West BC (1970–*).

MARGATE ALL SAINTS, WESTBROOK
EP Cr 1894 from Margate St John the Baptist AP, Westgate St James EP.[54] Westb. RDn (1894–1930), Thanet RDn (1930–*).

MARGATE ST JOHN THE BAPTIST
AP Chap in Minster AP, sep par *ca* 1200.[387] *LG* Ring. Hd, Lbty of Dover, non-corporate mbr Cq Pt of Dover, corporate mbr (from 1869), Isle of Thanet PLU, Margate MB (pt 1857–94, ent 1894–1974), pt Margate USD, pt Isle of Thanet RSD. Civ bdry: 1894 (the area of the MB extended to incl the greater pt of this par,[388] the pts not so incl lost to cr the 3 CPs of Garlinge, Northdown, Westgate on Sea[5]), 1913.[103] Abol civ 1935 to help cr Margate CP.[6] *Parl* E'rn Dv (1832–85), Isle of Thanet Dv (1885–1948). *Eccl* Seq 18. Eccl bdry: 1842 (cr Margate Trinity EP),[68] 1873 (cr Westgate St James EP),[54] 1874,[285] 1894 (help cr Margate All Saints, Westbrook EP),[54] 1957.[389]

MARGATE ST PAUL–Name used now for EP cr 1874 as 'Cliftonville', qv.

MARGATE TRINITY
EP Cr 1842 from Margate St John the Baptist AP.[68] Westb. RDn (1842–1930), Thanet RDn (1930–*). Bdry: 1874 (cr Cliftonville EP, now called 'Margate St Paul'),[215] 1874.[285]

MARK BEECH
EP Cr 1839 from Cowden AP, Hever AP.[224] Mall. RDn (1839–64), S Mall. RDn (1864–84), Tonbr. RDn (1884–*).

WEST MARSH
EP Cr 1849 from Ash AP.[27] Bridge RDn (1849–73), E Bridge RDn (1873–1967). Abol 1967 to help cr Ash with Westmarsh EP.[28]

MATFIELD
EP Cr 1875 from Brenchley AP.[111] S Mall. RDn (1875–1906), Tunbr. Wells RDn (1906–*).

THE MEAN
Land common to High Halstow AP, St Mary Hoo AP, in same civ and eccl organisation as those two pars, transf civ 1935 ent to the latter,[6] transf eccl 1949 ent to the former.[31]

MEOPHAM
AP *LG* Seq 9. Civ bdry: 1968.[390] *Parl* Seq 8. *Eccl* Shor. RDn (until 1862), Cob. RDn (1862–*).

MEREWORTH
AP *LG* Seq 5. Civ bdry: 1883,[8] 1888,[9] 1888.[391] *Parl* Seq 10. *Eccl* Seq 24.

MERSHAM
AP *LG* Orig pt Birch. Franchise, pt Chart & Longbr. Hd, ent Chart & Longbr. Hd by 19th cent[44] and Seq 24 thereafter. Civ bdry: 1934.[19] *Parl* Seq 5. *Eccl* Seq 10.

MERSTON–See MARESTON OTHERWISE MERSTON

MIDLEY
AP *LG* Orig St Martin Ivychurch Hd, later ent Rom. Marsh Lbty,[44] Rom. Marsh PLU, RSD, RD. Abol civ 1934 ent to Old Romney AP.[19] *Parl* E'rn Dv (1832–85), S'rn Dv (1885–1918), Ashf. Dv (1918–48). *Eccl* Lym. RDn (until 1864), S Lym. RDn (1864–1935). Abol eccl 1935 to help cr Old Romney with Midley EP.[25]

MILSTEAD
AP Usual eccl spelling; for civ before 1962 (at which time the par civ renamed 'Milstead'[392]) see following entry. *LG* Swale RD. *Parl* Fav. CC (1970–*). *Eccl* Seq 16.

MILSTED
AP Usual civ spelling until renamed 1962 'Milstead'[392]; for eccl and civ after 1962 see prev entry. *LG* Milton Hd, PLU, RSD, RD (1894–1934), Swale RD (1934–62). *Parl* E'rn Dv (1832–85), N-E'rn Dv (1885–1918), Fav. Dv/CC (1948–70).

MILTON
AP *LG* Westgate Hd, Bridge PLU, RSD, RD. Abol civ 1934 ent to Thanington Without CP.[150] *Parl* E'rn Dv (1832–1918), Canterb. Dv (1918–48). *Eccl* Canterb. RDn. Abol eccl 1884 to help cr Thanington and Milton EP.[408]

MILTON
AP Usual civ spelling; for eccl see 'Milton-next-Gravesend'. *LG* Tolt. Hd, Grav. & Milton PLU, Grav. MB, USD. Abol civ 1915 ent to Gravesend AP.[320] *Parl* W'rn Dv (1832–67), Grav. Parl Bor (1867–1918).

MILTON
AP Usual civ spelling; sometimes anc 'Milton-next-Sittingbourne'; for eccl see 'Milton Regis'. *LG* Milton Hd, PLU, Milton next Sitt. USD, UD (1894–1907), Milton Regis UD (1907–30). Abol civ 1930 pt to help cr Sittingbourne and Milton CP, pt to Bobbing AP.[103] *Parl* E'rn Dv (1832–1918), Fav. Dv (1918–48).

MILTON CHRIST CHURCH
EP Cr 1857 from Milton-next-Gravesend AP.[393] Sometimes 'Milton-next-Gravesend Christ Church'. Roch. RDn (1857–62), Grav. RDn (1862–*). Bdry: 1934,[171] 1936,[283] 1954,[170] 1957.[119]

MILTON HOLY TRINITY
EP Cr 1845 from Milton-next-Gravesend AP.[256] Sometimes 'Milton-next-Gravesend Holy Trinity'. Roch. RDn (1845–62), Grav. RDn (1862–1952). Bdry: 1936.[283] Abol 1952 ent to Gravesend St James EP.[323]

MILTON-NEXT-GRAVESEND
AP Usual eccl spelling; for civ see second 'Milton' above. *Eccl* Seq 33. Eccl bdry: 1845 (cr Milton Holy Trinity EP),[256] 1857 (cr Milton Christ Church EP),[393] 1879 (gains ex-par Denton, sometimes thereafter called 'Milton-next-Gravesend with Denton' though name not used now),[112] 1934,[171] 1936.[283]

MILTON-NEXT-GRAVESEND WITH DENTON–See prev entry

MILTON REGIS
AP Usual eccl spelling; for civ see third 'Milton' above. *Eccl* Seq 16. Eccl bdry: 1925 (cr Milton Regis St Mary EP).[394]

MILTON REGIS ST MARY
EP Cr 1925 from Milton Regis AP.[394] Sitt. RDn.

MINSTER
AP Incl chaps Margate, St Peters, St Lawrence (each sep par *ca* 1200[387]), ville Acol (sep CP 1866[3]). *LG* Ring. Hd, Thanet PLU, RSD, Isle of Thanet RD (1894–1935), Eastry RD (1935–74). Civ bdry: 1878,[395] 1894 (help cr Westgate on Sea CP),[5] 1935 (incl help cr Margate CP, help cr Sandwich CP).[6] *Parl* Seq 7. *Eccl* Seq 18. Eccl bdry: 1884 (help cr Westgate on Sea EP).[396]

MINSTER IN SHEPPEY
AP Sometimes 'Minster-in-Sheppy', or eccl before 1954, 'Minster in the Isle of Sheppey'. Incl Sheerness (sep EP 1851,[399] sep CP 1894 [the pt in Sheerness USD][122]). *LG* Perhaps orig Milton Hd,[397] Isle of Shep. Lbty, Shep. PLU, pt Sheerness USD, pt Shep. RSD, Shep. RD. Addtl civ bdry alt: 1912,[308] 1934.[199] Abol civ 1968 to help cr Queenborough-in-Sheppey MB and CP.[263] *Parl* E'rn Dv (1832–85), N-E'rn Dv (1885–1918), Fav. Dv/CC (1918–70). *Eccl* Seq 16. Addtl eccl bdry alt: 1954.[135]

MINSTER IN THE ISLE OF SHEPPEY–See prev entry

MINT
Ex-par place, sep CP 1858.[163] *LG* Westgate Hd, Bridge PLU (1858[120]–89), RSD. Abol 1889 ent to Harbledown AP.[334] *Parl* E'rn Dv (1867–1918).

MOLASH
Chap in Chilham AP, sep civ identity early, sep EP 1871.[4] *LG* Seq 28. Addtl civ bdry alt: 1968.[174] *Parl* Seq 5. *Eccl* Bridge RDn (until 1873), W Bridge RDn (1873–1928). Abol eccl 1928 to help cr Challock and Molash EP.[175]

GREAT MONGEHAM
AP *LG* Corn. Hd, Eastry PLU, RSD, RD. Civ bdry: 1901.[400] Abol civ 1935 pt to Deal AP, pt to Sholden CP.[6] *Parl* E'rn Dv (1832–1918), Dover Dv (1918–48). *Eccl* Seq 14. Eccl bdry: 1894,[401] 1963.[102]

LITTLE MONGEHAM
AP *LG* Corn. Hd, Eastry PLU, RSD, RD. Abol civ 1935 ent to Sutton AP.[6] *Parl* E'rn Dv (1832–1918), Dover Dv (1918–48). *Eccl* Sandw. RDn. Abol eccl 1970 ent to Sutton by Dover AP.[221]

MONKS HORTON
AP *LG* Seq 38. *Parl* Seq 2. *Eccl* Elham RDn (until 1895), N Lym. RDn (1895–*).

MONKTON
AP Incl chap Birchington (sep civ identity early, eccl united 1871 with Acol ville in Minster AP to cr Birchington with Acol EP[4]). *LG* Ring. Hd, Thanet PLU, RSD, Isle of Thanet RD (1894–1935), Eastry RD (1935–74). *Parl* Seq 7. *Eccl* Exempt from Archdeacon (until 1845), Seq 18.

MOTTINGHAM
Hmlt in Eltham AP, sep CP 1866,[3] sep EP

1884.[278] *LG* Blackh. Hd, Lewisham PLU (1836–87), Brom. PLU (1887–1930), Brom. RSD (1887–94), RD. Abol civ 1934 to help cr Chislehurst and Sidcup CP.[19] *Parl* West Dv (1867–85), W'rn Dv (1885–1918), Chisl. Dv (1918–45). *Eccl* Woolw. RDn (1884–1966), Greenw. RDn (1966–*). Eccl bdry: 1950,[370] 1952 (incl help cr Mottingham St Edward the Confessor EP),[369] 1960.[96]

MOTTINGHAM ST EDWARD THE CONFESSOR
EP Cr 1952 from Mottingham EP, Lee St Augustine, Grove Park EP.[369] Eltham RDn (1952–66), Greenw. RDn (1966–*).

MURSTON
AP *LG* Milton Hd, PLU, RSD, RD. Abol civ 1930 pt to help cr Sittingbourne and Milton CP, pt to Cuddenham AP.[33] *Parl* E'rn Dv (1832–85), N-E'rn Dv (1885–1918), Fav. Dv (1918–48). *Eccl* Seq 16. Eccl bdry: 1927,[185] 194 (help cr Luddenham and Stone EP),[117] 1957.[34]

NACKINGTON
AP *LG* Pt Canterb. Bor/MB/CP, orig pts outside Bor in Bridge & Petham Hd, Whit. Hd, by 19th cent pt outside Bor ent Bridge & Petham Hd,[44] Bridge PLU, pt Canterb. USD, pt Bridge RSD, Bridge RD. Civ bdry: 1894 (loses the pt in the CB to Canterbury St Mary Bredin AP).[42] Abol civ 1934 ent to Lower Hardres AP.[19] *Parl* Pt Canterb. Parl Bor (until 1918), pt E'rn Dv (1832–1918), Canterb. Dv (1918–48). *Eccl* Canterb. RDn. Abol eccl 1921 to help cr Lower Hardres and Nackington EP.[335]

NETTLESTEAD
AP Incl eccl West Barming (orig sep AP, civ deemed within East Barming AP[38]). *LG* Seq 10. Civ bdry: 1883,[8] 1888,[402] 1934.[19] *Parl* Seq 14. *Eccl* Seq 24. Eccl bdry: 1860 (help cr Paddock Wood EP).[115]

NEWCHURCH
AP *LG* Orig pt Aloesb. Hd, pt St Martin Ivychurch Hd, pt Newchurch Hd, pt Worth Hd, by 19th cent ent Rom. Marsh Lbty,[44] Seq 37 thereafter. Civ bdry: 1883,[8] 1934.[19] *Parl* Seq 6. *Eccl* Exempt from Archdeacon (until 1845), Seq 12.

NEWENDEN
AP *LG* Selbrit. Hd, Tent. PLU, RSD, RD. *Parl* Seq 11. *Eccl* Seq 5.

NEWINGTON
AP Usual civ spelling; for eccl see 'Newington next Hythe'. *LG* Orig Folk. Hd, by 19th cent pt Eastry Hd, pt Folk. Hd, pt Rom. Marsh Lbty,[44] Elham PLU, RSD, RD. Civ bdry: 1886,[377] 1886 (loses the pt in Hythe Parl Bor [not prev in Hythe MB] to St Leonard Hythe CP),[353] 1934.[19] *Parl* Pt Hythe Parl Bor (1832–1918), remainder and later, Seq 2.

NEWINGTON
AP Usual civ spelling; for eccl see 'Newington next Sittingbourne'. *LG* Seq 29. *Parl* Seq 4.

NEWINGTON NEXT HYTHE
AP Usual eccl spelling; for civ see 1st 'Newington' above. *Eccl* Seq 7. Eccl bdry: 1930.[351]

NEWINGTON NEXT SITTINGBOURNE
AP Usual eccl spelling; for civ see 2nd 'Newington' above. *Eccl* Seq 16.

NEWNHAM
AP *LG* Seq 27. Civ bdry: 1935.[6] *Parl* Seq 4. *Eccl* Seq 13.

NONINGTON
AP Area in Wingham AP, sep par 1282.[318] *LG* Orig pt Wingham Hd, pt Eastry Hd, ent Wingham Hd by 19th cent,[44] Seq 21 thereafter. Civ bdry: 1951 (cr Aylesham CP).[32] *Parl* Seq 3. *Eccl* Pec jurisd Wingham (until 1546), exempt from Archdeacon (1546–1845), Seq 1 thereafter.

NORTHBOURNE
AP Incl chap Sholden (sep civ identity early, sep EP 1849[403]). *LG* Orig ent Corn. Hd, by 19th cent pt Corn. Hd, pt Eastry Hd,[44] Eastry PLU, RSD, RD. Addtl civ bdry alt: 1935.[6] *Parl* Seq 3. *Eccl* Seq 14. Addtl eccl bdry alt: 1894,[69] 1940 (help cr Chillendon with Knowlton EP),[180] 1963,[102] 1970.[221]

NORTHDOWN
CP Cr 1894 from pt of the pt of Margate St John the Baptist AP not in Margate MB.[5] *LG* Thanet PLU, Isle of Thanet RD. Abol 1913 pt to Garlinge CP, pt to Margate St John the Baptist AP.[103]

NORTHFLEET
AP *LG* Tolt. Hd, N Ayl. PLU (1835–84), Strood PLU (1884–1930), Northfleet USD, UD. Civ bdry: 1935.[6] *Parl* Pt Grav. Parl Bor (1867–1918), remainder and later, Seq 8. *Eccl* Shor. RDn (until 1862), Grav. RDn (1862–*). Eccl bdry: 1871 (help cr Perry Street EP),[404] 1887,[357] 1939.[217]

NORTON
AP *LG* Seq 27. Civ bdry: 1935.[6] *Parl* Seq 4. *Eccl* Seq 13. Eccl bdry: 1963.[102]

NUNHEAD ST SILAS
EP Cr 1904 from Forest Hill St Augustine, Honor Oak Park EP, a Kent pt of Hatcham St Catherine EP (Kent, Surrey), Nunhead St Antholin EP (Surrey).[212] Camberwell RDn. Bdry: 1925 (incl gains another pt anc Surrey),[74] 1936.[60]

NURSTED
AP *LG* Tolt. Hd, N Ayl. PLU (1835–84), RSD (1875–84), Strood PLU (1884–1930), RSD (1884–94), Strood RD. Civ bdry: 1935.[6] *Parl* Seq 8. *Eccl* Seq 30. Eccl bdry: 1887,[357] 1939.[217]

OARE
AP *LG* Seq 27. Civ bdry: 1935.[6] *Parl* Seq 4. *Eccl* Ospr. RDn. Eccl bdry: 194 .[117] Abol eccl 1966 to help cr Oare and Luddenham EP.[375]

OARE AND LUDDENHAM
EP Cr 1966 by union Oare AP, Luddenham with Stone EP.[375] Ospr. RDn.

OFFHAM
AP *LG* Seq 4. Civ bdry: 1934.[19] *Parl* Seq 10. *Eccl* Seq 24. Eccl bdry: 1934.[10]

ORGARSWICK
AP *LG* Orig Worth Hd, by 19th cent ent Rom. Marsh Lbty,[44] Rom. Marsh PLU, RSD, RD.

Abol civ 1934 ent to Burmarsh AP.[19] *Parl* E'rn Dv (1832–85), S'rn Dv (1885–1918), Ashf. Dv (1918–48). *Eccl* Lym. RDn (until 1873), S Lym. RDn (1873–1963). Abol eccl 1963 ent to Burmarsh AP.[102]

ORLESTONE

AP *LG* Perhaps orig ent Ham Hd,[358] probably pt Ham Hd, pt Rom. Marsh Lbty as later, E Ashf. PLU (1836–1930), RSD, RD. Civ bdry: 1883,[8] 1935.[6] *Parl* Seq 5. *Eccl* Seq 10. Eccl bdry: 1962.[24]

ORPINGTON

AP Incl chap Downe (sep civ identity early, sep EP 1861[177]), chap St Mary Cray (sep civ identity early, sep EP 1867[228]). *LG* Ruxley Hd, Brom. PLU, RSD, RD (1894–1935), Orp. UD (1935–65). Addtl civ bdry alt: 1934 (incl help cr Chislehurst and Sidcup CP).[19] Transf 1965 to Gtr London (Brom. LB).[51] *Parl* W'rn Dv (1832–67), West Dv (1867–85), N-W'rn Dv (1885–1918), Chisl. Dv (1918–48), Orp. CC (1948–70), Gtr London thereafter. *Eccl* Shor. RDn (until 1864), W Dartf. RDn (1864–1909), Brom. RDn (1909–54), Orp. RDn (1954–*). Addtl eccl bdry alt: 1852 (from area chap St Mary Cray, cr Crocken Hill EP),[229] 1934 (cr Orpington St Andrew EP),[405] 1935 (help cr Petts Wood EP),[82] 1938,[203] 1940 (help cr Orpington Christ Church EP),[202] 1959 (cr Crofton St Paul EP).[233]

ORPINGTON CHRIST CHURCH

EP Cr 1940 from Chelsfield AP, Orpington AP.[202] Brom. RDn (1940–54), Orp. RDn (1954–*).

ORPINGTON ST ANDREW

EP Cr 1934 from Orpington AP.[405] Brom. RDn (1934–54), Orp. RDn (1954–*).

OSPRINGE

AP *LG* Fav. Hd, PLU, pt Fav. Bor/MB (until 1883), pt Fav. corporate mbr Cq Pt of Dover, pt Fav. USD (1875–83), Fav. RSD (pt 1875–83, ent 1883–94), Fav. RD (1894–1934), Swale RD (1934–74). Civ bdry: 1883,[8] 1935 (incl help cr Faversham CP).[6] *Parl* Seq 4. *Eccl* Seq 13. Eccl bdry: 1930,[295] 1947.[117]

OTFORD

Chap in Shoreham AP, sep civ identity early, sep EP 1723.[177] *LG* Seq 40. Civ bdry: 1908 (cr Dunton Green CP).[258] *Parl* Seq 20. *Eccl* Shor. RDn. Eccl bdry: 1890 (cr Dunton Green EP).[242]

OTHAM

AP *LG* Seq 2. *Parl* Seq 9. *Eccl* Seq 17. Eccl bdry: 1971,[48] 1972.[49]

OTTERDEN

AP *LG* Orig ent Eyhorne Hd, by 19th cent pt Eyhorne Hd, pt Fav. Hd,[44] Hollingb. PLU, RSD, RD. Civ bdry: 1883.[343] *Parl* Pt E'rn Dv (1832–85), pt W'rn Dv (1832–67), Mid Dv (pt 1867–85, ent 1885–1918), Maid. Dv/CC (1918–*). *Eccl* Seq 13.

OXNEY

Chap in Eythorne AP, sep civ identity early, no sep eccl identity. *LG* Corn. Hd, River PLU (renamed Dover in 1840s), Dover RSD, RD. Abol civ 1934 pt to East Langdon AP, pt to St Margaret's at Cliffe AP.[19] *Parl* E'rn Dv (1832–1918), Dover Dv (1918–48).

PADDLESWORTH

AP *LG* Seq 36. *Parl* Seq 2. *Eccl* Exempt from Archdeacon (until 1845), Seq 8.

PADDLESWORTH

AP Orig AP, destroyed church, civ incl early in Snodland AP (Larkf. Hd); eccl in Mall. RDn, deemed as ex-par after destruction, abol eccl 1934 to help cr Snodland with Paddlesworth EP.[81]

PADDOCK WOOD

EP Cr 1860 from Brenchley AP, Yalding AP, Nettlestead AP, Collier Street EP.[115] Mall. RDn (1860–64), S Mall. RDn (1864–1906), Tunbr. Wells RDn (1906–09), Tonbr. RDn (1909–*).

CP Cr 1955 from Brenchley AP.[114] *LG* Tonbr. RD. *Parl* Royal Tunbr. Wells CC (1970–*).

PATRIXBOURNE

AP Incl chap Bridge (sep civ identity early, no sep eccl identity hence this par eccl 'Patrixbourne with Bridge', qv). *LG* Bridge & Petham Hd, pt Canterb. Bor/MB/CB, Bridge PLU, pt Canterb. USD, pt Bridge RSD, Bridge RD. Civ bdry: 1894 (loses the pt in the CB to Canterbury St Paul AP).[42] *Parl* Pt Canterb. Parl Bor (until 1918), remainder and later, Seq 1.

PATRIXBOURNE WITH BRIDGE

AP Usual eccl spelling; for civ and civ sep chap Bridge, see prev entry. *Eccl* Seq 1.

EAST PECKHAM

AP *LG* Orig pt Twyford Hd, pt Littlef. Hd, ent Twyford Hd by 19th cent,[44] Seq 11 thereafter. Civ bdry: 1883,[8] 1888,[9] 1934.[19] *Parl* Seq 15. *Eccl* Seq 25. Dedication changed 1972 from St Michael to Holy Trinity.[372] Eccl bdry: 1843 (cr East Peckham Holy Trinity EP),[294] 1947 (gains back East Peckham Holy Trinity EP).[341]

EAST PECKHAM HOLY TRINITY

EP Cr 1843 from East Peckham AP.[394] Shor. RDn (1843–64), N Mall. RDn (1864–1906), Mall. RDn (1906–47). Abol eccl 1947 ent to East Peckham AP.[341]

WEST PECKHAM

AP *LG* Orig pt Hoo Hd, pt Littlef. Hd, ent Littlef. Hd by 19th cent,[44] Seq 5 thereafter. Civ bdry: 1888.[9] *Parl* Seq 10. *Eccl* Seq 24.

PEMBURY

AP *LG* Orig pt Twyford Hd, pt Washl. Hd, ent Washl. Hd by 19th cent,[44] Seq 12 thereafter. Civ bdry: 1883,[8] 1934.[19] *Parl* Seq 16. *Eccl* Seq 27. Eccl bdry: 1962.[409]

PENGE

CP Transf 1899 from Surrey to Kent.[190] *LG* Penge UD. Transf 1965 to Gtr London (Brom. LB).[51] *Parl* Surrey until 1918, Brom. Parl Bor (1918–48), Beck. BC (1948–70), Gtr London thereafter.

PENGE LANE

EP Cr 1878 from Beckenham AP.[56] W Dartf. RDn (1878–1909), Beck. RDn (1909–*). Bdry:

1936,[61] 1952.[410] Now called 'Beckenham Holy Trinity'.

PENSHURST

AP *LG* Pt Somerden Hd, pt Washl. Hd, Penshurst PLU (1835–1840s), Seven. PLU (1840s–1930), RSD, RD. Civ bdry: 1934.[19] *Parl* W'rn Dv (1832–67), pt West Dv, pt Mid Dv (1867–85), S-W'rn Dv (1885–1918), Seven. Dv/CC (1918–*). *Eccl* Seq 37. Eccl bdry: 1870 (cr Fordcombe EP),[301] 1906 (help cr Chiddingstone Causeway EP).[209]

PERRY HILL

EP Cr 1880 from Forest Hill Christ Church EP, Lewisham AP.[134] Greenw. RDn (1880–86), Lewisham RDn (1886–*). Bdry: 1900 (help cr Crofton Park EP).[100]

PERRY STREET

EP Cr 1871 from Rosherville EP, Northfleet EP.[404] Grav. RDn. Bdry: 1939,[217] 1951 (incl help cr Gravesend St Mary EP).[322]

PETHAM WITH WALTHAM

EP Cr 1698 by union Petham AP, Waltham AP.[411] Bridge RDn (1698–1873), W Bridge RDn (1873–*). Bdry: 1970.[244]

PETTS WOOD

EP Cr 1935 from Orpington AP, Chislehurst AP.[82] Brom. RDn (1935–36), Chisl. RDn (1936–54), Orp. RDn (1954–*). Bdry: 1957.[84]

PLAISTOW

EP Cr 1863, refounded 1864 from Bromley AP.[126] Dartf. RDn (1863–64), W Dartf. RDn (1864–1909), Brom. RDn (1909–*). Bdry: 1880 (help cr Bromley St John the Evangelist EP),[127] 1887,[128] 1907,[82] 1927 (cr Bromley St Andrew EP),[133] 1955 (help cr Bromley Christ Church EP).[131]

PLATT

Chap in Wrotham AP, sep EP 1846,[412] sep CP 1934.[19] *LG* Mall. RD. *Parl* Seven. CC (1948–70), Tonbr. & Mall. CC (1970–*). *Eccl* Shor. RDn. Eccl bdry: 1966.[331]

PLAXTOL

Area in Wrotham AP, sep EP 1844,[413] sep CP 1934.[19] *LG* Mall. RD. *Parl* Seven. CC (1948–70), Tonbr. & Mall. CC (1970–*). *Eccl* Shor. RDn.

PLUCKLEY

AP *LG* Seq 23. Civ bdry: 1935,[6] 1957.[178] *Parl* Seq 5. *Eccl* Seq 4. Eccl bdry: 1970.[181]

PLUMSTEAD

The following have 'Plumstead' in their names. Insofar as any existed at a given time: *LG* Lessness Hd, Lewisham PLU (1836–68), Woolw. PLU (1868–89), Plumstead Dist (Metrop Bd Wks). Transf 1889 to London.[190] *Parl* Pt W'rn Dv (1832–67), Greenw. Parl Bor (pt 1832–67, ent 1867–85), Woolw. Parl Bor (1885–1918), London thereafter. *Eccl* Dartf. RDn (until 1845), [London dioc 1845–68], Greenw. RDn (1861–68), Woolw. RDn (1868–1966), Greenw. RDn (1966–*).

AP1–PLUMSTEAD [ST MARGARET] –Incl chap East Wickham (sep civ identity early, sep EP 1854[414]). Addtl eccl bdry alt: 1864 (cr EP11),[132] 1865 (help cr EP3),[275] 1876 (cr EP1),[415] 1880 (cr EP4),[416] 1903 (help cr EP8),[280] 1905 (help cr EP2),[278] 1908,[417] 1925,[407] 1927,[68] 1935,[418] 1953 (incl help cr EP5).[419] Abol eccl 1968 to help cr EP9.[420]

EP1–PLUMSTEAD ALL SAINTS, SHOOTER'S HILL–Cr 1876 from AP1.[415] Bdry: 1900,[421] 1934,[136] 1935,[418] 1953 (incl help cr EP5).[189]

EP2–PLUMSTEAD THE ASCENSION–Cr 1905 from AP1, EP11.[278] Bdry: 1957.[21]

EP3–PLUMSTEAD CHRIST CHURCH, SHOOTER'S HILL–Cr 1865 from Eltham AP, AP1, Woolwich AP.[275] Bdry: 1900,[421] 1925,[407] 1934,[136] 1937,[188] 1957.[21]

EP4–PLUMSTEAD ST JAMES–Cr 1880 from AP1.[416] Bdry: 1908.[417] Abol eccl 1953 to help cr EP5.[419]

EP5–PLUMSTEAD ST JAMES WITH ST JOHN THE BAPTIST–Cr 1953 by union EP4, EP6, pt AP1, pt EP1, pt Woolwich AP.[419] Abol 1968 to help cr EP7.[420]

EP6–PLUMSTEAD ST JOHN THE BAPTIST–Cr 1885 from EP11.[422] Bdry: 1908.[417] Abol 1953 to help cr EP5.[419]

EP7–PLUMSTEAD ST JOHN WITH ST JAMES AND ST PAUL–Cr 1968 by union EP5, EP12.[420]

EP8–PLUMSTEAD ST MARK–Cr 1903 from EP11, AP1.[280] Abol 1968 to help cr EP9.[420]

EP9–PLUMSTEAD ST MARK AND ST MARGARET–Cr 1968 by union EP8, AP1.[420] Bdry: 1973 (help cr Thamesmead EP).[2]

EP10–PLUMSTEAD ST MICHAEL AND ALL ANGELS–Cr 1908 from EP11.[257] Bdry: 1927.[68] Renamed 1965 'Abbey Wood'.[1]

EP11–PLUMSTEAD ST NICHOLAS–Cr 1864 from AP1.[132] Bdry: 1885 (help cr EP6),[422] 1902 (cr EP12),[89] 1903 (help cr EP8),[280] 1905 (help cr EP2),[278] 1908,[417] 1908 (cr EP10).[257]

EP12–PLUMSTEAD ST PAUL–Cr 1902 from EP11.[89] Bdry: 1908.[417] Abol 1968 to help cr EP7.[420]

POSTLING

AP *LG* Seq 35. *Parl* Seq 2. *Eccl* Elham RDn (until 1914), N Lym. RDn (1914–*).

POULTON

AP *LG* Bewsb. Hd, River PLU (renamed Dover in 1840s), pt Dover Bor/MB, pt Dover USD, pt Dover RSD, Dover RD. Civ bdry: 1883,[8] 1894 (loses the pt in the MB to cr Poulton Within CP),[122] 1895,[141] 1930.[249] Abol civ 1934 pt to Dover CP, pt to Hougham Without CP.[19] *Parl* E'rn Dv (1832–1918), Dover Dv (1918–48). *Eccl* No church, eccl incl in Hougham AP.

POLUTON WITHIN

CP Cr 1894 from the pt of Poluton CP in Dover MB.[122] *LG* Dover PLU, MB. Abol 1896 to help cr Dover CP.[182]

PRESTON

AP Sometimes 'Preston next Wingham'. *LG* Preston Hd, Eastry PLU, RSD, RD. Civ bdry: 1935.[6]

Parl Seq 3. *Eccl* Seq 1.

PRESTON NEXT FAVERSHAM

AP *LG* Fav. Hd, PLU, pt Fav. MB (1889–94), pt Fav. USD (1889–94), Fav. RSD (ent 1875–89, pt 1889–94). Abol civ 1894 the pt in the MB to cr Preston Within CP, the remainder to cr Preston Without CP.[294] *Parl* E'rn Dv (1832–85), N-E'rn Dv (1885–1918). *Eccl* Seq 13. Eccl bdry: 1881 (help cr The Brents EP),[116] 1930,[295] 1947.[117]

PRESTON WITHIN

CP Cr 1894 from the pt of Preston next Faversham AP in Fav. MB.[294] *LG* Fav. PLU, MB. Abol 1935 to help cr Faversham CP.[6] *Parl* Fav. Dv (1918–48).

PRESTON WITHOUT

CP Cr 1894 from the pt of Preston next Faversham AP not in Fav. MB.[294] *LG* Fav. PLU, RD. Abol 1897 to cr the 2 CPs of North Preston Without, South Preston Without.[423]

NORTH PRESTON WITHOUT

CP Cr 1897 from pt of Preston Without CP.[423] *LG* Fav. PLU, RD. Abol 1935 to help cr Faversham CP.[6] *Parl* Fav. Dv (1918–48).

SOUTH PRESTON WITHOUT

CP Cr 1897 from pt of Preston Without CP.[423] *LG* Fav. PLU, RD. Abol 1935 pt to help cr Faversham CP, pt to Ospringe AP, pt to Sheldwich AP.[6] *Parl* Fav. Dv (1918–48).

QUEENBOROUGH

AP *LG* Isle of Shep. Lbty, Shep. PLU, Queenborough Bor, MB (1885–1968), USD (1885–94). Civ bdry: 1912,[398] 1934.[19] Enlarged 1968, gaining Sheerness UD & CP, Sheppey RD (see next entry for constituent pars), the whole renamed 'Queenborough-in-Sheppey' MB & CP.[263] *Parl* Queenborough Parl Bor (1572–1832), E'rn Dv (1832–85), N-E'rn Dv (1885–1918), Fav. Dv/CC (1918–70). *Eccl* Seq 16. Eccl bdry: 1954.[135]

QUEENBOROUGH-IN-SHEPPEY

CP Cr 1968 by union Queenborough MB & AP, Sheerness UD & CP, Shep. RD (Eastchurch AP, Emley AP, Harty AP, Leysdown-on-Sea CP, Minster in Sheppey AP, Warden AP).[263] *LG* Queenborough-in-Shep. MB. *Parl* Fav. CC (1970–*).

RAINHAM

AP *LG* Milton Hd, PLU, RSD, RD. Abol civ 1929 ent to Gillingham AP.[365] *Parl* W'rn Dv (1832–67), Mid Dv (1867–85), N-E'rn Dv (1885–1918), Fav. Dv (1918–48). *Eccl* Sitt. RDn (until 1939), Roch. RDn (1939–54), Gill. RDn (1954–*). Eccl bdry: 1938,[121] 1943,[111] 1956 (incl help cr Gillingham Holy Trinity EP),[316] 1956 (help cr Wigmore with Hempstead EP),[317] 1972 (help cr South Gillingham EP).[113]

RAMSGATE

The following have 'Ramsgate' in their names. Insofar as any existed at a given time: *LG* Ring. Hd, Thanet PLU, in Lbty of Sandw. and thus non-corporate mbr Cq Pt of Sandw., Ramsgate MB (1884–1974), USD (1884–94), Thanet RSD (1875–84). *Parl* E'rn Dv (1832–85), Isle of Thanet Dv/CC (1885–1970), Thanet East BC (1970–*). *Eccl* Westb. RDn (until 1930), Thanet RDn (1930–*).

CP1/EP1–RAMSGATE [ST GEORGE]–Area in St Lawrence AP (eccl, 'St Laurence in Thanet'), sep civ identity early, sep EP 1827.[424] Civ bdry: 1922 (gains ent St Lawrence Intra CP),[425] 1935 (incl help cr Broadstairs and St Peter's CP).[6] Eccl bdry: 1848 (cr EP2),[426] 1877,[303] 1887 (cr EP5),[427] 1958.[204]

EP2–RAMSGATE CHRIST CHURCH–Cr 1848 from EP1.[426] Bdry: 1877.[303]

EP3–RAMSGATE HOLY TRINITY–Cr 1845 from St Laurence in Thanet AP.[321] Bdry: 1875 (help cr EP4),[10] 1958.[204]

EP4–RAMSGATE ST LUKE–Cr 1875 from St Laurence in Thanet AP, EP3.[10]

EP5–RAMSGATE ST PAUL–Cr 1887 from EP1.[427] Abol 1958 pt to EP1, pt to EP3.[204]

RECULVER

AP Incl chap Hoath (sep civ identity early, no sep eccl identity). *LG* Bleang. Hd, Blean PLU, RSD, RD. Abol civ 1934 ent to Herne Bay CP.[19] *Parl* E'rn Dv (1832–1918), Canterb. Dv (1918–48). *Eccl* Exempt from Archdeacon (until 1845), Westb. RDn (until 1930), Canterb. RDn (1930–71), Recul. RDn (1971–*). Eccl bdry: 1960.[212]

RECULVER WITH HOATH–See prev entry

RIDLEY

AP *LG* Axton/Axton, Darenth & Wilm. Hd, Dartf. PLU, RSD, RD. Abol civ 1955 to help cr Ash-cum-Ridley CP, now called 'Ash-with-Ridley'.[29] *Parl* W'rn Dv (1832–67), West Dv (1867–85), N-W'rn Dv (1885–1918), Dartf. Dv (1918–48), Orp. CC (1948–70). *Eccl* Seq 32.

RINGWOULD

AP Incl hmlt Kingsdown (sep EP 1850 as 'Kingsdown St John'[56]). *LG* Corn. Hd, Dover PLU, in Lbty Dover and thus non-corporate mbr Cq Pt of Dover, Dover RD. *Parl* Seq 3. *Eccl* Sandw. RDn. Eccl bdry: 1963.[102] Abol eccl 1964 to help cr Ringwould with Oxney EP.[407]

RINGWOULD WITH OXNEY

EP Cr 1964 by union Ringwould AP, Oxney EP.[407] Sandw. RDn.

RIPPLE

AP *LG* Seq 17. Civ bdry: 1935.[6] *Parl* Seq 3. *Eccl* Seq 14. Eccl bdry: 1963.[102]

RIVER

AP *LG* Bewsb. Hd, River PLU (renamed Dover in 1840s), Dover RSD, RD. Civ bdry: 1894 (gains the pt of Buckland AP not in Dover MB),[140] 1895,[141] 1903,[249] 1921,[250] 1934,[19] 1951.[251] Abol civ 1960 pt to help cr Temple Ewell with River CP, pt to Whitfield AP.[288] *Parl* E'rn Dv (1832–1918), Dover Dv/CC (1918–70). *Eccl* Seq 6.

RIVERHEAD

Chap in Sevenoaks AP, sep EP 1832, refounded 1864,[132] sep CP 1894 (from pt of the pt of the par not in Seven. USD).[428] *LG* Seven. PLU, RD. Civ bdry: 1934.[19] *Parl* Seven. Dv/CC

(1918–*). *Eccl* Shor. RDn (1832–1909), Seven. RDn (1909–*). Eccl bdry: 1871,[371] 1877 (help cr Kippington EP).[362]

ROCHESTER

The following have 'Rochester' in their names. Insofar as any existed at a given time: *LG* Roch. Bor/MB, Medway PLU, Roch. USD. *Parl* Roch. Parl Bor (1295–1918), pt Roch., Chatham Parl Bor, pt Roch., Gill. Parl Bor (1918–48 [see Part III of the *Guide* for constitution by wards], Roch. & Chatham BC (1948–*). *Eccl* Roch. RDn.

CP1–ROCHESTER–Cr 1934 by union CP2, AP3, St Margaret Intra CP, Strood Intra CP, Frindsbury Intra CP, and pts of Frindsbury Extra CP, Strood Extra CP, Chatham AP.[19] Civ bdry: 1962.[216] Parl bdry: 1964.[480]

EP1–ROCHESTER–Cr 1972 by union pt AP3, pt EP5.[429]

CP2–ROCHESTER CASTLE PRECINCTS–Ex-par place, sep CP 1858.[163] *LG* Not in Bor (in Chatham & Gill. Hd), Roch. MB (1835–1934). Abol 1934 to help cr CP1.[19]

–ROCHESTER PRECINCTS OF THE CATHEDRAL CHURCH OF CHRIST AND THE BLESSED VIRGIN MARY–Eccl ex-par. Bdry: 1972.[429]

AP1–ROCHESTER ST CLEMENT–United 1549 with AP3, the union civ called as AP3, eccl as EP3.[479]

EP2–ROCHESTER ST JUSTUS–Cr 1956 from EP5.[430] Bdry: 1966.[31]

AP2–ROCHESTER ST MARGARET–Pt Roch. Bor/MB/USD, pt Chatham & Gill. Hd, pt Medway RSD. Abol civ 1894 the pt in the MB to cr St Margaret Intra CP, the remainder to cr St Margaret Extra CP.[431] Eccl bdry: 1860 (cr EP4),[255] 1901 (cr Borstal EP).[96] Abol eccl 1954 to help cr EP5.[382]

AP3–ROCHESTER ST NICHOLAS–Gains 1549 AP1, the union civ called as AP3, eccl as EP3.[479] Abol civ 1934 to help cr CP1.[19]

EP3–ROCHESTER ST NICHOLAS WITH ST CLEMENT–Eccl name for union 1549 of AP1, AP3 (civ called as AP3).[479] Abol eccl 1972 pt to help cr EP1, pt to ex-par Precincts of the Cathedral Church of Christ and the Blessed Virgin Mary.[429]

EP4–ROCHESTER ST PETER–Cr 1860 from AP1.[255] Bdry: 1954 (help cr Chatham St Stephen EP).[198] Abol 1954 to help cr EP5.[382]

EP5–ROCHESTER ST PETER AND ST MARGARET–Cr 1954 by union EP4, AP2.[382] Bdry: 1956 (cr EP3).[430] Abol 1972 pt to help cr EP1, pt to ex-par Precincts of the Cathedral Church of Christ and the Blessed Virgin Mary.[429]

RODMERSHAM

AP *LG* Seq 29. *Parl* Seq 4. *Eccl* Seq 16. Eccl bdry: 1927.[185]

ROLVENDEN

AP *LG* Rolv. Hd, Tent. PLU, RSD, RD. *Parl* Seq 11. *Eccl* Seq 5.

NEW ROMNEY

AP *LG* Orig pt St Martin Ivychurch Hd, pt Langport Hd, New Rom. Bor and Cq Pt of New Rom., by 19th cent pt New Rom. Bor & Cq Pt, pt Rom. Marsh Lbty, pt Langport Hd,[44] Rom. Marsh PLU, New Rom. MB (pt 1885–94, ent 1894–1974), pt New Rom. USD (1885–94), Rom. Marsh RSD (ent 1875–85, pt 1885–94). Civ bdry: 1883,[8] 1894 (loses the pt in the MB to cr St Martin's New Romney CP),[122] 1934.[19] *Parl* Pt New Rom. Parl Bor (1558–1832), Seq 6. *Eccl* Exempt from Archdeacon (until 1845), Lym. RDn. Abol eccl 1845 to help cr New Romney with Hope EP.[348]

NEW ROMNEY WITH HOPE

EP Cr 1845 by union New Romney AP, Hope AP.[348] Lym. RDn (1845–64), S Lym. RDn (1864–*). Bdry: 1963.[102]

ST MARTIN'S NEW ROMNEY

CP Cr 1894 from the pt of New Romney AP not in New Rom. MB.[122] *LG* Rom. Marsh PLU, RD. Abol 1934 pt to Old Romney AP, pt to St Mary in the Marsh AP.[19] *Parl* Ashf. Dv (1918–48).

OLD ROMNEY

AP *LG* Orig pt Langport Hd, pt St Martin Ivychurch Hd, pt Cq Pt of New Rom., by 19th cent pt Langport Hd, pt Cq Pt of New Rom.,[44] Seq 37 thereafter. Civ bdry: 1934.[19] *Parl* Seq 6. *Eccl* Lym. RDn (until 1864), S Lym. RDn (1864–1935). Abol eccl 1935 to help cr Old Romney with Midley EP.[25]

OLD ROMNEY WITH MIDLEY

EP Cr 1935 by union Old Romney AP, Midley AP.[25] S Lym. RDn.

ROSHERVILLE

EP Cr 1853 from Northfleet AP.[434] Roch. RDn (1853–62), Grav. RDn (1862–*). Bdry: 1880 (help cr Perry Street CP).[404]

RUCKINGE

AP *LG* Pt Ham Hd, pt Newchurch Hd, pt Rom. Marsh Lbty, E Ashf. PLU (1836–1930), RSD, RD. Civ bdry: 1935.[6] *Parl* Seq 5. *Eccl* Seq 10. Eccl bdry: 1962.[24]

RUSTHALL

EP Cr 1868 from Speldhurst AP.[432] S Mall. RDn (1868–1906), Tunbr. Wells RDn (1906–*). Bdry: 1889 (help cr Tunbridge Wells King Charles the Martyr EP),[2] 1928,[342] 1947,[433] 1971.[366]

RYARSH

AP *LG* Seq 4. Civ bdry: 1883,[8] 1888.[9] *Parl* Seq 10. *Eccl* Seq 24. Eccl bdry: 1934.[10]

ST COSMUS AND ST DAMIAN IN THE BLEAN

AP Usual civ spelling; for eccl see 'Blean'. *LG* Whit. Hd, Blean PLU, RSD, RD (1894–1934), Bridge-Blean RD (1934–74). Civ bdry: 1934.[150] *Parl* Seq 1.

ST DUNSTAN

AP Usual civ spelling; for eccl see 'Canterbury St Dunstan'. *LG* Pt Westgate Hd, pt Canterb. Bor/MB/CB, Blean PLU, pt Canterb. USD, pt

Blean RSD. Abol civ 1894 the pt in the CB to cr St Dunstan Within CP, the remainder to cr St Dunstan Without CP.[42] *Parl* Pt Canterb. Parl Bor (1295–1918), pt E'rn Dv (1832–1918).

ST DUNSTAN WITHIN

CP Cr 1894 from the pt of St Dunstan AP in Canterb. CB.[42] *LG* Blean PLU, Canterb. CB. Abol 1912 ent to Canterb. CB and CP.[149]

ST DUNSTAN WITHOUT

CP Cr 1894 from the pt of St Dunstan AP not in Canterb. CB.[42] *LG* Blean PLU, RD. Abol 1934 pt to Canterb. CB & CP, pt to St Cosmus and St Damian in the Blean AP.[150] *Parl* Canterb. Dv (1918–48).

ST GREGORY THE GREAT–See CANTERBURY ST GREGORY THE GREAT

ST LAURENCE IN THANET

AP Usual eccl spelling; for civ and origin of par see following entry. *Eccl* Seq 18. Eccl bdry: 1845 (cr Ramsgate Holy Trinity EP),[321] 1875 (help cr Ramsgate St Luke EP),[10] 1877.[303]

ST LAWRENCE

AP Usual civ spelling; for eccl see prev entry. Chap in Minster AP, sep par *ca* 1200.[387] *LG* Ring. Hd, Thanet PLU, pt Ramsgate MB (188 –94), pt Ramsgate USD (1884–94), Thanet RSD (ent 1875–84, pt 1884–94). Civ bdry: 1878.[395] Abol civ 1894 the pt in the MB to cr St Lawrence Intra CP, the remainder to cr St Lawrence Extra CP.[122] *Parl* E'rn Dv (1832–85), Isle of Thanet Dv (1885–1918).

ST LAWRENCE EXTRA

CP Cr 1894 from the pt of St Lawrence AP not in Ramsgate MB.[122] *LG* Thanet PLU, Isle of Thanet RD. Abol 1935 ent to Ramsgate CP.[6] *Parl* Isle of Thanet Dv (1918–48).

ST LAWRENCE INTRA

CP Cr 1894 from the pt of St Lawrence AP in Ramsgate MB.[122] *LG* Thanet PLU, Ramsgate MB. Abol 1922 ent to Ramsgate CP.[425] *Parl* Isle of Thanet Dv (1918–48).

ST MARGARET EXTRA

CP Cr 1894 from the pt of Rochester St Margaret AP not in Roch. MB.[431] *LG* Medway PLU, RD. Abol 1905 ent to Wouldham AP.[435]

ST MARGARET INTRA

CP Cr 1894 from the pt of Rochester St Margaret AP in Roch. MB.[431] *LG* Medway PLU, Roch. MB. Bdry: 1894 (gains the pt of Wouldham AP in Roch. MB).[436] Abol 1934 to help cr Rochester CP.[19] *Parl* Roch., Gill. Parl Bor (1918–48).

ST MARGARET AT CLIFFE

AP Usual eccl spelling; for civ see following entry. *Eccl* Exempt from Archdeacon (until 1845), Seq 6.

ST MARGARET'S AT CLIFFE

AP Usual civ spelling; for eccl see prev entry. *LG* Bewsb. Hd, River PLU (renamed Dover in 1840s), Dover RSD, RD. Civ bdry: 1934.[19] *Parl* Seq 3.

ST MARY IN THE MARSH

AP *LG* Orig pt Newchurch Hd, pt St Martin Ivychurch Hd, ent Rom. Marsh Lbty by 19th cent,[44] Rom. Marsh PLU, RSD, RD. Civ bdry: 1883,[8] 1934,[19] 1951,[260] *Parl* Seq 6. *Eccl* Seq 12. Eccl bdry: 1933,[261] 1963.[102]

ST NICHOLAS AT WADE

AP Gains by 16th cent Sarre (orig sep AP,[437] sep CP 1866[3]). *LG* Ring. Hd, pt Cq Pt of Sandw. (16th cent–1866, the area of Sarre until it regains independence), Thanet PLU, RSD, Isle of Thanet RD (1894–1935), Eastry RD (1935–74). *Parl* Seq 7. *Eccl* Exempt from Archdeacon (until 1845), Seq 18.

ST NICHOLAS HOSPITAL

Ex-par, sep CP 1858.[163] *LG* Westgate Hd, Bridge PLU (1858[120]–1930), RSD, RD. Abol 1934 ent to Harbledown AP.[150] *Parl* E'rn Dv (1867–1918), Canterb. Dv (1918–48).

ST PETER

CP Renaming 1914 of St Peter Intra CP when gains pt St Peter Extra CP.[312] *LG* Thanet PLU, Broadstairs and St Peter's UD. Abol 1935 pt to help cr Broadstairs and St Peter's CP, pt to help cr Margate CP, pt to Ramsgate CP.[6] *Parl* Isle of Thanet Dv (1918–48).

ST PETER EXTRA

CP Cr 1894 from the pt of St Peters AP not in Broadstairs & St Peter's USD.[122] *LG* Thanet PLU, Isle of Thanet RD. Bdry: 1913.[103] Abol 1914 pt to help cr St Peter CP, pt to Garlinge CP.[312]

ST PETER IN THANET

AP Usual eccl spelling; for civ and origin of par, see 'St Peters'. *Eccl* Seq 18. Eccl bdry: 1850 (cr Broadstairs EP).[119]

ST PETER INTRA

CP Cr 1894 from the pt of St Peters AP in Broadstairs & St Peter's USD.[122] *LG* Thanet PLU, Broadstairs & St Peter's UD. Renamed 1914 'St Peter' when gains pt St Peter Extra CP.[312]

ST PETERS

AP Usual civ spelling; for eccl see 'St Peter in Thanet'. Chap in Minster AP, sep par *ca* 1200.[387] *LG* Ring. Hd, in Lbty Dover and thus non-corporate mbr Cq Pt of Dover, Thanet PLU, pt Broadstairs & St Peter's USD, pt Thanet RSD. Abol civ 1894 the pt in the USD to cr St Peter Intra CP, the remainder to cr St Peter Extra CP.[122] *Parl* E'rn Dv (1832–85), Isle of Thanet Dv (1918–48).

SALTWOOD

AP Incl chap St Leonard Hythe (sep civ identity early, sep EP 1844[352]). *LG* Hayne Hd, Elham PLU, RSD, RD. Civ bdry: 1886 (loses the pt in Hythe Parl Bor [not prev in Hythe MB] to St Leonard Hythe CP),[353] 1934 (help cr Hythe CP).[19] *Parl* Pt Hythe Parl Bor (1832–1918), remainder and later, Seq 2. *Eccl* Exempt from Archdeacon (until 1845), Seq 8. Eccl bdry: 1930.[351]

SANDGATE

EP Cr 1823, refounded 1854 from Folkestone AP, Cheriton AP.[204] Dover RDn (1823–95), Elham RDn (1895–*). Bdry: 1938.[207]

CP Cr 1894 from the pt of Cheriton AP in Sandgate

USD.[122] *LG* Elham PLU, Sandgate UD. Abol 1934 pt to help cr Hythe CP, pt to Folkestone CP.[19] *Parl* Hythe Parl Bor (1918–48).

SANDHURST
AP *LG* Selbrit. Hd, Cranb. PLU, RSD, RD. Civ bdry: 1886.[339] *Parl* Seq 12. *Eccl* Seq 5. Eccl bdry: 1930.[185]

SANDWICH
The following have 'Sandwich' in their names. Insofar as any existed at a given time: *LG* Sandw. Bor/MB, Cq Pt of Sandw. Eastry PLU, Sandw. USD. *Parl* Sandw. Parl Bor (1369–1885), Isle of Thanet Dv (1885–1918), Dover Dv (1918–48), Isle of Thanet CC (1948–70), Dover & Deal CC (1970–*). *Eccl* Sandw. RDn.

CP1–SANDWICH–Cr 1935 by union AP1, AP2, AP3, CP2, Stonar AP, and pts Minster AP, Woodnesborough AP, Worth CP.[6]

EP1–SANDWICH–Cr 1948 by union AP1, AP2, AP3, Stonar AP, pt Worth EP.[264] Bdry: 1968.[378]

CP2–SANDWICH ST BARTHOLOMEW'S HOSPITAL–Ex-par, sep CP 1858.[163] *LG* Not in Bor, in MB from 1866. Abol 1935 to help cr CP1.[6]

AP1–SANDWICH ST CLEMENT–Abol civ 1935 to help cr CP1.[6] Abol eccl 1948 to help cr EP1.[264]

AP2–SANDWICH ST MARY–Civ bdry: 1883.[8] Abol civ 1935 to help cr CP1.[6] Abol eccl 1948 to help cr EP1.[264]

AP3–SANDWICH ST PETER–Abol civ 1935 to help cr CP1.[6] Abol eccl 1948 to help cr EP1.[264]

SARRE
AP Orig AP, by 16th cent incl in St Nicholas at Wade AP,[437] sep CP 1866.[3] *LG* Ring. Hd, Lbty & Cq Pt of Sandw. (retained 16th cent–1866 also when in St Nicholas at Wade AP), Thanet PLU, RSD, Isle of Thanet RD (1894–1935), Eastry RD (1935–74). *Parl* E'rn Dv (1867–85), Isle of Thanet Dv/CC (1885–1970), Thanet West BC (1970–*). *Eccl* Exempt from Archdeacon (until 16th cent).

SEAL
Chap in Kemsing AP, sep civ identity early, sep EP 1874.[438] *LG* Seq 40. Civ bdry: 1934.[19] *Parl* Seq 20. *Eccl* Shor. RDn (1874–1909), Seven. RDn (1909–*). Eccl bdry: 1877 (cr Underriver EP).[115]

SEAL ST LAURENCE
EP Cr 1867 from Kemsing AP.[359] Shor. RDn (1867–1909), Seven. RDn (1909–*).

SEASALTER
AP *LG* Whit. Hd, Blean PLU, RSD, RD. Abol civ 1894 pt to help cr Whitstable Urban CP, pt to help cr Whitstable cum Seasalter CP.[214] *Parl* E'rn Dv (1832–1918). *Eccl* Seq 20.

SELLINDGE
AP *LG* Orig. pt Street Hd, pt Stow. Hd, by 19th cent pt Street Hd, pt Rom. Marsh Lbty,[44] Elham PLU, RSD, RD. Civ bdry: 1886,[259] 1934.[19] *Parl* Seq 2. *Eccl* Seq 10. Eccl bdry: 1927.[201]

SELLING
AP *LG* Orig pt Fav. Hd, pt Bough. under Blean Hd, by 19th cent ent Bough. under Blean Hd,[44] Seq 22 thereafter. Civ bdry: 1935.[6] *Parl* Seq 4. *Eccl* Seq 13.

SEVENOAKS
AP *LG* Codsh. Hd, Seven. PLU, pt Seven. USD, pt Seven. RSD, Seven. UD. Civ bdry: 1894 (loses the pt not in the USD to cr 2 CPs of Riverhead, Sevenoaks Weald),[429] 1934.[19] *Parl* Seq 20. *Eccl* Seq 38. Eccl bdry: 1821 (cr Sevenoaks Weald EP, refounded 1861),[439] 1864 (cr Riverhead EP),[132] 1871,[371] 1877 (help cr Kippington EP),[362] 1878 (cr Sevenoaks St John EP).[119]

SEVENOAKS ST JOHN
EP Cr 1878 from Sevenoaks AP.[119] Shor. RDn (1878–1909), Seven. RDn (1909–*).

SEVENOAKS WEALD
Chap in Sevenoaks AP, sep EP 1821, refounded 1861,[439] sep CP 1894 (from pt of the pt of the par not in Seven. USD).[428] *LG* Seven. PLU, RD. *Parl* Seven. Dv/CC (1918–*). *Eccl* Shor. RDn (1821–1909), Seven. RDn (1909–*).

SEVINGTON
AP *LG* Seq 24. Civ bdry: 1934.[19] *Parl* Seq 5. *Eccl* Seq 10.

SHADOXHURST
AP *LG* Orig pt Blackb. Hd, pt Ham Hd, pt Chart & Longbr. Hd, by 19th cent ent Blackb. Hd,[44] W Ashf. PLU, RSD, RD. Civ bdry: 1883.[8] *Parl* Seq 11. *Eccl* Seq 11. Eccl bdry: 1962.[24]

SHEERNESS
Chap in Minster in Sheppey AP, sep EP 1851,[399] sep CP 1894 (from the pt of the par in Sheerness USD[122]). *LG* Shep. PLU, Sheerness UD. Civ bdry: 1934.[19] Abol civ 1968 to help cr Queenborough-in-Sheppey MB and CP.[263] *Parl* Fav. Dv/CC (1918–70). *Eccl* Sitt. RDn. Eccl bdry: 1873 (cr Sheerness St Paul EP).[203] Abol 1963 to help cr Sheerness Holy Trinity with St Paul EP.[2]

SHEERNESS HOLY TRINITY WITH ST PAUL
EP Cr 1963 by union Sheerness EP, Sheerness St Paul EP.[2] Sitt. RDn.

SHEERNESS ST PAUL
EP Cr 1873 from Sheerness EP.[203] Sitt. RDn. Abol 1963 to help cr Sheerness Holy Trinity with St Paul EP.[2]

SHELDWICH
AP *LG* Seq 27. Civ bdry: 1935.[6] *Parl* Seq 4. *Eccl* Seq 13.

SHEPHERDSWELL–See SIBERTSWOLD

SHEPHERDSWELL WITH COLDRED
EP Cr 1963 by union Sibertswold AP, Coldred AP.[219] Dover RDn.

SHIPBOURNE
Chap in Tonbridge AP, sep civ identity early, sep EP 1859.[177] *LG* Seq 13. Civ bdry: 1934.[19] *Parl* Seq 15. *Eccl* Mall. RDn (until 1864), N Mall. RDn (1864–91), Tonbr. RDn (1891–*). Eccl bdry: 1954.[134]

SHOLDEN
Chap in Northbourne AP, sep civ identity early, sep EP 1849.[403] *LG* Seq 17. Civ bdry: 1935.[6] *Parl* Seq 3. *Eccl* Sandw. RDn. Eccl bdry: 1963.[102]

SHOREHAM
AP Incl chap Otford (sep civ identity early, sep EP 1723[177]). *LG* Seq 40. Addtl civ bdry alt: 1956.[333] *Parl* Seq 20. *Eccl* Seq 35. Eccl bdry: 1850 (help cr Woodlands EP),[441] 1938.[203]

SHORNE
AP Incl early civ former AP Mareston otherwise Merston (sep eccl identity maintained, qv). *LG* Seq 8. Addtl civ bdry alt: 1963.[213] *Parl* Seq 8. *Eccl* Seq 30.

SHORTLANDS
EP Cr 1870 from Beckenham AP.[52] W Dartf. RDn (1870–1909), Brom. RDn (1909–36), Beck. RDn (1936–*). Bdry: 1907,[82] 1938,[83] 1966.[132]

SIBERTSWOLD
AP Sometimes 'Shepherdswell'. *LG* Bewsb. Hd, River PLU (renamed Dover in 1840s), Dover RSD, RD. Abol civ 1963 to help cr Shepherdswell with Coldred CP.[219] *Parl* E'rn Dv (1832–1918), Dover Dv/CC (1918–70). *Eccl* Sandw. RDn (until 1884), Dover RDn (1884–1970). Abol eccl 1970 to help cr Sibertswold with Coldred EP.[220]

SIBERTSWOLD WITH COLDRED
EP Cr 1970 by union Sibertswold AP, Coldred AP.[220] Dover RDn.

SIDCUP
CP Renaming 1925 of Foots Cray AP.[240] *LG* Brom. PLU, Sidcup UD. Abol 1934 to help cr Chislehurst and Sidcup CP.[19]

SIDCUP CHRIST CHURCH, LONGLANDS
EP Cr 1897 from Sidcup St John EP.[442] RDns as for Sidcup St John, from 1897. Bdry: 1937,[282] 1954.[166]

SIDCUP ST ANDREW
EP Cr 1969 from Lamorbey Holy Trinity EP, Bexley AP, North Cray AP, Foots Cray AP.[76] Sidcup RDn.

SIDCUP ST JOHN
EP Cr 1843, refounded 1844 from Chislehurst AP.[211] Dartf. RDn (1843–64), E Dartf. RDn (1864–1909), Dartf. RDn (1909–36), Chisl. RDn (1936–65), Sidcup RDn (1965–*). Bdry: 1863,[144] 1886,[321] 1897 (cr Sidcup Christ Church, Longlands EP),[442] 1938,[83] 1968.[227]

SISSINGHURST
EP Renaming 1973 of Sissinghurst (or Trinity, Cranbrook) EP.[445] W Char. RDn.

SISSINGHURST (OR TRINITY, CRANBROOK)
EP Cr 1842 from Cranbrook AP.[226] Char. RDn (1842–64), W Char. RDn (1864–1973). Renamed 1973 'Sissinghurst'.[445]

SITTINGBOURNE
AP *LG* Milton Hd, PLU, Sitt. USD, UD. Abol civ 1930 pt to help cr Sittingbourne and Milton CP, pt to Tunstall AP.[33] *Parl* E'rn Dv (1832–85), N-E'rn Dv (1885–1918), Fav. Dv (1918–48). *Eccl* Seq 16. Eccl bdry: 1869 (cr Sittingbourne Holy Trinity EP).[79]

SITTINGBOURNE AND MILTON
CP Cr 1930 by union pts of Milton AP, Sittingbourne AP, Murston AP, Bapchild AP, Borden AP, Tunstall AP.[33] *LG* Sitt. & Milton UD. Bdry: 1935.[6] *Parl* Fav. Dv/CC (1948–*).

SITTINGBOURNE HOLY TRINITY
EP Cr 1869 from Sittingbourne AP.[79] Sitt. RDn.

SLADE GREEN
EP Cr 1925 from Crayford AP, Erith Christ Church EP.[231] Dartf. RDn (1925–60), Erith RDn (1960–*). Bdry: 1971.[287]

SMALLHYTHE
EP Cr 1866 from Tenterden AP.[90] W Char. RDn.

SMARDEN
AP *LG* Orig pt Calehill Hd, pt Berkeley Hd, pt Blackb. Hd, by 19th cent pt Calehill Hd, pt Berkeley Hd,[44] W Ashf. PLU, RSD, RD. *Parl* Pt E'rn Dv (1832–85), pt W'rn Dv (1832–67), pt Mid Dv (1867–85), S'rn Dv (1885–1918), Ashf. Dv/CC (1918–*). *Eccl* Char. RDn (until 1864), W Char. RDn (1864–1914), E Char. RDn (1914–*).

SMEETH
Chap in Aldington AP, sep civ identity early, sep EP 1868.[13] *LG* Seq 32. Civ bdry: 1934.[19] *Parl* Seq 5. *Eccl* N. Lym. RDn.

SNARGATE
AP *LG* Orig ent Aloesb. Hd, by 19th cent pt Aloesb. Hd, pt Lbty Cq Pt of New Rom., pt Rom. Marsh Lbty,[44] Seq 37 thereafter. Civ bdry: 1934.[19] *Parl* Seq 6. *Eccl* Seq 12. Eccl bdry: 1962.[24]

SNAVE
AP *LG* Orig pt Aloesb. Hd, pt Ham Hd, pt Newchurch Hd, ent Rom. Marsh Lbty by 19th cent,[44] Rom. Marsh PLU, RSD, RD. Civ bdry: 1883.[8] Abol civ 1934 pt to Brenzett AP, pt to Ivychurch AP.[19] *Parl* E'rn Dv (1832–85), S'rn Dv (1885–1918), Ashf. Dv (1918–48). *Eccl* Seq 12. Eccl bdry: 1935,[25] 1962.[24]

SNODLAND
AP Gains civ early Paddlesworth (orig sep AP, eccl ex-par after destruction of church, abol eccl 1934 to help cr Snodland with Paddlesworth EP[81]). *LG* Seq 4. Civ bdry: 1888,[9] 1898.[93] *Parl* Seq 10. *Eccl* Roch. RDn (until 1862), Cob. RDn (1862–1934). Abol eccl 1934 to help cr Snodland with Paddlesworth EP.[81]

SNODLAND WITH PADDLESWORTH
EP Cr 1934 by union Snodland AP, Paddlesworth (orig AP, deemed eccl ex-par since destruction of church).[81] Cob. RDn.

SOUTHBOROUGH
The following have 'Southborough' in their names. Insofar as any existed at at given time: *LG* Tonbr. PLU, Southborough UD. *Parl* Tonbr. Dv/CC (1918–70), Royal Tunbr. Wells CC (1970–*). *Eccl* Mall. RDn (until 1864), S Mall. RDn (1864–1906), Tunbr. Wells RDn (1906–*).
CP1–SOUTHBOROUGH–Cr 1894 from the pt of Tonbridge AP in Southborough USD.[446] Civ

bdry: 1934.[19]

EP1–SOUTHBOROUGH ST MATTHEW–Cr 1899 from EP2, Tunbridge Wells St John EP.[447] Bdry: 1911 (help cr Tunbridge Wells St Luke EP),[448] 1962.[151] Abol 1968 to help cr EP3.[89]

EP2–SOUTHBOROUGH ST PETER–Cr 1847 from Tonbridge AP.[177] Sometimes called 'Southborough St Peter with Christ Church'. Bdry: 1860 (cr EP4, refounded 1871),[449] 1899 (help cr EP1),[447] 1962.[151] Abol 1968 pt to help cr EP3, pt to Tonbridge St Stephen EP, pt to Bidborough AP.[89]

EP3–SOUTHBOROUGH ST PETER WITH CHRIST CHURCH AND ST MATTHEW–Cr 1968 by union EP1, pt EP2, pt EP4.[89]

EP4–SOUTHBOROUGH ST THOMAS–Cr 1860, refounded 1871 from EP2.[449] Bdry: 1968 (incl help cr EP3).[89]

SOUTHFLEET

AP *LG* Seq 39. Civ bdry: 1955.[29] *Parl* Seq 17. *Eccl* Seq 33. Eccl bdry: 1939.[217]

SPELDHURST

AP *LG* Orig pt Washl. Hd, pt Somerden Hd, pt Codsh. Hd, by 19th cent pt Washl. Hd, pt Somerden Hd,[44] Tonbr. PLU, pt Tunbr. Wells MB (1888–94), pt Tunbr. Wells USD (1888–94), Tonbr. RSD (ent 1875–88, pt 1888–94), Tonbr. RD. Civ bdry: 1894 (loses the pt in the MB to help cr Tunbridge Wells CP),[450] 1900,[451] 1934.[19] *Parl* W'rn Dv (1832–67), pt Mid Dv, pt West Dv (1867–85), S-W'rn Dv (1885–1918), Tonbr. Dv/CC (1918–70), Royal Tunbr. Wells CC (1970–*). *Eccl* Seq 27. Eccl bdry: 1868 (cr Rusthall EP),[432] 1880 (cr Langton Green EP),[365] 1947.[433]

STALISFIELD

AP *LG* Seq 27. Civ bdry: 1935.[6] *Parl* Seq 4. *Eccl* Seq 13.

STANFORD

Chap in Lyminge AP, sep civ identity early, sep EP 1853.[376] *LG* Seq 38. *Parl* Seq 2. *Eccl* Elham RDn (1853–95), N Lym. RDn (1895–*).

STANSTED

Chap in Wrotham AP, sep civ identity early, sep EP 1844.[458] *LG* Seq 13. *Parl* Seq 10. *Eccl* Shor. RDn.

STAPLE

AP Incl chap Adisham (sep civ identity early, sep EP 1863[11]). *LG* Downh. Hd, Eastry PLU, RSD, RD. Civ bdry: 1935.[6] *Parl* Seq 3. *Eccl* Exempt from Archdeacon (until 1845), Bridge RDn (until 1873), E Bridge RDn (1873–*).

STAPLEGATE

Ex-par ville, sep CP 1858,[163] eccl abol 1959 ent to Canterbury St Alphege with St Margaret EP.[152] *LG* Westgate Hd, Blean PLU, Canterb. MB/CB, USD. Abol civ 1912 ent to Canterbury CP.[149] *Parl* Canterb. Parl Bor (1867–1918).

STAPLEHURST

AP *LG* Orig pt Maid. Hd, pt Cranb. Hd, pt Marden Hd, pt Eyhorne Hd, by 19th cent pt Cranb. Hd, pt Marden Hd,[44] Maid. PLU, RSD, RD. *Parl* Seq 13. *Eccl* Sutton RDn (until 1914), W Char. RDn (1914–*).

STELLING

Chap in Upper Hardres AP, sep civ identity early, no sep eccl identity. *LG* Orig pt Loningb. Hd, pt Stow. Hd, by 19th cent ent Stow. Hd,[44] Elham PLU, RSD, RD. Civ bdry: 1886.[272] Abol civ 1968 ent to Stelling Minnis CP.[452] *Parl* E'rn Dv (1832–1918), Canterb. Dv (1918–48), Folk. & Hythe CC (1948–70).

STELLING MINNIS

Ex-par, sep CP 1858.[163] *LG* Loningb. Hd, Elham PLU (1858[120]–1930), RSD, RD. Bdry: 1957,[273] 1968.[452] *Parl* E'rn Dv (1867–1918), Canterb. Dv/CC (1918–70), Folk. & Hythe CC (1970–*).

STOCKBURY

AP *LG* Pt Eyhorne Hd, pt Milton Hd, Holling. PLU, RSD, RD. *Parl* Pt E'rn Dv (1832–85), pt W'rn Dv (1832–67), Mid Dv (pt 1867–85, ent 1885–1918), Maid. Dv/CC (1918–*). *Eccl* Seq 16.

STODMARSH

AP *LG* Downh. Hd, pt Lbty Fordwich and thus pt Fordwich corporate mbr Cq Pt of Sandw., Bridge PLU, RSD, RD. Abol civ 1934 ent to Wickhambreux AP.[19] *Parl* E'rn Dv (1832–1918), Canterb. Dv (1918–48). *Eccl* Donative, Seq 1.

STOKE

AP *LG* Orig pt Hoo Hd, pt Shamw. Hd, by 19th cent ent Hoo Hd,[44] Seq 3 thereafter. Civ bdry: 1968.[213] *Parl* Seq 8. *Eccl* Seq 28.

STONAR

AP *LG* Ring. Hd, Thanet PLU, RSD, Isle of Thanet RD. Abol civ 1935 to help cr Sandwich CP.[6] *Parl* E'rn Dv (1832–85), Isle of Thanet Dv (1885–1948). *Eccl* Sandw. RDn. Abol eccl 1948 to help cr Sandwich EP.[264]

STONE

AP Usual civ spelling; for eccl see 'Stone-in-Oxney'. *LG* Oxney Hd, Tent. PLU, RSD. Abol civ 1894 to help cr Stone cum Ebony CP.[268] *Parl* E'rn Dv (1832–85), S'rn Dv (1885–1918).

STONE

AP Sometimes 'Stone next Faversham'. *LG* Seq 27. Civ bdry: 1935.[6] *Parl* Seq 4. *Eccl* Ospr. RDn. Abol eccl 1926 to help cr Luddenham with Stone EP.[117]

STONE

AP Sometimes 'Stone near Dartford' *LG* Seq 39. Civ bdry: 1955.[29] *Parl* W'rn Dv (1832–67), West Dv (1867–85), N-W'rn Dv (1885–1918), Dartf. Dv (1918–48), Chisl. CC (1948–55), Dartf. CC (1955–*). *Eccl* Roch. RDn (until 1862), Grav. RDn (1862–1936), Dartf. RDn (1936–*). Eccl bdry: 1857 (help cr Greenhithe EP),[325] 1899,[326] 1956 (help cr Dartford St Edmund, King and Martyr EP).[237]

STONE CUM EBONY

CP Cr 1894 by union Stone AP, Ebony CP.[268] *LG* Tent. PLU, RD. Bdry: 1934.[19] *Parl* Ashf. Dv/CC (1918–*).

STONE-IN-OXNEY

AP Usual eccl spelling; for civ see 1st 'Stone' above.

Eccl Lym. RDn (until 1864), S Lym. RDn (1864–1928). Eccl united 1928 with chap Ebony of of Appledore with Ebony AP to cr Stone with Ebony EP, sometimes called 'Stone-in-Oxney with Ebony'.[23]

STONE-IN-OXNEY WITH EBONY–See following entry

STONE WITH EBONY

EP Cr 1928 by union Stone-in-Oxney AP, chap Ebony of Appledore with Ebony AP.[23] S Lym. RDn. Sometimes called 'Stone-in-Oxney with Ebony'.

STOURMOUTH

AP *LG* Bleang. Hd, pt Lbty Fordwich and thus pt Fordwich corporate mbr Cq Pt of Sandw., Eastry PLU, RSD, RD. *Parl* Seq 3. *Eccl* Seq 1.

STOWTING

AP *LG* Seq 38. *Parl* Seq 2. *Eccl* Seq 9.

STROOD

The following have 'Strood' in their names. Insofar as any existed at a given time: *LG* Shamw. Hd, N Ayl. PLU (1835–84), Strood PLU (1884–94), other organisation sep noted. *Parl* Sep noted. *Eccl* Roch. RDn (until 1954), Strood RDn (1954–*).

AP1–STROOD [ST NICHOLAS]–Orig chap in Frindsbury AP, sep par *temp* Richard I.[309] *LG* Pt Roch. MB (1835–94), pt Roch. USD, pt N Ayl. RSD (1875–84), pt Strood RSD (1884–94). Abol civ 1894 the pt in the MB to cr CP2, the remainder to cr CP1.[310] *Parl* Pt Roch. Parl Bor (1832–1918), pt W'rn Dv (1832–67), pt Mid Dv (1867–1918). *Eccl* Donative. Eccl bdry: 1869 (help cr EP2),[170] 1935,[134] 1957,[153] 1958 (cr EP1),[453] 1972 (gains EP2, Frindsbury with Upnor EP, EP1).[311]

CP1–STROOD EXTRA–Cr 1894 from the pt of AP1 not in Roch. MB.[310] *LG* Strood RD. Abol 1934 pt to help cr Rochester CP, pt to Cuxton AP.[19] *Parl* Grav. Dv (1918–48).

CP2–STROOD INTRA–Cr 1894 from the pt of AP1 in Roch. MB.[310] *LG* Roch. MB. Abol 1934 to help cr Rochester CP.[19] *Parl* See Part III of the *Guide* for composition of Roch. Parl Bors 1918–48 by wards.

EP1–STROOD ST FRANCIS–Cr 1958 from AP1.[453] Abol 1972 ent to AP1.[311]

EP2–STROOD ST MARY–Cr 1896 from Frindsbury AP, AP1.[170] Bdry: 1935.[134] Abol 1972 ent to AP1.[311]

STURRY

AP *LG* Bleang. Hd, pt Fordwich Bor & Lbty Fordwich and thus pt Cq Pt of Sandw., pt Canterb. CB (1890–94), pt Canterb. USD (1890–94), Blean PLU, RSD (ent 1875–90, pt 1890–94), Blean RD (1894–1934), Bridge-Blean RD (1934–74). Civ bdry: 1894 (loses the pt in the CB to Canterbury St Mary North Gate AP).[42] *Parl* Seq 1. *Eccl* Seq 3.

SUNDRIDGE

AP *LG* Seq 40. *Parl* Seq 20. *Eccl* Shor. RDn (until 1909), Seven. RDn (1909–73). Eccl bdry: 1818 (cr Ide Hill EP, refounded 1852 with enlarged area from other pars).[208] Abol eccl 1973 to help cr Sundridge with Ide Hill EP.[356]

SUNDRIDGE WITH IDE HILL

EP Cr 1973 by union Sundridge AP, Ide Hill EP.[356] Seven. RDn.

SUTTON

AP Usual civ spelling; for eccl see 'Sutton by Dover'. *LG* Seq 17. Civ bdry: 1935.[6] *Parl* Seq 3.

CHART SUTTON

AP *LG* Seq 1. *Parl* Seq 9. *Eccl* Seq 17.

EAST SUTTON

Chap in Sutton Valence AP, sep civ identity early, no sep eccl identity hence this par eccl 'Sutton Valence with East Sutton', qv. *LG* Seq 1. *Parl* Seq 9.

SUTTON AT HONE

AP *LG* Seq 39. Civ bdry: 1955 (incl help cr Swanley CP).[29] *Parl* Seq 17. *Eccl* Seq 21. Eccl bdry: 1862 (cr Swanley St Paul EP),[454] 1969.[87]

SUTTON BY DOVER

AP Usual eccl spelling; for civ see 'Sutton'. *Eccl* Seq 14. Eccl bdry: 1963,[102] 1970 (gains Little Mongeham AP).[221]

SUTTON VALENCE

AP Incl chap East Sutton (sep civ identity early, no sep eccl identity hence this par eccl 'Sutton Valence with East Sutton', qv). *LG* Seq 1. *Parl* Seq 9.

SUTTON VALENCE WITH EAST SUTTON

AP Usual eccl spelling; for civ and civ sep chap East Sutton see prev entry. *Eccl* Seq 17. Eccl bdry: 1970.[106]

SWALECLIFFE

AP *LG* Orig Whit. Hd, by 19th cent Bleang. Hd,[44] Blean PLU, RSD, RD. Civ bdry: 1883.[8] Abol civ 1934 to help cr Whitstable CP.[19] *Parl* E'rn Dv (1832–1918), Canterb. Dv (1918–48). *Eccl* Seq 20. Eccl bdry: 1938.[331]

SWANLEY

CP Cr 1955 from Eynsford AP, Farmingham AP, Horton Kirby AP, Sutton at Hone AP, Wilmington AP.[29] *LG* Dartf. RD. *Parl* Seven. CC (1970–*).

SWANLEY ST MARY

EP Cr 1901 from Crocken Hill EP, Swanley St Paul EP.[232] E Dartf. RDn (1901–09), Brom. RDn (1909–36), Chisl. RDn (1936–65), Dartf. RDn (1965–*). Bdry: 1969.[87]

SWANLEY ST PAUL

EP Cr 1862 from Sutton at Hone AP.[454] Dartf. RDn (1862–64), E Dartf. RDn (1864–1909), Dartf. RDn (1909–*). Bdry: 1868,[27] 1901 (help cr Swanley St Mary EP),[232] 1969,[87] 1972.[77]

SWANSCOMBE

AP *LG* Axton/Axton, Dartf. & Wilm. Hd, Dartf. PLU, RSD, RD (1894–1926), Swanscombe UD (1926–74). *Parl* W'rn Dv (1832–67), West Dv (1867–85), N-W'rn Dv (1885–1918), Dartf. Dv (1918–45), Dartf. Parl Bor/BC (1945–55), CC (1955–*). *Eccl* Seq 33. Eccl bdry: 1857 (help cr Greenhithe EP),[325] 1883 (cr Swanscombe

All Saints EP),[183] 1899,[326] 1971,[439] 1971 (gains Swanscombe All Saints EP).[455]

SWANSCOMBE ALL SAINTS
EP Cr 1883 from Swanscombe AP.[183] Grav. RDn. Abol 1971 ent to Swanscombe AP.[455]

SWINGFIELD
AP *LG* Seq 34. Civ bdry: 1934.[19] *Parl* Seq 2. *Eccl* Seq 7.

SYDENHAM
The following have 'Sydenham' in their names. Insofar as any existed at a given time: *Eccl* [London dioc 1855–68], Greenw. RDn (1861–68), Lewisham RDn (1868–*).
EP1–SYDENHAM ALL SAINTS–Cr 1909 from EP5.[456] Bdry: 1960.[124]
EP2–SYDENHAM HOLY TRINITY–Cr 1866 from EP3, Forest Hill Christ Church EP.[304] Bdry: 1936.[101]
EP3–SYDENHAM ST BARTHOLOMEW–Cr 1855 from Lewisham AP.[303] Bdry: 1866 (help cr EP2),[304] 1869 (cr EP4),[457] 1879 (help cr EP5),[295] 1880,[130] 1936.[61]
EP4–SYDENHAM ST PHILIP–Cr 1869 from EP3.[457]
EP5–LOWER SYDENHAM–Cr 1879 from EP3, Forest Hill Christ Church EP, Lewisham AP.[295] Bdry: 1909 (cr EP1),[456] 1940 (help cr Bellingham EP),[64] 1960.[124]

TENTERDEN
AP *LG* Tent. Hd, Bor/MB, corporate mbr Anc Town Rye (Cq Pt), Tent. PLU, USD. Civ bdry: 1894.[268] *Parl* Seq 11. *Eccl* Seq 5. Eccl bdry: 1863 (cr Tenterden St Michael EP, refounded 1864),[460] 1866 (cr Smallhythe EP).[90]

TENTERDEN ST MICHAEL
EP Cr 1863, refounded 1864 from Tenterden AP.[460] W Char. RDn. Bdry: 1882.[459]

TESTON
AP *LG* Seq 10. *Parl* Seq 9. *Eccl* Seq 24.

TEYNHAM
AP Incl chap Iwade (sep civ identity early, sep EP 1730[177]). *LG* Seq 30. *Parl* Seq 4. *Eccl* Seq 13. Eccl bdry: 1957 (gains Buckland AP),[95] 1963.[10]

THAMESMEAD
EP Cr 1973 from Plumstead St Mark and St Margaret EP (dioc Swk), Abbey Wood EP (dioc Swk), Belvedere St Augustine EP (dioc Roch), to be Swk dioc.[2] Greenw. RDn.

THANINGTON
AP *LG* Westgate Hd, pt Canterb. Bor/MB/CB, pt Canterb. USD, Bridge PLU, pt Bridge RSD. Abol civ 1894 the pt in the CB to cr Thanington Within CP, the remainder to cr Thanington Without CP.[268] *Parl* Pt Canterb. Parl Bor (1295–1918), pt E'rn Dv (1832–1918). *Eccl* Canterb. RDn. Abol eccl 1884 to help cr Thanington and Milton EP.[408]

THANINGTON AND MILTON
EP Cr 1884 by union Thanington AP, Milton AP.[408] Canterb. RDn.

THANINGTON WITHIN
CP Cr 1894 from the pt of Thanington AP in Canterb. CB.[42] *LG* Bridge PLU, Canterb. CB. Abol 1912 ent to Canterbury CP.[149]

THANINGTON WITHOUT
CP Cr 1894 from the pt of Thanington AP not in Canterb. CB.[42] *LG* Bridge PLU, RD (1894–1934), Bridge-Blean RD (1934–74). Bdry: 1934 (incl loses pt to Canterb. CB & CP).[150] *Parl* Canterb. Dv/CC (1918–*).

THROWLEY
AP *LG* Seq 27. *Parl* Seq 4. *Eccl* Seq 13.

THURNHAM
AP Sometimes 'Thornham'. *LG* Seq 1. Civ bdry: 1883,[8] 1888,[45] 1889.[46] *Parl* Seq 9. *Eccl* Seq 17. Eccl bdry: 1940.[47]

TILMANSTONE
AP *LG* Seq 19. Civ bdry: 1935.[6] *Parl* Seq 3. *Eccl* Seq 14.

TONBRIDGE
The following have 'Tonbridge' in their names. Insofar as any existed at a given time: *LG* Tonbr. Lowey, pt Tonbr. Bor, Tonbr. PLU, other sep noted. *Parl* pt Tonbr. Parl Bor (1295 only), W'rn Dv (1832–67), Mid Dv (1867–85), S-W'rn Dv (1885–1918), Tonbr. Dv/CC (1918–70), Tonbr. & Mall. CC (1970–*). *Eccl* Mall. RDn (until 1864), S Mall. RDn (1864–84), Tonbr. RDn (1884–*).
AP1–TONBRIDGE [ST PETER AND ST PAUL]–Incl chap Shipbourne (sep civ identity early, sep EP 1859[177]). *LG* Pt Tonbr. USD, pt Southborough USD (1886–94), pt Tunbr. Wells MB (1888–94), pt Tunbr. Wells USD (1888–94), pt Tonbr. RSD (reduced pt 1888–94). Abol civ 1894 the pt in Southborough USD to cr Southborough CP, the pt in Tonbr. USD to cr CP3, an expanded pt[471] in Tunbr. Wells MB to help cr Tunbridge Wells CP, pt of the rural pt to cr Hildenborough CP,[347] the remainder to help cr CP2.[450] Eccl bdry: 1833 (cr Tunbridge Wells EP),[461] 1844 (help cr Hildenborough EP),[227] 1847 (cr Southborough St Peter EP),[177] 1853 (cr EP1),[462] 1954.[134]
CP1–TONBRIDGE–Cr 1934 by union CP3 and pts of CP2, Hadlow AP, Hildenborough CP.[19] *LG* Tonbr. UD.
CP2–TONBRIDGE RURAL–Cr 1894 from the Kent pt of Frant AP (Kent, Sussex)[308] and from the pt of AP1 not in any MB or UD[450] or used to cr Hildenborough CP.[347] *LG* Tonbr. RD. Bdry: 1900,[451] 1921,[463] 1928.[332] Abol 1934 pt to help cr CP1, pt to Capel CP, pt to Pembury AP, pt to Southborough CP, pt to Tunbridge Wells MB & CP.[19]
EP1–TONBRIDGE ST STEPHEN–Cr 1853 from AP1.[462] Bdry: 1968.[89]
CP3–TONBRIDGE URBAN–Cr 1894 from the pt of AP1 in Tonbr. USD.[450] *LG* Tonbr. UD. Bdry: 1921,[463] 1928.[332] Abol 1934 to help cr CP1.[19]

TONGE
AP *LG* Seq 29. Civ bdry: 1883,[8] 1935.[6] *Parl* Seq 4. *Eccl* Seq 16.

TOVIL

EP Cr 1841, refounded 1843 from Maidstone AP, Loose EP, East Farleigh AP.[292] Sutton RDn. Bdry: 1971,[106] 1971.[48]

TROTTISCLIFFE

AP *LG* Seq 4. Civ bdry: 1968.[390] *Parl* Seq 10. *Eccl* Seq 24. Eccl bdry: 1934.[10]

TUDELEY

AP Incl chap Capel (sep civ identity early, sep EP by 1868[472]). *LG* Pt Twyford Hd, pt Washl. Hd, Tonbr. PLU, RSD. Abol civ 1885 ent to Capel CP.[164] *Parl* W'rn Dv (1832–67), Mid Dv (1867–85), S-W'rn Dv (1885–1918). *Eccl* Seq 26. Eccl bdry: 1962.[409]

TUNBRIDGE WELLS

The following have 'Tunbridge Wells' in their names. Insofar as any existed at a given time: *LG* Tonbr. PLU, Tunbr. Wells MB (later, 'Royal Tunbr. Wells' MB). *Parl* Tonbr. Dv/CC (1918–70), Royal Tunbr. Wells CC (1970–*). *Eccl* Mall. RDn (1833–64), S Mall. RDn (1864–1906), Tunbr. Wells RDn (1906–*).

CP1–TUNBRIDGE WELLS–Cr 1894 from an expanded pt[464] of Tonbridge AP and from the pt of Speldhurst AP, both in Tunbr. Wells MB.[450] Bdry: 1900,[451] 1935 (incl gains Broadwater Down CP).[19]

EP1–TUNBRIDGE WELLS [HOLY TRINITY]–Cr 1833 from Tonbridge AP.[461] Bdry: 1856 (cr EP2),[465] 1859 (cr EP7),[466] 1862 (cr EP6),[185] 1876 (cr EP9).[467] Abol 1967 to help cr EP3.[28]

EP2–TUNBRIDGE WELLS CHRIST CHURCH–Cr 1856 from EP1.[465] Bdry: 1889.[2] Abol 1967 to help cr EP3.[28]

EP3–TUNBRIDGE WELLS HOLY TRINITY WITH CHRIST CHURCH–Cr 1967 by union EP1, EP2.[28]

EP4–TUNBRIDGE WELLS KING CHARLES THE MARTYR–Cr 1889 from EP2, Rusthall EP, Broadwater EP (Kent, Sussex).[2]

EP5–TUNBRIDGE WELLS ST BARNABAS–Cr 1881 from EP6.[109] Bdry: 1911 (help cr EP8).[448]

EP6–TUNBRIDGE WELLS ST JAMES–Cr 1862 from EP1.[185] Bdry: 1881 (cr EP5),[109] 1911 (help cr EP8),[448] 1962.[151]

EP7–TUNBRIDGE WELLS ST JOHN–Cr 1859 from EP1.[466] Bdry: 1899 (help cr Southborough St Matthew EP),[447] 1911 (help cr EP8),[448] 1928,[342] 1971.[366]

EP8–TUNBRIDGE WELLS ST LUKE–Cr 1911 from EP7, EP5, EP6, Southborough St Matthew EP.[448] Bdry: 1962.[151]

EP9–TUNBRIDGE WELLS ST PETER, WINDMILL FIELDS–Cr 1876 from EP1.[467]

TUNSTALL

AP *LG* Seq 29. Civ bdry: 1930 (incl help cr Sittingbourne and Milton CP),[33] 1935.[6] *Parl* Seq 4. *Eccl* Seq 16.

ULCOMBE

AP *LG* Orig pt Eyhorne Hd, pt Fav. Hd, by 19th cent ent Eyhorne Hd,[44] Seq 7 thereafter. Civ bdry: 1888.[343] *Parl* Seq 9. *Eccl* Seq 17.

UNDERRIVER

EP Cr 1877 from Seal EP.[115] Shor. RDn (1877–1909), Seven. RDn (1909–*).

UPCHURCH

AP *LG* Seq 29. Civ bdry: 1883.[8] *Parl* Seq 4. *Eccl* Seq 16. Eccl bdry: 1961.[75]

UPNOR

EP Cr 1878 from Frindsbury AP.[56] Roch. RDn (1878–1909), Cliffe at Hoo RDn (1909–54), Strood RDn (1954–67). Abol 1967 to help cr Frindsbury with Upnor EP.[28]

VICTORIA DOCKS ST MARY

EP Cr 1864 from Plaistow St Mary EP (Essex), East Ham AP (Essex), the pt of Woolwich AP north of the Thames,[478] the last of these used 1877 to help cr North Woolwich EP.[478] For other bdry alts not affecting Kent, and for eccl organisation, see main entry in Essex.

WALDERSHARE

AP *LG* Orig ent Eastry Hd, by 19th cent pt Eastry Hd, pt Corn. Hd, pt Bewsb. Hd,[44] Eastry PLU, RSD, RD. Abol civ 1935 pt to Ripple AP, pt to Tilmanstone AP.[6] *Parl* E'rn Dv (1832–1918), Dover Dv (1918–48). *Eccl* Seq 14. Eccl bdry: 1970.[221]

WALMER

AP *LG* Corn. Hd, Lbty Sandw. and thus non-corporate mbr Cq Pt of Sandw., Eastry PLU, Walmer USD, UD. Civ bdry: 1901.[400] Abol civ 1935 pt to Deal AP, pt to Sholden CP.[6] *Parl* Sandw. Parl Bor (1832–85), E'rn Dv (1885–1918), Dover Dv (1918–48). *Eccl* Seq 14. Eccl bdry: 1894,[401] 1963.[102]

WALTHAM

AP *LG* Orig pt Bridge & Petham Hd, pt Stow. Hd, pt Wye Hd, by 19th cent ent Bridge & Petham Hd,[44] Seq 16 thereafter. Civ bdry: 1889,[337] 1934.[19] *Parl* Seq 1. *Eccl* Bridge RDn. Abol eccl 1698 to help cr Petham with Waltham EP.[411]

WARDEN

AP *LG* Orig Milton Hd, then Isle of Shep. Lbty, Shep. PLU, RSD, RD. Abol civ 1968 to help cr Queenborough-in-Sheppey MB and CP.[263] *Parl* E'rn Dv (1832–85), N-E'rn Dv (1885–1918), Fav. Dv/CC (1918–70). *Eccl* Sitt. RDn. Abol eccl 1962 pt to Eastchurch AP, pt to Leysdown AP.[264]

WAREHORNE

AP *LG* Orig pt Blackb. Hd, pt Ham Hd, by 19th cent pt Ham Hd, pt Rom. Marsh Lbty,[44] E Ashf. PLU (1836–1930), RSD, RD. Civ bdry: 1833,[8] 1934,[19] 1935.[6] *Parl* Seq 5. *Eccl* Seq 12. Eccl bdry: 1962.[24]

WATERINGBURY

AP *LG* Seq 11. Civ bdry: 1888,[391] 1934.[19] *Parl* Seq 10. *Eccl* Seq 24.

WELLING ST JOHN

EP Cr 1926 from Bexley Heath EP (dioc Roch), Lamorbey Holy Trinity EP (dioc Roch), East Wickham EP (dioc Swk) to be in Roch dioc.[79] Dartf. RDn (1926–60), Erith RDn (1960–*). Bdry: 1934 (help cr Lamorbey Holy Redeemer

EP),[108] 1936 (help cr Bexley St John EP),[2] 1937,[282] 1961.[75]

WELLING ST MARY THE VIRGIN

EP Cr 1947 from East Wickham AP.[468] Woolw. RDn (1947–66), Greenw. RDn (1966–*).

WESTBERE

AP *LG* Bleang. Hd, pt Lbty Fordwich and thus pt Fordwich corporate mbr Cq Pt of Sandw., Blean PLU, RSD, RD (1894–1934), Bridge-Blean RD (1934–74). Civ bdry: 1934.[19] *Parl* Seq 1. *Eccl* Seq 19. Eccl bdry: 1960.[212]

WESTCOMBE PARK

EP Cr 1892 from East Greenwich Christ Church EP.[138] Greenw. RDn (1892–1954), Greenw. & Deptf. RDn (1954–66), Greenw. RDn (1966–*).

WESTERHAM

AP Incl chap Edenbridge (sep civ identity early, sep EP 1844[270]). *LG* Seq 42. *Parl* Seq 20. *Eccl* Mall. RDn (1844–55), Shor. RDn (1855–1901), Seven. RDn (1901–*). Eccl bdry: 1863 (cr Crockham Hill EP).[177]

WESTGATE ON SEA

EP Cr 1884 from Minster AP, Birchington with Acol EP, Westgate St James EP.[396] Westb. RDn (1884–1930), Thanet RDn (1930–*).

CP Cr 1894 from Acol CP, Minster AP, pt of the pt of Margate St John the Baptist AP not in Margate MB.[5] *LG* Thanet PLU, Isle of Thanet RD. Abol 1935 to help cr Margate CP.[6] *Parl* Isle of Thanet Dv (1918–48).

WESTGATE ST JAMES

EP Cr 1873 from Margate St John the Baptist AP.[159] Westb. RDn (1873–1930), Thanet RDn (1930–*). Bdry: 1884 (help cr Westgate on Sea EP),[396] 1894 (help cr Margate All Saints, Westbrook EP).[54]

WESTMARSH–See WEST MARSH

WESTWELL

AP *LG* Pt Calehill Hd, pt Wye Hd, W Ashf. PLU, RSD, RD. Civ bdry: 1957.[178] *Parl* Seq 5. *Eccl* Exempt from Archdeacon (until 1845), Seq 4. Eccl bdry: 1940,[180] 1970.[181]

WHITFIELD

AP Sometimes 'Beaufield'. *LG* Seq 14. Civ bdry: 1960 (incl help cr Temple Ewell with River CP).[288] *Parl* Seq 14. *Eccl* Dover RDn (until 1884), Sandw. RDn (1884–86), Dover RDn (1886–*).

WHITSTABLE

AP *LG* Orig pt Whit. Hd, pt Westgate Hd, by 19th cent ent Whit. Hd,[44] Blean PLU, RSD. Abol civ 1894 the pt constitued Whit. UD to help cr Whitstable Urban CP, the remainder to help cr Whitstable cum Seasalter CP.[214] *Parl* E'rn Dv (1832–1918). *Eccl* Seq 20. Eccl bdry: 1935 (cr Whitstable St Peter EP),[469] 1938.[331]

CP Cr 1934 by union Swalecliffe AP, Whitstable Urban CP, Whitstable cum Seasalter CP, and pts of Dunkirk CP, Graveney AP, Hernhill AP.[19] *LG* Whit. UD. *Parl* Canterb. CC (1948–*).

WHITSTABLE CUM SEASALTER

CP Cr 1894 from the pts of Whitstable AP and Seasalter AP not constituted Whit. UD.[214] *LG* Blean PLU, RD. Abol 1934 to help cr Whitstable CP.[19] *Parl* Canterb. Dv (1918–48).

WHITSTABLE ST PETER

EP Cr 1935 from Whitstable AP.[469] Canterb. RDn (1935–71), Recul. RDn (1971–*).

WHITSTABLE URBAN

CP Cr 1894 from the pts of Whitstable AP and Seasalter AP constituted Whit. UD.[214] *LG* Blean PLU, Whit. UD. Abol 1934 to help cr Whitstable CP.[19] *Parl* Canterb. Dv (1918–48).

WICHLING

AP Usual civ spelling; for eccl see 'Wychling'. *LG* Seq 1. Civ bdry: 1883.[8] *Parl* Seq 9.

EAST WICKHAM

Chap in Plumstead AP, sep civ identity early, sep EP 1854.[414] *LG* Lessness Hd, Dartf. PLU, RSD, RD. Abol civ 1902 ent to Bexley AP.[470] *Parl* W'rn Dv (1832–67), West Dv (1867–85), N-W'rn Dv (1885–1918). *Eccl* [London dioc 1854–68], Greenw. RDn (1861–68), Woolw. RDn (1868–1966), Greenw. RDn (1966–*). Eccl bdry: 1926 (help cr Welling St John EP),[79] 1947 (cr Welling St Mary the Virgin EP).[468]

WEST WICKHAM

AP *LG* Ruxley Hd, Brom. PLU, RSD, RD. Abol civ 1934 pt to Beckenham AP, pt to Bromley AP, pt to Orpington AP.[19] *Parl* W'rn Dv (1832–67), West Dv (1867–85), W'rn Dv (1885–1918), Chisl. Dv (1918–45). *Eccl* Dartf. RDn (until 1864), W Dartf. RDn (1864–73), Croydon RDn (1873–*). Eccl bdry: 1935 (cr West Wickham St Francis of Assisi EP),[473] 1938 (help cr West Wickham St Mary of Nazareth EP).[63]

WEST WICKHAM ST FRANCIS OF ASSISI

EP Cr 1935 from West Wickham AP.[473] Croydon RDn.

WEST WICKHAM ST MARY OF NAZARETH

EP Cr 1938 from West Wickham AP (dioc Canterb), Hayes AP (dioc Roch), Bromley AP (dioc Roch), Beckenham St Barnabas EP (dioc Roch), to be in Canterb dioc.[63] Croydon RDn.

WICKHAMBREAUX

AP Usual eccl spelling, civ spelling from 1957 of par prev civ spelled 'Wickhambreux'.[474] *LG* Bridge-Blean RD. *Parl* Canterb. CC (1970–*). *Eccl* Seq 1. Eccl bdry: 1930.[302]

WICKHAMBREUX

AP Usual civ spelling; for eccl spelling and civ spelling after renamed 1957,[474] see prev entry. *LG* Downh. Hd, pt Lbty Fordwich and thus pt Fordwich corporate mbr Cq pt of Sandw., Bridge PLU, RSD, RD (1894–1934), Bridge-Blean RD (1934–57). Civ bdry: 1889,[12] 1934.[19] *Parl* E'rn Dv (1832–1918), Canterb. Dv/CC (1918–70).

WIGMORE WITH HEMPSTEAD

EP Cr 1956 from Rainham AP, Luton EP, Gillingham AP.[317] Roch. RDn (1956–57), Gill. RDn (1957–72). Usually called 'Gillingham St Matthew'. Abol 1972 pt to help cr South Gillingham EP, pt to Gillingham St Augustine EP.[113]

WILLESBOROUGH

AP *LG* Chart & Longbr. Hd, E Ashf. PLU, RSD, RD. Civ bdry: 1883.[8] Abol civ 1934 pt to Ashford AP, pt to Hinxhill AP, pt to Mersham AP, pt to Sevington AP.[19] *Parl* E'rn Dv (1832–85), S'rn Dv (1885–1918), Ashf. Dv (1918–48). *Eccl* Lym. RDn (until 1873), N Lym. RDn (1873–1933), E Char. RDn (1933–*). Eccl bdry: 1959.[30]

WILMINGTON

AP *LG* Dartf. & Wilm. Hd/Axton, Dartf. & Wilm. Hd, Dartf. PLU, RSD, RD. Civ bdry: 1955 (incl help cr Swanley EP).[29] *Parl* Seq 17. *Eccl* Dartf. RDn (until 1864), E Dartf. RDn (1864–1909), Dartf. RDn (1909–*). Eccl bdry: 1972.[77]

WINGHAM

AP Incl chap Ash (sep par 1286[26]), areas of Goodnestone, Nonington, Womemswold (each sep par 1286[318] [the last eccl called 'Wymynswold']). *LG* Wingham Hd, pt Lbty Fordwich and thus pt Fordwich corporate mbr Cq Pt of Sandw., Eastry PLU, RSD, RD. Addtl civ bdry alt: 1935.[6] *Parl* Seq 3. *Eccl* Pec jurisd Wingham (until 1546), exempt from Archdeacon (1546–1845), Seq 1 thereafter.

WITTERSHAM

AP *LG* Oxney Hd, Tent. PLU, RSD, RD. *Parl* Seq 5. *Eccl* Exempt from Archdeacon (until 1845), Seq 12.

WOMENSWOLD

AP Usual civ spelling; for eccl see 'Wymynswold'. Area in Wingham AP, sep par 1286.[318] *LG* Wingham Hd, Bridge PLU, RSD, RD (1894–1934), Bridge-Blean RD (1934–74). Civ bdry: 1889.[12] *Parl* Seq 1.

WOODCHURCH

AP *LG* Blackb. Hd, Tent. PLU, RSD, RD. Civ bdry: 1883,[8] 1934.[19] *Parl* Seq 11. *Eccl* Exempt from Archdeacon (until 1845), Lym. RDn (until 1873), S Lym. RDn (1873–1933), E Char. RDn (1933–*). Eccl bdry: 1962.[24]

WOODLANDS

EP Chap in Wrotham AP, sep EP 1850, incl also area of Shoreham AP.[441] Shor. RDn.

WOODNESBOROUGH

AP *LG* Eastry Hd, pt Cq Pt of Sandw., Eastry PLU, RSD, RD. Civ bdry: 1935 (incl help cr Sandwich CP).[6] *Parl* Seq 3. *Eccl* Seq 14. Eccl bdry: 1965.[378]

WOOLWICH

The following have 'Woolwich' in their names. Insofar as any existed at a given time: *LG* Blackh. Hd, Greenw. PLU (1836–68), Woolw. PLU (1868–89), Woolw. Vestry (Metrop Bd Wks). Transf 1889 to London.[190] *Parl* Pt Greenw. Parl Bor (1832–85), pt W'rn Dv (1832–67), pt West Dv (1867–85), Woolw. Parl Bor (1885–1918), London thereafter. *Eccl* Dartf. RDn (until 1845), [London dioc 1845– 68], Greenw. RDn (1861–68), Woolw. RDn (1868–*).

AP1–WOOLWICH [ST MARY]–Eccl bdry: 1845 (cr EP5),[138] 1864 (help cr Victorian Docks St Mark EP [from the pt of the par north of the Thames; EP mostly Essex),[478] 1865 (help cr Plumstead Christ Church, Shooter's Hill EP),[275] 1869 (cr EP2),[475] 1879 (cr EP4),[476] 1881 (cr EP1),[477] 1900,[421] 1939 (gains EP2).[137] Abol eccl 1953 pt to help cr Plumstead St James with St John the Baptist EP, pt to help cr EP3).[419]

EP1–WOOLWOCH HOLY TRINITY–Cr 1881 from AP1.[477] Bdry: 1900.[421] Abol 1953 to help cr EP3.[189]

EP2–WOOLWICH ST JOHN–Cr 1869 from AP1.[475] Bdry: 1900.[421] Abol 1939 ent to AP1.[137]

EP3–WOOLWICH ST MARY WITH HOLY TRINITY–Cr 1953 by union EP1, pt AP1.[189]

EP4–WOOLWICH ST MICHAEL AND ALL ANGELS–Cr 1879 from AP1.[476] Bdry: 1926,[208] 1953.[189]

EP5–WOOLWICH ST THOMAS–Cr 1845 from AP1, Charlton next Woolwich AP.[138] Bdry: 1926,[208] 1935,[187] 1953.[187]

NORTH WOOLWICH

EP Cr 1877 from Victoria Docks St Luke EP (Essex, Kent [the pt of Woolwich AP north of the Thames used 1875 to cr the former]).[478] For organisation in RDns, see entry in Essex.

WOOTTON

AP *LG* Kingh. Hd, River PLU (renamed Dover in 1840s), Dover RSD, RD. Civ bdry: 1883,[8] 1934.[19] Abol civ 1963 to help cr Denton with Wootton CP.[219] *Parl* E'rn Dv (1832–1918), Dover Dv/CC (1918–70). *Eccl* Elham RDn (until 1895), Dover RDn (1895–late 1890s), Elham RDn (late 1890s–*). Eccl bdry: 1891.[36]

WORMSHILL

AP *LG* Seq 1. *Parl* Seq 9. *Eccl* Sutton RDn (until 1914), Sitt. RDn (1914–*).

WORTH

Chap in Eastry AP, sep civ identity early, sep EP 1854.[265] *LG* Seq 19. Civ bdry: 1935 (incl help cr Sandwich CP).[6] *Parl* Seq 3. *Eccl* Sandw. RDn. Eccl bdry: 1948 (help cr Sandwich EP),[264] 1968.[378]

WOULDHAM

AP *LG* Larkf. Hd, Mall. PLU, pt Roch. Bor/MB, pt Roch. USD, pt Mall. RSD, Mall. RD (pt 1894–96, ent 1896–1974). Civ bdry: 1896 (loses the pt in the MB to St Margaret Intra CP),[436] 1905 (gains St Margaret Extra CP).[435] *Parl* Seq 10. *Eccl* Seq 31.

WROTHAM

AP Incl chap Woodlands (sep EP 1850, incl pt Shoreham AP[441]), chap Stanstead (sep civ identity early, sep EP 1844[458]). *LG* Wrotham Hd, Mall. PLU, Wrotham USD, UD (1894–1934), Mall. RD (1934–74). Addtl civ bdry alt: 1934 (incl help cr Borough Green CP, cr Platt CP, cr Plaxtol CP).[19] *Parl* W'rn Dv (1832–67), Mid Dv (1867–1918), Seven. Dv/CC (1918–70), Tonbr. & Mall. CC (1970–*). *Eccl* Seq 35. Eccl bdry: 1844 (cr Plaxtol EP),[413] 1846 (cr Platt EP),[412] 1966,[331] 1974 (help cr

Borough Green EP).[104]

WYCHLING

AP Usual eccl spelling; for civ see 'Wichling' *Eccl* Sitt. RDn (until 1891), Sutton RDn (1891–1914), Ospr. RDn (1914–*).

WYE

AP *LG* Seq 31. Civ bdry: 1934,[19] 1968.[174] *Parl* Seq 5. *Eccl* Bridge RDn (until 1873), E Bridge RDn (1873–1969), W Bridge RDn (1969–*).

WYMYNSWOLD

AP Usual eccl spelling; for civ see 'Womenswold'. Area in Wingham AP, sep par 1286.[318] *Eccl* Pec jurisd Wingham (until 1546), exempt from Archdeacon (1546–1845), Seq 1 thereafter.

YALDING

AP *LG* Seq 10. Civ bdry: 1888,[391] 1888,[402] 1934.[19] *Parl* Seq 14. *Eccl* Seq 24. Eccl bdry: 1858 (cr Collier Street EP),[221] 1860 (help cr Paddock Wood EP).[115]

LONDON

PART I: THE CITY OF LONDON

Spelling of Parochial Names:
For APs, the spelling in Harben's *Dictionary of London* is generally used, as preferred by the Guildhall Library and the Corporation of London RO, with occasional exceptions noted. Thereafter the practice of the times is followed: an infrequent use of commas to mark off street designations for the 17th–19th centuries, a profuse use as in recent orders.

The word 'united' is used in lieu of 'abol' as elsewhere in the *Guide* for eccl unions before 1954, because some pars retained elements of independence even after amalgamation.

Numbering of Parochial Names:
Each par is given a number, so that long parochial names need not be repeated.

LG Organisation:
The principal unit was the ward, but wards were not constituted by pars (see Part II of the *Guide* for a list of the 26 wards).

All APs and CPs in existence in 1907 with 3 sep noted exceptions were alamgamated into the single CP 'London',[1] a fact not sep noted below for brevity's sake. In addition the following 'sequences' are used:
LG Seq 1: City of London PLU (1837–1907)
LG Seq 2: E London PLU (1837–69), City of London PLU (1869–1907)
LG Seq 3: W London PLU (1837–69), City of London PLU (1869–1907)

Parl Organisation:
With a few exceptions sep noted, London pars were within the following organisation: City of London Parl Bor (1295–1948), The Cities of London and Westminster BC (1948–70), The City of London and Westminster South BC (1970–*).

Eccl Organisation:
London AD was not divided into RDns until 1869, thereafter into East City RDn and West City RDn (1869–1954) [sep noted below], then united into The City RDn (1954–*). Pars in peculiars are sep noted (pec jurisds abol 1845); many also were subject to the Commissary of London (APs 1-2, 4, 8, 11, 15-18, 20, 27-31, 34-37, 40-41, 44-45, 54-56, 62-63, 65-68, 70, 73, 77, 82, 84, 86, 91-96, 100, 104-05, 107-08, 110 and unions formed therefrom).

THE PARISHES OF THE CITY OF LONDON

AP1–ALL HALLOWS BARKING–*LG* Seq 1. *Eccl* E City RDn. Eccl bdry: 1954 (gains pt EP21, ent ex-par Lbty of the Tower, loses pt to AP39).[2] Abol eccl 1960 to help cr EP1.[3]

EP1–ALL HALLOWS, BERKYNGCHIRCHE-BY-THE-TOWER, WITH ST DUNSTAN IN THE EAST–Cr 1960 by union AP1, pt AP39.[3]

AP2–ALL HALLOWS, BREAD STREET–*LG* Seq 1. *Eccl* Pec jurisd Archbp Canterb (The Arches). United eccl 1670 to help cr EP2.[4]

EP2–ALL HALLOWS BREAD STREET WITH ST JOHN THE EVANGELIST–Cr 1670 by union AP2, AP51.[4] W City RDn. United 1876 to help cr EP54.[5]

AP3–ALL HALLOWS THE GREAT–*LG* Seq 1. *Eccl* United eccl 1670 to help cr EP3.[4]

EP3–ALL HALLOWS THE GREAT AND ALL HALLOWS THE LESS–Cr 1670 by union AP3, AP5.[4] W City RDn. United 1893 to help cr EP63.[6]

AP4–ALL HALLOWS, HONEY LANE–*LG* Seq 1. *Eccl* United eccl 1670 to help cr EP53.[4]

AP5–ALL HALLOWS THE LESS–*LG* Seq 1. *Eccl* United eccl 1670 to help cr EP3.[4]

AP6–ALL HALLOWS, LOMBARD STREET–*LG* Seq 1. *Eccl* Pec jurisd Archbp Canterb (The Arches). United eccl 1864 to help cr EP4.[7]

EP4–ALL HALLOWS LOMBARD STREET WITH ST BENET GRACECHURCH AND ST LEONARD EASTCHEAP–Cr 1864 by union AP6, EP19.[7] E City RDn. United 1876 to help cr EP5.[8]

EP5–ALL HALLOWS LOMBARD STREET WITH ST BENET GRACECHURCH, ST LEONARD EASTCHEAP AND ST DIONIS BACKCHURCH–Cr 1876 by union EP4, AP38.[7] E City RDn. United 1937 to help cr EP27.[9]

AP7–ALL HALLOWS, LONDON WALL–Gains 1441 AP22.[10] *LG* Seq 1. *Eccl* E City RDn. Abol eccl 1954 pt to help cr EP41, pt to AP34, pt to EP33, pt to AP17, pt to EP21.[2]

AP8–ALL HALLOWS STAINING–*LG* Seq 1. *Eccl* E City RDn. United eccl 1870 to help cr EP71.[11]

EP6–ALL SAINTS BISHOPSGATE–Cr 1864 from AP34,[12] merged back 1869 into AP34.[13] E City RDn.

CP1–BARNARD'S INN–Ex-par place, sep CP 1858.[14] *LG* Seq 3.

–BRIDEWELL–Anc chap, ex-par, sep CP 1858[14] as 'Bridewell Precinct', qv, eccl united 1906 to help cr EP23.[17]

CP2–BRIDEWELL PRECINCT–Ex-par place (for eccl see prev entry), sep CP 1858.[14] *LG* Seq 3.

AP9–CHRIST CHURCH, NEWGATE STREET–Cr 1547 by union AP21, AP97,[15] the Middx pt of AP 107,[63] using Greyfriars as the par church. *LG* Seq 1. *Eccl* United eccl 1670 to help cr EP7.[4]

EP7–CHRIST CHURCH, NEWGATE STREET WITH ST LEONARD, FOSTER LANE–Cr 1670 by union AP9, AP58.[4] W City RDn. Abol 1954 pt to help cr EP17, pt to help cr EP75, pt to help cr EP82.[2]

CP3–FURNIVAL'S INN–Ex-par place, primarily Middx with small pt in City of London, sep CP 1858.[14] The pt in London lost 1899 to AP14 so that this par ent Middx thereafter.[20] For civ and eccl organisation see main entry in Middx.

EP8–HOLY TRINITY GOUGH SQUARE–Cr 1842 from AP35.[16] W City RDn. United eccl 1906, merged back into AP35 but the union called as EP23.[17]

AP10–HOLY TRINITY THE LESS–*LG* Seq 1. *Eccl* United eccl 1670 to help cr EP61.[4]

–INNER TEMPLE–Ex-par, not incl in a PLU, not abol civ 1907 and sep status maintained.

–LAND COMMON TO INNER TEMPLE AND MIDDLE TEMPLE–Not abol civ 1907 and sep status maintained.

CP4–LONDON–Cr 1907 by amalgamation of all APs and CPs in existence in the City of London except Inner Temple, Land Common to Inner Temple and Middle Temple, Middle Temple.[1]

–MIDDLE TEMPLE–Ex-par, not incl in a PLU, not abol civ 1907 and sep status maintained.

AP11–ST ALBAN, WOOD STREET–*LG* Seq 1. *Eccl* United eccl 1670 to help cr EP9.[4]

EP9–ST ALBAN WOOD STREET WITH ST OLAVE SILVER STREET–Cr 1670 by union AP11, AP101.[4] W City RDn. United 1894 to help cr EP10.[18]

EP10–ST ALBAN WOOD STREET WITH ST OLAVE SILVER STREET, ST MICHAEL WOOD STREET WITH ST MARY STAINING–Cr 1894 by union EP9, EP64.[18] W City RDn. Abol 1954 pt to help cr EP82, pt to help cr EP31.[4]

AP12–ST ALPHAGE LONDON WALL–Sometimes 'St Alphage, Sion College'. *LG* Seq 1. *Eccl* W City RDn. United eccl 1917 to help cr EP11.[19]

EP11–ST ALPHAGE LONDON WALL WITH ST MARY ALDERMANBURY–Cr 1917 by union AP12, AP70.[19] W City RDn. Abol 1954 pt to help cr EP31, pt to help cr EP82, pt to help cr EP41.[2]

–ST ALPHAGE, SION COLLEGE–See AP12

EP12–ST ANDREW BY THE WARDROBE WITH ST ANN BLACKFRIARS–Cr 1670 by union AP13, AP18.[4] W City RDn. Reconstituted 1954 as for EP13 following.[2]

–ST ANDREW BUDGE ROW–See AP15

AP13–ST ANDREW BY THE WARDROBE–*LG* Seq 1. *Eccl* United eccl 1670 to help cr EP12.[4]

EP13–ST-ANDREW-BY-THE-WARDROBE WITH ST ANN BLACKFRIARS–Reconstitution 1954 of EP12, gaining pts EP67, EP23, EP16, EP65, EP35, EP46.[2]

AP14–ST ANDREW HOLBORN–Pt Middx, pt London. Occasional eccl spelling 'Holborn' or 'Holborn St Andrew'. Bdry alt: 1723 (cr from the Middx pt St George the Martyr CP, eccl called 'Queen Square' or 'Holborn St George the Martyr').[21] The Middx pt civ united 1767 with the CP cr in 1723 to cr St Andrew Holborn Above the Bars with St George the Martyr CP,[22] so that St Andrew Holborn (sometimes thereafter called 'St Andrew Holborn Below the Bars') ent London thereafter. *LG* Seq 3. Addtl civ bdry alt: 1899 (gains the pt of CP3 in the City of London so that the latter ent Middx thereafter).[20] *Eccl* St Sepulchre RDn (1861–1901), Holborn RDn (1901–34), Finsbury & Holborn RDn (1934–52). Addtl eccl bdry alt affecting Middx area in 1839, 1839, 1862, 1952 (see entries in Middx). Abol eccl 1952 the pt in Holborn Metrop Bor to help cr Holborn St Alban the Martyr with Saffron Hill St Peter EP, pt to Kingsway Holy Trinity with Drury Lane St John EP.[23]

AP15–ST ANDREW HUBBARD–Or 'ST ANDREW BUDGE ROW'. *LG* Seq 1. *Eccl* United eccl 1670 to help cr EP50.[4]

AP16–ST ANDREW UNDERSHAFT–United 1562 to help cr united pt which retained as civ name 'St Andrew Undershaft', eccl as AP17.[23] *LG* Seq 1.

AP17–ST ANDREW UNDERSHAFT WITH ST MARY AXE–Cr 1562 by union AP16, AP73,[73] civ name retained as for AP16, eccl as for AP17. *Eccl* E City RDn. Reconstituted 1954 losing pt to EP70 and gaining pts AP7, EP24, EP70.[2]

AP18–ST ANN BLACKFRIARS–*LG* Seq 1. *Eccl* United eccl 1670 to help cr EP13.[4]

AP19–ST ANN AND ST AGNES–Sometimes 'St Anne and St Agnes Aldersgate'. *LG* Seq 1. *Eccl* Pec jurisd Dean & Chapter of Westminster. United eccl 1670 to help cr EP14.[4]

EP14–ST ANN AND ST AGNES WITH ST JOHN ZACHARY–Cr 1670 by union AP19, AP52.[4] W

City RDn. Abol 1954 pt to help cr EP17, pt to help cr EP82.[4]

AP20–ST ANTHOLIN–*LG* Seq 1. *Eccl* United eccl 1670 to help cr EP15.[4]

EP15–ST ANTHOLIN WITH ST JOHN THE BAPTIST UPON WALLBROOK–Cr 1670 by union AP20, AP50.[4] W City RDn. United 1873 to help cr EP49.[53]

AP21–ST AUDOEN–Sometimes 'St Ewen'. Destroyed at Dissolution, united 1547 with AP97 to help cr AP9.[15]

AP22–ST AUGUSTINE ON THE WALL–Sometimes 'St Augustine Papey'. United 1441 to AP7.[10]

AP23–ST AUGUSTINE WATLING STREET–*LG* Seq 1. *Eccl* United eccl 1670 to help cr EP16.[4]

EP16–ST AUGUSTINE WITH ST FAITH–Cr 1670 by union AP24, AP43.[4] W City RDn. Abol 1954 pt to help cr EP75, pt to help reconstitute EP13, pt to help cr EP55.[2]

AP24–ST BARTHOLOMEW BY THE EXCHANGE–*LG* Seq 1. *Eccl* United eccl 1839 to help cr EP43.[25]

AP25–ST BARTHOLOMEW THE GREAT–Sometimes 'St Bartholomew the Great, West Smithfield'. Orig priory church, rebuilt and made parochial 1544.[26] *LG* Seq 3. *Eccl* W City RDn. Abol eccl 1954 pt to help cr EP17, pt to help cr EP75.[4]

EP17–ST BARTHOLOMEW-THE-GREAT, SMITHFIELD–Cr 1954 by union pts AP25, AP32, AP107, EP14, EP7.[4] Bdry: 1963.[27]

AP26–ST BARTHOLOMEW THE LESS–Chap in St Bartholomew's Hospital, parochial 1547.[26] *LG* Seq 3. *Eccl* W City RDn. Eccl bdry: 1954 (gains pt AP32),[4] 1963.[27]

EP18–ST BARTHOLOMEW MOOR LANE–Cr 1850 from AP46.[28] W City RDn. Merged 1900 back into AP46.[29]

AP27–ST BENET FINK–*LG* Seq 1. *Eccl* United eccl 1842 to help cr EP73.[30]

AP28–ST BENET GRACECHURCH–Sometimes 'St Benet Gracechurch Street'. *LG* Seq 1. *Eccl* United 1670 to help cr EP19.[4]

EP19–ST BENET GRACECHURCH WITH ST LEONARD EASTCHEAP–Cr 1670 by union AP28, AP57.[4] E City RDn. United 1864 to help cr EP4.[7]

AP29–ST BENET PAUL'S WHARF–*LG* Seq 1. *Eccl* United eccl 1670 to help cr EP20.[31]

EP20–ST BENET PAUL'S WHARF WITH ST ST PETER PAUL'S WHARF–Cr 1670 by union AP29, AP104.[31] W City RDn. United 1879 to help cr EP67.[32]

AP30–ST BENET SHEREHOG–*LG* Seq 1. *Eccl* United eccl 1670 to help cr EP76.[4]

–ST BOTOLPH ALDERSGATE–See AP32

–ST BOTOLPH ALDGATE–See AP33

EP21–ST BOTOLPH ALDGATE AND HOLY TRINITY MINORIES–Cr 1893 by union AP33, Holy Trinity Minories AP (Middx).[35] E City RDn. Reconstituted 1954 gaining pts AP7, EP24, EP70, Spitalfields Christ Church with All Saints EP (anc Middx), Whitechapel St Paul with St Mark EP (anc Middx), losing pts to AP34, AP1.[36]

AP31–ST BOTOLPH BY BILLINGSGATE–*LG* Seq 1. *Eccl* United eccl 1670 to help cr EP30.[4]

AP32–ST BOTOLPH WITHOUT ALDERSGATE–Name preferred to Harben's 'St Botolph Aldersgate'. Pt London, pt Middx (area of Glasshouse Yard Lbty, sep jurisd in Middx and sep CP there 1899[20] so that St Botolph without Aldersgate ent London thereafter). *LG* Seq 2. *Eccl* W City RDn. Abol eccl 1954 pt to help cr EP82, pt to AP26, pt to help cr EP31.[4]

AP33–ST BOTOLPH WITHOUT ALDGATE–Name preferred to Harben's 'St Botolph Aldgate'. Pt London, pt Middx (often 'East Smithfield Lbty'), one par for eccl purposes but each a sep par for civ purposes in the respective co even though each with same name (see the CP in Middx entries for cr of Holy Trinity Minories AP, St Katherine by the Tower CP). Organisation for the pt in London: *LG* Seq 3. Civ bdry: 1899 (gains the pt of CP8 in City of London so that the latter ent Middx thereafter).[20] *Eccl* E City RDn. United eccl 1893 to help cr EP21.[35]

AP34–ST BOTOLPH WITHOUT BISHOPSGATE–*LG* Seq 2. *Eccl* E City RDn. Eccl bdry: 1864 (cr EP6),[12] 1869 (gains back EP6).[13] Reconstituted 1954 gaining pts AP108, AP7, EP21, AP42, AP108.[4]

AP35–ST BRIDE–*LG* Seq 3. *Eccl* W City RDn. Eccl bdry: 1842 (cr EP8),[16] 1906 (gains back EP8, gains eccl ex-par Bridewell Precinct and ex-par Whitefriars, the union called as EP23).[17]

EP22–ST BRIDE, FLEET STREET, WITH HOLY TRINITY, GOUGH SQUARE–Cr 1954 by union EP23, EP26.[4]

EP23–ST BRIDE FLEET STREET WITH HOLY TRINITY GOUGH SQUARE AND THE PRECINCTS OF BRIDEWELL AND WHITEFRIARS–Cr 1906 by union AP35, EP8, ex-par Bridewell Precinct, ex-par Whitefriars.[17] W City RDn. Abol 1954 pt to help cr EP22, pt to help cr EP75, pt to help cr EP13.[4]

–ST CATHERINE COLEMAN–See AP53

–ST CATHERINE CREE–See AP54

EP24–ST CATHERINE CREE WITH ST JAMES DUKE'S PLACE–Cr 1873 by reunion AP54, EP34,[37] the name as EP24. E City RDn. Abol 1954 pt to AP17, pt to EP21.[2]

AP36–ST CHRISTOPHER LE STOCKS–*LG* Seq 1. *Eccl* United eccl 1781 to help cr EP42.[38]

AP37–ST CLEMENT, EASTCHEAP–*LG* Seq 1. *Eccl* United eccl 1670 to help cr EP25.[4]

EP25–ST CLEMENT EASTCHEAP WITH ST MARTIN ORGAR–Cr 1670 by union AP37, AP65.[4] E City RDn. Reconstituted 1954 gaining pts EP47, EP27, exchanging pts with EP40, AP65, losing pts to help cr EP76, to help cr EP29.[2] Addtl bdry alt: 1955.[39]

AP38–ST DIONIS BACKCHURCH–*LG* Seq 1. *Eccl* Pec jurisd Archbp Canterb (The Arches). E City RDn. United eccl 1876 to help cr EP5.[8]

AP39–ST DUNSTAN IN THE EAST–*LG* Seq 1.

Eccl Pec jurisd Archbp Canterb (The Arches). E City RDn. Eccl bdry: 1954 (gains pt EP45, AP1, loses pt to EP70).[2] Abol eccl 1960 pt to help cr EP1, pt to help cr EP51, pt to EP70.[3]

AP40–ST DUNSTAN IN THE WEST–Pt London, pt Middx (Liberty of the Rolls, sep CP 1866[33] in Middx so that this par ent London thereafter). *LG* Seq 3. *Eccl* W City RDn. Eccl bdry: 1842 (cr EP78),[40] 1886 (gains back EP79, the union called as EP26).[41]

EP26–ST DUNSTAN IN THE WEST WITH ST THOMAS IN THE LIBERTY OF THE ROLLS–Cr 1886 when AP43 gains back EP79.[41] W City RDn. Abol 1954 to help cr EP22.[2]

AP41–ST EDMUND THE KING AND MARTYR–*LG* Seq 1. *Eccl* United eccl 1670 to help cr EP28.[4]

EP27–ST EDMUND THE KING AND ST NICHOLAS ACONS WITH ALL HALLOWS, LOMBARD STREET, ST BENET, GRACECHURCH, ST LEONARD, EASTCHEAP, AND ST DIONIS, BACKCHURCH–Cr 1937 by union EP28, EP5.[9] Abol 1953 to help cr EP29.[2]

EP28–ST EDMUND THE KING WITH ST NICHOLAS ACONS–Cr 1670 by union AP41, AP94.[4] E City RDn. United 1937 to help cr EP27.[9]

EP29–ST EDMUND-THE-KING, WITH ST NICHOLAS ACONS, ALL HALLOWS, LOMBARD STREET, ST BENET GRACECHURCH, ST LEONARD, EASTCHEAP, AND ST DIONIS, BACKCHURCH–Reconstitution 1954 of EP26, gaining pts EP58, EP45, EP25, EP47, losing pts to help cr EP76, to help cr EP25, to help cr EP51, pt to EP40.[2]

AP42–ST ETHELBURGA–Sometimes 'St Ethelburga Bishopsgate'. *LG* Seq 1. *Eccl* E City RDn. Abol eccl 1954 pt to AP34, pt to EP33.[2]

–ST EWEN–See AP21

AP43–ST FAITH UNDER ST PAUL'S–*LG* Seq 1. *Eccl* Pec jurisd Dean & Chapter of St Paul's, London. United eccl 1670 to help cr EP16.[4]

AP44–ST GABRIEL FENCHURCH–Orig 'All Hallows Fenchurch'. *LG* Seq 1. *Eccl* United eccl 1670 to help cr EP45.[4]

AP45–ST GEORGE BOTOLPH LANE–*LG* Seq 1. *Eccl* United eccl 1670 to help cr EP30.[4]

EP30–ST GEORGE BOTOLPH-LANE WITH ST BOTOLPH BILLINGSGATE–Cr 1670 by union AP45, AP31.[4] E City RDn. United 1901 to help cr EP51.[2]

–ST GILES CRIPPLEGATE–See AP46

–ST GILES CRIPPLESGATE WITH ST BARTHOLOMEW MOOR LANE–See AP46

EP31–ST GILES CRIPPLEGATE, WITH ST BARTHOLOMEW, MOOR LANE AND ST ALPHAGE, LONDON WALL–Cr 1954 by union pts AP46, EP11, AP32, EP10, EP38, AP108.[2] Abol 1966 to help cr EP32.[43]

EP32–ST GILES CRIPPLEGATE WITH ST BARTHOLOMEW, MOOR LANE, ST ALPHAGE LONDON WALL AND ST LUKE OLD STREET WITH ST MARY CHARTERHOUSE AND ST PAUL CLERKENWELL–Cr 1966 by union EP31, pt Old Street St Luke with Charterhouse St Mary and Charterhouse St Paul EP (anc Middx), pt Shoreditch St Michael EP (anc Middx), ent Lbty or Lordship of Glasshouse Yard (anc Middx).[2] Bdry: 1972.[44]

AP46–ST GILES WITHOUT CRIPPLEGATE–Sometimes 'St Giles Cripplegate'. Pt London, pt Middx (the area cr 1723 a CP/EP civ called 'St Luke', eccl 'Old Street St Luke',[42] so that St Giles Without Cripplegate ent London thereafter). *LG* Seq 2. *Eccl* W City RDn. Addtl eccl bdry alt: 1850 (cr EP18),[28] 1900 (gains back EP18, the united par sometimes thereafter 'St Giles Cripplegate with St Bartholomew Moor Lane').[29] Abol eccl 1954 pt to help cr EP31, pt to help cr EP82.[2]

AP47–ST GREGORY BY ST PAUL'S–*LG* Seq 1. *Eccl* Pec jurisd Dean & Chapter of St Paul's, London. United eccl 1670 to help cr EP56.[4]

AP48–ST HELEN BISHOPSGATE–Name preferred to Harben's 'St Helen's'. *LG* Seq 1. *Eccl* E City RDn. United eccl 1873 to help cr EP33.[37]

EP33–ST HELEN BISHOPSGATE WITH ST MARTIN OUTWICH–Cr 1873 by union AP48, AP66.[37] E City RDn. Bdry: 1954 (gains pts AP7, AP42, EP60).[2]

CP5/EP34–ST JAMES' DUKE'S PLACE–First mention 1572 in AP54, rebuilt and consecr 1622/23.[46] *LG* Seq 1. *Eccl* E City RDn. Merged 1873 back into AP54, the union called as EP24.[37]

AP49–ST JAMES GARLICKHITHE–*LG* Seq 1. *Eccl* W City RDn. United eccl 1875 to help cr EP35.[47]

EP35–ST JAMES GARLICKHITHE, WITH ST MICHAEL, QUEENHITHE, AND HOLY TRINITY THE LESS–Cr 1875 by union AP49, EP61.[47] W City RDn. Abol 1954 when reconstituted as for EP36,[2] qv.

EP36–ST JAMES, GARLICKHYTHE, WITH ST MICHAEL, QUEENHITHE, AND HOLY TRINITY-THE-LESS–Reconstitution 1954 of EP35 when gains pts EP63, EP67, EP49, EP78, losing pt to help reconstitute EP12 as EP13, pt to help cr EP55.[2]

AP50–ST JOHN THE BAPTIST, WALBROOK–*LG* Seq 1. *Eccl* United eccl 1670 to help cr EP15.[4]

AP51–ST JOHN THE EVANGELIST, FRIDAY STREET–Orig 'St Werburga'. *LG* Seq 1. *Eccl* Pec jurisd Archbp Canterb (The Arches). United eccl 1670 to help cr EP2.[4]

AP52–ST JOHN ZACHARY–*LG* Seq 1. *Eccl* United eccl 1670 to help cr EP14.[4]

AP53–ST KATHERINE COLEMAN–Sometimes 'St Catherine Coleman', orig 'All Hallows Coleman'. *LG* Seq 1. *Eccl* E City RDn. United eccl 1921 to help cr EP70.[55]

AP54–ST KATHERINE CREE–Sometimes 'St Katherine Creechurch' or 'St Catherine Cree'. Bdry: 1622/23 (cr CP5/EP34).[45] *LG* Seq 1. *Eccl* E City RDn. Regains 1873 EP34, the union called as EP24.[37]

AP55–ST LAWRENCE JEWRY–*LG* Seq 1. *Eccl* United eccl 1670 to help cr EP37.[4]

EP37–ST LAWRENCE JEWRY WITH ST MARY MAGDALENE MILK STREET–Cr 1670 by union

AP55, AP77.[4] W City RDn. United 1897 to help cr EP3.[48]

EP38–ST LAWRENCE JEWRY, WITH ST MARY MAGDALENE, MILK-STREET, AND ST MICHAEL BASSISHAW–Cr 1897 by union EP37, AP85.[48] W City RDn. Abol 1954 pt to help cr EP31, pt to help cr EP82, pt to help cr EP55, pt to help cr EP41.[2]

AP56–ST LAWRENCE POUNTNEY–*LG* Seq 1. *Eccl* United eccl 1670 to help cr EP47.[4]

AP57–ST LEONARD EASTCHEAP–*LG* Seq 1. *Eccl* Pec jurisd Archbp Canterb (The Arches). United eccl 1670 to help cr EP19.[4]

AP58–ST LEONARD FOSTER LANE–*LG* Seq 1. *Eccl* Pec jurisd Dean & Chapter of Westminster. United eccl 1670 to help cr EP7.[4]

AP59–ST MAGNUS THE MARTYR–*LG* Seq 1. *Eccl* United eccl 1670 to help cr EP39.[4]

EP39–ST MAGNUS THE MARTYR WITH ST MARGARET NEW FISH STREET–Cr 1670 by union AP59, AP62.[4] Abol 1831 to help cr EP40.[49]

EP40–ST MAGNUS THE MARTYR WITH ST MARGARET NEW FISH STREET AND ST MICHAEL CROOKED LANE–Cr 1831 by union EP39, AP87.[49] E City RDn. Bdry: 1954 (gains pts EP27, EP25, loses pt to help cr EP51, pt to EP2),[2] 1955.[39]

AP60–ST MARGARET LOTHBURY–*LG* Seq 1. *Eccl* United eccl 1781 to help cr EP42.[38]

EP41–ST MARGARET LOTHBURY AND ST STEPHEN, COLEMAN STREET, WITH ST CHRISTOPHER LE STOCKS, ST BARTHOLOMEW-BY-THE-EXCHANGE, ST OLAVE, OLD JEWRY, ST MARTIN POMEROY, ST MILDRED POULTRY, AND ST MARY COLECHURCH–Cr 1954 by union pts AP108, EP38, EP11, EP60, EP44.[2]

EP42–ST MARGARET LOTHBURY WITH ST CHRISTOPHER LE STOCKS–Cr 1781 by union AP60, AP36.[4] United 1839 to help cr EP43.[25]

EP43–ST MARGARET LOTHBURY WITH ST CHRISTOPHER LE STOCKS AND ST BARTHOLOMEW BY THE EXCHANGE–Cr 1839 by union EP42, AP24.[25] E City RDn. United 1886 to help cr EP44.[50]

EP44–ST MARGARET LOTHBURY WITH ST CHRISTOPHER LE STOCKS, ST BARTHOLOMEW BY THE EXCHANGE, ST OLAVE OLD JEWRY, ST MARTIN POMEROY, ST MILDRED POULTRY AND ST MARY COLECHURCH–Cr 1886 by union EP43, EP73.[50] E City RDn. Abol 1954 pt to help cr EP41, pt to help cr EP82, pt to help cr EP55, pt to help cr EP76, pt to EP60.[2]

AP61–ST MARGARET MOSES–*LG* Seq 1. *Eccl* United eccl 1670 to help cr EP65.[4]

AP62–ST MARGARET NEW FISH STREET–More common name (Harben, 'St Margaret Fish Street Hall'). *LG* Seq 1. *Eccl* United eccl 1670 to help cr EP39.[4]

AP63–ST MARGARET PATTENS–*LG* Seq 1. *Eccl* United eccl 1670 to help cr EP45.[4]

EP45–ST MARGARET PATTENS WITH ST GABRIEL FENCHURCH–Cr 1670 by union AP63, AP44.[4] E City RDn. Abol 1954 pt to help cr EP29, pt to help cr EP51, pt to AP39, pt to EP70.[2]

AP64–ST MARTIN LUDGATE–*LG* Seq 1. *Eccl* W City RDn. Abol eccl 1890 to help cr EP46.[31]

EP46–ST MARTIN LUDGATE, WITH ST MARY MAGDALENE, OLD FISH STREET, AND ST GREGORY WITH ST PAUL–Cr 1890 by union AP64, EP56.[51] W City RDn. Abol 1954 pt to help cr EP75, pt to help reconstitute EP12 as EP13.[2]

AP65–ST MARTIN ORGAR–*LG* Seq 1. *Eccl* United eccl 1670 to help cr EP25.[4]

AP66–ST MARTIN OUTWICH–*LG* Seq 1. *Eccl* E City RDn. United eccl 1873 to help cr EP33.[37]

AP67–ST MARTIN POMEROY–More common spelling (Harben, 'St Martin Pomary'). *LG* Seq 1. *Eccl* United eccl 1670 to help cr EP72.[30]

AP68–ST MARTIN VINTRY–*LG* Seq 1. *Eccl* United eccl 1670 to help cr EP62.[4]

AP69–ST MARY ABCHURCH–*LG* Seq 1. *Eccl* United eccl 1670 to help cr EP47.[4]

EP47–ST MARY ABCHURCH WITH ST LAWRENCE POUNTNEY–Cr 1670 by union AP69, AP56.[4] W City RDn. Abol 1954 pt to help cr EP36, pt to help cr EP76, pt to help cr EP29, pt to EP25.[2]

AP70–ST MARY ALDERMANBURY–*LG* Seq 1. *Eccl* W City RDn. United eccl 1917 to help cr EP11.[52]

AP71–ST MARY ALDERMARY–*LG* Seq 1. *Eccl* Pec jurisd Archbp Canterb (The Arches). United eccl 1670 to help cr EP48.[4]

EP48–ST MARY ALDERMARY WITH ST THOMAS THE APOSTLE–Cr 1670 by union AP71, AP111.[4] W City RDn. United 1873 to help cr EP49.[53]

EP49–ST MARY ALDERMARY WITH ST THOMAS APOSTLE, ST ANTHOLIN AND ST JOHN THE BAPTIST UPON WALBROOK–Cr 1873 by union EP48, EP15.[53] W City RDn. Abol 1954 pt to help cr EP55, pt to help cr EP36, pt to help cr EP76.[2]

AP72–ST MARY AT HILL–*LG* Seq 1. *Eccl* United eccl 1670 to help cr EP50.[4]

EP50–ST MARY AT HILL WITH ST ANDREW HUBBARD–Cr 1670 by union AP72, AP15.[4] E City RDn. United 1901 to help cr EP52.[54]

EP51–ST MARY-AT-HILL WITH ST ANDREW HUBBARD, EASTCHEAP, ST GEORGE, BOTOLPH LANE, AND ST BOTOLPH BY BILLINGSGATE–Cr 1954 when EP52 gains pts EP45, EP27, EP40.[2] Bdry: 1960.[3]

EP52–ST MARY-AT-HILL WITH ST ANDREW HUBBARD, ST GEORGE BOTOLPH-LANE AND ST BOTOLPH BILLINGSGATE–Cr 1901 by union EP50, EP30.[54] E City RDn. Abol 1954 to help cr EP51.[2]

AP73–ST MARY AXE–United 1562 to AP16, the union civ called as AP16, eccl as AP17.[23]

AP74–ST MARY BOTHAW–*LG* Seq 1. *Eccl* Pec jurisd Archbp Canterb (The Arches). United eccl 1670 to help cr EP78.[4]

AP75–ST MARY LE BOW–*LG* Seq 1. *Eccl* Pec jurisd Archbp Canterb (The Arches). United eccl 1670 to help cr EP53.[4]

EP53–ST MARY LE BOW AND ST PANCRAS SOPER LANE WITH ALL HALLOWS HONEY LANE–Cr 1670 by union AP75, AP102, AP4.[4] W City RDn. United 1876 to help cr EP54.[5]

EP54–ST MARY LE BOW, ST PANCRAS, SOPER LANE, ALL HALLOWS, HONEY LANE, ALL HALLOWS, BREAD STREET, AND ST JOHN THE EVANGELIST–Cr 1876 by union EP53, EP2.[5] W City RDn. Abol 1954 pt to help cr EP82, pt to help cr EP55.[2]

EP55–ST MARY-LE-BOW, WITH ST PANCRAS, SOPER LANE, ALL HALLOWS, HONEY LANE, ALL HALLOWS, BREAD STREET, ST JOHN-THE-EVANGELIST, WATLING STREET, ST AUGUSTINE WITH ST FAITH UNDER ST PAUL'S, AND ST MILDRED BREAD STREET WITH ST MARGARET MOYSES–Cr 1954 by union pts EP54, EP49, EP16, EP65, EP44, EP58, EP77, EP35, EP38, EP81.[2]

AP76–ST MARY COLECHURCH–*LG* Seq 1. *Eccl* United eccl 1670 to help cr EP66.[4]

AP77–ST MARY MAGDALENE, MILK STREET–*LG* Seq 1. *Eccl* United eccl 1670 to help cr EP37.[4]

AP78–ST MARY MAGDALENE, OLD FISH STREET–*LG* Seq 1. *Eccl* United eccl 1670 to help cr EP56.[4]

EP56–ST MARY MAGDALENE OLD FISH STREET WITH ST GREGORY BY ST PAUL–Cr 1670 by union AP78, AP47.[4] W City RDn. United 1890 to help cr EP46.[51]

AP79–ST MARY MOUNTHAW–*LG* Seq 1. *Eccl* United eccl 1670 to help cr EP57.[4]

AP80–ST MARY SOMERSET–*LG* Seq 1. *Eccl* United eccl 1670 to help cr EP57.[4]

EP57–ST MARY SOMERSET WITH ST MARY MOUNTHAW–Cr 1670 by union AP80, AP79.[4] W City RDn. United 1866 to help cr EP69.[56]

AP81–ST MARY STAINING–*LG* Seq 1. *Eccl* United eccl 1670 to help cr EP64.[4]

AP82–ST MARY WOOLCHURCH–Sometimes 'St Mary Woolchurch Haw'. *LG* Seq 1. *Eccl* United eccl 1670 to help cr EP58.[4]

AP83–ST MARY WOOLNOTH–*LG* Seq 1. *Eccl* United eccl 1670 to help cr EP58.[4]

EP58–ST MARY WOOLNOTH WITH ST MARY, WOOLCHURCH HAW–Cr 1670 by union AP83, AP82.[4] E City RDn. Abol 1954 pt to help cr EP76, pt to help cr EP29, pt to help cr EP55.[2]

AP84–ST MATTHEW FRIDAY STREET–*LG* Seq 1. *Eccl* United eccl 1670 to help cr EP59.[4]

EP59–ST MATTHEW FRIDAY STREET WITH ST PETER CHEAP–Cr 1670 by union AP84, AP106.[106] W City RDn. United 1882 to help cr EP81.[5]

AP85–ST MICHAEL BASSISHAW–*LG* Seq 1. *Eccl* W City RDn. United eccl 1897 to help cr EP38.[48]

AP86–ST MICHAEL CORNHILL–*LG* Seq 1. *Eccl* E City RDn. United eccl 1906 to help cr EP60.[57]

EP60–ST MICHAEL CORNHILL WITH ST PETER-LE-POER AND ST BENET FINK–Cr 1906 by union AP86, EP74.[57] E City RDn. Reconstituted 1954 exchanging pts with EP44, losing pt to EP33.[2]

AP87–ST MICHAEL CROOKED LANE–*LG* Seq 1. *Eccl* Pec jurisd Archbp Canterb (The Arches). United eccl 1831 to help cr EP40.[49]

AP88–ST MICHAEL QUEENHITHE–*LG* Seq 1. *Eccl* United eccl 1670 to help cr EP61.[4]

EP61–ST MICHAEL QUEENHITHE WITH HOLY TRINITY THE LESS–Cr 1670 by union AP88, AP10.[4] W City RDn. United eccl 1875 to help cr EP35.[47]

AP89–ST MICHAEL LE QUERNE–*LG* Seq 1. *Eccl* Pec jurisd Archbp Canterb (The Arches). United 1670 to help cr EP80.[4]

AP90–ST MICHAEL, PATERNOSTER ROYAL–Sometimes 'St Michael Royal'. *LG* Seq 1. *Eccl* Pec jurisd Archbp Canterb (The Arches). United eccl 1670 to help cr EP62.[4]

EP62–ST MICHAEL ROYAL WITH ST MARTIN VINTRY–Cr 1670 by union AP90, AP68.[4] W City RDn. United 1893 to help cr EP63.[6]

EP63–ST MICHAEL ROYAL, WITH ST MARTIN VINTRY, AND ALL HALLOWS THE GREAT AND LESS–Cr 1893 by union EP62, EP3.[6] W City RDn. Abol 1954 pt to help reconstitute EP35 as EP36, pt to help cr EP76.[2]

AP91–ST MICHAEL WOOD STREET–*LG* Seq 1. *Eccl* United eccl 1670 to help cr EP64.[4]

EP64–ST MICHAEL WOOD STREET WITH ST MARY STAINING–Cr 1670 by union AP91, AP81.[4] W City RDn. United 1894 to help cr EP10.[18]

AP92–ST MILDRED, BREAD STREET–*LG* Seq 1. *Eccl* United eccl 1670 to help cr EP65.[4]

EP65–ST MILDRED BREAD STREET WITH ST MARGARET MOSES–Cr 1670 by union AP92, AP61.[4] W City RDn. Abol 1954 pt to help reconstitute EP12 as EP13, pt to help cr EP55.[2]

AP93–ST MILDRED POULTRY–*LG* Seq 1. *Eccl* United eccl 1670 to help cr EP66.[4]

EP66–ST MILDRED POULTRY WITH ST MARY COLECHURCH–Cr 1670 by union AP93, AP76.[4] W City RDn. United 1871 to help cr EP73.[58]

AP94–ST NICHOLAS ACONS–More common spelling (Harben, 'St Nicholas Acon'). *LG* Seq 1. *Eccl* United eccl 1670 to help cr EP28.[4]

AP95–ST NICHOLAS COLE ABBEY–*LG* Seq 1. *Eccl* United eccl 1670 to help cr EP68.[4]

EP67–ST NICHOLAS, COLE ABBEY, ST NICHOLAS, OLAVE, ST MARY SOMERSET, AND ST MARY, MOUNTHAW, WITH ST BENET, PAUL'S WHARF, AND ST PETER, PAUL'S WHARF–Cr 1879 by union EP69, EP20.[32] W City RDn. Abol 1954 pt to help reconstitute EP12 as EP13, pt to help reconstitute EP35 as EP36.[2]

EP68–ST NICHOLAS COLE ABBEY WITH ST NICHOLAS OLAVE–Cr 1670 by union AP95, AP96.[4] W City RDn. United 1866 to help cr EP69.[59]

EP69–ST NICHOLAS COLE ABBEY WITH ST NICHOLAS OLAVE WITH ST MARY SOMERSET AND ST MARY MOUNTHAW–Cr 1866 by union EP68, EP57.[59] W City RDn. United 1879 to help cr EP67.[32]

AP96–ST NICHOLAS OLAVE–*LG* Seq 1. *Eccl* United eccl 1670 to help cr EP68.[4]

AP97–ST NICHOLAS SHAMBLES–Destroyed at Dissolution, united 1547 with AP21, using church of Greyfriars as par church, to cr AP9.[15]

AP98–ST OLAVE BREAD STREET–Disappeared by 1271 after Austin friars settled nearby.

AP99–ST OLAVE HART STREET–*LG* Seq 1. *Eccl* E City RDn. United eccl 1870 to help cr EP71.[4]

EP70–ST OLAVE HART STREET AND ALL HALLOWS STAINING WITH ST CATHERINE COLEMAN–Cr 1921 by union EP71, AP53.[53] E City RDn. Reconstituted 1954 gaining pts AP39, EP45, AP17, losing pt to help cr EP76, pt to help reconstitute AP17, pt to EP21.[2] Addtl eccl bdry alt: 1960.[3]

EP71–ST OLAVE HART STREET WITH ALL HALLOWS STAINING–Cr 1870 by union AP99, AP8.[11] E City RDn. United 1921 to help cr EP70.[60]

AP100–ST OLAVE OLD JEWRY–*LG* Seq 1. *Eccl* United eccl 1670 to help cr EP72.[4]

EP72–ST OLAVE OLD JEWRY WITH ST MARTIN POMEROY–Cr 1670 by union AP100, AP67.[4] W City RDn. United 1871 to help cr EP73.[61]

EP73–ST OLAVE OLD JEWRY WITH ST MARTIN POMEROY, ST MILDRED POULTRY AND ST MARY COLECHURCH–Cr 1871 by union EP72, EP66.[61] W City RDn. United 1886 to help cr EP44.[50]

AP101–ST OLAVE SILVER STREET–*LG* Seq 1. *Eccl* United eccl 1670 to help cr EP9.[4]

AP102–ST PANCRAS, SOPER LANE–*LG* Seq 1. *Eccl* Pec jurisd Archbp Canterb (The Arches). United eccl 1670 to help cr EP53.[4]

–ST PETER CHEAP–See AP106

AP103–ST PETER CORNHILL–*LG* Seq 1. *Eccl* E City RDn.

AP104–ST PETER PAUL'S WHARF–*LG* Seq 1. *Eccl* United eccl 1670 to help cr EP20.[4]

AP105–ST PETER LE POER–*LG* Seq 1. *Eccl* United eccl 1842 to help cr EP74.[4]

EP74–ST PETER LE POER WITH ST BENET FINK–Cr 1842 by union AP105, AP27.[30] E City RDn. United 1906 to help cr EP60.[57]

AP106–ST PETER WESTCHEAP–Sometimes 'St Peter Cheap'. *LG* Seq 1. *Eccl* United eccl 1670 to help cr EP59.[4]

AP107–ST SELPUCHRE–Pt London (eccl severed 1547 to help cr AP9[63]), pt Middx, each a sep par for civ purposes in the respective cos though with the same name, one par for eccl purposes. London pt: *LG* Seq 3. *Eccl* St Sepulchre RDn (1861–1901), W City RDn (1901–54). Abol eccl 1954 pt to help cr EP17, pt to help cr EP75.[2]

EP75–ST SEPULCHRE WITH CHRIST CHURCH, GREYFRIARS AND ST LEONARD, FOSTER LANE–Cr 1954 by union AP107, EP7, EP46, AP25, EP23, EP16, EP81.[2] Bdry: 1963.[27]

AP108–ST STEPHEN COLEMAN STREET–*LG* Seq 1. *Eccl* W City RDn. Abol 1954 pt to help cr EP31, pt to help cr EP41, pt to AP34.[2]

AP109–ST STEPHEN WALLBROOK–*LG* Seq 1. *Eccl* United eccl 1670 to help cr EP77.[4]

EP76–ST STEPHEN WALBROOK AND ST SWITHUN LONDON STONE, WITH ST BENET SHEREHOG AND ST MARY BOTHAW WITH ST LAURENCE, POUNTNEY–Cr 1954 by union pts EP77, EP47, EP79, EP44, EP58, EP27, EP25, EP70, EP49.[2]

EP77–ST STEPHEN WALBROOK WITH ST BENET SHEREHOG–Cr 1670 by union AP109, AP30.[4] W City RDn. Abol 1954 pt to help cr EP55, pt to help cr EP76.[2]

AP110–ST SWITHIN LONDON STONE–Sometimes 'St Swithun'. *LG* Seq 1. *Eccl* United eccl 1670 to help cr EP78.[4]

EP78–ST SWITHUN LONDON STONE WITH ST MARY BOTHAW–Cr 1670 by union AP110, AP74.[4] W City RDn. Abol 1954 pt to help cr EP36, pt to help cr EP76.[2]

AP111–ST THOMAS APOSTLE–*LG* Seq 1. *Eccl* United eccl 1670 to help cr EP48.[4]

EP79–ST THOMAS IN THE LIBERTY OF THE ROLLS–Cr 1842 from the Middx pt of AP40.[40] W City RDn. Merged 1886 back into AP40 and the union called as EP26.[41]

AP112–ST VEDAST FOSTER LANE–*LG* Seq 1. *Eccl* Pec jurisd Archbp Canterb (The Arches). United eccl 1670 to help cr EP80.[4]

EP80–ST VEDAST FOSTER LANE WITH ST MICHAEL-LE-QUERNE–Cr 1670 by union AP112, AP89.[4] W City RDn. United 1882 to help cr EP81.[5]

EP81–ST VEDAST FOSTER LANE WITH ST MICHAEL-LE-QUERNE AND ST MATTHEW FRIDAY STREET WITH ST PETER CHEAP–Cr 1882 by union EP81, EP59.[5] W City RDn. Abol 1954 pt to help cr EP75, pt to help cr EP82, pt to help cr EP55.[2]

EP82–ST VEDAST WITH ST MICHAEL-LE-QUERNE, ST MATTHEW, FRIDAY STREET, ST PETER, CHEAP, ST ALBAN, WOOD STREET, ST OLAVE, SILVER STREET, ST MICHAEL, WOOD STREET, ST MARY STAINING, ST ANNE AND ST AGNES, GRESHAM STREET, AND ST JOHN ZACHARY, GRESHAM STREET–Cr 1954 by union pts EP81, EP10, EP38, EP14, AP46, AP33, EP7, EP54, EP44, EP11.[2]

–ST WERBURGA–See AP51

CP6–SERJEANTS' INN–Ex-par place, sep CP 1858.[14] *LG* Seq 3.

CP7–THAVIE'S INN–Ex-par place, sep CP 1858.[14] *LG* Seq 3.

CP8/EP83–WHITECHAPEL–Cr early 17th cent from Stepney AP (Middx),[66] small pt in London, the latter transf 1900 to AP33,[20] and Whitechapel ent Middx thereafter, qv.

–WHITEFRIARS–Ex-par place, sep CP 1858 as CP9,[14] qv, eccl abol 1906 to help cr EP23.[17]

CP9–WHITEFRIARS PRECINCT–Ex-par place (for eccl see prev entry), sep CP 1858.[14] *LG* Seq 1.

PART II: LONDON ADMINISTRATIVE COUNTY, 1889[67]–1965[68]

PLAN FOR FOLLOWING ENTRIES

The county was formed in 1889 from the pts of Middx, Surrey and Kent which had been in the Metropolis from 1855. The entires below show only those APs and CPs which were pt of the civ composition of the county for 1889–1965, and of the parl composition for 1918–70. Unless specified otherwise in the entries, pars were pt of PLUs for the period 1889–1930, of Vestries and Dists in the Metrop Bd Wks for 1889–99, and of Metrop Bors for 1900–65. Consult the entries in anc Midd, Surrey and Kent for civ organisation before 1889, for parl constituencies before 1918, and for all details of eccl organisation (which are listed in the entries for the Anc Cos through 1 Apr 1974, even though the pars were civ transferred here). For civ organisation after 1965 and parl constituencies from 1970, see the entries in Part III below, Greater London.

NAMES OF PARISHES

The common practice was to place the dedication of the parish before the place name, whereas the principle adopted throughout the *Guide* reverses that order (e.g., 'St Olave Southwark', and 'Southwark St Olave'). The list below therefore reverses the more common order for the following parishes: Deptford St Nicholas, Deptford St Paul, Newington (usually 'St Mary Newington'), and all the pars in Southwark and Westminster.

ABBREVIATIONS

Batt.	Battersea
Berm.	Bermondsey
Beth. Gr.	Bethnal Green
Cambw.	Camberwell
Clap.	Clapham
Finsb.	Finsbury
Greenw.	Greenwich
Hack.	Hackney
Hamm.	Hammersmith
Hampst.	Hampstead
Holb.	Holborn
Isling.	Islington
Kens.	Kensington
Lamb.	Lambeth
Limeh.	Limehouse
Padd.	Paddington
St Panc.	St Pancras
Shored.	Shoreditch
Step.	Stepney
Swk.	Southwark
Tow. Hmlts.	Tower Hamlets
Wandsw.	Wandsworth
W'minst.	Westminster
Whitech.	Whitechapel
Woolw.	Woolwich

THE PARISHES OF LONDON COUNTY

BATTERSEA

AP Orig Surrey. *LG* Wandsw. & Clap. PLU (1889–1904), Batt. Par (poor, 1904–30), Wandsw. Dist (Metrop Bd Wks), Batt. Metrop Bor. Civ bdry: 1899.[69] Transf 1965 to Gtr London (Wandsw. LB).[68] *Parl* Pt Batt., North Parl Bor/BC, pt Batt., South Parl Bor/BC (1918–70). Parl bdry: 1949.[70]

BERMONDSEY

AP Orig Surrey. *LG* St Olave PLU (1889–1904), Berm. Par (poor, 1904–30), Vestry (Metrop Bd Wks), Metrop Bor. Civ bdry: 1899,[69] 1904 (gains Rotherhithe AP, Southwark St Olave and St Thomas CP, Southwark St John Horsleydown CP).[88] Transf 1965 to Gtr London (Swk. LB).[68] *Parl* Pt Berm., Rotherhithe Parl Bor, pt Berm., W Berm. Parl Bor (1918–48), Berm. BC (1948–70). Parl bdry: 1949.[70]

BETHNAL GREEN

AP Orig Middx (qv also for EP of this name). *LG* Beth. Gr. Par (poor), Vestry (Metrop Bd Wks), Metrop Bor. Civ bdry: 1899.[69] Transf 1965 to Gtr London (Tow. Hmlts. LB).[68] *Parl* Pt Beth. Gr., North East Parl Bor, pt Beth. Gr., South West Parl Bor (1918–48), Beth. Gr. BC (1948–70). Parl bdry: 1955.[71]

BOW

CP Orig Midd (qv also for EP of this name). Sometimes 'Stratford le Bow'. *LG* Poplar PLU, Dist (Metrop Bd Wks), Metrop Bor. Bdry: 1899.[69] Abol civ 1907 to help cr Poplar Borough CP.[72]

BROMLEY

AP Orig Middx. *LG* Poplar PLU, Dist (Metrop Bd Wks), Metrop Bor. Civ bdry: 1899.[69] Abol civ 1907 to help cr Poplar Borough CP.[72]

CAMBERWELL

AP Orig Surrey. *LG* Cambw. Par (poor), Vestry (Metrop Bd Wks), Metrop Bor. Civ bdry: 1899.[69] Transf 1965 to Gtr London (Swk. LB).[68] *Parl* Pt Cambw., Dulwich Parl Bor/BC (1918–70), pt Cambw., Peckham Parl Bor/BC (1918–70), pt Cambw., North Parl Bor (1918–48), pt Cambw., North-West Parl Bor (1918–48).

CHARLTON AND KIDBROOKE

CP Cr 1901 by union Charlton next Woolwich AP, Kidbrooke CP.[73] *LG* Woolw. PLU, Greenw.

Metrop Bor. Abol 1930 to help cr Borough of Greenwich CP.[74] *Parl* Greenw. Parl Bor (1918–48).

CHARLTON NEXT WOOLWICH

AP Orig Kent. *LG* Lewisham PLU, Plumstead Dist (Metrop Bd Wks, 1889–94), Lee Dist (Metrop Bd Wks, 1894–1900), Greenw. Metrop Bor. Civ bdry: 1899.[69] Abol civ 1901 to help cr Charlton and Kidbrooke CP.[73]

CHARTERHOUSE

CP Orig Middx (qv for EPs of this name). *LG* Holb. PLU, in no Metrop Bd Wks Dist, Finsb. Metrop Bor. Abol 1915 to help cr Finsbury CP.[75]

CHELSEA

AP Orig Middx. *LG* Chelsea Par (poor), Vestry (Metrop Bd Wks), Metrop Bor. Civ bdry: 1899.[69] Transf 1965 to Gtr London (Kens. & Chelsea LB).[68] *Parl* Chelsea Parl Bor/BC (1918–70).

CLAPHAM

AP Orig Surrey. *LG* Wandsw. & Clap. PLU, Wandsw. Dist (Metrop Bd Wks), Metrop Bor. Civ bdry: 1899.[69] Abol civ 1904 to help cr Wandsworth Borough CP.[76]

CLERKENWELL

AP Orig Middx. *LG* Holb. PLU, Clerkenwell Vestry (Metrop Bd Wks), Finsb. Metrop Bor. Civ bdry: 1899.[69] Abol civ 1915 to help cr Finsbury CP.[75]

CLOSE OF THE COLLEGIATE CHURCH OF ST PETER

CP Orig Middx. *LG* St George PLU (1889–1913), City of W'minst. PLU (1913–22), in no Metrop Bd Wks Dist, W'minst. Metrop Bor. Abol civ 1922 to help cr City of Westminster CP.[77] *Parl* See Part III of the *Guide* for composition of the 2 W'minst. Parl Bors by wards of the Metrop Bor.

DEPTFORD ST NICHOLAS

AP Orig Kent. *LG* Greenw. PLU, Dist (Metrop Bd Wks), Metrop Bor. Civ bdry: 1899.[69] Abol civ 1930 to help cr Borough of Greenwich CP.[74] *Parl* Greenw. Parl Bor (1918–48).

DEPTFORD ST PAUL

CP Orig Kent, Surrey (qv for EP of this name). *LG* Greenw. PLU, Dist (Metrop Bd Wks), Deptford Metrop Bor. Bdry: 1899.[69] Transf 1965 to Gtr London (Lewisham LB).[68] *Parl* Deptford Parl Bor/BC (1918–70).

ELTHAM

AP Orig Kent. *LG* Lewisham PLU, Plumstead Dist (Metrop Bd Wks, 1889–94), Lee Dist (Metrop Bd Wks, 1894–1900), Woolw. Metrop Bor. Civ bdry: 1899.[69] Abol civ 1930 to help cr Borough of Woolwich CP.[78] *Parl* See Part III of the *Guide* for composition of the 2 Woolw. Parl Bors by wards of the Metrop Bor.

FINSBURY

CP Cr 1915 by union Charterhouse CP, Clerkenwell AP, Glasshouse Yard CP, St Luke CP, St Sepulchre AP.[75] *LG* Holb. PLU, Finsb. Metrop Bor. Transf 1965 to Gtr London (Isling. LB).[68] *Parl* Finsb. Parl Bor (1918–48), Finsb. & Shored. BC (1948–70).

FULHAM

AP Orig Middx. *LG* Fulham PLU (1889–99), Par (poor, 1899–1930), Vestry (Metrop Bd Wks), Metrop Bor. Civ bdry: 1899.[69] Transf 1965 to Gtr London (Hamm. LB).[68] *Parl* Pt Fulham, East Parl Bor/BC, pt Fulham, West Parl Bor/BC (1918–55), pt Barons Court BC, pt Fulham BC (1955–70).

FURNIVAL'S INN

CP Orig pt City of London, pt Middx (London Adm Co from 1889), the former lost 1899 to St Andrew Holborn AP (City of London) and the par ent London Adm Co thereafter.[69] *LG* London Adm Co pt, Holb. PLU, in no Metrop Bd Wks Dist, Holb. Metrop Bor. Abol 1930 to help cr Holborn CP.[79] *Parl* Holb. Parl Bor (1918–48).

GLASSHOUSE YARD

Lbty in Middx (London Adm Co from 1889), made sep CP 1899.[73] *LG* As Lbty, then CP: Holb. PLU, Dist (Metrop Bd Wks), Finsb. Metrop Bor. Abol 1915 to help cr Finsbury CP.[75]

GRAY'S INN

CP Orig Middx. *LG* In no PLU or Metrop Bd Wks Dist, Holb. Metrop Bor. Abol 1932 ent to Holborn CP.[80] *Parl* Holb. Parl Bor (1918–48).

GREENWICH

AP Orig Kent. *LG* Greenw. PLU, Dist (Metrop Bd Wks), Metrop Bor. Civ bdry: 1899.[69] Abol civ 1930 to help cr Borough of Greenwich CP.[74] *Parl* Greenw. Parl Bor (1918–48).

BOROUGH OF GREENWICH

CP Cr 1930 by union Charlton and Kidbrooke CP, Greenwich AP, Deptford St Nicholas AP.[74] *LG* Greenw. Metrop Bor. Transf 1965 to Gtr London (Greenw. LB).[68] *Parl* Greenw. BC (1948–70).

HACKNEY

AP Orig Middx. *LG* Hack. PLU, Dist (Metrop Bd Wks, 1889–94), Hack. Vestry (Metrop Bd Wks, 1894–1900), Metrop Bor. Civ bdry: 1899,[69] 1908 (exchanges pts with Tottenham AP, Middx).[81] *Parl* Pt Hack., Central Parl Bor, pt Hack. North Parl Bor (1918–48), pt Hack., South Parl Bor/BC (1918–55), pt Hack., Central BC (1955–70), pt Stoke Newington & Hack. North BC (1948–70), pt Beth. Gr. BC (1955–70). Parl bdry: 1955.[71]

HAMMERSMITH

CP Orig Middx. *LG* Fulham PLU (1889–99), Hamm. Par (poor, 1899–1930), Hamm. Vestry (Metrop Bd Wks), Metrop Bor. Civ bdry: 1899.[69] Transf 1965 to Gtr London (Hamm. LB).[68] *Parl* Pt Hamm., North Parl Bor/BC (1918–70), pt Hamm., South Parl Bor/BC (1918–55), pt Barons Court BC (1955–70). Parl bdry: 1955.[82]

HAMPSTEAD

AP Orig Middx. *LG* Hampst. Par (poor), Vestry (Metrop Bd Wks), Metrop Bor. Civ bdry: 1899.[69] Transf 1965 to Gtr London (Camden LB).[68] *Parl* Hampst. Parl Bor/BC (1918–70).

HOLBORN
CP Cr 1930 by union Furnival's Inn CP, Liberty of Saffron Hill, Hatton Garden, Ely Rents and Ely Place CP, Staple Inn CP, St Andrew Holborn Above the Bars with St George the Martyr CP, St Giles in the Fields and St George Bloomsbury CP.[79] *LG* Holb. Metrop Bor. Bdry: 1932 (gains Gray's Inn CP, Lincoln's Inn CP).[80] Transf 1965 to Gtr London (Camden LB).[68] *Parl* Holb. & St Panc. South BC (1948–70).

HOLY TRINITY MINORIES
AP Orig. Middx. *LG* Whitech. PLU, Dist (Metrop Bd Wks). Abol civ 1895 ent to Whitechapel CP.[83]

ISLINGTON
AP Orig Middx. *LG* Isling. Par (poor), Vestry (Metrop Bd Wks), Metrop Bor. Civ bdry: 1899 (incl gains pt South Hornsey CP, Middx).[69] Transf 1965 to Gtr London (Isling. LB).[68] *Parl* Pt Isling, East Parl Bor/BC (1918–70), pt Isling., North Parl Bor/BC (1918–70), pt Isling., South Parl Bor (1918–48), pt Isling., South West Parl Bor/BC (1918–70), pt Isling., West Parl Bor (1918–48).

KENSINGTON
AP Orig Middx. *LG* Kens. Par (poor), Vestry (Metrop Bd Wks), Metrop Bor. Civ bdry: 1899.[69] Transf 1965 to Gtr London (Kens. & Chelsea LB).[68] *Parl* Pt Kens., North Parl Bor/BC (1918–70), pt Kens., South Parl Bor/BC (1918–70), pt Chelsea BC (1948–70).

KIDBROOKE
CP Orig Kent (qv for EP of this name). *LG* Woolw. PLU, Plumstead Dist (Metrop Bd Wks, 1889–94), Lee Dist (Metrop Bd Wks, 1894–1900), Greenw. Metrop Bor. Civ bdry: 1899.[69] Abol 1901 to help cr Charlton and Kidbrooke CP.[73]

LAMBETH
AP Orig Surrey. *LG* Lamb. Par (poor), Vestry (Metrop Bd Wks), Metrop Bor. Civ bdry: 1899.[69] Transf 1965 to Gtr London (Lamb. LB).[68] *Parl* Pt Lamb., Brixton Parl Bor/BC (1918–70), pt Lamb., Norwood Parl Bor/BC (1918–70), pt Lamb., Vauxhall BC (1948–70), pt Lamb., Kennington Parl Bor (1918–48), pt Lamb., North Parl Bor (1918–48).

LEE
AP Orig Kent. *LG* Lewisham PLU, Plumstead Dist (Metrop Bd Wks, 1889–94), Lee Dist (Metrop Bd Wks, 1894–1900), Lewisham Metrop Bor. Civ bdry: 1899.[69] Abol civ 1905 ent to Lewisham AP.[84]

LEWISHAM
AP Orig Kent. *LG* Lewisham PLU, Dist (Metrop Bd Wks), Metrop Bor. Civ bdry: 1899,[69] 1905 (gains Lee AP).[84] Transf 1965 to Gtr London (Lewisham LB).[68] *Parl* Pt Lewisham, East Parl Bor (1918–48), pt Lewisham North BC (1948–70), pt Lewisham South BC (1948–70), pt Lewisham, West Parl Bor/BC (1918–70).

LIBERTY OF THE ROLLS
CP Orig Middx (qv for 'St Thomas in the Liberty of the Rolls' EP). *LG* Strand PLU (1889–1913), City of W'minst. PLU (1913–22), Strand Dist (Metrop Bd Wks), W'minst. Metrop Bor. Bdry: 1899.[69] Abol 1922 to help cr City of Westminster CP.[77] *Parl* See Part III of the *Guide* for composition of the 2 W'minst. Parl Bors by wards of the Metrop Bor.

LIBERTY OF SAFFRON HILL, HATTON GARDEN, ELY RENTS, AND ELY PLACE
CP Orig Middx. *LG* Holb. PLU, Dist (Metrop Bd Wks), Metrop Bor. Bdry: 1899.[69] Abol 1930 to help cr Holborn CP.[79] *Parl* Holb. Parl Bor (1918–48).

LIMEHOUSE
CP Orig Middx. *LG* Step. PLU (1889–1921), Limeh. Par (poor, 1921–27), Limeh. Dist (Metrop Bd Wks), Step. Metrop Bor. Civ bdry: 1899,[69] 1921 (gains Ratcliff CP, Shadwell CP, Wapping CP).[85] Abol civ 1927 to help cr Stepney CP.[86] *Parl* See Part III of the *Guide* for composition of the 3 Step. Parl Bors by wards of the Metrop Bor.

LINCOLN'S INN
CP Orig Middx. *LG* In no PLU or Metrop Bd Wks Dist, Holb. Metrop Bor. Bdry: 1899.[69] Abol 1932 ent to Holborn CP.[80] *Parl* Holb. Parl Bor (1918–48).

MILE END NEW TOWN
CP Orig Middx (qv for EP of the same name). *LG* Whitech. PLU, Dist (Metrop Bd Wks), Step. Metrop Bor. Bdry: 1921.[69] Abol 1921 ent to Whitechapel CP.[85] *Parl* As for Limehouse CP.

MILE END OLD TOWN
CP Orig Middx (qv for EP of the same name). *LG* Mile End Old Town Par (poor, 1889–1925), Step. PLU (1925–27), Mile End Old Town Vestry (Metrop Bd Wks), Step. Metrop Bor. Bdry: 1899.[69] Abol 1927 to help cr Stepney CP.[86] *Parl* As for Limehouse CP.

NEWINGTON
AP Orig Surrey. *LG* St Saviour's PLU (1889–1901), Swk. PLU (1901–30), Newington St Mary Vestry (Metrop Bd Wks), Swk. Metrop Bor. Civ bdry: 1899.[69] Abol civ 1930 to help cr Southwark CP.[87] *Parl* See Part III of the *Guide* for composition of the 3 Swk. Parl Bors by wards of the Metrop Bor.

NORTON FOLGATE
CP Orig Middx. *LG* Whitech. PLU, Dist (Metrop Bd Wks), Step. Metrop Bor. Bdry: 1899.[69] Abol 1921 ent to Whitechapel CP.[85] *Parl* As for Limehouse CP.

OLD ARTILLERY GROUND
CP Orig Middx. *LG* Whitech. PLU, Dist (Metrop Bd Wks), Step. Metrop Bor. Abol 1921 ent to Whitechapel CP.[85] *Parl* As for Limehouse CP.

PADDINGTON
AP Orig Middx. *LG* Padd. Par (poor), Vestry (Metrop Bd Wks), Metrop Bor. Civ bdry: 1899.[69] Transf 1965 to Gtr London (City of W'minst. LB).[68] *Parl* Pt Padd., North Parl Bor/BC, pt Padd., South Parl Bor/BC (1918–70).

PLUMSTEAD
AP Orig Kent. *LG* Woolw. PLU, Plumstead Dist

(Metrop Bd Wks, 1889–94), Vestry (Metrop Bd Wks, 1894–1900), Woolw. Metrop Bor. Abol 1930 to help cr Borough of Woolwich CP.[78] *Parl* As for Eltham AP.

POPLAR

CP Orig Middx. *LG* Poplar PLU, Dist (Metrop Bd Wks), Metrop Bor. Bdry: 1899.[69] Abol 1907 to help cr Poplar Borough CP.[72]

POPLAR BOROUGH

CP Cr 1907 by union Bow CP, Bromley AP, Poplar CP.[72] *LG* Poplar Borough Par (poor), Poplar Metrop Bor. Transf 1965 to Gtr London (Tow. Hmlts. LB).[68] *Parl* Pt Poplar, Bow & Bromley Parl Bor, pt Poplar, S Poplar Parl Bor (1918–48), Poplar BC (1948–70).

PUTNEY

CP Orig Surrey (qv for EP of the same name). *LG* Wandsw. & Clap. PLU, Wandsw. Dist (Metrop Bd Wks), Metrop Bor. Bdry: 1899.[69] Abol 1904 to help cr Wandsworth Borough CP.[76]

RATCLIFF

CP Orig Middx (qv for EP of the same name). *LG* Step. PLU, Limeh. Dist (Metrop Bd Wks), Step. Metrop Bor. Abol 1921 ent to Limehouse CP.[85] *Parl* As for Limehouse CP.

ROTHERHITHE

AP Orig Surrey. *LG* St Olave PLU, Rotherhithe Vestry (Metrop Bd Wks), Berm. Metrop Bor. Civ bdry: 1899.[69] Abol civ 1904 ent to Bermondsey AP.[88]

ST ANDREW HOLBORN ABOVE THE BARS WITH ST GEORGE THE MARTYR

CP Orig Middx. *LG* Holb. PLU, Dist (Metrop Bd Wks), Metrop Bor. Bdry: 1899.[69] Abol 1930 to help cr Holborn CP.[79] *Parl* Holb. Parl Bor (1918–48).

ST ANNE WITHIN THE LIBERTY OF WESTMINSTER

CP Orig Middx (sometimes 'St Anne Soho'; see Middx for eccl as 'Soho St Anne'). *LG* W'minst. PLU (1889–1913), City of W'minst. PLU (1913–22), Strand Dist (Metrop Bd Wks), W'minst. Metrop Bor. Abol 1922 to help cr City of Westminster CP.[77] *Parl* As for Liberty of the Rolls CP.

ST BOTOLPH WITHOUT ALDGATE

CP Orig Middx (the Middx pt, sometimes 'East Smithfield Lbty' of the par which orig had pts in City of London, Middx, each a sep par for civ purposes though each with the same name). *LG* Whitech.PLU, Dist (Metrop Bd Wks), Step. Metrop Bor. Bdry: 1895 (gains St Katherine by the Tower CP, Old Tower Without CP),[89] 1901 (gains Tower of London CP).[90] Abol 1921 ent to Whitechapel CP.[85] *Parl* As for Limehouse CP.

ST CLEMENT DANES

AP Orig Middx. *LG* Strand PLU (1889–1913), City of W'minst. PLU (1913–22), Stand Dist (Metrop Bd Wks), W'minst. Metrop Bor. Civ bdry: 1899.[69] Abol civ 1922 to help cr City of Westminster CP.[77] *Parl* As for Liberty of the Rolls CP.

ST GEORGE HANOVER SQUARE

CP Orig Middx (qv for EP of the same name). *LG* St George's PLU (1889–1913), City of W'minst. PLU (1913–22), St George Hanover Square Vestry (Metrop Bd Wks), W'minst. Metrop Bor. Bdry: 1899.[69] Abol 1922 to help cr City of W'minst. CP.[77] *Parl* As for Liberty of the Rolls CP.

ST GEORGE IN THE EAST

CP Orig Middx (qv for EP 'St George St George in the East'). *LG* St George in the East Par (poor, 1889–1925), Step. PLU (1925–27), St George in the East Vestry (Metrop Bd Wks), Step. Metrop Bor. Abol 1927 to help cr Stepney CP.[86] *Parl* As for Limehouse CP.

ST GILES IN THE FIELDS AND ST GEORGE BLOOMSBURY

CP Orig Middx. *LG* St Giles in the Fields and St George Bloomsbury Par (poor, 1889–1914), Holb. PLU (1914–30), St Giles Dist (Metrop Bd Wks), Holb. Metrop Bor. Bdry: 1899,[69] 1891.[91] Abol 1930 to help cr Holborn CP.[79] *Parl* Holb. Parl Bor (1918–48).

ST KATHERINE BY THE TOWER

CP Orig Middx. *LG* Whitech. PLU, Dist (Metrop Bd Wks). Abol 1895 ent to St Botolph without Aldgate CP (London Adm Co).[89]

ST LUKE

CP Orig Middx (qv for EP 'Old Street St Luke'). *LG* Holb. PLU, St Luke Vestry (Metrop Bd Wks), Finsb. Metrop Bor. Bdry: 1899.[69] Abol 1915 to help cr Finsbury CP.[75]

ST MARTIN IN THE FIELDS

AP Orig Middx. *LG* Strand PLU (1889–1913), City of W'minst. PLU (1913–22), St Martin in the Fields Vestry (Metrop Bd Wks), W'minst. Metrop Bor. Civ bdry: 1899.[69] Abol civ 1922 to help cr City of Westminster CP.[77] *Parl* As for Liberty of the Rolls CP.

ST MARY LE STRAND

AP Orig Middx. *LG* Strand PLU (1889–1913), City of W'minst. PLU (1913–22), Strand Dist (Metrop Bd Wks), W'minst. Metrop Bor. Abol civ 1922 to help cr City of Westminster CP.[77] *Parl* As for Liberty of the Rolls CP.

ST MARYLEBONE

AP Orig Middx. *LG* St Marylebone Par (poor), Vestry (Metrop Bd Wks), Metrop Bor. Civ bdry: 1899.[69] Transf 1965 to Gtr London (City of W'minst. LB).[68] *Parl* St Marylebone Parl Bor/BC (1918–70).

ST PANCRAS

AP Orig Middx. *LG* St Panc. Par (poor), Vestry (Metrop Bd Wks), Metrop Bor. Civ bdry: 1891,[91] 1899.[69] Transf 1965 to Gtr London (Camden LB).[68] *Parl* Pt St Panc., North Parl Bor/BC (1918–70), pt St Panc., South East Parl Bor (1918–48), pt St Panc., South West Parl Bor (1918–48), pt Holb. & St Panc. South BC (1948–70).

ST PAUL COVENT GARDEN

CP Orig Middx (qv for EP 'Covent Garden St Paul'). *LG* Strand PLU (1889–1913), City of W'minst.

PLU (1913–22), Strand Dist (Metrop Bd Wks), W'minst. Metrop Bor. Abol 1922 to help cr City of Westminster CP.[77] *Parl* As for Liberty of the Rolls CP.

ST SEPULCHRE
AP Orig pt Middx, pt City of London, each a sep par for civ purposes in the respective counties though with the same name. Adm Co pt: *LG* Holb. PLU, Dist (Metrop Bd Wks), Finsb. Metrop Bor. Abol civ 1915 to help cr Finsbury CP.[75]

PRECINCT OF THE SAVOY
CP Orig Middx. *LG* Strand PLU (1889–1913), City of W'minst. PLU (1913–22), Strand Dist (Metrop Bd Wks), W'minst. Metrop Bor. Abol 1922 to help cr City of Westminster CP.[77] *Parl* As for Liberty of the Rolls CP.

SHADWELL
CP Orig Midd (qv for EP of the same name). *LG* Step. PLU, Limeh. Dist (Metrop Bd Wks), Step. Metrop Bor. Abol 1921 ent to Limehouse CP.[85] *Parl* As for Limehouse CP.

SHOREDITCH
AP Orig Middx. *LG* Shored. Par (poor), Vestry (Metrop Bd Wks), Metrop Bor. Civ bdry: 1899.[69] Transf 1965 to Gtr London (Hack. LB).[68] *Parl* Shored. Parl Bor (1918–48), Shored. & Finsb. BC (1948–70).

SOUTHWARK
CP Cr 1930 by union Southwark Christchurch CP, Southwark St Saviour AP, Southwark St George the Martyr AP, Newington AP.[87] *LG* Swk. Metrop Bor. Transf 1965 to Gtr London (Swk. LB).[68] *Parl* Swk. BC (1948–70).

SOUTHWARK CHRISTCHURCH
CP Orig Surrey (qv for EP of the same name). *LG* St Saviour's PLU (1889–1901), Swk. PLU (1901–30), St Saviour's Dist (Metrop Bd Wks), Swk. Metrop Bor. Civ bdry: 1899.[69] Abol 1930 to help cr Southwark CP.[87] *Parl* As for Newington AP.

SOUTHWARK ST GEORGE THE MARTYR
AP Orig Surrey. *LG* St Saviour's PLU (1889–1901), Swk. PLU (1901–30), Swk. St George the Martyr Vestry (Metrop Bd Wks), Swk. Metrop Bor. Civ bdry: 1899.[69] Abol civ 1930 to help cr Southwark CP.[87] *Parl* As for Newington AP.

SOUTHWARK ST JOHN HORSLEYDOWN
CP Orig Surrey (qv for EP of the same name). *LG* St Olave PLU, Dist (Metrop Bd Wks), Berm. Metrop Bor. Abol 1904 ent to Bermondsey AP.[88]

SOUTHWARK ST OLAVE
AP Orig Surrey. *LG* St Olave PLU, Dist (Metrop Bd Wks). Abol 1896 to help cr Southwark St Olave and St Thomas CP.[92]

SOUTHWARK ST OLAVE AND ST THOMAS
CP Cr 1896 by union Southwark St Olave AP, Southwark St Thomas AP.[92] *LG* St Olave PLU, Dist (Metrop Bd Wks), Berm. Metrop Bor. Civ bdry: 1899.[69] Abol 1904 ent to Bermondsey AP.[88]

SOUTHWARK ST SAVIOUR
AP Orig Surrey. *LG* St Saviour's PLU (1889–1901), Swk. PLU (1901–30), St Saviour's Dist (Metrop Bd Wks), Swk. Metrop Bor. Civ bdry: 1899.[69] Abol civ 1930 to help cr Southwark CP.[74] *Parl* As for Newington AP.

SOUTHWARK ST THOMAS
AP Orig Surrey. *LG* St Olave PLU, Dist (Metrop Bd Wks). Abol 1896 to help cr Southwark St Olave and St Thomas CP.[92]

SPITALFIELDS
CP Orig Middx (qv for EP of the same name). *LG* Whitech. PLU, Dist (Metrop Bd Wks), Step. Metrop Bor. Bdry: 1899.[69] Abol 1921 ent to Whitechapel CP.[85] *Parl* As for Limehouse CP.

STAPLE INN
CP Orig Middx. *LG* Holb. PLU, in no Metrop Bd Wks Dist, Holb. Metrop Bor. Abol 1930 to help cr Holborn CP.[79] *Parl* Holb. Parl Bor (1918–48).

STEPNEY
CP Cr 1927 by union Limehouse CP, Mile End Old Town CP, St George in the East CP, Whitechapel CP.[86] *LG* Step. Par (poor), Metrop Bor. Transf 1965 to Gtr London (Tow. Hmlts. LB).[68] *Parl* Step. BC (1948–70).

STOKE NEWINGTON
AP Orig Middx. *LG* Hack. PLU, Dist (Metrop Bd Wks, 1889–94), Stoke Newington Vestry (Metrop Bd Wks, 1894–1900), Metrop Bor. Civ bdry: 1899 (incl gains pt South Hornsey CP, Middx).[69] Transf 1965 to Gtr London (Hack. LB).[68] *Parl* Stoke Newington Parl Bor (1918–48), Stoke Newington & Hack. North BC (1948–70).

STREATHAM
AP Orig Surrey. *LG* Wandsw. & Clap. PLU, Wandsw. Dist (Metrop Bd Wks), Metrop Bor. Civ bdry: 1899.[69] Abol civ 1904 to help cr Wandsworth Borough CP.[76]

TOOTING GRAVENEY
AP Orig Surrey. *LG* Wandsw. & Clap. PLU, Wandsw. Dist (Metrop Bd Wks), Metrop Bor. Civ bdry: 1899.[69] Abol civ 1904 pt to help cr Wandsworth Borough CP,[76] pt to Mitcham AP (Surrey).[101]

TOWER OF LONDON
CP Orig Middx. *LG* Whitech. PLU, Dist (Metrop Bd Wks), Step. Metrop Bor. Abol 1901 ent to St Botolph Without Aldgate CP (London Adm Co).[90]

OLD TOWER WITHOUT
CP Orig Middx. *LG* Whitech. PLU, Dist (Metrop Bd Wks). Abol 1895 ent to St Botolph Without Aldgate CP (London Adm Co).[83]

WANDSWORTH
AP Orig Surrey. *LG* Wandsw. & Clap. PLU, Wandsw. Dist (Metrop Bd Wks), Metrop Bor. Civ bdry: 1899.[69] Abol civ 1904 to help cr Wandsworth Borough CP.[76]

WANDSWORTH BOROUGH
CP Cr 1904 by union Clapham AP, Putney CP, Streatham AP, pt Tooting Graveney AP, Wandsworth AP.[76] *LG* Wandsw. Par (poor), Metrop

Bor. Transf 1965 to Gtr London (pt to Lamb. LB, pt to Wandsw. LB).[68] *Parl* Pt Wandsw., Balham & Tooting Parl Bor (1918–48), pt Wandsw., Central Parl Bor/BC (1918–70), pt Wandsw., Clap. Parl Bor/BC (1918–70), pt Wandsw., Putney Parl Bor/BC (1918–70), pt Wandsw., Streatham Parl Bor/BC (1918–70).

WAPPING

CP Orig Middx (qv for EP of the same name). *LG* Step. PLU, Limeh. Dist (Metrop Bd Wks), Step. Metrop Bor. Abol 1921 ent to Limehouse CP.[85] *Parl* As for Limehouse CP.

CITY OF WESTMINSTER

CP Cr 1922 by union Close of the Collegiate Church of St Peter CP, Liberty of the Rolls CP, Precinct of the Savoy CP, St Anne Within the Liberty of Westminster CP, Westminster St Margaret and St John CP, St Martin in the Fields AP, St Mary le Strand AP, St Paul Covent Garden CP, St Clement Danes AP, St George Hanover Square CP, Westminster St James AP.[77] *LG* City of W'minst. Par (poor), W'minst. Metrop Bor. Transf 1965 to Gtr London (City of W'minst. LB).[68] *Parl* Cities of London & W'minst. BC (1948–70).

WESTMINSTER ST JAMES

CP Orig Middx (qv for EP of the same name; sometimes both civ and eccl 'St James Piccadilly'). *LG* W'minst. PLU (1889–1913), City of W'minst. PLU (1913–22), W'minst. St James Vestry (Metrop Bd Wks), W'minst. Metrop Bor. Abol civ 1922 to help cr City of Westminster CP.[77] *Parl* As for Liberty of the Rolls CP.

WESTMINSTER ST MARGARET AND ST JOHN

CP Orig Middx. *LG* St George's PLU (1889–1913), City of W'minst. PLU (1913–22), W'minst. Dist (Metrop Bd Wks), W'minst. Metrop Bor. Bdry: 1899.[69] Abol 1922 to help cr City of Westminster CP.[77] *Parl* As for Liberty of the Rolls CP.

WHITECHAPEL

CP Orig pt City of London, pt Middx, the former lost 1899 to St Botolph Without Aldgate AP (City of London),[69] and this par ent London Adm Co thereafter; see Middx for EP of the same name. London Adm Co pt: *LG* Whitech. PLU (1889–1921), Par (poor, 1921–25), Step. PLU (1925–27), Whitech. Dist (Metrop Bd Wks), Step. Metrop Bor. Addtl civ bdry alt: 1895 (gains Holy Trinity Minories AP),[83] 1921 (gains Mile End New Town CP, Norton Folgate CP, St Botolph Without Aldgate CP, Spitalfields CP, Old Artillery Ground CP.[85] Abol 1927 to help cr Stepney CP.[86] *Parl* As for Limehouse CP.

WOOLWICH

AP Orig Kent. *LG* Woolw. PLU, Vestry (Metrop Bd Wks), Metrop Bor. Abol 1930 to help cr Borough of Woolwich CP.[78] *Parl* Pt Woolw., East Parl Bor, pt Wool., West Parl Bor (1918–48).

BOROUGH OF WOOLWICH

CP Cr 1930 by union Eltham AP, Plumstead AP, Woolwich AP.[78] *LG* Woolw. Metrop Bor. Transf 1965 to Gtr London (pt to Greenw. LB, pt to Newham LB).[68] *Parl* Pt Woolw. East BC, pt Woolw. West BC (1948–70).

PART III: GREATER LONDON, 1965[68]–*

PLAN FOR FOLLOWING ENTRIES

The county was formed in 1965 from London Adm Co, Croydon CB, East Ham CB, West Ham CB, and from pts of Middx, Surrey, Kent, Essex and Herts. The London Government Act, 1963, specified that the county should be divided into London Boroughs and that no pt should be divided into parishes. Consult the entries in the respective constituent counties for civ organisation before 1965, for parl constituencies before 1970, and for all details of eccl organisation. Every LB was divided into 2 or more BCs from 1970; the constituencies are sep noted. For constituent wards of the BCs, see Part III of the *Guide*.

THE BOROUGHS OF GREATER LONDON

BARKING LB

Cr from Essex Adm Co, pt Barking MB, pt Dagenham MB. 2 BCs: Barking, Barking; Barking, Dagenham.

BARNET LB

Cr from Middx Adm Co, Finchley MB, Friern Barnet UD, Hendon MB, and from Herts Adm Co, Barnet UD, East Barnet UD. 4 BCs: Barnet, Chipping Barnet; Barnet, Finchley; Barnet, Hendon North; Barnet, Hendon South.

BEXLEY LB

Cr from Kent Adm Co, Bexley MB, pt Chislehurst and Sidcup UD, Crayford UD, Erith MB. 3 BCs: Bexley, Bexleyheath; Bexley, Erith and Crayford; Bexley, Sidcup.

BRENT LB

Cr from Middx Adm Co, Wembley MB, Willesden MB. 3 BCs: Brent East, Brent North, Brent South.

BROMLEY LB

Cr from Kent Adm Co, Beckenham MB, Bromley MB, pt Chislehurst and Sidcup UD, Orpington UD, Penge UD. 4 BCs: Bromley, Beckenham; Bromley, Chislehurst; Bromley, Orpington; Bromley, Ravensbourne, with redefinition of constituent wards in 1971.[93]

CAMDEN LB

Cr from London Adm Co, Hampstead Metrop Bor, Holborn Metrop Bor, St Pancras Metrop Bor. 3 BCs: Camden, Hampstead; Camden, Holborn & St Pancras South; Camden, St Pancras North, with redefinition of constituent wards in 1973.[94]

GREWNWICH LB
Cr from London Adm Co, Greenwich Metrop Bor, pt Woolwich Metrop Bor. 3 BCs: Greenwich, Greenwich; Greenwich, Woolwich East; Greenwich, Woolwich West.

HACKNEY LB
Cr from London Adm Co, Hackney Metrop Bor, Shoreditch Metrop Bor, Stoke Newington Metrop Bor. 3 BCs: Hackney Central, Hackney North and Stoke Newington, Hackney South and Shoreditch.

HAMMERSMITH LB
Cr from London Adm Co, Fulham Metrop Bor, Hammersmith Metrop Bor. 2 BCs: Hammersmith, Fulham; Hammersmith, North.

HARINGEY LB
Cr from Middx Adm Co, Hornsey MB, Tottenham MB, Wood Green MB. 3 BCs: Haringey, Hornsey; Haringey, Tottenham; Haringey, Wood Green.

CROYDON LB
Cr from Croydon CB (associated with Surrey) and from Surrey Adm Co, Coulsdon and Purley UD. Bdry alt: 1969 (help cr Chelsham and Farleigh CP, to be in Surrey, Godstone RD).[95] 4 BCs: Croydon Central, Croydon North East, Croydon North West, Croydon South.

EALING LB
Cr from Middx Adm Co, Acton MB, Ealing MB, Southall MB. 3 BCs: Ealing, Acton; Ealing North; Ealing, Southall.

ENFIELD LB
Cr from Middx Adm Co, Edmonton MB, Enfield MB, Southgate MB. 3 BCs: Enfield, Edmonton; Enfield North; Enfield, Southgate.

HARROW LB
Cr from Middx Adm Co, Harrow MB. 3 BCs: Harrow Central, Harrow East, Harrow West.

HAVERING LB
Cr from Essex Adm Co, Hornchurch UD, Romford MB. 3 BCs: Havering, Hornchurch; Havering, Romford; Havering, Upminster.

HILLINGDON LB
Cr from Middx Adm Co, Hayes and Harlington UD, Ruislip-Northwood UD, Uxbridge MB, Yiewsley and West Drayton UD. Bdry alt: 1968 (gains pt Hounslow LB),[96] 1969 (gains pt Hounslow LB).[97] 3 BCs: Hillingdon, Hayes and Harlington; Hillingdon, Ruislip-Northwood; Hillingdon, Uxbridge.

HOUNSLOW LB
Cr from Middx Adm Co, Brentwood and Chiswick MB, Feltham UD, Heston and Isleworth MB. Bdry alt: 1968 (loses pt to Hillingdon LB),[96] 1969 (loses pt to Hillingdon LB).[97] 2 BCs: Hounslow, Brentford and Isleworth; Hounslow, Feltham and Heston.

ISLINGTON LB
Cr from London Adm Co, Finsbury Metrop Bor, Islington Metrop Bor. 3 BCs: Islington Central, Islington North, Islington South and Finsbury.

KENSINGTON AND CHELSEA LB (also, 'ROYAL BOROUGH OF KENSINGTON AND CHELSEA')
Cr from London Adm Co, Chelsea Metrop Bor, Kensington Metrop Bor. 2 BCs: Kensington and Chelsea, Chelsea; Kensington and Chelsea, Kensington.

KINGSTON UPON THAMES LB
Cr from Surrey Adm Co, Kingston upon Thames MB, Malden and Coombe MB, Surbiton MB. 2 BCs: Kingston upon Thames, Kingston; Kingston upon Thames, Surbiton.

LAMBETH LB
Cr from London Adm Co, Lambeth Metrop Bor, pt Wandsworth Metrop Bor. 4 BCs: Lambeth Central; Lambeth, Norwood; Lambeth, Streatham; Lambeth, Vauxhall.

LEWISHAM LB
Cr from London Adm Co, Deptford Metrop Bor, Lewisham Metrop Bor. 3 BCs: Lewisham, Deptford; Lewisham East; Lewisham West.

CITY OF LONDON
Defined to be within Greater London, but independence maintained. It and Inner Temple, Middle Temple form pt of The City of London and Westminster South BC.

MERTON LB
Cr from Surrey Adm Co, Merton and Morden UD, Mitcham MB, Wimbledon MB. 2 BCs: Merton, Mitcham and Morden; Merton, Wimbledon.

NEWHAM LB
Cr from East Ham CB, West Ham CB (both associated with Essex), from Essex Adm Co, pt Barking MB, and from London Adm Co, pt Woolwich Metrop Bor. 3 BCs: Newham North-East, Newham North-West, Newham South.

REDBRIDGE LB
Cr from Essex Adm Co, pt Chigwell UD, pt Dangenham MB, Ilford MB, Wanstead and Woodford MB. 3 BCs: Redbridge, Ilford North; Redbridge, Ilford South; Redbridge, Wanstead and Woodford.

RICHMOND UPON THAMES LB
Cr from Surrey Adm Co, Barnes MB, Richmond MB, and from Middx Adm Co, Twickenham MB. Bdry alt: 1970 (exchanges pts with Esher AP [Esher UD, Surrey]).[98] 2 BCs: Richmond upon Thames, Richmond; Richmond upon Thames, Twickenham, with redefinition of constituent wards in 1971.[99]

SOUTHWARK LB
Cr from London Adm Co, Bermondsey Metrop Bor, Camberwell Metrop Bor, Southwark Metrop Bor. 3 BCs: Southwark, Bermondsey; Southwark, Dulwich; Southwark, Peckham, with redefinition of constituent wards in 1971.[100]

SUTTON LB
Cr from Surrey Adm Co, Beddington and Wallington MB, Carshalton UD, Sutton and Cheam MB. 2 BCs: Sutton: Sutton and Cheam; Sutton, Carshalton.

TOWER HAMLETS LB

Cr from London Adm Co, Bethnal Green Metrop Bor, Poplar Metrop Bor, Stepney Metrop Bor. 2 BCs: Tower Hamlets, Bethnal Green and Bow; Tower Hamlets, Stepney and Poplar.

WALTHAM FOREST LB

Cr from Essex Adm Co, Chingford MB, Leyton MB, Walthamstow MB. 3 BCs: Waltham Forest, Chingford; Waltham Forest, Leyton; Waltham Forest, Walthamstow.

WANDSWORTH LB

Cr from London Adm Co, Battersea Metrop Bor, pt Wandsworth Metrop Bor. 4 BCs: Wandsworth, Battersea North; Wandsworth, Battersea South; Wandsworth, Putney; Wandsworth, Tooting.

CITY OF WESTMINSTER LB

Cr from London Adm Co, Paddington Metrop Bor, St Marylebone Metrop Bor, Westminster Metrop Bor. 3 BCs: City of Westminster, Paddington; City of Westminster, St Marylebone; and forms pt of The City of London and Westminster South (together with City of London and Inner and Middle Temples).

MIDDLESEX

ABBREVIATIONS

Abbreviations particular to Middx follow. Those general abbreviations in use throughout the *Guide* are found on page xix.

Beth. Gr.	Bethnal Green
Brentf.	Brentford
Camd.	Camden
Chisw.	Chiswick
Edm.	Edmonton
Elth.	Elthorne
Enf.	Enfield
Finch.	Finchley
Finsb.	Finsbury
Hack.	Hackney
Hagg.	Haggerston
Hamm.	Hammersmith
Hampst.	Hampstead
Highg.	Highgate
Hilling.	Hillingdon
Holb.	Holborn
Islew.	Isleworth
Isling.	Islington
Kens.	Kensington
Marylb.	Marylebone
Newing.	Newington
Ossul.	Ossulstone
Padd.	Paddington
St Geo. Bloomsb.	St George Bloomsbury
St Geo. Hanov. Sq.	St George Hanover Square
St Mgt.('s)	St Margaret ('s)
St Marylb.	St Marylebone
St Panc.	St Pancras
Shored.	Shoreditch
Spitalf.	Spitalfields
Step.	Stepney
Stk. Newing.	Stoke Newington
Tott.	Tottenham
Tow. Hmlts.	Tower Hamlets
Twick.	Twickenham
Uxbr.	Uxbridge
Whitech.	Whitechapel
W'minst.	Westminster
Will.	Willesden

SEQUENCES

An abbreviated entry prefixed by 'Seq' is used in the parochial entries to avoid repeating often the names of superior units of administration. The content of each sequence is shown below.

Parliamentary Sequences ('Parl')

SEQ 1 Uxbr. Dv (1885–1918), Spelth. Dv (1918–70), Surrey thereafter.

Ecclesiastical Sequences ('Eccl')

SEQ 1 Ealing RDn (1858–1967), Ealing West RDn (1967–*)

SEQ 2 Enf. RDn (1858–*)
SEQ 3 Enf. RDn (1858–1901), Hornsey RDn (1901–67), Central Barnet RDn (1967–*)
SEQ 4 Hampton RDn (1858–*)
SEQ 5 Hampton RDn (1858–1953), Staines RDn (1953–*)
SEQ 6 Harrow RDn (1858–1901), Will. RDn (1901–14), Harrow RDn (1914–*)
SEQ 7 Staines RDn (1858–61), Hampton RDn (1861–1953), Staines RDn (1953–*)
SEQ 8 Staines RDn (1858–61), Uxbr. RDn (1861–1967), Hilling. RDn (1967–*)
SEQ 9 Uxbr. RDn (1858–1967), Hilling. RDn (1967–*)

DIOCESE AND ARCHDEACONRIES

Middx pars are in London dioc. All were in Middx AD before the cr of RDns in 1858 except for a few in London AD (Clerkenwell, Islington, Shoreditch and the EPs cr from those pars, and the chapels royal). The organisation in archdeaconries after 1858 follows.

HACKNEY AD (1951–*)
Beth. Gr. RDn (1951–66), Hack. RDn (1967–*), Hack. & Stk. Newing. RDn (1951–67), Isling. RDn, Poplar RDn (1951–66), Step. RDn (1951–66), Tow. Hmlts. RDn (1966–*)

HAMPSTEAD AD (1912–*)
Central Barnet RDn (1967–*), W Barnet RDn (1967–*), Brent RDn (1967–70), N Camd. (Hampst.) RDn (1967–*), S Camd. (Holb. & St Panc.) RDn (1967–*), Enf. RDn, Hampst. RDn (1912–67), E Haringey RDn (1967–*), W Haringey RDn (1967–*), Harrow RDn (1914–70), Hendon RDn (1934–67), Holb. RDn (1912–14), Hornsey RDn (1912–67), St Marylb. RDn (1912–67), St Panc. RDn (1912–67), Tott. RDn (1912–67), W'minst. (St Marylb.) RDn (1967–70), Will. RDn (1912–67)

LONDON AD
Beth. Gr. RDn (1901–51), The City RDn (1954–*), East City RDn (1869–1954), West City RDn (1869–1954), Enf. RDn (1900–12), Finsb. RDn (1901–34), Finsb. & Holb. RDn (1934–67), Hack. RDn (1861–1901), Hack. & Stk. Newing. RDn (1901–51), Holb. RDn (1901–12), Isling. RDn (1861–1951), Poplar RDn (1901–51), St Sepulchre RDn (1861–1901), Shored. RDn (1870–1967), Spitalf. RDn (1861–1901), Step. RDn (1861–1951), Tott. RDn (1901–12), W'minst. (Padd.) RDn (1970–*), W'minst. (St Marylb.) RDn (1970–*), W'minst. (St Mgt.'s) RDn (1970–*)

MIDDLESEX AD
Barnes & Hamm. RDn (1861–72), Chelsea RDn (1861–*), Ealing RDn (1858–1967), Ealing East RDn (1967–70), Ealing West RDn (1967–70), Enf. RDn (1858–1900), Fulham RDn (1858–1967), Hamm. RDn (1901–*), Hampst. RDn (1901–12), Hampton RDn, Harrow RDn (1858–1901), Highg. RDn (1875–1901), Hilling. RDn (1967–70), Hornsey RDn (1901–12), Hounslow RDn (1967–*), Kens. RDn (1861–*), Padd. RDn (1861–1967), St Geo. Bloomsb. RDn (1861–97), St Geo. Hanov. Sq. RDn (1861–1901), St James W'minst. RDn (1861–97), St John W'minst. RDn (1861–83), St Mgt. W'minst. RDn (1861–83), St Mgt. & St John W'minst. RDn (1883–1901), St Martin in the Fields RDn (1861–1901), St Marylb. RDn (1861–1912), St Panc. RDn (1858–1912), Staines RDn (1858–61), Staines RDn (1953–*), Uxbr. RDn (1858–1967), W'minst. RDn (1901–67), W'minst. (Padd.) RDn (1967–70), W'minst. (St Mgt.'s) RDn (1967–70), Will. RDn (1901–12)

NORTHOLT AD (1970–*)
Brent RDn, Ealing East RDn, Ealing West RDn, Harrow RDn, Hilling. RDn

THE PARISHES OF MIDDLESEX

ACTON
The following have 'Acton' in their names. Insofar as any existed at a given time: *LG* Ossul. Hd, Brentf. PLU, Acton USD, UD (1894–1921), MB (1921–65). Transf 1965 to Gtr London (Ealing LB).[1] *Parl* Ealing Dv (1885–1918), Acton Dv (1918–48), BC (1948–70). Gtr London thereafter. *Eccl* Pec jurisd Bp London (until 1845), Ealing RDn (1858–1934), Hamm. RDn (1934–67), Ealing East RDn (1967–*).

AP1–ACTON–Civ bdry: 1894,[2] 1895,[3] 1934.[4] Parl bdry: 1945.[202] Eccl bdry: 1873 (cr EP3),[5] 1875 (help cr Harlesden All Souls EP),[6] 1880 (cr EP1),[7] 1907 (help cr EP4),[8] 1931 (help cr EP2).[9]

EP1–EAST ACTON–Cr 1880 from AP1.[7] Bdry: 1891 (help cr Hammersmith St Saviour EP),[10] 1915 (cr EP7),[11] 1931 (help cr EP2),[9] 1951.[12]

EP2–NORTH ACTON–Cr 1931 from AP1, EP1.[9] Bdry: 1948 (help cr Ealing The Ascension, Hanger Hill EP),[13] 1951,[12] 1974.[14]

EP3–SOUTH ACTON–Cr 1873 from AP1.[5] Bdry: 1879 (help cr Bedford Park EP),[15] 1889 (help cr EP5),[16] 1906,[17] 1915 (help cr EP6),[18] 1921,[19] 1929 (help cr Gunnersbury EP).[20]

EP4–WEST ACTON–Cr 1907 from AP1, Ealing AP, Ealing Christ Church EP.[8]

EP5–ACTON GREEN ST ALBAN THE MARTYR–Cr 1889 from EP3, Ealing AP.[16] Bdry: 1906,[17] 1915 (help cr EP6),[18] 1921,[19] 1929,[21] 1935.[22]

EP6–ACTON GREEN ST PETER–Cr 1915 from EP3, Bedford Park EP, EP5.[18] Bdry: 1916,[23] 1921.[19]

EP7–ACTON VALE–Cr 1915 from EP1.[11]

AGAR TOWN

EP Cr 1862 from St Pancras AP, Camden Town EP, Kentish Town chap of St Pancras AP, Camden New Town St Paul EP.[24] St Panc. RDn. Abol 1954 pt to help cr Camden Town St Michael with All Saints and St Thomas EP, pt to St Pancras Old Church EP.[25]

ALEXANDRA PARK ST ANDREW

EP Cr 1900 from Wood Green EP, Clerkenwell AP.[27] Enf. RDn (1900–01), Hornsey RDn (1901–67), W Haringey RDn (1967–*).

ALEXANDRA PARK ST SAVIOUR

EP Cr 1904 from Wood Green EP.[28] Tott. RDn (1904–67), W Haringey RDn (1967–*).

ALPERTON

EP Cr 1904 from Wembley EP.[29] Will. RDn (1904–14), Harrow RDn (1914–67), Brent RDn (1967–*).

ASHFORD

Chap in Staines AP, sep civ identity early, some early distinct eccl status,[30] sep EP 1859.[31] *LG* Spelth. Hd, Staines PLU, RSD, RD (1894–1930), UD (1930–65). Civ bdry: 1934.[4] Transf 1965 to Surrey.[1] *Parl* Seq 1. *Eccl* Staines RDn 1858–1880s), Hampton RDn (1880s–1953), Staines RDn (1953–*). Eccl bdry: 1949,[32] 1951 (help cr Staines Christ Church EP),[33] 1973 (incl help cr Ashford St Hilda EP).[34]

ASHFORD ST HILDA

EP Cr 1973 from Ashford AP, Staines AP, Stanwell AP.[34] Staines RDn.

NORTH AUDLEY STREET

EP Cr 1835 from St George Hanover Square EP.[35] St Geo. Hanov. Sq. RDn (1866–1901), W'minst. RDn (1901–67), W'minst. (St Mgt.'s) RDn (1967–*). Bdry: 1938.[36]

BALL'S POND

EP Cr 1830 from Islington AP.[37] Isling. RDn. Bdry: 1849,[38] 1851 (cr Islington St Matthew EP),[29] 1856 (cr Islington St Jude, Mildmay Park EP),[39] 1871 (help cr Highbury New Park EP),[40] 1873 (cr Islington St John the Baptist EP),[41] 1893,[42] 1895,[44] 1953 (incl help cr Islington St Stephen with St Bartholomew and St Matthew EP).[9] This par sometimes called 'Islington St Paul, Ball's Pond'.

FRIERN BARNET

AP Chap of ease to priory of Clerkenwell, sep par 1549.[237] *LG* Ossul. Hd, Barnet PLU, Barnet RSD (1875–83), pt Hornsey USD (1883–91), Friern Barnet USD (pt 1883–91, ent 1891–94), Friern Barnet UD (1894–1965). Civ bdry: 1883,[159] 1934,[4] 1937.[222] Transf 1965 to Gtr London (Barnet LB).[43] *Parl* Enf. Dv (1885–1918), Finch. Dv (1918–48), BC (1948–70), Gtr London thereafter. Parl bdry: 1945.[202] *Eccl* Sometimes as 'Fryern Barnet', pec jurisd Dean & Chapter of St Paul's, London (until 1845), Seq 3 thereafter. Eccl bdry: 1873 (help cr New Southgate EP),[238] 1882 (cr Friern Barnet All Saints EP),[227] 1911 (cr Friern Barnet St Peter le Poer EP),[239] 1972 (gains pt New Southgate St Michael and All Angels EP, dioc St Alb).[240]

FRIERN BARNET ALL SAINTS

EP Cr 1882 from Friern Barnet AP.[227] Enf. RDn (1882–1901), Hornsey RDn (1901–67), Central Barnet RDn (1967–*).

FRIERN BARNET ST PETER LE POER

EP Cr 1911 from Friern Barnet AP.[239] Hornsey RDn (1911–67), W Haringey RDn (1967–*).

BARNSBURY

EP Cr 1862 from Lower Holloway EP.[46] Isling. RDn.

BARNSBURY ST ANDREW WITH ST THOMAS AND ST MATTHIAS

EP Cr 1955 by union Islington St Andrew with St Thomas EP, Islington St Matthias, Caledonian Road EP.[47] Isling. RDn.

BAYSWATER

EP Cr 1858 from Paddington AP.[48] Padd. RDn (1861–1967), W'minst. (Padd.) RDn (1967–*). Bdry: 1861.[49]

BEDFONT

AP Usual eccl spelling; for civ see following entry. *Eccl* Hampton RDn (1858–1953), Staines RDn (1953–67), Hounslow RDn (1967–*). Eccl bdry: 1973.[34]

EAST BEDFONT

AP Usual civ spelling; for eccl see prev entry. *LG* Spelth. Hd, Staines PLU, RSD, RD (1894–1930), Feltham UD (1930–65). Civ bdry: 1934.[4] Transf 1965 to Gtr London (Hounslow LB).[1] *Parl* Uxbr. Dv (1885–1918), Spelth. Dv/CC (1918–70), Gtr London thereafter.

BEDFORD NEW TOWN

EP Cr 1859 from St Pancras AP.[50] St Panc. RDn. Bdry: 1876 (help cr Camden Town St Michael EP),[51] 1877,[17] 1954.[25] Abol 1956 to help cr Old St Pancras with Bedford New Town St Matthew EP.[53]

BEDFORD PARK

EP Cr 1879 from Chiswick AP, South Acton EP, Old Brentford EP.[15] Ealing RDn (1879–1901), Hamm. RDn (1901–67), Hounslow RDn (1967–*). Bdry: 1915 (help cr Acton Green St Peter EP),[18] 1916,[23] 1935.[22]

BELMONT

EP Cr 1940 from Great Stanmore AP, Harrow Weald EP.[54] Harrow RDn.

BELSIZE PARK

EP Cr 1861 from Hampstead AP.[6] Enf. RDn (1861–75), Highg. RDn (1875–1901), Hampst. RDn (1901–67), N Camd. (Hampst.) RDn (1967–*).

BETHNAL GREEN

The following have 'Bethnal Green' in their names. Insofar as any existed at a given time: *LG* Ossul. Hd, Beth. Gr. PLU, Dist (Metrop Bd Wks). Transf 1889 to London.[43] *Parl* Tow. Hmlts. Parl Bor (1832–85), pt Beth. Gr. Parl Bor, N-E Dv, pt Beth. Gr. Parl Bor, S-W Dv (1885–1918), London thereafter. *Eccl* Spitalf. RDn (1861–1901), Beth. Gr. RDn (1901–66), Tow. Hmlts. RDn (1966–*).

CP/EP1–BETHNAL GREEN [ST MATTHEW]–Pt of Stepney AP, sep par 1743.[45] Eccl bdry: 1837 (cr EP8),[55] 1843 (cr EP2, EP7, EP13, EP15),[52] 1844 (cr EP4, EP5, EP10, EP11, EP18),[56] 1865 (help cr EP12),[23] 1951,[58] 1954,[39] 1958.[59]

EP2–BETHNAL GREEN ST ANDREW–Cr 1843 from EP1.[52] Abol 1958 ent to EP1.[59]

EP3–BETHNAL GREEN ST BARNABAS–Cr 1870 from EP7, EP16.[60]

EP4–BETHNAL GREEN ST BARTHOLOMEW–Cr 1844 from EP1.[56] Bdry: 1951.[58]

EP5–BETHNAL GREEN ST JAMES THE GREAT–Cr 1844 from EP1.[56] Abol 1951 to help cr EP6.[58]

EP6–BETHNAL GREEN ST JAMES THE GREAT WITH ST JUDE–Cr 1951 by union EP5, pt EP10.[58]

EP7–BETHNAL GREEN ST JAMES THE LESS–Cr 1843 from EP1.[52] Bdry: 1844 (cr EP16),[56] 1870 (help cr EP3),[60] 1871,[40] 1871 (help cr South Hackney Christ Church EP),[61] 1951.[58]

EP8–BETHNAL GREEN ST JOHN–Cr 1837 from EP1.[55] Bdry: 1871,[40] 1871 (help cr South Hackney EP).[61] Abol 1951 to help cr EP9.[58]

EP9–BETHNAL GREEN ST JOHN WITH ST SIMON–Cr 1951 by union EP8, EP17.[58]

EP10–BETHNAL GREEN ST JUDE–Cr 1844 from EP1.[56] Bdry: 1865 (help cr South Hackney St Michael and All Angels EP, help cr Haggerston St Stephen EP).[62] Abol 1951 pt to help cr EP6, pt to help cr EP14.[58]

EP11–BETHNAL GREEN ST MATTHIAS–Cr 1844 from EP1.[56] Abol 1951 ent to EP1.[58]

EP12–BETHNAL GREEN ST PAUL–Cr 1865 from EP1, EP18.[23] Abol 1951 ent to EP1.[58]

EP13–BETHNAL GREEN ST PETER–Cr 1843 from EP1.[52] Bdry: 1865 (help cr Haggerston St Stephen EP).[62] Abol 1951 to help cr EP14.[58]

EP14–BETHNAL GREEN ST PETER WITH ST THOMAS–Cr 1951 by union EP13, EP18, pt EP10.[58]

EP15–BETHNAL GREEN ST PHILIP–Cr 1843 from EP1.[52] Bdry: 1863,[63] 1931 (help cr Shoreditch Holy Trinity EP).[64] Abol 1951 ent to EP1.[58]

EP16–BETHNAL GREEN ST SIMON ZELOTES–Cr 1844 from EP7.[56] Bdry: 1870 (help cr EP3).[60] Abol 1936 to help cr EP17.[65]

EP17–BETHNAL GREEN ST SIMON ZELOTES WITH ST ANTHONY–Cr 1936 by union EP16, Stepney St Anthony EP.[65] Abol 1951 to help cr EP9.[58]

EP18–BETHNAL GREEN ST THOMAS–Cr 1844 from EP1.[56] Bdry: 1865 (help cr EP12).[23] Abol 1951 to help cr EP14.[58]

BLOOMSBURY ST GEORGE

Usual eccl name for par cr 1731 from St Giles in the Fields AP[66]; for civ see 'St George Bloomsbury'. *Eccl* St Geo. Bloomsb. RDn (1861–97), St Martin in the Fields RDn (1897–1901), Holb. RDn (1901–34), Finsb. & Holb. RDn (1934–52). Eccl bdry: 1867 (help cr Holborn St John the Evangelist EP),[69] 1902 (help cr Woburn Square EP),[68] 1902.[67] Abol eccl 1952 pt to help cr Bloomsbury St George with St John the Evangelist EP, pt to Holborn St George the Martyr EP, pt to St Giles in the Fields AP.[70]

BLOOMSBURY ST GEORGE WITH ST JOHN THE EVANGELIST

EP Cr 1952 by union Holborn St John the Evangelist EP, pt Bloomsbury St George EP, pt St Giles in the Fields AP.[70] Finsb. & Holb. RDn (1952–67), S Camd. (Holb. & St Panc.) RDn (1967–*).

BOUNDS GREEN

EP Cr 1906 from Wood Green EP, Southgate St Michael at Bowes EP, New Southgate EP.[71] Tott. RDn (1906–67), E Haringey RDn (1967–*).

BOW

Usual civ name for par cr 1719 from Stepney AP[72]; for eccl see 'Stratford Bow St Mary'. *LG* Ossul. Hd, Poplar PLU, Dist (Metrop Bd Wks). Transf 1889 to London.[43] *Parl* Tow. Hmlts. Parl Bor (1832–85), Tow. Hmlts. Parl Bor, Bow & Bromley Dv (1885–1918), London thereafter.

BOW ST MARY WITH BROMLEY ST LEONARD

EP Cr 1963 by union Stratford Bow St Mary EP, Bromley St Mary the Virgin with St Andrew EP.[73] Poplar RDn (1963–66), Tow. Hmlts. RDn (1966–*).

BOW COMMON

EP Cr 1951 by union pt Stepney St Paul EP, pt Mile End St Luke, Old Town EP.[74] Stepney RDn.

BRENTFORD

EP Cr 1907 from Old Brentford St Paul EP.[69] Ealing RDn (1907–67), Ealing West RDn (1967–*). Bdry: 1952 (incl help cr Brentford St Lawrence with St Paul EP).[46]

BRENTFORD ST LAWRENCE WITH ST PAUL

EP Cr 1952 by union pt New Brentford EP, pt Old Brentford St Paul EP, pt Brentford EP, pt Isleworth St Francis EP.[46] Ealing RDn. Abol 1961 to help cr Brentford St Paul with St Lawrence and St George EP.[75]

BRENTFORD ST PAUL WITH ST LAWRENCE AND ST GEORGE

EP Cr 1961 by union Brentford St Paul with St Lawrence EP, pt Old Brentford EP.[75] Ealing RDn (1961–67), Hounslow RDn (1967–*).

NEW BRENTFORD

Chap in Hanwell AP (from 12th cent), sep civ

identity early, sep EP 1721.[76] *LG* Elth. Hd, Brentf. PLU, USD, UD (1894–1927), Brentf. & Chisw. UD (1927–32), MB (1932–65). Civ bdry: 1934.[4] Transf 1965 to Gtr London (Hounslow LB).[1] *Parl* Brentf. Dv (1885–1918), Brentf. & Chisw. Dv (1918–48), BC (1948–70), Gtr London thereafter. Parl bdry: 1945.[202] *Eccl* Ealing RDn. Abol eccl 1952 pt to help cr Brentford St Lawrence with St Paul EP, pt to Brentford EP, pt to Hanwell St Thomas EP.[46]

OLD BRENTFORD

Chap in Ealing AP, sep EP 1828,[80] sep CP 1894.[78] *LG* Brentf. PLU, UD (1894–1927), Brentf. & Chisw. UD (1927–32), MB (1932–65). Civ bdry: 1912,[79] 1934.[4] Transf 1965 to Gtr London (Hounslow LB).[1] *Parl* Brentf. & Chisw. Dv (1918–48), BC (1948–70), Gtr London thereafter. Parl bdry: 1945.[202] *Eccl* Ealing RDn. Eccl bdry: 1864 (help cr Old Brentford St Paul EP),[81] 1865,[82] 1879 (help cr Bedford Park EP),[15] 1888 (help cr Gunnersbury EP),[20] 1929.[21] Abol eccl 1961 pt to help cr Brentford St Paul with St Lawrence and St George EP, pt to Brentford EP.[75]

OLD BRENTFORD ST PAUL

EP Cr 1864 from Old Brentford EP, Ealing AP.[81] Ealing RDn. Bdry: 1907 (cr Brentford EP).[69] Abol 1952 pt to help cr Brentford St Lawrence with St Paul EP, pt to Brentford EP.[46]

BROMLEY

The following have 'Bromley' in their names. Insofar as any existed at a given time: *LG* Ossul. Hd, Poplar PLU, Dist (Metrop Bd Wks). Transf 1889 to London.[43] *Parl* Tow. Hmlts. Parl Bor (1832–85), pt Tow. Hmlts. Parl Bor, Bow & Bromley Dv, pt Tow. Hmlts. Parl Bor, Poplar Dv (1885–1918), London thereafter. *Eccl* Stepney RDn (1861–1901), Poplar RDn (1901–66), Tow. Hmlts. RDn (1966–*).

AP1–BROMLEY–Eccl bdry: 1858 (help cr Stepney St Paul EP),[83] 1864 (cr EP5),[84] 1875 (cr EP1),[39] 1900 (cr EP3),[27] 1952 (incl help cr EP4).[70]

EP1–BROMLEY ALL HALLOWS–Cr 1875 from AP1.[39] Bdry: 1952.[70]

EP2–BROMLEY ST GABRIEL–Cr 1869 from EP5.[85] Abol 1952 to help cr Poplar St Saviour with St Gabriel and St Stephen EP.[70]

EP3–BROMLEY ST LEONARD, ST ANDREW–Cr 1900 from AP1.[27] Abol 1952 pt to help cr EP4, pt to EP5.[70]

EP4–BROMLEY ST MARY THE VIRGIN WITH ST ANDREW–Cr 1952 by union pt AP1, pt EP3, pt Stratford Bow St Mary EP.[70] Abol 1963 to help cr Bow St Mary with Bromley St Leonard EP.[73]

EP5–BROMLEY ST MICHAEL AND ALL ANGELS–Cr 1864 from AP1.[84] Bdry: 1869 (cr EP2),[85] 1879 (cr East India Docks EP),[86] 1914 (help cr Poplar St Frideswide EP),[87] 1952 (incl help cr Poplar All Saints with St Frideswide EP).[70] Abol 1971 to help cr Poplar EP.[18]

BROMPTON

EP Cr 1830 from Kensington AP.[77] Kens. RDn. Bdry: 1850 (cr West Brompton EP),[77] 1861 (cr Onslow Square EP),[88] 1953,[89] 1954.[90]

WEST BROMPTON

EP Cr 1850 from Brompton EP.[77] Kens. RDn (1861–1967), Chelsea RDn (1967–73). Bdry: 1867 (cr South Kensington St Peter EP),[36] 1869 (help cr Kensington St Augustine EP),[91] 1872 (help cr South Kensington St Jude EP),[92] 1874 (help cr South Kensington St Luke EP).[93] Abol 1973 to help cr West Brompton St Mary with St Peter EP.[94]

WEST BROMPTON ST MARY WITH ST PETER

EP Cr 1973 by union West Brompton EP, South Kensington St Peter EP.[94] Chelsea RDn.

BRONDESBURY CHRIST CHURCH

EP Cr 1867 from Willesden AP.[95] Harrow RDn (1867–1901), Will. RDn (1901–67), Brent RDn (1967–7). Bdry: 1898 (help cr Willesden Green EP),[50] 1905 (help cr Brondesbury St Anne EP),[96] 1908 (help cr Brondesbury St Laurence EP).[97] Abol 1971 to help cr Brondesbury Christ Church with St Laurence EP.[98]

BRONDESBURY CHRIST CHURCH WITH ST LAURENCE

EP Cr 1971 by union Brondesbury Christ Church EP, Brondesbury St Laurence EP.[98] Brent RDn.

BRONDESBURY ST ANNE

EP Cr 1905 from Brondesbury Christ Church EP, Kensal Green St John EP, Kilburn Holy Trinity EP.[96] Will. RDn. Abol 1955 to help cr Brondesbury St Anne with Kilburn Holy Trinity EP.[99]

BRONDESBURY ST ANNE WITH KILBURN HOLY TRINITY

EP Cr 1955 by union Brondesbury St Anne EP, Kilburn Holy Trinity EP.[99] Will. RDn (1955–67), Brent RDn (1967–*). Bdry: 1972 (incl help cr Kilburn St Augustine with St John EP).[100]

BRONDESBURY ST LAURENCE

EP Cr 1908 from Brondesbury Christ Church EP, Kensal Green St John EP.[97] Will. RDn (1908–67), Brent RDn (1967–71). Abol 1971 to help cr Brondesbury Christ Church with St Laurence EP.[98]

BROOKFIELD

EP Cr 1877 from Highgate Rise EP (commonly known as 'Brookfield St Anne'), Upper Holloway St John EP.[101] St. Panc. RDn (1877–1967), S Camd. (Holb. & St. Panc.) RDn (1967–*).

BROOKFIELD ST ANNE–See HIGHGATE RISE

BROWNSWOOD PARK

EP Cr 1875 from Hornsey AP.[102] Highg. RDn (1875–1901), Hack. & Stk. Newing. RDn (1901–67), Hack. RDn (1967–*). Bdry: 1881 (help cr Stroud Green EP),[99] 1916.[103]

BUCKINGHAM PALACE ROAD

EP Cr 1891 from Chester Square EP.[104] St Geo. Han. Sq. RDn (1891–1901), W'minst. RDn

(1901–53). Abol 1953 pt to help cr Chester Square St Michael with St Philip EP, pt to Pimlico St Gabriel EP.[89]

BURLEIGH STREET
EP Cr 1848 from St Martin in the Fields AP.[105] St Martin in the Fields RDn (1861–1901), W'minst. RDn (1901–05). Abol 1905 ent to Covent Garden St Paul EP.[460]

BUSH HILL PARK ST MARK
EP Cr 1903 from Enfield AP, Edmonton AP.[106] Enf. RDn.

BUSH HILL PARK ST STEPHEN
EP Cr 1909 from Edmonton AP.[107] Enf. RDn. Bdry: 1941.[108]

CAMDEN SQUARE
EP Cr 1852 from St Pancras AP.[109] St Panc. RDn. Bdry: 1862 (help cr Agar Town EP),[24] 1869 (help cr New Kentish Town EP).[114] Usually called 'Camden New Town St Paul'. Abol 1956 to help cr Camden Square St Luke Oseney Crescent with St Paul EP.[110]

CAMDEN SQUARE ST LUKE OSENEY CRESCENT WITH ST PAUL
EP Cr 1956 by union New Kentish Town EP, Camden Square EP (usually called 'Camden New Town St Paul').[110] St Panc. RDn (1956–67), S Camd. (Holb. & St Panc.) RDn (1967–*).

CAMDEN TOWN
EP Cr 1852 from St Pancras AP.[109] St Panc. RDn (1858–1954). Bdry: 1862 (help cr Agar Town EP),[24] 1863,[111] 1876 (help cr Camden Town St Michael EP),[51] 1877.[17] Abol 1954 pt to help cr Camden Town St Michael with All Saints EP, pt to St Pancras Old Church EP, pt to Bedford New Town St Matthew EP.[25]

CAMDEN TOWN ST MICHAEL
EP Cr 1876 from Camden Town EP, Haverstock Hill EP, Bedford New Town EP.[51] St Panc. RDn. Bdry: 1904.[112] Abol 1954 to help cr Camden Town St Michael with All Saints and St Thomas EP.[25]

CAMDEN TOWN ST MICHAEL WITH ALL SAINTS AND ST THOMAS
EP Cr 1954 by union Camden Town St Michael EP, pt Camden Town EP, pt Agar Town EP.[25] St Panc. RDn (1954–67), S Camd. (Holb. & St Panc.) RDn (1967–*).

CAMDEN NEW TOWN ST PAUL–See CAMDEN SQUARE

CAMPDEN HILL
EP Cr 1865 from Notting Hill St John EP, Kensington AP.[115] Kens. RDn. Abol 1954 to help cr Kensington St Mary Abbots with St George EP.[90]

CANONBURY
EP Cr 1971 by union Islington St Stephen with St Bartholomew and St Matthew EP, pt Islington St John the Baptist EP.[116] Isling. RDn.

UPPER CHARLOTTE STREET
EP Cr 1852 from St Pancras AP.[109] St Panc. RDn (1858–68). Renamed 1868 'Fitzroy Squre St John'.[117]

CHARTERHOUSE
Ex-par place, sep CP 1858,[118] eccl 1843 help cr Chartherhouse St Thomas EP.[25] *LG* Ossul. Hd, Holb. PLU (1877[119]–89). Transf 1889 to London.[43] *Parl* Finsb. Parl Bor (1832–85), Finsb. Parl Bor, East Dv (1885–1918), London thereafter.

CHARTERHOUSE ST MARY
EP Cr 1862 from Old Street St Luke EP, Charterhouse St Thomas EP.[120] St Sepulchre RDn (1862–1901), Finsb. RDn (1901–06). Abol 1906 to help cr Charterhouse St Mary with Charterhouse St Thomas EP.[122]

CHARTERHOUSE ST MARY WITH CHARTERHOUSE ST THOMAS
EP Cr 1906 by union Charterhouse St Mary EP, Charterhouse St Thomas EP.[122] Finsb. RDn. Abol 1932 to help cr Charterhouse St Mary with Finsbury St Paul EP.[121]

CHARTERHOUSE ST MARY WITH FINSBURY ST PAUL
EP Cr 1932 by union Finsbury St Paul EP, Charterhouse St Mary with Charterhouse St Thomas EP.[121] Finsb. RDn. Abol 1952 to help cr Old Street St Luke with Charterhouse St Mary and Clerkenwell St Paul EP.[123]

CHARTERHOUSE ST THOMAS
EP Cr 1843 from pt ex-par Charterhouse, Old Street St Luke EP.[25] St Sepulchre RDn (1861–1901), Finsb. RDn (1901–06). Bdry: 1862 (help cr Charterhouse St Mary EP).[120] Abol 1906 to help cr Charterhouse St Mary with Charterhouse St Thomas EP.[122]

CHELSEA
The following have 'Chelsea' in their names. Insofar as any existed at a given time: *LG* Ossul. Hd, Chelsea Par (poor purposes), Vestry (Metrop Bd Wks). Transf 1889 to London.[43] *Parl* Chelsea Parl Bor (1867–1918), London thereafter. *Eccl* Fulham RDn (1858–61), Chelsea RDn (1861–*).

AP1–CHELSEA [ST LUKE]–Eccl bdry: 1831 (cr EP6),[124] 1845 (help cr Kensal Green St John EP),[125] 1877 (cr EP4),[126] 1914 (help cr EP3),[129] 1951,[12] 1951 (help cr EP1).[127]

EP1–CHELSEA ALL SAINTS (CHELSEA OLD CHURCH)–Cr 1951 from AP1, EP3, EP2.[127]

EP2–CHELSEA CHRIST CHURCH–Cr 1859 from Highgate EP, Kentish Town chap of St Pancras AP.[128] Bdry: 1951,[12] 1951 (help cr EP1).[127]

EP3–CHELSEA ST ANDREW–Cr 1914 from AP1, EP4.[129] Bdry: 1951,[12] 1951 (help cr EP1).[127] Abol 1973 to help cr EP5.[130]

EP4–CHELSEA ST JOHN–Cr 1877 from AP1.[126] Bdry: 1914 (help cr EP3).[129] Abol 1973 to help cr EP5.[130]

EP5–CHELSEA ST JOHN WITH ST ANDREW–Cr 1973 by union EP4, EP3.[130]

EP6–UPPER CHELSEA–Cr 1831 from AP1.[124] Bdry: 1842 (cr EP8),[49] 1844 (cr EP7),[131] 1860 (help cr EP9),[132] 1951,[12] 1953.[89]

EP7–UPPER CHELSEA ST JUDE–Cr 1844 from

EP6.[131]

EP8–UPPER CHELSEA ST SAVIOUR–Cr 1842 from EP6.[49] Bdry: 1860 (help cr EP9).[132]

EP9–UPPER CHELSEA ST SIMON–Cr 1860 from EP6, EP8.[132]

CHESTER SQUARE

EP Cr 1846 from Pimlico St Peter EP.[133] St Geo. Han. Sq. RDn (1861–1901), W'minst. RDn (1901–53). Bdry: 1891 (cr Buckingham Palace Road EP).[104] Abol 1953 to help cr Chester Square St Michael with St Philip EP.[89]

CHESTER SQUARE ST MICHAEL WITH ST PHILIP

EP Cr 1953 by union Chester Square EP, pt Buckingham Palace Road EP, pt Pimlico St Peter EP.[89] W'minst. RDn (1953–67), W'minst. (St Mgt.'s) RDn (1967–*).

CHISWICK

The following have 'Chiswick' in their names. Insofar as any existed at a given time: *LG* Ossul. Hd, Brentf. PLU, Chisw. USD, UD (1894–1927), Brentf. & Chisw. UD (1927–32), MB (1932–65).Transf 1965 to Gtr London (Hounslow LB).[1] *Parl* Ealing Dv (1885–1918), Brentf. & Chisw. Dv (1918–48), BC (1948–70), Gtr London thereafter. *Eccl* Pec jurisd Dean & Chapter of St Paul's, London (until 1845), Ealing RDn (1858–1901), Hamm. RDn (1901–67), Hounslow RDn (1967–*).

AP1–CHISWICK [ST NICHOLAS]–Civ bdry: 1878,[134] 1912,[79] 1934.[4] Parl bdry: 1945.[202] Eccl bdry: 1845 (cr Turnham Green EP),[135] 1872 (help cr EP4),[136] 1879 (help cr Bedford Park EP),[15] 1894 (cr EP1),[137] 1906 (help cr EP2).[138] Abol eccl 1954 to help cr EP3.[139]

EP1–CHISWICK ST MARY MAGDALENE–Cr 1894 from AP1.[137] Abol 1954 to help cr EP3.[139]

EP2–CHISWICK ST MICHAEL–Cr 1906 from Turnham Green EP, AP1.[138] Bdry: 1907.[73]

EP3–CHISWICK ST NICHOLAS WITH ST MARY MAGDALENE–Cr 1954 by union AP1, EP1.[139]

EP4–CHISWICK ST PAUL, GROVE PARK–Cr 1872 from AP1, Turnham Green EP.[136]

CHITTS HILL

EP Cr 1907 from Tottenham AP, Wood Green EP.[140] Bdry: 1953,[141] 1973.[54]

CITY ROAD ST CLEMENT

EP Cr 1874 from Old Street St Luke EP, King Square EP, Old Street St Mark EP, Hoxton St John the Baptist EP.[93] St Sepulchre RDn (1874–1901), Finsb. RDn (1901–34), Finsb. & Holb. RDn (1934–52). Bdry: 1883.[142] Abol 1952 pt to help cr Old Street St Luke with Charterhouse St Mary and Clerkwenwell St Paul EP, pt to help cr Finsbury St Clement with St Barnabas and St Matthew EP.[123]

CITY ROAD ST MATTHEW

EP Cr 1848 from King Square EP.[143] St Sepulchre RDn (1861–1901), thereafter as for City Road St Clement. Abol 1952 pt to help cr Finsbury St Clement with St Barnabas and St Matthew EP, pt to Islington St Peter EP, pt to Clerkenwell St Mark EP.[123]

CLAPTON

The following have 'Clapton' in their names. Insofar as any existed at a given time: *Eccl* Hack. RDn (1861–1901), Hack. & Stk. Newing. RDn (1901–67), Hack. RDn (1967–*).

EP1–CLAPTON CHRIST CHURCH–Cr 1871 from West Hackney EP, EP2.[144] Abol 1953 pt to help cr EP3, pt to Stoke Newington Common EP.[93]

EP2–CLAPTON ST JAMES–Cr 1855, refounded 1863 from Hackney AP.[63] Bdry: 1866 (help cr EP4),[145] 1871 (help cr EP1),[144] 1880.[92] Abol 1953 pt to help cr EP3, pt to Stoke Newington Common EP.[93]

EP3–CLAPTON ST JAMES WITH CHRIST CHURCH–Cr 1953 by union EP2, pt EP1, pt Hackney AP.[93] Bdry: 1972 (help cr Hackney EP).[146]

EP4–UPPER CLACTON–Cr 1866 from Stamford Hill St Thomas EP, EP2.[145]

EP5–CLAPTON PARK ALL SAINTS–Cr 1873 from Hackney AP.[147] Bdry: 1885 (help cr EP6),[148] 1953,[93] 1972 (help cr Hackney EP).[146]

EP6–CLAPTON PARK ALL SOULS–Cr 1885 from EP5, Homerton EP.[148]

CLAY HILL

EP Cr 1867 from Enfield AP, Enfield Jesus Chapel EP.[14] Enf. RDn. Bdry: 1900 (cr Enfield St Luke EP).[149]

CLERKENWELL

The following have 'Clerkenwell' in their names. Insofar as any existed at a given time: *LG* Ossul. Hd, Holb. PLU, Clerkenwell Vestry (Metrop Bd Wks). Transf 1889 to London.[43] *Parl* Finsb. Parl Bor (1832–85), Finsb. Parl Bor, Central Dv (1885–1918), London thereafter. *Eccl* St Sepulchre RDn (1861–1901), Finsb. RDn (1901–34), Finsb. & Holb. RDn (1934–67), Isling. RDn (1967–*).

AP1–CLERKENWELL [ST JAMES] –Incl Clerkenwell St John [EP5] (former priory church, sep EP 1723[150]). Addtl eccl bdry alt: 1829 (cr EP6),[151] 1862 (cr Pentonville EP),[396] 1865 (help cr EP7),[106] 1871 (cr EP8),[152] 1900 (help cr Alexandra Park St Andrew EP[27]

EP1–CLERKENWELL THE HOLY REDEEMER–Cr 1882 from EP7.[111] Bdry: 1886.[152] Abol 1936 to help cr EP2.[153]

EP2–CLERKENWELL THE HOLY REDEEMER WITH ST PHILIP–Cr 1936 by union EP1, EP9.[153]

EP3–CLERKENWELL ST JAMES AND ST JOHN–Cr 1931 by union AP1, EP5.[154] Bdry: 1952.[123] Abol 1955 to help cr EP4.[80]

EP4–CLERKENWELL ST JAMES AND ST JOHN WITH ST PETER–Cr 1955 by union EP3, EP8.[80] Bdry: 1973.[58]

EP5–CLERKENWELL ST JOHN–Priory church,

sep EP 1723 from area of AP1.[150] Bdry: 1865 (help cr EP7).[100] Abol 1931 to help cr EP3.[154]

EP6–CLERKENWELL ST MARK–Cr 1829 from AP1.[151] Bdry: 1840 (cr EP9),[155] 1952.[123]

EP7–CLERKENWELL ST PAUL–Cr 1865 from Old Street St Luke EP, King Square EP, AP1, EP5.[100] Abol 1952 to help cr Old Street St Luke with Charterhouse St Mary and Clerkenwell St Paul EP.[123]

EP8–CLERKENWELL ST PETER–Cr 1871 from AP1.[61] Bdry: 1952.[123] Abol 1955 to help cr EP4.[80]

EP9–CLERKENWELL ST PHILIP–Cr 1840 from EP6.[155] Bdry: 1847,[156] 1882 (cr EP1).[111] Abol eccl 1936 to help cr EP2.[153]

CLOSE OF THE COLLEGIATE CHURCH OF ST PETER

Ex-par place, sep CP 1858.[118] *LG* City W'minst., St Geo. Hanov. Sq. PLU (1870–89). Transf 1889 to London.[43] *Parl* W'minst. Parl Bor (1867–1918), London thereafter.

COLINDALE

EP Cr 1951 from Hendon St Alphage EP, West Hendon EP.[157] Hendon RDn (1951–67), W Barnet RDn (1967–*).

COLNBROOK

EP Cr 1853 from Stanwell AP, Langley Marish chap of Wyrardisbury AP (Bucks), Horton AP (Bucks).[84] See entry in Bucks for RDns (Oxford dioc). Bdry: 1873.[147]

COVENT GARDEN ST PAUL

Usual eccl spelling for par cr 1645 from St Martin in the Fields AP[200]; for civ see 'St Paul Covent Garden'. *Eccl* St Martin in the Fields RDn (1861–1901), W'minst. RDn (1901–67), W'minst. (St Mgt.'s) RDn (1967–*). Bdry: 1905 (gains Burleigh Street EP),[460] 1953 (incl help cr St Mary le Strand with St Clement Danes EP).[89]

COWLEY

AP *LG* Elth. Hd, Uxbr. PLU, RSD, RD (1894–1929), UD (1929–38). Civ bdry: in pt intermixed with Hillingdon AP,[158] 1883,[159] 1896,[160] 1929.[161] Abol civ 1938 ent to Uxbridge CP.[162] *Parl* Uxbr. Dv (1885–1948). Parl bdry: 1945.[202] *Eccl* Seq 9. Eccl bdry: 1865 (help cr Hillingdon St Andrew EP),[163] 1884,[164] 1934 (help cr Hillingdon All Saints EP).[165]

CRANFORD

AP *LG* Elth. Hd, Staines PLU, RSD, RD (1894–1930), Hayes & Hilling. UD (1930–34). Abol civ 1934 pt to East Bedfont AP, pt to Harlington AP, pt to Heston and Isleworth CP.[4] *Parl* Uxbr. Dv (1885–1918), Spelth. Dv (1918–48). *Eccl* Hampton RDn (1861–1934), Uxbr. RDn (1934–67), Hounslow RDn (1967–*). Eccl bdry: 1965.[95]

CRICKLEWOOD ST MICHAEL

EP Cr 1910 from Willesden Green EP.[166] Will. RDn (1910–67), Brent RDn (1967–*).

CRICKLEWOOD ST PETER

EP Cr 1892 from Hendon All Saints, Child's Hill EP.[29] Harrow RDn (1892–1901), Hampst. RDn (1901–34), Hendon RDn (1934–67), W Barnet RDn (1967–*). Bdry: 1933,[167] 1956.[145]

CUBITT TOWN

EP Cr 1873 from Poplar Christ Church EP.[168] Step. RDn (1873–1901), Poplar RDn (1901–52). Abol 1952 to help cr Isle of Dogs Christ with St John and St Luke EP.[70]

CURTAIN ROAD

EP Cr 1841 from Shoreditch AP.[169] Sometimes 'Shoreditch St James, Curtain Road'. St Sepulchre RDn (1861–70), Shoreditch RDn (1870–1935). Bdry: 1872 (cr Shoreditch St Agatha EP),[6] 1915 (gains ent Shoreditch St Agatha EP),[170] 1930 (loses the area of former Shoreditch St Agatha to Shoreditch St Michael EP).[144] Abol 1935 ent to Shoreditch St Michael EP.[38]

DALSTON

The following have 'Dalston' in their names. Insofar as any existed at a given time: *Eccl* Hack. RDn (1861–1901), Hack. & Stk. Newing. RDn (1901–67), Hack. RDn (1967–*).

EP1–DALSTON [ST PHILIP]–Cr 1844, refounded 1848 from Hackney AP.[171] Bdry: 1872,[172] 1879 (help cr EP2),[15] 1880,[92] 1897 (help cr EP4).[173] Abol 1953 pt to help cr EP3, pt to Hackney AP.[93]

EP2–DALSTON HOLY TRINITY–Cr 1879 from EP1, EP5.[15] Abol 1953 to help cr EP3.[93]

EP3–DALSTON HOLY TRINITY WITH ST PHILIP–Cr 1953 by union EP2, pt EP1.[93]

EP4–DALSTON ST BARTHOLOMEW–Cr 1897 from EP5, EP1.[173] Abol 1953 to help cr EP6.[93]

EP5–DALSTON ST MARK–Cr 1871 from West Hackney EP, Hackney AP, Stoke Newington St Matthias EP.[125] Bdry: 1879 (help cr EP2),[15] 1880,[92] 1897 (help cr EP4),[173] 1929 (help cr Shacklewell EP).[201] Abol 1953 to help cr EP6.[93]

EP6–DALSTON ST MARK WITH ST BARTHOLOMEW–Cr 1953 by union EP5, EP4.[93]

DAVIES STREET ST ANSELM–See HANOVER CHAPEL

DAWLEY

EP Cr 1935 from Hillingdon AP, Hayes AP.[174] Uxbr. RDn (1935–67), Hilling. RDn (1967–*).

DeBEAUVOIR TOWN

EP Cr 1842 from West Hackney EP.[138] Hack. RDn (1861–1901), Hack. & Stk. Newing. RDn (1901–67), Hack. RDn (1967–*). Bdry: 1971.[116]

DOLLIS HILL

EP Cr 1939 from Neasden cum Kingsbury EP.[175] Will. RDn (1939–67), Brent RDn (1967–*).

WEST DRAYTON

AP *LG* Elth. Hd, Uxbr. PLU, RSD, RD (1894–1929), Yiewsley & W Drayton UD (1929–49). Abol civ 1949 to help cr Yiewsley and West Drayton CP.[176] *Parl* Uxbr. Dv/CC (1885–1970). *Eccl* Pec jurisd Dean & Chapter of St Paul's, London (beginning 15th cent–1550,

1678–1845[177]), Seq 8 thereafter.

DRURY LANE

EP Cr 1855 from St Martin in the Fields AP.[20] St Martin in the Fields RDn (1861–1901), W'minst. RDn (1901–38). Abol 1938 to help cr Kingsway Holy Trinity with Drury Lane St John EP.[99]

DUCHY OF LANCASTER

Lbty, sep CP 1866.[203] *LG* Ossul. Hd. Although sep identity gained, not sustained and incl soon afterwards in St Mary le Strand AP, in which transf 1899 to London.[43] *Parl* W'minst. Parl Bor (1832–1918).

EALING

The following have 'Ealing' in their names. Insofar as any existed at a given time: *LG* Ossul. Hd, Brentf. PLU, Ealing USD (ent 1875–85, pt 1885–94), pt Brentf. USD (1885–94), Ealing UD (1894–1901), MB (1901–65). Transf 1965 to Gtr London (Ealing LB).[1] *Parl* Pt Ealing Dv, pt Brentf. Dv (1885–1918), Ealing Parl Bor (1918–45), pt Ealing East Parl Bor, pt Ealing West Parl Bor (1945–48), pt Southall BC (1945–70), pt Ealing North BC, pt Ealing South BC (1948–70). *Eccl* Pec jurisd Bp London (until 1845), Ealing RDn (1858–1967), Ealing East RDn (1967–*).

AP1–EALING [ST MARY]–Incl chap Old Brentford (sep EP 1828,[80] sep CP 1894 [the pt in Brentf. USD][78]). Addtl civ bdry alt: 1878,[134] 1894,[2] 1926 (gains ent Greenford AP, Perivale AP, Hanwell AP, West Twyford CP),[178] 1928,[180] 1934 (incl help cr Harrow CP),[4] 1937.[179] Parl bdry: 1945.[202] Addtl eccl bdry alt: 1852 (cr EP3),[107] 1864 (help cr Old Brentford St Paul EP),[81] 1865,[82] 1876 (help cr EP12),[71] 1885 (help cr EP11),[148] 1885,[181] 1889 (help cr Acton Green St Alban the Martyr EP),[16] 1907 (help cr West Acton EP),[8] 1916 (help cr EP9),[18] 1929,[21] 1953 (cr EP1).[183]

EP1–EALING ALL SAINTS–Cr 1953 from AP1.[183]

EP2–EALING THE ASCENSION, HANGER HILL–Cr 1948 from EP3, North Acton EP.[13]

EP3–EALING CHRIST CHURCH–Cr 1852 from AP1.[107] Bdry: 1885,[181] 1885 (help cr EP11),[148] 1876 (cr EP12, EP 10),[71] 1894 (cr EP8),[185] 1907 (help cr West Acton EP),[8] 1916 (help cr EP9),[182] 1948 (help cr EP2).[13] Abol 1951 to help cr EP4.[184]

EP4–EALING CHRIST THE SAVIOUR–Cr 1951 by union EP3, EP9.[184]

EP5–EALING ST BARNABAS–Cr 1917 from EP10, EP8.[186]

EP6–EALING ST JAMES–Cr 1905 from EP12, Hanwell AP.[187]

EP7–EALING ST PAUL–Cr 1908 from EP12.[188]

EP8–EALING ST PETER, MOUNT PARK–Cr 1894 from EP3.[185] Bdry: 1917 (help cr EP5).[186]

EP9–EALING ST SAVIOUR–Cr 1916 from EP3, AP1.[182] Abol 1951 to help cr EP4.[184]

EP10–EALING ST STEPHEN, CASTLE HILL–Cr 1876 from EP3.[71] Bdry: 1917 (help cr EP5).[186]

EP11–EALING COMMON–Cr 1885 from EP3, AP1.[148]

EP12–EALING DEAN–Cr 1876 from AP1, EP3.[71] Bdry: 1885,[181] 1905 (help cr EP6),[187] 1908 (cr EP7).[188]

EARL'S COURT ST CUTHBERT WITH ST MATTHIAS

EP Cr 1954 by union Kensington St Cuthbert, Earl's Court EP, Kensington St Matthias, Earl's Court EP.[90] Kens. RDn.

EAST INDIA DOCKS

EP Cr 1879 from Bromley St Michael and All Angels EP.[86] Step. RDn (1879–1901), Poplar RDn (1901–52). Bdry: 1908.[23] Abol 1952 pt to help cr Poplar All Saints with St Frideswide EP, pt to Bromley St Michael and All Angels EP.[70]

EASTCOTE

EP Cr 1931 from Ruislip AP.[142] Uxbr. RDn (1931–67), Hilling. RDn (1967–*). Bdry: 1952 (help cr Northwood Hills EP).[189]

EDGWARE

Sometimes described as chap to Kingsbury AP, described as Donative from 1685, sep status sustained.[190] *LG* Gore Hd, Hendon PLU, RSD, RD. Abol civ 1931 ent to Hendon AP.[191] *Parl* Harrow Dv (1885–1918), Hendon Dv (1918–45). *Eccl* Harrow RDn (1858–1901), Will. RDn (1901–14), Harrow RDn (1914–31), Hendon RDn (1934–67), W Barnet RDn (1967–*).

EDMONTON

The following have 'Edmonton' in their names. Insofar as any existed at a given time: *LG* Edm. Hd, PLU, USD (ent 1875–81, pt 1881–94), pt Southgate USD (1881–94), pt Enf. USD (1883–94), Edm. UD (1894–1937), MB (1937–65). Transf 1965 to Gtr London (Enf. LB).[1] *Parl* Enf. Dv (1885–1918), Edm. Parl Bor/BC (1918–70), Gtr London thereafter. *Eccl* Seq 2.

AP1–EDMONTON [ALL SAINTS]–Civ bdry: 1779,[193] 1860,[193] 1883,[159] 1892,[193] 1894 (loses the pt in Southgate UD to cr Southgate CP),[78] 1894 (gains the pt of Tottenham AP in Southgate USD),[192] 1894 (presumably loses the pt in Enf. USD to Enfield AP),[219] 1927.[194] Eccl bdry: 1851 (cr Southgate EP, EP8, Winchmore Hill EP),[195] 1883 (cr EP4),[69] 1898 (cr EP7),[50] 1901 (cr EP6),[196] 1903 (help cr EP6),[196] 1903 (help cr Bush Hill Park St Mark EP, cr EP1),[106] 1909 (cr Bush Hill Park St Stephen EP),[107] 1911 (help cr EP3),[197] 1929,[173] 1941,[108] 1954 (cr EP2),[198] 1961.[138]

EP1–EDMONTON ST ALDHELM–Cr 1903 from AP1.[106] Bdry: 1929,[173] 1939 (help cr Tottenham St John the Baptist EP),[175] 1961.[199]

EP2–EDMONTON ST ALPHEGE–Cr 1954 from AP1.[198]

EP3–EDMONTON ST MARTIN–Cr 1911 from

AP1, EP4.[197]

EP4–EDMONTON ST MARY–Cr 1883 from AP1.[69] Bdry: 1911 (help cr EP3).[197] Abol 1954 to help cr EP5.[204]

EP5–EDMONTON ST MARY WITH ST JOHN–Cr 1955 by union EP9, EP4.[204]

EP6–EDMONTON ST MICHAEL–Cr 1901from AP1.[196]

EP7–LOWER EDMONTON–Cr 1898 from AP1.[50]

EP8–UPPER EDMONTON–Cr 1851 from AP1.[195] Bdry: 1906 (cr EP9).[205]

EP9–UPPER EDMONTON ST JOHN–Cr 1906 from EP8.[205] Abol 1954 to help cr EP5.[204]

ENDELL STREET

EP Cr 1845 from St Giles in the Fields AP.[206] St Geo. Bloomsb. RDn (1861–97), St Martin in the Fields RDn (1897–1901), Holb. RDn (1901–29). Abol 1929 ent to St Giles in the Fields AP.[207]

ENFIELD

The following have 'Enfield' in their names. Insofar as any existed at a given time: *LG* Edm. Hd, PLU, USD (ent 1875–83, pt 1883–94), pt E Barnet Valley USD (1888–94), Enf. UD (1894–1955), MB (1955–65). Transf 1965 to Gtr London (Enf. LB).[1] *Parl* Enf. Dv (1885–1948), pt Enf. East BC, pt Enf. West BC (1948–70), Gtr London thereafter. *Eccl* Seq 2.

AP1–ENFIELD [ST ANDREW]–Incl curacy Monken Hadley (sep civ identity early, eccl described as Donative but exemption ended 18th cent,[208] eccl status sustained). Addtl civ bdry alt: 1779,[211] 1860,[211] 1883,[159] 1894 (loses the pt in E Barnet Valley USD to Monken Hadley AP, Herts),[210] 1894 (presumably gains the pt of Edmonton AP in Enf. USD),[219] 1924,[209] 1927,[194] 1934.[4] Addtl eccl bdry alt: 1832 (cr EP4),[212] 1839 (cr EP1),[215] 1845 (cr EP2),[105] 1867 (help cr Clay Hill EP),[14] 1884 (cr EP8),[213] 1899 (help cr Ponders End EP),[147] 1903 (help cr Bush Hill Park St Stephen EP),[107] 1930 (cr EP6),[144] 1938,[217] 1941 (help cr Oakwood EP, help cr Grange Park EP).[214]

EP1–ENFIELD CHRIST CHURCH, TRENT PARK–Cr 1839 from AP1.[215]

EP2–ENFIELD JESUS CHAPEL–Cr 1845 from AP1.[105] Bdry: 1867 (help cr Clay Hill EP),[14] 1901 (help cr EP3),[216] 1938.[217]

EP3–ENFIELD ST GEORGE–Cr 1901 from EP4, EP2.[216] Bdry: 1938,[217] 1960.[54]

EP4–ENFIELD ST JAMES–Cr 1832, refounded 1834 from AP1.[212] Bdry: 1899 (help cr Ponders End EP),[147] 1901 (help cr EP3),[216] 1938,[217] 1951 (cr EP7),[218] 1960.[54]

EP5–ENFIELD ST LUKE–Cr 1900 from Clay Hill EP.[149] Bdry: 1938.[217]

EP6–ENFIELD ST MICHAEL AND ALL ANGELS–Cr 1930 from AP1.[144]

EP7–ENFIELD ST PETER AND ST PAUL–Cr 1951 from EP4.[218]

EP8–ENFIELD CHASE–Cr 1884 from AP1.[213]

FELTHAM

AP *LG* Spelth. Hd, Staines PLU, RSD, RD (1894–1904), Feltham UD (1904–65). Civ bdry: 1934,[4] 1936.[220] Transf 1965 to Gtr London (Hounslow LB).[1] *Parl* Uxbr. Dv (1885–1918), Spelth. Dv/CC (1918–55), Feltham BC (1955–70), Gtr London thereafter. *Eccl* Hampton RDn (1858–1953), Staines RDn (1953–67), Hounslow RDn (1967–*). Eccl bdry: 1966.[221]

FINCHLEY

The following have 'Finchley' in their names. Insofar as any existed at a given time: *LG* Ossul. Hd, Barnet PLU, Finch. USD, UD (1894–1933), MB (1933–65). Transf 1965 to Gtr London (Barnet LB).[1] *Parl* Hornsey Dv (1885–1918), Finch. Dv (1918–48), BC (1948–70), Gtr London thereafter. *Eccl* Pec jurisd Bp London (until 1845), Enf. RDn (1858–75), Highg. RDn (1875–1901), Hornsey RDn (1901–67), Central Barnet RDn (1967–*).

AP1–FINCHLEY [ST MARY]–Civ bdry: 1934,[4] 1937.[222] Eccl bdry: 1836 (cr Whetstone EP),[46] 1846 (cr EP2),[223] 1872 (help cr EP1),[224] 1886 (help cr EP4),[225] 1903 (help cr EP3),[64] 1923 (help cr Temple Fortune EP).[184]

EP1–FINCHLEY CHRIST CHURCH, NORTH END–Cr 1872 from AP1, Whetstone EP, EP2.[224] Bdry: 1886 (help cr EP4),[225] 1903,[226] 1914 (help cr Woodside Park EP).[141]

EP2–FINCHLEY HOLY TRINITY–Cr 1846 from AP1.[223] Bdry: 1872 (help cr EP1),[224] 1890,[41] 1900 (help cr EP5),[20] 1932.[84]

EP3–FINCHLEY ST LUKE–Cr 1903 from AP1, EP4.[64]

EP4–FINCHLEY ST PAUL, LONG LANE–Cr 1886 from AP1, EP1.[225] Bdry: 1903,[226] 1903 (help cr EP3),[64] 1903,[226] 1932.[227]

EP5–EAST FINCHLEY–Cr 1900 from EP2, Muswell Hill St James EP.[20]

FINSBURY ST CLEMENT WITH ST BARNABAS AND ST MATTHEW

EP Cr 1952 by union pt King Square EP, pt City Road St Clement EP, pt City Road St Matthew EP.[123] Finsb. & Holb. RDn (1952–67), Isling. RDn (1967–*). Bdry: 1955,[80] 1966.[228]

FINSBURY ST PAUL

EP Cr 1842 from Old Street St Luke EP.[229] St Sepulchre RDn (1861–1901), Finsb. RDn (1901–32). Abol 1932 to help cr Charterhouse St Mary with Finsbury St Paul EP.[121]

FINSBURY PARK

EP Cr 1888 from Tollington Park St Anne EP.[58] Isling. RDn.

FITZROY SQUARE ST JOHN

EP Renaming 1868 of Upper Charlotte Street EP.[117] St Panc. RDn. Abol 1904 to help cr Fitzroy Square St John with St Saviour EP.[29]

FITZROY SQUARE ST JOHN WITH ST SAVIOUR

EP Cr 1904 by union Fitzroy Square St John EP, Fitzroy Square St Saviour EP.[231] St Panc. RDn.

Bdry: 1925.[331] Abol 1952 pt to help cr St Marylebone All Souls with St Peter and St John EP, pt to St Giles in the Fields AP.[232]

FITZROY SQUARE ST SAVIOUR

EP Cr 1865 from Upper Charolotte Street EP.[230] St Panc. RDn. Abol 1904 to help cr Fitzroy Square St John with St Saviour EP.[231]

OLD FORD ST MARK, VICTORIA PARK

EP Cr 1873 from Old Ford St Stephen EP.[233] Step. RDn (1873–1901), Poplar RDn (1901–66), Tow. Hmlts. RDn (1966–*).

OLD FORD ST PAUL

EP Cr 1878 from Old Ford St Stephen EP.[234] Step. RDn (1878–1901), Poplar RDn (1901–66). Abol 1966 to help cr Old Ford St Paul with St Stephen EP.[235]

OLD FORD ST PAUL WITH ST STEPHEN

EP Cr 1966 by union Old Ford St Paul EP, pt Old Ford St Stephen EP.[235] Poplar RDn (1966), Tow. Hmlts. RDn (1966–*).

OLD FORD ST STEPHEN

EP Cr 1858 from Stratford Bow St Mary EP.[236] Step. RDn (1861–1901), Poplar RDn (1901–66). Bdry: 1873 (cr Old Ford St Mark, Victoria Park EP),[233] 1878 (cr Old Ford St Paul EP).[234] Abol 1966 pt to help cr Old Ford St Paul with St Stephen EP, pt to Stratford Bow St Mary AP.[235]

FULHAM

The following have 'Fulham' in their names. Insofar as any existed at a given time: *LG* Ossul. Hd, Fulham PLU, Dist (Metrop Bd Wks, 1855–86), Vestry (Metrop Bd Wks, 1866–89). Transf 1889 to London.[43] *Parl* Chelsea Parl Bor (1867–85), Fulham Parl Bor (1885–1918), London thereafter. *Eccl* Pec jurisd Bp London (until 1845), Fulham RDn (1858–1967), Hamm. RDn (1967–*).

AP1–FULHAM [ALL SAINTS]–Incl chap Hammersmith (sep par 1631[329]). Eccl bdry: 1835 (cr EP10, EP11),[241] 1868 (help cr EP9),[93] 1874 (help cr EP16),[23] 1883 (help cr EP15),[133] 1885 (help cr EP6),[242] 1886 (help cr EP5),[92] 1897 (help cr EP7).[173]

EP1–FULHAM CHRIST CHURCH–Cr 1903 from EP9, EP12.[20]

EP2–FULHAM ST ALBAN–Cr 1897 from EP16, Hammersmith St Paul EP.[201] Bdry: 1968.[243]

EP3–FULHAM ST AUGUSTINE–Cr 1901 from EP16, EP15, EP10.[244] Abol 1956 to help cr EP14.[245]

EP4–FULHAM ST AUGUSTINE–Renaming 1973 of EP14 after loses pts to EP10, EP16.[224]

EP5–FULHAM ST CLEMENT–Cr 1886 from AP1, EP16.[92] Bdry: 1902.[223] Abol 1968 pt to help cr EP8, pt to EP2, pt to Hammersmith St Paul EP.[243]

EP6–FULHAM ST DIONIS, PARSON'S GREEN–Cr 1885 from AP1, EP10.[242]

EP7–FULHAM ST ETHELDREDA–Cr 1897 from AP1, EP15.[173] Bdry: 1902.[223] Abol 1968 to help cr EP8.[243]

EP8–FULHAM ST ETHELDREDA WITH ST CLEMENT–Cr 1968 by union EP7, EP5.[243]

EP9–FULHAM ST JAMES, MOORE PARK–Cr 1868 from EP10, AP1.[93] Bdry: 1895 (cr EP12),[44] 1903 (help cr EP1).[20]

EP10–FULHAM ST JOHN, WALHAM GREEN–Cr 1835 from AP1.[241] Often called 'Walham Green St John'. Bdry: 1874 (help cr EP16),[23] 1885 (help cr EP6),[242] 1899 (help cr EP13),[246] 1901 (help cr EP3),[244] 1973.[224]

EP11–FULHAM ST MARY, NORTH END–Cr 1835 from AP1.[241] Bdry: 1874 (help cr EP16).[23]

EP12–FULHAM ST MATTHEW–Cr 1895 from EP9.[44] Bdry: 1903 (help cr EP1).[20]

EP13–FULHAM ST OSWALD–Cr 1899 from EP10, EP16.[246] Abol 1956 to help cr EP14.[245]

EP14–FULHAM ST OSWALD WITH ST AUGUSTINE–Cr 1956 by union EP13, EP3.[245] Renamed 1973 as EP4 when loses pts to EP10, EP16.[224]

EP15–FULHAM ST PETER–Cr 1883 from EP16, AP1.[133] Bdry: 1897 (help cr EP7),[173] 1901 (help cr EP3).[244]

EP16–FULHAM FIELDS–Cr 1874 from EP11, EP10, AP1.[23] Bdry: 1883 (help cr EP15),[133] 1886 (help cr EP5),[92] 1897 (help cr EP2),[201] 1899 (help cr EP13),[246] 1901 (help cr EP3),[244] 1973.[224]

FULWELL

EP Cr 1914 from Upper Teddington EP.[247] Hampton RDn.

FURNIVAL'S INN

Ex-par place, sep CP 1858,[118] abol eccl 1952 to help cr Holborn St Andrew the Martyr with Saffron Hill St Peter EP.[70] Pt City of London, pt Middx. *LG* Ossul. Hd, Holb. PLU (1858–89). The Middx pt transf 1889 to London[43] [the City of London pt transf 1899 to St Andrew Holborn AP so that the par ent London Adm Co thereafter; see entry in the latter county]. *Parl* The Middx pt, Finsb. Parl Bor (1832–85), Finsb. Parl Bor, Holb. Dv (1885–1918), London thereafter.

GLASSHOUSE YARD

Ex-par lbty or lordship, the Middx pt of St Botolph Without Aldersgate AP (City of London, Middx), sep CP 1866 in Middx,[203] so that the mother par ent City of London thereafter. *LG* Ossul. Hd, E London PLU (1866[248]–69), City of London PLU (1869–89), Holb. Dist (Metrop Bd Wks). Transf 1889 to London.[43] *Parl* Finsb. Parl Bor (1832–85), Finsb. Parl Bor, East Dv (1885–1918), London thereafter. Eccl bdry: 1966 (help cr St Giles Cripplegate with St Bartholomew Moor Lane and St Alphage London Wall EP).[228]

GOLDER'S GREEN ST ALBAN

EP Cr 1922 from Hendon All Saints, Child's Hill EP.[244] Hampst. RDn (1922–67), W Barnet RDn (1967–*).

GOLDER'S GREEN ST MICHAEL
EP Cr 1914 from Hendon AP.[249] Hampst. RDn (1914–67), W Barnet RDn (1967–*). Bdry: 1933,[167] 1956.[145]

GRANGE PARK
EP Cr 1941 from Enfield AP, Winchmore Hill EP.[214] Enf. RDn. Bdry: 1943.[250]

GRAY'S INN
Ex-par place, sep CP 1858.[118] *LG* Ossul. Hd, Holb. PLU. Transf 1889 to London.[43] *Parl* Finsb. Parl Bor (1832–85), Finsb. Parl Bor, Holb. Dv (1885–1918), London thereafter.

GRAY'S INN ROAD
EP Cr 1839 from Holborn St Andrew AP.[131] St Sepulchre RDn (1861–1901), Holb. RDn (1901–31). Bdry: 1862 (help cr Holborn St Alban EP).[24] Abol 1931 pt to help cr Holborn St George the Martyr with Holy Trinity EP, pt to Holborn St John the Evangelist EP.[251]

GRAY'S INN ROAD ST JUDE
EP Cr 1862 from St Pancras AP.[166] St Panc. RDn. Bdry: 1876 (help cr St Pancras Holy Cross EP).[9] Abol 1935 to help cr St Pancras Holy Cross with St Jude EP.[252]

GREENFORD
AP *LG* Elth. Hd, Brentf. PLU, RSD, Greenford UD. Civ bdry: before 1871,[253] 1883,[159] 1887.[254] Abol 1926 ent to Ealing AP.[178] *Parl* Ealing Dv (1885–1918), Harrow Dv (1918–45). *Eccl* Seq 1. Eccl bdry: 1949 (incl help cr North Greenford EP),[32] 1954,[204] 1964,[106] 1964 (help cr Southall Christ the Redeemer EP).[255]

NORTH GREENFORD
EP Cr 1949 from Greenford AP, Sudbury St Andrew EP, Wembley EP.[32] Ealing RDn (1949–67), Ealing West RDn (1967–*).

GREENHILL
EP Cr 1896 from Harrow on the Hill AP.[27] Harrow RDn (1896–1901), Will. RDn (1901–14), Harrow RDn (1914–*). Bdry: 1911 (help cr Headstone EP),[61] 1935 (help cr Kenton EP).[131]

GUNNERSBURY
EP Cr 1888 from Old Brentford EP, Turnham Green EP, South Acton EP.[20] Ealing RDn (1888–1901), Hamm. RDn (1901–67), Hounslow RDn (1967–*). Bdry: 1929.[21]

HACKNEY
The following have 'Hackney' in their names. Insofar as any existed at a given time: *LG* Ossul. Hd, Hack. PLU, Dist (Metrop Bd Wks). Transf 1889 to London.[43] *Parl* Tow. Hmlts. Parl Bor (1832–67), Hack. Parl Bor (1867–85), Hack. Parl Bor, pt Central Dv, pt North Dv, pt South Dv (1885–1918), London thereafter. *Eccl* Pec jurisd Bp London (until 1845), Hack. RDn (1861–1901), Hack. & Stk. Newing. RDn (1901–67), Hack. RDn (1967–*).

AP1–HACKNEY [ST JOHN]–Eccl bdry: 1825 (cr EP2, EP8),[102] 1828 (cr Stamford Hill St Thomas EP),[125] 1844 (cr Dalston EP),[171] 1846 (cr Homerton EP),[256] 1855 (cr Clapton St James EP),[63] 1871 (help cr Dalston St Mark EP),[125] 1873 (cr Clapton Park All Saints EP),[147] 1873 (help cr Homerton St Luke EP),[238] 1880,[92] 1953 (help cr Clapton St James with Christ Church EP, help cr EP5).[93] Abol eccl 1972 to help cr EP1.[146]

EP1–HACKNEY–Cr 1972 by union AP1, Clapton St James with Christ Church EP, Clapton Park EP.[146]

EP2–SOUTH HACKNEY [ST JOHN OF JERUSALEM]–Cr 1825 from AP1.[102] Bdry: 1865 (help cr EP6),[62] 1867 (cr EP4),[257] 1871 (help cr EP3),[61] 1873 (help cr Homerton St Luke EP).[238] Abol 1953 pt to help cr EP5, pt to help cr EP11.[93]

EP3–SOUTH HACKNEY CHRIST CHURCH–Cr 1871 from EP2, EP6, Bethnal Green St James the Less EP, Bethnal Green St John EP, Haggerston St Stephen EP.[61] Abol 1953 to help cr EP5.[93]

EP4–SOUTH HACKNEY ST AUGUSTINE–Cr 1867 from EP2.[257] Bdry: 1873 (help cr Homerton St Luke EP),[238] 1893 (help cr EP10),[195] 1909.[195] Abol 1953 pt to help cr EP11, pt to Homerton St Luke EP.[93]

EP5–SOUTH HACKNEY ST JOHN OF JERUSALEM WITH CHRIST CHURCH–Cr 1953 by union EP2, EP3, pt EP6, pt AP1, pt Homerton St Luke EP.[93]

EP6–SOUTH HACKNEY ST MICHAEL AND ALL ANGELS–Cr 1865 from EP2, Bethnal Green St Jude EP.[62] Bdry: 1871 (help cr EP3),[61] 1872,[172] 1953 (incl help cr EP5).[93] Abol 1971 to help cr EP7.[175]

EP7–SOUTH HACKNEY ST MICHAEL AND ALL ANGELS, LONDON FIELDS, WITH HACKNEY ST PAUL–Cr 1971 by union EP6, Haggerston St Paul EP.[175]

EP8–WEST HACKNEY–Cr 1825 from AP1.[102] Bdry: 1844 (cr DeBeauvoir Town EP),[128] 1863 (help cr Hoxton St Andrew EP),[155] 1871 (help cr Dalston St Mark EP),[125] 1871 (help cr Clapton Christ Church EP),[144] 1886 (help cr Stoke Newington Common EP),[300] 1929 (help cr Shacklewell EP).[173] Abol 1954 to help cr EP9.[259]

EP9–WEST HACKNEY ST BARNABAS–Cr 1954 by union EP8, Shacklewell EP.[259]

EP10–HACKNEY WICK–Cr 1893 from EP4, Homerton EP.[195] Bdry: 1909.[258] Abol 1953 to help cr EP11.[93]

EP11–HACKNEY WICK ST MARY OF ETON WITH ST AUGUSTINE–Cr 1953 by union EP10, pt EP4, pt EP2.[93]

MONKEN HADLEY
AP *LG* Edm. Hd, Barnet PLU, pt Barnet USD, pt E Barnet Valley USD (both primarily Herts). Civ bdry: 1779,[260] 1883.[159] Transf 1889 to Herts.[261] *Parl* Enf. Dv (1885–1918). See entry in Herts for this par 1889–1965 and Gtr London from 1965. *Eccl* Donative until 1771,[299] Enf. RDn (1858–1967), Central Barnet RDn (1967–*).

HAGGERSTON
The following have 'Haggerston' in their names.

Insofar as any existed at a given time: *Eccl* St Sepulchre RDn (1858–1901), Shored. RDn (1901–67), Hack. RDn (1967–*).

EP1–HAGGERSTON ALL SAINTS–Cr 1855, refounded 1858 from EP6.[262] Bdry: 1880.[92]

EP2–HAGGERSTON ST AUGUSTINE–Cr 1863 from EP6.[63] Bdry: 1865 (help cr EP9).[263] Abol 1953 to help cr EP3.[251]

EP3–HAGGERSTON ST AUGUSTINE WITH ST STEPHEN–Cr 1953 by union EP2, EP9.[251]

EP4–HAGGERSTON ST CHAD–Cr 1863 from EP6.[63] Abol 1953 to help cr EP7.[251]

EP5–HAGGERSTON ST COLUMBA–Cr 1863 from EP6.[63]

EP6–HAGGERSTON ST MARY–Cr 1830 from Shoreditch AP.[264] Bdry: 1855 (cr EP1),[262] 1861 (cr EP8),[265] 1863 (cr Hoxton St Andrew EP),[155] 1863 (cr EP2, EP4, EP5).[63] Abol 1953 to help cr EP7.[251]

EP7–HAGGERSTON ST MARY WITH ST CHAD–Cr 1953 by unon EP6, EP4.[251]

EP8–HAGGERSTON ST PAUL–Cr 1861 from EP6.[265] Bdry: 1872.[172] Abol 1971 to help cr South Hackney St Michael and All Angels, London Fields, with Hackney St Paul EP.[175]

EP9–HAGGERSTON ST STEPHEN–Cr 1865 from EP2, Bethnal Green St Jude EP, Bethnal Green St Peter EP.[62] Bdry: 1871 (help cr South Hackney Christ Church EP).[61] Abol 1953 to help cr EP3.[251]

HAMMERSMITH

The following have 'Hammersmith' in their names. Insofar as any existed at a given time: *LG* Ossul. Hd, Kens. PLU (1837–45), Fulham PLU (1845–89), Dist (Metrop Bd Wks, 1855–86), Hamm. Vestry (Metrop Bd Wks, 1886–89). Transf 1889 to London.[43] *Parl* Chelsea Parl Bor (1867–85), Hamm. Parl Bor (1885–1918), London thereafter. *Eccl* Pec jurisd Bp London (1631–1845), Fulham RDn (1858–61), Barnes & Hamm. RDn (1861–72), Fulham RDn (1872–1901), Hamm. RDn (1901–*).

CP/EP1–HAMMERSMITH [ST PAUL]–Chap in Fulham AP, sep par 1631.[329] Eccl bdry: 1836 (cr EP6),[266] 1845 (help cr Kensal Green St John EP),[125] 1850 (cr EP9),[216] 1860 (cr EP3),[267] 1872 (cr EP5),[6] 1890,[40] 1897 (help cr Fulham St Alban EP),[201] 1968.[243]

EP2–HAMMERSMITH HOLY INNOCENTS–Cr 1892 from EP3, EP6.[263]

EP3–HAMMERSMITH ST JOHN THE EVANGELIST–Cr 1860 from EP1.[267] Bdry: 1880 (help cr EP8),[269] 1886,[268] 1890,[40] 1892 (help cr EP2),[263] 1897.[270]

EP4–HAMMERSMITH ST LUKE–Cr 1872 from EP9.[92] Bdry: 1888 (cr Stamford Brook EP),[271] 1891 (help cr EP7),[10] 1922 (cr EP10).[238]

EP5–HAMMERSMITH ST MATTHEW–Cr 1872 from EP1.[6] Bdry: 1880 (help cr EP8).[269]

EP6–HAMMERSMITH ST PETER–Cr 1836 from EP1.[266] Bdry: 1892 (help cr EP2).[263]

EP7–HAMMERSMITH ST SAVIOUR–Cr 1891 from EP4, East Acton EP.[10]

EP8–HAMMERSMITH ST SIMON–Cr 1880 from EP5, EP3.[269] Bdry: 1886.[268]

EP9–HAMMERSMITH ST STEPHEN–Cr 1850 from EP1.[216] Bdry: 1867 (help cr Kensington St Barnabas EP),[257] 1872 (cr EP4),[92] 1875 (help cr Harlesden All Souls EP),[6] 1883 (cr Shepherd's Bush EP),[272] 1929.[69] Abol 1963 to help cr Shepherd's Bush St Stephen with St Thomas EP.[88]

EP10–NORTH HAMMERSMITH–Cr 1922 from EP4.[238] Bdry: 1929.[69]

HAMPSTEAD

The following have 'Hampstead' in their names. Insofar as any existed at a given time: *LG* Ossul. Hd, Edm. PLU (1837–48), Hampst. Par (poor law, 1848–89), Vestry (Metrop Bd Wks). Transf 1889 to London.[43] *Parl* Hampst. Parl Bor (1885–1918), London thereafter. *Eccl* Enf. RDn (1858–75), Highg. RDn (1875–1901), Hampst. RDn (1901–67), N Camd. (Hampst.) RDn (1967–*).

AP1–HAMPSTEAD [ST JOHN]–Chap in Hendon AP, sep par 1549.[273] Eccl bdry: 1852 (cr EP2),[274] 1856 (cr EP6),[275] 1860 (help cr EP4),[276] 1861 (cr Belsize Park EP),[6] 1865 (help cr EP1 [from pt in chap Kilburn St Mary]),[281] 1869 (cr Kilburn St Mary EP),[277] 1870 (cr EP5),[50] 1873 (help cr EP10),[278] 1896 (help cr EP9),[279] 1915.[280]

EP1–HAMPSTEAD ALL SOULS–Cr 1865 from EP4, Kilburn St Mary chap of AP1, St John's Wood EP.[281]

EP2–HAMPSTEAD CHRIST CHURCH–Cr 1852 from AP1.[274] Bdry: 1869,[282] 1915.[280]

EP3–HAMPSTEAD EMMANUEL, WEST END–Cr 1885 from EP10.[137] Bdry: 1896 (help cr EP9),[279] 1897.[270]

EP4–HAMPSTEAD ST PAUL–Cr 1860 from AP1, EP6.[276] Bdry: 1865 (help cr EP1),[281] 1865.[238] Abol 1957 to help cr Primrose Hill St Mary the Virgin with Avenue Road St Paul EP.[236]

EP5–HAMPSTEAD ST STEPHEN–Cr 1870 from AP1.[50] Bdry: 1915.[280]

EP6–SOUTH HAMPSTEAD–Cr 1856 from AP1.[275] Bdry: 1860 (help cr EP4),[276] 1865,[238] 1885 (cr Primrose Hill EP).[137]

EP7–WEST HAMPSTEAD ST CUTHBERT–Cr 1888 from EP10.[120]

EP8–WEST HAMPSTEAD ST JAMES–Cr 1888 from Kilburn St Mary EP.[33]

EP9–WEST HAMPSTEAD ST LUKE–Cr 1896 from AP1, EP3.[279] Bdry: 1897.[270]

EP10–WEST HAMPSTEAD THE TRINITY–Cr 1873 from AP1, Kilburn St Mary EP.[278] Bdry: 1885 (cr EP3),[137] 1888 (cr EP7).[120]

HAMPSTEAD GARDEN SUBURB

EP Cr 1911 from Hendon AP.[283] Hampst. RDn (1911–34), Hendon RDn (1934–67), W Barnet RDn (1967–*). Bdry: 1932.[84]

HAMPSTEAD ROAD

EP Cr 1864 from St Pancras AP.[39] St Panc. RDn.

Abol 1954 pt to help cr St Pancras with St James and Christ Church EP, pt to Munster Square EP, pt to Regent's Park Christ Church EP, pt to Bedford New Town St Matthew EP, pt to Somers Town EP.[25]

HAMPTON

AP Incl hmlt Hampton Wick (sep EP 1831,[285] sep CP 1866[284]). *LG* Spelth. Hd, Kingston PLU, Hampton USD, UD. Abol civ 1937 pt to Sunbury AP, pt to Twickenham AP.[286] *Parl* Uxbr. Dv (1885–1918), Spelth. Dv (1918–48). *Eccl* Seq 4. Addtl eccl bdry alt: 1864 (cr Hampton Hill EP),[29] 1929 (cr Hampton All Saints EP).[266]

HAMPTON ALL SAINTS

EP Cr 1929 from Hampton AP.[266] Hampton RDn. Bdry: 1972 (incl help cr Hanworth St Richard EP).[287]

HAMPTON HILL

EP Cr 1864 from Hampton AP.[29] Hampton RDn.

HAMPTON WICK

Hmlt in Hampton AP, sep EP 1831,[285] sep CP 1866.[284] *LG* Spelth. Hd, Kingston PLU, Hampton USD, UD. Civ bdry: 1912.[288] Abol civ 1937 ent to Twickenham AP.[286] *Parl* Uxbr. Dv (1885–1918), Spelth. Dv (1918–48). *Eccl* Hampton RDn.

HANGER LANE

EP Cr 1861 from Tottenham Holy Trinity EP.[289] Enf. RDn (1861–1901), Tott. RDn (1901–67), E Haringey RDn (1967–*). Bdry: 1885,[249] 1887 (cr Stamford Hill St John, Vartry Road EP),[290] 1889 (help cr Tottenham Christ Church, West Green EP),[291] 1892 (help cr Stoke Newington St Olave EP),[136] 1898 (help cr Hornsey St Peter EP),[292] 1903 (help cr Harringay EP),[70] 1903,[59] 1905 (help cr Stamford Hill St Bartholomew EP),[271] 1973.[54]

HANLEY ROAD ST SAVIOUR WITH ST PAUL

EP Cr 1953 by union Tollington Park St Saviour EP, pt Upper Holloway St Paul EP.[9] Isling. RDn.

HANOVER CHAPEL

EP Cr 1835 from St George Hanover Square EP.[35] Later called 'Davies Street St Anselm'. St Geo. Hanov. Sq. RDn (1861–1901), W'minst. RDn (1901–38). Abol 1938 pt to North Audley Street EP, pt to St George Hanover Square EP.[293]

HANWELL

The following have 'Hanwell' in their names. Insofar as any existed at a given time: *LG* Elth. Hd, Brentf. PLU, RSD (1875–85), Hanwell USD (1885–95), UD. Abol civ 1926 ent to Ealing AP.[178] *Parl* Pt Brentf. Dv, pt Ealing Dv (1885–1918), Harrow Dv (1918–48). *Eccl* Seq 7.

AP1–HANWELL [ST MARY]–Incl chap New Brentford (from 12th cent, sep civ identity early, sep EP 1721[76]). Addtl eccl bdry alt: 1905 (help cr Ealing St James EP),[187] 1908 (cr EP3),[188] 1933 (cr EP4),[61] 1951 (cr EP1).[294]

EP1–HANWELL ST CHRISTOPHER–Cr 1951 from AP1.[294]

EP2–HANWELL ST MARK–Cr 1919 from EP3.[295]

EP3–HANWELL ST MELLITUS–Cr 1908 from AP1.[188] Bdry: 1919 (cr EP2).[295]

EP4–HANWELL ST THOMAS–Cr 1933 from AP1.[61] Bdry: 1952.[46]

HANWORTH

AP *LG* Spelth. Hd, Staines PLU, RSD, RD (1894–1930), Feltham UD (1930–65). Civ bdry: 1934,[4] 1937.[286] Transf 1965 to Gtr London (Hounslow LB).[1] *Parl* Uxbr. Dv (1885–1918), Spelth. Dv (1918–55), Feltham BC (1955–70), Gtr London thereafter. *Eccl* Hampton RDn (1858–1967), Hounslow RDn (1967–*). Eccl bdry: 1957 (cr Hanworth All Saints EP),[296] 1966,[221] 1972 (incl help cr Hanworth St Richard EP).[287]

HANWORTH ALL SAINTS

EP Cr 1957 from Hanworth AP.[296] Hampton RDn (1957–67), Hounslow RDn (1967–*). Bdry: 1972 (incl help cr Hanworth St Richard EP).[287]

HANWORTH ST RICHARD

EP Cr 1972 from Hanworth AP, Hampton All Saints EP, Hanworth All Saints EP.[287] Hounslow RDn.

HAREFIELD

AP *LG* Elth. Hd, Uxbr. PLU, RSD, RD (1894–1929), UD (1929–38). Civ bdry: by 1871.[297] Abol civ 1938 ent to Uxbridge CP.[298] *Parl* Uxbr. Dv (1885–1948). *Eccl* Seq 9.

HARLESDEN ALL SOULS

EP Cr 1875 from Acton AP, Hammersmith St Stephen EP, Kensal Green St John EP.[6] Harrow RDn (1875–1901), Will. RDn (1901–67), Brent RDn (1967–*). Bdry: 1892 (help cr Stonebridge EP),[263] 1902 (help cr Willesden St Matthew EP),[68] 1915 (help cr Harlesden St Mark EP),[300] 1951,[12] 1974.[14]

HARLESDEN ST MARK

EP Cr 1915 from Harlesden All Souls EP, Kensal Green St John EP.[300] Will. RDn (1915–67), Brent RDn (1967–*).

HARLINGTON

AP *LG* Elth. Hd, Staines PLU, RSD, RD (1894–1930), Hayes & Harl. UD (1930–65). Civ bdry: early changes,[301] 1934.[4] Transf 1965 to Gtr London (Hilling. LB).[1] *Parl* Uxbr. Dv (1885–1918), Spelth. Dv (1918–48), Hayes & Harl. BC (1948–70), Gtr London thereafter. *Eccl* Seq 8.

HARMONDSWORTH

AP *LG* Elth. Hd, Staines PLU, RSD, RD (1894–1930), Yiewsley & W Drayton UD (1930–1949). Abol civ 1949 to help cr Yiewsley and West Drayton CP.[176] *Parl* Uxbr. Dv/CC (1885–1970). *Eccl* Seq 8.

HARRINGAY

EP Cr 1892 from Hornsey AP, Stroud Green EP, Hanger Lane EP.[70] Highg. RDn (1892–1901), Hornsey RDn (1901–67), E Haringey RDn (1967–*). Bdry: 1903.[59]

HARROW
The following have 'Harrow' in their names. Insofar as any existed at a given time: *LG* Gore Hd, Hendon PLU, pt Harrow USD, pt Hendon RSD, Harrow on the Hill UD (1894–1934), Harrow UD (1934–54), MB (1954–65). Transf 1965 to Gtr London (Harrow LB).[1] *Parl* Harrow Dv (1885–1945), pt Harrow East BC, pt Harrow West BC (1945–70), Gtr London thereafter. *Eccl* Pec jurisd Archbp Canterb (until 1845), Seq 6 thereafter.
EP1–HARROW–Cr 1913 from AP1.[302]
CP1–HARROW–Cr 1934 by union Great Stanmore AP, Little Stanmore AP, Pinner CP, pt AP1, Harrow Weald CP, pt Kingsbury AP, pt Wealdstone CP, pt Ealing AP, pt Wembley CP.[4]
EP2–NORTH HARROW–Cr 1937 from Pinner EP.[95] Bdry: 1953,[304] 1955 (help cr Roxbourne EP).[303]
EP3–SOUTH HARROW–Cr 1937 from Roxeth EP.[280] Bdry: 1953,[304] 1954,[204] 1955 (help cr Roxbourne EP).[303]
AP1–HARROW ON THE HILL–Incl chap Pinner (sep civ identity early, sep EP 1766[128]), dist Wembley (sep EP 1847,[128] sep CP 1894[306]). Addtl civ bdry alt: 1894 (cr CP2, Wealdstone CP),[306] 1895,[307] 1902,[308] 1928.[180] Abol civ 1934 pt to Ealing AP, pt to help cr CP1, pt to Wembley CP.[4] Addtl eccl bdry alt: 1841 (cr EP4),[309] 1863 (cr Roxeth EP),[63] 1882 (help cr Wealdstone EP),[271] 1896 (cr Greenhill EP),[27] 1913 (cr EP1),[302] 1923 (help cr Sudbury EP),[87] 1935 (incl help cr Kenton EP),[131] 1959 (help cr North Wembley EP).[304]
EP4–HARROW WEALD–Cr 1841, refounded 1845 from AP1.[309] Bdry: 1882 (help cr Wealdstone EP),[271] 1935 (help cr Kenton EP),[131] 1940 (help cr Belmont EP),[54] 1946,[310] 1958 (help cr EP5).[311]
CP2–HARROW WEALD–Cr 1894 from AP1.[306] *LG* Hendon PLU, RD. Abol 1934 to help cr CP1.[306] *Parl* Hendon Dv (1918–45).
EP5–HARROW WEALD ST MICHAEL AND ALL ANGELS–Cr 1958 from EP4, Wealdstone EP.[311]
HATCH END
EP Cr 1906 from Pinner EP.[312] Will. RDn (1906–14), Harrow RDn (1914–*). Bdry: 1911 (help cr Headstone EP).[61]
HAVERSTOCK HILL HOLY TRINITY
EP Cr 1852 from St Pancras AP.[109] St Panc. RDn. Bdry: 1864 (help cr Kentish Town St Martin EP),[80] 1865 (help cr Haverstock Hill St Andrew EP),[120] 1869 (help cr New Kentish Town EP),[114] 1876 (help cr Camden Town St Michael EP),[51] 1880 (help cr Kentish Town St Barnabas EP),[149] 1912 (help cr Kentish Town St Silas the Martyr EP).[313] Abol 1957 to help cr Haverstock Hill Holy Trinity with Kentish Town St Barnabas EP.[314]
HAVERSTOCK HILL HOLY TRINITY WITH KENTISH TOWN ST BARNABAS
EP Cr 1957 by union Haverstock Hill Holy Trinity EP, Kentish Town St Barnabas EP.[314] St Panc. RDn (1957–67), S Camd. (Holb. & St Panc.) RDn (1967–*).
HAVERSTOCK HILL ST ANDREW
EP Cr 1865 from Kentish Town EP, Haverstock Hill Holy Trinity EP.[120] St Panc. RDn. Bdry: 1894 (help cr North St Pancras EP),[245] 1912 (help cr Kentish Town St Silas the Martyr EP).[313] Abol 1953 pt to help cr Kentish Town St Martin with St Andrew EP, pt to Kentish Town St Silas EP.[140]
HAYES
AP Incl chap Norwood (*de facto* sep civ from middle ages,[331] sep EP 1725[332]). *LG* Elth. Hd, Uxbr. PLU, RSD, RD (1894–1904), Hayes UD (1904–30), Hayes & Harl. UD (1930–65). Addtl civ bdry alt: 1934.[4] Transf 1965 to Gtr London (Hilling. LB).[1] *Parl* Uxbr. Dv (1885–1948), Hayes & Harl. BC (1948–70), Gtr London thereafter. *Eccl* Pec jurisd Archbp Canterb (until 1845), Seq 9 thereafter. Addtl eccl bdry alt: 1929 (cr Hayes St Anselm EP),[6] 1935 (help cr Dawley EP).[174]
HAYES ST ANSELM
EP Cr 1929 from Hayes AP.[6] Uxbr. RDn (1929–67), Hilling. RDn (1967–*).
HEADSTONE
EP Cr 1911 from Hatch End EP, Greenhill EP.[61] Will. RDn (1911–14), Harrow RDn (1914–*).
HENDON
The following have 'Hendon' in their names. Insofar as any existed at a given time: *LG* Gore Hd, Hendon PLU, USD, UD (1894–1932), MB (1932–65). Transf 1965 to Gtr London (Barnet LB).[1] *Parl* Harrow Dv (1885–1918), Hendon Dv (1918–45), pt Hendon North BC, pt Hendon South BC (1945–70), Gtr London thereafter. *Eccl* Harrow RDn (1858–1901), Hampst. RDn (1901–34), Hendon RDn (1934–67), W Barnet RDn (1967–*).
AP1–HENDON [ST MARY]–Incl chap Hampstead (sep par 1549[273]). Addtl civ bdry alt: 1926 (loses pt to Shenley AP, Herts),[316] 1931 (gains Edgware CP).[317] Addtl eccl bdry alt: 1833 (cr Mill Hill St Paul [sometimes 'Hendon St Paul, Mill Hill'] EP),[370] 1857 (cr EP1),[318] 1876 (cr EP4),[246] 1896 (cr EP5),[188] 1911 (cr Hampstead Garden Suburb EP),[283] 1914 (cr Golder's Green St Michael EP),[249] 1923 (cr EP2),[319] 1923 (help cr Temple Fortune EP),[184] 1951,[184] 1956.[145]
EP1–HENDON ALL SAINTS, CHILD'S HILL–Cr 1857 from AP1.[318] Harrow RDn (1858–1901), Hampst. RDn (1901–67), W Barnet RDn (1967–*). Bdry: 1892 (help cr Cricklewood St Peter EP),[29] 1922 (cr Golder's Green St Alban EP),[244] 1933,[167] 1956.[145]
EP2–HENDON CHRIST CHURCH–Cr 1923 from AP1.[319] Bdry: 1956.[145]
EP3–HENDON ST ALPHAGE–Cr 1924 from EP5, Mill Hill St Paul EP.[199] Bdry: 1937 (help cr Mill Hill John Keble Church EP),[95] 1951 (help cr Colindale EP).[157]

EP4–HENDON ST BARNABAS–Cr 1876 from AP1.[246]

EP5–WEST HENDON–Cr 1896 from AP1.[188] Bdry: 1924 (help cr EP3),[199] 1951 (help cr Colindale EP),[157] 1956.[145]

HESTON

AP *LG* Islew. Hd, Brentf. PLU, Heston & Islew. USD, UD. Civ bdry: 1894.[321] Abol civ 1927 to help cr Heston and Isleworth CP.[320] *Parl* Brentf. Dv (1885–1918), Twick. Dv (1918–45). *Eccl* Ealing RDn (1858–1934), Hampton RDn (1934–53), Heston & Islew. RDn (1953–67), Hounslow RDn (1967–*). Eccl bdry: 1856 (help cr Spring Grove EP),[322] 1864 (help cr Hounslow EP),[111] 1871 (cr Hounslow Heath EP),[323] 1909,[324] 1965.[95]

HESTON AND ISLEWORTH

CP Cr 1927 by union Heston AP, Isleworth AP.[320] *LG* Brentf. PLU, Heston & Islew. UD (1927–30), MB (1932–65). Bdry: 1934.[4] Transf 1965 to Gtr London (Hounslow LB).[1] *Parl* Heston & Islew. Parl Bor/BC (ent 1945–55, pt 1955–70), pt Feltham BC (1955–70).

HIGHBURY CHRIST CHURCH

EP Cr 1849 from Islington St Mary EP.[64] Isling. RDn. Bdry: 1866 (cr Highbury St Saviour EP),[325] 1871 (help cr Highbury New Park EP),[40] 1882 (cr Highbury Vale EP),[271] 1895.[207]

HIGHBURY ST SAVIOUR

EP Cr 1866 from Highbury Christ Church EP.[325] Isling. RDn.

HIGHBURY NEW PARK

EP Cr 1871 from Highbury Christ Church EP, Ball's Pond EP.[40] Isling. RDn.

HIGHBURY VALE

EP Cr 1882 from Highbury Christ Church EP.[271] Isling. RDn.

HIGHGATE

EP Cr 1834 from Hornsey AP, St Pancras AP.[276] Pec jurisd Bp London (1834–45), Enf. RDn (1858–75), Highg. RDn (1875– 1901), Hornsey RDn (1901–67), W Haringey RDn (1967–*). Bdry: 1853 (help cr Highgate Rise EP),[123] 1859 (help cr Chelsea Christ Church EP),[128] 1874 (help cr Highgate All Saints EP),[326] 1898 (help cr Highgate St Augustine EP).[112]

HIGHGATE ALL SAINTS

EP Cr 1874 from Highgate EP, Hornsey AP, Muswell Hill St James EP.[326] RDns as for Highgate, from 1874. Bdry: 1898 (help cr Highgate St Augustine EP),[112] 1891.[89]

HIGHGATE ST AUGUSTINE

EP Cr 1898 from Highgate EP, Highgate All Saints EP.[112] RDns as for Highgate, from 1898.

HIGHGATE RISE

EP Cr 1853 from Highgate EP, St Pancras AP, Kentish Town chap of St Pancras AP.[123] St Panc. RDn (1858–1967), S Camd. (Holb. & St Panc.) RDn (1967–*). Bdry: 1877 (help cr Brookfield St Mary EP).[101]

HILLINGDON

AP Incl hmlt Uxbridge (sep EP 1827,[327] refounded 1842,[16] sep CP 1866[203]). *LG* Elth. Hd, Uxbr. PLU, RSD (ent 1875–83, pt 1883–94), pt Uxbr. USD (1883–94). Addtl civ bdry alt: 1883.[159] Abol civ 1894 the pt in the USD to cr Hillingdon West CP, the remainder to cr Hillingdon East CP.[78] *Parl* Uxbr. Dv (1885–1918). *Eccl* Seq 9. Addtl eccl bdry alt: 1842 (cr Uxbridge Moor EP),[16] 1865 (help cr Hillingdon St Andrew EP),[163] 1874 (cr Yiewsley EP),[181] 1884,[164] 1934 (help cr Hillingdon All Saints EP),[165] 1935 (help cr Dawley EP).[174]

HILLINGDON ALL SAINTS

EP Cr 1934 from Hillingdon AP, Ickenham AP, Cowley AP.[165] Hilling. RDn.

HILLINGDON EAST

CP Cr 1894 from the pt of Hillingdon AP not in Uxbr. USD.[78] *LG* Uxbr. PLU, RD (1894–1929), UD (1929–38). Bdry: 1896 (help cr Yiewsley CP),[328] 1896,[160] 1929.[161] Abol 1938 ent to Uxbridge CP.[298] *Parl* Uxbr. Dv (1918–48). Parl bdry: 1945.[202]

HILLINGDON ST ANDREW

EP Cr 1865 from Hillingdon AP, Cowley AP.[163] Uxbr. RDn (1865–1967), Hilling. RDn (1967–*).

HILLINGDON WEST

CP Cr 1894 from the pt of Hillingdon AP in Uxbr. USD.[78] *LG* Uxbr. PLU, UD. Abol 1938 ent to Uxbridge CP.[298] *Parl* Uxbr. Dv (1918–48).

HOLBORN

The following have 'Holborn' in their names. Insofar as any existed at a given time: *LG*, *Parl* See usual civ spelling, 'St Andrew Holborn'. *Eccl* St Sepulchre RDn (1861–1901), Holb. RDn (1901–34), Finsb. & Holb. RDn (1934–67), S Camd. (Holb. & St Panc.) RDn (1967–*).

AP1–HOLBORN–Usual eccl spelling, or 'Holborn St Andrew'; for civ see 'St Andrew Holborn'. Eccl bdry: 1723 (cr EP3, sometimes eccl called 'Queen Square', civ 'St George the Martyr', qv),[333] 1839 (cr Gray's Inn Road EP),[131] 1839 (cr Saffron Hill EP),[131] 1862 (help cr EP1).[24] Abol eccl 1952 pt (the pt in Holb. Metrop Bor) to help cr EP2, pt to Kingsway Holy Trinity with Drury Lane St John EP.[70]

EP1–HOLBORN ST ALBAN–Cr 1862 from AP1, Gray's Inn Road EP.[24] Abol 1952 to help cr EP2.[70]

EP2–HOLBORN ST ALBAN THE MARTYR WITH SAFFRON HILL ST PETER–Cr 1952 by union EP1, pt AP1 (the pt in Holb. Metrop Bor), ex-par Furnival's Inn, ex-par Staple Inn.[70]

EP3–HOLBORN ST GEORGE THE MARTYR–Cr 1723 from AP1 (civ, 'St George the Martyr', qv).[333] Sometimes 'Queen Square', or 'Holborn St George the Martyr, Queen Square'. Bdry: 1867 (help cr EP5).[69] Abol 1931 to help cr EP4.[251]

EP4–HOLBORN ST GEORGE THE MARTYR WITH HOLY TRINITY–Cr 1931 by union

EP3, pt Gray's Inn Road Holy Trinity EP.[251] Bdry: 1952.[70] Abol 1959 to help cr Queen Square St George the Martyr with Holborn Holy Trinity and Gray's Inn Road St Bartholomew EP.[334]

EP5–HOLBORN ST JOHN THE EVANGELIST–Cr 1867 from EP3, Bloomsbury St George EP.[69] Bdry: 1931.[251] Abol 1952 to help cr Bloomsbury St George with St John the Evangelist EP.[70]

HOLLOWAY

The following have 'Holloway' in their names. Insofar as any existed at a given time: *Eccl* Isling. RDn.

EP1–HOLLOWAY [EMMANUEL, HORNSEY ROAD]–Cr 1886 from Tollington Park St Mark EP, EP7, EP11.[152] Abol 1953 pt to help cr EP2, pt to Tufnell Park EP, pt to Tollington Park St Mark EP.[9]

EP2–HOLLOWAY EMMANUEL WITH HORNSEY ROAD ST BARNABAS–Cr 1953 by union EP1, pt Hornsey Road St Barnabas EP.[9]

EP3–HOLLOWAY ST MARY MAGDALENE WITH ST JAMES–Cr 1953 by union Islington St Mary Magdalene, Holloway Road EP, pt EP4, pt Hornsey Road St Barnabas EP.[9]

EP4–LOWER HOLLOWAY–Cr 1839 from Islington St Mary EP.[335] Bdry: 1846,[144] 1861 (help cr EP11),[6] 1862 (cr Barnsbury EP),[46] 1866 (help cr Hornsey Road EP).[185] Abol 1953 pt to help cr EP3, pt to EP10.[9]

EP5–UPPER HOLLOWAY ALL SAINTS–Cr 1885 from EP6, Tufnell Park EP.[242] Bdry: 1953.[9]

EP6–UPPER HOLLOWAY ST JOHN–Cr 1830 from Islington St Mary EP.[63] Bdry: 1846,[144] 1854 (cr Tollington Park St Anne EP),[167] 1861 (help cr EP11),[6] 1866 (help cr Hornsey Road EP),[185] 1868 (help cr Tufnell Park EP),[93] 1877 (help cr Brookfield St Mary EP),[101] 1880 (cr EP8),[257] 1881 (help cr EP9),[356] 1883,[337] 1897 (help cr Whitehall Park EP),[338] 1953.[9]

EP7–UPPER HOLLOWAY ST PAUL–Cr 1870 from EP6, Tollington Park St Mark EP, Hornsey Rise EP.[60] Bdry: 1886 (help cr EP1).[152] Abol 1953 pt to help cr Hanley Road St Saviour with St Paul EP, pt to Tufnell Park EP, pt to EP5.[9]

EP8–UPPER HOLLOWAY ST PETER–Cr 1880 from EP6.[257] Bdry: 1961.[61]

EP9–UPPER HOLLOWAY ST STEPHEN–Cr 1881 from EP6, Hornsey Rise EP.[336]

EP10–WEST HOLLOWAY ST DAVID–Cr 1869 from EP11.[91] Bdry: 1953.[9]

EP11–WEST HOLLOWAY ST LUKE–Cr 1861 from EP4, EP6.[6] Bdry: 1868 (help cr Tufnell Park EP),[93] 1869 (cr EP10),[91] 1886 (help cr EP1),[152] 1888 (help cr Islington St Matthias, Caledonian Road EP).[20]

HOLY TRINITY MINORIES

Orig priory church, in the Middx pt of St Botolph Without Aldgate AP, parochial from 1557.[461] *LG* Ossul. Hd, Whitech. PLU, Dist (Metrop Bd Wks). Transf 1889 to London.[43] *Parl* Tow. Hmlts. Parl Bor (1867–85), Tow. Hmlts. Parl Bor, Whitech. Dv (1885–1918), London thereafter. *Eccl* Royal pec (until 1730), E City RDn (1869–93). Abol eccl 1893 to help cr St Botolph Without Aldgate and Holy Trinity Minories EP[462] (qv in entries for City of London).

HOMERTON

EP Cr 1846 from Hackney AP.[256] Hack. RDn (1861–1901), Hack. & Stk. Newing. RDn (1901–67), Hack. RDn (1967–*). Bdry: 1873 (help cr Homerton St Luke EP),[238] 1885 (help cr Clapton Park All Souls EP),[148] 1889 (cr Lower Homerton EP),[156] 1893 (help cr Hackney Wick EP),[195] 1909,[258] 1953.[93]

HOMERTON ST LUKE

EP Cr 1873 from Hackney AP, Homerton EP, South Hackney EP, South Hackney St Augustine EP.[238] RDns as for Homerton, from 1873. Bdry: 1880,[92] 1953 (incl help cr South Hackney EP).[93]

LOWER HOMERTON

EP Cr 1889 from Homerton EP.[156] RDns as for Homerton, from 1889. Bdry: 1953.[93]

HORNSEY

The following have 'Hornsey' in their names. Insofar as any existed at a given time: *LG* Ossul. Hd, Edm. PLU, pt Hornsey USD, pt S Hornsey USD, pt S Hornsey UD (1894–96), Hornsey UD (pt 1894–96, ent 1896–1903), Hornsey MB (1903–65). Transf 1965 to Gtr London (Haringey LB).[1] *Parl* Hornsey Dv (1885–1918), Parl Bor/BC (1918–70), Gtr London thereafter. Eccl Pec jurisd Bp London (until 1845), Enf. RDn (1858–75), Highg. RDn (1875–1901), Hornsey RDn (1901–67), W Haringey RDn (1967–*).

AP1–HORNSEY [ST MARY]–Sometimes 'Haringay'. Civ bdry: 1883,[159] 1896 (loses the pt in S Hornsey UD to cr South Hornsey CP),[339] 1899 (gains pt Clerkenwell AP as the latter transf to London),[43] 1934,[4] 1937.[222] Parl bdry: 1945.[202] Eccl bdry: 1834 (help cr Highgate EP),[276] 1843 (cr Muswell Hill St James EP),[141] 1849 (help cr Stoke Newington St Matthias EP),[340] 1862 (cr EP1),[34] 1874 (help cr Highgate All Saints EP),[326] 1875 (cr Brownswood Park EP),[102] 1877 (cr EP2),[58] 1881 (help cr Stroud Green EP),[99] 1892 (help cr Harringay EP),[70] 1898 (help cr EP5),[292] 1910 (cr EP3).[136]

EP1–HORNSEY CHRIST CHURCH, CROUCH END–Cr 1862 from AP1.[54] Bdry: 1891,[89] 1903 (help cr EP4).[312]

EP2–HORNSEY HOLY INNOCENTS–Cr 1877 from AP1.[58] Bdry: 1881 (help cr Stroud Green EP),[99] 1903 (help cr EP4).[312]

EP3–HORNSEY ST GEORGE–Cr 1910 from AP1.[136]

EP4–HORNSEY ST LUKE–Cr 1903 from EP2, EP1, Stroud Green EP.[312]

EP5–HORNSEY ST PETER–Cr 1898 from AP1,

Noel Park EP, Tottenham Christ Church, West Green EP, Hangar Lane EP.[292]

CP1–SOUTH HORNSEY–Cr 1896 from the pt of AP1 in S Hornsey UD.[339] *LG* Edm. PLU, S Hornsey UD. Abol 1899 pt to Stoke Newington AP and Metrop Bor (London), pt to Islington AP and Metrop Bor (London).[43]

HORNSEY RISE

EP Cr 1865 from Tollington Park St Mark EP.[341] Isling. RDn. Bdry: 1870 (help cr Upper Holloway EP),[60] 1881 (help cr Upper Holloway St Stephen EP),[336] 1888 (help cr Tollington Park St Saviour EP),[20] 1897 (help cr Whitehall Park EP),[338] 1953.[9]

HORNSEY ROAD

EP Cr 1866 from Tollington Park St Mark EP, Islington St Mary EP, Lower Holloway EP, Upper Holloway St John EP.[185] Isling. RDn. Abol 1953 pt to help cr Holloway St Mary Magdalene with St James EP, pt to help cr Holloway Emmanuel with Hornsey Road St Barnabas EP.[9]

HOUNSLOW

EP Cr 1836 from Heston AP, Isleworth AP.[111] Ealing RDn (1858–1934), Hampton RDn (1934–53), Heston & Islew. RDn (1953–67), Hounslow RDn (1967–*). Bdry: 1856 (help cr Spring Grove EP),[322] 1864,[111] 1877 (help cr Hounslow St Stephhen EP),[342] 1909,[324] 1965.[95]

HOUNSLOW ST STEPHEN

EP Cr 1877 from Isleworth St John EP, Hounslow EP.[342] RDns as for Hounslow, from 1877. Bdry: 1902,[343] 1909,[324] 1954 (help cr Isleworth St Mary the Virgin EP),[344] 1955.[336]

HOUNSLOW HEATH

EP Cr 1871 from Heston AP.[323] RDns as for Hounslow, from 1871. Bdry: 1909,[324] 1965.[95]

HOXTON

The following have 'Hoxton' in their names. Insofar as any existed at a given time: *Eccl* St

EP1–HOXTON CHRIST CHURCH–Cr 1841 from EP7.[169] Bdry: 1862 (cr EP11).[24] Abol 1953 pt to help cr EP3, pt to help cr EP8.[251]

EP2–HOXTON HOLY TRINITY–Cr 1848 from EP7.[143] Bdry: 1865 (help cr EP9).[279] Abol 1953 to help cr EP3.[251]

EP3–HOXTON HOLY TRINITY WITH ST MARY–Cr 1953 by union EP2, EP9, pt EP1.[251]

EP4–HOXTON ST ANDREW–Cr 1863 from Haggerston St Mary EP, West Hackney St Peter EP.[155] Abol 1953 to help cr EP6.[251]

EP5–HOXTON ST ANNE–Cr 1865 from EP11, EP7.[53] Abol 1953 to help cr EP6.[251]

EP6–HOXTON ST ANNE WITH ST SAVIOUR AND ST ANDREW–Cr 1953 by union EP5, EP11, EP4.[251]

EP7–HOXTON ST JOHN–Cr 1830 from Shoreditch AP.[264] Bdry: 1841 (cr EP1),[169] 1848 (cr EP2, help cr Old Street St Mark EP),[143] 1865 (help cr EP5),[53] 1865 (help cr EP9),[279] 1869 (cr EP10),[335] 1874 (help cr City Road St Clement EP).[93] Abol 1953 to help cr EP8.[251]

EP8–HOXTON ST JOHN THE BAPTIST WITH CHRIST CHURCH–Cr 1953 by union EP7, pt EP1, pt Shoreditch AP.[251]

EP9–HOXTON ST MARY–Cr 1865 from Old Street St Luke EP, King Square EP, EP7, EP2.[279] Abol 1953 to help cr EP3.[251]

EP10–HOXTON ST PETER–Cr 1869 from EP7.[335] Abol 1937 ent to Shoreditch AP.[345]

EP11–HOXTON ST SAVIOUR–Cr 1862 from EP1.[24] Bdry: 1865 (help cr EP5).[53] Abol 1953 to help cr EP6.[251]

ICKENHAM

AP *LG* Elth. Hd, Uxbr. PLU, RSD, RD (1894–1929), UD (1929–38). Civ bdry: 1883,[159] 1934.[4] Abol civ 1938 ent to Uxbridge CP.[298] *Parl* Uxbr. Dv (1885–1948). *Eccl* Seq 9. Eccl bdry: 1934 (help cr Hillingdon All Saints EP).[165]

ISLE OF DOGS CHRIST AND ST JOHN WITH ST LUKE

EP Renaming 1965 of Isle of Dogs Christ Church with St John and St Luke EP.[165] Poplar RDn (1965–66), Tow. Hmlts. RDn (1966–*).

ISLE OF DOGS CHRIST CHURCH WITH ST JOHN AND ST LUKE

EP Cr 1952 by union Poplar Christ Church EP, Cubitt Town EP, Millwall EP.[70] Poplar RDn. Renamed 1965 Isle of Dogs Christ and St John with St Luke.[165]

ISLEWORTH

AP *LG* Islew. Hd, Brentf. PLU, Heston & Islew. USD, UD. Abol civ 1927 to help cr Heston and Isleworth CP.[320] *Parl* Brentf. Dv (1885–1918), Twick. Dv (1918–45). *Eccl* Ealing RDn (1858–1934), Hampton RDn (1934–53), Heston & Islew. RDn (1953–67), Hounslow RDn (1967–*). Eccl bdry: 1856 (help cr Spring Grove EP),[322] 1857 (cr Isleworth St John EP),[149] 1864 (help cr Hounslow EP),[111] 1898 (cr St Margaret's on Thames EP),[50] 1902,[343] 1935 (cr Isleworth St Francis EP).[73]

ISLEWORTH ST FRANCIS

EP Cr 1935 from Isleworth AP.[73] Hampton RDn (1935–53), Heston & Islew. RDn (1953–67), Hounslow RDn (1967–*). Bdry: 1952 (help cr Brentford St Lawrence with St Paul EP).[46]

ISLEWORTH ST JOHN

EP Cr 1857 from Isleworth AP.[149] RDns as for Isleworth AP, from 1858. Bdry: 1877 (help cr Hounslow St Stephen EP),[342] 1902,[343] 1954 (help cr Isleworth St Mary the Virgin EP).[344]

ISLEWORTH ST MARY THE VIRGIN

EP Cr 1954 from Isleworth St John the Baptist EP, Hounslow St Stephen EP.[344] Heston & Islew. RDn (1954–67), Hounslow RDn (1967–*). Bdry: 1955.[336]

ISLINGTON

The following have 'Islington' in their names. Insofar as any existed at a given time: *LG* Ossul. Hd, Isling. Par (poor relief, sep act until 1867, Bd Guardians 1867–89), Vestry (Metrop Bd Wks). Transf 1889 to London.[43] *Parl* Finsb.

Parl Bor (1832–85), from 1885–1918 divided into 3 Dvs (East, West, South) of Finsb. Parl Bor, London thereafter. *Eccl* Isling. RDn.

AP1–ISLINGTON [ST MARY]–Eccl bdry: 1830 (cr Upper Holloway St John EP, Ball's Pond EP, EP2),[63] 1836 (cr EP14),[335] 1839 (cr Portland Place EP, EP16, Lower Holloway EP),[335] 1849 (cr Highbury Christ Church EP),[64] 1858,[324] 1858 (help cr EP15),[249] 1866 (help cr Hornsey Road EP),[185] 1894 (cr EP10),[245] 1895.[44]

EP1–ISLINGTON ALL SAINTS–Cr 1839 from EP2.[24] Bdry: 1844 (help cr EP3),[155] 1868 (help cr Penton Street EP),[346] 1953.[9]

EP2–ISLINGTON HOLY TRINITY, CLOUDESLEY SQUARE–Cr 1830 from AP1.[63] Bdry: 1839 (cr EP1),[335] 1844 (help cr EP3),[155] 1862 (help cr EP19),[347] 1953.[9]

EP3–ISLINGTON ST ANDREW–Cr 1844 from EP2, EP1.[155] Bdry: 1862 (help cr EP19),[347] 1868 (cr EP13),[16] 1881,[99] 1888 (help cr EP12).[20] Abol 1953 to help cr EP4.[9]

EP4–ISLINGTON ST ANDREW WITH ST THOMAS–Cr 1953 by union EP3, pt EP19.[9] Abol 1955 to help cr Barnsbury St Andrew with St Thomas and St Matthias EP.[47]

EP5–ISLINGTON ST BARTHOLOMEW–Cr 1865 from EP16.[214] Abol 1938 to help cr EP17.[123]

EP6–ISLINGTON ST JAMES THE APOSTLE–Cr 1875 from EP15, EP14.[186] Abol 1953 to help cr EP7.[9]

EP7–ISLINGTON ST JAMES - THE - APOSTLE WITH ST PHILIP–Cr 1953 by union EP6, EP15, pt EP17 (the area of former EP5).[9]

EP8–ISLINGTON ST JOHN THE BAPTIST–Cr 1873 from Ball's Pond EP.[41] Bdry: 1953,[9] 1971 (incl help cr Canonbury EP).[116]

EP9–ISLINGTON ST JUDE, MILDMAY PARK–Cr 1856 from Ball's Pond EP.[39]

EP10–ISLINGTON ST MARY MAGDALENE, HOLLOWAY ROAD–Cr 1894 from AP1.[245] Bdry: 1849,[44] 1895.[207] Abol 1953 to help cr Holloway St Mary Magdalene with St James EP.[9]

EP11–ISLINGTON ST MATTHEW–Cr 1851 from Ball's Pond EP.[29] Abol 1953 pt to help cr EP18, pt to EP8.[9]

EP12–ISLINGTON ST MATTHIAS, CALEDONIAN ROAD–Cr 1888 from West Holloway St Luke EP, EP3.[29] Abol 1955 to help cr Barnsbury St Andrew with St Thomas and St Matthias EP.[47]

EP13–ISLINGTON ST MICHAEL–Cr 1856 from EP3.[16] Bdry: 1881.[99]

–ISLINGTON ST PAUL, BALL'S POND–Name sometimes used for Ball's Pond EP, qv.

EP14–ISLINGTON ST PETER–Cr 1836 from AP1.[335] Bdry: 1858,[324] 1875 (help cr EP6),[186] 1952.[123]

EP15–ISLINGTON ST PHILIP–Cr 1858 from AP1, EP16.[249] Bdry: 1875 (help cr EP6).[186] Abol 1953 to help cr EP7.[9]

EP16–ISLINGTON ST STEPHEN–Renaming 1849 of Portland Place EP.[348] Bdry: 1865 (cr EP5),[214] 1893,[42] 1895.[44] Abol 1938 to help cr EP17.[123]

EP17–ISLINGTON ST STEPHEN WITH ST BARTHOLOMEW–Cr 1938 by union EP16, EP5.[123] Abol 1953 pt to help cr EP7, pt to help cr EP18.[9]

EP18–ISLINGTON ST STEPHEN WITH ST BARTHOLOMEW AND ST MATTHEW–Cr 1953 by union pt EP17, pt EP11, pt Ball's Pond EP.[9] Bdry: 1971 (help cr Canonbury EP).[116]

EP19–ISLINGTON ST THOMAS–Cr 1862 from EP3, EP2.[347] Abol 1953 pt to help cr EP4, pt to EP2.[9]

KENSAL GREEN ST JOHN

EP Cr 1845 from Chelsea AP, Kensington AP, Hammersmith EP, Paddington AP, Willesden AP.[125] Padd. RDn (1861–1967), W'minst. (Padd.) RDn (1967–*). Bdry: 1871 (help cr Upper Westbourne Park EP),[338] 1875 (help cr Harlesden All Souls EP),[6] 1877 (help cr Kilburn St Luke the Evangelist EP),[101] 1879 (cr Kensal Green St Jude EP),[349] 1882 (help cr Notting Hill Christ Church EP),[271] 1890 (cr Kensal Town EP),[41] 1901 (cr Kensal Rise EP),[285] 1905 (help cr Brondesbury St Anne EP),[96] 1908 (help cr Brondesbury St Laurence EP),[97] 1915 (help cr Harlesden St Mark EP),[300] 1952,[232] 1953.[302]

KENSAL GREEN ST JUDE

EP Cr 1879 from Kensal Green St John EP.[349] Padd. RDn. Bdry: 1886 (help cr Paddington Emmanuel, Harrow Road EP),[92] 1892,[124] 1899 (help cr Paddington St Simon, Saltram Crescent EP).[283] Abol 1952 pt to help cr West Kilburn St Luke the Evangelist with St Simon and St Jude EP, pt to Kensal Green St John EP, pt to Paddington Emmanuel, Harrow Road EP.[232]

KENSAL RISE

EP Cr 1901 from Kensal Green St John EP.[285] Padd. RDn (1901), Will. RDn (1901–67), Brent RDn (1967–*).

KENSAL TOWN

EP Cr 1890 from Kensal Green St John EP.[41] Padd. RDn (1890–1901), Kens. RDn (1901–51). Abol 1951 to help cr Kensal Town St Thomas with St Andrew and St Philip EP.[74]

KENSAL TOWN ST THOMAS WITH ST ANDREW AND ST PHILIP

EP Cr 1951 by union Kensal Town EP, Upper Westbourne Park EP.[74] Kens. RDn.

KENSINGTON

The following have 'Kensington' in their names. Insofar as any existed at a given time: *LG* Ossul. Hd, Kens. PLU (1837–45), Par (poor law purposes, 1845–89), Vestry (Metrop Bd Wks). Transf 1889 to London.[43] *Parl* Chelsea Parl Bor (1867–85), pt Kens. Parl Bor, North Dv, pt Kens. Parl Bor, South Dv (1885–1918), London thereafter. *Eccl* Kens. RDn.

AP1–KENSINGTON [ST MARY ABBOTS]–Eccl bdry: 1830 (cr Brompton EP),[77] 1842 (cr

EP1),[350] 1845 (help cr Kensal Green St John EP),[125] 1845 (cr Notting Hill St John EP),[29] 1846 (cr Norlands EP),[346] 1858 (help cr EP9),[236] 1865 (help cr Campden Hill EP),[115] 1868 (cr EP15),[93] 1903,[87] 1904 (help cr EP16).[25] Abol eccl 1954 to help cr EP6.[90]

EP1–KENSINGTON ST BARNABAS–Cr 1842 from AP1.[350] Bdry: 1858 (help cr EP9),[236] 1867,[173] 1889 (help cr EP1),[243] 1903.[87]

EP2–KENSINGTON ST CLEMENT–Cr 1867 from Norlands EP, Hammersmith St Stephen EP, Notting Hill St Mary EP.[257] Usually called 'Kensington St Helen' in 20th cent. Bdry: 1875,[39] 1881,[351] 1884 (cr Notting Hill St Clement EP),[380] 1891.[188] Abol 1951 pt to help cr EP4, pt to Notting Hill St Michael and All Angels with Christ Church EP.[74]

EP3–KENSINGTON ST CUTHBERT, EARL'S COURT–Cr 1887 from EP9.[227] Abol 1954 to help cr Earl's Court St Cuthbert with St Matthias EP.[90]

–KENSINGTON ST HELEN–Usual name in 20th cent for par cr 1867 as 'Kensington St Clement', qv as EP2.

EP4–KENSINGTON ST HELEN WITH HOLY TRINITY–Cr 1951 by union Notting Hill Holy Trinity, Latimer Road EP, pt EP2, pt Notting Hill St Mark EP, pt Notting Hill St Michael and All Angels with Christ Church EP.[74]

EP5–KENSINGTON ST JOHN THE BAPTIST, HOLLAND ROAD–Cr 1889 from EP1, Hammersmith St Stephen EP.[243]

EP6–KENSINGTON ST MARY ABBOTS WITH ST GEORGE–Cr 1954 by union AP1, Campden Hill EP.[90]

EP7–KENSINGTON ST MATTHIAS, EARL'S COURT–Cr 1871 from EP8.[271] Bdry: 1872 (help cr EP12).[92] Abol 1954 pt to help cr Earl's Court St Cuthbert with St Matthias EP, pt to EP11.[90]

EP8–KENSINGTON ST PHILIP, EARL'S COURT–Cr 1858 from EP1, AP1.[236] Bdry: 1867,[173] 1871 (cr EP7),[271] 1887 (cr EP3).[227]

EP9–SOUTH KENSINGTON HOLY TRINITY WITH ALL SAINTS–Cr 1955 by union EP15, Knightsbridge All Saints EP.[60]

EP10–SOUTH KENSINGTON ST AUGUSTINE–Cr 1869 from West Brompton EP, Onslow Square EP.[91] Bdry: 1954.[90]

EP11–SOUTH KENSINGTON ST JUDE–Cr 1872 from EP14, West Brompton EP, EP7.[92] Kens. RDn (1872–1967), Chelsea RDn (1967–*). Bdry: 1954.[90]

EP12–SOUTH KENSINGTON ST LUKE–Cr 1874 from West Brompton EP.[93] RDns as for EP11, from 1874.

EP13–SOUTH KENSINGTON ST PETER–Cr 1867 from West Brompton EP.[36] Kens. RDn (1867–1967), Chelsea RDn (1967–73). Abol 1973 to help cr West Brompton St Mary with St Peter EP.[94]

EP14–SOUTH KENSINGTON ST STEPHEN–Cr 1868 from AP1.[93] Bdry: 1872 (help cr EP11),[92] 1954.[90]

EP15–KENSINGTON GORE–Cr 1904 from AP1, Knightsbridge All Saints EP.[25] Bdry: 1954.[90] Abol 1955 to help cr EP9.[60]

KENTISH TOWN

The following have 'Kentish Town' in their names. Insofar as any existed at a given time: *Eccl* St Panc. RDn (1858–1967), S Camd. (Holb. & St. Panc.) RDn (1967–*).

EP1–KENTISH TOWN [ST JOHN THE BAPTIST]–Cr 1863 from St Pancras AP.[111] Bdry: [while still chap] 1853 (help cr Highgate Rise EP),[123] 1859 (help cr Chelsea Christ Church EP),[128] 1862 (help cr Agar Town EP)[24]; [when sep par] 1864 (help cr EP4),[80] 1865 (help cr Haverstock Hill EP),[120] 1877 (help cr Brookfield EP),[101] 1880 (help cr EP2),[149] 1881 (cr EP3),[352] 1909.[145]

EP2–KENTISH TOWN ST BARNABAS–Cr 1880 from EP1, EP7, Haverstock Hill EP.[149] Bdry: 1884.[149] Abol 1957 to help cr Haverstock Hill Holy Trinity with Kentish Town St Barnabas EP.[314]

EP3–KENTISH TOWN ST BENET AND ALL SAINTS–Cr 1881 from EP1.[352] Bdry: 1909.[145]

EP4–KENTISH TOWN ST MARTIN–Cr 1864 from EP1, Haverstock Hill Holy Trinity EP.[80] Bdry: 1894 (help cr North St Pancras EP).[245] Abol 1953 to help cr EP5.[35]

EP5–KENTISH TOWN ST MARTIN WITH ST ANDREW–Cr 1953 by union EP4, pt Haverstock Hill St Andrew EP.[35]

EP6–KENTISH TOWN ST SILAS–Cr 1912 from Haverstock Hill St Andrew EP, Haverstock Hill Holy Trinity EP.[313] Bdry: 1953.[35]

EP7–NEW KENTISH TOWN–Cr 1869 from EP1, Camden Town St Paul EP, Haverstock Hill Holy Trinity EP.[114] Bdry: 1880,[149] 1884.[149] Abol 1956 to help cr Camden Square St Luke Oseney Crescent with St Paul EP.[110]

KENTON

EP Cr 1935 from Harrow on the Hill AP, Great Stanmore AP, Harrow Weald EP, Greenhill EP, Wembley Park EP.[131] Harrow RDn. Bdry: 1957 (help cr Preston EP).[353]

KILBURN

The following have 'Kilburn' in their names. The organisation in RDns differs and is sep noted.

EP1–KILBURN HOLY TRINITY–Cr 1867 from Willesden AP.[95] Harrow RDn (1867–1901), Will. RDn (1901–55). Bdry: 1872 (cr EP4),[354] 1877 (help cr EP5),[101] 1897 (help cr EP7),[338] 1905 (help cr Brondesbury St Anne EP),[96] 1935.[355] Abol 1955 to help cr Brondesbury St Anne with Kilburn Holy Trinity EP.[99]

EP2–KILBURN ST AUGUSTINE–Cr 1870 from EP6, St Marylebone St Mark EP, Paddington St Saviour EP.[19] Padd. RDn (1870–1967),

W'minst. (Padd.) RDn (1967–72). Abol 1972 to help cr EP3.[100]

EP3–KILBURN ST AUGUSTINE WITH ST JOHN–Cr 1972 by union EP2, pt EP4, pt Brondesbury St Anne with Kilburn Holy Trinity EP, pt Paddington St Saviour EP.[100] W'minst. (Padd.) RDn.

EP4–KILBURN ST JOHN THE EVANGELIST–Cr 1872 from EP1.[354] Harrow RDn (1872–1901), Will. RDn (1901–67), Brent RDn (1967–72). Bdry: 1892.[124] Abol 1972 pt to help cr EP3, pt to EP8, pt to Paddington St Saviour EP.[100]

EP5–KILBURN ST LUKE THE EVANGELIST–Cr 1877 from Kelsal Green St John, EP1.[101] Padd. RDn. Bdry: 1892.[124] Abol 1952 to help cr EP8.[302]

EP6–KILBURN ST MARY–Cr 1868 from Hampstead EP.[277] Enf. RDn (1868–75), Highg. RDn (1875–1901), Hampst. RDn (1901–67), N Camd. (Hampst.) RDn (1967–*). Bdry: [when still chap] 1865 (help cr Hampstead All Souls EP)[281]; [when sep par] 1870 (help cr EP2),[19] 1873 (help cr West Hampstead The Trinity EP),[278] 1888 (cr West Hampstead St James EP),[33] 1897 (help cr EP7),[338] 1935.[355]

EP7–KILBURN ST PAUL–Cr 1897 from EP1, EP6.[338] Harrow RDn (1897–1901), Will. RDn (1901–35). Abol 1935 pt to EP1, pt to EP6.[355]

EP8–WEST KILBURN ST LUKE THE EVANGELIST WITH ST SIMON AND ST JUDE–Cr 1952 by union EP5, pt Paddington St Simon, Saltram Crescent EP, pt Kensal Green St Jude EP.[302] Padd. RDn (1952–67), W'minst. (Padd.) RDn (1967–*). Bdry: 1972.[100]

KING SQUARE

EP Cr 1842 from Old Street St Luke EP.[356] Pec jurisd Dean & Chapter of St Paul's, London (1842–45), St Sepulchre RDn (1858–1901), Finsb. RDn (1901–34), Finsb. & Holb. RDn (1934–52). Bdry: 1848 (cr City Road St Matthew EP),[143] 1865 (help cr Hoxton St Barnabas EP),[279] 1865 (help cr Clerkenwell St Paul EP),[100] 1874 (help cr City Road St Clement EP).[93] Abol 1952 pt to help cr Finsbury St Clement with St Barnabas and St Matthew EP, pt to help cr Old Street St Luke with Charterhouse St Mary and Clerkenwell St Paul EP.[123]

KING'S CROSS

EP Cr 1849 from St Pancras AP.[20] St Panc. RDn. Abol 1868 to help cr Somers Town Christ Church EP.[63]

KINGSBURY

AP Edgware sometimes described as chap in this par (as Donative from 1685, sep status sustained[190]). *LG* Gore Hd, Hendon PLU, RSD, Wembley UD (1894–1900), Kingsbury UD (1900–34). Abol civ 1934 pt to help cr Harrow CP, pt to Wembley CP, pt to Willesden AP.[4] *Parl* Harrow Dv (1885–1918), Hendon Dv (1918–45). *Eccl* Harrow RDn (1861–1901), Will. RDn (1901–14), Harrow RDn (1914–34), Hendon RDn (1934–67), Brent RDn (1967–*). Eccl bdry: 1885 (help cr Neasden cum Kinsbury EP).[249]

KINGSBURY ST ANDREW

EP Cr 1932 from Neasden cum Kingsbury EP.[44] RDns as for Kingsbury, from 1932.

KINGSWAY HOLY TRINITY WITH DRURY LANE ST JOHN

EP Cr 1938 by union Drury Lane EP, Lincoln's Inn Fields EP.[99] Finsb. & Holb. RDn (1938–67), W'minst. (St Mgt.'s) RDn (1967–*). Bdry: 1952.[70]

KNIGHTSBRIDGE ALL SAINTS

EP Cr 1849 from Westminster St Margaret EP.[186] St Geo. Hanov. Sq. RDn (1861–1901), W'minst. RDn (1901–55). Bdry: 1866 (help cr Knightsbridge Holy Trinity EP),[149] 1904 (help cr Kensington Gore EP),[25] 1953.[89] Abol 1955 to help cr South Kensington Holy Trinity with All Saints EP.[60]

KNIGHTSBRIDGE HOLY TRINITY

EP Cr 1866 from Wilton Place EP, Knightsbridge All Saints EP.[149] St Mgt. W'minst. RDn (1866–83), St Mgt. & St John W'minst. RDn (1883–1901), W'minst. RDn (1901–60s), Chelsea RDn (1960s–*).

LALEHAM

Chap in Staines AP, sep civ identity by 1491,[30] sometimes sep eccl status,[30] sep EP 1859.[31] *LG* Spelth. Hd, Staines PLU, RSD, RD (1894–1930), UD (1930–65). Civ bdry: 1934.[4] Transf 1965 to Surrey.[1] *Parl* Seq 1. *Eccl* Seq 7. Eccl bdry: 1951 (help cr Staines Christ Church EP).[357]

LIBERTY OF THE ROLLS

Lbty, the Middx pt of St Dunstan in the West AP (otherwise City of London), sep CP 1866 in Middx,[203] so that the mother par ent City of London thereafter. *LG* Ossul. Hd, Strand Dist (Metrop Bd Wks). Transf 1889 to London.[43] *Parl* Finsb. Parl Bor (1867–85), Finsb. Parl Bor, Holb. Dv (1885–1918), London thereafter.

LIBERTY OF SAFFRON HILL, HATTON GARDEN, ELY RENTS AND ELY PLACE

Lbty, sep CP 1866.[203] *LG* Ossul. Hd, Holb. PLU, Dist (Metrop Bd Wks). Transf 1889 to London.[43] *Parl* Finsb. Parl Bor (1867–85), Finsb. Parl Bor, Holb. Dv (1885–1918), London thereafter.

LIMEHOUSE

The following have 'Limehouse' in their names. Insofar as any existed at a given time: *LG* Ossul. Hd, Stepney PLU, Limehouse Dist (Metrop Bd Wks). Transf 1889 to London.[43] *Parl* Tow. Hmlts. Parl Bor (1832–85), Tow. Hmlts. Parl Bor, Limehouse Dv (1885–1918), London thereafter. *Eccl* Stepney RDn (1861–1966), Tow. Hmlts. RDn (1966–*).

CP/EP1–LIMEHOUSE [ST ANNE]–Dist in Stepney AP, sep par 1725.[358] Eccl bdry: 1840 (help cr Ratcliffe EP),[337] 1853 (cr EP3),[136] 1858 (help cr Stepney St Paul EP),[83] 1872 (help cr Stepney St Matthew EP),[92] 1887 (help cr EP4),[59] 1951,[74] 1956.[359] Abol eccl 1971 to help cr EP2.[360]

EP2–LIMEHOUSE ST ANNE WITH ST PETER–Cr 1971 by union EP1, EP4.[360]

EP3–LIMEHOUSE ST JOHN THE EVANGELIST–Cr 1853 from EP1.[136] Bdry: 1872 (help cr Stepney St Matthew EP).[92] Abol 1951 to help cr EP5.[74]

EP4–LIMEHOUSE ST PETER–Cr 1887 from EP1, Poplar EP.[59] Step. RDn (1887–1952), Poplar RDn (1952–71). Bdry: 1951.[74] Abol 1971 to help cr EP2.[360]

EP5–LIMEHOUSE FIELDS ST JOHN WITH ST MATTHEW–Cr 1951 by union EP3, Stepney St Matthew EP, pt Stepney St Dunstan EP.[74] Abol 1956 pt to help cr Stepney St Dunstan with All Saints EP, pt to EP1.[359]

LINCOLN'S INN

Ex-par place, sep CP 1858.[361] *LG* Ossul. Hd, not in a PLU. Transf 1889 to London.[43] *Parl* Finsb. Parl Bor (1832–85), Finsb. Parl Bor, Holb. Dv (1885–1918), London thereafter.

LINCOLN'S INN FIELDS

EP Cr 1884 from St Giles in the Fields AP.[167] St Geo. Bloomsb. RDn (1884–97), St Martin in the Fields RDn (1897–1901), Holb. RDn (1901–34), Finsb. & Holb. RDn (1934–38). Abol 1938 to help cr Kingsway Holy Trinity with Drury Lane St John EP.[99]

LISSON GROVE

EP Cr 1838 from St Marylebone AP.[369] St Marylb. RDn. Abol 1952 pt to help cr Lisson Grove St Paul with St Matthew and Emmanuel EP, pt to St Marylebone St Cyprian EP.[232]

LISSON GROVE ST PAUL WITH ST MARYLEBONE ST MATTHEW AND EMMANUEL

EP Cr 1952 by union of pts of Lisson Grove EP, St Marylebone St Matthew EP, Maida Hill EP, St Marylebone Christ Church EP.[232] St Marylb. RDn (1952–67), W'minst. (St Marylb.) RDn (1967–71). Abol 1971 to help cr St Marylebone Christ Church and St Paul EP.[362]

LITTLETON

AP *LG* Spelth. Hd, Staines PLU, RSD, RD (1894–1930), Sunbury on Thames UD (1930–65). Civ bdry: 1934.[4] Transf 1965 to Surrey.[1] *Parl* Seq 1. *Eccl* Seq 5. Eccl bdry: 1949.[32]

LONDON DOCKS

EP Cr 1867 from St George in the East AP, Shadwell EP.[363] Step. RDn. Abol 1951 to help cr London Docks St Peter with Wapping St John EP.[74]

LONDON DOCKS ST PETER WITH WAPPING ST JOHN

EP Cr 1951 by union London Docks EP, Wapping EP, pt St George in the East St George EP, Whitechapel St Paul with St Mark EP, pt ex-par Precinct of St Katherine.[74] Step. RDn (1951–67), Tow. Hmlts. RDn (1967–*).

MAIDA HILL

EP Cr 1876 from St Marylebone Christ Church EP, Portland Town EP, Paddington St Saviour EP.[51] St Marylb. RD. Abol 1952 pt to help cr Lisson Grove St Paul with St Marylebone St Matthew and Emmanuel EP, pt to Portland Town EP.[232]

GREAT MARLBOROUGH STREET

EP Cr 1865 from Westminster St James AP, Westminster St Luke EP.[120] St Martin in the Fields RDn (1865–1901), W'minst. RDn (1901–37). Bdry: 1885.[64] Abol 1937 ent to Regent Street EP.[364]

MARYLEBONE ROAD

EP Cr 1872 from St Marylebone St Mary EP, St Marylebone St Luke, Nutford Place EP.[243] St Marylb. RDn. Abol 1952 to help cr St Marylebone St Mark with St Luke EP.[243]

MARYLEBONE ST PETER WITH ST THOMAS

EP Cr 1930 by union Portman Square EP, pt St Marylebone All Souls EP.[365] St Marylb. RDn. Abol 1952 to help cr St Marylebone All Souls with St Peter and St John EP.[232]

MAYFAIR

EP Cr 1865 from St George Hanover Square EP.[120] St Geo. Hanov. Sq. RDn (1865–1901), W'minst. RDn (1901–67), W'minst. (St Mgt.'s) RDn (1967–*).

MILE END NEW TOWN

Hmlt in Stepney AP, sep EP 1841 as 'Mile End New Town All Saints', qv,[173] sep CP 1866.[203] *LG* Ossul. Hd, Whitech. PLU, Dist (Metrop Bd Wks). Transf 1889 to London.[43] *Parl* Tow. Hmlts. Parl Bor (1867–85), Tow. Hmlts. Parl Bor, Whitech. Dv (1885–1918), London thereafter.

MILE END NEW TOWN ALL SAINTS

EP Cr 1841 from Stepney AP[173]; for civ see prev entry. Pec jurisd Bp London (1841–45), Step. RDn (1861–1914). Bdry: 1875 (cr Mile End New Town St Olave EP).[366] Abol 1914 to help cr Mile End New Town All Saints with St Olave EP.[367]

MILE END NEW TOWN ALL SAINTS WITH ST OLAVE

EP Cr 1914 by union Mile End New Town All Saints EP, Mile End New Town St Olave EP.[367] Step. RDn. Abol 1951 to help cr Spitalfields Christ Church with All Saints EP.[74]

MILE END NEW TOWN ST OLAVE

EP Cr 1875 from Mile End New Town All Saints EP.[366] Step. RDn. Abol 1914 to help cr Mile End New Town All Saints with St Olave EP.[367]

MILE END OLD TOWN

Hmlt in Stepney AP, sep EP 1841 as 'Mile End Old Town Holy Trinity', qv,[173] sep EP 1866.[203] *LG* Ossul. Hd, Step. PLU (1836–57), Hmlt of Mile End Old Town (poor law purposes, 1857–89), Mile End Old Town Vestry (Metrop Bd Wks). Transf 1889 to London.[43] *Parl* Tow. Hmlts. Parl Bor (1867–85), pt Tow. Hmlts. Parl Bor, Mile End Dv, pt Tow. Hmlts. Parl Bor, Step. Dv (1885–1918), London thereafter.

MILE END OLD TOWN HOLY TRINITY

EP Cr 1841 from Stepney AP[173]; for civ see prev

entry. Pec jurisd Bp London (1841–45), Step. RDn (1861–1966), Tow. Hmlts. RDn (1966–*). Bdry: 1858 (help cr Stepney St Paul EP),[83] 1870 (help cr Stepney St Benet EP),[368] 1870 (help cr Mile End Old Town St Luke EP).[95]

MILE END OLD TOWN ST LUKE

EP Cr 1870 from Stepney St Paul EP, Mile End Old Town Holy Trinity EP.[95] Step. RDn. Abol 1951 pt to help cr Bow Common St Paul with St Luke EP, pt to Mile End Old Town Holy Trinity EP, pt to Whitechapel St Paul with St Mark EP.[74]

MILL HILL JOHN KEBLE CHURCH

EP Cr 1937 from Mill Hill St Michael and All Angels EP, Hendon St Alphage EP, Mill Hill St Paul EP.[95] Hendon RDn (1937–67), W Barnet RDn (1967–*).

MILL HILL ST MICHAEL AND ALL ANGELS

EP Cr 1926 from Mill Hill St Paul EP.[185] Hampst. RDn (1924–34), Hendon RDn (1934–67), W Barnet RDn (1967–*). Bdry: 1937 (help cr Mill Hill John Keble Church EP).[95]

MILL HILL ST PAUL

EP Cr 1833 from Hendon AP.[370] Sometimes 'Hendon St Paul, Mill Hill'. Harrow RDn (1858–1901), Hampst. RDn (1901–34), Hendon RDn (1934–67), W Barnet RDn (1967–*). Bdry: 1924 (help cr Hendon St Alphage EP),[199] 1926 (cr Mill Hill St Michael and All Angels EP),[185] 1937 (help cr Mill Hill John Keble Church EP),[95] 1951.[184]

MILLWALL

EP Cr 1870 from Poplar Christ Church EP.[60] Step. RDn (1870–1901), Poplar RDn (1901–52). Abol 1952 to help cr Isle of Dogs Christ Church with St John and St Luke EP.[70]

SOUTH MIMMS

AP Usual civ spelling; for eccl see 'South Mymms'. Pt Middx (Edm. Hd), pt Herts (Cashio Hd). *LG* Barnet PLU, pt S Mimms RSD, pt Barnet RSD (1875–88), pt E Barnet Valley USD (1888–94), pt Barnet USD (the last 3 pts in Herts), S Mimms RD (1894–1934), Potter's Bar UD (1934–65). Civ bdry: 1781,[377] 1889,[371] 1894 (loses the pt in Barnet USD to cr South Mimms Urban CP to be in Herts, loses the pt in E Barnet Valley USD to Monken Hadley AP, Herts),[210] [par thus ent Middx 1894–1965], 1896 (loses pt to South Mimms Urban CP, Herts),[377] 1924,[209] 1926 (exchanges pts with Ridge AP, Herts).[316] Transf 1965 to Herts.[1] *Parl* Enf. Dv (1885–1948), Enf. West BC (1948–70), Herts thereafter. Parl bdry: 1945.[202]

MUNSTER SQUARE

EP Renaming 1868 of St Pancras St Mary Magdalene EP.[372] St Panc. RDn (1868–1967), S Camd. (Holb. & St Panc.) RDn (1967–*). Bdry: 1925,[231] 1954.[25]

MUSWELL HILL ST JAMES

EP Cr 1843 from Hornsey AP.[141] Enf. RDn (1858–75), Highg. RDn (1875–1901), Hornsey RDn (1901–67), W Haringey RDn (1967–*). Bdry: 1874 (help cr Highgate All Saints EP),[326] 1890,[41] 1900 (help cr East Finchley EP),[20] 1939 (cr Muswell Hill St Matthew EP).[242]

MUSWELL HILL ST MATTHEW

EP Cr 1939 from Muswell Hill St James EP.[242] Hornsey RDn (1939–67), W Haringey RDn (1967–*).

SOUTH MYMMS

AP Usual eccl spelling; for civ see 'South Mimms'. *Eccl* Seq 3. Eccl bdry: 1835 (cr Potter's Bar EP),[128] 1848 (cr South Mymms Christ Church EP),[379] 1949,[371] 1949 (help cr South Mymms King Charles the Martyr EP).[32]

SOUTH MYMMS CHRIST CHURCH

EP Cr 1848 from South Mymms AP.[379] Enf. RDn (1858–1901), Hornsey RDn (1901–67), Central Barnet RDn (1967–*).

SOUTH MYMMS KING CHARLES THE MARTYR

EP Cr 1949 from South Mymms AP, Potter's Bar EP.[32] Hornsey RDn (1949–67), Central Barnet RDn (1967–*).

SOUTH MYMMS ST MARY THE VIRGIN AND ALL SAINTS–See POTTER'S BAR

NEASDEN CUM KINGSBURY

EP Cr 1885 from Kingsbury AP, Willesden AP.[249] Harrow RDn (1885–1901), Will. RDn (1901–67), Brent RDn (1967–*). Bdry: 1932 (cr Kingsbury St Andrew EP),[44] 1939 (cr Dollis Hill EP).[175]

NOEL PARK

EP Cr 1889 from Wood Green EP.[47] Enf. RDn (1889–1901), Tott. RDn (1901–67), W Haringey RDn (1967–*). Bdry: 1898 (help cr Hornsey St Peter EP),[292] 1912 (help cr Tottenham St Benet Fink EP).[313]

NORLANDS

EP Cr 1846 from Kensington AP.[346] Kens. RDn. Bdry: 1867 (help cr Kensington St Clement EP),[257] 1875.[39]

NORTHOLT

AP *LG* Elth. Hd, Uxbr. PLU, RSD, RD. Civ bdry: before 1871,[253] 1883,[159] 1887.[254] Abol civ 1928 pt to Ealing AP, pt to Harrow on the Hill AP.[180] *Parl* Uxbr. Dv (1885–1948). *Eccl* Pec jurisd Bp London (until 1845), Ealing RDn (1858–1914), Harrow RDn (1914–48), Ealing RDn (1948–67), Ealing West RDn (1967–*). Eccl bdry: 1954,[204] 1954 (help cr Northolt Park EP),[373] 1964,[106] 1964 (help cr Southall Christ the Redeemer EP).[255]

NORTHOLT PARK

EP Cr 1954 from Sudbury St Andrew EP, Greenford AP, Northolt AP.[373] Ealing RDn (1954–67), Ealing West RDn (1967–*).

NORTHWOOD

EP Cr 1854 from Ruislip AP, Watford AP (Herts), Rickmansworth AP (Herts).[374] Uxbr. RDn (1858–1901), Will. RDn (1901–14), Harrow RDn (1914–*). Bdry: 1909 (cr Northwood Emmanuel EP).[354]

NORTHWOOD EMMANUEL

EP Cr 1909 from Northwood EP.[354] Will. RDn (1909–14), Harrow RDn (1914–*). Bdry: 1952 (help cr Northwood Hills EP).[189]

NORTHWOOD HILLS

EP Cr 1952 from Pinner EP, Eastcote EP, Northwood Emmanuel EP.[189] Harrow RDn.

NORTON FOLGATE

Ex-par lbty, sep CP 1858,[118] eccl abol 1911 to help cr Spitalfields Christ Church with St Mary and St Stephen EP.[430] *LG* Ossul. Hd, Whitech. PLU, Dist (Metrop Bd Wks). Transf 1889 to London.[43] *Parl* Tow. Hmlts. Parl Bor (1867–85), Tow. Hmlts. Parl Bor, Whitech. Dv (1885–1918), London thereafter.

NORWOOD

Chap in Hayes AP, *de facto* sep civ from middle ages,[331] sep EP 1725.[332] *LG* Elth. Hd, Uxbr. PLU, RSD (1875–91), Norwood USD (1891–94), Southall Norwood UD (1894–1936), Southall MB (1936–65). Civ bdry: 1894,[321] 1934.[4] Transf 1965 to Gtr London (Ealing LB).[1] *Parl* Brentf. Dv (1885–1918), Uxbr. Dv (1918–45), Southall BC (1945–70), Gtr London thereafter. *Eccl* Pec jurisd Archbp Canterb (1725–1845), Seq 1 thereafter. Eccl bdry: 1850 (cr Southall Green EP),[375] 1880.[376]

NOTTING HILL

The following have 'Notting Hill' in their names. Insofar as any existed at a given time: *Eccl* Kens. RDn.

EP1–NOTTING HILL ALL SAINTS–Cr 1861 from EP8.[338] Bdry: 1871 (cr EP10),[295] 1871 (help cr Upper Westbourne Park EP),[338] 1882 (help cr EP3),[271] 1902 (cr EP7).[68] Abol 1951 to help cr EP2.[74]

EP2–NOTTING HILL ALL SAINTS WITH ST COLUMB–Cr 1951 by union EP1, EP7.[74]

EP3–NOTTING HILL CHRIST CHURCH–Cr 1882 from EP1, Kensal Green St John EP, Upper Westbourne Park EP, Paddington St Luke EP.[271] Abol 1940 pt to EP11, pt to EP7.[49]

EP4–NOTTING HILL HOLY TRINITY, LATIMER ROAD–Cr 1885 from EP5.[380] Abol 1951 to help cr Kensington St Helen with Holy Trinity EP.[74]

EP5–NOTTING HILL ST CLEMENT–Cr 1884 from Kensington St Clement EP.[380] Bdry: 1885 (cr EP4),[380] 1951.[74] Abol 1972 to help cr EP6.[381]

EP6–NOTTING HILL ST CLEMENT AND ST MARK–Cr 1972 by union EP5, EP9.[381]

EP7–NOTTING HILL ST COLUMB–Cr 1902 from EP1.[68] Bdry: 1940.[49] Abol 1951 pt to help cr EP2, pt to EP11.[74]

EP8–NOTTING HILL ST JOHN–Cr 1845 from Kensington AP.[29] Bdry: 1857 (cr EP12),[382] 1861 (cr EP1),[338] 1864 (cr EP9),[39] 1865 (help cr Campden Hill EP).[115]

EP9–NOTTING HILL ST MARK–Cr 1864 from EP8.[39] Bdry: 1867 (help cr Kensington St Clement EP),[257] 1881,[351] 1890,[383] 1891,[188] 1951 (incl help cr Kensington St Helen with Holy Trinity EP).[74] Abol 1972 to help cr EP6.[381]

EP10–NOTTING HILL ST MICHAEL AND ALL ANGELS–Cr 1871 from EP1.[295] Bdry: 1890.[383] Abol 1940 pt to help cr EP11, pt to EP7.[49]

EP11–NOTTING HILL ST MICHAEL AND ALL ANGELS WITH CHRIST CHURCH–Cr 1940 by union EP10, EP3.[49] Bdry: 1951 (incl help cr Kensington St Helen with Holy Trinity EP).[74]

EP12–NOTTING HILL ST PETER–Cr 1857 from EP8.[382]

OAKLEY SQUARE–See BEDFORD NEW TOWN

OAKWOOD

EP Cr 1941 from Winchmore Hill EP, Enfield AP.[214] Enf. RDn.

OLD ARTILLERY GROUND

Lbty, sep CP 1866.[384] *LG* Ossul. Hd, Whitech. PLU, Dist (Metrop Bd Wks). Transf 1889 to London.[43] *Parl* Tow. Hmlts. Parl Bor (1867–85), Tow. Hmlts. Parl Bor, Whitech. Dv (1885–1918), London thereafter.

OLD STREET ST LUKE

Usual eccl name of par cr 1733 from St Giles Cripplegate AP[385]; for civ see 'St Luke'. *Eccl* Pec jurisd Dean & Chapter of St Paul's, London (1733–1845), St Sepulchre RDn (1861–1901), Finsb. RDn (1901–34), Finsb. & Holb. RDn (1934–52). Eccl bdry: 1842 (cr King Square EP, Finsbury St Paul EP),[229] 1843 (help cr Aldersgate Street EP),[26] 1848 (help cr Old Street St Mark EP),[143] 1865 (help cr Hoxton St Mary EP),[279] 1865 (help cr Clerkenwell St Paul EP),[100] 1874 (help cr City Road St Clement EP),[93] 1883,[142] 1919.[390] Abol eccl 1952 to help cr Old Street St Luke with Charterhouse St Mary and Clerkenwell St Paul EP.[123]

OLD STREET ST LUKE WITH CHARTERHOUSE ST MARY AND CLERKENWELL ST PAUL

EP Cr 1952 by union Old Street St Luke EP, Charterhouse St Mary with Finsbury St Paul EP, Clerkenwell St Paul EP, pt King Square EP, pt City Road St Clement EP.[123] Finsb. & Holb. RDn. Abol 1966 pt to Finsbury St Clement with St Barnabas and St Matthew EP, pt to help cr St Giles Cripplegate with St Bartholomew Moor Lane, St Alphage London Wall and St Luke Old Street with St Mary Charterhouse and St Paul Clerkenwell EP.[80]

OLD STREET ST MARK

EP Cr 1848 from Old Street St Luke EP, Shoreditch AP, Hoxton St John EP.[143] St Sepulchre RDn (1861–70), Shored. RDn (1870–1937). Bdry: 1874 (help cr City Road St Clement EP).[93] Abol 1937 pt to Shoreditch AP, pt to Shoreditch St Michael EP.[345]

ONSLOW SQUARE

EP Cr 1861 from Brompton EP.[88] Kens. RDn (1861–1967), Chelsea RDn (1967–*). Bdry: 1869 (help cr South Kensington St Augustine EP),[91] 1954.[90]

PADDINGTON

The following have 'Paddington' in their names. Insofar as any existed at a given time: *LG* Ossul.

Hd, Padd. Par (poor law purposes), Vestry (Metrop Bd Wks). Transf 1889 to London.[43] *Parl* Marylebone Parl Bor (1832–85), pt Padd. Parl Bor, North Dv, pt Padd. Parl Bor, South Dv (1885–1918), London thereafter. *Eccl* Pec jurisd Bp London (until 1845), Padd. RDn (1861–1967), W'minst. (Padd.) RDn (1967–*).

AP1–PADDINGTON [ST JAMES]–Eccl bdry: 1834 (cr EP6),[386] 1845 (cr EP9),[387] 1845 (cr Kensal Green St John EP),[125] 1846 (cr EP4),[221] 1848 (cr EP1),[388] 1856 (cr EP2),[68] 1856 (cr EP15, EP17),[175] 1858 (cr Bayswater EP),[48] 1861,[285] 1919,[390] 1965.[389]

EP1–PADDINGTON ALL SAINTS–Cr 1848 from AP1.[388] Abol 1919 pt to AP1, pt to help cr EP12.[390]

EP2–PADDINGTON CHRIST CHURCH–Cr 1856 from AP1.[68] Bdry: 1861.[285]

EP3–PADDINGTON EMMANUEL, HARROW ROAD–Cr 1886 from Kensal Green St Jude EP, EP14.[92] Bdry: 1952.[302]

EP4–PADDINGTON HOLY TRINITY–Cr 1846 from AP1.[221] Bdry: 1861,[49] 1864 (help cr EP10),[24] 1871 (cr EP14, help cr Upper Westbourne Park EP),[108] 1874 (cr EP13).[181] Abol 1952 pt to help cr EP5, pt to EP10.[302]

EP5–PADDINGTON HOLY TRINITY WITH ST PAUL–Cr 1952 by union EP4, EP13.[302]

EP6–PADDINGTON ST JOHN–Cr 1834 from AP1.[386] Bdry: 1844,[391] 1860 (cr EP11),[236] 1899 (help cr EP15).[283] Abol 1965 to help cr EP7.[389]

EP7–PADDINGTON ST JOHN WITH ST MICHAEL AND ALL ANGELS–Cr 1965 by union EP6, pt EP11.[389]

EP8–PADDINGTON ST LUKE–Cr 1868 from EP16.[188] Bdry: 1882 (help cr Notting Hill Christ Church EP).[271] Abol 1952 to help cr EP18.[302]

EP9–PADDINGTON ST MARY–Cr 1845 from AP1.[387]

EP10–PADDINGTON ST MARY MAGDALENE–Cr 1864 from EP4, EP15.[24] Bdry: 1952.[302]

EP11–PADDINGTON ST MICHAEL AND ALL ANGELS–Cr 1860, refounded 1864 from EP6.[236] Abol 1919 to help cr EP12.[390]

EP12–PADDINGTON ST MICHAEL AND ALL ANGELS WITH ALL SAINTS–Cr 1919 by union EP1, EP11.[390] Abol 1965 pt to help cr EP7, pt to AP1.[389]

EP13–PADDINGTON ST PAUL–Cr 1874 from EP4.[181] Abol 1952 pt to help cr EP5, pt to EP10.[302]

EP14–PADDINGTON ST PETER–Cr 1871 from EP4.[108] Bdry: 1886 (help cr EP3),[92] 1952.[302]

EP15–PADDINGTON ST SAVIOUR–Cr 1856 from AP1.[175] Bdry: 1864 (help cr EP10),[24] 1869,[392] 1870 (help cr Kilburn St Augustine EP),[19] 1876 (help cr Maida Hill EP),[51] 1972 (incl help cr Kilburn St Augustine with St John EP).[100]

EP16–PADDINGTON ST SIMON, SALTRAM CRESCENT–Cr 1899 from Kensal Green St Jude EP, EP6.[283] Abol 1952 pt to help cr West Kilburn St Luke the Evangelist with St Simon and St Jude EP, pt to EP14.[302]

EP17–PADDINGTON ST STEPHEN–Cr 1856 from AP1.[175] Bdry: 1868 (cr EP8).[188] Abol 1952 to help cr EP18.[302]

EP18–PADDINGTON ST STEPHEN WITH ST LUKE–Cr 1952 by union EP17, EP8.302

EP18–PADDINGTON ST STEPHEN WITH ST LUKE–Cr 1952 by union EP17, EP8.[302]

PALMER'S GREEN

EP Cr 1906 from Southgate EP, Winchmore Hill EP.[393] Enf. RDn. Bdry: 1953.[141]

PELL STREET

EP Cr 1860 from St George in the East AP.[279] Step. RDn. Bdry: 1870.[60] Abol 1890 ent to St George in the East AP.[394]

PENTON STREET

EP Cr 1868 from Pentonville EP, Islington All Saints EP.[346] Isling. RDn. Orig dedication 'St Silas'; renamed 1961 'Penton Street St Giles with All Saints'.[395]

PENTONVILLE

EP Cr 1862 from Clerkenwell AP.[396] St Sepulchre RDn (1862–1901), Finsb. RDn (1901–34), Finsb. & Holb. RDn (1934–67), Isling. RDn (1967–*). Bdry: 1868 (help cr Penton Street EP).[346]

PERIVALE

AP Sometimes anc 'Little Greenford'. *LG* Elth. Hd, Brentf. PLU, RSD, Greenford UD. Abol civ 1926 ent to Ealing AP.[178] *Parl* Ealing Dv (1885–1918), Harrow Dv (1918–45). *Eccl* Seq 1.

PIMLICO

The following have 'Pimlico' in their names. Insofar as any existed at a given time: *Eccl* St Geo. Hanov. Sq. RDn (1861–1901), W'minst. RDn (1901–67), W'minst. (St Mgt.'s) RDn (1967–*).

EP1–PIMLICO ST BARNABAS–Cr 1866 from Wilton Place EP.[186] Bdry: 1936,[142] 1951.[12]

EP2–PIMLICO ST GABRIEL–Cr 1853 from EP4.[216] Bdry: 1864 (cr EP6),[21] 1936,[142] 1953,[89] 1973.[397]

EP3–PIMLICO ST MARY, GRAHAM STREET–Cr 1909 from Wilton Place EP.[107] Bdry: 1936.[142]

EP4–PIMLICO ST PETER–Cr 1830 from St George Hanover Square EP.[185] Bdry: 1843 (cr Wilton Place EP),[58] 1846 (cr Chester Square EP),[133] 1853 (cr EP2).[216] Abol 1953 pt to help cr Chester Square St Michael with St Philip EP, pt to help cr EP5, pt to Westminster St Stephen with St John EP, pt to EP2, pt to Wilton Place EP.[89]

EP5–PIMLICO ST PETER WITH CHRIST CHURCH–Cr 1953 by union pt EP4, pt Westminster Christ Church, Broadway EP, pt Westminster St Andrew EP, pt Westminster St Stephen with St John EP.[89]

EP6–PIMLICO ST SAVIOUR–Cr 1864 from EP2.[21] Bdry: 1953,[89] 1954 (help cr Westminster St James the Less Holy Trinity EP).[398] Abol 1973 pt to help cr Westminster

St Saviour and St James the Less EP, pt to EP2.[397]

PINNER

Chap in Harrow on the Hill AP, sep civ identity early, sep EP 1766.[128] *LG* Gore Hd, Hendon PLU, RSD, RD. Abol civ 1934 to help cr Harrow CP.[4] *Parl* Harrow Dv (1885–1918), Hendon Dv (1918–45). *Eccl* Pec jurisd Archbp Canterb (1766–1845), Seq 6 thereafter. Eccl bdry: 1882 (help cr Wealdstone EP),[271] 1906 (cr Hatch End EP),[312] 1937 (cr North Harrow EP),[95] 1952 (help cr Northwood Hills EP).[189]

PONDERS END

EP Cr 1899 from Enfield St James EP, Enfield AP.[147] Enf. RDn.

POPLAR

The following have 'Poplar' in their names. Insofar as any existed at a given time: *LG* Ossul. Hd, Poplar PLU, Dist (Metrop Bd Wks). Transf 1889 to London.[43] *Parl* Tow. Hmlts. Parl Bor (1832–85), Tow. Hmlts. Parl Bor, Poplar Dv (1885–1918), London thereafter. *Eccl* Step. RDn (1861–1901), Poplar RDn (1901–66), Tow. Hmlts. RDn (1966–*).

CP/EP1–POPLAR [ALL SAINTS]–Dist in Stepney AP, chap from 1654, sep par 1817.[399] Eccl bdry: 1860 (cr EP4),[400] 1867 (cr EP6),[401] 1867 (cr EP9),[95] 1875 (cr EP7),[366] 1887 (help cr Limehouse St Peter EP).[59] Abol 1952 pt to help cr EP3, pt to help cr EP8, pt to Bromley St Michael and All Angels EP.[70]

EP2–POPLAR–Cr 1971 by union EP3, Bromley St Michael and All Angels EP, EP8.[18]

EP3–POPLAR ALL SAINTS WITH ST FRIDESWIDE–Cr 1952 by union pt EP1, pt EP5, pt East India Docks EP, pt Bromley St Michael and All Angels EP.[70] Abol 1971 to help cr EP2.[18]

EP4–POPLAR CHRIST CHURCH–Cr 1860 from EP1.[400] Bdry: 1870 (cr Millwall EP),[60] 1873 (cr Cubitt Town EP).[168] Abol 1952 to help cr Isle of Dogs Christ Church with St John and St Luke EP.[70]

EP5–POPLAR ST FRIDESWIDE–Cr 1914 from East India Docks EP, Bromley St Michael and All Angels EP.[87] Abol 1952 pt to help cr EP3, pt to Bromley St Michael and All Angels EP.[70]

EP6–POPLAR ST MATTHIAS–Cr 1867 from EP1.[401] Bdry: 1952.[70]

EP7–POPLAR ST SAVIOUR–Cr 1875 from EP1.[366] Abol 1952 to help cr EP8.[70]

EP8–POPLAR ST SAVIOUR WITH ST GABRIEL AND ST STEPHEN–Cr 1952 by union EP7, Bromley St Gabriel EP, pt EP9, pt EP1.[70] Abol 1971 to help cr EP2.[18]

EP9–POPLAR ST STEPHEN–Cr 1867 from EP1.[95] Abol 1952 pt to help cr EP8, pt to EP6.[70]

PORTLAND PLACE

EP Cr 1839 from Islington AP.[335] Renamed 1849 'Islington St Stephen',[348] qv.

PORTLAND TOWN

EP Cr 1849 from St Marylebone Christ Church EP.[142] St Marylb. RDn (1861–1952). Bdry: 1876 (help cr Maida Hill EP),[51] 1952.[232] Renamed 1952 'St John's Wood St Stephen' EP.[163]

PORTMAN SQUARE

EP Cr 1857 from St Marylebone AP.[106] St Marylb. RDn (1861–1930). Abol 1930 to help cr Marylebone St Peter with St Thomas EP.[365]

PORTMAN SQUARE ST PAUL

EP Cr 1901 from St Marylebone AP.[173] St Marylb. RDn (1901–67), W'minst. (St Marylb.) RDn (1967–*). Bdry: 1935.[355]

POTTER'S BAR

EP Cr 1835 from South Mymms AP.[128] Enf. RDn (1858–1901), Hornsey RDn (1901–67), Central Barnet RDn (1967–*). Orig church dedicated to St John burned 1911 and new church erected 1915 dedicated differently, so that from 1915 this par sometimes 'South Mymms St Mary the Virgin and All Saints'. Bdry: 1949,[371] 1949 (help cr South Mymms King Charles the Martyr EP).[32]

PRESTON

EP Cr 1957 from Wembley Park EP, Kenton EP.[353] Harrow RDn (1957–67), Brent RDn (1967–*).

PRIMROSE HILL

EP Cr 1885 from South Hampstead EP.[137] Highg. RDn (1885–1901), Hampst. RDn (1901–57). Abol 1957 to help cr Primrose Hill St Mary the Virgin with Avenue Road St Paul EP.[236]

PRIMROSE HILL ST MARY THE VIRGIN WITH AVENUE ROAD ST PAUL

EP Cr 1957 by union Primrose Hill EP, Hampstead St Paul EP.[236] Hampst. RDn (1957–67), N Camd. (Hampst.) RDn (1967–*).

QUEEN SQUARE ST GEORGE THE MARTYR WITH HOLBORN HOLY TRINITY AND GRAY'S INN ROAD ST BARTHOLOMEW

EP Cr 1959 by union Holborn St George the Martyr with Holy Trinity EP, pt St Pancras St Bartholomew EP.[334] Finsb. & Holb. RDn (1959–67), S Camd. (Holb. & St Panc.) RDn (1967–*).

QUEENSBURY

EP Cr 1941 from Little Stanmore AP, Great Stanmore AP.[5] Harrow RDn.

RATCLIFFE

Hmlt pt in Stepney AP, pt in Limehouse CP/EP (orig pt Stepney), sep EP 1840,[337] sep CP 1866.[203] *LG* Ossul. Hd, Step. PLU, Limehouse Dist (Metrop Bd Wks). Transf 1889 to London.[43] *Parl* Tow. Hmlts. Parl Bor (1867–85), Tow. Hmlts. Parl Bor, Limehouse Dv (1885–1918), London thereafter. *Eccl* Pec jurisd Bp London (1840–45), Step. RDn (1861–1951). Abol eccl 1951 pt to help cr Shadwell St Paul with Ratcliffe St James EP, pt to Limehouse EP, pt to Whitechapel St Paul with St Mark EP.[74]

REGENT SQUARE

EP Cr 1852 from St Pancras AP.[402] St Panc. RDn (1858–1954). Bdry: 1876 (help cr St Pancras Holy Cross EP),[9] 1902 (help cr Woburn Square EP),[68] 1902.[67] Abol 1954 pt to help cr St Pancras Holy Cross with St Jude and St Peter EP, pt to St Pancras St Bartholomew EP.[25]

REGENT STREET

EP Cr 1870 (formerly called Archbishop Tenison's chapel) from Westminster St James EP.[402] St Martin in the Fields RDn (1870–1901), W'minst. RDn (1901–53). Bdry: 1885,[64] 1937.[364] Abol 1953 to help cr Soho St Anne with St Thomas and St Peter EP.[89]

REGENT'S PARK

EP Cr 1853 from St Pancras AP.[88] St Panc. RDn (1858–1967), N Camd. (Hampst.) RDn (1967–*). Bdry: 1904.[112]

REGENT'S PARK CHRIST CHURCH–See ST PANCRAS CHRIST CHURCH

ROXBOURNE

EP Cr 1955 from South Harrow EP, North Harrow EP.[303] Harrow RDn.

ROXETH

EP Cr 1863 from Harrow on the Hill AP.[63] Harrow RDn (1863–1901), Will. RDn (1901–14), Harrow RDn (1914–*). Bdry: 1923 (help cr Sudbury EP),[87] 1937 (cr South Harrow EP),[280] 1954.[204]

RUISLIP

AP *LG* Elth. Hd, Uxbr. PLU, RSD, RD (1894–1904), Ruislip Northwood UD (1904–65). Civ bdry: 1934.[4] Transf 1965 to Gtr London (Hilling. LB).[1] *Parl* Uxbr. Dv (1885–1948), Ruislip-Northwood BC (1948–70), Gtr London thereafter. *Eccl* Seq 9. Eccl bdry: 1854 (help cr Northwood EP),[374] 1931 (cr Eastcote EP),[142] 1936 (cr Ruislip Manor EP).[403]

RUISLIP MANOR

EP Cr 1936 from Ruislip AP.[403] Uxbr. RDn (1936–67), Hilling. RDn (1967–*). Bdry: 1951 (cr Ruislip St Mary EP).[404]

RUISLIP ST MARY

EP Cr 1951 from Ruislip Manor EP.[404] Uxbr. RDn (1951–67), Hilling. RDn (1967–*).

SAFFRON HILL

EP Cr 1839 from Holborn AP.[131] St Sepulchre RDn (1861–1901), Holb. RDn (1901–34), Finsb. & Holb. RDn (1934–52). Abol 1952 to help cr Holborn St Andrew the Martyr with Saffron Hill St Peter EP.[70]

ST ANDREW HOLBORN

AP Usual civ spelling; for eccl see 'Holborn'. Bdry: 1723 (cr St George the Martyr CP, eccl 'Holborn St George the Martyr', sometimes eccl 'Queen Square').[333] Pt City of London, pt Middx (Ossul. Hd). The Middx pt abol civ 1767 to help cr St Andrew Holborn Above the Bars with St George the Martyr CP,[405] the union often called merely 'St Andrew Holborn'.

ST ANDREW HOLBORN ABOVE THE BARS WITH ST GEORGE THE MARTYR

CP Cr 1767 by union Middx pt St Andrew Holborn AP, St George the Martyr CP.[405] Sometimes called merely 'St Andrew Holborn'. *LG* Ossul. Hd, Holb. PLU, Dist (Metrop Bd Wks). Transf 1889 to London.[43] *Parl* Finsb. Parl Bor (1832–85), Finsb. Parl Bor, Holb. Dv (1885–1918), London thereafter.

ST ANNE SOHO

Usual eccl spelling of par cr 1687 from St Martin in the Fields AP,[406] more commonly eccl called 'Westminster St Anne Soho' in 20th cent; for civ see following entry. *Eccl* St Martin in the Fields RDn (1861–1901), W'minst. RDn (1901–53). Eccl bdry: 1856 (cr Westminster St Mary, Crown Street EP),[275] 1932 (gains ent Westminster St Mary, Crown Street EP),[227] 1935 (gains ent Westminster St Luke EP).[8] Abol eccl 1953 pt to help cr Soho St Anne with St Thomas and St Peter EP, pt to St Martin in the Fields AP.[89]

ST ANNE WITHIN THE LIBERTY OF WESTMINSTER

Usual civ spelling of par cr 1687 from St Martin in the Fields AP[406]; for eccl see prev entry. *LG* Lbty City W'minst., Strand PLU (1836–68), W'minst. PLU (1868–89), Strand Dist (Metrop Bd Wks). Transf 1889 to London.[43] *Parl* W'minst. Parl Bor (1832–85), Strand Parl Bor (1885–1918), London thereafter.

ST BOTOLPH ALDERSGATE

AP Sometimes 'St Botolph Without Aldersgate'. Pt Middx (the area of Glasshouse Yard, lbty with sep jurisd in Middx), pt City of London, the par ent City of London after the former achieves sep civ status 1866.[203] See main entry in City of London.

ST BOTOLPH ALDGATE–See ST BOTOLPH WITHOUT ALDGATE

ST BOTOLPH WITHOUT ALDERSGATE–See ST BOTOLPH ALDERSGATE

ST BOTOLPH WITHOUT ALDGATE

AP Pt City of London, pt Middx (an area sometimes called 'East Smithfield Lbty'), each a sep par for civ purposes in the respective counties though each with same name, but one par for eccl purposes. The Middx pt incl Holy Trinity Minories (orig priory church, parochial from 1557[463]), lbty St Katherine by the Tower (sep par 1866[203]). *LG* Ossul. Hd, Whitech. PLU, Dist (Metrop Bd Wks). Transf 1889 to London.[43] *Parl* Tow. Hmlts. Parl Bor (1832–85), Tow. Hmlts. Parl Bor, Whitech. Dv (1885–1918), London thereafter. *Eccl* East City RDn (1869–93). Abol eccl 1893 to help cr St Botolph Without Aldgate with Holy Trinity Minories EP.[462]

ST BOTOLPH WITHOUT ALDGATE WITH HOLY TRINITY MINORIES

EP Cr 1893 by union St Botolph without Aldgate AP, Holy Trinity Minories AP.[462] E City RDn (1893–1954), The City RDn (1954–*). Bdry: 1954.[330]

ST CLEMENT DANES

AP *LG* Pt Ossul. Hd, pt Lbty City W'minst., Strand PLU, Dist (Metrop Bd Wks). Transf 1889 to London.[43] *Parl* W'minst. Parl Bor (1832–85), Strand Parl Bor (1885–1918), London thereafter. *Eccl* St Martin in the Fields RDn (1861–1901), W'minst. RDn (1901–53). Abol eccl

1953 to help cr St Mary le Strand with St Clement Danes EP, pt to Covent Garden St Paul EP.[89]

ST DUNSTAN IN THE WEST

AP Pt City of London, pt Middx (area of the Liberty of the Rolls, sep CP 1866 in Middx,[203]), so that this par ent City of London from 1866, qv for main entry.

ST GEORGE BLOOMSBURY

Usual civ spelling for par cr 1731 from St Giles in the Fields AP[66]; for eccl see 'Bloomsbury St George'. *LG* Ossul. Hd. Abol civ 1774 to help cr St Giles in the Fields and St George Bloomsbury CP.[407]

ST GEORGE HANOVER SQUARE

Par cr 1724 from St Martin in the Fields AP.[408] *LG* Lbty City W'minst., St Geo.'s Governor & Directors of Poor (1789–1867), Guardians for Poor (1867–70), PLU (1870–89), St Geo. Hanov. Sq. Vestrry (Metrop Bd Wks). Transf 1889 to London.[43] *Parl* W'minst. Parl Bor (1832–85), St Geo. Hanov. Sq. Parl Bor (1885–1918), London thereafter. *Eccl* St Geo. Hanov. Sq. RDn (1861–1901), W'minst. RDn (1901–67), W'minst. (St Mgt.'s) RDn (1967–*). Eccl bdry: 1830 (cr Pimlico St Peter EP),[216] 1835 (cr Hanover Chapel EP, later called 'Davies Street St Anselm'),[216] 1865 (cr Mayfair EP),[120] 1938.[293]

ST GEORGE IN THE EAST

Usual civ spelling for par cr 1729 from Stepney AP[409]; for eccl see 'St George in the East St George'. *LG* Ossul. Hd, St Geo. in the East Par (poor law purposes), Vestry (Metrop Bd Wks). Transf 1889 to London.[43] *Parl* Tow. Hmlts. Parl Bor (1832–85), Tow. Hmlts. Parl Bor, St Geo. Dv (1885–1918), London thereafter.

ST GEORGE IN THE EAST CHRIST CHURCH

EP Cr 1842 from St George in the East St George EP.[410] Step. RDn (1861–1951). Bdry: 1850 (cr St George in the East St Mary EP),[411] 1871.[175] Abol 1951 pt to help cr Stepney St Augustine with St Philip EP, pt to help cr St George in the East with Christ Church and St John EP.[74]

ST GEORGE IN THE EAST ST GEORGE

Usual eccl spelling for par cr 1729 from Stepney AP[409]; for civ see 'St George in the East'. *Eccl* Step. RDn (1861–1951). Bdry: 1842 (cr St George in the East Christ Church EP),[410] 1860 (cr Pell Street EP),[279] 1867 (help cr London Docks EP),[363] 1870 (cr St John the Evangelist in the East EP),[88] 1870,[60] 1871,[175] 1890 (gains ent Pell Street EP).[394] Abol 1951 pt to help cr St George in the East with Christ Church and St John EP, pt to help cr London Docks St Peter with Wapping St John EP.[74]

ST GEORGE IN THE EAST ST MARY

EP Cr 1850 from St George in the East Christ Church EP.[411] Step. RDn (1861–1966), Tow. Hmlts. RDn (1966–*). Bdry: 1951.[174]

ST GEORGE IN THE EAST WITH CHRIST CHURCH AND ST JOHN

EP Cr 1951 by union St John the Evangelist in the East EP, pt St George in the East Christ Church EP, pt St George the East St George EP, pt Shadwell EP.[74] Step. RDn (1951–66), Tow. Hmlts. RDn (1966–71). Abol 1971 to help cr St George in the East with St Paul EP.[412]

ST GEORGE IN THE EAST WITH ST PAUL

EP Cr 1971 by union St George in the East with Christ Church and St John EP, Whitechapel St Paul with St Mark EP.[412] Tow. Hmlts. RDn.

ST GEORGE THE MARTYR

Cr 1723 as CP/EP from pt of the Middx pt of St Andrew Holborn AP (City of London, Middx).[333] Usual civ spelling; for eccl (sometimes 'Queen Square') see 'Holborn St George the Martyr'. *LG* Ossul. Hd. Abol civ 1767 to help cr St Andrew Holborn Above the Bars with St George the Martyr CP.[405]

ST GILES CRIPPLEGATE

AP Pt City of London, pt Middx, the latter cr CP/EP 1733 in Middx (civ usually 'St Luke', eccl 'Old Street St Luke'),[385] so that this par ent City of London thereafter, qv for main entry.

ST GILES IN THE FIELDS

AP Cr sep par 1547.[413] *LG* Ossul. Hd. Bdry alt: 1731 (cr St George Bloomsbury CP, eccl 'Bloomsbury St George').[66] Abol civ 1774 to help cr St Giles in the Fields and St George Bloomsbury CP.[407] *Eccl* St Geo. Bloomsb. RDn (1861–97), St Martin in the Fields RDn (1897–1901), Finsb. RDn (1901–34), Finsb. & Holb. RDn (1934–67), S Camd. (Holb. & St Panc.) RDn (1967–*). Addtl eccl bdry alt: 1845 (cr Endell Street EP),[206] 1884 (cr Lincoln's Inn Fields EP),[167] 1902 (help cr Woburn Square EP),[68] 1929 (gains Endell Street EP),[207] 1952,[232] 1952 (incl help cr Bloomsbury St George with St John the Evangelist EP).[70]

ST GILES IN THE FIELDS AND ST GEORGE BLOOMSBURY

CP Cr 1774 by union St Giles in the Fields AP, St George Bloomsbury CP.[407] *LG* Ossul. Hd, St Giles in the Fields and St Geo. Bloomsb. Par (poor law purposes), St Giles Dist (Metrop Bd Wks). Transf 1889 to London.[43] *Parl* Finsb. Parl Bor (1832–85), Finsb. Parl Bor, Holb. Dv (1885–1918), London thereafter.

ST JAMES PICCADILLY–See WESTMINSTER ST JAMES

ST JOHN THE EVANGELIST IN THE EAST

EP Cr 1870 from St George in the East EP.[88] Step. RDn. Abol 1951 to help cr St George in the East with Christ Church and St John EP.[74]

ST JOHN'S WOOD ALL SAINTS

EP Cr 1846 from St Marylebone AP.[415] St Marylb. RDn (1861–1967), W'minst. (St Marylb.) RDn (1967–*). Bdry: 1865 (help cr Hampstead All Souls EP).[281]

ST JOHN'S WOOD ST STEPHEN

EP Renaming 1952 of Portland Town St Stephen EP.[163] St Marylb. RDn (1952–67), W'minst.

(St Marylb.) RDn (1967–*).

ST KATHERINE BY THE TOWER

Usual civ spelling for precinct in the Middx par of St Botolph Without Aldgate AP, sep CP 1866[203]; for eccl see following entry. *LG* Ossul. Hd, Whitech. PLU, Dist (Metrop Bd Wks). Transf 1889 to London.[43] *Parl* Tow. Hmlts. Parl Bor (1867–85), Tow. Hmlts. Parl Bor, Whitech. Dv (1885–1918), London thereafter.

PRECINCT OF ST KATHERINE

Usual eccl spelling for ex-par precinct; for civ see prev entry. Bdry: 1951 (incl help cr London Docks St Peter with Wapping St John EP).[74]

ST LUKE

Usual civ spelling for par cr 1733 from the Middx pt of St Giles Cripplegate AP (London, Middx, ent London from 1733)[385]; for eccl see 'Old Stret St Luke'. *LG* Ossul. Hd, St Luke Par (poor relief, sep act until 1869), Holb. PLU (1869–89), St Luke Vestry (Metrop Bd Wks). Transf 1889 to London.[43] *Parl* Finsb. Parl Bor (1832–85), Finsb. Parl Bor, East Dv (1885–1918), London thereafter.

ST MARGARET'S ON THAMES

EP Cr 1898 from Isleworth AP.[50] Ealing RDn (1898–1934), Uxbr. RDn (1934–53), Hampton RDn (1953–67), Hounslow RDn (1967–*).

ST MARTIN IN THE FIELDS

AP Incl following, made sep CP/EP: St Paul Covent Garden in 1645 (eccl, 'Covent Garden St Paul'),[417] Westminster St James in 1685 (sometimes 'St James Piccadilly'),[416] St Anne Within the Liberty of Westminster in 1687 (eccl, 'St Anne Soho', or in 20th cent more often 'Westminster St Anne Soho'),[406] St George Hanover Square in 1724.[428] *LG* Lbty City W'minst., St Martin in the Fields Par (poor law purposes, 1835–68), Strand PLU (1868–89), St Martin in the Fields Vestry (Metrop Bd Wks). Transf 1889 to London.[43] *Parl* W'minst. Parl Bor (1832–85), Strand Parl Bor (1885–1918), London thereafter. *Eccl* St Martin in the Fields RDn (1861–1901), W'minst. RDn (1901–67), W'minst. (St Mgt.'s) RDn (1967–*). Addtl eccl bdry alt: 1848 (cr Burleigh Street EP),[105] 1855 (cr Drury Lane EP),[20] 1953.[89]

ST MARY LE STRAND

AP Taken down 1549, sep again 1723.[419] *LG* Lbty City W'minst., Strand PLU, Dist (Metrop Bd Wks). Transf 1889 to London.[43] *Parl* W'minst. Parl Bor (1832–85), Strand Parl Bor (1885–1918), London thereafter. *Eccl* St Martin in the Fields RDn (1861–1901), W'minst. RDn (1901–53). Abol eccl 1953 pt to help cr St Mary le Strand with St Clement Danes EP, pt to Covent Garden St Paul EP.[89]

ST MARY LE STRAND WITH ST CLEMENT DANES

EP Cr 1953 by union pt St Mary le Strand AP, pt St Clement Danes AP, pt Covent Garden St Paul EP.[89] W'minst RDn (1953–67), W'minst. (St Mgt.'s) RDn (1967–*).

ST MARYLEBONE

The following have 'St Marylebone' in their names. Insofar as any existed at a given time: *LG* Ossul. Hd, St Marylebone Par (for poor relief, 1775–1867), Par (poor law purposes, 1867–89), Vestry (Metrop Bd Wks). Transf 1889 to London.[43] *Parl* Marylb. Parl Bor (1832–85), pt Marylb. Parl Bor, East Dv, pt Marylb. Parl Bor, West Dv (1885–1918), London thereafter. *Eccl* St Marylb. RDn (1861–1967), W'minst. (St Marylb.) RDn (1967–*).

AP1–ST MARYLEBONE–Orig 'Tyburn'. Eccl bdry: 1825 (cr EP2, EP5, EP8, EP15),[290] 1838 (cr Lisson Grove EP),[369] 1846 (cr St John's Wood All Saints EP),[415] 1857 (cr Portman Square EP),[106] 1864 (cr EP12),[84] 1901 (cr Portman Square St Paul EP).[173] Abol eccl 1955 to help cr EP17.[24]

EP1–ST MARYLEBONE ALL SAINTS–Cr 1849 from EP2.[186] Bdry: 1952.[232]

EP2–ST MARYLEBONE ALL SOULS–Cr 1825 from AP1.[290] Bdry: 1844 (cr EP9),[37] 1849 (cr EP1),[186] 1930 (help cr Marylebone St Peter with St Thomas EP),[365] 1932 (gains ent EP9).[419] Abol 1952 pt to help cr EP3, pt to EP1, pt to St Giles in the Fields AP.[232]

EP3–ST MARYLEBONE ALL SOULS WITH ST PETER AND ST JOHN–Cr 1952 by union pt EP2, Marylebone St Peter with St Thomas EP, pt Fitzroy Square St John with St Saviour EP.[232] Bdry: 1957,[290] 1959.[138]

EP4–ST MARYLEBONE THE ANNUCIATION, BRYANSTON STREET–Cr 1894 from EP15.[245]

EP5–ST MARYLEBONE CHRIST CHURCH–Cr 1825 from AP1.[290] Bdry: 1849 (cr Portland Town EP),[142] 1850 (cr EP13),[216] 1853 (cr EP16),[411] 1866 (cr EP11),[420] 1866 (cr EP10),[90] 1876 (help cr Maida Hill EP).[51] Abol 1952 pt to help cr Lisson Grove St Paul with St Marylebone St Matthew and Emmanuel EP, pt to help cr EP7, pt to help cr EP14, pt to EP11, pt to Portland Town EP.[232]

EP6–ST MARYLEBONE CHRIST CHURCH AND ST PAUL–Cr 1971 by union EP7, Lisson Grove St Paul with St Marylebone St Matthew and Emmanuel EP.[362]

EP7–ST MARYLEBONE CHRIST CHURCH WITH ST BARNABAS–Cr 1952 by union pt EP5, pt EP10.[232]

EP8–ST MARYLEBONE HOLY TRINITY–Cr 1825 from AP1.[290]

EP9–ST MARYLEBONE ST ANDREW–Cr 1844 from EP2.[37] Abol 1932 ent to EP2.[419]

EP10–ST MARYLEBONE ST BARNABAS–Cr 1866 from EP5.[90] Often 'St Barnabas in St Marylebone'. Bdry: 1952 (incl help cr EP7, help cr EP14).[232]

EP11–ST MARYLEBONE ST CYPRIAN–Cr 1866 from EP5.[420] Bdry: 1952.[232]

EP12–ST MARYLEBONE ST LUKE, NUTFORD PLACE–Cr 1864 from AP1.[84] Bdry: 1872 (help cr Marylebone Road EP).[243] Abol 1952 to help cr EP14.[232]

EP13–ST MARYLEBONE ST MARK–Cr 1850 from EP5.[216] Bdry: 1869,[392] 1870 (help cr Kilburn St Augustine EP).[19]

EP14–ST MARYLEBONE ST MARK WITH ST LUKE–Cr 1952 by union Marylebone Road EP, EP12, pt EP5, pt EP10.[232]

EP15–ST MARYLEBONE ST MARY–Cr 1825 from AP1.[290] Bdry: 1872 (help cr Marylebone Road EP),[243] 1894 (cr EP4).[245]

EP16–ST MARYLEBONE ST MATTHEW–Cr 1853 from EP5.[411] Bdry: 1952 (help cr Lisson Grove St Paul with St Marylebone St Matthew and Emmanuel EP).[232]

EP17–ST MARYLEBONE WITH ST MARYLEBONE HOLY TRINITY–Cr 1955 by union AP1, EP8.[24] Bdry: 1957,[290] 1959.[138]

ST PANCRAS

The following have 'St Pancras' in their names. Insofar as any existed at a given time: *LG* Ossul. Hd, St Panc. Par (poor law purposes, 1867–89), Vestry (Metrop Bd Wks). Transf 1889 to London.[43] *Parl* Marylb. Parl Bor (1832–85), from 1885–1918 divided into 4 Dvs (North, South, East, West) of St Panc. Parl Bor, London thereafter. *Eccl* Pec jurisd Dean & Chapter of St Paul's, London (until 1845), St Panc. RDn (1858–1967), S Camd. (Holb. & St Panc.) RDn (1967–*).

AP1–ST PANCRAS–Civ bdry: 1891.[414] Eccl bdry: 1834 (cr Highgate EP),[276] 1837 (cr EP1),[421] 1852 (cr Camden Town EP, Upper Charlotte Street EP, Camden Square EP, Haverstock Hill Holy Trinity EP, Regent Square EP, EP5 [at first called 'Old St Pancras', later 'Parish Chapel' when refounded 1863,[111] later again 'Old St Pancras']),[109] 1852 (cr Somers Town EP),[423] 1853 (help cr Highgate Rise EP),[123] 1853 (cr Regent's Park EP, EP7),[88] 1859 (cr Bedford New Town EP, Oakley Square EP),[50] 1860 (cr EP6),[422] 1860 (cr Gray's Inn Road St Jude EP),[166] 1862 (cr Agar Town EP),[24] 1863 (cr Kentish Town EP),[111] 1864 (cr Hampstead Road EP),[39] 1865 (help cr EP9),[230] 1902 (help cr Woburn Square EP).[68] Abol eccl 1954 to help cr EP10.[25]

EP1–ST PANCRAS CHRIST CHURCH–Cr 1837 from AP1.[421] Sometimes 'Regent's Park Christ Church', or 'St Pancras Christ Church, Albany Street'. Bdry: 1852 (cr EP8),[420] 1954.[25]

EP2–ST PANCRAS HOLY CROSS–Cr 1876 from Gray's Inn Road St Jude EP, Regent Square EP.[9] Abol 1935 to help cr EP3.[252]

EP3–ST PANCRAS HOLY CROSS WITH ST JUDE–Cr 1935 by union Gray's Inn Road St Jude EP, EP2.[252] Abol 1954 to help cr EP4.[25]

EP4–ST PANCRAS HOLY CROSS WITH ST JUDE AND ST PETER–Cr 1954 by union EP3, pt Regent Square EP.[25] Bdry: 1959.[334]

EP5–ST PANCRAS OLD ST PANCRAS–Cr 1852 as 'Old St Pancras' from AP1,[109] refounded 1863 as 'Parish Chapel',[111] later again called 'Old St Pancras'. Bdry: 1868 (help cr Somers Town Christ Church EP),[63] 1954.[25] Abol 1956 to help cr EP12.[53]

–ST PANCRAS PARISH CHAPEL–See prev entry

EP6–ST PANCRAS ST BARTHOLOMEW–Cr 1860 from AP1.[422] Bdry: 1954.[25] Abol 1959 pt to EP4, pt to help cr Queen Square St George the Martyr with Holborn Holy Trinity and Gray's Inn Road St Bartholomew EP.[334]

EP7–ST PANCRAS ST MARK–Cr 1853 from AP1.[88]

EP8–ST PANCRAS ST MARY MAGDALENE–Cr 1852 from EP1.[420] Renamed 1868 'Munster Square' EP.[372]

EP9–ST PANCRAS ST SAVIOUR–Cr 1865 from AP1, Fitzroy Square St John EP.[230]

EP10–ST PANCRAS WITH ST JAMES AND CHRIST CHURCH–Cr 1954 by union AP1, pt Hampstead Road EP, pt Somers Town Christ Church EP.[25]

EP11–NORTH ST PANCRAS–Cr 1894 from Haverstock Hill St Andrew EP, Kentish Town St Martin EP.[245] St Panc. RDn (1894–1967), N Camd. (Hampst.) RDn (1967–72), S Camd. (Holb. & St Panc.) RDn (1972–*).

EP12–OLD ST PANCRAS WITH BEDFORD NEW TOWN–Cr 1956 by union EP5, Bedford New Town EP.[53]

ST PAUL COVENT GARDEN

Usual civ spelling for par cr 1645 from St Martin in the Fields AP, confirmed 1660[417]; for eccl see 'Covent Garden St Paul'. *LG* Lbty City W'minst., Strand PLU, Dist (Metrop Bd Wks). Transf 1899 to London (W'minst. Metrop Bor).[43] *Parl* W'minst. Parl Bor (1832–85), Strand Parl Bor (1885–1918), London thereafter.

ST SEPULCHRE

AP Pt City of London, pt Middx, each a sep par for civ purposes in their respective counties although each with the same name, one par for eccl purposes. *LG* Ossul. Hd, W London PLU (1837–45), Holb. PLU (1845–89), Dist (Metrop Bd Wks). Transf 1889 to London.[43] *Parl* Finsb. Parl Bor (1832–85), Finsb. Parl Bor, East Dv (1885–1918), London Adm Co thereafter. *Eccl* See main entry in City of London.

PRECINCT OF THE SAVOY

Lbty, sep CP 1866.[203] *LG* Lbty City W'minst., Strand PLU, Dist (Metrop Bd Wks). Transf 1889 to London.[43] *Parl* W'minst. Parl Bor (1867–85), Strand Parl Bor (1885–1918), London thereafter.

SHACKLEWELL

EP Cr 1929 from West Hackney EP, Dalston St Mark EP.[173] Hack. & Stk. Newing. RDn. Abol 1954 to help cr West Hackney St Barnabas EP.[259]

SHADWELL

Hmlt or precinct in Stepney AP, sep par

1670.[425] *LG* Ossul. Hd, Step. PLU, Limehouse Dist (Metrop Bd Wks). Transf 1889 to London.[43] *Parl* Tow. Hmlts. Parl Bor (1832–85), Tow. Hmlts. Parl Bor, Limehouse Dv (1885–1918), London thereafter. *Eccl* Pec jurisd Bp London (until 1845), Step. RDn (1861–1951). Eccl bdry: 1867 (help cr London Docks EP).[363] Abol eccl 1951 pt to help cr St George in the East with Christ Church and St John EP, pt to help cr Shadwell St Paul with Ratcliffe St James EP.[74]

SHADWELL ST PAUL WITH RATCLIFFE ST JAMES

EP Cr 1951 by union pt Shadwell EP, pt Ratcliffe EP.[74] Step. RDn (1951–66), Tow. Hmlts. RDn (1966–*).

SHEPHERD'S BUSH

EP Cr 1883 from Hammersmith St Stephen EP.[272] Fulham RDn (1883–1901), Hamm. RDn (1901–63). Abol 1963 to help cr Shepherd's Bush St Stephen with St Thomas EP.[88]

SHEPHERD'S BUSH ST STEPHEN WITH ST THOMAS

EP Cr 1963 by union Hammersmith St Stephen EP, Shepherd's Bush EP.[88] Hamm. RDn.

SHEPPERTON

AP *LG* Spelth. Hd, Staines PLU, RSD, RD (1894–1930), Sunbury on Thames UD (1930–65). Transf 1965 to Surrey.[1] *Parl* Seq 1. *Eccl* Seq 5. Eccl bdry: 1949.[32]

SHOREDITCH

The following have 'Shoreditch' in their names. Insofar as any existed at a given time: *LG* Ossul. Hd, Shored. Par (poor relief), Vestry (Metrop Bd Wks). Transf 1889 to London.[43] *Parl* Tow. Hmlts. Parl Bor (1832–67), Hack. Parl Bor (1867–85), pt Shored. Parl Bor, Hagg. Dv, pt Shored. Parl Bor, Hoxton Dv (1885–1918), London thereafter. *Eccl* St Sepulchre RDn (1858–70), Shored. RDn (1870–1967), Hack. RDn (1967–*).

AP1–SHOREDITCH [ST LEONARD]–Eccl bdry: 1830 (cr Haggerston St Mary EP, Hoxton St John EP),[264] 1841 (cr Curtain Road EP),[169] 1848 (help cr Old Street St Mark EP),[143] 1862 (crEP4),[120] 1863,[63] 1866 (help cr EP1),[64] 1937 (gains ent Hoxton St Peter EP, Old Street St Mark EP),[345] 1953 (help cr Hoxton St John the Baptist with Christ Church EP),[251] 1954.[39] Abol eccl 1972 to help cr EP3.[426]

EP1–SHOREDITCH HOLY TRINITY–Cr 1866 from AP1, Bethnal Green St Philip EP.[64]

EP2–SHOREDITCH ST AGATHA–Cr 1872 from Curtain Road EP.[6] Abol 1915 ent to Curtain Road EP.[170]

–SHOREDITCH ST JAMES–See CURTAIN ROAD

EP3–SHOREDITCH ST LEONARD WITH ST MICHAEL–Cr 1972 by union AP1, EP4.[426]

EP4–SHOREDITCH ST MICHAEL–Cr 1862 from AP1.[120] Bdry: 1930,[144] 1935 (gains ent Curtain Road EP),[38] 1937,[345] 1966 (help cr St Giles Cripplegate with St Bartholomew Moor Lane, St Alphage London Wall and St Luke Old Street with St Mary Charterhouse and St Paul Clerkenwell EP).[228] Abol 1972 to help cr EP3.[426]

SOHO ST ANNE–See ST ANNE SOHO

SOHO ST ANNE WITH ST THOMAS AND ST PETER

EP Cr 1953 by union Regent Street EP, Great Windmill Street EP, pt St Anne Soho EP.[89] W'minst. RDn (1953–67), W'minst. (St Mgt.'s) RDn (1967–*).

SOMERS TOWN

EP Cr 1852 from St Pancras AP.[423] St Panc. RDn (1858–1967), S Camd. (Holb. & St Panc.) RDn (1967–*). Bdry: 1868 (help cr Somers Town Christ Church EP),[63] 1954.[25]

SOMERS TOWN CHRIST CHURCH

EP Cr 1868 from ent King's Cross EP, pt Somers Town EP, pt St Pancras Old St Pancras EP.[63] St Panc. RDn. Abol 1954 pt to help cr St Pancras with St James and Christ Church EP, pt to Somers Town EP.[25]

SOUTHALL CHRIST THE REDEEMER

EP Cr 1964 from Greenford AP, Southall Holy Trinity EP, Northolt AP.[255] Ealing RDn (1964–67), Ealing West RDn (1967–*).

SOUTHALL HOLY TRINITY

EP Cr 1891 from Southall Green EP.[183] Ealing RDn (1891–1967), Ealing West RDn (1967–*). Bdry: 1906 (cr Southall St George EP),[17] 1964 (cr Southall Christ the Redeemer EP).[255]

SOUTHALL ST GEORGE

EP Cr 1906 from Southall Holy Trinity EP.[17] Ealing RDn (1906–67), Ealing West RDn (1967–*).

SOUTHALL GREEN

EP Cr 1850 from Norwood EP.[325] Ealing RDn (1858–1967), Ealing West RDn (1967–*). Bdry: 1880,[376] 1891 (cr Southall Holy Trinity EP).[183]

SOUTHGATE

Chap in Edmonton AP, sep EP 1851,[195] sep CP 1894 (the pt in Southgate USD).[78] *LG* Edm. PLU, Southgate UD (1894–1933), MB (1933–65). Civ bdry: 1934.[4] Transf 1965 to Gtr London (Enf. LB).[1] *Parl* Wood Green Dv (1918–48), Southgate BC (1948–70), Gtr London thereafter. *Eccl* Enf. RDn (1858–*). Eccl bdry: 1873 (cr New Southgate EP),[238] 1874 (help cr Southgate St Michael at Bowes EP),[326] 1906 (help cr Palmer's Green EP),[393] 1928 (cr Southgate St Andrew EP),[280] 1972 (gains pt New Southgate St Michael and All Angels EP, dioc St Alb),[240] 1974.[427]

SOUTHGATE ST ANDREW

EP Cr 1928 from Southgate EP.[280] Bdry: 1972 (gains pt New Southgate St Michael and All Angels EP, dioc St Alb),[240] 1974 (incl loses pt to East Barnet EP, dioc St Alb).[427]

SOUTHGATE ST MICHAEL AT BOWES

EP Cr 1874 from Southgate EP, Wood Green EP.[326] Enf. RDn. Bdry: 1906 (help cr Bounds Green EP),[71] 1953.[141]

NEW SOUTHGATE
EP Cr 1873 from Southgate EP, Friern Barnet AP.[238] Enf. RDn (1873–1901), Hornsey RDn (1901–67), Central Barnet RDn (1967–*). Bdry: 1906 (help cr Bounds Green EP),[71] 1972 (gains pt New Southgate St Michael and All Angels EP, dioc St Alb).[240]

SPITALFIELDS
Par cr 1729 from Stepney AP.[428] *LG* Ossul. Hd, Whitech. PLU, Dist (Metrop Bd Wks). Transf 1889 to London.[43] *Parl* Tow. Hmlts Parl Bor (1832–85), Tow. Hmlts. Parl Bor, Whitech. Dv (1885–1918), London thereafter. *Eccl* Spitalf. RDn (1861–1901), Step. RDn (1901–). Eccl bdry: 1854 (cr Spitalfields St Mary EP),[430] 1858 (cr Spitalfields St Stephen EP).[225] Abol eccl 1911 to help cr Spitalfields Christ Church with St Mary and St Stephen EP.[429]

SPITALFIELDS CHRIST CHURCH WITH ALL SAINTS
EP Cr 1951 by union Spitalfields Christ Church with St Mary and St Stephen EP, Mile End New Town All Saints with St Olave EP, pt Whitechapel St Mary with St Jude EP.[74] Step. RDn (1951–66), Tow. Hmlts. RDn (1966–*). Eccl bdry: 1954.[330]

SPITALFIELDS CHRIST CHURCH WITH ST MARY AND ST STEPHEN
EP Cr 1911 by union Spitalfields EP, Spitalfields St Mary EP, Spitalfields St Stephen EP, ex-par Norton Folgate.[429] Step. RDn. Abol 1951 to help cr Spitalfields Christ Church with All Saints EP.[74]

SPITALFIELDS ST MARY
EP Cr 1854 from Spitalfields EP.[430] Spitalf. RDn (1854–1901), Step. RDn (1901–11). Abol 1911 to help cr Spitalfields Christ Church with St Mary and St Stephen EP.[429]

SPITALFIELDS ST STEPHEN
EP Cr 1858 from Spitalfields EP.[225] RDns and abol as for Spitalfields EP.[429]

SPRING GROVE
EP Cr 1856 from Heston AP, Hounslow EP, Isleworth AP.[322] Ealing RDn (1858–1934), Hampton RDn (1934–53), Heston & Islew. RDn (1953–67), Hounslow RDn (1967–*).

STAINES
AP Incl chap Ashford (sep civ identity eary, sometimes sep eccl status,[30] sep EP 1859[31]), chap Laleham (sep civ status by 1491,[30] sometimes sep eccl status,[30] sep EP 1859[31]), chap Teddington (sep par 13th cent[431]). *LG* Spelth. Hd, Staines PLU, USD, UD. Addtl civ bdry alt: 1896.[432] Transf 1965 to Surrey.[1] *Parl* Seq 1. *Eccl* Seq 7. Addtl eccl bdry alt: 1894 (cr Staines St Peter EP),[33] 1973 (help cr Ashford St Hilda EP).[34]

STAINES CHRIST CHURCH
EP Cr 1951 from Staines St Peter EP, Laleham EP, Ashford AP.[357] Hampton RDn (1951–53), Staines RDn (1953–*).

STAINES ST PETER
EP Cr 1894 from Staines AP.[33] Hampton RDn (1894–1953), Staines RDn (1953–*). Bdry: 1951 (help cr Staines Christ Church EP).[357]

STAMFORD BROOK
EP Cr 1888 from Hammersmith St Luke EP.[271] Fulham RDn (1888–1901), Hamm. RDn (1901–*).

STAMFORD HILL ST ANNE–See HANGER LANE

STAMFORD HILL ST BARTHOLOMEW
EP Cr 1905 from Hanger Lane EP, Stamford Hill St Thomas EP.[271] Tott. RDn (1905–67), E Haringey RDn (1967–*). Bdry: 1949,[433] 1973.[434]

STAMFORD HILL ST JOHN, VARTRY ROAD
EP Cr 1887 from Hanger Lane EP.[290] Enf. RDn (1887–1901), Tott. RDn (1901–67), E Haringey RDn (1967–*). Bdry: 1892 (help cr Stoke Newington St Olave EP).[136]

STAMFORD HILL ST THOMAS
EP Cr 1828 from Hackney AP.[125] Hack. RDn (1861–1901), Hack. & Stk. Newing. RDn (1901–67), Hack. RDn (1967–*). Bdry: 1866 (help cr Upper Clapton EP),[145] 1883 (help cr Stoke Newington St Andrew EP),[435] 1885,[249] 1886 (help cr Stoke Newington Common EP),[300] 1905 (help cr Stamford Hill St Bartholomew EP),[271] 1917.[186]

GREAT STANMORE
AP *LG* Gore Hd, Hendon PLU, RSD, RD. Abol civ 1934 to help cr Harrow CP.[4] *Parl* Harrow Dv (1885–1918), Hendon Dv (1918–45). *Eccl* Seq 6. Eccl bdry: 1935 (help cr Kenton EP),[131] 1940 (help cr Belmont EP),[54] 1941 (help cr Queensbury EP),[5] 1955.[34]

LITTLE STANMORE
AP Sometimes anc 'Whitchurch'. *LG* Gore Hd, Hendon PLU, RSD, RD. Abol civ 1934 pt to help cr Harrow CP, pt to Wembley CP.[4] *Parl* Harrow Dv (1885–1918), Hendon Dv (1918–45). *Eccl* AP but donative in 18th cent,[436] Harrow RDn (1858–1901), Will. RDn (1901–14), Harrow RDn (1914–34), Hendon RDn (1934–67), Harrow RDn (1967–*). Eccl bdry: 1941 (help cr Queensbury EP),[5] 1955.[34]

STANWELL
AP *LG* Spelth. Hd, Staines PLU, RSD, RD (1894–1930), UD (1930–65). Civ bdry: 1896.[432] Transf 1965 to Surrey.[1] *Parl* Seq 1. *Eccl* Seq 7. Eccl bdry: 1853 (help cr Colnbrook EP [primarily Bucks, to be ent Oxford dioc]),[84] 1973 (incl help cr Ashford St Hilda EP).[34]

STAPLE INN
Ex-par place, sep CP 1858,[118] eccl abol 1952 to help cr Holborn St Andrew the Martyr with Saffron Hill St Peter EP.[70] *LG* Ossul. Hd, Holb. PLU (1858–89). Transf 1889 to London.[43] *Parl* Finsb. Parl Bor (1867–85), Finsb. Parl Bor, Holb. Dv (1885–1918), London thereafter.

STEPNEY
The following have 'Stepney' in their names. Insofar as any existed at a given time: *LG* Ossul. Hd. *Parl* Tow. Hmlts. Parl Bor (1832–67). *Eccl* Pec jurisd Bp London (until 1845), Step. RDn (1861–1966), Tow. Hmlts. RDn (1966–*).

AP1–STEPNEY [ST DUNSTAN]–Incl the following which were made sep pars: Whitechapel in early 17th cent (pt London, pt Middx),[442] Bow (eccl, 'Stratford Bow St Mary') in 1719,[72] Spitalfields in 1729,[428] Wapping in 1729,[441] Limehouse in 1729,[358] pt Ratcliffe in 1729,[358] St George in the East (eccl, 'St George in the East St George') in 1729,[409] Bethnal Green in 1743,[45] Whitechapel in 1780,[442] Poplar in 1817,[399] Mile End New Town (sep EP 1841 as 'Mile End New Town All Saints',[173] sep CP 1866[203]), Mile End Old Town (sep EP 1841 as 'Mile End Old Town Holy Trinity',[173] sep CP 1866[203]). The remainder of Ratcliffe added to the former CP 1866,[203] and Ratcliffe EP cr [incl pt from Limehouse EP] 1840.[337] From time dependent areas sep rated for poor, and from time the last recognised as CPs in 1866 'Stepney' has no further civ identity. Addtl eccl bdry alt: 1837 (cr EP13),[437] 1840 (cr EP11, EP14),[337] 1858 (help cr EP10),[83] 1866 (help cr EP5),[368] 1870 (help cr Mile End Old Town St Luke EP),[95] 1872 (help cr EP9),[92] 1877 (cr EP1),[132] 1879 (help cr EP2),[351] 1926 (cr EP8).[389] Abol eccl 1951 pt to help cr EP7, pt to help cr Limehouse Fields St John with St Matthew EP.[74]

EP1–STEPNEY CHRIST CHURCH–Cr 1877 from AP1.[132] Abol 1951 pt to help cr EP4, pt to help cr EP7.[74]

EP2–STEPNEY ST ANTHONY–Cr 1879 from AP1, EP11.[351] Abol 1936 to help cr Bethnal Green St Simon Zelotes with St Anthony EP.[65]

EP3–STEPNEY ST AUGUSTINE–Cr 1880 from EP13.[89] Abol 1951 to help cr EP4.[74]

EP4–STEPNEY ST AUGUSTINE WITH ST PHILIP–Cr 1951 by union EP3, EP13, pt Whitechapel St Mary with St Jude EP, pt EP1, pt EP14, pt St George in the East Christ Church EP.[74]

EP5–STEPNEY ST BENET–Cr 1870 from Mile End Old Town Holy Trinity EP, AP1, EP11.[368] Abol 1951 pt to help cr EP12, pt to help cr EP7.[74]

EP6–STEPNEY ST DUNSTAN AND ALL SAINTS–Cr 1956 by union EP7, pt Limehouse Fields St John with St Matthew EP.[359]

EP7–STEPNEY ST DUNSTAN AND ALL SAINTS WITH ST THOMAS AND ST FAITH–Cr 1951 by union EP8, pt AP1, pt EP14, pt EP1, pt EP5.[74] Abol 1956 to help cr EP6.[359]

EP8–STEPNEY ST FAITH–Cr 1926 from AP1.[389] Abol 1951 to help cr EP7.[74]

EP9–STEPNEY ST MATTHEW–Cr 1872 from AP1, Limehouse EP, Limehouse St John the Evangelist EP.[92] Abol 1951 to help cr Limehouse Fields St John with St Matthew EP.[74]

EP10–STEPNEY ST PAUL–Cr 1858 from AP1, Bromley AP, Limehouse EP, Mile End Old Town Holy Trinity EP.[83] Abol 1951 pt to help cr Bow Common St Paul with St Luke EP, pt to Limehouse EP.[74]

EP11–STEPNEY ST PETER–Cr 1840 from AP1.[337] Bdry: 1866 (help cr EP5),[368] 1879 (help cr EP2).[351] Abol 1951 to help cr EP12.[74]

EP12–STEPNEY ST PETER WITH ST BENET–Cr 1951 by union EP11, EP5.[74]

EP13–STEPNEY ST PHILIP THE APOSTLE–Cr 1837 from AP1.[437] Bdry: 1880 (cr EP3).[89] Abol 1951 to help cr EP4.[74]

EP14–STEPNEY ST THOMAS–Cr 1840 from AP1.[337] Abol 1951 pt to help cr EP4, pt to help cr EP7, pt to Whitechapel St Paul with St Mark EP.[74]

STOKE NEWINGTON

The following have 'Stoke Newington' in their names. Insofar as any existed at a given time: *LG* Ossul. Hd, Hack. PLU, Dist (Metrop Bd Wks). Transf 1889 to London.[43] *Parl* Finsb. Parl Bor (1832–85), Hack. Parl Bor, North Dv (1885–1918), London thereafter. *Eccl* Pec jurisd Dean & Chapter of St Paul's, London (until 1845), Hack. RDn (1861–1901), Hack. & Stk. Newing. RDn (1901–67), Hack. RDn (1967–*).

AP1–STOKE NEWINGTON [ST MARY]–Eccl bdry: 1849 (help cr EP6),[340] 1873 (help cr EP3),[5] 1873 (help cr EP3),[238] 1883 (help cr EP2),[435] 1885,[249] 1892 (help cr EP8),[136] 1956.[10]

EP1–STOKE NEWINGTON ALL SAINTS–Cr 1873 from EP6, AP1.[238] Abol 1956 pt to help cr EP5, pt to AP1.[10]

EP2–STOKE NEWINGTON ST ANDREW–Cr 1883 from AP1, Stamford Hill St Thomas EP.[435] Bdry: 1892 (help cr EP8),[136] 1917,[186] 1949.[433]

EP3–STOKE NEWINGTON ST FAITH–Cr 1873 from EP6, AP1.[5] Abol 1951 to help cr EP4.[438]

EP4–STOKE NEWINGTON ST FAITH WITH ST MATTHIAS–Cr 1951 by union EP3, EP6.[438] Abol 1956 to help cr EP5.[10]

EP5–STOKE NEWINGTON ST FAITH WITH ST MATTHIAS AND ALL SAINTS–Cr 1956 by union EP4, pt EP1.[10] Renamed 1974 as EP7.[439]

EP6–STOKE NEWINGTON ST MATTHIAS–Cr 1849 from Hornsey AP, AP1.[340] Bdry: 1871 (help cr Dalston St Mark EP),[125] 1873 (help cr EP3),[5] 1873 (help cr EP1).[238] Abol 1951 to help cr EP4.[438]

EP7–STOKE NEWINGTON ST MATTHIAS–Renaming 1974 of EP5.[439]

EP8–STOKE NEWINGTON ST OLAVE–Cr 1892 from AP1, EP2, Stamford Hill St John, Vartry Road EP, Hanger Lane EP.[136]

EP9–STOKE NEWINGTON COMMON–Cr 1886 from Stamford Hill St Thomas EP, West Hackney EP.[300] Bdry: 1953.[93]

STONEBRIDGE

EP Cr 1892 from Harlesden All Souls EP, Willesden AP.[263] Harrow RDn (1892–1901), Will. RDn

(1901–67), Brent RDn (1967–*).

STRATFORD BOW ST MARY

Usual eccl spelling for par cr 1719 from Stepney AP[72]; for civ see 'Bow'. *Eccl* Step. RDn (1861–1901), Poplar RDn (1901–63). Eccl bdry: 1858 (cr Old Ford St Stephen EP),[236] 1952 (incl help cr Bromley St Mary the Virgin with St Andrew EP),[70] 1966.[235] Abol eccl 1963 to help cr Bow St Mary with Bromley St Leonard EP.[73]

STROUD GREEN

EP Cr 1881 from Hornsey Holy Innocents EP, Brownswood Park EP, Hornsey AP.[99] Highg. RDn (1881–1901), Hornsey RDn (1901–67), W Haringey RDn (1967–*). Bdry: 1892 (help cr Harringay EP),[70] 1903 (help cr Hornsey St Luke EP),[312] 1916.[103]

SUDBURY

EP Cr 1923 from Harrow on the Hill AP, Roxeth EP, Wembley EP.[87] Harrow RDn (1923–67), Brent RDn (1967–*). Bdry: 1949 (incl help cr North Greenford EP),[32] 1954,[204] 1954 (help cr Northolt Park EP),[373] 1959 (help cr North Wembley EP).[304]

SUNBURY

AP Usual civ spelling; for eccl see following entry. *LG* Spelth. Hd, Staines PLU, RSD, Sunbury on Thames UD. Civ bdry: 1934,[4] 1936.[220] Transf 1965 to Surrey.[1] *Parl* Seq 1.

SUNBURY ON THAMES

AP Usual eccl spelling; for civ see prev entry. *Eccl* Seq 5. Eccl bdry: 1881 (cr Upper Sunbury EP),[440] 1896,[93] 1949.[32]

UPPER SUNBURY

EP Cr 1881 from Sunbury AP.[440] Hampton RDn (1881–1953), Staines RDn (1953–*). Bdry: 1896,[93] 1949.[32]

TEDDINGTON

AP Chap in Staines AP, sep par 13th cent.[431] *LG* Spelth. Hd, Kingston PLU, Teddington USD, UD. Civ bdry: 1912.[288] Abol civ 1937 ent to Twickenham AP.[286] *Parl* Uxbr. Dv (1885–1918), Spelth. Dv (1918–48). *Eccl* Seq 4. Eccl bdry: 1880 (cr Upper Teddington EP),[22] 1938 (cr Teddington St Mark EP).[217]

TEDDINGTON ST MARK

EP Cr 1938 from Tedddington AP.[217] Hampton RDn.

UPPER TEDDINGTON

EP Cr 1880 from Teddington AP.[22] Hampton RDn. Bdry: 1914 (cr Fulwell EP).[247]

TEMPLE FORTUNE

EP Cr 1923 from Hendon AP, Finchley AP.[184] Hampst. RDn (1923–34), Hendon RDn (1934–67), W Barnet RDn (1967–*).

TOKYNGTON

EP Cr 1933 from Wembley EP.[187] Harrow RDn (1933–67), Brent RDn (1967–*).

TOLLINGTON PARK ST ANNE

EP Cr 1871 from Tollington Park St Mark EP.[108] Isling. RDn. Bdry: 1888 (cr Finsbury Park EP).[58] Abol 1965 to help cr Tollington Park St Mark with St Anne EP.[22]

TOLLINGTON PARK ST MARK

EP Cr 1854 from Upper Holloway St John EP.[167] Isling. RDn. Bdry: 1865 (cr Hornsey Rise EP),[341] 1866 (help cr Hornsey Road EP),[185] 1870 (help cr Upper Holloway St Paul EP),[60] 1871 (help cr Tollington Park St Anne EP),[108] 1886 (help cr Holloway EP),[152] 1888 (help cr Tollington Park St Saviour EP),[20] 1896,[93] 1953.[9] Abol eccl 1965 to help cr Tollington Park St Mark with St Anne EP.[22]

TOLLINGTON PARK ST MARK WITH ST ANNE

EP Cr 1965 by union Tollington Park St Mark EP, Tollington Park St Anne EP.[22] Isling. RDn.

TOLLINGTON PARK ST SAVIOUR

EP Cr 1888 from Tollington Park St Mark EP, Hornsey Rise EP.[20] Isling. RDn. Bdry: 1896.[93] Abol 1953 to help cr Hanley Road St Saviour with St Paul EP.[9]

TOTHILL FIELDS

EP Cr 1841 from Westminster St John the Evangelist AP.[245] St John W'minst. RDn (1861–83), St Mgt. & St John W'minst. RDn (1883–1901), W'minst. RDn (1901–50). Bdry: 1862 (cr Westminster St James the Less, Upper Garden Street EP).[387] Church torn down after made pt of united benefice of Westminster St Stephen and St Mary, par abol 1950 to help cr Westminster St Stephen with St John EP.[445]

TOTTENHAM

The following have 'Tottenham' in their names. Insofar as any existed at a given time: *LG* Edm. Hd, PLU, Tott. USD (ent 1875–88, pt 1888–94), pt Wood Green USD (1888–94), pt Southgate USD (1888–94), Tott. UD (1894–1934), MB (1934–65). Transf 1965 to Gtr London (Haringey LB).[1] *Parl* Tott. Dv (1885–1918), pt Tott. North Parl Bor, pt Tott. South Parl Bor (1918–48), pt Tott. BC, pt Wood Green BC (1948–70), Gtr London thereafter. *Eccl* Enf. RDn (1858–1901), Tott. RDn (1901–67), E Haringey RDn (1967–*).

AP1–TOTTENHAM [ALL HALLOWS]–Civ bdry: 1894 (loses the pt in Wood Green USD to cr Wood Green CP,[78] loses the pt in Southgate USD to Edmonton AP[192]), 1908 (exchanges pts with Hackney AP, London),[451] 1934 (incl exchanges pts with Hackney AP, London).[4] Eccl bdry: 1844 (cr EP2),[447] 1859 (cr EP6),[448] 1866 (cr Wood Green EP),[149] 1888 (help cr EP5),[58] 1889 (help cr EP1),[291] 1907 (help cr Chitts Hill EP),[140] 1912 (help cr EP3),[313] 1932,[449] 1939 (help cr EP4),[175] 1973.[54]

EP1–TOTTENHAM CHRIST CHURCH, WEST GREEN–Cr 1889 from EP2, Wood Green EP, Hanger Lane EP, AP1.[291] Bdry: 1898 (help cr Hornsey St Peter EP),[292] 1907 (help cr EP7),[450] 1912 (help cr EP3),[313] 1973.[54]

EP2–TOTTENHAM HOLY TRINITY–Cr 1844 from AP1.[447] Bdry: 1861 (cr Hanger Lane EP),[289] 1888 (help cr EP5),[58] 1889 (help cr EP1),[291] 1900 (cr EP8),[312] 1907 (help cr

EP7),[450] 1973.[434]

EP3–TOTTENHAM ST BENET FINK–Cr 1912 from EP1, AP1, Noel Park EP.[313] Bdry: 1932.[449]

EP4–TOTTENHAM ST JOHN THE BAPTIST–Cr 1939 from AP1, Edmonton St Aldhelm EP.[175] Bdry: 1973.[54]

EP5–TOTTENHAM ST MARY THE VIRGIN–Cr 1888 from EP6, AP1, EP2.[58] Bdry: 1973.[54]

EP6–TOTTENHAM ST PAUL–Cr 1859 from AP1.[448] Bdry: 1973.[54]

EP7–TOTTENHAM ST PHILIP–Cr 1907 from EP2, EP1.[450] Bdry: 1973.[54]

EP8–SOUTH TOTTENHAM–Cr 1900 from EP2.[312] Abol 1973 pt to EP2, pt to Stamford Hill St Bartholomew EP.[434]

TOWER OF LONDON

Ex-par place, sep CP 1858,[118] eccl abol 1954 ent to All Hallows Barking AP.[330] *LG* Ossul. Hd, Whitech. PLU, Dist (Metrop Bd Wks). Transf 1889 to London.[43] *Parl* Tow. Hmlts. Parl Bor (1867–85), Tow. Hmlts. Parl Bor, Whitech. Dv (1885–1918), London thereafter.

OLD TOWER WITHOUT

Ex-par place, sep CP 1858.[118] *LG* Ossul. Hd, Whitech. PLU. Transf 1889 to London.[43] *Parl* Tow. Hmlts. Parl Bor (1867–85), Tow. Hmlts. Parl Bor, Whitech. Dv (1885–1918), London thereafter.

TUFNELL PARK

EP Cr 1868 from Upper Holloway St John EP, West Holloway St Luke EP.[93] Isling. RDn. Bdry: 1883,[337] 1885 (help cr Upper Holloway All Saints EP),[242] 1953.[9]

TURNHAM GREEN

EP Cr 1845 from Chiswick AP.[135] Ealing RDn (1858–1901), Hamm. RDn (1901–67), Hounslow RDn (1967–*). Bdry: 1872 (help cr Chiswick St Paul, Grove Park EP),[136] 1906 (help cr Chiswick St Michael EP),[138] 1907,[73] 1935.[22]

TWICKENHAM

The following have 'Twickenham' in their names. Insofar as any existed at a given time: *LG* Islew. Hd, Brentf. PLU, Twick. USD, UD (1894–1926), MB (1926–65). Transf 1965 to Gtr London (Richmond upon Thames LB).[1] *Parl* Brentf. Dv (1885–1918), Twick. Dv (1918–45), Twick. Parl Bor/BC (1945–70), Gtr London thereafter. *Eccl* Seq 4.

AP1–TWICKENHAM [ST MARY THE VIRGIN]–Civ bdry: 1934,[4] 1937.[286] Eccl bdry: 1842 (cr EP4),[452] 1862 (cr Whitton EP),[46] 1875 (cr EP3),[366] 1914 (cr EP2),[283] 1939 (cr EP1).[242]

EP1–TWICKENHAM ALL HALLOWS–Cr 1939 from AP1.[242]

EP2–TWICKENHAM ALL SAINTS–Cr 1914 from AP1.[283]

EP3–EAST TWICKENHAM–Cr 1875 from AP1.[366]

EP4–TWICKENHAM COMMON–Cr 1842 from AP1.[452]

TWYFORD ABBEY–See following entry

WEST TWYFORD

Chap in Willesden AP, sep CP 1866,[203] no sep eccl identity. Sometimes 'Twyford Abbey'. *LG* Ossul. Hd, Brentf. PLU, RSD, Greenford UD. Abol 1926 ent to Ealing AP.[178] *Parl* Harrow Dv (1885–1945).

UXBRIDGE

Hmlt and chap in Hillingdon AP, sep EP 1827,[327] refounded 1842,[16] sep CP 1866.[203] *LG* Elth. Hd, Uxbr. PLU, USD, UD (1894–1955), MB (1955–65). Civ bdry: 1883,[159] 1883,[453] 1938 (gains ent Cowley AP, Harefield AP, Ickenham AP, Hillingdon East CP, Hillingdon West CP).[298] Transf 1965 to Gtr London (Hilling. LB).[1] *Parl* Uxbr. Dv/CC (1885–1970), Gtr London thereafter. *Eccl* Uxbr. RDn (1858–1967), Hilling. RDn (1967–*).

UXBRIDGE MOOR

EP Cr 1842 from Hillingdon AP.[16] RDns as for Uxbridge.

VAUXHALL BRIDGE ROAD

EP Cr 1852 from Westminster St John the Evangelist EP.[201] St Mgt. W'minst. RDn (1861–83), St Mgt. & St John W'minst. RDn (1883–1901), W'minst. RDn (1901–53). Abol 1953 pt to help cr Westminster St Stephen with St John EP, pt to Pimlico St Saviour EP.[89]

WALHAM GREEN–See FULHAM ST JOHN, WALHAM GREEN

WAPPING

Hmlt in Stepney AP, sep par 1729.[428] *LG* Ossul. Hd, Step. PLU, Limehouse Dist (Metrop Bd Wks). Transf 1889 to London.[43] *Parl* Tow. Hmlts. Parl Bor (1832–85), Tow. Hmlts. Parl Bor, St Geo. Dv (1885–1918), London thereafter. *Eccl* Pec jurisd Bp London (1729–1845), Step. RDn (1861–1951). Eccl bdry: 1864 (help cr Whitechapel St Paul, Dock Street EP).[21] Abol eccl 1951 to help cr London Docks St Peter with Wapping St John EP.[74]

WEALDSTONE

Chap in Harrow on the Hill AP, sep EP (incl pts from Harrow Weald EP, Pinner EP) 1882,[271] sep CP 1894.[306] *LG* Hendon PLU, Wealdstone UD. Civ bdry: 1895,[307] 1902.[308] Abol civ 1934 pt to help cr Harrow CP, pt to Wembley CP.[4] *Parl* Harrow Dv (1918–45). *Eccl* Harrow RDn (1882–1901), Will. RDn (1901–14), Harrow RDn (1914–*). Eccl bdry: 1946,[310] 1958 (help cr Harrow Weald St Michael and All Angels EP).[311]

WEMBLEY

Dist in Harrow on the Hill AP, sep EP 1847,[128] sep CP 1894.[306] *LG* Hendon PLU, Wembley UD (1894–1937), MB (1937–65). Civ bdry: 1934 (incl help cr Harrow CP),[4] 1937,[179] 1938.[454] Transf 1965 to Gtr London (Brent LB).[1] *Parl* Harrow Dv (1918–45), pt Wembley North Parl Bor/BC, pt Wembley South Parl Bor/BC (1945–70), Gtr London thereafter. *Eccl* Harrow RDn (1861–1901), Will. RDn (1901–14), Harrow RDn (1914–67), Brent RDn (1967–*). Eccl bdry: 1904 (cr Alperton

EP),[29] 1923 (help cr Sudbury EP),[87] 1927 (cr Wembley Park EP),[21] 1927 (help cr Preston EP),[353] 1933 (help cr Tokyngton EP),[187] 1949 (incl help cr North Greenford EP).[32]

NORTH WEMBLEY

EP Cr 1959 from Harrow on the Hill AP, Sudbury EP.[304] Harrow RDn (1959–67), Brent RDn (1967–*).

WEMBLEY PARK

EP Cr 1927 from Wembley EP.[21] Harrow RDn (1927–67), Brent RDn (1967–*). Bdry: 1935 (help cr Kenton EP),[131] 1953.[304]

UPPER WESTBOURNE PARK

EP Cr 1871 from Notting Hill All Saints EP, Kensal Green St John EP, Paddington Holy Trinity EP.[338] Kens. RDn. Bdry: 1882 (help cr Notting Hill Christ Church EP).[271] Abol 1951 to help cr Kensal Town St Thomas with St Andrew and St Philip EP.[74]

WESTMINSTER

The following have 'Westminster' in their names. Insofar as any existed at a given time: *LG* Sep noted. Transf 1889 to London.[43] *Parl* Sep noted. *Eccl* RDns before 1901 sep noted, thereafter: W'minst. RDn (1901–67), W'minst. (St Mgt.'s) RDn (1967–*).

EP1–WESTMINSTER CHRIST CHURCH, BROADWAY–Cr 1844 from AP1.[82] St Mgt. W'minst. RDn (1861–83), St Mgt. & St John W'minst. RDn (1883–1901). Abol 1953 pt to help cr Pimlico St Peter with Christ Church EP, pt to EP9, pt to AP1.[89]

EP2–WESTMINSTER ST ANDREW–Cr 1856 from AP1.[175] RDns before 1901 as for EP1. Abol 1953 pt to help cr Pimlico St Peter with Christ Church EP, pt to EP14.[89]

–WESTMINSTER ST ANNE SOHO–See ST ANNE SOHO

CP1/EP3–WESTMINSTER ST JAMES–Cr 1685 from St Martin in the Fields AP.[416] Sometimes 'St James Piccadilly'. *LG* Lbty City W'minst., Par of St James (poor relief, 1762–(1868), W'minst. PLU (1868–89), W'minst. St James Vestry (Metrop Bd Wks). *Parl* W'minst. Parl Bor (1832–85), Strand Parl Bor (1885–1918), London thereafter. *Eccl* St James W'minst. RDn (1861–97), St Martin in the Fields RDn (1897–1901). Eccl bdry: 1841 (cr EP7),[449] 1865 (help cr Great Windmill Street EP),[230] 1865 (help cr Great Marlborough Street EP),[120] 1870 (cr Regent Street EP).[323]

EP4–WESTMINSTER ST JAMES THE LESS HOLY TRINITY–Renaming 1954 of EP5 when gains pt Pimlico St Saviour EP.[398] Abol 1973 to help cr EP10.[397]

EP5–WESTMINSTER ST JAMES THE LESS, UPPER GARDEN STREET–Cr 1862 from Tothill Fields EP.[387] St John W'minst. RDn (1862–83), St Mgt. & St John W'minst. RDn (1883–1901). Renamed 1954 as EP4 when gains pt Pimlico St Saviour EP.[398]

CP2/EP6–WESTMINSTER ST JOHN THE EVANGELIST–Cr 1727 from AP1,[456] sep par but governed by joint vestry with AP1 so that often 'Westminster St Margaret and St John the Evangelist'. *LG* City W'minst., Pars of St Mgt. and St John (poor relief, 1765–1867), St George's PLU (1867–89), W'minst. Dist (Metrop Bd Wks, 1855–87, renamed St Mgt. & St John Combined Vestry, 1887–89). *Parl* W'minst. Parl Bor (1727–1918). *Eccl* St John W'minst. RDn (1861–83), St Mgt. & St John W'minst. RDn (1883–1901). Eccl bdry: 1841 (help cr Tothill Fields EP),[245] 1847 (help cr EP11),[443] 1851 (cr EP9),[120] 1852 (cr Vauxhall Bridge Road EP).[201] Abol eccl 1950 pt to help cr EP12, pt to AP1.[445]

EP7–WESTMINSTER ST LUKE–Cr 1841 from EP3.[447] Sometimes 'Berwick Street' or 'Westminster St Luke, Berwick Street'. RDns as for EP3. Bdry: 1865 (help cr Great Windmill Street EP),[230] 1865 (help cr Great Marlborough Street EP).[120] Abol 1935 ent to St Anne Soho EP.[8]

AP1–WESTMINSTER ST MARGARET–Bdry: 1727 (cr CP2/EP6).[456] Because AP1 and CP2 administered by joint vestry, often 'Westminster St Margaret and St John'. *LG* As for CP2. *Parl* W'minst. Parl Bor (1586–1918). *Eccl* RDns before 1901 as for EP1. Addtl eccl bdry alt: 1844 (cr EP1),[82] 1847 (cr EP11),[443] 1849 (cr Knightsbridge All Saints EP),[186] 1856 (cr EP2).[175]

–WESTMINSTER ST MARGARET AND ST JOHN THE EVANGELIST–See AP1, CP2

EP8–WESTMINSTER ST MARY, CROWN STREET, SOHO–Cr 1856 from St Anne Soho EP.[275] St Martin in the Fields RDn (1861–1901). Abol 1932 ent to St Anne Soho EP, commonly called in 20th cent 'Westminster St Anne Soho'.[227]

EP9–WESTMINSTER ST MATTHEW–Cr 1851 from EP6.[120] RDns before 1901 as for EP1. Bdry: 1953,[89] 1974.[263]

EP10–WESTMINSTER ST SAVIOUR AND ST JAMES THE LESS–Cr 1973 by union pt Pimlico St Saviour EP, pt EP4, pt Pimlico St Gabriel EP.[397]

EP11–WESTMINSTER ST STEPHEN–Cr 1847 from AP1, EP6, Tothill Fields EP.[443] RDns before 1901 as for EP1. Abol 1950 to help cr EP12.[445]

EP12–WESTMINSTER ST STEPHEN WITH ST JOHN–Cr 1950 by union EP11, Tothill Fields EP, pt EP6.[445] Bdry: 1953.[89]

WHETSTONE

EP Cr 1833, refounded 1836 from Finchley AP.[46] Enf. RDn (1858–75), Highg. RDn (1875–1901), Hornsey RDn (1901–67), Central Barnet RDn (1967–*). Bdry: 1872 (help cr Finchley Christ Church, North End EP),[224] 1914 (help cr Woodside Park EP).[141]

WHITECHAPEL

The following have 'Whitechapel' in their names.

Insofar as any existed at a given time: *LG* Ossul. Hd, Whitech. PLU, Dist (Metrop Bd Wks). Transf 1889 to London.[43] *Parl* Tow. Hmlts. Parl Bor (1832–85), Tow. Hmlts. Parl Bor, Whitech. Dv (1885–1918), London thereafter. *Eccl* Pec jurisd Bp London (1780–1845), Spitalf. RDn (1861–1901), Step. RDn (1901–66), Tow. Hmlts. RDn (1966–*).

CP1/EP1–WHITECHAPEL [ST MARY]–Cr early 17th cent from Stepney AP.[442] Pt London, pt Middx (the former lost 1900 to St Botolph Without Aldgate AP, City of London; qv in entries for London Adm Co). Eccl bdry: 1841 (cr EP3),[455] before 1870 (cr EP2).[459] Abol 1923 to help cr EP4.[376]

EP2–WHITECHAPEL ST JUDE–Cr before 1870 from EP1.[446] Abol 1923 to help cr EP4.[376]

EP3–WHITECHAPEL ST MARK–Cr 1841 from EP1.[455] Abol 1926 to help cr EP6.[304]

EP4–WHITECHAPEL ST MARY WITH ST JUDE–Cr 1923 by union EP1, EP2.[376] Abol 1951 pt to help cr Spitalfields Christ Church with All Saints EP, pt to help cr Stepney St Augustine with St Philip EP.[74]

EP5–WHITECHAPEL ST PAUL, DOCK STREET–Cr 1864 from EP3, Wapping EP, Aldgate St Botolph EP.[21] Abol 1926 to help cr EP6.[304]

EP6–WHITECHAPEL ST PAUL WITH ST MARK–Cr 1926 by union EP5, EP3.[304] Bdry: 1951 (incl help cr London Docks St Peter with Wapping St John EP),[74] 1954,[398] 1954.[330]

WHITEHALL PARK

EP Cr 1897 from Upper Holloway St John EP, Hornsey Rise EP.[338] Isling. RDn.

WHITTON

EP Cr 1862 from Twickenham AP.[46] Hampton RDn. Bdry: 1955,[336] 1958 (cr Whitton St Augustine EP).[455]

WHITTON ST AUGUSTINE

EP Cr 1958 from Whitton EP.[455] Hampton RDn. Bdry: 1972.[287]

WILLESDEN

The following have 'Willesden' in their names. Insofar as any existed at a given time: *LG* Ossul. Hd, Hendon PLU (1835–96), Will. USD (pt 1875–83, ent 1883–94), pt Hendon RSD (1875–83), Will. UD (1894–1933), MB (1933–65). Transf 1965 to Gtr London (Brent LB).[1] *Parl* Harrow Dv (1885–1918), pt Will. East Parl Bor/BC, pt Will. West Parl Bor/BC (1918–70), Gtr London thereafter. *Eccl* Pec jurisd Dean & Chapter of St Paul's, London (until 1845), Harrow RDn (1861–1901), Will. RDn (1901–67), Brent RDn (1967–*).

AP1–WILLESDEN–Civ bdry: 1895,[3] 1934,[4] 1938.[454] Parl bdry: 1945.[202] Eccl bdry: 1845 (help cr Kensal Green St John EP),[125] 1867 (cr Kilburn Holy Trinity EP, Brondesbury Christ Church EP),[95] 1880 (cr EP1),[376] 1885 (help cr Neasden cum Kingsbury EP),[249] 1892 (help cr Stonebridge EP),[263] 1902 (cr EP2).[376]

EP1–WILLESDEN ST ANDREW–Cr 1880 from AP1.[376] Bdry: 1898 (help cr EP3),[50] 1933 (cr Gladstone Park EP).[61]

EP2–WILLESDEN ST MATTHEW–Cr 1902 from AP1, Harlesden All Souls EP.[68]

EP3–WILLESDEN GREEN–Cr 1898 from Brondesbury Christ Church EP, EP1.[50] Bdry: 1910 (cr Cricklewood St Michael EP).[166]

WILTON PLACE

EP Cr 1843 from Pimlico St Peter EP.[58] St Geo. Hanov. Sq. RDn (1861–1901), W'minst. RDn (1901–67), W'minst. (St Mgt.'s) RDn (1967–*). Bdry: 1846,[221] 1866 (help cr Knightsbridge Holy Trinity EP),[149] 1866 (cr Pimlico St Barnabas EP),[186] 1909 (cr Pimlico St Mary, Graham Street EP),[107] 1953.[89]

WINCHMORE HILL

EP Cr 1851 from Edmonton AP.[195] Enf. RDn. Bdry: 1906 (help cr Palmer's Green EP),[393] 1913 (cr Winchmore Hill Holy Trinity EP),[458] 1941 (help cr Oakwood EP, help cr Grange Park EP),[214] 1943.[250]

WINCHMORE HILL HOLY TRINITY

EP Cr 1913 from Winchmore Hill EP.[458] Enf. RDn.

GREAT WINDMILL STREET

EP Cr 1865 from Westminster St James EP, Westminster St Luke EP.[230] St James W'minst. RDn (1865–97), St Martin in the Fields RDn (1897–1901), W'minst. RDn (1901–53). Abol 1953 to help cr Soho St Anne with St Thomas and St Peter EP.[89]

WOBURN SQUARE

EP Cr 1902 from Bloomsbury St George EP, St Giles in the Fields AP, St Pancras AP, Gordon Square EP, Regent Square EP.[68] St Geo. Bloomsb. RDn (1861–97), St Martin in the Fields RDn (1897–1901), Holb. RDn (1901–34), Finsb. & Holb. RDn (1934–67), S Camd. (Holb. & St Panc.) RDn (1967–*).

WOOD GREEN

Chap in Tottenham AP, sep EP 1866,[149] sep CP 1894 (the pt in Wood Green USD).[78] *LG* Edm. PLU, Wood Green UD (1894–1933), MB (1933–65). Civ bdry: 1934.[4] Transf 1965 to Gtr London (Haringey LB).[1] *Parl* Wood Green Dv (1918–48), BC (1948–70), Gtr London thereafter. *Eccl* Enf. RDn (1866–1901), Tott. RDn (1901–67), E Haringey RDn (1967–*).

WOODSIDE PARK

EP Cr 1914 from Finchley Christ Church, North End EP, Whetstone EP.[141] Hornsey RDn (1914–67), Central Barnet RDn (1967–*). Bdry: 1932,[227] 1951.[184]

YIEWSLEY

Chap in Hillingdon AP, sep EP 1874,[181] sep CP 1896 (from Hillingdon East CP).[328] *LG* Uxbr. Eccl bdry: 1874 (help cr Southgate St Michael at Bowes EP),[326] 1889 (help cr Tottenham Christ Church, West Green EP),[291] 1889 (cr Noel Park EP),[47] 1900 (help cr Alexandra Park St Andrew EP),[27] 1904 (cr Alexandra Park St Saviour EP),[28] 1906 (help cr Bounds Green EP),[71] 1907 (help cr Chitts Hill EP),[140] 1932.[449]

PLU, RD (1896–1911), Yiewsley UD (1911–29), Yiewsley & W Drayton UD (1929–49). Civ bdry: 1929.[161] Abol civ 1949 to help cr Yiewsley and West Drayton CP.[176] *Parl* Uxbr. Dv/CC (1918–70). *Eccl* Uxbr. RDn (1874–1967), Hilling. RDn (1967–*).

YIEWSLEY AND WEST DRAYTON

CP Cr 1949 by union Yiewsley CP, West Drayton AP, Harmondsworth AP.[176] *LG* Yiewsley & W Drayton UD. Transf 1965 to Gtr London (Hilling LB).[1] *Parl* Gtr London from 1970.

NORFOLK

ABBREVIATIONS

Abbreviations particular to Norfolk follow. Those general abbreviations in use throughout the *Guide* are found on page xix.

Ayl.	Aylsham
Blof.	Blofield
Brecc.	Breccles
Breckl.	Breckland
Brisl.	Brisley
Brothc.	Brothercross
Burn.	Burnham
Clack.	Clackclose
Clav.	Clavering
Cranw.	Cranwich
Ctrl.	Central
Depw.	Depwade
Dock.	Docking
Down.	Downham
Earsh.	Earsham
Elm.	Elmham
Erp.	Erpingham
Eynsf.	Eynsford
Foreh.	Forehoe
Freebr.	Freebridge
Greenh.	Greenhoe
Guiltc.	Guiltcross
Hap.	Happing
Heach.	Heacham
Henst.	Henstead
Hingh.	Hingham
Humblyd.	Humbleyard
Ingw.	Ingworth
Laund.	Launditch
Lodd.	Loddon
K's Lynn	King's Lynn
Marshl.	Marshland
Mitf.	Mitford
Norw.	Norwich
Redenh.	Redenhall
Rockl.	Rockland
Shrop.	Shropham
Smallb.	Smallburgh
Smithd.	Smithdon
Spar.	Sparham
Swaff.	Swaffham
Tav.	Taverham
Thetf.	Thetford
Toft.	Toftrees
Tunst.	Tunstead
Walsing.	Walsingham
Wax.	Waxham
Wayl.	Wayland
(Gt) Yarm.	(Great) Yarmouth

SEQUENCES

An abbreviated entry prefixed by 'Seq' is used in the parochial entries to avoid repeating often the names of superior units of administration. The content of each sequence is shown below.

Local Government Sequences ('LG')

SEQ 1 Blof. Hd, PLU, RSD, RD (1894–1935), Blof. & Flegg RD (1935–74)
SEQ 2 Brothc. Hd, Dock. PLU, RSD, RD
SEQ 3 Clack. Hd, Down. PLU, RSD, RD
SEQ 4 Clav. Hd, Lodd. & Clav. PLU, RSD, RD (1894–1935), Lodd. RD (1935–74)
SEQ 5 Depw. Hd, PLU, RSD, RD
SEQ 6 Diss Hd, Depw. PLU, RSD, RD
SEQ 7 Diss Hd, Guiltc. PLU (1835–1902), RSD, Depw. PLU (1902–30), RD (1902–74)
SEQ 8 Earsh. Hd, Depw. PLU, RSD, RD
SEQ 9 N Erp. Hd, Erp. PLU, RSD, RD
SEQ 10 S Erp. Hd, Ayl. PLU, RSD, RD (1894–1935), Erp. RD (1935–74)
SEQ 11 S Erp. Hd, Ayl. PLU, RSD, RD (1894–1935), St Faith's & Ayl. RD (1935–74)
SEQ 12 S Erp. Hd, Ayl. PLU, RSD, RD (1894–1935), Smallb. RD (1935–74)
SEQ 13 S Erp. Hd, Erp. PLU, RSD, RD
SEQ 14 Eynsf. Hd, Ayl. PLU, RSD, RD (1894–1935), St Faith's & Ayl. RD (1935–74)
SEQ 16 Eynsf. Hd, Mitf. & Laund. PLU, RSD, RD
SEQ 17 Eynsf. Hd, St Faith's PLU, RSD, RD (1894–1935), St Faith's & Ayl. RD (1935–74)
SEQ 18 E Flegg Hd, E & W Flegg incorp for poor, RSD, RD (1894–1935), Blof. & Flegg RD (1935–74)
SEQ 19 W Flegg Hd, E & W Flegg incorp for poor, RSD, RD (1894–1935), Blof. & Flegg RD (1935–74)
SEQ 20 Foreh. Hd, incorp for poor/PLU, RSD, RD (1894–1935), Foreh. & Henst. RD (1935–74)
SEQ 21 Freebr. Lynn Hd, Dock. PLU, RSD, RD
SEQ 22 Freebr. Lynn Hd, PLU, RSD, RD
SEQ 23 Freebr. Marshl. Hd, Down. PLU, RSD, RD
SEQ 24 Freebr. Marshl. Hd, Wisbech PLU, RSD, Marsh. RD
SEQ 25 Gallow Hd, Dock. PLU, RSD, RD
SEQ 26 Gallow Hd, Walsing. PLU, RSD, RD
SEQ 27 N Greenh. Hd, Walsing. PLU, RSD, RD
SEQ 28 S Greenh. Hd, Swaff. PLU, RSD, RD
SEQ 29 Grimshoe Hd, Swaff. PLU, RSD, RD
SEQ 30 Grimshoe Hd, Thetf. PLU, RSD, RD (1894–1935), Down. RD (1935–74)
SEQ 31 Grimshoe Hd, Thetf. PLU, RSD, RD (1894–1935), Swaff. RD (1935–74)
SEQ 32 Guiltc. Hd, PLU (1835–1902), RSD, RD (1894–1902), Thetf. PLU (1902–30), RD (1902–35), Wayl. RD (1935–74)
SEQ 33 Guiltc. Hd, PLU (1835–1902), RSD, RD (1894–1902), Wayl. PLU (1902–30), RD (1902–74)
SEQ 34 Hap. Hd, Tunst. & Hap. incorp for poor (1780–1870), Smallb. PLU (1870–1930), RSD, RD
SEQ 35 Henst. Hd, PLU, RSD, RD (1894–1935), Foreh. & Henst. RD (1935–74)
SEQ 36 Holt Hd, Erp. PLU, RSD, RD
SEQ 37 Holt Hd, Walsing. PLU, RSD, RD
SEQ 38 Humblyd. Hd, Henst. PLU, RSD, RD (1894–1935), Foreh. & Henst. RD (1935–74)
SEQ 39 Laund. Hd, Mitf. & Laund. PLU, RSD, RD
SEQ 40 Lodd. Hd, Lodd. & Clav. PLU, RSD, RD (1894–1935), Lodd. RD (1935–74)
SEQ 41 Mitf. Hd, Mitf. & Laund. PLU, RSD, RD
SEQ 42 Shrop. Hd, Guiltc. PLU (1835–1902), RSD, RD (1894–1902), Wayl. PLU (1902–30), RD (1902–74)
SEQ 43 Shorp. Hd, Wayl. PLU, RSD, RD
SEQ 44 Smithd. Hd, Dock. PLU, RSD, RD
SEQ 45 Tav. Hd, St Faith's PLU, RSD, RD (1894–1935), St Faith's & Ayl. RD (1935–74)
SEQ 46 Tunst. Hd, Blof. PLU, RSD, RD (1894–1935), Blof. & Flegg RD (1935–74)
SEQ 47 Tunst. Hd, Tunst. & Hap. incorp for poor (1780–1870), Smallb. PLU (1870–1930), RSD, RD
SEQ 48 Walsham Hd, Blof. PLU, RSD, RD (1894–1935), Blof. & Flegg RD (1935–74)
SEQ 49 Wayl. Hd, Swaff. PLU, RSD, RD
SEQ 50 Wayl. Hd, PLU, RSD, RD

Parliamentary Sequences ('Parl')

SEQ 1 E'rn Dv (1832–67), N E Dv (1867–85), E'rn Dv (1885–1948), N Norfolk CC (1948–*)
SEQ 2 E'rn Dv (1832–67), N E Dv (1867–85), E'rn Dv (1885–1948), Yarm. CC (1948–*)
SEQ 3 E'rn Dv (1832–67), N E Dv (1867–85), E'rn Dv (1885–1918), N'rn Dv (1918–48), Ctrl. Norfolk CC (1948–70), N Norfolk CC (1970–*)
SEQ 4 E'rn Dv (1832–67), N E Dv (1867–85), E'rn Dv (1885–1918), N'rn Dv (1918–48), N Norfolk CC (1948–*)
SEQ 5 E'rn Dv (1832–67), N E Dv (1867–85), N'rn Dv (1885–1918), E'rn Dv (1918–48), Ctrl. Norfolk CC (1948–70), N Norfolk CC (1970–*)
SEQ 6 E'rn Dv (1832–67), N E Dv (1867–85), N'rn Dv (1885–1948), Ctrl. Norfolk CC (1948–70), N Norfolk CC (1970–*)
SEQ 7 E'rn Dv (1832–67), N E Dv (1867–85), N'rn Dv (1885–1948), N Norfolk CC (1948–*)
SEQ 8 E'rn Dv (1832–67), N E Dv (1867–85), N'rn Dv (1885–1948), N Norfolk CC

(1948–70), N W Norfolk CC (1970–*)
SEQ 9 E'rn Dv (1832–67), N E Dv (1867–85), N'rn Dv (1885–1918), S-W'rn Dv (1918–48), S W Norfolk CC (1948–*)
SEQ 10 E'rn Dv (1832–67), S E Dv (1867–85), E'rn Dv (1885–1948), Ctrl. Norfolk CC (1948–70), N Norfolk CC (1970–*)
SEQ 11 E'rn Dv (1832–67), S E Dv (1867–85), E'rn Dv (1885–1948), Yarm. CC (1948–*)
SEQ 12 E'rn Dv (1832–67), S E Dv (1867–85), Mid Dv (1885–1918), S'rn Dv (1918–48), Ctrl. Norfolk CC (1948–70), S Norfolk CC (1970–*)
SEQ 13 E'rn Dv (1832–67), S E Dv (1867–85), S'rn Dv (1885–1948), Ctrl. Norfolk CC (1948–70), S Norfolk CC (1970–*)
SEQ 14 E'rn Dv (1832–67), S E Dv (1867–85), S'rn Dv (1885–1948), S Norfolk CC (1948–*)
SEQ 15 E'rn Dv (1832–67), S E Dv (1867–85), S-W'rn Dv (1885–1918), E'rn Dv (1918–48), S Norfolk CC (1948–*)
SEQ 16 W'rn Dv (1832–67), N E Dv (1867–85), N'rn Dv (1885–1948), N Norfolk CC (1948–*)
SEQ 17 W'rn Dv (1832–67), N E Dv (1867–85), N'rn Dv (1885–1948), N W Norfolk CC (1948–*)
SEQ 18 W'rn Dv (1832–67), S E Dv (1867–85), Mid Dv (1885–1918), S'rn Dv (1918–48), S Norfolk CC (1948–*)
SEQ 19 W'rn Dv (1832–67), S E Dv (1867–85), Mid Dv (1885–1918), S-W'rn Dv (1918–48), S W Norfolk CC (1948–*)
SEQ 20 W'rn Dv (1832–67), W Dv (1867–85), Mid Dv (1885–1918), S-W'rn Dv (1918–48), S W Norfolk CC (1948–*)
SEQ 21 W'rn Dv (1832–67), W Dv (1867–85), N-W'rn Dv (1885–1918), K's Lynn Dv/CC (1918–70), N W Norfolk CC (1970–*)
SEQ 22 W'rn Dv (1832–67), W Dv (1867–85), N-W'rn Dv (1885–1918), K's Lynn Dv (1918–48), S W Norfolk CC (1948–*)
SEQ 23 W'rn Dv (1832–67), W Dv (1867–85), N-W'rn Dv (1885–1918), N'rn Dv (1918–48), N Norfolk CC (1948–*)
SEQ 24 W'rn Dv (1832–67), W Dv (1867–85), S-W'rn Dv (1885–1918), S'rn Dv (1918–48), S Norfolk CC (1948–*)
SEQ 25 W'rn Dv (1832–67), W Dv (1867–85), S-W'rn Dv (1885–1948), K's Lynn CC (1948–70), N W Norfolk CC (1970–*)
SEQ 26 W'rn Dv (1832–67), W Dv (1867–85), S-W'rn Dv (1885–1948), S W Norfolk CC (1948–*)

Ecclesiastical Sequences ('Eccl')

Orig Norfolk AD:
SEQ 1 Brooke RDn (until 1970), Depw. RDn (1970–*)
SEQ 2 Brooke RDn (until 1970), Lodd. RDn (1970–*)
SEQ 3 Brooke RDn (until 1918), Lodd. RDn (1918–*)
SEQ 4 Brooke RDn (until 1918), Lodd. RDn (1918–70), Depw. RDn (1970–*)
SEQ 5 Burn. RDn (until 1970), Burn. & Walsing. RDn (1970–*)
SEQ 6 Burn. RDn (until 1970), Heach. & Rising RDn (1970–*)
SEQ 7 Cranw. RDn (until 1918), Swaff. RDn (1918–70), Breckl. RDn (1970–*)
SEQ 8 Cranw. RDn (until 1918), Swaff. RDn (1918–70), Brisl. & Elm. RDn (1970–*)
SEQ 9 Cranw. RDn (until 1918), Swaff. RDn (1918–70), Hingh. & Mitf. RDn (1970–*)
SEQ 10 Cranw. RDn (until 1918), Thetf. RDn (1918–70), Breckl. RDn (1970–*)
SEQ 11 Depw. RDn
SEQ 12 Heach. RDn (until 1970), Heach. & Rising RDn (1970–*)
SEQ 13 Hingh. RDn (until 1970), Hingh. & Mitf. RDn (1970–*)
SEQ 14 Hingh. RDn (until 1970), Humblyd. RDn (1970–*)
SEQ 15 Hingh. RDn (until 1918), Mitf. RDn (1918–70), Hingh. & Mitf. RDn (1970–*)
SEQ 16 Humblyd. RDn
SEQ 17 Humblyd. RDn (until 1918), Norw. RDn (1918–70), Norw. (South) RDn (1970–*)
SEQ 18 Redenh. RDn
SEQ 19 S Repps RDn (until 1894), Repps RDn (1894–*)
SEQ 20 Rockl. RDn (until 1970), Thetf. & Rockl. RDn (1970–*)
SEQ 21 Rockl. RDn (until 1918), Harling RDn (1918–31), Rockl. RDn (1931–70), Redenh. RDn (1970–*)
SEQ 22 Rockl. RDn (until 1918), Harling RDn (1918–31), Rockl. RDn (1931–70), Thetf. & Rockl. RDn (1970–*)
SEQ 23 Rockl. RDn (until 1918), Thetf. RDn (1918–70), Thetf. & Rockl. RDn (1970–*)
SEQ 24 Wax. RDn
SEQ 25 Wax. RDn (until 1918), Tunst. RDn (1918–*)
SEQ 26 Wax. RDn (until 1918), Tunst. RDn (1918–70), Repps RDn (1970–*)

Orig Norw. AD:
SEQ 27 Blof. RDn
SEQ 28 Brecc. RDn (until 1970), Breckl. RDn (1970–*)
SEQ 29 Brisl. RDn (until 1970), Brisl. & Elm. RDn (1970–*)
SEQ 30 Brisl. RDn (until 1918), Elm. RDn (1918–70), Brisl. & Elm. RDn (1970–*)
SEQ 31 Flegg RDn
SEQ 32 Holt RDn
SEQ 33 Ingw. RDn
SEQ 34 Ingw. RDn (until 1970), Tunst. RDn (1970–*)
SEQ 35 Lynn RDn (until 1866), Lynn Marshl. RDn (1866–*)

SEQ 36 Lynn RDn (until 1866), Lynn Marshl. RDn (1866–1914), Lynn Norfolk RDn (1914–18), Rising RDn (1918–70), Heach. & Rising RDn (1970–*)
SEQ 37 Lynn RDn (until 1866), Lynn Marshl. RDn (1866–1914), Lynn Norfolk RDn (1914–18), Lynn RDn (1918–*)
SEQ 38 Lynn RDn (until 1866), Lynn Norfolk RDn (1866–1918), Lynn RDn (1918–*)
SEQ 39 Norw. RDn (until 1970), Norw. (East) RDn (1970–*)
SEQ 40 Spar. RDn
SEQ 41 Tav. RDn (until 1970), Blof. RDn (1970–*)
SEQ 42 Tav. RDn (until 1970), Norw. (North) RDn (1970–*)
SEQ 43 Thetf. RDn (until 1970), Thetf. & Rockl. RDn (1970–*)
SEQ 44 Toft. RDn (until 1918), Brisl. RDn (1918–70), Brisl. & Elm. RDn (1970–*)
SEQ 45 Toft. RDn (until 1918), Brisl. RDn (1918–70), Burn. & Walsing. RDn (1970–*)
SEQ 46 Walsing. RDn (until 1970), Burn. & Walsing. RDn (1970–*)
SEQ 47 Walsing. RDn (until 1970), Holt RDn (1970–*)

DIOCESES AND ARCHDEACONRIES

Norfolk pars were organised in dioceses and archdeaconries as follows.

ELY DIOC (1914–*)
IoE AD (1914–17): Fincham RDn, Lynn Marshl. RDn
Wisbech AD (1917–):* Feltwell RDn, Fincham RDn, Lynn Marshl. RDn

NORWICH DIOC
Lynn AD (1894–):* Brecc. RDn (1918–70), Breckl. RDn (1970–*), Brisl. RDn (1894–1970), Brisl. & Elm. RDn (1970–*), Burn. RDn (1894–1970), Burn. & Walsing. RDn (1970–*), Cranw. RDn (1894–1918), Elm. RDn (1918–70), Fincham RDn (1894–1914), Heach. RDn (1894–1970), Heach. & Rising RDn (1970–*), Holt RDn (1918–*), Lynn RDn (1918–*), Lynn Marshl. RDn (1894–1914), Lynn Norfolk RDn (1894–1918), Rising RDn (1918–70), Swaff. RDn (1918–70), Thetf. RDn (1894–1964), Toft. RDn (1894–1918), Walsing. RDn (1894–1970)
Norfolk AD: Brecc. RDn (1894–1918), Brooke RDn (until 1970), Burn. RDn (until 1894), Cranw. RDn (until 1894), Depw. RDn, Fincham RDn (until 1894), Harling RDn (1918–31), Heach. RDn (until 1894), Hingh. RDn (until 1970), Hingh. & Mitf. RDn (1970–*), Humblyd. RDn, Lodd. RDn (1918–*), Mitf. RDn (1918–70), Redenh. RDn, Repps RDn (until 1894), Rockl. RDn (until 1970), Spar. RDn (until 1846), Thetf. RDn (1964–70), Thetf. & Rockl. RDn (1970–*), Wax. RDn (until 1894)
Norwich AD: Blof. RDn, Brecc. RDn (until 1894), Brisl. RDn (until 1894), Flegg RDn, Holt RDn (until 1918), Ingw. RDn, Lynn RDn (until 1866), Lynn Marshl. RDn (1866–94), Lynn Norfolk RDn (1866–94), Norw. RDn (until 1970), Norw. (East) RDn (1970–*), Norw. (North) RDn (1970–*), Norw. (South) RDn (1970–*), Repps RDn (1894–*), Spar. RDn (1846–*), Tav. RDn (until 1970), Thetf. RDn (until 1894), Toft. RDn (until 1894), Tunst. RDn (1918–*), Walsing. RDn (until 1894), Wax. RDn (1894–*)

THE PARISHES OF NORFOLK

ACLE
AP *LG* Seq 48. Civ bdry: 1935.[1] *Parl* Seq 11. *Eccl* Seq 27.

SOUTH ACRE
AP *LG* Seq 28. *Parl* Seq 26. *Eccl* Seq 8.

WEST ACRE
AP Usual eccl spelling; for civ see 'Westacre'. *Eccl* Seq 37.

ALBURGH
AP *LG* Seq 8. *Parl* Seq 14. *Eccl* Seq 18.

ALBY
AP *LG* S Erp. Hd, Ayl. PLU, RSD. Abol civ 1884 to help cr Alby with Thwaite CP.[2] *Parl* E'rn Dv (1832–67), N E Dv (1867–85). *Eccl* Seq 33.

ALBY WITH THWAITE
CP Cr 1884 by union Alby AP, Thwaite AP.[2] *LG* S Erp. Hd, Ayl. PLU, RSD, RD (1894–1935), Erp. RD (1935–74). *Parl* N'rn Dv (1885–1948), N Norfolk CC (1948–*).

ALDBOROUGH
AP *LG* Seq 9. Civ bdry: 1935 (gains Thurgarton AP).[1] *Parl* Seq 7. *Eccl* Seq 19.

ALDEBY
AP *LG* Seq 4. *Parl* Seq 15. *Eccl* Seq 3.

ALDERFORD
AP *LG* Seq 17. *Parl* Seq 5. *Eccl* Seq 40.

ALETHORPE
Orig sep AP,[3] later deemed ex-par, sep CP 1858.[4] *LG* Gallow Hd, Walsing. PLU, RSD, RD. Abol 1935 ent to Little Snoring AP.[1] *Parl* W Dv (1867–85), N-W'rn Dv (1885–1918), N'rn Dv (1918–48).

ALPINGTON
AP *LG* Seq 40. *Parl* Seq 15. *Eccl* Brooke RDn, early in ruins, now eccl incl in Bergh Apton AP.

ANMER
AP *LG* Seq 21. *Parl* Seq 21. *Eccl* Seq 36.
ANTINGHAM
AP Orig 2 pars, St Mary, St Margaret, one for civ purposes, the latter eccl abol before 1845 and incl in the former. *LG* Seq 9. *Parl* Seq 7. *Eccl* Seq 19.
APPLETON
AP *LG* Freebr. Lynn Hd, abol civ early 18th cent to cr Flitcham with Appleton CP.[5] *Eccl* Lynn RDn (until 1866), Lynn Norfolk RDn (1866–1918), Rising RDn (1918–27). Abol eccl 1927 to help cr West Newton with Appleton EP.[6]
ARMINGHALL
AP *LG* Henst. Hd, PLU, RSD, RD. Abol civ 1935 ent to Bixley AP.[1] *Parl* E'rn Dv (1832–67), S E Dv (1867–85), S'rn Dv (1885–1948). *Eccl* Pec jurisd Dean & Chapter of Norw. (until 1847), Seq 2 thereafter.
ASHBY ST MARY
AP *LG* Seq 40. *Parl* Seq 15. *Eccl* Seq 2.
ASHBY WITH OBY
AP *LG* Seq 19. *Parl* Seq 2. *Eccl* Flegg RDn. Abol eccl 1604 to help cr Ashby with Oby and Thurne EP.[7]
ASHBY WITH OBY AND THURNE
EP Cr 1604 by union Ashby with Oby AP, Thurne AP.[7] *Eccl* Seq 31.
ASHILL
AP *LG* Seq 49. *Parl* Seq 26. *Eccl* Seq 28.
ASHMANHAUGH
AP *LG* Seq 47. Civ bdry: 1935 (gains Beeston St Lawrence AP).[1] *Parl* Seq 1. *Eccl* Seq 25.
ASHWELLTHORPE
AP *LG* Seq 5. Civ bdry: 1935 (gains Fundenhall AP).[1] *Parl* Seq 14. *Eccl* Depw. RDn (until 1918), Humblyd. RDn (1918–*).
ASHWICKEN
AP Gains after 1474 Leziate AP[8] (the latter regains sep civ identity early, the union sometimes eccl 'Ashwicken and Leziate'). *LG* Freebr. Lynn Hd, PLU, RSD, RD. Abol civ 1935 ent to Leziate AP.[1] *Parl* W'rn Dv (1832–67), W Dv (1867–85), N-W'rn Dv (1885–1918), K's Lynn Dv (1918–48). *Eccl* Seq 38. Eccl bdry: 1937.[9]
ASHWICKEN AND LEZIATE–See prev entry
ASLACTON
AP *LG* Seq 5. *Parl* Seq 14. *Eccl* Seq 11.
ATTLEBOROUGH
AP *LG* Seq 43. *Parl* Seq 18. *Eccl* Seq 20.
ATTLEBRIDGE
AP *LG* Seq 45. *Parl* Seq 10. *Eccl* Tav. RDn (until 1918), Spar. RDn (1918–*).
AYLMERTON
AP *LG* Seq 9. *Parl* Seq 7. *Eccl* Seq 19.
AYLSHAM
AP *LG* Seq 11. *Parl* Seq 5. *Eccl* Seq 33.
BABINGLEY
AP *LG* Freebr. Lynn Hd, PLU, RSD, RD. Abol civ 1935 ent to Sandringham AP.[1] *Parl* W'rn Dv (1832–67), W Dv (1867–85), N-W'rn Dv (1885–1918), K's Lynn Dv (1918–48). *Eccl* Seq 36.
BACONSTHORPE
AP *LG* Seq 13. *Parl* Seq 7. *Eccl* Ingw. RDn (until 1918), Holt RDn (1918–*).
BACTON
AP *LG* Seq 47. Civ bdry: 1885,[10] 1935 (gains Edingthorpe AP).[1] *Parl* Seq 1. *Eccl* Seq 25.
BAGTHORPE
AP *LG* Gallow Hd, Dock. PLU, RSD, RD. Abol civ 1935 to help cr Bagthorpe with Barmer CP.[1] *Parl* W'rn Dv (1832–67), W Dv (1867–85), N-W'rn Dv (1885–1918), K's Lynn Dv (1918–48). *Eccl* Seq 6.
BAGTHORPE WITH BARMER
CP Cr 1935 by union Bagthorpe AP, Barmer AP.[1] *LG* Dock. RD. *Parl* K's Lynn CC (1948–70), N W Norfolk CC (1970–*).
BALE
AP Sometimes anc 'Baithley'. *LG* Holt Hd, Walsing. PLU, RSD, RD. Abol civ 1935 ent to Gunthorpe AP.[1] *Parl* W'rn Dv (1832–67), N E Dv (1867–85), N'rn Dv (1885–1948). *Eccl* Seq 32.
BANHAM
AP *LG* Seq 33. *Parl* Seq 18. *Eccl* Seq 22.
BANNINGHAM
AP *LG* S Erp. Hd, Ayl. PLU, RSD, RD. Abol civ 1935 ent to Colby AP.[1] *Parl* E'rn Dv (1832–67), N E Dv (1867–85), N'rn Dv (1885–1948). *Eccl* Seq 34.
BARFORD
AP *LG* Seq 20. *Parl* Seq 12. *Eccl* Seq 13.
BARMER
AP *LG* Gallow Hd, Dock. PLU, RSD, RD. Civ bdry: 1885.[11] Abol civ 1935 to help cr Bagthorpe with Barmer CP.[1] *Parl* W'rn Dv (1832–67), W Dv (1867–85), N-W'rn Dv (1885–1918), K's Lynn Dv (1918–48). *Eccl* Seq 5.
BARNEY
AP *LG* N Greenh. Hd, Walsing. PLU, RSD, RD. Abol civ 1935 to help cr Fulmodeston CP.[1] *Parl* W'rn Dv (1832–67), N E Dv (1867–85), N'rn Dv (1885–1948). *Eccl* Seq 47.
BARNHAM BROOM
AP Orig 2 pars, St Peter and St Paul, St Michael, early united.[12] Gains 1680 Bixton AP.[13] *LG* Seq 20. *Parl* Seq 12. *Eccl* Seq 13.
LITTLE BARNINGHAM
AP *LG* Seq 10. *Parl* Seq 7. *Eccl* Seq 33.
BARNINGHAM NORWOOD
AP *LG* N Erp. Hd, Erp. PLU, RSD, RD. Abol civ 1935 ent to Gresham AP.[1] *Parl* E'rn Dv (1832–67), N E Dv (1867–85), N'rn Dv (1885–1948). *Eccl* Repps RDn. Abol eccl 1942 to help cr Barningham Winter with Barningham Norwood EP.[14]
BARNINGHAM WINTER
AP Usual eccl spelling; for civ see following entry. *Eccl* Repps RDn. Abol eccl 1942 to help cr Barningham Winter with Barningham Norwood EP.[14]
BARNINGHAM WINTER OR BARNINGHAM TOWN
AP Usual civ spelling; for eccl see prev entry. *LG* N Erp. Hd, Erp. PLU, RSD, RD. Civ bdry: 1884.[15]

Abol civ 1935 ent to Matlask AP.[1] *Parl* E'rn Dv (1832–67), N E Dv (1867–85), N'rn Dv (1885–1948). *Eccl* Repps RDn. Abol eccl 1942 to help cr Barningham Winter with Barningham Norwood EP.[14]

BARNINGHAM WINTER WITH BARNINGHAM NORWOOD
EP Cr 1942 by union Barningham Winter AP, Barningham Norwood AP.[14] Repps RDn.

BARSHAM
CP Cr 1935 by union North Barsham AP, East Barsham AP, West Barsham AP, Houghton St Giles AP.[1] *LG* Walsing. RD. *Parl* N Norfolk CC (1948–70), N W Norfolk CC (1970–*).

EAST BARSHAM
AP *LG* Gallow Hd, Walsing. PLU, RSD, RD. Abol civ 1935 to help cr Barsham CP.[1] *Parl* W'rn Dv (1832–67), W Dv (1867–85), N-W'rn Dv (1885–1918), N'rn Dv (1918–48). *Eccl* Seq 5.

NORTH BARSHAM
AP Organisation as for East Barsham.

WEST BARSHAM
AP Organisation as for East Barsham.

BARTON BENDISH
AP Orig 3 pars, Barton Bendish All Saints, Barton Bendish St Mary, Barton Bendish St Andrew, the first two united before 1845 as Barton Bendish St Mary and All Saints; the 2 remaining EPs united 1968 as 'Barton Bendish'.[16] *LG* Seq 3. Civ bdry: 1935 (help cr Beachamwell CP).[1] *Parl* Seq 26. *Eccl* Fincham RDn (1973–*).

BARTON BENDISH ALL SAINTS
AP One of 3 pars in Barton Bendish, forms with others one civ par (see prev entry). *Eccl* Fincham RDn. Abol eccl before 1845 to help cr Barton Bendish St Mary and All Saints EP.[16]

BARTON BENDISH ST ANDREW
AP One of 3 pars in Barton Bendish, forms with others one civ par (see 'Barton Bendish'). *Eccl* Fincham RD. Abol eccl 1968 to help cr Barton Bendish EP.[16]

BARTON BENDISH ST MARY
AP Organisation as for Barton Bendish All Saints.

BARTON BENDISH ST MARY AND ALL SAINTS
EP Cr before 1845 by union Barton Bendish St Mary AP, Barton Bendish All Saints AP. Fincham RDn. Abol 1968 to help cr Barton Bendish EP.[16]

BARTON TURF
AP *LG* Seq 47. Civ bdry: 1935 (gains Irstead AP).[1] *Parl* Seq 1. *Eccl* Wax. RDn (until 1932), Tunst. RDn (1932–*).

BARWICK
AP Orig sep AP, Heacham RDn, united 1511 to Stanhoe AP,[17] sep civ identity regained early. *LG* Seq 44. *Parl* Seq 21.

BAWBURGH
AP *LG* Seq 20. Civ bdry: 1968.[18] *Parl* Seq 12. *Eccl* Seq 14.

BAWDESWELL
AP *LG* Seq 16. *Parl* Seq 9. *Eccl* Seq 40.

BAWSEY
AP *LG* Seq 22. Civ bdry: 1935 (gains Mintlyn CP).[1] *Parl* Seq 21. *Eccl* Lynn RDn (until1866), Lynn Norfolk RDn (1866–1918), Lynn RDn (1918–37). Abol eccl 1937 pt to help cr Gaywood and Mintlyn EP, pt to Ashwicken AP.[9]

BAYFIELD
AP Orig sep AP, early civ united with Glandford AP to cr 'Glandford with Bayfield', qv. *Eccl* Holt RDn. Abol eccl 1935 to help cr Letheringsett with Bayfield EP.[19]

BEACHAMWELL
CP Cr 1935 by union Beechamwell AP, Shingham AP and pts of Barton Bendish AP, Marham AP.[1] *LG* Swaff. RD. *Parl* S W Norfolk CC (1948–*).

BEACHAMWELL ALL SAINTS WITH SHINGHAM
EP Union early of Beachamwell All Saints AP, Shingham AP. Fincham RDn. Reconstituted 1968 gaining Beachamwell St Mary with St John EP, but retaining name as above.[22]

BEACHAMWELL ST MARY WITH ST JOHN
EP Early union of Beachamwell St Mary AP, Beachamwell St John EP. Fincham RDn. Abol 1968 ent to Beachamwell All Saints with Shingham EP.[22]

EAST BECKHAM
AP *LG* Seq 9. Civ bdry: 1957.[20] *Parl* Seq 7. *Eccl* Repps RDn (until 1888), Ingw. RDn (1888–1918), Repps RDn (1918–61), Holt RDn (1961–*).

WEST BECKHAM
AP *LG* Seq 13. Civ bdry: 1883.[21] *Parl* Seq 7. *Eccl* Pec jurisd Dean & Chapter of Norwich (until 1847), Repps RDn (1847–1961), Holt RDn (1961–*).

BEDINGHAM
AP *LG* Seq 40. *Parl* Seq 15. *Eccl* Seq 4.

BEECHAMWELL
AP Orig 3 sep pars, All Saints, St John, St Mary, one for civ purposes as 'Beechamwell', the first united early with Shingham AP as 'Beachamwell with Shingham', the last two EPs united early as 'Beachamwell St Mary with St John', the 2 combined EPs united 1968 as 'Beachamwell All Saints with Shingham'.[22] *LG* Clack. Hd, Swaff. PLU, RSD, RD. Abol civ 1935 to help cr Beachamwell CP.[1] *Parl* W'rn Dv (1832–67), W Dv (1867–85), S-W'rn Dv (1885–1948).

BEESTON
AP Sep AP for eccl purposes, civ united with Bittering AP as 'Beeston with Bittering', qv. Sometimes 'Beeston next Mileham' or 'Beeston All Saints'. *Eccl* Seq 30.

BEESTON REGIS
AP *LG* Seq 9. Civ bdry: 1901 (loses pt to Sheringham AP to help constitute Sheringham UD),[23] 1914,[24] 1935,[1] 1957.[20] *Parl* Seq 7. *Eccl* Seq 19.

BEESTON ST ANDREW
AP *LG* Seq 45. *Parl* Seq 10. *Eccl* Sinecure rectory, Tav. RDn, eccl incl in Sprowston AP.

BEESTON ST LAWRENCE
AP *LG* Tunst. Hd, Tunst. & Hap. incorp for poor (1785–1870), Smallb. PLU (1870–1930), RSD, RD. Abol civ 1935 ent to Ashmanhaugh AP.[1] *Parl* E'rn Dv (1832–67), N E Dv (1867–85),

E'rn Dv (1885–1948). *Eccl* Seq 25.

BEESTON WITH BITTERING

CP One par for civ purposes; Beeston, Bittering each have sep eccl identity, qv. *LG* Seq 39. *Parl* Seq 20.

BEETLEY

AP *LG* Seq 39. Civ bdry: 1935 (gains East Bilney AP),[1] 1957.[25] *Parl* Seq 20. *Eccl* Seq 30. Eccl bdry: 1958.[26]

BEIGHTON

AP *LG* Seq 48. Civ bdry: 1935.[1] *Parl* Seq 11. *Eccl* Blof. RDn. Abol eccl 1921 to help cr Beighton with Moulton EP.[27]

BEIGHTON WITH MOULTON

EP Cr 1921 by union Beighton AP, Moulton St Mary AP.[27] Blof. RDn.

BELAUGH

AP *LG* Seq 11. *Parl* Seq 3. *Eccl* Seq 33.

BELTON

AP In E Suffolk (qv), transf 1974 to Norfolk.[28]

BERGH APTON

AP Orig 2 sep pars, St Peter and St Paul, St Martin, the latter abol 15th cent and incl in former.[29] *LG* Seq 4. *Parl* Seq 15. *Eccl* Incl eccl Holveston, Alpington (each orig sep AP and in ruins), Seq 2.

BESSINGHAM

AP *LG* N Erp. Hd, Erp. PLU, RSD, RD. Civ bdry: 1884.[15] Abol civ 1935 ent to Sustead AP.[1] *Parl* E'rn Dv (1832–67), N E Dv (1867–85), N'rn Dv (1885–1948). *Eccl* Seq 19.

BESTHORPE

AP *LG* Seq 43. *Parl* Seq 18. *Eccl* Seq 20.

BEXWELL

AP *LG* Clack. Hd, Down. PLU, RSD, RD. Abol civ 1935 ent to Ryston AP.[1] *Parl* W'rn Dv (1832–67), W Dv (1867–85), S-W'rn Dv (1885–1948). *Eccl* Fincham RDn.

BILLINGFORD

AP *LG* Earsh. Hd, Depw. PLU, RSD, RD. Abol civ 1935 ent to Scole AP.[1] *Parl* E'rn Dv (1832–67), S E Dv (1867–85), S'rn Dv (1885–1948). *Eccl* [St Leonard] Seq 18.

BILLINGFORD

AP *LG* Seq 16. *Parl* Seq 9. *Eccl* [St Peter] Spar. RDn (until 1924), Elm. RDn (1924–70), Brisl. & Elm. RDn (1970–*).

BILLOCKBY

AP *LG* W Flegg Hd, E & W Flegg incorp for poor, RSD, RD. Abol civ 1935 to help cr Fleggburgh CP.[1] *Parl* E'rn Dv (1832–67), N E Dv (1867–85), E'rn Dv (1885–1948). *Eccl* Seq 31.

EAST BILNEY

AP *LG* Laund. Hd, Mitf. & Laund. PLU, RSD, RD. Abol civ 1935 ent to Beetley AP.[1] *Parl* W'rn Dv (1832–67), W Dv (1867–85), Mid Dv (1885–1918), S-W'rn Dv (1918–48). *Eccl* Seq 30.

WEST BILNEY

AP *LG* Freebr. Lynn Hd, PLU, RSD, RD. Abol civ 1935 ent to East Winch AP.[1] *Parl* W'rn Dv (1832–67), W Dv (1867–85), N-W'rn Dv (1885–1918), K's Lynn Dv (1918–48). *Eccl* Seq 38.

BINHAM

AP *LG* Seq 27. Civ bdry: 1935 (gains Cockthorpe AP).[1] *Parl* Seq 17. *Eccl* Seq 47.

BINTREE

AP Sometimes 'Bintry'. *LG* Seq 16. *Parl* Seq 9. *Eccl* Seq 40.

BIRCHAM

CP Cr 1935 by union Bircham Newton AP, Bircham Tofts AP, Great Bircham AP.[1] *LG* Dock. RD. *Parl* K's Lynn CC (1948–70), N W Norfolk CC (1970–*).

GREAT BIRCHAM

AP *LG* Smithd. Hd, Dock. PLU, RSD, RD. Abol civ 1935 to help cr Bircham CP.[1] *Parl* W'rn Dv (1832–67), W Dv (1867–85), N-W'rn Dv (1885–1918), K's Lynn Dv (1918–48). *Eccl* Heach. RDn. Abol eccl 1935 to help cr Great Bircham with Bircham Newton and Bircham Tofts EP.[30]

GREAT BIRCHAM WITH BIRCHAM NEWTON AND BIRCHAM TOFTS

EP Cr 1935 by union Great Bircham AP, Bircham Newton AP, Bircham Tofts AP.[30] Heach. RDn (1935–70), Heach. & Rising RDn (1970–*).

BIRCHAM NEWTON

AP Organisation as for Great Bircham.

BIRCHAM TOFTS

AP Organisation as for Great Bircham.

BITTERING

AP Orig 2 sep pars, Bircham Magna (long in ruins and united to Gressenhall AP[31]), Bircham Parva (for eccl see following entry), the latter civ united with Beeston as one par 'Beeston with Bittering', qv.

BITTERING PARVA

AP For civ see prev entry. *Eccl* Brisl. RDn. Abol eccl 1930 to help cr Longham with Bittering Parva EP.[32]

EP Cr 1961 when Longham with Bittering Parva EP divided into 2 EPs of Longham, Bittering Parva.[33] Elm. RDn (1961–70), Brisl. & Elm. RDn (1970–*).

BIXLEY

AP *LG* Seq 35. Civ bdry: 1935 (gains Arminghall AP).[1] *Parl* Seq 13. *Eccl* Seq 2.

BIXTON

AP Foreh. Hd, Hingh. RDn, abol 1680 ent to Barnham Broom AP.[13]

BLAKENEY

AP *LG* Seq 37. *Parl* Seq 17. *Eccl* Holt RDn. Reconstituted eccl early 17th cent gaining Little Langham AP and afterward 'Blakeney with Little Langham',[34] qv.

BLAKENEY WITH LITTLE LANGHAM

EP Cr early 17th cent by union Blakeney AP, Little Langham AP.[34] *Eccl* Holt RDn (early 17th cent–1918), Walsing. RDn (1918–70), Holt RDn (1970–*).

BLICKLING

AP *LG* Seq 11. *Parl* Seq 5. *Eccl* Seq 33.

BLO' NORTON

AP Orig 2 sep pars, St Andrew, St Margaret, the

latter pulled down and united 1394 to the former.[35] *LG* Seq 32. *Parl* Seq 18. *Eccl* Seq 22.

BLOFIELD
AP *LG* Seq 1. Civ bdry: 1884.[36] *Parl* Seq 11. *Eccl* Seq 27.

BODHAM
AP *LG* Seq 36. Civ bdry: 1883.[21] *Parl* Seq 16. *Eccl* Seq 32.

BODNEY
AP *LG* S Greenh. Hd, Swaff. PLU, RSD, RD. Abol civ 1935 ent to Hilborough AP.[1] *Parl* W'rn Dv (1832–67), W Dv (1867–85), S-W'rn Dv (1885–1948). *Eccl* Seq 7.

BOOTTON
AP *LG* S Erp. Hd, St Faith's PLU, RSD, RD (1894–1935), St. Faith's & Ayl. RD (1935–74). *Parl* Seq 5. *Eccl* Ingw. RDn (until 1927), Spar. RDn (1927–*).

BOUGHTON
AP *LG* Seq 3. *Parl* Seq 26. *Eccl* Fincham RDn (until 1917), Feltwell RDn (1917–*).

BOWTHORPE
AP *LG* Foreh. Hd, incorp for poor/PLU, RSD, RD. Abol civ 1935 ent to Costessy AP.[1] *Parl* E'rn Dv (1832–67), S E Dv (1867–85), Mid Dv (1885–1918), S'rn Dv (1918–48). *Eccl* Orig rectory, sometimes later considered free chapel, Donative, Hingh. RDn. Abol eccl 1938 to help cr Earlham with Bowthorpe EP.[37]

BRACON ASH
AP *LG* Seq 38. Civ bdry: 1935.[1] *Parl* Seq 13. *Eccl* Seq 16.

BRADENHAM
CP Cr 1952 by union East Bradenham AP, West Bradenham AP.[38] *LG* Swaff. RD. *Parl* S W Norfolk CC (1970–*).

EAST BRADENHAM
AP *LG* S Greenh. Hd, Swaff. PLU, RSD, RD. Abol civ 1952 to help cr Bradenham CP.[38] *Parl* W'rn Dv (1832–67), W Dv (1867–85), S-W'rn Dv (1885–1948), S W Norfolk CC (1948–70). *Eccl* Seq 9.

WEST BRADENHAM
AP Organisation as for East Bradenham.

BRADESTON
AP Usual civ spelling; for eccl see 'Braydeston'. *LG* Blof. Hd, PLU, RSD. Abol civ 1884 pt to Brundall AP, pt to Strumpshaw AP.[39] *Parl* E'rn Dv (1832–67), S E Dv (1867–85).

BRADFIELD
AP *LG* Tunst. Hd, Tunst. & Hap. incorp for poor (1785–1870), Smallb. PLU (1870–1930), RSD, RD. Abol civ 1935 ent to Swafield AP.[1] *Parl* E'rn Dv (1832–67), N E Dv (1867–85), E'rn Dv (1885–1948). *Eccl* Seq 26.

BRADWELL
AP In E Suffolk (qv), transf 1974 to Norfolk.[28]

BRAMERTON
AP *LG* Seq 35. *Parl* Seq 13. *Eccl* Seq 2.

BRAMPTON
AP *LG* Seq 11. Civ bdry: 1935 (gains Oxnead AP).[1] *Parl* Seq 5. *Eccl* Seq 33.

BRANCASTER
AP *LG* Seq 44. Civ bdry: 1935 (gains Burnham Deepdale AP).[1] *Parl* Seq 21. *Eccl* Seq 12. Eccl bdry: 1931.[40]

BRANDISTON
AP Orig 2 sep pars, St Michael, St Swithun (in Gunton), the two early united hence this par eccl sometimes 'Brandiston with Gunton'. *LG* Seq 17. *Parl* Seq 5. *Eccl* Seq 40.

BRANDISTON WITH GUNTON–See prev entry

BRANDON
AP Sometimes 'Brandon Ferry'. Pt Norfolk (Foreh. Hd), pt Suffolk (Lackford Hd), made ent W Suffolk 1895.[41] *LG* Thetf. PLU, RSD, pt sep RD in Norfolk (1894–95). *Parl* Norfolk pt, E'rn Dv (1832–67), S E Dv (1867– 85), S-W'rn Dv (1885–1918). For later civ and for eccl organisation, see main entry in Suffolk.

BRANDON PARVA
AP *LG* Foreh. Hd, incorp for poor/PLU, RSD, RD. Abol civ 1935 ent to Runhall AP.[1] *Parl* E'rn Dv (1832–67), S E Dv (1867–85), Mid Dv (1885–1918), S'rn Dv (1918–48). *Eccl* Seq 13.

BRAYDESTON
AP Usual eccl spelling; for civ see 'Bradeston'. *Eccl* Seq 27.

BRECKLES
AP *LG* Wayl. Hd, PLU, RSD, RD. Abol civ 1935 ent to Stow Bedon AP.[1] *Parl* W'rn Dv (1832–67), W Dv (1867–85), S-W'rn Dv (1885–1918), S'rn Dv (1918–48). *Eccl* Seq 28.

BRESSINGHAM
AP *LG* Seq 7. Civ bdry: 1935 (gains Fersfield AP).[1] *Parl* Seq 14. *Eccl* Seq 18.

BRETTENHAM
AP *LG* Shrop. Hd, Thetf. PLU, RSD, RD (1894–1935), Wayl. RD (1935–74). Civ bdry: 1935 (gains Rusford AP, Great and Little Snarehill CP).[1] *Parl* Seq 18. *Eccl* Seq 23.

BRIDGHAM
AP *LG* Shrop. Hd, Guiltc. PLU (1835–1902), RSD, RD (1894–1902), Thetf. PLU (1902–30), RD (1902–35), Wayl. RD (1935–74). Civ bdry: 1956.[42] *Parl* Seq 18. *Eccl* Rockl. RDn (until 1918), Harling RDn (1918–23). Abol eccl 1923 to help cr Bridgham with Roudham EP.[43]

BRIDGHAM WITH ROUDHAM
EP Cr 1923 by union Bridgham AP, Roudham AP.[43] Harling RDn (1923–31), Rockl. RDn (1931–70), Thetf. & Rockl. RDn (1970–*).

BRININGHAM
AP *LG* Seq 37. *Parl* Seq 17. *Eccl* Seq 32.

BRINTON
AP *LG* Holt Hd, Brinton incorp for poor (1783–1860s), Walsing. PLU (1860s–1930), RSD, RD. Civ bdry: 1935 (gains Sharrington AP).[1] *Parl* Seq 17. *Eccl* Seq 32.

BRISLEY
AP *LG* Seq 39. *Parl* Seq 20. *Eccl* Seq 29.

BRISTON
AP *LG* Holt Hd, Erp. PLU, RSD, RD (1894–1935), Walsing. RD (1935–74). Civ bdry: 1884.[15] *Parl*

Seq 17. *Eccl* Seq 32.

BROCKDISH

AP *LG* Seq 8. Civ bdry: 1885,[44] 1935 (gains Thorpe Abbots AP).[1] *Parl* Seq 14. *Eccl* Seq 18.

BROOKE

AP *LG* Seq 4.[45] *Parl* Seq 15. *Eccl* Seq 1.

BROOME

AP *LG* Seq 40. *Parl* Seq 15. *Eccl* Seq 4.

BROOMSTHORPE

Orig sep AP, church destroyed before *temp* Eliz. I, thereafter ex-par, sep CP 1858.[4] *LG* Gallow Hd, Dock. PLU, RSD, RD. Abol 1935 ent to East Rudham AP.[1] *Parl* W Dv (1867–85), N-W'rn Dv (1885–1918), K's Lynn Dv (1918–48).

BRUMSTEAD

AP *LG* Seq 34. *Parl* Seq 1. *Eccl* Seq 24.

BRUNDALL

AP *LG* Seq 1. Civ bdry: 1884.[39] *Parl* Seq 11. *Eccl* Seq 27.

BUCKENHAM

AP *LG* Blof. Hd, PLU, RSD, RD. Abol civ 1935 ent to Strumpshaw AP.[1] *Parl* E'rn Dv (1832–67), S E Dv (1867–85), E'rn Dv (1885–1948). *Eccl* Blof. RDn. Abol eccl 1951 to help cr Buckenham with Hassingham EP.[46]

BUCKENHAM WITH HASSINGHAM

EP Cr 1951 by union Buckenham AP, Hassingham AP.[46] Blof. RDn.

NEW BUCKENHAM

AP *LG* New Buckenham Bor (status not sustained), Seq 42. *Parl* Seq 18. *Eccl* Seq 20.

OLD BUCKENHAM

AP Orig 2 sep pars, All Saints, St Andrew, the latter desecrated 16th cent and united to former.[47] *LG* Seq 42. *Parl* Seq 18. *Eccl* Seq 20.

BUCKENHAM PARVA

AP Usual eccl spelling; for civ see following entry. *Eccl* Cranw. RDn (until 1918), Thetf. RDn (1918–24). Abol eccl 1924 to help cr West Tofts with Buckenham Tofts EP.[48]

BUCKENHAM TOFTS

AP Usual civ spelling; for eccl see prev entry. *LG* Grimshoe Hd, Swaff. PLU, RSD, RD. Abol civ 1935 ent to Stanford AP.[1] *Parl* W'rn Dv (1832–67), W Dv (1867–85), S-W'rn Dv (1885–1948).

BUNWELL

AP *LG* Seq 5. *Parl* Seq 14. *Eccl* Seq 11.

BURGH

AP Sometimes eccl 'Burgh St Mary' or 'Burgh next Aylsham'. *LG* S Erp. Hd, Ayl. PLU, RSD, RD. Abol civ 1935 ent to Tuttington AP.[1] *Parl* E'rn Dv (1832–67), N E Dv (1867–85), N'rn Dv (1885–1948). *Eccl* Seq 33.

FLEGG BURGH–see BURGH ST MARGARET

WHEATACRE BURGH–See BURGH ST PETER

BURGH CASTLE

AP In E Suffolk (qv), transf 1974 to Norfolk.[28]

BURGH PARVA

AP Early united for civ purposes with Melton Constable AP. *Eccl* Seq 32.

BURGH ST MARGARET

AP Sometimes 'Flegg Burgh'. Orig 2 pars, St Margaret, St Mary, united 1550s.[49] *LG* W Flegg Hd, E & W Flegg incorp for poor, RSD, RD. Abol civ 1935 to help cr Fleggburgh CP.[1] *Parl* E'rn Dv (1832–67), N E Dv (1867–85), E'rn Dv (1885–1948). *Eccl* Seq 31.

BURGH ST MARY–See BURGH

BURGH ST PETER

AP Sometimes 'Wheatacre Burgh'. *LG* Seq 4. Civ bdry: 1935.[1] *Parl* Seq 15. *Eccl* Seq 3.

BURLINGHAM

CP Cr 1935 by union Burlingham St Edmund AP, Burlingham St Peter AP, pt Burlingham St Andrew AP.[1] *LG* Blof. & Flegg RD. *Parl* Yarm. CC (1948–*).

BURLINGHAM ST ANDREW

AP *LG* Blof. Hd, PLU, RSD, RD. Abol civ 1935 pt to help cr Burlingham CP, pt to Halvergate AP.[1] *Parl* E'rn Dv (1832–67), S E Dv (1867–85), E'rn Dv (1885–1948). *Eccl* Blof. RDn. Abol eccl 1935 to help cr Burlingham St Andrew and St Peter EP.[50]

BURLINGHAM ST ANDREW AND ST PETER

EP Cr 1935 by union Burlingham St Andrew AP, Burlingham St Peter AP.[50] Blof. RDn.

BURLINGHAM ST EDMUND

AP *LG* Blof. Hd, PLU, RSD, RD. Civ bdry: 1884.[36] Abol civ 1935 to help cr Burlingham CP.[1] *Parl* As for Burlingham St Andrew. *Eccl* Seq 27.

BURLINGHAM ST PETER

AP Organisation as for Burlingham St Andrew, except civ abol ent to help cr Burlingham CP.[1]

BURNHAM DEEPDALE

AP *LG* Brothc. Hd, Dock. PLU, RSD, RD. Abol civ 1935 ent to Brancaster AP.[1] *Parl* W'rn Dv (1832–67), W Dv (1867–85), N-W'rn Dv (1885–1918), K's Lynn Dv (1918–48). *Eccl* Seq 6. Eccl bdry: 1931.[40]

BURNHAM MARKET

CP Cr 1929 by union Burnham Sutton cum Burnham Ulph CP, Burnham Westgate AP.[51] *LG* Dock. PLU, RD. *Parl* K's Lynn CC (1948–70), N W Norfolk CC (1970–*).

BURNHAM NORTON

AP *LG* Seq 2. *Parl* Seq 21. *Eccl* Seq 5.

BURNHAM OVERY

AP Gains 1447 Burnham St Andrew AP.[52] Organisation as for Burnham Norton.

BURNHAM ST ANDREW

AP Burn. RDn, abol 1447 ent to Burnham Overy AP.[52]

BURNHAM SUTTON

AP *LG* Brothc. Hd. Abol prob 1729 to help cr Burnham Sutton cum Burnham Ulph CP.[53] *Eccl* Burn. RD. Abol eccl 1938 to help cr Burnham Sutton with Burnham Ulph EP.[54]

BURNHAM SUTTON CUM BURNHAM ULPH

CP Cr prob 1729 by union Burnham Sutton AP, Burnham Ulph AP.[53] *LG* Brothc. Hd, Dock. PLU, RSD, RD. Abol civ 1929 to help cr Burnham Market CP.[51] *Parl* W'rn Dv (1832–67), W Dv (1867–85), N-W'rn Dv (1885–1918), K's Lynn Dv (1918–48).

BURNHAM SUTTON WITH BURNHAM ULPH

EP Cr 1938 by union Burnham Sutton AP, Burnham Ulph AP.[54] Burn. RDn (1938–70), Burn. & Walsing. RDn (1970–*).

BURNHAM THORPE

AP Organisation as for Burnham Norton.

BURNHAM ULPH

AP Organisation as for Burnham Sutton.

BURNHAM WESTGATE

AP *LG* Brothc. Hd, Dock. PLU, RSD, RD. Abol civ 1929 to help cr Burnham Market CP.[51] *Parl* As for Burnham Sutton cum Burnham Ulph. *Eccl* Seq 5.

BURSTON

AP *LG* Seq 6. Civ bdry: 1935 (gains Shimpling AP).[1] *Parl* Seq 14. *Eccl* Seq 18.

BUXTON

AP *LG* S Erp. Hd, Ayl. PLU, RSD, RD. Abol civ 1935 to help cr Buxton with Lammas CP.[1] *Parl* E'rn Dv (1832–67), N E Dv (1867–85), N'rn Dv (1885–1948). *Eccl* Seq 33.

BUXTON WITH LAMMAS

CP Cr 1935 by union Buxton AP, Lammas with Little Hautbois AP.[1] *LG* St Faith's & Ayl. RD. *Parl* Ctrl. Norfolk CC (1948–70), N Norfolk CC (1970–*).

BYLAUGH

AP *LG* Seq 16. *Parl* Seq 9. *Eccl* Seq 40.

CAISTER

AP Usual eccl spelling; for civ see 'Caister next Yarmouth'. *Eccl* Seq 31.

EAST CAISTER

CP Cr 1926 from Caister next Yarmouth AP.[55] *LG* E & W Flegg incorp for poor, RD (1926–35), Blof. & Flegg RD (1935–54).Renamed 1954 'Caister-on-Sea'.[56] *Parl* Yarm. CC (1948–70).

WEST CAISTER

CP Cr 1926 from Caister next Yarmouth AP.[55] *LG* E & W Flegg incorp for poor, RD (1926–35), Blof. & Flegg RD (1935–74). *Parl* Yarm. CC (1948–*).

CAISTER NEXT YARMOUTH

AP Usual civ spelling; for eccl see 'Caister'. Orig 2 sep pars, St Edmund, Holt Trinity, united 1608.[57] *LG* E Flegg Hd, E & W Flegg incorp for poor, RD. Abol civ 1926 pt to cr East Caister CP, pt to cr West Caister CP, pt to Ormesby St Margaret with Scratby AP.[55] *Parl* E'rn Dv (1832–67), N E Dv (1867–85), E'rn Dv (1885–1948).

CAISTER-ON-SEA

CP Renaming 1954 of East Caister CP.[56] *LG* Blof. & Flegg RD. *Parl* Yarm. CC (1970–*).

CAISTER ST EDMUND

AP *LG* Henst. Hd, PLU, RSD, RD. Abol civ 1935 to help cr Caister St Edmunds CP.[1] *Parl* E'rn Dv (1832–67), S E Dv (1867–85), S'rn Dv (1885–1948). *Eccl* Brooke RDn. Gains eccl 1695 Markshall AP to cr Caister St Edmund with Markshall EP.[58]

CAISTER ST EDMUND WITH MARKSHALL

EP Cr 1695 by union Caister St Edmund AP, Markshall AP.[58] *Eccl* Seq 2.

CAISTER ST EDMUNDS

CP Cr 1935 by union Caister St Edmund AP, Markshall AP.[1] *LG* Foreh. & Henst. RD. Renamed 1955 'Caistor St Edmund'.[59] *Parl* Ctrl. Norfolk CC (1948–70).

CAISTOR ST EDMUND

CP Renaming 1955 of Caister St Edmunds AP.[59] *LG* Foreh. & Henst. RD. *Parl* S Norfolk CC (1970–*).

CALDECOTE

AP *LG* S Greenh. Hd, Swaff. PLU, RSD, RD. Abol civ 1935 ent to Oxborough AP.[1] *Parl* W'rn Dv (1832–67), W Dv (1867–85), S-W'rn Dv (1885–1948). *Eccl* Cranw. RDn (until 1918), Swaff. RDn (1918–35). Abol eccl 1935 to help cr Oxborough with Caldecote EP.[60]

CALTHORPE

AP *LG* S Erp. Hd, Ayl. PLU, RSD, RD. Abol civ 1935 ent to Erpingham AP.[1] *Parl* E'rn Dv (1832–67), N E Dv (1867–85), N'rn Dv (1885–1948). *Eccl* Seq 33.

CANTELOFF

AP Humblyd. RDn, united 1397 to Hethersett AP.[61]

CANTLEY

AP *LG* Seq 1. Civ bdry: 1935 (incl gains Limpenhoe AP, Southwood AP).[1] *Parl* Seq 11. *Eccl* Seq 27.

CARBROOKE

AP Orig 2 sep pars, Great Carbrooke, Little Carbrooke, united 1424 and latter pulled down.[62] *LG* Seq 50. *Parl* Seq 24. *Eccl* Seq 28.

EAST CARLETON

AP Orig 2 sep pars, St Mary, St Peter, the latter early in ruins, united 1550.[63] *LG* Seq 38. *Parl* Seq 13. *Eccl* Seq 16.

CARLETON FOREHOE

AP *LG* Foreh. Hd, incorp for poor/PLU, RSD, RD. Abol civ 1935 ent to Kimberley AP.[1] *Parl* E'rn Dv (1832–67), S E Dv (1867–85), Mid Dv (1885–1918), S'rn Dv (1918–48). *Eccl* Seq 13. Eccl bdry: 1873.[64]

CARLETON RODE

AP *LG* Seq 5. *Parl* Seq 14. *Eccl* Seq 11.

CARLETON ST PETER

AP *LG* Seq 40. *Parl* Seq 15. *Eccl* Seq 2.

CASTLE ACRE

AP Usual civ spelling; for eccl see 'Castleacre'. *LG* Seq 22. *Parl* Seq 21.

CASTLE RISING

AP *LG* Castle Rising Bor, Seq 22. *Parl* Castle Rising Parl Bor (1558–1832), Seq 21 thereafter. *Eccl* Pec jurisd Castle Rising (until 1847), Seq 36 thereafter.

CASTLEACRE

AP Usual eccl spelling; for civ see 'Castle Acre'. *Eccl* Lynn RDn (until 1866), Lynn Norfolk RDn (1866–1918), Swaff. RDn (1918–70), Brisl. & Elm. RDn (1970–*).

CASTON

AP *LG* Seq 50. *Parl* Seq 24. *Eccl* Seq 28.

CATFIELD

AP *LG* Seq 34. *Parl* Seq 1. *Eccl* Seq 24.

CATTON

AP *LG* Seq 45. Civ bdry: 1907 (loses pt to Norw. CB and CP),[65] 1959,[66] 1968 (incl loses pt to

Norw. CB and CP).[18] *Parl* Seq 10. *Eccl* Pec jurisd Dean & Chapter of Norw. (until 1847), Seq 42 thereafter. Eccl bdry: 1915 (help cr New Catton St Luke EP).[67]

NEW CATTON CHRIST CHURCH

EP Cr 1842 from Norwich St Clement AP.[68] Norw. RDn (1842–1970), Norw. (North) RDn (1970–*). Bdry: 1915 (help cr New Catton St Luke EP).[67]

NEW CATTON ST LUKE

EP Cr 1915 from New Catton Christ Church EP, Hellesdon AP, Catton AP.[67] Norw. RDn (1915–70), Norw. (North) RDn (1970–*). Bdry: 1932 (help cr Mile Cross EP),[48] 1940.[69]

CAWSTON

AP *LG* Seq 11. *Parl* Seq 5. *Eccl* Seq 33.

CHEDGRAVE

AP *LG* Seq 40. Civ bdry: 1935.[1] *Parl* Seq 15. *Eccl* Seq 3.

CHOSELEY

Ex-par place, sep CP 1858.[4] *LG* Smithd. Hd, Dock. PLU (1858[70]–1930), RSD, RD. *Parl* Seq 21.

CLAXTON

AP *LG* Seq 40. *Parl* Seq 15. *Eccl* Seq 2.

CLENCHWARTON

AP *LG* Seq 24. Civ bdry: 1885,[71] 1935 (incl help cr Marshland St James CP).[1] *Parl* Seq 21. *Eccl* Seq 35. Eccl bdry: 1922 (help cr Marshland St James EP).[72]

CLEY NEXT THE SEA

AP *LG* Seq 36. *Parl* Seq 16. *Eccl* Seq 32.

CLIPPESBY

AP *LG* W Flegg Hd, E & W Flegg incorp for poor, RSD, RD. Abol civ 1935 to help cr Fleggburgh CP.[1] *Parl* E'rn Dv (1832–67), N E Dv (1867–85), E'rn Dv (1885–1948). *Eccl* Seq 31.

COCKLEY CLEY

AP *LG* Seq 28. *Parl* Seq 26. *Eccl* Seq 7.

COCKTHORPE

AP *LG* N Greenh. Hd, Walsing. PLU, RSD, RD. Abol civ 1935 ent to Binham AP.[1] *Parl* W'rn Dv (1832–67), N E Dv (1867–85), N'rn Dv (1885–1948). *Eccl* Seq 32.

COLBY

AP *LG* Seq 10. Civ bdry: 1935 (gains Banningham AP).[1] *Parl* Seq 7. *Eccl* Seq 34.

COLKIRK

AP *LG* Seq 39. Civ bdry: 1935 (gains Oxwick and Pattesley CP).[1] *Parl* Seq 20. *Eccl* Toft. RDn (until 1918), Brisl. RDn (1918–40). Abol eccl 1940 to help cr Colkirk and Oxwick EP.[73]

COLKIRK AND OXWICK

EP Cr 1940 by union Colkirk AP, Oxwick AP.[73] Brisl. RDn (until 1970), Brisl. & Elm. RDn (1970–*).

COLNEY

AP *LG* Seq 38. Civ bdry: 1968 (loses pt to Norw. CB and CP).[18] *Parl* Seq 13. *Eccl* Humblyd. RDn (until 1970), Norw. (South) RDn (1970–*).

COLTISHALL

AP *LG* Seq 11. Civ bdry: 1935 (gains Great Hautbois AP).[1] *Parl* Seq 3. *Eccl* Seq 33.

COLTON

AP *LG* Foreh. Hd, incorp for poor/PLU, RSD, RD. Abol civ 1935 ent to Marlingford AP.[1] *Parl* E'rn Dv (1832–67), S E Dv (1867–85), Mid Dv (1885–1918), S'rn Dv (1918–48). *Eccl* Seq 13.

COLVESTON

AP *LG* Grimshoe Hd, Swaff. PLU, RSD, RD. Abol civ 1935 ent to Didlington AP.[1] *Parl* W'rn Dv (1832–67), W Dv (1867–85), S-W'rn Dv (1885–1948). *Eccl* Cranw. RDn. Early in ruins, now eccl incl in Cranwich AP.

CONGHAM

AP Orig 2 sep pars, St Andrew, St Mary, united 1684.[75] *LG* Seq 22. *Parl* Seq 21. *Eccl* Lynn RDn (until 1866), Lynn Norfolk RDn (1866–1918), Rising RDn (1918–70), Lynn RDn (1970–*).

CORPUSTY

AP *LG* Seq 10. Civ bdry: 1935 (gains Saxthorpe AP).[1] *Parl* Seq 7. *Eccl* Ingw. RDn. Abol eccl 1921 to help cr Saxthorpe with Corpusty EP.[74]

COSTESSY

AP *LG* Seq 20. Civ bdry: 1935 (gains Bowthorpe AP),[1] 1968 (incl loses pt to Norw. CB and CP).[18] *Parl* Seq 12. *Eccl* Hingh. RDn (until 1918), Tav. RDn (1918–70), Norw. (North) RDn (1970–*).

COSTON

AP *LG* Foreh. Hd, incorp for poor/PLU, RSD, RD. Abol civ 1935 ent to Runhall AP.[1] *Parl* E'rn Dv (1832–67), S E Dv (1867–85), Mid Dv (1885–1918), S'rn Dv (1918–48). *Eccl* Seq 13.

CRANWICH

AP *LG* Seq 31. *Parl* Seq 26. *Eccl* Incl eccl Colveston (orig AP long in ruins). Cranw. RDn (until 1918), Thetf. RDn (1918–*).

CRANWORTH

AP Gains 1547 Letton AP[76] (sep civ identity regained early). *LG* Seq 41. Civ bdry: 1935 (gains Letton CP, Southburgh AP, Woodrising AP).[1] *Parl* Seq 19. *Eccl* Seq 15.

NORTH CREAKE

AP *LG* Seq 2. *Parl* Seq 21. *Eccl* Seq 5.

SOUTH CREAKE

AP *LG* Seq 2. Civ bdry: 1935 (gains Waterden AP).[1] *Parl* Seq 21. *Eccl* Seq 5.

GREAT CRESSINGHAM

AP *LG* Seq 28. *Parl* Seq 26. *Eccl* Pec jurisd Great Cressingham (until 1847), Seq 7 thereafter.

LITTLE CRESSINGHAM

AP *LG* Seq 28. Civ bdry: 1935 (gains Threxton AP).[1] *Parl* Seq 26. *Eccl* Cranw. RDn (until 1918), Swaff. RDn (1918–25), Breccles RDn (1925–70), Breckl. RDn (1970–*).

CRIMPLESHAM

AP *LG* Seq 3. *Parl* Seq 26. *Eccl* Fincham RDn.

CRINGLEFORD

AP *LG* Seq 38. *Parl* Seq 13. *Eccl* Seq 16.

CROMER

AP *LG* N Erp. Hd, Erp. PLU, RSD (1875–84), Cromer USD (1884–94), UD. Civ bdry: 1896,[77] 1902,[78] 1953.[79] *Parl* Seq 7. *Eccl* Seq 19.

CROSTWICK
AP *LG* Seq 45. *Parl* Seq 10. *Eccl* Seq 42.
CROSTWIGHT
AP *LG* Tunst. Hd, Tunst. & Hap. incorp for poor (1785–1870), Smallb. PLU (1870–1930), RSD, RD. Abol civ 1935 ent to Honing AP.[1] *Parl* E'rn Dv (1832–67), N E Dv (1867–85), E'rn Dv (1885–1948). *Eccl* Seq 25.
CROWNTHORPE
AP *LG* Foreh. Hd, incorp for poor/PLU, RSD, RD. Abol civ 1935 ent to Wicklewood AP.[1] *Parl* E'rn Dv (1832–67), S E Dv (1867–85), Mid Dv (1885–1918), S'rn Dv (1918–48). *Eccl* Hingh. RDn. Abol eccl 1929 to help cr Wicklewood with Crownthorpe EP.[80]
CROXTON
AP *LG* Grimshoe Hd, Thetf. PLU, RSD, RD (1894–1935), Wayl. RD (1935–74). *Parl* W'rn Dv (1832–67), W Dv (1867–85), S-W'rn Dv (1885–1948), S Norfolk CC (1948–*). *Eccl* Cranw. RDn (until 1918), Thetf. RDn (1918–70), Thetf. & Rockl. RDn (1970–*).
DENTON
AP *LG* Seq 8. *Parl* Seq 14. *Eccl* Seq 18.
DENVER
AP *LG* Seq 3. Civ bdry: 1930 (help cr Nordelph CP),[81] 1935.[1] *Parl* Seq 26. *Eccl* Fincham RDn. Eccl bdry: 1909 (help cr Nordelph EP).[82]
DEOPHAM
AP *LG* Seq 20. Civ bdry: 1935 (gains Hackford AP).[1] *Parl* Seq 12. *Eccl* Seq 14.
EAST DEREHAM
AP Incl hmlt and chap Hooe (sep civ identity early, sep EP before 1845). *LG* Pt Mitf. Hd, pt Laund. Hd, Mitf. & Laund. PLU, E Dereham USD, UD. *Parl* W'rn Dv (1832–67), pt S E Dv, pt W Dv (1867–85), Mid Dv (1885–1918), S-W'rn Dv (1918–48), S W Norfolk CC (1948–*). *Eccl* Seq 15.
WEST DEREHAM
AP Orig 2 sep pars, St Andrew, St Peter, the latter early incl in former.[83] *LG* Seq 3. Civ bdry: 1957.[84] *Parl* Seq 26. *Eccl* Fincham RDn (until 1922), Feltwell RDn (1922–*).
DERSINGHAM
AP *LG* Seq 21. *Parl* Seq 21. *Eccl* Seq 36.
DICKLEBURGH
AP *LG* Seq 6. Civ bdry: 1935 (gains Rushall AP).[1] *Parl* Seq 14. *Eccl* Seq 18.
DIDLINGTON
AP *LG* Seq 28. Civ bdry: 1935 (gains Colveston AP),[1] 1957.[85] *Parl* Seq 26. *Eccl* Seq 10.
DILHAM
AP *LG* Seq 47. *Parl* Seq 1. *Eccl* Seq 25.
DISS
AP *LG* Diss Hd, Depw. PLU, Diss USD, UD. *Parl* Seq 14. *Eccl* Seq 18.
DITCHINGHAM
AP *LG* Seq 40. *Parl* Seq 15. *Eccl* Seq 4.
DOCKING
AP *LG* Seq 44. *Parl* Seq 21. *Eccl* Seq 12.
DOWNHAM MARKET
AP *LG* Clack. Hd, Down. PLU, pt Down. Market USD, pt Down. RSD, Down. Market UD. Civ bdry: 1884,[86] 1894 (loses the pt not in the USD to cr Downham West CP).[87] *Parl* Seq 26. *Eccl* Fincham RDn. Eccl bdry: 1909 (help cr Nordelph EP).[82]
DOWNHAM WEST
CP Cr 1894 from the pt of Downham Market AP not in Down. Market USD.[87] *LG* Down. PLU, RD. Bdry: 1930 (help cr Nordelph CP),[81] 1935.[1] *Parl* S-W'rn Dv (1918–48), S W Norfolk CC (1948–*).
DRAYTON
AP *LG* Seq 45. *Parl* Seq 10. *Eccl* Seq 42.
GREAT DUNHAM
AP *LG* Seq 39. *Parl* Seq 20. *Eccl* Seq 30.
LITTLE DUNHAM
AP *LG* Seq 39. *Parl* Seq 20. *Eccl* Seq 30.
DUNSTON
AP *LG* Humblyd. Hd, Henst. PLU, RSD, RD. Abol civ 1935 ent to Stoke Holy Cross AP.[1] *Parl* E'rn Dv (1832–67), S E Dv (1867–85), S'rn Dv (1885–1948). *Eccl* Humblyd. RDn (until 1922), Lodd. RDn (1922–*).
DUNTON
CP Cr 1935 by union Dunton cum Doughton AP, Shereford AP, Toftrees AP.[1] *LG* Walsing. RD. Bdry: 1958.[88] *Parl* N Norfolk CC (1948–70), N W Norfolk CC (1970–*).
DUNTON CUM DOUGHTON
AP *LG* Gallow Hd, Walsing. PLU, RSD, RD. Abol civ 1935 to help cr Dunton CP.[1] *Parl* W'rn Dv (1832–67), W Dv (1867–85), N-W'rn Dv (1885–1918), N'rn Dv (1918–48). *Eccl* Seq 5.
EARLHAM
AP *LG* Norw. Bor/MB/CB, USD. Abol civ 1889 to help cr Norwich CP.[89] *Parl* Norw. Parl Bor (1295–1918). *Eccl* Humblyd. RDn (until 1918), Norw. RDn (1918–38). Abol eccl 1938 to help cr Earlham with Bowthorpe EP.[37]
EARLHAM ST ANNE
EP Cr 1938 from Earlham with Bowthorpe EP.[90] Norw. RDn (1938–70), Norw. (South) RDn (1970–*). Bdry: 1954.[128]
EARLHAM WITH BOWTHORPE
EP Cr 1938 by union Earlham AP, Bowthorpe AP.[37] Humblyd. RDn (1938–70), Norw. (South) RDn (1970–*). Bdry: 1938 (cr Earlham St Anne EP).[9]
EARSHAM
AP Small pt in Suffolk (Wangford Hd), remainder in Norfolk, the former lost civ 1885 to Bungay St Mary AP, Suffolk, and the par ent Norfolk thereafter.[91] *LG* Norfolk pt, Seq 8. *Parl* Seq 14. *Eccl* Seq 18.
EASTON
AP *LG* Seq 20. Civ bdry: 1885.[92] *Parl* Seq 12. *Eccl* Seq 13.
EASTON
AP *LG* Norw. Bor/MB/CB, USD. Abol civ 1889 to help cr Norwich CP.[89] *Parl* Norw. Parl Bor (1295–1918). *Eccl* Pec jurisd Dean & Chapter of Norw. (until 1847), Seq 17 thereafter.

ECCLES

AP *LG* Shrop. Hd, Guiltc. PLU (1835–1902), RSD, RD (1894–1902), Wayl. PLU (1902–30), RD (1902–56). Civ bdry: 1935 (gains Hargham AP, Quidenham AP, Wilby AP).[1] Renamed civ 1956 'Quidenham'.[93] *Parl* W'rn Dv (1832–67), S E Dv (1867–85), Mid Dv (1885–1918), S'rn Dv (1918–48), S Norfolk CC (1948–70). *Eccl* Seq 22.

ECCLES

AP Sometimes 'Eccles next the Sea'. Church early lost into the sea, civ incl in 'Hempstead with Eccles', qv. *Eccl* Wax. RDn. Abol eccl 1923 to help cr Hempstead with Eccles next the Sea EP.[166]

EDGEFIELD

AP *LG* Seq 36. *Parl* Seq 16. *Eccl* Seq 32.

EDINGTHORPE

AP *LG* Tunst. Hd, Tunst. & Hap. incorp for poor (1785–1870), Smallb. PLU (1870–1930), RSD, RD. Civ bdry: 1885.[10] Abol civ 1935 ent to Bacton AP.[1] *Parl* E'rn Dv (1832–67), N E Dv (1867–85), E'rn Dv (1885–1948). *Eccl* Seq 25.

EGMERE

AP *LG* N Greeh. Hd, Walsing. PLU, RSD, RD. Abol civ 1935 ent to Great Walsingham AP.[1] *Parl* W'rn Dv (1832–67), N E Dv (1867–85), N'rn Dv (1885–1918), N Norfolk CC (1970–*). *Eccl* Walsing. RDn. Demolished 16th cent, eccl incl in Waterden AP.[95]

ELLINGHAM

AP *LG* Seq 4. *Parl* Seq 15. *Eccl* Seq 3.

GREAT ELLINGHAM

AP *LG* Seq 43. *Parl* Seq 18. *Eccl* Seq 20.

LITTLE ELLINGHAM

AP *LG* Perhaps orig pt Wayl. Hd, pt Foreh. Hd,[96] later ent Wayl. Hd and Seq 50 thereafter. *Parl* Seq 24. *Eccl* Brecc. RDn (until 1918), Rockl. RDn (1918–70), Thetf. & Rockl. RDn (1970–*).

NORTH ELMHAM

AP *LG* Seq 39. *Parl* Seq 20. *Eccl* Seq 30.

ELSING

AP *LG* Seq 16. *Parl* Seq 9. *Eccl* Seq 40.

EMNETH

Hmlt (Norfolk, Freebr. Marshl. Hd) and chap (pec jurisd Bp Ely) in Elm AP (o'wise IoE, Cambs), sep civ identity early in Norfolk, sep EP 1841.[97] *LG* Seq 24. Civ bdry: 1894 (the pt to be in Walsoken UD cr Walsoken Hungate CP),[87] 1934 (incl loses pt to Elm AP, IoE),[98] 1935 (help cr Marshland St James CP).[1] *Parl* Seq 21. *Eccl* Wisbech RDn. Eccl bdry: 1922 (help cr Marshland St James EP).[72]

ERPINGHAM

AP *LG* Seq 10. Civ bdry: 1935 (gains Calthorpe AP).[1] *Parl* Seq 7. *Eccl* Seq 33.

FAKENHAM

AP *LG* Seq 26. Civ bdry: 1958.[88] *Parl* Seq 23. *Eccl* Seq 5.

FELBRIGG

AP *LG* Seq 9. Civ bdry: 1902.[78] *Parl* Seq 7. *Eccl* Seq 19.

FELMINGHAM

AP *LG* Seq 47. *Parl* Seq 1. *Eccl* Seq 25.

FELTHORPE

AP *LG* Seq 45. *Parl* Seq 10. *Eccl* Tav. RDn (until 1970), Ingw. RDn (1970–*).

FELTWELL

AP Orig 2 sep pars St Nicholas, St Mary, early united. *LG* Seq 30. Civ bdry: 1929 (gains Feltwell Anchor CP).[99] *Parl* Seq 26. *Eccl* Cranw. RDn (until 1914), Fincham RDn (1914–17), Feltwell RDn (1917–*). Eccl bdry: 1866 (help cr Little Ouse EP).[100]

FELTWELL ANCHOR

Ex-par place, sep CP 1858.[4] *LG* Grimshoe Hd, Thetf. PLU (1858[70]–1929), RSD, RD. Abol 1929 ent to Feltwell AP.[99] *Parl* W Dv (1867–85), S-W'rn Dv (1885–1948).

FERSFIELD

AP *LG* Diss Hd, Guiltc. PLU (1835–1902), RSD, RD (1894–1902), Depw. PLU (1902–30), RD (1902–35). Abol civ 1935 ent to Bressingham AP.[1] *Parl* E'rn Dv (1832–67), S E Dv (1867–85), S'rn Dv (1885–1948). *Eccl* Seq 18.

FIELD DALLING

AP *LG* Seq 27. Civ bdry: 1935 (gains Saxlingham AP).[1] *Parl* Seq 17. *Eccl* Seq 32.

FILBY

AP *LG* Seq 18. *Parl* Seq 2. *Eccl* Seq 31.

FINCHAM

AP Orig 2 sep pars, St Martin, St Nicholas, united *ca* 1800.[101] *LG* Seq 3. *Parl* Seq 26. *Eccl* Fincham RDn.

FISHLEY

AP *LG* Walsham Hd, civ united early with Upton AP as 'Upton with Fishley', qv. *Eccl* Seq 27.

FLEGGBURGH

CP Cr 1935 by union Billockby AP, Burgh St Margaret AP, Clippesby AP.[1] *LG* Blof. & Flegg RD. *Parl* Yarm. CC (1948–*).

FLITCHAM

AP Freebr. Lynn Hd, Lynn RDn, united prob early 18th cent to help cr Flitcham with Appleton CP/EP.[5]

FLITCHAM WITH APPLETON

Union for civ and eccl purposes prob early 18th cent of Flitcham AP, Appleton AP.[5] *LG* Seq 22. *Parl* Seq 21. *Eccl* Seq 36.

FLORDON

AP *LG* Seq 38. *Parl* Seq 13. *Eccl* Seq 16.

FORDHAM

AP *LG* Seq 3. *Parl* Seq 26. *Eccl* Fincham RDn.

FORNCETT

CP Cr 1935 by union Forncett St Mary AP, Forncett St Peter AP.[1] *LG* Depw. RD. *Parl* S Norfolk CC (1948–*).

FORNCETT ST MARY

AP Incl Forncett St Peter (perhaps orig sep AP, deemed as chap from 1465,[102] regains sep civ identity early, sep EP 1845[103]). *LG* Depw. Hd, PLU, RSD, RD. Abol civ 1935 to help cr Forncett CP.[1] *Parl* E'rn Dv (1832–67), S E Dv (1867–85), S'rn Dv (1885–1948). *Eccl* Seq 11.

FORNCETT ST PETER
Perhaps orig sep AP, deemed chap in Forncett St Mary from 1465,[102] regains sep civ identity early, sep EP 1845.[103] *LG*, civ abol, *Parl* as for Forncett St Mary. *Eccl* Depw. RDn.

FOULDEN
AP *LG* Seq 28. *Parl* Seq 26. *Eccl* Seq 7.

FOULSHAM
AP *LG* Seq 14. Civ bdry: 1957.[104] *Parl* Seq 6. *Eccl* Seq 40.

FOXLEY
AP *LG* Seq 16. *Parl* Seq 9. *Eccl* Seq 40.

FRAMINGHAM PIGOT
AP *LG* Seq 35. *Parl* Seq 13. *Eccl* Seq 2.

FRAMINGHAM EARL
AP *LG* Seq 35. *Parl* Seq 13. *Eccl* Seq 2.

FRANSHAM
CP Cr 1935 by union Great Fransham AP, Little Fransham AP.[1] *LG* Mitf. & Laund. RD. *Parl* S W Norfolk CC (1948–*).

GREAT FRANSHAM
AP *LG* Laund. Hd, Mitf. & Laund. PLU, RSD, RD. Abol civ 1935 to help cr Fransham CP.[1] *Parl* W'rn Dv (1832–67), W Dv (1867–85), Mid Dv (1885–1918), S-W'rn Dv (1918–48). *Eccl* Seq 30.

LITTLE FRANSHAM
AP Organisation as for Great Fransham.

FREETHORPE
AP *LG* Seq 1. Civ bdry: 1935 (incl gains Wickhampton AP).[1] *Parl* Seq 11. *Eccl* Seq 27.

FRENZE
AP Diss Hd, civ united with Scole early and hence loses sep civ identity. *Eccl* Seq 18.

FRETTENHAM
AP Incl Stanninghill (orig sep AP, in ruins by 16th cent[105]). *LG* Seq 45. *Parl* Seq 10. *Eccl* Seq 42.

FRING
AP *LG* Seq 44. *Parl* Seq 21. *Eccl* Seq 12.

FRITTON
AP In E Suffolk (qv), transf 1974 to Norfolk incl gains the pt of Herringfleet AP (Suffolk) also transf to Norfolk.[28]

FRITTON
AP Usual civ spelling; for eccl see following entry. *LG* Depw. Hd, PLU, RSD, RD. Abol civ 1935 ent to Morning Thorpe AP.[1] *Parl* E'rn Dv (1832–67), S E Dv (1867–85), S'rn Dv (1885–1948).

FRITTON ST CATHERINE
AP Usual eccl spelling; for civ see prev entry. *Eccl* Seq 11.

FULMODESTON
CP Cr 1935 by union Barney AP, Fulmodeston cum Croxton AP, Thursfield AP.[1] *LG* Walsing. RD. Bdry: 1953 (cr Thursford CP).[106] *Parl* N Norfolk CC (1948–70), N W Norfolk CC (1970–*).

FULMODESTON CUM CROXTON
AP *LG* Gallow Hd, Walsing. PLU, RSD, RD. Abol civ 1935 to help cr Fulmodeston CP.[1] *Parl* W'rn Dv (1832–67), W Dv (1867–85), N-W'rn Dv (1885–1918), N'rn Dv (1918–48). *Eccl* Seq 5.

FUNDENHALL
AP *LG* Depw. Hd, PLU, RSD, RD. Abol civ 1935 ent to Ashwellthorpe AP.[1] *Parl* E'rn Dv (1832–67), S E Dv (1867–85), S'rn Dv (1885–1948). *Eccl* Seq 11.

GARBOLDISHAM
AP Orig 2 pars, St John, All Saints, united 1734.[107] *LG* Seq 32. *Parl* Seq 18. *Eccl* Seq 22.

GARVESTON
AP Sometimes 'Garvestone'. *LG* Seq 41. Civ bdry: 1935 (gains Reymerston AP, Thuxton AP).[1] *Parl* Seq 19. *Eccl* Seq 15.

GASTHORPE
AP *LG* Guiltc. Hd, PLU (1835–1902), RSD, RD (1894–1902), Thetf. PLU (1902–30), RD (1902–35). Abol civ 1935 ent to Riddlesworth AP.[1] *Parl* W'rn Dv (1832–67), S E Dv (1867–85), Mid Dv (1885–1918), S'rn Dv (1918–48). *Eccl* Rockl. RDn (until 1918), Harling RDn (1918–31), Rockl. RDn (1931–32). Abol eccl 1932 to help cr Riddlesworth with Gasthorpe and Knettishall EP.[108]

GATELEY
AP *LG* Seq 39. *Parl* Seq 20. *Eccl* Brisl. RDn (until 1970), Burn. & Walsing. RDn (1970–*).

GAYTON
AP *LG* Seq 22. Civ bdry: 1935 (gains Gayton Thorpe AP).[1] *Parl* Seq 21. *Eccl* Seq 38.

GAYTON THORPE
AP *LG* Freebr. Lynn Hd, PLU, RSD, RD. Abol civ 1935 ent to Gayton AP.[1] *Parl* W'rn Dv (1832–67), W Dv (1867–85), N-W'rn Dv (1885–1918), K's Lynn Dv (1918–48). *Eccl* Seq 38.

GAYWOOD
AP *LG* Freebr. Lynn Hd, PLU, RSD, RD. Abol civ 1935 to help cr King's Lynn CP.[1] *Parl* W'rn Dv (1832–67), W Dv (1867–85), N-W'rn Dv (1885–1918), K's Lynn Dv (1918–48). *Eccl* Lynn RDn (until 1866), Lynn Norfolk RDn (1866–1918), Lynn RDn (1918–37). Abol eccl 1937 to help cr Gaywood with Bawsey and Mintlyn EP.[9]

GAYWOOD WITH BAWSEY AND MINTLYN
EP Cr 1937 by union Gaywood AP, Bawsey AP, Mintlyn AP.[9] Lynn RDn.

GELDESTON
AP *LG* Seq 4. *Parl* Seq 15. *Eccl* Seq 3.

GILLINGHAM
Union for civ and eccl purposes 1748 of Gillingham St Mary AP, Gillingham All Saints AP.[109] *LG* Seq 4. *Parl* Seq 15. *Eccl* Seq 2.

GILLINGHAM ALL SAINTS
AP Gains 1440 Winston AP, Wyndale AP.[110] Clav. Hd, Brooke RDn. Abol 1748 to help cr Gillingham CP/EP.[109]

GILLINGHAM ST MARY
AP Clav. Hd, Brooke RDn. Abol 1748 to help cr Gillingham CP/EP.[109]

GIMINGHAM
AP *LG* Seq 9. *Parl* Seq 7. *Eccl* Seq 19.

GISSING
AP *LG* Seq 6. *Parl* Seq 14. *Eccl* Seq 18.

GLANDFORD
AP Holt RDn, early united for civ purposes with Bayfield as 'Glandford with Bayfield', qv, eccl incl as chap in Wiveton AP (thereafter known as 'Wiveton with Glandford'), sep eccl identity regained 1959.[111] *Eccl* Holt RDn (1959–*).

GLANDFORD WITH BAYFIELD
AP Early civ union of Glandford AP, Bayfield AP. *LG* Holt Hd, Erp. PLU, RSD, RD. Abol civ 1935 to help cr Letheringsett with Glandford CP.[1] *Parl* W'rn Dv (1832–67), N E Dv (1867–85), N'rn Dv (1885–1948).

GODWICK
AP Laund. Hd, Brisl. RDn, united 1630 to Tittleshall AP.[112]

GOODERSTONE
AP *LG* Seq 28. *Parl* Seq 26. *Eccl* Seq 7.

GORLESTON
AP In Suffolk (Mutford and Lothingland Hd). Incl chap Southtown (sep EP 1911,[114] so that this par eccl prev 'Gorleston with Southtown'). *LG* Yarm. PLU, Bor/MB, USD. Transf out of Suffolk 1889 when Gt Yarm. becomes CB. Civ bdry: 1894.[113] *Parl* (Gt) Yarm. Parl Bor (pt 1298–1832, ent 1832–1948), Yarm. CC (1948–*). *Eccl* See entry in Suffolk.

GORLESTON WITH SOUTHTOWN–See prev entry

GRESHAM
AP *LG* Seq 9. Civ bdry: 1935 (gains Barningham Norwood AP),[1] 1957.[20] *Parl* Seq 7. *Eccl* Seq 19.

GRESSENHALL
AP *LG* Seq 39. Civ bdry: 1883,[21] 1957.[25] *Parl* Seq 20. *Eccl* Seq 30. Eccl bdry: 1958.[26]

GRIMSTON
AP *LG* Seq 22. *Parl* Seq 21. *Eccl* Lynn RDn (until 1866), Lynn Norfolk RDn (1866–1918), Rising RDn (1918–70), Lynn RDn (1970–*).

GRISTON
AP *LG* Seq 50. *Parl* Seq 24. *Eccl* Seq 28.

GUESTWICK
AP *LG* Seq 14. Civ bdry: 1957.[104] *Parl* Seq 6. *Eccl* Seq 40.

GUIST
AP *LG* Seq 16. *Parl* Seq 9. *Eccl* Seq 40.

GUNTHORPE
AP *LG* Seq 37. Civ bdry: 1935 (gains Bale AP).[1] *Parl* Seq 17. *Eccl* Seq 32.

GUNTON
AP *LG* N Erp. Hd, Erp. PLU, RSD, RD. Abol civ 1935 ent to Hanworth AP.[1] *Parl* E'rn Dv (1832–67), N E Dv (1867–85), N'rn Dv (1885–1948). *Eccl* Seq 19.

GUNTON–See BRANDISTON

HACKFORD
AP Burned 1500 and united to Whitwell AP,[115] sep civ identity regained early, eccl 'Hackford with Whitwell', qv. *LG* Eynsf. Hd, Ayl. PLU, RSD, RD. Abol civ 1935 to help cr Reepham CP.[1] *Parl* E'rn Dv (1832–67), N E Dv (1867–85), N'rn Dv (1885–1948).

HACKFORD
AP *LG* Foreh. Hd, incorp for poor/PLU, RSD, RD. Abol civ 1935 ent to Deopham AP.[1] *Parl* E'rn Dv (1832–67), S E Dv (1867–85), Mid Dv (1885–1918), S'rn Dv (1918–48). *Eccl* Seq 14.

HACKFORD WITH WHITWELL
EP Cr 1500 by union Hackford AP, Whitwell AP (for civ see each sep).[115] Hingh. RDn. Abol eccl 1935 to help cr Reepham and Hackford with Whitwell and Kerdiston EP.[116]

HADDISCOE
AP *LG* Seq 4. Civ bdry: 1935 (incl gains Thorpe next Haddiscoe AP).[1] *Parl* Seq 15. *Eccl* Seq 3.

HAINFORD
AP Usual civ spelling; for eccl see 'Haynford'. *LG* Seq 45. *Parl* Seq 10.

HALES
AP *LG* Seq 4. *Parl* Seq 15. *Eccl* Brooke RDn (until 1918), Lodd. RDn (1918–70). Abol eccl 1970 to help cr Hales with Heckingham EP.[117]

HALES WITH HECKINGHAM
EP Cr 1970 by union Hales AP, Heckingham AP.[117] Lodd. RDn.

HALVERGATE
AP *LG* Seq 48. Civ bdry: 1935 (incl gains Tunstall AP).[1] *Parl* Seq 11. *Eccl* Seq 27.

HANWORTH
AP *LG* Seq 9. Civ bdry: 1935 (gains Gunton AP).[1] *Parl* Seq 7. *Eccl* Seq 19.

HAPPISBURGH
AP *LG* Seq 34. Civ bdry: 1935 (gains Walcot AP).[1] *Parl* Seq 1. *Eccl* Seq 24.

HAPTON
AP *LG* Depw. Hd, PLU, RSD, RD. Abol civ 1935 ent to Tharston AP.[1] *Parl* E'rn Dv (1832–67), S E Dv (1867–85), S'rn Dv (1885–1948). *Eccl* Depw. RDn (until 1937), Humblyd. RDn (1937–*).

HARDINGHAM
AP *LG* Seq 41. *Parl* Seq 19. *Eccl* Seq 15.

HARDLEY
AP *LG* Lodd. Hd, Lodd. & Clav. PLU, RSD, RD. Abol civ 1935 to help cr Langley with Hardley CP.[1] *Parl* E'rn Dv (1832–67), S E Dv (1867–85), S-W'rn Dv (1885–1918), E'rn Dv (1918–48). *Eccl* Seq 3.

HARDWICK
AP *LG* Depw. Hd, PLU, RSD, RD. Abol civ 1935 ent to Shelton AP.[1] *Parl* E'rn Dv (1832–67), S E Dv (1867–85), S'rn Dv (1885–1948). *Eccl* Seq 11.

HARGHAM
AP *LG* Shrop. Hd, Wayl. PLU, RSD, RD. Abol civ 1935 ent to Eccles AP.[1] *Parl* W'rn Dv (1832–67), S E Dv (1867–85), Mid Dv (1885–1918), S'rn Dv (1918–48). *Eccl* Seq 20.

HARLING
CP Cr 1935 by union East Harling AP, West Harling AP.[1] *LG* Wayl. RD. Bdry: 1956.[42] *Parl* S Norfolk CC (1948–*).

EAST HARLING
AP *LG* Gulitc. Hd, PLU (1835–1902), RSD, RD (1894–1902), Thetf. PLU (1902–30), RD (1902–35). Abol civ 1935 to help cr Harling CP.[1] *Parl* W'rn Dv (1832–67), S E Dv (1867–85), Mid Dv (1885–1918), S'rn Dv (1918–48).

Eccl Seq 22.
LITTLE HARLING
AP Rockl. RDn, abol 1543 ent to West Harling AP.[118]
WEST HARLING
AP Gains 1543 Little Harling AP.[118] Organisation o'wise as for East Harling.
HARPLEY
AP *LG* Seq 22. *Parl* Seq 21. *Eccl* Lynn RDn (until 1866), Lynn Norfolk RDn (1866–1918), Rising RDn (1918–70), Brisl. & Elm. RDn (1970–*).
HASSINGHAM
AP *LG* Blof. Hd, PLU, RSD, RD. Abol civ 1935 ent to Strumpshaw AP.[1] *Parl* E'rn Dv (1832–67), S E Dv (1867–85), E'rn Dv (1885–1948). *Eccl* Blof. RDn. Abol eccl 1951 to help cr Buckenham with Hassingham EP.[46]
GREAT HAUTBOIS
AP *LG* S Erp. Hd, Ayl. PLU, RSD, RD. Abol civ 1935 ent to Coltishall AP.[1] *Parl* E'rn Dv (1832–67), N E Dv (1867–85), E'rn Dv (1885–1918), N'rn Dv (1918–48). *Eccl* Seq 33.
LITTLE HAUTBOIS
AP Ingw. RDn, abol 1481 to help cr Lammas with Little Hautbois AP.[119]
HAVERINGLAND
AP *LG* Seq 17. *Parl* Seq 5. *Eccl* Spar. RDn (until 1927), Tav. RDn (1927–70), Ingw. RDn (1970–*).
HAYNFORD
AP Usual eccl spelling; for civ see 'Hainford'. *Eccl* Tav. RDn (until 1970), Ingw. RDn (1970–*).
HEACHAM
AP *LG* Seq 44. Civ bdry: 1902,[120] 1925,[121] 1928.[122] *Parl* Seq 21. *Eccl* Seq 12.
HECKINGHAM
AP *LG* Seq 4. *Parl* Seq 15. *Eccl* Brooke RDn (until 1918), Lodd. RDn (1918–73). Abol eccl 1973 to help cr Hales with Heckingham EP.[117]
HEDENHAM
AP *LG* Seq 40. *Parl* Seq 15. *Eccl* Seq 4.
HEIGHAM
The following have 'Heigham' in their names. Insofar as any existed at a given time: *LG* Norw. Bor/MB/CB, incorp for poor, CB. *Parl* Norw. Parl Bor. *Eccl* Humblyd. RDn (until 1918), Norw. RDn (1918–70), Norw. (South) RDn (1970–*).
AP1–HEIGHAM [ST BARTHOLOMEW]–Abol civ 1889 to help cr Norwich CP.[89] Eccl bdry: 1867 (cr EP1),[123] 1868 (cr EP3),[124] 1907 (cr EP2),[125] 1932 (help cr Mile Cross EP).[48]
EP1–HEIGHAM MOST HOLY TRINITY–Cr 1867 from AP1.[123] Bdry: 1889 (help cr EP4).[126]
EP2–HEIGHAM ST BARNABAS–Cr 1907 from AP1.[125]
EP3–HEIGHAM ST PHILIP–Cr 1868 from AP1.[124] Bdry: 1889 (help cr EP4).[126]
EP4–HEIGHAM ST THOMAS–Cr 1889 from EP3, EP1.[126]

HELHOUGHTON
AP *LG* Seq 26. *Parl* Seq 23. *Eccl* Toft. RDn (until 1918), Brisl. RDn (1918–27). Abol eccl 1927 to help cr Raynham with Helhoughton EP.[127]
HELLESDON
AP *LG* Tav. Hd, St Faith's PLU, pt Norw. Bor/MB/CB, pt Norw. USD, pt St Faith's RSD, St Faith's RD (1894–1935), St Faith's & Ayl. RD (1935–74). Civ bdry: 1889 (the pt in the CB lost to help cr Norwich CP),[89] 1959,[66] 1968 (incl loses pt to Norw. CB and CP).[18] *Parl* Pt Norw. Parl Bor (1295–1918), remainder and later, Seq 10. *Eccl* Seq 42. Eccl bdry: 1915 (help cr New Catton St Luke EP),[67] 1932 (help cr Mile Cross EP),[48] 1940,[69] 1954.[128]
HELLINGTON
AP *LG* Seq 40. *Parl* Seq 15. *Eccl* Seq 2.
HEMBLINGTON
AP *LG* Seq 48. *Parl* Seq 11. *Eccl* Seq 27.
HEMPNALL
AP *LG* Seq 5. *Parl* Seq 14. *Eccl* Seq 11.
HEMPSTEAD
AP *LG* Seq 36. *Parl* Seq 16. *Eccl* Seq 32.
HEMPSTEAD–See following entry
HEMPSTEAD WITH ECCLES
AP Hempstead AP gains civ early Eccles AP (eccl, 'Eccles next the Sea') when latter's church lost into sea, thereafter civ 'Hempstead with Eccles' but eccl 'Hempstead'. *LG* Hap. Hd, Tunst. & Hap. incorp for poor (1785–1870), Smallb. PLU (1870–1930), RSD, RD. Abol civ 1935 ent to Lessingham AP.[1] *Parl* E'rn Dv (1832–67), N E Dv (1867–85), E'rn Dv (1885–1948). *Eccl* Wax. RDn. Abol eccl 1923 to help cr Hempstead with Eccles next the Sea EP.[94]
HEMPSTEAD WITH ECCLES NEXT THE SEA
EP Cr 1923 by union Hempstead AP, Eccles next the Sea AP.[94] Wax. RDn.
HEMPTON
AP *LG* Seq 26. *Parl* Seq 23. *Eccl* Toft. RDn (until 1918), Brisl. RDn (1918–30). Abol eccl 1930 to help cr Hempton with Pudding Norton EP.[129]
HEMPTON WITH PUDDING NORTON
EP Cr 1930 by union Hempton AP, Pudding Norton AP.[129] Brisl. RDn (1930–70), Burn. & Walsing. RDn (1970–*).
HEMSBY
AP *LG* Seq 19. *Parl* Seq 2. *Eccl* Seq 31.
HETHEL
AP *LG* Humblyd. Hd, Henst. PLU, RSD, RD. Abol civ 1935 ent to Bracon Ash AP.[1] *Parl* E'rn Dv (1832–67), S E Dv (1867–85), S'rn Dv (1885–1948). *Eccl* Seq 16.
HETHERSETT
AP Gains 1397 Canteloff AP.[61] *LG* Seq 38. *Parl* Seq 13. *Eccl* Seq 16.
HEVINGHAM
AP *LG* Seq 11. *Parl* Seq 5. *Eccl* Seq 33.
HEYDON
AP *LG* Seq 11. *Parl* Seq 5. *Eccl* Incl eccl Irmingland AP (early in ruins), Seq 33.
HICKLING
AP *LG* Seq 34. Civ bdry: 1885.[10] *Parl* Seq 1. *Eccl*

Seq 24.
HILGAY
AP *LG* Seq 3. Civ bdry: 1885,[130] 1957.[131] *Parl* Seq 26. *Eccl* Fincham RDn. Eccl bdry: 1866 (help cr Little Ouse EP).[100]
HILBOROUGH
AP *LG* Seq 28. Civ bdry: 1935 (gains Bodney AP).[1] *Parl* Seq 26. *Eccl* Seq 7.
HILLINGTON
AP *LG* Seq 22. *Parl* Seq 21. *Eccl* Seq 36.
HINDOLVESTON
AP *LG* Seq 15. *Parl* Seq 8. *Eccl* Pec jurisd Dean & Chapter of Norw. (until 1847), Seq 40 thereafter.
HINDRINGHAM
AP *LG* Seq 27. *Parl* Seq 17. *Eccl* Seq 47.
HINGHAM
AP *LG* Seq 20. *Parl* Seq 12. *Eccl* Seq 13.
HOCKERING
AP *LG* Seq 41. *Parl* Seq 19. *Eccl* Seq 15.
HOCKHAM
AP *LG* Seq 43. *Parl* Seq 18. *Eccl* Seq 20.
HOCKWOLD
AP *LG* Grimshoe Hd. Abol civ *ca* 1720 to help cr Hockwold cum Wilton CP.[132] *Eccl* Cranw. RDn (until 1914), Fincham RDn (1914–17), Feltwell RDn (1917–72). Abol eccl 1972 to help cr Hockwold with Wilton EP.[133]
HOCKWOLD CUM WILTON
CP Cr *ca* 1720 by union Hockwold AP, Wilton AP.[132] *LG* Seq 30. *Parl* Seq 26.
HOCKWOLD WITH WILTON
EP Cr 1972 by union Hockwold AP, Wilton AP.[133] Feltwell RDn.
HOE
Hmlt and chap in East Dereham AP, sep civ identity early, sep EP before 1845. *LG* Seq 39. Civ bdry: 1935 (gains Worthing AP).[1] *Parl* Seq 20. *Eccl* Brisl. RDn (cr–1918), Mitf. RDn (1918–70), Hingh. & Mitf. RDn (1970–*).
HOLKHAM
AP *LG* Seq 27. Civ bdry: 1950.[134] *Parl* Seq 17. *Eccl* Seq 46.
HOLME HALE
AP *LG* Seq 28. *Parl* Seq 26. *Eccl* Seq 7.
HOLME NEXT THE SEA
AP *LG* Seq 44. *Parl* Seq 21. *Eccl* Seq 12.
HOLT
AP *LG* Seq 36. *Parl* Seq 16. *Eccl* Seq 32.
HOLVERSTON
AP *LG* Seq 35. *Parl* Seq 13. *Eccl* Brooke RDn. Early in ruins, now eccl incl in Bergh Apton AP.
HONING
AP *LG* Seq 47. Civ bdry: 1935 (gains Crostwright AP).[1] *Parl* Seq 1. *Eccl* Seq 25.
HONINGHAM
AP *LG* Foreh. Hd, St Faith's PLU, RSD, RD (1894–1935), St Faith's & Ayl. RD (1935–74). *Parl* E'rn Dv (1832–67), S E Dv (1867–85), Mid Dv (1885–1918), E'rn Dv (1918–48), Ctrl. Norfolk CC (1948–70), N Norfolk CC (1970–*). *Eccl* Seq 15.
HOPTON-ON-SEA
CP In E Suffolk (qv), transf 1974 to Norfolk incl gains the pt of Corton AP (Suffolk) also transf to Norfolk.[28]
HORNING
AP *LG* Seq 47. *Parl* Seq 1. *Eccl* Seq 25.
HORNINGTOFT
AP *LG* Seq 39. *Parl* Seq 20. *Eccl* Seq 29.
HORSEY
AP *LG* Seq 34. Civ bdry: 1885.[10] *Parl* Seq 1. *Eccl* Seq 24.
HORSFORD
AP *LG* Seq 45. Civ bdry: 1968.[18] *Parl* Seq 10. *Eccl* Seq 42.
HORSHAM ST FAITH AND NEWTON ST FAITH
CP Renaming 1955 of Horsham St Faith with Newton St Faith AP.[135] *LG* St Faith's & Ayl. RD. Bdry: 1968 (incl loses pt to Norw. CB and CP).[18] *Parl* N Norfolk CC (1970–*).
HORSHAM ST FAITH WITH NEWTON ST FAITH
AP *LG* Tav. Hd, St Faith's PLU, RSD, RD (1894–1935), St Faith's & Ayl. RD (1935–55). Renamed civ 1955 'Horsham St Faith and Newton St Faith'.[135] *Parl* E'rn Dv (1832–67), S E Dv (1867–85), E'rn Dv (1885–1948), Ctrl. Norfolk CC (1948–70). *Eccl* Seq 42.
HORSTEAD
AP Civ united 16th cent with Stanninghall AP to cr Horstead with Stanninghall,[136] qv. *Eccl* Tav. RDn (until 1970), Ingw. RDn (1970–*).
HORSTEAD WITH STANNINGHALL
AP Civ union 16th cent of Hortead AP, Stanninghall AP.[136] *LG* Seq 45. Civ bdry: 1885.[137] *Parl* Seq 10.
HOUGHTON
AP Sometimes 'New Houghton'. *LG* Seq 25. *Parl* Seq 21. *Eccl* Seq 5.
HOUGHTON ON THE HILL
AP *LG* S Greenh. Hd, Swaff. PLU, RSD, RD. Abol civ 1935 ent to North Pickenham AP.[1] *Parl* W'rn Dv (1832–67), W Dv (1867–85), S-W'rn Dv (1885–1948). *Eccl* Seq 7.
HOUGHTON ST GILES
AP Sometimes 'Houghton in the Dale' or 'Houghton next Walsingham'. *LG* N Greenh. Hd, Walsing. PLU, RSD, RD. Abol civ 1935 to help cr Barsham CP.[1] *Parl* W'rn Dv (1832–67), N E Dv (1867–85), N'rn Dv (1885–1948). *Eccl* Walsing. RD. Abol eccl 1969 to help cr Walsingham St Mary and All Saints with St Peter and Houghton St Giles EP.[138]
HOVETON
CP Cr 1935 by union Hoveton St John AP, Hoveton St Peter AP.[1] *LG* Smallb. RD. *Parl* N Norfolk CC (1948–*).
HOVETON ST JOHN
AP *LG* Tunst. Hd, Tunst. & Hap. incorp for poor (1785–1870), Smallb. PLU (1870–1930), RSD, RD. Abol civ 1935 to help cr Hoveton CP.[1] *Parl* E'rn Dv (1832–67), N E Dv (1867–85), E'rn Dv (1885–1948). *Eccl* Seq 25.
HOVETON ST PETER
AP Civ and parl organisation as for Hoveton St

John. *Eccl* Seq 25. Eccl bdry: 1936.[139]
HOWE
AP *LG* Seq 4. *Parl* Seq 15. *Eccl* Seq 2.
HUNSTANTON
AP Gains 16th cent Ringstead Parva AP.[140] *LG* Smithd. Hd, Dock. PLU, pt Hunstanton USD (1891–94), Dock. RSD (ent 1875–91, pt 1891–94), Dock. RD. Civ bdry: 1894 (the pt in the USD cr New Hunstanton CP),[87] 1902,[120] 1928.[122] Renamed civ 1953 'Old Hunstanton'.[141] *Parl* W'rn Dv (1832–67), W Dv (1867–85), N-W'rn Dv (1885–1918), K's Lynn Dv/CC (1918–70). *Eccl* Seq 12. Eccl bdry: 1904 (cr Hunstanton St Edmund EP).[142]
NEW HUNSTANTON
CP Cr 1894 from the pt of Hunstanton AP in Hunstanton USD.[87] *LG* Dock. PLU, Hunstanton UD (1894–96), New Hunstanton UD (1896–1954),[120] Hunstanton UD (1954–74). Bdry: 1902,[120] 1925,[121] 1928.[122] *Parl* K's Lynn Dv/CC (1918–70), N W Norfolk CC (1970–*).
OLD HUNSTANTON
CP Renaming 1953 of Hunstanton AP.[141] *LG* Dock. RD. *Parl* N W Norfolk CC (1970–*).
HUNSTANTON ST EDMUND
EP Cr 1904 from Hunstanton AP.[142] Heach. RDn (1904–70), Heach. & Rising RDn (1970–*).
HUNWORTH
AP *LG* Holt Hd, Erp. PLU, RSD, RD. Abol civ 1935 ent to Stody AP.[1] *Parl* W'rn Dv (1832–67), N E Dv (1867–85), N'rn Dv (1885–1918). *Eccl* Seq 32.
ICKBURGH
AP *LG* Seq 29. Civ bdry: 1935 (gains Langford AP).[1] *Parl* Seq 26. *Eccl* Seq 10.
ILLINGTON
AP *LG* Shrop. Hd, Wayl. PLU, RSD, RD. Abol civ 1935 to help cr Wretham CP.[1] *Parl* W'rn Dv (1832–67), S E Dv (1867–85), Mid Dv (1885–1918), S'rn Dv (1918–48). *Eccl* Rockl. RDn (until 1925), Thetf. RDn (1925–70), Thetf. & Rockl. RDn (1970–*).
INGHAM
AP *LG* Seq 34. *Parl* Seq 1. *Eccl* Seq 24.
INGOLDISTHORPE
AP *LG* Seq 44. *Parl* Seq 21. *Eccl* Seq 12.
INGWORTH
AP *LG* Seq 10. *Parl* Seq 7. *Eccl* Seq 33.
INTWOOD
AP *LG* Humblyd. Hd, Henst. PLU, RSD, RD. Abol civ 1935 ent to Keswick AP.[1] *Parl* E'rn Dv (1832–67), S E Dv (1867–85), S'rn Dv (1885–1948). *Eccl* Seq 16.
IRMINGLAND
AP *LG* S Erp. Hd, Ayl. PLU, RSD, RD. Abol civ 1935 ent to Oulton AP.[1] *Parl* E'rn Dv (1832–67), N E Dv (1867–85), N'rn Dv (1885–1918). *Eccl* Ingw. RDn. Early in ruins and eccl incl in Heydon AP.
IRSTEAD
AP *LG* Tunst. Hd, Tunst. & Hap. incorp for poor (1785–1870), Smallb. PLU (1870–1930), RSD, RD. Abol civ 1935 ent to Barton Turf AP.[1] *Parl* E'rn Dv (1832–67), N E Dv (1867–85), E'rn Dv (1885–1948). *Eccl* Wax. RDn (until 1932), Tunst. RDn (1932–*).
ISLINGTON
AP Usual eccl spelling; for civ see 'Tilney with Islington'. *Eccl* Lynn RDn (until 1866), Lynn Marshland RDn (1866–1971). Eccl bdry: 1922 (help cr Marshland St James EP).[72] Abol eccl 1971 to help cr Wiggenhall St Mary the Virgin with Islington EP.[143]
ITTERINGHAM
AP *LG* Seq 10. Civ bdry: 1935 (gains Mannington AP).[1] *Parl* Seq 7. *Eccl* Ingw. RDn. Abol eccl prob 1577 to help cr Itteringham with Mannington EP.[144]
ITTERINGHAM WITH MANNINGTON
EP Cr prob 1577 by union Itteringham AP, Mannington AP.[144] *Eccl* Seq 33.
KELLING
AP *LG* Seq 36. *Parl* Seq 16. *Eccl* Seq 32.
KEMPSTON
AP Usual eccl spelling; for civ see following entry. *Eccl* Seq 30.
KEMPSTONE
AP Usual civ spelling; for eccl see prev entry. *LG* Seq 39. *Parl* Seq 20.
KENINGHAM
AP Humblyd. RDn, united 1452 to Mulbarton AP.[145]
KENNINGHALL
AP *LG* Seq 33. *Parl* Seq 18. *Eccl* Seq 22.
KESWICK
AP *LG* Seq 38. Civ bdry: 1935 (gains Intwood AP).[1] *Parl* Seq 13. *Eccl* Seq 16.
KETTERINGHAM
AP *LG* Seq 38. *Parl* Seq 13. *Eccl* Seq 16.
KETTLESTONE
AP *LG* Seq 26. Civ bdry: 1935 (gains Pensthorpe AP),[1] 1958.[88] *Parl* Seq 23. *Eccl* Seq 5.
KILVERSTONE
AP *LG* Shrop. Hd, Thetf. PLU, RSD, RD (1894–1935), Wayl. RD (1935–74). *Parl* Seq 18. *Eccl* Seq 23.
KIMBERLEY
AP *LG* Seq 20. Civ bdry: 1935 (gains Carleton Forehoe AP).[1] *Parl* Seq 12. *Eccl* Seq 13.
KIRBY BEDON
AP Orig 2 pars, St Andrew, St Mary, early united. *LG* Seq 35. Civ bdry: 1935 (gains Whitlingham AP).[1] *Parl* Seq 13. *Eccl* Seq 2. Gains eccl *ca* 1630 Whitlingham AP,[146] the union often called 'Kirby Bedon with Whitlingham'.
KIRBY BEDON WITH WHITLINGHAM–See prev entry
KIRBY CANE
AP *LG* Seq 4. *Parl* Seq 15. *Eccl* Seq 3.
KIRSTEAD
AP Gains 1421 Langhale AP.[147] *LG* Seq 40. *Parl* E'rn Dv (1832–67), S E Dv (1867–85), S'rn Dv (1885–1918), E'rn Dv (1918–48), S Norfolk CC (1948–*). *Eccl* Sometimes as 'Kirstead with Langhale', Seq 2.
KIRSTEAD WITH LANGHALE–See prev entry

KNAPTON

AP *LG* N Erp. Hd, Erp. PLU, RSD, RD. Civ bdry: 1926.[148] Abol civ 1935 ent to Paston AP.[1] *Parl* E'rn Dv (1832–67), N E Dv (1867–85), N'rn Dv (1885–1948). *Eccl* Repps RDn (until 1924), Tunst. RDn (1924–*).

CP Cr 1950 from Paston AP.[1] *LG* Smallb. RD. *Parl* N Norfolk CC (1970–*).

LAKENHAM

AP *LG* Norw. Bor/MB/CB, incorp for poor, USD. Abol civ 1889 to help cr Norwich CP.[89] *Parl* Norw. Parl Bor (1295–1918). *Eccl* Pec jurisd Dean & Chapter of Norw. (until 1847), Norw. RDn (1847–1970), Norw. (South) RDn (1970–*). Eccl bdry: 1845 (cr Lakenham St Mark EP),[149] 1949 (help cr Lakenham St Alban EP),[150] 1969 (cr Tuckswood EP).[151]

LAKENHAM ST ALBAN

EP Cr 1949 by union Liberty of the Town Close ex-par place and pts Lakenham AP, Lakenham St Mark EP.[150] Norw. RDn (1949–70), Norw. (South) RDn (1970–*).

LAKENHAM ST MARK

EP Cr 1845 from Lakenham AP.[149] Norw. RDn (1845–1970), Norw. (East) RDn (1970–*). Bdry: 1949 (help cr Lakenham St Alban EP).[150]

LAMMAS

AP Ingw. RDn, abol 1481 to help cr Lammas with Little Hautbois AP.[119]

LAMMAS WITH LITTLE HAUTBOIS

AP Cr 1481 by union Lammas AP, Little Hautbois AP.[119] *LG* S Erp. Hd, Ayl. PLU, RSD, RD. Abol civ 1935 to help cr Buxton with Lammas CP.[1] *Parl* E'rn Dv (1832–67), N E Dv (1867–85), E'rn Dv (1885–1918), N'rn Dv (1918–48). *Eccl* Seq 33. Eccl bdry: 1973.[152]

LANGFORD

AP *LG* S Greenh. Hd, Swaff. PLU, RSD, RD. Abol civ 1935 ent to Ickburgh AP.[1] *Parl* W'rn Dv (1832–67), W Dv (1867–85), S-W'rn Dv (1885–1948).

LANGHALE

AP Brooke RDn, abol 1421 ent to Kirstead AP.[147]

LANGHAM

AP Usual civ spelling, sometimes civ 'Great Langham'; for eccl see 'Langham Episcopi'. *LG* Seq 37. *Parl* Seq 17.

GREAT LANGHAM—See prev entry

LITTLE LANGHAM

AP Holt Hd, Holt RDn, abol early 17th cent ent to Blakeney AP.[34]

LANGHAM EPISCOPI

AP Usual eccl spelling; for civ see 'Langham'. *Eccl* Seq 32.

LANGLEY

AP *LG* Lodd. Hd, Lodd. & Clav. PLU, RSD, RD. Abol civ 1935 pt to help cr Langley with Hardley CP, pt to Haddiscoe AP.[1] *Parl* E'rn Dv (1832–67), S E Dv (1867–85), S-W'rn Dv (1885–1918), E'rn Dv (1918–48). *Eccl* Seq 3.

LANGLEY WITH HARDLEY

CP Cr 1935 by union Hardley AP, pt Langley AP.[1] *LG* Lodd. RD. *Parl* S Norfolk CC (1948–*).

LARLING

AP *LG* Shrop. Hd, Wayl. PLU, RSD, RD. Abol civ 1935 ent to Roudham AP.[1] *Parl* W'rn Dv (1832–67), S E Dv (1867–85), Mid Dv (1885–1918), S'rn Dv (1918–48). *Eccl* Rockl. RDn (until 1918), Harling RDn (1918–30), Rockl. RDn (1930–70), Thetf. & Rockl. RDn (1970–*).

LESSINGHAM

AP *LG* Seq 34. *Parl* Seq 1. *Eccl* Seq 24.

LETHERINGSETT

AP *LG* Holt Hd, Erp. PLU, RSD, RD. Abol civ 1935 to help cr Letheringsett with Glandford CP.[1] *Parl* W'rn Dv (1832–67), N E Dv (1867–85), N'rn Dv (1885–1948). *Eccl* Holt RDn. Abol eccl 1925 to help cr Letheringsett with Bayfield EP.[19]

LETHERINGSETT WITH BAYFIELD

EP Cr 1925 by union Letheringsett AP, Bayfield AP.[19] Holt RDn.

LETHERINGSETT WTIH GLANDFORD

CP Cr 1935 by union Letheringsett AP, Glandford AP.[1] *LG* Erp. RD. *Parl* N Norfolk CC (1970–*).

LETTON

AP Hingh. RDn, abol 1547 ent to Cranworth AP,[76] sep civ identity regained early. *LG* Mitf. Hd, Mitf. & Laund. PLU, RSD, RD. Abol civ 1935 ent to Cranworth AP.[1] *Parl* W'rn Dv (1832–67), S E Dv (1867–85), Mid Dv (1885–1918), S-W'rn Dv (1918–48).

LEXHAM

CP Cr 1935 by union East Lexham AP, West Lexham AP.[1] *LG* Mitf. & Laund. RD. *Parl* S W Norfolk CC (1948–*).

EAST LEXHAM

AP *LG* Laund. Hd, Mitf. & Laund. PLU, RSD, RD. Abol civ 1935 to help cr Lexham CP.[1] *Parl* W'rn Dv (1832–67), W Dv (1867–85), Mid Dv (1885–1918), S-W'rn Dv (1918–48). *Eccl* Seq 30.

WEST LEXHAM

AP Organisation as for East Lexham.

LEZIATE

AP Lynn RDn, abol after 1474 to Ashwicken AP,[8] sep civ identity regained early. *LG* Seq 22. Civ bdry: 1935 (gains Ashwicken AP).[1] *Parl* Seq 21.

LIBERTY OF THE TOWN CLOSE

Ex-par place, sep CP 1858 as 'Norwich Liberty of the Town Close',[4] qv, eccl abol 1949 to help cr Lakenham St Alban EP.[150]

LIMPENHOE

AP *LG* Blof. Hd, PLU, RSD, RD. Civ bdry: 1884.[36] Abol civ 1935 ent to Cantley AP.[1] *Parl* E'rn Dv (1832–67), S E Dv (1867–85), E'rn Dv (1885–1948). *Eccl* Blof. RDn. Abol eccl 1934 to help cr Limpenhoe with Southwood EP.[153]

LIMPENHOE WITH SOUTHWOOD

EP Cr 1934 by union Limpenhoe AP, Southwood AP.[153] Blof. RDn.

LINGWOOD

AP *LG* Blof. Hd, PLU, RSD, RD. Civ bdry: 1884.[36] Abol civ 1935 to help cr Burlingham CP.[1] *Parl* E'rn Dv (1832–67), S E Dv (1867–85), E'rn

Dv (1885–1948). *Eccl* Seq 27.

LITCHAM

AP *LG* Seq 39. *Parl* Seq 20. *Eccl* Seq 30.

LODDON

AP *LG* Seq 40. Civ bdry: 1935.[1] *Parl* Seq 15. *Eccl* Seq 3.

LONGHAM

AP *LG* Seq 39. Civ bdry: 1883.[21] *Parl* Seq 20. *Eccl* Brisl. RDn (until 1918), Elm. RDn (1918–30). Abol eccl 1930 to help cr Longham with Bittering Parva EP.[32]

EP Cr 1961 when Longham with Bittering Parva EP divided into 2 EPs of Longham, Bittering Parva.[33] Elm. RDn (1961–70), Brisl. & Elm. RDn (1970–*).

LONGHAM WITH BITTERING PARVA

EP Cr 1930 by union Longham AP, Bittering Parva AP.[32] Elm. RDn. Bdry: 1958.[26] Abol eccl 1961, divided into 2 EPs of Longham, Bittering Parva.[33]

NORTH LOPHAM

AP *LG* Seq 32. *Parl* Seq 18. *Eccl* Seq 21.

SOUTH LOPHAM

AP *LG* Seq 32. *Parl* Seq 18. *Eccl* Seq 21.

LUDHAM

AP *LG* Seq 34. *Parl* Seq 1. *Eccl* Seq 24.

LYNFORD

AP *LG* Seq 31. Civ bdry: 1935 (gains Santon AP, West Tofts AP).[1] *Parl* Seq 26. *Eccl* Cranw. RDn (until 1918), Thetf. RDn (1918–24). Abol eccl 1924 to help cr Mundford and Lynford EP.[48]

LYNG

AP *LG* Seq 16. *Parl* Seq 9. *Eccl* Seq 40.

LYNN

The following have 'Lynn' in their names. Insofar as any existed at a given time: *LG* Freebr. Lynn Hd, K's Lynn PLU, remainder sep noted. *Parl* Sep noted. *Eccl* Lynn RDn (until 1866), Lynn Marshland RDn (1866–1914), Lynn Norfolk RDn (1914–18), Lynn RDn (1918–*). Orig called 'Lynn' or 'Bishop's Lynn'; since *temp* Henry VIII, 'King's Lynn', the latter used invariably below for convenience's sake.

CP1–KING'S LYNN–Cr 1935 by union Gaywood AP, AP1, AP2 and pts North Runcton AP, AP3, AP4.[1] *LG* K's Lynn MB. *Parl* K's Lynn CC (1948–70), N W Norfolk CC (1970–*).

–KING'S LYNN ALL SAINTS–See AP3

EP1–KING'S LYNN ST JOHN–Cr 1846 from AP1.[154]

AP1–KING'S LYNN ST MARGARET–Incl chap St Nicholas (no sep identity, hence this par eccl usually called 'King's Lynn St Margaret with St Nicholas'. *LG* K's Lynn Bor/MB, USD. Abol civ 1935 to help cr CP1.[1] *Parl* K's Lynn Parl Bor (1298–1918), K's Lynn Dv (1918–48). Eccl bdry: 1846 (cr EP1).[154]

–KING'S LYNN ST MARGARET WITH ST NICHOLAS–See AP1

AP2–NORTH LYNN [ST EDMUND] –*LG* Pt K's Lynn USD, pt K's Lynn RSD, Freebr. Lynn RD. Civ bdry: 1885.[71] Abol civ 1935 to help cr CP1.[1] *Parl* W'rn Dv (1832–67), W Dv (1867–85), N-W'rn Dv (1885–1918), K's Lynn Dv (1918–48).

AP3–SOUTH LYNN [ALL SAINTS] –*LG* K's Lynn Bor (from 1557)/MB, USD. Abol civ 1935 pt to help cr CP1, pt to Clenchwarton AP.[1] *Parl* As for AP1, from 1557. *Eccl* Called eccl 'King's Lynn All Saints'.

AP4–WEST LYNN [ST PETER] –*LG* K's Lynn RSD, RD. Civ bdry: 1885.[11] Abol civ 1935 pt to help cr CP1, pt to Clenchwarton AP.[1] *Parl* As for AP2.

MANNINGTON

AP *LG* S Erp. Hd, Ayl. PLU, RSD, RD. Abol civ 1935 ent to Itteringham AP.[1] *Parl* E'rn Dv (1832–67), N E Dv (1867–85), N'rn Dv (1885–1948). *Eccl* Seq 33.

MARHAM

AP Orig 2 pars, St Andrew, Holy Trinity, united prob 13th cent.[156] *LG* Seq 3. Civ bdry: 1935 (help cr Beachamwell CP).[1] *Parl* Seq 26. *Eccl* Fincham RDn.

MARKSHALL

AP *LG* Humblyd. Hd, Henst. PLU, RSD, RD. Abol civ 1935 to help cr Caister St Edmunds CP.[1] *Parl* E'rn Dv (1832–67), S E Dv (1867–85), S'rn Dv (1885–1948). *Eccl* Humblyd. RDn. Abol eccl 1695 to help cr Caister St Edmund with Markshall EP.[58]

MARLINGFORD

AP *LG* Seq 20. Civ bdry: 1885,[92] 1935 (gains Colton AP).[1] *Parl* Seq 12. *Eccl* Seq 14.

MARSHAM

AP *LG* Seq 11. *Parl* Seq 5. *Eccl* Seq 33.

MARSHLAND ST JAMES

EP Cr 1922 by union pts Walpole St Peter AP, Walpole St Andrew AP, Walsoken AP, West Walton AP, Clenchwarton AP, Emneth EP, Ilsington AP, Terrington St Clement AP, Terrington St John AP, Tilney All Saints with St Lawrence AP.[72] Lynn Marshland RDn.

CP Cr 1935 by union pts Clenchwarton AP, Emneth CP, Terrington St Clement AP, Terrington St John AP, Tilney All Saints AP, Tilney St Lawrence AP, Tilney with Islington AP, Walsoken AP, Walton AP.[1] *LG* Marshland RD. *Parl* K's Lynn CC (1948–70), N W Norfolk CC (1970–*).

MARTHAM

AP *LG* Seq 19. *Parl* Seq 2. *Eccl* Pec jurisd Dean & Chapter of Norw. (until 1847), Seq 31 thereafter.

GREAT MASSINGHAM

AP *LG* Seq 22. *Parl* Seq 21. *Eccl* Lynn RDn (until 1866), Lynn Norfolk RDn (1866–1918), Rising RDn (1918–70), Brisl. & Elm. RDn (1970–*).

LITTLE MASSINGHAM

AP Organisation as for Great Massingham.

MATLASK

AP Usual civ spelling; for eccl see following entry. *LG* Seq 9. Civ bdry: 1935 (gains Barningham Winter or Barningham Town AP).[1] *Parl* Seq 7.

MATLASKE

AP Usual eccl spelling; for civ see prev entry. *Eccl*

Seq 19.
MATTISHALL
AP *LG* Seq 41. Civ bdry: 1935 (gains Mattishall AP).[1] *Parl* Seq 19. *Eccl* Seq 15.
MATTISHALL BURGH
AP *LG* Mitf. Hd, Mitf. & Laund. PLU, RSD, RD. Abol civ 1935 ent to Mattishall AP.[1] *Parl* W'rn Dv (1832–67), S E Dv (1867–85), Mid Dv (1885–1918), S-W'rn Dv (1918–48). *Eccl* Seq 15.
MAUTBY
AP *LG* Seq 18. Civ bdry: 1935.[1] *Parl* Seq 2. *Eccl* Seq 31.
GREAT MELTON
AP Orig 2 pars, All Saints, St Mary, united 1728.[155] *LG* Seq 38. *Parl* Seq 13. *Eccl* Seq 16.
LITTLE MELTON
AP *LG* Seq 38. *Parl* Seq 13. *Eccl* Seq 16.
MELTON CONSTABLE
AP Incl civ Burgh Parva AP. *LG* Holt Hd, Brinton incorp for poor (1738–1860s), Walsing. PLU (1860s–1930), RSD, RD. *Parl* Seq 17. *Eccl* Seq 32.
MENDHAM
AP Pt Norfolk (Earsh. Hd), pt Suffolk (Hoxne Hd), the former lost 1885 to Rendenhall with Harleston AP and Mendham ent Suffolk thereafter.[157] Incl chap Needham (sep civ identity early in Norfolk, sep EP 1764[163]). *LG* Hoxne PLU, RSD. *Parl* Norfolk pt, E'rn Dv (1832–67), S E Dv (1867–85), S'rn Dv (1885–1918). For later civ and for eccl organisation, see main entry in Suffolk.
MERTON
AP *LG* Seq 50. Civ bdry: 1965.[158] *Parl* Seq 24. *Eccl* Seq 28.
METHWOLD
AP *LG* Seq 30. Civ bdry: 1954,[159] 1957.[131] *Parl* Seq 26. *Eccl* Cranw. RDn (until 1914), Fincham RDn (1914–18), Feltwell RDn (1918–*).
METTON
AP *LG* N Erp. Hd, Erp. PLU, RSD, RD. Abol civ 1935 ent to Sustead AP.[1] *Parl* E'rn Dv (1832–67), N E Dv (1867–85), N'rn Dv (1885–1948). *Eccl* Seq 19.
MIDDLETON
AP *LG* Seq 22. *Parl* Seq 21. *Eccl* Seq 38.
MILE CROSS
EP Cr 1932 from New Catton St Luke EP, Hellesdon AP, Heigham AP.[48] Norw. RDn (1932–70), Norw. (North) RDn (1970–*). Bdry: 1940,[69] 1954.[128]
MILEHAM
AP *LG* Seq 39. *Parl* Seq 20. *Eccl* Seq 30.
MINTLYN
Orig AP, later in ruins and considered civ expar, sep CP 1858.[4] *LG* Freebr. Lynn Hd, PLU, RSD, RD. Abol civ 1935 ent to Bawsey AP.[1] *Parl* W Dv (1867–85), N-W'rn Dv (1885–1918), K's Lynn Dv (1885–1918). *Eccl* Lynn RDn (until 1866), Lynn Norfolk RDn (1866–1918), Lynn RDn (1918–37). Abol eccl 1937 to help cr Gaywood with Bawsey and Mintlyn EP.[9]

MORLEY
CP Cr 1935 by union Morley St Botolph AP, Morley St Peter CP.[1] *LG* Foreh. & Henst. RD. *Parl* Ctrl. Norfolk CC (1948–70), S Norfolk CC (1970–*).
MORLEY ST BOTOLPH
AP Incl chap Morley St Peter (sep civ identity early, no sep eccl identity hence this par eccl 'Morley St Botolph with St Peter', qv). *LG* Foreh. Hd, incorp for poor/PLU, RSD, RD. Addtl civ bdry alt: 1885.[160] Abol civ 1935 to help cr Morley CP.[1] *Parl* E'rn Dv (1832–67), S E Dv (1867–85), Mid Dv (1885–1918), S'rn Dv (1918–48).
MORLEY ST BOTOLPH WITH ST PETER
AP Usual eccl spelling; for civ and civ sep chap Morley St Peter, see prev entry. *Eccl* Seq 14.
MORLEY ST PETER
Chap in Morley St Botolph AP, sep civ identity early, no sep eccl identity. *LG*, civ bdry alt, *Parl*, civ abol as for Morley St Botolph.
MORNING THORPE
AP Usual civ spelling; for eccl see following entry. *LG* Seq 5. Civ bdry: 1935 (gains Fritton AP).[1] *Parl* Seq 14.
MORNINGTHORPE
AP Usual eccl spelling; for civ see prev entry. *Eccl* Seq 11.
MORSTON
AP *LG* Seq 37. *Parl* Seq 17. *Eccl* Seq 32.
MORTON ON THE HILL
AP *LG* Seq 17. *Parl* Seq 5. *Eccl* Seq 40.
GREAT MOULTON
AP Usual eccl spelling; for civ see 'Moulton St Michael'. *Eccl* Depw. RDn. Abol eccl 1926 to help cr Great Moulton with Little Moulton EP.[162]
CP Renaming 1960 of Moulton St Michael AP.[161] *LG* Depw. RD. *Parl* S Norfolk CC (1970–*).
GREAT MOULTON WITH LITTLE MOULTON
EP Cr 1926 by union Great Moulton AP, Little Moulton AP.[162] Depw. RDn.
LITTLE MOULTON
AP Civ incl in Moulton St Michael AP (eccl, 'Great Moulton') from 1581.[165] *Eccl* Depw. RDn. Abol eccl 1926 to help cr Great Moulton with Little Moulton EP.[162]
MOULTON ST MARY
AP *LG* Walsham Hd, Blof. PLU, RSD, RD. Abol civ 1935 pt to Beighton AP, pt to Reedham AP.[1] *Parl* E'rn Dv (1832–67), S E Dv (1867–85), E'rn Dv (1885–1948). *Eccl* Blof. RDn. Abol eccl 1921 to help cr Beighton with Moulton EP.[27]
MOULTON ST MICHAEL
AP Usual civ spelling; for eccl see 'Great Moulton'. *LG* Civ incl Little Moulton from 1581.[165] Depw. Hd, PLU, RSD, RD. Renamed civ 1960 'Great Moulton'.[161] *Parl* E'rn Dv (1832–67), S E Dv (1867–85), E'rn Dv (1885–1918), S'rn Dv (1918–48), S Norfolk CC (1948–70).
MULBARTON
AP Gains 1452 Keningham AP.[145] *LG* Seq 38. *Parl*

Seq 13. *Eccl* Seq 16.

MUNDESLEY

AP *LG* Seq 9. Civ bdry: 1926.[148] *Parl* Seq 7. *Eccl* Seq 19.

MUNDFORD

AP *LG* Seq 31. *Parl* Seq 26. *Eccl* Cranw. RDn (until 1918), Thetf. RDn (1918–24). Abol eccl 1924 to help cr Mundford and Lynford EP.[48]

MUNDFORD AND LYNFORD

EP Cr 1924 by union Mundford AP, Lynford AP.[48] Thetf. RDn (1924–70), Breckland RDn (1970–*).

MUNDHAM

AP Orig 2 pars, St Peter (or Mundham Magna), St Ethelred, early united. *LG* Seq 40. *Parl* E'rn Dv (1832–67), S E Dv (1867–85), S'rn Dv (1885–1918), E'rn Dv (1918–48), S Norfolk CC (1948–*). *Eccl* Seq 3.

NARBOROUGH

AP *LG* Seq 28. *Parl* Seq 26. *Eccl* Cranw. RDn (until 1918), Swaff. RDn (1918–70), Lynn RDn (1970–*).

NARFORD

AP *LG* Seq 28. *Parl* Seq 26. *Eccl* Cranw. RDn (until 1918), Swaff. RDn (1918–70), Lynn RDn (1970–*).

NEATISHEAD

AP *LG* Seq 47. Civ bdry: 1936.[139] *Parl* Seq 1. *Eccl* Seq 25.

NECTON

AP *LG* Seq 28. *Parl* Seq 26. *Eccl* Seq 7.

NEEDHAM

Chap in Mendham AP (Suffolk, Norfolk), sep civ identity early in Norfolk, sep EP 1764.[163] *LG* Seq 8. *Parl* Seq 14. *Eccl* Redenh. RDn.

NELONDE

AP Humblyd. RDn, united 1406 to Little Wreningham AP.[164]

WEST NEWTON

AP *LG* Freebr. Lynn Hd, PLU, RSD, RD. Abol civ 1935 ent to Sandringham AP.[1] *Parl* W'rn Dv (1832–67), W Dv (1867–85), N-W'rn Dv (1885–1918), K's Lynn Dv (1918–48). *Eccl* Lynn RDn (until 1866), Lynn Norfolk (1866–1918), Rising RDn (1918–27). Abol eccl 1927 to help cr West Newton with Appleton EP.[6]

WEST NEWTON WITH APPLETON

EP Cr 1927 by union West Newton AP, Appleton AP.[6] Rising RDn (1927–70), Heach. & Rising RDn (1970–*).

NEWTON BY CASTLE ACRE

AP *LG* Seq 28. *Parl* Seq 26. *Eccl* Seq 8.

NEWTON FLOTMAN

AP *LG* Seq 38. *Parl* Seq 13. *Eccl* Seq 16.

NORDELPH

EP Cr 1909 from Upwell AP, Outwell AP, Stow Bardolph AP, Wimbotsham AP, Downham Market AP, Denver AP.[82] Fincham RDn.

CP Cr 1930 from Denver AP, Downham West CP, Stow Bardolph AP, Outwell AP, Upwell AP.[81] *LG* Down. RD. *Parl* S W Norfolk CC (1948–*).

NORTHREPPS

AP *LG* Seq 9. Civ bdry: 1906,[166] 1953.[167] *Parl* Seq 7. *Eccl* Seq 19.

NORTHWOLD

AP *LG* Seq 30. Civ bdry: 1954,[159] 1957.[85] *Parl* Seq 26. *Eccl* Cranw. RDn (until 1914), Fincham RDn (1914–18), Feltwell RDn (1918–*). Eccl bdry: 1874 (cr Whittington EP).[168]

NORTON SUBCOURSE

AP *LG* Seq 4. Civ bdry: 1935.[1] *Parl* Seq 15. *Eccl* Seq 3.

NORWICH

The following have 'Norwich' in their names. Insofar as any existed at a given time: *LG* Norw. Bor/MB/CB, incorp for poor, USD. *Parl* Norw. Parl Bor (1295–1948), Norw. North BC, Norw. South BC (1948–*)(see Part III of the *Guide* for compositions of the BCs by wards of the CB). *Eccl* Norw. RDn (until 1970), Norw. (East) RDn (1970–*).

CP1–NORWICH–Cr 1889 by union Earlham AP, Easton AP, Heigham AP, pt Hellesdon AP, Lakenham AP, AP1, CP2, CP3, AP3, AP4, AP6, AP9, AP13, AP15, AP16, AP17, AP18, AP19, AP20, AP21, AP24, AP25, AP26, AP27, AP28, AP29, AP32, AP33, AP34, AP35, AP39, AP40, AP41, AP44, AP45, AP46, AP47, AP48, AP49, AP50, AP51, AP52, pt Thorpe next Norwich AP, pt Trowse with Newton AP.[89] Civ bdry: 1907,[65] 1951,[169] 1968.[18] Parl bdry: 1951.[202]

pt Thorpe next Norwich AP, pt Trowse with Newton AP.[89] Civ bdry: 1907,[65] 1951,[169] 1958.[18] Parl bdry: 1951.[202]

AP1–NORWICH ALL SAINTS–Abol civ 1889 to help cr CP1.[89] Eccl bdry: 1882.[170] Abol eccl 1953 to help cr EP7.[171]

AP2–NORWICH ALL SAINTS IN FYEBRIDGE GATE–Gains early AP31.[172] Abol 16th cent ent to AP44.[172]

CP2–NORWICH COUNTY GAOL AND HOUSE OF CORRECTION–Ex-par place, sep CP 1858.[4] In MB from 1835, Parl Bor from 1832; not in incorp for poor. Abol civ 1889 to help cr CP1.[89]

CP3–NORWICH LIBERTY OF THE TOWN CLOSE–Ex-par place (for eccl see 'Liberty of the Town Close'), sep CP 1858.[4] Abol civ 1889 to help cr CP1.[89]

AP3–NORWICH ST ANDREW–Gains *temp* Henry III AP8,[173] gains 1551 AP11.[174] Abol civ 1889 to help cr CP1.[89]

AP4–NORWICH ST AUGUSTINE–Abol civ 1889 to help cr CP1.[89] Eccl bdry: 1880.[175] Abol eccl 1957 to help cr EP1.[176]

EP1–NORWICH ST AUGUSTINE WITH ST MARY COSLANY–Cr 1957 by union AP4 and pts AP34, AP32.[176]

AP5–NORWICH ST BARTHOLOMEW–Abol *temp* Edw. VI ent to AP25.[177]

AP6–NORWICH ST BENEDICT–Abol civ 1889 to help cr CP1.[89] Abol eccl 1957 to help cr EP6.[178]

AP7–NORWICH ST BOTOLPH IN FYEBRIDGE GATE–Abol 1548 ent to AP49.[179]

–NORWICH ST CATHERINE NEWGATE–See AP54

AP8–NORWICH ST CHRISTOPHER–Abol *temp* Henry III ent to AP3.[173]

AP9–NORWICH ST CLEMENT–Abol civ 1889 to help cr CP1.[89] Abol eccl 1937 to help cr EP2.[180]

AP10–NORWICH ST CLEMENT OF CONISFORD–Sometimes 'Norwich St Clement at the Wall'. Abol 1482 ent to AP27.[201]

EP2–NORWICH ST CLEMENT WITH ST GEORGE–Cr 1937 by union AP19, AP16.[180]

AP11–NORWICH ST CROSS–Abol 1551 pt to AP24, pt to AP3.[174]

AP12–NORWICH ST CUTHBERT–Abol 1492 ent to AP36.[181]

AP13–NORWICH ST EDMUND–Abol civ 1889 to help cr CP1.[89]

AP14–NORWICH ST EDWARD–Abol before 1305 ent to AP27.[193]

AP15–NORWICH ST ETHELDREDA–Abol civ 1889 to help cr CP1.[89] Donative, abol eccl 1953 to help cr EP3.[182]

EP3–NORWICH ST ETHELDREDA WITH ST PETER SOUTHGATE–Cr 1953 by union AP15, AP48.[182] Abol 1970 to help cr EP12.[183]

EP4–NORWICH ST FRANCIS, HEARTEASE–Cr 1969 from Sprowston AP, Thorpe AP, Thorpe St Matthew EP.[184]

AP16–NORWICH ST GEORGE COLEGATE–Gains 13th cent AP22,[187] gains 14th cent AP30,[186] gains 1546 AP43.[185] Abol civ 1889 to help cr CP1.[89] Abol eccl 1937 to help cr EP2.[180]

AP17–NORWICH ST GEORGE TOMBLAND–Gains 1542 AP36.[188] Abol civ 1889 to help cr CP1.[89] Abol eccl 1937 to help cr EP5.[189]

EP5–NORWICH ST GEORGE TOMBLAND WITH ST SIMON AND ST JUDE–Cr 1937 by union AP17, AP50.[189]

AP18–NORWICH ST GILES–Abol civ 1889 to help cr CP1.[89] Abol eccl 1549 to help cr EP6.[178]

EP6–NORWICH ST GILES WITH ST BENEDICT–Cr 1957 by union AP17, AP6.[178]

AP19–NORWICH ST GREGORY–Abol civ 1889 to help cr CP1.[89]

AP20–NORWICH ST HELEN–Abol civ 1889 to help cr CP1.[89] Pec jurisd Dean & Chapter of Norw. (until 1847).

AP21–NORWICH ST JAMES–Incl chap Pockthorpe (no sep identity, but this par eccl 'Norwich St James with Pockthorpe'). Abol civ 1889 to help cr CP1.[89] Pec jurisd Dean & Chapter of Norw. (until 1847). Eccl bdry: 1909 (cr EP8).[191] Abol eccl 1972 to help cr EP9.[190]

–NORWICH ST JAMES WITH POCKTHORPE–See prev entry

–NORWICH ST JOHN DE SEPULCHRE–See AP25

AP22–NORWICH ST JOHN THE BAPTIST–Abol 13th cent to AP16.[187]

AP23–NORWICH ST JOHN THE EVANGELIST IN SOUTHGATE–Abol *ca* 1300 ent to AP47.[192]

AP24–NORWICH ST JOHN MADDERMARKET–Gains 1551 pt AP11.[174] Abol civ 1889 to help cr CP1.[89]

AP25–NORWICH ST JOHN SEPULCHRE–Gains *temp* Edw. VI AP5.[177] Abol civ 1889 to help cr CP1.[89] Eccl 'Norwich St John de Sepulchre'.

AP26–NORWICH ST JOHN TIMBERHILL–Abol civ 1889 to help cr CP1.[89] Abol eccl 1953 to help cr EP7.[171]

EP7–NORWICH ST JOHN TIMBERHILL WITH ALL SAINTS–Cr 1953 by union AP26, AP1, AP40.[171]

AP27–NORWICH ST JULIAN–Gains before 1305 AP14,[193] gains 1482 AP10.[201] Abol civ 1889 to help cr CP1.[89] Abol eccl 1953 to help cr EP11.[171]

AP28–NORWICH ST LAWRENCE–Abol civ 1889 to help cr CP1.[89]

AP29–NORWICH ST MARGARET–Abol civ 1889 to help cr CP1.[89]

–NORWICH ST MARGARET AT COLEGATE–See following entry

AP30–NORWICH ST MARGARET AT NEW BRIDGE–Sometimes 'St Margaret at Colegate'. Abol 14th cent to AP16.[186]

AP31–NORWICH ST MARGARET IN FYEBRIDGE GATE–Abol early to AP2.[172]

AP32–NORWICH ST MARTIN AT OAK–Abol civ 1889 to help cr CP1.[89] Abol eccl 1957 pt to AP41, pt to help cr EP1.[176]

AP33–NORWICH ST MARTIN AT PALACE–Gains 1377 AP38.[194] Sometimes eccl 'St Martin of Tours at Palace'.

AP34–NORWICH ST MARY COSLANY–Abol civ 1889 to help cr CP1.[89] Abol eccl 1957 pt to help cr EP1, pt to AP41.[176]

AP35–NORWICH ST MARY IN THE MARSH–Sometimes 'Norwich Trinity'. St Faith's PLU. Abol civ 1889 to help cr CP1.[89]

AP36–NORWICH ST MARY THE LESS–Gains 1492 AP12.[181] Abol 1542 ent to AP17.[188]

AP37–NORWICH ST MARY UNBRENT–Abol 16th cent at Dissolution ent to AP49.[195]

EP8–NORWICH ST MARY MAGDALENE–Cr 1909 from AP21.[191] Abol 1972 to help cr EP9.[190]

EP9–NORWICH ST MARY MAGDALENE WITH ST JAMES–Cr 1972 by union EP8, AP21.[190]

AP38–NORWICH ST MATTHEW–Abol 1377 ent to AP33.[194]

AP39–NORWICH ST MICHAEL AT PLEA–Abol civ 1889 to help cr CP1.[89] Abol eccl 1932 to help cr EP10.[196]

EP10–NORWICH ST MICHAEL AT PLEA WITH ST PETER HUNGATE–Cr 1932 by union AP39, AP45.[196]

AP40–NORWICH ST MICHAEL AT THORN–Abol civ 1889 to help cr CP1.[89] Abol eccl 1953 to help cr EP7.[171]

AP41–NORWICH ST MICHAEL COSLANY–Abol civ 1889 to help cr CP1.[89] Eccl bdry: 1957.[176]

AP42–NORWICH ST MICHAEL IN CONISFORD–Abol early 19th cent ent to AP47.[197]

AP43–NORWICH ST OLAVE–Abol 1546 ent to AP16.[185]

AP44–NORWICH ST PAUL–Gains 16th cent AP2.[172] Abol civ 1889 to help cr CP1.[89] Pec jurisd Dean & Chapter of Norw. (until 1847). Abol eccl 1957 to help cr EP13.[178]

–NORWICH ST PAUL, TUCKSWOOD–See 'Tuckswood'.

AP45–NORWICH ST PETER HUNGATE–Abol civ 1889 to help cr CP1.[89] Abol eccl 1932 to help cr EP10.[196]

AP46–NORWICH ST PETER MANCROFT–Abol civ 1889 to help cr CP1.[89]

AP47–NORWICH ST PETER MOUNTERGATE–Gains *ca* 1300 AP23,[192] gains 1562 AP53,[198] gains early 19th cent AP42.[197] Abol civ 1889 to help cr CP1.[89] Eccl 'St Peter Parmentergate', abol eccl 1953 to help cr EP11.[171]

–NORWICH ST PETER PARMENTERGATE–See prev entry

EP11–NORWICH ST PETER PARMENTERGATE WITH ST JULIAN–Cr 1953 by union AP47, AP27.[171] Abol 1970 to help cr EP12.[183]

EP12–NORWICH ST PETER PARMENTERGATE WITH ST JULIAN WITH ST ST ETHELDREDA AND ST PETER SOUTHGATE–Cr 1970 by union EP11, EP3.[183]

AP48–NORWICH ST PETER SOUTHGATE–Abol civ 1889 to help cr CP1.[89] Eccl bdry: 1948.[199] Abol eccl 1953 to help cr EP3.[182]

AP49–NORWICH ST SAVIOUR–Gains 16th cent at Dissolution AP37,[195] gains 1548 AP7.[179] Abol civ 1889 to help cr CP1.[89] Abol eccl 1957 to help cr EP13.[178]

EP13–NORWICH ST SAVIOUR WITH ST PAUL–Cr 1957 by union AP49, AP44.[178]

AP50–NORWICH ST SIMON AND ST JUDE–Abol civ 1889 to help cr CP1.[89] Abol eccl 1937 to help cr EP5.[189]

AP51–NORWICH ST STEPHEN–Gains 16th cent AP54.[200] Abol civ 1889 to help cr CP1.[89]

AP52–NORWICH ST SWITHIN–Abol civ 1889 to help cr CP1.[89]

AP53–NORWICH ST VEDAST–Abol 1562 ent to AP47.[198]

AP54–NORWICH ST WINEWALOY–Sometimes 'St Catherine in Newgate'. Abol 16th cent ent to AP51.[200]

ORMESBY ST MARGARET WITH SCRATBY

AP Orig 2 pars, St Andrew, St Peter, united *ca* 1600[203]; Scratby is a hmlt. *LG* Seq 18. Civ bdry: 1926.[55] *Parl* Seq 2. *Eccl* Seq 31.

ORMESBY ST MICHAEL

AP *LG* Seq 18. *Parl* Seq 2. *Eccl* Seq 31.

OULTON

AP *LG* Seq 11. Civ bdry: 1935 (gains Irmingland AP).[1] *Parl* Seq 5. *Eccl* Seq 33.

LITTLE OUSE

EP Cr 1866 from Hilgay AP, Feltwell AP, Littleport AP (Cambs, IoE), ex-par area in Norfolk fens.[100] Ely RDn (dioc Ely). Bdry: 1878 (from area in IoE, cr Prickwillow EP).[207]

OUTWELL

AP Pt Norfolk (Clack. Hd), pt Cambs (IoE, Wisbech Hd). *LG* Wisbech PLU, RSD. Divided 1889 into 2 CPs, each 'Outwell', one in Norfolk, one in IoE.[206] *Parl* Norfolk pt, W'rn Dv (1832–67), W Dv (1867–85), S-W'rn Dv (1885–1918). *Eccl* Fincham RDn (until 1917), Wisbech RDn (1917–*). Eccl bdry: 1909 (help cr Nordelph EP).[82]

CP Cr 1889 from the pt of Outwell AP in Norfolk.[206] *LG* Wisbech PLU, Marshl. RD. Bdry: 1930 (help cr Nordleph CP),[81] 1934.[98] *Parl* S-W'rn Dv (1918–48), K's Lynn CC (1948–70), N W Norfolk CC (1970–*).

OVERSTRAND

AP *LG* Seq 9. Civ bdry: 1906,[166] 1932.[77] *Parl* Seq 7. *Eccl* Seq 19.

OVINGTON

AP *LG* Seq 50. *Parl* Seq 24. *Eccl* Seq 28.

OXBOROUGH

AP *LG* Seq 28. Civ bdry: 1935 (gains Caldecote AP).[1] *Parl* Seq 26. *Eccl* Cranw. RDn (until 1918), Swaff. RDn (1918–35). Abol eccl 1935 to help cr Oxborough with Caldecote EP.[60]

OXBOROUGH WITH CALDECOTE

EP Cr 1935 by union Oxborough AP, Caldecote AP.[60] Swaff. RDn (1935–70), Breckl. RDn (1970–*).

OXNEAD

AP *LG* S Erp. Hd, Ayl. PLU, RSD, RD. Abol civ 1935 ent to Brampton AP.[1] *Parl* E'rn Dv (1832–67), N E Dv (1867–85), N'rn Dv (1885–1948). *Eccl* Seq 33.

OXWICK

AP Gains early Pattesley AP, the union civ 'Oxwick and Pattesley', qv, eccl 'Oxwick'. *Eccl* Brisl. RDn. Abol eccl 1940 to help cr Colkirk and Oxwick EP.[73]

OXWICK AND PATTESLEY

AP Civ name for union early of Oxwick AP, Pattesley AP. *LG* Laund. Hd, Mitf. & Laund. PLU, RSD, RD. Abol civ 1935 ent to Colkirk AP.[1] *Parl* W'rn Dv (1832–67), W Dv (1867–85), Mid Dv (1885–1918), S-W'rn Dv (1918–48).

LITTLE PALGRAVE

AP Cranw. RDn, united by 1581 to Sporle to cr Sporle with Palgrave AP.[208]

PALLING

AP *LG* Hap. Hd, Tunst. & Hap. incorp for poor (1785–1870), Smallb. PLU (1870–1930), RSD, RD. Civ bdry: 1935 (gains Waxham AP).[1] Renamed civ 1948 'Sea Palling'.[209] *Parl* E'rn Dv (1832–67), N E Dv (1867–85), E'rn Dv (1885–1948), N Norfolk CC (1948–70). *Eccl* Seq 24.

SEA PALLING

CP Renaming 1948 of Palling AP.[209] *LG* Smallb. RD. *Parl* N Norfolk CC (1970–*).

PANXWORTH

AP Blof. RDn, early united with Panxworth as 'Ranworth with Panxworth'.

PASTON

AP *LG* Seq 47. Civ bdry: 1935 (gains Knapton AP),[1] 1950 (cr Knapton CP).[134] *Parl* Seq 1. *Eccl* Seq 25.

PATTESLEY

AP Hingh. RDn. United early with Oxwick AP, the union civ 'Oxwick and Pattesley', eccl 'Oxwick'.

PENSTHORPE

AP *LG* Gallow Hd, Walsing. PLU, RSD, RD. Abol civ 1935 ent to Kettlestone AP.[1] *Parl* W'rn Dv (1832–67), W Dv (1867–85), N-W'rn Dv (1885–1918), N'rn Dv (1918–48). *Eccl* Burn. RDn (until 1960s), Brisl. RDn (1960s–70), Brisl. & Walsing. RDn (1970–*).

PENTNEY

AP *LG* Seq 22. *Parl* Seq 21. *Eccl* Seq 38.

NORTH PICKENHAM

AP *LG* Seq 28. Civ bdry: 1935 (gains Houghton on the Hill AP).[1] *Parl* Seq 26. *Eccl* Seq 7.

SOUTH PICKENHAM

AP *LG* Seq 28. *Parl* Seq 26. *Eccl* Seq 7.

PLUMSTEAD

AP *LG* Seq 9. *Parl* Seq 7. *Eccl* Repps RDn (until 1940s), Holt RDn (1940s–*).

PLUMSTEAD, GREAT AND LITTLE

CP Cr 1935 by union Little Plumstead AP, pt Great Plumstead AP.[1] *LG* Blof. & Flegg RD. *Parl* Ctrl. Norfolk CC (1948–70), Yarm. CC (1970–*). Now usually called 'Great and Little Plumstead'.

GREAT PLUMSTEAD

AP *LG* Blof. Hd, PLU, RSD, RD. Abol civ 1935 pt to help cr Plumstead, Great and Little CP, pt to Postwick AP.[1] *Parl* E'rn Dv (1832–67), S E Dv (1867–85), S'rn Dv (1885–1948). *Eccl* Pec jurisd Dean & Chapter of Norw. (until 1847), Seq 27 thereafter.

GREAT AND LITTLE PLUMSTEAD–See PLUMSTEAD, GREAT AND LITTLE

LITTLE PLUMSTEAD

AP *LG* Blof. Hd, PLU, RSD, RD. Abol civ 1935 to help cr Plumstead, Great and Little CP.[1] *Parl* As for Great Plumstead. *Eccl* Seq 27.

PORINGLAND

AP Orig 2 pars, Great Poringland (or East Poringland), Little Poringland (or West Poringland), united 16th cent.[210] *LG* Seq 35. *Parl* Seq 13. *Eccl* Seq 2.

POSTWICK

AP *LG* Seq 1. Civ bdry: 1935 (gains Witton AP).[1] *Parl* E'rn Dv (1832–67), S E Dv (1867–85), E'rn Dv (1885–1948), Ctrl. Norfolk CC (1948–70), Yarm. CC (1970–*). *Eccl* Seq 27.

POTTER HEIGHAM

AP *LG* Seq 34. *Parl* Seq 1. *Eccl* Seq 24.

PUDDING NORTON

AP *LG* Seq 26. Civ bdry: 1935 (gains Testerton AP).[1] *Parl* Seq 23. *Eccl* Toft. RDn (until 1918), Brisl. RDn (1918–30). Abol eccl 1930 to help cr Hempton with Pudding Norton EP.[129]

PULHAM MARKET

Chap in Pulham St Mary the Virgin AP, sep civ identity early as 'Pulham St Mary Magdalene', qv, sep EP 1849.[213] *Eccl* Seq 18.

CP Renaming 1947 of Pulham St Mary Magdalene AP.[211] *LG* Depw. RD. *Parl* S Norfolk CC (1948–*).

PULHAM ST MARY

CP Renaming 1947 of Pulham St Mary the Virgin AP.[211] *LG* Depw. RD. *Parl* S Norfolk CC (1948–*).

PULHAM ST MARY MAGDALENE

Chap in Pulham St Mary the Virgin AP, sep civ identity early, sep EP 1849 as 'Pulham Market',[213] qv. *LG* Earsh. Hd, Depw. PLU, RSD, RD. Renamed civ 1947 'Pulham Market'.[211] *Parl* E'rn Dv (1832–67), S E Dv (1867–85), S'rn Dv (1885–1948).

PULHAM ST MARY THE VIRGIN

AP Incl chap Pulham St Mary Magdalene (sep civ identity early, sep EP 1847 as 'Pulham Market'[213]). *LG* Earsh. Hd, Depw. PLU, RSD, RD. Renamed civ 1947 'Pulham St Mary'.[211] *Parl* As for Pulham St Mary Magdalene. *Eccl* Seq 18.

QUARLES

Orig AP, not used after 14th cent and later considered ex-par, sep CP 1858.[4] *LG* N Greenh. Hd, Walsing. PLU (1858[70]–1930), RSD, RD. Abol 1935 ent to Great Walsingham AP.[1] *Parl* N E Dv (1867–85), N'rn Dv (1885–1918), S'rn Dv (1918–48).

QUIDENHAM

AP *LG* Guiltc. Hd, PLU (1835–1902), RSD, RD (1894–1902), Wayl. PLU (1902–30), RD (1902–35). Abol civ 1935 ent to Eccles AP.[1] *Parl* W'rn Dv (1832–67), S E Dv (1867–85), Mid Dv (1885–1918), S'rn Dv (1918–48). *Eccl* Seq 22.

CP Renaming 1956 of Eccles AP.[93] *LG* Wayl. RD. *Parl* S Norfolk CC (1970–*).

RACKHEATH

AP Orig 2 pars, Rackheath Magna, Rackheath Parva, early united.[214] *LG* Seq 45. *Parl* Seq 10. *Eccl* Seq 41.

RANWORTH

AP Blof. RDn, early united with Panxworth AP as 'Ranworth with Panxworth', qv.

RANWORTH WITH PANXWORTH

AP Early union of Ranworth AP, Panxworth AP. *LG* Walsham Hd, Blof. PLU, RSD, RD. Abol civ 1935 ent to Woodbastwick AP.[1] *Parl* E'rn Dv (1832–67), S E Dv (1867–85), E'rn Dv (1885–1948). *Eccl* Seq 27.

RAVENINGHAM

AP *LG* Seq 4. Civ bdry: 1935.[1] *Parl* Seq 15. *Eccl* Seq 3.

RAYNHAM

CP Cr 1935 by union East Raynham AP, South Raynham AP, West Raynham AP.[1] *LG* Walsing. RD. *Parl* N Norfolk CC (1948–70), N W Norfolk CC (1970–*).

EAST RAYNHAM

AP *LG* Gallow Hd, Walsing. PLU, RSD, RD. Abol

civ 1935 to help cr Raynham AP.[1] *Parl* W'rn Dv (1832–67), W Dv (1867–85), N-W'rn Dv (1885–1918), N'rn Dv (1918–48). *Eccl* Toft. RDn (until 1918), Brisl. RDn (1918–27). Abol eccl 1927 to help cr Raynham with Helhoughton EP.[127]

SOUTH RAYNHAM

AP Organisation as for East Raynham.

WEST RAYNHAM

AP Organisation as for East Raynham.

RAYNHAM WITH HELHOUGHTON

EP Cr 1927 by union East Raynham AP, West Raynham AP, South Raynham AP, Helhoughton AP.[127] Brisl. RDn (1927–70), Brisl. & Elm. RDn (1970–*).

REDENHALL WITH HARLESTON

AP Incl hmlt Wortwell (sep civ identity early, no sep eccl identity). *LG* Seq 8. Addtl civ bdry alt: 1885 (gains the pt in Norfolk of Mendham AP [Suffolk, Norfolk] so that Mendham ent Suffolk thereafter).[157] *Parl* Seq 14. *Eccl* Seq 18.

REDMERE

Ex-par place, sep CP 1858.[4] *LG* Clack. Hd, Ely PLU, RSD, sep RD in Norfolk (1894–95). Transf 1895 to IoE.[215] *Parl* Norfolk pt, W Dv (1867–85), S-W'rn Dv (1885–1918).

REEDHAM

AP *LG* Seq 48. Civ bdry: 1935,[1] 1974 (the par to be in Broadland Dist except pt to be in Gt Yarm. Dist [latter not to be in a par]).[28] *Parl* Seq 11. *Eccl* Seq 27.

REEPHAM

CP Cr 1935 by union Hackford AP, Reepham with Kerdiston AP, Whitwell AP.[1] *LG* St Faith's & Ayl. RD. *Parl* Ctrl. Norfolk CC (1948–70), N Norfolk CC (1970–*).

REEPHAM AND HACKFORD WITH WHITWELL AND KERDISTON

EP Cr 1935 by union Hackford with Whitwell EP, Reepham with Kerdiston AP.[116] Spar. RDn.

REYMERSTON

AP *LG* Mitf. Hd, Mitf. & Laund. PLU, RSD, RD. Abol civ 1935 ent to Garveston AP.[1] *Parl* W'rn Dv (1832–67), S E Dv (1867–85), Mid Dv (1885–1918), S-W'rn Dv (1918–48). *Eccl* Seq 15.

REEPHAM WITH KERDISTON

AP *LG* Eynsf. Hd, Ayl. PLU, RSD, RD. Abol civ 1935 to help cr Reepham CP.[1] *Parl* E'rn Dv (1832–67), S E Dv (1867–85), N'rn Dv (1885–1948). *Eccl* Spar. RDn. Abol eccl 1935 to help cr Reepham and Hackford with Whitwell and Kerdiston EP.[116]

REPPS WITH BASTWICK

AP *LG* Seq 19. *Parl* Seq 2. *Eccl* Seq 31.

RIDDLESWORTH

AP *LG* Seq 32. Civ bdry: 1935 (gains Gasthorpe AP).[1] *Parl* Seq 18. *Eccl* Rockl. RDn (until 1918), Harling RDn (1918–31), Rockl. RDn (1931–32). Abol eccl 1932 to help cr Riddlesworth with Gasthorpe and Knettishall EP.[108]

RIDDLESWORTH WITH GASTHORPE AND KNETTISHALL

EP Cr 1932 by union Riddlesworth AP, Gasthorpe AP, Knettishall AP (Suffolk).[108] Rockl. RDn (1932–70), Thetf. & Rockl. RDn (1970–*).

RIDLINGTON

AP *LG* Tunst. Hd, Tunst. & Hap. incorp for poor (1785–1870), Smallb. PLU (1870–1930), RSD, RD. Abol civ 1935 ent to Ridlington AP.[1] *Parl* E'rn Dv (1832–67), N E Dv (1867–85), E'rn Dv (1885–1948). *Eccl* Wax. RDn (until 1953), Tunst. RDn (1953–*).

RINGLAND

AP *LG* Seq 17. *Parl* Seq 5. *Eccl* Spar. RDn (until 1960), Tav. RDn (1960–70), Norw. (North) RDn (1970–*).

RINGSTEAD

AP Orig 2 pars, St Andrew, St Peter, united 1771.[216] Sometimes 'Great Ringstead'. *LG* Seq 44. *Parl* Seq 21. *Eccl* Seq 12.

RINGSTEAD PARVA

AP Heach. RDn, in ruins by 16th cent and incl in Hunstanton AP.[140]

ROCKLAND ALL SAINTS

AP *LG* Shrop. Hd, Wayl. PLU, RSD. Abol civ 1885 to help cr Rockland All Saints and St Andrew CP.[217] *Parl* W'rn Dv (1832–67), S E Dv (1867–85), Mid Dv (1885–1918). *Eccl* Gains eccl 1557 Rockland St Andrew EP.[218] Seq 20.

ROCKLAND ALL SAINTS AND ST ANDREW

CP Cr 1885 by union Rockland All Saints AP, Rockland St Andrew AP.[217] *LG* Wayl. PLU, RD. Abol 1935 to help cr Rocklands CP.[1] *Parl* S'rn Dv (1918–48).

ROCKLAND ST ANDREW

AP *LG* Shrop. Hd, Wayl. PLU, RSD. Abol civ 1885 to help cr Rockland All Saints and St Andrew CP.[217] *Parl* As for Rockland All Saints. *Eccl* Rockl. RDn. Abol eccl 1557 ent to Rockland All Saints AP.[218]

ROCKLAND ST MARY

AP *LG* Seq 35. *Parl* Seq 13. *Eccl* Seq 2.

ROCKLAND ST PETER

AP *LG* Wayl. Hd, PLU, RSD, RD. Abol civ 1935 to help cr Rocklands CP.[1] *Parl* W'rn Dv (1832–67), W Dv (1867–85), S-W'rn Dv (1885–1918), S'rn Dv (1918–48). *Eccl* Seq 20.

ROCKLANDS

CP Cr 1935 by union Rockland All Saints and St Andrew CP, Rockland St Peter AP.[1] *LG* Wayl. RD. *Parl* S Norfolk CC (1948–*).

ROLLESBY

AP *LG* Seq 19. *Parl* Seq 2. *Eccl* Seq 31.

ROUDHAM

AP *LG* Seq 43. Civ bdry: 1935 (gains Larling AP).[1] *Parl* Seq 18. *Eccl* Rockl. RDn (until 1918), Harling RDn (1918–23). Abol eccl 1923 to help cr Bridgham with Roudham EP.[43]

ROUGHAM

AP *LG* Seq 39. *Parl* Seq 20. *Eccl* Seq 29.

ROUGHTON

AP *LG* Seq 9. *Parl* Seq 7. *Eccl* Seq 19.

ROXHAM

AP *LG* Clack. Hd, Down. PLU, RSD, RD. Abol civ 1935 ent to Ryston AP.[1] *Parl* W'rn Dv (1832–67), W Dv (1867–85), S-W'rn Dv (1885–1948). *Eccl* Fincham RD. In ruins early and eccl incl in Ryston AP,[219] the latter thereafter 'Ryston with Roxham'.

ROYDON

AP *LG* Seq 7. *Parl* Seq 14. *Eccl* Seq 18.

ROYDON

AP *LG* Seq 22. *Parl* Seq 21. *Eccl* Pec jurisd Dean & Chapter of Norw. (until 1847), Seq 37 thereafter.

EAST RUDHAM

AP *LG* Seq 25. Civ bdry: 1935 (gains Broomsthorpe AP).[1] *Parl* Seq 21. *Eccl* Seq 5.

WEST RUDHAM

AP *LG* Seq 25. *Parl* Seq 21. *Eccl* Seq 5.

NORTH RUNCTON

AP Gains early Setchey (church lost before 16th cent, sep civ identity regained early). Incl hmlt Hardwicke (no sep identity) hence this par eccl 'North Runcton with Hardwicke and Setchey', qv. *LG* Seq 22. Civ bdry: 1935 (help cr King's Lynn CP).[1] *Parl* Seq 21.

NORTH RUNCTON WITH HARDWICKE AND SETCHEY

AP Usual eccl spelling; for civ and gain Setchey, see prev entry. *Eccl* Seq 38.

SOUTH RUNCTON

AP Incl chap and hmlt Runcton Holme (sep civ identity early), Wallington (orig sep AP, incl in this par by 16th cent), hmlt Thorpland (the last 2 sep civ identity early as 'Wallington with Thorpland'), hence this par eccl 'Runcton Holme with South Runcton, Wallington and Thorpeland', qv. *LG* Clack. Hd, Down. PLU, RSD, RD. Addtl civ bdry alt: 1935 (gains Runcton Holme CP, Wallington CP, Thorpland CP).[1] Renamed civ 1950 'Runcton Holme'.[221] *Parl* W'rn Dv (1832–67), W Dv (1867–85), S-W'rn Dv (1885–1948), S W Norfolk CC (1948–70).

RUNCTON HOLME

Chap and hmlt in South Runcton AP, sep civ identity early; for eccl see 'Runcton Holme with South Runcton, Wallington and Thorpeland'. *LG* Clack. Hd, Down. PLU, RSD, RD. Abol civ 1935 ent to South Runcton AP.[1] *Parl* W'rn Dv (1832–67), W Dv (1867–85), S-W'rn Dv (1885–1948).

CP Renaming 1950 of South Runcton CP.[221] *LG* Down. RD. *Parl* S W Norfolk CC (1970–*).

RUNCTON HOLME WITH SOUTH RUNCTON, WALLINGTON AND THORPELAND

AP One par for eccl purposes; for details of civ organisation, see 'South Runcton'. Fincham RDn.

RUNHALL

AP *LG* Seq 20. Civ bdry: 1935 (gains Brandon Parva AP, Corston AP, Welborne AP).[1] *Parl* Seq 12. *Eccl* Seq 13.

RUNHAM

AP *LG* E Flegg Hd, E & W Flegg incorp for poor, pt Great Yarm. CB (1889–94 [the pt first incl in Parl Bor from 1885]), E & W Flegg RSD (ent 1875–89, pt 1889–94), E & W Flegg RD. Civ bdry: 1889 (the pt in the Parl Bor incl in the CB),[206] 1894 (loses the pt in the CB to cr Runham Vauxhall CP).[222] Abol civ 1935 pt to Mautby AP, pt to Reedham AP.[1] *Parl* E'rn Dv (1832–67), N E Dv (1867–85), pt Gt Yarm. Parl Bor (1885–1918), E'rn Dv (pt 1885–1918, ent 1918–48). *Eccl* Seq 31.

RUNHAM VAUXHALL

CP Cr 1894 from the pt of Runham in Gt Yarm. CB.[222] *LG* E & W Flegg incorp for poor, Gt Yarm. CB. *Parl* Gt Yarm. Parl Bor (1918–48), Yarm. CC (1948–*).

RUNTON

AP *LG* Seq 9. *Parl* Seq 7. *Eccl* Seq 19.

RUSHFORD

AP Pt Norfolk (Guiltc. Hd), pt Suffolk (Babergh Hd), the latter transf 1894 to Euston AP (W Suffolk) and the par ent Norfolk thereafter.[224] *LG* Thetf. PLU, RSD, RD. Abol civ 1935 ent to Brettenham AP.[1] *Parl* Norfolk pt, W'rn Dv (1832–67), S E Dv (1867–85), Mid Dv (1885–1918), S'rn Dv (1918–48). *Eccl* Seq 23.

RUSHALL

AP *LG* Earsh. Hd, Depw. PLU, RSD, RD. Abol civ 1935 ent to Dickleburgh AP.[1] *Parl* E'rn Dv (1832–67), S E Dv (1867–85), S'rn Dv (1885–1948). *Eccl* Seq 18.

EAST RUSTON

AP *LG* Seq 34. *Parl* Seq 1. *Eccl* Seq 24.

GREAT RYBURGH

AP *LG* Seq 26. Civ bdry: 1886,[225] 1958.[88] *Parl* Seq 23. *Eccl* Toft. RDn (until 1918), Brisl. RDn (1918–25). Abol eccl 1925 to help cr Great Ryburgh with Little Ryburgh and Testerton EP.[226]

GREAT RYBURGH WITH LITTLE RYBURGH AND TESTERTON

EP Cr 1925 by union Great Ryburgh AP, Little Ryburgh AP, Testerton AP.[226] Brisl. RDn (1925–70), Burn. & Walsing. RDn (1970–*).

LITTLE RYBURGH

AP *LG* Seq 26. Civ bdry: 1958.[88] *Parl* Seq 23. *Eccl* Burn. RDn (until 1918), Brisl. RDn (1918–23). Abol eccl as for Great Ryburgh.

RYSTON

AP *LG* Seq 3. Civ bdry: 1935 (gains Bexwell AP, Roxham AP).[1] *Parl* Seq 26. *Eccl* Fincham RDn. Gains early eccl Roxham AP,[219] thereafter 'Ryston with Roxham', qv.

RYSTON WITH ROXHAM

EP Usual eccl spelling after union early of Ryston AP, Roxham AP; for civ see prev entry. *Eccl* Fincham RDn.

SAHAM TONEY

AP *LG* Seq 49. *Parl* Seq 26. *Eccl* Seq 28.

SALHOUSE

Chap in Wroxham AP, sep civ identity early, sep EP 1936.[139] *LG* Seq 45. *Parl* Seq 10. *Eccl* Tav. RDn (1936–70), Blof. RDn (1970–*).

SALL

AP Usual civ spelling; for eccl see following entry.

LG Seq 14. *Parl* Seq 6.

SALLE

AP Usual eccl spelling; for civ see prev entry. *Eccl* Seq 40.

SALTHOUSE

AP *LG* Seq 36. *Parl* Seq 16. *Eccl* Seq 32.

SANDRINGHAM

AP *LG* Seq 22. Civ bdry: 1935 (gains Babingley AP, West Newton AP, Wolferton AP).[1] *Parl* Seq 21. *Eccl* Seq 36.

SANTON

AP *LG* Grimshoe Hd, Thetf. PLU, RSD, RD. Abol civ 1935 ent to Lynford AP.[1] *Parl* W'rn Dv (1832–67), W Dv (1867–85), S-W'rn Dv (1885–1918). *Eccl* Cranw. RDn (until 1914), Mildenhall RDn (dioc St Edm & Ipsw, 1914–62). Abol eccl 1962, united with Santon Downham AP (Suffolk) to cr Santon and Santon Downham EP.[227]

SANTON AND SANTON DOWNHAM

EP Cr 1962 by union Santon AP (Norfolk), Santon Downham AP (Suffolk), to be in dioc St Edm & Ipsw (Sudbury AD, Mildenhall RDn).[227]

SAXLINGHAM

AP *LG* Holt Hd, Walsing. PLU, RSD, RD. Abol civ 1935 ent to Field Dalling AP.[1] *Parl* W'rn Dv (1832–67), N E Dv (1867–85), N'rn Dv (1885–1948). *Eccl* Seq 32.

SAXLINGHAM NETHERGATE

AP *LG* Seq 35. Civ bdry: 1883,[21] 1925 (gains Saxlingham Thorpe AP).[228] *Parl* Seq 13. *Eccl* Seq 1. Eccl bdry: 1740 (gains Saxlingham Thorpe AP).[229]

SAXLINGHAM THORPE

AP *LG* Henst. Hd, PLU, RSD, RD. Civ bdry: 1883.[21] Abol civ 1925 ent to Saxlingham Nethergate AP.[228] *Parl* E'rn Dv (1832–67), S E Dv (1867–85), S'rn Dv (1885–1948). *Eccl* Brooke RDn. Abol eccl 1740 ent to Nethergate AP.[229]

SAXTHORPE

AP *LG* S Erp. Hd, Ayl. PLU, RSD, RD. Abol civ 1935 ent to Corpusty AP.[1] *Parl* E'rn Dv (1832–67), N E Dv (1867–85), N'rn Dv (1885–1948). *Eccl* Ingw. RDn. Abol eccl 1921 to help cr Saxthorpe with Corpusty EP.[74]

SAXTHORPE WITH CORPUSTY

EP Cr 1921 by union Saxthorpe AP, Corpusty AP.[74] Ingw. RDn.

SCARNING

AP *LG* Seq 39. *Parl* Seq 20. *Eccl* Seq 30.

SCO' RUSTON

AP *LG* Tunst. Hd, Tunst. & Hap. incorp for poor (1785–1870), Smallb. PLU (1870–1930), RSD, RD. Abol civ 1935 ent to Tunstead AP.[1] *Parl* E'rn Dv (1832–67), N E Dv (1867–85), E'rn Dv (1885–1948). *Eccl* Wax. RDn. Early in ruins and incl in Tunstead AP.

SCOLE

AP Sometimes anc 'Osmundeston'. Incl for civ purposes Frenze (orig sep AP), incl for civ and eccl purposes Thorpe Parva (identity lost 15th cent[230]). *LG* Seq 6. Civ bdry: 1935 (gains Billingford AP, Thelveton AP).[1] *Parl* Seq 14. *Eccl* Seq 18.

SCOTTOW

AP *LG* Seq 12. *Parl* Seq 4. *Eccl* Seq 34. Eccl bdry: 1973.[152]

SCOULTON

AP *LG* Seq 50. *Parl* Seq 24. *Eccl* Seq 28.

SCULTHORPE

AP *LG* Seq 26. *Parl* Seq 23. *Eccl* Seq 5.

SEDGEFORD

AP *LG* Seq 44. *Parl* Seq 21. *Eccl* Pec jurisd Dean & Chapter of Norw. (until 1847), Seq 12 thereafter.

SEETHING

AP *LG* Seq 40. *Parl* Seq 15. *Eccl* Seq 3.

SETCHEY

AP Church lost before 16th cent, incl in North Runcton AP, sep civ identity regained early. *LG* Freebr. Lynn Hd, PLU, RSD, RD. Abol civ 1935 ent to West Winch AP.[1] *Parl* W'rn Dv (1832–67), W Dv (1867–85), N-W'rn Dv (1885–1918), K's Lynn Dv (1918–48). *Eccl* Lynn RDn.

SHARRINGTON

AP *LG* Holt Hd, Walsing. PLU, RSD, RD. Abol civ 1935 ent to Brinton AP.[1] *Parl* W'rn Dv (1832–67), N E Dv (1867–85), N'rn Dv (1885–1948). *Eccl* Seq 32.

SHELFANGER

AP *LG* Seq 7. *Parl* Seq 14. *Eccl* Seq 18.

SHELTON

AP *LG* Seq 5. Civ bdry: 1935 (gains Hardwick AP).[1] *Parl* Seq 14. *Eccl* Seq 11.

SHEREFORD

AP *LG* Gallow Hd, Walsing. PLU, RSD, RD. Abol civ 1935 to help cr Dunton CP.[1] *Parl* W'rn Dv (1832–67), W Dv (1867–85), N-W'rn Dv (1885–1918), N'rn Dv (1918–48). *Eccl* Seq 45.

SHERINGHAM

AP *LG* N Erp. Hd, Erp. PLU, RSD, RD (1894–1901), Sheringham UD (1901–74). Civ bdry: 1901 (loses the pt not to be in the UD to cr Upper Sheringham CP, gains pt Beeston Regis AP to help constitute the UD),[23] 1914,[24] 1935.[1] *Parl* Seq 7. *Eccl* Seq 19. Eccl bdry: 1953 (the pt not in the UD cr Upper Sheringham EP).[231]

UPPER SHERINGHAM

Cr civ 1901,[23] eccl 1953[231] from the pt of Sheringham AP at the time not in Sheringham UD. *LG* Erp. PLU, RD. *Parl* N'rn Dv (1918–48), N Norfolk CC (1948–*). *Eccl* Repps RDn.

SHERNBORNE

AP *LG* Seq 44. *Parl* Seq 21. *Eccl* Seq 12.

SHIMPLING

AP *LG* Diss Hd, Depw. PLU, RSD, RD. Abol civ 1935 ent to Burston AP.[1] *Parl* E'rn Dv (1832–67), S E Dv (1867–85), S'rn Dv (1885–1948). *Eccl* Seq 18.

SHINGHAM

AP *LG* Pt Clack. Hd, pt S Greenh. Hd, Swaff. PLU, RSD, RD. Abol civ 1935 to help cr Beachamwell CP.[1] *Parl* W'rn Dv (1832–67), W Dv (1867–85), S-W'rn Dv (1885–1948). *Eccl* Fincham

RDn. Early united with Beachamwell All Saints AP as 'Beachamwell All Saints with Shingham', qv.

SHIPDHAM

AP *LG* Seq 41. *Parl* Seq 19. *Eccl* Seq 15.

SHOTESHAM

CP Cr 1935 by union Shotesham All Saints AP, Shotesham St Mary AP.[1] *LG* Foreh. & Henst. RD. *Parl* Ctrl. Norfolk CC (1948–70), S Norfolk CC (1970–*).

SHOTESHAM ALL SAINTS

AP Sometimes 'High Shotesham'. *LG* Henst. Hd, PLU, RSD, RD. Civ bdry: 1883.[21] Abol civ 1935 to help cr Shotesham CP.[1] *Parl* E'rn Dv (1832–67), S E Dv (1867–85), S'rn Dv (1885–1948). *Eccl* Brooke RDn. Abol eccl 1552 ent to Shotesham St Mary AP.[232]

SHOTESHAM ST BOTOLPH

AP Brooke RDn, abol 16th cent ent to Shotesham St Mary AP.[233]

SHOTESHAM ST MARTIN

AP Henst. Hd, Brooke RDn, abol in 18th cent ent to Shotesham St Mary AP.[234]

SHOTESHAM ST MARY

AP Gains 16th cent Shotesham St Botolph AP,[233] gains 1552 Shotesham All Saints AP,[232] gains 18th cent Shotesham St Martin AP.[234] Sometimes 'Low Shotesham'. *LG* Henst. Hd, PLU, RSD, RD. Addtl civ bdry alt: 1883.[160] Abol civ 1935 to help cr Shotesham CP.[1] *Parl* As for Shotesham All Saints. *Eccl* Seq 1.

SHOULDHAM

AP Orig 2 pars, St Margaret, All Saints, the former disused by 16th cent. *LG* Seq 3. *Parl* Seq 26. *Eccl* Fincham RDn.

SHOULDHAM THORPE

AP *LG* Seq 3. *Parl* Seq 26. *Eccl* Fincham RDn.

SHROPHAM

AP *LG* Seq 43. *Parl* Seq 18. *Eccl* Seq 20.

SIDESTRAND

AP *LG* Seq 9. Civ bdry: 1906.[166] *Parl* Seq 7. *Eccl* Seq 19.

SISLAND

AP *LG* Seq 40. *Parl* Seq 15. *Eccl* Seq 3.

SKEYTON

AP *LG* Seq 12. *Parl* E'rn Dv (1832–67), N E Dv (1867–85), N'rn Dv (1885–1948), N Norfolk CC (1948–*). *Eccl* Seq 34.

SLOLEY

AP *LG* Seq 47. *Parl* Seq 1. *Eccl* Seq 25.

SMALLBURGH

AP *LG* Seq 47. *Parl* Seq 1. *Eccl* Seq 25.

GREAT AND LITTLE SNAREHILL

Ex-par place, sep CP 1858.[4] *LG* Guiltc. Hd, Thetf. PLU (1858[70]–1930), RSD, RD. Abol 1935 ent to Brettenham AP.[1] *Parl* S E Dv (1867–85), Mid Dv (1885–1918), S'rn Dv (1918–48).

SNETTERTON

AP Orig 2 pars, All Saints, St Andrew, the latter united 1453 to the former.[235] *LG* Seq 43. *Parl* Seq 18. *Eccl* Seq 20.

SNETTISHAM

AP *LG* Seq 44. *Parl* Seq 21. *Eccl* Seq 12.

GREAT SNORING

AP *LG* Seq 27. *Parl* Seq 17. *Eccl* Seq 46.

LITTLE SNORING

AP *LG* Seq 26. Civ bdry: 1935 (gains Alethorpe AP).[1] *Parl* Seq 23. *Eccl* Burn. RDn (until 1926), Walsing. RDn (1926–70), Burn. & Walsing. RDn (1970–*).

SOMERTON

CP Cr 1935 by union East Somerton CP, West Somerton AP.[1] *LG* Blof. & Flegg RD. *Parl* Yarm. CC (1948–*).

EAST SOMERTON

Chap in Winterton AP (sep civ identity early, no sep eccl identity). *LG* W Flegg Hd, E & W Flegg incorp for poor, RSD, RD. Abol civ 1935 to help cr Somerton CP.[1] *Parl* E'rn Dv (1832–67), N E Dv (1867–85), E'rn Dv (1885–1948). *Eccl* Seq 31.

WEST SOMERTON

AP An AP, organisation o'wise as for East Somerton.

SOUTHBURGH

AP *LG* Mitf. Hd, Mitf. & Laund. PLU, RSD, RD. Abol civ 1935 ent to Cranworth AP.[1] *Parl* W'rn Dv (1832–67), S E Dv (1867–85), Mid Dv (1885–1918), S-W'rn Dv (1918–48). *Eccl* Seq 15.

SOUTHERY

AP *LG* Seq 3. Civ bdry: 1885,[130] 1957.[131] *Parl* Seq 26. *Eccl* Fincham RDn.

SOUTHREPPS

AP *LG* Seq 9. *Parl* Seq 7. *Eccl* Seq 19.

SOUTHTOWN

Chap (Suffolk) in Gorleston AP (Suffolk until 1889, Gt Yarm. CB thereafter), sep EP 1911.[114] See entry in Suffolk.

SOUTHWOOD

AP *LG* Blof. Hd, PLU, RSD, RD. Civ bdry: 1884.[36] Abol civ 1935 ent to Cantley AP.[1] *Parl* E'rn Dv (1832–67), S E Dv (1867–85), E'rn Dv (1885–1948). *Eccl* Blof. RDn. Abol eccl 1934 to help cr Limpenhoe with Southwood EP.[153]

SPARHAM

AP *LG* Seq 16. *Parl* Seq 9. *Eccl* Seq 40.

SPIXWORTH

AP *LG* Seq 45. Civ bdry: 1968 (loses pt to Norw. CB and CP).[18] *Parl* Seq 10. *Eccl* Seq 42.

SPORLE

AP Cranw. RDn, abol 1581 to help cr Sporle with Palgrave AP.[208]

SPORLE WITH PALGRAVE

AP Cr 1581 by union Sporle AP, Palgrave AP.[208] *LG* Seq 28. *Parl* Seq 26. *Eccl* Seq 7.

SPROWSTON

AP *LG* Seq 45. Civ bdry: 1885,[137] 1907 (loses pt to Norw. CB and CP),[65] 1951 (loses pt to Norw. CB and CP),[169] 1959.[66] *Parl* Seq 10. Parl bdry: 1951.[202] *Eccl* Incl Beeston St Andrew AP, long in ruins. Pec jurisd Dean & Chapter of Norw. (until 1847), Seq 42 thereafter. Addtl eccl bdry alt: 1969 (help cr Norwich St Francis, Heartease EP).[184]

STALHAM
AP *LG* Seq 34. *Parl* Seq 1. *Eccl* Seq 24.
STANFIELD
AP *LG* Seq 39. *Parl* Seq 20. *Eccl* Brisl. RDn (until 1918), Elm. RDn (1918–25), Brisl. RDn (1925–70), Brisl. & Elm. RDn (1970–*).
STANFORD
AP *LG* Seq 29. Civ bdry: 1935 (gains Buckenham Tofts AP).[1] *Parl* Seq 26. *Eccl* Cranw. RDn (until 1918), Swaff. RDn (1918–70), Breckl. RDn (1970–*).
STANHOE
AP Gains 1511 Barwick AP[17] (sep civ identity regained early). *LG* Seq 44. *Parl* Seq 21. *Eccl* Seq 12.
STANNINGHALL
AP Tav. RDn, in ruins by 16th cent, civ united to Horstead AP to cr Horstead with Stanninghall AP,[136] eccl incl in Frettenham AP.
STARSTON
AP *LG* Seq 8. *Parl* Seq 14. *Eccl* Seq 18.
STIBBARD
AP *LG* Seq 26. Civ bdry: 1886.[225] *Parl* Seq 23. *Eccl* Seq 5.
STIFFKEY
AP *LG* Seq 27. *Parl* Seq 17. *Eccl* Seq 47.
STOCKTON
AP *LG* Seq 4. Civ bdry: 1935.[1] *Parl* Seq 15. *Eccl* Seq 3.
STODY
AP *LG* Seq 36. Civ bdry: 1884,[15] 1935 (gains Hunworth AP).[1] *Parl* Seq 16. *Eccl* Seq 32.
STOKE FERRY
AP *LG* Seq 3. Civ bdry: 1884,[236] 1957.[131] *Parl* Seq 26. *Eccl* Fincham RDn (until 1918), Feltwell RDn (1918–*).
STOKE HOLY CROSS
AP *LG* Seq 35. Civ bdry: 1935 (gains Dunston AP).[1] *Parl* Seq 13. *Eccl* Seq 2.
STOKESBY WITH HERRINGBY
AP *LG* Seq 18. *Parl* Seq 2. *Eccl* Seq 31.
STOW BARDOLPH
AP *LG* Seq 3. Civ bdry: 1883,[21] 1884,[237] 1930 (help cr Nordelph CP).[81] *Parl* Seq 26. *Eccl* Fincham RDn. Eccl bdry: 1909 (help cr Nordelph EP).[82]
STOW BEDON
AP *LG* Seq 50. Civ bdry: 1935 (gains Breckles AP).[1] *Parl* Seq 24. *Eccl* Seq 28.
STRADSETT
AP *LG* Seq 3. *Parl* Seq 26. *Eccl* Fincham RDn.
LONG STRATTON
CP Cr 1935 by union Stratton St Mary AP, Stratton St Michael AP.[1] *LG* Depw. RD. *Parl* S Norfolk CC (1948–*).
LONG STRATTON ST MARY
AP Usual eccl spelling; for civ see 'Stratton St Mary'. *Eccl* Seq 11.
LONG STRATTON ST MICHAEL
AP Usual eccl spelling; for civ see 'Stratton St Michael'. *Eccl* Gains 1449 Long Stratton St Peter AP.[238] Seq 11.
LONG STRATTON ST PETER
AP Depw. RDn, abol 1449 ent to Long Stratton St Michael AP.[238]
STRATTON ST MARY
AP Usual civ spelling; for eccl see 'Long Stratton St Mary'. *LG* Depw. Hd, PLU, RSD, RD. Civ bdry: 1885.[44] Abol civ 1935 to help cr Long Stratton CP.[1] *Parl* E'rn Dv (1832–67), S E Dv (1867–85), S'rn Dv (1885–1948).
STRATTON ST MICHAEL
AP Usual civ spelling; for eccl see 'Long Stratton St Michael'. *LG* Depw. Hd, PLU, RSD, RD. Abol civ 1935 to help cr Long Stratton CP.[1] *Parl* As for Stratton St Mary.
STRATTON STRAWLESS
AP *LG* Seq 11. *Parl* Seq 5. *Eccl* Ingw. RDn (until 1960s), Tav. RDn (1960s–70), Ingw. RDn (1970–*).
STRUMPSHAW
AP *LG* Seq 1. Civ bdry: 1884,[39] 1935 (gains Hassingham AP, Buckenham AP).[1] *Parl* Seq 11. *Eccl* Seq 27.
STURSTON
AP *LG* Seq 31. *Parl* Seq 26. *Eccl* Cranw. RDn. In ruins early, eccl incl in Tottington AP.
SUFFIELD
AP *LG* Seq 9. *Parl* Seq 7. *Eccl* Repps RDn (until 1960s), Tunst. RDn (1960s–*).
SURLINGHAM
AP Orig 2 pars, St Mary, St Saviour, the latter abol and incl in former *ca* 1705.[239] *LG* Seq 35. *Parl* Seq 13. *Eccl* Seq 2.
SUSTEAD
AP *LG* Seq 9. Civ bdry: 1935 (gains Bessingham AP, Metton AP).[1] *Parl* Seq 7. *Eccl* Seq 19.
SUTTON
AP *LG* Seq 34. Civ bdry: 1885.[10] *Parl* Seq 1. *Eccl* Seq 24.
SWAFFHAM
AP *LG* S Greenh. Hd, Swaff. PLU, USD, UD. *Parl* Seq 26. *Eccl* Seq 7.
SWAFIELD
AP *LG* Seq 47. Civ bdry: 1935 (gains Bradfield AP).[1] *Parl* Seq 1. *Eccl* Seq 26.
SWAINSTHORPE
AP *LG* Seq 38. *Parl* Seq 13. *Eccl* Seq 16.
SWANNINGTON
AP *LG* Seq 17. *Parl* Seq 5. *Eccl* Seq 40.
SWANTON ABBOT
AP *LG* Seq 12. *Parl* Seq 4. *Eccl* Seq 34.
SWANTON MORLEY
AP *LG* Seq 39. *Parl* Seq 20. *Eccl* Seq 30.
SWANTON NOVERS
AP *LG* Seq 37. *Parl* Seq 17. *Eccl* Seq 32.
SWARDESTON
AP *LG* Seq 38. *Parl* Seq 13. *Eccl* Seq 16.
SYDERSTONE
AP *LG* Seq 25. Civ bdry: 1885.[11] *Parl* Seq 21. *Eccl* Seq 5.
TACOLNESTON
AP *LG* Seq 5. *Parl* Seq 14. *Eccl* Seq 11.
TASBURGH
AP *LG* Seq 5. *Parl* Seq 14. *Eccl* Seq 11.

TATTERFORD

AP *LG* Gallow Hd, Walsing. PLU, RSD, RD. Abol civ 1935 ent to Tattersett AP.[1] *Parl* W'rn Dv (1832–67), W Dv (1867–85), N-W'rn Dv (1885–1918), N'rn Dv (1918–48). *Eccl* Seq 5.

TATTERSETT

AP *LG* Seq 26. Civ bdry: 1935 (gains Tatterford AP),[1] 1958.[88] *Parl* Seq 23. *Eccl* Seq 5.

TAVERHAM

AP *LG* Seq 45. *Parl* Seq 10. *Eccl* Seq 42.

TERRINGTON ST CLEMENT

AP Incl chap Terrington St John (sep civ identity early, sep EP 1843[240]). *LG* Seq 24. Addtl civ bdry alt: 1935 (incl help cr Marshland St James CP),[1] 1957 (gains pt Sutton Bridge AP, Lincs [Pt of Holland]).[241] *Parl* Seq 21. *Eccl* Seq 35. Addtl eccl bdry alt: 1922 (help cr Marshland St James EP).[72]

TERRINGTON ST JOHN

Chap in Terrington St Clement AP, sep civ identity early, sep EP 1843.[240] *LG* Seq 24. Civ bdry: 1935 (help cr Marshland St James CP).[1] *Parl* Seq 21. *Eccl* Seq 35. Eccl bdry: 1922 (help cr Marshland St James EP).[72]

TESTERTON

AP *LG* Gallow Hd, Walsing. PLU, RSD, RD. Abol civ 1935 ent to Pudding Norton AP.[1] *Parl* W'rn Dv (1832–67), W Dv (1867–85), N-W'rn Dv (1885–1918), N'rn Dv (1918–48). *Eccl* Toft. RDn (until 1918), Brisl. RDn (1918–25). Abol eccl 1925 to help cr Great Ryburgh with Little Ryburgh and Testerton EP.[226]

THARSTON

AP *LG* Seq 5. Civ bdry: 1935 (gains Hapton AP).[1] *Parl* Seq 14. *Eccl* Seq 11.

THELVETON

AP *LG* Diss Hd, Depw. PLU, RSD, RD. Abol civ 1935 ent to Scole AP.[1] *Parl* E'rn Dv (1832–67), S E Dv (1867–85), S'rn Dv (1885–1948). *Eccl* Seq 18.

THEMELTHORPE

AP *LG* Seq 14. *Parl* Seq 6. *Eccl* Seq 40.

THETFORD

The following have 'Thetford' in their names. In earlier times seven of the par churches were in Suffolk (APs 6, 7, 12, 13, 14, 16, 18 below), the remainder in Norfolk (Grimshoe Hd); in later times pts of AP5, AP16 were in Suffolk, the pars made ent Norfolk 1889.[206] Insofar as any par existed at a given time: *LG* Thetf. Bor/MB, PLU, USD. *Parl* Thetf. Parl Bor (1573–1918), S-W'rn Dv (1918–48), S Norfolk CC (1948–*). *Eccl* Thetf. RDn (until 1970), Thetf. & Rockl. RDn (1970–*).

CP1–THETFORD–Cr 1924 by union AP5, AP16, AP20.[244]

EP1–THETFORD–Cr 1972 by union AP5, AP16, AP20.[242]

AP1–THETFORD ALL SAINTS–Demolished in 16th cent.[244]

AP2–THETFORD HOLY TRINITY–Gains 11th cent AP15,[251] gains *temp* Rchd. II AP11.[247] Abol 1547 ent to AP5.[246]

AP3–THETFORD ST ANDREW–Abol 1546 ent to AP20.[249]

AP4–THETFORD ST BENNET–Demolished by *temp* Edw. III.[244]

AP5–THETFORD ST CUTHBERT–Gains 14th cent AP9,[249] gains 1547 AP2.[246] Abol civ 1924 to help cr CP1.[244] Abol eccl 1972 to help cr EP1.[242]

AP6–THETFORD ST EDMUND–In disuse by *temp* Henry IV.[244]

AP7–THETFORD ST ETHELDRED–Sometimes 'St Audry'. Abol 16th cent at Dissolution.[252]

AP8–THETFORD ST GEORGE–Early became priory church.[248]

AP9–THETFORD ST GILES–Abol 14th cent ent to AP5.[249]

AP10–THETFORD ST HELEN–Early demolished.[249]

AP11–THETFORD ST JOHN–Abol *temp* Rchd. II ent to AP2.[247]

AP12–THETFORD ST LAURENCE–Demolished after *temp* Edw. III.[248]

AP13–THETFORD ST MARGARET–Disused by *temp* Henry III.[247]

AP14–THETFORD ST MARTIN–Disused by *temp* Edw. III.[247]

AP15–THETFORD ST MARY [THE GREAT]–Abol 11th cent ent to AP2.[251]

AP16–THETFORD ST MARY [THE LESS]–Abol civ 1924 to help cr CP1.[244] Abol eccl 1972 to help cr EP1.[242]

AP17–THETFORD ST MARY MAGDALEN–Converted into hospital *temp* Henry III.[250]

AP18–THETFORD ST MICHAEL–Demolished before 16th cent.[248]

AP19–THETFORD ST NICHOLAS–Abol 1547 ent to AP20.[248]

AP20–THETFORD ST PETER–Gains 1547 AP3,[249] gains 1547 AP19.[248] Abol civ 1924 to help cr CP1.[244] Abol eccl 1972 to help cr EP1.[242]

THOMPSON

AP *LG* Seq 50. Civ bdry: 1965.[158] *Parl* Seq 24. *Eccl* Seq 28.

THORNAGE

AP *LG* Seq 36. *Parl* Seq 16. *Eccl* Seq 32.

THORNHAM

AP *LG* Seq 44. *Parl* Seq 21. *Eccl* Seq 12.

THORPE

AP Usual eccl spelling, sometimes 'Thorpe Episcopi'; for civ see 'Thorpe next Norwich'. *Eccl* Blof. RDn (until 1970), Norw. (East) RDn (1970–*). Eccl bdry: 1852 (cr Thorpe St Matthew EP),[253] 1 1969 (help c
1969 (help cr Norwich St Francis, Heartease EP).[184]

THORPE ABBOTS

AP *LG* Earsh. Hd, Depw. PLU, RSD, RD. Civ bdry: 1885.[44] Abol civ 1935 ent to Brockdish AP.[1] *Parl* E'rn Dv (1832–67), S E Dv (1867–85), N'rn Dv (1885–1918), S'rn Dv (1918–48). *Eccl* Seq 18.

THORPE MARKET
AP *LG* Seq 9. *Parl* Seq 7. *Eccl* Seq 19.
THORPE NEXT HADDISCOE
AP *LG* Clav. Hd, Lodd. & Clav. PLU, RSD, RD. Abol civ 1935 ent to Haddiscoe AP.[1] *Parl* E'rn Dv (1832–67), S E Dv (1867–85), S'rn Dv (1885–1918), E'rn Dv (1918–48). *Eccl* Seq 3.
THORPE NEXT NORWICH
AP Usual civ spelling; for eccl see 'Thorpe' (sometimes 'Thorpe Episcopi'). *LG* Blof. Hd, PLU, pt Norw. Bor/MB/CB, pt Norw. USD, pt Blof. RSD, Blof. RD (1894–1935), Blof. & Flegg RD (1935–55). Civ bdry: 1889 (loses the pt in the CB to help cr Norwich CP),[89] 1935,[1] 1951 (loses pt to Norw. CB and CP).[169] Renamed civ 1955 'Thorpe St Andrew'.[135] *Parl* Pt Norw. Parl Bor (1295–1918), pt E'rn Dv (1832–67), pt S E Dv (1867–85), E'rn Dv (pt 1885–1918, ent 1918–48), Ctrl. Norfolk CC (1948–70). Parl bdry: 1951.[202]
THORPE PARVA
AP Redenh. RDn, abol 15th cent ent to Scole AP.[230]
THORPE ST ANDREW
CP Renaming 1955 of Thorpe next Norwich AP.[135] *LG* Blof. & Flegg RD. Bdry: 1974 (par to be in Broadland Dist except pt to be in Norwich Dist [latter not to be in a par]).[28] *Parl* Yarm. CC (1970–*).
THORPE ST MATTHEW
EP Cr 1852 from Thorpe AP.[153] Blof. RDn (1852–1918), Norw. RDn (1918–70), Norw. (East) RDn (1970–*). Bdry: 1948,[199] 1969 (help cr Norwich St Francis, Heartease EP).[184]
THREXTON
AP *LG* Wayl. Hd, Swaff. PLU, RSD, RD. Abol civ 1935 ent to Little Cressingham AP.[1] *Parl* W'rn Dv (1832–67), W Dv (1867–85), S-W'rn Dv (1885–1948). *Eccl* Seq 28.
THRIGBY
AP *LG* E Flegg Hd, E & W Flegg incorp for poor, RSD, RD. Abol civ 1935 ent to Mautby AP.[1] *Parl* E'rn Dv (1832–67), N E Dv (1867–85), E'rn Dv (1885–1948). *Eccl* Seq 31.
THURGARTON
AP *LG* N Erp. Hd, Erp. PLU, RSD, RD. Abol civ 1935 ent to Aldborough AP.[1] *Parl* Seq 7. *Eccl* Seq 19.
THURLTON
AP *LG* Seq 4. Civ bdry: 1935.[1] *Parl* Seq 15. *Eccl* Seq 3.
THURNE
AP *LG* Seq 19. *Parl* Seq 2. *Eccl* Flegg RD. Abol eccl 1604 to help cr Ashby with Oby and Thurne EP.[7]
THURNING
AP *LG* Seq 15. *Parl* Seq 8. *Eccl* Seq 40.
THURSFORD
AP *LG* N Greenh. Hd, Walsing. PLU, RSD, RD. Abol civ 1935 to help cr Fulmodeston CP.[1] *Parl* W'rn Dv (1832–67), N E Dv (1867–85), N'rn Dv (1885–1948). *Eccl* Seq 47.
CP Cr 1954 from Fulmodeston CP.[106] *LG* Walsing. RD. *Parl* N W Norfolk CC (1970–*).
THURTON
AP *LG* Seq 40. *Parl* Seq 15. *Eccl* Seq 2.
THUXTON
AP *LG* Mitf. Hd, Mitf. & Laund. PLU, RSD, RD. Abol civ 1935 ent to Garveston AP.[1] *Parl* W'rn Dv (1832–67), S E Dv (1867–85), Mid Dv (1885–1918), S-W'rn Dv (1918–48). *Eccl* Seq 15.
THWAITE
AP *LG* S Erp. Hd, Lodd. & Clav. PLU, RSD. Abol civ 1884 to help cr Alby with Thwaite CP.[2] *Parl* E'rn Dv (1832–67), N E Dv (1867–85). *Eccl* Seq 33.
THWAITE
AP *LG* Seq 40. *Parl* Seq 15. *Eccl* Seq 2.
TIBENHAM
AP *LG* Seq 5. *Parl* Seq 14. *Eccl* Depw. RDn (until 1970), Redenh. RDn (1970–*).
TILNEY ALL SAINTS
AP Incl chap Tilney St Lawrence (sep civ identity early, no sep eccl identity hence this par eccl 'Tilney All Saints with St Lawrence', qv). *LG* Seq 24. Addtl civ bdry alt: 1935 (incl help cr Marshland St James CP).[1] *Parl* Seq 21.
TILNEY ALL SAINTS WITH ST LAWRENCE
AP Usual eccl spelling; for civ and civ sep chap Tilney St Lawrence, see prev entry. *Eccl* Seq 35. Eccl bdry: 1922 (help cr Marshland St James EP).[72]
TILNEY ST LAWRENCE
Chap in Tilney All Saints AP, sep civ identity early, no sep eccl identity. *LG* Seq 24. Civ bdry: 1935 (incl help cr Marshland St James CP).[1] *Parl* Seq 21.
TILNEY WITH ISLINGTON
AP Usual civ spelling; for eccl see 'Islington'. *LG* Freebr. Marshl. Hd, Wisbech PLU, RSD, Marshl. RD. Abol civ 1935 pt to help cr Marshland St James CP, pt to Tilney St Lawrence CP.[1] *Parl* W'rn Dv (1832–67), W Dv (1867–85), N-W'rn Dv (1885–1918), K's Lynn Dv (1918–48).
TITCHWELL
AP *LG* Seq 44. *Parl* Seq 21. *Eccl* Seq 12.
TITTLESHALL
AP Gains 1630 Godwick AP.[112] *LG* Seq 39. *Parl* Seq 20. *Eccl* Seq 29.
TIVETSHALL ST MARGARET
AP *LG* Seq 6. *Parl* Seq 14. *Eccl* Orig dependent on Tivetshall St Mary but sep pars.[254] Seq 18.
TIVETSHALL ST MARY
AP *LG* Seq 6. *Parl* Seq 14. *Eccl* Orig mother church to Tivetshall St Margaret but sep pars.[254] Seq 18.
TOFTREES
AP *LG* Gallow Hd, Walsing. PLU, RSD, RD. Abol civ 1935 to help cr Dunton CP.[1] *Parl* W'rn Dv (1832–67), W Dv (1867–85), N-W'rn Dv (1885–1918), N'rn Dv (1918–48). *Eccl* Seq 45.
WEST TOFTS
AP *LG* Grimshoe Hd, Thetf. PLU, RSD, RD. Abol civ 1935 ent to Lynford AP.[1] *Parl* W'rn Dv (1832–67), W Dv (1867–85), S-W'rn Dv (1885–1948). *Eccl* Cranw. RDn (until 1918),

Thetf. RDn (1918–24). Abol eccl 1924 to help cr West Tofts with Buckenham Parva EP.[48]

WEST TOFTS WITH BUCKENHAM PARVA

EP Cr 1924 by union West Tofts AP, Buckenham Parva AP.[48] Thetf. RDn (1924–70), Breckl. RDn (1970–*).

TOFTS MONKS

AP *LG* Seq 4. Civ bdry: 1935.[1] *Parl* Seq 15. *Eccl* Seq 3.

TOPCROFT

AP *LG* Seq 40. *Parl* Seq 15. *Eccl* Seq 4.

TOTTENHILL

AP *LG* Seq 3. *Parl* Seq 26. *Eccl* Fincham RDn.

TOTTINGTON

AP *LG* Seq 50. *Parl* Seq 24. *Eccl* Incl eccl Sturston AP, long in ruins. Seq 28.

TRIMINGHAM

AP *LG* Seq 9. *Parl* Seq 7. *Eccl* Seq 19.

TROWSE

AP Usual eccl spelling; for civ see following entry. *Eccl* Pec jurisd Dean & Chapter of Norw. (until 1847), Seq 2 thereafter.

TROWSE WITH NEWTON

AP Usual civ spelling; for eccl see prev entry. *LG* Henst. Hd, PLU, pt Norw. Bor/MB/CB, pt Norw. USD, pt Henst. RSD, Henst. RD (1894–1935), Foreh. & Henst. RD (1935–74). Civ bdry: 1889 (loses the pt in the CB to help cr Norwich CP),[89] 1935.[1] *Parl* Pt Norw. Parl Bor (1295–1918), remainder and later, Seq 13.

TRUNCH

AP *LG* N Erp. Hd, Erp. PLU, RSD, RD (1894–1935), Smallb. RD (1935–74). *Parl* Seq 7. *Eccl* Repps RDn (until 1960s), Tunst. RDn (1960s–70), Repps RDn (1970–*).

TUCKSWOOD

EP Cr 1969 from Lakenham AP.[151] Norw. RDn (1969–70), Norw. (South) RDn (1970–*). Sometimes called 'Norwich St Paul, Tuckswood'.

EAST TUDDENHAM

AP *LG* Seq 41. *Parl* Seq 19. *Eccl* Seq 15.

NORTH TUDDENHAM

AP *LG* Seq 41. *Parl* Seq 19. *Eccl* Seq 15.

TUNSTALL

AP *LG* Walsham Hd, Blof. PLU, RSD, RD. Abol civ 1935 ent to Halvergate AP.[1] *Parl* E'rn Dv (1832–67), S E Dv (1867–85), E'rn Dv (1885–1948). *Eccl* Seq 27.

TUNSTEAD

AP *LG* Seq 47. Civ bdry: 1935 (gains Sco' Ruston AP).[1] *Parl* Seq 1. *Eccl* Incl Sco' Ruston, long in ruins. Seq 25.

TUTTINGTON

AP *LG* Seq 11. Civ bdry: 1935 (gains Burgh AP).[1] *Parl* Seq 5. *Eccl* Seq 34.

TWYFORD

AP *LG* Seq 16. *Parl* Seq 9. *Eccl* Seq 40.

UPTON

AP *LG* Walsham Hd, early united civ with Fishley AP as 'Upton with Fishley', qv. *Eccl* Seq 27.

UPTON WITH FISHLEY

CP Union for civ purposes of Upton AP, Fishley AP. *LG* Seq 48. *Parl* Seq 11.

UPWELL

AP Pt Norfolk (Clack. Hd), pt Cambs (IoE, Wisbech Hd). Incl chap Welney (itself pt Norfolk, pt Cambs, prob of 17th cent origin, sep CP 1866[204] with pt in both cos, sep EP 1862[205]). *LG* Wisbech PLU, RSD. Addtl civ bdry alt: 1884.[255] Divided 1889 into 2 CPs, each 'Upwell', one in Norfolk, one in IoE.[206] *Parl* Norfolk pt, W'rn Dv (1832–67), W Dv (1867–85), S-W'rn Dv (1885–1918). *Eccl* Fincham RDn (until 1917), March RDn (1917–*). Eccl bdry: 1909 (help cr Nordelph EP).[82]

CP Cr 1889 from the pt of Upwell AP in Norfolk.[229] *LG* Wisbech PLU, Marshl. RD. Bdry: 1930 (help cr Nordelph CP),[81] 1934 (gains pt Upwell CP, IoE),[98] 1935.[1] *Parl* S-W'rn Dv (1918–48), K's Lynn CC (1948–70), N W Norfolk CC (1970–*).

WACTON

AP Orig 2 pars, Wacton Magna, Wacton Parva, united by 1500.[256] *LG* Seq 5. Civ bdry: 1885.[256] *Parl* Seq 14. *Eccl* Seq 11.

WALCOT

AP Usual eccl spelling; for civ see following entry. *Eccl* Seq 24.

WALCOTT

AP Usual civ spelling; for eccl see prev entry. *LG* Hap. Hd, Tunst. & Hap. incorp for poor (1785–1870), Smallb. PLU (1870–1930), RSD, RD. Abol civ 1935 ent to Happisburgh AP.[1] *Parl* E'rn Dv (1832–67), N E Dv (1867–85), E'rn Dv (1885–1948).

WALLINGTON WITH THORPLAND

Early civ union of Wallington AP (incl in South Runcton AP by 16th cent), Thorpland hmlt in South Runcton AP; for eccl see 'Runcton Holme with South Runcton, Wallington and Thorpeland'. *LG* Clack. Hd, Down. PLU, RSD, RD. Abol 1935 ent to South Runcton AP.[1] *Parl* W'rn Dv (1832–67), W Dv (1867–85), S-W'rn Dv (1885–1948).

WALPOLE ST ANDREW

AP *LG* Seq 24. Civ bdry: 1935 (help cr Marshland St James CP).[1] *Parl* Seq 21. *Eccl* Seq 35. Eccl bdry: 1922 (help cr Marshland St James EP).[72]

WALPOLE ST PETER

AP *LG* Seq 24. Civ bdry: 1934 (gains pt Tydd St Giles AP, Lincs [Pt of Holland]),[98] 1935 (help cr Marshland St James CP).[1] *Parl* Seq 21. *Eccl* Seq 35. Eccl bdry: 1922 (help cr Marshland St James EP).[72]

NORTH WALSHAM

AP *LG* Tunst. Hd, Tunst. & Hap. incorp for poor (1785–1930), Smallb. PLU (1870–1930), N Walsham USD, UD. *Parl* Seq 1. *Eccl* Seq 25.

SOUTH WALSHAM

CP Cr 1897 by union South Walsham St Lawrence AP, South Walsham St Mary AP.[257] *LG* Blof. PLU, RD (1894–1935), Blof. & Flegg. RD (1935–74). Bdry: 1935.[1] *Parl* E'rn Dv (1918–48), Yarm. CC (1948–*).

SOUTH WALSHAM ST LAWRENCE

AP *LG* Walsham Hd, Blof. PLU, RSD, RD. Abol civ

1897 to help cr South Walsham CP.[257] *Parl* E'rn Dv (1832–67), S E Dv (1867–85), E'rn Dv (1885–1918). *Eccl* Seq 27.

SOUTH WALSHAM ST MARY

AP Organisation as for South Walsham St Lawrence.

GREAT WALSINGHAM

AP *LG* Seq 27. Civ bdry: 1935 (gains Egmere AP, Quarles CP),[1] 1950.[134] *Parl* Seq 17. *Eccl* Walsing. RDn. Abol eccl 1969 to help cr Walsingham St Mary and All Saints with St Peter and Houghton St Giles EP.[138]

LITTLE WALSINGHAM

AP *LG* Seq 27. *Parl*, *Eccl*, eccl abol as for Great Walsingham.

WALSINGHAM ST MARY AND ALL SAINTS WITH ST PETER AND HOUGHTON ST GILES

EP Cr 1969 by union Great Walsingham AP, Little Walsingham AP, Houghton St Giles AP.[138] Walsing. RDn (1969–70), Burn. & Walsing. RDn (1970–*).

WALSOKEN

AP *LG* Freebr. Marshl. Hd, Wisbech PLU, Walsoken USD, UD (1894–1934), Marshl. RD (1934–74). Civ bdry: 1934 (gains Walsoken Hungate CP),[98] 1935 (incl help cr Marshland St James CP).[1] *Parl* Seq 21. *Eccl* Seq 35. Eccl bdry: 1922 (help cr Marshland St James EP).[72]

WALSOKEN HUNGATE

CP Cr 1894 from the pt of Emneth CP to be in Walsoken UD.[87] *LG* Wisbech PLU, Walsoken UD. Abol 1934 ent to Walsoken AP.[98] *Parl* K's Lynn Dv (1918–48).

EAST WALTON

AP *LG* Seq 22. *Parl* Seq 21. *Eccl* Seq 38.

WEST WALTON

AP *LG* Seq 24. Civ bdry: 1935 (help cr Marshland St James CP).[1] *Parl* Seq 21. *Eccl* Seq 35. Eccl bdry: 1922 (help cr Marshland St James EP).[72]

WARHAM

CP Cr 1935 by union Warham All Saints AP, Warham St Mary AP.[1] *LG* Walsing. RD. *Parl* N Norfolk CC (1948–70), N W Norfolk CC (1970–*).

WARHAM ALL SAINTS

AP *LG* N Greenh. Hd, Walsing. PLU, RSD, RD. Abol civ 1935 to help cr Warham CP.[1] *Parl* W'rn Dv (1832–67), N E Dv (1867–85), N'rn Dv (1885–1948). *Eccl* Seq 46.

WARHAM ST MARY

AP Organisation as for Warham All Saints.

WATERDEN

AP *LG* Brothc. Hd, Dock. PLU, RSD, RD. Abol civ 1935 ent to South Creake AP.[1] *Parl* W'rn Dv (1832–67), W Dv (1867–85), N-W'rn Dv (1885–1918), K's Lynn Dv (1918–48). *Eccl* Incl Egmere AP, in ruins by 16th cent.[95] Seq 5.

WATLINGTON

AP *LG* Seq 3. *Parl* Seq 26. *Eccl* Fincham RDn.

WATTON

AP *LG* Seq 50. *Parl* Seq 24. *Eccl* Seq 28.

WAXHAM

AP Orig 2 pars, Great Waxham, Little Waxham, the latter's church lost into sea at early date and the 2 united. *LG* Hap. Hd, Tunst. & Hap. incorp for poor (1785–1870), Smallb. PLU (1870–1930), RSD, RD. Civ bdry: 1885.[10] Abol civ 1935 ent to Palling AP.[1] *Parl* E'rn Dv (1832–67), N E Dv (1867–85), E'rn Dv (1885–1948). *Eccl* Seq 24.

WEASENHAM ALL SAINTS

Chap in Weasenham St Peter, sep civ identity early, no sep eccl identity. *LG* Seq 39. *Parl* Seq 20.

WEASENHAM ST PETER

AP Incl chap Weasenham All Saints (sep civ identity early, no sep eccl identity). *LG* Seq 39. *Parl* Seq 20. *Eccl* Seq 29.

WEETING

AP Orig 2 pars, All Saints, St Mary, united 1651,[258] so that this par eccl 'Weeting All Saints with St Mary', qv; incl area Bromehill, so that this par civ 'Weeting-with-Bromehill', qv.

WEETING ALL SAINTS WITH ST MARY

AP Usual eccl spelling of union 1651 of Weeting All Saints AP, Weeting St Mary AP.[258] Cranw. RDn (until 1914), Fincham RDn (1914–18), Feltwell RDn (1918–*).

WEETING-WITH-BROMEHILL

AP Usual civ spelling; for eccl see prev entries. *LG* Seq 31. *Parl* Seq 26.

WELBORNE

AP *LG* Foreh. Hd, incorp for poor/PLU, RSD, RD. Abol civ 1935 ent to Runhall AP.[1] *Parl* E'rn Dv (1832–67), S E Dv (1867–85), Mid Dv (1885–1918), S'rn Dv (1918–48). *Eccl* Seq 13.

WELLINGHAM

AP *LG* Seq 39. *Parl* Seq 20. *Eccl* Seq 29.

WELLS NEXT THE SEA

AP *LG* N Greenh. Hd, Walsing. PLU, Wells USD, UD (1894–1955), Wells next the Sea UD (1955–74). *Parl* Seq 17. *Eccl* Seq 6.

WELNEY

Chap (pt Norfolk [Clack. Hd], pt Cambs [IoE, Wisbech Hd]) in Upwell AP (itself pt Norfolk, pt Cambs), prob of 17th cent origin, sep CP 1866[204] with pt in both cos, sep EP 1862.[205] *LG* Down. PLU, RSD. Divided 1889 into 2 CPs, each 'Welney', one in Norfolk, one in IoE.[206] *Parl* W Dv (1867–85), S-W'rn Dv (1885–1918). *Eccl* Fincham RDn (1862–1917), March RDn (1917–*).

CP Cr 1889 from the pt of Welney CP in Norfolk.[206] *LG* Down. PLU, RD. Bdry: 1935.[1] *Parl* S-W'rn Dv (1918–48), S W Norfolk CC (1948–*).

WEST WELNEY

CP Orig cr 1889 as 'Welney' from the pt of Welney CP in IoE,[206] renamed 'West Welney' when transf 1895 to Norfolk.[259] *LG* Down. PLU, RD. Abol 1935 pt to Welney CP, pt to Upwell AP.[1] *Parl* S-W'rn Dv (1918–48).

WENDLING

AP *LG* Seq 39. *Parl* Seq 20. *Eccl* Seq 30.

WEREHAM

AP *LG* Seq 3. Civ bdry: 1884,[236] 1957.[131] *Parl* Seq 26. *Eccl* Fincham RDn (until 1918), Felt-

well RDn (1918–*).
WESTACRE
AP Usual civ spelling; for eccl see 'West Acre'. *LG* Seq 22. *Parl* Seq 21.
WESTFIELD
AP *LG* Mitf. Hd, Mitf. & Laund. PLU, RSD, RD. Abol civ 1935 ent to Whinburgh AP.[1] *Parl* W'rn Dv (1832–67), S E Dv (1867–85), Mid Dv (1885– 1918), S-W'rn Dv (1918–48). *Eccl* Seq 15.
WESTON LONGVILLE
AP *LG* Seq 17. *Parl* Seq 5. *Eccl* Seq 40.
WESTWICK
AP *LG* Seq 47. *Parl* Seq 1. *Eccl* Seq 25.
WEYBOURNE
AP *LG* Seq 36. *Parl* Seq 16. *Eccl* Seq 32.
WHEATACRE
AP *LG* Seq 4. Civ bdry: 1935.[1] *Parl* Seq 15. *Eccl* Sometimes as 'Wheatacre All Saints', Seq 3.
WHINBURGH
AP *LG* Seq 41. Civ bdry: 1935 (gains Westfield AP).[1] *Parl* Seq 19. *Eccl* Seq 15.
WHISSONSETT
AP *LG* Seq 39. *Parl* Seq 20. *Eccl* Seq 29.
WHITLINGHAM
AP *LG* Henst. Hd, PLU, RSD, RD. Abol civ 1935 ent to Kirby Bedon AP.[1] *Parl* E'rn Dv (1832–67), S E Dv (1867–85), S'rn Dv (1885–1948). *Eccl* Brooke RD. In ruins and *ca* 1630 united to Kirby Bedon AP,[146] the union often 'Kirby Bedon with Whitlingham'.
WHITTINGTON
EP Cr 1874 from Northwold AP.[168] Cranw. RDn (1874–1914), Fincham RDn (1914–18), Feltwell RDn (1918–*).
WHITWELL
AP Spar. RDn, gains 1500 Hackford AP[115] (sep civ identity regained early, the union eccl 'Hackford with Whitwell', qv). *LG* Eynsf. Hd, Ayl. PLU, RSD, RD. Abol civ 1935 to help cr Reepham CP.[1] *Parl* E'rn Dv (1832–67), N E Dv (1867–85), N'rn Dv (1885–1948).
WICKHAMPTON
AP *LG* Walsham Hd, Blof. PLU, RSD, RD. Civ bdry: 1884.[36] Abol civ 1935 ent to Freethorpe AP.[1] *Parl* E'rn Dv (1832–67), S E Dv (1867–85), E'rn Dv (1885–1948). *Eccl* Seq 27.
WICKLEWOOD
AP Orig 2 pars, All Saints, St Andrew, united 1367.[260] *LG* Seq 20. Civ bdry: 1935 (gains Crownthorpe AP).[1] *Parl* Seq 12. *Eccl* Hingh. RDn. Abol eccl 1929 to help cr Wickewood with Crownthorpe EP.[80]
WICKLEWOOD WITH CROWNTHORPE
EP Cr 1929 by union Wicklewood AP, Crownthorpe AP.[80] Humblyd. RDn.
WICKMERE
AP *LG* Seq 10. Civ bdry: 1935 (gains Wolterton AP).[1] *Parl* Seq 7. *Eccl* Ingw. RDn. Abol eccl 1971 to help cr Wickmere with Wolterton EP.[261]
WICKMERE WITH WOLTERTON
EP Cr 1971 by union Wickmere AP, Wolterton AP.[261] Ingw. RDn.
WIGGENHALL ST GERMAN
AP Usual civ spelling; for eccl see following entry. *LG* Freebr. Marshl. Hd, Down. PLU, RSD, RD. Abol civ 1935 to help cr Wiggenhall St Germans CP.[1] *Parl* W'rn Dv (1832–67), W Dv (1867–85), N-W'rn Dv (1885–1918), K's Lynn Dv (1918–48).
WIGGENHALL ST GERMANS
AP Usual eccl spelling; for civ see prev entry. *Eccl* Lynn RDn (until 1866), Lynn Marshl. RDn (1866–1928). Abol eccl 1928 to help cr Wiggenhall St Germans with St Peter EP.[262]
CP Cr 1935 by union Wiggenhall St German AP, Wiggenhall St Peter AP.[1] *LG* Down. RD. *Parl* S W Norfolk CC (1948–*).
WIGGENHALL ST GERMANS WITH ST PETER
EP Cr 1928 by union Wiggenhall St Germans AP, Wiggenhall St Peter AP.[262] Lynn Marshl. RDn.
WIGGENHALL ST MARY MAGDALEN
AP *LG* Seq 23. Civ bdry: 1883,[21] 1935.[1] *Parl* Seq 22. *Eccl* Seq 35.
WIGGENHALL ST MARY THE VIRGIN
AP *LG* Seq 23. Civ bdry: 1935.[1] *Parl* Seq 22. *Eccl* Lynn RDn (until 1866), Lynn Marshl. RDn (1866–1971). Abol eccl 1971 to help cr Wiggenhall St Mary the Virgin with Islington EP.[143]
WIGGENHALL ST MARY THE VIRGIN WITH ISLINGTON
EP Cr 1971 by union Wiggenhall St Mary the Virgin AP, Islington AP.[143] Lynn Marshl. RDn.
WIGGENHALL ST PETER
AP *LG* Freebr. Marshl. Hd, Down. PLU, RSD, RD. Civ bdry: 1883.[21] Abol civ 1935 to help cr Wiggenhall St Germans CP.[1] *Parl* As for Wiggenhall St German. *Eccl* Lynn RDn (until 1866), Lynn Marshl. RDn (1866–1928). Abol eccl 1928 to help cr Wiggenhall St Germans with St Peter EP.[262]
WIGHTON
AP *LG* Seq 27. *Parl* Seq 17. *Eccl* Seq 46.
WILBY
AP *LG* Shrop. Hd, Guiltc. PLU (1835–1902), RSD, RD (1894–1902), Wayl. PLU (1902–30), RD. Abol civ 1935 ent to Eccles AP.[1] *Parl* W'rn Dv (1832–67), S E Dv (1867–85), Mid Dv (1885–1918), S'rn Dv (1918–48). *Eccl* Seq 20.
WILTON
AP *LG* Grimshoe Hd. Abol civ *ca* 1720 to help cr Hockwold cum Wilton CP.[132] *Eccl* Cranw. RDn (until 1914), Fincham RDn (1914–17), Feltwell RDn (1917–72). Abol eccl 1972 to help cr Hockwold with Wilton EP.[133]
WIMBOTSHAM
AP *LG* Seq 3. Civ bdry: 1883.[21] *Parl* Seq 26. *Eccl* Fincham RDn. Eccl bdry: 1909 (help cr Nordelph EP).[82]
EAST WINCH
AP *LG* Seq 22. Civ bdry: 1935 (gains West Bilney AP).[1] *Parl* Seq 21. *Eccl* Seq 38.
WEST WINCH
AP *LG* Seq 22. Civ bdry: 1935 (gains Setchey AP).[1] *Parl* Seq 21. *Eccl* Seq 38.

WINFARTHING
AP *LG* Seq 7. *Parl* Seq 14. *Eccl* Seq 18.
WINSTON
AP Brooke RDn, abol 1440 ent to Gillingham All Saints AP.[110]
WINTERTON
AP Incl chap East Somerton (sep civ identity early, no sep eccl identity hence this par eccl 'Winterton with East Somerton', qv). *LG* W Flegg Hd, E & W Flegg incorp for poor, RSD, RD (1894–1935), Blof. & Flegg RD (1935–53). Renamed civ 1953 'Winterton-on-Sea'.[263] *Parl* E'rn Dv (1832–67), N E Dv (1867–85), E'rn Dv (1885–1948), Yarm. CC (1948–70).
WINTERTON-ON-SEA
CP Renaming 1953 of Winterton AP.[263] *LG* Blof. & Flegg RD. *Parl* Yarm. CC (1970–*).
WINTERTON WITH EAST SOMERTON
AP Usual eccl spelling; for civ and civ sep chap East Somerton, see 'Winterton'. *Eccl* Seq 31.
GREAT WITCHINGHAM
AP *LG* Seq 17. *Parl* Seq 5. *Eccl* Seq 40.
LITTLE WITCHINGHAM
AP *LG* Seq 17. *Parl* Seq 5. *Eccl* Seq 40.
WITTON
AP *LG* Seq 47. Civ bdry: 1935 (gains Ridlington AP).[1] *Parl* Seq 1. *Eccl* Seq 25.
WITTON
AP *LG* Blof. Hd, PLU, RSD, RD. Abol civ 1935 ent to Postwick AP.[1] *Parl* E'rn Dv (1832–67), S E Dv (1867–85), E'rn Dv (1885–1948). *Eccl* Seq 27.
WIVETON
AP Incl chap Glandford (no sep identity, hence this par eccl 'Wiveton with Glandford', qv). *LG* Seq 37. *Parl* Seq 17.
EP Cr 1959 when chap Glandford of Wiveton with Glandford AP severed to become sep EP, the remainder to be Wiveton.[111] Holt RDn.
WIVETON WITH GLANDFORD
AP Usual eccl spelling; for civ see 'Wiveton'. *Eccl* Holt RDn. Abol eccl 1959 when chap Glandford severed to be sep EP, the remainder to be Wiveton.[111]
WOLFERTON
AP *LG* Freebr. Lynn Hd, PLU, RSD, RD. Abol civ 1935 ent to Sandringham AP.[1] *Parl* W'rn Dv (1832–67), W Dv (1867–85), N-W'rn Dv (1885–1918), K's Lynn Dv (1918–48). *Eccl* Seq 36.
WOLTERTON
AP *LG* S Erp. Hd, Ayl. PLU, RSD, RD. Abol civ 1935 ent to Wickmere AP.[1] *Parl* E'rn Dv (1832–67), N E Dv (1867–85), N'rn Dv (1885–1948). *Eccl* Ingw. RD. Abol eccl 1971 to help cr Wickmere with Wolterton EP.[261]
WOOD DALLING
AP *LG* Seq 14. *Parl* Seq 6. *Eccl* Seq 40.
WOOD NORTON
AP *LG* Seq 15. *Parl* Seq 8. *Eccl* Seq 40.
WOODBASTWICK
AP *LG* Seq 48. Civ bdry: 1935 (gains Ranworth with Panxworth CP).[1] *Parl* Seq 11. *Eccl* Seq 27.
WOODRISING
AP *LG* Mitf. Hd, Mitf. & Laund. PLU, RSD, RD. Abol civ 1935 ent to Cranworth AP.[1] *Parl* W'rn Dv (1832–67), S E Dv (1867–85), Mid Dv (1885–1918), S-W'rn Dv (1918–48). *Eccl* Hingh. RDn (until 1918), Mitf. RDn (1918–25), Brecc. RDn (1925–70), Breckl. RDn (1970–*).
WOODTON
AP *LG* Seq 40. *Parl* Seq 15. *Eccl* Seq 4.
NORTH WOOTTON
AP *LG* Seq 22. *Parl* Seq 21. *Eccl* Pec jurisd Castle Rising (until 1847), Lynn RDn (1847–66), Lynn Norfolk RDn (1866–1918), Rising RDn (1918–64), Lynn RDn (1964–*).
SOUTH WOOTTON
AP *LG* Seq 22. *Parl* Seq 21. *Eccl* As for North Wootton.
WORMEGAY
AP *LG* Seq 3. *Parl* Seq 26. *Eccl* Fincham RDn.
WORSTEAD
AP *LG* Seq 47. *Parl* Seq 1. *Eccl* Seq 25.
WORTHING
AP *LG* Laund. Hd, Mitf. & Laund. PLU, RSD, RD. Abol civ 1935 ent to Hoe CP.[1] *Parl* W'rn Dv (1832–67), W Dv (1867–85), Mid Dv (1885–1918), S-W'rn Dv (1918–48). *Eccl* Seq 30.
WORTWELL
Hmlt in Redenhall with Harleston AP, sep civ identity early, no sep eccl identity. *LG* Seq 8. *Parl* Seq 14.
WRAMPLINGHAM
AP *LG* Seq 20. *Parl* Seq 12. *Eccl* Seq 13.
WRENINGHAM
AP Orig 2 pars, Great Wreningham, Little Wreningham, united 1414[264] (Little Wreningham had gained Nelonde AP 1406[164]). *LG* Seq 38. *Parl* Seq 13. *Eccl* Seq 16.
WRETHAM
CP Cr 1935 by union East Wretham AP, West Wretham AP, Illington AP.[1] *LG* Wayl. RD. *Parl* S Norfolk CC (1948–*).
EAST WRETHAM
AP *LG* Shrop. Hd, Thetf. PLU, RSD, RD. Abol civ 1935 to help cr Wretham CP.[1] *Parl* W'rn Dv (1832–67), S E Dv (1867–85), Mid Dv (1885–1918), S'rn Dv (1918–48). *Eccl* Seq 23.
WEST WRETHAM
AP Organisation as for East Wretham.
WRETTON
AP *LG* Seq 3. Civ bdry: 1884,[236] 1957.[159] *Parl* Seq 26. *Eccl* Fincham RDn (until 1918), Feltwell RDn (1918–*).
WROXHAM
AP Incl chap Salhouse (sep civ identity early, sep EP 1936[139]). *LG* Seq 45. *Parl* Seq 10. *Eccl* Tav. RDn (until 1970), Tunst. RDn (1970–*).
WYMONDHAM
AP *LG* Foreh. Hd, PLU, RSD, RD (1894–1935), Wymondham UD (1935–74). *Parl* E'rn Dv (1832–67), S E Dv (1867–85), Mid Dv (1885–1918), S'rn Dv (1918–48), S Norfolk CC (1948–*). *Eccl* Seq 14.

WYNDALE
AP Brooke RDn, abol 1440 ent to Gillingham All Saints AP.[110]

GREAT YARMOUTH
AP *LG* Yarm. Bor/MB, PLU, USD, Gt Yarm. CB. Civ bdry: 1894.[113] *Parl* Yarm. Parl Bor (1298–1948), Yarm. CC (1948–*). *Eccl* Seq 31. Eccl bdry: 1881.[223]

YAXHAM
AP *LG* Seq 41. *Parl* Seq 19. *Eccl* Seq 15.

YELVERTON
AP *LG* Henst. Hd, Lodd. & Clav. PLU, RSD, RD (1894–1935), Lodd. RD (1935–74). *Parl* Seq 15. *Eccl* Seq 2.

OXFORDSHIRE

ABBREVIATIONS

Abbreviations particular to Oxon follow. Those general abbreviations in use throughout the *Guide* are found on page xix.

Bamp.	Bampton
Banb.	Banbury
Bic.	Bicester
Binf.	Binfield
Blox.	Bloxham
Bull.	Bullingdon
Chadl.	Chadlington
Chip.	Chipping
Crowm.	Crowmarsh
Cudd.	Cuddesdon
Dedd.	Deddington
Dorch.	Dorchester
Ew.	Ewelme
Head.	Headington
Isl.	Islip
Langt.	Langtree
Lewk.	Lewknor
Nort.	Norton
Oxf.	Oxford
Plough.	Ploughley
Woods.	Woodstock
Woott.	Wootton

SEQUENCES

An abbreviated entry prefixed by 'Seq' is used in the parochial entries to avoid repeating often the names of superior units of administration. The content of each sequence is shown below.

Local Government Sequences ('LG')

SEQ 1 Bamp. Hd, Witney PLU, RSD, RD
SEQ 2 Banb. Hd, PLU, RSD, RD
SEQ 3 Banb. Hd, Bic. PLU, RSD, RD (1894–1932), Plough. RD (1932–74)
SEQ 4 Binf. Hd, Henley PLU, RSD, RD
SEQ 5 Blox. Hd, Banb. PLU, RSD, RD
SEQ 6 Bull. Hd, Bic. PLU, RSD, RD (1894–1932), Plough. RD (1932–74)
SEQ 7 Bull. Hd, Abingdon PLU, RSD, Culham RD (1894–1932), Bull. RD (1932–74)
SEQ 8 Bull. Hd, Head. PLU, RSD, RD (1894–1932), Bull. RD (1932–74)
SEQ 9 Chadl. Hd, Chip. Nort. PLU, RSD, RD
SEQ 10 Chadl. Hd, Witney PLU, RSD, RD
SEQ 11 Ew. Hd, Wallingford PLU, RSD, Crowm. RD (1894–1932), Bull. RD (1932–74)
SEQ 12 Ew. Hd, Henley PLU, RSD, RD
SEQ 13 Ew. Hd, Thame PLU, RSD, RD (1894–1932), Bull. RD (1932–74)
SEQ 14 Langt. Hd, Bradfield PLU, RSD, Goring RD (1894–1932), Henley RD (1932–74)
SEQ 15 Langt. Hd, Henley PLU, RSD, RD
SEQ 16 Lewk. Hd, Thame PLU, RSD, RD (1894–1932), Bull. RD (1932–74)
SEQ 17 Plough. Hd, Bic. PLU, RSD, RD (1894–1932), Plough. RD (1932–74).
SEQ 18 Pyrton Hd, Henley PLU, RSD, RD (1894–1932), Bull. RD (1932–74)
SEQ 19 Pyrton Hd, Thame PLU, RSD, RD (1894–1932), Bull. RD (1932–74)
SEQ 20 Thame Hd, PLU, RSD, RD (1894–1932), Bull. RD (1932–74)
SEQ 21 Woott. Hd, Chip. Nort. PLU, RSD, RD
SEQ 22 Woott, Hd, Witney PLU, RSD, RD
SEQ 23 Woott. Hd, Woods. PLU, RSD, RD (1894–1932), Banb. RD (1932–74)
SEQ 24 Woott. Hd, Woods. PLU, RSD, RD (1894–1932), Chip. Nort. RD (1932–74)
SEQ 25 Woott. Hd, Woods. PLU, RSD, RD (1894–1932), Plough. RD (1932–74)

Parliamentary Sequences ('Parl')

SEQ 1 Mid Dv (1885–1918), Banb. Dv/CC

(1918–*)
SEQ 2 Mid Dv (1885–1918), Banb. Dv/CC (1918–70), Mid-Oxon CC (1970–*)
SEQ 3 Mid Dv (1885–1918), Henley Dv/CC (1918–*)
SEQ 4 Mid Dv (1885–1918), Henley Dv/CC (1918–70), Banb. CC (1970–*)
SEQ 5 Mid Dv (1885–1918), Henley Dv/CC (1918–70), Mid-Oxon CC (1970–*)
SEQ 6 N'rn Dv (1885–1918), Banb. Dv/CC (1918–*)
SEQ 7 S'rn Dv (1885–1918), Henley Dv/CC (1918–*)
SEQ 8 S'rn Dv (1885–1918), Henley Dv/CC (1918–70), Mid-Oxon CC (1970–*)

Ecclesiastical Sequences ('Eccl')

SEQ 1 Aston RDn
SEQ 2 Bic. RDn (until 1956), Bic. & Isl. RDn (1956–*)
SEQ 3 Bic. RDn (until 1852), Isl. RDn (1852–1956), Bic. & Isl. RDn (1956–*)
SEQ 4 Cudd. RDn
SEQ 5 Cudd. RDn (until 1852), Isl. RDn (1852–1956), Cudd. RDn (1956–*)
SEQ 6 Dedd. RDn
SEQ 7 Henley RDn
SEQ 8 Chip. Nort. RDn
SEQ 9 Oxf. RDn
SEQ 10 Witney RDn
SEQ 11 Woods. RDn
SEQ 12 Pec jurisd Banb. (until 1846), Dedd. RDn (1846–*)
SEQ 13 Pec jurisd Dorch. (until 1846), Cudd. RDn (1846–*)

DIOCESES AND ARCHDEACONRY

With a few exceptions noted below in the parochial entries, Oxon pars were in Oxford AD which was in Lincoln dioc until 1542, in Osney dioc 1542–45, and thereafter in Oxford dioc when the see was transferred.

THE PARISHES OF OXFORDSHIRE

ABINGDON
CP In Berks, qv, transf 1974 to Oxon.[1]
ABINGDON ST HELEN WITHOUT
CP In Berks, qv, transf 1974 to Oxon.[1]
ADDERBURY
AP Incl tps East Adderbury, West Adderbury (each sep CP 1866[2]), chap Bodicote (sep EP 1855,[3] sep CP 1866[2]), chap Barford St John (sep CP 1866,[2] eccl severed 1890 to help cr Barford St Michael with Barford St John EP[4]), hmlt Milton (sep CP 1866,[2] no sep eccl identity hence this par eccl 'Adderbury with Milton', qv). *LG* Blox. Hd. Because each subordinate pt sep rated for poor and gains sep civ identity 1866, Adderbury loses sep civ status then.
CP Cr 1971 by union East Adderbury CP, West Adderbury CP.[4] *LG* Banb. RD.
EAST ADDERBURY
Tp in Adderbury AP, sep CP 1866.[2] *LG* Blox. Hd, Banb. PLU, RSD, RD. Bdry: 1966.[6] Abol 1971 to help cr Adderbury CP.[5] *Parl* Seq 6.
WEST ADDERBURY
Tp in Adderbury AP, sep CP 1866.[2] *LG* Blox. Hd, Banb. PLU, RSD, RD. Abol 1971 to help cr Adderbury CP.[5] *Parl* Seq 6.
ADDERBURY WITH MILTON
AP Usual eccl spelling; for civ, civ sep chap Milton and sep other units, see 'Adderbury'. *Eccl* Seq 6.
ADWELL
AP *LG* Seq 16. Civ bdry: 1954.[7] *Parl* Seq 7. *Eccl* Seq 1.
ALBURY
AP Incl hmlt Tiddington (sep CP 1866[2]). *LG* Bull. Hd, Thame PLU, RSD, RD. Abol civ 1932 to help cr Tiddington with Albury CP.[8] *Parl* S'rn Dv (1885–1918), Henley Dv (1918–48). *Eccl* Seq 4.
ALKERTON
AP *LG* Blox. Hd, Banb. PLU, RSD, RD. Abol civ 1970 to help cr Shenington with Alkerton CP.[9] *Parl* Seq 5. *Eccl* Seq 6.
ALVESCOT
AP *LG* Seq 1. Civ bdry: 1886,[11] 1954.[12] *Parl* Seq 2. *Eccl* Seq 10.
AMBROSDEN
AP Incl chap Piddington (sep par 1428[13]), hmlt Arncott (sep CP 1866[2]), hmlt Blackthorn (sep CP 1866[2]). *LG* Seq 6. Addtl civ bdry alt: 1932.[8] *Parl* Seq 3. *Eccl* Seq 2.
APPLEFORD
CP In Berks, qv, transf 1974 to Oxon.[1]
APPLETON WITH EATON
AP In Berks, qv, transf 1974 to Oxon.[1]
ARDINGTON
AP In Berks, qv, transf 1974 to Oxon.[1]
ARDLEY
AP *LG* Seq 17. Civ bdry: 1948.[14] *Parl* Seq 4. *Eccl* Bic. RDn. Abol eccl 1921 to help cr Ardley with Fewcott EP.[15]
ARDLEY WITH FEWCOTT
EP Cr 1921 by union Ardley AP, Fewcott EP.[15] Bic. RDn (1921–56), Bic. & Isl. RDn (1956–*).
ARNCOTT
Hmlt in Ambrosden AP, sep CP 1866.[2] *LG* Seq 6. *Parl* Seq 3.

ASCOTT
Hmlt in Great Milton AP, sep CP 1866.[2] *LG* Thame PLU, RSD, RD. Abol 1932 ent to Stadhampton AP.[8] *Parl* S'rn Dv (1885–1918), Henley Dv (1918–48).

ASCOTT-UNDER-WYCHWOOD
Chap in Shipton-under-Wychwood AP, sep civ identity early, sep EP 1763.[16] *LG* Seq 9. Civ bdry: 1954.[17] *Parl* Seq 6. *Eccl* Chip. Nort. RDn.

ASHBURY
AP In Berks, qv, transf 1974 to Oxon.[1]

ASTERLEIGH
AP Orig sep AP, united 1466 to Kiddington AP,[18] later civ considered ex-par, sep CP 1858.[19] *LG* Woott. Hd, Woods. PLU, RSD. Abol 1894 to help cr Kiddington with Asterleigh CP.[20] *Parl* Mid Dv (1885–1918).

ASTHALL
AP *LG* Seq 1. Civ bdry: 1883,[21] 1886,[11] 1932.[8] *Parl* Seq 2. *Eccl* Seq 10.

MIDDLE ASTON
Tp in Steeple Aston AP, sep CP 1866.[2] *LG* Seq 23. *Parl* Seq 6.

NORTH ASTON
AP *LG* Seq 23. *Parl* Seq 6. *Eccl* Seq 11.

STEEPLE ASTON
AP Incl tp Middle Aston (sep CP 1866[2]). *LG* Seq 23. *Parl* Seq 6. *Eccl* Seq 11.

ASTON AND COTE
Hmlts in Bampton AP, sep CP 1866,[2] eccl severed 1845 to help cr Bampton Aston with Shifford EP.[22] *LG* Bamp. Hd, Witney PLU, RSD, RD. Abol 1932 to help cr Aston Bampton CP.[8] *Parl* Mid Dv (1885–1918), Banb. Dv (1918–48).

ASTON BAMPTON
CP Cr 1932 by union Aston and Cote CP, Chimney CP.[8] *LG* Witney RD. Abol 1954 to help cr Aston Bampton and Shifford CP.[17] *Parl* Banb. CC (1948–70).

ASTON BAMPTON AND SHIFFORD
CP Cr 1954 by union Aston Bampton CP, Shifford CP.[17] *LG* Witney RD. *Parl* Mid-Oxon CC (1970–*).

ASTON ROWANT
AP Incl chap Stokenchurch (sep civ identity early, some sep eccl rights early,[23] sep EP 1844[24]). *LG* Seq 16. *Parl* Seq 7. *Eccl* Sometimes as 'Aston Rowant with Kingston Blount', Seq 1.

ASTON TIRROLD
AP In Berks, qv, transf 1974 to Oxon.[1]

ASTON UPTHORPE
CP In Berks, qv, transf 1974 to Oxon.[1]

ATTINGTON
Ex-par, sep CP 1858.[19] *LG* Thame Hd, PLU, RSD, RD. Abol 1932 ent to Tetsworth CP.[8] *Parl* S'rn Dv (1885–1918), Henley Dv (1918–48).

BADGEMORE
CP Cr 1894 from the pt of Henley-on-Thames AP not in Henley-on-Thames MB.[25] *LG* Henley PLU, RD. Bdry: 1932.[8] Abol 1952 pt to Bix AP, pt to Rotherfield Greys AP.[26] *Parl* Henley Dv/CC (1918–70).

MARSH BALDON
AP *LG* Bull. Hd, Abingdon PLU, RSD, Culham RD (1894–1932), Bull. RD (1932–74). Civ bdry: 1932.[8] *Parl* Seq 7. *Eccl* Pec jurisd Dorch. (until 1846), Cudd. RDn (1846–1972). Abol eccl 1972 to help cr Marsh and Toot Baldon with Nuneham Courtenay EP.[27]

MARSH AND TOOT BALDON WITH NUNEHAM COURTENAY
EP Cr 1972 by union Marsh Baldon AP, Toot Baldon AP, Nuneham Courtenay AP.[27] Cudd. RDn.

TOOT BALDON
AP Identical to Marsh Baldon AP in all respects.

BAMPTON
AP Incl hmlts Aston, Cote (one CP 1866[2] as 'Aston and Cote'), chap Shifford (sep CP 1866[2]), hmlt Brighthampton (sep CP 1866[2]), hmlt Chimney (sep CP 1866[2]), all of the prev eccl united 1845 to cr Bampton Aston with Shifford EP[22]; incl hmlt Lew (sep CP 1866,[2] sep EP 1845 as 'Bampton Lew'[22]); the remainder of the par reconstituted eccl 1845 as 'Bampton Proper'.[22] *LG* Seq 1. Addtl civ bdry alt: 1886.[11] *Parl* Seq 2. *Eccl* Witney RDn (until 1845).

BAMPTON ASTON WITH SHIFFORD
EP Cr 1845 by union pts Bampton AP: hmlts Aston, Cote, chap Shifford, hmlts Brighthampton, Chimney.[22] Witney RDn.

BAMPTON LEW
EP Cr 1845 from pt Bampton AP incl hmlt Lew.[22] Witney RDn.

BAMPTON PROPER
EP Cr 1845 from the pt of Bampton AP not cr Bampton Aston with Shifford EP or Bampton Lew EP.[22] Witney RDn.

BANBURY
AP Incl for eccl purposes tg Neithrop, chap Grimsbury (each for civ purposes in Northants, Neithrop civ incl in Warkworth AP [King's Sutton Hd], sep CP 1866 in Oxon[2]), Grimsbury cr sep CP 1894 in Oxon,[25] and Banbury made ent Oxon, Grimsbury sep EP 1921 from area South Banbury EP[34]). *LG* Pt Oxon (pt Banb. Hd, pt Blox. Hd), pt Northants (until 1894), Banb. PLU, Banb. Bor/MB (pt until 1866, ent 1866–1974), Banb. USD. Addtl civ bdry alt: 1932 (incl gains Grimsbury CP, Neithrop CP),[8] 1968.[28] *Parl* Banb. Parl Bor (pt *temp* Mary I–1832, ent 1832–85), Seq 6 thereafter. *Eccl* Seq 12. Eccl bdry: 1846 (cr South Banbury EP),[29] 1952,[30] 1966,[27] 1967 (gains South Banbury EP),[32] 1971.[33]

SOUTH BANBURY
EP Cr 1846 from Banbury AP.[29] Dedd. RDn. Bdry: 1852,[30] 1921 (cr Grimsbury EP).[34] Abol 1967 ent to Banbury AP.[32]

BARFORD ST JOHN
Chap in Adderbury AP, sometimes 'Little Barford', sep CP 1866,[2] eccl severed 1890 to help cr Barford St Michael with Barford St John EP.[4] *LG* Blox. Hd, Banb. PLU, RSD, RD. Abol 1932 to help cr Barford St John and St

Michael CP.[8] *Parl* N'rn Dv (1885–1918), Banb. Dv (1918–48).

BARFORD ST JOHN AND ST MICHAEL

CP Cr 1932 by union Barford St John CP, pt Barford St Michael AP, pt Deddington AP.[8] *LG* Banb. RD. *Parl* Banb. Dv/CC (1918–*).

BARFORD ST MICHAEL

AP *LG* Woott. Hd, Banb. PLU, RSD, RD. Civ bdry: 1889.[35] Abol civ 1932 pt to help cr Barford St John and St Michael CP, pt to Deddington AP.[8] *Parl* N'rn Dv (1885–1918), Banb. Dv (1918–48). *Eccl* Dedd. RDn. Abol eccl 1890 to help cr Barford St Michael with Barford St John EP.[4]

BARFORD ST MICHAEL WITH BARFORD ST JOHN

EP Cr 1890 by union Barford St Michael AP, chap Barford St John in Adderbury AP.[4] Dedd. RDn.

STEEPLE BARTON

AP *LG* Seq 24. Civ bdry: 1883,[21] 1932.[8] *Parl* Seq 6. *Eccl* Seq 11.

WESTCOTE BARTON

AP Usual eccl spelling; for civ see following entry. *Eccl* Seq 11.

WESTCOTT BARTON

AP Usual civ spelling; for eccl see prev entry. *LG* Seq 24. Civ bdry: 1883,[21] 1932.[8] *Parl* Seq 6.

BAULKING

CP In Berks, qv, transf 1974 to Oxon.[1]

BECKLEY

AP Incl hmlt Studley (orig Bucks [Ashendon Hd], transf to Oxon 1832 for parl purposes, 1844 for civ purposes,[60] in two pts, one sep civ identity early as 'Studley', the other as 'Horton cum Studley' sep CP 1866,[2] sep EP 1880[36]). *LG* Bull. Hd (pt until 1844, ent from 1844), Head. PLU, RSD, RD. Abol civ 1932 pt to help cr Beckley and Stowood CP, pt to Fencott and Murcott CP.[8] *Parl* Mid Dv (1885–1918), Henley Dv (1918–48). *Eccl* Seq 5.

BECKLEY AND STOWOOD

CP Cr 1932 by union Stowood AP, pt Beckley AP.[8] *LG* Bull. RD. *Parl* Henley Dv/CC (1918–70), Mid-Oxon CC (1970–*).

BEGBROKE

AP *LG* Seq 25. Civ bdry: 1883,[21] 1932,[8] 1948.[37] *Parl* Woods. Parl Bor (1832–85), Seq 1 thereafter. *Eccl* Seq 11. Eccl bdry: 1952.[38]

BENSON

AP *LG* Pt Ew. Hd, pt Dorch. Hd, Wallingford PLU, RSD, Crowm. RD (1894–1932), Bull. RD (1932–74). Civ bdry: 1932.[8] *Parl* Seq 7. *Eccl* Pec Dorch. (until 1846), Cudd. RDn (1846–52), Nettlebed RDn (1852–74), Cudd. RDn (1874–1915), Wallingford RDn (Berks AD, 1915–56), Cudd. RDn (1956–*).

BERINSFIELD

CP Cr 1964 from Dorchester AP.[40] *LG* Bull. RD. *Parl* Henley CC (1970–*).

BERRICK SALOME

Chap in Chalgrove AP, sep civ identity early, no sep eccl identity. *LG* Seq 11. Civ bdry: 1932.[8] *Parl* Seq 7.

BESSELSLEIGH

AP In Berks, qv, transf 1974 to Oxon.[1]

BICESTER

AP Incl chap Stratton Audley (sep par prob in 1455[41]), tps Bicester King's End, Bicester Market End (each sep CP 1866[2]). *LG* Plough. Hd. Because each tp sep rated for poor and gains sep civ identity 1866, Bicester loses sep civ status then. *Eccl* Seq 2.

CP Cr 1932 by union pts Bicester King's End CP, Bicester Market End CP, Caversfield AP.[8] *LG* Bic. UD. *Parl* Henley CC (1948–70), Banb. CC (1970–*).

BICESTER KING'S END

Tp in Bicester AP, sep CP 1866.[2] *LG* Plough. Hd, Bic. PLU, USD, UD. Abol 1932 pt to help cr Bicester CP, pt to Chesterton AP.[8] *Parl* Mid Dv (1885–1918), Henley Dv (1918–48).

BICESTER MARKET END

CP Identical to Bicester King's End, except that at abol 1932 pt to help cr Bicester CP, pt to Ambrosden AP, pt to Bucknell AP.[8]

BINSEY

AP *LG* Woott. Hd, Lbty and Bor/MB/CB Oxf., Abingdon PLU, Oxf. USD. Civ bdry: 1894.[42] Abol civ 1926 to help cr St Giles and St John CP.[43] *Parl* Oxf. Parl Bor (1295–1948). *Eccl* Donative, Seq 9.

BIX

AP Orig two sep pars, 'Bixbrand', 'Bixgwbbyn', long united. Incl pt chap Highmore (sep EP 1860,[44] sep CP 1952 as 'Highmoor'[26]). *LG* Seq 4. Addtl civ bdry alt: 1932.[8] *Parl* Seq 7. *Eccl* Henley RDn. Eccl bdry: 1953.[45] Abol eccl 1973 to help cr Bix with Pishill EP.[46]

BIX WITH PISHILL

EP Cr 1973 by union Bix AP, pt Pishill AP.[46] Henley RDn.

BIXBRAND, BIXGWBBYN–See BIX

BLACKTHORN

Hmlt in Ambrosden AP, sep CP 1866.[2] *LG* Seq 6. Bdry: 1932.[8] *Parl* Seq 3.

BLADON

AP Incl hmlt Hensington (sep CP 1866[2]). *LG* Woott. Hd, Woods. PLU, RSD, RD (1894–1932), Witney RD (1932–74). Civ bdry: 1954.[12] *Parl* Woods. Parl Bor (1832–85), Seq 2 thereafter. *Eccl* Woods. RDn. Reconstituted eccl 1877 when gains hmlt and chap Woodstock in Wootton AP to cr Woodstock with Bladon EP, sometimes 'Bladon with Woodstock'.[47]

BLADON WITH WOODSTOCK–See WOODSTOCK WITH BLADON

BLENHEIM

CP Cr 1954 by union Blenheim Park CP, pt Hensington Without CP.[12] *LG* Chip. Nort. RD. *Parl* Banb. CC (1970–*).

BLENHEIM PARK

Ex-par area, sep CP 1858.[19] *LG* Woott. Hd, Lbty Oxf., Woods. PLU, RSD, RD (1894–1932), Chip. Nort. RD (1932–54). Bdry: 1897.[48] Abol 1954 to help cr Blenheim CP.[12] *Parl* Woods. Parl Bor (1832–85), Mid Dv (1885–1918),

Banb. Dv/CC (1918–70).

BLETCHINGDON

AP *LG* Seq 17. *Parl* Seq 3. *Eccl* Seq 3.

BLEWBURY

AP In Berks, qv, transf 1974 to Oxon.[1]

BLOXHAM

AP Incl chap Milcombe (sep EP 1866,[2] sep EP 1854 [incl pt Wiggington AP][49]). *LG* Seq 5. *Parl* Seq 6. *Eccl* Seq 6.

BODICOTE

Chap in Adderbury AP, sep EP 1855,[3] sep CP 1866.[2] *LG* Seq 5. Civ bdry: 1884,[50] 1932,[8] 1966.[6] *Parl* Seq 5. *Eccl* Dedd. RDn. Eccl bdry: 1966,[27] 1971.[33]

BOURTON

Tp and chap (pec jurisd Banb.) in Cropredy AP, sep CP 1866,[2] sep EP 1872,[51] orig eccl 'Bourton' but later eccl 'Great Bourton'. *LG* Seq 2. Civ bdry: 1932.[8] *Parl* Seq 6. *Eccl* Dedd. RDn.

BOURTON

CP In Berks, qv, transf 1974 to Oxon.[1]

BLACK BOURTON

AP *LG* Bamp. Hd, Witney PLU, RSD, RD. Civ bdry: 1886,[11] 1954.[12] Abol civ 1971 to help cr Carterton and Black Bourton CP.[52] *Parl* Seq 3. *Eccl* Seq 10. Eccl bdry: 1963.[53]

GREAT BOURTON–See first BOURTON above

BRADWELL

EP Eccl reconstitution 1960 when Kelmscot chap severed from Bradwell (or Broadwell) with Kelmscot AP (civ 'Broadwell') to help cr Clanfield with Kelmscot EP, the remainder to be Bradwell.[54] Witney RDn.

BRADWELL (OR BROADWELL) WITH KELMSCOT

AP Usual eccl spelling; for civ, civ sep chap Kelmscot, and civ and eccl sep other units, see 'Broadwell'. *Eccl* Witney RDn. Reconstituted eccl 1960 when chap Kelmscot severed to help cr Clanfield with Kelmscot EP, the remainder to be Bradwell.[54]

BRIGHTHAMPTON

Hmlt in Bampton AP, sep CP 1866,[2] eccl severed 1845 to help cr Bampton Aston with Shifford EP.[22] *LG* Bamp. Hd, Witney PLU, RSD, RD. Bdry: 1883,[21] 1886.[11] Abol 1932 ent to Standlake AP.[8] *Parl* Mid Dv (1885–1918), Banb. Dv (1918–48).

BRIGHTWELL BALDWIN

AP *LG* Ew. Hd, Henley PLU, RSD, RD (1894–1932), Bull. RD (1932–74). *Parl* Seq 7. *Eccl* Seq 1.

BRIGHTWELL-CUM-SOTWELL

CP In Berks, qv, transf 1974 to Oxon.[1]

BRITWELL

CP Cr 1912 by union pts Britwell Prior CP, Britwell Salome AP.[55] *LG* Henley PLU, RD (1912–32), Bull. RD (1932–74). Bdry: 1932.[8] *Parl* Henley Dv/CC (1918–*).

BRITWELL PRIOR

Chap (pec jurisd) in Newington AP, sep CP 1866.[2] Sometimes 'Brightwell Prior'. *LG* Ew. Hd, Henley PLU, RSD, RD. Abol civ 1912 to help cr Britwell CP.[55] *Parl* S'rn Dv (1885–1918).

BRITWELL SALOME

AP Sometimes 'Brightwell Salome'. *LG* Lewk. Hd, Henley PLU, RSD, RD. Abol civ 1912 to help cr Britwell CP.[55] *Parl* S'rn Dv (1885–1918). *Eccl* Seq 1.

BROADWELL

AP Incl hmlt Filkins (sep EP 1858,[16] eccl refounded 1864,[56] sep CP 1896[57]), chap Holwell (sep EP 1850,[58] sep CP 1866[2]), tp and chap Kelmscot (sep CP 1866,[2] eccl severed 1960 to help cr Clanfield with Kelmscot EP,[54] so that this par eccl 'Bradwell (or Broadwell) with Kelmscot' before 1960, 'Bradwell' thereafter, qv). *LG* Seq 1. Addtl civ bdry alt: 1883,[21] 1886 (gains Filkins CP).[59] *Parl* Seq 2.

BROUGHTON

AP Incl tp North Newington (sep CP 1866[2]). *LG* Seq 5. *Parl* Seq 6. *Eccl* Seq 6.

BROUGHTON POGGS

AP *LG* Pt Oxon (Bamp. Hd), pt Glos (Great Lemhills Farm, Brightwells Barrow Hd), the latter transf to Glos and Lechlade AP 1832 for parl purposes, 1844 for civ purposes[60] so that this par ent Oxon thereafter. *LG* Witney PLU, RSD, RD. Addtl civ bdry alt: 1886 (loses pt to Lechlade AP, Glos).[61] Abol civ 1954 to help cr Filkins and Broughton Poggs CP.[17] *Parl* N'rn Dv (1885–1918), Banb. Dv/CC (1918–70). *Eccl* Sometimes as 'Broughton Pogis', Seq 10. Gains eccl 1855 hmlt Filkins[16] (sep EP 1858,[16] eccl refounded 1864[56]).

BRUERN

Ex-par place, sep CP 1858.[19] *LG* Seq 9. *Parl* Seq 6.

BUCKLAND

AP In Berks, qv, transf 1974 to Oxon.[1]

BUCKNELL

AP *LG* Seq 17. Civ bdry: 1932.[8] *Parl* Seq 4. *Eccl* Seq 2.

BURCOTT

Hmlt in Dorchester AP, sep CP 1866.[2] *LG* Dorch. Hd, Abingdon PLU, RSD, Culham RD. Abol 1932 ent to Clifton Hampden CP.[8] *Parl* S'rn Dv (1885–1918), Henley Dv (1918–48).

BURFORD

AP Gains *ca* 1215 Fulbrook AP[63] (regains sep civ identity early, but does not regain eccl identity). Incl hmlts Upton, Signet (sep CP 1866 as 'Upton and Signet'[2]). *LG* Bamp. Hd, Burford Bor (status not sustained), Witney PLU, RSD, RD. Addtl civ bdry alt: 1886.[11] Abol civ 1954 to help cr Burford and Upton and Signet CP.[17] *Parl* Burford Parl Bor (1306 only), Mid Dv (1885–1918), Banb. Dv/CC (1918–70). *Eccl* Seq 10.

BURFORD AND UPTON AND SIGNET

CP Cr 1954 by union Burford AP, Upton and Signet CP.[17] *LG* Witney RD. *Parl* Mid CC (1970–*).

BUSCOT

AP In Berks, qv, transf 1974 to Oxon.[1]

CADMORE END

EP Cr 1852,[64] refounded 1853[65] from Fingest AP

(Bucks), Lewknor AP (Oxon), Stokenchurch EP (Oxon). Aston RDn (1852–1973), Wycombe RDn (Bucks AD, 1973–*).

CARTERTON AND BLACK BOURTON

CP Cr 1971 by union Black Bourton AP, pt Brize Norton AP.[66] *LG* Witney RD.

CASSINGTON

AP *LG* Woott. Hd, Woods. PLU, RSD, RD (1894–1932), Witney RD (1932–74). *Parl* Seq 2. *Eccl* Seq 11.

CAVERSFIELD

AP In Bucks (Buckingham Hd), transf to Oxon (Plough. Hd) 1832 for parl purposes, 1844 for civ purposes.[60] *LG* Bic. PLU, RSD, RD (1894–1932), Plough. RD (1932–74). Civ bdry: 1886,[31] 1932 (help cr Bicester CP).[8] *Parl* Seq 4. *Eccl* Buckingham RDn (Bucks AD, until 1855), Bic. RDn (1855–1956), Bic. & Isl. RDn (1956–*). Eccl bdry: 1928.[67]

CAVERSHAM

AP *LG* Binf. Hd, Henley PLU, RSD (ent 1875–90, pt 1890–94), pt Caversham USD (1890–94), Caversham UD. Civ bdry: 1894 (the pt not in the USD cr Kidmore CP).[25] Abol civ 1911 pt to Reading CB and CP (associated with Berks), pt to Eye and Dunsden CP.[68] *Parl* S'rn Dv (1885–1918). *Eccl* Henley RDn (until 1915), Reading RDn (Berks AD, 1915–*). Eccl bdry: 1915 (help cr Kidmore End EP),[69] 1970.[70]

CHADLINGTON

Tg in Charlbury AP, sep CP 1866,[2] eccl severed 1963 to help cr Spelsbury with Chadlington EP.[71] *LG* Seq 9. *Parl* Seq 6.

CHALGROVE

AP Incl chap Berrick Salome (sep civ identity early, no sep eccl identity hence this par eccl 'Chalgrove with Berrick Salome', qv). *LG* Seq 13. Addtl civ bdry alt: 1932 (incl gains Warpsgrove AP).[8] *Parl* Seq 7.

CHALGROVE WITH BERRICK SALOME

AP Usual eccl spelling; for civ and civ sep chap Berrick Salome, see prev entry. *Eccl* Aston RDn (until 1956), Cudd. RDn (1956–*). Eccl bdry: 1929.[72]

EAST CHALLOW

CP In Berks, qv, transf 1974 to Oxon.[1]

WEST CHALLOW

CP In Berks, qv, transf 1974 to Oxon.[1]

CHARLBURY

AP Incl tg Chadlington (sep CP 1866,[2] eccl severed 1963 to help cr Spelsbury with Chadlington EP[71]), hmlts Fawler, Finstock (each sep CP 1866,[2] united eccl 1860 as Finstock and Fawler EP[74]), chap Chilson (sep CP 1866,[2] eccl as 'Shorthampton (or Chilson)' no sep eccl identity hence this par eccl 'Charlbury with Shorthampton (or Chilson)', qv). *LG* Pt Banb. Hd, pt Chadl. Hd, Chip. Nort. PLU, RSD, RD. Addtl civ bdry alt: 1968.[73] *Parl* Seq 6.

CHARLBURY WITH SHORTHAMPTON (OR CHILSON)

AP Usual eccl spelling; for civ, civ sep chap Chilson, and sep other units, see prev entry. *Eccl* Seq 8.

CHARLTON-ON-OTMOOR

AP Incl hmts Fencott, Murcott (united 1866 as Fencott and Murcott CP[2]). *LG* Seq 17. *Parl* Seq 3. *Eccl* Seq 3.

CHARNEY BASSETT

CP In Berks, qv, transf 1974 to Oxon.[1]

CHASTLETON

AP *LG* Seq 9. *Parl* Seq 6. *Eccl* Seq 8.

CHECKENDON

AP *LG* Seq 14. Civ bdry: 1952.[26] *Parl* Seq 7. *Eccl* Henley RDn (until 1852), Nettlebed RDn (1852–74), Henley RDn (1874–*).

CHESTERTON

AP *LG* Seq 17. Civ bdry: 1932.[8] *Parl* Seq 4. *Eccl* Seq 2.

CHILDREY

AP In Berks, qv, transf 1974 to Oxon.[1]

CHILSON

Chap in Charlbury AP, sep CP 1866.[2] *LG* Seq 9. *Parl* Seq 6.

CHILTON

AP In Berks, qv, transf 1974 to Oxon.[1]

CHINNOR

AP *LG* Chinnor Bor (status not sustained), Seq 16. Civ bdry: 1932,[8] 1954.[7] *Parl* Seq 7. *Eccl* Aston RDn. Abol eccl 1973 to help cr Chinnor with Emmington and Sydenham EP.[75]

CHINNOR WITH EMMINGTON AND SYDENHAM

EP Cr 1973 by union Chinnor AP, Emmington AP, Sydenham EP.[75] Aston RDn.

CHIPPINGHURST

Hmlt in Cuddesdon AP, sep CP 1866.[2] *LG* Bull. Hd, Head. PLU, RSD, RD. Abol 1932 ent to Denton CP.[8] *Parl* S'rn Dv (1885–1918), Henley RDn (1918–48).

CHISLEHAMPTON

Chap in Dorchester AP, sep civ identity early, sep EP 1750, fully independent eccl 1763.[76] *LG* Dorch. Hd, Abingdon PLU, RSD, Culham RD. Abol civ 1932 ent to Stadhampton AP.[8] *Parl* S'rn Dv (1885–1918), Henley Dv (1918–48). *Eccl* Pec jurisd Dorch. (1750–1841). Abol eccl 1841 to help cr Stadhampton with Chislehampton EP.[77]

CHOLSEY

AP In Berks, qv, transf 1974 to Oxon.[1]

CHURCHILL

AP *LG* Seq 9. Civ bdry: 1884.[129] *Parl* Seq 6. *Eccl* Chip. Nort. RDn. Abol eccl 1851 to help cr Sarsden with Churchill EP.[146]

CLANFIELD

AP *LG* Seq 1. Civ bdry: 1886,[11] 1954.[12] *Parl* Seq 2. *Eccl* Witney RDn. Abol eccl 1960 to help cr Clanfield with Kelmscot EP.[54]

CLANFIELD WITH KELMSCOT

EP Cr 1960 by union Clanfield AP, chap Kelmscot in Bradwell (or Broadwell) with Kelmscot AP, hmlt Radcot in Langford AP.[54] Witney RDn.

CLATTERCOT

Ex-par place, sep CP 1858.[19] *LG* Banb. Hd, PLU, RSD, RD. Abol 1932 to help cr Claydon with Clattercot CP.[8] *Parl* N'rn Dv (1885–1918), Banb. Dv (1918–48).

CLAYDON
Chap (pec jurisd Banb.) in Cropredy AP, sep CP 1866,[2] eccl united 1851 with chap Mollington in same par to cr Claydon with Mollington EP,[78] the latter divided 1863 into 2 EPs Claydon, Mollington.[79] *LG* Banb. Hd, PLU, RSD, RD. Abol civ 1932 to help cr Claydon with Clattercot CP.[8] *Parl* N'rn Dv (1885–1918), Banb. Dv (1918–48). *Eccl* Dedd. RDn.

CLAYDON WITH CLATTERCOT
CP Cr 1932 by union Claydon CP, Clattercot CP.[8] *LG* Banb. RD. *Parl* Banb. CC (1948–*).

CLAYDON WITH MOLLINGTON
EP Cr 1853 by union chaps Claydon, Mollington, each in Cropredy AP.[78] Dedd. RD. Abol 1863, divided into 2 EPs Claydon, Mollington.[79]

CLIFTON HAMPDEN
Chap in Dorchester AP, sep civ identity early, sep EP perhaps 1809,[16] certainly by 1819.[80] *LG* Dorch. Hd, Abingdon PLU, RSD, Culham RD (1894–1932), Bull. RD (1932–74). Civ bdry: 1932.[8] *Parl* Seq 7. *Eccl* Seq 13. Eccl bdry: 1960.[81]

COGGES
AP *LG* Woott. Hd, Witney PLU, RSD, RD. Civ bdry: 1898.[82] Abol civ 1932 pt to South Leigh CP, pt to Ducklington AP, pt to Witney AP.[8] *Parl* Mid Dv (1885–1918), Banb. Dv (1918–48). *Eccl* Seq 10.

COLESHILL
AP In Berks, qv, transf 1974 to Oxon.[1]

COMBE
AP Sometimes 'Long Combe'. *LG* Seq 24. *Parl* Woods. Parl Bor (1832–85), Seq 1 thereafter. *Eccl* Pec jurisd (until 1846), Seq 11 thereafter.

COMPTON BEAUCHAMP
AP In Berks, qv, transf 1974 to Oxon.[1]

CORNBURY AND WYCHWOOD
CP Cr 1949 by union Cornbury Park CP, pt Wychwood CP.[83] *LG* Chip. Nort. RD. Bdry: 1950.[84] *Parl* Banb. CC (1970–*).

CORNBURY PARK
Ex-par place, sep CP 1858.[19] *LG* Banb. Hd, Chip. Nort. PLU, RSD, RD. Abol 1949 to help cr Cornbury and Wychwood CP.[83] *Parl* N'rn Dv (1885–1918), Banb. Dv/CC (1918–70).

CORNWELL
AP *LG* Seq 9. *Parl* Seq 6. *Eccl* Seq 8.

COTTISFORD
AP *LG* Seq 17. Civ bdry: 1932 (gains territory of Land Common to Cottisford and Hethe pars).[8] *Parl* Seq 4. *Eccl* Seq 2.

GREAT COXWELL
AP In Berks, qv, transf 1974 to Oxon.[1]

LITTLE COXWELL
CP In Berks, qv, transf 1974 to Oxon.[1]

COWLEY
AP *LG* Bull. Hd, Head. PLU, pt Oxf. MB/CB (1835–94), pt Oxf. USD (pt larger than in MB), pt Head. RSD, Head. RD. Civ bdry: 1883,[21] 1885,[86] 1894 (loses the pt in the CB to help cr Cowley St John CP).[87] Abol civ 1929 ent to Oxf. CB and St Giles and St John CP.[88] *Parl* Pt Oxf. Parl Bor (1832–1918 [enlarged pt 1867–1918]), pt Mid Dv (1885–1918), Henley Dv (1918–48). *Eccl* Sometimes as 'Cowley St James', Cudd. RDn (until 1956), Cowley RDn (1956–*). Eccl bdry: 1868 (help cr Cowley St John EP),[89] 1877.[90]

COWLEY ST JOHN
EP Cr 1868 from Cowley AP, Oxford St Clement AP, Iffley AP.[89] Cudd. RDn (1868–1915), Oxf. RDn (1915–56), Cowley RDn (1956–*). Bdry: 1913.[91]
CP Cr 1894 from the pts of Cowley AP, Iffley AP in Oxf. CB.[87] *LG* Head. PLU, Oxf. CB. Abol 1926 to help cr St Giles and St John CP.[43] *Parl* Oxf. Parl Bor (1918–48).

CRAWLEY
Hmlt and chap in Witney AP, sep CP 1866,[2] eccl severed 1854 to help cr Hailey with Crawley EP.[92] *LG* Seq 1. Bdry: 1954.[12] *Parl* Seq 2.

CROPREDY
AP Incl chap Wardington (sep EP 1851,[78] sep CP 1866[2]), chap Claydon (sep CP 1866,[2] eccl severed 1851 to help cr Claydon with Mollington EP[78]), chap Mollington (pt Warws [Kington Hd], pt Oxon [Blox. Hd], sep CP 1866 with pt in ea co,[2] eccl severed 1851 to help cr Claydon with Mollington EP[78]), chap Bourton (sep CP 1866,[2] sep EP 1872 [orig eccl called 'Bourton' but later 'Great Bourton'][51]). *LG* Oxon (pt until 1866, in Banb. Hd, Blox. Hd [pt Mollington], ent Oxon from 1866), pt Warws (pt Mollington, until 1866), Banb. PLU, RSD, RD. Addtl civ bdry alt: 1883,[21] 1888.[93] *Parl* Seq 6. *Eccl* Seq 12.

CROWELL
AP *LG* Seq 16. *Parl* Seq 7. *Eccl* Seq 1.

CROWMARSH
CP Cr 1932 by union Crowmarsh Gifford AP, Newnham Murren CP, North Stoke AP, Mongewell AP.[8] *LG* Henley RD. Bdry: 1952 (incl help cr Stoke Row CP).[26] *Parl* Henley CC (1948–*).

CROWMARSH GIFFORD
AP *LG* Langt. Hd, Wallingford PLU, RSD, Culham RD. Abol civ 1932 to help cr Crowmarsh CP.[8] *Parl* S'rn Dv (1885–1918), Henley Dv (1918–48). *Eccl* Henley RDn (until 1852), Nettlebed RDn (1852–74), Henley RDn (1874–1907). Abol eccl 1907 to help cr Crowmarsh Gifford with Newnham Murren EP.[94]

CROWMARSH GIFFORD WITH NEWNHAM MURREN
EP Cr 1907 by union Crowmarsh Gifford AP, chap Newnham Murren in North Stoke EP.[94] Henley RDn.

CUDDESDON
AP Incl chap and hmlt Denton (sep CP 1866[2]), chap and hmlt Wheatley (sep EP 1745,[16] eccl refounded 1854,[95] sep CP 1866[2]), chap Chippinghurst (sep CP 1866[2]). *LG* Bull. Hd, Head. PLU, RSD, RD (1894–1932), Bull. RD (1932–62). Addtl civ bdry alt: 1878,[96] 1878,[97] 1932.[8] Abol civ 1962 to help cr Cuddesdon and Den-

ton CP.[98] *Parl* S'rn Dv (1885–1918), Henley Dv/CC (1918–70). *Eccl* Seq 4.

CUDDESDON AND DENTON
CP Cr 1962 by union Cuddesdon AP, Denton CP.[98] *LG* Bull. RD. *Parl* Henley CC (1970–*).

CULHAM
AP Pt Oxon (Dorch. Hd), pt Berks (Ock. Hd, with pt in Abingdon MB/USD 1890–94), the latter transf 1894 to Abingdon St Helen AP, Berks, and Culham ent Oxon thereafter.[99] *LG* Abingdon PLU, RSD (ent 1875–90, pt 1890–94), Culham RD (1894–1932), Bull. RD (1932–74). *Parl* Oxon pt, Seq 7. *Eccl* Seq 4.

CUMNOR
AP In Berks, qv, transf 1974 to Oxon.[1]

CURBRIDGE
Hmlt in Witney AP, sep CP 1866.[2] *LG* Seq 1. Bdry: 1883,[21] 1898,[82] 1932,[8] 1963.[100] *Parl* Seq 2.

CUTTESLOWE
Ex-par place, sep CP 1858.[19] *LG* Woott. Hd, Woods. PLU, RSD, RD. Bdry: 1929.[88] Abol 1932 ent to Gosford and Water Eaton CP.[8] *Parl* Mid Dv (1885–1918), Banb. Dv (1918–48).

CUXHAM
AP *LG* Ew. Hd, Henley PLU, RSD, RD. Abol civ 1932 to help cr Cuxham with Easington CP.[8] *Parl* S'rn Dv (1885–1918), Henley Dv (1918–48). *Eccl* Aston RDn. Abol eccl 1853 to help cr Cuxham with Easington EP.[101]

CUXHAM WITH EASINGTON
Cr eccl 1853,[101] civ 1932[8] by union Cuxham AP, Easington AP. *LG* Bull. RD. *Parl* Henley CC (1948–*). *Eccl* Aston RDn.

DEDDINGTON
AP *LG* Dedd. Bor (status not sustained), Seq 23. Civ bdry: 1883,[21] 1889,[35] 1932 (incl help cr Barford St John and St Michael CP).[8] *Parl* Dedd. Parl Bor (1302–04 only), Seq 6 thereafter. *Eccl* Seq 6.

DENCHWORTH
AP In Berks, qv, transf 1974 to Oxon.[1]

DENTON
Chap and hmlt in Cuddesdon AP, sep CP 1866.[2] *LG* Bull. Hd, Head. PLU, RSD, RD (1894–1932), Bull. RD (1932–62). Bdry: 1932.[8] Abol 1962 to help cr Cuddesdon and Denton CP.[98] *Parl* S'rn Dv (1885–1918), Henley Dv/CC (1918–70).

DIDCOT
AP In Berks, qv, transf 1974 to Oxon.[1]

DORCHESTER
AP Incl hmlt Burcott (sep CP 1866[2]), chap Chislehampton (sep civ identity early, sep EP 1750, fully independent eccl 1763[76]), chap Clifton Hampden (sep civ identity early, sep EP perhaps 1809,[16] certainly by 1819[90]), chap Drayton St Leonard (sep civ identity early, sep EP 1848[102]), chap Stadhampton (sep par before 16th cent[185]). *LG* Dorch. Hd, Wallingford PLU, RSD, Crowm. RD (1894–1932), Bull. RD (1932–74). Addtl civ bdry alt: 1964 (cr Berinsfield CP).[40] *Parl* Seq 7. *Eccl* Seq 13. Addtl eccl bdry alt: 1960.[81]

DRAYTON
AP *LG* Seq 5. Civ bdry: 1932.[8] *Parl* Seq 6. *Eccl* Seq 6.

DRAYTON
CP In Berks, qv, transf 1974 to Oxon.[1]

DRAYTON ST LEONARD
Chap (pec jurisd Dorch.) in Dorchester AP, sep civ identity early, sep EP 1848.[102] *LG* Dorch. Hd, Abingdon PLU, RSD, Crowm. RD (1894–1932), Bull. RD (1932–74). Civ bdry: 1932,[8] 1968.[28] *Parl* Seq 7. *Eccl* Cudd. RDn.

DUCKLINGTON
AP Incl chap Hardwick (sep CP 1866[2]). *LG* Seq 1. Addtl civ bdry alt: 1883,[21] 1886,[11] 1932,[8] 1967.[103] *Parl* Seq 2. *Eccl* Seq 10.

DUNSDEN
Chap in Sonning AP (Berks, Oxon), sep CP 1866[2] as 'Eye and Dunsden', qv, sep EP 1876 as 'Dunsden'.[104] Sonning RDn (Berks AD, 1876–1915), Henley RDn (1915–*).

EASINGTON
AP *LG* Ew. Hd, Thame PLU, RSD, RD. Abol civ 1932 to help cr Cuxham with Easington CP.[8] *Parl* S'rn Dv (1885–1918), Henley Dv (1918–48). *Eccl* Aston RDn. Abol eccl 1853 to help cr Cuxham with Easington EP.[101]

WATER EATON
Hmlt in Kidlington AP, sep CP 1866.[2] *LG* Woott. Hd, Woods. PLU, RSD, RD. Bdry: 1883,[2] 1929.[88] Abol 1932 to help cr Gosford and Water Eaton CP.[8] *Parl* Mid Dv (1885–1918), Banb. Dv (1918–48).

EATON HASTINGS
AP In Berks, qv, transf 1974 to Oxon.[1]

ELSFIELD
AP *LG* Seq 8. Civ bdry: 1929.[88] *Parl* Seq 5. *Eccl* Seq 5.

EMMINGTON
AP *LG* Lewk. Hd, Thame PLU, RSD, RD. Abol civ 1932 ent to Chinnor AP.[8] *Parl* S'rn Dv (1885–1918), Henley Dv (1918–48). *Eccl* Aston RDn. Abol eccl 1973 to help cr Chinnor with Emmington and Sydenham EP.[75]

ENSTONE
AP *LG* Seq 9. *Parl* Seq 6. *Eccl* Seq 8.

EPWELL
Tg in Swalcliff AP, sep CP 1866,[2] eccl severed 1842 to help cr Sibford EP.[16] *LG* Seq 2. *Parl* Seq 6.

EWELME
AP *LG* Seq 11. Civ bdry: 1932.[8] *Parl* Seq 7. *Eccl* Aston RDn (until 1852), Nettlebed RDn (1852–74), Aston RDn (1874–*).

EYE AND DUNSDEN
Lbty and chap in Sonning AP (Berks, Oxon) [the only pt in Oxon], sep CP 1866[2] in Oxon so that Sonning ent Berks thereafter, sep EP 1876 as 'Dunsden',[104] qv. *LG* Seq 4. Bdry: 1911,[105] 1952 (incl help cr Sonning Common CP).[26] *Parl* Seq 7.

EYNSHAM
AP *LG* Eynsham Bor (status not sustained), Seq 22. Civ bdry: 1932,[8] 1954.[12] *Parl* Seq 2. *Eccl* Seq 11. Eccl bdry: 1869 (cr Freeland EP),[106] 1966.[27]

GREAT FARINGDON
AP In Berks, qv, transf 1974 to Oxon.[1]

LITTLE FARINGDON
Tg and chap (situated in Berks) in Langford AP, area transf to Oxon 1832 for parl purposes, 1844 for civ purposes,[60] sep CP 1866[2] in Oxon, sep EP 1864.[107] *LG* Bamp. Hd, Faringdon PLU, RSD, Witney RD. *Parl* Seq 2. *Eccl* Witney RDn.

FAWLER
Hmlt in Charlbury AP, sep CP 1866,[2] eccl severed 1860 to help cr Finstock and Fawler EP.[74] *LG* Banb. Hd, Chip. Nort. PLU, RSD, RD. Bdry: 1968.[73] *Parl* Seq 6.

FENCOTT AND MURCOTT
Hmlts in Charlton-on-Otmoor AP, sep CP 1866.[2] *LG* Seq 17. Bdry: 1932.[8] *Parl* Seq 3.

FERNHAM
CP In Berks, qv, transf 1974 to Oxon.[1]

FEWCOTT
EP Cr 1907 from Stoke Lyne AP.[108] Bic. RDn. Abol 1921 to help cr Ardley with Fewcott EP.[15]

FIFIELD
Chap in Swimbrook AP, sep civ identity early, sep EP 1750.[16] *LG* Seq 9. *Parl* Seq 6. *Eccl* Chip. Nort. RDn. Abol eccl 1972 to help cr Fifield with Idbury EP.[109]

FIFIELD WITH IDBURY
EP Cr 1972 by union Fifield AP, Idbury EP.[109] Chip. Nort. RDn.

FILKINS
Hmlt in Broadwell AP (eccl, 'Bradwell (or Broadwell) with Kelmscot'), eccl transf 1855 to Broughton Poggs AP[16] from which sep EP 1858,[16] eccl refounded 1864,[56] sep CP 1866.[2] *LG* Bamp. Hd, Witney PLU, RSD. Abol civ 1886 ent to Broadwell AP,[59] but again sep CP 1896 from Broadwell,[57] Witney PLU, RD. Abol civ again 1954 to help cr Filkins and Broughton Poggs CP.[17] *Parl* Mid Dv (1885–1918), Banb. Dv/CC (1970–*). *Eccl* Witney RDn.

FILKINS AND BROUGHTON POGGS
CP Cr 1954 by union Filkins CP, Broughton Poggs AP.[17] *LG* Witney RD. *Parl* Mid-Oxon CC (1970–*).

FINMERE
AP *LG* Seq 17. *Parl* Seq 4. *Eccl* Seq 2.

FINSTOCK
Hmlt in Charlbury AP, sep CP 1866,[2] eccl severed 1860 to help cr Finstock and Fawler EP.[74] *LG* Banb. Hd, Chip. Nort. PLU, RSD, RD. Bdry: 1950.[84] *Parl* Seq 6.

FINSTOCK AND FAWLER
EP Cr 1860 by union hmlts Finstock, Fawler, each in Charlbury (each sep CP 1866[2]) AP.[74] Chip. Nort. RDn.

FOREST HILL
AP Chap in Stanton St John AP, sep perhaps in 1273, certainly by 1341.[110] *LG* Bull. Hd, Head. PLU, RSD. Civ bdry: 1878.[112] Abol civ 1881 to help cr Forest Hill with Shotover CP.[111] *Eccl* Cudd. RDn (until 1852), Isl. RDn (1852–1956), Cudd. RDn (1956–*).

FOREST HILL WITH SHOTOVER
CP Cr 1881 by union Forest Hill AP, Shotover CP.[111] *LG* Head. PLU, RSD, RD (1894–1932), Bull. RD (1932–74). Bdry: 1885,[85] 1929,[88] 1949,[113] 1954,[40] 1956 (cr Risinghurst and Sandhills CP).[114] *Parl* Mid Dv (1885–1918), Henley Dv/CC (1918–70), Mid-Oxon CC (1970–*).

FREELAND
EP Cr 1869 from Eynsham AP.[106] Woods. RDn. Bdry: 1966.[27]
CP Cr 1948 from Handborough AP.[115] *LG* Witney RD. *Parl* Mid-Oxon CC (1970–*).

FRILFORD
CP In Berks, qv, transf 1974 to Oxon.[1]

FRINGFORD
AP *LG* Seq 17. *Parl* Seq 4. *Eccl* Seq 2.

FRITWELL
AP *LG* Seq 17. Civ bdry: 1888,[31] 1953.[116] *Parl* Seq 4. *Eccl* Seq 2.

FULBROOK
AP Orig sep AP, united *ca* 1215 to Burford AP,[63] regains sep civ identity early. *LG* Seq 10. Bdry: 1886,[11] 1932.[8] *Parl* Seq 2.

FYFIELD AND TUBNEY
CP In Berks, qv, transf 1974 to Oxon.[1]

GARFORD
CP In Berks, qv, transf 1974 to Oxon.[1]

GARSINGTON
AP *LG* Seq 8. *Parl* Seq 7. *Eccl* Seq 4.

GLYMPTON
AP *LG* Seq 24. *Parl* Seq 1. *Eccl* Seq 11.

GODINGTON
AP *LG* Seq 17. Civ bdry: 1956 (gains pt Chetwode AP, Bucks).[117] *Parl* Seq 4. *Eccl* Seq 2.

GOOSEY
CP In Berks, qv, transf 1974 to Oxon.[1]

GORING
AP *LG* Seq 14. Civ bdry: 1952 (help cr Goring Heath CP, help cr Woodcote CP).[26] *Parl* Seq 7. *Eccl* Henley RDn (until 1852), Nettlebed RDn (1852–74), Henley RDn (1874–*).

GORING HEATH
CP Cr 1952 from Goring AP, Whitchurch AP.[26] *LG* Henley RD. *Parl* Henley CC (1970–*).

GOSFORD
Hmlt in Kidlington AP, sep CP 1866.[2] *LG* Woott. Hd, Woods. PLU, RSD, RD. Abol 1932 pt to help cr Gosford and Water Eaton CP, pt to help cr Hampton Gay and Poyle CP, pt to Kidlington AP.[8] *Parl* Mid Dv (1885–1918), Banb. Dv (1918–48).

GOSFORD AND WATER EATON
CP Cr 1932 by union Water Eaton CP, Cutteslowe CP, Land Common to Begbroke and Yarnton pars (Pixney Mead), and pts Gosford CP, Kidlington AP.[8] *LG* Plough. RD. *Parl* Banb. CC (1948–70), Mid-Oxon CC (1970–*).

GRAFTON
Tp in Langford AP, sep CP 1866.[2] *LG* Bamp. Hd, Faringdon PLU, RSD, Witney RD. Abol 1932 to help cr Grafton and Radcot CP.[8] *Parl* Mid Dv (1885–1918), Banb. Dv (1918–48).

GRAFTON AND RADCOT
CP Cr 1932 by union Grafton CP, Radcot CP.[8] *LG* Witney RD. *Parl* Banb. CC (1948–70), Mid-Oxon CC (1970–*).

GREYS
CP Cr 1894 from the pt of Rotherfield Greys AP in Henley-on-Thames MB.[25] *LG* Henley PLU, Henley-on-Thames MB. Abol 1905 ent to Henley-on-Thames AP.[118]

GRIMSBURY
Tg (Northants, King's Sutton Hd) in Banbury AP, sep CP 1894 in Oxon,[25] sep EP 1921 from South Banbury EP.[34] *LG* Banb. PLU, MB. Abol 1932 ent to Banbury AP.[8] *Parl* Banb. Parl Bor (1832–85), Dv (1918–48). *Eccl* Dedd. RDn.

GROVE
CP In Berks, qv, transf 1974 to Oxon.[1]

EAST HAGBOURNE
CP In Berks, qv, transf 1974 to Oxon.[1]

WEST HAGBOURNE
CP In Berks, qv, transf 1974 to Oxon.[1]

HAILEY
Chap in Witney AP, sep CP 1866,[2] sep EP 1761,[16] eccl abol 1854 to help cr Hailey with Crawley EP.[92] *LG* Seq 1. Civ bdry: 1898,[82] 1932,[8] 1954,[12] 1968.[119] *Parl* Seq 2. *Eccl* Witney RDn.

HAILEY WITH CRAWLEY
EP Cr 1854 by union Hailey EP, chap Crawley in Witney AP.[92] Witney RDn. Bdry: 1953.[120]

HAMPTON GAY
Orig appropriated chap, then free chap, sep civ identity early, sep eccl status by 19th cent.[147] *LG* Plough. Hd, Woods. PLU, RSD, RD. Abol civ 1932 to help cr Hampton Gay and Poyle CP.[8] *Parl* Woods. Parl Bor (1832–85), Mid Dv (1885–1918), Banb. Dv (1918–48). *Eccl* Bic. RDn (cr–1852, Isl. RDn (1852–1956), Woods. RDn (1956–*).

HAMPTON GAY AND POYLE
CP Cr 1932 by union Hampton Gay CP, Hampton Poyle AP, pts Gosford CP, Kidlington AP, Thrup CP.[8] *Parl* Banb. CC (1948–70), Mid-Oxon CC (1970–*).

HAMPTON POYLE
AP *LG* Plough. Hd, Woods. PLU, RSD, RD. Abol civ 1932 to help cr Hampton Gay and Poyle CP.[8] *Parl* Mid Dv (1885–1918), Banb. Dv (1918–48). *Eccl* Seq 3.

HANBOROUGH
AP Usual eccl spelling; for civ see 'Handborough'. *Eccl* Seq 11. Eccl bdry: 1966.[27]
CP Cr 1948 from Handborough AP.[115] *LG* Witney RD. *Parl* Mid-Oxon CC (1970–*).

HANDBOROUGH
AP Usual civ spelling; for eccl see 'Hanborough'. *LG* Woott. Hd, Witney PLU, RSD, RD. Civ bdry: 1932.[8] Abol civ 1948 pt to help cr Hanborough CP, pt to help cr Freeland CP.[115] *Parl* Woods. Parl Bor (1832–85), Mid Dv (1885–1918), Banb. Dv/CC (1918–70). *Eccl* Seq 11.

EAST HANNEY
CP In Berks, qv, transf 1974 to Oxon.[1]

WEST HANNEY
AP In Berks, qv, transf 1974 to Oxon.[1]

HANWELL
AP *LG* Seq 5. *Parl* Seq 6. *Eccl* Seq 6.

HARDWICK
AP *LG* Plough. Hd, Bic. PLU, RSD, RD. Civ bdry: 1886.[31] Abol civ 1932 to help cr Hardwick with Tusmore CP.[8] *Parl* Mid Dv (1885–1918), Henley Dv (1918–48). *Eccl* Bic. RDn. Abol eccl *ca* 1840 to help cr Hardwick-cum-Tusmore EP.[121]

HARDWICK
Chap in Ducklington AP, sep CP 1866.[2] *LG* Bamp. Hd, Witney PLU, RSD, RD. Bdry: 1886.[11] Abol 1932 pt to help cr Hardwick-with-Yelford CP, pt to Standlake AP.[8] *Parl* Mid Dv (1885–1918), Banb. Dv (1918–48).

HARDWICK-CUM-TUSMORE
EP Cr *ca* 1840 by union Hardwick AP, Tusmore AP.[121] Bic. RDn (*ca* 1840–1956), Bic. & Isl. RDn (1956–*).

HARDWICK WITH TUSMORE
CP Cr 1932 by union Hardwick AP, Tusmore AP.[8] *LG* Plough. RD. *Parl* Henley CC (1948–70), Banb. CC (1970–*).

HARDWICK-WITH-YELFORD
CP Cr 1932 by union Yelford AP and pts Hardwick CP, Ducklington AP, Standlake AP.[8] *LG* Witney RD. *Parl* Banb. CC (1948–70), Mid-Oxon CC (1970–*).

HARPSDEN
AP *LG* Seq 4. Civ bdry: 1932,[8] 1952.[26] *Parl* Seq 6. *Eccl* Seq 7. Eccl bdry: 1953.[122]

HARWELL
AP In Berks, qv, transf 1974 to Oxon.[1]

GREAT HASELEY
AP *LG* Seq 13. Civ bdry: 1932.[8] *Parl* Seq 6. *Eccl* Seq 4. Eccl bdry: 1939.[123]

HATFORD
AP In Berks, qv, transf 1974 to Oxon.[1]

HEADINGTON
AP *LG* Bull. Hd, Head. PLU, pt Oxf. CB (1889–94), pt Oxf. USD, pt Head. RSD, Head. RD. Civ bdry: 1894 (loses the pt in the CB to Oxford St Clement AP).[124] Abol civ 1929 pt to Oxf. CB and St Giles and St John CP, pt to Elsfield AP, pt to Horspath AP, pt to Forest Hill with Shotover CP, pt to Stowood AP.[88] *Parl* Pt Oxf. Parl Bor (1832–1918 [enlarged pt 1867–1918]), pt Mid Dv (1885–1918), Henley Dv (1918–48). *Eccl* Cudd. RDn (until 1852), Isl. RDn (1852–1956), Cowley RDn (1956–*). Eccl bdry: 1850 (cr Headington Quarry EP),[125] 1910 (cr Highfield EP).[126]

HEADINGTON QUARRY
EP Cr 1850 from Headington AP.[125] Cudd. RDn (1850–52), Isl. RDn (1852–1956), Cowley RDn (1956–*).

EAST HENDRED
AP In Berks, qv, transf 1974 to Oxon.[1]
WEST HENDRED
AP In Berks, qv, transf 1974 to Oxon.[1]
HENLEY HOLY TRINITY
EP Name commonly used for EP cr as 'Rotherfield Greys Holy Trinity', qv.
HENLEY-ON-THAMES
AP *LG* Binf. Hd, Henley PLU, Henley-on-Thames MB (pt 1883–94, ent 1894–1974), Henley RSD (ent 1875–83, pt 1883–94), pt Henley-on-Thames USD (1883–94). Civ bdry: 1894 (the pt not in the MB cr Badegmore CP),[25] 1905 (gains Greys CP),[118] 1932.[8] *Parl* Seq 7. *Eccl* Seq 7. Eccl bdry: 1849 (cr Rotherfield Greys Holy Trinity EP, now called 'Henley Holy Trinity'),[127] 1953.[45]
HENSINGTON
Hmlt in Bladon AP, sep CP 1866.[2] *LG* Woott. Hd, Woods. PLU, pt Woods. MB & USD (1886–94), Woods. RSD (ent 1875–86, pt 1886–94). Abol 1894 the pt in the MB cr Hensington Within CP, the remainder cr Hensington Without CP.[25] *Parl* Mid Dv (1885–1918).
HENSINGTON WITHIN
CP Cr 1894 from the pt of Hensington CP in Woods. MB.[25] *LG* Woods. PLU, MB. *Parl* Banb. Dv/CC (1918–*).
HENSINGTON WITHOUT
CP Cr 1894 from the pt of Hensington CP not in Woods. MB.[25] *LG* Woods. PLU, RD (1894–1932), Chip. Nort. RD (1932–74). Bdry: 1954 (incl help cr Blenheim CP).[12] *Parl* Banb. Dv/CC (1918–*).
HETHE
AP *LG* Seq 17. Civ bdry: 1888.[128] *Parl* Seq 4. *Eccl* Seq 2.
LOWER HEYFORD
AP *LG* Seq 17. *Parl* Seq 4. *Eccl* Seq 2.
UPPER HEYFORD
AP Usual civ spelling; for eccl see following entry. *LG* Seq 17. *Parl* Seq 4.
HEYFORD WARREN
AP Usual eccl spelling. for civ see prev entry. *Eccl* Seq 2.
HEYTHROP
AP *LG* Seq 21. Civ bdry: 1884.[129] *Parl* Seq 6. *Eccl* Seq 8.
HIGHFIELD
EP Cr 1910 from Headington AP.[126] Isl. RDn (1910–56), Cowley RDn (1956–*).
HIGHMORE
Chap in Bix AP, Rotherfield Greys AP, sep EP 1860,[44] sep CP 1952 as 'Highmoor',[26] qv. *Eccl* Henley RDn.
HIGHMOOR
Chap in Bix AP, Rotherfield Greys AP, sep EP 1860 as 'Highmore',[44] qv, sep CP 1952.[26] *LG* Henley RD. *Parl* Henley CC (1970–*).
NORTH HINKSEY
Chap in Cumnor AP (Berks), sep civ identity early in Berks (Hormer Hd), sep EP 1726.[148] *LG* Abingdon PLU, pt Oxf. CB (1889–94), pt Oxf. USD, pt Abingdon RSD. Civ bdry: 1885,[130] 1894 (loses the pt in the CB to Oxford St Thomas AP[131] so that North Hinksey ent Berks until transf 1974 to Oxon[1]). *Parl* In Berks. *Eccl* Oxf. RDn (but in Berks AD 1726–1915, in Oxf. AD 1915–*).
SOUTH HINKSEY
Chap in Cumnor AP (Berks), sep civ identity early in Berks (Hormer Hd), sep EP 1723,[149] eccl refounded 1885.[150] *LG* Abingdon PLU, pt Oxf. CB (1889–94), pt Oxf. USD (1889–94), Abingdon RSD (ent 1875–89, pt 1889–94). Civ bdry: 1885,[130] 1885,[151] 1894 (loses the pt in the CB to Oxford St Aldate AP,[131] so that South Hinksey ent Berks, qv for civ organisation and bdry alt). Transf 1974 to Oxon.[1] *Parl* Pt Oxf. Parl Bor (1867–1918), remainder in Berks, qv. *Eccl* As for North Hinksey.
HINTON WALDRIST
AP In Berks, qv, transf 1974 to Oxon.[1]
HOLTON
AP *LG* Seq 8. Civ bdry: 1878,[96] 1949,[113] 1954.[7] *Parl* Seq 8. *Eccl* Seq 4.
HOLWELL
Chap in Broadwell AP (eccl, 'Bradwell (or Broadwell) with Kelmscot'), sep EP 1850,[58] sep CP 1866.[2] *LG* Seq 1. *Parl* Seq 2. *Eccl* Witney RDn.
HOLYWELL
Chap in Oxford St Aldate AP, sep civ identity early, sep EP 1769 as 'Oxford St Cross or Holywell',[16] qv. *LG* Oxf. Bor/MB/CB, USD, incorp for poor. Civ bdry: 1894 (gains pt of the pt of Marston AP in the CB).[124] Abol civ 1926 to help cr Oxford CP.[43] *Parl* Oxf. Parl Bor (1295–1948).
HORLEY
AP *LG* Seq 5. Civ bdry: 1883.[21] *Parl* Seq 6. *Eccl* Seq 12.
HORNTON
AP Organisation and bdry alt as for Horley.
HORSPATH
AP *LG* Seq 8. Civ bdry: 1929,[88] 1954.[7] *Parl* Seq 8. *Eccl* Seq 4.
HORTON CUM STUDLEY
Hmlt and chap in Beckley AP, sep CP 1866,[2] sep EP 1880.[44] *LG* Bull. Hd, Head. PLU, RSD, RD (1894–1932), Plough. RD (1932–74). Civ bdry: 1932 (incl gains Studley CP).[8] *Parl* Seq 5. *Eccl* Isl. RDn (1880–1956), Cudd. RDn (1956–*).
IBSTONE
AP Pt Bucks (Desborough Hd), pt Oxon (Pyrton Hd). *LG* Wycombe PLU, RSD, pt sep RD in Oxon (1894–96), made ent Bucks 1896.[134] *Parl* Oxon pt, S'rn Dv (1885–1918). *Eccl* Aston RDn. Abol eccl 1853 to help cr Ibstone with Fingest EP.[135]
IBSTONE WITH FINGEST
EP Cr 1853 by union Ibstone AP, Fingest AP (Bucks).[135] Aston RDn (1853–65), Marlow RDn (1865–74), Wycombe RDn (1874–*)

(last 2 RDns in Bucks AD).

ICKFORD

AP Pt Bucks (Ashendon Hd), pt Oxon (Ew. Hd), the latter transf 1886 to Waterstock AP and Ickford ent Bucks thereafter.[152] *LG* Thame PLU, RSD. *Parl* Oxon pt, S'rn Dv (1885–1918). For later civ and for eccl organisation, see main entry in Bucks.

IDBURY

Chap in Swimbrook AP, sep civ identity early, sep EP 1750.[16] *LG* Seq 9. Civ bdry: 1884.[129] *Parl* Seq 6. *Eccl* Chip. Nort. RDn. Abol eccl 1972 to help cr Fifield with Idbury EP.[109]

IFFLEY

AP Incl pt chap Littlemore (sep EP 1847,[136] sep CP 1866[2]). *LG* Bull. Hd, Head. PLU, pt Oxf. CB & USD (1889–94), Head. RSD (ent 1875–89, pt 1889–94), Head. RD. Addtl civ bdry alt: 1883,[21] 1885,[137] 1886,[86] 1894 (loses the pt in the CB to help cr Cowley St John CP).[87] Abol civ 1929 pt to Oxf. CB and St Giles and St John CP, pt to Littlemore CP.[88] *Parl* Pt Oxf. Parl Bor (1867–1918), pt Mid Dv (1885–1918), Henley Dv (1918–48). *Eccl* Cudd. RDn (until 1956), Cowley RDn (1956–*). Addtl eccl bdry alt: 1898 (help cr Cowley St John EP),[89] 1877.[90]

IPSDEN

AP Incl pt chap Stoke Row (sep EP 1849,[138] sep CP 1952[26]). *LG* Seq 15. *Parl* Seq 7. *Eccl* Aston RDn (until 1928), Henley RDn (1928–*).

ISLIP

AP *LG* Seq 17. Civ bdry: 1883,[21] 1932.[8] *Parl* Seq 3. *Eccl* Seq 3.

KELMSCOT

Chap in Broadwell AP (eccl, 'Bradwell (or Broadwell) with Kelmscot' until 1960), sep CP 1866,[2] eccl severed 1960 to help cr Clanfield with Kelmscot EP (the remaidner to be Bradwell EP).[54] *LG* Seq 1. *Parl* Seq 2.

KENCOT

AP *LG* Seq 1. Civ bdry: 1886.[11] *Parl* Seq 2. *Eccl* Seq 10.

KENNINGTON

CP In Berks, qv, transf 1974 to Oxon.[1]

KIDDINGTON

AP Gains 1466 Asterleigh AP (later considered civ ex-par, sep CP 1858[19]). *LG* Woott. Hd, Woods. PLU, RSD. Abol civ 1894 to help cr Kiddington with Asterleigh CP.[20] *Parl* Mid Dv (1885–1918). *Eccl* Seq 11.

KIDDINGTON WITH ASTERLEIGH

CP Cr 1894 by union Kiddington AP, Asterleigh CP.[20] *LG* Woods. PLU, RD (1894–1932), Chip. Nort. RD (1932–74). *Parl* Banb. Dv/CC (1918–*).

KIDLINGTON

AP Incl hmlt Gosford (sep CP 1866[2]), hmlt Thrup (sep CP 1866[2]), hmlt Water Eaton (sep CP 1866[2]). *LG* Seq 25. Addtl civ bdry alt: 1883,[21] 1932,[8] 1948.[37] *Parl* Pt Woods. Parl Bor (1832–85), Seq 2 thereafter. *Eccl* Woods. RDn (until 1965), Oxf. RDn (1965–*). Addtl eccl bdry alt: 1952,[38] 1972.[140]

KIDMORE

CP Cr 1894 from the pt of Caversham AP not in Caversham UD.[25] *LG* Henley PLU, RD. Renamed civ 1902 'Kidmore End'.[141]

KIDMORE END

EP Cr 1854 from Caversham AP, Shiplake AP, Sonning AP (Berks, Oxon).[69] Henley RDn. Bdry: 1970.[70]

CP Renaming 1902 of Kidmore CP.[141] *LG* Henley PLU, RD. Bdry: 1912,[105] 1952 (help cr Sonning Common CP).[26] *Parl* Henley Dv/CC (1918–*).

KINGHAM

AP *LG* Seq 9. *Parl* Seq 6. *Eccl* Seq 8.

KINGSEY

AP Pt Oxon (Lewk. Hd), pt Bucks (Ashendon Hd). *LG* Thame PLU, RSD, pt sep RD in Bucks (1894–96), Thame RD (pt 1894–96, ent 1896–1933). Civ bdry: 1886 (loses pt to Ilmer AP, Bucks),[142] 1896 (made ent Oxon).[134] Transf 1933 to Bucks.[143] *Parl* Oxon pt, S'rn Dv (1885–1918), Henley Dv (1918–48). *Eccl* Waddesdon RDn (until 1874), Aylesbury RDn (1874–1925)(both in Bucks AD), Aston RDn (1925–*).

KINGSTON BAGPUIZE WITH SOUTHMOOR

CP In Berks, qv, transf 1974 to Oxon.[1]

KINGSTON LISLE

CP In Berks, qv, transf 1974 to Oxon.[1]

KIRTLINGTON

AP *LG* Seq 17. *Parl* Seq 4. *Eccl* Seq 2.

LAND COMMON TO BEGBROKE AND YARNTON (PIXEY MEAD)

In Woods. RD, abol civ 1932 to help cr Gosford and Water Eaton CP.[8]

LAND COMMON TO BEGBROKE AND YARNTON (YARNTON OR WEST MEAD, OXNEY MEAD)

In Woods. RD, abol civ 1932 ent to Yarnton CP.[8]

LAND COMMON TO COTTISFORD AND HETHE

In Bic. RD. abol civ 1932 ent to Cottisford CP.[8]

LANGFORD

AP Incl hmlt Radcot (sep CP 1866,[2] eccl severed 1960 to help cr Clanfield with Kelmscot EP[54]), tp Grafton (sep CP 1866[2]), chap Little Faringdon (in Berks, area transf to Oxon 1832 for parl purposes, 1844 for civ purposes,[60] sep CP 1866 in Oxon,[2] sep EP 1864[107]). *LG* Pt Berks (until 1844), Oxon (pt until 1844, ent from 1844; Bamp. Hd), Faringdon PLU, RSD, Witney RD. *Parl* Seq 2. *Eccl* Pec jurisd (until 1846), Seq 10 thereafter.

LANGLEY

Hmlt in Shipton-under-Wychwood AP, sep CP 1866.[2] *LG* Chadl. Hd, Chip. Nort. PLU, RSD, RD. Abol 1932 ent to Shipton-under-Wychwood AP.[8] *Parl* N'rn Dv (1885–1918), Banb. Dv (1918–48).

LAUNTON

AP *LG* Seq 17. *Parl* Seq 4. *Eccl* Seq 2.

LEAFIELD
Chap (founded *temp* Eliz I) in Shipton-under-Wychwood AP, sep EP 1745,[16] gains eccl 1860 ex-par Wychwood and sometimes thereafter eccl 'Leafield cum Wychwood',[144] sep CP 1866.[2] *LG* Seq 9. Civ bdry: 1932,[8] 1950.[84] *Parl* Seq 6. *Eccl* Chip. Nort. RDn.

NORTH LEIGH
AP *LG* Seq 22. Civ bdry: 1932 (gains Osney Hill CP, Wilcote AP),[8] 1954.[12] *Parl* Seq 2. *Eccl* Seq 11. Eccl bdry: 1953 (incl gains eccl ex-par Osney Hill).[120]

SOUTH LEIGH
Chap in Stanton Harcourt AP, sep civ identity early, sep EP 1868.[145] *LG* Seq 22. Civ bdry: 1883,[21] 1932,[8] 1967.[103] *Parl* Seq 2. *Eccl* Witney RDn.

LETCOMBE BASSETT
AP In Berks, qv, transf 1974 to Oxon.[1]

LETCOMBE REGIS
AP In Berks, qv, transf 1974 to Oxon.[1]

LEW
Hmlt in Bampton AP, sep CP 1866,[2] eccl severed 1845 to help cr Bampton Lew EP.[22] *LG* Seq 1. *Parl* Seq 2.

LEWKNOR
AP Incl 3 detached pts (sep CP 1866 as 'Lewknor Uphill',[2] pt Oxon [Lewk. Hd, area in Oxon enlarged when pt of the detached pts known as chap Ackhampstead transf from Bucks to Oxon 1832 for parl purposes, 1844 for civ purposes[60]], pt Bucks [Desborough Hd, reduced pt from 1844]). *LG* Seq 16. Addtl civ bdry alt: 1932,[8] 1954 (incl gains South Weston AP).[7] *Parl* Seq 7. *Eccl* Seq 1. Eccl bdry: 1852 (cr Cadmore End EP,[64] refounded 1853[65]), 1961.[163]

LEWKNOR UPHILL
Comprised of 3 detached pts in Lewknor AP, pt Oxon (Lewk. Hd), pt Bucks (Desborough Hd), the area of the former increased and the latter decreased when chap Ackhampstead transf from Bucks to Oxon 1832 for parl purposes, 1844 for civ purposes,[60] sep CP 1866 with area in ea co.[2] *LG* Wycombe PLU, RSD. Abol 1885 the pt in Oxon to Stokenchurch CP, the pt in Bucks to Great Marlow AP.[154] *Parl* Oxon pt, S'rn Dv (1885–1918).

LILLINGSTONE LOVELL
AP In Oxon (Plough. Hd, Buckingham PLU from 1835), transf to Bucks 1832 for parl purposes, 1844 for civ purposes.[60] For later civ organisation, see entry in Bucks. *Eccl* Bic. RDn (until 1920), Buckingham RDn (Bucks AD, 1920–*).

LITTLEMORE
Lbty and chap in Iffley AP, Oxford St Mary the Virgin AP, sep EP 1847,[137] sep CP 1866.[2] *LG* Bull. Hd, pt Oxf. MB/CB (1866–89), Head. PLU, pt Oxf. USD (1875–89), Head. RSD (pt 1875–89, ent 1889–94), Head. RD (1894–1932), Bull. RD (1932–74). Civ bdry: 1885,[85] 1886,[86] 1889 (loses pt in MB when Oxf. made CB), 1929,[88] 1957 (loses pt to Oxf. CB and CP).[155] *Parl* Pt Oxf. Parl Bor (1867–1918), remainder and later, Seq 7. Parl bdry: 1960.[193] *Eccl* Cudd. RDn (1847–1956), Cowley RDn (1956–*).

LITTLEWORTH
CP In Berks, qv, transf 1974 to Oxon.[1]

LOCKINGE
CP In Berks, qv, transf 1974 to Oxon.[1]

LONGCOTT
CP In Berks, qv, transf 1974 to Oxon.[1]

LONGWORTH
AP In Berks, qv, transf 1874 to Oxon.[1]

LYFORD
CP In Berks, qv, transf 1974 to Oxon.[1]

LYNEHAM
Chap and hmlt in Shipton-under-Wychwood AP, sep CP 1866,[2] eccl severed 1895 to help cr Milton-under-Wychwood EP.[156] *LG* Seq 9. *Parl* Seq 6.

MAPLEDURHAM
AP *LG* Seq 14. *Parl* Seq 7. *Eccl* Seq 7.

MARCHAM
AP In Berks, qv, transf 1974 to Oxon.[1]

MARSTON
AP *LG* Bull. Hd, Head. PLU, pt Oxf. CB (1889–94), pt Oxf. USD, pt Head. RSD, Head. RD. Civ bdry: 1894 (loses pt of the pt in the CB to Oxford St Clement AP, pt to Holywell CP),[124] 1929.[88] *Parl* Oxf. Parl Bor (pt 1832–67, ent 1867–1918), Henley Dv/CC (1918–70), Mid-Oxon CC (1970–*). *Eccl* Cudd. RDn (until 1852), Isl. RDn (1852–1956), Cowley RDn (1956–*).

MERTON
AP *LG* Seq 6. *Parl* Seq 3. *Eccl* Seq 2.

MIDDLETON STONEY
AP *LG* Seq 19. *Parl* Seq 4. *Eccl* Seq 2.

MILCOMBE
Chap in Bloxham AP, sep CP 1866,[2] sep EP 1854 (incl pt Wiggington AP).[49] *LG* Seq 5. *Parl* Seq 6. *Eccl* Dedd. RDn.

MILTON
Hmlt in Adderbury AP, sep CP 1866.[2] *LG* Seq 5. *Parl* Seq 6.

MILTON
AP In Berks, qv, transf 1974 to Oxon.[1]

GREAT MILTON
AP Incl chap Little Milton (sep civ identity early, sep EP 1844[157]), hmlt Chilworth (sep CP 1866[2]), hmlt Ascott (sep CP 1866[2]). *LG* Pt Bull. Hd (Chilworth, until 1866), Thame Hd (pt until 1866, ent from 1866), Thame PLU, RSD, RD (1894–1932), Bull. RD (1932–74). Addtl civ bdry alt: 1932,[8] 1954.[7] *Parl* Seq 8. *Eccl* Pec jurisd Thame (until 1846), Cudd. RDn (1846–*).

LITTLE MILTON
Chap in Great Milton AP, sep civ identity early, sep EP 1844.[157] *LG* Seq 20. *Parl* Seq 7. *Eccl* Pec jurisd Thame (1844–46), Cudd. RDn (1846–*).

MILTON-UNDER-WYCHWOOD
Chap and tp in Shipton-under-Wychwood AP, sep CP 1866,[2] sep EP 1895 (incl Lyneham

chap in same par).[156] *LG* Seq 9. *Parl* Seq 6. *Eccl* Chip. Nort. RDn. Eccl bdry: 1953.[158]

MINSTER LOVELL

AP *LG* Seq 10. *Parl* Seq 2. *Eccl* Seq 10.

MIXBURY

AP *LG* Seq 19. Civ bdry: 1888.[159] *Parl* Seq 4. *Eccl* Seq 2.

MOLLINGTON

Chap (pec jurisd Banb.) in Cropredy AP, sep CP 1866,[2] eccl severed 1851 to help cr Claydon with Mollington EP,[78] the latter divided 1863 into 2 EPs Claydon, Mollington.[79] *LG* Pt Oxon (Blox. Hd), pt Warws (Kington Hd), Banb. PLU, RSD. In 1894 becomes 2 sep pars, each 'Mollington',[160] one in Oxon (Banb. RD), one in Warws,[160] the latter abol 1896 ent to Mollington (Oxon).[161] *Parl* Oxon pt, Seq 6. *Eccl* Dedd. RDn.

MONGEWELL

AP *LG* Langt. Hd, Wallingford PLU, RSD, Crowm. RD. Abol civ 1932 pt to help cr Crowmarsh CP, pt to Rotherfield Greys CP.[8] *Parl* S'rn Dv (1885–1918), Henley Dv (1918–48). *Eccl* Henley RDn (until 1852), Nettlebed RDn (1852–74), Henley RDn (1874–1915), Wallingford RDn (Berks AD, 1915–28), Henley RDn (1928–*).

NORTH MORETON

AP In Berks, qv, transf 1974 to Oxon.[1]

SOUTH MORETON

AP In Berks, qv, transf 1974 to Oxon.[1]

MOULSFORD

CP In Berks, qv, transf 1974 to Oxon.[1]

NEITHROP

Tg (Oxon, Banb. Hd) in Warkworth AP (otherwise Northants, King's Sutton Hd) for civ purposes, Banbury AP for eccl purposes, sep CP 1866 in Oxon[2] so that Warkworth ent Northants thereafter. *LG* Banb. PLU, MB (1889–1932), USD (1889–94), RSD (1875–89). Abol 1932 ent to Banbury AP.[8] *Parl* N'rn Dv (1885–1918), Banb. Dv (1918–48).

NETTLEBED

AP *LG* Seq 12. Civ bdry: 1952.[26] *Parl* Seq 7. *Eccl* Donative, pec jurisd Dorch. (until 1846), Cudd. RDn (1846–52), Nettlebed RDn (1852–74), Henley RDn (1874–*). Eccl bdry: 1953.[45]

NEWINGTON

AP Incl chap Britwell Prior (sep CP 1866[2]). *LG* Seq 11. Civ bdry: 1932.[8] *Parl* Seq 7. *Eccl* Pec jurisd (until 1846), Seq 4 thereafter.

NORTH NEWINGTON

Tp in Broughton AP, sep CP 1866.[2] *LG* Seq 5. *Parl* Seq 6.

SOUTH NEWINGTON

AP *LG* Woott. Hd, Banb. PLU, RSD, RD. *Parl* Seq 6. *Eccl* Seq 6.

NEWNHAM MURREN

Chap in North Stoke AP, sep civ identity early, eccl severed 1907 to help cr Crowmarsh Gifford with Newnham Murren EP.[94] *LG* Langt. Hd, Wallingford PLU, RSD, Crowm. RD. Abol 1932 to help cr Crowmarsh CP.[8] *Parl* S'rn Dv (1885–1918), Henley Dv (1918–48).

NEWTON PURCELL

AP *LG* Plough. Hd, Bic. PLU, RSD, RD. Abol civ 1932 to help cr Newton Purcell with Shelswell CP.[8] *Parl* Mid Dv (1885–1918), Henley Dv (1918–48). *Eccl* Bic. RDn. Abol eccl 1850 to help cr Newton Purcell with Shelswell EP.[162]

NEWTON PURCELL WITH SHELSWELL

Cr eccl 1850,[162] civ 1932[8] by union Newton Purcell AP, Shelswell AP.[162] *LG* Plough. RD. *Parl* Banb. CC (1948–70), Mid-Oxon CC (1970–*). *Eccl* Bic. RDn (1850–1956), Bic. & Isl. RDn (1956–*).

NOKE

AP *LG* Seq 19. Civ bdry: 1883,[21] 1932.[8] *Parl* Seq 3. *Eccl* Cudd. RDn (until 1852), Isl. RDn (1852–1956), Bic. & Isl. RDn (1956–*).

NORTHMOOR

AP *LG* Seq 10. Civ bdry: 1886,[11] 1932.[8] *Parl* Seq 2. *Eccl* Seq 10.

BRIZE NORTON

AP *LG* Seq 1. Civ bdry: 1886,[11] 1932,[8] 1963,[53] 1971 (help cr Carterton and Black Bourton CP).[66] *Parl* Seq 2. *Eccl* Seq 10.

CHIPPING NORTON

AP Incl hmlt Over Norton (not in Chip. Nort. Bor/MB, sep CP 1866[2]). *LG* Chadl. Hd, Chip. Nort. PLU, Bor/MB (pt until 1866, ent 1866–1974), Chip. Nort. USD. Addtl civ bdry alt: 1932.[8] *Parl* Chip. Nort. Parl Bor (1302–04 only), Seq 6 thereafter. *Eccl* Seq 8.

HOOK NORTON

AP *LG* Chadl. Hd, Banb. PLU, RSD, RD. *Parl* Seq 6. *Eccl* Seq 8.

OVER NORTON

Hmlt in Chipping Norton AP, sep CP 1866.[2] *LG* Seq 9. Bdry: 1884,[129] 1932.[8] *Parl* Seq 6.

NUFFIELD

AP *LG* Seq 12. Civ bdry: 1932.[8] *Parl* Seq 7. *Eccl* Henley RDn (until 1852), Nettlebed RDn (1852–74), Henley RDn (1874–*).

NUNEHAM COURTENAY

AP *LG* Seq 7. *Parl* Seq 7. *Eccl* Cudd. RDn. Abol eccl 1972 to help cr Marsh and Toot Baldon with Nuneham Courtenay EP.[27]

ODDINGTON

AP *LG* Seq 17. *Parl* Seq 3. *Eccl* Seq 3.

NEW OSNEY

EP Cr 1873 from Oxford St Thomas the Martyr AP.[163] Oxf. RDn. Now called 'Oxford St Frideswide'.

OSNEY HILL

Ex-par place, sep CP 1858,[19] eccl abol 1953 ent to North Leigh CP.[8] *LG* Woott. Hd, Witney PLU (1858[164]–1930), RSD, RD. Abol 1932 ent to North Leigh CP.[8] *Parl* Mid Dv (1885–1918), Banb. Dv (1918–48).

OXFORD

The following have 'Oxford' in their names. Insofar as any existed at a given time: *LG* Oxf. Bor/MB/CB, incorp for poor, USD. *Parl* Oxf. Parl Bor (1295–*). *Eccl* Oxf. RDn.

CP1–OXFORD–Cr 1926 by union Holywell CP,

AP2, AP7, CP2, AP14, AP15, AP16, AP19, AP20, AP21, Oxf. University Colleges and Halls.[43] Bdry: 1934 (gains St Giles and St John CP),[165] 1957.[155] Parl bdry: 1960.[193]

AP1–OXFORD ALL SAINTS–Gains early AP8. Abol civ 1895 to help cr CP2.[166] Abol eccl 1896 to help cr EP9.[167]

EP1–OXFORD HOLY TRINITY–Cr 1844 from AP7.[168] Abol 1956 to help cr EP2.[169]

AP2–OXFORD ST ALDATE–Incl chap Holywell (sep civ identity early, sep EP 1769 as EP5[16]). *LG* Pt Oxon (Oxf. Bor/MB/CB, USD), pt Berks (tg Grandpont, in Oxf. USD), par made ent Oxon 1889.[170] Addtl civ bdry alt: 1885 (gains pt North Hinksey CP, pt South Hinksey CP, both Berks),[130] 1894 (gains pt South Hinksey CP, Berks).[131] Abol civ 1926 to help cr CP1.[43] *Parl* Oxon pt in Oxf. Parl Bor, tg Grandpont in the Parl Bor 1867–1918. Eccl bdry: 1913 (cr EP10).[171] Abol eccl 1956 to help cr EP2.[169]

EP2–OXFORD ST ALDATE WITH HOLY TRINITY–Cr 1956 by union AP2, EP1.[169]

AP3–OXFORD ST ANDREW–Early demolished

EP3–OXFORD ST ANDREW–Cr 1905 from EP14, Summertown EP.[172]

EP4–OXFORD ST BARNABAS–Cr 1869 from EP12.[173]

–OXFORD ST BARTHOLOMEW HOSPITAL–Ex-par, eccl abol 1913 ent to Cowley St John EP.[91]

AP4–OXFORD ST BENEDICT–Early demolished

AP5–OXFORD ST BUDOC–Early demolished

AP6–OXFORD ST CLEMENT–*LG* Pt Bull. Hd, Oxf. Bor/MB/CB (pt until 1894 [enlarged pt 1835–94], ent 1894–1926), Head. PLU, pt Oxf. USD, pt Head. RSD. Civ bdry: 1885,[85] 1894 (gains the pt of Headington AP and pt of the pt of Marston AP in Oxf. CB).[124] Abol civ 1924 to help cr St Giles and St John CP.[43] *Parl* Oxf. Parl Bor (pt 1295–1867 [enlarged pt 1835–67], ent 1867–1948). *Eccl* Oxf. RDn (until 1956), Cowley RDn (1956–*). Eccl bdry: 1868 (help cr Cowley St John EP).[89]

EP5–OXFORD ST CROSS OR HOLYWELL–Chap in AP2, sep civ identity early, as 'Holywell', sep EP 1769.[16] Abol eccl 1966 to help cr EP6.[133]

EP6–OXFORD ST CROSS AND ST PETER IN THE EAST WITH ST JOHN THE BAPTIST–Cr 1966 by union EP5, EP13.[131]

AP7–OXFORD ST EBBE–Abol civ 1926 to help cr CP1.[43] Eccl bdry: 1844 (cr EP1).[168] Abol eccl 1964 to help cr EP7.[174]

EP7–OXFORD ST EBBE WITH ST PETER-LE-BAILEY–Cr 1964 by union AP7, AP20.[174]

AP8–OXFORD ST EDWARD–Early demolished, incl in AP1

AP9–OXFORD ST FRIDESWIDE–Early demolished

–OXFORD ST FRIDESWIDE–Name used now for EP cr as New Osney, qv

AP10–OXFORD ST GEORGE–Early demolished

AP11–OXFORD ST GILES–*LG* Head. PLU. Civ bdry: 1894 (gains pt Wolvercott CP).[42] Abol civ 1926 to help cr St Giles and St John CP.[43] *Parl* Oxf. Parl Bor (pt 1295–1867, ent 1867–1948). Eccl bdry: 1833 (cr Summertown EP),[175] 1837 (help cr EP12),[176] 1863 (help cr EP14).[178]

AP12–OXFORD ST JOHN THE BAPTIST–*LG* Head. PLU. Abol civ 1926 to help cr St Giles and St John CP.[43] Abol eccl 1891 to help cr EP13.[178]

EP8–OXFORD ST MARGARET–Cr 1896 from EP14, Summertown EP.[179]

AP13–OXFORD ST MARTIN–Sometimes 'Carfax'. Abol civ 1895 to help cr CP2.[166] Abol eccl 1896 to help cr EP9.[167]

CP2/EP9–OXFORD ST MARTIN AND ALL SAINTS–Cr eccl 1896,[167] civ 1895[166] by union AP13, AP1. Abol civ 1926 to help cr CP1.[43] Abol eccl 1971 to help cr EP11.[180]

AP14–OXFORD ST MARY MAGDALENE–Abol civ 1926 to help cr CP1.[43]

AP15–OXFORD ST MARY THE VIRGIN–Incl pt chap Littlemore (sep EP 1847,[136] sep CP 1866[2]). Abol civ 1926 to help cr CP1.[43]

EP10–OXFORD ST MATTHEW, GRANDPONT–Cr 1913 from AP2.[171] Bdry: 1914.[132]

AP16–OXFORD ST MICHAEL–Abol civ 1926 to help cr CP1.[43] Abol eccl 1971 to help cr EP11.[180]

EP11–OXFORD ST MICHAEL AT THE NORTH GATE WITH ST MARTIN AND ALL SAINTS–Cr 1971 by union EP9, AP16.[180]

AP17–OXFORD ST MICHAEL SOUTHGATE–Early demolished

AP18–OXFORD ST MILDRED–Early demolished

–OXFORD ST NICHOLAS–See AP21

EP12–OXFORD ST PAUL–Cr 1837 from AP11, AP21.[176] Bdry: 1869 (cr EP4).[173]

AP19–OXFORD ST PETER IN THE EAST–Incl chap Wolvercott (sep civ identity early, sep EP 1759[16]). Abol civ 1926 to help cr CP1.[43] Abol eccl 1891 to help cr EP13.[178]

EP13–OXFORD ST PETER IN THE EAST WITH ST JOHN THE BAPTIST–Cr 1891 by union AP19, AP12.[178] Abol 1966 to help cr EP6.[133]

AP20–OXFORD ST PETER LE BAILEY–Abol civ 1926 to help cr CP1.[43] Abol eccl 1964 to help cr EP7.[174]

EP14–OXFORD ST PHILIP AND ST JAMES–Cr 1863 from AP11.[177] Bdry: 1896 (help cr EP8),[179] 1905 (help cr EP3).[172]

AP21–OXFORD ST THOMAS–Usual civ spelling; eccl 'Oxford St Thomas the Martyr', sometimes 'St Nicholas'. Civ bdry: 1894 (gains pt North Hinksey CP, Berks).[131] Abol civ 1926 to help cr CP1.[43] Eccl bdry: 1837 (help cr EP12),[176] 1873 (cr New Osney EP, now called 'Oxford St Frideswide').[163]

–OXFORD UNIVERSITY COLLEGES AND HALLS–Sep rated for poor law purposes but not considered sep CP individually or collectively but rather within the various Oxford pars; abol civ 1926 to help cr CP1.[43]

PIDDINGTON

AP Chap in Ambrosden AP, sep par 1428.[13] *LG* Seq 6. Civ bdry: 1956 (gains pt Marsh Gibbon AP, Bucks).[181] *Parl* Seq 3. *Eccl* Seq 2.

PISHILL

AP *LG* Pyrton Hd, Henley PLU, RSD, RD. Abol civ 1922 to help cr Pishill with Stonor CP.[182] *Parl* S'rn Dv (1885–1918), Henley Dv (1918–48). *Eccl* Pec jurisd Dorch. (until 1846), Cudd. RDn (1846–52), Nettlebed RDn (1852–74), Aston RDn (1874–1973). Abol eccl 1973 pt to help cr Bix with Pishill EP, pt to Swyncombe AP.[46]

PISHILL WITH STONOR

CP Cr 1922 by union Pishill AP, Stonor CP.[182] *LG* Henley PLU, RD. Bdry: 1932.[8] *Parl* Henley CC (1948–*).

PRESCOTE

Ex-par lordship, sep CP 1858.[19] *LG* Seq 2. *Parl* Seq 6.

PUSEY

AP In Berks, qv, transf 1974 to Oxon.[1]

PYRTON

AP *LG* Seq 18. Civ bdry: 1896 (cr Stonor CP),[17] 1932.[8] *Parl* Seq 7. *Eccl* Seq 1. Eccl bdry: 1939.[123]

RADCOT

Hmlt in Langford AP, sep CP 1866,[2] eccl severed 1960 to help cr Clanfield with Kelmscot EP.[54] *LG* Bamp. Hd, Faringdon PLU, RSD, Witney RD. Abol 1932 to help cr Grafton and Radcot CP.[8] *Parl* Mid Dv (1885–1918), Banb. Dv (1918–48).

RADLEY

CP In Berks, qv, transf 1974 to Oxon.[1]

RAMSDEN

Chap in Shipton-under-Wychwood AP, sep EP 1843,[16] eccl refounded 1861,[183] sep CP 1866.[2] *LG* Seq 10. *Parl* Seq 2. *Eccl* Chip. Nort. RDn.

RISINGHURST AND SANDHILLS

CP Cr 1956 from Forest Hill with Shotover CP.[114] *LG* Bull. RD. *Parl* Mid-Oxon CC (1970–*).

ROLLRIGHT

CP Cr 1932 by union Great Rollright AP, Little Rollright AP.[8] *LG* Chip. Nort. RD. *Parl* Banb. CC (1970–*).

GREAT ROLLRIGHT

AP *LG* Chadl. Hd, Chip. Nort. PLU, RSD, RD. Abol civ 1932 to help cr Rollright CP.[8] *Parl* N'rn Dv (1885–1918), Banb. Dv (1918–48). *Eccl* Seq 8.

LITTLE ROLLRIGHT

AP Organisation as for Great Rollright.

ROTHERFIELD GREYS

AP Incl pt chap Highmore (sep EP 1860,[44] sep CP 1952 as 'Highmoor'[26]). *LG* Binf. Hd, Henley PLU, pt Henley-on-Thames MB & USD (1883–94), Henley RSD (ent 1875–83, pt 1883–94), Henley RD. Addtl civ bdry: 1894 (the pt in the MB cr Greys CP),[25] 1932.[8] *Parl* Seq 7. *Eccl* Seq 7. Addtl eccl bdry alt: 1849 (help cr Rotherfield Greys Holy Trinity EP, now called 'Henley Holy Trinity').[127]

ROTHERFIELD GREYS HOLY TRINITY

EP Cr 1849 from Rotherfield Greys AP, Rotherfield Peppard AP, Henley-on-Thames AP.[127] Henley RDn. Bdry: 1953.[122] Now called 'Henley Holy Trinity'.

ROTHERFIELD PEPPARD

AP *LG* Seq 4. Civ bdry: 1932,[8] 1952.[26] *Parl* Seq 7. *Eccl* Seq 7. Eccl bdry: 1849 (help cr Rotherfield Greys Holy Trinity EP, now called 'Henley Holy Trinity').[127]

ROUSHAM

AP *LG* Seq 24. *Parl* Seq 6. *Eccl* Woods. RDn (until 1955), Bic. RDn (1955–56), Bic. & Isl. RDn (1956–*).

ST GILES AND ST JOHN

CP Cr 1926 by union Binsey AP, Cowley St John CP, Oxford St Clement AP, Oxford St Giles AP, Oxford St John the Baptist AP.[43] *LG* Head. PLU, Oxf. CB. Bdry: 1929 (incl gains Cowley AP, Unnamed CP [area after 1894 in Oxf. CB of Seacourt CP, remainder in Berks and sep CP in Berks from 1894]).[88] Abol 1933 ent to Oxford CP.[165]

SALFORD

AP *LG* Seq 9. *Parl* Seq 6. *Eccl* Seq 8.

SANDFORD-ON-THAMES

AP *LG* Seq 7. *Parl* Seq 7. *Eccl* Cudd. RDn (until 1956), Cowley RDn (1956–*).

SANDFORD ST MARTIN

AP *LG* Seq 24. *Parl* Seq 6. *Eccl* Seq 11.

SARSDEN

AP *LG* Seq 9. *Parl* Seq 6. *Eccl* Chip. Nort. RDn. Abol eccl 1851 to help cr Sarsden with Churhill EP.[146]

SARSDEN WITH CHURCHILL

EP Cr 1851 by union Sarsden AP, Churchill AP.[146] Chip. Nort. RDn. Bdry: 1953.[158]

SEACOURT

Church in ruins by 15th cent, treated later as free chapel then as ex-par place, sep CP 1858,[19] pt Oxon (Oxf. MB/CB), pt Berks (Hormer Hd), Abingdon PLU, pt Oxf. USD, pt Abingdon RSD. Made 2 sep CPs 1894, 'Seacourt' in Berks, 'Unnamed' (because no name assigned) in Oxon, qv).[192]

SHELLINGFORD

AP In Berks, qv, transf 1974 to Oxon.[1]

SHELSWELL

AP *LG* Plough. Hd, Bic. PLU, RSD, RD. Abol civ 1932 to help cr Newton Purcell with Shelswell CP.[8] *Parl* Mid Dv (1885–1918), Henley Dv (1918–48). *Eccl* Bic. RDn. Abol eccl 1850 to help cr Newton Purcell with Shelswell EP.[162]

SHENINGTON

AP In Glos (Tewkesbury Hd) though situated in Oxon, transf to Oxon 1832 for parl purposes, 1844 for civ purposes.[60] *LG* Blox. Hd, Banb. PLU, RSD, RD. Abol civ 1970 to help cr Shenington with Alkerton CP.[9] *Parl* Seq 6. *Eccl* In Worcester dioc until 1541 (Campden RDn),

Glouc dioc 1541–1837, Worcester dioc 1837–1900, Dedd. RDn (Oxford dioc, 1900–*).

SHENINGTON WITH ALKERTON

CP Cr 1970 by union Shenington AP, Alkerton AP.[9] *LG* Banb. RD.

SHIFFORD

Chap in Bampton AP, sep CP 1866,[2] eccl severed 1845 to help cr Bampton Aston with Shifford EP.[22] *LG* Bamp. Hd, Witney PLU, RSD, RD. Abol 1954 to help cr Aston Bampton and Shifford CP.[15] *Parl* Mid Dv (1885–1918), Banb. Dv (1918–48).

SHILTON

AP *LG* Pt Berks (Faringdon Hd), pt Oxon (Bamp. Hd), the former transf to Oxon 1832 for parl purposes, 1844 for civ purposes,[60] so that par ent Oxon thereafter. *LG* Witney PLU, RSD, RD. Addtl civ bdry alt: 1932.[8] *Parl* Seq 2. *Eccl* Seq 10.

SHIPLAKE

AP *LG* Seq 4. Civ bdry: 1952 (incl help cr Sonning Common CP).[26] *Parl* Seq 7. *Eccl* Seq 7. Eccl bdry: 1854 (help cr Kidmore End EP).[69]

SHIPTON-ON-CHERWELL

AP *LG* Woott. Hd, Woods. PLU, RSD, RD (1894–1932), Plough. RD (1932–55). Abol civ 1955 to help cr Shipton-on-Cherwell and Thrup CP.[184] *Parl* Woods. Parl Bor (1832–85), Mid Dv (1885–1918), Banb. Dv/CC (1918–70). *Eccl* Seq 11. Eccl bdry: 1952,[38] 1953.[158]

SHIPTON-ON-CHERWELL AND THRUP

CP Cr 1955 by union Shipton-on-Cherwell AP, Thrup CP.[184] *LG* Plough. RD. *Parl* Mid-Oxon CC (1970–*).

SHIPTON-UNDER-WYCHWOOD

AP Incl chap Ascott-under-Wychwood (sep civ identity early, sep EP 1763[16]), chap Ramsden (sep EP 1843,[16] eccl refounded 1861,[183] sep CP 1866[2]), chap Leafield (erected *temp* Eliz I, sep EP 1745,[16] gains eccl 1860 ex-par Wychwood and sometimes thereafter eccl 'Leafield cum Wychwood',[144] sep CP 1866 as 'Leafield'[2]), chap and hmlt Lyneham (sep CP 1866,[2] eccl severed 1895 to help cr Milton-under-Wychwood EP[156]), tp and chap Milton-under-Wychwood (sep CP 1866,[2] sep EP 1895 [incl chap Lyneham][156]). *LG* Seq 9. Addtl civ bdy alt: 1932 (gains Langley CP),[8] 1954.[12] *Parl* Seq 6. *Eccl* Seq 8.

SHIRBURN

AP *LG* Seq 19. *Parl* Seq 7. *Eccl* Seq 1.

SHOTOVER

Ex-par place, sep CP 1858.[19] *LG* Bull. Hd, Head. PLU (1858[164]–81), RSD. Bdry: 1881.[85] Abol 1881 to help cr Forest Hill with Shotover CP.[111]

SHRIVENHAM

AP In Berks, qv, transf 1974 to Oxon.[1]

SHUTFORD

Chap in Swalcliffe AP, divided for civ purposes into 2 tps of East Shutford, West Shutford, each sep CP 1866,[2] the chap a sep EP 1968.[39] Dedd. RDn.

CP Cr 1932 by union East Shutford CP, West Shutford CP.[8] *LG* Banb. RD. *Parl* Banb. CC (1948–*).

EAST SHUTFORD

Tp in Swalcliffe AP (pt of Shutford chap, qv for eccl organisation), sep CP 1866.[2] *LG* Banb. Hd, PLU, RSD, RD. Abol 1932 to help cr Shutford CP.[8] *Parl* N'rn Dv (1885–1918), Banb. Dv (1918–48).

WEST SHUTFORD

Organisation as for East Shutford.

SIBFORD

EP Cr 1842 by union tps Sibford Gower, Sibford Ferris, Epwell in Swalcliffe AP.[16] Pec jurisd (1842–46), Dedd. RDn (1846–*).

SIBFORD FERRIS

Tp (pec jurisd) in Swalcliffe AP (for eccl see 'Sibford'), sep CP 1866.[2] *LG* Seq 5. *Parl* Seq 6.

SIBFORD GOWER

Organisation as for Sibford Ferris.

SOMERTON

AP *LG* Seq 17. Civ bdry: 1888.[31] *Parl* Seq 4. *Eccl* Seq 2.

SONNING

AP Pt Berks (Sonning Hd), pt Oxon (Eye and Dunsden Lbty, Binf. Hd), the latter sep CP 1866 in Oxon[2] (eccl sep EP 1876 as 'Dunsden'[104]) so that Sonning ent Berks thereafter. *LG* Wokingham PLU. For later civ organisation and for eccl, see entry in Berks; Oxon area incl in cr 1854 of Kidmore End EP.[69]

SONNING COMMON

CP Cr 1952 from Eye and Dunsden CP, Kidmore End CP, Shiplake AP.[26] *LG* Henley RD. *Parl* Henley CC (1970–*).

SOULDERN

AP *LG* Seq 17. Civ bdry: 1953.[116] *Parl* Seq 4. *Eccl* Seq 2.

SPARSHOLT

AP In Berks, qv, transf 1974 to Oxon.[1]

SPELSBURY

AP *LG* Seq 9. *Parl* Seq 6. *Eccl* Chip. Nort. RDn. Abol eccl 1963 to help cr Spelsbury with Chadlington EP.[71]

SPELSBURY WITH CHADLINGTON

EP Cr 1963 by union Spelsbury AP, tg Chadlington in Charlbury AP.[71] Chip. Nort. RDn.

STADHAMPTON

AP Chap in Dorchester AP, sep par before 16th cent.[185] *LG* Seq 7. Civ bdry: 1932 (incl gains Chislehampton CP).[8] *Parl* Seq 7. *Eccl* Donative, pec jurisd Dorch. Abol eccl 1841 to help cr Stadhampton with Chislehampton EP.[77]

STADHAMPTON WITH CHISLEHAMPTON

EP Cr 1841 by union Stadhampton AP, Chislehampton EP.[77] Pec jurisd Dorch. (1841–46), Cudd. RDn (1846–*)

STANDLAKE

AP *LG* Seq 1. Civ bdry: 1886,[11] 1932.[8] *Parl* Seq 2. *Eccl* Seq 10.

STANFORD IN THE VALE

AP In Berks, qv, transf 1974 to Oxon.[1]

STANTON HARCOURT

AP Incl chap South Leigh (sep civ identity early,

sep EP 1868[145]). *LG* Seq 22. Civ bdry: 1886,[145] 1932.[8] *Parl* Seq 2. *Eccl* Woods. RDn (until 1952), Witney RDn (1952–*).

STANTON ST JOHN

AP Incl chap Forest Hill (sep par perhaps in 1273, certainly by 1341[110]). *LG* Seq 8. Civ bdry: 1932,[8] 1949.[113] *Parl* Seq 5. *Eccl* Seq 5.

STEVENTON

AP In Berks, qv, transf 1974 to Oxon.[1]

NORTH STOKE

AP Incl chap Newnham Murren (sep civ identity early, eccl severed 1928 to help cr Crowmarsh Gifford with Newnham Murren EP[94]). *LG* Langt. Hd, Wallingford PLU, RSD, Crowm. RD. Abol civ 1932 to help cr Crowmarsh CP.[8] *Parl* S'rn Dv (1885–1918), Henley Dv (1918–48). *Eccl* Henley RDn (until 1852), Nettlebed RDn (1852–74), Henley RDn (1874–*). Eccl bdry: 1849 (from area chap Newnham Murren, help cr Stoke Row EP).[138]

SOUTH STOKE

AP *LG* Dorch. Hd, Wallingford PLU, RSD, Crowm. RD (1894–1932), Henley RD (1932–74). Civ bdry: 1952.[26] *Parl* Seq 7. *Eccl* Henley RDn (until 1852), Nettlebed RDn (1852–74), Henley RDn (1874–*).

STOKE LYNE

AP *LG* Seq 17. Civ bdry: 1948.[37] *Parl* Seq 4. *Eccl* Seq 2. Eccl bdry: 1907 (cr Fewcot EP).[108]

STOKE ROW

EP Cr 1849 from Ipsden AP, Newnham Murren chap in North Stoke AP, Mongewell AP.[138] Henley RDn (1849–52), Nettlebed RDn (1852–74), Henley RDn (1874–*).

CP Cr 1952 from Crowmarsh CP, Ipsden AP.[26] *LG* Henley RD. *Parl* Henley CC (1970–*).

STOKE TALMAGE

AP *LG* Seq 19. *Parl* Seq 7. *Eccl* Seq 1.

STOKENCHURCH

Chap in Aston Rowant AP, sep civ identity early, some sep eccl rights early,[23] sep EP 1844.[24] *LG* Lewk. Hd, Wycombe PLU, RSD, sep RD in Oxon (1894–96). Transf 1896 to Bucks.[134] *Parl* S'rn Dv (1885–1918), Bucks thereafter. *Eccl* Aston RDn (1844–1973), Wycombe RDn (Bucks AD, 1973–*). Eccl bdry: 1852 (help cr Cadmore End EP,[64] refounded 1853[65]), 1961.[163]

STONESFIELD

AP *LG* Seq 24. *Parl* Woods. Parl Bor (1832–85), Seq 1 thereafter. *Eccl* Seq 11.

STONOR

CP Cr 1896 from Pyrton AP.[17] *LG* Henley PLU, RD. Abol 1922 to help cr Pishill with Stonor CP.[182] *Parl* Henley Dv (1918–48).

STOWE

AP In Bucks (Buckingham Hd), incl hmlt Boycott (Oxon, Plough. Hd), the latter transf to Bucks 1832 for parl purposes, 1844 for civ purposes,[60] so that Stowe ent Bucks thereafter. *LG* Buckingham PLU; for later and for eccl organisation, see main entry in Bucks.

STOWOOD

AP *LG* Bull. Hd, Head. PLU, RSD, RD. Civ bdry: 1929.[88] Abol civ 1932 to help cr Beckley and Stowood CP.[8] *Parl* Mid Dv (1885–1918), Henley Dv (1918–48).

STRATTON AUDLEY

AP Chap in Bicester AP, sep par prob 1455.[41] *LG* Pt Bucks (Buckingham Hd), pt Oxon (Plough. Hd), the former transf to Oxon 1832 for parl purposes, 1844 for civ purposes,[60] so that par ent Oxon thereafter, Seq 17. Addtl civ bdry alt: 1883,[21] 1886.[31] *Parl* Seq 4. *Eccl* Seq 2. Eccl bdry: 1928.[67]

STUDLEY

Hmlts (Bucks, Ashendon Hd), in Beckley AP (otherwise Oxon), transf to Oxon 1832 for parl purposes, 1844 for civ purposes,[60] in two pts, one 'Studley', the other 'Horton cum Studley' (qv, incl sep civ and eccl identity), Studley sep CP 1866.[2] *LG* Bull. Hd, Head. PLU, RSD, RD. Abol 1932 ent to Horton cum Studley CP.[8] *Parl* Mid Dv (1885–1918), Henley Dv (1918–48).

SUMMERTOWN

EP Cr 1833 from Oxford St Giles AP.[125] Oxf. RDn. Bdry: 1863 (help cr Oxford St Philip and St James EP),[177] 1896 (help cr Oxford St Margaret EP),[179] 1905 (help cr Oxford St Andrew EP).[172]

SUNNINGWELL

AP In Berks, qv, transf 1974 to Oxon.[1]

SUTTON COURTENAY

AP In Berks, qv, transf 1974 to Oxon.[1]

SWALCLIFFE

AP Incl chap Shutford (eccl severed *ca* 1840 to help cr Shenington with Alkerton and Shutford EP,[10] civ divided into 2 tps of East Shutford, West Shutford, each sep CP 1866[2]), tp Epwell (sep CP 1866,[2] eccl severed 1842 to help cr Sibford EP[16]), tps Sibford Ferris, Sibford Gower (each sep CP 1866,[2] each pec jurisd, eccl united 1842 with tp Epwell to cr Sibford EP[16]). *LG* Banb. Hd (pt until 1866, ent from 1866 [incl Epwell, Shutford], pt Blox. Hd (until 1866 [Sibford Ferris, Sibford Gower]), Banb. PLU, RSD, RD. *Parl* Seq 6. *Eccl* Seq 6.

SWERFORD

AP *LG* Seq 9. Civ bdry: 1932.[8] *Parl* Seq 6. *Eccl* Sometimes as 'Sweford with Showell', Seq 8.

SWINBROOK

AP Incl chaps Fifield, Idbury (each sep civ identity early, each sep CP 1750[131]). *LG* Chadl. Hd, Witney PLU, RSD, RD. Addtl civ bdry alt: 1883,[1] 1886.[11] Abol civ 1932 pt to Asthall AP, pt to Shilton AP, pt to help cr Swinbrook and Widford CP.[8] *Parl* Mid Dv (1885–1918), Banb. Dv (1918–48). *Eccl* Witney RDn. Abol eccl 1859 to help cr Swinbrook with Widford EP.[186]

SWINBROOK AND WIDFORD

CP Cr 1932 by union pts Swinbrook AP, Widford AP, Fulbrook CP, Shilton AP.[8] *LG* Witney RD. *Parl* Banb. CC (1948–70), Mid-Oxon CC (1970–*).

SWINBROOK WITH WIDFORD
EP Cr 1859 by union Swinbrook AP, Widford AP (dioc Glouc & Bristol), to be in dioc Oxon.[186] Witney RDn.

SWYNCOMBE
AP *LG* Seq 12. Civ bdry: 1952.[26] *Parl* Seq 7. *Eccl* Henley RDn (until 1852), Nettlebed RDn (1852–74), Aston RDn (1874–*). Eccl bdry: 1973.[46]

SYDENHAM
Chap in Thame AP, sep civ identity early, sep EP 1841.[187] *LG* Seq 16. Civ bdry: 1954.[7] *Parl* Seq 7. *Eccl* Pec jurisd Thame (1841–46), Aston RDn (1846–1973). Abol eccl 1973 to help cr Chinnor with Emmington and Sydenham EP.[75]

TACKLEY
AP *LG* Seq 24. *Parl* Woods. Parl Bor (1832–85), Seq 1 thereafter. *Eccl* Seq 11.

TADMARTON
AP *LG* Seq 5. *Parl* Seq 6. *Eccl* Seq 6.

TAYNTON
AP *LG* Seq 10. Civ bdry: 1886.[11] *Parl* Seq 2. *Eccl* Witney RDn (until 1929), Northleach RDn (dioc Gloucester, Cheltenham AD, 1929–*).

TETSWORTH
Chap in Thame AP, sep civ identity early, sep EP 1841.[187] *LG* Seq 20. Civ bdry: 1932 (gains Attington CP).[8] *Parl* Seq 7. *Eccl* Pec jurisd Thame (1841–46), Aston RDn (1846–*).

DUNS TEW
AP *LG* Seq 23. *Parl* Seq 6. *Eccl* Seq 11.

GREAT TEW
AP Incl chap Little Tew (sep civ identity early, sep EP 1855[188]), chap Nether Worton (sep civ identity early, sep EP 1745[16]). *LG* Seq 21. *Parl* Seq 6. *Eccl* Dedd. RDn (until 1930), Chip. Nort. RDn (1930–*).

LITTLE TEW
Chap in Great Tew AP, sep civ identity early, sep EP 1855.[188] *LG* Woott. Hd, Chip. Nort. PLU, RSD, RD. Civ bdry: 1932.[8] *Parl* Seq 6. *Eccl* Dedd. RDn (until 1915), Chip. Nort. RDn (1915–*).

THAME
AP Incl chaps Tetsworth, Sydenham (both in Oxon), chap Towersey (in Bucks) (each sep civ identity early in respective cos, each sep EP 1841[187]), chap Stokenchurch (sep civ identity early, sep EP 1844[24]). *LG* Thame Hd, Bor (status not sustained), PLU, USD, UD. Addtl civ bdry alt: 1932.[8] *Parl* Seq 7. *Eccl* Pec jurisd Thame (until 1846), Aston RDn (1846–*).

THOMLEY
Hmlt in Waterperry AP, sep CP 1866.[2] *LG* Bull. Hd, Thame PLU, RSD, RD (1894–1932), Bull. RD (1932–74). *Parl* Seq 8.

THRUP
Hmlt in Kidlington AP, sep CP 1866.[2] *LG* Woott. Hd, Woods. PLU, RSD, RD (1894–1932), Plough. RD (1932–55). Bdry: 1883,[21] 1932.[8] Abol 1955 to help cr Shipton-on-Cherwell and Thrup CP.[184] *Parl* Mid Dv (1885–1918), Banb. Dv/CC (1918–70).

TIDDINGTON
Hmlt in Albury AP, sep CP 1866.[2] *LG* Bull. Hd, Thame PLU, RSD, RD. Abol 1932 to help cr Tiddington with Albury CP.[8] *Parl* S'rn Dv (1885–1918), Henley Dv (1918–48).

TIDDINGTON WITH ALBURY
CP Cr 1932 by union Tiddington CP, Albury AP.[8] *LG* Bull. RD. Bdry: 1954.[7] *Parl* Henley CC (1948–70), Mid-Oxon CC (1970–*).

TOWERSEY
Chap in Thame AP, situated in Bucks and sep civ identity there early, sep EP 1841.[187] Transf 1933 from Bucks to Oxon,[143] Bull. RD. *Parl* In Bucks until 1948, Henley CC (1948–*). *Eccl* See entry in Bucks.

TUSMORE
AP *LG* Plough. Hd, Bic. PLU, RSD, RD. Abol civ 1932 to help cr Hardwick with Tusmore CP.[8] *Parl* Mid Dv (1885–1918), Henley Dv (1918–48). *Eccl* Bic. RDn. Abol eccl *ca* 1840 to help cr Hardwick-cum-Tusmore EP.[121]

UFFINGTON
AP In Berks, qv, transf 1974 to Oxon.[1]

UNNAMED
Cr 1894 when Seacourt CP (Berks, Oxon) becomes two sep CPs, Seacourt in Berks, this par (to which no name given) in Oxon.[192] *LG* Abingdon PLU, Oxf. CB. Abol 1929 ent to St Giles and St John CP.[88] *Parl* Oxf. Parl Bor (1918–48).

UPTON
CP In Berks, qv, transf 1974 to Oxon.[1]

UPTON AND SIGNET
Hmlts in Burford AP, united 1866 to cr this CP.[2] *LG* Bamp. Hd, Witney PLU, RSD, RD. Bdry: 1886.[11] Abol 1954 to help cr Burford and Upton and Signet CP.[17] *Parl* Mid Dv (1885–1918), Banb. Dv/CC (1918–70).

WALLINGFORD
CP In Berks, qv, transf 1974 to Oxon.[1]

WANTAGE
AP In Berks, qv, transf 1974 to Oxon.[1]

WARBOROUGH
AP *LG* Seq 11. Civ bdry: 1932.[8] *Parl* Seq 7. *Eccl* Pec jurisd Dorch. (until 1847), Cudd. RDn (1847–1915), Wallingford RDn (Berks AD, 1915–56). Cudd. RDn (1956–*).

WARDINGTON
Chap (pec jurisd Banb.) in Cropredy AP, sep EP 1851,[78] sep CP 1866.[2] *LG* Seq 2. Bdry: 1883,[21] 1888.[93] *Parl* Seq 6. *Eccl* Dedd. RDn.

WARKWORTH
AP Pt Northants (King's Sutton Hd, incl tg Neithrop), pt Oxon (chap Grimsbury), the former sep CP 1866 in Oxon,[2] the latter sep CP 1894 in Oxon[25] so that Warkworth ent Northants thereafter, Grimsbury sep EP 1921 from area South Banbury EP.[34] *LG* Banb. PLU, pt Banb. MB (Grimsbury, 1889–94), pt Banb. USD (Grimsbury, 1875–94), pt Banb. RSD. For later civ and for eccl organisation, see main entry in Northants.

WARPSGROVE
AP *LG* Ew. Hd, Thame PLU, RSD, RD. Abol civ 1932 ent to Chalgrove AP.[8] *Parl* S'rn Dv (1885–1918), Henley Dv (1918–48). *Eccl* Aston RDn.

WATCHFIELD
CP In Berks, qv, transf 1974 to Oxon.[1]

WATERPERRY
AP Incl hmlt Thomley (sep CP 1866[2]). *LG* Bull. Hd, Thame PLU, RSD, RD (1894–1932), Bull. RD (1932–74). *Parl* Seq 8. *Eccl* Seq 4.

WATERSTOCK
AP *LG* Seq 20. Civ bdry: 1886 (gains the pt of Ickford AP [Bucks, Oxon] in Oxon so that Ickford ent Bucks thereafter),[152] 1954.[7] *Parl* Seq 8. *Eccl* Seq 4.

WATLINGTON
AP *LG* Seq 18. Civ bdry: 1932.[8] *Parl* Seq 7. *Eccl* Seq 1.

WENDLEBURY
AP *LG* Seq 17. *Parl* Seq 3. *Eccl* Seq 2.

SOUTH WESTON
AP *LG* Pyrton Hd, Thame PLU, RSD, RD (1894–1932), Bull. RD (1932–54). Civ bdry: 1932.[8] Abol civ 1954 ent to Lewknor AP.[7] *Parl* S'rn Dv (1885–1918), Henley Dv/CC (1918–70). *Eccl* Seq 1.

WESTON-ON-THE-GREEN
AP *LG* Seq 17. Civ bdry: 1932.[8] *Parl* Seq 3. *Eccl* Seq 2.

WESTWELL
AP *LG* Seq 1. *Parl* Seq 2. *Eccl* Seq 10.

WHEATFIELD
AP *LG* Seq 19. *Parl* Seq 7. *Eccl* Seq 1. Eccl bdry: 1929.[72]

WHEATLEY
Hmlt and chap in Cuddesdon AP, sep EP 1745,[16] eccl refounded 1854,[95] sep CP 1866.[2] *LG* Bull.Hd, Head. PLU, Wheatley USD, UD (1894–1932), Bull. RD (1932–74). Civ bdry: 1932,[8] 1954.[7] *Parl* Seq 8. *Eccl* Cudd. RDn.

WHITCHURCH
AP *LG* Pt Oxon (Langt. Hd), pt Berks (Reading Hd), Bradfield PLU, RSD, Goring RD (1894–1932), Henley RD (1932–74). Civ bdry: 1883,[21] 1894 (the pt in Berks transf to Purley AP, Berks, and Whitchurch ent Oxon thereafter),[194] 1952.[26] *Parl* Oxon pt, Seq 7. *Eccl* Henley RDn (until 1852), Nettlebed RDn (1852–74), Henley RDn (1874–*).

WIDFORD
AP In Glos (Slaughter Hd) but situated in Oxon, transf to Oxon 1832 for parl purposes, 1844 for civ purposes.[60] *LG* Bamp. Hd, Witney PLU, RSD, RD. Abol civ 1932 pt to help cr Swinbrook and Widford CP, pt to Shilton AP.[8] *Parl* Mid Dv (1885–1918), Banb. Dv (1918–48). *Eccl* Stow RDn (dioc Worc [until 1541]/Glouc [1541–1836]/Glouc & Britsol [from 1836], Gloucester AD). Abol eccl 1859 to help cr Swinbrook with Widford EP, to be in dioc Oxf.[186]

WIGGINTON
AP *LG* Seq 5. *Parl* Seq 6. *Eccl* Seq 6. Eccl bdry: 1854 (help cr Milcombe EP).[49]

WILCOTE
AP *LG* Woott. Hd, Witney PLU, RSD, RD. Abol civ 1932 ent to North Leigh AP.[8] *Parl* Mid Dv (1885–1918), Banb. Dv (1918–48). *Eccl* Woods. RDn (until 1953), Chip. Nort. RDn (1953–*).

WITNEY
AP Incl hmlt Curbridge (sep CP 1866[2]), chap Hailey (sep EP 1761,[16] abol eccl 1854 to help cr Hailey with Crawley EP,[92] sep CP 1866[2]), hmlt and chap Crawley (sep CP 1866,[2] eccl severed 1854 and united with Crawley EP to cr Hailey with Crawley EP[92]). *LG* Bamp. Hd, Witney Bor (status not sustained), PLU, USD, RD. Addtl civ bdry alt: 1883,[21] 1898,[82] 1932,[8] 1963,[100] 1968.[119] *Parl* Witney Parl Bor (1304–06 only), Seq 2 thereafter. *Eccl* Seq 10.

LITTLE WITTNEHAM
AP In Berks, qv, transf 1974 to Oxon.[1]

LONG WITTENHAM
AP In Berks, qv, transf 1974 to Oxon.[1]

WOLVERCOTT
Chap in Oxford St Peter in the East AP, sep civ identity early, sep EP 1759.[16] *LG* Woott. Hd, Woodst. PLU, pt Oxf. Bor[194]/MB/CB, pt Oxf. USD, pt Woods. RSD, Woods. RD. Civ bdry: 1883,[1] 1894 (loses the pt in the CB pt to Binsey AP, pt to Oxford St Giles AP).[42] *Parl* Pt Oxf. Parl Bor (until 1918), pt Mid Dv (1885–1918), Banb. Dv (1918–48). *Eccl* Oxf. RDn. Eccl bdry: 1972.[140]

WOODCOTE
CP Cr 1952 from Goring AP, South Stoke AP.[26] *LG* Henley RD. *Parl* Henley CC (1970–*).

WOODEATON
AP *LG* Seq 8. *Parl* Seq 5. *Eccl* Cudd. RDn (until 1852), Isl. RDn (1852–1956), Bic. & Isl. RDn (1956–*).

WOODSTOCK
Hmlt, chap and bor in Wootton AP, sep civ identity early, eccl severed 1877 to help cr Woodstock with Bladon EP,[47] the latter sometimes 'Bladon with Woodstock'. *LG* Woott. Hd, Lbty Oxf., Woods. Bor, MB (1886–1974), USD (1886–94), PLU, RSD (1875–86). Bdry: 1897.[48] *Parl* Woods. Parl Bor (1302–04, 1571–1885), Mid Dv (1885–1918), Banb. Dv/CC (1918–*).

WOODSTOCK WITH BLADON
EP Cr 1877 by union chap Woodstock in Wootton AP, Bladon AP.[47] Woods. RDn. Bdry: 1951,[190] 1953.[158] Sometimes 'Bladon with Woodstock'.

OLD WOODSTOCK
CP Cr 1894 from the pt of Wootton AP in Woods. MB.[25] *LG* Woods. PLU, MB. *Parl* Banb. Dv/CC (1918–*).

WOOLSTONE
CP In Berks, qv, transf 1974 to Oxon.[1]

WOOTTON
AP Incl hmlt, chap and bor Woodstock (sep civ identity early, eccl severed 1877 to help cr Woodstock with Bladon EP,[47] sometimes 'Bla-

don with Woodstock'). *LG* Woott. Hd, Woods. PLU, pt Woods. MB & USD (1886–94), Woods. RSD (ent 1875–86, pt 1886–94), Woods. RD (1894–1932), Chip. Nort. RD (1932–74). Addtl civ bdry alt: 1894 (the pt in the MB cr Old Woodstock CP).[25] *Parl* Woods. Parl Bor (1832–85), Seq 1 thereafter. *Eccl* Seq 11. Addtl eccl bdry alt: 1951.[190]

WOOTTON

CP In Berks, qv, transf 1974 to Oxon.[1]

WORTON

CP Cr 1932 by union Nether Worton CP, Over Worton AP.[8] *LG* Chip. Nort. RD. *Parl* Banb. CC (1948–*).

NETHER WORTON

Chap in Great Tew AP, sep civ identity early, sep EP 1745.[16] *LG* Woott. Hd, Woods. PLU, RSD, RD. Abol civ 1932 to help cr Worton CP.[8] *Parl* N'rn Dv (1885–1918), Banb. Dv (1918–48). *Eccl* Dedd. RDn. Abol eccl 1928 to help cr Over with Nether Worton EP.[191]

OVER WORTON

AP *LG* Woott. Hd, Woods. PLU, RSD, RD. Civ abol, *Parl*, *Eccl* as for Over Worton.

OVER WITH NETHER WORTON

EP Cr 1928 by union Over Worton AP, Nether Worton EP.[191] Dedd. RDn.

WROXTON

AP Usual civ spelling; for eccl see following entry. *LG* Seq 5. *Parl* Seq 6.

WROXTON WITH BALSCOTE

AP Usual eccl spelling. for civ see prev entry. *Eccl* Seq 6.

WYCHWOOD

Ex-par forest, sep CP 1858,[19] eccl transf 1860 to Leafield EP,[144] the latter sometimes thereafter 'Leafield cum Wychwood'. *LG* Chadl. Hd, Chip. Nort. PLU, RSD, RD. Abol 1949 pt to help cr Cornbury and Wychwood CP, pt to Leafield CP.[83] *Parl* N'rn Dv (1885–1918), Banb. Dv/CC (1918–70).

WYTHAM

AP In Berks, qv, transf 1974 to Oxon.[1]

YARNTON

AP *LG* Seq 25. Civ bdry: 1883,[21] 1932 (incl gains Land Common to Begbroke and Yarnton pars [Oxey Mead, Yarnton (or West) Mead]).[8] *Parl* Seq 2. *Eccl* Seq 11.

YELFORD

AP *LG* Bamp. Hd, Witney PLU, RSD, RD. Civ bdry: 1883.[21] Abol civ 1932 to help cr Hardwick-with-Yelford CP.[8] *Parl* Mid Dv (1885–1918), Banb. Dv (1918–48). *Eccl* Seq 10.

SOMERSET

ABBREVIATIONS

Abbreviations particular to Somerset follow. Those general abbreviations in use throughout the *Guide* are found on page xix.

Abd. & Bulst.	Abdick and Bulstone
Andersf.	Andersfield
Axbr.	Axbridge
Bedm.	Bedminster
Bempst.	Bempstone
Bridgw.	Bridgwater
Brisl.	Brislington
Cann.	Cannington
Carhamp.	Carhampton
Clut.	Clutton
Crewk.	Crewkerne
Dulv.	Dulverton
Dunst.	Dunster
Exm.	Exmoor
Glaston.	Glastonbury
Hamp. & Clav.	Hampton and Claverton
Hartcl.	Hartcliffe
Houndsb., Barw. & Coker	Houndsborough, Barwick and Coker
Horeth.	Horethorne
Ilch.	Ilchester
Ilmin.	Ilminster
Keyn.	Keynsham
Kilm.	Kilmersdon
Kingsbr.	Kingsbridge
Langp.	Langport
Lock.	Locking
Mart.	Martock
Merst.	Merston
Mids. Nort.	Midsomer Norton
Milb.	Milborne
Peth.	Petherton
Portish.	Portishead
Quantk.	Quantock
Quantoxhd.	Quantoxhead
Redcl.	Redcliffe
Shept. Mal.	Shepton Mallet
Somert.	Somerton
Taun.	Taunton
W-s-M.	Weston-super-Mare
Welling.	Wellington
Willit & Freem.	Williton and Freemanors
Wincan.	Wincanton
Wivel.	Wiveliscombe
Yeov.	Yeovil

SEQUENCES

An abbreviated entry prefixed by 'Seq' is used in the parochial entries to avoid repeating often the names of superior units of administration. The content of each sequence is shown below.

Local Government Sequences ('LG')

SEQ 1 Abd. & Bulst. Hd, Chard PLU, RSD, RD
SEQ 2 Abd. & Bulst. Hd, Langp. PLU, RSD, RD
SEQ 3 Abd. & Bulst. Hd, Taun. PLU, RSD, RD
SEQ 4 Andersf. Hd, Bridgw. PLU, RSD, RD
SEQ 5 Bath Forum Hd, Bath PLU, RSD, RD (1894–1933), Bathavon RD (1933–74)
SEQ 6 Bath Forum Hd, Keyn. PLU, RSD, RD (1894–1933), Bathavon RD (1933–74)
SEQ 7 Bempst. Hd, Axbr. PLU, RSD, RD
SEQ 8 Brent with Wrington Hd, Axbr. PLU, RSD, RD
SEQ 9 Bruton Hd, Wincan. PLU, RSD, RD
SEQ 10 Cann. Hd, Bridgw. PLU, RSD, RD
SEQ 11 Carhamp. Hd, Willit. PLU, RSD, RD
SEQ 12 Catsash Hd, Langp. PLU, RSD, RD
SEQ 13 Catsash Hd, Wincan. PLU, RSD, RD
SEQ 14 Chew Hd, Clut. PLU, RSD, RD
SEQ 15 Chewton Hd, Bedm. PLU (1836–99), RSD, Long Ashton PLU (1899–1930), RD
SEQ 16 Chewton Hd, Clut. PLU, RSD, RD
SEQ 17 Crewk. Hd, Chard PLU, RSD, RD
SEQ 18 N Curry Hd, Taun. PLU, RSD, RD
SEQ 19 Frome Hd, PLU, RSD, RD
SEQ 20 Glaston. Twelve Hides Hd, Wells PLU, RSD, RD
SEQ 21 Hamp. & Clav. Hd, Bath PLU, RSD, RD (1894–1933), Bathavon RD (1933–74)
SEQ 22 Hartcl. with Bedm. Hd, Bedm. PLU (1836–99), RSD, Long Ashton PLU (1899–1930), RD
SEQ 23 Horeth. Hd, Wincan. PLU, RSD, RD
SEQ 24 Houndsb., Barw. & Coker Hd, Yeov. PLU, RSD, RD
SEQ 25 Keyn. Hd, Clut. PLU, RSD, RD
SEQ 26 Keyn. Hd, PLU, RSD, RD (1894–1933), Bathavon RD (1933–74)
SEQ 27 Kilm. Hd, Frome PLU, RSD, RD
SEQ 28 Kilm. Hd, Shept. Mal. PLU, RSD, RD
SEQ 29 E Kingsbury Hd, Chard PLU, RSD, RD
SEQ 30 W Kingsbury Hd, Taun. PLU, RSD, RD
SEQ 31 W Kingsbury Hd, Welling. PLU, RSD, RD
SEQ 32 Milverton Hd, Welling. PLU, RSD, RD
SEQ 33 Norton Ferris Hd, Wincan. PLU, RSD, RD
SEQ 34 N Petherton Hd, Bridgw. PLU, RSD, RD
SEQ 35 S Petherton Hd, Chard PLU, RSD, RD
SEQ 36 Pitney Hd, Langp. PLU, RSD, RD
SEQ 37 Portbury Hd, Bedm. PLU (1836–99), RSD, Long Ashton PLU (1899–1930), RD
SEQ 38 Somert. Hd, Langp. PLU, RSD, RD
SEQ 39 Somert. Hd, Yeov. PLU, RSD, RD
SEQ 40 Stone Hd, Yeov. PLU, RSD, RD
SEQ 41 Taun. & Taun. Dean Hd, Taun. PLU, RSD, RD
SEQ 42 Taun. & Taun. Dean Hd, Welling. PLU, RSD, RD
SEQ 43 Tintinhull Hd, Yeov. PLU, RSD, RD
SEQ 44 Wellow Hd, Bath PLU, RSD, RD (1894–1933), Bathavon RD (1933–74)
SEQ 45 Wellow Hd, Frome PLU, RSD, RD
SEQ 46 Wellow Hd, Keyn. PLU, RSD, RD (1894–1933), Batavon RD (1933–74)
SEQ 47 Wells Forum Hd, Shept. Mal. PLU, RSD, RD
SEQ 48 Wells Forum Hd, Wells PLU, RSD, RD
SEQ 49 Whitley Hd, Bridgw. PLU, RSD, RD
SEQ 50 Whitstone Hd, Shept. Mal. PLU, RSD, RD
SEQ 51 Willit. & Freem. Hd, Dulv. PLU, RSD, RD
SEQ 52 Willit. & Freem. Hd, Willit. PLU, RSD, RD
SEQ 53 Winterstoke Hd, Axbr. PLU, RSD, RD
SEQ 54 Winterstoke Hd, Bedm. PLU (1836–99), RSD, Long Ashton PLU (1899–1930), RD

Parliamentary Sequences ('Parl')

SEQ 1 E'rn Dv (1832–67), East Dv (1867–85), Frome Dv (1885–1948), N Somerset CC (1948–*)
SEQ 2 E'rn Dv (1832–67), East Dv (1867–85), Frome Dv (1885–1948), Wells CC (1948–*)
SEQ 3 E'rn Dv (1832–67), East Dv (1867–85), N'rn Dv (1885–1918), Frome Dv (1918–48), N Somerset CC (1948–*)
SEQ 4 E'rn Dv (1832–67), East Dv (1867–85), N'rn Dv (1885–1918), Wells Dv/CC (1918–*)
SEQ 5 E'rn Dv (1832–67), East Dv (1867–85), N'rn Dv (1885–1918), W-s-M Dv/CC (1918–70), N Somerset CC (1970–*)
SEQ 6 E'rn Dv (1832–67), East Dv (1867–85), N'rn Dv (1885–1918), W-s-M Dv/CC (1918–*)
SEQ 7 E'rn Dv (1832–67), East Dv (1867–85), Wells Dv (1885–1918), W-s-M Dv/CC (1918–*)
SEQ 8 E'rn Dv (1832–67), Mid Dv (1867–85), E'rn Dv (1885–1918), Wells Dv/CC (1918–*)
SEQ 9 E'rn Dv (1832–67), Mid Dv (1867–85), E'rn Dv (1885–1918), Yeov. Dv/CC (1918–*)
SEQ 10 E'rn Dv (1832–67), Mid Dv (1867–85), Frome Dv (1885–1948), Wells CC (1948–*)
SEQ 11 E'rn Dv (1832–67), East Dv (1867–85), Frome Dv (1885–1918), Wells Dv/CC (1918–*)
SEQ 12 E'rn Dv (1832–67), Mid Dv (1867–85), S'rn Dv (1885–1918), Wells Dv/CC (1918–*)

SEQ 13 E'rn Dv (1832–67), Mid Dv (1867–85), Wells Dv/CC (1885–*)
SEQ 14 W'rn Dv (1832–67), Mid Dv (1867–85), E'rn Dv (1885–1918), Wells Dv/CC (1918–*)
SEQ 15 W'rn Dv (1832–67), Mid Dv (1867–85), E'rn Dv (1885–1918), Yeov. Dv/CC (1918–*)
SEQ 16 W'rn Dv (1832–67), Mid Dv (1867–85), S'rn Dv (1885–1918), Yeov. Dv/CC (1918–*)
SEQ 17 W'rn Dv (1832–67), West Dv (1867–85), Bridgw. Dv/CC (1885–*)
SEQ 18 W'rn Dv (1832–67), West Dv (1867–85), Bridgw. Dv (1885–1918), Taun. Dv/CC (1918–*)
SEQ 19 W'rn Dv (1832–67), West Dv (1867–85), Bridgw. Dv (1885–1918), Yeov. Dv/CC (1918–*)
SEQ 20 W'rn Dv (1832–67), West Dv (1867–85), S'rn Dv (1885–1918), Yeov. Dv/CC (1918–*)
SEQ 21 W'rn Dv (1832–67), West Dv (1867–85), W'rn Dv (1885–1918), Bridgw. Dv/CC (1918–*)
SEQ 22 W'rn Dv (1832–67), West Dv (1867–85), W'rn Dv (1885–1918), Taun. Dv/CC (1918–*)

Ecclesiastical Sequences ('Eccl')

Orig Bath AD:
SEQ 1 Bath RDn
SEQ 2 Bath RDn (until 1858), Keyn. RDn (1858–*)
SEQ 3 Redcl. & Bedm. RDn (until 1847), Bath RDn (1847–*)
SEQ 4 Redcl. & Bedm. RDn (until 1847), Bath RDn (1847–58), Keyn. RDn (1858–*)
SEQ 5 Redcl. & Bedm. RDn (until 1847), Chew RDn (1847–58), Chew Magna RDn (1858–*)
SEQ 6 Redcl. & Bedm. RDn (until 1847), Chew RDn (1847–58), Portish. RDn (1858–*)

Orig Taunton AD:
SEQ 7 Bridgw. RDn
SEQ 8 Bridgw. RDn (until 1844), Quantoxhd. RDn (1884–1973), Quantk. RDn (1973–*)
SEQ 9 Crewk. RDn
SEQ 10 Crewk. RDn (until 1872), Ilmin. RDn (1872–*)
SEQ 11 Crewk. RDn (until 1872), Ilmin. RDn (1872–1955), Taun. RDn (1955–63), Taun. S RDn (1963–*)
SEQ 12 Dunst. RDn (until 1973), Exm. RDn (1973–*)
SEQ 13 Dunst. RDn (until 1872), Wivel. RDn (1872–1973), Exm. RDn (1973–*)
SEQ 14 Dunst. RDn (until 1951), Wivel. RDn (1951–73), Exm. RDn (1973–*)
SEQ 15 Dunst. RDn (until 1872), Wivel. RDn (1872–1951), Dunst. RDn (1951–73), Exm. RDn (1973–*)
SEQ 16 Dunst. RDn (until 1872), Wivel. RDn (1872–1951), Dunst. RDn (1951–73), Quantk. RDn (1973–*)
SEQ 17 Dunst. RDn (until 1872), Wivel. RDn (1872–1973), Tone RDn (1973–*)
SEQ 18 Taun. RDn (until 1963), Taun. N RDn (1963–*)
SEQ 19 Taun. RDn (until 1963), Taun. N RDn (1963–73), Tone RDn (1973–*)
SEQ 20 Taun. RDn (until 1963), Taun. S RDn (1963–*)
SEQ 21 Taun. RDn (until 1872), Welling. RDn (1872–1973), Tone RDn (1973–*)

Orig. Wells AD:
SEQ 22 Axbr. RDn
SEQ 23 Axbr. RDn (until 1872), Burnham RDn (1872–*)
SEQ 24 Axbr. RDn (until 1872), Lock. RDn (1872–*)
SEQ 25 Cary RDn
SEQ 26 Cary RDn (until 1872), Bruton RDn (1872–*)
SEQ 27 Cary RDn (until 1872), Shept. Mal. RDn (1872–*)
SEQ 28 Frome RDn
SEQ 29 Frome RDn (until 1872), Mids. Nort. RDn (1872–*)
SEQ 30 Frome RDn (until 185), Wells RDn (185 –58), Chew Magna RDn (1858–*)
SEQ 31 Merst. RDn
SEQ 32 Merst. RDn (until 1844), Milb. Port RDn (1884–1955), Merst. RDn (1955–*)
SEQ 33 Ilch. RDn
SEQ 34 Ilch. RDn (until 1872), Mart. RDn (1872–*)
SEQ 35 Pawlet RDn (until 1956), Bridgw. RDn (1956–*)
SEQ 36 Glaston. Jurisd

DIOCESES AND ARCHDEACONRIES

With a few exceptions noted below (particulary those pars in or near Bristol) in the parochial entries, Somerset pars are in Bath & Wells dioc. The organisation in dioceses and archdeaconries is as follows.

BATH AD
Bath RDn, Chew RDn (1847–55), Chew Magna RDn (1855–*), Frome RDn (1962–*), Keyn. RDn (1855–*), Mids. Nort. RDn (1962–*), Portish. RDn (1855–*), Redcl. & Bedm. RDn (until 1847)

TAUNTON AD

Bridgw. RDn, Crewk. RDn, Dunst. RDn (until 1973), Exm. RDn (1973–*), Ilmin. RDn (1872–*), Quantk. RDn (1973–*), Quantoxhd. RDn (1884–1973), Taun. RDn (until 1963), Taun. N RDn (1963–*), Taun. S RDn (1963–*), Tone RDn (1973–*), Welling. RDn (1872–1973), Wivel. RDn (1872–1973)

WELLS AD

Axbr. RDn, Bruton RDn (1872–*), Burnham RDn (1872–*), Cary RDn, Frome RDn (until 1962), Glaston. Jurisd, Ilch. RDn, Lock. RDn (1872–*), Mart. RDn (1872–*), Merst. RDn, Milb. Port RDn (1884–1955), Mids. Nort. RDn (1872–1962), Pawlett RDn (until 1856), Shept. Mal. RDn (1872–*), Wells RDn (1855–72)

THE PARISHES OF SOMERSET

AISHOLT

AP *LG* Cann. Hd, Bridgw. PLU, RSD, RD. Civ bdry: 1883,[1] 1885.[2] Abol civ 1933 ent to Spaxton AP.[3] *Parl* W'rn Dv (1832–67), West Dv (1867–85), Bridgw. Dv (1885–1948). *Eccl* Bridgw. RDn (until 1955), Quantoxhd. RDn (1955–73), Quantk. RDn (1973–74), Bridgw. RDn (1974–*).

ALCOMBE

EP Cr 1953 from Dunster AP.[4] Dunst. RDn (1953–73), Exm. RDn (1973–*).

ALFORD

AP *LG* Seq 13. Civ bdry: 1885.[5] *Parl* Seq 8. *Eccl* Seq 25.

ALLER

AP *LG* Seq 38. Civ bdry: 1886.[6] *Parl* Seq 15. *Eccl* Seq 33.

CHAPEL ALLERTON

AP *LG* Seq 7. Civ bdry: 1885.[7] *Parl* Seq 7. *Eccl* Pec jurisd Dean of Wells (until 1845), Seq 22 thereafter.

ANGERSLEIGH

AP *LG* Taun. & Taun. Dean Hd, Taun. PLU, RSD, RD. Civ bdry: 1883.[1] Abol civ 1933 ent to Pitminster AP.[3] *Parl* W'rn Dv (1832–67), West Dv (1867–85), W'rn Dv (1885–1918), Taun. Dv (1918–48). *Eccl* Seq 20.

ANSFORD

AP *LG* Seq 13. Civ bdry: 1886.[8] *Parl* Seq 8. *Eccl* Seq 25.

ASH

Chap in Martock AP, sep EP 1845,[9] sep CP 1895.[10] *LG* Yeov. PLU, RD. Civ bdry: 1957.[11] *Parl* Yeov. Dv/CC (1918–*). *Eccl* Ilch. RDn (1845–72), Mart. RDn (1872–*).

ASH PRIORS

AP *LG* Seq 30. Civ bdry: 1884.[12] *Parl* Seq 22. *Eccl* Seq 21.

ASHBRITTLE

AP *LG* Seq 32. Civ bdry: 1884.[13] *Parl* Seq 22. *Eccl* Seq 21.

ASHCOTT

Chap in Shapwick AP, sep civ identity early, no sep eccl identity. *LG* Seq 49. Civ bdry: 1883,[1] 1885.[2] *Parl* Seq 17.

ASHILL

AP *LG* Seq 1. Civ bdry: 1885.[15] *Parl* Seq 1. *Eccl* Pec jurisd (until 1845), Seq 10 thereafter. Eccl bdry: 1929.[16]

ASHINGTON

AP *LG* Stone Hd, Yeov. PLU, RSD, RD. Civ bdry: 1884.[17] Abol civ 1933 ent to Chilton Cantelo AP.[3] *Parl* W'rn Dv (1832–67), Mid Dv (1867–85), S'rn Dv (1885–1918), Yeov. Dv (1918–48). *Eccl* Seq 31.

LONG ASHTON

AP Incl chap Whitchurch (sometimes 'Filton', sep civ identity early, sep EP 1720[25]). *LG* Seq 22. Addtl civ bdry alt: 1896 (help cr South Bristol CP, to be in Bristol CB),[18] 1898 (loses pt to Bristol CB and South Bristol CP),[19] 1951,[20] 1966 (loses pt to Bristol CB and CP).[21] Transf 1974 to Avon.[22] *Parl* E'rn Dv (1832–67), East Dv (1867–85), N'rn Dv (1885–1918), W-s-M Dv (1918–48). N Somerset CC (1948–*). *Eccl* Seq 6. Eccl bdry: 1893 (cr Leigh Woods EP),[23] 1959.[24]

ASHWICK

Chap in Kilmersdon AP, sep civ identity early, sep EP 1826.[25] *LG* Seq 28. Civ bdry: 1897,[26] 1933.[3] *Parl* Seq 11. *Eccl* Frome RDn (1826–72), Mids. Nort. RDn (1872–1953), Shept. Mal. RDn (1953–*). Eccl bdry: 1866 (help cr Oakhill EP),[27] 1966.[28]

AXBRIDGE

AP *LG* Axbr. Bor (status not sustained), Seq 53. Civ bdry: 1897,[29] 1935.[30] *Parl* Axbr. Parl Bor (1295, 1313, 1319–25), Seq 7 thereafter. *Eccl* Seq 22.

BABCARY

AP *LG* Seq 12. *Parl* Seq 9. *Eccl* Seq 25.

BABINGTON

AP *LG* Kilm. Hd, Shept. Mal. PLU (1835–45), Frome PLU (1845–1930), RSD, RD. Civ bdry: 1883.[1] Abol civ 1949 pt to Kilmington AP, pt to help cr Coleford CP.[31] *Parl* E'rn Dv (1832–67), Mid Dv (1867–85), Frome Dv (1885–1948), Wells CC (1948–70). *Eccl* Seq 29. Eccl bdry: 1954.[32]

BACKWELL

AP *LG* Seq 22. Transf 1974 to Avon.[22] *Parl* E'rn Dv (1832–67), East Dv (1867–85), N'rn Dv (1885–1918), W-s-M Dv (1918–48), N Somerset CC (1948–*). *Eccl* Seq 6. Eccl bdry: 1873 (help cr Felton Common Hill EP).[33]

BADGWORTH

AP *LG* Perhaps Badgworth Bor[34] (status not sustained), Seq 53. Civ bdry: 1885,[7] 1933.[3] *Parl* Seq 7. *Eccl* Seq 23.

BAGBOROUGH
EP Renaming 1972 of West Bagborough AP.[35] Taun. N RDn.

WEST BAGBOROUGH
AP *LG* Seq 41. *Parl* Seq 22. *Eccl* Taun. RDn (until 1872), Welling. RDn (1872–1963), Taun. N RDn (1963–72). Renamed eccl 1972 'Bagborough'.[35]

BALTONSBOROUGH
Chap in Butleigh AP, sep civ identity early, sep EP 1895.[36] *LG* Seq 20. Civ bdry: 1884.[37] *Parl* Seq 8. *Eccl* Glaston. Jurisd.

BANWELL
AP Incl chap Churchill, chap Puxton (each sep civ identity early, each sep EP 1749[25]). *LG* Seq 53. Transf 1974 to Avon.[22] *Parl* Seq 7. *Eccl* Pec jurisd (until 1845), Seq 24 thereafter. Addtl eccl bdry alt: 1865 (help cr Congresbury St Ann EP, later called 'Hewlish St Ann').[117]

BARRINGTON
AP *LG* S Peth. Hd, Langp. PLU, RSD, RD. Civ bdry: 1885,[38] 1886.[6] *Parl* Seq 20. *Eccl* Crewk. RDn (until 1872), Ilmin. RDn (1872–*). Eccl bdry: 1844 (help cr Hambridge EP).[39]

NORTH BARROW
AP *LG* Seq 13. *Parl* Seq 8. *Eccl* Seq 25.

SOUTH BARROW
AP *LG* Seq 13. *Parl* Seq 8. *Eccl* Pec jurisd Dean & Chapter of Wells (until 1845), Seq 25 thereafter.

BARROW GURNEY
AP *LG* Seq 22. Transf 1974 to Avon.[22] *Parl* E'rn Dv (1832–67), East Dv (1867–85), N'rn Dv (1885–1918), W-s-M Dv (1918–48), N Somerset CC (1948–*). *Eccl* Donative, Redcl. & Bedm. RDn (until 1847), Chew RDn (1847–58), Portish. RDn (1858–*).

BARTON ST DAVID
AP *LG* Seq 12. *Parl* Seq 9. *Eccl* Seq 25.

BARTON HILL ST LUKE WITH CHRIST CHURCH
EP Reconstitution 1970 of Barton Hill St Luke with Christ Church EP (erected from territory in anc Glos), gaining ent Bedminster St Luke with St Silas EP (from anc Somerset).[40] Bitton RDn (dioc Bristol).

BARWICK
AP *LG* Seq 24. *Parl* Seq 16. *Eccl* Seq 31.

BATCOMBE
AP Incl chap Upton Noble (sep civ identity early, sep EP 1734[25]). *LG* Seq 50. *Parl* Seq 11. *Eccl* Seq 26.

BATH
The following have 'Bath' in their names. First are listed pars whose names consist of 'Bath' usually followed by a saint's name, then eccl renamings which include 'Bath' and then another place name, finally names in which 'Bath' is only pt of a compound name. Insofar as the first group existed at a given time: *LG* Bath Forum Hd, Bath Bor/MB/CB, PLU, USD. *Parl* Bath Parl Bor/BC (1295–*). *Eccl* Bath RDn.

CP1–BATH–Cr 1900 by unions of the pars in Bath CB: AP1, AP5, AP7, Bathwick AP, Lyncombe and Widcombe AP, Walcot AP.[41] Civ bdry: 1911,[42] 1951,[43] 1967.[44] Transf 1974 to Avon.[22] Parl bdry: 1951.[45]

–BATH ABBEY–See AP7

EP1–BATH ABBEY WITH ST JAMES–Cr 1956 by union AP7, AP1.[46]

EP2–BATH THE ASCENSION–Renaming 1967 of South Twerton EP.[47]

–BATH CHRIST CHURCH–Name used now for EP cr 1798 as 'Walcot Christ Church', qv

EP3–BATH HOLY TRINITY–Cr 1952 by union Walcot AP, pt EP8.[48]

EP4–BATH ST BARNABAS–Renaming 1967 of Twerton Hill EP.[47] Keyn. RDn.

EP5–BATH ST BARTHOLOMEW–Renaming 1972 of greater pt of Bath Lyncombe EP.[49]

AP1–BATH ST JAMES–Orig AP, sep civ identity maintained, later treated as chap in AP7, sep eccl identity regained 1861.[50] Abol civ 1900 to help cr CP1.[39] Eccl bdry: 1869 (help cr EP8).[51] Abol eccl 1956 to help cr EP1.[46]

EP6–BATH ST LUKE–Renaming 1967 of South Lyncombe EP.[47]

AP2–BATH ST MARY DE STALLS–Disused in 16th cent. Incl chap Widcombe (sep eccl identity early, civ united with Lyncombe as 'Lyncombe with Widcombe').

AP3–BATH ST MARY WITHIN THE WALLS–Disused in 16th cent.

AP4–BATH ST MARY WITHOUT THE WALLS–Disused by 1535.

AP5–BATH ST MICHAEL–Orig 'Bath St Michael Without the Walls'. Abol civ 1900 to help cr CP1.[39] Abol eccl 1952 to help cr EP7.[48]

EP7–BATH ST MICHAEL WITH ST PAUL–Cr 1952 by union AP5, pt EP8.[48]

AP6–BATH ST MICHAEL WITHIN THE WALLS–Disused by 16th cent.

–BATH ST MICHAEL WITHOUT THE WALLS–See AP5

EP8–BATH ST PAUL–Cr 1869 from Walcot Holy Trinity EP, AP1.[51] Abol 1952 pt to help cr EP3, pt to help cr EP7.[48]

AP7–BATH ST PETER AND ST PAUL–Parochial 16th cent on ruins of Abbey. Usual civ spelling; usual eccl 'Bath Abbey'. Gains as chap AP1 (sep civ identity maintained, eccl sep status regained 1861[50]). Abol civ 1900 to help cr CP1.[39] Abol eccl 1956 to help cr EP1.[46]

EP9–BATH ST SAVIOUR–Renaming 1967 of Walcot St Saviour EP.[47]

EP10–BATH ST STEPHEN–Renaming 1967 of Lansdown EP.[47]

AP8–BATH ST WERBURGH–Disused by 1535.

BATH BATHWICK ST JOHN
EP Renaming 1967 of Bathwick St John the Baptist EP.[47] Bath RDn.

BATH BATHWICK ST MARY WITH WOOLLEY
EP Renaming 1967 of Bathwick with Woolley AP.[47] Bath RDn.

BATH LYNCOMBE
EP Renaming 1967 of Lyncombe EP.[47] Bath RDn.

Bdry: 1972.[49]

BATH ODD DOWN

EP Renaming 1967 of Odd Down EP.[47] Bath RDn.

BATH TWERTON-ON-AVON

EP Renaming 1967 of Twerton-on-Avon AP.[47] Keyn. RDn.

BATH WALCOT

EP Renaming 1967 of Walcot AP.[47] Bath RDn.

BATH WESTON ALL SAINTS

EP Renaming 1967 of Weston AP.[47] Keyn. RDn.

BATH WESTON ST JOHN

EP Renaming 1967 of Weston St John EP.[47] Keyn. RDn.

BATH WIDCOMBE

EP Renaming 1967 of Widcombe EP.[47] Bath RDn. Bdry: 1972.[49]

BATHAMPTON

AP *LG* Seq 21. Transf 1974 to Avon.[22] *Parl* Seq 1. *Eccl* Seq 1.

BATHEALTON

AP *LG* Seq 32. Civ bdry: 1933.[3] *Parl* Seq 22. *Eccl* Seq 21.

BATHEASTON

AP Incl chap St Catherine (sep civ identity early, no sep eccl identity). *LG* Pt Bath Forum Hd, pt Hamp. & Clav. Hd, Bath PLU, RSD, RD (1894–1933), Bathavon RD (1933–74). Civ bdry: 1883,[1] 1967 (loses pt to Bath CB and CP).[44] Transf 1974 to Avon.[22] *Parl* Seq 1. *Eccl* Seq 2.

BATHFORD

AP *LG* Seq 5. Transf 1974 to Avon.[22] *Parl* Seq 1. *Eccl* Seq 2.

BATHWICK

AP *LG* Bath Forum Hd, Bath PLU, MB (1835–89), CB (1889–1900), USD. Abol civ 1900 to help cr Bath CP.[41] *Parl* Bath Parl Bor (1832–1918). *Eccl* Bath RDn. Abol eccl before 1535 to help cr Bathwick with Woolley EP.

BATHWICK ST JOHN THE BAPTIST

EP Cr 1871 from Bathwick with Woolley EP.[52] Bath RD. Renamed 1967 'Bath Bathwick'.[47]

BATHWICK WITH WOOLLEY

EP Cr before 1535 by union Bathwick AP, Woolley AP. Bath RD. Bdry: 1871 (cr Bathwick St John the Baptist EP).[52] Renamed 1967 'Bath Bathwick St Mary with Woolley'.[47]

BAWDRIP

AP *LG* Seq 34. *Parl* Seq 17. *Eccl* Seq 35.

BECKINGTON

AP *LG* Seq 19. Civ bdry: 1885.[53] *Parl* Seq 10. *Eccl* Frome RDn. Abol *ca* 1660 to help cr Beckington with Standerwick EP.[54]

BECKINGTON WITH STANDERWICK

EP Cr *ca* 1660 by union Beckington AP, Standerwick AP.[54] Frome RDn.

BEDMINSTER

The following have 'Bedminster' in their names. Insofar as any existed at a given time: *LG* Sep noted. *Parl* Seq noted. *Eccl* Redcl. & Bedm. RDn (dioc Bath & Wells, until 1845), thereafter in dioc Bristol: Bristol RDn (1845–66), Bristol (City Dv) RDn (1866–87), Bristol RDn (1887–1901), Bedm. RDn (1901–*).

AP1–BEDMINSTER [ST JOHN THE BAPTIST]–Incl chaps Abbots Leigh, Bristol St Mary Redcliffe, Bristol St Thomas (the first sep civ identity early in Somerset, the last two sep civ identity early in Bristol Bor/Co, each sep EP 1852[55]). *LG* Hartcl. & Bedm. Hd, Bedm. PLU, Bristol MB/CB (pt 1835–94, ent 1894–96), pt Bristol USD, pt Bristol RSD. Addtl civ bdry alt: 1894 (the pt not in the CB cr CP1).[56] Abol civ 1896 to help cr South Bristol CP.[18] *Parl* The pt in the MB/CB: Bristol Parl Bor (1832–85), pt Bristol Parl Bor, South Dv (1885–1918); the pt in Somerset: E'rn Dv (1832–67), East Dv (1867–85), N'rn Dv (1885–1918). Addtl eccl bdry alt: 1841 (cr EP7),[57] 1844 (cr Bishopsworth EP),[58] 1861 (help cr EP3),[59] 1883 (help cr Knowle Holy Nativity EP),[60] 1902 (help cr EP1),[61] 1902 (cr Windmill Hill EP),[62] 1935 (help cr Knowle St Barnabas EP).[63] Abol eccl 1965 pt to help cr Bristol St Mary Redcliffe with Bristol Temple and Bedminster St John the Baptist EP, pt to EP1, pt to help cr EP6.[64]

EP1–BEDMINSTER ST ALDHELM–Cr 1902 from AP1, EP7, Bishopsworth EP.[61] Bdry: 1929 (cr EP9),[65] 1929 (cr EP2),[66] 1951,[67] 1965.[64]

EP2–BEDMINSTER ST DUNSTAN–Cr 1929 from EP1.[66] Bdry: 1951.[67]

EP3–BEDMINSTER ST FRANCIS, ASHTON GATE–Cr 1883 from AP1, EP7.[59] Bdry: 1951.[67]

EP4–BEDMINSTER ST LUKE–Cr 1861 from AP1, Bristol St Mary Redcliffe EP.[68] Abol 1956 to help cr EP5.[69]

EP5–BEDMINSTER ST LUKE WITH ST SILAS–Cr 1956 by union EP4, pt Bristol St Silas EP, pt Bristol Temple AP.[69] Abol 1970 pt to Barton Hill St Luke with Christ Church EP, pt to Bristol St Mary Redcliffe with Bristol Temple and Bedminster St John the Baptist EP, pt to Knowle Holy Nativity EP.[70]

EP6–BEDMINSTER ST MICHAEL AND ALL ANGELS–Cr 1965 by union Windmill Hill EP, pt AP1.[64]

EP7–BEDMINSTER ST PAUL–Cr 1841 from AP1.[57] Bdry: 1883 (help cr EP3),[59] 1893 (cr EP8),[71] 1902 (help cr EP1).[61]

EP8–BEDMINSTER ST RAPHAEL THE ARCHANGEL–Cr 1893 from EP7.[71] Abol 1943 pt to Bristol St Mary Redcliffe EP, pt to Clifton Holy Trinity, St Andrew the Less and St Peter EP.[72]

EP9–BEDMINSTER DOWN–Cr 1929 from EP1.[65] Bdry: 1951.[67]

CP1–BEDMINSTER WITHOUT–Cr 1894 from the pt of AP1 not in Bristol CB.[56] *LG* Bedm. PLU, RD. Bdry: 1898 (loses pt to Bristol CB and CP).[73] Renamed soon after 'Bishopsworth'.[74]

BEER CROCOMBE

AP *LG* Seq 2. Civ bdry: 1885,[38] 1886.[6] *Parl* Seq 19. *Eccl* Sometimes as 'Beercrocombe', Crewk.

RDn (until 1872), Ilmin. RDn (1872–1955), Taun. RDn (1955–63), Taun. S RDn (1963–*). Eccl bdry: 1931.[89]

BERKLEY

AP *LG* Seq 19. Civ bdry: 1883,[1] 1886.[6] *Parl* Seq 20. *Eccl* Seq 28.

BERROW

AP *LG* Seq 8. Civ bdry: 1914.[75] *Parl* Seq 7. *Eccl* Seq 23.

BICKENHALL

Chap in Staple Fitzpaine AP, sep civ identity early, no sep eccl identity. *LG* Seq 3. Civ bdry: 1883,[1] 1884.[12] *Parl* Seq 18.

BICKNOLLER

Chap in Stogumber AP, sep civ identity early, sep EP 1770.[25] *LG* Seq 52. Civ bdry: 1885.[76] *Parl* Seq 21. *Eccl* Dunst. RDn (1770–1872), Wivel. RDn (1872–1951), Dunst. RDn (1951–73), Quantk. RDn (1973–*).

BIDDISHAM

AP *LG* Bempst. Hd, Axbr. PLU, RSD, RD. Abol civ 1933 ent to Badgworth AP.[3] *Parl* E'rn Dv (1832–67), East Dv (1867–85), Wells Dv (1885–1918), W-s-M Dv (1918–48). *Eccl* Pec jurisd Dean of Wells (until 1845), Seq 23 thereafter.

BINEGAR

AP *LG* Seq 47. Civ bdry: 1884,[77] 1933,[3] 1958.[78] *Parl* Seq 8. Parl bdry: 1960.[79] *Eccl* Pec jurisd Dean of Wells (until 1845), Frome RDn (1845–72), Mids. Nort. RDn (1872–1962), Shept. Mal. RDn (1962–*). Eccl bdry: 1966.[28]

BISHOPSWORTH

EP Cr 1852 from Bedminster AP.[58] Bristol RDn (1852–66), Bristol (City Dv) RDn (1866–87), Bristol RDn (1887–1901), Bedm. RDn (1901–*).

CP Renaming soon after 1898 of Bedminster Without CP.[74] *LG* Long Ashton PLU, RD. Civ bdry: 1929,[80] 1930 (loses pt to Bristol CB and CP),[81] 1933,[3] 1951.[82] Abol 1951 pt to Dundry CP, pt to Bristol CB and CP.[20] *Parl* W-s-M Dv/CC (1918–52[83]).

BLACKFORD

Chap in Maperton AP, sep civ identity early, sep EP 1852.[25] *LG* Whitley Hd, Wincan. PLU, RSD, RD. Civ bdry: 1885.[84] Abol civ 1933 ent to Compton Pauncefoot AP.[3] *Parl* W'rn Dv (1832–67), Mid Dv (1867–85), E'rn Dv (1885–1918), Wells Dv (1918–48). *Eccl* Cary RDn.

BLACKFORD

EP Cr 1844 from Wedmore AP.[85] Sometimes 'Blackford Holy Trinity'. Axbr. RDn (1844–72), Burnham RDn (1872–1956), Axbr. RDn (1956–*).

BLAGDON

AP *LG* Seq 53. Civ bdry: 1885,[86] 1933.[3] Pt transf 1974 to Avon to be 'Blagdon', the pt remaining in Somerset added to Priddy CP.[22] *Parl* Seq 7. *Eccl* Seq 24. Eccl bdry: 1960.[87]

BLEADON

AP *LG* Seq 53. Civ bdry: 1933.[3] Transf 1974 to Avon.[22] *Parl* Seq 7. *Eccl* Axbr. RDn (until 1872), Burnham RDn (1872–1956), Lock. RDn (1956–*). Eccl bdry: 1960 (help cr Weston-super-Mare St Andrew, Bournville EP).[88]

BRADFORD

AP *LG* Seq 42. Civ bdry: 1883.[1] *Parl* Seq 22. *Eccl* Seq 21.

MAIDEN BRADLEY

AP Pt Wilts (Mere Hd), pt Somerset (Norton Ferris Hd), made ent Wilts 1895.[90] *LG* Mere PLU, RSD, pt sep RD in Somerset (1894–95). Civ bdry: 1885.[115] *Parl* Somerset pt, E'rn Dv (1832–67), Mid Dv (1867–85), E'rn Dv (1885–1918). See main entry in Wilts for civ organisation after 1895 and for eccl organisation in Sarum dioc.

WEST BRADLEY

Chap in East Pennard AP, sep civ identity early, sep EP 1875.[91] *LG* Glaston. Twelve Hides Hd, Wells PLU (1836–82), RSD (1875–82), Wells PLU (1882–1930), RSD (1882–94), RD. Civ bdry: 1879,[92] 1884,[37] 1933.[3] *Parl* E'rn Dv (1832–67), Mid Dv (1867–85), Wells Dv/CC (1885–*). *Eccl* Glaston. Jurisd.

GOOSE BRADON

AP Orig AP, early sinecure, incl in South Bradon.

NORTH AND SOUTH BRADON

AP Usual eccl spelling; for civ and incl of Goose Bradon, see following entry. *Eccl* Crewk. RDn (until 1872), Ilmin. RDn (1872–1962). Abol eccl 1962 to help cr Puckington with Bradon EP.[94]

SOUTH BRADON

AP Usual civ spelling; for eccl see prev entry. Incl Goose Bradon (orig AP, long sincecure). *LG* Abd. & Bulst. Hd, Langp. PLU, RSD. Abol civ 1885 pt to Kingsbury Episcopi AP, pt to Puckington AP, pt to Isle Brewers AP.[93] *Parl* W'rn Dv (1832–67), West Dv (1867–85), Bridgw. Dv (1885–1918).

BRATTON ST MAUR

AP Usual eccl spelling; for civ see following entry. *Eccl* Seq 26.

BRATTON SEYMOUR

AP Usual civ spelling; for eccl see prev entry. *LG* Seq 33. Civ bdry: 1886.[95] *Parl* Seq 8.

BREAN

AP *LG* Seq 7. *Parl* Seq 7. *Eccl* As 'Breane', Seq 23. Eccl bdry: 1966,[96] 1967.[97]

BREANE–See prev entry

EAST BRENT

AP *LG* Seq 8. Civ bdry: 1885,[7] 1974 (gains the pt of Loxton AP not transf to Avon to be sep par 'Loxton' in that co).[22] *Parl* Seq 7. *Eccl* Seq 23.

SOUTH BRENT–See following entry.

BRENT KNOLL

AP Sometimes 'South Brent'. *LG* Seq 8. Civ bdry: 1885,[7] 1914.[75] *Parl* Seq 7. *Eccl* Seq 23.

BREWHAM

CP Cr 1933 by union North Brewham CP, South Brewham CP.[3] *LG* Wincan. RD. *Parl* Wells CC (1948–*).

NORTH BREWHAM

CP Sep civ identity early from Bruton AP, eccl pt

of one par 'South Brewham with North Brewham', qv. *LG* Bruton Hd, Wincan. PLU, RSD, RD. Civ bdry: 1885.[84] Abol 1933 to help cr Brewham CP.[3] *Parl* E'rn Dv (1832–67), Mid Dv (1867–85), E'rn Dv (1885–1918), Wells Dv (1918–48).

SOUTH BREWHAM

CP Sep civ identity early from Bruton AP, eccl pt of one par 'South Brewham with North Brewham', qv. *LG* Bruton Hd, Wincan. PLU, RSD, RD. Civ bdry: 1885.[98] Civ abol, *Parl* as for North Brewham.

SOUTH BREWHAM WITH NORTH BREWHAM

Chap in Bruton AP, sep EP before 1784,[116] 2 sep CPs of North Brewham, South Brewham, qv. *Eccl* Cary RDn (1784–1872), Bruton RDn (1872–*). Bdry: 1966 (gains ex-par places Brewham Lodge, Four Towers).[100]

BRIDGWATER

AP *LG* N Peth. Hd, Bridgw. Bor/MB (pt until 1894, ent 1894–1974), Bridgw. PLU, pt Bridgw. USD, pt Bridgw. RSD. Civ bdry: 1886,[101] 1887,[102] 1894 (the pt not in the MB cr Bridgwater Without CP),[56] 1896,[103] 1929,[80] 1933,[3] 1938,[104] 1952.[105] *Parl* Pt Bridgw. Parl Bor (1295–1867), pt W'rn Dv (1832–67), West Dv (1867–85), Bridgw. Dv/CC (1885–*). *Eccl* Seq 7. Eccl bdry: 1840 (help cr Burrowbridge EP),[106] 1841 (cr Bridgwater Holy Trinity EP),[107] 1846 (cr Eastover EP),[108] 1958,[109] 1961 (help cr Greenfield EP),[110] 1966.[111]

BRIDGWATER HOLY TRINITY

EP Cr 1841 from Bridgwater AP.[107] Bridgw. RDn. Abol 1958 ent to Bridgwater AP.[111]

BRIDGWATER HOLY TRINITY

EP Renaming 1972 of Greenfield EP.[112] Bridgw. RDn.

BRIDGWATER ST FRANCIS OF ASSISI

EP Cr 1965 from Eastover EP, Wembdon AP.[113] Bridgw. RDn.

BRIDGWATER ST JOHN THE BAPTIST

EP Renaming 1972 of Eastover EP.[114] Bridgw. RDn.

BRIDGWATER WITHOUT

CP Cr 1894 from the pt of Bridgwater AP not in Bridgw. MB.[56] *LG* Bridgw. PLU, RD. Civ bdry: 1896,[103] 1929,[80] 1933,[3] 1938,[104] 1952.[105] *Parl* Bridgw. Dv/CC (1918–*).

BRISLINGTON

The following have 'Brislington' in their names. Insofar as any existed at a given time: *LG* Keyn. Hd, PLU, RSD, RD. *Parl* E'rn Dv (1832–67), East Dv (1867–85), N'rn Dv (1885–1918), Frome Dv (1918–48). *Eccl* Redcl. & Bedm. RDn (cr–1847), Bath RDn (1847–1927), Bedm. RDn (1927–73), Brisl. RDn (1973–*).

CP1/EP1–BRISLINGTON [ST LUKE]–Chap and donative in Keynsham AP, sep civ identity early, sep EP before 1786.[99] Civ bdry: 1898 (loses pt to Bristol CB and CP),[73] 1930 (loses pt to Bristol CB and CP).[81] Abol civ 1933 ent to Bristol CB and CP.[3] Eccl bdry: 1909 (cr EP2),[118] 1930 (help cr EP4),[119] 1932,[120] 1932 (help cr EP3),[121] 1940 (help cr Hengrove EP),[122] 1973 (help cr Bristol Christ the Servant, Stockwood EP).[123]

EP2–BRISLINGTON ST ANNE–Cr 1909 from AP1.[118] Bdry: 1930 (help cr EP4),[119] 1932.[120]

EP3–BRISLINGTON ST CHRISTOPHER–Cr 1932 from AP1, EP3, Knowle Holy Nativity EP.[121] Bdry: 1940 (help cr Hengrove EP).[122]

EP4–BRISLINGTON ST CUTHBERT–Cr 1930 from AP1, EP2.[119]

BRISTOL

The following have 'Bristol' in their names and contain territory in anc Somerset; the majority of Bristol pars were in anc Glos, qv. Insofar as any existed at a given time: *LG* Bristol Bor/Co/MB/CB, incorp for poor, USD. *Parl* Bristol Parl Bor (1295–1885), Bristol Parl Bor, South Dv (1885–1918). *Eccl* Bristol RDn (until 1866), Bristol (City Dv) RDn (1866–87), Bristol RDn (1887–1901), Bedm. RDn (1901–*).

EP1–BRISTOL CHRIST THE SERVANT, STOCKWOOD–Cr 1973 from Hengrove EP, Whitchurch EP, Brislington EP (all dioc Bristol) and from Keynsham AP (dioc Bath & Wells).[125]

–BRISTOL HOLY CROSS–See AP2

EP2–BRISTOL HOLY CROSS INNS COURT–Cr 1959 from Knowle St Barnabas EP (dioc Bristol) and from Whitchurch AP (dioc Bath & Wells).[126]

EP3–BRISTOL ST ANDREW, HARTCLIFFE–Cr 1962 from Bishopsworth EP, EP2 (both dioc Bristol) and from Dundry EP, Chew Magna AP, Whitchurch EP (dioc Bath & Wells).[124]

CP1/EP4–BRISTOL ST MARY REDCLIFFE–Chap in Bedminster AP, sep civ identity early in Bristol Bor/Co, sep EP 1852.[55] Abol civ 1896 to help cr Central Bristol CP.[18] Abol eccl 1956 to help cr EP5.[127]

EP5–BRISTOL ST MARY REDCLIFFE WITH BRISTOL TEMPLE–Cr 1956 by union EP4, AP1, AP2.[127] Abol 1965 to help cr EP6.[64]

EP6–BRISTOL ST MARY REDCLIFFE WITH BRISTOL TEMPLE AND BEDMINSTER ST JOHN THE BAPTIST–Cr 1965 by union EP5, pt Bedminster EP.[64]

AP1–BRISTOL ST THOMAS–Abol civ 1896 to help cr Central Bristol CP.[18] Abol eccl 1956 to help cr EP5.[127]

AP2–BRISTOL TEMPLE–Sometimes 'Bristol Holy Cross'. Abol civ 1896 to help cr Central Bristol CP.[18] Abol eccl 1956 to help cr EP5.[127]

BROADWAY

AP Orig curacy to priory church. *LG* Seq 1. Civ bdry: 1885,[128] 1886.[129] *Parl* Seq 19. *Eccl* Crewk. RDn (until 1872), Ilmin. RDn (1872–*). Eccl bdry: 1928,[130] 1931,[89] 1958,[131] 1972.[141]

BROCKLEY

AP *LG* Seq 15. Civ bdry: 1885.[132] Transf 1974 to Avon.[22] *Parl* E'rn Dv (1832–67), East Dv

(1867–85), N'rn Dv (1885–1918), W-s-M Dv (1918–48), N Somerset CC (1948–*). *Eccl* Seq 6.

BROMPTON RALPH

AP *LG* Seq 52. Civ bdry: 1883.[1] *Parl* Seq 21. *Eccl* Dunst. RDn (until 1973), Quantk. RDn (1973–*).

BROMPTON REGIS

AP *LG* Seq 51. Civ bdry: 1884,[133] 1933.[3] *Parl* Seq 22. *Eccl* Dunst. RDn (until 1951), Wivel. RDn (1951–58). Abol eccl 1958 to help cr Brompton Regis with Withiel Florey EP.[134]

BROMPTON REGIS WITH WITHIEL FLOREY

EP Cr 1958 by union Brompton Regis AP, Withiel Florey EP.[134] Wivel. RDn (1958–73), Exm. RDn (1973–*). Bdry: 1959.[135]

BROOMFIELD

AP *LG* Seq 4. Civ bdry: 1887.[136] *Parl* Seq 17. *Eccl* Donative, pec jurisd Dean of Wells (until 1845), Bridgw. RDn (1845–1955),Taun. RDn (1955–63), Taun. N RDn (1963–*).

BRUSHFORD

AP *LG* Seq 51. Civ bdry: 1966 (exchanges pts with East Anstey AP, Devon).[137] *Parl* Seq 22. *Eccl* Seq 14. Eccl bdry: 1959.[135]

BRUTON

AP Orig monastery church, early parochial. Incl chap Pitcombe (sep civ identity early, sep EP 1784[25]), chap Redlynch (sep EP 1733[25]), chap South Brewham with North Brewham (sep EP 1784,[116] sep civ identity early in two CPs of North Brewham, South Brewham), chap Wyke Champflower (sep EP 1748[25]). *LG* Bruton Bor, Seq 9. Addtl civ bdry alt: 1883,[1] 1885.[138] *Parl* Seq 8. *Eccl* Cary RDn (until 1872), Bruton RDn (1872–1933). Abol eccl 1933 to help cr Bruton and Redlynch EP.[140]

BRUTON AND REDLYNCH

EP Cr 1933 by union Bruton AP, Redlynch EP, ex-par Eastrip.[140] Bruton RDn. Abol 1971 to help cr Bruton with Wyke Champflower and Redlynch EP.[142]

BRUTON WITH WYKE CHAMPFLOWER AND REDLYNCH

EP Cr 1971 by union Bruton and Redlynch EP, Wyke Champlower EP,[142] the name 'Champflower' not in the order but commonly used. Bruton RDn.

BRYMPTON

AP *LG* Seq 40. Civ bdry: 1884,[17] 1930,[143] 1933.[3] *Parl* Seq 16. *Eccl* Seq 34.

WEST BUCKLAND

Chap in Wellington AP (eccl, 'Wellington with West Buckland'), sep civ identity early, sep EP 1967[144] (the mother par thereafter eccl 'Wellington'). *LG* Seq 31. Civ bdry: 1933,[3] 1966 (gains pt Clayhidon AP, Devon).[137] *Parl* Seq 22. *Eccl* Welling. RDn (1967–73), Tone RDn (1973–*).

BUCKLAND DINHAM

AP *LG* Seq 27. *Parl* Seq 11. *Eccl* Pec jurisd (until 1845), Seq 28 thereafter.

BUCKLAND ST MARY

AP *LG* Pt Abd. & Bulst. Hd, pt Mart. Hd, pt S Peth. Hd, Chard PLU, RSD, RD. Civ bdry: 1885.[38] *Parl* Seq 19. *Eccl* Seq 10.

BURNETT

AP *LG* Keyn. Hd, PLU, RSD, RD. Abol civ 1933 ent to Compton Dando AP.[3] *Parl* E'rn Dv (1832–67), East Dv (1867–85), N'rn Dv (1885–1918), Frome Dv (1918–48). *Eccl* Seq 4.

BURNHAM

AP Usual civ spelling; for eccl see following entry. *LG* Bempst. Hd, Axbr. PLU, pt Burnham USD, pt Axbr. RSD, Burnham UD (1894–1917), Burnham-on-Sea UD (1917–33). Civ bdry: 1894 (the pt not in the USD cr Highbridge CP),[56] 1896,[145] 1914.[75] Abol civ 1933 to help cr Burnham-on-Sea CP.[3] *Parl* E'rn Dv (1832–67), East Dv (1867–85), Wells Dv (1885–1918), Bridgw. Dv (1918–48).

BURNHAM-ON-SEA

AP Usual eccl spelling; for civ see prev entry. *Eccl* Seq 23. Eccl bdry: 1860 (cr Highbridge EP).[146]

CP Cr 1933 by union Burnham AP, North Highbridge CP, South Highbridge CP.[3] *LG* Burnham-on-Sea UD. *Parl* Bridgw. Dv/CC (1948–*).

BURNHAM WITHOUT

CP Cr 1896 from Highbridge CP.[147] *LG* Axbr. PLU, RD. *Parl* W-s-M Dv/CC (1918–*).

BURRINGTON

Chap in Wrington AP, sep civ identity early, sep EP 1758.[25] *LG* Seq 8. Civ bdry: 1885.[148] Pt transf 1974 to Avon to be 'Burrington', the remainder in Somerset added to Priddy CP.[22] *Parl* Seq 7. *Eccl* Redcl. & Bedm. RDn (until 1847), Chew RDn (1847–58), Portish. RDn (1858–1956), Lock. RDn (1956–*). Eccl bdry: 1964.[87]

BURROWBRIDGE

EP Cr 1840 from Lyng AP, Othery AP, Westonzoyland EP, Middlezoy AP, Bridgwater AP, North Petherton AP, Stoke St Gregory EP.[106] Bridgw. RDn (1840–1956), Taun. RDn (1956–63) Taun. N RDn (1963–69), Bridgw. RDn (1969–*).

BURTLE

EP Cr 1856 from Chilton Polden EP, Edington EP.[149] Glaston. Jurisd.

BUTCOMBE

AP *LG* Hartcl. with Bedm. Hd, Axbr. PLU, RSD, RD. Civ bdry: 1885.[150] Transf 1974 to Avon.[22] *Parl* Seq 7. *Eccl* Seq 5.

BUTLEIGH

AP Incl chap Baltonsborough (sep civ identity early, sep EP 1895[36]). *LG* Whitley Hd, Wells PLU, RSD, RD. Addtl civ bdry alt: 1884,[151] 1885,[152] 1933.[3] *Parl* Seq 14. *Eccl* Seq 36.

NORTH CADBURY

AP *LG* Seq 13. Civ bdry: 1885.[153] *Parl* Seq 8. *Eccl* Seq 25.

SOUTH CADBURY

AP *LG* Seq 13. Civ bdry: 1933.[3] *Parl* Seq 8. *Eccl* Seq 25.

QUEEN CAMEL
AP Sometimes 'East Camel'. *LG* Seq 13. *Parl* Seq 12. *Eccl* Seq 31.
WEST CAMEL
AP *LG* Seq 39. Civ bdry: 1885.[153] *Parl* Seq 15. *Eccl* Seq 31.
CAMELEY
AP *LG* Seq 16. Civ bdry: 1956.[154] Transf 1974 to Avon.[22] *Parl* Seq 3. *Eccl* Frome RDn (until 1872), Mids. Nort. RDn (1872–1962), Chew Magna RDn (1962–*).
CANNINGTON
AP Incl hmlt Edstock and Beer (sep CP 1866[158]). *LG* Seq 10. Addtl civ bdry alt: 1878,[159] 1883,[1] 1884,[160] 1886.[161] *Parl* Seq 17. *Eccl* Seq 7.
CARHAMPTON
AP *LG* Seq 11. Civ bdry: 1883,[162] 1884,[163] 1886.[164] *Parl* Seq 21. *Eccl* Pec jurisd Dean of Wells (until 1845), Seq 15 thereafter. Eccl bdry: 1954.[165]
CASTLE CARY
AP *LG* Seq 13. *Parl* Seq 8. *Eccl* Seq 25.
CATCOTT
Chap in Moorlinch AP, sep CP 1866,[158] sep EP 1903.[25] *LG* Seq 49. Civ bdry: 1933.[3] *Parl* West Dv (1867–85), Bridgw. Dv/CC (1885–*). *Eccl* Glaston. Jurisd.
CAMERTON
AP Incl pt area Peasedown (sep EP 1874,[155] sep CP 1955 as 'Peasedown St John'[156]). *LG* Wellow Hd, Clut. PLU, RSD, RD (1894–1912), Bath RD (1912–33), Bathavon RD (1933–74). Addtl civ bdry alt: 1885.[157] Transf 1974 to Avon.[22] *Parl* Seq 1. *Eccl* Seq 29.
CHAFFCOMBE
AP *LG* Seq 35. *Parl* Seq 20. *Eccl* Seq 9.
CHANTRY
EP Cr 1845,[25] refounded 1846[166] from Whatley AP, Elm AP, Mells AP. Frome RDn.
CHARD
AP *LG* E Kingsbury Hd, pt Chard Bor/MB (until 1866, 1892–93), Chard PLU, pt Chard USD (1892–93), Chard RSD (ent 1875–92, pt 1892–93, ent 1893–94), Chard RD. Civ bdry: 1866 (the pt in the MB cr Chard Borough CP),[158] 1892 (pt added to Chard MB),[170] 1893 (loses the pt in the MB to Chard Borough CP),[158] 1933,[3] 1966 (gains pt Chardstock AP, exchanges pts with Thorncombe AP, both Devon).[137] *Parl* Pt Chard Parl Bor (1312–13, 1328 only), Seq 20. *Eccl* Seq 9. Eccl bdry: 1866 (cr Tatworth EP),[168] 1897 (cr Chard The Good Shepherd, Furnham EP).[169]
CHARD BOROUGH
CP Cr 1866 from the pt of Chard AP in Chard MB.[158] *LG* E Kingsbury Hd, Chard PLU, MB, USD. Bdry: 1893 (gains the pt of Chard AP in the MB),[167] 1933.[3] *Parl* West Dv (1867–85), S'rn Dv (1885–1918), Yeov. Dv/CC (1918–*).
CHARD THE GOOD SHEPHERD, FURNHAM
EP Cr 1897 from Chard AP.[169] Crewk. RDn.
CHARLCOMBE
AP *LG* Seq 21. Civ bdry: 1885,[171] 1911 (loses pt to Bath CB and CP),[39] 1933,[3] 1951 (loses pt to Bath CB and CP),[41] 1953,[172] 1967 (loses pt to Bath CB and CP).[44] Transf 1974 to Avon.[22] *Parl* Seq 1. Parl bdry: 1951.[173] *Eccl* Seq 2.
QUEEN CHARLTON
Chap in Keynsham AP, sep civ identity early, sep EP 1741.[25] *LG* Keyn. Hd, PLU, RSD, RD. Abol civ 1933 ent to Compton Dando AP.[3] *Parl* E'rn Dv (1832–67), East Dv (1867–85), N'rn Dv (1885–1918), Frome Dv (1918–48). *Eccl* Redcl. & Bedm. RDn (1741–1847), Bath RDn (1847–55), Keyn. RDn (1855–*).
CHARLTON ADAM
AP Sometimes anc 'East Charlton'. *LG* Somert. Hd, Langp. PLU, RSD, RD. Abol civ 1887 pt to Compton Dundon AP, pt to Charlton Mackrell AP, pt to Kingweston AP.[196] *Parl* W'rn Dv (1832–67), Mid Dv (1867–85), E'rn Dv (1885–1918). *Eccl* Seq 33. Eccl bdry: 1932.[174]
CHARLTON HORETHORNE
AP *LG* Seq 23. Civ bdry: 1885,[153] 1933.[3] *Parl* Seq 8. *Eccl* Seq 32. Eccl bdry: 1934.[175]
CHARLTON MACKRELL
AP Sometimes anc 'West Charlton'. *LG* Seq 38. Civ bdry: 1887.[173] *Parl* Seq 15. *Eccl* Seq 33.
CHARLTON MUSGROVE
AP *LG* Seq 33. Civ bdry: 1883,[1] 1884,[176] 1885,[177] 1886.[95] *Parl* Seq 14. *Eccl* Seq 26. Eccl bdry: 1929,[139] 1940.[178]
CHARLYNCH
AP *LG* Seq 10. Civ bdry: 1883,[1] 1885,[2] 1933.[3] *Parl* Seq 17. *Eccl* Seq 7.
CHARTERHOUSE
Ex-par place, sep CP 1858.[179] *LG* Winterstoke Hd, Axbr. PLU, RSD, RD. Civ bdry: 1885.[148] Abol 1933 pt to Blagdon AP, pt to Cheddar AP.[3] *Parl* East Dv (1867–85), Wells Dv (1885–1918), W-s-M Dv (1918–48).
CHEDDAR
AP *LG* Seq 53. Civ bdry: 1885,[148] 1897,[29] 1933,[3] 1935.[30] *Parl* Seq 7. *Eccl* Pec jurisd Dean & Chapter of Wells (until 1845), Seq 22 thereafter. Eccl bdry: 1862 (help cr Draycott EP).[180]
CHEDDON FITZPAINE
AP *LG* Seq 41. Civ bdry: 1932,[181] 1933,[3] 1958.[182] *Parl* Seq 18. *Eccl* Seq 18. Eccl bdry: 1967 (help cr Halcon EP).[295]
CHEDZOY
AP *LG* Seq 34. Civ bdry: 1885,[2] 1886.[161] *Parl* Seq 17. *Eccl* Seq 7. Eccl bdry: 1962.[183]
CHELVEY
AP *LG* Hartcl. with Bedm. Hd, Bedm. PLU, RSD. Abol civ 1885 ent to Brockley AP.[132] *Parl* E'rn Dv (1832–67), East Dv (1867–85), N'rn Dv (1885–1918). *Eccl* Seq 6.
CHELWOOD
AP *LG* Seq 25. Transf 1974 to Avon.[22] *Parl* Seq 3. *Eccl* Seq 5.
NORTH CHERITON
AP *LG* Seq 23. Civ bdry: 1885.[184] *Parl* Seq 8. *Eccl* Merston RDn (until 1884), Milb. Port RDn (1884–1955), Cary RDn (1955–*). Eccl bdry: 1957.[185]

CHEW MAGNA
AP Incl chap Dundry (sep civ identity early, sep EP 1855[186]), tg Norton Hawkfield (sep CP 1866[158]). *LG* Seq 14. Addtl civ bdry alt: 1883,[1] 1884,[187] 1949.[188] Transf 1974 to Avon.[22] *Parl* Seq 3. *Eccl* Seq 5. Eccl bdry: 1876 (cr Bishop's Sutton EP).[189]

CHEW STOKE
AP *LG* Seq 14. Transf 1974 to Avon.[22] *Parl* Seq 3. *Eccl* Seq 5.

CHEWTON MENDIP
AP Incl chap Emborough (sep civ identity early, no sep eccl identity hence this par eccl usually 'Chewton Mendip with Emborough', qv), chap Farrington Gurney, chap Ston Easton (each sep civ identity early, united eccl 1867 to cr Ston Easton with Farrington Gurney EP,[190] sometimes 'Ston Easton cum Farrington Gurney'), chap Paulton (sep civ identity early, sep EP 1841[191]), tg North Widcombe (sep CP 1866[158]). *LG* Chewton Hd, Wells PLU, RSD, RD. Addtl civ bdry alt: 1883,[1] 1884,[192] 1885.[194] *Parl* Seq 4.

CHEWTON MENDIP WITH EMBOROUGH
AP Usual eccl spelling; for civ and civ sep chap Emborough, and for sep of other chaps, see prev entry. *Eccl* Frome RDn (until 1872), Mids. Nort. RDn (1872–1962), Shept. Mal. RDn (1962–*). Addtl eccl bdry alt: 1862 (help cr Priddy EP),[194] 1966.[195]

CHILCOMPTON
AP *LG* Chewton Hd, Clut. PLU, pt Mids. Nort. USD (1883–Mar 1894[197]), Clut. RSD (ent 1875–83, pt 1883–Mar 1894, ent Mar 1894–apptd day 1894), Clut. RD. Civ bdry: 1883,[1] 1933,[3] 1958.[72] *Parl* E'rn Dv (1832–67), Mid Dv (1867– 85), N'rn Dv (1885–1918), Frome Dv (1918–48), N Somerset CC (1948–*). Parl bdry: 1960.[441] *Eccl* Pec jurisd Dean of Wells (until 1845), Frome RDn (1845–72), Mids. Nort. RDn (1872–*). Eccl bdry: 1966.[28]

CHILLINGTON
Chap in South Petherton AP, sep civ identity early, sep EP 1750.[25] *LG* Seq 35. *Parl* Seq 20. Parl bdry: 1960.[79] *Eccl* Crewk. RDn.

CHILTHORNE DOMER
AP *LG* Seq 40. Civ bdry: 1957.[11] *Parl* Seq 16. *Eccl* Seq 34. Eccl bdry: 1955.[198]

CHILTON CANTELO
AP *LG* Seq 24. Civ bdry: 1933.[3] *Parl* Seq 16. *Eccl* Seq 31. Eccl bdry: 1953.[199]

CHILTON COMMON
Ex-par place, sep CP 1858,[179] eccl abol 1966 ent to Chilton Trinity AP.[202] *LG* N Peth. Hd, Bridgw. PLU (1858[200]–1907), RSD, RD. Abol civ 1907 ent to Chilton Trinity AP.[201] *Parl* West Dv (1867–85), Bridgw. Dv (1885–1918).

CHILTON POLDEN
Chap in Moorlinch AP, sep EP 1828,[25] sep CP 1866.[158] Sometimes 'Chilton upon Polden'. *LG* Seq 49. Civ bdry: 1933.[3] *Parl* West Dv (1867–85), Bridgw. Dv/CC (1885–*). *Eccl* Glaston. Jurisd. Eccl bdry: 1856 (help cr Burtle EP).[149]

CHILTON TRINITY
AP *LG* Pt Andersf. Hd, pt N Peth. Hd, pt Whitley Hd, Bridgw. PLU, RSD, RD. Civ bdry: 1885,[2] 1886,[203] 1907,[201] 1933.[3] *Parl* Seq 17. *Eccl* Sometimes as 'Chilton', Seq 7. Eccl bdry: 1962,[183] 1966.[202]

EAST CHINNOCK
AP *LG* Seq 24. Civ bdry: 1957.[11] *Parl* Seq 16. *Eccl* Seq 34.

MIDDLE CHINNOCK
AP *LG* Houndsb., Barw. & Coker Hd, Yeov. PLU, RSD. United civ 1884 with West Chinnock CP, the union at first called 'Middle Chinnock' but within several years 'West Chinnock',[204] qv. *Parl* W'rn Dv (1832–67), Mid Dv (1867–85). *Eccl* Seq 34. Eccl bdry: 1970.[205]

WEST CHINNOCK
Chap in Chiselborough AP, sep civ identity early, sep EP 1970 (from pt of the area, the remainder eccl transf to Middle Chinnock AP).[205] *LG* Houndsb., Barw. & Coker Hd, Yeov. PLU, RSD. United civ 1884 with Middle Chinnock AP, the union at first called 'Middle Chinnock' but within several years 'West Chinnock'; par as reconstituted, Yeov. RSD, RD. *Parl* Seq 16. *Eccl* Mart. RDn.

CHIPSTABLE
AP *LG* Willit. & Freem. Hd, Welling. PLU, RSD, RD. Civ bdry: 1884,[206] 1933.[3] *Parl* Seq 22. *Eccl* Seq 17. Eccl bdry: 1971 (gains ent Raddington AP).[207]

CHISELBOROUGH
AP Incl chap West Chinnock (sep civ identity early, sep EP 1970 [from pt of area, remainder eccl transf to Middle Chinnock AP][205]). *LG* Seq 24. *Parl* Seq 16. *Eccl* As 'Chiselborough with West Chinnock' before 1970 and 'Chiselborough' thereafter, Ilch. RDn (until 1872), Mart. RDn (1872–*).

CHISELBOROUGH WTIH WEST CHINNOCK–See prev entry

CHRISTON
AP *LG* Winterstoke Hd, Axbr. PLU, RSD, RD. Abol civ 1933 ent to Loxton AP.[3] *Parl* E'rn Dv (1832–67), East Dv (1867–85), Wells Dv (1885–1918), W-s-M Dv (1918–48). *Eccl* Seq 22.

CHURCHILL
Chap in Banwell AP, sep civ identity early, sep EP 1749.[25] *LG* Seq 53. Civ bdry: 1935.[29] Transf 1974 to Avon.[22] *Parl* Seq 7. *Eccl* Pec jurisd (1749–1872), Axbr. RDn (1872–*). Eccl bdry: 1964.[87]

CHURCHSTANTON
AP In Devon, transf 1896 to Somerset.[208] *LG* Taun. PLU, sep RD in Devon (1894–96), Taun. RD (1896–1974). Civ bdry: 1966 (exchanges pts with Upottery AP, Devon).[137] *Parl* In Devon until 1918, Taun. Dv/CC (1918–*). *Eccl* Dunkeswell RDn (until 1875), Dunkeswell & Honiton RDn (1875–1902), Honiton RDn (1902–70)(all in dioc Exeter), Taun. S RDn (dioc Bath & Wells, 1970–*).

CLANDOWN
EP Cr 1849 from Midsomer Norton AP.[209] Frome RDn (1849–72), Mids. Nort. RDn (1872–*).
CLAPTON
AP Usual civ spelling; for eccl see following entry. *LG* Portbury Hd, Bedm. PLU (1836–99), RSD, Long Ashton PLU (1899–1930), RD. Civ bdry: 1844.[210] Abol civ 1954 to help cr Clapton-in-Gordano CP.[211] *Parl* E'rn Dv (1832–67), East Dv (1867–85), N'rn Dv (1885–1918), W-s-M Dv (1918–48), N Somerset CC (1948–70).
CLAPTON-IN-GORDANO
AP Usual eccl spelling; for civ see prev entry. *Eccl* Seq 6.
CP Cr 1954 by union Clapton AP, pt Portbury AP.[211] *LG* Long Ashton RD. Transf 1974 to Avon.[22] *Parl* N Somerset CC (1970–*).
CLATWORTHY
AP *LG* Seq 52. *Parl* Seq 21. *Eccl* Seq 17.
CLAVERTON
AP *LG* Seq 21. Civ bdry: 1951 (loses pt to Bath CB and CP).[41] Transf 1974 to Avon.[22] *Parl* Seq 1. Parl bdry: 1951.[173] *Eccl* Seq 1.
CLEEVE
Chap in Yatton AP, sep EP 1841 as 'Cleeve in Yatton',[25] eccl refounded 1843 as 'Cleeve'[212] although 'Cleeve in Yatton' commonly used, sep CP 1949.[213] *LG* Long Ashton RD. Transf 1974 to Avon.[22] *Parl* W-s-M CC (1951–*). Parl bdry: 1951.[173] *Eccl* Redcl. & Bedm. RDn (1841–47), Chew RDn (1847–55), Portish. RDn (1855–*).
CLEEVE IN YATTON–See prev entry
OLD CLEEVE
AP Incl chap Leighland (sep EP 1724,[25] refounded 1865[214]). *LG* Seq 52. Civ bdry: 1883,[1] 1884,[215] 1886.[164] *Parl* Seq 21. *Eccl* Seq 15.
CLEVEDON
The following have 'Clevedon' in their names. Insofar as any existed at a given time: *LG* Portbury Hd, Bedm. PLU (1836–99), Long Ashton PLU (1899–1930), Clevedon USD, UD. *Parl* E'rn Dv (1832–67), East Dv (1867–85), N'rn Dv (1885–1918), W-s-M Dv/CC (1918–*). *Eccl* Seq 6.
AP1–CLEVEDON [ST ANDREW]–Civ bdry: 1933,[3] 1951 (gains foreshore area from Bristol CB and CP).[20] Transf 1974 to Avon.[22] Parl bdry: 1952.[83] Eccl bdry: 1861 (cr EP3),[216] 1876 (cr EP4),[217] 1940 (cr EP1).[218]
–CLEVEDON ALL SAINTS–See EP3
EP1–CLEVEDON CHRIST CHURCH–Cr 1940 from AP1.[217]
EP2–CLEVEDON ST JOHN THE EVANGELIST–Renaming 1972 of EP4.[219]
EP3–EAST CLEVEDON–Cr 1861 from AP1.[216] Now usually called 'Clevedon All Saints'. Bdry: 1955.[220]
EP4–SOUTH CLEVEDON–Cr 1876 from AP1.[217] Renamed 1972 as EP2.[219]
CLIFTON HOLY TRINITY, ST ANDREW THE LESS AND ST PETER
EP Cr from territory in anc Glos, gains 1943 pt Bedminster St Raphael the Archangel EP (anc Somerset).[72] See main entry in Glos.
CLOFORD
AP *LG* Frome Hd, PLU, RSD, RD. Abol civ 1933 ent to Wanstrow AP.[3] *Parl* E'rn Dv (1832–67), Mid Dv (1867–85), Frome Dv (1885–1918), Wells Dv (1918–48). *Eccl* Frome RDn. Abol eccl 1974 to help cr Nunney with Wanstrow and Cloford EP.[221]
CLOSWORTH
AP *LG* Seq 24. Civ bdry: 1933.[3] *Parl* Seq 16. *Eccl* Seq 31.
CLUTTON
AP *LG* Seq 14. Civ bdry: 1956.[154] Transf 1974 to Avon.[22] *Parl* Seq 3. *Eccl* Seq 5.
EAST COKER
AP *LG* Seq 24. Civ bdry: 1930,[143] 1933.[3] *Parl* Seq 16. *Eccl* Seq 31. Eccl bdry: 1959.[222]
WEST COKER
AP *LG* Seq 24. Civ bdry: 1930.[143] *Parl* Seq 16. *Eccl* Seq 31.
COLEFORD
Chap in Kilmersdon AP, sep EP 1834,[25] eccl refounded 1843,[223] sep CP 1949 (from pt Kilmersdon, pt Babington AP).[31] *LG* Frome RD. *Parl* Wells CC (1970–*). *Eccl* Frome RDn (1843–72), Mids. Nort. RDn (1872–*). Eccl bdry: 1954.[32]
ABBAS AND TEMPLE COMBE
EP Renaming 1972 of Abbas Combe (or Templecombe)(civ, 'Abbas Combe').[224] Merston RDn.
ABBAS COMBE
AP Usual civ spelling; for eccl see following entry. *LG* Seq 23. *Parl* Seq 8.
ABBAS COMBE (OR TEMPLECOMBE)
AP Usual eccl spelling; for civ see prev entry. *Eccl* Merston RDn (until 1884), Milb. Port RDn (1884–1955), Merston RDn (1955–72). Renamed 1972 'Abbas and Temple Combe'.[224]
ENGLISH COMBE
AP Usual civ spelling; for eccl see 'Englishcombe'. *LG* Seq 44. Civ bdry: 1883,[1] 1885,[171] 1951 (loses pt to Bath CB and CP).[41] Transf 1974 to Avon.[22] *Parl* Seq 1. Parl bdry: 1951.[173]
MONKTON COMBE
AP Incl chap Combe Down (sep EP 1839,[25] refounded 1854[25]). *LG* Seq 5. Civ bdry: 1951 (loses pt to Bath CB and CP),[41] 1967 (loses pt to Bath CB and CP).[42] Transf 1974 to Avon.[22] *Parl* Seq 1. Parl bdry: 1951.[73] *Eccl* Seq 1.
COMBE DOWN
EP Cr 1839,[25] refounded 1854[225] from Monkton Combe AP. Bath RD. Bdry: 1901,[226] 1964.[227]
COMBE FLOREY
AP *LG* Seq 41. *Parl* Seq 22. *Eccl* Taun. RDn (until 1872), Welling. RDn (1872–1936), Taun. N RDn (1963–73), Tone RDn (1973–*).
COMBE HAY
AP *LG* Seq 44. Transf 1974 to Avon.[22] *Parl* Seq 1. *Eccl* Frome RDn (until 1872), Mids. Nort. RDn (1872–1956), Bath RDn (1956–*).
COMBE ST NICHOLAS
AP *LG* Seq 29. *Parl* Seq 20. *Eccl* Pec jurisd Dean &

Chapter of Wells (until 1845), Seq 9 thereafter. Eccl bdry: 1961.[228]

COMPTON BISHOP

AP *LG* Incl Rackley Bor (status not sustained), Seq 53. Civ bdry: 1897,[29] 1935.[30] *Parl* Seq 7. *Eccl* Pec jurisd (until 1845), Seq 22 thereafter.

COMPTON DANDO

AP *LG* Seq 26. Civ bdry: 1933,[3] 1938.[229] Transf 1974 to Avon.[22] *Parl* Seq 3. *Eccl* Seq 5.

COMPTON DUNDON

AP *LG* Pt Whitley Hd, pt Somert. Hd, Langp. PLU, RSD, RD. Civ bdry: 1887.[196] *Parl* Seq 15. *Eccl* Pec jurisd (until 1845), Seq 33 thereafter.

COMPTON MARTIN

AP Incl chap Nempnett Thrubwell (sep civ identity early, sep EP 1859[230]). *LG* Seq 16. Addtl civ bdry alt: 1884.[231] Pt transf 1974 to Avon to be Compton Martin par, the pt remaining in Somerset added to Priddy CP.[22] *Parl* Seq 3. *Eccl* Seq 5.

COMPTON PAUNCEFOOT

AP *LG* Seq 13. Civ bdry: 1933.[3] *Parl* Seq 8. *Eccl* Seq 25.

CONGRESBURY

AP Incl chap Wick St Lawrence (sep civ identity early, eccl severed 1954 to help cr Hewish St Ann and Wick St Lawrence EP[232]). *LG* Seq 53. Addtl civ bdry alt: 1885,[148] 1962.[233] Transf 1974 to Avon.[22] *Parl* Seq 7. *Eccl* Seq 24. Addtl eccl bdry alt: 1865 (help cr Congresbury St Ann EP, later called 'Hewish St Ann').[117]

CONGRESBURY ST ANN

EP Cr 1865 from Congresbury AP, Wick St Lawrence chap in Congresbury AP, Banwell AP, Puxton EP.[117] Later called 'Hewish St Ann'. Axbr. RDn (1865–72), Lock. RDn (1872–1954). Abol 1954 to help cr Hewish St Ann and Wick St Lawrence EP.[232]

CORFE

Chap in Taunton St Mary Magdalene AP, sep civ identity early, sep EP 1826.[25] *LG* Seq 41. Civ bdry: 1883,[1] 1887.[234] *Parl* Seq 18. *Eccl* Taun. RDn (1826–1963), Taun. S RDn (1963–*).

CORSTON

AP *LG* Seq 46. Transf 1974 to Avon.[22] *Parl* Seq 1. *Eccl* Seq 4.

CORTON DENHAM

AP *LG* Seq 23. Civ bdry: 1966 (loses pt to Sandford Orcas AP, Dorset).[137] *Parl* Seq 8. *Eccl* Seq 32.

COSSINGTON

AP *LG* Seq 49. Civ bdry: 1933.[3] *Parl* Seq 17. *Eccl* Seq 35.

COTHELSTONE

Chap in Kingston AP, sep civ identity early, sep EP 1729.[25] *LG* Seq 41. Civ bdry: 1883,[1] 1884.[12] *Parl* Seq 22. *Eccl* Taun. RDn (1729–1872), Welling. RDn (1872–1963), Taun. N RDn (1963–*).

COXLEY

EP Cr 1844 from Wells St Cuthbert AP.[236] Cary RDn (1844–72), Shept. Mal. RDn (1872–*).

CRANMORE

CP Cr 1933 by union Wast Cranmore CP, West Cranmore CP.[3] *LG* Shept. Mal. RD. *Parl* Wells CC (1948–*).

EAST CRANMORE

Chap in Doulting AP, sep civ identity early, no sep eccl identity. *LG* Lbty Cranmore, Frome Hd, Shept. Mal. PLU, RSD, RD. Abol 1933 to help cr Cranmore CP.[3] *Parl* E'rn Dv (1832–67), Mid Dv (1867–85), Frome Dv (1885–1918), Wells Dv (1918–48).

WEST CRANMORE

Chap in Doulting AP, sep civ identity early, no sep eccl identity. *LG* Lbty Cranmore, Wells Forum Hd, Shept. Mal. PLU, RSD, RD. Civ abol, *Parl* as for East Cranmore.

CREECH ST MICHAEL

AP *LG* Andersf. Hd, Taun. PLU, RSD, RD. Civ bdry: 1884.[12] *Parl* Seq 18. *Eccl* Seq 18. Eccl bdry: 1960.[237]

CREWKERNE

AP *LG* Crewk. Hd, Chard PLU, RSD, Crewk. UD. Civ bdry: 1885,[238] 1894 (the pt not constituted Crewk. UD cr West Crewkerne CP),[239] 1934.[240] *Parl* Seq 16. *Eccl* Seq 9. Eccl bdry: 1925 (gains Easthams reputed par).[241]

WEST CREWKERNE

CP Cr 1894 from the pt of Crewkerne AP not constituted Crewk. UD.[239] *LG* Chard PLU, RD. Bdry: 1933,[3] 1966 (gains pt Broadwindsor AP, Dorset).[137] *Parl* Yeov. Dv/CC (1918–*).

CRICKET MALHERBIE

AP *LG* Abd. & Bulst. Hd, Chard PLU, RSD, RD. Civ bdry: 1885.[238] Abol civ 1933 ent to Knowle St Giles CP.[3] *Parl* W'rn Dv (1832–67), West Dv (1867–85), S'rn Dv (1885–1918), Yeov. Dv (1918–48). *Eccl* Crewk. RDn. Abol eccl 1961 to help cr Knowle St Giles with Cricket Malherbie EP.[228]

CRICKET ST THOMAS

AP *LG* Seq 35. Civ bdry: 1886.[242] *Parl* Seq 20. *Eccl* Seq 9.

CROSCOMBE

AP *LG* Seq 50. Civ bdry: 1883,[1] 1884,[243] 1933.[3] *Parl* Seq 8. *Eccl* Seq 27. Eccl bdry: 1960.[244]

CROWCOMBE

AP *LG* Seq 52. *Parl* Seq 21. *Eccl* Bridgw. RDn (until 1884), Quantoxhd. RDn (1884–1955), Dunst. RDn (1955–73), Quant. RDn (1973–*).

CUCKLINGTON

AP *LG* Seq 33. *Parl* Seq 8. *Eccl* Seq 26.

CUDWORTH

AP Incl chap Knowle St Giles (sep civ identity early, sep EP 1731[25]). *LG* Seq 35. *Parl* Seq 20. *Eccl* Pec jurisd (until 1845), Seq 19 thereafter.

CULBONE

AP Sometimes anc 'Kitnor'. *LG* Carhamp. Hd, Willit. PLU, RSD, RD. Abol civ 1933 ent to Oare AP.[3] *Parl* W'rn Dv (1832–67), West Dv (1867–85), W'rn Dv (1885–1918), Bridgw. Dv (1918–48). *Eccl* Seq 12.

CURLAND

Chap in Curry Mallet AP, sep civ identity early,

eccl detached 1960 to help cr Staple Fitzpaine with Bickenhall and Curland EP.[245] *LG* Seq 3. Addtl civ bdry alt: 1883.[1] *Parl* Seq 18.

NORTH CURRY

AP Incl chap West Hatch (sep civ identity early, sep EP 1850,[25] eccl refounded 1856[246]), chap Stoke St Gregory (sep civ identity early, sep EP 1827[25]), bor Newport (status not sustained, no sep civ or eccl identity). *LG* Seq 18. Addtl civ bdry alt: 1885.[247] *Parl* Seq 18. *Eccl* Pec jurisd Dean & Chapter of Wells (until 1845), Seq 18 thereafter. Addtl eccl bdry alt: 1960.[237]

CURRY MALLET

AP Incl chap Curland (sep civ identity early, eccl detached 1960 to help cr Staple Fitzpaine with Bickenhall and Curland EP[245]). *LG* Seq 2. Addtl civ bdry alt: 1886.[6] *Parl* Seq 19. *Eccl* As 'Curry Mallet with Curland' until 1960 and 'Curry Mallet' thereafter, Crewk. RDn (until 1872), Ilmin. RDn (1872–*).

CURRY MALLET WITH CURLAND–See prev entry

CURRY RIVEL

AP Incl chap Earnshill (sep par by *temp* Henry VIII[248]). *LG* Seq 2. Civ bdry: 1885,[249] 1886,[6] 1933.[3] *Parl* Seq 20. *Eccl* Seq 10. Eccl bdry: 1844 (help cr Hambridge EP).[39]

CUTCOMBE

AP *LG* Seq 11. Civ bdry: 1883,[250] 1886.[164] *Parl* Seq 21. *Eccl* Seq 12.

DINDER

AP *LG* Seq 48. *Parl* Seq 13. *Eccl* Pec jurisd Dean of Wells (until 1845), Seq 27 thereafter. Eccl bdry: 1966.[28]

DINNINGTON

Chap in Seavington St Michael AP, sep civ identity early, eccl severed perhaps 1920s or 1930s to help cr Hinton St George with Dinnington EP.[251] *LG* Seq 35. Civ bdry: 1885.[238] *Parl* Seq 20.

DITCHEAT

AP *LG* Seq 50. Civ bdry: 1879,[92] 1885.[252] *Parl* Seq 8. *Eccl* Seq 27. Eccl bdry: 1875 (help cr West Bradley EP).[91]

DODINGTON

AP *LG* Willit. & Freem. Hd, Willit. PLU, RSD, RD. Civ bdry: 1883,[253] 1884,[254] 1886.[164] Abol civ 1933 ent to Holford AP.[3] *Parl* W'rn Dv (1832–67), West Dv (1867–85), W'rn Dv (1885–1918), Bridgw. Dv (1918–48). *Eccl* Seq 8.

DONYATT

AP *LG* Seq 1. *Parl* Seq 19. *Eccl* Seq 10. Eccl bdry: 1958.[131]

DOULTING

AP Incl chaps Downhead, East Cranmore, West Cranmore (each sep civ identity early, none with sep eccl identity, hence this par eccl 'Doulting with Downhead, East Cranmore and West Cranmore', qv), chap Stoke Lane (sep civ identity early, sep EP 1826[25]). *LG* Seq 50. Addtl civ bdry alt: 1883,[1] 1884,[255] 1933.[3] *Parl* Seq 8.

DOULTING WITH DOWNHEAD, EAST CRANMORE AND WEST CRANMORE

AP Usual eccl spelling; for civ, civ sep chaps Downhead, East Cranmore, West Cranmore, and for civ and eccl sep chap Stoke Lane, see prev entry. *Eccl* Seq 27. Addtl eccl bdry alt: 1960.[244]

WEST DOWLISH

AP *LG* Abd. & Bulst. Hd, Chard PLU, RSD, RD. Civ bdry: 1885.[238] Abol civ 1933 ent to Dowlish Wake AP.[3] *Parl* W'rn Dv (1832–67), West Dv (1867–85), S'rn Dv (1885–1918), Yeov. Dv (1918–48). *Eccl* Seq 9.

DOWLISH WAKE

AP Usual civ spelling; for eccl see following entry. *LG* Seq 35. Civ bdry: 1885,[238] 1933 (gains West Dowlish AP).[3] *Parl* Seq 20.

DOWLISHWAKE

AP Usual eccl spelling; for civ see prev entry. *Eccl* Seq 9.

DOWNHEAD

Chap in Doulting AP, sep civ identity early, no sep eccl identity. *LG* Seq 50. *Parl* Seq 11.

DOWNSIDE

EP Cr 1840,[25] refounded 1845[256] from Midsomer Norton AP. Frome RDn (1840–72), Mids. Nort. RDn (1872–*). Bdry: 1966.[28]

DRAYCOTT

EP Cr 1862 from Cheddar AP, Rodney Stoke AP, ent ex-par place Nyland.[180] Axbr. RDn.

DRAYTON

AP *LG* Pt Abd. & Bulst. Hd, pt E Kingsbury Hd, pt Pitney Hd, Langp. PLU, RSD, RD. Civ bdry: 1886.[6] *Parl* Seq 20. *Eccl* Seq 10. Eccl bdry: 1844 (help cr Hambridge EP).[39]

DULVERTON

AP *LG* Seq 51. Civ bdry: 1884,[133] 1966 (gains pt East Anstey AP, Devon).[137] *Parl* Seq 22. *Eccl* Seq 14. Eccl bdry: 1959.[135]

DUNDRY

Chap in Chew Magna AP, sep civ identity early, sep EP 1855.[186] *LG* Chew Hd, Bedm. PLU (1836–99), RSD, Long Ashton PLU (1899–1930), RD. Civ bdry: 1883,[1] 1884,[257] 1951.[20] Transf 1974 to Avon.[22] *Parl* Seq 3. Parl bdry: 1952.[83] *Eccl* Chew Magna RDn.

DUNKERTON

AP Incl pt area Peasdown (sep EP 1874,[155] sep CP 1955 as 'Peasdown St John'[156]). *LG* Seq 44. Civ bdry: 1885.[157] Transf 1974 to Avon.[22] *Parl* Seq 1. *Eccl* Frome RDn (until 1872), Mids. Nort. RDn (1872–1956), Bath RDn (1956–66), Mids. Nort. RDn (1966–*).

DUNSTER

AP *LG* Dunst. Bor (status not sustained), Seq 11. Civ bdry: 1884,[254] 1916.[258] *Parl* Dunst. Parl Bor (1360 only), Seq 21. *Eccl* Seq 12. Eccl bdry: 1852 (cr Road Hill EP),[259] 1953 (cr Alcombe EP),[4] 1954.[165]

DURLEIGH

AP *LG* Andersf. Hd, Bridgw. PLU, pt Bridgw. MB (1835–86), pt Bridgw. USD (1875–86), Bridgw. RSD (pt 1875–86, ent 1886–94) Bridgw. RD. Civ bdry: 1886 (loses the pt in the

MB to Bridgwater AP),[161] 1886,[260] 1887,[102] 1933,[3] 1952.[105] *Parl* Pt Bridgw. Parl Bor (1832–67), remainder and later, Seq 17. *Eccl* Seq 7. Eccl bdry: 1961 (help cr Greenfield EP),[110] 1958.[109]

DURSTON

AP *LG* N Peth. Hd, Taun. PLU, RSD, RD. Civ bdry: 1888.[261] *Parl* Seq 18. *Eccl* Donative, Bridgw. RDn (until 1963), Taun. N RDn (1963–*).

EARNSHILL

AP Chap in Curry Rivel AP, sep par by *temp* Henry VIII.[248] *LG* Abd. & Bulst. Hd, Langp. PLU, RSD, RD. Civ bdry: 1886.[6] Abol civ 1933 ent to Curry Rivel AP.[3] *Parl* W'rn Dv (1832–67), West Dv (1867–85), S'rn Dv (1885–1918), Yeov. Dv (1918–48). *Eccl* Crewk. RDn. Abol eccl 1844 to help cr Hambridge with Earnshill EP.[262]

EASTHAMS

Sinecure rectory in Crewk. RDn, eccl 'reputed par', no sep civ identity, abol eccl 1925 ent to Crewkerne AP.[241]

EASTON

EP Cr 1844 from Wells St Cuthbert AP.[263] Cary RDn (1844–72), Shept. Mal. RDn (1872–*). Eccl bdry: 1862 (help cr Priddy EP),[194] 1931,[264] 1973 (cr Wookey Hole EP).[265]

EASTON-IN-GORDANO

AP *LG* Seq 37. Civ bdry: 1884,[210] 1896 (help cr South Bristol CP to be in Bristol CB),[18] 1898 (loses pt to Bristol CB and South Bristol CP),[18] 1951 (gains pt Bristol CB and CP).[20] Transf 1974 to Avon.[22] *Parl* Seq 5. Parl bdry: 1952.[83] *Eccl* Pec jurisd (until 1845), Seq 6 thereafter. Eccl bdry: 1861 (help cr Pill EP),[267] 1957.[266]

EASTOVER

EP Cr 1846 from Bridgwater AP.[108] Bridgw. RDn. Bdry: 1962,[183] 1965 (help cr Bridgwater St Francis of Assisi EP).[113] Renamed 1972 'Bridgwater St John the Baptist'.[114]

EASTRIP

Ex-par place, sep CP 1858,[179] abol eccl 1933 to help cr Bruton with Wyke Champflower and Redlynch EP.[140] *LG* Bruton Hd, Wincan. PLU (1858[200]–85), RSD. Abol 1885 pt to South Brewham CP, pt to Bruton AP.[17] *Parl* Mid Dv (1867–85), E'rn Dv (1885–1918).

EDINGTON

Chap in Moorlinch AP, sep EP 1828,[25] sep CP 1866.[158] *LG* Seq 49. Civ bdry: 1933.[3] *Parl* West Dv (1867–85), Bridgw. Dv/CC (1885–*). *Eccl* Glaston. Jurisd. Eccl bdry: 1856 (help cr Burtle EP).[149]

EDSTOCK AND BEER

Hmlt in Cannington AP, sep CP 1866.[158] *LG* Cann. Hd, Bridgw. PLU, RSD. Abol 1886 pt to Cannington AP, pt to Otterhampton AP.[161] *Parl* West Dv (1867–85), Bridgw. Dv (1885–1918).

ELM

AP Sometimes 'Great Elm'. *LG* Seq 19. Civ bdry: 1883,[1] 1885.[53] *Parl* Seq 10. *Eccl* Seq 28. Eccl bdry: 1846 (help cr Chantry EP).[166]

ELWORTHY

AP *LG* Seq 52. Civ bdry: 1886.[164] *Parl* Seq 21. *Eccl* Dunst. RDn. Eccl bdry: 1967.[269] Abol eccl 1969 ent to Monksilver AP, the latter sometimes thereafter called 'Monksilver with Elworthy'.[270]

EMBOROUGH

Chap in Chewton Mendip AP, sep civ identity early, no sep eccl identity. *LG* Chewton Hd, Shept. Mal. PLU, RSD, RD. Bdry: 1883,[1] 1884,[271] 1885.[272] *Parl* Seq 4.

ENGLISHCOMBE

AP Usual eccl spelling; for civ see 'English Combe'. *Eccl* Seq 1.

ENMORE

AP *LG* Seq 4. Civ bdry: 1878,[273] 1887.[136] *Parl* Seq 17. *Eccl* Seq 7. Eccl bdry: 1957 (help cr Twerton Hill EP).[274]

EVERCREECH

AP Usual civ spelling; for eccl see following entry. *LG* Seq 47. *Parl* Seq 8.

EVERCREECH WITH CHESTERBLADE

AP Usual eccl spelling; for civ see prev entry. *Eccl* Pec jurisd Dean of Wells (until 1845), Seq 26 thereafter.

EXFORD

AP *LG* Carhamp. Hd, Dulv. PLU, RSD, RD. *Parl* Seq 22. *Eccl* Seq 14.

EXMOOR

Ex-par place, primarily in Somerset (Willit. & Freem. Hd), small uninhabited pt in Devon (S Molton Hd), the latter added 1884 to North Molton AP, Devon,[276] and ent Somerset thereafter; Exmoor sep CP 1858,[179] sep EP 1857.[275] *LG* Dulv. PLU (except Devon pt in S Molton PLU), Dulv. RSD, RD. *Parl* Somerset pt, West Dv (1867–85), W'rn Dv (1885–1918), Taun. Dv/CC (1918–*). *Eccl* Dunst. RDn (1857–1951), Wivel. RDn (1951–73), Exm. RDn (1973–*).

EXTON

AP *LG* Pt Carhamp. Hd, pt Willit. & Freem. Hd, Dulv. PLU, RSD, RD. *Parl* Seq 22. *Eccl* Seq 14.

FARLEIGH HUNGERFORD

AP *LG* Wellow Hd, Frome PLU, RSD, RD. Civ bdry: 1883,[1] 1878.[273] Abol civ 1933 ent to Norton St Philip AP.[3] *Parl* E'rn Dv (1832–67), East Dv (1867–85), Frome Dv (1885–1948). *Eccl* Frome RDn. Abol eccl 1972 to help cr Rode Major EP.[277]

FARMBOROUGH

AP *LG* Seq 25. Civ bdry: 1956.[154] Transf 1974 to Avon.[22] *Parl* Seq 3. *Eccl* Seq 3.

FARRINGTON GURNEY

Chap in Chewton Mendip AP, sep civ identity early, eccl combined 1867 with chap Ston Easton in same par to cr Ston Easton with Farrington Gurney EP (sometimes 'Ston Easton cum Farrington Gurney'),[190] detached 1973 to cr Farrington Gurney EP.[278] *LG* Seq 16. Transf 1974 to Avon.[22] *Parl* Seq 3. *Eccl* Mids. Nort. RDn (1973–*).

FELTON COMMON HILL
EP Cr 1873 from Winford AP, Backwell AP, Wrington AP.[33] Chew Magna RDn.

FIDDINGTON
AP *LG* Seq 10. Civ bdry: 1878,[279] 1884,[160] 1886.[161] *Parl* Seq 21. *Eccl* Seq 8. Eccl bdry: 1930.[280]

FILTON–See WHITCHURCH

FITZHEAD
Chap in Wiveliscombe AP, sep civ identity early, sep EP 1737.[25] *LG* Seq 31. *Parl* Seq 22. *Eccl* Pec jurisd Wiveliscombe (1737–1845), Dunst. RDn (1845–72), Wivel. RDn (1872–1966), Welling. RDn (1966–73), Tone RDn (1973–*).

FIVEHEAD
AP *LG* Pt Abd. & Bulst. Hd, pt Willit. & Freem. Hd, Langp. PLU, RSD, RD. Civ bdry: 1885,[38] 1886,[6] 1933.[3] *Parl* Seq 19. *Eccl* Seq 10.

FLAX BOURTON
Chap in Wraxall AP, sep civ identity early, eccl attached early to chap Nailsea in same par until 1801,[281] sep EP 1841.[282] Sometimes eccl 'Bourton'. *LG* Seq 37. Transf 1974 to Avon.[22] *Parl* Seq 5. *Eccl* Redcl. & Bedm. RDn (1844–47), Chew RDn (1847–55), Portish. RDn (1855–*). Eccl bdry: 1959.[24]

FOXCOTE
AP Sometimes 'Forscote' or 'Foxcote or Forscote'. *LG* Wellow Hd, Frome PLU, RSD, RD. Abol civ 1933 ent to Hemington AP.[3] *Parl* E'rn Dv (1832–67), Mid Dv (1867–85), Frome Dv (1885–1948). *Eccl* Frome RDn (until 1872), Mids. Nort. RDn (1872–1926). Abol eccl 1926 to help cr Foxcote with Shoscombe EP.[284]

FOXCOTE WITH SHOSCOMBE
EP Cr 1926 by union Foxcote AP, pt Wellow AP (incl area Shoscombe).[284] Mids. Nort. RDn.

FRESHFORD
AP *LG* Bath Forum Hd, Bradford PLU (1836–82), RSD (1875–82), Bath PLU (1882–1930), RSD (1882–94), Bath RD (1894–1933), Bathavon RD (1933–74). Transf 1974 to Avon.[22] *Parl* Seq 1. *Eccl* Seq 1.

FROME
The following have 'Frome' in their names. Insofar as any existed at a given time: *LG* Frome Hd, PLU, pt Frome USD, pt Frome RSD, Frome UD. *Parl* Pt Frome Parl Bor (1832–85), remainder and later, Seq 10. *Eccl* Frome RDn.

AP1–FROME [ST JOHN THE BAPTIST]–Incl chap Selwood (sep EP 1873 as EP3, now usually called 'Frome St Mary the Virgin',[285] sep CP 1894 [from the area not in the USD] as 'Selwood',[56] qv), chap Woodlands (sep civ identity early, sep EP 1872[286] from area EP3). Addtl civ bdry alt: 1883,[1] 1885,[53] 1897.[287] Addtl eccl bdry alt: 1819 (cr EP1,[25] refounded 1844[288]), 1840 (cr EP2,[25] refounded 1844[288]).

EP1–FROME CHRIST CHURCH–Cr 1819,[25] refounded 1844[288] from AP1.

EP2–FROME HOLY TRINITY–Cr 1840,[25] refounded[288] 1844 from AP1.

–FROME ST MARY THE VIRGIN–Name used now for EP cr 1873 as EP3, qv.

EP3–FROME SELWOOD–Chap in AP1 as 'Selwood', sep EP 1873 as 'Frome Selwood,[275] sep CP 1894 (the pt not in Frome USD) as 'Selwood',[156] qv. This par now usually eccl called 'Frome St Mary the Virgin'. Eccl bdry: 1872 (when still chap, cr Woodlands EP).[286]

GLASTONBURY
AP Incl Glastonbury St Benedict (sep EP 1726,[25] refounded 1844[289]), chap West Pennard (sep civ identity early, sep EP 1824[25]), Nyland cum Batcombe (orig sep AP, in this par before 1535,[393] sep civ identity regained early). *LG* Glaston. Twelve Hides Hd, Wells PLU. Glaston. Bor/MB (ent until 1883, pt 1883–94, ent 1894–1974), Glaston. USD (ent 1875–83, pt 1883–94), pt Street USD (1883–94), pt Wells RSD. Addtl civ bdry alt: 1883 (detached pt lost to Street AP and thus becomes pt Street USD, gains detached pt Street so that Glastonbury no longer ent in MB and pt Street in Glaston. MB and USD),[1] 1884,[290] 1894 (exchanges pts with Street AP),[291] 1894 (the pt not in a USD cr Sharpham CP).[56] *Parl* Summonded to parl in mediev period but did not send MPs, Seq 8. *Eccl* Seq 36.

GLASTONBURY ST BENEDICT
EP Cr 1726,[25] refounded 1844[289] from Glastonbury AP. Donative, pec jurisd Bp Bath & Wells (1726–1845), Glaston. Jurisd. thereafter.

GOATHILL
AP *LG* Horeth. Hd, Sherborne PLU, RSD, sep RD in Somerset (1894–95). Transf 1895 to Dorset.[90] *Parl* E'rn Dv (1832–67), Mid Dv (1867–85), E'rn Dv (1885–1918), Dorset thereafter. *Eccl* Merst. RDn (until 1884), Milb. Port RDn (1884–1955), Merst. RDn (1955–*).

GOATHURST
AP *LG* Seq 4. Civ bdry: 1883,[1] 1885,[2] 1886.[161] *Parl* Seq 17. *Eccl* Seq 7.

GODNEY
Chap in Meare AP, sep EP 1740,[25] eccl refounded 1869,[292] sep CP 1904.[293] *LG* Wells PLU, RD. *Parl* Wells Dv/CC (1918–*). *Eccl* Glaston. Jurisd (1740–1970), Shept. Mal. RDn (1970–*).

GREEN OARE
Ex-par place, sep CP 1858,[179] abol eccl 1966 ent to Chewton Mendip with Emborough AP.[28] *LG* Chewton Hd, Wells PLU (1858[200]–85), RSD. Abol 1885 ent to Chewton Mendip AP.[294] *Parl* East Dv (1867–85), N'rn Dv (1885–1918).

GREENFIELD
EP Cr 1961 from Bridgwater AP, Durleigh AP, North Petherton AP, Northmoor Green EP.[110] Bridgw. RDn. Renamed 1972 'Bridgwater Holy Trinity'.[112]

GREINTON
AP *LG* Seq 49. Civ bdry: 1883,[1] 1885.[2] *Parl* Seq 17. *Eccl* Pawlett RDn (until 1956), Glaston. Jurisd (1956–*).

HALCON
EP Cr 1967 from Taunton Holy Trinity EP, West Monkton AP, Taunton St James AP, Cheddon Fitzpaine AP.[295] Taun. S RDn. Renamed 1972 'Taunton All Saints'.[296]

HALSE
AP *LG* Willit. & Freem. Hd, Taun. PLU, RSD, RD. Civ bdry: 1883.[1] *Parl* Seq 22. *Eccl* Seq 21.

HIGH HAM
AP *LG* Pt Pitney Hd, pt Whitley Hd, pt Willit. & Freem. Hd, Langp. PLU, RSD, RD. Civ bdry: 1886.[6] *Parl* Seq 15. *Eccl* Sometimes as 'High Ham with Low Ham', Seq 33.

HAMBRIDGE WITH EARNSHILL
EP Cr 1844 by union Earnshill AP, ex-par Nidon, and pts Curry Rivel AP, Isle Brewers AP, Barrington EP, Drayton AP.[39] Crewk. RDn (1844–72), Ilmin. RDn (1872–*).

HARDINGTON
AP *LG* Kilm. Hd, Frome PLU, RSD, RD. Abol civ 1933 ent to Hemington AP.[3] *Parl* E'rn Dv (1832–67), Mid Dv (1867–85), Frome Dv (1885–1948). *Eccl* Frome RDn. Abol prob in 1748 to help cr Hemington with Hardington EP.[297]

HARDINGTON MANDEVILLE
AP *LG* Seq 24. *Parl* Seq 16. *Eccl* Seq 34.

EAST HARPTREE
AP *LG* Winterstoke Hd, Clut. PLU, RSD, RD. Pt transf 1974 to Avon to be East Harptree par, the pt remaining in Somerset added to Priddy CP.[22] *Parl* Seq 3. *Eccl* Frome RDn (until 1855), Wells RDn (1855–72), Mids. Nort. RDn (1872–*). Eccl bdry: 1862 (help cr Priddy EP).[194]

WEST HARPTREE
AP *LG* Seq 16. Civ bdry: 1933.[3] Pt transf 1974 to Avon to be West Harptree par, the pt remaining in Somerset added to Priddy CP.[22] *Parl* Seq 3. *Eccl* Seq 5. Eccl bdry: 1862 (help cr Priddy EP).[194]

HASLEBURY PLUCKNETT
AP *LG* Seq 24. *Parl* Seq 16. *Eccl* Pec jurisd (until 1845), Seq 34 thereafter.

WEST HATCH
Chap in North Curry AP, sep civ identity early, sep EP 1850,[25] eccl refounded 1856.[246] *LG* Seq 18. Civ bdry: 1883,[1] 1884,[12] 1885.[247] *Parl* Seq 18. *Eccl* Taun. RDn (1850–1963), Taun. S RDn (1963–*). Eccl bdry: 1960.[237]

HATCH BEAUCHAMP
AP *LG* Seq 3. Civ bdry: 1884,[12] 1885.[298] *Parl* Seq 18. *Eccl* Seq 11. Eccl bdry: 1931.[89]

HAWKRIDGE
AP Incl chap Withypool (sep civ identity early, no sep eccl identity hence this par eccl 'Hawkridge with Withypool', qv). *LG* Willit. & Freem. Hd, Dulv. PLU, RSD, RD. Addtl civ bdry alt: 1885.[299] Abol civ 1933 ent to Withypool CP.[3] *Parl* W'rn Dv (1832–67), West Dv (1867–85), W'rn Dv (1885–1918), Taun. Dv (1918–48).

HAWKRIDGE WITH WITHYPOOL
AP Usual eccl spelling; for civ and civ sep chap Withypool, see prev entry. *Eccl* Dunst. RDn (until 1951), Wivel. RDn (1951–73), Exm. RDn (1973–*).

HEATHFIELD
AP *LG* Taun. & Taun. Dean Hd, Taun. PLU, RSD, RD. Abol civ 1933 ent to Norton Fitzwarren AP.[3] *Parl* W'rn Dv (1832–67), West Dv (1867–85), W'rn Dv (1885–1918), Yeov. Dv (1918–48). *Eccl* Seq 21.

HEMINGTON
AP *LG* Seq 27. Civ bdry: 1933.[3] *Parl* Seq 11. *Eccl* Frome RDn. Abol eccl prob in 1748 to help cr Hemington with Hardington EP.[297]

HEMINGTON WITH HARDINGTON
EP Cr prob in 1748 by union Hemington AP, Hardington AP.[297] Frome RDn (1748–1872), Mids. Nort. RDn (1872–1962), Frome RDn (1962–*).

HENDFORD
EP Cr 1846 from Yeovil AP.[300] Merst. RDn. Bdry: 1846,[300] 1959.[222] Renamed 1972 'Yeovil Holy Trinity'.[302]

HENGROVE
EP Cr 1940 from Brislington EP, Brislington St Christopher EP.[122] Bedm. RDn (1940–73), Brisl. RDn (1973–*). Bdry: 1973 (help cr Bristol Christ the Servant, Stockwood EP).[125]

HENSTRIDGE
AP *LG* Seq 23. Civ bdry: 1966 (exchanges pts with Kington Magna AP, loses pt to Fifehead Magdalen AP, both Dorset).[137] *Parl* Seq 8. *Eccl* Pec jurisd (until 1845), Seq 32 thereafter.

HENTON
EP Cr 1848 from Wookey AP, Meare AP.[303] Axbr. RDn.

HEWISH ST ANN
EP Name commonly used for par cr 1865 as 'Congresbury St Ann', qv, incl abol 1954 to help cr Hewish St Ann and Wick St Lawrence EP.[232]

HEWISH ST ANN AND WICK ST LAWRENCE
EP Cr 1954 by union Congresbury St Ann EP (commonly called 'Hewish St Ann'), chap Wick St Lawrence in Congresbury AP.[232] Lock. RDn.

HIGHBRIDGE
Chap in Burnham AP (eccl, 'Burnham-on-Sea'), sep EP 1860,[146] sep CP 1894.[56] *LG* Axbr. PLU, RD. Civ bdry: 1894.[145] Abol civ 1896 the pt to help constitute Highbridge UD to cr North Highbridge CP, the remainder to cr Burnham Without CP.[147] *Eccl* Axbr. RDn (1860–72), Burnham RDn (1872–*).

NORTH HIGHBRIDGE
CP Cr 1896 from the pt of Highbridge CP to help constitute Highbridge UD.[147] *LG* Axbr. PLU, Highbridge UD. Abol 1933 to help cr Burnham-on-Sea CP.[3] *Parl* Bridgw. Dv (1918–48).

SOUTH HIGHBRIDGE
CP Cr 1896 from Huntspill AP.[147] *LG* Axbr. PLU, Highbridge UD. Abol 1933 to help cr Burnham-on-Sea CP.[3] *Parl* Bridgw. Dv (1918–48).

HILLFARRANCE

AP *LG* Taun. & Taun. Dean Hd, Welling. PLU, RSD. Civ bdry: 1883.[1] Abol civ 1884 pt to Milverton AP, pt to Oake AP, pt to Nynehead AP.[304] *Parl* W'rn Dv (1832–67), West Dv (1867–85). *Eccl* Sometimes as 'Hill Farrance', Taun. RDn (until 1872), Welling. RDn (1872–1973), Tone RDn (1973–*).

HINTON BLEWETT

AP Usual civ spelling; for eccl see following entry. *LG* Seq 16. Transf 1974 to Avon.[22] *Parl* Seq 3.

HINTON BLEWITT

AP Usual eccl spelling. for civ see prev entry. *Eccl* Redcl. & Bedm. RDn (until 1847), Chew RDn (1847–55), Chew Magna RDn (1855–1956), Mids. Nort. RDn (1956–62), Chew Magna RDn (1962–*).

HINTON CHARTERHOUSE

Chap in Norton St Philip AP, sep civ identity early, sep EP 1824.[25] *LG* Seq 44. Transf 1974 to Avon.[22] *Parl* Seq 1. *Eccl* Frome RDn.

HINTON ST GEORGE

AP *LG* Seq 17. *Parl* Seq 16. *Eccl* Crewk. RDn. Abol eccl perhaps in 1920s or 1930s to help cr Hinton St George with Dinnington EP.[251]

HINTON ST GEORGE WITH DINNINGTON

EP Cr perhaps in 1920s or 1930s by union Hinton St George AP, chap Dinnington in Seavington St Michael AP.[251] Crewk. RDn.

HOLCOMBE

AP *LG* Seq 28. Civ bdry: 1883,[1] 1884.[305] *Parl* Seq 11. *Eccl* Seq 29. Eccl bdry: 1953 (help cr Westfield EP).[306]

HOLFORD

AP *LG* Whitley Hd, Willit. PLU, RSD, RD. Civ bdry: 1884,[254] 1886,[307] 1933.[3] *Parl* Seq 21. *Eccl* Seq 8.

HOLTON

AP *LG* Whitley Hd, Wincan. PLU, RSD, RD. Civ bdry: 1885,[153] 1886.[95] *Parl* Seq 14. *Eccl* Cary RDn (until 1932), Bruton RDn (1932–*).

HOLWELL

AP In Somerset (Horeth. Hd) but situated in Dorset, transf to Dorset 1832 for parl purposes, 1844 for civ purposes.[308] See main entry in Dorset.

HORNBLOTTON

AP *LG* Whitstone Hd, Shept. Mal. PLU, RSD, RD. Civ bdry: 1885.[309] Abol civ 1933 ent to West Bradley CP.[3] *Parl* E'rn Dv (1832–67), Mid Dv (1867–85), E'rn Dv (1885–1918), Wells Dv (1918–48). *Eccl* Seq 25.

HORRINGTON

EP Cr 1844 from Wells St Cuthbert AP.[310] Cary RDn (1844–72), Shept. Mal. RDn (1872–*). Bdry: 1966.[28]

HORSINGTON

AP *LG* Seq 23. Civ bdry: 1883,[1] 1885,[153] 1886.[95] *Parl* Seq 8. *Eccl* Merst. RDn (until 1884), Milb. Port RDn (1884–1955), Bruton RDn (1955–*).

HUISH CHAMPFLOWER

AP *LG* Seq 51. Civ bdry: 1884.[206] *Parl* Seq 22. *Eccl* Seq 17.

HUISH EPISCOPI

AP Incl chap and bor Langport (bor status not sustained but parl representation 1304–07 only, no sep civ identity, sep EP 1876[349]). *LG* Pt Pitney Hd, pt E Kingsbr. Hd, pt Willit. & Freem. Hd, Langp. PLU, RSD, RD. Civ bdry: 1886.[6] *Parl* Seq 15. *Eccl* Pec jurisd (until 1845), Seq 33 thereafter.

BISHOP'S HULL

Chap in Taunton St Mary Magdalene AP, sep civ identity early, sep EP 1729.[25] *LG* Taun. & Taun. Dean Hd, Taun. PLU, pt Taun. USD, pt Taun. RSD. Civ bdry: 1883,[1] 1884.[304] Abol civ 1885 the pt in the USD to cr Bishop's Hull Within MB to be in newly incorp Taun. MB, the remainder to cr Bishop's Hull Without CP.[312] *Parl* Pt Taun. Parl Bor (1832–1918), pt W'rn Dv (1832–67), pt West Dv (1867–85), pt W'rn Dv (1885–1918). *Eccl* Taun. RDn (1729–1963), Taun. S RDn (1963–*). Eccl bdry: 1864 (help cr Bishop's Hull St John the Evangelist EP),[313] 1933,[314] 1969.[315]

BISHOP'S HULL ST JOHN THE EVANGELIST

EP Cr 1864 from Bishop's Hull EP, Wilton EP, Taunton St Mary Magdalene AP.[313] Taun. RDn (1864–1963), Taun. S RDn (1963–72). Bdry: 1933,[314] 1969.[315] Renamed 1972 'Taunton St John'.[316]

BISHOP'S HULL WITHIN

CP Cr 1885 from the pt of Bishop's Hull CP in Taun. USD.[312] *LG* Taun. PLU, MB, USD. Abol 1921 to help cr Taunton CP.[317] *Parl* Taun. Dv/CC (1918–48).

BISHOP'S HULL WITHOUT

CP Cr 1885 from the pt of Bishop's Hull CP not in Taun. USD.[312] *LG* Taun. PLU, RSD, RD. Bdry: 1921 (help cr Taunton CP).[317] *Parl* Taun. Dv/CC (1918–*).

HUNTSPILL

AP *LG* Huntspill & Puriton Hd, Bridgw. PLU, RSD, RD. Civ bdry: 1885,[318] 1896 (cr South Highbridge CP, to be in Highbridge UD),[147] 1933.[3] Abol civ 1949 pt to cr East Huntspill CP, pt to cr West Huntspill CP.[319] *Parl* W'rn Dv (1832–67), West Dv (1867–85), Bridgw. Dv/CC (1885–1970). *Eccl* Pawlett RDn (until 1956), Burnham RDn (1956–*). Eccl bdry: 1845 (cr Huntspill All Saints EP).[320]

HUNTSPILL ALL SAINTS

EP Cr 1845 from Huntspill AP.[320] Pawlett RDn (1845–1956), Burnham RDn (1956–72). Renamed 1972 'East Huntspill'.[321]

EAST HUNTSPILL

CP Cr 1949 from Huntspill AP.[319] *LG* Bridgw. RD. *Parl* Bridgw. CC (1970–*).

EP Renaming 1972 of Huntspill All Saints EP.[321] Burnham RDn.

WEST HUNTSPILL

CP Cr 1949 from Huntspill AP.[319] *LG* Bridgw. RD. *Parl* Bridgw. CC (1970–*).

HUTTON

AP *LG* Seq 53. Civ bdry: 1933.[3] Transf 1974 to Avon.[22] *Parl* Seq 7. *Eccl* Seq 24.

ILCHESTER
AP *LG* Ilch. Bor, Seq 43. Civ bdry: 1884,[17] 1885,[322] 1933,[3] 1957.[11] *Parl* Seq 16. *Eccl* Seq 33.

ILMINSTER
AP *LG* Abd. & Bulst. Hd, Chard PLU, RSD, RD (1894–99), Ilmin. UD (1899–1974). Civ bdry: 1886,[323] 1899 (the pt not constituted Ilmin. UD cr Ilminster Without CP).[324] *Parl* Seq 19. *Eccl* Royal pec jurisd of Ilmin. (until 1845), Seq 10 thereafter. Eccl bdry: 1928.[130]

ILMINSTER WITHOUT
CP Cr 1899 from the pt of Ilminster AP not constituted Ilmin. UD.[324] *LG* Chard PLU, RD. *Parl* Yeov. Dv/CC (1918–*).

ILTON
AP *LG* Seq 1. Civ bdry: 1885.[325] *Parl* Seq 19. *Eccl* Pec jurisd (until 1845), Seq 10 thereafter. Eccl bdry: 1875.[322]

ISLE ABBOTS
AP *LG* Seq 2. Civ bdry: 1885,[38] 1886.[6] *Parl* Seq 19. *Eccl* Sometimes as 'Ile Abbots', Seq 10. Eccl bdry: 1929,[16] 1931.[89]

ISLE BREWERS
AP *LG* Seq 2. Civ bdry: 1886.[6] *Parl* Seq 19. *Eccl* Sometimes as 'Ile Brewers', Seq 10. Eccl bdry: 1844 (help cr Hambridge EP).[39]

KEINTON MANDEVILLE
AP *LG* Seq 12. *Parl* Seq 9. *Eccl* Seq 25.

KELSTON
AP Anc 'Kelveston'. *LG* Seq 6. Civ bdry: 1953.[172] Transf 1974 to Avon.[22] *Parl* Seq 1. *Eccl* Seq 2.

KENN
Chap in Yatton AP, sep civ identity early, sep EP 1846.[326] *LG* Seq 54. Civ bdry: 1883,[1] 1884.[210] Transf 1974 to Avon.[22] *Parl* Seq 6. *Eccl* Redcl. & Bedm. RDn (1846–47), Chew RDn (1847–55), Portish. RDn (1855–*).

KEWSTOKE
AP *LG* Winterstoke Hd, Axbr. PLU, pt W-s-M USD (1893–94), Axbr. RSD (ent 1875–83, pt 1883–94), pt W-s-M UD (1894–96), Axbr. RD (pt 1894–96, ent 1896–1974) Civ bdry: 1883 (gains detached pt Weston-super-Mare AP in W-s-M USD),[1] 1885,[148] 1896 (made ent Axbr. RD),[327] 1902,[328] 1933.[3] Transf 1974 to Avon.[22] *Parl* Seq 7. *Eccl* Seq 24. Eccl bdry: 1964,[329] 1965 (help cr Milton EP).[330]

KEYNSHAM
AP Incl chap Queen Charlton (sep civ identity early, sep EP 1741[25]), chap Brislington (sep civ identity early, eccl donative, sep EP before 1786[99]). *LG* Keyn. Hd, PLU, RSD, RD (1894–1933), Bathavon RD (1933–38), Keyn. UD (1938–74). Addtl civ bdry alt: 1883,[1] 1884,[331] 1898 (loses pt to Bristol CB and CP),[73] 1938 (the pt not constituted Keyn. UD lost pt to Compton Dando AP, pt to Whitchurch AP, and remainder [a small pt] becomes 'Unnamed' CP, sometimes 'Unnaxed Area'),[229] 1966 (gains pt Bristol CB and CP).[21] Transf 1974 to Avon.[22] *Parl* Seq 3. *Eccl* Seq 4. Addtl eccl bdry alt: 1973 (help cr Bristol Christ the Servant, Stockwood EP).[123]

KILMERSDON
AP Incl chap Ashwick (sep civ identity early, sep EP 1826[25]), chap Coleford (sep EP 1834,[25] eccl refounded 1843,[223] sep CP 1949 [incl pt Babington AP][31]). *LG* Seq 27. Addtl civ bdry alt: 1883,[1] 1884,[333] 1885,[334] 1933 (incl help cr Norton Radstock CP).[3] *Parl* Seq 11. *Eccl* Frome RDn (until 1872), Mids. Nort. RDn (1872–*). Addtl eccl bdry alt: 1953 (help cr Westfield EP).[306]

KILMINGTON
AP *LG* Nort. Ferris Hd, Mere PLU, RSD, sep RD in Somerset (1894–96), transf 1896 to Wilts.[335] *Parl* E'rn Dv (1832–67), Mid Dv (1867–85), E'rn Dv (1885–1918), Wilts thereafter. *Eccl* Seq 26.

KILTON
AP *LG* Willit. & Freem. Hd, Willit. PLU, RSD. Abol civ 1886 pt to Holford AP, pt to Stringston AP, pt to help cr Kilton with Lilstock CP.[336] *Parl* W'rn Dv (1832–67), West Dv (1867–85), W'rn Dv (1885–1918). *Eccl* Seq 8. Eccl bdry: 1881 (gains chap Lilstock from Stogursey AP).[337]

KILTON WITH LILSTOCK
CP Cr 1886 by union Lilstock CP, pt Kilton AP.[336] *LG* Willit. & Freem. Hd, Willit. PLU, RSD, RD. Abol 1933 ent to Stringston AP.[3] *Parl* Bridgw. Dv (1918–48).

KILVE
AP *LG* Seq 52. Civ bdry: 1933.[3] *Parl* Seq 21. *Eccl* Seq 8.

KINGSBURY EPISCOPI
AP Civ incl East Lambrook (orig sep AP, eccl sep status maintained). *LG* E Kingsbr. Hd, Langp. PLU, RSD, RD. Civ bdry: 1885,[339] 1886.[6] *Parl* Seq 20. *Eccl* Pec jurisd (until 1845), Crewk. RDn (1845–1931). Abol eccl 1931 to help cr Kingsbury Episcopi with East Lambrook EP.[340]

KINGSBURY EPISCOPI WITH EAST LAMBROOK
EP Cr 1931 by union Kingsbury Episcopi AP, East Lambrook EP.[340] Crewk. RDn (1931–55), Ilmin. RDn (1955–*).

KINGSDON
AP *LG* Somert. Hd, Langp. PLU, RSD, RD. Civ bdry: 1885,[341] 1886.[342] *Parl* Seq 15. *Eccl* Seq 33.

KINGSTON
AP Usual civ spelling until renamed 1952 'Kingston St Mary',[344] the usual eccl spelling; see following entry. Incl chap Cothelstone (sep civ identity early, sep EP 1729[25]). *LG* Taun. & Taun. Dean Hd, Taun. PLU, RSD, RD. Addtl civ bdry alt: 1883,[1] 1884,[343] 1885,[238] 1933.[3] *Parl* W'rn Dv (1832–67), West Dv (1867–85), W'rn Dv (1885–1918), Taun. Dv/CC (1918–70).

KINGSTON PITNEY
Sinecure rectory, 'reputed par', no sep civ identity, Merst. RDn, eccl abol 1937 to help cr Yeovil with Preston Plucknett and Kingston Pitney EP.[345]

KINGSTON ST MARY

AP Usual eccl spelling, civ spelling from 1952 when 'Kingston' so renamed,[344] qv for earlier civ and for sep chap Cothelstone. *LG* Taun. RD. *Parl* Taun. CC (1970–*). *Eccl* Seq 18.

KINGSTON SEYMOUR

AP *LG* Seq 15. Transf 1974 to Avon.[22] *Parl* Seq 6. *Eccl* Seq 6.

KINGSTONE

AP *LG* Tintinhull Hd, Chard PLU, RSD, RD. *Parl* Seq 20. *Eccl* Seq 9.

KINGWESTON

AP *LG* Seq 12. Civ bdry: 1887.[196] *Parl* Seq 9. *Eccl* Seq 25. Eccl bdry: 1932.[174]

KITNOR–See Culbone

KITTISFORD

AP *LG* Milverton Hd, Welling. PLU, RSD, RD. Abol civ 1933 ent to Stawley AP.[3] *Parl* W'rn Dv (1832–67), West Dv (1867–85), W'rn Dv (1885–1918), Taun. Dv (1918–48). *Eccl* Seq 21.

KNOWLE HOLY NATIVITY

EP Cr 1883 from Bedminster St John EP.[60] Bristol (Rural Dv) RDn (1883–87), Bristol RDn (1887–1901), Bedm. RDn (1901–73), Brisl. RDn (1973–*). Bdry: 1906 (cr Knowle St Martin EP).[350]

KNOWLE ST BARNABAS

EP Cr 1935 from Bedminster AP, Knowle St Martin EP.[346] Bedm. RDn (1935–73), Brisl. RDn (1973–*). Bdry: 1959 (help cr Bristol Holy Cross Inns Court EP),[126] 1959.[347]

KNOWLE ST GILES

Chap in Cudworth AP, sep civ identity early, sep EP 1731.[25] *LG* Seq 35. Civ bdry: 1885,[238] 1933.[3] *Parl* Seq 20. *Eccl* Crewk. RDn. Abol eccl 1961 pt to help cr Knowle St Giles with Cricket Malherbie EP, pt to Combe St Nicholas AP, pt to Chard The Good Shepherd, Fulham EP.[228]

KNOWLE ST GILES WITH CRICKET MALHERBIE

EP Cr 1961 by union Cricket Malherbie AP, pt Knowle St Giles EP.[228] Crewk. RDn.

KNOWLE ST MARTIN

EP Cr 1906 from Knowle Holy Nativity EP.[350] Bedm. RDn (1906–73), Brisl. RDn (1973–*). Bdry: 1935 (help cr Knowle St Barnabas EP).[303]

EAST LAMBROOK

AP Civ incl early in Kingsbury Episcopi AP, qv. *Eccl* Crewk. RDn. Abol eccl 1931 to help cr Kingsbury Episcopi with East Lambrook EP.[139]

LAMYAT

AP *LG* Seq 50. *Parl* Seq 8. *Eccl* Seq 26.

LANGFORD BUDVILLE

Chap in Milverton AP, sep civ identity early, sep EP 1863.[348] *LG* Seq 32. Civ bdry: 1884,[13] 1933.[3] *Parl* Seq 22. *Eccl* Taun. RDn (1863–72), Welling. RDn (1872–1973), Tone RDn (1973–*).

LANGPORT

Chap and bor in Huish Episcopi AP, sep civ identity early but bor status not sustained (Langp. Parl Bor represented 1304–07 only), sep EP 1876.[349] *LG* Seq 36. *Parl* Seq 15. *Eccl* Ilch. RDn.

LANGRIDGE

AP *LG* Bath Forum Hd, Bath PLU, RSD, RD. Civ bdry: 1883,[1] 1885.[171] Abol civ 1933 ent to Charlcombe AP.[3] *Parl* E'rn Dv (1832–67), East Dv (1867–85), Frome Dv (1885–1948). *Eccl* Seq 2.

LANSDOWN

EP Cr 1881 from Walcot AP.[351] Bath RDn. Renamed 1967 'Bath St Stephen'.[47]

LAVERTON

AP *LG* Frome Hd, PLU, RSD, RD. Civ bdry: 1885.[53] Abol civ 1933 ent to Lullington AP.[3] *Parl* E'rn Dv (1832–67), Mid Dv (1867–85), Frome Dv (1885–1948). *Eccl* Seq 28.

ABBOTS LEIGH

Chap in Bedminster AP, sep civ identity early, sep EP 1852.[55] *LG* Seq 37. Addtl civ bdry alt: 1896 (loses pt to help cr South Bristol CP to be in Bristol CB).[18] Transf 1974 to Avon.[22] *Parl* Seq 5. *Eccl* Bristol RDn (1855–66), Bristol (Rural Dv) RDn (1866–87), Bristol RDn (1887–1901), Clifton RDn (1901–*).

LEIGH ON MENDIP–See following entry

LEIGH-UPON-MENDIP

Chap in Mells AP, sep civ identity early, sep EP 1860 as 'Leigh on Mendip'.[352] *LG* Seq 19. *Parl* Seq 10. *Eccl* Frome RDn (1860–1962), Shept. Mal. RDn (1962–*).

LEIGH WOODS

EP Cr 1893 from Long Ashton AP.[23] Portish. RDn.

LEIGHLAND

EP Cr 1724,[25] refounded 1865[214] from Old Cleeve AP. Dunst. RDn (1724–1872), Wivel. RDn (1872–1951), Dunst. RDn (1951–73), Exm. RDn (1973–*).

LILSTOCK

Chap in Stogursey AP, sep civ identity early, eccl severed 1881 and united to Kilton AP.[336] *LG* Willit. & Freem. Hd, Willit. PLU, RSD. Abol 1886 to help cr Kilton with Lilstock CP.[336] *Parl* W'rn Dv (1832–67), West Dv (1867–85), W'rn Dv (1885–1918).

LIMINGTON

AP *LG* Seq 40. Civ bdry: 1884.[17] *Parl* Seq 16. *Eccl* Seq 33.

HIGH LITTLETON

AP *LG* Seq 16. Civ bdry: 1956.[154] Transf 1974 to Avon.[22] *Parl* Seq 3. *Eccl* Seq 5.

LITTON

AP *LG* Wells Forum Hd, Clut. PLU, RSD, RD. Civ bdry: 1883,[1] 1884.[353] *Parl* Seq 3. *Eccl* Frome RDn (until 1855), Wells RDn (1855–72), Mids. Nort. RDn (1872–1962), Chew Magna RDn (1962–*).

LOCKING

AP *LG* Seq 53. Civ bdry: 1933.[3] Transf 1974 to Avon.[22] *Parl* Seq 7. *Eccl* Seq 24.

LONG LOAD

Chap in Martock AP, sep EP 1733,[25] eccl refounded 1867 as 'Long Load Christ Church',[354] renamed eccl 1972 'Long Load',[355] sep CP

1895.[10] *LG* Yeov. PLU, RD. *Parl* Yeov. Dv/CC (1918–*). *Eccl* Ilch. RDn (1867–72), Mart. RDn (1872–*).

LONG LOAD CHRIST CHURCH–See prev entry

LOPEN

Chap in South Petherton AP, sep civ identity early, sep EP 1747.[25] *LG* Seq 35. *Parl* Seq 16. *Eccl* Crewk. RDn.

LOVINGTON

AP *LG* Seq 13. Civ bdry: 1933.[3] *Parl* Seq 8. *Eccl* Pec jurisd Dean & Chapter of Wells (until 1845), Cary RDn (1845–*).

LOXTON

AP *LG* Seq 53. Civ bdry: 1933.[3] Pt transf 1974 to Avon to be Loxton par, the pt remaining in Somerset added to East Brent AP.[22] *Parl* Seq 7. *Eccl* Seq 22.

LUCCOMBE

AP *LG* Seq 11. Civ bdry: 1883,[356] 1886,[164] 1929,[357] 1933.[3] *Parl* Seq 21. *Eccl* Seq 12. Eccl bdry: 1952,[358] 1954.[165]

LUFTON

AP *LG* Stone Hd, Yeov. PLU, RSD, RD. Abol civ 1933 ent to Brympton AP.[3] *Parl* W'rn Dv (1832–67), Mid Dv (1867–85), S'rn Dv (1885–1918), Yeov. Dv (1918–48). *Eccl* Seq 34.

LULLINGTON

AP *LG* Seq 19. Civ bdry: 1933.[3] *Parl* Seq 10. *Eccl* Frome RDn.

LUXBOROUGH

AP *LG* Seq 11. Civ bdry: 1883.[1] *Parl* Seq 21. *Eccl* Seq 12.

BISHOP'S LYDEARD

AP *LG* Seq 30. Civ bdry: 1884.[12] *Parl* Seq 22. *Eccl* Pec jurisd Dean & Chapter of Wells (until 1845), Taun. RDn (1845–72), Welling. RDn (1872–1963), Taun. N RDn (1963–*).

LYDEARD ST LAWRENCE

AP *LG* Seq 41. *Parl* Seq 22. *Eccl* Taun. RDn (until 1872), Welling. RDn (1872–1963), Taun. N RDn (1963–73), Tone RDn (1973–*).

LYDFORD

CP Cr 1933 by union East Lydford AP, West Lydford AP.[3] *LG* Shept. Mal. RD. *Parl* Wells CC (1948–*).

EAST LYDFORD

AP *LG* Somert. Hd, Shept. Mal. PLU, RSD, RD. Civ bdry: 1884.[338] Abol civ 1933 to help cr Lydford CP.[3] *Parl* W'rn Dv (1832–67), Mid Dv (1867–85), E'rn Dv (1885–1918), Wells Dv (1918–48). *Eccl* Cary RDn. Abol eccl 1965 to help cr East Lydford with Wheathill EP.[360]

EAST LYDFORD WITH WHEATHILL

EP Cr 1965 by union East Lydford AP, Wheathill AP.[360] Cary RDn. Abol 1971 to help cr Lydford-on-Fosse EP.[142]

WEST LYDFORD

AP *LG* Catsash Hd, Shept. Mal. PLU, RSD, RD. Civ bdry: 1884.[359] Abol civ 1933 to help cr Lydford CP.[3] *Parl* E'rn Dv (1832–67), Mid Dv (1867–85), E'rn Dv (1885–1918), Wells Dv (1918–48). *Eccl* Pec jurisd (until 1845), Cary RDn (1845–1971). Abol eccl 1971 to help cr Lydford-on-Fosse EP.[142]

LYDFORD-ON-FOSSE

EP Cr 1971 by union East Lydford with Wheathill EP, West Lydford AP.[142] Cary RDn.

LYMPSHAM

AP *LG* Seq 8. *Parl* Seq 7. *Eccl* Seq 23.

LYNCOMBE

EP Cr 1856 from Widcombe AP (civ 'Lyncombe and Widcombe').[361] Bath RD. Bdry: 1868 (cr South Lyncombe EP),[362] 1901.[363] Renamed 1967 'Bath Lyncombe'.[47]

LYNCOMBE AND WIDCOMBE

AP Usual civ spelling; for eccl see 'Widcombe'. Orig chap in Bath St Mary de Stalls AP, sep identity early. *LG* Bath Forum Hd, Bath MB/CB, USD. Abol civ 1900 to help cr Bath CP.[39] *Parl* Bath Parl Bor (1832–1918).

SOUTH LYNCOMBE

EP Cr 1868 from Lyncombe EP.[362] Bath RDn. Bdry: 1901,[363] 1964,[227] 1964 (cr Odd Down EP).[364] Renamed 1967 'Bath St Luke'.[47]

LYNG

AP *LG* Lyng Bor (status not sustained), Seq 4. Civ bdry: 1883,[1] 1885,[365] 1886,[161] 1888.[261] *Parl* Seq 17. *Eccl* Bridgw. RDn (until 1956), Taun. RDn (1956–63), Taun. N RDn (1963–*). Eccl bdry: 1840 (help cr Burrowbridge EP).[106]

LYNGFORD

EP Cr 1957 from Rowbarton EP.[366] Taun. RDn (1957–63), Taun. N RDn (1963–72). Renamed 1972 'Taunton St Peter, Lyngford'.[367]

MAPERTON

AP *LG* Seq 13. Civ bdry: 1883,[1] 1886.[95] *Parl* Seq 8. *Eccl* Seq 25.

MARK

Chap in Wedmore AP, sep civ identity early, sep EP 1816.[25] *LG* Seq 7. Addtl civ bdry alt: 1885.[7] *Parl* Seq 7. *Eccl* Pec jurisd Dean of Wells (until 1845), Axbr. RDn (1845–72), Burnham RDn (1872–*).

MARKSBURY

AP *LG* Seq 26. Civ bdry: 1933.[3] Transf 1974 to Avon.[22] *Parl* Seq 3. *Eccl* Seq 3.

MARSTON BIGOT

AP *LG* Frome Hd, PLU, RSD, RD. Civ bdry: 1883,[1] 1885.[53] Abol civ 1933 ent to Nunney AP.[3] *Parl* Pt Frome Parl Bor (1832–85), pt E'rn Dv (1832–67), pt Mid Dv (1867–85), Frome Dv (1885–1918), Wells Dv (1918–48). *Eccl* Seq 28. Eccl bdry: 1973.[368]

MARSTON MAGNA

AP *LG* Horeth. Hd, Sherborne PLU (1835–94), RSD, Yeov. PLU (1894–1930), RD. Civ bdry: 1885.[153] *Parl* E'rn Dv (1832–67), Mid Dv (1867–85), S'rn Dv (1885–1918), Yeov. Dv/CC (1918–*). *Eccl* Seq 31.

MARTOCK

AP Incl chap Ash (sep EP 1845,[9] sep CP 1895[10]), chap Long Load (sep EP 1733,[25] eccl refounded 1867[354] as 'Long Load Christ Church', eccl renamed 1972 'Long Load',[355] sep CP 1895[10]). *LG* Mart. Hd, Yeov. PLU, RSD, RD. Addtl civ bdry alt: 1883,[1] 1885,[341] 1957.[11]

Parl Seq 16. *Eccl* Seq 34.

MEARE

AP Incl chap Godney (sep EP 1740,[25] eccl refounded 1869,[292] sep CP 1904[293]). *LG* Seq 20. Addtl civ bdry alt: 1884.[369] *Parl* E'rn Dv (1832–67), Mid Dv (1867–85), Wells Dv/CC (1885–*). *Eccl* Seq 36. Addtl eccl bdry alt: 1848 (help cr Henton EP).[303]

MELLS

AP Incl chap Leigh-upon-Mendip (sep civ identity early, sep EP 1860 as 'Leigh on Mendip'[352]). *LG* Seq 19. Addtl civ bdry alt: 1883,[1] 1885.[53] *Parl* Seq 10. *Eccl* Seq 28. Eccl bdry: 1846 (help cr Chantry EP),[166] 1852 (cr Vobster EP).[370]

MERRIOTT

AP *LG* Seq 17. Civ bdry: 1933,[3] 1934.[240] *Parl* Seq 16. *Eccl* Seq 9.

MIDDLEZOY

AP *LG* Seq 49. Civ bdry: 1883,[1] 1886.[371] *Parl* Seq 17. *Eccl* Seq 36. Eccl bdry: 1840 (help cr Burrowbridge EP).[106]

MILBORNE PORT

AP *LG* Milborne Port Bor (status not sustained), Seq 23. Civ bdry: 1885.[153] *Parl* Seq 8. *Eccl* Seq 32.

MILTON

EP Cr 1965 from Kewstoke AP, Worle AP, Weston-super-Mare Christ Church EP, Weston-super-Mare St Saviour EP.[330] Lock. RDn.

MILTON CLEVEDON

AP *LG* Bruton Hd, Shept. Mal. PLU, RSD, RD. *Parl* Seq 8. *Eccl* Seq 26.

MILVERTON

AP Incl chap Langford Budville (sep civ identity early, sep EP 1863[347]). *LG* Milverton Bor (status not sustained), pt Milverton Hd, pt Willit. & Freem. Hd, Welling. PLU, RSD, RD. Addtl civ bdry alt: 1884,[372] 1933.[3] *Parl* Seq 22. *Eccl* Seq 21.

MINEHEAD

AP *LG* Carhamp. Hd, Willit. PLU, RSD (ent 1875–91, pt 1891–94), pt Minehead USD (1891–94), Minehead UD. Civ bdry: 1883,[373] 1894 (the pt not in the USD cr Minehead Without CP),[56] 1916.[258] *Parl* Seq 21. *Eccl* Seq 12.

MINEHEAD WITHOUT

CP Cr 1894 from the pt of Minehead AP not in Minehead USD.[56] *LG* Willit. PLU, RSD, RD. Bdry: 1916.[258] *Parl* Bridgw. Dv/CC (1918–*).

MISTERTON

AP *LG* Crewk. Hd, Beaminster PLU (1835–96), RSD, Chard PLU (1896–1930), RD. Civ bdry: 1966 (gains pt South Perrott AP, Dorset).[137] *Parl* Seq 16. *Eccl* Seq 9.

MONKSILVER

AP *LG* Seq 52. Civ bdry: 1883,[1] 1884.[374] *Parl* Seq 21. *Eccl* Seq 16. Eccl bdry: 1967,[269] 1969 (gains Elworthy AP, the union sometimes thereafeter called 'Monksilver with Elworthy').[270]

MONKSILVER WITH ELWORTHY–See prev entry

WEST MONKTON

AP *LG* Whitley Hd, Taun. PLU, pt Taun. USD (1875–85), Taun. RSD (pt 1875–85, ent 1885–94), Taun. RD. Civ bdry: 1885 (loses the pt in the USD to help cr Taunton St Mary Magdalene Within CP to be in newly incorp Taun. MB),[375] 1895,[376] 1932,[181] 1958,[182] 1966.[377] *Parl* Pt Taun. Parl Bor (1832–1918), remainder and later, Seq 18. *Eccl* Seq 18. Eccl bdry: 1933,[314] 1967 (help cr Halcon EP).[295]

MONTACUTE

AP *LG* Montacute Bor (status not sustained), Seq 43. Civ bdry: 1885,[322] 1957.[11] *Parl* Montacute Parl Bor (1304–06 only), Seq 16. *Eccl* Seq 34.

MOORLINCH

AP Incl chap Chilton Polden (sep civ identity early, sep EP 1828[25]), chaps Stawell, Sutton Mallet (each with sep civ identity early, neither with sep eccl identity hence this par eccl 'Moorlinch with Stawell and Sutton Mallet', qv). *LG* Seq 49. Addtl civ bdry alt: 1933.[3] *Parl* Seq 17.

MOORLINCH WITH STAWELL AND SUTTON MALLET

AP Usual eccl spelling; for civ, civ and eccl sep chap Chilton Polden, and civ sep chaps Stawell, Sutton Mallet, see prev entry. *Eccl* Seq 36.

MUCHELNEY

AP *LG* Seq 36. *Parl* Seq 15. *Eccl* Seq 33.

MUDFORD

AP *LG* Seq 40. Civ bdry: 1884.[17] *Parl* Seq 16. *Eccl* Seq 31.

NAILSEA

Chap in Wraxall AP, sep civ identity early, sep EP 1811.[281] *LG* Seq 37. Civ bdry: 1883,[1] 1884.[210] Transf 1974 to Avon.[22] *Parl* Seq 5. *Eccl* Redcl. & Bedm. RDn (1811–47), Chew RDn (1847–55), Portish. RDn (1855–*). Eccl bdry: 1844 (cr Flax Bourton EP),[282] 1844 (cr Nailsea Christ Church EP).[378]

NAILSEA CHRIST CHURCH

EP Cr 1844 from Nailsea EP.[378] Redcl. & Bedm. RDn (1844–47), Chew RDn (1847–55), Portish. RDn (1855–*).

NEMPNETT THRUBWELL

Chap in Compton Martin AP, sep civ identity early, sep EP 1859.[230] *LG* Seq 25. Civ bdry: 1883,[1] 1884.[379] Transf 1974 to Avon.[22] *Parl* Seq 3. *Eccl* Chew Magna RDn.

NETTLECOMBE

AP *LG* Seq 52. Civ bdry: 1883.[380] *Parl* Seq 21. *Eccl* Seq 16.

NORTH NEWTON

EP Cr 1743,[25] refounded 1880[381] from North Petherton AP. Bridgw. RDn. Abol 1962 to help cr North Newton with St Michaelchurch EP.[382]

NORTH NEWTON WITH ST MICHAELCHURCH

EP Cr 1962 by union North Newton AP, St Michaelchurch EP.[382] Bridgw. RDn.

NEWTON ST LOE

AP *LG* Seq 46. Civ bdry: 1967 (loses pt to Bath CB and CP).[42] Transf 1974 to Avon.[22] *Parl* Seq 1. *Eccl* Seq 2.

NORTHMOOR GREEN

EP Cr 1845 from North Petherton AP.[383] Bridgw. RDn. Bdry: 1961 (help cr Greenfield EP),[110]

1962.[183]

NORTHOVER

AP *LG* Tintinhull Hd, Yeov. PLU, RSD, RD. Abol civ 1933 ent to Ilchester AP.[3] *Parl* W'rn Dv (1832–67), Mid Dv (1867–85), S'rn Dv (1885–1918), Yeov. Dv (1918–48). *Eccl* Seq 33.

MIDSOMER NORTON

AP Incl chap Downside (sep civ identity early, sep EP 1840,[25] eccl refounded 1845[256]). *LG* Chewton Hd, Clut. PLU, Mids. Nort. USD (ent 1875–83, pt 1883–94), Mids. Nort. UD. Addtl civ bdry alt: 1883 (gains detached pts from Chilcompton CP, Paulton CP, Ston Easton CP so that the par no longer ent USD),[1] 1884,[187] 1888,[384] 1894 (par made ent Mids. Nort. UD).[392] Abol civ 1933 pt to Paulton AP, pt to Ston Easton CP, pt to Starron-on-the-Fosse AP, pt to help cr Norton Radstock CP.[3] *Parl* W'rn Dv (1832–67), West Dv (1867–85), W'rn Dv (1885–1918), Taun. Dv (1918–48). *Eccl* Seq 29. Addtl eccl bdry alt: 1849 (cr Clandown EP),[209] 1953 (help cr Westfield EP),[306] 1966.[28]

NORTON FITZWARREN

AP *LG* Seq 41. Civ bdry: 1933.[3] *Parl* Seq 22. *Eccl* Seq 18.

NORTON HAWKFIELD

Tg in Chew Magna AP, sep CP 1866.[158] *LG* Chew Hd, Clut. PLU, RSD, RD. Civ bdry: 1883,[1] 1884.[365] Abol 1896 ent to Norton Malreward AP.[386] *Parl* East Dv (1867–85), N'rn Dv (1885–1918).

NORTON MALREWARD

AP *LG* Seq 14. Civ bdry: 1896.[386] Transf 1974 to Avon.[22] *Parl* Seq 3. *Eccl* Seq 5.

NORTON-RADSTOCK

CP Cr 1933 by union Radstock AP, pts Kilmersdon AP, Midsomer Norton AP, Writhlington AP.[3] *LG* Norton-Radstock UD. Transf 1974 to Avon.[22] *Parl* N Somerset CC (1948–*).

NORTON ST PHILIP

AP Incl chap Hinton Charterhouse (sep civ identity early, sep EP 1824[25]). *LG* Seq 45. Addtl civ bdry alt: 1933,[3] 1966 (loses pt to Wingfield AP, Wilts).[137] *Parl* Seq 2. *Eccl* Seq 28.

NORTON SUB HAMDON

AP *LG* Seq 24. Civ bdry: 1885,[322] 1957.[11] *Parl* Seq 16. *Eccl* Seq 34.

NUNNEY

AP *LG* Seq 19. Civ bdry: 1933,[3] 1951 (cr Trudoxhill CP).[213] *Parl* Seq 11. *Eccl* Frome RDn. Eccl bdry: 1973.[368] Abol eccl 1974 to help cr Nunney with Wanstrow and Cloford EP.[221]

NUNNEY WITH WANSTROW AND CLOFORD

EP Cr 1974 by union Nunney AP, Wanstrow AP, Cloford AP.[221] Frome RDn.

NYLAND CUM BATCOMBE

AP *LG* Glaston. Twelve Hides Hd, Axbr. PLU, RSD, RD. Civ bdry: 1885.[387] Abol civ 1933 ent to Cheddar AP.[3] *Parl* E'rn Dv (1832–67), Mid Dv (1867–85), N'rn Dv (1885–1918), W-s-M Dv/CC (1918–48). *Eccl* Glaston. Jurisd. Abol eccl before 1535 ent to Glastonbury AP.[393]

NYNEHEAD

AP *LG* Seq 42. Civ bdry: 1884,[388] 1933.[3] *Parl* Seq 22. *Eccl* Seq 21.

OAKE

AP *LG* Seq 42. Civ bdry: 1884.[388] *Parl* Seq 22. *Eccl* Seq 21.

OAKHILL

EP Cr 1866 from Shepton Mallet AP, Ashwick EP, Stoke Lane AP.[27] Cary RDn (1866–72), Shept. Mal. RDn (1872–*).

OARE

AP *LG* Seq 11. Civ bdry: 1933.[3] *Parl* Seq 21. *Eccl* Seq 12.

ODCOMBE

AP *LG* Seq 24. Civ bdry: 1884,[17] 1957.[11] *Parl* Seq 16. *Eccl* Seq 34.

ODD DOWN

EP Cr 1964 from South Lyncombe EP.[364] Bath RDn. Renamed 1967 'Bath Odd Down'.[47]

ORCHARD PORTMAN

AP *LG* Seq 41. Civ bdry: 1883,[1] 1933.[3] *Parl* Seq 18. *Eccl* Seq 20.

ORCHARDLEIGH

AP *LG* Frome Hd, PLU, RSD, RD. Abol civ 1933 ent to Lullington CP.[3] *Parl* E'rn Dv (1832–67), Mid Dv (1867–85), Frome Dv (1885–1948). *Eccl* Seq 28.

OTHERY

AP *LG* Seq 49. Civ bdry: 1883,[1] 1886.[161] *Parl* Seq 17. *Eccl* Seq 36. Eccl bdry: 1840 (help cr Burrowbridge EP).[106]

OTTERFORD

AP *LG* Seq 41. *Parl* Seq 22. *Eccl* Taun. RDn (until 1963), Taun. S RDn (1963–*).

OTTERHAMPTON

AP Usual civ spelling; for eccl see following entry. *LG* Seq 10. Civ bdry: 1883,[1] 1886,[161] 1933.[3] *Parl* Seq 17.

OTTERHAMPTON WITH COMBWICH

AP Usual eccl spelling; for civ see prev entry. *Eccl* Seq 8.

PAULTON

Chap in Chewton Mendip AP, sep civ identity early, sep EP 1841.[191] *LG* Seq 16. Addtl civ bdry alt: 1884,[389] 1888,[384] 1933,[3] 1956.[154] Transf 1974 to Avon.[22] *Parl* Seq 3. *Eccl* Frome RDn (1841–72), Mids. Nort. RDn (1872–*).

PAWLETT

AP *LG* Seq 34. *Parl* Seq 17. *Eccl* Seq 35.

PEASEDOWN—See following entry

PEASEDOWN ST JOHN

Dist pt in Wellow AP, pt in Dunkerton AP, pt in Camberton AP, sep EP 1874 as 'Peasedown',[155] sep CP 1955 as 'Peasedown St John'.[156] *LG* Bathavon RD. Transf 1974 to Avon.[22] *Parl* N Somerset CC (1970–*). *Eccl* Mids. Nort. RDn.

PENDOMER

AP *LG* Houndsb., Barw. & Coker Hd, Yeov. PLU, RSD, RD. Abol civ 1933 ent to Closworth AP.[3] *Parl* W'rn Dv (1832–67), Mid Dv (1867–85), S'rn Dv (1885–1918), Yeov. Dv (1918–48). *Eccl* Ilch. RDn (until 1872), Mart. RDn (1872–

1955), Merst. RDn (1955–69), Mart. RDn (1969–*).

EAST PENNARD

AP Incl chap West Bradley (sep civ identity early, sep EP 1875[91]). *LG* Seq 50. Addtl civ bdry alt: 1884.[390] *Parl* Seq 8. *Eccl* Seq 27.

WEST PENNARD

Chap in Glastonbury AP, sep civ identity early, sep EP 1824.[25] *LG* Seq 20. Civ bdry: 1884.[391] *Parl* Seq 8. *Eccl* Glaston. Jurisd.

PENSELWOOD

AP *LG* Seq 33. Civ bdry: 1885,[153] 1966 (gains pt Stourton with Gasper AP, Wilts).[137] *Parl* Seq 8. *Eccl* Sometimes as 'Pen-selwood', Seq 26.

PENSFORD

Chap in Stanton Drew AP, sep civ identity early as 'St Thomas in Pensford', qv, eccl severed perhaps in 1920s or 1930s to help cr Pensford with Publow EP.[394]

PENSFORD WITH PUBLOW

EP Cr perhaps in 1920s or 1930s by union Publow EP, chap Pensford (civ, 'St Thomas in Pensford').[394] Chew Magna RDn. Renamed 1972 'Publow with Pensford'.[395]

NORTH PERROT

AP *LG* Seq 24. *Parl* Seq 16. *Eccl* Seq 34.

NORTH PETHERTON

AP Incl chap St Michaelchurch (sep civ identity early, sep EP 1740[25]). *LG* Pt N Peth. Hd, pt Andersf. Hd, Bridgw. PLU, RSD, RD. Addtl civ bdry alt: 1883,[1] 1886,[101] 1933,[3] 1952.[105] *Parl* Seq 17. *Eccl* Seq 7. Addtl eccl bdry alt: 1743 (cr North Newton EP,[25] refounded 1880[381]), 1840 (help cr Burrowbridge EP),[106] 1845 (cr Northmoor Green EP),[383] 1961 (help cr Greenfield EP).[110]

SOUTH PETHERTON

AP Incl chap Chillington (sep civ identity early, sep EP 1750[25]), chap Lopen (sep civ identity early, sep EP 1747[25]). *LG* S Peth. Hd, Yeov. PLU, RSD, RD. Civ bdry: 1957.[11] *Parl* Seq 20. *Eccl* Seq 9.

PILL

EP Cr 1861 from Easton-in-Gordano AP, Portbury EP.[267] Portish. RDn. Bdry: 1957.[266]

PILTON

AP Incl chap North Wootton (sep civ identity early, sep EP 1845 [incl pt from Wells St Cuthbert AP][396]). *LG* Pt Glaston. Twelve Hides Hd, pt Whitstone Hd, Shept. Mal. PLU, RSD, RD. Addtl civ bdry alt: 1883.[1] *Parl* Seq 8. *Eccl* Pec jurisd (until 1845), Seq 27 thereafter. Addtl eccl bdry alt: 1960.[244]

PITCOMBE

Chap in Bruton AP, sep civ identity early, sep EP 1784.[25] *LG* Seq 9. Civ bdry: 1883,[1] 1885.[153] *Parl* Seq 8. *Eccl* Cary RDn (until 1872), Bruton RDn (1872–*).

PITMINSTER

AP *LG* Seq 41. Civ bdry: 1933.[3] *Parl* Seq 22. *Eccl* Seq 20. Eccl bdry: 1969.[315]

PITNEY

AP *LG* Seq 36. Civ bdry: 1886.[6] *Parl* Seq 15. *Eccl* Pec jurisd (until 1845), Seq 33 thereafter.

PODIMORE

AP Usual civ spelling, sometimes 'Podimore Milton'; for eccl see following entry. *LG* Whitley Hd, Yeov. PLU, RSD, RD. Abol civ 1933 ent to Yeovilton AP.[3] *Parl* W'rn Dv (1832–67), Mid Dv (1867–85), E'rn Dv (1885–1918), Yeov. Dv (1918–48).

PODYMORE

AP Usual eccl spelling; for civ see prev entry. *Eccl* Seq 33.

PORLOCK

AP *LG* Seq 11. Civ bdry: 1929.[357] *Parl* Seq 21. *Eccl* Seq 12. Eccl bdry: 1952.[358]

PORTBURY

AP *LG* Seq 37. Civ bdry: 1884,[210] 1896 (help cr South Bristol CP to be in Bristol CB),[18] 1898 (loses pt to Bristol CB and South Bristol CP),[19] 1954 (help cr Clapton-in-Gordano CP).[211] Transf 1974 to Avon.[22] *Parl* Seq 5. *Eccl* Seq 6. Eccl bdry: 1861 (help cr Pill EP).[267]

PORTISHEAD

AP *LG* Portbury Hd, Bedm. PLU (1836–99), RSD (ent 1875–92, pt 1892–94), pt Portish. USD (1892–94), Long Ashton PLU (1899–1930), Portish. UD. Civ bdry: 1894 (the pt not in the USD cr North Weston CP),[51] 1896 (help cr South Bristol CP to be in Bristol CB),[18] 1898 (loses pt to Bristol CB and South Bristol CP),[19] 1926 (loses pt to Bristol CB and CP),[398] 1930 (loses pt to Bristol CB and CP),[81] 1951 (gains pt Bristol CB and CP).[20] Transf 1974 to Avon.[22] *Parl* E'rn Dv (1832–67), East Dv (1867–85), N'rn Dv (1885–1918), W-s-M Dv (1918–48), N Somerset CC (1948–*). Parl bdry: 1952.[83] *Eccl* Seq 6.

POYNTINGTON

AP *LG* Horeth. Hd, Sherborne PLU, RSD, sep RD in Somerset (1894–95). Transf 1895 to Dorset.[90] *Parl* E'rn Dv (1832–67), Mid Dv (1867–85), E'rn Dv (1885–1918), Dorset thereafter. *Eccl* Merst. RDn (until 1929), Sherborne RDn (dioc Sarum, 1929–*).

PRESTON PLUCKNETT

Chap in Yeovil AP, sep civ identity early, no sep eccl identity. *LG* Stone Hd, Yeov. PLU, RSD, RD. Civ bdry: 1884,[17] 1903.[399] Abol 1930 pt to Yeovil AP, pt to Brympton AP, pt to West Coker AP.[143] *Parl* W'rn Dv (1832–67), Mid Dv (1867–85), S'rn Dv (1885–1918), Yeov. Dv (1918–48).

PRIDDY

Chap in Westbury AP, sep civ identity early, sep EP 1862 (incl pts from West Harptree AP, East Harptree AP, Chewton Mendip AP, Wells St Cuthbert AP, Wookey AP, Easton EP).[194] *LG* Seq 48. Civ bdry: 1974 (gains the pts of the following remaining in Somerset [the main pt of each par transf to Avon as par with respective name]: Blagdon AP, Burrington CP, Compton Martin AP, East Harptree AP, West Harptree AP, Ubley AP).[22] *Parl* Seq 13. *Eccl* Axbr. RDn.

PRISTON
AP *LG* Seq 26. Transf 1974 to Avon.[3] *Parl* Seq 3. *Eccl* Seq 3.

PUBLOW
Chap in Stanton Drew AP, sep civ identity early, sep EP 1864.[400] *LG* Seq 25. Civ bdry: 1948.[188] Transf 1974 to Avon.[22] *Parl* Seq 3. *Eccl* Chew Magna RDn. Abol eccl perhaps in 1920s or 1930s to help cr Pensford with Publow EP.[394]

PUBLOW WITH PENSFORD
EP Renaming 1972 of Pensford with Publow EP.[395] Chew Magna RDn.

PUCKINGTON
AP *LG* Seq 2. Civ bdry: 1885,[93] 1886.[401] *Parl* Seq 20. *Eccl* Crewk. RDn (until 1872), Ilmin. RDn (1872–1962). Abol eccl 1962 to help cr Puckington with Bradon EP.[94]

PUCKINGTON WITH BRADON
EP Cr 1962 by union Puckington AP, North and South Bradon AP.[94] Ilmin. RDn.

PURITON
AP *LG* Huntspill and Puriton Hd, Bridgw. PLU, RSD, RD. Civ bdry: 1933.[3] *Parl* Seq 17. *Eccl* Seq 35.

PUXTON
Chap in Banwell AP, sep civ identity early, sep EP 1749.[25] *LG* Seq 53. Civ bdry: 1885,[148] 1962.[232] Transf 1974 to Avon.[22] *Parl* Seq 7. *Eccl* Axbr. RDn (until 1872), Lock. RDn (1872–*). Eccl bdry: 1865 (help cr Congresbury St Ann EP, later called 'Hewish St Ann').[117]

PYLLE
AP *LG* Seq 50. Civ bdry: 1883,[1] 1884.[402] *Parl* Seq 8. *Eccl* Seq 27. Eccl bdry: 1960.[244]

EAST QUANTOXHEAD
AP *LG* Seq 52. *Parl* Seq 21. *Eccl* Seq 8.

WEST QUANTOXHEAD
AP Usual civ spelling; eccl 'St Audries (or West Quantoxhead', qv, renamed 1972 'West Quantoxhead'.[403] *LG* Seq 52. *Parl* Seq 21. *Eccl* Dunst. RDn (1972–73), Quantk. RDn (1973–*).

RADDINGTON
AP *LG* Willit. & Freem. Hd, Welling. PLU, RSD, RD. Abol civ 1933 ent to Chipstable AP.[3] *Parl* W'rn Dv (1832–67), West Dv (1867–85), W'rn Dv (1885–1918), Taun. Dv (1918–48). *Eccl* Dunst. RDn (until 1872), Wivel. RDn (1872–1971). Abol eccl 1971 ent to Chipstable AP.[207]

RADSTOCK
AP *LG* Kilm. Hd, Clut. PLU, Radstock USD, UD. Abol civ 1933 to help cr Norton Radstock CP.[3] *Parl* E'rn Dv (1832–67), Mid Dv (1867–85), Frome Dv (1885–1918). *Eccl* Frome RDn (until 1872), Mids. Nort. RDn (1872–1971). Eccl bdry: 1953 (help cr Westfield EP).[306] Abol eccl 1971 to help cr Radstock with Writhlington EP.[404]

RADSTOCK WITH WRITHLINGTON
EP Cr 1971 by union Radstock AP, Writhlington AP.[404] Mids. Nort. RDn.

REDLYNCH
Chap in Bruton AP, sep EP 1733.[25] Cary RDn (1773–1872), Bruton RDn (1872–1933). Abol 1933 to help cr Bruton and Redlynch EP.[140]

RIMPTON
AP *LG* Taun. & Taun. Dean Hd, Sherborne PLU (1835–96), RSD, Yeov. PLU (1896–1930), RD. *Parl* Seq 16. *Eccl* Seq 31.

ROAD
AP Usual civ spelling until 1919 when renamed 'Rode',[405] the latter the usual eccl spelling. See entries under 'Rode'.

ROCKWELL GREEN
EP Cr 1890 from Wellington AP.[406] Welling. RDn (1890–1973), Tone RDn (1973–*). Now usually called 'Wellington All Saints'.

RODDEN
Chap in Boyton AP (Wilts), sep civ identity early in Somerset, sep EP 1802.[25] *LG* Frome Hd, PLU, RSD, RD. Civ bdry: 1883.[1] Abol civ 1933 ent to Selwood CP.[3] *Parl* E'rn Dv (1832–67), Mid Dv (1867–85), Frome Dv (1885–1948). *Eccl* Frome RDn.

RODE
AP Usual eccl spelling, civ spelling from 1919 after 'Road' so renamed.[405] *LG* Seq 19. Civ bdry: 1883,[1] 1885,[53] 1937 (gains pt Southwick CP, Wilts).[407] *Parl* Seq 10. *Eccl* Frome RDn. Abol eccl 1972 to help cr Rode Major EP.[277]

RODE HILL–See ROAD HILL

RODE MAJOR
EP Cr 1972 by union Farleigh Hungerford AP, Tellisford AP, Rode AP, Road Hill EP (Wilts), Woolverton AP.[277] Frome RDn.

ROWBARTON
EP Cr 1879 from Taunton St James AP.[408] Taun. RDn (1879–1963), Taun. N RDn (1963–72). Bdry: 1936,[410] 1952,[411] 1957 (cr Lyngford EP).[366] Renamed 1972 'Taunton St Andrew'.[409]

ROWBERROW
AP *LG* Winterstoke Hd, Axbr. PLU, RSD, RD. Civ bdry: 1885.[148] Abol civ 1933 ent to Shipham AP.[3] *Parl* E'rn Dv (1832–67), East Dv (1867–85), Wells Dv (1885–1918), W-s-M Dv (1918–48). *Eccl* Seq 24.

RUISHTON
Chap in Taunton St Mary Magdalene AP, sep civ identity early, sep EP 1744.[25] *LG* Seq 41. *Parl* Seq 18. *Eccl* Taun. RDn (1744–1963), Taun. S RDn (1963–*).

RUNNINGTON
AP *LG* Milverton Hd, Welling. PLU, RSD, RD. Civ bdry: 1884.[13] Abol civ 1933 ent to Langford Budville CP.[3] *Parl* W'rn Dv (1832–67), West Dv (1867–85), W'rn Dv (1885–1918), Taun. Dv (1918–48). *Eccl* Seq 21.

ST AUDRIES (OR WEST QUANTOXHEAD)
AP Usual eccl spelling until renamed eccl 1972 'West Quantoxhead',[403] the latter the usual civ spelling, qv. *Eccl* Dunst. RDn (until 1872), Wivel. RDn (1872–1951), Dunst. RDn (1951–72).

ST CATHERINE
Chap in Batheaston AP, sep civ identity early, no sep eccl identity. *LG* Seq 5. Civ bdry: 1883.[1] Transf 1974 to Avon.[22] *Parl* Seq 1.

ST DECUMAN'S
AP Incl chap Williton (sep EP 1784,[25] sep CP as noted below), bor Watchet (status not sustained but parl representation 1302 only, sep CP as noted below). *LG* Willit. & Freem. Hd, Willit. PLU, RSD, RD. Addtl civ bdry alt: 1883,[412] 1886.[164] Abol civ 1902 pt to cr Watchet CP, pt to cr Williton CP.[413] *Parl* W'rn Dv (1832–67), West Dv (1867–85), W'rn Dv (1885–1918). *Eccl* Pec jurisd (until 1845), Seq 16 thereafter.

ST MICHAELCHURCH
Chap in North Petherton AP, sep civ identity early, sep EP 1740.[25] *LG* N Peth. Hd, Bridgw. PLU, RSD, RD. Abol civ 1933 ent to North Petherton AP.[3] *Parl* W'rn Dv (1832–67), West Dv (1867–85), Bridgw. Dv (1885–1948). *Eccl* Bridgw. RDn. Abol 1962 to help cr North Newton with St Michaelchurch EP.[382]

ST THOMAS IN PENSFORD
Chap in Stanton Drew AP, sep civ identity early, eccl severed perhaps in 1920s or 1930s to help cr Pensford with Publow EP.[394] *LG* Keyn. Hd, Clut. PLU, RSD, RD. Civ bdry: 1883.[1] Abol civ 1884 ent to Stanton Drew AP.[414] *Parl* E'rn Dv (1832–67), East Dv (1867–85).

SALTFORD
AP *LG* Keyn. Hd, PLU, RSD, RD (1894–1933), Bathavon RD (1933–38). Abol civ 1938 ent to Keynsham AP.[229] *Parl* E'rn Dv (1832–67), East Dv (1867–85), N'rn Dv (1885–1918), Frome Dv (1918–48). *Eccl* Seq 4.

SAMPFORD ARUNDEL
AP *LG* Seq 32. *Parl* Seq 22. *Eccl* Seq 21.

SAMPFORD BRETT
AP *LG* Seq 52. Civ bdry: 1883,[1] 1885.[415] *Parl* Seq 21. *Eccl* Seq 16. Eccl bdry: 1954,[416] 1967.[269]

SANDFORD ORCAS
AP *LG* Horeth. Hd, Sherborne PLU, RSD, sep RD in Somerset (1894–95). Transf 1895 to Dorset.[90] *Parl* E'rn Dv (1832–67), Mid Dv (1867–85), E'rn Dv (1885–1918), Dorset thereafter. *Eccl* Merst. RDn (until 1884), Milb. Port RDn (1884–1955), Merst. RDn (1955–73), Sherborne RDn (dioc Sarum, 1973–*).

SEABOROUGH
AP *LG* Crewk. Hd, Beaminster PLU, RSD, sep RD in Somerset (1894–95). Transf 1895 to Dorset.[90] *Parl* W'rn Dv (1832–67), Mid Dv (1867–85), S'rn Dv (1885–1918), Dorset thereafter. *Eccl* Seq 9.

SEAVINGTON ST MARY
AP *LG* Seq 35. Civ bdry: 1885.[238] *Parl* Seq 20. *Eccl* Seq 9.

SEAVINGTON ST MICHAEL
AP Incl chap Dinnington (sep civ identity early, eccl severed perhaps in 1920s or 1930s to help cr Hinton St George with Dinnington EP[251]). *LG* Seq 35. *Parl* Seq 20. *Eccl* Seq 9. Addtl eccl bdry alt: 1875.[417]

SELWOOD
Chap in Frome AP, sep EP 1873 as 'Frome Selwood',[285] qv, sep CP 1894 as 'Selwood'.[56] *LG* Frome PLU, RD. Civ bdry: 1901,[287] 1933.[3] *Parl* Frome Dv (1918–48), Wells CC (1948–*).

SELWORTHY
AP *LG* Seq 11. Civ bdry: 1883.[418] *Parl* Seq 21. *Eccl* Seq 12.

SHAPWICK
AP Incl chap Ashcott (sep civ identity early, no sep eccl identity). *LG* Seq 49. Addtl civ bdry alt: 1883,[1] 1885,[2] 1933.[3] *Parl* Seq 17. *Eccl* Seq 36.

SHARPHAM
CP Cr 1894 from the pt of Glastonbury AP not in Glaston. MB.[56] *LG* Wells PLU, RD. Bdry: 1933.[3] *Parl* Wells Dv/CC (1918–*).

SHEPTON BEAUCHAMP
AP *LG* Seq 35. Civ bdry: 1885.[38] *Parl* Seq 20. *Eccl* Seq 10.

SHEPTON MALLET
AP *LG* Whitstone Hd, Shept. Mal. PLU, USD (ent 1875–83, pt 1883–86, ent 1886–94), pt Shept. Mal. RSD (1883–86), Shept. Mal. UD. Civ bdry: 1883,[1] 1884,[419] 1897,[26] 1933.[3] *Parl* Seq 8. *Eccl* Seq 27. Eccl bdry: 1866 (help cr Oakhill EP),[27] 1960.[224]

SHEPTON MONTAGUE
AP *LG* Seq 33. Civ bdry: 1884,[176] 1885.[153] *Parl* Seq 8. *Eccl* Seq 26. Eccl bdry: 1929.[139]

SHIPHAM
AP *LG* Seq 53. Civ bdry: 1933.[3] *Parl* Seq 7. *Eccl* Seq 24.

SHOSCOMBE
Area in Wellow AP, sep CP 1955,[156] eccl severed 1926 to help cr Foxcote with Shoscombe EP.[284] *LG* Bathavon RD. *Parl* N Somerset CC (1948–*).

SKILGATE
AP *LG* Seq 51. *Parl* Seq 22. *Eccl* Seq 13.

SOCK DENNIS
Orig sep AP in Merst. RDn, long demolished and later considered ex-par, sep CP 1858.[179] *LG* Tintinhill Hd, Yeov. PLU (1858[200]–1930), PLU, RSD, RD. Bdry: 1885.[420] Abol 1957 pt to Ilchester AP, pt to Tintinhull AP.[11] *Parl* Mid Dv (1867–85), S'rn Dv (1885–1918), Yeov. Dv (1918–70).

SOMERTON
AP *LG* Somerton Bor (status not sustained), pt Pitney Hd, pt Somert. Hd, Lang. PLU, RSD, RD. Civ bdry: 1883,[1] 1886.[421] *Parl* Seq 15. *Eccl* Seq 33.

SPARKFORD
AP *LG* Seq 13. Civ bdry: 1933.[3] *Parl* Seq 12. *Eccl* Seq 25.

SPAXTON
AP *LG* Seq 10. Civ bdry: 1878,[422] 1880,[423] 1883,[1] 1885,[2] 1933.[3] *Parl* Seq 17. *Eccl* Seq 7. Eccl bdry: 1930.[280]

STANDERWICK
AP Orig AP in Frome RDn, church destroyed by *ca* 1660, sep civ identity retained, eccl united to help cr Beckington with Standerwick EP.[424] *LG* Frome Hd, PLU, RSD, RD. Civ bdry:

1883.[1] Abol 1885 pt to Frome AP, pt to Beckington AP, pt to Berkeley AP.[53] *Parl* E'rn Dv (1832–67), Mid Dv (1867–85), Frome Dv (1885–1918).

STANTON DREW

AP Incl chap Publow (sep civ identity early, sep EP 1864[400]), chap Pensford (sep civ identity early as 'St Thomas in Pensford' eccl severed perhaps in 1920s or 1930s to help cr Pensford with Publow EP[394]). *LG* Seq 25. Addtl civ bdry alt: 1883,[1] 1884,[414] 1948.[425] Transf 1974 to Avon.[22] *Parl* Seq 3. *Eccl* Seq 5.

STANTON PRIOR

AP *LG* Keyn. Hd, PLU, RSD, RD. Abol civ 1933 ent to Marksbury AP.[3] *Parl* E'rn Dv (1832–67), East Dv (1867–85), N'rn Dv (1885–1918), Frome Dv (1918–48). *Eccl* Bath RDn (until 1855), Keyn. RDn (1855–1966), Bath RDn (1966–*).

STAPLE FITZPAINE

AP Incl chap Bickenhall (sep civ identity early, no sep eccl identity hence this par eccl 'Staple Fitzpaine with Bickenhall', qv). *LG* Seq 3. Addtl civ bdry alt: 1883.[1] *Parl* Seq 18.

STAPLE FITZPAINE WITH BICKENHALL

AP Usual eccl spelling; for civ and civ sep chap Bickenhall, see prev entry. *Eccl* Crewk. RDn (until 1872), Ilmin. RDn (1872–1960). Reconstituted eccl 1960, gaining chap Curland of Curry Mallet with Curland AP to cr Staple Fitzpaine with Bickenhall and Curland EP.[245]

STAPLE FITZPAINE WITH BICKENHALL AND CURLAND

EP Cr 1960 by union Staple Fitzpaine with Bickenhall AP, chap Curland in Curry Mallet with Curland AP.[245] Ilmin. RDn.

STAPLEGROVE

AP *LG* Seq 41. Civ bdry: 1885,[426] 1895,[376] 1932,[181] 1958.[182] *Parl* Seq 22. *Eccl* Seq 18. Eccl bdry: 1952.[411]

STAWELL

Chap in Moorlinch AP (eccl 'Moorlinch with Stawell and Sutton Mallet'), sep CP 1866,[158] no sep eccl identity. *LG* Seq 49. Civ bdry: 1933.[3] *Parl* Seq 17.

STAWLEY

AP *LG* Seq 32. Civ bdry: 1884,[13] 1933.[3] *Parl* Seq 22. *Eccl* Seq 21.

STEEP HOLME ISLAND

Ex-par place, associated with Axbr. RD, civ transf 1974 to Avon,[22] eccl abol 1966 ent to Breane AP.[427]

STOCKLAND BRISTOL

AP Sometimes anc 'Stockland Gaunts'. *LG* Seq 10. Civ bdry: 1886.[161] *Parl* Seq 17. *Eccl* Seq 8. Eccl bdry: 1930.[280]

STOCKLINCH

CP Cr 1884 by union Stocklinch Magdalen AP, Stocklinch Ottersey AP.[428] *LG* Chard PLU, RSD, RD. *Parl* S'rn Dv (1885–1918), Yeov. Dv/CC (1918–*).

STOCKLINCH MAGDALEN

AP Usual civ spelling; for eccl see 'Stocklynch Magdalen'. *LG* Abd. & Bulst. Hd, Chard PLU, RSD, RD. Abol civ 1884 to help cr Stocklinch CP.[428] *Parl* W'rn Dv (1832–67), West Dv (1867–85).

STOCKLINCH OTTERSEY

AP Usual civ spelling; for eccl see 'Stocklynch Ottersey'. Organisation as for Stocklinch Magdalen.

STOCKLYNCH MAGDALEN

AP Usual eccl spelling; for civ see 'Stocklinch Magdalen'. *Eccl* Crewk. RDn (until 1872), Ilmin. RDn (1872–1931). Abol eccl 1931 to help cr Stocklynch Ottersey with Stocklynch Magdalen EP.[429]

STOCKLYNCH OTTERSEY

AP Usual eccl spelling; for civ see 'Stocklinch Ottersey'. *Eccl* As for Stocklynch Magdalen.

STOCKYLNCH OTTERSEY WITH STOCKLYNCH MAGDALEN

EP Cr 1931 by union Stocklynch Ottersey AP, Stocklynch Magdalen AP.[429] Ilmin. RDn.

STOGUMBER

AP Incl chap Bicknoller (sep civ identity early, sep EP 1770[25]). *LG* Seq 52. Addtl civ bdry alt: 1883,[1] 1884,[430] 1885,[431] 1886.[164] *Parl* Seq 21. *Eccl* Seq 16. Eccl bdry: 1954,[416] 1967.[269]

STOGURSEY

AP Anc 'Stoke Courcy'. Incl chap Lilstock (sep civ identity early, no sep eccl identity). *LG* Stogursey Bor (status not sustained), pt Cann. Hd, pt Willit. & Freem. Hd, Willit. PLU, RSD, RD. Addtl civ bdry alt: 1881,[337] 1885,[432] 1886.[260] *Parl* Stogursey Parl Bor (1360 only), Seq 21. *Eccl* Seq 8.

NORTH STOKE

AP *LG* Seq 6. Civ bdry: 1966 (loses pt to Bitton AP, Glos).[137] Transf 1974 to Avon.[22] *Parl* Seq 1. *Eccl* Seq 2.

RODNEY STOKE

AP Sometimes 'Stoke Gifford'. *LG* Winterstoke Hd, Wells PLU, RSD, RD. Civ bdry: 1885.[433] *Parl* Seq 10. *Eccl* Seq 22. Eccl bdry: 1862 (help cr Draycott EP).[180]

SOUTH STOKE

AP *LG* Seq 5. Civ bdry: 1884,[434] 1951 (loses pt to Bath CB and CP).[43] Transf 1974 to Avon.[22] *Parl* Seq 1. Parl bdry: 1951.[173] *Eccl* Seq 1.

STOKE LANE

Chap in Doulting AP, sep civ identity early, sep EP 1826.[25] *LG* Whitstone Hd, Shept. Mal. PLU, RSD, RD. Renamed civ 1955 'Stoke St Michael'.[442] *Parl* E'rn Dv (1832–67), East Dv (1867–85), Frome Dv (1885–1918), Wells Dv/CC (1918–70). *Eccl* Cary RDn (1826–72), Shept. Mal. RDn (1872–1972). Eccl bdry: 1866 (help cr Oakhill EP).[27] Renamed eccl 1972 'Stoke St Michael'.[436]

STOKE PERO

AP *LG* Carhamp. Hd, Willit. PLU, RSD, RD. Abol civ 1933 ent to Luccombe AP.[3] *Parl* W'rn Dv (1832–67), West Dv (1867–85), W'rn Dv (1885–1918), Bridgw. Dv (1918–48). *Eccl* Seq 12. Eccl bdry: 1952.[358]

STOKE ST GREGORY
Chap in North Curry AP, sep civ identity early, sep EP 1827.[25] *LG* Seq 18. Civ bdry: 1885.[435] *Parl* Seq 18. *Eccl* Pec jurisd Dean & Chapter of Wells (until 1845), Taun. RDn (1845–1963), Taun. N RDn (1963–*). Eccl bdry: 1840 (help cr Burrowbridge EP).[106]

STOKE ST MARY
AP *LG* Seq 41. Civ bdry: 1883,[1] 1884,[437] 1885,[375] 1932,[181] 1966.[377] *Parl* Seq 18. *Eccl* Seq 20.

STOKE ST MICHAEL
Renaming civ 1955,[442] eccl 1972[436] of Stoke Lane CP, EP respectively. *LG* Shept. Mal. RD. *Parl* Wells CC (1970–*). *Eccl* Shept. Mal. RDn.

STOKE SUB HAMDON
AP *LG* Seq 43. Civ bdry: 1884,[17] 1957.[11] *Parl* Seq 16. *Eccl* Seq 34.

STOKE TRISTER
AP *LG* Seq 33. Civ bdry: 1885,[153] 1886.[95] *Parl* Seq 8. *Eccl* Seq 26.

STON EASTON
Chap in Chewton Mendip AP, sep civ identity early, eccl united 1867 with chap Farrington Gurney in same par to cr Ston Easton with Farrington Gurney EP (sometimes 'Ston Easton cum Farrington Gurney')[190]; Farrington Gurney made sep EP 1973 and the eccl name of the remainder 'Ston Easton'.[438] *LG* Seq 16. Civ bdry: 1884,[439] 1933,[3] 1958.[78] *Parl* Seq 16. *Eccl* Mids. Nort. RDn (1973–*).

STON EASTON WITH FARRINGTON GURNEY
EP Cr 1867 by union chaps Ston Easton, Farrington Gurney, each in Chewton Mendip AP.[190] Sometimes 'Ston Easton cum Farrington Gurney'. Frome RDn (1867–72), Mids. Nort. RDn (1872–1973). Bdry: 1966.[24] Abol 1973 pt to cr Farrington Gurney EP, the remainder to be Ston Easton EP.[438]

STOURTON
AP Pt Wilts (Mere Hd), pt Somerset (Nort. Ferrers Hd). Sometimes 'Stourton with Gasper'. *LG* Mere PLU, RSD, pt sep RD in Somerset (1894–95). The par made ent Wilts 1895.[90] *Parl* Somerset pt, E'rn Dv (1832–67), Mid Dv (1867–85), E'rn Dv (1885–1918). See main entry in Wilts for organisation after 1895, and for eccl organisation in dioc Sarum.

STOWELL
AP *LG* Horeth. Hd, Wincan. PLU, RSD, RD. Civ bdry: 1885.[153] Abol civ 1933 ent to Charlton Horethorne AP.[3] *Parl* E'rn Dv (1832–67), Mid Dv (1867–85), E'rn Dv (1885–1918), Wells Dv (1918–48). *Eccl* Seq 31. Eccl bdry: 1934.[175]

STOWEY
AP *LG* Chew Hd, Clut. PLU, RSD, RD. Civ bdry: 1883,[1] 1884.[187] Abol civ 1949 pt to Chew Magna AP, pt to help cr Stowey-Sutton CP.[188] *Parl* E'rn Dv (1832–67), East Dv (1867–85), N'rn Dv (1885–1918), Frome Dv (1918–48), N Somerset CC (1948–70). *Eccl* Seq 5.

NETHER STOWEY
AP *LG* Nether Stowey Bor (status not sustained), Willit. & Freem. Hd, Bridgw. PLU, RSD, RD. Civ bdry: 1880,[423] 1886.[161] *Parl* Seq 21. *Eccl* Pec jurisd Dean of Wells (until 1845), Seq 8 thereafter. Eccl bdry: 1930.[280]

OVER STOWEY
AP *LG* Pt Cann. Hd, pt Willit. & Freem. Hd, Bridgw. PLU, RSD, RD. Civ bdry: 1880,[423] 1886.[161] *Parl* Seq 21. *Eccl* Seq 8.

STOWEY-SUTTON
CP Cr 1949 from Chew Magna AP, Stowey AP.[188] *LG* Clut. RD. Transf 1974 to Avon.[22] *Parl* N Somerset CC (1970–*).

STRATTON-ON-THE-FOSSE
AP *LG* Seq 28. Civ bdry: 1884,[440] 1885,[84] 1933,[3] 1958.[78] *Parl* Seq 11. Parl bdry: 1960.[441] *Eccl* Seq 29. Eccl bdry: 1953 (help cr Westfield EP),[306] 1966.[28]

STREET
AP Incl chap Walton (sep civ identity early, sep EP 1886[443]). *LG* Whitley Hd, Wells PLU, Street USD (ent 1875–83, pt 1883–94), pt Glaston. USD (1883–94), Street UD. Civ bdry: 1883 (gains detached pt of Glastonbury AP so that pt in Glaston. USD and no longer ent Street USD),[1] 1884,[444] 1894 (exchanges pts with Glastonbury AP),[291] 1933.[3] *Parl* Seq 14. *Eccl* Glaston. Jurisd.

STRINGTSON
AP *LG* Cann. Hd, Willit. PLU, RSD, RD. Civ bdry: 1883,[253] 1886,[445] 1933.[3] *Parl* Seq 21. *Eccl* Seq 8.

BISHOP'S SUTTON
EP Cr 1876 from Chew Magna AP.[189] Chew Magna RDn.

LONG SUTTON
AP *LG* Pt Pitney Hd, pt Somert. Hd, Langp. PLU, RSD, RD. Civ bdry: 1886.[6] *Parl* Seq 15. *Eccl* Pec jurisd Dean & Chapter of Wells (until 1845), Seq 33 thereafter.

SUTTON BINGHAM
AP *LG* Houndsb., Barw. & Coker Hd, Yeov. PLU, RSD, RD. Abol civ 1933 ent to Closworth AP.[3] *Parl* W'rn Dv (1832–67), Mid Dv (1867–85), S'rn Dv (1885–1918), Yeov. Dv (1918–48). *Eccl* Seq 31.

SUTTON MALLET
Chap in Moorlinch AP (eccl 'Moorlinch with Stawell and Sutton Mallet'), sep CP 1866,[158] no sep eccl identity. *LG* Whitley Hd, Bridgw. PLU, RSD, RD. Abol 1933 ent to Stawell AP.[3] *Parl* W'rn Dv (1867–85), Bridgw. Dv (1885–1948).

SUTTON MONTIS
AP *LG* Catsash Hd, Wincan. PLU, RSD, RD. Abol civ 1933 ent to South Cadbury AP.[3] *Parl* E'rn Dv (1832–67), Mid Dv (1867–85), E'rn Dv (1885–1918), Wells Dv (1918–48). *Eccl* Seq 25.

SWAINSWICK
AP *LG* Seq 5. Civ bdry: 1967 (loses pt to Bath CB and CP).[42] Transf 1974 to Avon.[22] *Parl* Seq 1. *Eccl* Seq 2.

SWELL
AP *LG* Abd. & Bulst. Hd, Langp. PLU, RSD, RD.

Civ bdry: 1885,[446] 1886.[6] Abol civ 1933 ent to Fivehead AP.[3] *Parl* W'rn Dv (1832–67), West Dv (1867–85), S'rn Dv (1885–1918), Yeov. Dv (1918–48). *Eccl* Seq 10.

TATWORTH

EP Cr 1866 from Chard AP.[168] Crewk. RDn.

TAUNTON

The following have 'Taunton' in their names. Insofar as any existed at a given time: *LG* Taun. & Taun. Dean Hd, Taun. PLU (Bor, MB [incorp 1885], USD, RSD sep noted). *Parl* Sep noted before 1918, Taun. Dv/CC (1918–*). *Eccl* Taun. RDn (until 1963), sep noted thereafter.

CP1–TAUNTON–Cr 1921 by union Bishop's Hull Within CP, CP2, CP4, Wilton CP, and pts of Bishop's Hull Without CP, West Monkton AP, CP3, Trull CP.[317] *LG* Taun. MB. Bdry: 1932,[181] 1958,[182] 1966.[377]

EP1–TAUNTON ALL SAINTS–Renaming 1972 of Halcon EP.[296] Taun. S RDn.

EP2–TAUNTON HOLY TRINITY–Cr 1842 from AP2.[274] Taun. S RDn. Bdry: 1933,[314] 1967 (help cr Halcon EP).[295]

EP3–TAUNTON ST ANDREW–Renaming 1972 of Rowbarton EP.[409] Taun. N RDn.

AP1–TAUNTON ST JAMES–*LG* Pt Taun. Bor, pt Taun. USD. pt Taun. RSD. Civ bdry: 1884.[447] Abol civ 1885 the pt in the USD to cr CP2, pt to cr CP3, pt to Staplegrove AP.[312] *Parl* Pt Taun. Parl Bor (1295–1918), pt W'rn Dv (1832–67), pt West Dv (1867–85), pt W'rn Dv (1885–1918). *Eccl* Seq 18. Eccl bdry: 1879 (cr Rowbarton EP),[408] 1936,[410] 1952,[411] 1967 (help cr Halcon EP).[295]

CP2–TAUNTON ST JAMES WITHIN–Cr 1885 from the pt of AP1 in Taun. USD.[312] *LG* Taun. MB, USD. Bdry: 1895.[376] Abol 1921 to help cr CP1.[317]

CP3–TAUNTON ST JAMES WITHOUT–Cr 1885 from the pt of AP1 not in Taun. USD.[312] *LG* Taun. RSD, RD. Bdry: 1895,[376] 1921 (help cr CP1).[317] Abol 1933 pt to CP1, pt to Cheddon Fitzpaine AP.[181]

EP4–TAUNTON ST JOHN–Renaming 1972 of Bishop's Hull St John the Evangelist EP.[316] Taun. S RDn.

AP2–TAUNTON ST MARY MAGDALENE–Incl chap Corfe (sep civ identity early, sep EP 1826[25]), chap Ruishton (sep civ identity early, sep EP 1744[25]), chap Wilton (sep civ identity early, sep EP 1739[25]), chap Bishop's Hull (sep civ identity early, sep EP 1729[25]), chap Thurlbear (sep civ identity early, sep EP before 1858 as 'Thurlbere'[449]). *LG* Pt Taun. Bor, pt Taun. USD, pt Taun. RSD. Addtl civ bdry alt: 1883,[1] 1884.[437] Abol civ 1885 the pt in the USD to help cr CP4, pt to cr CP5, pt to Stoke St Mary AP.[375] *Parl* As for AP1. *Eccl* Seq 20. Addtl eccl bdry alt: 1842 (cr EP2),[274] 1864 (help cr Bishop's Hull St John the Evangelist EP),[313] 1933.[314]

CP4–TAUNTON ST MARY MAGDALENE WITHIN–Cr 1885 from the pt of AP2 and the pts of West Monkton AP, Wilton CP in Taun. USD.[375] *LG* Taun. MB, USD. Bdry: 1887,[334] 1895.[376] Abol 1921 to help cr CP1.[317]

CP5–TAUNTON ST MARY MAGDALENE WITHOUT–Cr 1885 from pt of the pt of AP2 not in Taun. USD.[375] *LG* Taun. RSD, RD. Bdry: 1895.[376] Abol 1933 pt to CP1, pt to Stoke St Mary AP.[3]

EP5–TAUNTON ST PETER, LYNGFORD–Renaming 1972 of Lyngford EP.[367] Taun. N RDn.

TELLISFORD

AP *LG* Seq 45. Civ bdry: 1883,[1] 1885,[53] 1933.[3] *Parl* Seq 2. *Eccl* Frome RDn. Abol eccl 1972 to help cr Rode Major EP.[277]

THEALE

EP Cr 1828,[25] refounded 1844[448] from Wedmore AP. Axbr. RDn.

THORN FALCON

AP *LG* Seq 18. Civ bdry: 1883.[1] *Parl* Seq 18. *Eccl* Sometimes as 'Thornfalcon', Seq 20.

THORNE

AP Usual civ spelling; for eccl see following entry. *LG* Tintinhill Hd, Yeov. PLU, RSD, RD. Abol civ 1933 ent to Brympton AP.[3] *Parl* W'rn Dv (1832–67), Mid Dv (1867–85), S'rn Dv (1885–1918), Yeov. Dv (1918–48).

THORNE COFFIN

AP Usual eccl spelling; for civ see prev entry. *Eccl* Seq 34.

THORNE ST MARGARET

Orig chantry, parochial since Dissolution. *LG* Seq 32. Civ bdry: 1966 (gains pt Holcombe Rogus AP, Devon).[137] *Parl* Seq 22. *Eccl* Pec jurisd (until 1845), Taun. RDn (1845–72), Welling. RDn (1872–1973), Tone RDn (1973–*).

THURLBEAR

Chap in Taunton St Mary Magdalene AP, sep civ identity early, sep EP before 1858 as 'Thurlbere',[449] qv. *LG* N Curry Hd, Taun. PLU, RSD, RD. Abol civ 1933 ent to Orchard Portman AP.[3] *Parl* W'rn Dv (1832–67), West Dv (1867–85), Bridgw. Dv (1885–1918), Taun. Dv (1918–48).

THURLBERE

Chap in Taunton St Mary Magdalene AP, sep civ identity early as 'Thurlbear', qv, sep EP before 1858.[449] *Eccl* Seq 20.

THURLOXTON

AP *LG* Seq 34. *Parl* Seq 17. *Eccl* Bridgw. RDn (until 1973), Taun. N RDn (1973–*).

TICKENHAM

AP *LG* Seq 37. Transf 1974 to Avon.[22] *Parl* Seq 5. *Eccl* Seq 6.

TIMBERSCOMBE

AP *LG* Seq 11. Civ bdry: 1883,[450] 1884.[254] *Parl* Seq 21. *Eccl* Pec jurisd (until 1845), Seq 12 thereafter. Eccl bdry: 1954.[165]

TIMSBURY

AP *LG* Seq 14. Transf 1974 to Avon.[22] *Parl* Seq 3. *Eccl* Seq 3.

TINTINHULL

AP *LG* Seq 43. Civ bdry: 1883,[1] 1884,[17] 1885,[451]

1957.[11] *Parl* Seq 16. *Eccl* Seq 34.

TOLLAND

AP *LG* Seq 41. Civ bdry: 1883.[1] *Parl* Seq 22. *Eccl* Dunst. RDn (until 1963), Taun. N RDn (1963–73), Tone RDn (1973–*).

TREBOROUGH

AP *LG* Seq 11. *Parl* Seq 21. *Eccl* Seq 15.

TRENT

AP *LG* Horeth. Hd, Sherborne PLU, RSD, sep RD in Somerset (1894–95). Transf 1895 to Dorset.[90] *Parl* E'rn Dv (1832–67), Mid Dv (1867–85), S'rn Dv (1885–1918), Dorset thereafter. *Eccl* Merst. RDn (until 1973), Sherborne RDn (dioc Sarum, 1973–*).

TRUDOXHILL

CP Cr 1951 from Nunney AP.[213] *LG* Frome RD. *Parl* Wells CC (1970–*).

TRULL

AP *LG* Seq 41. Civ bdry: 1883,[1] 1884,[12] 1921,[317] 1958.[182] *Parl* Seq 22. *Eccl* Taun. RDn (until 1963), Taun. S RDn (1963–*). Eccl bdry: 1969.[315]

TWERTON OR TWIVERTON

AP Usual civ spelling; for eccl see 'Twerton-on-Avon'. *LG* Wellow Hd, Bath PLU, RSD, RD. Civ bdry: 1883,[1] 1885.[171] Abol civ 1911 ent to Bath CB and CP.[42] *Parl* E'rn Dv (1832–67), pt Bath Parl Bor (1867–1918), pt East Dv (1867–85), pt Frome Dv (1885–1918).

SOUTH TWERTON

EP Cr 1912 from Twerton-on-Avon AP.[452] Keyn. RDn. Bdry: 1964.[227] Renamed 1967 'Bath The Ascension'.[47]

TWERTON HILL

EP Cr 1957 from Twerton-on-Avon AP, Englishcombe AP.[453] Keyn. RDn. Renamed 1967 'Bath St Barnabas'.[47]

TWERTON-ON-AVON

AP Usual eccl spelling; for civ see 'Twerton or Twiverton'. *Eccl* Bath RDn (until 1855), Keyn. RDn (1855–1967). Eccl bdry: 1912 (cr South Twerton EP),[452] 1957 (help cr Twerton Hill EP).[453] Renamed 1967 'Bath Twerton-on-Avon'.[47]

UBLEY

AP *LG* Seq 16. Pt transf 1974 to Avon to be Ubley par, the pt remaining in Somerset added to Priddy CP.[22] *Parl* Seq 3. *Eccl* Seq 5.

UNANNEXED AREA–See following entry

UNNAMED

CP Cr 1938 from the pt of Keynsham AP neither constituted Keyn. UD, nor added to Compton Dando AP or Whitchurch AP.[332] Sometimes called 'Unannexed Area'. *LG* Bathavon RD. Transf 1974 to Avon.[22] *Parl* N Somerset CC (1948–*).

UPHILL

AP *LG* Winterstoke Hd, Axbr. PLU, pt W-s-M USD (1883–94), Axbr. RSD (ent 1875–83, pt 1883–94), Axbr. RD. Civ bdry: 1883 (pt added to W-s-M USD),[469] 1894 (loses the pt in the USD to Weston-super-Mare AP).[454] Abol civ 1933 ent to Weston-super-Mare AP.[3] *Parl* E'rn Dv (1832–67), East Dv (1867–85), Wells Dv (1885–1918), W-s-M Dv (1918–48). *Eccl* Seq 24. Eccl bdry: 1912 (help cr Weston-super-Mare St Paul EP),[455] 1960 (help cr Weston-super-Mare St Andrew, Bournville EP).[88]

UPTON

AP *LG* Seq 51. *Parl* Seq 22. *Eccl* Dunst. RDn (until 1872), Wivel. RDn (1872–1973), Exm. RDn (1973–*).

UPTON NOBLE

Chap in Batcombe AP, sep civ identity early, sep EP 1734.[25] *LG* Bruton Hd, Shept. Mal. PLU, RSD, RD (1894–1933), Frome RD (1933–74). *Parl* E'rn Dv (1832–67), Mid Dv (1867–85), Frome Dv (1885–1918), Wells Dv/CC (1918–*). *Eccl* Cary RDn (until 1872), Bruton RDn (1872–*).

VOBSTER

EP Cr 1852 from Mells AP.[370] Frome RDn.

WALCOT

AP *LG* Bath Forum Hd, Bath Bor/MB/CB (pt until 1885, ent 1885–1900), Bath PLU, Bath USD (pt 1875–85, ent 1885–94), pt Bath RSD (1875–85). Civ bdry: 1885.[171] Abol civ 1900 to help cr Bath CP.[38] *Parl* Pt Bath Parl Bor (1295–1918), pt E'rn Dv (1832–67), pt East Dv (1867–85), pt Frome Dv (1885–1918). *Eccl* Bath RDn. Eccl bdry: 1839 (cr Walcot St Saviour EP, cr Walcot Holy Trinity EP),[456] 1869 (help cr Bath St Paul EP),[51] 1881 (cr Lansdown EP).[357] Renamed 1967 'Bath Walcot'.[47]

WALCOT HOLY TRINITY

EP Cr 1839 from Walcot AP.[456] Bath RDn. Gains 1952 pt Bath St Paul EP and reconstituted as 'Bath Holy Trinity'.[46]

WALCOT ST SAVIOUR

EP Cr 1839 from Walcot AP.[456] Bath RDn. Renamed 1967 'Bath St Saviour'.[47]

WALTON

Chap in Street AP, sep civ identity early, sep EP 1886.[443] *LG* Whitley Hd, Wells PLU, RSD, RD. Civ bdry: 1885.[457] *Parl* Seq 14. *Eccl* Glaston. Jurisd.

WALTON-IN-GORDANO

AP *LG* Seq 37. Civ bdry: 1933,[3] 1951 (gains pt foreshore area of Bristol CB and CP).[25] Transf 1974 to Avon.[22] *Parl* Seq 5. Parl bdry: 1952.[83] *Eccl* Seq 6. Eccl bdry: 1955.[220]

WAMBROOK

AP In Dorset (Beaminster Hd), transf 1895 to Somerset.[90] *LG* Chard PLU, RSD, sep RD in Dorset (1894–95), Chard RD (1895–1974). Civ bdry: 1966 (gains pt Chardstock AP, Devon).[137] *Parl* In Dorset until 1918, Yeov. Dv/CC (1918–*). *Eccl* Pec jurisd Chapter of Sarum; see entry in Dorset for this and later eccl organisation.

WANSTROW

AP *LG* Seq 19. Civ bdry: 1933.[3] *Parl* Seq 11. *Eccl* Frome RDn. Abol eccl 1974 to help cr Nunney with Wanstrow and Cloford EP.[221]

WATCHET

CP Cr 1902 from St Decuman's AP.[413] *LG* Willit.

PLU, Watchet UD. *Parl* Bridgw. Dv/CC (1918–*).

WAYFORD

AP *LG* Seq 17. Civ bdry: 1885,[238] 1966 (loses pt to Broadwindsor AP, Dorset).[137] *Parl* Seq 16. *Eccl* Seq 9.

WEARE

AP *LG* Weare Bor (status not sustained), Seq 7. Civ bdry: 1883,[1] 1885.[7] *Parl* Weare Parl Bor (1304–07 only), Seq 7. *Eccl* Seq 23.

WEDMORE

AP Incl chap Mark (sep civ identity early, sep EP 1816[25]), chap Theale (sep civ identity early, sep EP 1844[23]), chap Blackford (sep civ identity early, sep EP 1825,[25] eccl refounded 1844[85]). *LG* Pt Bempst. Hd, pt Glaston. Twelve Hides Hd, Axbr. PLU, RSD, RD. Addtl civ bdry alt: 1885.[7] *Parl* Seq 7. *Eccl* Pec jurisd Dean of Wells (until 1845), Seq 22 thereafter.

WELLINGTON

AP Incl chap West Buckland (sep civ identity early, sep EP 1967[144] [this par eccl 'Wellington with West Buckland' before 1967, 'Wellington' thereafter]). *LG* Welling. Bor (status not sustained), W Kingsbr. Hd, Welling. PLU, USD, UD. Addtl civ bdry alt: 1933 (cr Wellington Without CP).[3] *Parl* Seq 22. *Eccl* Taun. RDn (until 1872), Welling. RDn (1872–1973), Tone RDn (1973–*). Addtl eccl bdry alt: 1890 (cr Rockwell Green EP, now usually called 'Wellington All Saints').[406]

WELLINGTON ALL SAINTS

EP Usual name now for EP cr 1890 as Rockwell Green, qv.

WELLINGTON WITH WEST BUCKLAND–See WELLINGTON

WELLINGTON WITHOUT

CP Cr 1933 from Wellington AP.[3] *LG* Welling. RD. Bdry: 1966 (gains pt Hemyock AP, Devon).[137] *Parl* Taun. CC (1948–*).

WELLOW

AP Incl pt dist Peasedown (sep EP 1874,[155] sep CP 1955 as 'Peasedown St John'[156]), area Shoscombe (sep CP 1955,[156] eccl severed 1926 to help cr Foxcote with Shoscombe EP[284]). *LG* Seq 44. Addtl civ bdry alt: 1955.[156] Transf 1974 to Avon.[22] *Parl* Seq 1. *Eccl* Seq 29.

WELLS

The following have 'Wells' in their names. Insofar as any existed at a given time: *LG* Wells Forum Hd, Wells PLU (Bor/MB, USD, RSD sep noted). *Parl* Sep noted before 1867, thereafter Mid Dv (1867–85), Wells Dv/CC (1885–*). *Eccl* Cary RDn (until 1855), Wells RDn (1855–72), Shept. Mal. RDn (1872–*).

CP1–WELLS–Cr 1933 by union CP2, CP3, pt CP4.[3] *LG* Wells MB.

CP2–WELLS ST ANDREW–Lbty and Cathedral (pec jurisd Dean & Chapter of Wells), sep CP 1866.[158] *LG* Wells MB, USD. Abol 1933 to help cr CP1.[3] *Parl* Wells Parl Bor (1295–1867).

AP1–WELLS ST CUTHBERT–*LG* Pt Wells Bor/MB. Abol civ 1866 pt of the pt in the MB cr CP3, the remainder (incl pt in MB) cr CP4.[158] *Parl* Pt Wells Parl Bor (1295–1867), pt E'rn Dv (1832–67). *Eccl* Pec jurisd Dean of Wells (until 1845). Eccl bdry: 1844 (cr Coxley EP, cr Easton EP, cr Horrington EP),[236] 1845 (help cr North Wootton EP),[396] 1858 (cr EP1, now usually called 'Wells St Thomas'),[458] 1862 (help cr Priddy EP),[194] 1931,[264] 1957.[459]

CP3–WELLS ST CUTHBERT IN–Cr 1866 from pt of the pt of AP1 in Wells MB.[158] *LG* Wells MB, USD. Bdry: 1884 (gains the pt of CP4 in Wells MB).[460] Abol 1933 to help cr CP1.[3]

CP4–WELLS ST CUTHBERT OUT–Cr 1866 from pt of the pt of AP1 in Wells MB and from the pt of the same par not in the MB.[158] *LG* Pt Wells MB (1866–84), pt Wells USD (1875–84), Wells RSD (pt 1875–84, ent 1884–94), Wells RD. Bdry: 1884 (loses the pt in the MB to CP3),[460] 1884,[461] 1933 (help cr CP1).[3]

–WELLS ST THOMAS–Name used now for EP1, qv.

EP1–EAST WELLS–Cr 1858 from AP1.[458] Now usually called 'Wells St Thomas'.

WEMBDON

AP *LG* N Peth. Hd, Bridgw. PLU, pt Bridgw. Bor/MB (until 1886), pt Bridgw. USD (1875–86), Bridgw. RSD (pt 1875–86, ent 1886–94), Bridgw. RD. Addtl civ bdry alt: 1886 (loses the pt in the MB to Bridgwater AP),[161] 1886,[260] 1896,[103] 1933.[3] *Parl* Pt Bridgw. Parl Bor (1295–1867), remainder and later, Seq 17. *Eccl* Seq 7. Eccl bdry: 1962,[183] 1965 (help cr Bridgwater St Francis of Assisi EP).[113]

WESTBURY

AP Incl chap Priddy (sep civ identity early, sep EP 1862 [incl pts from West Harptree AP, East Harptree AP, Chewton Mendip AP, Wells St Cuthbert AP, Wookey AP, Easton AP] [194]). *LG* Seq 48. *Parl* Seq 13. *Eccl* Pec jurisd (until 1845), Seq 22 thereafter.

WESTFIELD

EP Cr 1953 from Midsomer Norton AP, Radstock AP, Kilmersdon AP, Stratton-on-the-Fosse AP, Holcombe AP.[306] Mids. Nort. RDn.

WESTON

AP Incl chap Weston St John (sep EP 1841,[25] refounded 1879[462]). *LG* Bath Forum Hd, Bath PLU, RSD, RD (1894–1933), Bathavon RD (1933–54). Civ bdry: 1883,[1] 1885,[171] 1911 (loses pt to Bath CB and CP),[39] 1951 (loses pt to Bath CB and CP).[41] Abol civ 1953 pt to Charlcombe AP, pt to Kelston AP.[172] *Parl* E'rn Dv (1832–67), East Dv (1867–85), Frome Dv (1885–1948), N Somerset CC (1948–55). Parl bdry: 1951.[173] *Eccl* Bath RDn (until 1855), Keyn. RDn (1855–1967). Renamed 1967 'Bath Weston All Saints'.[47]

NORTH WESTON

CP Cr 1894 from the pt of Portishead AP not in Portish. USD.[56] *LG* Long Ashton PLU, RD. Bdry: 1951 (gains pt foreshore area of Bristol CB and CP).[20] Transf 1974 to Avon.[22] *Parl*

W-s-M Dv (1918–48), N Somerset CC (1948–*).

WESTON ST JOHN
EP Cr 1841,[25] refounded 1879[462] from Weston AP. Keyn. RDn. Renamed 1967 'Bath Weston St John'.[47]

WESTON BAMPFYLDE
AP *LG* Catsash Hd, Wincan. PLU, RSD, RD. Abol civ 1933 ent to Sparkford AP.[3] *Parl* E'rn Dv (1832–67), Mid Dv (1867–85), E'rn Dv (1885–1918), Wells Dv (1918–48). *Eccl* Seq 25.

WESTON-IN-GORDANO
AP *LG* Seq 37. Civ bdry: 1951 (gains pt foreshore area Bristol CB and CP).[20] Transf 1974 to Avon.[22] *Parl* Seq 5. *Eccl* Seq 6.

WESTON-SUPER-MARE
The following have 'Weston-super-Mare' in their names. Insofar as any existed at a given time: *LG* Winterstoke Hd, Axbr. PLU, W-s-M USD, UD (1894–1937), MB (1937–74). *Parl* Seq 7. *Eccl* Axbr. RDn (until 1872), Lock. RDn (1872–*).

AP1–WESTON-SUPER-MARE [ST JOHN THE BAPTIST]–Civ bdry: 1885,[148] 1894 (gains the pt of Uphill AP in W-s-M USD),[454] 1902,[328] 1933.[3] Transf 1974 to Avon.[22] Eccl bdry: 1847 (cr EP3),[464] 1855 (cr EP2),[465] 1862 (cr EP4),[466] 1902 (cr EP1).[463]

EP1–WESTON-SUPER-MARE ALL SAINTS–Cr 1902 from AP1.[463]

EP2–WESTON-SUPER-MARE CHRIST CHURCH –Cr 1855 from AP1.[465] Bdry: 1885,[467] 1903 (help cr EP7),[468] 1965 (help cr Milton EP).[330]

EP3–WESTON-SUPER-MARE EMMANUEL–Cr 1847 from AP1.[464] Bdry: 1903 (help cr EP7),[468] 1912 (help cr EP6).[455]

EP4–WESTON-SUPER-MARE HOLY TRINITY–Cr 1862 from AP1.[466]

EP5–WESTON-SUPER-MARE ST ANDREW, BOURNEVILLE–Cr 1960 from Bleadon AP, Uphill AP, EP6, EP7.[88]

EP6–WESTON-SUPER-MARE ST PAUL–Cr 1912 from EP3, Uphill AP.[455] Bdry: 1960 (help cr EP5).[88]

EP7–WESTON-SUPER-MARE ST SAVIOUR–Cr 1903 from EP3, EP2.[468] Bdry: 1960 (help cr EP5),[88] 1965 (help cr Milton EP).[330]

WESTONZOYLAND
AP *LG* Seq 49. Civ bdry: 1885,[2] 1886.[101] *Parl* Seq 17. *Eccl* Glaston. Jurisd (until 1962), Bridgw. RDn (1962–*). Eccl bdry: 1840 (help cr Burrowbridge EP),[105] 1962.[183]

WHATLEY
AP Incl chap Chantry (sep EP 1845,[25] refounded 1846[166]). *LG* Seq 19. Civ bdry: 1885.[53] *Parl* Seq 11. *Eccl* Seq 28.

WHEATHILL
AP *LG* Whitley Hd, Wincan. PLU, RSD, RD. Abol civ 1933 ent to Lovington CP.[3] *Parl* W'rn Dv (1832–67), Mid Dv (1867–85), E'rn Dv (1885–1918), Wells Dv (1918–48). *Eccl* Cary RDn. Abol eccl 1965 to help cr East Lydford with Wheathill EP.[360]

WHITCHURCH
Chap in Long Ashton AP, sep civ identity early, sep EP 1720.[25] Sometimes 'Filton'. *LG* Seq 26. Civ bdry: 1883,[1] 1930 (loses pt to Bristol CB and CP),[81] 1938,[229] 1951 (loses pt to Bristol CB and CP),[20] 1966 (loses pt to Bristol CB and CP).[21] Transf 1974 to Avon.[22] *Parl* Seq 3. Parl bdry: 1952.[83] *Eccl* Redcl. & Bedm. RDn (1720–1847), Chew RDn (1847–55), Chew Magna RDn (1855–*). Eccl bdry: 1959 (help cr Bristol Holy Cross Inns Court EP),[126] 1973 (help cr Bristol Christ the Servant, Stockwood EP).[125]

WHITELACKINGTON
AP *LG* Seq 1. Civ bdry: 1885,[15] 1886.[129] *Parl* Seq 20. *Eccl* Pec jurisd (until 1845), Seq 10 thereafter. Eccl bdry: 1928.[130]

WHITESTAUNTON
AP *LG* Seq 35. *Parl* Seq 19. *Eccl* Seq 9.

WICK ST LAWRENCE
Chap in Congresbury AP, sep civ identity early, eccl severed 1954 to help cr Hewlish St Ann and Wick St Lawrence EP.[232] *LG* Seq 53. Civ bdry: 1885.[148] Transf 1974 to Avon.[22] *Parl* Seq 7. Eccl bdry: 1862 (while still chap, help cr Congresbury St Ann EP, later called 'Hewish St Ann').[117]

WIDCOMBE
AP Chap in Bath St Mary de Stalls AP, sep identity early. Usual eccl spelling; for civ see 'Lyncombe and Widcombe'. *Eccl* Bath RDn. Eccl bdry: 1856 (cr Lyncombe EP),[361] 1901.[226] Renamed 1967 'Bath Widcombe'.[47]

NORTH WIDCOMBE
Tg in Chewton Mendip AP, sep CP 1866.[158] *LG* Chewton Hd, Clut. PLU, RSD, RD. Abol 1933 ent to West Harptree AP.[3] *Parl* East Dv (1867–85), N'rn Dv (1885–1918), Frome Dv (1918–48).

WILLITON
Chap in St Decuman's AP, sep EP 1784,[25] sep CP 1902.[413] *LG* Willit. PLU, RD. *Parl* Bridgw. Dv/CC (1918–*). *Eccl* Dunst. RDn (1784–1872), Wivel. RDn (1872–1951), Dunst. RDn (1951–73), Quantk. RDn (1973–*). Eccl bdry: 1954.[416]

WILTON
Chap in Taunton St Mary Magdalene AP, sep civ identity early, sep EP 1739.[25] *LG* Taun. & Taun. Dean Hd, Taun. PLU, pt Taun. USD (1875–85), Taun. RSD (pt 1875–85, ent 1885–94), Taun. RD. Civ bdry: 1885 (loses the pt in the USD to help cr Taunton St Mary Magdalene Within CP).[471] Abol civ 1921 to help cr Taunton CP.[317] *Parl* Pt Taun. Parl Bor (1832–1918), pt W'rn Dv (1832– 67), pt West Dv (1867–85), pt W'rn Dv (1885–1918), Taun. Dv (1918–48). *Eccl* Taun. RDn (1739–1963), Taun. S RDn (1963–*). Eccl bdry: 1864 (help cr Bishop's Hull St John the Evangelist EP),[313] 1933,[314] 1969.[315]

WINCANTON
AP *LG* Seq 33. Civ bdry: 1883,[1] 1884,[176] 1885,[184]

1966 (exchanges pts with Buckhorn Weston AP, Dorset).[137] *Parl* Seq 8. *Eccl* Cary RDn (until 1872), Bruton RDn (1872–*). Eccl bdry: 1957.[185]

WINDMILL HILL
EP Cr 1902 from Bedminster AP.[62] Bedm. RDn. Abol 1965 to help cr Bedminster St Michael and All Angels EP.[64]

WINFORD
AP *LG* Seq 22. Civ bdry: 1883,[1] 1884,[472] 1885.[473] Transf 1974 to Avon.[22] *Parl* Seq 5. *Eccl* Seq 5. Eccl bdry: 1873 (help cr Felton Common Hill EP).[33]

WINSCOMBE
AP *LG* Seq 53. Civ bdry: 1935.[29] Transf 1974 to Avon.[22] *Parl* Seq 7. *Eccl* Seq 24. Eccl bdry: 1964.[87]

WINSFORD
AP *LG* Seq 51. *Parl* Seq 22. *Eccl* Seq 14.

WINSHAM
AP *LG* Pt E Kingsbr. Hd, pt St Peth. Hd, Chard PLU, RSD, RD. Civ bdry: 1886,[247] 1966 (loses pt to Broadwindsor AP, Dorset).[137] *Parl* Seq 20. *Eccl* Pec jurisd Dean & Chapter of Wells (until 1845), Seq 9 thereafter.

WITHAM FRIARY
AP *LG* Witham Friary Lbty, Seq 19. *Parl* Seq 11. *Eccl* Pec jurisd (until 1845), Seq 28 thereafter.

WITHIEL FLOREY
AP Orig monastic church. *LG* Taun. & Taun. Dean Hd, Willit. PLU (1836–96), RSD, Dulv. PLU (1896–1930), RD. Civ bdry: 1883.[1] Abol civ 1933 ent to Brompton Regis AP.[3] *Parl* W'rn Dv (1832–67), West Dv (1867–85), W'rn Dv (1885–1918), Taun. Dv (1918–48). *Eccl* Dunst. RDn (until 1872), Wivel. RDn (1872–1958). Abol eccl 1958 to help cr Brompton Regis with Withiel Florey EP.[134]

WITHYCOMBE
AP *LG* Seq 11. Civ bdry: 1883,[1] 1884,[163] 1886.[164] *Parl* Seq 21. *Eccl* Seq 15. Eccl bdry: 1954.[165]

WITHYPOOL
Chap in Hawkridge AP, sep civ identity early, no sep eccl identity. *LG* Seq 51. Civ bdry: 1885,[299] 1933.[3] *Parl* Seq 22.

WIVELISCOMBE
AP Incl chap Fitzhead (sep civ identity early, sep EP 1737[25]). *LG* Wivel. Bor (status not sustained), W Kingsbr. Hd, Welling. PLU, pt Wivel. USD, pt Welling. RSD, Wivel. UD (1894–1933), Welling. RD (1933–74). Addtl civ bdry alt: 1894 (the pt not in the USD cr Wiveliscombe Without CP).[56] *Parl* Seq 22. *Eccl* Pec jurisd (until 1845), Seq 17 thereafter.

WIVELISCOMBE WITHOUT
CP Cr 1894 from the pt of Wiveliscombe AP not in Wivel. USD.[56] *LG* Welling. PLU, RD. *Parl* Taun. Dv/CC (1918–*).

WOODLANDS
EP Cr 1872 from chap Frome Selwood in Frome AP.[286] Frome RDn.

WOOKEY
AP *LG* Seq 48. Civ bdry: 1884,[474] 1933.[3] *Parl* Seq 13. *Eccl* Pec jurisd (until 1845), Axbr. RDn (1845–55), Wells RDn (1855–72), Axbr. RDn (1872–*). Eccl bdry: 1848 (cr Henton EP),[303] 1862 (help cr Priddy EP),[194] 1931.[264]

WOOKEY HOLE
EP Cr 1973 from Easton EP.[265] Shept. Mal. RDn.

WOOLAVINGTON
AP *LG* Seq 49. Civ bdry: 1885,[2] 1886.[161] *Parl* Seq 17. *Eccl* Seq 35. Eccl bdry: 1962.[183]

WOOLLEY
AP *LG* Bath Forum Hd, Bath PLU, RSD, RD. Abol civ 1933 ent to Charlcombe AP.[3] *Parl* E'rn Dv (1832–67), East Dv (1867–85), Frome Dv (1885–1948). *Eccl* Bath RDn. Abol eccl before 1535 to help cr Bathwick with Woolley EP.

WOOLVERTON
AP *LG* Frome Hd, PLU, RSD, RD. Civ bdry: 1883,[1] 1885.[53] Abol civ 1933 ent to Tellisford AP.[3] *Parl* E'rn Dv (1832–67), Mid Dv (1867–85), Frome Dv (1885–1948). *Eccl* Frome RDn. Abol eccl 1972 to help cr Rode Major EP.[247]

NORTH WOOTTON
Chap in Pilton AP, sep civ identity early, sep EP 1845 (incl pt Wells St Cuthbert AP).[396] *LG* Seq 20. Addtl civ bdry alt: 1883,[1] 1884.[475] *Parl* Seq 8. *Eccl* Cary RDn (1845–72), Shept. Mal. RDn (1872–*).

WOOTTON COURTENAY
AP Usual eccl spelling, civ spelling from 1961 at civ renaming 'Wootton Courtney'.[476] *LG* Seq 11. Civ bdry: 1883,[373] 1916.[258] *Parl* Seq 21. *Eccl* Seq 12.

WOOTTON COURTNEY–See prev entry

WORLE
AP *LG* Winterstoke Hd, Axbr. PLU, pt W-s-M USD (1883–94), Axbr. RSD (ent 1875–83, pt 1883–94), pt W-s-M UD (1894–96), Axbr. RD (pt 1894–96, ent 1896–1933). Civ bdry: 1883 (gains former detached pt of Weston-super-Mare in the USD),[1] 1885,[148] 1896 (made ent RD).[327] Abol civ 1933 pt to Weston-super-Mare AP, pt to Kewstoke AP, pt to Locking AP.[3] *Parl* E'rn Dv (1832–67), East Dv (1867–85), Wells Dv (1885–1918), W-s-M Dv (1918–48). *Eccl* Seq 24. Eccl bdry: 1964,[329] 1965 (help cr Milton EP).[330]

WRAXALL
AP Incl chap Nailsea (sep civ identity early, sep EP 1811[281]). *LG* Seq 37. Addtl civ bdry alt: 1883,[1] 1884.[210] Transf 1974 to Avon.[22] *Parl* Seq 5. *Eccl* Seq 6.

WRINGTON
AP Incl chap Burrington (sep civ identity early, sep EP 1758[25]). *LG* Seq 8. Transf 1974 to Avon.[22] *Parl* Seq 7. *Eccl* Seq 6. Eccl bdry: 1873 (help cr Felton Common Hill EP).[33]

WRITHLINGTON
AP *LG* Kilm. Hd, Frome PLU, RSD, RD. Abol civ 1933 pt to help cr Norton-Radstock CP, pt to Kilmersdon AP.[3] *Parl* E'rn Dv (1832–67), Mid Dv (1867–85), Frome Dv (1885–1948). *Eccl* Frome RDn (until 1872), Mids. Nort. RDn (1872–1971). Abol eccl 1971 to help cr Rad-

stock with Writhlington EP.[404]

WYKE CHAMPFLOWER

EP Chap in Bruton AP, sep EP 1748.[25] Cary RDn (1748–1872), Bruton RDn (1872–1971). Abol 1971 to help cr Bruton with Wyke Champflower and Redlynch EP, 'Champflower' not in order but commonly used.[142]

YARLINGTON

AP *LG* Seq 9. *Parl* Seq 8. *Eccl* Seq 25.

YATTON

AP Incl chap Cleeve (sep EP 1841 as 'Cleeve in Yatton',[25] eccl refounded 1843 as 'Cleeve'[245] although 'Cleeve in Yatton' commonly used, sep CP 1949[213]). *LG* Seq 54. Addtl civ bdry alt: 1883,[1] 1884,[210] 1962.[233] Transf 1974 to Avon.[22] *Parl* Seq 6. Parl bdry: 1951.[173] *Eccl* Seq 6. Addtl eccl bdry alt: 1865 (help cr Congresbury St Ann EP, later called 'Hewish St Ann').[117]

YEOVIL

AP Incl chap Preston Plucknett (sep civ identity early, no sep eccl identity hence this par eccl 'Yeovil with Preston Plucknett', qv). *LG* Stone Hd, Yeov. PLU, Yeov. Bor/MB (pt until 1894, ent 1894–1974), pt Yeov. USD, pt Yeov. RSD. Civ bdry: 1894 (the pt not in the MB cr Yeovil Without CP),[56] 1903,[399] 1930,[143] 1959,[477] 1967.[42] *Parl* Seq 16.

YEOVIL HOLY TRINITY

EP Renaming 1972 of Hendford EP.[302] Merst. RDn.

YEOVIL ST MICHAEL AND ALL ANGELS

EP Cr 1897 from Yeovil with Preston Plucknett AP.[479] Merst. RDn.

YEOVIL WITH PRESTON PLUCKNETT

AP Usual eccl spelling; for civ and civ sep chap Preston Plucknett, see 'Yeovil'. *Eccl* Merst. RDn. Eccl bdry: 1846 (cr Hendford EP),[250] 1872 (cr Yeovil Marsh EP),[478] 1897 (cr Yeovil St Michael and All Angels EP).[479] Abol eccl 1937 to help cr Yeovil with Preston Plucknett and Kingston Pitney EP.[345]

YEOVIL WITH PRESTON PLUCKNETT AND KINGSTON PITNEY

EP Cr 1937 by union Yeovil with Preson Plucknett AP, Kingston Pitney sinecure rectory, 'reputed par'.[345] Merst. RDn.

YEOVIL WITHOUT

CP Cr 1894 from the pt of Yeovil AP not in Yeov. MB.[56] *LG* Yeov. PLU, RD. Civ bdry: 1903,[399] 1930,[143] 1933,[3] 1957,[11] 1959,[477] 1967.[42] *Parl* Yeov. Dv/CC (1918–*).

YEOVIL MARSH

EP Cr 1872 from Yeovil with Preston Plucknett AP.[478] Merst. RDn (1872–1967), Mart. RDn (1967–*). Bdry: 1955.[198]

YEOVILTON

AP *LG* Seq 39. Civ bdry: 1933.[2] *Parl* Seq 15. *Eccl* Seq 33. Eccl bdry: 1953.[199]

SUFFOLK

ABBREVIATIONS

Abbreviations particular to Suffolk follow. Those general abbreviations in use throughout the *Guide* are found on page xix.

Aldb.	Aldeburgh
Bab.	Babergh
Bosm. & Clay.	Bosmere and Claydon
Bury St Edm.	Bury St Edmunds
Carlf.	Carlford
Coln.	Colneis
Cosf.	Cosford
Dunw.	Dunwich
Elm.	Elmham
Ford.	Fordwich
Gip.	Gipping
Hadl.	Hadleigh
Halesw.	Halesworth
Hart.	Hartismere
Horng.	Horningsheath
Horr.	Horringer
Ipsw.	Ipswich
Ixw.	Ixworth
Lackf.	Lackford
Lav.	Lavenham
Loth.	Lothingland
Lowest.	Lowestoft
Melf.	Melford
Mild.	Mildenhall
Mutf.	Mutford
Nwmkt.	Newmarket
Plom.	Plomesgate
Risb.	Risbridge
Samf.	Samford
Saxm.	Saxmundham
Stowm.	Stowmarket
Sudb.	Sudbury
Thedw.	Thedwastre
Thetf.	Thetford
Thred.	Thredling
Thurl.	Thurlow
Wainf.	Wainford
Wangf.	Wangford
Wilf.	Wilford
Woodb.	Woodbridge

SEQUENCES

An abbreviated entry prefixed by 'Seq' is used in the parochial entries to avoid repeating often the names of superior units of administration. The content of each sequence is shown below.

Local Government Sequences ('LG')

SEQ 1 Bab. Hd, Cosf. PLU, RSD, [W Suffolk] Cosf. RD

SEQ 2 Bab. Hd, Sudb. PLU, RSD, [W Suffolk] Melf. RD

SEQ 3 Blackbourn Hd, Stow PLU, RSD [W Suffolk] Thedw. RD

SEQ 4 Blackbourn Hd, Thetf. PLU, RSD, [W Suffolk] Brandon RD (1894–1935), Thingoe

RD (1935–74)
SEQ 5 Blackbourn Hd, Thingoe PLU (1836–1907), RSD, Bury St Edm. PLU (1907–30), [W Suffolk] Thingoe RD
SEQ 6 Blything Hd, PLU, RSD, [E Suffolk] Blything RD (1894–1934), Blyth RD (1934–74)
SEQ 7 Blything Hd, PLU, RSD, [E Suffolk] Blything RD (1894–1934), Loth. RD (1934–74)
SEQ 8 Blything Hd, PLU, RSD, [E Suffolk] Blything RD (1894–1934), Wainf. RD (1934–74)
SEQ 9 Bosm. & Clay. Hd, Bosm. PLU, RSD, [E Suffolk] Bosm. & Clay. RD (1894–1934), Gip. RD (1934–74)
SEQ 10 Carlf. Hd, Woodb. PLU, RSD, [E Suffolk] Woodb. RD (1894–1934), Deben RD (1934–74)
SEQ 11 Coln. Hd, Woodb. PLU, RSD, [E Suffolk] Woodb. RD (1894–1934), Deben RD (1934–74)
SEQ 12 Cosf. Hd, PLU, RSD, [W Suffolk] Cosf. RD
SEQ 13 Hart. Hd, PLU, RSD, [E Suffolk] Hart. RD
SEQ 14 Hoxne Hd, PLU (1835–1907), RSD, Hart. PLU (1907–30), [E Suffolk] Hoxne RD (1894–1934), Blyth RD (1934–74)
SEQ 15 Hoxne Hd, PLU (1835–1907), RSD, Hart. PLU (1907–30), [E Suffolk] Hoxne RD (1894–1934), Hart. RD (1934–74)
SEQ 16 Lackf. Hd, Mild. PLU, RSD, [W Suffolk] Mild. RD
SEQ 17 Lackf. Hd, Thetf. PLU, RSD, [W Suffolk] Brandon RD (1894–1935), Mild. RD (1935–74)
SEQ 18 Loes Hd, Plom. PLU, RSD, [E Suffolk] Plom. RD (1894–1934), Blyth RD (1934–74)
SEQ 19 Loes Hd, Plom. PLU, RSD, [E Suffolk] Plom. RD (1894–1934), Deben RD (1934–74)
SEQ 20 Mutf. & Loth. Hd, PLU, RSD, [E Suffolk] Mutf. & Loth. RD (1894–1934), Loth. RD (1934–74)
SEQ 21 Plom. Hd, PLU, RSD, [E Suffolk] Plom. RD (1894–1934), Blyth RD (1934–74)
SEQ 22 Plom. Hd, PLU, RSD, [E Suffolk] Plom. RD (1894–1934), Deben RD (1934–74)
SEQ 23 Risb. Hd, Nwmkt. PLU, RSD, [W Suffolk] Moulton RD (1894–1935), Clare RD (1935–74)
SEQ 24 Risb. Hd, Nwmkt. PLU, RSD, [W Suffolk] Moulton RD (1894–1935), Mild. RD (1935–74)
SEQ 25 Risb. Hd, PLU, RSD, [W Suffolk] Clare RD
SEQ 26 Risb. Hd, Thingoe PLU (1836–1907), RSD, Bury St Edm. PLU (1907–30), [W Suffolk] Thingoe RD
SEQ 27 Samf. Hd, PLU, RSD, [E Suffolk] Samf. RD
SEQ 28 Stow Hd, PLU, RSD, [E Suffolk] E Stow RD (1894–1934), Gip. RD (1934–74)
SEQ 29 Thedw. Hd, Stow PLU, RSD, [W Suffolk] Thedw. RD
SEQ 30 Thedw. Hd, Thingoe PLU (1836–1907), RSD, Bury St Edm. PLU (1907–30), [W Suffolk] Thingoe RD
SEQ 31 Thingoe Hd, PLU (1836–1907), RSD, Bury St Edm. PLU (1907–30), [W Suffolk] Thingoe RD
SEQ 32 Thred. Hd, Bosm. PLU, RSD, [E Suffolk] Bosm. & Clay. RD (1894–1934), Gip. RD (1934–74)
SEQ 33 Wangf. Hd, PLU, RSD, [E Suffolk] Wangf. RD (1894–1934), Wainf. RD (1934–74)
SEQ 34 Wilf. Hd, Woodb. PLU, RSD, [E Suffolk] Woodb. RD (1894–1934), Deben RD (1934–74)

Parliamentary Sequences ('Parl')

SEQ 1 E'rn Dv (1832–85), N'rn Dv (1885–1918), Eye Dv (1918–48), Lowest. CC (1948–*)
SEQ 2 E'rn Dv (1832–85), N'rn Dv (1885–1918), Lowest. Dv/CC (1918–*)
SEQ 3 E'rn Dv (1832–85), N-E'rn Dv (1885–1918), Eye Dv/CC (1918–*)
SEQ 4 E'rn Dv (1832–85), N-E'rn Dv (1885–1918), Eye Dv (1918–48), Sudb. & Woodb. CC (1948–*)
SEQ 5 E'rn Dv (1832–85), N-E'rn Dv (1885–1918), Woodb. Dv (1918–48), Eye CC (1948–*)
SEQ 6 E'rn Dv (1832–85), N-W'rn Dv (1885–1918), Bury St Edm. Dv/CC (1918–*)
SEQ 7 E'rn Dv (1832–85), S-E'rn Dv (1885–1918), Woodb. Dv (1918–48), Eye CC (1948–*)
SEQ 8 E'rn Dv (1832–85), S-E'rn Dv (1885–1918), Woodb. Dv (1918–48), Sudb. & Woodb. CC (1948–*)
SEQ 9 W'rn Dv (1832–85), N-E'rn Dv (1885–1918), Eye Dv/CC (1918–*)
SEQ 10 W'rn Dv (1832–85), N-W'rn Dv (1885–1918), Bury St Edm. Dv/CC (1918–*)
SEQ 11 W'rn Dv (1832–85), N-W'rn Dv (1885–1918), Eye Dv/CC (1918–*)
SEQ 12 W'rn Dv (1832–85), N-W'rn Dv (1885–1918), Sudb. Dv (1918–48), Bury St Edm. CC (1948–*)
SEQ 13 W'rn Dv (1832–85), South Dv (1885–1918), Sudb. Dv (1918–48), Bury St Edm. CC (1948–*)
SEQ 14 W'rn Dv (1832–85), South Dv (1885–1918), Sudb. Dv (1918–48), Sudb. & Woodb. CC (1948–*)
SEQ 15 W'rn Dv (1832–85), S-E'rn Dv (1885–1918), Eye Dv (1918–48), Sudb. & Woodb. CC (1948–*)
SEQ 16 W'rn Dv (1832–85), S-E'rn Dv (1885–1918), Woodb. Dv (1918–48), Eye CC (1948–*)

Ecclesiastical Sequences ('Eccl')

SEQ 1 Blackburne RDn (until 1972), Ixw. RDn (1972–*)
SEQ 2 Blackburne RDn (until 1884), Thedw. RDn (1884–1972), Lav. RDn (1972–*)
SEQ 3 Blackburne RDn (until 1884), Thingoe RDn (1884–*)
SEQ 4 Clare RDn
SEQ 5 Clare RDn (until 1884), Horng. RDn (1884–1914), Hor. RDn (1914–72), Thingoe RDn (1972–*)

Orig Sudbury AD:

SEQ 1 Blackburne RDn (until 1972), Ixw. RDn (1972–*)
SEQ 2 Blackburne RDn (until 1884), Thedw. RDn (1884–1972), Lav. RDn (1972–*)
SEQ 3 Blackburne RDn (until 1884), Thingoe RDn (1884–*)
SEQ 4 Clare RDn
SEQ 5 Clare RDn (until 1884), Horng. RDn (1884–1914), Hor. RDn (1914–72), Thingoe RDn (1972–*)
SEQ 6 Clare RDn (until 1884), Thurl. RDn (1884–1916), Nwmkt. RDn (1916–72), Clare RDn (1972–*)
SEQ 7 Clare RDn (until 1884), Thurl. RDn (1884–1916), Nwmkt. RDn (1916–72), Mild. RDn (1972–*)
SEQ 8 Ford. RDn (until 1862, Ford. (Suffolk) RDn (1862–84), Ford. RDn (1884–1914), Thurl. RDn (1914–16), Nwmkt. RDn (1916–72), Mild. RDn (1972–*)
SEQ 9 Ford. RDn (until 1862), Ford. (Suffolk) RDn (1862–84), Mild. RDn (1884–*)
SEQ 10 Hart. RDn (until 1897), Hart. (North) RDn (1897–1931), N Hart. RDn (1931–72), Hart. RDn (1972–*)
SEQ 11 Hart. RDn (until 1897), Hart. (South) RDn (1897–1931), S Hart. RDn (1931–72), Stowm. RDn (1972–*)
SEQ 12 Stow RDn (until 1972), Stowm. RDn (1972–*)
SEQ 13 Sudb. RDn (until 1864), Sudb. (E'rn) RDn (1864–84), Hadl. RDn (1884–*)
SEQ 14 Sudb. RDn (until 1864), Sudb. (E'rn) RDn (1864–84), Lav. RDn (1884–*)
SEQ 15 Sudb. RDn (until 1864), Sudb. (W'rn) RDn (1884–1914), Lav. RDn (1914–*)
SEQ 16 Sudb. RDn (until 1864), Sudb. (W'rn) RDn (1864–84), Sudb. RDn (1884–*)
SEQ 17 Thedw. RDn (until 1972), Clare RDn (1972–*)
SEQ 18 Thedw. RDn (until 1972), Lav. RDn (1972–*)
SEQ 19 Thedw. RDn (until 1884), Horng. RDn (1884–1914), Hor. RDn (1914–72), Lav. RDn (1972–*)
SEQ 20 Thedw. RDn (until 1884), Thingoe RDn (1884–*)
SEQ 21 Thingoe RDn
SEQ 22 Thingoe RDn (until 1884), Horng. RDn (1884–1914), Hor. RDn (1914–72), Thingoe RDn (1972–*)

Orig Suffolk AD:

SEQ 23 Bosm. RDn
SEQ 24 Bosm. RDn (until 1914), Clay. RDn (1914–72), Bosm. RDn (1972–*)
SEQ 25 Carlf. RDn (until 1972), Woodb. RDn (1972–*)
SEQ 26 Clay. RDn (until 1972), Bosm. RDn (1972–*)
SEQ 27 Clay. RDn (until 1972), Ipsw. RDn (1972–*)
SEQ 28 Clay. RDn (until 1972), Loes RDn (1972–*)
SEQ 29 Colneys RDn
SEQ 30 Dunw. RDn (until 1868), Dunw. (North) RDn (1868–1914), Beccles RDn (1914–72), Beccles & S Elm. RDn (1972–*)
SEQ 31 Dunw. RDn (until 1868), Dunw. (North) RDn (1868–1914, N Dunw. RDn (1914–72), Halesw. RDn (1972–*)
SEQ 32 Dunw. RDn (until 1868), Dunw. (South) RDn (1868–1914), S Dunw. RDn (1914–72), Saxm. RDn (1972–*)
SEQ 33 Dunw. RDn (until 1868), Dunw. (South) RDn (1868–1914), S Dunw. RDn (1914–72), Halesw. RDn (1972–*)
SEQ 34 S Elm. RDn (until 1972), Beccles & S Elm. RDn (1972–*)
SEQ 35 Hoxne RDn
SEQ 36 Ipsw. RDn
SEQ 37 Loes RDn
SEQ 38 Loes RDn (until 1914), Carlf. RDn (1914–72), Woodb. RDn (1972–*)
SEQ 39 Loes RDn (until 1914), Wilf. RDn (1914–72), Woodb. RDn (1972–*)
SEQ 40 Loth. RDn
SEQ 41 Orford RDn (until 1914), Saxm. RDn (1914–*)
SEQ 42 Orford RDn (until 1914), Wilf. RDn (1914–72), Woodb. RDn (1972–*)
SEQ 43 Samf. RDn
SEQ 44 Samf. RDn (until 1946), Hadl. RDn (1946–*)
SEQ 45 Wangf. RDn (until 1914), Beccles RDn (1914–72), Beccles & S Elm. RDn (1972–*)
SEQ 46 Wangf. RDn, early in S Elm. RDn (until 1972), Beccles & S Elm. RDn (1972–*)
SEQ 47 Wilf. RDn (until 1972), Woodb. RDn (1972–*)
SEQ 48 Wilf. RDn (until 1914), Carlf. RDn (1914–72), Woodb. RDn (1972–*)
SEQ 49 Wilf. RDn (until 1914), Loes RDn (1914–*)

DIOCESES AND ARCHDEACONRIES

Suffolk pars were organised in dioceses and archdeaconries as follows.

IPSWICH AD (1931–*)
Bosm. RDn, Clay. RDn (1931–72), Colneys RDn (1972–*), Hadl. RDn (1931–*), N Hart. RDn (1931–72), S Hart. RDn (1931–72), Ipsw. RDn, Samf. RDn, Stow RDn (1931–72), Stowm. RDn (1972–*), Woodb. RDn (1972–*)

SUDBURY AD
Blackburne RDn (until 1972), Clare RDn, Ford. RDn (until 1862), Ford. (Suffolk) RDn (1862–84), Hadl. RDn (1884–1931), Hart. RDn (until 1837), Horng. RDn (1884–1914), Hor. RDn (1914–72), Ixw. RDn (1972–*), Lav. RDn (1884–*), Mild. RDn (1884–*), Nwmkt. RDn (1916–72), Stow RDn (until 1837), Sudb. RDn (until 1864), Sudb. RDn (1884–*), Sudb. (E'rn) RDn (1864–84), Sudb. (W'rn) RDn (1864–84), Thedw. RDn (until 1972), Thingoe RDn, Thurl. RDn (1884–1916)

SUFFOLK AD
Beccles RDn (1916–72), Beccles & S Elm. RDn (1972–*), Bosm. RDn (until 1931), Carlf. RDn (until 1972), Clay. RDn (until 1931), Colneys RDn (until 1972), Dunw. RDn (until 1868), Dunw. (North) RDn (1868–1914), Dunw. (South) RDn (1868–1914), N Dunw. RDn (1914–72), S Dunw. RDn (1914–72), S Elm. RDn (until 1972), Halesw. RDn (1972–*), Hart. RDn (1837–97), Hart. RDn (1972–*), Hart. (North) RDn (1897–1931), Hart. (South) RDn (1897–1931), Hoxne alias Bishop's RDn, Ipsw. RDn (until 1931), Loes RDn, Loth. RDn (until 1914), Orford RDn (until 1914), Samf. RDn (until 1931), Saxm. RDn (1916–*), Stow RDn (1837–1931), Wangf. RDn (until 1914), Wilf. RDn (until 1972)

THE PARISHES OF SUFFOLK

ACTON
AP *LG* Seq 2. Civ bdry: 1883,[1] 1885,[2] 1885.[3] *Parl* Seq 14. *Eccl* Sudb. RDn (until 1864), Sudb. (W'rn) RDn (1864–1884), Lav. RDn (1884–1914), Sudb. RDn (1914–*).

AKENHAM
AP *LG* Seq 9. Civ bdry: 1952 (loses pt to Ipsw. CB and CP).[4] *Parl* Seq 7. Parl bdry: 1953.[5] *Eccl* Seq 27.

ALDEBURGH
AP Incl hmlt Hazlewood (sep CP 1866,[6] no sep eccl identity thus this par eccl 'Aldeburgh with Hazlewood', qv). *LG* Plom. Hd, Aldb. Bor, MB (1885–1974), Plom. PLU, RSD (1875–85), Aldb. USD (1885–94). [E Suffolk]. Civ bdry: 1934.[7] *Parl* Aldb. Parl Bor (1571–1832), Seq 16 thereafter.

ALDEBURGH WITH HAZLEWOOD
AP Usual eccl spelling; for civ and civ sep chap Hazlewood, see prev entry. *Eccl* Seq 41. Eccl bdry: 1958.[8]

ALDERTON
AP *LG* Wilf. Hd, Woodb. PLU, RSD, [E Suffolk] Woodb. RD (1894–1934), Deben RD (1934–74). *Parl* Seq 8. *Eccl* Seq 47.

ALDHAM
AP *LG* Seq 12. Civ bdry: 1883,[1] 1935.[9] *Parl* Seq 14. *Eccl* Seq 13.

ALDRINGHAM WITH THORPE
AP *LG* Seq 6. *Parl* Seq 3. *Eccl* Dunw. RDn (until 1868), Dunw. (South) RDn (1868–1914), Saxm. RDn (1914–*). Eccl bdry: 1958.[8]

ALNESBOURN PRIORY
Ex-par place, sep CP 1858,[10] abol eccl 1939 to help cr Ipswich All Hallows EP.[11] *LG* Coln. Hd, Woodb. PLU, RSD, [E Suffolk] Woodb. RD. Abol 1934 pt to Ipswich CB and CP, pt to Nacton AP.[12] *Parl* E'rn Dv (1867–85), S-E'rn Dv (1885–1918), Woodb. Dv (1918–48). Eccl bdry: 1928 (help cr Ipswich St Augustine EP).[13]

ALPHETON
AP *LG* Seq 2. *Parl* Seq 14. *Eccl* Sudb. RDn (until 1864), Sudb. (W'rn) RDn (1864–84), Sudb. RDn (1884–1926), Lav. RDn (1926–*).

AMPTON
AP *LG* Seq 30. *Parl* Seq 10. *Eccl* Thedw. RDn (until 1884), Thingoe RDn (1884–1946). Abol eccl 1946 to help cr Ampton with Little Livermere EP.[14]

AMPTON WITH LITTLE LIVERMERE
EP Cr 1946 by union Ampton AP, Little Livermere AP.[14] Thingoe RDn.

ASHBOCKING
AP Sometimes 'Ash Bocking'. *LG* Seq 9. *Parl* Seq 7. *Eccl* Seq 24.

ASHBY
AP *LG* Seq 20. *Parl* Seq 2. *Eccl* Loth. RDn (until 1970), Flegg RDn [also in Norw dioc] (1970–*).

GREAT ASHFIELD
AP *LG* Seq 3. *Parl* Seq 10. *Eccl* Seq 2.

ASHFIELD WITH THORPE
AP United before 1291 with Thorpe AP to cr Ashfield with Thorpe AP. *LG* Seq 32. *Parl* Seq 5. *Eccl* Seq 28.

ASPALL
AP *LG* Seq 13. *Parl* Seq 9. *Eccl* Hart. RDn (until 1897), Hart. (South) RDn (1897–1931), S Hart. RDn (1931–72), Loes RDn (1972–*).

ASSINGTON
AP *LG* Seq 2. Civ bdry: 1952 (help cr Leavenheath CP).[147] *Parl* Seq 14. *Eccl* Seq 16. Eccl bdry: 1863 (help cr Leavenheath EP).[146]

ATHELINGTON
AP *LG* Seq 15. *Parl* Seq 3. *Eccl* Seq 35.

BACTON
AP *LG* Seq 13. Civ bdry: 1883.[1] *Parl* Seq 9. *Eccl* Seq 11.

BADINGHAM
AP *LG* Seq 14. *Parl* Seq 3. *Eccl* Hoxne RDn (until 1914), Loes RDn (1914–*).

BADLEY
AP *LG* Seq 9. *Parl* Seq 7. *Eccl* Seq 23.

BADWELL ASH
AP *LG* Seq 3. *Parl* Seq 10. *Eccl* Seq 2.

BALLINGDON
AP Orig AP, church in ruins and eccl incl in Sudbury All Saints AP as below. Sometimes 'Ballingdon cum Brundon'. Pt Essex (Hinckford Hd), pt Suffolk (Bab. Hd), the par made ent Suffolk 1896, gaining at same time the pt of Bulmer AP (Essex) in Sudb. UD.[15] *LG* Sudb. PLU, the Suffolk pt in Sudb. MB (1892–96, ent 1896–1974), pt Sudb. USD (1892–94). Addtl civ bdry alt: 1883.[2] *Parl* Sudb. Parl Bor (1832–85), Suffolk pt, South Dv (1885–1918), Sudb. Dv (1918–48), Sudb. & Woodb. CC (1948–*). *Eccl* Sudb. RDn. Abol eccl 1847 to help cr Sudbury All Saints with Ballingdon and Brundon EP.[16]

BARDWELL
AP *LG* Seq 5. *Parl* Seq 10. *Eccl* Seq 1.

BARHAM
AP *LG* Seq 9. *Parl* Seq 7. *Eccl* Clay. RDn (until 1972), Bosm. RDn (1972–73). Eccl bdry: 1946.[14] Abol eccl 1973 to help cr Claydon and Barham EP.[17]

BARKING
AP Incl hmlt & chap Darmsden (sep rated as PLU unit but sep status not sustained as CP, no sep eccl identity thus this par eccl 'Barking with Darmsden', qv), hmlt Needham Market (sep EP 1901,[18] sep CP 1907[19]). *LG* Seq 9. Addtl civ bdry alt: 1884.[20] *Parl* Seq 7.

BARKING WITH DARMSDEN
AP Usual eccl spelling; for civ and sep of Needham Market see prev entry. *Eccl* Seq 23.

BARNARDISTON
AP *LG* Seq 25. *Parl* Seq 13. *Eccl* Seq 4. Eccl bdry: 1931 (gains ex-par Monks Risbridge).[21]

BARNBY
AP *LG* Seq 20. *Parl* Seq 2. *Eccl* Loth. RDn (until 1922), Beccles RDn (1922–72), Beccles & S Elm. RDn (1972–*).

BARNHAM
AP *LG* Seq 4. *Parl* Seq 10. *Eccl* Seq 1.

BARNINGHAM
AP *LG* Seq 4. *Parl* Seq 10. *Eccl* Blackburne RDn. Abol eccl 1802 to help cr Barningham with Coney Weston EP.[22]

BARNINGHAM WITH CONEY WESTON
EP Cr 1802 by union Barningham AP, Coney Weston AP.[22] Blackburne RDn (1802–1972), Ixw. RDn (1972–*).

BARROW
AP *LG* Seq 31. *Parl* Seq 10. *Eccl* Seq 21.

BARSHAM
AP *LG* Seq 33. Civ bdry: 1879.[23] *Parl* Seq 2. *Eccl* Seq 45.

GREAT BARTON
AP *LG* Seq 30. *Parl* Seq 10. *Eccl* Seq 20.

BARTON MILLS
AP *LG* Seq 16. *Parl* Seq 6. *Eccl* Seq 9.

BATTISFORD
AP *LG* Seq 9. *Parl* Seq 7. *Eccl* Seq 23.

BAWDSEY
AP *LG* Seq 34. *Parl* Seq 8. *Eccl* Seq 47. Eccl bdry: 1960.[24]

BAYLHAM
AP *LG* Seq 9. *Parl* Seq 7. *Eccl* Seq 23.

GREAT BEALINGS
AP *LG* Seq 10. *Parl* Seq 8. *Eccl* Seq 25.

LITTLE BEALINGS
AP *LG* Seq 10. *Parl* Seq 8. *Eccl* Seq 25.

BECCLES
AP *LG* Wangf. Hd, PLU, Beccles Bor/MB, USD. [E Suffolk]. *Parl* Seq 2. *Eccl* Seq 45.

BEDFIELD
AP *LG* Seq 15. *Parl* Seq 3. *Eccl* Seq 35.

BEDINGFIELD
AP *LG* Seq 15. *Parl* Seq 3. *Eccl* Hoxne RDn. Abol eccl 1951 to help cr Bedingfield with Southolt EP.[31]

BEDINGFIELD WITH SOUTHOLT
EP Cr 1951 by union Bedingfield AP, chap Southolt of Worlingworth with Southolt AP.[31] Hoxne RDn.

BELSTEAD
AP *LG* Samf. Hd, pt Ipsw. Bor/MB/CB, Samf. PLU, pt Ipsw. USD, pt Samf. RSD, [E Suffolk] Samf. RD. Civ bdry: 1894 (loses the pt in the CB to Ipswich St Mary Stoke AP),[26] 1934 (loses pt to Ipswich CB and CP).[7] *Parl* Pt Ipsw. Parl Bor (until 1918), remainder and later, Seq 8. *Eccl* Seq 43. Eccl bdry: 1959 (help cr Ipswich St Francis EP).[27]

BELTON
AP *LG* Seq 20. Transf 1974 to Norfolk.[25] *Parl* Seq 2. *Eccl* Loth. RDn (until 1970), Flegg RDn [also in Norw dioc] (1970–*).

BENACRE
AP *LG* Seq 7. *Parl* Seq 2. *Eccl* Seq 30. Eccl bdry: 1749 (gains Easton Bavents AP [church of the latter washed into the sea[28]] the par sometimes afterwards called 'Benacre with Easton Bavents').

BENHALL
AP *LG* Seq 21. *Parl* Seq 9. *Eccl* Seq 41.

BENTLEY
AP *LG* Seq 27. *Parl* Seq 8. *Eccl* Seq 43.

EAST BERGHOLT
Chap in Brantham AP, sep civ identity early, sep EP 1843.[29] *LG* Seq 27. Civ bdry: 1938 (exchanges pts with Dedham AP, Essex).[30] *Parl* Seq 8. *Eccl* Samf. RDn.

BEYTON
AP *LG* Thedw. Hd, Stow PLU, RSD, [W Suffolk] Thedw. RD. *Parl* Seq 10. *Eccl* Seq 18.

BILDESTON
AP *LG* Seq 12. Civ bdry: 1883,[1] 1935 (help cr Nedging with Naughton CP).[9] *Parl* Seq 14. *Eccl* Seq 13.

GREAT BLAKENHAM
AP *LG* Seq 9. *Parl* Seq 7. *Eccl* Seq 23.
LITTLE BLAKENHAM
AP *LG* Seq 9. *Parl* Seq 7. *Eccl* Seq 23.
BLAXHALL
AP *LG* Seq 22. *Parl* Seq 7. *Eccl* Seq 41.
BLUNDESTON
AP Incl chap Flixton ('free chapel' in 16th cent,[32] sep civ identity early, later deemed chap in this par, thus this par eccl 'Blundeston with Flixton', qv). *LG* Seq 20. *Parl* Seq 2.
BLUNDESTON WITH FLIXTON
AP Usual eccl spelling; for civ and civ sep chap Flixton, see prev entry. *Eccl* Seq 40.
BLYFORD
AP *LG* Seq 8. Civ bdry: 1884,[33] 1884.[34] *Parl* Seq 1. *Eccl* Seq 31. Eccl bdry: 1935.[35]
BLYTHBURGH
AP Incl chap Walberswick (sep civ identity early, no sep eccl identity thus this par eccl 'Blythburgh with Walberswick', qv). *LG* Seq 6. *Parl* Seq 3.
BLYTHBURGH WITH WALBERSWICK
AP Usual eccl spelling; for civ and civ sep chap Walberswick, see prev entry. *Eccl* Dunw. RDn (until 1868), Dunwich (South) RDn (1868–1914), N Dunw. RDn (1914–72), Halesw. RDn (1972–*).
BOTESDALE
Chap & hmlt in Redgrave AP, sep CP 1866,[6] no sep eccl identity. *LG* Seq 13. *Parl* W'rn Dv (1867–85), N-E'rn Dv (1885–1918), Eye Dv/CC (1918–*).
BOULGE
AP *LG* Seq 34. *Parl* Seq 7. *Eccl* Seq 38.
BOXFORD
AP Incl hmlt Hadleigh Hamlet, sep CP 1866.[6] *LG* Pt Bab. Hd, pt Cosf. Hd, Cosf. PLU, RSD, [W Suffolk] Cosf. RD. Addtl civ bdry alt: 1883,[2] 1885,[36] 1885,[3] 1935.[9] *Parl* Seq 14. *Eccl* Sudb. RDn (until 1864), Sudb. (W'rn) RDn (1864–84), Hadl. RDn (1884–1972), Sudb. RDn (1972–*). Eccl bdry: 1946.[37]
BOXTED
AP *LG* Seq 2. Civ bdry: 1883,[2] 1885.[3] *Parl* Seq 14. *Eccl* Sudb. RDn. Abol eccl before 1535 to help cr Hartest with Boxted EP.[32]
BOYTON
AP *LG* Seq 34. *Parl* Seq 8. *Eccl* Seq 47.
BRADFIELD COMBUST
AP *LG* Seq 30. Civ bdry: 1935.[9] *Parl* Seq 12. *Eccl* Seq 19.
BRADFIELD ST CLARE
AP *LG* Seq 30. *Parl* Seq 12. *Eccl* Seq 19.
BRADFIELD ST GEORGE
AP *LG* Seq 30. Civ bdry: 1884.[38] *Parl* Seq 12. *Eccl* Seq 19.
GREAT BRADLEY
AP *LG* Seq 25. *Parl* Seq 13. *Eccl* Seq 6.
LITTLE BRADLEY
AP *LG* Seq 25. *Parl* Seq 13. *Eccl* Seq 6.
BRADWELL
AP *LG* Seq 20. Transf 1974 to Norfolk.[25] *Parl* Seq 2. *Eccl* Loth. RDn (until 1970), Flegg RDn [also in Norw dioc] (1970–*).
BRAISEWORTH
AP *LG* Seq 13. *Parl* Eye Parl Bor (1832–85), N-E'rn Dv (1885–1918), Eye Dv/CC (1918–*). *Eccl* Seq 10.
BRAMFIELD
AP *LG* Seq 6. *Parl* Seq 3. *Eccl* Seq 33.
BRAMFORD
AP Incl chap Burstall (sep civ identity early, eccl severed 1962 to help cr Sproughton with Burstall EP,[39] so that this par eccl before 1962 'Bramford with Burstall'). *LG* Bosm. & Clay. Hd, pt Ipsw. Bor/MB/CB, Bosm. & Clay. PLU, pt Ipsw. USD, pt Bosm. & Clay. RSD, [E Suffolk] Bosm. & Clay. RD (1894–1934), Gip. RD (1934–74). Addtl civ bdry alt: 1894 (loses the two pts in the CB, one to Ipswich St Matthew AP, one to Whitton cum Thurleston AP),[26] 1934 (loses pt to Ipsw. CB and CP),[7] 1952 (loses pt to Ipsw. CB and CP).[4] *Parl* Pt Ipsw. Parl Bor (1295–1918), remainder and later, Seq 7. Parl bdry: 1953.[5] *Eccl* As 'Bramford with Burstall' before 1962 and 'Bramford' thereafter, Seq 7. Addtl eccl bdry alt: 1868 (help cr Ipswich All Saints EP).[40]
BRAMFORD WITH BURSTALL–See prev entry
BRAMPTON
AP *LG* Seq 8. *Parl* Seq 1. *Eccl* Seq 31.
BRANDESTON
AP *LG* Seq 18. Civ bdry: 1883.[2] *Parl* Seq 3. *Eccl* Seq 37.
BRANDON
AP Sometimes eccl 'Brandon Ferry'. Pt Norfolk (Forehoe Hd), pt Suffolk (Lackf. Hd), made ent Suffolk 1895.[41] *LG* Thetf. PLU, RSD, [W Suffolk] Brandon RD (pt 1894–95, ent 1895–1935), Mild. RD (1935–74). *Parl* Suffolk pt, Seq 6. *Eccl* Ford. RDn (until 1862), Ford. (Suffolk) RDn (1862–84), Mild. RDn (1884–1962). Abol eccl 1962 to help cr Brandon Ferry and Wangford EP.[42]
BRANDON FERRY–see BRANDON
BRANDON FERRY AND WANGFORD
EP Cr 1962 by union Brandon AP (sometimes 'Brandon Ferry'), Wangford AP.[42] Mild. RDn.
BRANTHAM
AP *LG* Seq 27. *Parl* Seq 8. *Eccl* Seq 43.
BREDFIELD
AP *LG* Pt Wilf. Hd, pt Loes Hd, Woodb. PLU, RSD, [E Suffolk] Woodb. RD (1894–1934), Deben RD (1934–74). *Parl* Seq 7. *Eccl* Seq 48.
BRETTENHAM
AP *LG* Seq 12. Civ bdry: 1885,[36] 1935.[9] *Parl* Seq 14. *Eccl* Seq 14.
GREAT BRICETT
AP *LG* Seq 9. *Parl* Seq 7. *Eccl* Seq 23.
LITTLE BRICETT
AP Orig AP, united before 1535 with Offton AP, the union civ called 'Offton', eccl 'Offton with Little Bricett'.
BRIGHTWELL
AP *LG* Seq 10. *Parl* Seq 8. *Eccl* Carlf. RDn. Abol

eccl *ca* 1530 to help cr Brightwell with Foxhall EP.[43]

BRIGHTWELL WITH FOXHALL
EP Cr *ca* 1530 by union Brightwell AP, Foxhall EP.[43] Carlf. RDn (*ca* 1530–1926), Colneys RDn (1926–*).

BROCKLEY
AP *LG* Seq 31. Civ bdry: 1885.[44] *Parl* Seq 13. *Eccl* Seq 22.

BROME
AP *LG* Seq 13. *Parl* Eye Parl Bor (1832–85), N-E'rn Dv (1885–1918), Eye Dv/CC (1918–*). *Eccl* Hart. RDn. Abol prob in 17th cent to help cr Brome with Oakley EP.[45]

BROME WITH OAKLEY
EP Cr prob in 17th cent by union Brome AP, Oakley AP.[45] Hart. RDn (17th cent–1897), Hart. (North) RDn (1897–1931), N Hart. RDn (1931–72), Hart. RDn (1972–*).

BROMESWELL
AP *LG* Seq 34. Civ bdry: 1956.[46] *Parl* Seq 8. *Eccl* Seq 47.

BRUISYARD
AP *LG* Seq 21. *Parl* Seq 9. *Eccl* Orford RDn (until 1914), Saxm. RDn (1914–*).

BRUNDISH
Chap in Tannington AP, sep civ identity early, eccl severed 1951 to help cr Wilby with Brundish EP.[31] *LG* Seq 15. *Parl* Seq 3.

BUCKLESHAM
AP *LG* Seq 11. *Parl* Seq 8. *Eccl* Seq 29.

BUNGAY
CP Cr 1910 by union Bungay Holy Trinity AP, Bungay St Mary AP.[47] *LG* [E Suffolk] Wangf. PLU, Bungay UD. *Parl* Lowest. Dv/CC (1918–*).

BUNGAY HOLY TRINITY
AP *LG* Wangf. Hd, PLU, RSD, [E Suffolk] Wangf. RD. Civ bdry: 1879.[48] Abol civ 1910 to help cr Bungay CP.[47] *Parl* E'rn Dv (1832–85), N'rn Dv (1885–1918). *Eccl* Seq 34.

BUNGAY ST MARY
AP *LG* Wangf. Hd, PLU, RSD, [E Suffolk] Wangf. RD. Civ bdry: 1879,[49] 1885 (gains the Suffolk pt of Earsham AP [Norfolk, Suffolk]).[50] Abol civ 1910 to help cr Bungay CP.[47] *Parl* As for Bungay Holy Trinity. *Eccl* Seq 34.

BUNGAY ST THOMAS
AP Prob destroyed at Dissolution when nunnery in Bungay fell.[51]

BURES ST MARY
AP Incl hmlt Bures (Essex, Hinckford Hd, sep CP 1866[6] in Essex so that this par ent Suffolk thereafter). *LG* Bab. Hd (pt until 1866, ent from 1866), Sudb. PLU, RSD, [W Suffolk] Melford RD. Addtl civ bdry alt: 1883,[2] 1885.[3] *Parl* Suffolk pt, Seq 14. *Eccl* Seq 16. The pt in Essex declared 1914 to be ent St Edm & Ipsw dioc.[52]

BURGATE
AP *LG* Seq 13. *Parl* Seq 9. *Eccl* Seq 10.

BURGH
AP *LG* Seq 10. *Parl* Seq 7. *Eccl* Seq 25.

BURGH CASTLE
AP *LG* Seq 20. Transf 1974 to Norfolk.[25] *Parl* Seq 2. *Eccl* Loth. RDn (until 1970), Flegg RDn [also Norw dioc] (1970–*).

BURSTALL
Chap in Bramford AP, sep civ identity early, eccl severed 1962 to help cr Sproughton with Burstall EP.[39] *LG* Seq 27. *Parl* Seq 8.

BURY ST EDMUNDS
The following have 'Bury St Edmunds' in their names. Insofar as any existed at a given time: *LG* Bury St Edm. Bor/MB, PLU, USD. *Parl* Bury St Edm. Parl Bor (1614–1918), Dv/CC (1918–*). *Eccl* Pec jurisd Bury St Edm. (until 1844),[53] Thingoe RDn (1844–*).

CP1–BURY ST EDMUNDS–Cr 1895 by union AP1, AP2.[54] Bdry: 1935.[9]

EP1–BURY ST EDMUNDS ALL SAINTS–Cr 1962 from AP1, EP3, Westley AP.[55]

EP2–BURY ST EDMUNDS ST GEORGE–Cr 1958 from Fornham All Saints AP, Westley AP.[56]

AP1–BURY ST EDMUNDS ST JAMES–Erected *temp* Edward VI.[57] Abol civ 1895 to help cr CP1.[54] Eccl bdry: 1846 (cr EP3),[58] 1962 (help cr EP1).[55]

EP3–BURY ST EDMUNDS ST JOHN–Cr 1846 from AP1.[58] Bdry: 1962 (help cr EP1).[55]

AP2–BURY ST EDMUNDS ST MARY–Abol civ 1895 to help cr CP1.[54]

BUTLEY
AP *LG* Seq 19. *Parl* Seq 8. *Eccl* Seq 47. Eccl bdry: *ca* 1530 (gains Capel St Andrew AP).[59]

BUXHALL
AP *LG* Seq 28. *Parl* Seq 11. *Eccl* Seq 12.

BUXLOW
AP Orig AP, Blything Hd, Dunw. RDn, abol 1721 ent to Knodishall AP,[60] the union civ called 'Knodishall', eccl 'Knodishall with Butley'.

CAMPSEA ASHE
AP Usual eccl spelling; for civ see following entry. *Eccl* Seq 37. Eccl bdry: 1934.[61]

CAMPSEY ASH
AP Usual civ spelling; for eccl see prev entry. *LG* Seq 19. *Parl* Seq 7.

CAPEL ST ANDREW
AP *LG* Seq 34. *Parl* Seq 8. *Eccl* Wilf. RDn. Abol eccl *ca* 1530 ent to Butley AP.[59]

CAPEL ST MARY
AP *LG* Seq 27. *Parl* Seq 8. *Eccl* Samf. RDn. Abol eccl 1786 to help cr Capel St Mary with Little Wenham EP.[62]

CAPEL ST MARY WITH LITTLE WENHAM
EP Cr 1786 by union Capel St Mary AP, Little Wenham AP.[62] Samf. RDn.

CARLTON
AP *LG* Hoxne Hd, Blything PLU, RSD. Civ bdry: 1883.[2] Abol civ 1885 to help cr Kelsale cum Carlton CP.[63] *Parl* E'rn Dv (1832–85), N-E'rn Dv (1885–1918). *Eccl* Dunw. RDn. Abol eccl before 1844 to help cr Kelsale with Carlton EP.[64]

CARLTON COLVILLE
AP *LG* Seq 20. Civ bdry: 1904 (help cr Oulton Broad CP),[65] 1934.[7] *Parl* Seq 2. *Eccl* Seq 40. Eccl bdry: 1964.[66]

CAVENDISH
AP *LG* Bab. Hd, Sudb. PLU, RSD, [W Suffolk] Melf. RD (1894–1935), Clare RD (1935–74). Civ bdry: 1883,[2] 1884,[67] 1885.[3] *Parl* Seq 13. *Eccl* Sudb. RDn (until 1864), Sudb. (W'rn) RDn (1864–84), Clare RDn (1884–*).

CAVENHAM
AP *LG* Seq 17. *Parl* Seq 6. *Eccl* Seq 9.

CHARSFIELD
AP *LG* Loes Hd, Woodb. PLU, RSD, [E Suffolk] Woodb. RD (1894–1934), Deben RD (1934–74). *Parl* Seq 7. *Eccl* Seq 37.

CHATTISHAM
AP *LG* Seq 27. *Parl* Seq 8. *Eccl* Seq 44.

CHEDBURGH
AP *LG* Seq 26. *Parl* Seq 13. *Eccl* Seq 5.

CHEDISTON
AP *LG* Seq 6. *Parl* E'rn Dv (1832–85), N'rn Dv (1885–1918), Eye Dv/CC (1918–*). *Eccl* Seq 31.

CHELMONDISTON
AP *LG* Seq 27. *Parl* Seq 8. *Eccl* Seq 43.

CHELSWORTH
AP *LG* Seq 12. *Parl* Seq 14. *Eccl* Sudb. RDn (until 1864), Sudb. (E'rn) Dv (1864–84), Hadl. RDn (1884–1928), Lav. RDn (1928–*).

CHEVINGTON
AP *LG* Seq 31. *Parl* Seq 13. *Eccl* Seq 22.

CHILLESFORD
AP *LG* Seq 22. *Parl* Seq 16. *Eccl* Seq 42.

CHILTON
AP *LG* Seq 2. Civ bdry: 1885.[3] *Parl* Seq 14. *Eccl* Seq 16.

CHIMNEY MILLS
Ex-par place, sep CP 1858.[10] *LG* Blackbourn Hd, Thingoe PLU, RSD, [W Suffolk] Thingoe RD. Abol 1897 ent to Culford AP.[68] *Parl* W'rn Dv (1832–85), N-W'rn Dv (1885–1918).

CLARE
AP *LG* Clare Bor (status not sustained), Seq 25. Civ bdry: 1884.[69] *Parl* Seq 13. *Eccl* Seq 4.

CLAYDON
AP *LG* Seq 9. *Parl* Seq 7. *Eccl* Clay. RDn (until 1972), Bosm. RDn (1972–73). Abol eccl 1973 to help cr Claydon and Barham EP.[17]

CLAYDON AND BARHAM
EP Cr 1973 by union Claydon AP, Barham AP.[17] Bosm. RDn.

CLOPTON
AP *LG* Seq 10. *Parl* Seq 7. *Eccl* Seq 25.

COCKFIELD
AP *LG* Seq 1. Civ bdry: 1935.[7] *Parl* Seq 14. *Eccl* Seq 14.

CODDENHAM
AP *LG* Seq 9. *Parl* Seq 7. *Eccl* Seq 24.

COMBS
AP *LG* Seq 28. Civ bdry: 1884,[70] 1934.[7] *Parl* Seq 11. *Eccl* Seq 12. Eccl bdry: 1934.[71]

COOKLEY
AP *LG* Seq 6. *Parl* Seq 3. *Eccl* Dunw. RDn. Abol eccl 1733 to help cr Huntingfield with Cookley EP.[72]

COPDOCK
AP *LG* Seq 27. *Parl* Seq 8. *Eccl* Seq 43.

GREAT CORNARD
AP *LG* Seq 2. Civ bdry: 1883,[2] 1885.[3] *Parl* Seq 14. *Eccl* Seq 16.

LITTLE CORNARD
AP *LG* Seq 2. Civ bdry: 1883,[2] 1885.[3] *Parl* Seq 14. *Eccl* Seq 16.

CORTON
AP *LG* Seq 20. Civ bdry: 1934,[7] 1974 (loses pt to Norfolk, united to Hopton-on-Sea CP also transf to Norfolk).[25] *Parl* Seq 2. *Eccl* Seq 40.

COTTON
AP *LG* Seq 13. Civ bdry: 1883,[2] 1884.[73] *Parl* Seq 9. *Eccl* Seq 11.

NORTH COVE
AP *LG* Seq 33. *Parl* Seq 2. *Eccl* Seq 45.

SOUTH COVE
AP *LG* Seq 7. *Parl* Seq 2. *Eccl* Seq 31.

COVEHITHE
AP Sometimes 'North Hales'. *LG* Seq 7. *Parl* Seq 2. *Eccl* Seq 30.

COWLINGE
AP *LG* Seq 25. *Parl* Seq 13. *Eccl* Seq 6.

CRANSFORD
AP *LG* Seq 21. *Parl* Seq 9. *Eccl* Seq 41.

CRATFIELD
AP *LG* Seq 6. Civ bdry: 1884.[74] *Parl* Seq 3. *Eccl* Dunw. RDn (until 1868), Dunw. (North) RDn (1868–1914), S Dunw. RDn (1914–72), Halesw. RDn (1972–*).

CREETING ALL SAINTS
AP *LG* Bosm. & Clay. Hd, Bosm. PLU, RSD. Abol civ 1884 ent to Creeting St Mary AP.[75] *Parl* E'rn Dv (1832–85). *Eccl* Bosm. RDn. Abol eccl 1712 to help cr Creeting All Saints with Creeting St Olave EP.[77]

CREETING ALL SAINTS WITH CREETING ST OLAVE
EP Cr 1712 by union Creeting All Saints AP, Creeting St Olave AP.[77] Bosm. RDn. Abol 1792 to help cr Creeting St Mary with Creeting All Saints and St Olave EP.[76]

CREETING ST MARY
AP *LG* Seq 9. Civ bdry: 1884,[20] 1884 (gains Creeting All Saints AP, Creeting St Olave AP),[75] 1907 (incl help cr Needham Market CP).[19] *Parl* Seq 7. *Eccl* Bosm. RDn. Abol eccl 1792 to help cr Creeting St Mary with Creeting All Saints and St Olave EP.[76]

CREETING ST MARY WITH CREETING ALL SAINTS AND ST OLAVE
EP Cr 1792 by union Creeting All Saints with Creeting St Olave EP, Creeting St Mary AP.[76] Bosm. RDn.

CREETING ST OLAVE
AP *LG* Bosm. & Clay. Hd, Bosm. PLU, RSD. Abol civ 1884 ent to Creeting St Mary AP.[75] *Parl*

E'rn Dv (1832–85). *Eccl* Bosm. RDn. Abol eccl 1712 to help cr Creeting All Saints with Creeting St Olave EP.[77]

CREETING ST PETER

AP Sometimes 'West Creeting'. *LG* Seq 28. Civ bdry: 1934.[7] *Parl* Seq 11. *Eccl* Stow RDn (until 1931), Bosm. RDn (1931–*).

WEST CREETING–See prev entry

CRETINGHAM

AP *LG* Seq 19. *Parl* Seq 3. *Eccl* Loes RDn (until 1931), Clay. RDn (1931–68), Loes RDn (1968–*).

CROWFIELD

AP *LG* Seq 9. *Parl* Seq 7. *Eccl* Bosm. RDn (until 1914), Clay. RDn (1914–31), Bosm. RDn (1931–*).

CULFORD

AP *LG* Seq 5. Civ bdry: 1897 (gains Chimney Mills CP).[68] *Parl* Seq 10. *Eccl* Sometimes as 'Culford with Culford Heath', Blackburne RDn (until 1884), Thingoe RDn (1884–*).

CULPHO

AP *LG* Seq 10. *Parl* Seq 8. *Eccl* Seq 25.

DALHAM

AP *LG* Seq 24. *Parl* Seq 10. *Eccl* Seq 7.

DALLINGHOO

AP *LG* Pt Wilf. Hd, pt Loes Hd, Woodb. PLU, RSD, [E Suffolk] Woodb. RD (1894–1934), Deben RD (1934–74). *Parl* Seq 7. *Eccl* Seq 49.

DALLINGHOO WIELD

Ex-par place, sep CP 1858.[10] *LG* Seq 34. *Parl* E'rn Dv (1867–85), S-E'rn Dv (1885–1918), Woodb. Dv (1918–48), Eye CC (1948–*).

DARMSDEN

Chap in Barking AP, sep rated orig as PLU unit in Bosm. PLU, but sep status not sustained, never a CP or EP.

DARSHAM

AP *LG* Seq 6. *Parl* Seq 3. *Eccl* Seq 32.

DEBACH

AP *LG* Seq 34. *Parl* Seq 7. *Eccl* Seq 38.

DEBENHAM

AP *LG* Seq 32. *Parl* Seq 5. *Eccl* Seq 28.

DENHAM

AP Usual civ spelling; for eccl see 'Denham St John'. *LG* Hoxne Hd, PLU (1835–1907), RSD, Hart. PLU (1907–30), [E Suffolk] Hoxne RD (1894–1934), Hart. RD (1934–74). *Parl* Seq 5.

DENHAM

AP Usual civ spelling; for eccl see 'Denham St Mary'. *LG* Seq 26. *Parl* Seq 10.

DENHAM ST JOHN

AP Usual eccl spelling; for civ see 1st 'Denham' above. *Eccl* Seq 35.

DENHAM ST MARY

AP Usual eccl spelling; for civ see 2nd 'Denham' above. *Eccl* Seq 5.

DENNINGTON

AP *LG* Seq 14. *Parl* Seq 3. *Eccl* Hoxne RDn (until 1914), Loes RDn (1914–72), Hoxne RDn (1972–*).

DENSTON

AP *LG* Seq 25. *Parl* Seq 13. *Eccl* Seq 4.

DEPDEN

AP *LG* Risb. Hd, Thingoe PLU (1836–1907), RSD, Bury St Edm. PLU (1907–30), [W Suffolk] Thingoe RD (1894–1935), Clare RD (1935–74). *Parl* Seq 13. *Eccl* Clare RDn (until 1914), Hor. RDn (1914–72), Thingoe RDn (1972–*).

WOOD DITTON

AP Cambs AP, incl chap Newmarket All Saints (sep civ identity early in Cambs, sep EP 1747[55]). See main entry in Cambs for early civ, and for parl and eccl organisation. Pt of this par made pt of Nwmkt. USD, so that in 1894 becomes 2 sep CPs, one in Cambs, one in W Suffolk, the latter (Nwmkt. UD) abol 1895 ent to Newmarket All Saints CP.[79]

DRINKSTONE

AP *LG* Seq 29. *Parl* Seq 10. *Eccl* Seq 18.

DUNNINGWORTH

AP In ruins by 16th cent, united with Tunstall AP late that cent,[80] the union civ called 'Tunstall', eccl 'Tunstall with Dunningworth'.

DUNWICH

AP Only Dunwich St James survived from the 18th cent, usually called 'Dunwich'. Earlier churches lost into the sea: St Felix, *temp* Edward the Confessor; St Leonard, by 14th cent; St Martin, last presentment 1335; St Nicholas, last presentment 1352; St John Baptist, pulled down 1540; All Saints, last appointment in 1628; St Peter, pulled down in 1702; doubtful early churches in addition, St Bartholomew, St Michael.[81] *LG* Dunw. Bor, Seq 6. Civ bdry: 1934.[7] *Parl* Dunw. Parl Bor (1298–1832), Seq 3 thereafter. *Eccl* Seq 32.

EASTON

AP *LG* Seq 19. *Parl* Seq 4. *Eccl* Seq 37.

EASTON BAVENTS

AP *LG* Seq 7. Civ bdry: 1934.[7] *Parl* Seq 2. *Eccl* Dunw. RDn. Abol eccl 1749 ent to Benacre AP, the union sometimes afterwards called 'Benacre with Easton Bavents'.[28]

EDWARDSTONE

AP *LG* Seq 1. Civ bdry: 1883,[2] 1885,[76] 1934.[7] *Parl* Seq 14. *Eccl* Seq 16. Eccl bdry: 1946.[37]

ELDEN–See ELVEDEN

BRENT ELEIGH

AP *LG* Seq 1. Civ bdry: 1935.[9] *Parl* Seq 14. *Eccl* Seq 14.

MONKS ELEIGH

AP *LG* Seq 1. Civ bdry: 1935.[7] *Parl* Seq 14. *Eccl* Pec jurisd Archbp Canterb (until 1847), Sudb. RDn (1847–64), Sudb. (E'rn) RDn (1864–84), Lav. RDn (1884–*).

ELLOUGH

AP *LG* Seq 33. *Parl* Seq 2. *Eccl* Wangf. RDn (until 1914), Beccles RDn (1914–72). Abol eccl 1972 to help cr Ellough and Weston EP.[84]

ELLOUGH AND WESTON

EP Cr 1972 by union Ellough AP, Weston AP.[84] Beccles & S Elm. RDn.

SOUTH ELMHAM

The following have 'South Elmham' in their names. Insofar as any existed at a given time:

LG Seq 33. *Parl* Seq 2. *Eccl* Seq 34.
AP1–SOUTH ELMHAM ALL SAINTS–Abol civ and eccl 1737 to help cr CP1/EP1.[82]
CP1/EP1–SOUTH ELMHAM ALL SAINTS AND ST NICHOLAS–Cr 1737 by union AP1, AP6.[82] Eccl bdry: 1931.[86]
AP2–SOUTH ELMHAM ST CROSS–Sometimes 'Sandcroft'. Abol eccl 1767 to help cr EP2.[83]
EP2–SOUTH ELMHAM ST CROSS WITH HOMERSFIELD–Cr 1767 by union AP2, Homersfield AP.[83]
AP3–SOUTH ELMHAM ST JAMES
AP4–SOUTH ELMHAM ST MARGARET
–SOUTH ELMHAM ST MARY–See HOMERSFIELD
AP5–SOUTH ELMHAM ST MICHAEL
AP6–SOUTH ELMHAM ST NICHOLAS–Abol civ and eccl 1737 to help cr CP1/EP1.[82]
AP7–SOUTH ELMHAM ST PETER

ELMSETT
AP *LG* Seq 12. Civ bdry: 1885,[85] 1935.[9] *Parl* Seq 14. *Eccl* Seq 13.

ELMSWELL
AP *LG* Seq 3. *Parl* Seq 10. *Eccl* Seq 2.

ELVEDEN
AP Sometimes 'Elden'. *LG* Seq 3. *Parl* Seq 10. *Eccl* Seq 9.

ERISWELL
AP *LG* Seq 16. *Parl* Seq 6. *Eccl* Seq 9.

ERWARTON
AP Sometimes 'Arwarton'. *LG* Seq 27. *Parl* Seq 8. *Eccl* Seq 43.

EUSTON
AP *LG* Seq 4. Civ bdry: 1886,[87] 1894 (gains the pt of Rushford AP [Norfolk, Suffolk] in Suffolk so that the latter ent Norfolk thereafter).[88] *Parl* Seq 10. *Eccl* Seq 1. Eccl bdry: before 1535 (gains Fakenham Parva AP).[89]

EXNING
AP *LG* Lackf. Hd, Exning Bor (status not sustained), Nwmkt. PLU, pt Nwmkt. USD, pt Nwmkt. RSD, [W Suffolk] Nwmkt. UD (pt 1894–95, ent 1895–1974), pt Moulton RD (1894–95). Civ bdry: 1895 (par made ent Nwmkt. UD).[90] *Parl* Seq 6. *Eccl* Seq 8. Eccl bdry: 1887 (help cr Exning St Agnes EP).[91]

EXNING ST AGNES
EP Cr 1887 from Exning AP, Newmarket St Mary AP.[91] Ford. RDn (1887–1914), Thurl. RDn (1914–16), Nwmkt. RDn (1916–*).

EYE
AP *LG* Hart. Hd, PLU, Eye Bor/MB, USD. [E Suffolk]. *Parl* Eye Parl Bor (1571–1885), N-E'rn Dv (1885–1918), Eye Dv/CC (1918–*). *Eccl* Seq 10.

EYKE
AP *LG* Seq 19. *Parl* Seq 7. *Eccl* Seq 39.

FAKENHAM
AP Usual eccl spelling; for civ see following entry. *Eccl* Seq 1. Eccl bdry: 1931 (gains ex-par Rymer).[92]

FAKENHAM MAGNA
AP Usual civ spelling; for eccl see prev entry. *LG* Seq 4. Civ bdry: 1885 (gains Rymer CP),[95] 1886.[87] *Parl* Seq 10.

FAKENHAM PARVA
AP Blackburne RDn. Abol before 1535, united with Euston AP.[89]

FALKENHAM
AP *LG* Seq 11. *Parl* Seq 8. *Eccl* Seq 29.

FARNHAM
AP *LG* Seq 21. *Parl* Seq 9. *Eccl* Seq 41.

FELAWS HOUSE–See IPSWICH FELAWS HOUSE

FELIXSTOWE
AP *LG* Coln. Hd, Woodb. PLU, Felixstowe & Walton USD (1887–94), Woodb. RSD (1875–87), [E Suffolk] Felixstowe & Walton UD (1894–1914), Felixstowe UD (1914–74). Civ bdry: 1914 (gains Walton AP).[93] *Parl* Seq 8. *Eccl* Seq 29. Eccl bdry: 1894 (cr Felixstowe St John the Baptist EP).[94]

FELIXSTOWE ST JOHN THE BAPTIST
EP Cr 1894 from Felixstowe AP.[94] Colneys RDn.

FELSHAM
AP *LG* Seq 29. Civ bdry: 1884.[70] *Parl* Seq 10. *Eccl* Seq 18.

GREAT FINBOROUGH
AP *LG* Seq 28. Civ bdry: 1884.[70] *Parl* Seq 11. *Eccl* Seq 12. Eccl bdry: 1934.[71]

LITTLE FINBOROUGH
AP *LG* Seq 28. Civ bdry: 1884.[70] *Parl* Seq 11. *Eccl* Stow RDn (until 1934), Bosm. RDn (1934–*). Eccl bdry: 1934.[71]

FINNINGHAM
AP *LG* Seq 13. *Parl* Seq 9. *Eccl* Seq 11.

FLEMPTON
AP *LG* Seq 31. *Parl* Seq 10. *Eccl* Thingoe RDn. Abol eccl 1589 to help cr Flempton with Hengrave EP.[96]

FLEMPTON WITH HENGRAVE
EP Cr 1589 by union Flempton AP, Hengrave AP.[96] Thingoe RDn.

FLIXTON
Free chap in 16th cent,[32] later deemed chap in Blundeston AP, sep civ identity early, no sep eccl identity. *LG* Seq 20. *Parl* Seq 2.

FLIXTON
AP *LG* Seq 33. *Parl* Seq 2. *Eccl* Seq 21.

FLOWTON
AP *LG* Seq 9. *Parl* Seq 7. *Eccl* Seq 23.

FORDLEY
AP Orig AP, united with Middleton AP before 1535, Fordley later considered hmlt to Middleton, no sep civ identity later, eccl union called 'Middleton with Fordley', qv.

FORNHAM ALL SAINTS
AP *LG* Seq 31. Civ bdry: 1935.[7] *Parl* Seq 10. *Eccl* Seq 21. Eccl bdry: 1958 (help cr Bury St Edmunds St George EP).[56]

FORNHAM ST GENEVIEVE
AP *LG* Seq 30. *Parl* Seq 10. *Eccl* Thedw. RDn (until 1837), Thingoe RDn (1837–1957). Abol eccl 1957 ent to Fornham St Martin AP.[97]

FORNHAM ST MARTIN
AP *LG* Seq 30. *Parl* Seq 10. *Eccl* Thedw. RDn (until 1837), Thingoe RDn (1837–*). Eccl bdry:

1957 (gains Fornham St Genevieve AP).[97]

FOXHALL

AP *LG* Seq 10. *Parl* Seq 8. *Eccl* Carlf. RDn. Abol *ca* 1530 to help cr Brightwell with Foxhall EP.[43]

FRAMLINGHAM

AP Incl chap Saxstead (sep civ identity early, no sep eccl identity thus this par eccl 'Framlingham with Saxstead', qv). *LG* Seq 18. *Parl* Seq 3.

FRAMLINGHAM WITH SAXSTEAD

AP Usual eccl spelling; for civ and civ sep chap Saxstead, see prev entry. *Eccl* Seq 37.

FRAMSDEN

AP *LG* Seq 32. *Parl* Seq 5. *Eccl* Seq 28.

FRECKENHAM

AP *LG* Seq 16. *Parl* Seq 6. *Eccl* Pec jurisd Freckenham (Bp Roch, until 1847), Ford. RDn (1847–62), Ford. (Suffolk) RDn (1862–84), Mild. RDn (1884–*). Eccl bdry: 1973.[98]

FRESSINGFIELD

AP *LG* Seq 15. *Parl* Seq 3. *Eccl* Seq 35.

FRESTON

AP *LG* Seq 27. *Parl* Seq 8. *Eccl* Seq 43.

FRISTON

AP *LG* Seq 21. Civ bdry: 1934.[7] *Parl* Seq 9. *Eccl* Orford RDn. Abol eccl 1785 to help cr Friston with Snape EP.[99]

FRISTON WITH SNAPE

EP Cr 1785 by union Friston AP, Snape AP.[99] Orford RDn (1785–1914), Saxm. RDn (1914–*). Bdry: 1958.[8]

FRITTON

AP *LG* Seq 20. Transf 1974 to Norfolk (gaining at same time the pt of Herringfleet AP also transf to Norfolk).[25] *Parl* Seq 2. *Eccl* Seq 40.

FROSTENDEN

AP *LG* Seq 7. *Parl* Seq 2. *Eccl* Seq 31.

GAZELEY

AP *LG* Pt Risb. Hd, pt Lackf. Hd (the hmlt of Higham Green, sep CP 1866[6] [sep EP 1861[100]]), so that Gazeley ent Risb. Hd from 1866, thereafter Seq 24. *Parl* Seq 10. *Eccl* Seq 7.

GEDDING

AP *LG* Seq 29. Civ bdry: 1884.[70] *Parl* Seq 10. *Eccl* Seq 18.

GEDGRAVE

Ex-par place, sep CP 1858.[10] *LG* Seq 22. *Parl* W'rn Dv (1867–85), S-E'rn Dv (1885–1918), Woodb. Dv (1918–48), Eye CC (1948–*).

GEORGE STREET–See IPSWICH GEORGE STREET

GIPPING

Chap & hmlt in Old Newton AP, sep CP 1866,[6] no sep eccl identity. *LG* Seq 28. *Parl* W'rn Dv (1867–85), N-W'rn Dv (1885–1918), Eye CC (1918–*).

GISLEHAM

AP *LG* Seq 20. Civ bdry: 1934.[7] *Parl* Seq 2. *Eccl* Seq 40.

GISLINGHAM

AP *LG* Seq 13. *Parl* Seq 9. *Eccl* Seq 10.

GREAT GLEMHAM

AP *LG* Seq 21. *Parl* Seq 9. *Eccl* Orford RDn. Abol eccl 1803 to help cr Great Glemham with Little Glemham EP.[101]

GREAT GLEMHAM WITH LITTLE GLEMHAM

EP Cr 1803 by union Great Glemham AP, Little Glemham AP.[101] Orford RDn (1803–1914), Saxm. RDn (1914–*).

LITTLE GLEMHAM

AP *LG* Seq 21. *Parl* Seq 9. *Eccl* Orford RDn. Abol eccl 1803 to help cr Great Glemham with Little Glemham EP.[101]

GLEMSFORD

AP *LG* Bab. Hd, Sudb. PLU, RSD, [W Suffolk] Melford RD (1894–96), Glemsford UD (1896–1935),[3] Melford RD (1935–74). Civ bdry: 1885.[3] *Parl* Seq 14. *Eccl* Seq 16.

GORLESTON

AP Incl chap Southtown (sep EP 1911.[102] this par prev called 'Gorleston with Southtown'). *LG* Mutf. & Loth. Hd, Yarmouth PLU, Great Yarmouth MB (1835–88). USD. Transf out of Suffolk 1889 when Great Yarmouth made CB. *Parl* Great Yarmouth Parl Bor (1832–1918), Norfolk thereafter. *Eccl* Loth. RDn (until 1970), Flegg RDn [also Norw dioc] (1970–*).

GOSBECK

AP *LG* Seq 9. *Parl* Seq 7. *Eccl* Bosm. RDn (until 1933), Clay. RDn (1933–72), Bosm. RDn (1972–*).

GROTON

AP *LG* Seq 1. Civ bdry: 1883,[2] 1885,[36] 1935.[9] *Parl* Seq 14. *Eccl* Sudb. RDn (until 1864), Sudb. (E'rn) RDn (1864–84), Hadl. RDn (1884–1926),[3] Sudb. RDn (1926–*). Eccl bdry: 1946.[37]

GRUNDISBURGH

AP *LG* Seq 10. *Parl* Seq 7. *Eccl* Seq 25.

GUNTON

AP *LG* Mutf. & Loth. Hd, PLU, pt Lowest. MB & USD (1890–94), Mutf. & Loth. RSD (ent 1875–90, pt 1890–94), [E Suffolk] Mutf. & Loth. RD. Civ bdry: 1894 (loses the pt in the MB to Lowestoft MB and AP).[103] *Parl* Seq 2. *Eccl* Seq 40. Eccl bdry: 1964.[66]

HACHESTON

AP *LG* Seq 18. *Parl* Seq 3. *Eccl* Loes RDn. Abol eccl before 1813 to help cr Parham with Hacheston EP.[104]

HADLEIGH

AP *LG* Cosf. Hd, PLU, Hadl. USD (ent 1875–83, pt 1883–94), Cosf. RSD (pt 1883–94 [this pt a detached pt of Aldham AP, gained 1883[2] by Hadleigh AP but not in the USD]), [W Suffolk] Hadl. UD (pt 1894–96, ent 1896–1974), pt Cosf. RD (1894–96). Addtl civ bdry alt: 1896 (the par made ent Hadl. UD).[105] *Parl* Seq 14. *Eccl* Pec jurisd Archbp Canterb (until 1847), Seq 13 thereafter.

HADLEIGH HAMLET

Hmlt in Boxford AP, sep CP 1866.[6] *LG* Cosf. Hd, PLU, RSD, [W Suffolk] Cosf. RD. Abol 1935 pt to Boxford AP, pt to Kersey AP.[7] *Parl* W'rn Dv (1867–85), South Dv (1885–1918), Sudb. Dv (1918–48).

HALESWORTH
AP *LG* Blything Hd, PLU, RSD, [E Suffolk] Blything RD (1894–1900), Halesw. UD (1900–74). Civ bdry: 1884,[2] 1934.[7] *Parl* Seq 1. *Eccl* Seq 31.
HARDWICK
Ex-par place, sep CP 1858,[10] eccl abol 1937 ent to Nowton AP.[106] *LG* Seq 31. *Parl* Seq 10.
HARGRAVE
AP *LG* Seq 31. Civ bdry: 1884.[107] *Parl* Seq 13. *Eccl* Seq 22. Eccl bdry: 1927 (gains ex-par Southwell).[108]
HARKSTEAD
AP *LG* Seq 27. *Parl* Seq 8. *Eccl* Seq 43.
HARLESTON
AP *LG* Seq 28. *Parl* Seq 11. *Eccl* Stow RDn. Abol eccl 1891 to help cr Onehouse with Harleston EP.[109]
HARTEST
AP *LG* Seq 2. Civ bdry: 1883.[2] *Parl* Seq 14. *Eccl* Sudb. RDn. Abol eccl before 1535 to help cr Hartest with Boxted EP.[32]
HARTEST WITH BOXTED
EP Cr before 1535 by union Hartest AP, Boxted AP.[32] *Eccl* Seq 16.
HASKETON
AP *LG* Seq 10. *Parl* Seq 8. *Eccl* Seq 25.
HAUGHLEY
AP Incl chap Shelland (sep par before 1535). *LG* Seq 28. Civ bdry: 1934.[110] *Parl* Seq 11. *Eccl* Seq 12.
HAVERGATE ISLAND
Ex-par place, sep CP 1858.[10] *LG* Seq 22. *Parl* W'rn Dv (1867–85), S-E'rn Dv (1885–1918), Woodb. Dv (1918–48), Sudb. & Woodb. Dv/CC (1948–*).
HAVERHILL
AP Pt Suffolk (Risb. Hd), pt Essex (Hinckford Hd), exchanges pts 1879 with Sturmer AP (Essex) so that the 2 pars ent within their respective counties.[111] *LG* Risb. PLU, Haverhill USD (ent 1875–83, pt 1883–94), pt Risb. RSD (1883–94 [a detached pt of Little Wratting AP gained 1883[2] but not in the USD]), Haverhill UD (pt 1894–96, ent 1896–1974). Addtl civ bdry alt: 1885,[112] 1896 (the par made ent Haverhill UD),[113] 1971.[114] *Parl* Suffolk pt, W'rn Dv (1832–85), South Dv (1885–1918), Subd. Dv (1918–48), Bury St Edm. CC (1948–*). *Eccl* Seq 4.
HAWKEDON
AP *LG* Risb. Hd, Sudb. PLU, RSD, [W Suffolk] Melf. RD (1894–1935), Clare RD (1935–74). *Parl* Seq 13. *Eccl* Seq 4.
HAWSTEAD
AP *LG* Seq 31. Civ bdry: 1883.[2] *Parl* W'rn Dv (1832–85), N-W'rn Dv (1885–1918), Sudb. Dv (1918–48), Bury St Edm. CC (1948–*). *Eccl* Thingoe RDn (until 1884), Horng. RDn (1884–1914), Hor. RDn (1914–72), Thingoe RDn (1972–*).
HAZLEWOOD
Chap in Aldeburgh AP, sep CP 1866,[6] no sep eccl identity. Sometimes 'Hazlewood Hamlet'. *LG* Plom. Hd, PLU, RSD, [E Suffolk] Plom. RD. Abol 1934 pt to Friston AP, pt to Aldb. MB and CP.[7] *Parl* W'rn Dv (1867–85), N-E'rn Dv (1885–1918), Eye Dv (1918–48).
HELMINGHAM
AP *LG* Seq 9. *Parl* Seq 7. *Eccl* Seq 26.
HEMINGSTONE
AP *LG* Seq 9. *Parl* Seq 7. *Eccl* Seq 24.
HEMLEY
AP *LG* Seq 11. *Parl* Seq 8. *Eccl* Colneys RDn. Abol eccl 1901 to help cr Waldringfield with Hemley EP.[215]
HENGRAVE
AP *LG* Seq 31. *Parl* Seq 10. *Eccl* Thingoe RDn. Abol eccl 1589 to help cr Flempton with Hengrave EP.[96]
HENHAM
Hmlt in Wangford AP, sep CP 1866,[6] no sep eccl identity. *LG* Seq 7. *Parl* Seq 1.
HENLEY
AP *LG* Seq 9. *Parl* Seq 7. *Eccl* Seq 26. Eccl bdry: 1929.[116]
HENSTEAD
AP *LG* Pt Blything Hd, pt Wangf. Hd, Blything PLU, RSD, [E Suffolk] Blything RD (1894–1934), Loth. RD (1934–74). *Parl* Seq 2. *Eccl* Seq 30.
HEPWORTH
AP *LG* Seq 4. *Parl* Seq 10. *Eccl* Seq 1.
HERRINGFLEET
AP *LG* Seq 20. Civ bdry: 1974 (loses pt to Norfolk, added to Fritton AP also transf to Norfolk).[25] *Parl* Seq 2. *Eccl* Donative, Seq 40.
HERRINGSWELL
AP *LG* Seq 16. *Parl* Seq 6. *Eccl* Seq 9. Eccl bdry: 1973.[98]
HESSETT
AP *LG* Seq 29. Civ bdry: 1884.[38] *Parl* Seq 10. *Eccl* Seq 18.
HEVENINGHAM
AP *LG* Seq 6. *Parl* Seq 3. *Eccl* Dunw. RDn (until 1868), Dunw. (South) RDn (1868–1914), S Dunw. RDn (1914–71). Abol eccl 1971 to help cr Heveningham and Ubbeston EP.[117]
HEVENINGHAM AND UBBESTON
EP Cr 1971 by union Heveningham AP, Ubbeston AP.[117] S Dunw. RDn (1971–72), Halesw. (1972–*).
HIGHAM
AP Usual civ spelling; for eccl see following entry. *LG* Seq 27. *Parl* Seq 8.
HIGHAM ST MARY
AP Usual eccl spelling; for civ see prev entry. *Eccl* Seq 44.
HIGHAM–See HIGHAM GREEN
HIGHAM GREEN
Hmlt in Gazeley AP, sep EP 1861,[100] sep CP 1866.[6] Civ sometimes 'Higham'. *LG* Risb. Hd, Nwmkt. PLU, RSD, [W Suffolk] Moulton RD (1894–1935), Mild. RD (1935–74). *Parl* W'rn Dv (1867–85), N-W'rn Dv (1885–1918), Bury St Edm. Dv/CC (1918–*). *Eccl* Clare RDn

(1861–84), Thurl. RDn (1884–1916), Nwmkt. RDn (1916–72), Mild. RDn (1972–*).

HINDERCLAY

AP *LG* Seq 3. *Parl* Seq 10. *Eccl* Seq 1.

HINTLESHAM

AP *LG* Seq 27. Civ bdry: 1884.[20] *Parl* Seq 8. *Eccl* Seq 44.

HITCHAM

AP *LG* Seq 12. Civ bdry: 1885,[34] 1935.[9] *Parl* Seq 14. *Eccl* Seq 14.

HOLBROOK

AP *LG* Seq 27. *Parl* Seq 8. *Eccl* Seq 43.

HOLLESLEY

AP *LG* Seq 34. *Parl* Seq 8. *Eccl* Seq 47. Eccl bdry: 1960.[24]

HOLTON

AP Usual civ spelling; for eccl see 'Holton St Peter'. *LG* Seq 8. Civ bdry: 1884,[33] 1934.[7] *Parl* Seq 1.

HOLTON ST MARY

AP *LG* Seq 27. *Parl* Seq 8. *Eccl* Samf. RDn (until 1931), Hadl. RDn (1931–*).

HOLTON ST PETER

AP Usual eccl spelling; for civ see 'Holton'. *Eccl* Seq 31. Eccl bdry: 1935.[35]

HOMERSFIELD

AP Sometimes 'Homersfield St Mary' or 'South Elmham St Mary'. *LG* Seq 33. *Parl* Seq 2. *Eccl* S Elm. RDn. Abol eccl 1767 to help cr South Elmham St Cross with Homersfield EP.[83]

HONINGTON

AP *LG* Seq 4. *Parl* Seq 10. *Eccl* Blackburne RDn (until 1972), Ixw. RDn (1972). Abol eccl 1972 to help cr Honington with Sapiston EP.[118]

HONINGTON WITH SAPISTON

EP Cr 1972 by union Honington AP, Sapiston AP.[118] Ixw. RDn.

HOO

AP *LG* Seq 19. *Parl* Seq 3. *Eccl* Seq 37.

HOPTON

AP *LG* Seq 4. *Parl* Seq 10. *Eccl* Seq 1.

HOPTON

AP *LG* Mutf. & Loth. Hd, PLU, RSD, [E Suffolk] Mutf. & Loth. RD (1894–1934), Loth. RD (1934–52). Renamed civ 1952 'Hopton-on-Sea' CP.[230] *Parl* E'rn Dv (1832–85), N'rn Dv (1885–1918), Lowest. Dv/CC (1918–70). *Eccl* Seq 40.

HOPTON-ON-SEA

CP Renaming 1952 of Hopton AP.[230] *LG* Loth. RD. Transf 1974 to Norfolk (incl gains the pt of Corton AP also transf to Norfolk).[25] *Parl* Lowest. CC (1970–*).

HORHAM

AP *LG* Seq 15. *Parl* Seq 3. *Eccl* Seq 35.

GREAT HORNINGSHEATH

AP Sometimes 'Great Horringer'. Thingoe Hd, Thingoe RD. Abol 1548, united with Little Horningsheath, the union civ 'Horringer', eccl 'Great and Little Horningsheath'.[121]

GREAT AND LITTLE HORNINGSHEATH

EP Eccl name for union 1548 of Great Horningsheath AP, Little Horningsheath AP (for civ see 'Horringer').[121] Thingoe RDn (1548–1884), Horng. RDn (1884–1914), Hor. RDn (1914–65). Abol eccl 1965 to help cr Horringer cum Ixworth AP.[120]

LITTLE HORNINGSHEATH

AP Sometimes 'Little Horringer'. Organisation as for Great Horningsheath.

HORRINGER

AP Civ name for union 1548 of Great Horningsheath AP, Little Horninghseath AP (for eccl see 'Great and Little Horningsheath').[187] *LG* Seq 31. *Parl* Seq 10.

GREAT HORRINGER, LITTLE HORRINGER–See GREAT HORNINGSHEATH, LITTLE HORNINGSHEATH

HORRINGER CUM ICKWORTH

EP Cr 1965 by union Great and Little Horningsheath EP, Ickworth AP.[120] Hor. RDn (1965–72), Thingoe RDn (1972–*).

HOXNE

AP *LG* Seq 15. Civ bdry: 1884.[122] *Parl* Eye Parl Bor (1832–85), N-E'rn Dv (1885–1918), Eye Dv/CC (1918–*). *Eccl* Seq 35. Eccl bdry: 1935.[130]

HUNDON

AP *LG* Seq 25. Civ bdry: 1885.[123] *Parl* Seq 13. *Eccl* Seq 4. Eccl bdry: 1931.[21]

HUNSTON

AP *LG* Seq 3. *Parl* Seq 10. *Eccl* Seq 2.

HUNTINGFIELD

AP *LG* Seq 6. *Parl* Seq 3. *Eccl* Dunw. RDn. Abol eccl 1733 to help cr Huntingfield with Cookley EP.[72]

HUNTINGFIELD WITH COOKLEY

EP Cr 1733 by union Huntingfield AP, Cookley AP.[72] Dunw. RDn (1733–1868), Dunw. (North) RDn (1868–1914), S Dunw. RDn (1914–72), Halesw. RDn (1972–*).

ICKLINGHAM

AP The two following pars, sep for eccl purposes, considered as the single civ unit 'Icklingham'. *LG* Seq 16. *Parl* Seq 6.

ICKLINGHAM ALL SAINTS

AP For civ see 'Icklingham'. *Eccl* Ford. RDn (until 1862), Ford. (Suffolk) RDn (1862–84), Mild. RDn (1884–1972). Abol eccl 1972 to help cr Icklingham All Saints with St James EP.[124]

ICKLINGHAM ALL SAINTS WITH ST JAMES

EP Cr 1972 by union Icklingham All Saints AP, Icklingham St James AP.[124] Mild. RDn.

ICKLINGHAM ST JAMES

AP For civ see 'Icklingham'. *Eccl* RDns and abol 1972 as for Icklingham All Saints.

ICKWORTH

AP *LG* Seq 31. *Parl* Seq 10. *Eccl* Thingoe RDn (until 1884), Horng. RDn (1884–1914), Hor. RDn (1914–65). Abol eccl 1965 to help cr Horringer cum Ickworth EP.[120]

IKEN

AP *LG* Seq 22. *Parl* Seq 16. *Eccl* Seq 42.

ILKETSHALL ST ANDREW

AP *LG* Seq 33. *Parl* Seq 2. *Eccl* Seq 46.

ILKETSHALL ST JOHN

AP As for Ilketshall St Andrew.

ILKETSHALL ST LAWRENCE
AP *LG* Seq 33. Civ bdry: 1879.[125] *Parl* Seq 2. *Eccl* Seq 46.

ILKETSHALL ST MARGARET
AP As for Ilketshall St Andrew.

INGHAM
AP *LG* Seq 5. *Parl* Seq 10. *Eccl* Seq 3.

IPSWICH
The following have 'Ipswich' in their names. Insofar as any existed at a given time: *LG* Ipsw. Bor/MB/CB, PLU, USD. *Parl* Ipsw. Parl Bor (1298–*). *Eccl* Ipsw. RDn.

CP1–IPSWICH–Cr 1903 by union AP2, AP5, AP7, AP8, AP9, AP10, AP11, AP12, AP13, AP15, AP16, AP18, Rushmere AP, Shire Hall Yard CP, Warren House CP, Westerfield in Ipswich CP, Whitton cum Thurleston AP.[126] Bdry: 1934,[110] 1952.[4]

EP1–IPSWICH ALL HALLOWS–Cr 1939 from AP2, ex-par Alnesbourn Priory.[11]

EP2–IPSWICH ALL SAINTS–Cr 1888 from AP13, Bramford AP, Sproughton AP.[40] Bdry: 1938 (cr EP12).[138]

–IPSWICH COLD DUNGHILLS–Ex-par place sep rated as PLU unit, sep civ status not sustained.

–IPSWICH FELAWS HOUSE–As for Ipswich Cold Dunghills.

–IPSWICH GEORGE STREET–As for Ipswich Cold Dunghills.

EP3–IPSWICH HOLY TRINITY–Cr 1838 from AP2.[127] Bdry: 1887,[128] 1894 (help cr EP6).[129]

EP4–IPSWICH ST ANDREW–Cr 1958 from EP8, AP5, Rushmere St Andrew AP.[131] Bdry: 1964.[132]

EP5–IPSWICH ST AUGUSTINE OF HIPPO–Cr 1926 from ex-par Purdis Farm, and from pts of ex-par Alnesbourn Priory, EP6, Rushmere St Andrew AP, Kesgrave AP.[13]

AP1–IPSWICH ST AUSTIN–Often called chap but parochial, last use in 15th cent.

EP6–IPSWICH ST BARTHOLOMEW, ROSE HILL–Cr 1894 from AP2, EP3.[129] Bdry: 1928 (help cr EP5),[13] 1964.[132]

AP2–IPSWICH ST CLEMENT–Abol civ 1903 to help cr CP1.[126] Eccl bdry: 1838 (cr EP3),[127] 1881 (help cr EP10),[133] 1887,[128] 1894 (help cr EP6),[129] 1939 (help cr EP1),[11] 1964.[132]

AP3–IPSWICH ST EDMUND A POUNTNEY–Early united with AP5.

EP7–IPSWICH ST FRANCIS–Cr 1959 from AP2, Belstead AP, Sproughton AP.[27]

AP4–IPSWICH ST GREGORY–Nothing known other than medieval impropriation.

AP5–IPSWICH ST HELEN–Gains early AP3. Abol civ 1903 to help cr CP1.[126] Eccl bdry: 1958 (help cr EP4),[131] 1964.[132]

EP8–IPSWICH ST JOHN–Cr 1879 from AP8.[134] Bdry: 1958 (help cr EP5).[131]

AP6–IPSWICH ST JOHN THE BAPTIST–Early abolished.

AP7–IPSWICH ST LAWRENCE–Abol civ 1903 to help cr CP1.[126] Eccl bdry: 1964.[132]

AP8–IPSWICH ST MARGARET–Abol civ 1903 to help cr CP1.[126] Eccl bdry: 1879 (cr EP8),[134] 1881 (help cr EP10),[133] 1964.[132]

AP9–IPSWICH ST MARY AT THE ELMS–Abol civ 1903 to help cr CP1.[126] Eccl bdry: 1964.[132]

AP10–IPSWICH ST MARY AT THE QUAY–Civ bdry: 1883.[2] Abol civ 1903 to help cr CP1.[126] Eccl bdry: 1945.[135] Abol eccl 1948 to help cr EP11.[136]

AP11–IPSWICH ST MARY AT THE TOWER (eccl, IPSWICH ST MARY-LE-TOWER)–Abol civ 1903 to help cr CP1.[126] Eccl bdry: 1964.[132]

AP12–IPSWICH ST MARY STOKE–Civ bdry: 1894 (gains the pt of Belstead AP in Ipsw. CB).[26] Abol civ 1903 to help cr CP1.[126] Eccl bdry: 1959 (help cr EP7),[27] 1964.[132] Abol eccl 1969 to help cr EP9.[137]

EP9–IPSWICH ST MARY STOKE WITH ST PETER AND ST MARY–Cr 1969 by union AP12, EP11.[137]

AP13–IPSWICH ST MATTHEW–Civ bdry: 1894 (gains the pts of Bramford AP, Sproughton AP in Ipsw. CB).[26] Abol civ 1903 to help cr CP1.[126] Eccl bdry: 1888 (help cr EP2).[40]

AP14–IPSWICH ST MICHAEL–Dilapidated by *temp* John.

EP10–IPSWICH ST MICHAEL–Cr 1881 from AP8, AP2.[133] Bdry: 1964.[132]

AP15–IPSWICH ST NICHOLAS–Civ bdry: 1883.[2] Abol civ 1903 to help cr CP1.[126] Eccl bdry: 1964.[132]

AP16–IPSWICH ST PETER–Abol civ 1903 to help cr CP1.[126] Abol eccl 1948 to help cr EP11.[136]

EP11–IPSWICH ST PETER WITH ST MARY AT THE QUAY–Cr 1948 by union AP16, AP10.[136] Bdry: 1964.[132]

AP17–IPSWICH ST SAVIOUR–Dilapidated by *temp* John.

AP18–IPSWICH ST STEPHEN–Abol civ 1903 to help cr CP1.[126] Eccl bdry: 1964.[132]

EP12–IPSWICH ST THOMAS–Cr 1938 from EP2.[138]

IXWORTH
AP *LG* Seq 5. *Parl* Seq 10. *Eccl* Blackburne RDn. Abol eccl 1968 to help cr Ixworth and Ixworth Thorpe EP.[139]

IXWORTH AND IXWORTH THORPE
EP Cr 1968 by union Ixworth AP, Ixworth Thorpe EP.[139] Blackburne RDn (1968–72), Ixw. RDn (1972–*).

IXWORTH THORPE
AP Sometimes 'Thorpe-by-Ixworth'. *LG* Seq 5. *Parl* Seq 10. *Eccl* Blackburne RDn. Abol eccl 1968 to help cr Ixworth and Ixworth Thorpe EP.[139]

KEDINGTON
AP Sometimes 'Ketton'. Pt Suffolk (Risb. Hd), pt Essex (Hinckford Hd), the par made ent Suffolk 1895.[140] *LG* Risb. PLU, RSD, [W Suffolk] Clare RD (pt 1894–95, ent 1895–1974), pt sep RD in Essex (1894–95). Addtl civ bdry alt: 1883 (gains pt Sturmer AP, Essex).[3] *Parl* Suf-

folk pt, Seq 13. *Eccl* Seq 4.

KELSALE

AP *LG* Hoxne Hd, Blything PLU, RSD. Civ bdry: 1883.[2] Abol civ 1885 to help cr Kelsale cum Carlton CP.[63] *Parl* E'rn Dv (1832–85), N-E'rn Dv (1885–1918). *Eccl* Dunw. RDn. Abol eccl before 1844 to help cr Kelsale with Carlton EP.[64]

KELSALE CUM CARLTON

CP Cr 1885 by union Kelsale AP, Carlton AP.[63] *LG* Hoxne Hd, Blything PLU, RSD, [E Suffolk] Blything RD (1894–1934), Blyth RD (1934–74). *Parl* Eye Dv/CC (1918–*).

KELSALE WITH CARLTON

EP Cr before 1844 by union Kelsale AP, Carlton AP.[64] Dunw. RDn (cr–1868), Dunw. (South) RDn (1868–1914), S Dunw. RDn (1914–72), Saxm. RDn (1972–*).

KENTFORD

AP *LG* Pt Lackf. Hd, pt Risb. Hd, Mild. PLU, RSD, [W Suffolk] Mild. RD. *Parl* Pt E'rn Dv, pt W'rn Dv (1832–85), Seq 10 thereafter. *Eccl* Seq 7.

KENTON–See KEDINGTON

KENTON

AP *LG* Loes Hd, Plom. PLU, RSD, [E Suffolk] Plom. RD (1894–1934), Hart. RD (1934–74). *Parl* Seq 3. *Eccl* Loes RDn (until 1914), Hoxne RDn (1914–72), Loes RDn (1972–*).

KERSEY

AP *LG* Seq 12. Civ bdry: 1935.[9] *Parl* Seq 14. *Eccl* Seq 13.

KESGRAVE

AP *LG* Seq 10. *Parl* Seq 7. *Eccl* Carlf. RDn (until 1972), Ipsw. RDn (1972–*). Eccl bdry: 1928 (help cr Ipswich St Augustine of Hippo EP).[13]

KESSINGLAND

AP *LG* Seq 20. *Parl* Seq 2. *Eccl* Seq 40.

KETTLEBASTON

AP *LG* Seq 12. Civ bdry: 1883,[2] 1885,[36] 1935.[9] *Parl* Seq 14. *Eccl* Seq 14.

KETTLEBURGH

AP *LG* Seq 18. *Parl* Seq 3. *Eccl* Wilf. RDn (until 1929), Loes RDn (1929–*).

KETTON–See KEDINGTON

KIRKLEY

AP *LG* Mutf. & Loth. Hd, PLU, Lowest. MB (1890–1907), USD (1890–94), Mutf. & Loth. RSD (1875–84). [E Suffolk]. Civ bdry: 1883.[2] Abol civ 1907 ent to Lowestoft MB and AP.[141] *Parl* E'rn Dv (1832–85), N'rn Dv (1885–1918). *Eccl* Loth. RDn. Abol eccl 1974 to help cr Kirkley with Lowestoft St John EP.[142]

KIRKLEY WITH LOWESTOFT ST JOHN

EP Cr 1974 by union Kirkley AP, Lowestoft St John EP.[142] Loth. RDn.

KIRTON

AP *LG* Seq 11. *Parl* Seq 8. *Eccl* Seq 29.

KNETTISHALL

AP *LG* Seq 4. *Parl* Seq 10. *Eccl* Blackburne RDn. Abol eccl 1932 to help cr Riddlesworth with Gasthorpe and Knettishall EP.[143]

KNODISHALL

AP *LG* Seq 6. Civ bdry: 1883.[2] *Parl* Seq 3. *Eccl* Dunw. RDn. Abol eccl 1721 to help cr Knodshall with Buxlow EP.[60]

KNODISHALL WITH BUXLOW

EP Cr 1721 by union Knodishall AP, Buxlow AP.[60] Dunw. RDn (1721–1868), Dunw. (South) RDn (1868–1914), Saxm. RDn (1914–*).

LACKFORD

AP *LG* Seq 31. *Parl* Seq 10. *Eccl* Seq 21.

LAKENHEATH

AP *LG* Seq 16. *Parl* Seq 6. *Eccl* Seq 9.

LANGHAM

AP *LG* Seq 3. *Parl* Seq 10. *Eccl* Seq 2.

LAVENHAM

AP *LG* Seq 1. Civ bdry: 1935.[9] *Parl* Seq 14. *Eccl* Seq 15.

LAWSHALL

AP *LG* Seq 2. Civ bdry: 1883,[2] 1935.[9] *Parl* Seq 14. *Eccl* Seq 15.

LAXFIELD

AP *LG* Seq 15. *Parl* Seq 3. *Eccl* Seq 35.

LAYHAM

AP *LG* Seq 12. Civ bdry: 1884,[144] 1935.[9] *Parl* Seq 14. *Eccl* Seq 13. Eccl bdry: 1933.[145]

LEAVENHEATH

Chap in Stoke by Nayland AP, sep CP 1952 (incl pts from Assington AP, Nayland with Wissington CP, Polstead AP),[147] sep EP 1863 (incl pts from Assington AP, Polstead AP, Wissington AP).[146] *LG* Melf. RD. *Parl* Sudb. & Woodb. CC (1970–*). *Eccl* Sudb. RDn (1863–64), Sudb. (W'rn) RDn (1864–84), Hadl. RDn (1914–*).

LEISTON

AP Usual civ spelling; for eccl see following entry. Sometimes civ 'Leiston cum Sizewell' though chap Sizewell never had sep civ or eccl identity. *LG* Blything Hd, PLU, RSD, [E Suffolk] Blything RD (1894–95), Leiston cum Sizewell UD (1895–1974). Civ bdry: 1934.[110] *Parl* Seq 3.

LEISTON WITH SIZEWELL

AP Usual eccl spelling; for civ see prev entry. *Eccl* Seq 32. Eccl bdry: 1958.[8]

LETHERINGHAM

AP *LG* Seq 19. *Parl* Seq 3. *Eccl* Seq 37.

LEVINGTON

AP *LG* Seq 11. *Parl* Seq 8. *Eccl* Colneys RDn. Abol eccl 1734 to help cr Nacton with Levington EP.[148]

LIDGATE

AP Usual civ spelling; for eccl see 'Lydgate'. *LG* Seq 23. *Parl* Seq 13.

LINDSEY

AP *LG* Seq 12. Civ bdry: 1885,[36] 1935.[9] *Parl* Seq 14. *Eccl* Seq 13.

LINSTEAD MAGNA

AP *LG* Seq 6. *Parl* Seq 3. *Eccl* Dunw. RDn (until 1868), Dunw. (North) RDn (1868–89). Abol eccl 1889 to help cr Linstead Magna with Linstead Parva EP.[149]

LINSTEAD MAGNA WITH LINSTEAD PARVA

EP Cr 1889 by union Linstead Magna AP, Linstead Parva AP.[149] Dunw. (North) RDn (1889–1914), N Dunw. RDn (1914–72), Halesw. RDn (1972–*).

LINSTEAD PARVA
AP As for Linstead Magna, incl eccl abol 1889.
GREAT LIVERMERE
AP *LG* Seq 30. *Parl* Seq 10. *Eccl* Thedw. RDn (until 1837), Blackburne RDn (1837–1972), Ixw. RDn (1972–*).
LITTLE LIVERMERE
AP *LG* Seq 5. *Parl* Seq 10. *Eccl* Blackburne RDn (until 1930), Thingoe RDn (1930–46). Abol eccl 1946 to help cr Ampton with Little Livermere EP.[14]
LOUDHAM
AP Orig AP, before 1535 sep status lost and later considered hmlt in Pettistree AP.
LOUND
AP *LG* Seq 20. *Parl* Seq 2. *Eccl* Seq 40.
LOWESTOFT
AP *LG* Mutf. & Loth. Hd, PLU, Lowest. MB (1885–1974), USD (1885–94), Mutf. & Loth. RSD (1875–85). [E Suffolk]. Civ bdry: 1894 (gains the pt of Gunton AP in Lowestoft MB),[103] 1907 (gains Kirkley AP),[141] 1919 (gains Oulton Broad CP),[150] 1934.[4] *Parl* E'rn Dv (1832–85), N'rn Dv (1885–1918), Lowest. Dv/CC (1918–*). *Eccl* Seq 40. Eccl bdry: 1854 (cr Lowestoft St John EP),[151] 1866 (cr Lowestoft Christ Church EP),[152] 1964,[66] 1965.[153]
LOWESTOFT CHRIST CHURCH
EP Cr 1866 from Lowestoft AP.[152] Loth. RDn. Bdry: 1964,[66] 1965.[153]
LOWESTOFT ST JOHN
EP Cr 1854 from Lowestoft AP.[151] Loth. RDn. Bdry: 1964,[66] 1965.[153] Abol 1974 to help cr Kirkley with Lowestoft St John EP.[142]
LYDGATE
AP Usual eccl spelling; for civ see 'Lidgate'. *Eccl* Seq 7.
MARLESFORD
AP *LG* Seq 18. *Parl* Seq 3. *Eccl* Seq 37.
MARTLESHAM
AP *LG* Seq 10. *Parl* Seq 8. *Eccl* Carlf. RDn (until 1972), Colneys RDn (1972–*).
LONG MELFORD
AP *LG* Seq 2. Civ bdry: 1883,[2] 1935.[7] *Parl* Seq 14. *Eccl* Seq 16.
MELLIS
AP *LG* Seq 13. *Parl* Seq 9. *Eccl* Seq 10.
MELTON
AP *LG* Seq 34. Civ bdry: 1956,[44] 1960.[154] *Parl* Seq 8. *Eccl* Seq 48.
MENDHAM
AP Incl chap & hmlt Mendham (Donative since 1570,[155] later considered distinct civ and eccl). Pt Suffolk (Hoxne Hd), pt Norfolk (Earsham Hd), the former lost 1885 to Rendlesham with Harleston AP, Norfolk, and the par ent Suffolk thereafter.[156] *LG* Suffolk pt, Seq 15. Addtl civ bdry alt: 1885.[157] *Parl* Suffolk pt, Seq 3. *Eccl* Seq 35.
MENDLESHAM
AP *LG* Seq 13. Civ bdry: 1883.[2] *Parl* Seq 9. *Eccl* Seq 11.
METFIELD
AP Chap & hmlt in Mendham AP, donative since 1570 and later considered distinct civ and eccl.[155] *LG* Seq 15. Civ bdry: 1885.[157] *Parl* Seq 3. *Eccl* Seq 35.
METTINGHAM
AP *LG* Seq 33. *Parl* Seq 2. *Eccl* Seq 46.
MICKFIELD
AP *LG* Seq 9. Civ bdry: 1883.[2] *Parl* Seq 7. *Eccl* Bosm. RDn. Abol eccl 1973 to help cr Aspal and Mickfield EP.[158]
MIDDLETON
AP Gains before 1535 Fordley AP, the union civ called Middleton (sometimes 'Middleton cum Fordley'), eccl 'Middleton with Fordley' qv. *LG* Seq 6. Civ bdry: 1885 (loses detached pt situated in Bulmer AP, Essex, to the latter).[3] *Parl* Seq 3.
MIDDLETON WITH FORDLEY
AP Usual eccl spelling; for civ and for early union of Middleton, Fordley, see prev entry. *Eccl* Seq 32.
MILDEN
AP *LG* Seq 1. *Parl* Seq 14. *Eccl* Seq 14.
MILDENHALL
AP *LG* Seq 16. *Parl* Seq 6. *Eccl* Seq 9.
MONEWDEN
AP *LG* Seq 19. Civ bdry: 1883.[2] *Parl* Seq 3. *Eccl* Seq 37.
MOULTON
AP *LG* Seq 24. *Parl* Seq 10. *Eccl* Pec jurisd Archbp Canterb (until 1847), Clare RDn (1847–84), Thurl. RDn (1884–1972), Mild. RDn (1972–*).
MUTFORD
AP *LG* Seq 20. *Parl* Seq 2. *Eccl* Seq 40.
NACTON
AP *LG* Seq 11. Civ bdry: 1934,[7] 1952 (loses pt to Ipswich CB and CP).[4] *Parl* Seq 8. Parl bdry: 1953.[5] *Eccl* Colneys RDn. Abol eccl 1734 to help cr Nacton with Levington EP.[148]
NACTON WITH LEVINGTON
EP Cr 1734 by union Nacton AP, Levington AP.[148] *Eccl* Seq 29.
NAUGHTON
AP *LG* Cosf. Hd, PLU, RSD, [W Suffolk] Cosf. RD. Civ bdry: 1883,[2] 1885.[36] Abol civ 1935 to help cr Nedging with Naughton CP.[9] *Parl* W'rn Dv (1832–85), South Dv (1885–1918), Sudb. Dv (1918–48). *Eccl* Seq 13. Eccl bdry: 1933.[159]
NAYLAND
Chap in Stoke by Nayland AP, sep civ identity early, sep EP before 1855.[161] *LG* Bab. Hd, Sudb. PLU, RSD. Abol civ 1884 to help cr Nayland with Wissington CP.[160] *Parl* W'rn Dv (1832–85). *Eccl* Seq 13.
NAYLAND WITH WISSINGTON
CP Cr 1884 by union Nayland CP, Wissington AP.[160] *LG* Bab. Hd, Sudb. PLU, RSD, [W Suffolk] Melf. RD. *Parl* South Dv (1885–1918), Sudb. Dv (1918–48), Sudb. & Woodb. CC (1948–*). Bdry: 1952 (help cr Leavenheath CP).[147]

NEDGING
AP *LG* Cosf. Hd, PLU, RSD, [W Suffolk] Cosf. RD. Civ bdry: 1883,[2] 1885.[36] Abol civ 1935 to help cr Nedging with Naughton CP.[9] *Parl* W'rn Dv (1832–85), South Dv (1885–1918), Sudb. Dv (1918–48). *Eccl* Seq 13. Eccl bdry: 1933.[159]

NEDGING WITH NAUGHTON
CP Cr 1935 by union Nedging AP, Naughton AP, pt Bildeston AP.[9] *LG* [W Suffolk] Cosf.RD. *Parl* Sudb. & Woodb. CC (1948–*).

NEEDHAM MARKET
Hmlt in Barking AP, sep CP 1901,[18] sep EP 1907 (from Barking AP, Creeting St Mary AP).[19] *LG* [E Suffolk] Bosm. & Clay. PLU, RD (1901–34), Gip. RD (1934–74). *Parl* Woodb. Dv (1918–48), Sudb. & Woodb. CC (1948–*). *Eccl* Bosm. RDn.

NETTLESTEAD
AP *LG* Seq 9. Civ bdry: 1884.[20] *Parl* Seq 7. *Eccl* Seq 23.

NEWBOURNE
AP *LG* Seq 10. *Parl* Seq 7. *Eccl* Carlf. RDn (until 1914), Colneys RDn (1914–*).

NEWMARKET ALL SAINTS
Chap in Wood Ditton AP, sep civ identity early in Cambs, sep EP 1747.[55] See Cambs for early civ organisation. Transf 1889 to Suffolk.[162] *LG* Nwmkt. PLU, USD, [W Suffolk] Nwmkt. UD. Civ bdry: 1895 (gains Wood Ditton CP [the pt of Wood Ditton AP in Nwmkt. USD, which became sep CP in Suffolk 1894]).[79] *Parl* Cambs until 1918, Bury St Edm. Dv/CC (1918–*). *Eccl* Ford. RDn (1747–1862), Ford. (Cambs) RDn (1862–84), Ford. RDn (1884–1914), Thurl. RDn (1914–16), Nwmkt. RDn (1916–*). Eccl bdry: 1870,[163] 1948 (gains pt Cheveley AP [dioc Ely]).[164]

NEWMARKET ST MARY
AP *LG* Pt Suffolk (Lackf. Hd), pt Cambs (Cheveley Hd), ent Suffolk from 1894. *LG* Nwmkt. PLU, USD, [W Suffolk] Nwmkt. UD. *Parl* Suffolk pt, Seq 6. *Eccl* Seq 8. Eccl bdry: 1866,[165] 1887 (help cr Exning St Anges EP).[91]

NEWTON
AP Sometimes 'Newton Green' or 'Newton (near Sudbury)'. *LG* Seq 2. Civ bdry: 1883,[2] 1885,[3] 1935.[9] *Parl* Seq 14. *Eccl* Sudb. RDn (until 1864), Sudb. (W'rn) RDn (1864–84), Sudb. RDn (1884–*).

OLD NEWTON
AP Incl hmlt and chap Gipping (sep CP 1866[6]). *LG* Seq 28. *Parl* Seq 11. *Eccl* Seq 12. Eccl bdry: 1968.[166]

NORTON
AP *LG* Seq 3. *Parl* Seq 10. *Eccl* Blackburne RDn (until 1884), Thedw. RDn (1884–1972), Lav. RDn (1972–*).

NOWTON
AP *LG* Seq 31. *Parl* Seq 10. *Eccl* Seq 2. Eccl bdry: 1937 (gains ex-par Hardwick).[106]

OAKLEY
AP Orig Oakley Magna, gains 1449 Oakley Parva,[167] thereafter called 'Oakley'. *LG* Seq 13. *Parl* Eye Parl Bor (1832–85), N-E'rn Dv (1885–1918), Eye Dv/CC (1918–*). *Eccl* Hart. RDn. Abol prob in 17th cent to help cr Brome with Oakley EP.[45]

OAKLEY PARVA
AP Hart. RDn. Abol 1449 ent to Oakley Magna AP, the united par called 'Oakley',[167] qv.

OCCOLD
AP *LG* Seq 13. *Parl* Eye Parl Bor (1832–85), N-E'rn Dv (1885–1918), Eye Dv/CC (1918–*). *Eccl* Seq 10.

OFFTON
AP Gains before 1535 Little Bricett AP, the union civ called 'Offton', eccl 'Offton with Little Bricett', qv. *LG* Seq 9. Civ bdry: 1885.[85] *Parl* Seq 7.

OFFTON WITH LITTLE BRICETT
AP Usual eccl name for union before 1535 of Offton AP, Little Bricett AP; for civ see prev entry. *Eccl* Seq 23.

ONEHOUSE
AP *LG* Seq 28. Civ bdry: 1934.[7] *Parl* Seq 11. *Eccl* Stow RDn. Abol eccl 1891 to help cr Onehouse with Harleston EP.[109]

ONEHOUSE WITH HARLESTON
EP Cr 1891 by union Onehouse AP, Harleston AP.[109] Stow RDn (1891–1972), Stowm. RDn (1972–*).

ORFORD
Chap in Sudbourne AP, sep civ identity early, no sep eccl identity. *LG* Orford Bor, Seq 22. *Parl* Orford Parl Bor (1529–1832), Seq 16 thereafter.

ORFORD WITH SUDBOURNE–See SUDBOURNE WITH ORFORD

OTLEY
AP *LG* Seq 10. *Parl* Seq 7. *Eccl* Seq 25.

OULTON
AP Incl Oulton Broad (sep CP 1904,[65] sep EP 1932[168]). *LG* Seq 20. Addtl civ bdry alt: 1934.[7] *Parl* Seq 2. *Eccl* Seq 40. Addtl eccl bdry alt: 1965.[153]

OULTON BROAD
Area in Oulton AP, sep CP 1904,[65] sep EP 1932.[168] *LG* Mutf. & Loth. PLU, [E Suffolk] Oulton Broad UD. Abol 1919 ent to Lowestoft MB and AP.[150] *Parl* Lowest. Dv (1918–48). *Eccl* Loth. RDn.

OUSDEN
AP *LG* Seq 23. *Parl* Seq 13. *Eccl* Seq 7.

PAKEFIELD
AP *LG* Mutf. & Loth. Hd, PLU, RSD, [E Suffolk] Mutf. & Loth. RD. Abol civ 1934 pt to Lowestoft MB and AP, pt to Carlton Colville AP, pt to Gisleham AP.[7] *Parl* E'rn Dv (1832–85), N'rn Dv (1885–1918), Lowest. Dv (1918–48). *Eccl* Seq 40.

PAKENHAM
AP *LG* Seq 30. *Parl* Seq 10. *Eccl* Seq 17.

PALGRAVE
AP *LG* Seq 13. *Parl* Seq 9. *Eccl* Seq 10.

PARHAM
AP *LG* Seq 21. *Parl* Seq 9. *Eccl* Loes RDn. Abol eccl before 1813 to help cr Parham with Hacheston EP.[104]

PARHAM WITH HACHESTON
EP Cr before 1813 by union Parham AP, Hacheston AP.[104] Loes RDn.

PEASENHALL
AP *LG* Seq 6. Civ bdry: 1885.[169] *Parl* Seq 3. *Eccl* Seq 32.

PETTAUGH
AP *LG* Seq 32. *Parl* Seq 5. *Eccl* Seq 28.

PETTISTREE
AP Gains before 1535 Loudham AP, the union sometimes eccl called 'Pettistree with Loudham'. *LG* Seq 34. *Parl* Seq 7. *Eccl* Wilf. RDn (until 1928), Loes RDn (1928–*).

PETTISTREE WITH LOUDHAM–See PETTISTREE

PLAYFORD
AP *LG* Seq 10. *Parl* Seq 8. *Eccl* Seq 25.

POLSTEAD
AP *LG* Seq 1. Civ bdry: 1884,[170] 1885,[36] 1935,[9] 1952 (help cr Leavenheath CP).[147] *Parl* Seq 14. *Eccl* Seq 13. Eccl bdry: 1863 (help cr Leavenheath EP),[146] 1930.[145]

POSLINGFORD
AP *LG* Seq 25. Civ bdry: 1883.[2] *Parl* Seq 13. *Eccl* Seq 4.

PRESTON
AP Usual eccl spelling, civ spelling until civ renamed 1957 'Preston St Mary'.[171] *LG* Bab. Hd, Cosf. PLU, RSD, [W Suffolk] Cosf. RD. Civ bdry: 1883,[2] 1885,[36] 1885.[172] *Parl* W'rn Dv (1832–85), South Dv (1885–1918), Sudb. Dv (1918–48), Sudb. & Woodb. CC (1948–70). *Eccl* Seq 14.

PRESTON ST MARY
CP Renaming 1957 of Preston AP.[171] *LG* [W Suffolk] Cosf. RD. *Parl* Sudb. & Woodb. CC (1970–*).

PURDIS FARM
Ex-par place, sep CP 1858,[10] eccl abol 1928 to help cr Ipswich St Augustine of Hippo EP.[13] *LG* Seq 11. Civ bdry: 1934 (loses pt to Ipsw. CB and CP),[7] 1952 (exchanges pts with Ipsw. CB and CP).[4] *Parl* E'rn Dv (1867–85), S-E'rn Dv (1885–1918), Woodb. Dv (1918–48), Sudb. & Woodb. CC (1948–*). Parl bdry: 1953.[5]

RAMSHOLT
AP *LG* Seq 34. *Parl* Seq 8. *Eccl* Seq 47.

RATTLESDEN
AP *LG* Seq 29. *Parl* Seq 10. *Eccl* Seq 18.

RAYDON
AP *LG* Seq 27. *Parl* Seq 8. *Eccl* Seq 44.

REDE
AP *LG* Seq 31. *Parl* Seq 13. *Eccl* Seq 22.

REDGRAVE
AP Incl hmlt & chap Botesdale (sep CP 1866,[6] no sep eccl identity thus this par eccl 'Redgrave with Botesdale', qv). *LG* Seq 13. *Parl* Seq 9.

REDGRAVE WITH BOTESDALE
AP Usual eccl spelling; for civ and civ sep chap & hmlt Botesdale, see prev entry. *Eccl* Seq 10.

REDISHAM
AP Usual civ spelling; for eccl see following entry. *LG* Seq 33. *Parl* Seq 2.

GREAT REDISHAM
AP Usual eccl spelling; for civ see prev entry. *Eccl* Seq 45.

LITTLE REDISHAM
Free chapel, annexed to Ringsfield AP by 1450 and consolidated with it by 1627 at which time the chap long in ruins.[173]

REDLINGFIELD
AP Former prioy church early parochial.[176] *LG* Seq 13. Civ bdry: 1883.[2] *Parl* Eye Parl Bor (1832–85), N-E'rn Dv (1885–1918), Eye Dv/CC (1948–*).

RENDHAM
AP *LG* Seq 21. *Parl* Seq 9. *Eccl* Seq 10.

RENDLESHAM
AP *LG* Seq 19. *Parl* Seq 7. *Eccl* Seq 41. Eccl bdry: 1934.[61]

REYDON
AP Incl chap Southwold (sep civ identity early, some parochial rights since 15th cent but EP 1752[174]). *LG* Seq 7. *Parl* Seq 2. *Eccl* Seq 39.

RICKINGHALL INFERIOR
AP *LG* Seq 3. *Parl* Seq 10. *Eccl* Blackburne RDn (until 1837), Hart. RDn (1837–97), Hart. (North) RDn (1897–1931), N Hart. RDn (1931–38). Abol eccl 1938 to help cr Rickinghall Inferior and Rickinghall Superior EP.[175]

RICKINGHALL INFERIOR AND RICKINGHALL SUPERIOR
EP Cr 1938 by union Rickinghall Inferior AP, Rickinghall Superior AP.[175] N Hart. RDn (1938–72), Hart. REn (1972–*).

RICKINGHALL SUPERIOR
AP *LG* Seq 13. *Parl* Seq 9. *Eccl* As for Rickinghall Inferior, incl eccl abol 1938.

RINGSFIELD
AP *LG* Gains by 1627 chap Little Redisham (annexed to this par from 1450, prev free chapel[173]). *LG* Seq 33. Addtl civ bdry alt: 1879.[23] *Parl* Seq 2. *Eccl* Seq 45.

RINGSHALL
AP *LG* Seq 9. *Parl* Seq 7. *Eccl* Seq 23.

MONKS RISBRIDGE
Ex-par place, sep CP 1858,[10] eccl abol 1931 ent to Barnardiston AP.[21] *LG* Risb. Hd, PLU, RSD, [W Suffolk] Clare RD. *Parl* W'rn Dv (1867–85), South Dv (1885–1918), Sudb. Dv (1918–48), Bury St Edm. CC (1948–*).

RISBY
AP *LG* Seq 31. *Parl* Seq 10. *Eccl* Seq 21.

RISHANGLES
AP *LG* Seq 13. *Parl* Seq 9. *Eccl* Hart. RDn (until 1897), Hart. (South) RDn (1897–1931), S Hart. RDn (1931–72), Stowm. RDn (1972). Abol eccl 1972 to help cr Thorndon with Rishangles EP.[177]

ROUGHAM
AP *LG* Seq 30. *Parl* Seq 10. *Eccl* Seq 18.

RUMBURGH
AP *LG* Seq 8. *Parl* Seq 1. *Eccl* Dunw. RDn (until

1868), Dunw. (North) RDn (1868–1957), S Elm. RDn (1957–72), Beccles & S Elm. RDn (1972–*). Eccl bdry: 1931.[86]

RUSHBROOKE
AP *LG* Seq 30. *Parl* Seq 10. *Eccl* Seq 19.

RUSHFORD
AP Pt Norfolk (Guiltcross Hd), pt Suffolk (Bab. Hd), the latter transf 1894 to Euston AP and the par ent Norfolk thereafter.[88] *LG* Thetf. PLU, RSD. *Parl* Suffolk pt, W'rn Dv (1832–85), N-W'rn Dv (1885–1918). For later civ and parl, and for all eccl organisation, see main entry in Norfolk.

RUSHMERE
AP *LG* Seq 20. *Parl* Seq 2. *Eccl* Seq 40.

RUSHMERE
AP Sometimes 'Rushmere St Andrew'. *LG* Carlf. Hd, Woodb. PLU, pt Ipsw. Bor/MB, Ipsw. CB (pt 1888–94, ent 1894–1903), pt Ipsw. USD, pt Woodb. RSD. Civ bdry: 1894 (loses the pt not in the CB to cr Rushmere St Andrew CP).[26] Abol civ 1903 to help cr Ipswich CP.[126] *Parl* Pt Ipsw. Parl Bor (1298–1918), pt E'rn Dv (1832–85), pt S-E'rn Dv (1885–1918). *Eccl* Carlf. RDn (until 1920), Ipsw. RDn (1920–*). Eccl bdry: 1928 (help cr Ipswich St Augustine of Hippo EP),[13] 1958 (help cr Ipswich St Andrew EP).[131]

RUSHMERE ST ANDREW
CP Cr 1894 from the pt of Rushmere AP not in Ipsw. CB.[26] *LG* [E Suffolk] Woodb. RD (1894–1934), Deben RD (1934–74). Bdry: 1934 (loses pt to Ipsw. CB and CP),[7] 1952 (exchanges pts with Ipsw. CB and CP).[4] *Parl* Woodb. Dv (1918–48), Sudb. & Woodb. CC (1948–*). Parl bdry: 1953.[5]

RYMER
Ex-par place, sep CP 1858.[10] Abol civ 1885,[95] eccl 1931,[178] in each case ent to Fakenham Magna AP (eccl, 'Fakenham'). *LG* Blackbourn Hd, Thetf. PLU, RSD. *Parl* W'rn Dv (1832–85), N-W'rn Dv (1885–1918).

SANDCROFT–See SOUTH ELMHAM ST CROSS

SANTON AND SANTON DOWNHAM
EP Cr 1962 by union Santon AP (Norfolk), Santon Downham AP.[179] Mild. RDn.

SANTON DOWNHAM
AP *LG* Seq 17. *Parl* Seq 6. *Eccl* Ford. RDn (until 1862), Ford. (Suffolk) RDn (1862–84), Mild. RDn (1884–1962). Abol eccl 1962 to help cr Santon and Santon Downham EP.[179]

SAPISTON
AP *LG* Seq 4. *Parl* Seq 10. *Eccl* Blackburne RDn. Abol eccl 1972 to help cr Honington with Sapiston EP.[118]

GREAT SAXHAM
AP *LG* Seq 31. *Parl* Seq 10. *Eccl* Seq 21.

LITTLE SAXHAM
AP *LG* Seq 31. *Parl* Seq 10. *Eccl* Seq 21.

SAXMUNDHAM
AP *LG* Plom. Hd, PLU, RSD, [E Suffolk] Plom. RD (1894–1900), Saxm. UD (1900–74). *Parl* Seq 9. *Eccl* Loes RDn (until 1914), Saxm. RDn (1914–*).

SAXSTEAD
Chap in Framlingham AP, sep civ identity early, no sep eccl identity. *LG* Seq 14. *Parl* Seq 3.

SEMER
AP *LG* Seq 12. Civ bdry: 1883,[2] 1885,[34] 1935.[9] *Parl* Seq 14. *Eccl* Seq 13.

SHADINGFIELD
AP *LG* Seq 33. *Parl* Seq 2. *Eccl* Seq 45.

SHELLAND
AP *LG* Seq 28. *Parl* Seq 11. *Eccl* Donative, Seq 12.

SHELLEY
AP *LG* Seq 27. Civ bdry: 1884.[180] *Parl* Seq 8. *Eccl* Seq 43. Eccl bdry: 1933.[145]

SHIMPLING
AP Usual civ spelling; for eccl see following entry. *LG* Seq 2. Civ bdry: 1885.[181] *Parl* Seq 14.

SHIMPLINGTHORNE
AP Usual eccl spelling; for civ see prev entry. *Eccl* Seq 15.

SHIPMEADOW
AP *LG* Seq 33. *Parl* Seq 2. *Eccl* Seq 45.

SHIRE YARD HALL
Ex-par place, sep CP 1858,[10] abol eccl 1945 ent to Ipswich St Mary at the Quay AP.[135] *LG* Ipsw. PLU, MB/CB, USD. Abol 1903 to help cr Ipswich CP.[126] *Parl* Ipsw. Parl Bor (1867–1918).

SHOTLEY
AP *LG* Seq 27. *Parl* Seq 8. *Eccl* Seq 43.

SHOTTISHAM
AP *LG* Seq 34. *Parl* Seq 8. *Eccl* Seq 47.

SIBTON
AP *LG* Seq 6. Civ bdry: 1885.[169] *Parl* Seq 3. *Eccl* Seq 32.

SNAPE
AP *LG* Seq 21. *Parl* Seq 9. *Eccl* Orford RDn. Abol eccl 1785 to help cr Friston with Snape EP.[99]

EARL SOHAM
AP *LG* Seq 19. *Parl* Seq 4. *Eccl* Bosm. RDn (until 1853), Loes RDn (1853–*).

MONK SOHAM
AP *LG* Seq 15. *Parl* Seq 3. *Eccl* Seq 35.

SOMERLEYTON
AP *LG* Seq 20. *Parl* Seq 2. *Eccl* Seq 40.

SOMERSHAM
AP *LG* Seq 9. Civ bdry: 1884.[20] *Parl* Seq 7. *Eccl* Seq 23.

SOMERTON
AP *LG* Seq 2. Civ bdry: 1883,[2] 1885.[3] *Parl* Seq 14. *Eccl* Sudb. RDn (until 1864), Sudb. (W'rn) RDn (1864–1884), Horng. RDn (1884–1914), Hor. RDn (1914–72), Sudb. RDn (1972–*).

SOTHERTON
AP *LG* Seq 8. *Parl* Seq 1. *Eccl* Seq 31.

SOTTERLEY
AP *LG* Seq 33. *Parl* Seq 2. *Eccl* Wangf. RDn (until 1914), Saxm. RDn (1914–69), Beccles RDn (1969–72), Beccles & S Elm. RDn (1972–*).

SOUTHOLT
Chap in Worlingworth AP, sep civ identity early, eccl severed 1951 to help cr Bedingfield with Southolt EP.[31] *LG* Seq 15. *Parl* Seq 3.

SOUTHTOWN
EP Cr 1911 from Gorleston with Southtown AP.[102] Loth. RDn (1911–70), Flegg RDn [also in Norw dioc] (1970–*).
SOUTHWELL PARK
Ex-par place, incl 1858 civ[10] and 1927 eccl[108] in Hargrave AP.
SOUTHWOLD
Chap in Reydon AP, some parochial rights from 15th cent, sep civ identity early, sep EP 1752.[174] *LG* Blything Hd, PLU, Southwold Bor/MB, USD. [E Suffolk]. Civ bdry: 1934.[7] *Parl* Seq 2. *Eccl* Seq 31.
SPEXHALL
AP *LG* Seq 8. Civ bdry: 1885,[3] 1934.[7] *Parl* Seq 1. *Eccl* Seq 31.
SPROUGHTON
AP *LG* Samf. Hd, PLU, pt Ipsw. Bor/MB/CB, pt Ipsw. USD, pt Samf. RSD, [E Suffolk] Samf. RD. Civ bdry: 1894 (loses the pt in the CB to Ipswich St Matthew AP),[26] 1934 (loses pt to Ipsw. CB and CP),[7] 1952 (loses pt to Ipswich CB and CP).[4] *Parl* Pt Ipsw. Parl Bor (until 1918), remainder and later, Seq 8. Parl bdry: 1953.[5] *Eccl* Samf. RDn (until 1914), Bosm. RD RDn (1914–31), Stow RDn (1931–62). Eccl bdry: 1858 (help cr Ipswich All Saints EP),[40] 1959 (help cr Ipswich St Francis EP).[27] Abol eccl 1962 to help cr Sproughton with Burstall EP.[39]
SPROUGHTON WITH BURSTALL
EP Cr 1962 by union Sproughton AP, chap Burstall of Bramford with Burstall AP.[39] Samf. RDn.
STANNINGFIELD
AP *LG* Seq 30. Civ bdry: 1884.[36] *Parl* Seq 12. *Eccl* Seq 19.
STANSFIELD
AP *LG* Seq 25. Civ bdry: 1883.[2] *Parl* Seq 13. *Eccl* Seq 4.
STANSTEAD
AP *LG* Seq 2. Civ bdry: 1885.[182] *Parl* Seq 14. *Eccl* Seq 16.
STANTON
Union prob in 17th cent of Stanton All Saints AP, Stanton St John the Baptist AP.[183] *LG* Seq 5. *Parl* Seq 10. *Eccl* Seq 1.
STANTON ALL SAINTS, STANTON ST JOHN THE BAPTIST–See prev entry
STERNFIELD
AP *LG* Seq 21. *Parl* Seq 9. *Eccl* Seq 41.
STOKE ASH
AP *LG* Seq 13. *Parl* Seq 9. *Eccl* Seq 11.
STOKE BY CLARE
AP *LG* Seq 25. Civ bdry: 1885.[184] *Parl* Seq 13. *Eccl* Seq 4.
STOKE BY NAYLAND
AP Incl chap Nayland (sep civ identity early, sep EP before 1855[161]), chap Leavenheath (sep CP 1952,[147] sep EP 1863[146] [in each case with pts from other pars; sep sep entry]). *LG* Seq 2. Addtl civ bdry alt: 1884,[185] 1935.[9] *Parl* Seq 14. *Eccl* Seq 13.
EARL STONHAM
AP *LG* Seq 9. *Parl* Seq 7. *Eccl* Seq 23.
LITTLE STONHAM
AP Usual civ spelling; for eccl see 'Stonham Parva'. Formerly 'Stonham Jernagens'. *LG* Seq 9. *Parl* Seq 7.
STONHAM ASPAL–See STONHAM ASPALL
STONHAM ASPAL AND MICKFIELD
EP Cr 1973 by union Stonham Aspal AP, Mickfield EP.[158] Bosm. RDn.
STONHAM ASPALL
AP Usual civ spelling; usual eccl, 'Stonham Aspal'. Formerly, 'Stonham Antegan'. *LG* Seq 9. Civ bdry: 1883.[2] *Parl* Seq 7. *Eccl* Bosm. RDn. Abol eccl 1973 to help cr Stonham Aspal and Mickfield EP.[158]
STONHAM PARVA
AP Usual eccl spelling; for civ see 'Little Stonham'. *Eccl* Seq 23.
STOVEN
AP *LG* Seq 8. *Parl* Seq 1. *Eccl* Seq 31.
WEST STOW
AP *LG* Seq 5. *Parl* Seq 10. *Eccl* Seq 20.
STOWLANGTOFT
AP *LG* Seq 3. *Parl* Seq 10. *Eccl* Seq 2.
STOWMARKET
AP Incl chap Stowupland (sep civ identity early, sep EP 1844[186]). *LG* Stow Hd, PLU, Stowm. USD, [E Suffolk] Stowm. UD. Addtl civ bdry alt: 1934.[7] *Parl* Seq 11. *Eccl* Seq 12. Addtl eccl bdry alt: 1926,[187] 1968.[166]
STOWUPLAND
Chap in Stowmarket AP, sep civ identity early, sep EP 1844.[186] *LG* Seq 28. Civ bdry: 1934.[7] *Parl* Seq 11. *Eccl* Stow RDn (1844–1972), Stowm. RDn (1972–*). Eccl bdry: 1926.[187]
STRADBROKE
AP *LG* Seq 15. *Parl* Seq 3. *Eccl* Seq 35.
STRADISHALL
AP *LG* Seq 25. *Parl* Seq 13. *Eccl* Seq 4.
STRATFORD ST ANDREW
AP *LG* Seq 21. *Parl* Seq 9. *Eccl* Seq 41.
STRATFORD ST MARY
AP *LG* Seq 27. *Parl* Seq 8. *Eccl* Seq 44.
STRATTON HALL
Ex-par place, sep CP 1858.[10] *LG* Seq 11. *Parl* E'rn Dv (1867–85), S-E'rn Dv (1885–1918), Woodb. Dv (1918–48), Sudb. & Woodb. CC (1948–*).
STUSTON
AP *LG* Seq 13. *Parl* Seq 9. *Eccl* Seq 10.
STUTTON
AP *LG* Seq 27. *Parl* Seq 8. *Eccl* Seq 43.
SUDBOURNE
AP Incl chap Orford, sep civ identity early, no sep eccl identity (thus this par eccl 'Sudbourne with Orford', qv [sometimes 'Orford with Sudbourne']). *LG* Seq 22. *Parl* Seq 16.
SUDBOURNE WITH ORFORD
AP Usual eccl spelling; for civ and civ sep chap Orford, see prev entry. Sometimes 'Orford with Sudbourne'. *Eccl* Seq 42.

SUDBURY
The following have 'Sudbury' in their names. Insofar as any existed at a given time: *LG* Thingoe Hd, Sudb. Bor, PLU, MB (1892–1974), Sudb. USD. [W Suffolk]. *Parl* Sudb. Parl Bor (1558–1885), South Dv (1885–1918), Sudb. Dv (1918–48), Sudb. & Woodb. CC (1948–*). *Eccl* Seq 16.
CP1–SUDBURY–Cr 1880s by union AP1, AP2, CP3.[188] Bdry: 1883,[2] 1935.[9]
AP1–SUDBURY ALL SAINTS–Abol civ in 1880s to help cr CP1.[188] Abol eccl 1847 to help cr EP1.[16]
EP1–SUDBURY ALL SAINTS WITH BALLINGDON AND BRUNDON–Cr 1847 by union AP1, Ballingdon AP.[16]
CP2–SUDBURY ST BARTHOLOMEW–Ex-par place, sep CP 1858.[10] Civ bdry: 1883.[2] Abol 1935 pt to CP1, pt to Long Melford AP.[9]
AP2–SUDBURY ST GREGORY–Incl chap Sudbury St Peter (sep civ identity early as CP3, sep EP perhaps in 1960s as EP3[189]). Abol civ in 1880s to help cr CP1.[188] Abol eccl 1972 to help cr EP2.[190]
EP2–SUDBURY ST GREGORY WITH ST PETER–Cr 1972 by union AP2, EP3.[190]
CP3/EP3–SUDBURY ST PETER–Chap in AP2, sep civ identity early, sep EP perhaps in 1960s.[188] Abol eccl 1972 to help cr EP1.[190]

SUTTON
AP *LG* Seq 34. *Parl* Seq 8. *Eccl* Seq 47.

SWEFLING
AP *LG* Seq 21. *Parl* Seq 9. *Eccl* Seq 41.

SWILLAND
AP *LG* Bosm. & Clay. Hd, PLU, RSD, [E Suffolk] Bosm. & Clay. RD (1894–1934), Gip. RD (1934–74). *Parl* Seq 7. *Eccl* Seq 26.

SYLEHAM
AP *LG* Seq 15. *Parl* Seq 3. *Eccl* Seq 35.

TANNINGTON
AP Incl chap Brundish (sep civ identity early, eccl severed 1951 to help cr Worlingworth with Tannington EP[31]). *LG* Seq 15. *Parl* Seq 3. *Eccl* Before 1951 as 'Tannington with Brundish', afterwards as 'Tannington', Seq 35.

TANNINGTON WITH BRUNDISH–See prev entry

TATTINGSTONE
AP *LG* Seq 27. *Parl* Seq 8. *Eccl* Seq 43.

THEBERTON
AP *LG* Seq 6. Civ bdry: 1934.[7] *Parl* Seq 3. *Eccl* Seq 32.

THELNETHAM
AP *LG* Seq 4. *Parl* Seq 10. *Eccl* Seq 1.

THETFORD
Six par churches in Thetford (primarily Norfolk) were in Suffolk but disappeared by the 16th cent (St Edmund, St Etheldred, St Laurence, St Margaret, St Martin, St Michael); full details including dates of abol are incl in the entries for Norfolk, qv. Pts of two others were in both Norfolk and Suffolk as follows:

THETFORD ST CUTHBERT
THETFORD ST MARY
Each of these two APs primarily Norfolk (Thetf. Bor/MB, USD), each pt Suffolk (Lackf. Hd), ent in Thetf. PLU, each par made ent Norfolk in 1894. *Parl* Thetf. Parl Bor (1553–1885), the Suffolk pt N-W'rn Dv (1885–1918), Norfolk thereafter. For later civ and parl, and ent eccl organisation, see main entry in Norfolk.

THORINGTON
AP *LG* Seq 6. *Parl* Seq 3. *Eccl* Dunw. RDn (until 1868), Dunw. (South) RDn (1868–1914), S Dunw. RDn (1914–36), N Dunw. RDn (1936–72), Halesw. RDn (1972–*).

THORNDON
AP *LG* Seq 13. *Parl* Eye Parl Bor (1832–85), N-E'rn Dv (1885–1918), Eye Dv/CC (1918–*). *Eccl* Hart. RDn (until 1897), Hart. (South) RDn (1897–1931), S Hart. RDn (1931–72). Abol eccl 1972 to help cr Thorndon with Rishangles EP.[177]

THORNDON WITH RISHANGLES
EP Cr 1972 by union Thorndon AP, Rishangles AP.[177] S Hart. RDn (1972), Hart. RDn (1972–*).

THORNHAM MAGNA
AP *LG* Seq 13. *Parl* Seq 9. *Eccl* Hart. RDn (until 1897), Hart. (South) RDn (1897–1931), S Hart. RDn (1931–72), Hart. RDn (1972–*).

THORNHAM PARVA
AP Organisation as for Thornham Magna.

THORPE MORIEUX
AP *LG* Seq 12. Civ bdry: 1885,[172] 1934.[7] *Parl* Seq 14. *Eccl* Seq 14.

THRANDESTON
AP *LG* Seq 13. *Parl* Eye Parl Bor (1832–85), N-E'rn Dv (1885–1918), Eye Dv/CC (1918–*). *Eccl* Seq 10.

GREAT THURLOW
AP *LG* Seq 25. *Parl* Seq 13. *Eccl* Seq 6.

LITTLE THURLOW
AP *LG* Seq 25. *Parl* Seq 13. *Eccl* Seq 6.

THURLESTON
AP Orig AP in Ipsw. Bor, in disuse late 16th cent and united with Whitton AP to cr Whitton cum Thurleston AP,[191] qv.

THURSTON
AP *LG* Seq 29. *Parl* Seq 10. *Eccl* Seq 17.

THWAITE
AP Sometimes 'Thwaite St George'. *LG* Seq 13. *Parl* Seq 9. *Eccl* Seq 11.

TIMWORTH
AP *LG* Seq 30. *Parl* Seq 10. *Eccl* Seq 3.

TOSTOCK
AP *LG* Seq 29. *Parl* Seq 10. *Eccl* Seq 17.

TRIMLEY ST MARTIN
AP *LG* Seq 11. Civ bdry: 1883.[192] *Parl* Seq 8. *Eccl* Seq 29.

TRIMLEY ST MARY
AP *LG* Seq 11. Civ bdry: 1883.[192] *Parl* Seq 8. *Eccl* Seq 29.

TROSTON
AP Usual civ spelling; for eccl see following entry. *LG* Seq 5. *Parl* Seq 10.
TROSTON ST MARY
AP Usual eccl spelling; for civ see prev entry. *Eccl* Seq 1.
TUDDENHAM
AP Sometimes 'Tuddenham St Martin'. *LG* Seq 10. Civ bdry: 1952 (loses pt to Ipsw. CB and CP).[4] *Parl* Seq 8. Parl bdry: 1953.[5] *Eccl* Seq 25.
TUDDENHAM
AP Sometimes 'Tuddenham St Mary'. *LG* Seq 16. *Parl* Seq 6. *Eccl* Seq 9.
TUNSTALL
AP Gains late 16th cent Dunningworth AP,[80] the union civ called 'Tunstall', eccl 'Tunstall with Dunningworth', qv. *LG* Seq 22. *Parl* Seq 16. *Eccl* Orford RDn. From later 16th cent, see following entry.
TUNSTALL WITH DUNNINGWORTH
EP Usual eccl name for union late 16th cent of Tunstall AP, Dunningworth AP[80]; for civ see prev entry. *Eccl* Seq 47.
UBBESTON
AP *LG* Seq 6. Civ bdry: 1884.[74] *Parl* Seq 3. *Eccl* Dunw. RDn (until 1868), Dunw. (South) RDn (1868–1914), S Dunw. RDn (1914–72). Abol eccl 1972 to help cr Heveningham and Ubbeston EP.[117]
UFFORD
AP *LG* Seq 34. *Parl* Seq 7. *Eccl* Wilf. RDn (until 1914), Carlf. RDn (1914–72), Woodb. RDn (1972–*).
UGGESHALL
AP *LG* Seq 7. *Parl* Seq 1. *Eccl* Seq 31.
WALBERSWICK
Chap in Blythburgh AP, sep civ identity early, no sep eccl identity. *LG* Seq 6. Civ bdry: 1934.[7] *Parl* Seq 3.
GREAT WALDINGFIELD
AP *LG* Seq 2. Civ bdry: 1883,[2] 1885,[3] 1885.[193] *Parl* Seq 14. *Eccl* Sudb. RDn (until 1864), Sudb. (W'rn) RDn (1864–84), Lav. RDn (1884–1972), Sudb. RDn (1972–*).
LITTLE WALDINGFIELD
AP *LG* Seq 2. Civ bdry: 1885.[3] *Parl* Seq 14. *Eccl* Sudb. RDn (until 1864), Sudb. (W'rn) RDn (1864–84), Lav. RDn (1884–1957), Sudb. RDn (1957–*).
WALDRINGFIELD
AP *LG* Seq 10. *Parl* Seq 8. *Eccl* Colneys RDn. Abol eccl 1901 to help cr Waldringfield with Hemley EP.[115]
WALDRINGFIELD WITH HEMLEY
EP Cr 1901 by union Waldringfield AP, Hemley AP.[115] Colneys RDn.
WALPOLE
AP *LG* Seq 6. *Parl* Seq 3. *Eccl* Seq 33.
WALSHAM-LE-WILLOWS
AP *LG* Seq 3. *Parl* Seq 10. *Eccl* Seq 1.
WALTON
AP *LG* Coln. Hd, Woodb. PLU, Felixstowe & Walton USD (1887–94), Woodb. RSD (1875–87), [E Suffolk] Felixstowe & Walton UD (1894–1914). Abol civ 1914 ent to Felixstowe UD and AP.[93] *Parl* E'rn Dv (1832–85), S-E'rn Dv (1885–1918). *Eccl* Seq 29.
WANGFORD
AP Incl chap Henham (sep CP 1866[6]). *LG* Seq 16. *Parl* Seq 6. *Eccl* Ford. RDn (until 1862), Ford. (Suffolk) RDn (1862–84), Mild. RDn (1884–1962). Abol eccl 1962 to help cr Brandon Ferry and Wangford EP.[42]
WANGFORD
AP *LG* Seq 7. *Parl* Seq 1. *Eccl* Seq 31.
WANTISDEN
AP *LG* Seq 22. *Parl* Seq 16. *Eccl* Seq 42.
WARREN HOUSE
Ex-par place, sep CP 1858.[10] *LG* Ipsw. MB/CB, PLU, USD. Abol 1903 to help cr Ipswich CP.[126] *Parl* Ipsw. Parl Bor (1867–1918).
WASHBROOK
AP *LG* Seq 27. Civ bdry: 1884.[20] *Parl* Seq 8. *Eccl* Seq 43.
WATTISFIELD
AP *LG* Seq 3. *Parl* Seq 10. *Eccl* Seq 1.
WATTISHAM
AP *LG* Seq 12. Civ bdry: 1883,[2] 1885,[36] 1935.[9] *Parl* Seq 14. *Eccl* Sudb. RDn (until 1864), Sudb. (E'rn) RDn (1864–84), Lav. RDn (1884–1931), Bosm. RDn (1931–72), Hadl. RDn (1972–*).
GREAT WELNETHAM
AP Usual civ spelling; for eccl see 'Great Whelnetham'. *LG* Seq 30. Civ bdry: 1884.[194] *Parl* Seq 12.
LITTLE WELNETHAM
AP Usual civ spelling; for eccl see 'Little Whelnetham'. *LG* Seq 30. *Parl* Seq 12.
GREAT WENHAM
AP *LG* Seq 27. *Parl* Seq 8. *Eccl* Samf. RDn (until 1946), Hadl. RDn (1946–*).
LITTLE WENHAM
AP *LG* Seq 27. *Parl* Seq 8. *Eccl* Samf. RDn. Abol eccl 1786 to help cr Capel St Mary with Little Wenham EP.[62]
WENHASTON
AP *LG* Sometimes as 'Wenhaston with Mells', Seq 6. *Parl* Seq 3. *Eccl* Seq 33.
WESTERFIELD
AP *LG* Bosm. & Clay. Hd, pt Ipsw. Bor/MB/CB (until 1894), Ipsw. PLU, pt Ipsw. USD, pt Ipsw. RSD, [E Suffolk] Woodb. RD (1894–1934), Deben RD (1934–74). Civ bdry: 1894 (loses the pt in the CB to cr Westerfield in Ipswich EP),[26] 1952 (loses pt to Ipswich CB and CP).[4] *Parl* Pt Ipsw. Parl Bor (until 1918), remainder and later, Seq 8. Parl bdry: 1953.[5] *Eccl* Seq 26.
WESTERFIELD IN IPSWICH
CP Cr 1894 from the pt of Westerfield AP in Ipsw. CB.[26] *LG* Ipsw. PLU, CB. Abol 1903 to help cr Ipswich CP.[126]
WESTHALL
AP *LG* Seq 8. *Parl* Seq 1. *Eccl* Seq 31.

WESTHORPE
AP *LG* Seq 13. *Parl* Seq 9. *Eccl* Seq 11.
WESTLETON
AP *LG* Seq 6. *Parl* Seq 3. *Eccl* Seq 32.
WESTLEY
AP *LG* Seq 31. Civ bdry: 1935.[9] *Parl* Seq 10. *Eccl* Seq 21. Eccl bdry: 1958 (help cr Bury St Edmunds St George EP),[56] 1962 (help cr Bury St Edmunds All Saints EP).[55]
WESTON
AP *LG* Seq 33. *Parl* Seq 2. *Eccl* Seq 45.
CONEY WESTON
AP *LG* Seq 4. *Parl* Seq 10. *Eccl* Blackburne RDn. Abol eccl 1802 to help cr Barningham with Coney Weston EP.[22]
MARKET WESTON
AP *LG* Seq 4. *Parl* Seq 10. *Eccl* Seq 1.
WETHERDEN
AP *LG* Seq 28. *Parl* Seq 11. *Eccl* Seq 12.
WETHERINGSETT
AP *LG* Sometimes as 'Wetheringsett cum Brockford', Seq 13. *Parl* Seq 9. *Eccl* Seq 10.
WEYBREAD
AP *LG* Seq 15. *Parl* Seq 3. *Eccl* Seq 35.
WHATFIELD
AP *LG* Seq 12. Civ bdry: 1883,[2] 1885,[36] 1935.[9] *Parl* Seq 14. *Eccl* Seq 13. Eccl bdry: 1933.[159]
GREAT WHELNETHAM
AP Usual eccl spelling; for civ see 'Great Welnetham'. *Eccl* Seq 19.
LITTLLE WHELNETHAM
AP Usual eccl spelling; for civ see 'Little Welnetham'. *Eccl* Seq 19.
WHEPSTEAD
AP *LG* Seq 31. Civ bdry: 1884,[194] 1885.[44] *Parl* Seq 13. *Eccl* Seq 22.
WHERSTEAD
AP *LG* Seq 27. *Parl* Seq 8. *Eccl* Seq 43.
WHITTON
AP Orig AP in Bosm. & Clay. Hd, Clay. RDn, gains late 16th cent Thurleston AP in Ipsw. Bor, the union called 'Whitton cum Thurleston', qv.
CP Cr 1894 from the pt of Whitton cum Thurleston AP not in Ipsw. CB.[26] *LG* Bosm. & Clay. PLU, [E Suffolk] Bosm. & Clay. RD (1894–1934), Gip. RD (1934–74). Civ bdry: 1952 (loses pt to Ipsw. CB & CP).[4] *Parl* Woodb. Dv (1918–48), Eye CC (1948–*). Parl bdry: 1953.[5]
WHITTON CUM THURLESTON
AP Cr late 16th cent by union Whitton AP, Thurleston AP. *LG* Pt Bosm. & Clay. Hd, pt Ipsw. Bor/MB, Ipsw. CB (pt 1888–94, ent 1894–1903), Ipsw. PLU, pt Ipsw. USD, pt Ipsw. RSD. Civ bdry: 1894 (loses the pt not in the CB to cr Whitton CP, gains pt of the pt of Bramford AP in the CB).[26] Abol civ 1903 to help cr Ipswich CP.[126] *Parl* Pt Ipsw. Parl Bor (until 1918), pt E'rn Dv (1832–85), pt S-E'rn Dv (1885–1918). *Eccl* Seq 27.
WICKHAMBROOK
AP *LG* Seq 25. *Parl* Seq 13. *Eccl* Seq 4.
WICKHAM MARKET
AP *LG* Wilf. Hd, Plom. PLU, RSD, [E Suffolk] Plom. RD (1894–1934), Deben RD (1934–74). *Parl* Seq 7. *Eccl* Seq 49.
WICKHAM SKEITH
AP *LG* Seq 13. Civ bdry: 1883.[2] *Parl* Seq 9. *Eccl* Seq 11.
WILBY
AP *LG* Seq 15. Civ bdry: 1884.[122] *Parl* Seq 3. *Eccl* Hoxne RDn. Eccl bdry: 1935.[130] Abol eccl 1951 to help cr Wilby with Brundish AP.[31]
WILBY WITH BRUNDISH
EP Cr 1951 by union Wilby AP, chap Brundish of Tannington with Brundish AP.[31] Hoxne RDn.
WILLINGHAM–See WILLINGHAM ST MARY
WILLINGHAM ALL SAINTS–See ELLOUGH
WILLINGHAM ST MARY
AP *LG* Seq 33. *Parl* Seq 2. *Eccl* Sometimes as 'Willingham', Wangf. RDn (until 1914), Beccles RDn (1914–72), Beccles & S Elm. RDn (1972–*).
WILLISHAM
AP *LG* Seq 9. Civ bdry: 1884.[20] *Parl* Seq 7. *Eccl* Seq 23.
WINGFIELD
AP *LG* Seq 15. *Parl* Seq 3. *Eccl* Seq 35.
WINSTON
AP *LG* Seq 32. *Parl* Seq 5. *Eccl* Seq 28.
WISSETT
AP *LG* Seq 8. Civ bdry: 1884,[67] 1934.[7] *Parl* Seq 1. *Eccl* Dunw. RDn (until 1868), Dunw. (North) RDn (1868–1914), N Dunw. RDn (1914–72), Halesw. RDn (1972–*).
WISSINGTON
AP Sometimes 'Wiston'. *LG* Bab. Hd, Sudb. PLU, RSD. Abol civ 1884 to help cr Nayland with Wissington CP.[160] *Parl* W'rn Dv (1832–85). *Eccl* Sudb. RDn (until 1864), Sudb. (W'rn) RDn (1864–84), Hadl. RDn (1884–*). Eccl bdry: 1863 (help cr Leavenheath EP).[146]
WISTON–See prev entry
WITHERSDALE
AP *LG* Hoxne Hd, PLU, RSD. Civ bdry: 1883.[2] Abol civ 1885 pt to Metfield AP, pt to Mendham AP, pt to Linstead Parva AP.[195] *Parl* E'rn Dv (1832–85), N-E'rn Dv (1885–1918).
WITHERSFIELD
AP *LG* Seq 25. Civ bdry: 1885,[112] 1971.[114] *Parl* Seq 13. *Eccl* Seq 4.
WITNESHAM
AP *LG* Seq 10. *Parl* Seq 7. *Eccl* Carlf. RDn (until 1931), Clay. RDn (1931–72), Bosm. RDn (1972–*).
WIXOE
AP *LG* Seq 25. Civ bdry: 1884,[196] 1885.[197] *Parl* Seq 13. *Eccl* Seq 4. Eccl bdry: 1931.[21]
WOODBRIDGE
AP *LG* Loes Hd, Woodb. PLU, USD (1894), Woodb. RSD (1875–Feb 1894), [E Suffolk] Woodb. UD. *Parl* Seq 8. *Eccl* Seq 48. Eccl bdry: 1854 (cr Woodbridge St John EP).[198]
WOODBRIDGE ST JOHN
EP Cr 1854 from Woodbridge AP.[198] Wilf. RDn (1854–1914), Carlf. RDn (1914–72), Woodb. RDn (1972–*).

WOOLPIT
AP *LG* Seq 29. *Parl* Seq 10. *Eccl* Seq 18.
WOOLVERSTONE
AP *LG* Seq 27. *Parl* Seq 8. *Eccl* Seq 43.
WORDWELL
AP *LG* Seq 5. *Parl* Seq 10. *Eccl* Seq 20.
WORLINGHAM
AP Cr 1492 by union Worlingham All Saints AP, Worlingham St Peter AP.[199] *LG* Seq 33. *Parl* Seq 2. *Eccl* Seq 45.
WORLINGHAM ALL SAINTS
AP Wangf. RDn. United 1492 with Worlingham St Peter AP, the union called 'Worlingham'.[199]
WORLINGHAM ST PETER
AP Wangf. RDn. United 1492 with Worlingham All Saints AP, the union called 'Worlingham'.[199]
WORLINGTON
AP *LG* Seq 16. *Parl* Seq 6. *Eccl* Seq 9.
WORLINGWORTH
AP Incl chap Southolt (sep civ identity early, eccl severed 1951 to help cr Bedingfield with Southolt EP,[31] so that this par eccl 'Worlingworth with Southolt' before 1951, 'Worlingworth' thereafter). *LG* Seq 15. *Parl* Seq 3. *Eccl* Seq 35.
WORLINGWORTH WITH SOUTHOLT—See prev entry
WORTHAM
AP *LG* Seq 13. *Parl* Seq 9. *Eccl* Seq 10.
GREAT WRATTING
AP *LG* Seq 25. *Parl* Seq 13. *Eccl* Clare RDn. Abol eccl 1819 to help cr Great Wratting with Little Wratting EP.[200]
GREAT WRATTING WITH LITTLE WRATTING
EP Cr 1819 by union Great Wratting AP, Little Wratting AP.[200] Clare RDn.
LITTLE WRATTING
AP *LG* Seq 25. Civ bdry: 1883.[2] 1885.[112] *Parl* Seq 13. *Eccl* Clare RDn. Abol eccl 1819 to help cr Great Wratting with Little Wratting EP.[200]
WRENTHAM
AP *LG* Seq 7. *Parl* Seq 2. *Eccl* Seq 30.
WYVERSTONE
AP *LG* Seq 13. *Parl* Seq 9. *Eccl* Seq 11.
YAXLEY
AP *LG* Seq 13. *Parl* Eye Parl Bor (1832–85), N-E'rn Dv (1885–1918), Eye Dv/CC (1918–*). *Eccl* Seq 10.
YOXFORD
AP *LG* Seq 6. *Parl* Seq 3. *Eccl* Seq 32.

SURREY

ABBREVIATIONS

Abbreviations particular to Surrey follow. Those general abbreviations in use throughout the *Guide* are found on page xix.

Batt.	Battersea
Bedd.	Beddington
Berm.	Bermondsey
Blackh.	Blackheath
Brix.	Brixton
Cambw.	Camberwell
Carsh.	Carshalton
Caterh.	Caterham
Chert.	Chertsey
Clap.	Clapham
Copth.	Copthorne
Cranl.	Cranleigh
Croy.	Croydon
Dork.	Dorking
Dulw.	Dulwich
Elmbr.	Elmbridge
Farn.	Farnham
Godalm.	Godalming
Godst.	Godstone
Guildf.	Guildford
Hambl.	Hambledon
Kenn.	Kennington
Kingst.	Kingston
Lamb.	Lambeth
Leath.	Leatherhead
Newing.	Newington
Reig.	Reigate
Richm.	Richmond
Spelth.	Spelthorne
Streath.	Streatham
Swk.	Southwark
Tandr.	Tandridge
Wall.	Wallington
Wandsw.	Wandsworth
Wimb.	Wimbledon
Wok.	Woking

SEQUENCES

An abbreviated entry prefixed by 'Seq' is used in the parochial entries to avoid repeating often the names of superior units of administration. The content of each sequence is show below.

Local Government Sequences ('LG')

SEQ 1 Blackh. Hd, Hambl. PLU, RSD, RD
SEQ 2 Godalm. Hd, Hambl. PLU, RSD, RD
SEQ 3 Godley Hd, Chert. PLU, RSD, RD (1894–1933), Bagshot RD (1933–74)
SEQ 4 Reig. Hd, PLU, RSD, RD (1894–1933), Dork. & Horley RD (1933–74)
SEQ 5 Reig. Hd, PLU, RSD, RD (1894–1933), Godst. RD (1933–74)
SEQ 6 Tandr. Hd, Godst. PLU, RSD, RD
SEQ 7 Wok. Hd, Guildf. PLU, RSD, RD
SEQ 8 Wotton Hd, Dork. PLU, RSD, RD (1894–1933), Dork. & Horley RD (1933–74)

Parliamentary Sequences ('Parl')

SEQ 1 E'rn Dv (1832–67), East Dv (1867–85),

N-E'rn Dv (1885–1918), E'rn Dv (1918–48), E Surrey CC (1948–*)

SEQ 2 E'rn Dv (1832–67), East Dv (1867–85), S-E'rn Dv (1885–1918), E'rn Dv (1918–48), Reig. CC (1948–70), E Surrey CC (1970–*)

SEQ 3 E'rn Dv (1832–67), East Dv (1867–85), S-E'rn Dv (1885–1918), E'rn Dv (1918–48), E Surrey CC (1948–*)

SEQ 4 E'rn Dv (1832–67), Mid Dv (1867–85), S-E'rn Dv (1885–1918), Reig. Dv (1918–48), Dork. CC (1948–*)

SEQ 5 E'rn Dv (1832–67), Mid Dv (1867–85), S-E'rn Dv (1885–1918), Reig. Dv/CC (1918–*)

SEQ 6 E'rn Dv (1832–67), Mid Dv (1867–85), S-E'rn Dv (1885–1918), Reig. Dv/CC (1918–70), E Surrey CC (1970–*)

SEQ 7 W'rn Dv (1832–85), Kingst. Dv (1885–1918), Chert. Dv (1918–48), Esher CC (1948–*)

SEQ 8 W'rn Dv (1832–85), Mid Dv (1885–1918), Epsom Dv/CC (1918–70), Epsom & Ewell CC (1970–*)

SEQ 9 W'rn Dv (1832–85), Mid Dv (1885–1918), Reig. Dv (1918–48), Dork. CC (1948–*)

SEQ 10 W'rn Dv (1832–85), N-W'rn Dv (1885–1918), Chert. Dv/CC (1918–70), N W Surrey CC (1970–*)

SEQ 11 W'rn Dv (1832–85), N-W'rn Dv (1885–1918), Chert. Dv (1918–48), Wok. CC (1948–*)

SEQ 12 W'rn Dv (1832–85), N-W'rn Dv (1885–1918), Guildf. Dv/CC (1918–*)

SEQ 13 W'rn Dv (1832–85), N-W'rn Dv (1885–1918), Guildf. Dv (1918–48), Dork. CC (1948–*)

SEQ 14 W'rn Dv (1832–85), S-E'rn Dv (1885–1918), Reig. Dv (1918–48), Dork. CC (1948–*)

SEQ 15 W'rn Dv (1832–85), S-W'rn Dv (1885–1918), Farn. Dv/CC (1918–*)

SEQ 16 W'rn Dv (1832–85), S-W'rn Dv (1885–1918), Guildf. Dv/CC (1918–*)

SEQ 17 W'rn Dv (1832–85), S-W'rn Dv (1885–1918), Guildf. Dv (1918–48), Dork. CC (1948–*)

SEQ 18 W'rn Dv (1832–85), S-W'rn Dv (1885–1918), Guildf. Dv (1918–48), Farn. CC (1948–*)

SEQ 19 Pt W'rn Dv (1832–85), pt E'rn Dv (1832–67), pt Mid Dv (1867–85), Kingst. Dv (1885–1918), Chert. Dv (1918–48), Esher CC (1948–*)

Ecclesiastical Sequences ('Eccl')

SEQ 1 Guildf. RDn (until *ca* 1535), Stoke RDn (*ca* 1535–1858), W Ewell RDn (1858–71), Leath. RDn (1871–*)

SEQ 2 Guildf. RDn (until *ca* 1535), Stoke RDn (*ca* 1535–1858), Guildf. RDn (1858–1928), Cranl. RDn (1928–*)

SEQ 3 Guildf. RDn (until *ca* 1535), Stoke RDn (*ca* 1535–1858), Guildf. RDn (1858–*)

SEQ 4 Guildf. RDn (until *ca* 1535), Stoke RDn (*ca* 1535–1858), Guildf. RDn (1858–71), S-W Stoke RDn (1871–78), Godalm. RDn (1878–1928), Cranl. RDn (1928–*)

SEQ 5 Guildf. RDn (until *ca* 1535), Stoke RDn (*ca* 1535–1858), N-E Stoke RDn (1858–78), Emly RDn (1878–*)

SEQ 6 Guildf. RDn (until *ca* 1535), Stoke RDn (*ca* 1535–1858), N-E Stoke RDn (1858–78), Wok. RDn (1878–*)

SEQ 7 Guildf. RDn (until *ca* 1535), Stoke RDn (*ca* 1535–1858), N-W Stoke RDn (1858–71), Emly RDn (1871–1946), Chert. RDn (1946–*)

SEQ 8 Guildf. RDn (until *ca* 1535), Stoke RDn (*ca* 1535–1858), N-W Stoke RDn (1858–71), Emly RDn (1871–78), Wok. RDn (1878–*)

SEQ 9 Guildf. RDn (until *ca* 1535), Stoke RDn (*ca* 1535–1858), N-W Stoke RDn (1858–61), N-E Stoke RDn (1861–78), Wok. RDn (1878–*)

SEQ 10 Guildf. RDn (until *ca* 1535), Stoke RDn (*ca* 1535–1858), S-E Stoke RDn (1858–78), Dork. RDn (1878–*)

SEQ 11 Guildf. RDn (until *ca* 1535), Stoke RDn (*ca* 1535–1858), S-W Stoke RDn (1858–78), Farn. RDn (1878–*)

SEQ 12 Guildf. RDn (until *ca* 1535), Stoke RDn (*ca* 1535–1858), S-W Stoke RDn (1858–78), Godalm. RDn (1878–*)

SEQ 13 Guildf. RDn (until *ca* 1535), Stoke RDn (*ca* 1535–1858), S-W Stoke RDn (1858–78), Godalm. RDn (1878–1928), Guildf. RDn (1928–*)

SEQ 14 Ewell RDn (until 1858), N-E Ewell RDn (1858–78), Bedd. RDn (1878–1966), Sutton RDn (1966–*)

SEQ 15 Ewell RDn (until 1858), N-E Ewell RDn (1858–71), Kingst. RDn (1871–79), Richm. RDn (1879–1922), Richm. & Barnes RDn (1922–*)

SEQ 16 Ewell RDn (until 1858), N-E Ewell RDn (1858–78), Leath. RDn (1878–1928), Epsom RDn (1928–*)

SEQ 17 Ewell RDn (until 1858), S-E Ewell RDn (1858–71), Bedd. RDn (1871–79), Catherh. RDn (1879–*)

SEQ 18 Ewell RDn (until 1858), S-E Ewell RDn (1858–71), S-W Ewell RDn (1871–79), Reig. RDn (1879–*)

SEQ 19 Ewell RDn (until 1858), S-E Ewell RDn (1858–71), Godst. RDn (1871–*)

SEQ 20 Ewell RDn (until 1858), S-E Ewell RDn (1858–71), Godst. RDn (1871–79), Caterh. RDn (1879–*)

SEQ 21 Swk. RDn (until 1858), N-E Ewell RDn (1858–79), Bedd. RDn (1879–1966), Sutton RDn (1966–*)

SEQ 22 Swk. RDn (until 1947), Swk. & Newing.

RDn (1947–*)

SEQ 23 Pec jurisd Archbp Canterb (Croy. RDn, until 1845), Barnes & Hammersmith RDn (1861–72), Barnes RDn (1872–1922), Richm. & Barnes RDn (1922–*)

DIOCESES AND ARCHDEACONRIES

Surrey pars have been in a number of dioceses and archdeaconries.
The organisation of RDns within each was as follows:

CANTERBURY DIOC
Croydon peculiar until 1845, RDn from 1873, AD and RDn from 1930

GUILDFORD DIOC (1927–*)
Dorking AD (1928–):* Chert. RDn, Dork. RDn, Emly RDn, Epsom RDn (1928–*), Leath. RDn, Wok. RDn
Surrey AD: Aldershot RDn, Chert. RDn (1927–28), Cranl. RDn (1928–*), Dork. RDn (1927–28), Emly RDn (1927–28), Farn. RDn, Godalm. RDn, Guildf. RDn, Leath. RDn (1927–28), Wok. RDn (1927–28)

LONDON DIOC (1845–77)
Middlesex AD: Barnes RDn (1872–77), Barnes & Hammersmith RDn (1861–72), Cambw. RDn (1871–77), Clap. RDn (1871–77), Lamb. RDn (1865–77), Newing. RDn (1870–77), Swk. RDn (1845–77), Streath. RDn (1865–77), Swk. RDn

ROCHESTER DIOC (1877–1905)
(In no AD 1877–78)
Kingston-upon-Thames AD (1879–1905): Barnes RDn, Bedd. RDn, Catherh. RDn (1901–05), Dulw. RDn (1901–05), Godst. RDn, Kingst. RDn, Reig. RDn, Richm. RDn (1901–05), Streath. RDn, Wandsw. RDn (1901–05)
Southwark AD (1878–1905): Barnes (1878–79), Batt. RDn (1879–1905), Cambw. RDn, Clap. RDn, Kenn. RDn (1879–1905), Kingst. RDn (1878–79), Lamb. RDn, Newing. RDn, Reig. RDn (1878–79), Swk. RDn, Streath. RDn (1878–79)

SOUTHWARK DIOC (1905–*)
Kingston-upon-Thames AD: Barnes RDn (1905–22), Bedd. RDn (1905–66), Caterh. RDn, Dulw. RDn (1905–06), Godst. RDn, Kingst. RDn, Merton RDn (1966–73), Reig. RDn, Richm. RDn (1905–22), Richm. & Barnes RDn (1922–73), Streath. RDn (1905–06), Sutton RDn (1966–*), Wandsw. RDn (1905–06), Wimb. RDn (1909–66)
Lewisham AD (1906–):* Cambw. RDn (1906–73), Dulw. RDn (1906–73)
Southwark AD: Batt. RDn (1905–73), Berm. RDn (1909–*), Brix. & Kenn. RDn (1935–47), Cambw. RDn (1905–06), Cambw. RDn (1973–*), Clap. RDn (1905–47), Clap. & Brix. RDn (1947–*), Dulw. RDn (1973–*), Kenn. RDn (1905–35), Lamb. RDn, Newing. RDn (1905–47), Streath. RDn (1906–58), Streath. RDn (1966–*), Streath. & Mitcham RDn (1958–66), Swk. RDn (1905–47), Swk. & Newing. RDn (1947–*), Tooting RDn (1966–73), Wandsw. RDn (1906–73)
Wandsworth AD (1973–):* Batt. RDn, Merton RDn, Richm. & Barnes RDn, Tooting RDn, Wandsw. RDn

WINCHESTER DIOC (until 1927)
Surrey AD: Dork. RDn (1878–1927), Emly RDn (1871–1927), Ewell RDn (until 1858), N-E Ewell RDn (1858–78), S-E Ewell RDn (1858–78), S-W Ewell RDn (1858–78), Farn. RDn (1878–1928), Godalm. RDn (1878–1927), Guildf. RDn (until *ca* 1535), Guildf. RDn (1858–1927), Leath. RDn (1871–1928), Stoke RDn (*ca* 1535–1858), N-E Stoke RDn (1858–78), N-W Stoke RDn (1858–78), S-E Stoke RDn (1858–78), S-W Stoke RDn (1858–78), Swk. RDn (until 1845), Wok. RDn (1878–1927)

THE PARISHES OF SURREY

ABINGER
AP *LG* Seq 8. Civ bdry: 1883,[1] 1879,[2] 1901,[3] 1934.[4] *Parl* Seq 14. *Eccl* Seq 10. Eccl bdry: 1853 (help refound Okewood EP),[5] 1878 (help cr Holmbury EP).[6]

ADDINGTON
AP *LG* Wall. Hd, Croy. Hd, RSD, RD (1894–1915), Godst. RD (1915–25). Abol civ 1925 ent to Croy. CB and AP.[7] *Parl* E'rn Dv (1832–67), East Dv (1867–85), N-E'rn Dv (1885–1918), E'rn Dv (1918–45). *Eccl* Ewell RDn (until 1837), Croy. RDn (1873–*). Eccl bdry: 1934 (help cr Selsdon EP),[8] 1952 (help cr Shirley St George EP),[9] 1958 (cr New Addington EP),[10] 1958 (cr Spring Park EP),[11] 1962.[76]

NEW ADDINGTON
EP Cr 1958 from Addington AP.[10] Croy. RDn.

ADDISCOMBE ST MARY MAGDALENE
EP Cr 1879 from Croydon Common EP.[12] Croy. RDn. Bdry: 1922 (help cr Addiscombe St Mildred EP),[14] 1930.[13]

ADDISCOMBE ST MILDRED
EP Cr 1922 from Addiscombe St Mary Magdalene EP, Shirley EP, Croydon St Luke, Woodside EP.[14]

ADDLESTONE
Chap in Chertsey AP, sep EP 1838.[15] Stoke RDn (1838–58), N-W Stoke RDn (1858–71), Emly RDn (1871–1946), Chert. RDn (1946–*). Bdry: 1865 (cr Ottershaw EP),[16] 1902 (help cr Woodham EP),[17] 1967,[18] 1972 (cr New Haw EP).[20]

ALBURY
AP *LG* Blackh. Hd, Guildf. PLU, RSD, RD. Civ bdry: 1880,[20] 1883,[21] 1933,[22] 1955.[23] *Parl* Seq 17. *Eccl* Seq 2.

ALFOLD
AP Pt Surrey (Blackh. Hd), pt Sussex (Bury Hd, Rape of Arundel). *LG* Hambl. PLU, RSD, RD. Civ bdry: 1880,[23] 1883,[21] 1884 (loses the pt in Sussex to Wisborough Green AP, Sussex),[24] 1933.[22] *Parl* Surrey pt, Seq 16. *Eccl* Seq 4.

ANGELL TOWN
EP Cr 1853 from Brixton St Matthew EP.[25] Swk. RDn (1853–71), Clap. RDn (1871–1935), Brix. & Kenn. RDn (1935–47), Clap. & Brix. RDn (1947–*). Bdry: 1877 (help cr Loughborough Park EP),[43] 1891,[26] 1905,[27] 1905 (gains ent Loughborough Park EP).[27]

ARTINGTON
Area in Guildford St Nicolas AP (the pt not in Guildf. Bor/MB), sep CP 1894.[28] *LG* Guildf. PLU, RD. Bdry: 1904,[29] 1922,[30] 1933.[4] *Parl* Guildf. Dv/CC (1918–*).

ASH
AP Usual eccl spelling; for civ and sep chap Frimley see 'Ash and Normandy'. *Eccl* Guildf. RDn (until *ca* 1535), Stoke RDn (*ca* 1535–1858), N-W Stoke RDn (1858–71), Guildf. RDn (1871–1922), Aldershot RDn (1922–*). Addtl eccl bdry alt: 1847 (help cr Wyke EP),[34] 1972 (cr Ash Vale EP).[14]
CP Cr 1955 when Ash and Normandy AP divided into 2 CPs of Ash, Normandy.[31] *LG* Guildf. RD. *Parl* Wok. CC (1970–*).

ASH AND NORMANDY
AP Usual civ spelling; for eccl see prev entry. Incl chap Frimley (sep CP 1866 in Godley Hd,[32] so that Ash and Normandy ent Wok. Hd thereafter, sep EP 1813 [refounded 1866][33]). *LG* Wok. Hd (pt until 1866, ent thereafter), pt Godley Hd (Frimley, until 1866), Farn. PLU (1869–1930), RSD, RD (1894–1933), Guildf. RD (1933–55). Divided 1955 into 2 CPs of Ash, Normandy.[31] *Parl* W'rn Dv (1832–85), S-W'rn Dv (1885–1918), Farn. Dv (1918–48), Wok. CC (1948–70).

ASH VALE
EP Cr 1972 from Ash AP.[14] Aldershot RDn.

ASHFORD
CP/EP transf 1965 from Middx.[35] *LG* Staines UD. *Parl* Spelth. BC (1970–*). *Eccl* See main entry in Middx.

ASHTEAD
AP *LG* Copth. Hd, Epsom PLU, RSD, RD (1894–1933), Leath. UD (1933–74). *Parl* Seq 8. *Eccl* Ewell RDn (until 1858), N-E Ewell RDn (1858–71), Leath. RDn (1871–1928), Epsom RDn (1928–66), Leath. RDn (1966–*).

BAGSHOT
EP Cr 1874 from Windlesham AP.[36] Emly RDn (1874–78), Wok. RDn (1878–*). Bdry: 1963,[37] 1963 (help cr Lightwater EP),[38] 1973.[39]

BALHAM
EP Cr 1901 from Streatham St Mary EP (commonly known as 'Balham St Mary'), Upper Tooting EP.[40] Streath. RDn (1901–58), Streath. & Mitcham RDn (1958–66), Tooting RDn (1966–*).

BALHAM HILL
EP Cr 1884 from Streatham St Mary EP, Clapham AP.[41] Streath. RDn (1884–1935), Clap. RDn (1935–47), Clap. & Brix. RDn (1947–66), Tooting RDn (1966–*). Bdry: 1895,[40] 1952.[42]

BALHAM ST MARY–See STREATHAM ST MARY

BANSTEAD
AP *LG* Copth. Hd, Epsom PLU, RSD, RD (1894–1933), Banstead UD (1933–74). Civ bdry: 1933,[22] 1969 (gains pt Croy. CB and AP).[44] *Parl* W'rn Dv (1832–85), Mid Dv (1885–1918), Epsom Dv (1918–45), Carsh. Dv/CC (1945–70), Reig. CC (1970–*). *Eccl* Seq 16. Eccl bdry: 1833 (help cr Kingswood EP),[47] 1931 (help cr Noak EP),[45] 1937 (help cr Burgh Heath EP),[46] 1937.[34]

BARNES
AP *LG* Brix. Hd, Richm. PLU, RSD (1875–93), Barnes USD (1893–94), UD (1894–1932), MB (1932–65). Civ bdry: 1901 (gains pt Putney CP, London),[48] 1957 (gains pt Wandsworth Borough CP, London).[49] Transf 1965 to Gtr London (Richm. upon Thames LB).[35] *Parl* E'rn Dv (1832–67), Mid Dv (1867–85), Richm. Parl Bor, Kingst. Dv (1885–1918), Richm. Parl Bor/BC (1918–70), Gtr London thereafter. *Eccl* Seq 23. Eccl bdry: 1888 (cr Barnes Holy Trinity EP),[50] 1919 (cr Barnes St Michael and All Angels EP).[51]

BARNES HOLY TRINITY
EP Cr 1888 from Barnes AP.[50] Barnes RDn (1888–1922), Richm. & Barnes RDn (1922–*).

BARNES ST MICHAEL AND ALL ANGELS
EP Cr 1919 from Barnes AP.[51] RDns as for Barnes Holy Trinity, from 1919.

BATTERSEA
The following have 'Battersea' in their names. Insofar as any existed at a given time: *LG* Brix. Hd, Wandsw. & Clap. PLU, Wandsw. Dist (Metrop Bd Wks, 1855–88), Batt. Vestry (Metrop Bd Wks, 1888–89). Transf 1889 to London.[53] *Parl* E'rn Dv (1832–67), Mid Dv (1867–85), Batt. & Clap. Parl Bor, pt Batt. Dv, pt Clap. Dv (1885–1918), London thereafter. *Eccl* Swk. RDn (until 1865), Streath. RDn (1865–79), Batt. RDn (1879–*).
AP1–BATTERSEA [ST MARY]–Incl detached hmlt Penge (sep EP 1851 as 'Penge St John',[52] sep CP 1866[32]). Addtl eccl bdry alt: 1831 (cr EP5, refounded 1853),[54] 1861 (cr EP1),[55] 1863 (help cr EP7),[56] 1871 (help cr EP14),[57]

1874,[58] 1883 (cr EP19),[59] 1883 (cr EP10),[8] 1884 (help cr EP17),[60] 1887 (help cr EP16),[6] 1889 (help cr Wandsworth Common EP),[61] 1895,[40] 1895 (help cr Clapham Common EP),[62] 1900 (cr EP8),[72] 1935 (cr EP9).[73]

EP1–BATTERSEA CHRIST CHURCH–Cr 1861 from AP1.[55] Bdry: 1871 (help cr EP14),[57] 1872 (help cr EP18),[63] 1874 (incl cr EP12),[58] 1887 (help cr EP16),[6] 1956.[64] Abol 1972 to help cr EP2.[65]

EP2–BATTERSEA CHRIST CHURCH AND ST STEPHEN–Cr 1972 by union EP1, EP16.[65]

EP3–BATTERSEA ST ANDREW–Cr 1886 from EP5.[66] Abol 1956 to help cr EP6.[67]

EP4–BATTERSEA ST BARTHOLOMEW–Cr 1906 from EP14, Clapham St Paul EP.[68] Bdry: 1956.[64] Abol 1973 to help cr EP15.[69]

EP5–BATTERSEA ST GEORGE–Cr 1831, refounded 1853 from AP1.[54] Bdry: 1871 (help cr EP14),[57] 1884 (help cr EP17),[60] 1886 (cr EP3).[66] Abol 1954 to help cr EP6.[67]

EP6–BATTERSEA ST GEORGE WITH ST ANDREW–Cr 1954 by union EP5, EP3.[67]

EP7–BATTERSEA ST JOHN–Cr 1863 from AP1, Wandsworth St Anne EP.[56] Bdry: 1884 (help cr Wandsworth St Faith EP),[12] 1939.[70] Renamed 1948 as EP11.[71]

EP8–BATTERSEA ST LUKE–Cr 1900 from AP1.[72] Batt. RDn (1900–35), Clap. RDn (1935–47), Batt. RDn (1947–*). Bdry: 1952,[42] 1956.[47]

EP9–BATTERSEA ST MARY LE PARK–Cr 1935 from AP1.[73]

EP10–BATTERSEA ST MICHAEL, WANDSWORTH COMMON–Cr 1883 from AP1.[8] Bdry: 1956.[74]

EP11–BATTERSEA ST PAUL–Renaming 1948 of EP7.[71] Bdry: 1950.[75] Abol 1973 to help cr EP13.[69]

EP12–BATTERSEA ST PETER–Cr 1874 from EP1.[58] Bdry: 1950.[75] Abol 1973 to help cr EP13.[69]

EP13–BATTERSEA ST PETER AND ST PAUL–Cr 1973 by union EP11, EP12.[69]

EP14–BATTERSEA ST PHILIP–Cr 1871 from EP1, EP5, AP1.[57] Bdry: 1875 (cr Lavender Hill EP),[76] 1884 (help cr EP17),[60] 1895 (help cr Clapham Common EP),[77] 1906 (help cr EP4).[68] Abol 1973 to help cr EP15.[69]

EP15–BATTERSEA ST PHILIP WITH ST BARTHOLOMEW–Cr 1973 by union EP14, EP4.[69]

EP16–BATTERSEA ST STEPHEN–Cr 1887 from AP1, EP18.[6] Bdry: 1956.[64] Abol 1972 to help cr EP2.[65]

EP16–BATTERSEA ST STEPHEN–Cr 1887 from AP1, EP18.[6] Bdry: 1956.[64] Abol 1972 to help cr EP2.[65]

EP17–BATTERSEA PARK ALL SAINTS–Cr 1884 from EP5, EP14, EP18, AP1.[60]

EP18–BATTERSEA PARK ST SAVIOUR–Cr 1872 from EP1.[63] Bdry: 1884 (help cr EP17),[60] 1887 (help cr EP16).[6]

EP19–BATTERSEA RISE–Cr 1883 from AP1.[59] Bdry: 1939,[70] 1956.[74]

BEDDINGTON

AP Incl hmlt and chap Wallington (sep CP 1866,[32] sep EP 1867[78]). *LG* Wall. Hd, Croy. PLU, RSD, RD (1894–1915), Bedd. & Wall. UD (1915–37), MB (1937–65). Addtl civ bdry alt: 1915,[79] 1933 (incl exchanges pts with Croy. CB and AP).[4] Transf 1965 to Gtr London (Sutton LB).[35] *Parl* E'rn Dv (1832–67), Mid Dv (1867–85), N-E'rn Dv (1885–1918), Mitcham Dv (1918–45), Parl Bor/BC (1945–70), Gtr London thereafter. Parl bdry: 1945.[413] *Eccl* Seq 21. Addtl eccl bdry alt: 1884 (help cr Purley Christ Church EP),[12] 1907 (help cr South Beddington EP),[80] 1911 (help cr Purley St Mark, Woodcote EP),[81] 1915 (help cr Coulsdon St Andrew EP),[82] 1934 (help cr North Beddington EP).[83]

NORTH BEDDINGTON

EP Cr 1934 from Beddington AP, Mitcham AP, Carshalton AP.[83] Bedd. RDn (1934–66), Sutton RDn (1966–69). Bdry: 1939.[64] Renamed 1969 'Hackbridge and North Beddington'.[84]

SOUTH BEDDINGTON

EP Cr 1907 from Beddington AP, Wallington AP.[80] Bedd. RDn (1907–66), Sutton RDn (1966–*).

BELMONT

EP Cr 1916 from Cheam AP, Sutton Christ Church EP.[85] Bedd. RDn (1916–66), Sutton RDn (1966–*). Bdry: 1965 (incl help cr Carshalton Beeches EP).[86]

BENHILTON

EP Cr 1863 from Sutton AP.[70] N-E Ewell RDn (1863–79), Bedd. RDn (1879–1966), Sutton RDn (1966–*). Bdry: 1884 (help cr Sutton New Town EP),[87] 1930 (help cr St Helier EP),[88] 1939.[64]

BERMONDSEY

The following have 'Bermondsey' in their names. Insofar as any existed at a given time: *LG* Brix. Hd, Berm. Par (poor law purposes, 1836–69), St Olave PLU (1869–99), Berm. Vestry (Metrop Bd Wks). Transf 1889 to London.[53] *Parl* Swk. Parl Bor (1832–85), Swk. Parl Bor, pt Rotherhithe Dv, pt Berm. Dv (1885–1918), London thereafter. *Eccl* Swk. RDn (until 1909), Berm. RDn (1909–*).

AP1–BERMONDSEY [ST MARY MAGDALEN]–Eccl bdry: 1840 (cr EP5),[89] 1846 (cr EP10),[90] 1885 (help cr EP7).[92] Abol eccl 1956 pt to help cr EP8, pt to Southwark St Stephen EP.[93]

EP1–BERMONDSEY CHRIST CHURCH–Cr 1845 from EP5.[94] Abol 1956 to help cr EP6.[93]

EP2–BERMONDSEY ST ANNE–Cr 1871 from EP5.[95] Bdry: 1876 (help cr Camberwell St Philip EP).[96]

EP3–BERMONDSEY ST CRISPIN–Cr 1875 from EP3.[98] Abol 1950 to help cr EP4.[75]

EP4–BERMONDSEY ST CRISPIN WITH CHRIST CHURCH–Cr 1950 by union EP3, Rotherhithe Christ Church EP.[75]

EP5–BERMONDSEY ST JAMES–Cr 1840 from AP1.[89] Bdry: 1845 (cr EP1),[94] 1871 (cr EP2),[95] 1875 (cr EP3),[98] 1878 (cr EP11),[91] 1885 (help cr EP7).[92] Abol 1956 to help cr EP6.[93]

EP6–BERMONDSEY ST JAMES WITH CHRIST CHURCH–Cr 1956 by union EP5, EP1.[93]

EP7–BERMONDSEY ST LUKE, ORANGE ROAD–Cr 1885 from AP1, EP5.[92] Abol 1964 pt to help cr EP9, pt to Walworth All Saints and St Stephen EP.[99]

EP8–BERMONDSEY ST MARY MAGDALEN WITH ST OLAVE AND ST JOHN–Cr 1956 by union AP1, Southwark St Olave and St John EP, pt Southwark St Mary EP.[93] Abol 1964 to help cr EP9.[99]

EP9–BERMONDSEY ST MARY MAGDALEN WITH ST OLAVE, ST JOHN AND ST LUKE–Cr 1964 by union EP8, pt EP7.[99]

EP10–BERMONDSEY ST PAUL–Cr 1846 from AP1.[90] Abol 1956 pt to help cr Southwark St Saviour with All Hallows EP, pt to Southwark St Stephen EP.[93]

EP11–SOUTH BERMONDSEY–Cr 1878 from EP6.[91] Bdry: 1888 (help cr Camberwell St Bartholomew EP).[100]

BETCHWORTH

AP *LG* Seq 4. Civ bdry: 1933 (cr Brockham CP).[4] *Parl* Seq 4. *Eccl* Ewell RDn (until 1858), S-E Stoke RDn (1858–79), Reig. RDn (1879–*). Eccl bdry: 1848 (cr Brockham Green EP),[101] 1971.[102]

BISLEY

AP *LG* Seq 3. Civ bdry: 1933.[4] *Parl* Seq 10. *Eccl* Seq 9. Eccl bdry: 1959.[103]

BLACKHEATH AND CHILWORTH

EP Cr 1937 from Wonersh AP, Shalford AP, St Martha AP.[78] Guildf. RDn.

BLENHEIM GROVE

EP Cr 1872 from Camberwell AP.[104] Camberw. RDn. Bdry: 1905.[105] Now called 'Camberwell All Saints'.

BLETCHINGLEY

AP Incl Horne (sep par 1705[106]). *LG* Bletchingley Bor, Seq 6. Addtl civ bdry alt: 1894,[107] 1933,[4] 1956.[108] *Parl* Bletchingley Parl Bor (1295–1832), Seq 2 thereafter. *Eccl* Seq 19. Addtl eccl bdry alt: 1870 (help cr Outwood EP),[109] 1890.[110]

BLINDLEY HEATH

EP Cr 1842 from Godstone AP.[15] Ewell RDn (1842–58), S-E Ewell RDn (1858–71), Godst. RDn (1871–*). Bdry: 1866 (help cr Felbridge EP).[63]

GREAT BOOKHAM

AP *LG* Effingham Hd, Epsom PLU, RSD, RD (1894–1933), Leath. UD (1933–74). Civ bdry: 1833,[21] 1933.[4] *Parl* Seq 8. *Eccl* Seq 1. Eccl bdry: 1860 (cr Ranmore EP).[111]

LITTLE BOOKHAM

AP Organisation as for Great Bookham.

BOTLEYS AND LYNE

EP Cr 1849 from Chertsey AP.[15] Stoke RDn (1849–58), N-W Stoke RDn (1858–71), Emly RDn (1871–1946), Chert. RDn (1946–*).

BOURNE

EP Cr 1875 from Farnham[113] AP.[112] Farn. RDn (1878–*). Bdry: 1957.[114]

BOWLING GREEN

Ex-par place, sep CP 1858.[115] *LG* Guildf. PLU, MB, USD. Abol 1883 ent to Guildford Holy Trinity AP.[116] *Parl* Guildf. Parl Bor (1867–85).

BRAMLEY

Chap in Shalford AP, sep civ identity early, sep EP 1847.[117] *LG* Seq 1. Civ bdry: 1883,[21] 1884,[118] 1933,[4] 1933.[22] *Parl* Seq 16. *Eccl* Stoke RDn (1847–58), Guildf. RDn (1858–1928), Cranl. RDn (1928–*). Eccl bdry: 1863 (help cr Grafham EP).[90]

BRIXTON

The following have 'Brixton' in their names. Insofar as any existed at a given time: *Eccl* Swk. RDn (until 1871), Clap. RDn (1871–1935), Brix. & Kenn. RDn (1935–47), Clap. & Brix. RDn (1947–*).

EP1–BRIXTON ST MATTHEW–Cr 1825 from Lambeth AP.[119] Bdry: 1848 (cr Denmark Hill EP),[120] 1853 (cr Angell Town EP),[25] 1856 (help cr Tulse Hill EP),[121] 1859 (help cr Clapham Park EP),[122] 1868 (help cr Stockwell Green EP),[123] 1869 (cr EP3),[112] 1876 (cr EP4),[124] 1877 (help cr Loughborough Park EP),[43] 1882 (cr EP2),[81] 1899 (help cr Upper Tulse Hill EP),[125] 1901,[112] 1917.[67]

EP2–BRIXTON ST PAUL–Cr 1882 from EP1.[81]

EP3–EAST BRIXTON–Cr 1869 from EP1.[112] Bdry: 1877,[126] 1877 (help cr Loughborough Park EP),[43] 1917.[67]

EP4–BRIXTON HILL–Cr 1876 from EP1.[124] Bdry: 1901.[112]

BRIXTON ROAD

EP Cr 1856 from Kennington St Mark EP.[127] Swk. RDn (1856–65), Lamb. RDn (1865–79), Kenn. RDn (1879–1935), Brix. & Kenn. RDn (1935–47), Lamb. RDn (1947–*). Bdry: 1872 (help cr Kennington St John the Divine EP),[128] 1874 (help cr Camberwell St James EP),[129] 1923.[130]

BROCKHAM

CP Cr 1933 from Betchworth AP.[4] *LG* Dork. UD. *Parl* Dork. CC (1948–*).

BROCKHAM GREEN

EP Cr 1848 from Betchworth AP.[101] Ewell RDn (1848–58), S-E Stoke RDn (1858–79), Reig. RDn (1879–*). Bdry: 1971.[131]

BUCKLAND

AP *LG* Seq 4. Civ bdry: 1883,[21] 1933.[4] *Parl* Seq 4. *Eccl* Seq 18. Eccl bdry: 1862 (help refound Sidlow Bridge EP).[132]

BURGH HEATH

EP Cr 1937 from Banstead AP, Kingswood EP.[46] Epsom RDn. Bdry: 1955 (help cr Tadworth EP, to be in Swk dioc).[133] Renamed 1967 'Tattenham Corner and Burgh Heath'.[134]

BURPHAM WITH SUTTON

EP Cr 1920 from Worplesdeon AP, Woking AP.[78]

Later usually called 'Burpham'. Guildf. RDn. Bdry: 1955.[135] Abol 1961 pt to help cr Guildford St Luke, Burpham EP, pt to Woking AP.[136]

BURSTOW

AP *LG* Seq 5. Civ bdry: 1933.[4] *Parl* Seq 6. *Eccl* Pec jurisd Archbp Canterb (Croy. RDn, until 1845), Ewell RDn (1845–58), S-E Ewell RDn (1858–60s), S-W Ewell RDn (1860s–71), Reig. RDn (1871–1901), Godst. RDn (1901–35), Reig. RDn (1935–*). Eccl bdry: 1870 (help cr Outwood EP),[109] 1881 (help cr Copthorne EP, to be in Chich dioc).[201]

BUSBRIDGE

EP Cr 1865 from Godalming AP.[137] S-W Stoke RDn (1865–78), Godalm. RDn (1878–*).

CP Cr 1933 from Godalming Rural CP, Hascombe AP.[4] *LG* Hambl. RD. *Parl* Guildf. CC (1948–*).

BYFLEET

AP *LG* Godley Hd, Chert. PLU, RSD, RD (1894–1933), Wok. UD (1933–74). Civ bdry: 1933,[4] 1936.[138] *Parl* Seq 11. *Eccl* Seq 6. Eccl bdry: 1917 (cr West Byfleet EP).[139]

WEST BYFLEET

EP Cr 1917 from Byfleet AP.[139] Wok. RDn. Bdry: 1953,[140] 1970.[19]

CAMBERLEY [ST MICHAEL]–See YORK TOWN

CAMBERLEY [ST PAUL]

EP Cr 1935 from Frimley AP, York Town EP.[141] Aldershot RDn.

CAMBERWELL

The following have 'Camberwell' in their names. Insofar as any existed at a given time: *LG* Brix. Hd, Cambw. Par (poor law purposes), Vestry (Metrop Bd Wks). Transf 1889 to London.[53] *Parl* Pt E'rn Dv (1832–67), pt East Dv (1867–85), pt Lamb. Parl Bor (1832–85), Cambw. Parl Bor, pt North Dv, pt Peckham Dv, pt Dulw. Dv (1885–1918), London thereafter. *Eccl* Swk. RDn (until 1871), Cambw. RDn (1871–*).

AP1–CAMBERWELL [ST GILES]–Eccl bdry: 1825 (cr EP5),[142] 1838 (cr EP2),[143] 1842 (cr EP3, cr Peckham St Mary Magdalen EP),[17] 1845 (help cr Herne Hill EP),[144] 1845 (cr EP1),[145] 1865 (cr East Dulwich St John the Evangelist EP),[146] 1868 (cr South Dulwich EP),[147] 1869,[112] 1872 (cr Blenheim Grove EP [now called 'Camberwell All Saints']),[104] 1884 (help cr Dulwich Common EP),[40] 1885 (help cr Peckham St Chrysostom EP),[148] 1892,[149] 1894 (cr Dulwich EP),[150] 1931,[56] 1960.[105]

–CAMBERWELL ALL SAINTS–Name commonly used for par cr 1872 as 'Blenheim Grove', qv.

EP1–CAMBERWELL CAMDEN CHAPEL–Cr 1845 from AP1.[145] Bdry: 1866 (help cr Peckham St Andrew EP),[152] 1878 (help cr EP7),[153] 1892 (help cr North Peckham EP),[17] 1960.[105]

EP2–CAMBERWELL CHRIST CHURCH–Cr 1838 from AP1.[143] Bdry: 1866 (help cr Peckham St Andrew EP),[152] 1880 (help cr Peckham St Jude EP),[154] 1888 (help cr EP4),[100] 1889.[61]

EP3–CAMBERWELL EMMANUEL–Cr 1842 from AP1.[17] Bdry: 1869,[112] 1872 (help cr Kennington St John the Divine EP),[128] 1874 (help cr EP6),[155] 1960.[105] Abol 1967 to help cr EP11.[152]

EP4–CAMBERWELL ST BARTHOLOMEW–Cr 1888 from EP2, Hatcham Park EP (Surrey, Kent), Rotherhithe All Saints EP, South Bermondsey EP.[100]

EP5–CAMBERWELL ST GEORGE–Cr 1825 from AP1.[142] Bdry: 1872 (help cr Kennington St John the Divine EP),[128] 1876 (help cr EP12),[96] 1878 (help cr EP7),[153] 1880 (help cr EP8),[34] 1883,[156] 1892 (help cr North Peckham EP),[17] 1893,[157] 1960,[105] 1972.[151]

EP6–CAMBERWELL ST JAMES–Cr 1874 from EP3, Kennington St John the Divine EP, Brixton Road EP, Herne Hill Road EP.[155] Cambw. RDn (1874–1935), Brix. & Kenn. RDn (1935–47), Clap. & Brix. RDn (1947–*). Bdry: 1924,[158] 1962.[159]

EP7–CAMBERWELL ST LUKE–Cr 1878 from EP5, EP1.[153] Bdry: 1892 (help cr North Peckham EP),[17] 1893,[157] 1960.[105]

EP8–CAMBERWELL ST MARK–Cr 1880 from EP5, Newington All Saints EP.[34] Abol 1965 to help cr EP13.[86]

EP9–CAMBERWELL ST MICHAEL AND ALL ANGELS–Cr 1922 from Kennington St John the Divine EP.[160] Kenn. RDn (1922–35), Cambw. RDn (1935–56). Abol 1956 to help cr EP10.[161]

EP10–CAMBERWELL ST MICHAEL AND ALL ANGELS WITH ALL SOULS–Cr 1956 by union EP9, Grosvenor Park EP.[161] Bdry: 1960.[105] Abol 1967 to help cr EP11.[152]

EP11–CAMBERWELL ST MICHAEL AND ALL ANGELS AND ALL SOULS WITH EMMANUEL–Cr 1967 by union EP10, EP3.[152] Cambw. RDn (1967–71), Swk. & Newing. RDn (1971–*). Bdry: 1972.[151]

EP12–CAMBERWELL ST PHILIP–Cr 1876 from EP5, Bermondsey St Anne EP.[96] Bdry: 1889.[61] Abol 1965 to help cr EP13.[86]

EP13–CAMBERWELL ST PHILIP AND ST MARK–Cr 1965 by union EP12, EP8.[86]

CAPEL

AP Chap in Dorking AP, sep par between 1291–1361.[162] *LG* Seq 8. Civ bdry: 1879,[163] 1894.[107] *Parl* Seq 14. *Eccl* Seq 10. Eccl bdry: 1848 (help cr Coldharbour EP).[62]

CARSHALTON

AP *LG* Wall. Hd, Epsom PLU, RSD (1875–83), Carsh. USD (1883–94), UD. Civ bdry: 1927,[164] 1933.[4] Transf 1965 to Gtr London (Sutton LB).[35] *Parl* E'rn Dv (1832–67), Mid Dv (1867–85), N-E'rn Dv (1885–1918), Mitcham Dv (1918–45), Carsh. Dv/CC (1945–70), Gtr London thereafter. *Eccl* Seq 14. Eccl bdry: 1884 (help cr Sutton New Town EP),[87] 1915 (help cr Coulsdon St Andrew EP),[165] 1930 (help cr St Helier EP),[88] 1932,[166] 1934 (help cr North

Dv (1918–48), E Surrey CC (1948–*). Parl bdry: 1945.[413] *Eccl* Ewell RDn (until 1858), S-E Ewell RDn (1858–71), S-W Ewell RDn (1871–79), Reig. RDn (1879–1935), Caterh. RDn (1935–*).

CHAMPION HILL

EP Cr 1881 from East Dulwich St John the Evangelist EP.[174] Dulw. RDn. Bdry: 1931.[56]

CHARLWOOD

AP *LG* Seq 4. Civ bdry: 1894,[107] 1974 (help cr Salfords and Sidlow CP).[175] *Parl* Seq 4. *Eccl* Pec jurisd Archbp Canterb (Croy. RDn, until 1845), Seq 18 thereafter.

CHEAM

AP *LG* Wall. Hd, Epsom PLU, RSD, RD (1894–1928), Sutton & Cheam UD (1928–34), MB (1934–49). Civ bdry: 1933.[4] Abol 1949 to help cr Sutton and Cheam CP.[176] *Parl* E'rn Dv (1832–67), Mid Dv (1867–1918), Epsom Dv (1918–45), Sutton & Cheam Parl Bor/BC (1945–70). *Eccl* Pec jurisd Archbp Canterb (Croy. RDn, until 1845), Seq 14 thereafter. Eccl bdry: 1906 (cr Cheam Common EP),[126] 1916 (help cr Belmont EP),[85] 1948.[177]

CHEAM COMMON

EP Cr 1906 from Cheam AP, Cuddington AP.[126] Bedd. RDn (1906–66), Sutton RDn (1966–*). Bdry: 1948,[177] 1948 (help cr Stoneleigh EP, to be in Guildf dioc).[178]

CHELSHAM

Chap in Warlingham AP, sep civ identity early, no sep eccl identity. *LG* Tandr. Hd, Godst. PLU, RSD, RD. Bdry: 1933.[4] Abol 1969 to help cr Chelsham and Farleigh CP.[44] *Parl* E'rn Dv (1832–67), East Dv (1867–85), N-E'rn Dv (1885–1918), E'rn Dv (1918–48), Reig. CC (1948–70).

Beddington EP),[83] 1965 (incl help cr Carshalton Beeches EP).[86]

CARSHALTON BEECHES

EP Cr 1965 from Carshalton AP, Wallington AP, Belmont EP, Sutton Christ Church EP.[86] Bedd. RDn (1965–66), Sutton RDn (1966–*).

CATERHAM

AP *LG* Tandr. Hd, Godst. PLU, RSD, RD (1894–99), Caterh. UD (1899–1929), Caterh. & Warlingham UD (1929–74). Civ bdry: 1929,[167] 1933.[4] *Parl* Seq 1. *Eccl* Seq 20. Eccl bdry: 1866 (help cr Caterham Valley St Luke EP),[168] 1884 (cr Caterham Valley St John the Evangelist EP).[169]

CATERHAM VALLEY ST JOHN THE EVANGELIST

EP Cr 1884 from Caterham AP.[169] Caterh. RDn. Bdry: 1910.[170]

CATERHAM VALLEY ST LUKE

EP Cr 1866 from Caterham AP, Warlingham AP, Coulsdon AP.[168] S-E Ewell RDn (1866–71), Godst. RDn (1871–79), Caterh. RDn (1879–1964). Bdry: 1885,[171] 1889 (help cr Kenley EP),[172] 1953.[173] Renamed 1964 'Whyteleafe' EP.[99]

CHALDON

AP *LG* Wall. Hd, Reig. PLU, RSD, RD (1894–1933), Caterh. & Warlingham UD (1933–74). Civ bdry: 1933.[4] *Parl* E'rn Dv (1832–67), Mid Dv (1867–85), S-E'rn Dv (1885–1918), Reig.

CHELSHAM AND FARLEIGH

CP Cr 1969 by union Chelsham CP, pt Croy. LB & AP (Gtr London).[44] *LG* Godst. RD. *Parl* E Surrey CC (1970–*).

CHERTSEY

AP Incl chap Addlestone (sep EP 1838[15]). *LG* Godley Hd, Chert. PLU, RSD, UD. Civ bdry: 1933.[4] *Parl* W'rn Dv (1832–85), N-W'rn Dv (1885–1918), Chert. Dv/CC (1918–70), Chert. & Walton CC (1970–*). *Eccl* Seq 7. Addtl eccl bdry alt: 1847 (cr Long Cross EP),[179] 1849 (cr Botley and Lyne EP).[15]

CHERTSEY CHRIST CHURCH–See LONG CROSS

CHESSINGTON

Chap in Malden AP, sep civ identity early, sep EP 1938 (earlier, 'Malden and Chessington').[170] *LG* Kingst. Hd (until 1610), Copth. Hd (from 1610), Epsom PLU, RSD, RD (1894–1933), Surbiton MB (1933–65). Civ bdry: 1884.[180] Transf 1965 to Gtr London (Kingst. upon Thames LB).[35] *Parl* W'rn Dv (1832–85), Mid Dv (1885–1918), Epsom Dv (1918–48), Kingst. upon Thames BC (1948–55), Surbiton BC (1955–70), Gtr London thereafter. *Eccl* Epsom RDn. Eccl bdry: 1965.[114]

CHIDDINGFOLD

AP Incl chap and bor Haslemere (sep civ identity early, sep EP 1869[181]). *LG* Godalm. Hd, Hambl. PLU, RSD, RD. Addtl civ bdry alt: 1884,[118] 1933.[4] *Parl* Seq 18. *Eccl* Seq 12. Addtl eccl bdry alt: 1900 (help cr Grayswood EP).[182]

CHILWORTH–See ST MARTHA

CHIPSTEAD

AP *LG* Reig. Hd, PLU, RSD, RD (1894–1933), Banstead UD (1933–74). Civ bdry: 1933.[4] *Parl* E'rn Dv (1832–67), Mid Dv (1867–85), S-E'rn Dv (1885–1918), Reig. Dv (1918–45), Carsh. Dv/CC (1945–70), Reig. CC (1970–*). *Eccl* Seq 18.

CHOBHAM

AP *LG* Seq 3. Civ bdry: 1936,[183] 1968 (cr West End CP).[184] *Parl* Seq 2. *Eccl* Guildf. RDn (until *ca* 1535), Stoke RDn (*ca* 1535–1858), N-W Stoke RDn (1858–71), Emly RDn (1871–78), Wok. RDn (1878–1956). Eccl bdry: 1868 (help cr Chobham St Saviour EP),[63] 1895 (cr Chobham Holy Trinity, West End EP).[40] Abol eccl 1956 to help cr Chobham with Valley End EP.[185]

CHOBHAM HOLY TRINITY, WEST END

EP Cr 1895 from Chobham AP.[40] Wok. RDn. Bdry: 1963 (help cr Lightwater EP).[38]

CHOBHAM ST SAVIOUR

EP Cr 1868 from Chobham AP, Windlesham AP.[63] N-W Stoke RDn (1868–71), Emly RDn (1871–78), Wok. RDn (1878–1956). Bdry: 1904.[186] Abol 1956 to help cr Chobham with Valley End EP.[185]

CHOBHAM WITH VALLEY END
EP Cr 1956 by union Chobham AP, Chobham St Saviour EP.[185] Wok. RDn.

CHURT
EP Cr 1865 from Frensham AP, Shottermill EP.[187] S-W Stoke RDn (1865–78), Farn. RDn (1878–*). Bdry: 1908 (help cr Hindhead EP).[188]

EAST CLANDON
AP *LG* Seq 7. *Parl* Seq 13. *Eccl* Guildf. RDn (until *ca* 1535), Stoke RDn (*ca* 1535–1858), Guildf. RDn (1858–71), Leath. RDn (1871–78), Guildf. RDn (1878–*).

WEST CLANDON
AP *LG* Seq 7. Civ bdry: 1933.[4] *Parl* Seq 13. *Eccl* Seq 3.

CLAPHAM
The following have 'Clapham' in their names. Insofar as any existed at a given time: *LG* Brix. Hd, Wandsw. & Clap. PLU, Wandsw. Dist (Metrop Bd Wks). Transf 1889 to London.[53] *Parl* E'rn Dv (1832–67), East Dv (1867–85), Batt. & Clap. Parl Bor, Clap. Dv (1885–1918), London thereafter. *Eccl* Swk. RDn (until 1871), Clap. RDn (1871–1947), Clap. & Brix. RDn (1947–*).

AP1–CLAPHAM [HOLY TRINITY]–Eccl bdry: 1843 (cr EP4),[189] 1854 (cr EP3),[190] 1861 (cr EP5),[191] 1862 (cr EP1),[131] 1884 (help cr Balham Hill EP),[41] 1892,[192] 1907,[89] 1913 (help cr EP2),[136] 1920 (cr EP6).[193]

EP1–CLAPHAM CHRIST CHURCH–Cr 1862 from AP1.[131] Bdry: 1907.[89]

EP2–CLAPHAM THE HOLY SPIRIT–Cr 1913 from AP1, EP3.[136]

EP3–CLAPHAM ST JAMES–Cr 1854 from AP1.[190] Bdry: 1859 (help cr EP8),[122] 1892,[192] 1905 (help cr EP9),[194] 1913 (help cr EP2).[136]

EP4–CLAPHAM ST JOHN–Cr 1843 from AP1.[189] Bdry: 1907,[89] 1950.[195]

EP5–CLAPHAM ST PAUL–Cr 1861 from AP1.[191] Bdry: 1906 (help cr Battersea St Bartholomew EP),[68] 1907.[89]

EP6–CLAPHAM ST PETER–Cr 1920 from AP1.[193]

EP7–CLAPHAM COMMON–Cr 1895 from Battersea AP, Battersea St Philip EP.[77] Batt. RDn (1895–1935), Clap. RDn (1935–47), Batt. RDn (1947–*). Bdry: 1956.[47]

EP8–CLAPHAM PARK ALL SAINTS–Cr 1859 from EP3, Brixton St Matthew EP.[122] Bdry: 1905 (help cr EP9),[194] 1906.[196]

EP9–CLAPHAM PARK ST STEPHEN–Cr 1905 from Streatham St Mary EP, EP8, EP3.[194] Clap. RDn (1905–47), Streath. RDn (1947–58), Streath. & Mitcham RDn (1958–66), Streath. RDn (1966–*).

CLAYGATE
EP Cr 1840 from Thames Ditton EP.[15] Ewell RDn (1840–58), N-E Ewell RDn (1858–71), Emly RDn (1871–*). Bdry: 1913 (help cr Oxshott EP).[197]

COBHAM
AP *LG* Elmbr. Hd, Epsom PLU, RSD, RD (1894–1933), Esher UD (1933–74). Civ bdry: 1933.[4] *Parl* Seq 7. *Eccl* Ewell RDn (until 1858), N-E Stoke RDn (1858–71), Leath. RDn (1871–*). Eccl bdry: 1913 (help cr Oxshott EP),[197] 1954.[198]

COLDHARBOUR
EP Cr 1848 from Capel AP, Dorking AP, Ockley AP, Wotton AP, Holmwood EP.[62] Stoke RDn (1848–58), S-E Stoke RDn (1858–78), Dork. RDn (1878–*).

COMPTON
AP *LG* Godalm. Hd, Guildf. PLU, RSD, RD. Civ bdry: 1933.[4] *Parl* Seq 16. *Eccl* Seq 13.

COOMBE
CP Cr 1894 from the pt of Kingston upon Thames AP not in Kingst. upon Thames MB.[28] *LG* Kingst. PLU, RD (1894–95), The Maldens & Coombe UD (1895–1936), Malden & Coombe MB (1936–65). Bdry: 1895,[199] 1933.[200] Transf 1965 to Gtr London (Kingst. upon Thames LB).[35] *Parl* Kingst. upon Thames Parl Bor (1918–48), Wimb. BC (1948–55), Kingst. upon Thames BC (1955–70), Gtr London thereafter.

COPTHORNE
EP Cr 1881 from Crawley Down EP (Sussex), Worth AP (Sussex), Burstow AP (Surrey), Horne EP (Surrey), to be ent in Chich dioc.[201] See main entry in Sussex.

COULSDON
AP *LG* Wall. Hd, Croy. PLU, RSD, RD (1894–1915), Coulsdon & Purley UD (1915–65). Civ bdry: 1915,[79] 1933 (incl loses pt to Croy CB and AP).[4] Transf 1965 to Gtr London (Croy. LB).[35] *Parl* E'rn Dv (1832–67), Mid Dv (1867–85), N-E'rn Dv (1885–1918), E'rn Dv (1918–48), E Surrey CC (1948–70), Gtr London thereafter. *Eccl* Ewell RDn (until *ca* 1535), Swk. RDn (*ca* 1535–1858), S-W Ewell RDn (1858–71), Bedd. RDn (1871–79), Caterh. RDn (1879–*). Eccl bdry: 1866 (help cr Catherham Valley St Luke EP),[168] 1884 (help cr Purley Christ Church EP),[12] 1885,[171] 1889 (help cr Kenley EP),[172] 1890,[109] 1911 (help cr Purley St Mark, Woodcote EP),[81] 1915 (help cr Coulsdon St Andrew EP),[165] 1925 (help cr Riddlesdown EP),[202] 1925,[82] 1953,[173] 1960,[203] 1966 (cr Purley St Barnabas EP).[351]

COULSDON ST ANDREW
EP Cr 1915 from Beddington AP, Coulsdon AP, Woodmansterne AP, Carshalton AP, Purley St Mark, Woodcote EP.[165] Catherh. RDn. Bdry: 1925,[82] 1961 (help cr Purley St Swithun EP).[204]

CRANLEIGH
AP *LG* Seq 1. Civ bdry: 1883,[21] 1884,[118] 1933,[4] 1933.[22] *Parl* Seq 16. *Eccl* Seq 2. Eccl bdry: 1878 (help cr Holmbury EP).[6]

CROWHURST
AP *LG* Seq 6. *Parl* Seq 2. *Eccl* Seq 19.

CROYDON

The following have 'Croydon' in their names. Insofar as any existed at a given time: *LG* Wall. Hd, Croy. PLU, USD (ent 1875–83, pt 1883–94), pt Croy. RSD (1883–94), Croy. MB (1883–88), CB (1888–1965). Transf 1965 to Gtr London (Croy. LB).[35] *Parl* E'rn Dv (1832–67), East Dv (1867–85), Croy. Parl Bor (1885–1918), pt Croy. South Parl Bor (1918–48), pt Croy. North Parl Bor/BC (1918–55), pt Croy. East BC (1948–55), pt Croy. West BC (1948–55), pt Croy. North East BC (1955–70), pt Croy. North West BC (1955–70), pt Croy. South BC (1955–70), Gtr London thereafter. Parl bdry: 1945.[413] *Eccl* Pec jurisd Archbp Canterb (Croy. RDn, until 1845), Croy. RDn (1873–*).

AP1–CROYDON [ST JOHN THE BAPTIST]–Civ bdry: 1883,[205] 1925,[206] 1925 (gains ent Addington AP),[7] 1933,[4] 1936.[207] Eccl bdry: 1845 (cr Norwood All Saints EP),[17] 1846 (cr Shirley EP),[148] 1853 (cr EP1, EP9, EP12),[208] 1861 (help cr EP3),[209] 1866 (cr EP7),[210] 1904,[17] 1930,[13] 1939.[64]

EP1–CROYDON CHRIST CHURCH, BROAD GREEN–Cr 1853 from AP1.[208] Bdry: 1912 (cr Norbury St Philip EP),[211] 1924 (cr Thornton Heath St Jude EP),[141] 1930.[13]

EP2–CROYDON HOLY TRINITY–Cr 1867 from EP12.[89] Bdry: 1927,[212] 1930.[213] Sometimes called 'Selhurst'.

EP3–CROYDON ST ANDREW–Cr 1861 from EP9, AP1.[209] Bdry: 1904,[17] 1930.[13]

EP4–CROYDON ST AUGUSTINE–Cr 1885 from EP9, Sanderstead AP.[72] Bdry: 1896 (help cr EP11),[214] 1904,[17] 1925 (help cr Sanderstead St Mary EP, to be in Swk dioc).[82]

EP5–CROYDON ST LUKE, WOODSIDE–Cr 1872 from EP12.[215] Bdry: 1922 (help cr Addiscombe St Mildred EP),[14] 1927 (help cr EP6),[216] 1962.[151]

EP6–CROYDON ST MARTIN–Cr 1927 from EP12, EP5.[216] Bdry: 1930.[217]

EP7–CROYDON ST MATTHEW–Cr 1866 from AP1.[210] Bdry: 1882,[218] 1927,[212] 1930.[217]

EP8–CROYDON ST MICHAEL AND ALL ANGELS–Cr 1871 from EP12.[219] Bdry: 1930.[13]

EP9–CROYDON ST PETER, SOUTH END–Cr 1853 from AP1.[208] Bdry: 1861 (help cr EP3),[209] 1884 (help cr Purley Christ Church EP),[12] 1885 (help cr EP4),[72] 1896 (help cr EP11),[214] 1904,[17] 1930,[13] 1934 (help cr Selsdon EP).[8]

EP10–CROYDON ST SAVIOUR–Cr 1867 from EP12.[89] Bdry: 1871 (help cr Thornton Heath St Paul EP),[220] 1907 (cr Norbury St Stephen EP),[221] 1930.[213]

EP11–SOUTH CROYDON–Cr 1896 from EP9, EP4.[214]

EP12–CROYDON COMMON–Cr 1853 from AP1.[208] Bdry: 1867 (cr EP2, EP10),[89] 1871 (cr EP8),[219] 1872 (cr EP5),[215] 1879 (cr Addiscombe St Mary Magdalene EP),[12] 1882,[218] 1927 (help cr EP6),[216] 1927.[212]

CUDDINGTON

AP *LG* Copth. Hd, Epsom PLU, RSD, RD (1894–1933), UD (1933–34), Epsom & Ewell UD (1934–37), MB (1937–74). Civ bdry: 1933.[4] *Parl* Seq 8. Parl bdry: 1945.[413] *Eccl* Seq 16. Eccl bdry: 1906 (help cr Cheam Common EP),[126] 1931 (help cr Nork EP),[45] 1948 (help cr Stoneleigh EP),[178] 1948 (incl help cr Ewell St Francis of Assisi, Ruxley Lane EP),[177] 1949.[216]

DENMARK HILL

EP Cr 1848 from Brixton St Matthew EP.[120] Swk. RDn (1848–71), Cambw. RDn (1871–79), Dulw. RDn (1879–1956). Bdry: 1868 (help cr Herne Hill Road EP).[85] Abol 1956 to help cr Ruskin Park St Saviour with St Matthew EP.[222]

DEPTFORD ST PAUL

CP/EP cr 1730 from the Surrey pt (Hatcham, in Brix. Hd) and from pt of the Kent pt (Blackheath Hd) of Deptford St Nicholas AP.[240] *LG* Greenwich PLU, Dist (Metrop Bd Wks). Transf 1889 to London.[53] *Parl* Greenwich Parl Bor (1832–85), Deptford Parl Bor (1885–1918), London thereafter. *Eccl* See main entry in Kent. Hatcham cr sep EP 1845 as 'Hatcham St James',[96] qv. Eccl bdry affecting Surrey pt: 1851[127]; for addtl EPs cr from the Kent pt, see main entry in Kent. Abol eccl 1921 to help cr Deptford St Paul with St Mark, qv in Kent.

DEPTFORD ST NICHOLAS

AP Pt Kent (Blackheath Hd), pt Surrey (Hatcham, in Brix. Hd). In 1730, Deptford St Paul CP/EP cr from the Surrey pt and pt of the Kent pt of this par, which thereafter was ent Kent.[240] See main entry in Kent.

LONG DITTON

AP *LG* Kingst. Hd, PLU, RSD, RD (1894–95), Esher & The Dittons UD (1895–1933), Esher UD (1933–74). Civ bdry: 1895 (cr Tolworth CP),[223] 1933.[4] *Parl* E'rn Dv (1832–67), Mid Dv (1867–85), Kingst. Dv (1885–1918), Chert. Dv (1918–45), Epsom Dv (1945–48), Esher CC (1948–*). *Eccl* Ewell RDn (until 1858), N-E Ewell RDn (1858–79), Bedd. RDn (1879–1909), Kingst. RDn (1909–*). Eccl bdry: 1876 (help cr Surbiton St Matthew EP),[224] 1964.[137]

THAMES DITTON

Chap in Kingston upon Thames AP, sep par 1769.[225] *LG* Pt Elmbr. Hd, pt Kingst. Hd, Kingst. PLU, RSD, RD (1894–95), Esher & The Dittons UD (1895–1933), Esher UD (1933–74). *Parl* Seq 19. *Eccl* Ewell RDn (1769–1858), N-E Ewell RDn (1858–71), Kingst. RDn (1871–78), Emly RDn (1878–*). Eccl bdry: 1840 (cr Claygate EP),[15] 1934 (cr Weston EP).[226]

DOCKENFIELD

Tg in Frensham AP (ex-par otherwise), situated in Hants and sep CP 1866[32] in Hants (Alton Hd), transf 1895 to Surrey.[227] *LG* Farn. PLU, RSD, sep RD in Hants (1894–95), Farn. RD

(1895–1933), Hambl. RD (1933–74). *Parl* Hants 1867–1918, Farn. Dv/CC (1918–*).

DORKING

AP Incl chap Capel (sep par between 1291–1361[162]), chap Holmwood (sep EP 1839,[15] sep CP 1933 [from Dorking Rural CP][11]). *LG* Wotton Hd, Dork. PLU, pt Dork. USD, pt Dork. RSD, Dork. UD. Addtl civ bdry alt: 1879,[229] 1894 (loses the pt not in the USD to cr Dorking Rural CP).[228] Addtl eccl bdry alt: 1848 (help cr Coldharbour EP),[62] 1852 (cr Westcott EP),[231] 1857 (cr Dorking St Paul EP),[232] 1860 (help cr Ranmore EP).[111]

DORKING RURAL

CP Cr 1894 from the pt of Dorking AP not in Dork. USD.[28] *LG* Dork. PLU, RD. Bdry: 1928.[230] Abol 1933 pt to help cr Milton CP, pt to Wotton AP, pt to help cr Holmwood CP.[4] *Parl* Reig. Dv (1918–48).

DORKING ST PAUL

EP Cr 1857 from Dorking AP.[232] Stoke RDn (1857–58), S-E Stoke RDn (1858–78), Dork. RDn (1878–*).

DORMANS LAND

EP Cr 1885 from Lingfield AP.[148] Godst. RDn. Bdry: 1921.[73]

DULWICH

The following have 'Dulwich' in their names. Insofar as any existed at a given time: *Eccl* Swk. RDn (until 1871), Cambw. RDn (1871–79), Dulw. RDn (1879–*).

EP1–DULWICH–Cr 1894 from Camberwell AP.[150] Bdry: 1899 (help cr EP5),[233] 1902.[234]

EP2–EAST DULWICH ST CLEMENT–Cr 1866 from EP3, EP8.[235] Bdry: 1902.[104]

EP3–EAST DULWICH ST JOHN THE EVANGELIST–Cr 1865 from Camberwell AP.[146] Bdry: 1866 (help cr EP2),[235] 1881 (cr Champion Hill EP),[174] 1884 (help cr EP8),[40] 1902,[234] 1931.[56]

EP4–SOUTH DULWICH–Cr 1868 from Camberwell AP.[147] Bdry: 1884 (help cr EP8),[40] 1899 (help cr EP5),[233] 1900.[236]

EP5–WEST DULWICH ALL SAINTS–Cr 1899 from Tulse Hill EP, Norwood EP, EP7, EP4, EP1.[233] Abol 1966 to help cr EP6.[133]

EP6–WEST DULWICH ALL SAINTS AND EMMANUEL–Cr 1966 by union EP5, EP7.[133] Dulw. RDn (1966), Streath. RDn (1966–*).

EP7–WEST DULWICH EMMANUEL–Cr 1878 from Norwood EP.[211] Clap. RDn (1878–79), Dulw. RDn (1879–1966). Bdry: 1899 (help cr EP5),[233] 1900.[236] Abol 1966 to help cr EP6.[133]

EP8–DULWICH COMMON–Cr 1884 from EP4, Camberwell AP, EP3.[40] Bdry: 1902,[17] 1921.[237]

DUNSFOLD

AP *LG* Seq 1. Civ bdry: 1883,[21] 1884.[118] *Parl* Seq 16. *Eccl* Seq 4. Eccl bdry: 1863 (help cr Grafham EP).[90]

EARLSFIELD ST ANDREW

EP Cr 1890 from Summers Town EP, Wandsworth St Anne EP.[12] Wandsw. RDn. Bdry: 1938 (cr Earlsfield St John the Divine EP),[133] 1939.[238]

EARLSFIELD ST JOHN THE DIVINE

EP Cr 1938 from Earlsfield St Andrew EP.[133] Wandsw. RDn.

EFFINGHAM

AP *LG* Effingham Hd, Dork. PLU, RSD, RD (1894–1933), Guildf. RD (1933–74). Civ bdry: 1934.[239] *Parl* Seq 9. *Eccl* Seq 1. Eccl bdry: 1860 (help cr Ranmore EP).[111]

EGHAM

AP Incl chap Thorpe (sep par 15th cent[241]). *LG* Godley Hd, Windsor PLU, RSD, Egham RD (1894–1906), Egham UD (1906–74). *Parl* Seq 10. *Eccl* Seq 7. Addtl eccl bdry alt: 1929 (cr Englefield Green EP),[242] 1930 (cr Egham Hythe EP).[160]

EGHAM CHRIST CHURCH–See VIRGINIA WATER

EGHAM HYTHE

EP Cr 1930 from Egham AP.[160] Emly RDn (1930–46), Chert. RDn (1946–*).

ELSTEAD

AP Chap in Farnham AP, sep par 1539.[217] *LG* Farn. Hd, Hambl. PLU, RSD, RD. Civ bdry: 1933 (help cr Hindhead and Churt CP, help cr Tilford CP).[4] *Parl* W'rn Dv (1832–85), S-W'rn Dv (1885–1918), Guildf. Dv (1918–48), Farn. CC (1948–*). *Eccl* Seq 12.

ENGLEFIELD GREEN

EP Cr 1929 from Egham AP.[242] Emly RDn (1929–46), Chert. RDn (1946–*).

EPSOM

AP *LG* Copth. Hd, Epsom PLU, USD, UD (1894–1934), Epsom & Ewell UD (1934–37), MB (1937–74). Civ bdry: 1933.[4] *Parl* Seq 8. *Eccl* Seq 16. Eccl bdry: 1874 (cr Epsom Common EP).[243]

EPSOM ST BARNABAS

EP Cr 1919 from Epsom Common EP.[244] Leath. RDn (1919–28), Epsom RDn (1928–*). Bdry: 1951.[244]

EPSOM COMMON

EP Cr 1874 from Epsom AP.[243] N-E Ewell RDn (1874–78), Leath. RDn (1878–1928), Epsom RDn (1928–*). Bdry: 1919 (cr Epsom St Barnabas EP),[135] 1951.[244]

ESHER

AP *LG* Pt Elmbr. Hd, pt Kingst. Hd, Kingst. PLU, RSD, RD (1894–95), Esher & The Dittons UD (1895–1933), Esher UD (1933–74). Civ bdry: 1957,[245] 1970 (exchanges pts with Twickenham AP, Gtr London).[246] *Parl* Seq 19. *Eccl* Ewell RDn (until 1858), N-E Ewell RDn (1858–71), Emly RDn (1871–*).

EWELL

AP Incl lbty Kingswood (detached pt in Reig. Hd, sep EP 1833 [from Ewell AP, Banstead AP],[47] sep CP 1866[32]). *LG* Pt Reig. Hd (Kingswood, until 1866), Copth. Hd (pt until 1866, ent from 1866), Epsom PLU, RSD, RD (1894–1933), UD (1933–34), Epsom & Ewell UD (1934–37), MB (1937–74). Addtl civ bdry alt: 1933.[4] *Parl*

Seq 8. *Eccl* Seq 16. Addtl eccl bdry alt: 1931 (help cr Nork EP),[45] 1948 (incl help cr Ewell St Francis of Assisi, Ruxley Lane EP),[177] 1948 (help cr Stoneleigh EP),[178] 1951,[244] 1952 (cr West Ewell EP).[247]

EWELL ST FRANCIS OF ASSISI, RUXLEY LANE
EP Cr 1948 from Cuddington AP, Ewell AP, Surbiton St Matthew EP.[177] Epsom RDn.

WEST EWELL
EP Cr 1952 from Ewell AP.[247] Epsom RDn.

EWHURST
AP *LG* Seq 1. Civ bdry: 1884,[118] 1933,[4] 1933.[22] *Parl* Seq 16. *Eccl* Seq 2. Eccl bdry: 1878 (help cr Holmbury EP).[6]

FARLEIGH
AP *LG* Tandr. Hd, Godst. PLU, RSD, RD (1894–1933), Coulsdon & Purley UD (1933–65). Civ bdry: 1936 (loses pt to Croy. CB and AP).[207] Transf 1965 to Gtr London (Croy. LB).[35] *Parl* E'rn Dv (1832–67), East Dv (1867–85), N-E'rn Dv (1885–1918), E'rn Dv (1918–48), E Surrey CC (1948–70), Gtr London thereafter. Parl bdry: 1945.[413] *Eccl* Seq 17. Eccl bdry: 1960.[135]

FARNCOMBE
EP Cr 1849 from Godalming AP.[15] Stoke RDn (1849–58), S-W Stoke RDn (1858–78), Godalm. RDn (1878–*).

FARNHAM
AP Incl chaps Elstead, Seale (each sep par 1539[217]), chap Frensham (sep par by 1553[217]), chap Bentley (in Hants, at times such as 1573 in Surrey for some purposes,[248] sep civ identity early in Hants, sep EP 1727[15]). *LG* Farn. Hd, Bor, PLU, pt Farn. USD (extended pt 1884–94), pt Farn. RSD (reduced pt 1884–94), Farn. UD. Addtl civ bdry alt: 1894 (loses the pt not in the USD to cr Farnham Rural CP),[28] 1902,[249] 1914,[250] 1924,[251] 1934.[4] *Parl* Seq 15. *Eccl* Guildf. RDn (until 1876[263]), Farn. RDn (1878–*). Addtl eccl bdry alt: 1840 (cr Wrecclesham EP),[113] 1845 (cr Hale EP),[252] 1865 (cr Tilford EP).[187]

FARNHAM RURAL
CP Cr 1894 from the pt of Farnham AP not in Farn. USD[28] and from ent Waverley CP.[253] *LG* Farn. PLU, RD. Bdry: 1902,[249] 1914,[250] 1924.[251] Abol 1933 pt to help cr Tilford CP, pt to Farnham AP.[4] *Parl* Farn. Dv (1918–48).

FELBRIDGE
EP Cr 1866 from Blindley Heath EP, East Grinstead AP (Sussex).[63] S-E Ewell RDn (1866–71), Godst. RDn (1871–*).
CP Cr 1953 from Godstone AP, Horne CP, Tandridge AP.[254] *LG* Godst. RD. *Parl* E Surrey CC (1970–*).

FETCHAM
AP *LG* Copth. Hd, Epsom PLU, RSD, RD (1894–1933), Leath. UD (1933–74). Civ bdry: 1883,[21] 1884,[180] 1933.[4] *Parl* Seq 8. *Eccl* Seq 1.

FRENSHAM
AP Chap in Farnham AP, sep par by 1553.[217] *LG* Pt Surrey (Farn. Hd), pt Hants (Dockenfield hmlt, Alton Hd, sep civ identity 1866[32] in Hants so this par ent Surrey thereafter). *LG* Farn. PLU, RSD, RD (1894–1933), Hambl. RD (1933–74). Addtl civ bdry alt: 1894 (cr Shottermill CP),[255] 1933 (incl help cr Hindhead and Churt EP).[4] *Parl* Seq 15. *Eccl* Seq 11. Eccl bdry: 1846 (cr Shottermill EP),[15] 1865 (help cr Churt EP),[187] 1871 (help cr Rowledge EP in Hants).[113]

FRIMLEY
Chap in Ash AP, sep EP 1813, refounded 1866,[33] sep CP 1866.[32] *LG* Godley Hd, Farn. PLU, RSD, Frimley UD. Civ bdry: 1936.[183] *Parl* Dv (1867–85), N-W'rn Dv (1885–1918), Farn. Dv (1918–48), Wok. CC (1948–70), N W Surrey CC (1970–*). *Eccl* Stoke RDn (1813–58), N-W Stoke RDn (1858–78), Wok. RDn (1878–1928), Aldershot RDn (1928–*). Eccl bdry: 1935 (help cr Camberley EP),[141] 1948 (cr Frimley Green EP).[256]

FRIMLEY GREEN
EP Cr 1948 from Frimley AP.[256] Aldershot RDn.

GATTON
AP *LG* Reig. Hd, Gatton Bor, Reig. PLU, RSD, (1894–1933), MB (1933–74). Civ bdry: 1899.[257] *Parl* Gatton Parl Bor (1450–1832), Seq 5 thereafter. *Eccl* Seq 18. Eccl bdry: 1899 (help cr South Mertsham EP),[258] 1956.[178]

GIPSEY HILL
EP Cr 1867 from Norwood EP.[259] Swk. RDn (1867–71), Clap. RDn (1871–79), Dulw. RDn (1879–1966), Streath. RDn (1966–*).

GODALMING
AP Incl chap Shackleford (sep EP 1866,[130] sep CP 1933 from Godalming Rural CP[4]). *LG* Godalm. Hd, Guildf. PLU, pt Godalm. Bor, pt Godalm. USD (extended pt 1892–94), pt Guildf. RSD (reduced pt 1892–94), Godalm. MB (pt 1835–94, ent 1894–1974). Addtl civ bdry alt: 1894 (loses the pt not in the MB to cr Godalming Rural CP),[28] 1929,[260] 1934.[4] *Parl* Seq 18. *Eccl* Seq 12. Addtl eccl bdry alt: 1849 (cr Farncombe EP),[15] 1865 (cr Busbridge EP).[137]

GODALMING RURAL
CP Cr 1894 from the pt of Godalming AP not in Godalm. MB.[28] *LG* Guildf. PLU, RD. Bdry: 1897,[261] 1929.[260] Abol 1933 pt to help cr Shackleford CP, pt to help cr Busbridge CP, pt to Godalming AP, pt to Artington CP, pt to Hascombe AP.[4] *Parl* Guildf. Dv (1918–48).

GODSTONE
AP *LG* Seq 6. Civ bdry: 1933,[4] 1953 (incl help cr Felbridge CP),[254] 1956.[108] *Parl* Seq 2. *Eccl* Seq 19. Eccl bdry: 1842 (cr Blindley Heath EP),[15] 1960.[135]

GRAFHAM
EP Cr 1863 from Dunsfold AP, Bramley EP.[90] Guildf. RDn (1863–1928), Cranl. RDn (1928–*).

GRAYSHOTT
EP Cr 1901 from Headley AP (Hants), Churt EP, Shottermill EP.[264] Godalm. RDn (1901–28),

Farn. RDn (1928–*). Bdry: 1908 (help cr Hindhead EP),[188] 1946.[265]

GRAYSWOOD

EP Cr 1900 from Witley EP, Chiddingfold AP, Haslemere EP, Thursley EP.[182] Godalm. RDn.

GROSVENOR PARK

EP Cr 1871 from Walworth St Peter EP.[45] Newing. RDn (1871–1947), Swk. & Newing. RDn (1947–56). Abol 1956 to help cr Camberwell St Michael and All Angels with All Souls EP.[161]

GUILDFORD

The following have 'Guildford' in their names. Insofar as any existed at a given time: *LG* Guildf. Bor/MB, PLU, USD. *Parl* Guildf. Parl Bor (1295–1885), S-W'rn Dv (1885–1918), Guildf. Dv/CC (1918–*). *Eccl* Guildf. RDn (until *ca* 1535), Stoke RDn (*ca* 1535–1858), Guildf. RDn (1858–*).

CP1–GUILDFORD–Cr 1908 by union CP2, AP1, AP2, AP3, CP3, Stoke CP.[266] Bdry: 1922,[30] 1933,[4] 1954.[267]

EP1–GUILDFORD ALL SAINTS–Renaming 1968 of Onslow Village EP.[268]

CP2–GUILDFORD CHRISTCHURCH–Renaming 1904 of Stoke Within CP.[269] Abol 1908 to help cr CP1.[266]

EP2–GUILDFORD CHRISTCHURCH–Cr 1936 from Stoke next Guildford AP.[270] Bdry: 1955.[135]

CP3–GUILDFORD THE FRIARY–Ex-par place, sep CP 1858,[115] eccl abol 1893 to help cr Stoke next Guildford St Saviour EP.[84] Abol 1908 to help cr CP1.[266]

AP1–GUILDFORD HOLY TRINITY–Civ bdry: 1880,[271] 1883 (gains ent Bowling Green CP).[116] Abol civ 1908 to help cr CP1.[266]

EP3–GUILDFORD ST FRANCIS, WESTBOROUGH–Cr 1958 from Worplesdon AP, AP3, Stoke next Guildford AP, Stoke next Guildford Emmanuel, Stoughton EP.[272]

EP4–GUILDFORD ST LUKE, BURPHAM–Cr 1961 from Burhpam with Sutton EP.[136] Bdry: 1972 (help cr Stoke Hill EP).[14]

AP2–GUILDFORD ST MARY–Civ bdry: 1894 (gains the pt of Shalford AP in Guildf. MB).[107] Abol civ 1908 to help cr CP1.[266]

AP3–GUILDFORD ST NICOLAS–*LG* Pt Guildf. Bor/MB (until 1894), pt Godalm. Hd (tg Artington), pt Guildf. USD (1886–94), Guildf. RSD (ent 1875–86, pt 1886–94). Civ bdry: 1894 (loses the pt not in the MB to cr Artington CP),[28] 1904.[29] Abol civ 1908 to help cr CP1.[266] *Parl* Pt Guildf. Parl Bor (1295–1885), pt W'rn Dv (1832–85), S-W'rn Dv (1885–1918). Eccl bdry: 1933 (cr Onslow Village EP),[45] 1956,[74] 1958,[273] 1958 (help cr EP3).[272]

EP5–GUILDFORD ST SAVIOUR–Renaming 1968 of Stoke next Guildford St Saviour EP.[126]

HACKBRIDGE AND NORTH BEDDINGTON

EP Renaming 1969 of North Beddington EP.[84] Sutton RDn.

HALE

EP Cr 1845 from Farnham AP.[252] Guildf. RDn (1845–78[263]), Farn. RDn (1878–*). Bdry: 1866 (help cr Tongham EP).[274]

HAM

Area in Kingston upon Thames AP, sep EP 1834,[275] sep CP 1866.[32] Eccl often called 'Ham St Andrew', civ called 'Ham with Hatch' in 19th cent, 'Ham' more commonly thereafter. *LG* Kingst. Hd, PLU, pt Ham Common USD, pt Kingst. USD, Ham UD (1894–1933), Richm. MB (1933–65). Civ bdry: 1894 (loses the pt in Kingst. USD to help cr Coombe CP),[107] 1933,[278] 1958.[279] Transf 1965 to Gtr London (Richm. upon Thames LB).[35] *Parl* Mid Dv (1867–85), Kingst. Dv (1885–1918), Richm. Parl Bor/ BC (1918–70), Gtr London thereafter. *Eccl* Ewell RDn (1834–58), N-E Ewell RDn (1858–61), N-W Ewell RDn (1861–71), Kingst. RDn (1871–*). Eccl bdry:1847 (help cr Robin Hood EP),[276] 1966 (cr Ham St Richard EP).[277]

HAM ST ANDREW–See prev entry

HAM ST RICHARD

EP Cr 1966 from Ham EP.[277] Richm. & Barnes RDn.

HAM WITH HATCH–See HAM

HAMBLEDON

AP *LG* Seq 2. Civ bdry: 1884,[118] 1897,[261] 1933.[22] *Parl* Seq 16. *Eccl* Seq 12.

HASCOMBE

AP *LG* Seq 1. Civ bdry: 1884,[118] 1933 (incl help cr Busbridge CP),[4] 1933.[22] *Parl* Seq 16. *Eccl* Guildf. RDn (until *ca* 1535), Stoke RDn (*ca* 1535–1858), Guildf. RDn (1858–78), Godalm. RDn (1878–*).

HASLEMERE

Chap in Chiddingfold AP, sep civ identity early, sep EP 1869.[181] *LG* Godalm. Hd, Haslemere Bor, Hambl. PLU, RSD, RD (1894–1913), Haslemere UD (1913–74). Civ bdry: 1884,[118] 1894,[107] 1933 (gains ent Shottermill CP).[4] *Parl* Haslemere Parl Bor (1584–1832), Seq 18 thereafter. *Eccl* S-W Stoke RDn (1869–78), Godalm. RDn (1878–*). Eccl bdry: 1900 (help cr Grayswood EP).[182]

HATCHAM ST JAMES

EP Cr 1845 from the Surrey pt of Deptford St Paul EP (Kent, Surrey).

HATCHAM ST JAMES

EP Cr 1845 from the Surrey pt of Deptford St Paul EP (Kent, Surrey).[96] Dartford RDn (1845–86), Greenw. RDn (1886–1954), thereafter as for Hatcham St Catherine. Bdry: 1851 (incl gains area in anc Kent),[127] 1872 (cr Hatcham Park EP),[281] 1886 (help cr Rotherhithe St Katherine EP).[281]

HATCHAM PARK

EP Cr 1872 from Hatcham St James EP (Surrey, Kent) and thus this par also pt Surrey, pt Kent.[281] RDns as for Hatcham St James, from 1872. Bdry: 1888 (help cr Camberwell St Bartholomew EP),[100] 1891 (help cr Hatcham

St Catherine EP),[187] 1960.[105]

NEW HAW

EP Cr 1972 from Addlestone EP.[14] Chert. RDn.

HEADLEY

AP *LG* Copth. Hd, Reig. PLU (1836–79), Epsom PLU (1879–1930), Reig. RSD (1875–79), Epsom RSD (1879–94), Epsom RD (1894–1933), Dork. & Horley RD (1933–74). *Parl* W'rn Dv (1832–85), Mid Dv (1885–1918), Epsom Dv (1918–45), Reig. Dv (1945–48), Dork. CC (1948–*). *Eccl* Ewell RDn (until 1858), W Ewell RDn (1858–71), Leath. RDn (1871–1928), Farn. RDn (1928–*). Eccl bdry: 1971.[131]

HERNE HILL

EP Cr 1845 from Camberwell AP, Lambeth AP.[144] Swk. RDn (1845–71), Cambw. RDn (1871–79), Dulw. RDn (1879–*). Bdry: 1877,[126] 1902.[234]

HERNE HILL ROAD

EP Cr 1868 from Denmark Hill EP.[85] Lamb. RDn (1868–71), Cambw. RDn (1871–79), Dulw. RDn (1879–1956). Bdry: 1874 (help cr Camberwell St James EP).[155] Abol 1956 to help cr Ruskin Park St Saviour with St Matthew EP.[222]

HERSHAM

EP Cr 1849, refounded 1851 from Walton-on-Thames AP.[282] Stoke RDn (1849–58), N-E Stoke RDn (1858–78), Emly RDn (1858–*). Bdry: 1869 (help cr Oatlands EP).[283]

HINCHLEY WOOD

EP Cr 1953 from Weston EP.[284] Emly RDn.

HINDHEAD

EP Cr 1908 from Churt EP, Grayshott EP.[188] Farn. RDn.

HINDHEAD AND CHURT

CP Cr 1933 from Elstead AP, Frensham AP.[4] *LG* Haslemere UD. *Parl* Farn. CC (1948–*).

HOLMBURY

EP Cr 1878 from Shere AP, Abinger AP, Ewhurst AP, Cranleigh AP, Ockley AP, Ockham AP.[6] Dork. RDn.

HOLMWOOD

Area in Dorking AP, sep EP 1839,[15] sep CP 1933 (from Dorking Rural CP).[4] *LG* Dork. & Horley RD. *Parl* Dork. CC (1948–*). *Eccl* Stoke RDn (1839–58), S-E Stoke RDn (1858–78), Dork. RDn (1878–*). Eccl bdry: 1848 (help cr Coldharbour EP),[62] 1874 (cr North Holmwood EP).[36]

NORTH HOLMWOOD

EP Cr 1874 from Holmwood EP.[36] S-E Stoke RDn (1874–78), Dork. RDn (1878–*).

HOOK

Hmlt in Kingston upon Thames AP, sep EP 1852,[15] sep CP 1866.[32] *LG* Kingst. Hd, PLU, RSD, RD (1894–95), Surbiton UD (1895–1936), MB (1936–65). Civ bdry: 1933.[4] Transf 1965 to Gtr London (Kingst. upon Thames LB).[35] *Parl* Mid Dv (1867–85), Kingst. Dv (1885–1918), Kingst. upon Thames Parl Bor/BC (1918–55), Surbiton BC (1955–70), Gtr London thereafter. *Eccl* Ewell RDn (1852–58), N-E Ewell RDn (1858–80), Kingst. RDn (1880–*). Bdry: 1963,[285] 1964,[137] 1965.[114]

HORLEY

AP *LG* Seq 4. Civ bdry: 1894,[107] 1933,[4] 1974 (help cr Salfords and Sidlow CP).[175] *Parl* Seq 4. *Eccl* Seq 18. Eccl bdry: 1861 (cr Sidlow Bridge EP, refounded 1862 with pts from other pars, qv),[132] 1870 (help cr Outwood EP),[109] 1952 (help cr Salfords EP).[286]

HORNE

Chap in Bletchingley AP, sep par 1705.[106] *LG* Seq 6. Civ bdry: 1894,[107] 1953 (incl help cr Felbridge CP).[254] *Parl* Seq 2. *Eccl* Seq 19. Eccl bdry: 1870 (help cr Outwood EP),[109] 1881 (help cr Copthorne EP, to be in Chich dioc).[201]

HORSELL

AP Chap in Woking AP, sep par from Dissolution in 16th cent.[287] *LG* Godley Hd, Chert. PLU, RSD, Wok. UD. Civ bdry: 1901,[288] 1933.[4] *Parl* W'rn Dv (1832–85), N-W'rn Dv (1885–1918), Farn. Dv (1918–48), Wok. CC (1948–*). *Eccl* Guildf. RDn (until *ca* 1535), Stoke RDn (*ca* 1535–1858), N-E Stoke RDn (1858–78), Wok. RDn (1878–94), Chert. RDn (1894–1907), Wok. RDn (1907–*).

EAST HORSLEY

AP *LG* Seq 7. *Parl* Seq 13. *Eccl* Pec jurisd Archbp Canterb (until 1845), Seq 1 thereafter.

WEST HORSLEY

AP *LG* Seq 7. Civ bdry: 1883.[289] *Parl* Seq 13. *Eccl* Seq 1.

HORSLEYDOWN ST JOHN–See SOUTHWARK ST JOHN HORSLEYDOWN

HORSLEYDOWN ST MARK

EP Cr 1844 from Southwark St John Horsleydown EP.[290] Swk. RDn. Abol 1885 ent to Southwark St John Horsleydown EP.[72]

HURST GREEN

EP Cr 1963 from Oxted AP, Limpsfield AP.[291] Godst. RDn. Bdry: 1969.[14]

KENLEY

EP Cr 1889 from Coulsdon AP, Caterham Valley St Luke EP.[172] Caterh. RDn. Bdry: 1890,[109] 1925 (help cr Riddlesdown EP),[202] 1953.[173]

KENNINGTON ST JAMES

EP Cr 1875 from Kennington St Mark EP.[113] Lamb. RDn (1875–79), Kenn. RDn (1879–1921). Taken down after cr UB 1921 with Lambeth St Mary EP (commonly called 'Lambeth St Mary the Less') and incorporated into it.[292]

KENNINGTON ST JOHN THE DIVINE

EP Cr 1872 from Camberwell Emmanuel EP, Camberwell St George EP, Brixton Road EP.[128] Lamb. RDn (1872–79), Kenn. RDn (1879–1935), Brix. & Kenn. RDn (1935–47), Lamb. RDn (1947–*). Bdry: 1874 (help cr Camberwell St James EP),[155] 1883,[156] 1922 (cr Camberwell St Michael and All Angels EP),[160] 1923,[130] 1962.[159]

KENNINGTON ST MARK

EP Cr 1825 from Lambeth AP.[293] Swk. RDn (1825–65), Lamb. RDn (1865–79), thereafter as for prev par. Bdry: 1851 (cr South Kennington EP),[16] 1856 (cr Brixton Road EP),[127] 1861,[55] 1868 (help cr Stockwell Green EP),[123] 1869 (cr South Lambeth St Anne EP),[161] 1875 (cr Kennington St James EP),[112] 1923,[130] 1937,[256] 1960.[105]

SOUTH KENNINGTON
EP Cr 1851 from Kennington St Mark EP.[16] Swk. RDn (1851–65), Lamb. RDn (1865–79), Kenn. RDn (1879–1935), Clap. RDn (1935–47), Lamb. RDn (1947–50). Bdry: 1874 (cr South Lambeth All Saints EP).[36] Abol 1950 pt to help cr South Lambeth All Saints and St Barnabas EP, pt to Clapham St John EP.[295]

KENNINGTON CROSS
EP Cr 1901 from Lambeth AP.[281] Lamb. RDn. Bdry: 1922,[296] 1966.[297] Abol 1974 to help cr North Lambeth EP.[298]

KENNINGTON PARK
EP Cr 1874 from Newington St Paul EP.[299] Newing. RDn (1874–1947), Swk. & Newing. RDn (1947–*). Bdry: 1960.[105]

KENT TOWN
EP Cr 1856 from East Molesey EP.[218] Ewell RDn (1856–58), N-E Ewell RDn (858–71), Kingst. RDn (1871–78), Emly RDn (1878–*). Sometimes 'East Molesey St Paul'.

KEW
Private chapel from 1522 in Kingston upon Thames AP, sep civ identity early, sep EP 1715,[15] eccl united 1769 with Petersham chap in Kingston upon Thames AP to cr Kew with Petersham EP,[300] the latter divided 1891 into the 2 EPs of Kew, Petersham.[301] *LG* Kingst. Hd, Richm. PLU, RSD (1875–92), MB (1892–1965), USD (1892– 94). Transf 1965 to Gtr London (Richm. upon Thames LB).[35] *Parl* E'rn Dv (1832–67), Mid Dv (1867–85), Kingst. Dv (1885–1918), Richm. Parl Bor/BC (1918–70), Gtr London thereafter. *Eccl* Seq 15.

KEW WITH PETERSHAM
EP Cr 1769 by union Kew EP, chap Petersham of Kingston upon Thames AP.[300] Ewell RDn. Divided 1891 into 2 EPs of Kew, Petersham.[301]

KINGSTON HILL
EP Cr 1881 from Norbiton EP.[302] Kingst. RDn. Bdry: 1890 (cr Kingston upon Thames St Luke EP).[96]

KINGSTON UPON THAMES
AP Incl chap Kew (private chapel from 1522, sep civ identity early, sep EP 1714[15]), chap Thames Ditton (sep par 1769[225]), chap East Molesley (sep par 1769[225]), chap Petersham (eccl severed 1769 to help cr Kew with Petersham EP[225]), area of Ham (sep EP 1834,[302] sep CP 1866[32] [called 'Ham with Hatch' in 19th cent, more commonly 'Ham' later]), hmlt Hook (sep EP 1852,[15] sep CP 1866[32]), area of Surbiton (sep EP 1895 as 'Surbiton St Mark',[309] sep CP 1894 [the area in Surbiton USD][28]), chap Richmond [anc, 'Sheen'], sep civ identity early, eccl united with Kingston upon Thames 1769 to cr Kingston upon Thames with Sheen EP,[225] divided 1849 into 2 EPs of Kingston upon Thames, Richmond.[307] *LG* Kingst. Hd, PLU, pt Kingst. Bor, Kingst. MB (pt 1835–94, ent 1894–1965), pt Kingst. USD, pt Kingst. RSD, pt Surbiton USD, pt New Malden USD. Addtl civ bdry alt: 1894 (loses the pt in Surbiton USD to cr Surbiton CP, the pt in New Malden USD to cr New Malden CP, the pt in the RSD to help cr Coombe CP).[28] Transf 1965 to Gtr London (Kingst. upon Thames LB).[35] *Parl* Kingst. upon Thames Parl Bor (1311–73 irregularly), E'rn Dv (1832–67), Mid Dv (1867–85), Kingst. Dv (1885–1918), Kingst. upon Thames Parl Bor/BC (1918–70), Gtr London thereafter. *Eccl* Ewell RDn (until 1858), N-E Ewell RDn (1858–61), N-W Ewell RDn (1861–71), Kingst. RDn (1871–*). Addtl eccl bdry alt: 1841 (cr Norbiton EP),[305] 1847 (help cr Robin Hood EP),[276] 1873 (help cr Kingston upon Thames St John the Evangelist EP).[306]

KINGSTON UPON THAMES ST JOHN THE EVANGELIST
EP Cr 1873 from Kingston upon Thames AP, Norbiton EP.[306] Kingst. RDn.

KINGSTON UPON THAMES ST LUKE
EP Cr 1890 from Kingston Hill EP.[96] Kingst. RDn.

KINGSTON UPON THAMES WITH SHEEN
EP Cr 1769 by union Kingston upon Thames AP, chap Sheen [Richmond] in that par,[225] divided 1849 into 2 EPs of Kingston upon Thames, Richmond.[307] Ewell RDn. Bdry: 1839 (cr Richmond Holy Trinity EP).[360]

KINGSTON VALE
EP Renaming 1970 of Robin Hood EP.[308] Kingst. RDn.

KINGSWOOD
Lbty in Ewell AP, sep CP 1866,[32] sep EP 1833 (from Ewell AP, Banstead AP).[47] *LG* Reig. Hd, PLU, RSD, RD (1894–1933), Banstead UD (1933–74). *Parl* Mid Dv (1867–85), S-E'rn Dv (1885–1918), Reig. Dv (1918–45), Carsh. Dv/CC (1945–70), Reig. CC (1970–*). *Eccl* Ewell RDn (1833–58), S-W Ewell RDn (1858–79), Reig. RDn (1879–*). Eccl bdry: 1937 (help cr Burgh Heath EP),[46] 1937,[34] 1955 (help cr Tadworth EP).[133]

KNAPHILL
EP Cr 1967 from Woking St John the Baptist EP.[309] Wok. RDn.

LALEHAM
CP/EP transf to Surrey 1965 from Middx.[35] *LG* Staines UD. *Parl* Spelth. BC (1970–*).

LAMBETH
The following have 'Lambeth' in their names. Insofar as any existed at a given time: *LG* Brix. Hd, Lamb. Par (poor law purposes), Vestry (Metrop Bd Wks). Transf 1889 to London.[53] *Parl* Pt E'rn Dv (1832–67), pt East Dv (1867–85), pt Lamb. Parl Bor (1832–85), Lamb. Parl Bor, in 4 Dvs of North, Kenn., Brix., and Norwood (1885–1918), London thereafter. *Eccl* Swk. RDn (until 1865), Lamb. RDn (1865–*).

AP1–LAMBETH [ST MARY]–Eccl bdry: 1825 (cr Norwood St Luke EP),[203] 1825 (cr Brixton St Matthew EP),[119] 1841 (cr EP3),[310] 1842 (cr EP8),[311] 1845 (help cr Herne Hill EP),[144] 1845 (cr Stockwell EP),[387] 1846 (cr Kennington St Mark EP),[293] 1864 (cr EP10),[312] 1869 (cr EP2),[114] 1887,[110] 1901 (cr Kennington Cross EP).[281] Abol eccl 1951 to help cr EP9.[156]

EP1–LAMBETH ALL SAINTS, LOWER MARSH–Cr 1845, refounded 1847 from EP6.[313] Pulled down *ca* 1910 for expansion of Waterloo Station, to help cr EP7.[314]

EP2–LAMBETH EMMANUEL–Cr 1869 from AP1.[114] Abol 1951 pt to help cr EP9, pt to EP8.[156]

EP3–LAMBETH HOLY TRINITY–Cr 1841 from AP1.[310] Abol 1951 to help cr EP9.[156]

EP4–LAMBETH ST ANDREW–Cr 1846 from EP6.[315] Swk. RDn (1846–65), Lamb. RDn (1865–1956). Abol 1956 pt to help cr EP5, pt to EP6.[316]

EP5–LAMBETH ST ANDREW WITH ST THOMAS–Cr 1956 by union EP11, EP4.[316]

EP6–LAMBETH ST JOHN THE EVANGELIST, WATERLOO ROAD–Cr 1825 from AP1.[203] Swk. RDn (1825–65), Lamb. RDn (1865–*ca* 1910). Bdry: 1845 (cr EP1, refounded 1847),[313] 1846 (cr EP4, EP11).[315] Abol *ca* 1910 to help cr EP7.[314]

EP7–LAMBETH ST JOHN THE EVANGELIST, WATERLOO ROAD WITH ALL SAINTS–Cr *ca* 1910 by union EP6, EP1.[314] Bdry: 1956.[316]

EP8–LAMBETH ST MARY–Cr 1842 from AP1.[311] Commonly called 'Lambeth St Mary the Less'. Bdry: 1861 (cr Vauxhall EP),[55] 1887,[110] 1921 (gains ent Kennington St James EP),[292] 1922,[296] 1951.[156] Abol 1966 ent to Kennington Cross EP.[297]

–LAMBETH ST MARY THE LESS–See EP8

EP9–LAMBETH ST MARY WITH HOLY TRINITY AND EMMANUEL–Cr 1951 by union AP1, EP3, pt EP2.[156] Renamed 1963 'St Mary-at-Lambeth'.[317]

EP10–LAMBETH ST PHILIP–Cr 1864 from AP1.[312] Abol 1974 to help cr EP12.[298]

EP11–LAMBETH ST THOMAS–Cr 1846 from EP6.[315] Abol 1956 pt to help cr EP5, pt to EP7.[316]

EP12–NORTH LAMBETH–Cr 1974 by union St Mary-at-Lambeth EP, EP10, Kennington Cross EP.[298]

EP13–SOUTH LAMBETH ALL SAINTS–Cr 1874 from South Kennington EP.[36] Lamb. RDn (1874–79), Kenn. RDn (1879–1935), Clap. RDn (1935–47), Lamb. RDn (1947–50). Abol 1950 pt to help cr EP14, pt to Clapham St John EP.[195]

EP14–SOUTH LAMBETH ALL SAINTS AND ST BARNABAS–Cr 1950 by union pt EP13, pt South Kennington EP.[195] Bdry: 1959.[214]

EP15–SOUTH LAMBETH ST ANNE–Cr 1869 from Kennington St Mark EP.[161] Lamb. RDn (1869–79), Kenn. RDn (1879–1935), Brix. & Kenn. RDn (1935–47), Lamb. RDn (1947–*). Bdry: 1937,[256] 1959,[214] 1966.[294]

EP16–SOUTH LAMBETH ST STEPHEN–Cr 1861 from Stockwell EP.[318] Clap. RDn (1861–79), Kenn. RDn (1879–1935), Brix. & Kenn. RDn (1935–47), Lamb. RDn (1947–*).

LAVENDER HILL

EP Cr 1875 from Battersea St Philip EP.[76] Streath. RDn (1875–79), Batt. RDn (1879–*). Bdry: 1956.[64]

LEATHERHEAD

AP *LG* Copth. Hd, Epsom PLU, RSD, Leath. UD. Civ bdry: 1884.[180] *Parl* Seq 8. *Eccl* Ewell RDn (until 1858), W Ewell RDn (1858–71), Leath. RDn (1871–*).

LEIGH

AP *LG* Seq 4. *Parl* Seq 4. *Eccl* Guildf. RDn (until *ca* 1535), Stoke RDn (*ca* 1535–1858), S-E Stoke RDn (1858–71), S-W Ewell RDn (1871–79), Reig. RDn (1879–*). Eccl bdry: 1862 (help refound Sidlow Bridge EP [cr 1861]).[132]

LIGHTWATER

EP Cr 1963 from Bagshot EP, Windlesham AP, Chobham Holy Trinity, West End EP.[38] Wok. RDn. Bdry: 1973.[39]

LIMPSFIELD

AP *LG* Seq 6. Civ bdry: 1956.[108] *Parl* Seq 2. *Eccl* Ewell RDn (until 1858), S-E Ewell RDn (1858–71), Godst. RDn (1871–1973). Eccl bdry: 1963 (help cr Hurst Green EP),[291] 1969.[14] Abol eccl 1973 to help cr Limpsfield and Titsey EP.[319]

LIMPSFIELD AND TITSEY

EP Cr 1973 by union Limpsfield AP, Titsey AP.[319] Godst. RDn.

LINGFIELD

AP *LG* Tandr. Hd, E Grinstead PLU (1836–97), RSD, Godst. PLU (1897–1930), RD. *Parl* Seq 2. *Eccl* Seq 19. Eccl bdry: 1885 (cr Dormans Land EP),[148] 1921.[73]

LITTLETON

AP Transf to Surrey 1965 from Middx.[35] *LG* Sunbury on Thames UD. *Parl* Spelth. BC (1970–*).

LONG CROSS

EP Cr 1847 from Chertsey AP.[179] Stoke RDn (1847–58), N-W Stoke RDn (1858–71), Emly RDn (1871–1946), Chert. RDn (1946–*). Sometimes 'Chertsey Christ Church'.

LOUGHBOROUGH PARK

EP Cr 1877 from Angell Town EP, East Brixton EP, Brixton St Matthew EP.[43] Clap. RDn. Abol 1905 ent to Angell Town EP.[27]

MALDEN

AP Incl chap Chessington (sep civ identity early, sep EP 1938[170] so that this par eccl 'Malden with Chessington' until 1938, qv, and 'Malden' thereafter). *LG* Kingst. Hd, PLU, RSD, RD (1894–95), The Maldens & Coombe UD (1895–1936), Malden & Coombe MB (1936–65). Addtl civ bdry alt: 1884,[180] 1933.[4] Transf

1965 to Gtr London (Kingst. upon Thames LB).[35] *Parl* E'rn Dv (1832–67), Mid Dv (1867–85), Kingst. Dv (1885–1918), Kingst. upon Thames Parl Bor (1918–48), Wimb. BC (1948–55), Kingst. upon Thames BC (1955–70), Gtr London thereafter. Parl bdry: 1945.[413] *Eccl* Kingst. RDn (1938–*).

MALDEN ST JAMES
EP Cr 1929 from New Malden and Coombe EP, Raynes Park EP.[80] Kingst. RDn. Bdry: 1932.[311]

MALDEN WITH CHESSINGTON
AP Usual eccl spelling; for civ and civ sep chap Chessington, see 'Malden'. *Eccl* Ewell RDn (until 1858), N-E Ewell RDn (1858–71), Bedd. RDn (1871–79), Kingst. RDn (1879–1938). Divided 1938 into 2 EPs of Malden, Chessington.[170]

NEW MALDEN
CP Cr 1894 from the pt of Kingston upon Thames AP in New Malden USD.[28] *LG* Kingst. PLU, New Malden UD (1894–95), The Maldens & Coombe UD (1895–1936), Malden & Coombe MB (1936–65). Transf 1965 to Gtr London (Kingst. upon Thames LB).[35] *Parl* Kingst. upon Thames Parl Bor (1918–48), Wimb. BC (1948–55), Kingst. upon Thames BC (1955–70), Gtr London thereafter.

NEW MALDEN AND COOMBE
EP Cr 1867 from Norbiton EP.[320] N-W Ewell RDn (1867–71), Kingst. RDn (1871–*). Bdry: 1929 (help cr Malden St James EP).[80]

MERROW
AP *LG* Wok. Hd, Guildf. PLU, RSD, RD. Abol civ 1933 pt to Guildford CP, pt to West Clandon AP.[4] *Parl* W'rn Dv (1832–85), S-W'rn Dv (1885–1918), Guildf. Dv (1918–48). *Eccl* Seq 3. Eccl bdry: 1955.[135]

MERSTHAM
AP *LG* Reig. Hd, PLU, RSD, RD (1894–1933), MB (1933–74). Civ bdry: 1899,[257] 1933.[4] *Parl* Seq 5. Parl bdry: 1945.[413] *Eccl* Pec jurisd Archbp Canterb (Croy. RDn, until 1845), Seq 18 thereafter. Eccl bdry: 1899 (help cr South Merstham EP).[258]

SOUTH MERSTHAM
EP Cr 1899 from Merstham AP, Gatton AP.[258] Reig. RDn.

MERTON
AP *LG* Brix. Hd, Croy. PLU, RSD, RD (1894–1907), Merton UD (1907–13), Merton & Morden UD (1913–65). Civ bdry: 1898,[321] 1933.[4] Transf 1965 to Gtr London (Merton LB).[35] *Parl* E'rn Dv (1832–67), Mid Dv (1867–85), N-E'rn Dv (1885–1918), Wimb. Parl Bor (1918–48), Merton & Morden BC (1948–70), Gtr London thereafter. Parl bdry: 1945.[413] *Eccl* Ewell RDn (until 1858), N-E Ewell RDn (1858–79), Bedd. RDn (1879–1909), Wimb. RDn (1909–66), Merton RDn (1966–*). Eccl bdry: 1907 (cr Raynes Park EP),[322] 1928 (cr Merton St John the Divine EP),[323] 1932,[311] 1951 (help cr Merton St James EP).[324]

MERTON ST JAMES
EP Cr 1951 from Merton AP, Raynes Park EP.[324] Wimb. RDn (1951–66), Merton RDn (1966–*).

MERTON ST JOHN THE DIVINE
EP Cr 1928 from Merton AP.[323] Wimb. RDn (1928–66), Merton RDn (1966–*).

MICKLEHAM
AP *LG* Copth. Hd, Dork. PLU, RSD, RD (1894–1933), Dork. UD (1933–74). Civ bdry: 1879,[229] 1933.[4] *Parl* Seq 9. *Eccl* Ewell RDn (until 1858), S-E Stoke RDn (1858–78), Dork. RDn (1878–*). Eccl bdry: 1860 (help cr Ranmore EP).[111]

MILFORD
EP Cr 1844 from Witley AP.[177] Stoke RDn (1844–58), S-W Stoke RDn (1858–78), Godalm. RDn (1878–*).

MILTON
CP Cr 1933 from Dorking Rural CP.[4] *LG* Dork. UD. *Parl* Dork. CC (1948–*).

MITCHAM
The following have 'Mitcham' in their names. Insofar as any existed at a given time: *LG* Wall. Hd, Croy. PLU, RSD, RD (1894–1915), Mitcham UD (1915–34), MB (1934–65). Transf 1965 to Gtr London (Merton LB).[35] *Parl* E'rn Dv (1832–67), Mid Dv (1867–85), N-E'rn Dv (1885–1918), Mitcham Dv (1918–45), Parl Bor/BC (1945–70), Gtr London thereafter. *Eccl* Sep noted.

AP1–MITCHAM [ST PETER AND ST PAUL]–Civ bdry: 1901 (loses pt to Tooting Graveney AP, London),[48] 1904 (exchanges pts with Tooting Graveney AP, London),[325] 1925 (incl exchanges pts with Croy. CB and AP),[206] 1933 (incl loses pts to Croy. CB and AP),[4] 1936 (exchanges pts with Croy. CB and AP).[207] *Eccl* Ewell RDn (until 1858), N-E Ewell RDn (1858–79), Bedd. RDn (1879–1958), Streath. & Mitcham RDn (1958–66), Merton RDn (1966–*). Eccl bdry: 1875 (cr EP2),[152] 1905 (cr EP4),[326] 1934 (help cr North Beddington EP).[83]

EP1–MITCHAM THE ASCENSION, POLLARD'S HILL–Cr 1953 from EP5.[327] Streath. RDn (1953–58), thereafter as for AP1.

EP2–MITCHAM CHRIST CHURCH–Cr 1875 from AP1.[152] Wimb. RDn (1875–1966), Merton RDn (1966–*). Bdry: 1914 (cr EP3),[82] 1923 (help cr Streatham St Paul, Furzedown EP).[328]

EP3–MITCHAM ST BARNABAS–Cr 1914 from EP2.[82] Wimb. RDn (1914–58), thereafter as for AP1. Bdry: 1930 (help cr Streatham Vale EP).[13]

EP4–MITCHAM ST MARK–Cr 1905 from AP1.[326] Streath. RDn (1905–58), thereafter as for AP1. Bdry: 1929 (cr EP5),[80] 1930 (help cr Streatham Vale EP).[13]

EP5–MITCHAM ST OLAVE–Cr 1929 from EP4.[80] Bedd. RDn (1929–35), Streath. RDn (1935–58), thereafter as for AP1. Bdry: 1953 (cr EP1).[327]

EAST MOLESEY
Chap in Kingston upon Thames AP, sep par 1769.[225] *LG* Elmbr. Hd, Kingst. PLU, E Molesey USD, UD (1894–95), E & W Molesey UD (1895–1933), Esher UD (1933–74). *Parl* Seq 7. *Eccl* Ewell RDn (1769–1858), N-E Ewell RDn (1858–61), N-W Ewell RDn (1861–71), Kingst. RDn (1871–78), Emly RDn (1878–*). Eccl bdry: 1856 (cr Kent Town EP).[218]

EAST MOLESEY ST PAUL–See KENT TOWN

WEST MOLESEY
Chap in Walton-on-Thames AP, sep civ identity early, sep EP 1726.[329] *LG* Elmbr. Hd, Kingst. PLU, RSD, RD (1894–95), E & W Molesey UD (1895–1933), Esher UD (1933–74). *Parl* Seq 7. *Eccl* RDns as for East Molesey.

MORDEN
AP *LG* Wall. Hd, Croy. PLU, RSD, RD (1894–1913), Merton & Morden UD (1913–65). Civ bdry: 1933.[4] Transf 1965 to Gtr London (Merton LB).[35] *Parl* E'rn Dv (1832–67), Mid Dv (1867–85), N-E'rn Dv (1885–1918), Wimb. Parl Bor (1918–48), Merton & Morden BC (1948–70), Gtr London thereafter. *Eccl* Ewell RDn (until 1858), N-E Ewell RDn (1858–79), Bedd. RDn (1879–1966), Merton RDn (1966–*). Eccl bdry: 1930 (help cr St Helier EP),[88] 1939.[64]

MORTLAKE
Chap in Wimbledon AP, sep civ identity early, sep EP and curacy from 17th cent.[330] *LG* Brix. Hd, Richm. PLU, RSD (ent 1875–92, pt 1892–93), pt Richm. MB and USD (1892–94), pt Barnes USD (1893–94), Barnes UD (1894–1932), MB (1932–65). Civ bdry: 1894 (loses the pt in Richm. MB to cr North Sheen CP).[28] Transf 1965 to Gtr London (Richm. upon Thames LB).[35] *Parl* E'rn Dv (1832–67), Mid Dv (1867–85), Kingst. Dv (1885–1918), Richm. Parl Bor/BC (1918–70), Gtr London thereafter. *Eccl* Seq 23. Eccl bdry: 1890 (help cr Richmond St Luke EP),[109] 1894 (help cr Richmond Christ Church EP).[331]

NEWDIGATE
AP *LG* Copth. Hd, Dork. PLU, RSD, RD (1894–1933), Dork. & Horley RD (1933–74). Civ bdry: 1879,[163] 1894.[107] *Parl* Seq 14. *Eccl* Seq 10.

NEWINGTON
The following have 'Newington' in their names. Insofar as any existed at a given time: *LG* Brix. Hd, Newing. Par (poor law purposes, 1836–69), St Saviour's PLU (1869–99), Newing. St Mary Vestry (Metrop Bd Wks). Transf 1889 to London.[53] *Parl* Lamb. Parl Bor (1832–85), Newing. Parl Bor, pt West Dv, pt Walworth Dv (1885–1918), London thereafter. *Eccl* Pec jurisd Archbp Canterb (until 1845), Newing. RDn (1870–1947), Swk. & Newing. RDn (1947–*).

AP1–NEWINGTON [ST MARY]–Eccl bdry: 1827 (cr Southwark Holy Trinity EP, sometimes called 'Newington Holy Trinity'),[63] 1827 (cr Walworth Common EP),[332] 1857 (cr EP4),[63] 1860 (cr Walworth St John EP),[333] 1866 (cr EP1),[63] 1868 (cr EP3),[334] 1960.[105]

EP1–NEWINGTON ALL SAINTS–Cr 1866 from AP1.[63] Bdry: 1880 (help cr EP8).[34] Abol 1956 pt to help cr Walworth All Saints with St Stephen EP, pt to help cr Walworth The Lady Margaret with St Mary Magdalene EP.[93]

–NEWINGTON HOLY TRINITY–See SOUTHWARK HOLY TRINITY

EP2–NEWINGTON ST ANDREW–Cr 1877 from Southwark Holy Trinity EP.[93] Abol 1956 pt to Southwark Holy Trinity EP, pt to Southwark St Stephen EP.[93]

EP3–NEWINGTON ST MATTHEW–Cr 1868 from AP1.[334] Bdry: 1956.[93] Abol 1974 to help cr Southwark Holy Trinity with St Matthew EP.[335]

EP4–NEWINGTON ST PAUL–Cr 1857 from AP1.[63] Bdry: 1874 (cr Kennington Park EP),[299] 1960.[105]

NORBITON
EP Cr 1842 from Kingston upon Thames AP.[305] Ewell RDn (1842–58), N-E Ewell RDn (1858–61), N-W Ewell RDn (1861–71), Kingst. RDn (1871–*). Bdry: 1847 (help cr Robin Hood EP),[276] 1867 (cr New Malden and Coombe EP),[320] 1873 (help cr Kingston upon Thames St John the Evangelist EP),[306] 1881 (cr Kingston Hill EP).[302]

NORBURY ST OSWALD
EP Cr 1934 from Norwood EP, Thornton Heath St Paul EP.[46] Croy. RDn.

NORBURY ST PHILIP
EP Cr 1912 from Croydon Christ Church, Broad Green EP.[211] Croy. RDn.

NORBURY ST STEPHEN
EP Cr 1907 from Croydon St Saviour EP.[221] Croy. RDn. Bdry: 1930.[213]

NORK
EP Cr 1931 from Banstead AP, Ewell AP, Cuddington AP.[45] Epsom RDn.

NORMANDY
CP Cr 1955 when Ash and Normandy AP divided into 2 CPs of Ash, Normandy.[31] *LG* Guildf. RD. *Parl* Wok. CC (1970–*).

NORWOOD
The following have 'Norwood' in their names. Insofar as any existed at a given time: *Eccl* Croy. RDn (1873–*).

EP1–NORWOOD ALL SAINTS–Cr 1845 from Croydon AP.[17] Bdry: 1859 (cr EP5),[6] 1871 (help cr Thornton Heath St Paul EP),[220] 1875 (help cr EP6),[6] 1904,[235] 1934 (help cr Norbury St Oswald EP).[46]

EP2–NORWOOD ST LUKE–Cr 1825 from Lambeth AP.[203] Swk. RDn (1825–71), Clap. RDn (1871–79), Dulw. RDn (1879–1966), Streath. RDn (1966–*). Bdry: 1856 (help cr Tulse Hill EP),[121] 1867 (cr Gipsey Hill EP),[259] 1870 (help cr Streatham St Peter EP),[337] 1878 (cr West Dulwich Emmanuel EP),[211] 1899 (help cr West Dulwich All

Saints EP),[233] 1900.[236]

EP3–SOUTH NORWOOD HOLY INNOCENTS–Cr 1949 from EP5.[297]

EP4–SOUTH NORWOOD ST ALBAN–Cr 1921 from EP6.[338] Bdry: 1930,[213] 1937.[114]

EP5–SOUTH NORWOOD ST MARK–Cr 1859 from EP1.[6] Bdry: 1875 (help cr EP6),[6] 1927,[212] 1930,[213] 1937.[114]

EP6–UPPER NORWOOD–Cr 1875 from EP1, EP5, Thornton Heath St Paul EP.[6] Bdry: 1904,[235] 1930,[213] 1937.[114]

NUNHEAD ST ANTHOLIN

EP Cr 1878 from Peckham St Mary Magdalene EP.[89] Cambw. RD. Bdry: 1925.[74] Renamed 1958 'Nunhead St Antony'.[135]

NUNHEAD ST ANTONY

EP Renaming 1958 of Nunhead St Antholin EP.[135] Cambw. RDn.

NUNHEAD ST SILAS

EP Cr 1904 from Forest Hill St Augustine Honor Oak Park EP (Kent).[283] Cambw. RDn. Gains pt Surrey pars in bdry alt: 1925,[74] 1936.[340]

NUTFIELD

AP *LG* Seq 5. Civ bdry: 1894,[107] 1933.[4] *Parl* Seq 6. *Eccl* Seq 18. Eccl bdry: 1870 (help cr Outwood EP),[109] 1889 (cr Lower Nutfield EP),[341] 1910.[342]

LOWER NUTFIELD

EP Cr 1889 from Nutfield AP.[341] Reig. RDn. Bdry: 1890,[110] 1910.[342]

OATLANDS

EP Cr 1869 from Walton-on-Thames AP, Hersham EP.[283] N-E Stoke RDn (1869–71), Emly RDn (1871–*).

OCKHAM

AP *LG* Seq 7. Civ bdry: 1883,[343] 1933.[22] *Parl* Seq 13. *Eccl* Guildf. RDn (until *ca* 1535), Stoke RDn (*ca* 1535–1858), N-E Stoke RDn (1858–78), Leath. RDn (1878–1935), Wok. RDn (1935–54), Leath. RDn (1954–*). Eccl bdry: 1878 (help cr Holmbury EP),[6] 1954.[198]

OCKLEY

AP *LG* Seq 8. Civ bdry: 1879,[344] 1901.[3] *Parl* Seq 14. *Eccl* Seq 10. Eccl bdry: 1848 (help cr Coldharbour EP),[62] 1853 (help refound Okewood EP [cr 1723]),[5] 1878 (help cr Holmbury EP).[6]

OKEWOOD

EP Cr 1723 from Wotton AP,[15] refounded 1853 from Wotton AP, Abinger AP, Ockley AP.[5] Stoke RDn (1723–1858), S-E Stoke RDn (1858–78), Dork. RDn (1878–1928), Cranl. RDn (1928–*).

ONSLOW VILLAGE

EP Cr 1933 from Guildford St Nicholas EP.[45] Guildf. RDn. Renamed 1968 'Guildford All Saints'.[345]

OTTERSHAW

EP Cr 1865 from Addlestone EP.[16] N-W Stoke RDn (1865–71), Emly RDn (1871–1946), Chert. RDn (1946–*). Bdry: 1967.[18]

OUTWOOD

EP Cr 1870 from Burstow AP, Nutfield AP, Horley AP, Blechingley AP, Horne EP.[109] S-E Ewell RDn (1870–71), Godst. RDn (1871–*).

OXSHOTT

EP Cr 1913 from Stoke D'Abernon AP, Cobham AP, Claygate EP.[197] Leath. RDn.

OXTED

AP *LG* Seq 6. Civ bdry: 1933,[4] 1956.[108] *Parl* Seq 2. *Eccl* Seq 19. Eccl bdry: 1963 (help cr Hurst Green EP).[291]

PARIS GARDEN–See SOUTHWARK CHRISTCHURCH

PECKHAM

The following have 'Peckham' in their names. Insofar as any existed at a given time: *Eccl* Swk. RDn (until 1871), Cambw. RDn (1871–*).

EP1–PECKHAM ST ANDREW–Cr 1866 from Camberwell Camden Chapel EP, Camberwell Christ Church EP.[152] Bdry: 1880 (help cr EP6),[154] 1885 (help cr EP3).[148] Abol 1956 to help cr EP2.[161]

EP2–PECKHAM ST ANDREW WITH ALL SAINTS–Cr 1956 by union EP1, EP10.[161] Bdry: 1960 (incl help cr EP4).[105]

EP3–PECKHAM ST CHRYSOSTOM–Cr 1885 from Camberwell AP, EP1, EP8.[148] Abol 1960 pt to help cr EP4, pt to EP8, pt to Camberwell St Luke EP.[105]

EP4–PECKHAM ST CHRYSOSTOM AND ST JUDE–Cr 1960 by union pt EP2, pt EP3, pt EP6, pt EP7.[105] Renamed 1966 as EP5.[309]

EP5–PECKHAM ST JOHN–Renaming 1966 of EP4.[309]

EP6–PECKHAM ST JUDE–Cr 1880 from EP1, EP8, Camberwell Christ Church EP.[154] Abol 1960 pt to help cr EP4, pt to Hatcham Park EP.[105]

EP7–PECKHAM ST MARK–Cr 1884 from EP8.[169] Abol 1960 pt to help cr EP4, pt to EP8.[105]

EP8–PECKHAM ST MARY MAGDALEN–Cr 1842 from Camberwell AP.[17] Bdry: 1878 (cr Nunhead St Antholin EP),[89] 1884 (cr EP7),[169] 1885 (help cr EP2),[148] 1960.[105]

EP9–NORTH PECKHAM–Cr 1892 from Camberwell St George EP, Camberwell St Luke EP, Camberwell Camden Chapel EP.[17] Abol 1956 to help cr EP2.[161]

PENGE

The following have 'Penge' in their names. Insofar as any existed at a given time: *LG* Brix. Hd, Croy. PLU, RSD, RD. Transf 1899 to Kent as Penge UD.[53] *Parl* East Dv (1867–85), Cambw. Parl Bor, Dulw. Dv (1885–1918), Kent thereafter. *Eccl* Swk. RDn (until 1871), Streath. RDn (1871–7), Cambw. RDn (187 –79), Dulw. RDn (1879–1905), thereafter in Roch dioc, W Dartford RDn (1905–55), Beckenham RDn (1955–*).

CP1–PENGE–Detached hmlt of Battersea AP, sep CP 1866,[32] sep EP 1851 as EP3, qv.

EP1–PENGE CHRIST CHURCH–Cr 1886 from EP3, EP2.[346] Bdry: 1952,[347] 1956.[348]

EP2–PENGE HOLY TRINITY–Cr 1873 from EP3, EP4.[194] Bdry: 1886 (help cr EP1),[346]

1936,[349] 1952.[347]

EP3–PENGE ST JOHN–Cr 1851 from Battersea AP[52]; for civ see CP1. Bdry: 1867 (cr EP4),[211] 1873 (help cr EP2),[194] 1880,[71] 1886 (help cr EP1),[346] 1952,[347] 1956.[348]

EP4–PENGE ST PAUL–Cr 1867 from EP3.[211] Bdry: 1873 (help cr EP2),[194] 1880,[71] 1936.[349]

PEPER HAROW

AP *LG* Seq 2. *Parl* Seq 18. *Eccl* Seq 12.

PETERSHAM

Chap in Kingston upon Thames AP, sep civ identity early, eccl severed 1769 to help cr Kew with Petersham EP,[225] qv, the latter divided 1891 into the 2 EPs of Kew, Petersham.[301] *LG* Kingst. Hd, Richm. PLU, RSD (1875–92), USD (1892–94), MB (1892–1965). Transf 1965 to Gtr London (Richm. upon Thames LB).[35] *Parl* E'rn Dv (1832–67), Mid Dv (1867–85), Kingst. Dv (1885–1918), Richm. Parl Bor/BC (1918–70), Gtr London thereafter. *Eccl* Richm. RDn (1891–1922), Richm. & Barnes RDn (1922–*).

PIRBRIGHT

Chap in Woking AP, sep par from Dissolution in 16th cent.[350] *LG* Seq 7. *Parl* W'rn Dv (1832–85), N-W'rn Dv (1885–1918), Farn. Dv (1918–48), Wok. CC (1948–*). *Eccl* Seq 9.

PURLEY CHRIST CHURCH

EP Cr 1884 from Coulsdon AP, Beddington AP, Sanderstead AP, Croydon St Peter, South End EP.[14] Catherh. RDn. Bdry: 1925 (help cr Riddlesdown EP),[202] 1925,[82] 1960,[203] 1961,[123] 1961 (help cr Purley St Swithun EP).[204]

PURLEY ST BARNABAS

EP Cr 1966 from Coulsdon AP.[351] Caterh. RDn.

PURLEY ST MARK, WOODCOTE

EP Cr 1911 from Beddington AP, Coulsdon AP.[81] Catherh. RDn. Bdry: 1915 (help cr Coulsdon St Andrew EP),[165] 1925,[82] 1961,[123] 1961 (help cr Purley St Swithun EP).[204]

PURLEY ST SWITHUN

EP Cr 1961 from Purley St Mark, Woodcote EP, Coulsdon St Andrew EP, Purley Christ Church EP.[204] Caterh. RDn.

PUTNEY

Chap in Wimbledon AP, sep civ identity early, sep EP and curacy from 17th cent.[352] *LG* Brix. Hd, Wandsw. & Clap. PLU, Wandsw. Dist (Metrop Bd Wks). Transf 1889 to London.[53] *Parl* E'rn Dv (1832–67), Mid Dv (1867–85), Wands. Parl Bor (1885–1918), London thereafter. *Eccl* Pec jurisd Archbp Canterb (until 1845), Barnes & Hammersmith RDn (1861–72), Barnes RDn (1872–1922), Richm. & Barnes RDn (1922–66), Wandsw. RDn (1966–*). Eccl bdry: 1845 (cr Roehampton EP),[353] 1923 (help cr Putney St Margaret EP),[178] 1953.[354]

PUTNEY ST MARGARET

EP Cr 1923 from Putney AP, Roehampton AP.[178] Richm. & Barnes RDn (1923–66), Wandsw. RDn (1966–*).

PUTTENHAM

AP *LG* Godalm. Hd, Guildf. PLU, RSD, RD. *Parl* Seq 16. *Eccl* Seq 13.

PYRFORD

Chap in Woking AP, transf before 1631 to be chap in Wisley AP,[355] sep civ identity early, no sep eccl identity. *LG* Godley Hd, Chert. PLU, RSD, RD (1894–1933), Wok. UD (1933–74). Bdry: 1933 (help cr Ripley CP).[4] *Parl* Seq 11.

RANMORE

EP Cr 1860 from Great Bookham AP, Little Bookham AP, Effingham AP, Dorking AP, Mickleham AP.[111] W Ewell RDn (1860–71), Leath. RDn (1871–78), Dork. RDn (1878–*).

RAYNES PARK

EP Cr 1907 from Merton AP.[322] Bedd. RDn (1907–09), Wimb. RDn (1909–66), Merton RDn (1966–*). Bdry: 1929 (help cr Malden St James EP),[80] 1951 (help cr Merton St James EP).[324]

REDHILL HOLY TRINITY

EP Cr 1907 from Redhill St Matthew EP.[356] Reig. RDn. Bdry: 1956.[178]

REDHILL ST MATTHEW

EP Cr 1867 from Redhill St John the Evangelist EP (Hants), Reigate St Mark EP, Reigate AP.[209] S-E Ewell RDn (1867–71), S-W Ewell RDn (1871–79), Reig. RDn (1879–*). Bdry: 1907 (cr Redhill Holy Trinity EP).[356]

REIGATE

The following have 'Reigate' in their names. Insofar as any existed at a given time: *LG* Reig. Hd, PLU, MB (1863–1974), USD (Bor sep noted). *Parl* Sep noted. *Eccl* Seq 18.

AP1–REIGATE [ST MARY MAGDALENE]–*LG* Pt in Reig. Bor (cr 1866 'Reigate Borough' CP[32]), pt not in the Bor (cr 'Reigate Foreign' CP[32]), both sep rated for poor so that this par has no sep civ identity after 1866, yet both the CPs in the MB. *Parl* Pt (area of Reigate Borough) Reig. Parl Bor (1295–1867), pt E'rn Dv (1832–67). Eccl bdry: 1860 (cr EP2),[357] 1862 (help refound Sidlow Bridge EP [cr 1861]),[132] 1867 (help cr Redhill St Matthew EP),[209] 1871 (cr EP1).[45]

CP1–REIGATE–Renaming 1899 of CP2.[358] Bdry: 1933.[4] *Parl* Reig. CC (1918–*).

CP1–REIGATE BOROUGH–The pt of AP1 in Reig. Bor, sep CP 1866.[32] Bdry: 1894 (gains ent CP3).[359] Renamed 1899 as CP1.[358] *Parl* Mid Dv (1867–85), S-E'rn Dv (1885–1918).

CP3–REIGATE FOREIGN–The pt of AP1 not in Reig. Bor, sep CP 1866,[32] but incl in Reig. MB. Abol 1894 ent to CP2.[359] *Parl* As for CP2.

EP1–REIGATE ST LUKE, SOUTH PARK–Cr 1871 from AP1.[45] Bdry: 1939,[127] 1954.[256]

EP2–REIGATE ST MARK–Cr 1860 from AP1.[357] Bdry: 1867 (help cr Redhill St Matthew EP).[209]

RICHMOND

The following have 'Richmond' in their names. Insofar as any existed a given time: *LG* Kingst. Hd, Richm. PLU, USD, MB (1890–1965).

Transf 1965 to Gtr London (Richm. upon Thames LB).[35] *Parl* E'rn Dv (1832–67), Mid Dv (1867–85), Kingst. Dv (1885–1918), Richm. Parl Bor/BC (1918–70), Gtr London thereafter. *Eccl* Seq 15.

CP1/EP1–RICHMOND [ST MARY MAGDALENE]–Chap in Kingston upon Thames AP, anc called 'Sheen', sep civ identity early, eccl united with Kingston upon Thames AP (at time some other chaps severed) to cr Kingston upon Thames with Sheen EP,[225] the latter divided 1849 into 2 EPs of Kingston upon Thames, Richmond.[307] Eccl bdry: 1876,[361] 1876.[96]

EP2–RICHMOND CHRIST CHURCH–Cr 1894 from EP4, Mortlake EP.[331] Bdry: 1951.[178]

EP3–RICHMOND HOLY TRINITY–Cr 1870 from EP4.[362] Bdry: 1876,[361] 1951.[178]

EP4–RICHMOND ST JOHN–Cr 1838 from EP1.[360] Bdry: 1852,[363] 1870 (cr EP3),[362] 1876,[361] 1876,[96] 1890 (help cr EP5),[109] 1894 (help cr EP2).[331]

EP5–RICHMOND ST LUKE–Cr 1890 from EP4, Mortlake EP.[109] Bdry: 1930 (cr North Sheen EP).[364]

RIDDLESDOWN

EP Cr 1925 from Coulsdon AP, Purley Christ Church EP, Kenley EP.[202] Catherh. RDn.

RIPLEY

Chap in Send and Ripley AP, sep EP 1878,[41] sep CP 1933 when Send and Ripley divided into 2 CPs of Send, Ripley,[22] gaining at same time pt Pyrford CP.[4] *LG* Guildf. RD. *Parl* Dork. CC (1948–*). *Eccl* Wok. RDn.

ROBIN HOOD

EP Cr 1847 from Kingston upon Thames AP, Ham EP, Norbiton EP.[276] Ewell RDn (1847–58), N-E Ewell RDn (1858–61), N-W Ewell RDn (1861–71), Kingst. RDn (1871–1970). Bdry: 1953.[354] Renamed 1970 'Kingston Vale'.[308]

ROEHAMPTON

EP Cr 1845 from Putney EP.[353] Pec jurisd Archbp Canterb (1845), Barnes & Hammersmith RDn (1861–72), Barnes RDn (1872–1922), Richm. & Barnes RDn (1922–66), Wandsw. RDn (1966–*). Bdry: 1923 (help cr Putney St Margaret EP),[178] 1953,[354] 1969.[365]

ROTHERHITHE

The following have 'Rotherhithe' in their names. Insofar as any existed at a given time: *LG* Brix. Hd, Rotherhithe Par (poor law purposes, 1836–69), St Olave PLU (1869–99), Rotherhithe Vestry (Metrop Bd Wks). Transf 1889 to London.[53] *Parl* Swk. Parl Bor (1832–85), Swk. Parl Bor, Rotherhithe Dv (1885–1918) London thereafter. *Eccl* Swk. RDn (until 1909), Berm. RDn (1909–*).

AP1–ROTHERHITHE [ST MARY]–Eccl bdry: 1840 (cr EP2),[15] 1840 (cr EP1, refounded 1843),[366] 1841 (cr EP3, refounded 1843),[367] 1873 (help cr EP4).[136] Abol eccl 1952 to help cr EP7.[368]

EP1–ROTHERHITHE ALL SAINTS–Cr 1840, refounded 1843 from AP1.[366] Bdry: 1873 (help cr EP4),[136] 1886 (help cr EP5),[281] 1888 (help cr Camberwell St Bartholomew EP).[100] Abol 1952 pt to help cr EP7, pt to EP4.[368]

EP2–ROTHERHITHE CHRIST CHURCH–Cr 1840 from AP1.[15] Abol 1950 to help cr Bermondsey St Crispin with Christ Church EP.[75]

EP3–ROTHERHITHE HOLY TRINITY–Cr 1841, refounded 1843 from AP1.[367]

EP4–ROTHERHITHE ST BARNABAS–Cr 1873 from AP1, EP1.[136] Bdry: 1886 (help cr EP5),[281] 1952.[368] Abol 1956 pt to help cr EP6, pt to help cr EP7.[368]

EP5–ROTHERHITHE ST KATHERINE–Cr 1886 from EP4, EP1, Hatcham St James EP.[281] Bdry: 1952.[368] Abol 1956 to help cr EP6.[369]

EP6–ROTHERHITHE ST KATHERINE WITH ST BARNABAS–Cr 1956 by union EP5, pt EP4.[369]

EP7–ROTHERHITHE ST MARY WITH ALL SAINTS–Cr 1952 by union AP1, pt EP1.[368] Bdry: 1956.[369]

ROWLEDGE

EP Cr 1871 from Binsted EP (Hants), Wrecclesham EP, Frensham AP.[113] S-W Stoke RDn (1871–78), Farn. RDn (1878–*).

RUSKIN PARK ST SAVIOUR WITH ST MATTHEW

EP Cr 1956 from Herne Hill Road EP, Denmark Hill EP.[222] Dulw. RDn. Bdry: 1960.[105]

ST HELIER

EP Cr 1930 from Morden AP, Carshalton AP, Benhilton EP.[88] Bedd. RDn (1930–66), Sutton RDn (1966–*). Bdry: 1932.[166]

ST MARTHA

AP Sometimes 'Chilworth', or 'St Martha (or Chilworth)'. *LG* Blackh. Hd, Hambl. PLU, RSD, RD (1894–1933), Guildf. RD (1933–74). Civ bdry: 1933.[4] *Parl* Seq 17. *Eccl* Guildf. RDn (until *ca* 1535), Stoke RDn (*ca* 1535–1858), S-E Stoke RDn (1858–71), Guildf. RDn (1871–1928), Cranl. RDn (1928–*). Bdry: 1937 (help cr Blackheath and Chilworth EP).[78]

ST MARY-AT-LAMBETH

EP Renaming 1963 of Lambeth St Mary with Holy Trinity and Emmanuel EP.[317] Lamb. RDn. Abol 1974 to help cr North Lambeth EP.[298]

SALFORDS

EP Cr 1952 from Horley AP, Redhill St John the Evangelist EP (Hants).[286] Reig. RDn. Orig dedication 'Christ Church', changed 1967 to 'Christ the King'.[310]

SALFORDS AND SIDLOW

CP Cr 1974 by union pts Charlwood AP, Horley AP.[175]

SANDERSTEAD

AP *LG* Wall. Hd, Croy. PLU, RSD, RD (1894–1915), Coulsdon & Purley UD (1915–65). Civ bdry: 1883,[205] 1929,[370] 1933,[4] 1936 (exchanges pts with Croy. CB and AP).[207] Transf

1965 to Gtr London (Croy. LB).[35] *Parl* E'rn Dv (1832–67), East Dv (1867–85), N-E'rn Dv (1885–1918), E'rn Dv (1918–48). E Surrey CC (1948–70), Gtr London thereafter. Parl bdry: 1945.[413] *Eccl* Ewell RDn (until 1858), N-E Ewell RDn (1858–71), Bedd. RDn (1871–79), Caterh. RDn (1879–*). Eccl bdry: 1884 (help cr Purley Christ Church EP),[12] 1885 (help cr Croydon St Augustine EP),[72] 1925 (incl help cr Sanderstead St Mary EP),[82] 1956.[182]

SANDERSTEAD ST MARY
EP Cr 1925 from Sanderstead AP, Croydon St Augustine EP.[82] Catherh. RDn.

SEALE
AP Chap in Farnham AP, sep par 1539.[217] *LG* Farn. Hd, PLU (1869–1930), RSD, RD (1894–1933), Guildf. RD (1933–63). Renamed civ 1963 'Seale and Tongham'.[371] *Parl* W'rn Dv (1832–85), S-W'rn Dv (1885–1918), Farn. Dv/CC (1918–70). *Eccl* Seq 11. Eccl bdry: 1866 (help cr Tongham EP).[274]

SEALE AND TONGHAM
CP Renaming 1963 of Seale AP.[371] *LG* Guildf. RD. *Parl* Farn. CC (1970–*).

SELHURST–See CROYDON HOLY TRINITY

SELSDON
EP Cr 1934 from Croydon St Peter, South End EP, Addington AP.[8] Croy. RDn Bdry: 1962.[76]

SEND
EP Name used eccl for 'Send and Ripley' AP after Ripley EP cr 1878 from latter.[41] Wok. RDn. Bdry: 1959.[103]
CP Cr 1933 when Send and Ripley AP divided (see following entry).[22] *LG* Guildf. RD. *Parl* Dork. CC (1948–*).

SEND AND RIPLEY
AP Incl chap Riley (sep EP 1878,[41] so that this par eccl 'Send' thereafter, sep CP as below). *LG* Wok. Hd, Guildf. PLU, RSD, RD. Abol civ 1933 pt to cr Send CP, pt to help cr Ripley CP,[22] pt to Guildford CP.[4] *Parl* W'rn Dv (1832–85), N-W'rn Dv (1885–1918), Guildf. Dv (1918–48). *Eccl* Guildf. RDn (until *ca* 1535), Stoke RDn (*ca* 1535–1858), N-E Stoke RDn (1858–78).

SHACKLEFORD
Chap in Godalming AP, sep EP 1866,[130] sep CP 1933 (from Godalming Rural CP).[4] *LG* Guildf. RD. *Parl* Guildf. CC (1948–*). *Eccl* S-W Stoke RDn (1866–78), Godalm. RDn (1878–*).

SHALFORD
AP Incl chap Bramley (sep civ identity early, sep EP 1847[117]). *LG* Blackh. Hd, Hambl. PLU, RSD (ent 1875–86, pt 1886–94), pt Guildf. MB & USD (1886–94), Hambl. RD (1894–1933), Guildf. RD (1933–74). Addtl civ bdry alt: 1833,[21] 1894 (loses the pt in the MB to Guildford St Mary AP),[107] 1933.[4] *Parl* Seq 16. *Eccl* Seq 3. Eccl bdry: 1937 (help cr Blackheath and Chilworth EP).[78]

SHAMLEY GREEN
EP Cr 1881 from Wonersh AP.[372] Guildf. RDn (1881–1928), Cranl. RDn (1928–*).

SHEEN–See RICHMOND

NORTH SHEEN
CP Cr 1894 from the pt of Mortlake CP in Richm. MB.[28] *LG* Richm. PLU, MB. Transf 1965 to Gtr London (Richm. upon Thames LB).[35] *Parl* Richm. Parl Bor/BC (1918–70), Gtr London thereafter.
EP Cr 1930 from Richmond St Luke EP.[364] Richm. & Barnes RDn.

SHEPPERTON
AP Transf 1965 to Surrey from Middx.[35] *LG* Sunbury on Thames UD. *Parl* Spelth. BC (1970–*).

SHERE
AP *LG* Blackh. Hd, Guildf. PLU, RSD, RD. Civ bdry: 1880,[373] 1884,[118] 1933,[22] 1955.[23] *Parl* Seq 17. *Eccl* Guildf. RDn (until *ca* 1535), Stoke RDn (*ca* 1535–1858), S-E Stoke RDn (1858–78), Dork. RDn (1878–1928), Cranl. RDn (1928–*). Eccl bdry: 1878 (help cr Holmbury EP).[6]

SHIRLEY
EP Cr 1846 from Croydon AP.[148] Croy. RDn (1873–*). Bdry: 1922 (help cr Addiscombe St Mildred EP),[14] 1952 (help cr Shirley St George EP).[9]

SHIRLEY ST GEORGE
EP Cr 1952 from Shirley AP, Addington AP.[9] Croy. RDn. Bdry: 1962.[151]

SHOTTERMILL
Area in Frensham AP, sep EP 1846,[15] sep CP 1896.[255] *LG* Farn. PLU, RD. Abol civ 1933 ent to Haslemere CP.[4] *Parl* Farn. Dv (1918–48). *Eccl* Stoke RDn (1846–58), S-W Stoke RDn (1858–78), Godalm. RDn (1878–*). Eccl bdry: 1865 (help cr Churt EP).[187]

SIDLOW BRIDGE
EP Cr 1861 from Horley AP, refounded 1862 from Horley AP, Charlwood AP, Buckland AP, Leigh AP, Reigate AP.[132] S-W Ewell RDn (1861–79), Reig. RDn (1879–*). Bdry: 1939,[127] 1954.[256]

SOUTHFIELDS
EP Cr 1922 from Wandsworth St Paul, Wimbledon Park EP.[16] Wandsw. RDn.

SOUTHWARK
The following have 'Southwark' in their names. Insofar as any existed at a given time: *LG* Brix. Hd, PLU sep noted, Swk. Bor, concurrent jurisd in City London from 1550 as Bridge Ward Without, Vestry or Dist in Metrop Bd Wks sep noted. Transf 1889 to London.[53] *Parl* Swk. Parl Bor (1832–85), Dv of Swk. Parl Bor (1885–1918) sep noted, London thereafter. *Eccl* Swk. RDn (until 1947), Swk. & Newing. RDn (1947–*).

EP1–SOUTHWARK ALL HALLOWS–Cr 1875 from AP5, EP2.[374] Abol 1956 pt to help cr EP14, pt to EP2.[374]

CP1/EP2–SOUTHWARK CHRISTCHURCH–Orig Paris Garden Lbty, cr sep par 1670.[375] *LG* St Saviour's PLU, Dist (Metrop Bd Wks). *Parl* Swk. Parl Bor, West Dv (1885–1918). Eccl bdry: 1875 (help cr EP1),[374] 1956.[93]

EP3–SOUTHWARK HOLY TRINITY–Cr 1827 from Newington AP.[63] Sometimes called 'Newington Holy Trinity'. Swk. RDn (1827–70), Newing. RDn (1870–1947), Swk. & Newing. RDn (1947–74). Bdry: 1877 (cr Newington St Andrew EP),[93] 1956.[93] Abol 1974 to help cr EP4.[335]

EP4–SOUTHWARK HOLY TRINITY WITH ST MATTHEW–Cr 1974 by union Newington St Matthew EP, EP3.[335]

EP5–SOUTHWARK ST ALPHEGE–Cr 1872 from AP1.[281]

AP1–SOUTHWARK ST GEORGE THE MARTYR–*LG* St George the Martyr Par (poor law purposes, 1835–69), St Saviour's PLU (1869–99), St George the Martyr Vestry (Metrop Bd Wks). *Parl* Swk. Parl Bor, pt West Dv, pt Berm. Dv (1885–1918). Eccl bdry: 1843 (cr EP9),[376] 1849 (help cr EP16),[377] 1850 (cr EP8),[378] 1858 (cr EP12),[379] 1867 (cr EP10),[209] 1872 (cr EP5),[281] 1956 (incl help cr EP14),[93] 1964.[196]

CP2/EP6–SOUTHWARK ST JOHN HORSLEYDOWN–Cr 1733 from AP4.[380] *LG* St Olave PLU, Dist (Metrop Bd Wks). Transf 1899 to London (Berm. Metrop Bor).[53] *Parl* Swk. Parl Bor, Rotherhithe Dv (1885–1918). Eccl bdry: 1844 (cr Horsleydown St Mark EP),[290] 1885 (gains ent Horsleydown St Mark EP).[72] Abol eccl 1947 to help cr EP11.[384]

EP7–SOUTHWARK ST JUDE–Renaming 1956 of EP8 when gains pt EP12.[316]

EP8–SOUTHWARK ST JUDE, ST GEORGE'S ROAD–Cr 1850 from AP1.[378] Renamed as EP7 when reconstituted 1956.[316]

AP2–SOUTHWARK ST MARGARET–Abol 1541 to help cr AP5.[381]

EP9–SOUTHWARK ST MARY–Cr 1843 from AP1.[376] Sometimes 'Southwark St Mary Magdalene'. Bdry: 1849 (help cr EP16).[377] Abol 1956 pt to help cr Bermondsey St Mary Magdalen with St Olave and St John EP, pt to help cr Walworth All Saints with St Stephen EP, pt to help cr Walworth The Lady Margaret with St Mary Magdalene EP, pt to EP16, pt to EP3.[93]

AP3–SOUTHWARK ST MARY MAGDALENE–Abol 1541 to help cr AP5.[381]

EP10–SOUTHWARK ST MICHAEL–Cr 1867 from AP1.[209] Abol 1956 ent to AP1.[93]

AP4–SOUTHWARK ST OLAVE–Bdry: *ca* 1550 (cr AP6 from the area of Archbp Canterb's hospital in this par),[383] 1733 (cr CP2/EP6).[380] *LG* St Olave PLU, Dist (Metrop Bd Wks). *Parl* Swk. Parl Bor, Rotherhithe Dv (1885–1918). Abol eccl 1947 to help cr EP11.[384]

EP11–SOUTHWARK ST OLAVE AND ST JOHN–Cr 1947 by union AP4, EP6.[384] Abol 1956 to help cr Bermondsey St Mary Magdalen with St Olave and St John EP.[93]

EP12–SOUTHWARK ST PAUL–Cr 1858 from AP1.[379] Abol 1956 pt to help cr Lambeth St Andrew with St Thomas EP, pt to help cr EP7.[316]

EP13–SOUTHWARK ST PETER–Cr 1843 from AP5.[15] Abol 1915 to help cr EP15.[385]

AP5–SOUTHWARK ST SAVIOUR–Cr 1541 by union AP2, AP3.[381] *LG* St Saviour's PLU, Dist (Metrop Bd Wks). *Parl* Swk. Parl Bor, West Dv (1885–1918). Eccl bdry: 1875 (help cr EP1),[374] 1898 (gains AP6).[386] Abol eccl 1915 to help cr EP15.[385]

EP14–SOUTHWARK ST SAVIOUR WITH ALL HALLOWS–Cr 1956 by union pt EP15, pt Bermondsey St Paul EP, pt EP1, pt AP1.[93]

EP15–SOUTHWARK ST SAVIOUR WITH ST PETER–Cr 1915 by union AP5, EP13.[385] Abol 1956 pt to AP1, pt to help cr EP14.[93]

EP16–SOUTHWARK ST STEPHEN–Cr 1849, refounded 1850 from AP1, EP9.[377] Bdry: 1956.[93] Abol 1956 pt to AP1, pt to Bermondsey St Mary Magdalen with St Olave and St John EP.[196]

AP6–SOUTHWARK ST THOMAS–Cr *ca* 1550 from the area of Archbp Canterb's hospital in AP4.[383] *LG* St Olave PLU, Dist (Metrop Bd Wks). *Parl* Swk. Parl Bor, Rotherhithe Dv (1885–1918). Abol eccl 1898 ent to AP5.[386]

SPRING PARK

EP Cr 1958 from Addington AP.[11] Croy. RDn.

STAINES

AP Transf to Surrey 1965 from Middx.[35] *LG* Staines UD. *Parl* Spelth. BC (1970–*).

STANWELL

AP Transf to Surrey 1965 from Middx.[35] *LG* Staines UD. *Parl* Spelth. BC (1970–*).

STOCKWELL

EP Cr 1845 from Lambeth AP.[387] Swk. RDn (1845–65), Lamb. RDn (1865–79), Kenn. RDn (1879–1935), Brix. & Kenn. RDn (1935–47), Lamb. RDn (1947–*). Bdry: 1861 (cr South Lambeth St Stephen EP),[318] 1861,[55] 1891.[26]

STOCKWELL GREEN

EP Cr 1868 from Kennington St Mark EP, Brixton St Matthew EP.[123] Lamb. RDn (1868–79), Kenn. RDn (1879–1935), Brix. & Kenn. RDn (1935–47), Lamb. RDn (1947–*). Bdry: 1891,[26] 1907.[89]

STOKE

AP Usual civ spelling; for eccl see 'Stoke next Guildford'. *LG* Wok. Hd, Guildf. PLU, pt Guildf. MB, pt Guildf. USD, pt Guildf. RSD. Civ bdry: 1880.[271] Abol civ 1894 the pt in the MB to cr Stoke Within CP, the remainder to cr Stoke next Guildford CP.[28] *Parl* Guildf. Parl Bor (pt 1832–67, ent 1867–85), S-W'rn Dv (1885–1918).

CP Renaming 1904 of Stoke next Guildford CP.[26] *LG* Guildf. PLU, MB. Abol 1908 to help cr Guildford CP.[266]

STOKE D'ABERNON

AP *LG* Elmbr. Hd, Epsom PLU, RSD, RD (1894–1933), Esher UD (1933–74). *Parl* Seq 7. *Eccl* Seq 1. Eccl bdry: 1913 (help cr Oxshott EP).[197]

STOKE HILL

EP Cr 1972 from Stoke next Guildford AP, Guildford St Luke EP, Burpham EP.[14] Guildf. RDn.

STOKE NEXT GUILDFORD

AP Usual eccl spelling; for civ see 'Stoke'. *Eccl* Seq 3. Eccl bdry: 1893 (help cr Stoke next Guildford St Saviour EP, cr Stoke next Guildford Emmanuel Stoughton EP),[84] 1936 (cr Guildford Christchurch EP),[270] 1956,[74] 1958 (help cr Guildford St Francis, Westborough EP),[272] 1972 (help cr Stoke Hill EP).[14]

CP Cr 1894 from the pt of Stoke AP not in Guildf. MB.[28] *LG* Guildf. PLU, RD. Abol 1904 pt to cr Stoke CP, pt to Worplesdon AP.[269]

STOKE NEXT GUILDFORD EMMANUEL STOUGHTON

EP Cr 1893 from Stoke next Guildford AP.[84] Guildf. RDn. Bdry: 1956,[74] 1958,[273] 1958 (help cr Guildford St Francis, Westborough EP).[272] Renamed 1968 'Stoughton Emmanuel'.[126]

STOKE NEXT GUILDFORD ST SAVIOUR

EP Cr 1893 from Stoke next Guildford AP, ent ex-par place Guildford The Friary.[84] Guildf. RDn. Renamed 1968 'Guildford St Saviour'.[126]

STOKE WITHIN

CP Cr 1894 from the pt of Stoke AP in Guildf. MB.[28] *LG* Guildf. PLU, MB. Renamed 1904 'Guildford Christchurch'.[269]

STONELEIGH

EP Cr 1948 from Cuddington AP, Ewell AP (both in Guildf dioc), Cheam Common EP (Swk dioc), to be ent Guildf dioc.[178] Epsom RDn.

STOUGHTON EMMANUEL

EP Renaming 1968 of Stoke next Guildford Emmanuel Stoughton EP.[126] Guildf. RDn.

STREATHAM

The following have 'Streatham' in their names. Insofar as any existed at a given time: *LG* Brix. Hd, Wandsw. & Clap. PLU, Wandsw. Dist (Metrop Bd Wks). Transf 1889 to London.[53] *Parl* E'rn Dv (1832–67), East Dv (1867–85), Wandsw. Parl Bor (1885–1918), London thereafter. *Eccl* Swk. RDn (until 1865), Streath. RDn (1865–1958), Streath. & Mitcham RDn (1958–66), Streath. RDn (1966–*).

AP1–STREATHAM [ST LEONARD]–Eccl bdry: 1844 (cr EP1),[243] 1855 (cr EP2),[196] 1855 (cr Upper Tooting EP, cr EP5 [commonly called 'Balham St Mary']),[388] 1888 (cr EP11),[18] 1898,[389] 1908 (help cr EP4),[390] 1909.[274]

EP1–STREATHAM CHRIST CHURCH–Cr 1844 from AP1.[243] Bdry: 1856 (help cr Tulse Hill EP),[121] 1870 (help cr EP7),[337] 1898,[389] 1901 (help cr EP10),[391] 1903 (cr Telford Park EP),[395] 1952.[213]

EP2–STREATHAM IMMANUEL–Cr 1855 from AP1.[196] Bdry: 1887 (cr EP8),[372] 1905 (help cr EP9),[94] 1909,[274] 1930 (help cr EP12),[13] 1930.[160] Abol 1952 pt to help cr EP3, pt to EP7.[213]

EP3–STREATHAM IMMANUEL WITH ST ANSELM–Cr 1952 by union pt EP2, pt EP4, pt EP7.[213]

EP4–STREATHAM ST ANSELM–Cr 1908 from AP1, EP7.[390] Abol 1952 pt to help cr EP3, pt to EP7.[213]

EP5–STREATHAM ST MARY–Cr 1855 from AP1.[388] Commonly known as 'Balham St Mary'. Swk. RDn (1855–65), Streath. RDn (1865–1958), Streath. & Mitcham RDn (1958–66), Tooting RDn (1966–*). Bdry: 1884 (help cr Balham Hill EP),[41] 1895,[40] 1901 (help cr Balham EP),[40] 1905 (help cr Clapham Park EP),[194] 1906,[196] 1952.[42]

EP6–STREATHAM ST PAUL, FURZEDOWN–Cr 1923 from EP11, Mitcham Christ Church EP, Tooting Graveney AP.[328] RDns as for EP5, from 1923.

EP7–STREATHAM ST PETER–Cr 1870 from EP1, Norwood St Luke EP.[337] Bdry: 1901 (help cr EP10),[391] 1908 (help cr EP4),[390] 1909,[274] 1930,[160] 1952 (incl help cr EP3).[213]

EP8–LOWER STREATHAM–Cr 1887 from EP2.[372] Bdry: 1909,[274] 1930 (help cr EP12),[13] 1930.[160]

EP9–WEST STREATHAM–Cr 1905 from EP2, EP11.[94] RDns as for EP5, from 1905. Bdry: 1930.[160]

EP10–STREATHAM HILL–Cr 1901 from EP1, EP7.[391] Bdry: 1952.[213]

EP11–STREATHAM PARK–Cr 1888 from AP1.[18] RDns as for EP5, from 1888. Bdry: 1905 (help cr EP9),[94] 1923 (help cr EP6).[328]

EP12–STREATHAM VALE–Cr 1930 from EP2, EP8, Mitcham St Mark EP, Mitcham St Barnabas EP.[13]

SUMMERS TOWN

EP Cr 1845 from Wandsworth AP.[392] Swk. RDn (1845–65), Streath. RDn (1865–79), Wandsw. RDn (1879–*). Bdry: 1883,[156] 1890 (help cr Earlsfield St Andrew EP),[14] 1956.[74]

SUNBURY

AP Transf to Surrey 1965 from Middx.[35] Usual civ spelling; for eccl and eccl organisation, see 'Sunbury upon Thames' in Middx. *LG* Sunbury on Thames UD. *Parl* Spelth. BC (1970–*).

SURBITON

The following have 'Surbiton' in their names. Insofar as any existed at a given time: *LG* Kingst. PLU, RD (1894–95), Surbiton UD (1895–1936), MB (1936–65). Transf 1965 to Gtr London (Kingst. upon Thames LB).[35] *Parl* Kingst. upon Thames Parl Bor (1918–55), Surbiton BC (1955–70), Gtr London thereafter. *Eccl* Ewell RDn (until 1858), N-E Ewell RDn (1858–61), N-W Ewell RDn (1861–71), Kingst. RDn (1871–*).

CP1–SURBITON–Cr 1894 from the pt of Kingston upon Thames AP in Surbiton USD.[28] Bdry: 1895,[199] 1933.[278]

EP1–SURBITON ST ANDREW–Cr 1933 from EP2.[56]

EP2–SURBITON ST MARK–Cr 1845 from Kingston upon Thames AP.[304] Bdry: 1863 (cr EP4),[393] 1931,[394] 1933 (cr EP1).[56]

EP3–SURBITON ST MATTHEW–Cr 1876 from

EP4, Long Ditton AP.[224] Bdry: 1931,[394] 1948 (help cr Ewell St Francis of Assisi, Ruxley Lane EP),[177] 1949,[216] 1963.[285]

EP4–SURBITON HILL–Cr 1863 from EP2.[393] Bdry: 1876 (help cr EP3),[224] 1931.[394]

SUTTON

AP *LG* Wall. Hd, Epsom PLU, RSD (1875–82), Sutton USD (1882–94), UD (1894–1928), Sutton & Cheam UD (1928–34), MB (1934–49). Civ bdry: 1933.[4] Abol civ 1949 to help cr Sutton and Cheam CP.[176] *Parl* E'rn Dv (1832–67), Mid Dv (1867–1918), Epsom Dv (1918–45), Sutton & Cheam Parl Bor/BC (1945–70). *Eccl* Seq 21. Eccl bdry: 1863 (cr Benhilton EP),[70] 1884 (help cr Sutton New Town EP),[87] 1888 (cr Sutton Christ Church EP).[50]

SUTTON AND CHEAM

CP Cr 1949 by union Sutton AP, Cheam AP.[176] *LG* Sutton & Cheam MB. Transf 1965 to Gtr London (Sutton LB).[35]

SUTTON CHRIST CHURCH

EP Cr 1888 from Sutton AP.[50] Bedd. RDn (1888–1966), Sutton RDn (1966–*). Bdry: 1916 (help cr Belmont EP),[85] 1965 (incl help cr Carshalton Beeches EP).[86]

SUTTON NEW TOWN

EP Cr 1884 from Sutton AP, Benhilton EP, Carshalton AP.[87] Bedd. RDn (1884–1966), Sutton RDn (1966–*).

TADWORTH

EP Cr 1955 from Kingswood EP (Swk dioc), Burgh Heath EP (Guildf dioc) to be ent Swk dioc.[133] Reig. RDn.

TANDRIDGE

AP *LG* Seq 6. Civ bdry: 1933,[4] 1953 (incl help cr Felbridge CP).[254] *Parl* Seq 2. *Eccl* Seq 19. Eccl bdry: 1910.[170]

TATSFIELD

AP *LG* Seq 6. *Parl* Seq 2. *Eccl* Seq 19.

TATTENHAM CORNER AND BURGH HEATH

EP Renaming 1967 of Burgh Heath EP.[134] Epsom RDn.

TELFORD PARK

EP Cr 1903 from Streatham Christ Church EP.[395] Streath. RDn (1903–58), Streath. & Mitcham RDn (1958–66), Streath. RDn (1966–*). Bdry: 1906.[196]

THORNTON HEATH ST JUDE

EP Cr 1921 from Croydon Christ Church, Broad Green EP.[141] Croy. RDn.

THORNTON HEATH ST PAUL

EP Cr 1871 from Croydon St Saviour EP, Norwood All Saints EP.[220] Croy. RDn (1873–*). Bdry: 1875 (help cr Upper Norwood EP),[6] 1904,[235] 1930,[213] 1934 (help cr Norbury St Oswald EP).[46]

THORPE

AP Chap in Egham AP, sep par 15th cent.[241] *LG* Godley Hd, Windsor PLU (1835–94), RSD, Chert. PLU (1894–1930), RD (1894–1933), Egham UD (1933–74). *Parl* Seq 10. *Eccl* Seq 7.

THURSLEY

Chap in Witley AP, sep civ identity early, sep EP 1850.[396] *LG* Seq 2. Civ bdry: 1894,[107] 1933.[4] *Parl* W'rn Dv (1832–85), S-W'rn Dv (1885–1918), Guildf. Dv (1918–48), Farn. CC (1948–*). *Eccl* Stoke RDn (1850–58), S-W Stoke RDn (1858–78), Godalm. RDn (1878–*). Eccl bdry: 1900 (help cr Grayswood EP).[182]

TILFORD

EP Cr 1865 from Farnham AP.[187] Farn.[263] RDn. Bdry: 1957.[114]

CP Cr 1933 from Elstead AP, Farnham Rural CP.[4] *LG* Hambl. RD. *Parl* Farn. CC (1948–*).

TITSEY

AP *LG* Seq 6. *Parl* Seq 2. *Eccl* Ewell RDn (until 1858), S-E Ewell RDn (1858–71), Godst. RDn (1871–1973). Abol eccl 1973 to help cr Limpsfield and Titsey EP.[319]

TOLWORTH

CP Cr 1895 from Long Ditton AP.[223] *LG* Kingst. PLU, Surbiton UD (1895–1936), MB (1936–65). Bdry: 1933.[4] Transf 1965 to Gtr London (Kingst. upon Thames LB).[35] *Parl* Kingst. upon Thames Parl Bor (1918–55), Surbiton BC (1955–70), Gtr London thereafter.

TONGHAM

EP Cr 1866 from Seale AP, Hale EP.[274] S-W Stoke RDn (1866–78), Farn. RDn (1878–19), Aldershot RDn (19 –*).

TOOTING

The following have 'Tooting' in their names. Insofar as any existed at a given time: *LG* Brix. Hd, Wandsw. & Clap. PLU, Wandsw. Dist (Metrop Bd Wks). Transf 1889 to London.[53] *Parl* E'rn Dv (1832–67), Wandsw. Parl Bor (1885–1918), London thereafter. *Eccl* Swk. RDn (until 1865), Streath. RDn (1865–1958), Streath. & Mitcham RDn (1958–66), Tooting RDn (1966–*).

EP1–TOOTING ALL SAINTS–Cr 1903 from AP1.[85] Bdry: 1911.[124]

AP1–TOOTING GRAVENEY–Eccl bdry: 1903 (cr EP1),[85] 1923 (help cr Streatham St Paul, Furzedown EP),[328] 1926 (help cr EP2).[397]

EP2–TOOTING ST AUGUSTINE–Cr 1926 from EP3, AP1.[397] Bdry: 1956.[74]

EP3–UPPER TOOTING–Cr 1855 from Streatham AP.[388] Bdry: 1883,[156] 1895,[40] 1901 (help cr Balham EP),[40] 1911,[124] 1926 (help cr EP2).[397]

TULSE HILL

EP Cr 1856 from Norwood St Luke EP, Brixton St Matthew EP, Streatham Christ Church EP.[121] Swk. RDn (1856–71), Clap. RDn (1871–1935), Brix. & Kenn. RDn (1935–47), Clap. & Brix. RDn (1947–*). Bdry: 1899 (help cr West Dulwich All Saints EP),[233] 1899 (help cr Upper Tulse EP),[125] 1902.[234]

UPPER TULSE HILL

EP Cr 1899 from Tulse Hill EP, Brixton St Matthew EP, Brixton Hill EP.[125] Clap. RDn (1899–1935), Brix. & Kenn. RDn (1935–47), Clap. & Brix. RDn (1947–*).

VAUXHALL

EP Cr 1861 from Lambeth St Mary EP.[55] Lamb.

RDn.

VIRGINIA WATER

EP Cr 1839 from Egham AP.[15] Stoke RDn (1839–58), N-W Stoke RDn (1858–71), Emly RDn (1871–1946), Chert. RDn (1946–*). Sometimes 'Egham Christ Church'.

WALLINGTON

Hmlt & chap in Beddington AP, sep CP 1866,[32] sep EP 1867.[78] *LG* Wall. Hd, Croy. PLU (1866–1930), RSD, RD (1894–1915), Bedd. & Wall. UD (1915–37), MB (1937–65). Civ bdry: 1927,[164] 1933.[4] Transf 1965 to Gtr London (Sutton LB).[35] *Parl* Mid Dv (1867–85), Kingst. Dv (1885–1918), Mitcham Dv (1918–45), BC (1945–70), Gtr London thereafter. *Eccl* N-E Ewell RDn (1867–79), Bedd. RDn (1879–1966), Sutton RDn (1966–*). Eccl bdry: 1907 (help cr South Beddington EP),[80] 1965 (incl help cr Carshalton Beeches EP).[86]

WALTON ON THE HILL

AP *LG* Copth. Hd, Reig. PLU, RSD, RD (1894–1933), Banstead UD (1933–74). Civ bdry: 1933.[4] *Parl* W'rn Dv (1832–67), Mid Dv (1867–85), Reig. Dv (1918–45), Carsh. Dv/CC (1945–70), Reig. CC (1970–*). *Eccl* Ewell RDn (until 1858), W Ewell RDn (1858–71), Leath. RDn (1871–1920s), Epsom RDn (1920s–*).

WALTON-ON-THAMES

AP Usual eccl spelling; for civ and sep chap West Molesey see following entry. *Eccl* Seq 5. Addtl eccl bdry alt: 1849 (cr Hersham EP),[282] 1869 (help cr Oatlands EP).[283]

WALTON UPON THAMES

AP Incl chap West Molesey (sep civ identity early, sep EP 1726[329]). Usual civ spelling; for eccl see prev entry. *LG* Elmbr. Hd, Chert. PLU, RSD, Walton upon Thames UD (1894–1933), Walton & Weybridge UD (1933–74). Addtl civ bdry alt: 1933,[4] 1936,[138] 1957.[245] *Parl* W'rn Dv (1832–85), Kingst. Dv (1885–1918), Chert. Dv/CC (1918–70), Chert. & Walton CC (1970–*).

WALWORTH

The following have 'Walworth' in their names. Insofar as any existed at a given time: *Eccl* Pec jurisd Archbp Canterb (until 1845), Newing. RDn (1870–1947), Swk. & Newing. RDn (1947–*).

EP1–WALWORTH ALL SAINTS WITH ST STEPHEN–Cr 1956 by union pt Newington All Saints EP, pt EP8, pt EP6, pt Southwark St Mary EP.[93] Bdry: 1964.[99]

EP2–WALWORTH THE LADY MARGARET–Cr 1890 from EP4.[398] Abol 1956 to help cr EP3.[93]

EP3–WALWORTH THE LADY MARGARET WITH ST MARY MAGDALENE–Cr 1956 by union EP2, pt Southwark St Mary EP, pt Newington All Saints EP, pt EP5, pt EP4.[93]

EP4–WALWORTH ST JOHN–Cr 1860 from Newington AP.[333] Bdry: 1890 (cr EP2),[398] 1956 (incl help cr EP3).[93]

EP5–WALWORTH ST MARK, EAST STREET–Cr 1870 from EP6.[342] Bdry: 1872.[209] Abol 1956 pt to help cr EP3, pt to EP6, pt to EP4.[93]

EP6–WALWORTH ST PETER–Cr 1827 from Newington AP.[93] Bdry: 1870 (cr EP5, EP8),[342] 1871 (cr Grosvenor Park EP),[45] 1872,[209] 1956 (incl help cr EP1).[93]

EP7–WALWORTH COMMON–Cr 1827 from Newington AP.[363] Bdry: 1907.[322] Abol 1956 pt to help cr EP1, pt to EP6.[93]

EP8–WALWORTH COMMON ST STEPHEN–Cr 1870 from EP6.[342] Abol 1956 pt to help cr EP3, pt to EP6.[93]

WANBOROUGH

AP *LG* Seq 7. *Parl* Seq 12. *Eccl* Sometimes Donative, disused nearly 200 yrs, sep status maintained.[400] Guildf. RDn (until *ca* 1535), Stoke RDn (*ca* 1535–1858), S-W Stoke RDn (1858–78), Godalm. RDn (1878–1928), Guildf. RDn (1928–*). Eccl bdry: 1847 (help cr Wyke EP),[34] 1945.[399]

WANDSWORTH

The following have 'Wandsworth' in their names. Insofar as any existed at a given time: *LG* Brix. Hd, Wandsw. & Clap. PLU, Wandsw. Dist (Metrop Bd Wks). Transf 1889 to London.[53] *Parl* E'rn Dv (1832–67), Mid Dv (1867–85), Wandsw. Parl Bor (1885–1918), London thereafter. *Eccl* Swk. RDn (until 1865), Streath. RDn (1865–79), Wandsw. RDn (1879–*).

AP1–WANDSWORTH [ALL SAINTS]–Eccl bdry: 1845 (cr Summers Town EP),[392] 1847 (cr EP1),[401] 1877 (cr EP4),[161] 1878 (cr EP5),[37] 1898 (cr EP3),[73] 1901,[318] 1969.[326]

EP1–WANDSWORTH ST ANNE–Cr 1847 from AP1.[401] Bdry: 1863 (help cr Battersea St John EP),[56] 1884 (help cr EP2),[12] 1889 (help cr EP6),[61] 1890 (help cr Earlsfield St Andrew EP),[12] 1895,[40] 1939,[238] 1939,[70] 1956,[74] 1969.[326]

EP2–WANDSWORTH ST FAITH–Cr 1884 from EP1, Battersea St John EP.[12]

EP3–WANDSWORTH ST MICHAEL AND ALL ANGELS, SOUTHFIELDS–Cr 1898 from AP1.[73] Bdry: 1901,[318] 1969.[326]

EP4–WANDSWORTH ST PAUL, WIMBLEDON PARK–Cr 1877 from AP1.[161] Bdry: 1922 (cr Southfields EP),[16] 1969.[326]

EP5–WANDSWORTH ST STEPHEN–Cr 1878 from AP1.[37]

EP6–WANDSWORTH COMMON–Cr 1889 from EP1, Battersea AP.[61] Wandsw. RDn (1889–1966), Tooting RDn (1966–*). Bdry: 1956.[74]

–WANDSWORTH COMMON ST MICHAEL–See BATTERSEA ST MICHAEL, WANDSWORTH COMMON

WARLINGHAM

AP Incl chap Chelsham (sep civ identity early, no sep eccl identity so this par eccl 'Warlingham with Chelsham', qv). *LG* Tandr. Hd, Godst. PLU, RSD, RD (1894–1929), Caterh. & Warlingham UD (1929–74). Addtl civ bdry alt: 1929,[370] 1929,[167] 1933.[4] *Parl* Seq 1.

WARLINGHAM WITH CHELSHAM

AP Usual eccl spelling; for civ and civ sep chap Chelsham, see prev entry. *Eccl* Seq 17. Eccl bdry: 1866 (help cr Caterham Valley St Luke EP),[168] 1956,[182] 1960.[135]

WAVERLEY

Ex-par place, sep CP 1858.[115] *LG* Farn. Hd, PLU (1858[402]–94), RSD. Abol 1894 ent to help cr Farnham Rural CP.[353] *Parl* W'rn Dv (1867–85), S-W'rn Dv (1885–1918).

WEST END

CP Cr 1968 from Chobham AP.[184] *LG* Bagshot RD. *Parl* N W Surrey CC (1970–*).

WESTCOTT

EP Cr 1852 from Dorking AP.[231] Stoke RDn (1852–58), S-E Stoke RDn (1858–78), Dork. RDn (1878–*).

WESTON

EP Cr 1934 from Thames Ditton EP.[226] Emly RDn. Bdry: 1953 (cr Hinchley Wood EP).[284]

WEYBRIDGE

AP *LG* Elmbr. Hd, Chert. PLU, RSD, Weybridge UD (1894–1933), Walton & Weybridge UD (1933–74). Civ bdry: 1933.[4] *Parl* W'rn Dv (1832–85), N-W'rn Dv (1885–1918), Chert. Dv (1918–48), Esher CC (1948–70), Chert. & Walton CC (1970–*). *Eccl* Seq 5.

WHYTELEAFE

EP Renaming 1964 of Caterham Valley St Luke EP.[99] Caterh. RDn.

WIMBLEDON

The following have 'Wimbledon' in their names. Insofar as any existed at a given time: *LG* Brix. Hd, Kingst. PLU, Wimb. USD, UD (1894–1905), MB (1905–65). Transf 1965 to Gtr London (Merton LB).[35] *Parl* E'rn Dv (1832–67), Mid Dv (1867–85), N-E'rn Dv (1885–1918), Wimb. Parl Bor/BC (1918–70), Gtr London thereafter. *Eccl* Pec jurisd Archbp Canterb (until 1845), Barnes & Hammersmith RDn (1861–72), Barnes RDn (1872–1909), Wimb. RDn (1909–66), Merton RDn (1966–*).

AP1–WIMBLEDON [ST MARY]–Incl chap Mortlake (sep civ identity early, sep EP from 17th cent[330]), chap Putney (sep civ identity early, sep EP from 17th cent[352]). Addtl civ bdry alt: 1898,[321] 1933.[4] Parl bdry: 1945.[413] Addtl eccl bdry alt: 1872 (cr EP3),[63] 1910 (cr EP1),[403] 1961 (cr EP6).[123]

EP1–WIMBLEDON ST LUKE–Cr 1910 from AP1.[403]

EP2–SOUTH WIMBLEDON ALL SAINTS–Cr 1892 from EP3.[25] Bdry: 1912 (help cr EP5).[404]

EP3–SOUTH WIMBLEDON HOLY TRINITY–Cr 1872 from AP1.[63] Bdry: 1892 (cr EP2),[25] 1910 (cr EP4),[405] 1912 (help cr EP5).[404]

EP4–SOUTH WIMBLEDON ST ANDREW–Cr 1910 from EP3.[405]

EP5–SOUTH WIMBLEDON ST PETER–Cr 1912 from EP2, EP3.[404]

EP6–WEST WIMBLEDON–Cr 1961 from AP1.[123]

WINDLESHAM

AP *LG* Wok. Hd, Chert. PLU, RSD, RD (1894–1909), Windlesham UD (1909–33), Bagshot RD (1933–74). Civ bdry: 1936.[183] *Parl* W'rn Dv (1832–85), N-W'rn Dv (1885–1918), Farn. Dv (1918–48), Chert. Dv (1948–70), N W Surrey CC (1970–*). *Eccl* Seq 8. Eccl bdry: 1868 (help cr Chobham St Saviour EP),[63] 1874 (cr Bagshot EP),[36] 1963,[37] 1963 (help cr Lightwater EP),[38] 1973.[39]

WISLEY

AP Incl chap Pyrford (from 1631, chap in Woking AP prev[355]; sep civ identity early, no sep eccl identity so this par eccl 'Wisley with Pyrford', qv). *LG* Seq 7. Addtl civ bdry alt: 1883,[406] 1933.[22] *Parl* Seq 13.

WISLEY WITH PYRFORD

AP Usual eccl spelling; for civ and civ sep chap Pyrford see prev entry. *Eccl* Seq 6.

WITLEY

AP Incl chap Thursley (sep civ identity early, sep EP 1850[396]). *LG* Seq 2. Addtl civ bdry alt: 1884,[118] 1897,[261] 1929,[260] 1933,[4] 1933.[22] *Parl* Seq 18. *Eccl* Seq 12. Addtl eccl bdry alt: 1844 (cr Milford EP),[177] 1900 (help cr Grayswood EP).[182]

WOKING

The following have 'Woking' in their names. Insofar as any existed at a given time: *LG* Wok. Hd, Guildf. PLU, RSD (1875–93), Wok. USD (1893–94), UD. *Parl* W'rn Dv (1832–85), N-W'rn Dv (1885–1918), Farn. Dv (1918–48), Wok. CC (1948–*). *Eccl* Seq 6.

AP1–WOKING [ST PETER]–Incl chap Horsell (sep par from Dissolution 16th cent[287]), chap Pirbright (sep par from Dissolution 16th cent[350]), chap Pyrford (transf by 1631 to be chap in Wisley AP,[355] qv for later civ sep). Addtl civ bdry alt: 1901.[288] Addtl eccl bdry alt: 1886,[409] 1920 (help cr Burpham with Sutton EP),[78] 1959 (incl help cr EP4),[103] 1961.[136]

EP1–WOKING CHRIST CHURCH–Cr 1893 from EP2.[84] Bdry: 1923 (help cr EP2),[407] 1953,[140] 1959 (incl help cr EP4).[103]

EP2–WOKING ST JOHN THE BAPTIST–Cr 1884 from AP1.[408] Bdry: 1886,[409] 1893 (cr EP1),[84] 1923 (help cr EP3),[407] 1959,[103] 1967 (cr Knaphill EP).[309]

EP3–WOKING ST MARY OF BETHANY–Cr 1923 from EP1, EP2.[407] Bdry: 1959.[103]

EP4–WOKING ST PAUL–Cr 1959 from EP1, AP1.[103]

WOLDINGHAM

AP *LG* Tandr. Hd, Godst. PLU, RSD, RD (1894–1933), Caterh. & Warlingham UD (1933–74). Civ bdry: 1933.[4] *Parl* Seq 3. *Eccl* Donative 13th–19th cent. Seq 20. Eccl bdry: 1960,[135] 1969.[14]

WONERSH

AP *LG* Seq 1. Civ bdry: 1883,[21] 1884,[118] 1933,[4] 1933.[22] *Parl* Seq 16. *Eccl* Seq 3. Addtl eccl bdry alt: 1881 (cr Shamley Green EP),[372] 1937 (help cr Blackheath and Chilworth EP).[78]

WOODHAM

EP Cr 1902 from Addlestone EP, Horsell AP.[17] Emly RDn (1902–08), Wok. RDn (1908–*). Bdry: 1953.[140]

WOODMANSTERNE

AP *LG* Wall. Hd, Croy. PLU, RSD, RD (1894–1915), Epsom RD (1915–33), Banstead UD (1933–74). Civ bdry: 1915,[79] 1933.[4] *Parl* E'rn Dv (1832–67), Mid Dv (1867–85), N-E'rn Dv (1885–1918), Epsom Dv (1918–45), Carsh. Dv/CC (1945–70), Reig. CC (1970–*). *Eccl* Seq 14. Eccl bdry: 1915 (help cr Coulsdon St Andrew EP).[165]

WORPLESDON

AP *LG* Seq 7. Civ bdry: 1880,[410] 1904,[269] 1933,[4] 1954,[267] 1962.[336] *Parl* Seq 12. *Eccl* Guildf. RDn (until *ca* 1535), Stoke RDn (*ca* 1535–1858), N-W Stoke RDn (1858–61), N-E Stoke RDn (1861–78), Guildf. RDn (1878–*). Eccl bdry: 1847 (help cr Wyke EP),[34] 1920 (help cr Burpham with Sutton EP),[78] 1956,[74] 1958 (help cr Guildford St Francis, Westborough EP).[272]

WOTTON

AP *LG* Seq 8. Civ bdry: 1879,[411] 1879,[412] 1901,[3] 1933,[4] 1934.[239] *Parl* Seq 14. *Eccl* Seq 10. Eccl bdry: 1723 (help cr Okewood EP, refounded 1853 [from other pars as well, qv]),[5] 1848 (help cr Coldharbour EP).[62]

WRECCLESHAM

EP Cr 1840 from Farnham AP.[113] Stoke RDn (1840–58), Guildf. RDn (1858–78),[263] Farn. RDn (1878–*). Bdry: 1871 (help cr Rowledge EP in Hants),[113] 1875 (cr Bourne EP).[113]

WYKE

EP Cr 1847 from Worplesdon AP, Ash AP, Wanborough EP.[34] Stoke RDn (1847–58), N-W Stoke RDn (1858–66), Guildf. RDn (1866–71), N-E Stoke RDn (1871–78), Guildf. RDn (1878–*). Bdry: 1945.[399]

YORK TOWN

EP Cr 1851 from Ash AP.[15] Stoke RDn (1851–58), N-W Stoke RDn (1858–71), N-E Stoke RDn (1871–78), Wok. RDn (1878–1928), Aldershot RDn (1928–*). Bdry: 1935 (help cr Camberley EP).[141] Sometimes called 'Camberley St Michael'.

SUSSEX

ABBREVIATIONS

Abbreviations particular to Sussex follow. Those general abbreviations in use throughout the *Guide* are found on page xix.

Aldw.	Aldwick
Arund.	Arundel
Avisf.	Avisford
Bishopst.	Bishopstone
Bogn. (Reg.)	Bognor (Regis)
Box & Stockb.	Box and Stockbridge
Boxg.	Boxgrove
Brigh.	Brighton
Brightf.	Brightford
Buttg.	Buttinghill
Chanct.	Chanctonbury
Chich.	Chichester
Cuckf.	Cuckfield
Dall.	Dallington
Dumpf.	Dumpford
Easeb.	Easebourne
Easw.	Easwrith
E'bourne.	Eastbourne
Etch.	Etchingham
Fishg.	Fishergate
Flexb.	Flexborough
Grin.	Grinstead
Hast.	Hastings
Holm.	Holmstrow
Long.	Longbridge
Loxf.	Loxfield
Manh.	Manhood
Midh.	Midhurst
Newh.	Newhaven
Petw.	Petworth
Pev.	Pevensey
Rothb.	Rotherbridge
Shor.	Shoreham
Singl.	Singleton
Stapl.	Staplehurst
Stey.	Steyning
Stockb.	Stockbridge
Storr.	Storrington
Thak.	Thakenham
Ticeh.	Ticehurst
Uckf.	Uckfield
W'bourne.	Westbourne
W'hamp.	Westhampnett
Whaleb.	Whalebone

SEQUENCES

An abbreviated entry prefixed by 'Seq' is used in the parochial entries to avoid repeating often the names of superior units of administration. The content of each sequence is shown below.

Local Government Sequences ('LG')

Sequenced pars orig in Rapes of Arundel, Bramber, Chichester were in W Sussex Adm Co from 1894; the others were in E Sussex Adm Co.

Rape of Arundel:

SEQ 1 Avisf. Hd, E Preston incorp for poor (1791 [later addition sep noted] –1869), E Preston PLU (1869–1930), RSD, RD (1894–1933), Chich. RD (1933–74)
SEQ 2 Avisf. Hd, W'hamp. PLU, RSD, RD (1894–1933), Chich. RD (1933–74)
SEQ 3 Bury Hd, Sutton incorp for poor (1791 [later addition sep noted] –1869), Petw. PLU (1869–1930), RSD, RD
SEQ 4 W Easw. Hd, Horsham PLU, RSD, RD
SEQ 5 W Easw. Hd, Thak. PLU, RSD, RD (1894–1933), Chanct. RD (1933–74)
SEQ 6 Poling Hd, E Preston incorp for poor (1791 [later addition sep noted] –1869), E Preston PLU (1869–1930), RSD, RD (1894–1933), Worthing RD (1933–74)
SEQ 7 Rothb. Hd, Midh. PLU, RSD, RD
SEQ 8 Rothb. Hd, Petw. PLU, RSD, RD

Rape of Bramber:

SEQ 9 Brightf. Hd, Steyn, PLU, RSD, Steyn. W RD (1894–1933), Worthing RD (1933–74)
SEQ 10 E Easw. Hd, Thak. PLU, RSD, RD (1894–1933), Chanct. RD (1933–74)
SEQ 11 W Grin. Hd, Horsham PLU, RSD, RD
SEQ 12 Singl. Hd, Horsham PLU, RSD, RD

Rape of Chichester:

SEQ 13 Aldw. Hd, W'hamp. PLU, RSD, RD (1894–1933), Chich. RD (1933–74)
SEQ 14 Bosham Hd, W'bourne PLU, RSD, RD (1894–1933), Chich. RD (1933–74)
SEQ 15 Box & Stockb. Hd, W'hamp. PLU, RSD, RD (1894–1933), Chich. RD (1933–74)
SEQ 16 Dumpf. Hd, Midh. PLU, RSD, RD
SEQ 17 Easeb. Hd, Midh. PLU, RSD, RD
SEQ 18 Manh. Hd, W'hamp. PLU, RSD, RD (1894–1933), Chich. RD (1933–74)
SEQ 19 W'bourne & Singl. Hd, W'bourne PLU, RSD, RD (1894–1933), Chich. RD (1933–74)

Rape of Hastings:

SEQ 20 Baldstow Hd, Battle PLU, RSD, RD
SEQ 21 Foxearle Hd, Hailsham PLU, RSD, RD
SEQ 22 Goldspur Hd, Rye PLU, RSD, RD (1894–1934), Battle RD (1934–74)
SEQ 23 Gostrow Hd, Rye PLU, RSD, RD (1894–1934), Battle RD (1934–74)
SEQ 24 Guestling Hd, Hast. PLU, RSD, RD (1894–1934), Battle RD (1934–74)
SEQ 25 Hawkesborough Hd, Hailsham PLU, RSD, RD
SEQ 26 Henhurst Hd, Ticeh. PLU, RSD, RD (1894–1934), Battle RD (1934–74)
SEQ 27 Netherfield Hd, Battle PLU, RSD, RD
SEQ 28 Ninfield Hd, Hailsham PLU, RSD, RD

Rape of Lewes:

SEQ 29 Barcombe Hd, Chailey PLU (1835–98), RSD, Lewes PLU (1898–1930), Chailey RD
SEQ 30 Buttg. Hd, Cuckf. PLU, RSD, RD
SEQ 31 Buttg. Hd, E Grin. PLU, RSD, RD (1894–1934), Cuckf. RD (1934–74)
SEQ 32 Holmstrow Hd, Newh. PLU, RSD, RD (1894–1934), Chailey RD (1934–74)
SEQ 33 Poynings Hd, Cuckf. PLU, RSD, RD
SEQ 34 Street Hd, Chailey PLU (1835–98), RSD, Lewes PLU (1898–1930), Chailey RD
SEQ 35 Swanborough Hd, Newh. PLU, RSD, RD (1894–1934), Chailey RD (1934–74)

Rape of Pevensey:

SEQ 36 Alciston Hd, E'bourne PLU, RSD, RD (1894–1934), Hailsham RD (1934–74)
SEQ 37 Dill Hd, Hailsham PLU, RSD, RD
SEQ 38 Hartfield Hd, E Grin. PLU, RSD, RD (1894–1934), Uckf. RD (1934–74)
SEQ 39 Longb. Hd, E'bourne PLU, RSD, RD (1894–1934), Hailsham RD (1934–74)
SEQ 40 Loxf. Dorset Hd, Uckf. PLU, RSD, RD
SEQ 41 Pev. Lowey, E'bourne PLU, RSD, RD (1894–1934), Hailsham RD (1934–74)
SEQ 42 Ringmer Hd, W Firle PLU (1835–98), RSD, Lewes PLU (1898–1930), Uckf. RD
SEQ 43 Rushmonden Hd, Uckf. PLU, RSD, RD
SEQ 44 Shiplake Hd, Hailsham PLU, RSD, RD
SEQ 45 Shiplake Hd, W Firle PLU (1835–98), RSD, Hailsham PLU (1898–1930), RD
SEQ 46 Shiplake Hd, Uckf. PLU, RSD, RD (1894–1934), Hailsham RD (1934–74)
SEQ 47 Willingdon Hd, E'bourne PLU, RSD, RD (1894–1934), Hailsham RD (1934–74)

Parliamentary Sequences ('Parl')

SEQ 1 E'rn Dv (1832–1918), E'bourne Dv/CC (1918–55), Rye CC (1955–*)
SEQ 2 E'rn Dv (1832–1918), E Grin. Dv/CC (1918–*)
SEQ 3 E'rn Dv (1832–85), Mid Dv (1885–1918), E Grin. Dv (1918–48), Lewes CC (1948–70), Mid-Sussex CC (1970–*)

SEQ 4 E'rn Dv (1832–85), Mid Dv (1885–1918), Lewes Dv/CC (1918–*)
SEQ 5 E'rn Dv (1832–85), N'rn Dv (1885–1918), E Grin. Dv/CC (1918–*)
SEQ 6 E'rn Dv (1832–85), N'rn Dv (1885–1918), E Grin. Dv/CC (1918–70), Mid-Sussex CC (1970–*)
SEQ 7 E'rn Dv (1832–1918), Rye Dv (1918–48), E Grin. CC (1948–*)
SEQ 8 E'rn Dv (1832–1918), Rye Dv (1918–48), E Grin. CC (1948–55), Rye CC (1955–*)
SEQ 9 E'rn Dv (1832–1918), Rye Dv (1918–48), Hast. BC (1948–55), Rye CC (1955–*)
SEQ 10 E'rn Dv (1832–85), S'rn Dv (1885–1918), E'bourne Dv/CC (1918–*)
SEQ 11 E'rn Dv (1832–85), S'rn Dv (1885–1918), E'bourne Dv (1918–48), Lewes CC (1948–55), E'bourne CC (1955–70), Lewes CC (1970–*)
SEQ 12 E'rn Dv (1832–85), S'rn Dv (1885–1918), Lewes Dv/CC (1918–*)
SEQ 13 E'rn Dv (1832–85), S'rn Dv (1885–1918), Rye Dv (1918–48), Lewes CC (1948–55), Rye CC (1955–*)
SEQ 14 Midh. Parl Bor (1832–85), N-W'rn Dv (1885–1918), Chich. Dv (1918–48), Horsham CC (1948–70), Chich. CC (1970–*)
SEQ 15 Pt Midh. Parl Bor, pt W'rn Dv (1832–85), N-W'rn Dv (1885–1918), Chich. Dv (1918–48), Horsham CC (1948–70), Chich. CC (1970–*)
SEQ 16 Rye Parl Bor (1832–85), E'rn Dv (1885–1918), Rye Dv (1918–48), Hast. BC (1948–55), Rye CC (1955–*)
SEQ 17 Pt Rye Parl Bor, pt E'rn Dv (1832–85), E'rn Dv (1885–1918), Rye Dv (1918–48), Hast. BC (1948–55), Rye CC (1955–*)
SEQ 18 New Shor. Parl Bor (1832–85), Mid Dv (1885–1918), Horsham & Worthing Dv (1918–45), Horsham Dv (1945–48), Arund. & Shor. CC (1948–70), Shor. CC (1970–*)
SEQ 19 New Shor. Parl Bor (1832–85), Mid Dv (1885–1918), Horsham & Worthing Dv (1918–45), Worthing Dv (1945–48), Arund. & Shor. CC (1948–70), Shor. CC (1970–*)
SEQ 20 New Shor. Parl Bor (1832–85), N-W'rn Dv (1885–1918), Horsham & Worthing Dv (1918–45), Horsham Dv/CC (1945–70), Horsham & Crawley CC (1970–*)
SEQ 21 New Shor. Parl Bor (1832–85), S-W'rn Dv (1885–1918), Horsham & Worthing Dv (1918–45), Horsham Dv (1945–48), Arund. & Shor. CC (1948–70), Shor. CC (1970–*)
SEQ 22 W'rn Dv (1832–85), Mid Dv (1885–1918), Horsham & Worthing Dv (1918–45), Horsham Dv (1945–48), Arund. & Shor. CC (1948–70), Shor. CC (1970–*)
SEQ 23 W'rn Dv (1832–85), N-W'rn Dv (1885–1918), Chich. Dv (1918–48), Horsham CC (1948–70), Chich. CC (1970–*)
SEQ 24 W'rn Dv (1832–85), N-W'rn Dv (1885–1918), Horsham & Worthing Dv (1918–45), Horsham Dv/CC (1945–70), Chich. CC (1970–*)
SEQ 25 W'rn Dv (1832–85), S-W'rn Dv (1885–1918), Chich. Dv/CC (1918–*)
SEQ 26 W'rn Dv (1832–85), S-W'rn Dv (1885–1918), Chich. Dv/CC (1918–70), Arund. CC (1970–*)
SEQ 27 W'rn Dv (1832–85), S-W'rn Dv (1885–1918), Chich. Dv (1918–48), Arund. & Shor. CC (1948–70), Arund. CC (1970–*)
SEQ 28 W'rn Dv (1832–85), S-W'rn Dv (1885–1918), Horsham & Worthing Dv (1918–45), Horsham Dv (1945–48), Arund. & Shor. CC (1948–70), Shor. CC (1970–*)

Orig Chich. AD:

SEQ 1 Arund. RDn (until 1871), Arund. I RDn (1871–1913), Arund. I RDn (1913–*)
SEQ 2 Arund. RDn (until 1871), Arund. II RDn (1871–1913), Arund. RDn (1913–*)
SEQ 3 Arund. RDn (until 1871), Arund. II RDn (1871–1913), Selsey RDn (1913–43), Bogn. Reg. RDn (1943–*)
SEQ 4 Boxg. RDn (until 1871), Arund. II RDn (1871–1913), Selsey RDn (1913–43), Chich. RDn (1943–*)
SEQ 5 Boxg. RDn (until 1871), Boxg. I RDn (1871–1913), Boxg. RDn (1913–29), Chich. RDn (1929–*)
SEQ 6 Boxg. RDn (until 1871), Boxg. II RDn (1871–1913), W'bourne RDn (1913–*)
SEQ 7 Boxg. RDn (until 1871), Boxg. III RDn (1871–1913), Selsey RDn (1913–43), Chich. RDn (1943–*)
SEQ 8 Boxg. RDn (until 1871), Boxg. III RDn (1871–1913), Selsey RDn (1913–29), Chich. RDn (1929–*)
SEQ 9 Midh. RDn (until 1871), Midh. I RDn (1871–1913), Midh. RDn (1913–*)
SEQ 10 Midh. RDn (until 1871), Midh. II RDn (1871–1913), Midh. RDn (1913–*)
SEQ 11 Midh. RDn (until 1871), Midh. II RDn (1871–1913), Petw. RDn (1913–*)
SEQ 12 Midh. RDn (until 1871), Midh. III RDn (1871–1913), Petw. RDn (1913–*)
SEQ 13 Storr. RDn (until 1871), Storr. I RDn (1871–1913), Storr. RDn (1913–*)
SEQ 14 Storr. RDn (until 1871), Storr. II RDn (1871–1913), Horsham RDn (1913–*)
SEQ 15 Storr. RDn (until 1871), Storr. III RDn (1871–1913), Horsham RDn (1913–*)
SEQ 16 Storr. RDn (until 1871), Storr. III RDn (1871–1913), Storr. RDn (1913–*)
SEQ 17 Storr. RDn (until 1871), Storr. III RDn (1871–79), Storr. IV RDn (1879–1913), Worthing RDn (1913–*)
SEQ 18 Tarring RDn (pec jurisd until 1846, within AD 1846–71), Arund. I RDn (1871–79), Storr. IV RDn (1879–1913), Worthing

RDn (1913–*)

Orig Lewes AD:
SEQ 19 Dall. RDn
SEQ 20 Dall. RDn (until 1858), Hast. I RDn (1858–1913), Hast. RDn (1913–31), Battle & Bexhill RDn (1931–*)
SEQ 21 Dall. RDn (until 1858), Hast. II RDn (1858–1913), Rye RDn (1913–*)
SEQ 22 Dall. RDn (until 1913), Etch. RDn (1913–*)
SEQ 23 Hast. RDn (until 1858), Hast. I RDn (1858–1913), Hast. RDn (1913–*)
SEQ 24 Hast. RDn (until 1858), Hast. II RDn (1858–1913), Rye RDn (1913–*)
SEQ 25 Lewes RDn (until 1858), Lewes I RDn (1858–1913), Lewes RDn (1913–*)
SEQ 26 Lewes RDn (until 1858), Lewes I RDn (1858–1913), Brigh. RDn (1913–55), Kemp Town RDn (1955–*)
SEQ 27 Lewes RDn (until 1858), Lewes II RDn (1858–1913), Hove RDn (1913–*)
SEQ 28 Lewes RDn (until 1858), Lewes II RDn (1858–1913), Hurst RDn (1913–*)
SEQ 29 Lewes RDn (until 1858), Lewes III RDn (1858–1913), Cuckf. RDn (1913–*)
SEQ 30 Lewes RDn (until 1858), Lewes IV RDn (1858–1913), Hurst RDn (1913–*)
SEQ 31 Lewes RDn (until 1858), Pev. III RDn (1858–1913), Uckf. RDn (1913–*)
SEQ 32 Pev. RDn (until 1858), Pev. I RDn (1858–1913), E'bourne RDn (1913–*)
SEQ 33 Pev. RDn (until 1858), Pev. I RDn (1858–1913), Seaford RDn (1913–*)
SEQ 34 Pev. RDn (until 1858), Pev. II RDn (1858–1913), Seaford RDn (1913–*)
SEQ 35 Pev. RDn (until 1858), Pev. III RDn (1858–1913), Uckf. RDn (1913–*)
SEQ 36 Pev. RDn (until 1858), Pev. IV RDn (1858–1913), E Grin. RDn (1913–*)
SEQ 37 S Mall. RDn (pec jurisd until 1846, within AD 1846–58), Lewes I RDn (1858–1913), Lewes RDn (1913–*)
SEQ 38 S Mall. RDn (pec jurisd until 1846, within AD 1846–58), Pev. III RDn (1858–1913), Uckf. RDn (1913–*)

DIOCESE AND ARCHDEACONRIES

With a few exceptions noted below in the parochial entries, Sussex pars are in Chichester dioc. The organisation of rural deaneries in archdeaconries follows.

CHICHESTER AD
Arund. RDn (until 1871), Arund. RDn (1913–*), Arund. I RDn (1871–1913), Arund. II RDn (1871–1913), Bogn. Reg. RDn (1943–*), Boxg. RDn (until 1871), Boxg. RDn (1913–29), Boxg. I RDn (1871–1913), Boxg. II RDn (1871–1913), Boxg. III RDn (1871–1913), Chich. RDn, Horsham RDn (1913–*), Midh. RDn (until 1871), Midh. RDn (1913–*), Midh. I RDn (1871–1913), Midh. II RDn (1871–1913), Midh. III RDn (1871–1913), Pagham RDn (1846–71), Petw. RDn (1913–*), Selsey RDn (1913–43), Storr. RDn (until 1871), Storr. RDn (1913–*), Storr. I RDn (1871–1913), Storr. II RDn (1871–1913), Storr. III RDn (1871–1913), Storr. IV RDn (1871–1913), Tarring RDn (1846–71)

HASTINGS AD (1912–*)
Battle & Bexhill RDn (1931–*), Dall. RDn, E'bourne RDn (1913–*), Etch. RDn (1913–*), Hast. RDn (1913–*), Hast. I RDn (1912–13), Hast. II RDn (1912–13), Pev. I RDn (1912–13), Pev. II RDn (1912–13), Rye RDn (1913–*), Seaford RDn (1913–*)

LEWES AD
Brigh. RDn (1913–*), Cuckf. RDn (1913–*), Dall. RDn (until 1912), E Grin. RDn (1913–*), Hast. RDn (until 1858), Hast. I RDn (1858–1912), Hast. II RDn (1858–1912), Hove RDn (1913–*), Hurst RDn (1913–*), Kemp Town RDn (1955–*), Lewes RDn (until 1858), Lewes RDn (1913–*), Lewes I RDn (1858–1913), Lewes II RDn (1858–1913), Lewes III RDn (1858–1913), Lewes IV RDn (1858–1913), Lewes V RDn (1858–1913), S Mall. RDn (1846–58), Pev. RDn (until 1858), Pev. I RDn (1858–1912), Pev. II RDn (1858–1912), Pev. III RDn (1858–1913), Pev. IV RDn (1858–1913), Preston RDn (1955–*), Uckf. RDn (1913–*)

THE PARISHES OF SUSSEX

ALBOURNE
AP *LG* Tipnoak Hd, Cuckf. PLU, RSD, RD [in W Sussex 1889–1908, in E Sussex 1908[1]–74, transf 1974 to W Sussex[128]]. *Parl* New Shor. Parl Bor (1832–85), Mid Dv (1885–1918), E Grin. Dv (1918–48), Lewes CC (1948–70), Mid-Sussex CC (1970–*). *Eccl* Seq 30.

ALCISTON
AP *LG* Alciston Hd, W Firle PLU (1835–98), RSD, E'bourne PLU (1898–1930), [E Sussex] E'bourne RD (1894–1934), Hailsham RD (1934–74). Civ bdry: 1883,[2] 1934.[3] *Parl* Seq 11. *Eccl* Seq 34.

ALDINGBOURNE
AP *LG* Seq 15. *Parl* Seq 26. *Eccl* Boxg. RDn (until 1871), Boxg. I RDn (1871–1913), Boxg. RDn (1913–29), Selsey RDn (1929–43), Bogn. Reg. RDn (1943–*).

ALDRINGTON
AP *LG* Fishg. Hd, Stey. PLU, RSD (1875–93), Hove USD (1893–94), [W Sussex] Hove UD (1894–98), MB (1898–1974). Civ bdry: 1883.[2] *Parl* W'rn Dv (1832–85), Mid Dv (1885–1918), Brigh. Parl Bor (1918–48), Hove BC (1948–*). *Eccl* Seq 27. Eccl bdry: 1911 (cr Aldrington St Philip EP),[4] 1935,[5] 1939 (help cr Hove Bishop Hannington Memorial Chapel EP),[6] 1955.[7]

ALDRINGTON ST PHILIP
EP Cr 1911 from Aldrington AP.[4] Lewes II RDn (1911–13), Hove RDn (1913–49). Bdry: 1935.[5] Renamed 1949 'Hove St Philip', losing pt at same time to Hove Bishop Hannington Memorial Chapel EP.[8]

ALDWICK
EP Cr 1935 from Pagham AP.[9] Selsey RDn (1935–43), Bogn. Reg. RDn (1943–*).

ALFOLD
AP Pt Sussex (Bury Hd), pt Surrey (Blackheath Hd), the former lost 1884 to Wisborough Green AP, Sussex, and the par ent Surrey thereafter.[10] *LG* Hambledon PLU, RSD. *Parl* Sussex pt, W'rn Dv (1832–85). For later civ organisation, and for eccl organisation, see main entry in Surrey.

ALFRISTON
AP *LG* Seq 36. Civ bdry: 1934.[3] *Parl* Seq 11. *Eccl* Pev. RDn (until 1858), Pev. I RDn (1858–1913), Seaford RDn (1913–26). Abol eccl 1926 to help cr Alfriston with Lullington EP.[99]

ALFRISTON WITH LULLINGTON
EP Cr 1926 by union Alfriston AP, Lullington AP.[99] Seaford RDn.

ALMODINGTON
AP Boxg. RDn, abol before 1535 and absorbed in Earnley AP.[11]

AMBERLEY
AP Incl hmlt Rackham (sep CP 1866[12]), chap Houghton (sep civ identity early, eccl severed 1935 to help cr Bury with Houghton EP,[13] so that this par eccl 'Amberley with Houghton', qv, before 1935, 'Amberley' thereafter). *LG* W Easw. Hd, E Preston incorp for poor (1791–1869), Thak. PLU (1869–1930), RSD, [W Sussex] Thak. RD (1894–1933), Chanct. RD (1933–74). Addtl civ bdry alt: 1933 (incl gains North Stoke AP).[14] *Parl* Seq 28. *Eccl* Storr. RDn (1935–*).

AMBERLEY WITH HOUGHTON
AP Usual eccl spelling before eccl loses 1935 chap Houghton (for that, and for earlier civ sep of the chap, see prev entry; after 1935, eccl 'Amberley', qv). *Eccl* Arund. RDn (until 1871), Storr. I RDn (1871–1913), Storr. RDn (1913–35). Addtl eccl bdry alt: 1898.[15]

NORTH AMBERSHAM
Tg in Steep AP (Hants), transf to Selham AP, Sussex 1832 for parl purposes, 1844 for civ purposes,[16] sep CP 1866 in Sussex,[12] no sep eccl identity, transf 1916 from dioc Winch to dioc Chich.[17] *LG* Seq 17. Bdry: 1879.[18] *Parl* Hants until 1832, pt Midh. Parl Bor, pt W'rn Dv (1832–85), N-W'rn Dv (1885–1918), Chich. Dv (1918–48), Horsham CC (1948–70), Chich. CC (1970–*).

SOUTH AMBERSHAM
Tg in Steep AP (Hants), transf to Selham AP, Sussex 1832 for parl purposes, 1844 for civ purposes,[16] sep CP 1866 in Sussex,[12] no sep eccl identity, transf 1916 from dioc Winch to dioc Chich.[17] *LG* Seq 17. *Parl* Seq 14.

ANGMERING
AP Union 1573 of East Angmering AP, West Angmering AP[19]; usual civ spelling, eccl early 'East Angmering with Angmering', later sometimes 'Angmering with Ham and Bargham'. *LG* Seq 6 [E Preston incorp for poor 1806–69]. Civ bdry: 1877,[20] 1878,[21] 1883,[2] 1933.[14] *Parl* Seq 27. *Eccl* Arund. RDn (1573–1871), Storr. III RDn (1871–80), Storr. IV RDn (1880–1913), Arund. RDn (1913–*).

ANGMERING WITH HAM AND BARGHAM–See prev entry

EAST ANGMERING
AP Arund RDn, abol 1573 to help cr Angmering AP.[19]

WEST ANGMERING
AP Organisation as for East Angmering.

APPLEDRAM
AP Usual civ spelling; for eccl see following entry. *LG* Seq 15. *Parl* Seq 25.

APULDRAM
AP Usual eccl spelling; for civ see prev entry. *Eccl* Seq 8.

ARDINGLY
AP *LG* Seq 30. Civ bdry: 1934.[3] Transf 1974 to W Sussex.[128] *Parl* Seq 6. *Eccl* Seq 29. Eccl bdry: 1896 (help cr Turner's Hill EP).[22]

ARLINGTON
AP *LG* Longb. Hd, Hailsham PLU, RSD, [E Sussex] Hailsham RD. *Parl* Seq 11. *Eccl* Seq 34. Eccl bdry: 1845 (help cr Upper Dicker Common EP),[23] 1956.[24]

ARUNDEL
AP *LG* Arund. Honour in Avisf. Hd, Arund. Bor/MB, USD, incorp for poor (18th cent–1869), E Preston PLU (1869–1930). [W Sussex]. Civ bdry: 1902.[25] *Parl* Arund. Parl Bor (1295–1867), Seq 27 thereafter. *Eccl* Seq 1.

ASHBURNHAM
AP *LG* Foxearle Hd, Battle PLU, RSD, [E Sussex] Battle RD. Civ bdry: 1887.[26] *Parl* Seq 9. *Eccl* Seq 19.

ASHINGTON
AP Usual civ spelling; for eccl see following entry. *LG* W Grin. Hd, Thak. PLU, RSD, [W Sussex] Thak. RD (1894–1933), Chanct. RD (1933–74). Civ bdry: 1883,[2] 1933 (incl gains Warminghurst CP),[14] 1960.[27] *Parl* Seq 21.

ASHINGTON WITH BUNCTON
AP Usual eccl spelling; for civ see prev entry. *Eccl* Storr. RDn (until 1871), Storr. I RDn (1871–80), Storr. III RDn (1880–1913), Storr. RDn (1913–*).

ASHURST
AP Chap in Steyning AP, sep par 1580.[28] *LG* W

Grin. Hd, Stey. PLU, RSD, [W Sussex] Stey. W RD (1894–1933), Chanct. RD (1933–74). Civ bdry: 1883,[2] 1933.[14] *Parl* Seq 18. *Eccl* Seq 15.

BALCOMBE

AP *LG* Pt Buttg. Hd, pt Street Hd, Cuckf. PLU, RSD, [E Sussex] Cuckf. RD. Civ bdry: 1934,[3] 1957.[29] Transf 1974 to W Sussex.[128] *Parl* Seq 6. *Eccl* Seq 29.

BARCOMBE

AP *LG* Seq 29. Civ bdry: 1883,[2] 1934.[3] *Parl* Seq 4. *Eccl* Lewes RDn (until 1858), Pev. III RDn (1858–1913), Uckf. RDn (1913–31), Lewes RDn (1931–*).

BARLAVINGTON

AP *LG* Rothb. Hd, Sutton incorp for poor (1804–69), Petw. PLU (1869–1930), [W Sussex] Petw. RD. *Parl* Seq 23. *Eccl* Seq 11.

BARNHAM

AP *LG* Seq 2. Civ bdry: 1883.[2] *Parl* Seq 26. *Eccl* Seq 3. Eccl bdry: 1973.[122]

BATTLE

AP *LG* Battle Hd, Bor (status not sustained), PLU, USD, [E Sussex] Battle UD (1894–1934), RD (1934–74). Civ bdry: 1958.[30] *Parl* Seq 9. *Eccl* Pec jurisd Dean of Battle (until 1846), Seq 20 thereafter. Eccl bdry: 1862 (help cr Netherfield EP),[31] 1960.[119]

BECKLEY

AP *LG* Seq 22. *Parl* Seq 9. *Eccl* Seq 21.

BEDDINGHAM

AP *LG* Totnore Hd, W Firle PLU (1835–98), RSD, Lewes PLU (1898–1930), [E Sussex] Chailey RD. Civ bdry: 1934.[3] *Parl* Seq 12. *Eccl* Pev. RDn (until 1858), Pev. II RDn (1858–1913), Lewes RDn (1913–*).

LOWER BEEDING

Detached chap of Upper Beeding AP, sep EP 1838,[32] sep CP 1866.[12] *LG* Burbeach Hd, Horsham PLU, RSD, [W Sussex] Horsham RD. Civ bdry: 1933,[14] 1956 (exchanges pts with Crawley AP [the pt lost to help constitute Crawley UD]).[33] *Parl* New Shor. Parl Bor (1867–85), N-W'rn Dv (1885–1918), Horsham & Worthing Dv (1918–45), Horsham Dv/CC (1945–70), Horsham & Crawley CC (1970–*). *Eccl* Lewes RDn (1838– 58), Lewes IV RDn (1858–1913), Hurst RDn (1913–43), Horsham RDn (1943–*). Eccl bdry: 1871 (help cr Colgate EP).[34]

UPPER BEEDING

AP Anc 'Sele' or 'Sela'. Incl detached chap Lower Beeding (sep EP 1838,[32] sep CP 1866[12]). *LG* Burbeach Hd, Stey. PLU, RSD, [W Sussex] Stey. W RD (1894–1933), Chanct. RD (1933–74). Addtl civ bdry alt: 1883,[2] 1933 (gains Edburton AP).[14] *Parl* Seq 18. *Eccl* Lewes RDn (until 1858), Lewes IV RDn (1858–70s), Storr. RDn (1870s–1913), Hove RDn (1913–*). Addtl eccl bdry alt: 1871 (help cr Colgate EP).[34]

BEPTON

AP *LG* Seq 17. Civ bdry: 1879.[18] *Parl* Seq 15. *Eccl* Seq 15. Eccl bdry: 1931.[35]

BERSTED

AP Usual civ spelling, though sometimes 'South Bersted'; for eccl see following entry. Incl Bognor (sep EP 1828,[36] sep CP 1894 [the pt in Bogn. USD][37]). *LG* Aldw. Hd, Sutton incorp for poor (1791–1869), W'hamp. PLU (1869–1930), pt Bogn. USD, pt W'hamp. RSD, [W Sussex] W'hamp. RD (1894–1933), Chich. RD (1933–74). Addtl civ bdry alt: 1900,[38] 1913,[39] 1933.[14] *Parl* Seq 26.

SOUTH BERSTED

AP Usual eccl spelling, sometimes civ spelling; for usual civ, see prev entry. *Eccl* Pagham RDn (pec jurisd until 1846, in AD 1846–71), Arund. I RDn (1871–80), Arund. II RDn (1880–1913), Selsey RDn (1913–43), Bogn. Reg. RDn (1943–*). Eccl bdry: 1915.[40]

BERWICK

AP *LG* Longb. Hd, W Firle PLU (1835–98), RSD, E'bourne. PLU (1898–1930), [E Sussex] E'bourne. RD (1894–1934), Hailsham RD (1934–74). *Parl* Seq 11. *Eccl* Seq 34.

BEXHILL

The following have 'Bexhill' in their names. Insofar as any existed at a given time: *LG* Bexhill Hd, Battle PLU, pt Bexhill USD (1884–94), pt Battle RSD (1875–84); the pt of the par known as Lbty of the Sluice in Hast. Bor, MB, Cq Pt, CB (1889–94), USD; [E Sussex] Bexhill UD (1894–1902), MB (1902–74). *Parl* Pt [Lbty of the Sluice] Hast. Parl Bor (until 1885), remainder E'rn Dv (1832–85), thereafter ent par E'rn Dv (1885–1918), Rye Dv (1918–48), E'bourne. CC (1948–55), Rye CC (1955–*). *Eccl* Hast. RDn (until 1858), Hast. I RDn (1858–1913), Hast. RDn (1913–31), Battle & Bexhill RDn (1931–*).

AP1–BEXHILL [ST PETER]–Civ bdry: 1894 (loses the pt in the CB to Hastings St Mary Bulverhythe CP).[41] Eccl bdry: 1857 (cr EP3),[42] 1891 (cr EP2),[43] 1900 (cr EP4),[44] 1930 (cr Sidley EP).[45]

EP1–BEXHILL ST AUGUSTINE–Cr 1934 from EP2, EP3.[46] Bdry: 1952,[47] 1958.[48]

EP2–BEXHILL ST BARNABAS–Cr 1891 from AP1.[43] Bdry: 1934 (help cr EP1).[46]

EP3–BEXHILL ST MARK–Cr 1857 from AP1.[42] Bdry: 1925,[49] 1934 (help cr EP1),[46] 1958,[48] 1970.[50]

EP4–BEXHILL ST STEPHEN–Cr 1900 from AP1.[44] Bdry: 1925,[49] 1952.[47]

BIGNOR

AP *LG* Seq 3. Civ bdry: 1883,[2] 1889.[51] *Parl* Seq 15. *Eccl* Seq 11.

BILLINGSHURST

AP *LG* W Easw. Hd, Petw. PLU (1835–70), Horsham PLU (1870–1930), RSD, [W Sussex] Horsham RD. Civ bdry: 1933.[14] *Parl* Seq 24. *Eccl* Seq 14. Eccl bdry: 1935.[52]

BINDERTON

AP Orig had sep parochial rights, sep civ identity retained, eccl later considered within West Dean AP. *LG* W'bourne. & Singl. Hd, W'hamp. PLU,

RSD, [W Sussex] W'hamp. RD. Abol civ 1933 ent to West Dean AP.[14] *Parl* W'rn Dv (1832–85), S-W'rn Dv (1885–1918), Chich. Dv (1918–48). *Eccl* Pev. RDn.

BINSTED
AP *LG* Avisf. Hd, W'hamp. PLU, RSD, [W Sussex] W'hamp. RD. Abol civ 1833 ent to Tortington AP.[14] *Parl* W'rn Dv (1832–85), S-W'rn Dv (1885-1918), Chich. Dv (1918–48). *Eccl* Seq 1.

BIRDHAM
AP *LG* Seq 18. *Parl* Seq 25. *Eccl* Seq 7. Eccl bdry: 1935.[53]

BISHOPSTONE
AP *LG* Bishopst. Hd, Newh. PLU, RSD, [E Sussex] Newh. RD. Abol civ 1934 pt to Newhaven AP, pt to East Blatchington AP, pt to South Heighton AP.[3] *Parl* E'rn Dv (1832–85), S'rn Dv (1885–1918), Lewes Dv (1918–48). *Eccl* Seq 34.

BLACKLANDS
EP Cr 1881 from Hastings St Mary in the Castle AP.[54] Hast. I RDn (1881–1913), Hast. RDn (1913–70). Bdry: 1891,[55] 1938.[56] Abol 1970 to help cr Blacklands Christ Church and Hastings St Andrew EP.[57]
CP Cr 1894 from the pt of Ore AP in Hast. CB.[58] *LG* Hast. PLU, CB. Renamed 1897 'Hastings St Helens' when extended to incl pt Ore AP.[59]

BLACKLANDS CHRIST CHURCH AND HASTINGS ST ANDREW
EP Cr 1970 by union Blacklands EP, Hastings St Andrew AP.[57] Hast. RDn.

EAST BLATCHINGTON
AP *LG* Flexb. Hd, Newh. PLU, RSD (1875–83), Seaford USD (1883–94), [E Sussex] Seaford UD. Civ bdry: 1934.[3] *Parl* Seq 12. *Eccl* Lewes RDn (until 1858), Pev. II RDn (1858–1913), Seaford RDn (1913–*).

WEST BLATCHINGTON
AP *LG* Whaleb. Hd, Stey. PLU, RSD, [E Sussex] Stey. E RD (1894–1928), Hove MB (1928–74). Civ bdry: 1928 (loses pt to Brigh. CB and AP).[62] *Parl* E'rn Dv (1832–85), Mid Dv (1885–1918), Lewes Dv (1918–48), Hove BC (1948–*). *Eccl* Lewes RDn (until 1858), Lewes V RDn (1858–1913), Brigh. RDn (1913–43), Hove RDn (1943–*). Eccl bdry: 1939 (help cr Hove Bishop Hannington Memorial Chapel EP),[6] 1949.[8]

BODIAM
AP *LG* Stapl. Hd, Ticeh. PLU, RSD, [E Sussex] Ticeh. RD (1894–1934), Battle RD (1934–74). *Parl* Seq 9. *Eccl* Seq 22.

BODLE STREET GREEN
EP Cr 1855 from Herstmonceux AP, Warbleton AP, Dallington AP.[60] Dall. RDn (1855–71), Pev. I RDn (1871–1913), Dall. RDn (1913–*). Bdry: 1958.[61]

BOGNOR
Area in Bersted AP (eccl and sometimes civ, 'South Bersted'), sep EP 1828,[36] sep CP 1894 (from the pt in Bogn. USD).[37] Called 'Bognor Regis' from 1929. *LG* [W Sussex] W'hamp. PLU, Bogn. UD (1894–1929), Bogn. Reg. UD (1929–*). Civ bdry: 1900,[38] 1933.[14] *Parl* Chich. Dv/CC (1918–70), Arund. CC (1970–*). *Eccl* Pagham RDn (pec jurisd 1828–46, in AD 1846–71), Arund. I RDn (1871–79), Arund. II RDn (1879–1913), Selsey RDn (1913–43), Bogn. Reg. RDn (1943–*). Eccl bdry: 1915,[40] 1935.[63]

BOGNOR REGIS–See prev entry

BOLNEY
AP *LG* Seq 30. Civ bdry: 1934.[3] Transf 1974 to W Sussex.[128] *Parl* Seq 6. *Eccl* Lewes RDn (until 1858), Lewes IV RDn (1858–1913), Cuckf. RDn (1913–*). Eccl bdry: 1965.[64]

BOSHAM
AP *LG* Seq 14. Civ bdry: 1933.[14] *Parl* Seq 25. *Eccl* Boxg. RDn (until 1871), Boxg. III RDn (1871–1913), W'bourne. RDn (1913–*). Eccl bdry: 1957,[121] 1971.[23]

BOTOLPHS
AP *LG* Stey. Hd, PLU, RSD, [W Sussex] Stey. W RD. Abol civ 1933 ent to Bramber AP.[14] *Parl* New Shor. Parl Bor (1832–85), Mid Dv (1885–1918), Horsham & Worthing Dv (1918–45). *Eccl* Storr. RDn. Abol eccl 1530 to help cr Bramber with Botolphs EP.[65]

BOXGROVE
AP *LG* Seq 15. Civ bdry: 1933.[14] *Parl* Seq 25. *Eccl* Boxg. RDn (until 1871), Arund. II RDn (1871–80), Boxg. I RDn (1880–1913), Boxg. RDn (1913–29), Chich. RDn (1929–43), Bogn. Reg. RDn (1943–*).

BRAMBER
AP *LG* Stey. Hd, Bramber Bor (status not sustained), Stey. PLU, RSD, [W Sussex] Stey. W RD (1894–1933), Chanct. RD (1933–74). Civ bdry: 1933 (gains Botolphs AP).[14] *Parl* Bramber Parl Bor (1295 and often irregularly, sometimes returned with Steyning, regularly by itself 1369–1832), Seq 18 thereafter. *Eccl* Storr. RDn. Abol eccl 1530 to help cr Bramber with Botolphs EP.[65]

BRAMBER WITH BOTOLPHS
EP Cr 1530 by union Bramber AP, Botolphs AP[65] (each retains sep civ identity). Storr. RDn (1530–1871), Storr. III RDn (1871–1913), Horsham RDn (1913–29), Hove RDn (1929–*).

BRAMSHOTT
AP Pt Hants (orig Alton Hd, Finchdean Hd from 1830s), pt Sussex (Dumpf. Hd), the par made ent Hants 1895.[66] *LG* Headley incorp for poor (until 1869), Petersfield PLU (1869–1930), RSD, pt sep RD in W Sussex (1894–95). Bdry: 1832 for parl purposes, 1844 for civ purposes (Hants pt of par enlarged by gaining pt of the par prev in Sussex).[16] *Parl* Sussex pt, W'rn Dv (1832–85), N-W'rn Dv (1885–1918). For later civ organisation, and for eccl organisation, see main entry in Hants.

BREDE
AP *LG* Seq 23. Civ bdry: 1876,[67] 1934,[3] 1958.[30] *Parl* Seq 17. *Eccl* Dall. RDn (until 1858), Hast. II RDn (1858–1913), Rye RDn (1913–*).

BRIGHTLING
AP *LG* Seq 27. Civ bdry: 1887.[68] *Parl* Seq 9. *Eccl* Hast. RDn (until 1858), Dall. RDn (1858–*).

BRIGHTON
The following have 'Brighton' in their names. Insofar as any existed at a given time: *LG* Whaleb. Hd, Brigh. Town (some sep governmental rights from 1580, augmented by later acts[69]), Brigh. incorp for poor, USD, MB (1854–89), CB (1889–1974). Made pt 1974 of E Sussex.[128] *Parl* Brigh. Parl Bor (1832–1948), pt Brigh., Kemptown BC, pt Brigh., Pavillion BC (1948–*) [see Pt III of the *Guide* for composition of these constituencies by wards of the CB]. *Eccl* Lewes RDn (until 1858), Lewes V RDn (1858–1913), Brigh. RDn (1913–*).

AP1–BRIGHTON–Orig AP was St Nicholas, in 1873 status as mother church given to St Peter and St Nicolas then accounted as sep EP,[74] qv. The par orig called 'Brightelmston'. Civ bdry: 1928 (gains ent Ovingdean AP, Rottingdean AP, Preston AP, exchanges pts with Hove AP, gains pts of Falmer AP, West Blatchington AP, Patcham AP),[62] 1952.[70] Eccl bdry: 1834 (cr EP2,[36] refounded 1883[71]), 1849 (cr Kemp Town EP,[36] refounded 1930 [incl area from Rottingdean AP][72]), 1872 (cr EP12),[9] 1873 (cr EP23),[73] 1873 (cr EP22),[74] 1875 (cr EP15),[75] 1876 (cr EP11),[76] 1879 (help cr EP16),[77] 1880 (cr EP3),[9] 1881 (cr EP10),[78] 1884 (cr EP18),[79] 1884 (cr EP19),[80] 1885 (cr EP13),[71] 1887,[81] 1897 (cr EP4),[82] 1907 (cr EP25),[83] 1917 (cr EP1),[84] 1920,[85] 1921 (cr EP8),[86] 1922 (help cr EP26),[87] 1922,[88] 1924 (help cr EP21),[91] 1935 (cr EP14),[92] 1956 (gains EP18),[89] 1968.[90]

EP1–BRIGHTON ALL SAINTS–Cr 1917 from AP1.[84] Abol 1956 ent to EP21.[89]

EP2–BRIGHTON ALL SOULS–Cr 1834,[36] refounded 1883[71] from AP1. Lewes RDn (1834–58), Lewes V RDn (1858–1913), Brigh. RDn (1913–55), Kemp Town RDn (1955–67). Abol 1967 to help cr Kemp Town St Mary EP.[93]

EP3–BRIGHTON THE ANNUNCIATION–Cr 1880 from AP1.[9]

EP4–BRIGHTON THE CHAPEL ROYAL–Cr 1897 from AP1.[82]

EP5–BRIGHTON CHRIST CHURCH–Cr 1956 by union EP25, EP14.[89]

EP6–BRIGHTON THE GOOD SHEPHERD, PRESTON–Cr 1922 from Preston AP, Prestonville EP.[94] Brigh. RDn (1922–55), Preston RDn (1955–*). Bdry: 1927 (help cr Hove St Agnes EP),[95] 1949.[8]

EP7–BRIGHTON ST ALBAN, PRESTON–Cr 1915 from Preston AP.[96] Bdry: 1920,[85] 1968.[97]

EP8–BRIGHTON ST ANNE–Cr 1921 from AP1.[86] Brigh. RDn (1921–55), Kemp Town RDn (1955–*). Bdry: 1968.[90]

EP9–BRIGHTON ST AUGUSTINE, PRESTON–Cr 1898 from Preston AP.[81] Lewes V RDn (1898–1913), Brigh. RDn (1913–55), Preston RDn (1955–*).

EP10–BRIGHTON ST BARTHOLOMEW–Cr 1881 from AP1.[78]

EP11–BRIGHTON ST JAMES–Cr 1876 from AP1.[76] Abol 1956 to help cr EP17.[89]

EP12–BRIGHTON ST JOHN THE EVANGELIST–Cr 1840,[36] refounded 1872[9] from AP1. Bdry: 1879 (help cr EP16),[77] 1968.[90]

EP13–BRIGHTON ST LUKE–Cr 1885 from AP1.[71] Lewes V RDn (1885–1913), Brigh. RDn (1913–55), Kemp Town RDn (1955–*). Bdry: 1922 (help cr EP26),[87] 1968.[90]

EP14–BRIGHTON ST MARGARET–Cr 1935 from AP1.[92] Abol 1956 to help cr EP5.[89]

EP15–BRIGHTON ST MARTIN–Cr 1875 from AP1.[75] Bdry: 1920.[85]

EP16–BRIGHTON ST MARY–Cr 1879 from AP1, EP12.[77] Abol 1956 to help cr EP17.[89]

EP17–BRIGHTON ST MARY AND ST JAMES–Cr 1956 by union EP16, EP11.[89] Kemp Town RDn. Abol 1967 to help cr Kemp Town St Mary EP.[93]

EP18–BRIGHTON ST MARY MAGDALEN–Cr 1884 from AP1.[79] Abol 1956 ent to AP1.[89]

EP19–BRIGHTON ST MATTHEW–Cr 1884 from AP1.[80] Lewes V RDn (1884–1913), Brigh. RDn (1913–55), Kemp Town RDn (1955–67). Abol 1967 to help cr Kemp Town St Mark and St Matthew EP.[93]

EP20–BRIGHTON ST MATTHIAS, PRESTON–Cr 1912 from Preston AP.[98] Lewes V RDn (1912–13), Brigh. RDn (1913–55), Preston RDn (1955–*). Bdry: 1952.[118]

EP21–BRIGHTON ST MICHAEL AND ALL ANGELS–Cr 1924 from AP1, EP22, EP25.[91] Bdry: 1956 (gains EP1),[89] 1957.[100]

EP22–BRIGHTON ST NICOLAS–Orig mother church of Brighton until that status given 1873 to St Peter, qv as AP1.[74] Bdry: 1887,[81] 1924 (help cr EP21).[91]

EP23–BRIGHTON ST PAUL–Cr 1873 from AP1.[73] Bdry: 1887.[81]

EP24–BRIGHTON ST SAVIOUR, PRESTON–Cr 1888 from Preston AP.[101] Lewes V RDn (1888–1913), Brigh. RDn (1913–55), Preston RDn (1955–*).

EP25–BRIGHTON ST STEPHEN–Cr 1907 from AP1.[83] Bdry: 1922,[88] 1924 (help cr EP21).[91] Abol 1956 to help cr EP5.[89]

EP26–BRIGHTON ST WILFRID–Cr 1922 from AP1, EP13.[87] Bdry: 1937 (help cr Whitehawk EP).[96]

BROADWATER
AP *LG* Brightf. Hd, E Preston incorp for poor (1799–1869), PLU (1869–1902), pt Worthing MB (1890–94), pt Worthing USD, pt E Preston RSD, [W Sussex] E Preston RD (1894–1902). Civ bdry: 1879,[102] 1894 (the pt in the MB to cr Worthing CP).[58] Abol civ 1902 pt to Durrington AP, pt to Sompting AP, pt to Worthing

CP.[103] *Parl* New Shor. Parl Bor (1832–85), Mid Dv (1885–1918). *Eccl* Seq 17. Eccl bdry: 1855 (cr Worthing Christ Church EP),[104] 1868 (cr Worthing St George EP),[123] 1884 (help cr Worthing Holy Trinity EP),[105] 1888 (help cr Worthing St Andrew EP),[101] 1894 (help cr Worthing St Paul EP),[106] 1957.[107]

BROADWATER ST MARK
EP Cr 1867 from Frant AP (Sussex, Kent), Eridge Green EP.[108] Pev. IV RDn (1867–1913), Etch. RDn (1913–*). Bdry: 1921.[109]

BROOMHILL
AP Pt Kent (Lbty Cq Pt of New Romney), pt Sussex (Goldspur Hd, in Anc Town/Cq Pt of Winchelsea), the par made ent E Sussex 1895.[66] Bdry: 16th cent (loses marshlands in the par to help cr East Guldeford AP).[310] *LG* Rye PLU, RSD, pt sep RD in Kent (1894–95), [E Sussex] Rye RD (pt 1894–95, ent 1895–1934), Battle RD (1934–56). Abol civ 1956 to help cr Camber CP.[311] *Parl* Sussex pt, E'rn Dv (1832–1918), Rye Dv (1918–48), Hast. BC (1948–55), Rye CC (1955–70). *Eccl* Lympne RDn in dioc Canterb; early destroyed and incl in Lydd AP (Kent), qv for eccl organisation incl cr of Rye Harbour EP.

BURGESS HILL
EP Cr 1902 from St John's Common EP, Ditchling AP.[90] Lewes II RDn (1902–13), Hurst RDn (1913–*). Bdry: 1965.[64]
CP Cr 1934 by union Clayton Urban CP, Keymer Within CP, and pts Clayton AP, Ditchling AP, Wivelsfield AP.[3] *LG* Burgess Hill UD. Transf 1974 to W Sussex.[128] *Parl* Lewes CC (1948–70), Mid-Sussex CC (1970–*).

BURPHAM
AP *LG* Burpham Bor (status not sustained), Seq 6. Civ bdry: 1933.[14] *Parl* Seq 27. *Eccl* Seq 1.

BURTON
AP *LG* Rothb. Hd, Sutton incorp for poor (1791–1869), Petw. PLU (1869–1930), RSD, [W Sussex] Petw. RD. Civ bdry: 1833.[2] Abol civ 1933 pt to East Lavington AP, pt to Sutton AP, pt to Duncton AP.[14] *Parl* W'rn Dv (1832–85), N-W'rn Dv (1885–1918), Chich. Dv (1918–48). *Eccl* Midh. RDn. Abol before 1535 (sep civ identity retained) to cr Burton with Coates EP.[110]

BURTON WITH COATES
EP Cr before 1535 by union Burton AP, Coates AP (each retains sep civ identity).[110] *Eccl* Seq 11.

BURWASH
AP *LG* Pt Shoyswell Hd, pt Henhurst Hd, Ticeh. PLU, RSD, [E Sussex] Ticeh. RD (1894–1934), Battle RD (1934–74). *Parl* Seq 8. *Eccl* Seq 22. Eccl bdry: 1872 (help cr Burwash Weald EP).[77]

BURWASH WEALD
EP Cr 1877 from Burwash AP, Mayfield AP, Heathfield AP.[77] Dall. RDn.

BURY
AP *LG* Seq 3. Civ bdry: 1883,[2] 1933.[14] *Parl* Seq 23. *Eccl* Arund. RDn (until 1871), Midh. II RDn (1871–1913), Petw. RDn (1913–35). Abol eccl 1935, united with chap Houghton of Amberley with Houghton AP to cr Bury with Houghton EP.[13]

BURY WITH HOUGHTON
EP Cr 1935 by union Bury AP, chap Houghton of Amberley with Houghton AP.[13] Petw. RDn.

BUXTED
AP Incl chap Uckfield (sep civ identity early, sep EP 1846[111]), pt Hadlow Down (sep EP 1837,[112] sep CP 1905[113]). *LG* Seq 40. *Parl* Seq 5. *Eccl* Seq 38. Addtl eccl bdry alt: 1871 (cr Highhurst Wood EP),[34] 1844 (cr Buxted St Mary EP),[114] 1901 (help cr Fairwarp EP),[115] 1957,[116] 1969.[117]

BUXTED ST MARY
EP Cr 1884 from Buxted AP.[114] Pev. III RDn (1884–1913), Uckf. RDn (1913–*). Bdry: 1957.[116]

CAMBER
CP Cr 1956 by union Broomhill AP, St Thomas the Apostle, Winchelsea AP.[311] *LG* [E Sussex] Battle RD. *Parl* Rye CC (1970–*).
EP Cr 1973 from Rye Harbour EP.[104] Rye RDn.

CAMELSDALE
EP Cr 1938 from Fernhurst AP, Lynchmere AP.[125] Midh. RDn.

CATSFIELD
AP *LG* Orig pt Ninfield Hd, pt Netherfield Hd, later ent Ninfield Hd, Battle PLU, RSD, [E Sussex] Battle RD. Civ bdry: 1887.[126] *Parl* Seq 9. *Eccl* Seq 20.

CHAILEY
AP *LG* Seq 34. Civ bdry: 1883,[2] 1934.[3] *Parl* Seq 4. *Eccl* Seq 31.

CHALVINGTON
AP *LG* Seq 45. Civ bdry: 1934.[3] *Parl* Seq 11. *Eccl* Pev. RDn (until 1858), Pev. II RDn (1858–1913), Seaford RDn (1913–53). Abol eccl 1953 to help cr Ripe with Chalvington EP.[309]

NORTH CHAPEL
Area in Petworth AP, sep CP/EP 1692.[127] *LG* Rothb. Hd, Midh. PLU (1835–69), Petw. PLU (1869–1930), RSD, [W Sussex] Petw. RD. *Parl* Seq 23. *Eccl* Seq 12.

CHICHESTER
The following have 'Chichester' in their names. Insofar as any existed at a given time: *LG* Chich. Bor/MB, incorp for poor (1753–1930), USD. [W Sussex]. *Parl* Chich. Parl Bor (1295–1885), S-W'rn Dv (1885–1918), Chich. Dv/CC (1918–*). *Eccl* Pec jurisd Dean of Chich. (until 1846), Chich. RDn (1846–*).
CP1–CHICHESTER–Cr 1896 by union AP1, CP2, CP3, AP2, AP4, CP4, AP5, AP7, AP8, AP9, AP10, Portfield CP, Rumboldswyke AP.[129] Bdry: 1933.[14]
AP1–CHICHESTER ALL SAINTS–Abol civ 1896 to help cr CP1.[129] *Eccl* Pec jurisd Pagham

RDn (until 1846), Chich. RDn (1846–1952). Abol eccl 1952 ent to AP9.[130]

CP2–CHICHESTER THE CLOSE–Ex-par area (eccl in pec jurisd Dean of Chich. until 1846), sep CP 1858.[131] Not in Bor, but area in MB from 1835, Parl Bor from 1832. Abol civ 1896 to help cr CP1.[129]

CP3–CHICHESTER NEWTOWN, OR ST JOHN–Chap deemed ex-par, endowed as PC 1826[36] but later not considered parochial, sep CP 1858,[131] eccl abol 1952 pt to AP9, pt to AP8.[130] Abol civ 1896 to help cr CP1.[129]

AP2–CHICHESTER ST ANDREW [IN THE MARKET or IN THE OX-MARKET]–Abol civ 1896 to help cr CP1.[129] Abol eccl 1952 pt to AP9, pt to AP4, pt to AP8.[130]

AP3–CHICHESTER ST ANDREW IN THE PALLANT–Early demolished

AP4–CHICHESTER ST BARTHOLOMEW–Early double dedication, that of 'St Sepulchre' dropped 16th cent. *LG* Not in Bor but in Box & Stockb. Hd, Chich. MB (pt 1835–94, ent 1894–96), pt Chich. USD, pt Chich. RSD. Civ bdry: 1894 (the pt not in the MB cr St Bartholomew Rural CP),[132] 1895 (gains St Bartholomew Rural CP).[133] Abol civ 1896 to help cr CP1.[129] *Parl* Pt Chich. Parl Bor, pt W'rn Dv (1832–85), S-W'rn Dv (1885–1918). Eccl bdry: 1876,[134] 1952.[130] Abol eccl 1959 to help cr EP3.[135]

CP4–CHICHESTER ST JAMES–Ex-par place, orig hospital, sep CP 1858,[136] eccl abol 1952 ent to AP8.[130] *LG* Not in Bor, MB (1835–96). Abol civ 1896 to help cr CP1.[129] *Parl* Chich. Parl Bor (1835–85), S-W'rn Dv (1885–1918).

AP5–CHICHESTER ST MARTIN–Abol civ 1896 to help cr CP1.[129] Abol eccl 1899 to help cr EP1.[137]

AP6–CHICHESTER ST MARY IN THE MARKET–In ruins by end 16th cent, united to AP9.[138]

AP7–CHICHESTER ST OLAVE–Abol civ 1896 to help cr CP1.[129] Abol eccl 1899 to help cr EP1.[137]

EP1–CHICHESTER ST OLAVE WITH ST MARTIN–Cr 1899 by union AP5, AP7.[137] Abol 1952 ent to AP9.[130]

AP8–CHICHESTER ST PANCRAS–*LG* Pt Chich. Bor, pt Box & Stockb. Hd, Chich. MB (enlarged pt 1835–94, ent 1894–96), pt Chich. USD, pt Chich. RSD. Civ bdry: 1894 (the pt not in the MB cr St Pancras Rural CP).[132] Abol civ 1896 to help cr CP1.[129] *Parl* Pt Chich. Parl Bor (1295–1885), pt W'rn Dv (1832–85), S-W'rn Dv (1885–1918). *Eccl* Pt pec jurisd Pagham RDn, pt pec jurisd Dean of Chich. (until 1846), Chich. RDn (1846–*). Eccl bdry: 1952 (incl gains Chichester St James [area of CP4]).[130]

EP2–CHICHESTER ST PAUL–Cr 1837 from AP9.[139] Bdry: 1876,[134] 1952.[130] Abol 1959 to help cr EP3.[135]

EP3–CHICHESTER ST PAUL AND ST BARTHOLOMEW–Cr 1959 by union EP2, AP4.[135] Bdry: 1969.[73]

AP9–CHICHESTER ST PETER THE GREAT OR SUB-DEANERY–Gains 16th cent AP6.[138] *LG* Pt Chich. Bor, pt Box & Stockb. Hd, Chich. MB (enlarged pt 1835–94, ent 1894–96), pt Chich. USD, pt Chich. RSD. Civ bdry: 1882,[2] 1894 (the pt not in the MB cr Sub-Deanery Rural CP),[132] 1895.[133] Abol civ 1896 to help cr CP1.[129] *Parl* Pt Chich. Parl Bor (1295–1885), pt W'rn Dv (1832–85), S-W'rn Dv (1885–1918). Eccl bdry: 1837 (cr EP2),[139] 1876,[134] 1952 (incl gains EP1),[130] 1969.[73]

AP10–CHICHESTER ST PETER THE LESS–Gains 16th cent AP11.[138] Addtl civ bdry alt: 1883.[2] Abol civ 1896 to help cr CP1.[129] Abol eccl 1952 pt to AP9, pt to EP2.[130]

AP11–CHICHESTER ST PETER SUB CASTRO–Abol 16th cent, united to AP10.[138]

CHIDDINGLY

AP *LG* Seq 44. Civ bdry: 1951 (help cr Horam CP).[140] *Parl* Seq 11. *Eccl* Pev. RDn (until 1858), Pev. II RDn (1858–1913), Dall. RDn (1913–*). Eccl bdry: 1845 (help cr Upper Dicker Common EP).[23]

CHIDHAM

AP *LG* Seq 14. *Parl* Seq 25. *Eccl* Seq 6. Eccl bdry: 1957.[121]

EAST CHILTINGTON

Chap (pec jurisd S Mall.) and hmlt in Westmeston AP, sep CP 1866,[12] no sep eccl identity, eccl united 1909 to Plumpton AP.[141] *LG* Seq 34. Bdry: 1934.[3] *Parl* Seq 4.

WEST CHILTINGTON

AP *LG* Pt W Easw. Hd, pt E Easw. Hd, Thak. PLU, RSD, [W Sussex] Thak. RD (1894–1933), Chanct. RD (1933–74). Civ bdry: 1883.[2] *Parl* Pt New Shor. Parl Bor, pt W'rn Dv (1832–85), Mid Dv (1885–1918), Horsham & Worthing Dv (1918–45), Horsham Dv (1945–48), Arund. & Shor. CC (1948–70), Shor. CC (1970–*). *Eccl* Seq 13. Eccl bdry: 1960.[120]

CHITHURST

Chap in Iping AP, sep civ identity early, eccl severed 1957 to help cr Trotton with Chithurst EP.[143] *LG* Seq 16. Civ bdry: 1879.[18] *Parl* Seq 14.

CLAPHAM

AP *LG* Brightf. Hd, Sutton incorp for poor (1791–1869), E Preston PLU (1869–1930), RSD, [W Sussex] E Preston RD (1894–1933), Worthing RD (1933–74). Civ bdry: 1933.[14] *Parl* New Shor. Parl Bor (1832–85), Mid Dv (1885–1918), Chich. Dv (1918–48), Arund. & Shor. CC (1948–70), Arund. CC (1970–*). *Eccl* Arund. RDn (until 1871), Arund. I RDn (1871–80), Storr. IV RDn (1880–1913), Worthing RDn (1913–*).

CLAYTON

AP *LG* Buttg. Hd, Cuckf. PLU, pt Burgess Hill USD, pt Cuckf. RSD, [E Sussex] Cuckf. RD. Civ bdry: 1894 (the pt in Burgess Hill USD cr Clayton Urban CP),[58] 1934 (incl help cr Burgess Hill CP).[3] Transf 1974 to W Sussex.[128] *Parl* Seq 3. *Eccl* Always held eccl with Keymer AP as 'Clayton with Keymer',[144] qv.

CLAYTON URBAN

CP Cr 1894 from the pt of Clayton AP in Burgess Hill USD.[58] *LG* [E Sussex] Cuckf. PLU, Burgess Hill UD. Abol 1934 to help cr Burgess Hill CP.[3] *Parl* E Grin. Dv (1918–48).

CLAYTON WITH KEYMER

EP One par for eccl purposes[144]; for civ see Clayton AP, Keymer AP. *Eccl* Seq 28. Eccl bdry: 1865 (cr St John's Common EP).[145]

CLIMPING

AP Usual civ spelling; for eccl see following entry. Bdry: perhaps soon after 1546 (gains Cudlow AP).[147] *LG* Seq 1 (E Preston incorp for poor from 1799). Addtl civ bdry alt: 1880,[148] 1933.[14] *Parl* Seq 26.

CLYMPING

AP Usual eccl spelling; for civ and 16th cent gain of Cudlow AP, see prev entry. *Eccl* Seq 2.

COATES

AP *LG* Bury Hd, Sutton incorp for poor (1791–1869), Petw. PLU (1869–1930), RSD, [W Sussex] Petw. RD. Abol civ 1933 ent to Fittleworth AP.[14] *Parl* W'rn Dv (1832–85), N-W'rn Dv (1885–1918), Chich. Dv (1918–48). *Eccl* Midh. RDn. Abol eccl before 1535 (sep civ identity retained) to help cr Burton with Coates EP.[110]

COCKING

AP Incl chap Linchmere (eccl, 'Lynchmere'; sep civ identity early [sep perhaps in 1568[149]], sep eccl no later than 1724[36]). *LG* Seq 17. *Parl* Seq 14. *Eccl* Seq 10. Addtl eccl bdry alt: 1931.[35]

COLDWALTHAM

AP Usual civ spelling; for eccl see 'Cold Waltham'. *LG* Bury Hd, Sutton incorp for poor (1804–35), Thak. PLU (1835–1930), RSD, [W Sussex] Thak. RD (1894–1933), Chanct. RD (1933–74). Civ bdry: 1933 (gains Hardham AP).[14] *Parl* Seq 22.

COLEMAN'S HATCH

EP Cr 1912 from Hartfield AP.[92] Pev. IV RDn (1912–13), E Grin. RDn (1913–*).

COLGATE

EP Cr 1871 from Upper Beeding AP, Lower Beeding EP, Horsham AP.[34] Lewes IV RDn (1871–1913), Hurst RDn (1913–29), Horsham RDn (1929–*). Bdry: 1952.[150]

COMPTON

AP Incl chap Up Marden (sep civ identity early, no sep eccl identity hence this par eccl 'Compton with Up Marden', qv). *LG* Seq 19. Addtl civ bdry alt: 1880,[151] 1933 (gains Up Marden CP).[14] *Parl* Seq 25.

COMPTON WITH UP MARDEN

AP Usual eccl spelling; for civ and civ sep chap Up Marden, see prev entry. *Eccl* Seq 6. Eccl bdry: 1856 (help cr Stansted EP from area of the chap).[152]

COOMBES

AP *LG* Stey. Hd, PLU, RSD, [W Sussex] Stey. W RD (1894–1933), Worthing RD (1933–74). *Parl* Seq 19. *Eccl* Seq 17.

COPTHORNE

EP Cr 1881 from Crawley Down EP, Worth AP (both Sussex, dioc Chich), and from Horne EP, Burstow AP (both Surrey, dioc Roch).[81] Lewes III RDn (1881–1913), E Grin. RDn (1913–*).

COWFOLD

AP *LG* Windham & Ewhurst Hd, Cuckf. PLU (1835–97), RSD, Horsham PLU (1897–1930), [W Sussex] Horsham RD. Civ bdry: 1933.[14] *Parl* Seq 20. *Eccl* Seq 30.

CRAWLEY

AP Orig free chapel, considered parochial by 16th cent,[153] sometimes afterward considered chap to Slaugham AP, sep eccl identity maintained. Bdry: *ca* 1510 (gains Shelley AP).[154] *LG* Buttg. Hd, E Grin. PLU (1835–80), RSD (1875–80), Horsham PLU (1880–1930), RSD (1880–94), [E Sussex 1889–95[66], W Sussex 1895–1974] Horsham RD (1894–1956), Crawley UD (1956–74). Addtl civ bdry alt: 1933 (incl gains Ifield AP),[14] 1953 (gains pts Slaugham AP, Worth AP, both E Sussex),[155] 1956 (exchanges pts with Lower Beeding CP, loses pt to Rusper AP, the altered par constituted Crawley UD).[33] *Parl* E'rn Dv (1832–85), N-W'rn Dv (1885–1918), Horsham & Worthing Dv (1918–45), Horsham Dv/CC (1945–70), Horsham & Crawley CC (1970–*). *Eccl* Lewes RDn (16th cent–1858), Lewes III RDn (1858–1913), Cuckf. RDn (1913–29), Horsham RDn (1929–*). Addtl eccl bdry alt: 1952,[150] 1955 (gains West Crawley EP),[156] 1959 (cr Southgate EP),[157] 1959.[158]

WEST CRAWLEY

EP Cr 1901 from Ifield AP.[159] Lewes III RDn (1901–13), Cuckf. RDn (1913–29), Horsham RDn (1929–55). Bdry: 1952.[150] Abol eccl 1955 ent to Crawley AP.[156]

CRAWLEY DOWN

EP Cr 1862 from Worth AP.[31] Lewes III RDn (1862–1913), E Grin. RDn (1913–*). Bdry: 1881 (help cr Copthorne EP),[81] 1896 (help cr Turner's Hill EP).[22]

CROWBOROUGH

Hmlt in Rotherfield AP, sep EP 1880,[160] sep CP 1905.[161] *LG* [E Sussex] Uckf. PLU, RD. *Parl* E Grin. Dv/CC (1918–*). *Eccl* Pev. IV RDn (1880–1913), E Grin. RDn (1913–*).

CROWHURST

AP *LG* Seq 20. Civ bdry: 1938.[162] *Parl* Seq 9. *Eccl* Seq 20.

CUCKFIELD

AP *LG* Buttg. Hd, Cuckf. PLU, pt Hayward's Heath USD, pt Cuckf. USD, pt Cuckf. RSD, [E Sussex] Cuckf. UD. Civ bdry: 1894 (the pt in Hayward's Heath CP cr Hayward's Heath CP, the pt not in a USD cr Cuckfield Rural CP),[58] 1934.[3] Transf 1974 to W Sussex.[128] *Parl* E'rn Dv (1832–85), N'rn Dv (1885–1918), E Grin. Dv/CC (1918–

70), Mid-Sussex CC (1970–*). *Eccl* Seq 29. Eccl bdry: 1848 (cr Staplefield Common EP),[163] 1866 (cr Hayward's Heath St Wilfrid, Cuckfield EP[164] [soon afterward called 'Cuckfield St Wilfrid' until renamed 1944 'Hayward's Heath St Wilfrid' gaining at same time pt Wivelsfield AP[99]]), 1911,[165] 1965.[64]

CUCKFIELD RURAL

CP Cr 1894 from the pt of Cuckfield AP not in a USD.[58] *LG* [E Sussex] Cuckf. PLU, RD. Bdry: 1934,[3] 1957.[29] Transf 1974 to W Sussex.[128] *Parl* E Grin. Dv/CC (1918–70), Mid-Sussex CC (1970–*).

CUCKFIELD ST WILFRID

EP Name commonly used for EP cr 1866 as 'Hayward's Heath St Wilfrid, Cuckfield' (qv for RDns and bdry alts) until renamed 1944 'Hayward's Heath St Wilfrid' gaining at same time pt Wivelsfield AP.[99]

CUDLOW

AP Storr. RDn, abol prob soon after 1546 and absorbed into Climping AP (eccl, 'Clymping').[147]

DALLINGTON

AP *LG* Pt Netherfield Hd, pt Hawkesborough Hd, Battle PLU, RSD, [E Sussex] Battle RD. Civ bdry: 1883,[2] 1887.[26] *Parl* Seq 9. *Eccl* Seq 19. Eccl bdry: 1855 (help cr Bodle Street Green EP).[60]

DANEHILL

Chap in Fletching AP, Horsted Keynes AP, sep EP 1851,[166] sep CP 1898.[167] *LG* [E Sussex] Uckf. PLU, RD. *Parl* E Grin. Dv/CC (1918–*). *Eccl* Pev. RDn (1851–58), Pev. III RDn (1858–1913), Uckf. RDn (1913–*).

EAST DEAN

AP [E Sussex]. *LG* Seq 47. Civ bdry: 1938 (loses pt to E'bourne CB and AP).[168] *Parl* Seq 10. *Eccl* Seq 32.

EAST DEAN

AP [W Sussex]. *LG* W'bourne & Singl. Hd, W'hamp. PLU, RSD, RD (1894–1933), Chich. RD (1933–74). *Parl* Seq 25. *Eccl* Boxg. RDn (until 1871), Boxg. II RDn (1871–80), Boxg. I RDn (1880–1913), Boxg. RDn (1913–29), Chich. RDn (1929–50), W'bourne RDn (1950–*).

WEST DEAN

AP [E Sussex]. *LG* Seq 47. *Parl* E'rn Dv (1832–85), S'rn Dv (1885–1918), E'bourne Dv (1918–48), Lewes CC (1948–55), E'bourne CC (1955–*). *Eccl* Pev. RDn (until 1858), Pev. I RDn (1858–1913), E'bourne RDn (1913–30), Seaford RDn (1930–*).

WEST DEAN

AP [W Sussex]. *LG* Seq 19. Civ bdry: 1933 (gains Binderton AP).[14] *Parl* Seq 25. *Eccl* Seq 6. Eccl bdry: early gains eccl Binderton AP (orig sep AP, sep civ identity maintained until 1933).

DENTON

AP *LG* Bishopst. Hd, Newh. PLU, RSD (ent 1875–81, pt 1881–94), pt Newh. USD (1881–94), [E Sussex] Newh. RD. Civ bdry: 1894 (the pt in the USD cr Denton Urban CP).[58] Abol civ 1934 pt to Newhaven AP, pt to South Heighton AP.[3] *Parl* E'rn Dv (1832–85), S'rn Dv (1885–1918), Lewes Dv (1918–48). *Eccl* Seq 34. Eccl bdry: 1930.[169]

DENTON URBAN

CP Cr 1894 from the pt of Denton AP in Newh. USD.[58] *LG* [E Sussex] Newh. PLU, UD. Abol 1934 ent to Newhaven AP.[3] *Parl* Lewes Dv (1918–48).

UPPER DICKER COMMON

EP Cr 1845 from Arlington AP, Hellingly AP, Chiddingly AP.[23] Pev. RDn (1845–58), Pev. II RDn (1858–1913), Seaford RDn (1913–*). Sometimes called 'Upper Dicker'.

DIDLING

AP *LG* Dumpf. Hd, Midh. PLU, RSD, [W Sussex] Midh. RD. Abol civ 1933 ent to Treyford AP.[14] *Parl* Midh. Parl Bor (1832–85), N-W'rn Dv (1885–1918), Chich. Dv (1918–48). *Eccl* Midh. RDn. Abol 1503 to help cr Elsted with Treyford and Didling EP.[170]

DITCHLING

AP Incl chap Wivelsfield (gained as chap by end 12th cent[171]; sep par perhaps at Dissolution in 16th cent, sep civ identity early, sep eccl no later than 1773[36]), Burgess Hill (sep EP 1902,[90] sep CP 1934[3] [qv for other pars drawn on to constitute the CP]). *LG* Seq 34. Addtl civ bdry alt: 1934.[3] *Parl* Seq 4. *Eccl* Seq 28. Addtl eccl bdry alt: 1965.[64]

DONNINGTON

AP *LG* Seq 15. Civ bdry: 1883,[2] 1896 (gains St Pancras Rural CP),[172] 1933.[14] *Parl* Seq 25. *Eccl* Seq 8. Eccl bdry: 1969.[73]

DUNCTON

CP/EP cr 1692 from Petworth AP.[127] *LG* Rothb. Hd, Sutton incorp for poor (1791–1869), Petw. PLU (1869–1930), RSD, [W Sussex] Petw. RD. Civ bdry: 1883,[2] 1933.[14] *Parl* Seq 23. *Eccl* Seq 11. Eccl bdry: 1865.[173]

DURRINGTON

Area in West Tarring AP, sep civ identity early, sep EP 1914.[174] *LG* Brightf. Hd, E Preston incorp for poor (1803–69), PLU (1869–1930), RSD, [W Sussex] E Preston RD (1894–1929). Civ bdry: 1902,[103] 1902.[25] Abol civ 1929 ent to Worthing CP.[175] *Parl* New Shor. Parl Bor (1832–85), Mid Dv (1885–1918), Chich. Dv (1918–48). *Eccl* Worthing RDn. Eccl bdry: 1957.[107]

EARNLEY

AP Bdry: before 1535 (gains Almodington AP[11], the union civ called 'Earnley', eccl 'Earnley and Almodington', qv). *LG* Seq 18. Addtl civ bdry alt: 1933.[14] *Parl* Seq 25.

EARNLEY AND ALMODINGTON

AP Usual eccl spelling of par cr before 1535 by union Earnley AP, Almodington AP[11]; for civ spelling see prev entry. *Eccl* Seq 7.

EARTHAM

AP Sometimes anc 'Bowden'. *LG* Seq 15. *Parl* Seq 25. *Eccl* Boxg. RDn (until 1871), Boxg. I RDn (1871–1913), Boxg. RDn (1913–29), Arund. RDn (1929–*).

EASEBOURNE
AP Incl chap Lodsworth (sep civ identity early, sep EP 1773[36]), chap and bor Midhurst (sep civ identity early, sep EP 1725[36]). *LG* Seq 17. Addtl civ bdry alt: 1889.[51] *Parl* Seq 14. *Eccl* Seq 9. Addtl eccl bdry alt: 1931,[35] 1958.[48]

EASTBOURNE
The following have 'Eastbourne' in their names. Insofar as any existed at a given time: *LG* E'bourne Hd, PLU, USD, MB (1883–1911), CB (1911–74). Made pt 1974 of E Sussex.[128] *Parl* Seq 10. *Eccl* Pev. RDn (until 1858), Pev. I RDn (1858–1931), E'bourne RDn (1913–*).

AP1–EASTBOURNE [ST MARY] –Civ bdry: 1899 (gains Norway CP),[176] 1912 (gains Hampden Park CP),[177] 1926,[178] 1938.[168] Eccl bdry: 1847 (cr EP4),[179] 1870 (help cr Meads EP),[86] 1883 (help cr EP6),[180] 1911,[181] 1911 (cr EP8),[97] 1927,[182] 1935 (help cr EP7).[183]

EP1–EASTBOURNE ALL SAINTS–Cr 1882 from EP11.[6] Bdry: 1899,[184] 1956.[185]

EP2–EASTBOURNE ALL SOULS–Cr 1881 from EP4.[78] Bdry: 1890.[139]

EP3–EASTBOURNE CHRIST CHURCH–Cr 1859,[36] refounded 1864[186] from EP4. Bdry: 1873,[187] 1890,[139] 1917 (cr EP5),[188] 1925 (help cr EP10).[49]

EP4–EASTBOURNE HOLY TRINITY–Cr 1847 from AP1.[179] Bdry: 1859 (cr EP3,[36] refounded 1864[186]), 1867 (cr EP11),[189] 1870 (help cr Meads EP),[86] 1881 (cr EP2),[78] 1882 (help cr EP1),[6] 1883 (help cr EP6).[180]

EP5–EASTBOURNE ST ANDREW–Cr 1917 from EP3.[188] Bdry: 1951,[190] 1953 (help cr Hampden Park EP),[191] 1957,[192] 1969 (cr Langney EP).[117]

EP6–EASTBOURNE ST ANNE, UPPERTON–Cr 1883 from AP1, EP4.[180] Bdry: 1925 (help cr EP10).[49] Abol 1956 pt to EP9, pt to EP8, pt to EP1, pt to EP10.[185]

EP7–EASTBOURNE ST ELISABETH–Cr 1935 from AP1, Willingdon AP, EP8.[183]

EP8–EASTBOURNE ST MICHAEL AND ALL ANGELS, OCKLYNGE–Cr 1911 from AP1.[97] Bdry: 1925 (help cr EP10),[49] 1927,[182] 1935 (help cr EP7),[183] 1951,[190] 1953 (help cr Hampden Park EP),[193] 1956.[185]

EP9–EASTBOURNE ST PETER–Cr 1896 from EP11.[194] Bdry: 1920,[195] 1956.[185]

EP10–EASTBOURNE ST PHILIP–Cr 1925 from EP3, EP8, EP6.[49] Bdry: 1956.[185] Abol 1971 to help cr EP12.[144]

EP11–EASTBOURNE ST SAVIOUR–Cr 1867 from EP4.[189] Bdry: 1882 (help cr EP1),[6] 1892,[197] 1896 (cr EP9),[194] 1920.[195] Abol 1971 to help cr EP12.[196]

EP12–EASTBOURNE ST SAVIOUR WITH ST PHILIP–Cr 1971 by union EP11, EP10.[196]

EASTERGATE
AP *LG* Seq 2. *Parl* Seq 26. *Eccl* Seq 3.

EBERNOE
EP Cr 1875 from Kirdford AP.[198] Midh. III RDn (1875–1913), Petw. RDn (1913–*).

EDBURTON
AP [Pt E Sussex (Poynings Hd), pt W Sussex (Burbeach Hd) until 1894, ent W Sussex thereafter]. *LG* Stey. PLU, RSD, Stey. W RD. Civ bdry: 1894 (the pt in E Sussex cr Fulking CP and this par ent W Sussex thereafter).[199] Abol civ 1933 ent to Upper Beeding AP.[14] *Parl* Pt New Shor. Parl Bor, pt E'rn Dv (1832–85), Mid Dv (1885–1918), Horsham & Worthing Dv (1918–48). *Eccl* S Mall. RDn (pec jurisd until 1846, in AD 1846–58), Lewes II RDn (1858–1913), Hurst RDn (1913–*).

EGDEAN
AP *LG* Rothb. Hd, Sutton incorp for poor (1792–1869), Petw. PLU (1869–1930), RSD, [W Sussex] Petw. RD. Abol civ 1933 ent to Petworth AP.[14] *Parl* W'rn Dv (1832–85), N-W'rn Dv (1885–1918), Chich. Dv (1918–48). *Eccl* Seq 12.

ELSTED
AP *LG* Seq 16. *Parl* Seq 23. *Eccl* Midh. RDn. Abol eccl 1503 (sep civ identity maintained) to help cr Elsted with Treyford and Didling EP.[170]

ELSTED WITH TREYFORD AND DIDLING
EP Cr 1503 by union Elsted AP, Treyford AP, Didling AP (each retains sep civ identity).[170] *Eccl* Seq 9.

ERIDGE GREEN
EP Cr 1856 from Frant AP, Rotherfield AP.[200] Pev. RDn (1856–58), Pev. IV RDn (1858–1913), Etch. RDn (1913–*). Bdry: 1867 (help cr Broadwater St Mark EP),[108] 1872.[201]

ETCHINGHAM
AP Incl pt Hurst Green (sep EP 1907,[203] sep CP 1952[202]). *LG* Pt Henhurst Hd, pt Shoyswell Hd, Ticeh. PLU, RSD, [E Sussex] Ticeh. RD (1894–1934), Battle RD (1934–74). Addtl civ bdry alt: 1886 (incl gains Sussex pt of Hawkhurst AP [Kent, Sussex]),[204] 1952.[202] *Parl* Seq 8. Parl bdry: 1953 (the pt lost to cr Hurst Green CP transf to Hast. BC).[205] *Eccl* Seq 22.

EWHURST
AP *LG* Staple Hd, Battle PLU, RSD, [E Sussex] Battle RD. Civ bdry: 1958.[30] *Parl* Seq 9. *Eccl* Seq 21.

FAIRLIGHT
AP *LG* Seq 24. Civ bdry: 1897,[59] 1938 (loses pt to Hast. CB and CP),[162] 1952.[206] *Parl* Seq 9. *Eccl* Seq 23.

FAIRWARP
EP Cr 1901 from Maresfield AP, Buxted AP, Highhurst Wood EP.[115] Pev. III RDn (1901–13), Uckf. RDn (1913–*).

FALMER
AP *LG* Younsmere Hd, Newh. PLU, RSD, [E Sussex] Newh. RD (1894–1934), Chailey RD (1934–74). Civ bdry: 1928 (loses pt to Brigh. CB and AP),[62] 1934,[3] 1952 (incl loses pt to Brigh. CB and AP).[70] *Parl* Seq 4. *Eccl* Lewes RDn (until 1858), Lewes I RDn (1858–1913), Lewes RDn (1913–56). Eccl bdry: 1931 (help cr Moulsecoomb EP),[207] 1952 (help cr South Patcham EP).[191] Abol eccl 1956 to help cr

Stanmer-with-Falmer and Moulsecoomb EP.[89]

FELPHAM

AP *LG* Avisf. Hd, W'hamp. PLU, RSD, [W Sussex] W'hamp. RD. Civ bdry: 1913.[39] Abol civ 1933 pt to Bognor Regis CP, pt to Yapton AP, pt to Middleton AP.[14] *Parl* W'rn Dv (1832–85), S-W'rn Dv (1885–1918), Chich. Dv (1918–48). *Eccl* Seq 3.

FERNHURST

Chap in Linch AP (eccl, 'Lynch'), sep civ identity early, sep EP 1773.[36] *LG* Seq 17. Civ bdry: 1879.[18] *Parl* Seq 23. *Eccl* Midh. RDn (1773–1871), Midh. I RDn (1871–1913), Midh. RDn (1913–*). Eccl bdry: 1916,[208] 1938 (help cr Camelsdale EP),[125] 1958.[48]

FERRING

AP *LG* Seq 6. *Parl* Seq 27. *Eccl* Arund. RDn (until 1871), Storr. III RDn (1871–80), Storr. IV RDn (1880–1913), Worthing RDn (1913–*). Eccl incl Kingston AP (sep civ identity maintained, church lost into sea and remainder of area incl in this par).[209]

FINDON

AP *LG* Brightf. Hd, Thak. PLU, RSD, [W Sussex] Thak. RD (1894–1933), Worthing RD (1933–74). Civ bdry: 1933.[14] *Parl* New Shor. Parl Bor (1832–85), S-W'rn Dv (1885–1918), Horsham & Worthing Dv (1918–45), Worthing Dv (1945–48), Arund. & Shor. CC (1948–70), Shor. CC (1970–*). *Eccl* Seq 17. Eccl bdry: 1957.[107]

FIRLE

CP Renaming 1971 of West Firle AP.[210] *LG* [E Sussex] Chailey RD.

WEST FIRLE

AP *LG* Totnore Hd, W Firle PLU (1835–98), RSD, [E Sussex] Lewes PLU (1898–1930), Chailey RD (1894–1971). Renamed civ 1971 'Firle'.[210] *Parl* Seq 12. *Eccl* Pev. RDn (until 1858), Pev. II RDn (1858–1913), Lewes RDn (1913–*).

NEW FISHBOURNE

AP *LG* Box & Stockb. Hd, W'hamp. PLU, RSD, [W Sussex] W'hamp. RD. Civ bdry: 1896 (gains Sub-Deanery Rural CP).[172] Abol civ 1933 pt to Chichester CP, pt to Bosham CP, pt to Funtington AP.[14] *Parl* W'rn Dv (1832–85), S-W'rn Dv (1885–1918), Chich. Dv (1918–48). *Eccl* Pec jurisd Dean of Chich. (until 1846), Chich. RDn (1846–71), Boxg. II RDn (1871–80), Boxg. III RDn (1880–1913), Chich. RDn (1913–*). Eccl bdry: 1969,[73] 1971.[23]

FITTLEWORTH

AP *LG* Seq 3. Civ bdry: 1933 (gains Coates AP).[14] *Parl* Seq 23. *Eccl* Seq 12.

FLETCHING

AP Incl pt Danehill (sep EP 1851,[52] sep CP 1898[167]). *LG* Seq 43. *Parl* Seq 5. *Eccl* Seq 35.

FLIMWELL

EP Name used now for EP cr 1860 as 'Ticehurst St Augustine', qv.

FOLKINGTON

AP *LG* Seq 39. Civ bdry: 1883,[2] 1888.[211] *Parl* Seq 11. *Eccl* Pev. RDn (until 1858), Pev. I RDn (1858–1913), E'bourne RDn (1913–60s), Seaford RDn (1960s–*). Eccl bdry: 1937 (help cr Polegate EP),[212] 1962.[142]

FORD

AP *LG* Seq 1 (E Preston incorp for poor from 1799). *Parl* Seq 26. *Eccl* Seq 2.

FOREST ROW

Chap and hmlt in East Grinstead AP, sep EP 1850,[213] sep CP 1894 (the pt not in E Grin. USD).[58] *LG* [E Sussex] E Grin. PLU, RD (1894–1934), Uckf. RD (1934–74). Civ bdry: 1934.[3] *Parl* E Grin. Dv/CC (1918–*). *Eccl* Lewes RDn (1850–58), Lewes III RDn (1858–80), Pev. IV RDn (1880–1913), E Grin. RDn (1913–*). Eccl bdry: 1968.[214]

FOREST SIDE–See STANSTED

FRAMFIELD

AP *LG* Seq 40. *Parl* Seq 5. *Eccl* Seq 38.

FRANT

AP Pt Kent (Washlingstone Hd), pt Sussex (Rotherfield Hd), the former transf to Kent 1894 to cr 2 CPs of Broadwater Down, Tonbridge Rural,[58] and Frant ent E Sussex thereafter. *LG* Ticeh. PLU, pt of the Kent pt in Tunbridge Wells MB (1889–94), Ticeh. RSD (ent 1875–89, pt 1889–94), Ticeh. RD (1894–1934), Uckf. RD (1934–74). Addtl civ bdry alt: 1900 (loses pt to Broadwater Down CP, Kent).[215] *Parl* Sussex pt, Seq 7. *Eccl* Pev. RDn (until 1858), Pev. IV RDn (1858–1913), Etch. RDn (1913–*). Eccl bdry: 1856 (help cr Eridge Green EP),[200] 1867 (help cr Broadwater St Mark EP),[108] 1872,[201] 1921.[109]

FRISTON

AP *LG* Seq 47. Civ bdry: 1938 (loses pt to E'bourne. CB and AP).[168] *Parl* Seq 10. *Eccl* Seq 32.

FULKING

CP Cr 1894 from the pt of Edburton AP (E Sussex, W Sussex) in E Sussex.[199] *LG* Stey. PLU, Stey. E RD (1894–1928), Cuckf. RD (1928–74). Transf 1974 to W Sussex.[128] *Parl* Lewes Dv/CC (1918–70), Mid-Sussex CC (1970–*).

FUNTINGTON

AP *LG* Seq 14. Civ bdry: 1933 (incl gains West Stoke AP).[14] *Parl* Seq 25. *Eccl* Boxg. RDn (until 1858), Boxg. II RDn (1858–1913), W'bourne. RDn (1913–30). Eccl bdry: 1829 (cr Sennicotts EP).[216] Abol eccl 1930 to help cr Funtington with Sennicotts EP.[217]

FUNTINGTON WITH SENNICOTTS

EP Cr 1930 by union Funtington AP, Sennicotts EP.[217] W'bourne. RDn.

GLYNDE

AP *LG* Seq 42. *Parl* Seq 12. *Eccl* S Mall. RDn (pec jurisd until 1846, in AD 1846–58), Pev. II RDn (1858–1913), Lewes RDn (1913–*).

GORING BY SEA

AP *LG* Poling Hd, E Preston incorp for poor (1791–1869), PLU (1869–1929), RSD, [W Sussex] E Preston RD. Civ bdry: 1902.[103] Abol civ 1929 ent to Worthing CP.[175] *Parl* W'rn Dv (1832–85), Mid Dv (1885–1918), Chich. Dv (1918–48). *Eccl* Seq 17.

GRAFFHAM
AP *LG* Easeb. Hd, W'hamp. PLU (1835–69), Midh. PLU (1869–1930), RSD, [W Sussex] Midh. RD. Civ bdry: 1933 (gains Selham AP).[14] *Parl* Seq 14. *Eccl* Midh. RDn (until 1871), Midh. II RDn (1871–1913), Petw. RDn (1913–72). Abol eccl 1972 to help cr Graffham with Woolavington EP.[145]
GRAFFHAM WITH WOOLAVINGTON
EP Cr 1972 by union Graffham AP, Woolavington AP.[145] Petw. RDn.
GREATHAM
AP *LG* E Easw. Hd, Sutton incorp for poor (1791–1869), Thak. PLU (1869–1930), RSD, [W Sussex] Thak. RD. Abol civ 1933 ent to Parham AP.[14] *Parl* W'rn Dv (1832–85), Mid Dv (1885–1918), Horsham & Worthing Dv (1918–45). *Eccl* Storr. RDn. Abol eccl 1510 (civ identity maintained to help cr Greatham with Wiggonholt EP.[218]
GREATHAM WITH WIGGONHOLT
EP Cr 1510 by union Greatham AP, Wiggonholt AP (each retains sep civ identity).[218] Storr. RDn (1510–1871), Storr. I RDn (1871–1913), Storr. RDn (1913–*).
EAST GRINSTEAD
AP Incl chap and hmlt Forest Row (sep EP 1850,[213] sep CP 1894 [the pt not in E Grin. USD][58]). *LG* E Grin. Hd, Bor, PLU, RSD (ent 1875–84, pt 1884–94), pt E Grin. USD (1884–94), [E Sussex] E Grin. UD. Transf 1974 to W Sussex.[128] *Parl* E Grin. Parl Bor (1307–1832), Seq 5 thereafter. *Eccl* Pt pec jurisd S Mall. RDn (until 1846), remainder and later, Lewes RDn (until 1858), Lewes III RDn (1858–80), Pev. IV RDn (1880–1913), E Grin. RDn (1913–*). Addtl eccl bdry alt: 1880 (help cr Hammerwood EP),[219] 1905 (cr East Grinstead St Mary the Virgin EP).[220]
EAST GRINSTEAD ST MARY THE VIRGIN
EP Cr 1905 from East Grinstead AP.[220] Pev. IV RDn (1905–13), E Grin. RDn (1913–*). Bdry: 1953.[222]
WEST GRINSTEAD
AP *LG* Seq 11. Civ bdry: 1883.[2] *Parl* Seq 20. *Eccl* Seq 15.
NEW GROOMBRIDGE
EP Cr 1886 from Withyam AP.[23] Pev. IV RDn (1886–1913), E Grin. RDn (1913–*).
GUESTLING
AP *LG* Seq 24. Civ bdry: 1938 (loses pt to Hast. CB and CP),[162] 1952,[206] 1958.[30] *Parl* Seq 9. *Eccl* Seq 24.
EAST GULDEFORD
AP Cr 16th cent from marshlands in Playdon AP, Broomhill AP.[310] *LG* Seq 22. Civ bdry: 1934.[3] *Parl* Seq 16. *Eccl* Seq 24.
THE GUMBER
Ex-par area surrounded by Slindon AP and other pars, civ incl in Slindon AP 1858,[131] eccl into that par 1934.[139]
HADLOW DOWN
Chap in Buxted AP, Mayfield AP, sep EP 1837,[112] sep CP 1905.[113] *LG* [E Sussex] Uckf. PLU, RD. Civ bdry: 1949.[223] *Parl* E Grin. Dv/CC (1918–*). *Eccl* S Mall. RDn (pec jurisd 1837–46, in AD 1846–58), Pev. III RDn (1858–1913), Uckf. RDn (1913–*).
HAILSHAM
AP *LG* Pt Pev. corporate mbr Cq Pt of Hast., Seq 37. Civ bdry: 1937,[224] 1939 (help cr Polegate CP).[225] *Parl* Seq 11. *Eccl* Seq 32. Eccl bdry: 1937 (help cr Polegate EP).[212]
HALTON IN HASTINGS–See HASTINGS ST CLEMENT, HALTON
HAMMERWOOD
EP Cr 1880 from East Grinstead AP, Hartfield AP.[219] Pev. IV RDn (1880–1913), E Grin. RDn (1913–*). Bdry: 1968.[214]
HAMPDEN PARK
CP Cr 1911 from Willingdon AP.[226] *LG* E'bourne. PLU, CB. Abol 1912 ent to Eastbourne AP.[177]
EP Cr 1953 from Willingdon AP, Westham AP, Eastbourne St Andrew EP, Eastbourne St Michael and All Angels, Ocklynge EP.[193] E'bourne RDn.
HAMSEY
AP *LG* Seq 29. Civ bdry: 1934.[3] *Parl* Seq 4. *Eccl* Seq 25.
HANGLETON
AP *LG* Fishg. Hd, Stey. PLU, RSD, [E Sussex] Stey. E RD (1894–1928), Hove MB (1928–74). *Parl* E'rn Dv (1832–85), Mid Dv (1885–1918), Lewes Dv (1918–48), Hove BC (1948–*). *Eccl* Seq 27. Eccl bdry: 1939 (help cr Hove Bishop Hannington Memorial Chapel EP),[6] 1949,[8] 1955.[7]
HARDHAM
AP *LG* Bury Hd, Thak. PLU, RSD, [W Sussex] Thak. RD. Abol civ 1933 ent to Coldwaltham AP.[14] *Parl* W'rn Dv (1832–85), N-W'rn Dv (1885–1918), Horsham & Worthing Dv (1918–45). *Eccl* Midh. RDn (until 1871), Midh. II RDn (1871–1913), Storr. RDn (1913–*).
HARTFIELD
AP *LG* Seq 38. *Parl* Seq 5. *Eccl* Pec jurisd S Mall. (until 1846), Seq 36 thereafter. Eccl bdry: 1880 (help cr Hammerwood EP),[219] 1912 (cr Coleman's Hatch EP).[92]
HARTING
AP *LG* Seq 16. *Parl* Seq 23. *Eccl* Seq 9.
HASTINGS
The following have 'Hastings' in their names. Insofar as any existed at a given time: *LG* Baldstrow Hd, Hast. PLU (inclusion in Bor, MB, CB, USD, Cq Pt sep noted). Made pt 1974 of E Sussex.[128] *Parl* Hast. Parl Bor/BC (1369–*). *Eccl* Hast. RDn (until 1858), Hast. I RDn (1858–1913), Hast. RDn (1913–*).
CP1–HASTINGS–Cr 1909 by union AP1, AP2, AP3, AP4, CP2, AP5, CP3, AP6, AP7, CP4, AP8.[227] *LG* Hast. CB. Bdry: 1925 (gains Hollington St John CP),[228] 1938.[162]
EP1–HASTINGS ALL SOULS, CLIVE VALE–Cr 1889 from AP1.[156]
EP2–HASTINGS CHRIST CHURCH–Cr 1885

from AP7, AP5.[122] Sometimes 'St Leonards-on-Sea Christ Church'. Bdry: 1929 (cr St Leonards-on-Sea St Ethelburga EP).192

AP1–HASTINGS ALL SAINTS–*LG* Hast. Bor/MB, CB, USD, Cq Pt. Civ bdry: 1897.[59] Abol civ 1909 to help cr CP1.[227] Eccl bdry: 1889 (help cr EP1).[156]

EP3–HASTINGS EMMANUEL–Cr 1875 from AP6.[186] Abol 1970 to help cr EP4.[229]

EP4–HASTINGS EMMANUEL AND ST MARY IN THE CASTLE–Cr 1970 by union EP3, AP6.[229]

AP2–HASTINGS HOLY TRINITY–*LG* Hast. Bor, MB, CB, USD, Cq Pt. Abol civ 1909 to help cr CP1.[227] Eccl gains 1882 AP8.[230]

AP3–HASTINGS ST ANDREW–Depopulated & disused by 1440, sep civ identity maintained, eccl functions assumed by AP6,[230] eccl refounded as sep par 1870.[34] *LG* Hast. Bor/MB, CB, USD, Cq Pt. Abol civ 1909 to help cr CP1.[227] Abol eccl 1970 to help cr Blacklands Christ Church and Hastings St Andrew EP.[57]

AP4–HASTINGS ST CLEMENT–*LG* Hast. Bor/MB, CB, USD, Cq Pt. Abol civ 1909 to help cr CP1.[227] Eccl bdry: 1839 (cr EP5),[231] 1970 (gains EP5).[229]

EP5–HASTINGS ST CLEMENT, HALTON–Cr 1839 from AP4.[231] Sometimes 'Halton in Hastings'. Bdry: 1951.[106] Abol 1970 ent to AP4.[229]

CP2–HASTINGS ST HELENS–Renaming 1897 of Blacklands CP when extended to incl pt Ore AP.[59] *LG* Hast. CB. Abol 1909 to help cr CP1.[227]

AP5–HASTINGS ST LEONARDS–Depopulated by 15th cent, sep civ identity maintained, eccl free chapel in Hollington AP, eccl refounded as sep par 1869 (incl pt AP7).[232] *LG* Pt Hast. Bor, pt Hast. MB, pt Hast. USD, pt Hast. RSD, pt Cq Pt (the pt known as Petit Iham also in the Cq Pt), Hast. CB (pt 1889–94, ent 1894–99). Civ bdry: 1883,[2] 1894 (the pt not in the CB to help cr CP4),[41] 1897.[59] Abol civ 1909 to help cr CP1.[227] *Parl* Hast. Parl Bor (pt 1369–1867), ent 1867–85, pt 1885–1918), pt E'rn Dv (1832–67), pt E'rn Dv [Petit Iham] (1885–1918). Eccl bdry: 1870 (cr Silverhill EP),[108] 1881 (cr Upper St Leonards EP),[74] 1885 (help cr EP2).[122]

–HASTINGS ST MARGARET–See AP7

CP3–HASTINGS ST MARY BULVERHYTHE–Orig chap in AP8, sep civ identity early, in ruins by late 14th cent, deemed eccl ex-par,[233] abol eccl 1929 to help cr St Leonards-on-Sea St Ethelburga EP.[192] *LG* Hast. Bor/MB, CB, USD, Cq Pt. Bdry: 1894 (gains the pt of Bexhill AP [Lbty of the Sluice] in the CB).[41] Abol 1909 to help cr CP1.[227]

AP6–HASTINGS ST MARY IN THE CASTLE–Assumed eccl functions, prob in 15th cent, of AP3 though latter's sep civ identity maintained[230]; this par in ruins and long eccl disused, eccl refounded 1885.[234] *LG* Pt Hast. Bor, pt Hast. MB, pt Hast. USD, pt Hast. RSD, pt Cq Pt, Hast. CB (pt 1889–94, ent 1894–1909). Civ bdry: 1894 (the pt not in the CB to help cr CP4).[41] Abol civ 1909 to help cr CP1.[227] *Parl* Hast. Parl Bor (pt 1369–1867, ent 1867–1918), pt E'rn Dv (1832–67). Eccl bdry: 1875 (cr EP3),[186] 1881 (cr Blacklands EP),[54] 1902.[90] Abol eccl 1970 to help cr EP4.[229]

AP7–HASTINGS ST MARY MAGDALEN–Seems to have been substitute dedication for church orig known as 'Hastings St Margaret'.[230] *LG* Hast. Bor, MB, CB, USD, Cq Pt. Abol civ 1909 to help cr CP1.[227] Eccl bdry: 1870 (cr EP6),[235] 1885 (help cr EP2).[122]

CP4–HASTINGS ST MATTHEW–Cr 1894 from the pt of AP5 and the pt of AP6 not in Hast. CB.[41] *LG* Hast. PLU, RD. Bdry: 1897 (help cr Hollington St John CP, help cr Hollington Rural CP).[59] Abol civ 1909 to help cr CP1.[227]

AP8–HASTINGS ST MICHAEL [ON THE ROCK]–Lost to depredations of pirates in 13th cent, sep civ identity maintained, eccl joined 1882 to AP2.[230] Incl chap Hastings St Mary Bulverhythe (sep civ identity early [as CP3], in ruins by late 14th cent, deemed eccl ex-par,[233] abol eccl 1929 to help cr St Leonards-on-Sea St Ethelburga EP[192]). *LG* Hast. Bor/MB, CB, USD, Cq Pt. Abol civ 1909 to help cr CP1.[227]

EP6–HASTINGS ST PAUL–Cr 1870 from AP7.[235] Bdry: 1890 (cr EP7),[80] 1910.[80] Abol 1963 to help cr St Leonards-on-Sea St Peter and St Paul EP.[236]

EP7–HASTINGS ST PETER–Cr 1890 from EP6.[80] Bdry: 1910.[115] Abol 1963 to help cr St Leonards-on-Sea St Peter and St Paul EP.[236]

HAWKHURST

AP *LG* Pt Kent (orig E Barnfield Hd, pt Cranbrook Hd, pt Selbrittenden Hd, by 19th cent ent E Barnfield Hd[237]), pt Sussex (Henhurst Hd), the latter lost 1886 to Etchingham AP and this par ent Kent thereafter.[204] *LG* Cranbrook PLU, RSD. *Parl* Sussex pt, E'rn Dv (1832–1918). For later civ organisation, and for eccl organisation in dioc Canterb (incl eccl bdry alt), see main entry in Kent.

HAYWARD'S HEATH

CP Cr 1934 from the pt of Cuckfield AP in Hayward's Heath USD.[78] Now commonly 'Haywards Heath'. *LG* [E Sussex] Cuckf. PLU, Hayward's Heath UD (1894–1934), Cuckf. UD (1934–74). Bdry: 1934.[3] Transf 1974 to W Sussex.[128] *Parl* E Grin. Dv/CC (1918–70), Mid-Sussex CC (1970–*).

HAYWARD'S HEATH ST RICHARD

EP Cr 1939 from Hayward's Heath St Wilfrid, Cuckfield EP (commonly called 'Cuckfield St Wilfrid'), Lindfield AP.[238] Cuckf. RDn. Bdry: 1965.[64]

HAYWARD'S HEATH ST WILFRID

EP Renaming 1944 of EP known as 'Cuckfield St Wilfrid' (cr 1873 as 'Hayward's Heath St Wilfrid,

Cuckfield', qv), gaining at same time pt Wivelsfield AP.[99] Cuckf. RDn. Bdry: 1965.[64]

HAYWARD'S HEATH ST WILFRID, CUCKFIELD
EP Cr 1873 from Cuckfield AP,[164] soon afterwards commonly called 'Cuckfield St Wilfrid', renamed 1944 'Hayward's Heath St Wilfrid', gaining at same time pt Wivelsfield AP.[99] Lewes III RDn (1866–1913), Cuckf. RDn (1913–44). Bdry: 1894,[14] 1911,[200] 1939 (cr Hayward's Heath St Richard EP).[238]

HEATHFIELD
AP *LG* Pt Hawkesborough Hd, pt Dill Hd, Hailsham PLU, RSD, [E Sussex] Hailsham RD. Civ bdry: 1951 (help cr Horam CP).[140] *Parl* Seq 13. *Eccl* Seq 19. Eccl bdry: 1877 (help cr Burwash Weald EP),[77] 1960 (help cr Heathfield St Richard EP),[45] 1963 (help cr Horam EP).[239]

HEATHFIELD ST RICHARD
EP Cr 1960 from Heathfield AP, Waldron AP.[45] Dall. RDn.

HEENE
Area (anc chap, long demolished) in West Tarring AP, sep civ identity early, sep EP 1875.[240] *LG* Brightf. Hd, Worthing PLU, RSD (1875–90), Worthing MB (1890–1902), USD (1890–94). [W Sussex]. Abol civ 1902 ent to Worthing CP.[103] *Parl* New Shor. Parl Bor (1832–85), Mid Dv (1885–1918). *Eccl* Storr. IV RDn (1871–1913), Worthing RDn (1913–*). Bdry: 1955 (incl help cr West Worthing EP),[125] 1957.[107]

SOUTH HEIGHTON
AP *LG* Flexb. Hd, Newh. PLU, RSD, [E Sussex] Newh. RD (1894–1934), Chailey RD (1934–74). Civ bdry: 1934.[3] *Parl* Seq 12. *Eccl* Seq 34.

HELLINGLY
AP *LG* Seq 37. Civ bdry: 1951 (help cr Horam CP).[140] *Parl* Seq 11. *Eccl* Pev. RDn (until 1858), Pev. I RDn (1858–1913), Dall. RDn (1913–*). Eccl bdry: 1845 (help cr Upper Dicker Common EP),[23] 1963 (help cr Horam EP).[239]

HENFIELD
AP *LG* Tipnoak Hd, Stey. PLU, RSD, [W Sussex] Stey. W RD (1894–1933), Chanct. RD (1933–74). Civ bdry: 1883.[2] *Parl* Seq 18. *Eccl* Seq 30.

HERSTMONCEUX
AP *LG* Seq 21. Civ bdry: 1886.[241] *Parl* Seq 13. *Eccl* Dall. RDn (until 1858), Pev. I RDn (1858–1913), Dall. RDn (1913–*). Bdry: 1855 (help cr Bodle Street Green EP),[60] 1958.[61]

HEYSHOTT
AP Orig sep AP, united with Stedham before 1342,[242] sep civ identity regained early, sep EP 1882.[243] *LG* Seq 17 (date of inclusion in Sutton incorp uncertain). *Parl* Seq 14. *Eccl* Midh. RDn.

HIGHBROOK
EP Cr 1882 from West Hoathly AP.[130] Lewes III RDn (1882–1913), Cuckf. RDn (1913–*).

HIGHHURST WOOD
EP Cr 1871 from Buxted AP.[34] Pev. III RDn (1871–1913), Uckf. RDn (1913–*). Bdry: 1901 (help cr Fairwarp EP).[115]

EAST HOATHLY
AP *LG* Seq 46. *Parl* E'rn Dv (1832–85), S'rn Dv (1885–1918), E Grin. Dv (1918–48), Lewes CC (1948–55), E'bourne CC (1955–70), Lewes CC (1970–*). *Eccl* Seq 35.

WEST HOATHLY
AP *LG* Seq 31. Civ bdry: 1938,[244] 1958.[245] Transf 1974 to W Sussex.[128] *Parl* Seq 6. *Eccl* Seq 29. Eccl bdry: 1882 (cr Highbrook EP),[130] 1896 (help cr Turner's Hill EP).[22]

HOLLINGTON
AP *LG* Baldstrow Hd, Battle PLU, RSD (ent 1875–80s, pt 1880s–94), pt Hast. MB/CB (1880s–97). Abol civ 1897 the pt in the CB to cr Hollington St John CP, the remainder to cr Hollington Rural CP.[59] *Parl* E'rn Dv (1832–1918). *Eccl* Seq 23. Eccl bdry: 1870 (cr Hollington St John the Evangelist EP),[78] 1951.[246]

HOLLINGTON RURAL
CP Cr 1897 from the pt of Hollington AP not in Hast. CB and from pt Hastings St Matthew CP.[59] *LG* [E Sussex] Battle PLU, RD. Abol 1937 pt to Hast. CB and CP, pt to Crowhurst AP, pt to Westfield AP.[162] *Parl* Rye Dv (1918–48).

HOLLINGTON ST JOHN
CP Cr 1897 from the pt of Hollington AP in Hast. CB and from pt Hastings St Matthew CP.[59] *LG* Battle PLU, Hast. CB. Abol 1925 ent to Hastings CP.[228] *Parl* Rye Dv (1918–48).

HOLLINGTON ST JOHN THE EVANGELIST
EP Cr 1870 from Hollington AP.[78] Hast. I RDn (1870–1913), Hast. RDn (1913–*). Bdry: 1902,[90] 1938,[56] 1951.[246]

HOOE
AP *LG* Seq 28. *Parl* Seq 1. *Eccl* Dall. RDn (until 1858), Lewes II RDn (1858–80), Hast. I RDn (1880–1913), Hast. RDn (1913–31), Battle & Bexhill RDn (1931–*).

HORAM
CP Cr 1951 from Chiddingly AP, Heathfield AP, Hellingly AP, Waldron AP.[140] *LG* [E Sussex] Hailsham RD. *Parl* Rye CC (1955–*).
EP Cr 1963 from Heathfield AP, Hellingly AP, Waldron AP.[239] Dall. RDn.

HORSHAM
AP *LG* Singlecross Hd, Horsham Bor, PLU, pt Horsham USD, pt Horsham RSD, [W Sussex] Horsham UD. Civ bdry: 1878,[102] 1894 (the pt not in the USD cr Horsham Rural CP),[58] 1901,[247] 1927.[248] *Parl* Horsham Parl Bor (pt 1295–1832, ent 1832–85), N-W'rn Dv (1885–1918), Horsham & Worthing Dv (1918–45), Horsham Dv/CC (1945–70), Horsham & Crawley CC (1970–*). *Eccl* Pt pec jurisd Pagham (until 1846), remainder and later, Storr. RDn (until 1871), Midh. III RDn (1871–80), Storr. II RDn (1880–1913), Horsham RDn (1913–*). Eccl bdry: 1853 (help cr Southwater EP),[249]

1871 (help cr Colgate EP),[34] 1878 (cr Roffey EP [orig 'Roughley or Roffey']).[192]

HORSHAM RURAL

CP Cr 1894 from the pt of Horsham AP not in Horsham USD.[58] *LG* [W Sussex] Horsham PLU, RD. Bdry: 1901,[247] 1927,[248] 1933.[14] *Parl* Horsham & Worthing Dv (1918–45), Horsham Dv/CC (1945–70), Horsham & Crawley CC (1970–*).

HORSMONDEN

AP Pt Kent (orig pt Brenchley & Horsmonden Hd, pt Larkfield Hd [pt also in Town of Aylesford], by 19th cent ent in Brenchley & Horsmonden Hd[237]), pt Sussex (Loxfield Pelham Hd), the par made ent Kent 1895.[66] *LG* Tonbridge PLU, RSD, pt sep RD in E Sussex (1894–95). *Parl* Sussex pt, E'rn Dv (1832–1918). For later civ organisation, and for eccl organisation, see main entry in Kent.

LITTLE HORSTED

AP Usual civ spelling; for eccl see 'Horsted Parva'. *LG* Seq 43. *Parl* Seq 5.

HORSTED KEYNES

AP Incl pt chap Danehill (sep EP 1851,[166] sep CP 1898[167]). *LG* Danehill Horsted Hd, Cuckf. PLU, RSD, [E Sussex] Cuckf. RD. Addtl civ bdry alt: 1938.[244] Transf 1974 to W Sussex.[128] *Parl* Seq 6. *Eccl* Pev. RDn (until 1858), Pev. III RDn (1858–1913), Cuckf. RDn (1913–*).

HORSTED PARVA

AP Usual eccl spelling; for civ see 'Little Horsted'. *Eccl* Seq 35.

HOUGHTON

Chap in Amberley AP, sep civ identity early, eccl severed 1935 to help cr Bury with Houghton EP.[13] *LG* Bury Hd, E Preston incorp for poor (1803–69), PLU (1869–1930), RSD, [W Sussex] E Preston RD (1894–1933), Worthing RD (1933–74). Civ bdry: 1883.[2] *Parl* W'rn Dv (1832–85), S-W'rn Dv (1885–1918), Chich. Dv (1918–48), Arund. & Shor. CC (1948–70), Shor. CC (1970–*).

HOVE

The following have 'Hove' in their names. Insofar as any existed at a given time: *LG* Preston Hd, Stey. PLU, Hove USD, [E Sussex] Hove UD (1894–98), MB (1898–1974). *Parl* Brigh. Parl Bor (1832–1948), Hove BC (1948–*). *Eccl* Pev. RDn (until 1858), Lewes V RDn (1858–1913), Hove RDn (1913–*).

AP1–HOVE [orig ST ANDREW, later ALL SAINTS]–Civ bdry: 1928 (exchanges pts with Brigh. CB and AP),[62] 1928 (gains Preston Rural CP, pt Patcham AP).[250] Eccl bdry: 1883 (cr EP4),[35] 1885 (cr EP6),[17] 1924 (help cr EP8),[114] 1943,[251] 1957 (cr EP3),[252] 1966 (cr EP5).[253]

EP1–HOVE BISHOP HANNINGTON MEMORIAL CHAPEL–Cr 1939 from Aldrington AP, West Blatchington AP, Hangleton AP, EP2.[6] Bdry: 1949.[8]

EP2–HOVE ST AGNES–Cr 1927 from EP4, Brighton The Good Shepherd, Preston EP.[95] Bdry: 1939 (help cr EP1),[6] 1943.[251]

EP3–HOVE ST ANDREW (OLD CHURCH)–Cr 1957 from AP1.[252]

EP4–HOVE ST BARNABAS–Cr 1883 from AP1.[35] Bdry: 1927 (help cr EP2).[95]

EP5–HOVE ST JOHN THE BAPTIST–Cr 1966 from AP1.[253]

EP6–HOVE ST PATRICK–Cr 1885 from AP1.[17] Bdry: 1924 (help cr EP8).[114]

EP7–HOVE ST PHILIP–Renaming 1949 of Aldrington St Philip EP, at same time losing pt to EP1.[8]

EP8–HOVE ST THOMAS–Cr 1924 from EP6, AP1.[114] Bdry: 1957.[100]

HUNSTON

AP *LG* Seq 15. *Parl* Seq 25. *Eccl* Seq 4.

HURST GREEN

EP Cr 1907 from Etchingham AP, Salehurst AP.[203] Dall. RDn (1907–13), Etch. RDn (1913–*).

CP Cr 1952 from Etchingham AP, Salehurst AP, Ticehurst AP.[202] *LG* [E Sussex] Battle RD. *Parl* Hast. BC (1953[205]–55), Rye CC (1955–*).

HURSTPIERPOINT

AP *LG* Seq 30. Civ bdry: 1934.[3] Transf 1974 to W Sussex.[128] *Parl* Seq 3. *Eccl* Seq 28. Eccl bdry: 1881 (cr Sayer's Common EP).[7]

ICKLESHAM

AP *LG* Guestling Hd, Rye PLU, RSD, pt Anc Town/Cq Pt Winchelsea, [E Sussex] Rye RD (1894–1934), Battle RD (1934–74). Civ bdry: 1883,[2] 1952.[206] *Parl* Seq 16. *Eccl* Seq 24. Eccl bdry: 1905 (help cr Rye Harbour EP),[254] 1966.[255]

IDEN

AP *LG* Seq 22. *Parl* Seq 16. *Eccl* Seq 21.

IFIELD

AP *LG* Burbeach Hd, Horsham PLU, RSD, [W Sussex] Horsham RD. Abol civ 1933 ent to Crawley AP.[14] *Parl* New Shor. Parl Bor (1832–85), N-W'rn Dv (1885–1918), Horsham & Worthing Dv (1918–45). *Eccl* Lewes RDn (until 1858), Lewes III RDn (1858–1913), Cuckf. RDn (1913–29), Horsham RDn (1929–*). Eccl bdry: 1901 (cr West Crawley EP),[159] 1952.[150]

IFORD

AP *LG* Seq 35. Civ bdry: 1934.[3] *Parl* Seq 4. *Eccl* Seq 25.

IPING

AP Incl chap Chithurst (sep civ identity early, eccl severed 1956 to help cr Trotton with Chithurst EP[142]). *LG* Seq 17. Addtl civ bdry alt: 1879,[18] 1922.[256] *Parl* Pt Midh. Parl Bor, pt W'rn Dv (1832–85), N-W'rn Dv (1885–1918), Chich. Dv (1918–48), Horsham CC (1948–70), Chich. CC (1970–*). *Eccl* Midh. RDn (until 1871), Midh. I RDn (1871–1913), Midh. RDn (1913–57). Eccl bdry: 1956 (incl help cr Trotton with Chithurst EP).[142] Abol eccl 1957 pt to help cr Stedham with Iping EP, pt to help cr Lynch with Iping Marsh EP.[143]

ISFIELD

AP *LG* Seq 40. *Parl* Seq 5. *Eccl* Seq 38.

WEST ITCHENOR

AP *LG* Seq 18. *Parl* Seq 25. *Eccl* Seq 7. Eccl bdry:

1932.[53]

ITCHINGFIELD

AP *LG* E Easw. Hd, Horsham PLU, RSD, [W Sussex] Horsham RD. *Parl* Seq 20. *Eccl* Seq 14.

JARVIS BROOK

EP Cr 1934 from Rotherfield AP.[101] E Grin. RDn. Bdry: 1969.[257]

JEVINGTON

AP *LG* Seq 47. Civ bdry: 1883,[2] 1888,[211] 1937,[224] 1938 (loses pt to E'bourne. CB and AP),[168] 1939 (help cr Polegate CP).[225] *Parl* Seq 10. *Eccl* Seq 32. Eccl bdry: 1937 (help cr Polegate EP),[212] 1962.[142]

KEMP TOWN

EP Cr 1849,[36] refounded 1930 from Brighton AP, Rottingdean AP.[72] Lewes RDn (1849–58), Lewes V RDn (1858–1913), Brigh. RDn (1913–55), Kemp Town RDn (1955–67). Bdry: 1937 (help cr Whitehawk EP).[96] Abol 1967 to help cr Kemp Town St Mark and St Matthew EP.[93]

KEMP TOWN ST MARK AND ST MATTHEW

EP Cr 1967 by union Kemp Town EP, Brighton St Matthew EP.[93] Kemp Town RDn. Bdry: 1968.[90]

KEMP TOWN ST MARY

EP Cr 1967 by union Brighton All Souls EP, Brighton St Mary and St James EP.[93] Kemp Town RDn. Bdry: 1968.[90]

KEYMER

AP *LG* Buttg. Hd, Cuckf. PLU, pt Burgess Hill USD, pt Cuckf. RSD, [E Sussex] Cuckf. RD. Civ bdry: 1894 (the pt in the USD cr Keymer Urban CP),[58] 1934.[3] Transf 1974 to W Sussex.[128] *Parl* Seq 3. *Eccl* Held with Clayton AP as single EP Clayton with Keymer,[144] qv.

KEYMER URBAN

CP Cr 1894 from the pt of Keymer AP in Burgess Hill USD.[58] *LG* [E Sussex] Cuckf. PLU, Burgess Hill UD. Abol 1934 to help cr Burgess Hill CP.[3] *Parl* E Grin. Dv (1918–48).

KINGSTON

AP Church lost into sea, remaining area eccl incl in Ferring AP,[209] sep civ identity maintained. *LG* Poling Hd, not in PLU before 1869, E Preston PLU (1869–1930), RSD, [W Sussex] E Preston RD (1894–1933), Worthing RD (1933–74). *Parl* Seq 27.

KINGSTON

AP Usual civ spelling; for eccl see 'Kingston near Lewes'. *LG* Swanborough Hd, Newh. PLU, pt Lewes MB (1881–94), pt Lewes USD (1881–94), Newh. RSD (ent 1875–81, pt 1881–94). Abol civ 1894 the pt in the MB cr Kingston Urban CP, the remainder cr Kingston near Lewes CP.[58] *Parl* Pt Lewes Parl Bor, pt E'rn Dv (1832–85), Mid Dv (1885–1918).

KINGSTON BY SEA

AP *LG* Fishg. Hd, Stey. PLU, RSD, [W Sussex] Stey. W RD (1894–1910), Shor.-by-Sea UD (1910–74). *Parl* New Shor. Parl Bor (1832–85), Mid Dv (1885–1918), Horsham & Worthing Dv (1918–45), Horsham Dv (1945–48), Arund. & Shor. CC (1948–70), Shor. CC (1970–*). *Eccl* Seq 27.

KINGSTON NEAR LEWES

AP Usual eccl spelling; for civ see 2nd 'Kingston' above. *Eccl* Seq 25. Eccl bdry: 1932.[258]

CP Cr 1894 from the pt of Kingston AP (eccl, 'Kingston near Lewes') not in Lewes MB.[58] *LG* [E Sussex] Newh. PLU, RD (1894–1934), Chailey RD (1934–74). Bdry: 1934.[3] *Parl* Lewes Dv/CC (1918–*).

KINGSTON URBAN

CP Cr 1894 from the pt of Kingston AP (eccl, 'Kingston near Lewes') in Lewes MB.[58] *LG* [E Sussex] Newh. PLU, Lewes MB. Abol 1934 ent to Lewes CP.[3] *Parl* Lewes Dv (1918–48).

KIRDFORD

AP Incl chap Plaistow (sep CP 1951,[259] no sep eccl identity hence this par eccl sometimes 'Kirdford with Plaistow'). *LG* Seq 8. Addtl civ bdry alt: 1879.[10] *Parl* Seq 23. *Eccl* Pt (Plaistow) in pec jurisd Pagham RDn (until 1846), remainder and later, Seq 12. Eccl bdry: 1875 (cr Ebernoe EP).[198]

KIRDFORD WITH PLAISTOW—See prev entry

LAMBERHURST

AP Pt Kent (Brenchley & Horsmonden Hd), pt Sussex (Loxfield Pelham Hd), the par made ent Kent 1895.[66] *LG* Ticeh. PLU, RSD, pt sep RD in E Sussex (1894–95). *Parl* Sussex pt, E'rn Dv (1832–1918). For later civ organisation, and for eccl organisation (incl pec jurisd in Roch dioc), see main entry in Kent.

LANCING

AP *LG* Brightf. Hd, Worthing PLU (1835–69), Stey. PLU (1869–1930), RSD, [W Sussex] Stey. W RD (1894–1933), Worthing RD (1933–74). Civ bdry: 1910 (help cr Shoreham-by-Sea CP),[260] 1927.[261] *Parl* Seq 19. *Eccl* Seq 17. Eccl bdry: 1931 (cr Lancing St Michael and All Angels EP),[262] 1934 (help cr Southwick St Peter EP),[46] 1955.[213]

LANCING ST MICHAEL AND ALL ANGELS

EP Cr 1931 from Lancing AP.[262] Worthing RDn. Bdry: 1955,[213] 1973 (cr Shoreham Beach EP).[263]

LANGNEY

EP Cr 1969 from Eastbourne St Andrew EP.[117] E'bourne. RDn.

LAUGHTON

AP *LG* Seq 44. *Parl* Seq 11. *Eccl* Pev. RDn (until 1858), Pev. II RDn (1858–1913), Seaford RDn (1913–43), Lewes RDn (1943–65), Dall. RDn (1965–*).

LAVANT

Cr civ 1872,[264] eccl 1971,[75] by union East Lavant AP, Mid Lavant AP. *LG* W'bourne. & Singl. Hd, W'hamp. PLU, RSD, [W Sussex] W'hamp. RD (1894–1933), Chich. RD (1933–74). *Parl* S-W'rn Dv (1885–1918), Chich. Dv/CC (1918–*). *Eccl* Chich. RDn.

EAST LAVANT

AP *LG* Aldw. Hd, W'hamp. PLU, RSD. Abol civ 1872 to help cr Lavant CP.[264] *Parl* W'rn Dv (1832–85). *Eccl* Pagham RDn (pec jurisd until

1846, in AD 1846–71), Boxg. I RDn (1871–1913), Boxg. RDn (1913–29), Chich. RDn (1929–71). Abol eccl 1971 to help cr Lavant EP.[75]

MID LAVANT

AP *LG* W'bourne. & Singl. Hd, W'hamp. PLU, RSD. Abol civ 1872 to help cr Lavant CP.[264] *Parl* W'rn Dv (1832–85). *Eccl* Boxg. RDn (until 1871), Boxg. I RDn (1871–1913), Boxg. RDn (1913–29), Chich. RDn (1929–71). Abol eccl 1971 to help cr Lavant EP.[75]

EAST LAVINGTON

AP Usual civ spelling; for eccl see 'Woolavington'. Incl chap West Lavington (sep EP 1850,[265] sep CP 1866[12]). *LG* Rothb. Hd, Midh. PLU, RSD, [W Sussex] Midh. RD. Civ bdry: 1933.[14] *Parl* Seq 23.

WEST LAVINGTON

Chap in East Lavington AP (eccl, 'Woolavington'), sep EP 1850,[265] sep CP 1866.[12] *LG* Rothb. Hd, Midh. PLU (1866[285]–1930), RSD, [W Sussex] Midh. RD. *Parl* Seq 14. *Eccl* Midh. RDn (1850–71), Midh. II RDn (1871–1913), Midh. RDn (1913–*).

LEWES

The following have 'Lewes' in their names. Insofar as any existed at a given time: *LG* Lewes PLU (inclusion in Bor, MB [incorporated 1881], USD sep noted). *Parl* Lewes Parl Bor (1295–1885), Mid Dv (1885–1918), Lewes Dv/CC (1918–*). *Eccl* Lewes RDn (until 1858), Lewes I RDn (1858–1913), Lewes RDn (1913–*).

CP1–LEWES–Cr 1913 by union AP1, CP2, AP4, AP5, AP6, AP10, AP15, South Malling AP.[226] *LG* Lewes MB. Bdry: 1934 (incl gains Kingston Urban CP).[3]

AP1–LEWES ALL SAINTS–*LG* Lewes Bor, MB, USD. Abol civ 1913 to help cr CP1.[266]

CP2–LEWES THE CASTLE PRECINCTS–Ex-par place, sep CP 1858.[131] *LG* Not in Bor, in MB, USD. Abol 1913 to help cr CP1.[226]

AP2–LEWES HOLY TRINITY–*LG* Lewes Bor. In ruins by 1319.[267]

AP3–LEWES ST ANDREW–*LG* Lewes Bor. Abol 1545 ent to AP10.[268]

AP4–LEWES ST ANN–Usual civ spelling; usual eccl 'Lewes St Anne'. Name used from 16th cent for united par formed by union AP9, AP13,[268] sometimes 'Lewes St Mary Westout with St Peter Westout'. *LG* Pt Lewes Bor, Lewes MB (enlarged pt 1881–94, ent 1894–1913), pt Lewes USD, pt Lewes RSD. Civ bdry: 1894 (the pt not in the MB cr CP3).[58] Abol civ 1913 to help cr CP1.[266] *Parl* Pt Lewes Parl Bor (1295–1885), pt E'rn Dv (1832–85).

CP3–LEWES ST ANN WITHOUT–Cr 1894 from the pt of AP4 not in Lewes MB.[58] *LG* Chailey RD. Bdry: 1934.[3]

AP5–LEWES ST JOHN THE BAPTIST, SOUTHOVER–*LG* Pt Lewes Bor, Lewes MB (pt 1881–94, ent 1894–1913), pt Lewes USD, pt Lewes RSD. Civ bdry: 1894 (the pt not in the MB cr Southover Without CP).[58] Abol civ 1913 to help cr CP1.[266] *Parl* Pt Lewes Parl Bor (1295–1885), pt E'rn Dv (1832–85). Eccl bdry: 1932.[258]

–LEWES ST JOHN SUB CASTRO–See AP6

AP6–LEWES ST JOHN UNDER THE CASTLE–Usual civ spelling; usual eccl 'Lewes St John sub Castro'. Gains 1538 AP8.[268] *LG* Pt Lewes Bor, Lewes MB (pt 1881–94, ent 1894–1913), pt Lewes USD, pt Lewes RSD. Civ bdry: 1894 (the pt not in the MB cr CP4).[58] Abol civ 1913 to help cr CP1.[266] *Parl* Pt Lewes Parl Bor (1295–1885), pt E'rn Dv (1832–85).

CP4–LEWES ST JOHN WITHOUT–Cr 1894 from the pt of AP6 not in Lewes MB.[58] *LG* Chailey RD. Bdry: 1934.[3]

AP7–LEWES ST MARTIN–*LG* Lewes Bor. Lost by 16th cent.[268]

AP8–LEWES ST MARY [IN THE MARKET]–*LG* Lewes Bor. Abol 1538 ent to AP6.[268]

AP9–LEWES ST MARY WESTOUT–*LG* Not in the Bor. United 1539 to AP13, the union sometimes called 'Lewes St Mary Westout with St Peter Westout', but more commonly as AP4.[268]

–LEWES ST MARY WESTOUT WITH ST PETER WESTOUT–See AP4

AP10–LEWES ST MICHAEL–Gains 1545 AP3.[268] *LG* Lewes Bor, MB, USD. Abol civ 1913 to help cr CP1.[266]

AP11–LEWES ST NICHOLAS–*LG* Lewes Bor. In ruins prob late 15th cent.[267]

AP12–LEWES ST PETER [THE LESS]–*LG* Lewes Bor. In ruins by 1319.[267]

AP13–LEWES ST PETER WESTOUT–*LG* Orig outside Bor, then in Bor. United 1539 to AP9, the union sometimes called 'Lewes St Mary Westout with St Peter Westout', but more commonly as AP4.[268]

AP14–LEWES ST SEPULCHRE–*LG* Lewes Bor. Prob disued from 13th cent.[267]

AP15–LEWES ST THOMAS A BECKET, CLIFFE–Usual civ spelling; usual eccl 'Lewes St Thomas at Cliffe'. *LG* Lewes Bor, MB, USD. Abol civ 1913 to help cr CP1.[266] *Eccl* Seq 37.

–LEWES ST THOMAS AT CLIFFE–See AP15

LINCH

AP Usual civ spelling; for eccl see 'Lynch'. Incl chap Farnhurst (sep civ identity early, sep EP 1773[36]). *LG* Seq 17. Addtl civ bdry alt: 1879.[18] *Parl* Seq 15.

LINCHMERE

AP Usual civ spelling; for eccl see 'Lynchmere'. Chap in Cocking AP, sep par perhaps in 1568,[149] sep civ identity early, eccl sep no later than 1724.[36] *LG* Seq 17. Civ bdry: 1879.[18] *Parl* Seq 23.

LINDFIELD

AP *LG* Pt Street Hd, pt Burleigh Arches Hd, Cuckf. PLU, RSD, [E Sussex] Cuckf. RD (1894–

1934), Cuckf. UD (1934–74). Civ bdry: 1934 (pt transf to Cuckf. UD, the remainder cr Cuckfield Rural CP).[3] Transf 1974 to W Sussex.[128] *Parl* Seq 6. *Eccl* Pec jurisd S Mall. (until 1846), Pev. RDn (1846–58), Lewes III RDn (1858–1913), Cuckf. RDn (1913–*). Eccl bdry: 1911,[200] 1929 (cr Scaynes Hill EP),[269] 1939 (help cr Hayward's Heath St Richard EP),[238] 1953,[222] 1965.[64]

LINDFIELD RURAL
CP Cr 1934 from the pt of Lindfield AP not transf to Cuckf. UD.[3] *LG* [E Sussex] Cuckf. RD. Transf 1974 to W Sussex.[128] *Parl* E Grin. CC (1948–70), Mid-Sussex CC (1970–*).

LITLINGTON
AP *LG* Seq 39. Civ bdry: 1934.[3] *Parl* Seq 11. *Eccl* Seq 33.

LITTLEHAMPTON
AP *LG* Poling Hd, E Preston incorp for poor (1791–1869), PLU (1869–1930), Littlehampton USD, [W Sussex] Littlehampton UD. Civ bdry: 1880,[148] 1933.[14] *Parl* Seq 27. *Eccl* Seq 1. Eccl bdry: 1929 (cr Littlehampton St James EP).[270]

LITTLEHAMPTON ST JAMES
EP Cr 1929 from Littlehampton AP.[270] Arund. RDn. Bdry: 1954.[271]

LODSWORTH
Chap in Easebourne AP, sep civ identity early, sep EP 1773.[36] *LG* Seq 17. Civ bdry: 1879.[18] *Parl* Seq 15. *Eccl* Midh. RDn (1773–1871), Midh. II RDn (1871–1913), Midh. RDn (1913–*).

LORDINGTON
AP Boxg. RDn, united 1440 with Racton AP, the union civ called 'Racton', eccl 'Racton with Lordington'.[272]

LOXWOOD
Chap in Wisborough Green AP, sep EP 1873,[114] sep CP 1938.[273] *LG* [W Sussex] Petw. RD. Civ bdry: 1960.[274] *Parl* Horsham CC (1948–70), Chich. CC (1970–*). *Eccl* Midh. III RDn (1873–80), Storr. I RDn (1880–1913), Horsham RDn (1913–*).

LULLINGTON
AP *LG* Seq 36. Civ bdry: 1934.[3] *Parl* Seq 11. *Eccl* Pev. RDn (until 1858), Pev. I RDn (1858–1913), Seaford RDn (1913–26). Abol eccl 1926 to help cr Alfriston with Lullington EP.[99]

LURGASHALL
AP *LG* Seq 7. Civ bdry: 1879.[18] *Parl* Seq 23. *Eccl* Seq 12.

LYMINSTER
AP Incl tg Warningcamp (sep CP 1866[12]), area Wick (sep CP 1901,[275] sep EP 1973[276]). *LG* Seq 6. Addtl civ bdry alt: 1877.[277] *Parl* Seq 27. *Eccl* Seq 1. Addtl eccl bdry alt: 1954.[271]

LYNCH
AP Usual eccl spelling; for civ and sep (civ and eccl) chap Farnhurst, see 'Linch'. *Eccl* Midh. RDn (until 1871), Midh. I RDn (1871–1913), Midh. RDn (1913–56). Addtl eccl bdry alt: 1885,[278] 1931.[35] Abol eccl 1957 to help cr Lynch with Iping Marsh EP.[143]

LYNCH WITH IPING MARSH
EP Cr 1957 by union Lynch AP, pt Iping AP.[143] Midh. RDn.

LYNCHMERE
AP Usual eccl spelling; for civ see 'Linchmere'. Chap in Cocking AP, sep par perhaps in 1568,[149] sep civ identity early, eccl sep no later than 1724.[36] *Eccl* Donative, Seq 9. Eccl bdry: 1931,[35] 1938 (help cr Camelsdale EP).[125]

MADEHURST
AP *LG* Seq 2. *Parl* Seq 26. *Eccl* Arund. RDn (until 1871), Storr. I RDn (1871–1913), Arund. RDn (1913–*).

SOUTH MALLING
AP *LG* Ringmer Hd, Lewes PLU, Lewes MB (pt 1881–94, ent 1894–1913), pt Lewes USD (1881–94), Lewes RSD (ent 1875–81, pt 1881–94). [E Sussex]. Civ bdry: 1894 (the pt not in Lewes MB cr South Malling Without CP).[58] Abol civ 1913 to help cr Lewes CP.[266] *Parl* Pt Lewes Parl Bor, pt E'rn Dv (1832–85), Mid Dv (1885–1918). *Eccl* Donative, Seq 37.

SOUTH MALLING WITHOUT
CP Cr 1894 from the pt of South Malling AP not in Lewes MB.[58] *LG* [E Sussex] Lewes PLU, Chailey RD. Bdry: 1934.[3] *Parl* Lewes Dv/CC (1918–*).

MARDEN
CP Cr 1933 by union East Marden AP, North Marden AP.[14] *LG* [W Sussex] Chich. RD. *Parl* Chich. CC (1948–*).

EAST MARDEN
AP *LG* W'bourne. & Singl. Hd, W'bourne. PLU, RSD, [W Sussex] W'bourne. RD. Civ bdry: 1880.[151] Abol civ 1933 to help cr Marden CP.[14] *Parl* W'rn Dv (1832–85), S-W'rn Dv (1885–1918), Chich. Dv (1918–48). *Eccl* Seq 6.

NORTH MARDEN
AP *LG* As for East Marden AP, with no civ bdry alt. Abol civ 1933 to help cr Marden CP.[14] *Parl* As for East Marden. *Eccl* Seq 6.

UP MARDEN
Chap in Compton AP, sep civ identity early, no sep eccl identity (area reduced 1856 to help cr Stanstead EP[152]). *LG* As for East Marden AP, with no civ bdry alt. Abol 1933 ent to Compton AP.[14] *Parl* As for East Marden.

MARESFIELD
AP *LG* Seq 43. *Parl* Seq 5. *Eccl* Seq 35. Eccl bdry: 1847 (cr Nutley EP),[279] 1901 (help cr Fairwarp EP).[115]

MARK CROSS
EP Cr 1874 from Rotherfield AP, Wadhurst AP, Tidebrook EP.[280] Pev. IV RDn (1874–1913), E Grin. RDn (1913–*).

MAYFIELD
AP Incl pt chap Hadlow Down (sep EP 1837,[112] sep CP 1905[113]). *LG* Pt Loxf. Pelham Hd, pt Hawkesborough Hd, Uckf. PLU, RSD, [E Sussex] Uckf. RD. Addtl civ bdry alt: 1949.[223] *Parl* Seq 2. *Eccl* S Mall. RDn (pec jurisd until 1846, in AD 1846–58), Pev. IV RDn (1858–80), Dall. RDn (1880–*). Addtl eccl bdry alt:

1858 (help refound Tidebrook EP),[281] 1877 (help cr Burwash Weald EP).[77]

MEADS

EP Cr 1870 from Eastbourne AP, Eastbourne Holy Trinity EP.[86] Pev. I RDn (1870–1913), E'bourne. RDn (1913–*). Bdry: 1882 (help cr Eastbourne All Saints EP),[6] 1892,[197] 1899,[184] 1911.[181]

MERSTON

AP *LG* Box & Stockb. Hd, W'hamp. PLU, RSD, [W Sussex] W'hamp. RD. Abol civ 1933 ent to Oving AP.[14] *Parl* W'rn Dv (1832–85), S-W'rn Dv (1885–1918), Chich. Dv (1918–48). *Eccl* Boxg. RDn (until 1871), Arund. II RDn (1871–1913), Selsey RDn (1913–31), Chich. RDn (1913–43), Bogn. Reg. RDn (1943–*).

MIDDLETON

AP *LG* Avisf. Hd, W'hamp. PLU, RSD, [W Sussex] W'hamp. RD (1894–1933), Chich. RD (1933–34). Civ bdry: 1933.[14] Renamed civ 1934 'Middleton-on-Sea'.[282] *Parl* W'rn Dv (1832–85), S-W'rn Dv (1885–1918), Chich. Dv (1918–48). *Eccl* Seq 3.

MIDDLETON-ON-SEA

CP Renaming 1934 of Middleton AP.[282] *LG* [W Sussex] Chich. RD. *Parl* Chich. CC (1948–70), Arund. CC (1970–*).

MIDHURST

Chap in Easebourne AP, sep civ identity early, sep EP 1725.[36] *LG* Midh. Bor, Seq 17. *Parl* Midh. Parl Bor (1310–11, 1512–1885), Seq 14 thereafter. *Eccl* Donative, Midh. RDn (1725–1871), Midh. II RDn (1871–80), Midh. I RDn (1880–1913), Midh. RDn (1913–*). Eccl bdry: 1931.[35]

MILLAND

EP Name used now for EP cr 1863 as 'Tuxlith', qv.

MOULSECOOMB

EP Cr 1931 from Patcham AP, Falmer AP.[207] Brigh. RDn. Abol 1956 to help cr Stanmer-with-Falmer and Moulsecoomb EP.[89]

MOUNTFIELD

AP *LG* Seq 27. Civ bdry: 1886,[204] 1958.[30] *Parl* Seq 9. *Eccl* Dall. RDn (until 1858), Hast. II RDn (1858–80), Dall. RDn (1880–1913), Etch. RDn (1913–60s), Battle & Bexhill RDn (1960s–*). Eccl bdry: 1960.[119]

NORTH MUNDHAM

AP *LG* Seq 15. Civ bdry: 1897.[283] *Parl* Seq 25. *Eccl* Seq 4. Eccl bdry: 1891.[284]

NETHERFIELD

EP Cr 1862 from Battle AP.[31] Hast. I RDn (1862–1913), Hast. RDn (1913–31), Battle & Bexhill RDn (1931–*).

NEW TOWN–See CHICHESTER NEWTOWN

NEWHAVEN

AP Sometimes anc 'Meeching'. *LG* Holm. Hd, Newh. PLU, RSD (1875–81), USD (1881–94), [E Sussex] Newh. UD. Civ bdry: 1934.[3] *Parl* Seq 12. *Eccl* Seq 25. Eccl bdry: 1930.[169]

NEWICK

AP *LG* Seq 29. Civ bdry: 1934.[3] *Parl* Seq 4. *Eccl* Seq 31.

NEWTIMBER

AP *LG* Seq 33. Transf 1974 to W Sussex.[128] *Parl* Seq 3. *Eccl* Seq 28.

NINFIELD

AP *LG* Seq 28. Civ bdry: 1887.[126] *Parl* Seq 1. *Eccl* Seq 20.

NORTHIAM

AP *LG* Staple Hd, Rye PLU, RSD, [E Sussex] Rye RD (1894–1934), Battle RD (1934–74). Civ bdry: 1883.[2] *Parl* Seq 9. *Eccl* Seq 21.

NORWAY

CP Cr 1894 from the pt of Willingdon AP in E'bourne. MB.[58] *LG* [E Sussex] E'bourne. PLU, MB. Abol 1899 ent to Eastbourne AP.[176]

NUTHURST

AP *LG* Seq 12. Civ bdry: 1877,[102] 1933.[14] *Parl* Seq 20. *Eccl* Seq 14.

NUTLEY

EP Cr 1847 from Maresfield AP.[279] Pev. RDn (1847–58), Pev. III RDn (1858–1913), Uckf. RDn (1913–*).

ODIMORE–See UDIMORE

ORE

AP *LG* Baldstrow Hd, Hast. PLU, pt Hast. Bor/MB/CB, pt Hast. USD, pt Hast. RSD, [E Sussex] Hast. RD (1894–1934), Battle RD (1934–58). Civ bdry: 1894 (the pt in Hast. CB cr Blacklands CP),[58] 1897 (help cr Hastings St Helens CP [renaming of Blacklands CP when extended to incl pt of this par]),[59] 1938 (loses pt to Hast. CB and CP).[162] Abol civ 1958 pt to Guestling AP, pt to Wivelsfield AP.[30] *Parl* Hast. Parl Bor (pt 1369–1867, ent 1867–1918), pt E'rn Dv (1832–67), Rye Dv (1918–48), Hast. BC (1948–55), Rye CC (1955–70). *Eccl* Seq 23. Eccl bdry: 1887 (cr Ore Christ Church EP),[85] 1891,[55] 1938.[56]

ORE CHRIST CHURCH

EP Cr 1887 from Ore AP.[85] Hast. I RDn (1887–1913), Hast. RDn (1913–*). Bdry: 1951.[106]

OVING

AP Incl area Porthfield (sep EP 1871,[286] sep CP 1894 [the pt in Chich. MB][37]). *LG* Box & Stockb. Hd, W'hamp. PLU, pt Chich. MB (1835–94), pt Chich. USD, pt W'hamp. RSD, [W Sussex] W'hamp. RD (1894–1933), Chich. RD (1933–74). Addtl civ bdry alt: 1894 (gains the pt of Rumboldswyke AP not in Chich. MB),[37] 1933 (gains Merston AP).[14] *Parl* Chich. Parl Bor (pt 1832–67, ent 1867–85), pt W'rn Dv (1832–67), S-W'rn Dv (1885–1918), Chich. Dv/CC (1918–*). *Eccl* Boxg. RDn (until 1871), Boxg. I RDn (1871–1913), Boxg. RDn (1913–29), Chich. RDn (1929–43), Bogn. Reg. RDn (1943–*). Addtl eccl bdry alt: 1873.[73]

OVINGDEAN

AP *LG* Younsmere Hd, Newh. PLU, RSD, [E Sussex] Newh. RD. Abol civ 1928 ent to Brigh. CB and AP.[62] *Parl* E'rn Dv (1832–85), Mid Dv (1885–1918), Lewes Dv (1918–45). *Eccl* Seq 26. Eccl bdry: 1937 (help cr Whitehawk EP),[96] 1952,[150] 1953 (help cr Woodingdean EP),[287] 1968.[287]

PAGHAM
AP *LG* Seq 13. Civ bdry: 1897,[283] 1900,[38] 1933.[14] *Parl* Seq 26. *Eccl* Pagham RDn (pec jurisd until 1846, in AD 1846–58), Boxg. II RDn (1871–80), Arund. II RDn (1880–1913), Selsey RDn (1913–43), Bogn. Reg. RDn (1943–*). Eccl bdry: 1891,[284] 1935,[63] 1935 (cr Aldwick EP).[9]

PARHAM
AP *LG* Seq 5. Civ bdry: 1933 (gains Greatham AP, Rackham AP, Wiggonholt AP).[14] *Parl* Seq 22. *Eccl* Seq 13. Eccl bdry: 1898.[15]

PATCHAM
AP *LG* Whaleb. Hd (until late 17th or early 18th cent), Dean Hd (thereafter), Stey. PLU, RSD, [E Sussex] Stey. E RD. Abol civ 1928 pt to Brigh. CB and AP,[62] pt to Hove AP.[250] *Parl* E'rn Dv (1832–85), Mid Dv (1885–1918), Lewes Dv (1918–45). *Eccl* Lewes RDn (until 1858), Lewes II RDn (1858–1913), Brigh. RDn (1913–55), Preston RDn (1955–*). Eccl bdry: 1931 (help cr Moulsecoomb EP),[207] 1952,[99] 1952 (help cr South Patcham EP).[191]

SOUTH PATCHAM
EP Cr 1952 from Patcham AP, Falmer AP.[191] Brigh. RDn (1952–55), Preston RDn (1955–*).

PATCHING
AP *LG* Patching Hd, Sutton incorp for poor (1791–1869), E Preston PLU (1869–1930), RSD, [W Sussex] E Preston RD (1894–1933), Worthing RD (1933–74). Civ bdry: 1933.[14] *Parl* New Shor. Parl Bor (1832–85), S-W'rn Dv (1885–1918), Chich. Dv (1918–48), Arund. & Shor. CC (1948–70), Arund. CC (1970–*). *Eccl* Seq 18.

PEACEHAVEN
Area in Piddinghoe AP, sep EP 1927,[31] sep CP 1929.[288] *LG* [E Sussex] Newh. PLU, RD (1929–34), Chailey RD (1934–74). *Parl* Lewes CC (1948–*). *Eccl* Lewes RDn.

PEASMARSH
AP *LG* Seq 22. Civ bdry: 1883,[2] 1934.[3] *Parl* Seq 16. *Eccl* Seq 21.

PENHURST
AP *LG* Seq 27. *Parl* Seq 9. *Eccl* Seq 19.

PETT
AP *LG* Pt Anc Town/Cq Pt of Winchelsea, Seq 24. Civ bdry: 1952.[206] *Parl* Seq 9. *Eccl* Seq 24. Eccl bdry: 1966.[255]

PETWORTH
AP Incl North Chapel, Duncton (each made sep par 1692[127]). *LG* Seq 8. Addtl civ bdry alt: 1933 (gains Egdean AP).[14] *Parl* Seq 23. *Eccl* Seq 12. Eccl bdry: 1865.[173]

PEVENSEY
AP *LG* Pev. Bor, corporate mbr Cq Pt of Hast., Seq 41. *Parl* Seq 10. *Eccl* Seq 32. Eccl bdry: 1970.[50]

PIDDINGHOE
AP Incl area Peacehaven (sep EP 1927,[31] sep CP 1929[288]). *LG* Seq 32. Addtl civ bdry alt: 1934.[3] *Parl* Seq 4. *Eccl* Seq 25.

PLAISTOW
CP Chap (pec jurisd Pagham) in Kirdford AP, sep CP 1951 (no sep eccl identity).[259] *LG* [W Sussex] Petw. RD. Bdry: 1960.[274] *Parl* Chich. CC (1970–*).

PLAYDEN
AP Bdry: 16th cent (loses marshlands in this par to help cr East Guldeford AP).[310] *LG* Seq 22. Addtl civ bdry alt: 1934.[3] *Parl* Seq 16. *Eccl* Seq 21.

PLUMPTON
AP *LG* Seq 34. *Parl* Seq 4. *Eccl* Lewes RDn (until 1858), Lewes II RDn (1858–1913), Lewes RDn (1913–*). Eccl bdry: 1909 (gains hmlt East Chiltington from Westmeston AP).[141]

POLEGATE
EP Cr 1937 from Hailsham AP, Willingdon AP, Westham AP, Jevington AP, Wilmington AP, Folkington AP.[212] E'bourne. RDn.
CP Cr 1939 from Hailsham AP, Jevington AP, Westham AP, Willingdon AP.[225] *LG* [E Sussex] Hailsham RD. *Parl* E'bourne. CC (1948–*).

POLING
AP *LG* Seq 6 (E Preston incorp for poor from 1806). Civ bdry: 1877,[289] 1883.[2] *Parl* Seq 27. *Eccl* Seq 1.

PORTFIELD
Area in Oving AP, sep EP 1871,[286] sep CP 1894 (the pt of Oving AP in Chich. MB).[129] *LG* [W Sussex] W'hamp. PLU, Chich. MB. Abol 1896 to help cr Chichester CP.[129] *Eccl* Boxg. I RDn (1871–1913), Chich. RDn (1913–*). Eccl bdry: 1873,[73] 1952.[130]

PORTSLADE
AP *LG* Fishg. Hd, Stey. PLU, RSD, [E Sussex] Stey. E RD. Civ bdry: 1883,[2] 1898 (pt constituted Portslade by Sea UD and CP).[291] Abol civ 1928 ent to Portslade by Sea CP.[290] *Parl* E'rn Dv (1832–85), Mid Dv (1885–1918), Lewes Dv (1918–45). *Eccl* Seq 27. Eccl bdry: 1876 (cr Portslade by Sea EP),[292] 1935,[5] 1955.[7]

PORTSLADE BY SEA
Area cr EP 1876,[292] CP 1898 (the pt constituted Portslade by Sea UD),[291] from Portslade AP. *LG* [E Sussex] Stey. PLU, Portslade by Sea UD. Civ bdry: 1928 (gains Portslade AP).[290] *Parl* Lewes Dv (1918–48), Hove BC (1948–*). *Eccl* Lewes II RDn (1876–1913), Hove RDn (1913–*). Eccl bdry: 1934 (help cr Southwick St Peter EP).[46]

POYNINGS
AP *LG* Poynings Hd, Stey. PLU, RSD, [E Sussex] Stey. E RD (1894–1928), Cuckf. RD (1928–74). Transf 1974 to W Sussex.[128] *Parl* E'rn Dv (1832–85), Mid Dv (1885–1918), Lewes Dv/CC (1918–70), Mid-Sussex CC (1970–*). *Eccl* Seq 28.

PRESTON
AP *LG* Preston Hd, Stey. PLU, Brigh. MB/CB (pt 1854–94, ent 1894–1928), pt Brigh. USD, pt Stey. RSD. [pt E Sussex 1889–94]. Civ bdry: 1894 (the pt not in Brigh. CB cr Preston Rural CP).[58] Abol civ 1928 ent to Brighton AP.[62] *Parl* E'rn Dv (1832–67), Brigh. Parl Bor (1867–1948). *Eccl* Lewes RDn (until 1858), Lewes II RDn (1858–71), Lewes V RDn (1871–1913), Brigh. RDn (1913–55), Preston (1955–*). Eccl

bdry: 1878 (cr Prestonville EP),[293] 1888 (cr Brighton St Saviour, Preston EP),[101] 1898 (cr Brighton St Augustine, Preston EP),[81] 1912 (cr Brighton St Matthias, Preston EP),[98] 1915 (cr Brighton St Alban, Preston EP),[96] 1922 (help cr Brighton The Good Shepherd, Preston EP),[42] 1952.[99]

EAST PRESTON

AP *LG* Seq 6. Civ bdry: 1877.[294] *Parl* Seq 27. *Eccl* Arund. RDn (until 1871), Storr. III RDn (1871–80), Storr. IV RDn (1880–1913), Worthing RDn (1913–*).

PRESTON RURAL

CP Cr 1894 from the pt of Preston AP not in Brigh. CB.[58] *LG* [E Sussex] Stey. PLU, Stey. E RD. Abol 1928 ent to Hove AP.[250] *Parl* Lewes Dv (1918–48).

PRESTONVILLE

EP Cr 1878 from Preston AP.[293] Lewes V RDn (1878–1913), Brigh. RDn (1913–55), Preston RDn (1955–*). Bdry: 1922 (help cr Brighton The Good Shepherd, Preston EP),[94] 1957.[100]

PULBOROUGH

AP *LG* Seq 5. Civ bdry: 1933.[14] *Parl* Seq 22. *Eccl* Seq 13. Eccl bdry: 1935.[52]

PYECOMBE

AP *LG* Seq 33. Transf 1974 to W Sussex.[128] *Parl* Seq 3. *Eccl* Seq 28.

RACKHAM

Hmlt in Amberley AP, sep CP 1866.[12] *LG* W Easw. Hd, not in PLU before 1848, Thak. PLU (1848–1930), RSD, [W Sussex] Thak. RD. Abol civ 1933 ent to Parham AP.[14] *Parl* W'rn Dv (1867–85), S-W'rn Dv (1885–1918), Horsham & Worthing Dv (1918–45).

RACTON

AP Bdry: 1440 (gains Lordington AP, the union civ called 'Racton', eccl 'Racton with Lordington', qv).[272] *LG* W'bourne. & Singl. Hd, W'bourne. PLU, RSD, [W Sussex] W'bourne. RD. Abol civ 1933 ent to Stoughton AP.[14] *Parl* W'rn Dv (1832–85), S-W'rn Dv (1885–1918), Chich. Dv (1918–48).

RACTON WITH LORDINGTON

AP Usual eccl name for union 1440 of Racton AP, Lordington AP[272]; union civ called 'Racton', qv. *Eccl* Seq 6.

RINGMER

AP *LG* Ringmer Hd, Chailey PLU (1835–98), RSD, [E Sussex] Lewes PLU (1898–1930), Chailey RD. *Parl* Seq 12. *Eccl* Seq 37.

RIPE

AP *LG* Seq 45. *Parl* Seq 11. *Eccl* Pev. RDn (until 1858), Pev. II RDn (1858–1913), Seaford RDn (1913–53). Abol eccl 1953 to help cr Ripe with Chalvington EP.[309]

RIPE WITH CHALVINGTON

EP Cr 1953 by union Ripe AP, Chalvington AP.[309] Seaford RDn.

RODMELL

AP *LG* Seq 32. *Parl* Seq 4. *Eccl* Seq 25.

ROFFEY

EP Cr 1878 as 'Roughley or Roffey' from Horsham AP,[192] 'Roffey' more commonly used. Storr. II RDn (1878–1913), Horsham RDn (1913–*).

ROGATE

AP Pt Sussex (Dumpf. Hd), pt Hants (Rogate Bonhunt Farm in Alton Hd), the latter transf to Sussex 1832 for parl purposes, 1844 for civ purposes,[16] so that this par ent Sussex thereafter. *LG* After 1844, Seq 16. Addtl civ bdry alt: 1894,[295] 1959.[27] *Parl* After 1832, Seq 23. *Eccl* Seq 9. Eccl bdry: 1877,[5] 1956.[142]

ROTHERFIELD

AP Incl hmlt Crowborough (sep EP 1880,[160] sep CP 1905[161]). *LG* Rotherfield Hd, Uckf. PLU, RSD, [E Sussex] Uckf. RD. Addtl civ bdry alt: 1949.[296] *Parl* Seq 2. *Eccl* Seq 36. Addtl eccl bdry alt: 1856 (help cr Eridge Green EP),[201] 1874 (help cr Mark Cross EP),[280] 1934 (cr Jarvis Brook EP).[101]

ROTTINGDEAN

AP *LG* Younsmere Hd, Newh. PLU, RSD, [E Sussex] Newh. RD. Abol civ 1928 ent to Brigh. CB and AP.[62] *Parl* E'rn Dv (1832–85), Mid Dv (1885–1918), Lewes Dv (1918–45). *Eccl* Seq 26. Eccl bdry: 1930 (help refound Kemp Town EP),[72] 1952,[150] 1953 (help cr Woodingdean EP),[287] 1963,[297] 1967 (cr Saltdean EP).[298]

ROUGHLEY–See ROFFEY

RUDGWICK

AP *LG* W Easw. Hd, Petw. PLU (1835–69), Horsham PLU (1869–1930), RSD, [W Sussex] Horsham RD. *Parl* Seq 24. *Eccl* Seq 14.

RUMBOLDSWYKE

AP *LG* Box & Stockb. Hd, W'hamp. PLU, Chich. Bor/MB (pt 1835–94, ent 1894–96), pt Chich. USD, pt W'hamp. RSD. [W Sussex]. Civ bdry: 1894 (loses the pt not in Chich. MB to Oving AP),[37] Abol civ 1896 to help cr Chichester CP.[129] *Parl* Chich. Parl Bor (pt 1832–67, ent 1867–85), pt W'rn Dv (1832–67), S-W'rn Dv (1885–1918). *Eccl* Pec jurisd Dean of Chich. (until 1846), Chich. RDn (1846–*). Eccl bdry: 1952.[130]

RUSPER

AP *LG* Seq 12. Civ bdry: 1956.[33] *Parl* Seq 20. *Eccl* Seq 14.

RUSTINGTON

AP *LG* Seq 6 (E Preston incorp for poor from 1806). Civ bdry: 1877,[277] 1878,[148] 1933.[14] *Parl* Seq 27. *Eccl* Seq 1.

RYE

AP *LG* Goldspur Hd, pt Rye Anc Town/Cq Pt, Rye Bor/MB (pt until 1894, ent 1894–1974), Rye PLU, pt Rye USD, pt Rye RSD. [E Sussex]. Civ bdry: 1883,[2] 1894 (the pt not in the MB cr Rye Foreign CP),[58] 1934.[3] *Parl* Rye Parl Bor (pt 1295–1832, ent 1832–85), Rye Dv (1918–48), Hast. BC (1948–55), Rye CC (1955–*). *Eccl* Seq 24.

RYE FOREIGN

CP Cr 1894 from the pt of Rye AP not in Rye MB.[58] *LG* [E Sussex] Rye PLU, RD (1894–1934), Battle RD (1934–74). Bdry: 1934.[3] *Parl* Rye Dv (1918–48), Hast. BC (1948–55),

Rye CC (1955–*).

RYE HARBOUR

EP Cr 1905 from Icklesham AP, St Thomas the Apostle, Winchelsea AP, Lydd AP (Kent, incl area of destroyed church of Broomhill, Sussex).[254] Hast. II RDn (1905–13), Rye RDn (1913–*). Bdry: 1966,[255] 1973 (cr Camber EP).[124]

ST BARTHOLOMEW RURAL

CP Cr 1894 from the pt of Chichester St Bartholomew AP not in Chich. MB.[132] *LG* [W Sussex] Chich. incorp for poor, W'hamp. RD. Abol 1895 ent to Chichester St Bartholomew AP.[133]

ST GILES, WINCHELSEA

AP Winchelsea Bor, Anc Town/Cq Pt of Winchelsea, Hast. RDn, burned 1413 and considered in St Thomas the Apostle, Winchelsea AP by 1500.[29]

ST JOHN'S COMMON

EP Cr 1865 from Clayton with Keymer AP.[145] Lewes II RDn (1865–1913), Hurst RDn (1913–*). Bdry: 1894,[71] 1902 (help cr Burgess Hill EP),[90] 1965.[64]

ST-LEONARDS-ON-SEA CHRIST CHURCH–See HASTINGS CHRIST CHURCH

ST LEONARDS-ON-SEA ST ETHELBURGA

EP Cr 1929 from Hastings Christ Church EP (sometimes 'St Leonards-on-Sea Christ Church'), eccl ex-par Hastings St Mary Bulverhythe.[192] Hast. RDn. Bdry: 1951.[246]

ST LEONARDS-ON-SEA ST PETER AND ST PAUL

EP Cr 1963 by union Hastings St Peter EP, Hastings St Paul EP.[236] Hast. RDn.

UPPER ST LEONARDS

EP Cr 1881 from Hastings St Leonards AP.[74] Hast. I RDn (1881–1913), Hast. RDn (1913–*).

ST PANCRAS RURAL

CP Cr 1894 from the pt of Chichester St Pancras AP not in Chich. MB.[133] *LG* [W Sussex] Chich. incorp for poor, W'hamp. RD. Bdry: 1895.[133] Abol 1896 ent to Donnington AP.[172]

ST THOMAS AT CLIFFE–See LEWES ST THOMAS AT CLIFFE

ST THOMAS THE APOSTLE, WINCHELSEA

AP Gains by 1500 St Giles, Winchelsea AP (burned 1413).[299] *LG* Anc Town/Cq Pt of Winchelsea, Winchelsea Bor, Rye PLU, RSD, [E Sussex] Rye RD (1894–1934), Battle RD (1934–56). Addtl civ bdry alt: 1883.[2] Abol civ 1956 to help cr Camber CP.[311] *Parl* Winchelsea Parl Bor (1369–1832), Rye Parl Bor (1832–85), E'rn Dv (1885–1918), Lewes Dv (1918–48), Hast. BC (1948–55), Rye CC (1955–*). *Eccl* Seq 24. Addtl eccl bdry alt: 1905 (help cr Rye Harbour EP),[254] 1966.[99]

SALEHURST

AP Incl pt Hurst Green (sep EP 1907,[203] sep CP 1952[202]). *LG* Seq 26. Addtl civ bdry alt: 1958.[30] *Parl* Seq 9. *Eccl* Seq 22.

SALTDEAN

EP Cr 1967 from Rottingdean AP.[298] Kemp Town RDn.

SAYER'S COMMON

EP Cr 1881 from Hurstpierpoint AP.[7] Lewes II RDn (1881–1913), Hurst RDn (1913–*). Bdry: 1965.[64]

SCAYNES HILL

EP Cr 1929 from Lindfield AP.[269] Cuckf. RDn.

SEAFORD

AP *LG* Flexb. Hd, Seaford Bor, Seaford corporate mbr Cq Pt of Hast., E'bourne. PLU, RSD (1875–83), Seaford USD (1883–94), [E Sussex] Seaford UD. *Parl* Seaford Parl Bor (1298–1398, *temp* Edw. IV–1832), Seq 12 thereafter. *Eccl* Seq 34.

SEDLESCOMBE

AP *LG* Pt Battle Hd, pt Staple Hd, Battle PLU, RSD, [E Sussex] Battle RD. Civ bdry: 1958.[30] *Parl* Seq 9. *Eccl* Dall. RDn (until 1858), Hast. II RDn (1858–1913), Hast. RDn (1913–31), Battle & Bexhill RDn (1931–*). Bdry: 1960.[119]

SELE or SELA–See UPPER BEEDING

SELHAM

AP Gains tgs North Ambersham, South Ambersham from Steep AP (Hants) 1832 for parl purposes, 1844 for civ purposes[16] (each sep CP in Sussex 1866[12]; no sep eccl identity, transf 1916 from dioc Winch to dioc Chich[17]). *LG* Easeb. Hd, Midh. PLU, RSD, [W Sussex] Midh. RD. Addtl civ bdry alt: 1879.[18] Abol civ 1933 ent to Graffham AP.[14] *Parl* Pt Midh. Parl Bor, pt W'rn Dv (1832–85), N-W'rn Dv (1885–1918), Chich. Dv (1918–48). *Eccl* Seq 10.

SELMESTON

AP *LG* Danehill Horsted Hd, W Firle PLU (1835–98), RSD, [E Sussex] E'bourne. PLU (1898–1930), RD (1894–1934), Hailsham RD (1934–74). Civ bdry: 1883,[2] 1934.[3] *Parl* Seq 11. *Eccl* Seq 34.

SELSEY

AP *LG* Seq 18. Civ bdry: 1933.[14] *Parl* Seq 25. *Eccl* Seq 7.

SENNICOTTS

EP Cr 1829 from Funtington AP.[216] Boxg. RDn (1829–58), Boxg. II RDn (1858–1913), W'bourne. RDn (1913–30). Abol 1930 to help cr Funtington with Sennicotts EP.[217]

SHERMANBURY

AP *LG* Windham & Ewhurst Hd, Stey. PLU, RSD, [W Sussex] Stey. W RD (1894–1933), Chanct. RD (1933–74). *Parl* Seq 18. *Eccl* Seq 30.

SHIPLEY

AP *LG* Seq 11. *Parl* Seq 20. *Eccl* Seq 14. Eccl bdry: 1853 (help cr Southwater EP).[249]

NEW SHOREHAM

AP *LG* Fishg. Hd, Shor. Bor, Stey. PLU, New Shor. USD, [W Sussex] New Shor. UD. Abol civ 1910 to help cr Shoreham-by-Sea UD and CP.[300] *Parl* New Shor. Parl Bor (1295–1885), Mid Dv (1885–1918). *Eccl* Seq 27.

OLD SHOREHAM

AP *LG* Fishg. Hd, Stey. PLU, RSD, [W Sussex] Stey. W RD (1894–1933), Shor.-by-Sea UD (1933–74). Civ bdry: 1910 (help cr Shoreham-by-Sea UD and CP).[300] *Parl* New Shor. Parl Bor

(1832–85), Mid Dv (1885–1918), Horsham & Worthing Dv (1918–45), Horsham Dv (1945–48), Arund. & Shor. CC (1948–70), Shor. CC (1970–*). *Eccl* Seq 27.

SHOREHAM BEACH

EP Cr 1973 from Lancing St Michael and All Angels EP.[263] Hove RDn.

SHOREHAM-BY-SEA

CP Cr 1910 by union New Shoreham AP and pts of Lancing AP, Old Shoreham AP.[300] *LG* [W Sussex] Stey. PLU, Shor.-by-Sea UD. Bdry: 1927.[261] *Parl* Horsham & Worthing Dv (1918–45), Horsham Dv (1945–48), Arund. & Shor. CC (1948–70), Shor. CC (1970–*).

SIDLESHAM

AP *LG* Seq 18. Civ bdry: 1883.[2] *Parl* Seq 25. *Eccl* Seq 7.

SIDLEY

EP Cr 1930 from Bexhill AP.[45] Hast. RDn (1930–31), Battle & Bexhill RDn (1931–*).

SILVERHILL

EP Cr 1870 from Hastings St Leonards AP.[108] Hast. I RDn (1870–1913), Hast. RDn (1913–*). Bdry: 1902.[90]

SINGLETON

AP *LG* W'bourne. & Singl. Hd, W'hamp. PLU, RSD, [W Sussex] W'hamp. RD (1894–1933), Chich. RD (1933–74). *Parl* Seq 25. *Eccl* Seq 6.

SLAUGHAM

AP Sometimes Crawley considered chap in this par (orig free chapel, considered parochial by 16th cent[153]). *LG* Seq 30. Civ bdry: 1953 (loses pt to Crawley AP, W Sussex),[155] 1957,[29] 1974 (the pt in Crawley New Town to be in Crawley Dist but in no par, the remainder to be 'Slaugham' par in Mid Sussex Dist, so that this par ent W Sussex from 1974).[128] *Parl* Pt New Shor. Parl Bor, pt E'rn Dv (1832–85), N'rn Dv (1885–1918), E Grin. Dv/CC (1918–70), Mid-Sussex CC (1970–*). *Eccl* Seq 29. Eccl bdry: 1952.[150]

SLINDON

AP Gains ex-par place The Gumber civ 1858,[131] eccl 1934.[221] *LG* Aldw. Hd, Sutton incorp for poor (1792–1858), W'hamp. PLU (1858–1930), RSD, [W Sussex] W'hamp. RD (1894–1933), Chich. RD (1933–74). *Parl* Seq 26. *Eccl* Pagham RDn (pec jurisd until 1846, in AD 1846–71), Boxg. I RDn (1871–1913), Boxg. RDn (1913–29), Arund. RDn (1929–*).

SLINFOLD

AP *LG* Pt E Easw. Hd, pt W Easw. Hd, Horsham PLU, RSD, [W Sussex] Horsham RD. *Parl* Seq 24. *Eccl* Seq 14.

SOMPTING

AP *LG* Seq 9. Civ bdry: 1902,[103] 1933.[14] *Parl* Seq 19. *Eccl* Seq 17.

SOUTHBOURNE

Chap in Westbourne AP, sep EP 1878,[293] sep CP 1968.[301] *LG* Chich. RD. *Parl* Chich. CC (1970–*). *Eccl* Boxg. II RDn (1878–1913), W'bourne. RDn (1913–*). Eccl bdry: 1957.[121]

SOUTHEASE

AP *LG* Seq 32. *Parl* Seq 4. *Eccl* Seq 25.

SOUTHGATE

EP Cr 1959 from Crawley AP.[157] Horsham RDn.

SOUTHOVER WITHOUT

CP Cr 1894 from the pt of Lewes St John the Baptist, Southover AP not in Lewes MB.[58] *LG* [E Sussex] Lewes PLU, Chailey RD. Abol 1934 pt to Lewes CP, pt to Iford AP.[3] *Parl* Lewes Dv (1918–48).

SOUTHWATER

EP Cr 1853 from Horsham AP, Shipley AP.[249] Storr. RDn (1853–71), Midh. III RDn (1871–80), Storr. II RDn (1880–1913), Horsham RDn (1913–*).

SOUTHWICK

AP *LG* Fishg. Hd, Stey. PLU, RSD, [W Sussex] Stey. W RD (1894–99), Southwick UD (1899–1974). *Parl* Seq 18. *Eccl* Seq 27. Eccl bdry: 1934 (help cr Southwick St Peter EP),[46] 1965.[302]

SOUTHWICK ST PETER

EP Cr 1934 from Southwick AP, Lancing AP, Portslade by Sea EP.[46] Hove RDn. Bdry: 1965.[302]

STANMER

AP *LG* Ringmer Hd, Newh. PLU, RSD, [E Sussex] Newh. RD (1894–1934), Chailey RD (1934–58). Civ bdry: 1934.[3] Abol civ 1958 pt to Brigh. CB and AP, pt to Falmer AP.[70] *Parl* E'rn Dv (1832–85), Mid Dv (1885–1918), Lewes Dv/CC (1918–70). *Eccl* S Mall. RDn (pec jurisd until 1846, in AD 1846–58), Lewes I RDn (1858–1913), Lewes RDn (1913–56). Abol eccl 1956 to help cr Stanmer-with-Falmer and Moulsecoomb EP.[89]

STANMER-WITH-FALMER AND MOULSECOOMB

EP Cr 1956 by union Stanmer AP, Falmer AP, Moulsecoomb EP.[89] Brigh. RDn. Bdry: 1968.[97]

STANSTED

EP Cr 1856 by union pts Stoughton AP, chap Up Marden of Compton with Up Marden AP.[152] Boxg. RDn (1856–71), Boxg. II RDn (1871–1913), W'bourne. RDn (1913–*). Commonly called 'Forest Side [with Stansted chap]'.

STAPLEFIELD COMMON

EP Cr 1848 from Cuckfield AP.[163] Lewes RDn (1848–58), Lewes III RDn (1858–1913), Cuckf. RDn (1913–*).

STEDHAM

AP Incl Heyshott (orig sep AP, united to this par before 1342,[242] sep civ identity regained early, sep EP 1882[243]). *LG* Seq 17. Addtl civ bdry alt: 1879.[16] *Parl* Seq 15. *Eccl* Midh. RDn (until 1871), Midh. II RDn (1871–80s), Midh. I RDn (1880s–1913), Midh. RDn (1913–57). Eccl bdry: 1885,[278] 1956.[142] Abol eccl 1957 to help cr Stedham with Iping EP.[236]

STEDHAM WITH IPING

EP Cr 1957 by union pt Stedham AP, pt Iping AP.[236] Midh. RDn.

STEEP

AP In Hants, incl tgs North Ambersham, South Ambersham, both transf to Sussex 1832 for parl purposes, 1844 for civ purposes[16] (each a sep CP 1866 in Sussex[12]; see the respective pars for transf from dioc Winch to dioc Chich), so that Steep ent Hants from 1844; see main entry in Hants.

STEYNING

AP Incl chap Ashurst (sep par 1580[28]). *LG* Stey. Hd, Bor, PLU, RSD [W Sussex] Stey. W RD (1894–1933), Chanct. RD (1933–74). Addtl civ bdry alt: 1883,[2] 1933.[14] *Parl* Stey. Parl Bor (sometimes returned with Bramber, itself *temp* Edw. I–1832), Seq 18 thereafter. *Eccl* Storr. RDn (until 1871), Storr. III RDn (1871–1913), Horsham RDn (1913–29), Worthing RDn (1929–*).

NORTH STOKE

AP *LG* Poling Hd, in no PLU before 1869, Thak. PLU (1869–1930), RSD, [W Sussex] Thak. RD. Abol civ 1933 ent to Amberley AP.[14] *Parl* W'rn Dv (1832–85), S-W'rn Dv (1885–1918), Horsham & Worthing Dv (1918–45). *Eccl* Arund. RDn (until 1871), Arund. I RDn (1871–80), Storr. I RDn (1880–1913), Arund. RDn (1913–29), Storr. RDn (1929–*).

SOUTH STOKE

AP *LG* Avisf. Hd, in no PLU before 1869, E Preston PLU (1869–1930), RSD, [W Sussex] E Preston RD (1894–1933), Worthing RD (1933–74). *Parl* Seq 27. *Eccl* Seq 1.

WEST STOKE

AP *LG* Bosham Hd, W'hamp. PLU, RSD, [W Sussex] W'hamp. RD. Abol civ 1933 ent to Funtington AP.[14] *Parl* W'rn Dv (1832–85), S-W'rn Dv (1885–1918), Chich. Dv (1918–48). *Eccl* Seq 6.

STONEGATE

EP Cr 1838 from Ticehurst AP.[303] Dall. RDn (1838–1913), Etch. RDn (1913–*).

STOPHAM

AP *LG* Rothb. Hd, Thak. PLU (1835–69), Petw. PLU (1869–1930), RSD, [W Sussex] Thak. RD. *Parl* Seq 23. *Eccl* Seq 12.

STORRINGTON

AP *LG* Seq 5. *Parl* Seq 28. *Eccl* Storr. RDn (until 1871), Storr. III RDn (1871–80), Storr. I RDn (1880–1913), Storr. RDn (1913–*).

STOUGHTON

AP *LG* Seq 19. Civ bdry: 1880,[151] 1933 (gains Racton AP).[14] *Parl* Seq 25. *Eccl* Seq 6. Eccl bdry: 1856 (help cr Stansted EP).[152]

STREAT

AP Sometimes 'Street'. *LG* Seq 34. *Parl* Seq 4. *Eccl* Seq 28.

STREET–See prev entry

SUB-DEANERY RURAL

CP Cr 1894 from the pt of Chichester St Peter the Great or Sub-Deanery AP not in Chich. MB.[132] *LG* [W Sussex] Chich. incorp for poor, W'hamp. RD. Bdry: 1895.[133] Abol 1896 ent to New Fishbourne AP.[172]

SULLINGTON

AP *LG* Seq 10. Civ bdry: 1878.[304] *Parl* Seq 21. *Eccl* Seq 13.

SUTTON

AP *LG* Rothb. Hd, Sutton incorp for poor (1791–1869), Petw. PLU (1869–1930), RSD, [W Sussex] Petw. RD. Bdry: 1883,[2] 1933.[14] *Parl* Seq 23. *Eccl* Seq 11.

TANGMERE

AP *LG* Seq 13. *Parl* Seq 25. *Eccl* Pagham RDn (pec jurisd until 1846, in AD 1846–71), Boxg. I RDn (1871–1913), Boxg. RDn (1913–29), Chich. RDn (1929–43), Bogn. Reg. RDn (1943–*).

WEST TARRING

AP Incl area Durrington (sep civ identity early, sep EP 1914[174]). *LG* Tarring Hd, E Preston incorp for poor (1803–69), PLU (1869–1902), RSD, [W Sussex] E Preston RD. Abol civ 1902 pt to Goring by Sea AP, pt to Durrington CP, pt to Worthing CP.[103] *Parl* New Shor. Parl Bor (1832–85), Mid Dv (1885–1918). *Eccl* Seq 18. Addtl eccl bdry alt: 1955 (incl help cr West Worthing EP),[125] 1957.[107]

TARRING NEVILLE

AP *LG* Danehill Horsted Hd, Newh. PLU, RSD, [E Sussex] Newh. RD (1894–1934), Chailey RD (1934–74). Civ bdry: 1934.[3] *Parl* Seq 12. *Eccl* Seq 34.

TELSCOMBE

AP *LG* Seq 32. *Parl* Seq 4. *Eccl* Seq 25. Eccl bdry: 1963.[297]

TERWICK

AP *LG* Dumpf. Hd, Midh. PLU, RSD, [W Sussex] Midh. RD. Civ bdry: 1879.[18] Abol civ 1959 pt to Rogate AP, pt to Trotton AP.[305] *Parl* W'rn Dv (1832–85), N-W'rn Dv (1885–1918), Chich. Dv (1918–48). *Eccl* Seq 9. Eccl bdry: 1956 (incl help cr Trotton with Chithurst EP).[142]

THAKENHAM

AP *LG* Seq 10. Civ bdry: 1883,[2] 1933.[14] *Parl* Seq 21. *Eccl* Storr. RDn (until 1871), Storr. III RDn (1871–1913), Storr. RDn (1913–60). Abol eccl 1960 pt to help cr Thakenham with Warminghurst EP, pt to West Chiltington AP.[120]

THAKENHAM WITH WARMINGHURST

EP Cr 1960 by union Warminghurst AP, pt Thakenham AP.[120] Storr. RDn.

WEST THORNEY

AP *LG* Seq 14. *Parl* Seq 25. *Eccl* Seq 6.

TICEHURST

AP *LG* Shoyswell Hd, Ticeh. PLU, RSD, [E Sussex] Ticeh. RD (1894–1934), Battle RD (1934–74). Civ bdry: 1952 (incl help cr Hurst Green CP).[202] *Parl* Seq 8. Parl bdry: 1953 (the pt lost to help cr Hurst Green CP transf to Hast. BC).[205] *Eccl* Seq 22. Eccl bdry: 1838 (cr Stonegate EP),[303] 1860 (cr Ticehurst St Augustine EP,[36] now called 'Flimwell').

TICEHURST ST AUGUSTINE

EP Cr 1860 from Ticehurst AP.[36] Dall. RDn (1860–1913), Etch. RDn (1913–*). Now called 'Flimwell'.

TIDEBROOK

EP Cr 1857 from Wadhurst AP,[36] refounded 1858

from Wadhurst AP, Mayfield AP.[281] Pev. RDn (1857–58), Pev. IV RDn (1858–1912), Dall. RDn (1912–13), Etch. RDn (1913–*). Bdry: 1874 (help cr Mark Cross EP).[280]

TILLINGTON

AP *LG* Seq 7. *Parl* Seq 23. *Eccl* Seq 12.

TORTINGTON

AP *LG* Seq 1 [E Preston incorp for poor from 1799]. Civ bdry: 1902,[25] 1933 (gains Binsted AP).[14] *Parl* Seq 26. *Eccl* Seq 1.

TREYFORD

AP *LG* Seq 16. Civ bdry: 1933 (gains Didling AP).[14] *Parl* Seq 23. *Eccl* Midh. RDn. Abol eccl 1503 (sep civ identity maintained) to help cr Elsted with Treyford and Didling EP.[170]

TROTTON

AP *LG* Pt Dumpf. Hd, pt Easeb. Hd, Midh. PLU, RSD, [W Sussex] Midh. RD. Civ bdry: 1879,[18] 1922,[256] 1959.[27] *Parl* Pt Midh. Parl Bor, pt W'rn Dv (1832–85), N-W'rn Dv (1885–1918), Chich. Dv (1918–48), Horsham CC (1948–70), Chich. CC (1970–*). *Eccl* Midh. RDn (until 1871), Midh. I RDn (1871–1913), Midh. RDn (1913–56). Eccl bdry: 1862 (cr Tuxlith EP, now called 'Milland').[306] Abol eccl 1956 pt to help cr Trotton with Chithurst EP, pt to Tuxlith EP, pt to Iping AP.[142]

TROTTON WITH CHITHURST

EP Cr 1956 by union chap Chithurst of Iping AP and pts Trotton AP, Terwick AP.[142] Midh. RDn.

TURNER'S HILL

EP Cr 1896 from Worth AP, Ardingley AP, West Hoathly AP, Crawley Down EP.[22] Lewes III RDn (1896–1913), E Grin. RDn (1913–*).

TUXLITH

EP Cr 1862 from Trotton AP.[306] Midh. RDn (1863–71), Midh. I RDn (1871–1913), Midh. RDn (1913–*). Bdry: 1877,[5] 1956.[142] Now called 'Milland'.

TWINEHAM

AP *LG* Seq 30. Transf 1974 to W Sussex.[128] *Parl* Seq 3. *Eccl* Seq 30.

UCKFIELD

Chap in Buxted AP, sep civ identity early, sep EP 1846.[111] *LG* Loxf. Dorset Hd, Uckf. PLU, USD, [E Sussex] Uckf. UD (1894–1934), RD (1934–74). *Parl* Seq 5. *Eccl* S Mall. RDn (1846–58), Pev. III RDn (1858–1913), Uckf. RDn (1913–*). Eccl bdry: 1969.[117]

UDIMORE

AP Sometimes 'Odimore'. *LG* Seq 23. Civ bdry: 1876,[67] 1934,[3] 1958.[30] *Parl* Seq 17. *Eccl* Seq 21.

WADHURST

AP *LG* Pt Loxf. Pelham Hd, pt Hawkesborough Hd, Ticeh. PLU, RSD, [E Sussex] Ticeh. RD (1894–1934), Uckf. RD (1934–74). *Parl* Seq 7. *Eccl* S Mall. RDn (pec jurisd until 1846, in AD 1846–58), Pev. IV RDn (1858–1912), Dall. RDn (1912–13), Etch. RDn (1913–*). Eccl bdry: 1857 (cr Tidebrook EP,[36] refounded 1858 [incl pt Mayfield EP][281]), 1874 (help cr Mark Cross EP).[280]

WALBERTON

AP *LG* Seq 2. Civ bdry: 1883.[2] *Parl* Seq 26. *Eccl* Arund. RDn (until 1871), Arund. II RDn (1871–80), Arund. I RDn (1880–1913), Arund. RDn (1913–*). Eccl bdry: 1929.[307]

WALDRON

AP Incl pt area Horam (sep CP 1951,[140] sep EP 1963[239]). *LG* Seq 46. *Parl* E'rn Dv (1832–85), S'rn Dv (1885–1918), E Grin. Dv (1918–48), Lewes CC (1948–55), Rye CC (1955–*). *Eccl* Pev. RDn (until 1858), Dall. RDn (1858–*). Addtl eccl bdry alt: 1960 (help cr Heathfield St Richard EP).[45]

COLD WALTHAM

AP Usual eccl spelling; for civ see 'Coldwaltham'. *Eccl* Midh. RDn (until 1871), Midh. II RDn (1871–1913), Storr. RDn (1913–*).

UP WALTHAM

AP *LG* Seq 15. *Parl* Seq 25. *Eccl* Boxg. RDn (until 1871), Boxg. I RDn (1871–1913), Petw. RDn (1913–*).

WARBLETON

AP *LG* Seq 25. Civ bdry: 1887.[126] *Parl* Seq 13. *Eccl* Seq 19. Eccl bdry: 1855 (help cr Bodle Street Green EP).[60]

WARMINGHURST

AP *LG* E Easw. Hd, Thak. PLU, RSD, [W Sussex] Thak. RD. Abol civ 1933 ent to Ashington AP.[14] *Parl* New Shor. Parl Bor (1832–85), S-W'rn Dv (1885–1918), Horsham & Worthing Dv (1918–45). *Eccl* Orig dependent on Duke of Norfolk, Storr. RDn (until 1871), Storr. III RDn (1871–1913), Storr. RDn (1913–60). Abol eccl 1960 to help cr Thakenham with Warminghurst EP.[120]

WARNHAM

AP *LG* Seq 12. Civ bdry: 1933.[14] *Parl* Seq 20. *Eccl* Seq 14.

WARNINGCAMP

Tg in Lyminster AP, sep CP 1866.[12] *LG* Poling Hd, Sutton incorp for poor (1866[285]–69), E Preston PLU (1869–1930), RSD, [W Sussex] E Preston RD (1894–1933), Worthing RD (1933–74). *Parl* W'rn Dv (1867–85), S-W'rn Dv (1885–1918), Chich. Dv (1918–48), Arund. & Shor. CC (1948–70), Arund. CC (1970–*).

WARTLING

AP *LG* Seq 21. Civ bdry: 1886.[241] *Parl* E'rn Dv (1832–85), S'rn Dv (1885–1918), Rye Dv (1918–48), E'bourne. CC (1948–55), Rye CC (1955–*). *Eccl* Dall. RDn (until 1858), Pev. I RDn (1858–1913), Dall. RDn (1913–*).

WASHINGTON

AP *LG* Stey. Hd, Thak. PLU, RSD, [W Sussex] Thak. RD (1894–1933), Chanct. RD (1933–74). Civ bdry: 1883,[2] 1933,[14] 1960.[27] *Parl* Seq 21. *Eccl* Storr. RDn (until 1871), Storr. I RDn (1871–80), Storr. III RDn (1880–1913), Storr. RDn (1913–*).

WESTBOURNE

AP Incl chap Southbourne (sep EP 1878,[293] sep CP 1968[301]). *LG* Seq 19. *Parl* Seq 25. *Eccl* Seq 6. Addtl eccl bdry: 1957.[121]

WESTFIELD
AP *LG* Seq 20. Civ bdry: 1938,[162] 1958.[30] *Parl* Seq 9. *Eccl* Dall. RDn (until 1858), Hast. I RDn (1858–1913), Hast. RDn (1913–*). Eccl bdry: 1960.[119]

WESTHAM
AP Incl pt area Polegate (sep EP 1937,[212] sep CP 1939[225]). *LG* Pev. corporate mbr Cq Pt of Hast., Seq 41. Addtl civ bdry alt: 1938 (loses pt to E'bourne. CB and AP).[168] *Parl* Seq 10. *Eccl* Seq 32. Addtl eccl bdry alt: 1953 (help cr Hampden Park EP),[193] 1957.[192]

WESTHAMPNETT
AP *LG* Seq 15. Civ bdry: 1933.[14] *Parl* Seq 25. *Eccl* Seq 5.

WESTMESTON
AP Incl hmlt East Chiltington (sep CP 1866,[12] eccl severed 1909 and transf to Plumpton AP[141]). *LG* Seq 34. Addtl civ bdry alt: 1934.[3] *Parl* Seq 4. *Eccl* Seq 28.

WHATLINGTON
AP *LG* Battle Hd, PLU, RSD, [E Sussex] Battle RD. Civ bdry: 1958.[30] *Parl* Seq 9. *Eccl* Dall. RDn (until 1858), Hast. II RDn (1858–70s), Dall. RDn (1870s–1913), Etch. RDn (1913–25), Hast. RDn (1925–31), Battle & Bexhill RDn (1931–*). Eccl bdry: 1960.[119]

WHITEHAWK
EP Cr 1937 from Ovingdean AP, Kemp Town EP, Brighton St Wilfrid EP.[96] Brigh. RDn (1937–55), Kemp Town RDn (1955–*).

WICK
Area in Lyminster AP, sep CP 1901,[275] sep EP 1973.[276] *LG* [W Sussex] E Preston PLU, Littlehampton UD. *Parl* Chich. Dv (1918–48), Arund. & Shor. CC (1948–70), Arund. CC (1970–*). *Eccl* Arund. RDn.

WIGGONHOLT
AP *LG* W Easw. Hd, Worthing PLU (1836–69), Thak. PLU (1869–1930), RSD, [W Sussex] Thak. RD. Abol civ 1933 ent to Parham AP.[14] *Parl* W'rn Dv (1832–85), Mid Dv (1885–1918), Horsham & Worthing Dv (1918–45). *Eccl* Storr. RDn. Abol eccl 1510 (sep civ identity maintained) to help cr Greatham with Wiggonholt EP.[218]

WILLINGDON
AP Incl pt area Polegate (sep EP 1937,[212] sep CP 1939[225]), pt area Hampden Park (sep CP 1911,[226] sep EP 1953[193]). *LG* Willingdon Hd, E'bourne PLU, pt E'bourne MB/CB (1883–94), pt E'bourne USD (1883–94), E'bourne RSD (ent 1875–83, pt 1883–94), [E Sussex] E'bourne. RD (1894–1934), Hailsham RD (1934–74). Addtl civ bdry alt: 1888,[211] 1894 (the pt in the MB cr Norway CP),[58] 1926 (loses pt to E'bourne. CB and AP),[178] 1938 (loses pt to E'bourne. CB and AP).[168] *Parl* Seq 10. *Eccl* Seq 32. Addtl eccl bdry alt: 1873,[187] 1935 (help cr Eastbourne St Elisabeth EP),[183] 1951.[190]

WILMINGTON
AP *LG* Seq 39. Civ bdry: 1888.[211] *Parl* Seq 11. *Eccl* Seq 33. Eccl bdry: 1937 (help cr Polegate EP),[212] 1956,[24] 1962.[142]

WINCHELSEA–See ST GILES, WINCHELSEA and ST THOMAS THE APOSTLE, WINCHELSEA

WISBOROUGH GREEN
AP Incl chap Loxwood (sep EP 1873,[114] sep CP 1938[273]). *LG* Pt W Easw. Hd, pt Rothb. Hd, Petw. PLU, RSD, [W Sussex] Petw. RD. Addtl civ bdry alt: 1884 (gains the pt of Alfold AP [Surrey, Sussex] in Sussex, so that the latter ent Surrey thereafter).[10] *Parl* Seq 23. *Eccl* Storr. RDn (until 1871), Midh. III RDn (1871–80), Storr. I RDn (1880–1913), Horsham RDn (1913–62), Petw. RDn (1962–*).

WISTON
AP *LG* Stey. Hd, Thak. PLU, RSD, [W Sussex] Thak. RD (1894–1933), Chanct. RD (1933–74). Civ bdry: 1883,[2] 1933,[14] 1960.[27] *Parl* Seq 21. *Eccl* Storr. RDn (until 1871), Storr. III RDn (1871–1913), Horsham RDn (1913–29), Storr. RDn (1929–*).

WITHYHAM
AP *LG* Seq 38. Civ bdry: 1949.[296] *Parl* Seq 5. *Eccl* Pec jurisd S Mall. (until 1846), Seq 36 thereafter. Eccl bdry: 1871 (cr Withyham St John EP).[34]

WITHYHAM ST JOHN
EP Cr 1871 from Withyham AP.[34] Pev. IV RDn (1871–1913), E Grin. RDn (1913–*). Bdry: 1886 (cr New Groombridge EP).[23]

EAST WITTERING
AP *LG* Seq 18. Civ bdry: 1883,[2] 1933.[14] *Parl* Seq 25. *Eccl* Seq 7. Eccl bdry: 1973.[308]

WEST WITTERING
AP *LG* Seq 18. Civ bdry: 1883.[2] *Parl* Seq 25. *Eccl* Seq 7. Eccl bdry: 1973.[308]

WIVELSFIELD
Chap in Ditchling AP before end 12th cent[171]; sep par perhaps at Dissolution in 16th cent, sep civ identity early, sep eccl no later than 1773.[36] *LG* Seq 34. Civ bdry: 1934 (incl help cr Burgess Hill CP).[3] *Parl* E'rn Dv (1832–85), N'rn Dv (1885–1918), Lewes Dv/CC (1918–*). *Eccl* Pec jurisd S Mall. (until 1846), Seq 29 thereafter. Eccl bdry: 1894,[71] 1944 (loses pt to Cuckfield St Wilfrid EP at same time latter renamed 'Hayward's Heath St Wilfrid').[99]

WOODINGDEAN
EP Cr 1953 from Rottingdean AP, Ovingdean AP.[287] Brigh. RDn (1953–55), Kemp Town RDn (1955–*).

WOODMANCOTE
AP *LG* Tipnoak Hd, Stey. PLU, RSD, [W Sussex] Stey. W RD (1894–1933), Chanct. RD (1933–74). *Parl* Seq 18. *Eccl* Seq 30.

WOOLAVINGTON
AP Usual eccl spelling; for civ see 'East Lavington'. Incl chap West Lavington (sep EP 1850,[265] sep CP 1866[12]). *Eccl* Midh. RDn (until 1871), Midh. II RDn (1871–1913), Petw. RDn (1913–72). Addtl eccl bdry alt: 1931.[35] Abol eccl 1972 to help cr Graffham with Woolavington EP.[145]

WOOLBEDING
AP *LG* Seq 17. Civ bdry: 1879.[18] *Parl* Seq 15. *Eccl* Seq 9. Eccl bdry: 1885.[278]

WORTH
AP *LG* Seq 31. Civ bdry: 1953 (incl loses pt to Crawley AP, W Sussex),[155] 1958,[245] 1974 (the pt in Crawley New Town to be in Crawley Dist but in no par, the remainder to be 'Worth' par in Mid Sussex Dist so that this par ent W Sussex from 1974).[128] *Parl* Seq 6. *Eccl* Seq 29. Eccl bdry: 1862 (cr Crawley Down EP),[31] 1881 (help cr Copthorne EP),[81] 1896 (help cr Turner's Hill EP),[22] 1952.[150]

WORTHING
The following have 'Worthing' in their names. Insofar as any existed at a given time: *LG* [W Sussex] E Preston PLU, Worthing MB. *Parl* Horsham & Worthing Dv (1918–45), Worthing Dv (1945–48), Worthing BC (1948–*). *Eccl* Storr. RDn (cr–1858), Storr. IV RDn (1858–1913), Worthing RDn (1913–*).

CP1–WORTHING–Cr 1894 from the pt of Broadwater AP in Worthing MB.[58] Bdry: 1902,[103] 1902,[25] 1929 (gains Durrington CP, Goring by Sea AP),[175] 1933.[14]

EP1–WORTHING CHRIST CHURCH–Cr 1855 from Broadwater AP.[104] Bdry: 1884 (help cr EP2),[105] 1888 (help cr EP3).[101]

EP2–WORTHING HOLY TRINITY–Cr 1884 from EP1, Broadwater AP.[105] Bdry: 1888 (help cr EP3),[101] 1957.[61]

EP3–WORTHING ST ANDREW–Cr 1888 from EP2, EP1, Broadwater AP.[101]

EP4–WORTHING ST GEORGE–Cr 1868 from Broadwater AP.[123] Bdry: 1894 (help cr EP5).[106]

EP5–WORTHING ST PAUL–Cr 1894 from Broadwater AP, EP4.[106]

EP6–WEST WORTHING–Cr 1955 from West Tarring AP, Heene AP.[125]

YAPTON
AP *LG* Seq 2. Civ bdry: 1883,[2] 1933.[14] *Parl* Seq 26. *Eccl* Arund. RDn (until 1871), Arund. II RDn (1871–80), Arund. I RDn (1880–1913), Arund. RDn (1913–*). Eccl bdry: 1929,[307] 1973.[122]

WILTSHIRE

ABBREVIATIONS

Abbreviations particular to Wilts follow. Those general abbreviations in use throughout the *Guide* are found on page xix.

Aldb.	Alderbury
Amesb.	Amesbury
Aveb.	Avebury
Bradf.	Bradford
Cann.	Cannings
Cawd. & Cad.	Cawden and Cadworth
Chip.	Chippenham
Crickl.	Cricklande
Dam.	Damerham
Deviz.	Devizes
Down.	Downton
Elst. & Ev.	Elstub and Everleigh
Enf.	Enford
Frust.	Frustfield
Heytb.	Heytesbury
Highw.	Highworth
Kingsbr.	Kingsbridge
Kinw.	Kinwardstone
Malm.	Malmesbury
Marlb.	Marlborough
Melk.	Melksham
Pott.	Potterne
Ramsb.	Ramsbury
Salisb.	Salisbury
Selk.	Selkley
Swanb.	Swanborough
Swind.	Swindon
Tisb.	Tisbury
Und.	Underditch
Warm.	Warminster
W'bury	Westbury
Whorw.	Whorwellsdown
Woot. Bas.	Wootton Bassett

SEQUENCES

An abbreviated entry prefixed by 'Seq' is used in the parochial entries to avoid repeating often the names of superior units of administration. The content of each sequence is shown below.

Local Government Sequences ('LG')

SEQ 1 Aldb. Hd, PLU (1835–95), RSD, RD (1894–1934), Salisb. PLU (1895–1930), Salisb. & Wilton RD (1934–74)
SEQ 2 Amesb. Hd, PLU, RSD, RD
SEQ 3 Amesb. Hd, Pewsey PLU, RSD, RD
SEQ 4 Bradf. Hd, PLU (1835–95), RSD, Bradf.-on-Avon PLU (1895–1930), RD (1894–1934), Bradf. & Melk. RD (1934–74)
SEQ 5 Branch & Dole Hd, Amesb. PLU, RSD, RD
SEQ 6 Branch & Dole Hd, Wilton PLU, RSD, RD (1894–1934), Salisb. & Wilton RD (1934–74)
SEQ 7 Calne Hd, PLU, RSD, RD (1894–1934), Calne & Chip. RD (1934–74)
SEQ 8 Cawd. & Cad. Hd, Aldb. PLU (1835–95), RSD, Salisb. PLU (1895–1930), Salisb. RD (1894–1934), Salisb. & Wilton RD (1934–74)
SEQ 9 Cawd. & Cad. Hd, Wilton PLU, RSD, RD (1894–1934), Salisb. & Wilton RD (1934–74)
SEQ 10 Chalk Hd, Tisb. PLU, RSD, RD (1894–1934), Mere & Tisb. RD (1934–74)
SEQ 11 Chalk Hd, Wilton PLU, RSD, RD (1894–

1934), Salisb. & Wilton RD (1934–74)
SEQ 12 Chip. Hd, PLU, RSD, RD (1894–1934), Calne & Chip. RD (1934–74)
SEQ 13 Chip. Hd, Malm. PLU, RSD, RD
SEQ 14 Dam. Hd, Chip. PLU, RSD, RD (1894–1934), Calne & Chip. RD (1934–74)
SEQ 15 Down. Hd, Tisb. PLU, RSD, RD (1894–1934), Mere & Tisb. RD (1934–74)
SEQ 16 Dunworth Hd, Tisb. PLU, RSD, RD (1894–1934), Mere & Tisb. RD (1934–74)
SEQ 17 Elst. & Ev. Hd, Pewsey PLU, RSD, RD
SEQ 18 Frust. Hd, Aldb. PLU (1835–95), RSD, Salisb. PLU (1895–1930), RD (1894–1934), Salisb. & Wilton RD (1934–74)
SEQ 19 Heytb. Hd, Warm. PLU, RSD, RD (1894–1934), Warm. & W'bury RD (1934–74)
SEQ 20 Highw., Crickl. & Staple Hd, Crickl. & Woot. Bas. PLU, RSD, RD
SEQ 21 Highw., Crickl. & Staple Hd, Highw. & Swindon PLU (1836–99), RSD, Swindon & Highw. PLU (1899–1930), Highw. RD
SEQ 22 Kingsbr. Hd, Crickl. & Woot. Bas. PLU, RSD, RD
SEQ 23 Kingsbr. Hd, Highw. & Swind. PLU (1835–96), Swind. & Highw. PLU (1896–1930), Highw. RD
SEQ 24 Kinw. Hd, Hungerford PLU (1835–96), RSD, Hungerford & Ramsb. PLU (1896–1930), Ramsb. RD (1894–1934), Marlb. & Ramsb. RD (1934–74)
SEQ 25 Kinw. Hd, Pewsey PLU, RSD, RD
SEQ 26 Malm. Hd, Chip. PLU, RSD, RD (1894–1934), Calne & Chip. RD (1934–74)
SEQ 27 Malm. Hd, PLU, RSD, RD
SEQ 28 Melk. Hd, Deviz. PLU, RSD, RD
SEQ 29 Mere Hd, PLU, RSD, RD (1894–1934), Mere & Tisb. RD (1934–74)
SEQ 30 Pott. & Cann. Hd, Deviz. PLU, RSD, RD
SEQ 31 Ramsb. Hd, Hungerford PLU (1835–96), RSD, Hungerford & Ramsb. PLU (1896–1930), Ramsb. RD (1894–1934), Marlb. & Ramsb. RD (1934–74)
SEQ 32 Selk. Hd, Marlb. PLU, RSD, RD (1894–1934), Marlb. & Ramsb. RD (1934–74)
SEQ 33 Swanb. Hd, Deviz. PLU, RSD, RD
SEQ 34 Swanb. Hd, Pewsey PLU, RSD, RD
SEQ 35 Und. Hd, Amesb. PLU, RSD, RD
SEQ 36 Warm. Hd, PLU, RSD, RD (1894–1934), Warm. & W'bury RD (1934–74)
SEQ 37 Whorw. Hd, W'bury & Whorw. PLU, RSD, RD (1894–1934), Warm. & W'bury RD (1934–74)

Parliamentary Sequences ('Parl')

SEQ 1 Crickl. Parl Bor (1832–85), N'rn Dv (1885–1918), Chip. Dv/CC (1918–*)
SEQ 2 Crickl. Parl Bor (1832–85), N'rn Dv (1885–1918), Swind. Dv (1918–48), Deviz. CC (1948–*)
SEQ 3 Crickl. Parl Bor (1832–85), N-W'rn Dv (1885–1918), Chip. Dv/CC (1918–*)
SEQ 4 N'rn Dv (1832–1918), Deviz. Dv/CC (1918–*)
SEQ 5 N'rn Dv (1832–85), E'rn Dv (1885–1918), Deviz. Dv/CC (1918–*)
SEQ 6 N'rn Dv (1832–85), N-W'rn Dv (1885–1918), Chip. Dv/CC (1918–*)
SEQ 7 N'rn Dv (1832–85), W'rn Dv (1885–1918), W'bury Dv/CC (1918–*)
SEQ 8 S'rn Dv (1832–85), E'rn Dv (1885–1918), Deviz. Dv/CC (1918–*)
SEQ 9 S'rn Dv (1832–1918), Salisb. Dv/CC (1918–*)
SEQ 10 S'rn Dv (1832–1918), Salisb. Dv (1918–48), W'bury CC (1948–*)
SEQ 11 S'rn Dv (1832–1918), W'bury Dv/CC (1918–*)
SEQ 12 S'rn Dv (1832–85), W'rn Dv (1885–1918), W'bury Dv/CC (1918–*)
SEQ 13 Wilton Parl Bor (1832–85), S'rn Dv (1885–1918), Salisb. Dv/CC (1918–*)

Ecclesiastical Sequences ('Eccl')

Orig Sarum AD:

SEQ 1 Amesb. RDn (until 1872), Amesb. RDn First Dv/Aldb. (1872–*)
SEQ 2 Amesb. RDn (until 1872), Amesb. RDn Second Dv/Amesb. (1872–1951), Aldb. RDn (1951–*)
SEQ 3 Amesb. RDn (until 1872), Amesb. RDn Second Dv/Amesb. (1872–1951), Avon RDn (1951–*)
SEQ 4 Chalke RDn (until 1872), Chalke RDn First Dv/Chalke (1872–*)
SEQ 5 Chalke RDn (until 1872), Chalke RDn Second Dv/Tisb. (1872–1973), Shaft. & Tisb. RDn (1973–*)
SEQ 6 Pott. RDn (until 1872), Pott. RDn First Dv/Pott. (1872–1951), Deviz. RDn (1951–*)
SEQ 7 Pott. RDn (until 1872), Pott. RDn Second Dv/Enf. (1872–1951), Avon RDn (1951–*)
SEQ 8 Pott. RDn (until 1872), Pott. RDn Second Dv/Enf. (1872–1951), Deviz. RDn (1951–*)
SEQ 9 Pott. RDn (until 1872), Pott. RDn Third Dv/Bradf. (1872–*)
SEQ 10 Salisb. Sub-deanery RDn (until 1872), Salisb. & Wilton RDn (1872–1971), Salisb. RDn (1971–*)
SEQ 11 Wilton RDn (until 1872), Salisb. & Wilton RDn (1872–1971), Salisb. RDn (1971–*)
SEQ 12 Wylye RDn (until 1872), Wylye RDn First Dv/Wylye (1872–1971), Wylye & Wilton RDn (1971–*)
SEQ 13 Wylye RDn (until 1872), Wylye RDn Second Dv/Heytb. RDn (1872–*)

Orig Wilts AD:

SEQ 14 Aveb. RDn (until 1872), Aveb. RDn First Dv/Aveb. (1872–1974), Calne RDn (1974–*)

SEQ 15 Aveb. RDn (until 1872), Aveb. RDn First Dv/Aveb. (1872–1974), Marlb. RDn (1974–*)
SEQ 16 Aveb. RDn (until 1872), Aveb. RDn Second Dv/Cann. (1872–1951), Aveb. RDn (1951–74), Calne RDn (1974–*)
SEQ 17 Aveb. RDn (until 1872), Aveb. RDn Second Dv/Cann. (1872–1951), Deviz. RDn (1951–*)
SEQ 18 Aveb. RDn (until 1872), Aveb. RDn Second Dv/Cann. (1872–1951), Marlb. RDn (1951–*)
SEQ 19 Aveb. RDn (until 1872), Aveb. RDn Second Dv/Cann. (1872–1951), Pewsey RDn (1951–*)
SEQ 20 Crickl. RDn
SEQ 21 Malm. RDn (until 1866), Malm. North RDn (1866–87), Malm. RDn (1887–*)
SEQ 22 Malm. RDn (until 1866), Malm. South RDn (1866–87), Chip. RDn (1887–*)
SEQ 23 Marlb. RDn (until 1872), Marlb. RDn First Dv/Marlb. (1872–*)
SEQ 24 Marlb. RDn (until 1872), Marlb. RDn Second Dv/Pewsey (1872–*)

DIOCESES AND ARCHDEACONRIES

Wilts pars were organised in dioceses and archdeaconries as follows.

BRISTOL DIOC (1897–*)
Bristol AD (1897–1904): Chip. RDn, Crickl. RDn, Malm. RDn
Swindon AD (1919–):* Chip. RDn, Crickl. RDn, Malm. RDn
North Wilts AD (1904–19): Chip. RDn, Crickl. RDn, Malm. RDn

GLOUCESTER AND BRISTOL DIOC (1837–97)
Bristol AD: Chip. RDn (1887–97), Crickl. RDn, Malm. RDn (1837–66), Malm. RDn (1887–97), Malm. North RDn (1866–87), Malm. South RDn (1866–87)
SARUM DIOC
Dorset AD: Shaft. & Tisb. RDn (1973–*)
Sarum AD: Aldb. RDn (1872–*), Amesb. RDn (until 1872), Amesb. RDn (1872–1951), Avon RDn (1951–*), Chalke RDn (until 1872), Chalke RDn (1872–*), Heytb. RDn (1872–*), Salisb. Sub-deanery RDn (until 1872), Salisb. RDn (1971–*), Tisb. RDn (1872–1973), Wilton RDn (until 1872), Wilton RDn (1872–1971), Wylye RDn (until 1872), Wylye RDn (1872–1971), Wylye & Wilton RDn (1971–*)
Wilts AD: Aveb. RDn (until 1872), Aveb. RDn (1872–1974), Bradf. RDn (1872–*), Calne RDn (1974–*), Cann. RDn (1872–1951), Crickl. RDn (until 1837), Deviz. RDn (1951–*), Enf. RDn (1872–1951), Malm. RDn (until 1837), Marlb. RDn (until 1872), Marlb. RDn (1872–*), Pewsey RDn (1872–*), Pott. RDn (until 1872), Pott. RDn (1872–1951)

Note: From 1872 until well into 20th cent RDns in Sarum were known both as divisions of the orig RDns and by the names used invariably later; the seq numbers above use the former, the organisation of RDns in ADs and the parochial entries the latter. The double names may be paired as follows:
Amesb. First–Second Dvs: Aldb., Amesb., respectively
Aveb. First–Second Dvs: Aveb., Cann., respectively
Chalke First–Second Dvs: Chalke, Tisb., respectively
Pott. First–Third Dvs: Pott., Enf., Bradf., respectively
Marlb. First–Second Dvs: Marlb., Pewsey, respectively
Wylye First–Second Dvs: Wylye, Heytb., respectively

THE PARISHES OF WILTSHIRE

ALDBOURNE
AP *LG* Selk. Hd, Hungerford PLU (1835–96), RSD, Hungerford & Ramsb. PLU (1896–1930), Ramsb. RD (1894–1934), Marlb. & Ramsb. RD (1934–74). Civ bdry: 1934.[1] *Parl* Seq 5. *Eccl* Seq 23. Eccl bdry: 1971.[2]

ALDERBURY
AP Incl chaps Piton, Farley, sep CP 1866 as 'Pitton and Farley',[3] sep EP 1874 as 'Farley with Pitton'.[4] *LG* Seq 1. *Parl* Seq 9. *Eccl* Pec jurisd Treasurer in Prebend of Calne (until 1847), Seq 1 thereafter. Eccl bdry: 1969.[5]

ALDERTON
AP *LG* Chip. Hd, Malm. PLU, RSD, RD. Abol civ 1934 ent to Luckington AP.[1] *Parl* N'rn Dv (1832–85), N-W'rn Dv (1885–1918), Chip. Dv (1918–48). *Eccl* Malm. RDn (until 1866), Malm. South RDn (1866–87), Chip. RDn (1887–1955), Malm. RDn (1955–*).

ALLINGTON
AP *LG* Seq 2. Civ bdry: 1934.[1] *Parl* Seq 9. *Eccl* Amesb. RDn (until 1951), Aldb. RDn (1951–70). Abol eccl 1970 to help cr Allington with Boscombe EP.[6]

ALLINGTON
Tg in All Cannings AP, sep CP 1866.[3] *LG* Swanb. Hd, Deviz. PLU, RSD, RD. Abol 1934 ent to All Cannings AP.[1] *Parl* N'rn Dv (1867–85), W'rn Dv (1885–1918), Deviz. Dv (1918–48).

ALLINGTON WITH BOSCOMBE
EP Cr 1970 by union Allington AP, Boscombe AP.[6] Aldb. RDn.

ALTON
CP Cr 1934 by union Alton Barnes AP, Alton Priors CP.[1] *LG* Pewsey RD. *Parl* Deviz. CC (1948–*).

ALTON BARNES
AP *LG* Swanb. Hd, Deviz. PLU, RSD, RD. Civ bdry: 1885.[7] Abol civ 1934 to help cr Alton CP.[1] *Parl* N'rn Dv (1832–85), W'rn Dv (1885–1918), Deviz. Dv (1918–48). *Eccl* Seq 19. Eccl bdry: 1932 (incl gains chap Alton Priors of Overton AP).[8]

ALTON PRIORS
Chap in Overton AP, sep CP 1866,[3] eccl reduced 1892 to help refound Oare EP,[198] eccl severed 1932 and united to Alton Barnes AP.[8] *LG* Elst. & Ev. Hd, Pewsey PLU, RSD, RD. Bdry: 1885,[7] 1885.[9] Abol 1934 to help cr Alton CP.[1] *Parl* S'rn Dv (1867–85), E'rn Dv (1885–1918), Deviz. Dv (1918–48).

ALVEDISTON
Chap in Broad Chalke AP, sep civ identity early, sep EP 1861.[10] *LG* Seq 10. *Parl* Seq 10. *Eccl* Chalke RDn. Abol eccl 1970 to help cr Ebbesborne Wake with Fifield Bavant and Alvediston EP.[11]

AMESBURY
AP *LG* Amesb. Bor (status not sustained), Seq 2. *Parl* Seq 9. *Eccl* Seq 3.

ANSTY
AP *LG* Seq 16. Civ bdry: 1883,[12] 1885.[13] *Parl* Seq 10. *Eccl* Seq 5.

ASHLEY
AP *LG* Malm. Hd, Tetbury PLU, RSD, RD. Transf 1930 to Glos.[285] *Parl* Crickl. Parl Bor (1832–85), N-W'rn Dv (1885–1918), Chip. Dv (1918–48). *Eccl* Seq 22.

STEEPLE ASHTON
AP Incl chap Semington (sep CP 1866,[3] no sep eccl identity hence this par eccl 'Steeple Ashton with Semington', qv), tg West Ashton (sep CP 1866,[3] sep EP 1847[14]), tg Great Hinton (sep CP 1866[3]). *LG* Seq 37. Addtl civ bdry alt: 1897.[15] *Parl* Seq 7.

STEEPLE ASHTON WITH SEMINGTON
AP Usual eccl spelling; for civ and civ and eccl sep of other units, see prev entry. *Eccl* Seq 9. Addtl eccl bdry alt: 1954.[16]

WEST ASHTON
Tg in Steeple Ashton AP, sep EP 1847,[14] sep CP 1866.[3] *LG* Seq 37. *Parl* N'rn Dv (1867–85), W'rn Dv (1885–1918), W'bury Dv/CC (1918–*). *Eccl* Pott. RDn (1847–72), Bradf. RDn (1872–*).

ASHTON KEYNES
AP Incl chap Leigh (sep CP 1866,[3] no sep eccl identity hence this par eccl 'Ashton Keynes with Leigh', qv). *LG* Seq 20. Addtl civ bdry alt: 1883,[12] 1884.[17] *Parl* Pt Crickl. Parl Bor (1832–85), remainder and later, Seq 1.

ASHTON KEYNES WITH LEIGH
AP Usual eccl spelling; for civ and civ sep chap Leigh, see prev entry. *Eccl* Seq 20.

ATWORTH
Chap in Bradford-on-Avon AP, sep CP 1884 (incl area from other par and ex-par places, qv),[8] eccl united 1846 with chap South Wraxall in same par to cr Atworth with South Wraxall EP.[19] *LG* Bradf. Hd, PLU (1885–95), RSD, Bradf.-on-Avon PLU (1895–1930), RD (1894–1934), Bradf. & Melk. RD (1934–74). *Parl* W'bury Dv/CC (1918–*).

ATWORTH WITH SOUTH WRAXALL
EP Cr 1846 by union chaps Atworth, Wraxall in Bradford-on-Avon AP.[19] Pott. RDn (1846–72), Bradf. RDn (1872–*). Eccl bdry: 1965.[20]

AVEBURY
AP *LG* Seq 32. *Parl* Seq 5. *Eccl* Aveb. RDn. Abol eccl 1970 to help cr Avebury with Winterbourne Monkton and Berwick Bassett EP.[21]

AVEBURY WITH WINTERBOURNE MONKTON AND BERWICK BASSETT
EP Cr 1970 by union Avebury AP, Winterbourne Monkton with Berwick Bassett EP.[21] Aveb. RDn (1970–74), Marlb. RDn (1974–*).

AVON
Tg (orig chap, destroyed prob 16th cent) in Christian Malford AP, sep CP 1866.[3] *LG* Chip. Hd, PLU, RSD, RD. Abol 1895 to help cr Kellaways CP.[22] *Parl* N'rn Dv (1867–85), N-W'rn Dv (1885–1918).

BARFORD ST MARTIN
AP *LG* Seq 9. Civ bdry: 1884,[23] 1934.[1] *Parl* Seq 13. *Eccl* Seq 4.

BAVERSTOCK
AP *LG* Cawd. & Cad. Hd, Wilton PLU, RSD, RD. Civ bdry: 1884.[23] Abol civ 1934 ent to Dinton AP.[1] *Parl* S'rn Dv (1832–1918), Salisb. Dv (1918–48). *Eccl* Seq 4.

BAYDON
Chap in Ramsbury AP, sep civ identity early, sep EP 1793.[24] *LG* Seq 31. Civ bdry: 1934.[1] *Parl* Seq 5. *Eccl* Pec jurisd Dean of Sarum (until 1847), Seq 23 thereafter.

GREAT BEDWYN
AP Incl Little Bedwyn (sep par 1405[25]), tg Grafton (sep CP 1866,[3] sep EP 1844 as 'East Grafton'[26]). *LG* Great Bedwyn Bor, Seq 24. *Parl* Great Bedwyn Parl Bor (1295–1832), Seq 8 thereafter. *Eccl* Pec jurisd Lord Warden of Savernake Forest and Dean of Sarum (until 1847), Marlb. RDn (1847–86), Pewsey RDn (1886–*). Eccl bdry: 1864 (help cr Savernake Forest EP).[27]

LITTLE BEDWYN
AP Orig in Great Bedwyn AP, sep par 1405.[25] *LG* Perhaps in Chisbury Bor,[28] Seq 24. *Parl* Seq 8. *Eccl* Organisation as for Great Bedwyn. Eccl bdry: 1864 (help cr Savernake Forest EP).[27]

BEECHINGSTOKE
AP *LG* Seq 33. *Parl* Seq 5. *Eccl* Seq 19. Eccl bdry: 1967.[29]

BEMERTON
Chap in Fugglestone St Peter AP, sep CP 1894 (the pt not in Wilton USD),[30] sep EP 1972 (from par by then renamed 'Bemerton with Fugglestone', qv).[31] *LG* Wilton PLU, RD. Civ bdry: 1927.[32] Abol civ 1934 pt to help cr Quidhampton CP, pt to Wilton AP.[1] *Parl* Salisb. Dv (1918–48). *Eccl* Salisb. RDn.

BEMERTON WITH FUGGLESTONE
EP Renaming 1969 of Fugglestone with Bemerton AP.[33] Wilton RDn (1969–71), Salisb. RDn (1971–72). Abol 1972 when Fugglestone severed to help cr Wilton with Netherhampton and Fugglestone EP, the remainder to be Bemerton.[31]

BERWICK BASSETT
Chap in Calne AP, sep civ identity early, sep EP 1844.[34] *LG* Calne Hd, Marlb. PLU, RSD, RD (1894–1934), Marlb. & Ramsb. RD (1934–74). *Parl* Seq 5. *Eccl* Pec jurisd Treasurer in Prebend of Calne (until 1847), Aveb. RDn (1847–65). Abol eccl 1865 to help cr Winterbourne Monkton with Berwick Bassett EP.[35]

BERWICK ST JAMES
AP *LG* Seq 6. Civ bdry: 1884.[23] *Parl* Seq 9. *Eccl* Pec jurisd Bp of Sarum (until 1847), Seq 12 thereafter.

BERWICK ST JOHN
AP *LG* Seq 10. Civ bdry: 1884.[36] *Parl* Seq 10. *Eccl* Seq 5.

BERWICK ST LEONARD
AP Incl chap Sedgehill (sep civ identity early, sep EP 1916[24]). *LG* Seq 16. Addtl civ bdry alt: 1934.[1] *Parl* Seq 10. *Eccl* Chalke RDn (until 1872), Tisb. RDn (1872–1966). Abol eccl 1966 to help cr Berwick St Leonard with Fonthill Bishop EP.[37]

BERWICK ST LEONARD WITH FONTHILL BISHOP
EP Cr 1966 by union Berwick St Leonard AP, Fonthill Bishop AP.[37] Tisb. RDn. Renamed 1971 'Fonthill Bishop with Berwick St Leonard'.[175]

BIDDESTONE
CP Cr 1885 by union Biddestone St Peter AP, Biddestone St Nicholas AP.[38] *LG* Chip. PLU, RSD, RD (1894–1934), Calne & Chip. RD (1934–74). Bdry: 1934 (gains Slaughterford AP).[1] *Parl* Chip. Dv/CC (1918–*).
EP Usual name after 1719 when Biddestone St Nicholas AP gains Biddestone St Peter AP, in ruins.[40] Malm. RDn (1719–1866), Malm. South RDn (1866–87), Chip. RDn (1887–*).

BIDDESTONE ST NICHOLAS
AP *LG* Chip. Hd, PLU, RSD, RD. Civ bdry: 1884.[39] Abol civ 1885 to help cr Biddestone CP.[38] *Parl* N'rn Dv (1832–85), N-W'rn Dv (1885–1918). *Eccl* Malm. RDn. Gains eccl 1719 Biddestone St Peter AP, in ruins,[40] the union thereafter usually 'Biddestone', qv.

BIDDESTONE ST PETER
AP *LG* Chip. Hd, PLU, RSD, RD. Abol civ 1885 to help cr Biddestone CP.[38] *Parl*, *Eccl* as for Biddestone St Nicholas.

BISHOPSTONE
AP *LG* Down. Hd, Wilton PLU, RSD, RD (1894–1934), Salisb. & Wilton RD (1934–74). *Parl* Pt Wilton Parl Bor (1832–85), remainder and later, Seq 9. *Eccl* Pec jurisd Prebend of Bishopstone and Dean of Sarum (until 1847), Seq 4 thereafter.

BISHOPSTONE
AP *LG* Ramsb. Hd, Highw. & Swind. PLU (1836–99), RSD, Swind. & Highw. PLU (1899–1930), Highw. RD. Civ bdry: 1934.[1] *Parl* Seq 4. *Eccl* Crickl. RDn. Abol eccl 1946 to help cr Bishopstone with Hinton Parva EP.[41]

BISHOPSTONE WITH HINTON PARVA
EP Cr 1946 by union Bishopstone AP, Hinton Parva AP.[41] Crickl. RDn.

BISHOPSTROW
AP *LG* Seq 36. Civ bdry: 1883,[12] 1884.[18] *Parl* Seq 12. *Eccl* Wylye RDn (until 1872), Heytb. RDn (1872–1956). Renamed 1956 'Bishopstrow and Boreham' when gains pts Warminster AP, Warminster Christ Church EP.[42]

BISHOPSTROW AND BOREHAM
EP Renaming 1956 of Bishopstrow AP when gains pts Warminster AP, Warminster Christ Church EP.[42] Heytb. RDn.

BLACKLAND
AP *LG* Calne Hd, PLU, RSD. Abol civ 1890 to help cr Calne Without CP.[43] *Parl* Pt Calne Parl Bor, pt N'rn Dv (1832–85), N-W'rn Dv (1885–1918). *Eccl* Seq 16.

BLUNSDON ST ANDREW
AP *LG* Seq 21. Civ bdry: 1894,[44] 1934.[1] *Parl* Seq 2. *Eccl* Seq 20.

BROAD BLUNSDON
EP Chap (pec jurisd Prebend of Highworth and Dean of Sarum) in Highworth AP, sep EP 1864.[45] Crickl. RDn. Bdry: 1940.[46]

BOSCOMBE
AP *LG* Amesb. Hd, PLU, RSD, RD. Abol civ 1934 ent to Allington AP.[1] *Parl* S'rn Dv (1832–1918), Salisb. Dv (1918–48). *Eccl* Amesb. RDn (until 1951), Aldb. RDn (1951–70). Abol eccl 1970 to help cr Allington with Boscombe EP.[6]

BOWDEN HILL
EP Cr 1863 from Lacock EP.[47] Malm. RDn (1863–66), Malm. RDn South Dv (1866–87), Chip. RDn (1887–1955). Abol eccl 1955 to help cr Lacock with Bowden Hill EP.[48]

BOWOOD
Ex-par lbty, sep EP 1858,[49] abol eccl 1841 to help cr Derry Hill EP.[50] *LG* Calne Hd, PLU, RSD. Abol 1890 to help cr Calne Without CP.[43] *Parl* N'rn Dv (1867–85), N-W'rn Dv (1885–1918).

BOX
AP *LG* Seq 12. Civ bdry: 1884 (gains Ditteridge AP).[51] *Parl* Seq 6. *Eccl* Seq 21.

BOYTON
AP *LG* Seq 19. Civ bdry: 1884.[52] *Parl* Seq 12. *Eccl* Seq 12. Eccl bdry: 1956.[42]

BRADENSTOKE CUM CLACK

EP Cr 1866 from Lyneham AP, Christian Malford AP.[53] Aveb. RDn. Abol 1954 to help cr Lyneham with Bradenstoke EP.[54]

BRADFORD-ON-AVON

AP Incl chap Westwood (sep civ identity early, sep EP 1846[19]), chap Holt, dist Winsley, area Limpley Stoke (each a sep CP 1894 [from Bradford Without CP],[56] each a sep EP 1846[19]), chap Atworth (sep CP 1885 [incl area from other pars, qv] [18]), chap South Wraxall (sep CP 1894 [from Bradford Without CP] [56]), the last 2 eccl united 1846 to cr Atworth with South Wraxall EP[19]). *LG* Bradf. Hd, PLU (1835–95), Bradf.-on-Avon Bor, PLU (1895–1930), pt Bradf.-on-Avon USD, pt Bradf. RSD, Bradf.-on-Avon UD. Addtl civ bdry alt: 1883,[12] 1894 (loses the pt not in the USD to cr Bradford Without CP),[58] 1899,[57] 1934.[1] *Parl* Bradf.-on-Avon Parl Bor (1295 only), Seq 7 thereafter. *Eccl* Seq 9. Addtl eccl bdry alt: 1843 (cr Bradford-on-Avon Christ Church EP).[59]

BRADFORD-ON-AVON CHRIST CHURCH

EP Cr 1843 from Bradford-on-Avon AP.[59] Pott. RDn (1843–72), Bradf. RDn (1872–*).

BRADFORD WITHOUT

CP Cr 1894 from the pt of Bradford-on-Avon AP not in Bradf,-on-Avon USD.[58] *LG* Bradf. PLU (1894–95), Bradf.-on-Avon PLU (1895–1930), RD. Bdry: 1894 (cr 4 CPs of Holt, Limpley Stoke, South Wraxall, Winsley),[56] 1899.[57] Abol 1934 pts to Bradford-on-Avon AP, Trowbridge AP, Holt CP, South Wraxall CP, Westwood CP, Wingfield CP.[1] *Parl* W'bury Dv (1918–48).

MAIDEN BRADLEY WITH YARNFIELD

AP Pt Wilts (Mere Hd), pt Somerset (Norton Ferris Hd), made ent Wilts 1895.[60] *LG* Mere PLU, RSD, pt sep RD in Somerset (1894–95), Mere RD (pt 1894–95, ent 1895–1934), Mere & Tisb. RD (1934–74). Addtl civ bdry alt: 1885.[61] *Parl* Wilts pt, S'rn Dv (1832–85), W'rn Dv (1885–1918), W'bury Dv/CC (1918–*).

NORTH BRADLEY

AP Orig chap in Edington AP, sep par by 16th cent.[195] Incl tg Southwick (sep CP 1866[3]). *LG* Seq 37. Civ bdry: 1885.[62] *Parl* Seq 7. *Eccl* Seq 9. Eccl bdry: 1825 (cr North Bradley Christ Church EP,[24] refounded 1852 as Road Hill EP[63]), 1973.[64]

NORTH BRADLEY CHRIST CHURCH

EP Cr 1825 from North Bradley AP.[24] Pott. RDn. Refounded 1852 as Road Hill EP,[63] qv.

BRAMSHAW

AP Pt Wilts (Cawd. & Cad. Hd), pt Hants (New Forest Hd [until 1834], Redbridge Hd [from 1834]), made 1889 2 sep CPs, each 'Bramshaw', one in ea co,[80] the Wilts par transf 1895 to Hants and renamed East Bramshaw.[65] *LG* New Forest PLU, RSD, sep RD in Wilts (1894–95). *Parl* Wilts pt, S'rn Dv (1832–1918). *Eccl* Pec jurisd Dean & Chapter of Sarum (until 1847), Seq 1 thereafter. Eccl bdry: 1955 (gains ex-par No Man's Land).[66]

BRATTON

Chap (pec jurisd Precenter of Sarum) in Westbury AP, sep EP 1845,[67] sep CP 1894.[68] *LG* W'bury & Whorw. PLU, RD. *Parl* W'bury Dv/CC (1918–*). *Eccl* Wylye RDn (1847–72), Heytb. RDn (1872–*).

BRAYDON

Hmlt in Purton AP, sep CP 1866.[3] *LG* Seq 20. *Parl* Seq 1.

BREMHILL

AP Incl chap Highway (sep civ identity early, eccl severed 1952 to help cr Hilmarton and Highway EP,[71] so that this par eccl 'Bremhill with Foxham and Highway' before 1952, 'Bremhill with Foxham' thereafter, qv). *LG* Chip. Hd, Calne PLU, RSD, RD (1894–1934), Calne & Chip. RD (1934–74). Civ bdry: 1883,[12] 1883,[14] 1884,[69] 1885,[70] 1890 (help cr Calne Without CP).[43] *Parl* Seq 6.

BREMHILL WITH FOXHAM

EP Renaming 1952 of Bremhill with Foxham and Highway when chap Highway severed to help cr Hilmarton and Highway EP.[71] Aveb. RDn (1952–74), Calne RDn (1974–*).

BREMHILL WITH FOXHAM AND HIGHWAY

AP Usual eccl spelling; for civ and civ sep chap Highway, see 'Bremhill'. *Eccl* Aveb. RDn. Eccl bdry: 1841 (help cr Derry Hill EP).[50] Abol eccl 1952 when chap Highway severed to help cr Hilmarton and Highway EP, the remainder to be Bremhill with Foxham.[71]

BREMILHAM

AP *LG* Malm. Hd, PLU, RSD. Abol civ 1884 pt to Westport St Mary AP, pt to Brokenborough AP, pt to Foxley AP.[72] *Parl* Malm. Parl Bor (1832–85). *Eccl* Seq 21.

BRINKWORTH

AP *LG* Seq 27. Civ bdry: 1884.[73] *Parl* Seq 3. *Eccl* Seq 22. Eccl bdry: 1973 (gains pt Wootton Bassett AP, dioc Sarum).[74]

BRITFORD

AP Incl chap East Harnham (sep EP 1855,[75] sep CP 1896[76]). *LG* Seq 8. Addtl civ bdry alt: 1885,[77] 1904 (help cr Harnham CP),[78] 1934,[1] 1954.[79] *Parl* Seq 13. *Eccl* Pec jurisd Dean & Chapter of Sarum (until 1847), Seq 4 thereafter.

BROAD TOWN

Hmlt and chap in Clyffe Pypard AP, sep CP 1866,[3] sep EP 1846 (incl pt Broad Hinton AP).[81] *LG* Seq 22. *Parl* Crickl. Parl Bor (1867–85), N'rn Dv (1885–1918), Chip. Dv/CC (1918–*). *Eccl* Aveb. RDn (1846–1974), Calne RDn (1974–*).

BROKENBOROUGH

Chap in Westport St Mary AP, sep civ identity early, eccl severed 1879, combined with chap Charlton in same par to cr Charlton with Brokenborough EP.[82] *LG* Malm. Hd, PLU, pt Malm. MB and USD (1886–94), Malm. RSD (ent 1875–86, pt 1886–94). Bdry: 1883,[12] 1884,[73] 1884.[72] Abol 1894 the pt in the MB to cr Brokenborough Within CP, the remainder to cr Brokenborough Without CP.[83] *Parl* Malm. Parl Bor (1832–85), N-W'rn Dv (1885–1918).

CP Renaming 1897 of Brokenborough Without CP.[84] *LG* Malm. PLU, RD. Bdry: 1934 (help cr Malmesbury CP),[1] 1956,[85] 1966.[86] *Parl* Chip. Dv/CC (1918–*).

BROKENBOROUGH WITHIN

CP Cr 1894 from the pt of Brokenborough CP in Malm. MB.[83] *LG* Malm. PLU, MB. Abol 1897 ent to Westport St Mary Within CP.[87]

BROKENBOROUGH WITHOUT

CP Cr 1894 from the pt of Brokenborough CP not in Malm. MB.[83] *LG* Malm. PLU, RD. Renamed 1897 'Brokenborough'.[84]

BROMHAM

AP *LG* Seq 30. Civ bdry: 1884,[88] 1884,[89] 1934.[1] *Parl* Seq 5. *Eccl* Seq 17. Eccl bdry: 1846 (help cr Chittoe EP),[90] 1847,[91] 1973.[92]

BROUGHTON GIFFORD

AP *LG* Seq 4. Civ bdry: 1934.[1] *Parl* Seq 7. *Eccl* Seq 9.

BULFORD

AP *LG* Seq 2. *Parl* Seq 9. *Eccl* Seq 3.

BULKINGTON

Tg in Keevil AP, sep CP 1866,[3] sep EP 1883.[93] *LG* Melk. Hd, W'bury & Whorw. PLU, RSD, RD (1894–1934), Warm. & W'bury RD (1934–74). *Parl* N'rn Dv (1867–85), W'rn Dv (1885–1918), W'bury Dv/CC (1918–*). *Eccl* Pott. RDn (1883–1951), Bradf. RDn (1951–*).

BURBAGE

AP *LG* Seq 25. *Parl* Seq 8. *Eccl* Pec jurisd Prebend of Hurstbourne and Burbage and Dean of Sarum (until 1847), Seq 24 thereafter. Eccl bdry: 1864 (help cr Savernake Forest EP),[27] 1971.[94]

BURCOMBE

AP *LG* Cawd. & Cad. Hd, Wilton PLU, pt Wilton MB and USD (1885–94), Wilton RSD (ent 1875–85, pt 1885–94). Civ bdry: 1883,[12] 1884.[23] Abol civ 1894 the pt in the MB to cr Burcombe Within CP (by the same order immediately incl in Wilton AP), the remainder to cr Burcombe Without CP.[30] *Parl* Wilton Parl Bor (1832–85), S'rn Dv (1885–1918). *Eccl* Wilton RDn (until 1971), Chalke RDn (1971–*). Eccl bdry: 1971,[95] 1972.[96]

BURCOMBE WITHIN

CP Cr 1894 from the pt of Burcombe AP in Wilton MB but immediately by same order incl in Wilton AP.[30]

BURCOMBE WITHOUT

CP Cr 1894 from the pt of Burcombe AP not in Wilton MB.[30] *LG* Wilton PLU, RD (1894–1934), Salisb. & Wilton RD (1934–74). Bdry: 1934.[1] *Parl* Salisb. Dv/CC (1918–*).

BUTTERMERE

AP *LG* Seq 24. *Parl* Seq 8. *Eccl* Marlb. RDn (until 1886), Pewsey RDn (1886–1958). Abol eccl 1958 ent to Ham AP.[97]

CALNE

AP Incl chap Berwick Bassett (sep civ identity early, sep EP 1844[34]). *LG* Calne Hd, PLU, pt Calne Bor/MB, pt Calne USD, pt Calne RSD. Addtl civ bdry alt: 1883.[98] Abol civ 1890 the pt in the MB to cr Calne Within CP, the remainder to help cr Calne Without CP.[43] *Parl* Calne Parl Bor (pt 1295–1832, ent 1832–85), N-W'rn Dv (1885–1918). *Eccl* Pec jurisd Treasurer in Prebend of Calne (until 1847), Seq 14 thereafter. Addtl eccl bdry alt: 1841 (help cr Derry Hill EP),[50] 1844 (cr Cherhill EP),[93] 1879,[100] 1887,[101] 1973.[102]

CALNE WITHIN

CP Cr 1890 from the pt of Calne AP in Calne MB.[43] *LG* Calne PLU, MB. Bdry: 1934.[1] *Parl* Chip. Dv/CC (1918–*).

CALNE WITHOUT

CP Cr 1890 by union Blackland AP, Bowood CP, Calstone Wellington AP and pts Calne AP (the pt not in the MB), Bremhill AP.[43] *LG* Calne PLU, RD (1894–1934), Calne & Chip. RD (1934–74). Bdry: 1934.[1] *Parl* Chip. Dv/CC (1918–*).

CALSTONE WELLINGTON

AP *LG* Calne Hd, PLU, RSD. Civ bdry: 1883.[98] Abol civ 1890 to help cr Calne Without CP.[43] *Parl* Pt Calne Parl Bor (1832–85), N'rn Dv (pt 1832–85, ent 1885–1918). *Eccl* Seq 16. Eccl bdry: 1887.[101]

ALL CANNINGS

AP Incl tg Allington (sep CP 1866[3]), chap Etchilhampton (sep CP 1866,[3] no sep eccl identity hence this par eccl 'All Cannings with Etchilhampton', qv). *LG* Seq 33. Addtl civ bdry alt: 1934.[1] *Parl* Seq 5.

ALL CANNINGS WITH ETCHILHAMPTON

AP Usual eccl spelling; for civ and civ sep Etchilhampton and other area, see prev entry. *Eccl* Seq 17.

BISHOPS CANNINGS

AP Incl chap Southbroom or Devizes St James (sep EP 1832 as 'Southbroom',[24] sep CP 1866 as 'Devizes St James'[3]), tg and chap Chittoe (sep CP 1866,[3] sep EP 1846 [incl pt Bromham AP][90]). *LG* Seq 30. *Parl* Seq 5. *Eccl* As 'Bishop's Cannings', pec jurisd Dean and Chapter of Sarum (until 1847), Seq 17 thereafter. Addtl eccl bdry alt: 1841 (help cr Derry Hill EP),[50] 1970.[99]

CASTLE COMBE

AP *LG* Seq 12. *Parl* Seq 6. *Eccl* Pec jurisd Castle Combe (until 1847), Seq 21 thereafter.

CASTLE EATON

AP *LG* Seq 21. Civ bdry: 1934.[1] *Parl* Seq 2. *Eccl* Seq 20. Eccl bdry: 1952.[103]

GREAT CHALFIELD

AP Incl eccl as chap Little Chalfield (orig sep AP 14th and 15th cent, then chap in this par, pulled down 17th cent and thereafter deemed ex-par both civ and eccl,[104] sep CP 1858,[49] eccl one with Cottles [see 'Little Chalfield and Cottles']). *LG* Bradf. Hd, PLU, RSD. Abol civ 1885 to help cr Atworth CP.[18] *Parl* N'rn Dv (1832–1918). *Eccl* Seq 9. Eccl bdry: 1965.[20]

LITTLE CHALFIELD

AP Orig sep AP 14th and 15th cent, then deemed chap in Great Chalfield AP, pulled down 17th cent and thereafter ex-par civ and eccl,[104] sep CP 1858,[49] eccl with Cottles as 'Little Chalfield and Cottles', qv. *LG* Bradf. Hd, PLU, RSD. Abol 1885 to help cr Atworth CP.[18] *Parl* N'rn Dv (1867–1918).

LITTLE CHALFIELD AND COTTLES

Single eccl ex-par place (for civ and for earlier status of Little Chalfield, see Little Chalfield, Cottles), eccl abol 1965 pt to Atworth and South Wraxall EP, pt to Great Chalfield AP.[20]

BOWER CHALKE

Chap in Broad Chalke AP, sep civ identity early, sep EP 1720,[24] eccl refounded 1880.[105] *LG* Seq 11. Civ bdry: 1885.[106] *Parl* Seq 9. *Eccl* Chalke RDn.

BROAD CHALKE

AP Incl chap Bower Chalke (sep civ identity early, sep EP 1720,[24] eccl refounded 1880[105]), chap Alvediston (sep civ identity early, sep EP 1861[10]). *LG* Seq 11. *Parl* Seq 9. *Eccl* Seq 4.

CHAPMANSLADE

CP Cr 1934 from Corsley AP, Dilton Marsh CP, Upton Scudamore AP.[1] *LG* Warm. & W'bury RD. *Parl* W'bury CC (1948–*).

CHARLTON

AP *LG* Seq 34. *Parl* Seq 5. *Eccl* Pott. RDn (until 1872), Enf. RDn (1872–1951), Avon RDn (1951–56), Deviz. RDn (1956–*).

CHARLTON

Chap in Westport St Mary AP, sep civ identity early, eccl united 1879 with chap Brokenborough in same par to cr Charlton with Brokenborough EP,[82] qv. *LG* Seq 27. *Parl* Malm. Parl Bor (1832–85), N-W'rn Dv (1885–1918), Chip. Dv/CC (1918–*).

CHARLTON ALL SAINTS

EP Cr 1851 from Downton AP.[107] Wilton RDn (1851–1951), Aldb. RDn (1951–*). Bdry: 1969.[5]

CHARLTON WITH BROKENBOROUGH

EP Cr 1879 by union chaps Charlton, Brokenborough, both in Westport St Mary AP.[82] Malm. North RDn (1879–87), Malm. RDn (1887–*).

CHERHILL

Chap (pec jurisd Treasurer in Prebend of Calne) in Calne AP, sep civ identity early, sep EP 1844.[24] *LG* Seq 7. Civ bdry: 1883,[98] 1934.[1] *Parl* Seq 6. *Eccl* Aveb. RDn (1847–1974), Calne RDn (1974–*). Eccl bdry: 1879.[100]

CHEVERELL MAGNA

AP Sometimes 'Great Cheverell'. *LG* Seq 33. *Parl* Seq 5. *Eccl* Seq 6.

LITTLE CHEVERELL

AP Sometimes 'Little Cheverell'. *LG* Seq 33. *Parl* Seq 5. *Eccl* Seq 6.

CHICKLADE

AP *LG* Seq 16. Civ bdry: 1934.[1] *Parl* Seq 10. *Eccl* Chalke RDn (until 1872), Tisb. RDn (1872–1922). Abol eccl 1922 to help cr Chicklade and Pertwood EP.[108]

CHICKLADE AND PERTWOOD

EP Cr 1922 by union Chicklade AP, Pertwood AP.[108] Tisb. RDn. Abol 1972 to help cr Hindon with Chicklade and Pertwood EP.[109]

CHILMARK

AP *LG* Seq 16. Civ bdry: 1885.[110] *Parl* Seq 10. *Eccl* Seq 5.

CHILTON FOLIAT

AP Pt Wilts (Kinw. Hd), pt Berks (Kintbury Eagle Hd), the latter transf 1895 to Hungerford AP (Berks) and the par ent Wilts thereafter.[111] *LG* Hungerford PLU (1835–96), RSD, Hungerford & Ramsb. PLU (1896–1930), Ramsb. RD (pt 1894–95, ent 1895–1934), Marlb. & Ramsb. RD (1934–74). *Parl* Wilts pt, Seq 8. *Eccl* Seq 23.

CHIPPENHAM

AP Usual civ spelling; for eccl see 'Chippenham with Tytherton Lucas'. *LG* Chip. Hd, PLU, pt Chip. Bor/MB, pt Chip. USD, pt Chip. RSD. Civ bdry: 1883,[12] 1884,[39] 1884.[88] Abol civ 1894 the pt in the MB to cr Chippenham Within CP, the remainder to cr Chippenham Without CP.[112] *Parl* Chip. Parl Bor (pt 1295–1832, ent 1832–85), N-W'rn Dv (1885–1918).

CHIPPENHAM ST PAUL

EP Cr 1855 from Chippenham with Tytherton Lucas AP, Langley Burrell AP, Hardenhuish AP, Kington St Michael AP.[113] Malm. RDn (1855–66), Malm. South RDn (1866–87), Chip. RDn (1887–1965). Abol 1965 to help cr Chippenham St Paul with Langley Burrell EP.[114]

CHIPPENHAM ST PAUL WITH LANGLEY BURRELL

EP Cr 1965 by union Chippenham St Paul EP, Langley Burrell AP.[114] Chip. RDn. Bdry: 1969 (help cr Chippenham St Peter EP).[115]

CHIPPENHAM ST PETER

EP Cr 1969 from Chippenham with Tytherton Lucas AP, Chippenham St Paul with Langley Burrell AP, Hardenhuish AP.[115] Chip. RDn.

CHIPPENHAM WITH TYTHERTON LUCAS

AP Usual eccl spelling; for civ see 'Chippenham'. *Eccl* Seq 21. Eccl bdry: 1841 (help cr Derry Hill EP),[50] 1855 (help cr Chippenham St Paul EP),[113] 1969 (incl help cr Chippenham St Peter EP).[115]

CHIPPENHAM WITHIN

CP Cr 1894 from the pt of Chippenham AP in Chip. MB.[112] *LG* Chip. PLU, MB. Bdry: 1914,[116] 1934,[1] 1952.[117] *Parl* Chip. Dv/CC (1918–*).

CHIPPENHAM WITHOUT

CP Cr 1894 from the pt of Chippenham AP not in Chip. MB.[112] *LG* Chip. PLU, RD (1894–1934), Calne & Chip. RD (1934–74). Bdry: 1896,[118] 1914,[116] 1934,[1] 1952,[117] 1971.[119] *Parl* Chip. Dv/CC (1918–*).

CHIRTON

AP *LG* Seq 33. *Parl* Seq 5. *Eccl* Seq 8.

CHISELDON

AP *LG* Seq 23. Civ bdry: 1894,[120] 1928,[32] 1934,[1] 1969.[121] *Parl* Crickl. Parl Bor (1832–85), N'rn

Dv (1885–1918), Deviz. Dv/CC (1918–*). Parl bdry: 1971.[283] *Eccl* Marlb. RDn. Abol eccl 1923 to help cr Chiseldon with Draycot Foliat EP.[122]

CHISELDON WITH DRAYCOT FOLIAT
EP Cr 1923 by union Chiseldon AP, Draycot Foliat AP.[122] Marlb. RDn. Bdry: 1971,[2] 1972 (help cr Swindon St Paul, Covingham EP to be in dioc Bristol).[123]

CHITTERNE
Cr civ 1907,[124] eccl 1971[125] by union Chitterne All Saints AP, Chitterne St Mary AP. *LG* Warm. PLU, RD (1894–1934), Warm. & W'bury RD (1934–74). *Parl* W'bury Dv/CC (1918–*). *Eccl* Wylye & Wilton RDn.

CHITTERNE ALL SAINTS
AP *LG* Heytb. Hd, Warm. PLU, RSD RD. Abol civ 1907 to help cr Chitterne CP.[124] *Parl* S'rn Dv (1832–85), W'rn Dv (1885–1918). *Eccl* Wylye RDn (until 1971), Wylye & Wilton RDn (1971). Abol eccl 1971 to help cr Chitterne EP.[125]

CHITTERNE ST MARY
AP Organisation as for Chitterne All Saints.

CHITTOE
Tg and chap in Bishops Cannings AP (eccl, 'Bishop's Cannings'), sep CP 1866,[3] sep EP 1846 [incl pt Bromham AP][90]). *LG* Pott. & Cann. Hd, Deviz. PLU, RSD, RD. Civ bdry: 1884.[89] Abol civ 1934 ent to Bromham AP.[1] *Parl* N'rn Dv (1867–85), E'rn Dv (1885–1918), Deviz. Dv (1918–48). *Eccl* Aveb. RDn (1846–72), Cann. RDn (1872–1951), Deviz. RDn (1951–*). Eccl bdry: 1864,[91] 1932.[126]

CHOLDERTON
AP *LG* Seq 2. *Parl* Seq 9. *Eccl* Seq 2. Eccl bdry: 1955 (gains pt Quarley AP, dioc Winch).[127]

CHRISTIAN MALFORD
AP Incl tg Avon (orig chap, destroyed prob 16th cent, sep CP 1866[3]). *LG* Pt Chip. Hd, pt Dam. Hd, Chip. PLU, RSD, RD (1894–1934), Calne & Chip. RD (1934–74). Addtl civ bdry alt: 1884,[69] 1885.[70] *Parl* Seq 6. *Eccl* Seq 21. Eccl bdry: 1866 (help cr Bradenstoke cum Clack EP).[53]

CHUTE
AP *LG* Kinw. Hd, Andover PLU (1835–79), RSD (1875–79), Pewsey PLU (1879–1930), RSD (1879–94), Pewsey RD. *Parl* Seq 8. *Eccl* Pec jurisd Prebend of Chute and Chisenbury and Dean of Sarum (until 1847), Marlb. RDn (1847–72), Pewsey RDn (1872–1954). Abol eccl 1954 to help cr Chute with Chute Forest EP.[128]

CHUTE FOREST
Ex-par place, sep CP 1858,[49] sep EP 1875.[129] *LG* As for Chute. *Parl* S'rn Dv (1867–85), E'rn Dv (1885–1918), Deviz. Dv/CC (1918–*). *Eccl* Pewsey RDn. Abol eccl 1954 to help cr Chute with Chute Forest EP.[128]

CHUTE WITH CHUTE FOREST
EP Cr 1954 by union Chute AP, Chute Forest EP.[128] Pewsey RDn.

CLARENDON PARK
Ex-par lbty, sep CP 1858.[49] *LG* Seq 1. *Parl* S'rn Dv (1867–1918), Salisb. Dv/CC (1918–*).

CLATFORD PARK
Ex-par place, sep CP 1858,[49] eccl abol 1971 ent to Preshute AP.[131] *LG* Selk. Hd, Marlb. PLU (1858[153]–96), RSD. Bdry: 1895.[49] *Parl* N'rn Dv (1867–85), E'rn Dv (1885–1918).

CLYFFE PYPARD
AP Incl hmlt Broad Town (sep CP 1866,[3] sep EP 1846 [incl pt Broad Hinton AP][81]). *LG* Seq 22. Addtl civ bdry alt: 1884.[132] *Parl* Pt Crickl. Parl Bor (1832–85), N'rn Dv (pt 1832–85, ent 1885–1918), Chip. Dv/CC (1918–*). *Eccl* Seq 14.

CODFORD
CP Cr 1934 by union Codford St Mary AP, Codford St Peter AP.[1] *LG* Warm. & W'bury RD. *Parl* W'bury CC (1948–*).

CODFORD ST MARY
AP *LG* Heytb. Hd, Warm. PLU, RSD, RD. Civ bdry: 1883.[12] Abol civ 1934 to help cr Codford CP.[1] *Parl* S'rn Dv (1832–85), W'rn Dv (1885–1918), W'bury Dv (1918–48). *Eccl* Seq 12.

CODFORD ST PETER
AP *LG* Heytb. Hd, Warm. PLU, RSD, RD. Civ bdry: 1883,[12] 1884.[52] Abol civ 1934 to help cr Codford CP.[1] *Parl*, *Eccl* organisation as for Codford St Mary. Eccl bdry: 1930.[133]

COLERNE
AP *LG* Seq 12. Civ bdry: 1971.[119] *Parl* Seq 6. *Eccl* Seq 21.

COLESHILL
AP Pt Wilts (Highw., Crickl. & Staple Hd), pt Berks (Shrivenham Hd), the former transf 1881 to Inglesham AP (Wilts) so that the par ent Berks thereafter.[154] *LG* Faringdon PLU, RSD. *Parl* Wilts pt, Crickl. Parl Bor (1832–85). *Eccl* Oxf dioc; see entry in Berks. Eccl bdry: 1940 (help cr Highworth with Sevenhampton and Inglesham EP).[135]

COLLINGBOURNE DUCIS
AP *LG* Seq 17. Civ bdry: 1934.[1] *Parl* Seq 8. *Eccl* Pec jurisd Lord Warden of Savernake Forest and Bp of Sarum (until 1847), Seq 24 thereafter.

COLLINGBOURNE KINGSTON
AP *LG* Pt Elst. & Ev. Hd, pt Kinw. Hd, Pewsey PLU, RSD, RD. Civ bdry: 1934.[1] *Parl* Seq 8. *Eccl* Seq 24.

COMPTON BASSETT
AP *LG* Seq 7. Civ bdry: 1883,[98] 1934.[1] *Parl* Seq 6. *Eccl* Seq 14.

COMPTON CHAMBERLAYNE
AP *LG* Dam. Hd, Wilton PLU, RSD, RD (1894–1934), Salisb. & Wilton RD (1934–74). *Parl* Seq 9. *Eccl* Seq 4.

COOMBE BISSETT
AP Incl chap West Harnham (sep civ identity early, eccl severed 1881 to help cr East Harnham with West Harnham EP[136]). *LG* Seq 8. Addtl civ bdry alt: 1883,[12] 1885,[77] 1934.[1] *Parl* Pt Wilton Parl Bor, pt S'rn Dv (1832–85), S'rn Dv (1885–

1918), Salisb. Dv/CC (1918–*). *Eccl* Pec jurisd Prebend of Coombe Bisset and Harnham and Dean of Sarum (until 1847), Chalke RDn (1847–1972). Abol eccl 1972 to help cr Coombe Bissett with Homington EP.[137]

COOMBE BISSETT WITH HOMINGTON
EP Cr 1972 by union Coombe Bissett AP, Homington AP.[137] Chalke RDn.

CORSHAM
AP *LG* Seq 12. Civ bdry: 1884,[88] 1952.[117] *Parl* Seq 6. *Eccl* Pec jurisd Vicar of Corsham and Bp of Sarum (until 1847), Seq 21 thereafter. Eccl bdry: 1841 (help cr Derry Hill EP),[50] 1869 (cr Neston EP).[138]

CORSLEY
AP *LG* Seq 36. Civ bdry: 1883,[12] 1884,[52] 1934 (incl help cr Chapmanslade CP).[1] *Parl* Seq 12. *Eccl* Sometimes as 'Corsley with Chapmanslade', Seq 13. Eccl bdry: 1954,[139] 1959.[140]

CORSTON WITH RODBOURNE
EP Cr 1881 from Malmesbury EP.[141] Malm. North RDn (1881–87), Malm. RDn (1887–*).

COTTLES
Ex-par place, sep CP 1858,[49] eccl forms pt of ex-par Little Chalfield and Cottles, qv. *LG* Bradf. Hd, PLU, RSD. Abol 1885 to help cr Atworth CP.[18] *Parl* N'rn Dv (1867–1918).

EAST COULSTON
AP *LG* Seq 37. Civ bdry: 1934.[1] *Parl* Seq 7. *Eccl* Seq 6. Eccl bdry: 1934.[142]

CRICKLADE
CP Cr 1899 by union Cricklade St Mary AP, Cricklade St Sampson AP.[1] *LG* Crickl. & Woott. Bas. PLU, RD. Bdry: 1934.[1] *Parl* Chip. Dv/CC (1918–*).
EP Cr 1952 by union Cricklade St Mary AP, Cricklade St Sampson AP, pt Latton with Eisey EP.[103] Crickl. RDn.

CRICKLADE ST MARY
AP *LG* Highw., Crickl. & Staple Hd, Crickl. Bor, Crickl. & Woot. Bas. PLU, RSD, RD. Abol civ 1899 to help cr Cricklade CP.[143] *Parl* Crickl. Parl Bor (1295–1885), N'rn Dv (1885–1918). *Eccl* Crickl. RDn. Abol eccl 1952 to help cr Cricklade EP.[103]

CRICKLADE ST SAMPSON
AP Organisation as for Cricklade St Mary, and also eccl bdry: 1940.[46]

CRUDWELL
AP *LG* Seq 27. *Parl* Seq 3. *Eccl* Seq 22.

DAMERHAM
AP Sometimes 'South Damerham'. Incl chap Martin (sep civ identity early, sep EP 1854[240]). *LG* Dam. Hd, Fordingbridge PLU, RSD, sep RD in Wilts (1894–95). Transf 1895 to Hants.[65] *Parl* S'rn Dv (1832–1918). *Eccl* Seq 4.

DAUNTSEY
AP *LG* Seq 27. Civ bdry: 1884.[73] *Parl* Seq 3. *Eccl* Seq 22.

WEST DEAN
AP Incl chap East Grimstead (sep CP 1866,[3] no sep eccl identity hence this par eccl 'West Dean with East Grimstead', qv). Pt Wilts (Aldb. Hd), pt Hants (Thorngate Hd), the latter lost 1883 to West Tytherley AP (Hants) and the par ent Wilts thereafter.[144] *LG* Stockbridge PLU (1835–83), RSD (1875–83), Aldb. PLU (1883–95), RSD (1883–94), Salisb. PLU (1895–1930), RD (1894–1934), Salisb. & Wilton RD (1934–74). Addtl civ bdry alt: 1934.[1] *Parl* Wilts pt, Seq 9.

WEST DEAN WITH EAST GRIMSTEAD
AP Usual eccl spelling; for civ see prev entry. *Eccl* Seq 1.

DERRY HILL
EP Cr 1841 from Calne AP, Bremhill AP, Bishop's Cannings AP, Chippenham with Tytherton Lucas AP, Corsham AP, ent ex-par places Bowood, Pewsham.[50] Aveb. RDn (1841–1974), Calne RDn (1974–*). Bdry: 1864,[91] 1973.[102]

BRIXTON DEVERILL
AP *LG* Seq 19. *Parl* Seq 12. *Eccl* Wylye RDn (until 1872), Heytb. RDn (1872–1972). Abol eccl 1972 to help cr The Deverills EP.[145]

HILL DEVERILL
AP *LG* Heytb. Hd, Warm. PLU, RSD, RD. Civ bdry: 1884,[52] 1885.[146] Abol civ 1934 ent to Longbridge Deverill AP.[1] *Parl* S'rn Dv (1832–85), W'rn Dv (1885–1918), W'bury Dv (1918–48). *Eccl* Wylye RDn (until 1872), Heytb. RDn (1872–96). Abol eccl 1896 to help cr Longbridge Deverill with Crockerton and Hill Deverill EP.[147]

KINGSTON DEVERILL
AP *LG* Pt Mere Hd, pt Dam. Hd, Mere PLU, RSD, RD (1894–1934), Warm. & W'bury RD (1934–74). Civ bdry: 1885,[146] 1934 (incl gains Monkton Deverill CP).[1] *Parl* Seq 11. *Eccl* Wylye RDn (until 1872), Heytb. RDn (1872–92). Abol eccl 1892 to help cr Kingston Deverill with Monkton Deverill EP.[148]

KINGSTON DEVERILL WITH MONKTON DEVERILL
EP Cr 1892 by union Kingston Deverill AP, chap Monkton Deverill of Longbridge Deverill AP.[148] Heytb. RDn. Abol 1972 to help cr The Deverills EP.[145]

LONGBRIDGE DEVERILL
AP Usual civ spelling; for eccl see following entry. Incl chap Monkton Deverill (sep civ identity early, eccl severed 1892 to help cr Kingston Deverill with Monkton Deverill EP[148]). *LG* Dam. Hd, Warm. PLU, RSD, RD (1894–1934), Warm. & W'bury RD (1934–74). Addtl civ bdry alt: 1884,[52] 1934 (incl gains Kingston Deverill AP).[1] *Parl* Seq 12.

LONGBRIDGE DEVERILL WITH CROCKERTON
AP Usual eccl spelling; for civ see prev entry. *Eccl* Wylye RDn (until 1872), Heytb. RDn (1872–96). Abol eccl 1896 to help cr Longbridge Deverill with Crockerton and Hill Deverill EP.[145]

LONGBRIDGE DEVERILL WITH CROCKERTON AND HILL DEVERILL
EP Cr 1896 by union Longbridge Deverill with Crockerton AP, Hill Deverill AP.[145] Heytb.

RDn. Bdry: 1959.[140] Abol 1972 to help cr The Deverills EP.[145]

MONKTON DEVERILL
Chap in Longbridge Deverill AP, sep civ identity early, eccl severed 1892 to help cr Kingston Deverill with Monkton Deverill EP.[148] *LG* Dam. Hd, Mere PLU, RSD, RD. Abol civ 1934 ent to Kingston Deverill AP.[1] *Parl* S'rn Dv (1832–1918), W'bury Dv (1918–48).

THE DEVERILLS
EP Cr 1972 by union Brixton Deverill AP, Kingston Deverill with Monkton Deverill EP, Longbridge Deverill with Crockerton and Hill Deverill EP.[145] Heytb. RDn.

DEVIZES
The following have 'Devizes' in their names. Insofar as any existed at a given time: *LG* Pott. Hd, Deviz. PLU, Bor/MB, USD. *Parl* Deviz. Parl Bor (1295–1885), E'rn Dv (1885–1918), Deviz. Dv/CC (1918–*). *Eccl* Pott. RDn (until 1951), Deviz. RDn (1951–*).

CP1–DEVIZES–Cr 1934 by union CP2, AP1, AP2, Rowde Within CP, and pts Potterne AP, Roundway CP, Rowde AP.[1]

CP2–DEVIZES ST JAMES–Chap in Bishops Cannings AP (eccl, 'Bishop's Cannings'), sep CP 1866,[3] sep EP 1842 as 'Southbroom',[32] qv. *LG* Deviz. MB (pt 1835–94, ent 1894–1934), pt Deviz. USD, pt Deviz. RSD. Bdry: 1884,[151] 1894 (loses the pt not in the MB to cr Roundway CP).[150] Abol 1934 to help cr CP1.[1] *Parl* Pt Deviz. Parl Bor (1832–85), pt N'rn Dv (1832–85), E'rn Dv (1885–1918), Deviz. Dv (1918–48).

AP1–DEVIZES ST JOHN THE BAPTIST–Incl for eccl purposes AP2, the 2 held as one single eccl unit but with sep civ identity.[194] Abol civ 1934 to help cr CP1.[1] Pec jurisd Bp of Sarum (until 1847).

AP2–DEVIZES ST MARY THE VIRGIN–Sep for civ purposes, sometimes deemed chap in AP1 with which forms one par for eccl purposes.[194] Abol civ 1934 to help cr CP1.[1]

EP1–DEVIZES ST PETER–Cr 1867 from Rowde AP, Southbroom EP.[155] Aveb. RDn (1867–72), thereafter as other Devizes pars. Bdry: 1886,[156] 1927,[157] 1952.[152]

DILTON MARSH
Chap (pec jurisd Precenter of Sarum) in Westbury AP, sep EP 1845 as 'Diltons Marsh',[67] sep CP 1894.[68] *LG* W'bury & Whorw. PLU, RD. Civ bdry: 1934 (help cr Chapmanslade CP).[1] *Parl* W'bury Dv/CC (1918–*). *Eccl* Wylye RDn (1845–72), Heytb. RDn (1872–*). Eccl bdry: 1954,[139] 1973.[158]

DILTONS MARSH–See prev entry

DINTON
AP Incl chap Teffont Magna (sep civ identity early, eccl severed 1922 to help cr Teffont Evias with Teffont Magna EP,[159] so that this par 'Dinton with Teffont Magna' before 1922, 'Dinton' thereafter). *LG* Warm. Hd, Wilton PLU, RSD, RD (1894–1934), Salisb. & Wilton RD (1934–74). Addtl civ bdry alt: 1934.[1] *Parl* Seq 9. *Eccl* Seq 4.

DINTON WITH TEFFONT MAGNA–See prev entry

DITTERIDGE
AP *LG* Chip. Hd, PLU, RSD. Abol civ 1884 ent to Box AP.[51] *Parl* N'rn Dv (1832–85). *Eccl* Seq 21.

DONHEAD ST ANDREW
AP *LG* Seq 16. Civ bdry: 1883,[12] 1884.[36] *Parl* Seq 10. *Eccl* Seq 5.

DONHEAD ST MARY
AP Usual civ spelling; for eccl see following entry. *LG* Seq 16. Civ bdry: 1883,[12] 1884.[36] *Parl* Seq 10.

DONHEAD ST MARY WITH CHARLTON
AP Usual eccl spelling; for civ see prev entry. *Eccl* Seq 5.

DOWNTON
Incl chap Nunton and Bodenham (sep civ identity early, eccl severed 1916 to help cr Odstock with Nunton and Bodenham EP[160]), chap Redlynch (sep EP 1836, eccl refounded 1841,[24] sep CP 1896[161]), area Standlynch (sep civ identity early, no sep eccl identity). *LG* Down. Hd, Bor, Aldb. PLU (1836–95), RSD, Salisb. PLU (1895–1930), RD (1894–1934), Salisb. & Wilton RD (1934–74). Addtl civ bdry alt: 1885,[77] 1894,[120] 1897 (cr Standlynch with Charlton All Saints CP when gains Standlynch CP),[87] 1923 (cr Morgan's Vale and Woodfalls CP),[162] 1934.[1] *Parl* Down. Parl Bor (1295–1832), Seq 9 thereafter. *Eccl* Wilton RDn (until 1951), Aldb. RDn (1951–*). Addtl eccl bdry alt: 1851 (cr Charlton All Saints EP),[107] 1915 (help cr Morgan's Vale EP).[163]

DRAYCOT CERNE
AP *LG* Malm. Hd, Chip. PLU, RSD, RD. Civ bdry: 1883,[12] 1884.[39] Abol civ 1934 ent to Sutton Benger AP.[1] *Parl* Crickl. Parl Bor (1832–85), N-W'rn Dv (1885–1918), Chip. Dv (1918–48). *Eccl* Seq 21.

DRAYCOT FOLIAT
AP *LG* Kingsbr. Hd, Highw. & Swind. PLU (1836–94), RSD. Abol civ 1894 ent to Chiseldon AP.[120] *Parl* Crickl. Parl Bor (1832–85), N'rn Dv (1885–1918). *Eccl* Marlb. RDn. Abol eccl 1923 to help cr Chiseldon with Draycot Foliat EP.[122]

DURNFORD
AP *LG* Seq 2. Civ bdry: 1885.[164] *Parl* Pt Wilton Parl Bor, pt S'rn Dv (1832–85), S'rn Dv (1885–1918), Salisb. Dv/CC (1918–*). *Eccl* Pec jurisd Prebend of Durnford and Dean of Sarum (until 1847), Seq 3 thereafter.

DURRINGTON
AP *LG* Seq 2. Civ bdry: 1885.[164] *Parl* Seq 9. *Eccl* Seq 3.

EARLDOMS
Ex-par place, sep CP 1858.[49] *LG* Frust. Hd, Aldb. PLU (1836–95), RSD, Salisb. PLU (1895–96), RD (1894–96). Abol 1896 ent to Landford AP.[165] *Parl* S'rn Dv (1867–1918).

EASTERTON
CP Tg in East Lavington AP, sep CP 1866.[3] *LG*

Seq 33. Bdry: 1934.[1] *Parl* N'rn Dv (1867–85), E'rn Dv (1885–1918), Deviz. Dv/CC (1918–*).
EP Cr 1874 from West Lavington AP, Market Lavington AP, Urchfont AP.[166] Pott. RDn (1874–1951), Deviz. RDn (1951–*).

EASTON GREY
AP *LG* Pt Malm. Hd, pt Chip. Hd, Malm. PLU, RSD, RD. *Parl* Pt Crickl. Parl Bor (1832–85), remainder and later, Seq 6. *Eccl* Seq 22.

EASTON ROYAL
AP *LG* Seq 25. *Parl* Seq 8. *Eccl* Seq 24. Eccl bdry: 1871.[94]

EBBESBOURNE WAKE
AP *LG* Seq 11. Civ bdry: 1894.[120] *Parl* Seq 9. *Eccl* Chalke RDn. Abol eccl 1923 to help cr Ebbesbourne Wake with Fifield Bavant EP.[167]

EBBESBOURNE WAKE WITH FIFIELD BAVANT
EP Cr 1923 by union Ebbesbourne Wake AP, Fifield Bavant AP.[167] Chalke RDn. Abol 1970 to help cr Ebbesbourne Wake with Fifield Bavant and Alvediston EP.[11]

EBBESBOURNE WAKE WITH FIFIELD BAVAND AND ALVEDISTON
EP Renaming 1970 of Ebbesbourne Wake with Fifield Bavant and Alvediston EP.[196] Chalke RDn.

EBBESBOURNE WAKE WITH FIFIELD BAVANT AND ALVEDISTON
EP Cr 1970 by union Ebbesbourne Wake with Fifield Bavant EP, Alvediston AP.[11] Chalke RDn. Renamed 1970 'Ebbesbourne Wake with Fifield Bavand and Alvediston'.[196]

EDINGTON
AP Incl chap North Bradley (sep par by 16th cent[195]). *LG* Seq 37. Civ bdry: 1934.[1] *Parl* Seq 7. *Eccl* Pott. RDn (until 1951), Heytb. RDn (1951–54). Eccl bdry: 1934.[142] Abol eccl 1954 to help cr Edington and Imber EP.[168]

EDINGTON AND IMBER
EP Cr 1954 by union Edington AP, Imber AP.[168] Deviz. RDn.

EISEY
AP *LG* Highw., Crickl. & Staple Hd, Crickl. & Woot. Bas. PLU, RSD, RD. Abol civ 1896 ent to Latton AP.[118] *Parl* Crickl. Parl Bor (1832–85), N'rn Dv (1885–1918). *Eccl* Crickl. RDn. Abol eccl 1952 pt to help cr Latton with Eisey EP, pt to Castle Eaton AP.[103]

ENFORD
AP *LG* Seq 17. Civ bdry: 1885.[9] *Parl* Seq 8. *Eccl* Seq 7.

ERLESTOKE
Sometimes 'Earlestoke'. Chap in Melksham AP, sep civ identity early, sep EP 1877.[169] *LG* Seq 28. *Parl* Seq 5. *Eccl* Pott. RDn (1877–1951), Deviz. RDn (1951–*).

ETCHILHAMPTON
Chap in All Cannings AP, sep CP 1866.[3] *LG* Swanb. Hd, Deviz. PLU, RSD, RD. *Parl* N'rn Dv (1867–85), E'rn Dv (1885–1918), Deviz. Dv (1918–*).

EVERLEIGH
AP *LG* Seq 17. *Parl* Seq 8. *Eccl* Seq 24.

FARLEY WITH PITTON
EP Cr 1874 by union chaps Farley, Pitton in Alderbury AP (for civ see 'Pitton with Farley').[4] Aldb. RDn.

FIFIELD BAVANT
AP *LG* Chalk Hd, Wilton PLU, RSD, RD. Civ bdry: 1885.[106] Abol civ 1894 ent to Ebbesbourne Wake AP.[120] *Parl* S'rn Dv (1832–1918). *Eccl* Chalke RDn. Abol eccl 1923 to help cr Ebbesbourne Wake with Fifield Bavant EP.[167]

FIGHELDEAN
AP *LG* Seq 2. Civ bdry: 1885.[164] *Parl* Seq 9. *Eccl* Pec jurisd Treasurer of Prebend of Calne (until 1847), Seq 3 thereafter.

FISHERTON ANGER
AP *LG* Branch & Dole Hd, Aldb. PLU, pt Salisb. MB (1835–94), pt Salisb. USD, pt Aldb. RSD. Abol civ 1894 the pt in the MB to cr Fisherton Anger Within CP, the remainder to cr Fisherton Anger Without CP.[170] *Parl* Pt Wilton Parl Bor (1832–85), pt S'rn Dv (1832–67), pt Salisb. Parl Bor (1867–85), S'rn Dv (1885–1918). *Eccl* Seq 11. Eccl bdry: 1938 (help cr Salisbury St Michael and All Angels EP),[171] 1973.[172]

FISHERTON ANGER WITHIN
CP Cr 1894 from the pt of Fisherton Anger AP in Salisb. MB.[170] *LG* Aldb. PLU (1894–95), Salisb. PLU (1896–1905), Salisb. MB. Abol 1905 to help cr New Sarum CP.[173]

FISHERTON ANGER WITHOUT
CP Cr 1894 from the pt of Fisherton Anger AP not in Salisb. MB.[170] *LG* Aldb. PLU (1894–95), Salisb. PLU (1895–1905), RD. Abol 1905 to help cr New Sarum CP.[173]

FISHERTON DE LA MARE
AP Usual civ spelling; for eccl see following entry. *LG* Warm. Hd, Wilton PLU, RSD, RD. Abol civ 1934 pt to Wylye AP, pt to Stockton AP.[1] *Parl* S'rn Dv (1832–1918), Salisb. Dv (1918–48).

FISHERTON DELAMERE
AP Usual eccl spelling; for civ see prev entry. *Eccl* Seq 12. Eccl bdry: 1930.[174]

FITTLETON
AP *LG* Seq 17. *Parl* Seq 8. *Eccl* Seq 7.

FONTHILL BISHOP
AP *LG* Seq 15. *Parl* Seq 10. *Eccl* Chalke RDn (until 1872), Tisb. RDn (1872–1966). Abol eccl 1966 to help cr Berwick St Leonard with Fonthill Bishop EP.[37]

FONTHILL BISHOP WITH BERWICK ST LEONARD
EP Renaming 1971 of Berwick St Leonard with Fonthill Bishop EP.[175] Tisb. RDn (1971–72), Shaft. & Tisb. RDn (1972–*).

FONTHILL GIFFORD
AP *LG* Seq 16. Civ bdry: 1934.[1] *Parl* Seq 10. *Eccl* Seq 5.

FOSBURY
EP Cr 1856 from Tidcombe AP, Shalbourne AP.[176] Marlb. RDn (1856–86), Pewsey RDn (1886–*).

FOVANT
AP *LG* Seq 9. *Parl* Seq 9. *Eccl* Seq 4.

FOXLEY
AP *LG* Malm. Hd, PLU, RSD, RD. Civ bdry: 1884,[72] 1884.[73] Abol civ 1934 ent to Norton AP.[1] *Parl* Malm. Parl Bor (1832–85), N-W'rn Dv (1885–1918), Chip. Dv (1918–48). *Eccl* Seq 21.

FROXFIELD
AP *LG* Seq 24. *Parl* Seq 8. *Eccl* Seq 23.

FUGGLESTONE ST PETER
AP Incl chap Bemerton (sep CP 1894 [the pt not in Wilton USD],[30] sep EP 1972 [from par by then renamed 'Bemerton with Fugglestone', qv][31]). Usual civ name; usual eccl before 1969 'Fugglestone with Bemerton', qv. *LG* Branch & Dole Hd, Wilton PLU, pt Wilton MB and USD (1885–94), Wilton RSD (ent 1875–86, pt 1886–94). Abol civ 1894 the pt in the USD to Wilton AP, the remainder to cr Bemerton CP.[30] *Parl* Wilton Parl Bor (1832–85), S'rn Dv (1885–1918).

FUGGLESTONE WITH BEMERTON
AP Usual eccl spelling; for civ and sep chap Bemerton, see prev entry. *Eccl* Wilton RDn. Eccl bdry: 1938 (help cr Salisbury St Michael and All Angels EP),[171] 1957.[212] Renamed eccl 1969 'Bemerton with Fugglestone'.[33]

FULLAWAY
Ex-par place, sep CP 1858.[49] *LG* Swanb. Hd, Deviz. PLU, RSD. Abol 1894 ent to Stert CP.[120] *Parl* N'rn Dv (1867–85), E'rn Dv (1885–1918) .

FYFIELD
Chap in Overton AP, sep civ identity early, no sep eccl identity. *LG* Elst. & Ev. Hd, Marlb. PLU, RSD, RD (1894–1934), Marlb. & Ramsb. RD (1934–74). Addtl civ bdry alt: 1896.[118] *Parl* Seq 8.

GARSDON
AP *LG* Malm. Hd, PLU, RSD, RD. Civ bdry: 1883.[12] Abol civ 1934 ent to Lea and Calverton AP.[1] *Parl* Malm. Parl Bor (1832–85), N-W'rn Dv (1885–1918), Chip. Dv (1918–48). *Eccl* Seq 22.

GRAFTON
Tg and chap in Great Bedwyn AP, sep EP 1844 as 'East Grafton',[26] qv, sep CP 1866.[3] *LG* Kinw. Hd, Hungerford PLU (1835–96), RSD, Hungerford & Ramsb. PLU (1896–1930), Ramsb. RD (1894–1934), Marlb. & Ramsb. RD (1934–74). *Parl* S'rn Dv (1867–85), E'rn Dv (1885–1918), Deviz. Dv/CC (1918–*).

EAST GRAFTON
Tg and chap in Great Bedwyn AP, sep EP 1844,[26] sep CP 1866 as 'Grafton',[3] qv. Marlb. RDn (1844–86), Pewsey RDn (1886–*).

GRIMSTEAD
CP Cr 1934 by union East Grimstead CP, West Grimstead AP.[1] *LG* Salisb. & Wilton RD. *Parl* Salisb. CC (1948–*).

EAST GRIMSTEAD
Chap in West Dean AP, sep CP 1866.[3] *LG* Aldb. PLU (1836–95), RSD, Salisb. PLU (1895–1930), RD. Abol 1934 to help cr Grimstead CP.[1] *Parl* S'rn Dv (1867–1918), Salisb. Dv (1918–48).

WEST GRIMSTEAD
AP Incl chap Plaitford (sep civ identity early, sep EP 1865[178]). *LG* Aldb. Hd, PLU (1836–95), RSD, Salisb. PLU (1895–1930), RD. Abol civ 1934 to help cr Grimstead CP.[1] *Parl* S'rn Dv (1832–1918), Salisb. Dv (1918–48). *Eccl* Seq 1.

GRITTLETON
AP *LG* Seq 14. Civ bdry: 1934.[1] *Parl* Seq 6. *Eccl* Malm. RDn (until 1866), Malm. South RDn (1866–87), Chip. RDn (1887–1968), Malm. RDn (1968–*).

GROVELEY WOOD
Ex-par place, sep CP 1858,[49] eccl abol 1952 ent to Wishford Magna AP.[179] *LG* Cawd. & Cad. Hd, Wilton PLU, RSD, RD. Abol 1934 ent to Barford St Martin AP.[1] *Parl* Pt Wilton Parl Bor, pt S'rn Dv (1832–85), S'rn Dv (1885–1918), Salisb. Dv (1918–48).

HAM
AP *LG* Elst. & Ev. Hd, Hungerford PLU (1835–96), RSD, Hungerford & Ramsb. PLU (1896–1930), Ramsb. RD (1894–1934), Marlb. & Ramsb. RD (1934–74). *Parl* Seq 8. *Eccl* Marlb. RDn (until 1956), Pewsey RDn (1956–*). Eccl bdry: 1958 (gains Buttermere AP).[97]

HANKERTON
AP *LG* Seq 27. Civ bdry: 1883.[12] *Parl* Seq 3. *Eccl* Malm. RDn (until 1866), Malm. South RDn (1866–87), Chip. RDn (1887–1954), Malm. RDn (1954–*).

HANNINGTON
AP *LG* Seq 21. Civ bdry: 1934.[1] *Parl* Seq 2. *Eccl* Seq 20.

HARDENHUISH
AP *LG* Chip. Hd, PLU, RSD, RD. Civ bdry: 1884,[39] 1896,[118] 1914.[116] Abol civ 1934 ent to Langley Burrell Without CP.[1] *Parl* Chip. Parl Bor (1832–85), N-W'rn Dv (1885–1918), Chip. Dv (1918–48). *Eccl* Seq 21. Eccl bdry: 1855 (help cr Chippenham St Paul EP),[113] 1969 (help cr Chippenham St Peter EP).[115]

HARNHAM
CP Cr 1904 from Britford AP, East Harnham CP.[78] *LG* Salisb. PLU, RD. Abol 1905 to help cr New Sarum CP.[173]

EAST HARNHAM
Chap in Britford AP, sep EP 1855,[75] sep CP 1896.[76] *LG* Salisb. PLU, RD. Abol 1904 pt to help cr Harnham CP, pt to Britford AP.[78] *Eccl* Chalke RDn. Abol 1881 to help cr East Harnham with West Harnham EP.[136]

EAST HARNHAM WITH HARNHAM
EP Cr 1881 by union East Harnham EP, West Harnham chap in Coombe Bissett AP.[136] Chalke RDn (1881–1956), Wilton RDn (1956–72). Renamed 1972 'Harnham St George and All Saints'.[180]

EAST HARNHAM WITH WEST HARNHAM
EP Cr 1881 by union East Harnham EP, West Harnham chap in Coombe Bissett AP.[136] Chalke

WEST HARNHAM
Chap (pec jurisd Prebend of Coombe Bissett and Harnham and Dean of Sarum) in Coombe

Bissett AP, sep civ identity early, eccl severed 1881 to help cr East Harnham with West Harnham EP.[136] *LG* Cawd. & Cad. Hd, Aldb. PLU (1836–95), RSD, Salisb. PLU (1895–1930), RD. Bdry: 1904,[78] 1927.[181] Abol 1934 ent to Netherhampton CP.[1] *Parl* Wilton Parl Bor (1832–85), S'rn Dv (1885–1918), Salisb. Dv (1918–48).

HARNHAM ST GEORGE AND ALL SAINTS

EP Renaming 1972 of East Harnham with West Harnham EP.[180] Wilton RDn. Bdry: 1973.[172]

HAYDON WICK

CP Cr 1928 from the pt of Rodbourne Cheney AP not transf to Swindon AP.[32] *LG* Swind. & Highw. PLU, Highw. RD. *Parl* Deviz. CC (1948–*).

HEDDINGTON

AP *LG* Seq 7. *Parl* Seq 6. *Eccl* Seq 16. Eccl bdry: 1887.[101]

HEYTESBURY

AP Incl chap Knook (sep civ identity early, sep EP 1782[24]), chap Tytherington (sep civ identity early, no sep eccl identity hence this par eccl 'Heytesbury with Tytherington', qv). *LG* Heytb. Bor, Seq 19. Addtl civ bdry alt: 1884,[52] 1885.[182] *Parl* Heytb. Parl Bor (1450–1832), Seq 12 thereafter.

HEYTESBURY WITH TYTHERINGTON

AP Usual eccl spelling; for civ and sep other units, see prev entry. *Eccl* Pec jurisd Dean of Sarum (until 1847), Wylye RDn (1847–72), Heytb. RDn (1872–1970). Addtl eccl bdry alt: 1959.[140] Abol eccl 1970 to help cr Heytesbury with Tytherington and Knook EP.[183]

HEYTESBURY WITH TYTHERINGTON AND KNOOK

EP Cr 1970 by union Heytesbury with Tytherington AP, Knook EP.[183] Heytb. RDn.

HEYWOOD

Chap in Westbury AP, sep EP 1849,[184] sep CP 1894.[68] *LG* W'bury & Whorw. PLU, RD. *Parl* W'bury Dv/CC (1918–*). *Eccl* Wylye RDn (1849–72), Heytb. RDn (1872–1962), Bradf. RDn (1962–*).

HIGHWAY

Chap in Bremhill AP, sep civ identity early, eccl severed 1952 to help cr Hilmarton and Highway EP.[71] *LG* Pott. & Cann. Hd, Calne PLU, RSD. Abol civ 1890 ent to Hilmarton AP.[43] *Parl* N'rn Dv (1832–85), N-W'rn Dv (1885–1918).

HIGHWORTH

AP Incl chap South Marston (sep EP 1889,[187] sep CP 1894[186]). Usual civ spelling; for eccl see following entry. *LG* Highw. Bor, Seq 21. Addtl civ bdry alt: 1883,[12] 1884.[44] *Parl* Highw. Parl Bor (1298, 1311 only), Seq 2 thereafter.

HIGHWORTH WITH SEVENHAMPTON

AP Usual eccl spelling; for civ and sep other unit, see prev entry. *Eccl* Pec jurisd Prebend of Highworth and Dean of Sarum (until 1847), Crickl. RDn (1847–1940). Eccl bdry: 1864 (cr Broad Blunsdon EP).[45] Abol eccl 1940 to help cr Highworth with Sevenhampton and Inglesham EP.[135]

HIGHWORTH WITH SEVENHAMPTON AND INGLESHAM

EP Cr 1940 by union Highworth with Sevenhampton AP, Inglesham AP, pt Coleshill AP.[135] Crickl. RDn.

HILMARTON

AP *LG* Pt Kingsbr. Hd, pt Selk. Hd, Calne PLU, RSD, RD (1894–1934), Calne & Chip. RD (1934–74). Civ bdry: 1883,[98] 1890.[43] *Parl* Pt Crickl. Parl Bor (1832–85), remainder and later, Seq 6. *Eccl* Aveb. RDn. Abol eccl 1952 to help cr Hilmarton and Highway EP.[71]

HILMARTON AND HIGHWAY

EP Cr 1952 by union Hilmarton AP, pt Bremhill with Foxham and Highway AP.[71] Aveb. RDn (1952–74), Calne RDn (1974–*).

HILPERTON

AP *LG* Melk. Hd, PLU (1835–98), RSD, Trowbridge & Melk. PLU (1898–1930), Melk. RD (1894–1934), Bradf. & Melk. RD (1934–74). Civ bdry: 1884,[189] 1884,[190] 1897.[188] *Parl* Seq 7. *Eccl* Pott. RDn. Abol eccl 1854 to help cr Hilperton with Whaddon EP.[191]

HILPERTON WITH WHADDON

EP Cr 1854 by union Hilperton AP, Whaddon AP.[191] Pott. RDn (1854–72), Bradf. RDn (1872–*). Bdry: 1955.[192]

HINDON

Chap and bor (status not sustained) in East Knoyle AP, sep civ identity early, sep EP 1821,[24] eccl refounded 1869.[193] *LG* Seq 15. Civ bdry: 1934.[1] *Parl* Hindon Parl Bor (1449–1832), Seq 10 thereafter. *Eccl* Chalke RDn (until 1872), Tisb. RDn (1872–1972). Abol eccl 1972 to help cr Hindon with Chicklade and Pertwood EP.[109]

HINDON WITH CHICKLADE AND PERTWOOD

EP Cr 1972 by union Hindon EP, Chicklade and Pertwood EP.[109] Tisb. RDn (1972–73), Shaft. & Tisb. RDn (1973–*).

BROAD HINTON

AP *LG* Seq 32. Civ bdry: 1884.[132] *Parl* Pt Crickl. Parl Bor, pt N'rn Dv (1832–85), pt E'rn Dv, pt N'rn Dv (1885–1918), Deviz. Dv/CC (1918–*). *Eccl* Seq 15. Eccl bdry: 1846 (help cr Broad Town EP).[81]

GREAT HINTON

Tg in Steeple Ashton AP, sep CP 1866.[3] *LG* Seq 37. Bdry: 1884.[190] *Parl* N'rn Dv (1867–85), W'rn Dv (1885–1918), W'bury Dv/CC (1918–*).

LITTLE HINTON

AP Usual civ spelling; for eccl see following entry. *LG* Elst. & Ev. Hd, Highw. & Swind. PLU (1836–99), RSD, Swind. & Highw. PLU (1899–1930), Highw. RD. Civ bdry: 1884.[44] Abol civ 1934 ent to Bishopstone AP.[1] *Parl* S'rn Dv (1832–85), N'rn Dv (1885–1918), Deviz. Dv (1918–48).

HINTON PARVA

AP Usual eccl spelling; for civ see prev entry. *Eccl* Crickl. RDn. Abol eccl 1946 to help cr Bishopstone with Hinton Parva EP.[41]

HIPPENSCOMBE

Ex-par place, sep CP 1858[49] (Kinw. Hd, Hungerford PLU, RSD) sep civ identity not sustained and civ incl in Tidcombe AP, eccl abol 1879 ent to Tidcombe AP.[197]

HOLT

Chap in Bradford-on-Avon AP, sep EP 1846,[19] sep CP 1894 (from Bradford Without CP).[56] *LG* Bradf. PLU (1894–95), Bradf.-on-Avon PLU (1895–1930), RD (1894–1934), Bradf. & Melk. RD (1934–74). Civ bdry: 1934.[1] *Parl* W'bury Dv/CC (1918–*). *Eccl* Pott. RDn (1846–72), Bradf. RDn (1872–*).

HOMINGTON

AP *LG* Cawd. & Cad. Hd, Aldb. PLU (1836–95), RSD, Salisb. PLU (1895–1930), RD. Civ bdry: 1883,[12] 1885.[27] Abol civ 1934 ent to Coombe Bissett AP.[1] *Parl* Wilton Parl Bor (pt 1832–67, ent 1867–85), S'rn Dv (pt 1832–67, ent 1885–1918), Salisb. Dv (1918–48). *Eccl* Pec jurisd Dean & Chapter of Sarum (until 1847), Chalke RDn (1847–1972). Abol eccl 1972 to help cr Coombe Bissett with Homington EP.[137]

HORNINGSHAM

AP *LG* Seq 19. Civ bdry: 1884,[52] 1885.[61] *Parl* Seq 12. *Eccl* Pec jurisd Dean of Sarum (until 1847), Seq 13 thereafter.

HUISH

AP *LG* Seq 34. Civ bdry: 1885.[9] *Parl* Seq 5. *Eccl* Marlb. RDn (until 1872), Pewsey RDn (1872–1972). Eccl bdry: 1892 (help refound Oare EP).[198] Abol eccl 1972 to help cr Huish and Oare EP.[199]

HUISH AND OARE

EP Cr 1972 by union Huish AP, Oare EP.[199] Pewsey RDn.

HULLAVINGTON

AP *LG* Pt Malm. Hd, pt Chip. Hd, Malm. PLU, RSD, RD. Civ bdry: 1884,[73] 1934.[1] *Parl* Seq 3. *Eccl* Seq 22.

HUNGERFORD

AP Prob pt of Kintbury AP, sep par early.[215] Pt Berks (Kintbury Eagle Hd, Hungerford Bor [status not sustained]), pt Wilts (Kinw. Hd), the par made ent Berks 1895.[60] *LG* Hungerford PLU, RSD, pt sep RD in Wilts (1894–95). *Parl* Wilts pt, S'rn Dv (1832–85), E'rn Dv (1885–1918). *Eccl* Pec jurisd Dean & Canons of Windsor (until 1847), Newbury RDn (dioc Oxford, 1847–1952). Abol eccl 1952 to help cr Hungerford and Denford EP.[216]

HURST

Parochial chap in Sonning AP, sep civ identity early, sep EP 1831.[217] Pt Berks (Sonning Hd, Charlton Hd), pt Wilts (Broad Hinton Lbty in Amesb. Hd), the latter transf to Berks 1832 for par purposes, 1844 for civ purposes.[200] See main entry in Berks, incl other units incl within this par.

IDMISTON

AP Usual civ spelling; for eccl see following entry. *LG* Aldb. Hd, Amesb. PLU, RSD, RD. Civ bdry: 1883,[12] 1885.[202] *Parl* Seq 9.

IDMISTON WITH PORTON

AP Usual eccl spelling; for civ see prev entry. *Eccl* Amesb. RDn (until 1872), Aldb. RDn (1872–1973). Eccl bdry: 1973 (help cr Winterbourne Earls and Dauntsey EP).[203] Renamed 1973 'Idmiston with Porton and Gomeldon'.[201]

IDMISTON WITH PORTON AND GOMELDON

EP Renaming 1973 of Idmiston with Porton EP.[201] Aldb. RDn. Bdry: 1973.[204]

IMBER

AP *LG* Pt Heytb. Hd, pt Swanb. Hd, Warm. PLU, RSD, RD (1894–1934), Warm. & W'bury RD (1934–74). *Parl* Pt N'rn Dv, pt S'rn Dv (1832–85), W'rn Dv (1885–1918), W'bury Dv/CC (1918–*). *Eccl* Pott. RDn (until 1951), Deviz. RDn (1951–54). Abol eccl 1954 to help cr Edington and Imber EP.[168]

INGLESHAM

AP Pt Wilts (Amesb. Hd), pt Berks (Faringdon Hd), the latter transf to Wilts 1832 for parl purposes, 1844 for civ purposes.[200] *LG* Highw. & Swind. PLU, RSD, Swind. & Highw. PLU (1899–1930), Highw. RD. Civ bdry: 1879,[134] 1881 (gains the pt of Coleshill AP [Wilts, Berks] in Wilts so that Coleshill ent Berks thereafter).[154] *Parl* Crickl. Parl Bor (1832–85), N'rn Dv (1885–1918), Swind. Dv (1918–48), Deviz. CC (1948–*). *Eccl* Crickl. RDn. Abol eccl 1940 to help cr Highworth with Sevenhampton and Inglesham EP.[135]

KEEVIL

AP Incl tg Bulkington (sep CP 1866,[3] sep EP 1883[93]). *LG* Pt Whorw. Hd, pt Melk. Hd, W'bury & Whorw. PLU, RSD, RD (1894–1934), Warm. & W'bury RD (1934–74). *Parl* Seq 7. *Eccl* Pott. RDn (until 1951), Bradf. RDn (1951–*).

KELLAWAYS

CP Cr 1895 by union Avon CP, Tytherton Kellaways AP.[22] *LG* Chip. PLU, RD. Abol 1934 ent to Langley Burrell Without CP.[1] *Parl* Chip. Dv (1918–48).

KEMBLE

AP *LG* Malm. Hd, Cirencester PLU, RSD, sep RD in Wilts (1894–97). Transf 1897 to Glos.[206] *Parl* Crickl. Parl Bor (1832–85), N-W'rn Dv (1885–1918). *Eccl* Malm. RDn (until 1866), Malm. North RDn (1866–87), Malm. RDn (1887–97), Cirencester RDn (Cirencester AD, 1897–*).

EAST KENNETT

AP *LG* Seq 32. *Parl* Seq 5. *Eccl* Seq 18.

POOLE KEYNES

AP *LG* Malm. Hd, Cirencester PLU, RSD, sep RD in Wilts (1894–97). Transf 1897 to Glos.[206] *Parl* Crickl. Parl Bor (1832–85), N-W'rn Dv (1885–1918). *Eccl* Malm. RDn (until 1866), Malm. North RDn (1866–87), Malm. RDn (1887–97), Cirencester RDn (Cirencester AD, 1897–*).

SOMERFORD KEYNES

AP *LG* Highw., Crickl. & Staple Hd, Cirencester

PLU, RSD, sep RD in Wilts (1894–97). Transf 1897 to Glos.[206] *Parl* As for Poole Keynes. *Eccl* Crickl. RDn. Abol eccl 1881 to help cr Somerford Keynes with Sharncote EP.[205]

SOMERFORD KEYNES WITH SHARNCOTE
EP Cr 1881 by union Somerford Keynes AP, Sharncote AP.[205] Crickl. RDn (1881–97), Cirencester RDn (Cirencester AD, 1897–*).

KILMINGTON
AP In Somerset (qv), transf 1896 to Wilts.[207] *LG* Mere PLU, RSD, sep RD in Somerset (1894–96), Mere RD (1896–1934), Mere & Tisb. RD (1934–74). *Parl* In Somerset until 1918, W'bury Dv/CC (1918–*). *Eccl* See entry in Somerset.

WEST KINGTON
AP *LG* Chip. Hd, PLU, RSD, RD. Abol civ 1934 ent to Nettleton AP.[1] *Parl* N'rn Dv (1832–85), N-W'rn Dv (1885–1918), Chip. Dv (1918–48). *Eccl* Seq 21.

KINGTON LANGLEY
Tg and chap in Kington St Michael AP, sep CP 1866 as 'Kington Langley',[3] sep EP 1865 as 'Langley Fitzurse',[208] qv. *LG* Seq 14. Civ bdry: 1883,[12] 1884.[39] *Parl* N'rn Dv (1867–85), N-W'rn Dv (1885–1918), Chip. Dv/CC (1918–*).

KINGTON ST MICHAEL
AP Incl tg and chap Kington Langley (sep CP 1866,[3] sep EP 1865 as 'Langley Fitzurse'[208]). *LG* Seq 14. Addtl civ bdry alt: 1883,[12] 1971.[119] *Parl* Pt Crickl. Parl Bor (1832–85), remainder and later, Seq 6. *Eccl* Seq 21. Addtl eccl bdry alt: 1885 (help cr Chippenham St Paul EP).[113]

KINGSWOOD
AP In Wilts (Chip. Hd), transf to Glos 1832 for parl purposes, 1844 for civ purposes.[200] See main entry in Glos.

KNOOK
Chap in Heytesbury AP, sep civ identity early, sep EP 1782.[24] *LG* Seq 19. Civ bdry: 1885.[102] *Parl* Seq 12. *Eccl* Pec jurisd Dean of Sarum (until 1847), Wylye RDn (1847–72), Heytb. RDn (1872–1970). Abol eccl 1970 to help cr Heytesbury with Tytherington and Knook EP.[183]

EAST KNOYLE
AP Incl chap and bor Hindon (sep civ identity early, sep bor status not sustained, sep EP 1869[193]). *LG* Down. Hd, Mere PLU, RSD, RD (1894–1934), Mere & Tisb. RD (1934–74). Addtl civ bdry alt: 1885.[209] *Parl* Pt Hindon Parl Bor (1449 until Hindon gains sep civ identity), Seq 11. *Eccl* Seq 5.

WEST KNOYLE
AP *LG* Seq 29. *Parl* Seq 11. *Eccl* Chalke RDn (until 1872), Tisb. RDn (1872–1953), Heytb. RDn (1953–*).

LACOCK
AP *LG* Lacock Bor (status not sustained), Seq 12. Civ bdry: 1914,[116] 1952.[117] *Parl* Seq 6. *Eccl* Malm. RDn (until 1866), Malm. South RDn (1866–87), Chip. RDn (1887–1955). Eccl bdry: 1863 (cr Bowden Hill EP).[47] Abol eccl 1955 to help cr Lacock with Bowden Hill EP.[48]

LACOCK WITH BOWDEN HILL
EP Cr 1955 by union Lacock AP, Bowden Hill EP.[48] Chip. RDn.

LAND COMMON TO MELKSHAM WITHOUT AND BROUGHTON
For Hd, PLU, RSD, see sep pars. *LG* Melk. RD (1894–1934), Bradf. & Melk. RD (1934–74).

LANDFORD
AP *LG* Seq 18. Civ bdry: 1896.[165] *Parl* Seq 9. *Eccl* Seq 1.

LITTLE LANGFORD
AP *LG* Branch & Dole Hd, Wilton PLU, RSD, RD. Abol civ 1934 ent to Steeple Langford AP.[1] *Parl* S'rn Dv (1832–1918), Salisb. Dv (1918–48). *Eccl* Wylye RDn (until 1971), Wylye & Wilton RDn (1971–73). Abol eccl 1973 to help cr The Langfords EP.[210]

STEEPLE LANGFORD
AP *LG* Branch & Dole Hd, Wilton PLU, RSD, RD (1894–1934), Salisb. & Wilton RD (1934–74). Civ bdry: 1934.[1] *Parl* Seq 9. *Eccl* As for Little Langford.

THE LANGFORDS
EP Cr 1973 by union Steeple Langford AP, Little Langford AP.[210] Wylye & Wilton RDn.

LANGLEY BURRELL
AP *LG* Chip. Hd, PLU, pt Chip. MB (1889–94), pt Chip. USD, pt Chip. RSD. Civ bdry: 1883,[12] 1884.[39] Abol civ 1894 the pt in the MB to cr Langley Burrell Within CP, the remainder to cr Langley Burrell Without CP.[112] *Parl* Chip. Parl Bor (1832–85), N-W'rn Dv (1885–1918). *Eccl* Malm. RDn (until 1866), Malm. South RDn (1866–87), Chip. RDn (1887–1965). Eccl bdry: 1855 (help cr Chippenham St Paul EP).[113] Abol eccl 1965 to help cr Chippenham St Paul with Langley Burrell EP.[114]

LANGLEY BURRELL WITHIN
CP Cr 1894 from the pt of Langley Burrell AP in Chip. MB.[112] *LG* Chip. PLU, MB. Bdry: 1914.[116] Abol 1934 ent to Chippenham Within CP.[1] *Parl* Chip. Dv (1918–48).

LANGLEY BURRELL WITHOUT
CP Cr 1894 from the pt of Langley Burrell AP not in Chip. MB.[112] *LG* Chip. PLU, RD (1894–1934), Calne & Chip. RD (1934–74). Bdry: 1896,[118] 1914,[116] 1934,[1] 1952.[117] *Parl* Chip. Dv/CC (1918–*).

LANGLEY FITZURSE
Chap in Kington St Michael AP, sep EP 1865,[208] sep CP 1866 as 'Kington Langley',[3] qv. Malm. RDn (1865–66), Malm. South RDn (1866–87), Chip. RDn (1887–*).

LANGLEY WOOD
Ex-par place, sep CP 1858.[49] *LG* Down. Hd, Aldb. PLU, RSD. Abol 1894 ent to Downton AP.[120] *Parl* S'rn Dv (1867–1918).

LATTON
AP *LG* Seq 20. Civ bdry: 1896.[118] *Parl* Seq 1. *Eccl* Crickl. RDn. Abol eccl 1952 to help cr Latton with Eisey EP.[103]

LATTON WITH EISEY
EP Cr 1952 by union Latton AP, pt Eisey AP.[103] Crickl. RDn. Bdry: 1952 (help cr Cricklade EP).[103]

LAVERSTOCK
AP Sometimes 'Laverstock and Ford'. *LG* Seq 1. Civ bdry: 1883,[12] 1885,[130] 1885,[202] 1904,[78] 1928,[181] 1954.[78] *Parl* Seq 9. *Eccl* Amesb. RDn (until 1951), Wilton RDn (1951–70), Salisb. RDn (1970–*). Eccl bdry: 1973,[211] 1973 (help cr Winterbourne Earls and Dauntsey EP).[203]

EAST LAVINGTON–See MARKET LAVINGTON

BISHOPS LAVINGTON–See WEST LAVINGTON

MARKET LAVINGTON
AP Sometimes 'East Lavington'. *LG* Swanb. Hd, Deviz. PLU, RSD, RD. Civ bdry: 1884.[89] *Parl* Seq 5. *Eccl* Seq 6. Eccl bdry: 1874 (help cr Easterton EP).[166]

WEST LAVINGTON
AP Sometimes 'Bishops Lavington'. *LG* Seq 30. Civ bdry: 1884.[89] *Parl* Seq 5. *Eccl* Pec jurisd Bp of Sarum (until 1847), Seq 6 thereafter. Eccl bdry: 1874 (help cr Easterton EP).[166]

LEA AND CLEVERTON
AP *LG* Seq 27. Civ bdry: 1883,[12] 1934.[1] *Parl* Malm. Parl Bor (1832–85), N-W'rn Dv (1885–1918), Chip. Dv/CC (1918–*). *Eccl* Seq 22.

LEIGH
Chap in Ashton Keynes AP, sep CP 1866,[3] no sep eccl identity. *LG* Seq 20. Bdry: 1883,[12] 1884.[17] *Parl* Crickl. Parl Bor (1867–85), N'rn Dv (1885–1918), Chip. Dv/CC (1918–*).

LEIGH DELAMERE
AP *LG* Chip. Hd, PLU, RSD, RD. Abol civ 1934 ent to Grittleton AP.[1] *Parl* N'rn Dv (1832–85), N-W'rn Dv (1885–1918), Chip. Dv (1918–48). *Eccl* Malm. RDn (until 1866), Malm. South RDn (1866–87), Chip. RDn (1887–1968), Malm. RDn (1968–*).

LIDDINGTON
AP *LG* Seq 23. Civ bdry: 1884,[212] 1969.[121] *Parl* Crickl. Parl Bor (1832–85), N'rn Dv (1885–1918), Deviz. Dv/CC (1918–*). Parl bdry: 1971.[283] *Eccl* Sometimes as 'Lyddington', Seq 20. Eccl bdry: 1972 (incl help cr Swindon St Paul, Covingham EP).[123]

LIMPLEY STOKE
Area in Bradford-on-Avon AP, sep EP 1846,[19] sep CP 1894 (from Bradford Without CP).[56] *LG* Bradf. PLU (1894–95), Bradf.-on-Avon PLU (1895–1930), RD (1894–1934), Bradf. & Melk. RD (1934–74). *Parl* W'bury Dv/CC (1918–*). *Eccl* Pott. RDn (1846–72), Bradf. RDn (1872–1972), Bath RDn (Bath & Wells dioc, Bath AD, 1972–*).

LITTLETON DREW
AP *LG* Chip. Hd, PLU, RSD, RD. Abol civ 1934 ent to Grittleton AP.[1] *Parl* N'rn Dv (1832–85), N-W'rn Dv (1885–1918), Chip. Dv (1918–48). *Eccl* Seq 21.

LUCKINGTON
AP *LG* Seq 13. Civ bdry: 1883,[12] 1884,[73] 1934.[1] *Parl* Seq 6. *Eccl* Seq 22.

LUDGERSHALL
AP *LG* Amesb. Hd, Ludgershall Bor, Andover PLU (1835–79), RSD (1875–79), Pewsey PLU (1879–1930), RSD (1879–94), RD. *Parl* Ludgershall Parl Bor (1295–1832), Seq 8 thereafter. *Eccl* Seq 3.

LYDDINGTON–See LIDDINGTON

LYDIARD MILLICENT
AP Sometimes 'North Lydiard'. *LG* Seq 20. Civ bdry: 1928.[32] *Parl* Seq 1. *Eccl* Seq 20.

LYDIARD TREGOZ
AP Usual eccl spelling; for civ see following entry. *Eccl* Seq 20. Eccl bdry: 1973 (loses pt to Wootton Bassett AP, dioc Sarum).[213]

LYDIARD TREGOZE
AP Usual civ spelling; for eccl see prev entry. *LG* Seq 22. Civ bdry: 1928,[32] 1934.[1] *Parl* Crickl. Parl Bor (1832–85), N'rn Dv (1885–1918), pt Chip. Dv, pt Deviz. Dv (1918–48), Chip. CC (1948–*).

LYNEHAM
AP *LG* Seq 22. Civ bdry: 1969.[214] *Parl* Seq 1. *Eccl* Aveb. RDn. Eccl bdry: 1866 (help cr Bradenstoke cum Clack EP).[53] Abol eccl 1954 to help cr Lyneham with Bradenstoke EP.[54]

LYNEHAM WITH BRADENSTOKE
EP Cr 1954 by union Lyneham AP, Bradenstoke cum Clack EP.[54] Aveb. RDn (1954–74), Calne RDn (1974–*). Bdry: 1963.[217]

MADDINGTON
AP *LG* Branch & Dole Hd, Amesb. PLU, RSD, RD. Civ bdry: 1885.[164] Abol civ 1934 ent to Shrewton AP.[1] *Parl* S'rn Dv (1832–1918), Salisb. Dv (1918–48). *Eccl* Wylye RDn. Abol eccl 1970 ent to Shrewton AP.[218]

MALMESBURY
The following have 'Malmesbury' in their names. Insofar as any existed at a given time: *LG* Malm. Hd, Bor, MB (1886–1974), PLU, USD. *Parl* Malm. Parl Bor (1295–1885), N-W'rn Dv (1885–1918), Chip. Dv/CC (1918–*). *Eccl* Malm. RDn (until 1866), Malm. North RDn (1866–87), Malm. RDn (1887–*).

CP1–MALMESBURY–Cr 1934 by union AP1, CP2, Westport St Mary Within CP, pt Brokenborough CP.[1] Bdry: 1956.[85]

EP1–MALMESBURY–Single par for eccl purposes comprising AP1 (parochial since Dissolution), AP2 (long in ruins, church taken down 1852). Bdry: 1881 (cr Corston with Rodbourne EP).[141] Abol eccl 1946 to help cr EP2.[219]

AP1–MALMESBURY THE ABBEY–Orig abbey church, parochial since Dissolution, now eccl forms one par with AP2 (long in ruins, taken down 1852) as EP1, qv. Abol civ 1934 to help cr CP1.[1]

AP2–MALMESBURY ST PAUL–Incl chap Long Newnton (sep par by 1248[220]). Long in ruins, taken down 1852, now forms one par for eccl purposes with AP1 as EP1, qv. *LG* Malm. Bor, MB (ent 1835–83, pt 1883–94), Malm. USD (ent 1875–83, pt 1883–94), pt Malm.

RSD (1883–94). Civ bdry: 1883,[12] 1884.[73] Abol civ 1894 the pt in the MB to cr CP2, the remainder to cr CP3.[83]

CP2–MALMESBURY ST PAUL WITHIN–Cr 1894 from the pt of AP2 in Malm. MB.[83] Abol 1934 to help cr CP1.[1]

CP3–MALMESBURY ST PAUL WITHOUT–Cr 1894 from the pt of AP2 not in Malm. MB.[83] *LG* Malm. RD. Bdry: 1896,[118] 1956.[85]

EP2–MALMESBURY WITH WESTPORT ST MARY–Cr 1946 by union EP1, Westport St Mary AP.[219] Malm. RDn.

MANNINGFORD

CP Cr 1934 by union Manningford Abbots AP, Manningford Bohune CP, Manningford Bruce AP.[1] *LG* Pewsey RD. *Parl* Deviz. CC (1948–*).

MANNINGFORD ABBAS

AP Usual eccl spelling; for civ see following entry. *Eccl* Seq 24.

MANNINGFORD ABBOTS

AP Usual civ spelling; for eccl see prev entry. *LG* Swanb. Hd, Pewsey PLU, RSD, RD. Abol civ 1934 to help cr Manningford CP.[1] *Parl* N'rn Dv (1832–85), E'rn Dv (1885–1918), Deviz. Dv (1918–48).

MANNINGFORD BOHUNE

Tg and chap in Wilsford AP, sep CP 1866,[3] sep EP 1859[24] but sep eccl status not sustained, eccl severed 1939 pt to help cr Woodborough with Manningford Bohune EP, pt to Manningford Bruce AP.[221] *LG* Swanb. Hd, Pewsey PLU, RSD, RD. Abol civ 1934 to help cr Manningford CP.[1] *Parl* As for Manningford Abbots.

MANNINGFORD BRUCE

AP *LG*, civ abol, *Parl* as for Manningford Abbots. *Eccl* Seq 24. Eccl bdry: 1939.[221]

MARDEN

AP *LG* Seq 33. *Parl* Seq 5. *Eccl* Seq 8. Eccl bdry: 1967.[29]

MARLBOROUGH

The following have 'Marlborough' in their names. Insofar as any existed at a given time: *LG* Selk. Hd, Marlb. Bor/MB, PLU, USD. *Parl* Marlb. Parl Bor (1295–1885), E'rn Dv (1885–1918), Deviz. Dv/CC (1918–*). *Eccl* Marlb. RDn (until 1872), Pewsey RDn (1872–*).

CP1–MARLBOROUGH–Cr 1925 by union AP1, AP2, Preshute Within CP.[1] Bdry: 1934.[1]

AP1–MARLBOROUGH ST MARY THE VIRGIN–Abol civ 1925 to help cr CP1.[223] Abol eccl 1952 to help cr EP1.[224]

EP1–MARLBOROUGH ST MARY THE VIRGIN WITH ST PETER AND ST PAUL–Cr 1952 by union AP1, AP2, pt Preshute AP.[224] Eccl bdry: 1971.[254]

AP2–MARLBOROUGH ST PETER AND ST PAUL–Abol civ 1925 to help cr CP1.[223] Abol eccl 1952 to help cr EP1.[224]

MARSTON

Tg in Potterne AP, sep CP 1866.[3] *LG* Seq 30. *Parl* N'rn Dv (1867–85), E'rn Dv (1885–1918), Deviz. Dv/CC (1918–*).

SOUTH MARSTON

Chap (pec jurisd Prebend of Highw. and Dean of Sarum) in Highworth AP, sep EP 1889,[225] sep CP 1894.[186] *LG* Highw. & Swind. PLU (1894–99), Swind. & Highw. PLU (1899–1930), Highw. RD. *Parl* Swind. Dv (1918–48), Deviz. CC (1948–*). *Eccl* Crickl. RDn.

MARSTON MEYSEY

AP *LG* Highw., Crickl. & Staple Hd, Cirencester PLU (1836–81), RSD (1875–81), Crickl. & Woot. Bas. PLU (1881–1930), RSD (1881–94), RD. *Parl* Seq 1. *Eccl* Fairford RDn (Bristol AD until 1882, Cirencester AD 1882–1919, Cheltenham AD 1919–*).

MARTIN

Chap in Damerham AP, sep civ identity early, sep EP 1854.[240] *LG* Dam. Hd, Fordingbridge PLU, RSD, sep RD in Wilts (1894–95). Transf 1895 to Hants.[65] *Parl* S'rn Dv (1867–1918). *Eccl* Chalke RDn.

MELCHET PARK

Ex-par place, sep CP 1858.[49] *LG* Aldb. Hd, Romsey PLU, RSD, sep RD in Wilts (1894–95). Transf 1895 to Hants.[65] *Parl* S'rn Dv (1867–1918).

MELKSHAM

AP Incl chap Seend (sep civ identity early, sep EP 1873[226]), chap Erlestoke (sep civ identity early, sep EP 1877[169]). *LG* Melk. Hd, PLU, pt Melk. USD, pt Melk. RSD. Abol civ 1894 the pt in the USD to cr Melksham Within CP, the remainder to cr Melksham Without CP.[227] *Parl* N'rn Dv (1832–85), W'rn Dv (1885–1918). *Eccl* Seq 9. Eccl bdry: 1843 (cr Shaw EP),[228] 1954.[16]

MELKSHAM WITHIN

CP Cr 1894 from the pt of Melksham AP in Melk. USD.[227] *LG* Melk. PLU (1894–98), UD, Trowbridge & Melk. PLU (1898–1930). Bdry: 1896,[229] 1914,[230] 1934,[1] 1954.[231] *Parl* W'bury Dv/CC (1918–*).

MELKSHAM WITHOUT

CP Cr 1894 from the pt of Melksham AP not in Melk. USD.[227] *LG* Melk. PLU (1894–98), RD (1894–1934), Trowbridge & Melk. PLU (1898–1930), Bradf. & Melk. RD (1934–74). Bdry: 1896,[229] 1914,[230] 1934,[1] 1954.[231] *Parl* W'bury Dv/CC (1918–*).

MERE

AP Incl chap Zeals (sep EP 1848,[232] sep CP 1896[233]). *LG* Mere Bor (status not sustained), Seq 29. *Parl* Mere Parl Bor (1304–07 only), Seq 11. *Eccl* Pec jurisd Dean of Sarum (until 1847), Seq 13 thereafter.

MILDENHALL

AP *LG* Seq 32. Civ bdry: 1901,[234] 1934.[1] *Parl* Seq 5. *Eccl* Seq 23.

MILFORD

Tg (pec jurisd Sub-Dean of Sarum and Bp of Sarum) in Salisbury St Martin AP, sep CP 1866.[3] *LG* Und. Hd, Aldb. PLU, pt Salisb. MB (1835–94), pt Salisb. USD, pt Aldb. RSD.

Bdry: 1883,[12] 1885.[202] Abol 1894 the pt in the MB to cr Milford Within CP, the remainder to cr Milford Without CP.[170] *Parl* Salisb. Parl Bor (1832–1918).

CP Cr 1904 by union Milford Without CP, pt Stratford sub Castle AP.[78] *LG* Salisb. PLU, RD. Abol 1905 to help cr New Sarum CP.[173]

MILFORD WITHIN

CP Cr 1894 from the pt of Milford CP in Salisb. MB.[170] *LG* Aldb. PLU (1894–95), Salisb. PLU (1895–1905), MB. Bdry: 1897 (gains the pt of Stratford sub Castle AP in Salisb. MB).[235] Abol 1905 to help cr New Sarum CP.[173]

MILFORD WITHOUT

CP Cr 1894 from the pt of Milford CP not in Salisb. MB.[170] *LG* Aldb. PLU (1894–95), Salisb. PLU (1895–1904), RD. Bdry: 1897.[235] Abol 1904 to help cr Milford CP.[78]

MILSTON

AP *LG* Seq 2. *Parl* Seq 9. *Eccl* Seq 5.

MILTON LILBOURNE

AP *LG* Seq 25. *Parl* Seq 8. *Eccl* Seq 24.

MINETY

AP In Glos (Crowthorne & Minety Hd), situated in Wilts and transf to Wilts 1832 for parl purposes, 1844 for civ purposes.[200] *LG* Seq 27. Civ bdry: 1884.[73] *Parl* Pt Crickl. Parl Bor (1832–85), pt N'rn Dv (1832–85), N-W'rn Dv (1885–1918), Chip. Dv/CC (1918–*). *Eccl* Seq 22.

MONKTON FARLEIGH

AP *LG* Seq 4. *Parl* Seq 7. *Eccl* Seq 9.

MORGAN'S VALE

EP Cr 1915 from Downton AP, Redlynch EP.[163] Wilton RDn (1915–51), Aldb. RDn (1951–*).

MORGAN'S VALE AND WOODFALLS

CP Cr 1923 from Downton AP.[162] *LG* Salisb. PLU, RD. Abol 1934 ent to Redlynch CP.[1]

NESTON

EP Cr 1869 from Corsham AP.[138] Malm. South RDn (1869–87), Chip. RDn (1887–*).

NETHERAVON

AP *LG* Seq 17. Civ bdry: 1885.[9] *Parl* Seq 8. *Eccl* Pec jurisd Prebend of Netheravon and Dean of Sarum (until 1847), Seq 7 thereafter.

NETHERHAMPTON

Chap in Wilton AP, sep civ identity early, no sep eccl identity. *LG* Seq 9. Civ bdry: 1934,[1] 1954.[79] *Parl* Seq 13.

NETTLETON

AP *LG* Seq 14. Civ bdry: 1934,[1] 1971.[119] *Parl* Seq 6. *Eccl* Seq 21.

LONG NEWNTON

Chap in Malmesbury St Paul AP, sep par by 1248.[220] *LG* Malm. Hd, Tetbury PLU, RSD, RD. Transf 1930 to Glos.[285] *Parl* Crickl. Parl Bor (1832–85), N-W'rn Dv (1885–1918), Chip. Dv (1918–48). *Eccl* Seq 22.

NORTH NEWNTON

AP *LG* Seq 34. Civ bdry: 1885.[9] *Parl* Seq 5. *Eccl* Aveb. RDn (until 1872), Cann. RDn (1872–1951), Avon RDn (1951–56), Deviz. RDn (1956–*). Eccl bdry: 1892 (help refound Oare EP).[198]

SOUTH NEWTON

AP *LG* Branch & Dole Hd, Wilton PLU, pt Wilton MB and USD (1885–94), Wilton RSD (ent 1875–85, pt 1885–94). Civ bdry: 1884.[23] Abol civ 1894 the pt in the MB to cr South Newton Within CP (by same order incl ent in Wilton AP), the remainder to cr South Newton Without CP (immediately called 'South Newton' since South Newton Within did not sustain sep civ identity).[30] *Parl* Wilton Parl Bor (1832–85), S'rn Dv (1885–1918). *Eccl* Wilton RDn (until 1951), Wylye RDn (1951–71), Wylye & Wilton RDn (1971–*).

CP Name used for par cr 1894 as 'South Newton Without' from the pt of South Newton AP not in Wilton MB.[30] *LG* Wilton PLU, RD (1894–1934), Salisb. & Wilton RD (1934–74). Bdry: 1934.[1] *Parl* Salisb. Dv/CC (1918–*).

SOUTH NEWTON WITHIN, SOUTH NEWTON WITHOUT–See SOUTH NEWTON

NEWTON TONEY

AP *LG* Seq 2. *Parl* Seq 9. *Eccl* As 'Newton Tony', Seq 2.

NO MAN'S LAND

Ex-par place, sep CP 1858,[49] eccl abol 1955 ent to Bramshaw AP.[66] *LG* Down. Hd, Aldb. PLU (1836–95), RSD, Salisb. PLU (1895–1930), RD. Abol 1934 ent to Redlynch CP.[1] *Parl* S'rn Dv (1867–1918), Salisb. Dv (1918–48).

NORTON

AP Sometimes 'Norton Coleparle'. *LG* Seq 27. Civ bdry: 1884,[73] 1934.[1] *Parl* Seq 3. *Eccl* Seq 22.

NORTON BAVANT

AP *LG* Seq 36. Civ bdry: 1884.[52] *Parl* Seq 12. *Eccl* Seq 13. Eccl bdry: 1959.[140]

NORTON COLEPARLE–See NORTON

NUNTON AND BODENHAM

Chap in Downton AP, sep civ identity early, eccl severed 1916 to help cr Odstock with Nunton and Bodenham EP.[160] *LG* Down. Hd, Aldb. PLU (1836–95), RSD, Salisb. PLU (1895–1930), RD. Abol 1934 ent to Britford AP.[1] *Parl* S'rn Dv (1832–1918), Salisb. Dv (1918–48).

OAKSEY.

AP *LG* Seq 27. Civ bdry: 1884.[73] *Parl* Seq 3. *Eccl* Seq 22.

OARE

EP Cr 1858 from Wilcot AP,[24] refounded eccl 1892 from Wilcot AP, Alton Priors chap in Overton AP, North Newnton AP, Huish AP.[198] Marlb. RDn (1858–72), Pewsey RDn (1872–1972). Abol 1972 to help cr Huish and Oare EP.[199]

ODSTOCK

AP *LG* Seq 8. Civ bdry: 1934.[1] *Parl* Seq 9. *Eccl* Chalke RDn. Abol 1916 to help cr Odstock with Nunton and Bodenham EP.[160]

ODSTOCK WITH NUNTON AND BODENHAM

EP Cr 1916 by union Odstock AP, chap Nunton and Bodenham in Downton AP.[160] Chalke RDn (1916–51), Aldb. RDn (1951–*).

OGBOURNE ST ANDREW
AP *LG* Seq 32. *Parl* Seq 5. *Eccl* Pec jurisd Dean & Canons of Windsor (until 1847), Seq 23 thereafter.

OGBOURNE ST GEORGE
AP Organisation as for Ogbourne St Andrew.

ORCHESTON
Cr civ 1934,[1] eccl 1971[237] by union Orcheston St Mary AP, Orcheston St George AP. *LG* Amesb. RD. *Parl* Salisb. CC (1948–*). *Eccl* Wylye & Wilton RDn.

ORCHESTON ST GEORGE
AP *LG* Heytb. Hd, Amesb. PLU, RSD, RD. Civ bdry: 1885.[164] Abol civ 1934 to help cr Orcheston CP.[1] *Parl* S'rn Dv (1832–1918), Salisb. Dv (1918–48). *Eccl* Wylye RDn (until 1970), Wylye & Wilton RDn (1970–71). Abol eccl 1971 to help cr Orcheston EP.[237]

ORCHESTON ST MARY
AP Organisation and civ bdry alt as for Orcheston St George.

OVERTON WITH FYFIELD
AP Usual eccl spelling; for civ see 'West Overton'. Incl chap Alton Priors (sep civ identity early, eccl reduced 1892 to help refound Oare EP,[198] eccl severed 1932 ent to Alton Barnes AP[8]), chap Fyfield (sep civ identity early, no sep eccl identity hence this par eccl 'Overton with Fyfield'). *Eccl* Seq 18.

WEST OVERTON
AP Usual civ spelling; for eccl and sep chaps see prev entry. *LG* Pt Selk. Hd, pt Elst. & Ev. Hd, Marlb. PLU, RSD, RD (1894–1934), Marlb. & Ramsb. RD (1934–74). *Parl* Pt N'rn Dv, pt S'rn Dv (1832–85), E'rn Dv (1885–1918), Deviz. Dv/CC (1918–*).

OVERTON HEATH
Ex-par place, sep CP 1858,[49] eccl abol 1971 ent to Preshute AP.[131] *LG* Selk. Hd, Marlb. PLU, RSD, RD. Abol 1895 ent to Clatford AP.[238] *Parl* N'rn Dv (1867–85), E'rn Dv (1885–1918).

PATNEY
AP *LG* Elst. & Ev. Hd, Deviz. PLU, RSD, RD. *Parl* S'rn Dv (1832–85), E'rn Dv (1885–1918), Deviz. Dv/CC (1918–*). *Eccl* Seq 8.

PENHILL
EP Cr 1957 from Upper Stratton EP, Rodbourne Cheney AP.[239] Crickl. RDn. Now called 'Swindon St Peter, Penhill'.

PERTWOOD
AP Usual eccl spelling; for civ see following entry. *Eccl* Wylye RDn (until 1872), Heytb. RDn (1872–1922). Abol eccl 1922 to help cr Chicklade and Pertwood EP.[108]

UPPER PERTWOOD
AP Usual civ spelling; for eccl see prev entry. *LG* Warm. Hd, Mere PLU, RSD. Abol civ 1885 pt to Sutton Veney AP,[236] pt to East Knoyle AP.[209] *Parl* S'rn Dv (1832–1918).

PEWSEY
AP *LG* Seq 25. *Parl* Seq 8. *Eccl* Seq 24.

PEWSHAM
Ex-par place, sep CP 1858,[49] abol eccl 1841 to help cr Derry Hill EP.[50] *LG* Seq 12. Bdry: 1884,[39] 1884,[88] 1934.[1] *Parl* Chip. Parl Bor (1832–85), N-W'rn Dv (1885–1918), Chip. Dv/CC (1918–*).

PITTON AND FARLEY
Chaps in Alderbury AP, sep CP 1866[3] (sep EP 1874 as 'Farley with Pitton'.[4] qv). *LG* Seq 1. *Parl* S'rn Dv (1867–1918), Salisb. Dv/CC (1918–*).

PLAITFORD
Chap in West Grimstead AP, sep civ identity early, sep EP 1865.[178] *LG* Aldb. Hd, Romsey PLU, RSD, sep RD in Wilts (1894–95). Civ bdry: 1885.[241] Transf 1895 to Hants.[65] *Parl* S'rn Dv (1832–1918). *Eccl* Amesb. RDn (1865–72), Aldb. RDn (1872–*).

POTTERNE
AP Incl tg Marston (sep CP 1866[3]), tg and chap Worton (sep EP 1852,[242] sep CP 1866[3]). *LG* Seq 30. Addtl civ bdry alt: 1884,[151] 1884,[89] 1934.[1] *Parl* Seq 5. *Eccl* Pec jurisd Bp of Sarum (until 1847), Seq 6 thereafter.

POULSHOT
AP *LG* Seq 28. Civ bdry: 1884.[89] *Parl* Seq 5. *Eccl* Seq 6. Eccl bdry: 1932.[126]

POULTON
AP In Wilts (Highw., Crickl. & Staple Hd), transf to Glos 1832 for parl purposes, 1844 for civ purposes.[200] For civ organisation thereafter, see main entry in Glos. *Eccl* Crickl. RDn (until 1887), Fairford RDn (1887–*).

PRESHUTE
AP *LG* Selk. Hd, Marlb. PLU, RSD, RD. Abol civ 1901 the pt to be in Marlb. MB cr Preshute Within CP, pt to cr Preshute Without CP, the remainder to Mildenhall AP, North Savernake CP.[234] *Parl* Marlb. Parl Bor (1832–85), E'rn Dv (1885–1918). *Eccl* Marlb. RDn (until 1872), Pewsey RDn (1872–88), Marlb. RDn (1888–*). Eccl bdry: 1854 (help cr Savernake EP),[243] 1952 (help cr Marlborough St Mary the Virgin with St Peter and St Paul EP),[224] 1971,[254] 1971 (gains ex-par Clatford Park, Overton Heath).[131]
CP Renaming 1925 of Preshute Without CP.[223] *LG* Marlb. PLU, RD. Bdry: 1934.[1] *Parl* Deviz. CC (1948–*).

PRESHUTE WITHIN
CP Cr 1901 from the pt of Preshute AP to be in Marlb. MB.[234] *LG* Marlb. PLU, MB. Abol 1925 to help cr Marlborough CP.[223] *Parl* Deviz. Dv (1918–48).

PRESHUTE WITHOUT
CP Cr 1901 from the pt of Preshute AP not to be in Marlb. MB.[234] *LG* Marlb. PLU, RD. Renamed 1925 'Preshute'.[223] *Parl* Deviz. Dv (1918–48).

PURTON
AP Incl hmlt Braydon (sep CP 1866[3]). *LG* Seq 20. *Parl* Pt Crickl. Parl Bor, pt N'rn Dv (1832–85),

N'rn Dv (1885–1918), Chip. Dv/CC (1918–*). *Eccl* Seq 20. Eccl bdry: 1952.[103]

QUIDHAMPTON

CP Cr 1934 from Bemerton CP.[1] *LG* Salisb. & Wilton RD. Bdry: 1954.[79] *Parl* Salisb. CC (1948–*).

RAMSBURY

AP Usual civ spelling; for eccl see following entry. *LG* Seq 31. *Parl* Seq 5.

RAMSBURY WITH AXFORD

AP Usual eccl spelling; for civ see prev entry. *Eccl* Pec jurisd Dean of Sarum (until 1847), Seq 23 thereafter.

REDLYNCH

Chap in Downton AP, sep EP 1838,[14] eccl refounded 1841,[161] sep CP 1896.[161] *LG* Salisb. PLU, RD (1896–1934), Salisb. & Wilton RD (1934–74). Civ bdry: 1934.[1] *Parl* Salisb. Dv/CC (1918–*). *Eccl* Wilton RDn (1838–1951), Aldb. RDn (1951–*). Eccl bdry: 1915 (help cr Morgan's Vale EP).[163]

ROAD HILL

EP Cr 1825 from North Bradley AP as 'North Bradley Christ Church',[24] refounded 1852 as 'Road Hill'[63] though usually called 'Rode Hill'. Pott. RDn (1825–72), Bradf. RDn (1872–1923), Frome RDn (Bath & Wells dioc, 1923–*).

RODBOURNE CHENEY

AP *LG* Highw., Crickl. & Staple Hd, Highw. & Swind. PLU (1836–99), Swind. & Highw. PLU (1899–1930), pt Swind. New Town USD (1875–90), Highw. & Swind RSD (pt 1875–90, ent 1890–94), Highw. RD. Civ bdry: 1890 (loses the pt in the USD to Swindon AP).[245] Abol civ 1928 pt to cr Haydon Wick CP, pt to Swindon AP.[32] *Parl* Crickl. Parl Bor (1832–85), N'rn Dv (1885–1918), Swind. Dv (1918–48). *Eccl* Seq 20. Eccl bdry: 1908 (help cr Swindon St Augustine EP),[247] 1930 (help cr Swindon All Saints EP),[246] 1957 (help cr Penhill EP,[239] now called 'Swindon St Peter, Penhill').

RODE HILL–See ROAD HILL

ROLLESTONE

AP *LG* Elst. & Ev. Hd, Amesb. PLU, RSD, RD. Civ bdry: 1885.[164] Abol civ 1934 ent to Shrewton AP.[1] *Parl* S'rn Dv (1832–1918), Salisb. Dv (1918–48). *Eccl* Wylye RDn. Abol eccl 1970 ent to Shrewton AP.[218]

ROUNDWAY

CP Cr 1894 from the pt of Devizes St James CP not in Deviz. MB.[150] *LG* Deviz. PLU, RD. Bdry: 1934,[1] 1956.[149] *Parl* Deviz. Dv/CC (1918–*).

ROWDE

AP *LG* Pott. & Cann. Hd, Deviz. PLU, pt Deviz. MB (1835–94), pt Deviz. USD, pt Deviz. RSD, Deviz. RD. Civ bdry: 1894 (loses the pt in the MB to cr Rowde Within CP),[150] 1934.[1] *Parl* Pt Deviz. Parl Bor (1832–85), remainder and later, Seq 5. *Eccl* Seq 17. Eccl bdry: 1867 (help cr Devizes St Peter EP),[155] 1886,[156] 1927,[157] 1973.[92]

ROWDE WITHIN

CP Cr 1894 from the pt of Rowde AP in Deviz. MB.[150] *LG* Deviz. PLU, MB. Abol 1934 to help cr Devizes CP.[1] *Parl* Deviz. Dv (1918–48).

RUSHALL

AP *LG* Seq 34. *Parl* Seq 5. *Eccl* Seq 7.

SALISBURY

The following have 'Salisbury' in their names. Insofar as any existed at a given time: *LG*, *Parl* sep noted. *Eccl* Salisb. Sub-deanery RDn (until 1872), Wilton RDn (1872–1970), Salisb. & Wilton RDn (1970–*).

CP1–SALISBURY THE CLOSE OF THE CANONS OF THE CATHEDRAL CHURCH–Ex-par area not in Salisb. Bor, sep CP 1858,[49] loses area eccl 1973 to AP2.[211] *LG* Aldb. PLU (1836–99), Salisb. MB (1835–1905), PLU (1895–1905), USD. Bdry: 1897.[235] Abol 1905 to help cr New Sarum CP.[173] *Parl* Salisb. Parl Bor (1832–1918). *Eccl* Pec jurisd Dean of Sarum (until 1847).

AP1–SALISBURY ST EDMUND–*LG* Salisb. incorp for poor (1770–1869), Aldb. PLU (1869–95), Salisb. Bor/MB, USD, PLU (1895–1905). Abol civ 1905 to help cr New Sarum CP.[173] *Parl* Salisb. Parl Bor (1295–1918). Eccl bdry: 1960.[248] Abol eccl 1974 to help cr EP4.[249]

EP1–SALISBURY ST FRANCIS–Cr 1937 from Stratford sub Castle AP, EP2.[250] Bdry: 1968.[253]

EP2–SALISBURY ST MARK–Cr 1899 from AP2.[251] Bdry: 1937 (help cr EP1),[250] 1960.[248]

AP2–SALISBURY ST MARTIN–Incl tg Milford (not in Bor/MB but in Und. Hd, sep CP 1866[3]). *LG* Salisb. incorp for poor (1770–1869), Aldb. PLU (1869–95), pt Salisb. Bor, Salisb. MB (pt 1835–66, ent 1866–1905), Salisb. USD, PLU (1895–1905). Abol civ 1905 to help cr New Sarum CP.[173] *Parl* Salisb. Parl Bor (pt 1295–1832, ent 1832–1918). Eccl bdry: 1899 (cr EP2),[251] 1973 (incl gains pt eccl area of the Close [as CP1 when cr]).[211]

EP3–SALISBURY ST MICHAEL–Cr 1938 from Fugglestone with Bemerton AP, Fisherton Anger AP.[171]

AP3–SALISBURY ST THOMAS–*LG* As for AP1. Abol civ 1905 to help cr New Sarum CP.[173] *Parl* As for AP1. Eccl bdry: 1973.[172] Abol eccl 1974 to help cr EP4.[249]

EP4–SALISBURY ST THOMAS AND ST EDMUND–Cr 1974 by union AP3, AP1.[249]

NEW SARUM

CP Cr 1905 by union Fisherton Anger Within CP, Fisherton Anger Without CP, Harnham CP, Milford CP, Milford Within CP, Salisbury St Edmund AP, Salisbury St Martin AP, Salisbury St Thomas AP, Salisbury The Close of the Canons of the Cathedral Church CP.[173] *LG* Salisb. PLU, MB. Bdry: 1927,[181] 1954.[79] *Parl* Salisb. Dv/CC (1918–*).

OLD SARUM
Ex-par place, sep CP 1858,[49] eccl abol 1953 ent to Stratford sub Castle AP.[252] *LG* Und. Hd, Aldb. PLU, RSD. Abol 1894 ent to Stratford sub Castle AP.[120] *Parl* Old Sarum Parl Bor (1295–1832), Wilton Parl Bor (1832–85), S'rn Dv (1885–1918).

SAVERNAKE
EP Cr 1854 by union ex-par Savernake, pt Preshute AP.[243] Marlb. RDn. Bdry: 1971,[94] 1971.[254] Renamed 1973 'Savernake Christchurch'.[255]
CP Cr 1934 by union North Savernake CP, South Savernake with Brimslade and Cadley CP.[1] *LG* Marlb. & Ramsb. RD. *Parl* Deviz. CC (1948–*).

NORTH SAVERNAKE
Ex-par place, sep CP 1858.[49] *LG* Kinw. Hd, Marlb. PLU, RSD, RD. Bdry: 1901.[234] Abol 1934 pt to help cr Savernake CP, pt to Marlborough CP.[1] *Parl* S'rn Dv (1867–85), E'rn Dv (1885–1918), Deviz. Dv (1918–48).

SOUTH SAVERNAKE WITH BRIMSLADE AND CADLEY
Ex-par place, sep CP 1858.[49] Organisation as for North Savernake.

SAVERNAKE CHRISTCHURCH
EP Renaming 1973 of Savernake EP.[255] Pewsey RDn.

SAVERNAKE FOREST
EP Cr 1864 from Great Bedwyn AP, Little Bedwyn AP, Burbage AP.[27] Marlb. RDn (1864–1959), Pewsey RDn (1959–*).

SEAGRY
AP *LG* Malm. Hd, Chip. PLU, RSD, RD. Abol civ 1934 ent to Sutton Benger AP.[1] *Parl* Crickl. Parl Bor (1832–85), N-W'rn Dv (1885–1918), Chip. Dv (1918–48). *Eccl* Malm. RDn (until 1866), Malm. South RDn (1866–87), Chip. RDn (1887–1967), Malm. RDn (1967–*).
CP Cr 1971 from Sutton Benger AP.[256] *LG* Calne & Chip. RD.

SEEND
Chap in Melksham AP, sep CP 1866,[3] sep EP 1873.[226] *LG* Melk. Hd, PLU (1835–98), RSD, Trowbridge & Melk. PLU (1898–1930), Melk. RD (1894–1934), Deviz. RD (1934–74). *Parl* N'rn Dv (1867–85), W'rn Dv (1885–1918), W'bury Dv (1918–48), Deviz. CC (1948–*). *Eccl* Bradf. RDn (1873–1951), Deviz. RDn (1951–*).

SEDGEHILL
Chap in Berwick St Leonard AP, sep civ identity early, sep EP 1916.[24] *LG* Dunworth Hd, Mere PLU, RSD, RD (1894–1934), Mere & Tisb. RD (1934–74). *Parl* Seq 11. *Eccl* Tisb. RDn (1916–73), Shaft. & Tisb. RDn (1973–*).

SEMINGTON
Chap in Steeple Ashton AP, sep CP 1866.[3] *LG* Whorw. Hd, Melk. PLU (1835–98), RSD, Trowbridge & Melk. PLU (1898–1930), Melk. RD (1934–74), Bradf. & Melk. RD (1934–74). Bdry: 1884,[189] 1894.[120] *Parl* N'rn Dv (1867–85), W'rn Dv (1885–1918), W'bury Dv (1918–48).

SEMLEY
AP *LG* Seq 10. *Parl* Seq 10. *Eccl* Seq 5.

SHALBOURNE
AP Pt Wilts (Kinw. Hd), pt Berks (Kintbury Eagle Hd), the par made ent Wilts 1895.[60] *LG* Hungerford PLU (1835–96), RSD, Hungerford & Ramsb. PLU (1896–1930), Ramsb. RD (1894–1934), Marlb. & Ramsb. RD (1934–74). Addtl civ bdry alt: 1934.[1] *Parl* Wilts pt, Seq 8. *Eccl* Pec jurisd Dean & Canons of Windsor (until 1847), Newbury RDn (dioc Oxford, 1847–1956), Pewsey RDn (1956–*). Eccl bdry: 1856 (help cr Fosbury EP).[176]

SHARNCOTE
AP Usual eccl spelling; for civ see 'Shorncott'. *Eccl* Crickl. RDn. Abol eccl 1881 to help cr Somerford Keynes with Sharncote EP.[205]

SHAW
EP Cr 1843 from Melksham AP.[228] Pott. RDn (1843–72), Bradf. RDn (1872–1972). Renamed 1972 'Shaw and Witley'.[258]

SHAW AND WHITLEY
EP Renaming 1972 of Shaw EP.[258] Bradf. RDn.

SHERRINGTON
AP *LG* Branch & Dole Hd, Warm. PLU, RSD, RD (1894–1934), Warm. & W'bury RD (1934–74). Civ bdry: 1884.[52] *Parl* Seq 12. *Eccl* Seq 12. Eccl bdry: 1930.[133]

SHERSTON
CP Cr 1896 by union Sherston Magna AP, Sherston Pinkney AP.[118] *LG* Malm. PLU, RD. Bdry: 1966.[86] *Parl* Chip. Dv/CC (1918–*).

SHERSTON MAGNA
AP *LG* Chip. Hd, Malm. PLU, RSD, RD. Civ bdry: 1883,[12] 1884.[86] Abol civ 1896 to help cr Sherston CP.[118] *Parl* N'rn Dv (1832–85), N-W'rn Dv (1885–1918). *Eccl* Malm. RDn. Incl by 1640 Sherston Parva AP, thereafter 'Sherston Magna with Sherston Parva', qv.

SHERSTON MAGNA WITH SHERSTON PARVA
EP Cr by 1640 by union Sherston Magna AP, Sherston Parva AP (in ruins). *Eccl* Seq 21.

SHERSTON PINKNEY
AP Usual civ spelling; eccl usually 'Sherston Parva', united eccl by 1640 with Sherston Magna AP as 'Sherston Magna with Sherston Parva', qv. *LG*, civ abol, *Parl* as for Sherston Magna.

SHINFIELD
AP Pt Berks (Charlton Hd, Theale Hd), pt Wilts (tg Didnam, Amesb. Hd), the latter transf to Berks 1832 for parl purposes, 1844 for civ purposes.[200] See main entry in Berks.

SHORNCOTT
AP Usual civ spelling; for eccl see 'Sharncote'. *LG* Highw., Crickl. & Staple Hd, Cirencester PLU, RSD. Abol civ 1894 ent to Somerford Keynes AP.[257] *Parl* Crickl. Parl Bor (1832–85), N-W'rn Dv (1885–1918).

SHREWTON
AP *LG* Seq 5. Civ bdry: 1885,[52] 1934 (gains Maddington AP, Rollestone AP).[1] *Parl* Seq 9. *Eccl* Seq 12. Eccl bdry: 1970 (gains Maddington AP, Rollestone AP).[218]

SLAUGHTERFORD
AP *LG* Chip. Hd, PLU, RSD, RD. Civ bdry: 1883,[12] 1884.[39] Abol civ 1934 ent to Biddestone AP.[1] *Parl* N'rn Dv (1832–85), N-W'rn Dv (1885–1918), Chip. Dv (1918–48). *Eccl* Seq 22.

GREAT SOMERFORD
AP *LG* Seq 27. Civ bdry: 1883.[12] *Parl* Malm. Parl Bor (1832–85), N-W'rn Dv (1885–1918), Chip. Dv/CC (1918–*). *Eccl* Seq 22.

LITTLE SOMERFORD
AP Organisation as for Great Somerford, incl civ bdry alt.

SOPWORTH
AP *LG* Seq 13. Civ bdry: 1966.[86] *Parl* Seq 6. *Eccl* Seq 21.

SOUTHBROOM
Chap (pec jurisd Dean & Chapter of Sarum) in Bishops Cannings AP (eccl, 'Bishop's Cannings'), sep EP 1832,[24] sep CP 1866 as 'Devizes St James',[3] qv. *Eccl* Aveb. RDn (1832–72), Cann. RDn (1872–1951), Deviz. RDn (1951–*). Eccl bdry: 1871 (help cr Devizes St Peter EP),[155] 1886,[156] 1952,[152] 1970.[99]

SOUTHWICK
Tg in North Bradley AP, sep CP 1866.[3] *LG* Seq 37. Bdry: 1885,[62] 1937.[259] *Parl* N'rn Dv (1867–85), W'rn Dv (1885–1918), W'bury Dv/CC (1918–*).

STANDLYNCH
Area in Downton AP, sep civ identity early, no sep eccl identity. *LG* Down. Hd, Aldb. PLU (1836–95), RSD, Salisb. PLU (1895–97), RD. Abol 1897 ent to Downton AP.[87] *Parl* S'rn Dv (1832–1918).

STANDLYNCH WITH CHARLTON ALL SAINTS
CP Cr 1897 from Downton AP.[87] *LG* Salisb. PLU, RD. Abol 1934 ent to Downton AP.[1] *Parl* Salisb. Dv (1918–48).

STANTON FITZWARREN
AP *LG* Seq 21. Civ bdry: 1883,[12] 1884.[44] *Parl* Seq 2. *Eccl* Seq 20.

STANTON ST BERNARD
AP *LG* Seq 33. *Parl* Seq 5. *Eccl* Seq 19.

STANTON ST QUINTIN
AP *LG* Seq 26. Civ bdry: 1883.[12] *Parl* Seq 3. *Eccl* Seq 22.

STAPLEFORD
AP *LG* Seq 6. Civ bdry: 1884.[23] *Parl* Seq 9. *Eccl* Seq 12.

STAVERTON
Chap (pec jurisd Bp of Sarum) in Trowbridge AP, sep EP 1839,[260] sep CP 1894 (the pt not in Trowbridge USD).[227] *LG* Melk. PLU (1894–98), RD (1894–1934), Trowbridge & Melk. PLU (1898–1930), Bradf. & Melk. RD (1934–74). *Parl* W'bury Dv/CC (1918–*). *Eccl* Pott. RDn (1847–72), Bradf. RDn (1872–*). Eccl bdry: 1870 (help cr Trowbridge St Thomas EP),[261] 1955.[192]

STERT
Tg in Urchfont AP, sep CP 1866.[3] *LG* Seq 33. Bdry: 1894.[120] *Parl* N'rn Dv (1867–85), E'rn Dv (1885–1918), Deviz. Dv/CC (1918–*).

STOCKTON
AP *LG* Elst. & Ev. Hd, Warm. PLU, RSD, RD (1894–1934), Warm. & W'bury RD (1934–74). Civ bdry: 1934.[1] *Parl* Seq 12. *Eccl* Seq 12. Eccl bdry: 1930.[174]

UPPER STOUR
EP Cr 1973 by union Bourton AP (Dorset), Zeals EP, Stourton with Gasper AP.[262] Heytb. RDn.

STOURTON WITH GASPER
AP Pt Somerset (Norton Ferris Hd), pt Wilts (Mere Hd), the par made ent Wilts 1895.[60] *LG* Mere PLU, RSD, RD (pt 1894–95, ent 1895–1934), Mere & Tisb. RD (1934–74). Addtl civ bdry alt: 1966.[86] *Parl* Wilts pt, Seq 11. *Eccl* Wylye RDn (until 1872), Heytb. RDn (1872–1973). Abol eccl 1973 to help cr Upper Stour EP.[262]

STRATFORD SUB CASTLE
AP *LG* Und. Hd, Aldb. PLU (1836–95), pt Salisb. Bor/MB (until 1897), pt Salisb. USD, pt Aldb. RSD, Salisb. PLU (1895–1930), Salisb. RD (pt 1894–97, ent 1897–1934), Salisb. & Wilton RD (1934–54). Civ bdry: 1894,[120] 1897 (loses the pt in the MB to Milford Within CP),[235] 1904,[78] 1927.[181] Abol civ 1954 pt to New Sarum CP, pt to Laverstock AP.[79] *Parl* Salisb. Parl Bor (pt 1832–67, ent 1885–1918), Wilton Parl Bor (pt 1832–67, ent 1867–85), Salisb. Dv/CC (1918–70). *Eccl* Seq 10. Eccl bdry: 1937 (help cr Salisbury St Francis EP),[250] 1953 (gains ex-par Old Sarum),[252] 1957,[217] 1968.[253]

STRATFORD TONY
AP *LG* Seq 8. Civ bdry: 1883,[12] 1885.[77] *Parl* Pt Wilton Parl Bor (1832–85), S'rn Dv (pt 1832–85, ent 1885–1918), Salisb. Dv/CC (1918–*). *Eccl* Seq 4.

UPPER STRATTON
EP Cr 1932 from Stratton St Margaret AP.[263] Crickl. RDn. Bdry: 1957 (help cr Penhill EP, now called 'Swindon St Peter, Penhill').[239]

STRATTON ST MARGARET
AP *LG* Highw., Crickl. & Staple Hd, Highw. & Swind. PLU (1836–99), Swind. & Highw. PLU (1899–1930), pt Swind. New Town USD (1875–90), Highw. & Swind. RSD (pt 1875–90, ent 1890–94), Highw. RD. Civ bdry: 1890 (loses the pt in the USD to Swindon AP),[245] 1928,[32] 1952.[264] *Parl* Seq 2. Parl bdry: 1951.[284] *Eccl* Pec jurisd Vicar of Corsham and Bp of Sarum (until 1847), Seq 20 thereafter. Eccl bdry: 1890 (cr New Swindon St Barnabas, Gorse Hill EP),[265] 1932 (cr Upper Stratton EP),[263] 1972 (help cr Swindon St Paul, Covingham EP).[123]

STUDLEY
EP Cr 1858 from Trowbridge Holy Trinity EP.[266] Pott. RDn (1858–72), Bradf. RDn (1872–*). Bdry: 1922.[267]

SUTTON BENGER
AP *LG* Seq 26. Civ bdry: 1883,[12] 1884,[39] 1934 (gains Seagry AP),[1] 1971 (cr Seagry CP).[256] *Parl* Seq 3. *Eccl* Seq 21.

SUTTON MANDEVILLE

AP *LG* Cawd. & Cad. Hd, Tisb. PLU, RSD, RD (1894–1934), Mere & Tisb. RD (1934–74). *Parl* Seq 10. *Eccl* Chalke RDn (until 1872), Tisb. RDn (1872–1959), Chalke RDn (1959–*).

SUTTON VENY

AP *LG* Seq 36. Civ bdry: 1884,[52] 1885,[236] 1934.[1] *Parl* Seq 12. *Eccl* Seq 13. Eccl bdry: 1959.[140]

SWALLOWCLIFFE

AP *LG* Seq 16. *Parl* Seq 10. *Eccl* Pec jurisd Dean of Sarum (until 1847), Seq 5 thereafter.

SWALLOWFIELD

AP Pt Berks (Charlton Hd), pt Wilts (Amesb Hd), the par made ent Berks 1832 for parl purposes, 1844 for civ purposes.[200] See main entry in Berks.

SWINDON

The following have 'Swindon' in their names. Insofar as any existed at a given time: *LG* Kingsbr. Hd, Highw. & Swind. PLU (1836–99), Swind. & Highw. PLU (1899–1930), pt Old Swind. USD, pt Swind. New Town USD, pt Old Swind. UD, pt Swind. New Town UD (1894–1900), Swind. MB (1900–74). *Parl* Crickl. Parl Bor (1832–85), N'rn Dv (1885–1918), Swind. Dv (1918–48), Swind. BC (1948–*). *Eccl* Crickl. RDn.

AP1–SWINDON–Civ bdry: 1884,[212] 1890 (gains the pts of Rodbourne Cheney AP, Stratton St Margaret AP in Swind. New Town USD),[245] 1928,[32] 1934,[1] 1952,[264] 1969.[121] Parl bdry: 1951,[284] 1971.[283] Eccl bdry: 1846 (cr EP2).[268]

EP1–SWINDON ALL SAINTS–Cr 1930 from Rodbourne Cheney AP, EP2.[246]

EP2–SWINDON NEW TOWN–Cr 1846 from AP1.[270] Bdry: 1881 (cr EP6),[269] 1908 (help cr EP3),[247] 1930 (cr EP1),[246] 1965 (gains EP6).[271]

EP3–SWINDON ST AUGUSTINE–Cr 1908 from Rodbourne Cheney AP, EP2.[247]

EP4–SWINDON ST BARNABAS, GORSE HILL–Cr 1890 from Stratton St Margaret AP.[265]

EP5–SWINDON ST PAUL, COVINGHAM–Cr 1972 from Stratton St Margaret AP, Wanborough AP, Liddington AP (all three in dioc Bristol), Chiseldon with Draycott Foliatt EP (Sarum), to be in Bristol dioc.[123]

–SWINDON ST PETER, PENHILL–Name used now for EP cr as 'Penhill', qv.

EP6–NEW SWINDON ST PAUL–Cr 1881 from EP2.[269] Abol 1965 ent to EP2.[271]

TEFFONT

CP Cr 1934 by union Teffont Evias AP, Teffont Magna CP.[1] *LG* Mere & Tisb. RD. *Parl* W'bury CC (1948–*).

TEFFONT EVIAS

AP *LG* Dunworth Hd, Tisb. PLU, RSD, RD. Abol civ 1934 to help cr Teffont CP.[1] *Parl* S'rn Dv (1832–1918), Salisb. Dv (1918–48). *Eccl* Chalke RDn. Abol eccl 1922 to help cr Teffont Evias with Teffont Magna EP.[159]

TEFFONT EVIAS WITH TEFFONT MAGNA

EP Cr 1922 by union Teffont Evias AP, chap Teffont Magna of Dinton with Teffont Magna AP.[159] Chalke RDn.

TEFFONT MAGNA

Chap in Dinton AP (eccl, 'Dinton with Teffont Magna' before 1922), sep civ identity early, eccl severed 1922 to help cr Teffont Evias with Teffont Magna EP.[159] *LG* Warm. Hd, Tisb. PLU, RSD, RD. Abol civ 1934 to help cr Teffont CP.[1] *Parl* As for Teffont Evias.

TIDCOMBE–See following entry

TIDCOMBE AND FOSBURY

AP *LG* Seq 24. Civ bdry: 1934.[1] *Parl* Seq 8. *Eccl* Marlb. RDn (until 1886), Pewsey RDn (1886–*). Eccl bdry: 1856 (cr Fosbury EP [hence this par eccl 'Tidcombe and Fosbury' before 1856, 'Tidcombe' thereafter]),[176] 1879 (gains ex-par Hippenscombe).[197]

TIDWORTH

EP Cr 1972 by union North Tidworth AP, South Tidworth AP (Hants), to be in Sarum dioc.[272] Avon RDn.

NORTH TIDWORTH

AP *LG* Amesb. Hd, Andover PLU (1835–79), RSD (1875–79), Pewsey PLU (1879–1930), RSD (1879–94), RD. *Parl* Seq 8. *Eccl* Amesb. RDn (until 1951), Avon RDn (1951–72). Abol eccl 1972 to help cr Tidworth EP.[272]

TISBURY

AP *LG* Dunworth Hd, perhaps Tisbury Bor.[281] Abol civ 1834 to cr 3 CPs of East Tisbury, West Tisbury, Wardour.[273] *Parl* S'rn Dv (1832–67). *Eccl* Seq 5.

CP Cr 1927 by union East Tisbury CP, Wardour CP.[274] *LG* Tisb. PLU, RD (1927–34), Mere & Tisb. RD (1934–74). *Parl* W'bury CC (1948–*).

EAST TISBURY

CP Cr 1834 from Tisbury AP.[273] *LG* Dunworth Hd, Tisb. PLU, RSD, RD. Bdry: 1883,[12] 1885.[110] Abol 1927 to help cr Tisbury CP.[274] *Parl* S'rn Dv (1867–1918), Salisb. Dv (1918–48).

WEST TISBURY

CP Cr 1834 from Tisbury AP.[273] *LG* Seq 16. *Parl* S'rn Dv (1867–1918), Salisb. Dv/CC (1918–*).

TILSHEAD

AP *LG* Tilshead Bor (status not sustained), pt Branch & Dole Hd, pt Whorw. Hd, Amesb. PLU, RSD, RD. *Parl* Pt N'rn Dv, pt S'rn Dv (1832–85), E'rn Dv (1885–1918), Salisb. Dv/CC (1918–*). *Eccl* Seq 12.

TOCKENHAM

AP *LG* Seq 22. Civ bdry: 1969.[214] *Parl* Seq 1. *Eccl* Seq 14. Eccl bdry: 1963.[217]

TOLLARD ROYAL

AP Pt Wilts (Chalk Hd), pt Dorset (Cranborne Hd), made ent Wilts in 1860s.[282] *LG* Tisb. PLU, RSD, RD (1894–1934), Mere & Tisb. RD (1934–74). *Parl* Wilts pt, Seq 10. *Eccl* Chalke RDn (until 1872), Tisb. RDn (1872–1951), Blandf. RDn (1951–70), Milton & Blandf. RDn (1970–*) (last 2 in Dorset AD).

TOYD FARM WITH ALLENFORD
Ex-par place, sep CP 1858.[49] *LG* Dam. Hd, Fordingbridge PLU (1858[153]–1930), RSD, sep RD in Wilts (1894–95), Transf 1895 to Hants.[65] *Parl* S'rn Dv (1867–1918).

TROWBRIDGE
AP Incl chap Staverton (sep EP 1839,[260] sep CP 1894 [the pt not in Trowbridge USD][227]). *LG* Melk. Hd, PLU (1835–98), Trowbridge Bor, pt Trowbridge USD, pt Melk. RSD, Trowbridge & Melk. PLU (1898–1930), Trowbridge UD. Addtl civ bdry alt: 1883,[12] 1897,[15] 1897,[188] 1934.[1] *Parl* Seq 7. *Eccl* Pec jurisd Bp of Sarum and pec of Trowbridge (until 1847), Seq 9 thereafter. Addtl eccl bdry alt: 1839 (cr Trowbridge Holy Trinity EP),[260] 1870 (help cr Trowbridge St Thomas EP),[261] 1954.[16]

TROWBRIDGE HOLY TRINITY
EP Cr 1839 from Trowbridge AP.[260] Pott. RDn (1839–72), Bradf. RDn (1872–*). Bdry: 1858 (cr Studley EP),[266] 1922.[267]

TROWBRIDGE ST THOMAS
EP Cr 1870 from Trowbridge AP, Staverton EP.[261] Pott. RDn (1870–72), Bradf. RDn (1872–*).

TYTHERINGTON
Chap in Heytesbury AP, sep civ identity early (Heytb. Hd, Warm. PLU) but sep civ status not sustained and incl in Heytesbury AP, no sep eccl identity.

TYTHERTON KELLAWAYS
AP *LG* Chip. Hd, PLU, RSD, RD. Civ bdry: 1883,[12] 1884,[39] 1884.[69] Abol civ 1895 to help cr Kellaways CP.[22] *Parl* N'rn Dv (1832–85), N-W'rn Dv (1885–1918). *Eccl* Seq 21.

UPAVON
AP *LG* Seq 34. *Parl* Seq 5. *Eccl* Seq 7.

UPTON LOVELL
AP *LG* Seq 19. *Parl* Seq 12. *Eccl* Wylye RDn (until 1872), Heytb. RDn (1872–1954), Wylye RDn (1954–71), Wylye & Wilton RDn (1971–*).

UPTON SCUDAMORE
AP *LG* Seq 36. Civ bdry: 1883,[12] 1884,[52] 1934 (help cr Chapmanslade CP).[1] *Parl* Seq 12. *Eccl* Seq 13. Eccl bdry: 1954,[139] 1959.[140]

URCHFONT
AP Incl tg Stert (sep civ identity early, no sep eccl identity hence this par eccl 'Urchfont with Stert', qv). *LG* Seq 33. Addtl civ bdry alt: 1934.[1] *Parl* Seq 5.

URCHFONT WITH STERT
AP Usual eccl spelling; for civ and civ sep chap Stert, see prev entry. *Eccl* Seq 8. Eccl bdry: 1874 (help cr Easterton EP).[166]

WANBOROUGH
AP *LG* Seq 23. Civ bdry: 1884,[44] 1969.[121] *Parl* Crickl. Parl Bor (1832–85), N'rn Dv (1885–1918), Deviz. Dv/CC (1918–*). Parl bdry: 1971.[283] *Eccl* Seq 20. Eccl bdry: 1972 (incl help cr Swindon St Paul, Covingham EP).[123]

WARDOUR
CP Cr 1834 from Tisbury AP.[273] *LG* Dunworth Hd, Tisb. PLU, RSD, RD. Bdry: 1885.[13] Abol civ 1927 to help cr Tisbury CP.[274] *Parl* S'rn Dv (1867–1918), Salisb. Dv (1918–48).

WARMINSTER
AP *LG* Warm. Hd, PLU, pt Warm. Bor,[275] Warm. USD (ent 1875–83, pt 1883–85, ent 1885–94), Warm. UD. Civ bdry: 1883,[12] 1884,[52] 1934.[1] *Parl* Seq 12. *Eccl* Seq 13. Eccl bdry: 1838 (cr Warminster Christ Church EP),[276] 1868,[203] 1956 (incl loses pt to help reconstitute Bishopstrow AP as Bishopstrow and Boreham EP),[42] 1959.[140]

WARMINSTER CHRIST CHURCH
EP Cr 1838 from Warminster AP.[276] Wylye RDn (1838–72), Heytb. RDn (1872–*). Bdry: 1868,[203] 1956 (help reconstitute Bishopstrow AP as Bishopstrow and Boreham EP),[42] 1959.[203]

WEST WELLOW
Tg (in Wilts, Amesbury Hd) in East Wellow AP (o'wise Hants, Thorngate Hd), sep civ identity early in Wilts, no sep eccl identity. *LG* Romsey PLU, RSD, sep RD in Hants (1894–95). Transf 1895 to Hants.[65] *Parl* S'rn Dv (1832–1918).

WESTBURY
AP Incl chap Dilton Marsh (sep CP 1894,[68] sep EP 1845 as 'Diltons Marsh'[67]), chap Heywood (sep CP 1894,[68] sep EP 1894[184]), chap Bratton (sep CP 1894,[68] sep EP 1845[67]). *LG* W'bury Hd, pt W'bury Bor,[275] W'bury PLU, RSD, RD (1894–99), UD (1899–1974). Addtl civ bdry alt: 1883,[12] 1909.[185] *Parl* W'bury Parl Bor (pt 1448–1832, ent 1832–85), W'rn Dv (1885–1918), W'bury Dv/CC (1918–*). *Eccl* Pec jurisd Precenter of Sarum (until 1847), Seq 13 thereafter.

WESTPORT ST MARY
AP Incl chaps Charlton, Brokenborough (each sep civ identity early, sep EP 1879 as 'Charlton with Brokenborough'[82]). *LG* Malm. Hd, PLU, pt Malm. MB & USD (1886–94), Malm. RSD (ent 1875–86, pt 1886–94). Addtl civ bdry alt: 1883,[12] 1884,[73] 1884.[72] Abol civ 1894 the pt in the MB to cr Westport St Mary Within CP, the remainder to cr Westport St Mary Without CP.[83] *Parl* Malm. Parl Bor (1832–85), N-W'rn Dv (1885–1918). *Eccl* Malm. RDn (until 1866), Malm. North RDn (1866–87), Malm. RDn (1887–1946). Abol eccl 1946 to help cr Malmesbury with Westport St Mary EP.[219]

WESTPORT ST MARY WITHIN
CP Cr 1894 from the pt of Westport St Mary AP in Malm. MB.[83] *LG* Malm. PLU, MB. Bdry: 1896,[118] 1897.[87] Abol 1934 to help cr Malmesbury CP.[1] *Parl* Chip. Dv (1918–48).

WESTPORT ST MARY WITHOUT
CP Cr 1894 from the pt of Westport St Mary AP not in Malm. MB.[83] *LG* Malm. PLU, RD. Abol 1896 ent to Malmesbury St Paul Without CP.[118]

WESTWOOD
Chap in Bradford-on-Avon AP, sep civ identity early, sep EP 1876.[55] *LG* Elst. & Ev. Hd, Bradf. PLU (1835–95), RSD, Bradf.-on-Avon PLU (1895–1930), RD (1894–1934), Bradf. &

Melk. RD (1934–74). Civ bdry: 1883,[12] 1885,[277] 1934.[1] *Parl* Seq 12. *Eccl* Bradf. RDn.

WHADDON

AP *LG* Melk. Hd, PLU, RSD. Civ bdry: 1884.[189] Abol civ 1894 ent to Semington CP.[120] *Parl* N'rn Dv (1832–85), W'rn Dv (1885–1918). *Eccl* Pott. RDn. Abol eccl 1854 to help cr Hilperton with Whaddon EP.[191]

WHITEPARISH

AP *LG* Seq 18. Civ bdry: 1885.[241] *Parl* Seq 9. *Eccl* Seq 1.

WHITSBURY

AP *LG* Cadw. & Cad. Hd, Fordingbridge PLU, RSD, sep RD in Wilts (1894–95). Transf 1895 to Hants.[65] *Parl* S'rn Dv (1832–1918). *Eccl* In dioc Winch; see entry in Hants.

WILCOT

AP *LG* Seq 34. Civ bdry: 1885.[9] *Parl* Seq 5. *Eccl* Seq 24. Eccl bdry: 1858 (cr Oare EP,[24] re-founded 1892[198]), 1932.[8]

WILSFORD

AP Incl tg and chap Manninford Bohune (sep CP 1866,[3] sep EP 1859[24] but sep eccl status not sustained, eccl severed 1939 pt to help cr Woodborough with Manningford Bohune EP, pt to Manningford Bruce AP[221]). *LG* Seq 34. Addtl civ bdry alt: 1885.[164] *Parl* Seq 5. *Eccl* Pott. RDn (until 1872), Enf. RDn (1872–1951), Avon RDn (1951–56), Deviz. RDn (1956–*).

WILSFORD CUM LAKE

AP *LG* Seq 35. *Parl* Seq 9. *Eccl* Amesb. RDn (until 1956), Deviz. RDn (1956–*).

WILTON

AP Incl chap Netherhampton (sep civ identity early, no sep ecc identity hence this par eccl 'Wilton with Netherhampton', qv). *LG* Pt Branch & Dole Hd, pt Cawd. & Cad. Hd, pt Wilton Bor, Wilton PLU, RSD (1875–85), Wilton MB (1885–1974). Civ bdry: 1883,[12] 1894 (gains Burcombe Within CP, South Newton Within CP, pt Fugglestone St Peter AP),[30] 1934.[1] *Parl* Wilton Parl Bor (pt 1295–1832, ent 1832–85), S'rn Dv (1885–1918), Salisb. Dv/CC (1918–*).

WILTON WITH NETHERHAMPTON

AP Usual eccl spelling; for civ and civ sep chap Netherhampton, see prev entry. *Eccl* Wilton RDn (until 1971), Wylye & Wilton RDn (1971–72). Abol eccl 1972 to help cr Wilton with Netherhampton and Fugglestone EP.[31]

WILTON WITH NETHERHAMPTON AND FUGGLESTONE

EP Cr 1972 by union Wilton with Netherhampton AP, pt Bemerton with Fugglestone EP.[31] Wylye & Wilton RDn.

WINGFIELD

AP *LG* Seq 4. Civ bdry: 1883,[12] 1885,[277] 1885,[278] 1934,[1] 1966.[86] *Parl* Seq 7. *Eccl* Seq 9.

WINSLEY

Chap in Bradford-on-Avon AP, sep EP 1846,[19] sep CP 1894 (from Bradford Without CP).[56] *LG* Bradf. PLU (1894–95), Bradf.-on-Avon PLU (1895–1930), RD (1894–1934), Bradf. & Melk. RD (1934–74). Civ bdry: 1934.[1] *Parl* W'bury Dv/CC (1918–*). *Eccl* Pott. RDn (1846–72), Bradf. RDn (1872–*).

WINTERBOURNE

CP Cr 1934 by union Winterbourne Dauntsey AP, Winterbourne Earls AP, Winterbourne Gunner AP.[1] *LG* Amesb. RD. *Parl* Salibs. CC (1948–*).

WINTERBOURNE BASSETT

AP *LG* Seq 32. *Parl* Seq 5. *Eccl* Aveb. RDn (until 1974), Marlb. RDn (1974–*).

WINTERBOURNE DAUNTSEY

AP *LG* Aldb. Hd, Amesb. PLU, RSD, RD. Civ bdry: 1885.[202] Abol civ 1934 to help cr Winterbourne CP.[1] *Parl* S'rn Dv (1832–1918), Salisb. Dv (1918–48). *Eccl* Pec jurisd Prebend of Chute and Chisenbury and Dean of Sarum (until 1847), Amesb. RDn (1847–72), Aldb. RDn (1872–1973). Eccl bdry: 1956.[279] Abol eccl 1973 to help cr Winterbourne Earls and Dauntsey EP.[203]

WINTERBOURNE EARLS

AP As for Winterbourne Dauntsey except not in pec jurisd (Amesb. RDn until 1872).

WINTERBOURNE EARLS AND DAUNTSEY

EP Cr 1973 by union Winterbourne Earls AP, Winterbourne Dauntsey AP, pts Laverstock AP, Idmiston with Porton AP, Winterbourne Gunner AP.[203] Aldb. RDn.

WINTERBOURNE GUNNER

AP *LG* Aldb. Hd, Amesb. PLU, RSD, RD. Civ bdry: 1885.[202] Abol civ 1934 to help cr Winterbourne CP.[1] *Parl* As for Winterbourne Dauntsey. *Eccl* Seq 1. Eccl bdry: 1973 (help cr Winterbourne Earls and Dauntsey EP).[203]

WINTERBOURNE MONKTON

AP *LG* Seq 32. *Parl* Seq 5. *Eccl* Aveb. RDn. Abol eccl 1865 to help cr Winterbourne Monkton with Berwick Bassett EP.[35]

WINTERBOURNE MONKTON WITH BERWICK BASSETT

EP Cr 1865 by union Winterbourne Monkton AP, Berwick Bassett EP.[35] Aveb. RDn. Abol eccl 1970 to help cr Avebury with Winterbourne Monkton and Berwick Bassett EP.[21]

WINTERBOURNE STOKE

AP *LG* Seq 5. Civ bdry: 1885.[164] *Parl* Seq 9. *Eccl* Seq 12.

WINTERSLOW

AP *LG* Seq 1. Civ bdry: 1883,[12] 1883,[280] 1934.[1] *Parl* Seq 9. *Eccl* Seq 1. Eccl bdry: 1956,[279] 1973.[203]

GREAT WISHFORD

AP Usual civ spelling; for eccl see following entry. *LG* Seq 6. *Parl* Seq 13.

WISHFORD MAGNA

AP Usual eccl spelling; for civ see prev entry. *Eccl* Seq 12. Eccl bdry: 1952 (gains ex-par Groveley Wood).[211]

WOKINGHAM

AP Pt Wilts (Amesb. Hd), pt Berks (Sonning Hd), the former transf to Berks 1832 for parl purposes, 1844 for civ purposes.[200] See main entry in Berks.

WOODBOROUGH
AP *LG* Seq 34. *Parl* Seq 5. *Eccl* Aveb. RDn (until 1872), Cann. RDn (1872–1939). Abol eccl 1939 to help cr Woodborough with Manningford Bohune EP.[222]

WOODBOROUGH WITH MANNINGFORD BOHUNE
EP Cr 1939 by union Woodborough AP, pt chap Manningford Bohune in Wilsford with Manningford Bohune AP.[222] Cann. RDn (1939–51 [but Manningford Bohune remains Enf. RDn this period]), Pewsey RDn (1951–*).

WOODFORD
AP *LG* Seq 35. *Parl* Seq 13. *Eccl* Pec jurisd Prebend of Wilsford and Woodford and Dean of Sarum (until 1847), Seq 3 thereafter.

WOOTTON BASSETT
AP *LG* Woot. Bas. Bor, Seq 22. *Parl* Woot. Bas. Parl Bor (1447–1832), Seq 1 thereafter. *Eccl* Seq 14. Eccl bdry: 1973 (gains pt Lydiard Tregoz AP, loses pt to Brinkworth AP, both Bristol dioc).[74]

WOOTTON RIVERS
AP *LG* Seq 25. *Parl* Seq 8. *Eccl* Seq 24. Eccl bdry: 1971.[254]

WORTON
Tg and chap in Potterne AP, sep EP 1852,[242] sep CP 1866.[3] *LG* Seq 30. Civ bdry: 1884,[89] 1934.[1] *Parl* N'rn Dv (1867–85), E'rn Dv (1885–1918), Deviz. Dv/CC (1918–*). *Eccl* Pott. RDn (1852–1951), Deviz. RDn (1951–*).

NORTH WRAXALL
AP *LG* Seq 12. Civ bdry: 1971.[119] *Parl* Seq 6. *Eccl* Seq 21.

SOUTH WRAXALL
Chap in Bradford-on-Avon AP, sep CP 1894 (from Bradford Without CP),[56] combined eccl 1846 with chap Atworth in same par to cr Atworth with South Wraxall EP.[19] *LG* Bradf. PLU (1894–95), Bradf.-on-Avon PLU (1895–1930), RD (1894–1934), Bradf. & Melk. RD (1934–74). Bdry: 1934.[1] *Parl* W'bury Dv/CC (1918–*).

WROUGHTON
AP *LG* Elst. & Ev. Hd, Highw. & Swind. PLU (1836–99), RSD, Swind. & Highw. PLU (1899–1930), Highw. RD. Civ bdry: 1928,[32] 1934.[1] *Parl* Pt Crickl. Parl Bor (1832–85), remainder and later, Seq 4. *Eccl* Seq 6.

WYLYE
AP *LG* Seq 6. Civ bdry: 1934.[1] *Parl* Seq 10. *Eccl* Seq 12.

YATESBURY
AP *LG* Calne Hd, PLU, RSD, RD. Abol civ 1934 ent to Cherhill CP.[1] *Parl* N'rn Dv (1832–85), N-W'rn Dv (1885–1918), Chip. Dv (1918–48). *Eccl* Seq 14.

YATTON KEYNELL
AP *LG* Seq 12. *Parl* Seq 6. *Eccl* Seq 21.

ZEALS
Chap in Mere AP, sep EP 1848,[232] sep CP 1896.[233] *LG* Mere PLU, RD (1896–1934), Mere & Tisb. RD (1934–74). *Parl* W'bury Dv/CC (1918–*). *Eccl* Wylye RDn (1848–72), Heytb. RDn (1872–1973). Abol eccl 1973 to help cr Upper Stour EP.[262]

Part II: Local Government Units

AVON

NON-METROPOLITAN COUNTY

As constituted 1 Apr 1974, defined in terms of Adm Co units as of 31 Mar.

BATH DIST
Bath CB
BRISTOL DIST
Bristol CB
KINGSWOOD DIST
From Glos: Kingswood UD, Mangotsfield UD, Warmley RD
NORTHAVON DIST
From Glos: pt Sodbury RD (all except Alderley), pt Thornbury RD (Almondsbury, Alveston Aust, Charfield, Cromhall, Falfield, Hill, Oldbury upon Severn, Olveston, Patchway, Pilning and Severn Beach, Rangeworthy, Rockhampton, Thornbury, Tortworth, Tytherington)
WANDSDYKE DIST
From Somerset: Bathavon RD, pt Clutton RD (Cameley, Chelwood, Chew Magna, Chew Stoke, Clutton, Compton Martin,[1] Farmborough, Farrington Gurney, East Harptree,[1] West Harptree,[1] Hinton Blewett, High Littleton, Nempnett Thrubwell, Norton Malreward, Paulton, Publow, Stanton Drew, Stowey-Sutton, Timsbury, Ubley[1]), Keynsham UD, Norton-Radstock UD, unannexed area adjacent to Kensham UD
WOODSPRING DIST
From Somerset: Long Ashton RD, pt Axbridge RD (Banwell, Blagdon,[1] Bleadon, Burrington,[1] Butcombe, Churchill, Congresbury, Hutton, Kewstoke, Locking, Loxton,[2] Puxton, Wick St Lawrence, Winscombe, Wrington), Clevedon UD, Portishead UD, Steep Holme Island, Weston-super-Mare MB

BEDFORDSHIRE

ALTERATIONS IN COUNTY BOUNDARIES

As noted by year below, Beds pars gained territory from or lost it to pars in adjoining counties or county borough, or were entirely transferred to them. Details of these alterations are noted in Part I of the *Guide* under Beds.

ANCIENT COUNTY (until 1889: Hds, Bors, MBs, PLUs, RSDs, USDs)
1844 Everton, Ickleford, Meppershall, Studham. *1885* Aspley Heath.

ADMINISTRATIVE COUNTY (1889–1974: Hds,[1] PLUs, MBs, RDs, UDs, with Luton CB associated 1964–74)
1894 Caddington, Studham. *1896* Swineshead, Tilbrook. *1897* Caddington, Holwell, Houghton Regis, Humbershoe, Kensworth, Shillington, Studham, Whipsnade. *1907* Caddington, Hyde, Shillington, Studham. *1947* Arlesey. *1956* Arlesey, Aspley Guise, Hulcote and Salford. *1964* Caddington, Hyde, Luton, Streatley, Sundon, Toddington. *1965* Aspley Heath, Caddington, Eaton Socon, Everton, Hyde, Leighton Buzzard, Melchbourne and Yelden, Stotford, Tempsford, Wymington.

NON-METROPOLITAN COUNTY (from 1974: Dists)

ASSOCIATED COUNTY BOROUGH

Luton MB was made a CB in 1964. There were no bdry alts 1964–74.

HUNDREDS[1]

BARFORD HD
Great Barford, Colmworth, Eaton Socon, Goldington, Ravensden, Renhold, Roxton, Wilden

BIGGLESWADE HD
Astwick, Little Barford, Biggleswade,[2] Dunton, Edworth, pt Everton (ent from 1844), Eyeworth, Cockayne Hatley, Langford, Potton, pt Sandy, Sutton, Tempsford, Wrestlingworth

CLIFTON HD
Arlesey, Campton, Chicksands (from 1858), Clifton, Henlow, Holwell, pt Ickleford (until 1844), pt Meppershall (ent from 1844), Shefford (from 1866), Shefford Hardwick (from 1858), pt Shillington, Upper Stondon, Stotfold

FLITT HD
Barton in the Clay, pt Caddington, Clophill, Flitton, Lower Gravenhurst, Upper Gravenhurst, Haynes, Higham Gobion, Luton,[2] Pulloxhill, pt Shillington, Silsoe (from 1866), Streatley, Sundon

MANSHEAD HD
Aspley Guise, Aspley Heath (from 1883), Battlesden, Billington (from 1866), Chalgrave, Dunstable,[2] Eaton Bray, Eggington (from 1866), Eversholt, Harlington, Heath and Reach (from 1866), Hockliffe, Holcot, Houghton Regis, Humbershoe (from 1866), Husborne Crawley, Leighton Buzzard,[2] Milton Bryan, Potsgrove, Salford, Stanbridge (from 1866), pt Studham, Tilsworth, Tingrith, Toddington,[2] Totternhoe, Westoning, pt Whipsnade, Woburn

REDBORNSTOKE HD
Ampthill, Cranfield, Elstow, Flitwick, Houghton Conquest, Kempston, Lidlington, Marston Moretaine, Maulden, Milbrook, Ridgmont, Steppingley, Wilshamstead, Wotton

STODDEN HD
Bolnhurst, Clapham, Dean, Keysoe, Knotting, Melchbourne, Milton Ernest, Oakley, Pertenhall, Riseley, Shelton, Little Staughton, Tilbrook, Yelden

WILLEY HD[3]
Biddenham, Bletsoe, Bromham, Carlton, Chellington, pt Farndish (until 1844), Felmersham, Harrold, Odell, Pavenham, Podington, Sharnbrook, Souldrop, Stagsden, Stevington, Thurleigh, Turvey, Wymington

BOROUGHS

Units with some degree of burghal character[4] are denominated 'Bor'.
Those which did not sustain that status until the 19th cent are in italics.
Municipal Boroughs were established by the Municipal Corporations Act, 1835,[5] or by later charter.

BEDFORD BOR/MB
Bedford (1934–74), Bedford All Saints (until 17th cent), Bedford St Cuthbert (until 1934), Bedford St John (until 1934), Bedford St Mary (until 1934), Bedford St Paul (until 1934), Bedford St Peter (until 1934), Bedford St Peter Dunstable (until 1545)

BIGGLESWADE BOR[6]
Biggleswade

DUNSTABLE BOR, MB (1864[7]–1974)
Dunstable

LEIGHTON BUZZARD BOR[8]
Leighton Buzzard

LUTON BOR,[9] MB (1876[10]–1964), CB (1964[11]–74)
pt Luton (1876–94), Luton (1896–1974), Luton Urban (1894–96)

TODDINGTON BOR[12]
Toddington

POOR LAW UNIONS[13]

In Bedfordshire Poor Law County:[14]

AMPTHILL PLU[15]
Ampthill, Aspley Guise (1899–1930), Aspley Heath (1899–1930), Battlesden (1899–1930), Clophill, Cranfield, Eversholt (1899–1930), Flitton, Flitwick, Gravenhurst (1888–1930), Lower Gravenhurst (1835–88), Upper Gravenhurst (1835–88), Harlington (1899–1930), Haynes, Higham Gobion, Holcot (1899–1930), Houghton Conquest, Husborne Crawley (1899–1930), Lidlington, Marston Moretaine, Maulden, Millbrook, Milton Bryan (1899–1930), Potsgrove (1899–1930), Pulloxhill, Ridgmont (1899–1930), Salford (1899–1930), Shillington, Silsoe, Steppingley, Tingrith (1899–1930), Toddington (1899–1930), Westoning, Woburn (1899–1930)

BEDFORD PLU
Great Barford, Bedford St Cuthbert, Bedford St John, Bedford St Mary, Bedford St Paul, Bedford St Peter, Biddenham, Bletsoe, Bolnhurst, Bromham, Cardington, Carlton, Chellington, Clapham, Colmworth, Colworth Farm (1858–95), Cople, Eastcotts, Elstow, Felmersham, Goldington, Harrold, Kempston, Kempston Rural (1896–1930), Keysoe, Knotting, Melchbourne, Milton Ernest, Oakley, Odell, Pavenham, Ravensden, Renhold, Riseley, Roxton, Sharnbrook, Souldrop, Stagsden, Stevington, Thurleigh, Turvey, Wilden, Willington, Wilshamstead, Wootton, Yelden

BIGGLESWADE PLU
Arlesey, Astwick, Biggleswade, Blunham, Campton, Chicksands (1858–1930), Clifton, Dunton, Edworth, Everton, Eyeworth, Cockayne Hatley, Henlow, Langford, Meppershall, Moggerhanger, Northill, Potton, Sandy, Shefford, Shefford Hardwick, Southill, Upper Stondon, Stotfold, Sutton, Tempsford, Old Warden, Wrestlingworth

LEIGHTON BUZZARD PLU[15]
Billington, Chalgrave (1899–1930), Eaton Bray (18 –1930), Eggington, Heath and Reach, Hockliffe (1899–1930), Leighton Buzzard, Stanbridge, Tilsworth (1899–1930)

LUTON PLU
Barton in the Clay, Caddington, Dunstable, Eaton Bray (1835–40s), Houghton Regis, Humbershoe (1835–97), Hyde (1896–1930), Kensworth, Leagrave (1896–1928), Limbury (1896–1928), Luton (1835–94), Luton (1896–1930), Luton Rural (1894–96), Luton Urban (1894–96), Streatley, Stopsley (1896–1930), Studham, Sundon, Totternhoe, Whipsnade

WOBURN PLU[15]
Aspley Guise, Aspley Heath (1883–99), Battlesden, Chalgrave, Eversholt, Harlington, Hockliffe, Holcot, Husborne Crawley, Milton Bryan, Potsgrove, Ridgmont, Salford, Tilsworth, Tingrith, Toddington, Woburn

In Other Poor Law Counties:

HITCHIN PLU[16] (Herts)
Holwell

ST NEOTS PLU[17] (Hunts)
Little Barford, Dean, Eaton Socon, Pertenhall, Shelton, Little Staughton, Tilbrook

WELLINGBOROUGH PLU (Northants)
Farndish (1835–84), Podington, Wymington

SANITARY DISTRICTS

AMPTHILL RSD
same as PLU less Ampthill (1893–94)
AMPTHILL USD[18] (1893–94)
Ampthill
BEDFORD RSD
same as PLU less the Bedford pars
BEDFORD USD
Bedford St Cuthbert, Bedford St John, Bedford St Mary, Bedford St Paul, Bedford St Peter
BIGGLESWADE RSD
same as PLU less Biggleswade (1892–94)
BIGGLESWADE USD[19] (1892–94)
Biggleswade
DUNSTABLE USD
Dunstable

HITCHIN RSD
same as PLU for Beds par
LEIGHTON BUZZARD RSD
same as PLU less Leighton Buzzard (1891–94)
LEIGHTON BUZZARD USD[20] (1891–94)
Leighton Buzzard
LUTON RSD
same as PLU less Dunstable, Luton (ent 1875–76, pt 1876–94)
LUTON USD
Luton (ent 1875–76, pt 1876–94)
ST NEOTS RSD
same as PLU for Beds pars
WELLINGBOROUGH RSD
same as PLU for Beds pars
WOBURN RSD
same as PLU

ADMINISTRATIVE COUNTY

For CB and MBs, see BOROUGHS earlier in this Part of the *Guide*.

AMPTHILL RD
Aspley Guise, Aspley Heath, Battlesden, Clophill, Cranfield, Eversholt, Flitton, Flitwick, Gravenhurst, Harlington, Haynes, Higham Gobion, Holcot (1894–1933), Houghton Conquest, Hulcote and Salford (1933–74), Husborne Crawley, Lidlington, Marston Moretaine, Maulden, Millbrook, Milton Bryan, Potsgrove, Pulloxhill, Ridgmont, Salford (1894–1933), Shillington, Silsoe, Steppingley, Tingrith, Toddington (1894–1933), Westoning, Woburn
AMPTHILL UD
Ampthill
BEDFORD RD
Great Barford, Little Barford (1934–74), Biddenham, Bletsoe, Bolnhurst (1894–1934), Bolnhurst and Keysoe (1934–74), Bromham, Cardington, Carlton (1894–1934), Carlton and Chellington (1934–74), Chellington (1894–1934), Clapham, Colmworth, Colworth Farm (1894–95), Cople, Dean and Shelton (1934–74), Eastcotts, Eaton Socon (1934–65), Elstow, Felmersham, Goldington (1894–1934), Harrold, Kempston (1894–96), Kempston Rural (1896–1974), Keysoe (1894–1934), Knotting (1894–1934), Knotting and Souldrop (1934–74), Melchbourne (1894–1934), Melchbourne and Yelden (1934–74), Milton Ernest, Oakley, Odell, Pavenham, Pertenhall (1934–74), Podington, Ravensden, Renhold, Riseley, Roxton, Sharnbrook, Souldrop (1894–1934), Stagsden, Staploe (1965–74), Little Staughton (1934–74), Stevington, Stewartby (1934–74), Swineshead (1934–74), Thurleigh, Turvey, Wilden, Willington, Wilshamstead, Wootton, Wymington, Yelden (1894–1934)

BIGGLESWADE RD
Arlesey, Astwick, Blunham, Campton, Chicksands, Clifton, Dunton, Edworth, Everton, Eyeworth, Cockayne Hatley, Henlow, Langford, Meppershall, Moggerhanger, Northill, Potton, Sandy (1894–1927), Shefford, Shefford Hardwick (1894–1933), Southill, Upper Stondon, Stotfold, Sutton, Tempsford, Old Warden, Wrestlingworth
BIGGLESWADE UD
Biggleswade
EATON BRAY RD (1894–1933[21])
Billington, Chalgrave, Eaton Bray, Eggington, Heath and Reach, Hockliffe, Stanbridge, Tilsworth
EATON SOCON RD (1894–1934[22])
Little Barford, Dean, Eaton Socon, Pertenhall, Shelton, Little Staughton, Swineshead
KEMPSTON UD (1896[23]–1974)
Kempston
LEIGHTON BUZZARD UD (1894–1965[24])
Leighton Buzzard
LEIGHTON-LINSLADE UD (1965[24]–74)
Leighton-Linslade
LUTON RD
Barton in the Clay (1894–1956), Barton-le-Cley (1956–74), Billinggton (1933–74), Caddington, Chalgrave (1933–74), Eaton Bray (1933–74), Eggington (1933–74), Heath and Reach (1933–74), Hockliffe (1933–74), Houghton Regis, Humbershoe (1894–97), Hyde (1896–1974), Kensworth, Leagrave (1896–1928), Limbury (1896–1928), Luton Rural (1894–96), Stanbridge (1933–74), Stopsley (1896–1933), Streatley, Studham, Suundon, Tilsworth (1933–74), Toddington (1933–74), Totternhoe, Whipsnade
SANDY UD (1927[25]–74)
Sandy

NON-METROPOLITAN COUNTY

As constituted 1 Apr 1974, defined in terms of Adm Co units as of 31 Mar.

BEDFORD DIST
Bedford MB, Berford RD, Kempston UD

LUTON DIST
Luton CB

MID BEDFORDSHIRE DIST
Ampthill RD, Ampthill UD, Biggleswade RD, Biggleswade UD, Sandy UD

SOUTH BEDFORDSHIRE DIST
Dunstable MB, Leighton-Linslade UD, Luton RD

BERKSHIRE

ALTERATIONS IN COUNTY BOUNDARIES

As noted by year below, Berks pars gained territory from or lost it to pars in adjoining counties or county boroughs, or were entirely transferred to them. Details of these alterations are noted in Part I of the *Guide* under Berkshire.

ANCIENT COUNTY (until 1889: Hds, Bors, MBs, PLUs, RSDs, USDs)
1844 Great Baringdon, Hurst, Shalbourne, Shingfield, Wokingham. *1866* Sonning, Stratfield Mortimer, Stratfield Saye. *1881* Coleshill. *1885* North Hinksey, South Hinksey.

ADMINISTRATIVE COUNTY (1889–1974: Hds,[1] PLUs, MBs, RDs, UDs, with Reading CB associated)

NON-METROPOLITAN COUNTY (from 1974: Dists)
1974 Abingdon, Abingdon St Helen Without, Appleford, Appleton with Eaton, Ardington, Ashbury, Aston Tirrold, Aston Upthorpe, Baulking, Besslesleigh, Blewbury, Bourton, Brightwell-cum-Sotwell, Britwell, Buckland, Buscot, East Challow, West Challow, Charney Bassett, Childrey, Chilton, Cholsey, Coleshill, Compton Beauchamp, Great Coxwell, Little Coxwell, Cumnor, Datchet, Denchworth, Didcot, Drayton, Eaton Hastings, Eton, Great Faringdon, Fernham, Frilford, Fyfield and Tubney, Garford, Goosey, Grove, East Hagbourne, West Hagbourne, East Hanney, West Hanney, Harwell, Hatford, East Hendred, West Hendred, North Hinksey, South Hinksey, Hinton Waldrist, Horton, Kennington, Kingston Bagpuize with Southmoor, Kingston Lisle, Letcombe Bassett, Letcombe Regis, Littleworth, Lockinge, Longcott, Longworth, Lyford, Marcham, Milton, North Moreton, South Moreton, Moulsford, Pusey, Radley, Shellingford, Shrivenham, Slough, Sparsholt, Stanford in the Vale, Steventon, Sunningwell, Sutton Courtenay, Uffington, Upton, Wallingford, Wantage, Watchfield, Wexham Court, Little Wittenham, Long Wittenham, Woolstone, Wootton, Wraysbury, Wytham
1889 Burghfield, Earley, Oxford St Aldate, Shinfield, Sonning, Tilehurst. *1894* Abingdon St Nicholas, Culham, North Hinksey, South Hinksey, Seacourt, Whitchurch. *1895* Chilton Foliat, Combe, Hungerford, Shalbourne. *1911* Theale, Tilehurst.

ASSOCIATED COUNTY BOROUGH

READING CB
Bdry: 1889 (gains the pts of non-Reading pars in the CB), 1911 (gains pt Berks pars of Theale, Tilehurst, ent Caversham UD [Oxon])

HUNDREDS[1]

BEYNHURST HD
Bisham, Hurley, Remenham, Shottesbrooke, White Waltham

BRAY HD
Bray[2]

CHARLTON HD
Barkham, Broad Hinton (from 1866), Earley[2] (from 1866), Finchampstead, pt Hurst (1844–66), pt Shinfield[2] (ent from 1844), pt Sonning[2] (until 1866), pt Swallowfield, Whistley (from 1866)

COMPTON HD
Adlworth, Catmore, Chilton, Compton, Farnborough, East Ilsley, West Ilsley

COOKHAM HD
Binfield, Cookham,[2] Sunninghill

FAIRCROSS HD
Beedon, pt Boxford, Brightwalton, Brimpton, Chieveley, Frilsham, Greenham[2] (from 1866), Hampstead Norris, Leckhampstead (from 1866), Midgham, Newbury,[2] Peasemore, Sandleford (from 1858), Shaw cum Donnington, pt Speen,[2] Stanford Dingley, pt Thatcham (until 1866), Wasing, Welford, Winterbourne (from 1866), Yattendon

FARINGDON HD
pt Great Barrington (until 1844), Great Coxwell,[2] Little Coxwell (from 1866), pt Great Faringdon,[2] pt Inglesham (until 1844), pt Langford (until 1844), pt Shilton (until 1844)

GANFIELD HD
Buckland, Charney Bassett (from 1866), Hatford, Hinton Waldrist, pt Longworth (ent from 1866), Pusey, Shellingford, pt Stanford in the Vale (ent from 1866)

HORMER HD
Abingdon St Helen,[2] Abingdon St Nicholas,[2] Bagley Wood (from 1858), Besselsleigh, Chandlings Farm (from 1858), Cumnor, North Hinksey,[2] South Hinksey,[2] pt Oxford St Aldate,[2] Radley, Seacourt (from 1858), Sunningwell, Wootton, Wytham

KINTBURY EAGLE HD
Avington, pt Boxford, Chaddldworth, East Challow (from 1866), West Challow (from 1866), pt Chilton Foliat, Enborne, Fawley, Hampstead Marshall, pt Hungerford,[2] Inkpen, Kintbury, Letcombe Bassett, Letcombe Regis, pt Shalbourn, East Shefford, West Shefford, pt Speen, West Woodhay

LAMBOURN HD
pt East Garston, Lambourn[2]

MORETON HD
Ashampstead, Aston Tirrold, Aston Upthorpe (from 1866), Basildon, pt Blewbury (until 1866), Brightwell, Didcot, pt East Garston, Hagbourne (until 1866), East Hagbourne (from 1866), West Hagbourne (from 1866), Harwell, North Moreton, South Moreton, Moulsford, Sotwell, Streatley, Upton (from 1866), Wallingford All Hallows,[2] Wallingford Castle Precincts[2] (from 1858), Wallingford St Leonard,[2] Wallingford St Mary le More,[2] Wallingford St Peter[2]

OCK HD
Appleford (from 1866), Appleton with Eaton, pt Culham, pt Denchworth (from 1831), Draycot Moor (from 1866), Drayton, Frilford (from 1866), Fyfield, Garford (from 1866), Goosey (from 1866), pt West Hanney (until 1866), Kingston Bagpuize, pt Longworth (until 1866), Lyford (from 1866), Marcham, Milton, pt Stanford in the Vale (until 1866), Steventon, Sutton Courtenay, Sutton Wick[2] (from 1866), Tubney, Little Wittenham, Long Wittenham

READING HD
Beech Hill (from 1866), Beenham, pt Blewbury (ent from 1866), Bucklebury, Cholsey, Grazelev (from 1866), Pangbourne, Reading St Giles,[2] Reading St Lawrence,[2] Reading St Mary,[2] pt Stratfield Mortimer (until mid 17th cent), pt Stratfield Saye (until 1866), Sulhamstead Abbots, pt Swallowfield, pt Thatcham[2] (ent from 1866), Tilehurst,[2] pt Whitchurch

RIPPLESMERE HD
Clewer,[2] Easthampstead, New Windsor,[2] Old Windsor,[2] Winkfield

SHRIVENHAM HD
Ashbury, Baulking (from 1866), Bourton (from 1866), Buscot, pt Coleshill (ent from 1881), Compton Beauchamp, Eaton Hastings, pt Great Faringdon, [2] Ferhham (from 1866), Kingston Lisle (from 1866), Longcott (from 1866), Shrivenham, pt Sparsholt (until 1866), Uffington, Watchfield (from 1866), Woolstone (from 1866)

SONNING HD
Arborfield, pt Hurst (until 1866), Newland (from 1866), Ruscombe, Sandhurst, pt Sonning,[2] Winnersh (from 1866), pt Wokingham[2] (ent from 1844), Woodley and Sandford (from 1866)

THEALE HD
Aldermaston,[2] Bradfield, Burghfield,[2] Englefield, Padworth, Purley, Purley, pt Shinfield, pt Stratfield Mortimer (from mid 17th cent, ent from 1866), Sulham, Sulhamstead Bannister (until 1866), Sulhamstead Bannister Lower End (from 1866), Sulhamstead Bannister Upper End (from 1866), Tidmarsh, Ufton Nervet, Wokefield (from 1866), Woolhampton

WANTAGE HD
Ardington, Charlton (from 1866), Childrey, Denchworth (ent to 1831, pt from 1831), pt East Garston, Grove (from 1866), East Hanney (from 1866), pt West Hanney (ent from 1866), East Hendred, West Hendred, East Lockinge, West Lockinge (from 1866), pt Sparsholt (ent from 1866), Wantage

WARGRAVE HD
Waltham St Lawrence, Warfield, Wargrave[2]

BOROUGHS

Units with some degree of burghal character[3] are denominated 'Bor'. Those which did not sustain that status until the 19th cent are in italics. MBs were established by the Municipal Corporations Act, 1835,[4] or by later charter.

ABINGDON BOR/MB
Abingdon (1894–1974), pt Abingdon St Helen (until 1894), Abingdon St Nicholas (ent until 1883, pt 1883–94), pt Culham (1890–94), pt Sutton Wick (1890–94)

ALDERMASTON BOR (until 16th cent[5])
Aldermaston

BRAY BOR (perhaps mediev bor[6])
Bray

FARINGDON BOR[7]
Great Faringdon

HUNGERFORD BOR[8]
Hungerford

LAMBOURN BOR (until 15th cent[9])
Lambourn

MAIDENHEAD BOR/MB
pt Bray (until 1894), pt Cookham (until 1894), Maidenhead (1894–1974)

NEWBURY BOR/MB
pt Greenham (1878–94), Newbury, pt Speen (1878–94)

READING BOR/MB/CB (1888–1974)
pt Burghfield (1887–89), pt Earley (1887–89), Reading (1905–74), Reading St Giles (pt until 1887, ent 1887–1905), Reading St Lawrence (until 1905), Reading St Mary (pt until 1887, ent

1887–1905), pt Shinfield (1887–89), pt Sonning (1887–89), pt Tilehurst (1887–89)

THATCHAM BOR[10]

Thatcham

WALLINGFORD BOR/MB

Wallingford (1919–74), Wallingford All Hallows (pt until 1894, ent 1894–1919), pt Wallingford Castle Precincts (1866–94), Wallingford St Leonard (until 1919), Wallingford St Mary le More (until 1919), Wallingford St Peter (until 1919)

WINDSOR BOR/MB (usually styled 'New Windsor' until 19th cent, now 'Royal Bor of Windsor')

pt Clewer (1835–94), Clewer Within (1894–1974), Clewer Without (1920–74), New Windsor (pt until 1880s, ent 1880s–1974), pt Windsor Castle (1886–1974)

OLD WINDSOR BOR (perhaps mediev bor[11])

Old Windsor

WOKINGHAM BOR, MB (188 –1974)

pt Wokingham (Bor, the pt in Berks; MB, pt until 1894), Wokingham Within (1894–1974)

POOR LAW UNIONS

In Berkshire Poor Law County:[12]

ABINGDON PLU (Berks, Oxon)

Abingdon (1894–1930), Abingdon St Helen (1835–94), Abingdon St Helen Without (1894–1930), Abingdon St Nicholas (1835–94), Appleford, Appleton with Eaton, Bagley Wood (1835–1900), Besselsleigh, Chandlings Farm (1835–1900), Culham, Cumnor, Draycot Moor, Drayton, Frilford, Fyfield, Garford, North Hinksey, South Hinksey, Kingston Bagpuize, Lyford, Marcham, Milton, Radley, Seacourt, Steventon, Sunningwell, Sutton Courtenay, Sutton Wick, Tubney, Wootton, Wytham

BRADFIELD PLU (Berks, Oxon)

Aldermaston, Ashampstead, Basildon, Beech Hill, Beenham, Bradfield, Bucklebury, Burghfield, Englefield, Frilsham, Grazeley, Padworth, Pangbourne, Purley, Stanford Dingley, Stratfield Mortimer, Streatley, Sulham, Sulhamstead Abbots, Sulhamstead Bannister Lower End, Sulhamstead Bannister Upper End, Theale (1894–1930), Tidmarsh, Tilehurst, Ufton Nervet, Whitchurch, Wokefield, Yattendon

COOKHAM PLU (renamed 1899 'MAIDENHEAD')

Bisham, Bray, Cookham, Hurley, Maidenhead (1894–1930), Shottesbrooke, White Waltham, Waltham St Lawrence

EASTHAMPSTEAD PLU

Binfield, Crowthorne (1894–1930), Easthampstead, Sandhurst, Warfield, Winkfield

FARINGDON PLU (Berks, Oxon, Glos)

Ashbury, Baulking, Bourton, Buckland, Buscot, Charney Bassett, Coleshill, Compton Beauchamp, Great Coxwell, Little Coxwell, Eaton Hastings, Great Faringdon, Fernham, Hatford, Hinton Waldrist, Kingston Lisle, Longcott, Longworth, Pusey, Shellingford, Shrivenham, Stanford in the Vale, Uffington, Watchfield, Woolstone

HUNGERFORD PLU (Berks, Wilts, renamed 1896 'HUNGERFORD AND RAMSBURY')

Avington, Chilton Foliat,[13] Combe,[14] East Garston, Hungerford, Inkpen, Kintbury, Lambourn, Shalbourn, East Shefford, West Shefford, West Woodhay

MAIDENHEAD PLU–renaming 1899 of COOKHAM PLU, qv

NEWBURY PLU

Boxford, Brimpton, Chieveley, Cold Ash (1894–1930), Enborne, Greenham, Hamstead Marshall, Leckhampstead, Midgham, Newbury, Sandleford, Shaw cum Donnington, Speen, Thatcham, Wasing, Welford, Winterbourne, Woolhampton

READING PLU

Reading (1905–30), Reading St Giles (1835–1905), Reading St Lawrence (1835–1905), Reading St Mary (1835–1905)

WALLINGFORD PLU

Aston Tirrold, Aston Upthorpe, Brightwell, Cholsey, Clapcot (1894–1930), Didcot, East Hagbourne, West Hagbourne, North Moreton, South Moreton, Moulsford, Sotwell, Wallingford (1919–30), Wallingford All Hallows (1835–1919), Wallingford Castle Precincts (1858–94), Wallingford St Leonard (1835–1919), Wallingford St Mary le More (1835–1919), Wallingford St Peter (1835–1919), Little Wittenham, Long Wittenham

WANTAGE PLU

Aldworth, Ardington, Beedon, Blewbury, Brightwalton, Catmore, Chaddleworth, East Challow, West Challow, Charlton, Childrey, Chilton, Compton, Denchworth, Farnborough, Fawley, Goosey, Grove, Hampstead Norris, East Hanney, West Hanney, Harwell, East Hendred, West Hendred, East Ilsley, West Ilsley, Letcombe Bassett, Letcombe Regis, East Lockinge, West Lockinge, Peasemore, Sparsholt, Upton, Wantage

WINDSOR PLU

Clewer (1835–94), Clewer Within (1894–1930), Clewer Without (1894–1930), Sunningdale (1894–1930), Sunninghill, New Windsor, Old Windsor, pt Windsor Castle (1866–1930)

WOKINGHAM PLU

Arborfield, Barkham, Earley, Finchampstead, Broad Hinton, Hurst St Nicholas (1894–1930), Newland, Remenham (1894–1930), Ruscombe, Shinfield, Sonning, Swallowfield (1894–1930), East Swallowfield (1866–94), West Swallowfield (1866–94), Twyford (1894–1930), Wargrave, Whistley (1835–94), Winnersh, Wokingham (1835–94), Wokingham Within (1894–1930), Wokingham Without (1894–1930)

In Other Poor Law Counties:

HENLEY PLU (Oxon)

Remenham (1835–94)

ADMINISTRATIVE COUNTY

For MBs and associated CB, see BOROUGHS earlier in this Part of the *Guide*.

ABINGDON RD

Abingdon St Helen Without, Appleford, Appleton with Eaton, Bagley Wood (1894– 1900), Besselsleigh, Chandlings Farm (1894–1900), pt Culham (until Nov 1894), Cumnor, Draycot Moor (1894–1971), Drayton, Frilford, Fyfield (1894–1952), Fyfield and Tubney (1952–74), Garford, North Hinksey (pt to Nov 1894, ent Nov 1894–1974), South Hinksey (pt to Nov 1894, ent Nov 1894–1974), Kennington (1936–74), Kingston Bagpuize (1894– 1971), Kingston Bagpuize with Southmoor (1971–74), Lyford, Marcham, Milton, Radley, Seacourt (1894–1900), Steventon, Sunningwell, Sutton Courtenay, Sutton Wick (1894–1934), Tubney (1894–1952), Wootton, Wytham

BRADFIELD RD

Aldermaston, Ashampstead, Basildon, Beech Hill, Beenham, Bradfield, Bucklebury, Burghfield, Englefield, Frilsham, Grazeley, Padworth, Pangbourne, Purley, Stanford Dingley, Stratfield Mortimer, Streatley, Sulham, Sulhamstead (1934–74), Sulhamstead Abbots (1894–1934), Sulhamstead Bannister (1934–74), Sulhamstead Bannister Lower End (1894–1934), Sulhamstead Bannister Upper End (1894–1934), Theale, Tidmarsh,Tilehurst, Ufton Nervet, Wokefield, Yattendon

COOKHAM RD

Bisham, Bray, Cookham, Hurley, Shottesbrooke, White Waltham, Waltham St Lawrence

EASTHAMPSTEAD RD

Binfield, Bracknell (1955–74), Crowtherne, Easthampstead, Sandhurst, Warfield, Winkfield

FARINGDON RD (Berks, Glos until 1934, ent Berks thereafter)

Ashbury, Baulking, Bourton, Buckland, Buscot, Charney Bassett, Coleshill, Compton Beauchamp, Great Coxwell, Little Coxwell, Eaton Hastings, Great Faringdon, Fernham, Hatford, Hinton Waldrist, Kingston Lisle, Littleworth (1952–74), Longcott, Longworth, Pusey, Shellingford, Shrivenham, Stanford in the Vale, Uffington, Watchfield, Woolstone

HUNGERFORD RD

Avington (1894–1934), pt Chilton Foliat (1894–95), Combe (1895–1974), East Garston, Hungerford (pt until 1895, ent 1895–1974), Inkpen, Kintbury, Lambourn, pt Shalbourn (1894–95), East Shefford, West Shefford, West Woodhay

NEWBURY RD

Boxford, Brimpton, Chieveley, Cold Ash, Enborne, Greenham, Hamstead Marshall, Leckhampstead, Midgham, Sandleford (1894–1934), Shaw cum Donnington, Speen, Thatcham, Wasing, Welford, Winterbourne, Woolhampton

WALLINGFORD RD

Aston Tirrold, Aston Upthorpe, Brightwell (1894–1948), Brightwell-cum-Sotwell (1948–74), Cholsey, Clapcot (1894–1934), Didcot, East Hagbourne, West Hagbourne, North Moreton, South Moreton, Moulsford, Sotwell (1894–1948), Little Wittenham, Long Wittenham

WANTAGE RD

Aldworth, Ardington, Beedon, Blewbury, Brightwalton, Catmore, Chaddleworth, East Challow, West Challow, Charlton (1894–1934), Childrey, Chilton, Compton, Denchworth, Farnborough, Fawley, Goosey, Grove, Hampstead Norris (1894–1969), Hampstead Norreys (1969–74), East Hanney, West Hanney, Harwell, East Hendred, West Hendred, Hermitage (1948–74), East Ilsley, West Ilsley, Letcombe Bassett, Letcombe Regis, Lockinge (1934–74), East Lockinge (1894–1934), West Lockinge (1894–1934), Peasemore, Sparsholt, Upton

WANTAGE UD

Wantage

WINDSOR RD

Clewer Without (1894–1920), Sunningdale, Sunninghill, Old Windsor

WOKINGHAM RD

Arborfield (1894–1948), Arborfield and Newland (1948–74), Barkham, Charvil (1970–74), Earley, Finchampstead, Hurst St Nicholas, Newland (1894–1948), Remenham, Ruscombe, Shinfield, Sonning, Swallowfield, Twyford, Wargrave, Winnersh, Wokingham Without, Woodley and Sandford

NON-METROPOLITAN COUNTY

As constituted 1 Apr 1974, defined in terms of Adm Co units as of 31 Mar. A considerable pt of Berks Adm Co was transferred to Oxon Non-Metropolitan Co, qv.

BRACKNELL DIST
Easthampstead RD

NEWBURY DIST
Bradfield RD, Hungerford RD, Newbury MB, Newbury RD, pt Wantage RD (Aldworth, Beedon, Brightwalton, Catmore, Chaddleworth, Compton, Farnborough, Fawley, Hampstead Norreys, Hermitage, East Ilsley, West Ilsley, Peasemore)

READING DIST
Reading CB

SLOUGH DIST
pt Eton RD (Bucks: pt Burnham [cr Britwell CP], pt Wexham [cr Wexham Court CP]), Slough MB (Bucks)

WINDSOR AND MAIDSTONE DIST
Cookham RD, pt Eton RD (Bucks: Datchet, Horton, Wraysbury), Eton UD (Bucks), Maidstone MB, Windsor RD, New Windsor MB

WOKINGHAM DIST
Wokingham MB, Wokingham RD

BUCKINGHAMSHIRE

ALTERATIONS IN COUNTY BOUNDARIES

As noted by year below, Bucks pars gained territory from or lost it to pars in adjoining cos, or were entirely transferred to them. Details of these alterations are noted in Part I of the *Guide* under Buckinghamshire.

ANCIENT COUNTY (until 1889: Hds, Bors, MBs, PLUs, RSDs, USDs)

1844 Beckley, Caversfield, Lewknor, Luffield Abbey, Lillingstone Lovell, Stowe. *1883* Drayton Beauchamp, Marsworth. *1884* Biddlesden. *1885* Edlesborough, Lewknor Uphill, Wavendon. *1886* Ickford, Ilmer. *1888* Marsworth.

ADMINISTRATIVE COUNTY (1889–1974: Hds,[1] PLUs, MBs, RDs, UDs)

1894 Hanslope. *1895* Ivinghoe, Kingsey, Nettleden, Stokenchurch. *1896* Ibstone. *1907* Ashley Green, Chalfont St Peter, Chenies, Denham, Edlesborough, Gerrard's Cross, Hawridge, Latimer. *1933* Towersey. *1956* Chetwode, Marsh Gibbon, Wavendon. *1965* Linslade, Wavendon, Woburn Sands.

NON-METROPOLITAN COUNTY (from 1974: Dists)

1974 Burnham, Datchet, Eton, Horton, Slough, Wexham, Wraysbury.

HUNDREDS[1]

ASHENDON HD

Ashendon, Aston Sandford, pt Beckley (until 1844), Boarstall, Brill, Chearsley, Chilton, East Claydon, Middle Claydon, Long Crendon, pt Dinton-with-Ford and Upton, Dorton, Granborough, Grendon Underwood, Hogshaw, pt Ickford, Ilmer, pt Kingsey, Kingswood (from 1866), Ludgershall, Fleet Marston, Oakley,[2] Oving, Pitchcott, Quainton, Quarrendon, Shabbington, Shipton Lee (from 1866), Towersey, Waddesdon, Westcott (from 1866), Lower Winchendon, Upper Winchendon, Woodham (from 1866), Worminghall, Wotton Underwood

AYLESBURY HD

Aston Clinton, Aylesbury,[2] Bierton with Broughton, Bledlow, Buckland, Cuddington, pt Dinton-with-Ford and Upton, Ellesborough, Haddenham, Halton, Great Hampden (until 1885), Great and Little Hampden (from 1885), Little Hampden (until 1885), Hartwell, Horsenden, Hulcott, Great Kimble (until 1885), Great and Little Kimble (from 1885), Little Kimble (until 1885), Lee, Great Missenden, Little Missenden, Monk's Risborough, Princes Risborough, Stoke Mandeville, Stone, Wendover,[2] Weston Turville

BUCKINGHAM HD

Addington, Adstock, Akeley, Barton Hartshorn, Beachampton, Biddlesden, Buckingham,[2] Caversfield (until 1844), Charndon (from 1866), Chetwode, Steeple Claydon, Edgcott, Foscott, Hillesden, Leckhampstead, Lillingstone Dayrell, Lillingstone Lovell (from 1844), Luffield Abbey (from 1858), Marsh Gibbon, Maids' Moreton, Padbury, Poundon (from 1866), Preston Bissett, Radclive-cum-Chackmore, Shalstone, Stowe, Water Stratford, pt Stratton Audley (until 1844), Thornborough, Thornton, Tingewick, Turweston, Twyford, Westbury

BURNHAM HD

pt Amersham[2] (ent from 1844), Beaconsfield, Boveney (from 1866), Burnham, Chalfont St Giles, Chalfont St Peter, Chenies, Chesham, Chesham Bois, Coleshill (from 1866), Dorney, Farnham Royal, Hedgerley Dean (from 1866), Hitcham, Penn, Seer Green (from 1866), Taplow

COTTESLOE HD

Aston Abbots, Cheddington, Cholesbury, Creslow, Cublington, Drayton Beauchamp, Drayton Parslow, Dunton, Edlesborough, Grove, Hardwick, Hawridge, Hoggeston, Great Horwood, Little Horwood, Ivinghoe, Linslade, Marsworth, Mentmore, Mursley, Nash (from 1866), Nettleden (from 1866), Pitstone, pt Shenley (until 1866), Shenley Brook End (from 1866), Slapton, Soulbury, Stewkley, Swanbourne, Tattenhoe, Weedon (from 1866), Whaddon, Whitchurch, Wing, Wingrave with Rowsham, Winslow

DESBOROUGH HD

Bradenham, pt Dinton-with-Ford and Upton, Fawley, Fingest, Hambleden, Hedsor, Hughenden, pt Ibstone, pt Lewknor (1844–66), pt Lewknor Uphill (1866–85), Great Marlow,[2] Little Marlow, Medmenham, Radnage, Saunderton, Turville, Wooburn, Wycombe (from 1866),[2] Chepping Wycombe,[2] West Wycombe

NEWPORT HD

Astwood, Bletchley,[2] Bradwell, Bradwell Abbey (from 1858), Cold Brayfield, Bow Brickhill, Great Brickhill, Little Brickhill, Broughton, Calverton, Castlethorpe, Chicheley, Clifton Reynes, North Crawley, Emberton, Filgrave (until 1639), Gayhurst, pt Hanslope, Hardmead, Haversham, Lathbury, Lavendon, Great Linford, Little Linford, Loughton, Milton Keynes, Moulsoe, Newport Pagnell,[2] Newton Blossomville, Newton Longville, Olney,[2] Olney Park Farm (from 1858), Petsoe Manor (from 1858), Ravenstone, pt Shenley (until 1866), Shenley Church End (from 1866), Sherington, Simpson,[2] Stantonbury, Stoke Goldington, Stoke Hammond, Fenny Stratford (from 1866), Stony Stratford (until late 18th cent), Stony Stratford East (from late 18th cent), Stony Stratford West (from late 18th cent), Tyringham (until 1639), Tyringham with Filgrave (from 1639), Walton, Warrington (from 1866), Water Eaton (from 1866), Wavendon, Weston Underwood, Willen, Wolverton, Great Woolstone, Little Woolstone, Woughton on the Green

STOKE HD

Datchet, Denham, Eton, Fulmer, Hedgerley, Horton, Iver, Langley Marish, Stoke Poges, Upton cum Chalvey, Wexham, Wyrardisbury

BOROUGHS

Units with some degree of burghal character[3] are denominated 'Bor'.
Those which did not sustain that status until the 19th cent are in italics.
MBs were established by the Municipal Corporations
Act, 1835,[4] or by later charter.

AMERSHAM BOR
Amersham

AYLESBURY BOR, MB (1917[5]–74)
Aylesbury (pt until 1835, ent thereafter)

BRILL BOR
pt Oakley

BUCKINGHAM BOR/MB
Buckingham

GREAT MARLOW BOR/MB
Great Marlow

NEWPORT PAGNELL BOR
Newport Pagnell

OLNEY BOR
Olney

SLOUGH MB (1938[6]–74)
Slough

FENNY STRATFORD BOR
pt Bletchely, pt Simpson

WENDOVER BOR
Wendover

CHEPPING WYCOMBE BOR/MB (1832–1946[7])
Wycombe (1866–94), pt Chepping Wycombe (until 1894, enlarged pt 1832–94), Chepping Wycombe Urban (1894–96), High Wycombe (1896–1946)

HIGH WYCOMBE MB (1946[7]–74)
High Wycombe

POOR LAW UNIONS

In Buckinghamshire Poor Law County:[9]

AMERSHAM PLU

Amersham, Ashley Green (1897–1930), Beaconsfield, Chalfont St Giles, Chalfont St Peter, Chartridge (1899–1930), Chenies, Chesham, Chesham Bois, Coleshill, Latimer (1899–1930), Lee (1838–1930), Great Missenden (1838–1930), Little Missenden (1901–30), Penn, Seer Green

AYLESBURY PLU

Ashendon, Aston Abbots, Aston Clinton, Aston Sandford, Aylesbury, Bierton with Broughton, Buckland, Chearsley, Cholesbury, Creslow, Cublington, Cuddington, Dinton-with-Ford and Upton, Drayton Beauchamp, Grendon Underwood, Haddenham, Halton, Hardwick, Hartwell, Hawridge, Hulcott, Kingswood, Ludgershall, Fleet Marston, Oving, Pitchcott, Quainton, Quarrendon, Shipton Lee (1835–86), Stone, Waddesdon, Weedon, Westcott, Weston Turville, Whitchurch, Lower Winchendon, Upper Winchendon, Wingrave with Rowsham, Woodham, Wotton Underwood

BUCKINGHAM PLU

Addington, Adstock, Akeley, Barton Hartshorn, Beachampton, Charndon, Chetwode, Middle Claydon, Steeple Claydon, Edgcott, Foscott, Hillesden, Leckhampstead, Lillingstone Dayrell, Lillingstone Lovell,[10] Luffield Abbey (1858–1930), Marsh Gibbon, Maids' Moreton, Padbury, Poundon, Preston Bissett, Radclive-cum-Chackmore, Shalstone, Stowe, Water Stratford, Thornborough, Thornton, Tingewick, Twyford

ETON PLU

Boveney, Burnham, Datchet, Denham, Dorney, Eton, Eton Wick (1894–1930), Farnham Royal, Fulmer, Gerrard's Cross (1895–1930), Hedgerley, Hedgerley Dean, Hitcham, Horton, Iver, Langley Marish, Slough (1894-1930), Stoke in Slough (1894–96), Stoke Poges, Taplow, Upton cum Chalvey (1835–1901), Wexham, Wyrardisbury

NEWPORT PAGNELL PLU

Astwood, Bletchley, Bradwell, Bradwell Abbey (1861-1930), New Bradwell (1919–30), Cold Brayfield, Bow Brickhill, Great Brickhill, Little Brickhill, Broughton, Castlethorpe, Chicheley, Clifton Reynes, North Crawley, Emberton, Gayhurst, Hanslope, Hardmead, Haversham, Lathbury, Lavendon, Great Linford, Little Linford, Loughton, Milton Keynes, Moulsoe, Newport Pagnell, Newton Blossonville, Newton Longville, Olney, Olney Park Farm (1861–1930), Petsoe Manor (1861–1930), Ravenstone, Shenley Church End, Sherington, Stantonbury, Stoke Goldington, Fenny Stratford,

Tyringham with Filgrave, Warrington, Water Eaton, Wavendon, Weston Underwood, Woughton on the Green

WINSLOW PLU

East Claydon, Drayton Parslow, Dunton, Granborough, Hoggeston, Hogshaw, Great Horwood, Little Horwood, North Marston, Mursley, Nash, Shenley Brook End, Stewkley, Swanbourne, Tattenhoe, Whaddon, Winslow

WYCOMBE PLU

Bledlow, Bradenham, Ellesborough, Fawley (1835–45), Fingest, Hambledon (1835–45), Great Hampden (1835–85), Great and Little Hampden (1885–1930), Little Hampden (1835–85), Hedsor, Horsenden, Hughenden, Ibstone, Ilmer, Great Kimble (1835–85), Great and Little Kimble (1885–1930), Little Kimble (1835–85), Lewknor Uphill (1866–85), Great Marlow, Little Marlow, Marlow Urban (1896–1930), Medmenham (1835–45), Little Missenden (1835–1901), Radnage, Monk's Risborough, Princes Risborough, Saunderton, Stoke Mandeville, Stokenchurch,[10] Turville, Wendover, Wooburn, Wycombe (1866–96), Chepping Wycombe (1835–94), Chepping Wycombe Rural (1894–1930), Chepping Wycombe Urban (1894–96), High Wycombe (1896–1930), West Wycombe

In Other Poor Law Counties:

BERKHAMPSTEAD PLU (Herts)

Marsworth, Nettleden,[11] Pitstone (1835–1923)

BICESTER PLU (Oxon)

Boarstall

LEIGHTON BUZZARD PLU (Beds)

Cheddington, Edlesborough, Grove, Ivinghoe, Linslade, Mendmore, Pitstone (1923–30), Slapton, Soulbury, Stoke Hammond, Wing

BRACKLEY PLU[12] (Northants)

Biddlesden, Turweston, Westbury

HENLEY PLU[13] (Oxon)

Fawley, Hambleden, Medmenham

POTTERSPURY PLU[14] (Northants)

Calverton, Stony Stratford East, Stony Stratford West, Wolverton

THAME PLU (Oxon)

Brill, Chilton, Long Crendon, Dorton, Granborough, Ickford, Kingsey,[15] Oakley, Shabbington, Worminghall

SANITARY DISTRICTS

AMERSHAM RSD

same as PLU less Beaconsfield, Chesham (1884–94)

AYLESBURY RSD

same as PLU less Aylesbury

AYLESBURY USD

Aylesbury

BEACONSFIELD USD

Beaconsfield

BERKHAMPSTEAD RSD

same as PLU for Bucks pars

BICESTER RSD

Boarstall only Bucks par

BRACKLEY RSD

same as PLU for Bucks pars

BUCKINGHAM RSD

same as PLU less Buckingham

BUCKINGHAM USD

Buckingham

CHESHAM USD (1884[16]–94)

Chesham

ETON RSD

same as PLU less pt Eton, pt Stoke Poges, pt Upton cum Chalvery

ETON USD

pt Eton

HENLEY RSD

same as PLU for Bucks pars

LEIGHTON BUZZARD RSD

same as PLU for Bucks pars

NEWPORT PAGNELL RSD

same as PLU

POTTERSPURY RSD

same as PLU for Bucks pars

SLOUGH USD

pt Stoke Poges, pt Upton cum Chalvey

THAME RSD

same as PLU for Bucks pars

WINSLOW RSD

same as PLU

WYCOMBE RSD

same as PLU less Wycombe, pt Chepping Wycombe

CHEPPING WYCOMBE USD

Wycombe, pt Chepping Wycombe

ADMINISTRATIVE COUNTY

For MBs see BOROUGHS earlier in this Part of the *Guide*.

AMERSHAM RD

Amersham, Ashley Green (1897–1974), Chalfont St Giles, Chalfont St Peter, Chartridge (1899–1974), Chenies, Chesham Bois, Cholesbury cum St Leonards (1934–74), Coleshill, Latimer (1899–1974), Lee (1894–1954), The Lee (1954–74), Great Missenden, Little Missenden (1901–74), Penn, Seer Green

AYLESBURY RD

Ashendon, Aston Abbots (1894–1934), Aston Clinton, Aston Sandford, Bierton with Broughton, Boarstall (1934–74), Great Brickhill (1894–1934),

Brill (1934–74), Buckland, Chearsley, Chilton (1934–74), Cholesbury (1894–1934), Long Crendon (1934–74), Creslow, Cublington (1894–1934), Cuddington, Dinton-with-Ford and Upton, Dorton (1934–74), Drayton Beauchamp, Granborough (1934–74), Grendon Underwood, Haddenham, Halton, Hardwick, Hartwell, Hawridge (1894–1934), Hulcott, Ickford (1934–74), Kingsey (1933–74), Kingswood, Ludgershall, Fleet Marston, Oakley (1934–74), Oving, Pitchcott, Quainton, Quarrendon, Shabbington (1934–74), Stoke Mandeville, Stone, Waddesdon, Weedon, Wendover, Westcott, Weston Turville, Whitchurch, Lower Winchendon, Upper Winchendon, Wingrave with Rowsham (1894–1934), Woodham, Worminghall (1934–74), Wotton Underwood

AYLESBURY UD (1894–1917[17])
Aylesbury

BEACONSFIELD UD
Beaconsfield

BLETCHLEY UD (1911[18]–74)
Bletchley, Simpson (1911–34), Fenny Stratford (1911–34)

BUCKINGHAM RD
Addington, Adstock, Akeley, Barton Hartshorn, Beachampton, Biddlesden, Charndon, Chetwode, Middle Claydon, Steeple Claydon, Edgcott, Foscott, Hillesden, Leckhampstead, Lillingstone Dayrell, Lillingstone Lovell, Luffield Abbey, Marsh Gibbon, Maids' Moreton, Padbury, Poundon, Preston Bissett, Radclive-cum-Chackmore, Shalstone, Stowe, Water Stratford, Thornborough, Thornton, Tingewick, Turweston, Twyford, Westbury

CHESHAM UD
Chesham

LONG CRENDON RD (1894–1934)
Boarstall , Brill, Chilton, Long Crendon, Dorton, Granborough, Ickford, Oakley, Shabbington, Towersey, Worminghall

ETON RD
Boveney (1894–1934), Burnham, Datchet, Denham, Dorney, Eton Wick (1894–1934), Farnham Royal, Fulmer, Gerrard's Cross (1895–1974), Hedgerley, Hedgerley Dean (1894–1934), Hitcham (1894–1934), Horton, Iver, Langley Marish (1894–1934), Stoke Poges, Taplow, Upton cum Chalvey (1894–1901), Wexham, Wyrardisbury

ETON UD
Eton

HAMBLEDEN RD (1894–1934)
Fawley, Hambleden, Medmenham

LINSLADE UD (1897[20]–1965[21])
Linslade

MARLOW UD (1896[22]–1974)
Marlow Urban

GREAT MARLOW UD (1896[23]–97[22])
Marlow Urban

NEWPORT PAGNELL RD
Astwood, Bletchley (1894–98), Bradwell, Bradwell Abbey, Cold Brayfield, Bow Brickhill, Great Brickhill (1894–1934), Little Brickhill, Broughton, Castlethorpe, Chicheley, Clifton Reynes, North Crawley, Emberton, Gayhurst, Hanslope, Hardmead, Haversham (1894–1934), Haversham cum Little Linford (1934–74), Lathbury, Lavendon, Great Linford, Little Linford (1894–1934), Loughton, Milton Keynes, Moulsoe, Newport Pagnell (1894–97), Newton Blossomville, Newton Longville, Olney, Olney Park Farm, Petsoe Manor, Ravenstone, Shenley Church End, Sherington, Simpson (1894–95), Stantonbury, Stoke Goldington, Fenny Stratford (1894–95), Tyringham with Filgrave, Walton, Warrington, Water Eaton (1894–1934), Wavendon, Weston Underwood, Willen (1894–1934), Woburn Sands (1907–74), Great Woolstone (1894–1934), Little Woolstone (1894–1934), Woolstone cum Willen (1934–74), Woughton on the Green

NEWPORT PAGNELL UD (1897[24]–1974)
Newport Pagnell

SLOUGH UD (1894–1938[25])
Slough, Stoke in Slough (1894–96)

FENNY STRATFORD UD (1895[26]–1911[19])
Bletchley (1898–1911), Simpson, Fenny Stratford

STRATFORD AND WOLVERTON RD (1894–1919[27])
Calverton, Stony Stratford East, Stony Stratford West, Wolverton

STRATFORD AND WOLVERTON UD (1919[27]–20[28])
New Bradwell, Calverton, Stony Stratford East, Stony Stratford West, Wolverton

WING RD
Aston Abbots (1934–74), Great Brickhill (1934–74), Cheddington, Cublington (1934–74), Edlesborough, Grove, Ivinghoe, Linslade (1894–97), Marsworth, Mentmore, Pitstone, Slapton, Soulbury, Stoke Hammond, Wing, Wingrave with Rowsham (1934–74)

WINSLOW RD
East Claydon, Drayton Parslow, Dunton, Granborough, Hoggeston, Hogshaw, Great Horwood, Little Horwood, North Marston, Mursley, Nash, Newton Longville (1934–74), Shenley Brook End, Stewkley, Swanbourne, Tattenhoe, Whaddon, Winslow

WOLVERTON UD (1920[28]–74)
New Bradwell (1920–34), Calverton (1920–27), Stony Stratford East (1920–27), Stony Stratford West (1920–27), Wolverton

WYCOMBE RD
Bledlow (1894–1934), Bledlow cum Saunderton (1934–74), Bradenham, Ellesborough, Fawley (1934–74), Fingest (1894–1937), Fingest and Lane End (1934–74), Hambleden (1934–74), Great and Little Hampden, Hedsor, Horsenden (1894–1934), Hughenden, Ibstone, Ilmer (1894–1934), Great and Little Kimble, Lacey Green (1934–74), Longwick cum Ilmer (1934–74), Great Marlow, Little Marlow, Medmenham (1934–74), Little Missenden (1894–1901), Radnage, Monk's Risborough (1894–1934), Princes Risborough, Saunderton (1894–1934), Stokenchurch (1895–1974), Turville, Upton cum Chalvey (1894–1901), Wooburn, Chepping Wycombe (1949–74), Chepping Wycombe Rural (1894–1949), West Wycombe

(1894–1934), West Wycombe Rural (1934–74)

NON-METROPOLITAN COUNTY

As constituted 1 Apr 1974, defined in terms of Adm Co units as of 31 Mar. Pt of Bucks was transf to Berks.[31]

AYLESBURY VALE DIST
Aylesbury MB, Aylesbury RD, Buckingham MB, Buckingham RD, Wing RD, pt Winslow RD[30]

BEACONSFIELD DIST
Beaconsfield UD, pt Eton RD[30]

CHILTERN DIST
Amersham RD, Chesham UD

MILTON KEYNES DIST
Bletchley UD, Newport Pagnell RD, Newport Pagnell UD, pt Winslow RD,[29] Wolverton UD

WYCOMBE DIST
Marlow UD, Wycombe RD, High Wycombe MB

CAMBRIDGESHIRE

ALTERATIONS IN COUNTY BOUNDARIES

As noted by year below, pars in Cambs and the IoE gained territory from or lost in to pars in adjoining counties, or were entirely transferred to them. Details of these alterations are noted in Part I of the *Guide* under Cambs.

CAMBS ANCIENT COUNTY (until 1889: Hds, Bors, MBs, PLUs, RSDs, USDs)
1860s Ramsey. *1883* Stanground. *1884* Upwell, Welney. *1885* Helion Bumpstead, Castle Camps, Littleport.

CAMBS ADMINISTRATIVE COUNTY (1889–1965: Hds,[1] PLUs, MBs, RDs, UDs)
1889 Newmarket All Saints. *1894* Wood Ditton. *1895* Great Chishill, Little Chishill, Wood Ditton, Heydon, Papworth St Agnes. *1896* Bassingbourn, Kneesworth, Melbourn, Royston.

ISLE OF ELY ADMINISTRATIVE COUNTY (1889–1965: Hds,[1] PLUs, MBs, RDs, UDs)
1889 Outwell, Upwell, Welney. *1895* Redmere, Welney. *1905* Stanground, Stanground North. *1934* Elm, Leverington, Outwell, Parson Drove, Tydd St Giles, Upwell, Wisbech St Peter.

CAMBS AND ISLE OF ELY ADMINISTRATIVE COUNTY (1965–74: MBs, RDs, UDs)
1965 Bartlow, Benwick, Castle Camps, Chatteris, Great Chishill, Duxford, Fowlmere, Gamlingay, Heydon, Ickleton, Linton. *1966* Gamlingay.

CAMBS NON-METROPOLITAN COUNTY (From 1974: Dists)

HUNDREDS[1]

In Cambridgeshire proper:

ARMINGFORD HD
Abington Pigotts, Bassingbourn, Croydon, East Hatley, Kneesworth (from 1866), Litlington, Melbourn, Meldreth, Guilden Morden, Steeple Morden, pt Royston, Shingay,Tadlow, Wendy, Whaddon

CHESTERTON HD
Chesterton, Childerley, Cottenham, Dry Drayton, Histon (from late 18th cent), Histon St Andrew (until late 18th cent), Histon St Etheldreda (until late 18th cent), pt Oakington (until 1866), Westwick (from 1866)

CHEVELEY HD
Ashley, Cheveley, Wood Ditton, Kirtling, Newmarket All Saints

CHILFORD HD
Great Abington, Little Abington, Babraham, Bartlow, pt Helion Bumpstead (until 1885), Castle Camps, Shudy Camps, Hildersham, Horseheath, Linton,[2] Pampisford, West Wickham

FLENDISH HD[3]
Fen Ditton, Fulbourn (from 1765), Fulbourn All Saints (until 1765), Fulbourn St Vigoris (until 1765), Cherry Hinton, Horningshea, Teversham

LONGSTOW HD
Bourn, Caldecote, Caxton, Croxton, Eltisley, Great Eversden, Little Eversden, Gamlingay, Little Gransden, Hardwick, Hatley St George, Kingston, Longstowe, Toft

NORTHSTOW HD
Girton, Impington, Landbeach, Lolworth, Madingley, Milton, Oakington (pt until 1866, ent from 1866), Rampton, Long Stanton All Saints, Long Stanton St Michael, Waterbeach

PAPWORTH HD
Boxworth, Conington, Fen Drayton, Elsworth, Graveley, Knapwell, Over, Papworth Everard, pt Papworth St Agnes, Swavesey,[2] Willingham

RADFIELD HD
Balsham, Brinkley, Burrough Green, Carlton, Dullingham, Stetchworth, Westley Waterless, Weston Colville, West Wratting

STAINE HD
Bottisham, Stow cum Quy, Swaffham Bulbeck, Swaffham Prior (from 1667), Swaffham Prior St Cyriac and St Jolitta (until 1667), Swaffham Prior St Mary (until 1667), Great Wilbraham, Little Wilbraham

STAPLOE HD
Burwell (from 17th or 18th cent), Burwell St Andrew (until 17th or 18th cent), Burwell St Mary (until 17th or 18th cent), Chippenham, Fordham, Isleham, Kennett, Landwade, Snailwell, Soham, Wicken

THRIPLOW HD
Fowlmere, Foxton, Harston, Hauxton, Newton, Great Shelford, Little Shelford, Stapleford, Thriplow, Trumpington

WETHERLEY HD
Arrington, Barrington, Barton, Comberton, Coton,

Grantchester, Harlton, Haslingfield, Orwell, Shepreth, Wimpole
WITTLESFORD HD
Duxford, Hinxton, Ickleton, Sawston, Whittlesford

In Isle of Ely:
ELY HD
Downham, Ely College (from 1858), Ely St Mary,[2] Ely Trinity,[2] Littleport
WISBECH HD
Elm, Leverington, Newton, pt Outwell, Parson Drove (from 1866), Thorney, Tydd St Giles, pt Upwell, pt Welney (from 1866), Wisbech St Mary, Wisbech St Peter[2]
NORTH WITCHFORD HD
Benwick (from 1866), Chatteris, Doddington, March (from 1866), pt Ramsey (until 1860s), pt Stanground, Whittlesey St Andrew (until 1850), Whittlesey St Mary (until 1850), Whittlesey St Mary and St Andrew (from 1850), Wimblington (from 1866)
SOUTH WITCHFORD HD
Coveney, Grunty Fen (from 1858), Haddenham, Manea (from 1866), Mepal, Stretham, Sutton, Thetford (from 1866), Welches Dam (from 1858), Wentworth, Wilburton, Witcham, Witchford

BOROUGHS

Units with some degree of burghal character[4] are denomiated 'Bor'. Those which did not sustain that status until the 19th cent are in italics. Municipal Boroughs were established by the Municipal Corporations Act, 1835,[5] or by later charter.

CAMBRIDGE BOR/MB (City from 1951[6])
Cambridge (1900–74), Cambridge All Saints (until 1900), Cambridge Holy Sepulchre (until 1900), Cambridge Holy Trinity (until 1900), Cambridge St Andrew the Great (until 1900), Cambridge St Andrew the Less (until 1900), Cambridge St Benedict (until 1900), Cambridge St Botolph (until 1900), Cambridge St Clement (until 1900), Cambridge St Edward (until 1900), Cambridge St Giles (until 1900), Cambridge St Mary the Great (until 1900), Cambridge St Mary the Less (until 1900), Cambridge St Michael (until 1900), Cambridge St Peter (until 1886), Cambridge Without (1912–23), Chesterton (1912–23)
ELY BOR
Ely St Mary, Ely Trinity
LINTON BOR
Linton
SWAVESEY BOR
Swavesey
WISBECH BOR/MB
Wisbech St Peter

POOR LAW UNIONS

In Cambridge Poor Law County[7]
CAMBRIDGE PLU
Cambridge (1900–30), Cambridge All Saints (until 1900), Cambridge Holy Sepulchre (until 1900), Cambridge Holy Trinity (until 1900), Cambridge St Andrew the Great (until 1900), Cambridge St Andrew the Less (until 1900), Cambridge St Benedict (until 1900), Cambridge St Botolph (until 1900), Cambridge St Clement (until 1900), Cambridge St Edward (until 1900), Cambridge St Giles (until 1900), Cambridge St Mary the Great (until 1900), Cambridge St Mary the Less (until 1900), Cambridge St Michael (until 1900), Cambridge St Peter (until 1886)
CAXTON PLU (Cambs, Hunts)
Arrington, Bourn, Caldecote, Caxton, Croxton, Croydon, Elsworth, Eltisley, Great Eversden, Little Eversden, Hardwick, East Hatley, Hatley St George, Kingston, Knapwell, Longstowe, Orwell, Papworth Everard, Papworth St Agnes, Tadlow, Toft, Wimpole
CHESTERTON PLU
Barton, Cambridge Without (1912–23), Cherry Hinton, Chesterton, Childerley, Comberton, Coton, Cottenham, Fen Ditton, Dry Drayton, Fulbourn, Girton, Grantchester, Harlton, Harston, Haslingfield, Hauxton, Histon, Horningsea, Impington, Landbeach, Madingley, Milton, Newton, Oakington, Rampton, Great Shelford, Little Shelford, Long Stanton All Saints, Long Stanton St Michael, Stapleford, Stow cum Quy, Teversham, Trumpington, Waterbeach, Westwick (1866[8]–1930), Great Wilbraham, Little Wilbraham, Willingham
ELY PLU (Cambs/IoE, Norfolk)
Coveney, Downham, Ely College (1858[8]–1930), Ely St Mary, Ely Trinity, Grunty Fen (1858[8]–1930), Haddenham, Littleport, Mepal, Redmere,[9] Stretham, Sutton, Thetford, Wentworth, Wilburton, Witcham, Witcham Gravel (1894–1930), Witchford
LINTON PLU (Cambs, Essex)
Great Abington, Little Abington, Babraham, Balsham, Bartlow, Castle Camps, Shudy Camps, Carlton, Duxford, Hildersham, Hinxton, Horseheath, Ickleton, Linton, Pampisford, Sawston, Weston Colville, Whittlesford, West Wickham, West Wratting
NEWMARKET PLU (Cambs, Suffolk/W Suffolk)
Ashley, Bottisham, Brinkley, Burrough Green, Burwell, Cheveley, Chippenham, Wood Ditton, Dullingham, Fordham, Isleham, Kennett, Kirtling,

Landwade, Newmarket All Saints,[10] Snailwell, Soham, Stetchworth, Swaffham Bulbeck, Swaffham Prior, Westley Waterless, Wicken

WHITTLESEY PLU

Whittlesey (1926–30), Whittlesey Rural (1894–1926), Whittlesey St Andrew (1836–50), Whittlesey St Mary (1836–50), Whittlesey St Mary and St Andrew (1850–94), Whittlesey Urban (1894–1926)

WISBECH PLU (Cambs/IoE, Norfolk)

Elm, Leverington, Newton, Outwell,[11] Parson Drove, Tydd St Giles, Upwell,[11] Wisbech St Mary, Wisbech St Peter

NORTH WITCHFORD PLU

Benwick, Chatteris, Doddington, Manea, March, Welches Dam, Wimblington

In Other Poor Law Counties:

DOWNHAM PLU (Norfolk)

Welney[11]

PETERBOROUGH PLU (Northants)

Stanground,[12] Stanground North (1905–30), Thorney

ROYSTON PLU (Herts[13])

Abington Pigotts, Barrington, Bassingbourn, Great Chishill,[14] Little Chishill,[14] Fowlmere, Foxton, Heydon,[14] Kneesworth, Litlington, Melbourn, Meldreth, Guilden Morden, Steeple Morden, Royston,[15] Shepreth, Shingay, Thriplow, Wendy, Whaddon

ST IVES PLU (Hunts)

Boxworth, Conington, Fen Drayton, Lolworth, Over, Swavesey

ST NEOTS PLU (Hunts)

Graveley

SANITARY DISTRICTS

CAMBRIDGE RSD

same as PLU less the Cambridge pars

CAMBRIDGE USD

Cambridge All Saints, Cambridge Holy Sepulchre, Cambridge Holy Trinity, Cambridge St Andrew the Great, Cambridge St Andrew the Less, Cambridge St Benedict, Cambridge St Botolph, Cambridge St Clement, Cambridge St Edward, Cambridge St Giles, Cambridge St Mary the Great, Cambridge St Mary the Less, Cambridge St Michael, Cambridge St Peter (1875–86)

CAXTON RSD

same as PLU

CHATTERIS USD

Chatteris

CHESTERTON RSD

same as PLU less Chesterton

CHESTERTON USD

Chesterton

DOWNHAM RSD

same as PLU for the Cambs par

ELY RSD

same less the Ely pars

ELY USD

Ely College, Ely St Mary, Ely Trinity

LINTON RSD

same as PLU

MARCH USD

March

NEWMARKET RSD

same as PLU for Cambs pars less pt Wood Ditton

NEWMARKET USD

primarily Suffolk, incl pt Wood Ditton

PETERBOROUGH RSD

same as PLU for the Cambs pars

ROYSTON RSD

same as PLU for the Cambs pars

ST IVES RSD

same as PLU for the Cambs pars

ST NEOTS RSD

same as PLU for the Cambs par

WHITTLESEY RSD

pt Whittlesey St Mary and St Andrew

WHITTLESEY USD

pt Whittlesey St Mary and St Andrew

WISBECH RSD

same as PLU less Wisbech St Peter

WISBECH USD

Wisbech St Peter

ADMINISTRATIVE COUNTIES

For MBs, see BOROUGHS earlier in this Part of the *Guide*.

SOUTH CAMBRIDGESHIRE RD (Cambs 1934–65, Cambs & IoE 1965–74)

Great Abington, Little Abington, Abington Pigotts, Arrington, Babraham, Balsham, Barrington, Bartlow, Bassingbourn (1934–66), Bassingbourn cum Kneesworth (1966–74), Castle Camps, Shudy Camps, Carlton, Great Chishill (1934–68), Great and Little Chishill (1968-74), Little Chishill (1934–68), Croydon, Duxford, Great Eversden, Little Eversden, Fowlmere, Foxton, Gamlingay, Hatley (1957–74), East Hatley (1934–57), Hatley St George (1934–57), Heydon, Hildersham, Hinxton, Horseheath, Ickleton, Kingston, Kneesworth (1934–66), Linton, Litlington, Longstowe, Melbourn, Meldreth, Guilden Morden, Steeple Morden, Orwell, Pampisford, Sawston, Shepreth, Shingay (1934–57), Shingay cum Wendy (1957–74), Tadlow, Thriplow, Wendy (1934–57), Weston Colville,

Whaddon, Whittlesford, West Wickham, Wimpole, West Wratting

CAXTON AND ARRINGTON RD (Cambs 1894–1934)
Arrington, Bourn, Caldecote, Caxton, Croxton, Croydon, Elsworth, Eltisley, Great Eversden, Little Eversden, Gamlingay, Little Gransden, Hardwick, East Hatley, Hatley St George, Kingston, Knapwell, Longstowe, Orwell, Papworth Everard, Papworth St Agnes (pt 1894–95, ent 1895–1934), Taplow, Toft, Wimpole

CHATTERIS UD (IoE 1894–1965, Cambs & IoE 1965–74)
Chatteris

CHESTERTON RD (Cambs 1894–1965, Cambs & IoE 1965–74)
Bar Hill (1966–74), Barton, Bourn (1934–74), Boxworth (1934–74), Caldecote (1934–74), Cambridge Without (1912–23), Caxton (1934–74), Cherry Hinton, Childerley, Comberton, Conington (1934–74), Coton, Cottenham, Croxton (1934–74), Fen Ditton, Dry Drayton (1934–74), Fen Drayton (1934–74), Elsworth (1934–74), Eltisley (1934–74), Fulbourn, Girton, Grantchester, Graveley (1934–74), Hardwick (1934–74), Harlton, Harston, Haslingfield, Hauxton, Histon, Horningsea, Impington, Knapwell (1934–74), Landbeach, Lolworth (1934–74), Longstanton (1953–74), Madingley, Milton, Newton, Oakington, Over (1934–74), Papworth Everard (1934–74), Papworth St Agnes (1934–74), Rampton, Great Shelford, Little Shelford, Long Stanton All Saints (1894–1953), Long Stanton St Michael (1894–1953), Stapleford, Stow cum Quy, Swavesey (1934–74), Teversham, Toft (1934–74), Trumpington (1894–1934), Waterbeach, Westwick, Great Wilbraham, Little Wilbraham, Willingham

CHESTERTON UD (Cambs 1894–1965, Cambs & IoE 1965–74)
Chesterton

ELY RD (IoE 1894–1965, Cambs & IoE 1965–74)
Coveney, Downham, Grunty Fen (1894–1933), Haddenham, Littleport, Mepal, Redmere (1895–1933), Stretham, Sutton, Thetford, Wentworth, Wilburton, Witcham, Witchford

ELY UD (IoE 1894–1965, Cambs & IoE 1965–74)
Ely College, Ely Holy Trinity with St Mary (1933–74), Ely St Mary (1894–1933), Ely Trinity (1894–1933), Land Common to Ely St Mary and Ely Trinity (1894–1933), Witcham Gravel (1894–1933)

LINTON RD (Cambs 1894–1934)
Great Abington, Little Abington, Babraham, Balsham, Bartlow, Castle Camps, Shudy Camps, Carlton, Duxford, Hildersham, Hinxton, Horseheath, Ickleton, Linton, Pampisford, Sawston, Weston Colville, Whittlesford, West Wickham, West Wratting

MARCH UD (IoE 1894–1965, Cambs & IoE 1965–74)
March

MELBOURN RD (Cambs 1894–1934)
Abington Pigotts, Barrington, Bassingbourn, Great Chishill (1895–1934), Little Chishill (1895–1934), Fowlmere, Foxton, Heydon (1895–1934), Kneesworth, Litlington, Melbourn, Meldreth, Guilden Morden, Steeple Morden, Shepreth, Shingay, Thriplow, Wendy, Whaddon

NEWMARKET RD (Cambs 1894–1965, Cambs & IoE 1965–74)
Ashley, Bottisham, Brinkley, Burrough Green, Burwell, Cheveley, Chippenham, Wood Ditton, Dullingham, Fordham, Isleham, Kennett, Kirtling, Landwade (1894–1953), Lode, Reach (1954–74), Snailwell, Soham, Stetchworth, Swaffham Bulbeck, Swaffham Prior, Westley Waterless, Wicken

SWAVESEY RD (Cambs 1894–1934)
Boxworth, Conington, Fen Drayton, Lolworth, Over, Swavesey

THORNEY RD (IoE 1894–1965, Cambs & IoE 1965–74)
pt Stanground (1894–1905), Stanground North (1905–74), Thorney

WHITTLESEY RD (IoE 1894–1926)
Whittlesey Rural

WISBECH RD (IoE 1894–1965, Cambs & IoE 1965–74)
Elm, Leverington, Newton, Outwell, Parson Drove, Tydd St Giles, Upwell, Wisbech St Mary

NORTH WITCHFORD RD (IoE 1894–1965, Cambs & IoE 1965–74)
Benwick, Doddington, Manea, Welches Dam (1894–1960), Wimblington

NON-METROPOLITAN COUNTY

As constituted 1 Apr 1974, defined in terms of Adm Co units as of 31 Mar.

CAMBRIDGE DIST
Cambridge MB

EAST CAMBRIDGESHIRE DIST
Ely RD, Ely UD, Newmarket RD

SOUTH CAMBRIDGESHIRE DIST
Chesterton RD, South Cambridgeshire RD

FENLAND DIST
Chatteris UD, March UD, Whittlesey UD, North Witchford RD, Wisbech MB, Wisbech RD

HUNTINGDON DIST
from Hunts & Peterb: Huntingdon RD, Huntingdon & Godmanchester MB, pt Norman Cross RD,[16] Ramsey UD, St Ives MB, St Ives RD, St Neots RD, St Neots UD

PETERBOROUGH DIST
from Hunts & Peterb: Barnack RD, Old Fletton UD, pt Norman Cross RD,[16] Peterborough MB, Peterborough RD, Thorney RD

CORNWALL

ALTERATIONS IN COUNTY BOUNDARIES

As noted by year below, Cornw pars gained territory from or lost it to pars in Devon, or Cornw gained ent pars from Devon. Details of these alterations are noted in Part I of the *Guide* under Cornw.

ANCIENT COUNTY (until 1889: Hds, Bors, MBs, PLUs, RSDs, USDs)
1844 Bridgerule, St John, Maker, North Petherwin, North Tamerton, Werrington.

ADMINISTRATIVE COUNTY (1889–1974: Hds,[1] PLUs, MBs, UDs, RDs)
1894 St Budeaux. *1966* Boyton, Calstock, Kilkhampton, Launcells, Morwenstow, North Petherwin, St Stephens by Launceston Rural, Stoke Climsland, North Tamerton, Werrington, Whitstone.

NON-METROPOLITAN COUNTY (from 1974: Dists)

HUNDREDS[1]

EAST HD
Antony, Botus Fleming, Callington, Calstock, Egloskerry, North Hill, South Hill, Landrake with St Erney, Landulph, Laneast, Lawhitton, Lewannick, Lezant, Linkinhorne, pt Maker, Menheniot, South Petherwin, Pillaton, Quethiock, Rame, pt St Budeaux, St Dominick, St Germans, St Ive, pt St John, St Mary Magdalene, St Mellion, St Stephens, St Stephens, St Thomas the Apostle, St Thomas Street (from 1866), Saltash (from 1866), Sheviock, Stoke Climsland, Tremaine, Tresmeer, Trewen

KERRIER HD
Breage, Budock, Constantine, Cury, Falmouth (from 1664), Falmouth Borough (from 1866), Germoe, Grade, Gunwalloe, Gwennap, Helston (from 1866), Landewednack, Mabe, Manaccan, Mawgan in Meneage, Mawnan, Mullion, Mylor, Penryn (from 1866), Perranarworthal, Ruan Major, Ruan Minor, St Anthony in Meneage, St Gluvias, St Keverne, St Martin in Meneage, Sithney, Stithians, Wendron

LESNEWTH HD
Advent, Altarnun, Davidstow, Forrabury, Lanteglos, Lesnewth, Marazion (from 1866), Michaelstow, Minster, Otterham, Penzance (from 1866), Poundstock, St Clether, St Gennys, St Juliot, Tintagel, Treneglos, Trevalga, Warbstow

PENWITH HD
Camborne, Crowan, Gulval, Gwinear, Gwithian, Illogan, Ludgvan, Madron, Morvah, Paul, Perranuthnoe, Phillack, Redruth, St Buryan, St Erth, St Hilary, St Ives, St Just in Penwith, St Levan, Sancreed, Sennen, Towednack, Uny Lelant, Zennor

POWDER HD
Cornelly, Creed, Cuby, Feock, Fowey, Gerrans, Gorran, Grampound (from 1866), Kea, Kenwyn, Ladock, Lamorran, Lanlivery, Lostwithiel, Luxulyan, Merther, Mevagissey, Philleigh, Probus, Roche, Ruan Lanihorne, St Allen, St Anthony in Roseland, St Austell, St Blazey, St Clement, St Dennis, pt St Enoder (until 19th cent), St Erme, St Ewe, St Just in Roseland, St Mewan, St Michael Carhays, St Michael Penkevil, St Sampson, St Stephen in Brannel, Tregavethan (from 1866), Tregony (from 1866), Truro St Mary, Tywardreath, Veryan

PYDER HD
Colan, Crantock, Cubert, Lanhydrock, Lanivet, Mawgan in Pyder, Newlyn, Padstow, Perranzabuloe, Little Petherick, St Agnes, St Breock, St Columb Major, St Columb Minor, St Enoder (pt until 19th cent, ent thereafter), St Ervan, St Eval, St Issey, St Merryn, St Wenn, Withiel

STRATTON HD
pt Boyton, pt Bridgerule, Jacobstow, Kilkhampton, Launcells, Marhamchurch, Morwenstow, Poughill, Stratton, North Tamerton (pt until 1844, ent thereafter), Week St Mary, Whitstone

TRIGG HD
Blisland, Bodmin, Bodmin Borough (from 1866), Egloshayle, Helland, St Breward, St Endellion, St Kew, St Mabyn, St Minver (until 1866), St Minver Highlands (from 1866), St Minver Lowlands (from 1866), St Teath, St Tudy, Temple

WEST HD
Boconnoc, Broadoak, Cardinham, Duloe, Lanreath, Lansallos, Lanteglos, Liskeard, Liskeard Borough (from 1866), East Looe (from 1866), West Looe (from 1866), Morval, Pelynt, St Cleer, St Keyne, St Martin, St Michael's Mount (from 1858), St Neot, St Pinnock, St Veep, St Winnow, Talland, Warleggan

BOROUGHS

Units with some degree of burghal character[2] are denominated 'Bor'.
Those which did not sustain that status until the 19th cent are in italics.
Municipal Boroughs were established by the Municipal Corporations
Act, 1835,[3] or by later charter.

BODMIN BOR/MB
pt Bodmin (until 1866), Bodmin Borough (1866–1974)

BOSCASTLE BOR
pt Minster

BOSSINEY BOR
pt Tintagel

CALLINGTON BOR
Callington (from time had sep civ identity), pt South Hill (earlier)

CAMELFORD BOR
pt Lanteglos

CRAFTHOLE BOR
pt Sheviock

CUDDENBEAK BOR
pt St Germans

DUNHEVED BOR[4]
pt St Mary Magdalene

FALMOUTH BOR/MB
pt Budock (1892[16]–94), Budock Urban (1894–1920), Falmouth (pt until 1866, 1892[16]–1974), Falmouth Borough (1866–1920)

FOWEY BOR, MB (1913[24]–1968[23])
Fowey, pt Lanteglos (in Bor only, not in MB)

GRAMPOUND BOR
pt Creed, pt Probus

HELSTON BOR/MB
Helston (1866–1974), pt Wendron (until 1866)

KILKHAMPTON BOR
Kilkhampton

LAUNCESTON (OTHERWISE DUNHEVED) BOR/MB[5]
Launceston (otherwise Dunheved)(1922–74), Lawhitton (pt until 1835, ent 1835–89), pt 1889–94), Lawhitton Urban (1894–1922), St Mary Magdalene (until 1922), St Stephens (ent 1835–89, pt 1889–94), St Stephens by Launceston Urban (1894–1922), St Thomas the Apostle (pt until 1835, ent 1835–89, pt 1889–94), St Thomas the Apostle Urban (1894–1922), St Thomas Street (1866–1922)

LISKEARD BOR/MB
pt Liskeard (enlarged pt 1587–1884), Liskeard Borough (1866–1974), pt St Cleer (until 1884)

EAST LOOE BOR
pt St Martin

WEST LOOE BOR
pt Talland

LOSTWITHIEL BOR,[8] MB (1885[6]–1968[7])
pt Lanlivery (until 1894), Lanlivery Urban (1894–96), Lostwithiel

MARAZION BOR
pt St Hilary

MICHELL BOR
pt Newlyn, pt St Enoder

MOUSEHOLE BOR
pt Paul

NEWPORT BOR
pt St Stephens

PADSTOW BOR
Padstow

PENKNETH BOR[8]
pt Lanlivery

PENRYN BOR/MB
Penryn (1866–1974), pt St Gluvias (until 1866)

PENZANCE BOR/MB
pt Madron (until 1894), Madron in Penzance (1894–1934), Penzance (ent 1866–75, pt 1875–94, ent 1894–1974)

ST AUSTELL WITH FOWEY MB (1968[23]–74)
Fowey, St Austell, Tywardreath

ST IVES BOR/MB
St Ives

ST MAWES BOR
pt St Just in Roseland

SALTASH BOR, MB (1885[9]–1974)
pt St Stephens (when Bor), Saltash (when MB)

TREGONY BOR
pt Cuby

TREMATON BOR
pt St Stephens

TRURO BOR/MB
pt Kenwyn (enlarged pt 1835–94), Kenwyn Urban (1894–1934), pt St Clement (1835–94), St Clement Urban (1894–1934), Truro (1934–74), Truro St Mary (until 1934)

WEEK ST MARY BOR
Week St Mary

POOR LAW UNIONS

In Cornwall Poor Law County:[10]

BODMIN PLU
Blisland, Bodmin, Bodmin Borough, Cardinham, Egloshayle, Helland, Lanhydrock, Lanivet, Lanlivery (1837–94), Lanlivery Rural (1894–1930), Lanlivery Urban (1894–96), Lostwithiel, Luxulyan, St Endellion, St Kew, St Mabyn, St Minver Highlands, St Minver Lowlands, St Tudy, St Winnow, Temple, Wadebridge (1898–1930), Warleggan, Withiel

CAMELFORD PLU
Advent, Davidstow, Forrabury (1837–1919), Forrabury and Minster (1919–30), Lanteglos, Lesnewth, Michaelstow, Minster (1837–1919), Otterham, St Breward, St Clether, St Juliot, St Teath, Tintagel, Trevalga

FALMOUTH PLU
Budock (1837–94), Budock Rural (1894–1930), Budock Urban (1894–1920), Constantine, Falmouth, Falmouth Borough (1837–1920), Mabe, Mawnan, Mylor, Penryn, Perranarworthal, St Gluvias

HELSTON PLU
Breage, Crowan, Cury, Germoe, Gunwalloe, Grade, Helston, Landewednack, Manaccan, Mawgan in Meneage, Ruan Major, Ruan Minor, St Anthony in Meneage, St Keverne, St Martin in Meneage, Sithney, Wendron

LAUNCESTON PLU (Cornwall, Devon)
Altarnun, Boyton,[11] Egloskerry, North Hill, Laneast, Launceston (otherwise Dunheved)(1922–30), Lawhitton (1837–94), Lawhitton Rural (1894–1930), Lawhitton Urban (1894–1922), Lewannick, Lezant, South Petherwin, St Mary Magdalene (1837–1922), St Stephens (1837–94), St Stephens by Launceston Rural (1894–1930), St Stephens by Launceston Urban (1894–1922), St Thomas the Apostle (1837–94), St Thomas the Apostle Rural (1894–1930), St Thomas the Apostle Urban (1894–1930), St Thomas Street (1837–1922), Tremaine, Treneglos, Tresmeer, Trewen, Warbstow

LISKEARD PLU
Boconnoc, Broadoak, Callington (1894–1901), Duloe, South Hill, Lanreath, Lansallos, Lanteglos, Lanteglos, Linkinhorne, Liskeard, Liskeard Borough, East Looe (1894–1930), West Looe (1894–1930), Menheniot, Morval, Pelynt, St Cleer, St Dominick, St Ive, St Keyne, St Martin, St Neot, St Pinnock, St Veep, Talland

PENZANCE PLU
Gulval, Ludgvan, Madron, Madron in Penzance (1894–1930), Marazion, Morvah, Paul, Penzance, Penzance in Madron (1894–1930), Perranuthnoe, St Buryan, St Erth (1837–94), St Erth Rural (1894–1930), St Erth Urban (1894–1930), St Hilary, St Ives, St Just in Penwith, St Levan, St Michael's Mount (1858[12]–1930), Sancreed, Senned, Towednack, Uny Lelant, Wolfe Rock Lighthouse, Zennor

REDRUTH PLU
Camborne, Gwennap, Gwinear, Gwithian, Illogan, Phillack (1837–94), East Phillack (1894–1930), West Phillack (1894–1930), Redruth

ST AUSTELL PLU
Creed, Fowey (1894–1930), Gorran, Grampound, Mevagissey, Roche, St Austell (1837–94), St Austell Rural (1894–1930), St Austell Urban (1894–1930), St Blazey, St Dennis, St Ewe, St Mewan, St Michael Carhays, St Sampson, St Stephen in Brannel, Tywardreath

ST COLUMB MAJOR PLU
Colan, Crantock (1837–94), Crantock Rural (1894–1930), Crantock Urban (1894–1902), Cubert, Mawgan in Pyder, Newquay (1894–1930), Padstow (1837–94), Padstow Rural (1894–1930), Padstow Urban (1894–1930), Little Petherick, St Breock, St Columb Major, St Columb Minor (1837–94), St Columb Minor Rural (1894–1930), St Enoder, St Ervan, St Eval, St Issey, St Merryn, St Wenn

ST GERMANS PLU (Cornwall, Devon)
Antony, Botus Fleming, Landrake with St Erney, Landulph, Maker,[11] Millbrook (1896–1930), Pillaton, Quethiock, Rame, St Germans, St John,[11] St Mellion, St Stephens, Saltash, Sheviock, Torpoint (1904–30)

ISLES OF SCILLY PLU[13]
Bryher, St Agnes, St Martin's, St Mary's, Tresco

STRATTON PLU
Jacobstow, Kilkhampton, Launcells, Marhamchurch, Morwenstow, Poughill, Poundstock, St Gennys, Stratton, Stratton and Bude (1900–30), Week St Mary, Whitstone

TRURO PLU
Cornelly, Cuby, Feock, Gerrans, Kea, Kenwyn (1837–94), Kenwyn Rural (1894–1930), Kenwyn Urban (1894–1930), Ladock, Lamorran, Merther, Perranzabuloe, Philleigh, Probus, Ruan Lanihorne, St Agnes, St Allen, St Anthony in Roseland, St Clement (1837–94), St Clement Rural (1894–1930), St Clement Urban (1894–1930), St Erme, St Just in Roseland, St Michael Penkevil, Tregavethan, Tregony, Truro St Mary, Veryan

In Other Poor Law Counties:

HOLSWORTHY PLU (Devon)
North Tamerton[11]

PLYMPTON ST MARY (Devon)
St Budeaux[14]

TAVISTOCK PLU (Devon)
Calstock[15]

SANITARY DISTRICTS

BODMIN RSD
same as PLU less Bodmin, pt Lanlivery (1885[17]–94), Lostwithiel (1885[17]–94)

BODMIN USD
Bodmin Borough

CAMBORNE USD
Camborne

CAMELFORD RSD
same as PLU

FALMOUTH RSD
same as PLU less pt Budock (1892[16]–94), Falmouth, Falmouth Borough, Penryn

FALMOUTH USD[16]
pt Budock (1892–94), Falmouth (1892–94), Fal-

mouth Borough
FALMOUTH PARISH USD (1875–92[16])
Falmouth
HAYLE USD
pt Phillack, pt St Erth
HELSTON RSD
same as PLU less Helston
HELSTON USD
Helston
HOLSWORTHY RSD
same as PLU for the Cornw par
LAUNCESTON RSD
same as PLU less pars and pts of pars in Launc. USD
LAUNCESTON USD
pt Lawhitton, St Mary Magdalene, pt St Stephens, pt St Thomas the Apostle, St Thomas Street
LISKEARD RSD
same as PLU less pt Liskeard (1875–84), Liskeard Borough, Ludgvan, pt St Cleer (1875–84)
LISKEARD USD
pt Liskeard (1875–84), Liskeard Borough, pt St Cleer (1875–84)
LOSTWITHIEL USD (1885[17]–94)
pt Lanlivery, Lostwithiel
LUDGVAN USD
Ludgvan
MADRON USD
pt Madron, pt Penzance
NEWQUAY USD
pt Crantock (1892[18]–94), pt St Columb Minor
PADSTOW USD
pt Padstow
PAUL USD (1891[19]–94)
Paul
PENRYN USD
Penryn
PENZANCE RSD
same as PLU less Madron, Paul (1891[19]–94), Penzance, pt St Erth, St Ives
PENZANCE USD
pt Madron, pt Penzance
PHILLACK USD
pt Phillack
REDRUTH USD
Redruth
ST AUSTELL RSD
same as PLU less pt St Austell
ST AUSTELL USD
pt St Austell
ST COLUMB MAJOR RSD
same as PLU less pt Crantock (1892[18]–94), pt Padstow, pt St Columb Minor
ST GERMANS RSD
same as PLU less Saltash
ST IVES USD
St Ives
ISLES OF SCILLY RSD[13]
same as PLU
SALTASH USD
Saltash
STRATTON RSD
same as PLU
TAVISTOCK RSD
same as PLU for Cornw par
TRURO RSD
same as PLU less par and pts of pars in Truro USD
TRURO USD
pt Kenwyn, pt St Clement, Truro St Mary

ADMINISTRATIVE COUNTY

For MBs, see BOROUGHS earlier in this Part of the *Guide*.

BODMIN RD (1894–1934)
Blisland, Bodmin, Cardinham, Egloshayle, Helland, Lanhydrock, Lanivet, Lanlivery Rural, Luxulyan, St Endellion, St Kew, St Mabyn, St Minver Highlands, St Minver Lowlands, St Tudy, St Winnow, Temple, Warleggan, Withiel
BUDE-STRATTON UD (1934–74)
Bude-Stratton
CALLINGTON UD (1901[20]–34)
Callington
CALSTOCK RD (1894–1934)
Calstock
CAMBORNE UD (1894–1934)
Camborne
CAMBORNE-REDRUTH UD (1934–74)
Camborne-Redruth
CAMELFORD RD
Advent, Camelford (1934–74), Davidstow, Forrabury (1894–1919), Forrabury and Minster (1919–74), Lanteglos (1894–1934), Lesnewth, Michaelstow, Minster (1894–1919), Otterham, St Breward, St Clether, St Juliot, St Teath, Tintagel, Trevalga
HAYLE UD (1894–1934)
West Phillack, St Erth Urban
HELSTON RD (1894–1934)
Breage, Crowan, Cury, Germoe, Grade, Gunwalloe, Landewednack, Manaccan, Mawgan in Meneage, Mullion, Ruan Major, Ruan Minor, St Anthony in Meneage, St Keverne, St Martin in Meneage, Sithney, Wendron
HOLSWORTHY RD (Devon, Cornwall)[21]
North Tamerton (1894–1934)
KERRIER RD (1934–74)
Breage, Budock, Constantine, Crowan, Cury, Germoe, Grade-Ruan, Gunwalloe, Landewednack, Mabe, Manaccan, Mawgan in Meneage, Mawnan, Mullion, St Anthony in Meneage, St Gluvias, St Keverne, St Martin in Meneage, Sithney, Stithians, Wendron
EAST KERRIER RD (1894–1934)
Budock Rural, Constantine, Mabe, Mawnan, Mylor, Perranarworthal, St Gluvias

LAUNCESTON RD
Altarnun, Boyton, Egloskerry, North Hill, Laneast, Lawhitton Rural, Lewannick, North Petherwin (1966–74), South Petherwin, St Stephens by Launceston Rural, St Thomas the Apostle Rural, Stoke Climsland, Tremaine, Treneglos, Tresmeer, Trewen, Warbstow, Werrington (1966–74)

LISKEARD RD
Boconnoc, Broadoak, Duloe, South Hill, Lanreath, Lansallos, Lanteglos, Linkinhorne, Liskeard, Menheniot, Morval, Pelynt, St Cleer, St Dominick (1894–1934), St Ive, St Keyne, St Martin, St Neot, St Pinnock, St Veep, St Winnow (1934–74), Talland (1894–1934), Warleggan (1934–74)

LOOE UD (1898[22]–1974)
Looe (1934–74), East Looe (1898–1934), West Looe (1898–1934)

LUDGVAN UD (1894–1934)
Ludgvan

MADRON UD (1894–1934)
Madron, Penzance in Madron

NEWQUAY UD
Crantock Urban (1894–1902), Newquay

PADSTOW UD (1894–1968[25])
Padstow Urban

PAUL UD (1894–1934)
Paul

WEST PENWITH RD
Gulval (1894–1934), Gwinear-Gwithian (1934–74), Hayle (1934–74), Ludgvan (1934–74), Madron (1934–74), Marazion, Morvah, Paul (1934–74), Perranuthnoe, West Phillack (1934–38), St Buryan, St Erth (1934–74), St Erth Rural (1894–1934), St Hilary, St Just in Penwith (1894–97), St Levan, St Michael's Mount, Sancreed, Sennen, Towednack, Uny Lelant (1894–1934), Wolfe Rock Lighthouse, Zennor

PHILLACK UD (1894–1934)
East Phillack

REDRUTH RD (1894–1934)
Gwennap, Gwinear, Gwithian, Illogan, Stithians

REDRUTH UD (1894–1934)
Redruth

ST AUSTELL RD
Colan (1934–74), Creed, Gorran, Grampound, Lanlivery (1934–74), Lostwithiel (1968–74), Luxulyan (1934–74), Mawgan in Pyder (1934–74), Mevagissey (1894–1934), Roche, St Austell Rural (1894–1934), St Blazey (1894–1934), St Columb Major (1934–74), St Dennis, St Enoder (1934–74), St Ewe, St Mewan, St Michael Carhays, St Sampson, St Stephen in Brannel, St Wenn (1934–74), Tywardreath (1894–1934)

ST AUSTELL UD (1894–1968[23])
St Austell (1934–68), St Austell Urban (1894–1934), Tywardreath

ST COLUMB MAJOR RD (1894–1934)
Colan, Crantock Rural, Cubert, Mawgan in Pyder, Newlyn, Padstow Rural, Little Petherick, St Breock, St Columb Major, St Columb Minor Rural, St Enoder, St Ervan, St Eval, St Issey, St Merryn, St Wenn

ST GERMANS RD
Antony, Botus Fleming, Callington (1934–74), Calstock (1934–74), Landrake with St Erney, Landulph, Maker (1894–1950), Maker with Rame (1950–74), Millbrook (1896–1974), Pillaton, Quethiock, Rame (1894–1950), St Dominick (1934–74), St Germans, St John, St Mellion, St Stephens (1894–1934), Sheviock

ST JUST UD (1897[26]–1974)
St Just in Penwith

ISLES OF SCILLY RD (1890[13]–1974)
Bryher, St Agnes, St Martin's, St Mary's, Tresco

STRATTON RD
Jacobstow, Kilkhampton, Launcells, Marhamchurch, Morwenstow, Poughill (1894–1934), Poundstock, St Gennys, Stratton (1894–1934), North Tamerton (1934–74), Week St Mary, Whitstone

STRATTON AND BUDE UD (1900[27]–1934)
Stratton and Bude

TORPOINT UD (1904[28]–1974)
Torpoint

TRURO RD
Chacewater (1934–74), Cornelly (1894–1934), Cubert (1934–74), Cuby, Feock, Gerrans, Gwennap (1934–74), Kea, Kenwyn (1934–74), Kenwyn Rural (1894–1934), Ladock, Lamorran (1894–1934), Land Common to Philleigh and Ruan Lanihorne (1894–1934), Merther (1894–1934), Mylor (1934–74), Newlyn (1934–74), Perranarworthal (1934–74), Perranzabuloe, Philleigh, Probus, Ruan Lanihorne, St Agnes, St Allen, St Anthony in Roseland (1894–1934), St Clement (1934–74), St Clement Rural (1894–1934), St Erme, St Just in Roseland, St Michael Penkevil, Tregavethan (1894–1934), Tregony, Veryan

WADEBRIDGE RD (1934–1968[25])
Blisland, Bodmin Rural (1934–39), Cardinham, Egloshayle, Helland, Lanhydrock, Lanivet, St Breock, St Endellion, St Ervan, St Eval, St Issey, St Kew, St Mabyn, St Merryn, St Minver Highlands, St Minver Lowlands, St Tudy, Wadebridge (1934–68), Withiel

WADEBRIDGE AND PADSTOW RD (1968[25]–74)
Same as Wadebridge RD less Bodmin Rural, adding Padstow

WADEBRIDGE UD (1898[29]–1934)
Wadebridge

NON-METROPOLITAN COUNTY

As constituted 1 Apr 1974, defined in terms of Adm Co units as of 31 Mar.

CARADON DIST
Liskeard MB, Liskeard RD, Looe UD, St Germans RD, Saltash MB, Torpoint UD
CARRICK DIST
Falmouth MB, Penryn MB, Truro MB, Truro RD
NORTH CORNWALL DIST
Bodmin MB, Bude-Stratton UD, Camelford RD, Launceston (otherwise Dunheved) MB, Launceston RD, Stratton RD, Wadebridge and Padstow RD
KERRIER DIST
Camborne-Redruth UD, Helston MB, Kerrier RD
PENWITH DIST
West Penwith RD, Penzance MB, St Ives MB, St Just UD, Wolfe Rock Lighthouse
RESTORMEL DIST
Newquay UD, St Austell RD, St Austell with Fowey MB

DEVON

ALTERATIONS IN COUNTY BOUNDARIES

As noted by year below, Devon pars gained territory from or lost it to pars in adjoining cos or county boroughs, or were entirely transferred to them. Details of these alterations are noted in Part I of the *Guide* under Devon.

ANCIENT COUNTY (until 1889: Hds, Bors, MBs, PLUs, RSDs, USDs)
1844 Axminster, Boyton, Bridgerule, Maker, North Petherwin, St John, St Stephens, Stockland, North Tamerton, Thorncombe, Werrington. *1884* Exmoor, Membury.

ADMINISTRATIVE COUNTY (1889–1974: Hds,[1] PLUs, MBs, RDs, UDs, with Devonport CB, Exeter CB, Plymouth CB, Torbay CB associated)
1889 Pennycross, St Budeaux, Stoke Damerel. *1894* St Budeaux. *1895* St Stephens. *1896* Egg Buckland, Chardstock, Churchstanton, Compton Gifford, Hawkchurch, Laira Green, Pennycross. *1897* Plymstock. *1898* Pennycross, St Budeaux. *1899* St Budeaux. *1900* St Thomas the Apostle, Weston Peverell. *1913* Heavitree, Topsham. *1914* East Stonehouse. *1937* Alphington. *1939* Egg Buckland, Compton Gifford, Plymstock, St Budeaux, Tamerton Foliot. *1940* Alphington, Brampford Speke, Exminster, Pinhoe, Sowton, Stoke Canon, Topsham, Upton Pyne, Whitestone. *1951* Bickleigh, St Budeaux, Tamerton Foliot. *1963* Devon County Buildings Area, Devon Prison and Constabulary Barracks. *1966* Alphington, East Anstey, Bradworthy, Bridgerule, Brixton, Chardstock, Clayhidon, Dunterton, Exminster, Hawkchurch, Hemyock, Holcombe Rogus, Huxham, Lamerton, Luffincott, Milton Abbot, Pancrasweek, North Petherwin, Pinhoe, Plympton St Mary, Plympton St Maurice, Plymstock, Poltimore, Pyworthy, St Giles on the Heath, Sowton, Sydenham Damerel, Tetcott, Topsham, Upottery, Werrington. *1967* Brixham, Churston Ferrers, Coffinswell, Kerswells, Marldon, Paignton.

NON-METROPOLITAN COUNTY (from 1974: Dists)

ASSOCIATED COUNTY BOROUGHS

For constituent pars see listing for BOROUGHS in this Part of the *Guide*.

DEVONPORT CB (1889–1914)
Bdry: 1898,[2] 1900.[3] Abol 1914 and constituent par of Devonport transf to Plymouth CB.[4]

EXETER CB
Bdry: 1900,[5] 1913,[6] 1937,[9] 1940,[7] 1966.[8]

PLYMOUTH CB
Bdry: 1896,[10] 1897,[59] 1899,[60] 1914,[56] 1914,[4] 1939,[11] 1951,[12] 1966.[13]

TORBAY CB (1967–74)
Cr 1967[14] from several pars (see Torbay CP in Part I of the *Guide*). No bdry alt 1967–74.

HUNDREDS[1]

AXMINSTER HD
Axminster[15] (pt until 1844, ent from 1844), Axmouth, Combe Raleigh, Combpyne, Dalwood (from 1866), Honiton,[15] Kilmington, Luppitt, Membury, Musbury, Rousdon, Stockland (from 1844), Thorncombe (until 1844), Uplyme, Upottery, Yarcombe

BAMPTON HD
Bampton,[15] pt Burlescombe, Clayhanger, Hockworthy, Holcombe Rogus, Morebath, Uffculme

BRAUNTON HD
Ashford, Barnstaple,[15] Berrynarbor, Bittadon, Bratton Fleming, Braunton, East Buckland, West Buckland, Combe Martin,[15] East Down, West Down, Filleigh, Georgeham, Goodleigh, Heanton Punchardon, Ilfracombe,[15] Kentisbury, Marwood, Mortehoe, Pilton,[15] Trentishoe

EAST BUDLEIGH HD
Aylesbeare,[15] Bicton, East Budleigh, Clyst Honiton, Clyst St George, Clyst St Mary, Colaton Raleigh, Dotton (from 1858), Farringdon, Gittisham, Harpford, Littleham, Lympstone,[15] Otterton, Venn Ottery, Rockbeare, Salcombe Regis, Sidbury, Sidmouth,[15] Withycombe Raleigh, Woodbury[15]

WEST BUDLEIGH HD
Cheriton Fitzpaine, Poughill, Shobrooke, Stockleigh English, Stockleigh Pomeroy, Upton Hellions, Washfield

CLISTON HD
Butterleigh, Broad Clyst, Clyst Hidon, Clyst St Lawrence, Whimple

COLERIDGE HD
Ashprington, Blackawton, Buckland Tout Saints

(from 1866), Charleton, Chivelstone, Cornworthy, Dittisham, Dodbrooke,[15] Halwell, Harberton, pt Loddiswell, South Pool, East Portlemouth, St Petrox,[15] St Saviour,[15] Sherford, Slapton, Stoke Fleming,[15] Stokenham,[15] Totnes,[15] Townstall[15]

COLYTON HD

Branscombe, Colyton,[15] Cotleigh, Farway, Monkton, Northleigh, Offwell, Seaton and Beer, Shute,[15] Southleigh,[15] Widworthy

CREDITON HD

Colebrooke, Crediton,[15] Kennerleigh, Morchard Bishop, Newton St Cyres, Sandford, Sherwood Villa (from 1858)

ERMINGTON HD

Aveton Gifford,[15] Bigbury, Cornwood, Ermington, Harford, Holbeton, Kingston, Modbury, Newton Ferrers,[15] Ringmore, Ugborough

EXMINSTER HD

Ashcombe, Ashton, Bishopsteignton,[15] Chudleigh,[15] Dawlish, Doddiscombsleigh, Dunchideock, Exminster, Ide, Kenn,[15] Kenton,[15] Mamhead, Modbury,[15] Powderham, Shillingford St George, East Teignmouth,[15] West Teignmouth,[15] Trusham

FREMINGTON HD

Alverdiscott, Fremington,[15] Horwood, Huntshaw, Instow, Newton Tracey, Roborough, St Giles in the Wood, Tawstock, Great Torrington,[15] Westleigh

HALBERTON HD

pt Burlescombe, Halberton, Sampford Peverell,[15] pt Uplowman, Willand

HARTLAND HD

Clovelly, Hartland,[15] Woolfardisworthy, Yarnscombe

HAYRIDGE HD

Bickleigh, Blackborough (until 19th cent), Bradninch,[15] Broadhembury, Cadbury, Cadeleigh, Cullompton,[15] Nether Exe, Feniton, Kentisbeare, Payhembury, Plymtree, pt Rewe, Sheldon, Silverton,[15] Talaton, Thorverton

HAYTOR HD

Abbotskerswell, Berry Pomeroy,[15] Brixham, Broadhempston, Buckland in the Moor, Churston Ferrers, Cockington, Coffinswell, Denbury,[15] Little Hempston, Ipplepen, Kingskerswell, Kingswear, Marldon, Paignton,[15] St Mary Church, Staverton, Stoke Gabriel, Torbryan, Tormoham,[15] Widecombe in the Moor, Wolborough,[15] Woodland (from 1866)

HEMYOCK HD

Awliscombe, Buckerell, Churchstanton, Clayhidon, Culmstock, Dunkeswell, Hemyock

LIFTON HD

Bradstone, Bratton Clovelly, Bridestowe, Broadwoodwidger, Coryton, Dunterton, Germansweek, Kelly, Lamerton, Lewtrenchard, Lifton, Lydford,[15] Marystow, Marytavy, pt Okehampton,[15] pt Petertavy, Sourton, Stowford, Sydenham Damerel, Thrushelton, Virginstow

SOUTH MOLTON HD

East Anstey, West Asntey, Chittlehamholt (from 1866), Chittlehampton, pt Exmoor (1858–84), Knowstone, Landkey, Molland, North Molton,[15] South Molton,[15] George Nympton, Satterleigh, Swimbridge, Bishop's Tawton,[15] Twitchen, Warkleigh

OTTERY ST MARY HD

Ottersy St Mary

PLYMPTON HD

Brixton,[15] Chelson Meadow[15] (from 1858), Plympton St Mary,[15] Plympton St Maurice,[15] Plymstock, Revelstoke,[15] Shaugh Prior, Wembury, Yealmpton[15]

ROBOROUGH HD

Bere Ferrers,[15] Bickleigh, Egg Buckland, Buckland Monachorum, Compton Gifford (from 1866), Devonport[15] (from 1824), Laira Green (from 1858), pt Maker (until 1844), Meavy, Pennycross (from 1866), pt Petertavy, Plymouth Charles,[15] Plymouth St Andrew,[15] pt St Budeaux, pt St John (until 1844), pt St Stephens, Sampford Spiney, Sheepstor, Stoke Damerel,[15] East Stonehouse,[15] Tamerton Foliot,[15] Walkhampton, Whitchurch

SHEBBEAR HD

Abbotsham, Alwington, Beaford, Bideford,[15] Buckland Brewer, Buckland Filleigh, Bulkworthy, Frithelstock, Huish, Iddesleigh, Landcross, Langtree, Littleham, Lundy Island, Meeth, Merton, Monkleigh, Newton St Petrock, Northam, Parkham, Peters Marland, Petrockstow, East Putford, Shebbear,[15] Sheepwash,[15] Little Torrington, Weare Giffard

SHIRWELL HD

Arlington, High Bray, Brendon, Challacombe, Charles, Countisbury, Loxhore, Lynton, Martinhoe, Parracombe, Shirwell, Stoke Rivers

STANBOROUGH HD

East Allington, West Alvington,[15] South Brent, Buckfastleigh, Churchstow, Dartington, Dean Prior, Diptford, Holne, North Huish, South Huish, Kingsbridge,[15] pt Loddiswell, Malborough,[15] South Milton, Moreleigh, Rattery, Thurlestone, Woodleigh

TAVISTOCK HD

Brentor, Milton Abbot, Tavistock[15]

NORTH TAWTON AND WINKLEIGH HD[16]

Ashreigny, Atherington, High Bickington, Bondleigh, Bow,[15] Brushford, Burrington, Chawleigh,[15] Clannaborough, Coldridge, Dolton, Dowland, Down St Mary, Eggesford, Lapford, Broad Nymet (until 1820/50), Nymet Rowland, North Tawton,[15] Wembworthy, Winkleigh,[15] Zeal Monachorum

TEIGNBRIDGE HD

Ashburton,[15] Bickington, North Bovey, Bovey Tracey,[15] Hennock, Highweek, Ideford, Ilsington, Kingsteignton,[15] Lustleigh, Manaton, Moretonhampstead,[15] Teigngrace

TIVERTON HD

Calverleigh, Huntsham, Loxbeare, Tiverton,[15] pt Uplowman

BLACK TORRINGTON HD

Ashbury, Ashwater, Beaworthy, Belstone, Abbots Bickington, pt Boyton (until 1866), Bradford, Bradworthy, Bridgerule (pt until 1844, ent 1844–66), Bridgerule East (from 1866), Bridgerule West (from 1866), Broadwood Kelly, Clawton, Cookbury, Exbourne, Halwill, Hatherleigh,[15] Highampton, Hollacombe, Holsworthy,[15] Honeychurch, Inwardleigh, Jacobstowe, Luffincott, Milton Damerel, Northcott (from 1866), Northlew, pt Okehampton,[15] Monk Okehampton, Pancrasweek, North Petherwin (from 1844), West Putford, Pyworthy, St Giles on the Heath, Sampford Courtenay, Sutcombe, Tetcott, Thornbury, Black Torrington, Werrington

WITHERIDGE HD

Cheldon, Chumleigh,[15] Creacombe, Cruwys Morchard, Highley St Mary (from 1858), Mariansleigh, Meshaw, Bishop's Nympton, King's Nympton, Oakford, Puddington, Rackenford,[15] Romansleigh, Rose Ash, Stoodleigh, Templeton, Thelbridge, Washford Pyne, Witheridge,[15] Woolfardisworthy, East Worlington, West Worlington

WONFORD HD[17]

Alphington,[15] Brampford Speke, Bridford, Chagford, Cheriton Bishop, Christow, Combe in Teignhead (until 1885), Drewsteignton, Dunsford, Gidleigh, Haccombe (until 1885), Haccombe with Combe (from 1885), Heavitree, Hittisleigh, Holcombe Burnell, Huxham, East Ogwell, West Ogwell, Pinhoe, Poltimore, pt Rewe, St Leonard,[15] St Nicholas, St Thomas the Apostle, Sowton, Spreyton, Stoke Canon, Stokeinteignhead, South Tawton,[15] Tedburn St Mary, Throwleigh, Topsham,[15] Upton Pyne, Whitestone

BOROUGHS

Units with some degree of burghal character[18] are denominated 'Bor'.
Those which did not sustain that status until the 19th cent are in italics.
MBs were established by the Municipal Corporations
Act, 1835,[19] or by later charter.

ALPHINGTON BOR
Alphington

WEST ALVINGTON BOR
West Alvington

ASHBURTON BOR
Ashburton

AVETON GIFFORD BOR
Aveton Gifford

AXMINSTER BOR
pt Axminster

BAMPTON BOR
Bampton

BARNSTAPLE BOR/MB
Barnstaple

BERE ALSTON BOR
pt Bere Ferrers

BIDEFORD BOR/MB
Bideford

BOVEY TRACEY BOR
Bovey Tracey

BOW BOR
Bow

BRADNINCH BOR
Bradninch, pt Cullompton

BRIDGETOWN POMEROY BOR
pt Totnes

CHAWLEIGH BOR
Chawleigh

CHILLINGTON BOR
pt Stokenham

CHUDLEIGH BOR
Chudleigh

CHUMLEIGH BOR
Chumleigh

COLYFORD BOR
pt Colyton

COMBE MARTIN BOR
Combe Martin

CREDITON BOR
Crediton

CULLOMPTON BOR[20]
pt Cullompton

DARTMOUTH BOR/MB [CLIFTON DARTMOUTH HARDNESS]
Dartmouth (1891–1974), St Petrox (until 1891), St Saviour (until 1891), Stoke Fleming (1835–85), pt Townstall (until 1891)

DENBURY BOR
Denbury

DEVONPORT MB (1837–89), CB (1889–1914[4])
Devonport, Stoke Damerel (1837–98)

DODBROOKE BOR
Dodbrooke

EXETER BOR/MB/CB
Bradninch (until 1901), Close of St Peter's Cathedral (until 1901), Devon Prison and Constabulary Barracks (until 1963), Exeter (1901–74), Exeter Allhallows, Goldsmith Street (until 1901), Exeter Allhallows on the Walls (until 1901), Exeter Bedford Circus (1858–1901), Exeter Castle Yard (1858–1963), Exeter Holy Trinity (until 1901), Exeter St David (until 1901), Exeter St Edmund (until 1901), Exeter St George the Martyr (until 1901), Exeter St John (until 1901), Exeter St Kerrian (until 1901), Exeter St Lawrence (until 1901), Exeter St Martin (until 1901), Exeter St Mary Arches (until 1901), Exeter St Mary Major (until 1901), Exeter St Mary Steps (until 1901), Exeter St Olave (until 1901), Exeter St Pancras (until 1901), Exeter St Paul (until 1901), Exeter St Petrock (until 1901), Exeter St Sidwell (until 1901), Exeter St Stephen (until 1901), St Leonard (1900–74), St Thomas the Apostle (1900–74)

NORTH FORD BOR
pt Dartington

FREMINGTON BOR
Fremington

HARTON BOR
pt Hartland

HATHERLEIGH BOR
Hatherleigh
HOLSWORTHY BOR
Holsworthy
HONITON BOR, MB (1846–1974)
Honiton
ILFRACOMBE BOR
Ilfracombe
KENNFORD BOR
pt Kenn
KENTON BOR
Kenton
KINGSBRIDGE BOR
Kingsbridge
LYDFORD BOR
Lydford
LYMPSTONE BOR
Lympstone
MALBOROUGH BOR[21]
pt West Alvington
MODBURY BOR
Modbury
NORTH MOLTON BOR
North Molton
SOUTH MOLTON BOR/MB (1835–1967[22])
South Molton (disputed whether ent or pt in MB 1835–94)
MORETONHAMPSTEAD BOR
Moretonhampstead
NEWPORT BOR
pt Bishop's Tawton
NEWTON ABBOT BOR
pt Wolborough
NEWTON BUSHEL BOR
pt Wolborough
NEWTON FERRERS BOR
Newton Ferrers
NEWTON POPPLEFORD BOR
pt Aylesbeare
NOSS MAYO BOR
pt Yealmpton
OKEHAMPTON BOR, MB (1885–1974)
Okehampton (ent in Bor, pt in MB 1885–94, ent 1894–1974)
PAIGNTON BOR
Paignton
PILTON BOR
Pilton
PLYMOUTH BOR (1439[23]–1835), MB, CB
Plymouth (1898–1974), Plymouth Charles (1641–1898), Plymouth St Andrew (until 1898)
PLYMPTON [EARLE] BOR
pt Brixton, Chelson Meadow, pt Plympton St Mary, Plympton St Maurice
RACKENFORD BOR
Rackenford
SAMPFORD PEVERELL BOR
Sampford Peverell
SHEEPWASH BOR
pt Shebbear
SHUTE BOR
pt Colyton
SIDMOUTH BOR
Sidmouth
SILVERTON BOR
Silverton
SUTTON PRIOR BOR (until 1439[23])
Plymouth St Andrew
TAMERTON FOLIOT BOR
Tamerton Foliot
TAVISTOCK BOR
Tavistock
NORTH TAWTON BOR
North Tawton
EAST TEIGNMOUTH BOR
pt Dawlish
WEST TEIGNMOUTH BOR
pt Bishopsteignton
TIVERTON BOR/MB
Tiverton
TOPSHAM BOR
Topsham
TORBAY CB (1967[14]–74)
Torbay
TORQUAY MB (1892–1967[14])
St Mary Church (1900–24), Tormoham (1892–1924), Torquay (1924–67)
TORRINGTON BOR/GREAT TORRINGTON MB
Great Torrington (pt until 1617, ent 1617–1974)
TOTNES BOR/MB
Berry Pomeroy (1835–94), Totnes[24]
LITTLE TOTNES BOR
pt Totnes
WHITFORD BOR
pt Colyton
WINKLEIGH BOR
Winkleigh
WISCOMBE BOR
pt Southleigh
WITHERIDGE BOR
Witheridge
WOODBURY BOR
Woodbury
SOUTH ZEAL BOR
pt South Tawton

POOR LAW UNIONS

In Devon Poor Law County:[25]
AXMINSTER PLU (Devon, Dorset)
Axminster (1836–1915),[26] Axminster Hamlets (1915–30), Axminster Town (1915–30), Axmouth, Beer (1894–1930), Chardstock,[27] Colyton, Combpyne, Dalwood,[28] Hawkchurch,[27] Kilmington, Membury, Musbury, Rousdon, Seaton (1894–1930), Seaton and Beer (1836–94), Shute, Stockland,[28] Thorncombe[29] (1836–94), Uplyme
BARNSTAPLE PLU
Arlington, Ashford, Atherington, Barnstaple, Berrynarbor, Bittadon, Bratton Fleming, Braunton,

High Bray, Brendon, Challacombe, Combe Martin, Countisbury, East Down, West Down, Fremington, Georgeham, Goodleigh, Heanton Punchardon, Horwood, Ilfracombe, Instow, Kentisbury, Landkey, Loxhore, Lynton, Martinhoe, Marwood, Mortehoe, Newton Tracey, Parracombe, Pilton (1835–94), East Pilton (1894–1930), West Pilton (1894–1930), Shirwell, Stoke Rivers, Swimbridge, Tawstock, Bishop's Tawton, Trentishoe, Westleigh

BIDEFORD PLU

Abbotsham, Alwington, Bideford, Bradworthy (1835–before 1850), Buckland Brewer, Bulkworthy, Clovelly, Hartland, Landcross, Littleham, Lundy Island, Monkleigh, Newton St Petrock, Northam, Parkham, East Putford, West Putford (1835–97), Welcombe, Woolfardisworthy

CREDITON PLU

Bow, Brushford, Chawleigh, Cheriton Bishop, Cheriton Fitzpaine, Clannaborough, Coldridge, Colebrooke, Crediton (1836–94), Crediton Hamlets (1894–1930), Crediton Town (1894–1930), Down St Mary, Eggesford, Hittisleigh, Kennerleigh, Lapford, Morchard Bishop, Newton St Cyres, Nymet Rowland, Poughill, Puddington, Sandford, Sherwood Villa (1858[30]–94), Shobrooke, Stockleigh English, Stockleigh Pomeroy, Thelbridge, Upton Hellions, Washford Pyne, Wembworthy, Woolfardisworthy, Zeal Monachorum

DEVONPORT PARISH (1898[31]–1930)

Devonport

EXETER INCORPORATION (1697–1930)

As for Exeter Bor/MB/CB (see listing above for BOROUGHS) less Devon Prison and Constabulary Barracks, St Leonard, St Thomas the Apostle

HOLSWORTHY PLU (Devon, Cornwall)

Ashwater, Abbots Bickington, Bradford, Bradworthy (before 1850–1930), Bridgerule East, Bridgerule West,[32] Broadwoodwidger (1837–52), Clawton, Cookbury, Halwill, Hollacombe, Holsworthy, Holsworthy Hamlets (1901–30), Luffincott, Milton Damerel, Northcott (1837–52), Pancrasweek, West Putford (1897–1930), Pyworthy, St Giles on the Heath (1837–52), Sutcombe, Tetcott, Thornbury, Black Torrington, Virginstow (1837–52)

HONITON PLU

Awliscombe, Branscombe, Broadhembury, Buckerell, Combe Raleigh, Cotleigh, Dunkeswell, Farway, Feniton, Gittisham, Harpford, Honiton, Luppitt, Monkton, Northleigh, Offwell, Ottery St Mary, Venn Ottery, Payhembury, Plymtree, Salcombe Regis, Sheldon, Sidbury, Sidmouth, Southleigh, Talaton, Upottery, Widworthy, Yarcombe (1894–1930)

KINGSBRIDGE PLU

East Allington, West Alvington, Aveton Gifford, Bigbury, Blackawton, Buckland Tout Saints, Charleton, Chivelstone, Churchstow, Dodbrooke (1836–93), South Huish, Kingsbridge (1836–93), Kingsbridge and Dodbrooke (1893–1930), Kingston, Loddiswell, Malborough, South Milton, Modbury, South Pool, East Portlemouth, Ringmore, Salcombe, Sherford, Slapton, Stoke Fleming, Stokenham, Thurlestone, Woodleigh

SOUTH MOLTON PLU (Devon, Somerset)

East Anstey, West Anstey, East Buckland, West Buckland, Burrington, Charles, Cheldon, Chittlehamholt (1866[30]–1930), Chittlehampton, Chumleigh, Creacombe, Exmoor,[33] Filleigh, Knowstone, Mariansleigh, Meshaw, Molland, North Molton, South Molton, Bishop's Nympton, George Nympton, King's Nympton, Queensnympton (1894–1930), Rackenford, Romansleigh, Rose Ash, Satterleigh (1835–94), Satterleigh and Warkleigh (1894–1930), Twitchen, Warkleigh (1835–94), Witheridge, East Worlington, West Worlington (1835–85)

NEWTON ABBOT PLU

Abbotskerswell, Ashburton, Bickington, Bishopsteignton, North Bovey, Bovey Tracey, Broadhempston, Buckland in the Moor, Chudleigh, Cockington (1836–1928), Coffinswell, Combe in Teignhead (1836–85), Dawlish (1836–94), East Dawlish (1894–1930), West Dawlish (1894–1930), Denbury (1836–94), Haccombe (1836–85), Haccombe with Combe (1885–1930), Hennock, Highweek, Ideford, Ilsington, Ipplepen, Kingskerswell, Kingsteignton, Lustleigh, Manaton, Milber (1901–30), Moretonhampstead, Ogwell (1894–1930), East Ogwell (1836–94), West Ogwell (1836–94), St Mary Church (1836–1924), St Nicholas, Stokeinteignhead, Teignmouth (1909–30), East Teignmouth (1836–1909), West Teignmouth (1836–1909), Teigngrace, Torbryan, Tormoham (1836–1924), Torquay (1924–30), Trusham, Widecombe in the Moor, Wolborough, Woodland

OKEHAMPTON PLU

Ashworthy, Beaworthy, Belstone, Bondleigh, Bratton Clovelly, Bridestowe, Broadwood Kelly, Chagford, Drewsteignton, Exbourne, Germansweek, Gidleigh, Hatherleigh, Highampton, Honeychurch, Iddesleigh, Inwardleigh, Jacobstow, Meeth, Northlew, Okehampton, Okehampton Hamlets (1894–1930), Monk Okehampton, Sampford Courtenay, Sourton, Spreyton, North Tawton, South Tawton, Throwleigh

PLYMOUTH INCORPORATION (1708-1930)

Plymouth (1898–1930), Plymouth Charles (1708–1898), Plymouth St Andrew (1708–1898)

PLYMPTON ST MARY PLU

Bickleigh, Brixton, Egg Buckland, Chelson Meadow (1858[30]–94), Compton Gifford, Cornwood, Ermington, Harford, Holbeton, Ivybridge (1894–1930), Laira Green (1858[30]–96), Newton Ferrers, Pennycross (1836–98), Plympton St Mary, Plympton St Maurice, Plymstock, Revelstoke, St Budeaux,[34] Shaugh Prior, Tamerton Foliot, Wembury, Weston Peverell (1899–1930), Yealmpton

ST THOMAS PLU

Alphington, Ashcombe, Ashton, Aylesbeare, Bicton, Brampford Speke, Bridford, East Budleigh, Budleigh Salterton (1894–1930), Christow, Broad Clyst, Clyst Honiton, Clyst Hydon, Clyst St George, Clyst St Lawrence, Clyst St Mary, Colaton Raleigh, Doddiscombsleigh, Dotton (1858[30]–94), Dunchideock, Dunsford, Nether Exe, Exminster, Farringdon, Heavitree, Holcombe Burnell, Huxham, Ide, Kenn, Kenton, Littleham, Lympstone, Mamhead, Newton Poppleford (1898–1930), Otterton, Pinhoe, Poltimore, Powderham, Rewe, Rockbeare, St Leonard, St Thomas the Apostle, Shillingford St George, Sowton, Stoke Canon, Tedburn St Mary, Topsham, Upton Pyne, Whimple, Whitestone, Withycombe Raleigh, Woodbury

STOKE DAMEREL INCORPORATION (until 1898[31])
Stoke Damerel

EAST STONEHOUSE PLU
East Stonehouse

TAVISTOCK PLU (Devon, Cornwall)
Bere Ferrers, Bradstone, Brentor, Buckland Monachorum, Coryton, Dunterton, Kelly, Lamerton, Lewtrenchard, Lifton, Lydford, Marystow, Marytavy, Meavy, Milton Abbot, Petertavy, Sampford Spiney, Sheepstor, Stowford, Sydenham Damerel, Tavistock, Tavistock Hamlets (1898–1930), Thrushelton, Walkhampton, Whitchurch

TIVERTON PLU
Bampton, Bickleigh, Blackborough,[35] Bradninch (1835–1901), Butterleigh, Cadbury, Cadeleigh, Calverleigh (1835–85), Clayhanger, Cruwys Morchard, Cullompton, Halberton, Highley St Mary (1858[30]–94), Hockworthy, Holcombe Rogus (1835–before 1850), Huntsham, Kentisbeare, Loxbeare, Morebath (1835–56 and 1894–1930), Oakford, Sampford Peverell, Silverton, Stoodleigh, Templeton, Thorverton, Tiverton, Uffculme, Uplowman, Washfield, Willand

TORRINGTON PLU
Alverdiscott, Ashreigney, Beaford, High Bickington, Buckland Filleigh, Dolton, Dowland, Frithelstock, Huish, Huntshaw, Langtree, Merton, Peters Marland, Petrockstow, Roborough, St Giles in the Wood, Shebbear, Sheepwash, Great Torrington, Little Torrington, Weare Giffard, Winkleigh, Yarnscombe

TOTNES PLU
Ashprington, Berry Pomeroy, South Brent, Brixham, Buckfastleigh (1836–94), East Buckfastleigh (1894–1930), West Buckfastleigh (1894–1930), Churston Ferrers, Cornworthy, Dartington, Dartmouth (1891–1930), Dean Prior, Diptford, Dittisham, Halwell, Harberton, Little Hempston, Holne, North Huish, Kingswear, Marldon, Moreleigh, Paignton, Rattery, St Petrox (1836–91), St Saviour (1836–91), Staverton, Stoke Gabriel, Totnes, Townstall (1836–91), Ugborough

In Other Poor Law Counties:

CHARD PLU (Somerset)
Yarcombe (1836–94)

DULVERTON PLU (Somerset)
Morebath (1856–94)

LAUNCESTON PLU (Cornwall)
Broadwoodwidger (1852–1930), Northcott (1852–1930), North Petherwin, St Giles on the Heath (1852–1930), Virginstow (1852–1930), Werrington

TAUNTON PLU (Somerset)
Churchstanton[36]

WELLINGTON PLU (Somerset)
Burlescombe, Clayhidon, Culmstock, Hemyock, Holcombe Rogus (before 1850–1930)

SANITARY DISTRICTS

AXMINSTER RSD
same as PLU less pt Seaton and Beer

BAMPTON USD
pt Bampton

BARNSTAPLE RSD
same as PLU less Barnstaple, Ilfracombe, Lynton, pt Pilton, pt Bishop's Tawton

BARNSTAPLE USD
Barnstaple, pt Pilton, pt Bishop's Tawton

BIDEFORD RSD
same as PLU less Bideford, Northam

BIDEFORD USD
Bideford

LOWER BRIXHAM USD
pt Brixham

BUCKFASTLEIGH USD (Jan[37]–apptd day 1894)
pt Buckfastleigh

BUDLEIGH SALTERTON USD
pt East Budleigh

CHARD RSD
same as PLU for the Devon par

COCKINGTON USD (Jan[38]–apptd day 1894)
Cockington

COMPTON GIFFORD USD
Compton Gifford

CREDITON RSD
same as PLU less pt Crediton

CREDITON USD
pt Crediton

DARTMOUTH USD
Dartmouth (1891–94), St Petrox (1875–91), St Saviour (1875–91), pt Stoke Fleming (1875–85), Townstall (1875–91)

DAWLISH USD
pt Dawlish

DEVONPORT USD
Devonport, Stoke Damerel

DULVERTON RSD
same as PLU for the Devon par

EXETER USD
same as Exeter incorp for poor

EXMOUTH USD
pt Littleham, pt Withycombe Raleigh

HOLSWORTHY RSD
same as PLU for the Devon pars

HONITON RSD
same as PLU less Honiton, Ottery St Mary, Sidmouth

HONITON USD
Honiton

ILFRACOMBE USD
Ilfracombe
IVYBRIDGE USD
pt Cornwood, pt Ermington, pt Harford, pt Ugborough
KINGSBRIDGE RSD
same as PLU less pt Cornwood, Kingsbridge (1893), Kingsbridge and Dodbrooke (1893–94), pt Malborough, pt Stoke Fleming
KINGSBRIDGE USD (1893[39]–94)
Kingsbridge and Dodbrooke
KINGSBRIDGE AND DODBROOKE USD (1893[39])
Kingsbridge and Dodbrooke
LAUNCESTON RSD
same as PLU for Devon pars
LYNTON USD
Lynton
SOUTH MOLTON RSD
same as PLU less South Molton, pt Bishop's Tawton
SOUTH MOLTON USD
South Molton
NEWTON ABBOT RSD
same as PLU less pt Bishopsteignton, Cockington, pt Dawlish, pt St Mary Church, St Nicholas, pt Stokeinteignhead, East Teignmouth, West Teignmouth, Tormoham
NORTHAM USD
Northam
OKEHAMPTON RSD
same as PLU less pt Okehampton (1885–94)
OKEHAMPTON USD (1885–94)
pt Okehampton
OTTERY ST MARY USD
Ottery St Mary
PAIGNTON USD
Paignton
PLYMOUTH USD
Plymouth Charles, Plymouth St Andrew
PLYMPTON ST MARY RSD
same as PLU less Compton Gifford, pt Ermington, pt Harford
ST MARY CHURCH USD
pt St Mary Church
ST THOMAS RSD
same as PLU less pt East Budleigh, pt Littleham, St Thomas the Apostle, pt Withycombe Raleigh
ST THOMAS THE APOSTLE USD
St Thomas the Apostle
SALCOMBE USD
pt Malborough
SEATON USD
pt Seaton and Beer
SIDMOUTH USD
Sidmouth
TAUNTON RSD
same as PLU for the Devon par
TAVISTOCK RSD
same as PLU
TEIGNMOUTH USD
pt Bishopsteignton, pt Dawlish, St Nicholas, pt Stokeinteignhead, East Teignmouth, West Teignmouth
TIVERTON RSD
same as PLU less pt Bampton, Tiverton
TIVERTON USD
Tiverton
TORQUAY USD
Tormoham
TORRINGTON RSD
same as PLU less Great Torrington
GREAT TORRINGTON USD
Great Torrington
TOTNES RSD
same as PLU less pt Berry Pomeroy, pt Brixham, pt Buckfastleigh, Paignton, St Petrox, St Saviour, Totnes, Townstall, pt Ugborough
TOTNES USD
pt Berry Pomeroy, Totnes
WELLINGTON RSD
same as PLU for the Devon pars
WOLBOROUGH USD
pt East Ogwell, Wolborough

ADMINISTRATIVE COUNTY

For MBs see BOROUGHS, and for CBs see ASSOCIATED COUNTY BOROUGHS, both earlier in this Part of the *Guide*.

ASHBURTON UD (1898[40]–1974)
Ashburton
AXMINSTER UD (1915[41]–53[42])
Axminster Town
AXMINSTER RD
Axminster (1894–1915), Axminster (1953–74), Axminster Hamlets (1915–62), Axmouth, Beer, Chardstock (1896–1974), Colyton, Combpyne (1894–1939), Combpyne Rousdon (1939–74), Dalwood, Hawkchurch (1896–1974), Kilmington, Land Common to Axminster and Kilmington (1894–1915), Land Common to Axminster Hamlets and Kilmington (1915–74), Membury, Musbury, Rousdon (1894–1939), Shute, Stockland, Thorncombe (1894–96), Uplyme
BAMPTON UD (1894–1935)
Bampton
BARNSTAPLE RD
Arlington, Ashford, Atherington, Berrynarbor, Bittadon, Bratton Fleming, Braunton, High Bray, Brendon, Challcombe, Combe Martin, Countisbury, East Down, West Down, Fremington, Georgeham, Goodleigh, Heanton Punchardon, Horwood, Instow, Kentisbury, Landkey, Loxhore, Martinhoe, Marwood, Mortehoe, Newton Tracey, Parracombe, West Pilton, Shirwell, Stoke Rivers, Swimbridge, Tawstock, Bishop's Tawton, Trentishoe, Westleigh

BIDEFORD RD
Abbotsham, Alwington, Buckland Brewer, Bulkworthy, Clovelly, Hartland, Landcross, Littleham, Lundy Island, Monkleigh, Newton St Petrock, Parkham, East Putford, Welcombe, Woolfardisworthy

BRIXHAM UD (1895[43]–1967[44])
Brixham

LOWER BRIXHAM UD (1894–95[43])
Brixham

BROADWOODWIDGER RD (1894–1966[45])
Broadwoodwidger, Northcott, North Petherwin, St Giles on the Heath, Virginstow, Werrington

BUCKFASTLEIGH UD
East Buckfastleigh

BUDLEIGH SALTERTON UD
Budleigh Salterton

COCKINGTON UD (1894–1900[46])
Cockington

COMPTON GIFFORD UD (1894–96[47])
Compton Gifford

CREDITON UD
Crediton Town

CREDITON RD
Bow, Brushford, Chawleigh, Cheriton Bishop, Cheriton Fitzpaine, Clannaborough, Coldridge, Colebrooke, Crediton Hamlets, Down St Mary, Eggesford, Hittisleigh, Kennerleigh, Lapford, Morchard Bishop, Newton St Cyres, Nymet Rowland, Poughill, Puddington, Sandford, Shobrooke, Stockleigh English, Stockleigh Pomeroy, Thelbridge, Upton Hellions, Washford Pyne, Wembworthy, Woolfardisworthy, Zeal Monachorum

CULMSTOCK RD (1894–1935)
Burlescombe, Clayhidon, Culmstock, Hemyock, Holcombe Rogus

DAWLISH UD
East Dawlish, West Dawlish (1935–74)

EXMOUTH UD
Littleham, Withycombe Raleigh

HEAVITREE UD (1896[48]–1913[49])
Heavitree

HOLSWORTHY RD[50]
Ashwater, Abbots Bickington, Bradford, Bradworthy, Bridgerule (1950–74), Bridgerule East (1894–1950), Bridgerule West (1894–1950), Broadwoodwidger (1966–74), Clawton, Cookbury, Halwill, Hollacombe, Holsworthy (1894–1900), Holsworthy (1964–74), Holsworthy Hamlets (1901–74), Luffincott, Milton Damerel, Pancrasweek, West Putford, Pyworthy, St Giles on the Heath (1966–74), Sutcombe, Tetcott, Thornbury, Black Torrington, Virginstow (1966–74)

HOLSWORTHY UD (1900[52]–64[53])
Holsworthy

HONITON RD
Awliscombe, Branscombe, Broadhembury, Buckerell, Combe Raleigh, Cotleigh, Dunkeswell, Farway, Feniton, Gittisham, Harpford (1894–1935), Luppitt, Monkton, Northleigh, Offwell, Venn Ottery (1894–1935), Payhembury, Plymtree, Salcombe Regis (1894–1935), Sheldon, Sidbury (1894–1935), Southleigh, Talaton, Upottery, Widworthy, Yarcombe

ILFRACOMBE UD
Ilfracombe

IVYBRIDGE UD (1894–1935)
Ivybridge

KINGSBRIDGE RD
East Allington, West Alvington, Aveton Gifford, Bigbury, Blackawton, Buckland Tout Saints, Charleton, Chivelstone, Churchstow, South Huish, Kingston, Loddiswell, Malborough, South Milton, Modbury, South Pool, East Portlemouth, Ringmore, Sherford, Slapton, Stoke Fleming, Stokenham, Strete (1935–74), Thurlestone, Woodleigh

KINGSBRIDGE UD
Kingsbridge and Dodbrooke

LYNTON UD
Lynton

SOUTH MOLTON RD
East Anstey, West Anstey, East Buckland, West Buckland, Burrington, Charles, Cheldon, Chittlehamholt, Chittlehampton, Chumleigh, Creacombe, Filleigh, Knowstone, Mariansleigh, Meshaw, Molland, North Molton, South Molton (1967–74), Bishop's Nympton, George Nympton, King's Nympton, Queensnympton, Rackenford, Romansleigh, Rose Ash, Satterleigh and Warkleigh, Twitchen, Witheridge, East Worlington

NEWTON ABBOT RD
Abbotskerswell (1894–1935), Ashburton (1894–98), Bickington, Bishopsteignton, North Bovey, Bovey Tracey, Broadhempston, Buckland in the Moor, Chudleigh, Cockington (1900–28), Coffinswell, West Dawlish (1894–1935), Haccombe with Combe, Hennock, Highweek (1894–1901), Ideford, Ilsington, Ipplepen, Kingskerswell (1894–1935), Kerswells (1935–74), Kingsteignton, Lustleigh, Manaton, Moretonhampstead, Ogwell, Stokeinteignhead, Teigngrace, Torbryan, Trusham, Widecombe in the Moor, Woodland

NEWTON ABBOT UD (1894[51]–1974)
Highweek (1901–74), Milber (1901–74), Wolborough

NORTHAM UD
Northam

OKEHAMPTON RD
Ashbury, Beaworthy, Belstone, Bondleigh, Bratton Clovelly, Bridestowe, Broadwood Kelly, Chagford, Drewsteignton, Exbourne, Germansweek, Gidleigh, Hatherleigh, Highampton, Iddesleigh, Inwardleigh, Jacobstowe, Land Common to Bridestowe and Sourton, Meeth, Northlew, Monk Okehampton, Okehampton Hamlets, Sampford Courtenay, Sourton, Spreyton, North Tawton, South Tawton, Throwleigh

OTTERY ST MARY UD
Ottery St Mary

PAIGNTON UD (1894–1967[44])
Paignton

PLYMPTON ST MARY RD
Bickleigh, Brixton, Egg Buckland (1894–1939), Compton Gifford (1896–1939), Cornwood, Ermington, Harford, Holbeton, Ivybridge (1935–74), Laira Green (1894–96), Newton and Noss (1935–74), Newton Ferrers (1894–1935), Pennycross

(1894–98), Plympton St Mary (1894–1966), Plympton St Maurice (1894–1966), Plymstock (1894–1966), Revelstoke (1894–1935), St Budeaux (1894–1951), Shaugh Prior, Sparkwell (1966–74), Tamerton Foliot (1894–1951), Weston Peverell (1899–1935), Wembury, Yealmpton

ST MARY CHURCH UD (1894–1900[54])
St Mary Church

ST THOMAS RD
Alphington, Ashcombe, Ashton, Aylesbeare, Bicton, Brampford Speke, Bridford, East Budleigh, Christow, Broad Clyst, Clyst Honiton, Clyst Hydon, Clyst St George, Clyst St Lawrence, Clyst St Mary, Colaton Raleigh, Doddiscombsleigh, Dunchideock, Dunsford, Nether Exe, Exminster, Farringdon, Harpford (1935–68), Heavitree (1894–96), Holcombe Burnell, Huxham, Ide, Kenn, Kenton, pt Littleham (1894–96), Lympstone, Mamhead, Newton Poppleford (1898–1935), Newton Poppleford and Harpford (1968–74), Otterton, Pinhoe (1894–1966), Poltimore, Powderham, Rewe, Rockbeare, St Leonard (1894–1900), Shillingford St George, Sowton, Stoke Canon, Tedburn St Mary, Topsham (1894–1966), Upton Pyne, Whimple, Whitestone, Woodbury

ST THOMAS THE APOSTLE UD (1894–1900[55])
St Thomas the Apostle

SALCOMBE UD
Salcombe

SEATON UD
Seaton

SIDMOUTH UD
Sidmouth

EAST STONEHOUSE UD (1894–1914[56])
East Stonehouse

TAVISTOCK RD
Bere Ferrers, Bradstone, Brentor, Buckland Monachorum, Coryton, Dunterton, Horrabridge (1950–74), Kelly, Lamerton, Lewtrenchard, Lifton, Lydford, Marystow, Marytavy, Meavy, Milton Abbot, Petertavy, Sampford Spiney, Sheepstor, Stowford, Sydenham Damerel, Tavistock (1894–98), Tavistock (1966–74), Tavistock Hamlets (1898–1974), Thrushelton, Walkhampton, Whitchurch

TAVISTOCK UD (1898[57]–1966[58])
Tavistock

TEIGNMOUTH UD
St Nicholas, Teignmouth (1909–74), East Teignmouth (1894–1909), West Teignmouth (1894–1909)

TIVERTON RD
Bampton (1935–74), Bickleigh, Bradninch, Burlescombe (1935–74), Butterleigh, Cadbury, Cadeleigh, Clayhanger, Clayhidon (1935–74), Cruwys Morchard, Cullompton, Culmstock (1935–74), Halberton, Hemyock (1935–74), Hockworthy, Huntsham, Holcombe Rogus (1935–74), Kentisbeare, Loxbeare, Morebath, Oakford, Sampford Peverell, Silverton, Stoodleigh, Templeton, Thorverton, Uffculme, Uplowman, Washfield, Willand

TORRINGTON RD
Alverdiscott, Ashreigney, Beaford, High Bickington, Buckland Filleigh, Dolton, Dowland, Frithelstock, Huish, Huntshaw, Langtree, Merton, Peters Marland, Petrockstow, Roborough, St Giles in the Wood, Shebbear, Sheepwash, Little Torrington, Weare Giffard, Winkleigh, Yarnscombe

TOTNES RD
Ashprington, Berry Pomeroy, South Brent, West Buckfastleigh, Churston Ferrers (1894–1967), Cornworthy, Dartington, Dean Prior, Diptford, Dittisham, Halwell, Harberton, Little Hempston, Holne, North Huish, Kingswear, Marldon, Moreleigh, Rattery, Staverton, Stoke Gabriel, Ugborough

WOLBOROUGH UD (1894[51])
Wolborough

NON-METROPOLITAN COUNTY

As constituted 1 Apr 1974, defined in terms of Adm Co units as of 31 Mar.

EAST DEVON DIST
Axminster RD, Budleigh Salterton UD, Exmouth UD, Honiton MB, Honiton RD, Ottery St Mary UD, pt St Thomas RD (the pars not in Teignbridge Dist), Seaton UD, Sidmouth UD

NORTH DEVON DIST
Barnstaple MB, Barnstaple RD, Ilfracombe UD, Lynton UD, South Molton RD

WEST DEVON DIST
Okehampton MB, Okehampton RD, Tavistock RD

EXETER DIST
Exeter CB, Devon County Buildings Area

SOUTH HAMS DIST
Dartmouth MB, Kingsbridge RD, Kingsbridge UD, Plympton St Mary RD, Salcombe UD, Totnes MB, Totnes RD

PLYMOUTH DIST
Plymouth CB, Plymouth Breakwater (Fort and Lighthouse)

TEIGNBRIDGE DIST
Ashburton UD, Buckfastleigh UD, Dawlish UD, Newton Abbot RD, Newton Abbot UD, pt St Thomas RD (Alphington, Ashcombe, Ashton, Bridford, Christow, Doddiscombsleigh, Dunchideock, Dunsford, Exminster, Holcombe Burnell, Ide, Kenn, Kenton, Mamhead, Powderham, Shillingford St George, Tedburn St Mary, Whitstone), Teignmouth UD

TIVERTON DIST
Crediton RD, Crediton UD, Tiverton MB, Tiverton RD

TORBAY DIST
Torbay CB

TORRIDGE DIST
Bideford MB, Bideford RD, Holsworthy RD, Lundy Island, Northam UD, Torrington RD, Great Torrington MB

DORSET

ALTERATIONS IN COUNTY BOUNDARIES

As noted by year below, Dorset pars gained territory from or lost it to pars in adjoining counties, or were entirely transferred to them. Details of these alterations are noted in Part I of the *Guide* under Dorset.

ANCIENT COUNTY (until 1889: Hds, Bors, MBs, PLUs, RSDs, USDs)
1844 Axminster, Holwell, Stockland, Thorncombe. *1860s* Hampreston. *1880s* Tollard Royal. *1884* Chardstock.

ADMINISTRATIVE COUNTY (1889–1974: Hds,[1] PLUs, MBs, UDs, RDs)
1895 Goathill, Poyntington, Sandford Orcas, Seaborough, Trent, Wambrook. *1896* Chardstock, Hawkchurch. *1931* Kinson. *1947* West Parley. *1966* Broadwindsor, Buckhorn Weston, Fifehead Magdalen, Kington Magna, Marshwood, South Perrott, Sandford Orcas, Thorncombe, Whitechurch Canonicorum.

NON-METROPOLITAN COUNTY (from 1974: Dists)
1974 Burton, Hurn, St Leonards and St Ives.

HUNDREDS[1]

ALTON PANCRAS LBTY
Alton Pancras

BADBURY HD
Chalbury, Moor Crichel, Gussage St Michael, Hinton Parva, Hinton Martell, Horton, Shapwick, Tarrant Crawford, Wimborne Minster[2]

BEAMINSTER HD
Beaminster, Cheddington, Chardstock, Corscombe, Netherbury, Stoke Abbott, Wambrook

BEAMINSTER FORUM AND REDHONE HD
Bradpole,[2] Mapperton, Mosterton, South Perrot, North Poorton, pt Toller Porcorum

BERE REGIS HD
Bere Regis, Milborne Stileham (from 1866), Winterborne Kingston

BINDON LBTY
Chaldon Herring, pt Edmondsham, West Lulworth, pt Moreton, pt Pulham, Wool

BROADWINDSOR LBTY
Broadwindsor

BROWNSHALL HD
Stourton Caundle, Holwell (from 1844), Stalbridge, Stock Gaylard

BUCKLAND NEWTON HD
Buckland Newton, Mappowder, pt Pulham, Glanvilles Wootton

CERNE, TOTBURY AND MODBURY HD
Cattistock, Nether Cerne, Cerne Abbas, West Compton, Godmanston, pt Hawkchurch, Hillfield

COGDEAN HD
Canford Magna,[2] Charlton Marshall, Corfe Mullen, Hamworthy,[2] Kinson (from 1866), Longfleet[2] (from 1866), Lytchett Matravers, Lytchett Minster, Parkstone[2] (from 1866), Sturminster Marshall

COOMBS DITCH HD
Anderson, Blandford Forum,[2] Blandford St Mary, Bloxworth, Winterborne Clenston, Winterborne Tomson, Winterborne Whitechurch

CORFE CASTLE HD
Corfe Castle[2]

CRANBORNE HD
Ashmore, Bellchalwell, pt Cranborne, pt Edmondsham, Farnham, pt Hampreston, West Parley, Pentridge, Shillingstone, Tarrant Gunville, Tarrant Rushton, pt Tollard Royal, Turnworth, Withcampton, East Woodyates (from 1858)

CULLIFORD TREE HD
Broadway, Buckland Ripers, pt West Chickerell, West Knighton, Melcombe Regis,[2] Osmington, Radipole,[2] West Stafford, pt Upwey, Whitcombe, pt Winterborne Came, Winterborne Herringston, Winterborne Monkton

DEWLISH LBTY
Dewlish, pt Milborne St Andrew

EGGERTON HD
Askerswell, Long Bredy, Hooke, pt Powerstock, Winterbourne Abbas, Wraxall

FORDINGTON LBTY
Fordington,[2] Hermitage, pt Minterne Magna, pt Stockland (until 1844)

FRAMPTON LBTY
Bettiscombe, Bincombe, Burton Bradstock,[2] Compton Valence, Frampton, pt Winterborne Came

GEORGE HD
Bradford Peverell, Broadmayne, Charminster, Frome Whitfield (until 1610), Stinsford, Stratton, Winterborne St Martin

GILLINGHAM LBTY
Bourton (from 1866), Gillingham, Motcombe

GODDERTHORNE HD
Allington,[2] Shipton George, Walditch[2]

HALSTOCK LBTY
Halstock
HASILOR HD
Arne, Church Knowle, East Holme, Kimmeridge, Poole St James,[2] Steeple, Tyneham
HUNDREDSBARROW HD
Affpuddle, Turnerspuddle
KNOWLTON HD
Long Crichel, Gussage All Saints, Woodlands
LOOSEBARROW HD
Almer, Morden, Spetisbury
LODERS AND BOTHENHAMPTON LBTY
Bothenhampton,[2] Loders
MONKTON UP WIMBORNE HD[3]
Chettle, pt Cranborne, Tarrant Monkton
OWERMOIGNE LBTY
Owermoigne
PIDDLEHINTON LBTY
Piddlehinton
PIDDLETRENTHIDE LBTY
Gorewood (from 1858), pt Minterne Magna, Piddletrenthide
PIMPERNE HD
Bryanston, Durweston, Fifehead Neville, Hammoon, Hazelbury Bryan, Iwerne Steepleton, Langton Long Blandford, Pimperne, Stourpaine, Tarrant Hinton, Tarrant Keynston, Tarrant Launceston, Tarrant Rawston, Winterborne Houghton, Winterborne Stickland
ISLE OF PORTLAND LBTY
Portland
POWERSTOCK LBTY
pt Powerstock
PUDDLETOWN HD
Athelhampton, Burleston, pt Milborne St Andrew, Puddletown, Tincleton, Tolpuddle
REDLAND HD
Buckhorn Weston, Fifehead Magdalen, Hanford (from 1858), Iwerne Courtney, Kington Magna, Manston, Childe Okeford, Silton, East Stour, West Stour, Sutton Waldron, Todber
ROWBERROW HD
Langton Matravers, Studland, Swanage, Worth Matravers
RUSHMORE HD
Winterborne Zelston
RYME INTRINSECA LBTY
Ryme Intrinseca
SHERBORNE HD
Beer Hacket, Bradford Abbas, Castleton,[2] Bishop's Caundle, Purse Caundle, Caundle Marsh, Up Cerne, Nether Compton, Over Compton, Folke, Haydon, Holnest, Lillington, Longburton, Oborne, Sherborne,[2] Thornford, North Wootton
SIXPENNY HADLEY HD
Cann, Compton Abbas, Fontmell Magna, Sixpenny Hadley, Iwerne Minster, Melbury Abbas, East Orchard, West Orchard
STOUR PROVOST LBTY
Stour Provost
STURMINSTER NEWTON HD
Hinton St Mary, Margaret Marsh, Marnhull, Okeford Fitzpaine, Sturminster Newton
SUTTON POYNTZ LBTY
pt West Chickerell, Preston, Stockwood
SYDLING ST NICHOLAS LBTY
Sydling St Nicholas
TOLLERFORD HD
East Chelborough, West Chelborough, Chilfrome, Evershot, Frome St Quintin, Frome Vauchurch, Maiden Newton, Melbury Sampford, Rampisham, Toller Fratrum, pt Toller Porcorum, Wynford Eagle
UGGSCOMBE HD[4]
Abbotsbury, Chilcombe, Fleet, pt Hawkchurch, Kingston Russell, Langton Herring, Littlebredy, Litton Cheney, Portesham, Puncknowle, Swyre, Weymouth,[2] Winterborne Steepleton
WABYHOUSE LBTY
pt Upwey
WHITCHURCH CANONICORUM HD
Bridport,[2] Burstock, Catherston Leweston, Charmouth,[2] Chideock, Lyme Regis,[2] Marshwood, Pilsdon, pt Stockland (until 1844), Stanton St Gabriel, Symondsbury,[2] Thorncombe (until 1844), Whitechurch Canonicorum,[2] Wootton Fitzpaine
WHITEWAY HD
Cheselbourne, Hinton, Ibberton, Melcombe Horsey, Milton Abbas, Stoke Wake, Wolland
WIMBORNE ST GILES HD
Wimborne All Saints (until 1732), Wimborne St Giles, West Woodyates (from 1858)
WINFRITH HD[5]
Combe Keynes, East Lulworth, pt Moreton, Poxwell, East Stoke, Warmwell, Watercombe (from 1858), Winfrith Newburgh, Woodsford
WYKE REGIS AND ELWELL LBTY
Wyke Regis
YETMINSTER HD
Batcombe, Chetnole (from 1866), Clifton Maybank, Leigh (from 1866), Melbury Bubb, Melbury Osmond, Yetminster

BOROUGHS

Units with some degree of burghal character[6] are denominated 'Bor'. Those which did not sustain that status until the 19th cent are in italics. Municipal Boroughs were established by the Municipal Corporations Act, 1835,[7] or by later charter.

BLANDFORD FORUM BOR/MB
Blandford Forum (pt until 1896, ent 1896–1974)

BRIDPORT BOR/MB
pt Allington (1835–94), pt Bothenhampton

(1835–94), pt Bradpole (1835–94), Bridport, pt Burton Bradstock (1835–94), pt Symondsbury (1835–94), pt Walditch (1835–94)

CASTLETON BOR
pt Oborne

CHARMOUTH BOR
Charmouth

CORFE CASTLE BOR
Corfe Castle

DORCHESTER BOR[8]/MB
Dorchester (1927–74), Dorchester All Saints (until 1927), Dorchester Holy Trinity (pt until 1835, enlarged pt 1835–94), Dorchester St Peter,[9] pt Fordington (1835–94)

LYME REGIS BOR/MB
Lyme Regis (pt until 1889, ent 1889–1974)

MELCOMBE REGIS BOR (until 1571)
pt Radipole

NEWTON BOR
pt Studland

POOLE BOR/MB
pt Canford Magna (1835–66), Hamworthy (1835–1905), Longfleet (1866–1905), Parkstone (1866–1905), Poole (1905–74), Poole St James (until 1905)

SHAFTESBURY BOR/MB
Shaftesbury (1894–1974), pt Shaftesbury Holy Trinity (until 1894), pt Shaftesbury St James (until 1894), pt Shaftesbury St Peter (until 1894)

SHERBORNE BOR
pt Sherborne

STOBOROUGH BOR
pt Wareham Holy Trinity

WAREHAM BOR, MB (1886–1974)
pt Wareham Holy Trinity (until 1894), Wareham Lady St Mary (pt until 1886, ent 1886–1974), pt Wareham St Martin (until 1894)

WEYMOUTH BOR (until 1571)
pt Wyke Regis

WEYMOUTH AND MELCOMBE REGIS BOR (1571–1835)/MB
Bor: Melcombe Regis (when gains sep civ identity), pt Radipole (until Melcombe Regis gains sep civ identity), Weymouth (when gains sep civ identity), pt Wyke Regis (until Weymouth gains sep civ identity)
MB: Melcombe Regis, pt Radipole (1835–94), Weymouth, pt Wyke Regis (1835–94)

WHITECHURCH CANONICORUM BOR
Whitechurch Canonicorum

WIMBORNE MINSTER BOR
Wimborne Minster

POOR LAW UNIONS

In Dorset Poor Law County:[11]

BEAMINSTER PLU (Dorset, Somerset until 1896, ent Dorset thereafter)
Beaminster, Bettiscombe, Broadwinsor, Burstock, Chedington, East Chelborough, West Chelborough, Corscombe, Evershot, Halstock, Hooke, Mapperton, Marshwood, Melbury Osmund, Melbury Sampford, Mosterton, Netherbury, South Perrot, North Poorton, Pilsdon, Powerstock, Rampisham, Seaborough,[12] Stoke Abbot, Thorncombe[13] (1894–1930)

BLANDFORD PLU
Almer (1835–94), Anderson, Blandford Forum, Blandford St Mary, Bryanston, Charlton Marshall, Chettle (1894–1930), Durweston, Farnham (1894–1930), Hilton, Iwerne Courtney, Iwerne Steepleton, Langton Long Blandford, Milborne St Andrew, Milborne Stileham, Milton Abbas, Pimperne, Spetisbury, Stourpaine, Tarrant Crawford, Tarrant Gunville, Tarrant Hinton, Tarrant Keyneston, Tarrant Launceston, Tarrant Monkton, Tarrant Rawston, Tarrant Rushton, Turnworth, Winterborne Clenston, Winterborne Houghton, Winterborne Kingston, Winterborne Stickland, Winterborne Tomson, Winterborne Whitechurch, Winterborne Zelston

BRIDPORT PLU
Allington, Askerswell, Bothenhampton, Bradpole, Bridport, Burton Bradstock, Catherston Leweston, Charmouth (1894–1930), Chideock, Chilcombe, Litton Cheney, Loders, Stratton St Gabriel, Swyre, Symondsbury, Walditch, Whitechurch Canonicorum, Wootton Fitzpaine

CERNE PLU
Alton Pancras, Batcombe, Buckland Newton, Cattistock, Nether Cerne, Up Cerne, Cerne Abbas, Cheselbourne, Frome St Quintin, Godmanston, Gorewood, Hermitage, Hillfield, Mappowder, Melbury Bubb, Melcombe Horsey, Minterne Magna, Piddletrenthide, Pulham, Sydling St Nicholas, Glanvilles Wootton

CRANBORNE PLU (Mar–Aug 1836, then incl in WIMBORNE PLU to cr WIMBORNE AND CRANBORNE PLU, qv where pars orig in this PLU are indicated)

DORCHESTER PLU
Athelhampton, Long Bredy, Bradford Peverell, Broadmayne, Burleston, Compton Abbas, Charminster, Chilfrome, Compton Valence, Dewlish, Dorchester (1927–30), Dorchester All Saints (1836–1927), Dorchester Holy Trinity (1836–1927), Dorchester St Peter (1836–1927), Fordington (1836–1900), Frampton, Frome Vauchurch, Kingston Russell, West Knighton, Littlebredy, Maiden Newton, Piddlehinton, Puddletown, West Stafford, Stinsford, Stratton, Tincleton, Toller Fratrum, Toller Porcorum, Tolpuddle, Warmwell, Watercombe, Whitcombe, Winterborne Came, Winterborne Herringston, Winterborne Monkton, Winterborne St Martin, Winterborne Steepleton, Winterbourne Abbas, Woodsford, Wynford Eagle

POOLE PLU
Branksome (1894–1905), Canford Magna, Hamworthy (1835–1905), Kinson, Longfleet (1835–

PURBECK PLU (Mar–Sept 1836, then incl in WAREHAM PLU to cr WAREHAM AND PURBECK PLU, qv where pars orig in this PLU are indicated)

SHAFTESBURY INCORPORATION (until 1880s) See notes in following entry

1905), Lytchett Matravers, Lytchett Minster, Parkstone (1835–1905), Poole (1905–30), Poole St James (1835–1905)

SHAFTESBURY PLU

Alcester (1894–1921), Ashmore, Bourton (1894–1930), Buckhorn Weston (1894–1930), Cann, Compton Abbas, Fontmell Magna, Gillingham, Iwerne Minster, Kington Magna (1894–1930), Margaret Marsh, Melbury Abbas, Motcombe, East Orchard, West Orchard, Shaftesbury (1894–1930), Shaftesbury Holy Trinity,[14] Shaftesbury St James,[14] Shaftesbury St Peter,[14] Silton (1894–1930), East Stour, West Stour, Stour Provost, Sutton Waldron, Todber

SHERBORNE (Dorset, Somerset until 1896, ent Dorset thereafter)

Beer Hacket, Bradford Abbas, Castleton, Bishop's Caundle, Purse Caundle, Caundle Marsh, Chetnole, Clifton Maybank, Nether Compton, Over Compton, Folke, Goathill,[12] Haydon, Holnest, Holwell, Leigh, Leweston, Lillington, Longburton, Oborne, Poyntington,[12] Ryme Intrinseca, Sandford Orcas,[12] Sherborne, Stockwood, Thornford, Trent,[12] North Wootton, Yetminster

STURMINSTER PLU

Bellchalwell (1835–84), Stourton Caundle, Fifehead Magdalen, Fifehead Neville, Hammoon, Hanford (1858[15]–1930), Hazelbury Bryan, Hinton St Mary, Ibberton, Lydlinch, Manston, Marnhull, Childe Okeford, Okeford Fitzpaine, Shillingstone, Stalbridge, Stock Gaylard (1835–84), Stoke Wake, Sturminster Newton, Wooland

WAREHAM AND PURBECK PLU (pars in Purbeck PLU Mar–Sept 1836 only are indicated †)

Affpuddle, Arne, Bere Regis, Bloxworth, Chaldon Herring, Church Knowle†, Coombe Keynes, Corfe Castle†, East Holme, Kimmeridge†, East Lulworth, West Lulworth, Langton Matravers†, Moreton, Morden, St Martin (1894–1930), Steeple†, East Stoke, Studland†, Swanage†, Turners Puddle, Tyneham†, Wareham Holy Trinity, Wareham Lady St Mary, Wareham St Martin, Winfrith Newburgh, Wool, Worth Matravers†

WEYMOUTH PLU

Abbotsbury, Bincombe, Broadway, Buckland Ripers (1836–94), Chickerell, Fleet, Langton Herring, Melcombe Regis (1836–1920), Owermoigne, Portesham, Portland, Poxwell, Preston, Radipole, Upwey, Weymouth, Wyke Regis

WIMBORNE AND CRANBORNE PLU (pars in Cranborne PLU Mar–Aug 1836 only are indicated†)

Alderholt (1894–1930), Almer (1894–1930), Chalbury, Chettle†, Colehill (1896–1930), Corfe Mullen, Cranborne†, Long Crichel†, Moor Crichel†, Edmondsham†, Farnham† (1835–94), Gussage All Saints†, Gussage St Michael†, Hampreston, Sixpenny Handley†, Hinton Martell, Hinton Parva, Holt (1894–1930), Horton†, Pamphill (1894–1930), West Parley, Pentridge†, Shapwick, Sturminster Marshall, Verwood (1894–1930), Wimborne Minster, Wimborne St Giles†, Witchampton, Woodlands†, East Woodyates (1858[15]–1930), West Woodyates

In Other Poor Law Cos:

AXMINSTER PLU (Devon)

Chardstock,[16] Charmouth (1836–94), Hawkchurch,[16] Lyme Regis, Thorncombe (1836–94)

CHARD PLU (Somerset)

Wambrook[17]

MERE PLU (Wilts)

Bourton (1835–94), Silton (1835–94)

WINCANTON PLU (Somerset)

Buckhorn Weston (1835–94), Kington Magna (1835–94)

SANITARY DISTRICTS

AXMINSTER RSD[19]

same as PLU for Dorset pars less Lyme Regis

BEAMINSTER RSD

same as PLU

BLANDFORD RSD

same as PLU less pt Bladford Forum, pt Blandford St Mary, pt Bryanston

BLANDFORD FORUM USD

pt Blandford Forum, pt Blandford St Mary, Bryanston

BRIDPORT RSD

same as PLU less par and pts of pars in Bridport USD

BRIDPORT USD

pt Allington, pt Bothenhampton, pt Bradpole, Bridport, pt Burton Bradstock, pt Symondsbury, pt Walditch

CERNE RSD

same as PLU

CHARD RSD

same as PLU for the Dorset par

DORCHESTER RSD

same as PLU less pars and pts of pars in Dorchester USD

DORCHESTER USD

Dorchester All Saints, pt Dorchester Holy Trinity, Dorchester St Peter, pt Fordington

KINSON USD (1892[18]–94)

pt Kinson

LYME REGIS USD

Lyme Regis[20]

MERE RSD

same as PLU for the Dorset par

POOLE RSD

same as PLU less Hamworthy, Longfleet, Melcombe Regis, Parkstone, Poole St James, Portland, pt Radipole, Weymouth, pt Wyke Regis

POOLE USD
Hamworthy, Longfleet, Parkstone, Poole St James

PORTLAND USD
Portland

SHAFTESBURY RSD
same as PLU less pts of pars in Shaftesbury USD

SHAFTESBURY USD
pt Shaftesbury Holy Trinity, pt Shaftesbury St James, pt Shaftesbury St Peter

SHERBORNE RSD
same as PLU less pts of pars in Sherborne USD

SHERBORNE USD
pt Castleton, pt Sherborne

STURMINSTER RSD
same as PLU

SWANAGE USD
Swanage

WAREHAM AND PURBECK RSD
same as PLU less Swanage, pt Wareham Holy Trinity, Wareham Lady St Mary (pt 1875–86, ent 1886–94), pt Wareham St Martin

WAREHAM USD
pt Wareham Holy Trinity, Wareham Lady St Mary (pt 1875–86, ent 1886–94), pt Wareham St Martin

WEYMOUTH RSD
same as PLU less Melcombe Regis, Portland, pt Radipole, Weymouth, pt Wyke Regis

WEYMOUTH AND MELCOMBE REGIS USD
Melcombe Regis, pt Radipole, Weymouth, pt Wyke Regis

WIMBORNE AND CRANBORNE RSD
same as PLU less pt Wimborne Minster (1892–94)

WIMBORNE MINSTER UD (1892[21]–94)
pt Wimborne Minster

WINCANTON RSD
same as PLU for Dorset pars

ADMINISTRATIVE COUNTY

For MBs see listing for BOROUGHS earlier in this Part of the *Guide*.

BEAMINSTER RD
Beaminster, Bettiscombe, Broadwindsor, Burstock, Chedington, East Chelborough, West Chelborough, Corscombe, Evershot, Halstock, Hooke, Kinson (1894–1931), Mapperton, Marshwood, Melbury Osmond, Melbury Sampford, Mosterton, Netherbury, South Perrott, Pilsdon, North Poorton, Powerstock, Rampisham, Seaborough (1895–1974), Stoke Abbott, Thorncombe (1896–1974)

BLANDFORD RD
Anderson, Blandford St Mary (pt 1894–96, ent 1896–1974), Bryanston (pt 1894–96, ent 1896–1974), Catherston Leweston, Charlton Marshall, Chideock, Durweston, Farnham (1933–74), Fifehead Neville, Hammoon, Hazelbury Bryan, Hilton, Iwerne Courtney, Iwerne Steepleton, Langton Long Blandford, Milborne (1933–74), Milborne St Andrew (1894–1933), Milborne Stileham (1894–1933), Milton Abbas, Pimperne, Spetisbury, Stanton St Gabriel, Stourpaine, Tarrant Crawford, Tarrant Gunville, Tarrant Hinton, Tarrant Monkton, Tarrant Keyneston, Tarrant Launceston, Tarrant Rawston, Tarrant Rushton, Turnworth, Whitechurch Canonicorum, Winterborne Clenston, Winterborne Houghton, Winterborne Kingston, Winterborne Stickland, Winterborne Tompson (1894–1933), Winterborne Zelston, Winterborne Whitechurch, Wootton Fitzpaine

BRANKSOME UD (1894–1905[10])
Branksome

BRIDPORT RD
Allington, Askerswell, Bothenhampton, Bradpole, Burton Bradstock, Catherston Leweston, Charmouth, Chideock, Chilcombe, Litton Cheney, Loders, Puncknowle, Shipton George, Stanton St Gabriel, Swyre, Symondsbury, Whitechurch Canonicorum, Wootton Fitzpaine

CERNE RD (1894–1933)
Alton Pancras, Batcombe, Buckland Newton, Cattistock, Nether Cerne, Up Cerne, Cerne Abbas, Cheselbourne, Frome St Quintin, Godmanston, Gorewood, Hermitage, Hilfield, Melbury Bubb, Melcombe Horsey, Minterne Magna, Piddletrenthide, Pulham, Sydling St Nicholas, Glanvilles Wootton

DORCHESTER RD
Abbotsbury (1933–74), Alton Pancras (1933–74), Athelhampton, Bincombe (1933–74), Bradford Peverell, Long Bredy, Broadmayne, Buckland Newton (1933–74), Burleston, Cattistock (1933–74), Nether Cerne (1933–74), Up Cerne (1933–74), Cerne Abbas (1933–74), Charminster, Cheselbourne (1933–74), Chickerell (1933–74), Chilfrome, Compton Valence, Dewlish, Fleet (1933–74), Fordington (1894–1900), Frampton, Frome St Quintin (1933–74), Frome Vauchurch, Godmanston (1933–66), Godmanstone (1966–74), Kingston Russell, West Knighton, Langton Herring (1933–74), Littlebredy, Maiden Newton, Melcombe Horsey (1933–74), Minterne Magna (1933–74), Osmington (1933–74), Owermoigne (1933–74), Piddlehinton, Piddletrenthide (1933–74), Portesham (1933–74), Poxwell (1933–74), Puddletown, West Stafford, Stinsford, Stratton, Sydling St Nicholas (1933–74), Tincleton, Toller Fratrum, Toller Porcorum, Tolpuddle, Warmwell, Watercombe, Whitcombe, Winterborne Came, Winterborne Herringston, Winterborne Monkton, Winterborne St Martin, Winterborne Steepleton, Winterbourne Abbas, Woodsford, Glanvilles Wootton, Wynford Eagle

POOLE RD (1894–1933)
Branksome (1894–1905), Canford Magna, Lytchett Matravers, Litchett Minster

PORTLAND UD
Portland
SHAFTESBURY RD
Alcester (1894–1921), Ashmore, Buckhorn Weston, Cann, Compton Abbas, Fontmell Magna, Gillingham, Iwerne Minster, Kington Magna, Margaret Marsh, Melbury Abbas, Mere, Motcombe, East Orchard, West Orchard, Silton, East Stour, West Stour, Stour Prevost, Sutton Waldron, Todber
SHERBORNE RD
Batcombe (1933–74), Beer Hacket, Bradford Abbas, Castleton, Bishop's Caundle, Purse Caundle, Caundle Marsh, Chetnole, Clifton Maybank, Nether Compton, Over Compton, Folke, Goathill (1895–1974), Haydon, Hermitage (1933–74), Hilfield (1933–74), Holnest, Holwell, Leigh, Leweston, Lillington, Longburton, Melbury Bubb (1933–74), Oborne, Poyntington (1895–1974), Ryme Intrinseca, Sandford Orcas (1895–1974), Stockwood, Thornford, Trent (1895–1974), North Wootton, Yetminster
SHERBORNE UD
Sherborne
STURMINSTER RD
Stourton Caundle, Durweston, Fifehead Magdalen, Fifehead Neville, Hammoon, Hanford, Hazelbury Bryan, Hinton St Mary, Ibberton, Iwerne Steepleton, Langton Long Blandford, Lydlinch, Manston, Mappowder (1933–74), Marnhull, Childe Okeford, Okeford Fitzpaine, Pimperne, Pulham (1933–74), Shillingstone, Stalbridge, Stoke Wake, Stourpaine, Sturminster Newton, Tarrant Hinton, Tarrant Keynston, Tarrant Launceston, Tarrant Rawston, Winterborne Houghton, Winterborne Stickland, Wolland, Glanvilles Wootton (1933–74)
SWANAGE UD
Swanage
WAREHAM AND PURBECK RD
Affpuddle, Arne, Bere Regis, Bloxworth, Chaldon Herring, Church Knowle, Coombe Keynes, Corfe Castle, East Holme, Kimmeridge, East Lulworth, West Lulworth, Langton Matravers, Lytchett Matravers (1933–74), Lytchett Minster (1933–74), Morden, Moreton, Steeple, East Stoke, Studland, Turners Puddle, Tyneham, Winfrith Newburgh, Wool, Worth Matravers
WEYMOUTH RD (1894–1933)
Abbotsbury, Bincombe, Broadway, Chickerell, Fleet, Langton Herring, Osmington, Owermoigne, Portesham, Poxwell, Preston, East Radipole (1894–95), Upwey, Wyke Regis
WIMBORNE AND CRANBORNE RD
Alderholt, Almer, Chalbury, Corfe Mullen, Cranborne, Long Crichel, Moor Crichel, Edmondsham, Gussage All Saints, Gussage St Michael, Hampreston, Sixpenny Hadley, Hinton Martell, Hinton Parva, Holt, Horton, Pamphill, West Parley, Pentridge, Shapwick, Sturminster Marshall, Verwood, Wimborne St Giles, Witchampton, Woodlands, East Woodyates (1894–1933), West Woodyates (1894–1933)
WIMBORNE MINSTER UD
Wimborne Minster

NON-METROPOLITAN COUNTY

As constituted 1 Apr 1974, defined in terms of Adm Co units as of 31 Mar.

BOURNEMOUTH DIST
Bournemouth CB
CHRISTCHURCH DIST
from Hants: Christchurch MB, pt Ringwood and Fordingbridge RD[22]
NORTH DORSET DIST
Blandford RD, Blandford Forum MB, Shaftesbury MB, Shaftesbury RD, Sturminster RD
WEST DORSET DIST
Beaminster RD, Bridgport MB, Bridport RD, Dorchester MB, Dorchester RD, Lyme Regis MB, Sherborne RD, Sherborne UD
POOLE DIST
Poole MB
PURBECK DIST
Swanage UD, Wareham MB, Wareham and Purbeck RD
WEYMOUTH AND PORTLAND DIST
Portland UD, Weymouth and Melcombe Regis MB
WIMBORNE DIST
from Dorset: Wimborne and Cranborne RD, Wimborne Minster UD
from Hants: pt Ringwood and Fordingbridge RD[23]

ESSEX

ALTERATIONS IN COUNTY BOUNDARIES

As noted by year below, Essex pars gained territory from or lost it to pars in adjoining counties or county boroughs, or were entirely transferred to them. Details of these alterations are noted in Part I of the *Guide* under Essex.

ANCIENT COUNTY (until 1889: Hds, Bors, MBs, PLUs, RSDs, USDs)
1866 Bures, Bures St Mary. *1879* Haverhill, Sturmer. *1883* Kedington, Sturmer. *1884* Sturmer. *1885* Helion Bumpstead, Sturmer.

ADMINISTRATIVE COUNTY (1889–1974: Hds,[1] PLUs, MBs, RDs, UDs, with East Ham CB, West Ham CB, Southend on Sea CB associated)
1895 Great Chishill, Little Chishill, Heydon, Kedington. *1896* Ballingdon. *1914* Southend on Sea. *1915* East Ham. *1933* Eastwood, North Shoebury, Shoebury, Shopland, Southend on Sea, Great Wakering. *1934* Great Parndon. *1965* Ashdon, Barking, Helion Bumpstead, Cann Hall, Great Chesterford, Chigwell, Chingford, Chrishall, Cranham, Dagenham, Hadstock, Havering-atte-Bower, Hempstead, Hornchurch, Ilford, Leyton, Noak Hill, Radwinter, Rainham, Romford, Upminster, Walthamstow, Wanstead, Great Warley, Wennington, Woodford.

NON-METROPOLITIAN COUNTY (from 1974: Dists)

ASSOCIATED COUNTY BOROUGHS

For constituent pars see listing for BOROUGHS in this Part of the *Guide*.

EAST HAM CB (1915–1965)
Cr 1915 when East Ham MB made a CB.[2] Abol 1965 when transf to Gtr London to help constitute Newham LB.[3]

WEST HAM CB (1889–1965)
Abol 1965 when transf to Gtr London to help constitute Newham LB.[3]

SOUTHEND ON SEA CB (1914–1974)
Cr 1914 when Southend on Sea MB made a CB.[4] Bdry: 1933.[5]

HUNDREDS[1]

BARSTABLE HD
Basildon (from 1866), North Benfleet, South Benfleet, Bowers Gifford, Bulphan, Great Burstead, Little Burstead, pt Canvey Island (from 1880), Chadwell St Mary, Corringham, Doddinghurst, Downham, Dunton, Fobbing, East Horndon, West Horndon, Horndon on the Hill, Hutton, Ingrave, Laindon, Langdon Hills, Lee Chapel (from 1858), Mucking, Nevendon, Orsett, Pitsea, Ramsden Bellhouse, Ramsden Crays, Shenfield, Stanford le Hope, pt Thundersley, Little Thurrock, East Tilbury, West Tilbury, Vange, Wickford

BECONTREE HD
Barking, Dagenham, East Ham, West Ham,[6] Ilford (from 1866), Little Ilford, Leyton, Walthamstow, Wanstead, Woodford

CHAFFORD HD
Aveley, Brentwood (from 1866), Childerditch, Cranham, North Ockendon, South Ockendon, Rainham, Stifford, Grays Thurrock, West Thurrock, Upminster, Great Warley, Little Warley, South Weald, Wennington

CHELMSFORD HD
Great Baddow, Little Baddow, Blackmore, Boreham, Broomfield, Buttsbury, Chelmsford,[6] Chignall (from 1888), Chignall St James (until 1888), Chignall Smealy (until 1888), Danbury, Fryerning, East Hanningfield, South Hanningfield, West Hanningfield, Ingatestone, pt Great Leighs, Little Leighs, Margaretting, Mountnessing, Rettendon, Roxwell, Runwell, Sandon, Springfield, Stock, Great Waltham, Little Waltham, Widford, Woodham Ferrers, Writtle[6]

CLAVERING HD
Berden,[6] Clavering, Farnham, pt Henham, Langley, Manuden, pt Stanstead Mountfitchett, Ugley

DENGIE HD[7]
Althorne, Asheldham, Bradwell on Sea, Burnham, Creeksea, Dengie, North Fambridge, Hazeleigh, Latchingdon, Mayland, Mundon, Cold Norton, Pur-

leigh, St Lawrence, Snoreham (until mid 18th cent), Southminster, Steeple, Stow Maries, Tillingham, Woodham Mortimer, Woodham Walter

DUNMOW HD

Barnston, Broxted, Great Canfield, Little Canfield, Chickney, Great Dunmow, Little Dunmow, Good Easter, High Easter, Great Easton, Little Easton, Lindsell, Mashbury, Pleshey,[6] pt Abbess Roding, Aythorpe Roding, Berners Roding, High Roding, Leaden Roding, Margaret Roding, White Roding, Shellow Bowells, Thaxted,[6] Tilty, Willingale Doe, Willingale Spain

FRESHWELL HD

Ashdon, Great Bardfield,[6] Little Bardfield, Bardfield Saling, Bartlow End (from 1866), Helion Bumpstead (pt until 1885, ent from 1885), Hadstock, Hempstead, Radwinter, Great Sampford, Little Sampford

HARLOW HD

Great Hallingbury, Little Hallingbury, Harlow,[6] Hatfield Broad Oak, Latton, Matching, Netteswell, Great Parndon, Little Parndon, pt Roydon, Sheering, pt North Weald Bassett

HAVERING-ATTE-BOWER LBTY

Havering-atte-Bower, Hornchurch, Romford

HINCKFORD HD

Alphamstone, Ashen, pt Ballingdon, Belchamp Otten, Belchamp St Paul, Belchamp Walter, Birdbrook, Bocking, Borley, Braintree, Bulmer, Steeple Bumpstead, Bures (from 1866), pt Bures St Mary (until 1866), Felsted, Finchingfield, Foxearth, Gestingthorpe, Gosfield, Halstead, pt Haverhill (until 1879), Castle Hedingham, Sible Hedingham, Great Henny, Little Henny, pt Kedington, Lamarsh, Liston, Great Maplestead, Little Maplestead, Middleton, Ovington, Panfield, Pebmarsh, Pentlow, Rayne, Ridgewell, Great Saling, Shalford, Stambourne, Stebbing, Stisted, Sturmer, Tilbury juxta Clare, Toppesfield, Twinstead, Wethersfield, Wickham St Paul, North Wood (from 1858), Great Yeldham, Little Yeldham

LEXDEN HD[8]

Aldham, West Bergholt, Birch (from 1816), Great Birch (until 1816), Little Birch (until 1816), Boxted, Mount Bures, Chappel, Great Coggeshall, Earls Colne, Wakes Colne, White Colne, Colne Engaine, Copford, Dedham, East Donyland, Easthorpe, Feering, Fordham, Great Horkesley, Little Horkesley, Inworth, Langham, Markshall, Messing, Pattiswick, Stanway, Great Tey, Little Tey, Marks Tey, Wivenhoe, Wormingford

ONGAR HD

Bobbingworth, Chigwell, Fyfield, Greenstead, Kelvedon Hatch, Lambourne, High Laver, Little Laver, Magdalen Laver, Loughton, Moreton, Navestock, Norton Mandeville, Chipping Ongar, High Ongar, pt Abbess Roding, Beauchamp Roding, Shelley, Stanford Rivers, Stapleford Abbotts, Stapleford Tawney, Stondon Massey, Theydon Bois, Theydon Garnon, Theydon Mount, pt North Weald Bassett

ROCHFORD HD

Ashingdon, Barling, Canewdon, pt Canvey Island (from 1880), Eastwood, South Fambridge, Foulness, Hadleigh, Havengore (from 1858), Hawkwell, Hockley, Leigh, Paglesham, Prittlewell, Rawreth, Rayleigh, Rochford, North Shoebury, South Shoebury, Shopland, Southchurch, Great Stambridge, Little Stambridge, Sutton, pt Thundersley, Great Wakering, Little Wakering

TENDRING HD[9]

Alresford, Ardleigh, Beaumont (until 1678), Beaumont cum Moze (from 1678), Great Bentley, Little Bentley, Bradfield,[6] Brightlingsea, Great Bromley, Little Bromley, Great Clacton, Little Clacton, Elmstead, Frating, Frinton, Great Holland, Little Holland, Kirby le Soken, Lawford, Manningtree,[6] Mistley,[6] Moze (until 1678), Great Oakley, Little Oakley, Ramsey, St Osyth, Tendring, Thorpe le Soken, Thorrington, Walton le Soken, Weeley, Wix, Wrabness

THURSTABLE HD

Goldhanger, Heybridge, Langford, Tollesbury, Tolleshunt d'Arcy, Tolleshunt Knights, Tolleshunt Major, Great Totham, Little Totham, Wickham Bishops

UTTLESFORD HD

Arkesden, Birchanger, Great Chesterford, Little Chesterford, Great Chishill, Little Chishill, Chrishall, Debden, Elmdon, Elsenham, pt Henham, Heydon, Littlebury, Newport,[6] Quendon, Rickling, Saffron Walden,[6] pt Stanstead Mountfitchet, Strethall, Takeley, Great Wenden (until 1662), Little Wenden (until 1662), Wendens Ambo (from 1662), Wendon Lofts, Wicken Bonhunt, Widdington, Wimbish

WALTHAM HD

Chingford, Epping, Nazeing, pt Roydon, Waltham Holy Cross[6]

WINSTREE HD

Abberton, Fingringhoe, Langenhoe, Layer Breton, Layer de la Haye, Layer Marney, East Mersea, West Mersea, Peldon, Salcot, Virley, Great Wigborough, Little Wigborough

WITHAM HD

Bradwell, Great Braxted, Little Braxted, Little Coggeshall, Cressing, Fairstead, Faulkbourne, Hatfield Peverel, Kelvedon, pt Great Leighs, Black Notley, White Notley, Rivenhall, Terling, Ulting, Witham[6]

BOROUGHS

Units with some degree of burghal character[10] are denominated 'Bor'.
Those which did not sustain that status until the 19th cent are in italics.
Municipal Boroughs were established by the Municipal Corporations Act, 1835,[11] or by later charter.

GREAT BARDFIELD BOR
Great Bardfield
BARKING MB (1931–65[3])
Barking
BERDEN BOR
Berden
CHELMSFORD BOR, MB (1888–1974)
Chelmsford
CHINGFORD MB (1938–65[3])
Chingford
COLCHESTER BOR/MB
Berechurch (1536–1897), Colchester (1897–1974), Colchester All Saints (until 1897), Colchester Holy Trinity (until 1897), Colchester St Botolph (until 1897), Colchester St Giles (until 1897), Colchester St James (until 1897), Colchester St Leonard (until 1897), Colchester St Martin (until 1897), Colchester St Mary at the Walls (until 1897), Colchester St Mary Magdalen (until 1897), Colchester St Nicholas (until 1897), Colchester St Peter (until 1897), Colchester St Runwald (until 1897), Greenstead (until 1897), Lexden (until 1897), Mile End St Michael (until 1897)
DAGENHAM MB (1938–65[3])
Dagenham
EAST HAM MB (1904–15[2]), CB (1915[2]–65[3])
East Ham
WEST HAM MB (1886–88), CB (1888–65[3])
West Ham, pt Wanstead (1886–94)
HARLOW BOR
Harlow
HARWICH BOR/MB
Dovercourt (until 1925), Harwich (1925–74), Harwich St Nicholas (until 1925)
HATFIELD REGIS BOR
Hatfield Broad Oak
ILFORD MB (1926–65[3])
Ilford
LEYTON MB (1926–65[3])
Cann Hall, Leyton
MALDON BOR/MB
Maldon (1934–74), Maldon All Saints (until 1934), Maldon St Mary (until 1934), Maldon St Peter (until 1934)
MANNINGTREE BOR
pt Bradfield, pt Mistley
NEWPORT BOR
Newport
PLESHEY BOR
Pleshey
ROMFORD MB (1937–65[3])
Havering-atte-Bower, Noak Hill, Romford
SAFFRON WALDEN MB (184 –1974)
Saffron Walden
SOUTHEND ON SEA MB (1892–1914[4]), CB (1914[4]–74)
Prittlewell (1892–1913), Southchurch (1892–1913), Southend on Sea (1913–74)
THAXTED BOR
Thaxted
WALTHAM BOR
Waltham Holy Cross
WALTHAMSTOW MB (1926–65[3])
Walthamstow
WANSTEAD AND WOODFORD MB (1937–65[3])
Wanstead, Woodford
WITHAM BOR
Witham
WRITTLE BOR
Writtle

POOR LAW UNIONS

In Essex Poor Law County:[12]
BILLERICAY PLU
Basildon, North Benfleet, South Benfleet, Bowers Gifford, Brentwood, Great Burstead, Little Burstead, Childerditch, Downham, Dunton, East Horndon, West Horndon, Hutton, Ingrave, Laindon, Lee Chapel (1858[13]–1930), Mountnessing, Nevendon, Pitsea, Ramsden Bellhouse, Ramsden Crays, Shenfield, Thundersley (1835–), Vange, Great Warley, Little Warley, South Weald, Wickford
BRAINTREE PLU
Bocking, Bradwell, Braintree, Great Coggeshall (1883–1930), Little Coggeshall (1883–1930), Cressing, Fairstead (1883–1930), Faulkbourne (1883–1930), Feering (1883–1930), Finchingfield, Hatfield Peverel (1883–1930), Kelvedon (1883–1930), Markshall (1883–1930), Black Notley, White Notley, Panfield, Pattiswick, Rayne, Rivenhall (1883–1930), Great Saling, Shalford, Stisted, Terling (1883–1930), Wethersfield, Witham (1883–1930)
CHELMSFORD PLU
Great Baddow, Little Baddow, Boreham, Broomfield, Buttsbury, Chelmsford, Chignall (1888–1930), Chignall St James (1835–88), Chignall Smealy (1835–88), Danbury, Good Easter, High Easter, Fryerning, East Hanningfield, South Hanningfield, West Hanningfield, Ingatestone, Great Leighs,[14] Little Leighs,[14] Margaretting, Mashbury, Pleshey, Rettendon,[14] Roxwell, Run-

well,[14] Sandon, Springfield, Stock, Great Waltham, Little Waltham, Widford, Woodham Ferrers,[14] Writtle

COLCHESTER PLU

Berechurch (1835–97), Colchester (1897–1930), Colchester All Saints (1835–97), Colchester Holy Trinity (1835–97), Colchester St Botolph (1835–97), Colchester St Giles (1835–97), Colchester St James (1835–97), Colchester St Leonard (1835–97), Colchester St Martin (1835–97), Colchester St Mary at the Walls (1835–97), Colchester St Mary Magdalen (1835–97), Colchester St Nicholas (1835–97), Colchester St Peter (1835–97), Colchester St Runwald (1835–97), Greenstead (1835–97), Lexden (1835–97), Mile End St Michael (1835–97)

DUNMOW PLU

Great Bardfield, Little Bardfield, Bardfield Saling, Barnston, Broxted, Great Canfield, Little Canfield, Chickney, Great Dunmow, Little Dunmow, High Easter, Great Easton, Little Easton, Felsted, Hatfield Broad Oak, Lindsell, Aythorpe Roding, High Roding, Leaden Roding, Margaret Roding, [Morrel Roding[15]], White Roding,[15] Stebbing, Takeley, Thaxted, Tilty

EPPING PLU

Buckhurst Hill (1894–1930), Chigwell, Chingford, Epping, Epping Upland (1896–1930), Harlow, Latton, Magdalen Laver, Loughton, Matching, Nazeing, Netteswell, Great Parndon, Little Parndon, Roydon,[16] Sheering, Theydon Bois, Theydon Garnon, North Weald Bassett

HALSTEAD PLU

Earls Colne, White Colne, Colne Engaine, Gosfield, Halstead (1835–94), Halstead Rural (1894–1930), Halstead Urban (1894–1930), Castle Hedingham, Sible Hedingham, Great Maplestead, Little Maplestead, Pebmarsh, Ridgewell, Stambourne, Tilbury juxta Clare, Toppesfield, Great Yeldham, Little Yeldham

WEST HAM PLU

Cann Hall (1894–1930), East Ham, West Ham, Little Ilford (1836–1900), Leyton, Walthamstow, Wanstead, Woodford

LEXDEN AND WINSTREE PLU

Abberton, Aldham, West Bergholt, Birch, Boxted, Brightlingsea (1836–80), Mount Bures, Chappel, Wakes Colne, Copford, Dedham, East Donyland, Easthorpe, Fingringhoe, Fordham, Great Horkesley, Little Horkesley, Inworth (1883–1930), Langenhoe, Langham, Layer Breton, Layer de la Haye, Layer Marney, East Mersea, West Mersea, Messing (1883–1930), Peldon, Salcot, Stanway, Great Tey, Little Tey, Marks Tey, Virley, Great Wigborough, Little Wigborough, Wivenhoe, Wormingford

MALDON PLU

Althorne, Asheldham, Bradwell on Sea, Great Braxted (1883–1930), Little Braxted (1883–1930), Burnham, Creeksea, Dengie, North Fambridge, Goldhanger, Hazeleigh, Heybridge, Langford, Latchingdon, Maldon All Saints, Maldon St Mary, Maldon St Peter, Mayland, Mundon, Cold Norton, Purleigh, St Lawrence, Southminster, Steeple, Stow Maries, Tillingham, Tollesbury, Tolleshunt d'Arcy, Tolleshunt Knights, Tolleshunt Major, Great Totham, Little Totham, Ulting (1883–1930), Wickham Bishops (1883–1930), Woodham Mortimer, Woodham Walter

ONGAR PLU

Blackmore, Bobbingworth, Doddinghurst, Fyfield, Greenstead, Kelvedon Hatch, Lambourne, High Laver, Little Laver, Moreton, Navestock, Norton Mandeville, Chipping Ongar, High Ongar, Abbess Roding, Beauchamp Roding, Berners Roding, Shelley, Shellow Bowells, Stanford Rivers, Stapleford Abbotts, Stapleford Tawney, Stondon Massey, Theydon Mount, Willingale Doe, Willingale Spain

ORSETT PLU

Aveley, Bulphan, Chadwell St Mary, Corringham, Fobbing, Horndon on the Hill, Langdon Hills, Mucking, North Ockendon, South Ockendon, Orsett, Stanford le Hope, Stifford, Grays Thurrock, Little Thurrock, West Thurrock, East Tilbury, West Tilbury

ROCHFORD PLU (Essex, Suffolk)

Ashingdon, Barling, South Benfleet (1847–1930), Canewdon, Canvey Island (1880[13]–1930), Eastwood, South Fambridge, Foulness,[14] Hadleigh, Havengore (1858[13]–1930), Hawkwell, Hockley, Leigh (1885–1913), Paglesham, Prittlewell (1835–1913), Rawreth, Rayleigh, Rochford, North Shoebury, South Shoebury, Shopland, Southchurch (1835–1913), Southend on Sea (1913–30), Great Stambridge, Little Stambridge, Sutton, Thundersley (1847–1930), Great Wakering, Little Wakering

ROMFORD PLU

Barking, Cranham, Dagenham, Havering-atte-Bower, Hornchurch, Ilford,[13] Noak Hill (1895–1930), Rainham, Romford (1836–94), Romford (1900–30), Romford Rural (1894–1900), Romford Urban (1894–1900), Upminster, Great Warley, Wennington

SAFFRON WALDEN PLU

Arkesden, Ashdon, Great Chesterford, Little Chesterford, Chrishall, Clavering, Debden, Elmdon, Hempstead, Langley, Littlebury, Newport, Quendon, Radwinter, Ricking, Saffron Walden, Great Sampford, Little Sampford, Strethall, Wendens Ambo, Wendon Lofts, Wicken Bonhunt, Widdington, Wimbish

TENDRING PLU

Alresford, Ardleigh, Beaumont cum Moze, Great Bentley, Little Bentley, Bradfield, Brightlingsea (1838–1930), Great Bromley, Little Bromley, Great Clacton, Little Clacton, Dovercourt (1838–1925), Elmstead, Frating, Frinton, Harwich (1925–30), Harwich St Nicholas (1838–1925), Great Holland, Little Holland, Kirby le Soken, Lawford, Manningtree, Mistley, Great Oakley, Little Oakley, Ramsey, St Osyth, Thorpe le Soken, Tendring, Thorrington, Walton le Soken, Weeley, Wix, Wrabness

WITHAM PLU (1835–83)

Great Braxted, Little Braxted, Great Coggeshall, Little Coggeshall, Fairstead, Faulkbourne, Feering, Hatfield Peverel, Inworth, Kelvedon, Markshall,

Messing, Rivenhall, Terling, Ulting, Witham, Wickham Bishops

In Other Poor Law Counties:
EDMONTON PLU (Middx)
Waltham Holy Cross
LINTON PLU (Cambs)
Bartlow End,[14] Hadstock
RISBRIDGE PLU (Suffolk)
Ashen, Birdbrook, Helion Bumpstead,[20] Steeple Bumpstead, Haverhill,[17] Kedington,[18] Ovington, Sturmer
ROYSTON PLU (Herts, Cambs)
Great Chishill,[19] Little Chishill,[19] Heydon[19]
BISHOP'S STORTFORD PLU (Herts)
Berden, Birchanger, Elsenham, Farnham, Great Hallingbury, Little Hallingbury, Henham, Manuden, Stanstead Mountfitchet, Ugley
SUDBURY PLU (Suffolk)
Alphamstone, Belchamp Otten, Belchamp St Paul, Belchamp Walter, Borley, Bulmer, Bures, Foxearth, Gestingthorpe, Great Henny, Little Henny, Lamarsh, Liston, Middleton, Pentlow, Twinstead, Wickham St Paul, North Wood

SANITARY DISTRICTS

BARKING TOWN USD (1882[21]–94)
Barking (pt 1882–85, ent 1885[22]–94)
BILLERICAY RSD
same as PLU
BRAINTREE RSD
same as PLU less Braintree, pt Stisted (1883–89)
BRAINTREE USD
Braintree, pt Stisted (1883–89)
CHELMSFORD RSD
same as PLU less Chelmsford
CHELMSFORD USD
Chelmsford
GREAT CLACTON USD (1891[23]–94)
Great Clacton
COLCHESTER USD
same as MB for 1875–94
DUNMOW RSD
same as PLU
EDMONTON RSD
no Essex pars
EPPING RSD
same as PLU
HALSTEAD RSD
same as PLU less pt Halstead
HALSTEAD USD
pt Halstead
EAST HAM USD
East Ham, Little Ilford (1886[26]–94)
WEST HAM RSD
Little Ilford (1875–86)
WEST HAM USD
West Ham
HARWICH USD
Dovercourt, Harwich St Nicholas
ILFORD USD (1890[24]–94)
Ilford
LEXDEN AND WINSTREE RSD
same as PLU
LEYTON USD
Leyton (ent 1875–83, pt 1883[27]–87,[28] ent 1887–94), pt Wanstead (1883–94)
MALDON RSD
same as PLU less Maldon All Saints, Maldon St Mary, Maldon St Peter
MALDON USD
Maldon All Saints, Maldon St Mary, Maldon St Peter
ONGAR RSD
same as PLU
ORSETT RSD
same as PLU less Grays Thurrock (1886–94)
RISBRIDGE RSD
same as PLU for the Essex pars
ROCHFORD RSD
same as PLU less Prittlewell, Southcurch
ROMFORD RSD
same as PLU less Barking (pt 1882–85, ent 1885–94), Ilford (1890–94), Leyton, pt Romford, Walthamstow, Wanstead, Woodford
ROMFORD USD
pt Romford
ROYSTON RSD
same as PLU for the Essex pras
SAFFRON WALDEN RSD
same as PLU less Saffron Walden
SAFFRON WALDEN USD
Saffron Walden
BISHOP'S STORTFORD RSD
same as PLU for the Essex pars
SOUTHEND ON SEA USD
Prittelwell, Southchurch
SUDBURY RSD
same as PLU for the Essex pars
TENDRING RSD
same as PLU less Great Clacton (1892–94), Dovercourt, Harwich St Nicholas, Walton le Soken
GRAYS THURROCK USD (1886[25]–94)
Grays Thurrock
WALTHAM HOLY CROSS USD
Waltham Holy Cross
WALTHAMSTOW USD
Walthamstow
WALTON ON THE NAZE USD
Walton le Soken
WANSTEAD USD
pt Leyton (1883[27]–87[28]), Wanstead (ent 1875–83, pt 1883–94)
WITHAM RSD
same as PLU less Witham
WITHAM USD
Witham
WOODFORD USD
Woodford

ADMINISTRATIVE COUNTY

For MBs see BOROUGHS, and for CBs see ASSOCIATED COUNTY BOROUGHS, both earlier in this Part of the *Guide*.

BARKING TOWN UD (1894–1931[29])
Barking
BASILDON UD (1955[30]–74)
Billericay
BELCHAMP RD (1894–1934)
Alphamstone, pt Ballingdon (1894–95), Belchamp Otten, Belchamp St Paul, Belchamp Walter, Borley, Bulmer, Bures, Foxearth, Gestingthorpe, Great Henny, Little Henny, Lamarsh, Liston, Middleton, Pentlow, Twinstead, Wickham St Paul, North Wood
BENFLEET UD (1929[31]–74)
South Benfleet, Hadleigh, Thundersley
BILLERICAY RD (1894–1934)
Basildon, North Benfleet, Bowers Gifford, Great Burstead, Little Burstead, Childerditch, Downham, Dunton, East Horndon, West Horndon, Hutton, Ingrave, Laindon, Lee Chapel, Mountnessing, Nevendon, Pitsea, Ramsden Bellhouse, Ramsden Crays, Shenfield, Vange, Little Warley, South Weald, Wickford
BILLERICAY UD (1934–55[30])
Basildon (1934–37), North Benfleet (1934–37), Billericay (1937–55), Bowers Gifford (1934–37), Great Burstead (1934–37), Little Burstead (1934–37), Laindon (1934–37), Lee Chapel (1934–37), Nevendon (1934–37), Vange (1934–37), Wickford (1934–37)
BRAINTREE RD
Great Bardfield (1934–74), Bardfield Saling (1934–74), Bocking (1894–1934), Bradwell, Coggeshall (1949–74), Great Coggeshall (1894–1949), Little Coggeshall (1894–1949), Cressing, Fairstead, Faulkbourne, Feering, Finchingfield, Hatfield Peverel, Kelvedon, Markshall (1894–1949), Black Notley, White Notley, Panfield, Pattiswick (1894–1949), Rayne, Rivenhall (1894–1933), Great Saling, Shalford, Stisted, Terling, Unnamed (1894–1903), Wethersfield
BRAINTREE UD (1894–1934)
Braintree
BRAINTREE AND BOCKING UD (1934–74)
Braintree and Bocking
BRENTWOOD UD (1899[33]–1974)
Brentwood
BRIGHTLINGSEA UD (1896[34]–1974)
Brightlingsea
BUCKHURST HILL UD (1894[35]–1933[36])
Buckhurst Hill
BUMPSTEAD RD (1894–1934)
Ashen, Birdbrook, Helion Bumpstead, Steeple Bumpstead, Ovington, Sturmer
BURNHAM ON CROUCH UD (1898[37]–1974)
Burnham
CANVEY ISLAND UD (1926[38]–74)
Canvey Island
CHELMSFORD RD
Great Baddow, Little Baddow, Boreham, Broomfield, Buttsbury (1894–1935), Chignall, Danbury, Good Easter, East Hanningfield, South Hanningfield, West Hanningfield, Highwood (1954–74), Ingatestone and Fryerning, Great Leighs (1894–1949), Great and Little Leighs (1949–74), Little Leighs (1894–1949), Margaretting, Mashbury, Mountnessing (1934–74), Pleshey, Rettendon, Roxwell, Runwell, Sandon, Springfield, Stock, Great Waltham, Little Waltham, Widford (1894–1934), Woodham Ferrers, Writtle
CHIGWELL UD (1933[36]–74)
Buckhurst Hill, Chigwell, Loughton
CHINGFORD UD (1894[39]–1938[40])
Chingford
CLACTON UD (orig GREAT CLACTON UD, soon renamed)
Great Clacton
GREAT CLACTON UD–See prev entry
DAGENHAM UD (1926[41]–38[40])
Dagenham
DUNMOW RD
Great Bardfield (1894–1934), Little Bardfield, Bardfield Saling (1894–1934), Barnston, Broxted, Great Canfield, Little Canfield, Chickeney, Great Dunmow, Little Dunmow, High Easter, Great Easton, Little Easton, Felsted, Great Hallingbury (1934–74), Little Hallingbury (1934–74), Hatfield Broad Oak, Lindsell, Aythorpe Roding, High Roding, Leaden Roding, Margaret Roding, White Roding, Stebbing, Takeley, Thaxted, Tilty
EPPING RD (1894–1955[42])
Chigwell (1894–1933), Epping (1894–96), Epping Upland (1896–1955), Harlow, Latton (1894–1949), Magdalen Laver, Loughton (1894–1900), Matching, Nazeing, Netteswell, Great Parndon, Little Parndon (1894–1949), Roydon, Sheering, Theydon Bois, Theydon Garnon, North Weald Basset
EPPING UD (1896[43]–1974)
Epping
EPPING AND ONGAR RD (1955[42]–74)
Blackmore, Bobbingworth, Doddinghurst, Epping Upland, Fyfield, Greenstead (1955–65), Kelvedon Hatch, Lambourne, High Laver, Little Laver, Magdalen Laver, Matching, Moreton, Navestock, Nazeing, Norton Mandeville (1955–68), Ongar (1965–74), Chipping Ongar (1955–65), High Ongar, Abbess Beauchamp and Berners Roding, Roydon, Sheering, Shelley (1955–65), Stanford Rivers, Stapleford Abbotts, Stapleford Tawney, Stondon Massey, Theydon Bois, Theydon Garnon, Theydon Mount, North Weald Bassett, Willingale
FRINTON AND WALTON UD (1934–74)
Frinton and Walton
FRINTON ON SEA UD (1901[44]–34)
Frinton
HALSTEAD RD
Alphamstone (1934–74), Ashen (1934–74), Bel-

champ Otten (1934–74), Belchamp St Paul (1934–74), Belchamp Walter (1934–74), Birdbrook (1934–74), Borley (1934–74), Bulmer (1934–74), Helion Bumpstead (1934–74), Steeple Bumpstead (1934–74), Bures (1934–74), Earls Colne, White Colne, Colne Engaine, Foxearth (1934–74), Gestingthorpe (1934–74), Gosfield, Halstead Rural, Castle Hedingham, Sible Hedingham, Great Henny (1934–74), Little Henny (1934–74), Lamarsh (1934–74), Liston (1934–74), Great Maplestead, Little Maplestead, Middleton (1934–74), Ovington (1934–74), Pebmarsh, Pentlow (1934–74), Ridgewell, Stambourne, Sturmer (1934–74), Tilbury juxta Clare, Toppesfield, Twinstead (1934–74), Wickham St Paul (1934–74), North Wood (1934–46), Great Yeldham, Little Yeldham

HALSTEAD UD
Halstead Urban

EAST HAM UD (1894–1904[45])
East Ham, Little Ilford (1894–1900)

HARLOW UD (1955[42]–74)
Harlow

HORNCHURCH UD (1926[46]–65[3])
Cranham (1934–65), Hornchurch, Rainham (1934–65), Upminster (1934–65), Great Warley (1934–65), Wennington (1934–65)

ILFORD UD (1894–1926[47])
Ilford

LEIGH ON SEA UD (1897[48]–1913[49])
Leigh

LEXDEN AND WINSTREE RD
Abberton, Aldham, West Bergholt, Birch, Boxted, Mount Bures, Chappel, Wakes Colne, Copford, Dedham, East Donyland, Easthorpe (1894–1949), Eight Ash Green (1949–74), Fingringhoe, Fordham, Great Horkesley, Little Horkesley, Inworth (1894–1934), Langenhoe, Langham, Layer Breton, Layer de la Haye, Layer Marney, East Mersea, West Mersea (1894–1926), Messing (1894–1949), Messing cum Inworth (1934–74), Peldon, Salcot, Stanway, Great Tey, Little Tey (1894–1949), Marks Tey, Tiptree (1934–74), Virley, Great Wigborough (1894–1953), Great and Little Wigborough (1953–74), Little Wigborough (1894–1953), Wivenhoe (1894–96), Wormingford

LEYTON UD (1894–1926[47])
Cann Hall, Leyton

LOUGHTON UD (1900[50]–33[36])
Loughton

MALDON RD
Althorne, Asheldham, Bradwell on Sea, Great Braxted, Little Braxted, Burnham (1894–98), Creeksea (1894–1934), Dengie, North Fambridge, Goldhanger, Hazeleigh, Heybridge (1894–1934), Langford, Latchingdon, Mayland, Mundon, Cold Norton, Purleigh, St Lawrence, Southminster, Steeple, Stow Maries, Tillingham, Tollesbury, Tolleshunt d'Arcy, Tolleshunt Knights, Tolleshunt Major, Great Totham, Little Totham, Ulting, Wickham Bishops, Woodham Mortimer, Woodham Walter

WEST MERSEA UD (1926[51]–74)
West Mersea

ONGAR RD (1894–1955[42])
Blackmore, Bobbingworth, Doddinghurst, Fyfield, Greenstead, Kelvedon Hatch, Lambourne, High Laver, Little Laver, Moreton, Navestock, Norton Mandeville, Chipping Ongar, High Ongar, Abbess Roding (1894–1946), Abbess Beauchamp and Berners Roding (1946–55), Beauchamp Roding (1894–1946), Berners Roding (1894–1946), Shelley, Shellow Bowells (1894–1946), Stanford Rivers, Stapleford Abbotts, Stapleford Tawney, Stondon Massey, Theydon Mount, Willingale (1946–55), Willingale Doe (1894–1946), Willingale Spain (1894–1946)

ORSETT RD (1894–1936[53])
Aveley (1894–1929), Bulphan, Chadwell St Mary (1894–1912), Corringham, Fobbing, Horndon on the Hill, Langdon Hills, Mucking, North Ockendon, South Ockendon, Orsett, Stanford le Hope, Stifford, Little Thurrock, West Thurrock (1894–1929), East Tilbury, West Tilbury

PURFLEET UD (1929[52]–36[53])
Aveley, South Ockendon, West Thurrock

RAYLEIGH UD (1929[31]–74)
Rawreth, Rayleigh

ROCHFORD RD
Ashingdon, Barling (1894–1946), Barling Magna (1946–74), South Benfleet (1894–1929), Canewdon, Canvey Island (1894–1926), Eastwood (1894–1926), South Fambridge (1894–1949), Foulness, Hadleigh (1894–1929), Havengore (1894–1946), Hawkwell, Hockley, Hullbridge (1964–74), Leigh (1894–97), Paglesham, Rawreth (1894–1929), Rayleigh (1894–1929), Rochford, North Shoebury (1894–1933), Shopland (1894–1933), Stambridge (1934–74), Great Stambridge (1894–1934), Little Stambridge (1894–1934), Sutton, Thundersley (1894–1929), Great Wakering, Little Wakering (1894–1946)

ROMFORD RD (1894–1934)
Cranham, Dagenham (1894–1926), Havering-atte-Bower, Hornchurch (1894–1926), Noak Hill (1895–1934), Rainham, Romford Rural (1894–1900), Upminster, Great Warley, Wennington

ROMFORD UD (1894–1937[47])
Havering-atte-Bower (1934–37), Noak Hill (1934–37), Romford (1900–37), Romford Urban (1894–1900)

SAFFRON WALDEN RD
Arkesden, Ashdon, Bartlow End (1894–1946), Berden (1934–74), Birchanger (1934–74), Great Chesterford, Little Chesterford, Chrishall, Clavering, Debden, Elmdon, Elsenham (1934–74), Farnham (1934–74), Hadstock, Hempstead, Henham (1934–74), Langley, Littlebury, Manuden (1934–74), Newport, Quendon (1894–1946), Quendon and Rickling (1946–74), Radwinter, Rickling (1946–74), Great Sampford, Little Sampford, Stanstead Mountfitchet (1934–74), Strethall, Ugley (1934–74), Wendens Ambo, Wendon Lofts, Wicken Bonhunt, Widdington, Wimbish

SOUTH SHOEBURY UD–See following entry
SHOEBURYNESS UD (1894[54] [orig cr as SOUTH SHOEBURY UD, soon renamed SHOEBURYNESS] –1933[55])
South Shoebury
STANSTEAD RD (1894–1934)
Berden, Birchanger, Elsenham, Farnham, Great Hallingbury, Little Hallingbury, Henham, Manuden, Stanstead Mountfitchet, Ugley
TENDRING RD
Alresford, Ardleigh, Beaumont cum Moze, Great Bentley, Little Bentley, Bradfield, Brightlingsea (1894–96), Great Bromley, Little Bromley, Little Clacton, Elmstead, Frating, Frinton (1894–1901), Great Holland (1894–1934), Little Holland (1894–1934), Kirby le Soken (1894–1934), Lawford, Manningtree, Mistley, Great Oakley, Little Oakley, Ramsey, St Osyth, Thorpe le Soken, Tendring, Thorrington, Weeley, Wix, Wrabness
THURROCK UD (1936[55]–74)
Thurrock
GRAYS THURROCK UD (1894–1936[55])
Grays Thurrock
TILBURY UD (1912[56]–36[55])
Chadwell St Mary
WALTHAM HOLY CROSS UD
Waltham Holy Cross
WALTHAMSTOW UD (1894–1926[47])
Walthamstow
WALTON ON THE NAZE UD (1894–1934)
Walton le Soken
WANSTEAD UD (1894–1934)
Wanstead
WANSTEAD AND WOODFORD UD (1934–37[47])
Wanstead, Woodford
WITHAM UD
Witham
WIVENHOE UD (1898[57]–1974)
Wivenhoe
WOODFORD UD (1894–1934)
Woodford

NON-METROPOLITAN COUNTY

As constituted 1 Apr 1974, defined
in terms of Adm Co units as of 31 Mar.

BASILDON DIST
Basildon UD, pt Thurrock UD (the pt in Basildon New Town)
BRAINTREE DIST
Braintree RD, Braintree and Bocking UD, Halstead RD, Halstead UD, Witham UD
BRENTWOOD DIST
Brentwood UD, pt Chelmsford RD (Ingatestone and Fryerning, Mountnessing), pt Epping and Ongar RD (Blackmore, Doddinghurst, Kelvedon Hatch, Navestock, Stondon Massey)
CASTLE POINT DIST
Benfleet UD, Canvey Island UD
CHELMSFORD DIST
Chelmsford MB, pt Chelmsford RD (the pars not in Brentwood Dist)
COLCHESTER DIST
Colchester MB, Lexden and Winstree RD, West Mersea UD, Wivenhoe UD
EPPING FOREST DIST
Chigwell UD, Epping UD, pt Epping and Ongar RD (the pars not in Brentwood Dist), Waltham Holy Cross UD
HARLOW DIST
Harlow UD
MALDON DIST
Burnham on Crouch UD, Maldon MB, Maldon RD
ROCHFORD DIST
Rayleigh UD, Rochford RD
SOUTHEND ON SEA DIST
Southend on Sea CB
TENDRING DIST
Brightlingsea UD, Clacton UD, Frinton and Walton UD, Harwich MB, Tendring RD
THURROCK DIST
pt Thurrock UD (all except the pt in Basildon Dist)
UTTLESFORD DIST
Dunmow RD, Saffron Walden MB, Saffron Walden RD

GLOUCESTERSHIRE

ALTERATIONS IN COUNTY BOUNDARIES

As noted by year below, Glos pars gained territory from or lost it to pars in adjoining counties or county boroughs, or were entirely transferred to them. Details of these alterations are noted in Part I of the *Guide* under Glos.

ANCIENT COUNTY (until 1889: Hds, Bors, MBs, PLUs, RSDs, USDs)
1844 Alstone, Great Barrington, Broughton Poggs, Little Compton, Icomb, Church Icomb, Kingswood, Lea, Lea Bailey, Lechlade, Minety, Newland, Overbury, Poulton, Shenington, Sutton-under-Brailes. Little Washbourne, Widford. *1880s* Welford, Weston-on-Avon. *1886* Lechlade.

ADMINISTRATIVE COUNTY (1889–1974: Hds,[1] PLUs, MBs, RDs, UDs, with associated CBs of Britsol, Gloucester)
1890 Blaisdon. *1894* Ilmington. *1896* Batsford, Blaisdon, Henbury, St Nicholas Without, Shirehampton. *1897* Kemble, Poole Keynes, Somerford Keynes. *1898* Stapleton. *1900* Barnwood, Hempsted, Matson, Tuffley, Upton St Leonards. *1901* Henbury, Shirehampton. *1902* Henbury, Shirehampton. *1904* Henbury, Horfield, Shirehampton, Westbury-on-Trym. *1910* Wotton Vill. *1931* Ashley, Ashton under Hill, Aston Somerville, Beckford, Blockley, Chaceley, Child's Wickham, Clifford Chambers, Cutsdean, Daylesford, Dorsington, Evenlode, Hinton on the Green, Cow Honeybourne, Kemerton, Marston Sicca, Long Newnton, Pebworth, Preston on Stour, Quinton, Redmarley d'Abitot, Staunton, Teddington, Welford, Weston-on-Avon. *1935* Adminton, Barnwood, Clopton, Filton, Hempsted, Henbury, Longford, Maisemore, Matson, Quedgeley, Stoke Gifford, Upton St Leonards, Whaddon, Winterbourne, Wotton St Mary Without. *1951* Barnwood, Brookthorpe, Hempsted, Longlevens, Quedgeley, Wotton Vill. *1957* Upton St Leonards. *1965* Ashchurch, English Bicknor, Chipping Campden, Chaceley, Dumbleton, Drybrook, Forthampton, Kempley, Longhope, Mitcheldean, Newent, Redmarley d'Abitot, Staunton, Teddington, Tewkesbury, Weston Subedge, Willersey. *1966* Almondsbury, Barnwood, Bitton, Didmarton, Filton, Hempsted, Highnam, Hucclecote, Kingswood, Longford, Longlevens, Maisemore, Mangotsfield Urban, Minsterworth, Long Newnton, Stoke Gifford, Upton St Leonards, Westonbirt, Winterbourne.

NON-METROPOLITAN COUNTY (from 1974: Dists)
1974 Iron Acton, Acton Turville, Almondsbury, Alveston, Cold Ashton, Aust, Great Badminton, Bitton, Charfield, Cromhall, Dodington, Doynton, Dyrham and Hinton, Falfield, Filton, Frampton Cotterell, Hanham Abbots, Hawkesbury, Hill, Horton, Kingswood, Mangotsfield Rural, Mangotsfield Urban, Oldbury upon Severn, Oldland, Patchway, Pilning and Severn Beach, Pucklechurch, Rangeworthy, Rockhampton, Siston, Sodbury, Little Sodbury, Stoke Gifford, Thornbury, Tormarton, Tortworth, Tytherington, Westerleigh, Wick and Abson, Wickwar, Winterbourne, Yate

ASSOCIATED COUNTY BOROUGHS

For constituent pars see listing for BOROUGHS in this Part of the *Guide*.

BRISTOL CB
Bdry: 1896,[2] 1898,[3] 1898,[4] 1898,[5] 1901,[6] 1902,[7] 1904,[8] 1918,[9] 1933,[10] 1935,[11] 1951,[12] 1966.[13] Transf 1974 to Avon Non-Metrop Co.[14]

GLOUCESTER CB
Bdry: 1900,[15] 1910,[16] 1935,[11] 1951,[17] 1957,[18] 1966.[19] Transf 1974 to Glos Non-Metrop Co.[14]

HUNDREDS[1]

BARTON REGIS HD
Bristol St George (from 1756), pt Bristol St James (until 1866), Bristol St James and St Paul Out (from 1866), pt Bristol St Paul (until 1866), pt Bristol St Philip and St Jacob (until 1866), Bristol St Philip and St Jacob Out (from 1866), Clifton,[20] Mangotsfield, Stapleton

BERKELEY HD[21]
Alkington (from 1866), pt Almondsbury, Arlingham, Ashleworth, Berkeley,[20] Beverstone, Bread-

stone (from 1866), Cam, Coaley, Cromhall, Dursley,[20] Elberton, Filton, Ham and Stone (from 1866), Hamfallow (from 1866), pt Henbury, Hill, Hinton (from 1866), Horfield, Kingscote, Kingswood (from 1844), Newington Bagpath, North Nibley, Nympsfield, Owlpen, Ozleworth, pt Rockhampton, Slimbridge, Stinchcombe, Uley, Wotton under Edge

BISLEY HD

Bisley, Edgeworth, Miserden, Painswick,[20] Sapperton, Stroud, Winstone

BLEDISLOE HD

Alvington, Awre, Aylburton (from 1866), Lydney

BOTLOE HD

Bromsberrow, Dymock,[20] Kempley, Newent,[20] Oxenhall, Pauntley, pt Rudford, Taynton, Upleadon

BRADLEY HD

Aston Blank, pt Bibury, Coln Rogers, Compton Abdale, Dowdeswell, Eastington (from 1866), Farmington, Hampnett, Hasleton, pt Naunton, Nortleach,[20] Notgrove, Salperton, Sevenhampton, Shipton (from 1871), Shipton Oliffe (until 1871), Shipton Sollars (until 1871), Stowell, Turkdean, Whittington, Winson (from 1866), Withington, Yanworth (from 1866)

BRIGHTWELLS BARROW HD[22]

Aldsworth, Bransley, pt Bibury, Coln St Aldwyn, Eastleach Martin, Eastleach Turville, Fairford,[20] Hatherop, Kempsford, Lechlade,[20] Quenington, Southrop

CHELTENHAM HD

Charlton Kings, Cheltenham,[20] Leckhampton, Swindon

CLEEVE (or BISHOP'S CLEEVE) HD

Bishop's Cleeve, Gotherington (from 1866), Southam and Brockhampton (from 1866), Stoke Orchard (from 1866), Woodmancote (from 1866)

CROWNTHORNE AND MINETY HD

Down Ampney, Ampney Crucis, Ampney St Mary, Ampney St Peter, Bagendon, Baunton, South Cerney, Cirencester,[20] Coates, Daglingworth, Driffield, pt Duntisbourne Abbots, Duntisbourne Rouse, Harnhill, Meysey Hampton, Minety (until 1844), Poulton (from 1844), Preston, Siddington, Stratton

DEERHURST HD

Coln St Dennis, Little Compton (until 1844), pt Deerhurst, pt Elmstone Hardwicke, pt Leigh, Prestbury,[20] Preston on Stour, Staverton, pt Tirley, Uckington (from 1866), pt Welford, Woolstone

DUCHY OF LANCASTER HD[21]

Bulley, Huntley, Longhope, Minsterworth, Tibberton, pt Westbury on Severn

DUDSTONE AND KING'S BARTON HD[23]

Badgeworth, Barnwood, Brockworth, Brookthorpe, Churchdown, pt Churcham, Elmore, pt Gloucester Barton St Mary[20] (1866–85), pt Gloucester Barton St Michael[20] (1866–85), pt Gloucester South Hamlet[20] (1858–85), pt Gloucester St Catherine[20] (until 1885), pt Gloucester St Mary de Lode[20] (until 1866), pt Gloucester St Michael[20] (until 1866), Harescombe, Hartpury, Down Hatherley, Up Hatherley, Hempsted, Highleadon (from 1866), Highnam Over and Linton (from 1866), Hucclecote (from 1866), Lassington, Longford (from 1885), pt Longford St Catherine[20] (1866–85), pt Longford St Mary[20] (1866–85), Maisemore, Matson, Norton, Pitchcombe, Preston, Prinknash Park (from 1858), pt Quedgeley, pt Rudford, Sandhurst, Shurdington, Tuffley (from 1866), Twigworth (from 1866), Upton St Leonards, Whaddon, Great Witcombe, pt Wotton St Mary[20] (1866–85), pt Wotton St Mary Within[20] (from 1885), Wotton St Mary Without (from 1885)

GRUMBALDS ASH HD[24]

pt Iron Acton, Acton Turville, Alderley, Great Badminton, Boxwell with Leighterton, Charfield, Didmarton, Dodington, Dyrham and Hinton, Hawkesbury, Horton, West Littleton, Oldbury on the Hill, Chipping Sodbury,[20] Little Sodbury, Old Sodbury, Tormarton, Tortworth, Wapley and Cordington, Wickwar[20]

HENBURY HD[24]

Aust (from 1866), Compton Greenfield, pt Henbury, Redwick and Northwick (from 1866), Shirehampton (from 1866), Stoke Gifford, pt Tytherington, Westbury-on-Trym, Yate

KIFTSGATE HD

Admington (from 1866), Alstone (from 1866), Aston Somerville, Aston Subedge, Batsford, Buckland, Child's Wickham, Chipping Campden,[20] Charlton Abbots, Clopton (from 1866), pt Condicote, Didbrook, Dorsington, Dumbelton, Ebrington, Temple Guiting, Guiting Power, Hailes, Hawling, Hidcote Bartrim (from 1866), Cow Honeybourne, pt Ilmington, Longborough, Marston Sicca, Mickleton, Pebworth, Pinnock and Hyde (from 1866), Quinton, Roel (from 1858), Saintbury, Sezincote, Snowshill, Stanley Pontlarge, Stanton, Sudeley Manor, Upper Swell, Toddington, Twyning, Little Washbourne (from 1866), pt Weston on Avon, Weston Subedge, Willersey, Winchcombe,[20] Wormington

LANGLEY AND SEINEHEAD HD

pt Almondsbury, Alveston, Bitton, Doynton, Frampton Cotterell, Hanham (from 1866), Littleton upon Severn, Oldland (from 1866), Olveston, pt Rockhampton, Winterbourne

LONGTREE HD

Avening, Cherington, Horsley, Lasborough (until mid 17th cent), Minchinhampton,[20] Nailsworth (from 1866), Rodborough, Rodmarton, Shipton Moyne, Tetbury,[20] Weston Birt, Woodchester

PUCKLECHURCH HD

Cold Ashton, Pucklechurch, Siston, Westerleigh, Wick and Abson

RAPSGATE HD

Brimpsfield, North Cerney, Chedworth, Coberley, Colesbourne, Cowley, Cranham, pt Duntisbourne Abbots, Elkstone, Rendcombe, Syde

ST BRIAVELS HD[22]

Abenhall, English Bicknor, East Dean (from 1844), West Dean (from 1844), Flaxley, Hewelsfield, Hinders Lane and Dockham (1858–84), pt Lea (until 1844), Lea Bailey (from 1866), Littledean, Mitcheldean, Newland, Ruardean, St Briavels,[20] Staunton

SLAUGHTER HD
Adlestrop, Great Barrington (pt until 1844, ent 1844, ent from 1844), Church Icomb (from 1866), Maugersbury (from 1866), pt Naunton, Oddington, Great Rissington, Little Rissington, Wick Rissington, Sherborne, Lower Slaughter, Upper Slaughter, Stow on the Wold,[20] Lower Swell, Westcote, Widford (until 1844), Windrush

TEWKESBURY HD
Alderton, Ashchurch, pt Boddington, pt Bourton on the Hill, Clifford Chambers, Forthampton, Kemerton, Lower Lemington, Oxenton, Prescott (from 1858), Shenington (until 1844), Stanway, Tewkesbury,[20] Tredington, Walton Cardiff, Great Washbourne

THORNBURY HD
pt Iron Acton, pt Almondsbury, Marshfield,[20] Rangeworthy (from 1866), Thornbury,[20] pt Tytherington

TIBALDSTONE HD[25]
Ashton under Hill, Beckford, Hinton on the Green

WESTBURY HD[26]
Blaisdon, pt Churcham, Lancaut (from 1866), Newnham,[20] Tidenham, pt Westbury on Severn, Woolaston

WESTMINSTER HD
pt Boddington, pt Bourton on the Hill, Corse, pt Deerhurst, pt Elmstone Hardwicke, Hasfield, pt Leigh, Moreton in Marsh,[20] Sutton-under-Brailes (until 1844), pt Tirley, Todenham

WHITSTONE HD
Eastington, Frampton on Severn, Fretherne, Frocester, Hardwicke, Haresfield, Haywards Field (from 1858), Longney, Moreton Valence, pt Quedgeley, Randwick, Saul, Standish, King's Stanley,[20] Leonard Stanley, Stonehouse, Wheatenhurst

BOROUGHS

Units with some degree of burghal character[27] are denominated 'Bor'.
Those which did not sustain that status until the 19th cent are in italics.
Municipal Boroughs were established by the Municipal Corporations Act, 1835,[28] or by later charter.

BERKELEY BOR
Berkeley

BRISTOL BOR/MB/CB (Glos pars[29])
Bristol (1898–1974), Central Bristol (1896–98), North Bristol (1896–98), Bristol All Saints (until 1896), Bristol Castle Precincts (1858–96), Bristol Christ Church (until 1896), Bristol St Augustine (until 1896), Bristol St Ewen (until 1896), pt Bristol St James (until 1866), Bristol St James In (1866–96), Bristol St James and St Paul Out (1868–96), Bristol St John the Baptist (until 1896), Bristol St Lawrence (until 1578), Bristol St Leonard (until 1896), Bristol St Mary le Port (until 1896), Bristol St Michael (until 1896), Bristol St Nicholas (until 1896), pt Bristol St Paul (until 1866), Bristol St Paul In (1866–96), Bristol St Peter (until 1896), pt Bristol St Philip and St Jacob (until 1720), Bristol St Philip and St Jacob In (1720–1896), Bristol St Philip and St Jacob Out (1868–96), Bristol St Stephen (until 1896), Bristol St Werburgh (until 1878), Clifton (1868–96), Redland (1894–96), pt Westbury-onTrym (1880s–94)

CHIPPING CAMPDEN BOR
Chipping Campden

CIRENCESTER BOR
Cirencester

DURSLEY BOR
Dursley

DYMOCK BOR
Dymock

FAIRFORD BOR
Fairford

GLOUCESTER BOR/MB/CB
Gloucester (1896–1974), Gloucester All Saints (early destroyed), Gloucester Barton St Mary (pt 1866–85, ent 1885–96), pt Gloucester Barton St Michael (1866–85), Gloucester Holy Trinity (until 1896), Gloucester North Hamlet (1858–85), Gloucester Pool Meadow (1858–96), Gloucester South Hamlet (pt 1858–85, ent 1885–96), Gloucester St Aldate (until 1896), Gloucester St Audonei (early destroyed), Gloucester St Catherine (pt until 1885, ent 1885–96), Gloucester St John the Baptist (until 1896), Gloucester St Mary de Crypt (until 1896), Gloucester St Mary de Grace (until 1896), Gloucester St Mary de Lode (pt until 1866, ent 1866–96), Gloucester St Michael (pt until 1866, ent 1866–96), Gloucester St Nicholas (until 1896), Gloucester St Owen (until 1896), Littleworth (1858–96), pt Longford St Catherine (1866–85), pt Longford St Mary (1866–85), pt Wotton St Mary (1866–85), Wotton St Mary Within (pt 1885–94, ent 1894–96)

LECHLADE BOR
Lechlade

MARSHFIELD BOR
Marshfield

MINCHINHAMPTON BOR
Minchinhampton

MORETON IN MARSH BOR
Moreton in Marsh

NEWENT BOR
Newent

NEWNHAM BOR
Newnham

NORTHLEACH BOR
Northleach

PAINSWICK BOR
Painswick

PRESTBURY BOR
Prestbury

ST BRIAVELS BOR
St Briavels
CHIPPING SODBURY BOR
Chipping Sodbury
KING'S STANLEY BOR
King's Stanley
STOW ON THE WOLD BOR
Stow on the Wold
TETBURY BOR
Tetbury

TWEKESBURY BOR/MB
Tewkesbury
THORNBURY BOR
Thornbury
WICKWAR BOR
Wickwar
WINCHCOMBE BOR
Winchcombe
WOTTON UNDER EDGE BOR
Wotton under Edge

POOR LAW UNIONS

In Glos Poor Law County:[30]

BARTON REGIS PLU (1836–1904 [called CLIFTON PLU 1840s–80s])
Bristol St George (1836–98), Bristol St James and St Paul Out (1836–96), Bristol St Philip and St Jacob Out (1836–96), Clifton (1836–96), Compton Greenfield (1836–86), Filton, Henbury (1836–1904), Horfield (1836–1904), Shirehampton (1836–1904), Stapleton (1836–98), Stoke Gifford (1836–1904), Westbury-on-Trym (1836–1904), Winterbourne (1836–1904)

BRISTOL INCORPORATION (Glos, Somerset[29])
Bristol (1898–1930), Central Bristol (1896–98), North Bristol (1896–98), Bristol All Saints (until 1896), Bristol Castle Precincts (until 1896), Bristol Christ Church (until 1896), Bristol St Augustine (until 1896), Bristol St Ewen (until 1896), Bristol St James (until 1866), Bristol St James In (1866–96), Bristol St John the Baptist (until 1896), Bristol St Leonard, Bristol St Mary le Port, Bristol St Michael, Bristol St Nicholas, Bristol St Paul (until 1866), Bristol St Paul In (1866–96), Bristol St Peter, Bristol St Philip and St Jacob In, Bristol St Stephen, Bristol St Werburgh (until 1878), Filton (192 –30), Redland (1894–96)

CHELTENHAM PLU
Badgeworth, Charlton Kings, Cheltenham, Coberley, Cowley, Up Hatherley, Leckhampton, Prestbury, Shurdington, Staverton, Swindon, Uckington, Great Witcombe

CIRENCESTER PLU (Glos, Wilts)
Down Ampney, Ampney Crucis, Ampney St Mary, Ampney St Peter, Bagendon, Barnsley, Baunton, Brimpsfield, North Cerney, South Cerney, Cirencester, Coates, Colesbourne, Daglingworth, Driffield, Duntisbourne Abbots, Duntisbourne Rouse, Edgeworth, Elkstone, Fairford, Harnhill, Hatherop, Kempsford, Meysey Hampton, Poulton, Preston, Quenington, Rendcombe, Rodmarton, Sapperton, Siddington, Stratton, Syde, Winstone

DURSLEY PLU
Cam, Coaley, Dursley, Kingswood, North Nibley, Nympsfield, Owlpen, Slimbridge, Stinchcombe, Uley, Wotton under Edge

GLOUCESTER PLU
Ashleworth, Barnwood, Brockworth, Churchdown, Elmore, Gloucester (1896–1930), Gloucester Barton St Mary (until 1896), Gloucester Barton St Michael (until 1885), Gloucester Holy Trinity (until 1896), Gloucester North Hamlet (until 1885), Gloucester South Hamlet (until 1896), Gloucester Pool Meadow (until 1896), Gloucester St Aldate (until 1896), Gloucester St Catherine (until 1896), Gloucester St John the Baptist (until 1896), Gloucester St Mary de Crypt (until 1896), Gloucester St Mary de Grace (until 1896), Gloucester St Mary de Lode (until 1896), Gloucester St Michael (until 1896), Gloucester St Nicholas (until 1896), Gloucester St Owen (until 1896), Down Hatherley, Hempsted, Highnam Over and Linton, Hucclecote, Lassington, Littleworth (until 1896), Longford (1885–1930), Longford St Catherine (1866–85), Longford St Mary (1866–85), Maisemore, Matson, Norton, Prinknash Park, Quedgeley, Sandhurst, Tuffley (until 1900), Twigworth, Upton St Leonards, Whaddon, Ville of Wotton (from 1885), Wotton St Mary (until 1885), Wotton St Mary Within (1885–98), Wotton St Mary Without (1885–1930), Wotton Vill (1894–1930)

NEWENT PLU
Bromsberrow, Corse, Dymock, Hartpury, Highleadon, Kempley, Newent, Oxenhall, Pauntley, Preston, Rudford, Taynton, Tibberton, Upleadon

NORTHLEACH PLU
Aldsworth, Aston Black, Little Barrington, Bibury, Chedworth, Coln Rogers, Coln St Aldwyn, Coln St Dennis, Compton Abdale, Dowdeswell, Eastington, Eastleach Martin, Eastleach Turville, Farmington, Hampnett, Hasleton, Northleach, Salperton, Sevenhampton, Sherborne, Shipton, Southrop, Stowell, Turkdean, Winson, Whittington, Windrush, Withington, Yanworth

CHIPPING SODBURY PLU
Iron Acton, Acton Turville, Alderley, Cold Ashton, Great Badmington, Dodington, Doynton, Dyrham and Hinton, Filton (1894–1930), Frampton Cotterell, Hawkesbury, Horton, West Littleton, Marshfield, Pucklechurch, Chipping Sodbury, Little Sodbury, Old Sodbury, Stoke Gifford (1894–1930), Tormarton, Wapley and Cordrington, Westerleigh, Wick and Abson, Wickwar, Winterbourne (1894–1930), Yate

STOW ON THE WOLD PLU
Adlestrop, Great Barrington, Bledington, Bourton on the Water, Broadwell, Clapton, Condicote, Donnington, Eyford, Icomb, Church Icomb, Longborough, Maugersbury, Naunton, Notgrove, Od-

dington, Great Rissington, Little Rissington, Wick Rissington, Sezincote, Lower Slaughter, Upper Slaughter, Stow-on-the-Wold, Lower Swell, Upper Swell, Westcote

STROUD PLU
Avening, Bisley (1836–94), Bisley with Lypiatt (1894–1930), Cainscross (1894–1930), Chalford (1894–1930), Cranham, Haywards Field (1858–84), Horsley, Minchinhampton, Miserden, Nailsworth, Painswick, Pitchcombe, Randwick, Rodborough, King's Stanley, Leonard Stanley, Stonehouse, Stroud, Thrupp (1894–1930), Uplands (1894–1930), Whiteshill (1894–1930), Woodchester

TETBURY PLU
Beverstone, Boxwell with Leighterton, Cherington, Didmarton, Kingscote, Newington Bagpath, Oldbury on the Hill (1836– 83), Ozleworth, Shipton Moyne, Tetbury, Tetbury Upton (1894–1930), Weston Birt

TEWKESBURY PLU
Ashchurch, Beddington, Deerhurst, Elmstone Hardwicke, Forthampton, Hasfield, Kemerton, Leigh, Oxenton, Stoke Orchard, Tewkesbury, Tirley, Tredington, Twyning, Walton Cardiff, Woolstone

THORNBURY PLU
Alkington, Almondsbury, Alveston, Aust, Berkeley, Breadstone, Charfield, Cromhall, Elberton, Falfield (1894–1930), Ham and Stone, Hamfallow, Hill, Hinton, Littleton upon Severn, Oldbury upon Severn (1894–1930), Olveston, Rangeworthy, Redwick and Northwick, Rockhampton, Thornbury, Tortworth, Tytherington

WESTBURY ON SEVERN PLU
Abenhall, Awre, Blaisdon, Bulley, Churcham, East Dean, Flaxley, Hinders Lane and Dockham (1858–84), Huntley, Littledean, Longhope, Minsterworth, Mitcheldean, Newnham, Westbury on Severn

WHEATENHURST PLU
Arlington, Brookthorpe, Eastington, Frampton on Severn, Fretherne (1836–84), Fretherne with Saul (1884–1930), Frocester, Hardwicke, Harescombe, Haresfield, Longney, Moreton Valence, Saul (1836–84), Standish, Wheatenhurst

WINCHCOMBE PLU
Alderton, Alstone, Beckford, Buckland, Charlton Abbots, Bishop's Cleeve, Didbrook, Dumbleton, Gotherington, Temple Guiting, Guiting Power, Hailes, Hawling, Pinnock and Hyde, Prescott, Roel, Snowshill, Southam and Brockhampton, Stanley Pontlarge, Stanton, Stanway, Sudeley Manor, Toddington, Great Washbourne, Little Washbourne, Winchcombe, Woodmancote, Wormington

In Other Poor Law Counties:

CHEPSTOW PLU (Monmouth)
Alvington, Aylburton, Hewelsfield, Lancaut, Lydney, St Briavels, Tidenham, Woolaston

FARINGDON PLU (Berks)
Lechlade

EVESHAM PLU (Worcs)
Ashton under Hill, Aston Somerville, Aston Subedge, Child's Wickham, Hinton on the Green, Cow Honeybourne, Pebworth, Saintbury, Weston Subedge, Willersley

KEYNSHAM PLU (Somerset)
Bittton, Hanham (1836–94), Hanham Abbots (1894–1930), Kingswood (1894–1930), Mangotsfield (1836–1927), Mangotsfield Rural (1927–30), Mangotsfield Urban (1927–30), Oldland, Siston

MONMOUTH PLU (Monmouth)
English Bicknor, West Dean, Newland, Staunton

ROSS PLU (Hereford)
Lea Bailey (1836–90), Ruardean

SHIPSTON ON STOUR PLU (Warws)
Admington, Batsford, Bourton on the Hill, Chipping Campden, Clopton, Ebrington, Hidcote Bartrim, Ilmington,[31] Lower Lemington, Mickleton, Moreton in Marsh, Quinton, Todenham

STRATFORD ON AVON PLU (Warws)
Clifford Chambers, Dorsington, Marston Sicca, Preston on Stour, Welford, Weston on Avon

SANITARY DISTRICTS

AWRE USD
Awre

BARTON REGIS RSD
same as PLU less Bristol St George, Horfield (pt 1875–81, ent 1881–94), Stapleton

BISLEY USD
Bisley (ent 1875–83, pt 1883–94), pt Cranham (1883–94), pt Miserden (1883–94)

BRISTOL USD
same as Bristol MB for 1875–94

CHARLTON KINGS USD
Charlton Kings (ent 1875–92, pt 1892–94)

CHELTENHAM RSD
same as PLU less Charlton Kings, Cheltenham, pt Leckhampton

CHELTENHAM USD
pt Charlton Kings (1892–94), Cheltenham

CIRENCESTER RSD
same as PLU less Cirencester

CIRENCESTER USD
Cirencester

COLEFORD USD
pt Newland

DURSLEY RSD
same as PLU

EVESHAM RSD
same as PLU for the Glos pars

GLOUCESTER RSD
same as PLU less the pars in Gloucester MB for 1875–94

GLOUCESTER USD
same as Gloucester MB for 1875–94

HORFIELD USD[32]
Horfield (pt 1875–81, ent 1881–94)

KEYNSHAM RSD
same as PLU for the Glos pars less pt Hanham, pt Mangotsfield (1890–94), pt Oldland
KINGSWOOD USD[33]
pt Hanham, pt Mangotsfield (1890–94), pt Oldland
LECKHAMPTON USD
pt Leckhampton
MONMOUTH RSD
same as PLU for Glos pars less pt Coleford
NEWENT RSD
same as PLU
NEWNHAM USD
Newnham
NORTHLEACH RSD
same as PLU
ROSS RSD
same as PLU for the Glos pars
ST GEORGE USD
Bristol St George
SHIPSTON ON STOUR RSD
same as PLU for the Glos pars
CHIPPING SODBURY RSD
same as PLU
STAPLETON USD
Stapleton
STOW ON THE WOLD RSD
same as PLU less pt Maugersbury, Stow on the Wold
STOW ON THE WOLD USD
pt Maugersbury, Stow on the Wold
STRATFORD ON AVON RSD
same as PLU for the Glos pars
STROUD RSD
same as PLU less Bisley (ent 1875–83, pt 1883–94), pt Cranham (1883–94), pt Miserden (1883–94), pt Painswick (1883–94), pt Stroud
STROUD USD[34]
pt Painswick (1883–94), pt Stroud
TETBURY RSD
same as PLU less pt Tetbury
TETBURY USD
pt Tetbury
TEWKESBURY RSD
same as PLU less Tewkesbury
TEWKESBURY USD
Tewkesbury
THORNBURY RSD
same as PLU
WESTBURY ON SEVERN RSD
same as PLU less Awre, pt Littledean (1883–94), Newnham, Westbury on Severn (ent 1875–83, pt 1883–94)
WESTBURY ON SEVERN USD
pt Littledean (1883–94), Westbury on Severn (ent 1875–83, pt 1883–94)
WHEATENHURST RSD
same as PLU
WINCHCOMBE RSD
same as PLU

ADMINISTRATIVE COUNTY

For MBs and the associated CBs see BOROUGHS.

AWRE UD (1894–1935)
Awre
BARTON REGIS RD (1894–1904[35])
Filton, Henbury, Shirehampton, Stoke Gifford, Westbury-on-Trym, Winterbourne
CAMPDEN RD (1894–1935)
Admington, Aston Subedge (1931–35), Batsford, Blockley (1931–35), Bourton on the Hill, Chipping Campden, Clopton, Ebrington, Hidcote Bartrim, Lower Lemington, Mickleton, Moreton in Marsh, Quinton, Saintbury (1931–35), Todenham, Weston Subedge (1931–35), Willersey (1931–35)
CHARLTON KINGS UD
Charlton Kings
CHELTENHAM RD
Alderton (1935–74), Ashchurch (1935–74), Badgeworth, Boddington (1935–74), Buckland (1935–74), Bishop's Cleeve (1935–74), Coberly, Cowley, Deerhurst (1935–74), Dumbelton (1935–74), Elmstone Hardwicke (1935–74), Gotherington (1935–74), Up Hatherley, Hawling (1935–74), Leckhampton, Leigh (1935–74), Oxenton (1935–74), Prescott (1935–74), Prestbury, Shurdington, Snowshill (1935–74), Southam (1935–74), Stanton (1935–74), Stanway (1935–74), Staverton, Stoke Orchard (1935–74), Swindon, Sudeley (1935–74), Teddington (1935–74), Toddington (1935–74), Twyning (1935–74), Uckington, Walton Cardiff (1935–74), Winchcombe (1935–74), Great Witcombe, Woodmancote (1935–74)
CIRENCESTER RD
Down Ampney, Ampney Crucis, Ampney St Mary, Ampney St Peter, Bagendon, Barnsley, Baunton, Brimpsfield, North Cerney, South Cerney, Coates, Colesbourne, Daglingworth, Driffield, Duntisbourne Abbots, Duntisbourne Rouse, Edgeworth, Elkstone, Fairford, Harnhill (1894–1935), Hatherop, Kemble (1897–1974), Kempsford, Poole Keynes (1897–1974), Somerford Keynes (1897–1974), Lechlade (1935–74), Meysey Hampton, Poulton, Preston, Quenington, Rendcombe, Rodmarton, Sapperton, Siddington, Stratton (1894–1935), Syde, Winstone
CIRENCESTER UD
Cirencester
COLEFORD UD (1894–1935)
Coleford
NORTH COTSWOLD RD (1935–74)
Adlestrop, Aston Subedge, Batsford, Bledington, Blockley, Bourton on the Hill, Bourton on the Water, Broadwell, Chipping Campden, Clapton, Condicote, Cutsdean, Donnington, Ebrington, Evenlode, Temple Guiting, Guiting Power, Icomb, Longborough, Maugersbury, Mickleton, Moreton in Marsh, Naunton, Oddington, Great Rissington,

Little Rissington, Wick Rissington, Saintbury, Sezincote, Lower Slaughter, Upper Slaughter, Stow-on-the-Wold, Swell, Todenham, Westcote, Weston Subedge, Willersley

EAST DEAN RD (1935–74)

Awre, Blaisdon, Churcham, Cinderford (1953–74). East Dean (1935–53), Drybrook (1953–74), Huntley, Littledean, Longhope, Mitcheldean, Ruardean, Ruspidge (1953–74)

EAST DEAN AND UNITED PARISHES RD (1894–1935)

Abenhall, Blaisdon, Bulley, Churcham, East Dean, Flaxley, Huntley, Littledean, Longhope, Mitcheldean, Minsterworth, Ruardean

WEST DEAN RD

English Bicknor, Coleford (1935–74), West Dean, Lydbrook (1935–74), Newland, Staunton

DURSLEY RD

Cam, Coaley, Dursley, Kingswood, North Nibley, Nympsfield, Owlpen, Slimbridge, Stinchcombe, Uley, Wotton under Edge

FARINGDON (Berks, Glos [ent Berks from 1935])

Lechlade (1894–1935)

GLOUCESTER RD

Arlingham (1935–74), Ashleworth, Barnwood (1894–1966), Brockworth, Brookthorpe (1935–56), Brookthorpe-with-Whaddon (1956–74), Chaceley (1935–74), Churchdown, Eastington (1935–74), Elmore, Forthampton (1935–74), Frampton on Severn (1935–74), Fretherne with Saul (1935–74), Frocester (1935–74), Hardwicke (1935–74), Harescombe (1935–74), Haresfield (1935–74), Hasfield (1935–74), Down Hatherley, Hempsted (1894–1966), Highnam (1935–74), Highnam Over and Linton (1894–1935), Hucclecote, Innsworth (1967–74), Lassington (1894–1935), Longford, Longlevens (1935–67), Longney (1935–74), Maisemore, Matson (1894–1935), Minsterworth (1935–74), Moreton Valence (1935–74), Newnham (1935–74), Norton, Prinknash Park (1894–1935), Quedgeley, Sandhurst, Standish (1935–74), Tirley (1935–74), Twigworth, Upton St Leonards, Westbury on Severn (1935–74), Whaddon (1894–1935), Wheatenhurst (1935–45), Whitminster (1945–74), Wotton St Mary Without (1894–1935), Wotton Vill (1894–1951)

HORFIELD UD (1894–1904[35])

Horfield

KINGSWOOD UD

Kingswood

LYDNEY RD

Alvington, Aylburton, Hewelsfield, Lancaut (1894–1935), Lydney, St Briavels, Tidenham, Woolaston

MARSTON SICCA RD (1894–1931[36])

Clifford Chambers, Dorsington, Marston Sicca, Preston on Stour, Welford, Weston on Avon

MANGOTSFIELD UD (1927[37]–74)

Mangotsfield Urban

NAILSWORTH UD (1894[38]–1974)

Nailsworth

NEWENT RD

Bromsberrow, Corse, Dymock, Hartpury, Highleadon (1894–1935), Kempley, Newent, Oxenhall, Pauntley, Preston (1894–1935), Redmarley d'Abitot (1931–74), Rudford, Staunton (1931–74), Taynton, Tibberton, Upleadon

NEWNHAM UD (1894–1935)

Newnham

NORTHLEACH RD

Aldsworth, Andoversford (1956–74), Aston Blank, Barrington (1935–74), Little Barrington (1894–1935), Bibury, Chedworth, Coln Rogers (1894–1935), Coln St Aldwyn (1894–1959), Coln St Aldwyns (1959–74), Coln St Dennis, Compton Abdale, Dowdeswell, Eastington (1894–1950), Eastleach (1935–74), Eastleach Martin (1894–1935), Eastleach Turville (1894–1935), Farmington, Hampnett, Hasleton, Northleach (1894–1950), Northleach with Eastington (1950–74), Notgrove (1935–74), Salperton (1894–1935), Sevenhampton, Sherborne, Shipton, Southrop, Stowell (1894–1935), Turkdean, Whittington, Windrush, Winson, Withington, Yanworth

PEBWORTH RD (1894–1931[37])

Ashton under Hill, Aston Somerville, Aston Subedge, Child's Wickham, Hinton on the Green, Cow Honeybourne, Pebworth, Saintbury, Weston Subedge, Willersey

ST GEORGE UD (1894–98[39])

Bristol St George

SODBURY RD (1935–74)

Iron Acton, Acton Turville, Alderley, Cold Ashton, Great Badminton, Dodington, Doynton, Dyrham and Hinton, Filton, Frampton Cotterell, Hawkesbury, Horton, Marshfield, Pucklechurch, Sodbury (1946–74), Chipping Sodbury (1935–46), Little Sodbury, Old Sodbury (1935–46), Stoke Gifford, Tormarton, Westerleigh, Wick and Abson, Wickwar, Winterbourne, Yate

CHIPPING SODBURY RD (1894–1935)

Iron Acton, Acton Turville, Alderley, Cold Ashton, Great Badminton, Dodington, Doynton, Dyrham and Hinton, Filton (1904–35), Frampton Cotterell, Hawkesbury, Horton, West Littleton, Marshfield, Pucklechurch, Chipping Sodbury, Little Sodbury, Old Sodbury, Stoke Gifford (1904–35), Tormarton, Wapley and Cordrington, Westerleigh, Wick and Abson, Wickwar, Winterbourne (1904–35), Yate

STAPLETON UD (1894–98[39])

Stapleton

STOW ON THE WOLD RD (1894–1935) [pt Glos, pt Worcs[40] until 1931, ent Glos 1931–35]

Adlestrop, Great Barrington, Bledington, Bourton on the Water, Broadwell, Clapton, Condicote, Daylesford (1931–35), Donnington, Evenlode (1931–35), Eyford, Icomb, Church Icomb, Longborough, Maugersbury, Naunton, Notgrove, Oddington, Great Rissington, Little Rissington, Wick Rissington, Sezincote, Lower Slaughter, Upper Slaughter, Lower Swell, Upper Swell, Westcote

STOW ON THE WOLD UD (1894–1935)

Stow-on-the-Wold

STROUD RD

Bisley with Lypiatt, Cainscross (1894–1936), Chalford, Cranham, Horsley, Minchinhampton, Miserden, Painswick, Pitchcombe, Randwick, Rodborough, King's Stanley, Leonard Stanley, Stonehouse, Thrupp, Whiteshill, Woodchester

STROUD UD

Stroud, Uplands (1894–1936)

TETBURY RD [pt Glos, pt Wilts[41] until 1930, ent Glos 1930–74]

Ashley (1930–74), Avening, Beverstone, Boxwell with Leighterton, Cherington, Didmarton, Kingscote, Newington Bagpath, Long Newnton (1930–74), Ozleworth, Shipton Moyne, Tetbury (1935–74), Tetbury Upton, Weston Birt

TETBURY UD (1894–1935)

Tetbury

TEWKESBURY RD (1894–1935) [pt Glos, pt Worcs[42]]

Ashchurch, Boddington, Chaceley (1931–35), Deerhurst, Elmstone Hardwicke, Forthampton, Hasfield, Kemerton (1894–1931), Leigh, Oxenton, Stoke Orchard, Teddington (1931–35), Tirley, Tredington, Twyning, Walton Cardiff, Woolstone

THORNBURY RD

Alkington, Almondsbury, Alveston, Aust, Berkeley, Breadstone (1894–1935), Charfield, Cromhall, Elberton (1894–1935), Falfield, Ham and Stone, Hamfallow, Henbury (1904–35), Hill, Hinton, Littleton upon Severn (1894–1935), Oldbury upon Severn, Olveston, Patchway (1953–74), Pilning and Severn Beach (1965–74), Rangeworthy, Redwick and Northwick (1894–1965), Rockhampton, Thornbury, Tortworth, Tytherington

WARMLEY RD

Bitton, Hanham Abbots, Mangotsfield (1894–1927), Mangotsfield Rural (1927–74), Oldland, Siston

WESTBURY ON SEVERN UD (1894–1935)

Westbury on Severn

WHEATENHURST RD (1894–1935)

Arlingham, Brookthorpe, Eastington, Harescombe, Frampton on Severn, Fretherne with Saul, Frocester, Hardwicke, Haresfield, Longney, Moreton Valence, Standish, Wheatenhurst

WINCHCOMBE RD (1894–1935) [pt Glos, pt Worcs[43]]

Alderton, Alstone, Beckford (1894–1931), Buckland, Charlton Abbots, Bishop's Cleeve, Cutsdean (1931–35), Didbrook, Dumbleton, Gotherington, Temple Guiting, Guiting Power, Hailes, Hawling, Pinnock and Hyde, Prescott, Roel, Snowshill, Southam and Brockhampton, Stanley Pontlarge, Stanton, Stanway, Sudeley Manor, Toddington, Great Washbourne, Little Washbourne, Winchcombe, Woodmancote, Wormington

NON-METROPOLITAN COUNTY

As constituted 1 Apr 1974, defined in terms of Adm Co units as of 31 Mar.

CHELTENHAM DIST

Charlton Kings UD, Cheltenham MB

COTSWOLD DIST

Cirencester RD, Cirencester UD, North Cotswold RD, Northleach RD, Tetbury RD

FOREST OF DEAN DIST

East Dean RD, West Dean RD, pt Gloucester RD (Newnham, Westbury-on-Severn), Lydney RD, Newent RD

GLOUCESTER DIST

Gloucester CB

STROUD DIST

Dursley RD, pt Gloucester RD (all except the pars in Forest of Dean Dist and in Tewkesbury Dist), Nailsworth UD, pt Sodbury RD (Alderley), Stroud RD, Stroud UD, pt Thornbury RD (Alkington, Berkeley, Ham and Stone, Hamfallow, Hinton)

TEWKESBURY DIST

Cheltenham RD, pt Gloucester RD (Ashleworth, Brockworth, Chaceley, Churchdown, Forthampton, Hasfield, Down Hatherley, Highnam, Hucclecote, Innsworth, Longford, Maisemore, Minsterworth, Norton, Sandhurst, Tirley, Twigworth), Tewkesbury MB

HAMPSHIRE

ALTERATIONS IN COUNTY BOUNDARIES

As noted by year below, Hants pars gained territory from or lost it to pars in adjoining counties or county boroughs, or were entirely transferred to them. Details of these alterations are noted in Part I of the *Guide* under Hants.

ANCIENT COUNTY (until 1889: Hds, Bors, MBs, PLUs, RSDs, USDs)

1844 Bramshott, Steep. *1860s* Hampreston. *1866* Dockenfield, Frensham, Stratfield Mortimer, Stratfield Saye. *1883* West Dean, West Tytherley.

HAMPSHIRE ADMINISTRATIVE COUNTY (1889–1974: Hds,[2] PLUs, MBs, RDs, UDs, with associated CBs of Bournemouth [1900–74], Portsmouth, Southampton) (also incl Isle of Wight 1889–90 until latter became sep Adm Co)

1894 Bramshaw. *1895* East Bramshaw, Bramshott, Combe, Damerham, Dockenfield, Martin, Melchet Park, Plaitford, Shirley, Toyd Farm and Allenford, West Wellow, Whitsbury. *1900* Bournemouth, Portsea, Great Salterns. *1901* Holdenhurst. *1902* Hurn, Pokesdown, Southbourne, Winton. *1904* Cosham. *1914* Holdenhurst. *1920* Bitterne, Cosham, Itchen, North Stoneham, South Stoneham. *1922* Alverstoke. *1931* Holdenhurst. *1932* Christchurch. Farlington, Portchester. *1940* Alverstoke. *1954* Christchurch, Hound, Millbrook, Nursling and Rownhams, West End. *1967* Nursling and Rownhams.

ISLE OF WIGHT ADMINISTRATIVE COUNTY (1890–1974: Hds,[2] PLUs, MBs, RDs, UDs)

unaltered in area

HAMPSHIRE NON-METROPOLITAN COUNTY (from 1974: Dists)

1974 Christchurch, Christchurch East, Hurn, St Leonards and St Ives, Sopley

ISLE OF WIGHT NON-METROPOLITAN COUNTY (from 1974: Dists)

ASSOCIATED COUNTY BOROUGHS

For constituent pars see listing for BOROUGHS in this Part of the *Guide*.

BOURNEMOUTH CB (1900–74)

Cr 1900 when Bournemouth MB made a CB.[3] Bdry: 1901,[4] 1902,[5] 1904,[6] 1914,[7] 1931 (incl gains Kinson AP, Dorset),[8] 1932.[9] Transf 1974 to Dorset.[10]

PORTSMOUTH CB

Bdry: 1895,[61] 1900,[11] 1904,[12] 1904,[13] 1920,[14] 1922,[15] 1932,[16] 1940.[17]

SOUTHAMPTON CB

Bdry: 1895,[18] 1920,[19] 1925,[20] 1954,[21] 1967.[22]

HUNDREDS[2]

ALTON HD

Alton,[23] Binsted, pt Bramshott (until 1834), Chawton, Coldred (from 1858), Dockenfield (from 1866), pt Frensham (until 1866), Froyle, Greatham (until 1834), Hartley Mauditt, Headley (from 1834), Holybourne, Kingsley, Neatham (from 1834), Shalden (from 1834), pt East Tisted (until 1834), East Worldham, West Worldham

ALVERSTOKE LBTY

Alverstoke

ANDOVER HD

pt Abbots Ann (until 1834), Amport, Andover,[23] Appleshaw, Upper Clatford (until 1834), Knights Enham, Foxcott, Fyfield, Grately, Kimpton, Monxton, Penton Grafton, Penton Mewsey, Quarley, Shipton Bellinger (from 1834), Tangley (from 1834), Thruxton (until 1834), South Tedworth

BARTON STACEY HD

Barton Stacey, Colemore (until 1834), Priors Dean (until 1834), Pamber (until 1834), Wonston (until 1834), Headbourne Worthy (until 1834), Kings Worthy (until 1834)

BASINGSTOKE HD

Andwell (from 1858), pt Basing, Basingstoke,[23] Bramley, Cliddesden, Eastrop,[23] Mapledurwell, Up Nateley, Nateley Scures, Newnham, Pamber (from 1834), Monk Sherborne (from 1834), Sherborne St John, Sherfield-on-Loddon (from 1834), Steventon (until 1834), Tunworth, Winslade, Wootton St Lawrence (from 1834), Worting

(from 1834)
BEAULIEU LBTY
Beaulieu, Denny Lodge (from 1868)
BENTLEY LBTY
Bentley
BERMONDSPIT HD
Bentworth (from 1834), Bradley (from 1834), Preston Candover, Dunmer, Ellisfield, Farleigh Wallop, Herriard (pt until 1834, ent from 1834), Lasham (from 1834), Nutley, Popham (from 1834), Upton Grey, South Warnborough (until 1834), Weston Corbett (from 1858), Weston Patrick (from 1834)
BOSMERE HD
North Hayling, South Hayling, Warblington
BOUNTISBOROUGH HD
Godsfield (from 1858), Itchen Abbas, Itchen Stoke, Swarraton (until 1834)
BREAMORE LBTY
Breamore
BUDDLESGATE HD
Ashley (from 1834), Chilbolton (until 1834), Compton, Crawley, Houghton (until 1834), Hunton (from 1866), Hursley, Lainston (from 1858), Littleton, Michelmersh (until 1834), Millbrook (until 1834), Nursling (until 1834), Otterbourne, St Faith,[23] Little Somborne (from 1834), Sparsholt, Stoke Charity, Weeke,[23] Wonston (from 1834)
CHRISTCHURCH HD[24]
pt Boldre, Christchurch[23] (ent until 1834, pt from 1834), Hordle, pt Milford, Milton, pt Rhinefield (from 1868), Sopley
CHUTELEY HD
Hannington, Oakley, Monk Sherborne (until 1834), Wootton St Lawrence (until 1834), Worting (until 1834)
CRONDALL HD
Aldershot, Cove (from 1866), Crondall, Farnborough, Hawley with Minely (from 1866), Long Sutton, Yateley
DIBDEN LBTY
Calshot (from 1858), Dibden, Fawley (from late 18th cent)
EVINGAR HD
Ashmansworth, Baughurst, pt Burghclere,[23] Ecchinswell, Freefolk Manor, Highclere, Hurstbourne Priors, Newtown,[23] St Mary Bourne, Tufton (from 1834), Whitchurch,[23] East Woodhay
FAREHAM HD
Fareham[23]
FAWLEY HD
New Alresford,[23] Old Alresford, Avington, Beauworth, Bishopstoke, Cheriton, Chilcomb,[23] Easton, Exton (until 1834), Hinton Ampner, Kilmiston, Medstead (until 1834), West Meon (until 1834), Morestead, Ovington, Owslebury, Privett (until 1834), Tichborne, Twyford, pt Upham (from 1834), Wield (until 1834), Winnall,[23] Headbourne Worthy (from 1834), pt Kings Worthy (from 1834), Martyr Worthy
FINCHDEAN HD
Blendworth, pt Bramshott (from 1834), Buriton, Catherington, Chalton, Clanfield, Greatham (from 1834), Idsworth (from 1866), Liss (from 1834), Petersfield,[23] Sheet (from 1866)
FORDINGBRIDGE HD
Ashley Walk (from 1868), Broomy (from 1868), North Charford, South Charford, Ellingham (until 1834), Fordingbridge, Hale, Ibsley, Rockbourne, Woodgreen (from 1858)
NEW FOREST HD
pt Boldre, pt Bramshaw (until 1834), Brockenhurst, Burley (from 1868), Exbury (until late 18th cent), pt Fawley (1662–late 18th cent), Lyndhurst (until 1834), Lymington,[23] Minstead (until 1834), pt Rhinefield (from 1868), Sway (from 1866)
HAMBLEDON HD
Hambledon
HAVANT LBTY
Havant
HOLDSHOT HD
pt Eversley (until 1834), Hartley Wespall, Heckfield, Mattingly (from 1866), pt Odiham (until 1834), Mortimer West End (from 1866), Silchester, pt Stratfield Mortimer (from 1866), Stratfield Saye (pt until 1866, ent from 1866), Stratfield Turgis, North Waltham (from 1834), Woodmancott (from 1834)
KINGSCLERE HD
pt Burghclere,[23] Ewhurst, Kingsclere (pt until 1866, ent from 1866), Litchfield, Sydmonton, Wolverton
MAINSBROUGH HD
Brown Candover, Chilton Candover, Woodmancott until 1834)
MAINSBRIDGE HD
North Baddesley (until 1834), Botley, Bursledon (from 1834), Chilworth, Hamble le Rice, Hound, Millbrook (from 1834), St Mary Extra, North Stoneham, South Stoneham[23]
EAST MEON HD
Colemore (from 1834), Priors Dean (from 1834), Froxfield, East Meon, Privett[23] (from 1834), Steep (pt until 1844, ent from 1844)
MEONSTOKE HD
Corhampton, Exton (from 1834), West Meon (from 1834), Meonstoke, Soberton, pt Upham (from 1834), Warnford
MICHELDEVER HD
Farley Chamberlayne (from 1834), Micheldever, Northington, Popham (until 1834), East Stratton, Swarraton (from 1834), pt Kings Worthy (from 1834)
ODIHAM HD
Bentworth (until 1834), Bramshill [par from 1866] (from 1834), Dogmersfield, Elvetham, Eversley (pt until 1866, ent from 1866), Greywell, Hartley Wintney, pt Herriard (until 1834), Lasham (until 1834), Liss (until 1834), Loddon (until 1834), Odiham (pt until 1834, ent from 1834), Rotherwick, Shalden (until 1834), Sherfield-on-Loddon (until 1834), South Warnborough (from 1834), Weston Patrick (until 1834), Winchfield

OVERTON HD
Ashe, Bradley (until 1834), Deane, Laverstoke, Overton,[23] Steventon (until 1834), Tadley, North Waltham (until 1834)
PASTROW HD
Upper Clatford (from 1834), Combe, Crux Easton, Vernhams Dean, Faccombe, Hurstbourne Tarrant, Linkenholt, Tangley (until 1834), Thruxton (from 1834), Woodcott
PORTSDOWN HD
Bedhampton, Boarhunt, Farlington, Portchester,[23] pt Portsea,[23] Great Salterns (from 1858), Southwick, Waterloo (from 1858), Widley, Wymering
PORTSMOUTH AND PORTSEA ISLAND LBTY
pt Portsea,[23] Portsmouth[23]
REDBRIDGE HD
pt Bramshaw (from 1834), pt Eling, pt Fawley (until 1834), Nursling (from 1834)
RINGWOOD HD
pt Christchurch[23] (from 1834), Ellingham (from 1834), Harbridge, pt Milford, Ringwood
SELBORNE HD
Empshott, Farringdon, Hawkley, Newton Valence, Selborne, East Tisted (pt until 1834, ent from 1834)
KING'S SOMBORNE HD
Ashley (until 1834), North Baddesley (from 1834), Upper Eldon (from 1858), Farley Chamberlayne (until 1834), Houghton (from 1834), Leckford (until 1834), Longstock (until 1834), Romsey[23] (until 1866), Romsey Extra[23] (from 1866), Romsey Infra[23] (from 1866), Kings Somborne, Little Somborne (until 1834), Stockbridge[23] (until 1834), Timsbury
BISHOP'S SUTTON HD
Bighton, Bramdean, Headley (until 1834), Medstead (from 1834), Ropley, Bishops Sutton, West Tisted, Wield (from 1834)
THORNGATE HD
Bossington, Broughton, Buckholt (from 1858), Crown Farm (from 1858), East Dean, pt West Dean (until 1883), Dunwood (from 1858), pt Eling, Frenchmoor (from 1866), Leckford (from 1834), Lockerley, Longstock (from 1834), Lyndhurst (from 1834), Michelmersh (from 1834), Minstead (from 1834), Mottisfont, Sherfield English, Shipton Bellinger (until 1834), Stockbridge[23] (from 1834), East Tytherley, West Tytherley, Nether Wallop, Over Wallop, East Wellow
TITCHFIELD HD
Rowner, Titchfield, Wickham
BISHOP'S WALTHAM HD
Bursledon (until 1834), Droxford, Exbury (from late 18th cent), pt Fawley (1662–late 18th cent), Upham (until 1834), Bishops Waltham
WESTOVER LBTY[24]
Christchurch[23] (ent until 1834, pt from 1834), pt Hampreston (until 1860s), Holdenhurst[23]
WHERWELL HD
Abbots Ann (pt until 1834, ent from 1834), Bullington, Chilbolton (from 1834), Goodworth Clatford, Longparish, Tufton (until 1834), Wherwell

In Isle of Wight:
EAST MEDINA HD/LBTY
Arreton, Binstead, Bonchurch, Brading,[23] Godshill, Newchurch, Niton, Ryde[23] (from 1866), St Helens,[23] St Lawrence, Shanklin, Ventnor (from 1866), Whippingham,[23] Whitwell, Wootton, Yaverland
WEST MEDINA HD/LBTY
Brixton, Brook, Calbourne,[23] Carisbrooke,[23] Chale, Freshwater, Gatcombe, Kingston, Mottistone, Newport,[23] Northwood,[23] St Nicholas,[23] Shalfleet, Shorwell, Thorley, Yarmouth[23]

BOROUGHS

Units with some degree of burghal character[25] are denominated 'Bor'.
Those which did not sustain that status until the 19th cent are in italics.
Municipal Boroughs were established by the Municipal Corporations Act, 1835,[26] or by later charter.

ALDERSHOT MB (1922[27]–74)
Aldershot
NEW ALRESFORD BOR
New Alresford
ALTON BOR
Alton
ANDOVER BOR/MB
Andover (ent until 1883, pt 1883–94, ent 1894–1974)
BASINGSTOKE BOR/MB
Basingstoke, Eastrop (1879–91)
BOURNEMOUTH MB (1890[28]–1900), CB (1900[3]–74)
Bournemouth (1894–1974), pt Christchurch (1890–94), pt Holdenhurst (1890–94), Pokesdown (1901[4]–02), Winton (1901[4]–02)
BRADING BOR [ISLE OF WIGHT]
Brading
CHRISTCHURCH BOR (sometimes earlier, 'TWINEHAM' or 'CHRISTCHURCH TWINEHAM'), MB (1886[29]–1974)
Christchurch (pt when Bor, pt 1886–94, ent 1894–1974)
EASTLEIGH MB (1936[27]–74)
Eastleigh
FAREHAM BOR
Fareham
GOSPORT[30] MB (1922[31]–74)
Alverstoke, Lee on the Solent (1930–32)
LYMINGTON BOR/MB
pt Boldre (until Lymington gained sep civ identity), Lymington (pt until 1889, ent 1889–1974)

NEWPORT BOR/MB [ISLE OF WIGHT]
pt Carisbrooke (until 1894), Newport, pt Northwood (until 1876[32]), pt St Nicholas (until 1894), pt Whippingham (until 1894)

NEWTOWN BOR
pt Burghclere (until Newtown gained sep civ identity), Newtown

NEWTOWN BOR [ISLE OF WIGHT] (Sometimes, 'FRANCHEVILLE')
pt Calbourne

OVERTON BOR
Overton

PETERSFIELD BOR
pt Buriton (until Petersfield gained sep civ identity), pt Petersfield

PORTCHESTER BOR
Portchester

PORTSMOUTH BOR/MB/CB
Portsea (pt until 1835, ent 1835–1900), Portsmouth, Great Salterns (1895–1900)

ROMSEY BOR/MB
pt Romsey (until 1866), pt Romsey Extra (1866–94), Romsey Infra (1866–94)

RYDE MB (1868[33]–1974) [ISLE OF WIGHT]
Ryde (pt 1868–94, ent 1894–1974), pt St Helens (1868–94)

SOUTHAMPTON[34] BOR/MB/CB
Bitterne (1920–25), Itchen (1920–25), Portswood (1894–1912), Shirley (1895–1912), Southampton (1912–74), Southampton All Saints (until 1912), Southampton Holy Rood (until 1912), Southamp-

STOCKBRIDGE BOR
pt Kings Somborne (until Stockbridge gained sep civ identity), Stockbridge

TWINEHAM–See CHRISTCHURCH

WHITCHURCH BOR
Whitchurch

WICKHAM BOR
Wickham

WINCHESTER BOR/MB[35]
pt Chilcombe (1835–94), Chilcombe Within (1894–1902), Milland (ent 1835–89, pt 1889–94, ent 1894–1902), pt St Faith (until 1894), St Faith Within (1894–1902), Winchester (1902–74), Winchester St Bartholomew Hyde (pt until 1894, ent 1894–1902), Winchester St George (until 1615), Winchester St John (pt until 1894, ent 1894–1902), Winchester St Lawrence (until 1902), Winchester St Mary de Worde (until 1615), Winchester St Mary Kalendar (until 1902), Winchester St Maurice (until 1902), Winchester St Michael (until 1902), Winchester St Peter Cheesehill (pt until 1894, ent 1894–1902), Winchester St Peter Colebrook (until 1902), Winchester St Swithin (until 1902), Winchester St Thoms (until 1902), pt Weeke (until 1894), Weeke Within (1894–1902), Winnall (pt 1835–94, ent 1894–1902)

YARMOUTH BOR [ISLE OF WIGHT]
Yarmouth

ton St John (until 1912), Southampton St Lawrence (until 1912), Southampton St Mary (until 1912), Southampton St Michael (until 1912), Southampton St Nicholas (1920–25), pt South Stoneham (until 1894)

POOR LAW UNIONS

In Hants Poor Law County:[36]

ALRESFORD PLU
New Alresford, Old Alresford, Beauworth, Bighton, Bramdean, Brown Candover, Chilton Candover, Cheriton, Godsfield (1858[37]–1930), Hinton Ampner, Itchen Stoke, Kilmiston, Northington, Ovington, Ropley, Bishops Sutton, Swarraton, Tichborne, West Tisted

ALTON PLU
Alton, Bentley, Bentworth, Binstead, Chawton, Coldrey, Farringdon, Froyle, Grayshott (1902–30), Hartley Mauditt, Headley (1869–1930), Holybourne, Kingsley (1869–1930), Lasham, Medstead, Neatham, Newton Valence, Selborne, Shalden, East Tisted, Whitehill (1929–30), Wield, East Worldham, West Worldham

ALVERSTOKE INCORP (1799–1852), PLU (1852–1930)
Alverstoke

ANDOVER PLU (Hants, Wilts)
Abbots Ann, Amport, Andover, Appleshaw, Barton Stacey, Bullington, Chilbolton, Goodworth Clatford, Upper Clatford, Vernhams Dean, Knights Enham (1894–1930), Faccombe, Foxcott, Fyfield, Grateley, Hurstbourne Tarrant, Kimpton, Linkenholt, Longparish, Monxton, *Park House*,[40] Penton Grafton, Penton Mewsey, Quarley, Shipton Bellinger, Tangley, Thruxton, South Tedworth, Wherwell

BASINGSTOKE PLU (Hants, Berks)
Andwell, Basing, Basingstoke, Bradley, Bramley, Preston Candover, Cliddesden, Deane, Dummer, Eastrop, Ellisfield, Farleigh Wallop, Hartley Wespall, Herriard, Mapledurwell, Mortimer West End (1866[37]–1930), Nateley Scures, Up Nateley, Newnham, Nutley, Oakley, Pamber, Popham, Monk Sherborne, Sherborne St John, Sherfield-on-Loddon, Silchester, Steventon, Stratfield Turgis, Tunworth, Upton Grey, North Waltham, Weston Corbett, Weston Patrick, Winslade, Woodmancott, Wootton St Lawrence, Worting

BOURNEMOUTH PAR (1900–30)
Bournemouth

BOURNEMOUTH AND CHRISTCHURCH PLU (1835–1900)
Bournemouth, Christchurch, Christchurch East (1894–1900), Highcliffe (1894–1900), Holdenhurst, Hurn (1894–1900), Pokesdown (1894–1900), Sopley, Southbourne (1894–1900), Winton (1894–1900)

CATHERINGTON PLU
Blendworth, Catherington, Chalton, Clanfield, Ids-

worth, Waterloo (1910–30)
CHRISTCHURCH PLU (1900–30)
Christchurch, Christchurch East, Highcliffe, Holdenhurst, Hurn, Pokesdown (1900–02), Sopley, Southbourne (1900–02), Winton (1900–02)
DROXFORD PLU
Corhampton, Curdridge (1894–1930), Droxford, Durley, Exton, Hambledon, West Meon, Meonstoke, Soberton, Upham, Shedfield (1894–1930), Swanmore (1894–1930), Bishops Waltham, Warnford
EASTLEIGH PLU (1920–30)
Bishopstoke, Botley, Burlesdon, Chilworth, Eastleigh, Hamble le Rice, Hedge End, Hound, Millbrook, North Stoneham (ent 1920–24, pt 1924–30), West End
FAREHAM PLU
Boarhunt, Cosham (1894–1921), Crofton (1894–1930), Fareham, Hook with Warsash (1894–1930), Portchester, Rowner, Sarisbury (1894–1930), Southwick, Titchfield, Wickham, Widley (1835–94), Widley (1921–30), Wymering (1835–94)
FARNBOROUGH INCORP[38] (1794–1869)
Cove, Farnborough, Hawley with Minley, Yateley
FORDINGBRIDGE PLU (Hants, Wilts until 1895, ent Wilts thereafter)
Ashley Walk (1868–1930), Breamore, North Charford, South Charford, Damerham,[39] Fordingbridge, Hale, Martin,[39] Rockbourne, Toyd Farm and Allenford,[39] Whitsbury,[39] Woodgreen
NEW FOREST PLU (Hants, Wilts)
Beaulieu, Bramshaw (Hants, Wilts, 1835–94), Bramshaw (Hants, 1894–1930), Bramshaw (Wilts, 1894–95), East Bramshaw (1895–1930), *Calshot*,[40] Colbury (1894–1930), Copythorne (1894–1930), Denny Lodge (1868–1930), Dibden, Eling, Exbury, Fawley, Lyndhurst, Marchwood (1894–1930), Minstead, Netley Marsh (1894–1930)
HAVANT PLU
Bedhampton, Farlington, Havant, North Havant (1902–30), North Hayling, South Hayling, Warblington
HARTLEY WINTNEY PLU
Bramshill, Cove (1869–1930), Crondall, Crookham (1894–1930), Dogmersfield, Elvetham, Eversley, Farnborough (1869–1930), Fleet (1894–1930), Greywell, Hartley Wintney, Hawley with Minley (1869–1930), Heckfield, Mattingley, Odiham, Rotherwick, Long Sutton (1869–1930), South Warnborough, Winchfield, Yateley (1869–1930)
HURSLEY PLU
Ampfield (1894–1930), North Baddesley, Chandlers Ford (1894–1930), Farley Chamberlayne, Hursley, Otterbourne
KINGSCLERE PLU
Ashmansworth, Baughurst, Burghclere, Crux Easton, Ecchinswell, Ewhurst, Hannington, Highclere, Kingsclere, Litchfield, Newtown (1894–1930), Sydmonton, Tadley, Wolverton, Woodcott, East Woodhay
LYMINGTON PLU
Boldre, East Boldre (1929–30), Brockenhurst, Hordle, Lymington, Milford (1835–1911), Milford on Sea (1911–30), Milton, Pennington (1911–30), Rhinefield, Sway (1866[37]–1930)
PETERSFIELD PLU
Bramshott[41] (1869–1930), Buriton, Colemore, Priors Dean, Empshott, Froxfield, Greatham, Hawkley, Langrish (1894–1930), Liss, East Meon, Petersfield, Privett, Sheet, Steep
PORTSEA ISLAND PLU (1836–1900)
Portsea, Portsmouth, Great Salterns (1858[37]–1930)
PORTSMOUTH PAR (1900–30)
Portsmouth
RINGWOOD PLU
Broomy (1868–1930), Burley (1868–1930), Ellingham, Harbirdge, Ibsley, Ringwood
ROMSEY PLU (Hants, Wilts until 1895, ent Hants thereafter)
East Dean, Dunwood (1858[37]–1930), Lockereley, Melchet Park,[39] Michelmersh, Mottisfont, Nursling, Plaitford,[39] Romsey Extra, Romsey Infra, Rownhams (1897–1930), Sherfield English, Timsbury, East Wellow, West Wellow[39]
SOUTHAMPTON INCORP (1772–1909), PLU (1909–30)
Bitterne (1924–30), Portswood (1908–12), Shirley (1908–12), pt North Stoneham (1924–30), Southampton (1912–30), Southampton All Saints (1772–1912), Southampton Holy Rood (1772–1912), Southampton St John (1772–1912), Southampton St Lawrence (1772–1912), Southampton St Mary (1772–1912), Southampton St Michael (1772–1912), Southampton St Nicholas (1920–25)
STOCKBRIDGE PLU (Hants, Wilts until 1894, ent Hants thereafter)
Ashley, Bossington, Broughton, Buckholt, Crown Farm (1858[37]–83), West Dean[43] (1835–94), Upper Eldon, Frenchmoor, Houghton, Leckford, Longstock, Kings Somborne, Little Somborne, Stockbridge, East Tytherley, West Tytherley, Nether Wallop, Over Wallop
SOUTH STONEHAM PLU (1835–1920)
Bitterne (1894–1920), Botley, Bursledon, Chilworth, Eastleigh (1894–1920), Hamble le Rice, Hedge End (1894–1920), Hound, Itchen (1903–20), Millbrook, Portswood (1894–1908), St Mary Extra (1835–1903), Shirley (1894–1908), Sholing (1894–1903), North Stoneham, South Stoneham, West End (1894–1920)
WHITCHURCH PLU
Ashe, Freefolk Manor, Hurstbourne Priors, Laverstoke, Overton, St Mary Bourne, Tufton, Whitchurch
WINCHESTER PLU
Abbots Barton (1894–1930), Avington, Bishop-

stoke, Chilcombe (1835–94), Chilcombe Within (1894–1902), Chilcombe Without (1894–1930), Compton, Crawley, Easton, Fair Oak (1894–1930), Hunton, Itchen Abbas, Lainston, Littleton, Micheldever, Milland (1835–1902), Morestead, Owslebury, St Faith (1835–94), St Faith Within (1894–1902), St Faith Without (1894–1900), Sparsholt, Stoke Charity, Stoke Park (1899–1930), East Stratton, Twyford, Weeke (1835–94), Weeke Within (1894–1902), Weeke Without (1894–1930), Winchester (1902–30), Winchester St Bartholomew Hyde (1835–1902), Winchester St John (1835–1902), Winchester St Lawrence (1835–1902), Winchester St Mary Kalendar (1835–1902), Winchester St Maurice (1835–1902), Winchester St Michael (1835–1902), Winchester St Peter Cheesehill (1835–1902), Winchester St Peter Colebrook (1835–1902), Winchester St Swithin (1835–1902), Winchester St Thomas (1835–1902), Winnall (1835–1902), Wonston, Headbourne Worthy, Kings Worthy, Martyr Worthy

In Isle of Wight (Hants until 1890, Isle of Wight Adm Co (1890–1930):

ISLE OF WIGHT INCORP (1770–1865), PLU (1865–1930)
Arreton (1865–94), Ashey (1894–1930), Bambridge (1896–1930), Binstead, Bonchurch, Brading, Brixton, Brook, Calbourne, Carisbrooke, Chale, Cowes (1894–1930), East Cowes (1894–1930), Freshwater, Gatcombe, Godshill, Kingston, Mottistone, Newchurch, Newport, Niton, Northwood, Ryde, St Helens, St Lawrence, St Nicholas (1770–1894), Sandown (1894–1930), Shalfleet, Shanklin, East Shanklin (1894–98), Shorwell, Thorley, Totland (1894–1930), Ventnor, Whippingham, Whitwell, Wootton (1770–1894), Yarmouth, Yaverland

In Other Poor Law Counties:

ASH INCORP (Surrey, Hants) (until 1846)
Long Sutton
FARNHAM PLU (Surrey, Hants)
Aldershot, Dockenfield
HUNGERFORD PLU (Berks, Hants, Wilts)
Coombe
NEWBURY PLU (Berks, Hants)
Newtown
WIMBORNE PLU (Dorset, Hants until 1860s, ent Dorset thereafter)
Hampreston

SANITARY DISTRICTS

ALDERSHOT USD
Aldershot
ALRESFORD RSD
same as PLU
ALTON RSD
same as PLU less Alton
ALTON USD
Alton
ALVERSTOKE USD (1875–91[44])
Alverstoke (ent 1875–83, pt 1883–91), pt Rowner (1883–91)
ANDOVER RSD
same as PLU less Andover (ent 1875–83, pt 1883–94)
ANDOVER USD
Andover (ent 1875–83, pt 1883–94)
BASINGSTOKE RSD
same as PLU less Basingstoke, pt Eastrop (1879–91)
BASINGSTOKE USD
Basingstoke, pt Eastrop (1879[47]–91)
BOURNEMOUTH USD[48]
pt Christchurch (extended pt 1884–94), pt Holdenhurst (extended pt 1884–94)
BOURNEMOUTH AND CHRISTCHURCH RSD
same as PLU less pt Christchurch (1875–84, extended pt 1884–94), pt Holdenhurst (1875–84, extended pt 1884–94)
CATHERINGTON RSD
same as PLU
CHRISTCHURCH USD (1886[45]–94)
pt Christchurch
EAST COWES USD [ISLE OF WIGHT]
pt Whippingham
WEST COWES USD[49] [ISLE OF WIGHT]
pt Northwood (extended pt 1882–94)
DROXFORD RSD
same as PLU
EASTLEIGH USD (1893[53]–94)
pt South Stoneham
FAREHAM RSD
same as PLU less Aldershot, Fareham, Rowner (ent 1875–83, pt 1883–94)
FAREHAM USD
Fareham
FARNHAM RSD
same as PLU for Hants pars
FORDINGBRIDGE RSD
same as PLU
NEW FOREST RSD
same as PLU
GOSPORT AND ALVERSTOKE USD (1891[44]–94)
pt Alverstoke, pt Rowner
HARTLEY WINTNEY RSD
same as PLU
HAVANT RSD
same as PLU less Havant
HAVANT USD
Havant
HUNGERFORD RSD
same as PLU for Hants par
HURSLEY RSD
same as PLU
ISLE OF WIGHT RSD
same as PLU less pt Brading, pt Carisbrooke, Newport, pt Northwood (1875–76, reduced pt 1876–

82, extended pt 1882–94), pt Ryde, pt St Helens, pt St Nicholas, pt Shanklin, pt Ventnor, pt Whippingham
KINGSCLERE RSD
same as PLU
LYMINGTON RSD
same as PLU less Lymington (pt 1875–89, ent 1889–94)
LYMINGTON USD[50]
Lymington (pt 1875–89, ent 1889–94)
NEWBURY RSD
same as PLU for Hants par
NEWPORT USD [ISLE OF WIGHT]
pt Carisbrooke, Newport, pt Northwood (1875–76[51]), pt St Nicholas, pt Whippingham
PETERSFIELD RSD
same as PLU less pt Buriton (1893–94), Petersfield (1893–94), pt Sheet (1893–94)
PETERSFIELD USD (1893[46]–94)
pt Buriton, Petersfield, pt Sheet
PORTSEA ISLAND RSD
Great Salterns
PORTSMOUTH USD
Portsea, Portsmouth
RINGWOOD RSD
same as PLU
ROMSEY RSD
same as PLU less pt Romsey Extra, Romsey Infra
ROMSEY USD
pt Romsey Extra, Romsey Infra
RYDE USD [ISLE OF WIGHT]
pt Ryde, pt St Helens
ST HELENS USD [ISLE OF WIGHT]
pt St Helens
SANDOWN USD [ISLE OF WIGHT]
pt Brading
SHANKLIN USD [ISLE OF WIGHT]
pt Brading, pt Shanklin
SHIRLEY USD (1875–81[52])
pt Millbrook
SHIRLEY AND FREEMANTLE USD (1881[52]–94)
pt Millbrook
SOUTHAMPTON USD
Southampton All Saints, Southampton Holy Rood, Southampton St John, Southampton St Lawrence, Southampton St Mary, Southampton St Michael, pt South Stoneham
STOCKBRIDGE RSD
same as PLU
SOUTH STONEHAM RSD
same as PLU less pt Millbrook (extended pt 1881–94), pt South Stoneham
VENTNOR USD [ISLE OF WIGHT]
pt Ventnor
WHITCHURCH RSD
same as PLU
WINCHESTER USD
pt Chilcombe, Milland (ent 1875–89, pt 1889–94), pt St Faith, pt Weeke, pt Winchester St Bartholomew Hyde, pt Winchester St John, Winchester St Lawrence, Winchester St Mary Kalendar, Winchester St Maurice, pt Winchester St Peter Cheesehill, Winchester St Peter Colebrook, Winchester St Swithin, Winchester St Thomas, pt Winnall
NEW WINCHESTER RSD
same as Winchester PLU less pars and pts of pars in Winchester USD

HAMPSHIRE ADMINISTRATIVE COUNTY

For the MBs and the associated CBs, see BOROUGHS.

ALDERSHOT UD (1894–1922[27])
Aldershot
ALRESFORD RD (1894–1932)
New Alresford, Old Alresford, Beauworth, Bighton, Bramdean, Brown Candover, Chilton Candover, Cheriton, Godsfield, Hinton Ampner, Itchen Stoke, Kilmiston, Northington, Ovington, Ropley, Bishops Sutton, Swarraton, Tichborne, West Tisted
ALTON RD
Bentley, Bentworth, Binsted, Chawton, Coldrey (1894–1932), Grayshott (1902–74), Farringdon, Four Marks (1932–74), Froyle, Hartley Mauditt (1894–1932), Headley, Holybourne (1894–1932), Kingsley, Lasham, Medstead, Neatham (1894–1932), Newton Valence, Ropley (1932–74), Selborne, Shalden, East Tisted, West Tisted (1932–74), Whitehill (1929–74), Wield, Worldham (1932–74), East Worldham (1894–1932), West Worldham (1894–1932)
ALTON UD
Alton
ANDOVER RD
Abbots Ann, Amport, Appleswaw, Barton Stacey, Bullington, Chilbolton, Goodworth Clatford, Upper Clatford, Vernhams Dean, Knights Enham (1894–1932), Faccombe, Foxcott (1894–1932), Fyfield, Grateley, Hurstbourne Tarrant, Kimpton, Linkenholt, Longparish, Monxton, Penton Grafton, Penton Mewsey, Quarley, Shipton Bellinger, Smannel (1932–74), Tangley, Thruxton, South Tedworth, Wherwell
BASINGSTOKE RD
Andwell (1894–1932), Basing, Bradley, Bramley, Preston Candover, Candovers (1932–74), Cliddesden, Deane, Dummer, Ellisfield, Farleigh Wallop, Hartley Wespall, Herriard, Mapledurwell (1894–1932), Mapledurwell and Up Nately (1932–74), Mortimer West End, Nately Scures (1894–1932), Up Nately (1894–1932), Newnham, Nutley, Oakley, Pamber, Popham, Monk Sherborne, Sherborne St John, Sherfield-on-Loddon, Silchester, Steventon, Stratfield Saye, Stratfield Turgis, Tunworth,

Upton Grey, North Waltham, Weston Corbett, Weston Patrick, Winslade, Woodmancott, Wootton St Lawrence, Worting (1894–1932)
CATHERINGTON RD (1894–1932)
Blendworth, Catherington, Chalton, Clanfield, Idsworth, Waterloo
CHRISTCHURCH RD (1894–1932)
Christchurch East, Highcliffe (1897–1932), Holdenhurst, Hurn, Pokesdown (1894–1895), Sopley, Soutbourne (1894–1902), Winton (1894–1902)
DROXFORD RD
Boarhunt (1932–74), Corhampton (1894–1932), Corhampton and Meonstoke (1932–74), Curbridge (1932–52), Curdridge, Denmead (1932–74), Droxford, Durley, Exton, Hambledon, West Meon, Meonstoke (1894–1932), Shedfield, Soberton, Southwick and Widley (1932–74), Swanmore, Upham, Bishops Waltham, Warnford, Wickham (1932–74)
EASTLEIGH UD (1894–99[54])
Eastleigh
EASTLEIGH UD (1932–36[27])
Eastleigh
EASTLEIGH AND BISHOPSTOKE UD (1899[54]–1932)
Bishopstoke, Eastleigh
FAREHAM RD (1894–1932)
Boarhunt, Cosham (1894–1921), Crofton, Hook with Warsash, Portchester, Rowner, Sarisbury, Southwick, Titchfield, Wickham, Widley (1921–32)
FAREHAM UD
Fareham
FARNBOROUGH UD (1896[55]–74)
Farnborough
FLEET UD (1904[56]–74)
Fleet
FORDINGBRIDGE RD (1894–1932)
Ashley Walk, Breamore, North Charford, South Charford, Damerham (1895–1932), Fordingbridge, Hale, Martin (1895–1932), Rockbourne, Toyd Farm and Allenford (1895–1932), Whitsbury (1895–1932), Woodgreen
NEW FOREST RD
Beaulieu, Boldre (1932–74), Bramshaw, East Bramshaw (1895–1932), Brockenhurst (1932–74), Colbury (1894–1934), Copythorne, Denny Lodge, Dibden, Eling, Exbury, Fawley, Lyndhurst, Marchwood, Minstead, Netley Marsh, Rhinefield (1932–74), Sway (1932–74)
GOSPORT AND ALVERSTOKE UD (1894–1922[31])
Alverstoke
HARTLEY WINTNEY RD
Bramshill, Cove (1894–1932), Crondall, Crookham (1894–1932), Crookham Village (1952–74), Dogmersfield, Elvetham (1894–1932), Eversley, Farnborough (1894–96), Fleet (1894–1904), Greywell, Hartley Wintney, Hawley (1932–74), Hawley with Minley (1894–1932), Heckfield, Hook (1932–74), Mattingley, Odiham, Rotherwick, Long Sutton, South Warnborough, Winchfield, Yateley
HAVANT RD (1894–1932)
Bedhampton, Farlington, North Havant (1902–32), North Hayling, South Hayling
HAVANT UD (1894–1932)
Havant
HAVANT AND WATERLOO UD (1932–74)
Havant
HURSLEY RD (1894–1932)
Ampfield, North Baddesley, Chandlers Ford (1897–1932), Farley Chamberlayne, Hursley, Otterbourne
ITCHEN UD (1898[57]–1920[20])
Itchen (1903–20), St Mary Extra (1898–1903), Sholing (1898–1903)
KINGSCLERE RD (1894–1932)
Ashmansworth, Baughurst, Burghclere, Crux Easton, Ecchinswell, Ewhurst, Hannington, Highclere, Kingsclere, Litchfield, Newtown, Sydmonton, Tadley, Wolverton, Woodcott
KINGSCLERE AND WHITCHURCH RD (1932–74)
Ashmansworth, Baughurst, Burghclere, Ecchinswell and Sydmonton, Highclere, Hurstbourne Priors, Kingsclere, Laverstoke, Litchfield and Woodcott, Newtown, Overton, St Mary Bourne, Tadley, Whitchurch, East Woodhay
LYMINGTON RD (1932–74)
Boldre, East Boldre (1929–32), Brockenhurst, Hordle, Milford (1894–1911), Milford on Sea (1911–32), Milton, Pennington (1911–32), Rhinefield, Sway
MILTON UD (1926[58]–1932)
Milton
PETERSFIELD RD
Bramshott (pt 1894–95, ent 1895–1974), Buriton, Clanfield (1932–74), Colemore (1894–1932), Colemore and Priors Dean (1932–74), Priors Dean (1894–1932), Empshott (1894–1932), Froxfield, Greatham, Hawkley, Horndean (1932–74), Langrish, Liss, East Meon, Privett (1894–1932), Rowlands Castle (1932–74), Sheet (1894–1932), Steep
PETERSFIELD UD
Petersfield
POKESDOWN UD (1895[59]–1901[60])
Pokesdown
PORTSEA ISLAND RD (1894–95[61])
Great Salterns
RINGWOOD RD (1894–1932)
Broomy, Burley, Ellingham, Harbridge, Ibsley, Ringwood
RINGWOOD AND FORDINGBRIDGE RD (1932–74)
Breamore, Burley, Christchurch East, Damerham, Ellingham, Fordingbridge, Hale, Harbridge and Ibsley (1932–74), Hurn, Martin, Ringwood, Rockbourne, St Leonards and St Ives (1932–74), Sopley, Whitsbury, Woodgreen
ROMSEY RD (1894–1932)
East Dean, Dunwood, Lockerley, Melchet Park (1895–1932), Michelmersh, Mottisfont, Nursling, Plaitford (1895–1932), Romsey Extra, Rownhams (1897–1932), Sherfield English, Timsbury, East Wellow, West Wellow (1895–1932)

ROMSEY AND STOCKBRIDGE RD (1932–74)
Ampfield, Ashley (1932–33), North Baddesley, Bossington, Braishfield (1951–74), Broughton, Buckholt, Chilworth, East Dean, Frenchmoor, Houghton, Leckford, Lockerley, Longstock, Melchet Park and Plaitford (1932–74), Michelmersh, Millbrook (1932–54), Mottisfont, Nursling and Rownhams (1932–74), Romsey Extra, Sherfield English, Kings Somborne, Little Somborne, Stockbridge, East Tytherley, West Tytherley, Nether Wallop, Over Wallop, Wellow (1932–74)

SHIRLEY AND FREEMANTLE UD (1894–95[18])
Shirley

STOCKBRIDGE RD (1894–1932)
Ashley, Bossington, Broughton, Buckholt, Upper Eldon, Frenchmoor, Houghton, Leckford, Longstock, Kings Somborne, Little Somborne, Stockbridge, East Tytherley, West Tytherley, Nether Wallop, Over Wallop

SOUTH STONEHAM RD (1894–1932)
Bitterne (1894–1925), Botley, Bursledon, Chilworth, Eastleigh (1894–1932), Hamble le Rice, Hedge End, Hound, Millbrook, St Mary Extra (1894–98), Sholing (1894–98), North Stoneham, South Stoneham (1894–1920), West End

WARBLINGTON UD (1894[62]–1932)
Warblington

WHITCHURCH RD (1894–1932)
Ashe, Freefolk Manor, Hurstbourne Priors, Laverstoke, Overton, St Mary Bourne, Tufton, Whitchurch

WINCHESTER RD (1905[63]–1974), renaming of NEW WINCHESTER RD (1894–1905[63])
Abbots Barton, New Alresford (1932–74), Old Alresford (1932–74), Avington (1894–1932), Beauworth (1932–74), Bighton (1932–74), Bishopstoke (1894–99), Botley (1932–74), Bramdean (1932–74), Bursledon (1932–74), Cheriton (1932–74), Chilcombe (1932–74), Chilcombe Without (1894–1932), Colden Common (1932–74), Compton, Crawley, Easton (1894–1932), Fair Oak, Hamble le Rice (1932–74), Hedge End (1932–74), Hound (1932–74), Hunton (1894–1932), Hursley (1932–74), Itchen Abbas (1894–1932), Itchen Stoke and Ovington (1932–74), Itchen Valley (1932–74), Kilmiston (1932–74), Lainston (1894–1932), Littleton, Micheldever, Morestead (1894–1932), Northington (1932–74), Olivers Battery (1956–74), Owslebury, St Faith Without (1894–1900), Sparsholt, Stoke Charity (1894–1932), Stoke Park (1899–1932), East Stratton (1894–1932), Bishops Sutton (1932–74), Tichborne (1932–74), Twyford, West End (1932–74), Headbourne Worthy, Kings Worthy, Martyr Worthy (1894–1932), Weeke Without (1894–1932), Wonston

NEW WINCHESTER RD–See WINCHESTER RD

WINTON UD (1898[64]–1901[60])
Winton

ISLE OF WIGHT ADMINISTRATIVE COUNTY

For the MBs, see BOROUGHS.

COWES UD
Cowes

EAST COWES UD (1894–1933)
East Cowes

ISLE OF WIGHT RD
North Arreton (1894–1907), South Arreton, Ashey (1894–1933), Brading, Binsted, Bonchurch (1894–1933), Brixton, Brook (1894–1933), Calbourne, Carisbrooke (1894–1933), Chale, Freshwater, Gatcombe, Godshill, Kingston (1894–1933), Mottistone (1894–1933), Newchurch, Niton, Northwood (1894–1933), St Lawrence (1894–1933), Shalfleet, Shorwell, Thorley (1894–1933), Whippingham (1894–1933), Whitwell (1894–1933), Wroxall (1894–1933), Yarmouth, Yaverland (1894–1933)

ST HELENS UD (1894–1933)
St Helens

SANDOWN UD (1894–1933)
Sandown

SANDOWN-SHANKLIN UD (1933–74)
Sandown-Shanklin

SHANKLIN UD (1894–1933)
Shanklin, East Shanklin (1894–98)

VENTNOR UD
Ventnor

HAMPSHIRE NON-METROPOLITAN COUNTY

As constituted 1 Apr 1974, defined in terms of Adm Co units as of 31 Mar.

BASINGSTOKE DIST
Basingstoke MB, Basingstoke RD, Kingsclere and Whitchurch RD

EASTLEIGH DIST
Eastleigh MB, pt Winchester RD (the pars of Botley, Bursledon, Fair Oak, Hamble le Rice, Hedge End, Hound, West End)

FAREHAM DIST
Fareham UD

NEW FOREST DIST
New Forest RD, Lymington MB, pt Ringwood and Fordingbridge RD[65]
GOSPORT DIST
Gosport MB
HARTLEY WINTNEY DIST
Fleet UD, Hartley Wintney RD
HAVANT DIST
Havant and Waterloo UD
PETERSFIELD DIST
Alton RD, Alton UD, Petersfield RD, Petersfield UD
PORTSMOUTH DIST
Portsmouth CB
RUSHMOOR DIST
Aldershot MB, Farnborough UD
SOUTHAMPTON DIST
Southampton CB
TEST VALLEY DIST
Andover MB, Andover RD, Romsey MB, Romsey and Stockbridge RD
WINCHESTER DIST
Droxford RD, Winchester MB, pt Winchester RD (the pars not in Eastleigh Dist)

ISLE OF WIGHT NON-METROPOLITAN COUNTY

As constituted 1 Apr 1974, defined in terms of Adm Co units as of 31 Mar.

MEDINA DIST
Cowes UD, Newport MB, Ryde MB
SOUTH WEST DIST
Isle of Wight RD, Sandown-Shanklin UD, Ventnor UD

HERTFORDSHIRE

ALTERATIONS IN COUNTY BOUNDARIES

As noted by year below, Herts pars gained territory from or lost it to pars in adjoining counties, or were entirely transferred to them. Details of these alterations are noted in Part I of the *Guide* under Herts.

ANCIENT COUNTY (until 1889: Hds, Bors, MBs, PLUs, RSDs, USDs)
1844 Amersham, Ickleford, Meppershall, Studham. *1883* Tring. *1895* Little Gaddesden. *1888* Puttenham.

ADMINISTRATIVE COUNTY (1889–1974: Hds,[1] PLUs, MBs, RDs, UDs)
1889 Enfield, Monken Hadley. *1894* Caddington, Enfield, Monken Hadley, South Mimms, Studham. *1895* Little Gaddesden, Nettleden. *1896* South Bassingbourn, South Kneesworth, South Melbourn, Royston, North Royston. *1897* Caddington, Flamstead, Holwell, Kensworth, Markyate, Pirton, Shillington, Studham, Whipsnade. *1907* Bovingdon, Chorleywood, Flamstead, Flaunden, Little Gaddesden, Harpenden Rural, Markyate, Northchurch, Offley, Rickmansworth Rural, Wiggington. *1926* Ridge, Shenley. *1935* Eastwick, Gilston. *1947* Ickleford. *1956* Ickleford. *1965* Arkley, Chipping Barnet, East Barnet, Barnet Vale, Flamstead, Hadley, Monken Hadley, South Mimms, South Mimms Urban Rowley, Totteridge.

NON-METROPOLITAN COUNTY (from 1974: Dists)

HUNDREDS[1]

BRAUGHING HD
Braughing, Eastwick, Gilston, Hunsdon, Sawbridgeworth, Standon,[2] Stanstead Abbots,[2] Bishop's Stortford,[2] Thorley, Thundridge, Ware,[2] Westmill, Widford

BROADWATER HD
Aston, Ayot St Lawrence, Ayot St Peter, Baldock,[2] Benington, Datchworth, Digswell, Graveley, Bishop's Hatfield, Knebworth, Letchworth, Great Munden, Little Munden, Sacombe, Stevenage, Totteridge, Walkern, Watton at Stone, Welwyn, Weston, Willian, Great Wymondley, Little Wymondley

CASHIO HD
pt Aldenham, Chipping Barnet, East Barnet, Bramfield, Codicote, Elstree, Hexton, Abbots Langley, pt South Mimms, Newnham, Northaw, Norton, Redbourn, Rickmansworth, Ridge, St Albans,[2] St Albans St Michael,[2] St Albans St Peter,[2] St Stephen,[2] Sandridge,[2] Sarratt, Shephall, St Paul's Walden, Watford[2]

DACORUM HD
Aldbury, pt Aldenham, pt Amersham (until 1844), Berkhampstead,[2] Bovingdon (from 1866), Bushey, pt Caddington, Flamstead, Flaunden (from 1866), Great Gaddesden, Little Gaddesden, Harpenden, Hemel Hempstead,[2] Kensworth, King's Langley, pt Meppershall (until 1844), North Mimms, Northchurch, Puttenham, Shenley, pt Studham, Tring, Wheathampstead, pt Whipsnade, Wigginton

EDWINSTREE HD
Albury, Anstey, Ardeley (from 1843), Aspenden, Barkway, Barley (until 1841), Buckland, Little Hadham, Much Hadham, Great Hormead, Little Hormead, Layston, Meesden, Nuthampstead (from 1866), Brent Pelham, Furneux Pelham, Stocking Pelham, Throcking, Wakeley (from 1858), Wyddial

HERTFORD HD
Great Amwell,[2] Little Amwell,[2] Bayford, Bengeo,[2] Little Berkhampstead, Brickendon[2] (from 1866), Broxbourne, Cheshunt, Essendon, Hertford All Saints,[2] Hertford St Andrew,[2] Hertford St John,[2] Hertingfordbury, Hoddesdon (from 1866), Stanstead St Margaret, Stapleford, Tewin, Wormley

HITCHIN AND PIRTON HD
Hitchin,[2] Ickeford (pt until 1844, ent from 1844), Ippollitts, Kimpton, Lilley, Offley, Pirton, King's Walden

ODSEY HD
Ardley (from 1843), Ashwell,[2] Barley (from 1841), Broadfield (from 1858), Bygrave, Caldecote, Clothall, Cottered, Hinxworth, Kelshall, Radwell, Reed, pt Royston, Rushden, Sandon, Therfield, Wallington

BOROUGHS

Units with some degree of burghal character[3] are denominated 'Bor'. Those which did not sustain that status until the 19th cent are in italics. Municipal Boroughs were established by the Municipal Corporations Act, 1835,[4] or by later charter.

ASHWELL BOR
Ashwell
BALDOCK BOR
Baldock
BERKHAMPSTEAD BOR
Berkhampstead
HEMEL HEMPSTEAD BOR, MB (1898[5]–1974)
Hemel Hempstead
HERTFORD BOR/MB
pt Great Amwell (1885–97), pt Little Amwell (1835–94), pt Bengeo (1868–94), Bengeo Urban (1894–1900), pt Brickendon (1866–94), Brickendon Urban (1894–1900), Hertford (1900–74), Hertford All Saints (pt until 1866, ent 1866–1900), pt Hertford St Andrew (until 1894), pt Hertford St John (until 1894), Hertford St Mary (until 15th cent), Hertford St Nicholas (until 15th cent), St Andrew Urban (1894–1900), St John Urban (1894–1900), pt Ware (1888–97)
HITCHIN BOR
Hitchin
ST ALBANS BOR/MB (City since 1877)
St Albans, pt St Albans St Michael (until 1894), pt St Albans St Peter (until 1894), St Michael Urban (1894–98), St Peter Urban (1894–98), pt St Stephen (1835–94), pt Sandridge (1877–94), Sandridge Urban (1894–98)
STANDON BOR
Standon
STANSTEAD ABBOTS BOR[6]
Stanstead Abbots
BISHOP'S STORTFORD BOR
Bishop's Stortford
WARE BOR
Ware
WATFORD BOR, MB (1922[7]–74)
Oxhey (1922–35), Watford (mediev period, 1935–74), Watford Urban (1922–35)

POOR LAW UNIONS

In Hertfordshire Poor Law County:[9]
BARNET PLU (Herts, Middx)
Arkley (1894–1930), Chipping Barnet, East Barnet, Barnet Vale (1894–1930), Elstree, Hadley (1894–1930), Monken Hadley,[10] South Mimms,[11] South Mimms Urban (1894–1930), Ridge, Shenley, Totteridge
BERKHAMPSTEAD PLU
Aldbury, Berkhampstead (1835–98), Great Berkhampstead Rural (1898–1930), Great Berkhampstead Urban (1898–1930), Little Gaddesden, Nettleden,[12] Northchurch, Puttenham, Tring (1835–94), Tring Rural (1894–1930), Tring Urban (1894–1930), Wigginton
BUNTINGFORD PLU
Anstey, Ardeley, Aspenden, Broadfield, Buckland, Cottered, Great Hormead, Little Hormead, Layston, Meesden, Rushden, Sandon, Throcking, Wallington, Westmill, Wyddial
HATFIELD PLU
Essendon, Bishop's Hatfield, North Mimms, Northaw
HEMEL HEMPSTEAD PLU
Bovingdon, Flamstead, Flaunden, Great Gaddesden, Hemel Hempstead, King's Langley, Markyate (1897–1930)
HERTFORD PLU
Little Amwell (1866[13]–1930), Aston, Bayford, Bengeo (1835–94), Bengeo Rural (1894–1930), Bengeo Urban (1894–1900), Benington, Little Berkhampstead, Bramfield, Brickendon (1835–94), Brickendon Liberty (1929–30), Brickendon Rural (1894–1929), Brickendon Urban (1894–1900), Datchworth, Hertford (1900–30), Hertford All Saints (1835–1900), Hertford St Andrew (1835–94), Hertford St John (1835–94), Hertingfordbury, Sacombe, St Andrew Rural (1894–1924), St Andrew Urban (1894–1900), St John Rural (1894–1929), St John Urban (1894–1900), Stapleford, Tewin, Unnamed (1894–1900), Walkern, Watton at Stone
HITCHIN PLU
Baldock, Bygrave, Caldecote, Clothall, Codicote, Graveley, Hexton, Hitchin (1835–94), Hitchin Urban (1894–1930), Holwell,[14] Ickleford, Ippollitts, Kimpton, Knebworth, Langley (1894–1930), Letchworth, Lilley, Newnham, Norton (1835–1908), Offley, Pirton, Preston (1894–1930), Radwell, Shephall, Stevenage, King's Walden, St Paul's Walden, Walsworth (1894–1922), Weston, Willian, Great Wymondley, Little Wymondley
ROYSTON PLU (Herts, Cambs, Essex)
Ashwell, Barkway, Barley, South Bassingbourn (1896–97), Hinxworth, Kelsall, South Kneesworth (1896–97), South Melbourn (1896–97), Nuthampstead, Reed, Royston, North Royston (1896–97), Therfield
ST ALBANS PLU
Harpenden (1835–98), Harpenden Rural (1898–1930), Harpenden Urban (1898–1930), Redbourn, St Albans, St Albans St Michael (1835–94), St Albans St Peter (1835–94), St Michael Rural (1894–1930), St Michael Urban (1894–98), St

Peter Rural (1894–1930), St Peter Urban (1894–98), St Stephen, Sandridge (1835–94), Sandridge Rural (1894–1930), Sandridge Urban (1894–98), Wheathampstead

BISHOP'S STORTFORD PLU
Albury, Braughing, Little Hadham, Much Hadham, Brent Pelham, Furneux Pelham, Stocking Pelham, Sawbridgeworth, Bishop's Stortford, Thorley, High Wych (1901–30)

WARE PLU
Great Amwell, Broxbourne, Eastwick, Gilston, Hoddesdon (1835–94), Hoddesdon Rural (1894–1930), Hoddesdon Urban (1894–1930), Hunsdon, Great Munden, Little Munden, Standon, Stanstead Abbots, Stanstead St Margaret, Thundridge, Ware (1835–94), Ware Rural (1894–1930), Ware Urban (1894–1930), Widford, Wormley

WATFORD PLU
Aldenham, Bushey (1835–94), Bushey (1906–30), Bushey Rural (1894–1906), Bushey Urban (1894–1906), Chorleywood (1898–1930), Abbots Langley, Oxhey (1906–30), Rickmansworth (1835–98), Rickmansworth Rural (1898–1930), Rickmansworth Urban (1898–1930), Sarratt, Watford (1835–94), Watford Rural (1894–1930), Watford Urban (1894–1930)

WELWYN PLU
Ayot St Lawrence, Ayot St Peter, Digswell, Welwyn, Welwyn Garden City (1921–30)

In Other Poor Law Counties:

AMPTHILL PLU (Beds)
Shillington[15]

EDMONTON PLU (Middx)
Cheshunt, Enfield[16]

LUTON PLU (Beds)
Caddington,[17] Kensworth,[18] Studham,[19] Whipsnade[15]

SANITARY DISTRICTS

AMPTHILL RSD
Shillington only par pt in Herts

BALDOCK USD
Baldock

BARNET RSD
same as PLU less pt Chipping Barnet, East Barnet, pt Monken Hadley, pt South Mimms

BARNET USD
pt Chipping Barnet, pt Monken Hadley, pt South Mimms

EAST BARNET VALLEY USD
pt Chipping Barnet, East Barnet, pt Enfield (Middx, 1888[20]–94), pt Monken Hadley, pt South Mimms (1888[20]–94)

BERKHAMPSTEAD RSD
same as PLU less pt Berkhampstead, pt Tring

GREAT BERKHAMPSTEAD USD
pt Berkhampstead

BUNTINGFORD RSD
same as PLU

CHESHUNT USD
Cheshunt

HATFIELD RSD
same as PLU

HEMEL HEMPSTEAD RSD
same as PLU

HERTFORD RSD
same as PLU less pt Little Amwell, pt Bengeo, pt Brickendon, Hertford All Saints, pt Hertford St Andrew, pt Hertford St John

HERTFORD USD
pt Great Amwell (1885[21]–94), pt Little Amwell, pt Bengeo, pt Brickendon, Hertford All Saints, pt Hertford St Andrew, pt Hertford St John, pt Ware (1885[21]–94)

HITCHIN RSD
same as PLU less Baldock, pt Hitchin, Stevenage

HITCHIN USD
pt Hitchin

HODDESDON USD
pt Hoddesdon

LUTON RSD
same as PLU for Herts pars

ROYSTON RSD
same as PLU for Herts pars

ST ALBANS RSD
same as PLU less St Albans, pt St Albans St Michael, pt St Albans St Peter, pt St Stephen, pt Sandridge

ST ALBANS USD
St Albans, pt St Albans St Michael, pt St Albans St Peter, pt St Stephen, pt Sandridge

STEVENAGE USD
Stevenage

BISHOP'S STORTFORD RSD
same as PLU less Bishop's Stortford

BISHOP'S STORTFORD USD
Bishop's Stortford

TRING USD
pt Tring

WARE RSD
same as PLU less pt Great Amwell (reduced pt 1885[21]–94), pt Hoddesdon, pt Ware (reduced pt 1885[21]–94)

WARE USD
pt Great Amwell, pt Ware

WATFORD RSD
same as PLU less pt Bushey, pt Watford (reduced pt 1892[22]–94)

WATFORD USD
pt Bushey, pt Watford (enlarged pt 1892[22]–94)

WELWYN RSD
same as PLU

ADMINISTRATIVE COUNTY

For MBs see BOROUGHS earlier in this Part of the *Guide*.

ASHWELL RD (1894–1935)
Ashwell, Barkway, Barley, South Bassingbourn (1896–97), Hinxworth, Kelshall, South Kneesworth (1896–97), South Melbourn (1896–97), Nuthampstead, Reed, North Royston (1896–97), Therfield

BALDOCK UD
Baldock

BARNET RD (1894–1941[23])
Arkley (1894–1905), Elstree, Ridge, Shenley, Totteridge (1894–1914)

BARNET UD (1894–1965[24])
Arkley (1905–65), Chipping Barnet, Hadley, South Mimms Urban, Rowley (1935–65), Totteridge (1914–65)

EAST BARNET UD (1935[25]–65[24])
East Barnet, Barnet Vale, Monken Hadley

EAST BARNET VALLEY UD (1894–1935[25])
East Barnet, Barnet Vale, Monken Hadley

BERKHAMPSTEAD RD (1894–1937[26])
Aldbury, pt Berkhampstead (1894–98), Great Berkhampstead Rural (1898–1937), Little Gaddesden, Nettleden (1895–1937), Northchurch, Puttenham, Tring Rural, Wigginton

GREAT BERKHAMPSTEAD UD (1894–1937[27])
pt Berkhampstead (1894–98), Great Berkhampstead Urban (1898–1937)

BERKHAMSTED RD (1937[26]–74)
Aldbury, Little Gaddesden, Nettleden with Potten End, Northchurch, Puttenham (1937–64), Tring Rural, Wigginton

BERKHAMSTED URBAN UD (1937[27]–74)
Berkhamsted Urban

BRAUGHING RD (1935–74)
Albury, Anstey, Ardeley, Aspenden, Braughing, Broadfield (1935–55), Buckland, Buntingford (1937–74), Cottered, Little Hadham, Much Hadham, Hormead (1937–74), Great Hormead (1935–37), Little Hormead (1935–37), Layston (1935–37), Meesden, Brent Pelham, Furneux Pelham, Stocking Pelham, Thorley, Throcking (1935–55), Westmill, High Wych, Wyddial

BUNTINGFORD RD (1894–1935)
Anstey, Ardeley, Aspenden, Broadfield, Buckland, Cottered, Great Hormead, Little Hormead, Layston, Meesden, Rushden, Sandon, Throcking, Wallington, Westmill, Wyddial

BUSHEY UD (1906[28]–74)
Bushey

CHESHUNT UD
Cheshunt

CHORLEYWOOD UD (1913[29]–74)
Chorleywood

ELSTREE RD (1941[23]–74)
Elstree, Ridge, Shenley

HADHAM RD (1895[30]–1935)
Albury, South Bassingbourn (1896–97), Braughing, Little Hadham, Much Hadham, South Kneesworth (1896–97), South Melbourn (1896–97), Brent Pelham, Furneux Pelham, Stocking Pelham, North Royston (1896–97), Thorley, High Wych (1901–35)

HARPENDEN UD (1898[31]–1974)
Harpenden Urban

HATFIELD RD
Essendon, Hatfield (1951–74), Bishop's Hatfield (1894–1951), North Mimms, Northaw

HEMEL HEMPSTEAD RD
Bovingdon, Caddington (1894–97), Chipperfield (1958–74), Flamstead, Flaunden, Great Gaddesden, Hemel Hempstead (1894–98), King's Langley, Markyate (1897–1974)

HERTFORD RD
Little Amwell, Aston, Bayford, Bengeo Rural, Benington, Little Berkhampstead, Bramfield, Brickendon Liberty (1929–74), Brickendon Rural (1894–1929), Datchworth, Hertingfordbury, Sacombe, St Andrew Rural (1894–1929), St John Rural (1894–1929), Stapleford, Tewin, Walkern, Watton at Stone

HITCHIN RD
Ashwell (1935–74), Barkway (1935–74), Barley (1935–74), Bygrave, Caldecote, Clothall, Codicote, Graveley, Hexton, Hinxworth (1935–74), Holwell (1897–1974), Ickleford, Ippollitts, Kelshall (1935–74), Kimpton, Knebworth, Langley, Letchworth (1894–1919), Lilley, Newnham, Norton (1894–1908), Nuthampstead (1935–74), Offley, Pirton, Preston, Radwell, Reed (1935–74), Rushden (1935–74), Sandon (1935–74), Shephall (1894–1935), Therfield (1935–74), King's Walden, St Paul's Walden, Wallington (1935–74), Walsworth (1894–1921), Weston, Willian (1894–1935), Wymondley (1937–74), Great Wymondley (1894–1937), Little Wymondley (1894–1937)

HITCHIN UD
Hitchin Urban

HODDESDON UD
Hoddesdon (1935–74), Hoddesdon Urban (1894–1935)

LETCHWORTH UD (1919[32]–74)
Letchworth

POTTERS BAR UD (1965[33]–74)
South Mimms

RICKMANSWORTH UD (1898[34]–74)
Rickmansworth Urban

ROYSTON UD (1897[35]–1974)
Royston

ST ALBANS RD
London Colney (1947–74), Colney Heath (1947–74), Harpenden (1894–98), Harpenden Rural (1898–1974), Redbourn, St Michael Rural, St

Peter Rural (1894–1947), St Stephen, Sandridge (1957–74), Sandridge Rural (1894–1957), Wheathampstead
SAWBRIDGEWORTH UD (1901[36]–74)
Sawbridgeworth
STEVENAGE UD
Shephall (1953–74), Stevenage
BISHOP'S STORTFORD RD (1894–95[30])
Albury, Braughing, Little Hadham, Much Hadham, Brent Pelham, Furneux Pelham, Stocking Pelham, Sawbridgeworth, Thorley
BISHOP'S STORTFORD UD
Bishop's Stortford
TRING UD
Tring Urban
WARE RD
Great Amwell (pt 1894–97, ent 1897–1974), Broxbourne (1894–1935), Eastwick, Gilston, Hoddesdon Rural (1894–1935), Hunsdon, Great Munden, Little Munden, Standon, Stanstead Abbots, Stanstead St Margaret, Thundridge, Ware Rural, Widford, Wormley (1894–1935)
WARE UD
Unnamed (1894–1904), Ware Urban
WATFORD RD
Aldenham, Bushey Rural (1894–1906), Chorleywood (1898–1913), Abbots Langley, Rickmansworth (1894–98), Rickmansworth Rural (1898–1935), Sarratt, Watford Rural
WATFORD UD (1894–1922[7])
Bushey Urban (1894–1906), Oxhey (1906–22), Watford Urban
WELWYN RD
Ayot St Lawrence, Ayot St Peter, Digswell (1894–1935), Welwyn, Welwyn Garden City (1894–1927)
WELWYN GARDEN CITY (1927[37]–74)
Welwyn Garden City

NON-METROPOLITAN COUNTY

As constituted 1 Apr 1974, defined in terms of Adm Co units as of 31 Mar.

BROXBOURNE DIST
Cheshunt UD, Hoddesdon UD
DACORUM DIST
Berkhamsted RD, Berkhamsted UD, Hemel Hempstead MB, Hemel Hempstead RD, pt St Albans RD,[38] Tring UD, pt Watford RD[39]
EAST HERTFORDSHIRE DIST
Braughing RD, Hertford MB, pt Hertford RD,[40] Sawbridgeworth UD, Bishop's Stortford UD, Ware RD, Ware UD
NORTH HERTFORDSHIRE DIST
Baldock UD, Hitchin RD, Hitchin UD, Letchworth UD, Royston UD
HERTSMERE DIST
Bushey UD, Elstree RD, Potters Bar UD, pt Watford RD[39]
ST ALBANS DIST
Harpenden UD, St Albans MB, pt St Albans RD[38]
STEVENAGE DIST
pt Hertford RD,[40] Stevenage UD
THREE RIVERS DIST
Chorleywood UD, Rickmansworth UD, pt Watford RD[39]
WATFORD DIST
Watford MB
WELWYN HATFIELD DIST
Hatfield RD, Welwyn RD, Welwyn Garden City UD

HUNTINGDONSHIRE

ALTERATIONS IN COUNTY BOUNDARIES

As noted by year below, Hunts pars gained territory from or lost it to pars in adjoining counties, or were entirely transferred to them. Details of these alterations are noted in Part I of the *Guide* under Hunts.

HUNTS ANCIENT COUNTY (until 1889: Hds, Bors, MBs, PLUs, RSDs, USDs)
1840s Elton. *1844* Everton, Tetworth. *1860s* Ramsey.

HUNTS ADMINISTRATIVE COUNTY (1889–1965: Hds,[1] PLUs, MBs, RDs, UDs)
1889 Fletton, Woodston. *1894* Fletton, Old Fletton, Woodston, Woodston Rural. *1895* Luddington in the Brook, Lutton, Papworth St Agnes, Thurning, Winwick. *1896* Swineshead, Tilbrook. *1905* Stanground, Stanground South. *1956* Alwalton, Chesterton, Orton Longueville.

HUNTS AND PETERBOROUGH ADMINISTRATIVE COUNTY (1965–74: MBs, RDs, UDs)
1965 Brington and Molesworth, Bythorn and Keyston, Denton and Caldecote, Elton, Great Gidding, Morborne, Ramsey, St Neots, Somersham, Tetworth, Waresley, Winwick.

HUNTS AND PETERBOROUGH ADM CO abol 1974 and made part of Cambs Non-Metropolitan County.

HUNDREDS[1]

HURSTINGSTONE HD[2]
Bluntisham cum Earith, Broughton, Bury, Colne, Hartford,[3] Holywell cum Needingworth, Houghton, Old Hurst, Pidley cum Fenton, Ramsey (pt until 1860s, ent thereafter),[4] Great Raveley, Little Raveley, Abbots Ripton, Kings Ripton,[3] St Ives,[3] Somersham, Great Stukeley, Little Stukeley, Upwood, Warboys, Wistow, Woodhurst, Wyton

LEIGHTONSTONE HD
Alconbury,[3] Alconbury Weston,[3] Barham, Brampton,[3] Brington, Buckworth, Bythorn, Catworth (from 1885), Great Catworth (until 1885), Little Catworth (until 1885), Coppingford, Covington, Easton, Ellington, Great Gidding, Little Gidding, Steeple Gidding, Grafham, Hamerton, Keyston, Kimbolton, Leighton, pt Luddington in the Brook, Molesworth, Spaldwick, Stow, Swineshead, pt Thurning, Upton, Old Weston, pt Winwick, Woolley

NORMAN CROSS HD
Alwalton, Botolphbridge (until 1702), Caldecote, Chesterton, Conington, Denton, Elton (pt until 1840s, ent thereafter),[4] Farcet (from 1866), Fletton,[3] Folkesworth, Glatton,[3] Haddon, Holme (from 1866),[3] pt Lutton, Morborne, Orton Longueville, Orton Waterville, Sawtry All Saints (until 1886), Sawtry All Saints and St Andrew (from 1866), Sawtry St Andrew (until 1886), Sawtry St Judith (from 1858), Sibson cum Stibbington, pt Stanground, Stilton, Wood Walton, Washingley, Water Newton, Woodston,[3] Yaxley

TOSELAND HD
Abbotsley, Buckden, Diddington, pt Everton (until 1810), Eynesbury, Fenstanton,[3] Godmanchester,[3] Great Gransden, Hemingford Abbots, Hemingford Grey,[3] Hilton, Midloe (from 1858), Offord Cluny,[3] Offord D'Arcy, pt Papworth St Agnes, Great Paxton, Little Paxton, St Neots, Southoe, Great Staughton, Tetworth (pt 1810–44, ent from 1844), Toseland, Waresley, Hail Weston, Yelling

BOROUGHS

Units with some degree of burghal character[5] are denominated 'Bor'. Those which did not sustain that status until the 19th cent are in italics. Municipal Boroughs were established by the Municipal Corporations Act, 1835,[6] or by later charter.

ALCONBURY WESTON BOR (perhaps a bor[7])
pt Alconbury

BRAMPTON BOR (perhaps a bor[7])
Brampton

GODMANCHESTER BOR, MB (18 –1961[8])
Godmanchester
HARTFORD BOR (perhaps a bor[7])
Hartford
HOLME BOR
pt Glatton
HUNTINGDON BOR[9]/MB (1835–1961[8])
Huntingdon (1921–61), Huntingdon All Saints (until 1921), Huntingdon St Benedict (until 1921), Huntingdon St John (until 1921), Huntingdon St Mary (until 1921)

HUNTINGDON AND GODMANCHESTER MB (1961[8]–74)
Huntingdon and Godmanchester
OFFORD CLUNY BOR (perhaps a bor[10])
Offord Cluny
PETERBOROUGH MB[9]
pt Fletton (1874–94), pt Woodston (1874–94)
KINGS RIPTON BOR (perhaps a bor[10])
Kings Ripton
ST IVES MB (1874–1974)
Eynesbury (pt 1874–95, ent 1895–1974), St Neots (pt 1874–95, ent 1895–1974)

POOR LAW UNIONS

In Hunts Poor Law County:[11]
HUNTINGDON PLU
Alconbury, Alconbury Weston, Barham, Brampton, Buckworth, Conington, Coppingford, Easton, Ellington, Steeple Gidding, Godmanchester, Hamerton, Hartford, Huntingdon (1921–30), Huntingdon All Saints (1836–1921), Huntingdon St Benedict (1836–1921), Huntingdon St John (1836–1921), Huntingdon St Mary (1836–1921), Leighton, Ramsey,[20] Great Raveley, Little Raveley, Abbots Ripton, Kings Ripton, Sawtry All Saints (1836–86), Sawtry All Saints and St Andrew (1886–1930), Sawtry St Andrew (1836–86), Sawtry St Judith, Spaldwick, Great Stukeley, Little Stukeley, Upton, Upwood, Wood Walton, Woolley
ST IVES PLU (Hunts, Cambs)
Bluntisham cum Earith, Broughton, Bury, Colne, Fenstanton, Hemingford Abbots, Hemingford Grey, Hilton, Holywell cum Needingworth, Houghton, Old Hurst, Pidley cum Fenton, St Ives, Somersham, Warboys, Wistow, Woodhurst, Wyton
ST NEOTS PLU (Hunts, Beds, Cambs)
Abbotsley, Buckden, Catworth (1885–1930), Great Catworth (1835–85), Little Catworth (1835–85), Diddington, Eynesbury, Eynesbury Hardwicke (1895–1930), Grafham, Kimbolton, Midloe, Offord Cluny, Offord D'Arcy, Great Paxton, Little Paxton, St Neots, St Neots Rural (1895–1930), Southoe, Great Staughton, Stow, Swineshead,[12] Tetworth, Tilbrook,[13] Toseland, Waresley, Hail Weston

In Other Poor Law Counties:
CAXTON PLU (Cambs)
Great Gransden, Papworth St Agnes,[14] Yelling
OUNDLE PLU (Northants)
Elton,[21] Great Gidding, Little Gidding, Luddington in the Brook,[15] Lutton,[15] Thurning,[15] Winwick[16]
PETERBOROUGH PLU (Northants, Cambs/IoE, Lincs)
Alwalton, Caldecote, Chesterton, Denton, Farcet, Fletton (1835–94),[17] Fletton Rural (1894–1930), Folksworth, Glatton, Haddon, Holme, Morborne, Orton Longueville, Orton Waterville, Stanground (1835–1905),[18] Stanground South (1905–30), Stilton, Washingley, Water Newton, Woodston (1835–94),[19] Woodston Rural (1894–1930), Yaxley
STAMFORD PLU (Lincs)
Sibson cum Stibbington
THRAPSTON PLU (Northants)
Brington, Bythorn, Covington, Keyston, Molesworth, Old Weston

SANITARY DISTRICTS

CAXTON RSD
same as PLU for Hunts pars
GODMANCHESTER USD
Godmanchester
HUNTINGDON RSD
same as PLU less Godmanchester, Huntingdon All Saints, Huntingdon St Benedict, Huntingdon St John, Huntingdon St Mary, Ramsey
HUNTINGDON USD
Huntingdon All Saints, Huntingdon St Benedict, Huntingdon St John, Huntingdon St Mary
OUNDLE RSD
same as PLU for Hunts pars
PETERBOROUGH RSD
same as PLU for Hunts pars less pt Fletton, pt Woodston

PETERBOROUGH USD
for Hunts, pt Fletton, pt Woodston
RAMSEY USD
Ramsey
ST IVES RSD
same as PLU less pt Fenstanton (1889–94), pt Hemingford Grey (1889–94), St Ives
ST IVES USD
pt Fenstanton (1889–94), pt Hemingford Grey (1889–94), St Ives
ST NEOTS RSD
same as PLU less pt Eynesbury, pt St Neots
ST NEOTS USD
pt Eynesbury, pt St Neots
STAMFORD RSD
same as PLU for the Hunts par
THRAPSTON RSD
same as PLU for the Hunts pars

ADMINISTRATIVE COUNTIES

HUNTS ADM CO (1888–1965[23])
HUNTS AND PETERB ADM CO (1965[23]–74)

For MBs see BOROUGHS earlier in this part of the *Guide*.

BARNACK RD[23] (1965–74)
Bainton, Barnack, St Martin's Without, Southorpe, Thornhaugh, Ufford, Wansford, Wittering, Wothorpe

OLD FLETTON UD (1905[22]–74)
Fletton (1938–74), Fletton Rural (1905–38), Stanground South, Woodston (1938–74), Woodston Rural (1905–38)

HUNTINGDON RD
Alconbury, Alconbury Weston, Barham (1894–1935), Barham and Woolley (1935–74), Brampton, Brington and Molesworth (1935–74), Buckworth, Bythorn and Keyston (1935–74), Conington, Coppingford (1894–1935), Easton, Ellington, Great Gidding (1935–74), Little Gidding (1935–74), Steeple Gidding, Hamerton, Hartford (1894–1935), Leighton, Great Raveley (1894–1935), Little Raveley (1894–1935), Abbots Ripton, Kings Ripton, Sawtry (1935–74), Sawtry All Saints and St Andrew (1894–1935), Sawtry St Judith (1894–1935), Spaldwick, Great Stukeley (1894–1935), Little Stukeley (1894–1935), The Stukeleys (1935–74), Upton (1894–1935), Upton and Coppingford (1935–74), Upwood (1894–1935), Upwood and the Raveleys (1935–74), Wood Walton, Old Weston (1935–74), Winwick (1935–74), Woolley (1894–1935)

OUNDLE RD[24] (1894–1935)
Elton, Great Gidding, Little Gidding, Winwick

PETERBOROUGH RD[23] (1965–74)
Ailsworth, Borough Fen, Castor, Deeping Gate, Etton, Eye, Glinton, Helpston, Marholm, Maxey, Newborough, Northborough, Peakirk, Sutton, Upton

NORMAN CROSS RD
Alwalton, Caldecote (1894–1935), Chesterton, Denton (1894–1935), Denton and Caldecote (1935–74), Elton (1935–74), Farcet, Fletton Rural (1894–1905), Folksworth (1894–1935), Folksworth and Washingley (1935–74), Glatton, Haddon, Holme, Morborne, Orton Longueville, Orton Waterville, Sibson cum Stibbington (1935–74), pt Stanground (1894–1905), Stilton, Washingley (1894–1935), Water Newton, Woodston Rural (1894–1905), Yaxley

RAMSEY UD
Ramsey

ST IVES RD
Bluntisham (1948–74), Bluntisham cum Earith (1894–1948), Broughton, Bury, Colne, Earith (1948–74), Fenstanton (pt 1894–96, ent 1896–1974), Hemingford Abbots, Hemingford Grey (pt 1894–96, ent 1896–1974), Hilton, Holywell cum Needingworth, Houghton (1894–1935), Houghton and Wyton (1935–74), Old Hurst, Pidley cum Fenton, Somersham, Warboys, Wistow, Woodhurst, Wyton (1894–1935)

ST NEOTS RD
Abbotsley, Buckden, Catworth, Covington (1935–74), Diddington, Eynesbury Hardwicke (1895–1974), Grafham, Great Gransden, Kimbolton, Midloe (1894–1935), Offord Cluny, Offord D'Arcy, Great Paxton, Little Paxton, St Neots Rural (1895–1974), Great Staughton, Southoe (1894–1935), Southoe and Midloe (1935–74), Stow (1894–1955), Stow Longa (1955–74), Tetworth, Tilbrook, Toseland, Waresley, Hail Weston, Old Weston, Yelling

ST NEOTS UD
Eynesbury (pt 1894–95, ent 1895–1974), St Neots (pt 1894–95, ent 1895–1974)

THORNEY RD[25] (1965–74)
Stanground North, Thorney

THRAPSTON RD[24] (1894–1935)
Brington, Bythorn, Covington, Keyston, Molesworth, Old Weston

UNNAMED RD[26] (1894–1935)
Sibson cum Stibbington

KENT

ALTERATIONS IN COUNTY BOUNDARIES

As noted by year below, Kent pars gained territory from or lost it to pars in adjoining counties or county boroughs, or were entirely transferred to them. Details of these alterations are noted in Part I of the *Guide* under Kent.

ANCIENT COUNTY (until 1889: Hds, Bors, MBs, PLUs, RSDs, USDs, Vestry and Dists in Metrop Bd Wks)
1730 Deptford St Nicholas, Deptford St Paul. *1886* Hawkhurst.

ADMINISTRATIVE COUNTY (1889–1974: Hds,[1] PLUs, MBs, RDs, UDs, with Canterbury CB associated)
1889 Charlton next Woolwich, Deptford St Nicholas, Deptford St Paul, Eltham, Greenwich, Kidbrooke, Lee, Lewisham, Plumstead, Woolwich. *1894* Frant. *1895* Broomhill, Horsmonden, Lamberhurst. *1899* Penge. *1934* Hackington, Harbledown, St Dunstan Without, Thanington Without. *1965* Beckenham, Bexley, Bromley, Chislehurst and Sidcup, Crayford, Erith, Orpington, Penge. *1969* Knockholt.

NON-METROPOLITAN COUNTY (from 1974: Dists)

HUNDREDS[1]

Because the composition of Hds by pars varied greatly from the 16th to 19th centuries, pars which in whole or pt belonged to different Hds at the two times are noted below in italics; reference should be made to the explanatory notes in Part I of the *Guide* for elaboration.

Lathe of St Augustine:[2]

BEWSBOROUGH HD
Buckland,[3] Charlton,[3] West Cliffe, Coldred, *Deal*,[3] Temple Ewell, Guston,[3] pt Hougham,[3] West Langdon, *Lydden*, Poulton,[5] River, St Margaret's at Cliffe, Sibertswold, *pt Waldershare*, Whitfield

BLEANGATE HD
Chislet,[4] *Hackington*, Herne, Hoath, Reculver, Stourmouth,[4] Sturry,[3] *Swalecliffe*, Westbere[4]

BRIDGE AND PETHAM HD
Bekesbourne,[3] Bridge, *Chartham*, *Hackington*, Lower Hardres, *Upper Hardres*, *Nackington*, Patrixbourne,[5] Petham, *Waltham*

CORNILLO HD
pt Deal.[3] East Langdon, Great Mongeham, Little Mongeham, *Northbourne*, *Oxney*, Ringwould,[4] Ripple, Sholden, Sutton, Walmer,[3] *Waldershare*

DOWNHAMFORD HD
Adisham, Fordwich,[3] *Hackington*,[5] Ickham and Well, Littlebourne,[6] Staple, Stodmarsh,[4] Wickhambreux[4]

EASTRY HD
Barfreston, Betteshanger, Chillenden, Denton,[5] Eastry,[5] Eythorne, Ham, Knowlton, *pt Newington*, *Nonington*, *Northbourne*, Tilmanstone, *Waldershare*, Woodnesborough, Worth

KINGHAMFORD HD
Barham, Bishopsbourne, pt Denton, Kingston, Wootton

PRESTON HD
Elmstone, Preston

RINGSLOW HD (sometimes THANET HD)
Acol (from 1866),[4] Birchington,[3] Margate St John the Baptist,[3] Minster, Monkton, Ramsgate,[3] St Lawrence,[5] St Nicholas at Wade,[4] St Peters, Sarre (from 1866),[4] Stonar

WESTGATE HD
pt Canterbury Holy Cross Westgate, *Chartham*, Dunkirk (from 1858), *pt Hackington*,[5] Harlbedown, Mint (from 1858), pt St Dunstan,[6] Staplegate[5] (from 1858), Thanington,[6] *Westbere*, *Whitstable*

WHITSTABLE HD
Nackington,[6] St Cosmus and St Damian in the Blean, Seasalter, *Swalecliffe*, *Whitstable*

WINGHAM HD
Ash, pt Eastry, Goodnestone, *Nonington*, Wingham,[4] Womenswold

Lathe of Aylesford:[7]

WAST BARNFIELD (the pt of the Hd in this Lathe)
Goudhurst

BRENCHLEY AND HORSMONDEN HD
Brenchley, pt Horsmonden, pt Lamberhurst
CHATHAM AND GILLINGHAM HD
Chatham,[6] Gillingham,[6] *Isle of Grain*, Grange[4] (from 1866), Lidsing (from 1866), Rochester Castle Precincts,[6] pt Rochester St Margaret[6]
EYHORNE HD
Bearsted, *Bicknor*, Boughton Malherbe, *Boughton Monchelsea*, Bredhurst, Broomfield, Frinsted, Harrietsham, *Headcorn*, Hollingbourne, Hucking, Langley, Leeds, *Lenham*, *Marden*, Otham, *Otterden*, *Staplehurst*, Chart Sutton, East Sutton, Sutton Valence, Thurnham, *Ulcombe*, Wichling, Wormshill
HOO HD
Allhallows, *Cobham*, High Halstow, Hoo, St Mary Hoo, *Isle of Grain*, *West Peckham*, *Stoke*
LARKFIELD HD
Addington, Allington, Aylesford, Birling, Burham, Ditton, *Horsmonden*, *Hunton*, Leybourne, East Malling, West Malling, Offham, Ryarsh, Snodland, Trottiscliffe, Wouldham[6]
LITTLEFIELD HD
Hadlow, Mereworth, *East Peckham*, *West Peckham*
MAIDSTONE HD
East Barming, West Barming (from 1866), *Bearsted*, *Boughton Monchelsea*, Boxley, Detling, East Farleigh, *Hunton*, Linton, Loose, *Marden*, *Staplehurst*
SHAMWELL HD
Chalk, Cliffe at Hoo, *Cobham*, Cooling, Cuxton, Denton, Frindsbury,[6] Halling, Higham, Mareston otherwise Merston (status not sustained[8]), Shorne, *Stoke*, Strood[6]
TOLTINGTROUGH HD
Gravesend,[6] Ifield, Luddesdown, Meopham, Milton,[6] Northfleet, Nurstead
TONBRIDGE LOWEY
pt Capel, *Hadlow*, Tonbridge[6]
TWYFORD HD
Brenchley, *Capel*, West Farleigh, *Hunton*, *Marden*, Nettlestead, *East Peckham*, *Pembury*, Teston, pt Tudeley, Wateringbury, Yalding
WASHLINGSTONE HD
Ashurst, Bidborough, pt Capel, pt Frant,[6] *Leigh*, *Pembury*, pt Penshurst, pt Speldhurst, pt Tudeley
WROTHAM HD
Ightham, Shipbourne, Stansted, Wrotham[6]
Lathe of Scray:[9]

The Hds of Calehill, Chart and Longbridge, Felborough, Wye were in this Lathe at least through 16th cent, thereafter in Shepway[10]; they are listed for convenience's sake only in this Lathe. Hasted listed the 'neutral' Hd of Bircholt Barony in this Lathe, but others and this list place it in Shepway.

EAST BARNFIELD HD (the pt of the Hd in this Lathe)
Cranbrook, pt Hawkhurst
BERKELEY HD
Benenden, *Biddenden*, *Cranbrook*, *Frittenden*, *Headcorn*, pt High Halden, pt Smarden
BLACKBOURNE HD
pt Appledore,[3] *Bethersden*, pt High Halden, pt Kenardington,[4] *Shadoxhurst*, *Smarden*, *Warehorne*, Woodchurch
BOUGHTON UNDER BLEAN HD
Boughton under Blean, Graveney, Hernhill, *Selling*
CALEHILL HD
Bethersden, Charing, *Great Chart*, Little Chart, Egerton, *Headcorn*, *Hothfield*, *Lenham*, Pluckley, pt Smarden, pt Westwell
CHART AND LONGBRIDGE HD
Ashford, *Bethersden*, *Brook*, *Great Chart*, Hinxhill, *Hothfield*, Kennington, Kingsnorth, *Mersham*, Sevington, *Shadoxhurst*, Willesborough
CRANBROOK HD
Benenden, *Biddenden*, *Cranbrook*, *Frittenden*, pt Goudhurst, *Hawkchurch*, *Headcorn*, pt Staplehurst
FAVERSHAM HD
Badlesmere, Buckland, Davington, Eastling, Faversham,[3] Goodnestone, Harty, Leaveland, Luddenham, Newnham, Norton, Oare, Ospringe,[3] *Otterden*, Preston next Faversham,[6] *Selling*, Sheldwich, Stalisfield, Stone, Throwley, *Ulcombe*
FELBOROUGH HD
Challock, pt Chartham, Chilham, Godmersham, Molash
MARDEN HD
pt Goudhurst, *Marden*, Staplehurst
MILTON HD
Bapchild, *Bicknor*, Bobbing, Borden, Bredgar, Eastchurch,[11] *Elmley*, Lower Halstow, Hartlip, Iwade,[5] Kingsdown, Milsted, Milton, *Minster in Sheppey*,[11] Murston, Newington, Rainham, Rodmersham, Sittingbourne, pt Stockbury, Tonge, Tunstall, Upchurch, *Warden*[11]
ROLVENDEN HD
Benenden, Rolvenden
SELBRITTENDEN HD
Benenden, *Hawkchurch*, Newenden, Sandhurst
ISLE OF SHEPPEY LIBERTY
Bicknor, *Eastchurch*,[11] *Elmley*, Leysdown, *Minster in Sheppey*,[11] Queenborough,[6] Warden[11]
TENTERDEN HD
pt Ebony,[6] Tenterden[6]
TEYNHAM HD
Doddington, *Headcorn*, Iwade,[5] Lynsted, Teynham
WYE HD
Boughton Aluph, *Brabourne*, *Brook*, Crundale, Eastwell, *Waltham*, pt Westwell, Wye
Lathe of Shepway:

See notes at head of entries for Lathe of Scray, applicable here also.

ALOESBRIDGE HD
Brenzett,[4] *Brookland*,[4] Fairfield, *Ivychurch*, *Newchurch*, *Snargate*,[4] *Snave*
BIRCHOLT BARONY[12]/later BIRCHOLT FRANCHISE AND BARONY
Bircholt, *Brabourne*, Hastingleigh
BIRCHOLT FRANCHISE[12]/later BIRCHOLT FRANCHISE AND BARONY
pt Aldington,[4] *Mersham*, Smeeth
FOLKESTONE HD
pt Acrise, Alkham, Capel-le-Ferne, Cheriton, Folkestone,[3] Hawkinge, pt Hougham,[3] *Lydden*, *Newington*, Swingfield

HAM HD
Kenardington,[4] pt Orlestone,[5] pt Ruckinge,[4] *Shadoxhurst*, *Snave*, pt Warehorne
HAYNE HD
Lympne, Postling, Saltwood
HYTHE HD
St Leonard Hythe,[3] *West Hythe*[3]
LANGPORT LIBERTY (ent incl in Rom. Marsh Lbty or Cq Pt of New Rom. by 19th cent)
pt Hope All Saints, Lydd,[3] pt New Romney,[3] pt Old Romney
LONINGBOROUGH HD
pt Acrise, Elham, *Upper Hardres*, Lyminge, Paddlesworth, *Stelling*, Stelling Minnis (from 1858)
ST MARTIN IVYCHURCH HD (sometimes POUNTNEY HD; ent incl in Rom. Marsh Lbty or Cq Pt of New Rom. by 19th cent)
pt Hope All Saints, pt Ivychurch,[4] Midley, *pt Newchurch*, *pt New Romney*,[3] *pt Old Romney*,[4] *pt St Mary in the Marsh*
NEWCHURCH HD
pt Bilsington, *Newchurch*, pt Ruckinge,[4] *St Mary in the Marsh*, *Snave*
OXNEY HD
pt Ebony,[3] Stone, Wittersham
ROMNEY MARSH LBTY (the listing below is the 19th cent organisation; see Part I of the *Guide* under each par for organisation in Bors and for earlier organisation in Hds and/or the Lbty)
pt Aldington, pt Appledore, pt Bilsington, Blackstone, pt Bonnington, pt Brenzett, pt Brookland, Burmarsh, Dymchurch, Eastbridge, Hope All Saints, pt Hurst, pt West Hythe, pt Ivychurch, pt Kenardington, pt Lympne, Newchurch, pt Newington, Orgarswick, pt Orlestone, pt New Romney, pt Ruckinge, St Mary in the Marsh, Sellindge, pt Snargate, Snave
STOWTING HD
Elmsted, Monks Horton, *Sellindge*, Stanford, *Stelling*, Stowting, *Waltham*
STREET HD
Bonnington, pt Hurst, pt Lympne, pt Sellindge
WORTH HD (ent incl in Rom. Marsh Lbty or Cq Pt of New Rom. by 19th cent)
Blackmanstone, Burmarsh, Dymchurch, Eastbridge, pt West Hythe,[6] pt Lympne, pt Newchurch, Orgarswick

Lathe of Sutton at Hone:

AXTON HD/later AXTON, DARTFORD AND WILMINGTON HD
Ash, *Cowden*, Darenth, Eynsford, Farningham, Fawkham, Hartley, Horton Kirby, pt Kingsdown, Longfield, Lullingstone, Ridley, Southfleet, Stone, Sutton at Hone, Swanscombe
BLACKHEATH HD
Charlton next Woolwich, *Chislehurst*, Deptford St Nicholas (pt until 1730, ent from 1730), pt Deptford St Paul (from 1730), Eltham, Greenwich, Lee, Lewisham, Mottingham (from 1866), Woolwich
BROMLEY AND BECKENHAM HD
Beckenham, Bromley
CODSHEATH HD
Bexley, *Brasted*, *Chevening*, Halstead, Kensing, pt Kingsdown, pt Leigh, Otford, Seal, Sevenoaks, Shoreham, *Speldhurst*, Sundridge
DARTFORD AND WILMINGTON HD/later AXTON, DARTFORD AND WILMINGTON HD
Dartford, Wilmington
LESSNESS HD (orig LITTLE AND LESSNESS HD)
Bexley, Crayford, Erith, Plumstead, East Wickham
LITTLE AND LESSNESS HD–See LESSNESS HD
RUXLEY HD
Bexley, Chelsfield, *Chiddingstone*, *Chislehurst*, Foots Cray, North Cray, St Mary Cray, St Paul's Cray, Cudham, Downe, Farnborough, Hayes, *Hever*, Keston, Knockholt, Orpington, West Wickham
SOMERDEN HD
Chiddingstone
Chiddingstone, *Chevening*, pt Cowden, *Edenbridge*,[5] *Hever*, pt Leigh, pt Penshurst, pt Speldhurst
WESTERHAM HD (orig WESTERHAM AND EDENBRIDGE HD)
Brasted, pt Cowden, *Edenbridge*,[5] Westerham

BOROUGHS

Units with some degree of burghal character[13] are denominated 'Bor'.
Those which did not sustain that status until the 19th cent are in italics.
Municipal Boroughs were established by the Municipal Corporations Act, 1835,[14] or by later charter.

BECKENHAM MB (1935[15]–65[16])
Beckenham
BEXLEY MB (1937[15]–65[16])
Bexley
BROMLEY MB (1903[17]–65[16])
Bromley
CANTERBURY BOR/MB/CB
pt Bekesbourne (1868–94), Canterbury (1897–1974), Canterbury All Saints (until 1897), Canterbury The Archbishop's Palace Precincts (1835–1912), Canterbury Black Prince's Chantry (1835–97), Canterbury Christchurch (1835–1912), Canterbury East Bridge Hospital (1835–97), Canterbury Old Castle (1835–97), pt Canterbury Holy Cross Westgate (until 1894), Canterbury St Alphege (until 1897), Canterbury St Andrew (until 1897), Canterbury St Augustine (1835–97), Canterbury St Edmund (until 1349), Canterbury St George the Martyr (until 1897), Canterbury St Gregory the Great (1835–1912), Canterbury St John (until 1349), Canterbury St John's Hospital (1835–97), Canterbury St Margaret (until 1897), Canterbury

St Martin (until 1897), Canterbury St Mary Bredin (until 1897), Canterbury St Mary Bredman (until 1897), Canterbury St Mary de Castro (until 1684), Canterbury St Mary Magdalen (until 1897), Canterbury St Mary North Gate (until 1897), Canterbury St Mary Queengate (until before 1381), Canterbury St Michael Burgate (until late medieval period), Canterbury St Mildred (until 1897), Canterbury St Paul (until 1897), Canterbury St Peter (until 1897), Canterbury White Friars (1835–97), pt Fordwich (until 1894), pt Hackington (until 1894), Holy Cross Westgate Within (1894–97), pt Littlebourne (until 1894), pt Nackington (until 1894), pt Patrixbourne (until 1894), pt St Dunstan (until 1894), St Dunstan Within (1894–1912), Staplegate (1858–1912), pt Sturry (1890–94), pt Thanington (until 1894), Thanington Within (1894–1912)

CHATHAM MB (1890[18]–1974)
Chatham (pt 1880–1934, ent 1934–74), pt Gillingham (1880–94)

DEAL BOR/MB
Deal

DOVER BOR/MB
Buckland (pt until 1894, ent 1894–96), Charlton (pt until 1894, ent 1894–96), East Cliffe (1835–96), Dover (1896–1974), Dover Castle (1814–1934), Dover St James the Apostle (until 1896), Dover St John (early destroyed), Dover St Martin the Greater (early destroyed), Dover St Martin the Less (early destroyed), Dover St Mary the Virgin (until 1896), Dover St Nicholas (early destroyed), Dover St Peter (early destroyed), pt Guston (until 1894), Hougham (pt until 1894, ent 1894–96), pt Poulton (until 1894), Poulton Within (1894–96)

ERITH MB (1938[15]–65[16])
Erith

FAVERSHAM BOR/MB
pt Faversham (until 1894), Faversham (1935–74), Faversham Within (1894–1935), pt Ospringe (until 1883), pt Preston next Faversham (1888–94), Preston Within (1894–1935)

FOLKESTONE BOR/MB
pt Folkestone (until 1886), Folkestone (before 1891–1974), Folkestone Town (1886–before 1891)

FORDWICH BOR
pt Fordwich

GILLINGHAM MB (1903[17]–74)
pt Chatham (1903–06), Gillingham, Grange (1903–06), Lidsing (1903–13)

GRAVESEND MB
Gravesend, Milton (1835–1915)

HYTHE BOR/MB
pt Aldington (until 1888), pt Cheriton (1835–86), Hythe (1934–74), St Leonard Hythe (until 1934), pt West Hythe (until 1888), pt Newington (1835–86), pt Saltwood (1835–86)

LYDD BOR, MB (1885[19]–1974)
Lydd

MAIDSTONE BOR/MB
Maidstone

MARGATE MB (1857[20]–1974)
Margate (1935–74), Margate St John the Baptist (pt 1857–94, ent 1894–1935)

QUEENBOROUGH BOR, MB (1885[24]–1968[21])
Queenborough

QUEENBOROUGH-IN-SHEPPEY MB (1968[21]–74)
Queenborough-in-Sheppey

RAMSGATE MB (1884[22]–1974)
Ramsgate, pt St Lawrence (1884–94), St Lawrence Intra (1894–1922)

ROCHESTER BOR/MB
pt Chatham (until 1934), pt Frindsbury (1835–94), Frindsbury Intra (1894–1934), Rochester (1934–74), Rochester Castle Precincts (1835–1974), pt Rochester St Margaret (until 1894), Rochester St Nicholas (until 1934), St Margaret Intra (1894–1934), pt Strood (1835–94), Strood Intra (1894–1934), pt Wouldham (until 1896)

NEW ROMNEY BOR, MB (1885[25]–1974)
New Romney (pt 1885–94, ent 1894–1974)

SANDWICH BOR/MB
Sandwich (1935–74), Sandwich St Bartholomew's Hospital (until 1935), Sandwich St Clement (until 1935), Sandwich St Mary (until 1935), Sandwich St Peter (until 1935)

TENTERDEN BOR/MB
pt Ebony (until 1894), Tenterden

TONBRIDGE BOR
pt Tonbridge

TUNBRIDGE WELLS MB (1888[26]–1974) (later called 'ROYAL TUNBRIDGE WELLS')
pt Frant (1888–94), pt Speldhurst (1888–94), pt Tonbridge (1888–94), Tunbridge Wells (1894–1974)

CINQUE PORTS

The Anc Town/Cq Pt of Winchelsea is ent in Sussex; the greater pt of Hastings Cq Pt and Rye Anc Town/Cq Pt are in Sussex, and a pt of Sandwich Cq Pt is in Essex. See the respective counties for those entries. Kent pars in these are shown below, an +

indicating a corporate mbr (which status may exist because a par was in a Lbty of a corporate town) either ent or in pt.

DOVER CQ PT[28]
Acol, Birchington, pt Buckland+, pt Charlton+, East Cliffe+, Dover Castle+, Dover St James the Apostle+, Dover St Mary the Virgin+, pt Faversham+, pt Folkestone+, pt Guston+, pt Hougham+, Margate St John the Baptist+, Ringwould, St Peters
HASTINGS CQ PT
Bekesbourne, , Grange
HYTHE CQ PT
pt Aldington+, St Leonard Hythe+, pt West Hythe+
NEW ROMNEY CQ PT
pt Appledore+, pt Brenzett+, pt Broomhill+ (the Kent pt of the par[27]), pt Brookland+, pt Ivychurch+, pt Kenardington+, pt Lydd+, pt New Romney+, pt Old Romney+, pt Snargate+
RYE ANC TOWN/CQ PT
pt Ebony+, Tenterden+
SANDWICH CQ PT
pt Chislet+, Deal+, Fordwich+, Ramsgate, pt St Nicholas at Wade (when incl Sarre 16th cent–1866), Sandwich St Bartholomew's Hospital+, Sandwich St Clement+, Sandwich St Mary+, Sandwich St Peter+, Sarre (before 16th cent and from 1866 when again independent of St Nicholas at Wade), pt Stodmarsh+, pt Stourmouth+, pt Sturry+, Walmer, pt Westbere+, pt Wickhambreux+, pt Wingham+

POOR LAW UNIONS

In Kent Poor Law County:[32]
EAST ASHFORD PLU
Aldington, Bilsington, Bircholt, Bonnington, Boughton Aluph, Brabourne, Brook, Challock, Chilham, Crundale, Eastwell, Godmersham, Hastingleigh, Hinxhill, Hurst, Kennington, Mersham, Molash, Orlestone (1836–1930), Ruckinge (1836–1930), Sevington, Smeeth, Warehorne (1836–1930), Willesborough, Wye
WEST ASHFORD PLU
Ashford (1836–1930), Bethersden, Charing, Great Chart, Little Chart (1836–1930), Egerton, Hothfield, Kingsnorth, Pluckley, Shadoxhurst, Smarden, Westwell
NORTH AYLESFORD PLU (1835–84), renamed STROOD PLU (1884–1930)
Chalk, Cliffe at Hoo, Cobham, Cuxton, Denton, Frindsbury (1835–94), Frindsbury Extra (1894–1930), Frindsbury Intra (1894–1930), Halling, Higham, Ifield, Luddesdown, Meopham, Northfleet, Nursted, Shorne, Strood (1835–94), Strood Extra (1894–1930), Strood Intra (1894–1930)
BLEAN PLU
Canterbury The Archbishop's Palace Precincts (1835–1912), Canterbury Christchurch (1835–1912), Canterbury St Gregory the Great (1835–1912), Chislet, Hackington, Herne, Herne Bay (1894–1930), Hoath, Reculver, St Cosmus and St Damian in the Blean, St Dunstan (1835–94), St Dunstan Within (1894–1912), St Dunstan Without (1894–1930), Seasalter (1835–94), Staplegate (1835–1912), Sturry, Swalecliffe, Westbere, Whitstable (1835–94), Whitstable cum Seasalter (1894–1930), Whitstable Urban (1894–1930)
BRIDGE PLU
Adisham, Barham, Bekesbourne, Bishopsbourne, Bridge, pt Canterbury Holy Cross Westgate (1835–94), Chartham, Fordwich, Harbledown, Lower Hardres, Upper Hardres, Holy Cross Westgate Without (1894–1912), Ickham and Well, Kingston, Littlebourne, Mint (1858[33]–89), Nackington, Patrixbourne, Petham, St Nicholas Hospital (1858[33]–1930), Stodmarsh, Thanington (1835–94), Thanington Within (1894–1912), Thanington Without (1894–1930), Waltham, Wickhambreux, Womenswold
BROMLEY PLU
Beckenham, Bromley, Chelsfield, Chislehurst, Foots Cray (1836–1925), North Cray, St Mary Cray, St Paul's Cray, Cudham, Downe, Farnborough, Hayes, Keston, Knockholt, Mottingham (1887–1930), Orpington, Sidcup (1925–30), West Wickham
CANTERBURY INCORPORATION
Canterbury (1897–1930), Canterbury All Saints (until 1897), Canterbury Black Prince's Chantry (until 1897)), Canterbury East Bridge Hospital (until 1897), Canterbury Old Castle (until 1897), pt Canterbury Holy Cross Westgate (until 1894), Canterbury St Alphege (until 1897), Canterbury St Andrew (until 1897), Canterbury St Augustine (until 1897), Canterbury St George the Martyr (until 1897), Canterbury St John's Hospital (until 1897), Canterbury St Margaret (until 1897), Canterbury St Martin (until 1897), Canterbury St Mary Bredin (until 1897), Canterbury St Mary Bredman (until 1897), Canterbury St Mary Magdalen (until 1897), Canterbury St Mary North Gate (until 1897), Canterbury St Mildred (until 1897), Canterbury St Paul (until 1897), Canterbury St Peter (until 1897), Canterbury White Friars (until 1897), Holy Cross Westgate Within (1894–97)
CRANBROOK PLU
Benenden, Cranbrook, Frittenden, Goudhurst, Hawkhurst,[35] Sandhurst
DARTFORD PLU
Ash, Bexley, Crayford, Darenth, Dartford, Erith, Eynsford, Farningham, Fawkham, Hartley, Horton Kirby, Kingsdown, Longfield, Lullingstone, Ridley, Southfleet, Stone, Sutton at Hone, Swanscombe, East Wickham (1836–1902), Wilmington

DOVER PLU (renaming in 1840s of RIVER PLU)
Alkham, Buckland (1835–96), Capel-le-Ferne, Charlton (1835–96), East Cliffe (1835–96), West Cliffe, Coldred, Denton, Dover (1896–1930), Dover Castle, Dover St James the Apostle (1835–96), Dover St Mary the Virgin (1835–96), Temple Ewell, Guston, Hougham (1835–96), Hougham Without (1894–1930), East Langdon, West Langdon, Lydden, Oxney, Poulton, Poulton Within (1894–96), Ringwould, River, St Margaret's at Cliffe, Sibertswold, Whitfield, Wootton

EASTRY PLU
Ash, Barfreston, Betteshanger, Chillenden, Deal (1836–1930), Eastry, Elmstone, Eythorne, Goodnestone, Ham, Knowlton, Great Mongeham, Little Mongeham, Nonington, Northbourne, Preston, Ripple, Sandwich St Bartholomew's Hospital (1836–1930), Sandwich St Clement (1836–1930), Sandwich St Mary (1836–1930), Sandwich St Peter (1836–1930), Sholden, Staple, Stourmouth, Sutton, Tilmanstone, Waldershare, Walmer, Wingham, Woodnesborough, Worth

ELHAM PLU
Acrise, Cheriton, Elham, Elmsted, Folkestone (1835–86), Folkestone (before 1891–1930), Folkestone next Sandgate (1894–1930), Folkestone Town (1886–before 1891), Hawkinge, St Leonard Hythe (1836–1930), Lyminge, Lympne, Monks Horton, Newington, Paddlesworth, Postling, Saltwood, Sandgate (1894–1930), Sellindge, Stanford, Stelling, Stelling Minnis (1858[33]–1930), Stowting, Swingfield

FAVERSHAM PLU
Badlesmere, Boughton under Blean, Buckland, Davington, Doddington, Dunkirk, Eastling, Faversham (1835–94), Faversham Within (1894–1930), Faversham Without (1894–1930), Goodnestone, Graveney, Hernhill, Leaveland, Luddenham, Lynsted, Newham, Norton, Oare, Ospringe, Preston next Faversham (1835–94), Preston Within (1894–1930), Preston Without (1894–97), North Preston Without (1897–1930), South Preston Without (1897–1930), Selling, Sheldwich, Stalisfield, Stone, Teynham, Throwley

GARVESEND AND MILTON PLU
Gravesend, Milton

GREENWICH PLU (1836–89[29])
Deptford St Nicholas, Deptford St Paul,[30] Greenwich, Woolwich (1836–68)

HOLLINGBOURNE PLU
Bicknor, Boughton Malherbe, Boxley, Bredhurst, Broomfield, Detling, Frinsted, Harrietsham, Headcorn, Hollingbourne, Hucking, Langley, Leeds, Lenham, Otterden, Stockbury, Chart Sutton, East Sutton, Sutton Valence, Thurnham, Ulcombe, Wichling, Wormshill

HOO PLU
Allhallows, Cooling, High Halstow, Hoo, St Mary Hoo, Isle of Grain, Stoke

LEWISHAM PLU (1836–89[29])
Charlton (1836–68), Eltham, Kidbrooke (1836–68), Lee, Lewisham, Mottingham (1836–87), Plumstead (1836–68)

MAIDSTONE PLU
East Barming, West Barming (1866[33]–1930), Bearsted, Boughton Monchelsea, East Farleigh, West Farleigh, Hunton, Linton, Loose, Maidstone, Marden, Nettlestead, Otham, Staplehurst, Teston, Yalding

MALLING PLU
Addington, Allington, Aylesford, Birling, Burham, Ditton, Ightham, Leybourne, East Malling, West Malling, Mereworth, Offham, East Peckham, West Peckham, Ryarsh, Shipbourne, Snodland, Stanstead, Trottiscliffe, Wateringbury, Wouldham, Wrotham

MEDWAY PLU
Chatham, Gillingham, Grange (1835–1906), Lidsing, Rochester Castle Precincts, Rochester St Nicholas, Rochester St Margaret (1835–94), St Margaret Extra (1894–1905), St Margaret Intra (1894–1930)

MILTON PLU
Bapchild, Bobbing, Borden, Bredgar, Lower Halstow, Hartlip, Iwade, Kingsdown, Milsted, Milton, Murston, Newington, Rainham (1835–1929), Rodmersham, Sittingbourne, Tonge, Tunstall, Upchurch

PENSHURST PLU (1835–1840s[34])
Chiddingstone, Cowden, Edenbridge, Hever, Leigh, Penshurst

RIVER PLU–renamed in 1840s DOVER PLU, qv above

ROMNEY MARSH PLU
Blackmanstone, Brenzett, Brookland, Burmarsh, Dymchurch, Eastbridge, Fairfield, Hope All Saints, West Hythe (1835–88), Ivychurch, Lydd, Midley, Newchurch, Orgarswick, New Romney, St Martin's New Romney (1894–1930), Old Romney, St Mary in the Marsh, Snargate, Snave

SEVENOAKS PLU
Brasted, Chevening, Chiddingstone (1840s–1930), Cowden (1840s–1930), Dunton Green (1908–30), Edenbridge (1840s–1930), Halstead, Hever (1840s–1930), Kemsing, Leigh (1840s–1930), Otford, Penshurst (1840s–1930), Riverhead (1894–1930), Seal, Sevenoaks, Sevenoaks Weald (1894–1930), Shoreham, Sundridge, Westerham

SHEPPEY PLU
Eastchurch, Elmley, Harty, Leysdown, Minster in Sheppey, Queenborough, Sheerness (1894–1930), Warden

STROOD PLU–renaming 1884 of NORTH AYLESFORD PLU, qv above where all pars for period 1835–1930 are listed

TENTERDEN PLU
Appledore, Biddenden, Ebony (1835–94), High Halden, Kenardington, Newenden, Rolvenden, Stone (1835–94), Stone cum Ebony (1894–1930), Tenterden, Wittersham, Woodchurch

THANET PLU (sometimes ISLE OF THANET)
Acol, Birchington, Garlinge (1894–1930), Margate St John the Baptist (1836–1930), Minster, Monkton, Northdown (1894–1913), Ramsgate (1836–1930), St Lawrence (1835–94), St Lawrence Extra (1894–1930), St Lawrence Intra

(1894–1922), St Nicholas at Wade, St Peter (1914–30), St Peter Extra (1894–1914), St Peter Intra (1894–1914), St Peters (1835–94), Sarre, Stonar, Westgate on Sea (1894–1930)
TONBRIDGE PLU
Ashurst, Bidborough, Brenchley, Capel, Hadlow, Hildenborough (1894–1930), Horsmonden, Pembury, Southborough (1894–1930), Speldhurst, Tonbridge (1835–94), Tonbridge Rural (1894–1930), Tonbridge Urban (1894–1930), Tudeley (1835–85), Tunbridge Wells (1894–1930)
WOOLWICH PLU (1868–89[29])
Charlton, Kidbrooke, Plumstead, Woolwich

In Other Poor Law Counties:
RYE PLU (Sussex, Kent)
Broomhill[36]
TICEHURST PLU (Sussex, Kent)
Frant[37]

SANITARY DISTRICTS

ASHFORD USD
Ashford
EAST ASHFORD RSD
same as PLU
WEST ASHFORD RSD
same as PLU less Ashford
NORTH AYLESFORD RSD (1875–84), renamed STROOD RSD (1884–94)
same as PLU less Northfleet
BECKENHAM USD
Beckenham
BEXLEY USD
Bexley
BLEAN RSD
same as PLU less Canterbury The Archbishop's Palace Precincts, Canterbury Christchurch, Canterbury St Gregory the Great, pt Hackington, pt Herne, pt St Dunstan, Staplegate, pt Sturry (1890–94)
BRIDGE RSD
same as PLU less pt Beakesbourne, pt Canterbury Holy Cross Westgate Without, pt Fordwich, pt Littlebourne, pt Nackington, pt Patrixbourne, pt Thanington
BROADSTAIRS AND ST PETERS USD
pt St Peters
BROMLEY RSD
same as PLU less Beckenham, Bromley
BROMLEY USD
Bromley
CANTERBURY USD
same as MB/CB for period 1875–94
CHATHAM USD
pt Chatham, pt Gillingham
CRANBROOK RSD
same as PLU
DARTFORD RSD
same as PLU less Bexley, Dartford, Erith
DARTFORD USD
Dartford
DEAL USD
Deal
DOVER RSD
same as PLU less pt Buckland, pt Charlton, East Cliffe, Dover Castle, Dover St James the Apostle, Dover St Mary the Virgin, pt Guston, pt Hougham, pt Poulton (188 –94)
DOVER USD
pt Buckland, pt Charlton, East Cliffe, Dover Castle, Dover St James the Apostle, Dover St Mary the Virgin, pt Guston, pt Hougham, pt Poulton
EASTRY RSD
same as PLU less Deal, Sandwich St Bartholomew's Hospital, Sandwich St Clement, Sandwich St Mary, Sandwich St Peter, Walmer
ELHAM RSD
same as PLU less pt Folkestone (1875–86), pt Folkestone (before 1891–94), Folkestone Town (1886–before 1891), St Leonard Hythe
ERITH USD
Erith
FAVERSHAM RSD
same as PLU less pt Faversham, pt Preston next Faversham
FAVERSHAM USD
pt Faversham, pt Preston next Faversham
FOLKESTONE USD
pt Folkestone (1875–86), pt Folkestone (before 1891–94), Folkestone Town (1886–before 1891)
GILLINGHAM USD
pt Chatham, pt Gillingham
GRAVESEND USD
Gravesend, Milton
HERNE BAY USD
pt Herne
HOLLINGBOURNE RSD
same as PLU
HOO RSD
same as PLU
HYTHE USD
pt Aldington (until 1888), St Leonard Hythe, pt West Hythe (until 1888)
LYDD USD (1885–94)
Lydd
MAIDSTONE RSD
same as PLU less Maidstone
MAIDSTONE USD
Maidstone
MALLING RSD
same as PLU less Wrotham
MARGATE USD
pt Margate St John the Baptist
MEDWAY RSD
same as PLU less pt Chatham, pt Frindsbury, pt Gillingham, Rochester Castle Precincts, Rochester St Nicholas, pt Rochester St Margaret, pt Strood
MILTON RSD
same as PLU less Milton, Sittingbourne

MILTON NEXT SITTINGBOURNE USD
Milton
NORTHFLEET USD
Northfleet
QUEENBOROUGH USD (1885–94)
Queenborough
RAMSGATE USD (1884–94)
Ramsgate, pt St Lawrence
ROCHESTER USD
pt Chatham, pt Frindsbury, Rochester Castle Precincts, Rochester St Nicholas, pt Rochester St Margaret, pt Strood, pt Wouldham
NEW ROMNEY USD (1885–94)
pt New Romney
ROMNEY MARSH RSD
same as PLU less pt Aldington (until 1888), pt West Hythe (until 1888), Lydd (1885–94), pt New Romney (1885–94)
RYE RSD
same as PLU for Kent par
SANDGATE USD
pt Folkestone (an area in Folkestone MB)
SANDWICH USD
Sandwich St Bartholomew's Hospital, Sandwich St Clement, Sandwich St Mary, Sandwich St Peter
SEVENOAKS RSD
same as PLU less pt Sevenoaks
SEVENOAKS USD
pt Sevenoaks
SHEERNESS USD
pt Minster in Sheppey
SHEPPEY RSD
same as PLU less pt Minster in Sheppey, Queenborough
SITTINGBOURNE USD
Sittingbourne
SOUTHBOROUGH USD (1886[38]–94)
pt Tonbridge
STROOD RSD–renaming 1884 of NORTH AYLESFORD RSD, qv above where all pars for period 1875–94 are listed
TENTERDEN RSD
same as PLU less pt Ebony, Tenterden
TENTERDEN USD
pt Ebony, Tenterden
THANET RSD (sometimes ISLE OF THANET)
same as PLU less pt Margate St John the Baptist, Ramsgate (188 –94), pt St Lawrence, pt St Peters
TICEHURST RSD
same as PLU for Kent par less pt Frant (188 –94)
TONBRIDGE RSD
same as PLU less pt Speldhurst, pt Tonbridge
TONBRIDGE USD
pt Tonbridge
TUNBRIDGE WELLS USD (188 –94)
pt Frant, pt Speldhurst, pt Tonbridge
WALMER USD
Walmer
WROTHAM USD
Wrotham

KENT PARISHES IN THE METROPOLIS, 1855–89[29]

Par Under Vestry:
Woolwich

Pars Within Dists:
GREENWICH DIST
Deptford St Nicholas, Deptford St Paul,[30] Greenwich
LEWISHAM DIST[31]
Lewisham
PLUMSTEAD DIST
Charlton next Woolwich, Eltham, Kidbrooke, Lee, Plumstead

ADMINISTRATIVE COUNTY

For the MBs and the associated CB, see BOROUGHS.

ASHFORD UD
Ashford
EAST ASHFORD RD
Aldington, Bilsington, Bircholt (1894–1934), Bonnington, Boughton Aluph, Brabourne, Brook, Challock, Chilham, Crundale, Eastwell, Godmersham, Hastingleigh, Hinxhill, Hurst (1894–1934), Kennington (1894–1934), Mersham, Molash, Orlestone, Ruckinge, Sevington, Smeeth, Warehorne, Willesborough (1894–1934), Wye
WEST ASHFORD RD (1894–1934)
Bethersden, Charing, Great Chart, Little Chart, Egerton, Hothfield, Kingsnorth, Pluckley, Shadoxhurst, Smarden, Westwell
BECKENHAM UD (1894–1935[15])
Beckenham
BEXLEY UD (1894–1937[15])
Bexley
BLEAN RD (1894–1934)
Chislet, Hackington, Herne, Hoath, Reculver, St Cosmus and St Damian in the Blean, St Dunstan Without, Sturry, Swalecliffe, Westbere, Whitstable cum Seasalter
BRIDGE RD (1894–1934)
Adisham, Barham, Bekesbourne, Bishopsbourne, Bridge, Chartham, Fordwich, Harbledown, Lower Hardres, Upper Hardres, Holy Cross Westgate Without (1894–1912), Ickham and Well, Kingston,

Littlebourne, Milton, Nackington, Patrixbourne, Petham, St Nicholas Hospital, Stodmarsh, Thanington Without, Waltham, Wickhambreux, Womenswold

BRIDGE-BLEAN RD (1934–74)
Adisham, Barham, Bekesbourne, Bishopsbourne, Bridge, Chartham, Chislet, Fordwich, Hackington, Harbledown, Lower Hardres, Upper Hardres, Hoath, Ickham and Well, Kingston, Littlebourne, Patrixbourne, Petham, St Cosmus and St Damian in the Blean, Sturry, Thanington Without, Waltham, Westbere, Wickhambreaux (1957–74), Wickhambreux (1934–57), Womenswold

BROADSTAIRS AND ST PETER'S UD
Broadstairs and St Peter's (1935–74) St Peter (1914–35), St Peter Intra (1894–1914)

BROMLEY RD (1894–1934)
Chelsfield, Chislehurst (1894–1900), Foots Cray (1894–1902), North Cray, St Mary Cray, St Paul's Cray, Cudham, Downe, Farnborough, Hayes, Keston, Knockholt, Mottingham, Orpington, West Wickham

BROMLEY UD (1894–1903[17])
Bromley

CHERITON UD (1898[39]–1934)
Cheriton

CHISLEHURST UD (1900[40]–1934)
Chislehurst

CHISLEHURST AND SIDCUP UD (1934–65[16])
Chislehurst and Sidcup

CRANBROOK RD
Benenden, Cranbrook, Frittenden, Goudhurst, Hawkhurst, Sandhurst

FOOTS CRAY UD (1902[41]–21[42]) (sometimes FOOTSCRAY UD)
Foots Cray

CRAYFORD UD (1920[43]–65[16])
Crayford

DARTFORD RD
Ash (1894–1955), Ash-cum-Ridley [later called Ash-with-Ridley] (1955–74), Crayford (1894–1920), Darenth, Eynsford, Farningham, Fawkham, Hartley, Horton Kirby, Kingsdown (1894–1948), West Kingsdown (1948–74), Longfield, Lullingstone (1894–1955), Ridley (1894–1955), Southfleet, Stone, Sutton at Hone, Swanley (1955–74), Swanscombe (1894–1926), East Wickham (1894–1902), Wilmington

DARTFORD UD (1894–1933[15])
Dartford

DOVER RD
Alkham, Capel-le-Ferne, West Cliffe (1894–1934), Coldred (1894–1963), Denton (1894–1963), Denton with Wootton (1963–74), Temple Ewell (1894–1960), Temple Ewell with River (1960–74), Guston, pt Hougham (1894–96), Hougham Without, Langdon (1963–74), East Langdon (1894–1963), West Langdon (1894–1963), Lydden, Oxney (1894–1934), Poulton (1894–1934), Ringwould, River (1894–1960), St Margaret's at Cliffe, Shepherdswell with Coldred (1963–74), Sibertswold (1894–1963), Whitfield, Wootton (1894–1963)

EASTRY RD
Acol (1935–74), Ash, Aylesham (1951–74), Barfreston (1894–1935), Betteshanger (1894–1935), Chillenden (1894–1935), Eastry, Elmstone (1894–1935), Eythorne, Goodnestone, Ham (1894–1935), Knowlton (1894–1935), Minster (1935–74), Great Mongeham (1894–1935), Little Mongeham (1894–1935), Monkton (1935–74), Nonington, Northbourne, Preston, Ripple, St Nicholas at Wade (1935–74), Sarre (1935–74), Sholden, Staple, Stourmouth, Sutton, Tilmanstone, Waldershare (1894–1935), Wingham, Woodnesborough, Worth

ELHAM RD
Acrise, Cheriton (1894–98), Elham, Elmsted, Hawkinge, Lyminge, Lympne, Monks Horton, Newington, Paddlesworth, Postling, Saltwood, Sellindge, Stanford, Stelling (1894–1968), Stelling Minnis, Stowting, Swingfield

ERITH UD (1894–1938[15])
Erith

FAVERSHAM RD (1894–1934)
Badlesmere, Boughton under Blean, Buckland, Davington, Doddington, Dunkirk, Eastling, Faversham Without, Goodnestone, Graveney, Hernhill, Leaveland, Luddenham, Lynsted, Newham, Norton, Oare, Ospringe, Preston Without (1894–97), North Preston Without (1897–1934), South Preston Without (1897–1934), Selling, Sheldwich, Stalisfield, Stone, Teynham, Throwley

GILLINGHAM UD (1894–1903[17])
pt Chatham, Gillingham

HERNE BAY UD
Herne Bay

HOLLINGBOURNE RD
Bicknor, Boxley, Bredhurst, Broomfield, Boughton Malherbe, Detling, Frinsted, Harrietsham, Headcorn, Hollingbourne, Hucking, Langley, Leeds, Lenham, Otterden, Stockbury, Chart Sutton, East Sutton, Sutton Valence, Thurnham, Ulcombe, Wichling, Wormshill

HOO RD (1894–1935)
Allhallows, Cooling, High Halstow, Hoo, St Mary Hoo, Isle of Grain, Land Common to High Halstow and St Mary Hoo [The Mean], Stoke

MAIDSTONE RD
Barming (1934–74), East Barming (1894–1934), West Barming (1894–1934), Bearsted, Boughton Monchelsea, East Farleigh, West Farleigh, Hunton, Linton, Loose, Marden, Nettlestead, Otham, Staplehurst, Teston, Yalding

MALLING RD
Addington, Allington (1894–1934), Aylesford, Birling, Borough Green (1934–74), Burham, Ditton, Ightham, Leybourne, East Malling (1894–1962), East Malling and Larkfield (1962–74), West Malling, Mereworth, Offham, East Peckham, West Peckham, Platt (1934–74), Plaxtol (1934–74), Ryarsh, Shipbourne, Snodland, Stansted, Trottiscliffe, Wateringbury, Wouldham, Wrotham (1934–74)

MEDWAY RD (1894–1905[44])
Grange (1894–1903), Lidsing (1894–1903), St Margaret Extra (1894–1905)

MILTON RD (1894–1934)
Bapchild, Bobbing, Borden, Bredgar, Lower Halstow, Hartlip, Iwade, Kingsdown, Milsted, Murston (1894–1930), Newington, Rainham (1894–1929), Rodmersham, Tonge, Tunstall, Upchurch
MILTON NEXT SITTINGBOURNE UD (1894–1907[45])
Milton
MILTON REGIS UD (1907[45]–30[46])
Milton
NORTHFLEET UD
Northfleet
ORPINGTON UD (1934–65[16])
Orpington
PENGE UD (1899[47]–1965[16])
Penge
ROMNEY MARSH RD
Blackmanstone (1894–1934), Brenzett, Brookland, Burmarsh, Dymchurch, Eastbridge (1894–1934), Fairfield (1894–1934), Hope All Saints (1894–1934), Ivychurch, Midley (1894–1934), Newchurch, Orgarswick (1894–1934), St Martin's New Romney (1894–1934), Old Romney, St Mary in the Marsh, Snargate, Snave (1894–1934)
SANDGATE UD (1894–1934)
pt Folkestone next Sandgate, Sandgate
SEVENOAKS RD
Brasted, Chevening, Chiddingstone, Cowden, Dunton Green (1908–74), Edenbridge, Halstead, Hever, Kemsing, Knockholt (1969–74), Leigh, Otford, Penshurst, Riverhead, Seal, Sevenoaks Weald, Shoreham, Sundridge, Westerham
SEVENOAKS UD
Sevenoaks
SHEERNESS UD (1894–1968[21])
Sheerness
SHEPPEY RD (1894–1968[21])
Eastchurch, Elmley, Harty, Leysdown (1894–1949), Leysdown-on-Sea (1949–68), Minster in Sheppey, Warden
SIDCUP UD (1921[42]–34)
Foots Cray (1921–25), Sidcup (1925–34)
SITTINGBOURNE UD (1894–1930[46])
Sittingbourne
SITTINGBOURNE AND MILTON UD (1930[46]–74)
Sittingbourne and Milton
SOUTHBOROUGH UD
Southborough
STROOD RD
Allhallows (1935–74), Chalk (1894–1935), Cliffe, Cobham, Cooling (1935–74), Cuxton, Denton (1894–1935), Frindsbury Extra, Halling, High Halstow (1935–74), Higham, Hoo (1935–68), Hoo St Werburgh (1968–74), St Mary Hoo (1935–74), Ifield (1894–1935), Isle of Grain (1935–74), Luddesdown, Meopham, Nursted, Shorne, Stoke (1935–74), Strood Extra (1894–1934)
SWALE RD (1934–74)
Badlesmere, Bapchild, Bobbing, Borden, Bredgar, Boughton under Blean, Buckland, Doddington, Dunkirk, Eastling, Faversham Without, Goodnestone, Graveney, Lower Halstow, Hartlip, Hernhill, Iwade, Kingsdown, Leaveland, Luddenham, Lynsted, Milstead (1962–74), Milsted (1934–62), Newington, Newham, Norton, Oare, Ospringe, Rodmersham, Selling, Sheldwich, Stalisfield, Stone, Teynham, Throwley, Tonge, Tunstall, Upchurch
SWANSCOMBE UD (1926[48]–74)
Swanscombe
TENTERDEN RD
Appledore, Biddesden, High Halden, Kenardington, Newenden, Rolvenden, Stone cum Ebony, Wittersham, Woodchurch
ISLE OF THANET RD (1894–1935)
Acol, Birchington, Garlinge, Minster, Monkton, Northdown (1894–1913), St Lawrence Extra, St St Nicholas at Wade, St Peter Extra (1894–1914), Sarre, Stonar, Westgate on Sea
TONBRIDGE RD
Ashurst, Bidborough, Brenchley, Capel, Hadlow, Hildenborough, Horsmonden (pt 1894–95, ent 1895–1974), Lamberhurst (pt 1894–95, ent 1895–1974), Paddock Wood (1955–74), Pembury, Speldhurst, Tonbridge Rural (1894–1934)
TONBRIDGE UD
Tonbridge (1934–74), Tonbridge Urban (1894–1934)
WALMER UD (1894–1934)
Walmer
WHITSTABLE UD (1894[49]–1974)
Whitstable (1934–74), Whitstable Urban (1894–1934)
WROTHAM UD (1894–1934)
Wrotham

NON-METROPOLITAN COUNTY

As constituted 1 Apr 1974, defined in terms of Adm Co units as of 31 Mar.

ASHFORD DIST
Ashford UD, East Ashford RD, West Ashford RD, Tenterden MB, Tenterden RD
CANTERBURY DIST
Bridge-Blean RD, Canterbury CB, Herne Bay UD, Whitstable UD
DARTFORD DIST
Dartford MB, pt Dartford RD (Darenth, Southfleet, Stone, Sutton at Hone, Wilmington), Swanscombe UD
DOVER DIST
Deal MB, Dover MB, Dover RD, pt Eastry RD (all except the pars in Thanet Dist), Sandwich MB
GILLINGHAM DIST
Gillingham MB

GRAVESHAM DIST
Gravesend MB, Northfleet UD, pt Strood RD (Cobham, Higham, Luddesdown, Meopham, Shorne)

MAIDSTONE DIST
Hollingbourne RD, Maidstone MB, Maidstone RD

MEDWAY DIST
Chatham MB, Rochester MB, pt Strood RD (all except the pars in Gravesham Dist)

SEVENOAKS DIST
pt Dartford RD (all except the pars in Dartford Dist), Sevenoaks RD, Sevenoaks UD

SHEPWAY DIST
Elham RD, Folkestone MB, Hythe MB, Lydd MB, New Romney MB, Romney Marsh RD

SWALE DIST
Faversham MB, Queenborough-in-Sheppey MB, Sittingbourne and Milton UD, Swale RD

THANET DIST
Boadstairs and St Peter's UD, pt Eastry RD (Acol, Minster, Monkton, St Nicholas at Wade, Sarre), Margate MB, Ramsgate MB

TONBRIDGE AND MALLING DIST
Malling RD, pt Tonbridge RD (Hadlow, Hildenborough), Tonbridge UD

TUNBRIDGE WELLS DIST
Cranbrook RD, Southborough UD, pt Tonbridge RD (all except the pars in Tonbridge and Malling Dist), Royal Tunbridge Wells MB

LONDON

PART I: THE CITY OF LONDON

ALTERATIONS IN BOUNDARIES

The boundaries of the City of London were altered in the years indicated below; see Part I of the *Guide* under the par noted for details of the alteration. In addition, the pars of St Botolph Aldgate and St Sepulchre each had a pt in Middx which had sep civ jurisdiction, and thus formed pars of the same names in Middx (London Adm Co from 1899).

1723 St Giles Without Cripplegate. *1767* St Andrew Holborn. *1866* St Botolph Without Aldersgate, St Dunstan in the West. *1899* Furnival's Inn, St Andrew Holborn, St Botolph Without Aldersgate, Whitechapel.

THE WARDS OF THE CITY OF LONDON

As of final elaboration in mid-16th cent. The wards were not defined in terms of parishes.

Aldersgate, Aldgate, Bassishaw, Billingsgate, Bishopsgate, Bread Street, Bridge Within, Bridge Without, Broad Street, Candlewick, Castle Baynard, Cheap, Coleman Street, Cordwainer, Cornhill, Cripplegate, Cowgate, Farringdon Within, Farringdon Without, Langbourn, Lime Street, Portsoken, Queenhithe, Tower, Vintry, Walbrook.

THE PARISHES OF THE CITY OF LONDON

from 1907: London, Inner Temple, Middle Temple.
until 1907: All Hallows Barking; All Hallows, Bread Street; All Hallows the Great; All Hallows, Honey Lane; All Hallows the Less; All Hallows, Lombard Street; All Hallows, London Wall; All Hallows Staining; Barnard's Inn[1]; Bridewell Precinct[1]; Christ Church, Newgate Street (1547–1907), pt Furnival's Inn[1] (until 1899); Holy Trinity the Less; Inner Temple; Middle Temple; St Alban, Wood Street; St Alphage London Wall; St Andrew by the Wardrobe; St Andrew Holborn (pt until 1767, ent 1767–1907); St Andrew Hubbard; St Andrew Undershaft; St Ann Blackfriars; St Ann and St Agnes; St Antholin; St Audoen (until 1547); St Augustine on the Wall (until 1441); St Augustine Watling Street; St Bartholomew by the Exchange; St Batholomew the Great; St Bartholomew the Less; St Benet Fink; St Benet Gracechurch; St Benet Paul's Wharf; St Benet Sherehog; St Botolph by Billingsgate; St Botolph Without Aldersgate (pt until 1866, ent 1866–1907); St Botolph Without Aldgate[2]; St Botolph Without Bishopsgate; St Bride; St Christopher le Stocks; St Clement, Eastcheap; St Dionis, Backchurch; St Dunstan in the East; St Dunstan in the West (pt until 1866, ent 1866–1907); St Edmund The King and Martyr; St Ethelburga; St Faith Under St Paul's; St Gabriel Fenchurch; St George Botolph Lane; St Giles Without Cripplegate (pt until 1723, ent 1723–1907); St Gregory by St Paul's; St Helen Bishopsgate; St James Duke's Place (1623–1907); St James Garlickhithe; St John the Baptist, Walbrook; St John the Evangelist; St John Zachary; St Katherine Coleman; St Katherine Cree; St Lawrence Jewry; St Lawrence Pountney; St Leonard Eastcheap; St Leonard Foster Lane; St Magnus the Martyr; St Margaret Lothbury; St Margaret Moses; St Margaret New Fish Steet; St Margaret Pattens; St Martin Ludgate; St Martin Orgar; St Martin Outwich; St Martin Pomeroy; St Martin Vintry; St Mary Abchurch; St Mary Aldermanbury; St Mary Aldermary; St Mary at Hill; St Mary Axe (until 1562)· St Mary Bothaw; St Mary le Bow; St Mary Colechurch; St Mary Magdalene, Old Fish Street; St Mary Mounthaw; St Mary Somerset; St Mary Staining; St Mary Woolchurch; St Mary Woolnoth; St Matthew Friday Street; St Michael Bassishaw; St Michael Cornhill; St Michael Crooked Lane; St Michael Queenhithe; St Michael le Querne; St Michael, Paternoster Royal; St Michael, Wood Street; St Mildred, Bread Street; St Mildred Poultry; St Nicholas Acons; St Nicholas Cole Abbey; St Nicholas Olave; St Nicholas Shambles (until 1547); St Olave Bread Street (until before 1271); St Olave Hart Street; St Olave Old Jewry; St Olave Silver Street; St Pancras, Soper Lane; St Peter Cornhill: St Peter Paul's Wharf; St Peter le Poer; St Peter Westcheap; St Sepulchre[2]; St Stephen Coleman Street; St Stephen Walbrook; St Swithun London Stone; St Thomas Apostle; St Vedast Foster Lane;

Serjeants' Inn[1]; Thavie's Inn[1]; pt Whitechapel (1780[3]–1899); Whitefriars Precinct[1]

POOR LAW UNIONS

CITY OF LONDON PLU (1837–1930)
from 1907: London
1837–1907: All Hallows Barking; All Hallows, Bread Street; All Hallows the Great; All Hallows, Honey Lane; All Hallows the Less; All Hallows, Lombard Street; All Hallows, London Wall; All Hallows Staining; Barnard's Inn (1869–1907); Bridewell Precinct (1869–1907); Christ Church, Newgate Street; Holy Trinity the Less; St Alban, Wood Street; St Alphage London Wall; St Andrew by the Wardrobe; St Andrew Holborn (1869–1907); St Andrew Hubbard; St Andrew Undershaft; St Ann Blackfriars; St Ann and St Agnes; St Antholin; St Augustine Watling Street; St Bartholomew by the Exchange; St Bartholomew the Great (1869–1907); St Bartholomew the Less (1869–1907); St Benet Fink; St Benet Gracechurch; St Benet Paul's Wharf; St Benet Sherehog; St Botolph Aldersgate (1869–1907), St Botolph by Billingsgate; St Botolph Without Aldersgate (1869–1907); St Botolph Without Aldgate (1869–1907); St Botolph Without Bishopsgate; St Bride (1869–1907); St Christopher le Stocks; St Clement, Eastcheap; St Dionis Backchurch; St Dunstan in the East; St Dunstan in the West (1869–1907); St Edmund The King and Martyr; St Ethelburga; St Faith Under St Paul's; St Gabriel Fenchurch; St George Botolph Lane; St Giles Without Cripplegate (1869–1907); St Gregory by St Paul's; St Helen Bishopsgate; St James Duke's Place; St James Garlickhithe; St John the Baptist, Walbrook; St John the Evangelist; St John Zachary; St Katherine Coleman; St Katherine Cree; St Lawrence Jewry; St Lawrence Pountney; St Leonard Eastcheap; St Leonard Foster Lane, St Magnus the Martyr; St Margaret Lothbury; St Margaret Moses; St Margaret New Fish Street; St Margaret Pattens; St Martin Ludgate; St Martin Orgar; St Martin Outwich; St Martin Pomeroy; St Martin Vintry; St Mary Abchurch; St Mary Aldermanbury; St Mary Aldermary; St Mary at Hill; St Mary Bothaw; St Mary le Bow; St Mary Colechurch; St Mary Magdalene, Old Fish Street; St Mary Mounthaw; St Mary Somerset; St Mary Staining; St Mary Woolchurch; St Mary Woolnoth; St Matthew Friday Street; St Michael Bassishaw; St Michael Cornhill; St Michael Crooked Lane; St Michael Queenhithe; St Michael le Querne; St Michael, Paternoster Royal; St Michael, Wood Street; St Mildred, Bread Street; St Mildred Poultry; St Nicholas Acons; St Nicholas Cole Abbey; St Nicholas Olave; St Olave Hart Street; St Olave Old Jewry; St Olave Silver Street; St Pancras, Soper Lane; St Peter Cornhill; St Peter Paul's Wharf; St Peter le Poer; St Peter Westcheap; St Sepluchre (1869–1907); St Stephen Coleman Street; St Stephen Walbrook; St Swithin London Stone; St Thomas Aspostle; St Vedast Foster Lane; Serjeants' Inn (1869–1907); Thavie's Inn (1869–1907); Whitefriars Precinct

EAST LONDON PLU (1837–69) (City of London, Middx)
St Botolph Without Aldersgate; St Botolph Without Aldgate; St Botolph Without Bishopsgate; St Giles Without Cripplegate

WEST LONDON PLU (1837–69)
Barnard's Inn; Bridewell Precinct; St Andrew Holborn; St Bartholomew the Great; St Bartholomew the Less; St Bride; St Dunstan in the West; Serjeants' Inn; Thavie's Inn

PART II: LONDON ADMINISTRATIVE COUNTY

ALTERATIONS IN BOUNDARIES

The boundaries of London Administrative County were altered in the years indicated below. See Part I of the *Guide* under the par noted for details of the alterations.

1899 Furnival's Inn, Islington, Stoke Newington, Whitechapel. *1904* Tooting Graveney. *1908* Hackney.

POOR LAW UNIONS

The alterations in PLUs and Pars (poor) below were consequent upon the amalgamation of pars, for details of which see Part I of the *Guide*. Otherwise the PLUs or Pars existed 1889–1930. For earlier years, see Middx, Surrey and Kent.

BATTERSEA PAR (1904–30)
Battersea

BERMONDSEY PAR (1904–30)
Bermondsey

BETHNAL GREEN PAR
Bethnal Green

CAMBERWELL PAR
Camberwell

CHELSEA PAR
Chelsea

FULHAM PAR (1899–1930)
Fulham

FULHAM PLU (1889–99)
Fulham, Hammersmith

GREENWICH PLU
Deptford St Nicholas, Deptford St Paul, Greenwich

HACKNEY PLU
Hackney, Stoke Newington

HAMMERSMITH PAR (1899–1930)
Hammersmith

HAMPSTEAD PAR
Hampstead

HOLBORN PLU
Chartherhouse (1889–1915), Clerkenwell (1899–

1915), Finsbury (1915–30), Furnival's Inn, Glasshouse Yard (1901–15); Liberty of Saffron Hill, Hatton Garden, Ely Rents and Ely Place; St Andrew Holborn Above the Bars with St George the Martyr, St Giles in the Fields and St George Bloomsbury (1914–30), St Luke (1889–1915), St Sepulchre (1889–1915), Staple Inn

ISLINGTON PAR
Islington

KENSINGTON PAR
Kensington

LAMBETH PAR
Lambeth

LEWISHAM PLU
Eltham, Lee (1889–1905), Lewisham

MILE END OLD TOWN PAR (1889–1925)
Mile End Old Town

PADDINGTON PAR
Paddington

POPLAR BOROUGH PAR (1907–30)
Poplar Borough

POPLAR PLU (1889–1907)
Bow, Bromley, Poplar

ST GEORGE IN THE EAST PAR (1889–1925)
St George in the East

ST GEORGE'S PLU (1889–1913)
The Close of the Collegiate Church of St Peter, St George Hanover Square, Westminster St Margaret and St John

ST OLAVE PLU (1889–1904)
Bermondsey, Rotherhithe, Southwark St John Horsleydown, Southwark St Olave (1889–96), Southwark St Olave and St Thomas (1896–1904), Southwark St Thomas (1889–96)

ST PANCRAS PAR
St Pancras

ST SAVIOUR'S PLU (1889–1901)
Newington, Southwark Christchurch, Southwark St George the Martyr, Southwark St Saviour

SHOREDITCH PAR
Shoreditch

SOUTHWARK PLU (1901–30)
Newington, Southwark Christchurch, Southwark St George the Martyr, Southwark St Saviour

STEPNEY PAR (1927–30)
Stepney

STEPNEY PLU (1889–1921)
Limehouse, Ratcliff, Shadwell, Wapping

STEPNEY PLU (1925–27)
Mile End Old Town, St George in the East, Whitechapel

STRAND PLU (1899–1913)
Liberty of the Rolls, St Clement Danes, St Martin in the Fields, St Mary le Strand, St Paul Covent Garden, Precinct of the Savoy

WANDSWORTH PAR (1904–30)
Wandsworth Borough

WANDSWORTH AND CLAPHAM PLU (1889–1904)
Battersea, Clapham, Streatham, Tooting Graveney, Wandsworth

WESTMINSTER PLU (1889–1913)
St Anne Within the Liberty of Westminster, Westminster St James

CITY OF WESTMINSTER PAR (1922–30)
City of Westminster

CITY OF WESTMINSTER PLU (1913–22)
The Close of the Collegiate Church of St Peter, Liberty of the Rolls, St Anne Within the Liberty of Westminster, St Clement Danes, St George Hanover Square, St Martin in the Fields, St Mary le Strand, St Paul Covent Garden, Precinct of the Savoy, Westminster St James, Westminster St Margaret and St John

WHITECHAPEL PAR (1921–25)
Whitechapel

WHITECHAPEL PLU (1889–1921)
Holy Trinity Minories (1889–95), Mile End New Town, Norton Folgate, Old Artillery Ground, St Botolph Without Aldgate, St Katherine by the Tower (1889–95), Spitalfields, Tower of London (1889–1901), Old Tower Without (1889–95), Whitechapel

WOOLWICH PLU
Charlton and Kidbrooke (1901–30), Charlton next Woolwich (1889–1901), Kidbrooke (1889–1901), Plumstead, Woolwich

METROPOLITAN BOARD OF WORKS, 1889–1900

Pars Under Vestries:
Bermondsey, Bethnal Green, Camberwell, Chelsea, Clerkenwell, Fulham, Hackney (1894–99), Hammersmith, Hampstead, Islington, Kensington, Lambeth, Mile End Old Town, Newington, Paddington, Plumstead (1894–99), Rotherhithe, St George Hanover Square, St George in the East, St Luke, St Martin in the Fields, St Marylebone, St Pancras, Shoreditch, Southwark St George the Martyr, Stoke Newington (1894–99), Westminster St James, Woolwich

Pars in Dists:

GREENWICH DIST
Deptford St Nicholas, Deptford St Paul, Greenwich

HACKNEY DIST (1889–94)
Hackney, Stoke Newington

HOLBORN DIST
Glasshouse Yard; Liberty of Saffron Hill, Hatton Garden, Ely Rents and Ely Place; St Andrew Holborn Avove the Bars with St George the Martyr, St Sepulchre

LEE DIST (1894–99)
Charlton next Woolwich, Eltham, Kidbrooke, Lee

LEWISHAM DIST
Lewisham

LIMEHOUSE DIST
Limehouse, Ratcliff, Shadwell, Wapping

PLUMSTEAD DIST (1889–94)
Charlton next Woolwich, Eltham, Kidbrooke, Lee, Plumstead

POPLAR DIST
Bow, Bromley

ST GILES DIST
St Giles in the Fields and St George Bloomsbury

ST OLAVE DIST
Southwark St John Horsleydown, Southwark St Olave (1889–96), Southwark St Olave and St Thomas (1896–99), Southwark St Thomas (1889–96)
ST SAVIOUR'S DIST
Southwark Christchurch, Southwark St Saviour
STRAND DIST
Liberty of the Rolls, St Anne Within the Liberty of Westminster, St Clement Danes, St Mary le Strand, St Paul' Covent Garden, Precinct of the Savoy
WANDSWORTH DIST
Battersea, Clapham, Putney, Streatham, Tooting Graveney, Wandsworth
WESTMINSTER DIST
Westminster St Margaret and St John
WHITECHAPEL DIST
Mile End New Town, Norton Folgate, Old Artillery Ground, St Botolph Without Aldgate, Spitalfields, Whitechapel

METROPOLITAN BOROUGHS 1900–1965

BATTERSEA METROP BOR
Battersea
BERMONDSEY METROP BOR
Bermondsey, Rotherhithe (1900–04), Southwark St John Horsleydown (1900–04), Southwark St Olave and St Thomas
BETHNAL GREEN METROP BOR
Bethnal Green
CAMBERWELL METROP BOR
Camberwell
CHELSEA METROP BOR
Chelsea
DEPTFORD METROP BOR
Deptford St Paul
FINSBURY METROP BOR
Charterhouse (1900–15), Clerkenwell (1900–15), Finsbury (1915–65), Glasshouse Yard (1900–15), St Luke (1900–15), St Sepulchre (1900–15)
FULHAM METROP BOR
Fulham
GREENWICH METROP BOR
Charlton and Kidbrooke (1901–30), Charlton next Woolwich (1900–01), Deptford St Nicholas (1900–30), Greenwich (1900–30), Borough of Greenwich (1930–65), Kidbrooke (1900–01)
HACKNEY METROP BOR
Hackney
HAMMERSMITH METROP BOR
Hammersmith
HAMPSTEAD METROP BOR
Hampstead
HOLBORN METROP BOR
Furnival's Inn (1900–30), Gray's Inn (1900–32), Holborn (1930–65); Liberty of Saffron Hill, Hatton Garden, Ely Rents and Ely Place (1900–30; Lincoln's Inn (1900–32), St Andrew Holborn Above the Bars with St George the Martyr (1900–30), St Giles in the Fields and St George Bloomsbury (1900–30), Staple Inn (1900–30)
ISLINGTON METROP BOR
Islington
KENSINGTON METROP BOR
Kensington
LAMBETH METROP BOR
Lambeth
LEWISHAM METROP BOR
Lee (1900–30), Lewisham
PADDINGTON METROP BOR
Paddington
POPLAR METROP BOR
Bow (1900–07), Bromley (1900–07), Poplar (1900–07), Poplar Borough (1907–65)
ST MARYLEBONE METROP BOR
St Marylebone
ST PANCRAS METROP BOR
St Pancras
SHOREDITCH METROP BOR
Shoreditch
SOUTHWARK METROP BOR
Newington (1900–30), Southwark (1930–65), Southwark Christchurch (1900–30), Southwark St George the Martyr (1900–30), Southwark St Saviour (1900–30)
STEPNEY METROP BOR
Limehouse (1900–21), Mile End New Town (1900–21), Mile End Old Town (1900–27), Norton Folgate (1900–21), Old Artillery Ground (1900–21), Ratcliff (1900–21), St Botolph Without Aldgate (1900–21), St George in the East (1900–21), Shadwell (1900–21), Spitalfields (1900–21), Stepney (1927–65), Tower of London (1900–01), Wapping (1900–21), Whitechapel (1900–27)
STOKE NEWINGTON METROP BOR
Stoke Newington
WANDSWORTH METROP BOR
Clapham (1900–04), Putney (1900–04), Streatham (1900–04), Tooting Graveney (1900–04), Wandsworth (1900–04), Wandsworth Borough (1904–65)
WESTMINSTER METROP BOR
Close of the Collegiate Church of St Peter (1900–22), Liberty of the Rolls (1900–22), St Anne Within the Liberty of Westminster (1900–22), St Clement Danes (1900–22), St George Hanover Square (1900–22), St Martin in the Fields (1900–22), St Mary le Strand (1900–22), St Paul Covent Garden (1900–02), Precinct of the Savoy (1900–22), City of Westminster (1922–65), Westminster St James (1900–22), Westminster St Margaret and St John (1900–22)
WOOLWICH METROP BOR
Eltham (1900–30), Plumstead (1900–30), Woolwich (1900–30), Borough of Woolwich (1930–65)

PART III: GREATER LONDON

ALTERATIONS IN BOUNDARIES

The boundaries of Greater London were altered only in 1969; see Part I of the *Guide* under Croydon for details of the alteration.

COMPOSITION OF THE COUNTY

The county is composed of London Boroughs, none of which are divided into pars. See Part I of the *Guide* under Greater London for composition of the London Boroughs.

MIDDLESEX

ALTERATIONS IN COUNTY BOUNDARIES

As noted by year below, Middx pars gained territory from or lost it to pars in adjoining counties, or were entirely transferred to them. Details of these alterations are noted in Part I of the *Guide* under Middx. The county was abolished in 1965.

ANCIENT COUNTY (until 1888: Hds, Bors, MBs, PLUs, RSDs, USDs, Vestries and Dists in Metrop Bd Wks)

1733 St Giles Cripplegate. *1767* St Andrew Holborn. *1866* St Botolph Aldersgate, St Dunstan in the West.

ADMINISTRATIVE COUNTY (1889–1965: Hds,[1] PLUs, MBs, RDs, UDs)

1889 Bethnal Green, Bow, Bromley, Charterhouse, Chelsea, Clerkenwell, Close of the Collegiate Church of St Peter, Fulham, Furnival's Inn, Glasshouse Yard, Gray's Inn, Hackney, Monken Hadley, Hammersmith, Hampstead, Holy Trinity Minories, South Hornsey, Islington, Kensington, Liberty of the Rolls; Liberty of Saffron Hill, Hatton Garden, Ely Rents and Ely Place; Limehouse, Lincoln's Inn, Mile End New Town, Mile End Old Town, Norton Folgate, Old Artillery Ground, Paddington, Poplar, Ratcliffe, St Andrew Holborn Above the Bars with St George the Martyr, St Anne Within the Liberty of Westminster, St Botolph Without Aldgate, St Clement Danes, St George Hanover Square, St George in the East, St Giles in the Fields and St George Bloomsbury, St Katherine by the Tower, St Luke's, St Martin in the Fields, St Paul Covent Garden, St Sepulchre, Precinct of the Savoy, Shadwell, Shoreditch, Spitalfields, Staple Inn, Stoke Newington, Tower of London, Old Tower Without, Wapping, Westminster St James, Westminster St Margaret and St John the Evangelist. *1894* Enfield, South Mimms. *1899* Furnival's Inn, Whitechapel. *1900* Whitechapel. *1908* Tottenham. *1926* Hendon. *1934* Tottenham. *1965 Transf to Herts:* South Mimms. *Transf to Surrey:* Ashford, Laleham, Littleton, Shepperton, Staines, Stanwell, Sunbury. *Transf to Gtr London:* Acton, Friern Barnet, East Bedfont, New Brentford, Old Brentford, Chiswick, Ealing, Edmonton, Enfield, Feltham, Finchley, Hanworth, Harlington, Harrow, Hayes, Hendon, Heston and Isleworth, Hornsey, Norwood, Ruislip, Southgate, Tottenham, Twickenham, Uxbridge, Wembley, Willesden, Wood Green, Yiewsley and West Drayton.

HUNDREDS[1]

EDMONTON HD

Edmonton, Enfield, Monken Hadley, South Mimms, Tottenham

ELTHORNE HD

New Brentford, Cowley, Cranford, West Drayton, Greenford, Hanwell, Harefield, Harlington, Harmondsworth, Hayes, Hillingdon, Ickenham, Northolt, Norwood, Perivale, Ruislip, Uxbridge (from 1866)

GORE HD

Edgware, Harrow, Hendon, Kingsbury, Pinner, Great Stanmore, Little Stanmore

ISLEWORTH HD

Heston, Isleworth, Twickenham

OSSULSTONE HD

Acton, Bethnal Green[2] (from 1743), Bow[2] (from 1719), Bromley,[2] Charterhouse[2] (from 1858), Chelsea,[2] Chiswick, Clerkenwell,[2] Duchy of Lancaster[2] (from 1866, not sustained), Ealing, Finchley, Friern Barnet, Fulham,[2] pt Furnival's Inn[2] (from 1858), Glasshouse Yard[2] (from 1866), Gray's Inn[2] (from 1858), Hackney,[2] Hammersmith[2] (from 1631), Holy Trinity Minories,[2] Hornsey,[2] Islington,[2] Hampstead,[2] Kensington,[2] Liberty of the Rolls[2] (from 1866); Liberty of Saffron Hill, Hatton Garden, Ely Rents and Ely Place[2] (from 1866); Limehouse[2] (from 1729), Lincoln's Inn[2] (from 1858), Mile End New Town[2] (from 1866), Mile End Old Town[2] (from 1866), Norton Folgate[2] (from 1866), Old Artillery Ground[2] (from 1866), Paddington,[2] Poplar[2] (from 1817), Ratcliffe[2] (pt from 1729, ent from 1866), pt St Andrew Holborn (until 1767), St Andrew Holborn Above the Bars with St George the Martyr[2] (from 1767), pt St Botolph Aldersgate[2] (until 1866), St Botolph Without Aldgate,[2] pt St Clement Danes,[2] pt St George Bloomsbury (1731–74), St George in the East[2] (from 1729), St George the Martyr (1733–67), pt St Giles Cripplegate (until 1733), St Giles in the Fields (until 1774), St Giles in the Fields and St George Bloomsbury[2] (from 1774), St Katherine by the Tower[2] (from 1866), St Luke[2] (from 1733), St Marylebone,[2] St Pancras,[2] St Paul Covent Garden[2] (from 1645), St Sepulchre,[2] Precinct of the Savoy[2] (from 1866), Shadwell[2] (from 1670), Shoreditch,[2] Spitalfields[2] (from 1729), Staple Inn[2] (from 1858), Stepney[2] (until 1866), Stoke Newington,[2] Tower of London[2] (from 1858), Old Tower Without[2] (from 1858), West Twyford, Wapping[2] (from 1729), pt Whitechapel[2] (from 1780), Willesden

SPELTHORNE HD
Ashford, East Bedfont, Feltham, Hampton, Hampton Wick (from 1866), Hanworth, Laleham, Littleton, Shepperton, Staines, Stanwell, Sunbury, Teddington

CITY OF WESTMINSTER AND ITS LIBERTY[2]
Close of the Collegiate Church of St Peter[3] (from 1858), St Anne Within the Liberty of Westminster (from 1687), pt St Clement Danes, St George Hanover Square (from 1724), St Martin in the Fields, St Mary le Strand, St Paul Covent Garden (from 1645), Westminster St James (from 1685), Westminster St John the Evangelist[3] (from 1727), Westminster St Margaret[3]

BOROUGHS

Units with some degree of burghal character[4] are denominated 'Bor'.
Those which did not sustain that status until the 19th cent are in italics.
Municipal Boroughs were established by the Municipal Corporations Act, 1835,[5] or by later charter.

ACTON MB (1921[6]–65)
Acton

BRENTFORD AND CHISWICK MB (1932[6]–65)
New Brentford, Old Brentford, Chiswick

EALING MB (1901[7]–65)
Ealing

EDMONTON MB (1937[6]–65)
Edmonton

ENFIELD MB (1955[8]–65)
Enfield

FINCHLEY MB (1933[6]–65)
Finchley

HARROW MB (1954[9]–65)
Harrow

HENDON MB (1932[6]–65)
Hendon

HESTON AND ISLEWORTH MB (1932[6]–65)
Heston and Isleworth

HORNSEY MB (1903[10]–65)
Hornsey

SOUTHALL MB (1936[6]–65)
Norwood

SOUTHGATE MB (1933[6]–65)
Southgate

TOTTENHAM MB (1934[6]–65)
Tottenham

TWICKENHAM MB (1926[6]–65)
Twickenham

UXBRIDGE BOR,[11] MB (1955[8]–65)
pt Hillingdon (in Bor), Uxbridge (in MB)

WEMBLEY MB (1937[6]–65)
Wembley

WESTMINSTER BOR/MB (City) (1586–1889)[12]
Close of the Collegiate Church of St Peter (1866–89), Westminster St John the Evangelist (1727–1889), Westminster St Margaret

WILLESDEN MB (1933[6]–65)
Willesden

WOOD GREEN MB (1933[6]–65)
Wood Green

POOR LAW UNIONS

In Middx Poor Law County:[13]

BRENTFORD PLU
Acton, New Brentford, Old Brentford (1894–1930), Chiswick, Ealing, Greenford, Hanwell (1836–1926), Heston (1836–1927), Heston and Isleworth (1927–30), Isleworth (1836–1927), Perivale (1836–1926), Twickenham, West Twyford (1836–1926)

EDMONTON PLU (Middx, Essex, Herts)
Edmonton, Enfield, Hampstead (1837–48), Hornsey, Southgate (1894–1930), Tottenham, Wood Green (1894–1930)

HENDON PLU
Edgware, Harrow on the Hill, Harrow Weald (1894–1930), Hendon, Kingsbury, Pinner, Great Stanmore, Little Stanmore, Wealdstone (1894–1930), Wembley (1894–1930), Willesden (1835–96)

STAINES PLU
Ashford, East Bedfont, Cranford, Feltham, Hanworth, Harlington, Harmondsworth, Laleham, Littleton, Shepperton, Staines, Stanwell, Sunbury

UXBRIDGE PLU
Cowley, West Drayton, Harefield, Hayes, Hillingdon (1836–94), Hillingdon East (1894–1930), Hillingdon West (1894–1930), Ickenham, Northolt (1836–1928), Norwood, Ruislip, Uxbridge, Yiewsley (1896–1930)

WILLESDEN PAR[14] (1896–1930)
Willesden

In Other Poor Law Counties;

BARNET PLU (Herts, Middx)
Friern Barnet, Finchley, Monken Hadley,[15] South Mimms[16]

KINGSTON PLU (Surrey, Middx)
Hampton, Hampton Wick, Teddington

Middx Poor Law County, in Metropolis (1855–89), London Poor Law County thereafter:

BETHNAL GREEN PAR
Bethnal Green
CHELSEA PAR
Chelsea
CLERKENWELL PAR[18] (until 1869)
Clerkenwell
FULHAM PLU (1845–89)
Fulham, Hammersmith
HACKNEY PLU
Hackney, Stoke Newington
HAMPSTEAD PAR (1848–89)
Hampstead
HOLBORN PLU
Charterhouse (1877–89), Clerkenwell (1869–89), Furnival's Inn (1858–89), Gray's Inn (1858–89), Holborn St Andrew Above the Bars with St George the Martyr; Liberty of Saffron Hill, Hatton Garden, Ely Rents and Ely Place; St Sepulchre (1845–89), St Luke (1869–89), Staple Inn (1858–89)
ISLINGTON PAR[19]
Islington
KENSINGTON PLU (1837–45), PAR (1845–89)
Fulham (1837–45), Hammersmith (1837–45), Kensington, Paddington (1837–89)
CITY OF LONDON PLU (London, Middx)
Glasshouse Yard (1869–89)
EAST LONDON PLU (London, Middx)
pt St Botolph Aldersgate (1837–66), Glasshouse Yard (1866–69)
HMLT/PAR OF MILE END OLD TOWN (1857–89)
Mile End Old Town
PADDINGTON PAR (1845–89)
Paddington
POPLAR PLU
Bow, Bromley, Poplar
ST GEORGE'S PAR,[21] PLU (1870–89)
Close of the Collegiate Church of St Peter (1870–89), St George Hanover Square, Westminster St John the Evangelist, Westminster St Margaret
ST GEORGE IN THE EAST PAR
St George in the East
ST GILES IN THE FIELDS AND ST GEORGE BLOOMSBURY PAR[22]
St Giles in the Field and St George Bloomsbury
ST JAMES PAR[23] (until 1868)
Westminster St James
ST LUKE PAR[24] (until 1869)
St Luke
ST MARGARET AND ST JOHN PARS,[25] PLU (1867–70)
Westminster St John the Evalgelist, Westminster St Margaret
ST MARTIN IN THE FIELDS PAR (1835–68)
St Martin in the Fields
ST MARYLEBONE PAR[25]
St Marylebone
ST PANCRAS PAR
St Pancras
SHOREDITCH PAR[23]
Shoreditch
STEPNEY PLU
Limehouse, Mile End Old Town (1836–57), Ratcliffe, Shadwell, Wapping
STRAND PLU
Liberty of the Rolls, St Anne Within the Liberty of Westminster (1837–68), St Clement Danes, St Martin in the Fields (1868–99), St Mary le Strand, St Paul Covent Garden, Precinct of the Savoy
WESTMINSTER PLU (1868–89)
St Anne Within the Liberty of Westminster, Westminster St James
WHITECHAPEL PLU
Holy Trinity Minories, Mile End New Town, Norton Folgate, Old Artillery Ground, St Botolph Without Aldgate, St Katherine by the Tower, Spitalfields, Tower of London, Whitechapel

SANITARY DISTRICTS

In Middx:
ACTON USD
Acton
BARNET RSD
same as PLU for Middx pars less Friern Barnet (1883–94)
FRIERN BARNET USD (1883[26]–94)
Friern Barnet (pt 1883–91, ent 1891–94)
BRENTFORD RSD
same as PLU less Acton, New Brentford, Chiswick, Ealing, Hanwell (1885–94), Heston, Isleworth, Twickenham
BRENTFORD USD
New Brentford, pt Ealing (1885–94)
CHISWICK USD
Chiswick
EALING USD
Ealing (ent 1875–85, pt 1885–94)
EDMONTON USD
Edmonton (pt 1875–81, pt 1881–94)
ENFIELD USD
pt Edmonton (1883–94), Enfield (ent 1875–83, pt 1883–94)
FINCHLEY USD
Finchley
HANWELL USD (1885[27]–94)
Hanwell
HARROW USD
pt Harrow on the Hill
HENDON RSD
same as PLU less pt Harrow on the Hill, Hendon, Willesden
HENDON USD
Hendon
HESTON AND ISLEWORTH USD
Heston, Isleworth
HORNSEY USD
pt Friern Barnet (1883–91), pt Hornsey
SOUTH HORNSEY USD
pt Hornsey

KINGSTON RSD
same as PLU for Middx pars less Teddington
NORWOOD USD (1891[28]–94)
Norwood
SOUTHGATE USD (1881[29]–94)
pt Edmonton, pt Tottenham (1881–92)
STAINES RSD
same as PLU less Staines
STAINES USD
Staines
TEDDINGTON USD
Teddington
TOTTENHAM USD
Tottenham (ent 1875–88, pt 1888–94)
TWICKENHAM USD
Twickenham
UXBRIDGE RSD
same as PLU less Norwood (1891–94), Uxbridge
UXBRIDGE USD
pt Hillingdon, Uxbridge
WILLESDEN USD
Willesden (pt 1875–83, ent 1883–94)
WOOD GREEN USD (1888[30]–94)
pt Tottenham

MIDDLESEX PARISHES IN THE METROPOLIS, 1855–99[29]

Pars Under Vestries:
Bethnal Green, Chelsea, Clerkenwell, Fulham (1886[30]–99), Hackney (1894–99), Hammersmith (1886[30]–99), Hampstead, Ilsington, Kensington, Mile End Old Town, Paddington, St George Hanover Square, St George in the East, St Luke, St Martin in the Fields, St Marylebone, St Pancras, Shoreditch, Stoke Newington (1894–99), Westminster St James, Westminster St Margaret and St John Combined Vestry (1887[31]–99)

Pars Within Districts:
FULHAM DIST (1855–86[30])
Fulham, Hammersmith
HACKNEY DIST (1855–94)
Hackney, Stoke Newington
HOLBORN DIST
Glasshouse Yard; Liberty of Saffron Hill, Hatton Garden, Ely Rent and Ely Place; St Andrew Holborn Above the Bars with St George the Martyr, St Sepulchre
LIMEHOUSE DIST
Limehouse, Ratcliffe, Shadwell, Wapping
POPLAR DIST
Bow, Bromley, Poplar
ST GILES DIST
St Giles in the Fields and St George Bloomsbury
STRAND DIST
Liberty of the Rolls, St Anne Within the Liberty of Westminster, St Clement Danes, St Mary le Strand, St Paul Covent Garden, Precinct of the Savoy
WESTMINSTER DIST (1855–87[31])
Westminster St John the Evangelist, Westminster St Margaret
WHITECHAPEL DIST
Holy Trinity Minories, Mile End New Town, Norton Folgate, Old Artillery Ground, Precinct of St Katherine, St Botolph Without Aldgate, Spitalfields, Tower of London, Whitechapel

ADMINISTRATIVE COUNTY

For MBs see BOROUGHS. The pars in the Metropolis were in Middx 1888–99, and in London thereafter.

ACTON UD (1894–1921[32])
Acton
FRIERN BARNET UD
Friern Barnet
BRENTFORD UD (1894–1927[33])
New Brentford, Old Brentford
BRENTFORD AND CHISWICK UD (1927[33]–32[32])
New Brentford, Old Brentford, Chiswick
CHISWICK UD (1894–1927[33])
Chiswick
EALING UD (1894–1901[32])
Ealing
EDMONTON UD (1894–1937[32])
Edmonton
ENFIELD UD (1894–1955[32])
Enfield
FELTHAM UD (1904[34]–65)
East Bedfont (1934–65), Feltham, Hanworth (1934–65)
FINCHLEY UD (1894–1933[32])
Finchley
GREENFORD UD (1894[35]–1926[36])
Greenford, Perivale, West Twyford
HAMPTON UD (1894–1937[37])
Hampton
HAMPTON WICK UD (1894–1937[37])
Hampton Wick
HANWELL UD (1894–1926[36])
Hanwell
HARROW UD (1934[38]–54[32])
Harrow
HARROW ON THE HILL UD (1894–1934[38])
Harrow on the Hill
HAYES UD (1904[39]–1930[40])
Hayes

HAYES AND HARLINGTON UD (1930[40]–65)
Cranford (1930–34), Hayes, Harlington
HENDON RD (1894–1934[38])
Edgware (1894–1931), Pinner, Great Stanmore, Little Stanmore, Harrow Weald
HENDON UD (1894–1932[32])
Hendon
HESTON AND ISLEWORTH UD (1894–1932[32])
Heston (1894–1927), Heston and Isleworth (1927–32), Isleworth (1894–1927)
HORNSEY UD (1894–1903[32])
Hornsey
SOUTH HORNSEY UD (1894–99[41])
pt Hornsey (1894–96), South Hornsey (1896–99)
KINGSBURY UD (1900[42]–34[38])
Kingsbury
SOUTH MIMMS RD (1894–1934[38])
South Mimms
POTTER'S BAR UD (1934[38]–65)
South Mimms
RUISLIP NORTHWOOD UD (1904[43]–65)
Ruislip
SOUTHALL NORWOOD UD (1894–1936[44])
Norwood
SOUTHGATE UD (1894–1933[32])
Southgate
STAINES RD (1894–1930[40])
Ashford, East Bedfont, Cranford, Feltham (1894–1930), Hanworth, Harlington, Harmondsworth, Laleham, Littleton, Shepperton, Stanwell
STAINES UD
Ashford (1930–65), Laleham (1930–65), Staines (1930–65), Stanwell
SUNBURY ON THAMES UD (1894[45]–1965)
Littleton (1930–65), Shepperton (1930–65), Sunbury
TEDDINGTON UD (1894–1937[37])
Teddington
TOTTENHAM UD (1894–1934[32])
Tottenham
TWICKENHAM UD (1894–1926[32])
Twickenham
UXBRIDGE RD (1894–1929[49])
Cowley, West Drayton, Harefield, Hayes (1894–1904), Hillingdon East, Ickenham, Northolt (1894–1928), Ruislip (1894–1904), Yiewsley (1894–1911)
UXBRIDGE UD (1894–1955[32])
Cowley (1929–38), Harefield (1929–38), Hillingdon East (1929–38), Hillingdon West (1929–38), Ickenham (1929–38), Uxbridge
WEALDSTONE UD (1894[46]–1934[38])
Wealdstone
WEMBLEY UD (1894[46]–1937[32])
Wembley
WILLESDEN UD (1894–1933[32])
Willesden
WOOD GREEN UD (1894–1933[32])
Wood Green
YIEWSLEY UD (1911[47]–29[47])
Yiewsley
YIEWSLEY AND WEST DRAYTON UD (1929[47]–65)
West Drayton (1929–49), Harmondsworth (1929–49), Yiewsley (1929–49), Yiewsley and West Drayton (1949–65)

NORFOLK

ALTERATIONS IN COUNTY BOUNDARIES

As noted by year below, Norfolk pars gained territory from or lost it to pars in adjoining counties or county boroughs, or were entirely transferred to them. Details of these alterations are noted in Part I of the *Guide* under Norfolk.

ANCIENT COUNTY (until 1889: Hds, Bors, MBs, PLUs, RSDs, USDs)
1885 Earsham, Mendham.

ADMINISTRATIVE COUNTY (1889–1974: Hds,[1] PLUs, MBs, RDs, UDs, with Norwich CB and Great Yarmouth CB associated)
1889 Outwell, Runham, Thetford St Cuthbert, Thetford St Mary, Upwell, Welney. *1894* Rushford. *1895* Redmere, West Welney. *1907* Catton, Sprowston. *1934* Emneth, Upwell, Walpole St Peter. *1951* Sprowston, Thorpe next Norwich. *1957* Terrington St Clement. *1968* Catton, Colney, Costessy, Hellesdon, Horsham St Faith and Newton St Faith, Spixworth.

NON-METROPLOLITAN COUNTY (from 1974: Dists
1974 Belton, Bradwell, Burgh Castle, Fritton, Hopton-on-Sea.

ASSOCIATED COUNTY BOROUGHS

NORWICH CB
Bdry: 1907,[30] 1951,[31] 1968.[32]

GREAT YARMOUTH CB
No bdry alt 1889–1974.

HUNDREDS[1]

BLOFIELD HD
Blofield, Bradeston (until 1884), Brundall, Buckenham, Burlingham St Andrew, Burlingham St Edmund, Burlingham St Peter, Cantley, Freethorpe, Hassingham, Limpenhoe, Lingwood, Great Plumstead, Little Plumstead, Postwick, Southwood, Strumpshaw, Thorpe next Norwich,[2] Witton

BROTHERCROSS HD
Burnham Deepdale, Burnham Norton, Burnham Overy, Burnham Sutton (until 1729), Burnham Sutton cum Burnham Ulph (from 1729), Burnham Thorpe, Burnham Ulph (until 1729), Burnham Westgate, North Creake, South Creake, Waterden

CLACKCLOSE HD
Barton Bendish, Beechamwell, Bexwell, Boughton, Crimplesham, Denver, West Dereham, Downham Market, Fincham (from *ca* 1800), Fincham St Martin (until *ca* 1800), Fincham St Michael (until *ca* 1800), Fordham, Hilgay, Marham, pt Outwell, Redmere (from 1858), Roxham, South Runcton, Runcton Holme, Ryston, pt Shingham, Shouldham, Shouldham Thorpe, Southery, Stoke Ferry, Stow Bardolph, Stradsett, Tottenhill, Wallington with Thorpland, pt Upwell, Watlington, pt Welney (from 1866), Wereham, Wimbotsham, Wormegay, Wretton

CLAVERING HD
Aldeby, Bergh Apton, Brooke, Burgh St Peter, Ellingham, Geldeston, Gillingham (from 1748), Gillingham All Saints (until 1748), Gillingham St Mary (until 1748), Haddiscoe, Hales, Heckingham, Howe, Kirby Cane, Norton Subcourse, Raveningham, Stockton, Thorpe next Haddiscoe, Thurlton, Toft Monks, Wheatacre

DEPWADE HD
Ashwellthorpe, Aslacton, Bunwell, Carleton Rode, Forncett St Mary, Forncett St Peter, Fritton, Fundenhall, Hapton, Hardwick, Hempnall, Morning Thorpe, Moulton St Mary, Moulton St Michael, Stratton St Mary, Stratton St Michael, Shelton, Tacolneston, Tasburgh, Tharston, Tibebham, Wacton

DISS HD
Bressingham, Burston, Diss, Dickleburgh, Fersfield, Frenze, Gissing, Roydon, Scole, Shelfanger, Shimpling, Thelveton, Tivetshall St Margaret, Tivetshall St Mary, Winfarthing

EARSHAM HD
Alburgh, Billingford, Brockdish, Denton, Earsham (pt until 1885, ent from 1885), pt Mendham (until 1885), Needham, Pulham St Mary Magdalen, Pulham St Mary the Virgin, Redenham with Harleston, Rushall, Starston, Thorpe Abbots, Wortwell

NORTH ERPINGHAM HD
Aldborough, Antingham, Aylmerton, Barningham Norwood, Barningham Winter or Barningham Town, East Beckham, Beeston Regis, Bessingham, Cromer, Felbrigg, Gimingham, Gresham, Gunton, Hanworth, Knapton, Matlask, Metton, Mundesley, Northrepps, Overstrand, Plumstead, Roughton,

Runton, Sheringham, Sidestrand, Southrepps, Suffield, Sustead, Thorpe Market, Thurgarton, Trimingham, Trunch

SOUTH ERPINGHAM HD
Alby (until 1884), Alby with Thwaite (from 1884), Aylsham, Baconsthorpe, Banningham, Little Bargham, West Beckham, Belaugh, Blickling, Booton, Brampton, Burgh, Buxton, Calthorpe, Cawston, Colby, Coltishall, Corpusty, Erpingham, Great Hautbois, Hevingham, Heydon, Ingworth, Irmingland, Itteringham, Lammas with Little Hautbois, Mannington, Marsham, Oulton, Oxnead, Saxthorpe, Scottow, Skeyton, Stratton Strawless, Swanton Abbot, Thwaite (until 1884), Tuttington, Wickmere, Wolterton

EYNESFORD HD
Alderford, Bawdeswell, Billingford, Bintree, Brandiston, Bylaugh, Elsing, Foulsham, Foxley, Guestwick, Guist, Hackford, Haveringland, Hindolveston, Lyng, Morton on the Hill, Reepham with Kerdiston, Ringland, Sall, Sparham, Swannington, Themelthorpe, Thurning, Twyford, Weston Longville, Whitwell, Great Witchingham, Little Witchingham, Wood Dalling, Wood Norton

EAST FLEGG HD
Caister next Yarmouth, Filby, Mautby, Ormesby St Margaret with Scratby, Ormesby St Michael, Runham, Stokesby with Herringby, Thrigby

WEST FLEGG HD
Ashby with Oby, Billockby, Burgh St Margaret, Clippesby, Hemsby, Martham, Repps with Bastwick, Rollesby, East Somerton, West Somerton, Thurne, Winterton

FOREHOE HD[3]
Barford, Barnham Broom, Bawburgh, Bixton (until 1680), Bowthorpe, Brandon Parva, Carleton Forehoe, Colton, Costessey, Coston, Crownthorpe, Deopham, Easton, Hackford, Hingham, Honingham, Kimberley, Marlingford, Morley St Botolph, Morley St Peter, Runhall, Welborne, Wicklewood, Wramplingham, Wymondham

FREEBRIDGE LYNN HD[4]
Appleton (until early 18th cent), Anmer, Ashwicken, Babingley, Bawsey, West Bilney, Castle Acre, Castle Rising,[2] Congham (from 1684), Congham St Andrew (until 1684), Congham St Mary (until 1684), Dersingham, Flitcham (until early 18th cent), Flitcham with Appleton (from early 18th cent), Gayton, Gayton Thorpe, Gaywood, Grimston, Harpley, Hillington, Leziate, Great Massingham, Little Massingham, Middleton, Mintlyn, West Newton, Pentney, Roydon, North Runcton, Sandringham, Setchey, East Walton, Westacre, East Winch, West Winch, Wolverton, North Wootton, South Wootton

FREEBRIDGE MARSHLAND HD[4]
Clenchwarton, Emneth, North Lynn, West Lynn, Terrington St Clement, Terrington St John, Tilney All Saints, Tilney St Lawrence, Tilney with Islington, Walpole St Andrew, Walpole St Peter, Walsoken, Walsoken Hungate (from 1866), East Walton, Wiggenhall St German, Wiggenhall St Mary Magdalen, Wiggenhall St Mary the Virgin, Wiggenhall St Peter

GALLOW HD
Alethorpe (from 1858), Bagthorpe, Barmer, East Barsham, North Barsham, West Barsham, Broomsthorpe (from 1858), Dunton cum Doughton, Fakenham, Fulmodeston cum Croxton, Helhoughton, Hempton, Houghton, Kettlestone, Pensthorpe, Pudding Norton, East Raynham, South Raynham, West Raynham, East Rudham, West Rudham, Great Ryburgh, Little Ryburgh, Sculthorpe, Shereford, Little Snoring, Stibbard, Syderstone, Tatterford, Tattersett, Testerton, Toftrees

NORTH GREENHOE HD
Barney, Binham, Cockthorpe, Egmere, Field Dalling, Hindringham, Houghton St Giles, Holkham, Quarles (from 1858), Great Snoring, Stiffkey, Thursford, Great Walsingham, Little Walsingham, Warham All Saints, Warham St Mary, Wells next the Sea, Wighton

SOUTH GREENHOE HD
South Acre, Bodney, East Bradenham, West Bradenham, Caldecote, Cockley Cley, Great Cressingham, Little Cressingham, Didlington, Foulden, Gooderstone, Hilborough, Holme Hale, Houghton on the Hill, Langford, Narborough, Narford, Necton, Newton by Castle Acre, Oxborough, North Pickenham, South Pickenham, Sporle with Palgrave, pt Shingham, Swaffham

GRIMSHOE HD[5]
Buckenham Tofts, Colveston, Cranwich, Croxton, Feltwell, Feltwell Anchor (from 1858), Hockwold (until 1720), Hockwold cum Wilton (from 1720), Ickburgh, Lynford, Methwold, Mundford, Northwold, Santon, Stanford, Sturston, West Tofts, Weeting All Saints (until 1651), Weeting St Mary (until 1651), (until 1651), Weeting-with-Bromehill (from 1651), Wilton (until 1720)

GUILTCROSS HD
Banham, Blo' Norton, Garboldisham (from 1734), Garboldisham All Saints (until 1734), Garboldisham St John (until 1734), Gasthorpe, East Harling, West Harling, Kenninghall, North Lopham, South Lopham, Quidenham, Riddlesworth, pt Rushford, Great and Little Snarehill (from 1858)

HAPPING HD
Brumstead, Catsfield, Happisburgh, Hempstead with Eccles, Hickling, Horsey, Ingham, Lessingham, Ludham, Palling, Potter Heigham, East Ruston, Stalham, Sutton, Walcott, Waxham

HENSTEAD HD
Arminghall, Bixley, Bramerton, Caister St Edmund, Framingham Earl, Framingham Pigot, Holverston, Kirby Bedon, Poringland, Rockland St Mary, Saxlingham Nethergate, Saxlingham Thorpe, Shotesham All Saints, Shotesham St Mary, Stoke Holy Cross, Surlingham (from *ca* 1705), Surlingham St Mary (until *ca* 1705), Surlingham St Saviour (until *ca* 1705), Trowse with Newton,[2] Whitlingham, Yelverton

HOLT HD
Bale, Blakeney, Bodham, Briningham, Brinton, Briston, Cley next the Sea, Edgefield, Glandford with Bayfield, Gunton, Hempstead, Holt, Hun-

worth, Kelling, Langham, Little Langham (until early 17th cent), Letheringsett, Melton Constable, Morston, Salthouse, Saxlingham, Sharrington, Stody, Swanton Novers, Thornage, Weybourne, Wiveton

HUMBLEYARD HD
Bracon Ash, East Carleton, Colney, Cringleford, Dunston, Flordon, Hethel, Hethersett, Intwood, Keswick, Ketteringham, Markshall, Great Melton (from 1728), Great Melton All Saints (until 1728), Great Melton St Mary (until 1728), Little Melton, Mulbarton, Newton Flotman, Swainsthorpe, Swardeston, Wreningham

LAUNDITCH HD
Beeston with Bittering, Beetley, East Bilney, Brisley, Colkirk, pt East Dereham, Great Dunham, Little Dunham, North Elmham, Great Fransham, Little Fransham, Gateley, Godwick (until 1630), Gressenhall, Hoe, Horningtoft, Kempstone, East Lexham, West Lexham, Litcham, Longham, Mileham, Oxwick and Pattesley, Rougham, Scarning, Stanfield, Swanton Morley, Titteshall, Weasenham All Saints, Weasebham St Peter, Wellingham, Wendling, Whissonsett, Worthing

LODDON HD
Alpington, Ashby St Mary, Bedingham, Broome, Carleton St Peter, Chedgrave, Claxton, Ditchingham, Hardley, Hedenham, Hellington, Kirstead, Langley, Loddon, Mundham, Seething, Sisland, Thurton, Thwaite, Topcroft, Woodton

MITFORD HD
Cranworth, pt East Dereham, Garveston, Hardingham, Hockering, Letton, Mattishall, Mattishall Burgh, Reymerston, Shipdham, Southburgh, Thuxton, East Tuddenham, North Tuddenham, Westfield, Whinburgh, Woodrising, Yaxham

SHROPHAM HD
Attleborough, Besthorpe, Brettenham, Bridgham, New Buckenham,[2] Old Buckenham, Eccles, Great Ellingham, Hargham, Hockham, Illington, Kilverstone, Larling, Rockland All Saints (until 1885), Rockland All Saints and St Andrew (from 1885), Rockland St Andrew (until 1885), Roudham, Shropham, Snetterton, Wilby, East Wretham, West Wretham

SMITHDON HD
Barwick, Great Bircham, Bircham Newton, Bircham Tofts, Brancaster, Choseley (from 1858), Docking, Fring, Heacham, Holme next the Sea, Hunstanton, Ingoldisthorpe, Ringstead (from 1771), Ringstead St Andrew (until 1771), Ringstead St Peter (until 1771), Sedgeford, Shernborne, Snettisham, Stanhoe, Thornham, Titchwell

TAVERHAM HD
Attlebridge, Beeston St Andrew, Catton, Crostwick, Drayton, Felthorpe, Frettenham, Hainford, Hellesdon,[2] Horsford, Horsham St Faith with Newton St Faith, Horstead with Stanninghall, Rackheath, Salhouse, Spixworth, Sprowston, Taverham, Wroxham

TUNSTEAD HD
Ashmanhaugh, Bacton, Barton Turf, Beeston St Lawrence, Bradfield, Crostwight, Dilham, Edingthorpe, Felmingham, Honing, Horning, Hoveton St John, Hoveton St Peter, Irstead, Neatishead, Paston, Ridlington, Sco' Ruston, Sloley, Smallburgh, Swafield, Tunstead, North Walsham, Westwick, Witton, Worstead

WALSHAM HD
Acle, Beighton, Halvergate, Hemblington, Moulton St Mary, Ranworth with Panxworth, Reedham, Tunstall, Upton with Fishley, Walsham St Lawrence, Walsham St Mary, Wickhampton, Woodbastwick

BOROUGHS

Units with some degree of burghal character[33] are denominated 'Bor'.
Those which did not sustain that status until the 19th cent are in italics.
Municipal Boroughs were established by the Municipal Corporations Act, 1835,[34] or by later charter.

NEW BUCKENHAM BOR
New Buckenham

CASTLE RISING BOR
Castle Rising

KING'S LYNN BOR[6]
King's Lynn (1935–74), King's Lynn St Margaret (until 1935), South Lynn (1557–1935)

NORWICH BOR/MB/CB[7]
until 1889: Earlham, Easton, Heigham, pt Hellesdon, Lakenham, Norwich All Saints, Norwich Liberty of the Town Close, Norwich St Andrew, Norwich St Augustine, Norwich St Benedict, Norwich St Clement, Norwich St Edmund, Norwich St Etheldreda, Norwich St George Colegate, Norwich St George Tombland, Norwich St Giles, Norwich St Gregory, Norwich St Helen, Norwich St James, Norwich St John Maddermarket, Norwich St John Sepulchre, Norwich St John Timberhill, Norwich St Julian, Norwich St Lawrence, Norwich St Margaret, Norwich St Martin at Oak, Norwich St Martin at Palace, Norwich St Mary Coslany, Norwich St Mary in the Marsh, Norwich St Michael at Plea, Norwich St Michael at Thorn, Norwich St Michael Coslany, Norwich St Paul, Norwich St Peter Hungate, Norwich St Peter Mancroft, Norwich St Peter Mountergate, Norwich St Peter Southgate, Norwich St Saviour, Norwich St Simon and St Jude, Norwich St Stephen, Norwich St Swithin, pt Thorpe next Norwich, pt Troswe with Newton
1889–1974: Norwich

THETFORD BOR/MB[7] (Norfolk, Suffolk until 1889, ent Norfolk 1889–1974[8])
Thetford (1924–74), Thetford St Cuthbert (until 1924), Thetford St Mary (until 1924), Thetford St Peter (until 1924)

GREAT YARMOUTH BOR/MB/CB[6] (Norfolk, Suffolk until 1889, sep and associated with Norfolk thereafter)
Gorleston (pt until 1835, ent 1835–1974), pt Runham (1889–94), Runham Vauxhall (1894–1974), Great Yarmouth

POOR LAW UNIONS

In Norwich Poor Law County:[9]

AYLSHAM PLU
Alby (1836–84), Alby with Thwaite (1885–1930), Aylsham, Banningham, Little Barningham, Belaugh, Blickling, Brampton, Burgh, Buxton, Calthorpe, Cawston, Colby, Coltishall, Corpusty, Erpingham, Foulsham, Guestwick, Hackford, Great Hautbois, Hevingham, Heydon, Hindolveston, Ingworth, Irmingland, Itteringham, Lammas with Little Hautbois, Mannington, Marsham, Oulton, Oxnead, Reepham with Kerdiston, Sall, Saxthorpe, Scottow, Skeyton, Stratton Strawless, Swanton Abbot, Themelthorpe, Thurning, Thwaite, Tuttington, Whitwell, Wickmere, Wolterton, Wood Dalling, Wood Norton

BLOFIELD PLU
Acle, Beighton, Blofield, Bradeston (1835–84), Brundall, Buckenham, Burlingham St Andrew, Burlingham St Edmund, Burlingham St Peter, Cantley, Freethorpe, Halvergate, Hassingham, Hemblington, Limpenhoe, Lingwood, Moulton St Mary, Great Plumstead, Little Plumstead, Postwick, Ranworth with Panxworth, Reedham, Southwood, Strumpshaw, Thorpe next Norwich, Tunstall, Upton with Fishley, South Walsham (1897–1930), South Walsham St Mary (1835–97), South Walsham St Lawrence (1835–97), Wickhampton, Witton, Woodbastwick

BRINTON INCORPORATION (1738–1860s)
Brinton, Melton Constable

DEPWADE PLU
Alburgh, Ashwellthorpe, Aslacton, Billingford, Bressingham (1902–30), Brockdish, Bunwell, Burston, Carleton Rode, Denton, Dickleburgh, Diss, Earsham, Fersfield (1902–30), Forncett St Mary, Forncett St Peter, Fritton, Fundenhall, Gissing, Hapton, Hardwick, Hempnall, Morning Thorpe, Moulton St Michael, Needham, Pulham St Mary Magdalen, Pulham St Mary the Virgin, Redenham with Harleston, Roydon (1902–30), Rushall, Scole, Shelfanger (1902–30), Shelton, Shimpling, Starston, Stratton St Mary, Stratton St Michael, Tacolneston, Tasburgh, Tharston, Thelveton, Thorpe Abbots, Tibenham, Tivetshall St Margaret, Tivetshall St Mary, Wacton, Winfarthing (1902–30), Wortwell

DOCKING PLU
Anmer, Bagthorpe, Barmer, Barwick, Great Bircham, Bircham Newton, Bircham Tofts, Brancaster, Broomsthorpe, Burnham Deepdale, Burnham Market (1929–30), Burnham Norton, Burnham Overy, Burnham Sutton cum Burnham Ulph (1835–1929), Burnham Thorpe, Burnham Westgate (1835–1929), Choseley (1858[10]–1930), North Creake, South Creake, Dersingham, Docking, Fring, Heacham, Holme next the Sea, Houghton, Hunstanton, New Hunstanton (1894–1930), Ingoldisthorpe, Ringstead, East Rudham, West Rudham, Sedgeford, Shernborne, Snettisham, Stanhoe, Syderstone, Thornham, Waterden, Titchwell

DOWNHAM PLU (Norfolk, Cambs/IoE until 1889, ent Norfolk thereafter)
Barton Bendish, Bexwell, Boughton, Crimplesham, Denver, West Dereham, Downham Market, Downham West (1894–1930), Fincham, Fordham, Hilgay, Marham, Roxham, South Runcton, Runcton Holme, Ryston, Shouldham, Shouldham Thorpe, Southery, Stoke Ferry, Stow Bardolph, Stradsett, Tottenhill, Wallington with Thorpland, Watlington, Welney,[11] West Welney[12] (1895–1930), Wereham, Wiggenhall St German, Wiggenhall St Mary Magdalen, Wiggenhall St Mary the Virgin, Wiggenhall St Peter, Wimbotsham, Wormegay, Wretton

ERPINGHAM PLU
Aldborough, Antingham, Aylmerton, Baconsthorpe, Barningham Norwood, Barningham Winter or Barningham Town, East Beckham, West Beckham, Beeston Regis, Bessingham, Bodham, Briston, Cley next the Sea, Cromer, Edgefield, Felbrigg, Gimingham, Glandford with Bayfield, Gresham, Gunton, Hanworth, Hempstead, Holt, Hunworth, Kelling, Knapton, Letheringsett, Matlask, Metton, Mundesley, Northrepps, Overstrand, Plumstead, Roughton, Runton, Salthouse, Sheringham, Upper Sheringham (1901–30), Sidestrand, Southrepps, Stody, Suffield, Sustead, Thorpe Market, Thornage, Thurgarton, Trimingham, Trunch, Weybourne

EAST AND WEST FLEGG INCORP
Ashby with Oby, Billockby, Burgh St Margaret, Caister next Yarmouth, Clippesby, Filby, Hemsby, Martham, Mautby, Ormesby St Margaret with Scratby, Ormesby St Michael, Repps with Bastwick, Rollesby, Runham, Runham Vauxhall (1894–1930), East Somerton, West Somerton, Stokesby with Herringby, Thurne, Winterton

FOREHOE INCORP/PLU
Barford, Barnham Broom, Bawburgh, Bowthorpe, Brandon Parva, Carleton Forehoe, Colton, Costessey, Coston, Crownthorpe, Deopham, Easton, Hackford, Hingham, Kimberley, Marlingford, Morley St Botolph, Morley St Peter, Runhall, Welborne, Wicklewood, Wramplingham

GUILTCROSS PLU (1835–1902)
Banham, Blo' Norton, Bressingham, Bridgham, New Buckenham, Old Buckenham, Eccles, Fersfield, Garboldisham, Gasthorpe, East Harling, West Harling, Kenninghall, North Lopham, South Lopham,

Quidenham, Riddlesworth, Roydon, Shelfanger, Wilby, Winfarthing

HENTEAD PLU

Arminghall, Bixley, Bracon Ash, Bramerton, Caister St Edmund, East Carleton, Colney, Cringleford, Flordon, Framingham Earl, Framingham Pigot, Hethel, Hethersett, Holverston, Intwood, Keswick, Ketteringham, Kirby Bedon, Markshall, Great Melton, Little Melton, Mulbarton, Newton Flotman, Poringland, Rockland St Mary, Saxlingham Nethergate, Saxlingham Thorpe, Shotesham All Saints, Shotesham St Mary, Stoke Holy Cross, Surlingham, Swainsthorpe, Swardeston, Trowse with Newton, Whitlingham, Wreningham

LODDON AND CLAVERING PLU

Aldeby, Alpington, Ashby St Mary, Bedingham, Bergh Apton, Brooke, Broome, Burgh St Peter, Carleton St Peter, Chedgrave, Claxton, Ditchingham, Ellingham, Geldeston, Gillingham, Haddiscoe, Hales, Hardley, Heckingham, Hedenham, Hellington, Howe, Kirby Cane, Kirstead, Langley, Loddon, Mundham, Norton Subcourse, Raveningham, Seething, Sisland, Stockland, Thorpe next Haddiscoe, Thurlton, Thurton, Thwaite, Toft Monks, Topcroft, Wheatacre, Woodton, Yelverton

FREEBRIDGE LYNN PLU

Ashwicken, Babingley, Bawsey, West Bilney, Castle Acre, Castle Rising, Congham, Flitcham with Appleton, Gayton, Gayton Thorpe, Gaywood, Grimston, Harpley, Hillington, Leziate, Great Massingham, Little Massingham, Middleton, Mintlyn, West Newton, Pentney, Roydon, North Runcton, Sandringham, Setchey, West Walton, Westacre, East Winch, West Winch, Wolferton, North Wootton, South Wootton

KING'S LYNN PLU

King's Lynn St Margaret, North Lynn, South Lynn, West Lynn

MITFORD AND LAUNDITCH PLU

Bawdeswell, Beeston with Bittering, Beetley, Billingford, East Bilney, Bintree, Brisley, Bylaugh, Colkirk, Cranworth, East Dereham, Great Dunham, Little Dunham, North Elmham, Elsing, Foxley, Great Fransham, Little Fransham, Garveston, Gateley, Gressenhall, Guist, Hardingham, Hockering, Hoe, Horningtoft, Kempstone, Letton, East Lexham, West Lexham, Litcham, Longham, Lyng, Mattishall, Mattishall Burgh, Mileham, Oxwick with Pattesley, Reymerston, Rougham, Scarning, Shipdham, Southburgh, Sparham, Stanfield, Swanton Morley, Tittleshall, East Tuddenham, North Tuddenham, Twyford, Weasenham All Saints, Weasenham St Peter, Wellingham, Wendling, Westfield, Whinburgh, Whissonsett, Woodrising, Worthing, Yaxham

ST FAITH'S PLU

Alderford, Attlebridge, Beeston St Andrew, Booton, Brandiston, Catton, Crostwick, Drayton, Felthorpe, Frettenham, Hainford, Haveringland, Hellesdon, Honingham, Horsford, Horsham St Faith with Newton St Faith, Horstead with Stanninghall, Morton on the Hill, Norwich St Mary in the Marsh (1836–89), Rackheath, Ringland, Salhouse, Spixworth, Sprowston, Swannington, Taverham, Weston Longville, Great Witchingham, Little Witchingham, Wroxham

SMALLBURGH PLU–Renaming 1870 of TUNSTEAD AND HAPPING INCORP, qv where all pars are listed for both

SWAFFHAM PLU

South Acre, Ashill, Beechamwell, Bodney, East Bradenham, West Bradenham, Buckenham Tofts, Caldecote, Cockley Cley, Colveston, Great Cressingham, Little Cressingham, Didlington, Foulden, Gooderstone, Hilborough, Houghton on the Hill, Holme Hale, Ickburgh, Langford, Narborough, Narford, Necton, Newton by Castle Acre, Oxborough, North Pickenham, South Pickenham, Saham Toney, Shingham, Sporle with Palgrave, Stanford. Swaffham, Threxton

THETFORD PLU (Norolk, Suffolk)

Blo' Norton (1902–30), Brettenham, Bridgham (1902–30), Cranwich, Croxton, Feltwell, Feltwell Anchor (1858[10]–1929, Garboldisham (1902–30), Gasthorpe (1902–30), East Harling (1902–30), West Harling (1902–30), Hockwold cum Wilton, Kilverstone, North Lopham (1902–30), South Lopham (1902–30), Lynford, Methwold, Mundford, Northwold, Riddlesworth (1902–30), Rushford, Santon, Great and Little Snarehill (1858[10]–1930), Sturston, Thetford (1924–30), Thetford St Cuthbert[13] (1835–1924), Thetford St Mary[13] (1835–1924), Thetford St Peter (1835–1924), West Tofts, Weeting-with-Bromehill, East Wretham, West Wretham

TUNSTEAD AND HAPPING INCORP (Renamed 1870 SMALLBURGH PLU; pars listed here only for brevity's sake)

Ashmanhaugh, Bacton, Barton Turf, Beeston St Lawrence, Bradfield, Brumstead, Catfield, Crostwight, Dilham, Edingthorpe, Felmingham, Happisburgh, Hempstead with Eccles, Hickling, Honing, Horning, Horsey, Hoveton St John, Hoveton St Peter, Ingham, Irstead, Lessingham, Ludham, Neatishead, Palling, Paston, Potter Heigham, Ridlington, East Ruston, Sco' Ruston, Sloley, Smallburgh, Stalham, Sutton, Swafield, Tunstead, Walcott, North Walsham, Waxham, Westwick, Witton, Worstead

WALSINGHAM PLU

Bale, Barney, East Barsham, North Barsham, West Barsham, Binham, Blakeney, Briningham, Brinton (1860s–1930), Cockthorpe, Dunton cum Doughton, Egmere, Fakenham, Field Dalling, Fulmodeston cum Croxton, Gunthorpe, Helhoughton, Hempton, Hindringham, Holkham, Houghton St Giles, Kettlesbaston, Langham, Melton Constable (1860s–1930), Morston, Pensthorpe, Pudding Norton, Quarles (1858[10]–1930), East Raynham, South Raynham, West Raynham, Great Ryburgh, Little Ryburgh. Saxlingham, Sculthorpe, Sharrington, Shereford, Great Snoring, Little Snoring, Stibbard, Stiffkey, Swanton Novers, Tatterford, Tattersett, Testerton, Thursford, Toftrees, Great Walsingham, Little Walsingham, Warham All Saints, Warham St Mary, Wells next the Sea, Wighton, Wiveton

WAYLAND PLU
Attleborough, Banham (1902–30), Besthorpe, Breckles, New Buckenham (1902–30), Old Buckenham (1902–30), Carbrooke, Caston, Eccles (1902–30), Great Ellingham, Little Ellingham, Griston, Hargham, Hockham, Illington, Kenninghall (1902–30), Larling, Merton, Ovington, Quidenham (1902–30), Rockland All Saints (1835–85), Rockland All Saints and St Andrew (1885–1930), Rockland St Andrew (1835–85), Rockland St Peter, Roudham, Scoulton, Shropham, Snetterton, Stow Bedon, Thompson, Tottington, Watton, Wilby (1903–30)

YARMOUTH PLU (Norfolk, Suffolk until 1889, Great Yarmouth CB 1889–1930)
Gorleston,[16] Great Yarmouth

In Other Poor Law Counties:
ELY (Cambs/IoE)
Redmere[14] (1858[10]–1930)
HOXNE PLU (Suffolk)
Mendham[15]
WISBECH PLU (Cambs/IoE)
Clenchwarton, Emneth, Outwell,[16] Terrington St Clement, Terrington St John, Tilney All Saints, Tilney St Lawrence, Tilney with Islington, Upwell,[16] Walpole St Andrew, Walpole St Peter, Walsoken, Walsoken Hungate (1894–1930), West Walton

SANITARY DISTRICTS

AYLSHAM RSD
same as PLU
BLOFIED RSD
same as PLU less pt Thorpe next Norwich (1835–89)
CROMER USD (1884[18]–94)
Cromer
EAST DEREHAM USD
East Dereham
DEPWADE RSD
same as PLU less Diss
DISS USD
Diss
DOCKING RSD
same as PLU less pt Hunstanton (1891–94)
DOWNHAM RSD
same as PLU for Norfolk less pt Downham Market
DOWNHAM MARKET USD
pt Downham Market
ELY RSD
same as PLU for the Norfolk par
ERPINGHAM RSD
same as PLU less Cromer (1884–94)
EAST AND WEST FLEGG RSD
same as PLU less pt Runham (1889–94)
FOREHOE RSD
same as PLU
GUILTCROSS RSD
same as PLU
HENSTEAD RSD
same as PLU less pt Trowse with Newton (1835–89)
HOXNE RSD
same as PLU for the pt of the par in Norfolk
HUNSTANTON USD (1891[19]–94)
pt Hunstanton
FREEBRIDGE LYNN RSD
same as PLU
KING'S LYNN RSD
same as PLU less King's Lynn St Margaret, pt North Lynn, South Lynn
KING'S LYNN USD
King's Lynn St Margaret, pt North Lynn, South Lynn
MITFORD AND LAUNDITCH RSD
same as PLU less East Dereham
NORWICH USD
same as Norwich MB/CB for 1875–94
ST FAITH'S PLU
same as PLU less pt Hellesdon (1836–89), Norwich St Mary in the Marsh (1836–89)
SMALLBURGH RSD
same as PLU less North Walsham
SWAFFHAM RSD
same as PLU less Swaffham
SWAFFHAM USD
Swaffham
THETFORD RSD
same as PLU less the pars in Thetford USD
THETFORD USD (Norfolk, Suffolk)
Thetford St Cuthbert,[13] Thetford St Mary,[13] Thetford St Peter
NORTH WALSHAM USD
North Walsham
WALSINGHAM RSD
same as PLU less Wells next the Sea
WALSOKEN USD
Walsoken
WELLS USD
Wells next the Sea
WISBECH RSD
same as PLU less Walsoken
GREAT YARMOUTH USD (Norfolk, Suffolk until 1889, Great Yarmouth CB 1889–94)
same as MB for 1889–94

ADMINISTRATIVE COUNTY

For MBs and the associated CBs, see BOROUGHS earlier in this part of the *Guide*.

AYLSHAM RD (1894–1935)

Alby with Thwaite, Aylsham, Banningham, Little Barningham, Belaugh, Blickling, Brampton, Burgh, Buxton, Calthorpe, Cawston, Colby, Coltishall, Corpusty, Erpingham, Foulsham, Guestwick, Hackford, Great Hautbois, Hevingham, Heydon, Hindolveston, Ingworth, Irmingland, Itteringham, Lammas with Little Hautbois, Mannington, Marsham, Oulton, Oxnead, Reepham with Kerdiston, Sall, Saxthorpe, Scottow, Skeyton, Stratton Strawless, Swanton Abbot, Themelthorpe, Thurning, Tuttington, Whitwell, Wickmere, Wolterton, Wood Dalling, Wood Norton

BLOFIELD RD (1894–1935)

Acle, Beighton, Blofield, Buckenham, Burlingham St Andrew, Burlingham St Edmund, Burlingham St Peter, Brundall, Cantley, Freethorpe, Halvergate, Hassingham, Hemblington, Limpenhoe, Lingwood, Moulton St Mary, Great Plumstead, Little Plumstead, Postwick, Ranworth with Panxworth, Reedham, Southwood, Strumpshaw, Thorpe next Norwich, Tunstall, Upton with Fishley, South Walsham (1897–1935), South Walsham St Lawrence (1894–97), South Walsham St Mary (1894–97), Wickhampton, Witton, Woodbastwick

BLOFIELD AND FLEGG RD (1935–74)

Acle, Ashby with Oby, Beighton, Blofield, Brundall, Burlingham, East Caister (1935–54), West Caiste , Caister-on-Sea (1954–74), Cantley, Filby, Fleggburgh, Freethorpe, Halvergate, Hemblington, Hemsby, Martham, Mautby, Ormesby St Margaret with Scratby, Ormesby St Michael; Plumstead, Great and Little; Postwick, Reedham, Repps with Eastwick, Rollesby, Somerton, Stokesby with Herringby, Strumpshaw, Thorpe next Norwich (1935–55), Thorpe St Andrew (1955–74), Thurne, Upton with Fishley, South Walsham, Winterton (1935–53), Winterton-on-Sea (1953–74), Woodbastwick

CROMER UD

Cromer

DEPWADE RD

Alburgh, Ashwellthorpe, Aslacton, Billingford (1894–1935), Bressingham (1902–74), Brockdish, Bunwell, Burston, Carleton Rode, Denton, Dickleburgh, Earsham, Fersfield (1902–35), Forncett (1935–74), Forncett St Mary (1894–1935), Forncett St Peter (1894–1935), Fritton (1894–1935), Fundenhall (1894–1935), Gissing, Hapton (1894–1935), Hardwick (1894–1935), Hempnall, Morning Thorpe, Great Moulton (1960–74), Moulton St Michael (1894–1960), Needham, Pulham Market (1947–74), Pulham St Mary (1947–74), Pulham St Mary Magdalene (1894–1947), Pulham St Mary the Virgin (1894–1947), Redenham with Harleston, Roydon (1902–74), Rushall (1894–1935), Scole, Shimpling (1894–1935), Shelfanger (1902–74), Shelton, Starston, Long Stratton (1935–74), Stratton St Mary (1894–1935), Stratton St Michael (1894–1935), Tacolneston, Tasburgh, Tharston, Thelveton (1894–1935), Thorpe Abbots (1894–1935), Tibenham, Tivetshall St Margaret, Tivetshall St Mary, Wacton, Winfarthing (1902–74), Wortwell

EAST DEREHAM UD

East Dereham

DISS UD

Diss

DOCKING RD

Anmer, Bagthorpe (1894–1935), Bagthorpe with Barmer (1935–74), Barmer (1894–1935), Barwick, Bircham (1935–74), Great Bircham (1894–1935), Bircham Newton (1894–1935), Bircham Tofts (1894–1935), Brancaster, Broomsthorpe (1894–1935), Burnham Deepdale (1894–1935), Burnham Market (1929–74), Burnham Norton, Burnham Sutton cum Burnham Ulph (1894–1929), Burnham Thorpe, Burnham Westgate (1894–1929), Choseley, North Creake, South Creake, Dersingham, Docking, Fring, Heacham, Holme next the Sea, Houghton, Hunstanton (1894–1953), Old Hunstanton (1953–74), Ingoldisthorpe, Ringstead, East Rudham, West Rudham, Sedgeford, Shernborne, Snettisham, Stanhoe, Syderstone, Thornham, Titchwell, Waterden (1894–1953)

DOWNHAM RD

Barton Bendish, Bexwell (1894–1935), Boughton, Crimplesham, Denver, West Dereham, Downham West, Feltwell (1935–74), Fincham, Fordham, Hilgay, Hockwold cum Wilton (1935–74), Marham, Methwold (1935–74), Nordelph (1930–74), Northwold (1935–74), Roxham (1894–1935), South Runcton (1894–1950), Runcton Holme (1950–74), Ryston, Shouldham, Shouldham Thorpe, Southery, Stoke Ferry, Stow Bardolph, Stradsett, Tottenhill, Wallington with Thorpland (1894–1935), Watlington, Welney, West Welney (1895–1935), Wereham, Wiggenhall St German (1894–1935), Wiggenhall St Germans (1935–74), Wiggenhall St Mary Magdalen, Wiggenhall St Mary the Virgin, Wiggenhall St Peter (1894–1935), Wimbotsham, Wormegay, Wretton

DOWNHAM MARKET UD

Downham Market

ERPINGHAM RD

Alby with Thwaite (1935–74), Aldborough, Antingham, Aylmerton, Baconsthorpe, Little Barningham (1935–74), Barningham Norwood (1894–1935), Barningham Winter or Barningham Town (1894–1935), East Beckham, West Beckham, Beeston Regis, Bessingham (1894–1935), Bodham, Briston (1894–1935), Cley next the Sea, Colby (1935–74), Corpusty (1935–74), Edgefield, Erpingham (1935–74), Felbrigg, Gimingham, Glandford with Bayfield (1894–1935), Gresham, Gunton (1894–1935), Hanworth, Hempstead,

Holt, Hunworth (1894–1935), Ingworth (1935–74), Itteringham (1935–74), Kelling, Knapton (1894–1935), Letheringsett (1894–1935), Letheringsett with Glandford (1935–74), Matlask, Mundesley, Northrepps, Overstrand, Plumstead, Roughton, Runton, Salthouse, Sheringham (1894–1901), Upper Sheringham (1901–74), Sidestrand, Southrepps, Stody, Suffield, Sustead, Thorpe Market, Thornage, Thurgarton (1894–1935), Trimingham, Trunch (1894–1935), Weybourne, Wickmere (1935–74)

EAST AND WEST FLEGG RD (1894–1935)
Ashby with Oby, Billockby, Burgh St Margaret, East Caister (1926–35), West Caister (1926–35), Caister next Yarmouth (1894–1926), Clippesby, Filby, Hemsby, Martham, Mautby, Ormesby St Margaret with Scratby, Ormesby St Michael, Repps with Bastwick, Rollesby, Runham, East Somerton, West Somerton, Stokesby with Herringby, Thrigby, Thurne, Winterton

FOREHOE RD (1894–1935)
Barford, Barnham Broom, Bawburgh, Bowthorpe, Brandon Parva, Carleton Forehoe, Colton, Costessey, Coston, Crownthorpe, Deopham, Easton, Hackford, Hingham, Kimberley, Marlingford, Morley St Botolph, Morley St Peter, Runhall, Welborne, Wicklewood, Wramplingham, Wymondham

FOREHOE AND HENSTEAD RD (1935–74)
Barford, Barnham Broom, Bawburgh, Bracon Ash, Bramerton, Caister St Edmunds (1935–55), Caistor St Edmund (1955–74), East Carleton, Colney, Costessey, Cringleford, Deopham, Easton, Flordon, Framingham Earl, Framingham Pigot, Hethersett, Hingham, Holverston, Keswick, Ketteringham, Kimberley, Kirby Bedon, Marlingford, Great Melton, Little Melton, Morley, Mulbarton, Newton Flotman, Poringland, Rockland St Mary, Runhall, Saxlingham Nethergate, Shotesham, Stoke Holy Cross, Surlingham, Swainsthorpe, Swardeston, Trowse with Newton, Wicklewood, Wramplingham, Wreningham

GUILTCROSS RD (1894–1902[20])
Banham, Blo' Norton, Bressingham, Bridgham, New Buckenham, Old Buckenham, Eccles, Fersfield, Garboldisham, Gasthorpe, East Harling, West Harling, Kenninghall, North Lopham, South Lopham, Quidenham, Riddlesworth, Roydon, Shelfanger, Wilby, Winfarthing

HENSTEAD RD (1894–1935)
Arminghall, Bixley, Bracon Ash, Bramerton, Caister St Edmund, East Carleton, Conley, Cringleford, Dunston, Flordon, Framingham Earl, Framingham Pigot, Hethel, Hethersett, Holverston, Intwood, Keswick, Ketteringham, Kirby Bedon, Markshall, Great Melton, Little Melton, Mulbarton, Newton Flotman, Poringland, Rockland St Mary, Saxlingham Nethergate, Saxlingham Thorpe (1894–1925), Shotesham All Saints, Shotesham St Mary, Stoke Holy Corss, Surlingham, Swainsthorpe, Swardeston, Trowse with Newton, Whitlingham, Wreningham

HUNSTANTON UD (1894–96[21])
New Hunstanton

HUNSTANTON UD (1954[22]–74)
New Hunstanton

NEW HUNSTANTON UD (1896[21]–1954[22])
New Hunstanton

LODDON RD (1935–74)
Aldeby, Alpington, Ashby St Mary, Bedingham, Bergh Apton, Brooke, Broome, Burgh St Peter, Carleton St Peter, Chedgrave, Claxton, Ditchingham, Ellingham, Geldeston, Gillingham, Haddiscoe, Hales, Heckingham, Hedenham, Hellington, Howe, Kirby Cane, Langley with Hardley, Kirstead, Loddon, Mundham, Norton Subcourse, Raveningham, Seething, Sisland, Stockton, Thurlton, Thurton, Thwaite, Toft Monks, Topcroft, Wheatacre, Woodton, Yelverton

LODDON AND CLAVERING RD (1894–1935)
Aldeby, Alpington, Ashby St Mary, Bedingham, Bergh Apton, Brooke, Broome, Burgh St Peter, Carleton St Peter. Chedgrave, Claxton, Ditchingham, Ellingham, Geldeston, Gillingham, Haddiscoe, Hales, Hardley, Heckingham, Hedenham, Hellington, Howe, Kirby Cane, Kirstead, Langley, Loddon, Mundham, Norton Subcourse, Raveningham, Seething, Sisland, Stockton, Thorpe next Haddiscoe, Thurlton, Thurton, Thwaite, Toft Monks, Topcroft, Wheatacre, Woodton, Yelverton

FREEBRIDGE LYNN RD
Ashwicken (1894–1935), Babingley (1894–1935), Bawsey, West Bilney (1894–1935), Castle Acre, Castle Rising, Congham, Flitcham with Appleton, Gayton, Gayton Thorpe (1894–1935), Gaywood (1894–1935), Grimston, Harpley, Hillington, Leziate, North Lynn (1894–1935), Great Massingham, Little Massingham, Middleton, Mintlyn (1894–1935), West Newton (1894–1935), Pentney, Roydon, North Runcton, Sandringham, Setchey (1894–1935), East Walton, Westacre, East Winch, West Winch, Wolferton (1894–1935), North Wootton, South Wootton

KING'S LYNN RD (1894–1935)
West Lynn

MARSHLAND RD
Clenchwarton, Emneth, Marshland St James (1935–74), Outwell, Terrington St Clement, Terrington St John, Tilney All Saints, Tilney St Lawrence, Tilney with Islington (1894–1935), Upwell, Walpole St Andrew, Walpole St Peter, Walsoken (1934–74), West Walton

MITFORD AND LAUNDITCH RD
Bawdeswell, Beeston with Bittering, Beetley, Billingford, East Bilney (1894–1935), Bintree, Brisley, Bylaugh, Colkirk, Cranworth, Great Dunham, Little Dunham, North Elmham, Elsing, Foxley, Fransham (1935–74), Great Fransham (1894–1935), Little Fransham (1894–1935), Garveston, Gateley, Gressenhall, Guist, Hardingham, Hockering, Hoe, Horningtoft, Kempstone, Letton (1894–1935), Lexham (1935–74), East Lexham (1894–1935), West Lexham (1894–1935), Litcham, Longham, Lyng, Mattishall, Mattishall Burgh (1894–1935), Mileham, Oxwick and Pattesley (1894–1935), Reymerston (1894–1935), Rougham, Scarning, Shipdham, Southburgh (1894–

1935), Sparham, Stanfield, Swanton Morley, Thuxton (1894–1935), Tittleshall, East Tuddenham, North Tuddenham, Twyford, Weasenham All Saints, Weasenham St Peter, Wellingham, Wendling, Westfield (1894–1935), Whinburgh, Whissonsett, Woodrising (1894–1935), Worthing, Yaxham

ST FAITH'S RD (1894–1935)

Alderford, Attlebridge, Beeston St Andrew, Booton, Brandiston, Catton, Crostwick, Drayton, Felthorpe, Frettenham, Hainford, Haveringland, Hellesdon, Honingham, Horsford, Horsham St Faith with Newton St Faith, Horstead with Stanninghall, Morton on the Hill, Rackheath, Ringland, Salhouse, Spixworth, Sprowston, Swannington, Taverham, Weston Longville, Great Witchingham, Little Witchingham, Wroxham

ST FAITH'S AND AYLSHAM RD (1935–74)

Alderford, Attlebridge, Aylsham, Beeston St Andrew, Belaugh, Blickling, Booton, Brampton, Brandiston, Buxton with Lammas, Catton, Cawston, Coltishall, Crostwick, Drayton, Felthorpe, Foulsham, Frettenham, Guestwick, Hainford, Haveringland, Hevingham, Heydon, Honingham, Horsford, Horsham St Faith and Newton St Faith (1955–74), Horsham St Faith with Newton St Faith (1935–54), Horstead with Stanninghall, Marsham, Morton on the Hill, Oulton, Rackheath, Reepham, Ringland, Salhouse, Sall, Spixworth, Sprowston, Stratton Strawless, Swannington, Taverham, Themelthorpe, Tuttington, Weston Longville, Great Witchingham, Little Witchingham, Wood Dalling, Wroxham

SHERINGHAM UD (1901[23]–74)

Sheringham

SMALLBURGH RD

Ashmanhaugh, Bacton, Barton Turf, Beeston St Lawrence (1894–1935), Bradfield (1894–1935), Brumstead, Catfield, Crostwight (1894–1935), Dilham, Edingthorpe (1894–1935), Felmingham, Happisburgh, Hempstead with Eccles (1894–1935), Hickling, Honing, Horning, Horsey, Hoveton (1935–74), Hoveton St John (1894–1935), Hoveton St Peter (1894–1935), Ingham, Irstead, Knapton (1950–74), Lessingham, Ludham, Neatishead, Palling (1894–1948), Sea Palling (1948–74), Paston, Potter Heigham, Ridlington (1894–1935), East Ruston, Sco' Ruston (1894–1935), Scottow (1935–74), Skeyton (1935–74), Sloley, Smallburgh, Stalham, Sutton, Swafield, Swanton Abbot (1935–74), Trunch (1935–74), Tunstead, Walcott (1894–1935), Waxham (1894–1935), Westwick, Witton, Worstead

SWAFFHAM RD

South Acre, Ashill, Beachamwell (1935–74), Beechamwell (1894–1935), Bodney (1894–1935), Bradenham (1935–74), East Bradenham (1894–1952), West Bradenham (1894–1952), Buckenham Tofts (1894–1935), Caldecote (1894–1935), Cockley Cley, Colveston (1894–1935), Cranwich (1935–74), Great Cressingham, Little Cressingham, Didlington, Foulden, Gooderstone, Hilborough, Holme Hale, Houghton on the Hill (1894–1935), Ickburgh, Langford (1894–1935), Lynford (1935–74), Mundford (1935–74), Narborough, Narford, Necton, Newton by Castle Acre, Oxborough, North Pickenham, South Pickenham, Saham Toney, Shingham, Sporle with Palgrave, Stanford, Sturston (1935–74), Threxton (1894–1935), Weeting-with-Bromehill (1935–74)

SWAFFHAM UD

Swaffham

THETFORD RD (1894–1935)

Blo' Norton (1902–35), Brettenham, Bridgham (1902–35), Cranwich, Croxton, Feltwell, Feltwell Anchor (1894–1929), Garboldisham (1902–35), Gasthorpe (1902–35), East Harling (1902–35), West Harling (1902–35), Hockwold cum Wilton, Kilverstone, North Lopham (1902–35), South Lopham (1902–35), Methwold, Mundford, Northwold, Riddlesworth (1902–35), Rushford, Santon, Great and Little Snarehill, Sturston, West Tofts, Weeting-with-Bromehill, East Wretham, West Wretham

NORTH WALSHAM UD

North Walsham

WALSINGHAM RD

Alethorpe (1894–1935), Bale (1894–1935), Barney (1894–1935), Barsham (1935–74), East Barsham (1894–1935), North Barsham (1894–1935), West Barsham (1894–1935), Binham, Blakeney, Briningham, Brinton, Briston (1935–74), Cockthorpe (1894–1935), Dunton (1935–74), Dunton cum Doughton (1894–1935), Egmere (1894–1935), Fakenham, Field Dalling, Fulmodeston (1935–74), Fulmodeston cum Croxton (1894–1935), Gunthorpe, Helhoughton, Hempton, Hindolveston (1935–74), Hindringham, Holkham, Houghton St Giles (1894–1935), Kettlestone, Langham, Melton Constable, Morston, Pensthorpe (1894–1935), Pudding Norton, Quarles (1894–1935), Raynham (1935–74), East Raynham (1894–1935), South Raynham (1894–1935), West Raynham (1894–1935), Great Ryburgh, Little Ryburgh, Saxlingham (1894–1935), Sculthorpe, Sharrington (1894– 1935), Shereford (1894–1935), Great Snoring, Little Snoring, Stibbard, Stiffkey, Swanton Novers, Tatterford (1894–1935), Tattersett, Testerton (1894–1935), Thurning (1935–74), Thursford (1894–1935), Thursford (1954–74), Toftrees (1894–1935), Great Walsingham, Little Walsingham, Warham (1935–74), Warham All Saints (1894–1935), Warham St Mary (1894–1935), Wighton, Wiveton

WALSOKEN UD (1894–1934[24])

Walsoken, Walsoken Hungate

WAYLAND RD

Attleborough, Banham (1902–35), Beesthorpe, Blo' Norton (1935–74), Breckles (1894–1935), Brettenham (1935–74), Bridgham (1935–74), New Buckenham (1902–35), Old Buckenham (1902–35), Carbrooke, Caston, Croxton (1935–74), Eccles (1902–56), Great Ellingham, Little Ellingham, Garboldisham (1935–74), Griston, Hargham (1894–1935), Harling (1935–74), Hockham, Illington (1894–1935), Kenninghall (1902–35), Kilverstone (1935–74), Larling

(1894–1935), North Lopham (1935–74), South Lopham (1935–74), Merton, Ovington, Quidenham (1902–35), Quidenham (1956–74), Riddlesworth (1935–74), Rockland All Saints and St Peter (1894–1935), Rockland St Andrew (1894–1935), Rocklands (1935–74), Roudham, Scoulton, Shropham, Snetterton, Stow Bedon, Thompson, Tottington, Watton, Wilby (1902–35), Wretham (1935–74)

NON-METROPOLITAN COUNTY

As constituted 1 Apr 1974, defined
in terms of Adm Co units as of 31 Mar.

BRECKLAND DIST
East Dereham UD, Mitford and Launditch RD, Swaffham RD, Swaffham UD, Thetford MB, Wayland RD

BROADLAND DIST
pt Blofield and Flegg RD (the pars not in Norwich Dist or Great Yarmouth Dist), St Faith's and Aylsham RD

NORTH NORFOLK DIST
Cromer UD, Erpingham RD, Sheringham UD, Smallburgh RD, North Walsham UD, Walsingham RD, Wells next the Sea UD

SOUTH NORFOLK DIST
Depwade RD, Diss UD, Forehoe and Henstead RD, Loddon RD, Wymondham UD

WEST NORFOLK DIST
Docking RD, Downham RD, Downham Market UD, Hunstanton UD, Freebridge Lynn RD, King's Lynn MB, Marshland RD

NORWICH DIST
pt Blofield and Flegg RD (pt Thorpe St Andrew[26]), Norwich CB

GREAT YARMOUTH DIST
Great Yarmouth CB, pt Blofield and Flegg RD (Ashby with Oby, West Caister, Caister-on-Sea, Filby, Fleggburgh, Hemsby, Martham, Mautby, Ormesby St Margaret with Scratby, Ormesby St Michael, pt Reedham,[27] Repps with Bastwick, Rollesby, Somerton, Stokesby Herringby, Thurne, Winterton-on-Sea), pt East Suffolk (pt Lothingland RD: Belton, Bradwell, Burgh Castle, Fritton,[28] Hopton on Sea[29])

OXFORDSHIRE

ALTERATIONS IN COUNTY BOUNDARIES

As noted by year below, Oxon pars gained territory from or lost it to pars in adjoining counties or county boroughs, or were entirely transferred to them. Details of these alterations are noted in Part I of the *Guide* under Oxon.

ANCIENT COUNTY (until 1889: Hds, Bors, MBs, PLUs, RSDs, USDs)

1844 Beckley, Broughton Poggs, Caversfield, Little Faringdon, Langford, Lewknor, Lillingstone Lovell, Sherington, Shilton, Stowe, Stratton Audley, Studley, Widford. *1866* Cropredy, Kingsey, Neithrop, Sonning, Warkworth. *1885* North Hinksey, South Hinksey, Lewknor Uphill. *1886* Broughton Poggs, Ickford.

ADMINISTRATIVE COUNTY (1889–1974: Hds,[1] PLUs, MBs, RDs, UDs, with Oxford CB associated)

1889 Headington, North Hinksey, South Hinksey, Marston. *1894* Banbury, Culham, Grimsbury, Mollington, Whitchurch. *1911* Caversham. *1926* Cowley, Headington. *1929* Cowley, Headington, Iffley, Wolvercott. *1933* Kingsey, Towersey. *1956* Godington, Piddington. *1957* Littlemore.

NON-METROPOLITAN COUNTY (from 1974: Dists)

1974 Abingdon, Abingdon St Helen Without, Appleford, Appleton with Eaton, Ardington, Ashbury, Aston Tirrold, Aston Upthorpe, Baulking, Besselsleigh, Blewbury, Bourton, Brightwell-cum-Sotwell, Buckland, Buscot, East Challow, West Challow, Charney Bassett, Childrey, Chilton, Cholsey, Coleshill, Compton Beauchamp, Great Coxwell, Little Coxwell, Cumnor, Denchworth, Didcot, Drayton, Eaton Hastings, Great Faringdon, Fernham, Frilford, Fyfield and Tubney, Garford, Goosey, Grove, East Hagbourne, West Hagbourne, East Hanney, West Hanney, Harwell, Hatford, East Hendred, West Hendred, North Hinksey, South Hinksey, Hinton Waldrist, Kennington, Kingston Bagpuize with Southmoor, Kingston Lisle, Letcombe Bassett, Letcombe Regis, Littleworth, Lockinge, Longcott, Longworth, Lyford, Marcham, Milton, North Moreton, South Moreton, Moulsford, Pusey, Radley, Shellingford, Shrivenham, Sparsholt, Stanford in the Vale, Steventon, Sunningwell, Sutton Courtenay, Uffington, Upton, Wallingford, Wantage, Watchfield, Little Wittenham, Long Wittenham, Woolstone, Wootton, Wytham.

ASSOCIATED COUNTY BOROUGH

For constituent pars see listing for BOROUGHS in this part of the *Guide*.

OXFORD CB

Bdry: 1889,[2] 1894,[3] 1929,[4] 1957.[5] Transf 1974 to Oxon.

HUNDREDS[1]

BAMPTON HD

Alvescot, Ashtall, Aston and Cote (from 1866), Bampton, Black Bourton, Brighthampton (from 1866), Broadwell, Broughton Poggs (pt until 1844, ent from 1844), Burford,[6] Chimney (from 1866), Clanfield, Crawley (from 1866), Curbridge (from 1866), Ducklington, Little Faringdon[7] (from 1866), Filkins (from 1866), Grafton (from 1866), Hailey (from 1866), Hardwick, Holwell (from 1866), Kelmscott (from 1866), Kencot, Langford[7] (pt until 1844, ent from 1844), Lew (from 1866), Brize Norton, Radcot (from 1866), Shifford (from 1866), Shilton (pt until 1844, ent from 1844), Standlake, Upton and Signet (from 1866), Westwell, Widford (from 1844), Witney,[6] Yelford

BANBURY HD

pt Banbury,[6] pt Charlbury, Bourton, Clattercott (from 1858), Claydon (from 1866), Cornbury Park (from 1858), Cropredy (pt until 1866, ent from 1866), Epwell (from 1866), Fawler (from 1866), Finstock (from 1866), pt Mollington (from 1866), Neithrop[8] (from 1866), Prescote (from 1858), East Shutford (from 1866), West Shutford (from 1866), Swalcliffe (pt until 1866, ent from 1866), Wardington (from 1866)

BINFIELD HD
Bix, Caversham, Eye and Dunsden (from 1866), Harpsden, Henley-on-Thames,[6] Rotherfield Greys,[6] Rotherfield Peppard, Shiplake, pt Sonning (until 1866)

BLOXHAM HD
Adderbury (until 1866), East Adderbury (from 1866), West Adderbury (from 1866), Alkerton, pt Banbury,[6] Barford St John (from 1866), Bloxham, Bodicote (from 1866), Broughton, pt Cropredy (until 1866), Drayton, Hanwell, Horley, Hornton, Milcombe (from 1866), Milton (from 1866), pt Mollington (from 1866), North Newington (from 1866), Shenington (from 1844), Sibford Ferris (from 1866), Sibford Gower (from 1866), pt Swalcliffe (until 1866), Tadmarton, Wigginton, Wroxton

BULLINGDON HD[9]
Albury, Ambrosden, Arncott (from 1866), Marsh Baldon, Toot Baldon, pt Beckley[10] (until 1866), Blackthorn (from 1866), Chilworth (from 1866), Chippinghurst (from 1866), Cowley, Cuddesdon, Denton (from 1866), Elsfield, Forest Hill, Garsington, Headington,[6] Holton, Horspath, Horton cum Studley (from 1866), Iffley, Littlemoor[6] (from 1866), Marston,[6] Merton, pt Great Milton, Oxford St Clement,[6] Piddington, Sandford-on-Thames, Shotover (from 1858), Stanton St John, Stowood, Studley[10] (from 1866), Thomley (from 1866), Tiddington (from 1866), Waterperry, Wheatley (from 1866), Woodeaton

CHADLINGTON HD
Ascott-under-Wychwood, Bruern (from 1858), Chadlington (from 1866), pt Charlbury, Chastleton, Chilson (from 1866), Churchill, pt Little Compton, Cornwell, Enstone, Fifield, Fulbrook, Idbury, Kingham, Langley (from 1866), Leafield (from 1866), Lyneham (from 1866), Milton-under-Wychwood (from 1866), Minster Lovell, Northover, Chipping Norton,[6] Hook Norton, Over Norton (from 1866), Ramsden (from 1866), Great Rollright, Salford, Sarsden, Shipton-under-Wychwood, Spelsbury, Swerford, Swinbrook, Taynton

DORCHESTER HD
pt Benson (until 1866), Burcott (from 1866), Chislehampton, Clifton Hampden, pt Culham, Dorchester, Drayton St Leonard, Stadhampton, South Stoke

EWELME HD
Benson (pt until 1866, ent from 1866), Berrick Salome, Brightwell Baldwin, Britwell Prior (from 1866), Chalgrove, Cuxham, Easington, Ewelme, Great Haseley, pt Ickford (until 1886), Nettlebed, Newington, Nuffield, Swyncombe, Warborough, Warpsgrove

LANGTREE HD
Checkendon, Crowmarsh Gifford, Goring, Ipsden Mapledurham, Mongewell, Newnham Murren, North Stoke, pt Whitchurch

LEWKNOR HD
Adwell, Aston Rowant, Britwell Salome, Chinnor,[6] Crowell, Emmington, pt Kingsey, Lewknor[11] (pt until 1866, ent from 1866), pt Lewknor Uphill[11] (1866–85), Stokenchurch, Sydenham

PLOUGHLEY HD
Ardley, Bicester (until 1866), Bicester King's End (from 1866), Bicester Market End (from 1866), Bletchington, Bucknell, Caversfield (from 1844), Charlton-on-Otmoor, Chesterton, Fencott and Murcott, Finmere, Fringford, Fritwell, Godington, Hampton Gay, Hampton Poyle, Hardwick, Hethe, Lower Heyford, Upper Heyford, Islip, Kirtlington, Launton, Lillingstone Lovell (until 1844), Middleton Stoney, Mixbury, Newton Purcell, Noke, Oddington, Shelswell, Somerton, Souldern, Stoke Lyne, pt Stowe (until 1844), Stratton Audley (pt until 1844, ent from 1844), Tusmore, Wendlebury, Weston-on-the-Green

PYRTON HD
pt Ibstone, Pishill, Pyrton, Shirburn, Stoke Talmage, Watlington, South Weston, Wheatfield

THAME HD
Ascott, Attington (from 1858), Great Milton (pt until 1866, ent from 1866), Little Milton, Tetsworth, Thame,[6] Waterstock

WOOTTON HD
Asterleigh (from 1858), Middle Aston (from 1866), North Aston, Steeple Aston, Barford St Michael, Steeple Barton, Westcott Barton, Begbroke, Binsey,[12] Bladon, Blenheim Park[13] (from 1858), Cassington, Cogges, Combe, Cutteslowe (from 1858), Deddington,[6] Eynsham,[6] Glympton, Gosford (from 1866), Handborough, Hensington[6] (from 1866), Heythrop, Kiddington, Kidlington, North Leigh, South Leigh, South Newington, Rousham, Sandford St Martin, Shipton-on-Cherwell, Stanton Harcourt, Stonesfield, Tackley, Duns Tew, Great Tew, Little Tew, Thrup (from 1866), Water Eaton (from 1866), Wilcote, Wolvercott,[6] Woodstock,[14] Wootton,[6] Nether Worton, Over Worton, Yarnton

BOROUGHS

Units with some degree of burghal character[15] are denominated 'Bor'.
Those which did not sustain that status until the 19th cent are in italics.
Municipal Boroughs were established by the Municipal Corporations Act, 1835,[16] or by later charter.

BANBURY BOR/MB[17]
Banbury (pt until 1866, ent 1866–1974), Grimsbury (1894–1932), Neithrop (1889[18]–1932)

BURFORD BOR
Burford

CHINNOR BOR
Chinnor

DEDDINGTON BOR
Deddington
EYNSHAM BOR
Eynsham
HENLEY-ON-THAMES BOR, MB (1883[19]–1974)
Bor: pt Henley-on-Thames
MB: Greys (1894–1905), Henley-on-Thames (pt 1883–94, ent 1894–1974), pt Rotherfield Greys (1883–94)
CHIPPING NORTON BOR/MB
Chipping Norton (pt until 1866, ent 1866–1974)
OXFORD BOR[20]/MB/CB
Binsey (until 1926), pt Cowley (until 1894), Cowley St John (1894–1926), pt Headington (until 1894), pt North Hinksey (until 1894), pt South Hinksey (1885–94), Holywell[21] (until 1926), pt Littlemore[22] (1886–94), pt Marston (until 1894), Oxford (1926–74), Oxford All Saints (until 1895), Oxford St Aldate (pt until 1889, ent 1889–1926), Oxford St Clement (pt until 1894, ent 1894–1926), Oxford St Ebbe (until 1926), Oxford St Giles (until 1926), Oxford St John the Baptist (until 1926), Oxford St Martin (until 1895), Oxford St Martin and All Saints (1895–1926), Oxford St Mary Magdalene (until 1926), Oxford St Mary the Virgin (until 1926), Oxford St Michael (until 1926), Oxford St Peter in the East (until 1926), Oxford St Peter le Bailey (until 1926), Oxford St Thomas (until 1926), *Oxford University Colleges and Halls,*[23] St Giles and St John (1926–33), Seacourt[24] (pt until 1894), Unnamed[24] (1894–1929), pt Wolvercott[25] (until 1894)
THAME BOR
Thame
WITNEY BOR
Witney
WOODSTOCK BOR, MB (1886[26]–1974)
Bor: pt Wootton (until Woodstock gains sep civ identity), pt Woodstock (thereafter)
MB: pt Hensington (1886–94), Hensington Within (1884–1974), Woodstock, Old Woodstock (1894–1974), pt Wootton (1886–94)

POOR LAW UNIONS

In Oxon Poor Law Co:[27]
BANBURY PLU (Oxon, Northants, Glos, Warws)
East Adderbury, West Adderbury, Alkerton, Banbury,[28] Barford St John, Barford St Michael, Bloxham, Bodicote, Bourton, Broughton, Clattercott, Claydon, Cropredy, Drayton, Epwell, Grimsbury (1894–1930), Hanwell, Horley, Hornton, Milcombe, Milton, Mollington,[29] Neithrop,[30] North Newington, South Newington, Hook Norton, Prescote, Shenington, East Shutford, West Shutford, Sibford Ferris, Sibford Gower, Swalcliffe, Tadmarton, Wardington, Wigginton, Wroxton
BICESTER PLU (Oxon, Bucks)
Ambrosden, Ardley, Arncott, Bicester King's End, Bicester Market End, Blackthorn, Bletchingdon, Bucknell, Caversfield,[31] Charlbury, Chalton-on-Otmoor, Chesterton, Cottisford, Fawler, Fencott and Murcott, Finmere, Finstock, Fringford, Fritwell, Godington, Hardwick, Hethe, Lower Heyford, Upper Heyford, Islip, Kirtlington, Launton, Merton, Middleton Stoney, Mixbury, Newton Purcell, Noke, Oddington, Piddington, Shelswell, Somerton, Souldern, Stoke Lyne, Stratton Audley,[32] Tusmore, Wendlebury, Weston-on-the-Green
HEADINGTON PLU (Oxon, Bucks until 1844, ent Oxon thereafter)
Beckley,[33] Chippinghurst, Cowley (1836–1929), Cowley St John (1894–1926), Cuddesdon, Denton, Elsfield, Forest Hill (1836–81), Forest Hill with Shotover (1881–1930), Garsington, Headington, Holton, Horspath, Horton cum Studley, Iffley, Littlemore, Marston, Oxford St Clement (1836–1926), Oxford St Giles (1836–1926), Oxford St John the Baptist (1836–1926), St Giles and St John (1926–30), Shotover (1858[34]–81), Stanton St John, Stowood, Studley,[33] Wheatley, Woodeaton
HENLEY PLU (Oxon, Berks, Bucks)
Badgemore (1894–1930), Bix, Brightwell Baldwin, Britwell (1912–30), Britwell Prior (1835–1912), Britwell Salome (1835–1912), Caversham, Checkendon, Cuxham, Eye and Dunsdem, Greys (1894–1905), Harpsden, Henley-on-Thames, Ipsden, Kidmore (1894–1902), Kidmore End (1902–30), Nettlebed, Nuffield, *Pepton,*[35] Pishill (1835–1922), Pishill with Stonor (1922–30), Pyrton, Rotherfield Greys, Rotherfield Peppard, Shiplake, Stonor (1896–1922), Swyncombe, Watlington
CHIPPING NORTON PLU (Oxon, Glos, Warws)
Ascott-under-Wychwood, Bruern, Chadlington, Charlbury, Chastleton, Chilson, Churchill, Cornbury Park, Cornwell, Enstone, Fawler, Fifield, Finstock, Heythrop, Idbury, Kingham, Langley, Leafield, Lyneham, Milton-under-Wychwood, Chipping Norton, Over Norton, Great Rollright, Little Rollright, Salford, Sarsden, Shipton-under-Wychwood, Spelsbury, Swerford, Great Tew, Little Tew, Wychwood
OXFORD INCORPORATION (Oxon/Oxf. CB, Berks until 1889, ent Oxf. CB thereafter)
Holywell (until 1926), Oxford (1926–30), Oxford All Saints (until 1895), Oxford St Aldate[36] (until 1926), Oxford St Ebbe (until 1926), Oxford St Martin (until 1895), Oxford St Martin and All Saints (1895–1926), Oxford St Mary Magdalene (until 1926), Oxford St Mary the Virgin (until 1926), Oxford St Michael (until 1926), Oxford St Peter in the East (until 1926), Oxford St Peter le Bailey (until 1926), Oxford St Thomas (until 1926)
THAME PLU (Oxon, Bucks)
Adwell, Albury, Ascott, Aston Rowant, Attington,

Chalgrove, Chilworth, Chinnor, Crowell, Easington, Emmington, Great Haseley, Ickford,[37] Kingsey, Lewknor,[38] Great Milton, Little Milton, Shirburn, Stoke Talmage, Sydenham, Tetsworth, Thame, Thomley, Tiddington, Warpsgrove, Waterstock, Waterperry, South Weston, Wheatfield

WITNEY PLU (Oxon, Glos, Berks until 1844, ent Oxon thereafter)
Alvescot, Asthall, Aston and Cote, Bampton, Black Bourton, Brighthampton, Broadwell, Broughton Poggs,[39] Burford, Chimney, Clanfield, Cogges, Crawley, Curbridge, Ducklington, Eynsham, Filkins (1835–86), Filkins (1896–1930), Fulbrook, Hailey, Handborough, Hardwick, Holwell, Kelmscot, Kencot, North Leigh, South Leigh, Lew, Minster Lovell, Northmoor, Brize Norton, Osney Hill (1858[34]–1930), Ramsden, Shifford, Shilton,[40] Standlake, Stanton Harcourt, Swinbrook, Taynton, Upton and Signet, Westwell, Widford,[41] Wilcote, Witney, Yelford
WOODSTOCK PLU
Asterleigh (1835–94), Middle Aston, North Aston, Steeple Aston, Steeple Barton, Westcott Barton, Begbroke, Bladon, Blenheim Park, Cassington, Clifton Hampden, Combe, Cutteslowe (1858[34]–1930), Deddington, Glympton, Gosford, Hampton Gay, Hampton Poyle, *Hempton*,[42] Hensington (1835–94), Hensington Within (1894–1930), Hensington Without (1894–1930), Kiddington (1835–94), Kiddington with Asterleigh (1894–1930), Kidlington, Rousham, Sandford St Martin, Shipton-on-Cherwell, Stonesfield, Tackley, Duns Tew, Thrup, Water Eaton, Wolvercott, Woodstock, Old Woodstock (1894–1930), Nether Worton, Over Worton, Wootton, Yarnton

In Other Poor Law Cos:
ABINGDON PLU (Berks, Oxon)
Marsh Baldon, Toot Baldon, Binsey, Burcott, Chislehampton, Clifton Hampden, Culham, Drayton St Leonard, Nuneham Courtenay, Sandford-on-Thames, Seacourt[24] (1836–94), Stadhampton, Unnamed[24] (1894–1929)
BRACKLEY PLU (Northants, Oxon)
Finmere, Mixbury
BRADFIELD PLU (Berks, Oxon)
Goring, Mapledurham, Whitchurch[43]
BUCKINGHAM PLU (Bucks, Oxon until 1844, ent Bucks thereafter)
Lillingstone Lovell,[44] pt Stowe (Boycott)[44]
FARINGDON PLU (Berks, Oxon)
Little Faringdon,[45] Grafton, Langford,[45] Radcot
WALLINGFORD PLU (Berks, Oxon)
Benson, Berrick Salome, Crowmarsh Gifford, Dorchester, Ewelme, Mongewell, Newington, Newnham Murren, North Stoke, South Stoke, Warborough
WYCOMBE PLU (Bucks, Oxon)
Chinnor, Ibstone,[46] Lewknor Uphill[47] (1835–85), Stokenchurch

SANITARY DISTRICTS

ABINGDON RSD
same as PLU for Oxon pars less Binsey, pt North Hinksey, pt South Hinksey, pt Seacourt
BANBURY RSD
same as PLU for Oxon pars less Banbury, Neithrop
BANBURY USD[17]
Banbury, Neithrop
BICESTER RSD
same as PLU for Oxon pars less Bicester King's End, Bicester Market End
BICESTER USD
Bicester King's End, Bicester Market End
BRACKLEY RSD
same as PLU for Oxon pars
BRADFIELD RSD
same as PLU for Oxon pars
CAVERSHAM USD (1890[48]–94)
pt Caversham
FARINGDON RSD
same as PLU for Oxon pars
HEADINGTON RSD
same as PLU less pt Cowley, pt Headington, pt Littlemore, pt Marston, pt Oxford St Clement, Oxford St Giles, Oxford St John the Baptist, Wheatley
HENLEY RSD
same as PLU for Oxon pars less pt Caversham (1890–94), pt Henley-on-Thames (1883–94), pt Rotherfield Greys (1883–94)
HENLEY-ON-THAMES USD (1883[19]–94)
pt Henley-on-Thames, pt Rotherfield Greys
CHIPPING NORTON RSD
same as PLU for Oxon pars less Chipping Norton
CHIPPING NORTON USD
Chipping Norton
OXFORD USD
Binsey, pt Cowley, pt Headington, pt North Hinksey, pt South Hinksey (1885–94), Holywell, pt Littlemore, pt Marston, Oxford All Saints, Oxford St Aldate (pt until 1889, ent 1889–94), pt Oxford St Clement, Oxford St Ebbe, Oxford St Giles, Oxford St John the Baptist, Oxford St Martin, Oxford St Mary Magdalene, Oxford St Mary the Virgin, Oxford St Michael, Oxford St Peter in the East, Oxford St Peter le Bailey, Oxford St Thomas, *Oxford University Colleges and Halls*,[23] pt Seacourt, pt Wolvercott
THAME RSD
same as PLU for Oxon pars less Thame
THAME USD
Thame
WALLINGFORD RSD
same as PLU for Oxon pars
WHEATLEY USD
Wheatley
WITNEY RSD
same as PLU less Witney

WITNEY USD
Witney
WOODSTOCK RSD
same as PLU less pt Hensington (1886–94), pt Wolvercott, Woodstock (1886–94), pt Wootton (1886–94)
WOODSTOCK USD (1886[26]–94)
pt Hensington, Woodstock, pt Wootton

WYCOMBE RSD
same as PLU for Oxon pars
hampton, Clifton Hampden, Culham, Drayton St Leonard, North Hinksey,[48] South Hinksey,[49] Nuneham Courtenay, Sandford-on-Thames, Seacourt[24] (1836–94), Stadhampton, Unnamed[24] (1894–1927)

ADMINISTRATIVE COUNTY

For MBs and the associated CB, see BOROUGHS earlier in this Part of the *Guide*.

BANBURY RD
Adderbury (1971–74), East Adderbury (1894–1971), West Adderbury (1894–1971), Alkerton (1894–1970), Middle Aston (1932–74), North Aston (1932–74), Steeple Aston (1932–74), Barford St John (1894–1932), Barford St John and St Michael (1932–74), Barford St Michael (1894–1932), Bloxham, Bodicote, Bourton, Broughton, Clattercot (1894–1932), Claydon (1894–1932), Claydon with Clattercot (1932–74), Cropredy, Deddington (1932–74), Drayton, Epwell, Hanwell, Horley, Hornton, Milcombe, Milton, Mollington, North Newington, South Newington, Hook Norton, Prescote, Shenington (1894–1970), Shenington with Alkerton (1970–74), Shutford (1932–74), East Shutford (1894–1932), West Shutford (1894–1932), Sibford Ferris, Sibford Gower, Swalcliffe, Tadmarton, Duns Tew (1932–74), Wardington, Wigginton, Wroxton
BICESTER RD (1894–1932)
Ambrosden, Ardley, Arncott, Blackthorn, Bletchingdon, Bucknell, Caversfield, Charlton-on-Otmoor, Chesterton, Cottisford, Fencott and Murcott, Finmere, Fringford, Fritwell, Godington, Hardwick, Hethe, Lower Heyford, Upper Heyford, Islip, Kirtlington, Land Common to Cottisford and Hethe, Launton, Merton, Middleton Stoney, Mixbury, Newton Purcell, Noke, Oddington, Piddington, Shelswell, Somerton, Souldern, Stoke Lyne, Stratton Audley, Tusmore, Wendlebury, Weston-on-the-Green
BICESTER UD
Bicester King's End, Bicester Market End
BULLINGDON RD (1932–74)
Adwell, Aston Rowant, Toot Baldon, Marsh Baldon, Beckley and Stowood, Benson, Berinsfield (1964–74), Berrick Salome, Brightwell Baldwin, Britwell, Chalgrove, Chinnor, Clifton Hampden, Crowell, Cuddesdon (1932–62), Cuddesdon and Denton (1962–74), Culham, Cuxham with Easington, Denton (1932–62), Dorchester, Drayton St Leonard, Elsfield, Ewelme, Forest Hill with Shotover, Garsington, Great Haseley, Holton, Horspath, Kingsey (1932–33), Lewknor, Littlemore, Marston, Great Milton, Little Milton, Newington, Nuneham Courtenay, Pyrton, Risinghurst and Sandhills (1956–74), Sandford-on-Thames, Shirburn, Stadhampton, Stanton St John, Stoke Talmage, Sydenham, Tetsworth, Thomley, Tiddington with Albury, Towersey (1933–74), Warborough, Waterperry, Waterstock, Watlington, South Weston (1932–54), Wheatfield, Wheatley, Woodeaton
CAVERSHAM UD (1894–1911[50])
Caversham
CROWMARSH RD (1894–1932)
Benson, Berrick Salome, Crowmarsh Gifford, Dorchester, Ewelme, Mongewell, Newnham Murren, Newington, North Stoke, South Stoke, Warborough
CULHAM RD (1894–1932)
Marsh Baldon, Toot Baldon, Burcot, Chislehampton, Clifton Hampden, Culham, Drayton St Leonard, Nuneham Courtenay, Sandford-on-Thames, Stadhampton
GORING RD (1894–1932)
Goring, Mapledurham, Whitchurch
HEADINGTON RD (1894–1932)
Beckley, Chippinghurst, Cowley (1894–1929), Cuddesdon, Denton, Elsfield, Forest Hill with Shotover, Garsington, Headington (1894–1929), Holton, Horspath, Horton cum Studley, Iffley (1894–1929), Littlemore, Marston, Stanton St John, Stowood, Studley, Woodeaton
HENLEY RD
Badgemore (1894–1952), Bix, Brightwell Baldwin (1894–1932), Britwell (1912–32), Britwell Pri
HENLEY RD
Badgemore (1894–1952), Bix, Brightwell Baldwin (1894–1932), Britwell (1912–32), Britwell Prior (1894–1912), Britwell Salome (1894–1912), Checkendon, Crowmarsh (1932–74), Cuxham (1894–1932), Eye and Dunsden, Goring (1932–74), Goring Heath (1952–74), Harpsden, Highmoor (1952–74), Ipsden, Kidmore (1894–1902), Kidmore End (1902–74), Mapledurham (1932–74), Nettlebed, Nuffield, Pishill (1894–1922), Pishill with Stonor (1922–74), Pyrton (1894–1932), Rotherfield Greys, Rotherfield Peppard, Shiplake, Sonning Common (1952–74), South Stoke (1932–74), Stoke Row (1952–74), Stonor (1896–1922), Swyncombe, Watlington (1894–1932), Whitchurch (1932–74), Woodcote (1952–74)
CHIPPING NORTON RD
Ascott-under-Wychwood, Steeple Barton (1932–74), Westcott Barton (1932–74), Blenheim (1954–

74), Blenheim Park (1932–54), Bruern, Chadlington, Charlbury, Chastleton, Chilson, Churchill, Combe (1932–74), Cornbury and Wychwood (1950–74), Cornbury Park (1894–1950), Cornwell, Enstone, Fawler, Fifield, Finstock, Glympton (1932–74), Hensington Without (1932–74), Heythrop, Idbury, Kiddington with Asterleigh, Kingham, Langley (1894–1932), Leafield, Lyneham, Milton-under-Wychwood, Over Norton, Rollright (1932–74), Great Rollright (1894–1932), Little Rollright (1894–1932), Rousham (1932–74), Salford, Sandford St Martin (1932–74), Sarsden, Shipton-under-Wychwood, Spelsbury, Stonefield (1932–74), Swerford, Tackley (1932–74), Great Tew, Little Tew, Wootton (1932–74), Worton (1932–74), Wychwood (1894–1950)

PLOUGHLEY RD (1932–74)
Ambrosden, Ardley, Arncott, Begbroke, Blackthorn, Bletchingdon, Bucknell, Caversfield, Charlton-on-Otmoor, Chesterton, Cottisford, Fencott and Murcott, Finmere, Fringford, Fritwell, Godington, Gosford and Water Eaton, Hampton Gay and Poyle, Hardwick with Tusmore, Hethe, Lower Heyford, Upper Heyford, Horton cum Studley, Islip, Kidlington, Kirtlington, Launton, Merton, Middleton Stoney, Mixbury, Newton Purcell with Shelswell, Noke, Oddington, Piddington, Shipton-on-Cherwell (1932–55), Shipton-on-Cherwell and Thrup (1955–74), Somerton, Souldern, Stoke Lyne, Stratton Audley, Thrup (1932–55), Wendlebury, Weston-on-the-Green, Yarnton

THAME RD (1894–1932)
Adwell, Albury, Ascott, Aston Rowant, Attington, Chalgrove, Chilworth, Chinnor, Crowell, Easington, Emmington, Great Haseley, Kingsey, Lewknor, Great Milton, Little Milton, Shirburn, Stoke Talmage, Sydenham, Tetsworth, Thomley, Tiddington, Warpsgrove, Waterperry, Waterstock, South Weston, Wheatfield

THAME UD
Thame

WHEATLEY UD (1894–1932)
Wheatley

WITNEY RD
Alvescot, Asthall, Aston and Cote (1894–1932), Aston Bampton (1932–54), Aston Bampton and Shifford (1954–74), Bampton, Bladon (1932–74), Black Bourton (1894–1971), Brighthampton (1894–1932), Broadwell, Broughton Poggs (1894–1954), Burford (1894–1954), Burford and Upton and Signet (1954–74), Carterton and Black Bourton (1971–74), Cassington (1932–74), Chimney, Clanfield, Cogges (1894–1932), Crawley, Curbridge, Ducklington, Eynsham, Little Faringdon, Filkins (1896–1954), Filkins and Broughton Poggs (1954–74), Freeland (1948–74), Fulbrook, Grafton (1894–1932), Grafton and Radcot (1932–74), Hailey, Hanborough (1948–74), Handborough (1894–1948), Hardwick (1894–1932), Hardwick with Yelford (1932–74), Holwell, Kelmscot, Kencot, Langford, North Leigh, South Leigh, Lew, Minster Lovell, Northmoor, Brize Norton, Osney Hill (1894–1932), Radcot (1894–1932), Ramsden, Shifford (1894–1954), Shilton, Standlake, Stanton Harcourt, Swinbrook (1894–1932), Swinbrook and Widford (1932–74), Taynton, Upton and Signet (1894–1954), Westwell, Widford (1894–1932), Wilcote (1894–1932), Yelford (1894–1932)

WITNEY UD
Witney

WOODSTOCK RD (1894–1932)
Middle Aston, North Aston, Steeple Aston, Steeple Barton, Westcott Barton, Begbroke, Bladon, Blenheim Park, Cassington, Combe, Cutteslowe, Deddington, Glympton, Gosford, Hampton Gay, Hampton Poyle, Hensington Without, Kiddington with Asterleigh, Kidlington, Land Common to Begbroke and Yanton (Oxney Mead, Yarnton or West Mead), Land Common to Begbroke and Yarnton (Pixey Mead), Rousham, Sandford St Martin, Shipton-on-Cherwell, Stonesfield, Tackley, Duns Tew, Thrup, Water Eaton, Wolvercott (1894–1929), Wootton, Nether Worton, Over Worton, Yarnton

NON-METROPOLITAN COUNTY

As constituted 1 Apr 1974, defined in terms of Adm Co units as of 31 Mar. Units transf from Berks Adm Co are marked †.

CHERWELL DIST
Banbury MB, Banbury RD, Bicester UD, Ploughley RD

OXFORD DIST
Oxford CB

WEST OXFORDSHIRE DIST
Chipping Norton MB, Chipping Norton RD, Witney RD, Witney UD, Woodstock MB

VALE OF WHITE HORSE DIST†
Abingdon MB, Abingdon RD, Faringdon RD, pt Wantage RD (Ardington, Blewbury, East Challow, West Challow, Childrey, Chilton, Denchworth, Goosey, Grove, East Hanney, West Hanney, Harwell, East Hendred, West Hendred, Letcombe Bassett, Letcombe Regis, Lockinge, Sparsholt, Upton), Wantage UD

WALLINGFORD DIST
Bullingdon RD, Henley RD, Henley-on-Thames MB, Thame UD, Wallingford MB,† Wallingford RD†

SOMERSET

ALTERATIONS IN COUNTY BOUNDARIES

As noted by year below, Somerset pars gained territory from or lost it to pars in adjoining counties or county boroughs, or were entirely transferred to them. Details of these alterations are noted in Part I of the *Guide* under Somerset.

ANCIENT COUNTY (until 1889: Hds, Bors, MBs, PLUs, RSDs, USDs)

1844 Holwell. *1884* Exmoor.

ADMINISTRATIVE COUNTY (1889–1974: Hds,[1] PLUs, MBs, RDs, UDs, with Bath CB associated)

1895 Maiden Bradley, Goathill, Poyntington, Sandford Orcas, Seaborough, Stourton, Trent, Wambrook. *1896* Long Ashton, Bedminster, Churchstanton, Easton-in-Gordano, Kilmington, Abbots Leigh, Portbury, Portishead. *1898* Long Ashton, Bedminster Without, Brislington, Easton-in-Gordano, Keynsham, Portbury, Portishead. *1911* Charlcombe, Twerton or Twiverton, Weston. *1926* Portsihead. *1930* Bishopsworth, Brislington, Portishead, Whitchurch. *1933* Brislington. *1937* Rode. *1951* Bishopsworth, Charlcombe, Claverton, Clevedon, English Combe, Monkton Combe, Easton-in-Gordano, Portishead, South Stoke, Walton-in-Gordano, Weston, North Weston, Weston-in-Gordano, Whitchurch. *1966* Long Ashton, Brushford, West Buckland, Chard, Churchstanton, Corton Denham, West Crewkerne, Dulverton, Henstridge, Keynsham, Misterton, Norton St Philip, Penselwood, North Stoke, Thorne St Margaret, Wambrook, Wayford, Wellington Without, Whitchurch, Wincanton, Winsham. *1967* Batheaston, Charlcombe, Monkton Combe, Newton St Loe, Swainswick.

NON-METROPOLITAN COUNTY (from 1974: Dists)

1974 Long Ashton, Backwell, Banwell, Barrow Gurney, Bathampton, Batheaston, Bathford, Blagdon, Bleadon, Brockley, Burrington, Butcombe, Cameley, Camerton, Charlcombe, Chelwood, Chew Magna, Chew Stoke, Churchill, Clapton-in-Gordano, Claverton, Cleeve, Clevedon, Clutton, English Combe, Monkton Combe, Combe Hay, Compton Dando, Compton Martin, Congresbury, Corston, Dundry, Dunkerton, Easton-in-Gordano, Farmborough, Farrington Gurney, Flax Bourton, Freshford, East Harptree, West Harptree, Hinton Blewett, Hinton Charterhouse, Hutton, Kelston, Kenn, Kewstoke, Keynsham, Kingston Seymour, Abbots Leigh, High Littleton, Locking, Loxton, Marksbury, Nailsea, Nempnett Thrubwell, Newton St Loe, Norton Malreward, Norton Radstock, Paulton, Peasedown St John, Portbury, Portishead, Priston, Publow, Puxton, St Catherine, Stanton Drew, Steep Holme Island, North Stoke, South Stoke, Stowey-Sutton, Swainswick, Tickenham, Timsbury, Ubley, Unnamed, Walton-in-Gordano, Wellow, North Weston, Weston-in-Gordano, Weston-super-Mare, Whitchurch, Wick St Lawrence, Winford, Winscombe, Wrington, Yatton

ASSOCIATED COUNTY BOROUGH

For constituent pars see listing for BOROUGHS in this part of the *Guide*.

BATH CB

Bdry: 1911,[2] 1951,[3] 1967.[4] Transf 1974 to Avon.[5]

HUNDREDS[1]

ABDICK AND BULSTONE HD

Ashill, Beer Crocombe, Bickenhall, South Bradon (until 1885), Broadway, pt Buckland St Mary, Cricket Malherbie, Curland, Curry Mallet, Curry Rivel, Donyatt, West Dowlish, pt Drayton, Earnshill, pt Fivehead, Hatch Beauchamp, Ilminster, Ilton,[6] Isle Abbots, Isle Brewers, Puckington, Staple Fitzpaine, Stocklinch (from 1884), Stocklinch Magdalene (until 1884), Stocklinch Ottersey (until 1884), Swell, Whitelackington

ANDERSFIELD HD

Broomfield, pt Chilton Trinity, Creech St Michael, Durleigh,[6] Enmore, Goathurst, Lyng,[6] pt North Petherton

BATH FORUM HD[7]

Bath St James,[6] Bath St Michael,[6] Bath St Peter and St Paul,[6] pt Batheaston, Bathford, Bathwick,[6] Monkton Combe, Freshford, Kelston, Langridge,

Monkton Combe, Freshford, Kelston, Langridge, Lyncombe and Widcombe,[6] St Catherine, North Stoke, South Stoke, Swainswick, Walcot,[6] Weston, Woolley

BEMPSTONE HD

Chapel Allerton, Biddisham, Brean, Burnham, Mark, Weare,[6] pt Wedmore

BRENT WITH WRINGTON HD

Berrow, East Brent, Brent Knoll, Burrington, Lympsham, Wrington

BRUTON HD

North Brewham, South Brewham, Bruton,[6] Eastrip (from 1866), Milton Clevedon, Pitcombe, Upton Noble, Yarlington

CANNINGTON HD

Aisholt, Cannington, Charlynch, Edstock and Beer (1866–86), Fiddington, Otterhampton, Spaxton, Stockland Bristol, pt Stogursey,[6] pt Over Stowey, Stringston

CARHAMPTON HD

Carhampton, Culbone, Cutcombe, Dunster,[6] Exford, pt Exton, Luccombe, Luxborough, Minehead, Oare, Porlock, Selworthy, Stoke Pero, Timberscombe, Treborough, Withycombe, Wootton Courtney

CATSASH HD

Alford, Ansford, Babcary, North Barrow, South Barrow, Barton St David, North Cadbury, South Cadbury, Queen Camel, Castle Cary, Compton Pauncefoot, Keinton Mandeville, Kingweston, Lovington, West Lydford, Maperton, Sparkford, Sutton Montis, Weston Bampfylde

CHEW HD

Chew Magna, Chew Stoke, Clutton, Dundry, Norton Hawkfield (from 1866), Norton Malreward, Stowey,[6] Timsbury

CHEWTON HD

Brockley, Cameley, Chewton Mendip, Chilcompton, Compton Martin, Emborough, Farrington Gurney, Green Oare (1858–85), West Harptree, Hinton Blewett, Kingston Seymour, High Littleton, Midsomer Norton, Paulton, Ston Easton, Ubley

CREWKERNE HD

Crewkerne, Hinton St George, Merriott, Misterton, Seaborough, Wayford

NORTH CURRY HD

North Curry,[6] West Hatch, Stoke St Gregory, Thorn Falcon, Thurlbear

FROME HD

Beckington, Berkley, Cloford, East Cranmore, Elm, Four Towers (1858–85), Frome, Laverton, Leigh-upon-Mendip,[9] Lullington, Marston Bigot, Mells,[9] Nunney, Orchardleigh, Road, Rodden, Standerwick (until 1885), Wanstrow, Whatley, Witham Friary,[8] Woolverton

GLASTONBURY TWELVE HIDES HD

Baltonsborough, West Bradley, Glastonbury,[6] Meare, Nyland cum Batcombe, West Pennard, pt Pilton, pt Wedmore, North Wootton

HAMPTON AND CLAVERTON HD

Bathampton, pt Batheaston, Charlcombe, Claverton

HARTCLIFFE WITH BEDMINSTER HD

Long Ashton, Backwell, Barrow Gurney, Bedminster,[6] Butcombe, Chelvey (until 1885), Winford

HORETHORNE HD

Charlton Horehtorne (until 1887), North Cheriton, Abbas Combe, Corton Denham, Goathill, Henstridge, Holwell (until 1844), Horsington, Marston Magna, Milborne Port,[6] Poyntington, Sandford Orcas, Stowell, Trent

HOUNDSBOROUGH, BARWICK AND COKER HD

Barwick, Chilton Cantelo, East Chinnock, Middle Chinnock[10] (until 1884), West Chinnock,[10] Chiselborough, Closworth, East Coker, West Coker, Hardington Mandeville, Haslebury Plucknett, Norton sub Hamdon, Odcombe, Pendomer, North Perrott, Sutton Bingham

HUNTSPILL AND PURITON HD

Huntspill, Puriton

KEYNSHAM HD

Brislington, Burnett, Queen Charlton, Chelwood, Compton Dando, Farmborough, Keynsham, Marksbury, Newmpnett Thrubwell, Priston, Publow, St Thomas in Pensford (until 1884), Saltford, Stanton Drew, Stanton Prior, Whitchurch

KILMERSDON HD

Ashwick, Babington, Buckland Dinham, Hardington, Hemington, Holcombe, Kilmersdon, Radstock, Stratton-on-the-Fosse, Writhtlington

EAST KINGSBURY HD

Chard,[6] Chard Borough[6] (from 1866), Combe St Nicholas, pt Drayton, pt Huish Episcopi,[6] Kingsbury Episcopi, pt Winsham

WEST KINGSBURY HD

Ash Priors, West Buckland, Fitzhead, Bishop's Lydeard, Wellington,[6] Wiveliscombe[6]

MARTOCK HD

pt Buckland St Mary, Martock

MILVERTON HD

Ashbrittle, Bathealton, Kittisford, Langford Budville, pt Milverton,[6] Runnington, Sampford Arundel, Stawley, Thorne St Margaret

NORTON FERRIS HD

pt Maiden Bradley, Bratton Seymour, Charlton Musgrove, Cucklington, Kilmington, Penselwood, Shepton Montague, Stoke Trister, pt Stourton, Wincanton

NORTH PETHERTON HD

Bawdrip, Bridgwater,[6] Chedzoy, Chilton Common (from 1858), pt Chilton Trinity, Durston, Pawlett, pt North Petherton, St Michaelchurch, Thurloxton, Wembdon[6]

SOUTH PETHERTON HD

Barrington, pt Buckland St Mary, Chaffcombe, Chillington, Cricket St Thomas, Cudworth, Dinnington, Dowlish Wake, Knowle St Giles, Lopen, South Petherton, Seavington St Mary, Seavington St Michael, Shepton Beauchamp, Whitestaunton, pt Winsham

PITNEY HD

pt Drayton, pt High Ham, pt Huish Episcopi,[6] Langport,[6] Muchelney, Pitney, pt Somerton,[6] pt Long Sutton

PORTBURY HD

Clapton, Clevedon, Easton-in-Gordano, Flax Bourton, Abbots Leigh, Nailsea, Portbury, Portishead,

Tickenham, Walton-in-Gordano, Weston-in-Gordano, Wraxall

SOMERTON HD

Aller, West Camel, Charlton Adam, Charlton Mackerell, pt Compton Dundon, pt Huish Episcopi,[6] Kingsdon, East Lydford, pt Somerton,[6] pt Long Sutton, Yeovilton

STONE HD

Ashington, Brympton, Chilthorne Domer, Limington, Lufton, Mudford, Preston Plucknett, Yeovil[6]

TAUNTON AND TAUNTON DEAN HD

Angersleigh, West Bagborough, Bradford, Cheddon Fitzpaine, Combe Florey, Corfe, Cothelstone, Heathfield, Hillfarrance (until 1884), Bishops's Hull,[6] Kingston, Lydeard St Lawrence, Norton Fitzwarren, Nynehead, Oake, Orchard Portman, Otterford, Pitminster, Rimpton, Ruishton, Staplegrove, Stoke St Mary, Taunton St James[6] (until 1885), Taunton St James Within[6] (from 1885), Taunton St James Without (from 1885), Taunton St Mary Magdalene[6] (until 1885), Taunton St Mary Magdalene Within[6] (from 1885), Taunton St Mary Magdalene Without (from 1885), Tolland, Trull, Wilton,[6] Withiel Florey

TINTINHULL HD

Ilchester,[6] Kingstone, Montacute,[6] Northover, Stoke sub Hamdon, Thorne, Tintinhull

WELLOW HD

Camerton, English Combe, Combe Hay, Corston, Dunkerton, Farleigh Hungerford, Foxcote, Hinton Charterhouse, Newton St Loe, Norton St Philip, Tellisford, Twerton or Twiverton, Wellow

WELLS FORUM HD

Binegar, West Cranmore, Dinder, Evercreech, Litton, Priddy, Wells St Andrew,[6] Wells St Cuthbert[6] (until 1866), Wells St Cuthbert In[6] (from 1866), Wells St Cuthbert Out[6] (from 1866), Westbury, Wookey

WHITLEY HD

Ashcott, Blackford, Butleigh, Catcott (from 1866), Chilton Polden (from 1866), pt Chilton Trinity, pt Compton Dundon, Cossington, Edington (from 1866), Greinton, pt High Ham, Holford, Holton, Middlezoy, West Monkton,[6] Moorlinch, Othery, Podimore, Shapwick, Stawell (from 1866), Street, Sutton Mallet (from 1866), Walton, Westonzoyland, Wheathill, Woolavington

WHITSTONE HD

Batcombe, Croscombe, Ditcheat, Doulting, Downhead, Hornblotton, Lamyat, East Pennard, pt Pilton, Pylle, Shepton Mallet, Stoke Lane

WILLITON AND FREEMANORS HD

Bicknoller, Brompton Ralph, Brompton Regis, Brushford, Chipstable, Clatworthy, Old Cleeve, Crowcombe, Dodington, Dulverton, Elworthy, Exmoor (pt until 1884, ent from 1884), pt Exton, pt Fivehead, Halse, pt High Ham, Hawkridge, Huish Champflower, Kilton (until 1886), Kilton with Lilstock (from 1886), Kilve, Lilstock (until 1886), pt Milverton,[6] Monksilver, Nettlecombe, East Quantoxhead, West Quantoxhead, Raddington, St Decuman's, Sampford Brett, Skilgate, Stogumber, pt Stogursey,[6] Nether Stowey, pt Over Stowey, Upton, Winsford, Withypoole

WINTERSTOKE HD

Axbridge,[6] Badgworth,[6] Banwell, Blagdon, Bleadon, Charterhouse (from 1866), Cheddar, Christon, Churchill, Compton Bishop,[6] Congresbury, East Harptree, Hutton, Kenn, Kewstoke, Locking, Loxton, Puxton, Rowberrow, Shipham, Rodney Stoke, Uphill, Weston-super-Mare, Wick St Lawrence, Winscombe, Worle, Yatton

BOROUGHS

Units with some degree of burghal character[11] are denominated 'Bor'.
Those which did not sustain that status until the 19th cent are in italics.
Municipal Boroughs were established by the Municipal Corporations Act, 1835,[12] or by later charter.

AXBRIDGE BOR

Axbridge

BADGWORTH BOR

Badgworth

BATH BOR/MB/CB[7]

Bath (1900–74), Bath St James (until 1900), Bath St Michael (until 1900), Bath St Peter and St Paul (until 1900), Bathwick (1835–1900), Lyncombe and Widcombe (1835–1900), Walcot (pt until 1835, ent 1835–1900)

BRIDGWATER BOR/MB

Bridgwater (pt until 1894, ent 1894–1974), pt Durleigh (1835–86), pt Wembdon (1835–86)

BRISTOL BOR/MB/CB[13]

Bedminster (pt 1835–94, ent 1894–96)

BRUTON BOR

Bruton

CHARD BOR/MB

pt Chard (until 1866 and 1892–93), Chard Borough (1866–1974)

DOWN END BOR

DUNSTER BOR

Dunster

GLASTONBURY BOR/MB

Glastonbury (ent until 1883, pt 1883–94, ent 1894–1974)

ILCHESTER BOR

Ilchester

LANGPORT BOR

pt Huish Episcopi

LYNG BOR

Lyng

MERRYFIELD BOR[14]

pt Ilton

MILBORNE PORT BOR
Milborne Port
MILVERTON BOR
Milverton
MONTACUTE BOR
Montacute
NEWPORT BOR
pt North Curry
RACKLEY BOR
pt Compton Bishop
SOMERTON BOR
Somerton
STOFORD BOR

STOGURSEY BOR
Stogursey
NETHER STOWEY BOR
Nether Stowey
TAUNTON BOR, MB (1885–1974)
Bor: pt Taunton St James, pt Taunton St Mary Magdalene
MB: Taunton (1921–74), Bishop's Hull Within (1885–1921), Taunton St James Within (1885–1921), Taunton St Mary Magdalene Within (1885–1921)
WATCHET BOR
Watchet
WEARE BOR
Weare
WELLINGTON BOR
Wellington
WELLS BOR/MB
Wells (1933–74), Wells St Andrew (1835–1933), pt Wells St Cuthbert (until 1866), Wells St Cuthbert In (1866–1933), pt Wells St Cuthbert Out (1866–84)
WESTON-SUPER-MARE MB (1937[15]–74)
Weston-super-Mare
WIVELISCOMBE BOR
Wiveliscombe
YEOVIL BOR, MB (18 –1974)
Yeovil (pt in Bor, pt MB 18 –94, ent 1894–1974)

POOR LAW UNIONS

In Somerset Poor Law County:[16]
LONG ASHTON PLU (1899[17]–1930, renaming of BEDMINSTER PLU, qv)
AXBRIDGE PLU
Chapel Allerton, Axbridge, Badgworth, Banwell, Berrow, Biddisham, Blagdon, Bleadon, Brean, East Brent, Brent Knoll, Burnham, Burhham Without (1896–1930), Burrington, Butcombe, Charterhouse, Cheddar, Christon, Churchill, Compton Bishop, Congresbury, Highbridge (1894–96), North Highbridge (1896–1930), South Highbridge (1896–1930), Hutton, Kewstoke, Locking, Loxton, Lympsham, Mark, Nyland cum Batcombe, Puxton, Rowberrow, Shipham, Uphill, Weare, Wedmore, Weston-super-Mare, Wick St Lawrence, Winscombe, Worle, Wrington
BATH PLU
Bath (1900–30), Bath St James (1836–1900), Bath St Michael (1836–1900), Bath St Peter and St Paul (1836–1900), Bathampton, Batheaston, Bathford, Bathwick (1836–1900), Charlcombe, Claverton, English Combe, Monkton Combe, Combe Hay, Dunkerton, Freshford (1882–1930), Hinton Charterhouse, Langridge, Lyncombe and Widcombe (1836–1900), St Catherine, South Stoke, Swainswick, Twerton or Twiverton (1836–1911), Walcot (1836–1900), Wellow, Weston, Wooley
BEDMINSTER PLU (1836–99[17], renamed LONG ASHTON PLU [as such 1899–1930])
Long Ashton, Backwell, Barrow Gurney, Bedminster (1836–96), Bedminster Without (1894–late 1890s[18]), Bishopsworth (late 1890s[18]–1930), Brockley, Chelvey (1836–96), Clapton, Clevedon, Dundry, Easton-in-Gordano, Flax Bourton, Kenn, Kingston Seymour, Abbots Leigh, Nailsea, Portbury, Portishead, Tickenham, Walton-in-Gordano, North Weston (1894–1930), Weston-in-Gordano, Winford, Wraxall, Yatton
BRIDGWATER PLU
Aisholt, Ashcott, Bawdrip, Bridgwater, Bridgwater Without (1894–1930), Broomfield, Cannington, Catcott, Charlynch, Chedzoy, Chilton Common (1858[19]–1907), Chilton Polden, Chilton Trinity, Cossington, Durleigh, Edington, Edstock and Beer (1836–86), Enmore, Fiddington, Goathurst, Greinton, Huntspill, Lyng, Middlezoy, Moorlinch, Othery, Otterhampton, Pawlett, North Petherton, Puriton, St Michaelchurch, Shapwick, Spaxton, Stawell, Stockland Bristol, Nether Stowey, Over Stowey, Sutton Mallet, Thurloxton, Wembdon, Westonzoyland, Woolavington
CHARD PLU (Somerset, Devon, Dorset)
Ashill, Broadway, Buckland St Mary, Chaffcombe, Chard, Chard Borough, Chillington, Combe St Nicholas, Crewkerne, West Crewkerne (1894–1930), Cricket Malherbie, Cricket St Thomas, Cudworth, Dinnington, Donyatt, West Dowlish, Dowlish Wake, Hinton St George, Ilminster, Ilminster Without (1899–1930), Ilton, Kingstone, Knowle St Giles, Lopen, Merriot, Misterton (1896–1930), Seavington St Mary, Seavington St Michael, Shepton Beauchamp, Stocklinch (1884–1930), Stocklinch Magdalen (1836–84), Stocklinch Ottersey (1836–84), Wambrook,[20] Wayford, Whitelackington, Whitestaunton, Winsham
CLUTTON PLU
Cameley, Camerton, Chelwood, Chew Magna, Chew Stoke, Chilcompton, Clutton, Compton Martin, Farmborough, Farrington Gurney, East Harptree, West Harptree, Hinton Blewitt, High Littleton, Litton, Nempnett Thrubwell, Midsomer Norton, Norton Hawkfield (1836–96), Norton Malreward, Paulton, Publow, St Thomas in Pensford (1836–84), Stanton Drew, Ston Easton, Stowey, Tims-

bury, Ubley, North Widcombe
BEAMINSTER RSD
same as PLU for Somerset pars
BEDMINSTER RSD
same as PLU less pt Bedminster, Clevedon, pt Portishead (1892–94)
BRIDGWATER RSD
same as PLU less pt Bridgwater, pt Durleigh (1875–86), pt Wembdon (1875–86)
BRIDGWATER USD
pt Bridgwater, pt Durleigh (1875–86[26]), pt Wembdon (1875–86[26])
BRISTOL USD[13]
pt Bedminster
BURNHAM USD
pt Burnham
CHARD RSD
same as PLU less pt Chard (1892–93), Chard Borough
CHARD USD
pt Chard (1892[27]–93[28]), Chard Borough
CLEVEDON USD
Clevedon
CLUTTON RSD
same as PLU less pt Chilcompton (1883–94), Midsomer Norton (ent 1875–83, pt 1883–94), Radstock
DULVERTON RSD
same as PLU
FROME RSD
same as PLU less Frome (ent 1875–83, pt 1883–94)
FROME USD
Frome (ent 1875–83, pt 1883–94)
GLASTONBURY USD
Glastonbury (ent 1875–83, pt 1883–94)
KEYNSHAM RSD
same as PLU
LANGPORT RSD
same as PLU
MERE RSD
same as PLU for Somerset par
MINEHEAD USD (1891[28]–94)
pt Minehead
SOUTH MOLTON RSD
same as PLU for pt Somerset par[21]
MIDSOMER NORTON USD
pt Chilcompton (1883–94), Midsomer Norton (ent 1875–83, pt 1883–94)
PORTISHEAD USD (1892[30]–94)
pt Portishead
RADSTOCK USD
Radstock
SHEPTON MALLET RSD
same as PLU less Shepton Mallet (ent 1875–83, pt 1883–86, ent 1886–94)
SHEPTON MALLET USD
Shepton Mallet (ent 1875–83, pt 1883–86,[31] ent 1886[31]–94)
SHERBORNE RSD
same as PLU for Somerset pars
STREET USD
pt Glastonbury (1883–94), Street (ent 1875–83, pt 1883–94)
TAUNTON RSD
same as PLU less pars in Taunton USD
TAUNTON USD
pt Bishop's Hull (1875–85), Bishop's Hull Within (1885–94), pt West Monkton (1875–85), pt Taunton St James (1875–83), Taunton St James Within (1885–94), pt Taunton St Mary Magdalene (1875–85), Taunton St Mary Magdalene Within (1885–94), pt Wilton (1875–85)
WELLINGTON RSD
same as PLU less Wellington, pt Wiveliscombe
WELLINGTON USD
Wellington
WELLS RSD
same as PLU less pt Glastonbury (1883–94), Street, Wells St Andrew, Wells St Cuthbert In, pt Wells St Cutbert Out (1875–86)
WELLS USD
Wells St Andrew, Wells St Cuthbert In, pt Wells St Cuthbert Out (1875–86)
WESTON-SUPER-MARE USD
pt Kewstoke (1883–94), pt Uphill (1883[32]–94), Weston-super-Mare, pt Worle (1883–94)
WILLITON RSD
same as PLU less pt Minehead (1891–94)
WINCANTON RSD
same as PLU
WIVELISCOMBE USD
pt Wiveliscombe
YEOVIL RSD
same as PLU less pt Yeovil
YEOVIL USD
pt Yeovil

ADMINISTRATIVE COUNTY

For MBs and associated CB, see BOROUGHS earlier in this Part of the *Guide*.

LONG ASHTON RD
Long Ashton, Backwell, Barrow Gurney, Bedminster Without (1894–late 1890s[18]), Bishopsworth (late 1890s[18]–1951), Brockley, Clapton (1894–1954), Clapton-in-Gordano (1954–74), Cleeve (1949–74), Dundry, Easton-in-Gordano (1894–1918), Flax Bourton, Kenn, Kingston Seymour, Abbots Leigh, Nailsea, Portbury, Tickenham, Walton-in-Gordano, North Weston, Weston-in-Gordano, Winford, Wraxall, Yatton
AXBRIDGE RD
Chapel Allerton, Axbridge, Badgworth, Banwell,

Berrow, Biddisham (1894–1933), Blagdon, Bleadon, Brean, East Brent, Brent Knoll, Burnham Without (1896–1974), Burrington, Butcombe, Charterhouse (1894–1933), Cheddar, Christon (1894–1933), Churchill, Compton Bishop, Congresbury, Hutton, Kewstoke (pt 1894–96, ent 1896–1974), Locking, Loxton, Lympsham, Mark, Nyland cum Batcombe (1894–1933), Puxton, Rowberrow (1894–1933), Shipham, Steep Holme Island, Uphill (1894–1933), Wedmore, Weare, Wick St Lawrence, Winscombe, Worle (pt (1894–96, ent 1896–1933), Wrington

BATH RD (1894–1933)

Bathampton, Batheaston, Bathford, Camerton (1912–33), Charlcombe, Claverton, English Combe, Monkton Combe, Combe Hay, Dunkerton, Freshford, Hinton Charterhouse, Langridge (1894–1933), St Catherine, South Stoke, Swainswick, Twerton or Twiverton (1894–1911), Wellow, Weston, Woolley (1894–1933)

BATHAVON RD (1933–74)

Bathampton, Batheaston, Bathford, Camerton, Charlcombe, Claverton, English Combe, Monkton Combe, Combe Hay, Compton Dando, Corston, Dunkerton, Freshford, Hinton Charterhouse, Kelston, Keynsham (1933–38), Marksbury, Newton St Loe, Peasedown St John (1955–74), Priston, St Catherine, Saltford (1933–38), Shoscombe (1955–74), North Stoke, South Stoke, Swainswick, Unnamed (1938–74), Wellow, Weston (1933–53), Whitchurch

BRIDGWATER RD

Aisholt (1894–1933), Ashcott, Bawdrip, Bridgwater Without, Broomfield, Cannington, Catcott, Charlynch, Chedzoy, Chilton Common (1894–1907), Chilton Polden, Chilton Trinity, Cossington, Durleigh, Edington, Enmore, Fiddington, Goathurst, Greinton, Huntspill (1894–1949), East Huntspill (1949–74), West Huntspill (1949–74), Lyng, Middlezoy, Moorlinch, Othery, Otterhampton, Pawlett, North Petherton, Puriton, St Michaelchurch (1894–1933), Shapwick, Spaxton, Stawell, Stockland Bristol, Nether Stowey, Over Stowey, Sutton Mallet (1894–1933), Thurloxton, Wembdon, Westonzoyland, Woolavington

DULVERTON PLU

Brompton Regis, Brushford, Dulverton, Exford, pt Exmoor,[21] Exton, Hawkridge, Huish Champflower, Skilgate, Upton, Winsford, Withiel Florey (1896–1930), Withypool

FROME PLU

Babington (1845–1930), Beckington, Berkley, Buckland Dinham, Cloford, Elm, Farleigh Hungerford, Foxcote, Frome, Hardington, Hemington, Kilmersdon, Laverton, Leigh-upon-Mendip, Lullington, Marston Bigot, Mells, Norton St Philip, Nunney, Orchardleigh, Rodden, Rode, Selwood (1894–1930), Standerwick (1836–85), Tellisford, Wanstrow, Whatley, Witham Friary, Woolverton, Writhlington

KEYNSHAM PLU (Somerset, Glos)

Brislington, Burnett, Queen Charlton, Compton Dando, Corston, Kelston, Keynsham, Marksbury, Newton St Loe, Priston, Saltford, Stanton Prior, North Stoke, Whitchurch

LANGPORT PLU

Aller, Babcary, Barrington, Barton St David, Beer Crocombe, South Bradon (1836–85), Charlton Adam (1836–87), Charlton Mackerell, Compton Dundon, Curry Mallet, Curry Rivel, Drayton, Earnshill, Fivehead, High Ham, Huish Episcopi, Isle Abbots, Isle Brewers, Keinton Mandeville, Kingsbury Episcopi, Kingsdon, Kingweston, Langport, Muchelney, Pitney, Puckington, Somerton, Long Sutton, Swell

SHEPTON MALLET PLU

Ashwick, Babington (1835–45), Batcombe, Binegar, West Bradley (1882–1930), East Cranmore, West Cranmore, Croscombe, Ditcheat, Doulting, Downhead, Emborough, Evercreech, Holcombe, Hornblotton, Lamyat, East Lydford, West Lydford, Milton Clevedon, East Pennard, Pilton, Pylle, Shepton Mallet, Stoke Lane, Stratton-on-the-Fosse, Upton Noble

TAUNTON PLU (Somerset, Devon until 1896, ent Somerset thereafter)

Angersleigh, Ash Priors, West Bagborough, Bickenhall, Cheddon Fitzpaine, Churchstanton,[22] Combe Florey, Corfe, Cothelstone, Creech St Michael, Curland, North Curry, Durston, Halse, West Hatch, Hatch Beauchamp, Heathfield, Bishop's Hull (1836–85), Bishop's Hull Within (1885–1921), Bishop's Hull Without (1885–1930), Kingston, Bishop's Lydeard, Lydeard St Lawrence, West Monkton, Norton Fitzwarren, Orchard Portman, Otterford, Pitminster, Ruishton, Stoke Fitzpaine, Staplegrove, Stoke St Gregory, Stoke St Mary, Taunton St James (1836–85), Taunton St James Within (1885–1921), Taunton St James Without (1885–1930), Taunton St Mary Magdalene (1836–85), Taunton St Mary Magdalene Within (1885–1921), Taunton St Mary Magdalene Without (1885–1930), Thorn Falcon, Thurlbear, Tolland, Trull, Wilton (1836–1921)

WELLINGTON PLU (Somerset, Devon)

Ashbrittle, Bathealton, Bradford, West Buckland, Chipstable, Fitzhead, Hillfarrance (1836–84), Kittisford, Langford Budville, Milverton, Nynehead, Oake, Raddington, Runnington, Sampford Arundel, Stawley, Thorne St Margaret, Wellington, Wiveliscombe, Wiveliscombe Without (1894–1930)

WELLS PLU

Baltonsborough, West Bradley (1836–82), Butleigh, Chewton Mendip, Dinder, Glastonbury, Godney (1904–30), Green Oare (1858[19]–85), Meare, West Pennard, Priddy, Sharpham (1894–1930), Rodney Stoke, Street, Walton, Wells St Andrew, Wells St Cuthbert In, Wells St Cuthbert Out, Westbury, Wookey, North Wootton

WILLITON PLU

Bicknoller, Brompton Ralph, Carhampton, Clatworthy, Old Cleeve, Crowcombe, Culbone, Cutcombe, Dodington, Dunster, Elworthy, Holford, Kilton (1836–86), Kilton with Lilstock (1886–1930), Kilve, Lilstock (1836–86), Luccombe, Luxborough, Minehead, Minehead Without (1894–

1930), Monksilver, Nettlecombe, Oare, Porlock, East Quantoxhead, West Quantoxhead, St Decuman's (1836–1902), Sampford Brett, Selworthy, Stogumber, Stogursey, Stoke Pero, Stringston, Timberscombe, Treborough, Watchet (1902–30), Williton (1902–30), Withiel Florey (1836–96), Withycombe, Wootton Courtney

WINCANTON PLU (Somerset, Dorset until 1896, ent Somerset thereafter)
Alford, Ashford, North Barrow, South Barrow, Blackford, Bratton Seymour, North Brewham, South Brewham, Bruton, North Cadbury, South Cadbury, Queen Camel, Castle Cary, Charlton Horethorne, Charlton Musgrove, North Cheriton, Abbas Combe, Compton Pauncefoot, Corton Denham, Cucklington, Eastrip (1858[19]–85), Four Towers (1858[19]–85), Henstridge, Holton, Horsington, Lovington, Maperton, Milborne Port, Penselwood, Pitcombe, Shepton Montague, Sparkford, Stoke Trister, Stowell, Sutton Montis, Weston Bampfylde, Wheathill, Wincanton, Yarlington

YEOVIL PLU
Ash (1895–1930), Ashington, Barwick, Brympton, West Camel, Chilthorne Domer, Chilton Cantelo, East Chinnock, Middle Chinnock[10] (1836–84), West Chinnock,[10] Chiselborough, Closworth, East Coker, West Coker, Hardington Mandeville, Haselbury Plucknett, Ilchester, Limington, Long Load (1895–1930), Lufton, Marston Magna (1894–1930), Martock, Montacute, Mudford, Northover, Norton sub Hamdon, Odcombe, Pendomer, North Perrott, South Petherton, Podimore, Preston Plucknett, Rimpton (1896–1930), Sock Dennis (1858[19]–1930), Stoke sub Hamdon, Sutton Bingham, Thorne, Tintinhull, Yeovil, Yeovil Without (1894–1930), Yeovilton

In Other Poor Law Counties:

BEAMINSTER PLU (Dorset, Somerset until 1896, ent Dorset thereafter)
Misterton (1836–96), Seaborough[23]

BRADFORD PLU (Wilts, Somerset until 1882, ent Wilts thereafter)
Freshford (1836–82)

MERE PLU (Wilts, Somerset until 1896, ent Wilts thereafter)
Maiden Bradley,[24] Kilmington,[25] Stourton[24]

SOUTH MOLTON PLU (Devon, Somerset until 1884, ent Devon thereafter)
pt Exmoor[21]

SHERBORNE PLU (Dorset, Somerset until 1896, ent Dorset thereafter)
Goathill,[23] Marston Magna (1836–94), Poyntington,[23] Rimpton (1836–96), Sandford Orcas,[23] Trent[23]

SANITARY DISTRICTS

AXBRIDGE RSD
same as PLU less pt Burnham, pt Kewstoke (1883–94), pt Uphill, Weston-super-Mare, pt Worle (1883–94)

BATH RSD
same as PLU less pars in Bath USD

BATH USD
Bath St James, Bath St Michael, Bath St Peter and St Paul, Bathwick, Lyncombe and Widcombe, Walcot

BURNHAM UD (1894–1917[33])
Burnham

BURNHAM-ON-SEA UD (1917[33]–74)
Burnham (1917–33), Burnham-on-Sea (1933–74)

CHARD RD
Ashill, Broadway, Buckland St Mary, Chaffcombe, Chard, Chillington, Combe St Nicholas, West Crewkerne, Cricket Malherbie (1894–1933), Cricket St Thomas, Cudworth, Dinnington, Donyatt, West Dowlish (1894–1933), Dowlish Wake, Hinton St George, Ilminster (1894–99), Ilminster Without (1899–1974), Ilton, Kingstone, Knowle St Giles, Lopen, Merriott, Misterton, Seavington St Mary, Seavington St Michael, Shepton Beauchamp, Stocklinch, Wambrook, Wayford, Whitelackington, Whitestaunton, Winsham

CLEVEDON UD
Clevedon

CLUTTON RD
Cameley, Camerton (1894–1912), Chelwood, Chew Magna, Chew Stoke, Chilcompton, Clutton, Compton Martin, Farmborough, Farrington Gurney, East Harptree, West Harptree, Hinton Blewett, High Littleton, Litton, Newpnett Thrubwell, Norton Hawkfield (1894–96), Norton Malreward, Paulton, Publow, Stanton Drew, Ston Easton, Stowey (1894–1949), Stowey-Sutton (1949–74), Timsbury, Ubley, North Widcombe (1894–1933)

CREWKERNE UD (1894[34]–1974)
Crewkerne

DULVERTON RD
Brompton Regis, Brushford, Dulverton, Exford, Exmoor, Exton, Hawkridge (1894–1933), Huish Champflower, Skilgate, Upton, Winsford, Withiel Florey (1894–1933), Withypool

FROME RD
Babington (1894–1949), Beckington, Berkley, Buckland Dinham, Cloford (1894–1933), Coleford (1949–74), Elm, Farleigh Hungerford (1894–1933), Foxcote (1894–1933), Hardington (1894–1933), Hemington, Kilmersdon, Laverton (1894–1933), Leigh-upon-Mendip, Lullington, Marston Bigot (1894–1933), Mells, Norton St Philip, Nunney, Orchardleigh (1894–1933), Rodden (1894–1933), Rode, Selwood, Tellisford, Trudoxhill (1951–74), Upton Noble (1933–74), Wanstrow, Whatley, Witham Friary, Woolverton (1894–1933), Writhlington (1894–1933)

FROME UD
Frome

HIGHBRIDGE UD (1896[35]–1933)
North Highbridge, South Highbridge

ILMINSTER UD (1899[36]–1974)
Ilminster
KEYNSHAM RD (1894–1933)
Brislington, Burnett, Queen Charlton, Compton Dando, Corston, Kelston, Keynsham, Marksbury, Newton St Loe, Priston, Saltford, Stanton Prior, North Stoke, Whitchurch
KEYNSHAM UD (1938[37]–74)
Keynsham
LANGPORT RD
Aller, Babcary, Barrington, Barton St David, Beer Crocombe, Charlton Mackrell, Compton Dundon, Curry Mallet, Curry Rivel, Drayton, Earnshill (1894–1933), Fivehead, High Ham, Huish Episcopi, Isle Abbots, Isle Brewers, Keinton Mandeville, Kingsbury Episcopi, Kingsdon, Kingweston, Langport, Muchelney, Pitney, Puckington, Somerton, Long Sutton, Swell (1894–1933)
MINEHEAD UD
Minehead
MIDSOMER NORTON UD (1894–1933)
Midsomer Norton
NORTON-RADSTOCK UD (1933–74)
Norton-Radstock
PORTISHEAD UD
Portishead
RADSTOCK UD (1894–1933)
Radstock
SHEPTON MALLET RD
Ashwick, Batcombe, Binegar, West Bradley, Cranmore (1933–74), East Cranmore (1894–1933), West Cranmore (1894–1933), Croscombe, Ditcheat, Doulting, Downhead, Emborough, Evercreech, Holcombe, Hornblotton (1894–1933), Lamyat, Lydford (1933–74), East Lydford (1894–1933), West Lydford (1894–1933), Milton Clevedon, East Pennard, Pilton, Pylle, Stoke Lane (1894–1955), Stoke St Michael (1955–74), Stratton-on-the-Fosse, Upton Noble (1894–1933)
SHEPTON MALLET UD
Shepton Mallet
STREET UD
Street
TAUNTON RD
Angersleigh (1894–1933), Ash Priors, West Bagborough, Bickenhall, Cheddon Fitzpaine, Churchstanton (1896–1974), Combe Florey, Corfe, Cothelstone, Creech St Michael, Curland, North Curry, Durston, Halse, West Hatch, Hatch Beauchamp, Heathfield (1894–1933), Bishop's Hull Without, Kingston (1894–1952), Kingston St Mary (1952–74), Bishop's Lydeard, Lydeard St Lawrence, West Monkton, Norton Fitzwarren, Orchard Portman, Otterford, Pitminster, Ruishton, Staple Fitzpaine, Staplegrove, Stoke St Gregory, Stoke St Mary, Taunton St James Without (1894–1933), Taunton St Mary Magdalene Without (1894–1933), Thorn Falcon, Thurlbear (1894–1933), Tolland, Trull, Wilton (1894–1921)
WATCHET UD (1902[38]–74)
Watchet
WELLINGTON RD
Ashbrittle, Beathealton, Bradford, West Buckland, Chipstable, Fitzhead, Kittisford (1894–1933), Langford Budville, Milverton, Nynehead, Oake, Raddington (1894–1933), Runnington (1894–1933), Sampford Arundel, Stawley, Thorne St Margaret, Wellington Without (1933–74), Wiveliscombe (1933–74), Wiveliscombe Without
WELLINGTON UD
Wellington
WELLS RD
Baltonsborough, Butleigh, Chewton Mendip, Dinder, Godney (1904–74), Meare, West Pennard, Priddy, Sharpham, Rodney Stoke, Walton, Wells St Cuthbert Out, Westbury, Wookey, North Wootton
WESTON-SUPER-MARE UD (1894–1937[15])
pt Kewstoke (1894–96), pt Worle (1894–96), Weston-super-Mare
WILLITON RD
Bicknoller, Brompton Ralph, Carhampton, Clatworthy, Old Cleeve, Crowcombe, Culbone (1894–1933), Cutcombe, Dodington (1894–1933), Dunster, Elworthy, Holford, Kilton with Lilstock (1894–1933), Kilve, Luccombe, Luxborough, Minehead Without, Monksilver, Nettlecombe, Oare, Porlock, East Quantoxhead, West Quantoxhead, St Decuman's (1894–1902), Sampford Brett, Selworthy, Stogumber, Stogursey, Stoke Perro (1894–1933), Stringston, Timberscombe, Treborough, Williton, Withycombe, Wootton Courtenay (1894–1961), Wootton Courtney (1894–1961)
WINCANTON RD
Alford, Ansford, North Barrow, South Barrow, Blackford (1894–1933), Bratton Seymour, Brewham (1933–74), North Brewham (1894–1933), South Brewham (1894–1933), Bruton, North Cadbury, South Cadbury, Queen Camel, Castle Cary, Charlton Horethorne, Charlton Musgrove, North Cheriton, Abbas Combe, Compton Pauncefoot, Corton Denham, Cucklington, Henstridge, Holton, Horsington, Lovington, Maperton, Milborne Port, Penselwood, Pitcombe, Shepton Montague, Sparkford, Stoke Trister, Stowell (1894–1933), Sutton Montis (1894–1933), Weston Bampfylde (1894–1933), Wheathill (1894–1933), Wincanton, Yarlington
WIVELISCOMBE UD (1894–1933)
Wiveliscombe
YEOVIL RD
Ash (1895–1974), Ashington (1894–1933), Barwick, Brympton, West Camel, Chilthorne Domer, Chilton Cantelo, Chiselborough, East Chinnock, West Chinnock, Closworth, East Coker, West Coker, Hardington Mandeville, Haselbury Plucknett, Ilchester, Limington, Long Load (1895–1974), Lufton (1894–1933), Marston Magna, Martock, Montacute, Mudford, Northover (1894–1933), Norton sub Hamdon, Odcombe, Pendomer (1894–1933), North Perrott, South Petherton, Podimore (1894–1933), Rimpton, Sock Dennis (1894–1957), Stoke sub Hamdon, Sutton Bingham (1894–1933), Thorne (1894–1933), Tintinhull, Yeovil Without, Yeovilton

NON-METROPOLITAN COUNTY

As constituted 1 Apr 1974, defined in terms of Adm Co units as of 31 Mar. A considerable pt of Somerset Adm Co was transferred to help cr Avon Non-Metropolitan Co, qv.

MENDIP DIST
pt Axbridge RD (the pts not in Sedgemoor Dist or transf to Avon, and pts of pars retained in Somerset[39]), pt Clutton RD (the pts not transf to Avon and pts of pars retained in Somerset[40]), Frome RD, Frome UD, Glastonbury MB, Shepton Mallet RD, Shepton Mallet UD, Street UD, Wells MB, Wells RD

SEDGEMOOR DIST
pt Axbridge RD (Chapel Allerton, Axbridge, Badgworth, Berrow, Brean, East Brent, Brent Knoll, Burnham Without, Cheddar, Compton Bishop, Lympsham, Mark, Shipham, Weare, Wedmore, and pt of par retained in Somerset[41]), Bridgwater MB, Bridgwater RD, Burnham-on-Sea UD

WEST SOMERSET DIST
Dulverton RD, Minehead UD, Watchet UD, Williton RD

TAUNTON DEANE DIST
Taunton MB, Taunton RD, Wellington RD, Wellington UD

YEOVIL DIST
Chard MB, Chard RD, Crewkerne UD, Ilminster UD, Langport RD, Wincanton RD, Yeovil MB, Yeovil RD

SUFFOLK

ALTERATIONS IN COUNTY BOUNDARIES

As noted by year below, Suffolk pars gained territory from or lost it to pars in adjoining counties or county boroughs, or were entirely transferred to them. Details of these alterations are noted in Part I of the *Guide* under Suffolk.

ANCIENT COUNTY (until 1889: Hds, Bors, MBs, PLUs, RSD, USDs)
1866 Bures St Mary. *1879* Haverhill. *1883* Kedington. *1885* Earsham, Mendham, Middleton.

EAST SUFFOLK ADMINISTRATIVE COUNTY (1889–1974: Hds,[1] PLUs, MBs, RDs, UDs, with Ipswich CB associated)
1889 Gorleston. *1894* Belstead, Bramford, Rushford, Sproughton, Whitton cum Thurleston. *1934* Alnesbourn Priory, Belstead, Bramford, Purdis Farm, Rushmere St Andrew, Sproughton. *1938* East Bergholt. *1952* Akenham, Bramford, Nacton, Purdis Farm, Rushmere St Andrew, Spoughton, Tuddenham, Westerfield, Whitton.

WEST SUFFOLK ADMINISTRATIVE COUNTY (1889–1974: Hds,[1] PLUs, MBs, RDs, UDs)
1889 Newmarket All Saints. *1894* Wood Ditton, Newmarket St Mary, Thetford St Cuthbert, Thetford St Mary. *1895* Brandon, Kedington. *1896* Ballingdon.

SUFFOLK NON-METROPOLITAN COUNTY (from 1974: Dists)
1974 Belton, Bradwell, Burgh Castle, Fritton, Herringfleet, Hopton-on-Sea.

ASSOCIATED COUNTY BOROUGH

For constituent pars see listing for BOROUGHS in this Part of the *Guide*.

IPSWICH CB
Bdry: 1894,[2] 1934,[3] 1952.[4]

HUNDREDS[1]

BABERGH HD
Acton, Alpheton, Assington, pt Ballingdon,[5] pt Boxford, Boxted, Bures St Mary (pt until 1866, ent from 1866), Cavendish, Chilton, Cockfield, Great Cornard, Little Cornard, Edwardstone, Brent Eleigh, Monks Eleigh, Glemsford, Groton, Hartest, Lavenham, Lawshall, Long Melford, Milden, Nayland (until 1884), Nayland with Wissington (from 1884), Newton, Polstead, Preston St Mary, Shimpling, Somerton, Stanstead, Stoke by Nayland, Sudbury[5] (from 1880s), Sudbury All Saints[5] (until 1880s), Sudbury St Bartholomew[5] (from 1858), Sudbury St Gregory[5] (until 1880s), Sudbury St Peter[5] (until 1880s), Great Waldingfield, Little Waldingfield, Wissington (until 1884)

BLACKBOURN HD
Great Ashfield, Badwell Ash, Bardwell, Barnham, Barningham, Chimney Mills (from 1858), Culford, Elmswell, Euston, Fakenham Magna, Hepworth, Hinderclay, Honington, Hopton, Hunston, Ingham, Ixworth, Ixworth Thorpe, Knettishall, Langham, Little Livermere, Norton, Rickinghall Inferior, pt Rushford, Rymer (from 1858), Sapiston, Stanton (prob from 17th cent), Stanton All Saints (prob until 17th cent), Stanton St John the Baptist (prob until 17th cent), West Stow, Stowlangtoft, Thelnetham, Troston, Walsham-le-Willows, Wattisfield, Coney Weston, Market Weston, Wordwell

BLYTHING HD
Aldringham with Thorpe, Benacre, Blyford, Blythburgh, Bramfield, Brampton, Buxlow (until 1721), Chediston, Cookley, South Cove, Covehithe, Cratfield, Darsham, Dunwich,[6] Easton Bavants, Frostenden, Halesworth, Henham (from 1866), pt Henstead, Heveningham, Holton, Huntingfield, Knoddishall, Leiston, Linstead Magna, Linstead Parva, Middleton, Peasenhall, Reydon, Rumburgh, Sibton, Sotherton, Southwold,[5] Spexhall, Stoven, Theberton, Thorington, Ubbeston, Uggeshall, Walberswick, Walpole, Wangford, Wenhaston, Westhall, Westleton, Wissett, Wrentham, Yoxford

BOSMERE AND CLAYDON HD
Akenham, Ashbocking, Badley, Barham, Barking, Battisford, Baylham, Great Blakenham, Little Blakenham, Bramford,[5] Great Bricett, Claydon, Coddenham, Creeting All Saints (until 1884),

Creeting St Mary, Creeting St Olave (until 1884), Crowfield, Flowton, Gosbeck, Helmingham, Hemingstone, Henley, Mickfield, Needham Market (from 1866), Nettlestead, Offton, Ringshall, Somersham, Earl Stonham, Little Stonham, Stonham Aspall, Swilland, Westerfield,[5] Whitton cum Thurleston,[5] Willisham

CARLFORD HD

Great Bealings, Little Bealings, Brightwell, Burgh, Clopton, Culpho, Foxhall, Grundisburgh, Hasketon, Kesgrave, Martlesham, Newbourne, Otley, Playford, Rushmere,[5] Tuddenham, Waldringfield, Witnesham

COLNEIS HD

Alnesbourn Priory (from 1858), Bucklesham, Falkenham, Felixstowe, Hemley, Kirton, Levington, Nacton, Purdis Farm (from 1858), Stratton Hall (from 1858), Trimley St Martin, Trimley St Mary, Walton

COSFORD HD

Aldham, Bildeston, pt Boxford, Brettenham, Chelsworth, Elmsett, Hadleigh, Hadleigh Hamlet (from 1866), Hitcham, Kersey, Kettlebaston, Layham, Lindsey, Naughton, Nedging, Semer, Thorpe Morieux, Wattisham, Whatfield

HARTISMERE HD

Aspall, Bacton, Botesdale (from 1866), Braiseworth, Brome, Burgate, Cotton, Eye,[5] Finningham, Gislingham, Mellis, Mendlesham, Oakley, Occold, Palgrave, Redgrave, Redlingfield, Rickinghalll Superior, Rishangles, Stoke Ash, Stuston, Thorndon, Thornham Magna, Thornham Parva, Thrandeston, Thwaite, Westhorpe, Wetheringsett cum Brockford, Wickham Skeith, Wortham, Wyverstone, Yaxley

HOXNE HD

Athelington, Badingham, Bedfield, Bedingfield, Brundish, Carlton (until 1885), Denham, Dennington, Fressingfield, Horham, Hoxne, Kelsale (until 1885), Kelsale cum Carlton (from 1885), Laxfield, Mendham (pt until 1885, ent from 1885), Metfield, Saxstead, Monk Soham, Southolt, Stradbroke, Syleham, Tannington, Weybread, Wilby, Wingfield, Withersdale (until 1885), Worlingworth

LACKFORD HD

Barton Mills, pt Brandon, Cavenham, Elveden, Eriswell, Exning,[5] Freckenham, Herringswell, Icklingham, pt Kentford, Lakenheath, Mildenhall, pt Newmarket St Mary, Santon Downham, pt Thetford St Cuthbert,[5] pt Thetford St Mary,[5] Tuddenham, Wangford, Worlington

LOES HD

Brandeston, pt Bredfield, Butley, Campsey Ash, Charsfield, Cretingham, pt Dallinghoo, Easton, Eyke, Framlingham, Hacheston, Hoo, Kenton, Kettleburgh, Letheringham, Marlesford, Monewden, Rendlesham, Earl Soham, Woodbridge

MUTFORD AND LOTHINGLAND HD

Ashby, Barnby, Belton, Blundeston, Bradwell, Burgh Castle, Carlton Colville, Corton, Flixton, Fritton, Gisleham, Gorleston,[5] Gunton, Herringfleet, Hopton, Kessingland, Kirkley, Lound, Lowestoft,[5] Mutford, Oulton, Pakefield, Rushmere, Somerleyton

PLOMESGATE HD

Aldeburgh,[5] Benhall, Blaxhall, Bruisyard, Chillesford, Cransford, Farnham, Friston, Gedgrave (from 1858), Great Glemham, Little Glemham, Havergate Island (from 1858), Hazlewood (from 1866), Iken, Orford,[5] Parham, Rendham, Saxmundham, Snape, Sternfield, Stratford St Andrew, Sudbourne, Swefling, Tunstall, Wantisden

RISBRIDGE HD

Barnardiston, Great Bradley, Little Bradley, Chedburgh, Clare,[5] Cowlinge, Dalham, Denham, Denston, Depden, Gazeley, pt Haverhill, Hawkedon, Higham Green (from 1866), Hundon, pt Kedington, pt Kentford, pt Kentford, Lidgate, Moulton, Ousden, Poslingford, Monks Risbridge (from 1858), Stansfield, Stoke by Clare, Stradishall, Great Thurlow, Little Thurlow, Wickhambrook, Withersfield, Wixoe, Great Wratting, Little Wratting

SAMFORD HD

Belstead, Bentley, East Bergholt, Brantham, Burstall, Capel St Mary, Chattisham, Chelmondiston, Copdock, Erwarton, Freston, Harkstead, Higham, Hintlesham, Holbrook, Holton St Mary, Raydon, Shelly, Shotley, Sproughton,[5] Stratford St Mary, Stutton, Tattingstone, Washbrook, Great Wenham, Little Wenham, Wherstead, Woolverstone

STOW HD

Buxhall, Combs, Creeting St Peter, Great Finborough, Little Finborough, Gipping (from 1866), Harleston, Haughley, Old Newton, Onehouse, Shelland, Stowmarket, Stowupland, Wetherden

THEDWASTRE HD

Ampton, Great Barton, Beyton, Bradfield Combust, Bradfield St Clare, Bradfield St George, Drinkstone, Felsham, Fornham St Genevieve, Fornham St Martin, Gedding, Hessett, Great Livermere, Pakenham, Rattlesden, Rougham, Rushbrooke, Stanningfield, Thurston, Timworth, Tostock, Great Welnetham, Little Welnetham, Woolpit

THINGOE HD

Barrow, Brockley, Chevington, Flempton, Fornham All Saints, Hardwick (from 1858), Hargrave, Hawstead, Hengrave, Horringer, Ickworth, Lackford, Nowton, Rede, Risby, Great Saxham, Little Saxham, Westley, Whepstead

THREDLING HD

Ashfield with Thorpe, Debenham, Framsden, Pettaugh, Winston

WANGFORD HD

Barsham, Beccles,[5] Bungay Holy Trinity,[5] Bungay St Mary,[5] North Cove, pt Earsham (until 1885), South Elmham All Saints (until 1737), South Elmham All Saints and St Nicholas (from 1737), South Elmham St Cross, South Elmham St James, South Elmham St Margaret, South Elmham St Michael, South Elmham St Nicholas (until 1737), South Elmham St Peter, Ellough, Flixton, pt Henstead, Homersfield, Ilketshall St Andrew, Ilketshall St John, Ilketshall St Lawrence, Ilketshall St Margaret, Mettingham, Redisham, Ringsfield, Shadingfield, Shipmeadow, Sotterley, Weston, Willingham, Worlingham

WILFORD HD
Alderton, Bawdsey, Boulge, Boyton, pt Bredfield, Bromeswell, Capel St Andrew, pt Dallinghoo, Dallinghoo Wield (from 1858), Debach, Hollesley, Melton, Pettistree, Ramsholt, Shottisham, Sutton, Ufford, Wickham Market

BOROUGHS

Units with some degree of burghal character[7] are denominated 'Bor'. Those which did not sustain that status until the 19th cent are in italics. Municipal Boroughs were established by the Municipal Corporations Act, 1835,[8] or by later charter. MBs in existence pt or all of the period 1889–1974 have [East] or [West] shown to indicate inclusion in East Suffolk or West Suffolk, respectively.

ALDEBURGH BOR, MB (1885–1974) [East]
Aldeburgh
BECCLES BOR/MB [East]
Beccles
BUNGAY BOR
Bungay Holy Trinity, Bungay St Mary
BURY ST EDMUNDS BOR/MB [West]
Bury St Edmunds (1895–1974), Bury St Edmunds St James (*temp* Edw VI–1895), Bury St Edmunds St Mary (until 1895)
CLARE BOR
Clare
DUNWICH BOR[6]
Dunwich
EXNING BOR
Exning
EYE BOR/MB [East]
Eye
IPSWICH BOR/MB/CB
pt Belstead (until 1894), pt Bramford (until 1894), Ipswich (1903–74), Ipswich St Clement (until 1903), Ipswich St Helen (until 1903), Ipswich St Lawrence (until 1903), Ipswich St Margaret (until 1903), Ipswich St Mary at the Elms (until 1903), Ipswich St Mary at the Quay (until 1903), Ipswich St Mary at the Tower (until 1903), Ipswich St Mary Stoke (until 1903), Ipswich St Matthew (until 1903), Ipswich St Nicholas (until 1903), Ipswich St Peter (until 1903), Ipswich St Stephen (until 1903), Rushmere (pt until 1894, ent 1894–1903), Shire Hall Yard (1858–1903), pt Sproughton (until 1894), Warren House (1858–1903), pt Westerfield (until 1894), Westerfield in Ipswich (1894–1903), Whitton cum Thurleston[9] (pt until 1894, ent 1894–1903)
LOWESTOFT MB (1885–1974) [East]
pt Gunton (1890–94), Kirkley (1890–1907), Lowestoft
ORFORD BOR
Orford
SOUTHWOLD BOR/MB [East]
Southwold
SUDBURY BOR, MB (1892–1974) [West]
Ballingdon (pt 1892–96, ent 1894–1974), pt Bulmer [Essex] (1892–96), Sudbury (1880s–1974), Sudbury All Saints (until 1880s), Sudbury St Bartholomew (1858–1935), Sudbury St Gregory (until 1880s), Sudbury St Peter (until 1880s)
THETFORD BOR/MB (Norfolk)
ent Norfolk but incl Suffolk pts of Thetford St Cuthbert, Thetford St Mary, both made ent Norfolk 1894

POOR LAW UNIONS

In Suffolk Poor Law County:[10]
BLYTHING PLU
Aldringham with Thorpe, Benacre, Blyford, Blythburgh, Bramfield, Brampton, Carlton (1835–85), Chediston, Cockley, South Cove, Covehithe, Cratfield, Darsham, Dunwich, Easton Bavants, Frostenden, Halesworth, Henham, Henstead, Heveningham, Holton, Huntingfield, Kelsale (1835–85), Kelsale cum Carlton (1885–1930), Knodishall, Leiston, Linstead Magna, Linstead Parva, Middleton, Peasenhall, Reydon, Rumburgh, Sibton, Sotherton, Southwold, Spexhall, Stoven, Theberton, Thorington, Ubbeston, Uggeshall, Walberswick, Walpole, Wangford, Wenhaston, Westhall, Westleton, Wissett, Wrentham, Yoxford
BOSMERE AND CLAYDON PLU
Akenham, Ashbocking, Ashfield with Thorpe, Badley, Barham, Barking, Battisford, Baylham, Great Blakenham, Little Blakenham, Bramford, Great Bricett, Claydon, Coddenham, Creeting All Saints (1835–84), Creeting St Mary, Creeting St Olave (1835–84), Crowfield, Darmsden (orig sep rated, status not sustained), Debenham, Flowton, Framsden, Gosbeck, Helmingham, Hemingstone, Henley, Mickfield, Needham Market (1907–30), Nettlestead, Offton, Pettaugh, Ringshall, Somersham, Earl Stonham, Little Stonham, Stonham Aspall, Swilland, Whitton (1894–1930), Willisham, Winston
BURY ST EDMUNDS PLU
In 1907 this PLU gained all the pars of Thingoe PLU (qv); prev this PLU contained Bury St Edmunds (1895–1930), Bury St Edmunds St James (1835–95), Bury St Edmunds St Mary (1835–95)
COSFORD PLU
Aldham, Bildeston, Boxford, Brettenham, Chelsworth, Cockfield, Edwardstone, Brent Eleigh, Monks Eleigh, Elmsett, Groton, Hadleigh, Hadleigh

Hamlet, Hitcham, Kersey, Kettlebaston, Lavenham, Layham, Lindsey, Milden, Naughton, Nedging, Polstead, Preston St Mary, Semer, Thorpe Morieux, Wattisham, Whatfield

HARTISMERE PLU

Aspall, Athelington (1907–30), Bacton, Badingham (1907–30), Bedfield (1907–30), Bedingfield (1907–30), Botesdale, Braiseworth, Brome, Brundish (1907–30), Burgate, Cotton, Denham (1907–30), Dennington (1907–30), Eye, Finningham, Fressingfield (1907–30), Gislingham, Horham (1907–30), Hoxne (1907–30), Laxfield (1907–30), Mellis, Mendham (1907–30), Mendlesham, Metfield (1907–30), Oakley, Occold, Palgrave, Redlingfield, Rickinghall Superior, Rishangles, Saxstead (1907–30), Monk Soham (1907–30), Southolt (1907–30), Stoke Ash, Stradbroke (1907–30), Stuston, Syleham (1907–30), Tannington (1907–30), Thorndon, Thornham Magna, Thornham Parva, Thrandeston, Thwaite, Westhorpe, Wetheringsett cum Brockford, Weybread (1907–30), Wickham Skeith, Wilby (1907–30), Wingfield (1907–30), Worlingworth (1907–30), Wortham, Wyverstone, Yaxley

HOXNE PLU (1835–1907)

Athelington, Badingham, Bedfield, Bedingfield, Brundish, Denham, Dennington, Fressingfield, Horham, Hoxne, Laxfield, Mendham,[11] Metfield, Saxstead, Monk Soham, Southolt, Stradbroke, Syleham, Tannington, Weybread, Wilby, Wingfield, Withersdale (1835–85), Worlingworth

IPSWICH PLU

Ipswich (1903–30), Westerfield (1835–94), Westerfield in Ipswich (1894–1903), Whitton cum Thurleston (1835–1903), and the following pars in Ipswich, all in the PLU 1835–1903: St Clement, St Helen, St Lawrence, St Margaret, St Mary at the Elms, St Mary at the Quay, St Mary at the Tower, St Mary Stoke, St Matthew, St Nicholas, St Peter, St Stephen

MILDENHALL PLU

Barton Mills, Cavenham, Elveden, Eriswell, Freckenham, Herringswell, Icklingham, Kentford, Lakenheath, Mildenhall, Tuddenham, Wangford, Worlington

MUTFORD AND LOTHINGLAND PLU

Ashby, Barnby, Belton, Blundeston, Bradwell, Burgh Castle, Carlton Colville, Corton, Flixton, Fritton, Gisleham, Gunton, Herringfleet, Hopton, Kessingland, Kirkley (1835–1907), Lound, Lowestoft, Mutford, Oulton, Oulton Broad (1907–19), Pakefield, Rushmere, Somerleyton

NEWMARKET PLU (Suffolk, Cambs)

Dalham, Wood Ditton,[12] Exning, Gazeley, Higham Green, Lidgate, Moulton, Newmarket All Saints,[13] Newmarket St Mary,[14] Ousden

PLOMESGATE PLU

Aldeburgh, Benhall, Blaxhall, Brandeston, Bruisyard, Butley, Campsey Ash, Chillesford, Cransford, Cretingham, Easton, Eyke, Farnham, Framlingham, Friston, Gedgrave, Great Glemham, Little Glemham, Hacheston, Havergate Island, Hazlewood, Hoo, Iken, Kenton, Kettleburgh, Letheringham, Marlesford, Monewden, Orford, Parham, Rendham, Rendlesham, Saxmundham, Snape, Earl Soham, Sternfield, Stratford St Andrew, Sudbourne, Swefling, Tunstall, Wantisden, Wickham Market

RISBRIDGE PLU (Suffolk, Essex)

Barnardiston, Great Bradley, Little Bradley, Clare, Cowlinge, Denston, Hundon, Haverhill,[15] Kedington,[16] Poslingford, Monks Risbridge, Stansfield, Stoke by Clare, Stradishall, Great Thurlow, Little Thurlow, Wickhambrook, Withersfield, Wixoe, Great Wratting, Little Wratting

SAMFORD PLU

Belstead, Bentley, East Bergholt, Brantham, Burstall, Capel St Mary, Chattisham, Chelmondiston, Copdock, Erwarton, Freston, Harkstead, Higham, Hintlesham, Holbrook, Holton St Mary, Raydon, Shelly, Shotley, Sproughton, Stratford St Mary, Stutton, Tattingstone, Washbrook, Great Wenham, Little Wenham, Wherstead, Woolverstone

STOW PLU

Great Ashfield, Badwell Ash, Boyton, Buxhall, Combs, Creeting St Peter, Drinkstone, Elmswell, Felsham, Great Finborough, Little Finborough, Gedding, Gipping, Harleston, Haughley, Hessett, Hinderclay, Hunston, Langham, Old Newton, Norton, Onehouse, Rattlesden, Rickinghall Inferior, Shelland, Stowlangtoft, Stowmarket, Stowupland, Thurston, Tostock, Walsham-le-Willows, Wattisfield, Wetherden, Woolpit

SUDBURY PLU (Suffolk, Essex)

Acton, Alpheton, Assington, Ballingdon,[17] Boxted, Bures St Mary,[18] Cavendish, Chilton, Great Cornard, Little Cornard, Glemsford, Hartest, Hawkedon, Lawshall, Long Melford, Nayland (1835–84), Nayland with Wissington (1884–1930), Newton, Shimpling, Somerton, Stanstead, Stoke by Nayland, Sudbury (1880s–1930), Sudbury All Saints (1835–80s), Sudbury St Bartholomew, Sudbury St Gregory (1835–80s), Sudbury St Peter (1835–80s), Great Waldingfield, Little Waldingfield, Wissington (1835–84)

THINGOE PLU (1836–1907)

Ampton, Bardwell, Barrow, Great Barton, Bradfield Combust, Bradfield St Clare, Bradfield St George, Brockley, Chedburgh, Chimney Mills (1858–97), Chevington, Culford, Denham, Depden, Flempton, Fornham All Saints, Fornham St Genevieve, Fornham St Martin, Hardwick, Hargrave, Hawstead, Hengrave, Horningsheath, Ickworth, Ingham, Ixworth, Ixworth Thorpe, Lackford, Great Livermere, Little Livermere, Nowton, Pakenham, Rede, Risby, Rougham, Rushbrooke, Great Saxham, Little Saxham, Stanningfield, Stanton, West Stow, Timworth, Troston, Great Welnetham, Little Welnetham, Westley, Whepstead, Wordwell

WANGFORD PLU

Barsham, Beccles, Bungay (1910–30), Bungay Holy Trinity (1835–1910), Bungay St Mary (1835–1910), North Cove, South Elmham All Saints and St Nicholas, South Elmham St Cross, South Elmham St James, South Elmham St Margaret, South Elmham St Michael, South Elmham St Peter, Ellough, Flixton, Homersfield, Ilketshall St Andrew, Ilketshall St John, Ilketshall St Lawrence, Ilketshall St Margaret, Mettingham, Redisham, Ringsfield, Shadingfield, Shipmeadow, Sotterley, Weston, Willingham, Worlingham

WOODBRIDGE PLU

Alderton, Alnesbourn Priory, Bawdsey, Great Bealings, Little Bealings, Boulge, Boyton, Bredfield, Brightwell, Bromeswell, Bucklesham, Burgh, Capel St Andrew, Charsfield, Clopton, Culpho, Dallinghoo, Dallinghoo Wield, Debach, Falkenham, Felixstowe, Foxhall, Grundisburgh, Hasketon, Hemley, Hollesley, Kesgrave, Kirtton, Levington, Martlesham, Melton, Nacton, Newbourne, Otley, Pettistree, Playford, Purdis Farm, Ramsholt, Rushmere (1836–1903), Rushmere St Andrew (1894–1930), Shottisham, Stratton Hall, Sutton, Trimley St Martin, Trimley St Mary, Tuddenham, Ufford, Waldringfield, Walton (1835–1914), Witnesham, Woodbridge

In Other Poor Law Counties:

DEPWADE PLU (Norfolk)

Earsham[19]

THETFORD PLU (Norfolk)

Barham, Barningham, Brandon, Euston, Fakenham Magna, Hepworth, Honington, Hopton, Kenttishall, Rushford,[20] Rymer (1835–81), Santon Downham, Sapiston, Thelnetham, Thetford St Cuthbert,[20] Thetford St Mary,[20] Coney Weston, Market Weston

YARMOUTH PLU (Norfolk)

Gorleston[21]

SANITARY DISTRICTS

ALDEBURGH USD (1885[23]–94)
Aldeburgh

BECCLES USD
Beccles

BLYTHING RSD
same as PLU less Southwold

BOSMERE AND CLAYDON RSD
same as PLU less pt Bramford

BURY ST EDMUNDS USD
Bury St Edmunds St James, Bury St Edmunds St Mary

COSFORD RSD
same as PLU less Hadleigh (ent 1875–83, pt 1883–94)

DEPWADE RSD
same as PLU for pt of Suffolk par

EYE USD
Eye

FELIXSTOWE AND WALTON USD (1887[22]–94)
Felixstowe, Walton

HADLEIGH USD
Hadleigh (ent 1875–83, pt 1883–94)

HARTISMERE RSD
same as PLU less Eye

HAVERHILL USD
Haverhill (ent 1875–83, pt 1883–94)

HOXNE RSD
same as PLU

IPSWICH RSD
the pts of Ipswich PLU not in Ipswich MB

IPSWICH USD
same as Ipswich MB

LOWESTOFT USD (1885[23]–94)
pt Gunton (1890[24]–94), Kirkley (1890[24]–94), Lowestoft

MILDENHALL RSD
same as PLU

MUTFORD AND LOTHINGLAND RSD
same as PLU less pt Gunton (1890–94), Kirkley (1890–94), Lowestoft (1885–94)

NEWMARKET RSD
same as PLU for Suffolk pars less pt Wood Ditton, pt Exning, Newmarket All Saints, Newmarket St Mary

NEWMARKET USD (Suffolk, Cambs)
pt Wood Ditton, pt Exning, Newmarket All Saints, Newmarket St Mary

PLOMESGATE RSD
same as PLU less Aldeburgh (1885–94)

RISBRIDGE RSD
same as PLU less Haverhill (ent 1875–83, pt 1883–94)

SAMFORD RSD
same as PLU less pt Belstead, pt Sproughton

SOUTHWOLD USD
Southwold

STOW RSD
same as PLU less Stowmarket

STOWMARKET USD
Stowmarket

SUDBURY RSD
same as PLU less pt Ballingdon, all the Sudbury pars

SUDBURY USD (Suffolk, Essex)
pt Ballingdon, pt Bulmer [Essex], Sudbury (1880s–94), Sudbury All Saints (1875–80s), Sudbury St Bartholomew, Sudbury St Gregory (1875–80s), Sudbury St Peter (1875–80s)

THETFORD RSD
same as PLU for the Suffolk pars less pt Thetford St Cuthbert, pt Thetford St Mary

THETFORD USD (Norfolk, Suffolk)
ent Norfolk and also pt Thetford St Cuthbert, pt Thetford St Mary

THINGOE RSD
same as PLU

WANGFORD RSD
same as PLU less Beccles

WOODBRIDGE RSD
same as PLU less Felixstowe (1887–94), pt Rushmere, Walton (1887–94), Woodbridge (1894)

WOODBRIDGE USD (1894[32])
Woodbridge

YARMOUTH USD (Norfolk, Suffolk)
ent Norfolk and also Gorleston

EAST SUFFOLK ADMINISTRATIVE COUNTY

For MBs and the associated CB see BOROUGHS.

BLYTH RD (1934–74)
Aldringham with Thorpe, Badingham, Benhall, Blythburgh, Bramfield, Brandeston, Bruisyard, Chediston, Cookley, Cransford, Cratfield, Darsham, Dennington, Dunwich, Easton, Farnham, Framlingham, Friston, Great Glemham, Little Glemham, Hacheston, Heveningham, Huntingfield, Kelsale cum Carlton, Kettleburgh, Knodishall, Linstead Magna, Linstead Parva, Marlesford, Middleton, Parham, Peasenhall, Rendham, Saxstead, Sibton, Snape, Earl Soham, Sternfield, Stratford St Andrew, Swefling, Theberton, Thorington, Ubbeston, Walberswick, Walpole, Wenhaston, Westleton, Yoxford

BLYTHING RD (1894–1934)
Aldringham with Thorpe, Benacre, Blyford, Blythburgh, Bramfield, Brampton, Chediston, Cookley, South Cove, Covehithe, Cratfield, Darsham, Dunwich, Easton Bavents, Frostenden, Halesworth (1894–1900), Henham, Henstead, Heveningham, Holton, Huntingfield, Kelsale cum Carlton, Knodishall, Linstead Magna, Linstead Parva, Middleton, Peasenhall, Reydon, Rumburgh, Sibton, Sotherton, Spexhall, Stoven, Theberton, Thorington, Ubbeston, Uggeshall, Walberswick, Walpole, Wangford, Wenhaston, Westhall, Westleton, Wissett, Wrentham, Yoxford

BOSMERE AND CLAYDON RD (1894–1934)
Akenham, Ashbocking, Ashfield with Thorpe, Badley, Barhan, Barking, Battisford, Baylham, Great Blakenham, Little Blakenham, Bramford, Great Bricett, Claydon, Coddenham, Creeting St Mary, Crowfield, Debenham, Flowton, Framsden, Gosbeck, Helmingham, Hemingstone, Henley, Mickfield, Needham Market (1907–34), Nettlestead, Offton, Pettaugh, Ringshall, Somersham, Earl Stonham, Little Stonham, Stonham Aspall, Swilland, Whitton, Willisham, Winston

BUNGAY UD (1910[25]–74)
Bungay

DEBEN RD (1934–74)
Alderton, Bawdsey, Great Bealings, Little Bealings, Blaxhall, Boulge, Boyton, Bredfield, Brightwell, Bromeswell, Bucklesham, Burgh, Butley, Campsey Ash, Capel St Andrew, Charsfield, Chillesford, Clopton, Cretingham, Dallinghoo, Dallinghoo Wield, Debach, Easton, Eyke, Falkenham, Foxhall, Grundisburgh, Hasketon, Havergate Island, Hemley, Holbrook, Hollesley, Hoo, Iken, Kesgrave, Kirton, Letheringham, Levington, Martlesham, Melton, Monewden, Nacton, Newbourne, Orford, Otley, Pettistree, Playford, Plomesgate, Ramsholt, Rendlesham, Shottisham, Earl Soham, Stratton Hall, Sudbourne, Sutton, Swilland, Trimley St Martin, Trimley St Mary, Tuddenham, Tunstall, Ufford, Waldringfield, Wantisden, Westerfield, Wickham Market, Witnesham

FELIXSTOWE UD (1914[26]–74)
Felixstowe

FELIXSTOWE AND WALTON UD (1894–1914[26])
Felixstowe, Walton

GIPPING RD (1934–74)
Akenham, Ashbocking, Ashfield with Thorpe, Badley, Barham, Barking, Battisford, Baylham, Great Blakenham, Litttle Blakenham, Bramford, Great Bricett, Buxhall, Claydon, Coddenham, Combs, Creeting St Mary, Creeting St Peter, Crowfield, Debenham, Great Finborough, Little Finborough, Flowton, Framsden, Gipping, Gosbeck, Harleston, Haughley, Helmingham, Hemingstone, Henley, Mickfield, Needham Market, Nettlestead, Old Newton, Offton, Onehouse, Pettaugh, Ringshall, Shelland, Somersham, Earl Stonham, Little Stonham, Stonham Aspall, Stowupland, Wetherden, Whitton (1934–52), Willisham, Winston

HALESWORTH UD (1900[27]–94)
Halesworth

HARTISMERE RD
Aspall, Athelington (1934–74), Bacton, Bedfield (1934–74), Bedingfield (1934–74), Botesdale, Braiseworth, Brome, Brundish (1934–74), Burgate, Cotton, Denham (1934–74), Finningham, Fressingfield (1934–74), Gislingham, Horham (1934–74), Hoxne (1934–74), Kenton (1934–74), Laxfield (1934–74), Mellis, Mendham (1934–74), Mendlesham, Metfield (1934–74), Oakley, Occold, Palgrave, Redgrave, Redlingfield, Rickinghall Superior, Rishangles, Monk Soham (1934–74), Southolt (1934–74), Stoke Ash, Stradbroke (1934–74), Stuston, Syleham (1934–74), Tannington (1934–74), Thorndon, Thornham Magna, Thornham Parva, Thrandeston, Thwaite, Westhorpe, Wetheringsett cum Brockford, Weybread (1934–74), Wickham Skeith, Wilby (1934–74), Wingfield (1934–74), Worlingworth (1934–74), Wortham, Wyverstone, Yaxley

HOXNE RD (1894–1934)
Athelington, Badingham, Bedfield, Bedingfield, Brundish, Denham, Dennington, Fressingfield, Horham, Hoxne, Laxfield, Mendham, Metfield, Saxstead, Monk Soham, Southolt, Stradbroke, Syleham, Tannington, Weybread, Wilby, Wingfield, Worlingworth

LEISTON CUM SIZEWELL UD (1895[28]–1974)
Leiston

LOTHINGLAND RD (1934–74)
Ashby, Barnby, Belton, Benacre, Blundeston, Bradwell, Burgh Castle, Carlton Colville, Corton, South Cove, Covehithe, Easton Bavants, Flixton, Fritton, Frostenden, Gisleham, Henham, Henstead, Herringfleet, Hopton (1934–52), Hopton-on-Sea (1952–74), Kessingland, Lound, Mutford, Oulton, Reydon, Rushmere, Somerleyton, Uggeshall, Wangford, Wrentham

MUTFORD AND LOTHINGLAND RD (1894–1934)
Ashby, Barnby, Belton, Blundeston, Bradwell, Burgh Castle, Carlton Colville, Corton, Flixton, Fritton, Gisleham, Gunton, Herringfleet, Hopton, Kessingland, Kirkley (1894–1907), Lound, Mutford, Oulton, Pakefield, Rushmere, Somerleyton

OULTON BROAD UD (1904[29]–19[30])
Oulton Broad

PLOMESGATE RD (1894–1934)
Benhall, Blaxhall, Brandeston, Bruisyard, Butley, Campsey Ash, Chillesford, Cransford, Cretingham, Easton, Eyke, Farnham, Framlingham, Friston, Gedgrave, Great Glemham, Little Glemham, Havergate Island, Hacheston, Hazlewood, Hoo, Iken, Kenton, Kettleburgh, Letheringham, Marlesford, Monewden, Orford, Parham, Rendham, Rendlesham, Saxmundham (1894–1900), Snape, Earl Soham, Sternfield, Stratford St Andrew, Sudbourne, Swefling, Tunstall, Wantisden, Wickham Market

SAMFORD RD
Belstead, Bentley, East Bergholt, Brantham, Burstall, Capel St Mary, Chattisham, Chelmondiston, Copdock, Erwarton, Freston, Harkstead, Higham, Hintlesham, Holbrook, Holton St Mary, Raydon, Shelly, Shotley, Sproughton, Stratford St Mary, Stutton, Tattingstone, Washbrook, Great Wehham, Little Wenham, Wherstead, Woolverstone

SAXMUNDHAM UD (1900[31]–74)
Saxmundham

EAST STOW RD (1894–1934)
Buxhall, Combs, Creeting St Peter, Great Finborough, Little Finborough, Gipping, Harleston, Haughley, Old Newton, Onehouse, Shelland, Stowupland, Wetherden

STOWMARKET UD
Stowmarket

WAINFORD RD (1934–74)
Alderton, Barhsam, Blyford, Brampton, North Cove, South Elmham All Saints and St Nicholas, South Elmham St Cross, South Elmham St James, South Elmham St Margaret, South Elmham St Michael, South Elmham St Peter, Ellough, Flixton, Holton, Homersfield, Ilketshall St Andrew, Ilketshall St John, Ilketshall St Lawrence, Ilketshall St Margaret, Mettingham, Redisham, Ringsfield, Rumburgh, Shadingfield, Shipmeadow, Sotherton, Sotterley, Spexhall, Stoven, Westhall, Weston, Wissett, Worlingham

WANGFORD RD (1894–1934)
Barsham, Bungay Holy Trinity (1894–1910), Bungay St Mary (1894–1910), North Cove, South Elmham All Saints and St Nicholas, South Elmham St Cross, South Elmham St James, South Elmham St Margaret, South Elmham St Michael, South Elmham St Peter, Ellough, Flixton, Homersfield, Ilketshall St Andrew, Ilketshall St John, Ilketshall St Lawrence, Ilketshall St Margaret, Mettingham, Redisham, Ringsfield, Shadingfield, Shipmeadow, Sotterley, Weston, Wingham, Worlingham

WOODBRIDGE RD (1894–1934)
Alderton, Alnesbourn Priory, Bawdsey, Great Bealings, Little Bealings, Boulge, Boyton, Bredfield, Brightwell, Bromeswell, Bucklesham, Burgh, Capel St Andrew, Charsfield, Clopton, Culpho, Dallinghoo, Dallinghoo Wield, Debach, Falkenham, Foxhall, Grundisburgh, Hasketon, Hemley, Hollesley, Kesgrave, Kirton, Levington, Martlesham, Melton, Nacton, Newbourne, Otley, Pettistree, Playford, Purdis Farm, Ramsholt, Rushmere St Andrew, Shottisham, Stratton Hall, Sutton, Trimley St Martin, Trimley St Mary, Tuddenham, Ufford, Waldringfield, Westerfield, Witnesham

WOODBRIDGE UD
Woodbridge

WEST SUFFOLK ADMINISTRATIVE COUNTY

For MBs see BOROUGHS.

BRANDON RD (1894–1935)
Barham, Carningham, Brandon, Euston, Fakenham Magna, Hepworth, Honington, Hopton, Knettishall, Santon Downham, Sapiston, Thelnetham, Coney Weston, Market Weston

CLARE RD
Barnardiston, Great Bradley, Little Bradley, Cavendish (1935–74), Clare, Cowlinge, Denston, Depden (1935–74), Hawkedon (1935–74), Hundon, Kedington, Lidgate (1935–74), Ousden (1935–74), Poslingford, Monks Risbridge, Stansfield, Stoke by Clare, Stradishall, Great Thurlow, Little Thurlow, Wickhambrook, Withersfield, Wixoe, Great Wratting, Little Wratting

COSFORD RD
Aldham, Bildeston, Boxford, Brettenham, Chelsworth, Cockfield, Edwardstone, Brent Eleigh, Monks Eleigh, Elmsett, Groton, pt Hadleigh (1894–96), Hadleigh Hamlet (1894–1935), Hitcham, Kersey, Kettlebaston, Lavenham, Layham, Lindsey, Milden, Naughton (1894–1935), Nedging (1894–1935), Nedging with Naughton (1935–74), Polstead, Preston (1894–1957), Preston St Mary (1957–74), Semer, Thorpe Morieux, Wattisham, Whatfield

GLEMSFORD UD (1896[33]–1935)
Glemsford

HADLEIGH UD
Hadleigh

HAVERHILL UD
Haverhill (pt 1894–96, ent 1896–1974)

MELFORD RD
Acton, Alpheton, Assington, Boxted, Bures St Mary, Cavendish (1894–1935), Chilton, Great Cornard, Little Cornard, Glemsford (1894–96 and 1935–74), Hartest, Hawkedon (1894–1935), Law-

shall, Leavenheath (1952–74), Long Melford, Nayland with Wissington, Newton, Shimpling, Somerton, Stanstead, Stoke by Nayland, Great Waldingfield, Little Waldingfield

MILDENHALL RD

Barton Mills, Brandon (1935–74), Cavenham, Dalham (1935–74), Elveden, Eriswell, Freckenham, Gazeley (1935–74), Herringswell, Higham Green (1935–74), Icklingham, Kentford, Lakenheath, Mildenhall, Moulton (1935–74), Santon Downham (1935–74), Tuddenham, Wangford, Worlington

MOULTON RD (1894–1935)

Dalham, pt Exning (1894–95), Gazeley, Higham Green, Lidgate, Moulton, Ousden

NEWMARKET UD

Exning (pt 1894–95, ent 1895–1974), Newmarket All Saints, Newmarket St Mary

THEDWASTRE RD

Great Ashfield, Badwell Ash, Beyton, Drinkstone, Elmswell, Felsham, Gedding, Hessett, Hinderclay, Hunston, Langham, Norton, Rattlesden, Rickinghall Inferior, Stowlangtoft, Thurston, Tostock, Walsham-le-Willows, Wattisfield, Woolpit

THINGOE RD

Ampton, Bardwell, Barnham (1935–74), Barningham (1935–74), Barrow, Great Barton, Bradfield Combust, Bradfield St Clare, Bradfield St George, Brockley, Chedburgh, Chevington, Chimney Mills (1894–97), Culford, Denham, Depden (1894–1935), Euston (1935–74), Fakenham Magna (1935–74), Flempton, Fornham All Saints, Fornham St Genevieve, Fornham St Martin, Hardwick, Hargrave, Hawstead, Hengrave, Hepworth (1935–74), Honington (1935–74), Hopton (1935–74), Horningsheath, Ickworth, Ingham, Ixworth, Ixworth Thorpe, Knettishall (1935–74), Lackford, Great Livermere, Little Livermere, Nowton, Pakenham, Rede, Risley, Rougham, Rushbrooke, Sapiston (1935–74), Great Saxham, Little Saxham, Stanningfield, Stanton, West Stow, Thelnetham (1935–74), Timworth, Troston, Great Welnetham, Little Welnetham, Westley, Coney Weston (1935–74), Market Weston (1935–74), Whepstead, Wordwell

NON-METROPOLITAN COUNTY

As constituted 1 Apr 1974, defined
in terms of Adm Co units as of 31 Mar.

BABERGH DIST

From East Suffolk: Samford RD. *From West Suffolk:* Cosford RD, Hadleigh UD, Melford RD, Sudbury MB

FOREST HEATH DIST

From West Suffolk: Mildenhall RD, Newmaket UD

IPSWICH DIST

Ipswich CB

ST EDMUNDSBURY DIST

From West Suffolk: Bury St Edmunds MB, Clare RD, Haverhill UD, Thingoe RD

MID SUFFOLK DIST

From East Suffolk: Eye MB, Gipping RD, Hartismere RD, Stowmarket UD. *From West Suffolk:* Thedwastre RD

SUFFOLK COASTAL DIST

From East Suffolk: Aldeburgh MB, Blyth RD, Deben RD, Felixstowe UD, Leiston cum Sizewell UD, Saxmundham UD, Woodbridge UD

WAVENEY DIST

From East Suffolk: Beccles MB, Bungay UD, Halesworth UD, pt Lothingland RD (all except the pars and pts of pars transf to Norfolk[34]), Lowestoft MB, Southwold MB, Wainford RD

SURREY

ALTERATIONS IN COUNTY BOUNDARIES

As noted by year below, Surrey pars gained territory from or lost it to pars in adjoining cos or county boroughs, or were entirely transferred to them. Details of these alterations are noted in Part I of the *Guide* under Surrey.

ANCIENT COUNTY (until 1889: Hds, Bors, MBs, PLUs, RSDs, USDs, Vestries and Dists in Metrop Bd Wks)
1730 Deptford St Nicholas. *1866* Dockenfield, Frensham. *1884* Alfold.

ADMINISTRATIVE COUNTY (1889–1974: Hds,[1] PLUs, MBs, RDs, UDs, with Croydon CB associated (1889–1965)
1889 Battersea, Bermondsey, Camberwell, Clapham, Croydon, Deptford St Paul, Lambeth, Newington, Putney, Rotherhithe, Southwark Christchurch, Southwark St George the Martyr, Southwark St John Horsleydown, Southwark St Olave, Southwark St Saviour, Southwark St Thomas, Streatham, Tooting Graveney, Wandsworth. *1895* Dockenfield. *1899* Penge. *1901* Barnes, Mitcham. *1904* Mitcham. *1925* Addington, Mitcham. *1933* Beddington, Coulsdon, Mitcham. *1936* Farleigh, Mitcham, Sanderstead. *1957* Barnes. *1965* Ashford, Barnes, Beddington, Carshalton, Chessington, Coombe, Coulsdon, Farleigh, Ham, Hook, Kew, Kingston upon Thames, Laleham, Littleton, Malden, New Malden, Merton, Mitcham, Morden, Mortlake, Petersham, Richmond, Sanderstead, North Sheen, Shepperton, Staines, Stanwell, Sunbury, Surbiton, Sutton and Cheam, Tolworth, Wallington, Wimbledon. *1969* Banstead, Chelsham and Farleigh. *1970* Esher.

NON-METROPOLITAN COUNTY (from 1974: Dists)
1974 Charlwood, Horley.

ASSOCIATED COUNTY BOROUGH

For constituent par see listing for BOROUGHS in this Part of the *Guide*.

CROYDON CB (1889–1965)
Bdry: 1925,[2] 1925,[3] 1933,[4] 1936.[5] Transf 1965 to Gtr London to help constitute Croydon LB.[6]

HUNDREDS[1]

BLACKHEATH HD
Albury, Alfold (pt until 1884, ent from 1884), Bramley, Cranleigh, Dunsfold, Ewhurst, Hascombe, St Martha, Shalford,[8] Shere, Wonersh

BRIXTON HD[7]
Barnes, Battersea, Bermondsey, Camberwell, Clapham, pt Deptford St Paul (from 1730), pt Deptford St Nicholas (until 1730), Lambeth, Merton, Mortlake,[8] Newington, Penge (from 1866), Putney, Rotherhithe, Streatham, Tooting Graveney, Wandsworth, Wimbledon

COPTHORNE HD
Ashtead, Banstead, Chessington (from 1610), Cuddington, Epsom, Ewell (pt until 1866, ent from 1866), Fetcham, Headley, Leatherhead, Mickleham, Newdigate, Walton on the Hill

EFFINGHAM HD
Great Bookham, Little Bookham, Effingham

ELMBRIDGE HD
Cobham, pt Thames Ditton (from 1769), pt Esher, East Molesey (from 1769), West Molesey, Stoke d'Abernon, Walton upon Thames, Weybridge

FARNHAM HD
Elstead, Farnham,[8] Frensham (pt until 1866, ent from 1866), Seale, Waverley (from 1858)

GODALMING HD
Chiddingfold, Compton, Godalming,[8] pt Guildford St Nicholas[9] (until 1866), Hambledon, Haslemere,[8] Peper Harow, Puttenham, Thursley, Witley

GODLEY HD
pt Ash and Normandy (until 1866), Bisley, Byfleet, Chertsey, Chobham, Egham, Frimley (from 1866), Horsell, Pyrford, Thorpe

KINGSTON HD
Chessington (until 1610), Long Ditton, pt Thames Ditton (from 1769), pt Esher, Ham with Hatch (from 1866), Hook (from 1866), Kew,[8] Kingston upon Thames,[8] Malden, Petersham,[8] Richmond[8]

REIGATE HD
Betchworth, Buckland, Burstow, Charlwood, Chip-

stead, pt Ewell (until 1866), Gatton,[8] Horley, Kingswood (from 1866), Leigh, Mertsham, Nutfield, Reigate[8] (until 1866), Reigate Borough[8] (from 1866), Reigate Foreign[8] (from 1866)

TANDRIDGE HD
Bletchingley,[8] Caterham, Chelsham, Crowhurst, Farleigh, Godstone, Horne, Limpsfield, Lingfield, Oxted, Tandridge, Tatsfield, Titsey, Warlingham, Woldingham

WALLINGTON HD
Addington, Beddington, Carshalton, Chaldon, Cheam, Coulsdon, Croydon,[8] Mitcham, Morden, Sanderstead, Sutton, Wallington (from 1866), Woodmansterne

WOKING HD
Ash and Normandy (pt until 1866, ent from 1866), East Clandon, West Clandon, East Horsley, West Horsley, Merrow, Ockham, Pirbright, Send and Ripley, Stoke,[8] Wanborough, Windlesham, Wisley, Woking, Worplesdon

WOTTON HD
Abinger, Capel, Dorking, Ockley, Wotton

BOROUGHS

Units with some degree of burghal character[10] are denominated 'Bor'.
Those which did not sustain that status until the 19th cent are in italics.
MBs were established by the Municipal Corporations
Act, 1835,[11] or by later charter.

BARNES MB (1932[12]–65[6])
Barnes, Mortlake

BEDDINGTON AND WALLINGTON MB (1937[12]–65[6])
Beddington, Wallington

BLETCHINGLEY BOR
Bletchingley

CROYDON MB (1883[18]–89), CB (1889–1965[6])
Croydon (pt 1883–94, ent 1894–1965)

EASHING BOR
pt Godalming

EPSOM AND EWELL MB (1937[12]–74)
Cuddington, Epsom, Ewell

FARNHAM BOR
Farnham

GATTON BOR
Gatton

GODALMING BOR, MB (1875–1974)
Godalming (pt until 1892, extended pt 1892–94, ent 1894–1974)

GUILDFORD BOR/MB
Bowling Green (1858–83), Guildford (1908–74), Guildford Christchurch (1904–08), Guildford The Friary (1858–1908), Guildford Holy Trinity (until 1908), Guildford St Mary (until 1908), Guildford St Nicolas (pt until 1894, ent 1894–1908), pt Shalford (1886–94), pt Stoke (1886–94), Stoke Within (1894–1904)

HASLEMERE BOR
Haslemere

KINGSTON UPON THAMES BOR/MB (1835–1965[6])
Kingston upon Thames (pt until 1894, ent 1894–1965)

MALDEN AND COOMBE MB (1936[14]–65[6])
Coombe, Malden, New Malden

MITCHAM MB (1934[12]–65[6])
Mitcham

REIGATE BOR, MB (1863–1974)
in Bor: pt Reigate
in MB: Gatton (1933–74), Merstham (1933–74), Reigate (1899–1974), Reigate Borough (1863–99), Reigate Foreign (1863–94)

RICHMOND MB (1890–1965[6])
Ham (1933–65), Kew (1892–1965), pt Mortlake (1892–94), Petersham (1892–1965), Richmond, North Sheen (1894–1965)

SOUTHWARK BOR[15]
Southwark St George the Martyr, Southwark St John Horsleydown (from 1733), Southwark St Margaret (until 1541), Southwark St Mary Magdalene (until 1541), Southwark St Olave, Southwark St Saviour (from 1541), Southwark St Thomas (from *ca* 1550)

SURBITON MB (1936[12]–65[6])
Chessington, Hook, Surbiton, Tolworth

SUTTON AND CHEAM MB (1934[12]–65[6])
Cheam (1934–49), Sutton (1934–49), Sutton and Cheam (1949–65)

WIMBLEDON MB (1905[12]–65[6])
Wimbledon

POOR LAW UNIONS

In Surrey Poor Law County:[16]

ASH PAR (local act, until 1846)
Ash and Normandy, Dockenfield, Frensham, Frimley, Seale

CHERTSEY PLU
Bisley, Byfleet, Chertsey, Chobham, Horsell, Pyrford, Thorpe (1894–1930), Walton upon Thames, Weybridge, Windlesham

CROYDON PLU
Addington, Beddington, Coulsdon, Croydon, Merton, Mitcham, Morden, Penge, Sanderstead, Wallington (1866–1930), Woodmansterne

DORKING PLU
Abinger, Capel, Dorking, Dorking Rural (1894–1930), Effingham, Mickleham, Newdigate, Ockley, Wotton

EPSOM PLU
Ashtead, Banstead, Great Bookham, Little Bookham, Carshalton, Cheam, Chessington, Cobham, Cuddington, Epsom, Ewell, Fetcham, Headley (1879–1930), Leatherhead, Stoke d'Abernon, Sutton

FARNHAM PLU (1846–1930) (Surrey, Hants)
Ash and Normandy, Dockenfield,[17] Farnham, Farnham Rural (1894–1930), Frensham, Frimley, Seale, Shottermill (1896–1930), Waverley (1858–94)

GODSTONE PLU
Bletchingley, Caterham, Chelsham, Crowhurst, Farleigh, Godstone, Horne, Limpsfield, Lingfield (1894–1930), Oxted, Tandridge, Tatsfield, Titsey, Warlingham, Woldingham

GUILDFORD PLU
Albury, Artington (1894–1930), Bowling Green (1858–83), East Clandon, West Clandon, Compton, Godalming, Godalming Rural (1894–1930), Guildford (1908–30), Guildford Christchurch (1904–08), Guildford The Friary (1858–1908), Guildford Holy Trinity (1836–1908), Guildford St Mary (1836–1908), Guildford St Nicolas (1836–1908), East Horsley, West Horsley, Merrow, Ockham, Pirbright, Puttenham, Send and Ripley, Shere, Stoke (1836–94), Stoke (1904–08), Stoke next Guildford (1894–1904), Stoke Within (1894–1904), Wanborough, Wisley, Woking, Worplesdon

HAMBLEDON PLU
Alfold,[18] Bramley, Chiddingfold, Cranleigh, Dunsfold, Elstead, Ewhurst, Hambledon, Hascombe, Haslemere, Peper Harow, St Martha, Shalford, Thursley, Witley, Wonersh

KINGSTON PLU
Coombe (1894–1930), Long Ditton, Thames Ditton, Esher, Ham with Hatch, Hook, Kingston upon Thames, Malden, New Malden (1894–1930), East Molesey, West Molesey, Surbiton (1894–1930), Tolworth (1895–1930), Wimbledon

REIGATE PLU
Betchworth, Buckland, Burstow, Chaldon, Charlwood, Chipstead, Gatton, Headley (1836–79), Horley, Kingswood, Leigh, Mertsham, Nutfield, Reigate (1899–1930), Reigate Borough (1836–99), Reigate Foreign (1836–94), Walton on the Hill

RICHMOND PLU
Barnes, Kew, Mortlake, Petersham, Richmond, North Sheen (1894–1930)

In Other Poor Law Counties:

EAST GRINSTEAD PLU (Sussex, Surrey)
Lingfield (1836–97)

WINDSOR PLU (Berks, Surrey)
Egham, Thorpe (1835–94)

Surrey Poor Law County, in Metropolis (1855–89), London Poor Law County thereafter:

BERMONDSEY PAR
Bermondsey

CAMBERWELL PAR
Camberwell

LAMBETH PAR
Lambeth

NEWINGTON ST MARY PAR
Newington

ROTHERHITHE PAR
Rotherhithe

ST OLAVE PLU
Southwark St John Horsleydown, Southwark St Olave, Southwark St Thomas

ST SAVIOUR'S PLU
Southwark Christchurch, Southwark St Saviour

SOUTHWARK ST GEORGE THE MARTYR PAR
Southwark St George the Martyr

WANDSWORTH AND CLAPHAM PLU
Battersea, Clapham, Putney, Streatham, Tooting Graveney, Wandsworth

SANITARY DISTRICTS

BARNES USD (1893[19]–94)
Barnes, pt Mortlake

CARSHALTON USD (1883[20]–94)
Carshalton

CHERTSEY RSD
same as PLU

CROYDON RSD
same as PLU less Croydon (ent 1875–83, pt 1883–94)

CROYDON USD (1883[13]–94)
Croydon (ent 1875–83, pt 1883–94)

DORKING RSD
same as PLU less pt Dorking

DORKING USD
pt Dorking

EPSOM RSD
same as PLU less Carshalton, Epsom, Sutton (1882–94)

EPSOME USD
Epsom

FARNHAM RSD
same as PLU less pt Farnham (enlarged pt 1884–94)

FARNHAM USD
pt Farnham (enlarged pt 1884–94)

GODALMING USD
pt Godalming (enlarged pt 1892–94)

GODSTONE RSD
same as PLU

EAST GRINSTEAD RSD
same as PLU for Surrey par

GUILDFORD RSD
same as PLU less Bowling Green (1875–83), pt Godalming (enlarged pt 1892–94), Guildford The Friary, Guildford Holy Trinity, Guildford St Mary, pt Guildford St Nicholas, pt Stoke (1886–94)

GUILDFORD USD
Bowling Green (1875–83), Guildford The Friary, Guildford Holy Trinity, Guildford St Mary, pt Guildford St Nicholas, pt Shalford (1886–94), pt Stoke (1886–94), Woking (1893–94)
HAM COMMON USD
pt Ham with Hatch
HAMBLEDON RSD
same as PLU less pt Shalford (1886–94)
KINGSTON RSD
same as PLU less pt Ham with Hatch, Kingston upon Thames, East Molesey, Wimbledon
KINGSTON UPON THAMES USD
pt Kingston upon Thames
NEW MALDEN USD
pt Kingston upon Thames
EAST MOLESEY USD
East Molesey
REIGATE RSD
same as PLU less Reigate Borough, Reigate Foreign
REIGATE USD
Reigate Borough, Reigate Foreign
RICHMOND RSD
same as PLU less Barnes, Kew (1892–94), pt Mortlake (1892–93, enlarged pt 1893–94), Richmond, Petersham (1892–94)
SURBITON USD
pt Kingston upon Thames
SUTTON USD (1882[21]–94)
Sutton
WIMBLEDON USD
Wimbledon
WINDSOR RSD
same as PLU for Surrey pars
WOKING USD (1893[50]–94)
Woking

SURREY PARISHES IN THE METROPOLIS, 1855–89[22]

Pars under Vestries:
Bermondsey, Camberwell, Lambeth, Newington, Rotherhithe, Southwark St George the Martyr

Pars within Districts:
GREENWICH DIST
ent Kent except the pt of Deptford St Paul (the area of Hatcham) in Surrey
ST OLAVE DIST
Southwark St John Horsleydown, Southwark St Olave, Southwark St Thomas
ST SAVIOUR'S DIST
Southwark Christchurch, Southwark St Saviour
WANDSWORTH DIST
Battersea, Clapham, Putney, Streatham, Tooting Graveney, Wandsworth

ADMINISTRATIVE COUNTY

For MBs and the associated CB see BOROUGHS.

BAGSHOT RD (1933–74)
Bisley, Chobham, West End (1968–74), Windlesham
BANSTEAD UD (1933–74)
Banstead, Chipstead, Kingswood, Walton on the Hill, Woodmansterne
BARNES UD (1894–1932[12])
Barnes, Mortlake
BEDDINGTON AND WALLINGTON UD (1915[23]–37[12])
Beddington, Wallington
CARSHALTON UD (1894–1965[6])
Carshalton
CATERHAM UD (1899[24]–1929[25])
Caterham
CATERHAM AND WARLINGHAM UD (1929[25]–74)
Caterham, Chaldon (1933–74), Warlingham, Woldingham (1933–74)
CHERTSEY RD (1894–1933)
Bisley, Byfleet, Chobham, Horsell (1894–1907), Pyrford, Thorpe, Windlesham (1894–1909)
CHERTSEY UD (1894[32]–1974)
Chertsey
COULSDON AND PURLEY UD (1915[26]–65[6])
Coulsdon, Farleigh (1933–65), Sanderstead
CROYDON RD (1894–1915[33])
Addington, Beddington, Coulsdon, Merton (1894–1907), Mitcham, Morden (1894–1913), Sanderstead, Wallington, Woodmansterne
DORKING RD (1894–1933)
Abinger, Capel, Dorking Rural, Effingham, Mickleham, Newdigate, Ockley, Wotton
DORKING UD
Brockham (1933–74), Dorking, Mickleham (1933–74), Milton (1933–74)
DORKING AND HORLEY RD (1933–74)
Abinger, Betchworth, Buckland, Capel, Charlwood, Headley, Holmwood, Horley, Leigh, Newdigate, Ockley, Wotton
EGHAM RD (1894–1906[27])
Egham
EGHAM UD (1906[27]–74)
Egham, Thorpe (1933–74)
EPSOM RD (1894–1933)
Ashtead, Banstead, Great Bookham, Little Bookham, Cheam (1894–1928), Chessington, Cobham, Cuddington, Ewell, Fetcham, Headley, Stoke d'Abernon, Woodmansterne (1915–33)
EPSOM UD (1894–1934[28])
Cuddington (1933–34), Epsom, Ewell (1933–34)

EPSOM AND EWELL UD (1934[28]–37[12])
Cuddington, Epsom, Ewell
ESHER UD (1933–74)
Cobham, Long Ditton, Thames Ditton, Esher, East Molesey, West Molesey, Stoke d'Abernon
ESHER AND THE DITTONS UD (1895[29]–1933)
Long Ditton, Thames Ditton, Esher
FARNHAM RD (1894–1933)
Ash and Normandy, Dockenfield (1895–1933), Farnham Rural, Frensham, Seale, Shottermill
FARNHAM UD
Farnham
FRIMLEY UD (1894[30]–1929[31])
Frimley
FRIMLEY AND CAMBERLEY UD (1929[31]–74)
Frimley
GODSTONE RD
Addington (1915–25), Bletchingley, Burstow (1933–74), Caterham (1894–99), Chelsham (1894–1969), Chelsham and Farleigh (1969–74), Crowhurst, Farleigh (1894–1933), Felbridge (1953–74), Godstone, Horne, Limpsfield, Lingfield, Nutfield (1933–74), Oxted, Tandridge, Tatsfield, Titsey, Warlingham (1894–1929), Woldingham (1894–1933)
GUILDFORD RD
Albury, Artington, Ash (1955–74), Ash and Normandy (1933–55), East Clandon, West Clandon, Compton, Effingham (1933–74), Godalming Rural (1894–1933), East Horsley, West Horsley, Merrow (1894–1933), Normandy (1955–74), Ockham, Pirbright, Puttenham, Ripley (1933–74), St Martha (1933–74), Seale (1933–63), Seale and Tongham (1963–74), Send (1933–74), Send and Ripley (1894–1933), Shackleford (1933–74), Shalford (1933–74), Shere, Stoke next Guildford (1894–1904), Wanborough, Wisley, Worplesdon
HAM UD (1894[34]–1933)
Ham [with Hatch]
HAMBLEDON RD
Alfold, Bramley, Busbridge (1933–74), Chiddingfold, Cranleigh, Dockenfield (1933–74), Dunsfold, Elstead, Ewhurst, Frensham (1933–74), Hambledon, Hascombe, Haslemere (1894–1913), Peper Harow, St Martha (1894–1933), Shalford (1894–1933), Thursley, Tilford (1933–74), Witley, Wonersh
HASLEMERE UD (1913[35]–74)
Haslemere, Hindhead and Churt (1933–74)
KINGSTON RD (1894–95[36])
Coombe,[38] Long Ditton,[37] Thames Ditton,[37] Esher,[37] Hook,[39] Malden,[38] West Molesey, Surbiton[39]
LEATHERHEAD UD (1894[40]–1974)
Ashstead (1933–74), Great Bookham (1933–74), Little Bookham (1933–74), Fetcham (1933–74), Leatherhead
THE MALDENS AND COOMBE UD (1895[41]–1936[14])
Coombe, Malden, New Malden
NEW MALDEN UD (1894–95[41])
New Malden
MERTON UD (1907[42]–1913[43])
Merton
MERTON AND MORDEN UD (1913[43]–65[6])
Merton, Morden
MITCHAM UD (1907[44]–34[12])
Mitcham
EAST MOLESEY UD (1894–95[36])
East Molesey
EAST AND WEST MOLESEY UD (1895[36]–1933)
East Molesey, West Molesey
REIGATE RD (1894–1933)
Betchworth, Buckland, Burstow, Chaldon, Charlwood, Chipstead, Gatton, Horley, Kingswood, Leigh, Mertsham, Nutfield, Walton on the Hill
STAINES UD (1965[45]–74)
Ashford, Laleham, Staines, Stanwell
SUNBURY ON THAMES UD (1965[45]–74)
Littleton, Shepperton, Sunbury
SURBITON UD (1894–1936[12])
Chessington (1933–36), Hook (1895–1936), Surbiton, Tolworth (1895–1936)
SUTTON UD (1894–1928[46])
Sutton
SUTTON AND CHEAM UD (1928[46]–34[12])
Cheam, Sutton
WALTON AND WEYBRIDGE UD (1933–74)
Walton upon Thames, Weybridge
WALTON UPON THAMES UD (1894[47]–1933)
Walton upon Thames
WEYBRIDGE UD (1894[48]–1933)
Weybridge
WIMBLEDON UD (1894–1905[12])
Wimbledon
WINDLESHAM UD (1909[49]–33)
Windlesham
WOKING UD
Byfleet (1933–74), Horsell (1907–74), Pyrford (1933–74), Woking

NON-METROPOLITAN COUNTY

As constituted 1 Apr 1974, defined in terms of Adm Co units as of 31 Mar.

ELMBRIDGE DIST
Esher UD, Walton and Weybridge UD
EPSOM AND EWELL DIST
Epsom and Ewell MB
GUILDFORD DIST
Guildford MB, Guildford RD
MOLE VALLEY DIST
Dorking UD, pt Dorking and Horley RD,[51] Leather-

head UD
REIGATE AND BANSTEAD DIST
Banstead UD, pt Dorking and Horley RD[51] (Horley, Salfords and Sidlow[51]), Reigate MB
RUNNYMEDE DIST
Chertsey UD, Egham UD
SPELTHORNE DIST
Staines UD, Sunbury on Thames UD
SURREY HEATH DIST
Bagshot RD, Frimley and Camberley UD
TANDRIDGE DIST
Caterham and Warlingham UD, Godstone RD
WAVERLEY DIST
Farnham UD, Godalming MB, Hambledon RD, Haslemere UD
WOKING DIST
Woking UD

SUSSEX

ALTERATIONS IN COUNTY BOUNDARIES

As noted by year below, Sussex pars gained territory from or lost it to pars in adjoining counties or county boroughs, or were entirely transferred to them. Details of these alterations are noted in Part I of the *Guide* under Sussex.

ANCIENT COUNTY (until 1889: Hds, Bors, MBs, PLUs, RSDs, USDs)
1844 North Ambersham, South Ambersham, Bramshott, Rogate, Selham, Steep. *1884* Alfold, Wisborough Green. *1886* Hawkhurst.

EAST SUSSEX ADMINISTRATIVE COUNTY (1889–1974: Hds,[1] PLUs, MBs, RDs, UDs, with CBs of Brighton, Eastbourne, Hastings associated)
1894 Edburton, Frant, Hastings St Leonards, Hastings St Mary in the Castle, Preston. *1895* Broomhill, Crawley, Horsmonden, Lamberhurst, Ore. *1897* Ore. *1900* Frant. *1908* Albourne. *1909* Hastings St Matthew. *1926* Willingdon. *1928* West Blatchington, Falmer, Hove, Ovingdean, Patcham, Preston, Rottingdean. *1938* Fairlight, Friston, Guestling, Hollington Rural, Jevington, Ore, Willingdon. *1952* Falmer, Stanmer. *1953* Slaugham, Worth.

WEST SUSSEX ADMINISTRATIVE COUNTY (1889–1974: Hds,[1] PLUs, MBs RDs, UDs)
1894 Edburton. *1895* Bramshott, Crawley. *1908* Albourne. *1953* Crawley.

EAST SUSSEX NON-METROPOLITAN COUNTY (from 1974: Dists)
1974 Albourne, Ardingly, Balcombe, Bolney, Burgess Hill, Clayton, Cuckfield, Cuckfield Rural, Fulking, Hayward's Heath, East Grinstead, West Hoathly, Horsted Keynes, Hurstpierpoint, Keymer, Lindfield, Lindfield Rural, Newtimber, Poynings, Pyecombe, Slaugham, Twineham, Worth.

WEST SUSSEX NON-METROPOLITAN COUNTY (from 1974: Dists)
1974 Albourne, Ardingly, Balcombe, Bolney, Burgess Hill, Charlwood, Clayton, Cuckfield, Cuckfield Rural, Fulking, Hayward's Heath, East Grinstead, West Hoathly, Horley, Horsted Keynes, Hurstpierpoint, Keymer, Lindfield, Lindfield Rural, Newtimber, Poynings, Pyecombe, Slaugham, Twineham, Worth.

ASSOCIATED COUNTY BOROUGHS

These CBs were associated with E Sussex Adm Co, and became pt of E Sussex Non-Metropolitan Co. For constituent pars see listing for BOROUGHS in this Part of the *Guide.*

BRIGHTON CB
Bdry: 1928,[2] 1952.[3]

EASTBOURNE CB (1911[4]–74)
Bdry: 1912,[5] 1926,[6] 1938.[7]

HASTINGS CB
Bdry: 1897,[8] 1938.[9]

HUNDREDS[1]

Rape of Arundel:

AVISFORD HD
Arundel,[10] Barnham, Binsted, Climping, Eastergate, Felpham, Ford, Madehurst, Middleton, South Stoke, Tortington, Walberton, Yapton

BURY HD
pt Alfold (until 1884), Bignor, Bury, Coates, Coldwaltham, Fittleworth, Hardham, Houghton, pt Wisborough Green

WEST EASWRITH HD
Amberley, Billingshurst, pt West Chiltington, Greatham, Parham, Pulborough, Rackham (from 1866), Rudgwick, pt Slinfold, Storrington, Wiggonholt, pt Wisborough Green

POLING HD
Angmering, Burpham,[10] Ferring, Goring by Sea, Kingston, Littlehampton, Lyminster, Poling, East Preston, Rustington, North Stoke, Warningcamp

(from 1866)
ROTHERBRIDGE HD
Barlavington, Burton, North Chapel (from 1692), Duncton (from 1692), Egdean, Kirdford, East Lavington, West Lavington (from 1866), Lurgashall, Petworth, Stopham, Sutton, Tillington, pt Wisborough Green

Rape of Bramber:
BRIGHTFORD HD
Broadwater, Clapham, Durrington, Findon, Heene, Lancing, Sompting
BURBEACH HD
Lower Beeding (from 1866), Upper Beeding, pt Edburton, Ifield
EAST EASWRITH HD
pt West Chiltington, Itchingfield, pt Slinfold, Sullington, Thakenham, Warminghurst
FISHERGATE HD
Kingston by Sea, New Shoreham,[10] Old Shoreham, Southwick
WEST GRINSTEAD HD
Ashington, Ashurst, West Grinstead, Shipley
PATCHING HD
Patching
SINGLECROSS HD
Horsham,[10] Nuthurst, Rusper, Warnham
STEYNING HD
Bramber,[10] Botolphs, Coombes, Steyning,[10] Washington, Wiston
TARRING HD
West Tarring
TIPNOAK HD
Albourne, Henfield, Woodmancote
WINDHAM AND EWHURST HD
Cowfold, Shermanbury

Rape of Chichester:
ALDWICK HD
Bersted, East Lavant, Pagham, Slindon, Tangmere
BOSHAM HD
Bosham, Chidham, Funtington, West Stoke, West Thorney
BOX AND STOCKBRIDGE HD[11]
Aldingbourne, Appledram, Boxgrove, Donnington, Eartham, New Fishbourne, Hunston, Merston, North Mundham, Oving,[10] Rumboldswyke,[10] Up Waltham, Westhampnett
DUMPFORD HD
pt Bramshott (until 1844), Chithurst, Didling, Elsted, Harting, Rogate (pt until 1844, ent from 1844), Terwick, Treyford, pt Trotton
EASEBOURNE HD
North Ambersham[12] (from 1866), South Ambersham[12] (from 1866), Bepton, Cocking, Easebourne,[10] Fernhurst, Graffham, Heyshott, Iping, Linch, Linchmere, Lodsworth, Midhurst,[10] Selham, Stedham, pt Trotton, Woolbeding
MANHOOD HD
Birdham, Earnley, West Itchenor, Selsey, Sidlesham, East Wittering, West Wittering
WESTBOURNE AND SINGLETON HD
Binderton, Compton, East Dean, West Dean, Lavant (from 1872), Mid Lavant (until 1872), East Marden, North Marden, Up Marden, Racton, Singleton, Stoughton, Westbourne

Rape of Hastings:[13]
BALDSTROW HD[14]
Crowhurst, Hollington, Ore,[10] Westfield
BATTLE HD
Battle,[10] pt Sedlescombe, Whatlington
BEXHILL HD
Bexhill
FOXEARLE HD
Ashburnham, Herstmonceux, Wartling
GOLDSPUR HD[13]
Beckley, pt Broomhill, East Guldeford, Iden, Peasmarsh, Playden
GOSTROW HD[13]
Brede, Udimore
GUESTLING HD
Fairlight, Guestling, Icklesham, Pett
HAWKESBOROUGH HD
pt Burwash, pt Dallington, pt Heathfield, pt Mayfield, pt Wadhurst, Warbleton
HENHURST HD
pt Burwash, pt Etchingham, pt Hawkhurst (until 1886), Salehurst
NETHERFIELD HD
Brightling, pt Dallington, pt Catsfield (orig, later ent Ninfield Hd), Mountfield, Penhurst
NINFIELD HD
Catsfield (orig pt, later ent this Hd), Hooe, Ninfield
SHOYSWELL HD
pt Burwash, pt Etchingham, Ticehurst
STAPLE HD
Bodiam, Ewhurst, Northiam, pt Sedlescombe

Rape of Lewes:
BARCOMBE HD
Barcombe, Hamsey, Newick
BUTTINGHILL HD
Ardingly, pt Balcombe, Bolney, Clayton, Crawley, Cuckfield, West Hoathly, Hurstpierpoint, Keymer, Slaugham, Twineham, Worth
DEAN HD (from late 17th or early 18th cent)[15]
Patcham
FISHERGATE HD
Aldrington, Hangleton, Portslade
HOLMSTROW HD
Newhaven, Piddinghoe, Rodmell, Southease, Telscombe
POYNINGS HD
pt Edburton, Newtimber, Pyecombe
PRESTON HD
Hove, Preston[10]
STREET HD
pt Balcombe, Chailey, East Chiltington (from 1866), Ditchling, pt Lindfield, Plumpton, Street, Westmeston, Wivelsfield
SWANBOROUGH HD[16]
Iford, Kingston
WHALEBONE HD
West Blatchington, Brighton,[10] Patcham (until late 17th or early 18th cent)[15]

YOUNSMERE HD
Falmer, Ovingdean, Rottingdean

Rape of Pevensey:
ALCISTON HD
Alciston, Alfriston, Lullington
BISHOPSTONE HD
Bishopstone, Denton
BURLEIGH ARCHES HD
pt Lindfield
DANEHILL HORSTED HD
Horsted Keynes, Selmeston, Tarring Neville
DILL HD
Hailsham, pt Heathfield, Hellingly
EASTBOURNE HD
Eastbourne[10]
FLEXBOROUGH HD
East Blatchington, South Heighton, Seaford[10]
EAST GRINSTEAD HD
East Grinstead[10]
HARTFIELD HD
Hartfield, Withyham
LONGBRIDGE HD
Arlington, Berwick, Folkington, Litlington, Wilmington
LOXFIELD DORSET HD
Buxted, Framfield, Isfield, Uckfield
LOXFIELD PELHAM HD
pt Horsmonden, pt Lamberhurst, pt Mayfield, pt Wadhurst
PEVENSEY LOWEY
Pevensey,[10] Westham
RINGMER HD[16]
Glynde, South Malling,[10] Ringmer, Stanmer
ROTHERFIELD HD
pt Frant, Rotherfield
RUSHMONDEN HD
Fletching, Little Horsted, Maresfield
SHIPLAKE HD
Chalvington, Chiddingly, East Hoathly, Laughton, Ripe, Waldron
TOTNORE HD
Beddingham, West Firle
WILLINGDON HD
East Dean, West Dean, Friston, Jevington, Willingdon[10]

BOROUGHS

Units with some degree of burghal character[17] are denominated 'Bor'. Those which did not sustain that status until the 19th cent are in italics. Municipal Boroughs were established by the Municipal Corporations Act, 1835,[18] or by later charter.

ARUNDEL BOR/MB
Arundel
BATTLE BOR
Battle
BEXHILL MB (1902[19]–74)
Bexhill
BRAMBER BOR
Bramber
BURPHAM BOR
Burpham
BRIGHTON MB (1854[20]–89), CB (1889–1974)
Brighton, Preston (1854–1928)
CHICHESTER BOR[21]/MB
Chichester (1896–1974), Chichester All Saints (until 1896), Chichester The Close (1835–96), Chichester Newtown, or St John (until 1896), Chichester St Andrew (until 1896), Chichester St Bartholomew (pt 1835–94, ent 1894–96), Chichester St James (1835–96), Chichester St Martin (until 1896), Chichester St Olave (until 1896), Chichester St Pancras (pt until 1894 [enlarged pt 1835–94], ent 1894–96), Chichester St Peter the Great or Sub-Deanery (pt until 1894 [enlarged pt 1835–94], ent 1894–96), Chichester St Peter the Less (until 1896), pt Oving (1835–94), Portfield (1894–96), Rumboldswyke (pt 1835–94, ent 1894–96)
EASTBOURNE MB (1883[22]–1911), CB (1911[23]–74)
Eastbourne, Hampden Park (1911–12), Norway (1894–99), pt Willingdon (1883–94)
EAST GRINSTEAD BOR
East Grinstead
HASTINGS BOR[21]/MB/CB
pt Bexhill (until 1894), Blacklands (1894–97), Hastings (1909–74), Hastings All Saints (until 1909), Hastings Holy Trinity (until 1909), Hastings St Andrew (until 1909), Hastings St Clement (until 1909), Hastings St Helens (1897–1909), Hastings St Leonards (pt until 1894, ent 1894–1909), Hastings St Mary Bulverhythe (until 1909), Hastings St Mary in the Castle (pt until 1894, ent 1894–1909), Hastings St Mary Magdalen (until 1909), Hastings St Michael (until 1909), Hollington (1880s–97), Hollington St John (1897–1925), pt Ore (until 1894)
HORSHAM BOR
Horsham
HOVE MB (1898[24]–1974)
Aldrington, West Blatchington (1928–74), Hangleton (1928–74), Hove
LEWES BOR,[21] MB (1881[25]–1974)
pt Kingston (1881–94), Kingston Urban (1894–1934), Lewes (1913–74), Lewes All Saints (until 1913), Lewes The Castle Precincts (1881–1913), Lewes St Ann (pt until 1894 [enlarged pt 1881–94], ent 1894–1913), Lewes St John the Baptist, Southover (pt until 1894, ent 1894–1913), Lewes St John under the Castle (pt until 1894, ent 1894–1913), Lewes St Michael (until 1913), Lewes St

Thomas a Becket, Cliffe (until 1913), South Malling (pt 1881–94, ent 1894–1913)
MIDHURST BOR
pt Easebourne (until Midhurst gains sep civ identity), Midhurst (thereafter)
PEVENSEY BOR
Pevensey
RYE BOR/MB
Rye (pt until 1894, ent 1894–1974)
SEAFORD BOR
Seaford
SHOREHAM BOR
New Shoreham
STEYNING BOR
Steyning
WINCHELSEA BOR[21]
St Thomas the Apostle, Winchelsea
WORTHING MB (1890[26]–1974)
pt Broadwater (1890–94), Heene (1890–1902), Worthing (1894–1974)

CINQUE PORTS

The Anc Town/Cq Pt of Winchelsea is ent in Sussex. The greater pts of Anc Town/Cq Pt of Rye and of Hastings Cq Pt are in Sussex, the remainder of each in Kent; see the entries in Kent for those. Of the remaining Cq Pts, Dover, Hythe and New Romney are ent in Kent, and Sandwich in Kent and Essex. In the entries below, an + indicates that the par is included as pt of the Lbty of a corporate town, ent or in pt.

HASTINGS CQ PT
pt Bexhill+ [Lbty of the Sluice], pt Hailsham+, Hastings All Saints+, Hastings Holy Trinity+, Hastings St Andrew+, Hastings St Clement+, Hastings St Leonards (pt in Bor+, the pt outside [Petit Iham] also in the Cq Pt), Hastings St Mary Bulverhythe+, pt Hastings St Mary in the Castle+, Hastings St Mary Magdalen+, Hastings St Michael+, pt Ore+, Pevensey+, Seaford+, Westham+
RYE ANC TOWN/CQ PT
pt Rye+
WINCHELSEA ANC TOWN/CQ PT[21]
pt Broomhill+ (the pt in Sussex), pt Icklesham+, pt Pett+, St Thomas the Apostle, Winchelsea+

POOR LAW UNIONS

In Sussex Poor Law County:[27]
ARUNDEL INCORP (18th cent–1869)
Arundel
BATTLE PLU
Ashburnham, Battle, Bexhill, Brightling, Catsfield, Crowhurst, Dallington, Ewhurst, Hollington (1835–97), Hollington Rural (1897–1930), Hollington St John (1897–1925), Mountfield, Penhurst, Sedlescombe, Westfield, Whatlington
BRIGHTON INCORP (1810[28]–1930)
Brighton
CHAILEY PLU (1835–98)
Barcombe, Chailey, East Chiltington, Ditchling, Hamsey, Plumpton, Newick, Ringmer, Streat, Westmeston, Wivelsfield
CHICHESTER INCORP (1753–1930)
Chichester (1896–1930), Chichester All Saints (until 1896), Chichester The Close (until 1896), Chichester Newtown, or St John (until 1896), Chichester St Andrew (until 1896), Chichester St Bartholomew (until 1896), Chichester St James (until 1896), Chichester St Martin (until 1896), Chichester St Olave (until 1896), Chichester St Pancras (until 1896), Chichester St Peter the Great or Sub-Deanery (until 1896), Chichester St Peter the Less (until 1896), St Bartholomew Rural (1894–95), St Pancras Rural (1894–96), Sub-Deanery Rural (1894–96)
CUCKFIELD PLU
Albourne, Ardingly, Balcombe, Bolney, Clayton, Clayton Urban (1894–1930), Cowfold (1835–97), Cuckfield, Cuckfield Rural (1894–1930), Hayward's Heath (1894–1930), Horsted Keynes, Hurstpierpoint, Keymer, Keymer Urban (1894–1930), Lindfield, Newtimber, Pyecombe, Slaugham, Twineham
EASTBOURNE PLU
Alciston (1898–1930), Alfriston, Berwick (1898–1930), East Dean, West Dean, Eastbourne, Folkington, Friston, Hampden Park (1911–12), Jevington, Litlington, Lullington, Norway (1894–99), Pevensey, Seaford, Selmeston (1898–1930), Westham, Willingdon, Wilmington
WEST FIRLE PLU (1835–98)
Alciston, Beddingham, Berwick, Chalvington, West Firle, Glynde, Ripe, Selmeston
EAST GRINSTEAD PLU (Sussex, Surrey 1836–97, ent Sussex 1897–1930)

Crawley (1835–80), Forest Row. (1894–1930), East Grinstead, Hartfield, West Hoathly, Withyham, Worth

HAILSHAM PLU

Arlington, Chalvington (1898–1930), Chiddingly, Hailsham, Heathfield, Hellingly, Herstmonceux, Hooe, Laughton, Ninfield, Ripe (1898–1930), Warbleton, Wartling

HASTINGS PLU

Blacklands (1894–97), Fairlight, Guestling, Hastings (1909–30), Hastings All Saints (1835–1909), Hastings Holy Trinity (1835–1909), Hastings St Andrew (1835–1909), Hastings St Clement (1835–1909), Hastings St Leonards (1835–1909), Hastings St Mary Bulverhythe (1835–1909), Hastings St Mary in the Castle (1835–1909), Hastings St Mary Magdalen (1835–1909), Hastings St Michael (1835–1909), Ore, Pett

HORSHAM PLU

Lower Beeding, Billingshurst (1870–1930), Cowfold (1897–1930), Crawley (1880–1930), West Grinstead, Horsham, Horsham Rural (1894–1930), Ifield, Itchingfield, Nuthurst, Rudgwick (1869–1930), Rusper, Shipley, Slinfold, Warnham

LEWES PLU

Barcombe (1898–1930), Beddingham (1898–1930), Chailey (1898–1930), Chalvington, East Chiltington (1898–1930), Ditchling (1898–1930), West Firle (1898–1930), Glynde (1898–1930), Hamsey (1898–1930), Lewes (1913–30), Lewes All Saints (1835–1913), Lewes The Castle Precincts (1858[29]–1913), Lewes St Ann (1835–1913), Lewes St Ann Without (1894–1930), Lewes St John the Baptist, Southover (1835–1913), Lewes St John under the Castle (1835–1913), Lewes St John Without (1894–1930), Lewes St Michael (1835–1913), Lewes St Thomas a Becket, Cliffe (1835–1913), South Malling (1835–1913), South Malling Without (1894–1930), Newick (1898–1930), Plumpton (1898–1930), Ringmer (1898–1930), Southover Without (1894–1930), Streat (1898–1930), Westmeston (1898–1930), Wivelsfield (1898–1930)

MIDHURST PLU (Sussex, Hants until 1844, ent Sussex 1844–1930)

North Ambersham,[30] South Ambersham,[30] Bepton, North Chapel (1835–69), Chithurst, Cocking, Didling, Easebourne, Elsted, Fernhurst, Graffham (1869–1930), Harting, Heyshott, Iping, East Lavington, West Lavington (1866[29]–1930), Linch, Linchmere, Lodsworth, Lurgashall, Midhurst, Rogate,[31] Selham, Stedham, Terwick, Tillington, Treyford, Trotton, Woolbeding

NEWHAVEN PLU

Bishopstone, East Blatchington, Denton, Denton Urban (1894–1930), Falmer, South Heighton, Iford, Kingston (1835–94), Kingston near Lewes (1894–1930), Kingston Urban (1894–1930), Newhaven, Ovingdean, Peacehaven (1929–30), Piddinghoe, Rodmell, Rottingdean, Southease, Stanmer, Tarring Neville, Telscombe

PETWORTH PLU

Barlavington (1869–1930), Bignor (1869–1930), Billingshurst (1835–70), Burton (1869–1930), Bury (1869–1930), North Chapel (1869–1930), Coates (1869–1930), Duncton, Egdean (1869–1930), Fittleworth (1869–1930), Kirdford, Petworth, Rudgwick (1835–69), Stopham (1869–1930), Sutton, Wisborough Green

EAST PRESTON INCORP (1791–1869), PLU (1869–1930)

Amberley (1791–1869), Angmering (1806–1930), Arundel (1869–1930), Broadwater (1799–1902), Burpham, Clapham (1869–1930), Climping (1799–1930), Durrington (1803–1929), Ferring, Ford (1799–1930), Goring by Sea (1791–1929), Heene (1869–1902), Houghton (1803–1930), Kingston (1869–1930), Lancing (1799–1869), Littlehampton, Lyminster, Patching (1869–1930), Poling (1806–1930), East Preston, Rustington (1806–1930), South Stoke (1869–1930), West Tarring (1803–1930), Tortington (1799–1930), Warningcamp (1869–1930), Wick (1901–30), Wigginholt (1803–69), Worthing (1894–1930)

RYE PLU (Sussex, Kent until 1895, ent Sussex 1895–1930)

Breckley, Brede, Broomhill,[32] East Guldeford, Icklesham, Iden, Northiam, Peasmarsh, Playden, Rye, Rye Foreign (1894–1930), Udimore; St Thomas the Apostle, Winchelsea

STEYNING PLU

Aldrington, Ashurst, Upper Beeding, West Blatchington, Botolphs, Bramber, Coombes, Edburton, Fulking (1894–1930), Hangleton, Henfield, Hove, Kingston by Sea, Lancing (1869–1930), Patching (1835–1928), Portslade (1835–1928), Portslade by Sea (1898–1930), Poynings, Preston (1835–1928), Preston Rural (1894–1928), Shermanbury, New Shoreham, Old Shoreham, Shoreham-by-Sea (1910–30), Sompting, Southwick, Steyning, Woodmancote

SUTTON INCORP (1791–1869)

Barlavington (1804–69), Bersted (1792–1869), Bignor, Burton, Bury, Clapham, Coates, Coldwaltham (1804–35), Duncton, Egdean (1792–1869), Fittleworth (1804–69), Greatham (1804–69), Heyshott (date of inclusion uncertain), Patching, Slindon (1792–1858), Sutton, Warningcamp (1866[29]–69)

THAKENHAM PLU

Amberley (1869–1930), Ashington, West Chiltington, Coldwaltham, Findon, Greatham (1869–1930), Hardham, Parham, Pulborough, Rackham (1848–1930), North Stoke (1869–1930), Storrington, Stopham (1835–69), Sullington, Thakenham, Warminghurst, Washington, Wigginholt (1869–1930), Wiston

TICEHURST PLU (Sussex, Kent)

Bodiam, Burwash, Etchingham, Frant,[33] Lamberhurst,[34] Salehurst, Ticehurst, Wadhurst

UCKFIELD PLU

Buxted, Crowborough (1905–30), Danehill (1898–1930), Fletching, Framfield, Hadlow Down (1905–30), East Hoathly, Little Horsted, Isfield, Maresfield, Mayfield, Rotherfield, Uckfield, Waldron

WESTBOURNE PLU
Bosham, Chidham, Compton, West Dean, Funtington, East Marden, North Marden, Up Marden, Racton, Stoughton, West Thorney, Westbourne
WESTHAMPNETT PLU
Aldingbourne, Appledram, Barnham, Bersted (1869–1930), Binderton, Binsted, Birdham, Bognor (1894–1930 [called Bognor Regis from 1929]), Boxgrove, East Dean, Donnington, Earnley, Eartham, Eastergate, Felpham, New Fishbourne, Hunston, West Itchenor, Lavant (1872–1930), East Lavant (1835–72), Mid Lavant (1835–72), Madehurst, Merston, Middleton, North Mundham, Oving, Pagham, Portfield (1894–96), Rumboldswyke (1835–96), Selsey, Sidlesham, Singleton, Slindon (1858–1930), West Stoke, Tangmere, Walberton, Up Waltham, Westhampnett, East Wittering, West Wittering, Yapton

In Other Poor Law Counties:
CRANBROOK PLU (Kent, Sussex)
Hawkhurst[35]
HAMBLEDON PLU (Surrey, Sussex)
Alfold[36]
HEADLEY INCORP (Hants, Sussex)
Bramshott[37] (18th cent–1869)
PETERSFIELD PLU (Hants, Sussex)
Bramshott[37] (1869–1930)
TONBRIDGE PLU
Horsmonden[34]

SANITARY DISTRICTS

ARUNDEL USD
Arundel
BATTLE RSD
same as PLU less Battle, Bexhill (pt 1875–84, ent 1884–94), pt Hollington (1880s–94)
BATTLE USD
Battle
BEXHILL USD (1884[38]–94)
Bexhill
BOGNOR USD
pt Bersted
BRIGHTON USD
Brighton, pt Preston
BURGESS HILL USD
pt Clayton, pt Keymer
CHAILEY RSD
same as PLU
CHICHESTER RSD
same as PLU less pars in Chichester USD
CHICHESTER USD
Chichester All Saints, Chichester The Close, Chichester Newtown, or St John, Chichester St Andrew, pt Chichester St Bartholomew, Chichester St James, Chichester St Martin, Chichester St Olave, pt Chichester St Pancras, pt Chichester St Peter the Great or Sub-Deanery, Chichester St Peter the Less, pt Oving, pt Rumboldswyke
CRANBROOK RSD
same as PLU for pt of Sussex par
CUCKFIELD RSD
same as PLU less pt Clayton, pt Cuckfield, pt Keymer
CUCKFIELD USD
pt Cuckfield
EASTBOURNE RSD
same as PLU less Eastbourne, Seaford (1883–94), pt Willingdon (1883–94)
EASTBOURNE USD
Eastbourne, pt Willingdon (1883–94)
WEST FIRLE RSD
same as PLU
EAST GRINSTEAD RSD
same as PLU less pt East Grinstead (1884–94)
EAST GRINSTEAD USD (1884[39]–94)
pt East Grinstead
HAILSHAM RSD
same as PLU
HAMBLEDON RSD
same as PLU for pt of Sussex par
HASTINGS RSD
same as PLU less pars in Hastings USD
HASTINGS USD
pt Bexhill, Hastings All Saints, Hastings Holy Trinity, Hastings St Andrew, Hastings St Clement, pt Hastings St Leonards, Hastings St Mary Bulverhythe, pt Hastings St Mary in the Castle, Hastings St Mary Magdalen, Hastings St Michael, pt Hollington (1880s–94), pt Ore
HAYWARD'S HEATH USD
pt Cuckfield
HORSHAM RSD
same as PLU less Horsham
HORSHAM USD
Horsham
HOVE USD
Aldrington (1893[43]–94), Hove
LEWES RSD
same as PLU less pars in Lewes USD
LEWES USD
pt Kingston (1881–94), Lewes All Saints, Lewes The Castle Precincts, pt Lewes St Ann; Lewes St John the Baptist, Southover; pt Lewes St John under the Castle, Lewes St Michael, Lewes St Thomas a Becket, Cliffe, pt South Malling
LITTLEHAMPTON USD
Littlehampton
MIDHURST RSD
same as PLU
NEWHAVEN RSD
same as PLU less East Blatchington (1883–94), pt Denton (1881–94), Newhaven (1881–94)
NEWHAVEN USD (1881[40]–94)
pt Denton, Newhaven
PETERSFIELD RSD
same as PLU for pt of Sussex par
PETWORTH RSD
same as PLU

EAST PRESTON RSD
same as PLU less Arundel, pt Broadwater, Heene (1890–94), Littlehampton
RYE RSD
same as PLU less pt Rye
RYE USD
pt Rye
SEAFORD USD (1883[41]–94)
East Blatchington, Seaford
NEW SHOREHAM USD
New Shoreham
STEYNING RSD
same as PLU less Aldrington (1893–94), Hove, pt Preston, New Shoreham
THAKENHAM RSD
same as PLU
TICEHURST RSD
same as PLU
TONBRIDGE RSD
same as PLU for pt of Sussex par
UCKFIELD RSD
same as PLU less Uckfield
UCKFIELD USD
Uckfield
WESTBOURNE RSD
same as PLU
WESTHAMPNETT RSD
same as PLU less pt Bersted, pt Chichester St Bartholomew, pt Chichester St Pancras, pt Chichester St Peter the Great, pt Oving, pt Rumboldswyke
WORTHING USD
pt Broadwater, Heene (1890[42]–94)

EAST SUSSEX ADMINISTRATIVE COUNTY

For the MBs and the associated CBs, see BOROUGHS.

BATTLE RD
Ashburnham, Battle (1934–74), Beckley (1934–74), Bodiam (1934–74), Brede (1934–74), Brightling, Broomhill (1934–74), Burwash (1934–74), Camber (1956–74), Catsfield, Crowhurst, Dallington, Etchingham (1934–74), Ewhurst, Fairlight (1934–74), Guestling (1934–74), East Guldeford (1934–74), Hollington Rural (1897–1937), Icklesham (1934–74), Iden (1934–74), Mountfield, Northiam (1934–74), Ore (1934–58), Peasmarsh (1934–74), Penhurst, Pett (1934–74), Playden (1934–74), Rye Foreign (1934–74); St Thomas the Apostle, Winchelsea (1934–74); Salehurst (1934–74), Sedlescombe, Ticehurst (1934–74), Udimore (1934–74), Westfield, Whatlington
BATTLE UD (1894–1934)
Battle
BEXHILL UD (1894–1902[19])
Bexhill
BURGESS HILL UD
Burgess Hill (1934–74), Clayton Urban (1894–1934), Keymer Urban (1894–1934)
CHAILEY RD
Barcombe, Beddingham, Chailey, East Chiltington, Ditchling, Falmer (1934–74), Firle (1971–74), West Firle (1894–1971), Glynde, Hamsey, South Heighton (1934–74), Iford (1934–74), Kingston near Lewes (1934–74), Lewes St Ann Without, Lewes St John Without, South Malling Without, Newick, Peacehaven (1934–74), Piddinghoe (1934–74), Plumpton, Ringmer, Rodmell (1934–74), Southease (1934–74), Southover Without (1894–1934), Stanmer (1934–52), Streat, Tarring Neville (1934–74), Telscombe (1934–74),Westmeston, Wivelsfield
CUCKFIELD RD (pt E Sussex, pt W Sussex until 1908, ent E Sussex 1908[44]–74)
Albourne,[44] Ardingly, Balcombe, Bolney, Clayton, Cuckfield Rural, Fulking (1928–74), West Hoathly (1934–74), Horsted Keynes, Hurstpierpoint, Keymer, Lindfield (1894–1934), Lindfield Rural (1934–74), Newtimber, Poynings (1928–74), Pyecombe, Slaugham, Twineham, Worth (1934–74)
CUCKFIELD UD
Cuckfield, Hayward's Heath (1934–74), Lindfield (1934–74)
EASTBOURNE RD (1894–1934)
Alciston, Alfriston, Berwick, East Dean, West Dean, Folkington, Friston, Jevington, Litlington, Lullington, Pevensey, Selmeston, Westham, Willingdon, Wilmington
EAST GRINSTEAD RD (1894–1934)
Forest Row, Hartfield, West Hoathly, Withyham, Worth
EAST GRINSTEAD UD
East Grinstead
HAILSHAM RD
Alciston (1934–74), Alfriston (1934–74), Arlington, Berwick (1934–74), Chalvington, Chiddingly, East Dean (1934–74), West Dean (1934–74), Folkington (1934–74), Friston (1934–74), Hailsham, Heathfield, Hellingly, Herstmonceux, East Hoathly (1934–74), Hooe, Horam (1951–74), Jevington (1934–74), Laughton, Litlington (1934–74), Lullington (1934–74), Ninfield, Pevensey (1934–74), Polegate (1939–74), Ripe, Selmeston (1934–74), Waldron (1934–74), Warbleton, Wartling, Westham (1934–74), Willingdon (1934–74), Wilmington (1934–74)
HASTINGS RD (1894–1934)
Fairlight, Guestling, Ore, Pett, Hastings St Matthew (1894–1909)
HAYWARD'S HEATH UD (1894–1934)
Hayward's Heath
HOVE UD (1894–98[24])
Aldrington, Hove
NEWHAVEN RD (1894–1934)
Bishopstone, Denton, Falmer, South Heighton,

Iford, Kingston near Lewes, Ovingdean (1894–1928), Peacehaven (1929–34), Piddinghoe, Rodmell, Rottingdean (1894–1928), Southease, Stanmer, Tarring Neville, Telscombe

NEWHAVEN UD
Denton Urban (1894–1934), Newhaven

PORTSLADE BY SEA UD (1898[45]–1974)
Portslade by Sea

RYE RD (1894–1934)
Beckley, Brede, Broomhill (pt 1894–95, ent 1895–1934), East Guldeford, Icklesham, Iden, Northiam, Peasmarsh, Playden, Rye Foreign; St Thomas the Apostle, Winchelsea; Udimore

SEAFORD UD
East Blatchington, Seaford

STEYNING EAST RD (1894–1928[46])
West Blatchington, Fulking, Hangleton, Patcham, Portslade, Poynings, Preston Rural

TICEHURST RD (1894–1934)
Bodiam, Burwash, Etchingham, Frant, pt Lamberhurst (1894–95), Salehurst, Ticehurst, Wadhurst

UCKFIELD RD
Buxted, Crowborough (1905–74), Danehill (1898–1974), Fletching, Forest Row (1934–74), Framfield, Frant (1934–74), Hadlow Down (1905–30), Hartfield (1934–74), East Hoathly (1894–1934), Little Horsted, Isfield, Maresfield, Mayfield, Rotherfield, Uckfield (1934–74), Wadhurst (1934–74), Waldron (1894–1934), Withyham (1934–74)

UCKFIELD UD (1894–1934)
Uckfield

WEST SUSSEX ADMINISTRATIVE COUNTY

For the MBs see BOROUGHS.

BOGNOR UD (1894–1929[47])
Bognor

BOGNOR REGIS UD (1929[74]–74)
Bognor Regis

CHANCTONBURY RD (1933–74)
Amberley, Ashington, Ashurst, Upper Beeding, Bramber, West Chiltington, Coldwaltham, Henfield, Parham, Pulborough, Shermanbury, Steyning, Storrington, Sullington, Thakenham, Washington, Wiston, Woodmancote

CHICHESTER RD (1933–74)
Aldingbourne, Appledram, Barnham, Bersted, Birdham, Bosham, Boxgrove, Chidham, Climping, Compton, East Dean, West Dean, Donnington, Earnley, Eartham, Eastergate, Ford, Huntington, Hunston, West Itchenor, Lavant, Madehurst, Marden, Middleton (1933–34), Middleton-on-Sea (1934–74), North Mundham, Oving, Pagham, Selsey, Sidlesham, Singleton, Slindon, Stoughton, Tangmere, West Thorney, Tortington, Walberton, Up Waltham, Westbourne, Westhampnett, East Wittering, West Wittering, Yapton

CRAWLEY UD (1956[48]–74)
Crawley

CUCKFIELD RD (pt E Sussex, pt W Sussex until 1908, ent E Sussex 1908[44]–74)
Albourne[44]

HORSHAM RD
Lower Beeding, Billingshurst, Cowfold, Crawley (1894–1956), West Grinstead, Horsham Rural, Ifield (1894–1933), Itchingfield, Nuthurst, Rudgwick, Rusper, Shipley, Slinfold, Warnham

HORSHAM UD
Horsham

LITTLEHAMPTON UD
Littlehampton, Wick

MIDHURST RD
North Ambersham, South Ambersham, Bepton, Chithurst, Cocking, Didling (1894–1933), Easebourne, Elsted, Fernhurst, Graffham, Harting, Heyshott, Iping, East Lavington, West Lavington, Linch, Linchmere, Lodsworth, Lurgashall, Midhurst, Rogate, Selham (1894–1933), Stedham, Terwick (1894–1933), Tillington, Treyford, Trotton, Woolbeding

PETWORTH RD
Barlavington, Bignor, Burton (1894–1933), Bury, North Chapel, Coates, Duncton, Egdean (1894–1933), Fittleworth, Kirdford, Loxwood (1938–74), Petworth, Plaistow (1951–74), Stopham, Sutton, Wisborough Green

EAST PRESTON RD (1894–1933)
Angmering, Broadwater (1894–1902), Burpham, Clapham, Climping, Durrington (1894–1929), Ferring, Ford, Goring by Sea (1894–1929), Houghton, Kingston, Lyminster, Patching, Poling, East Preston, Rustington, South Stoke, West Tarring (1894–1902), Tortington, Warningcamp

NEW SHOREHAM UD (1894–1910[49])
New Shoreham

SHOREHAM-BY-SEA UD (1910[49]–74)
Kingston by Sea, Old Shoreham (1933–74), Shoreham-by-Sea

SOUTHWICK UD (1899[50]–1974)
Southwick

STEYNING WEST RD (1894–1933)
Ashurst, Upper Beeding, Botolphs, Bramber, Coombes, Edburton, Henfield, Kingston by Sea (1894–1910), Lancing, Shermanbury, Old Shoreham, Sompting, Southwick (1894–99), Steyning, Woodmancote

THAKENHAM RD (1894–1933)
Amberley, Ashington, West Chiltington, Coldwaltham, Findon, Greatham, Hardham, Parham, Pulborough, Rackham, North Stoke, Storrington, Sullington, Thakenham, Warminghurst, Washington, Wiggonholt, Wiston

WESTBOURNE RD (1894–1933)
Bosham, Chidham, Compton, West Dean, Funtington, East Marden, North Marden, Up Marden, Racton, Stoughton, West Thorney, Westbourne

WESTHAMPNETT RD (1894–1933)
Aldingbourne, Appledram, Barnham, Bersted, Binderton (1894–1933), Binsted, Birdham, Boxgrove, East Dean, Donnington, Earnley, Eartham, Eastergate, Felpham, New Fishbourne, Hunston, West Itchenor, Lavant, Madehurst, Merston, Middleton, North Mundham, Oving, Pagham, St Bartholomew Rural (1894–95), St Pancras Rual (1894–96), Selsey, Sidlesham, Singleton (1894–1933), Slindon, West Stoke, Sub-Deanery Rural (1894–96), Tangmere, Walberton, Up Waltham, Westhampnett, East Wittering, West Wittering, Yapton

WORTHING RD (1933–74)
Angmering, Burpham, Clapham, Coombes, Ferring, Findon, Houghton, Kingston, Lancing, Lyminster, Patching, Poling, East Preston, Rustington, Sompting, South Stoke, Warninngcamp

EAST SUSSEX NON-METROPOLITAN COUNTY

As constituted 1 Apr 1974, defined in terms of Adm Co units in East Sussex and the associated CBs, as of 31 Mar.

BRIGHTON DIST
Brighton CB

EASTBOURNE DIST
Eastbourne CB

HASTINGS DIST
Hastings CB

HOVE DIST
Hove MB, Portslade by Sea UD

LEWES DIST
Chailey RD, Lewes MB, Newhaven UD, Seaford UD

ROTHER DIST
Battle RD, Bexhill MB, Rye MB

WEALDEN DIST
Hailsham RD, Uckfield RD

WEST SUSSEX NON-METROPOLITAN COUNTY

As constituted 1 Apr 1974, defined in terms of Adm Co units from the indicated counties, as of 31 Mar.

ADUR DIST
From W Sussex: Shoreham-by-Sea UD, Southwick UD, pt Worthing RD (the pars of Coombes, Lancing, Sompting)

ARUN DIST
From W Sussex: Arundel MB, Bognor Regis UD, pt Chichester RD (the pars of Aldringbourne, Barnham, Bersted, Climping, Eastergate, Ford, Madehurst, Middleton-on-Sea, Pagham, Slindon, Tortington, Walberton Yapton), Littlehampton UD, pt Worthing RD (all except the pars in Adur Dist)

CHICHESTER DIST
From W Sussex: Chichester MB, pt Chichester RD (all except the pars in Arun Dist), Midhurst RD, Petworth RD

CRAWLEY DIST
From E Sussex: pt Cuckfield RD (pt of the pars of Slaugham,[51] Worth[51]).
From W Sussex: Crawley UD

HORSHAM DIST
From W Sussex: Chanctonbury RD, Horsham RD, Horsham UD

MID SUSSEX DIST
From E Sussex: Burgess Hill UD, pt Cuckfield RD (all except pt Slaugham,[52] pt Worth[52])

WORTHING DIST
From W Sussex: Worthing MB

WILTSHIRE

ALTERATIONS IN COUNTY BOUNDARIES

As noted by year below, Wilts pars gained territory from or lost it to pars in adjoining counties, or were entirely transferred to them. Details of these alterations are noted in Part I of the *Guide* under Wilts.

ANCIENT COUNTY (from 1889: Hds, Bors, MBs, PLUs, RSD, USDs)
1844 Hurst, Inglesham, Kingswood, Minety, Poulton, Shinfield, Swallowfield, Wokingham. *1880s* Tollard Royal. *1881* Coleshill. *1883* West Dean.

ADMINISTRATIVE COUNTY (1889–1974: Hds,[1] PLUs, MBs, RDs, UDs)
1889 Bramshaw. *1895* Maiden Bradley with Yarnfield, Bramshaw, Chilton Foliat, Damerham, Hungerford, Martin, Melchet Park, Plaitford, Shalbourne, Stourton with Gasper, Toyd Farm with Allenford, West Wellow, Whitsbury. *1896* Kilmington. *1897* Kemble, Poole Keynes, Somerford Keynes. *1930* Ashley, Long Newnton. *1937* Southwick.

NON-METROPOLITAN COUNTY (from 1974: Dists)

HUNDREDS[1]

ALDERBURY HD
Alderbury, Clarendon Park (from 1858), West Dean (pt until 1883, ent from 1883), East Grimstead (from 1866), West Grimstead, Idmiston, Laverstock, Melchet Park (from 1858), Pitton and Farley (from 1866), Plaitford, Winterbourne Dauntsey, Winterbourne Earls, Winterbourne Gunner, Winterslow

AMESBURY HD
Allington, Amesbury,[2] Boscombe, Bulford, Cholderton, Durnford, Durrington, Figheldean, pt Hurst (until 1844), Inglesham (pt until 1844, ent from 1844), Ludgershall,[2] Milston, Newton Tony, pt Shinfield (until 1844), pt Swallowfield (until 1844), North Tidworth, West Wellow, pt Wokingham (until 1844)

BRADFORD HD
Atworth (from 1885), Bradford-on-Avon,[2] Broughton Gifford, Great Chalfield, Little Chalfield (from 1858), Cottles (from 1858), Monkton Farleigh, Wingfield

BRANCH AND DOLE HD
Berwick St James, Fisherton Anger,[2] Fugglestone St Peter, Little Langford, Steeple Langford, Maddington, South Newton, Orcheston St Mary, Sherrington, Shrewton, Stapleford, pt Tilshead,[2] pt Wilton,[2] Winterbourne Stoke, Great Wishford, Wylye

CALNE HD
Berwick Bassett, Blackland, Bowood (from 1858), Calne,[2] Calstone Wellington, Cherhill, Compton Bassett, Heddington, Yatesbury

CAWDEN AND CADWORTH HD
Baverstock, Barford St Martin, pt Bramshaw, Britford, Burcombe,[2] Coombe Bissett, Fovant, Groveley Wood (from 1858), West Harnham, Homington, Netherhampton, Odstock, Stratford Toney, Sutton Mandeville, Whitsbury, pt Wilton[2]

CHALK HD
Alvediston, Berwick St John, Bower Chalke, Broad Chalke, Ebbesbourne Wake, Fifield Bavant, Semley, Tollard Royal (pt until 1880s, ent from 1880s)

CHIPPENHAM HD
Alderton, Avon (from 1866), Biddestone St Nicholas, Biddestone St Peter, Box, Bremhill, Castle Combe, Chippenham,[2] pt Christian Malford, Colerne, Corsham, Ditteridge, pt Easton Grey, Hardenhuish, pt Hullavington, Kingswood, West Kington, Lacock,[2] Langley Burrell,[2] Leigh Delamere, Littleton Drew, Luckington, Pewsham (from 1858), Sherston Magna, Sherston Pinkney, Slaughterford, Sopworth, Tytherton Kellaways, North Wraxall, Yatton Keynell

DAMERHAM HD[3]
pt Christian Malford, Compton Chamberlayne, Damerham, pt Kingston Devereill, Longbridge Deverill, Monkton Deverill, Grittleton, Kington Langley (from 1866), Kington St Michael, Martin, Nettleton, Toyd Farm with Allenford (from 1858)

DOWNTON HD
Bishopstone, Downton,[2] Fonthill Bishop, Hindon,[2] East Knoyle,[2] Langley Wood (from 1858), No Man's Land (from 1858), Nunton and Bodenham, Standlynch

DUNWORTH HD
Anstey, Berwick St Leonard, Chilmark, Chicklade, Donhead St Andrew, Donhead St Mary, Fonthill Gifford, Sedgehill, Teffont Evias, Swallowcliffe, Tisbury (until 1834), East Tisbury (from 1834), West Tisbury (from 1834), Wardour (from 1834)

ELSTUB AND EVERLEIGH HD
Alton Priors (from 1866), Collingbourne Ducis, pt Collingbourne Kingston, Enford, Everleigh, Fittle-

ton, Fyfield, Ham, Little Hinton, Netheravon, pt West Overton, Patney, Rolleston, Stockton, Westwood, Wroughton

FRUSTFIELD HD
Earldoms (from 1858), Landford, Whiteparish

HEYTESBURY HD
Boyton, Chitterne All Saints, Chitterne St Mary, Codford St Mary, Codford St Peter, Brixton Deverill, Hill Deverill, Heytesbury,[2] Horningsham, pt Imber, Knook, Orcheston St George, Tytherington, Upton Lovell

HIGHWORTH, CRICKLADE AND STAPLE HD
Ashton Keynes, Blunsdon St Andrew, Braydon (from 1866), Castle Eaton, pt Coleshill (until 1881), Cricklade St Mary,[2] Cricklade St Sampson,[2] Eisey, Hannington, Highworth,[2] Somerford Keynes, Latton, Leigh (from 1866), Lydiard Millicent, Marston Meysey, Poulton (until 1844), Purton, Rodbourne Cheney, Shorncott, Stanton Fitzwarren, Stratton St Margaret

KINGSBRIDGE HD
Broad Town (from 1866), Chiseldon, Clyffe Pypard, Draycott Foliat, pt Hilmarton, Liddington, Lydiard Tregoze, Lyneham, Swindon, Tockenham, Wanborough, Wootton Bassett[2]

KINWARDSTONE HD
Great Bedwyn,[2] Little Bedwyn,[2] Burbage, Buttermere, pt Chilton Foliat, pt Collingbourne Kingston, Chute, Chute Forest (from 1858), Easton, Froxfield, Grafton (from 1866), Hippenscombe (from 1858), pt Hungerford, Milton Lilbourne, Pewsey, North Savernake (from 1858), South Savernake (from 1858), pt Shalbourne, Tidcombe and Fosbury, Wootton Rivers

MALMESBURY HD
Ashley, Bremilham, Brinkworth, Brokenborough,[2] Charlton, Crudwell, Dauntsey, Draycot Cerne, pt Easton Grey, Foxley, Garsdon, Hankerton, pt Hullavington, Kemble, Poole Keynes, Lea and Cleverton, Malmesbury The Abbey,[2] Malmesbury St Paul,[2] Minety (from 1844), Long Newnton, Norton, Oaksey, Seagry, Great Somerford, Little Somerford, Stanton St Quintin, Sutton Benger, Westport St Mary[2]

MERE HD
pt Maiden Bradley with Yarnfield, pt Kingston Deverill, West Knoyle, Mere,[2] pt Stourton with Gasper

POTTERNE AND CANNINGS HD[4]
Bromham, Bishops Cannings, Chittoe (from 1866), Highway, West Lavington, Marston (from 1866), Potterne, Rowde,[2] Worton (from 1866)

RAMSBURY HD
Baydon, Bishopstone, Ramsbury

SELKLEY HD[5]
Aldbourne, Avebury, Clatford Park (from 1858), pt Hilmarton, Broad Hinton, East Kennett, Mildenhall, Ogbourne St Andrew, Ogbourne St George, pt West Overton, Overton Heath (from 1858), Preshute, Winterbourne Bassett, Winterbourne Monkton

SWANBOROUGH HD
Allington (from 1866), Alton Barnes, Beechingstoke, All Cannings, Charlton, Cheverell Magna, Cheverell Parva, Chirton, Easterton (from 1866), Etchilhampton (from 1866), Fullaway (from 1858), Huish, pt Imber, Market Lavington, Manningford Abbots, Manningford Bohune (from 1866), Manningford Bruce, Marden, North Newnton, Rushall, Stanton St Bernard, Stert (from 1866), Upavon, Urchfont, Wilcot, Wilsford, Woodborough

UNDERDITCH HD
Milford[2] (from 1866), pt Salisbury St Martin[2] (until 1866), Old Sarum (from 1858), Stratford sub Castle,[2] Wilsford cum Lake, Woodford

WARMINSTER HD
North Bavant, Bishopstrow, Corsley, Dinton, Fisherton de la Mere, Upper Pertwood, Sutton Veny, Teffont Magna, Upton Scudamore, Warminster[2]

WESTBURY HD
Westbury[2]

WHORWELLSDOWN HD
Steeple Ashton, West Ashton (from 1866), North Bradley, East Coulston, Edington, Great Hinton (from 1866), pt Keevil, Semington (from 1866), Southwick (from 1866), pt Tilshead[2]

MELKSHAM HD
Bulkington (from 1866), Erlestoke, Hilperton, pt Keevil, Melksham, Poulshot, Seend (from 1866), Trowbridge,[2] Whaddon

BOROUGHS

Units with some degree of burghal character[6] are denominated 'Bor'.
Those which did not sustain that status until the 19th cent are in italics.
Municipal Boroughs were established by the Municipal Corporations Act, 1835,[7] or by later charter.

AMESBURY BOR
Amesbury

GREAT BEDWYN BOR
Great Bedwyn

BRADFORD-ON-AVON BOR
Bradford-on-Avon

CALNE BOR/MB
pt Calne (until 1890), Calne Within (1890–1974)

CHIPPENHAM BOR/MB
pt Chippenham (until 1894), Chippenham Within (1894–1974), pt Langley Burrell (1889–94), Langley Burrell Within (1894–1934)

CHISBURY BOR[8]
pt Little Bedwyn

CRICKLADE BOR
Cricklade St Mary, Cricklade St Sampson

DEVIZES BOR/MB
Devizes (1934–74), Devizes St James (pt 1835–94, ent 1894–1934), Devizes St John the Baptist (until 1934), Devizes St Mary the Virgin (until 1934), pt Rowde (1835–94), Rowde Within (1894–1934)
DOWNTON BOR
Downton
HEYTESBURY BOR
Heytesbury
HIGHWORTH BOR
Highworth
HINDON BOR
Hindon (when gains sep civ identity), pt East Knoyle (until Hindon gains sep civ identity)
LACOCK BOR
Lacock
LUDGERSHALL BOR
Ludgershall
MALMESBURY BOR, MB (1886[9]–1974)
pt Brokenborough (1886–94), Brokenborough Within (1894–97), Malmesbury (1934–74), Malmesbury The Abbey (until 1934), Malmesbury St Paul (ent until 1883, pt 1883–94), Malmesbury St Paul Within (1894–1934), pt Westport St Mary (1886–94), Westport St Mary Within (1894–1934)
MARLBOROUGH BOR/MB
Marlborough (1925–74), Marlborough St Mary the Virgin (until 1925), Marlborough St Peter and St Paul (until 1925), Preshute Within (1901–25)
MERE BOR
Mere
SALISBURY BOR/MB
pt Fisherton Anger (1835–94), Fisherton Anger Within (1894–1905), pt Milford (1835–94), Milford Within (1894–1905), Salisbury The Close of the Canons of the Cathedral Church (1835–1905), Salisbury St Edmund (until 1905), Salisbury St Martin (pt 1835–66, ent 1866–1905), Salisbury St Thomas (until 1905), New Sarum (1905–74), pt Stratford sub Caslte (until 1897)
OLD SARUM BOR
Old Sarum
SWINDON MB (1900[10]–74)
Swindon
TILSHEAD BOR
Tilshead
TROWBRIDGE BOR
Trowbridge
WARMINSTER BOR
Warminster
WESTBURY BOR
Westbury
WILTON BOR, MB (1885[11]–1974)
pt Burcombe (1885–94), pt Fugglestone St Peter (1885–94), pt South Newton (1885–94), Wilton
WOOTTON BASSETT BOR
Wootton Bassett

POOR LAW UNIONS

In Wilts Poor Law Co.[12]
ALDERBURY PLU (1836–95), renamed 28 May 1895 SALISBURY PLU (1895–1930)
Alderbury, Alderton, Britford, Clarendon Park, Coombe Bissett, West Dean (1883–1930), Downton, Earldoms (1836–96), Fisherton Anger (1836–94), Fisherton Anger Within (1894–1905), Fisherton Anger Without (1894–1905), East Grimstead, West Grimstead, Harnham (1904–05), East Harnham (1896–1904), West Harnham, Homington, Landford, Langley Wood (1836–94), Laverstock and Ford, Milford (1836–94), Milford Within (1894–1905), Milford Without (1894–1904), Morgans's Vale and Woodfalls (1923–30), No Man's Land, Nunton and Bodenham, Odstock, Pitton and Farley, Redlynch (1896–1930), Salisbury The Close of the Canons of the Cathedral Church (1836–1905), Salisbury St Edmund (1869–1905), Salisbury St Martin (1869–1905), Salisbury St Thomas (1869–1905), New Sarum (1905–30), Old Sarum (1836–94), Standlynch (1836–97), Standlynch with Charlton All Saints (1894–1930), Stratford sub Castle, Stratford Tony, Whiteparish, Winterslow
AMESBURY PLU
Allington, Amesbury, Boscombe, Bulford, Cholderton, Durnford, Durrington, Figheldean, Idmiston, Maddington, Milston, Newton Tony, Orcheston St George, Orcheston St Mary, Rollestone, Shrewton, Tilshead, Wilsford cum Lake, Winterbourne Dauntsey, Winterbourne Earls, Winterbourne Gunner, Winterbourne Stoke, Woodford
BRADFORD PLU (1835–95), renamed 5 July 1895 BRADFORD-ON-AVON PLU (1895–1930) (Wilts, Somerset until 1882, ent Wilts 1882–1930)
Atworth (1885–1930), Bradford-on-Avon, Bradford Without (1894–1930), Broughton Gifford, Great Chalfield (1835–85), Little Chalfield (1835–85), Cottles (1835–85), Holt (1894–1930), Limpley Stoke (1894–1930), Monkton Farleigh, Westwood (1894–1930), Wingfield, Winsley (1894–1930), South Wraxall (1894–1930)
BRADFORD-ON-AVON PLU–See BRADFORD
CALNE PLU
Blackland (1835–90), Bowood (1835–90), Bremhill, Calne (1835–90), Calne Within (1890–1930), Calne Without (1890–1930), Calstone Wellington (1835–90), Cherhill, Compton Bassett, Heddington, Highway (1835–90), Hilmarton, Yatesbury
CHIPPENHAM PLU
Avon (1835–95), Biddestone (1885–1930), Biddestone St Nicholas (1835–85), Biddestone St Peter (1835–95), Box, Castle Combe, Chippenham (1835–94), Chippenham Within (1894–1930), Chippenham Without (1894–1930), Christian Malford, Colerne, Corsham, Ditteridge (1835–84), Draycot Cerne, Grittleton, Hardenhuish, Kellaways (1895–1930), West Kington, Kington Langley, Kington St Michael, Lacock,

Langley Burrell (1835–94), Langley Burrell Within (1894–1930), Langley Burrell Without (1894–1930), Leigh Delamere, Littleton Drew, Nettleton, Pewsham, Seagry, Slaughterford, Stanton St Quintin, Sutton Benger, Tytherton Kellaways (1835–95), North Wraxall, Yatton Keynell

CRICKLADE AND WOOTTON BASSETT PLU

Ashton Keynes, Braydon, Broad Town, Clyffe Pypard, Cricklade (1899–1930), Cricklade St Mary (1835–99), Cricklade St Sampson (1835–99), Eisey (1835–96), Latton, Leigh, Lydiard Millicent, Lydiard Tregoze, Lyneham, Marston Meysey (1881–1930), Purton, Tockenham, Wootton Bassett

DEVIZES PLU

Allington, Alton Barnes, Beechingstone, Bromham, All Cannings, Bishops Cannings, Cheverell Magna, Cheverell Parva, Chirton, Chittoe, Devizes St James, Devizes St John the Baptist, Devizes St Mary the Virgin, Easterton, Erlestoke, Etchilhampton, Fullaway (1835–94), Market Lavington, West Lavington, Marden, Marston, Patney, Potterne, Poulshot, Roundway (1894–1930), Rowde, Rowde Within (1894–1930), Stanton St Bernard, Stert, Urchfont, Worton

HIGHWORTH AND SWINDON PLU (1835–98), renamed 24 Mar 1889 SWINDON AND HIGHWORTH PLU (1899–1930)

Bishopstone, Blunsdon St Andrew, Castle Eaton, Chiseldon, Draycot Foliat (1835–94), Hannington, Haydon Wick (1928–30), Highworth, Little Hinton, Inglesham,[13] Liddington, South Marston (1894–1930), Rodbourne Cheney (1835–1928), Stanton Fitzwarren, Stratton St Margaret, Swindon, Wanborough, Wroughton

MALMESBURY PLU (Wilts, Glos until 1844, ent Wilts 1844–1930)

Brinkworth, Brokenborough (1835–94), Brokenborough (1897–1930), Brokenborough Within (1894–97), Brokenborough Without (1894–97), Charlton, Crudwell, Dauntsey, Easton Grey, Foxley, Garsdon, Hankerton, Hullavington, Lea and Cleverton, Luckington, Malmesbury The Abbey, Malmesbury St Paul (1835–94), Malmesbury St Paul Within (1894–1930), Malmesbury St Paul Without (1894–96), Minety,[14] Norton, Oaksey, Sherston (1896–1930), Sherston Magna (1835–96), Sherston Pinkney (1835–96), Great Somerford, Little Somerford, Sopworth, Westport St Mary (1835–94), Westport St Mary Within (1894–1930), Westport St Mary Without (1894–1930)

MARLBOROUGH PLU

Avebury, Berwick Bassett, Clatford Park (1858[15]–96), Broad Hinton, Fyfield, East Kennett, Marlborough (1925–30), Marlborough St Mary the Virgin (1835–1925), Marlborough St Peter and St Paul (1835–1925), Mildenhall, Ogbourne St Andrew, Ogbourne St George, West Overton, Overton Heath (1835–95), Preshute (1835–1901), Preshute (1925–30), Preshute Within (1901–25), Preshute Without (1901–25), North Savernake, South Savernake with Brimslade and Cadley, Winterbourne Bassett, Winterbourne Monkton

MELKSHAM PLU (1835–98), renamed 16 Sept 1898 TROWBRIDGE AND MELKSHAM PLU (1898–1930)

Hilperton, Melksham (1835–94), Melksham Within (1894–1930), Melksham Without (1894–1930), Seend, Semington, Staverton (1894–1930), Trowbridge, Whaddon (1935– 94)

MERE PLU (Wilts, Somerset, Dorset until 1896, ent Wilts 1896–1930)

Maiden Bradley with Yarnfield,[16] Kingston Deveтill, Monkton Deverill, Kilmington,[17] East Knoyle, West Knoyle, Mere, Upper Pertwood (1835–85), Sedgehill, Stourton with Gasper,[16] Zeals (1896–1930)

PEWSEY PLU

Alton Priors, Burbage, Chute (1879–1930), Chute Forest (1879–1930), Collingbourne Ducis, Collingbourne Kingston, Easton, Enford, Everleigh, Fittleton, Huish, Ludgershall (1879–1930), Manningford Abbots, Manningford Bohune, Manningford Bruce, Milton Lilbourne, Netheravon, North Newnton, Pewsey, Rushall, North Tidworth (1879–1930), Upavon, Wilcot, Wilsford, Woodborough, Wootton Rivers

SALISBURY INCORPORATION (1770–1869)

Salisbury St Edmund, pt Salisbury St Martin, Salisbury St Thomas

SALISBURY PLU–See ALDERBURY PLU

SWINDON AND HIGHWORTH PLU–See HIGHWORTH AND SWINDON PLU

TISBURY PLU (Wilts, Dorset until 1880s, ent Wilts thereafter)

Alvediston, Ansty, Berwick St John, Berwick St Leonard, Chicklade, Chilmark, Donhead St Andrew, Donhead St Mary, Fonthill Bishop, Fonthill Gifford, Hindon, Semley, Sutton Mandeville, Swallowcliffe, Teffont Evias, Teffont Magna, Tisbury (1927–30), East Tisbury (1835–1927), West Tisbury, Tollard Royal,[18] Wardour (1835–1927)

TROWBRIDGE AND MELKSHAM PLU–See MELKSHAM PLU

WARMINSTER PLU

Bishopstrow, Boyton, Chitterne (1907–30), Chitterne All Saints (1835–1907), Chitterne St Mary (1835–1907), Codford St Mary, Codford St Peter, Corsley, Brixton Deverill, Hill Deverill, Longbridge Deverill, Heytesbury, Horningsham, Imber, Knook, Norton Bavant, Sherrington, Stockton, Sutton Veney, Tytherington, Upton Lovell, Upton Scudamore, Warminster

WESTBURY AND WHORWELLSDOWN PLU

Steeple Ashton, West Ashton, North Bradley, Bratton (1894–1930), Bulkington, East Coulston, Dilton Marsh (1894–1930), Edington, Heywood (1894–1930), Great Hinton, Keevil, Southwick, Westbury

WILTON PLU

Barford St Martin, Baverstock, Bemerton (1894–1930), Berwick St James, Bishopstone, Burcombe (1835–94), Burcombe Without (1894–1930), Bower Chalke, Broad Chalke, Compton Chamberlayne, Dinton, Ebbesbourne Wake, Fifield Bavant (1835–94), Fisherton de la Mere, Fovant, Fugglestone St Peter (1835–94), Groveley Wood, Little Langford, Steeple Langford, Netherhampton, South Newton (1835–94), South Newton (1894–1930), Stapleford, Wilton, Great Wishford, Wylye

In Other Poor Law Counties:

ANDOVER PLU (Hants)
Chute (1835–79), Chute Forest (1835–79), Ludgershall (1835–79), North Tidworth (1835–79)

CIRENCESTER PLU (Glos)
Kemble,[19] Poole Keynes,[19] Somerford Keynes,[19] Marston Meysey (1835–81), Poulton,[20] Shorncott (1835–94)

DURSLEY PLU (Glos)
Kingswood[20]

FARINGDON PLU (Berks)
Coleshill[21]

FORDINGBRIDGE PLU (Hants)
Damerham,[22] Martin,[22] Toyd Farm with Allenford[22] (from 1858), Whitsbury[22]

NEW FOREST (Hants)
Bramshaw[25]

HUNGERFORD PLU (Berks) (1835–96), renamed 4 June 1896 HUNGERFORD AND RAMSBURY PLU (1896–1930)
Aldbourne, Baydon, Great Bedwyn, Little Bedwyn, Buttermere, Chilton Foliat,[23] Froxfield, Grafton, Ham, Hippenscombe, Hungerford,[24] Ramsbury, Shalbourne,[23] Tidcombe and Fosbury

ROMSEY PLU (Hants)
Melchet Park,[22] Plaitford,[22] West Wellow[22]

STOCKBRIDGE (Hants)
West Dean (1835–83)

TETBURY PLU (Glos)
Ashley, Long Newnton

WOKINGHAM PLU (Berks)
Hurst,[26] Shinfield,[26] Swallowfield,[26] Wokingham[26]

SANITARY DISTRICTS

ALDERBURY RSD
same as PLU less pt Fisherton Anger, pt Milford, Salisbury The Close of the Canons of the Cathedral Church, Salisbury St Edmund, Salisbury St Martin, Salisbury St Thomas, pt Stratford sub Castle

AMESBURY RSD
same as PLU

ANDOVER RSD
same as PLU for Wilts pars

BRADFORD RSD
same as PLU less pt Bradford-on-Avon

BRADFORD-ON-AVON USD
pt Bradford-on-Avon

CALNE RSD
same as PLU less pt Calne (1875–90), Calne Within (1890–94)

CALNE USD[27]
pt Calne (1875–90), Calne Within (1890–94)

CHIPPENHAM RSD
same as PLU less pt Chippenham, pt Langley Burrell

CHIPPENHAM USD
pt Chippenham, pt Langley Burrell

CIRENCESTER RSD
same as PLU for Wilts pars

CRICKLADE AND WOOTTON BASSETT RSD
same as PLU

DEVIZES RSD
same as PLU less pt Devizes St James, Devizes St John the Baptist, Devizes St Mary the Virgin, pt Rowde

DEVIZES USD
pt Devizes St James, Devizes St John the Baptist, Devizes St Mary the Virgin, pt Rowde

FARINGDON RSD
same as PLU for the pt of the Wilts par

FORDINGBRIDGE RSD
same as PLU for Wilts pars

NEW FOREST RSD
same as PLU for the pt of the Wilts par

HIGHWORTH AND SWINDON RSD
same as PLU less pt Rodbourne Cheney (1875–90)pt Stratton St Margaret (1875–90), Swindon

HUNGERFORD RSD
same as PLU for Wilts pars

MALMESBURY RSD
same as PLU less pt Brokenborough (1886–94), Malmesbury The Abbey, Malmesbury St Paul (ent 1875–83, pt 1883–94), pt Westport St Mary (1886–94)

MALMESBURY USD
pt Brokenborough (1886–94), Malmesbury The Abbey, Malmesbury St Paul (ent 1875–83, pt 1883–94), pt Westport St Mary (1886–94)

MARLBOROUGH RSD
same as PLU less Marlborough St Mary the Virgin, Marlborough St Peter and St Paul

MARLBOROUGH USD
Marlborough St Mary the Virgin, Marlborough St Peter and St Paul

MELKSHAM RSD
same as PLU less pt Melksham, pt Trowbridge

MELKSHAM USD
pt Melksham

MERE RSD
same as PLU

ROMSEY RSD
same as PLU for Wilts pars

SALISBURY USD
pt Fisherton Anger, pt Milford, Salisbury The Close of the Canons of the Cathedral Church, Salisbury St Edmund, Salisbury St Martin, Salisbury St Thomas, pt Stratford sub Castle

STOCKBRIDGE RSD
same as PLU for the pt of the Wilts par

OLD SWINDON USD
pt Swindon

SWINDON NEW TOWN USD[28]
pt Rodbourne Cheney (1875–90), pt Stratton St Margaret (1875–90), pt Swindon
TETBURY RSD
same as PLU for the Wilts pars
TISBURY RSD
same as PLU
TROWBRIDGE USD
pt Trowbridge
WARMINSTER RSD
same as PLU less Warminster
WARMINSTER USD
Warminster
WESTBURY AND WHORWELLSDOWN RSD
same as PLU
WILTON RSD
same as PLU less pt Burcombe (1885–94), pt Fugglestone St Peter (1885–94), pt South Newton (1885–94), Wilton
WILTON USD
pt Burcombe (1885–94), pt Fugglestone St Peter (1885–94), pt South Newton (1885–94), Wilton

ADMINISTRATIVE COUNTY

For MBs see BOROUGHS earlier in this Pt of the *Guide*.

AMESBURY RD
Allington, Amesbury, Boscombe (1894–1934), Bulford, Cholderton, Durnford, Durrington, Figheldean, Idmiston, Maddington (1894–1934), Milston, Newton Tony, Orcheston (1934–74), Orcheston St George (1894–1934), Orcheston St Mary (1894–1934), Rollestone (1894–1934), Shrewton, Tilshead, Wilsford cum Lake, Winterbourne (1934–74), Winterbourne Dauntsey (1894–1934), Winterbourne Earls (1894–1934), Winterbourne Gunner (1894–1934), Winterbourne Stoke, Woodford
BRADFORD AND MELKSHAM RD (1934–74)
Atworth, Broughton Gifford, Hilperton, Holt, Land Common to Broughton Gifford and Melksham Without, Limpley Stoke, Melksham Without, Monkton Farleigh, Semington, Staverton, Westwood, Wingfield, Wingsley
BRADFORD-ON-AVON RD (1894–1934)
Atworth, Bradford Without, Broughton Gifford, Holt, Limpley Stoke, Monkton Farleigh, Westwood, Wingfield, Winsley, South Wraxall
BRADFORD-ON-AVON UD
Bradford-on-Avon
CALNE RD (1894–1934)
Bremhill, Calne Without, Cherhill, Compton Bassett, Heddington, Hilmarton, Yatesbury
CALNE AND CHIPPENHAM RD (1934–74)
Biddestone, Box, Bremhill, Calne Without, Castle Combe, Cherhill, Chippenham Without, Christian Malford, Colerne, Compton Bassett, Corsham, Grittleton, Heddington, Hilmarton, Kington Langley, Kington St Michael, Lacock, Langley Burrell Without, Nettleton, Pewsham, Seagry (1971–74), Stanton St Quintin, Sutton Benger, North Wraxall, Yatton Keynell
CHIPPENHAM RD (1894–1934)
Avon (1894–95), Biddestone, Box, Castle Combe, Chippenham Without, Christian Malford, Colerne, Corsham, Draycot Cerne, Grittleton, Hardenhuish, Kellaways (1895–1934), West Kington, Kington Langley, Kington St Michael, Lacock, Langley Burrell Without, Leigh Delamere, Littleton Drew, Nettlesham, Pewsham, Seagry, Slaughterford, Stanton St Quintin, Sutton Benger, Tytherton Kellaways (1894–95), North Wraxall, Yatton Keynell
CRICKLADE AND WOOTTON BASSETT RD
Ashton Keynes, Braydon, Broad Town, Clyffe Pypard, Cricklade (1899–1974), Cricklade St Mary (1894–99), Cricklade St Sampson (1894–99), Eisey (1894–96), Latton, Leigh, Lydiard Millicent, Lydiard Tregoze, Lyneham, Marston Meysey, Purton, Tockenham, Wootton Bassett
DEVIZES RD
Allington (1894–1934), Alton Barnes (1894–1934), Beechingstoke, Bromham, All Cannings, Bishops Cannings, Cheverell Magna, Cheverell Parva, Chirton, Chittoe (1894–1934), Easterton, Erlestoke, Etchilhampton, Market Lavington, West Lavington, Marden, Marston, Patney, Potterne, Poulshot, Roundway, Rowde, Seend (1934–74), Stanton St Bernard, Stert, Urchfont, Worton
HIGHWORTH RD
Blunsdon St Andrew, Bishopstone, Castle Eaton, Chiseldon, Hannington, Haydon Wick, Highworth, Little Hinton (1894–1934), Inglesham, Liddington, South Marston, Stanton Fitzwarren, Stratton St Margaret, Wanborough, Wroughton
MALMESBURY RD
Alderton (1894–1934), Brinkworth, Brokenborough (1897–1974), Brokenborough Without (1894–97), Charlton, Crudwell, Dauntsey, Easton Grey, Foxley (1894–1934), Garsdon (1894–1934), Hankerton, Hullavington, Lea and Cleverton, Luckington, Malmesbury St Paul Without, Minety, Norton, Oaksey, Sherston (1896–1974), Sherston Magna (1894–96), Sherston Pinkney (1894–96), Great Somerford, Little Somerford, Sopworth, Westport St Mary Without (1894–96)
MARLBOROUGH RD (1894–1934)
Avebury, Berwick Bassett, Fyfield, Broad Hinton, East Kennett, Mildenhall, West Overton, Overton Heath (1894–95), Ogbourne St Andrew, Ogbourne St George, Preshute (1894–1901), Preshute (1925–34), Preshute Without (1901–25), North Savernake, South Savernake with Brimslade and Cadley, Winterbourne Bassett, Winterbourne Monkton
MARLBOROUGH AND RAMSBURY RD (1934–74)
Aldbourne, Avebury, Baydon, Berwick Bassett,

Great Bedwyn, Little Bedwyn, Buttermere, Chilton Foliat, Froxfield, Fyfield, Grafton, Ham, Broad Hinton, East Kennett, Mildenhall, Ogbourne St Andrew, Ogbourne St George, West Overton, Preshute, Ramsbury, Savernake, Shalbourne, Tidcombe and Fosbury, Winterbourne Bassett, Winterbourne Monkton

MELKSHAM RD (1894–1934)
Hilperton, Land Common to Broughton Gifford and Melksham Without, Melksham Without, Seend, Semington, Staverton

MELKSHAM UD
Melksham Within

MERE RD (1894–1934)
Maiden Bradley with Yarnfield (pt 1894–95, ent 1895–1934), Kingston Deverill, Monkton Deverill, East Knoyle, West Knoyle, Kilmington (1896–1934), Mere, Sedgehill, Stourton with Gasper (pt 1894–95, ent 1895–1934), Zeals (1896–1934)

MERE AND TISBURY RD (1934–74)
Alvediston, Anstey, Berwick St John, Berwick St Leonard, Maiden Bradley with Yarnfield, Chilmark, Chicklade, Donhead St Andrew, Donhead St Mary, Fonthill Bishop, Fonthill Gifford, Hindon, Kilmington, East Knoyle, West Knoyle, Mere, Sedgehill, Semley, Stourton with Gasper, Swallowcliffe, Sutton Mandeville, Teffont, Tisbury, West Tisbury, Tollard Royal, Zeals

PEWSEY RD
Alton (1934–74), Alton Priors (1894–1934), Burbage, Charlton, Chute, Chute Forest, Collingbourne Ducis, Collingbourne Kingston, Easton, Enford, Everleigh, Fittleton, Huish, Ludgershall, Manningford (1934–74), Manningford Abbots (1894–1934), Manningford Bohune (1894–1934), Manningford Bruce (1894–1934), Milton Lilbourne, Netheravon, North Newnton, Pewsey, Rushall, North Tidworth, Upavon, Wilcot, Wilsford, Woodborough, Wootton Rivers

RAMSBURY RD (1894–1934)
Aldbourne, Baydon, Great Bedwyn, Little Bedwyn, Buttermere, Chilton Foliat (pt 1894–95, ent 1895–1934), Froxfield, Grafton, Ham, Ramsbury, Shalbourne (pt 1894–95, ent 1895–1934), Tidcombe and Fosbury

SALISBURY RD (1894–1934)
Alderbury, Britford, Clarendon Park, Coombe Bissett, West Dean, Downton, Earldoms (1894–96), Fisherton Anger Without (1894–1905), East Grimstead, West Grimstead, Harnham (1904–05), East Harnham (1896–1904), West Harnham, Homington, Landford, Laverstock, Morgan's Vale and Woodfalls (1923–34), No Man's Land, Nunton and Bodenham, Odstock, Pitton and Farley, Redlynch (1896–1934), Standlynch (1894–97), Standlynch with Charlton All Saints (1897–1934), Stratford sub Castle, Stratford Tony, Whiteparish, Winterslow

SALISBURY AND WILTON RD (1934–74)
Alderbury, Braford St Martin, Berwick St James, Bishopstone, Britford, Burcombe Without, Bower Chalke, Broad Chalke, Clarendon Park, Compton Chamberlayne, Coombe Bissett, West Dean, Dinton, Downton, Ebbesbourne Wake, Fovant, Grimstead, Landford, Steeple Langford, Laverstock, Netherhampton, South Newton, Odstock, Pitton and Farley, Quidhampton, Redlynch, Stapleford, Stratford sub Castle (1934–54), Stratford Tony, Whiteparish, Winterslow, Great Wishford, Wylye

OLD SWINDON UD (1894–1900[10])
pt Swindon

SWINDON NEW TOWN UD (1894–1900[10])
pt Swindon

TETBURY RD (Glos, Wilts until 1930, ent Glos thereafter[30])
Ashley, Long Newton

TISBURY RD (1894–1934)
Alvediston, Anstey, Berwick St John, Berwick St Leonard, Chilmark, Chicklade, Donhead St Andrew, Donhead St Mary, Fonthill Bishop, Fonthill Gifford, Hindon, Semley, Sutton Mandeville, Swallowcliffe, Teffont Evias, Teffont Magna, Tisbury (1927–30), East Tisbury (1894–1927), West Tisbury, Tollard Royal, Wardour (1894–1927)

TROWBRIDGE UD
Trowbridge

WARMINSTER RD (1894–1934)
Norton Bavant, Bishopstrow, Boyton, Chitterne (1907–34), Chitterne All Saints (1894–1907), Chitterne St Mary (1894–1907), Codford St Mary, Codford St Peter, Corsley, Brixton Deverill, Hill Deverill, Longbridge Deverill, Heytesbury, Horningsham, Imber, Knook, Sherrington, Stockton, Sutton Veny, Upton Lovell, Upton Scudamore

WARMINSTER UD
Warminster

WARMINSTER AND WESTBURY RD (1934–74)
Steeple Ashton, West Ashton, Norton Bavant, Bishopstrow, Boyton, North Bradley, Bratton, Bulkington, Chapmanslade, Chitterne, Codford, Corsley, East Coulston, Brixton Deverill, Kingston Deverill, Longbridge Deverill, Dilton Marsh, Edington, Heytesbury, Heywood, Great Hinton, Horningsham, Imber, Keevil, Knook, Sherrington, Southwick, Stockton, Sutton Veny, Upton Lovell, Upton Scudamore

WESTBURY UD (1899[29]–1974)
Westbury

WESTBURY AND WHORWELLSDOWN RD (1894–1934)
Steeple Ashton, West Ashton, North Bradley, Bratton, Bulkington, East Coulston, Dilton Marsh, Edington, Heywood, Great Hinton, Keevil, Southwick

WILTON RD (1894–1934)
Barford St Martin, Baverstock, Bemerton, Berwick St James, Bishopstone, Burcombe Without, Bower Chalke, Broad Chalke, Compton Chamberlayne, Dinton, Ebbesbourne Wake, Fisherton de la Mere, Fovant, Groveley Wood, Little Langford, Steeple Langford, Netherhampton, South Newton, Stapleford, Great Wishford, Wylye

NON-METROPOLITAN COUNTY

As constitued 1 Apr 1974, defined in terms of Adm Co units as of 31 Mar.

KENNET DIST
Devizes MB, Devizes RD, Marlborough MB, Marlborough and Ramsbury RD, Pewsey RD

SALISBURY DIST
Amesbury RD, Mere and Tisbury RD, Salisbury MB, Salisbury and Wilton RD, Wilton MB

THAMESDOWN DIST
Highworth RD, Swindon MB

NORTH WILTSHIRE DIST
Calne MB, Calne and Chippenham RD, Chippenham MB, Cricklade and Wootton Baseett RD, Malmesbury MB, Malmesbury RD

WEST WILTSHIRE DIST
Bradford and Melksham RD, Bradford-on-Avon UD, Melksham UD, Trowbridge UD, Warminster UD, Warminster and Westbury RD, Westbury UD

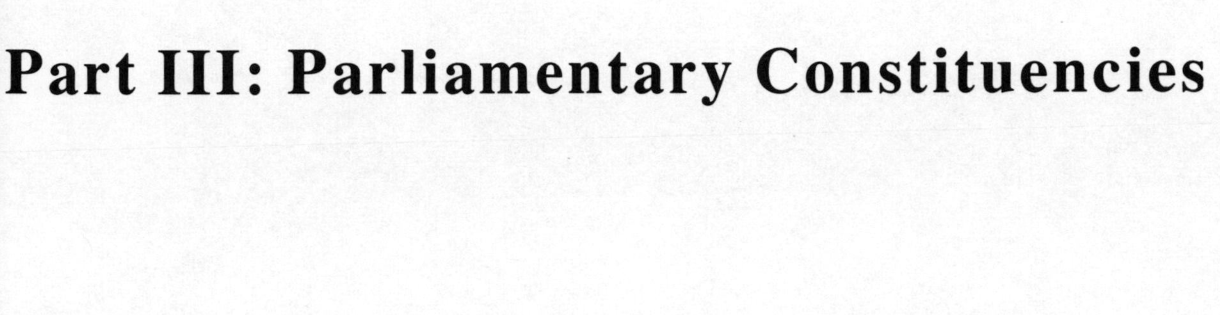

Part III: Parliamentary Constituencies

BEDFORDSHIRE

BOROUGH CONSTITUENCIES[1]

BEDFORD (1295–1885)
Bedford All Saints (until 17th cent), Bedford St Cuthbert, Bedford St John, Bedford St Mary, Bedford St Paul, Bedford St Peter, Bedford St Peter Dunstable (until 1545)

DUNSTABLE (1312 only)
Dunstable

LUTON (1948–70)
Luton MB less the wards of Leagrave, Limbury

LUTON EAST (1970–*)
pt of Luton CB (the wards of Central, Crawley, High Town, South, Stopsley, Wardown)

LUTON WEST (1970–*)
pt of Luton CB (the wards of Dallow, Icknelld, Leagrave, Limbury, Sundon Park)

COUNTY CONSTITUENCIES

Beds was undivided for parl purposes until 1885.

1885–1918

NORTHERN OR BIGGLESWADE DIVISION
pt Ampthill PSD, Bedford MB, Bedford PSD, Biggleswade PSD, Sharnbrook PSD, *viz.*, Ampthill, Arlesey, Astwick, Great Barford, Little Barford, Biddenham, Biggleswade, Bletsoe, Blunham, Bolnhurst, Bromham, Campton, Cardington, Carlton, Chellington, Chicksands, Edworth, Elstow, Eyeworth, Felmersham, Goldington, Harrold, Cockayne Hatley, Haynes, Henlow, Holwell, Houghton Conquest, Kempston, Keysoe, Knotting, Langford, Lidlington, Marston Moretaine, Maulden, Melchbourne, Meppershall, Millbrook, Milton Ernest, Moggerhanger, Northill, Oakley, Odell, Pavenham, Pertenhall, Podington, Potton, Ravensden, Renhold, Riseley, Roxton, Sandy, Sharnbrook, Shefford, Shefford Hardwick, Shelton, Souldrop, Southill, Stagsden, Little Staughton, Stevington, Upper Stondon, Stotfold, Sutton, Tempsford, Thurleigh, Tilbrook, Turvey, Old Warden, Wilden, Willington, Wilshamstead, Wootton, Wrestlingworth, Wymington, Yelden

SOUTHERN OR LUTON DIVISION
pt Ampthill PSD, Dunstable MB, Leighton Buzzard PSD, Luton MB, Luton PSD, Woburn PSD, *viz.*, Aspley Guise, Aspley Heath, Barton in the Clay, Battlesden, Billington, pt Caddington, Chalgrave, Dunstable, Eaton Bray, Eggington, Eversholt, Flitton, Flitwick, Lower Gravenhurst, Upper Gravenhurst, Harlington, Heath and Reach, Higham Gobion, Hockliffe, Holcot, Houghton Regis, Humbershoe, Husborne Crawley, Leighton Buzzard, Luton, Milton Bryan, Potsgrove, Pulloxhill, Ridgmont, Salford, Shillington, Silsoe, Stanbridge, Steppingley, Streatley, pt Studham, Sundon, Tilsworth, Tingrith, Toddington, Totternhoe, Westoning, pt Whipsnade, Woburn

1918–1948

BEDFORD DIVISION
Bedford MB, Bedford RD, Eaton Socon RD, Kempston UD

LUTON DIVISION
Dunstable MB, Luton MB, Luton RD

MID BEDFORDSHIRE DIVISION
Ampthill RD, Ampthill UD, Biggleswade RD, Biggleswade UD, Eaton Bray RD, Leighton Buzzard UD

1948–1970

BEDFORD COUNTY CONSTITUENCY
Bedford MB, pt Bedford RD[2] (the pars not in Mid-Bedfordshire CC), Kempston UD

MID-BEDFORDSHIRE COUNTY CONSTITUENCY
Ampthill RD, Ampthill UD, pt Bedford RD[2] (Great Barford, Little Barford, Cardington, Colmworth, Cople, Eastcotts, Eaton Socon, Elstow, Kempston Rural,[2] Renhold, Roxton, Stagsden,[2] Stewartby, Wilden, Willington, Wilshamstead, Wootton), Biggleswade RD, Biggleswade UD, Sandy UD

SOUTH BEDFORDSHIRE COUNTY CONSTITUENCY
Dunstable MB, Leighton Buzzard UD, pt Luton MB (the wards of Leagrave, Limbury), Luton RD

*1970–**

BEDFORD COUNTY CONSTITUENCY
Bedford MB, pt Bedford RD (the pars not in Mid-Bedfordshire CC), Kempston UD

MID-BEDFORDSHIRE COUNTY CONSTITUENCY
Ampthill RD, Ampthill UD, pt Bedford RD (Great Barford, Little Barford, Cardington, Colmworth, Cople, Eastcotts, Elstow, Kempston Rural, Renhold, Roxton, Stagsden, Staploe, Stewartby, Wilden, Wilshamstead, Wootton), Biggleswade RD, Biggleswade UD, Sandy UD

SOUTH BEDFORDSHIRE COUNTY CONSTITUENCY
Dunstable MB, Leighton-Linslade UD, Luton RD

BERKSHIRE

BOROUGH CONSTITUENCIES[1]

ABINGDON (1558–1885)
pt Abingdon St Helen,[2] Abingdon St Nicholas, pt Sutton Courtenay (1867–85)

NEWBURY (1302 only)
Newbury

READING (1295–1948 [1 mbr, 1885–1948])
Reading (1918–48, pt Reading St Giles (until 1918), Reading St Lawrence (until 1918), pt Reading St Mary (until 1918)

READING[3] (1955–70)
pt Reading CB (the wards of Abbey, Battle, Castle, Caversham [1960–70], Caversham East [1955–60], Caversham West [1955–60], Christchurch [1960–70], Church [1955–60], Katesgrove, Minster, Redlands, Thames [1960–70], Victoria [1955–60], West [1955–60], Whitley [1960–70])

READING NORTH (1948–55)
pt Reading CB (the wards of Abbey, Battle, Castle, Caversham East, Caversham West, Tilehurst, Victoria)

READING NORTH (1970–*)
pt Reading CB (the wards of Abbey, Battle, Castle, Caversham, Katesgrove, Minster, Norcot, Thames, Tilehurst)

READING SOUTH (1948–55)
pt Reading CB (the wards of Church, East, Katesgrove, Minster, Redlands, West)

WALLINGFORD (1295–1885 [1 mbr, 1832–85])
Aston Tirrold (1832–85), Aston Upthorpe (1832–85), Benson (Oxon, 1832–85), Brightwell (1832–85), pt Cholsey (1832–85), Crowmarsh (Oxon, 1832–85), North Moreton (1832–85), South Moreton (1832–85), Newnham Murren (Oxon, 1832–85), Sotwell (1832–85), Wallingford All Hallows (pt until 1832, ent 1832–85), Wallingford Castle Precincts (pt until 1832, ent 1832–85), Wallingford St Leonard, Wallingford St Mary le More, Wallingford St Peter

WINDSOR[4] (1302–1918 [1 mbr, 1867–1918])
pt Clewer[5] (1832–1918), pt Eton (Bucks, 1867–1918), New Windsor (pt until 1868, ent 1868–1918), pt Windsor Castle (1832– 1918)

COUNTY CONSTITUENCIES

Berks was undivided for parl purposes until 1885.

1885–1918

EASTERN OR WOKINGHAM DIVISION
Maidenhead PSD, pt Reading PSD, Windsor PSD, pt Wokingham PSD, *viz.*, Arborfield, Barkham, Binfield, Bisham, Bray, pt Clewer, Cookham, Easthampstead, Eaton Hastings, Finchampstead, Broad Hinton, Hurley, Newland, Remenham, Ruscombe, Sandhurst, Shottesbrooke, Sonning, Sunninghill, East Swallowfield, West Swallowfield, White Waltham, Waltham St Lawrence, Warfield, Wargrave, Whistley, Old Windsor, Winkfield, Winnersh, Wokingham, Woodley and Sandford

NORTHERN OR ABINGDON DIVISION
Abingdon PSD, Berks pt of Abingdon MB, Faringdon PSD, Berks pt of Oxford CB, Wallingford PSD, Wallingford MB, Wantage PSD, *viz.*, Abingdon St Helen, Abingdon St Nicholas, Appleford, Appleton with Eaton, Ardington, Ashbury, Aston Tirrold, Aston Upthorpe, Bagley Wood, Baulking, Besselsleigh, Bourton, Brightwell, Buckland, Biscot, Chaddleworth, East Challow, West Challow, Chandlings Farm, Charlton, Charney Bassett, Childrey, Cholsey, Compton Beauchamp, Great Coxwell, Little Coxwell, pt Culham, Denchworth, Didcot, Draycot Moor, Drayton, Great Faringdon, Fawley, Fernham, Frilford, Fyfield, Garford, Goosey, Grove, East Hagbourne, West Hagbourne, East Hanney, West Hanney, Harwell, Hatford, East Hendred, West Hendred, North Hinksey, South Hinksey, Hinton Waldrist, Kingston Bagpuize, Kingston Lisle, Letcombe Bassett, Letcombe Regis, East Lockinge, West Lockinge, Longworth, Lyford, Marcham, Milton, North Moreton, South Moreton, Moulsford, Pusey, Radley, pt Seacourt, Shellingford, Shrivenham, Sotwell, Sparsholt, Stanford in the Vale, Steventon, Sunningwell, Sutton Courtenay, Sutton Wick, Tubney, Uffington, Upton, Wallingford All Hallows, Wallingford Castle Precincts, Wallingford St Leonard, Wallingford St Mary le More, Wallingford St Peter, Wantage, Watchfield, Little Wittenham, Long Wittenham, Woolstone, Wootton, Wytham

SOUTHERN OR NEWBURY DIVISION
Ilsley PSD, Lambourn PSD, Newbury MB, Newbury PSD, pt Reading PSD, pt Wokingham PSD, *viz.*, Aldermaston, Aldworth, Ashampstead, Avington, Basildon, Beech Hill, Beedon, Beenham, Boxford, Bradfield, Brightwalton, Brimpton, Bucklebury, Catmore, Chieveley, Chilton, Compton, Earley, Enborne, Englefield, Farnborough, Frilsham, East

Garston, Grazeley, Greenham, Hampstead Marshall, Hampstead Norris, pt Hungerford, East Ilsley, West Ilsley, Inkpen, Kintbury, Lambourn, Leckhampstead, Midgham, Newbury, Padworth, Pangbourne, Peasemore, Purley, pt Reading St Giles, pt Reading St Mary, Sandleford, pt Shalbourne, Shaw cum Donnington, East Shefford, West Shefford, Shinfield, Speen, Stanford Dingley, Stratfield Mortimer, Streatley, Sulham, Sulhamstead Abbots, Sulhamstead Bannister Lower End, Sulhamstead Bannister Upper End, Thatcham, Tidmarsh, Tilehurst, Ufton Nervet, Wasing, Welford, Winterbourne, Wokefield, West Woodhay, Woolhampton, Yattendon

1918–1948

ABINGDON DIVISION

Abingdon MB, Abingdon RD, pt Bradfield RD (Ashamptstead, Basildon, Frilsham, Streatley, Yattendon), Faringdon RD, Wallingford MB, Wallingford RD, Wantage RD, Wantage UD

NEWBURY DIVISION

pt Bradfield RD (the pars not in Abingdon Dv), Hungerford RD, Newbury MB, Newbury RD, Wokingham MB, pt Wokingham RD (the pars not in Windsor Dv)

WINDSOR DIVISION

Cookham RD, Easthampstead RD, Maidenhead MB, Windsor MB, Windsor RD, pt Wokingham RD (Remenham, Ruscombe, Twyford, Wargrave)

1948–70[6]

ABINGDON COUNTY CONSTITUENCY

Abingdon MB, Abingdon RD, Faringdon RD, Wallingford MB, Wallingford RD, Wantage RD, Wantage UD

NEWBURY COUNTY CONSTITUENCY[6]

Bradfield RD, Hungerford RD, Newbury MB, Newbury RD. pt Reading CB (the ward of Norcot [1960–70], ward of Tilehurst [1955–70])

WINDSOR COUNTY CONSTITUENCY

Cookham RD, Maidenhead MB, Windsor MB, Windsor RD

WOKINGHAM COUNTY CONSTITUENCY[6]

Easthampstead RD, pt Reading CB (the ward of East [1955–60], ward of Park [1960–70]), Wokingham MB, Wokingham RD

*1970–**[7]

ABINGDON COUNTY CONSTITUENCY[7]

Abingdon MB, Abingdon RD, Faringdon RD, Wallingford MB, Wallingford RD, Wantage RD, Wantage UD

NEWBURY COUNTY CONSTITUENCY[7]

Bradfield RD, Hungerford RD, Newbury MB, Newbury RD

READING SOUTH COUNTY CONSTITUENCY

pt Reading CB (the wards of Christchurch, Park, Redlands, Whitley), pt Wokingham RD (the pars not in Wokingham CC)

WINDSOR AND MAIDENHEAD COUNTY CONSTITUENCY

Cookham RD, Maidenhead MB, Windsor MB, Windsor RD

WOKINGHAM COUNTY CONSTITUENCY

Easthampstead RD, Wokingham MB, pt Wokingham RD (Hurst St Nicholas, Remenham, Ruscombe, Twyford, Wargrave, Wokingham Without)

BUCKINGHAMSHIRE

BOROUGH CONSTITUENCIES[1]

AMERSHAM (1300–09, 1624–1832)
Amersham
AYLESBURY (1554–1885)
until 1804: pt Aylesbury
1804[2]–85: Aston Clinton, Aylesbury, Bierton with Broughton, Bledlow, Buckland, Cuddington, Dinton-with Ford and Upton (pt 1804–67, ent 1867–85), Ellesborough, Haddenham, Halton, Great Hampden, Little Hampden, Hartwell, Horsenden, Hughended, Hulcott, Great Kimble, Little Kimble, Lee, Great Missenden, Little Missenden, Monk's Risborough, Princes Risborough, Stoke Mandeville, Stone, Walton, Wendover, Weston Turville
BUCKINGHAM (1529–1885 [1 mbr, 1867–85])
Buckingham, and the following each ent in the Parl Bor (1832–85) only: Hillesden, Maids' Moreton, Padbury, Preston Bissett, Radclive-cum-Chackmore, Thornborough, Tingewick
ETON AND SLOUGH (1948–*)
Eton UD, Slough MB
GREAT MARLOW (1300–09, 1624–1885 [1 mbr, 1867–85])
Great Marlow, and the following each ent in the Parl Bor (1832–85) only: Bisham (Berks), Little Marlow, Medmenham
WENDOVER (1300–09, 1625–1832)
Wendover
WYCOMBE (1300–1885 [1 mbr, 1867–85])
Wycombe (1866–85), Chepping Wycombe (pt 1300–1832, ent 1832–85)

BUCKS PARS IN BOROUGH CONSTITUENCIES PRIMARILY IN OTHER COUNTIES

ABINGDON (primarily Berks)
pt Abingdon St Helen (until 1885)
OLD WINDSOR (primarily Berks)
pt Eton (1867–1918)

COUNTY CONSTITUENCIES

Bucks was undivided for parl purposes until 1885.

1885–1918
MID OR AYLESBURY DIVISION
Aylesbury PSD, Chesham PSD, pt Desborough PSD, Linslade PSD, pt Winslow PSD, *viz.*, Addington, Aston Abbots, Aston Clinton, Aston Sandford, Aylesbury, Bierton with Broughton, Bledlow, Bradenham, Buckland, Cheddington, Chenies, Chesham, Chesham Bois, Cholesbury, Creslow, Cublington, Cuddington, Dinton-with-Ford and Upton, Drayton Beauchamp, Edlesborough, Ellesborough, Grove, Haddenham, Halton, Great Hampdem, Little Hampden, Hardwick, Hartwell, Hawridge, Horsendon, Hughenden, Hulcott, Ilmer, Ivinghoe, Great Kimble, Little Kimble, pt Kingsey, Lee, Lewknor Uphill, Linslade, Fleet Marston, Marsworth, Mentmore, Great Missenden, Little Missenden, Nettleden, Oving, Pitchcott, Pitstone, Quainton, Qaurrendon, Radnage, Monk's Risborough, Princes Risborough, Saunderton, Shipton Lee, Slapton, Soulbury, Stewkley, Stoke Mandeville, Stone, Towersey, Waddesdon, Weedon, Wendover, Westcott, Weston Turville, Whitchurch, Lower Winchendon, Upper Winchendon, Wing, Wingrave with Rowsham

NORTHERN OR BUCKINGHAM DIVISION
Ashendon PSD, Buckingham MB, Buckingham PSD, Newport PSD, Stony Stratford PSD, pt Winslow PSD, *viz.*, Adstock, Akeley, Amersham, Ashendon, Astwood, Barton Hartshorn, Beachampton, Biddlesden, Bletchley, Boarstall, Bradwell, Bradwell Abbey, Cold Brayfield, Bow Brickhill, Great Brickhill, Little Brickhill, Brill, Broughton, Buckingham, Calverton, Castlethorpe, Charndon, Chearsley, Chetwode, Chicheley, Chilton, East Claydon, Middle Claydon, Steeple Claydon, North Crawley, Long Crendon, Dorton, Drayton Parslow, Dunton, Edgcott, Emberton, Foscott, Granborough, Grendon Underwood, pt Hanslope, Hardmead, Haversham, Hillesden, Hoggeston, Hogshaw, Great Horwood, Little Horwood, pt Ickford, Kingswood, Lathbury, Lavendon, Leckhampstead, Lillingstone Dayrell, Lillingstone Lovell, Great Linford, Little Linford, Loughton, Ludgershall, Luffield Abbey, Marsh Gibbon, North Marston, Milton Keynes, Maids' Moreton, Moulsoe, Nash, Newport Pagnell, Newton Blossomville, Newton Longville, Oakley, Olney, Olney Park Farm, Padbury, Petsoe Manor, Poun-

don, Preston Bissett, Radclive-cum-Chackmore, Ravenstone, Shabbington, Shalstone, Shenley Brook End, Shenley Church End, Sherington, Simpson, Stantonbury, Stoke Goldington, Stoke Hammond, Stowe, Fenny Stratford, Stony Stratford East, Stony Stratford West, Water Stratford, Swanbourne, Tattenhoe, Thornborough, Thornton, Tingewick, Turweston, Twyford, Tyringham with Filgrave, Walton, Warrington, Water Eaton, Wavendon, Westbury, Weston Underwood, Whaddon, Willen, Winslow, Wolverton, Woodham, Great Woolstone, Little Woolstone, Workinghall, Wotton Underwood, Woughton on the Green

SOUTHERN OR WYCOMBE DIVISION

Burnham PSD, pt Desborough PSD, Stoke PSD, Chepping Wycombe MB, *viz.*, Beaconsfield, Boveney, Burnham, Chalfont St Giles, Chalfont St Peter, Coleshill, Datchet, Denham, Dorney, pt Eton, Farnham Royal, Fawley, Fingest, Fulmer, Hambleden, Hedgerley, Hedgerley Dean, Hedsor, Hitcham, Horton, Iver, Langley Marish, Great Marlow, Little Marlow, Medmenham, Penn, Seer Green, Stoke Poges, Taplow, Turville, Upton cum Chalvey, Wexham, Wooburn, Wycombe, Chepping Wycombe, West Wycombe. Wyrardisbury

AYLESBURY DIVISION[3]

Amersham RD, Aylesbury MB, pt Aylesbury RD (the pars not in Buckingham Dv), Beaconsfield UD, Chesham UD, pt Long Crendon RD (Towersey), pt Wycombe RD (1918–45: Bledlow, Brandenham, Ellesborough, Great and Little Hampden, Radnage, Monk's Risborough, Princes Risborough, Saunderton, Wendover)

BUCKINGHAM DIVISION

pt Aylesbury RD (Ashendon, Chearsley, Grendon Underwood, Kingswood, Ludgershall, Woodham, Wotton Underwood), Bletchley UD, Buckingham MB, Buckingham RD, pt Long Crendon RD (the pars not in Aylesbury Dv), Linslade UD, Newport Pagnell RD, Newport Pagnell UD, Stratford and Wolverton RD, Wing RD, Winslow RD, Wolverton RD

ETON AND SLOUGH DIVISION (1945–48)

Eton RD, Eton UD, Slough MB

WYCOMBE DIVISION[3]

Eton RD (1918–45), Eton UD (1918–45), Hambleden RD, Marlow UD, Slough UD (1918–45), Wycombe RD (pt 1918–45: the pars not in Aylesbury Dv; ent 1945–48), Chepping Wycombe MB

1948–1970

AYLESBURY COUNTY CONSTITUENCY

pt Amersham RD (Ashley Green, Chartridge, Cholesbury cum St Leonards, Latimer, Lee, Great Missenden, Little Missenden), Aylesbury MB, Aylesbury RD, Chesham UD

BUCKINGHAM COUNTY CONSTITUENCY

Bletchley UD, Buckingham MB, Buckingham RD, Linslade UD, Newport Pagnell RD, Newport Pagnell UD, Wing RD, Winslow RD, Wolverton UD

SOUTH BUCKINGHAMSHIRE COUNTY CONSTITUENCY

pt Amersham RD (Amersham, Chalfont St Giles, Chalfont St Peter, Chenies, Chesham Bois, Coleshill, Penn, Seer Green), Beaconsfield UD, Eton RD

WYCOMBE COUNTY CONSTITUENCY

Marlow UD, Wycombe RD, High Wycombe MB

*1970–**

AYLESBURY COUNTY CONSTITUENCY

Aylesbury MB, Aylesbury RD, pt Wycombe RD (Bledlow cum Saunderton, Bradenham, Ellesborough, Great and Little Hampden, Ibstone, Great and Little Kimble, Lacey Green, Longwick cum Ilmer, Radnage, Princes Risborough, Stokenchurch)

BEACONSFIELD COUNTY CONSTITUENCY

Beaconsfield UD, Eton RD, pt Wycombe RD (Hedsor, Wooburn)

BUCKINGHAM COUNTY CONSTITUENCY

Bletchley UD, Buckingham MB, Buckingham RD, Newport Pagnell RD, Newport Pagnell UD, Wing RD, Winslow RD, Wolverton UD

CHESHAM AND AMERSHAM COUNTY CONSTITUENCY

Amersham RD, Chesham UD

WYCOMBE COUNTY CONSTITUENCY

Marlow UD, pt Wycombe RD (Fawley, Fingest and Lane End, Hambleden, Hughenden, Great Marlow, Little Marlow, Medmenham, Turville, Chepping Wycombe, West Wycombe Rural), High Wycombe MB

CAMBRIDGESHIRE

BOROUGH CONSTITUENCIES[1]

CAMBRIDGE (1295–* [1 member 1885–*])
Cambridge (1918–*), Cambridge All Saints (until 1918), Cambridge Holy Sepulchre (until 1918), Cambridge Holy Trinity (until 1918), Cambridge St Andrew the Great (until 1918), Cambridge St Andrew the Less (until 1918), Cambridge St Benedict (until 1918), Cambridge St Botolph (until 1918), Cambridge St Clement (until 1918), Cambridge St Edward (until 1918), Cambridge St Giles (until 1918), Cambridge St Mary the Great (until 1918), Cambridge St Mary the Less (until 1918), Cambridge St Michael (until 1918), Cambridge St Peter (until 1918), pt Chesterton (1867–1918)

ELY (1295 only)
Ely St Mary, Ely Trinity

COUNTY CONSTITUENCIES

Cambs was undivided for parl purposes until 1885. From 1918–70 the Adm Co of Cambs and the Adm Co of the Isle of Ely were each an undivided co constituency.

1885–1918

EASTERN OR NEWMARKET DIVISION
Bottisham PSD, pt Ely PSD, Linton PSD, Newmarket PSD, *viz.*, Great Abington, Little Abington, Ashley, Babraham, Balsham, Bottisham, Brinkley, Burrough Green, Burwell, Castle Camps, Shudy Camps, Carlton, Cherry Hinton, Cheveley, Chippenham, Fen Ditton, Wood Ditton, Duxford, Ely College, Ely St Mary, Ely Trinity, Fordham, Fulbourn, Hildersham, Hinxton, Horningsea, Horseheath, Ickleton, Isleham, Kennett, Kirtling, Landwade, Linton, Newmarket All Saints, Pampisford, Sawston, Snailwell, Soham, Stetchworth, Stow cum Quy, Swaffham Bulbeck, Swaffham Prior, Teversham, Westley Waterless, Weston Colville, Whittlesford, Wicken, West Wickham, Great Wilbraham, Little Wilbraham, West Wratting

NORTHERN OR WISBECH DIVISION
pt Ely PSD, Whittlesea PSD, North Witchford PSD, Wisbech MB, Wisbech PSD, *viz.*, Benwick, Chatteris, Coveney, Doddington, Downham, Elm, Leverington, Littleport, Manea, March, Newton, pt Outwell, Parson Drove, pt Stanground, Thorney, Tydd St Giles, pt Upwell, Welches Dam, pt Welney, Whittlesey St Mary and St Andrew, Wimblington, Wisbech St Mary, Wisbech St Peter

WESTERN OR CHESTERTON DIVISION
Arrington and Melbourn PSD, Cambridge PSD, Caxton PSD, pt Ely PSD, *viz.*, Abington Piggots, Arrington, Barrington, Bartlow, Barton, Bassingbourn, Bourn, Boxworth, Caldecote, Caxton, Chesterton, Childerley, Comberton, Conington, Coton, Cottenham, Croxton, Croydon, Dry Drayton, Elsworth, Eltisley, Great Eversden, Little Eversden, Fowlmere, Foxton, Gamlingay, Girton, Little Gransden, Grantchester, Graveley, Grunty Fen, Haddenham, Hardwick, Harlton, Harston, Haslingfield, East Hatley, Hatley St George, Hauxton, Histon, Impington, Kingston, Knapwell, Kneesworth, Landbeach, Litlington, Lolworth, Longstowe, Madingley, Melbourn, Meldreth, Mepal, Milton, Guilden Morden, Steeple Morden, Newton, Oakington, Orwell, Over, Papworth Everard, pt Papworth St Agnes, Rampton, pt Royston, Great Shelford, Little Shelford, Shepreth, Shingay, Long Stanton All Saints, Long Stanton St Michael, Stapleford, Stretham, Sutton, Swavesey, Tadlow, Thetford, Thriplow, Toft, Trumptington, Waterbeach, Wendy, Wentworth, Westwick, Whaddon, Wilburton, Willingham, Wimpole, Witcham, Witchford

*1970–**

CAMBRIDGESHIRE COUNTY CONSTITUENCY
South Cambridgeshire RD, Chesterton RD, Newmarket RD

ISLE OF ELY COUNTY CONSTITUENCY
Chatteris UD, Ely RD, Ely UD, March UD, Whittlesey UD, Wisbech MB, Wisbech RD, North Witchford RD

CORNWALL

BOROUGH CONSTITUENCIES[1]

BODMIN (1295–1885 [1 mbr 1867–85])
pt Bodmin (1295–1867), Bodmin Borough (1867–85), Helland (1832–85), Lanhydrock (1832–85), Lanivet (1832–85)

BOSSINEY (1553–1832)
pt Tintagel

CALLINGTON (1584–1832)
Callington

CAMELFORD (1553–1832)
pt Lanteglos

FOWEY (1572–1832)
Fowey, pt Lanteglos

GRAMPOUND (1553–1824[2])
pt Creed, pt Probus

HELSTON (1298–1885 [1 mbr, 1832–85])
Sithney (1832–85), pt Wendron (1298–1832, enlarged pt 1832–85)

LAUNCESTON (1295–1885 [1 mbr 1832–85])
Lawhitton (pt 1295–1832, ent 1832–85), South Petherwin (pt 1295–1832, ent 1832–85), St Mary Magdalene, St Stephens (1832–85), St Thomas the Apostle (pt 1295–1832, ent 1832–85), St Thomas Street (1867–85)

LISKEARD (1295–1885 [1 mbr 1832–85])
Liskeard (pt 1295–1587, enlarged pt 1587–1832, ent 1832–85), pt St Cleer

EAST LOOE (1563–1832)
pt St Martin

WEST LOOE (1553–1832)
pt Talland

LOSTWITHIEL (1304–1832)
pt Lanlivery, Lostwithiel

MICHELL (1553–1832)
pt Newlyn, pt St Enoder

NEWPORT (1553–1832)
pt St Stephens

PENRYN (1553–1832)
pt St Gluvias

PENRYN AND FALMOUTH (1832–1918 [1 mbr 1885–1918])
pt Budock, Falmouth, Falmouth Borough (1867–1918), Penryn (1867–1918), pt Mylor (1867–1918), pt St Gluvias (until 1867)

ST GERMANS (1563–1832)
St Germans

ST IVES (1558–1885 [1 mbr 1832–85])
St Ives, Towednack (1832–85), Uny Lelant (1832–85)

ST MAWES (1563–1832)
pt St Just in Penwith

SALTASH (1553–1832)
pt St Stephens

TREGONY (1295–1307, 1563–1832)
pt Cuby

TRURO (1295–1885)
pt Kenwyn (enlarged pt 1832–85), pt St Clement (1832–85), Truro St Mary

COUNTY CONSTITUENCIES

1832–1885

EASTERN DIVISION
Hundreds of East, Lesnewth, pt Powder (Fowey, Gorran, Ladock, Lanlivery, Lostwithiel, Luxulyan, Mevagissey, Roche, St Austell, St Blazey, St Dennis, St Ewe, St Mewan, St Michael Carhays, St Sampson, St Stephen in Brannel, Tywardreath), pt Pyder (the pars not in W'rn Dv), Stratton, Trigg, West

WESTERN DIVISION
Hundreds of Kerrier, Penwith, pt Powder (the pars not in E'rn Dv), pt Pyder (Crantock, Cubert, Newlyn, Perranzabuloe, St Agnes, St Enoder), the Isles of Scilly

1885–1918

MID OR ST AUSTELL DIVISION
Powder (East) PSD, Powder (South) PSD, pt Powder (Tywardreath) PSD, Pydar PSD, *viz.*, Colan, Cornelly, Crantock, Creed, Cubert, Cuby, Gerrans, Gorran, Grampound, Ladock, Lamorran, Mawgan in Pyder, Merther, Mevagissey, Newlyn, Padstow, Perranzabuloe, Little Petherick, Philleigh, Probus, Roche, Ruan Lanihorne, St Anthony in Roseland, St Austell, St Blazey, St Breock, St Columb Major, St Columb Minor, St Dennis, St Enoder, St Ervan, St Eval, St Ewe, St Issey, St Just in Roseland, St Merryn, St Mewan, St Michael Carhays, St Stephen in Brannel, St Wenn, Tregony, Veryan, Withiel

NORTH-EASTERN OR LAUNCESTON DIVISION
East (Middle) PSD, East (North) PSD, pt Trigg PSD, *viz.*, Advent, Altarnun, Blisland, Boyton, Callington, Calstock, Davidstow, Egloshayle, Egloskerry, Forrabury, North Hill, South Hill, Jacobstow, Kilkhampton, Laneast, Launcells, Lanteglos, Lawhitton, Lesnewth, Lewannick, Lezant, Linkinhorne, Marhamchurch, Michaelstow, Minster, Morwenstow, Otterham, South Petherwin, Pillaton, Poughill, Poundstock, Quethiock, St Breward, St Clether, St Dominick, St Endellion, St Gennys, St Ive, St Juliot, St Kew, St Mabyn, St Mellion, St Minver Highlands, St Minver Lowlands, St Mary Magdalene, St Stephens, St Teath, St Thomas the Apostle, St Thomas Street, St Tudy, Stoke Climsland, Stratton, North Tamerton, Temple, Tintagel, Tremaine, Treneglos, Tresmeer, Trevalga, Trewen, Warbstow, Week St Mary, Whitstone

NORTH-WESTERN OR CAMBORNE DIVISION
Pt Kerrier (East) PSD, pt Penwith (East) PSD, pt Powder (West) PSD, *viz.*, Camborne, Crowan, Gwennap, Gwinear, Gwithian, Illogan, Phillack, Redruth

SOUTH-EASTERN OR BODMIN DIVISION
Bodmin MB, East (South) PSD, Liskeard MB, pt Powder (Tywardreath) PSD, pt Trigg PSD, West Hundred PSD, *viz.*, Antony, Boconnoc, Bodmin, Bodmin Borough, Botus Fleming, Broadoack, Cardinham, Duloe, Fowey, Helland, Landrake with St Erney, Landulph, Lanhydrock, Lanivet, Lanlivery, Lanreath, Lansallos, Lanteglos, Liskeard, Liskeard Borough, East Looe, West Looe, Lostwithiel, Luxulyan, Maker, Menheniot, Morval, Pelynt, Rame, pt St Budeaux, St Cleer, St Germans, St John, St Keyne, St Neot, St Pinnock, St Sampson, St Stephens, St Veep, St Winnow, Saltash, Sheviock, Talland, Tywardreath, Warleggan

TRURO DIVISION
Helston MB, pt Kerrier (East) PSD, Kerrier (West) PSD, pt Powder (West) PSD, Truro MB, *viz.*, Breage, pt Budock, Constantine, Cury, Feock, Germoe, Grade, Gunwalloe, Helston, Kea, pt Kenwyn, Landewednack, Mabe, Manaccan, Mawgan in Meneage, Mawnan, Mullion, pt Mylor, Perranarworthal, Ruan Major, Ruan Minor, St Allen, St Anthony in Meneage, pt St Clement, St Gluvias, St Keverne, St Martin in Meneage, St Michael Penkevil, Sithney, Stithians, Tregavethan, Truro St Mary, Wendron

WESTERN OR ST IVES DIVISION
Pt Penwith (East) PSD, Penwith (West) PSD, Penzance MB, St Ives MB, Isles of Scilly, *viz.*, Bryher, Gulval, Ludgvan, Madron, Marazion, Morvah, Paul, Penzance, Perranuthnoe, St Agnes, St Buryan, St Erme, St Erth, St Hilary, St Ives, St Just, St Levan, St Martin's, St Mary's, St Michael's Mount, Sancreed, Sennen, Towednack, Tresco, Uny Lelant, Zennor

1918-1948

BODMIN DIVISION
Bodmin MB, pt Bodmin RD (the pars not in N'rn Dv), Callington UD, Fowey MB, Liskeard MB, Liskeard RD, Looe UD, Lostwithiel MB, pt St Austell RD (St Sampson, Tywardreath), St Germans RD, Saltash MB, Torpoint UD

CAMBORNE DIVISION
Camborne UD, Hayle UD, Helston MB, pt Helston RD (Crowan, Wendron), pt East Kerrier RD (Constantine, Mabe, Perranarworthal), Phillack UD, Redruth RD, Redruth UD, pt Truro RD (Kea, Kenwyn Rural, Perranzabuloe, St Agnes, St Allen, Tregavethan)

NORTHERN DIVISION
Pt Bodmin RD (Egloshayle, St Endellion, St Kew, St Minver Highlands, St Minver Lowlands), Calstock RD, Camelford RD, pt Holsworthy RD (the Cornw par), Launceston MB, Launceston RD, Newquay UD, Padstow UD, St Columb Major RD, Stratton RD, Stratton and Bude UD, Wadebridge UD

PENRYN AND FALMOUTH DIVISION
Falmouth MB, pt East Kerrier RD (the pars not in Camb. Dv), Penryn MB, St Austell UD, pt St Austell RD (the pars not in Bodm. Dv), Truro MB, pt Truro RD (the pars not in Camb. Dv)

ST IVES DIVISION
pt Helston RD (the pars not in Camb. Dv), Ludgvan UD, Madron UD, Paul UD, West Penwith RD, Penzance MB, St Ives MB, St Just UD, Isles of Scilly

1948–1970

BODMIN COUNTY CONSTITUENCY
Bodmin MB, Fowey MB, Liskeard MB, Liskeard RD, Lostwithiel MB, Looe UD, pt St Austell RD (Lanlivery, Luxulyan, St Sampson), St Germans RD, Saltash MB, Torpoint UD, pt Wadebridge RD (Blisland, Cardinham, Helland, Lanhydrock, Lanivet, Withiel)

NORTH CORNWALL COUNTY CONSTITUENCY
Bude-Stratton UD, Camelford RD, Launceston MB, Launceston RD, Newquay UD, Padstow UD, pt St Austell RD (Colan, Mawgan in Pyder, St Columb Major, St Enoder, Wenn), Stratton RD, pt Wadebridge RD (the pars not in Bodm. CC)

FALMOUTH AND CAMBORNE COUNTY CONSTITUENCY
Camborne-Redruth UD, Falmouth MB, pt Kerrier RD (Budock, Constantine, Crowan, Mabe, Mawnan, St Gluvias, Stithians, Wendron), Penryn MB, pt West Penwith RD (Gwinear-Gwithian, Hayle), pt Truro RD (Gwennap)

ST IVES COUNTY CONSTITUENCY
Helston MB, pt Kerrier RD (the pars not in Falm. & Camb. CC), pt West Penwith RD (the pars not in Falm. & Camb. CC), Penzance MB, St Ives MB, St Just UD, Isles of Scilly

TRURO COUNTY CONSTITUENCY
St Austell UD, pt St Austell RD (the pars not in Bodm. CC or N Cornw CC), Truro MB, pt Truro RD (the pars not in Falm. & Camb. CC)

*1970–**

BODMIN COUNTY CONSTITUENCY
Bodmin MB, Liskeard MB, Liskeard RD, Looe UD, pt St Austell RD (Lanlivery, Lostwithiel, Luxulyan, St Sampson), St Germans RD, Saltash MB, Torpoint UD, pt Wadebridge and Padstow RD (Blisland, Cardinham, Helland, Lanhydrock, Lanivet, Withiel)

NORTH CORNWALL COUNTY CONSTITUENCY
Bude-Stratton UD, Camelford RD, Launceston MB, Launceston RD, Newquay UD, pt St Austell RD (Colan, Mawgan in Pyder, St Columb Major, St Enoder, St Wenn), Stratton RD, pt Wadebridge and Padstow RD (the pars not in Bodm. CC)

FALMOUTH AND CAMBORNE COUNTY CONSTITUENCY
same composition as for 1948–70

ST IVES COUNTY CONSTITUENCY
same composition as for 1948–70

TRURO COUNTY CONSTITUENCY
pt St Austell RD (Creed, Gorran, Grampound, Roche, St Dennis, St Ewe, St Mewan, St Michael Carhays, St Stephen in Brannel), St Austell with Fowey MB, Truro MB, pt Truro RD (entire RD less Gwennap)

DEVON

BOROUGH CONSTITUENCIES[1]

ASHBURTON (1298, 1407–1918 [1 mbr, 1832–1918])
Ashburton

BARNSTAPLE (1295–1885)
Barnstaple, pt Pilton (1832–85), pt Bishop's Tawton (1832–85)

BERE ALSTON (1584–1832)
pt Bere Ferrers

BRADNINCH (1313 only)[2]
Bradninch

CREDITON (1307 only)
Crediton

DARTMOUTH (1298–1918 [1 mbr, 1832–1918])
St Petrox, St Saviour, pt Stoke Fleming (1832–1918), Townstall

DEVONPORT (1832–1918)
Devonport, Stoke Damerel, East Stonehouse

EXETER (1295–* [1 mbr, 1885–*])
Bradninch (until 1918), Close of St Peter's Cathedral (until 1918), Devon County Buildings Area (1970–*), Devon Prison and Constabulary Barracks (until 1970), Exeter (1918–*), Exeter Allhallows, Goldsmith Street (until 1918), Exeter Allhallows on the Wall (until 1918), Exeter Bedford Circus (until 1918), Exeter Castle Yard (until 1970), Exeter Holy Trinity (until 1918), Exeter St David (until 1918), Exeter St Edmund (until 1918), Exeter St George the Martyr (until 1918), Exeter St John (until 1918), Exeter St Kerrian (until 1918), Exeter St Lawrence (until 1918), Exeter St Martin (until 1918), Exeter St Mary Arches (until 1918), Exeter St Mary Major (until 1918), Exeter St Mary Steps (until 1918), Exeter St Olave (until 1918), Exeter St Pancras (until 1918), Exeter St Paul (until 1918), Exeter St Petrock (until 1918), Exeter St Sidwell (until 1918), Exeter St Stephen (until 1918), Heavitree (1832–1918), St Leonard (1832–*), St Thomas the Apostle (1832–*)

FREMINGTON (1332 only)
Fremington

HONITON (1300–11, 1640–1867)
Honiton

LYDFORD (1300 only)
Lydford

MODBURY (1360 only)
Modbury

SOUTH MOLTON (1302 only)
South Molton

OKEHAMPTON (1300–13, 1640–1832)
Okehampton

PLYMOUTH (1298–1328, 1442–1918)
Plymouth Charles (1641–1918), Plymouth St Andrew

PLYMOUTH DEVONPORT (1918–*)[3]
pt Plymouth CB (the wards of Drake [1955–70], Ernesettle [1951–*], Ford, Keynsham [1918–51], Molesworth [1918–70], Mount Edgcumbe [1948–51], Nelson [1918–70], Pennycross [1948–51], Peverell [1951–55], St Andrew [1955–*], St Aubyn, St Budeaux, St Peter [1948–*], Stoke [1948–*], Tamerton [1951–55], Trelawney [1951–70]), Tamerton Foliot (1948–51)

PLYMOUTH DRAKE (1918–48)
pt Plymouth CB (the wards of Drake's, Mount Edgcumbe, Mutley, Pennycross, St Peter's, Stoke, Valletort)

PLYMOUTH DRAKE (1970–*)
pt Plymouth CB (the wards of Compton, Drake, Honicknowle, Pennycross, Tamerton, Trelawny, Whitleigh)

PLYMOUTH SUTTON (1918–*)[4]
Bickleigh (1948–70), pt Plymouth CB (the wards of Charles [1918–70], Compton [1918–70], Crownhill [1948–*], Drake [1948–55], Efford [1951–*], Friary [1918–70], Laira [1918–51], Mount Gold [1951–*], Mutley [1948–51], Peverell [1955–70], Plympton Earle [1970–*], Plympton St Mary [1970–*], Plymstock Dunstone [1970–*], Plymstock Radford [1970–*], St Andrew [1918–55], Sutton, Tamerton [1955–70], Trelawney [1955–70], Vintry [1918–51])

PLYMPTON [EARLE] (1295–1832)
pt Brixton, Chelson Meadow, pt Plympton St Mary, Plympton St Maurice

TAVISTOCK (1295–1885)
pt Tavistock

TIVERTON (1621–1885)
Tiverton

TORBAY (1970–*)
Torbay

TORQUAY (1948–70)
Brixham, Churston Ferrers, Kingswear, Paignton, Torquay

TORRINGTON (1295–1330)
Great Torrington

TOTNES (1295–1918)
pt Berry Pomeroy (1832–1918), Totnes (pt until 1832, ent 1832–1918)

COUNTY CONSTITUENCIES

1832–1867

NORTHERN DIVISION

Hundreds of Bampton, Braunton, West Budleigh, Crediton, Fremington, Halberton, Hartland, Hayridge, Hemyock, South Molton, Shebbear, Shirwell, North Tawton and Winkleigh, Tiverton, Black Torrington, Witheridge

SOUTHERN DIVISION

Exeter Castle Yard and the Hundreds of Axminster, East Budleigh, Cliston, Coleridge, Colyton, Ermington, Exminster, Haytor, Lifton, Ottery St Mary, Plympton, Roborough, Stanborough, Tavistock, Teignbridge, Wonford

1867–1885

EAST DIVISION

Exeter Castle Yard and the Hundreds of Axminster, East Budleigh, Cliston, Colyton, Exminster, Haytor, Ottery St Mary, Teignbridge, Wonford

NORTH DIVISION

Hundreds of Bampton, Braunton, West Budleigh, Crediton, Fremington, Halberton, Hartland, Hayridge, Hemyock, South Molton, Shebbear, Shirwell, North Tawton and Winkleigh, Tiverton, Witheridge

SOUTH DIVISION

Hundreds of Coleridge, Ermington, Lifton, Plympton, Roborough, Stanborough, Tavistock, Black Torrington

1885–1918

EASTERN OR HONITON DIVISION

Axminster PSD, Honiton PSD, Ottery PSD, Woodbury PSD, *viz.*, Awliscombe, Axminster, Axmouth, Aylesbeare, Bicton, Branscombe, Buckerell, East Budleigh, Churchstanton, Clyst Honiton, Clyst St George, Clyst St Mary, Colaton Raleigh, Colyton, Combe Raleigh, Combpyne, Cotleigh, Dalwood, Dotton, Dunkeswell, Farringdon, Farway, Feniton, Gittisham, Harpford, Honiton, Kilmington, Luppitt, Lympstone, Membury, Monkton, Musbury, Northleigh, Offwell, Otterton, Ottery St Mary, Venn Ottery, Rockbeare, Rousdon, Salcombe Regis, Seaton and Beer, Sheldon, Shute, Sidbury, Sidmouth, Southleigh, Sowton, Stockland, Talaton, Thorncombe, Uplyme, Upottery, Whimple, Widworthy, Withycombe Raleigh, Woodbury, Yarcombe

MID OR ASHBURTON DIVISION

Crockenwell PSD, Teignbridge PSD, *viz.*, Abbotskerswell, Bickington, Bishopsteignton, North Bovey, Bovey Tracey, Bridford, Broadhempston, Buckland in the Moor, Chagford, Cheriton Bishop, Chudleigh, Coffinswell, Combe in Teignhead, Dawlish, Denbury, Drewsteignton, Dunsford, Gidleigh, Haccombe, Hennock, Highweek, Hittisleigh, Holne, Ideford, Ilsington, Ipplepen, Kingskerswell, Kingsteignton, Lustleigh, Manaton, Moretonhampstead, East Ogwell, West Ogwell, St Nicholas, Spreyton, Staverton, Stokeinteignhead, North Tawton, Tedburn St Mary, Teigngrace, East Teignmouth, West Teignmouth, Throwleigh, Torbryan, Trusham, Widecombe in the Moor, Wolborough, Woodland

NORTHERN OR SOUTH MOLTON DIVISION

Crediton PSD, South Molton MB, South Molton PSD, Great Torrington PSD, *viz.*, Alverdiscott, East Anstey, West Anstey, Ashreigney, Beaford, High Bickington, Bondleigh, Bow, Brushford, East Buckland, West Buckland, Buckland Filleigh, Burrington, Charles, Chawleigh, Cheldon, Cheriton Fitzpaine, Chittlehamholt, Chittlehampton, Chumleigh, Clannaborough, Coldridge, Colebrooke, Creacombe, Crediton, Dolton, Dowland, Down St Mary, Eggesford, Filleigh, Frithelstock, Huish, Huntshaw, Kennerleigh, Knowstone, Langtree, Lapford, Mariansleigh, Merton, Meshaw, Molland, North Molton, South Molton, Morchard Bishop, Newton St Cyres, Nymet Rowland, Bishop's Nympton, George Nympton, King's Nympton, Peters Marland, Petrockstow, Poughill, Puddington, Rackenford, Roborough, Romansleigh, Rose Ash, St Giles in the Wood, Sandford, Satterleigh, Shebbear, Sherwood Villa, Shobrooke, Stockleigh English, Stockleigh Pomeroy, North Tawton, Thelbridge, Great Torrington, Little Torrington, Twitchen, Upton Hellions, Warkleigh, Washford Pyne, Weare Giffard, Wembworthy, Winkleigh, Witheridge, Woolfardisworthy, East Worlington, West Worlington, Yarnscombe, Zeal Monachorum

NORTH-EASTERN OR TIVERTON DIVISION

Cullompton PSD, Tiverton MB, Wonford PSD, *viz.*, Alphington, Ashcombe, Ashton, Bampton, Bradninch, Brampford Speke, Broadhembury, Burlescombe, Butterleigh, Cadbury, Cadeleigh, Calverleigh, Christow, Clayhanger, Clayhidon, Broad Clyst, Clyst Hydon, Clyst St Lawrence, Cruwys Morchard, Cullompton, Culmstock, Doddiscombsleigh, Dunchideock, Nether Exe, Exminster, Halberton, Heavitree, Hemyock, Highley St Mary, Hockworthy, Holcombe Burnell, Holcome Rogus, Huntsham, Huxham, Ide, Kenn, Kentisbeare, Kenton, Littleham, Loxbeare, Mamhead, Morebath, Oakford, Payhembury, Pinhoe, Plymtree, Poltimore, Powderham, Rewe, St Leonard, St Thomas the Apostle, Sampford Peverell, Shillingford St George, Stoke Canon, Stoodleigh, Templeton, Thorverton, Tiverton, Topsham, Uffculme, Uplowman, Upton Pyne, Washfield, Whitestone, Willand

NORTH-WESTERN OR BARNSTAPLE DIVISION

Barnstaple MB, Bideford MB, Bideford PSD, Braunton PSD, *viz.*, Abbotsham, Alwington, Arlington, Ashford, Atherington, Barnstaple, Berrynarbor, Bickleigh, Bideford, Bittadon, Bratton Fleming, Braunton, High Bray, Brendon, Buckland Brewer, Bulkworthy, Challacombe, Clovelly, Combe Martin, Countisbury, East Down, West Down, Fremington, Georgeham, Goodleigh, Hartland, Heanton Punchardon, Horwood, Ilfracombe, Instow, Kentisbury, Landcross, Landkey, Littleham, Loxhore, Lynton, Martinhoe, Marwood, Morthoe, Newton St Petrock, Newton Tracey, Northam, Parkham, Parracombe, East Putford, Shirwell, Stoke Rivers, Swimbridge, Tawstock, Bishop's Tawton, Trentishoe, Welcombe, Westleigh, Woolfardisworthy

SOUTHERN OR TOTNES DIVISION
Ermington and Plympton PSD, Stanborough and Coleridge PSD, *viz.*, East Allington, West Alvington, Ashprington, Aveton Gifford, pt Berry Pomeroy, Bigbury, Blackawton, South Brent, Brixton, Buckfastleigh, Buckland Tout Saints, Charleton, Chelson Meadow, Chivelstone, Churchstow, Cornwood, Cornworthy, Dartington, Dean Prior, Diptford, Dittisham, Dodbrooke, Ermington, Halwell, Harberton, Harford, Little Hempston, Holbeton, North Huish, South Huish, Kingsbridge, Kingston, Loddiswell, Malborough, South Milton, Modbury, Moreleigh, Newton Ferrers, Plympton St Mary, Plympton St Maurice, Plymstock, South Pool, East Portlemouth, Rattery, Revelstoke, Ringmore, Sherford, Slapton, Stokenham, Thurlestone, Ugborough, Wembury, Woodleigh, Yealmpton

TORQUAY DIVISION
Paignton PSD, *viz.*, Brixham, Churston Ferrers, Cockington, Kingswear, Marldon, Paignton, St Mary Church, Stoke Gabriel, Tormoham

WESTERN OR TAVISTOCK DIVISION
Hatherleigh PSD, Holsworthy PSD, Lifton PSD, Roborough PSD, Midland Roborough PSD, Tavistock PSD, *viz.*, Ashbury, Ashwater, Beaworthy, Belstone, Bere Ferrers, Abbots Bickington, Bickleigh, Bradford, Bradstone, Bradworthy, Bratton Clovelly, Brentor, Bridestowe, Bridgerule East, Bridgerule West, Broadwood Kelly, Broadwoodwidger, Egg Buckland, Buckland Monachorum, Clawton, Compton Gifford, Cookbury, Coryton, Dunterton, Exbourne, Germansweek, Halwill, Hatherleigh, Highampton, Hollacombe, Holsworthy, Honeychurch, Iddesleigh, Inwardleigh, Jacobstowe, Kelly, Laira Green, Lamerton, Lewtrenchard, Lifton, Luffincott, Lydford, Marystow, Marytavy, Meavy, Meeth, Milton Abbot, Milton Damerel, Northcott, Northlew, Okehampton, Monk Okehampton, Pancrasweek, Petertavy, North Petherwin, West Putford, Pyworthy, pt St Budeaux, St Giles on the Heath, pt St Stephens, Sampford Courtenay, Sampford Spiney, Shaugh Prior, Sheepstor, Sheepwash, Sourton, pt Stoke Fleming, East Stonehouse, Stowford, Sutcombe, Sydenham Damerel, Tamerton Foliot, Tavistock, Tetcott, Thornbury, Thrushelton, Black Torrington, Virginstow, Walkhampton, Werrington, Weston Peverell, Whitchurch

1918–1948

BARNSTAPLE DIVISION
Barnstaple MB, Barnstaple RD, Bideford MB, Bideford RD, Ilfracombe UD, Lynton UD, Northam UD

HONITON DIVISION
Axminster RD, Axminster UD, Budleigh Salterton UD, Exmouth UD, Honiton MB, Honiton RD, Ottery St Mary UD, pt St Thomas RD (Aylesbeare, Bicton, East Budleigh, Clyst Honiton, Clyst St George, Colaton Raleigh, Farringdon,Lympstone, Newton Poppleford, Otterton, Rockbeare, Sowton, Woodbury), Seaton UD, Sidmouth UD

SOUTH MOLTON DIVISION
Crediton RD, Crediton UD, South Molton MB, South Molton RD, Okehampton MB, Okehampton RD, Great Torrington MB

TAVISTOCK DIVISION
Broadwoodwidger RD, the Devon pars in Holsworthy RD, Holsworthy UD, Ivybridge UD, Plympton St Mary RD, Tavistock RD, Tavistock UD

TIVERTON DIVISION
Bampton UD, Culmstock RD, Dawlish UD, pt Newton Abbot RD (West Dawlish), pt St Thomas RD (the pars not in Honiton Dv), Tiverton MB, Tiverton RD

TORQUAY DIVISION
Brixham UD, Dartmouth MB, pt Newton Abbot RD (Cockington, Stokeinteignhead), Paignton UD, Torquay MB, pt Totnes RD (Churston Ferrers, Kingswear, Marldon, Stoke Gabriel)

TOTNES DIVISION
Ashburton UD, Buckfastleigh UD, Kingsbridge RD, Kingsbridge UD, pt Newton Abbot RD (the pars not in Torquay Dv), Newton Abbot UD, Salcombe UD, Teignmouth UD, pt Totnes RD (the pars not in Torquay Dv)

1948–1970

NORTH DEVON COUNTY CONSTITUENCY
Barnstaple MB, Barnstaple RD, Ilfracombe UD, Lynton UD, South Molton MB, South Molton RD

HONITON COUNTY CONSTITUENCY
Axminster RD, Axminster UD, Budleigh Salterton UD, Exmouth UD, Honiton MB, Honiton RD, Ottery St Mary UD, pt St Thomas RD (Aylesbeare, Bicton, East Budleigh, Clyst Honiton, Clyst St George, Clyst St Mary, Colaton Raleigh, Farringdon, Harpford, Lympstone, Otterton, Rockbeare, Sowton, Topsham, Woodbury), Seaton UD, Sidmouth UD

TAVISTOCK COUNTY CONSTITUENCY[4]
Broadwoodwidger RD, Holsworthy RD, Holsworthy UD, pt Plympton St Mary RD (Brixton, Cornwood, Ermington, Harford, Holberton, Ivybridge, Newton and Noss, Plympton St Mary, Plympton St Maurice, Plymstock, St Budeaux, Shaugh Prior, Wembury, Yealmpton), Tavistock RD, Tavistock UD

TIVERTON COUNTY CONSTITUENCY
Dawlish UD, pt St Thomas RD (the pars not in Honiton CC), Teignmouth UD, Tiverton MB, Tiverton RD

TORRINGTON COUNTY CONSTITUENCY[5]
Bideford MB, Bideford RD, Crediton RD, Crediton UD, Northam UD, Okehampton MB, Okehampton RD, Torrington RD, Great Torrington MB

TOTNES COUNTY CONSTITUENCY
Ashburton UD, Buckfastleigh UD, Dartmouth MB, Totnes MB, pt Totnes RD (Ashprington, Berry Pomeroy, South Brent, West Buckfastleigh, Cornworthy, Dartington, Dean Prior, Diptford, Dittisham, Halwell, Harberton, Little Hempston, Holne, North Huish, Marldon, Moreleigh, Rattery, Staverton, Stoke Gabriel, Ugborough)

*1970–**

NORTH DEVON COUNTY CONSTITUENCY
Barnstaple MB, Barnstaple RD, Bideford MB, Bideford RD, Ilfracombe UD, Lynton UD, Northam UD, South Molton RD

WEST DEVON COUNTY CONSTITUENCY
Holsworthy RD, Okehampton MB, Okehampton RD, Plympton St Mary RD, Tavistock RD, Torrington RD, Great Torrington MB

HONITON COUNTY CONSTITUENCY
Axminster RD, Budleigh Salterton UD, Exmouth UD, Honiton MB, Honiton RD, Ottery St Mary UD, pt St Thomas RD (Aylesbeare, Bicton, East Budleigh, Clyst Honiton, Clyst St George, Clyst St Mary, Colaton Raleigh, Farringdon, Lympstone, Newton Poppleford and Harpford, Otterton, Rockbeare, Sowton, Woodbury), Seaton UD, Sidmouth UD

TIVERTON COUNTY CONSTITUENCY
Crediton RD, Crediton UD, Dawlish UD, pt St Thomas RD (the pars not in Honiton CC), Teignmouth UD, Tiverton MB, Tiverton RD

TOTNES COUNTY CONSTITUENCY
Ashburton UD, Buckfastleigh UD, Dartmouth MB, Kingsbridge RD, Kingsbridge UD, Newton Abbot RD, Newton Abbot UD, Salcombe UD, Totnes RD

DORSET

BOROUGH CONSTITUENCIES[1]

BLANDFORD (1304–49)
pt Blandford Forum
BRIDPORT (1295–1867 [1 mbr, 1867–85])
Bridport
CORFE CASTLE (1572–1832)
Corfe Castle
DORCHESTER (1295–1885 [1 mbr, 1867–85])
Dorchester All Saints, pt Dorchester Holy Trinity, Dorchester St Peter, pt Fordington (1832–85)
LYME REGIS (1295–1885 [1 mbr, 1832–85])
Charmouth (1832–85), Lyme Regis (pt 1295–1832, ent 1832–85)
MELCOMBE REGIS (1304, 1328–1832)
Melcombe Regis (1606–1832), pt Radipole (until 1606)
POOLE (1362–1867 [1 mbr, 1832–67])
pt Canford Magna (1832–67), Hamworthy (1832–85), Poole St James
POOLE (1948–*)
Poole MB
SHAFTESBURY (1295–1885 [1 mbr, 1832–85]) (Dorset until 1832, Dorset, Wilts 1832–85)
until 1832: pt Shaftesbury Holy Trinity, pt Shaftesbury St James, pt Shaftesbury St Peter
1832–85: Cann, Compton Abbas, Donhead St Mary [Wilts], pt Fontmell Magna, Margaret Marsh, Melbury Abbas, Motcombe, Shaftesbury Holy Trinity, Shaftesbury St James, Shaftesbury St Peter, East Stour, Stour Prevost, Todber
SHERBORNE (1338 only)
pt Sherborne
WAREHAM (1302–1885 [1 mbr, 1832–85])
until 1832: pt Wareham Holy Trinity, pt Wareham Lady St Mary, pt Wareham St Martin
1832–85: Arne, Bere Regis, Corfe Castle, pt East Stoke, Wareham Holy Trinity, Wareham Lady St Mary, Wareham St Martin
WEYMOUTH (1348–1832)
Weymouth (when gains sep civ identity), pt Wyke Regis (until Weymouth gains sep civ identity)
WEYMOUTH AND MELCOMBE REGIS (1832–85)
Melcombe Regis, pt Radipole, Weymouth, pt Wyke Regis

COUNTY CONSTITUENCIES

Dorset was undivided for parl purposes until 1885.

1885–1918

EASTERN DIVISION
Poole MB, pt Wareham PSD, Wimborne PSD, *viz.*, Almer, Arne, Athelhampton, Bere Regis, Bloxworth, Canford Magna, Chalbury, Church Knowle, Corfe Castle, Corfe Mullen, Cranborne, Long Crichel, Moor Crichel, Edmondsham, Gussage All Saints, Gussage St Michael, Hampreston, Hamworthy, Sixpenny Handley, Hinton Martell, Hinton Parva, East Holme, Horton, Kimmeridge, Kinson, Langton Matravers, Longfleet, Lytchett Matravers, Lytchett Minster, Morden, Parkstone, West Parley, Pentridge, Poole St James, Shapwick, Steeple, East Stoke, Studland, Sturminster Marshall, Swanage, Tarrant Crawford, Tarrant Rushton, Tyneham, Wareham Holy Trinity, Wareham Lady St Mary, Wareham St Martin, Wimborne Minster, Wimborne St Giles, Winterborne Kingston, Witchampton, Woodlands, East Woodyates, West Woodyates, Worth Matravers

NORTHERN DIVISION
Blandford PSD, Shaftesbury PSD, pt Sherborne PSD, Sturminster PSD, *viz.*, Abbotsbury, Anderson, Ashmore, Beer Hackett, Blandford Forum, Blandford St Mary, Bourton, Bradford Abbas, Bryanston, Buckhorn Weston, Cann, Castleton, Bishop's Caundle, Purse Caundle, Stourton Caundle, Caundle Marsh, Charlton Marshall, Chettle, Clifton Maybank, Nether Compton, Over Compton, Durweston, Farnham, Fifehead Magdalen, Fifehead Neville, Folke, Fontmell Magna, Gillingham, Hammoon, Hanford, Haydon, Hazelbury Bryan, Hilton, Hinton St Mary, Holnest, Holwell, Ibberton, Iwerne Courtney, Iwerne Minster, Iwerne Steepleton, Kington Magna, Langton Long Blandford, Leweston, Lillington, Longburton, Lydlinch, Manston, Margaret Marsh, Marnhull, Melbury Abbas, Milborne St Andrew, Milborne Stileham, Milton Abbas, Motcombe, Oborne, Childe Okeford, Okeford Fitzpaine, East Orchard, West Orchard, Pimperne, Shaftesbury Holy Trinity, Shaftesbury St James, Shaftesbury St Peter, Sherborne, Shillingstone, Silton, Spetisbury, Stalbridge, Stock Gaylard, Stoke Wake, East Stour, West Stour, Stour Provost, Stourpaine, Sturminster Newton, Sutton Waldron, Tarrant Gunville, Tarrant Hinton, Tarrant Keyneston, Tarrant Launceston, Tarrant Monkton, Tarrant Rawston, Thornford, Todber, Turnworth, Winterborne Clenston, Winterborne Houghton, Winterborne Stickland, Winterborne Tomson, Winterborne Whitechurch, Winterborne Zelston, Wolland, North Wootton

SOUTHERN DIVISION

Dorchester MB, pt Dorchester PSD, pt Wareham PSD, Weymouth and Melcombe Regis MB, *viz.*, Affpuddle, Bincombe, Bradford Peverell, Broadmayne, Broadway, Buckland Ripers, Burleston, Chaldon Herring, Charminster, Chickerell, Coombe Keynes, Dewlish, Dorchester All Saints, Dorchester Holy Trinity, Dorchester St Peter, Fleet, Fordington, West Knighton, East Lulworth, West Lulworth, Melcombe Regis, Moreton, Osmington, Owermoigne, Piddlehinton, Portland, Poxwell, Preston, Puddletown, Radipole, West Stafford, Stinsford, Stratton, Tincleton, Tolpuddle, Turners Puddle, Upwey, Warmwell, Watercombe, Weymouth, Whitcombe, Winfrith Newburgh, Winterborne Herringston, Winterborne Came, Winterborne Monkton, Winterborne St Martin, Woodsford, Wool, Wyke Regis

WESTERN DIVISION

Bridport MB, Bridport PSD, Cerne PSD, pt Dorchester PSD, Lyme Regis MB, pt Sherborne PSD, *viz.*, Allington, Alton Pancras, Askerswell, Batcombe, Beaminster, Bettiscombe, Bothenhampton, Bradpole, Long Bredy, Bridport, Broadwindsor, Buckland Newton, Burstock, Burton Bradstock, Catherston Leweston, Cattistock, Nether Cerne, Up Cerne, Cerne Abbas, Chardstock, Charmouth, Chedington, East Chelborough, West Chelborough, Cheselbourne, Chetnole, Chideock, Chilcombe, Chilfrome, West Compton, Compton Valence, Corscombe, Evershot, Frampton, Frome St Quintin, Frome Vauchurch, Godmanston, Gorewood, Halstock, Hawkchurch, Hermitage, Hilfield, Hooke, Kingston Russell, Langton Herring, Leigh, Littlebredy, Litton Cheney, Loders, Lyme Regis, Maiden Newton, Mapperton, Mappowder, Marshwood, Melbury Bubb, Melbury Osmond, Melbury Sampford, Melcombe Horsey, Minterne Magna, Mosterton, Netherbury, South Perrott, Piddletrenthide, Pilsdon, North Poorton, Portesham, Powerstock, Pulham, Puncknowle, Rampisham, Ryme Intrinseca, Shipton George, Stanton St Gabriel, Stockwood, Stoke Abbott, Swyre, Sydling St Nicholas, Symondsbury, Toller Fratrum, Toller Porcorum, Walditch, Wambrook, Whitechurch Canonicorum, Winterborne Steepleton, Winterbourne Abbas, Glanvilles Wootton, Wootton Fitzpaine, Wraxall, Wynford Eagle, Yetminster

1918–1948

EASTERN DIVISION

Poole MB, Poole RD, pt Wimborne and Cranborne RD (Almer, Charlbury, Colehill, Corfe Mullen, Moor Crichel, Hampreston, Hinton Martell, Hinton Parva, Holt, Pamphill, West Parley, Shapwick, Sturminster Marshall), Wimborne Minster UD

NORTHERN DIVISION

Blandford RD, Blandford Forum MB, Shaftesbury MB, Shaftesbury RD, Sherborne RD, Sherborne UD, Sturminster RD, pt Wimborne and Cranborne RD (the pars not in E'rn Dv)

SOUTHERN DIVISION

Portland UD, Swanage UD, Wareham MB, Wareham and Purbeck RD, pt Weymouth RD (the pars not in W'rn Dv), Weymouth and Melcombe Regis MB

WESTERN DIVISION

Beaminster RD, Bridport MB, Bridport RD, Cerne RD, Dorchester MB, Dorchester RD, Lyme Regis MB, pt Weymouth RD (Abbotsbury, Langton Herring, Portisham)

1948–1970

NORTH DORSET COUNTY CONSTITUENCY

Blandford RD, Blandford Forum MB, Shaftesbury MB, Shaftesbury RD, Sturminster RD, Wimborne and Cranborne RD, Wimborne Minster UD

SOUTH DORSET COUNTY CONSTITUENCY

pt Dorchester RD (Bincombe, Chickerell, Fleet, Osmington, Owermoigne, Poxwell), Portland UD, Swanage UD, Wareham MB, Wareham and Purbeck RD, Weymouth and Melcombe Regis MB

WEST DORSET COUNTY CONSTITUENCY

Beaminster RD, Bridport MB, Bridport RD, Dorchester MB, pt Dorchester RD (the pars not in South Dorset CC), Lyme Regis MB, Sherborne RD, Sherborne UD

*1970–**

NORTH DORSET COUNTY CONSTITUENCY

Blandford RD, Blandford Forum MB, Shaftesbury MB, Shaftesbury RD, Wimborne and Cranborne RD, Wimborne Minster UD

SOUTH DORSET COUNTY CONSTITUENCY

pt Dorchester RD (Bincombe, Chickerell, Fleet, Osmington, Owermoigne, Poxwell), Portland UD, Swanage UD, Wareham MB, Wareham and Purbeck RD, Weymouth and Melcombe Regis MB

WEST DORSET COUNTY CONSTITUENCY

Beaminster RD, Bridport MB, Bridport RD, Dorchester MB, pt Dorchester RD (the pars not in South Dorset CC), Lyme Regis MB, Sherborne RD, Sherborne UD

ESSEX

BOROUGH CONSTITUENCIES[1]

BARKING (1945–70)
Barking MB
BASILDON (1970–*)
Basildon UD
CHELMSFORD (1337 only)
Chelmsford
COLCHESTER (1295–1918 [1 mbr, 1885–1918])
Berechurch, Colchester All Saints, Colchester Holy Trinity, Colchester St Botolph, Colchester St Giles, Colchester St James, Colchester St Leonard, Colchester St Martin, Colchester St Mary at the Walls, Colchester St Mary Magdalen, Colchester St Nicholas, Colchester St Peter, Colchester St Runwald, Greenstead, Lexden, Mile End St Michael
DAGENHAM (1945–70)
Dagenham MB
EAST HAM NORTH (1918–70)
pt E Ham CB (the wards of Little Ilford [1948–70], Kensington [1948–70], Manor Park, Plashet [1948–70], Plashet East [1918–48], Plashet West [1918–48], Woodgrange [1948–70])
EAST HAM SOUTH (1918–70)
pt E Ham CB (the wards of Beackton and North Woolwich [1918–48], Castle [1948–70], Central [1948–70], Central East [1918–48], Central West [1918–48], Greatfield [1948–70], South [1948–70], Wall End [1948–70])
WEST HAM NORTH (1885–1918)
the pt of West Ham par north of a line described in the act
WEST HAM NORTH (1948–70)
pt W Ham CB (the wards of Broadway, Forest Gate, West Ham, High Street, Newtown, Park, Plashet Road, Upton)
WEST HAM PLAISTOW (1918–48)
pt W Ham CB (the wards of Hudsons, Plaistow, pt of ward of Canning Town)
WEST HAM SILVERTOWN (1918–48)
pt W Ham CB (the wards of Custom House and Silvertown, Tidal Basin, pt of ward of Canning Town)
WEST HAM SOUTH (1885–1918)
the pt of West Ham par south of a line described in the act
WEST HAM SOUTH (1948–70)
pt W Ham CB (the wards of Beckton Road, Bemersyde, Canning Town and Grange, Custom House and Silvertown, Hudsons, Ordnance, Plaistow, Tidal Basin)
WEST HAM STRATFORD (1918–48)
pt W Ham CB (the wards of Broadway, Forest Gate, High Street, New Town)
WEST HAM UPTON (1918–48)
pt W Ham CB (the wards of West Ham, Park, Upton)
HARWICH (1604–1885 [1 mbr, 1867–85])
Dovercourt, Harwich St Nicholas
HORNCHURCH (1948–70)
Hornchurch UD
ILFORD (1918–45)
Ilford MB
ILFORD NORTH[2] (1945–70)
pt Ilford MB (the wards of Barkingside, Clayhall [1948–70], Fairlop [1948–70], North Hainault, South Hainault, Seven Kings)
ILFORD SOUTH[2] (1945–70)
pt Ilford MB (the wards of Clementswood, Cranbrook, Goodmayes, Loxford, Mayfield [1948–70], Park)
LEYTON (1948–70)
Leyton MB
LEYTON EAST (1918–48)
pt Leyton UD (the wards of Cann Hall, Grove Green, Harrow Green, Leytonstone, Wanstead Slip)
LEYTON WEST (1918–48)
pt Leyton UD (the wards of Central, Forest, Lea Bridge, Leyton)
MALDON (1334–1885 [1 mbr, 1867–85])
Heybridge (1832–85), Maldon All Saints, Maldon St Mary, Maldon St Peter
ROMFORD[4] (1945–70)
Brentwood UD (1948–55), Romford MB
SOUTHEND ON SEA (1918–48)
Southend on Sea CB
SOUTHEND EAST[3] (1948–*)
Rochford RD (1948–70), pt Southend on Sea CB (the wards of All Saints, Pier, Shoebury, Southchurch, Thorpe)
SOUTHEND WEST[3] (1948–*)
pt Southend on Sea CB (the wards of Chalkwell, Eastwood, Leigh, Milton, Prittlewell, St Clements, Victoria, Westborough)
THURROCK (1970–*)
Thurrock UD
WALTHAMSTOW EAST (1918–70)
pt Walthamstow UD [1918]/MB [1948] (the wards of Hale End, Hoe Street, Wood Street)
WALTHAMSTOW WEST (1918–70)
pt Walthamstow UD [1918]/MB [1948] (the wards of High Street, Higham Hill, St James Street)
WANSTEAD AND WOODFORD (1964–70)
Renaming 1964 of following constituency, no alt in units involved
WOODFORD[5] (1945–64)
Chigwell UD (1945–55), Wanstead and Woodford MB

COUNTY CONSTITUENCIES

1832–1867

NORTHERN DIVISION

Hundreds of Clavering, Dunmow, Freshwell, Hinckford, Lexden, Tendring, Thurstable, Uttlesford, Winstree, Witham

SOUTHERN DIVISION

Liberty of Havering-atte-Bower and hundreds of Barstable, Becontree, Chafford, Chelmsford, Dengie, Harlow, Ongar, Rochford, Waltham

1867-1885

NORTH–EAST DIVISION

Hundreds of Dengie, Hinckford, Lexden, Tendring, Thurstable, Winstree, Witham

NORTH–WEST DIVISION

Hundreds of Chelmsford, Clavering, Dunmow, Freshwell, Harlow, Ongar, Uttlesford, Waltham

SOUTH DIVISION

Liberty of Havering-atte-Bower and hundreds of Barstable, Becontree, Chafford, Rochford

1885–1918

EASTERN OR MALDON DIVISION

Hinckford South (Braintree Bench) PSD, pt Hinckford South (Halstead Bench) PSD, pt Lexden and Winstree PSD, Maldon MB, Witham PSD, *viz.*, Aldham, Alphamstone, Bocking, Bradwell, Braintree, Great Braxted, Little Braxted, Great Coggeshall, Little Coggeshall, Earls Colne, Cressing, Easthorpe, Fairstead, Faulkbourne, Feering, Felsted, Goldhanger, Halstead, Hatfield Peverel, Inworth, Kelvedon, Langford, Markshall, Messing, Black Notley, White Notley, Panfield, Pattiswick, Rayne, Rivenhall, Great Saling, Shalford, Stisted, Terling, Great Tey, Little Tey, Marks Tey, Tollesbury, Tolleshunt d'Arcy, Tolleshunt Knights, Tolleshunt Major, Great Totham, Little Totham, Ulting, Wethersfield, Wickham Bishops, Witham

MID OR CHELMSFORD DIVISION

pt Brentwood PSD, Chelmsford PSD, *viz.*, Great Baddow, Little Baddow, Basildon, North Benfleet, Boreham, Bowers Gifford, Brentwood, Broomfield, Great Burstead, Little Burstead, Buttsbury, Chelmsford, Chignall St James, Chignall Smealy, Childerditch, Cranham, Danbury, Doddinghurst, Downham, Dunton, Good Easter, Fryerning, East Hanningfield, South Hanningfield, West Hanningfield, East Horndon, West Horndon, Hutton, Ingatestone, Ingrave, Laindon, Great Leighs, Little Leighs, Margaretting, Mashbury, Nevendon, Pitsea, Ramsden Bellhouse, Ramsden Crays, Rettendon, Roxwell, Runwell, Sandon, Shenfield, Springfield, Stock, Upminster, Vange, Great Waltham, Little Waltham, Great Warley, Little Warley, South Weald, Wickford, Widford, Woodham Ferrers, Writtle

NORTHERN OR SAFFRON WALDEN DIVISION

pt Dunmow PSD, Freshwell PSD, Hinckford (North) PSD, pt Hinckford South (Halstead Bench) PSD, Saffron Walden MB, Walden PSD, *viz.*, Arkesden, Ashdon, Ashen, pt Ballingdon, Great Bardfield, Little Bardfield, Bardfield Saling, Bartlow End, Belchamp Otten, Belchamp St Paul, Belchamp Walter, Berden, Birchanger, Birdbrook, Borley, Bulmer, pt Helion Bumpstead, Steeple Bumpstead, Bures, Great Chesterford, Little Chesterford, Great Chishill, Little Chishill, Chrishall, Clavering, White Colne, Colne Engaine, Debden, Elmdon, Elsenham, Farnham, Finchingfield, Foxearth, Gestingthorpe, Gosfield, Hadstock, Castle Hedingham, Sible Hedingham, Hempstead, Henham, Great Henny, Little Henny, Heydon, pt Kedington, Langley, Liston, Littlebury, Manuden, Great Maplestead, Little Maplestead, Middleton, Newport, Ovington, Pebmarsh, Pentlow, Quendon, Radwinter, Rickling, Ridgewell, Saffron Walden, Great Sampford, Little Sampford, Stambourne, Stansted Mountfitchet, Strethall, Sturmer, Thaxted, Tilbury juxta Clare, Toppesfield, Twinstead, Ugley, Wendens Ambo, Wendon Lofts, Wicken Bonhunt, Wickham St Paul, Widdington, Wimbish, North Wood, Great Yeldham, Little Yeldham

NORTH–EASTERN OR HARWICH DIVISION

Harwich MB, pt Lexden and Winstree PSD, Tendring PSD, *viz.*, Alresford, Ardleigh, Beaumont cum Moze, Great Bentley, Little Bentley, West Bergholt, Birch, Boxted, Bradfield, Brightlingsea, Great Bromley, Little Bromley, Mount Bures, Great Clacton, Little Clacton, Wakes Colne, Copford, Dedham, East Donyland, Dovercourt, Elmstead, Fingringhoe, Fordham, Frating, Frinton, Harwich St Nicholas, Great Holland, Little Holland, Great Horkesley, Little Horkesley, Kirby le Soken, Langenhoe, Langham, Lawford, Layer Breton, Layer de la Haye, Layer Marney, Manningtree, East Mersea, West Mersea, Mistley, Great Oakley, Little Oakley, Peldon, Ramsey, St Osyth, Salcot, Stanway, Tendring, Thorpe le Soken, Thorrington, Virley, Walton le Soken, Weeley, Great Wigborough, Little Wigborough, Wivenhoe, Wix, Wormingford, Wrabness

SOUTHERN OR ROMFORD DIVISION

pt Becontree PSD, Havering-atte-Bower Lbty, *viz.*, Barking, Dagenham, East Ham, Havering-atte-Bower, Hornchurch, Ilford, Little Ilford, Mountnessing, Romford, Wanstead

SOUTH–EASTERN DIVISION

pt Brentwood PSD, Dengie PSD, Orsett PSD, Rochford PSD, *viz.*, Althorne, Asheldham, Ashingdon, Aveley, Barling, South Benfleet, Bradwell on Sea, Bulphan, Burnham, Canewdon, Canvey Island, Chadwell St Mary, Corringham, Creeksea, Dengie, Eastwood, North Fambridge, South Fambridge, Fobbing, Foulness, Hadleigh, Hawkwell, Hazeleigh, Heybridge, Hockley, Horndon on the Hill, Langdon Hills, Latchingdon, Leigh, Mayland, Mucking, Mundon, Cold Norton, North Ockendon, South Ockendon, Orsett, Paglesham, Prittlewell, Purleigh, Rainham, Rawreth, Rayleigh, Rochford, St Lawrence, North Shoebury, South Shoebury, Shopland, Southchurch, Southminster, Great Stambridge, Little Stambridge, Stanford le Hope, Steeple, Stifford, Stow Maries, Sutton, Thundersley, Grays Thurrock, Little Thurrock, West Thurrock, East Tilbury, West Tilbury, Tillingham, Great Wakering, Little Wakering, Wennington, Woodham Mortimer, Woodham Walter

SOUTH–WESTERN OR WALTHAMSTOW DIVISION

pt Becontree PSD, *viz.*, Leyton, Walthamstow, Woodford

WESTERN OR EPPING DIVISION

pt Dunmow PSD, Epping PSD, Harlow PSD, Ongar PSD, *viz.*, Barnston, Blackmore, Bobbingworth, Broxted, Great Canfield, Little Canfield, Chickney, Chigwell, Chingford, Great Dunmow, Little Dunmow, High Easter, Great Easton, Little Easton, Epping, Fyfield, Great Hallingbury, Little Hallingbury, Harlow, Hatfield Broad Oak, Kelvedon Hatch, Lambourne, Latton, High Laver, Little Laver, Magdalen Laver, Lindsell, Loughton, Matching, Moreton, Navestock, Nazeing, Netteswell, Norton Mandeville, Chipping Ongar, High Ongar, Great Parndon, Little Parndon, Pleshey, Abbess Roding, Aythorpe Roding, Beauchamp Roding, Berners Roding, High Roding, Leaden Roding, Margaret Roding, White Roding, Roydon, Sheering, Shelley, Shellow Bowells, Stanford Rivers, Stapleford Abbotts, Stapleford Tawney, Stebbing, Stondon Massey, Takeley, Theydon Bois, Theydon Garnon, Theydon Mount, Tilty, Waltham Holy Cross, North Weald Bassett, Willingale Doe, Willingale Spain

1918–1948[6]

CHELMSFORD DIVISION[6]

pt Billericay RD (Hutton, Mountnessing, Shenfield, South Weald), Brentwood UD, Chelmsford MB, Chelmsford RD, Ongar RD

COLCHESTER DIVISION

Colchester MB, pt Lexden and Winstree RD (all except a detached pt of Inworth)

EPPING DIVISION

Buckhurst Hill UD (1918–45), Chingford UD/MB, Epping RD, Epping UD, Loughton UD (1918–45), Waltham Holy Cross UD, Wanstead UD (1918–45), Woodford UD (1918–45)

HARWICH DIVISION

Brightlingsea UD, Clacton UD, Frinton on Sea UD, Harwich MB, Tendring RD, Walton on the Naze UD, Wivenhoe UD

HORNCHURCH DIVISION (1945–48)

Hornchurch UD

MALDON DIVISION[6]

Braintree RD, Braintree UD, Burnham on Crouch UD, pt Lexden and Winstree RD (the detached pt of Inworth), Maldon MB, Maldon RD, Witham UD

ROMFORD DIVISION[6]

Barking Town UD (1918–45), Romford RD, Romford UD

SAFFRON WALDEN DIVISION

Belchamp RD, Bumpstead RD, Dunmow RD, Halstead RD, Halstead UD, Saffron Walden MB, Saffron Walden RD, Stansted RD

SOUTH–EASTERN DIVISION[6]

Benfleet UD (1945–48), pt Billericay RD (1918–45, the pars not in Chelmsford Dv), Billericay UD (1945–48), Canvey Island UD (1945–48), Orsett RD (1918–45), Rayleigh UD (1945–48), Rochford RD, Shoeburyness UD (1918–45), pt Southend on Sea CB[7] (1945–48), Grays Thurrock UD (1918–45), Tilbury UD (1918–45)

THURROCK DIVISION (1945–48)

Thurrock UD

1948–1970

BILLERICAY COUNTY CONSTITUENCY[4]

Benfleet UD (1948–55), Billericay UD, Brentwood UD (1955–70), Canvey Island UD (1948–55), Rayleigh UD (1948–55)

CHELMSFORD COUNTY CONSTITUENCY[8]

Chelmsford MB, Chelmsford RD, Ongar RD (1948–55)

CHIGWELL COUNTY CONSTITUENCY (1955[8]–70)

Chigwell UD, Ongar RD

COLCHESTER COUNTY CONSTITUENCY[9]

Colchester MB, Lexden and Winstree RD, West Mersea UD

EPPING COUNTY CONSTITUENCY

Chingford MB, Epping RD, Epping UD, Waltham Holy Cross UD

HARWICH COUNTY CONSTITUENCY

Brightlingsea UD, Clacton UD, Frinton and Walton UD, Harwich MB, Tendring RD, Wivenhoe UD

MALDON COUNTY CONSTITUENCY[9]

pt Braintree RD (the pars not in Saffron Walden CC), Braintree and Bocking UD, Burnham on Crouch UD, Maldon MB, Maldon RD, Witham UD

SAFFRON WALDEN COUNTY CONSTITUENCY[9]

pt Braintree RD (Great Bardfield, Bardfield Saling), Dunmow RD, Halstead RD, Halstead UD, Saffron Walden MB, Saffron Walden RD

SOUTH EAST ESSEX COUNTY CONSTITUENCY (1955[4]–70)

Benfleet UD, Canvey Island UD, Rayleigh UD

THURROCK COUNTY CONSTITUENCY

Thurrock UD

*1970–**

BRAINTREE COUNTY CONSTITUENCY

Braintree RD, Braintree and Bocking UD, pt Chelmsford RD (Boreham, Broomfield, Chignall, Good Easter, Great and Little Leighs, Mashbury, Pleshey, Roxwell, Springfield, Great Waltham, Little Waltham, Writtle), Witham UD

BRENTWOOD AND ONGAR COUNTY CONSTITUENCY

Brentwood UD, pt Epping and Ongar RD (Blackmore, Bobbingworth, Doddinghurst, Fyfield, Kelvedon Hatch, Lambourne, High Laver, Little Laver, Moreton, Navestock, Ongar, High Ongar, Abbess Beauchamp and Berners Roding, Stanford Rivers, Stapleford Abbotts, Stapleford Tawney, Stondon Massey, Theydon Mount, Willingale)

CHELMSFORD COUNTY CONSTITUENCY

Chelmsford MB, pt Chelmsford RD (the pars not in Braintree CC)

COLCHESTER COUNTY CONSTITUENCY

Colchester MB, Lexden and Winstree RD, West Mersea UD

EPPING FOREST COUNTY CONSTITUENCY
Chigwell UD, Epping UD, pt Epping and Ongar RD (Epping Upland, Theydon Bois, Theydon Garnon), Waltham Holy Cross UD

HARLOW COUNTY CONSTITUENCY
pt Epping and Ongar RD (Magdalen Laver, Matching, Nazeing, Roydon, Sheering, North Weald Bassett), Harlow UD

HARWICH COUNTY CONSTITUENCY
Brightlingsea UD, Clacton UD, Frinton and Walton UD, Harwich MB, Tendring RD, Wivenhoe UD

MALDON COUNTY CONSTITUENCY
Burnham on Crouch UD, Maldon MB, Maldon RD, Rochford RD

SAFFRON WALDEN COUNTY CONSTITUENCY
Dunmow RD, Halstead RD, Halstead UD, Saffron Walden MB, Saffron Walden RD

SOUTH EAST ESSEX COUNTY CONSTITUENCY
Benfleet UD, Canvey Island UD, Rayleigh UD

GLOUCESTERSHIRE

BOROUGH CONSTITUENCIES[1]

BRISTOL[2] (1295–1885) (Glos, Somerset)
Bristol All Saints, Bristol Castle Precincts, Bristol Christ Church, Bristol St Augustine, Bristol St Ewen, pt Bristol St James (1295–1867), Bristol St James In (1867–85), Bristol St James and St Paul Out (1867–85), Bristol St John the Baptist, Bristol St Leonard, Bristol St Mary le Port, Bristol St Michael, Bristol St Nicholas, pt Bristol St Paul (1295–1867), Bristol St Paul In (1867–85), Bristol St Peter, pt Bristol St Philip and St Jacob (1295–1720), Bristol St Philip and St Jacob In (1720–1885), Bristol St Philip and St Jacob Out (1867–85), Bristol St Stephen, Bristol St Werburgh, Clifton (1867–85)

BRISTOL CENTRAL[3] (1918–70)
pt Bristol CB (the wards of Central East [1918–48], Central West [1918–48], Easton [1948–70], Knowle [1948–70], Redcliffe [1918–55], St Augustine [1918–48], St James [1918–48], St Paul, St Philip and St Jacob [1955–70], St Philip and Jacob North [1948–55], St Philip and Jacob South [1918–55], Windmill Hill [1955–70])

BRISTOL, EAST DIVISION (1885–1918)
pt Bristol MB (the wards of pt St Philip and St Jacob North, St Philip and St Jacob South), Bristol St George

BRISTOL EAST (1918–48)
pt Bristol CB (the wards of pt Easton, St George East, St George West, pt Somerset)

BRISTOL, NORTH DIVISION (1885–1918)
pt Bristol MB (the wards of District, St James, St Paul, pt St Philip and St Jacob North), Stapleton

BRISTOL NORTH (1918–48)
pt Bristol CB (the wards of District, pt Easton, St Philip and St Jacob North, Stapleton)

BRISTOL NORTH EAST[3] (1948–*)
pt Bristol CB (the wards of District [1948–70], Easton [1970–*], Eastville, Hillfields, St Paul [1970–*], St Philip and St Jacob [1970–*], Stapleton), Mangotsfield UD (1955–70)

BRISTOL NORTH WEST[3] (1948–*)
pt Bristol CB (the wards of Avon, Durdham [1948–55], Henbury [1955–*], Horfield, Southmead [1955–*], Westbury-on-Trym)

BRISTOL, SOUTH DIVISION[4] (1885–1918) (Glos, Somerset)
pt Bristol MB (the wards of Bedminster East, Bedminster West, Bristol, Redcliffe)

BRISTOL SOUTH[5] (1918–*)
pt Bristol CB (the wards of Bedminster [1948–*], Bedminster East [1918–48], Bedminster West [1918–48], Bishopsworth [1955–*], Hengrove [1955–*], Somerset [pt 1918–48, ent 1948–*], Southville, Windmill Hill [1948–55])

BRISTOL SOUTH EAST[5] (1948–*)
pt Bristol CB (the wards of Brislington, Hengrove [1948–55], Knowle [1970–*], St George East, St George West, Stockwood [1955–*], Windmill Hill [1970–*]), Kingswood UD (1955–70)

BRISTOL, WEST DIVISION (1885–1918)
pt Bristol MB (the wards of Clifton, St Augustine, St Michael, Westbury), Horfield

BRISTOL WEST[3] (1918–*)
pt Bristol CB (the wards of Bishopston [1948–*], Cabot [1955–*], Clifton [1948–*], Clifton North [1918–48], Clifton South [1918–48], District [1970–*], Durdham [1955–*], Horfield [1918–48], Redland, St Augustine [1948–55], St James [1948–55], St Michael, Westbury-on-Trym [1918–48])

CHELTENHAM (1832–*)
Charlton Kings (1885–*), Cheltenham, pt Leckhampton (1867–1918)

CIRENCESTER (1572–1885 [1 mbr, 1867–85])
Cirencester, Stratton (1867–85)

GLOUCESTER[6] (1295–* [1 mbr, 1885–*])
until 1918: Gloucester Barton St Mary (1867–1918), Gloucester Barton St Michael (1867–1918), Gloucester Holy Trinity, pt Gloucester North Hamlet (1867–1918), Gloucester South Hamlet (1867–1918), Gloucester Pool Meadow (1867–1918), Gloucester St Aldate, Gloucester St Catherine (pt 1295–1867, ent 1867–1918), Gloucester St John the Baptist, Gloucester St Mary de Crypt, Gloucester St Mary de Grace, Gloucester St Mary de Lode (pt 1295–1867, ent 1867–1918), Gloucester St Michael, Gloucester St Nicholas, Gloucester St Owen, pt Hempsted (1867–85), Littleworth (1867–1918), pt Longford St Catherine (1867–1918), pt Longford St Mary (1867–1918), pt Upton St Leonards (1867–85), Ville of Wotton (1867–1918), pt Wotton St Mary (1867–1918)
since 1918: Gloucester CB, pt Gloucester RD (1948–70: Barnwood, Brockworth, Hempsted, Hucclecote, Wotton Vill [1948–51])

STROUD (1832–85)
Avening, Bisley, pt Brookthorpe (1867–85), Horsley, Minchinhampton, Painswick, Pitchcombe, Randwick, Rodborough, pt Standish (1867–85), King's Stanley, pt Leonard Stanley, Stonehouse, Stroud, Woodchester

TEWKESBURY (1604–1885 [1 mbr, 1867–85])
Tewkesbury (pt 1604–1832, ent 1832–85)

COUNTY CONSTITUENCIES

1832–1885

EASTERN DIVISION

Hds of Bisley, Bradley, Brightwells Barrow, Cheltenham, Cleeve, Crowthorne and Minety, Deerhurst, Dudstone and King's Barton, Kiftsgate, Longtree, Rapsgate, Slaughter, Tewkesbury, Tibaldstone, Westminster

WESTERN DIVISION

Hds of Barton Regis, Berkeley, Bledisloe, Botloe, Duchy of Lancaster, Grumbalds Ash, Henbury, Langley and Swinehead, Pucklechurch, St Briavels, Thornbury, Westbury

1885–1918

EASTERN OR CIRENCESTER DIVISION

Campden PSD, Cirencester PSD, Fairford PSD, Moreton in Marsh PSD, Northleach PSD, Stow PSD, Tetbury PSD, *viz.*, Adlestrop, Admington, Aldsworth, Down Ampney, Ampney Crucis, Ampney St Mary, Ampney St Peter, Aston Blank, Aston Subedge, Bagendon, Barnsley, Great Barrington, Little Barrington, pt Batsford, Baunton, Beverstone, Bibury, Bledington, Bourton on the Hill, Bourton on the Water, Boxwell with Leighterton, Brimpsfield, Broadwell, Chipping Campden, North Cerney, South Cerney, Chedworth, Cherington, Cirencester, Clapton, Clifford Chambers, Clopton, Coates, Colesbourne, Coln Rogers, Coln St Aldwyn, Coln St Dennis, Compton Abdale, Condicote, Daglingworth, Didmarton, Dorsington, Dowdeswell, Driffield, Duntisbourne Abbots, Duntisbourne Rouse, Eastington, Eastleach Martin, Eastleach Turville, Ebrington, Edgeworth, Elkstone, Eyford, Fairford, Farmington, Hampnett, Harnhill, Haselton, Hatherop, Hidcote Bartrim, Cow Honeybourne, Icomb, Church Icomb, Kempsford, Kingscote, Lechlade, Lower Lemington, Longborough, Marston Sicca, Maugersbury, Meysey Hampton, Mickleton, Moreton in Marsh, Naunton, Newington Bagpath, Northleach, Notgrove, Oddington, Ozleworth, Pebworth, Poulton, Preston, Preston, Preston on Stour, Quenington, Quinton, Rendcombe, Great Rissington, Little Rissington, Wick Rissington, Rodmarton, Saintbury, Salperton, Sapperton, Sevenhampton, Sezincote, Sherborne, Shipton Moyne, Siddington, Lower Slaughter, Upper Slaughter, Southrop, Stow-on-the-Wold, Stowell, Stratton, Lower Swell, Upper Swell, Syde, Tetbury, Todenham, Turkdean, Welford, Westcote, Weston-on-Avon, Weston Subedge, Westonbirt, Whittington, Willersley, Windrush, Winson, Winterbourne, Withington, Yanworth

FOREST OF DEAN DIVISION

Coleford PSD, Lydney PSD, Newent PSD, Newnham PSD, *viz.*, Abenhall, Alvington, Ashchurch, Awre, Aylburton, English Bicknor, Blaisdon, Bromesberrow, Corse, East Dean, West Dean, Dymock, Flaxley, Hewelsfield, Highleadon, Huntley, Kempley, Lancaut, Lea Bailey, Littledean, Longhope, Lydney, Mitcheldean, Newent, Newland, Newnham, Oxenhall, Pauntley, Ruardean, St Briavels, Staunton, Taynton, Tibberton, Tidenham, Upleadon, Westbury-on-Severn, Woolaston

MID OR STROUD DIVISION

pt Dursley PSD, Horsley PSD, Stroud PSD, pt Whitminster PSD, Wotton under Edge PSD, *viz.*, Avening, Bisley, Bitton, Cam, Charfield, Coaley, Cranham, Cromhall, Dursley, Eastington, Frocester, Horsley, Minchinhampton, Miserden, Nailsworth, North Nibley, Nympsfield, Owlpen, Painswick, Pitchcombe, Randwick, Rodborough, Slimbridge, King's Stanley, Leonard Stanley, Stinchcombe, Stonehouse, Stroud, Tortworth, Uley, Woodchester, Wotton under Edge

NORTHERN OR TEWKESBURY DIVISION

Berkeley PSD, Cheltenham PSD, pt Dursley PSD, Gloucester PSD, Tewkesbury MB, Tewkesbury PSD, pt Whitminster PSD, Winchcombe PSD, *viz.*, Alderton, Alkington, Alstone, Arlingham, Ashelworth, Ashton under Hill, Aston Somerville, Badgeworth, Barnwood, Beckford, Berkeley, Boddington, Breadstone, Brockworth, Brookthorpe, Buckland, Bulley, Charlton Abbots, Child's Wickham, Churcham, Churchdown, Bishop's Cleeve, Coberley, Cowley, Deerhurst, Didbrook, Dumbleton, Elmore, Elmstone Hardwicke, Forthampton, Frampton on Severn, Fretherne with Saul, Gotherington, Temple Guiting, Guiting Power, Hailes, Ham and Stone, Hamfallow, Hardwicke, Harescombe, Haresfield, Hartpury, Hasfield, Down Hatherley, Up Hatherley, Hawling, Hempsted, Highnam Over and Linton, Hinton, Hinton on the Green, Hucclecote, Ilmington, Kemerton, Kingswood, Lassington, pt Leckhampton, Leigh, pt Longford St Catherine, pt Longford St Mary, Longney, Maisemore, Matson, Minsterworth, Moreton Valence, Norton, Oxenton, Pinnock and Hyde, Prestbury, Prescott, Prinknash Park, Quedgeley, Roel, Rudford, Sandhurst, Shipton, Shurdington, Snowshill, Southam and Brockhampton, Standish, Stanley Pontlarge, Stanton, Stanway, Staverton, Stoke Orchard, Sudeley Manor, Swindon, Tewkesbury, Tirley, Toddington, Tredington, Tuffley, Twigworth, Twyning, Uckington, Upton St Leonards, Walton Cardiff, Great Washbourne, Little Washbourne, Whaddon, Wheatenhurst, Winchcombe, Great Witcombe, Woodmancote, Woolstone, Wormington, pt Wotton St Mary

SOUTHERN OR THORNBURY DIVISION

pt Lawford's Gate PSD, Sodbury PSD, Thornbury PSD, *viz.*, Iron Acton, Acton Turville, Alderley, Almondsbury, Alveston, Cold Ashton, Aust, Great Badminton, Compton Greenfield, Doddington, Doynton, Dyrham and Hinton, Elberton, Filton, Frampton Cotterell, Hanham, Hawkesbury, Henbury Hill, Horton, West Littleton, Littleton upon Severn, Mangotsfield, Marshfield, Oldland, Olveston, Pucklechurch, Rangeworthy, Redwick and Northwick, Rockhampton, Shirehampton, Siston, Chipping Sodbury, Little Sodbury, Old Sodbury, Stoke Gifford, Thornbury, Tormarton, Tytherington, Wapley and Codrington, Westbury-on-Trym,

Westerleigh, Wick and Abson, Wickwar, Yate

1918–1948

CIRENCESTER AND TEWKESBURY DIVISION
Campden RD, pt Cheltenham RD (Prestbury, Swindon, Uckington), Cirencester RD, Cirencester UD, the Glos par of Faringdon RD, Marston Sicca RD, Northleach RD, Pebworth RD, the Glos pars of Stow on the Wold RD, Stow on the Wold UD, the Glos pars of Tetbury RD, Tetbury UD, Tewkesbury MB, the Glos pars of Tewkesbury RD, the Glos pars of Winchcombe RD

FOREST OF DEAN DIVISION
Awre UD, Coleford UD, East Dean and United Parishes RD, West Dean RD, pt Gloucester RD (Ashleworth, Highnam Over and Linton, Lassington, Maisemore), Lydney RD, Newent RD, Newnham UD, Westbury-on-Severn UD

STROUD DIVISION
pt Cheltenham RD (the pars not in Cirencester and Tewkesbury Dv), Dursley RD, pt Gloucester RD (the pars not in Forest of Dean Dv), Nailsworth UD, Stroud RD, Stroud UD, Wheatenhurst RD

THORNBURY DIVISION
Kingswood UD, Chipping Sodbury RD, Thornbury RD, Warmley RD

1948–1970[3]

CIRENCESTER AND TEWKESBURY COUNTY CONSTITUENCY
Cheltenham RD, Cirencester RD, Cirencester UD, North Cotswold RD, Northleach RD, Tetbury RD (1948–55), Tewkesbury MB

SOUTH GLOUCESTERSHIRE COUNTY CONSTITUENCY
Kingswood UD (1948–55), Mangotsfield UD (1948–55), Sodbury RD, Thornbury RD (1955–70), Warmley RD

WEST GLOUCESTERSHIRE COUNTY CONSTITUENCY[7]
East Dean RD, West Dean RD, pt Gloucester RD (Ashleworth, Chaceley, Churchdown, Forthampton, Hasfield, Down Hatherley, Highnam, Longford, Longlevens, Maisemore, Minsterworth, Newnham, Norton, Sandhurst, Tirley, Twigworth, Westbury-on-Severn), Lydney RD, Newent RD

STROUD COUNTY CONSTITUENCY[8] (1955–70)
Dursley RD, pt Gloucester RD (the pars prev in Stroud and Thornbury CC 1948–55), Nailsworth UD, Stroud RD, Stroud UD, Tetbury RD

STROUD AND THORNBURY COUNTY CONSTITUENCY[7] (1948–55)
Dursley RD, pt Gloucester RD (Arlingham, Brookthorpe, Eastington, Elmore, Frampton on Severn, Fretherne with Saul, Frocester, Hardwicke, Harescombe, Haresfield, Longney, Moreton Valence, Quedgeley, Standish, Upton St Leonards, Whitminster), Nailsworth UD, Stroud RD, Stroud UD, Thornbury RD

*1970–**

CIRENCESTER AND TEWKESBURY COUNTY CONSTITUENCY
Cheltenham RD, Cirencester RD, Cirencester UD, North Cotswold RD, Northleach RD, Tewkesbury MB

SOUTH GLOUCESTERSHIRE COUNTY CONSTITUENCY
Sodbury RD, Thornbury RD

WEST GLOUCESTERSHIRE COUNTY CONSTITUENCY
East Dean RD, West Dean RD, pt Gloucester RD (Ashleworth, Brockworth, Chaceley, Churchdown, Forthampton, Hasfield, Down Hatherley, Highnam, Hucclecote, Innsworth, Longford, Maisemore, Minsterworth, Newnham, Norton, Sandhurst, Tirley, Twigworth, Westbury-on-Severn), Lydney RD, Newent RD

KINGSWOOD COUNTY CONSTITUENCY
Kingswood UD, Mangotsfield UD, Warmley RD

STROUD COUNTY CONSTITUENCY
Dursley RD, pt Gloucester RD (the pars not in West Gloucestershire CC), Nailsworth UD, Stroud RD, Stroud UD, Tetbury RD

HAMPSHIRE

BOROUGH CONSTITUENCIES[1]

NEW ALRESFORD (1295, 1300–01, 1306, 1306–07)
New Alresford
ALTON (1295 only)
Alton
ANDOVER (1295, 1302–07, 1586–1885 [1 mbr, 1867–85])
Andover, Knights Enham (1832–85), Foxcott (1832–85)
BASINGSTOKE (1295, 1302, 1306)
Basingstoke
BOURNEMOUTH (1918–48)
Bournemouth
BOURNEMOUTH EAST (1970–*)
pt Bournemouth CB (the wards of Boscombe East, Boscombe West, King's Park, Moordown North, Moordown South, Queen's Park, Southbourne, West Southbourne)
BOURNEMOUTH EAST AND CHRISTCHURCH[2] (1948–70)
pt Bournemouth CB (the wards of Boscombe East, Boscombe West, King's Park, Queen's Park, Southbourne, West Southbourne), Christchurch MB
BOURNEMOUTH WEST (1948–*)
pt Bournemouth CB (the wards of Central, East Cliff, West Cliff, Kinson [1948–70], Kinson North [1970–*], Kinson South [1970–*], Moordown North [1948–70], Moordown South [1948–70], Redhill Park, Westbourne, Winton)
CHRISTCHURCH (1571–1918 [1 mbr, 1832–1918])
pt Christchurch (extended pt 1832–1918), Holdenhurst (1832–1918)
CHRISTCHURCH AND LYMINGTON[3] (1970–*)
Christchurch MB, Lymington MB
FAREHAM (1306 only)
Fareham
FAREHAM (1970–*)
Fareham UD
GOSPORT (1970–*)
Gosport MB
GOSPORT AND FAREHAM (1948–70)
Fareham UD, Gosport MB
HAVANT AND WATERLOO (1970–*)
Havant and Waterloo UD
LYMINGTON (1584–1885 [1 mbr, 1867–85])
pt Boldre (1832–85), Lymington (pt 1584–1832, ent 1832–85)
NEWPORT (IoW, 1295 jointly with Yarmouth, 1584–1885 alone [1 mbr, 1867–85])
pt Carisbrooke (extended pt 1867–85), Newport, pt Northwood (1584–1867), pt St Nicholas, pt Whippingham (extended pt 1867–85)
NEWTOWN (1584–1832)
pt Burghclere (until Newtown gains sep civ identity), Newtown (thereafter)
PETERSFIELD (1306–07, 1553–1885 [1 mbr, 1832–85])
Buriton (1832–85), Froxfield (1832–85), Liss (1832–85), pt East Meon (1832–85), Petersfield, Steep (pt 1832–67, ent 1867–85)
PORTSMOUTH (1295–1918)
Portsea (1832–1918), Portsmouth
PORTSMOUTH CENTRAL (1918–48)
pt Portsmouth CB (the wards of Buckland, Fratton, Kingston, St Mary, Town Hall)
PORTSMOUTH LANGSTONE[4] (1948–70)
Havant and Waterloo UD, pt Portsmouth CB (the wards of Cosham, Farlington [1955–70], Meredith, Paulsgrove [1955–70])
PORTSMOUTH NORTH (1918–48)
pt Portsmouth CB (the wards of Charles Dickens, Mile End, North End, Portsea)
PORTSMOUTH NORTH (1970–*)
pt Portsmouth CB (the wards of Cosham, Farlington, Meredith, Nelson, North End, Paulsgrove, Portsea, St Mary and Guildhall)
PORTSMOUTH SOUTH[4] (1918–*)
pt Portsmouth CB (the wards of Buckland [1970–*], Fratton [1970–*], Havelock, Highland, Kingston [1948–*], St Jude [1955–*, incl for 1970–* Spitbank Fort and Horse Sand Fort], St Paul [1918–55], St Simon, St Thomas)
PORTSMOUTH WEST[4] (1948–70)
pt Portsmouth CB (the wards of Buckland, Charles Dickens [1948–55], Fratton, Guildhall [1948–55], Nelson, North End, Portsea, St Mary [1948–55], St Mary and Guildhall [1955–70])
SOUTHAMPTON (1295–1948)
Bitterne (1918–48), Itchen UD (1918–48), Southampton (1918–48), Southampton All Saints (1295–1918), Southampton Holy Rood (1295–1918), Southampton St John (1295–1918), Southampton St Lawrence (1295–1918), Southampton St Mary (1295–1918), Southampton St Michael (1295–1918), pt South Stoneham (Portswood, 1295–1918)
SOUTHAMPTON ITCHEN[4] (1948–*)
pt Southamton CB (the wards of Bevois [1948–55], Bitterne [1955–*], Bitterne and Peartree [1948–55], Bitterne and Sholing [1948–55], Harefield [1955–*], Newtown [1948–55], Northam [1948–55], Peartree and Bitterne Manor [1955–*], Portswood [1948–55], St Denys [1948–55], St Denys and Bitterne Park [1955–*], St Luke's [1955–*], St Mary's, Sholing [1955–*], Sway-

thling [1955–*], Trinity [1948–55], Woolston)
SOUTHAMPTON TEST[4] (1948–*)
Millbrook (1948–55), pt Southampton CB (the wards of All Saints [1948–55], Banister, Bargate [1955–*], Bassett [1955–*], Coxford [1955–*], Freemantle, Millbrook, Portswood [1955–*], Redbridge [1955–*], St Nicholas [1948–55], Shirley, Town [1948–55])
STOCKBRIDGE (1563–1832)
Stockbridge
WHITCHURCH (1586–1832)
Whitchurch
WINCHESTER[5] (1295–1918 [1 mbr, 1885–1918])
pt Chilcombe (1832–1918), Milland (1832–1918), pt St Faith, pt Winchester St Bartholomew Hyde, pt Winchester St John, Winchester St Lawrence, Winchester St Mary Kalendar, Winchester St Maurice, Winchester St Michael, pt Winchester St Peter Cheesehill, Winchester St Peter Colebrook, Winchester St Swithun, Winchester St Thomas, pt Weeke, pt Winnall (1832–1918)
YARMOUTH (1295 jointly with Newport, Yarmouth alone 1584–1832)
Yarmouth

COUNTY CONSTITUENCIES

1832–1867
NORTHERN DIVISION
Bentley Lbty and the Hds of Alton, Andover, Barton Stacey, Basingstoke, Bermondspit, Bountisborough, Buddlesgate, Chuteley, Crondall, Evingar, Fawley, Finchdean, Hambledon, Holdshot, Kingsclere, Mainsborough, East Meon, Meonstoke, Micheldever, Odiham, Overton, Pastrow, Selborne, Bishop's Sutton, pt Thorngate (the pars of Leckford, Longstock, Stockbridge, Nether Wallop, Over Wallop), Bishop's Waltham, Wherwell
SOUTHERN DIVISION
Liberties of Alverstoke, Beaulieu, Breamore, Dibden, Havant, Portsmouth and Portsea Island, Westover, and the Hds of Bosmere, Christchurch, Fareham, Fordingbridge, New Forest, Mainsbridge, Portsdown, Redbridge, Ringwood, King's Somborne, pt Thorngate (the pars not in N'rn Dv), Titchfield
ISLE OF WIGHT DIVISION
The Hds/Liberties of East Medina, West Medina

1885–1918
EASTERN OR PETERSFIELD DIVISION
Alton PSD, Droxford PSD, Petersfield PSD, pt Winchester PSD, *viz.*, New Alresford, Old Alresford, Alton, Beauworth, Bentley, Bentworth, Bighton, Binsted, Blendworth, Bramdean, Bramshott, Buriton, Brown Candover, Chilton Candover, Catherington, Chalton, Chawton, Cheriton, Clanfield, Coldrey, Colemore, Corhampton, Priors Dean, Dockenfield, Droxford, Durley, Empshott, Exton, Faringdon, Froxfield, Froyle, Godsfield, Greatham, Hambledon, Hartley Mauditt, Hawkley, Headley, Hinton Ampner, Holybourne, Idsworth, Itchen Stoke, Kilmiston, Kingsley, Lasham, Liss, Medstead, East Meon, West Meon, Meonstoke, Neatham, Newton Valence, Northington, Ovington, Petersfield, Privett, Ropley, Selborne, Shalden, Sheet, Soberton, Steep, Bishops Sutton, Swarraton, Tichborne, East Tisted, West Tisted, Upham, Bishops Waltham, Warnford, Wield, East Worldham, West Worldham
NEW FOREST DIVISION
Lymington PSD, Ringwood PSD, Romsey MB, pt Romsey PSD, pt Southampton PSD, *viz.*, Ashley Walk, North Baddesley, Beaulieu, Boldre, Bramshaw, Breamore, Brockenhurst, Broomy, Burley, North Charford, South Charford, Chilworth, Christchurch, East Dean, Denny Lodge, Dibden, Dunwood, Eling, Ellingham, Exbury, Fawley, Fordingbridge, Hale, Harbridge, Holdenhurst, Hordle, Ibsley, Lockerley, Lymington, Lyndhurst, Michelmersh, Milford, Milton, Minstead, Mottisfont, Nursling, Rhinefield, Ringwood, Rockbourne, Romsey Extra, Romsey Infra, Sherfield English, Sopley, North Stoneham, Sway, Timsbury, East Wellow, Woodgreen
NORTHERN OR BASINGSTOKE DIVISION
Basingstone MB, Basingstoke PSD, Odiham PSD, *viz.*, Aldershot, Andwell, Basing, Basingstoke, Bradley, Bramley, Bramshill, Preston Candover, Cliddesden, Cove, Crondall, Deane, Dogmersfield, Dummer, Eastrop, Ellisfield, Elvetham, Eversley, Farleigh Wallop, Farnborough, Greywell, Hartley Westpall, Hartley Wintney, Hawley with Minley, Heckfield, Herriard, Mapledurwell, Mattingly, Mortimer West End, Up Nately, Nately Scures, Newnham, Nutley, Oakley, Odiham, Pamber, Popham, Rotherwick, Monk Sherborne, Sherborne St John, Sherfield-on-Loddon, Silchester, Stratfield Saye, Stratfield Turgis, Long Sutton, Tunworth, Upton Grey, North Waltham, South Warnborough, Weston Corbett, Weston Patrick, Winchfield, Winslade, Woodmancott, Wootton St Lawrence, Worting, Yateley
SOUTHERN OR FAREHAM DIVISION
Fareham PSD, pt Southampton PSD, *viz.*, Alverstoke, Bedhampton, Boarhunt, Botley, Bursledon, Fareham, Farlington, Hamble le Rice, Havant, North Hayling, South Hayling, Hound, Millbrook, Portchester, Rowner, St Mary Extra, Great Salterns, Southwick, pt South Stoneham, Titchfield, Warblington, Waterloo, Wickham, Widley, Wymering
WESTERN DIVISION
Andover MB, Andover PSD, Kingsclere PSD, pt Romsey PSD, pt Winchester PSD, *viz.*, Abbots Ann, Amport, Andover, Appleshaw, Ashe, Ashley, Ashmansworth, Avington, Barton Stacey, Baughurst, Bishopstoke, Bossington, Broughton, Buckholt, Bullington, Burghclere, Chilbolton, pt Chilcomb, Goodworth Clatford, Upper Clatford, Combe, Compton, Crawley, Crown Farm, Crux Easton, Vernhams Dean, Easton, Ecchinswell, Upper Eldon, Knights Enham, Ewhurst, Faccombe, Farley Cham-

berlayne, Foxcott, Freefolk Manor, Frenchmoor, Fyfield, Grately, Hannington, Highclere, Houghton, Hunton, Hursley, Hurstbourne Priors, Hurstbourne Tarrant, Itchen Abbas, Kimpton, Kingsclere, Lainston, Laverstoke, Leckford, Linkenholt, Litchfield, Littleton, Longparish, Longstock, Micheldever, Monxton, Morestead, Newtown, Otterbourne, Overton, Owslebury, Penton Grafton, Penton Mewsey, Quarley, pt St Faith, St Mary Bourne, Shipton Bellinger, Kings Somborne, Little Somborne, Sparsholt, Steventon, Stockbridge, Stoke Charity, East Stratton, Sydmonton, Tadley, Tangley, South Tedworth, Thruxton, Tufton, Twyford, East Tytherley, West Tytherley, Nether Wallop, Over Wallop, pt Weeke, Wherwell, Whitchurch, pt Winchester St Bartholomew Hyde, pt Winchester St John, pt Winchester St Peter Cheesehill, pt Winnall, Wolverton, Wonston, Woodcott, East Woodhay, Headbourne Worthy, Kings Worthy, Martyr Worthy

ISLE OF WIGHT DIVISION

Arreton, Binsted, Bonchurch, Brading, Brixton, Brook, Calbourne, Carisbrooke, Chale, Freshwater, Gatcombe, Godshill, Kingston, Mottistone, Newchurch, Newport, Niton, Northwood, Ryde, St Helens, St Lawrence, St Nicholas, Shalfleet, Shanklin, Shorwell, Thorley, Ventnor, Whippingham, Whitwell, Wootton, Yarmouth, Yaverland

hams), pt Winchester RD (Botley, Bursldeon, Hamble le Rice, Hedge End, Hound, West End)

NEW FOREST COUNTY CONSTITUENCY[6]

Lymington MB, New Forest RD (ent 1948–55, pt 1955–70 [all except Eling, Netley Marsh]), Ringwood and Fordingbridge RD

PETERSFIELD COUNTY CONSTITUENCY

Alton RD, Alton UD, Petersfield RD, Petersfield UD, pt Winchester RD (1948–55, Botley, Bursledon, Hamble le Rice, Hedge End, Hound, West End)

WINCHESTER COUNTY CONSTITUENCY[4]

Eastleigh MB (1948–55), Romsey MB, pt Romsey and Stockbridge RD (1948–55, Ampfield, North Baddesley, Chilworth, East Dean, Lockerley, Melchet Park and Plaitford, Michelmersh, Mottisfont, Nursling and Rownhams, Romsey Extra, Sherfield England, Wellow; 1955–70, all except the pars in Eastleigh CC), Winchester RD (1948–55, entire; 1955–70, all except the pars in Eastleigh CC)

*1970–**

ALDERSHOT COUNTY CONSTITUENCY

Aldershot MB, Farnborough UD, Fleet UD, pt Hartley Wintney RD (Crondall, Crookham Village, Hawley, Yateley)

BASINGSTOKE COUNTY CONSTITUENCY

Basingstoke MB, Basingstoke RD, pt Hartley Wintney RD (the pars not in Aldershot CC), Kingsclere and Whitchurch RD

EASTLEIGH COUNTY CONSTITUENCY

Eastleigh MB, Romsey MB, pt Romsey and Stockbridge RD (Ampfield, North Baddesley, Braishfield, Chilworth, Melchet Park and Plaitford, Michelmersh, Nursling and Rownhams, Romsey Extra, Sherfield English, Wellow), pt Winchester RD (Botley, Bursledon, Hamble le Rice, Hedge End, Hound, West End)

NEW FOREST COUNTY CONSTITUENCY[3]

New Forest RD, Ringwood and Fordingbridge RD

PETERSFIELD COUNTY CONSTITUENCY

Alton RD, Alton UD, Droxford RD, Petersfield RD, Petersfield UD

WINCHESTER COUNTY CONSTITUENCY

Andover MB, Andover RD, pt Romsey and Stockbridge RD (the pars not in Eastleigh CC), pt Winchester RD (the pars not in Eastleigh CC)

1918–1948

ALDERSHOT DIVISION

Aldershot UD, Farnborough UD, Fleet UD, Hartley Wintney RD

BASINGSTOKE DIVISION

Andover MB, Andover RD, Basingstoke MB, Basingstoke RD, Kingsclere RD, Stockbridge RD, Whitchurch RD

FAREHAM DIVISION

Fareham RD, Fareham UD, Gosport and Alverstoke UD, Havant RD, Havant UD, Warblington UD

NEW FOREST AND CHRISTCHURCH DIVISION

Christchurch MB, Christchurch RD, Fordingbridge RD, New Forest RD, Lymington MB, Lymington RD, Ringwood RD, Romsey MB, Romsey RD

PETERSFIELD DIVISION

Alresford RD, Alton RD, Alton UD, Catherington RD, Droxford RD, Petersfield RD, Petersfield UD

WINCHESTER DIVISION

Eastleigh and Bishopstoke UD, Hursley RD, pt South Stoneham RD (all except Bitterne), Winchester MB, Winchester RD

1948–1970

ALDERSHOT COUNTY CONSTITUENCY

Aldershot MB, Farnborough UD, Fleet UD, Hartley Wintney RD

BASINGSTOKE COUNTY CONSTITUENCY[4]

Andover MB, Andover RD, Basingstoke MB, Basingstoke RD, Kingsclere and Whitchurch RD, pt Romsey and Stockbridge RD (1948–55, Ashley, Bossington, Broughton, Buckholt, Frenchmoor, Houghton, Leckford, Longstock, Kings Somborne, Little Somborne, Stockbridge, East Tytherley, West Tytherley, Nether Wallop, Over Wallop)

EASTLEIGH COUNTY CONSTITUENCY (1955[4]–70)

Eastleigh MB, pt New Forest RD (Eling, Netley Marsh), pt Romsey and Stockbridge RD (Ampfield, North Baddesley, Chilworth, Nursling and Rown-

HERTFORDSHIRE

BOROUGH CONSTITUENCIES

HERTFORD (1298–1376 irregularly, 1624–1885 [1 mbr, 1867–85])
pt Little Amwell (1866–85), pt Bengeo (1867–85), pt Brickendon(1866–85), Hertford All Saints (pt until 1866, ent 1866–85), pt Hertford St Andrew, pt Hertford St John

ST ALBANS (1300-36, 1553–1852[1])
St Albans, pt St Albans St Michael, pt St Albans St Peter, pt St Stephen (1832–52)

BISHOP'S STORTFORD (1311–41)
Bishop's Stortford

WATFORD (1948–*)
Watford

COUNTY CONSTITUENCIES

Herts was undivided for parl purposes until 1885.

1885–1918

EASTERN OR HERTFORD DIVISION
pt Albury PSD, Cheshunt PSD, pt Hertford PSD, Hertford MB, Bishop's Stortford PSD, pt Ware PSD, *viz.*, Great Amwell, Little Amwell, Bayford, Bengeo, Little Berkhampstead, Bramfield, Brickendon, Broxbourne, Cheshunt, Eastwick, Gilston, Little Hadham, Much Hadham, Hertford All Saints, Hertford St Andrew, Hertford St John, Hertingfordbury, Hoddesdon, Hunsdon, Northaw, Sawbridgeworth, Stapleford, Bishop's Stortford, Standon, Stanstead Abbots, Stanstead St Margaret, Tewin, Thorley, Thundridge, Ware, Widford, Wormley

MID OR ST ALBANS DIVISION
Barnet PSD, pt Dacorum PSD, St Albans PSD, St Albans MB, pt Watford PSD, *viz.*, Aldenham, Chipping Barnet, East Barnet, pt Caddington, Elstree, Essendon, Flamstead, Great Gaddesden, Little Gaddesden, Harpenden, Bishop's Hatfield, Kensworth, North Mimms, pt South Mimms, Redbourn, Ridge, St Albans, St Albans St Michael, St Albans St Peter, St Stephen, Sandridge, Shenley, pt Studham, Totteridge, Wheathampstead, pt Whipsnade

NORTHERN OR HITCHIN DIVISION
pt Albury PSD, Buntingford PSD, Hitchin PSD, Odsey PSD, Stevenage PSD, pt Ware PSD, Welwyn PSD, *viz.*, Albury, Anstey, Ardeley, Ashwell, Aspenden, Aston, Ayot St Lawrence, Ayot St Peter, Baldock, Barkway, Barley, Bennington, Braughing, Broadfield, Buckland, Bygrave, Caldecote, Clothall, Codicote, Cottered, Datchworth, Digswell, Graveley, Hexton, Hinxworth, Hitchin, Great Hormead, Little Hormead, Ickleford, Ippolyts, Kelshall, Kimpton, Knebworth, Layston, Letchworth, Lilley, Meesden, Great Munden, Little Munden, Newnham, Norton, Nuthampstead, Offley, Brent Pelham, Furneux Pelham, Stocking Pelham, Pirton,. Radwell, Reed, Royston, Rushden, Sacombe, Sandon, Shephall, pt Shillington, Stevenage, Therfield, Throcking, King's Walden, St Paul's Walden, Walkern, Wallington, Watton at Stone, Welwyn, Westmill, Weston, Willian, Wyddial, Great Wymondley, Little Wymondley

WESTERN OR WATFORD DIVISION
pt Dacorum PSD, pt Watford PSD, *viz.*, Aldbury, Berkhampstead, Bovingdon, Bushey, Flaunden, Hemel Hempstead, Abbots Langley, King's Langley, Northchurch, Pottenham, Rickmansworth, Sarratt, Tring, Watford, Wiggington

1918–1948

BARNET DIVISION (1945–48)
Barnet UD, East Barnet UD, Elstree RD

HEMEL HEMPSTEAD DIVISION[2]
Berkhampstead RD, Great Berkhampstead UD, Harpenden UD, Hemel Hempstead MB, Hemel Hempstead RD, pt St Albans RD (Harpenden Rural, Redbourn, Wheathampstead), Tring UD, pt Watford RD (Abbots Langley, Sarratt)

HERTFORD DIVISION[3]
Cheshunt UD, Hadham RD, Hertford MB, pt Hertford RD (the pars not in Hitchin Dv), Hoddesdon UD, Sawbridgeworth UD, Bishop's Stortford UD, Ware RD, Ware UD

HITCHIN DIVISION[4]
Ashwell RD, Baldock UD, Buntingford RD, pt Hertford RD (Aston, Bennington, Datchworth, Sacombe, Walkern, Watton at Stone), Hitchin RD, Hitchin UD, Royston UD, Stevenage UD, Welwyn RD

ST ALBANS DIVISION
Barnet RD (1918–45), Barnet UD (1918–45), East Barnet Valley UD (1918–45), pt St Albans RD (1918–45: the pars not in Hemel Hempstead Dv; 1945–48: the pars of St Michael Rural, St Peter Rural, St Stephen, Sandridge Rural), Welwyn Garden City UD (1945–48)

WATFORD DIVISION
Bushey UD, Chorleywood UD, Rickmansworth UD, pt Watford RD (the pars not in Hemel Hemp-

stead Dv), Watford UD

1948–1970[5]

BARNET COUNTY CONSTITUENCY

Barnet UD, East Barnet UD, Elstree RD, Hatfield RD (1948–55)

HEMEL HEMPSTEAD COUNTY CONSTITUENCY

Berkhamsted RD, Berkhamsted UD, Harpenden UD, Hemel Hempstead MB, Hemel Hempstead RD, pt St Albans RD (Harpenden Rural, Redbourn)

HERTFORD COUNTY CONSTITUENCY

pt Braughing RD (1948–55, the pars not in Hitchin CC), Cheshunt UD (1948–55), Hatfield RD (1955–70), Hertford MB, Hertford RD (pt 1948–55 [the pars not in Hitchin CC], ent 1955–70), Hoddesdon UD (1948–55), Sawbridgeworth UD (1948–55), Bishop's Stortford UD (1948–55), Ware RD (1948–55), Ware UD (1948–55), Welwyn RD (1955–70), Welwyn Garden City UD (1955–70)

EAST HERTFORDSHIRE COUNTY CONSTITUENCY (1955–70)

Braughing RD, Cheshunt UD, Hoddesdon UD, Sawbridgeworth UD, Bishop's Stortford UD, Ware RD, Ware UD

SOUTH WEST HERTFORDSHIRE COUNTY CONSTITUENCY

Bushey UD, Chorleywood UD, Rickmansworth UD, Watford RD

HITCHIN COUNTY CONSTITUENCY

Baldock UD, pt Braughing RD (1948–55, Anstey, Ardeley, Aspenden, Broadfield, Buckland, Buntingford, Cottered, Meesden, Throcking, Westmill, Wyddial), pt Hertford RD (1948–55, Aston, Bennington, Datchworth, Sacombe, Walkern, Watton at Stone), Hitchin RD, Hitchin UD, Letchworth UD, Royston UD, Stevenage UD

ST ALBANS COUNTY CONSTITUENCY

St Albans MB, pt St Albans RD (London Colney, Colney Heath, St Michael Rural, St Stephen, Sandridge Rural, Wheathampstead), Welwyn RD (1948–55), Welwyn Garden City UD (1948–55)

*1970–**

HEMEL HEMPSTEAD COUNTY CONSTITUENCY

Berkhamsted RD, Berkhamsted UD, Hemel Hempstead MB, Hemel Hempstead RD, Tring UD

HERTFORD AND STEVENAGE COUNTY CONSTITUENCY

Hertford MB, Hertford RD, Stevenage UD, Ware UD

EAST HERTFORDSHIRE COUNTY CONSTITUENCY

Braughing RD, Cheshunt UD, Hoddesdon UD, Sawbridgeworth UD, Bishop's Stortford UD, Ware RD

SOUTH HERTFORDSHIRE COUNTY CONSTITUENCY

Elstree RD, Potters Bar UD, pt St Albans RD (London Colney, Colney Heath, St Stephen), pt Watford RD (Aldenham)

SOUTH WEST HERTFORDSHIRE COUNTY CONSTITUENCY

Bushey UD, Chorleywood UD, Rickmansworth UD, pt Watford RD (Abbots Langley, Sarratt, Watford Rural)

HITCHIN COUNTY CONSTITUENCY

Baldock UD, Hitchin RD, Hitchin UD, Letchworth UD, Royston UD

ST ALBANS COUNTY CONSTITUENCY

Harpenden UD, St Albans MB, pt St Albans RD (Harpenden Rural, Redbourn, St Michael Rural, Sandridge, Wheathampstead)

WELWYN AND HATFIELD COUNTY CONSTITUENCY

Hatfield RD, Welwyn RD, Welwyn Garden City UD

HUNTINGDONSHIRE

BOROUGH CONSTITUENCY[1]

HUNTINGDON (1295–1885 [1 member 1867–85]) Godmanchester (1832–85), Huntingdon All Saints, Huntingdon St Benedict, Huntingdon St John, Huntingdon St Mary

COUNTY CONSTITUENCIES

Hunts was undivided for par purposes until 1885. From 1918–70 the Adm Co was an undivided parl county, and from 1970–* it was a single county constituency in Hunts & Peterb Parl County.

1885–1918

NORTHERN OR RAMSEY DIVISION
Hurstingstone PSD, Norman Cross PSD, Ramsey PSD, *viz.*, Alwalton, Bluntisham cum Earith, Broughton, Bury, Caldecote, Chesterton, Colne, Conington, Denton, Elton, Farcet, Fenstanton, Fletton, Folksworth, Glatton, Haddon, Hemingford Abbots, Hemingford Grey, Hilton, Holme, Holywell cum Needingworth, Houghton, Old Hurst, pt Luddington in the Brook, pt Lutton, Morborne, Orton Longueville, Orton Waterville, pt Papworth St Agnes, Pidley cum Fenton, Ramsey, Great Raveley, Little Raveley, Abbots Ripton, Kings Ripton, St Ives, Sawtry All Saints, Sawtry St Andrew, Sawtry St Judith, Sibson cum Stibbington, Somersham, pt Stanground, Stilton, pt Thurning, Upwood, Wood Walton, Warboys, Washingley, Water Newton, pt Winwick, Wistow, Woodhurst, Woodston, Wyton, Yaxley

SOUTHERN OR HUNTINGDON DIVISION
Leightonstone PSD, Toseland PSD, *viz.*, Abbotsley, Alconbury, Alconbury Weston, Barham, Brampton, Brington, Buckden, Buckworth, Bythorn, Great Catworth, Little Catworth, Coppingford, Covington, Diddington,, Easton, Ellington, Eynesbury, Great Gidding, Little Gidding, Steeple Gidding, Godmanchester, Grafham, Great Gransden, Hamerton, Hartford, Huntingdon All Saints, Huntingdon St Benedict, Huntingdon St John, Huntingdon St Mary, Keyston, Kimbolton, Leighton, Midloe, Molesworth, Offord Cluny, Offord D'Arcy, Great Paxton, Little Paxton, St Neots, Southoe, Spaldwick, Great Staughton, Stow, Great Stukeley, Little Stukeley, Swineshead, Tetworth, Toseland, Upton, Waresley, Hail Weston, Old Weston, Woolley, Yelling

KENT

BOROUGH CONSTITUENCIES[1]

Entirely in Kent:

BECKENHAM (1948–70)
Beckenham MB, Penge UD

BEXLEY (1945–70)
Bexley MB

BROMLEY (1918–70)
Beckenham UD (1918–48), Bromley MB, Penge UD (1918–70)

CANTERBURY[2] (1295–1918 [1 mbr, 1885–1918])
pt Bekesbourne (1867–1918), Canterbury All Saints, Canterbury The Archbishop's Palace Precincts (1832–1918), Canterbury Black Prince's Chantry (1832–1918), Canterbury Christchurch (1832–1918), Canterbury East Bridge Hospital (1832–1918), Canterbury Old Castle (1832–1918), pt Canterbury Holy Cross Westgate, Canterbury St Alphege, Canterbury St Andrew, Canterbury St Augustine (1832–1918), Canterbury St George the Martyr, Canterbury St Gregory the Great (1832–1918), Canterbury St John's Hospital (1832–1918), Canterbury St Margaret, Canterbury St Martin, Canterbury St Mary Bredin, Canterbury St Mary Bredman, Canterbury St Mary Magdalen, Canterbury St Mary North Gate, Canterbury St Mildred, Canterbury St Paul, Canterbury St Peter, Canterbury White Frairs (1832–1918), pt Fordwich, pt Hackington, pt Littlebourne, pt Nackington, pt Patrixbourne, pt St Dunstan, Staplegate (1867–1918), pt Thanington

CHATHAM[3] (1832–1918)
pt Chatham, pt Gillingham

DARTFORD (1945–55[4])
Crayford UD, Dartford MB, Erith MB

DOVER (1558–1918 [1 mbr, 1885–1918])
pt Buckland, pt Charlton, East Cliffe (1832–1918), Dover Castle (1814–1918), Dover St James the Apostle, Dover St Mary the Virgin, pt Guston, pt Hougham

ERITH AND CHATHAM (1955[4]–70)
Crayford UD, Erith MB

GILLINGHAM (1948–*)
Gillingham MB

GRAVESEND (1867–1918)
Gravesend, Milton, pt Northfleet

HYTHE (1558–1948 [1 mbr, 1832–1948])
until 1918: pt Aldington, Cheriton (1832–1918), Folkestone (1832–1918), St Leonard Hythe, West Hythe (pt 1558–1832, ent 1832–1918), pt Newington (1832–1918), Saltwood (1832–1918); after 1918: Cheriton UD, Folkestone MB, Hythe MB, the pt of Sandgate UD not in Folkestone MB

MAIDSTONE (1553, 1572–1918 [1 mbr, 1885–1918])
Maidstone

QUEENBOROUGH (1572–1832)
Queenborough

ROCHESTER (1295–1918 [1 mbr, 1885–1918])
pt Chatham, pt Frindsbury (1832–1918), Rochester Castle Precincts (1832–1918), pt Rochester St Margaret, pt Strood (1832–1918), pt Wouldham (1885–1918)

ROCHESTER AND CHATHAM[5] (1948–*)
Chatham MB, Rochester MB

ROCHESTER, CHATHAM (1918–48)
pt Chatham MB (the wards of Luton, St John), pt Rochester MB (pt of the ward of St Peter's)

ROCHESTER, GILLINGHAM (1918–48)
pt Chatham MB (the ward of St Mary), pt Rochester MB (all except pt of the ward of St Peter's)

NEW ROMNEY (1558–1832)
pt New Romney

SANDWICH (1369–1885[6])
Deal (1832–85), Sandwich St Bartholomew's Hospital, Sandwich St Clement, Sandwich St Mary, Sandwich St Peter, Walmer (1832–85)

THANET EAST (1970–*)
Broadstairs and St Peter's UD, Ramsgate MB

THANET WEST (1970–*)
pt Eastry RD (the pars of Acol, Minster, Monkton, St Nicholas at Wade, Sarre), Margate MB

TONBRIDGE (1295 only)
Tonbridge

Kent Parl Bors in Metropolis civ 1855–89, in London Adm Co from 1889, in London Parl Co from 1918:

DEPTFORD[7] (1885–1918)
Deptford St Paul

GREENWICH (1832–1918 [1 mbr, 1885–1918])
Charlton next Woolwich (pt 1832–67, ent 1867–1918), Deptford St Nicholas, Deptford St Paul[7] (1832–85), Greenwich (pt 1832–85, ent 1885–1918), Kidbrooke (1885–1918), Plumstead (pt 1832–67, ent 1867–85), pt Woolwich (1832–85)

LEWISHAM (1885–1918)
Lee, Lewisham

WOOLWICH (1885–1918)
Eltham, Plumstead, Woolwich

COUNTY CONSTITUENCIES

1832–1867

EASTERN DIVISION

The Lathes of St Augustine, Shepway, the upper division of the Lathe of Scray (the Hds of Boughton under Blean, Calehill, Chart and Longbridge, Faversham, Felborough, Milton, Teynham, Wye, and Isle of Sheppey Liberty)

WESTERN DIVISION

The Lathes of Aylesford, Sutton at Hone, the lower division of the Lathe of Scray (the Hds of East Barnfield, Berkeley, Blackbourn, Cranbrook, Marden, Rolvenden, Selbrittenden, Tenterden)

1867–1885

EASTERN DIVISION

As defined for 1832–1867

MID KENT

The Lathe of Aylesford, the lower division of the Lathe of Scray (see definition in 1832–1867)

WEST KENT

The Lathe of Sutton at Hone

1885–1918

EASTERN OR ST AUGUSTINE'S DIVISION

Elham PSD, Home PSD, Wingham PSD, Deal MB, Folkestone MB, pt Romney Marsh Liberty and other pars, *viz.*, Acrise, Adisham, pt Aldington, Alkham, Ash, Barfreston, Barham, Bekesbourne, Betteshanger, Bishopsbourne, Bridge, pt Buckland, Capel-le-Ferne, pt Charlton, Chartham, pt Cheriton, Chillenden, Chislet, West Cliffe, Coldred, Deal, Denton, Eastry, Elham, Elmsted, Elmstone, Temple Ewell, Eythorne, Folkestone, pt Fordwich, Goodnestone, pt Guston, pt Hackington, Ham, Harbledown, Lower Hardres, Upper Hardres, Hawkinge, Herne, Hoath, pt Hougham, Hurst, West Hythe, Ickham and Well, Kingston, Knowlton, East Langdon, West Langdon, pt Littlebourne, Lydden, Lyminge, Lympne, Milton, Milton, Mint, Great Mongeham, Little Mongeham, Monks Horton, pt Nackington, pt Newington, Nonington, Northbourne, Oxney, Paddlesworth, pt Patrixbourne, Petham, Postling, Poulton, Preston, Reculver, Ringwould, Ripple, River, St Cosmus and St Damian in the Blean, pt St Dunstan, St Margaret's at Cliffe, St Nicholas Hospital, Saltwood, Seasalter, Sellindge, Sholden, Sibertswold, Stanford, Staple, Stelling, Stelling Minnis, Stodmarsh, Stourmouth, Stowting, Sturry, Sutton, Swalecliffe, Swingfield, pt Thanington, Tilmanstone, Waldershare, Walmer, Waltham, Westbere, Whitstable, Wickhambreux, Wingham, Womenswold, Woodnesborough, Wootton, Worth

MID OR MEDWAY DIVISION

Bearstead PSD, pt Malling PSD, pt Rochester PSD, *viz.*, Addington, Allhallows, Allington, Aylesford, East Barming, West Barming, Bearsted, Bicknor, Birling, Boughton Malherbe, Boughton Monchelsea, Boxley, Bredhurst, Broomfield, Burham, Chalk, pt Chatham, Cliffe, Cobham, Cooling, Cuxton, Denton, Detling, Ditton, East Farleigh, West Farleigh, pt Frindsbury, Frinsted, pt Gillingham, Isle of Grain, Grange, Halling, High Halstow, Harrietsham, Headcorn, Higham, Hollingbourne, Hoo, St Mary Hoo, Hucking, Ifield, Ightham, Langley, Leeds, Lenham, Leybourne, Lidsing, Linton, Loose, Luddesdown, East Malling, West Malling, Meopham, Mereworth, pt Northfleet, Nursted, Offham, Otham, Otterden, West Peckham, Ryarsh, Shorne, Snodland, Stansted, Stockbury, Stoke, pt Strood, Chart Sutton, East Sutton, Sutton Valence, Teston, Thurnham, Trottiscliffe, Ulcombe, Wateringbury, Wichling, Wormshill, Wouldham, Wrotham

NORTH-EASTERN OR FAVERSHAM DIVISION

Faversham MB, Faversham PSD, Queenborough MB, *viz.*, Badlesmere, Bapchild, Bobbing, Borden, Bredgar, Boughton under Blean, Buckland, Davington, Doddington, Dunkirk, Eastling, Elmley, Faversham, Goodnestone, Graveney, Lower Halstow, Hartlip, Harty, Hernhill, Iwade, Kingsdown, Leaveland, Leysdown, Luddenham, Lynsted, Milsted, Minster in Sheppey, Murston, Newington, Newnham, Norton, Oare, Ospringe, Preston next Faversham, Queenborough, Rainham, Rodmersham, Selling, Sheldwich, Sittingbourne, Stalisfield, Stone, Teynham, Throwley, Tonge, Tunstall, Upchurch, Warden

NORTH-WESTERN OR DARTFORD DIVISION

pt Bromley PSD, Dartford PSD, *viz.*, Ash, Beckenham, Foots Cray, North Cray, St Mary Cray, St Paul's Cray, Crayford, Darenth, Dartford, Erith, Eynsford, Farningham, Fawkham, Hartley, Horton Kirby, Kingsdown, Longfield, Lullingstone, Orpington, Ridley, Southfleet, Stone, Sutton at Hone, Swanscombe, East Wickham, Wilmington

SOUTHERN OR ASHFORD DIVISION

Ashford PSD, Crayford PSD, Lydd MB, New Romney MB, pt Romney Marsh Liberty, *viz.*, Appledore, Ashford, Benenden, Bethersden, Biddesden, Bilsington, Bircholt, Bonnington, Boughton Aluph, Brabourne, Brenzett, Brook, Brookland, pt Broomhill, Burmarsh, Challock, Charing, Great Chart, Little Chart, Chilham, Cranbrook, Crundale, Dymchurch, Eastbridge, Eastwell, Ebony, Egerton, Fairfield, Frittenden, Godmersham, Goudhurst, High Halden, Hastingleigh, pt Hawkhurst, Hinxhill, Hope All Saints, pt Horsmonden, Hothfield, Ivychurch, Kenardington, Kennington, Kingsnorth, Lydd, Marden, Mersham, Midley, Molash, Newchurch, Newenden, Orgarswick, Orlestone, Pluckley, Rolvenden, New Romney, Old Romney, Ruckinge, St Mary in the Marsh, Sandhurst, Sevington, Shadoxhurst, Smarden, Smeeth, Snargate, Snave, Staplehurst, Stone, Tenterden, Warehorne, Westwell, Willesborough, Wittersham, Woodchurch, Wye

ISLE OF THANET DIVISION

Margate MB, Ramsgate PSD, Sandwich MB, and other pars, *viz.*, Acol, Birchington, Margate St John the Baptist, Minster, Monkton, Ramsgate, St Lawrence, St Nicholas at Wade, St Peters, Sandwich St Bartholomew's Hospital, Sandwich St Clement, Sandwich St Mary, Sandwich St Peter, Sarre,

Stonar

SOUTH-WESTERN OR TONBRIDGE DIVISION
pt Malling PSD, Tonbridge PSD, Tunbridge Wells PSD, *viz.*, Ashurst, Bidborough, Brenchley, Capel, Chiddingstone, Cowden, Edenbridge, pt Frant, Hadlow, Hever, Hunton, pt Lamberhurst, Leigh, Nettlestead, East Peckham, Pembury, Penshurst, Shipbourne, Speldhurst, Tonbridge, Tudeley, Whitfield, Yalding

WESTERN OR SEVENOAKS DIVISION
pt Bromley PSD, Sevenoaks PSD, the par of Mottingham, *viz.*, Bexley, Brasted, Bromley, Chelsfield, Chevening, Chislehurst, Cudham, Downe, Farnborough, Halstead, Hayes, Kemsing, Keston, Knockholt, Mottingham, Otford, Seal, Sevenoaks, Shoreham, Sundridge, Westerham, West Wickham

1918–1948

ASHFORD DIVISION
Ashford UD, East Ashford RD, West Ashford RD, Cranbrook RD, Lydd MB, New Romney MB, Romney Marsh RD, Tenterden MB, Tenterden RD

CANTERBURY DIVISION
Blean RD, Bridge RD, Canterbury CB, Eltham RD, pt Faversham RD (detached pts of Dunkirk, Hernhill), Herne Bay UD, Whitstable UD

CHISLEHURST DIVISION
Bromley RD (1918–45), Chislehurst UD (1918–45), Chislehurst and Sidcup UD (1945–48), Foots Cray UD (1918–45), Dartford RD (pt 1918–45, ent 1945–48), Swanscombe UD (1945–48)

DARTFORD DIVISION (1918–45)
Bexley UD, pt Dartford RD (Crayford, Stone, Swanscombe), Dartford UD, Erith UD

DOVER DIVISION
Deal MB, Dover MB, Dover RD, Eastry RD, Walmer UD

FAVERSHAM DIVISION
Faversham MB, pt Faversham RD (all except the detached pts of pars in Canterbury Dv), Milton RD, Milton Regis UD, Queenborough MB, Sheerness UD, Sheppey RD, Sittingbourne UD

GRAVESEND DIVISION
Gravesend MB, Hoo RD, Northfleet UD, Strood RD

MAIDSTONE DIVISION
Hollingbourne RD, Maidstone MB, Maidstone RD

ORPINGTON DIVISION (1945–48)
Beckenham MB, Bromley MB, Orpington UD

SEVENOAKS DIVISION[8]
Malling RD, Sevenoaks RD, Sevenoaks UD, Wrotham UD

ISLE OF THANET DIVISION
Broadstairs and St Peter's UD, Margate MB, Ramsgate MB, Sandwich MB, Isle of Thanet RD

TONBRIDGE DIVISION
Southborough UD, Tonbridge RD, Tonbridge UD, Tunbridge Wells MB

1948–1970

ASHFORD COUNTY CONSTITUENCY
Ashford UD, East Ashford RD, West Ashford RD, Cranbrook RD, Tenterden MB, Tenterden RD

CANTERBURY COUNTY CONSTITUENCY
Bridge-Blean RD, Canterbury CB, Herne Bay UD, Whitstable UD

CHISLEHURST COUNTY CONSTITUENCY[9]
Chislehurst and Sidcup UD, pt Dartford RD (Darenth, Stone, Sutton at Hone, Wilmington, 1948–55 only)

DARTFORD COUNTY CONSTITUENCY (1955[9]–70)
Dartford MB, Dartford RD, Swanscombe UD

DOVER COUNTY CONSTITUENCY
Deal MB, Dover MB, Dover RD, pt Eastry RD (all except the pars in Isle of Thanet CC), Sandwich MB

FAVERSHAM COUNTY CONSTITUENCY
Faversham MB, Queenborough MB, Sheerness UD, Sheppey RD, Sittingbourne and Milton UD, Swale RD

FOLKESTONE AND HYTHE COUNTY CONSTITUENCY
Elham RD, Folkestone MB, Hythe MB, Lydd MB, New Romney MB, Romney Marsh RD

GRAVESEND COUNTY CONSTITUENCY[10]
Gravesend MB, Northfleet UD, Strood RD, Swanscombe UD (1948–55)

MAIDSTONE COUNTY CONSTITUENCY
Hollingbourne RD, Maidstone MB, Maidstone RD

ORPINGTON COUNTY CONSTITUENCY[9]
pt Dartford RD (all except the pt in Chislehurst CC, 1948–55 only), Orpington UD

SEVENOAKS COUNTY CONSTITUENCY
Malling RD, Sevenoaks RD, Sevenoaks UD

ISLE OF THANET COUNTY CONSTITUENCY
Broadstairs and St Peter's UD, pt Eastry RD (Acol, Minster, Monkton, St Nicholas at Wade, Sarre), Margate MB, Ramsgate MB

TONBRIDGE COUNTY CONSTITUENCY
Southborough UD, Tonbridge UD, Tonbridge RD, Royal Tunbridge Wells MB

*1970–**

ASHFORD COUNTY CONSTITUENCY
Ashford UD, East Ashford RD, West Ashford RD, Tenterden MB, Tenterden RD

CANTERBURY COUNTY CONSTITUENCY
As defined 1948–1970

DARTFORD COUNTY CONSTITUENCY
Dartford MB, pt Dartford RD (Darenth, Southfleet, Stone, Sutton at Hone, Wilmington), Swanscombe UD

DOVER AND DEAL COUNTY CONSTITUENCY
Deal MB, Dover MB, Dover RD, pt Eastry RD (all except pars in Isle of Thanet CC), Sandwich MB

FAVERSHAM COUNTY CONSTITUENCY
Faversham MB, Queenborough-in-Sheppey MB, Sittingbourne and Milton UD

FOLKESTONE AND HYTHE COUNTY CONSTITUENCY
As defined 1948–1970

GRAVESEND COUNTY CONSTITUENCY
Gravesend MB, Northfleet UD, Strood RD

MAIDSTONE COUNTY CONSTITUENCY
As defined 1948–1970

SEVENOAKS COUNTY CONSTITUENCY

pt Dartford RD (Ash-cum-Ridley, Eynsford, Farningham, Fawkham, Hartley, Horton Kirby, West Kingsdown, Longfield, Swanley), Sevenoaks RD,[11] Sevenoaks UD

TONBRIDGE AND MALLING COUNTY CONSTITUENCY

Malling RD, pt Tonbridge RD (Hadlow, Hildenborough), Tonbridge UD

ROYAL TUNBRIDGE WELLS COUNTY CONSTITUENCY

Cranbrook RD, Southborough UD, pt Tonbridge RD (Bidborough, Brenchley, Capel, Horsmonden, Lamberhurst, Paddock Wood, Pembury, Speldhurst), Royal Tunbridge Wells MB

LONDON

PART I: THE CITY OF LONDON

The composition of the Parl Bor was identical to that of the City; see Part II of the *Guide*. The City formed the City of London Parl Bor (1295–1948), pt of The Cities of London and Westminster BC (1948–70) and pt of The City of London and Westminster South BC (1970–*).

PART II: LONDON ADMINISTRATIVE COUNTY

Entirely in Parl Bors (1918–48) and BCs (1948–70). For the period before 1918 see Middx, Surrey and Kent; for constituencies from 1970, see Part III below, Greater London.

BARONS COURT (1955[1]–70)
pt Fulham Metrop Bor (the wards of Barons Court, Margravine, Lillie), pt Hammersmith Metrop Bor (the wards of Broadway, Brook Green, Grove, Ravenscourt)

BATTERSEA NORTH[2]
pt Battersea Metrop Bor (the wards of Church, Latchmere, Newtown [1949–70], Nine Elms, Park, Queenstown [1949–70], Vicarage [1949–70]), Winstanley [1948–70])

BATTERSEA SOUTH[2]
pt Battersea Metrop Bor (the wards of Bolingbroke, Broomwood, Lavender [1949–70], Nightingale [1949–70], St John, Shaftesbury, Stormont [1949–70], Thornton [1949–70], Winstanley [1918–48])

BERMONDSEY (1948–70)
Bermondsey Metrop Bor

BERMONDSEY, ROTHERHITHE (1918–48)
pt Bermondsey Metrop Bor (the Bermondsey wards of St John, St Olave and St Thomas, numbers Five, Six; and the Rotherhithe wards of numbers One, Two, Three)

BERMONDSEY, WEST BERMONDSEY (1918–48)
pt Bermondsey Metrop Bor (the Bermondsey wards of One, Two, Three, Four)

BETHNAL GREEN[3] (1948–70)
Bethnal Green Metrop Bor, pt Hackney Metrop Bor (the wards of Trinagle, Victoria [1955–70])

BETHNAL GREEN, NORTH EAST (1918–48)
pt Bethnal Green Metrop Bor (the wards of North, East)

BETHNAL GREEN, SOUTH WEST (1918–48)
pt Bethnal Green Metrop Bor (the wards of South, West)

CAMBERWELL, DULWICH
pt Camberwell Metrop Bor (the wards of Alleyn, College [1918–48], The College [1948–70], Hamlet [1918–48], The Hamlet [1948–70], Lyndhurst [1948–70], Nunhead [1948–70], Ruskin, The Rye [1948–70], Rye Lane [1948–70], St John's)

CAMBERWELL, NORTH (1918–48)
pt Camberwell Metrop Bor (the wards of Coburg, Marlborough, North Peckham, St George's)

CAMBERWELL, NORTH-WEST (1918–48)
pt Camberwell Metrop Bor (the wards of Adding-

ton, Lyndhurst, St Giles, Town Hall, West)

CAMBERWELL, PECKHAM
pt Camberwell Metrop Bor (Addington [1948–70], Clifton, Coburg [1948–70], Goldsmith, Marlborough [1948–70], Nunhead [1918–48], North Peckham [1948–70], The Rye [1918–48], Rye Lane [1918–48], St George's [1948–70], St Giles [] 1948–70], St Mary's, The West [1948–70], Town Hall [1948–70])

CHELSEA
Chelsea Metrop Bor, pt Kensington Metrop Bor (the ward of Brompton [1948–70])

DEPTFORD
Deptford Metrop Bor

FINSBURY (1918–48)
Finsbury Metrop Bor

FULHAM (1955[1]–70)
pt Fulham Metrop Bor (the wards of Hurlingham, Munster, Sands End, Town, Walham)

FULHAM, EAST (1918–55[1])
pt Fulham Metrop Bor (the wards of Barons Court, Lillie, Sands End, Walham)

FULHAM, WEST (1918–55[1])
pt Fulham Metrop Bor (the wards of Hurlingham, Margravine, Munster, Town)

GREENWICH
Greenwich Metrop Bor

HACKNEY, CENTRAL (1918–48)
pt Hackney Metrop Bor (the wards of Downs, Hackney, Kingsland, and pt West Hackney)

HACKNEY CENTRAL (1955[3]–70)
pt Hackney Metrop Bor (the wards of Albion, Chatham, Kenninghall, Kingsland, Kingsmead, Lenbridge, Pembury, Rushmore, Town Hall)

HACKNEY, NORTH (1918–48)
pt Hackney Metrop Bor (the ward of Stamford Hill, pts of wards of Clapton Park, West Hackney)

HACKNEY, SOUTH (1918–55[3])
for 1918–48: pt Hackney Metrop Bor (the wards of South Hackney, Homerton, pt Clapton Park)
for 1948–55: the pt of Hackney Metrop Bor not in Stoke Newington and Hackney North BC

HAMMERSMITH, NORTH[1]
for 1918–48: pt Hammersmith Metrop Bor (the wards of Four, Five, Six, Seven)
for 1948–70: pt Hammersmith[4] Metrop Bor (the wards of Addison [1955–70], College Park and Latimer, Coningham, Old Oak, Olympia [1955–70], St Stephen's [1955–70], Starch Green, White City, Wormholt)

HAMMERSMITH, SOUTH (1918–55[1])
for 1918–48: pt Hammersmith Metrop Bor (the wards of One, Two, Three)
for 1948–55: pt Hammersmith[4] Metrop Bor (the wards of Addison, Broadway, Brook Green, Grove, Olympia, Ravenscourt, St Stephen's)

HAMPSTEAD
Hampstead Metrop Bor

HOLBORN (1918–48)
Holborn Metrop Bor

HOLBORN AND ST PANCRAS SOUTH (1948–70)
Holborn Metrop Bor, pt St Pancras Metrop Bor (the wards of 5, 6, 7, 8)

ISLINGTON, EAST
pt Islington Metrop Bor (the wards of Canonbury, Highbury, Mildmay)

ISLINGTON, NORTH
pt Islington Metrop Bor (the wards of Upper Holloway, Tollington, Tufnell)

ISLINGTON, SOUTH (1918–48)
pt Islington Metrop Bor (the wards of Barnsbury, St Mary, St Peter)

ISLINGTON SOUTH WEST (1948–70)
pt Islington Metrop Bor (the wards of Barnsbury, Lower Holloway, St Mary, St Peter, Thornhill)

ISLINGTON, WEST (1918–48)
pt Islington Metrop Bor (the wards of Lower Holloway, Thornhill)

KENSINGTON, NORTH
pt Kensington Metrop Bor (the wards of Golborne, Norland, Pembridge, St Charles)

KENSINGTON, SOUTH
pt Kensington Metrop Bor (the wards of Brompton [1918–48], Earls Court, Holland, Queens Gate, Redcliffe)

LAMBETH, BRIXTON
pt Lambeth Metrop Bor (the wards of

LAMBETH, BRIXTON
pt Lambeth Metrop Bor (the wards of Angell [1948–70], Stockwell, Town Hall [1948–70], Vassal [1948–70], and pts Brixton [1918–48], Herne Hill [1918–48], Tule Hill [1918–48])

LAMBETH, KENNINGTON (1918–48)
pt Lambeth Metrop Bor (the wards of Vauxhall, pts Brixton, Prince's)

LAMBETH, NORTH (1918–48)
pt Lambeth Metrop Bor (the wards of Bishops, Marsh, pt Prince's)

LAMBETH, NORWOOD
pt Lambeth Metrop Bor (the wards of Herne Hill [pt 1918–48, ent 1948–70], Knight's Hill [1948–70], Norwood [1918–48], Tulse Hill [pt 1918–48, ent 1948–70])

LAMBETH, VAUXHALL (1948–70)
pt Lambeth Metrop Bor (the wards of Bishops, Marsh, Oval, Prince's, Vauxhall)

LEWISHAM, EAST (1918–48)
pt Lewisham Metrop Bor (the wards of Blackheath, Church, Lewisham Park, Manor, South, pts Catford, Lewisham Village)

LEWISHAM NORTH (1948–70)
pt Lewisham Metrop Bor (the wards of Blackheath and Church Lee, Ladywell, Lewisham Park, Lewisham Village, Manor Lee, South Lee)

LEWISHAM SOUTH (1948–70)
pt Lewisham Metrop Bor (the wards of Bellingham, Catford, Downham, Hither Green)

LEWISHAM, WEST
pt Lewisham Metrop Bor (the wards of Brockley, Forest Hill, Honor Oak Park [1948–70], Sydenham [1918–48], Sydenham East [1948–70], Sydenham West [1948–70], and pts Catford [1918–48], Lewisham Village [1918–48])

CITIES OF LONDON AND WESTMINSTER (1948–70)
The City of London, Inner Temple, Middle Temple,

Westminster Metrop Bor
PADDINGTON, NORTH
pt Paddington Metrop Bor (the wards of Harrow Road, Maida Vale, Queen's Park, Town [1948–70], and pt Church [1918–48])
PADDINGTON, SOUTH
pt Paddington Metrop Bor (the wards of Church [pt 1918–48, ent 1948–70], Hyde Park, Lancaster Gate East, Lancaster Gate West, Westbourne)
POPLAR (1948–70)
Poplar Metrop Bor
POPLAR, BOW AND BROMLEY (1918–48)
pt Poplar Metrop Bor (the wards of Bow Central, Bow North, Bow South, Bow West, Bromley North East, Bromley North West, Bromley South West)
POPLAR, SOUTH POPLAR (1918–48)
pt Poplar Metrop Bor (the wards of Bromley Central, Bromley South East, Poplar Cubitt Town, Poplar East, Poplar Millwall, Poplar North West, Poplar West)
ST MARYLEBONE
St Marylebone Metrop Bor
ST PANCRAS, NORTH
pt St Pancras Metrop Bor (the wards of One, Two, Three [pt 1918–48, ent 1948–70], Four [1948–70])
ST PANCRAS, SOUTH EAST (1918–48)
pt St Pancras Metrop Bor (the wards of Six, Eight, pt Three)
ST PANCRAS, SOUTH WEST (1918–48)
pt St Pancras Metrop Bor (the wards of Four, Five, Seven)
SHOREDITCH (1918–48)
Shoreditch Metrop Bor
SHOREDITCH AND FINSBURY (1948–70)
Finsbury Metrop Bor, Shoreditch Metrop Bor
SOUTHWARK (1948–70)
Southwark Metrop Bor
SOUTHWARK, CENTRAL (1918–48)
pt Southwark Metrop Bor (the wards of St Mary's, St Paul's, Trinity, and pt St George's)
SOUTHWARK, NORTH (1918–48)
pt Southwark Metrop Bor (the wards of Christchurch, St Jude's, St Michael's, St Saviour, pt St George's)
SOUTHWARK, SOUTH EAST (1918–48)
pt Southwark Metrop Bor (the wards of St John's, St Peter's, pt St George's)
STEPNEY (1948–70)
Stepney Metrop Bor
STEPNEY, LIMEHOUSE (1918–48)
pt Stepney Metrop Bor (the wards of Limehouse North, Limehouse South, Mile End Old Town North East, Mile End Old Town South East, Ratcliffe)
STEPNEY, MILE END (1918–48)
pt Stepney Metrop Bor (the wards of Mile End Old Town Centre, Mile End Old Town North, Mile End Old Town South, Mile End Old Town West, Whitechapel East)
STEPNEY, WHITECHAPEL AND ST GEORGE'S (1918–48)
pt Stepney Metrop Bor (the wards of Mile End New Town, St George in the East North, St George in the East South, Shadwell, Spitalfields East, Spitalfields West, Whitechapel Middle, Whitechapel South, Tower)
STOKE NEWINGTON (1918–48)
Stoke Newington Metrop Bor
STOKE NEWINGTON AND HACKNEY NORTH[3] (1948–70)
pt Hackney Metrop Bor (the wards of Leaside [1948–55], Maury [1948–55], Northfield [1955–70], Northwold [1955–70], Rectory [1955–70], Southwold [1948–55] Springfield, Stamford [1948–55]), Stoke Newington Metrop Bor
WANDSWORTH, BALHAM AND TOOTING (1918–48)
pt Wandsworth Metrop Bor (the ward of Tooting, pt Balham)
WANDSWORTH, CENTRAL (1918–48)
pt Wandsworth Metrop Bor (the wards of Fairfield [1918–48], Springfield, Tooting [1948–70], pt Balham [1948–70])
WANDSWORTH, CLAPHAM
pt Wandsworth Metrop Bor (the wards of North, Clapham South, pt Balham)
WANDSWORTH, PUTNEY
pt Wandsworth Metrop Bor (the wards of Fairfield [1948–70], Putney, Southfields)
WANDSWORTH, STREATHAM
pt Wandsworth Metrop Bor (the ward of Streatham)
WESTMINSTER, ABBEY (1918–48)
pt Westminster Metrop Bor (the wards of Covent Garden, Great Marlborough, Pall Mall, Regent, St Anne, St John, St Margaret, Strand, pt Charing Cross)
WESTMINSTER, ST GEORGE'S (1918–48)
pt Westminster Metrop Bor (the wards of Conduit, Grosvenor, Hamlet of Knightsbridge, Knightsbridge St George's, Victoria, pt Charing Cross)
WOOLWICH, EAST[5]
pt Woolwich Metrop Bor (the wards of Abbey Wood [1948–70], Burrage, Central, Dockyard [1948–55], Glyndon, River [1948–70], St Margaret's, St Mary's [1948–70], St Nicholas, Slade [1955–70], Winn's Common [1955–70])
WOOLWICH, WEST[5]
pt Woolwich Metrop Bor (the wards of Avery Hill [1948–70], Coldharbour [1955–70], Dockyard [1918–48], Eltham [1918–48], New Eltham [1955–70], Eltham Green [1955–70], Falconwood [1955–70], Herbert, Horn Park [1955–70], Middle Park [1955–70], St George's, St Mary's [1918–48], Sherard [1948–70], Shooters Hill [1955–70], West Hall [1948–70])

PART III: GREATER LONDON

Entirely in BCs (1970–*). For the period before 1970 see London Admin Co, Croydon CB, East Ham CB, West Ham CB, Middx, Surrey, Kent, Essex and Herts.

BARKING, BARKING
pt Barking LB (the wards of Abbey, Cambell, Gascoigne, Longbridge, Manor)
BARKING, DAGENHAM
pt Barking LB (the wards of Chadwell Heath, Eastbrook, Fanshawe, Heath, River, Valence, Village)
BARNET, CHIPPING BARNET
pt Barnet LB (the wards of Arkley, East Barnet, Brunswick Park, Hadley, Totteridge)
BARNET, FINCHLEY
pt Barnet LB (the wards of Friern Barnet, Finchley, East Finchley, St Paul's, Woodhouse)
BARNET, HENDON NORTH
pt Barnet LB (the wards of Burnt Oak, Colindale, Edgware, Hale, Mill Hill)
BARNET, HENDON SOUTH
pt Barnet LB (the wards of Childs Hill, Garden Suburb, Golders Green, Hendon, West Hendon)
BEXLEY, BEXLEYHEATH
pt Bexley LB (the wards of Brampton, Christ Church, Danson, Falcolnwood, St Michael's, Upton, East Wickham)
BEXLEY, ERITH AND CRAYFORD
pt Bexley LB (the wards of Belvedere, Bostall, Crayford North, Crayford Town, Crayford West, Erith Town, Northumberland Heath)
BEXLEY, SIDCUP
pt Bexley LB (the wards of North Cray, Lamorbey East, Lamorbey West, St Mary's, Sidcup East, Sidcup West)
BRENT EAST
pt Brent LB (the wards of Brentwater, Brondesbury Park, Carlton, Church End, Cricklewood, Gladstone, Kilburn, Mapesbury, Queen's Park, Willesden Green)
BRENT NORTH
pt Brent LB (the wards of Fryent, Kenton, Kingsbury, Preston, Queensbury, Roe Green, Sudbury, Sudbury Court, Tokyngton, Town Hall, Wembley Park)
BRENT SOUTH
pt Brent LB (the wards of Alperton, Barham, Chamberlayne, Harlesden, Kensal Rise, Manor, Roundwood, St Raphael's, Stonebridge, Wembley Central)
BROMLEY, BECKENHAM[6]
pt Bromley LB (the wards of Anerley, Clock House, Copers Cope, Eden Park, Lawrie Park and Kent House, Manor House, Penge, Shortlands)
BROMLEY, CHISLEHURST[6]
pt Bromley LB (the wards of Bickley, Chislehurst, St Paul's Cray, Mottingham, Plaistow and Sundridge)
BROMLEY, ORPINGTON[7]
pt Bromley LB (the wards of Biggin Hill, Chelsfield, St Mary Cray, Darwin, Farnborough, Goddington, Petts Wood)
BROMLEY, RAVENSBOURNE
pt Bromley LB (the wards of Bromley Common, Keston and Hayes, Martin's Hill and Town, West Wickham North, West Wickham South)
CAMDEN, HAMPSTEAD[8]
pt Camden LB (the wards of Adelaide, Belsize, Hampstead Central [1970–73], Hampstead Town, Kilburn, Priory, Swiss Cottage [1973–*], West End)
CAMDEN, HOLBORN AND ST PANCRAS SOUTH
pt Camden LB (the wards of Bloomsbury, Euston, Holborn, King's Cross, Regent's Park, St Pancras)
CAMDEN, ST PANCRAS NORTH[8]
pt Camden LB (the wards of Camden, Chalk Farm, Gospel Oak, Grafton, Highgate, St John's)
CROYDON CENTRAL[7]
pt Croydon LB (the wards of New Addington, Broad Green, Central, Shirley, Waddon)
CROYDON NORTH EAST
pt Croydon LB (the wards of Addiscombe, East, South Norwood, Thornton Heath, Woodside)
CROYDON NORTH WEST
pt Croydon (the wards of Bensham Manor, Norbury, Upper Norwood, West Thornton, Whitehorse Manor)
CROYDON SOUTH[7]
pt Croydon LB (the wards of Coulsdon East, Purley, Sanderstead and Selsdon, Sanderstead North, Woodcote and Coulsdon West)
EALING, ACTON
pt Ealing LB (the wards of Central, East, Hanger Hill, Heathfield, Southfield, Springfield)
EALING NORTH
pt Ealing LB (the wards of Brent, Cleveland, Horsenden, Mandeville, Perivale, Ravenor, West End)
EALING, SOUTHALL
pt Ealing LB (the wards of Dormers Wells, Elthorne, Glebe, Northcote, Northfields, Walpole, Waxlow Manor)
ENFIELD, EDMONTON
pt Enfield LB (the wards of Angel Road, Bush Hill South, Church Street, Craig Park, Jubilee, New Park, Pymmes, St Alphege, St Peter's, Silver Street)
ENFIELD NORTH
pt Enfield LB (the wards of Bullsmoor, Bush Hill, Cambridge Road, Chase, Enfield Wash, Green Street, Ordnance, Ponders End, Town, Willow)
ENFIELD, SOUTHGATE
pt Enfield LB (the wards of Arnos, Bowes, Cockfosters, Grange, Highfield, Oakwood, Palmers Green, Southgate Green, West, Winchmore Hill)
GREENWICH, GREENWICH
pt Greenwich LB (the wards of Blackheath, Charl-

ton. Eastcombe, Hornfair, Kidbrooke, Marsh, Park, Trafalgar, Vanburgh, West)

GREENWICH, WOOLWICH EAST
pt Greenwich LB (the wards of Abbey Wood, Eynsham, St Margaret's, St Mary's, St Nicholas, Slade, Woolwich)

GREENWICH, WOOLWICH WEST
pt Greenwich LB (the wards of Academy, Coldharbour, Eltham, New Eltham, Horn Park, Middle Park, St George's, Sherard, Shooters Hill, Well Hall)

HACKNEY CENTRAL
pt Hackney LB (the wards of Chatham, Downs, Kingsmead, Leabridge, Rectory, Wick)

HACKNEY NORTH AND STOKE NEWINGTON
pt Hackney LB (the wards of Brownswood, Clissold, Defoe, New River, Northfield, Northwold, Springfield)

HACKNEY SOUTH AND SHOREDITCH
pt Hackney (the wards of Dalston, De Beauvoir, Haggerston, Moorfields, Queensbridge, Victoria, Wenlock)

HAMMERSMITH, FULHAM
pt Hammersmith LB (the wards of Avonmore, Colehill, Crabtree, Gibbs Green, Halford, Margravine, Parson's Green, Sandford, Sherbrooke, Sulivan, Town)

HAMMERSMITH NORTH
pt Hammersmith LB (the wards of Addison, Broadway, Brook Green, College Park and Old Oak), Coningham, Grove, St Stephen's, Starch Green, White City, Wormholt)

HARINGEY, HORNSEY
pt Haringey LB (the wards of Central Hornsey, South Hornsey, Crouch End, Fortis Green, Highgate, Muswell Hill, Stroud Green, Turnpike)

HARINGEY, TOTTENHAM
pt Haringey LB (the wards of Bruce Grove, Green Lanes, High Cross, Seven Sisters, South Tottenham, Tottenham Central, West Green)

HARINGEY, WOOD GREEN
pt Haringey LB (the wards of Alexandra-Bowes, Coleraine, Noel Park, Park, Town Hall)

HARROW CENTRAL
pt Harrow LB (the wards of West Harrow, Harrow-on-the-Hill and Greenhill, Kenton, Wealdstone North, Wealdstone South)

HARROW EAST
pt Harrow LB (the wards of Belmont, Harrow Weald, Queensbury, Stanmore North, Stanmore South)

HARROW WEST
pt Harrow LB (the wards of Hatch End, Headstone North, Headstone South, Pinner, Pinner West, Rayners Lane, Ridgeway, Roxbourne)

HAVERING, HORNCHURCH
pt Havering LB (the wards of Elm Park, Hacton, South Hornchurch, Hylands, Rainham, St Andrew's)

HAVERING, ROMFORD
pt Havering LB (the wards of Bedfords, Central, Collier Row, Gidea Park, Heath Park, Mawney, Oldchurch)

HAVERING, UPMINSTER
pt Havering LB (the wards of Cranham, Emerson Park, Gooshays, Harold Wood, Heaton, Hilldene, Upminster)

HILLINGDON, HAYES AND HARLINGTON
pt Hillingdon LB (the wards of Belmore, Frogmore, Hayes, South, Yealding)

HILLINGDON, RUISLIP-NORTHWOOD
pt Hillingdon LB (the wards of Eastcote, Haydon, Manor, Northwood, Ruislip, South Ruislip)

HILLINGDON, UXBRIDGE
pt Hillingdon LB (the wards of Colham-Crowley, Harefield, Hillingdon East, Hillingdon West, Ickenham, Uxbridge, Yiewsley)

HOUNSLOW, BRENTFORD AND ISLEWORTH
pt Hounslow LB (the wards of Clifden, Gunnersbury, Homefields, Hounslow Central, Hounslow South, Isleworth North, Isleworth South, Riverside, Spring Grove, Turnham Green)

HOUNSLOW, FELTHAM AND HESTON
pt Hounslow LB (the wards of East Bedfont, Cranford, Feltham Central, Feltham North, Feltham South, Hanworth, Heston East, Heston West, Hounslow Heath, Hounslow West)

ISLINGTON CENTRAL
pt Islington LB (the wards of Canonbury, Highbury, Holloway, Mildmay, Quadrant)

ISLINGTON NORTH
pt Islington LB (the wards of Highview, Hillmarton, Hillrise, Junction, Parkway, St George's, Station)

ISLINGTON SOUTH AND FINSBURY
pt Islington LB (the wards of Barnsbury, Bunhill, Clerkenwell, Pentonville, St Mary, St Peter, Thornhill)

KENSINGTON AND CHELSEA, CHELSEA
pt Kensington and Chelsea LB (the wards of Brompton, Cheyne, Church, Earls Court, Hans Town, Redcliffe, Royal Hospital, North Stanley, South Stanley)

KENSINGTON AND CHELSEA, KENSINGTON
pt Kensington and Chelea LB (the wards of Golborne, Holland, Norland, Pembridge, Queen's Gate, St Charles)

KINGSTON UPON THAMES, KINGSTON
pt Kingston upon Thames LB (the pt not in the following BC)

KINGSTON UPON THAMES, SURBITON
pt Kingston upon Thames LB (the former Surbiton MB)

LAMBETH CENTRAL
pt Lambeth LB (the wards of Angell, Clapham Town, Ferndale, Larkhall, Town Hall)

LAMBETH, NORWOOD
pt Lambeth LB (the wards of Herne Hill, Knight's Hill, Leigham, Thurlow Park, Tulse Hill)

LAMBETH, STREATHAM
pt Lambeth LB (the wards of Clapham Park, St Leonard's, Streatham South, Streatham Wells, Thornton)

LAMBETH, VAUXHALL
pt Lambeth LB (the wards of Bishop's, Oval, Prince's, Stockwell, Vassall)

LEWISHAM, DEPTFORD
pt Lewisham LB (the wards of Brockley, Deptford, Drake, Grinling, Gibbons, Ladywell, Marlowe, Pepys)
LEWISHAM EAST
pt Lewisham LB (the wards of Blackheath and Lewisham Village, Grove Park, Manor Lee, St Mildred Lee, South Lee, Lewisham Park, St Andrew, Southend, Whitefoot)
LEWISHAM WEST
pt Lewisham LB (the wards of Bellingham, Culverley, Forest Hill, Honor Oak Park, Rushey Green, Sydenham East, Sydenham West)
THE CITY OF LONDON AND WESTMINSTER SOUTH
The City of London, Inner Temple, Middle Temple, pt City of Westminster LB (the wards of Charing Cross, Churchill, Knightsbridge, Millbank, Regent Street, Victoria Street, Warwick)
MERTON, MITCHAM AND MORDEN
pt Merton LB (the wards of Mitcham Central, Mitcham East, Mitcham North, Mitcham South, Mitcham West, Morden, Ravensbury)
MERTON, WIMBLEDON
pt Merton LB (the wards of West Barnes, Cannon Hill, Priory, Wimbledon East, Wimbledon North, Wimbledon South, Wimbledon West)
NEWHAM NORTH-EAST
pt Newham LB (the wards of Castle, Central, Greatfield, Little Ilford, Kensington, Manor Park, St Stephens, Wall End, Woodgrange)
NEWHAM NORTH-WEST
pt Newham LB (the wards of Forest Gate, West Ham, New Town, Park, Plashet, Stratford, Upton)
NEWHAM SOUTH
pt Newham LB (the wards of Beckton, Bemersyde, Canning Town and Grange, Custom House and Silvertown, Hudsons, Ordnance, Plaistow, South)
REDBRIDGE, ILFORD NORTH
pt Redbridge LB (the wards of Aldborough, Barkingside, Chadwell, Fairlop, Hainault, Seven Kings)
REDBRIDGE, ILFORD SOUTH
pt Redbridge LB (the wards of Clementswood, Cranbrook, Goodmayes, Ilford, Mayfield, Park)
REDBRIDGE, WANSTEAD AND WOODFORD
pt Redbridge LB (the wards of Bridge, Clayhall, Snaresbrook, Wanstead, Woodford)
RICHMOND UPON THAMES, RICHMOND
pt Richmond upon Thames LB (the wards of Barnes, Ham-Petersham, Kew, Mortlake, Palewell, Richmond Hill, Richmond Town, North Sheen)
RICHMOND UPON THAMES, TWICKENHAM[9]
pt Richmond upon Thames LB (the wards of Hampton, Hampton Hill, Hampton Wick, Heathfield, Teddington, Central Twickenham, East Twickenham, South Twickenham, West Twickenham, Whitton)
SOUTHWARK, BERMONDSEY[10]
pt Southwark LB (the wards of Abbey, Bricklayers, Browning, Cathedral, Chaucer, Dockyard, Riverside, Rotherhithe)
SOUTHWARK, DULWICH[10]
pt Southwark LB (the wards of Alleyn, Bellenden, College, The Lane, Lyndhurst, Ruskin, Rye, Waverley)
SOUTHWARK, PECKHAM[10]
pt Southwark LB (the wards of Brunswick, Burgess, Consort, Faraday, Friary, Newington, St Giles)
SUTTON, CARSHALTON
pt Sutton LB (the wards of Beddington North, Beddington South, Carshalton Central, Carshalton North East, Carshalton North West, Carshalton St Helier North, Carshalton St Helier South, Carshalton St Helier West, Carshalton South East, Carshalton South West, Wallington Central, Wallington North, Wallington South)
SUTTON, SUTTON AND CHEAM
pt Sutton LB (the wards of Belmont, Cheam North, Cheam South, Cheam West, Sutton Central, Sutton East, Sutton North, Sutton North East, Sutton South, Sutton South East, Worcester Park North, Worcester Park South)
TOWER HAMLETS, BETHNAL GREEN AND BOW
pt Tower Hamlets LB (the wards of Bethnal Green Central, Bethnal Green East, Bethnal Green North, Bethnal Green South, Bethnal Green West, Bow North, Bow South, Bromley, Holy Trinity, Spitalfields)
TOWER HAMLETS, STEPNEY AND POPLAR
pt Tower Hamlets LB (the wards of Limehouse, Poplar East, Poplar Millwall, Poplar South, Poplar West, Redcoat, St Dunstan's, St Katherine's, St Mary's, Shadwell)
WALTHAM FOREST, CHINGFORD
pt Waltham Forest LB (the wards of Chapel End, Chingford Central, Chingford North West, Chingford South and Hale End)
WALTHAM FOREST, LEYTON
pt Waltham Forest LB (the wards of Cann Hall, Central, Forest, Lea Bridge, Leyton, Leytonstone)
WALTHAM FOREST, WALTHAMSTOW
pt Waltham Forest (the wards of High Street, Higham Hill, Hoe Street, St James Street, Wood Street)
WANDSWORTH, BATTERSEA NORTH
pt Wandsworth LB (the wards of Latchmere, Queenstown, St John, St Mary's Park, Shaftesbury)
WANDSWORTH, BATTERSEA SOUTH
pt Wandsworth LB (the wards of Balham, Earlsfield, Fairfield, Nightingale, Northcote)
WANDSWORTH, PUTNEY
pt Wandsworth LB (the wards of Putney, Roehampton, Southfield, Thamesfield, West Hill)
WANDSWORTH, TOOTING
pt Wandsworth LB (the wards of Bedford, Furzedown, Graveney, Springfield, Tooting)
CITY OF WESTMINSTER, PADDINGTON
pt City of Westminster LB (the wards of Harrow Road, Hyde Park, Lancaster Gate, Maida Vale, Queen's Park, Westbourne)
CITY OF WESTMINSTER, ST MARYLEBONE
pt City of Westminster LB (the wards of Baker Street, Cavendish, Church Street, Lords, Regent's Park)

MIDDLESEX

BOROUGH CONSTITUENCIES[1]

Entirely in Middx:

ACTON (1948–70)
Acton MB

BRENTFORD AND CHISWICK (1948–70)
Brentford and Chiswick MB

EALING (1918–45)
Ealing MB

EALING EAST (1945–48)
pt Ealing MB (the wards of Castlebar, Drayton, Grange, Grosvenor, Lammas, Manor, Mount Park)

EALING NORTH (1948–70)
pt Ealing MB (the wards of Greenford Central, Greenford North, Greenford South, Hanger Hill, Northolt, Perivale)

EALING SOUTH (1948–70)
pt Ealing MB (the wards as in Ealing East Parl Bor 1945–48)

EALING WEST (1945–48)
pt Ealing MB (the wards of Greenford North, Greenford South, Hanwell North, Hanwell South, Northolt)

EDMONTON (1918–70)
Edmonton UD/MB

ENFIELD EAST (1948–70)
pt Enfield UD/MB (the wards of Central, North East, South East)

ENFIELD WEST (1948–70)
pt Enfield UD/MB (the wards of South West, West), Potter's Bar UD

FELTHAM (1955–70)
Feltham UD, pt Heston and Isleworth MB (the wards of Cranford, Hounslow Heath)

FINCHLEY (1948–70)
Friern Barnet UD, Finchley MB

HARROW CENTRAL[2] (1948–70)
pt Harrow UD/MB (the wards of Harrow on the Hill and Greenhill, Headstone [1948–55], West Harrow, Kenton [1955–70], Wealdstone North, Wealdstone South)

HARROW EAST[2] (1945–70)
pt Harrow UD/MB (the wards of Belmont [1949–70], Harrow Weald [pt 1945–49, ent 1949–70], Kenton [1945–55], Queensbury [1949–70], Stanmore North, Stanmore South, Wealdstone North [1945–48], Wealdstone South [1945–48])

HARROW WEST[2] (1945–70)
pt Harrow UD/MB (the wards of Harrow on the Hill and Greenhill [1945–48], Harrow Weald [pt 1945–49], West Harrow [1945–48], Headstone [1945–48 and 1955–70], Pinner North [1945–49], Pinner North and Hatch End [1949–70], Pinner South, Roxeth, Roxbourne [1949–70])

HAYES AND HARLINGTON (1948–70)
Hayes and Harlington UD

HENDON NORTH (1945–70)
pt Hendon MB (the wards of Burnt Oak, Edgware, Mill Hill, West Henton)

HENDON SOUTH (1945–70)
pt Hendon MB (the wards of Central Hendon, Child's Hill, Garden Suburb, Golders Green Park)

HESTON AND ISLEWORTH (1945–70)
Heston and Isleworth MB (ent 1945–55, pt 1955–70 [the wards of Heston, Hounslow Central, Hounslow South, Hounslow West, Isleworth North, Isleworth South, Spring Grove])

HORNSEY (1918–70)
Hornsey MB

RUISLIP-NORTHWOOD (1948–70)
Ruislip-Northwood UD

SOUTHALL (1945–70)
pt Ealing MB (the wards of Hanwell North, Hanwell South), Hayes and Harlington MB (1945–48), Southall MB

SOUTHGATE (1948–70)
Southgate MB

TOTTENHAM (1948–70)
pt Tottenham MB (all, except the pt in Wood Green BC)

TOTTENHAM NORTH (1918–48)
pt Tottenham UD (the wards of Lower, Middle, West Green)

TOTTENHAM SOUTH (1918–48)
pt Tottenham UD (the wards of Harringay, High Cross, St Ann's)

TWICKENHAM (1945–70)
Twickenham MB

WEMBLEY NORTH (1945–70)
pt Wembley MB (the wards of Chalkhill, Fryent, Kenton, Preston, Roe Green, The Hyde)

WEMBLEY SOUTH (1945–70)
pt Wembley MB (the wards of Alperton, Central, Sudbury, Sudbury Court, Tokyngton, Wembley Park)

WILLESDEN EAST[3] (1918–70)
pt Willesden UD/MB (the wards of Brondesbury Park, Carlton [1948–70], Cricklewood, Kensal Rise [1918–48], Kilburn [1948–70], Mid Kilburn [1918–48], North Kilburn [1918–48], South Kilburn [1918–48])

WILLESDEN WEST[3] (1918–70)
pt Willesden UD/MB (the wards of Church End, Harlesden, Kensal Rise [1948–70], Manor [1948–70], Roundwood, Stonebridge, Willesden Green)

WOOD GREEN (1948–70)
pt Tottenham MB (the wards of Coleraine, Park, White Hart Lane), Wood Green MB

In Middx but within Metropolis 1855–89 and in London Adm Co from 1889, in Middx for parl purposes until 1918 and in London thereafter:

BETHNAL GREEN, NORTH-EAST DV (1885–1918)
pt Bethnal Green (the wards of North, East)

BETHANL GREEN, SOUTH-WEST DV (1885–1918)
pt Bethnal Green (the wards of South, West)

CHELSEA (1867–1918)
Chelsea, Fulham (1867–85), Hammersmith (1867–85), Kensington (1867–85)

FINSBURY (1832–85)
Charterhouse, pt Clerkenwell, pt Furnival's Inn, Glasshouse Yard, Gray's Inn, Islington, Liberty of the Rolls; Liberty of Saffron Hill, Hatton Garden, Ely Rent and Ely Place; Lincoln's Inn, St Andrew Holborn Above the Bars and St George the Martyr, St Giles in the Fields and St George Bloomsbury, St Luke, St Sepulchre, Staple Inn, Stoke Newington

FINSBURY, CENTRAL DV (1885–1918)
Clerkenwell

FINSBURY, EAST DV (1885–1918)
Charterhouse, Glasshouse Yard, St Luke, St Sepulchre

FINSBURY, HOLBORN DV (1885–1918)
pt Furnival's Inn, Gray's Inn; Liberty of Saffron Hill, Hatton Garden, Ely Rents and Ely Place; Lincoln's Inn, St Andrew Holborn Above the Bars with St George the Martyr, Staple Inn

FULHAM (1885–1918)
Fulham

HACKNEY (1867–85)
Bethnal Green, Hackney, Shoreditch

HACKNEY, CENTRAL DV (1885–1918)
pt Hackney (the wards of Dalston [no. 4], DeBeauvoir [no. 3], pt Hackney [no. 5])

HACKNEY, NORTH DV (1885–1918)
pt Hackney (the wards of Stamford Hill [no. 1], West Hackney [no. 2], pt Hackney [no. 5])

HACKNEY, SOUTH DV (1885–1918)
pt Hackney (the wards of South Hackney [no. 7], Homerton [no. 6], pt Hackney [no. 5])

HAMMERSMITH (1885–1918)
Hammersmith

ISLINGTON, EAST DV (1885–1918)
pt Islington (the wards of Highbury, Canonbury)

ISLINGTON, NORTH DV (1885–1918)
pt Islington (the ward of Upper Holloway)

ISLINGTON, SOUTH DV (1885–1918)
pt Islington (the wards of Barnsbury, St Mary, St Peter)

ISLINGTON, WEST DV (1885–1918)
pt Islington (the wards of Lower Holloway, Thornhill)

KENSINGTON, NORTH DV (1885–1918)
pt Kensington (as defined in act)

KENSINGTON, SOUTH DV (1885–1918)
pt Kensington (as defined in act)

MARYLEBONE (1832–85)
Paddington, St Marylebone, St Pancras

MARYLEBONE, EAST DV (1885–1918)
pt St Marylebone (the wards of St John's Wood Terrace, Regent Square and Regent's Park, Portland Place, Cavendish Square)

MARYLEBONE, WEST DV (1885–1918)
pt St Marylebone (the wards of Hamilton Terrace, New Church Street, Bryanstone, Portman)

PADDINGTON, NORTH DV (1885–1918)
pt Paddington (the ward of no. 2)

PADDINGTON, SOUTH DV (1885–1918)
pt Paddington (the wards of nos. 1, 3, 4)

ST GEORGE HANOVER SQUARE (1885–1918)
St George Hanover Square

ST PANCRAS, EAST DV (1885–1918)
pt St Pancras (the wards of nos. 3, 6)

ST PANCRAS, NORTH DV (1885–1918)
pt St Pancras (the ward of no. 1)

ST PANCRAS, SOUTH DV (1885–1918)
pt St Pancras (the wards of nos. 7, 8)

ST PANCRAS, WEST DV (1885–1918)
pt St Pancras (the wards of nos. 2, 4, 5)

SHOREDITCH, HAGGERSTON DV (1885–1918)
pt Shoreditch (the wards of Acton, Haggerston, Kingsland, Whitmore)

SHOREDITCH, HOXTON DV (1885–1918)
pt Shoreditch (the wards of Moorfields, Hoxton, Church, Wenlock)

STRAND (1885–1918)
Liberty of the Rolls, St Anne Within the Liberty of Westminster, St Clement Danes, St Mary le Strand, St Paul Covent Garden, Precinct of the Savoy

TOWER HAMLETS (1832–85)
Bethnal Green (1832–67), Bow, Bromley, Hackney (1832–67), Holy Trinity Minories (1867–85), Limehouse, Mile End New Town (1867–85), Mile End Old Town (1867–85), Norton Folgate (1867–85), Old Artillery Ground (1867–85), Poplar, Ratcliffe (1867–85), St Botolph Without Aldgate, St George in the East, St Katherine by the Tower (1867–85), Shoreditch (1832–67), Spitalfields, Tower of London, Old Tower Without, Wapping, pt Whitechapel

TOWER HAMLETS, BOW AND BROMLEY DV (1885–1918)
Bow, pt Bromley (as defined in act)

TOWER HAMLETS, LIMEHOUSE DV (1885–1918)
Limehouse, Ratcliffe, Shadwell

TOWER HAMLETS, MILE END DV (1885–1918)
pt Mile End Old Town (the wards of North, East)

TOWER HAMLETS, POPLAR DV (1885–1918)
pt Bromley (as defined in act), poplar

TOWER HAMLETS, ST GEORGE DV (1885–1918)
St George in the East, Wapping

TOWER HAMLETS, STEPNEY DV (1885–1918)
pt Mile End Old Town (the wards of Centre, West, South)

TOWER HAMLETS, WHITECHAPEL DV (1885–1918)
Holy Trinity Minories, Mile End New Town, Norton Folgate, Old Artillery Ground, St Botolph Without Aldgate, St Katherine by the Tower, Spitalfields, Tower of London, Old Tower Without, pt Whitechapel

WESTMINSTER (1586–1918)
Close of the Collegiate Church of St Peter (1832–

1918), Duchy of Lancaster (1832–1918 [civ status not sustained]), St Anne Within the Liberty of Westminster, St Clement Danes, St George Hanover Square (1867–1918), St Martin in the Fields (1832–1918), St Mary le Strand (1832–1918), St Paul Covent Garden (1832–1918), Precinct of the Savoy (1832–1918), Westminster St James (1832–1918), Westminster St John the Evangelist (1727–1918), Westminster St Margaret

COUNTY CONSTITUENCIES

Middx was undivided for parl purposes until 1885.

1885–1918

BRENTFORD DIVISION
New Brentford, pt Ealing, pt Hanwell, Heston, Isleworth, Norwood, Twickenham

EALING DIVISION
Acton, Chiswick, pt Ealing, Greenford, Perivale, pt Hanwell

ENFIELD DIVISION
Friern Barnet, Edmonton, Enfield, Monken Hadley, South Mimms

HARROW DIVISION
Edgware, Harrow on the Hill, Hendon, Kingsbury, Pinner, Great Stanmore, Little Stanmore, West Twyford, Willesden

HORNSEY DIVISION
Finchley, Hornsey

TOTTENHAM DIVISION
Tottenham

UXBRIDGE DIVISION
Ashford, East Bedfont, Cowley, Cranford, West Drayton, Feltham, Hampton, Hampton Wick, Hanworth, Harefield, Harlington, Harmondsworth, Hayes, Hillingdon, Ickenham, Laleham, Littleton, Northolt, Ruislip, Shepperton, Staines, Stanwell, Sunbury, Teddington, Uxbridge

1918–1948

ACTON DIVISION
Acton UD

BRENTFORD AND CHISWICK DIVISION[4]
Brentford UD, Chiswick UD

ENFIELD DIVISION[5]
Enfield UD, South Mimms RD

FINCHLEY DIVISION[6]
Friern Barnet UD, Finchley UD

HARROW DIVISION (1918–45)
Greenford UD, Hanwell UD, Harrow on the Hill UD, Wealdstone UD, Wembley UD

HENDON DIVISION (1918–45)
Hendon RD, Hendon UD, Kingsbury UD

SPELTHORNE DIVISION
Feltham UD, Hampton UD, Hampton Wick UD, Staines RD, Staines UD, Sunbury on Thames UD, Teddington UD

TWICKENHAM DIVISION (1918–45)
Heston and Isleworth UD, Twickenham UD

UXBRIDGE DIVISION
Hayes UD (1918–45), Ruislip Northwood UD, Southall Norwood UD (1918–45), Uxbridge RD (1918–45), Uxbridge UD, Yiewsley UD (1918–45)

WOOD GREEN DIVISION
Southgate UD, Wood Green UD

1948–1970

SPELTHORNE COUNTY CONSTITUENCY[7]
Feltham UD (1948–55), Staines UD, Sunbury on Thames UD

UXBRIDGE COUNTY CONSTITUENCY
Uxbridge UD, Yiewsley and West Drayton UD

NORFOLK

BOROUGH CONSTITUENCIES[1]

CASTLE RISING (1558–1832)
Castle Rising
KING'S LYNN[2] (1298–1918 [1 mbr, 1885–1918])
King's Lynn St Margaret, South Lynn (1557–1918)
NORWICH[3] (1295–1948)
1295–1918: Earlham, Easton, Heigham, pt Hellesdon, Lakenham, Norwich All Saints, Norwich County Gaol and House of Correction (1832–1918), Norwich Liberty of the Town Close, Norwich St Andrew, Norwich St Augustine, Norwich St Benedict, Norwich St Clement, Norwich St Edmund, Norwich St Etheldreda, Norwich St George Colegate, Norwich St George Tombland, Norwich St Giles, Norwich St Gregory, Norwich St Helen, Norwich St James, Norwich St John Maddermarket, Norwich St John Sepulchre, Norwich St John Timberhill, Norwich St Julian, Norwich St Lawrence, Norwich St Margaret, Norwich St Martin at Oak, Norwich St Martin at Palace, Norwich St Mary Coslany, Norwich St Mary in the Marsh, Norwich St Michael at Plea, Norwich St Michael at Thorn, Norwich St Michael Coslany, Norwich St Paul, Norwich St Peter Hungate, Norwich St Peter Mancroft, Norwich St Peter Mountergate, Norwich St Peter Southgate, Norwich St Saviour, Norwich St Simon and St Jude, Norwich St Stephen, Norwich St Swithin, pt Thorpe next Norwich, pt Trowse with Newton

1918–1948: Norwich
NORWICH NORTH[4] (1948–*)
pt Norwich CB (the wards of Catton, Coslany, Crome [1970–*], Fye Bridge [1948–70], Heigham, Mancroft [1973–*)], Mousehold, Thorpe, Westwick [1948–73])
NORWICH SOUTH[5] (1948–*)
pt Norwich CB (the wards of Ber Street [1948–70], Bowthorpe [1970–*], Conesford [1948–70], Earlham, Eaton, Lakenham, Mancroft [1970–73], Nelson, St Stephen, Town Close, University [1973–*])
THETFORD[3] (Norfolk, Suffolk[6]) (1573–1918 [1 mbr, 1867–1918])
Thetford St Cuthbert, Thetford St Mary, Thetford St Peter
GREAT YARMOUTH[7] (Norfolk, Suffolk[6]) (1298–1948)
Gorleston (pt 1298–1832, ent 1832–1948), pt Runham (1885–1918), Runham Vauxhall (1918–48), Great Yarmouth

COUNTY CONSTITUENCIES

1832–1867
EASTERN DIVISION
Hds of Blofield, Clavering, Depwade, Diss, Earsham, North Erpingham, South Erpingham, Eynesford, East Flegg, West Flegg, Forehoe, Happing, Henstead, Humbleyard, Loddon, Taversham, Tunstead, Walsham
WESTERN DIVISION
Hds of Brothercross, Clackclose, Freebridge Lynn, Freebridge Marshland, Gallow, North Greenhoe, South Greenhoe, Grimshoe, Guiltcross, Holt, Launditch, Mitford, Shropham, Smithdon, Wayland

1867–1885
NORTH EAST DIVISION
Hds of North Erpingham, South Erpingham, Eynesford, East Flegg, West Flegg, North Greenhoe, Happing, Holt, Tunstead
SOUTH EAST DIVISION
Hds of Blofield, Clavering, Depwade, Diss, Earsham, Forehoe, Guiltcross, Henstead, Humbleyard, Loddon, Mitford, Shropham, Taversham, Walsham
WEST DIVISION
Hds of Brothercross, Clackclose, Freebridge Lynn, Freebridge Marshland, Gallow, South Greenhoe, Grimshoe, Launditch, Smithdon, Wayland

1885–1918
EASTERN DIVISION
Blofield and Walsham PSD, pt South Erpingham PSD, East and West Flegg PSD, Taverham PSD, Tunstead and Happing PSD, *viz.*, Acle, Ashby with Oby, Ashmanhaugh, Attlebridge, Bacton, Barton Turf, Beeston St Andrew, Beeston St Lawrence, Beighton, Belaugh, Billockby, Blofield, Bradfield, Brumstead, Brundall, Buckenham, Burgh St Margaret, Burlingham St Andrew, Burlingham St Edmund, Burlingham St Peter, Caister next Yarmouth, Cantley, Catfield, Catton, Clippesby, Coltishall, Crostwick, Crostwight, Dilham, Drayton, Edingthorpe, Felmingham, Felthorpe, Filby, Freethorpe, Frettenham, Gillingham, Hainford, Halvergate, Happisburgh, Hassingham, Great Hautbois, pt Hellesdon, Hemblington, Hempstead with Eccles, Hemsby, Hickling, Honing, Horning, Horsey, Horsford, Horsham St Faith with Newton St Faith,

Horstead with Stanninghall, Hoveton St John, Hoveton St Peter, Ingham, Irstead, Lammas with Little Hautbois, Lessingham, Limpenhoe, Lingwood, Ludham, Martham, Mautby, Moulton St Mary, Moulton St Michael, Neatishead, Ormesby St Margaret with Scratby, Ormesby St Michael, Palling, Paston, Postwick, Potter Heigham, Rackheath, Ranworth with Panxworth, Reedham, Repps with Bastwick, Ridlington, Rollesby, pt Runham, East Ruston, Salhouse, Sco' Ruston, Scottow, Sloley, Smallburgh, East Somerton, West Somerton, Southwood, Spixworth, Sprowston, Stalham, Stokesby with Herringby, Strumpshaw, Sutton, Swafield, Swanton Abbot, Taverham, pt Thorpe next Norwich, Thrigby, Thurne, Tunstall, Tunstead, Upton with Fishley, Walcott, North Walsham, South Walsham St Lawrence, South Walsham St Mary, Waxham, Westwick, Wickhampton, Winterton, Witton, Witton, Woodbastwick, Worstead, Wroxham

MID DIVISION

Forehoe PSD, Guiltcross and Shropham PSD, Mitford and Launditch PSD, *viz.*, Attleborough, Banham, Barford, Barnham Broom, Bawburgh, Beeston with Bittering, Beetley, Besthorpe, East Bilney, Blo' Norton, Bowthorpe, Brandon Parva, Brettenham, Bridgham, Brisley, New Buckenham, Old Buckenham, Carleton Forehoe, Colkirk, Colton, Costessey, Coston, Cranworth, Crownthorpe, Deopham, East Dereham, Great Dunham, Little Dunham, Easton, Eccles, Great Ellingham, North Elmham, Great Fransham, Little Fransham, Garboldisham, Garveston, Gasthorpe, Gateley, Gressenhall, Hackford, Hardingham, Hargham, East Harling, West Harling, Hingham, Hockering, Hockham, Hoe, Honingham, Horningtoft, Illington, Kempstone, Kenninghall, Kilverstone, Kimberley, Larling, Letton, East Lexham, West Lexham, Litcham, Longham, North Lopham, South Lopham, Marlingford, Mattishall, Mattishall Burgh, Mileham, Morley St Botolph, Morley St Peter, Oxwick and Pattesley, Quidenham, Reymerston, Riddlesworth, Rockland All Saints, Rockland St Andrew, Roudham, Rougham, Runhall, pt Rushford, Scarning, Shipdham, Shropham, Great and Little Snarehill, Snetterton, Southburgh, Stanfield, Swanton Morley, Thuxton, Tittleshall, East Tuddenham, North Tuddenham, Weasenham All Saints, Weasenham St Peter, Welborne, Wellingham, Wendling, Westfield, Whinburgh, Whissonsett, Wicklewood, Wilby, Woodrising, Worthing, Wramplingham, East Wretham, West Wretham, Wymondham, Yaxham

NORTHERN DIVISION

North Erpingham PSD, pt South Erpingham PSD, Eynesford PSD, North Greenhoe PSD, Holt PSD, *viz.*, Alby with Thwaite, Aldborough, Alderford, Antingham, Aylmerton, Aylsham, Baconsthorpe, Bale, Banningham, Barney, Little Barningham, Barningham Norwood, Barningham Winter or Barningham Town, Bawdeswell, East Beckham, West Beckham, Beeston Regis, Bessingham, Billingford, Binham, Bintree, Blakeney, Blickling, Bodham, Booton, Brampton, Brandiston, Brinningham, Brinton, Briston, Burgh, Buxton, Bylaugh, Calthorpe, Cawston, Cley next the Sea, Cockthorpe, Colby, Corpusty, Cromer, pt Earsham, Edgefield, Egmere, Elsing, Erpingham, Felbrigg, Field Dalling, Foulden, Foulsham, Foxley, Gimingham, Glandford with Bayfield, Gresham, Guestwick, Guist, Gunthorpe, Gunton, Hackford, Hanworth, Haveringland, Hempstead, Hevingham, Heydon, Hindolveston, Hindringham, Holkham, Holt, Houghton St Giles, Hunworth, Ingworth, Irmingland, Itteringham, Kelling, Knapton, Langham, Letheringsett, Lyng, Mannington, Marsham, Matlask, Melton Constable, Metton, Morston, Morton on the Hill, Mundesley, Northrepps, Oulton, Overstrand, Oxnead, Plumstead, Quarles, Reepham with Kerdiston, Ringland, Roughton, Runton, Sall, Salthouse, Saxlingham, Saxthorpe, Sharrington, Sheringham, Sidestrand, Skeyton, Great Snoring, Southrepps, Sparham, Stiffkey, Stody, Stratton Strawless, Suffield, Sustead, Swannington, Swanton Novers, Themelthorpe, Thornage, Thorpe Abbots, Thorpe Market, Thurgarton, Thurning, Thursford, Trimingham, Trunch, Tuttington, Twyford, Great Walsingham, Little Walsingham, Warham All Saints, Warham St Mary, Wells next the Sea, Weston Longville, Weybourne, Whitwell, Wickmere, Wighton, Great Witchingham, Little Witchingham, Wiveton, Wolterton, Wood Dalling, Wood Norton

NORTH-WESTERN DIVISION

Freebridge Lynn PSD, Freebridge Marshland PSD, Gallow PSD, Smithdon and Brothercross PSD, *viz.*, Alethorpe, Anmer, Ashwicken, Babingley, Bagthorpe, Barmer, East Barsham, North Barsham, West Barsham, Bariwck, Bawsey, West Bilney, Great Bircham, Bircham Newton, Bircham Tofts, Brancaster, Broomsthorpe, Burnham Deepdale, Burnham Norton, Burnham Overy, Burnham Sutton cum Burnham Ulph, Burnham Thorpe, Burnham Westgate, Castle Acre, Castle Rising, Choseley, Clenchwarton, Congham, North Creake, South Creake, Dersingham, Docking, Dunton cum Doughton, Emneth, Fakenham, Flitcham with Appleton, Fring, Fulmodeston cum Croxton, Gayton, Gayton Thorpe, Gaywood, Grimston, Harpley, Heacham, Hempton, Hillington, Holme next the Sea, Houghton, Hunstanton, Ingoldisthorpe, Kettlestone, Leziate, North Lynn, West Lynn, Great Massingham, Little Massingham, Middleton, Mintlyn, West Newton, Pensthorpe, Pentney, Pudding Norton, East Raynham, South Raynham, West Raynham, Ringstead, Roydon, East Rudham, West Rudham, North Runcton, Great Ryburgh, Little Ryburgh, Sandringham, Sculthorpe, Sedgeford, Setchey, Shereford, Shernborne, Snettisham, Little Snoring, Stanhoe, Stibbard, Syderstone, Tatterford, Tattersett, Terrington St Clement, Terrington St John, Testerton, Thornham, Tilney All Saints, Tilney St Lawrence, Tilney with Islington, Titchwell, Toftrees, Walpole St Andrew, Walpole St Peter, Walsoken, East Walton, West Walton, Waterden, Westacre. Wiggenhall St German, Wiggenhall St Mary the Virgin, Wiggenhall St Peter, East Winch, West Winch, Wolferton, North Wootton, South

Wootton

SOUTHERN DIVISION

Depwade PSD, Diss PSD, Earsham PSD, Loddon and Clavering PSD, Swainsthorpe PSD, *viz.*, Alburgh, Arminghall, Ashwellthorpe, Aslacton, Billingford, Bixley, Bracon Ash, Bramerton, Bressingham, Brockdish, Bunwell, Burston, Caister St Edmund, East Carleton, Carleton Rode, Colney, Cringleford, Denton, Dickleburgh, Diss, Dunston, Fersfield, Flordon, Forncett St Mary, Forncett St Peter, Framingham Pigot, Framingham Earl, Fritton, Fundenhall, Gissing, Hapton, Hardwick, Hempnall, Hethel, Hethersett, Holverston, Intwood, Keswick, Ketteringham, Kirby Bedon, Kirstead, Markshall, Great Melton, Little Melton, pt Mendham, Morning Thorpe, Mulbarton, Mundham, Needham, Newton Flotman, Great Plumstead, Little Plumstead, Poringland, Pulham St Mary Magdalene, Pulham St Mary the Virgin, Redenhall with Harleston, Rockland St Mary, Roydon, Rushall, Saxlingham Nethergate, Saxlingham Thorpe, Scole, Shelfanger, Shelton, Shimpling, Shotesham All Saints, Shotesham St Mary, Starston, Stoke Holy Cross, Stratton St Mary, Stratton St Michael, Surlingham, Swainsthorpe, Swardeston, Tacolneston, Tasburgh, Tharston, Thelveton, Thorpe next Haddiscoe, Tibenham, Tivetshall St Margaret, Tivetshall St Mary, pt Trowse with Newton, Wacton, Whitlingham, Winfarthing, Wortwell, Wreningham

SOUTH-WESTERN DIVISION

Clackclose PSD, South Greenhoe PSD, Grimshoe PSD, Wayland PSD, *viz.*, South Acre, Aldeby, Alpington, Ashby St Mary, Ashill, Barton Bendish, Beechamwell, Bedingham, Bergh Apton, Bexwell, Bodney, Boughton, East Bradenham, West Bradenham, pt Brandon, Breckles, Brooke, Broome, Buckenham Tofts, Burgh St Peter, Caldecote, Carbrooke, Carleton St Peter, Caston, Chedgrave, Claxton, Cockley Cley, Colveston, Cranwich, Great Cressingham, Little Cressingham, Crimplesham, Croxton, Denver, West Dereham, Didlington, Ditchingham, Downham Market, Ellingham, Little Ellingham, Feltwell, Feltwell Anchor, Fincham, Fordham, Geldeston, Gooderstone, Griston, Haddiscoe, Hales, Hardley, Heckingham, Hedenham, Helhoughton, Hellington, Hilgay, Hilborough, Hockwold cum Wilton, Holme Hale, Houghton on the Hill, Howe, Ickburgh, Kirby Cane, Langford, Langley, Loddon, Lynford, Marham, Merton, Methwold, Mundford, Narborough, Narford, Necton, Newton by Castle Acre, Northwold, Norton Subcourse, pt Outwell, Ovington, Oxborough, North Pickenham, South Pickenham, Raveningham, Redmere, Rockland St Peter, Roxham, South Runcton, Runcton Holme, Ryston, Saham Toney, Santon, Scoulton, Seething, Shingham, Shouldham, Shouldham Thorpe, Sisland, Southery, Sporle with Palgrave, Stanford, Stockton, Stoke Ferry, Stow Bardolph, Stow Bedon, Stradsett, Sturston, Swaffham, Thompson, Threxton, Thurlton, Thurton, Thwaite, West Tofts, Toft Monks, Topcroft, Tottenhill, Tottington, pt Upwell, Wallington with Thorpland, Watlington, Watton, Weeting-with-Bromehill, pt Welney, Wereham, Wheatacre, Wimbotsham, Woodton, Wormegay, Wretton, Yelverton

1918–1948

EASTERN DIVISION[8]

Blofield RD, East and West Flegg RD, Loddon and Clavering RD, St Faith's RD, Smallburgh RD, North Walsham UD

KING'S LYNN DIVISION

Docking RD, pt Downham RD (Wiggenhall St German, Wiggenhall St Mary Magdalen, Wiggenhall St Mary the Virgin, Wiggenhall St Peter), Freebridge Lynn RD, New Hunstanton UD, King's Lynn MB, King's Lynn RD, pt Marshland RD (the pars not in S-W'rn Dv), Walsoken UD

NORTHERN DIVISION

Aylsham RD, Cromer UD, Erpingham RD, Sheringham UD, Walsingham RD, Wells UD

SOUTHERN DIVISION

Depwade RD, Diss UD, Forehoe RD, Henstead RD, pt Thetford RD (the pars not in S-W'rn Dv), Wayland RD

SOUTH-WESTERN DIVISION

East Dereham UD, pt Downham RD (the pars not in King's Lynn Dv), Downham Market UD, pt Marshland RD (Outwell, Upwell), Mitford and Launditch RD, Swaffham RD, Swaffham UD, Thetford MB, pt Thetford RD (Cranwich, Feltwell, Feltwell Anchor, Hockwold cum Wilton, Lynford, Methwold, Mundford, Northwood, Santon, West Tofts, Weeting with Bromehill)

1948–1970

KING'S LYNN COUNTY CONSTITUENCY

Docking RD, New Hunstanton UD, Freebridge Lynn RD, King's Lynn MB, Marshland RD

CENTRAL NORFOLK COUNTY CONSTITUENCY[9]

pt Blofield and Flegg RD (Plumstead, Great and Little; Postwick, Thorpe next Norwich), Forehoe and Henstead RD, St Faith's and Aylsham RD

NORTH NORFOLK COUNTY CONSTITUENCY

Cromer UD, Erpingham RD, Sheringham UD, Smallburgh RD, North Walsham UD, Walsingham RD, Wells next the Sea UD

SOUTH NORFOLK COUNTY CONSTITUENCY

Depwade RD, Diss UD, Loddon RD, Thetford MB, Wayland RD, Wymondham UD

SOUTH WEST NORFOLK COUNTY CONSTITUENCY

East Dereham UD, Downham RD, Downham Market UD, Mitford and Launditch RD, Swaffham RD, Swaffham UD

YARMOUTH COUNTY CONSTITUENCY

pt Blofield and Flegg RD (the pars not in Central Norfolk CC), Great Yarmouth CB

*1970–**

NORTH NORFOLK COUNTY CONSTITUENCY

Cromer UD, Erpingham RD, St Faith's and Aylsham RD, Sheringham UD, Smallburgh RD, North Walsham UD

NORTH WEST NORFOLK COUNTY CONSTITUENCY
Docking RD, Hunstanton UD, Freebridge Lynn RD, King's Lynn MB, Marshland RD, Walsingham RD, Wells next the Sea UD

SOUTH NORFOLK
Depwade RD, Diss UD, Forehoe and Henstead RD, Loddon RD, Thetford MB, Wayland RD, Wymondham UD

SOUTH WEST NORFOLK COUNTY CONSTITUENCY
East Dereham UD, Downham RD, Downham Market UD, Mitford and Launditch RD, Swaffham RD, Swaffham UD

YARMOUTH COUNTY CONSTITUENCY
Blofield and Flegg RD, Great Yarmouth CB

OXFORDSHIRE

BOROUGH CONSTITUENCIES[1]

BANBURY (*temp* Mary I–1885)(Oxon, Northants)
Banbury[2] (pt until 1832, ent 1832–85)
BURFORD (1306 only)
Burford
DEDDINGTON (1302–04 only)
Deddington
CHIPPING NORTON (1302–04 only)
Chipping Norton
OXFORD[3] (1295–* [1 mbr, 1885–*])(Oxon, Berks)
Binsey (until 1926), pt Cowley (1835–94), Cowley St John (1894–1926), pt Headington (1889–94), pt North Hinksey (1889–94), pt South Hinksey (1889–94), Holywell[21] (until 1926), pt Littlemore[22] (1866–94), pt Marston (1889– Binsey (until 1948), pt Cowley (1832–1918 [enlarged pt 1867–1918]), pt Headington (1832–1918), pt South Hinksey[4] (1867–1918), Holywell (1295–1948), pt Littlemore (1867–1918), Marston (pt 1832–67, ent 1867–1918), Oxford (1948–*), Oxford All Saints (1295–1918), Oxford St Aldate[4] (1295–1948), Oxford St Clement (pt 1295–1867, ent 1867–1918), Oxford St Ebbe (1295–1948), Oxford St Giles (pt 1295–1867, ent 1867–1948), Oxford St John the Baptist (1295–1948), Oxford St Martin (1295–1918), Oxford St Martin and All Saints (1918–48), Oxford St Mary Magdalene (1295–1948), Oxford St Mary the Virgin (1295–1948), Oxford St Michael (1295–1948), Oxford St Peter in the East (1295–1948), Oxford St Peter le Bailey (1295–1948), Oxford St Thomas (1295–1948), pt Seacourt[4] (until 1918), Unnamed (1918–48), pt Wolvercott (until 1918)
WITNEY (1304–06 only)
Witney
WOODSTOCK (1302–04, 1571–1885)
until 1835: pt Wootton (until Woodstock gains sep civ identity), Woodstock (thereafter)
1835–85: Begbroke, Bladon, Blenheim Park, Combe, Hampton Gay, Handborough, pt Kidlington, Shipton-on-Cherwell, Stonesfield, Tackley, Woodstock, Wootton

COUNTY CONSTITUENCIES

Oxon was undivided for parl purposes until 1885.

MID DIVISION
Bampton East PSD, Bampton West PSD, pt Bullingdon PSD, Ploughley PSD, Wootton South PSD, *viz.*, Alvescot, Ambrosden, Ardley, Arncott, Asterleigh, Asthall, Aston and Cote, Bampton, Beckley, Begbroke, Bicester King's End, Bicester Market End, Blackthorn, Bladon, Blenheim Park, Bletchingdon, Black Bourton, Brighthampton, Broadwell, Bucknell, Burford, Cassington, Caversfield, Charlton-on-Otmoor, Chesterton, Chimney, Clanfield, Cogges, Combe, Cottisford, pt Cowley, Crawley, Curbridge, Cutteslowe, Ducklington, Water Eaton, Elsfield, Eynsham, Little Faringdon, Fencott and Murcott, Filkins, Finmere, Forest Hill with Shotover, Fringford, Fritwell, Fulbrook, Glympton, Godington, Gosford, Grafton, Hailey, Hampton Gay, Hampton Poyle, Handborough, Hardwick, Hardwick, pt Headington, Hensington, Hethe, Lower Heyford, Upper Heyford, Holwell, Horton cum Studley, Iffley, Islip, Kelmscot, Kencot, Kiddington, Kidlington, Kirtlington, Langford, Launton, North Leigh, South Leigh, Lew, pt Marston, Merton, Middleton Stoney, Minster Lovell, Mixbury, Newton Purcell, Noke, Northmoor, Brize Norton, Oddington, Osney Hill, Piddington, Radcot, Ramsden, Shelswell, Shifford, Shilton, Shipton-on-Cherwell, Somerton, Souldern, Standlake, Stanton Harcourt, Stanton St John, Stoke Lyne, Stonesfield, Stowood, Stratton Audley, Studley, Swinbrook, Tackley, Taynton, Thrup, Tusmore, Upton and Signet, Wendlebury, Weston-on-the-Green, Westwell, Widford, Wilcote, Witney, Woodeaton, pt Wolvercott, Woodstock, Wootton, Yarnton, Yelford
NORTHERN DIVISION
Banbury MB, Banbury and Bloxham PSD, Chadlington PSD, Wootton North PSD, *viz.*, East Adderbury, West Adderbury, Alkerton, Ascott-under-Wychwood, Middle Aston, North Aston, Steeple Aston, Banbury,[2] Barford St John, Barford St Michael, Steeple Barton, Westcott Barton, Bloxham, Bodicote, Bourton, Broughton, Broughton Poggs, Bruern, Chadlington, Charlbury, Chastleton, Chilson, Churchill, Clattercott, Claydon, Cornbury Park, Cornwell, Cropredy, Deddington, Drayton, Enstone, Epwell, Fawler, Fifield, Finstock, Hanwell, Heythrop, Horley, Hornton, Idbury, Kingham, Langley, Leafield, Lyneham, Milcombe, Milton, Milton-under-Wychwood, Mollington, Neithrop, North Newington, South Newington, Chipping Norton, Hook Norton, Over Norton, Prescote, Great Rollright, Little Rollright, Rousham, Salford, Sandford St Martin, Sarsden, Shenington, Shipton-

under-Wychwood, East Shutford, West Shutford, Sibford Ferris, Sibford Gower, Spelsbury, Swalcliffe, Swerford, Tadmarton, Duns Tew, Great Tew, Little Tew, Wardington, Wigginton, Nether Worton, Over Worton, Wroxton, Wychwood

SOUTHERN DIVISION

pt Bullingdon PSD, Henley PSD, Henley-on-Thames MB, Waltlington PSD, *viz.*, Adwell, Albury, Ascott, Aston Rowant, Attington, Marsh Baldon, Toot Baldon, Benson, Berrick Salome, Bix, Brightwell Baldwin, Britwell Prior, Britwell Salome, Burcott, Caversham, Chalgrove, Checkendon, Chilworth, Chinnor, Chippinghurst, Chislehampton, Clifton Hampden,[5] Crowell, Crowmarsh Gifford, Cuddesdon, Culham, Cuxham, Denton, Dorchester, Drayton St Leonard, Easington, Emmington, Ewelme, Eye and Dunsden, Garsington, Goring, Harpsden, Great Haseley, Henley-on-Thames, Holton, Horspath, Ibstone, pt Ickford, Ipsden, pt Kingsey, Lewknor, pt Lewknor Uphill, pt Littlemore, Mapledurham, Great Milton, Little Milton, Mongewell, Nettlebed, Newington, Newnham Murren, Nuffield, Nuneham Courtenay, Pishill, Pyrton, Rotherfield Greys, Rotherfield Peppard, Sandford-on-Thames, Shiplake, Shirburn, Stadhampton, North Stoke, South Stoke, Stoke Talmage, Stokenchurch, Swyncombe, Sydenham, Tetsworth, Thame, Thomley, Tiddington, Warborough, Warpsgrove, Waterperry, Waterstock, Watlington, South Weston, Wheatfield, Wheatley, Whitchurch

1918–1948

BANBURY DIVISION

Banbury MB, Banbury RD, Chipping Norton MB, Chipping Norton RD, Witney RD, Witney UD, Woodstock MB, Woodstock RD

HENLEY DIVISION

Bicester RD, Bicester UD, Crowmarsh RD, Culham RD, Goring RD, Headington RD, Henley RD, Henley-on-Thames MB, Thame RD, Thame UD, Wheatley UD

1948–1970

BANBURY COUNTY CONSTITUENCY

Banbury MB, Banbury RD, Chipping Norton MB, Chipping Norton RD, pt Ploughley RD (Begbroke, Gosford and Water Eaton, Hampton Gay and Poyle, Kidlington, Shipton-on-Cherwell, Thrup, Yarnton), Witney RD, Witney UD, Woodstock MB

HENLEY COUNTY CONSTITUENCY[3]

Bicester UD, Bullingdon RD, Henley RD, Henley-on-Thames MB, pt Ploughley RD (the pars not in Banbury CC), Thame UD

*1970–**

BANBURY COUNTY CONSTITUENCY

Banbury MB, Banbury RD, Bicester UD, Chipping Norton MB, Chipping Norton RD, pt Ploughley RD (Ardley, Bucknell, Caversfield, Chesterton, Cottisford, Finmere, Fringford, Fritwell, Godington, Hardwick with Tusmore, Hethe, Lower Heyford, Upper Heyford, Kirtlington, Launton, Middleton Stoney, Mixbury, Newton Purcell with Shelswell, Somerton, Souldern, Stoke Lyne, Stratton Audley), Woodstock MB

HENLEY COUNTY CONSTITUENCY

pt Bullingdon RD (Adwell, Aston Rowant, Marsh Baldon, Toot Baldon, Benson, Berinsfield, Berrick Salome, Brightwell Baldwin, Britwell, Chalgrove, Chinnor, Clifton Hampden, Crowell, Cuddesdon and Denton, Culham, Cuxham with Easington, Dorchester, Drayton St Leonard, Ewelme, Garsington, Great Haseley, Lewknor, Littlemore, Little Milton, Newington, Nuneham Courtenay, Pyrton, Sandford-on-Thames, Shirburn, Stadhampton, Stoke Talmage, Sydenham, Tetsworth, Towersey, Warborough, Watlington, Wheatfield), Henley RD, Henley-on-Thames MB, Thame UD

MID-OXON COUNTY CONSTITUENCY

pt Bullingdon RD (the pars not in Henley CC), pt Ploughley RD (the pars not in Banbury CC), Witney RD, Witney UD

SOMERSET

BOROUGH CONSTITUENCIES[1]

AXBRIDGE (1295, 1313, 1319–25 only)
Axbridge

BATH[2] (1295–*)
Bath (1918–74), Bath St James (1295–1918), Bath St Peter and St Paul (1295–1918), Bath St Michael (1295–1918), Bathwick (1832–1918), Lyncombe and Widcombe (1832–1918), pt Twerton or Twiverton (1867–1918), pt Walcot (1295–1918)

BRIDGWATER (1295–1867)
pt Bridgwater, pt Durleigh (1832–67), pt Wembdon

BRISTOL[3] (Glos, Somerset) (1295–1885)
pt Bedminster (1832–85), Bristol St Mary Redcliffe, Bristol St Thomas, Bristol Temple

BRISTOL, SOUTH DIVISION[3] (Glos/Bristol CB, Somerset) (1885–1918)
pt Bedminster, Bristol St Mary Redcliffe, Bristol St Thomas, Bristol Temple

CHARD (1312–13, 1328 only)
pt Chard

DUNSTER (1360 only)
Dunster

FROME (1832–85)
pt Frome, pt Marston Bigot

LANGPORT (1304–07 only)
pt Huish Episcopi

MONTACUTE (1304–06 only)
Montacute

STOGURSEY (1360 only)
Stogursey

TAUNTON (1295–1918 [1 mbr, 1885–1918])
pt Bishop's Hull (1832–1918), pt West Monkton (1832–1918), pt Taunton St James, pt Taunton St Mary Magdalene, pt Wilton

WATCHET (1302 only)
pt St Decuman's

WEARE (1304–07 only)
Weare

WELLS (1295–1867)
Wells St Andrew, pt Wells St Cuthbert

COUNTY CONSTITUENCIES

1832–1867

EASTERN DV
Lbty of Mells and Leigh and the Hds of Bath Forum, Bempstone, Brent with Wrington, Bruton, Catsash, Chew, Chewton, Frome, Glaston Twelve Hides, Hampton and Claverton, Hartcliffe with Bedminster, Horethorne, Keynsham, Kilmersdon, Norton Ferris, Portbury, Wellow, Wells Forum, Whitstone, Winterstoke

WESTERN DV
Hds of Abdick and Bulstone, Andersfield, Cannington, Carhampton, Catsash, Crewkerne, North Curry; Houndsborough, Barwick and Coker; Huntspill and Puriton, East Kingsbury, West Kingsbury, Martock, Milverton, North Petherton, South Petherton, Pitney, Somerton, Stone, Taunton and Taunton Dean, Tintinhull, Whitley, Williton and Freemanors

1867–1885

EAST DV
Long Ashton PSD, Axbridge PSD, Keynsham PSD, Temple Cloud PSD, Weston PSD, *viz.*, Chapel Allerton, Long Ashton, Axbridge, Backwell, Badgworth, Banwell, Barrow Gurney, Bathampton, Batheaston, Bathford, pt Bedminster, Berrow, Biddisham, Blagdon, Bleadon, Brean, East Brent, Brent Knoll, Brislington, Brockley, Burnett, Burnham, Burrington, Butcombe, Cameley, Camerton, Charlcombe, Queen Charlton, Charterhouse, Cheddar, Chelvey, Chelwood, Chew Magna, Chew Stoke, Chewton Mendip, Christon, Churchill, Clapton, Claverton, Clevedon, Clutton, English Combe, Monkton Combe, Combe Hay, Compton Bishop, Compton Dando, Compton Martin, Congresbury, Corston, Dundry, Dunkerton, Easton-in-Gordano, Emborough, Farleigh Hungerford, Farmborough, Farrington Gurney, Flax Bourton, Freshford, Green Oare, East Harptree, West Harptree, Hinton Blewitt. Hinton Charterhouse, Hutton, Kelston, Kenn, Kewstoke, Keynsham, Kingston Seymour, Langridge, Abbots Leigh, High Littleton, Litton, Locking, Loxton, Lympsham, Mark, Marksbury, Nailsea, Nempnett Thrubwell, Newton St Loe, Midsomer Norton, Norton St Philip, Norton Hawkfield, Norton Malreward, Paulton, Portbury, Portishead, Priston, Publow, Puxton, Rowberrow, St Catherine, St Thomas in Pensford, Saltford, Shipham, Stanton Drew, Stanton Prior, North Stoke, South Stoke, Ston Easton, Stowey, Swainswick, Tellisford, Tickenham, Timsbury, pt Twerton or Twiverton, Ubley, Uphill, pt Walcot, Walton in Gordano, Weare, Wedmore, Wellow, Weston, Weston in Gordano, Weston super Mare, Whitchurch, Wick St Lawrence, North Widcombe, Winford, Winscombe, Woolley, Worle, Wraxall, Wrington, Yatton

MID DV
Crewkerne PSD, Frome PSD, Kilmersdon PSD, Shepton Mallet PSD, Somerton PSD, Wells PSD, Wincanton PSD, Yeovil PSD, *viz.*, Alford, Aller,

Ansford, Ashington, Ashwick, Babcary, Babington, Balstonsborough, North Barrow, South Barrow, Barton St David, Barwick, Batcombe, Beckington, Berkley, Binegar, Blackford, Maiden Bradley, West Bradley, Bratton Seymour, North Brewham, South Brewham, Bruton, Brympton, Buckland Dinham, Butleigh, North Cadbury, South Cadbury, Queen Camel, West Camel, Castle Cary, Charlton Adam, Charlton Horethorne, Charlton Mackrell, Charlton Musgrove, North Cheriton, Chilcompton, Chilthorne Domer, Chilton Canteloe, East Chinnock, Middle Chinnock, West Chinnock, Chiselborough, Cloford, Closworth, East Coker, West Coker, Abbas and Temple Combe, Compton Dundon, Compton Pauncefoot, Corton Denham, East Cranmore, West Cranmore, Crewkerne, Croscombe, Cucklington, Dinder, Ditcheat, Doulting, Downhead, Eastrip, Elm, Evercreech, Four Towers, Foxcote, pt Frome, Glastonbury, Goathill, High Ham, Hardington, Hardington Mandeville, Haslebury Plucknett, Hemington, Henstridge, Hinton St George, Holcombe, Holton, Hornblotton, Horsington, Huish Episcopi, Ilchester, Keinton Mandeville, Kilmersdon, Kilmington, Kingsdon, Kingweston, Lamyat, Langport, Laverton, Leigh upon Mendip, Limington, Lopen, Lovington, Lufton, Lullington, East Lydford, West Lydford, Maperton, pt Marston Bigot, Marston Magna, Martock, Meare, Mells, Merriott, Milborne Port, Milton Clevedon, Misterton, Montacute, Muchelney, Mudford, Northover, Norton sub Hamdon, Nunney, Nyland cum Batcombe, Odcombe, Orchardleigh, Pendomer, East Pennard, West Pennard, Penselwood, North Perrott, Pilton, Pitcombe, Pitney, Podimore, Poyntington, Preston Plucknett, Priddy, Pylle, Radstock, Rimpton, Road, Rodden, Sandford Orcas, Seaborough, Shepton Mallett, Shepton Montague, Sock Dennis, Somerton, Sparkford, Standerwick, Rodney Stoke, Stoke Lane, Stoke sub Hamdon, Stoke Trister, Stourton, Stowell, Stratton on the Fosse, Street, Long Sutton, Sutton Bingham, Sutton Montis, Thorne, Tintinhull, Trent, Upton Noble, Walton, Wanstrow, Wayford, Wells St Andrew, Wells St Cuthbert In, Wells St Cuthbert Out, Westbury, Weston Bampfylde, Whatley, Wheathill, Wincanton, Witham Friary, Woolverton, North Wootton, Wookey, Writhlington, Yarlington, Yeovil, Yeovilton

WEST DV

Bridgwater PSD, Dulverton PSD, Dunster PSD, Ilminster PSD, Bishop's Lydeard PSD, Taunton PSD, Wellington PSD, Williton PSD, Wiveliscombe PSD, *viz.*, Aisholt, Angersleigh, Ash Priors, Ashbrittle, Ashcott, Ashill, West Bagborough, Barrington, Bathealton, Bawdrip, Beer Crocombe, Bickenhall, Bicknoller, Bradford, South Bradon, Bridgwater, Broadway, Brompton Ralph, Brompton Regis, Broomfield, Brushford, West Buckland, Buckland St Mary, Cannington, Carhampton, Catcott, Chaffcombe, Chard, Chard Borough, Charlynch, Cheddon Fitzpaine, Chedzoy, Chillington, Chilton Common, Chilton Polden, Chilton Trinity, Chipstable, Clatworthy, Old Cleeve, Combe Florey, Combe St Michael, Corfe, Cossington, Cothelstone, Creech St Michael, Cricket Malherbie, Cricket St Thomas, Crowcombe, Cudworth, Culbone, Curland, North Curry, Curry Mallet, Curry Rivel, Cutcombe, Dinnington, Dodington, Donyatt, West Dowlish, Dowlish Wake, Drayton, Dulverton, Dunster, Durleigh, Durston, Earnshill, Edington, Edstock and Beer, Elworthy, Enmore, Exford, pt Exmoor, Exton, Fiddington, Fitzhead, Fivehead, Goathurst, Greinton, Halse, West Hatch, Hatch Beauchamp, Hawkridge, Heathfield, Hillfarrance, Holford, Huish Champflower, pt Bishop's Hull, Huntspill, Ilminster, Ilton, Isle Abbots, Isle Brewers, Kilton, Kilve, Kingsbury Episcopi, Kingston, Kingstone, Kittisford, Knowle St Giles, Langford Budville, Lilstock, Luccombe, Luxborough, Bishop's Lydeard, Lydeard St Lawrence, Lyng, Middlezoy, Milverton, Minehead, Monksilver, pt West Monkton, Moorlinch, Nettlecombe, Norton Fitzwarren, Nynehead, Oake, Oare, Orchard Portman, Othery, Otterford, Otterhampton, Pawlett, North Petherton, South Petherton, Pitminster, Porlock, Puckington, Puriton, East Quantoxhead, West Quantoxhead, Raddington, Ruishton, Runnington, St Decumans, St Michael Church, Sampford Arundel, Sampford Brett, Seavington St Mary, Seavington St Michael, Selworthy, Shapwick, Shepton Beauchamp, Skilgate, Spaxton, Staple Fitzpaine, Staplegrove, Stawell, Stawley, Stockland Bristol, Stocklinch Magdalen, Stocklinch Ottersey, Stogumber, Stogursey, Stoke Pero, Stoke St Gregory, Stoke St Mary, Nether Stowey, Over Stowey, Stringston, Sutton Mallet, Swell, pt Taunton St James, pt Taunton St Mary Magdalene, Thorn Falcon, Thorne St Margaret, Thurlbear, Thurloxton, Timberscombe, Tolland, Treborough, Trull, Upton, Wellington, Wembdon, Westonzoyland, Whitelackington, Whitestaunton, pt Wilton, Winsford, Winsham, Withiel Florey, Withycombe, Withypool, Wiveliscombe, Woolavington, Wootton Courtney

1885–1918

BRIDGWATER DV

Bridgwater PSD, Bridgwater MB, pt Taunton PSD, *viz.*, Aisholt, Ashcott, Ashill, Bawdrip, Beer Crocombe, Bickenhall, South Bradon, Bridgwater, Broadway, Broomfield, Buckland St Mary, Cannington, Catcott, Charlynch, Cheddon Fitzpaine, Chedzoy, Chilton Common, Chilton Polden, Chilton Trinity, Combe St Michael, Corfe, Cossington, Creech St Michael, Curland, North Curry, Curry Mallet, Donyatt, Durleigh, Durston, Edington, Edstock and Beer, Enmore, Fivehead, Goathurst, Greinton, West Hatch, Hatch Beauchamp, Hillfarrance, Huntspill, Ilminster, Ilton, Isle Abbots, Isle Brewers, Lyng, Middlezoy, pt West Monkton, Moorlinch, Orchard Portman, Othery, Otterhampton, Pawlett, North Petherton, Puriton, Ruishton, St Michaelchurch, Shapwick, Spaxton, Staple Fitzpaine, Stawell, Stockland Bristol, Stoke St Gregory, Stoke St Mary, Sutton Mallet, Thorn Falcon,

Thurlbear, Thurloxton, Wembdon, Westonzoyland, Whitestaunton, Woolavington

EASTERN DV

pt Shepton Mallet PSD, Somerton PSD, pt Wells PSD, Wincanton PSD, *viz.*, Alford, Aller, Ansford, Babcary, Baltonsborough, North Barrow, South Barrow, Barton St David, Maiden Bradley, Bratton Seymour, North Brewham, South Brewham, Bruton, Butleigh, North Cadbury, South Cadbury, West Camel, Castle Cary, Charlton Adam, Charlton Horethorne, Charlton Mackerell, Charlton Musgrove, North Cheriton, Abbas and Temple Combe, Compton Dundon, Compton Pauncefoot, Corton Denham, East Cranmore, West Cranmore, Croscombe, Cucklington, Ditcheat, Doulting, Eastrip, Evercreech, Four Towers, Glastonbury, Goathill, High Ham, Henstridge, Holton, Hornblotton, Horsington, Huish Episcopi, Keinton Mandeville, Kilmington, Kingsdon, Kingweston, Lamyat, Langport, Lovington, East Lydford, West Lydford, Maperton, Milborne Port, Milton Clevedon, Muchelney, East Pennard, West Pennard, Penselwood, Pilton, Pitcombe, Pitney, Podimore, Poyntington, Pylle, Sandford Orcas, Shepton Mallet, Shepton Montague, Somerton, Stoke Trister, Stourton, Stowell, Street, Long Sutton, Sutton Montis, Walton, Weston Bampfylde, Wheathill, Wincanton, North Wootton, Yarlington, Yeovilton

FROME DV

Frome PSD, pt Kilmersdon PSD, pt Shepton Mallet PSD, Weston PSD, *viz.*, Ashwick, Babington, Batcombe, Bathampton, Batheaston, Bathford, Beckington, Berkley, Blackford, Buckland Dinham, Camerton, Charlcombe, Claverton, Cloford, English Combe, Monkton Combe, Combe Hay, Corston, Downhead, Dunkerton, Elm, Farleigh Hungerford, Foxcote, Freshford, Frome, Hardington, Hemington, Hinton Charterhouse, Holcombe, Kelston, Kilmersdon, Langridge, Laverton, Leigh upon Mendip, Lullington, Marston Bigot, Mells, Newton St Loe, Norton St Philip, Nunney, Orchardleigh, Radstock, Road, Rodden, St Catherine, Standerwick, Rodney Stoke, North Stoke, South Stoke, Stoke Lane, Stratton on the Fosse, Swainswick, Tellisford, pt Twerton or Twiverton, Upton Noble, pt Walcot, Wanstrow, Wellow, Weston, Whatley, Witham Friary, Woolley, Woolverton, Writhlington

NORTHERN DV

Long Ashton PSD, Keynsham PSD, pt Kilmersdon PSD, Temple Cloud PSD, pt Wells PSD, *viz.*, Long Ashton, Backwell, Barrow Gurney, pt Bedminster, Binegar, Brislington, Brockley, Burnett, Cameley, Queen Charlton, Chelvey, Chelwood, Chew Magna, Chew Stoke, Chewton Mendip, Chilcompton, Clapton, Clevedon, Clutton, Compton Dando, Compton Martin, Dinder, Dundry, Easton in Gordano, Emborough, Farmborough, Farrington Gurney, Flax Bourton, Green Oare, East Harptree, West Harptree, Hinton Blewitt, Kenn, Keynsham, Kingston Seymour, Abbots Leigh, High Littleton, Litton, Marksbury, Nailsea, Nempnett Thrubwell, Midsomer Norton, Norton Hawkfield, Norton Malreward, Nyland cum Batcombe, Paulton, Portbury, Portishead, Priddy, Priston, Publow, Saltford, Stanton Drew, Stanton Prior, Ston Easton, Stowey, Tickenham, Timsbury, Ubley, Walton in Gordano, Westbury, Weston in Gordano, Whitchurch, North Widcombe, Winford, Wookey, Wraxall, Yatton

SOUTHERN DV

Crewkerne PSD, pt Ilminster PSD, Yeovil MB, Yeovil PSD, *viz.*, Ashington, Barrington, Barwick, Brympton, Queen Camel, Chaffcombe, Chard, Chard Borough, Chillington, Chilthorne Domer, Chilton Canteloe, East Chinnock, West Chinnock, Chiselborough, Closworth, East Coker, West Coker, Crewkerne, Cricket Malherbie, Cricket St Thomas, Cudworth, Curry Rivel, Dinnington, West Dowlish, Dowlish Wake, Drayton, Earnshill, Hardington Mandeville, Haslesbury Plucknett, Hinton St George, Ilchester, Kingsbury Episcopi, Kingstone, Knowle St Giles, Limington, Lopen, Lufton, Marston Magna, Martock, Merriott, Misterton, Montacute, Mudford, Northover, Norton sub Hamdon, Odcombe, Pendomer, North Perrott, South Petherton, Preston Plucknett, Puckington, Rimpton, Seaborough, Seavington St Mary, Seavington St Michael, Shepton Beauchamp, Sock Dennis, Sparkford, Stocklinch Magdalen, Stocklinch Ottersey, Stoke sub Hamdon, Sutton Bingham, Swell, Thorne, Tintinhull, Trent, Wayford, Whitelackington, Winsham, Yeovil

WELLS DV

Axbridge PSD, pt Wells PSD, *viz.*, Chapel Allerton, Axbridge, Badgworth, Banwell, Berrow, Biddisham, Blagdon, Bleadon, West Bradley, Brean, East Brent, Brent Knoll, Burnham, Burrington, Butcombe, Charterhouse, Cheddar, Christon, Churchill, Compton Bishop, Congresbury, Hutton, Kewstoke, Locking, Loxton, Lympsham, Mark, Meare, Puxton, Rowberrow, Shipham, Uphill, Wells St Andrew, Wells St Cuthbert In, Wells St Cuthbert Out, Weare, Wedmore, Weston super Mare, Wick St Lawrence, Winscombe, Worle, Wrington

WESTERN OR WELLINGTON DV

Dulverton PSD, Dunster PSD, Bishop's Lydeard PSD, pt Taunton PSD, Wellington PSD, Williton PSD, Wiveliscombe PSD, *viz.*, Angersleigh, Ash Priors, Ashbrittle, West Bagborough, Bathealton, Bicknoller, Bradford, Brompton Ralph, Brompton Regis, Brushford, West Buckland, Carhampton, Chipstable, Clatworthy, Old Cleeve, Combe Florey, Cothelstone, Crowcombe, Culbone, Cutcombe, Dodington, Dulverton, Dunster, Elworthy, Exford, Exmoor, Exton, Fiddington, Fitzhead, Halse, Hawkridge, Heathfield, Holford, Huish Champflower, pt Bishop's Hull, Kilton, Kilve, Kingston, Kittisford, Langford Budville, Lilstock, Luccombe, Luxborough, Bishop's Lydeard, Lydeard St Lawrence, Milverton, Minehead, Monksilver, Nettlecombe, Norton Fitzwarren, Nynehead, Oake, Oare, Otterford, Pitminster, Porlock, East Quantoxhead, West Quantoxhead, Raddington, Runnington, St Decuman's, Sampford Arundel, Sampford Brett, Selworthy, Skilgate, Staplegrove, Stawley, Stogumber, Stogursey, Stoke Pero, Nether Stowey, Over Stowey, Stringston, pt Taunton St James, pt Taunton St Mary Magdalene, Thorne St Margaret, Timberscombe, Tolland, Treborough, Trull, Upton, Wellington, pt Wilton, Winsford, Withiel Florey, Withycombe, Withypool, Wiveliscombe, Wootton Courtney

1918–1948

BRIDGWATER DIVISION

Bridgwater MB, Bridgwater RD, Burnham-on-Sea UD, Highbridge UD, Minehead UD, Watchet UD, Williton RD

FROME DIVISION

Bath RD, Clutton RD, pt Frome RD (the pars not in Wells Dv), Frome UD, Keynsham RD, Midsomer Norton UD, Radstock UD

TAUNTON DIVISION

Dulverton RD, Taunton MB, Taunton RD, Wellington RD, Wellington UD, Wiveliscombe UD

WELLS DIVISION

pt Frome RD (Cloford, Marston Bigot, Nunney, Wanstrow, Whatley, Witham Friary), Glastonbury MB, Shepton Mallet RD, Shepton Mallet UD, Street UD, Wells MB, Wells RD, Wincanton RD

WESTON-SUPER-MARE DIVISION

Long Ashton RD, Axbridge RD (including Steep Holme Island), Clevedon UD, Portishead UD, Weston-super-Mare UD

YEOVIL DIVISION

Chard MB, Chard RD, Crewkerne UD, Ilminster UD, Langport RD, Yeovil MB, Yeovil RD

1948–1970

BRIDGWATER COUNTY CONSTITUENCY

Bridgwater MB, Bridgwater RD, Burnham-on-Sea UD, Minehead UD, Watchet UD, Williton RD

NORTH SOMERSET COUNTY CONSTITUENCY[4]

Long Ashton RD (the pars not in Weston-super-Mare CC), Bathavon RD, Clutton RD, Keynsham UD, Norton-Radstock UD, Portishead UD

TAUNTON COUNTY CONSTITUENCY

Dulverton RD, Taunton MB, Taunton RD, Wellington RD, Wellington UD

WELLS COUNTY CONSTITUENCY[5]

Frome RD, Frome UD, Glastonbury MB, Shepton Mallet RD, Shepton Mallet UD, Street UD, Wells MB, Wells RD, Wincanton RD

WESTON-SUPER-MARE COUNTY CONSTITUENCY[6]

pt Long Ashton RD (Cleeve [1951–70], Kenn, Kingston Seymour, Yatton), Axbridge RD (including Steep Holme Island), Clevedon UD, Weston-super-Mare MB

YEOVIL COUNTY CONSTITUENCY

Chard MB, Chard RD, Crewkerne UD, Ilminster UD, Langport RD, Yeovil MB, Yeovil RD

*1970–**

BRIDGWATER COUNTY CONSTITUENCY

Bridgwater MB, Bridgwater RD, Burnham-on-Sea UD, Minehead UD, Watchet UD, Williton RD

NORTH SOMERSET COUNTY CONSTITUENCY

pt Long Ashton RD (the pars not in Weston-super-Mare CC), Bathavon RD, Clutton RD, Keynsham UD, Norton-Radstock UD, Portishead UD

TAUNTON COUNTY CONSTITUENCY

Dulverton RD, Taunton MB, Taunton RD, Wellington RD, Wellington UD

WELLS COUNTY CONSTITUENCY

Frome RD, Frome UD, Glastonbury MB, Shepton Mallet RD, Shepton Mallet UD, Street UD, Wells MB, Wells RD, Wincanton RD

WESTON-SUPER-MARE COUNTY CONSTITUENCY

pt Long Ashton RD (Cleeve, Kenn, Kingston Seymour, Yatton), Axbridge RD (including Steep Holme Island), Clevedon UD, Weston-super-Mare MB

YEOVIL COUNTY CONSTITUENCY

Chard MB, Chard RD, Crewkerne UD, Ilminster UD, Langport RD, Yeovil MB, Yeovil RD

SUFFOLK

BOROUGH CONSTITUENCIES[1]

Entirely or Primarily in Suffolk:
ALDEBURGH (1571–1832)
Aldeburgh
BURY ST EDMUNDS (1614–1918 [1 mbr, 1885–1918]
Bury St Edmunds St James, Bury St Edmunds St Mary
DUNWICH[2] (1298–1832)
Dunwich
EYE (1571–1885)
Eye, and the following for the period 1832–85 only: Braiseworth, Brome, Denham, Hoxne, Oakley, Occold, Redlingfield, Thorndon, Thrandeston, Yaxley
IPSWICH (1298–*)
until 1918: pt Belstead, pt Bramford, Ipswich St Clement, Ipswich St Helen, Ipswich St Lawrence, Ipswich St Margaret, Ipswich St Mary at the Elms, Ipswich St Mary at the Quay, Ipswich St Mary at the Tower, Ipswich St Mary Stoke, Ipswich St Matthew, Ipswich St Nicholas, Ipswich St Peter, Ipswich St Stephen, pt Rushmere, Shire Hall Yard (1867–1918), pt Sproughton, Warren House (1867–1918), pt Westerfield, pt Whitton cum Thurleston[3]
since 1918: Ipswich CB[4]
ORFORD (1298, restored 1529–1832)
Orford
SUDBURY (1558–1885)(Suffolk, Essex)
Ballington ([Suffolk, Essex], 1832–85), Sudbury All Saints, Sudbury St Bartholomew (1867–85), Sudbury St Gregory, Sudbury St Peter

Primarily in Norfolk:
THETFORD (1553–1885)
pt Thetford St Cuthbert, pt Thetford St Mary
GREAT YARMOUTH
Gorleston (1832–85) [par in Norfolk thereafter]

COUNTY CONSTITUENCIES

1832–1885
EASTERN DIVISION
Hds of Blything, Bosmere and Claydon, Carlford, Colneis, Hoxne, Lackford, Loes, Mutford and Lothingland, Samford, Thredling, Wangford, Wilford
WESTERN DIVISION
Hds of Babergh, Blackbourn, Cosford, Hartismere, Plomesgate, Risbridge, Stow, Thedwastre, Thingoe

1885–1918
NORTHERN OR LOWESTOFT DIVISION
Beccles PSD, pt Blything PSD, Bungay PSD, Mutford and Lothingland PSD, Southwold MB, *viz.*, Ashby, Barnby, Barsham, Beccles, Belton, Benacre, Blundeston, Blyford, Bradwell, Brampton, Bungay Holy Trinity, Bungay St Mary, Burgh Castle, Carlton Colville, Chediston, Corton, North Cove, South Cove, Covehithe, Easton Bavants, South Elmham All Saints and St Nicholas, South Elmham St Cross, South Elmham St James, South Emlham St Margaret, South Elmham St Michael, South Elmham St Peter, Ellough, Flixton, Flixton, Fritton, Frostenden, Gisleham, Gunton, Halesworth, Henham, Henstead, Herringfleet, Holton St Mary, Homersfield, Hopton, Ilketshall St Andrew, Ilketshall St John, Ilketshall St Lawrence, Ilketshall St Margaret, Kessingland, Kirkley, Lound, Lowestoft, Mettingham, Mutford, Oulton, Pakefield, Redisham, Reydon, Ringsfield, Rumburgh, Rushmere, Shadingfield, Shipmeadow, Somerleyton, Sotherton, Southwold, Spexhall, Stoven, Uggeshall, Wangford, Westhall, Weston, Wissett, Willingham, Worlingham, Wrentham
NORTH-EASTERN OR EYE DIVISION
pt Blything PSD, Eye MB, Framlingham PSD, Hartismere PSD, Hoxne PSD, *viz.*, Aldringham with Thorpe, Ashfield with Thorpe, Aspall, Athelington, Bacton, Badingham, Bedfield, Bedingfield, Benhall, Blythburgh, Botesdale, Braiseworth, Bramfield, Brandeston, Brome, Bruisyard, Brundish, Burgate, Carlton, Cookley, Cotton, Cransford, Cratfield, Cretingham, Darsham, Debenham, Denham, Dennington, Drinkstone, Easton, Eye, Farnham, Finningham, Framlingham, Framsden, Fressingfield, Friston, Gislingham, Great Glemham, Little Glemham, Hacheston, Hazlewood, Heveningham, Hoo, Horham, Hoxne, Huntingfield, Kelsale, Kenton, Kettleburgh, Knodishall, Laxfield, Leiston, Letheringham, Linstead Magna, Linstead Parva, Marlesford, Mellis, Mendham, Mendlesham, Metfield, Middleton, Monewden, Oakley, Occold, Palgrave, Parham, Peasenhall, Pettaugh, Redgrave, Redlingfield, Rendham, Rickinghall Superior, Rishangles, Saxmundham, Saxstead, Sibton, Snape, Earl Soham, Monk Soham, Southolt, Sternfield, Stoke Ash, Stradbroke, Stratford St Andrew, Stuston, Swefling, Syleham, Tannington, Theberton, Thorington, Thorndon, Thornham Magna, Thornham Parva, Thwaite, Ubbeston, Walberswick, Walpole, Wenhaston, Westleton, Westhorpe, Wetheringsett cum Brockford, Wickham Skeith, Wilby, Wing-

field, Winston, Withersdale, Worlingworth, Wortham, Wyverstone, Yaxley, Yoxford

NORTH-WESTERN OR STOWMARKET DIVISION

Blackbourn PSD, Lackford PSD, pt Newmarket PSD, Stowmarket PSD, pt Thingoe and Thedwastre PSD, *viz.*, Ampton, Great Ashfield, Badwell Ash, Bardwell, Barnham, Barningham, Barrow, Great Barton, Barton Mills, Beyton, Bradfield Combust, Bradfield St Clare, Bradfield St George, Brandon, Buxhall, Cavenham, Chimney Mills, Combs, Creeting St Peter, Culford, Dalham, Denham, Drinkstone, Elmswell, Elveden, Eriswell, Euston, Exning, Fakenham Magna, Felsham, Great Finborough, Little Finborough, Flempton, Fornham All Saints, Fornham St Genevieve, Fornham St Martin, Freckenham, Gazeley, Gedding, Gipping, Hardwick, Harleston, Haughley, Hengrave, Hepworth, Herringswell, Hessett, Higham Green, Hinderclay, Honington, Hopton, Horringer, Huntingfield, Icklingham, Ickworth, Ingham, Ixworth, Ixworth Thorpe, Kentford, Knettishall, Lackford, Lakenheath, Langham, Great Livermere, Little Livermere, Mildenhall, Moulton, pt Newmarket St Mary, Old Newton, Norton, Nowton, Onehouse, Pakenham, Rattlesden, Rickinghall Inferior, Risby, Rougham, Rushbrooke, Rushford, Santon Downham, Sapiston, Great Saxham, Little Saxham, Shelland, Stanningfield, Stanton, West Stow, Stowlangtoft, Stowmarket, Stowupland, Thelnetham, Thurston, Timworth, Tostock, Troston, Tuddenham, Walsham-le-Willows, Wangford, Wattisfield, Great Welnetham, Little Welnetham, Westley, Coney Weston, Market Weston, Wetherden, Woolpit, Wordwell, Worlington

SOUTH OR SUDBURY DIVISION

Boxford PSD, Hadleigh or Cosford PSD, Melford PSD, pt Newmarket PSD, Risbridge PSD, Sudbury MB, pt Thedwastre and Thingoe PSD, *viz.*, Acton, Aldham, Alpheton, Assington, pt Ballingdon, Barnardiston, Bildeston, Boxford, Boxted, Great Bradley, Little Bradley, Brettenham, Brockley, Bures St Mary, Cavendish, Chedburgh, Chevington, Chilton, Clare, Cockfield, Great Cornard, Little Cornard, Cowlinge, Denston, Depden, Edwardstone, Brent Eleigh, Monks Eleigh, Elmsett, Glemsford, Groton, Hadleigh, Hadleigh Hamlet, Hargrave, Hartest, Haverhill, Hawkedon, Hitcham, Hundon, pt Kedington, Kersey, Kettlebaston, Lavenham, Lawshall, Layham, Lidgate, Lindsey, Long Melford, Milden, Naughton, Nayland with Wissington, Nedging, Newton, Ousden, Polstead, Poslingford, Preston, Rede, Monks Risbridge, Semer, Shimpling, Somerton, Stansfield, Stanstead, Stoke by Clare, Stoke by Nayland, Stradishall, Sudbury, Sudbury St Bartholomew, Thorpe Morieux, Great Thurlow, Little Thurlow, Great Waldingfield, Little Waldingfield, Wattisham, Whatfield, Whepstead, Wickhambrook, Withersfield, Wixoe, Great Wratting, Little Wratting

SOUTH-EASTERN OR WOODBRIDGE DIVISION

Aldeburgh MB, Bosmere and Claydon PSD, Samford PSD, Woodbridge PSD, *viz.*, Akenham, Aldeburgh, Alderton, Alnesbourn Priory, Ashbocking, Badley, Barham, Barking, Battisford, Bawdsey, Baylham, Great Bealings, Little Bealings, pt Belstead, Bentley, East Bergholt, Great Blakenham, Little Blakenham, Blaxhall, Boulge, Boyton, pt Bramford, Brantham, Bredfield, Great Bricett, Brightwell, Bromeswell, Bucklesham, Burgh, Burstall, Butley, Campsey Ash, Capel St Andrew, Capel St Mary, Charsfield, Chattisham, Chelmondiston, Chillesford, Claydon, Clopton, Coddenham, Copdock, Creeting St Mary, Crowfield, Culpho, Dallinghoo, Dallinghoo Wield, Debach, Erwarton, Eyke, Falkenham, Felixstowe, Flowton, Foxhall, Freston, Gedgrave, Gosbeck, Grundisburgh, Harkstead, Hasketon, Havergate Island, Helmingham, Hemingstone, Hemley, Henley, Higham, Hintlesham, Holbrook, Hollesley, Holton St Mary, Iken, Kesgrave, Kirton, Layham, Levington, Martlesham, Melton, Mickfield, Nacton, Nettlestead, Newbourne, Offton, Orford, Otley, Pettistree, Playford, Purdis Farm, Ramsholt, Raydon, Rendlesham, Ringshall, Rushmere, Shelley, Shotley, Shottisham, Somersham, Sproughton, Earl Stonham, Little Stonham, Stonham Aspall, Stratford St Mary, Stutton, Sudbourne, Sutton, Swilland, Tattingstone, Stratton Hall, Trimley St Martin, Trimley St Mary, Tuddenham, Tunstall, Ufford, Waldringfield, Walton, Wantisden, Washbrook, Great Wenham, Little Wenham, Wherstead, pt Whitton cum Thurleston, Wickham Market, Willisham, Witnesham, Woolbridge, Woolverstone

1918–1948

East Suffolk:

EYE DIVISION

pt Blything RD (all except the pars in Lowestoft Dv), Eye MB, Halesworth UD, Hartismere RD, Hoxne RD, Leiston cum Sizewell UD, pt Plomesgate RD (all except the pars in Woodbridge Dv), Saxmundham UD, East Stow RD, Stowmarket UD

LOWESTOFT DIVISION

Beccles MB, pt Blything RD (Benacre, South Cove, Covehithe, Easton Bavants, Frostenden, Henstead, Reydon, Wrentham), Bungay UD, Lowestoft MB, Oulton Broad UD, Mutford and Lothingland RD, Southwold MB, Wangford RD

WOODBRIDGE DIVISION

Aldeburgh MB, Bosmere and Claydon RD, Felixstowe UD, pt Plomesgate RD (Blaxhall, Butley, Campsey Ash, Chillesford, Eyke, Gedgrave, Havergate Island, Iken, Orford, Rendlesham, Sudbourne, Tunstall, Wantisden, Wickham Market), Samford RD, Woodbridge RD, Woodbridge UD

West Suffolk:

BURY ST EDMUNDS DIVISION

Brandon RD, Bury St Edmunds MB, Mildenhall RD, pt Moulton RD (all except the pars in Sudbury Dv), Newmarket UD, Thedwastre RD, pt Thingoe RD (all except the pars in Sudbury Dv)

SUDBURY DIVISION

Clare RD, Cosford RD, Glemsford UD, Hadleigh UD, Haverhill UD, Melford RD, pt Moutlon RD (Lidgate, Ousden), Sudbury MB, pt Thingoe RD (Bradfield Combust, Bradfield St Clare, Bradfield

St George, Brockley, Chedburgh, Chevington, Depden, Hargrave, Hawstead, Rede, Stanningfield, Great Welnetham, Little Welnetham, Whepstead)

*1948–**

Not divided by Adm Co, but treated as one Parl Co:

BURY ST EDMUNDS COUNTY CONSTITUENCY

Bury St Edmunds MB, Clare RD, Haverhill UD, Mildenhall RD, Newmarket UD, Thedwastre RD, Thingoe RD

EYE COUNTY CONSTITUENCY[4]

Aldeburgh MB, Blyth RD, pt Deben RD (Blaxhall, Boulge, Bredfield, Burgh, Campsey Ash, Charsfield, Chillesford, Clopton, Cretingham, Dallinghoo, Dallinghoo Wield, Debach, Eyke, Gedgrave, Grundisburgh, Hoo, Iken, Letheringham, Monewden, Orford, Otley, Pettistree, Rendlesham, Sudbourne, Swilland, Tunstall, Ufford, Wantisden, Wickham Market, Witnesham), Eye MB, Gipping RD, Hartismere RD, Leiston cum Sizewell UD, Saxmundham UD, Stowmarket UD

LOWESTOFT COUNTY CONSTITUENCY

Beccles MB, Bungay UD, Halesworth UD, Lothingland RD, Lowestoft MB, Southwold MB, Wainford RD

SUDBURY AND WOODBRIDGE COUNTY CONSTITUENCY[4]

Cosford RD, pt Deben RD (all except the pars in Eye CC), Felixstowe UD, Hadleigh UD, Melford RD, Samford RD, Sudbury MB, Woodbridge UD

SURREY

BOROUGH CONSTITUENCIES[1]

Entirely in Surrey:

BLETCHINGLEY (1295–1832)
Bletchingley

CHERTSEY AND WALTON (1970–*)
Chertsey and Walton UD, Weybridge UD

CROYDON (1885–1918)
Croydon MB

CROYDON EAST (1948–55)[2]
pt Croydon CB (the wards of Addington, Addiscombe, East, South Norwood, Woodside)

CROYDON NORTH (1918–55)[2]
pt Croydon CB (the wards of Bensham Manor [1918–55], Norbury [1948–55], North [1918–48], South Norwood [1918–48], Upper Norwood, West Thornton [1948–55], Thornton Heath [1948–55])

CROYDON NORTH EAST (1955–70)[2]
pt Croydon CB (the wards of Addiscombe, East, South Norwood, Thornton Heath, Woodside)

CROYDON NORTH WEST (1955–70)[2]
pt Croydon CB (the wards of Bensham Manor, Norbury, Upper Norwood, West Thornton, Whitehorse Manor)

CROYDON SOUTH (1918–48)[3]
pt Croydon CB (the wards of Central, East, South, West)

CROYDON SOUTH (1955–70)[2]
pt Croydon CB (the wards of Addington, Broad Green, Central, Shirley, South, Waddon)

CROYDON WEST (1948–55)[2]
pt Croydon CB (the wards of Broad Green, Central, South, Waddon, Whitehorse Manor)

EPSOM AND EWELL (1970–*)
Epsom and Ewell MB, Leatherhead UD

ESHER (1970–*)[4]
Esher UD

FARNHAM (1311, 1460 only)
Farnham

GATTON (1450–1832)
Gatton

GUILDFORD (1295–1885 [1 mbr, 1867–85])
Bowling Green (1867–85), Guildford The Friary (1867–85), Guildford Holy Trinity (pt 1295–1832, ent 1832–85), Guildford St Mary, pt Guildford St Nicholas, pt Stoke (1832–85)

HASLEMERE (1584–1832)
Haslemere (orig pt Chiddingfold)

In Surrey until 1918, areas within Metropolis 1855–89, London Adm Co from 1889, in London for parl purposes after 1918:

KINGSTON UPON THAMES (1311–73 irregularly, 1918–70)[5]
in 14th cent: pt Kingston upon Thames; from 1918: Kingston upon Thames MB, Malden and Coombe MB (1955–70), The Maldens and Coombe UD (1918–48), Surbiton UD (1918–55)

MERTON AND MORDEN (1948–70)[2]
Merton and Morden UD

MITCHAM (1948–70)[2]
Beddington and Wallington MB, Mitcham MB

REIGATE (1295–1885 [1 mbr, 1832–85])
pt Reigate (until 1867), Reigate Borough (1867–85), Reigate Foreign (1867–85)

REIGATE (1970–*)
Banstead UD,[9] Reigate MB

RICHMOND (1918–70)
Barnes UD/MB, Ham UD (1918–48), Richmond MB

SPELTHORNE (1970–*)
Staines UD, Sunbury on Thames UD

SURBITON (1955–70)[5]
Surbiton MB

SUTTON AND CHEAM (1948–70)[2]
Sutton and Cheam MB

WIMBLEDON (1918–70)[5]
Malden and Coombe MB (1948–55), Merton and Morden UD (1918–48), Wimbledon MB

BATTERSEA AND CLAPHAM, BATTERSEA DIVISION (1885–1918)
pt Battersea (the wards of No. 2, No. 3, pt of the ward of No. 4)

BATTERSEA AND CLAPHAM, CLAPHAM DIVISION (1885–1918)
pt Battersea (the ward of No. 1, pt of the ward of No. 4), Clapham

CAMBERWELL, DULWICH DIVISION (1885–1918)
pt Camberwell (the ward of Camberwell and Dulwich)

CAMBERWELL, NORTH DIVISION (1885–1918)
pt Camberwell (the wards of St George's East, St George's West, Camden)

CAMBERWELL, PECKHAM DIVISION (1885–1918)
pt Camberwell (the wards of North Peckham, South Peckham)

DEPTFORD (1885–1918)
ent Kent except the pt of Deptford St Paul (the area of Hatcham) in Surrey

LAMBETH (1832–85)
pt Camberwell, pt Lambeth, pt Newington

LAMBETH, BRIXTON DIVISION (1885–1918)
pt Lambeth (pt of each of the wards of Brixton, Stockwell, Vauxhall)

LAMBETH, KENNINGTON DIVISION (1885–1918)
pt Lambeth (the ward of Prince's and pt of the ward of Vauxhall)

LAMBETH, NORTH DIVISION (1885–1918)
pt Lambeth (the wards of Bishop's, North Marsh, South Marsh)
LAMBETH, NORWOOD DIVISION
pt Lambeth (the ward of Norwood, pt of the wards of Brixton, Stockwell)
NEWINGTON, WALWORTH DIVISION (1885–1918)
pt Newington (the ward of St Peter's, pt of the ward of St Mary's)
NEWINGTON, WEST DIVISION (1885–1918)
pt Newington (the wards of Trinity, St Paul's, pt of the ward of St Mary's)
SOUTHWARK (1295–1885)
Bermondsey (1832–85), Rotherhithe (1832–85), Southwark Christchurch (1832–85), Southwark St George the Martyr, Southwark St John Horsleydown (1733–1885), Southwark St Margaret (until 1541), Southwark St Mary Magdalen (until 1541), Southwark St Olave, Southwark St Saviour (pt 1541–1832, ent 1832–85), Southwark St Thomas (*ca* 1550–1885)
WANDSWORTH (1885–1918)
Putney, Streatham, Tooting Graveney, Wandsworth

COUNTY CONSTITUENCIES

1832–1867
EASTERN DIVISION
Hundreds of Brixton, Kingston, Reigate, Tandridge, Wallington
WESTERN DIVISION
Hundreds of Blackheath, Copthorne, Effingham, Elmbridge, Farnham, Godalming, Godley, Woking, Wotton
1867–1885
EAST DIVISION
pt Brixton Hd (Camberwell, Clapham, pt Lambeth, Penge, Streatham, Tooting Graveney), Tandridge Hd, pt Wallington Hd (Addington, Croydon, Sanderstead)
MID DIVISION
pt Brixton Hd (Barnes, Battersea, Merton, Mortlake, Putney, Wandsworth, Wimbledon), Kingston Hd, Reigate Hd, pt Wallington Hd (Beddington, Carshalton, Chaldon, Cheam, Coulsdon, Mitcham, Morden, Sutton, Wallington, Woodmansterne)
WESTERN DIVISION
same Hds as for 1832–1867
1885–1918
KINGSTON DIVISION
pt Kingston PSD, Kingston upon Thames MB, Richmond PSD, *viz*., Cobham, Long Ditton, Thames Ditton, Esher, Ham, Hook, Kew, Kingston upon Thames, Malden, East Molesey, West Molesey, Petersham, Richmond, Stoke d'Abernon, Wallington, Walton upon Thames
MID OR EPSOM DIVISION
pt Dorking PSD, Epsom PSD, pt Kingston PSD, *viz*., Ashtead, Banstead, Great Bookham, Little Bookham, Cheam, Chessington, Cuddington, Effingham, Epsom, Ewell, Fetcham, Headley, Leatherhead, Mickleham, Mortlake, Sutton, Walton on the Hill
NORTH–EASTERN OR WIMBLEDON DIVISION
pt Croydon PSD, pt Godstone PSD, pt Wandsworth PSD, *viz*., Addington, Beddington, Carshalton, Caterham, Chelsham, Coulsdon, Farleigh, Merton, Mitcham, Morden, Sanderstead, Warlingham, Wimbledon, Woodmansterne
NORTH–WESTERN OR CHERTSEY DIVISION
Chertsey PSD, pt Farnham PSD, pt Guildford PSD, *viz*., Bisley, Byfleet, Chertsey, East Clandon, West Clandon, Egham, Frimley, Horsell, East Horsley, West Horsley, Ockham, Pirbright, Pyrford, Send and Ripley, Thorpe, Wanborough, Weybridge, Windlesham, Wisley, Woking, Worplesdon
SOUTH–EASTERN OR REIGATE DIVISION
pt Dorking PSD, pt Godstone PSD, Reigate MB, Reigate PSD, *viz*., Abinger, Betchworth, Bletchingley, Buckland, Burstow, Capel, Chaldon, Charlwood, Chipstead, Chobham, Crowhurst, Dorking, Gatton, Godstone, Horley, Horne, Kingswood, Leigh, Limpsfield, Lingfield, Merstham, Newdigate, Nutfield, Ockley, Oxted, Reigate Borough, Reigate Foreign, Tandridge, Tatsfield, Titsey, Woldingham, Wotton
SOUTH–WESTERN OR GUILDFORD DIVISION
pt Farnham PSD, Godalming MB, Guildford MB, pt Guildford PSD, *viz*., Albury, Alfold, Ash and Normandy, Bramley, Chiddingfold, Compton, Cranleigh, Dunsfold, Elstead, Ewhurst, Farnham, Frensham, Godalming, Guildford The Friary, Guildford Holy Trinity, Guildford St Mary, Guildford St Nicholas, Hambledon, Hascombe, Haslemere, Merrow, Peper Harow, Puttenham, St Martha, Seale, Shalford, Shere, Stoke, Thursley, Waverley, Witley, Wonersh
1918–1948
CARSHALTON DIVISION (1945–48)
Banstead UD, Carshalton UD
CHERTSEY DIVISION
Chertsey RD, Chertsey UD, Egham UD, Esher and the Dittons UD, East and West Molesey UD, Walton upon Thames UD, Weybridge UD
EASTERN DIVISION[7]
Caterham UD, Coulsdon and Purley UD, Godstone RD
EPSOM DIVISION[7]
Epsom RD (ent 1918–45, pt 1945–48 [less Banstead, Cheam, Sutton, and bdry alts in other pars[7]]), Epsom UD, Leatherhead UD, Sutton UD (1918–45)
FARNHAM DIVISION
Farnham RD, Farnham UD, Frimley UD, pt Guildford RD (Pirbright), Windlesham UD, Woking UD
GUILDFORD DIVISION
Godalming MB, Guildford MB, pt Guildford RD (all except the par in Epsom Dv), Hambledon RD, Haslemere UD

MITCHAM DIVISION (1918–45)
Beddington and Wallington UD, Carshalton UD, Mitcham UD
REIGATE DIVISION[7]
Dorking RD, Dorking UD, Reigate MB, Reigate RD

1948–1970

CARSHALTON COUNTY CONSTITUENCY
Banstead UD, Carshalton UD
CHERTSEY COUNTY CONSTITUENCY
Bagshot RD, Chertsey UD, Egham UD
DORKING COUNTY CONSTITUENCY
Dorking UD, Dorking and Horley RD, pt Guildford RD (Albury, East Clandon, West Clandon, Effingham, East Horsley, West Horsley, Ockham, Ripley, St Martha, Send, Shere, Wisley)
EPSOM COUNTY CONSTITUENCY
Epsom and Ewell MB, Leatherhead UD
ESHER COUNTY CONSTITUENCY
Esher UD, Walton and Weybridge UD
FARNHAM COUNTY CONSTITUENCY
Farnham UD, Godalming MB, pt Guildford RD (Seale), pt Hambledon RD (Chiddingfold, Dockenfield, Elstead, Frensham, Peper Harow, Thursley, Tilford, Witley), Haslemere UD
GUILDFORD COUNTY CONSTITUENCY[8]
Guildford MB, pt Guildford RD (Artington, Compton, Puttenham, Shackleford, Shalford, Wanborough, Worplesdon), pt Hambledon RD (Alfold, Bramley, Busbridge, Cranleigh, Dunsfold, Ewhurst, Hambledon, Hascombe, Wonersh)
REIGATE COUNTY CONSTITUENCY
Godstone RD, Reigate MB
WOKING COUNTY CONSTITUENCY[8]
Frimley and Camberley UD, pt Guildford RD (Ash and Normandv, Pirbright), Woking UD
EAST SURREY COUNTY CONSTITUENCY
Caterham and Warlingham UD, Coulsdon and Purley UD

*1970–**

DORKING COUNTY CONSTITUENCY
Dorking UD, Dorking and Horley RD, pt Guildford RD (Albury, East Clandon, West Clandon, Effingham, East Horsley, West Horsley, Ockham, Ripley, St Martha, Send, Shere, Wisley)
FARNHAM COUNTY CONSTITUENCY
Farnham UD, Godalming MB, pt Guildford RD (Seale and Tongham), pt Hambledon RD (Chiddingfold, Dockenfield, Elstead, Frensham, Peper Harow, Thursley, Tilford, Witley), Haslemere UD
GUILDFORD COUNTY CONSTITUENCY
Guildford MB, pt Guildford RD (Artington, Compton, Puttenham, Shackleford, Shalford, Wanborough, Worplesdon), pt Hambledon RD (Alfold, Bramley, Busbridge, Cranleigh, Dunsfold, Ewhurst, Hambledon, Hascombe, Wonersh)
EAST SURREY COUNTY CONSTITUENCY
Caterham and Warlingham UD, Godstone RD[9]
NORTH WEST SURREY COUNTY CONSTITUENCY
Bagshot RD, Egham UD, Frimley and Camberley UD
WOKING COUNTY CONSTITUENCY
pt Guildford RD (Ash, Normandy, Pirbright), Woking UD

SUSSEX

BOROUGH CONSTITUENCIES[1]

ARUNDEL (1295–1867 [1 mbr, 1832–67])
Arundel
BRAMBER (1295 and often irregularly, sometimes returned with Steyning, regularly 1369–1832)
Bramber
BRIGHTON (1832–1948)
1832–1948: Brighton, Hove, Preston (1867–1948)
1918–48: Brighton CB, Hove MB
BRIGHTON, KEMPTOWN[2] (1948–*)
pt Brighton CB (the wards of Elm Grove, Falmer [1955–70], Hanover, King's Cliff, Lewes Road, Moulsecoomb, Pier, Queen's Park, Rottingdean, St John's [1948–55], Warren [1955–70])
BRIGHTON, PAVILION[2] (1948–*)
pt Brighton CB (the wards of Hollingbury, Montpelier, Patcham, Pavilion [1948–55], Preston, Preston Park, Regency, St Nicholas, St Peter's, Stanmer [1955–70], West [1948–55])
CHICHESTER[3] (1295–1885 [1 mbr, 1867–85])
Chichester All Saints, Chichester The Close (1867–85); Chichester Newtown, or St John; Chichester St Andrew, pt Chichester St Bartholomew, Chichester St James (1832–85), Chichester St Martin, Chichester St Olave, pt Chichester St Pancras, pt Chichester St Peter the Great or Sub-Deanery, Chichester St Peter the Less, Oving (pt 1832–67, ent 1867–85), Rumboldswyke (pt 1832–67, ent 1867–85)
EAST GRINSTEAD (1307–1832)
East Grinstead
HASTINGS[3] (1369–* [1 mbr, 1885–*)])
until 1918: pt Bexhill, Hastings All Saints, Hastings Holy Trinity, Hastings St Andrew, Hastings St Clement, Hastings St Leonards (pt until 1867, ent 1867–85, pt[4] 1885–1918), Hastings St Mary Bulverhythe, Hastings St Mary in the Castle (pt until 1867, ent 1867–1918), Hastings St Mary Magdalen, Hastings St Michael, Ore (pt until 1867, ent 1867–1918)
1918–:* pt Battle RD (1948–55: all except the pars of Burwash, Etchingham, Ticehurst; incl Hurst Green 1953[5]–55), Hastings CB, Rye MB (1948–55)
HORSHAM (1295–1885 [1 mbr, 1832–85])
Horsham (pt until 1832, ent 1832–85)
HOVE (1948–*)
Hove MB, Portslade by Sea UD
LEWES[3] (1295–1885 [1 mbr 1867–85])
pt Kingston(1832–85), Lewes All Saints, Lewes The Castle Precincts (1867–85), pt Lewes St Ann; pt Lewes St John the Baptist, Southover; pt Lewes St John under the Castle, Lewes St Michael; Lewes St Thomas a Becket, Cliffe; pt South Malling (1832–85)
MIDHURST (1310–1885 [1 mbr, 1832–85])
until 1832: Midhurst
1832–85: pt North Ambersham, South Ambersham, pt Bepton, pt Bignor, Chithurst, Cocking, Didling, Easebourne, Graffham, Heyshott, pt Iping, West Lavington, pt Linch, pt Lodsworth, Midhurst, pt Selham, pt Stedham, pt Trotton, pt Woolbeding
RYE (1295–1885 [1 mbr, 1832–85])
until 1832: pt Rye
1832–85: pt Brede, East Guldeford, Icklesham, Iden, Peasmarsh, Playden, Rye, pt Udimore; St Thomas the Apostle, Winchelsea
SEAFORD (1298–1398, *temp* Edw IV–1832)
Seaford
NEW SHOREHAM (1295–1885)
until 1832: New Shoreham
1832–85: Albourne, Ashington, Ashurst, Lower Beeding (1867–85), Upper Beeding, Botolphs, Bramber, Broadwater, pt West Chiltington, Clapham, Coombes, Cowfold, Durrington, pt Edburton, Findon, West Grinstead, Heene, Henfield, Ifield, Itchingfield, Kingston by Sea, Lancing, Nuthurst, Patching, Rusper, Shermanbury, Shipley, New Shoreham, Old Shoreham, pt Slaugham, Sompting, Southwick, Steyning, Sullington, West Tarring, Thakenham, Warminghurst, Warnham, Washington, Wiston, Woodmancote
STEYNING (*temp* Edw I–1832, sometimes returned with Bramber)
Steyning
WINCHELSEA[3] (1369–1832)
St Thomas the Apostle, Winchelsea
WORTHING (1948–*)
Worthing MB

COUNTY CONSTITUENCIES

1832–1885
EASTERN DIVISION
Rapes of Lewes, Hastings, Pevensey
WESTERN DIVISION
Rapes of Arundel, Bramber, Chichester

1885–1918
EASTERN OR RYE DIVISION
Battle PSD, Burwash PSD, Frant PSD, Hastings PSD, Rye MB, Rye PSD, Anc Town Winchelsea, *viz.,* Ashburnham, Battle, Beckley, Bexhill, Bodiam,

Brede, Brightling, pt Broomhill, Burwash, Catsfield, Crowhurst, Dallington, Etchingham, Ewhurst, Fairlight, Frant, Guestling, East Guldeford, pt Hastings St Leonards (Petit Iham), pt Hawkhurst, Hollington, Hooe, pt Horsmonden, Icklesham, Iden, pt Lamberhurst, Mayfield, Mountfield, Ninfield, Northiam, Ore, Peasmarsh, Penhurst, Pett, Playden, Rotherfield, Rye, Salehurst, Sedlescombe, Ticehurst, Udimore, Wadhurst, Westfield, Whatlington; St Thomas the Apostle, Winchelsea

MID OR LEWES DIVISION

Hove PSD, pt Lewes PSD, pt Steyning PSD, Worthing PSD, *viz.*, Albourne, Aldrington, Ashurst, Barcombe, Upper Beeding, West Blatchington, Botolphs, Bramber, Broadwater, Chailey, East Chiltington, Clapham, Coombes, Ditchling, Durrington, Edburton, Falmer, Goring by Sea, Hamsey, Hangleton, Heene, Henfield, Hove, Iford, Kingston, Kingston by Sea, Lancing, Lewes All Saints, Lewes The Castle Precincts, Lewes St Ann; Lewes St John the Baptist, Southover; Lewes St John under the Castle, Lewes St Michael; Lewes St Thomas a Becket, Cliffe; South Malling, Newick, Newtimber, Ovingdean, Patcham, Piddinghoe, Plumpton, Portslade, Poynings, Preston, Pyecombe, Rodmell, Rottingdean, New Shoreham, Old Shoreham, Sompting, Southease, Southwick, Stanmer, Steyning, Streat, West Tarring, Telescombe, Westmeston, Woodmancote

NORTHERN OR EAST GRINSTEAD DIVISION

pt Cuckfield PSD, East Grinstead PSD, pt Uckfield PSD, *viz.*, Ardingly, Balcombe, Bolney, Buxted, Clayton, Cuckfield, Fletching, Framfield, East Grinstead, Hartfield, West Hoathly, Little Horsted, Horsted Keynes, Hurstpierpoint, Isfield, Keymer, Lindfield, Maresfield, Slaugham, Twineham, Uckfield, Withyham, Wivelsfield, Worth

NORTH-WESTERN OR HORSHAM DIVISION

pt Cuckfield PSD, Horsham PSD, Midhurst PSD, Petworth PSD, *viz.*, North Ambersham, South Ambersham, Barlavington, Lower Beeding, Bepton, Bignor, Billingshurst, pt Bramshott, Burton, Bury, North Chapel, West Chiltington, Chithurst, Coates, Cocking, Coldwaltham, Cowfold, Crawley, Didling, Duncton, Easebourne, Egdean, Elsted, Fernhurst, Fittleworth, Graffham, Greatham, West Grinstead, Hardham, Harting, Heyshott, Horsham, Ifield, Iping, Itchingfield, Kirdford, East Lavington, West Lavington, Linch, Linchmere, Lodsworth, Lurgashall, Midhurst, Nuthurst, Parham, Petworth, Pulborough, Rogate, Rudgwick, Rusper, Selham, Shermanbury, Shipley, Slinfold, Stedham, Stopham, Sutton, Terwick, Tillington, Treyford, Trotton, Warnham, Wiggonholt, Wisborough Green, Woolbeding

SOUTHERN OR EASTBOURNE DIVISION

Hailsham PSD, pt Lewes PSD, pt Uckfield PSD, Pevensey, Seaford, *viz.*, Alciston, Alfriston, Arlington, Beddingham, Berwick, Bishopstone, East Blatchington, Chalvington, Chiddingly, East Dean, West Dean, Eastbourne, West Firle, Folkington, Friston, Glynde, Hailsham, Heathfield, South Heighton, Hellingly, Herstmonceux, East Hoathly, Jevington, Laughton, Litlington, Lullington, Newhaven, Pevensey, Ringmere, Ripe, Seaford, Selmeston, Tarring Neville, Waldron, Warbleton, Wartling, Westham, Willingdon, Wilmington

SOUTH-WESTERN OR CHICHESTER DIVISION

Arundel PSD, Chichester MB, Chichester PSD, pt Steyning PSD, *viz.*, Aldringbourne, Amberley, Angmering, Appledram, Arundel, Ashington, Barnham, Bersted, Bidderton, Binsted, Birdham, Bosham, Boxgrove, Burpham, Chichester All Saints, Chichester The Close; Chichester Newtown, or St John; Chichester St Andrew, Chichester St Bartholomew, Chichester St James, Chichester St Martin, Chichester St Olave, Chichester St Pancras, Chichester St Peter the Great or Sub-Deanery, Chichester St Peter the Less, Chidham, Climping, Compton, East Dean, West Dean, Donnington, Earnley, Eartham, Eastergate, Felpham, Ferring, Findon, New Fishbourne, Ford, Funtington, Houghton, Hunston, West Itchenor, Kingston, Lavant, Littlehampton, Lyminster, Madehurst, East Marden, North Marden, Up Marden, Merston, Middleton, North Mundham, Oving, Pagham, Patching, Poling, East Preston, Rackham, Racton, Rumboldswyke, Rustington, Selsey, Sidlesham, Singleton, North Stoke, South Stoke, West Stoke, Storrington, Stoughton, Sullington, Tangmere, Thakenham, West Thorney, Tortington, Walberton, Up Waltham, Warminghurst, Warningcamp, Washington, Westbourne, Westhampnett, Wiston, East Wittering, West Wittering, Yapton

1918–1948

East Sussex:

EASTBOURNE DIVISION

Eastbourne CB, Eastbourne RD, pt Hailsham RD (Arlington, Chalvington, Chiddingly, Hailsham, Hellingly, Laughton, Ripe)

EAST GRINSTEAD DIVISION

Burgess Hill UD, Cuckfield RD, Cuckfield UD, East Grinstead RD, East Grinstead UD, Hayward's Heath UD, Uckfield RD, Uckfield UD

LEWES DIVISION

Chailey RD, Lewes MB, Newhaven RD, Newhaven UD, Portslade by Sea UD, Seaford UD, Steyning East RD

RYE DIVISION

Battle RD, Battle UD, Bexhill MB, pt Hailsham RD (all except the pars in Eastbourne Dv), Hastings RD, Rye MB, Rye RD, Ticehurst RD

West Sussex:

CHICHESTER DIVISION

Arundel MB, Bognor UD, Chichester MB, Littlehampton UD, East Preston RD, Midhurst RD, Petworth RD, Westbourne RD, Westhampnett RD

HORSHAM DIVISION (1945–48)

Chanctonbury RD, Horsham RD, Horsham UD, Shoreham-by-Sea UD, Southwick UD

HORSHAM AND WORTHING DIVISION (1918–45)

Horsham RD, Horsham UD, Shoreham-by-Sea UD, Southwick UD, Steyning West RD, Thakenham RD, Worthing MB

WORTHING DIVISION (1945–48)
Worthing MB, Worthing RD

1948–1970
East Sussex:[6]
EASTBOURNE COUNTY CONSTITUENCY
Bexhill MB (1948–55), Eastbourne CB, pt Hailsham RD (1948–55: East Dean, Friston, Hooe, Jevington, Ninfield, Pevensey, Polegate, Wartling, Westham, Willingdon; 1955–70: all except the pars in Rye CC)
EAST GRINSTEAD COUNTY CONSTITUENCY
pt Battle RD (1948–55: Burwash, Etchingham, Ticehurst), pt Cuckfield RD (Ardingly, Balcombe, Bolney, Cuckfield Rural, West Hoathly, Horsted Keynes, Lindfield Rural, Slaugham, Worth), Cuckfield UD, East Grinstead UD, Uckfield RD
LEWES COUNTY CONSTITUENCY
Burgess Hill UD, Chailey RD, pt Cuckfield RD (Albourne, Clayton, Fulking, Hurstpierpoint, Keymer, Newtimber, Poynings, Pyecombe, Twineham), pt Hailsham RD (1948–55: all except the pars in Eastbourne CC), Lewes MB, Newhaven UD, Seaford UD
RYE COUNTY CONSTITUENCY (1955–70)
Battle RD, Bexhill MB, pt Hailsham RD (Heathfield, Herstmonceux, Hooe, Horam, Ninfield, Waldron, Warbleton, Wartling), Rye MB

West Sussex:
ARUNDEL AND SHOREHAM COUNTY CONSTITUENCY
Arundel MB, Chanctonbury RD, Littlehampton UD, Shoreham-by-Sea UD, Southwick UD, Worthing RD
CHICHESTER COUNTY CONSTITUENCY
Bognor Regis UD, Chichester MB, Chichester RD
HORSHAM COUNTY CONSTITUENCY
Horsham RD, Horsham UD, Midhurst RD, Petworth RD

*1970–**
East Sussex:
EASTBOURNE COUNTY CONSTITUENCY
Eastbourne CB, pt Hailsham RD (East Dean, West Dean, Friston, Jevington, Pevensey, Polegate, Westham, Willingdon)
EAST GRINSTEAD COUNTY CONSTITUENCY
East Grinstead UD, Uckfield RD
LEWES COUNTY CONSTITUENCY
Chailey RD, pt Hailsham RD (Alciston, Alfiston, Arlington, Berwick, Chalvington, Chiddingly, Folkington, Hailsham, Hellingly, East Hoathly, Laughton, Litlington, Lullington, Ripe, Selmeston, Wilmington), Lewes MB, Newhaven UD, Seaford UD
MID-SUSSEX COUNTY CONSTITUENCY
Burgess Hill UD, Cuckfield RD, Cuckfield UD
RYE COUNTY CONSTITUENCY
Battle RD, Bexhill MB, pt Hailsham RD (Heathfield, Herstmonceux, Hooe, Horam, Ninfield, Waldron, Warleton, Wartling), Rye MB

West Sussex:
ARUNDEL COUNTY CONSTITUENCY
Arundel MB, Bognor Regis UD, pt Chichester RD (Aldringbourne, Barnham, Bersted, Climping, Eastergate, Ford, Madehurst, Middleton-on-Sea, Pagham, Slindon, Tortington, Walberton, Yapton), Littlehampton UD, pt Worthing RD (Angmering, Burpham, Clapham, Ferring, Kingston, Lyminster, Patching, Poling, East Preston, Rustington, South Stoke, Warningcamp)
CHICHESTER COUNTY CONSTITUENCY
Chichester MB, pt Chichester RD (the pars not in Arundel CC), Midhurst RD, Petworth RD
HORSHAM AND CRAWLEY COUNTY CONSTITUENCY
Crawley UD, Horsham RD, Horsham UD
SHOREHAM COUNTY CONSTITUENCY
Chanctonbury RD, Shoreham-by-Sea UD, Southwick UD, pt Worthing RD (the pars not in Arundel CC)

WILTSHIRE

BOROUGH CONSTITUENCIES[1]

GREAT BEDWYN (1295–1832)
Great Bedwyn
BRADFORD-ON-AVON (1295 only)
Bradford-on-Avon
CALNE (1295–1885 [1 mbr, 1832–85])
pt Blackland (1832–85), Calne (pt 1295–1832, ent 1832–85), pt Calstone Wellington (1832–85)
CHIPPENHAM (1295–1885 [1 mbr, 1867–85])
Chippenham (pt 1295–1832, ent 1832–85), Hardenhuish (1832–85), Langley Burrell (1832–85), Pewsham (1832–85)
CRICKLADE (1295–1885) (Wilts, Glos[2])
until 1832: Cricklade St Mary, Cricklade St Sampson
1832–85: Ashley, pt Ashton Keynes, Blunsdon St Andrew, Braydon, Brinkworth, Castle Eaton, Chiseldon, pt Clyffe Pypard, pt Coleshill, Cricklade St Mary, Cricklade St Sampson, Crudwell, Dauntsey, Draycot Cerne, Draycot Foliat, Eisey, Hankerton, Hannington, Highworth, pt Hilmarton, pt Broad Hinton, Hullavington, Inglesham, Kemble, Poole Keynes, Somerford Keynes, pt Kington St Michael, Latton, Leigh, Lydiard Millicent, Lydiard Tregoze, Liddington, Lyneham, Marston Meysey, pt Minety, Long Newnton, Norton, Oaksey, pt Purton, Rodbourne Cheney, Seagry, Shorncott, Stanton Fitzwarren, Stanton St Quintin, Stratton St Margaret, Sutton Benger, Swindon, Tockenham, Wanborough, Wootton Bassett, pt Wroughton
DEVIZES (1295–1885 [1 mbr, 1867–85])
pt Devizes St James (1832–85), Devizes St John the Baptist, Devizes St Mary the Virgin, pt Rowde (1832–85)
DOWNTON (1295–1832)
Downton
HEYTESBURY (1450–1832)
Heytesbury
HIGHWORTH (1298, 1311 only)
Highworth
HINDON (1449–1832)
Hindon (when gains sep civ identity), pt East Knoyle (until Hindon gains sep civ identity)
LUDGERSHALL (1295–1832)
Ludgershall
MALMESBURY (1295–1885 [1 mbr, 1832–85])
until 1832: Malmesbury The Abbey, Malmesbury St Paul
1832–85: Bremilham, Brokenborough, Charlton, Foxley, Garsdon, Lea and Claverton, Great Somerford, Little Somerford, Westport St Mary
MARLBOROUGH (1295–1885 [1 mbr, 1832–85])
Marlborough St Mary, Marlborough St Peter and St Paul, Preshute (1832–85)
MERE (1304–07 only)
Mere
SALISBURY (1295–1918 [1 mbr, 1885–1918])
pt Fisherton Anger (1867–1918), Milford (1832–1918), Salisbury The Close of the Canons of the Cathedral Church (1832–1918), Salisbury St Edmund, Salisbury St Martin (pt 1295–1832, ent 1832–1918), Salisbury St Thomas
OLD SARUM (1295–1832)
Old Sarum
SWINDON[3] (1948–*)
Swindon
WESTBURY (1448–1885 [1 mbr, 1832–85])
Westbury (pt 1448–1832, ent 1832–85)
WILTON (1295–1885 [1 mbr, 1832–85])
until 1832: pt Wilton
1832–85: Barford St Martin, pt Bishopstone, Britford, Burcombe, pt Coombe Bissett, pt Durnford, pt Fisherton Anger, Fugglestone St Peter, pt Groveley Wood, West Harnham, Homington, Netherhampton, South Newton, Old Sarum, Stratford sub Castle, pt Stratford Tony, Wilton, Woodford
WOOTTON BASSETT (1447–1832)
Wootton Bassett

COUNTY CONSTITUENCIES

1832–1885
NORTHERN DIVISION
Hds of Bradford, Calne, Chippenham, pt Damerham (pt Christian Malford, Grittleton, Kington Langley [1867–85], Kington St Michael, Nettleton), Melksham, Potterne and Cannings, Ramsbury, Selkley, Swanborough, Whorwellsdown
SOUTHERN DIVISION
Hds of Alderbury, Amesbury, Branch and Dole, Cawden and Cadworth, Chalk, pt Damerham (the pars not in N'rn Dv), Downton, Dunworth, Elstub and Everleigh, Frustfield, Heytesbury, Kinwardstone, Mere, Underditch, Warminster, Westbury

1885–1918
EASTERN OR DEVIZES DIVISION
Devizes MB, Devizes PSD, pt Everley and Pewsey PSD, Marlborough MB, Marlborough and Ramsbury PSD, *viz.*, Aldbourne, Alton Priors, Avebury, Baydon, Great Bedwyn, Little Bedwyn, Beechingstoke, Berwick Bassett, Bromham, Burbage, Buttermere, All Cannings, Bishops Cannings, Charlton,

Cheverell Magna, Cheverell Parva, pt Chilton Foliat, Chirton, Chittoe, Chute, Chute Forest, Clatford Park, Collingbourne Ducis, Collingbourne Kingston, Devizes St James, Devizes St John the Baptist, Devizes St Mary the Virgin, Easterton, Easton Grey, Enford, Erlestoke, Etchilhampton, Everleigh, Fittleton, Froxfield, Fullaway, Fyfield, Grafton, Ham, Huish, pt Hungerford, East Kennett, Market Lavington, West Lavington, Ludgershall, Manningford Abbots, Manningford Bohune, Manningford Bruce, Marden, Marlborough St Mary the Virgin, Marlborough St Peter and St Paul, Marston, Mildenhall, Milton Lilbourne, Netheravon, North Newnton, Ogbourne St Andrew, Ogbourne St George, West Overton, Overton Heath, Patney, Pewsey, Potterne, Poulshot, Preshute, Ramsbury, Rowde, Rushall, North Savernake, South Savernake with Brimslade and Cadley, pt Shalbourne, Stanton St Bernard, Stert, Tidcombe and Fosbury, North Tidworth, Tilshead, Upavon, Urchfont, Wilcot, Wilsford, Winterbourne Bassett, Winterbourne Monkton, Woodborough, Wootton Rivers, Worton

NORTHERN OR CRICKLADE DIVISION

Cricklade PSD, Swindon PSD, *viz.*, Ashton Keynes, Bishopstone, Blunsdon St Andrew, Braydon, Broad Town, Calstone Wellington, Castle Eaton, Great Chalfield, Little Chalfield, Chiseldon, Clyffe Pypard, Cottles, Cricklade St Mary, Cricklade St Sampson, Draycot Foliat, Eisey, Hannington, Highworth, Broad Hinton, Little Hinton, Inglesham, Latton, Leigh, Liddington, Lydiard Millicent, Lydiard Tregoze, Lyneham, Marston Meysey, Purton, Rodbourne Cheney, Stanton Fitzwarren, Stratton St Margaret, Swindon, Tockenham, Wanborough, Wootton Bassett, Wroughton

NORTH-WESTERN OR CHIPPENHAM DIVISION

Calne PSD, Chippenham PSD, Malmesbury PSD, *viz.*, Alderton, Ashley, Avon, Biddestone St Nicholas, Biddestone St Peter, Blackland, Bowood, Box, Bremhill, Brinkworth, Brokenborough, Calne, Castle Combe, Charlton, Cherhill, Chippenham, Christian Malford, Colerne, Compton Bassett, Corsham, Crudwell, Dauntsey, Draycot Cerne, Easton Royal, Foxley, Garsdon, Grittleton, Hankerton, Hardenhuish, Heddington, Highway, Hilmarton, Hullavington, Kemble, Poole Keynes, Somerford Keynes, West Kington, Kington Langley, Kington St Michael, Lacock, Langley Burrell, Lea and Claverton, Leigh Delamere, Littleton Drew, Luckington, Malmesbury The Abbey, Malmesbury St Paul, Minety, Nettleton, Long Newnton, Norton, Oaksey, Pewsham, Seagry, Sherston Magna, Sherston Pinkney, Shorncott, Slaughterford, Great Somerford, Little Somerford, Sopworth, Stanton St Quintin, Sutton Benger, Tytherton Kellaways, Westport St Mary, North Wraxall, Yatesbury, Yatton Keynell

SOUTHERN OR WILTON DIVISION

pt Elstub and Pewsey PSD, Hindon PSD, Salisbury MB, Salisbury and Amesbury PSD, pt Warminster PSD, *viz.*, Alderbury, Allington, Alvediston, Amesbury, Ansty, Barford St Martin, Baverstock, Berwick St James, Berwick St John, Berwick St Leonard, Bishopstone, Boscombe, Bramshaw, Britford, Bulford, Burcombe, Bower Chalke, Broad Chalke, Chicklade, Chilmark, Cholderton, Clarendon Park. Codford St Mary, Codford St Peter, Compton Chamberlayne, Coombe Bissett, Damerham, pt West Dean, Kingston Deverill, Monkton Deverill, Dinton, Donhead St Andrew, Donhead St Mary, Downton, Durnford, Durrington, Earldoms, Ebbesbourne Wake, Fifield Bavant, Figheldean, pt Fisherton Anger, Fisherton de la Mere, Fonthill Bishop, Fonthill Gifford, Fovant, Fugglestone St Peter, East Grimstead, West Grimstead, Groveley Wood, West Harnham, Hindon, Homington, Idmiston, East Knoyle, West Knoyle, Landford, Little Langford, Steeple Langford, Langley Wood, Laverstock, Maddington, Martin, Melchet Park, Mere, Milston, Netherhampton, South Newton, Newton Tony, No Man's Land, Nunton and Bodenham, Odstock, Orcheston St George, Orcheston St Mary, Upper Pertwood, Pitton and Farley, Plaitford, Rollestone, Old Sarum, Sedgehill, Semley, Shrewton, Standlynch, Stapleford, Stourton with Gasper, Stratford Tony, Sutton Mandeville, Swallowcliffe, Teffont Evias, Teffont Magna, East Tisbury, West Tisbury, Tollard Royal, Toyd Farm with Allenford, Wardour, West Wellow, Whiteparish, Whitsbury, Wilford cum Lake, Wilton, Winterbourne Dauntsey, Winterbourne Earls, Winterbourne Gunner, Winterbourne Stoke, Winterslow, Great Wishford, Woodford, Wylye

WESTERN OR WESTBURY DIVISION

Bradford PSD, Melksham PSD, Trowbridge and Westbury PSD, pt Warminister PSD, Whorwelsdown PSD, *viz.*, Allington, Alton Barnes, Steeple Ashton, West Ashton, Bishopstrow, Boyton, Bradford-on-Avon, pt Maiden Bradley with Yarnfield, North Bradley, Broughton Gifford, Bulkington, Chitterne All Saints, Chitterne St Mary, Corsley, East Coulston, Brixton Deverill, Hill Deverill, Longbridge Deverill, Edington, Heytesbury, Hilperton, Great Hinton, Horningsham, Imber, Keevil, Knook, Melksham, Monkton Farleigh, Norton Bavant, Seend, Semington, Sherrington, Southwick, Stockton, Sutton Veny, Trowbridge, Upton Lovell, Upton Scudamore, Warminster, Westbury, Westwood, Whaddon, Wingfield

1918–1948

CHIPPENHAM DIVISION

Calne MB, Calne RD, Chippenham MB, Chippenham RD, pt Cricklade and Wootton Baseett RD (all except a detached pt of Lydiard Tregoze), Malmesbury MB, Malmesbury RD, the pt of Tetbury RD in Wilts

DEVIZES DIVISION

pt Cricklade and Wootton Bassett RD (the detached pt of Lydiard Tregoze), Devizes MB, Devizes RD, pt Highworth RD (Bishopstone, Chisledon, Little Hinton, Liddington, Wanborough, Wroughton), Marlborough MB, Marlborough RD, Pewsey RD, Ramsbury RD

SALISBURY DIVISION

Amesbury RD, Salisbury MB, Salisbury RD, Tisbury RD, Wilton MB, Wilton RD

SWINDON DIVISION

pt Highworth RD (all except the pars in Devizes Dv), Swindon MB

WESTBURY DIVISION

Bradford-on-Avon RD, Bradford-on-Avon UD, Melksham RD, Melksham UD, Mere RD, Trowbridge UD, Warminster RD, Warminster UD, Westbury RD, Westbury and Whorwellsdown RD, Westbury UD

1948–1970

CHIPPENHAM COUNTY CONSTITUENCY

Calne MB, Calne and Chippenham RD, Chippenham MB, Cricklade and Wootton Bassett RD, Malmesbury MB, Malmesbury RD

DEVIZES COUNTY CONSTITUENCY[4]

Devizes MB, Devizes RD, Highworth RD, Marlborough MB, Marlborough and Rasmbury RD, Pewsey RD

SALISBURY COUNTY CONSTITUENCY

Amesbury RD, Salisbury MB, Salisbury and Wilton RD, Wilton MB

WESTBURY COUNTY CONSTITUENCY

Bradford and Melksham RD, Bradford-on-Avon UD, Melksham UD, Mere and Tisbury RD, Trowbridge UD, Warminster UD, Warminster and Westbury RD, Westbury UD

*1970–**

CHIPPENHAM COUNTY CONSTITUENCY

DEVIZES COUNTY CONSTITUENCY[5]

SALISBURY COUNTY CONSTITUENCY

WESTBURY COUNTY CONSTITUENCY

Each of the four CCs defined by units (as constituted at time of the order) with identical names by which defined for 1948–70.

Part IV: The Dioceses of England

BATH AND WELLS

Primarily Somerset.

ORGANISATION IN ARCHDEACONRIES AND RURAL DEANERIES

BATH AD
Bath, Chew (1847–55), Chew Magna (1855–*), Frome (1962–*), Keynsham (1855–*), Midsomer Norton (1962–*), Portishead (1855–*), Redcliffe and Bedminster (until 1847)

TAUNTON AD
Bridgwater, Crewkerne, Dunster (until 1973), Exmoor (1973–*), Ilminster (1872–*), Quantock (1973–*), Quantoxhead (1884–1973), Taunton (until 1963), Taunton North (1963–*), Taunton South (1963–*), Tone (1973–*), Wellington (1872–1973), Wiveliscombe (1872–1973)

WELLS AD
Axbridge, Bruton (1872–*), Burnham (1872–*), Cary, Frome (until 1962), Glastonbury Jurisdiction, Ilchester, Locking (1872–*), Martock (1872–*), Merston, Milborne Port (1884–1955), Midsomer Norton (1872–1962), Pawlett (until 1956), Shepton Mallet (1872–*), Wells (1855–72)

ALTERATIONS IN ARCHDEACONRIES AND RURAL DEANERIES

In 1847,[1] 1848,[2] 1855,[3] 1872,[3] 1884,[3] 1951,[4] 1955,[5] 1956,[6] 1962,[7] 1963,[8] 1966,[9] 1973,[10] 1974.[11]

BRISTOL

Cr 1542[1] from Bristol RDn of Gloucester dioc, Dorset AD of Sarum dioc. Abol 1836[2] to help cr Gloucester and Bristol dioc.

ORGANISATION IN ARCHDEACONRY AND RURAL DEANERIES

Bristol RDn (not in an AD)

DORSET AD
Bridport, Dorchester, Pimperne, Shaftesbury, Whitchurch

BRISTOL

Cr 1897[1] from Gloucester and Bristol dioc. Primarily Glos, incl pt Wilts.

ORGANISATION IN ARCHDEACONRIES AND RURAL DEANERIES

BRISTOL AD
Almondsbury (1927–73), Bedminster (1901–*), Bitton, Birslington (1973–*), Bristol (1897–1901), Bristol City (1901–*), East Bristol (1901–49), Chippenham (1897–1904), Clifton (1901–*), Cricklade (1897–1904), Horfield (1973–*), Malmesbury (1897–1904), Stapleton (1897–1927), Stapleton (1949–*), Westbury and Severnside (1973–*)

SWINDON AD (1919–*)
Chippenham, Cricklade, Malmesbury

NORTH WILTS AD (1904–19)
Chippenham, Cricklade, Malmesbury

ALTERATIONS IN ARCHDEACONRIES AND RURAL DEANERIES

In 1897,[2] 1898,[3] 1901,[4] 1904,[5] 1919,[6] 1949,[7] 1973.[8]

CANTERBURY

Primarily Kent, pt Surrey (orig peculiar of the Archbp)

ORGANISATION IN ARCHDEACONRIES AND RURAL DEANERIES

CANTERBURY AD
Bridge (until 1873), East Bridge (1873–*), West Bridge (1873–*), Canterbury, Charing (until 1841), Dover, Elham, Lympne (until 1864), North Lympne (1864–1914), South Lympne (1864–1914), Ospringe, Reculver (1971–*), Sandwich, Sittingbourne (until 1841), Sutton (until 1841), Thanet (1930–*), Westbere (until 1930)

CROYDON AD (1930–*)
Croydon

MAIDSTONE AD (1841–*)
Charing (1841–64), East Charing (1864–*), West Charing (1864–*), Croydon (1873–1930), Dartford (1845–64), East Dartford (1864–1905), West Dartford (1864–1905), North Lympne (1914–*), South Lympne (1914–*), Malling (1845–64), North Malling (1864–1905), South Malling (1864–1905), Shoreham (1845–1905), Sittingbourne, Sutton, Tonbridge (1884–1905)

ALTERATIONS IN ARCHDEACONRIES AND RURAL DEANERIES

In 1837,[1] 1841,[2] 1845,[3] 1845,[4] 1864,[5] 1873,[5] 1884,[6] 1886,[7] 1891,[8] 1895,[9] 1905,[10] 1906,[11] 1914,[12] 1930,[13] 1933,[14] 1962,[15] 1971.[16]

CHELMSFORD

Cr 1914[1] from St Albans dioc. Primarily Essex.

ORGANISATION IN ARCHDEACONRIES AND RURAL DEANERIES

COLCHESTER AD
Belchamp, Braintree, Coggeshall and Tey, Colchester, Dedham, Dunmow, Halstead and Hedingham, Harwich, Newport and Stanstead, Saffron Walden, St Osyth, Witham

ESSEX AD (1914–22)
Barking, Barstable otherwise Brentwood, Canewdon and Southend, Chafford otherwise Romford, Chelmsford, Chigwell, Dengie, West Ham, Harlow, Leyton (1916–22), Maldon, Ongar, Orsett and Grays, Roding, Walthamstow and Chingford (1916–22), Walthamstow and Leyton (1914–16), Wanstead and Woodford (1916–22), Wickford

WEST HAM AD (1922–*)
Barking, Chafford otherwise Romford (1922–66), Chigwell, West Ham (1922–66), Harlow (1952–*), Havering (1966–*), Leyton (1922–66), Newham (1966–*), Ongar (1952–*), Orsett and Grays (1922–52), Redbridge (1966–*), Walthamstow and Chingford (1922–66), Wanstead and Woodford (1922–66), Waltham Forest (1966–*)

SOUTHEND AD (1922–*)
Barstable otherwise Brentwood, Basildon (1955–*), Canewdon and Southend, Chelmsford, Dengie, Harlow (1922–52), Maldon, Ongar (1922–52), Orsett and Grays, Roding, Wickford

ALTERATIONS IN ARCHDEACONRIES AND RURAL DEANERIES

In 1914,[2] 1916,[3] 1922,[4] 1952,[5] 1955,[6] 1956,[7] 1964,[8] 1966,[9] 1967,[10] 1972.[11]

CHICHESTER

Primarily Sussex. There is evidence in diocesan records that the ancient rural deaneries were divided as early as 1845, but the *Clergy List* cites no divisions earlier than 1858; the latter is used for consistency with the remainder of the *Guide*. There is also evidence in diocesan records of a rearrangements of rural deaneries in 1899 and of a renaming of them in 1910, but these changes were ignored by the Ecclesiastical Commissioners in their order of 1913, and thus are not noted below.[1]

ORGANISATION IN ARCHDEACONRIES AND RURAL DEANERIES

CHICHESTER AD
Arundel (until 1871), Arundel (1913–*), Arundel I (1871–1913), Arundel II (1871–1913), Bognor Regis (1943–*), Boxgrove (until 1871), Boxgrove (1913–29), Boxgrove I (1871–1913), Boxgrove II (1871–1913), Boxgrove III (1871–1913), Chichester, Horsham (1913–*), Midhurst (until 1871), Midshurst (1913–*), Midhurst I (1871–1913), Midhurst II (1871–1913), Midhurst III (1871–1913), Pagham (1846–71), Petworth (1913–*), Selsey (1913–43), Storrington (until 1871), Storrington (1913–*), Storrington I (1871–1913), Storrington II (1871–1913), Storrington III (1871–1913), Storrington IV (1871–1913), Tarring (1846–71)

HASTINGS AD (1912–*)
Battle and Bexhill (1931–*), Dalling, Eastbourne (1913–*), Etchingham (1913–*), Hastings (1913–*), Hastings I (1912–13), Hastings II (1912–13), Pevensey I (1912–13), Pevensey II (1912–13), Rye (1913–*), Seaford (1913–*)

LEWES AD
Brighton (1913–*), Cuckfield (1913–*), Dallington (until 1912), East Grinstead (1913–*), Hastings (until 1858), Hastings I (1858–1912), Hastings II (1858–1912), Hove (1913–*), Hurst (1913–*), Kemp Town (1955–*), Lewes (until 1858), Lewes I (1858–1913), Lewes II (1858–1913), Lewes III (1858–1913), Lewes IV (1858–1913), Lewes V (1858–1913), South Malling (1846–58), Pevensey (until 1858), Pevensey I (1858–1912), Pevensey II (1858–1912), Pevensey III (1858–1912), Pevensey IV (1858–1913), Preston (1955–*), Uckfield (1913–*)

ALTERATIONS IN ARCHDEACONRIES AND RURAL DEANERIES

In 1858,[2] 1871,[2] 1912,[3] 1913,[4] 1929,[5] 1931,[6] 1943,[7] 1950,[8] 1955,[9] 1962,[10] 1965.[11]

ELY

Primarily Cambs. Incl Bedford 1837–1914, Huntingdon from 1837, a major pt of Suffolk 1837–1914 and pt Norfolk from 1914.

ORGANISATION IN ARCHDEACONRIES AND RURAL DEANERIES

BEDFORD AD (1837–1914)
Ampthill (1880–1914), Bedford (1837–66), Bedford (1880–1914), Bedford First Dv (1866–80), Bedford Second Dv (1866–80), Biggleswade (1880–1914), Clapham (1837–66), Clapham E'rn Dv (1866–80), Clapham W'rn Dv (1866–80), Dunstable (1837–66), Dunstable (1880–1914), Dunstable First Dv (1866–80), Dunstable Second Dv (1866–80), Felmersham (1880–1914), Haynes (1880–1914), Eaton (1837–66), Eaton (1880–1914), Eaton N'rn Dv (1866–80), Eaton S'rn Dv (1866–80), Fleete (1837–66), Fleete (1880–1914), Fleete E'rn Dv (1866–80), Fleete W'rn Dv (1866–80), Luton (1880–1914), Riseley (1880–1914), Shefford (1837–66), Shefford (1880–1914), Shefford E'rn Dv (1866–80), Shefford W'rn Dv (1866–80)

ELY AD
Abingdon (until 13th cent), Barton [orig Harston], Bourn, Cambridge, Camps (13th cent–1837), Camps First Dv (1877–99), Camps Second Dv (1877–99), Chesterton, (until 1899), Cheveley (1917–*), Fordham (1914–*), Knapwell [orig Papworth] (until 13th cent), Quy (1899–*), Shingay, North Stowe (1899–*), Wilbraham (until 13th cent)

HUNTINGDON AD (1837–*)
Huntingdon, Kimbolton (1878–1964), Leightonstone (1837–63), Leightonstone (1878–*), Leightonstone First Dv (1863–78), Leightonstone Second Dv (1863–78), St Ives, St Neots, Yaxley

ISLE OF ELY AD (1884–1915)
Ely, Fincham (1914–15), Lynn Marshland (1914–15), March, Wisbech

SUDBURY AD (1837–1914)
Blackburne, Camps (1837–62), Camps First Dv (1862–77), Camps Second Dv (1862–77), Clare, Fordham (1837–62), Fordham (1884–1914), Fordham Cambridge Dv (1862–84), Fordham Suffolk Dv (1862–84), Hadleigh (1884–1914), Horningsheath (1884–1914), Lavenham (1884–1914), Mildenhall (1884–1914), Sudbury (1837–64), Sudbury (1884–1914), Sudbury E'rn Dv (1864–84), Sudbury W'rn Dv (1864–74), Thedwastre, Thingoe, Thurlow (1884–1914)

WISBECH AD (1915–*)
Ely, Feltwell (1917–*), Fincham, Lynn Marshland, March, Wisbech

ALTERATIONS IN ARCHDEACONRIES AND RURAL DEANERIES

By 1291,[1] in 1837,[2] 1839,[3] 1844,[4] 1862,[5] 1863,[6] 1864,[5] 1866,[6] 1877,[7] 1878,[8] 1880,[9] 1884,[10] 1899,[11] 1914,[12] 1914,[13] 1914,[14] 1915,[15] 1917,[16] 1961,[17] 1964,[18] 1971.[19]

EXETER

Primarily Devon, incl Cornwall until 1876; Scilly Islands declared to be in this dioc in 1838.[1]

ORGANISATION IN ARCHDEACONRIES AND RURAL DEANERIES

BARNSTAPLE AD
Barnstaple, Chumleigh, Hartland, Holsworthy (1848–1918), South Molton, Plymtree (until 1875), Shirwell, Torrington

CORNWALL AD (until 1876)
Bodmin (1875–76), Carnmarth (1875–76), East, Kerrier, Penwith, Powder, Pydar, St Austell (1875–76), Stratton (1875–76), Trigg Major, Trigg Minor, West

EXETER AD
Aylesbeare, Cadbury, Christianity, Cullompton (1902–*), Dunkeswell (until 1875), Dunkeswell and Honiton (1875–1902), Dunsford (until 1875), Honiton (until 1875), Honiton (1902–*), Kenn, Ottery (1875–*), Tiverton (until 1875), Tiverton (1902–*), Tiverton East (1875–1902), Tiverton West (1875–1902)

PLYMOUTH AD (1918–*)
Plymouth (1954–*), Plympton, Tavistock, Three Towns (1918–54)

TOTNES
Holsworthy (until 1848), Holsworthy (1918–*), Ipplepen, Moreton, Okehampton, Plympton (until 1918), Tamerton (until 1875), Tavistock (until 1918), Three Towns (1875–1918), Totnes, Woodleigh

ALTERATIONS IN ARCHDEACONRIES AND RURAL DEANERIES

In 1836,[2] 1848,[3] 1875,[4] 1876,[5] 1902,[6] 1918,[7] 1972,[8] 1973.[9]

GLOUCESTER

Cr 1541[1] from RDns in Hereford dioc (Forest, Ross, Irchingfield) and RDns in Worcester dioc (the remainder). Primarily Glos. Abol 1836[2] to help cr Gloucester and Bristol dioc.

ORGANISATION IN ARCHDEACONRIES AND RURAL DEANERIES

GLOUCESTER AD
Bristol (1541–42), Campden, Cirencester, Dursley, Fairford, Gloucester, Hawkesbury, Stonehouse, Stow, Winchcombe

HEREFORD AD
Forest

ALTERATIONS IN ARCHDEACONRIES AND RURAL DEANERIES

In 1542.[2]

GLOUCESTER

Cr 1897[1] from Gloucester and Bristol dioc. Primarily Glos.

ORGANISATION IN ARCHDEACONRIES AND RURAL DEANERIES

CHELTENHAM AD (1919–*)
Campden, Cheltenham, Cirencester, Fairford, Northleach, Stow, Tetbury, Winchcombe

CIRENCESTER AD (1897–1919):
Campden, Cirencester, Fairford, Northleach, Stow, Winchcombe (1907–19)

GLOUCESTER AD
Bisley, Cheltenham (1897–1919), Dursley, Forest North, Forest South, Gloucester (1897–1952), Gloucester City (1952–*), Gloucester North (1952–*), Gloucester South (1952–*), Hawkesbury, Stonehouse, Tetbury (1907–19), Tewkesbury (1907–*), Winchcombe (1897–1907)

ALTERATIONS IN ARCHDEACONRIES AND RURAL DEANERIES

In 1898,[2] 1907,[3] 1919,[4] 1919,[5] 1920,[6] 1922,[7] 1948,[8] 1951,[9] 1952.[10]

GLOUCESTER AND BRISTOL

Cr 1836[1] by union Gloucester dioc, Bristol RDn of Bristol dioc. Primarily Glos, pt Wilts from 1837. Abol 1897,[2] pt to cr Gloucester dioc, pt to help cr Bristol dioc.

ORGANISATION IN ARCHDEACONRIES AND RURAL DEANERIES

BRISTOL AD
Bitton (1887–97), Bristol (1836–66), Bristol (1887–97), Bristol (City Dv) (1866–87), Bristol (Rural Dv) (1866–87), Chippenham (1887–97), Cirencester (1836–82), Cricklade (1837–97), Fairford (1836–82), Hawkesbury (1836–66), Hawkesbury (1887–97), Hawkesbury North (1866–87), Hawkesbury South (1866–87), Malmesbury (1837–66), Malmesbury (1887–97), Malmesbury North (1866–87), Malmesbury South (1866–87), Stapleton (1887–97)

CIRENCESTER AD (1882–97)
Campden, Cirencester, Fairford, Stow, Northleach (1887–97), Northleach North (1882–87)

GLOUCESTER AD
Bisley (1887–97), Campden (1836–82), Cheltenham (1887–97), Dursley, Forest (1836–66), Forest North (1866–97), Forest South (1866–97), Gloucester, Northleach (1836–66), Northleach North (1866–82), Northleach South (1866–87), Stonehouse (1836–66), Stonehouse (1887–97), Stonehouse North (1866–87), Stonehouse South (1866–87), Stow (1836–82), Winchcombe (1836–66), Winchcombe (1887–97), Winchcombe North (1866–87), Winchcombe South (1866–87)

ALTERATIONS IN ARCHDEACONRIES AND RURAL DEANERIES

In 1837,[3] 1848,[4] 1866,[5] 1882,[6] 1887.[7]

GUILDFORD

Cr 1927[1] from Winchester dioc. Primarily Surrey, incl pt Hants.

ORGANISATION IN ARCHDEACONRIES AND RURAL DEANERIES

DORKING AD (1928–*)
Chertsey (1946–*), Dorking, Emly, Epsom, Leatherhead, Woking

SURREY AD
Aldershot, Cranleigh (1928–*), Dorking (1927–28), Emly (1927–28), Farnham, Godalming, Guildford, Leatherhead (1927–28), Woking (1927–28)

ALTERATIONS IN ARCHDEACONRIES AND RURAL DEANERIES

In 1928,[2] 1935,[3] 1946.[4]

HEREFORD

Primarily comprised of counties included in Volume II of the *Guide*. Incl pt Glos (rural deaneries of Forest, Ross, Irchingfield), eccl severed 1541[1] to help cr Gloucester dioc.

LINCOLN

Primarily comprised of counties included in Volume II of the *Guide*. Incl Oxford until 1542,[1] Huntingdon until 1837,[2] and until 1845,[3] Bedford, Buckingham and pt Hertfordshire.

ORGANISATION IN ARCHDEACONRIES AND RURAL DEANERIES

BEDFORD AD (until 1837)
Bedford, Clapham, Dunstable, Eaton, Fleete, Shefford

BUCKINGHAM AD (until 1845)
Buckingham, Burnham, Mursley, Newport, Waddesdon, Wendover, Wycombe

HUNTINGDON AD (until 1845)
Baldock, Berkhampstead, Hertford, Hitchin, Huntingdon (until 1837), Leightonstone (until 1837), St Ives (until 1837), St Neots (until 1837), Yaxley (until 1837)

OXFORD AD (until 1542)
Aston, Bicester, Cuddesdon, Deddington, Henley, Chipping Norton, Oxford, Witney, Woodstock

ALTERATIONS IN ARCHDEACONRIES AND RURAL DEANERIES

In 1839.[4]

LONDON

Primarily City of London and Middx. Incl Essex until 1846,[1] pt Essex 1846–67[2]; pt Hertfordshire until 1845[3]; pt Surrey 1845[4]–77[5]; pt Kent 1845[3]–68[6].

ORGANISATION IN ARCHDEACONRIES AND RURAL DEANERIES

COLCHESTER AD (until 1846)
Colchester, Hedingham (1845–46), Lexden, Newport, Sampford, Tendring, Jurisd Waltham

ESSEX AD (until 1846)
Barking, Barstable, Billericay (1845–46), Canewdon (1845–46), Chafford, Chelmsford, Danbury (1845–46), Dengie, Dunmow (1845–46), Harlow (1845–46), Ingatestone (1845–46), Lambourne (1845–46), Maldon (1845–46), Ongar, Orsett (1845–46), Rochford

HACKNEY AD (1951–*)
Bethnal Green (1951–66), Hackney (1967–*), Hackney and Stoke Newington (1951–67), Islington, Poplar (1951–66), Stepney (1951–66), Tower Hamlets (1966–*)

HAMPSTEAD AD (1912–*)
Central Barnet (1967–*), West Barnet (1967–*), Brent (1967–70), North Camden (Hampstead) (1967–*), South Camden (Holborn and St Pancras) (1967–*), Enfield, Hampstead (1912–67), East Haringey (1967–*), West Haringey (1967–*), Harrow (1914–70), Hendon (1934–67), Holborn

(1912–14), Hornsey (1912–67), St Marylebone (1912–67), St Pancras (1912–67), Tottenham (1912–67), Westminster (St Marylebone) (1967–70), Willesden (1912–67)

LONDON AD
Not divided into RDns until 1861, incompletely then.
Bethnal Green (1901–51), The City (1954–*), East City (1869–1954), West City (1869–1954), Enfield (1900–12), Finsbury (1901–34), Finsbury and Holborn (1934–67), Hackney (1861–1901), Hackney and Stoke Newington (1901–51), Holborn (1900–12), Islington (1861–1951), Poplar (1901–51), St Sepulchre (1861–1901), Shoreditch (1870–1967), Spitalfields (1861–1901), Stepney (1861–1951), Tottenham (1901–12), Westminster (Paddington) (1970–*), Westminster (St Marylebone) (1970–*), Westminster (St Margaret's) (1970–*)

MIDDLESEX AD
Only Essex and Hertfordshire[7] pars divided into RDns before 1845; one Surrey RDn from 1845; all others from 1858, incompletely then.
pt Barking (1846–67), Barnes (1872–77), Barnes and Hammersmith (1861–72), Braughing[7] (until 1845), Camberwell (1871–77), Chelsea (1861–*), Clapham (1871–77), Dunmow (until 1845), Ealing (1858–1967), Ealing East (1967–70), Ealing West (1967–70), Enfield (1858–1900), Fulham (1858–1967), Greenwich (1861–68), Hammersmith (1901–*), Hampstead (1901–12), Hampton, Harlow (until 1845), Harrow (1858–1901), Hedingham (until 1845), Highgate (1875–1901), Hillingdon (1967–70), Hornsey (1901–12), Hounslow (1967–*), Kensington (1861–*), Lambeth (1865–77), Newington (1870–77), Paddington (1861–1967), St George Bloomsbury (1861–97), St George Hanover Square (1861–1901), St James Westminster (1861–97), St John Westminster (1861–83), St Margaret Westminster (1861–83), St Margaret and St John Westminster (1883–1901), St Martin in the Fields (1861–1901), St Marylebone (1861–1912), St Pancras (1858–1912), Southwark (1845–77), Staines (1858–61), Staines (1953–*), Streatham (1865–77), Uxbridge (1858–1967), Westminster (1901–67), Westminster (Paddington) (1967–70), Westminster (St Margaret's) (1967–70), Willesden (1901–12)

NORTHOLT AD (1970–*)
Brent, Ealing East, Ealing West, Harrow, Hillingdon

ALTERATIONS IN ARCHDEACONRIES AND RURAL DEANERIES

In 1858,[7] 1861,[7] 1869,[7] 1870,[7] 1871,[7] 1872,[7] 1875,[7] 1883,[7] 1897,[8] 1900,[7] 1901,[9] 1912,[10] 1914,[11] 1934,[12] 1948,[13] 1951,[14] 1951,[15] 1953,[16] 1954,[17] 1966,[18] 1967,[19] 1970,[20] 1972.[21]

NORWICH

Primarily Norfolk, incl Suffolk and pt Cambridgeshire until 1837, a major pt of Suffolk 1837–1914 and a small pt of Suffolk since 1914.

ORGANISATION IN ARCHDEACONRIES AND RURAL DEANERIES

LYNN AD (1894–*)
Breccles (1918–70), Breckland (1970–*), Brisley (1894–1970), Brisley and Elmham (1970–*), Burnham (1894–1970), Burnham and Walsingham (1970–*), Cranwich (1894–1918), Elmham (1918–70), Fincham (1894–1914), Heacham (1894–1970), Heacham and Rising (1970–*), Holt (1918–*), Lynn (1918–*), Lynn Marshland (1894–1914), Lynn Norfolk (1894–1918), Rising (1918–70), Swaffham (1918–70), Thetford (1894–1964), Toftrees (1894–1918), Walsingham (1894–1970)

NORFOLK AD
Breccles (1894–1918), Brooke (until 1970), Burnham (until 1894), Cranwich (until 1894), Depwade, Fincham (until 1894), Harling (1918–31), Heacham (until 1894), Hingham (until 1970), Hingham and Mitford (1970–*), Humbleyard, Loddon (1918–*), Lothingland (1914–*), Mitford (1918–70), Redenhall, Repps (until 1894), Rockland (until 1970), Sparham (until 1846), Thetford (1964–70), Thetford and Rockland (1970–*), Waxham (until 1894)

NORWICH AD
Blofield, Breccles (until 1894), Brisley (until 1894), Flegg, Holt (until 1918), Ingworth, Lynn (until 1866), Lynn Marshland (1866–94), Lynn Norfolk (1866–94), Norwich (until 1970), Norwich (East) (1970–*), Norwich (North) (1970–*), Norwich (South) (1970–*), Repps (1894–*), Sparham (1846–*), Taverham (until 1970), Thetford (until 1894), Toftrees (until 1894), Tunstead (1918–*), Walsingham (until 1894), Waxham (1894–*)

SUDBURY AD (until 1837)
Blackburne, Clare, Fordham, Hartismere, Stow, Sudbury, Thedwastre, Thingoe

SUFFOLK AD (until 1914)
Bosmere, Carlford, Claydon, Colneys, Dunwich (until 1868), Dunwich (North) (1868–1914), Dunwich (South) (1868–1914), South Elmham, Hartismere (1837–97), Hartismere (North) (1897–1914), Hartismere (South) (1897–1914), Hoxne alias Bishop's, Ipswich, Loes, Lothingland, Orford, Samford, Stow (1837–1914), Wangford, Wilford

In 1837,[1] 1846,[2] 1866,[2] 1868,[3] 1897,[3] 1894,[4] 1914,[5] 1914,[6] 1918,[7] 1931,[8] 1964,[9] 1964,[10] 1970.[11]

OXFORD

Cr 1542 as Osney from Lincoln dioc, becomes Oxford 1545 when see transferred there.[1] Primarily Oxon, incl Berkshire from 1836 and Buckinghamshire from 1845.

ORGANISATION IN ARCHDEACONRIES AND RURAL DEANERIES

BERKSHIRE AD (1836–*)
Abingdon, Bradfield (1865–*), Maidenhead (1865–*), Newbury, Reading, Sonning (1874–*), Vale of the White Horse (1865–*), Wallingford, Wantage (1865–*)

BUCKINGHAM AD (1845–*)
Amersham (1855–*), Aylesbury (1865–*), Bletchley (1874–*), Buckingham (1845–55), Buckingham (1874–*), Buckingham First Dv (1855–74), Buckingham Second Dv (1855–74), Burnham, Claydon (1855–*), Ivinghoe (1874–1964), Marlow (1865–74), Milton Keynes (1970–*), Mursley (1845–55), Mursley (1874–*), North Mursley (1855–74), South Mursley (1855–74), Newport (1845–55), Newport (1874–*), Newport First Dv (1855–74), Newport Second Dv (1855–74), Stony Stratford (1855–65), Waddesdon, Wendover (1845–55), Wendover (1874–*), Wendover First Dv (1855–74), Wendover Second Dv (1855–65), Wolverton (1915–70), Wycombe (1845–55), Wycombe (1874–*)

OXFORD AD
Aston, Bicester (1542–1956), Bicester and Islip (1956–*), Cowley (1956–*), Cuddesdon, Deddington, Henley, Islip (1852–1964), Nettlebed (1852–74), Chipping Norton, Oxford, Witney, Woodstock

ALTERATIONS IN ARCHDEACONRIES AND RURAL DEANERIES

In 1836,[2] 1837,[3] 1845,[4] 1846,[5] 1855,[6] 1865,[7] 1869,[8] 1874,[7] 1875,[9] 1915,[10] 1919,[11] 1920,[12] 1921,[13] 1922,[14] 1925,[15] 1952,[16] 1953,[17] 1956,[18] 1959,[19] 1964,[20] 1965,[21] 1966,[22] 1970,[23] 1973,[24] 1973,[25] 1973.[26]

PORTSMOUTH

Cr 1927[1] from Winchester dioc. Primarily Hants and Isle of Wight.

ORGANISATION IN ARCHDEACONRIES AND RURAL DEANERIES

PORTSMOUTH AD
Alverstoke, Havant, Petersfield, Portsmouth, Bishop's Waltham

ISLE OF WIGHT AD
East Wight, West Wight

ALTERATIONS IN ARCHDEACONRIES AND RURAL DEANERIES

In 1959,[2] 1970.[3]

ROCHESTER

Primarily Kent, incl most of Essex 1846–77, most of Hertfordshire 1845–77, pt of Surrey 1877–1905.

ORGANISATION IN ARCHDEACONRIES AND RURAL DEANERIES

BROMLEY AD (1955–*)
Beckenham, Bromley, Chislehurst (1955–65), Dartford (1955–65), Erith (1960–*), Orpington, Sidcup (1965–*)

COLCHESTER AD (1845–77)
Ardleigh (1847–77), Braintree (1847–77), Colchester, Dedham (1847–77), Halstead (1847–77), Harwich (1847–77), Hatfield Peverell (1847–77), Hedingham, Lexden (1845–47), Mersea (1847–77), Newport, Saffron Walden (1847–77), St Osyth (1847–77), Sampford, Tendring (1845–47), Jurisd Waltham (1845–47), Yeldham (1847–77)

ESSEX AD (1845–77)
Barking (pt 1845–67, ent 1867–77), Barstable, Billericay, Canewdon, Chafford, Chelmsford, Danbury, Dengie, Dunmow, Epping (1845–62), Harlow, Ingatestone, Lambourne, Maldon, Ongar, Orsett, Rochford, Roding (1862–77), Romford (1862–77)

KINGSTON-UPON-THAMES AD (1879–1905)
Barnes, Beddington, Caterham (1901–05), Dulwich (1901–05), Godstone, Kingston, Reigate, Richmond (1901–05), Streatham, Wandsworth (1901–05)

ROCHESTER AD (until 1845)
Dartford, Malling, Rochester

ROCHESTER AD (1877–*)
Beckenham (1909–55), Bromley (1909–55), Chislehurst (1936–55), Cliffe at Hoo (1909–54), Cobham (1909–54), Dartford (1909–55), Dartford (1965–*), East Dartford (1905–09), West Dartford (1905–09), Deptford (1879–86), Gillingham (1954–*), Gravesend, Greenwich (1877–1905), Lewisham (1886–1905), North Malling (1905–06), South Malling (1905–06), Orpington (1954–55), Rochester, Shoreham (1905–06), Strood (1954–*), Tonbridge (1905–06), Woolwich (1877–1905)

ROCHESTER AND ST ALBANS AD (1863–77)
Baldock, Barnet, Bennington, Berkhampstead, Buntingford, Cobham, Gravesend, Greenwich (1868–77), Hertford, Hitchin, Rochester, St Albans, Bishop's Stortford, Ware, Watford, Welwyn, Woolwich (1868–77)

ST ALBANS AD (1845–63)
Baldock, Barnet, Bennington, Berkhampstead, Buntingford, Hertford, Hitchin, St Albans, Bishop's Stortford, Ware, Watford, Welwyn

SOUTHWARK AD (1878–1905)
The Surrey pars in this dioc were not in an AD in 1877–78
Barnes (1878–79), Battersea (1879–1905), Camberwell, Clapham, Kennington (1879–1905), Kingston (1878–79), Lambeth, Newington, Reigate (1878–79), Southwark, Streatham (1878–79)

TONBRIDGE AD (1906–*)
Malling, Sevenoaks (1909–*), Shoreham, Tonbridge, Tunbridge Wells

ALTERATIONS IN ARCHDEACONRIES AND RURAL DEANERIES

In 1845,[1] 1845,[2] 1862,[3] 1862,[4] 1863,[5] 1868,[4] 1877,[6] 1877,[7] 1877,[8] 1878,[9] 1879,[10] 1879,[11] 1886,[12] 1895,[13] 1901,[14] 1905,[15] 1905,[16] 1906,[17] 1909,[18] 1914,[19] 1936,[20] 1954,[21] 1955,[22] 1957,[23] 1960,[24] 1965,[25] 1970,[26] 1973.[27]

ST. ALBANS

Cr 1877 from Rochester dioc.[1] Primarily Hertfordshire, incl Essex 1877–1914 and Bedfordshire from 1914.

ORGANISATION IN ARCHDEACONRIES AND RURAL DEANERIES

BEDFORD AD (1914–*)
Ampthill, Bedford, Biggleswade, Dunstable, Eaton (1914–17), Felmersham (1914–70), Haynes (1914–18), Luton, Riseley (1914–70), Sharnbrook (1970–*), Shefford

COLCHESTER AD (1877–1914)
Ardleigh (1877–95), Ardleigh and Harwich (1895–1907), Belchamp (1907–14), Braintree, Coggeshall (1877–1907), Coggeshall and Tey (1907–14), Colchester, Dedham, Dunmow (1907–14), Halstead (1877–1907), Halstead and Hedingham (1907–14), Harwich (1877–1905), Harwich (1907–14), Hatfield Peverell (1877–1907), Hedingham (1877–1907), Mersea (1877–1907), Newport (1877–1907), Newport and Stanstead (1907–14), Saffron Walden, St Osyth, Sampford (1877–1907), Witham, Yeldham (1877–1907)

ESSEX AD (1877–1914)
Barking (1877–95), Barking (1907–14), North Barking (1895–1907), South Barking (1895–1907), West Barking (1895–1907), Barstable (1877–1907), Barstable otherwise Brentwood (1907–14), Billericay (1877–95), Canewdon (1877–1907), Canewdon and Southend (1907–14), Chafford (1877–1907), Chafford otherwise Romford (1907–14), Chelmsford, Chigwell (1883–1914), Danbury (1877–1907), Dengie, Dunmow (1877–1907), West Ham (1907–14), Harlow, Ingatestone (1877–1907), Lambourne (1877–1907), Maldon, Ongar, Orsett (1877–1907), Orsett and Grays (1907–14), Rochford (1877–1907), Roding, Romford (1862–68), Walthamstow and Leyton (1907–14), Wickford (1907–14)

ST ALBANS AD
Aldenham (1970–*), Baldock (1877–1970), Barnet, Bennington (1877–82), Bennington (1892–1922), Bennington and Buntingford (1882–92), Berkhampstead (1877–1970), Berkhamstead (1970–*), Buntingford (1877–82), Buntingford (1892–*), Cheshunt (1970–*), Hatfield (1970–*), Hertford, Hitchin, Rickmansworth (1970–*), St Albans, Stevenage (1970–*), Bishop's Stortford, Ware (1877–1970), Watford, Welwyn (1877–1970), Wheathampstead (1970–*)

ALTERATIONS IN ARCHDEACONRIES AND RURAL DEANERIES

In 1862,[2] 1877,[3] 1882,[4] 1883,[2] 1892,[4] 1895,[5] 1907,[6] 1914,[7] 1914,[8] 1917,[9] 1918,[10] 1922,[11] 1930,[12] 1960,[13] 1970,[14] 1974.[15]

ST. EDMUNDSBURY AND IPSWICH

Cr 1914 from Norwich dioc, Ely dioc.[1] Primarily Suffolk.

ORGANISATION IN ARCHDEACONRIES AND RURAL DEANERIES

IPSWICH AD (1931–*)
Bosmere, Claydon (1931–72), Colneys (1972–*), Hadleigh, North Hartismere (1931–72), South Hartismere (1931–72), Ipswich, Samford, Stow (1931–72), Stowmarket (1972–*), Woodbridge (1972–*)

SUDBURY AD
Blackburne (1914–72), Clare, Hadleigh (1914–31), Horringer (1914–72), Ixworth (1972–*), Lavenham, Mildenhall, Newmarket (1916–72), Sudbury, Thedwastre (1914–72), Thingoe, Thurlow (1914–16)

SUFFOLK AD
Breccles (1916–72), Breccles and South Elmham (1972–*), Bosmere (1914–31), Carlford (1914–72), Claydon (1914–31), Colneys (1914–72), North Dunwich (1914–72), South Dunwich (1914–72), South Elmham (1914–72), Halesworth (1972–*), Hartismere (1972–*), Hartismere (North) (1914–31), Hartismere (South) (1914–31), Hoxne alias Bishop's, Ipswich (1914–31), Loes, Samford (1914–31), Saxmundham (1916–*), Stow (1914–31), Wilford (1914–72)

ALTERATIONS IN ARCHDEACONRIES AND RURAL DEANERIES

In 1914,[2] 1914,[3] 1931,[4] 1946,[5] 1972.[6]

SARUM

Primarily Wilts (ent until 1837, most from 1837), incl Dorset until 1542 and again from 1836, and Berkshire until 1836. For a long period the rural dearneries were known both as divisions of the original rural deanries and by the names that were used invariably later. For a key to the paired names, see Part I under Dorset and Wilts.

ORGANISATION IN ARCHDEACONRIES AND RURAL DEANERIES

BERKSHIRE AD (until 1836)
Abingdon, Newbury, Reading, Wallingford

DORSET AD (until 1542)
Bridport, Dorchester, Pimperne, Shaftesbury, Whitchurch

DORSET AD (1836–*)
Abbotsbury (1872–1916), Beaminster (1872–1916), Bere Regis (1872–1916), Blackmore Vale (1973–*), Blandford (1872–1970), Bridport (1836–72), Bridport (1872–1916), Cerne (1872–1916), Dorchester (1836–72), Dorchester (1872–1916), Lyme (1872–1916), Milton (1872–1970), Milton and Blandford (1970–*), Pimperne (1836–72), Poole (1872–*), Purbeck (1872–*), Shaftesbury (1836–72), Shaftesbury (1872–1972), Shaftesbury and Tisbury (1973–*), Sherborne (1872–1916), Stalbridge (1872–1954), Sturminster Newton (1872–1972), Weymouth (1872–1916), Whitchurch (until 1872), Wimborne (1872–*)

SARUM AD
Alderbury (1872–*), Amesbury (until 1872), Amesbury (1872–1951), Avon (1951–*), Chalke (until 1872), Chalke (1872–*), Heytesbury (1872–*), Salisbury Sub-deanery (until 1872), Salisbury (1971–*), Tisbury (1872–1973), Wilton (until 1872), Wilton (1872–1971), Wylye (until 1872), Wylye (1872–1971), Wylye and Wilton (1971–*)

SHERBORNE AD (1916–*)
Abbotsbury (1916–70), Beaminster, Bere Regis, Bridport (1916–70), Cerne (1916–54), Dorchester, Lyme (1916–70), Lyme Bay (1970–*), Sherborne, Weymouth

WILTS AD
Avesbury (until 1872), Avebury (1872–1974), Bradford (1872–*), Calne (1974–*), Cannings (1872–1951), Cricklande (until 1837), Devizes (1951–*), Enford (1872–1951), Malmesbury (until 1837), Marlborough (until 1872), Marlborough (1872–*), Pewsey (1872–*), Potterne (until 1872), Potterne (1872–1951)

ALTERATIONS IN ARCHDEACONRIES AND RURAL DEANERIES

In 1542,[1] 1836,[2] 1837,[3] 1846,[4] 1869,[5] 1872,[6] 1887,[7] 1916,[8] 1919,[9] 1949,[10] 1951,[11] 1954,[12] 1954,[13] 1955,[14] 1956,[15] 1959,[16] 1962,[17] 1971,[18] 1973,[19] 1973,[20] 1974.[21]

SOUTHWARK

Cr 1905 from Rochester dioc.[1] Primarily Surrey, incl pt Kent.

ORGANISATION IN ARCHDEACONRIES AND RURAL DEANERIES

KINGSTON-UPON-THAMES AD
Barnes (1905–22), Beddington (1905–66), Caterham, Dulwich (1905–06), Godstone, Kingston, Merton (1966–73), Reigate, Richmond (1905–22), Richmond and Barnes (1922–73), Streatham (1905–06), Sutton (1966–*), Wandsworth (1905–06), Wimbledon (1909–66)

LEWISHAM AD (1906–*)
The Kent pars in this dioc were not in an AD in 1905–06
Camberwell (1906–73), Dulwich (1906–73), Eltham (1962–66), Greenwich (1906–54), Greenwich (1966–*), Greenwich and Deptford (1954–66), Lewisham, Woolwich

SOUTHWARK AD
Battersea (1905–73), Bermondsey (1909–*), Brixton and Kennington (1935–47), Camberwell (1905–06), Camberwell (1973–*), Clapham (1905–47), Clapham and Brixton (1947–*), Dulwich (1973–*), Kennington (1905–35), Lambeth, Newington (1905–47), Streatham (1906–58), Streatham (1966–*), Streatham and Mitcham (1958–66), Southwark (1905–47), Southwark and Newington (1947–*), Tooting (1966–73), Wandsworth (1906–73)

WANDSWORTH AD (1973–*)
Battersea, Merton, Richmond and Barnes, Tooting, Wandsworth

ALTERATION IN ARCHDEACONRIES AND RURAL DEANERIES

In 1905,[2] 1906,[3] 1909,[4] 1922,[5] 1935,[6] 1947,[7] 1950,[8] 1954,[9] 1958,[10] 1966,[11] 1973.[12]

TRURO

Cr 1876 from Exeter dioc.[1] Primarily Cornwall.

ORGANISATION IN ARCHDEACONRIES AND RURAL DEANERIES

BODMIN AD (1878–*)
Bodmin, East, Stratton, Trigg Major, Trigg Minor, West

TRURO AD
Bodmin (1876–78), Carnmarth (1876–1915), Carnmarth North (1915–*), Carnmarth South (1915–*), East (1876–78), Kerrier, Penwith, Powder, Pydar, St Austell, Stratton (1876–78), Trigg Major (1876–78), Trigg Minor (1876–78), West (1876–78)

ALTERATION IN ARCHDEACONRIES AND RURAL DEANERIES

In 1877,[2] 1878,[3] 1915,[4] 1924,[5] 1964,[6] 1964,[7] 1972.[8]

WESTMINISTER

Cr 1540 from London dioc, suppressed 1550. Because of its short span of existence, there is no mention of this dioc in Part I of the *Guide*.

WINCHESTER

Primarily Hants (ent until 1927, pt from 1927), incl Surrey (ent until 1845, reduced pt progressively 1845–1927) and Isle of Wight until 1927.

ORGANISATION IN ARCHDEACONRIES AND RURAL DEANERIES

BASINGSTOKE AD (1927–*)
Aldershot (1927), Alresford (1948–*), Alton, Andover, Basingstoke, Kingsclere (1927–28), Odiham (1928–*), Silchester (1927–28), Whitchurch (1928–*)

PORTSMOUTH AD (1925–27)
Alverstoke, Havant, Peterfield, Portsmouth, Bishop's Waltham

ISLE OF WIGHT AD (1871–1927)
East Medine (1871–72), North-East Medine (1872–92), South-East Medine (1872–92), West Medine (1871–92), East Wight (1892–1927), West Wight (1892–1927)

SURREY AD (until 1927)
Dorking (1878–1927), Emly (1871–1927), Ewell (until 1858), North-East Ewell (1858–78), South-East Ewell (1858–78), South-West Ewell (1858–78), Farnham (1878–1927), Godalming (1878–1927), Guildford (until *ca* 1535), Guildford (1858–1927), Leatherhead (1871–1927), Stoke (*ca* 1535–1858), North-East Stoke (1858–78), North-West Stoke (1858–78), South-East Stoke (1858–78), South-West Stoke (1858–78), Southwark (until 1845), Woking (1878–1927)

WINCHESTER AD
Aldershot (1892–1927), Alresford (until 1948), Alton (until 1856), Alton (1892–1927), East Alton (1856–71), West Alton (1856–92), Alverstoke (1879–1925), Alverstoke and Portsea Island (1871–79), Andover (until 1856), Andover (1892–1927), North Andover (1871–92), North-East Andover (1856–71), North-West Andover (1856–71), South Andover (1871–92), South-West Andover (1856–71), West Andover (1871–92), Basingstoke (until 1856), Basingstoke (1892–1927), North-East Basingstoke (1856–92), South-West Basingstoke (1856–92), Bournemouth (1928–*), Chilbolton (1856–71), Christchurch (1892–*), Droxford (until 1856), North-East Droxford (1856–71), North-West Droxford (1856–71), South-East Droxford (1856–71), Fawley (1856–92), Fordingbridge (until 1856), East Fording-

bridge (1856–92), West Fordingbridge [sometimes 'Vale of Avon' after 1871] (1856–92), Havant (1871–92), Havant (1900–25), Kingsclere (1892–1927), Landport (1892–1900), Lyndhurst (1892–*), East Medine (1850–71), West Medine (1850–71), West Meon (1856–71), Micheldever (1856–71), Odiham (1856–92), Peterfield (1871–1925), Portsea Island (1879–92), Portsmouth (1892–1925), Ringwood (1908–12), Romsey (1871–*), Silchester (1892–1927), Somborne (until 1856), South-West Somborne (1856–71), Southampton, Stockbridge (1892–1922), Bishop's Waltham (1871–1925), Isle of Wight (until 1850), Winchester

ALTERATIONS IN ARCHDEACONRIES AND RURAL DEANERIES

By 1535,[1] in 1837,[2] 1845,[3] 1856,[4] 1858,[4] 1869,[5] 1871,[4] 1871,[6] 1872,[4] 1877,[7] 1878,[8] 1879,[9] 1892,[10] 1900,[11] 1908,[12] 1912,[13] 1922,[14] 1925,[15] 1927,[16] 1927,[17] 1928,[18] 1948,[19] 1949.[20]

WORCESTER

Primarily comprised of counties included in Volume II of the *Guide*.
Incl pt Glos, eccl severed 1541 to cr Gloucester dioc,[1] qv.

Notes for Entries

PART I: THE PARISHES OF ENGLAND

BEDFORDSHIRE

[1]13 Aug, MHealth Decl. [2]28 Sept, MHousLG Decl. [3]24 June, LGBO 15338. [4]1 Apr, MHealthO 77050. [5]21 Dec, MHousLG Decl. [6]12 Jan, SI 1965/24. [7]25 Mar, LGBO 18187. [8]*VCH Beds* III, 206. [9]9 Nov, *Lond Gaz*. [10]25 May, MHealth Decl. [11]28 Dec, MHousLG Decl. [12]23 Mar, *Lond Gaz*. [13]1 MHealthO 77888. [14]1 Apr, SI 1967/1786. [15]*VCH Beds* III, 30. [16]27 Oct, *Lond Gaz*. [17]23 May, *Lond Gaz*. [18]29 Sept (lic min, *Lond Gaz* 10 May 1955). [19]PC QAB. [20]20 July, *Lond Gaz*. [21]4 Dec, *Lond Gaz*. [22]7 May, *Lond Gaz*. [23]23 Aug, *Lond Gaz*. [24]6 Dec, *Lond Gaz*. [25]18 Jan (lic min, *Lond Gaz* 6 Dec 1955). [26]15 Sept, LGBO 66502. [27]29 & 30 Vict., *c* 113. [28]13 Nov, *Lond Gaz*. [29]13 Mar, *Lond Gaz*. [30]26 Mar, *Lond Gaz*. [31]12 June, *Lond Gaz*. [32]20 June (lic min, *Lond Gaz* 18 May 1954). [33]1 July (*Lond Gaz* 29 June). [34]1 Apr, MHealthO 76927. [35]30 Oct, *Lond Gaz*. [36]9 Oct, LGBO 6982. [37]1 Apr, MHealthO 10768. [38]5 June, MHousLG Decl. [39]56 & 57 Vict., *c* 73. [40]30 Sept, LGBProvO 1312. [41]6 Feb, SI 1964/169. [42]19 Jan, SI 1955/2. [43]30 May, *Lond Gaz*. [44]23 Mar, *Lond Gaz*. [45]17 Aug, *Lond Gaz*. [46]1 Oct, MHousO 73341. [47]22 Dec, *Lond Gaz*. [48]1 Jan, 20 Vict., *c* 19. [49]*VCH Beds* III, 131-32. [50]*VCH Beds* II, 212. [51]1 Apr, LGBO 32662. [52]*VCH Beds* III, 361. [53]1 Apr, 6 Edw. VII, *c* cxx. [54]1 Apr, SI 1954/314. [55]*VCH Hunts* II, 370. [56]2 & 3 Wm. IV, *c* 64 and 7 & 8 Vict., *c* 61. [57]25 Mar, 45 & 46 Vict., *c* 58. [58]30 June, *Lond Gaz*. [59]24 Mar, LGBO 16417. [60]22 Dec, *Lond Gaz*. [61]29 Nov, reported in *Parl Papers* 1872, XLVI, 21. [62]3 Feb, *Lond Gaz*. [63]24 Mar, LGBO 22219. [64]1 Sept (*Lond Gaz* 17 Aug 1972). [65]*VCH Beds* II, 335. [66]1 Nov, *Lond Gaz*. [67]*Guide to the Bedfordshire Record Office*, 27. [68]30 Sept, 60 & 61 Vict., *c* lxxv. [69]30 Sept, LGB ProvO 1313. [70]1 Oct, 18 & 19 Geo. V, *c* xiii. [71]13 June (lic min, *Lond Gaz* 16 Apr 1965). [72]2 Feb, reported in *Parl Papers* 1872, XLVI, 20. [73]1 Apr, 2 & 3 Geo. V, *c* xi. [74]1 Apr, LGBO 33504. [75]30 May, *Lond Gaz*. [76]*VCH Beds* III, 142. [77]1 Oct, MHealthO 92505. [78]15 Sept, LGBO 66502. [79]1 Apr, LGBO 33979. [80]16 Apr, *Lond Gaz*. [81]22 Jan, SI 1965/23. [82]8 Feb, *Lond Gaz*. [83]Co Council Naming O, on authority of 56 & 57 Vict., *c* 73. [84]8 Feb, *Lond Gaz*. [85]27 Mar, *Lond Gaz*. [86]17 May, *Lond Gaz*. [87]29 July, *Lond Gaz*. [88]12 Sept (lic min, *Lond Gaz* 1 May 1951). [89]12 Sept, *Lond Gaz*. [90]13 Sept, *Lond Gaz*. [91]24 Mar, *Lond Gaz*. [92]23 May, *Lond Gaz*. [93]22 Dec, *Lond Gaz*. [94]9 Nov, LGB ProvO 1095. [95]15 Mar (lic min, *Lond Gaz* 6 Aug 1955). [96]Presumed incl in PLU when became CP, not orig rated in PLU. [97]16 Apr, *Lond Gaz*. [98]30 Oct, *Lond Gaz*. [99]30 Sept, 60 & 61 Vict., *c* lxxv. [100]23 Dec, *Lond Gaz*. [101]*VCH Beds* III, 267. [102]8 June, LGBO 61842. [103]9 Oct, LGBO 6980, 6981, 6982. [104]1 Apr, MHealthO 76928. [105]*VCH Beds* III, 267. [106]OC 19 Oct. [107]*VCH Beds* I, 324. [108]9 Oct, LGBO 6980. [109]30 Sept, 60 & 61 Vict., *c* lxxv. [110]1 Apr, SI 1964/366, 367. [111]24 Mar, LGBO 22218. [112]*VCH Beds* III, 318. [113]30 Sept, 60 & 61 Vict., *c* lxxv. [114]5 Nov, *Lond Gaz*. [115]23 Aug, *Lond Gaz*.

BERKSHIRE

[1]Apptd day, LGBO 31930. [2]Apptd day, LGBO 31901. [3]1 Apr, MHealthO 77733. [4]1 Apr, 14 & 15 Geo. VI, *c* xxx. [5]1 Apr, 20 & 21 Eliz. II, *c* 70. [6]4 Nov, reported in *Parl Papers* 1872, XLVI, 22. [7]19 May, *Lond Gaz*. [8]17 May, reported in *Parl Papers* 1872, XLVI, 22. [9]9 Nov, 53 & 54 Vict., *c* lxxviii [10]25 Mar, 45 & 46 Vict., *c* 58. [11]25 Mar, LGBO 18177. [12]*VCH Berks* IV, 447. [13]*VCH Berks* III, 387-88. [14]29 & 30 Vict., *c* 113. [15]*VCH Berks* IV, 397. [16]23 Feb, *Lond Gaz*. [17]*VCH Berks* III, 203. [18]1 Apr, MHealthO 107591. [19]24 Mar, LGBO 20688, 29690, 20690. [20]4 Feb, *Lond Gaz*. [21]10 Mar, *Lond Gaz*. [22]*VCH Berks* III, 452. [23]27 Feb, reported in *Parl Papers* 1872, XLVI, 18. [24]7 June, reported in *Parl Papers* 1872, XLVI, 21. [25]1 Jan, 20 Vict., *c* 19. [26]1 Apr, LGBO 40662. [27]2 & 3 Wm. IV, *c* 64 and 7 & 8 Vict., *c* 61. [28]30 May, Instr CBC. [29]15 Apr, reported in *Parl Papers* 1872, XLVI, 19. [30]24 Mar, LGBO 21438. [31]First noted in *Clergy List*. [32]31 Jan, *Lond Gaz*. [33]*VCH Berks* IV, 43. [34]1 Apr, MHousLGO 4809. [35]29 Aug, *Lond Gaz*. [36]26 June, reported in *Parl Papers* 1872, XLVI, 22. [37]PC QAB, refounded 10 Apr 1858, *Lond Gaz*. [38]18 Nov, *Lond Gaz*. [39]24 Oct, *Lond Gaz*. [40]20 Nov, *Lond Gaz*. [41]1 Apr, MHousLGO 18058. [42]1 Apr, MHousLGO 34262. [43]Apptd day, LGBO 31898. [44]PC QAB, refounded 1 Mar 1867, *Lond Gaz*. [45]Beresford & Finberg, 67. [46]22 Aug, *Lond Gaz*. [47]19 Mar, *Lond Gaz*. [48]2 Dec, *Lond Gaz*. [49]*VCH Berks* III, 464. [50]1 Apr, MHealthO 107590. [51]First appearance in *Clergy List*. [52]23 June, *Lond Gaz*. [53]25 Nov, *Lond Gaz*. [54]1 Apr, MHousLGO 41456. [55]5 Jan, SI 1971/2106. [56]24 Mar, LGBO 23869. [57]24 Mar, LGBO 20689. [58]First appearance *Clergy List*. [59]4 Mar, *Lond Gaz*. [60]First appearance *Crockford's Clerical Directory*. [61]1 Apr, MHousLGO 45533. [62]*VCH Berks* IV, 84. [63]29 Dec, *Lond Gaz*. [64]12 July, *Lond Gaz*. [65]28 Mar, 56 & 57 Vict., *c* lxxiii. [66]26 Apr, reported in *Parl Papers* 1872, XLVI, 18. [67]1 Apr, MHealthO 107400. [68]3 Aug, *Lond Gaz*. [69]Apptd day, LGBO 31900. [70]21 Dec, LGBO 8920. [71]Apptd day, LGBO 31899. [72]10 Nov, reported in *Parl Papers* 1872, XLVI, 18. [73]18 Oct, *Lond Gaz*. [74]9 Nov, 10 & 11 Geo. V, *c* xxxv. [75]12 Sept, *Lond Gaz*. [76]Apptd day, LGBO 32022. [77]6 Nov, *Lond Gaz*. [78]20 Dec, LGBO 13156. [79]19 July, *Lond Gaz*. [80]50 & 51 Vict., *c* lxiii. [81]2 Jan, *Lond Gaz*. (OC 23 Dec 1845). [82]14 Feb, *Lond Gaz*.

[83]18 Nov, *Lond Gaz.* [84]11 Mar, *Lond Gaz.* [85]30 Sept, LGBO 31571. [86]10 July, *Lond Gaz.* [87]5 Mar, reported in *Parl Papers* 1890-91, LXI, 54. [88]*VCH Berks* IV, 267. [89]22 Oct, Instr CBC. [90]22 July, *Lond Gaz.* [91]1 Apr, MHealthO 81345. [92]12 Nov, *Lond Gaz.* [93]1 Apr, Dept EnvirnO 3711. [94]PC QAB. [95]17 July, *Lond Gaz.* [96]1 Jan, *Lond Gaz.* [97]22 May, *Lond Gaz.* [98]1 July (*Lond Gaz* 14 June). [99]22 Mar, *Lond Gaz.* [100]Effective this year, after date in *Lond Gaz* (28 June). [101]*VCH Berks* IV, 178. [102]19 May, reported in *Parl Papers* 1872, XLVI, 18. [103]1 Apr, MHousLGO 1303. [104]5 Sept, *Lond Gaz.* [105]16 May, *Lond Gaz.* [106]30 Dec, *Lond Gaz.* [107]20 Mar, reported *Parl Papers* 1872, XLVI, 20. [108]25 Oct, *Lond Gaz.* [109]Apptd day, LGBO 31902. [110]24 Feb, *Lond Gaz.* [111]1 Apr, LGBO 107451. [112]11 July, *Lond Gaz.* [113]13 Mar, *Lond Gaz.* [114]7 Aug, *Lond Gaz.* [115]25 Mar, LGBO 18178. [116]PC QAB, refounded 1885, reported *Parl Papers* 1890-91, LXI, 54. [117]25 Mar, LGBO 18177, 18178, 18180. [118]1 Apr, MHealthO 84971. [119]30 Sept, LGBO 31527. [120]Apptd day, LGBO 32021. [121]*VCH Berks* IV, 197-98. [122]First appearance *Clergy List.* [123]24 Mar, reported in *Parl Papers* 1890-91, LXI, 54. [124]1 Apr, MHousLGO 1417. [125]20 Feb, *Lond Gaz.* [126]12 May, *Lond Gaz.* [127]6 June, *Lond Gaz.* [128]3 Jan (OC 29 Dec 1853). [129]*VCH Berks* IV, 353. [130]21 Mar, *Lond Gaz.* [131]9 Mar, *Lond Gaz.* [132]*VCH Berks* IV, 151-52. [133]20 Jan, Instr CBC. [134]1 Dec, *Lond Gaz.* [135]9 May, *Lond Gaz.* [136]7 Apr, reported in *Parl Papers* 1872, XLVI, 21. [137]3 July, *Lond Gaz.* [138]1 Apr, MHousLGO 1457. [139]24 Mar, LGBO 20688. [140]Year vac (*Lond Gaz* 2 Apr 1926). [141]First appearance *Clergy List.* [142]*VCH Berks* IV, 134-35. [143]Effective this year after date *Lond Gaz* (20 Feb). [144]LGB ProvO 623. [145]Apptd day, LGBO 31931. [146]*VCH Berks* IV, 416. [147]31 Mar, LGBO 46554. [148]9 Nov, 1 & 2 Geo. V, *c* xlviii. [149]1 Apr, LGBO 63865. [150]30 Aug, *Lond Gaz.* [151]6 Sept, *Lond Gaz.* [152]30 Oct, *Lond Gaz.* [153]29 Oct, *Lond Gaz.* [154]6 Sept, *Lond Gaz.* [155]16 Jan, *Lond Gaz.* [156]18 Dec, *Lond Gaz.* [157]11 Oct, *Lond Gaz.* [158]Date uncertain. [159]Note cancelled. [160]*VCH Berks* IV, 185-87. [161]22 June, *Lond Gaz.* [162]*VCH Berks* III, 209. [163]56 & 57 Vict., *c* 73. [164]1 Apr, LGBO 40661. [165]30 Sept, 58 & 59 Vict., *c* xci. [166]Year vac (*Lond Gaz* 27 July 1926). [167]1 Mar (*Lond Gaz* 20 Feb). [168]27 Nov, reported in *Parl Papers* 1872, XLVI, 20. [169]9 Oct, LGBO 7056, 7057. [170]*VCH Berks* III, 170. [171]*VCH Berks* III, 232 [172]10 May, *Lond Gaz.* [173]26 May, *Lond Gaz.* [174]1 Apr, LGBO 23869. [175]14 Sept, *Lond Gaz.* [176]2 May, *Lond Gaz.* [177]*VCH Berks* III, 385. [178]18 Mar, *Lond Gaz.* [179]24 Dec, Instr Bps Oxford, Winch. [180]25 Mar, LGBO 29565. [181]24 June, *Lond Gaz.* [182]21 Dec, LGBO 8921. [183]24 Mar, LGBO 20690. [184]Apptd day, LGBO 32176. [185]*VCH Berks* III, 312. [186]Authority for cr not found. [187]Apptd day, LGBO 31427. [188]18 July, *Lond Gaz.* [189]21 Dec, *Lond Gaz.* [190]First noted in *Clergy List.* [191]*VCH Berks* III, 443. [192]1 Apr, LGBO 65053. [193]1 May, *Lond Gaz.* [194]*VCH Berks* III, 543. [195]*VCH Berks* III, 544. [196]*VCH Berks* III, 541. [197]1 May (*Lond Gaz* 16 Apr). [198]*VCH Berks* III, 542. [199]9 Oct, LGBO 7056, 7057. [200]Beresford & Finberg, 69. [201]Sep civ identity not regained. [202]Beresford & Finberg, 68. [203]*VCH Berks* II, 11. [204]*VCH Berks* IV, 380-81. [205]Apptd day, LGBO 31903. [206]28 July, *Lond Gaz.* [207]28 Mar, *Lond Gaz.* [208]1 Oct, 17 & 18 Geo. V, *c* xlviii. [209]21 Sept, *Lond Gaz.*

BUCKINGHAMSHIRE

[1]2 & 3 Wm. IV, *c* 64 and 7 & 8 Vict., *c* 61. [2]29 & 30 Vict., *c* 113. [3]1 Apr, MHealthO 77936. [4]1 Apr, MHousLGO 5943. [5]1 May (*Lond Gaz* 26 Apr). [6]5 Feb, *Lond Gaz.* [7]16 Aug, *Lond Gaz.* [8]Year vac (*Lond Gaz* 22 July 1921). [9]29 Oct, *Lond Gaz.* [10]1 Apr, LGBO 34772. [11]1 Oct, LGBO 41337. [12]1 Apr, 6 Edw. VII, *c* cxx. [13]28 Aug, *Lond Gaz.* [14]25 Mar, LGBO 18130. [15]12 Feb, MHousLG Decl. [16]*VCH Bucks* III, 18. [17]*VCH Bucks* II, 326. [18]2 Sept, reported in *Parl Papers* 1872, XLVI, 20. [19]Instr 1846, MSS Oxon C1340/2, supplied by Bucks RO. [20]25 Mar, 45 & 46 Vict., *c* 58. [21]25 Mar, LGBO 19622. [22]1 Oct, LGBO 35052. [23]1 Oct, LGBO 32795. [24]PC QAB, refounded 9 Apr 1852, *Lond Gaz.* [25]1 Nov, *Lond Gaz.* [26]*VCH Bucks* IV, 148-49. [27]Authority not found. [28]24 Mar, LGBO 15986, 15987. [29]13 May, reported in *Parl Papers* 1890-91, LXI, 54. [30]25 Mar, LGBO 17940. [31]6 Aug, Instr as Part Dist. [32]1 May (*Lond Gaz* 3 Apr). [33]PC QAB. [34]1 Jan (*Lond Gaz* 18 Dec 1973). [35]1 Apr, MHousLGO 3741. [36]12 Oct, *Lond Gaz.* [37]4 Sept, *Lond Gaz.* [38]United 16th cent as curacies, George Lipscomb, *The History and Antiquities of the County of Buckingham* (1847) (hereafter, Lipscomb), I, 109, PC QAB in 1740. [39]29 Jan, *Lond Gaz.* [40]OC 25 May, *VCH Bucks* III, 183. [41]25 Mar, LGBO 17936. [42]1 Apr, LGBO 65026. [43]1 Apr, LGBO 71580. [44]OC 1857, MSS Oxon C1356, supplied by Bucks RO. [45]28 Mar, *Lond Gaz.* [46]1 Jan, 20 Vict., *c* 19. [47]Incl in PLU only from 1861. [48]1 Apr, LGBO 71580. [49]*VCH Bucks* IV, 327. [50]30 Dec, *Lond Gaz.* [51]25 Mar, LGBO 19611. [52]21 Dec, MHousLG Decl. [53]PC QAB, refounded 4 Nov 1862, *Lond Gaz.* [54]28 Sept, MHousLG Decl. [55]1 Apr, 20 & 21 Eliz II, *c* 70; name declared in SI 1973/688. [56]31 Mar, MHealthO 74085. [57]1 Oct, LGBO 39609, 39611, 42617. [58]23 Jan, *Lond Gaz.* [59]24 Apr, *Lond Gaz*, refounded 24 Oct, reported in *Parl Papers* 1872, XLVI, 20. [60]PLU to take effect 20 May 1835 but Bucks pars added effective 28 Sept. [61]1 Apr, MHealthO 75180. [62]29 Nov, *Lond Gaz.* [63]16 Apr, *Lond Gaz.* [64]29 Aug, *Lond Gaz.* [65]20 July, MHousLG Decl. [66]Effective in year after *Lond Gaz* 28 June. [67]1 Apr, LGBO 38750. [68]23 Feb, Lipscomb I, 123. [69]24 Mar, LGBO 16583, 16584. [70]*VCH Bucks* III, 220-21. [71]15 May, *Lond Gaz.* [72]23 Aug, *Lond Gaz.* [73]19 Apr, *Lond Gaz.* [74]Lipscomb III, 7. [75]26 Oct, MHousLG Decl. [76]27 Nov, MHousLG Decl. [77]17 Apr, MHousLG Decl. [78]*VCH Bucks* IV, 56. [79]*VCH Bucks* IV, 32. [80]21 Dec, *Lond Gaz.* [81]14 June, *Lond Gaz.* [82]18 July, *Lond Gaz.* [83]*VCH Bucks* III, 338. [84]13 Aug, reported in *Parl Papers* 1872, XLVI, 20. [85]*VCH Bucks* III, 278. [86]19 Nov, *Lond Gaz.* [87]21 Sept, MHousLG Decl. [88]25 Mar, LGBO 16585. [89]Apptd day, Co Council Naming Order

and 56 & 57 Vict., *c* 73. [90] 1 Apr, LGBO 66946. [91] 1 Oct, LGBO 39609. [92] 27 Feb, reported in *Parl Papers* 1872, XLVI, 19. [93] *VCH Bucks* IV, 485. [94] Aug, MHealth Decl. [95] 5 Feb, *Lond Gaz.* [96] 17 Aug, *Lond Gaz.* [97] 15 May, *Lond Gaz.* [98] *Liber Regis*, 499. [99] 16 Apr, *Lond Gaz.* [100] 1 Apr, MHealthO 77936. [101] Lipscomb I, 249. [102] 28 Dec, MHousLG Decl. [103] 1 Feb (*Lond Gaz* 23 Jan). [104] 25 Mar, LGBO 17935. [105] 28 June, reported in *Parl Papers* 1897, LXVII, 174. [106] Apptd day, LGBO 31794. [107] 24 Mar, LGBO 19624. [108] 13 Feb. *Lond Gaz.* [109] 1 Oct (*Lond Gaz* 7 Sept). [110] 1 & 2 Wm. IV, *c* 38. [111] 15 Sept, *Lond Gaz.* [112] *VCH Bucks* III, 378-79. [113] 1 Apr, 17 & 18 Geo. V, *c* lxxxiii. [114] 31 Dec, *Lond Gaz.* [115] 25 Mar, LGBO 17937. [116] 31 Mar, 58 & 59 Vict., session 2, *c* viii. [117] 25 Mar, LGBO 19618. [118] 25 Mar, LGBO 19612. [119] 22 July, *Lond Gaz.* [120] 24 Mar, LGBO 16583, 16584, 16586. [121] 25 Mar, LGBO 16585, 19427. [122] 30 Sept, 58 & 59 Vict., session 2, *c* xi. [123] 26 July (*Lond Gaz* 18 Mar 1932, supplemented by *Lond Gaz* 27 June 1939). [124] 23 Jan, *Lond Gaz.* [125] 13 May, reported in *Parl Papers* 1897, LXVII, 173. [126] 1 Apr, 23 & 24 Geo. V, *c* iii. [127] PC QAB, refounded 1 Aug 1851, *Lond Gaz.* [128] *VCH Bucks* III, 300. [129] 30 Jan, reported in *Parl Papers* 1872, XLVI, 20. [130] 1 Oct, LGBO 39611. [131] 24 Mar, reported in *Parl Papers* 1890-91, LXI, 51. [132] 25 Feb, MHousLG Decl. [133] Incl in PLU from 1838. [134] 1 Apr, LGBO 55186. [135] 25 Mar, LGBO 17934. [136] 16 Dec, LGBO 7687. [137] 2 Oct, MHousLG Decl. [138] 22 Jan, SI 1965/23. [139] PC QAB, refounded 11 May 1866, *Lond Gaz.* [140] *VCH Bucks* IV, 395. [141] 1 Oct, LBGO 34210. [142] 7 May, *Lond Gaz.* [143] 20 Feb, *Lond Gaz.* [144] 21 June, *Lond Gaz.* [145] 24 Mar, LGBO 21701. [146] 11 Jan, *Lond Gaz.* [147] *VCH Bucks* IV, 248. [148] 31 July, *Lond Gaz.* [149] 1 Oct, MHousLG Decl. [150] PC QAB; see also *VCH Bucks* IV, 502. [151] *VCH Bucks* IV, 432. [152] 6 Mar, reported in *Parl Papers* 1903, L, 595-96. [153] MHealthO 68474. [154] 24 Mar, LGBO 16586. [155] 25 Mar, LGBO 19623. [156] *VCH Bucks* III, 95. [157] 25 Mar, LGBO 17936. [158] 25 Mar, LGBO 16584, 19427. [159] 13 Dec, *Lond Gaz.* [160] 26 Mar, LGBO 34075. [161] 22 Jan, SI 1965/23. [162] 1 Apr, SI 1958/460. [163] 23 May, reported in *Parl Papers* 1872, XLVI, 18. [164] 30 Sept, 58 & 59 Vict., session 2, *c* viii. [165] *VCH Bucks* IV, 476. [166] 8 Mar, *Lond Gaz.* [167] 25 Mar, LGBO 14671. [168] 24 Aug, *Lond Gaz.* [169] 17 Feb, *Lond Gaz.* [170] *VCH Oxon* VI, 330. [171] *VCH Bucks* III, 435. [172] 18 Mar, *Lond Gaz.* [173] 29 Nov, *Lond Gaz.* [174] *VCH Oxon* VII, 200. [175] 1 Apr, 23 & 24 Geo. V, *c* iii, and 1 Apr, MHealth O 77936. [176] 6 Dec, *Lond Gaz.* [177] 1 Oct, LGBO 39609, 39611, 42617. [178] 1 Oct, LGBO 42605. [179] 25 Mar, LGBO 18187. [180] 1 Apr, LGBO 50115. [181] 12 Jan, SI 1965/24. [182] 24 Mar, LGBO 15987. [183] *VCH Bucks* II, 346-47. [184] 31 July, *Lond Gaz.* [185] PC QAB, refounded 29 May 1846, *Lond Gaz.* [186] 23 June, *Lond Gaz.* [187] 24 Dec, *Lond Gaz.* [188] 30 Sept, LGBO 34583. [189] 24 Feb, MHousLG Decl. [190] 9 Nov, 1 Edw. VII, *c* cxlviii. [191] 5 Mar, *Lond Gaz.* [192] 1 Apr, *Lond Gaz.* [193] 26 May, *Lond Gaz.* [194] 1 Apr, 20 & 21 Eliz. II, *c* 70. [195] Presumed incl in PLU when became sep CP; not orig rated in the PLU.

CAMBRIDGESHIRE

[1] Orig Harston RDn, called Barton by mid–13th cent. [2] Orig Papw. RDn, called Knap. by mid–13th cent. [3] Ely RDn, Wisb. RDn were not in an AD but rather in pec jurisd of Bp Ely; an AD of 'Isle of Ely' was erected 1 July 1884 (*Lond Gaz*) but when Wisb. AD cr 5 Feb 1915 (*Lond Gaz*) the order stated that no prev AD existed. [4] March RDn cr 1884. [5] Incl other RDns with Suffolk pars, and many in list above incl Suffolk pars as well. This AD in Norw dioc until 1837, Ely dioc 1837–1914, St Edm & Ipsw thereafter. [6] Before *Valor Eccl.* [7] 1 Apr, LGO 23774. [8] SI 1964/366. [9] 29&30 Vict., *c* 113. [10] 32 Henry VIII, *c* 44. [11] 30 Sept, LGB ProvO 1173. [12] 1 Apr, MHousLGO 22509. [13] 8 Feb, reported in *Parl Papers* 1890–91, LXI, 57. [14] On death of rector of Doddington, under provisions of 19 & 20 Vict., *c* i (1856), amending 10 & 11 Vict., *c* iii. [15] PC QAB, refounded 1 May 1863, *Lond Gaz.* [16] Apptd day, LGBO 32005. [17] 1 Apr, MHealthO 108931. [18] 25 Mar, LGBO 19043. [19] 25 Mar, LGBO 16610. [20] I have been unable to determine the date of the union. [21] 1 Apr, MHousLGO 3703. [22] 28 Apr, *Lond Gaz.* [23] 1 Nov (*Lond Gaz*, 27 Oct). [24] 26 Mar, LGBO 40017. [25] 1 Apr, 12 & 13 Geo. V, *c* clxxxviii. [26] 1 Apr, MHealthO 78023. [27] *VCH Cambs* III, 123. [28] *VCH Cambs* III, 124. [29] Year of vac (*Lond Gaz*, 23 Jan 1973). [30] 25 Mar, 45 & 46 Vict., *c* 58. [31] 18 June, *Lond Gaz.* [32] 25 Mar, LGBO 18181. [33] 4 July, *Lond Gaz.* [34] *VCH Cambs* III, 126. [35] 21 Dec, *Lond Gaz.* [36] 28 June, *Lond Gaz.* [37] 24 Oct, *Lond Gaz.* [38] 17 Feb, *Lond Gaz.* [39] 3 Sept, lic min (*Lond Gaz*, 30 Apr). [40] *VCH Cambs* III, 129. [41] 25 Mar, LGBO 18183. [42] 14 May, *Lond Gaz.* [43] 29 Oct, *Lond Gaz.* [44] 1 Nov (*Lond Gaz*, 27 Oct). [45] 20 July, *Lond Gaz.* [46] 30 Apr, *Lond Gaz.* [47] 1 Apr, 1 & 2 Geo. V, *c* lxxxv. [48] United before *Valor Eccl.* [49] 1 Apr, IoE (Par of Welches Dam) O, 1959. [50] 21 May, *Lond Gaz.* [51] 1 Apr, *Lond Gaz.* [52] 29 Nov, *Lond Gaz.* [53] 26 Apr, *Lond Gaz.* [54] 25 Mar, *Lond Gaz.* [55] PC QAB. [56] 27 June, reported in *Parl Papers* 1890-91, XLI, 55. [57] 11 Mar, *Lond Gaz.* [58] 26 Jan, O Cambs Co Council. [59] 30 Sept, 58 & 59 Vict., session 2, *c* viii. [60] 1 Apr, MHousLGO 34452. [61] After *Valor Eccl.* [62] PC QAB, refounded 9 July 1850, *Lond Gaz.* [63] 10 July, *Lond Gaz.* [64] *VCH Cambs* V, 194. [65] 19 July, reported in *Parl Papers* 1890–91, LXI, 54. [66] 24 Mar, LGBO 15876, 15878. [67] 20 July, MHousLG Decl (Alt of Watercourses). [68] Made a city by letters patent, 21 Mar. [69] Apptd day, 56 & 57 Vict., *c* 73. [70] Year church erected, per statutory auth as in note 14. [71] On death of rector of Doddington, per statutory auth as in note 14; rectory the following year, *VCH Cambs* IV, 119. [72] 1 Apr, MHealthO 76490. [73] 2 July, *Lond Gaz.* [74] 12 May, reported in *Parl Papers* 1890–91, LXI, 51. [75] Date and authority for union not found. [76] 1 Apr, 23 & 24 Geo. V, *c* lxv. [77] 3 July, *Lond Gaz.* [78] 1 Jan, 20 Vict., *c* 19. [79] Presumed incl in PLU when made CP; not orig rated at cr PLU. [80] 5 Apr, *Lond Gaz.* [81] 24 June, *Lond Gaz.* [82] 1 Apr,

MHealthO 77445. [83]24 Mar, LGBO 15876. [84]25 Mar, LGBO 19516. [85]1 Apr, MHousLGO 3115. [86]5 Geo. III, *c* 49. [87]21 July, reported in *Parl Papers* 1890–91, LXI, 51. [88]1 Apr, MHousLGO 7208. [89]SI 1964/367. [90]1 Apr, MHealthO 78163. [91]1 Apr, MHousLGO 3104. [92]1 Apr, MHousLGO 4141. [93]27 June, *Lond Gaz.* [94]33 & 34 Vict., *c* xlv. [95]See *VCH Cambs* V, 96. [96]PC QAB from the area of chap Wisbech St Mary, refounded 28 Mar 1871, *Lond Gaz.* [97]1 Apr, MHousLGO 6510. [98]25 Mar, LGBO 19041. [99] Date and authority not found. [100]25 Mar, LGBO 18936. [101]1 Oct, LGBO 59200. [102] Bereford & Finberg, 72. [103]25 Mar, LGBO 17216. [104] 13 Nov, *Lond Gaz.* [105]1 Apr, MHousLGO 3157. [106]24 Mar, LGBO 15879. [107]1 Apr, MHousLGO 4728. [108]1Oct, LGBO 33509. [109]59 Vict., session 2, *c* ix. [110]Date death of rector of Outwell per authority 9 & 10 Vict., *c* vii. [111]51 & 52 Vict., *c* 41. [112]8 Oct, LGBO 47289. [113]30 Sept, 58 & 59 Vict., *c* lxxxix. [114]18 Sept, *Lond Gaz.* [115]*VCH Cambs* IV, 212. [116]Before *Valuation of Norwich.* [117]24 Mar, LGBO 15898. [118]1 Apr, MHousLGO 6501. [119]I have not found the authority for this cr; noted in *VCH Cambs* IV, 200. [120]25 Mar, LGBO 19414. [121]1 Oct, LGBO 47601. [122]31 July, *Lond Gaz.* [123]18 & 19 Chas. II, *c* 26. [124]I have not found the authority for this union. [125]Beresford & Finberg, 73. [126]24 Mar, LGBO 16517. [127]On death of rector of Upwell, per 9 & 10 Vict., *c* vii. [128]10 Aug, *Lond Gaz.* [129]Before *Valor Eccl.* [130]24 Mar, LGBO 15878, 15879. [131]Apptd day, 56 & 57 Vict., *c* 73 and Co Council Naming O. [133]12 & 13 Vict., *c* xxxii; on the customary union earlier, see *VCH Cambs*, IV, 129. [134]21 Jan, *Lond Gaz.* [135]11 Aug, reported in *Parl Papers* 1872, XLVI, 20. [136]24 Mar, LGBO 15876, 15879. [137]I have not found the date or auth for this change which occured between dates of the 1861 and 1871 census. [138]17 July, *Lond Gaz.*

CORNWALL

[1]4 May, *Lond Gaz.* [2]PC QAB, refounded 1873, *Lond Gaz.* [3]1 Apr, LGBO 46041. [4]12 Apr, *Lond Gaz.* [5]1 Jan, *Lond Gaz.* [6]1 Apr, MHealthO 77816. [7]1 Nov (*Lond Gaz* 27 Oct). [8]10 Aug, 29 & 30 Vict., *c* 113. [9]1 Apr, MHealthO 100217. [10]24 Dec, *Lond Gaz.* [11]PC QAB. [12]2 & 3 Wm. IV, *c* 64 and 7 & 8 Vict., *c* 61. [13]PC QAB. [14]3 July, *Lond Gaz.* [15]17 Mar, *Lond Gaz.* [16]21 Mar, reported in *Parl Papers* 1890-91, LXI, 54. [17]Apptd day, 56 & 47 Vict., *c* 73 and Co Council Naming O. [18]3 July, *Lond Gaz.* [19]29 July, *Lond Gaz.* [20]22 Feb, *Lond Gaz.* [21]2 Aug, *Lond Gaz.* [22]1 Oct, LGBO 66051. [23]Not made MB, disfranchised by 46 & 47 Vict., *c* 18. [24]8 Dec, SI 1965/2086. [25]3 June, *Lond Gaz.* [26]4 July, *Lond Gaz.* [27]1 Jan, *Lond Gaz.* [28]18 Dec (lic min, *Lond Gaz* 12 Oct 1948). [29]3 Oct, *Lond Gaz.* [30]9 Jan, *Lond Gaz.* [31]23 Dec, *Lond Gaz.* [32]24 Nov, *Lond Gaz.* [33]1 Nov, *Lond Gaz.* [34]PC QAB, refounded 11 July 1837, *Lond Gaz.* [35]24 July, *Lond Gaz.* [36]15 Sept, *Lond Gaz.* [37]*Liber Regis*, 310 (PC 1810). [38]1 Apr, LGBO 42498. [39]Year vac (*Lond Gaz* 16 Nov 1973). [40]Year vac (*Lond Gaz* 7 Aug 1973). [41]17 Jan, *Lond Gaz.* [42]5 Dec, *Lond Gaz.* [43]1 Apr, LGBO 37984. [44]PC QAB. [45]*Parochial History of Cornwall* [hereafter, *Paroch. Hist.*], I, 397. [46]10 July, *Lond Gaz.* [47]1 Apr, LGBO 64886. [48]13 May, *Lond Gaz.* [49]Authority not found. [50]Year vac (*Lond Gaz* 3 May 1963). [51]PC QAB, refounded 14 Aug 1835, *Lond Gaz.* [52]3 Dec, *Lond Gaz.* [53]1 Apr, MHealthO 94995. [54]5 June, *Lond Gaz.* [55]8 Feb, *Lond Gaz.* [56]1 Oct, MHealthO 83152. [57]1 Apr, MHealthO 100217. [58]5 Dec, *Lond Gaz.* [59]26 Mar, *Lond Gaz.* [60]27 Nov, *Lond Gaz.* [61]14 July, *Lond Gaz.* [62]21 May, *Lond Gaz.* [63]24 Mar, LGBO 14847, 17848. [64]23 Aug, reported in *Parl Papers* 1890-91, LXI, 54. [65]11 Aug, *Lond Gaz.* [66]10 Jan, *Lond Gaz.* [67]19 Feb, *Lond Gaz.* [68]*Paroch. Hist.*, III, 133. [69]21 Dec, *Lond Gaz.* [70]25 Mar, LGBO 34901. [71]1 Apr, MHealthO 67670. [72]11 Aug, reported in *Parl Papers* 1903, L, 596. [73]24 Mar, LGBO 16548. [74]8 July, *Lond Gaz.* [75]27 June, *Lond Gaz.* [76]1 Apr, LGBO 37818. [77]Not made MB. [78]19 June, reported in *Parl Papers* 1872, XLVI, 22. [79]28 Mar, *Lond Gaz.* [80]3 Mar, *Lond Gaz.* [81]14 May, *Lond Gaz.* [82]1 Apr, LGBO 34060. [83]1 Apr, MHealthO 109970. [84]23 Aug, *Lond Gaz.* [85]Year vac (*Lond Gaz* 20 June 1941). [86]13 May, *Lond Gaz.* [87]Perhaps in 16th cent, *Paroch. Hist.*, III, 328. [88]20 Aug, *Lond Gaz.* [89]20 Jan, *Lond Gaz.* [90]Note cancelled. [91]9 Jan, *Lond Gaz.* [92]2 Dec, *Lond Gaz.* [93]14 Feb, *Lond Gaz.* [94]2 Dec, *Lond Gaz.* [95]Year vac (*Lond Gaz* 31 May 1973). [96]Note cancelled. [97]25 Feb, reported in *Parl Papers* 1872, XLVI, 18. [98]Apptd day, LGBO 31778. [99]11 Oct, *Lond Gaz.* [100]13 June, *Lond Gaz.* [101]1 Apr, LGBO 39878. [102]9 Jan, *Lond Gaz.* [103]16 Apr, *Lond Gaz.* [104]Authority not found. [105]1 Apr, MHealthO 69695. [106]30 Nov, *Lond Gaz.* [107]7 Oct, reported in *Parl Papers* 1872, XLVI, 18. [108]3 Jan, SI 1968/6. [109]1 Apr, LGBO 32169. [110]Pec jurisd of St Buryan abol 1430. [111]7 Feb, *Lond Gaz.* [112]*Paroch. Hist.*, III, 328. [113]3 Dec, *Lond Gaz.* [114]First appearance *Clergy List.* [115]1 Apr, Dept EnvirnO 3706. [116]*Paroch. Hist.*, I, 339. [117]Presumed sep at Dissolution in 16th cent. [118]3 Aug, *Lond Gaz.* [119]14 Aug, information supplied by Cornw RO. [120]*Paroch. Hist.*, III, 272. [121]10 May, *Lond Gaz.* [122]Presumed incl in PLU when became sep CP; not orig rated in the PLU. [123]*Paroch. Hist.*, II, 95. [124]1 Apr, LGBO 32169. [125]Not made MB. [126]1 Apr, MHousLGO 27912. [127]10 May, *Lond Gaz.* [128]10 May, *Lond Gaz.* [129]53 54 Vict., *c* [not found]. [130]24 Aug, *Lond Gaz.* [131]11 Aug, reported in *Parl Papers* 1903, L, 596. [132]26 Mar, *Lond Gaz.* [133]26 Jan, *Lond Gaz.* [134]First appearance *Crockford's Clerical Directory.* [135]7 Feb, *Lond Gaz.* [136]25 Mar, LGBO 36955.

DEVON

[1]1 Apr, MHealthO 78580. [2]29 Dec, *Lond Gaz.* [3]24 Mar, LGBO 16545. [4]9 Nov, 3 & 4 Geo. V, *c* cxxxv. [5]1 Oct, MHealthO 92269. [6]1 Apr, 2 & 3 Geo. VI, *c* xv. [7]21 Feb, MHousLGO 22749. [8]11 July, reported in *Parl Papers* 1890-91, LXI, 54. [9]Beresford & Finberg, 94. [10]11 July, reported in *Parl Papers* 1890-91, LXI, 54. [11]PC QAB. [12]26

June, reported in *Parl Papers* 1890-91, LXI, 54.[13] 24 Mar, LGBO 16312. [14] Apptd day, LGBO 31803. [15] 25 June, LGBO 34675. [16] 8 Dec, SI 1965/2086. [17] PC QAB, refounded 23 May 1844, *Lond Gaz.* [18] Year vac (*Lond Gaz* 24 June 1938). [19] 5 Aug, reported in *Parl Papers* 1872, XLVI, 21. [20] Date and authority not found. [21] Year vac (*Lond Gaz* 2 June 1939). [22] 24 Mar, LGBO 16308. [23] 24 Mar, LGBO 16368, 16545. [24] 25 Mar, LGBO 19440. [25] 24 Mar, LGBO 16349. [26] 22 Dec, OC. [27] 2 & 3 Wm. IV, *c* 64 and 7 & 8 Vict., *c* 61. [28] 24 Mar, LGBO 15946. [29] 24 Mar, LGBO 15945. [30] 1 Apr, LGBO 62969. [31] 1 Apr, MHousLGO 3409. [32] 1 Apr, MHousLGO 9423. [33] 1 Apr, MHealthO 99547. [34] 25 Mar, *Lond Gaz.* [35] 1 Apr, LGBO 37175. [36] 15 May, *Lond Gaz.* [37] Information supplied by Cornw RO. [38] Apptd day, LGBO 31878. [39] 25 Mar, LGBO 15901. [40] 9 Nov, LGB ProvO 1507. [41] 14 Sept, *Lond Gaz.* [42] 4 Apr, cr Part Dist, Instr CBC. [43] 12 Mar, *Lond Gaz.* [44] 15 Dec, *Lond Gaz.* [45] 3 Apr, *Lond Gaz.* [46] 31 May (lic min, *Lond Gaz* 7 Aug 1953). [47] 56 & 57 Vict., *c* 73. [48] 15 Dec, *Lond Gaz.* [49] Year vac (*Lond Gaz* 28 June 1927). [50] Apptd day, LGBO 31879. [51] 9 Nov, LGB ProvO 1353. [52] 19 July, *Lond Gaz.* [53] 13 July, *Lond Gaz.* [54] 24 Mar, LGBO 14972. [55] 1 Apr, 1 & 2 Geo. VI, *c* lxi. [56] 1 Apr, SI 1951/432. [57] 1 Apr, 14 Geo. VI, *c* xlviii. [58] 10 Dec, reported in *Parl Papers* 1890-91, LXI, 53. [59] Year vac (*Lond Gaz* 21 Mar 1924). [60] 22 May, *Lond Gaz.* [61] Year vac (*Lond Gaz* 12 Oct 1923). [62] 11 Aug, reported in *Parl Papers* 1872, XLVI, 18. [63] Former detached pt West Teignmouth. [64] Presumed; subject to revision. [65] 6 Feb, *Lond Gaz.* [66] 17 Dec, *Lond Gaz.* [67] 22 July, *Lond Gaz.* [68] 24 Mar, LGBO 16310. [69] 24 Mar, LGBO 16404. [70] 8 May, *Lond Gaz.* [71] 25 Mar, LGBO 16337. [72] 25 Mar, 45 & 46 Vict., *c* 58. [73] 25 Mar, LGBO 16367. [74] 1 Apr, MHousLGO 6537. [75] 27 Feb, *Lond Gaz.* [76] 29 Nov, *Lond Gaz.* [77] 12 Oct, *Lond Gaz.* [78] 24 Mar, LGBO 14687. [79] Information supplied by Devon RO. [80] PC QAB. [81] 29 & 30 Vict., *c* 113. [82] 16 Feb, *Lond Gaz.* [83] 7 Apr, *Lond Gaz.* [84] Exact date not found. [85] 25 Mar, LGBO 16406. [86] 5 Aug, *Lond Gaz.* [87] Year vac (*Lond Gaz* 1 July 1927). [88] 1 Apr, MHealthO 109917. [89] 2 Dec, *Lond Gaz.* [90] Authority not found. [91] 25 Mar, LGBO 15033. [92] 28 May, reported in *Parl Papers* LXI, 54. [93] 24 Mar, LGBO 16405. [94] 1 Apr, MHealthO 109916. [95] 24 Mar, LGBO 14689. [96] Date and authority not found. [97] Apptd day, LGBO 32149. [98] 16 Feb, MHousLGO 25066. [99] 20 Sept, *Lond Gaz.* [100] 30 Apr, *Lond Gaz.* [101] 1 Jan, *Lond Gaz* (OC 22 Dec 1953). [102] 24 Mar, LGBO 16318. [103] 28 Dec, MHousLGO 23517. [104] Year vac (*Lond Gaz* 13 Sept). [105] 24 Mar, LGBO 16309. [106] 2 Aug, *Lond Gaz.* [107] 25 Mar, LGBO 16403. [108] 24 Mar, LGBO 15034. [109] 9 Nov, LGB ProvO 1257. [110] 18 Dec, *Lond Gaz.* [111] 1 Nov, *Lond Gaz.* [112] 24 Mar, LGBO 16344. [113] 25 Mar, LGBO 14829. [114] 21 May, *Lond Gaz.* [115] 1 Oct, MHealthO 110854. [116] 23 July, *Lond Gaz.* [117] 29 & 30 Vict., *c* 113. [118] 29 Apr, *Lond Gaz.* [119] 30 Jan, reported in *Parl Papers* 1872, XLVI, 19. [120] 22 May, *Lond Gaz.* [121] 1 Apr, LGBO 32746. [122] 25 Mar, LGBO 14830. [123] 24 Mar, LGBO 16383. [124] 25 Mar, LGBO 16307. [125] 7 July, *Lond Gaz.* [126] 2 July, 59 & 60 Vict., *c* lxxv. [127] 24 Mar, LGBO 15947. [128] Year vac (*Lond Gaz* 29 May 1931). [129] 1 Jan, 20 Vict., *c* 19. [130] Apptd day, LGBO 31983. [131] 24 Mar, LGBO 16552, 16553. [132] 13 Apr, *Lond Gaz.* [133] Year vac (*Lond Gaz* 16 Mar 1886). [134] 9 May, *Lond Gaz.* [135] Presumed incl in PLU when became sep CP; not orig rated in the PLU. [136] PC QAB, refounded 28 July 1839, *Lond Gaz.* [137] 25 Mar, LGBO 16436. [138] Year vac (*Lond Gaz* 29 May 1931). [139] 24 Mar, LGBO 16552. [140] 28 May, Part Dist., Instr CBC. [141] 24 Oct, *Lond Gaz.* [142] 13 Mar, *Lond Gaz.* [143] 9 Nov, LGB ProvO 1643. [144] 1 Oct, 18 & 19 Geo. V, [chapter not found]. [145] 23 Dec, *Lond Gaz.* [146] 5 Feb, *Lond Gaz.* [147] Apptd day, LGBO 31983. [148] 4 Dec, *Lond Gaz.* [149] 24 Mar, LGBO 16048. [150] 3 Aug, *Lond Gaz.* [151] 8 Mar, reported in *Parl Papers* 1872, XLVI, 22. [152] White (1878). [153] 22 Dec, *Lond Gaz.* [154] 25 Mar, LGBO 16371. [155] 22 Dec, *Lond Gaz.* [156] 29 & 30 Vic., *c* 113. [157] 2 Apr, *Lond Gaz.* [158] 18 Oct, *Lond Gaz.* [159] 11 Aug, *Lond Gaz.* [160] 15 Dec, *Lond Gaz.* [161] 21 Oct, *Lond Gaz.* [162] Authority not found. [163] 5 Feb, *Lond Gaz.* [164] 18 Sept, Part Dist, Instr CBC. [165] Apptd day, LGBO 31841. [166] 7 May, reported in *Parl Papers* 1872, XLVI, 20. [167] Authority not found. [168] 15 June, *Lond Gaz.* [169] 24 Mar, LGBO 16408, 16552. [170] Apptd day, LGBO 32150. [171] 24 Mar, LGBO 16553. [172] Beresford & Finberg, 90. [173] Devon Co Council, confirmed by LGBO 26400. [174] 25 Mar, LGBO 16546. [175] 1 Apr, MHealthO 72402. [176] 25 Mar, LGBO 16369. [177] 9 Nov, 63 & 64 Vict., *c* cclxii. [178] 5 Dec, *Lond Gaz.* [179] 11 Mar, *Lond Gaz.* [180] 12 Aug, *Lond Gaz.* [181] 13 Aug, *Lond Gaz.* [182] 26 Mar, *Lond Gaz.* [183] 26 May, *Lond Gaz.* [184] 30 May, *Lond Gaz.* [185] 28 July, *Lond Gaz.* [186] 13 Aug, *Lond Gaz.* [187] 23 June, *Lond Gaz.* [188] 3 Mar, *Lond Gaz.* [189] 15 Dec, *Lond Gaz.* [190] 20 May, *Lond Gaz.* [191] 16 Aug, *Lond Gaz.* [192] 6 Dec (date church consec, *Lond Gaz* 1 Nov 1957). [193] 30 Aug, *Lond Gaz.* [194] 27 June, *Lond Gaz.* [195] 22 Sept, *Lond Gaz.* [196] 26 Mar, LGBO 19274. [197] First appearance *Clergy List.* [198] 25 Mar, LGBO 16407. [199] Year vac (*Lond Gaz* 13 Aug 1926). [200] 3 June, *Lond Gaz.* [201] 1 Feb, *Lond Gaz.* [202] 4 Aug, *Lond Gaz.* [203] 23 Dec, *Lond Gaz.* [204] Year vac (*Lond Gaz* 30 Aug 1973). [205] 24 Apr (church consecr, *Lond Gaz* 4 Dec 1956). [206] First appearance *Clergy List.* [207] 16 Apr, *Lond Gaz.* [208] 11 Dec, Part Dist, Instr CBC. [209] 1 Apr, SI 1966/135. [210] 63 & 64 Vict., *c* ccxxxii. [211] Year vac (*Lond Gaz* 26 Oct 1973). [212] 1 Nov (*Lond Gaz* 12 Oct). [213] 7 Feb, *Lond Gaz.* [214] 24 Apr, *Lond Gaz.* [215] 29 Apr, *Lond Gaz.* [216] 8 Apr, *Lond Gaz.* [217] 1 July, *Lond Gaz.* [218] Year vac (*Lond Gaz* 12 Oct 1934). [219] 4 Sept, *Lond Gaz.* [220] 24 Apr, *Lond Gaz.* [221] 27 Mar, *Lond Gaz.* [222] 8 July, *Lond Gaz.* [223] 3 Mar, *Lond Gaz.* [224] 24 Apr, *Lond Gaz.* [225] 24 Apr, *Lond Gaz.* [226] 26 Nov (lic min, *Lond Gaz* 4 Sept). [227] 28 June, *Lond Gaz.* [228] 14 Oct, *Lond Gaz.* [229] 24 Mar, LGBO 16348. [230] Authority not found. [231] 4 Dec, *Lond Gaz.* [232] 24 Mar, LGBO 14970. [233] 25 Mar, LGBO 14830, 14831. [234] 24 Mar, LGBO 15900. [235] 1 Apr, LGBO 26400. [236] 24 Mar, LGBO 16308, 16310. [237] 24 Mar, LGBO 16306,

16308. [238] 31 Mar, *Lond Gaz.* [239] 1 May, MHous LG Renaming O. [240] 59 & 60 Vict., *c* lxxv. [241] 8 Apr, LGBO 8540. [242] 14 Sept, *Lond Gaz.* [243] 11 Nov, *Lond Gaz.* [244] 24 Mar, LGBO 16488. [245] Apptd day, LGBO 31983. [246] 9 July, reported in *Parl Papers* 1872, XLVI, 21. [247] 1 May, *Lond Gaz.* [248] 24 Mar, LGBO 16305. [249] 1 Apr, LGBO 39010. [250] 4 Dec, *Lond Gaz.* [251] 1 May, *Lond Gaz.* [252] 5 Feb, *Lond Gaz.* [253] 18 May, *Lond Gaz.* [254] 17 May, *Lond Gaz.* [255] 19 Mar, *Lond Gaz.* [256] 5 Mar, *Lond Gaz.* [257] 24 Mar, LGBO 16370. [258] 4 Dec 1829 (OC 24 Nov 1828). [259] 24 Mar, LGBO 16372. [260] 24 June, *Lond Gaz.* [261] 16 Aug, *Lond Gaz.* [262] 24 June, *Lond Gaz.* [263] 23 Dec, *Lond Gaz.* [264] 26 Mar, *Lond Gaz.* [265] 24 Mar, LGBO 14970, 14971. [266] 25 Mar, LGBO 16345. [267] 4 Mar, *Lond Gaz.* [268] 31 May, *Lond Gaz.* [269] 25 Mar, LGBO 15033. [270] Apptd day, LGBO 31840. [271] 29 July, *Lond Gaz.* [272] 25 Mar, LGBO 14691. [273] 1 Apr, SI 1951/327. [274] 11 Oct, *Lond Gaz.* [275] 14 May, *Lond Gaz.* [276] 1 Apr, LGBO 34060. [277] 1 Apr, LGBO 34396. [278] Date and authority not found. [279] 24 Mar, LGBO 15947, 15948. [280] First appearance *Crockford's Clerical Directory.* [281] 24 Mar, LGBO 16312, 16313. [282] 29 Nov, *Lond Gaz.* [283] 24 Mar, LGBO 16348. [284] Year vac (*Lond Gaz* 8 Mar 1940). [285] 23 Aug, *Lond Gaz.* [286] 24 Mar, LGBO 16314. [287] 29 May, *Lond Gaz.* [288] 25 Apr, *Lond Gaz.* [289] 2 July, *Lond Gaz.* [290] Date and authority not found. [291] 25 Mar, LGBO 14831. [292] 1 Apr, MHous LGO 27912. [293] 11 Aug, reported in *Parl Papers* 1890-91, LXI, 54. [294] Apptd day, LGBO 31983. [295] 16 July, *Lond Gaz.* [296] Year vac (*Lond Gaz* 17 Apr 1923). [297] 22 Feb, *Lond Gaz.* [298] First appearance *Crockford's Clerical Directory.* [299] 24 Mar, LGBO 14690. [300] 8 Feb, *Lond Gaz.* [301] 9 Nov, LGB ProvO 1462. [302] 1 May, *Lond Gaz.* [303] 24 Mar, LGBO 14971. [304] Beresford & Finberg, 96. [305] 25 Mar, *Lond Gaz.* [306] 61 & 62 Vict., *c* cxxxix. [307] 14 May, *Lond Gaz.* [308] 21 Apr, Letters Patent, 16 Chas. I, *c* 9. [309] 60 & 61 Vict., *c* l [fifty]. [310] 3 June, *Lond Gaz.* [311] 5 Mar, *Lond Gaz.* [312] 4 May, *Lond Gaz.* [313] 11 Sept, *Lond Gaz.* [314] 6 Mar, *Lond Gaz.* [315] 13 Aug, *Lond Gaz.* [316] 13 Nov, *Lond Gaz.* [317] 16 May, *Lond Gaz.* [318] PC QAB, refounded 8 Aug 1851. [319] Information supplied by Devon RO. [320] 11 July, *Lond Gaz.* [321] Year vac (*Lond Gaz* 13 Aug 1924). [322] Information supplied by Devon RO. [323] 29 Nov, *Lond Gaz.* [324] 1 Apr, *Lond Gaz.* [325] 29 Nov, *Lond Gaz.* [326] 31 Jan, *Lond Gaz.* [327] 15 Aug, *Lond Gaz.* [328] Year vac (*Lond Gaz* 29 May 1931). [329] 9 May, *Lond Gaz.* [330] 16 Apr, *Lond Gaz.* [331] 30 Jan, reported in *Parl Papers* 1872, XLVI, 20. [332] 1 Apr, LGBO 32169. [333] 1 Sept (*Lond Gaz* 3 Aug). [334] 1 Apr, LGBO 32169. [335] 1 June, *Lond Gaz.* [336] Apptd day, LGBO 31829. [337] 12 Nov, *Lond Gaz.* [338] 13 & 14 Geo. V, *c* cii. [339] 20 Dec (church consec, *Lond Gaz* 25 June 1954). [340] 24 Mar, LGBO 16373. [341] 25 Mar, LGBO 19441. [342] 29 May, LGB ProvO 549. [343] 63 & 64 Vict., *c* ccxxxii. [344] 12 Nov, *Lond Gaz.* [345] 1 Apr, LGBO 39011. [346] Authority not found. [347] 14 Jan, Part Dist, Instr CBC. [348] 11 Aug, reported in *Parl Papers* 1890-91, LXI, 54. [349] 24 Mar, LGBO 16552, 16553. [350] 1 Nov (*Lond Gaz* 26 Oct). [351] 25 July, *Lond Gaz.* [352] 21 Dec, *Lond Gaz.* [353] Note cancelled. [354] Note cancelled. [355] 1 Apr, LGBO 36290. [356] 1 Apr, LGBO 55341. [357] 23 Feb, *Lond Gaz.* [358] 2 June, *Lond Gaz.* [359] 1 Apr, LGBO 53217. [360] 30 Sept, 59 & 60 Vict., *c* lxxv. [361] 14 Sept, *Lond Gaz.* [362] 30 May, *Lond Gaz.* [363] 25 Mar, LGBO 16367, 16369. [364] 9 Nov, 63 & 64 Vict., *c* clxxxiii. [365] 30 July, 18 & 19 Vict., *c* lxxxiv. [366] 22 Nov, *Lond Gaz.* [367] 8 Oct, *Lond Gaz.* [368] 4 Dec, *Lond Gaz.* [369] 9 Dec, *Lond Gaz.* [370] 24 Mar, LGBO 14687, 14688, 14689. [371] 24 Mar, LGBO 16368. [372] 24 Mar, LGBO 16306. [373] 3 July, *Lond Gaz.* [374] 25 Mar, LGBO 16345, 16347. [375] 25 Mar, LGBO 16347. [376] 24 Mar, LGBO 15947.

DORSET

[1] 30 Sept, LGBO 31530. [2] 1 Apr, MHealthO 77049. [3] 30 July, *Lond Gaz.* [4] 9 Feb, *Lond Gaz.* [5] Apptd day, LGBO 31568. [6] 9 Nov, 11 & 12 Geo. V, *c* lviii. [7] 13 Nov, *Lond Gaz.* [8] Apptd day, LGBO 32025. [9] 24 Mar, LGBO 16570. [10] Apptd day, LGBO 31494. [11] Edward Boswell, *The Ecclesiastical Divisions of the Diocese of Bristol* (hereafter, Boswell), 34. [12] 15 Feb, *Lond Gaz.* [13] 1 June (*Lond Gaz* 2 May). [14] John Hutchins, *The History and Antiquities of the County of Dorset* (hereafter, Hutchins), I, 162. [15] Apptd day, LGBO 31566. [16] 1 Oct, Wareham (Extension) Act, 1931. [17] 13 Oct, *Lond Gaz.* [18] 1 May, reported in *Parl Papers* 1872, XLVI, 18. [19] 24 Mar, LGBO 16450. [20] 29 Jan, *Lond Gaz.* [21] 17 Aug, *Lond Gaz.* [22] 29 & 30 Vict., *c* 113. [23] 30 June, reported in *Parl Papers* 1890-91, LXI, 57. [24] 25 Mar, 45 & 46 Vict., *c* lviii. [25] 24 Mar, LGBO 16569. [26] Boswell, 32. [27] 15 Dec, *Lond Gaz.* [28] 1 Nov (*Lond Gaz* 22 Oct). [29] 25 Mar, LGBO 19158. [30] 28 Feb, LGBO 34065. [31] 30 Sept, LGBO 31555. [32] 1 Oct, 20 &21 Geo. V, *c* xlv. [33] 4 Aug, *Lond Gaz.* [34] Hutchins, I, 167. [35] 24 Mar, LGBO 19157. [36] 22 Dec, OC. [37] 2 & 3 Wm. IV, *c* 64 and 7 & 8 Vict., *c* 61. [38] 13 May, *Lond Gaz.* [39] 11 May, *Lond Gaz.* [40] 11 Aug, *Lond Gaz.* [41] 15 May, *Lond Gaz.* [42] 13 Feb, *Lond Gaz.* [43] 3 Aug, *Lond Gaz.* [44] 25 Mar, LGBO 16467. [45] Boswell, 44. [46] 20 July, *Lond Gaz.* [47] 27 May, *Lond Gaz.* [48] Apptd day, LGBO 31962. [49] 9 Nov, LGB ProvO 1546. [50] 9 Nov, 1 Edw. VII, *c* cxlviii. [51] 13 Feb, *Lond Gaz.* [52] 1 Jan (*Lond Gaz* 28 Dec 1970). [53] 30 Sept, LGBO 31582. [54] 9 Nov, Purbeck (Extension) O, 1905. [55] 30 Dec, *Lond Gaz.* [56] 2 Feb, *Lond Gaz.* [57] 20 Nov, *Lond Gaz.* [58] 30 June, *Lond Gaz.* [59] 25 Jan, *Lond Gaz.* [60] 8 Feb, *Lond Gaz.* [61] Note cancelled. [62] Hutchins II, 189. [63] 1 Oct, 13 & 14 Geo. V, *c* xlv. [64] 22 May, *Lond Gaz.* [65] 28 Nov, *Lond Gaz.* [66] 1 Nov (*Lond Gaz* 22 Oct). [67] 1 Mar (*Lond Gaz* 11 Feb). [68] 1 Apr, LGBO 35469. [69] Year vac (*Lond Gaz* 1 Apr 1930). [70] Apptd day, LGBO 31567. [71] 18 Dec, *Lond Gaz.* [72] Year vac (*Lond Gaz* 13 May 1927). [73] 10 Aug, *Lond Gaz.* [74] 15 Aug, Instr Bp Bristol. [75] 12 Mar (lic min, *Lond Gaz* 28 Feb). [76] Hutchins, I, 47 and Boswell, 50. [77] 7 Mar, *Lond Gaz.* [78] 1 Dec, *Lond Gaz.* [79] PC QAB. [80] Apptd day, LGBO 31897. [81] 1 Apr, MHealthO 72863. [82] 25 Mar, LGBO 19097. [83] 1 Dec (*Lond Gaz* 1 Nov). [84] 29 June, *Lond Gaz.* [85] 25 Mar, LGBO

19084. [86]Hutchins I, 344. [87]24 Mar, LGBO 15947. [88]30 Sept, 59 & 60 Vict., *c* lxxv. [89]13 Apr, *Lond Gaz.* [90]Some sources place in Beam. Forum & Redhorne Hd. [91]31 Dec, *Lond Gaz.* [92]In 1291 in Dorch. RDn. [93]25 Mar, LGBO 17602. [94]29 Oct, LGBO 11355. [95]14 June, *Lond Gaz.* [96]28 Feb, *Lond Gaz.* [97]26 June, reported in *Parl Papers* 1890-91, LXI, 54. [98]1 Apr, MHealthO 59792. [99]1 Apr, MHealthO 66673. [100]9 Nov, *Lond Gaz.* [101]2 July, *Lond Gaz.* [102]15 Jan, *Lond Gaz.* [103]30 Apr, reported in *Parl Papers* 1890-91, LXI, 54. [104]3 Feb, reported in *Parl Papers* 1872, XLVI, 20. [105]31 Mar, MHealthO 73972. [106]24 Mar, LGBO 16567. [107]1 Aug, *Lond Gaz.* [108]Year vac (*Lond Gaz* 15 June 1928). [109]14 Jan, reported in *Parl Papers* 1890-91, LXI, 54. [110]24 Oct, *Lond Gaz.* [111]5 Aug, *Lond Gaz.* [112]Hutchins, I, xxxii. [113]1 Apr, LGBO 34066. [114]25 Mar, LGBO 19023. [115]1 Oct, MHealthO 71944. [116]Year vac (*Lond Gaz* 3 Apr 1973). [117]30 July, *Lond Gaz.* [118]7 James I. [119]19 Feb, *Lond Gaz.* [120]16 May (lic min, *Lond Gaz* 14 Apr). [121]1 June, *Lond Gaz.* [122]25 Mar, LGBO 18148. [123]Boswell, 36, 38. [124]5 Sept, *Lond Gaz.* [125]1 Aug (*Lond Gaz* 28 July). [126]Boswell, 36. [127]25 Mar, LGBO 17603. [128]10 Feb, *Lond Gaz.* [129]23 Aug, reported in *Parl Papers* 1890-91, LXI, 54. [130]30 Sept, 58 & 59 Vict., *c* xci. [131]1 Jan, 20 Vict., *c* 19. [132]2 July, *Lond Gaz.* [133]1 Nov (*Lond Gaz* 29 Oct). [134]Authority and date not found; between censuses of 1861, 1871. [135]24 Mar, LGBO 21393. [136]Boswell, 44. [137]13 Dec, reported in *Parl Papers* 1890-91, LXI, 57. [138]Year vac (*Lond Gaz* 5 May 1925). [139]11 Feb, *Lond Gaz.* [140]22 Jan, *Lond Gaz.* [141]30 Jan, reported in *Parl Papers* 1872, XLVI, 19. [142]25 Mar, LGBO 17623. [143]20 Mar, reported in *Parl Papers* 1872, XLVI, 21. [144]Priory church, curacy since Dissolution in 16th cent, refounded 1886. [145]30 June, *Lond Gaz.* [146]30 Sept, LGBO 31575. [147]23 Dec, *Lond Gaz.* [148]1 Apr, MHealthO 63167. [149]14 Feb, *Lond Gaz.* [150]10 Oct, *Lond Gaz.* [151]1 Apr, 20 & 21 Geo. V, *c* lxxxi. [152]Boswell. [153]25 Mar, *Lond Gaz.* [154]25 June, *Lond Gaz.* [155]Boswell, 42. [156]30 July, reported in *Parl Papers* 1872, XLVI, 19. [157]22 Mar, *Lond Gaz.* [158]Effective this year after *Lond Gaz* 18 Apr. [159]Year lic min (*Lond Gaz* 19 Apr 1946). [160]15 May, *Lond Gaz.* [161]3 Feb, reported in *Parl Papers* 1872, XLVI, 21. [162]24 Mar, LGBO 20319. [163]24 Mar, LGBO 16451. [164]1 Apr, *Lond Gaz.* [165]30 June, *Lond Gaz.* [166]23 Jan, *Lond Gaz.* [167]9 Nov, LGB ProvO 1080. [168]1 Apr, MHealthO 66673. [169]22 Jan, *Lond Gaz.* [170]29 Oct, LGBO 11355, 11356. [171]23 Feb, *Lond Gaz.* [172]23 Aug, *Lond Gaz.* [173]*Temp* Jas. I. [174]7 Mar, *Lond Gaz.* [175]1 Apr, MHousLGO 5845. [176]Apptd day, LGBO 32026. [177]10 Jan, *Lond Gaz.* [178]1 Apr, SI 1954/318. [179]1 Apr, SI 1965/2086. [180]1 Apr, MHousLGO 3416. [181]16 July, MHousLG Decl. [182]13 May, MHousLG Decl. [183]24 Mar, LGBO 16449. [184]24 Mar, LGBO 16449, 16450. [185]29 Apr, *Lond Gaz.* [186]29 Oct, LGBO 11356. [187]8 Dec, *Lond Gaz.* [188]7 Feb, *Lond Gaz.* [189]10 Feb, *Lond Gaz.* [190]Year vac (*Lond Gaz* 22 June 1928). [191]Year vac (*Lond Gaz* 16 May 1930). [192]24 Mar, LGBO 19157, 19158. [193]Year vac (*Lond Gaz* 30 Mar 1928). [194]11 Oct, *Lond Gaz.* [195]PC QAB, refounded 9 Aug 1861 by Bp. [196]24 Mar, LGBO 16568. [197]11 Feb, *Lond Gaz.* [198]23 Dec, *Lond Gaz.* [199]8 June, *Lond Gaz.* [200]12 Oct, *Lond Gaz.* [201]3 May, *Lond Gaz.* [202]25 Mar, LGBO 19024. [203]24 Oct, *Lond Gaz.* [204]3 Feb, *Lond Gaz.* [205]24 Oct, *Lond Gaz.* [206]24 Mar, LGBO 21392, 21394. [207]20 Oct, *Lond Gaz.* [208]1 Apr, MHealthO 72863. [209]MHousLG Decl. [210]5 Dec, *Lond Gaz.* [211]30 Sept, LGBO 31581. [212]24 Mar, LGBO 21392, 21393. [213]24 Mar, LGBO 21395. [214]Year vac (*Lond Gaz* 30 Mar 1928). [215]Year vac (*Lond Gaz* 30 Mar 1928). [216]Hutchins, III, 574. [217]24 Mar, LGBO 21394, 21395. [218]30 Sept, 59 & 60 Vict., *c* lxxv. [219]24 Mar, LGBO 15945. [220]Authority not found. [221]First appearance *Clergy List.* [222]Boswell, 34. [223]Boswell, 40. [224]Boswell, 48. [225]Authority not found. [226]4 Dec, *Lond Gaz.* [227]29 Apr, *Lond Gaz.* [228]13 Dec, *Lond Gaz.* [229]29 Oct, *Lond Gaz.* [230]24 Mar, LGBO 16569, 16570. [231]10 Geo. II, *c* 9 and Boswell, 40. [232]Presumed incl in PLU when became sep CP; not orig rated in the PLU. [233]Hutchins, III, 607. [234]Hutchins II, 519. [235]18 Aug, MHealth Decl. [236]1 Apr, MHealthO 104955.

ESSEX

[1]27 June, *Lond Gaz.* [2]13 Jan, *Lond Gaz.* [3]6 July, *Lond Gaz.* [4]27 July, *Lond Gaz.* [5]14 Mar, *Lond Gaz.* [6]22 July (lic min, *Lond Gaz* 27 May). [7]24 Mar, LGBO 22363. [8]25 Mar, 45 & 46 Vict., *c* 58. [9]1 Apr, MHealthO 108754. [10]28 Aug, *Lond Gaz.* [11]15 Aug, *Lond Gaz.* [12]2 Aug, *Lond Gaz.* [13]14 Feb, *Lond Gaz.* [14]28 Aug, *Lond Gaz.* [15]24 Mar, LGBO 16461. [16]1 Apr, MHealthO 107430. [17]1 Apr, MHealthO 77918. [18]12 Apr, *Lond Gaz.* [19]29 & 30 Vict., *c* 113. [20]1 Apr, MHealthO 104866. [21]1 Apr, SI 1964/366. [22]24 Mar, LGBO 22354. [23]25 Mar, LGBO 16612, 16608. [24]1 Apr, MHealthO 83994. [25]5 May (lic min, *Lond Gaz* 8 Apr 1958). [26]20 Oct, *Lond Gaz.* [27]30 Sept, 59 & 60 Vict., *c* ccxxxvi. [28]Philip Morant, *The History and Antiquities of the County of Essex* (hereafter, Morant), II, 522-34. [29]24 Mar, LGBO 22326. [30]1 Apr, MHousLGO 4784. [31]24 Mar, LGBO 22340. [32]29 & 30 Vict., *c* 113. [33]27 Apr, *Lond Gaz.* [34]26 Mar, LGBO 29177. [35]9 Nov, East Ham, Barking Town and Ilford O, 1907. [36]1 Apr, Barking Corporation Act, 1934. [37]1 Apr, London Government Act, 1963. [38]27 Jan, *Lond Gaz.* [39]29 May, *Lond Gaz.* [40]25 May, *Lond Gaz.* [41]6 July, *Lond Gaz.* [42]17 Aug, *Lond Gaz.* [43]19 July, *Lond Gaz.* [44]6 Nov, *Lond Gaz.* [45]8 Nov, *Lond Gaz.* [46]6 May, *Lond Gaz.* [47]1 Mar (*Lond Gaz* 20 Feb). [48]6 Mar, *Lond Gaz.* [49]5 May, *Lond Gaz.* [50]30 May, *Lond Gaz.* [51]30 Mar, *Lond Gaz.* [52]30 Mar, *Lond Gaz.* [53]9 Apr, *Lond Gaz.* [54]28 Apr (lic min, *Lond Gaz* 29 Nov 1957). [55]Information supplied by Essex RO. [56]1 Jan, MHealthO 87970. [57]18 Sept (lic min, *Lond Gaz* 25 June 1957). [58]Richard Newcourt, *Repertorium Ecclesiasticum Parochiale Londinense* (hereafter, Newcourt), II, 41. [59]13 Aug, *Lond Gaz.* [60]Lic min later in year after *Lond Gaz* 1 July. [61]29 May, *Lond Gaz.* [62]25 Aug, *Lond Gaz.* [63]7 Dec, authority

not found. [64]2 Aug, *Lond Gaz.* [65]5 Dec, *Lond Gaz.* [66]Not orig in the PLU, incl by early 1840s. [67]24 Mar, LGBO 21886. [68]28 May, *Lond Gaz.* [69]11 Mar, LGBO 10518. [70]PC QAB, refounded 1881 as reported in *Parl Papers* 1890-91, LXI, 56. [71]17 July (lic min, *Lond Gaz* 1 Oct 1963). [72]3 July, *Lond Gaz.* [73]Morant, I, 139. [74]26 Mar, LGBO 36224. [75]14 Oct, MHealth Decl. [76]1 Apr, MHousLGO 4566. [77]PC QAB, refounded 14 Sept 1844, *Lond Gaz.* [78]6 Nov, reported in *Parl Papers* 1890-91, LXI, 56. [79]27 Jan, *Lond Gaz.* [80]1 Jan, MHealthO 88877. [81]56 Geo. III, *c* xxxi. [82]F. G. Emmison (ed.), *Catalogue of Essex Parish Records* (hereafter, EPR), 55. [83]Authority not found. [84]8 July, *Lond Gaz.* [85]18 May, *Lond Gaz.* [86]1 June (*Lond Gaz* 30 May). [87]24 Mar, LGBO 21887. [88]PC QAB, refounded 1881 as reported in *Parl Papers* 1890-91, LXI, 54. [89]10 Nov, reported *Parl Papers* 1872, XLVI, 17. [90]43 & 44 Vict., *c* 93. [91]25 Mar, LGBO 16608. [92]8 Feb, Instr CBC. [93]24 Mar, LGBO 22339. [94]28 Sept, MHousLG Decl. [95]PC QAB. [96]14 Feb, *Lond Gaz.* [97]11 July (lic min, *Lond Gaz* 28 Feb 1961). [98]1 Oct, LGBO 51878. [99]24 Mar, LGBO 22419, 22421. [100]7 July LGBO 23834. [101]24 Mar, LGBO 23834. [102]30 Jan, reported in *Parl Papers* 1897, LXVII, pt I, 174. [103]2 Dec, *Lond Gaz.* [104]22 Dec (lic min, *Lond Gaz* 25 Nov 1958). [105]17 Nov, *Lond Gaz.* [106]14 Dec, *Lond Gaz.* [107]Apptd day, LGBO 32112. [108]25 Mar, LGBO 16610. [109]1 Apr, SI 1964/366. [110]24 Mar, LGBO 16463. [111]1 Apr, MHealthO 83994. [112]30 Mar, *Lond Gaz.* [113]10 Mar, *Lond Gaz.* [114]1 Apr, MHealthO 108729. [115]2 & 3 Wm. IV, *c* 64 and 7 & 8 Vict., *c* 61. [116]8 Jan, *Lond Gaz.* [117]3 Mar, *Lond Gaz.* [118]22 Aug, *Lond Gaz.* [119]31 Jan, *Lond Gaz.* [120]Presumed incl in PLU when became sep CP; not orig rated in the PLU. [121]8 Dec, *Lond Gaz.* [122]20 Aug, *Lond Gaz.* [123]4 May, *Lond Gaz.* [124]28 June, *Lond Gaz.* [125]Morant, II, 209. [126]9 Nov, Chelmsford (Extension) O, 1907. [127]9 Nov, LGB ProvO 1332. [128]11 Sept, *Lond Gaz.* [129]18 Mar, *Lond Gaz.* [130]5 Oct, *Lond Gaz.* [131]5 Oct, *Lond Gaz.* [132]1 Apr, MHousLGO 3953. [133]24 Mar, LGBO 22421. [134]30 Oct, *Lond Gaz.* [135]29 Nov, *Lond Gaz.* [136]7 Dec, *Lond Gaz.* [137]11 Aug, *Lond Gaz.* [138]23 Feb, *Lond Gaz.* [139]30 Sept, 58 & 59 Vict., session 2, *c* viii. [140]James H. Silvester, *The Parish Church of Great Clacton.* [141]12 July, *Lond Gaz.* [142]31 Dec, *Lond Gaz.* [143]4 Feb, reported in *Parl Papers* 1890-91, LXI, 53. [144]15 Apr, *Lond Gaz.* [145]EPR, 84. [146]1 May, *Lond Gaz.* [147]Year vac (*Lond Gaz* 8 Nov 1929). [148]30 Sept (lic min, *Lond Gaz* 6 Oct 1953). [149]Conscr church [exact date in year not found], *Lond Gaz* 26 May 1950. [150]9 Dec (lic min, *Lond Gaz* 6 Oct). [151]26 May, *Lond Gaz.* [152]26 Aug, *Lond Gaz.* [153]3 May (lic min, *Lond Gaz* 15 Apr). [154]1 May (*Lond Gaz* 6 Apr). [155]25 Mar, LGBO 16612. [156]22 Oct, *Lond Gaz.* [157]24 Mar, LGBO 22351. [158]30 Nov, *Lond Gaz.* [159]30 Nov (lic min, *Lond Gaz* 1 Nov 1957). [160]18 Oct, MHealth Decl. [161]Effective later in year after *Lond Gaz* 1 July 1969. [162]4 Nov, *Lond Gaz.* [163]24 Mar, LGBO 22355. [164]Year vac (*Lond Gaz* 10 May 1929). [165]14 Jan, reported in *Parl Papers* 1872, XLVI, 22. [166]1 Oct, MHealthO 70164. [167]24 Mar, LGBO 22422. [168]24 Mar, LGBO 22419, 22420, 22423. [169]24 Mar, LGBO 22327, 22423. [170]20 Nov, reported in *Parl Papers* 1890-91, LXI, 56. [171]Speed's map early 17th cent places this in Ongar Hd. [172]1 Apr, MHealthO 70548. [173]9 Nov, 3 & 4 Geo, V, *c* cv. [174]19 Nov (lic min, *Lond Gaz* 3 Aug). [175]8 Dec (lic min, *Lond Gaz* 22 Oct). [176]1 Mar (lic min, *Lond Gaz* 26 Sept 1961). [177]22 Jan (lic min, *Lond Gaz* 20 Nov 1951). [178]22 Nov (lic min, *Lond Gaz* 2 Nov). [179]3 July, *Lond Gaz.* [180]1 Apr, LGBO 36270. [181]1 Apr, LGBO 34234. [182]25 June, *Lond Gaz.* [183]1 Apr, MHousLGO 4915. [184]1 Oct, MHealthO 77525. [185]Newcourt, II, 464. [186]28 Mar, *Lond Gaz.* [187]3 Dec, *Lond Gaz.* [188]22 July, *Lond Gaz.* [189]15 Aug, *Lond Gaz.* [190]20 Aug, *Lond Gaz.* [191]2 Feb, *Lond Gaz.* [192]9 Mar, *Lond Gaz.* [193]10 Aug, *Lond Gaz.* [194]13 Dec, *Lond Gaz.* [195]9 June, *Lond Gaz.* [196]8 Feb, *Lond Gaz.* [197]28 July, *Lond Gaz.* [198]Authority not found. [199]24 Mar, LGBO 22330. [200]1 Apr, LGBO 46178. [201]24 Mar, LGBO 22331. [202]24 Mar, LGBO 22420. [203]EPR, 108. [204]15 Aug, *Lond Gaz.* [205]7 Dec, *Lond Gaz.* [206]1 Apr, MHousLGO 19070. [207]30 Dec, *Lond Gaz.* [208]20 Mar (church consecr, *Lond Gaz* 28 Feb 1956). [209]25 Sept, *Lond Gaz.* [210]3 June, *Lond Gaz.* [211]30 Dec, *Lond Gaz.* [212]1 Apr, The County of Essex (Halstead UD) O, 1954. [213]1 Apr, LGBO 41593. [214]26 Mar, LGBO 40568. [215]5 Feb, *Lond Gaz.* [216]3 Jan, *Lond Gaz.* [217]15 Mar, *Lond Gaz.* [218]10 July, *Lond Gaz.* [219]22 Feb, *Lond Gaz.* [220]2 Mar, *Lond Gaz.* [221]24 Mar, LGBO 20403. [222]20 Aug, *Lond Gaz.* [223]3 Dec, *Lond Gaz.* [224]4 Aug, *Lond Gaz.* [225]2 Mar, *Lond Gaz.* [226]11 Feb, *Lond Gaz.* [227]26 Sept, *Lond Gaz.* [228]28 Mar, *Lond Gaz.* [229]24 Mar, LGBO 22419. [230]1 Apr, MHousLGO 4883. [231]8 Spet, *Lond Gaz.* [232]7 July, *Lond Gaz.* [233]26 June, *Lond Gaz.* [234]25 June, *Lond Gaz.* [235]13 Oct (lic min, *Lond Gaz* 11 Sept). [236]19 Mar (lic min, *Lond Gaz* 27 Jan). [237]2 Aug, *Lond Gaz.* [238]9 Mar, *Lond Gaz.* [239]1 Feb (*Lond Gaz* 29 Jan). [240]17 June, LGBO 9214. [241]25 Mar, LGBO 17924. [242]EPR, 128. [243]27 Jan, *Lond Gaz.* [244]Year vac (*Lond Gaz* 29 July 1921). [245]3 Aug, *Lond Gaz.* [246]18 Oct, *Lond Gaz.* [247]29 Oct, *Lond Gaz.* [248]1 Apr, MHousLGO 4046. [249]1 Apr, MHousLGO 8410. [250]1 Apr, MHousLGO 13730. [251]24 Mar, LGBO 22331. [252]1 Oct, MHealthO 73676. [253]24 July, *Lond Gaz.* [254]1 May (lic min, *Lond Gaz* 26 Feb). [255]27 July, *Lond Gaz.* [256]20 July, *Lond Gaz.* [257]27 June, *Lond Gaz.* [258]1 June (*Lond Gaz* 2 May). [259]10 Anne, *c* 35. [260]1 Apr, LGBO 54633. [261]22 Oct, *Lond Gaz.* [262]27 Nov, MHousLG Decl. [263]13 Dec, *Lond Gaz.* [264]12 May, *Lond Gaz.* [265]17 Apr, *Lond Gaz.* [266]25 Feb, *Lond Gaz.* [267]26 Mar, LGBO 40568. [268]1 Oct, MHealthO 110873. [269]24 June, *Lond Gaz.* [270]1 Apr, MHousLGO 5504. [271]24 Mar, LGBO 21887, 22351. [272]25 June, *Lond Gaz.* [273]24 Mar, LGBO 22341. [274]EPR, 143. [275]23 Aug, MHealth Decl. [276]20 Dec, *Lond Gaz.* [277]31 Aug, *Lond Gaz.* Notes 278-87 not used. [288]Between 1950-51 (information supplied by Essex RO) (*Lond Gaz* 6 June 1941). [289]EPR, 125. [290]Presumed a result of 51 & 52 Vict., *c* 41. [291]Exact date not found; after 1768 ed of Morant and before Silvester (note 40). [292]EPR, 181. [293]24 Jan, *Lond Gaz.* [294]17 May, *Lond Gaz.* [295]3 Aug, *Lond Gaz.* [296]11 Feb, *Lond Gaz.* [297]11 Feb, *Lond Gaz.* [298]8 Nov, *Lond Gaz.* [299]22 Jan, *Lond Gaz.* [300]2 Feb, *Lond Gaz.* [301]5 Mar, reported in *Parl Papers* 1890-91, LXI, 56. [302]12 Aug, *Lond Gaz.* [303]23 Aug, *Lond Gaz.* [304]10 June, *Lond Gaz.* [305]14 Nov, *Lond Gaz.* [306]11 June, *Lond Gaz.* [307]14 Feb, *Lond Gaz.* [308]23 Aug, *Lond Gaz.* [309]3 Jan, *Lond Gaz.* [310]30 June, *Lond Gaz.* [311]1 Jan, 20 Vict., *c* 113. [312]5 July, reported in *Parl Papers* 1890-91, LXI, 57. [313]21 Jan, *Lond Gaz.* [314]27 June, *Lond Gaz.* [315]EPR, 152. [316]16 Feb, *Lond Gaz.* [317]24 Mar, LGBO 22327. [318]26 May, *Lond Gaz.* [319]28 Feb, *Lond Gaz.* [320]24 Mar, LGBO 22350. [321]18 Jan, *Lond Gaz.* [322]1 May (*Lond Gaz* 3 Apr). [323]23 Aug, MHealth Decl. [324]1 Apr, MHousLGO 4619. [325]1 Apr, MHousLGO 4915. [326]1 Apr, MHousLGO 8314. [327]1 Oct, LGBO 32961. [328]*VCH Essex* IV, 152-53. [329]1 Apr, MHousLGO 34453. [330]20 Feb, *Lond Gaz.* [331]1 Apr, MHousLGO 19070. [332]17 Dec, LGBO 13052. [333]18 Sept, MHealth Decl. [334]7 Nov, *Lond Gaz.* [335]14 May, *Lond Gaz.* [336]1 Apr, LGBO 41046. [337]6 Oct, Part Dist, Instr CBC. [338]26 Oct, *Lond Gaz.* [339]8 Feb, *Lond Gaz.* [340]10 Oct, *Lond Gaz.* [341]24 Nov, *Lond Gaz.* [342]6 Oct, *Lond Gaz.* [343]1 Apr (*Lond Gaz* 29 Mar). [344]1 Aug (*Lond Gaz* 23 July). [345]30 July (lic min, *Lond Gaz* 31 May 1963). [346]1 Apr, MHousLGO 5823. [347]*VCH Essex* IV, 188. [348]24 Mar, LGBO 22423. [349]Morant, II, 171 and *VCH Essex* IV, 188. [350]17 July, *Lond Gaz.* [351]12 June, *Lond Gaz.* [352]31 Mar, LGBO 41102. [353]22 Nov, *Lond Gaz.* [354]31 Mar, LGBO 41102. [355]25 June (church consecr, *Lond Gaz* 29 Feb). [356]Essex RO, MSS D/DU 693. [357]Morant, I, 424. [358]16 Dec, LGBO 8885, 8886. [359]Year vac (*Lond Gaz* 12 Aug 1924). [360]27 July, *Lond Gaz.* [361]27 July, *Lond Gaz.* [362]21 Oct, *Lond Gaz.* [363]2 Feb, *Lond Gaz.* [364]24 Jan, *Lond Gaz.* [365]8 Feb, *Lond Gaz.* [366]17 Apr, *Lond Gaz.* [367]31 Oct, *Lond Gaz.* [368]17 June, *Lond Gaz.* [369]1 Aug, *Lond Gaz.* [370]12 Sept, *Lond Gaz.* [371]24 Mar, LGBO 16609. [372]25 Mar, LGBO 17924. [373]1 Jan, MHealthO 88877. [374]25 Mar, LGBO 29312. [375]27 Feb, *Lond Gaz.* [376]25 Mar, LGBO 16612, 17924. [377]19 Feb, *Lond Gaz.* [378]28 Feb, *Lond Gaz.* [379]24 Mar, LGBO 22356. [380]24 Mar, LGBO 22364. [381]1 Apr, MHousLGO 4078. Notes 382-88 not used. [389]EPR, 211. [390]27 May, LGBO 45011. [391]13 Oct, *Lond Gaz.* [392]13 Dec, *Lond Gaz.* [393]29 Oct, *Lond Gaz.* [394]13 Feb, *Lond Gaz.* [395]10 Dec, *Lond Gaz.* [396]1 Dec, LGBO 7348. [397]14 Sept, *Lond Gaz.* [398]28 Jan, *Lond Gaz.* [399]17 May, *Lond Gaz.* [400]8 Dec, *Lond Gaz.* [401]28 Oct, *Lond Gaz.* [402]28 Mar, *Lond Gaz.* [403]5 Sept, *Lond Gaz.* [404]10 Oct, *Lond Gaz.* [405]16 Feb, *Lond Gaz.* [406]16 Aug, *Lond Gaz.* [407]30 May, *Lond Gaz.* [408]29 Oct, *Lond Gaz.* [409]5 Apr, LGB ProvO 86. [410]25 Apr, LGB ProvO 491. [411]1 Apr, LGBO 39466. [412]8 May, *Lond Gaz.* [413]Dec, *Lond Gaz.* [414]26 Feb (lic min, *Lond Gaz* 19 Dec 1962). [415]31 Mar, LGBO 46157. [416]Morant, II, 592. [417]1 Apr, LGBO 41592. [418]1 Mar (*Lond Gaz* 11 Feb). [419]19 Dec, *Lond Gaz.* [420]10 Oct, *Lond Gaz.* [421]1 Dec (*Lond Gaz* 16 Nov). [422]24 Mar, LGBO 23834, 22419. [423]1 Apr, MHealthO 70548. [424]15 June, SI 1956/820. [425]*VCH Essex* II, 348, sep CP 1858 [as in note 311]. [426]11 June, SI 1945/701. [427]30 Mar, SI 1960/454. [428]19 Jan, SI 1955/8.

GLOUCESTERSHIRE

[1]25 Mar, LGBO 14762. [2]1 Apr, MHealthO 80904. [3]25 Mar, 46 & 47 Vict., *c* 58. [4]20 & 21 Eliz. II, *c* 70. [5]Sir Robert Atkyns, *The Ancient and Present State of Glostershire* (hereafter, Atkyns), 205. [6]5 Feb, reported in *Parl Papers* 1872, XLVI, 22. [7]Atkyns, 206. [8]Year vac (*Lond Gaz* 8 May). [9]29 & 30 Vict., *c* 113. [10]1 Apr, MHealthO 80904. [11]25 Mar, LGBO 18108. [12]1 Apr, MHousLGO 6462. [13]PC QAB. [14]Year vac (*Lond Gaz* 2 Nov 1928). [15]24 Mar, LGBO 16227. [16]1 Apr, MHousLGO 3411. [17]18 Feb, MHousLGO 21193. [18]1 Apr, MHousLGO 45729. [19]2 Sept, *Lond Gaz.* [20]16 Oct, *Lond Gaz.* [21]2 & 3 Wm. IV, *c* 64 and 7 & 8 Vict., *c* 61. [22]10 Nov, reported in *Parl Papers* 1872, XLVI, 17. [23]8 Feb, *Lond Gaz.* [24]Note cancelled. [25]Apptd day, LGBO 32064. [26]1 Apr, MHousLGO 5807. [27]13 Feb, *Lond Gaz.* [28]*VCH Glos* VIII, 18485. [29]1 Apr, SI 1965/223. [30]1 Apr, 21 & 22 Geo. V, *c* ix. [31]Authority not found. [32]Year vac (*Lond Gaz* 2 Aug 1930). [33]25 Mar, LGBO 18160. [34]20 July, *Lond Gaz.* [35]1 Apr, MHousLGO 3293. [36]26 Aug, *Lond Gaz.* [37]15 Sept, reported in *Parl Papers* 1890-91, LXI, 54. [38]*Guide to Bristol Parish Records* (hereafter, GBPR), 165. [39]Apptd day, LGBO 32064. [40]28 July, *Lond Gaz.* [41]Year vac (*Lond Gaz* 28 July 1933). [42]9 Nov, LGB ProvO 1649. [43]25 Mar, LGBO 16525. [44]28 Dec, MHousLGO 23995. [45]1 Apr, SI 1951/324. [46]1 Apr, Gloucester (Extension) Act, 1951. [47]30 Dec, *Lond Gaz.* [48]12 Apr, *Lond Gaz.* [49]31 Dec, *Lond Gaz.* [50]*VCH Glos* VI, 24. [51]2 & 3 Wm. IV, *c* 64 and 7 & 8 Vict., *c* 61. [52]*VCH Glos* VI, 16. [53]25 Mar, LGBO 14578. [54]30 Sept, 59 & 60 Vict., *c* lxxiv. [55]1 Oct, MHealthO 84989. [56]15 Sept, reported in *Parl Papers* 1890-91, 57. [57]23 Aug, *Lond Gaz.* [58]1 Jan, 20 Vict., *c* 19. [59]22 July, *Lond Gaz.* [60]*VCH Glos* VIII, 259. [61]20 Apr, *Lond Gaz.* [62]1 Nov (*Lond Gaz* 27 Oct). [63]29 Aug, Part Dist, CBC. [64]Apptd day, LGBO 32127. [65]25 Mar, LGBO 16222. [66]29 Aug, *Lond Gaz.* [67]10 Aug, *Lond Gaz.* [68]9 Mar, *Lond Gaz.* [69]1 Apr, MHealthO 84026. [70]1 Apr, MHousLGO 7075. [71]4 Mar, reported in *Parl Papers* 1872, XLVI, 18. [72]1 Apr, SI 1965/2086. [73]21 Nov, *Lond Gaz.* [74]25 Mar, LGBO 14581, 14582. [75]24 Mar, LGBO 23880. [76]1 Apr, 21 & 22 Geo. V, *c* ix. [77]Authority not found; date from diocesan directory. [78]16 June, *Lond Gaz.* [79]Note cancelled. [80]1 Nov, *Lond Gaz.* [81]18 June, *Lond Gaz.* [82]1 Oct, LGBO 38597. [83]1 Oct, 1 Edw. VII, *c* cclxiv. [84]1 Oct, 1 Edw. VII, *c* cxlii. [85]18 Oct, 4 Edw. VII, *c* ccxxiii. [86]8 & 9 Geo. V, *c* xlii. [87]1 Apr, MHealthO 77130. [88]1 Apr, Somerset and Bristol (Alteration of Boundary) O, 1951. [89]30 Sept, LGBO 34794. [90]1 Apr, LGBO 37475. [91]1 Apr, 60 & 61 Vict., *c* ccxxx. [92]9 Dec, *Lond Gaz.* [93]Date and authority not

but date noted in Bristol diocesan directory. [94] 1 Apr, *Lond Gaz.* [95] 16 Oct, *Lond Gaz.* [96] 3 June, Lond Gaz. [97] 24 Aug, *Lond Gaz.* [98] 20 May, *Lond Gaz.* [99] 4 June, *Lond Gaz.* [100] 31 Aug, *Lond Gaz.* [101] Year vac (*Lond Gaz* 30 Mar 1956). [102] 13 Jan, *Lond Gaz.* [103] 24 Sept, *Lond Gaz.* [104] Year vac (*Lond Gaz* 30 Mar 1956). [105] 20 Nov, *Lond Gaz.* [106] Year vac (*Lond Gaz* 5 June 1936). [107] 25 Nov, by the Bp. [108] 10 May, *Lond Gaz.* [109] 3 May, *Lond Gaz.* [110] 6 July, *Lond Gaz.* [111] 12 Feb, *Lond Gaz.* [112] Date as per Bristol Diocesan Directory. [113] 19 Aug, *Lond Gaz.* [114] 22 Feb, *Lond Gaz.* [115] 6 Feb, *Lond Gaz.* [116] 15 Aug, *Lond Gaz.* [117] 28 July, *Lond Gaz.* [118] PC QAB, refounded 19 Aug 1870, *Lond Gaz.* [119] 10 Dec, *Lond Gaz.* [120] Authority not found. [121] 10 Dec, *Lond Gaz.* [122] Year vac (*Lond Gaz* 10 Nov 1936). [123] Authority not found. [124] 18 Oct (lic min, *Lond Gaz* 30 May 1961). [125] 22 Oct, *Lond Gaz.* [126] 17 Jan, *Lond Gaz.* [127] Authority not found. [128] 24 Geo. II, *c* 32. [129] 23 June, *Lond Gaz.* [130] Year vac (*Lond Gaz* 10 Nov 1936). [131] 28 Feb, *Lond Gaz.* [132] 39 & 40 Vict., *c* clxxxviii. [133] 11 May, *Lond Gaz.* [134] 8 Feb, *Lond Gaz.* [135] Year vac (*Lond Gaz* 4 June 1954). [136] 30 Apr, *Lond Gaz.* [137] 24 Mar, LGBO 15264. [138] 25 Mar, LGBO 16495, 16525. [139] 3 July, MHousLG Decl. [140] 16 Jan, reported in *Parl Papers* 1890-91, LXI, 55. [141] 17 Jan, *Lond Gaz.* [142] 12 Aug, reported in *Parl Papers* 1890-91, LXI, 55. [143] Year vac (*Lond Gaz* 18 Mar 1932). [144] PC QAB. [145] 26 Mar, LGBO 30889. [146] 25 Mar, LGBO 14746. [147] 1 Apr, MHealthO 11131. [148] 14 Aug, *Lond Gaz.* [149] 1 Apr, MHousLGO 7715. [150] 25 Mar, LGBO 14695. [151] Apptd day, LGBO 31814. [152] 22 Sept, *Lond Gaz.* [153] Apptd day, LGBO 31814, 31815. [154] 28 Oct, *Lond Gaz.* [155] 1 Sept, *Lond Gaz.* [156] 8 May, *Lond Gaz.* [157] 22 July, *Lond Gaz.* [158] 4 Apr, *Lond Gaz.* [159] 25 May, *Lond Gaz.* [160] 16 Apr, *Lond Gaz.* [161] 2 Dec, *Lond Gaz.* [162] 6 June, *Lond Gaz.* [163] 15 Feb, *Lond Gaz.* [164] 27 Feb, *Lond Gaz.* [165] 13 Oct, *Lond Gaz.* [166] 14 May, *Lond Gaz.* [167] 26 May, *Lond Gaz.* [168] 29 Aug, *Lond Gaz.* [169] 19 May, *Lond Gaz.* [170] 1 June, *Lond Gaz.* [171] 27 June, *Lond Gaz.* [172] 24 Dec, *Lond Gaz.* [173] Authority not found. [174] 1 Apr, MHousLGO 3111. [175] 13 Aug, *Lond Gaz.* [176] 18 Apr, *Lond Gaz.* [177] 8 July, *Lond Gaz.* [178] Year vac (*Lond Gaz* 31 Dec 1929). [179] 14 Nov, *Lond Gaz.* [180] 1 Apr, MHealthO 110233. [181] 1 Apr, MHousLGO 3111. [182] *VCH Glos* VIII, 19. [183] 20 Nov, *Lond Gaz.* [184] 12 Nov, Instr CBC. [185] Reported in *Parl Papers* 1872, XLVI, 81. [186] 25 Oct, *Lond Gaz.* [187] 20 Nov, *Lond Gaz.* [188] 14 Mar, *Lond Gaz.* [189] 30 Oct, *Lond Gaz.* [190] 23 Dec, *Lond Gaz.* [191] 11 Mar, *Lond Gaz.* [192] 15 Sept, *Lond Gaz.* [193] 27 June, *Lond Gaz.* [194] 19 Mar, *Lond Gaz.* [195] 11 Mar, *Lond Gaz.* [196] 3 May, *Lond Gaz.* [197] Year vac (*Lond Gaz* 1 Apr 1938). [198] 8 Dec, *Lond Gaz.* [199] 29 Apr, *Lond Gaz.* [200] 25 Mar, LGBO 14746. [201] 29 Apr, *Lond Gaz.* [202] 12 June, *Lond Gaz.* [203] 14 May, *Lond Gaz.* [204] 19 Oct, MHous LG Decl. [205] 25 Mar, LGBO 18127. [206] *VCH Glos* VII, 70. [207] 1 Apr, MHousLGO 4861. [208] 25 Mar, LGBO 14583. [209] 24 Mar, LGBO 14580. [210] 6 July, Instr Bp Glouc & Bristol. [211] PC QAB. [212] 18 Sept, *Lond Gaz.* [213] 13 Apr, *Lond Gaz.* [214] *VCH Glos* VIII, 58. [215] *VCH Glos* VIII, 65. [216] *VCH Glos* VIII, 93. [217] *VCH Glos* VIII, 103. [218] *VCH Glos* VIII, 108. [219] *VCH Glos* VIII, 288. [220] *VCH Glos* VIII, 45. [221] GBPR, 159. [222] 25 Mar, LGBO 14751. [223] Authority not found. [224] 5 May, *Lond Gaz.* [225] Authority not found. [226] 12 May, reported in *Parl Papers* 1890-91, LXI, 53. [227] 6 June, *Lond Gaz.* [228] 1 Apr, MHousLGO 6589. [229] 1 Nov (*Lond Gaz* 27 Oct). [230] Year vac (*Lond Gaz* 26 July 1927). [231] 25 Mar, LGBO 14747. [232] 17 July, reported in *Parl Papers* 1890-91, LXI, 55. [233] 24 Mar, LGBO 15258. [234] 31 May, *Lond Gaz.* [235] 15 Mar, *Lond Gaz.* [236] 24 Mar, LGBO 14764. [237] 24 Mar, LGBO 15263. [238] 25 Mar, LGBO 16525. [239] 23 Aug, Part Dist. [240] GBPR, 137. [241] 15 Sept, *Lond Gaz.* [242] Apptd day, LGBO 32055. [243] 25 Mar, LGBO 18125. [244] 1 Oct, MHousLGO 1227. [245] 17 Dec, *Lond Gaz.* [246] 14 Dec, *Lond Gaz.* [247] 17 Nov, *Lond Gaz.* [248] 27 Aug, *Lond Gaz.* [249] 28 Mar, *Lond Gaz.* [250] 25 Mar, LGBO 14581, 14582, 14584. [251] 1 Apr, 21 & 22 Geo. V, *c* ix. [252] Year vac (*Lond Gaz* 13 Oct 1933). [253] 12 Aug, *Lond Gaz.* [254] 26 July, *Lond Gaz.* [255] Year vac (*Lond Gaz* 13 Oct 1933). [256] 26 Mar, 57 & 58 Vict., *c* xci. [257] Authority not found. [258] 26 May, *Lond Gaz.* [259] Year vac (*Lond Gaz* 5 July 1927). [260] 1 Apr, 14 & 15 Geo. VI, *c* ii. [261] 30 Nov, *Lond Gaz.* [262] Year vac (*Lond Gaz* 27 Feb 1934). [263] Authority not found. [264] 10 July, *Lond Gaz.* [265] 13 Aug, reported in *Parl Papers* 1890-91, LXI, 55. [266] Year lic min (*Lond Gaz* 3 Aug 1967). [267] 9 Oct, *Lond Gaz* (date of supplemental order making effective orig order 5 July 1927). [268] Authority not found. [269] 23 June, Instr CBC. [270] 10 Feb, *Lond Gaz.* [271] Authority not found. [272] 18 Apr, *Lond Gaz.* [273] 22 Oct, *Lond Gaz.* [274] 7 May, *Lond Gaz.* [275] 20 May, *Lond Gaz.* [276] 13 Aug, *Lond Gaz.* [277] 27 July, *Lond Gaz.* [278] *Liber Regis.* [279] Year vac (*Lond Gaz* 31 Oct 1930). [280] 29 Sept, *Lond Gaz.* [281] 25 Mar, LGBO 16495. [282] 24 Mar, LGBO 15260. [283] 25 Mar, LGBO 16229. [284] *Liber Regis,* 326. [285] 24 Mar, LGBO 16225. [286] 1 Apr, MHous LGO 4069. [287] 1 Oct, 4 Edw. VII, *c* ccxxiii. [288] 2 Feb, *Lond Gaz.* [289] 2 Apr, *Lond Gaz.* [290] 25 Mar, LGBO 18125. [291] 25 Mar, LGBO 18127. [292] 21 Dec, *Lond Gaz.* [293] Authority not found. [294] 25 June, *Lond Gaz.* [295] 26 Feb, *Lond Gaz.* [296] 21 July, reported in *Parl Papers* 1872, XLVI, 18. [297] 27 June, *Lond Gaz.* [298] Year vac (*Lond Gaz* 26 May 1922). [299] 25 Mar, LGBO 14639. [300] Authority not found. [301] 24 June, reported in *Parl Papers* 1890-91, LXI, 57. [302] 30 May, *Lond Gaz.* [303] 14 Sept, MHousLG Decl. [304] 30 Sept, 59 & 60 Vict., *c* ccxxxvi. [305] Authority not found. [306] Apptd day, LGBO 31776. [307] 25 Mar, LGBO 14750. [308] 31 Oct, *Lond Gaz.* [309] 12 May, reported in *Parl Papers* 1890-91, LXI, 55. [310] Authority not found. [311] Apptd day, LGBO 31815. [312] 14 May, *Lond Gaz.* [313] Authority not found. [314] Year vac (*Lond Gaz* 17 July 1928). [315] 25 Mar, LGBO 14584. [316] 25 Mar, LGBO 14636. [317] 1 July, *Lond Gaz.* [318] Year lic min (*Lond Gaz* 19 Dec 1952). [319] 1 Apr, MHousO 70989. [320] Year vac (*Lond Gaz* 22 Mar 1927). [321] 28 June, reported in *Parl Papers* 1890-91, LXVII, 173. [322] Apptd day,

LGBO 31861. [323]1 Apr, MHealthO 98242. [324]26 May, *Lond Gaz.* [325]24 Mar, LGBO 15262. [326]25 Mar, LGBO 19483. [327]24 Mar, LGBO 14749. [328]25 Mar, LGBO 14748. [329]15 Sept, *Lond Gaz.* [330]Apptd day, LGBO 32055. [331]28 June, *Lond Gaz.* [332]25 Mar, LGBO 18160. [333]25 Mar, LGBO 14638. [334]PC QAB. [335]17 Dec, *Lond Gaz.* [336]1 July, MHouLG Decl. [337]24 Mar, LGBO 15261. [338]9 July, *Lond Gaz.* [339]3 Aug, *Lond Gaz.* [340]26 Mar, LGBO 27790. [341]Presumed as result of 57 & 59 Vict., *c* 58. [342]Apptd day, LGBO 32063. [343]*VCH Glos* X, 115. [344]*VCH Glos* XI, 283. [345]*VCH Glos* VI, 219. [346]24 Mar, LGBO 15259. [347]26 Mar, LGBO 30890. [348]Authority not found; date from Bristol Diocesan Directory. [349]24 Feb, *Lond Gaz.* [350]11 Aug, reported in *Parl Papers* 1872, XLVI, 17. [351]Year vac (*Lond Gaz* 23 June 1922). [352]*VCH Glos* X, 167. [353]28 Nov, *Lond Gaz.* [354]*VCH Glos* X, 98. [355]*VCH Glos* VI, 248. [356]*VCH Glos* X, 214. [357]25 Mar, LGBO 14629. [358]*VCH Glos* X, 46. [359]*VCH Glos* X, 175. [360]25 Feb, reported in *Parl Papers* 1872, 18. [361]Curacy from 16th cent (*VCH Glos* VIII, 226), PC QAB 1746. [362]17 Dec, *Lond Gaz.* [363]Sep par, later deemed chap, PC QAB 1766. [364]*VCH Glos* X,2 222. [365]PC QAB; see *VCH Glos* X, 187. [366]4 May, *Lond Gaz.* [367]Local act, 1871. [368]3 Sept, reported in *Parl Papers* 1872, 8. [369]See *VCH Glos* XI, 136. [370]24 Mar, LGBO 14637. [371]1 Apr, MHealthO 104708. [372]14 July, *Lond Gaz.* [373]24 Mar, LGBO 16226, 16227. [374]24 Dec, *Lond Gaz.* [375]24 Mar, LGBO 16226. [376]24 Mar, LGBO 16224. [377]20 May, *Lond Gaz.* [378]2 Feb, *Lond Gaz.* [379]Apptd day, LGBO 32067. [380]4 Mar, *Lond Gaz.* [381]3 July, *Lond Gaz.* [382]*VCH Glos* VI, 32-33. [383]28 Dec, LGBO 32255. [384]1 Apr, MHousLGO 4926. [385]*VCH Glos* VII, 234. [386]*VCH Glos* VIII, 241. [387]3 Feb, *Lond Gaz.* [388]25 Dec, *Lond Gaz.* [389]27 June, reported in *Parl Papers* 1890-91, LXI, 55. [390]Authority not found. [391]Exact date not found. [392]14 Nov, *Lond Gaz.* [393]25 Mar, LGBO 19129. [394]6 Aug, *Lond Gaz.* [395]Exact date not found. [396]9 Nov, The Wheatenhurst (Change of Name) O, 1945. [397]23 July, Instr CBC. [398]23 June, *Lond Gaz.* [399]6 Aug, *Lond Gaz.* [400]29 Oct, *Lond Gaz.* [401]31 Mar, MHealthO 74051. [402]Presumed result of 57 & 58 Vict., *c* 58. [403]24 Mar, LGBO 15262, 15258. 15260, 15261. [404]25 Mar, LGBO 16525, 16229.

HAMPSHIRE

[1]1 Apr, MHealthO 76235. [2]9 Jan (lic min, *Lond Gaz* 6 Dec 1955). [3]57 & 58 Vict., *c* 58 and Co Council Naming O. [4]9 Nov, LGB ProvO 1604. [5]1 Apr, MHousLGO 41650. [6]*VCH Hants* IV, 195. [7]PC QAB. [8]7 Nov, Part Dist, Instr CBC. [9]31 Jan, *Lond Gaz.* [10]12 Dec, reported in *Parl Papers* 1872, XLVI, 19. [11]*VCH Hants* III, 349. [12]30 Aug, reported in *Parl Papers* 1872, XLVI, 21. [13]19 Mar, *Lond Gaz.* [14]25 June, *Lond Gaz.* [15]25 Jan, *Lond Gaz.* [16]25 Mar, 45 & 46 Vict., *c* 58. [17]25 Mar, LGBO 18581. [18]24 Sept, 9 & 10 Geo. V, *c* cxxii. [19]20 & 21 Geo. V, *c* xxi. [20]1 Apr, 2 & 3 Geo. VI, *c* xxiv. [21]7 Sept, *Lond Gaz.* [22]3 Sept, *Lond Gaz.* [23]23 Dec, *Lond Gaz.* [24]15 Aug, *Lond Gaz.* [25]Apptd day, LGBO 31851. [26]1 Oct, LGBO 36892. [27]1 Apr, MHousLGO 10419. [28]4 Dec, *Lond Gaz.* [29]3 June, *Lond Gaz.* [30]26 Apr, reported in *Parl Papers* 1872, LXI, 21. [31]7 Apr, *Lond Gaz.* [32]1 Jan, 20 Vict., *c* 19. [33]8 Dec, LGBO 10096. [34]21 Nov, *Lond Gaz.* [35]11 Nov, *Lond Gaz.* [36]Apptd day, LGBO 32029. [37]1 Apr, LGBO 50177. [38]1 Apr, LGBO 32507. [39]1 Apr, LGBO 36848. [40]22 July, *Lond Gaz.* [41]25 Mar, LGBO 14723. [42]1 Apr, MHealthO 76986. [43]23 Nov, Order Poor Law Board. [44]*VCH Hants* IV, 275. [45]11 Aug, reported in *Parl Papers* 1890-91, LXI, 54. [46]24 Mar, LGBO 22376. [47]26 Oct, *Lond Gaz.* [48]11 Apr, *Lond Gaz.* [49]1 Oct, LGBO 36648. [50]1 Apr, MHousLGO 4045. [51]1 Apr, MHousLGO 10417. [52]3 Aug, *Lond Gaz.* [53]21 Feb, *Lond Gaz.* [54]19 Apr, *Lond Gaz.* [55]14 Feb, *Lond Gaz* (OC 10 Dec 1842). [56]*VCH Hants* IV, 138. [57]8 Dec, LGBO 10101, 10097, 10098. [58]30 Sept, LGBO 31791. [59]9 Oct, *Lond Gaz.* [60]27 June, *Lond Gaz.* [61]4 June, *Lond Gaz.* [62]8 Dec, LGBO 10097. [63]9 Nov, 54 & 55 Vict., *c* ccx. [64]1 Apr, MHousLGO 19584. [65]1 Apr, Dept EnvirnO 3595. [66]27 Oct, *Lond Gaz.* [67]1 Apr, MHousLGO 5888. [68]10 Mar, *Lond Gaz.* [69]1 Apr (*Lond Gaz* 13 Mar). [70]25 Dec, *Lond Gaz.* [71]4 Feb, reported in *Parl Papers* 1890-91, LXI, 54. [72]24 Mar, LGBO 22374. [73]1 Apr, LGBO 41721. [74]29 Aug, *Lond Gaz.* [75]11 Jan, *Lond Gaz* (OC 31 Dec 1883). [76]1 Apr, LGBO 32375. [77]*VCH Surrey* II, 581. [78]*VCH Hants* III, 526. [79]14 Dec, *Lond Gaz.* [80]8 Mar, *Lond Gaz.* [81]Authority not found. [82]22 Aug, *Lond Gaz.* [83]Apptd day, LGBO 32030. [84]1 Apr, LGBO 39518. [85]9 Aug, *Lond Gaz.* [86]Apptd day, LGBO 32031. [87]9 Nov, LGB ProvO 1135. [88]1 Apr, MHealthO 69719. [89]8 Aug, *Lond Gaz.* [90]30 June, *Lond Gaz.* [91]8 Jan, *Lond Gaz.* [92]30 Sept, *Lond Gaz.* [93]2 Mar, *Lond Gaz.* [94]18 Apr, *Lond Gaz.* [95]5 Nov, *Lond Gaz.* [96]9 Nov, *Lond Gaz.* [97]Year vac (*Lond Gaz* 11 Feb 1955). [98]11 Feb, *Lond Gaz.* [99]25 Mar, LGBO 18579. [100]Information supplied by Hants RO. [101]Information supplied by Hants RO. [102]29 & 30 Vict., *c* 113. [103]7 Oct, reported in *Parl Papers* 1872, XLVI, 22. [104]23 Jan, *Lond Gaz.* [105]1 Apr, MHealthO 73183. [106]25 Sept, LGBO 8578. [107]25 Nov, reported in *Parl Papers* 1872, XLVI, 20. [108]30 Aug, *Lond Gaz.* [109]Perhaps considered rectory 19th cent, *VCH Hants* IV, 92. [110]25 Mar, LGBO 14726, 14727. [111]29 Feb, *Lond Gaz.* [112]24 Mar, LGBO 16412. [113]12 May, reported in *Parl Papers* 1872, XLVI, 55. [114]Apptd day, LGBO 32066. [115]9 Nov, The Bournemouth (Extension) O, 1901. [116]30 Sept, LGBO 44497. [117]9 Nov, 3 & 4 Geo. V, *c* cxxix. [118]1 Apr, 20 & 21 Geo. V, *c* clxxxi. [119]1 Apr, MHealthO 76234. [120]11 Nov, Part Dist, Instr CBC & Bp Winch. [121]24 Feb, *Lond Gaz.* [122]20 Mar, *Lond Gaz.* [123]28 July, *Lond Gaz.* [124]15 May, *Lond Gaz.* [125]19 Oct, *Lond Gaz.* [126]14 Oct, *Lond Gaz.* [127]18 Aug, *Lond Gaz.* [128]26 Oct (*Lond Gaz* 26 Apr). [129]Year lic min (*Lond Gaz* 9 Oct 1951). [130]19 Aug, *Lond Gaz.* [131]25 Feb, *Lond Gaz.* [132]14 Aug, *Lond Gaz.* [133]28 Feb, *Lond Gaz.* [134]23 Aug, *Lond Gaz.* [135]24 Dec, *Lond Gaz.* [136]18 Dec, *Lond Gaz.* [137]3 Mar, *Lond Gaz.* [138]15 May, *Lond Gaz.* [139]13 Feb, *Lond Gaz.*

[140]25 Sept, *Lond Gaz.* [141]1 Apr, 20 & 21 Eliz. II, *c* 70. [142]30 Sept, LGBO 33501. [143]30 Sept, LGBO 40087. [144]1 Apr, MHousLG Planning O 576. [145]30 Sept, 58 & 59 Vict., *c* xci. [146]8 Dec, LGBO 10098. [147]2 & 3 Wm. IV, *c* 64 and 7 & 8 Vict., *c* 61. [148]10 Aug, *Lond Gaz.* [149]24 Mar, LGBO 22388. [150]24 Mar, LGBO 22428. [151]1 Oct, MHealthO 79081, 79082. [152]*VCH Hants* IV, 497. [153]25 Mar, LGBO 14725, 14726. [154]16 May, *Lond Gaz.* [155]25 Mar, LGBO 14727. [156]*VCH Hants* IV, 410. [157]*VCH Hants* IV, 453. [158]26 Mar, *Lond Gaz.* [159]3 Aug, reported in *Parl Papers* 1890-91, LXI, 54. [160]Apptd day, LGBO 31924. [161]30 Nov, LGBO 5847. [162]14 Mar, Part Dist, Instr CBC. [163]Apptd day, LGBO 31850. [164]1 Apr, LGBO 51814. [165]1 Oct, MHous LGO 5415. [166]27 Nov, *Lond Gaz.* [167]13 Feb, *Lond Gaz.* [168]28 July, reported in *Parl Papers* 1872, XLVI, 22. [169]18 Jan, reported in *Parl Papers* 1872, XLVI, 18. [170]*VCH Hants* IV, 186. [171]*VCH Hants* III, 376. [172]13 Nov, reported in *Parl Papers* 1872, XLVI, 20. [173]30 Sept, LGBO 31448. [174]27 Feb, *Lond Gaz.* [175]4 Apr, *Lond Gaz.* [176]10 May, *Lond Gaz.* [177]22 Nov, *Lond Gaz.* [178]*VCH Hants* IV, 563. [179]1 Aug (*Lond Gaz* 31 July). [180]9 Feb, Part Dist. [181]24 Mar, LGBO 22375. [182]26 May, *Lond Gaz.* [183]26 Mar, LGBO 43701. [184]30 Sept, LGBO 31853. [185]1 Apr, SI 1954/408. [186]1 Oct, LGBO 36613. [187]15 Aug, LGBO 6705, 6772, 6773. [188]29 Sept, LGBO 28249. [189]Apptd day, LGBO 32017. [190]Apptd day, LGBO 32020. [191]1 Apr, 1 & 2 Geo. V, *c* lxxxiv. [192]1 Apr, MHealthO 76235. [193]1 Apr, MHousLGO 9009. [194]1 Apr, Dept EnvirnO 3708. [195]26 June, reported in *Parl Papers* 1872, XLVI, 22. [196]17 June, *Lond Gaz.* [197]14 July, *Lond Gaz.* [198]22 Mar, *Lond Gaz.* [199]18 Nov, *Lond Gaz.* [200]12 Feb (lic min, *Lond Gaz* 18 Nov 1969). [201]*VCH Hants* IV, 147. [202]13 Aug, *Lond Gaz.* [203]30 Sept, LGBO 31374. [204]1 Oct, MHealthO 79081. [205]1 Oct, MHealthO 79082. [206]18 Sept, *Lond Gaz.* [207]17 Nov, *Lond Gaz.* [208]28 Mar, 56 & 57 Vict., *c* lxxiii. [209]1 Oct, MHousLGO 6255. [210]*VCH Hants* III, 253, qv for later details. [211]24 Mar, LGBO 16411. [212]Apptd day, LGBO 31852. [213]9 Nov, 4 Edw. VII, *c* cxv. [214]1 Oct, Portsmouth Corporation Act, 1920. [215]13 Nov, *Lond Gaz.* [216]4 Nov, *Lond Gaz.* [217]1 Apr, MHealthO 68246. [218]1 Oct, LGBO 36884. [219]1 Nov (*Lond Gaz* 2 Oct). [220]14 Jan, reported in *Parl Papers* 1872, XLVI, 22. [221]30 Sept, LGBO 31927. [222]*VCH Hants* IV, 26. [223]30 Sept, LGBO 31424. [224]1 Apr, MHousLGO 1403. [225]26 July, *Lond Gaz.* [226]16 Mar, *Lond Gaz.* [227]19 Feb, *Lond Gaz.* [228]2 Oct, *Lond Gaz.* [229]Presumed incl in PLU when became sep CP; not orig rated in the PLU. [230]1 Apr, MHousLGO 1379. [231]30 Mar, *Lond Gaz.* [232]30 Sept, LGBO 31647. [233]1 Apr, MHousLGO 28127. [234]28 Jan, *Lond Gaz.* [235]30 Dec, reported in *Parl Papers* 1890-91, LXI, 54. [236]24 Mar, LGBO 22250. [237]25 Mar, LGBO 14730. [238]Year vac (*Lond Gaz* 23 Mar 1928). [239]1 Apr, MHousLGO 6984. [240]16 Mar, Order Poor Law Board. [241]1 Apr, 3 & 4 Geo. V, *c* cxxix. [242]18 Mar, *Lond Gaz.* [243]30 Sept, 58 & 59 Vict., session 2, *c* xi. [244]30 Sept, LGBO 31854. [245]21 Apr, *Lond Gaz.* [246]24 Mar, LGBO 16412, 16413. [247]8 Dec, LGBO 10105. [248]30 Oct, *Lond Gaz.* [249]28 Oct, *Lond Gaz.* [250]12 Dec, OC (information supplied by Hants RO). [251]26 Mar, LGBO 30279. [252]1 Apr, LGBO 37196. [253]16 Apr, *Lond Gaz.* [254]18 Aug, reported in *Parl Papers* 1872, XLVI, 19. [255]*VCH Hants* IV, 479. [256]29 Aug, *Lond Gaz.* [257]14 Mar (OC 22 Dec 1836). [258]29 Oct, *Lond Gaz.* [259]1 Oct, LGBO 70238. [260]3 Aug, *Lond Gaz.* [261]6 Aug, *Lond Gaz.* [262]Year vac (*Lond Gaz* 30 May 1924). [263]1 Nov (*Lond Gaz* 26 Oct). [264]5 Aug, *Lond Gaz.* [265]20 Mar, reported in *Parl Papers* 1872, XLVI, 21. [266]19 May, reported in *Parl Papers* 1903, L, 595. [267]27 Feb, Part Dist, Instr CBC. [268]24 Apr, *Lond Gaz.* [269]17 Apr (lic min, *Lond Gaz* 14 Feb 1956). [270]25 Mar, LGBO 18580. [271]2 Aug, *Lond Gaz.* [272]1 Feb, *Lond Gaz.* [273]1 Apr, MHousLGO 3459. [274]10 July, *Lond Gaz.* [275]21 Dec, *Lond Gaz.* [276]12 Feb, *Lond Gaz.* [277]*VCH Hants* IV, 580. [278]1 Apr, MHousLGO 10418. [279]13 Dec, Part Dist, Instr CBC. [280]24 Mar, LGBO 22251. [281]*VCH Hants* IV, 284. [282]6 June, *Lond Gaz.* [283]30 Sept, LGBO 31660. [284]4 Nov, Part Dist. [285]20 Dec, reported in *Parl Papers* 1872, XLVI, 22. [286]1 Apr, Dept Envirn O 3594. [287]7 Nov, *Lond Gaz.* [288]12 Oct, *Lond Gaz.* [289]Apptd day, LGBO 31436. [290]5 Dec, *Lond Gaz.* [291]26 Feb, reported in *Parl Papers* 1872, XLVI, 22. [292]1 Apr, LGBO 33968. [293]1 Apr, LGBO 36948. [294]19 July, *Lond Gaz.* [295]19 Dec, *Lond Gaz.* [296]After census of 1861. [297]1 Oct, LGBO 43777. [298]2 Aug, *Lond Gaz.* [299]1 Apr, MHealthO 73155. [300]7 Dec, *Lond Gaz.* [301]10 Dec, reported in *Parl Papers* 1903, L, 595. [302]1 Oct, LGBO 44456. [303]1 Oct, MHealth O 70181. [304]1 Apr, MHousLGO 1378. [305]*VCH Hants* V, 133. [306]Year vac (*Lond Gaz* 7 Oct 1932). [307]22 Dec, LGBO 10327. [308]30 Jan, *Lond Gaz.* [309]1 Oct, LGBO 43721. [310]1 Oct, LGBO 43720. [311]1 Apr, MHousLGO 1470. [312]1 Apr, MHousLGO 14331. [313]23 Nov, reported in *Parl Papers* 1872, XLVI, 21. [314]Not used. [315]1 Apr, MHousLGO 6984. [316]But see *VCH Hants* VIII, 134. [317]Note cancelled. [318]13 Jan, *Lond Gaz.* [319]30 Nov, *Lond Gaz.* [320]5 July, *Lond Gaz.* [321]4 Nov, reported in *Parl Papers* 1872, XLVI, 22. [322]15 Aug, LGBO 6705, 6772. [323]Apptd day, LGBO 32020. [324]9 Nov, LGB ProvO 1144. [325]22 Mar, *Lond Gaz.* [326]17 Dec, reported in *Parl Papers* 1872, XLVI, 21. [327]1 Oct, LGBO 48188. [328]14 June, *Lond Gaz.* [329]12 Aug, reported in *Parl Papers* 1890-91, LXI, 54. [330]15 June, *Lond Gaz.* [331]Year vac (*Lond Gaz* 3 Sept 1954). [332]16 Mar, *Lond Gaz.* [333]26 Mar, LGBO 44465. [334]*VCH Hants* IV, 181. [335]27 Mar, *Lond Gaz.* [336]31 Dec (*Lond Gaz* 15 Nov). [337]Apptd day, LGBO 32028. [338]*VCH Hants* IV, 86. [339]6 Feb, *Lond Gaz.* [340]17 Nov, *Lond Gaz.* [341]24 Mar, LGBO 22329. [342]1 Apr (*Lond Gaz* 22 Mar). [343]31 July, *Lond Gaz.* [344]1 Apr, LGBO 43702. [345]25 June, reported in *Parl Papers* 1890-91, LXI, 53. [346]3 May, reported in *Parl Papers* 1903, L, 595. [347]18 Jan, OC (information supplied by Hants RO). [348]29 May, *Lond Gaz.* [349]24 Mar, LGBO 23328. [350]1 Feb (*Lond Gaz* 3 Jan). [351]Information supplied by Hants RO. [352]1 Apr, LGBO 56291. [353]Information supplied by Hants RO. [354]9 Nov, LGB

ProvO 1135. [355] 15 Dec, *Lond Gaz.* [356] 1 Oct, LGBO 71087. [357] 15 Jan, *Lond Gaz.* [358] 12 June, Part Dist, Instr CBC. [359] *VCH Hants* III, 199. [360] 11 May, *Lond Gaz.* [361] 23 Feb, *Lond Gaz.* [362] 7 June, *Lond Gaz.* [363] 21 Mar, *Lond Gaz.* [364] Information supplied by Hants RO. [365] First appearance *Clergy List.* [366] *VCH Hants* IV, 518. [367] 8 Dec, LGBO 10100, 10096. [368] 8 Dec, LGBO 10100, 10101, 10102. [369] 29 & 30 Vict., *c* cxi. [370] 30 Sept, LGBO 31700. [371] 8 Dec, LGBO 10102. [372] 23 May, *Lond Gaz.* [373] 24 July, *Lond Gaz.* [374] 1 May (*Lond Gaz* 3 Apr). [375] 2 Mar, MHousLGO 29473. [376] *VCH Hants* III, 376. [377] 26 Apr, *Lond Gaz.* [378] 1 Apr, MHousLGO 33821. [379] 14 Aug, reported in *Parl Papers* 1890-91, LXI, 54. [380] 8 July, *Lond Gaz.* [381] 1 Apr, MHousLGO 5889. [382] 13 Apr (lic min, *Lond Gaz* 18 Mar). [383] 7 Jan, reported in *Parl Papers* 1872, XLVI, 21. [384] 20 May, *Lond Gaz.* [385] 29 Apr, *Lond Gaz.* [386] 29 Nov (lic min, *Lond Gaz* 29 July). [387] 25 Mar, LGBO 18151. [388] 19 Aug, *Lond Gaz.* [389] 31 Mar, 62 & 63 Vict., *c* cclvii. [390] 5 May, *Lond Gaz.* [391] 3 Dec, *Lond Gaz.* [392] 2 May, *Lond Gaz.* [393] 4 Oct, *Lond Gaz.* [394] 29 Jan, Part Dist, Instr Eccl Commissioners. [395] 24 Aug, *Lond Gaz.* [396] 1 July (*Lond Gaz* 29 June). [397] 8 Nov, *Lond Gaz.* [398] 21 July, *Lond Gaz.* [399] 23 Mar, MHousLGO 28062. [400] 22 Feb, *Lond Gaz.* [401] 31 Mar, LGBO 53725. [402] 5 Feb, *Lond Gaz.* [403] 24 July, *Lond Gaz.* [404] 29 & 30 Vict., *c* 66. [405] 17 July, *Lond Gaz.* [406] 30 Sept, LGBO 31711. [407] 25 July, reported in *Parl Papers* 1890-91, LXI, 54. [408] *VCH Surrey* II, 595. [409] 30 Sept, LGBO 31426. [410] 30 May, *Lond Gaz.* [411] 15 Feb, *Lond Gaz.* [412] 15 Aug, MHealth Decl. [413] *VCH Hants* III, 297. [414] 1 Mar, *Lond Gaz.* [415] 6 Dec, *Lond Gaz.* [416] 14 Mar, *Lond Gaz.* [417] Perhaps pt of the par in Alton Hd, as in list (1791) of Justices of the Peace. [418] 30 Sept, LGBO 37511. [419] 8 Oct, *Lond Gaz.* [420] 28 Jan, *Lond Gaz.* [421] 8 Dec, LGBO 10099. [422] 29 Sept, *Lond Gaz.* [423] 1 Feb, *Lond Gaz* OC 10 Dec 1842). [424] 6 Apr (lic min, *Lond Gaz* 28 Feb). [425] 28 Oct, *Lond Gaz.* [426] 7 May, OC (information supplied by Hants RO). [427] 24 Mar, LGBO 16413. [428] 10 Dec, reported in *Parl Papers* 1872, LXI, 18. [429] 25 Mar, LGBO 14723, 14728, 14729, 14730. [430] 25 Mar, LGBO 14729. [431] 15 Aug, LGBO 6773. [432] Letters Patent. [433] 8 Feb, *Lond Gaz.* [434] 31 May, *Lond Gaz.* [435] *VCH Hants* III, 529. [436] 9 Nov, 10 & 11 Geo. V, *c* cxvi. [437] 12 Mar, *Lond Gaz.* [438] Information from Hants RO. [439] 25 Mar, LGBO 18579, 18580. [440] Year lic min (*Lond Gaz* 6 Nov 1951). [441] 25 Mar, LGBO 14728. [442] 31 Jan, *Lond Gaz.* [443] 24 Mar, LGBO 22250, 22251. [444] 18 Aug, *Lond Gaz.* [445] 25 Mar, LGBO 14725, 14726, 14727. [446] 14 Oct, *Lond Gaz.* [447] 28 Nov, *Lond Gaz.* [448] *VCH Hants* V, 76. [449] 8 Dec, LGBO 10104. [450] 7 Aug, Part Dist. [451] 31 Jan, *Lond Gaz.* [452] Information from Hants RO and from *VCH.* There are a number of other units which may have been pars in the mediev period, but for which identification is not certain. [453] 3 May, *Lond Gaz.* [454] 3 Apr, *Lond Gaz.* [455] 24 Nov, *Lond Gaz.* [456] 2 Feb, *Lond Gaz.* [457] 13 Oct, *Lond Gaz.* [458] 21 June, *Lond Gaz.* [459] 24 Mar, LGBO 22192. [460] 13 Oct, MHealthO 71087. [461] 11 Mar, SI 1964/274. [462] 29 Mar, SI 1973/607. [463] Information from Hants RO. [464] Information from Hants RO. [465] Copy order in Hants RO, Southwick Cartulary III, 270 (information from Hants RO).

HERTFORDSHIRE

[1] 24 Mar, LGBO 21700. [2] 1 Apr, MHealthO 88225. [3] 21 June, *Lond Gaz.* [4] 1 Apr, MHealthO 80108. [5] 1 Apr, MHousLGO 1452. [6] 1 Apr, MHous LGO 34368. [7] 8 Dec, *Lond Gaz.* [8] 12 Dec, *Lond Gaz.* [9] 2 & 3 Wm. IV, *c* 64 and 7 & 8 Vict., *c* 61. [10] 2 Jan, *Lond Gaz.* [11] 29 & 30 Vict., *c* 113. [12] *VCH Herts* III, 472. [13] 25 Mar, 45 & 46 Vict., *c* 58. [14] Apptd day, LGBO 31764. [15] Apptd day, LGBO 31686. [16] 30 Sept, LGBO 36587. [17] 1 Oct, LGBO 47327. [18] 7 Sept, *Lond Gaz.* [19] 2 Aug, *Lond Gaz.* [20] 26 Oct, *Lond Gaz.* [21] 25 Feb, *Lond Gaz.* [22] *VCH Herts* III, 409-10. [23] Presumed incl in PLU when became sep CP; not orig rated in the PLU. [24] 24 Mar, LGBO 22216. [25] Apptd day, LGBO 31896. [26] 9 Nov, 10 & 11 Geo. V, *c* cxviii. [27] 1 Apr, MHousLGO 7703. [28] May, *Lond Gaz.* [29] 15 Oct, *Lond Gaz.* [30] 28 Sept, (*Lond Gaz* 12 Apr). [31] 28 July, *Lond Gaz.* [32] Apptd day, Co Council Naming O and 56 & 57 Vict., *c* 73. [33] 25 June, LGBO 35608. [34] 20 & 21 Eliz. II, *c* 70. [35] 10 Feb, *Lond Gaz.* [36] 19 Feb, *Lond Gaz.* [37] *VCH Herts* IV, 25. [38] 1 Jan, 20 Vict., *c* 19. [39] 25 Mar, LGBO 14396. [40] 1 Apr, MHealthO 88226. [41] 1 Apr, MHousLGO 1455. [42] 5 Apr, *Lond Gaz.* [43] *VCH Herts* III, 199-200. [44] 24 Mar, LGBO 22215. [45] 1 Apr, MHousLGO 3452. [46] 6 May, *Lond Gaz.* [47] 16 Apr, *Lond Gaz.* [48] 1 Apr, MHousLG PlanningO 648. [49] *VCH Herts* III, 66. [50] *VCH Herts* III, 66-68. [51] 20 Dec, LGBO 13027. [52] 1 Apr, LGBO 53029, 598606. [53] 1 Apr, LGBO 58329. [54] 1 Apr, MHealthO 72211. [55] 32 Henry VIII, *c* 44. [56] 14 Sept, reported in *Parl Papers* 1872, XLVI 22. [57] 15 Jan, *Lond Gaz.* [58] 18 July, *Lond Gaz.* [59] 19 June, *Lond Gaz.* [60] 10 Oct, *Lond Gaz.* [61] 1 June (*Lond Gaz* 2 May). [62] 29 Jan, *Lond Gaz.* [63] 4 May, *Lond Gaz.* [64] 30 Sept, LGB ProvO 1173. [65] 1 Oct, LGBO 36608. [66] 17 May, reported in *Parl Papers* 1872, XLVI, 22. [67] July, *Lond Gaz.* [68] 18 June, *Lond Gaz.* [69] 6 Oct, *Lond Gaz.* [70] 1 Sept (*Lond Gaz* 7 Aug). [71] 1 Apr, MHealthO 88227. [72] 30 Sept, LGBO 41369. [73] 24 Mar, LGBO 22215, 22216. [74] *VCH Herts* II, 163-64. [75] 15 Apr, LGBO 37522. [76] 8 Oct, reported in *Parl Papers* 1879, LXVII, 173. [77] 1 Apr, LGBO 51336. [78] Co Council Naming O. [79] 1 Apr, MHousLGO 8947. [80] 26 Feb, *Lond Gaz.* [81] 15 Dec (lic min, *Lond Gaz* 19 Feb 1957). [82] 1 Apr, MHealthO 72680. [83] PC QAB. [84] Note cancelled. [85] 1 Apr, MHealthO 72680. [86] *VCH Herts* III, 209. [87] 1 Apr, MHousLGO 4856. [88] 16 July, *Lond Gaz.* [89] *VCH Herts* II, 179. [90] 23 Dec, *Lond Gaz.* [91] 9 July, *Lond Gaz.* [92] 5 Sept, *Lond Gaz.* [93] 1 Apr, LGBO 48979. [94] 1 Apr, LGBO 48979. [95] Apptd day, 56 & 57 Vict., *c* 73. [96] 30 Sept, LGB ProvO 1312, confirmed by 60 & 61 Vict., *c* lxxv. [97] 5 Oct, *Lond Gaz.* [98] 4 July, *Lond Gaz.* [99] 30 June, *Lond Gaz.* [100] 1 Apr, MHousLGO 3452. [101] 29 June, *Lond Gaz.* [102] 28 June, *Lond Gaz.* [103] 1 Oct, MHealthO 98795.

[104]31 July, *Lond Gaz.* [105]1 Apr, MHealthO 88230. [106]21 Apr, *Lond Gaz.* [107]15 Apr, MHealthO 106432. [108]1 Apr, MHousLGO 9402. [109]18 Oct, *Lond Gaz.* [110]4 Dec, *Lond Gaz.* [111]28 July (lic min, *Lond Gaz* 21 May). [112]1 Apr, LGBO 55929. [113]1 Apr, MHousLGO 14582. [114]23 May, *Lond Gaz.* [115]1 Oct, MHealthO 67266. [116]11 June, *Lond Gaz.* [117]1 Apr, MHealthO 88233. [118]1 Nov, *Lond Gaz.* [119]1 Apr, MHousLG PlanningO 563. [120]1 Apr, MHousLGO 6506. [121]Apptd day, LGBO 32062. [122]*VCH Middx* V, 207. [123]*VCH Middx* V, 270. [124]*VCH Herts* II, 199. [125]30 Sept, 60 & 61 Vict., *c* lxxv. [126]1 Apr, 6 Edw. VII, *c* cxx. [127]1 Apr, SI 1965/24. [128]24 Mar, reported in *Parl Papers* 1890-91, LXI, 51. [129]27 Sept, *Lond Gaz.* [130]13 Aug, *Lond Gaz.* [131]8 Nov, *Lond Gaz.* [132]25 Mar, LGBO 16585. [133]30 Sept, LGB ProvO 1170, confirmed by 58 & 59 Vict., *c* xi. [134]27 June, *Lond Gaz.* [135]*VCH Herts* III, 90. [136]1 Apr, MHousLGO 4535. [137]1 Apr, MHousLGO 41735. [138]*VCH Herts* IV, 58. [139]31 Mar, reported in *Parl Papers* 1872, XLVI, 20. [140]*VCH Middx* V, 26. [141]*VCH Middx* V, 267. [142]22 Oct, reported in *Parl Papers* 1872, XLVI, 20. [143]15 Apr, LGBO 37507. [144]10 Nov, *Lond Gaz.* [145]29 July, *Lond Gaz.* [146]1 Apr, MHealthO 88231. [147]1 Oct, MHousLG ProvO 1149. [148]4 Nov, *Lond Gaz.* [149]17 Dec, *Lond Gaz.* [150]18 Aug, reported in *Parl Papers* 1897, LXVII, 173. [151]1 Oct, MHousLG ProvO 1149. [152]3 Feb, *Lond Gaz.* [153]16 Aug, *Lond Gaz.* [154]2 Feb, *Lond Gaz.* [155]*VCH Herts* II, 215-17. [156]19 May, charter incorp. [157]27 Sept, *Lond Gaz.* [158]*VCH Herts* II, 409. [159]*VCH Herts* III, 509. [160]29 Apr, *Lond Gaz.* [161]1 Apr, MHealthO 68775. [162]24 Mar, *Lond Gaz.* [163]8 July, *Lond Gaz.* [164]*VCH Herts* III, 186. [165]*VCH Herts* III, 28. [166]*VCH Herts* III, 6-7. [167]Apptd day, LGBO 32107. [168]19 July, *Lond Gaz.* [169]1 Apr, MHealthO 66416. [170]10 Feb, *Lond Gaz.* [171]*VCH Herts* III, 439. [172]30 Sept, LGB ProvO 1313, confirmed by 60 & 61 Vict., *c* lxxv. [173]1 Oct, LGBO 42779. [174]28 Sept, MHealth Decl. [175]24 Mar, LGBO 22217. [176]3 Nov, *Lond Gaz.* [177]*VCH Herts* III, 24. [178]30 Sept, LGB ProvO 1313, confirmed by 60 & 61 Vict., *c* lxxv. [179]13 Aug, MHealth Decl. [180]1 Apr, MHousLGO 4541. [181]30 May, *Lond Gaz.* [182]30 Sept, LGB ProvO 1773. [183]6 Nov, *Lond Gaz.* [184]18 Aug, *Lond Gaz.* [185]12 Oct, *Lond Gaz.* [186]25 Mar, 45 & 46 Vict., *c* 58 and LGBO 14396, 14397, 14398, 14399. [187]21 June, *Lond Gaz.* [188]6 Sept, *Lond Gaz.* [189]17 Feb, *Lond Gaz.* [190]30 Apr (lic min, *Lond Gaz* 28 Feb). [191]1 Apr, LGBO 51691. [192]18 Jan, *Lond Gaz.* [193]1 Apr, MHealthO 88229. [194]12 Sept, *Lond Gaz.* [195]30 Oct, *Lond Gaz.* [196]18 Nov, *Lond Gaz.* [197]23 Dec, *Lond Gaz.* [198]Apptd day, LGBO 31921 and 30 Sept, LGB ProvO 1260, confirmed by 59 & 60 Vict., *c* ccxxxvi. [199]1 Apr, MHealth O 88232. [200]1 Apr, MHousLGO 7572. [201]24 Mar, LGBO 22216, 22217. [202]13 Aug, *Lond Gaz.* [203]*VCH Herts* II, 359-60. [204]19 Oct, *Lond Gaz.* [205]16 June, *Lond Gaz.* [206]28 Mar, *Lond Gaz.* [207]24 Mar, LGBO 21701. [208]1 Apr, MHousLGO 14034. [209]MHealthO 58329. [210]1 Apr, MHealthO 68983. [211]*VCH Herts* II, 391. [212]1 Oct, 16 & 17 Geo. V. *c* lix. [213]8 Feb, *Lond Gaz.* [214]*VCH Herts* II, 510. [215]Disfranchised for corruption, 15 Vict., *c* 9. [216]Apptd day, LGBO 31895. [217]30 Sept, LGBO 38655. [218]9 Nov, 3 & 4 Geo. V, *c* cxxxvi. [219]23 June, Part Dist, Instr CBC. [220]21 Dec, *Lond Gaz.* [221]1 Nov (*Lond Gaz* 23 Oct). [222]15 Mar, *Lond Gaz.* [223]3 June, *Lond Gaz.* [224]28 Feb, *Lond Gaz.* [225]31 July, *Lond Gaz.* [226]9 Oct, LGBO 6831. [227]13 Jan, *Lond Gaz.* [228]MHealth Decl. [229]25 Mar, *Lond Gaz.* [230]1 Apr, LGBO 41642. [231]*VCH Beds* II, 335. [232]*VCH Herts* III, 348-49. [233]1 Apr, MHousLGO 1456. [234]*VCH Herts* III, 366. [235]1 Jan (*Lond Gaz* 22 Dec 1970). [236]1 Apr, LGBO 54014. [237]5 Jan, *Lond Gaz.* [238]1 May (*Lond Gaz* 3 Apr). [239]30 Sept, 60 & 61 Vict., *c* lxxv. [240]25 Mar, LGBO 14397, 14399. [241]*VCH Herts* III, 379-80. [242]30 Apr, *Lond Gaz.* [243]*VCH Herts* II, 317. [244]25 Mar, LGBO 14395. [245]29 Jan, *Lond Gaz.* [246]*VCH Herts* III, 383. [247]30 Apr, *Lond Gaz.* [248]1 Apr, MHousLGO 8871. [249]Beresford & Finberg, 126. [250]17 May, *Lond Gaz.* [251]8 Aug, *Lond Gaz.* [252]12 Aug, *Lond Gaz.* [253]3 Dec (lic min, *Lond Gaz* 12 Oct). [254]1 Feb (*Lond Gaz* 31 Jan). [255]16 Feb, *Lond Gaz.* [256]1 Apr, LGBO 41644. [257]1 Apr, LGBO 45486. [258]1 Apr, LGBO 53410. [259]1 Apr, MHealthO 66995. [260]1 Apr, 14 & 15 Geo. V, *c* xix. [261]*VCH Beds* III, 318. [262]25 Mar, LGBO 14398. [263]*VCH Herts* III, 191. [264]11 June, SI 1945/701. [265]5 Jan, SI 1971/2110.

HUNTINGDONSHIRE

[1]Beresford & Finberg, 126. [2]26 Sept, MHousLG Decl. [3]*VCH Hunts* III, 12. [4]PC QAB. [5]1 Apr, MHealthO 79915. [6]26 Mar, *Lond Gaz.* [7]1 Apr, MHealthO 106313. [8]24 Mar, LGBO 15914. [9]25 Mar, LGBO 17765. [10]*VCH Hunts* III, 190. [11]Year vac (*Lond Gaz* 2 Dev 1930). [12]*VCH Hunts* III, 102. [13]1 Apr, SI 1964/367. [14]8 Mar, *Lond Gaz.* [15]*VCH Hunts* II, 187. [16]*VCH Hunts* II, 167-68. [17]PC QAB but status as donative retained until 1867, *VCH Hunts* II, 202. [18]24 Mar, LGBO 15913. [19]Authority not found. [20]25 Mar, LGBO 18132. [21]*VCH Hunts* III, 28. [22]9 Oct, LGBO 6984. [23]*VCH Hunts* III, 38. [24]Ent Hunts in census of 1851; authority for change not found. [25]*VCH Hunts* II, 370. [26]2 & 3 Wm. IV, *c* 64 and 7 & 8 Vict., *c* 61. [27]1 Apr, LGBO 32508. [28]1 Apr, MHousLGO 33808. [29]17 July, *Lond Gaz.* [30]29 & 30 Vict., *c* 113. [31]Presumed incl in PLU when became sep CP; not orig rated in the PLU. [32]25 Mar, LGBO 19414. [33]17 July, reported in *Parl Papers* 1890-91, LXI, 53. [34]26 Mar, LGBO 32254. [35]57 & 58 Vict., *c* 58 and Co Council Naming O. [36]1 Apr, authority not found. [37]30 Oct, *Lond Gaz.* [38]20 Mar, reported in *Parl Papers* 1872, XLVI, 22. [39]20 Oct, *Lond Gaz.* [40]*VCH Hunts* I, 172. [41]1 Oct, LGBO 56410. [42]*VCH Hunts, II, 145.*
172. [41]1 Oct, LGBO 56410. [42]*VCH Hunts,* II, 145.
[43]*VCH Hunts* II, 142. [44]30 Sept, 58 & 59 Vict., *c* lxxxix. [45]*VCH Hunts* III, 229. [46]1 Jan, 20 Vict., *c* 19. [47]Beresford & Finberg, 127. [48]30 Sept, 58 & 59 Vict., *c* lxxxix. [49]18 Sept, *Lond Gaz.* [50]6 July, *Lond Gaz.* [51]Ent Hunts in census of 1871; authority for change not found. [52]1 Apr, SI 1964/366. [53]18

Sept, *Lond Gaz.* [54]25 Mar, LGBO 17146. [55]29 June, *Lond Gaz.* [56]1 Oct (*Lond Gaz* 5 Sept). [57]9 May, *Lond Gaz.* [58]1 Oct, LGBO 47601. [59]1 Apr, MHousLG Decl. [60]30 Sept, 59 & 60 Vict., *c* ccxxxvi. [61]1 Apr, MHousLGO 8963.

KENT

[1]16 Apr, *Lond Gaz.* [2]31 May, *Lond Gaz.* [3]29 & 30 Vict., *c* 113. [4]16 May, reported in *Parl Papers* 1872, XLVI, 22. [5]Apptd day, LGBO 31744. [6]1 Apr, SI 1935/1337. [7]The County of Kent (Pars of Acrise and Elham) O, 1959. [8]25 Mar, 45 & 46 Vict., *c* 58. [9]24 Mar, LGBO 21672. [10]17 Aug, *Lond Gaz.* [11]28 Apr, reported in *Parl Papers* 1872, XLVI, 21. [12]24 Mar, LGBO 23641. [13]19 June, reported in *Parl Papers* 1872, XLVI, 22. [14]24 Mar, LGBO 20657. [15]1 Apr, SI 1935/1337. [16]1 Apr, MHousLGO 8270. [17]1 Apr, MHousLGO 10334. [18]1 Apr, The Canterbury O, 1932. [19]1 Apr, SI 1934/261. [20]24 Oct, *Lond Gaz.* [21]29 Nov, *Lond Gaz.* [22]5 Feb, *Lond Gaz.* [23]23 Mar, *Lond Gaz.* [24]26 Jan, *Lond Gaz.* [25]Year vac (*Lond Gaz* 19 July 1935). [26]Edward Hasted, *The History and Topographical Survey of the County of Kent* (hereafer, Hasted), IX, 223. [27]10 July, *Lond Gaz.* [28]17 Nov, *Lond Gaz.* [29]1 Apr, MHousLG O 4833. [30]27 Nov, *Lond Gaz.* [31]8 Mar, *Lond Gaz.* [32]1 Apr, MHousLGO 681. [33]31 Mar, MHealthO 73566. [34]28 May, *Lond Gaz.* [35]20 Nov, reported in *Parl Papers* 1872, XLVI, 18. [36]24 Nov, reported in *Parl Papers* 1897, LXVII, Pt VI, 174. [37]28 June (lic min, *Lond Gaz* 26 May). [38]*Liber Regis*, 855. [39]28 Feb, *Lond Gaz.* [40]6 Aug, *Lond Gaz.* [41]5 Oct, *Lond Gaz.* [42]Apptd day, LGBO 31649. [43]1 Apr, MHous LGO 6985. [44]Earlier organisation as in Hasted and in Richard Kilburne, *A Topographie or Survey of the County of Kent* (1659); later organisation as in 19th cent censuses. [45]24 Mar, LGBO 21675. [46]24 Mar, LGBO 20930. [47]Year vac (*Lond Gaz* 26 Mar 1937). [48]1 Mar (*Lond Gaz* 12 Feb). [49]12 Sept, *Lond Gaz.* [50]1 Oct, LGBO 43880. [51]1 Apr, 11 & 12 Eliz. II, *c* 33. [52]3 Nov, Part Dist, Instr Ecclesiastical Commissioners and Archbp Canterb. [53]28 June, *Lond Gaz.* [54]4 May, *Lond Gaz.* [55]27 Aug, *Lond Gaz.* [56]30 Aug, *Lond Gaz.* [57]11 Aug, *Lond Gaz.* [58]24 Dec, *Lond Gaz.* [59]27 June, *Lond Gaz.* [60]14 July, *Lond Gaz.* [61]10 Nov, *Lond Gaz.* [62]Authority not found. [63]18 Mar, *Lond Gaz.* [64]19 Jan, *Lond Gaz.* [65]8 Aug, Part Dist, Instr. [66]24 Apr, *Lond Gaz.* [67]26 Apr, *Lond Gaz.* [68]Lic min later in year after *Lond Gaz* 13 Sept. [69]23 Aug, reported in *Parl Papers* 1897, LXVII, Pt VI, 174. [70]20 Feb, *Lond Gaz.* [71]1 Oct, LGBO 54400. [72]1 Apr, MHealthO 89460. [73]13 Apr, *Lond Gaz.* [74]6 Nov, *Lond Gaz.* [75]28 Mar, *Lond Gaz.* [76]5 Jan (lic min, *Lond Gaz* 18 Oct 1968). [77]7 Jan, *Lond Gaz.* [78]Lic min later in year after *Lond Gaz* 13 Sept. [79]19 Mar, *Lond Gaz.* [80]27 July, *Lond Gaz.* [81]6 July, *Lond Gaz.* [82]16 July, *Lond Gaz.* [83]23 Dec, *Lond Gaz.* [84]29 Nov, *Lond Gaz.* [85]Hasted places the par in Milton Hd, Kilburne in Isle of Sheppey Lbty. [86]Authority not found. [87]30 May, *Lond Gaz.* [88]25 Mar, LGBO 18152. [89]13 June, *Lond Gaz.* [90]11 May, *Lond Gaz.* [91]16 Sept, *Lond Gaz.* [92]2 Nov, *Lond Gaz.* [93]1 Apr, LGBO 37403. [94]24 Jan, *Lond Gaz.* [95]19 Apr, *Lond Gaz.* [96]13 Dec, *Lond Gaz.* [97]4 Sept, *Lond Gaz.* [98]15 June, *Lond Gaz.* [99]PC QAB, refounded 31 Jan 1868, *Lond Gaz.* [100]28 Sept, *Lond Gaz.* [101]4 Feb, *Lond Gaz.* [102]1 Oct, *Lond Gaz.* [103]9 Nov, 3 & 4 Geo. V, *c* cxliv. [104]29 Mar, *Lond Gaz.* [105]24 Mar, LGBO 20931. [106]25 Aug, *Lond Gaz.* [107]Authority not found. [108]2 Mar, *Lond Gaz.* [109]10 May, *Lond Gaz.* [110]Hasted, V, 590. [111]29 Oct, *Lond Gaz.* [112]17 May, reported in *Parl Papers* 1890-91, LXI, 55. [113]1 Dec (*Lond Gaz* 30 Nov). [114]1 Apr, MHousLGO 4842. [115]30 Oct, *Lond Gaz.* [116]26 July, *Lond Gaz.* [117]7 Dec, *Lond Gaz.* [118]1 Mar, *Lond Gaz.* [119]27 Sept, *Lond Gaz.* [120]Presumed incl in PLU when became sep CP; not orig rated in the PLU. [121]8 Nov, *Lond Gaz.* [122]57 & 57 Vict., *c* 58 and Co Council NamingO. [123]21 June, *Lond Gaz.* [124]9 Dec, *Lond Gaz.* [125]PC QAB 1842, refounded 8 Aug 1843, *Lond Gaz.* [126]5 Feb, *Lond Gaz.* [127]31 Dec, *Lond Gaz.* [128]15 July, *Lond Gaz.* [129]22 May, *Lond Gaz.* [130]27 Feb, *Lond Gaz.* [131]29 Sept (lic min, *Lond Gaz* 13 Sept). [132]PC QAB 1832, refounded 2 Aug 1864, *Lond Gaz.* [133]8 Feb, *Lond Gaz.* [134]7 May, *Lond Gaz.* [135]27 Apr, *Lond Gaz.* [136]18 May, *Lond Gaz.* [137]15 Sept, *Lond Gaz.* [138]13 May, *Lond Gaz.* [139]13 Aug, *Lond Gaz.* [140]30 Sept, LGBO 31658. [141]9 Nov, LGB ProvO 1128. [142]26 Mar, LGBO 33921. [143]22 Dec (*Lond Gaz* 17 Dec). [144]24 Mar, LGBO 22337. [145]But an OC in 1884 says this par prev not in a RDn. [146]30 Sept, 58 & 59 Vict., *c* lxxvi. [147]9 Nov, LGB ProvO 1626. [148]26 Mar, LGBO 35274. [149]1 Apr, LGBO 58189. [150]Authority not found. [151]24 May, *Lond Gaz.* [152]10 Apr, *Lond Gaz.* [153]11 Oct, *Lond Gaz.* [154]7 Feb, reported in *Parl Papers* 1890-91, LXI, 52. [155]Hasted, XI, 240. [156]30 June, reported in *Parl Papers* 1872, XLVI, 19. [157]15 Sept, reported in *Parl Papers* 1890-91, LXI, 57. [158]Hasted, XI, 271-72. [159]11 Feb, *Lond Gaz.* [160]Hasted, XI, 211. [161]Hasted, XI, 272-73. [162]Hasted, XI, 273. [163]1 Jan, 20 Vict., *c* 19. [164]25 Mar, LGBO 18153. [165]21 Mar, *Lond Gaz.* [166]9 Nov, *Lond Gaz.* [167]14 Aug, *Lond Gaz.* [168]1 June (*Lond Gaz* 31 May). [169]24 Mar, LGBO 20632. [170]10 Aug, *Lond Gaz.* [171]6 Mar, *Lond Gaz.* [172]13 Mar (lic min, *Lond Gaz* 24 Feb). [173]23 June, reported in *Parl Papers* 1872, XLVI, 22. [174]1 Apr, MHousLGO 34744. [175]Year vac (*Lond Gaz* 12 Aug 1927). [176]3 Dec, *Lond Gaz.* [177]PC QAB. [178]1 Apr, MHousLGO 6523. [179]24 Feb, *Lond Gaz.* [180]13 Sept, *Lond Gaz.* [181]22 Sept, *Lond Gaz.* [182]26 Mar, LGBO 33921. [183]18 Dec, *Lond Gaz.* [184]1 July (*Lond Gaz* 30 June). [185]4 Nov, *Lond Gaz.* [186]2 July, *Lond Gaz.* [187]12 Nov, *Lond Gaz.* [188]8 Jan, *Lond Gaz.* [189]1 Dec (*Lond Gaz* 27 Nov). [190]62 & 63 Vict., *c* 14. [191]11 July, Part Dist, Instr CBC and Bp Roch. [192]30 Sept, LGBO 31633. [193]1 Oct, LGBO 49866. [194]15 May, *Lond Gaz.* [195]PC QAB refounded 22 Oct 1852, *Lond Gaz.* [196]22 Oct, *Lond Gaz.* [197]23 Feb, *Lond Gaz.* [198]19 Feb (lic min, *Lond Gaz* 5 Feb). [199]15 July (lic min, *Lond Gaz* 27 May 1954). [200]17 May, reported in *Parl Papers* 1890-91, LXI, 54. [201]5 Aug, *Lond Gaz.* [202]9 Aug, *Lond Gaz.* [203]25 Mar, *Lond Gaz.* [204]31

Jan, *Lond Gaz.* [205] 25 Mar, LGBO 19009. [206] 23 Aug, *Lond Gaz.* [207] 8 Apr, *Lond Gaz.* [208] PC QAB, refounded 29 June 1852, *Lond Gaz.* [209] 12 Jan, *Lond Gaz.* [210] 7 July (lic min, *Lond Gaz* 11 Nov 1956). [211] PC QAB, refounded 7 Oct 1844, Part Dist, Instr CBC and Bp Roch. [212] 28 Oct, *Lond Gaz.* [213] 1 Apr, MHealthO 10334. [214] Apptd day, LGBO 31823. [215] 20 Mar, *Lond Gaz.* [216] 1 Apr, MHousLGO 9415. [217] 10 Mar, *Lond Gaz.* [218] Year vac (*Lond Gaz* 8 Mar 1949). [219] 1 Apr, MHousLGO 10215. [220] Authority not found. [221] 1 July (*Lond Gaz* 4 June). [222] 31 Aug, *Lond Gaz.* [223] 24 Mar, LGBO 20633. [224] 12 Apr, Part Dist, Instr CBC. [225] 1 Apr, MHousLGO 10523. [226] Authority not found. [227] 18 Oct, *Lond Gaz.* [228] 20 Dec, reported in *Parl Papers* 1872, LXI, 22. [229] 20 Apr, *Lond Gaz.* [230] 2 Apr, *Lond Gaz.* [231] 24 July, *Lond Gaz.* [232] 13 Aug, *Lond Gaz.* [233] 14 Mar (consecr church, *Lond Gaz* 4 May 1951). [234] 1 July (*Lond Gaz* 6 Oct). [235] 13 Mar, *Lond Gaz.* [236] 29 Apr, *Lond Gaz.* [237] 20 Nov (lic min, *Lond Gaz* 10 Aug). [238] 9 Apr, *Lond Gaz.* [239] 20 Nov, reported in *Parl Papers* 1890-91, LXI, 55. [240] 1 Oct, The Kent (Sidcup) O, 1925. [241] Kilburne places the par ent in Eastry Hd, Hasted and later authorities, in both Hds as shown. [242] 4 July, *Lond Gaz.* [243] 11 Oct, Part Dist, Instr CBC. [244] 22 Dec, *Lond Gaz.* [245] 18 Apr, *Lond Gaz.* [246] 3 Geo. II, *c* 33. [247] Hasted, IV, 358-59. [248] 4 July, *Lond Gaz.* [249] 9 Nov, The Dover (Extension) 0, 1903. [250] 9 Nov, 11 & 12 Geo. V, *c* xlvii. [251] 1 Apr, 14 & 15 Geo. V, *c* xxxviii. [252] 21 July, *Lond Gaz.* [253] 18 Aug, *Lond Gaz.* [254] 4 June, *Lond Gaz.* [255] 28 Aug, *Lond Gaz.* [256] 15 Aug, *Lond Gaz.* [257] 4 Aug, *Lond Gaz.* [258] 1 Oct, LGBO 52046. [259] 25 Mar, LGBO 19013. [260] 1 Apr, MHousLGO 629. [261] 10 Feb, *Lond Gaz.* [262] Hasted places the par in Milton Hd, others in Isle of Sheppey Lbty. [263] 1 Apr, MHousLGO 34431. [264] 26 Oct, *Lond Gaz.* [265] 30 Jan, reported in *Parl Papers* 1872, XLVI, 20. [266] Kilburne says the par ent in Eastry Hd. [267] 1 Apr (*Lond Gaz* 3 Mar). [268] Apptd day, LGBO 31657. [269] Kilburne say the par pt Somerden Hd, pt Westerham Hd. [270] Authority not found. [271] According to Hasted. [272] 25 Mar, LGBO 19010. [273] 1 Apr, MHousLGO 6503. [274] 25 Mar, LGBO 19008. [275] 6 July, Part Dist, Instr Bp London and Eccl Commissioners. [276] 18 Nov, Instr Eccl Commissioners and Bp Roch. [277] 20 July, Instr Eccl Commissioners and Bp Roch. [278] 11 July, *Lond Gaz.* [279] 26 Feb, *Lond Gaz.* [280] 3 July, *Lond Gaz.* [281] 13 Nov, *Lond Gaz.* [282] 9 Feb, *Lond Gaz.* [283] 1 May, *Lond Gaz.* [284] 12 Oct, *Lond Gaz.* [285] 20 Oct, *Lond Gaz.* [286] 21 Nov, *Lond Gaz.* [287] 1 Dec (*Lond Gaz* 25 Nov). [288] 1 Apr, MHousLGO 8270. [289] 11 Nov, *Lond Gaz.* [290] 29 Jan, *Lond Gaz.* [291] 24 Mar, LGBO 20929. [292] PC QAB, refounded 28 Feb 1843, *Lond Gaz.* [293] 1 May (*Lond Gaz* 16 Apr). [294] Apptd day, LGBO 31634. [295] 31 Oct, *Lond Gaz.* [296] PC QAB, refounded 28 Jan 1851, Part Dist, Instr CBC and Archbp Canterb. [297] 21 Aug, *Lond Gaz.* [298] 7 July, reported in *Parl Papers* 1890-91, LXI, 55. [299] 18 July, *Lond Gaz.* [300] 6 Aug, Instr Archbp Canterb and Eccl Commissioners. [301] 20 May, *Lond Gaz.* [302] Year vac (*Lond Gaz* 16 May 1930). [303] 13 Feb, *Lond Gaz.* [304] 20 Dec, Instr Bp London. [305] 10 Dec, Instr Eccl Commissioners, Bp Roch and Bp Winch. [306] 2 Dec, *Lond Gaz.* [307] 25 Feb, *Lond Gaz.* [308] Apptd day, LGBO 31985. [309] Hasted, III, 558-59. [310] 30 Sept, LGBO 31648. [311] 1 July (*Lond Gaz* 30 June). [312] 1 Apr, 3 & 4 Geo. V, *c* lxxiii. [313] 1 Apr, LGBO 48727. [314] 1 Oct, LGBO 60249. [315] 1 Apr, 18 & 19 Geo. V, *c* lx. [316] 11 June (lic min, *Lond Gaz* 25 May). [317] 30 Oct (lic min, *Lond Gaz* 12 Oct). [318] Hasted, IX, 239-40. [319] 1 Mar (*Lond Gaz* 20 Feb). [320] 1 Apr, LGBO 62747. [321] 20 Aug, *Lond Gaz.* [322] 16 Mar, *Lond Gaz.* [323] 4 Jan, *Lond Gaz.* [324] 19 Dec, *Lond Gaz.* [325] 13 Jan, *Lond Gaz.* [326] 17 Oct, *Lond Gaz.* [327] PC QAB, refounded 15 Oct 1861, *Lond Gaz.* [328] 21 May, *Lond Gaz.* [329] 12 Aug, *Lond Gaz.* [330] 17 Apr, *Lond Gaz.* [331] 24 June, *Lond Gaz.* [332] 1 Oct, MHealthO 72775. [333] 1 Apr, MHous LGO 5938. [334] 24 Mar, LGBO 23642. [335] 6 May, *Lond Gaz.* [336] Kilburne says the par pt in Bircholt Barony, pt in Bircholt Franchise. [337] 24 Mar, LGBO 23643. [338] 1 Dec, *Lond Gaz.* [339] 25 Mar, LGBO 18118. [340] 25 June, *Lond Gaz.* [341] 19 July, *Lond Gaz.* [342] 23 Nov, *Lond Gaz.* [343] 24 Mar, LGBO 21674. [344] 1 Apr, LGBO 40438. [345] 12 Jan, Part Dist, Instr CBC. [346] 5 June, *Lond Gaz.* [347] Apptd day, LGBO 31781. [348] Authority not found. [349] 23 Sept, Instr Archbp Canterb. [350] 25 Mar, LGBO 19012. [351] 27 May, *Lond Gaz.* [352] 31 Jan, reported in *Parl Papers* 1872, XLVI, 18. [353] 25 Mar, LGBO 19009. [354] 30 Sept, LGBO 27315. [355] 24 Mar, LGBO 22337. [356] 1 Nov (*Lond Gaz* 30 Oct). [357] 7 Mar, reported in *Parl Papers* 1890-91, LXI, 57. [358] According to Kilburne. [359] 5 Nov, *Lond Gaz.* [360] 4 Mar, *Lond Gaz.* [361] 1 Aug, The West Kingsdown (Name of Par) O, 1948. [362] First appearance *Clergy List.* [363] 10 Feb, *Lond Gaz.* [364] 1 Apr, SI 1968/2020. [365] 21 Sept, *Lond Gaz.* [366] 1 Jan (*Lond Gaz* 2 Dec 1970). [367] 26 Nov, Instr Eccl Commissioners and Bp London. [368] 11 Jan, *Lond Gaz.* [369] 18 May (lic min, *Lond Gaz* 29 Feb). [370] 10 Oct, *Lond Gaz.* [371] 1 Aug, *Lond Gaz.* [372] 30 June, *Lond Gaz.* [373] 1 Mar, The Leysdown-on-Sea (Name of Par) O, 1949. [374] 25 Mar, LGBO 14186. [375] 1 Mar (*Lond Gaz* 24 Feb). [376] 7 Feb, reported in *Parl Papers* 1872, XLVI, 20. [377] 25 Mar, LGBO 19011. [378] 28 Nov, *Lond Gaz.* [379] 30 Mar, *Lond Gaz.* [380] 10 Feb, *Lond Gaz.* [381] Year vac (*Lond Gaz* 16 Dec 1932). [382] 20 July, *Lond Gaz.* [383] 21 Feb, *Lond Gaz.* [384] 1 June, *Lond Gaz.* [385] 16 Apr, *Lond Gaz.* [386] 19 Apr, MHousLG Decl. [387] Hasted, X, 351. [388] 9 Nov, 57 & 58 Vict., *c* cxxiv. [389] 14 May, *Lond Gaz.* [390] 1 Apr, MHousLGO 34123. [391] 24 Mar, LGBO 21673. [392] 1 Oct, MHousLG Decl. [393] 9 Jan, *Lond Gaz.* [394] 28 July, *Lond Gaz.* [395] 25 Jan, LGBO 7480. [396] 16 Sept, *Lond Gaz.* [397] According to Hasted. [398] 9 Nov, 2 & 3 Geo. V, *c* cxxiii. [399] 14 Feb, *Lond Gaz.* [400] 1 Oct, LGBO 41388. [401] 29 Jan, reported in *Parl Papers* 1897, LXVII, Pt VI, 74. [402] 24 Mar, LGBO 20932. [403] 21 May, reported in *Parl Papers* 1872, XLVI, 19. [404] 19 May, *Lond Gaz.* [405] 21 Dec, *Lond Gaz.* [406] Note cancelled. [407] 16 Oct, *Lond Gaz.* [408] 17 Oct, reported in *Parl Papers* 1890-91, LXI, 52. [409] 25 May. *Lond Gaz.* [410] 1 Jan, *Lond Gaz.* [411] *Liber*

Regis, 24. [412]3 Feb, *Lond Gaz.* [413]17 Apr, reported in *Parl Papers* 1872, XLVI, 18. [414]13 Sept, reported in *Parl Papers* 1872, XLVI, 20. [415]2 May, *Lond Gaz.* [416]27 May, Part Dist, Instr Eccl Commissioners and Bp Roch. [417]14 Apr, *Lond Gaz.* [418]11 June, *Lond Gaz.* [419]1 Dec (*Lond Gaz* 27 Nov). [420]19 July, *Lond Gaz.* [421]9 Mar, *Lond Gaz.* [422]30 Jan, *Lond Gaz.* [423]1 Apr, LGBO 35396. [424]Authority not found. [425]1 Oct, 12 & 13 Geo. V, *c* lxxxv. [426]14 June, Instr. [427]15 Mar, *Lond Gaz.* [428]30 Sept, LGBO 31663. [429]1 Jan (*Lond Gaz* 31 Dec 1971). [430]9 Nov (consecr church, *Lond Gaz* 11 Feb 1955). [431]30 Sept, LGBO 31627. [432]12 Apr, *Lond Gaz.* [433]18 Feb, *Lond Gaz.* [434]Authority not found. [435]1 Apr, LGBO 47729. [436]26 Mar, LGBO 33741. [437]Hasted, X, 250-52. [438]6 Aug, reported in *Parl Papers* 1890-91, LXI, 53. [439]PC QAB, refounded 15 Oct 1861, *Lond Gaz.* [440]PC QAB, refounded 2 Aug 1864. [441]14 Aug, reported in *Parl Papers* 1872, XLVI, 19. [442]9 July, *Lond Gaz.* [443]PC QAB, refounded 7 Oct 1844, Part Dist, Instr CBC. [444]22 May, *Lond Gaz.* [445]1 Nov (*Lond Gaz* 30 Oct). [446]Apptd day, LGBO 31656. [447]3 Mar, *Lond Gaz.* [448]4 Apr, *Lond Gaz.* [449]7 Nov, *Lond Gaz.* [450]Apptd day, LGBO 31656. [451]9 Nov, 63 & 64 Vict., *c* clxxix. [452]1 Apr, MHousLGO 33911. [453]Year lic min (*Lond Gaz* 1 Oct 1957). [454]7 Feb, *Lond Gaz.* [455]1 July (*Lond Gaz* 8 June). [456]29 June, *Lond Gaz.* [457]15 Jan, *Lond Gaz.* [458]17 Apr, reported in *Parl Papers* 1872, XLVI, 18. [459]6 Feb, reported in *Parl Papers* 1890-91, LXI, 55. [460]12 July, *Lond Gaz.* [461]1 Jan, *Lond Gaz* (OC 2 May 1832). [462]PC QAB, refounded 5 Apr 1863, *Lond Gaz.* [463]1 Apr, LGBO 66912. [464]9 Nov, 57 & 58 Vict., *c* cxxiv. [465]7 Mar, *Lond Gaz.* [466]18 Jan, *Lond Gaz.* [467]25 July, *Lond Gaz.* [468]12 Aug, *Lond Gaz.* [469]1 Jan, *Lond Gaz.* [470]1 Oct, LGBO 44211. [471]9 Nov, 57 & 58 Vict., *c* cxxiv. [472]Authority not found. [473]16 Aug, *Lond Gaz.* [474]4 Mar, MHousLG Decl. [475]8 Oct, *Lond Gaz.* [476]26 Aug, *Lond Gaz.* [477]11 Mar, *Lond Gaz.* [478]5 Feb, *Lond Gaz.* [479]2 & 3 Edw. VI [chapter not found]. [480]11 Mar, SI 1964/277. [481]11 June, SI 1945/701.

LONDON

THE CITY OF LONDON, LONDON ADMINISTRATIVE COUNTY AND GREATER LONDON

[1]7 Edw. VII, *c* cxl. [2]22 Feb, *Lond Gaz.* [3]2 Feb, *Lond Gaz.* [4]22 Chas. II, *c* 11. [5]4 Aug, *Lond Gaz.*
[1]7 Edw. VII, *c* cxl. [2]22 Feb, *Lond Gaz.* [3]2 Feb, *Lond Gaz.* [4]22 Chas. II, *c* 11. [5]4 Aug, *Lond Gaz.* [6]19 May, *Lond Gaz.* [7]4 Nov, *Lond Gaz.* [8]27 Oct, *Lond Gaz.* [9]23 Apr, *Lond Gaz.* [10]*VCH London*, 400. [11]Authority not found. [12]4 Mar, *Lond Gaz.* [13]32 & 33 Vict., *c* lxvii. [14]1 Jan, 20 Vict., *c* 61. [15]*VCH London*, 401. [16]11 Oct, *Lond Gaz.* [17]3 July, *Lond Gaz.* [18]14 Aug, *Lond Gaz.* [19]15 Apr, *Lond Gaz.* [20]62 & 63 Vict., *c* 14. [21]9 Geo. I, [chapter not found]. [22]6 Geo. III, *c* 100. [23]Letters patent 4 Eliz. I, cited *VCH London*, 431. [24]Note cancelled. [25]2 & 3 Vict., *c* cvii. [26]Henry Andrade Harben, *A Dictionary of London* (hereafter, Harben), 49. [27]25 Oct, *Lond Gaz.* [28]21 June, *Lond Gaz.* [29]10 Aug, *Lond Gaz.* [30]5 & 6 Vict., *c* ci. [31]22 Chas. II, *c* 11. [32]8 July, *Lond Gaz.* [33]29 & 30 Vict., *c* 113. [34]Harben, 590. [35]19 May, *Lond Gaz.* [36]9 Nov, *Lond Gaz.* [37]6 May, *Lond Gaz.* [38]21 Geo. III, *c* 71. [39]4 Mar, *Lond Gaz.* [40]*VCH London*, 403. [41]23 Apr, *Lond Gaz.* [42]6 Geo. II, [chapter not found]. [43]11 Jan, *Lond Gaz.* [44]23 Nov, *Lond Gaz.* [45]*VCH London*, 401. [46]*VCH London*, 401. [47]10 Aug, *Lond Gaz.* [48]4 May, *Lond Gaz.* [49]1 Wm. IV, *c* iii. [50]17 Dec, *Lond Gaz.* [51]27 May, *Lond Gaz.* [52]15 Apr, *Lond Gaz.* [53]18 July, *Lond Gaz.* [54]1 Oct, *Lond Gaz.* [55]Authority not found. [56]13 Nov, *Lond Gaz.* [57]18 May, *Lond Gaz.* [58]22 Aug, *Lond Gaz.* [59]13 Nov, *Lond Gaz.* [60]Authority not found. [61]22 Aug, *Lond Gaz.* [62]Note cancelled. [63]Harben, 524. [64]Note cancelled. [65]1 Oct, LGBO 32663. [66]Registers from 1619. [67]51 & 52 Vict., *c* 41. [68]11 & 12 Eliz. II, *c* 33. [69]Series of orders, prob ranging over several years after statutory authority of 62 & 63 Vict., *c* 14. [70]10 Aug, SI 1949/1440. [71]19 Jan, SI 1955/20. [72]1 Apr, The Borough of Poplar (Union of Parishes) Scheme, 1907. [73]1 Apr, 62 & 63 Vict., *c* 14. [74]31 Mar, MHealthO 74156. [75]1 Apr, LGBO 63338. [76]1 Apr, The Borough of Woolwich (Union of Parishes) Scheme, 1903. [77]1 Apr, 11 & 12 Geo. V, *c* xxviii. [78]31 Mar, MHealthO 74156. [79]31 Mar, MHealthO 74153. [80]31 Mar, 21 & 22 Geo. V, *c* lix. [81]1 Apr, The Cos of London and Middx (Hackney and Tottenham) O, 1907. [82]15 Feb, SI 1955/165. [83]1 Oct, LGBO 32663. [84]1 Apr, *Lond Gaz* (OC 23 June 1904). [85]1 Apr, LGBO 66936. [86]1 Apr, MHealthO 71715. [87]31 Mar, MHealthO 74155. [88]1 Apr, The Borough of Bermondsey (Union of Parishes) Scheme, 1903. [89]1 Oct, LGBO 32663. [90]15 June, The Borough of Stepney (Tower of London) Scheme, 1901. [91]24 Mar, LGBO 26577. [92]26 Mar, LGBO 32683. [93]5 Jan, SI 1971/2112. [94]12 Apr, SI 1973/605. [95]1 Apr, SI 1968/2020. [96]1 Apr, MHousLGO 34497. [97]1 Apr, MHousLGO 40507. [98]1 Apr, MHousLGO 47801. [99]5 Jan, SI 1971/2114. [100]5 Jan, SI 1971/2113. [101]1 Apr, The Counties of London and Surrey (Wandsworth and Mitcham) O, 1903.

MIDDLESEX

[1]11 & 12 Eliz. II, *c* 33. [2]25 June, LGBO 31108. [3]1 Oct, LGBO 32900. [4]1 Apr, MHealthO 78096. [5]27 June, *Lond Gaz.* [6]14 May, *Lond Gaz.* [7]2 Apr, *Lond Gaz.* [8]16 July, *Lond Gaz.* [9]25 Aug, *Lond Gaz.* [10]27 Nov, *Lond Gaz.* [11]24 Sept, *Lond Gaz.* [12]1 May, *Lond Gaz.* [13]30 Nov, *Lond Gaz.* [14]22 Mar, *Lond Gaz.* [15]31 Oct, *Lond Gaz.* [16]12 Apr, *Lond Gaz.* [17]26 Oct, *Lond Gaz.* [18]8 June, *Lond Gaz.* [19]25 Feb, *Lond Gaz.* [20]14 Aug, *Lond Gaz.* [21]30 Aug, *Lond Gaz.* [22]7 May, *Lond Gaz.* [23]1 Dec, *Lond Gaz.* [24]4 Nov, *Lond Gaz.* [25]2 Feb, *Lond Gaz.* [26]13 June, Part Dist, Instr CBC. [27]4 Dec, *Lond Gaz.* [28]15 July, *Lond Gaz.* [29]12 Aug, *Lond Gaz.* [30]*VCH Middx* III, 13. [31]11 Jan, reported in *Parl Papers* 1872, XLVI, 20. [32]3 May, *Lond Gaz.* [33]3 July, *Lond Gaz.* [34]1

Nov (*Lond Gaz* 26 Oct). [35]23 June, *Lond Gaz.* [36]25 Feb, *Lond Gaz.* [37]14 Sept, *Lond Gaz.* [38]29 May, *Lond Gaz.* [39]5 Feb, *Lond Gaz.* [40]28 Mar, *Lond Gaz.* [41]6 May, *Lond Gaz.* [42]3 Feb, *Lond Gaz.* [43]62 & 63 Vict., *c* 14. [44]16 Aug, *Lond Gaz.* [45]16 Geo. II, *c* 28. [46]5 Sept, *Lond Gaz.* [47]6 Dec, *Lond Gaz.* [48]31 Aug, *Lond Gaz.* [49]22 Nov, *Lond Gaz.* [50]20 May, *Lond Gaz.* [51]27 Oct, *Lond Gaz.* [52]20 June, *Lond Gaz.* [53]10 June, *Lond Gaz.* [54]13 Sept, *Lond Gaz.* [55]31 Mar, *Lond Gaz.* [56]3 June, *Lond Gaz.* [57]1 Dec, *Lond Gaz.* [58]23 Nov, *Lond Gaz.* [59]9 Dec, *Lond Gaz.* [60]29 Nov, *Lond Gaz.* [61]22 Dec, *Lond Gaz.* [62]4 Apr, *Lond Gaz.* [63]15 Sept, *Lond Gaz.* [64]10 July, *Lond Gaz.* [65]Effective later in year after *Lond Gaz* (8 May). [66]Consecr 1731, one of 'fifty new' churches. [67]25 Nov, *Lond Gaz.* [68]7 Mar, *Lond Gaz.* [69]23 Aug, *Lond Gaz.* [70]1 July, *Lond Gaz.* [71]23 Oct, *Lond Gaz.* [72]Consecr 1719. [73]19 July, *Lond Gaz.* [74]17 July, *Lond Gaz.* [75]18 Apr, *Lond Gaz.* [76]PC QAB but *VCH Middx* III, 230 says 1330s. [77]19 Jan, *Lond Gaz.* [78]Apptd day, 57 & 58 Vict., *c* 58 and Co Council Naming O. [79]1 Apr, 1 & 2 Geo. V, *c* cxii. [80]18 Nov, *Lond Gaz.* [81]12 July, *Lond Gaz.* [82]20 Nov, *Lond Gaz.* [83]7 Sept, *Lond Gaz.* [84]14 June, *Lond Gaz.* [85]22 June, *Lond Gaz.* [86]22 Aug, *Lond Gaz.* [87]13 Mar, *Lond Gaz.* [88]28 June, *Lond Gaz.* [89]27 Feb, *Lond Gaz.* [90]29 June, *Lond Gaz.* [91]13 July, *Lond Gaz.* [92]13 Aug, *Lond Gaz.* [93]15 Mar, *Lond Gaz.* [94]1 Jan (*Lond Gaz* 29 Dec 1972). [95]6 Aug, *Lond Gaz.* [96]11 July, *Lond Gaz.* [97]31 Jan, *Lond Gaz.* [98]3 Aug, *Lond Gaz.* [99]10 May, *Lond Gaz.* [100]1 Jan (*Lond Gaz* 31 Dec 1971). [101]21 Dec, *Lond Gaz.* [102]19 Mar, *Lond Gaz.* [103]8 Dec, *Lond Gaz.* [104]16 Jan, *Lond Gaz.* [105]26 Dec, *Lond Gaz.* [106]30 June, *Lond Gaz.* [107]19 Oct, *Lond Gaz.* [108]17 Jan, *Lond Gaz.* [109]9 Jan, *Lond Gaz.* [110]Year vac (*Lond Gaz* 9 Dec 1955). [111]28 July, *Lond Gaz.* [112]8 Mar, *Lond Gaz.* [113]9 Jan, *Lond Gaz* (OC 26 Dec 1851). [114]22 June, *Lond Gaz.* [115]19 May, *Lond Gaz.* [116]1 Nov (*Lond Gaz* 28 Oct). [117]9 Jan, *Lond Gaz* (OC 26 Dec 1851). [118]1 Jan, 20 Vict., *c* 19. [119]Information supplied by Gtr London RO. [120]8 Aug, *Lond Gaz.* [121]Effective vac (between Mar-July) after *Lond Gaz* 18 Mar. [122]First appearance *Clergy List*; authority not found. [123]24 June, *Lond Gaz.* [124]2 Dec, *Lond Gaz.* [125]4 July, *Lond Gaz.* [126]20 Feb, *Lond Gaz.* [127]18 Dec (lic min, *Lond Gaz* 20 Nov). [128]PC QAB. [129]27 Jan, *Lond Gaz.* [130]1 Apr (*Lond Gaz* 13 Mar). [131]12 Nov, *Lond Gaz.* [132]30 Oct, *Lond Gaz.* [133]11 Sept, *Lond Gaz.* [134]23 Dec, LGBO 8931. [135]29 Apr, *Lond Gaz.* [136]9 Aug, *Lond Gaz.* [137]28 Aug, *Lond Gaz.* [138]31 July, *Lond Gaz.* [139]26 Nov, *Lond Gaz.* [140]17 May, *Lond Gaz.* [141]6 Oct, *Lond Gaz.* [142]13 Nov, *Lond Gaz.* [143]15 Feb, *Lond Gaz.* [144]7 Nov, *Lond Gaz.* [145]25 May, *Lond Gaz.* [146]In 1st half of the year after *Lond Gaz* 3 Jan. [147]18 July, *Lond Gaz.* [148]2 Jan, *Lond Gaz.* [149]6 Feb, *Lond Gaz.* [150]Samuel Lewis, *A Topographical Dictionary of England*, I (under 'Clerkenwell'). [151]13 Jan, *Lond Gaz* (OC 19 Mar 1928). [152]12 Mar, *Lond Gaz.* [153]Year vac (*Lond Gaz* 14 May 1935). [154]2 June, *Lond Gaz.* [155]24 Mar, *Lond Gaz.* [156]4 June, *Lond Gaz.* [157]19 July (lic min, *Lond Gaz* 3 July). [158]*VCH Middx* III, 170-71. [159]25 Mar, 45 & 46 Vict., *c* 58. [160]1 Apr, LGBO 32938. [161]31 Mar, MHealthO 73109. [162]1 Apr, MHealthO 92516. [163]9 Sept, *Lond Gaz.* [164]30 Dec, reported in *Parl Papers* 1890-91, LXI, 56. [165]18 May, *Lond Gaz.* [166]22 July, *Lond Gaz.* [167]15 Aug, *Lond Gaz.* [168]25 Mar, *Lond Gaz.* [169]3 Sept, *Lond Gaz.* [170]5 Mar, *Lond Gaz.* [171]PC QAB, refounded 25 Apr 1848, *Lond Gaz.* [172]25 Apr, *Lond Gaz.* [173]9 July, *Lond Gaz.* [174]11 June, *Lond Gaz.* [175]1 Aug, *Lond Gaz.* [176]1 Apr, MHealthO 108895. [177]*VCH Middx* III, 202. [178]1 Oct, 16 & 17 Geo. V, *c* lxii. [179]MHealth ProvO Confirmation (Ealing Extension) Act, 1937. [180]18 & 19 Geo. V, *c* xii. [181]30 Jan, *Lond Gaz.* [182]29 Feb, *Lond Gaz.* [183]7 Aug, *Lond Gaz.* [184]12 Oct, *Lond Gaz.* [185]27 July, *Lond Gaz.* [186]10 Aug, *Lond Gaz.* [187]21 Mar, *Lond Gaz.* [188]4 Aug, *Lond Gaz.* [189]1 Nov (lic min, *Lond Gaz* 5 Sept). [190]*VCH Middx* IV, 163. [191]1 Apr, The Hendon UD Council Act, 1929. [192]30 Sept, LGBO 31425. [193]*VCH Middx* V, 130. [194]1 Apr, MHealthO 71702. [195]29 Aug, *Lond Gaz.* [196]13 Dec, *Lond Gaz.* [197]12 May, *Lond Gaz.* [198]18 Jan (lic min, *Lond Gaz* 4 May 1951). [199]30 May, *Lond Gaz.* [200]Built 1640, sep par 1645, confirmed in 1660 (12 Chas. II, *c* 37). [201]9 July, *Lond Gaz.* [202]11 June, SI 1945/701. [203]29 & 30 Vict., *c* 113. [204]11 Oct (lic min, *Lond Gaz* 18 May 1954). [205]7 June, *Lond Gaz.* [206]Authority not found. [207]17 Dec, *Lond Gaz.* [208]*VCH Middx* V, 260, 267. [209]1 Apr, MHealthO 69066. [210]Apptd day, 57 & 58 Vict., *c* 58. [211]17 Geo. III, *c* 17; see also *VCH Middx* V, 130. [212]PC QAB 1832, refounded 22 July 1834, *Lond Gaz.* [213]19 Aug, *Lond Gaz.* [214]12 Dec, *Lond Gaz.* [215]Authority not found. [216]21 June, *Lond Gaz.* [217]5 Aug, *Lond Gaz.* [218]10 Sept (lic min, *Lond Gaz* 3 Aug). [219]Authority not found. [220]1 Apr, The Middx (Feltham and Sunbury on Thame UDs) Confirmation O, 1936. [221]17 Nov, *Lond Gaz.* [222]1 Apr, SI 1937/361. [223]19 Dec, *Lond Gaz.* [224]31 May, *Lond Gaz.* [225]28 Sept, *Lond Gaz.* [226]13 Oct, *Lond Gaz.* [227]16 Dec, *Lond Gaz.* [228]11 Jan, *Lond Gaz.* [229]4 Jan, *Lond Gaz.* [230]7 Feb, *Lond Gaz.* [231]13 Feb, *Lond Gaz.* [232]11 Mar, *Lond Gaz.* [233]2 Sept, *Lond Gaz.* [234]31 Dec, *Lond Gaz.* [235]Year vac (*Lond Gaz* 30 May 1961). [236]PC QAB 1860, refounded 2 Aug 1864, *Lond Gaz.* [237]Prob at Dissolution. [238]5 Sept, *Lond Gaz.* [239]24 Jan, *Lond Gaz.* [240]1 June (*Lond Gaz* 2 May). [241]25 Dec, *Lond Gaz.* [242]15 Dec, *Lond Gaz.* [243]18 Oct, *Lond Gaz.* [244]13 Dec, *Lond Gaz.* [245]20 July, *Lond Gaz.* [246]26 May, *Lond Gaz.* [247]23 Jan, *Lond Gaz.* [248]Presumed incl in PLU when became sep CP; not orig rated in the PLU. [249]21 July, *Lond Gaz.* [250]2 July, *Lond Gaz.* [251]17 Feb, *Lond Gaz.* [252]Year vac (*Lond Gaz* 28 Apr 1933). [253]*VCH Middx* III, 206. [254]24 Mar, LGBO 20644. [255]25 Sept (lic min, *Lond Gaz* 30 June 1964). [256]16 Jan, *Lond Gaz* (OC 23 Dec 1845). [257]24 Dec, *Lond Gaz.* [258]26 Feb, *Lond Gaz.* [259]1 Oct, *Lond Gaz.* [260]*VCH Middx* V, 207. [261]*VCH Middx* V, 26. [262]10 Apr, *Lond Gaz.* [263]12 Feb, *Lond Gaz.* [264]6 Apr, *Lond Gaz.* [265]16 Apr, *Lond Gaz.* [266]8 Nov, *Lond Gaz.* [267]12 June, *Lond*

Gaz. [268]20 Aug, *Lond Gaz.* [269]23 Apr, *Lond Gaz.* [270]3 Dec, *Lond Gaz.* [271]10 Feb, *Lond Gaz.* [272]24 July, *Lond Gaz.* [273]*VCH Middx* V, 33. [274]15 Nov, Instr CBC and Bp London. [275]24 Oct, *Lond Gaz.* [276]3 Aug, *Lond Gaz.* [277]13 Jan, *Lond Gaz.* [278]11 Feb, *Lond Gaz.* [279]10 Mar, *Lond Gaz.* [280]15 June, *Lond Gaz.* [281]1 June, authority not found. [282]11 & 12 Vict., *c* 37. [283]11 Aug, *Lond Gaz.* [284]29 & 30 Vict., *c* 113 but *VCH Middx* II, 319 says 1831. [285]26 July, *Lond Gaz.* [286]The Middx (Feltham and Sunbury on Thames UDs) Confirmation O, 1936. [287]30 May, *Lond Gaz.* [288]1 Oct, LGBO 58598. [289]8 Aug, Instr CBC. [290]29 Mar, *Lond Gaz.* [291]30 July, *Lond Gaz.* [292]25 Oct, *Lond Gaz.* [293]25 Feb, *Lond Gaz.* [294]3 July (lic min, *Lond Gaz* 1 June). [295]22 Aug, *Lond Gaz.* [296]28 Sept (consec church, *Lond Gaz* 10 Oct 1950). [297]*VCH Middx* III, 237. [298]1 Apr, MHealthO 92516. [299]*VCH Middx* V, 267. [300]9 Feb, *Lond Gaz.* [301]*VCH Middx* III, 258. [302]13 June, *Lond Gaz.* [303]13 Nov (lic min, *Lond Gaz* 4 Nov). [304]First appearance *Crockford's Clerical Directory.* [305]PC QAB. [306]Apptd day, LGBO 31845. [307]1 Oct, LGBO 33399. [308]24 Sept, LGBO 44414. [309]PC QAB refounded 9 July 1845, *Lond Gaz.* [310]7 July, *Lond Gaz.* [311]Year lic min (*Lond Gaz* 7 June 1946). [312]22 May, *Lond Gaz.* [313]20 Dec, *Lond Gaz.* [314]25 June, *Lond Gaz.* [315]PC QAB 1725 but *VCH Middx* IV, 40 says 1770. [316]1 Oct, 16 & 17 Geo. V, *c* lix. [317]The Hendon UD Council Act, 1929. [318]27 Aug, *Lond Gaz.* [319]26 June, *Lond Gaz.* [320]1 Apr, MHealthO 71724. [321]30 Sept, LGBO 31372. [322]19 Dec, Part Dist, Instr CBC. [323]8 Feb, *Lond Gaz.* [324]13 Apr, *Lond Gaz.* [325]8 Nov, Part Dist, Instr CBC. [326]20 Oct, *Lond Gaz.* [327]*VCH Middx* IV, 88, 90. [328]1 Apr, LGBO 33467. [329]Authority not found. [330]Henry Andrade Harben, *A Dictionary of London* (hereafter, Harben), 590. [331]*VCH Middx* IV, 40. [332]PC QAB but *VCH Middx* IV, 40 says 1859. [333]4 Geo. III, *c* 39. [334]7 Apr, *Lond Gaz.* [335]8 Oct, *Lond Gaz.* [336]15 Apr, *Lond Gaz.* [337]27 Mar, *Lond Gaz.* [338]15 Oct, *Lond Gaz.* [339]26 Mar, LGBO 33601. [340]5 Jan, *Lond Gaz* (OC 16 Dec 1848). [341]19 May, *Lond Gaz.* [342]30 Apr, *Lond Gaz.* [343]16 Sept, *Lond Gaz.* [344]12 June (consecr church, *Lond Gaz* 5 May 1951). [345]Year vac (*Lond Gaz* 6 Aug 1937). [346]6 Mar, *Lond Gaz.* [347]7 Jan, *Lond Gaz.* [348]27 May, *Lond Gaz.* [349]23 May, *Lond Gaz.* [350]15 Nov, *Lond Gaz.* [351]23 Dec, *Lond Gaz.* [352]4 Mar, *Lond Gaz.* [353]14 Sept (consecr church, *Lond Gaz* 4 May 1951). [354]23 Feb, *Lond Gaz.* [355]7 May, *Lond Gaz.* [356]4 Jan, *Lond Gaz* (OC 21 Oct 1841). [357]13 July (lic min, *Lond Gaz* 3 July). [358]3 Geo. II, *c* 17. [359]21 Feb, *Lond Gaz.* [360]1 Nov (*Lond Gaz* 28 Oct). [361]1 Jan, 20 Vict., *c* 19. [362]Effective later in year after *Lond Gaz* 3 Aug. [363]1 Jan, *Lond Gaz* (OC 28 Dec 1866). [364]11 June, *Lond Gaz.* [365]Effective later in year after *Lond Gaz* 17 June. [366]29 Oct, *Lond Gaz.* [367]Authority not found. [368]29 Nov (intended in 1866, as per *Lond Gaz* 16 Nov 1866). [369]Authority not found. [370]*VCH Middx* V, 35. [371]1 Apr, *Lond Gaz.* [372]St Pancras Act, 1868. [373]23 June (lic min, *Lond Gaz* 4 June). [374]16 June, *Lond Gaz.* [375]24 Apr, Part Dist, Instr CBC. [376]17 Sept, *Lond Gaz.* [377]*VCH Middx* V, 271. [378]51 & 52 Vict., *c* 41. [379]PC QAB, refounded 1884, *VCH Middx* V, 301. [380]18 Aug, *Lond Gaz.* [381]1 Feb (*Lond Gaz* 3 Jan). [382]1 Sept, *Lond Gaz.* [383]28 Oct, *Lond Gaz.* [384]Harben, 446. [385]Authority not found. [386]23 Sept, *Lond Gaz.* [387]4 Nov, *Lond Gaz.* [388]21 Apr, *Lond Gaz.* [389]2 Mar, *Lond Gaz.* [390]First appearance *Clergy List.* [391]9 Apr, *Lond Gaz.* [392]15 Jan, *Lond Gaz.* [393]12 Jan, *Lond Gaz.* [394]10 Mar, *Lond Gaz.* [395]28 Feb, *Lond Gaz.* [396]PC QAB. [397]1 Jan (*Lond Gaz* 29 Dec 1972). [398]22 Oct, *Lond Gaz.* [399]57 Geo. III, *c* xxxiv. [400]24 Feb, *Lond Gaz.* [401]14 Mar, Part Dist. [402]9 Jan, *Lond Gaz* (OC 26 Dec 1851). [403]14 July, *Lond Gaz.* [404]10 Sept (lic min, *Lond Gaz* 3 Aug). [405]6 Geo. III, *c* 100. [406]On authority 1 Jas. II, *c* 20. [407]14 Geo. III, *c* 62. [408]9 Anne, *c* 22. [409]One of 'fifty new churches'. [410]21 Jan, *Lond Gaz* (OC 10 Dec 1841). [411]19 Apr, *Lond Gaz.* [412]1 Dec (*Lond Gaz* 16 Nov). [413]J. Northouck, *A New History of London* (hereafter, Northouck), 740. [414]24 Mar, LGBO 26577. [415]8 Aug, *Lond Gaz.* [416]1 Jas. II, *c* 22. [417]16 Chas. II, *c* 37. [418]Northouck, 734. [419]18 Mar, *Lond Gaz.* [420]11 May, *Lond Gaz.* [421]Authority not found. [422]16 May, *Lond Gaz.* [423]20 Aug, *Lond Gaz.* [424]9 Mar, *Lond Gaz.* [425]21 Chas. II, [chapter not found]. [426]11 Mar (*Lond Gaz* 11 Feb). [427]29 Jan, *Lond Gaz.* [428]2 Geo. II, *c* 10. [429]First appearance *Clergy List*; authority not found. [430]First appearance *Clergy List.* [431]*VCH Middx* III, 27. [432]1 Apr, LGBO 33502. [433]30 Sept, *Lond Gaz.* [434]1 Aug (*Lond Gaz* 20 July). [435]11 Nov, *Lond Gaz.* [436]*VCH Middx* V, 122. [437]18 Apr (*Lond Gaz* 29 June 1836). [438]First appearance *Crockford's Clerical Directory.* [439]14 Feb, *Lond Gaz.* [440]6 Sept, *Lond Gaz.* [441]On authority 2 Geo. II, *c* 30. [442]20 Geo. III, *c* 66. [443]28 May, *Lond Gaz.* [444]Year vac (*Lond Gaz* 27 Apr 1923). [445]24 Nov, *Lond Gaz.* [446]*VCH Middx* V, 308. [447]10 Dec, *Lond Gaz.* [448]10 June, *Lond Gaz.* [449]29 Apr, *Lond Gaz.* [450]19 Feb, *Lond Gaz.* [451]1 Apr, The Counties of London and Middx (Hackney and Tottenham) O, 1907. [452]11 Jan, Part Dist, Instr CBC. [453]3 Aug, LGBO 15531. [454]28 Oct, MHealth Decl. [455]28 May, *Lond Gaz.* [456]1 Geo. II, [chapter not found]. [457]Note cancelled. [458]13 May, *Lond Gaz.* [459]First appearance *Clergy List.* [460]Authority not found. [461]Harben, 590. [462]Authority not found. [463]Harben, 590. [464]1 Oct, The Counties of London and Middx (Hackney and Tottenham) O, 1907.

NORFOLK

[1]1 Apr, MHealthO 78830. [2]24 Mar, LGBO16489. [3]Francis Blomefield, *An Essay Towards a Topographical History of the County of Norfolk* (hereafter, Blomefield), VII, 97. [4]1 Jan, 20 Vict., *c* 19. [5]Blomefield, VIII, 332. [6]1 July, *Lond Gaz.* [7]*White's Directory of Norfolk* (1845), (hereafter, White's), 300. [8]Blomefield, VIII, 340. [9]Year vac (*Lond Gaz* 27 July 1934). [10]25 Mar, LGBO 17028. [11]25 Mar, LGBO 17944. [12]Blomefield, II, 378. [13]Blomefield, II, 375. [14]23 Jan, *Lond Gaz.* [15]24 Mar, LGBO 16488. [16]14 May, *Lond Gaz.* [17]Blomefield, X, 297.

[18] 1 Apr, SI 1968/68. [19] 10 Feb, *Lond Gaz.* [20] 1 Apr, MHousLGO 6512. [21] 25 Mar, 45 & 46 Vict., *c* 58. [22] 14 May, *Lond Gaz.* [23] 1 Oct, LGBO 42599. [24] 1 Oct, LGBO 61238. [25] 1 Apr, MHousLGO 6466. [26] 9 May, *Lond Gaz.* [27] 11 Mar, *Lond Gaz.* [28] 1 Apr, 20 & 21 Eliz. II, *c* 70. [29] White's, 807. [30] Year vac (*Lond Gaz* 2 Feb 1926). [31] Blomefield, IX, 459. [32] Year vac (*Lond Gaz* 10 Feb 1925). [33] 30 May, *Lond Gaz.* [34] Blomefield, XI, 411. [35] Blomefield, I, 246. [36] 24 Mar, LGBO 16484. [37] 5 Apr, *Lond Gaz.* [38] 1 Apr, MHousLGO 1479. [39] 24 Mar, LGBO 16485. [40] 17 Feb, *Lond Gaz.* [41] 30 Sept, 58 & 59 Vict., session 2, *c* lxxxix. [42] 21 Dec, MHousLG Decl. [43] 30 Nov, *Lond Gaz.* [44] 25 Mar, LGBO 16486. [45] Blomefield places this par in Loddon Hd. [46] 16 Mar, *Lond Gaz.* [47] Blomefield, I, 390. [48] 11 Nov, *Lond Gaz.* [49] Blomefield XI, 156. [50] 7 June, *Lond Gaz.* [51] 1 Apr, MHealthO 73205. [52] Blomefield VII, 29. [53] Blomefield, VII, 31. [54] 23 Dec, *Lond Gaz.* [55] 1 Oct, MHealthO 71236. [56] 2 Jan, MHousLG Decl. [57] Blomefield, XI, 211. [58] Blomefield, X, 48. [59] 1 Jan, MHous LG Decl. [60] 2 Apr, *Lond Gaz.* [61] Blomefield, V, 33. [62] Blomefield, II, 331. [63] Blomefield, V, 99. [64] 4 Aug, OC. [65] 9 Nov, The Norwich (Extension) O, 1907. [66] 1 Apr, MHousLGO 7527. [67] 30 July, *Lond Gaz.* [68] 26 July, *Lond Gaz.* [69] 27 Feb, *Lond Gaz.* [70] Presumed incl in PLU when became sep CP; not orig rated in the PLU. [71] 25 Mar, LGBO 17476. [72] 26 May, *Lond Gaz.* [73] 29 Oct, *Lond Gaz.* [74] 9 Sept, *Lond Gaz.* [75] Blomefield, VIII, 389. [76] Blomefield, V, 233. [77] 1 Jan, LGBO 33742. [78] 1 Oct, LGBO 44367. [79] 1 Apr, MHousLGO 3209. [80] 8 Nov, *Lond Gaz.* [81] 1 Oct, MHealthO 74835. [82] 10 Aug, *Lond Gaz.* [83] Blomefield, VII, 327. [84] 9 Aug, MHousLG Decl. [85] 1 Apr, MHousLG Decl. [86] 24 Mar, LGBO 16515. [87] 57 & 58 Vict., *c* 58 and Co Council Naming O. [88] 16 May, MHousLG Decl. [89] 52 & 53 Vict., *c* clxxxvii. [90] 2 Aug, *Lond Gaz.* [91] Apptd day, LGBO 31704. [92] 25 Mar, LGBO 18137. [93] 16 May, MHousLG Decl. [94] 3 Apr, *Lond Gaz.* [95] Blomefield, XI, 224. [96] Blomefield, II, 490. [97] Authority not found. [98] 1 Apr, MHealth ProvO Confirmation (Ely, Holland and Norfolk) Act, 1934. [99] 1 Oct, MHealthO 73470. [100] 13 Nov, *Lond Gaz.* [101] Blomefield, VII, 363. [102] Blomefield, V, 260. [103] Authority not found. [104] 1 Apr, MHousLGO 6196. [105] Blomefield, X, 467. [106] 1 Apr, MHousLGO 3686. [107] Blomefield, I, 267. [108] 26 Apr, *Lond Gaz.* [109] White's, 809. [110] Blomefield, VIII, 69-70. [111] 20 Oct, *Lond Gaz.* [112] Blomefield IX, 510. [113] 25 Mar, LGBO 17591. [114] 26 May, *Lond Gaz.* [115] Blomefield, VIII, 225. [116] Year vac (*Lond Gaz* 4 Nov 1930). [117] 31 May, *Lond Gaz.* [118] Blomefield, I, 315. [119] Blomefield, VI, 294. [120] 1 Apr, LGBO 43635. [121] 1 Apr, MHealthO 69703. [122] 1 Apr, MHealthO 72347. [123] 5 Nov, *Lond Gaz.* [124] 31 Mar, *Lond Gaz.* [125] 16 July, *Lond Gaz.* [126] 22 Feb, *Lond Gaz.* [127] Year vac (*Lond Gaz* 4 Nov 1927). [128] 3 Dec, *Lond Gaz.* [129] 1 Apr, *Lond Gaz.* [130] 25 Mar, LGBO 17216. [131] 9 Aug, MHousLG Decl. [132] Blomefield, II, 177. [133] 26 Oct, *Lond Gaz.* [134] 1 Apr, MHealthO 110200. [135] 2 July, MHousLG Decl. [136] Blomefield, X, 467. [137] 25 Mar, LGBO 18135. [138] 1 Aug (*Lond Gaz* 1 July). [139] Year vac (*Lond Gaz* 5 Feb 1929). [140] Blomefield, X, 348. [141] 10 June, MHousLG Decl. [142] 8 Mar, *Lond Gaz.* [143] 3 Aug, *Lond Gaz.* [144] Blomefield, VI, 466. [145] Blomefield, X, 74. [146] White's, 795. [147] Blomefield, X, 165. [148] 1 Apr, MHealthO 70351. [149] 20 Aug, *Lond Gaz.* [150] 30 Sept, *Lond Gaz.* [151] 5 Oct (lic min, *Lond Gaz* 1 July). [152] 18 Jan, *Lond Gaz.* [153] Year vac (*Lond Gaz* 6 July 1934). [154] 17 Mar, *Lond Gaz.* [155] Statute cited by Blomefield, V, 18. [156] Blomefield, VII, 382. [157] 25 Mar, LGBO 16487. [158] 1 Apr, MHousLGO 18057. [159] 1 Apr, MHealthO 4173. [160] 25 Mar, LGBO 18139. [161] 7 Dec, MHousLG Decl. [162] Year vac (*Lond Gaz* 18 Apr 1924). [163] PC QAB. [164] Blomefield, V, 115. [165] Blomefield, V, 209. [166] 1 Apr, LGBO 49238. [167] 1 Apr, MHousLGO 3209. [168] 10 July, *Lond Gaz.* [169] 1 Apr, 14 & 15 Geo. VI, *c* xliii. [170] 28 Dec, *Lond Gaz.* [171] 10 Feb, *Lond Gaz.* [172] Blomefield, IV, 439. [173] Blomefield, IV, 319. [174] Blomefield, IV, 300. [175] 28 June, *Lond Gaz.* [176] 1 Jan (OC 19 Oct and 28 Dec 1956). [177] Blomefield, IV, 137. [178] 1 Jan (OC 19 Oct and 28 Dec 1956). [179] Blomefield, IV, 443. [180] 26 Mar, *Lond Gaz.* [181] Blomefield, IV, 116. [182] 10 Feb, *Lond Gaz.* [183] 1 Jan (*Lond Gaz* 5 Dec 1969). [184] 30 Oct (lic min, *Lond Gaz* 30 May). [185] Blomefield, IV, 475. [186] Blomefield, IV, 474. [187] Blomefield, IV, 335. [188] Blomefield, IV. 118. [189] 26 Oct, *Lond Gaz.* [190] 1 June (*Lond Gaz* 2 May). [191] 21 May, *Lond Gaz.* [192] Blomefield, IV, 102. [193] Blomefield, IV, 69. [194] Blomefield, IV, 375. [195] Blomefield IV, 450. [196] 16 Dec, *Lond Gaz.* [197] Blomefield, IV, 85. [198] Blomefield, IV, 106. [199] 12 Oct, *Lond Gaz.* [200] Blomefield, IV, 149. [201] Blomefield, IV, 78. [202] 1 Apr, SI 1951/325. [203] Blomefield, XI, 239. [204] 29 & 30 Vict., *c* 113. [205] Death of rector of Outwell, per authority 9 & 10 Vict., *c* vii. [206] 51 & 52 Vict., *c* 41. [207] 5 Apr, *Lond Gaz.* [208] Blomefield, VI, 127. [209] 2 Oct, The County of Norfolk (Rural Pars–Change of Name) O, 1948. [210] Blomefield, V, 447. [211] 1 Mar, The County of Norfolk (Rural Pars–Change of Name) O, 1948. [212] Blomefield, IX, 248. [213] 21 May, reported in *Parl Papers* 1872, XLVI, 19. [214] Blomefield, X, 452. [215] 58 & 59 Vict., session 2, *c* viii. [216] White's, 642. [217] 25 Mar, LGBO 18138. [218] Blomefield, I, 474. [219] Blomefield, VI, 393. [220] White's, 604. [221] 1 July, The County of Norfolk (Rural Pars–Change of Name), O, 1950. [222] 57 & 58 Vict., *c* 58. [223] 15 July, *Lond Gaz.* [224] Apptd day, LGBO 31938. [225] 25 Mar, LGBO 18128. [226] 16 Oct, *Lond Gaz.* [227] 31 July, *Lond Gaz.* [228] 1 Apr, MHealthO 69602. [229] Blomefield, V, 502. [230] Blomefield, I, 138. [231] 13 Mar, *Lond Gaz.* [232] Blomefield, V, 514. [233] Blomefield, V, 518. [234] Blomefield, V, 519. [235] Blomefield, I, 422. [236] 24 Mar, LGBO 16516. [237] 24 Mar, LGBO 16515. [238] Blomefield, V, 198. [239] Blomefield, V, 463. [240] White's, 572. [241] 1 Apr, SI 1957/414. [242] 1 Aug (*Lond Gaz* 28 July). [243] 57 & 58 Vict., *c* 58. [244] 1 Apr, MHealthO 69005. [245] Blomefield, II, 73. [246] Blomefield, II, 71. [247] Blomefield, II, 72. [248] Blomefield, II, 74. [249] Blomefield, II, 75. [250] Blomefield, II, 76. [251] Blomefield, II, 60. [252] Blomefield, II, 69.

[253]9 Mar, *Lond Gaz.* [254]Blomefield, I, 208. [255]24 Mar, LGBO 16517. [256]Blomefield, V, 297. [257]30 Sept, LGBO 36824. [258]Blomefield, II, 173. [259]58 & 59 Vict., session 2, *c* viii. [260]Blomefield, II, 461. [261]1 July (*Lond Gaz* 8 June). [262]7 Feb, *Lond Gaz.* [263]3 Oct, MHousLG Decl. [264]Blomefield, V, 120-21.

OXFORDSHIRE

[1]1 Apr, 20 & 21 Eliz. II, *c* 70. [2]29 & 30 Vict., *c* 113. [3]19 Oct, reported in *Parl Papers* 1872, XLVI, 20. [4]15 Aug, reported in *Parl Papers* 1890-91, LXI, 57. [5]1 Apr, Dept EnvirnO 3597. [6]1 Apr, MHousLGO 23092. [7]1 Apr, MHousLGO 3412. [8]1 Apr, MHealthO 76241. [9]1 Apr, MHousLGO 45759. [10]Note cancelled. [11]25 Mar, LGBO 19543. [12]1 Apr, MHousLGO 3881. [13]*VCH Oxon* V, 256. [14]1 Apr, MHealthO 107346. [15]31 Dec, *Lond Gaz.* [16]PC QAB. [17]1 Oct, LGBO 34646. [18]*Gardiner's Dictionary of Oxfordshire* (1852), 679. [19]1 Jan, 20 Vict., *c* 19. [20]1 Oct, LGBO 33012. [21]25 Mar, 45 & 46 Vict., *c* 58. [22]23 Dec, OC. [23]*VCH Oxon* VIII, 37-38. [24]23 May, reported in *Parl Papers* 1872, XLVI, 18. [25]57 & 58 Vict., *c* 58 and Co Council Naming O. [26]1 Apr, MHousLGO 1354. [27]1 Nov (*Lond Gaz* 27 Oct). [28]1 Apr, MHousLGO 34152. [29]20 Jan, *Lond Gaz* (OC 30 Dec 1845). [30]10 Feb, *Lond Gaz.* [31]24 Mar, LGBO 21435. [32]31 Aug, *Lond Gaz.* [33]1 Oct, *Lond Gaz.* [34]11 Feb, *Lond Gaz.* [35]24 Mar, LGBO 22226. [36]3 Aug, *Lond Gaz.* [37]1 Apr, MHealthO 107345. [38]5 Sept, *Lond Gaz.* [39]Information supplied by Diocesan Archivist. [40]1 Apr, MHousLGO 13793. [41]*VCH Oxon* VI, 330. [42]Apptd day, LGBO 31877. [43]1 Apr, 15 & 16 Geo. V, *c* xxviii. [44]3 Aug, *Lond Gaz.* [45]5 May, *Lond Gaz.* [46]1 Feb (*Lond Gaz* 23 Jan). [47]20 Mar, reported in *Parl Papers* 1890-91, LXI, 55. [48]1 Apr, LGBO 35928. [49]8 June, reported in *Parl Papers* 1872, XLVI, 20. [50]24 Mar, LGBO 15250. [51]6 Feb, *Lond Gaz.* [52]1 Apr, Dept EnvirnO 3707. [53]29 Nov, *Lond Gaz.* [54]13 Sept, *Lond Gaz.* [55]1 Oct, MHealthO 59587. [56]7 Jan, reported in *Parl Papers* 1872, XLVI, 21. [57]26 Mar, LGBO 33607. [58]8 Jan, reported in *Parl Papers* 1872, XLVI, 19. [59]25 Mar, LGBO 19542. [60]2 & 3 Wm. IV, *c* 64 and 7 & 8 Vict., *c* 61. [61]25 Mar, LGBO 19547. [62]*Kelly's Directory of Oxfordshire* (1883) (hereafter, Kelly's), 628. [63]Kelly's, 628. [64]26 Apr, *Lond Gaz.* [65]24 Oct, reported in *Parl Papers* 1872, XLVI, 20. [66]1 Apr, Dept Envirn 3707. [67]7 Feb, *Lond Gaz.* [68]9 Nov, LGB ProvO 2219. [69]3 Jan, *Lond Gaz* (OC 20 Dec 1853). [70]21 Nov, *Lond Gaz.* [71]1 Mar, *Lond Gaz.* [72]Year vac (*Lond Gaz* 8 May 1928). [73]1 Apr, MHousLGO 34302. [74]30 Oct, *Lond Gaz.* [75]1 Aug (*Lond Gaz* 31 July). [76]*VCH Oxon* VII, 87. [77]8 May, reported in *Parl Papers* 1872, XLVI, 12. [78]14 Nov, reported in *Parl Papers* 1872, XLVI, 19. [79]9 Jan, reported in *Parl Papers* 1872, XLVI, 20. [80]*VCH Oxon* VII, 23. [81]13 May, *Lond Gaz.* [82]1 Apr, LGBO 37371. [83]1 Apr, MHealthO 108911. [84]1 Apr, MHealthO 110279. [85]25 Mar, LGBO 18179. [86]25 Mar, LGBO 19430. [87]Apptd day, LGBO 31868. [88]18 & 19 Geo. V, *c* lxxxiv. [89]4 Apr, *Lond Gaz.* [90]11 July, reported in *Parl Papers* 1872, XLVI, 55. [91]14 Oct, *Lond Gaz.* [92]11 Aug, reported in *Parl Papers* 1872, XLVI, 20. [93]24 Mar, LGBO 22225. [94]Information supplied by Diocesan Archivist. [95]11 Dec, reported in *Parl Papers* 1872, XLVI, 20. [96]21 Dec, LGBO 7867. [97]24 Dec, LGBO 7868. [98]1 Apr, MHousLGO 99394. [99]Apptd day, LGBO 31930. [100]1 Apr, MHousLGO 10524. [101]29 Dec, reported in *Parl Papers* 1872, XLVI, 13. [102]PC QAB but *VCH Oxon* VII, 78 says 1747. [103]1 Apr, MHousLGO 28090. [104]26 May, *Lond Gaz.* [105]1 Nov, LGBO 58897. [106]8 July, Part Dist. [107]7 Apr, reported in *Parl Papers* 1872, XLVI, 21. [108]5 Nov, *Lond Gaz.* [109]30 Nov, *Lond Gaz.* [110]*VCH Oxon* VII, 87. [111]17 Dec, LGBO 12641. [112]24 Dec, LGBO 15137. [113]1 Apr, MHealthO 108356. [114]1 Apr, MHousLGO 5883. [115]1 Apr, MHealthO 107347. [116]1 Apr, MHousLGO 3421. [117]26 Oct, MHousLG Decl. [118]2 Aug, Oxon Co Council, confirmed by The County of Oxford (Henley-upon-Thames) Confirmation Order, 1905 (information supplied by Oxfordshire RO). [119]1 Apr, MHousLGO 34470. [120]7 Aug, *Lond Gaz.* [121]*VCH Oxon* III, 337. [122]29 May, *Lond Gaz.* [123]15 May, *Lond Gaz.* [124]Apptd day, LGBO 31868. [125]10 Sept, *Lond Gaz.* [126]9 June, Part Dist, Instr Bp Oxford and CBC. [127]9 Mar, *Lond Gaz.* [128]24 Mar, LGBO 21435, 21436. [129]24 Mar, LGBO 16162. [130]25 Mar, LGBO 18178. [131]Apptd day, LGBO 31930. [132]23 June, *Lond Gaz.* [133]4 Feb, *Lond Gaz.* [134]LGB ProvO Confirmation (No 14) Act, 1895. [135]24 Oct, reported in *Parl Papers* 1872, XLVI, 13. [136]30 July, *Lond Gaz.* [137]25 Mar, LGBO 18179, 18180. [138]4 Apr, *Lond Gaz.* [139]Note cancelled. [140]24 Aug, *Lond Gaz.* [141]31 Mar, Oxon Co Council O. [142]25 Mar, LGBO 19612. [143]1 Apr, 23 & 24 Geo. V, *c* iii. [144]Kelley's. [145]28 Mar, reported in *Parl Papers* 1872, XLVI, 22. [146]17 July, reported in *Parl Papers* 1872, XLVI, 13. [147]*VCH Oxon* VI, 158-59. [148]PC QAB. [149]PC QAB, refounded 1885 as reported in *Parl Papers* 1890-91, LXI, 54. [150]5 Mar, reported in *Parl Papers* 1890-91, LXI, 54. [151]25 Mar, LGBO 18180. [152]25 Mar, LGBO 19618. [153]18 Apr, *Lond Gaz.* [154]25 Mar, LGBO 17934. [155]1 Apr, SI 1957/462. [156]23 July, *Lond Gaz.* [157]18 Oct, *Lond Gaz.* [158]6 Oct, *Lond Gaz.* [159]24 Mar, LGBO 21436. [160]57 & 58 Vict., *c* 58. [161]30 Sept, LGB ProvO 1159. [162]13 July, reported in *Parl Papers* 1872, XLVI, 12. [163]17 Jan, *Lond Gaz.* [164]Presumed incl in PLU when became sep CP; not orig rated in the PLU. [165]1 Apr, 23 & 24 Geo. V, *c* xxi. [166]15 Apr, 52 Vict., *c* xv. [167]Information supplied by Oxford Diocesan Archivist. [168]14 Sept, *Lond Gaz.* [169]27 Apr, *Lond Gaz.* [170]LGB ProvO 623 (information supplied by Oxon RO). [171]13 June, *Lond Gaz.* [172]21 Nov, *Lond Gaz.* [173]14 Dec, *Lond Gaz.* [174]Year vac (*Lond Gaz* 27 June 1961). [175]9 Dec, OC. [176]11 July, *Lond Gaz.* [177]24 Mar, *Lond Gaz.* [178]Information supplied by Oxford Diocesan Archivist. [179]7 Aug, *Lond Gaz.* [180]1 May (*Lond Gaz* 16 Apr). [181]5 June, MHousLG Decl. [182]1 Oct, MHealthO 67810. [183]30 Nov, reported in *Parl Papers* 1890-91, LXI, 21. [184]1 Apr, MHousLGO 4846. [185]*VCH Oxon* VII, 87. [186]13 May, reported in *Parl Papers* 1872, XLVI, 14.

[187] *VCH Oxon* VII, 200. [188] 21 May, reported in *Parl Papers* 1872, XLVI, 20. [189] 24 Mar, LGBO 15250. [190] 12 Oct, *Lond Gaz.* [191] 30 Mar, *Lond Gaz.* [192] 57 & 58 Vict., *c* 58. [193] 30 Mar, SI 1960/459. [194] Presumed incl in Bor because of origin in Oxford St Peter in the East AP.

SOMERSET

[1] 25 Mar, 45 & 46 Vict., *c* 58. [2] 25 Mar, LGBO 18100. [3] 1 Apr, MHealthO 77130. [4] 25 July (lic min, *Lond Gaz* 23 June 1953). [5] 25 Mar, LGBO 17921, 17931. [6] 25 Mar, LGBO 17645. [7] 25 Mar, LGBO 17341. [8] 25 Mar, LGBO 18996. [9] 19 Dec, *Lond Gaz.* [10] 1 Apr, LGBO 32210. [11] 1 Apr, MHousLGO 6578. [12] 24 Mar, LGBO 16397. [13] 24 Mar, LGBO 16381. [14] Note cancelled. [15] 25 Mar, LGBO 16420, 17647, 17648. [16] 23 Aug, *Lond Gaz.* [17] 24 Mar, LGBO 16443. [18] 30 Sept, LGBO 34794. [19] 1 Apr, 60 & 61 Vict., *c* ccxxx. [20] 1 Apr, SI 1951/563. [21] 18 Feb, MHousLGO 21193. [22] 1 Apr, 20 & 21 Eliz. II, *c* 70. [23] 28 Nov, *Lond Gaz.* [24] 23 Oct, *Lond Gaz.* [25] PC QAB. [26] 1 Apr, LGBO 35339. [27] 11 May, *Lond Gaz.* [28] 24 June, *Lond Gaz.* [29] 30 Sept, LGBO 36707. [30] 1 Apr, MHealthO 81129. [31] 1 Apr, MHealthO 108888. [32] 5 Feb, *Lond Gaz.* [33] 6 May, *Lond Gaz.* [34] Beresford & Finberg, 154. [35] 10 Feb, *Lond Gaz.* [36] 11 May, reported in *Parl Papers* 1897, LXVII, Pt VI, 173. [37] 24 Mar, LGBO 16339. [38] 25 Mar, LGBO 17648. [39] 11 Oct, *Lond Gaz.* [40] 30 Apr, *Lond Gaz.* [41] 26 Mar, LGBO 40983. [42] 9 Nov, 1 & 2 Geo. V, *c* xxxv. [43] 1 Apr, 14 Geo. VI, *c* lxiv. [44] 1 Jan, MHousLG O 23994. [45] 1 Apr, SI 1951/431. [46] 27 Nov, *Lond Gaz.* [47] 13 Nov, *Lond Gaz.* [48] 30 May, *Lond Gaz.* [49] 1 Nov (*Lond Gaz* 26 Oct). [50] 11 Oct, reported in *Parl Papers* 1872, XLVI, 21. [51] 5 Feb, *Lond Gaz.* [52] 30 June, *Lond Gaz.* [53] 25 Mar, LGBO 16087. [54] Authority not found. [55] Somerset RO, Bath & Wells Dioc MSS Book, 14. [56] Apptd day, 57 & 58 Vict., *c* 58 and Co Council Naming O. [57] 31 Dec, Part Dist, Instr CBC. [58] 18 Aug, reported in *Parl Papers* 1872, XLVI, 19. [59] 20 July, *Lond Gaz.* [60] 29 May, *Lond Gaz.* [61] 25 Mar, *Lond Gaz.* [62] 25 Mar, *Lond Gaz.* [63] 22 Nov, *Lond Gaz.* [64] 21 Sept, *Lond Gaz.* [65] 26 Mar, *Lond Gaz.* [66] 8 Nov, *Lond Gaz.* [67] 12 Oct, *Lond Gaz.* [68] 14 Mar, Part Dist, Instr CBC. [69] 28 Feb, *Lond Gaz.* [70] 30 Apr, *Lond Gaz.* [71] 21 July, *Lond Gaz.* [72] 23 Apr, *Lond Gaz.* [73] 1 Oct, LGBO 38597. [74] Before census of 1901. [75] 1 Apr, LGBO 60946. [76] 25 Mar, LGBO 14612. [77] 24 Mar, LGBO 16326, 16327. [78] 1 Apr, MHousLGO 7244. [79] 30 Mar, SI 1960/458. [80] 1 Apr, 18 & 19 Geo. V, *c* cvi. [81] 1 Apr, 20 & 21 Geo. V, *c* clxxx. [82] 1 Apr, Somerset & Bristol (Alteration of Boundary) O, 1951. [83] 17 Mar, SI 1952/452. [84] 25 Mar, LGBO 16580. [85] 11 Oct, *Lond Gaz.* [86] 25 Mar, LGBO 17339, 17340. [87] 18 Mar, *Lond Gaz.* [88] 15 Aug (*Lond Gaz* 6 Dec 1955). [89] 10 July, *Lond Gaz.* [90] 58 & 59 Vict., *c* xci. [91] 29 Oct, *Lond Gaz.* [92] 19 Dec, LGBO 10252. [93] 25 Mar, LGBO 17646. [94] Year vac (*Lond Gaz* 30 Nov 1962). [95] 25 Mar, LGBO 18995. [96] 23 Dec, *Lond Gaz.* [97] 23 Dec, *Lond Gaz.* [98] 25 Mar, LGBO 16580, 16581, 17929. [99] Authority not found. [100] 25 Mar, LGBO 17929. [101] 25 Mar, LGBO 18100, 18101. [102] 24 Mar, LGBO 20642. [103] 9 Nov, LGB ProvO 1160. [104] 1 Oct, 1 & 2 Geo. VI, *c* xv. [105] 1 Apr, SI 1952/590. [106] 1 July, Part Dist, Instr CBC. [107] 2 Mar, *Lond Gaz.* [108] Year lic min (*Lond Gaz* 25 Nov 1958). [109] 6 June, *Lond Gaz.* [110] Year lic min (*Lond Gaz* 25 Nov 1958). [111] 6 June, *Lond Gaz.* [112] 18 Jan, *Lond Gaz.* [113] Year lic min (*Lond Gaz* 28 Aug 1962). [114] 10 Feb, *Lond Gaz.* [115] 25 Mar, LGBO 16466. [116] Authority and date not found. [117] 30 June, *Lond Gaz.* [118] 29 June, *Lond Gaz.* [119] 4 Nov, *Lond Gaz.* [120] 22 Mar, *Lond Gaz.* [121] 12 Aug, *Lond Gaz.* [122] Authority not found. [123] 1 May (*Lond Gaz* 3 Apr). [124] Authority not found. [125] 1 May (*Lond Gaz* 3 Apr). [126] 7 Dec (lic min, *Lond Gaz* 20 Oct). [127] Somerset RO, Bath & Wells Dioc MSS Book, 14. [128] 25 Mar, LGBO 16420, 17648, 17649, 17649. [129] 25 Mar, LGBO 19583. [130] 15 June, *Lond Gaz.* [131] 1 Aug, *Lond Gaz.* [132] 25 Mar, LGBO 14991. [133] 24 Mar, LGBO 15943. [134] 6 June, *Lond Gaz.* [135] 3 Apr, *Lond Gaz.* [136] 24 Mar, LGBO 20641. [137] 1 Apr, SI 1965/2086. [138] 25 Mar, LGBO 16580, 16582. [139] Year vac (*Lond Gaz* 9 July 1929). [140] Year vac (*Lond Gaz* 9 July 1929). [141] 23 Jan, *Lond Gaz.* [142] 16 Nov, *Lond Gaz.* [143] 31 19 & 20 Geo. V, *c* xxiv. [144] 21 Dec, *Lond Gaz.* [145] 1 Apr, LGBO 34419. [146] 28 Aug, *Lond Gaz.* [147] 1 Oct, LGBO 35270. [148] 25 Mar, LGBO 17338. [149] Authority of bp (information supplied by Somerset RO). [150] 25 Mar, LGBO 17339. [151] 24 Mar, LGBO 15662. [152] 25 Mar, LGBO 15665. [153] 25 Mar, LGBO 16580. [154] 1 Apr, MHealthO 5833. [155] 11 Aug, *Lond Gaz.* [156] 1 Apr, MHousLGO 4628. [157] 25 Mar, LGBO 18115. [158] 29 & 30 Vict., *c* 113. [159] 20 Dec, LGBO 7767. [160] 24 Mar, LGBO 15083. [161] 25 Mar, LGBO 18101. [162] 25 Mar, LGBO 14601. [163] 24 Mar, LGBO 14599. [164] 25 Mar, LGBO 19060. [165] 22 Oct, *Lond Gaz.* [166] 31 Aug, Part Dist, Instr CBC. [167] 30 Sept, LGBO 29765. [168] 18 Sept, *Lond Gaz.* [169] 19 Jan, *Lond Gaz.* [170] 9 Nov, LGB ProvO Confirmation (No 6) Act, 1892. [171] 25 Mar, LGBO 18114. [172] 1 Apr, MHousLGO 3424. [173] 1 Apr, SI 1951/431. [174] Year vac (*Lond Gaz* 27 May 1930). [175] Year vac (*Lond Gaz* 17 June 1930). [176] 24 Mar, LGBO 16581. [177] 25 Mar, LGBO 16580. [178] Year vac (*Lond Gaz* 15 Nov 1932). [179] 1 Jan, 20 Vict., *c* 19. [180] 25 Mar, *Lond Gaz.* [181] 1 Apr, 21 & 22 Geo. V, *c* cii. [182] 1 SI 1958/461. [183] 28 Aug, *Lond Gaz.* [184] 25 Mar, LGBO 16580, 17930. [185] 29 Mar, *Lond Gaz.* [186] 10 Mar, reported in *Parl Papers* 1872, XLVI, 20. [187] 24 Mar, LGBO 15678. [188] 1 Apr, MHousLGO 108890. [189] 28 Mar, *Lond Gaz.* [190] 26 June, reported in *Parl Papers* 1872, XLVI, 22. [191] 10 Dec, reported in *Parl Papers* 1872, XLVI, 17. [192] 24 Mar, LGBO 15679, 15681, 15682, 15684, 15685, 16325. [193] 25 Mar, LGBO 18162, 18163. [194] 21 Mar, reported in *Parl Papers* 1872, XLVI, 21. [195] 24 June, *Lond Gaz.* [196] 24 Mar, LGBO 19585. [197] 1 Apr, LGBO 30567. [198] 2 Aug, *Lond Gaz.* [199] 29 May, *Lond Gaz.* [200] Presumed incl in PLU when became sep CP; not orig rated in the PLU. [201] 1 Apr, LGBO 50552. [202] 23 Dec, *Lond Gaz.* [203] 25 Mar, LGBO 18101, 18102. [204] 24 Mar, LGBO 16444. [205] 1 May, *Lond Gaz.* [206] 24 Mar, LGBO 15944. [207] 1 June (*Lond Gaz* 5

May). [208] 30 Sept, 59 & 60 Vict., *c* lxxv. [209] 6 July, *Lond Gaz.* [210] 24 Mar, LGBO 16500. [211] 1 Apr, MHousLGO 4080. [212] 25 July, *Lond Gaz.* [213] 1 Apr, MHousLGO 108877. [214] 4 Apr, *Lond Gaz.* [215] 24 Mar, LGBO 14606. [216] 3 May, *Lond Gaz.* [217] 15 Feb, *Lond Gaz.* [218] 26 Mar, *Lond Gaz.* [219] 10 Feb, *Lond Gaz.* [220] 6 Dec, *Lond Gaz.* [221] 1 Feb (*Lond Gaz* 15 Jan). [222] 23 Jan, *Lond Gaz.* [223] 4 Apr, *Lond Gaz.* [224] 10 Feb, *Lond Gaz.* [225] 8 Aug, *Lond Gaz.* [226] 26 July, *Lond Gaz.* [227] 30 June, *Lond Gaz.* [228] 20 Jan, *Lond Gaz.* [229] 1 Apr, MHealthO 88217. [230] 3 Mar, reported in *Parl Papers* 1872, XLVI, 20. [231] 24 Mar, LGBO 15684. [232] 27 Apr, *Lond Gaz.* [233] 1 Apr, MHousLGO 9359. [234] 24 Mar, LGBO 19987. [235] 26 Feb, *Lond Gaz.* [236] 14 Sept, *Lond Gaz.* [237] 23 Dec, *Lond Gaz.* [238] 25 Mar, LGBO 16420. [239] Apptd day, LGBO 30631. [240] 1 Oct, MHealthO 79286. [241] 24 July, *Lond Gaz.* [242] 25 Mar, LGBO 19582. [243] 24 Mar, LGBO 16331, 16334, 16335, 16337. [244] 28 Oct, *Lond Gaz.* [245] 28 Oct, *Lond Gaz.* [246] 21 Aug, reported in *Parl Papers* 1872, XLVI. 20. [247] 25 Mar, LGBO 17650. [248] John Collinson, *History and Antiquities of the County of Somerset* (1791) (hereafter, Collinson), I, 31. [249] 25 Mar, LGBO 17648, 17653. [250] 25 Mar, LGBO 14615. [251] Authority not found. [252] 25 Mar, LGBO 17921, 17931, 18996. [253] 25 Mar, LGBO 14613. [254] 25 Mar, LGBO 14602. [255] 24 LGBO 16335, 16336. [256] 4 July, *Lond Gaz.* [257] 24 Mar, LGBO 15680, 16500. [258] 1 Apr, LGBO 63033. [259] PC QAB 1825 as North Bradley Christ Church, refounded 16 Apr 1852, *Lond Gaz.* [260] 25 Mar, LGBO 18102. [261] 24 Mar, LGBO 20643. [262] 11 Oct, *Lond Gaz.* [263] 14 Sept, *Lond Gaz.* [264] 29 May, *Lond Gaz.* [265] 1 Nov (*Lond Gaz* 26 Oct). [266] 19 Feb, *Lond Gaz.* [267] 15 Oct, *Lond Gaz.* [268] Reported in *Parl Papers* 1872, XLVI, 26. [269] 16 Feb, *Lond Gaz.* [270] Year vac (*Lond Gaz* 23 Sept 1966). [271] 24 Mar, LGBO 16325, 16326, 16327. [272] 25 Mar, LGBO 18163. [273] 20 Dec, LGBO 7749. [274] 26 Feb, *Lond Gaz.* [275] Authority not found. [276] 24 Mar, LGBO 16348. [277] 1 Dec (*Lond Gaz* 30 Nov). [278] 31 May, *Lond Gaz.* [279] 20 Dec, LGBO 7765, 7767. [280] 8 July, *Lond Gaz.* [281] 51 Geo. III [chapter not found]. [282] 19 June, reported in *Parl Papers* 1872, XLVI, 18. [283] 25 Mar, LGBO 17929 [284] 4 June, *Lond Gaz.* [285] 25 Mar, *Lond Gaz.* [286] 13 Aug, *Lond Gaz.* [287] 1 Apr, LGBO 41991. [288] 14 Sept, *Lond Gaz.* [289] 3 Sept, reported in *Parl Papers* 1872, XLVI, 18. [290] 24 Mar, LGBO 15661, 15662, 15663, 15664. [291] 26 Mar, LGBO 30668. [292] 8 Oct, *Lond Gaz.* [293] 1 Apr, LGBO 46219. [294] 25 Mar, LGBO 18162. [295] Information supplied by Somerset RO. [296] 10 Feb, *Lond Gaz.* [297] Information supplied by Somerset RO. [298] 25 Mar, LGBO 17649, 17651. [299] 25 Mar, LGBO 15942. [300] 10 Feb, *Lond Gaz.* [301] 22 Sept, *Lond Gaz.* [302] 10 Feb, *Lond Gaz.* [303] 3 July, *Lond Gaz.* [304] 24 Mar, LGBO 16603, 16397. [305] 24 Mar, LGBO 16328, 16329, 16330, 16331. [306] Later in year after *Lond Gaz* 15 Sept. [307] 25 Mar, LGBO 19060, 19061, 19063. [308] 2 & 3 Wm. IV, *c* 64 and 7 & 8 Vict., *c* 61. [309] 25 Mar, LGBO 17931. [310] 14 Sept, *Lond Gaz.* [311] 24 Mar, reported in *Parl Papers* 1890-91, LXI, 54. [312] 25 Mar, LGBO 18142. [313] 29 Apr, *Lond Gaz.* [314] 14 Nov, *Lond Gaz.* [315] 29 Apr, *Lond Gaz.* [316] 10 Feb, *Lond Gaz.* [317] 9 Nov, 11 & 12 Geo. V, *c* lix. [318] 25 Mar, LGBO 18100, 18103. [319] 1 Apr, MHealthO 108815. [320] 2 May, *Lond Gaz.* [321] 10 Feb, *Lond Gaz.* [322] 25 Mar, LGBO 17652. [323] 25 Mar, LGBO 19583, 19584. [324] 15 Apr, LGBO 34490. [325] 25 Mar, LGBO 16420, 17647. [326] 30 Jan, reported in *Parl Papers* 1872, XLVI, 18. [327] 1 Apr, LGBO 34014. [328] 1 Apr, LGBO 42992. [329] 24 Nov, *Lond Gaz.* [330] Authority not found. [331] 24 Mar, LGBO 16409. [332] 1 Apr, MHealthO 88217. [333] 24 Mar, LGBO 16328, 16330, 16331, 16332, 16333. [334] 25 Mar, LGBO 16087, 16881. [335] 59 & 60 Vict., *c* lxxv. [336] 25 Mar, LGBO 19063. [337] 1 Apr, reported in *Parl Papers* 1890-91, LXI, 56. [338] Note cancelled. [339] 25 Mar, LGBO 17646, 17648, 17653. [340] Year vac (*Lond Gaz* 23 Aug 1929). [341] 25 Mar, LGBO 17653. [342] 25 Mar, LGBO 17645, 19586. [343] 24 Mar, LGBO 16397, 16399. [344] 25 Mar, LGBO 18104. [345] Effective later in year after *Lond Gaz* 8 Jan 1937. [346] 22 Nov, *Lond Gaz.* [347] 20 Oct, *Lond Gaz.* [348] 27 July, reported in *Parl Papers* 1872, XLVI, 21. [349] 24 Mar, reported in *Parl Papers* 1890-91, LXI, 54. [350] 31 July, *Lond Gaz.* [351] 6 Dec, *Lond Gaz.* [352] 23 Jan, reported in *Parl Papers* 1872, XLVI, 21. [353] 24 Mar, LGBO 15682. [354] 23 Aug, *Lond Gaz.* [355] 1 June (*Lond Gaz* 2 May). [356] 25 Mar, LGBO 14604. [357] 1 Oct, 16 & 17 Geo. V, *c* 99. [358] 5 Sept, *Lond Gaz.* [359] 24 Mar, LGBO 16340. [360] 2 Feb, *Lond Gaz.* [361] 12 Feb, *Lond Gaz.* [362] 31 Mar, *Lond Gaz.* [363] 26 July, *Lond Gaz.* [364] 5 Aug (lic min, *Lond Gaz* 30 June). [365] 25 Mar, LGBO 18104. [366] 3 Dec, *Lond Gaz.* [367] 10 Feb, *Lond Gaz.* [368] 13 Dec, *Lond Gaz.* [369] 24 Mar, LGBO 15656, 15657, 15664. [370] 9 Jan, *Lond Gaz* (OC 26 Dec 1851). [371] 25 Mar, LGBO 18101, 18102. [372] 24 Mar, LGBO 16603, 16381. [373] 25 Mar, LGBO 14605. [374] 24 Mar, LGBO 14606, 14607. [375] 25 Mar, LGBO 18141. [376] 9 Nov, LGB ProvO 1127. [377] 1 Apr, MHousLGO 22150. [378] 12 Apr, *Lond Gaz.* [379] 24 Mar, LGBO 14613. [380] 25 Mar, 45 & 46 Vict., *c* 58 and LGBO 14609. [381] 23 Mar, *Lond Gaz.* [382] 31 July, *Lond Gaz.* [383] 11 Feb, *Lond Gaz.* [384] 24 Mar, LGBO 21481. [385] 24 Mar, LGBO 15680. [386] 1 Apr, LGBO 33993. [387] 25 Mar, LGBO 17340, 17342. [388] 24 Mar, LGBO 16603, 16381. [389] 24 Mar, LGBO 15678, 15681. [390] 24 Mar, LGBO 16337, 16338. [391] 24 Mar, LGBO 15659, 16333, 16334, 16337, 16339. [392] 57 & 58 Vict., *c* 58. [393] Before *Valor Eccl.* [394] Authority not found. [395] 10 Feb, *Lond Gaz.* [396] 30 June, reported in *Parl Papers* 1872, XLVI, 18. [397] 24 Mar, LGBO 15660, 15664, 16334, 16335, 16337. [398] 1 Apr, 16 & 17 Geo. V, *c* xcix. [399] 9 Nov, 3 Edw. VII, *c* cxxxvii. [400] 30 Aug, *Lond Gaz.* [401] 25 Mar, LGBO 17645, 19584. [402] 24 Mar, LGBO 16335, 16338. [403] 10 Feb, *Lond Gaz.* [404] 1 July (*Lond Gaz* 25 June). [405] 30 Aug, Co Council NamingO. [406] 20 Feb, Instr CBC and Bp Bath & Wells. [407] 1 Apr, 1 Edw. VIII and 1 Geo. VI, *c* xiii. [408] 31 Oct, *Lond Gaz.* [409] 10 Feb, *Lond Gaz.* [410] Year vac (*Lond Gaz* 9 Oct 1934). [411] 26 Oct, *Lond Gaz.* [412] 25 Mar, 45 & 46 Vict., *c* 58 and LGBO 14609. [413] 1 Apr, LGBO 43667. [414] 24 Mar, LGBO 15683. [415] 25 Mar, LGBO 14611.

[416] 9 Mar, *Lond Gaz.* [417] 13 May, reported in *Parl Papers* 1890-91, LXI, 55. [418] 25 Mar, LGBO 14615. [419] 24 Mar, LGBO 16335, 16336, 16337. [420] 25 Mar, LGBO 17652. [421] 25 Mar, LGBO 17645, 19586. [422] 20 Dec, LGBO 7749, 7765. [423] 3 June, LGBO 10612. [424] Authority not found. [425] 1 Apr, MHealthO 107530. [426] 25 Mar, LGBO 18140. [427] 23 Dec, *Lond Gaz.* [428] 24 Mar, LGBO 16421. [429] Year vac (*Lond Gaz* 25 Aug 1931). [430] 24 Mar, LGBO 14607. [431] 25 Mar, LGBO 14611, 14612. [432] 25 Mar, LGBO 18103. [433] 25 Mar, LGBO 17338, 17340, 17342. [434] 24 Mar, LGBO 15662. [435] 25 Mar, LGBO 17648, 17650, 17651, 18104. [436] 10 Feb, *Lond Gaz.* [437] 24 Mar, LGBO 16400. [438] 31 May, *Lond Gaz.* [439] 24 Mar, LGBO 15679, 15685. [440] 24 Mar, LGBO 16329, 16331, 16333. [441] 30 Mar, SI 1960/458. [442] 2 Feb, MHousLG Decl. [443] 6 May, reported in *Parl Papers* 1890-91, LXI, 54. [444] 24 Mar, LGBO 15661. [445] 25 Mar, LGBO 19060, 19063. [446] 25 Mar, LGBO 17648, 17651. [447] 24 Mar, LGBO 16399. [448] 11 Oct, *Lond Gaz.* [449] Authority not found. [450] 25 Mar, LGBO 14601, 14604, 14615. [451] 25 Mar, LGBO 17652, 17653. [452] 2 July, *Lond Gaz.* [453] 9 Jan, *Lond Gaz.* [454] Apptd day, LGBO 32082. [455] 12 Dec, Instr Eccl Commissioners and Bp Bath & Wells. [456] 19 Nov, *Lond Gaz.* [457] 25 Mar, LGBO 15665. [458] 10 Apr, *Lond Gaz.* [459] 29 Jan, *Lond Gaz.* [460] 24 Mar, LGBO 15658. [461] 24 Mar, LGBO 15657, 16327. [462] 4 July, *Lond Gaz.* [463] 13 June, *Lond Gaz.* [464] Authority not found. [465] 24 Sept, Instr CBC. [466] 2 May, *Lond Gaz.* [467] 12 May, *Lond Gaz.* [468] 31 Mar, *Lond Gaz.* [469] 22 May, LGB ProvO 1150. [470] 24 Mar, LGBO 16398. [471] 25 Mar, LGBO 18141, 18142. [472] 25 Mar, LGBO 14992, 16409. [473] 25 Mar, LGBO 17340. [474] 24 Mar, LGBO 15656. [475] 24 Mar, LGBO 15659, 15660, 15664, 16334, 16337. [476] 6 Jan, MHousLG Decl. [477] 1 Apr, MHousLGO 7707. [478] 22 Mar, *Lond Gaz.* [479] 6 Aug, *Lond Gaz.*

SUFFOLK

[1] 11 Sept, *Lond Gaz.* [2] 25 Mar, 45 & 46 Vict., *c* 58. [3] 25 Mar, LGBO 16461. [4] 1 Apr, The E Suffolk and Ipswich (Alt of Boundaries) O, 1952. [5] 7 May, SI 1953/744. [6] 29 & 30 Vict., *c* 113. [7] 1 Apr, MHealthO 77717. [8] 23 Dec, *Lond Gaz.* [9] 1 Apr, MHealthO 79349. [10] 1 Jan, 20 Vict., *c* 19. [11] 30 May, *Lond Gaz.* [12] 1 Apr, MHealthO 77717. [13] 14 Feb, *Lond Gaz.* [14] Year vac (*Lond Gaz* 28 Feb 1930). [15] 30 Sept, 59 & 60 Vict., *c* ccxxxvi. [16] Information supplied by Suffolk RO (Ipswich Branch). [17] 22 June, *Lond Gaz.* [18] 13 Aug, *Lond Gaz.* [19] 1 Apr, LGBO 50455. [20] 24 Mar, LGBO 16477. [21] 30 Oct, *Lond Gaz.* [22] Norfolk and Norwich RO (hereafter, NNRO), Faculty Book 5, Book 8, 26*d*-28*d*. [23] 8 Mar, LGBO 7784. [24] 9 Feb, *Lond Gaz.* [25] 1 Apr, 11 & 12 Eliz. II, *c* 70. [26] Apptd day, LGBO 31679. [27] 6 June (lic min, *Lond Gaz* 15 May). [28] 24 June, NNRO Faculty Book 2, Book 2, 156-57. [29] 4 Jan, OC. [30] 14 Oct, MHealth Decl. [31] Year vac (*Lond Gaz* 16 Feb 1932). [32] *Valor Eccl.* [33] 24 Mar, LGBO 16440. [34] 24 Mar, LGBO 16436. [35] 2 Apr, *Lond Gaz.* [36] 24 Mar, LGBO 14858. [37] Year vac (*Lond Gaz* 26 Feb 1926). [38] 24 Mar, LGBO 16513. [39] 30 Nov, *Lond Gaz.* [40] 6 Jan, *Lond Gaz.* [41] 30 Sept, 58 & 59 Vict., session 2, *c* lxxix. [42] 31 July, *Lond Gaz.* [43] [John Kirby], *A Topographical and Historical Description of the County of Suffolk* (1829) (hereafter, Kirby), 81-82. [44] 25 Mar, LGBO 14856. [45] Before 1705, *Liber Regis.* [46] 28 Dec, MHousLG Decl. [47] 1 Apr, LGBO 54513. [48] 8 Mar, LGBO 7785, 7786, 7787. [49] 8 Mar, LGBO 7785, 7786. [50] 25 Mar, LGBO 17591. [51] Alfred Suckling, *The History and Antiquities of the County of Suffolk* (1846, 1848) (hereafter, Suckling), I, 152. [52] 7 Apr, *Lond Gaz.* [53] 3 Sept, OC. [54] 30 Sept, LGBO 33020. [55] Year consecr church (*Lond Gaz* 28 Nov 1961). [56] 26 Jan (lic min, *Lond Gaz* 20 Dec 1957). [57] Kirby, 252. [58] 7 Apr, Part Dist, Instr CBC. [59] Authority not found. [60] 22 Nov, NNRO, Faculty Book 1, Book 1, 562. [61] Year vac (*Lond Gaz* 10 Mar 1931). [62] 8 Nov, NNRO, Faculty Book 3, Book 5, 319-21. [63] 25 Mar, LGBO 16439. [64] Information supplied by Suffolk RO (Ipswich Branch). [65] 1 Apr, LGBO 45965. [66] 24 Nov, *Lond Gaz.* [67] 24 Mar, LGBO 16465. [68] 1 Oct, LGBO 36350. [69] 24 Mar, LGBO 14465. [70] 24 Mar, LGBO 16512. [71] 27 Feb, *Lond Gaz.* [72] 22 June, NNRO, Faculty Book 1, Book 1, 620*d*-621. [73] 24 Mar, LGBO 16514. [74] 24 Mar, LGBO 16437. [75] 27 July, *Lond Gaz.* [76] 20 Nov, NNRO, Faculty Book 4, Book 6, 321-33*d*. [77] 2 Apr, NNRO, Faculty Book 1, Book 1, 502. [78] PC QAB. [79] 1 Oct, LGBO 33509. [80] Kirby, 152. [81] Suckling I, 246, 269-79. [82] Suckling I, 186. [83] 19 June, NNRO, Faculty Book 3, Book 4, 63*d*-65*d*. [84] 30 May, *Lond Gaz.* [85] 25 Mar, LGBO 16479. [86] Authority not found. [87] 25 Mar, LGBO 19038. [88] Apptd day, LGBO 31938. [89] Before *Valor Eccl.* [90] 1 Oct, LGBO 33509. [91] 15 Sept, OC. [92] Year vac (*Lond Gaz* 18 Dec 1931). [93] 1 Apr, LGBO 61509. [94] 19 Dec, *Lond Gaz.* [95] 17 Dec, LGBO 12574. [96] Authority not found. [97] 25 June, *Lond Gaz.* [98] 1 Apr (*Lond Gaz* 24 Mar). [99] 20 Jan, NNRO, Faculty Book 3, Book 5, 257*d*-60. [100] 11 Oct, OC. [101] 16 Dec, NNRO, Faculty Book 5, Book 8, 47*d*-50. [102] 26 May, *Lond Gaz.* [103] Apptd day, LGBO 31872. [104] Information supplied by Suffolk RO (Ipswich Branch). [105] 1 Oct, LGBO 34741. [106] Year vac (*Lond Gaz* 5 Jan 1934). [107] 24 Mar, LGBO 14859. [108] 12 Aug, *Lond Gaz.* [109] 24 Nov, OC. [110] 8 Nov, *Lond Gaz.* [111] 17 June, LGBO 9214. [112] 20 June, *Lond Gaz.* [113] Apptd day, LGBO 31993. [114] 1 Apr, Dept EnvirnO 3725. [115] 30 Jan, OC. [116] 8 Nov, *Lond Gaz.* [117] 3 Aug, *Lond Gaz.* [118] 1 Dec (*Lond Gaz* 30 Nov). [119] 25 July, MHousLG Decl. [120] 26 Mar, *Lond Gaz.* [121] Kirby, 404. [122] 24 Mar, LGBO 16496. [123] 25 Mar, LGBO 16608. [124] 28 July, *Lond Gaz.* [125] 8 Mar, LGBO 7787. [126] 25 Mar, LGBO 44972. [127] 2 Jan, *Lond Gaz.* [128] 9 Dec, *Lond Gaz.* [129] 14 Aug, *Lond Gaz.* [130] 29 Oct, *Lond Gaz.* [131] 31 Mar (lic min, *Lond Gaz* 31 Jan). [132] 30 June, *Lond Gaz.* [133] 22 July, *Lond Gaz.* [134] 31 Oct, *Lond Gaz.* [135] Year vac (*Lond Gaz* 9 Apr 1940). [136] 27 Feb, *Lond Gaz.* [137] 1 Dec (*Lond Gaz* 18 Nov). [138] Authority not found. [139] 18 Oct, *Lond Gaz.* [140] 30 Sept, 58 & 59 Vict., session 2, *c* viii. [141] 1 Apr, LGBO 50454. [142] 3 Jan, *Lond Gaz.* [143] Autho-

rity not found. [144]24 Mar, LGBO 16470. [145]Year vac (*Lond Gaz* 28 Apr 1933). [146]13 Jan, *Lond Gaz.* [147]Authority not found. [148]17 May, NNRO, Faculty Book 1, Book 1, 638-38*d.* [149]19 Feb, *Lond Gaz.* [150]9 Nov, LGB ProvO Confirmation (No 5), Act, 1919. [151]19 Dec, *Lond Gaz.* [152]13 Nov, *Lond Gaz.* [153]24 Nov, *Lond Gaz.* [154]1 Apr, MHousLGO 8402. [155]Authority not found. [156]25 Mar, LGBO 16487. [157]25 Mar, LGBO 16497, 16498. [158]18 Apr, *Lond Gaz.* [159]28 July, *Lond Gaz.* [160]24 Mar, LGBO 16462. [161]Authority not found. [162]Authority not found. [163]12 Dec, OC. [164]11 Mar, *Lond Gaz.* [165]10 Nov, OC. [166]28 Nov, *Lond Gaz.* [167]Kirby, 306. [168]13 Nov, *Lond Gaz.* [169]25 Mar, LGBO 16438. [170]24 Mar, LGBO 16464. [171]MHousLG Decl. [172]25 Mar, LGBO 18104. [173]Suckling, I, 66-67. [174]PC QAB. [175]10 May, *Lond Gaz.* [176]Authority not found. [177]3 Jan, *Lond Gaz.* [178]18 Dec, *Lond Gaz.* [179]31 July, *Lond Gaz.* [180]24 Mar, LGBO 16470. [181]25 Mar, LGBO 18105. [182]25 Mar, LGBO 18105. [183]Implied in *Liber Regis.* [184]25 Mar, LGBO 16608. [185]24 Mar, LGBO 16462, 16464. [186]10 Dec, *Lond Gaz.* [187]Year vac (*Lond Gaz* 27 July 1926). [188]Authority not found. [189]Authority not found. [190]30 May, *Lond Gaz.* [191]Kirby, 55. [192]25 Mar, LGBO 14674. [193]25 Mar, LGBO 18106. [194]24 Mar, LGBO 14857. [195]25 Mar, LGBO 16498. [196]24 Mar, LGBO 16609. [197]25 Mar, LGBO 16608. [198]Authority not found. [199]Suckling, I, 108. [200]18 Oct, NNRO, Faculty Book 5, Book 9, 239-242*d.*

SURREY

[1]25 Mar, LGBO 14281. [2]5 Dec, LGBO 9951, 9952. [3]1 Oct, LGBO 42609. [4]1 Apr, MHealthO 76890. [5]PCQAB, refounded 9 Aug 1853, *Lond Gaz.* [6]27 Sept, *Lond Gaz.* [7]1 Apr, 17 & 18 Geo. V, *c* cvi. [8]21 Dec, *Lond Gaz.* [9]Lic min later in year after *Lond Gaz* 24 Oct). [10]8 Oct (consecr church, *Lond Gaz* 3 June 1955). [11]8 Nov (*Lond Gaz* 29 Feb 1952). [12]1 July, *Lond Gaz.* [13]27 May, *Lond Gaz.* [14]30 May, *Lond Gaz.* [15]PC QAB. [16]7 Feb, *Lond Gaz.* [17]12 Aug, *Lond Gaz.* [18]24 Feb, *Lond Gaz.* [19]28 Apr, *Lond Gaz.* [20]2 Dec, LGBO 10920, 10921. [21]25 Mar, 45 & 46 Vict., *c* 58. [22]1 Apr, MHealthO 77146. [23]2 Dec, LGBO 10920. [24]24 Mar, LGBO 16533. [25]9 Aug, *Lond Gaz.* [26]27 Feb, *Lond Gaz.* [27]13 Jan, *Lond Gaz.* [28]57 & 58 Vict., *c* 58 and Co Council NamingO. [29]9 Nov, The Guildford (Extension) O, 1904. [30]1 Oct, 12 & 13 Geo. V, *c* xliv. [31]1 Apr, MHousLGO 4884. [32]29 & 30 Vict., *c* 113. [33]PC QAB, refounded 18 Sept 1866, *Lond Gaz.* [34]26 Nov, *Lond Gaz.* [35]1 Apr, 11 & 12 Eliz. II, *c* 33. [36]11 Aug, *Lond Gaz.* [37]30 Aug, *Lond Gaz.* [38]Lic min later in year after *Lond Gaz* 30 Aug. [39]25 Jan, *Lond Gaz.* [40]8 Feb, *Lond Gaz.* [41]31 Dec, *Lond Gaz.* [42]18 Apr, *Lond Gaz.* [43]4 May, *Lond Gaz.* [44]1 Apr, SI 1968/2020. [45]22 Dec, *Lond Gaz.* [46]6 July, *Lond Gaz.* [47]11 Sept, *Lond Gaz.* [48]26 Mar, consequent on 62 & 63 Vict., *c* 14. [49]1 Apr, 4 & 5 Eliz. II, *c* lxxvii. [50]14 Aug, *Lond Gaz.* [51]27 June, *Lond Gaz.* [52]2 Aug, Part Dist, Instr Bp Winch. [53]62 & 63 Vict., *c* 14. [54]PC QAB, refounded 9 Aug 1853, *Lond Gaz.* [55]15 Oct, *Lond Gaz.* [56]28 July, *Lond Gaz.* [57]16 May, *Lond Gaz.* [58]20 Oct, *Lond Gaz.* [59]16 Feb, *Lond Gaz.* [60]11 July, *Lond Gaz.* [61]9 July, *Lond Gaz.* [62]2 July, *Lond Gaz.* [63]6 Feb, *Lond Gaz.* [64]10 Feb, *Lond Gaz.* [65]1 Nov (*Lond Gaz* 27 Oct). [66]5 Jan, *Lond Gaz.* [67]16 Mar, *Lond Gaz.* [68]23 Feb, *Lond Gaz.* [69]1 Jan (*Lond Gaz* 29 Dec 1972). [70]15 Sept, *Lond Gaz.* [71]27 Feb, *Lond Gaz.* [72]22 May, *Lond Gaz.* [73]19 July, *Lond Gaz.* [74]6 Nov, *Lond Gaz.* [75]14 Apr, *Lond Gaz.* [76]29 June, *Lond Gaz.* [77]2 July, *Lond Gaz.* [78]24 Dec, *Lond Gaz.* [79]1 Apr, LGBO 62791. [80]8 Nov, *Lond Gaz.* [81]12 May, *Lond Gaz.* [82]17 Aug, *Lond Gaz.* [83]27 Mar, *Lond Gaz.* [84]3 Oct, *Lond Gaz.* [85]31 Mar, *Lond Gaz.* [86]2 Nov, *Lond Gaz.* [87]2 May, *Lond Gaz* (Part Dist, 3 Apr 1884, Instr Eccl Commissioners and Bp Winch). [88]30 Dec, *Lond Gaz.* [89]23 Aug, *Lond Gaz.* [90]24 Mar, *Lond Gaz.* [91]1 Aug, Part Dist. [92]15 Dec, *Lond Gaz.* [93]20 July, *Lond Gaz.* [94]8 Aug, *Lond Gaz.* [95]17 Jan, *Lond Gaz.* [96]4 July, *Lond Gaz.* [97]Note cancelled. [98]14 May, *Lond Gaz.* [99]29 Sept, *Lond Gaz.* [100]23 Nov, *Lond Gaz.* [101]4 Feb, Part Dist, Instr CBC. [102]27 June, *Lond Gaz.* [103]3 Apr, *Lond Gaz.* [104]25 July, Part Dist. [105]9 Dec, *Lond Gaz.* [106]Authority not found. [107]Apptd day, LGBO 31855. [108]1 Apr, MHousLGO 5824. [109]19 Aug, *Lond Gaz.* [110]20 May, *Lond Gaz.* [111]*VCH Surrey* III, 334. [112]19 Mar, *Lond Gaz.* [113]*VCH Surrey* II, 595. [114]16 Apr, *Lond Gaz.* [115]1 Jan, 20 Vict., *c* 19. [116]25 Mar, LGBO 14284. [117]27 Feb, reported in *Parl Papers* 1872, XLVI, 19. [118]24 Mar, LGBO 16532. [119]29 Mar, *Lond Gaz.* [120]28 Sept, Part Dist, Instr Bp Winch. [121]19 Apr, Part Dist, Instr CBC and Bp Winch. [122]10 Feb, Part Dist, Instr. [123]4 Aug, *Lond Gaz.* [124]9 May, *Lond Gaz.* [125]31 Oct, *Lond Gaz.* [126]20 Feb, *Lond Gaz.* [127]14 Mar, *Lond Gaz.* [128]22 Mar, *Lond Gaz.* [129]15 May, *Lond Gaz.* [130]13 Mar, *Lond Gaz.* [131]10 June, *Lond Gaz.* [132]PC QAB, refounded 7 Feb 1862, *Lond Gaz.* [133]2 Aug, *Lond Gaz.* [134]13 Oct, *Lond Gaz.* [135]18 Mar, *Lond Gaz.* [136]27 June, *Lond Gaz.* [137]30 June, *Lond Gaz.* [138]1 Apr, MHealthO 84423. [139]2 Jan, *Lond Gaz.* [140]23 June, *Lond Gaz.* [141]22 Feb, *Lond Gaz.* [142]17 Sept, *Lond Gaz.* [143]15 Dec, Instr Bp Winch. [144]28 Jan, *Lond Gaz.* [145]5 Mar, Part Dist, Instr CBC. [146]18 May, Part Dist, Instr Bp Winch. [147]3 Dec, Part Dist, Instr Bp Winch. [148]10 Mar, *Lond Gaz.* [149]18 Aug, *Lond Gaz.* [150]28 Aug, *Lond Gaz.* [151]26 Oct, *Lond Gaz.* [152]10 Aug, *Lond Gaz.* [153]7 May, *Lond Gaz.* [154]23 Apr, *Lond Gaz.* [155]15 May, *Lond Gaz.* [156]24 Aug, *Lond Gaz.* [157]17 Mar, *Lond Gaz.* [158]18 Jan, *Lond Gaz.* [159]26 Oct, *Lond Gaz.* [160]19 Dec, *Lond Gaz.* [161]13 July, *Lond Gaz.* [162]*VCH Surrey* III, 140. [163]5 Dec, LGBO 9913. [164]1 June, MHealthO 71885. [165]17 Aug, *Lond Gaz.* [166]16 Dec, *Lond Gaz.* [167]1 Oct, MHealthO 73618. [168]6 Dec, Part Dist, Instr. [169]15 Aug, *Lond Gaz.* [170]11 Nov, *Lond Gaz.* [171]24 July, *Lond Gaz.* [172]31 May, *Lond Gaz.* [173]29 May, *Lond Gaz.* [174]2 Sept, *Lond Gaz.* [175]1 Apr, 20 & 21 Eliz. II, *c* 70, amended by 22 & 23 Eliz. II, *c* xi. [176]1 Apr, MHealthO 108617. [177]14 Sept, *Lond Gaz.* [178]12 Oct, *Lond Gaz.* [179]*VCH Surrey* III, 413. [180]24 Mar, LGBO 16490. [181]17 Mar, reported in

Parl Papers 1872, XLVI, 22. [182]4 Dec, *Lond Gaz.* [183]1 Apr, MHealthO 84431. [184]1 Apr, MHousLGO 33843. [185]Year vac (*Lond Gaz* 1 Nov 1955). [186]24 June, *Lond Gaz.* [187]1 Dec, *Lond Gaz.* [188]3 Jan, *Lond Gaz.* [189]31 Jan, *Lond Gaz.* [190]9 June, *Lond Gaz.* [191]3 May, *Lond Gaz.* [192]29 Nov, *Lond Gaz.* [193]12 Mar, *Lond Gaz.* [194]21 Nov, *Lond Gaz.* [195]1 Jan (*Lond Gaz* 23 Dec 1949). [196]10 Apr, *Lond Gaz.* [197]17 Oct, *Lond Gaz.* [198]9 Nov, *Lond Gaz.* [199]1 July, LGBO 32897. [200]1 Apr, MHealthO 76974. [201]19 July, *Lond Gaz.* [202]5 May, *Lond Gaz.* [203]29 Mar, *Lond Gaz.* [204]14 Oct (lic min, *Lond Gaz* 4 Aug). [205]25 Mar, LGBO 14709. [206]1 Apr, 14 & 15 Geo. V, *c* xcviii. [207]1 Apr, MHealthO 84021. [208]5 Apr, *Lond Gaz.* [209]28 June, *Lond Gaz.* [210]18 Sept, *Lond Gaz.* [211]21 May, *Lond Gaz.* [212]4 Nov, *Lond Gaz.* [213]1 Apr, *Lond Gaz.* [214]18 Aug, *Lond Gaz.* [215]18 Oct, *Lond Gaz.* [216]29 July, *Lond Gaz.* [217]*VCH Surrey* II, 582. [218]5 Dec, *Lond Gaz.* [219]1 Aug, *Lond Gaz.* [220]22 Aug, *Lond Gaz.* [221]16 July, *Lond Gaz.* [222]13 Nov, *Lond Gaz.* [223]1 Apr, LGBO 32638. [224]2 May, *Lond Gaz.* [225]9 Geo. III, *c* lxv. [226]5 Jan, *Lond Gaz.* [227]30 Sept, LGB ProvO Confirmation (No 14), Act, 1895. [228]1 Oct, LGBO 34997. [229]5 Dec, LGBO 9949. [230]1 Oct, MHealthO 72791. [231]9 Aug, Part Dist, Instr CBC. [232]10 Dec, *Lond Gaz.* [233]18 July, *Lond Gaz.* [234]13 June, *Lond Gaz.* [235]12 Feb, *Lond Gaz.* [236]5 Jan, *Lond Gaz.* [237]25 Feb, *Lond Gaz.* [238]7 Apr, *Lond Gaz.* [239]1 Apr, MHealthO 77665. [240]3 Geo. II, *c* 33. [241]*VCH Surrey* III, 440. [242]17 Dec, *Lond Gaz.* [243]10 July, *Lond Gaz.* [244]7 Dec, *Lond Gaz.* [245]16 June, MHous LG Decl. [246]1 Apr, MHousLGO 47801. [247]Lic min later in year after *Lond Gaz* 5 Sept. [248]*VCH Surrey* II, 581. [249]1 Apr, LGBO 43079. [250]1 Apr, LGBO 61330. [251]1 Oct, MHealthO 69366. [252]7 Feb, *Lond Gaz.* [253]Apptd day, LGBO 31936. [254]1 Apr, MHous LGO 3263. [255]1 Oct, LGBO 34997. [256]6 Aug, *Lond Gaz.* [257]1 Oct, LGBO 39880. [258]29 Dec, *Lond Gaz.* [259]20 June, Part Dist. [260]1 Apr, 18 & 19 Geo. V, *c* lxii. [261]1 Apr, LGBO 35710. [262]*VCH Hants* IV, 29. [263]OC 1878 says this par not prev in a RDn, seemingly in error. [264]2 Feb, *Lond Gaz.* [265]4 July, Part Dist, Instr Bp Winch. [266]1 Apr, LGBO 51092. [267]1 Apr, SI 1954/273. [268]28 Nov, *Lond Gaz.* [269]9 Nov, The Guildford (Extension) O, 1904. [270]Information supplied by Surrey RO. [271]5 Dec, LGBO 10924. [272]19 Dec (lic min, *Lond Gaz* 24 Oct). [273]24 Oct, *Lond Gaz.* [274]13 Apr, *Lond Gaz.* [275]25 July, *Lond Gaz.* [276]22 June, Part Dist, Instr CBC. [277]16 May (lic min, *Lond Gaz* 26 Apr). [278]1 Apr, MHealthO 76974. [279]1 Apr, SI 1958/462. [280]14 July, *Lond Gaz.* [281]13 Aug, *Lond Gaz.* [282]4 Dec, *Lond Gaz.* [283]15 Jan, *Lond Gaz.* [284]Year lic min (*Lond Gaz* 30 Sept 1949). [285]31 May, *Lond Gaz.* [286]Lic min later in year after *Lond Gaz* 29 Feb. [287]*VCH Surrey* III, 430. [288]1 Apr, LGBO 41688. [289]25 Mar, LGBO 14283. [290]3 June, *Lond Gaz.* [291]24 Dec, *Lond Gaz.* [292]14 Oct, *Lond Gaz.* [293]Year vac (*Lond Gaz* 29 Mar 1825). [294]26 Apr, *Lond Gaz.* [295]23 Dec, *Lond Gaz.* [296]31 Jan, *Lond Gaz.* [297]8 Mar, *Lond Gaz.* [298]Exact date not found; *Lond Gaz* 18 Dec 1973. [299]20 Mar, *Lond Gaz.* [300]PC QAB; 9 Geo. III, *c* 65. [301]Authority not found. [302]11 Jan, *Lond Gaz.* [303]25 July, *Lond Gaz.* [304]4 July, Part Dist, Instr Bp Winch. [305]11 Oct, *Lond Gaz.* [306]6 May, *Lond Gaz.* [307]12 & 13 Vict., *c* 42. [308]5 June, *Lond Gaz.* [309]17 Nov, *Lond Gaz.* [310]3 Aug, *Lond Gaz.* [311]12 Apr, *Lond Gaz.* [312]5 Feb, *Lond Gaz.* [313]PC QAB 1845, refounded 19 Oct 1847, *Lond Gaz.* [314]*VCH Surrey* IV, 62. [315]17 Apr, *Lond Gaz.* [316]27 Nov, *Lond Gaz.* [317]29 Mar, *Lond Gaz.* [318]26 July, *Lond Gaz.* [319]1 Aug (*Lond Gaz* 20 July). [320]1 Mar, *Lond Gaz.* [321]1 Oct, LGBO 38288. [322]17 May, *Lond Gaz.* [323]15 June, *Lond Gaz.* [324]4 July (lic min, *Lond Gaz* 1 June). [325]1 Apr, The Counties of London and Surrey (Wandsworth and Mitcham) O, 1903. [326]14 Feb, *Lond Gaz.* [327]9 May (consecr church, *Lond Gaz* 29 July 1947). [328]31 July, *Lond Gaz.* [329]PC QAB; *VCH Surrey* III, 456 says independent in 1843. [330]*VCH Surrey* IV, 74. [331]23 Oct, *Lond Gaz.* [332]6 Feb, *Lond Gaz.* [333]30 Oct, *Lond Gaz.* [334]6 Mar, *Lond Gaz.* [335]1 Feb (*Lond Gaz* 29 Jan). [336]1 Apr, MHousLGO 9358. [337]14 July, Part Dist, Instr Eccl Commissioners and Bp Winch. [338]22 July, *Lond Gaz.* [339]28 Oct, *Lond Gaz.* [340]14 July, *Lond Gaz.* [341]1 Jan (Instr Bp Roch 22 Nov 1888). [342]29 Nov, *Lond Gaz.* [343]25 Mar, LGBO 14281, 14282, 14283. [344]5 Dec, LGBO 9950, 9951. [345]28 Nov, *Lond Gaz.* [346]11 May, *Lond Gaz.* [347]1 Jan, *Lond Gaz.* [348]25 May, *Lond Gaz.* [349]10 Nov, *Lond Gaz.* [350]*VCH Surrey* III, 365. [351]Year lic min (*Lond Gaz* 29 Mar 1960). [352]Owen Manning (ed. William Bray), *The History and Antiquities of Surrey* (1804-14), III, 300. [353]25 Nov, *Lond Gaz.* [354]1 May, *Lond Gaz.* [355]*VCH Surrey* III, 436. [356]19 Feb, *Lond Gaz.* [357]14 June, Part Dist. [358]19 May, LGBO 39822. [359]30 Sept, LGBO 31143. [360]18 Jan, *Lond Gaz.* [361]4 Apr, *Lond Gaz.* [362]30 June, Part Dist. [363]18 June, *Lond Gaz.* [364]7 Nov, *Lond Gaz.* [365]7 Aug, *Lond Gaz.* [366]PC QAB 1840, refounded 31 Jan 1843, *Lond Gaz.* [367]PC QAB 1841, refounded 31 Jan 1843, *Lond Gaz.* [368]4 Jan, *Lond Gaz.* [369]8 June, *Lond Gaz.* [370]1 Oct, MHealthO 73738. [371]30 July, MHousLG Decl. [372]6 Dec, *Lond Gaz.* [373]2 Dec, LGBO 10921. [374]29 Oct, *Lond Gaz.* [375]22 & 23 Chas. II, local act. [376]24 Nov, *Lond Gaz.* [377]PC QAB, refounded 22 Mar 1850, *Lond Gaz.* [378]26 Nov, Part Dist, Instr CBC. [379]27 Apr, *Lond Gaz.* [380]6 Geo. II, *c* xi. [381]31 & 32 Henry VIII. [382]22 Jan, London Co CouncilO. [383]*VCH Surrey* IV, 158-59. [384]Authority not found. [385]Authority not found. [386]61 & 62 Vict., *c* 116. [387]PC QAB. [388]31 Aug, *Lond Gaz.* [389]22 July, *Lond Gaz.* [390]3 Mar, *Lond Gaz.* [391]15 Mar, *Lond Gaz.* [392]20 Dec, Part Dist, Instr Bp Winch and CBC. [393]26 Nov, Part Dist, Instr Bp Winch and CBC. [394]17 Feb, *Lond Gaz.* [395]17 July, *Lond Gaz.* [396]12 Dec, reported in *Parl Papers* 1872, XLVI, 19. [397]27 July, *Lond Gaz.* [398]25 Mar, *Lond Gaz.* [399]Year vac (*Lond Gaz* 3 July 1941). [400]*VCH Surrey* III, 375. [401]15 Jan, *Lond Gaz.* [402]Presumed incl in PLU when became sep CP; not orig rated in the PLU. [403]29 Apr, *Lond Gaz.* [404]5 July, *Lond Gaz.* [405]5 Aug, *Lond Gaz.* [406]25 Mar, LGBO 14282. [407]30 Nov, *Lond Gaz.* [408]7 Mar, *Lond Gaz.* [409]6 Apr, *Lond Gaz.* [410]2 Dec,

LGBO 10925. [411]5 Dec, LGBO 9952. [412]5 Dec, LGBO 9950. [413]SI 1945/701.

SUSSEX

[1]1 Apr, 7 Edw. VII, *c* clvi. [2]25 Mar, 45 & 46 Vict., *c* 58. [3]1 Apr, MHealthO 77841. [4]7 July, *Lond Gaz.* [5]13 Aug, OC. [6]9 May, *Lond Gaz.* [7]15 Apr, *Lond Gaz.* [8]8 Mar, *Lond Gaz.* [9]13 Aug, *Lond Gaz.* [10]24 Mar, LGBO 16533. [11]James Dallaway, *A History of the Western Division of the County of Sussex* (hereafter, Dallaway), I, 26. [12]29 & 30 Vict., *c* 113. [13]Year vac (*Lond Gaz* 7 June 1935). [14]1 Apr, MHealthO 77136. [15]19 May, OC. [16]2 & 3 Wm. IV, *c* 64 and 7 & 8 Vict., *c* 61. [17]18 Aug, *Lond Gaz.* [18]19 Dec, LGBO 10297. [19]9 Apr, by the Bp, W Sussex RO Cap. I/27/1, folios 103-07. [20]20 Dec, LGBO 7429, 7442. [21]21 Dec, LGBO 7534. [22]10 Mar, *Lond Gaz.* [23]20 Aug, *Lond Gaz.* [24]14 Feb, *Lond Gaz.* [25]9 Nov, The Arundel (Extension) O, 1902. [26]24 Mar, LGBO 19652, 19657. [27]1 Apr, MHousLGO 8409. [28]Information supplied by W Sussex RO. [29]1 Apr, MHousLGO 6556. [30]1 Apr, MHousLGO 7247. [31]4 Nov, *Lond Gaz.* [32]Authority not found. [33]1 Apr, MHousLGO 5861. [34]22 Dec, *Lond Gaz.* [35]1 Oct, LGBO 41494. [36]PC QAB. [37]Apptd day, LGBO 31762. [38]1 Oct, LGBO 36551. [39]1 Oct, LGBO 61024. [40]22 Dec, OC. [41]Apptd day, LGBO 31743. [42]8 Sept, *Lond Gaz.* [43]26 June, *Lond Gaz.* [44]10 Oct, *Lond Gaz.* [45]2 Dec, *Lond Gaz.* [46]6 July, *Lond Gaz.* [47]5 Sept, *Lond Gaz.* [48]1 Aug, *Lond Gaz.* [49]26 May, *Lond Gaz.* [50]1 Nov (*Lond Gaz* 20 Oct). [51]24 Mar, LGBO 23839. [52]29 Mar, OC. [53]Year vac (*Lond Gaz* 22 July 1932). [54]21 July, *Lond Gaz.* [55]27 Feb, *Lond Gaz.* [56]23 Dec, *Lond Gaz.* [57]11 Mar (*Lond Gaz* 6 Feb). [58]57 & 58 Vict., *c* 58 and Co Council Naming O. [59]9 Nov, LGB ProvO 1388. [60]16 Oct, *Lond Gaz.* [61]6 June, *Lond Gaz.* [62]1 Apr, 17 & 18 Vict., *c* lxxxi. [63]3 Oct, OC. [64]26 Mar, *Lond Gaz.* [65]Dallaway, II-1, 284, and II-2, 215. [66]30 Sept, 58 & 59 Vict., *c* lxxxvi. [67]*VCH Sussex* IX, 172. [68]24 Mar, LGBO 19657. [69]*VCH Sussex* VII, 252. [70]1 Apr, 14 & 15 Geo. VI, *c* xxix. [71]28 Aug, *Lond Gaz.* [72]27 May, *Lond Gaz.* [73]25 Mar, *Lond Gaz.* [74]2 Sept, *Lond Gaz.* [75]29 Oct, *Lond Gaz.* [76]28 Mar, *Lond Gaz.* [77]31 Oct, *Lond Gaz.* [78]22 July, *Lond Gaz.* [79]11 July, *Lond Gaz.* [80]19 Aug, *Lond Gaz.* [81]19 July, *Lond Gaz.* [82]19 Jan, *Lond Gaz.* [83]23 Aug, *Lond Gaz.* [84]10 Oct, *Lond Gaz.* [85]27 July, *Lond Gaz.* [86]11 Feb, *Lond Gaz.* [87]28 Apr, *Lond Gaz.* [88]21 Nov, *Lond Gaz.* [89]3 Jan (*Lond Gaz* 29 Dec 1955). [90]13 June, *Lond Gaz.* [91]12 Aug, *Lond Gaz.* [92]2 Apr, *Lond Gaz.* [93]24 Feb, *Lond Gaz.* [94]13 Oct, *Lond Gaz.* [95]29 July, *Lond Gaz.* [96]9 Feb, *Lond Gaz.* [97]4 Apr, *Lond Gaz.* [98]29 Mar, *Lond Gaz.* [99]Year vac (*Lond Gaz* 11 Aug 1922). [100]1 Nov, *Lond Gaz.* [101]18 May, *Lond Gaz.* [102]20 Dec, LGBO 7427. [103]9 Nov, The Worthing (Extension) O, 1902. [104]31 July, *Lond Gaz.* [105]25 Apr, *Lond Gaz.* [106]4 May, *Lond Gaz.* [107]22 Feb, *Lond Gaz.* [108]28 June, *Lond Gaz.* [109]13 Dec, *Lond Gaz.* [110]Before *Valor Eccl* and Dallaway II-2, 715. [111]Authority not found. [112]11 Aug, *Lond Gaz.* [113]1 Oct, LGBO 47948. [114]15 Aug, *Lond Gaz.* [115]26 July, *Lond Gaz.* [116]25 June, *Lond Gaz.* [117]30 May, *Lond Gaz.* [118]29 Feb, *Lond Gaz.* [119]10 June, *Lond Gaz.* [120]24 June, *Lond Gaz.* [121]20 Dec, *Lond Gaz.* [122]22 May, *Lond Gaz.* [123]11 Dec, *Lond Gaz.* [124]1 Feb (*Lond Gaz* 23 Jan). [125]4 Mar, *Lond Gaz.* [126]24 Mar, LGBO 19652. [127]4 & 5 Wm. & Mary, parl 2, session 4, *c* xiii. [128]1 Apr, SI 1972/2039 on authority of 20 & 21 Eliz. II, *c* 70. [129]26 Mar, LGBO 34011. [130]5 Dec, *Lond Gaz.* [131]1 Jan, 20 Vict., *c* 19. [132]Apptd day, LGBO 32032. [133]9 Nov, LGB ProvO 1142. [134]24 Mar, OC. [135]15 May, *Lond Gaz.* [136]Statute requiring it to remaing ex-par cited in Dallaway, I, 198-99; sep CP 1858 by 20 Vict., *c* 19. [137]26 Oct, reported in *Parl Papers* 1903, L, 595-96. [138]*VCH Sussex* III, 166. [139]4 July, *Lond Gaz.* [140]1 Apr, MHousLG PlanningO 517. [141]*VCH Sussex* VII, 102. [142]21 Dec, *Lond Gaz.* [143]Year vac (*Lond Gaz* 22 Dec 1956). [144]*VCH Sussex* VII, 174. [145]30 June, *Lond Gaz.* [146]14 July, *Lond Gaz.* [147]Dallaway, II-1, 16-17. [148]16 June, LGBO 10436. [149]*VCH Sussex* IV, 70. [150]24 Oct, *Lond Gaz.* [151]27 Nov, LGBO 11288, 11289. [152]12 Feb, *Lond Gaz.* [153]*VCH Sussex* VII, 146. [154]*VCH Sussex* VII, 147. [155]19 Feb, SI 1953/518. [156]12 July, *Lond Gaz.* [157]23 Jan, *Lond Gaz.* [158]27 Nov, *Lond Gaz.* [159]8 Nov, *Lond Gaz.* [160]17 Sept, *Lond Gaz.* [161]1 Apr, LGBO 47656. [162]1 Edw. VIII and 1 Geo. VI, *c* lxiv. [163]19 Dec, *Lond Gaz.* [164]20 Feb, *Lond Gaz.* [165]5 May, *Lond Gaz.* [166]11 Mar, *Lond Gaz.* [167]Apptd day, LGBO 36014. [168]1 Edw. VIII and 1 Geo. VI, *c* lxxvi. [169]Year vac (*Lond Gaz* 2 Nov 1928). [170]Dallaway, I, 201. [171]*VCH Sussex* VII, 123. [172]26 Mar, LGBO 34010. [173]8 Aug, OC. [174]17 July, *Lond Gaz.* [175]1 Apr, 18 & 19 Geo. V, *c* lix. [176]26 Mar, LGBO 39222. [177]1 Apr, LGBO 58158. [178]1 Apr, 16 & 17 Geo. V, *c* xcv. [179]25 June, *Lond Gaz.* [180]20 July, *Lond Gaz.* [181]24 Jan, *Lond Gaz.* [182]26 Apr, *Lond Gaz.* [183]12 Nov, *Lond Gaz.* [184]3 Mar, *Lond Gaz.* [185]6 Apr, *Lond Gaz.* [186]5 Feb, *Lond Gaz.* [187]16 Dec, *Lond Gaz.* [188]17 Apr, *Lond Gaz.* [189]6 Aug, *Lond Gaz.* [190]12 Oct, *Lond Gaz.* [191]Effective lic min later in year after *Lond Gaz* (29 Feb). [192]31 Dec, *Lond Gaz.* [193]24 Oct (lic min, *Lond Gaz* 12 Oct). [194]4 Aug, *Lond Gaz.* [195]12 Mar, *Lond Gaz.* [196]Year vac (*Lond Gaz* 8 Aug 1971). [197]13 May, *Lond Gaz.* [198]14 May, *Lond Gaz.* [199]Apptd day, LGBO 31816. [200]5 May, *Lond Gaz.* [201]23 Apr, *Lond Gaz.* [202]1 Apr, MHousLGO 1306. [203]17 May, *Lond Gaz.* [204]25 Mar, LGBO 18118. [205]7 May, SI 1953/745. [206]1 Apr, MHousLGO 1375. [207]2 June, *Lond Gaz.* [208]18 Aug, OC. [209]Dallaway, II-1, 31. [210]8 Mar, Dept Envirn Decl. [211]24 Mar, LGBO 22206. [212]26 Oct, *Lond Gaz.* [213]11 Jan, *Lond Gaz.* [214]18 Oct, *Lond Gaz.* [215]9 Nov, LGB ProvO 1626. [216]*VCH Sussex* IV, 192. [217]30 Dec, *Lond Gaz.* [218]Dallaway, II-1, 272. [219]9 July, *Lond Gaz.* [220]15 Dec, *Lond Gaz.* [221]Year vac (*Lond Gaz* 18 Mar 1932). [222]8 May, *Lond Gaz.* [223]1 Apr, MHealthO 108747. [224]1 Apr, MHealthO 89197. [225]1 Apr, MHealthO 100207. [226]1 Apr, 10 Edw. VII & 1 Geo. V, *c* cxxiii. [227]1 Oct, LGBO 52001. [228]14 & 15 Geo. V, *c* lxxxviii. [229]1 July (*Lond Gaz* 4 June). [230]*VCH Sussex* IX,

27. [231] 28 June, OC. [232] 7 Oct, OC. [233] *VCH Sussex* IX, 21. [234] 2 Jan, *Lond Gaz* (and also 31 Dec 1884, *Lond Gaz* immediately preceeding). [235] 23 June, OC. [236] 1 Oct, *Lond Gaz.* [237] Earlier organisation as in Edward Hasted, *The History and Topographical Survey of the County of Kent* and in Richard Kilburne, *A Topographie or Survey of the County of Kent*; later as in 19th cent censuses. [238] 14 Mar, *Lond Gaz.* [239] Lic min later in year after *Lond Gaz* (29 May). [240] 17 Mar, OC. [241] 25 Mar, LGBO 19641. [242] Dallaway, I, 207. [243] *VCH Sussex* IV, 63. [244] 1 Apr, MHealthO 85133. [245] 1 Apr, MHousLGO 7246. [246] 3 Aug, *Lond Gaz.* [247] 1 Oct, LGBO 42098. [248] 1 Apr, MHealthO 71600. [249] 21 Jan, *Lond Gaz.* [250] 1 Apr, MHealth ProvO Confirmation (Hove Extension) Act, 1927. [251] 2 July, *Lond Gaz.* [252] 29 Nov, *Lond Gaz.* [253] 4 Feb, *Lond Gaz.* [254] 10 Feb, *Lond Gaz.* [255] 17 Nov, *Lond Gaz.* [256] 1 Oct, MHealthO 67960. [257] 29 Apr, *Lond Gaz.* [258] 16 Aug, *Lond Gaz.* [259] 1 Apr, MHousLG PlanningO 553. [260] 1 Oct, LGBO 54317. [261] 1 Oct, MHealthO 71927. [262] 29 May, *Lond Gaz.* [263] 1 July (*Lond Gaz* 22 June). [264] Authority not found. [265] 27 June, *Lond Gaz.* [266] 1 Apr, LGBO 57514. [267] *VCH Sussex* VII, 40. [268] *VCH Sussex* VII, 41. [269] 17 Dec, *Lond Gaz.* [270] 1 Jan, *Lond Gaz* (OC 21 Dec 1928). [271] 22 Oct, *Lond Gaz.* [272] Authority not found. [273] 1 Apr, MHealthO 93992. [274] 1 Apr, MHousLGO 8414. [275] 1 Apr, LGBO 41338. [276] 1 June (*Lond Gaz* 31 May). [277] 20 Dec, LGBO 7441. [278] 12 Dec, OC. [279] 22 June, *Lond Gaz.* [280] 10 July, *Lond Gaz.* [281] 27 Apr, *Lond Gaz.* [282] 1 Oct, MHealth Decl. [283] 1 Oct, LGBO 36551. [284] 24 Nov, OC. [285] Presumed incl in PLU when became sep par; not orig rated in the PLU. [286] 17 Jan, *Lond Gaz.* [287] 12 Jan (lic min, *Lond Gaz* 24 Oct 1952). [288] 1 Apr, LGBO 73137. [289] 20 Dec, LGBO 7442. [290] 31 Mar, 17 & 18 Geo. V, *c* lxxxi. [291] 1 Apr, LGBO 37456. [292] 27 Oct, *Lond Gaz.* [293] 26 Feb, *Lond Gaz.* [294] 20 Dec, LGBO 7429. [295] Apptd day, LGBO 31959. [296] 1 Apr, MHealthO 108923. [297] 24 Dec, *Lond Gaz.* [298] Lic min later in year after *Lond Gaz* (29 May). [299] *VCH Sussex* IX, 74. [300] 1 Oct, LGBO 54317. [301] 1 Apr, MHousLGO 34300. [302] 2 Nov, *Lond Gaz.* [303] *VCH Sussex* IX, 257. [304] 26 July, LGBO 8301. [305] 1 Apr, MHousLGO 7740. [306] Authority not found. [307] Year vac (*Lond Gaz* 5 Mar 1929). [308] 26 Mar, *Lond Gaz.* [309] Information supplied by W Sussex RO. [310] *VCH Sussex* IX, 142. [311] 1 Apr, MHousLGO 5787.

WILTSHIRE

[1] 1 Apr, MHealthO 77934. [2] 9 Nov, *Lond Gaz.* [3] 29 & 30 Vict., *c* 113. [4] 28 Nov, reported in *Parl Papers* 1890-91, LXI, 53. [5] 14 Feb, *Lond Gaz.* [6] 2 Oct, *Lond Gaz.* [7] 25 Mar, LGBO 16453. [8] 2 Mar, *Lond Gaz.* [9] 25 Mar, LGBO 17960. [10] 16 Apr, reported in *Parl Papers* 1872, XLVI, 21. [11] 10 Mar, *Lond Gaz.* [12] 25 Mar, 45 & 46 Vict., *c* 58. [13] 25 Mar, LGBO 17593. [14] 3 Mar, Part Dist, Instr CBC. [15] 1 Oct, LGBO 36449. [16] 31 Aug, *Lond Gaz.* [17] 24 Mar, LGBO 16422. [18] 25 Mar, LGBO 18189. [19] 18 Mar, reported in *Parl Papers* 1872, XLVI, 18. [20] 2 Nov, *Lond Gaz.* [21] 1 Nov (*Lond Gaz* 22 Oct). [22] 1 Apr, LGBO 32465. [23] 24 Mar, LGBO 15870. [24] PC QAB. [25] *The Topographical Collections of John Aubrey* (ed John Edward Jackson) (hereafter, Aubrey), 380. [26] 20 Aug, *Lond Gaz.* [27] 12 Apr, *Lond Gaz.* [28] Beresford & Finberg, 180. [29] 14 Apr, *Lond Gaz.* [30] 30 Sept, LGBO 31825. [31] 1 Nov (*Lond Gaz* 27 Oct). [32] 1 Oct, MHealth ProvO Confirmation (Swindon Extension) Act, 1928. [33] 25 Mar, *Lond Gaz.* [34] 19 June, reported in *Parl Papers* 1872, XLVI, 18. [35] 18 May, reported in *Parl Papers* 1872, XLVI, 14. [36] 24 Mar, LGBO 16476. [37] 25 Nov, *Lond Gaz.* [38] 25 Mar, LGBO 18133. [39] 24 Mar, LGBO 16526. [40] Aubrey, 53-54. [41] Year vac (*Lond Gaz* 27 Feb 1940). [42] 14 Feb, *Lond Gaz.* [43] 26 Mar, LGBO 25403. [44] 24 Mar, LGBO 16482. [45] 30 Aug, *Lond Gaz.* [46] 5 Jan, *Lond Gaz.* [47] 6 Feb, *Lond Gaz.* [48] 10 May, *Lond Gaz.* [49] 20 Vict., *c* 19. [50] 16 Nov, *Lond Gaz.* [51] 24 Mar, LGBO 16527. [52] 24 Mar, LGBO 16519. [53] 29 June, *Lond Gaz.* [54] Year vac (*Lond Gaz* 27 Apr 1954). [55] 28 Nov, reported in *Parl Papers* 1890-91. LXI, 54. [56] Apptd day, LGBO 32118. [57] 1 Oct, LGBO 39284. [58] 30 Sept, LGBO 31681. [59] 21 Feb, *Lond Gaz.* [60] LGB ProvO Confirmation (No 12), Act, 1895. [61] 25 Mar, LGBO 16466. [62] 25 Mar, LGBO 17881. [63] 16 Apr, *Lond Gaz.* [64] 17 Apr, *Lond Gaz.* [65] 58 & 59 Vict., *c* xci. [66] 4 Feb, *Lond Gaz.* [67] 9 May, *Lond Gaz.* [68] Apptd day, LGBO 31891. [69] 24 Mar, LGBO 16528. [70] 25 Mar, LGBO 18134. [71] 22 July, *Lond Gaz.* [72] 24 Mar, LGBO 16511. [73] 24 Mar, LGBO 16510. [74] 30 Oct, *Lond Gaz.* [75] 13 Feb, *Lond Gaz.* [76] 1 Oct, LGBO 34691. [77] 25 Mar, LGBO 18149. [78] 9 Nov, The New Sarum (Extension) O, 1904. [79] 1 Apr, SI 1954/316. [80] 51 & 52 Vict., *c* 41. [81] 21 July, *Lond Gaz.* [82] 22 Feb, reported in *Parl Papers* 1890-91, LXI, 54. [83] 30 Sept, LGBO 31683. [84] 31 Mar, LGBO 35447. [85] 1 Apr, SI 1956/371. [86] 1 Apr, SI 1965/2086. [87] 1 Apr, LGBO 35447. [88] 24 Mar, LGBO 16529. [89] 24 Mar, LGBO 16452. [90] 5 June, *Lond Gaz.* [91] 14 June, *Lond Gaz.* [92] 15 Oct, *Lond Gaz.* [93] First appearance *Clergy List.* [94] 28 Sept, *Lond Gaz.* [95] 5 Oct, *Lond Gaz.* [96] 5 May, *Lond Gaz.* [97] 31 Jan, *Lond Gaz.* [98] 25 Mar, LGBO 14451. [99] 3 Feb, *Lond Gaz.* [100] 14 Aug, reported in *Parl Papers* 1890-91, LXI, 56. [101] 28 Nov, reported in *Parl Papers* 1890-91, LXI, 57. [102] 3 Aug, *Lond Gaz.* [103] 24 Oct, *Lond Gaz.* [104] *VCH Wilts* VII, 65. [105] 6 Sept, reported in *Parl Papers* 1890-91, LXI, 54. [106] 25 Mar, LGBO 17500. [107] 1 Aug, *Lond Gaz.* [108] 18 Aug, *Lond Gaz.* [109] 30 May, *Lond Gaz.* [110] 25 Mar, LGBO 17592. [111] 28 Mar, 56 & 57 Vict., *c* lxxiii. [112] 30 Sept, LGBO 31682. [113] 19 June, Part Dist, Instr CBC. [114] Year vac (*Lond Gaz* 24 Nov 1964). [115] 30 May, *Lond Gaz.* [116] 9 Nov, 4 & 5 Geo. V, *c* cxxx. [117] 1 Apr, SI 1952/587. [118] 1 Oct, LGBO 34400. [119] 1 Apr, Dept EnvirnO 3732. [120] Apptd day LGBO 31776. [121] 1 Apr, MHousLGO 41814. [122] 12 Oct, *Lond Gaz.* [123] 1 June (*Lond Gaz* 30 May). [124] 1 Apr, LGBO 47951. [125] 1 Aug (*Lond Gaz* 29 July). [126] 29 May, *Lond Gaz.* [127] 24 June, *Lond Gaz.* [128] 16 Apr, *Lond Gaz.* [129] 17 June, Part Dist. [130] 25 Mar, LGBO 18150. [131] 16 Nov, *Lond Gaz.* [132] 24 Mar, LGBO

16423. [133]29 July, *Lond Gaz.* [134]LGBO 13156. [135]19 July, *Lond Gaz.* [136]26 Aug, reported in *Parl Papers* 1890-91, LXI, 56. [137]17 Aug, *Lond Gaz.* [138]16 Feb, *Lond Gaz.* [139]22 Oct, *Lond Gaz.* [140]15 May, *Lond Gaz.* [141]11 Jan, *Lond Gaz.* [142]Year vac (*Lond Gaz* 12 Aug 1927). [143]1 Apr, LGBO 39263. [144]25 Mar, LGBO 14730, 14731. [145]1 Dec (*Lond Gaz* 17 Nov). [146]25 Mar, LGBO 17894. [147]29 June, reported in *Parl Papers* 1897, LXVII, pt VI, 173. [148]28 June, reported in *Parl Papers* 1897, LXVII, pt VI, 174. [149]1 Apr, SI 1956/369. [150]Apptd day, LGBO 31904. [151]24 Mar, LGBO 16454. [152]14 Mar, *Lond Gaz.* [153]Presumed incl in PLU when became sep CP; not orig rated in the PLU. [154]20 Dec, LGBO 13156. [155]23 Aug, *Lond Gaz.* [156]2 July, *Lond Gaz.* [157]26 Apr, *Lond Gaz.* [158]17 Apr, *Lond Gaz.* [159]31 Oct, *Lond Gaz.* [160]Authority not found. [161]1 Apr, LGBO 33907. [162]1 Apr, MHealthO 68146. [163]9 Feb, *Lond Gaz.* [164]25 Mar, LGBO 17947. [165]1 Oct, LGBO 34125. [166]1 Dec, *Lond Gaz.* [167]12 Oct, *Lond Gaz.* [168]Year vac (*Lond Gaz* 7 Dec 1951). [169]20 Mar, reported in *Parl Papers* 1890-91, LXI, 54. [170]30 Sept, LGBO 31680. [171]5 Aug, *Lond Gaz.* [172]21 Dec, *Lond Gaz.* [173]1 Oct, LGBO 48109. [174]Year vac (*Lond Gaz* 20 Dec 1929). [175]Presumed effective 5 Oct, *Lond Gaz* although may be later. [176]11 Dec, Part Dist, Instr CBC. [177]Authority not found. [178]7 Jan, reported in *Parl Papers* 1872, XLVI, 21. [179]18 Apr, *Lond Gaz.* [180]14 Mar, *Lond Gaz.* [181]1 Oct, MHealth ProvO (New Swindon) Act, 1921. [182]25 Mar, LGBO 17893. [183]1 Nov (*Lond Gaz* 2 Oct). [184]6 July, *Lond Gaz.* [185]1 Apr, LGBO 53467. [186]Apptd day, LGBO 31889. [187]28 May, reported in *Parl Papers* 1890-91, LXI, 54. [188]1 Oct, LGBO 36447. [189]24 Mar, LGBO 16493. [190]24 Mar, LGBO 16494. [191]27 Nov, reported in *Parl Papers* 1872, XLVI, 14. [192]1 Nov, *Lond Gaz.* [193]22 June, *Lond Gaz.* [194]*VCH Wilts* X, 285-88. [195]*VCH Wilts,* VIII, 247. [196]7 Aug, *Lond Gaz* (corrected 11 Aug). [197]17 May, reported in *Parl Papers* 1890-91, LXI, 56. [198]18 Mar, *Lond Gaz.* [199]1 Apr (*Lond Gaz* 31 Mar). [200]2 & 3 Wm. IV, *c* 64 and 7 & 8 Vict., *c* 61. [201]3 Apr, *Lond Gaz.* [202]25 Mar, LGBO 17948. [203]31 May, *Lond Gaz.* [204]28 June, *Lond Gaz.* [205]Authority not found. [206]59 & 60 Vict., *c* ccxxxvi. [207]59 & 60 Vict., *c* lxxv. [208]10 Jan, *Lond Gaz.* [209]25 Mar, LGBO 16468. [210]16 Nov, *Lond Gaz.* [211]8 May, *Lond Gaz.* [212]24 Mar, LGBO 16483. [213]30 Oct, *Lond Gaz.* [214]1 Apr, MHousLGO 41529. [215]*VCH Berks* IV, 197-98. [216]22 July, *Lond Gaz.* [217]29 Nov, *Lond Gaz.* [218]4 June, *Lond Gaz.* [219]1 Nov, *Lond Gaz.* [220]Aubrey, 272. [221]Year vac (*Lond Gaz* 30 May 1924). [222]Not used. [223]1 Oct, MHealthO 70058. [224]5 Sept, *Lond Gaz.* [225]28 May, reported in *Parl Papers* 1890-91, LXI, 54. [226]5 May, reported in *Parl Papers* 1890-91, 53. [227]30 Sept, LGBO 31684. [228]24 Jan, *Lond Gaz* (OC 2 Nov 1842). [229]25 Mar, LGBO 34090. [230]1 Oct, MHealthO 61944. [231]1 Apr, MHousLGO 4171. [232]3 July, *Lond Gaz.* [233]31 Mar, LGBO 32760. [234]9 Nov, The Marlborough (Extension) O, 1901. [235]1 Apr, LGBO 35106. [236]25 Mar, LGBO 16463. [237]1 Aug (*Lond Gaz* 29 July). [238]1 Apr, LGBO 32465. [239]26 Feb, *Lond Gaz.* [240]7 Nov, Part Dist, Instr CBC. [241]25 Mar, LGBO 18151. [242]18 June, *Lond Gaz.* [243]12 Sept, *Lond Gaz.* [244]16 Mar, *Lond Gaz.* [245]30 Sept, LGBO 25937. [246]21 Jan, *Lond Gaz.* [247]12 June, *Lond Gaz.* [248]13 May, *Lond Gaz.* [249]1 Mar (*Lond Gaz* 12 Feb). [250]16 Apr, *Lond Gaz.* [251]11 Aug, *Lond Gaz.* [252]13 Feb, *Lond Gaz.* [253]20 Feb, *Lond Gaz.* [254]22 Nov, *Lond Gaz.* [255]1 May (*Lond Gaz* 3 Apr). [256]1 Apr, Dept Envirn O 3710. [257]Apptd day, LGBO 31776. [258]1 Aug, *Lond Gaz.* [259]1 Apr, 1 Edw. VIII & 1 Geo. VI, *c* xiii. [260]25 June, *Lond Gaz.* [261]8 Feb, *Lond Gaz.* [262]1 May (*Lond Gaz* 26 Apr). [263]29 Apr, *Lond Gaz.* [264]1 Apr, 14 & 15 Geo. VI, *c* xi. [265]14 Feb, *Lond Gaz.* [266]10 Sept, *Lond Gaz.* [267]14 Feb, *Lond Gaz.* [268]30 Jan, *Lond Gaz.* [269]2 Sept, *Lond Gaz.* [270]30 Jan, *Lond Gaz.* [271]Year vac (*Lond Gaz* 28 July 1964). [272]1 Sept (*Lond Gaz* 17 Aug). [273]Act parl (not found). [274]1 Apr, MHealthO 71541. [275]Bdry of bor in early period in dispute. [276]21 Dec, *Lond Gaz.* [277]25 Mar, LGBO 18190. [278]25 Mar, LGBO 18072. [279]2 Nov, *Lond Gaz.* [280]25 Mar, LGBO 14731. [281]Beresford & Finberg, 180. [282]Between census of 1861 and 1871. [283]5 Jan, SI 1971/2116. [284]25 July, SI 1952/1349. [285]31 Mar, MHealthO 74051.

PART II: LOCAL GOVERNMENT UNITS

AVON

[1]Pt of this par retained in Somerst, added to Priddy CP. [2]Pt of this par retained in Somerset, added to East Brent AP.

BEDFORDSHIRE

[1]Pars within hundreds from late 16th cent only and not shown after cr of Adm Co in 1889. [2]At some time pt or ent in a Borough; see BOROUGHS. [3]Incl Bedford pars. [4]Based on Beresford & Finberg *Hand-List* with no additional research. [5]5 & 6 Wm. IV, *c* 76. [6]*VCH Beds* II, 212. [7]Bor status lost at Dissolution. [8]*VCH Beds* III, 401-02. [9]*VCH Beds* III, 349-50. [10]Charter incorp. [11]SI 1964/169. [12]*VCH Beds* III, 441. [13]All effective 1835. [14]Not co-terminous with anc or adm co. [15]Woburn PLU abol 29 Sept 1899 and pars distributed to Ampthill and Leighton Buzzard. [16]Holwell transf 1897 to Herts. [17]Tillbrook transf 1896 to Hunts. [18]18 Feb, LGBO 29291. [19]22 Feb, LGBO 27859. [20]8 July, LGBO 27128. [21]1 Apr, MHealthO 77050. [22]1 Apr, MHealthO 77788. [23]1 Apr, LGBO 33504. [24]22 Jan, SI 1965/23. [25]1 Apr, MHealthO 71634.

BERKSHIRE

[1]Pars within hundreds from late sixteenth cent only, and not shown after cr of Adm Co in 1888. Pars which existed before but did not survive until late 16th cent are nevertheless listed in Part I of the *Guide.* [2]At some time pt or ent in a Bor; see BOROUGHS listing. [3]Based on Beresford & Finberg

handlist and secondary sources, not on original research. [4]5 & 6 Wm. IV, *c* 76. [5] *VCH Berks* III, 387–88. [6]Beresford & Finberg, 67. [7] *VCH Berks* IV, 491–92. [8] *VCH Berks* IV, 185–87. [9] *VCH Berks* IV, 251–52. [10] *VCH Berks* III, 312. [11]Beresford & Finberg, 68. [12]Not co-terminous with Anc or Adm Co. If a PLU contained pars of another co the fact is noted; see the other co for addtl members of the PLU. [13]Pt Berks, pt Wilts until 1895, ent Wilts thereafter. [14]Hants until 1895, Berks thereafter.

BUCKINGHAMSHIRE

[1]Pars within hundreds from late 16th cent only and not shown after 1889. [2]At some time pt or ent in a Bor; see BOROUGHS. [3]Based on Beresford & Finberg *Hand-List* and not on original research. [4]5 & 6 Wm. IV, *c* 76. [5]1 Jan, charter of incorp. [6]Slough UD made MB, charter of incorp. [7]1 Aug, The High Wycombe Corporation Act, 1946. [8]All effective in 1835. [9]Not co-terminous with anc or adm co. [10]Transf 1895 from Oxon to Bucks. [11]Transf 1895 to Herts. [12]No Bucks pars at first. [13]Orig in Wycombe PLU. [14]Bucks pars added Sept 1835. [15]Transf 1895 to Oxon. [16]LGBO [not found]. [17]1 Apr, MHealthO 77936. [18]1 Jan, charter of incorp. [19]16 May, Co Council NamingO. [20]1 Oct, LGBO 36631. [21]22 Jan, SI 1965/23. [22]Authority not found. [23]1 Oct, LGBO 34210. [24]1 Oct, LGBO 36352. [25]UD made MB by charter of incorp. [26]1 July, LGBO 32776. [27]1 Apr, LGBO 65026. [28]12 Feb, Co Council NamingO. [29]All except Shenley Brook End as augmented. [30]All transf to Berks except pt Burnham (cr Britwell CP), pt Wexham (cr Wexham Court CP).

CAMBRIDGESHIRE

[1]Pars within hundreds from late sixteenth cent only, and not shown after cr of Adm Co in 1889 Pars which existed before but did not survive until late 16th cent are nevertheless listed in Part I of the *Guide*. [2]At some time pt or ent in a Bor; see BOROUGHS listing. [3]Incl Cambridge pars. [4]Based on Beresford & Finberg handlist and secondary sources, not on original research. [5]5 & 6 Wm. IV, *c* 76. [6]By letters patent 21 Mar. [7] Not co-terminous with Anc or Admin Co. If a PLU contained pars of another co the fact is noted; see the other co for addtl members of the PLU. [8]Presumed joined the PLU when became a CP; not orig rated in the PLU. [9]Transf from Norfolk to IoE 1895. [10]Transf from Cambs to W Suffolk 1889. [11]Became 2 sep CPs, one in each co, in 1894 and PLU incl both as long as each existed. [12]Pt IoE, pt Hunts until 1905. [13]Incl Essex pars also. [14]Transf from Essex to Cambs 1895. [15]Pt Cambs, pt Herts until former transf to Herts 1895. [16]A reconstituted Orton Waterville CP (cr from pt Orton Waterville AP, Orton Longueville AP, pt Alwalton AP) to be in Peterborough Dist, the remainder of Norman Cross RDto be in Huntingdon Dist (the pts of Orton Longueville, Orton Waterville not in Peterborough Dist added to Alwalton par in Huntingdon Dist).

CORNWALL

[1]Pars within hundreds from late 16th cent only and not shown after cr of Adm Co in 1889. [2]Based on Beresford & Finberg *Hand-List* and other secondary sources with no additional research. [3]5 & 6 Wm. IV, *c* 76. [4]Dunheved Bor absorbed into Launceston Bor at an early date. [5]Absorbed Dunheved at an early date; changes in 1889 effective 9 Nov, LGB ProvO 620. [6]12 Aug, charter of incorp. [7]1 Apr, MHousLGO 2795. [8]Penkneth Bor absorbed into Lostwithiel Bor at an early date. [9]12 Dec, charter of incorp. [10]Not co-terminous with anc or adm co. [11]Pt Devon, pt Cornw, ent Cornw from 1844. [12]Presumed incl in PLU when became sep CP; not orig rated in the PLU. [13]Not an actual pt of Cornw. [14]Pt Cornw until 1894 after which ent Devon. [15]Sometimes listed sep for poor law purposes; prob always in this PLU. [16]LGB ProvO 822. [17]Authority not found. [18]4 Feb, LGBO 27789. [19]1 Apr, LGBO 26688. [20]1 Oct, LGBO 42499. [21]Remainder of pars in Devon; North Tamerton transf 1934 to Stratton RD and RD ent Devon thereafter. [22]1 Apr, LGBO 37818. [23]1 Apr, MHousLGO 32682. [24]10 Nov, charter of incorp. [25]1 Apr, MHousLGO 32701. [26]1 Apr, LGBO 35360. [27]1 Apr, LGBO 39878. [28]1 Apr, LGBO 46041. [29]1 Apr, LGBO 37894.

DEVON

[1]Pars within hundreds from late sixteenth cent only, and not shown after cr of Adm Co in 1889. Pars which existed before but did not survive until late 16th cent are nevertheless listed in Part I of the *Guide*. [2]Apptd day, LGBO 31841. [3]9 Nov, 63 & 64 Vict., *c* cclxii. [4]9 Nov, 4 & 5 Geo. V, *c* clxxxiii. [5]9 Nov, 63 & 64 Vict., *c* ccxxxii. [6]9 Nov, 3 & 4 Geo. V, *c* cxxxv. [7]1 Apr, 2 & 3 Geo. VI, *c* xv. [8]21 Feb, MHousLGO 22749. [9]1 Oct, MHealthO 92269. [10]9 Nov, LGB ProvO 1257. [11]1 Apr, 1 & 2 Geo. V, *c* lxi. [12]1 Apr, 14 & 15 Geo. VI, *c* lxi. [13]28 Dec, MHousLGO 23517. [14]16 Feb, MHousLGO 25066. [15]At some time pt or ent in a Bor; see BOROUGHS listing. [16]Some sep distinction between North Tawton Hd, Winkleigh Hd still maintained until late 16th cent, though common as one then (e.g., Speed's map). [17]Exeter pars situated in this Hd. [18]Based on Beresford & Finberg handlist and on secondary sources, not on original research. [19]5 & 6 Wm. IV, *c* 76. [20]Perhaps 17th cent bor; see Beresford & Finberg, 90. [21]Perhaps 17th cent bor; see Beresford & Finberg, 94. [22]1 Apr, MHousLGO 27912. [23]Sutton Prior bor incorp as 'Plymouth'. [24]Ent in this Bor once lesser bors in the par lose bor status. [25]Not co-terminous with Anc or Adm Co. [26]Pt Devon, pt Dorset until 1844, ent Devon thereafter. [27]Transf 1896 from Dorset to Devon. [28]Transf 1844 from Dorset to Devon. [29]Transf 1896 from Devon to Dorset. [30]Presumed incl in PLU when cr CP; not orig rated in PLU. [31]Stoke Damerel incorp becomes Devonport incorp when Stoke Damerel expanded and renamed 'Devonport'. [32]The pt of Bridgerule AP

transf 1844 from Cornw to Devon. [33]Pt Devon, pt Somerset until 1844, ent Somerset thereafter. [34]Pt Devon, pt Cornw until 1894, ent Devon thereafter. [35]Sep rated orig in PLU, but sep civ status lost soon after and civ incl thereafter in Kentisbeare AP. [36]Transf 1896 from Devon to Somerset. [37]1 Jan, LGBO 30499. [38]3 Jan. LGBO 30361. [39]Kingsbridge and Dodbrooke USD cr 4 Mar 1893, Order of Co Council, the two pars of Kingsbridge, Dodbrooke united 26 Mar and USD renamed 'Kingsbridge' 17 May. [40]1 Apr, LGBO 37817. [41]1 Apr, LGBO 62969. [42]1 Apr, MHousLGO 3409. [43]14 June, Lower Brixham UD renamed 'Brixham', Order Co Council. [44]16 Feb, MHousLGO 25066. [45]1 Jan, SI 1965/2087. [46]9 Nov, 63 & 64 Vict., *c* clxxxiii. [47]9 Nov, 59 & 60 Vict., *c* ccxxxvii. [48]25 June, LGBO 34702. [49]9 Nov, 3 & 4 Geo. V, *c* cxxxv. [50]This RD also contained one Cornw par (North Tamerton) 1894–1934. [51]Wolborough UD renamed 'Newton Abbot' UD 4 Aug, LGBO 31470. [52]1 Apr, LGBO 39010. [53]1 Apr, MHousLGO 13963. [54]9 Nov, 63 & 64 Vict., *c* clxxxiii. [55]9 Nov, 63 & 64 Vict., *c* ccxxxii. [56]9 Nov, 4 & 5 Geo. V, *c* clxxxiii. [57]1 Apr, LGBO 36290. [58]1 Apr, MHousLGO 23089.[59]60 & 61 Vict., *c* 1 [fifty, local]. [60]61 & 62 Vict., *c* cxxxix.

DORSET

[1]Pars within hundreds from late 16th cent only and not shown after cr of Adm Co in 1889. [2]At some time pt or ent in a Bor; see BOROUGHS. [3]Incl Shaftesbury. [4]Incl Dorchester. [5]Incl Bridport. [6]Based on Beresford & Finberg's *Hand-List* and other secondary sources, not on additional research. [7]5 & 6 Wm. IV, *c* 76. [8]Bdry of bor in dispute. [9]A small meadowland pt of this par not in the Bor. [10]The Poole (Extension) Order, 1905. [11]Not co-terminous with anc or adm co. [12]Transf 1895 from Somerset to Dorset. [13]In Dorset until 1844, Devon 1844-96, Dorset thereafter. [14]Date for abol of incorp and incl in PLU not found. [15]Presumed incl in the PLU when became sep CP; not orig rated in the PLU. [16]Transf 1896 to Devon. [17]Transf 1895 to Somerset. [18]27 July, Dorset Co CouncilO confirmed by LGBO 28427. [19]Note cancelled. [20]Extension 9 Nov 1889, LGB ProvO Confirmation (No 9) Act, 1889. [21]5 July, LGBO 28303. [22]Gains Hurn, pt Christchurch East (cr Burton CP), pt Sopley (added to Hurn). [23]Gains St Leonards and St Ives.

ESSEX

[1]Pars within hundreds from late 16th cent only, and not shown after cr of Adm Co in 1888. Pars which existed before but did not survive until late 16th cent are nevertheless listed in Part I of the *Guide*. [2]East Ham MB cr CB 1 Apr, 4 & 5 Geo. V, *c* iii. [3]Transf 1 Apr 1965 to Gtr London. [4] 1 Apr, 4 & 5 Geo. V, *c* cv. [5]1 Apr, MHealthO 83994. [6]At some time pt or ent in a Bor; see BOROUGHS listing. [7]Incl Maldon pars. [8]Incl the pars in Colchester Bor: the Colchester pars and Berechurch, Greenstead, Lexden, Mile End St Michael. [9]Incl the pars in Harwich Bor: Dovercourt, Harwich St Nicholas. [10]Based on Beresford & Finberg handlist and on secondary sources, not on original research. [11]5 & 6 Wm. IV, *c* 76. [12]Not co-terminous with Anc or Adm Co. [13]Not orig rated in the PLU; presumed incl when became a sep CP. [14]Not orig rated in the PLU, but incl by early 1840s. [15]Morrel Roding orig rated in the PLU but sep identity as par lost soon after and incl within White Roding. [16]Incl Roydon hmlt, orig sep rated in the PLU but sep identity not sustained. [17]Pt Essex, pt Suffolk, ent Suffolk from 1879. [18]Pt Essex, pt Suffolk, ent W Suffolk from 1895. [19]Transf 1895 from Essex to Cambs. [20]Pt Essex, pt Cambs, ent Essex from 1885. [21]14 Oct, LGBO 14192. [22]21 May, LGB ProvO 378. [23]17 June, LGBO 27026. [24]8 Aug, Essex Co Council O, conf by LGBO 25837. [25]20 Apr, LGBO 20057. [26]20 May, LGB ProvO 441. [27]20 May, LGB ProvO 86. [28]5 Apr, LGB ProvO 491. [29]9 Nov, chartered MB as 'Barking'. [30]1 Apr, Billericay UD renamed Basildon UD, MHealth Decl. [31]1 Oct, MHealthO 73676. [32]1 Apr, LGBO 37665. [33]1 Apr, LGBO 39045. [34]1 Oct, LGBO 34368. [35]Apptd day, LGBO 32112. [36]1 Oct, MHealthO 77525. [37]1 Apr, LGBO 36861. [38]1 Apr, MHealthO 70563. [39]Apptd day, LGBO 32113. [40]9 Nov, charter of incorp. [41]1 Apr, MHealthO 70562. [42]1 Apr, MHousLGO 4915. [43]1 Apr, LGBO 34234. [44]1 Oct, LGBO 42991. [45]10 Aug, cr MB. [46]1 Apr, MHealthO 70560. [47]9 Nov, charter of incorp. [48]1 Apr, LGBO 35841. [49]1 Apr, made pt of Southend on Sea MB, 3 & 4 Geo. V, *c* cv. [50]1 Apr, LGBO 40549. [51]1 Apr, MHealthO 70561.[52]1 Apr, MHealthO 72814. [53]1 Apr, MHealthO 83994. [54]Apptd day, LGBO 31574. [55]1 Apr, MHealthO 83994. [56]1 Apr, LGBO 57469.

GLOUCESTERSHIRE

[1]Pars within hundreds from late 16th cent only and not shown after cr of Adm Co in 1889. [2]30 Sept, LGBO 34794. [3]1 Apr, 60 & 61 Vict., *c* ccxxx. [4]1 Apr, LGBO 37475. [5]1 Oct, LGBO 38597. [6]1 Oct, 1 Edw. VII, *c* cclxiv. [7]1 Edw. VII, *c* cxlii. [8]18 Oct, 4 Edw. VII, *c* ccxxiii. [9]8 & 9 Geo. V, *c* xlii. [10]1 Apr, MHealthO 77130. [11]1 Apr, MHealthO 80904. [12]1 Apr, Somerset and Bristol (Alteration of Boundary) O, 1951. [13]SI 1966/134. [14]20 & 21 Eliz. II, *c* 70. [15]9 Nov, LGB ProvO 1649. [16]1 Apr, MHousLGO 3411. [17]1 Apr, Gloucester (Extension) Act, 1951. [18]1 Apr, 14 & 15 Geo. VI, *c* ii. [19]28 Dec, MHousLGO 23995. [20]At some time pt or ent in a Bor; see BOROUGHS. [21]Speed's map places in Duchy Lancaster Hd. [22]Speed's map has in St Briavels Hd. [23]Within Gloucester Bor & Co of itself 1483–1672; incl Gloucester pars. [24]Note cancelled. [25]Hmlt Stoke Orchard in this Hd until end 18th cent; *VCH Glos* VII, 186. [26]For 17th cent changes see *VCH Glos* X, 1. [27]Based on Beresford & Finberg's *Hand-List* and other secondary sources and not on additional research. [28]5 & 6 Wm. IV, *c* 76. [29]See also entries in Somerset for pars in its anc territory but within the Bor/MB/CB. [30]Not co-terminous with anc or adm co. [31] Pt Glos, pt Warws until 1894, ent

Warws thereafter. [32]Extended 29 Sept, LGB ProvO 12186 confirmed by 44 & 45 Vict., *c* xcix. [33]Authority not found. [34]Gains Painswick 21 May, LGB ProvO 166. [35]1 Oct, 4 Edw. VII, *c* ccxxiii. [36]1 Apr, 21 & 22 Geo. V, *c* ix. [37]1 Apr, MHealthO 70989. [38]Apptd day, LGBO 31997. [39]1 Apr, 60 & 61 Vict., *c* ccxxx. [40]The Worcs members of this RD (Daylesford, Evenlode) transf to Glos so that RD ent Glos 1931–35. [41]The Wilts members (Ashley, Long Newton) transf to Glos so that RD ent Glos. [42]Worcs members (Chaceley, Teddington, Kemerton) transf to Glos so that RD ent Glos thereafter. [43]Worcs members (Cutsdean, Beckford) transf to Glos so that RD ent Glos thereafter.

HAMPSHIRE

[1]1 Apr, MHousLG Decl. [2]Pars within hundreds from late 16th cent only and not shown after cr of Adm Co in 1889. [3]1 Apr, LGB ProvO 1508. [4]9 Nov, 1 Edw. VII, *c* clxviii. [5]30 Sept, LGBO 44497. [6]Note cancelled. [7]9 Nov, 3 & 4 Geo. V, *c* cxxix. [8]1 Apr, 20 & 21 Geo. V, *c* clxxxi. [9]1 Apr, MHealthO 76234. [10]1 Apr, 20 & 21 Eliz. II, *c* 70. [11]31 Mar, 62 & 63 Vict., *c* cclvi. [12]9 Nov, 4 Edw, VII, *c* cxv. [13]Note cancelled. [14]1 Oct, Plymouth Corporation Act, 1920. [15]24 Sept, 9 & 10 Geo. V, *c* cxxii. [16]1 Apr, MHealthO 76234. [17]1 Apr, 2 & 3 Geo. VI, *c* xxiv. [18]9 Nov, 59 Vict., *c* x. [19]9 Nov, 10 & 11 Geo. V, *c* cxvi. [20]1 Apr, MHealthO 69719. [21]1 Apr, SI 1954/408. [22]2 Mar, MHousLGO 29473. [23]At some time pt or ent in a Bor; see BOROUGHS. [24]Christchurch Hd deemed sometimes to incl Westover Lbty, the latter detached by 1620; *VCH Hants* V, 133. [25]Based on Beresford & Finberg's *Hand-List* and other secondary sources, not on additional research. [26]5 & 6 Wm. IV, *c* 76. [27] UD made MB by charter of incorp, 9 Nov. [28]Charter of incorp. [29]Charter of incorp. [30]Gosport claimed to be a bor and was temporarily incl in Portsmouth at one time; *VCH Hants* III, 205-06. [32]39 & 40 Vict., *c* 61. [33]Incl Ryde MB. [34]See *VCH Hants* III, 492-94 on disputed boundaries. [35]Pars from late 16th cent only; pars which existed earlier are nevertheless listed in Part I of the *Guide*. [36]Not co-terminous with anc or adm co. [37]Presumed incl in PLU when became sep CP; not orig rated in the PLU. [38]Other pars incl before 1834 (Eversley and Bramhill for 1802-06, Hartley Wintney 1798-1827). [39]Wilts until 1895, Hants thereafter. [40]Orig sep rated in PLU but sep civ status not sustained; see Part I. [41]Pt Sussex, pt Hants until 1895, ent Hants thereafter. [42]Pt Hants, pt Sussex until 1844, ent Hants thereafter. [43]Pt Wilts, pt Hants until 1883, ent Wilts thereafter. [44]USD renamed 1891. [45]Authority not found. [46]13 Feb, LGBO 28893. [47]Authority not found. [48]Authority for extension not found. [49]Authority for extension not found. [50]Authority for extension not found. [51]Authoroty for removal of Northwood not found. [52]Renaming 1881. [53]23 Mar, LGBO 29254. [54]1 Apr, LGBO 39518. [55]1 Jan, LGBO 33823. [56]1 Apr, LGBO 46259. [57]1 Apr, LGBO 37124. [58]1 Oct, MHealthO 71087. [59]1 Oct, LGBO 32827. [60]1 Edw. VII, *c* clxviii. [61]59 Vict., *c* v. [62]Apptd day, LGBO 32188. [63]20 May, Hants Co CouncilO. [64]1 Oct, LGBO 38387. [65]All except the pt transf to Dorset (Hurn [which gains the pt of Sopley to be in Dorset], St Leonards and St Ives, pt Christchurch East [cr Burton CP in Dorset] [the pt of Christchurch East to remain in Hants cr Bransgore CP]).

HERTFORDSHIRE

[1]Pars within hundreds from late 16th cent only, and not shown after cr of Adm Co in 1888. Pars which existed before but did not survive until late 16th cent are nevertheless listed in Part I of the *Guide*. [2]At some time pt or ent in a Bor; see BOROUGHS listing. [3]Based on Beresford & Finberg handlist and secondary sources, not on original research. [4]5 & 6 Wm. IV, *c* 76. [5]19 May, charter of incorp. [6]Perhaps mediev bor; see Beresford & Finberg, 125. [7]9 Nov, charter of incorp. [8]Note cancelled. [9]Not co-terminous with Anc or Adm Co. [10]In Middx, but see Part I for bdry alts with Herts. [11]Pt in Herts until 1894, ent Middx thereafter. [12]Transf 1895 from Bucks to Herts. [13]Presumed incl in PLU when cr CP; not orig rated in PLU. [14]Transf 1897 from Beds to Herts. [15]Shillington, Whipsnade each pt in Herts until 1897, ent Beds thereafter. [16]In Middx, but see Part I for bdry alts with Herts. [17]Two CPs cr 1894, one for ea county, both in PLU until Herts CP united 1897 with Beds CP and par ent Beds thereafter. [18]Transf 1897 to Beds. [19]Two CPs cr 1894, one for ea county, both in PLU until Herts CP abol 1897 and Caddington ent Beds thereafter. [20]Authority not found. [21]27 Aug, LGBO 19120. [22]7 Apr, LGBO 28119. [23]28 July, Barnet RD renamed Elstree RD. [24]Transf 1 Apr 1965 to Gtr London. [25]1 Apr, Co Council Naming O. [26]1 Nov, Berkhampstead RD renamed Berkhamsted RD. [27]1 Apr, Great Berkhampstead UD renamed Berkhamsted UD. [28]1 Apr, LGBO 48979. [29]1 Apr, LGBO 58323. [30]Bishop's Stortford RD renamed Hadham RD. [31]15 Apr, LGBO 37507. [32]1 Apr, LGBO 64963. [33]Transf 1 Apr 1965 from Middx to Herts. [34]15 Apr, LGBO 36629. [35]1 Oct, LGBO 36608. [36]1 Apr, LGBO 41642. [37]1 Apr, MHealthO 71611. [38]All of St Albans RD to be in St Albans Dist except the pts of Redbourn, St Michael Rural in Hemel Hempstead New Town (in Dacorum Dist) which cease to be in any par; the remainder of St Michael Rural in St Albans Dist renamed 'St Michael'. [39]Aldenham to be in Hertsmere Dist, remainder of Watford RD to be in Three Rivers Dist except the pt of Abbots Langley in Hemel Hempstead New Town (in Dacorum Dist, the latter cr Nash Mills CP). [40]All of Hertford RD to be in East Hertfordshire Dist except the pts of Aston, Datchworth in Stevenage New Town (in Stevenage Dist) which cease to be in any par.

HUNTS

[1]Pars within hundreds from late 16th cent

only, and not shown after cr of Adm Co in 1888. Pars which existed before but did not survive until late 16th cent are nevertheless listed in Part I of the *Guide*. [2]Incl Huntingdon pars. [3]At some time pt or ent in a Bor or MB; see BOROUGHS listing. [4]Authority not found for the loss of the small area of this par not in Hunts. [5]Based on Beresford & Finberg handlist and on secondary sources, not on original research. [6]5 & 6 Wm. IV, *c* 76. [7]Beresford & Finberg, 126. [8]1 Apr, MHousLGO 8963. [9]APs in the Bor which did not survive are not listed; see Part I of the *Guide* for a list of all pars in Huntingdon. [10]Beresford & Finberg, 127. [11]Not co-terminous with Anc or Adm Co. [12]Hunts until 1888, Beds thereafter. [13]Pt Hunts, pt Northants until 1895, ent Northants thereafter. [14]Pt Hunts, pt Cambs until 1895, ent Cambs thereafter. [15]Pt Hunts, pt Northants until 1895, ent Northants thereafter. [16] Pt Hunts, pt Northants until 1895, ent Hunts thereafter. [17]Pt Soke of Peterb 1888–94, divided 1894 into 2 pars in the respective counties. [18]Pt Hunts, pt Cambs/IoE until 1905, divided 1905 into 2 pars in the respective counties. [19]Pt Soke of Peterborough 1888–94, divided 1894 into 2 pars in the respective counties. [20]Pt Hunts, pt Cambs, ent Hunts from the 1860s. [21]Pt Hunts, pt Northants, ent Hunts from the 1840s. [22]1 Apr, LGBO 47601. [23]1 Apr, SI 1964/367. Barnack RD, Peterborough RD prev in Soke of Peterb Adm Co; see Vol. II of the *Guide*. [24]Pt of this RD in Northants. [25]Thorney RD prev in IoE Adm Co. [26]Administered by Barnack RD Council, Soke of Peterb.

KENT

[1]Pars within hundreds from late 16th cent only and not shown after cr of Adm Co in 1889. [2]Incl Bors of Dover, Canterbury, Sandwich. [3]At some time pt or ent in a Bor or MB and in a Cq Pt. [4]At some time pt or ent in a Cq Pt. [5]See note for this par in Part I of the *Guide*. [6]At some time pt or ent in a Bor or MB. [7]Incl Bors Maidstone, Rochester. [8]Later incl in Shorne AP. [9]Incl Bor Faversham. [10]Hasted and later place in Isle of Sheppey Lbty, Lambarde in Scray. [11]Hasted lists several pars in this hundred while others place in Isle of Sheppey Lbty. [12]The distinction into Franchise and Barony follows Kilburne; Hasted places in Lathe of Scray. [13]Based on Beresford & Finberg's *Hand-List* and on other secondary sources, not on additional research. [14]5 & 6 Wm. IV, *c* 76. [15]9 Nov, charter of incorp makes the UD a MB. [16]Transf to Gtr London 1965, 20 & 21 Eliz. II, *c* 70. [17]10 Aug, charter of incorp, UD made MB. [18]18 Oct, charter of incorp. [19]12 Aug, charter of incorp. [20]29 July, charter of incorp. [21]1 Apr, MHousLGO ,4431. [22]4 Mar, charter of incorp. [23]Concurrent jurisd in co of Kent from 1811. [24]Charter of incorp. [25]Charter of incorp. [26]17 Dec, charter of incorp. [27]The pt of this par in Sussex was in Winchelsea Anc Town/Cq Pt. [28]Pars from late 16th cent only; for earlier see Part I of the *Guide*. [29]Transf 1889 to London Adm Co, 62 & 63 Vict., *c* 14. [30]Pt in Surrey. [31]Incl Penge. [32]Not co-terminous with anc or adm co. [33]Presumed incl in PLU when became sep CP; not orig rated in the PLU. [34]Penshurst to Sevenoaks in 1840s. [35]Pt Kent, pt Sussex until 1886, ent Kent thereafter. [36]Pt Kent, pt Sussex until 1895, ent E Sussex thereafter. [37]Pt Sussex, pt Kent until 1894, ent E Sussex thereafter. [38]LGB ProvO 432. [39]1 Oct, LGBO 37899. [40]1 Apr, LGBO 40686. [41]1 Apr, LGBO 43476. [42]Renamed 1 Jan, Kent Co Council NamingO. [43]1 Oct, LGBO 66336. [44]1 Apr, LGBO 47729. [45]Renaming 5 Nov, Kent Co Council NamingO. [46]31 Mar, MHealthO 73566. [47]Transf 1899 from Surrey to Kent. [48]1 Apr, MHealthO 70252. [49]Apptd day, LGBO 31823.

MIDDLESEX

[1]Pars within hundreds from late 16th cent only, and not shown after cr Adm Co in 1889. [2]In Metropolis 1855-99, London Adm Co thereafter. [3]In City of Westminster. [4]Based on Beresford & Finberg *Hand-List* and secondary sources and not on additional research. [5]5 & 6 Wm. IV, *c* 76. [6]9 Nov, charter of incorp. [7]13 May, OC. [8]23 May, charter of incorp. [9]24 May, charter of incorp. [10]10 Aug, OC. [11]Status not sustained. [12]Transf 1899 to London Adm Co. [13]Not co-terminous with anc or adm co. [14]Sep Board of Guardians. [15]Transf 1889 to Herts. [16]Pt Middx, pt Herts, ent Middx from 1894. [17]Note cancelled. [18]Local act, in Holborn PLU from 1869. [19]Local act, own Board of Guardians from 1869. [20]Pt not in London poor law co. [21]Local act, own Board of Guardians 1867–70, PLU from 1870. [22]Local act. [23]Local act, own Board of Guardians from 1868. [24]Local act. [25]Local act, own Board of Guardians from 1869. [26]Authority not found. [27]27 May, LGBO 19120. [28]Middx Co Council O, confirmed 16 Jan, LGBO 26598. [29]Middx Co CouncilO, confirmed 8 Jan, LGBO 27860. [30]48 & 49 Vict., *c* 33. [31]50 & 51 Vict., *c* 17. [32]9 Nov, charter of incorp, UD made MB. [33]9 Nov, charter of incorp, UD made MB. [34]1 Apr, LGBO 45930. [35]Apptd day, LGBO 31817. [36]1 Oct, 16 & 17 Geo. V, *c* lxii. [37]1 Apr, The Middx (Feltham and Sunbury on Thames UDs) Confirmation O, 1936. [38]1 Apr, MHealthO 78096. [39]1 Oct, LGBO 47144. [40]31 Mar, MHealthO 74042. [41]62 & 63 Vict., *c* 14. [42]16 Apr, LGBO 41093. [43]30 Sept, LGBO 47041. [44]Southall Norwood UD made Southall MB, charter of incorp, 9 Nov. [45]Apptd day, LGBO 31845. [46]Apptd day, LGBO 31845. [47]1 Apr, LGBO 56481. [48]1 Apr, MHealthO 108895. [49]31 Mar, MHealthO 74041.

NORFOLK

[1]Pars within hundreds from late 16th cent only, and not shown after cr of Adm Co in 1889. Pars which existed before but did not survive until late 16th cent are nevertheless listed in Part I of the *Guide*. [2]At some time pt or ent in a Bor; see listing for BOROUGHS. [3]Little Ellingham perhaps orig pt Forehoe Hd, pt Wayland Hd. [4]Freebridge Lynn, Freebridge Marshland orig one Hd; incl area King's Lynn Bor. [5]Incl the Norfolk pt of Thetford Bor.

[6]The name 'Lynn' used for the Bor until *temp* Henry VIII and 'King's Lynn' thereafter; the names 'Yarmouth' and 'Great Yarmouth' used alternatively in earlier periods, the latter invariably later. Gorleston was in anc Suffolk. [7]Pars from late 16th cent only; for earlier which did not survive until then, see Part I of the *Guide*. [8]See Part I for indication of pts of Thetford Bor/MB in Suffolk. [9]Not co-terminous with Anc or Adm Co. [10]Presumed incl in PLU when became a sep CP; not orig rated in the PLU. [11]Pt Norfolk, pt Cambs until 1889; ent Norfolk thereafter. [12]Cr 1889 as 'Welney' CP in IoE, transf 1895 to Norfolk as 'West Welney'. [13]Pt Norfolk, pt Suffolk until 1889, ent Norfolk thereafter. [14]Transf 1895 from Norfolk to IoE. [15]Pt Norfolk, pt Suffolk, ent Suffolk from 1885. [16]Pt Norfolk, pt Cambs until 1889, then divided into 2 CPs, one Norfolk, one IoE, each with same name. [17]Suffolk until 1889. [18]23 Feb, LGBO 16865. [19]Norfolk Co CouncilO, confirmed 20 Mar, LGBO 26660. [20]1 Oct, LGBO 44423. [21]18 Feb, Norfolk Co CouncilO. [22]19 Nov, LG Decl. [23]1 Oct, LGBO 42599. [24]1 Apr, MHealth ProvO Confirmation (Ely, Holland and Norfolk) Act, 1933. [25]2 July, MHousLG Decl. [26]Not to be in any par. [27]Not to be in any par. [28]Renamed Fritton and St Olaves. [29]Gains pt Corton. [30]9 Nov, The Norwich (Extension) O, 1907. [31]1 Apr, 14 & 15 Geo. VI, *c* xliii. [32]1 Apr, SI 1968/68. [33]Based on Beresford & Finberg's *Hand-List* and secondary sources, not on additional research. [34]5 & 6 Wm. IV, *c* 76.

OXFORDSHIRE

[1]Pars within hundreds from late 16th cent only and not shown after cr of Adm Co in 1889. [2]LGB ProvO 623. [3]LGBO 31868, 31877, 31930. [4]1 Apr, 18 & 19 Geo. V, *c* lxxxiv. [5]1 Apr, SI 1957/462. [6]At some time pt or ent in a Bor; see BOROUGHS. [7]In Berks until 1844 as pt Langford AP, Oxon thereafter. [8]Northants until 1866, in Banbury MB from 1889. [9]Incl area Oxford pars; pars only ptly in the MB listed sep in the Hd. [10]Studeley hmlt in Beckley in Bucks until 1844, Oxon thereafter. [11]Lewknor Uphill (in Lewknor AP until 1866, sep CP from 1866) pt Bucks, pt Oxon until abol 1885. [12]In Lbty Oxford and Oxford Bor/MB/CB. [13]In Lbty Oxford. [14]In Lbty Oxford and Woodstock Bor, MB. [15]Based on Beresford & Finberg's *Hand-List* and other secondary sources and not on additional research. [16]5 & 6 Wm. IV, *c* 76. [17]Pt Northants: pt Banbury (until 1894), Neithrop (until 1866). [18]9 Nov, LGB ProvO Confirmation (No 15) Act, 1889. [19]19 July, charter of incorp. [20]Pars from late 16th cent only. [21]Holywell chap in Oxford St Nicholas. [22]Littlemore orig pt Iffley, pt Oxford St Mary the Virgin. [23]Orig sep rated in PLU but sep civ status not sustained. [24]Divided 1894 into 2 CPs, the pt in Berks called 'Seacourt', the pt in Oxford CB 'Unnamed'. [25]Wolvercot orig pt Oxford St Peter in the East. [26]Charter of incorp. [27]Not co-terminous with anc or adm co. [28]Pt Oxon, pt Berks (incl pt at some time in Abingdon MB) until 1894, ent Oxon thereafter. [29]57 & 58 Vict., *c* 58. [30]Tg (Oxon) in Warkworth (o'wise Northants). [31]Transf 1844 from Bucks to Oxon. [32]Pt Bucks, pt Oxon until 1894, ent Oxon thereafter. [33]Hmlt (Bucks) in Beckley (o'wise Oxon), transf 1844 to Oxon. [34]Presumed incl in PLU when became sep CP; not orig rated in the PLU. [35]Orig rated in the PLU, sep civ status not sustained. [36]Pt Oxon, pt Berks until 1889, ent Oxford CB thereafter. [37]Pt Bucks, pt Oxon until 1886, ent Bucks thereafter. [38]Pt Oxon, pt Bucks until 1844, ent Oxon thereafter. [39]Pt Glos, pt Oxon until 1844, ent Oxon thereafter. [40]Pt Berks, pt Oxon until 1844, ent Oxon thereafter. [41]Transf 1844 from Glos to Oxon. [42]Orig rated in the PLU, sep civ status not sustained. [43]Pt Berks, pt Oxon until 1894, ent Oxon thereafter. [44]Pt Bucks, pt Oxon until 1844, ent Bucks thereafter. [45]Transf 1844 from Bucks to Oxon. [46]Pt Bucks, pt Oxon until 1896, ent Bucks thereafter. [47]Transf 1844 from Glos to Oxon. [48]Pt Berks, pt Oxon until 1894, ent Berks thereafter. [49]Loses pt to Oxford CB 1889. [50]9 Nov, LGB ProvO 2219.

SOMERSET

[1]Pars within hundreds from late 16th cent only and not shown after cr of Adm Co in 1889. [2]1 & 2 Geo. V, *c* xxxv. [3]1 Apr, 14 Geo. VI, *c* lxiv. [4]1 Jan, MHousLGO 23994. [5]Transf 1 Apr 1974 from Somerset to help cr Avon, 20 & 21 Eliz. II, *c* 70. [6]At some time pt or ent in a Bor; see BOROUGHS. [7]Pars from later 16th cent only; for earlier pars see Part I of the *Guide*. [8]In Witham Friary Lbty. [9]In Mells & Leigh Lbty. [10]When Middle Chinnock and West Chinnock united 1884 the union at first called 'Middle Chinnock', but within several years 'West Chinnock'. [11]Based on Beresford & Finberg's *Hand-List* and on other secondary sources, not on additional research. [12]5 & 6 Wm. IV, *c* 76. [13]Bristol primarily anc Glos, qv. [14]Uncertain identification, Beresford & Finberg, 156. [15]9 Nov, charter of incorp. [16]Not co-terminous with anc or adm co. [17]PLU abol 25 Mar. [18]Between 1898-1901. [19]Presumed incl in PLU when became sep CP; not orig rated in the PLU. [20]Transf 1895 from Dorset to Somerset. [21]Pt Somerset, pt Devon until 1884, ent Somerset thereafter. [22]Transf 1896 from Devon to Somerset. [23]Transf 1895 to Dorset. [24]Pt Wilts, pt Somerset until 1895, ent Wilts thereafter. [25]Transf 1896 to Wilts. [26]25 Mar, LGBO 18101. [27]9 Nov, LGB ProvO Confirmation (No 6) Act, 1892. [28]Authority not found. [29]Somerset Co CouncilO, confirmed 27 Apr, LGBO 26856. [30]Somerset Co CouncilO, confirmed 3 Aug, LGBO 28481. [31]6 Jan, LGB ProvO 366. [32]22 May, LGBO 1150. [33]2 Jan, Somerset Co Council NamingO. [34]Apptd day, LGBO 30631. [35]1 Oct, LGBO 35270. [36]15 Apr, LGBO 39490. [37]The Co of Somerset (Keynsham UD) Order, 1936. [38]1 Apr, LGBO 43667. [39]Main pt of Blagdon and of Burrington transf to Avon to be pars there by respective names, remainder of each left in Somerset added to Priddy. [40]Chilcompton, Litton, Ston Easton remain in Somerset. The remainder of each of the following left in Somerset and added to

Priddy, while main pt of each to Avon to be par of respective name: Compton Martin, East Harptree, West Harptree, Ubley. [41]Pars of Axbridge, Badgworth, Berrow, Brean, East Brent, Brent Knoll, Burnham Without, Chapel Allerton, Cheddar, Compton Bishop, Lympsham, Mark, Shipham, Weare, Wedmore remain in Somerset; main pt of Loxton transf to Avon to be Loxton par there, the remainder left in Somerset added to East Brent.

SUFFOLK

[1]Pars within hundreds from late 16th cent only and not shown after cr of Adm Co in 1889. [2]Apptd day, LGBO 31679. [3]1 Apr, MHealthO 77717. [4]The E Suffolk and Ipswich (Alteration of Boundary) O, 1952. [5]At some time pt or ent in a Bor or MB; see BOROUGHS. [6]Pars from late 16th cent only; see Part I for earlier pars. [7]Based on Beresford & Finberg's *Hand-List* and other secondary sources and not on additional research. [8]5 & 6 Wm. IV, *c* 76. [9]Union late 16th cent of Whitton, Thurleston. [10]Not co-terminous with anc or adm co. [11]Pt Suffolk, pt Norfolk until 1885, ent Suffolk thereafter. [12]Pt Cambs, pt Suffolk, each made a sep CP 1894. [13]Transf 1889 from Cambs to W Suffolk. [14]Pt Cambs, pt Suffolk, ent W Suffolk from 1894. [15]Pt Suffolk, pt Essex, ent Suffolk from 1879. [16]Pt Suffolk, pt Essex, ent W Suffolk from 1895. [17]Pt Suffolk, pt Essex, ent W Suffolk from 1896. [18]Pt Essex, pt Suffolk, ent Suffolk from 1866. [19]Pt Norfolk, pt Suffolk, ent Norfolk from 1885. [20]Pt Norfolk, pt Suffolk, ent Norfolk from 1894. [21]Suffolk par transf out of co when Great Yarmouth CB 1889. [22]20 Apr, LGBO 21423. [23]When incorp as MB. [24]Extended 9 Nov, LGB ProvO 77, confirmed by LGB ProvO Confirmation (No. 9) Act, 1890. [25]1 Apr, LGBO 54513. [26]1 Apr, LGBO 61509. [27]1 Apr, LGBO 40418. [28]1 Oct, LGBO 33386. [29]1 Apr, LGBO 45965. [30]9 Nov, LGB ProvO Confirmation (No 5), Act, 1919. [31]1 Oct, LGBO 41276. [32]2 Feb, LGBO 30653. [33]1 Oct, LGBO 35026. [34]Belton, Bradwell, Burgh Castle, Fritton (gaining at same time the pt of Herringfleet transf to Norfolk), Hopton-on-Sea (gaining at same time the pt of Corton transf to Norfolk).

SURREY

[1]Pars within hundreds from late 16th cent only and not shown after cr of Adm Co in 1889. [2]1 Apr, 14 & 15 Geo. V, *c* xcviii. [3]1 Apr, 14 & 15 Geo. V, *c* cxcviii. [4]1 Apr, MHealthO 76890. [5]1 Apr, MHealthO 84021. [6]20 & 21 Eliz. II, *c* 70. [7]Incl Southwark pars. [8]At some time pt or ent in a Bor or MB; see BOROUGHS. [9]Artington is the pt not in the Bor. [10]Based on Beresford & Finberg's *Hand-List* and other secondary sources, not on additional research. [11]5 & 6 Wm. IV, *c* 76. [12]9 Nov, charter of incorp made UD a MB. [13]14 Feb, charter of incorp. [14]9 Nov, charter of incorp made The Maldens and Coombe UD Malden and Coombe MB. [15]City of London had concurrent jursid from 1550, Southwark treated as Bridge Without Ward. [16]Not co-terminous with anc or adm co. [17]Hants until 1895, Surrey thereafter. [18]Pt Sussex, pt Surrey, ent Surrey from 1884. [19]27 Mar, LGBO 29249. [20]Authority not found. [21]Authority not found. [22]Transf 1889 to London. [23]1 Apr, LGBO 62292. [24]1 Apr, LGBO 39147. [25]1 Oct, MHealthO 73618. [26]1 Apr, LGBO 62791. [27]1 Oct, LGBO 47956. [28]1 July, Surrey Co CouncilO. [29]1 Apr, LGBO 32638. [30]Apptd day, LGBO 31572. [31]Renaming 15 Apr by Surrey Co Council. [32]Apptd day, LGBO 31528. [33]1 Apr, LGBO 62598, 62599. [34]Apptd day, LGBO 31792. [35]1 Apr, LGBO 59890. [36]1 Oct, LGBO 32605. [37]Transf to Esher and the Dittons UD 1 Apr 1895, LGBO 32638. [38]Transf 1 July 1895 to The Maldens and Coombe, LGBO 30731. [39]Transf 1 July 1895 to Surbiton UD, LGBO 32897. [40]1 July, LGBO 31532. [41]1 Oct, LGBO 50390. [42]1 July, LGBO 30731. [43]1 Apr, LGBO 58201. [44]1 Apr, LGBO 61725. [45]Gained 1965 from Middx. [46]1 Apr, MHealthO 72455. [47]Apptd day, LGBO 31858. [48]Apptd day, LGBO 31544. [49]1 Apr, LGBO 52209. [50]1 Aug, LGBO 29987. [51]See 22 & 23 Eliz. II, *c* 11 for amendments to the Local Government Act, 1972, re-arranging Surrey Dists.

SUSSEX

[1]Pars within hundreds from late 16th cent only and not shown after cr of Adm Cos in 1889. [2]1 Apr, 17 & 18 Geo. V, *c* lxxxi. [3]1 Apr, 14 & 15 Geo. V, *c* xxix. [4]1 Apr, 10 Edw. VII and 1 Geo. V, *c* cxxiii. [5]26 Mar, LGBO 39222. [6]1 Apr, 16 & 17 Geo. V, *c* xcv. [7]1 Edw. VIII and 1 Geo. VI, *c* lxxvi. [8]9 Nov, LGB ProvO 1388. [9]1 Edw. VIII and 1 Geo. VI, *c* lxiv. [10]At some time pt or ent in a Bor or MB; see BOROUGHS. [11]Incl Chichester pars. [12]Area transf 1844 from Hants to Sussex; the unit became sep CP 1866. [13]Incl area Anc Town/Cq Pt of Winchelsea, pt Anc Town/Cq Pt of Rye, pt Hastings Cq Pt. [14]Incl Hastings pars. [15]See *VCH Sussex*. [16]Lewes pars in Swanborough Hd except Lewes St Thomas a Becket, Cliffe in Ringmer. [17]Based on Beresford & Finberg's *Hand-List* and other secondary sources, not on additional research. [18]5 & 6 Wm. IV, *c* 76. [19]24 Mar, OC, UD made MB. [20]Charter of incorp. [21]Pars from late 16th cent only; for a full list of earlier pars, see Part I of the *Guide*. [22]Charter of incorp. [23]1 Apr, 10 Edw. VII and 1 Geo. V, *c* cxxiii. [24]18 July, OC, UD made MB. [25]Charter of incorp. [26]Charter of incorp. [27]Not co-terminous with anc or adm co. [28]Local act; see *VCH Sussex* VII. [29]Presumed incl in PLU when became sep CP; not orig rated in the PLU. [30]Hants until 1844, Sussex thereafter. [31]Pt Hants, pt Sussex until 1844, ent Sussex thereafter. [32]Pt Sussex, pt Kent until 1895, ent E Sussex thereafter. [33]Pt Sussex, pt Kent until 1894, ent E Sussex thereafter. [34]Pt [E] Sussex, pt Kent until 1895, ent Kent thereafter. [35]Pt Kent, pt Sussex until 1886, ent Kent thereafter. [36]Pt Surrey, pt Sussex until 1884, ent Surrey thereafter. [37]Pt Hants, pt [W] Sussex until 1895, ent Hants thereafter. [38]7 May, LGBO 17054.

[39]20 June, LGBO 17090. [40]1 June, LGBO 12198. [41]10 July, LGBO 15599. [42]When Worthing incorp MB. [43]26 Mar, LGBO 30228. [44]Albourne only W Sussex par in the RD, transf 1908 to E Sussex (1 Apr, 7 Edw. VII, *c* clvi) so RD ent E Sussex thereafter. [45]1 Apr, LGBO 37456. [46]31 Mar, 17 & 18 Geo. V, *c* lxxxi. [47]26 July, W Sussex Co CouncilO. [48]1 Apr, MHousLGO 5861. [49]1 Oct, LGBO 54317. [50]1 Oct, LGBO 39616. [51]Not to be in any par. [52]To be sep pars under respective names even though area diminished.

WILTSHIRE

[1]Pars within hundreds from late 16th cent only, and not shown after cr of Adm Co in 1889. Pars which existed before but did not survive until late 16th cent are nevertheless listed in Part I of the *Guide*. [2]At some time pt or ent in a Bor; see BOROUGHS listing. [3]Damerham Hd was divided into a northern and southen division; see Part III where these are detailed (as belonging to different parl divisions 1832–85). [4]Incl area of Devizes pars. [5]Incl area of Marlbrough pars. [6]Based on Beresford & Finberg handlist and on secondary sources, not on original research. [7]5 & 6 Wm. IV, *c* 76. [8]Perhaps a bor but uncertain; see Beresford & Finberg, 177, 180. [9]16 Aug, charter of incorp. [10]Swindon New Town UD and New Swindon UD amalgamated into Swindon MB by charter of incorp, 27 Dec. [11]24 June, charter of incorp. [12]Not co-terminous with Anc or Adm Co. [13]Pt Wilts, pt Berks until 1844, ent Wilts thereafter. [14]Transf 1844 from Glos to Wilts. [15]Presumed incl in PLU when became sep CP; not orig rated in the PLU. [16]Pt Wilts, pt Somerset until 1895, ent Wilts thereafter. [17]Transf 1896 from Somerset to Wilts. [18]Pt Wilts, pt Dorset until 1880s (between censuses of 1881, 1891), ent Wilts thereafter. [19]Transf 1897 from Wilts to Glos. [20] Transf 1844 from Wilts to Glos. [21]Pt Wilts, pt Berks until 1881, ent Berks thereafter. [22]Transf 1895 from Wilts to Hants. [23]Pt Wilts, pt Berks until 1895, ent Wilts thereafter. [24]Pt Wilts, pt Berks until 1895, ent Berks thereafter. [25]Pt Wilts, pt Hants, each a sep CP 1889 in the respective cos, the Wilts par transf 1895 to Hants as 'East Bramshaw'. [26]Pt Wilts, pt Berks until 1844, ent Berks thereafter. [27]Enlarged 9 Nov 1889, LGB ProvO 612. [28]Bdry alt 1890, 24 Sept, LGBO 25937. [29]1 Oct, LGBO 39695. [30]31 Mar, MHealth O 74051.

PART III: PARLIAMENTARY CONSTITUENCIES

BEDFORDSHIRE

[1]Date of medieval representation from list of MPs in *Parliamentary Papers* with no additional research.

BERKSHIRE

[1]Dates of medieval representation from list of MPs in *Parl Papers* with no additional research. [2]Enlarged pt 1867–85. [3]The remaining wards of the CB assigned to Newbury CC, Wokingham CC, qv. [4]Called 'New Windsor' generally until mid-20th cent. [5]Enlarged pt 1867–1918. [6]The major pt of Reading CB in Reading Parl Bor 1955–70, qv. [7]The alt in 1972 to bring parl units into accord with civ bdry alt effective 1969 per MHousLGO 41456 (affected Bucklebury, Chieveley, Hampstead Norreys, Hermitage).

BUCKINGHAMSHIRE

[1]Dates of medieval representation taken from list of MPs in *Parliamentary Papers* with no additional research. [2]44 Geo. III, *c* lx.

CAMBRIDGESHIRE

[1]Dates of medieval representation from list of MPs in *Parl Papers* with no additional research.

CORNWALL

[1]Dates of medieval representation taken from list of MPs in *Parliamentary Papers* with no additional research. [2]Disfranchised for corruption

DEVON

[1]Dates of medieval representation taken from list of MPs in *Parl Papers* with no additional research. [2]Excused from sending MPs *temp* Henry VII; information from County Record Office. [3]Changes in wards: 1951, SI 1951/32; 1955, SI 1955/6. [4]Changes in wards in 1951 and 1955 as per note 3 the former involving also alt in Tavistock CC because of expansion of Plymouth CB (per civ bdry alt 1949, as in Part I of the *Guide*). [5]Lundy Island not explicitly mentioned in schedule of act in 1948, the omission corrected by supp order effective 1 April 1951 per SI 1951/327.

DORSET

[1]Dates of medieval representation from list of MPs in *Parl Papers* with no additional research.

ESSEX

[1]Dates of medieval representation taken from list of MPs in *Parl Papers* with no additional research. [2]Parl bdry alt effective 3 Mar 1960 between pars of Ilford, Woodford to bring parl bdry into agreement with civ changes in 1956, per SI 1960/454. [3]See SI 1955/8 for details of parl bdry alt for the 2 Southend on Sea BCs. [4]Changes effective 19 Jan 1955, per SI 1955/8. [5]Changes in 1955 effective 19 Jan (as per note 4), for 1960 effective 3 Mar (as per note 2). [6]The order in 1945 defined the divisions of Epping,

Hornchurch, South East, and Thurrock; bdry alts were made for Chelmsford Dv and for Maldon Dv affecting the pars of Cranham, Mountnessing, Stambridge, Upminster, Great Warley). The new Parl Bors of Barking, Dagenham, Romford were drawn from Romford Dv as defined in 1918, and Woodford from Epping Dv. [7]This pt of Southend on Sea CB was in this Dv as defined in 1918. [8]Changes effective 15 Feb 1955, per SI 1955/9. [9]Parl bdry alt effective 15 June 1956 (affecting West Bergholt, Wormingford) per SI 1956/80, to bring parl bdry into agreement with civ changes in 1955.

GLOUCESTERSHIRE

[1]Dates of medieval representation from list of MPs in *Parl Papers* with no additional research. [2]See Somerset for pars in Bristol Bor/MB but in territory orig Somerset Anc Co. Pars from late 16th cent only; for earlier pars see Part I of the *Guide*. [3]Rearrangement of constituencies 1955 effective 19 Jan, SI 1955/10. [4]Includes pt Bedminster, Somerset. [5]Rearrangement of constitencies as in note 3; bdry alt affecting Bristol South BC, Bristol South-East BC when each gains pt Somerset, qv for pars affected, effective 17 Mar, SI 1952/452. [6]Pars from late 16th cent only; for earlier pars see Part I of the *Guide*. Bdry alt 1951 affecting Gloucester BC (Gloucester), Stroud and Thornbury CC (Brookthorpe, Quedgeley) and West Gloucestershire CC (Longlevens), effective 1 .Apr, SI 1951/324. Bdry alt 1960 affecting Gloucester BC (Gloucester) and Stroud CC (Upton St Leonards), effective 30 Mar, SI 1960/452. [7]Bdry alt 1951 as in note 6. [8]Bdry alt 1960 as in note 6.

HAMPSHIRE

[1]Dates of medieval representation from list of MPs in *Parl Papers* with no additional research. [2]Bdry alt 1964 affecting Christchurch, Christchurch East, effective 11 Mar, SI 1964/274. [3]Bdry alt 1973 afffecting Christchurch, Hurn, effective 29 Mar, SI 1973/607. [4]Rearrangement of constituencies effective 19 Jan, SI 1955/11. [5]Pars listed from mid-17th cent only; for earlier pars see Part I of the *Guide*. [6]Rearrangement of constituenceis as in note 4 and bdry alt 1964 as in note 2.

HERTFORDSHIRE

[1]Disfranchised for corruption, 15 Vict., *c* 9. [2]Bdry alt 1945 affects Abbots Langley, Sarratt, Wheathampstead. [3]Bdry alt 1945 affects Braughing, Ware Urban. [4]Bdry alt 1945 affects Hormead, Westmill. [5]Changes in 1955 effective 19 Jan, SI 1955/12.

HUNTINGDONSHIRE

[1]Dates of medieval representation taken from list of MPs in *Parliamentary Papers* with no additional research.

KENT

[1]Dates of medieval representation taken from list of MPs in *Parliamentary Papers* with no additional research. [2]Pars from late 16th cent only; for earlier see Part I of the *Guide*. [3]Enlarged 1867, composition by pars not affected. [4]19 Jan, SI 1955/13. [5]1 Mar, SI 1964/277. [6]Disfranchised for corruption. [7]Incl pt Surrey. [8]11 June, SI 1945/701. [9]19 Jan, SI 1955/13. [10]Changes in 1955 as per note 8; in 1964, SI 1964/227. [11]As defined in SI 1968/2020.

LONDON

[1]19Jan, SI 1955/21. [2]Changes in 1949 effeective 10 Aug, SI 1949/440. [3]Changes in 1955 effective 19 Jan, SI 1955/20. [4]Constituent wards as defined by SI 1948/729. [5]Changes in 1955 effective 15 Feb, SI 1955/165. [6]Composition redefined 1972 (effective 5 Jan) in terms of wards as altered by SI 1970/1888. [7]Constituent wards as defined by SI 1968/202; also altered in 1972 as per note 6. [8]Composition redefined 1973 (effective 29 Mar) in terms of wards as altered by SI 1973/605. [9]Bdry alt 1972 (effective 5 Jan) to bring parl constituencies into agreement with civ bdry alt in SI 1971/2114. [10]Bdry alt 1972 (effective 5 Jan) to bring parl constituencies into agreement with civ bdry alt in SI 1971/2113.

MIDDLESEX

[1]Dates of medieval representation taken from list in *Parl Papers* with no additional research. [2]Changes in constitution by wards in 1949 effective 10 Aug, SI 1949/1441; in 1955, effective 15 Feb, SI 1955/167. [3]Bdry alt 1945 affecting Willesden. [4]Bdry alt 1945 affecting New Brentford, Old Brentford. [5]Bdry alt 1945 affecting South Mimms. [6]Bdry alt 1945 affecting Friern Barnet. [7]Changes 1955 effective 15 Feb, SI 1955/166.

NORFOLK

[1]Dates of medieval representation taken from list of MPs in *Parl Papers* with no additional research. [2]Called 'Lynn' before *temp* Henry VIII and 'King's Lynn' thereafter. [3]Pars from late 16th cent only; for earlier pars which did not survive until then, see Part I of the *Guide*. [4]Alteration of constituencies by wards effective 12 Apr 1973, SI 1973/608; bdry alt 1951 affecting Norwich CP and Norwich North BC and the pars of Sprowston, Thorpe next Norwich (both Cenral Norfolk CC) effective 1 Apr, SI1951/325. [5]Alteration of constituencies by wards in 1973 as per note 4. [6]Pt of Thetford St Cuthbert, Thetford St Mary in Thetford Parl Bor until 1918; Gorleston (Suffolk until 1889, Great Yarmouth CB thereafter) in (Great) Yarm. Parl Bor until 1832, ent 1832–1948. [7]Name alternatively 'Yarmouth' and/or 'Great Yarmouth' in early years, the latter invariably later. [8]Incl area of Norwich County Gaol and associated buildings. [9]Bdry alt 1951 as in note 4.

OXFORDSHIRE

[1]Dates of medieval representation from list of MPs in *Parl Papers* with no additional research. [2]Pars listed from late 16th cent only; for earlier pars see Part I of the *Guide*; also affected by bdry alt as in note 3. [3]Bdry alt 1960 affecting Oxford, Littlemore, effective 30 Mar, SI 1960/459. [4]Pt in Berks.

SOMERSET

[1]Dates of medieval representation taken from list of MPs in *Parl Papers* with no additional research.[2]Pars from late 16th cent only; for earlier pars see Part I of the *Guide*. Bdry alt 1951 affecting Bath BC (Bath), North Somerset CC (Charlcombe, Claverton, English Combe, Monkton Combe, South Stoke, Weston) and Weston-super-Mare CC (Cleeve [cr civ 1949 and now added to the CC], Yatton), effective 1 Apr, SI 1951/431. [3]Mostly Glos, later Bristol CB; see entries for Glos. [4]Bdry alt 1951 as in note 2, bdry alt 1952 as in note 6, bdry alt 1960 as in note 5. [5]Bdry alt 1960 affecting North Somerset CC (Chilcompton) and Wells CC (Binegar, Stratton-on-the-Fosse), effective 30 Mar, SI 1960/458. [6]Bdry alt 1951 as in note 2; bdry alt 1952 affecting Bristol constituencies (see Glos), Weston-super-Mare CC (Clevedon) and North Somerset CC (Bishopsworth, Dundry, Easton-in-Gordano, Portishead, Walton-in-Gordano, North Weston, Weston-in-Gordano, Whitchurch), effective 17 Mar, SI 1952/452.

SUFFOLK

[1]Dates of medieval representation taken from list of MPs in *Parl Papers* with no additional research. [2]A number of Dunwich pars existed, many washed into the sea at varying times; for their existence and inclusion in this Parl Bor, see Part I of the *Guide*. [3]Whitton was without the Parl Bor, Thurleston within, so that the united par from late 16th cent was pt within, pt without. [4]Bdry alt effective 7 May 1953, SI 1953/744, altered parl boundaries to coincide with civ enlargement of Ipswich CB 1951, affecting Akenham, Bramford, Nacton, Prudis Farm, Rushmere St Andrew, Sproughton, Tuddenham, Westerfield, Whitton, enlarging Ipswich Parl Bor and reducing the other pars respective CCs.

SURREY

[1]Dates of medieval representation taken from list of MPs in *Parl Papers* with no additional research. [2]Cr and abol of Croydon BCs, 15 Feb, SI 1955/174. [3]Bdry alt in 1945. [4]Bdry alt in 1972, 5 Jan, SI 1955/2114. [5]Bdry alt in 1945, and in 1955, 15 Feb, SI 1955/175. [6]Cr 1955, 15 Feb, SI 1955/175. [7]Bdry alt in 1945, affecting Eastern Dv (Addington, Farleigh, Sanderstead), Epsom Dv (Cuddington), Reigate Dv (Chaldon, Mertsham) in addition to noted transfers of Banstead, Cheam, Sutton to Parl Bors. [8]Bdry alt in 1964, 11 Mar, SI 1964/276. [9]As defined in SI 1968/2020.

SUSSEX

[1]Dates of medieval representation from list of MPs in *Parl Papers* with no additional research. [2]Rearrangement of constituencies 1955 effective 15 Feb, SI 1955/176. [3]Pars from late 16th cent only; for earlier pars see Part I of the *Guide*. [4]Excluding Petit Iham, Lbty of the Sluice. [5]Hurst Green (cr civ 1952 from Etchingham, Ticehurst [East Grinstead CC] and from Salehurst [Hastings BC]) made pt Hastings BC 1953, effective 7 May, SI 1953/745. [6]Rearrangement of constituencies 1955 as in note 2; East Grinstead CC affected 1953 as in note 5.

WILTSHIRE

[1]Dates of medieval representation from list of MPs in *Parl Papers* with no additional research. [2]Incl Poulton in Glos. [3]Affected by bdry alt 1951 (as in note 4) and 1971 (as in note 5). [4]Bdry alt 1951 affecting Swindon BC (Swindon) and Devizes CC (Stratton St Margaret), SI 1952/349, effective 25 July. [5]Bdry alt 1971 affecting Swindon BC (Swindon) and Devizes CC (Chiseldon, Liddington, Wanborough), SI 1971/2116, effective 5 Jan.

PART IV: THE DIOCESES OF ENGLAND

BATH AND WELLS

[1]17 Aug, *Lond Gaz.* [2]3 July, *Lond Gaz.* [3]First appearance *Clergy List.* [4]1 June, *Lond Gaz.* [5]15 Apr, *Lond Gaz.* [6]29 June, *Lond Gaz.* [7]30 Nov, *Lond Gaz.* [8]3 May, *Lond Gaz.* [9]14 June, *Lond Gaz.* [10]1 June (*Lond Gaz* 6 Apr). [11]29 Jan, *Lond Gaz.*

BRISTOL (1542–1836)

[1]4 June, Letters Patent, Rymer, *Foedera*, XIV, 748. [2]8 Oct, *Lond Gaz.*

BRISTOL (1897–*)

[1]9 July, *Lond Gaz.* [2]9 July, *Lond Gaz.* [3]8 Feb, *Lond Gaz.* [4]13 Aug, *Lond Gaz.* [5]12 Aug, *Lond Gaz.* [6]30 May, *Lond Gaz.* [7]3 June, *Lond Gaz.* [8]26 Mar, *Lond Gaz.*

CANTERBURY

[1]Reported *VCH Surrey* II, 52. [2]4 June, *Lond Gaz.* [3]20 Aug, *Lond Gaz.* [4]30 Dec, *Lond Gaz.* [5]First appearance *Clergy List.* [6]11 Jan, *Lond Gaz.* [7]2 July, *Lond Gaz.* [8]7 Aug, *Lond Gaz.* [9]8 Aug, *Lond Gaz.*

[10]11 Aug, *Lond Gaz.* [11]6 Mar, *Lond Gaz.* [12]17 July, *Lond Gaz.* [13]1 Apr, *Lond Gaz.* [14]10 Feb, *Lond Gaz.* [15]23 May, *Lond Gaz.* [16]15 July, *Lond Gaz.*

CHELMSFORD

[1]23 Jan, *Lond Gaz.* [2]7 Apr, *Lond Gaz.* [3]4 Feb, *Lond Gaz.* [4]17 Mar, *Lond Gaz.* [5]1 Feb, *Lond Gaz.* [6]18 Mar, *Lond Gaz.* [7]4 Dec, *Lond Gaz.* [8]28 Feb, *Lond Gaz.* [9]17 Nov, *Lond Gaz.* [10]17 Nov, *Lond Gaz.* [11]12 June, *Lond Gaz.*

CHICHESTER

[1]Information supplied by West Sussex RO. [2]First appearance *Clergy List.* [3]28 June, *Lond Gaz.* [4]13 June, *Lond Gaz.* [5]27 Aug, *Lond Gaz.* [6]29 May, *Lond Gaz.* [7]23 July, *Lond Gaz.* [8]4 Apr, *Lond Gaz.* [9]4 Jan, *Lond Gaz.* [10]30 Mar, *Lond Gaz.* [11]18 May, *Lond Gaz.*

ELY

[1]Before *Taxatio* of 1291. [2]30 May, *Lond Gaz.* [3]23 Apr, *Lond Gaz.* [4]24 Sept and 1 Oct, *Lond Gaz.* [5]Ely diocesan records. [6]First appearance *Clergy List.* [7]29 May, *Lond Gaz.* [8]23 Aug, *Lond Gaz.* [9]26 Feb, *Lond Gaz.* [10]1 July, *Lond Gaz.* [11]11 Aug, *Lond Gaz.* [12]23 Jan, *Lond Gaz.* [13]7 Aug, *Lond Gaz.* [14]21 Aug, *Lond Gaz.* [15]5 Feb, *Lond Gaz.* [16]16 Nov, *Lond Gaz.* [17]27 June, *Lond Gaz.* [18]30 June, *Lond Gaz.* [19]May be effective later than 21 Jan, *Lond Gaz.*

EXETER

[1]24 Aug, *Lond Gaz.* [2]16 Mar, *Lond Gaz.* [3]22 Feb, *Lond Gaz.* [4]10 Aug, *Lond Gaz.* [5]15 Dec, *Lond Gaz.* [6]13 June, *Lond Gaz.* [7]22 Mar, *Lond Gaz.* [8]27 Nov, *Lond Gaz.* [9]14 Sept, *Lond Gaz.*

GLOUCESTER (1541–1836)

[1]3 Sept, Letters Patent, Rymer, *Foedera,* XIV, 724. Suppressed by Mary I, re-erected by Eliz. I. [2]8 Oct, *Lond Gaz.*

GLOUCESTER (1897–*)

[1]9 July, *Lond Gaz.* [2]8 Feb, *Lond Gaz.* [3]17 May, *Lond Gaz.* [4]1 Aug, *Lond Gaz.* [5]31 Oct, *Lond Gaz.* [6]21 May, *Lond Gaz.* [7]14 Feb, *Lond Gaz.* [8]4 June, *Lond Gaz.* [9]10 Apr, *Lond Gaz.* [10]1 Feb, *Lond Gaz.*

GLOUCESTER AND BRISTOL

[1]8 Oct, *Lond Gaz.* [2]9 July, *Lond Gaz.* [3]18 Aug, *Lond Gaz.* [4]3 July, *Lond Gaz.* [5]First appearance *Clergy List.* [6]8 Dec, *Lond Gaz.* [7]7 July, *Lond Gaz.*

GUILDFORD

[1]1 May (*Lond Gaz* 26 Apr). [2]17 Aug, *Lond Gaz.* [3]11 June, *Lond Gaz.* [4]9 Aug, *Lond Gaz.*

LINCOLN

[1]1 Sept, Letters Patent, Rymer, *Foedera,* XIV, 754 (transf to Oxford 9 June 1845, Rymer, *Foedera,* XV, 75). [2]30 May, *Lond Gaz.* [3]Year vac (*Lond Gaz* 30 May 1837).

LONDON

[1]20 Aug, *Lond Gaz.* [2]26 & 27 Vict., *c* 36. [3]20 Aug, *Lond Gaz.* [4]20 Aug, *Lond Gaz:* Southwark pars, Battersea, Bermondsey, Camberwell, Clapham, Lambeth, Merton, Rotherhithe, Streatham, Tooting. [5]17 July, *Lond Gaz.* [6]Kent pars to Roch dioc. [7]First appearance *Clergy List.* [8]3 Dec, *Lond Gaz.* [9]13 Dec, *Lond Gaz.* [10]23 July, *Lond Gaz.* [11]13 Mar, *Lond Gaz.* [12]9 Nov, *Lond Gaz.* [13]27 Feb, *Lond Gaz.* [14]2 Mar, *Lond Gaz.* [15]17 July, *Lond Gaz.* [16]5 June, *Lond Gaz.* [17]2 Feb, *Lond Gaz.* [18]12 July, *Lond Gaz.* [19]30 June, *Lond Gaz.* [20]6 Oct, *Lond Gaz.* [21]31 Aug, *Lond Gaz.*

NORWICH

[1]12 Apr, *Lond Gaz.* [2]First appearance *Clergy List.* [3]Noted in Norwich dioc records. [4]28 Aug, *Lond Gaz.* [5]23 Jan, *Lond Gaz.* [6]21 Aug, *Lond Gaz.* [7]25 Jan, *Lond Gaz.* [8]17 Feb, *Lond Gaz.* [9]29 Sept, *Lond Gaz.* [10]21 Nov, *Lond Gaz.* [11]24 Mar, *Lond Gaz.*

OXFORD

[1]Cr 1 Sept, Letters Patent, Rymer, *Foedera,* XIV, 754; transf to Oxford 9 June 1845, Rymer, *Foedera,* XV, 75. [2]10 Oct and 7 Oct, *Lond Gaz.* [3]18 Apr, *Lond Gaz.* [4]Year vac (*Lond Gaz* 10 and 7 Oct 1837). [5]1 Jan (*Lond Gaz* 20 Aug 1845). [6]29 Sept, *Lond Gaz.* [7]First appearance *Clergy List.* [8]30 Apr, *Lond Gaz.* [9]5 Feb, *Lond Gaz.* [10]10 Dec, *Lond Gaz.* [11]31 Oct, *Lond Gaz.* [12]21 May, *Lond Gaz.* [13]18 Mar, *Lond Gaz.* [14]14 Feb, *Lond Gaz.* [15]20 Mar, *Lond Gaz.* [16]5 Feb, *Lond Gaz.* [17]20 Nov, *Lond Gaz.* [18]21 Dec, *Lond Gaz.* [19]3 Apr, *Lond Gaz.* [20]24 Nov, *Lond Gaz.* [21]18 May, *Lond Gaz.* [22]17 Nov, *Lond Gaz.* [23]4 June, *Lond Gaz.* [24]29 Jan, *Lond Gaz.* [25]13 Mar (2 orders), *Lond Gaz.* [26]14 June, *Lond Gaz.*

PORTSMOUTH

[1]1 May (*Lond Gaz* 26 Apr). [2]23 Jan, *Lond Gaz.* [3]6 Oct, *Lond Gaz.*

ROCHESTER

[1]20 Aug, *Lond Gaz.* [2]30 Dec, *Lond Gaz.* [3]25 & 26 Vict., *c* 36. [4]First appearance *Clergy List.* [5]26 & 27 Vict., *c* 36. [6]4 May, *Lond Gaz.* [7]13 July, *Lond Gaz.* [8]38 & 39 Vict., *c* 34. [9]3 May, *Lond Gaz.* [10]10 Jan, *Lond Gaz.* [11]22 Aug, *Lond Gaz.* [12]27 July, *Lond Gaz.* [13]23 Aug, *Lond Gaz.* [14]21 May, *Lond Gaz.* [15]21 May, *Lond Gaz.* [16]7 Aug, *Lond Gaz.* [17]10

Apr, *Lond Gaz.* [18]13 Apr, *Lond Gaz.* [19]23 Jan, *Lond Gaz.* [20]6 Mar, *Lond Gaz.* [21]23 Feb, *Lond Gaz.* [22]4 Jan, *Lond Gaz.* [23]29 Mar, *Lond Gaz.* [24]13 Sept, *Lond Gaz.* [25]6 Aug, *Lond Gaz.* [26]1 Dec, *Lond Gaz.* [27]26 Oct, *Lond Gaz.*

ST ALBANS

[1]4 May, *Lond Gaz.* [2]First appearance *Clergy List.* [3]11 July, *Lond Gaz.* [4]Deanery magazine in dioc archives. [5]23 Aug, *Lond Gaz.* [6]17 May, *Lond Gaz.* [7]21 Jan, *Lond Gaz.* [8]7 Apr, *Lond Gaz.* [9]20 Apr, *Lond Gaz.* [10]20 Dec, *Lond Gaz.* [11]10 Mar, *Lond Gaz.* [12]4 Nov, *Lond Gaz.* [13]12 Apr, *Lond Gaz.* [14]13 Feb (*Lond Gaz* 10 Feb). [15]24 Jan, *Lond Gaz.*

ST EDMUNDSBURY AND IPSWICH

[1]23 Jan, *Lond Gaz.* [2]7 Apr, *Lond Gaz.* [3]21 Aug, *Lond Gaz.* [4]22 Dec, *Lond Gaz.* [5]12 July, *Lond Gaz.* [6]13 June (may be slightly later date than *Lond Gaz* that date).

SARUM

[1]4 June, Letters Patent, Rymer, *Foedera*, XIV, 748. [2]10 and 7 Oct, *Lond Gaz.* [3]18 Aug, *Lond Gaz.* [4]29 Sept, *Lond Gaz.* [5]30 Apr, *Lond Gaz.* [6]First appearance *Clergy List.* [7]7 Jan, *Lond Gaz.* [8]31 Mar, *Lond Gaz.* [9]30 May, *Lond Gaz.* [10]1 Nov, *Lond Gaz.* [11]13 Apr, *Lond Gaz.* [12]25 June, *Lond Gaz.* [13]10 Aug, *Lond Gaz.* [14]24 June, *Lond Gaz.* [15]10 Aug, *Lond Gaz.* [16]20 Oct, *Lond Gaz.* [17]14 Mar, *Lond Gaz.* [18]1 Jan (*Lond Gaz* 220 Dec 1970). [19]1 Jan (*Lond Gaz* 26 Sept 1972). [20]1 Jan (*Lond Gaz* 9 Nov). [21]1 Jan (*Lond Gaz* 1 Nov).

SOUTHWARK

[1]21 Mar, *Lond Gaz.* [2]11 Aug, *Lond Gaz.* [3]6 Mar, *Lond Gaz.* [4]19 Oct, *Lond Gaz.* [5]23 June, *Lond Gaz.* [6]22 Feb, *Lond Gaz.* [7]17 Oct, *Lond Gaz.* [8]10 Oct, *Lond Gaz.* [9]9 Mar, *Lond Gaz.* [10]9 May, *Lond Gaz.* [11]23 Sept, *Lond Gaz.* [12]1 Apr (*Lond Gaz* 9 Mar).

TRURO

[1]15 Dec, *Lond Gaz.* [2]4 May, *Lond Gaz.* [3]21 May, *Lond Gaz.* [4]27 Aug, *Lond Gaz.* [5]15 Aug, *Lond Gaz.* [6]5 June, *Lond Gaz.* [7]30 June, *Lond Gaz.* [8]21 Nov, *Lond Gaz.*

WINCHESTER

[1]Before *Valor Eccl.* [2]Noted in *VCH Surrey* III, 52. [3]20 Aug, *Lond Gaz.* [4]First appearance *Clergy List.* [5]30 Apr, *Lond Gaz.* [6]22 Dec, *Lond Gaz.* [7]11 July and 17 July, *Lond Gaz.* [8]7 May, *Lond Gaz.* [9]14 Feb, *Lond Gaz.* [10]13 May, *Lond Gaz.* [11]14 Aug, *Lond Gaz.* [12]6 June, *Lond Gaz.* [13]26 July, *Lond Gaz.* [14]24 Mar, *Lond Gaz.* [15]6 Feb, *Lond Gaz.* [16]1 May (*Lond Gaz* 26 Apr). [17]26 July, *Lond Gaz.* [18]20 July, *Lond Gaz.* [19]27 Jan, *Lond Gaz.* [20]30 Sept, *Lond Gaz.*